SOMATOFORM DISORDERS

Somatization Disorder
Conversion Disorder
Hypochondriasis
Body Dysmorphic Disorder
Pain Disorder

FACTITIOUS DISORDERS

Factitious Disorder

DISSOCIATIVE DISORDERS

Dissociative Amnesia
Dissociative Fugue
Dissociative Identity Disorder (Multiple Personality Disorder)
Depersonalization Disorder

SEXUAL AND GENDER IDENTITY DISORDERS

Sexual Dysfunctions
Sexual Desire Disorders: Hypoactive Sexual Desire Disorder; Sexual Aversion Disorder / Sexual Arousal Disorders: Female Sexual Arousal Disorder; Male Erectile Disorder / Orgasmic Disorders: Female Orgasmic Disorder (Inhibited Female Orgasm); Male Orgasmic Disorder (Inhibited Male Orgasm); Premature Ejaculation / Sexual Pain Disorders: Dyspareunia; Vaginismus / Sexual Dysfunction Due to a General Medical Condition / Substance-induced Sexual Dysfunction
Paraphilias
Exhibitionism / Fetishism / Frotteurism / Pedophilia / Sexual Masochism / Sexual Sadism / Voyeurism / Transvestic Fetishism
Gender Identity Disorders
Gender Identity Disorder: in Children; in Adolescents or Adults (Transsexualism)

EATING DISORDERS

Anorexia Nervosa
Bulimia Nervosa

SLEEP DISORDERS

Primary Sleep Disorders
Dyssomnias: Primary Insomnia; Primary Hypersomnia; Narcolepsy; Breathing-related Sleep Disorder; Circadian Rhythym Sleep Disorder (Sleep-Wake Schedule Disorder) / Parasomnias; Nightmare Disorder (Dream Anxiety Disorder); Sleep Terror Disorder; Sleepwalking Disorder / Sleep Disorders Related to Another Mental Disorder
Sleep Disorder Due to a General Medical Condition
Substance-induced Sleep Disorder

IMPULSE CONTROL DISORDERS NOT ELSEWHERE CLASSIFIED

Intermittent Explosive Disorder
Kleptomania
Pyromania
Pathological Gambling
Trichotillomania

ADJUSTMENT DISORDERS

Adjustment Disorder
With Anxiety / with Depressed Mood / with Disturbance of Conduct / with Mixed Disturbance of Emotions and Conduct / with Mixed Anxiety and Depressed Mood

Axis II

Mental Retardation
Mild Mental Retardation / Moderate Mental Retardation / Severe Mental Retardation / Profound Mental Retardation

PERSONALITY DISORDERS

Paranoid Personality Disorder
Schizoid Personality Disorder
Schizotypal Personality Disorder
Antisocial Personality Disorder
Borderline Personality Disorder
Histrionic Personality Disorder
Narcissistic Personality Disorder
Avoidant Personality Disorder
Dependent Personality Disorder
Obsessive-Compulsive Personality Disorder

OTHER CONDITIONS THAT MAY BE A FOCUS OF CLINICAL ATTENTION

Psychological Factors Affecting Medical Condition
Medication-induced Movement Disorders
Relational Problems
Relational Problem Related to a Mental Disorder or General Medical Condition / Parent-Child Relational Problem / Partner Relational Problem / Sibling Relational Problem
Problems Related to Abuse or Neglect
Physical Abuse of Child / Sexual Abuse of Child / Neglect of Child / Physical Abuse of Adult / Sexual Abuse of Adult
Additional Conditions That May Be a Focus of Clincal Attention
Bereavement / Borderline Intellectual Functioning / Academic Problem / Occupational Problem / Child or Adolescent Antisocial Behavior / Adult Antisocial Behavior / Malingering / Phase of Life Problem / Noncompliance with Treatment / Identity Problem / Religious or Spiritual Problem / Acculturation Problem / Age-related Cognitive Decline

Abnormal Psychology
Ninth Edition
With Cases

Gerald C. Davison

University of Southern California

John M. Neale

State University of New York at Stony Brook

Ann M. Kring

University of California at Berkeley

WILEY

John Wiley & Sons, Inc.

EXECUTIVE EDITOR   Ryan Flahive
SENIOR DEVELOPMENTAL EDITOR   Ellen Ford
EDITORIAL ASSISTANT   Deepa Chungi
MARKETING MANAGER   Kate Stewart
MEDIA EDITOR   Tom Kulesa
PRODUCTION MANAGER   Jeanine Furino
PRODUCTION EDITOR   Sandra Dumas
SENIOR DESIGNER   Harold Nolan
COVER DESIGNER   Howard Grossman
INTERIOR DESIGN   Laura Ierardi/LCI Design
PHOTO EDITOR   Jennifer MacMillan
PHOTO RESEARCHER   Elyse Rieder
COVER PHOTOS BY   Andy Washnik
SENIOR ILLUSTRATION EDITOR   Anna Melhorn
PRODUCTION MANAGEMENT SERVICES   Suzanne Ingrao

Oltmanns, T. F., Neale, J. M., Davison, G. C., *Case Studies in Abnormal Behavior, 6th edition,* © 2003, John Wiley & Sons, Inc. This material used by permission of John Wiley & Sons, Inc.

This book was set in 10.5/12 Berkeley Book by LCI Design and printed and bound by Von Hoffmann Corporation. The cover was printed by Von Hoffmann Corporation.

The paper in this book was manufactured by a mill whose forest management programs include sustained yield harvesting of its timberlands. Sustained yield harvesting principles ensure that the number of trees cut each year does not exceed the amount of new growth.

This book is printed on acid-free paper. ∞

Gerald C. Davison, John M. Neale, Ann M. Kring.
Abnormal Psychology, Ninth Edition with Cases

ISBN 0-471-47958-6

Printed in the United States of America

10 9 8 7 6 5 4 3 2 1

To

Kathleen C. Chambers, Eve H. Davison, and Asher Davison

Gail and Sean Neale

Barbara Jean Beck

About the Authors

Gerald C. Davison received his B.A. from Harvard in 1961, studied in Germany on a Fulbright the following year, earned his Ph.D. from Stanford in 1965, and was a postdoctoral fellow in clinical psychology at the Palo Alto Veterans Administration Hospital from 1965 to 1966. He is Professor and Chair of the Department of Psychology at the University of Southern California, where he was also Director of Clinical Training from 1979 to 1984 and Department Chair from 1984 to 1990. From 1994 to 1996 he served as Interim Dean of the USC Annenberg School for Communication. Previously he was on the psychology faculty at the State University of New York at Stony Brook (1966–1979).

In 1988 Davison received an outstanding achievement award from APA's Board of Social and Ethical Responsibility; in 1989 was the recipient of the Albert S. Raubenheimer Distinguished Faculty Award from USC's College of Letters, Arts, and Sciences; in 1993 won the Associates Award for Excellence in Teaching, a university-wide prize; in 1995 received the Distinguished Psychologist Award from the Los Angeles County Psychological Association; and in 1997 was given the Outstanding Educator Award of the Association for Advancement of Behavior Therapy. At USC he is a Faculty Fellow in the Center for Excellence in Teaching.

Among his more than 120 publications, his book *Clinical Behavior Therapy*, co-authored in 1976 with Marvin Goldfried and reissued in expanded form in 1994, is one of two publications that have been recognized as Citation Classics by the Social Sciences Citation Index; it appears in German and Spanish translation. Other books are *Case Studies in Abnormal Psychology, Sixth edition* (2004) with Oltmanns and Neale and *Exploring Abnormal Psychology* (1996) with Neale and Haaga. Davison is on the editorial board of several professional journals, including *Behavior Therapy*, *Cognitive Therapy and Research*, *Journal of Cognitive Psychotherapy*, *Journal of Psychotherapy Integration*, *Journal of Clinical Psychology*, and *In Session: Psychotherapy in Practice*. His publications emphasize experimental and philosophical analyses of psychopathology, assessment, and therapeutic change. His current research program focuses on the relationships between cognition and a variety of behavioral and emotional problems via his articulated thoughts in simulated situations paradigm. He is also licensed as a psychologist in California and listed in the National Register of Health Service Providers in Psychology.

John M. Neale is Professor Emeritus of Psychology at the State University of New York at Stony Brook, where he regularly taught the undergraduate course in abnormal psychology. He received his B.A. from the University of Toronto and his M.A. and Ph.D. from Vanderbilt University. His internship in clinical psychology was as a Fellow in Medical Psychology at the Langley Porter Neuropsychiatric Institute. In 1975 he was a Visiting Fellow at the Institute of Psychiatry, London, England. In 1974 he won the American Psychological Association's Early Career Award for his research on cognitive processes in schizophrenia. In 1991 he won a Distinguished Scientist Award from the American Psychological Association's Society for a Science of Clinical Psychology. He has been on the editorial boards of several journals and has been associate editor of the Journal of Abnormal Psychology. Besides his numerous articles in professional journals, he has published books on the effects of televised violence on children, research methodology, schizophrenia, case studies in abnormal psychology, and psychological influences on health. Schizophrenia was a major focus of his research and he also conducted research on the influence of stress on health.

Ann M. Kring is Associate Professor of Psychology at the University of California at Berkeley, where she is also currently the Director of the Clinical Science Program and Psychology Clinic. She received a B.S. from Ball State University and her M.A. and Ph.D. from the State University of New York at Stony Brook. Her internship in Clinical Psychology was completed at Bellevue Hospital and Kirby Forensic Psychiatric Center, in New York. Before moving to Berkeley, she was on the psychology faculty at Vanderbilt University (1991–1998). She is on the editorial board of the *Journal of Abnormal Psychology* and was formerly an Associate Editor for *Cognition and Emotion*. In 1997 she was awarded a Young Investigator award from the National Alliance for Research on Schizophrenia and Depression. Her current research focus is on emotion and psychopathology, with a specific interest in the emotional features of schizophrenia, the linkage between attention and emotion in schizophrenia, and the social and emotional features of social anxiety and depression. A second major focus of Kring's research is on the origins and consequences of individual differences in emotional expressivity and how gender and social context shape the experience and expression of emotion.

Preface

We have chosen a kaleidoscope theme for the cover and the chapter openers to highlight the vibrant excitement and variety of challenges in the study of abnormal behavior. As a kaleidoscope is made up of numerous pieces of colored glass, which, when moved even slightly, provide an extensive array of patterns, so too are the elements that contribute to the study of abnormal psychology. This discipline consists of an almost limitless variety of influential factors, perceptions, points of view, and an ever-changing search for answers to complex questions. The human mind presents a challenging mix of pieces that we struggle to understand. By working with the pieces and seeing how they interact with each other, we are able to come to conclusions as we strive to gain an understanding of how and why we act the way we do.

We are pleased in this new edition to be joined by Ann Kring. She brings to our collaboration an interest and expertise in emotion and psychopathology, as well as an emphasis on gender, ethnicity, and culture across different mental disorders. Furthermore, her work is at the cutting edge as it draws from other disciplines as well as other areas of psychology to understand the causes and manifestations of psychopathology. For example, her work on schizophrenia incorporates research and theory from basic studies in emotion, linguistics, and cognitive neuroscience. This translational approach to research reflects, we believe, the wave of the future in the study of abnormal behavior, and we are excited to have this approach further represented in the book.

Goals of the Book

It has been more than thirty years since Davison and Neale sat down to share our experiences teaching the undergraduate abnormal psychology course at Stony Brook. Arising from that conversation was the outline of a textbook on which we decided to collaborate, one that was different from the texts available at the time in its balance and blending of the clinical and the empirical/experimental; in its use of paradigms as an organizing principle; and in its effort to involve the reader in the problem solving engaged in by clinicians and scientists. As young academics, we had no idea how our colleagues and their undergraduate students would react to our proposed effort. We were therefore surprised and delighted at the favorable reception our first edition received when it was published in 1974, and our pleasure has only been enhanced by the continuing acceptance of the succeeding editions. Our conservative estimate is that

over 1 million students have now learned about the field of abnormal psychology using our text.

With each new edition, we update, make changes, and streamline features to enhance both the scholarly and didactic characteristics of the book. We also devote considerable effort to couching complex concepts in prose that is lucid and vivid. The domains of psychopathology and intervention have become increasingly multifaceted and technical. Therefore a good abnormal psychology textbook must engage the careful and focused attention of students so that they can acquire a deep and critical understanding of the issues and the material. They deserve nothing less. We believe that this ninth edition maintains a proper balance between undiluted discussion of a complex subject matter and a student-friendly presentation that is both engaging and informative. Feedback that we have received over the years from both instructors and their students indicates that we have been succeeding in this effort.

In contemporary abnormal psychology there are few hard and fast answers. Indeed, the very way the field should be conceptualized and the kinds of questions that should be asked are hotly debated issues. In this book we have tried to present glimpses of possible answers to two primary questions: What causes psychopathology? and Which treatments are most effective in preventing or reducing psychological suffering?

Our goals in writing this textbook are not only to present up-to-date theories and research in psychopathology and intervention but also to convey some of the intellectual excitement that is associated with the search for answers to some of the most puzzling questions facing humankind. A reviewer of an earlier edition once said that our book reads like a detective story, for we do more than just state the problem and then its solution. Rather, we try to involve the student in the search for clues, the follow-up of hunches, and the evaluation of evidence that are part and parcel of the science and art of the field. We try to encourage students to participate with us in a process of discovery as we sift through the evidence on the origins of psychopathology and the effectiveness of specific interventions.

Scientific Clinical Approach

As in the preceding eight editions of this book, we share a strong commitment to a scientific approach, but at the same time we appreciate the often uncontrollable nature of the subject matter and the importance of clinical findings. It has become commonplace in psychology to recognize the selective nature of perception, and we sound this theme throughout the book. We encourage readers to think critically and to consider the merits of our own and others' points of view. We believe we have succeeded in presenting fairly and comprehensively the major alternative conceptualizations in contemporary psychopathology.

Paradigms as an Organizing Principle

A recurrent theme in the book is the importance of major points of view, perspectives, or, to use Kuhn's (1962) phrase, paradigms. Our experience in teaching undergraduates has made us very much aware of the importance of making explicit the unspoken assumptions underlying any quest for knowledge. In our handling of the paradigms, we have tried to make their premises clear. Long after specific facts are forgotten, the student should retain a grasp of the basic problems in the field of psychopathology and should understand that the answers one arrives at are, in an important but often subtle way, constrained by the questions one poses and the methods employed to ask those questions. Throughout the book we discuss four major paradigms: psychoanalytic, learning (behavioral), cognitive, and biological (often referred to nowadays as neuroscientific). When therapy is discussed, we also describe the humanistic and existential paradigm.

A related issue is the use of more than one paradigm in studying abnormal psychology. Rather than force an entire field into, for example, a biological paradigm, we argue from the available information that different problems in psychopathology are amenable to analyses within different frameworks. For instance, biological processes must be considered when examining mental retardation and schizophrenia; but for other disorders, such as depression, cognitive factors are essential as well; and for still others, for example, dissociative disorders, psychoanalytic theories can enhance our understanding. Over the course of our several revisions the importance of a diathesis-stress approach has become increasingly evident. Emerging data indicate that many, perhaps most, disorders arise from subtle interactions between somatic or psychological predispositions and stressful life events. Our coverage continues to reflect these hypotheses and findings, strengthening the basic position we took in our very first edition that a diathesis-stress paradigm is necessary for understanding most psychopathologies.

Organization of the Ninth Edition

In Chapters 1 through 5 we place the field in historical context, present the concept of paradigms in science, describe the major paradigms in psychopathology and intervention, review the text revision of the fourth edition of the Diagnostic and Statistical Manual of Mental Disorders (DSM-IV-TR), discuss critically its validity and reliability, provide an overview of major approaches and techniques in clinical assessment, and then describe the major research methods of the field. These chapters are the foundation upon which the later chapters can be interpreted and understood. As in previous editions, specific disorders and

their treatment are discussed in Chapters 6 through 16. Our chapter on aging in our third edition in 1982 was the first such chapter in a book of this kind, and our current Chapter 16 remains the most comprehensive discussion of this important and still inadequately studied set of topics in an abnormal psychology textbook. Then in Chapter 17 we discuss process and outcome research on treatment and controversial issues surrounding the therapy enterprise. In Chapter 18 we have continued to update and strengthen our chapter on legal and ethical issues, which we believe is the most current and analytical introduction to mental health law available in this kind of textbook. This closing chapter is devoted to an in-depth study of the complex interplay between scientific findings and theories, on the one hand, and the role of ethics and the law, on the other. A core issue in this regard is the dialectical tension between what science can tell us and what use is properly made of science in controlling the everyday lives of people.

Throughout the book we have included considerable material on cultural and ethnicity factors in the study of psychopathology and intervention as well as discussion of the different ways abnormal behavior is conceptualized in cultures other than our own. For example, we examine in depth the ways that DSM-IV-TR sensitizes clinicians and researchers to the role of culture in shaping abnormal behavior as well as the ways psychological abnormality is manifested in different parts of the world. In the anxiety disorders chapter (6), for example, we discuss kayak-angst, a form of panic disorder found among seal hunters who spend a great deal of time alone at sea. In the clinical assessment chapter (4), we have extended our earlier discussions of cultural bias in assessment and ways to guard against this selectivity in perception. Cultural influences are explored in the eating disorders chapter (9), where societal conceptions of what is beautiful and desirable in body shape are presented as contributing factors in the extremes to which people will go to control their weight, and the prevailing conception that eating disorders are primarily a Western phenomenon is critically examined in a new section on ethnic differences. We have expanded and updated information on ethnicity with respect to substance abuse and dependence in Chapter 12 (Substance Related Disorders). And in Chapter 17 we have enhanced our discussion of cultural and racial factors in psychological interventions.

Our book continues to pay major attention to biological factors in both etiology and treatment. Ongoing advances in neuroscience are producing new and important knowledge about the origins of psychopathology and about better ways to prevent and treat it. Of particular note are biological findings bearing on the origins of obsessive-compulsive disorder, schizophrenia, mood disorders, conduct disorder, attention-deficit/hyperactivity disorder, autistic disorder, and Alzheimer's disease. However, as the saying goes, anatomy is not destiny, and we endeavor to avoid the unwarranted extremes of biological determinism and reductionism as we maintain our focus on a diathesis-stress point of view. Thus, while improved twin and adoption studies as well as new neurochemical findings enhance our appreciation for the somatic contributions to abnormal behavior, considerable variance remains unexplained by these factors. Therefore, we must continue to explore the myriad and complex ways that biological predispositions interact with environmental factors, especially stressors that await us all as we negotiate our way.

Case Studies

The Case Edition of *Abnormal Psychology*, Ninth Edition expands upon the short chapter-opening and in-text cases to provide additional detailed descriptions of a variety of clinical problems. There are eleven (11) cases included, one for each of the disorder chapters. These longer, in-depth case studies provide a foundation on which to organize and further discuss the material in the chapter. The cases are all based on actual clinical situations and focus on problems of specific interest to students. The organization of each case allows students to examine each situation from a variety of perspectives, examine social history, evaluate etiological considerations, and consider alternate theories and treatment approaches when relevant to the case. Discussion and Review sections help the student to review the theoretical content of the chapter in terms of a real world application and offer the students more relevant information on treatment and follow up. This allows for valuable in-class discussion based on the readings.

New to This Edition

The ninth edition has undergone substantial change to the look and layout of the text. You will notice that the book is now formatted in a more open, one-column design with wider margins for placement of photos, illustrations and tables. We believe this will be more inviting and will enhance student readability, thereby making it easier for students to study and take notes.

With over 100 new photos in this edition, we think that student interest will be promoted through being able to see real-world examples and applications of abnormal psychology. Clear and colorful illustrations and tables provide additional visual clarification and explanation for more complex material.

A new feature in this edition is the addition of *DSM-IV-TR Criteria Tables*. These tables, found in margins in Chapters 6–16, provide succinct, bulleted lists of the major criteria cited in the DSM for diagnosing specific disorders. These tables should make it easier for students to remember and distinguish among different conditions.

New and Expanded Coverage

Some of the major new material in this ninth edition includes:

Chapter 1:
New focus on discovery box on harmful dysfunction as an attempt to define mental disorder
Historical evidence that Pinel did not actually free the patients at La Bicêtre

Chapter 4:
New information on ethnic influences on psychological test scores
Stereotype threat as a factor in performance on tests of ability

Chapter 6:
New data on the genetics of phobias
New psychological theories of the etiology of panic attacks
Latest information on the Multisite Comparative Study for the Treatment of Panic Attacks
New material on the etiology of childhood phobias
Emerging data on the potential harmfulness of critical incident stress debriefing

Chapter 7:
Latest information on therapies for somatoform disorders

Chapter 8:
Importance of positive emotions in alleviating the effects of stress
Allostatic load and the risk for illness
Expanded coverage of socioeconomic status, ethnicity, and health
New section on gender and health

Chapter 9:
Updated information on anorexia and depression
Latest details on the role of genetics in eating disorders
Expanded coverage of the relation of serotonin and eating disorders
Self-objectification theory and eating disorders
Expanded coverage of gender, ethnicity, and eating disorders

Chapter 10:
The seriousness of dysthymia
Research on emotion bearing on mood disorders
Recent research on cognitive theories of depression
New material on the interpersonal theory of depression
The behavioral activation system in bipolar disorder
New material on cognitive treatments for depression, including Mindfulness and Behavioral Activation Therapies

Chapter 11:
Latest on etiology of schizophrenia, including clues from early childhood home movies
New information on the possibility that the main brain dysfunction in schizophrenia is a failure of various brain areas to be adequately connected.
The appropriateness of different therapies for different stages of the illness
Latest information on the newer drugs for schizophrenia
New research on cognitive behavior therapy for improving cognitive and social functioning

Chapter 12:
The effects of drugs, especially addicting ones, on the brain
New data on Ecstasy and depletion of serotonin bearing on impairments in learning and memory
Expanded and updated coverage on gender and ethnicity
New data on the pernicious effects of methamphetamine
New biological therapies for substance abuse, e.g., Campral for alcohol abuse
Recent evidence supporting the effectiveness of AA

Recent mass media prevention efforts aimed at youth to discourage cigarette smoking

Chapter 13:
Possible links between schizotypal personality disorder and schizophrenia
The importance of impulsivity in psychopathy
Possible effectiveness of psychotherapy for psychopathy

Chapter 14:
New material on therapies for the paraphilias
Feminist critique of the DSM's views of female sexuality

Chapter 15:
New information on ADHD in girls and differences from boys
Recent evidence on effectiveness of Ritalin in ADHD
Peer influences in the course of ADHD and conduct disorder
Long-term outcomes for different types of conduct disorder
fMRI data on brain dysfunctions in dyslexia and autistic disorder
New data on theory of mind difficulties in autism

Chapter 16:
More evidence on the heritability of some forms of Alzheimer's disease
Emerging evidence of superiority and greater safety of cognitive behavioral and interpersonal psychotherapies over drugs in treating depression in older adults
PTSD in older adults traceable to traumas as long as fifty years earlier

Chapter 17:
Therapist variables in randomized clinical trials research
Aligning practice with science rather than aligning research with practice
Stepped care
New research on countertransference
Equivalence of cognitive therapy and SSRIs in alleviating severe depression
New research in minority mental health

Chapter 18:
Thorough updating of laws bearing on civil and criminal commitment

Special Features for the Student Reader

Several features of this book are designed to make it easier for students to master and enjoy the material; all these elements are designed to make it user friendly.

Focus on Discovery Boxes. There are many in-depth discussions of selected topics encased in Focus boxes throughout the book. This feature allows us to involve the reader in specialized topics in a way that does not detract from the flow of the regular text. Sometimes a Focus box expands on a point in the text; sometimes it deals with an entirely separate but relevant issue, often a controversial one. Reading these boxes with care will deepen the reader's understanding of the subject matter. (For a complete list of Focus boxes, see p. xix.)

Chapter-Opening Cases. The syndrome chapters, 6 through 16, open with extended case illustrations. These accounts provide a clinical context for the theories and research that occupy most of our attention in the chapter and help make vivid the real-life implications of the empirical work of psychopathologists and clinicians.

In-Text Cases. Many case examples are provided throughout the chapters in order to further illustrate some of the concepts.

Chapter Summaries. Summaries, which appear at the end of each chapter, have been completely rewritten in bulleted form. We believe this format will make it easier for readers to review and remember the material. We suggest that the student read it before beginning the chapter itself in order to get a good sense of what lies ahead. Then re-reading the summary after completing the chapter itself will enhance the student's understanding and provide an immediate sense of what has been learned in just one reading of the chapter.

Glossary. When an important term is introduced, it is boldfaced and defined or discussed immediately. Most such terms appear again later in the book, in which case they will not be highlighted in this way. All of these terms are listed again at the end of each chapter and definitions appear at the end of the book in a glossary.

DSM-IV-TR Table. The endpapers of the book contain a summary of the current psychiatric nomenclature found in the text revision of the fourth edition of the Diagnostic and Statistical Manual of Mental Disorders, known as DSM-IV-TR. This provides a handy guide to where particular disorders appear in the "official" taxonomy or classification. We make considerable use of DSM-IV-TR, though in a selective and sometimes critical vein. Sometimes we find it more effective to discuss theory and research on a particular problem in a way that is different from DSM's conceptualization.

References. Our commitment to current and forward-looking scholarship is reflected in the inclusion of more than 1000 new references.

Ancillaries

Several ancillaries have been prepared to enhance and facilitate teaching from this textbook; they are available free to adopters of the text. For details contact your Wiley sales representative or John Wiley and Sons, Inc., Marketing Department. These ancillaries are as follows:

Abnormal Psychology Videotapes, completely updated and revised for the ninth edition, feature short video clips of actual patients, their problems, and the professional care they receive. These interviews cover several of the major disorders discussed in the text.

Instructor's Resource Manual, written by Michael Gann of the Arizona Community Protection and Treatment Center, includes chapter summaries, lecture launchers, perspectives on the causes and treatment of each disorder, key points students should know, key terms, discussion stimulators, and guides to instructional films.

Instructor's Resource CD ROM contains figures from the text, the Instructor's Resource Manual, the Test Bank, and Lecture Notes. This allows the instructor to create a custom classroom presentation.

Test Bank, written by Dean McKay and Steven Tsao of Fordham University, contains nearly 2000 multiple choice questions. It is available in printed form as well as on disc.

Computerized Test Bank (Diploma for Windows; Exam for Mac), an easy-to-use computerized test bank that contains the same questions as the printed version. Instructors can customize exams by adding new questions or editing existing ones.

Study Guide, written by Douglas Hindman of Eastern Kentucky University, can be ordered from Wiley for sale to students. Each chapter includes a summary of the chapter, a list of key concepts, important study questions, and practice tests written in collaboration with the Test Bank author to ensure consistency and to encourage active reading and learning. Students find it to be a very helpful study guide.

Book Web Site (http://www.wiley.com/college/davison) includes an on-line Instructor Resource section and an on-line Student Resource section, as well as active learning links to several interesting sites related to the field of abnormal psychology. On-line Student Quizzes for which students can receive immediate feedback are also on the site.

Transparencies include all figures from the text in a four-color acetate set.

Acknowledgments

It is a pleasure to acknowledge the contributions of a number of colleagues to this ninth edition. Their thoughtful comments and expert feedback have helped us to refine and improve the book. A special thank you goes out to:

David Arnold, *University of Massachusetts*
Jack J. Blanchard, *University of Maryland*
John Burns, *Chicago Medical School*
Laura Heatherington, *Williams College*
Sheri Johnson, *University of Miami*
John Kassel, *University of Illinois at Chicago*
Joni Mihura, *University of Toledo*
Judith Moskowitz, *University of California, San Francisco*
Brady Phelps, *South Dakota State University*
Kathleen M. Pike, *Columbia University*
Judy Rauenzahn, *Kutztown University*
Melanie Domenech Rodriguez, *Utah State University*

Randall Salekin, *University of Alabama*
Carol Terry, *University of Oklahoma*

In addition, we recognize the following reviewers of previous editions, for it was with their assistance that the ninth edition had the strong base on which to build:

Mary Pat Kelly, *University of California-Irvine*; Judith LeMaster, *Scripps College*; David Greenway, *University of Southwestern Louisiana*; Drew Gouvier, *Louisiana State University-Baton Rouge*; Michael R. Hufford, *University of Montana*; C. Chrisman Wilson, *Tulane University*; Kathy Hoff, *Utah State University*; Jose M. Lafosse, *University of Colorado-Denver*; Kent Hutchinson, *University of Colorado*; Tibor Palfai, *Boston University*; Daniel L. Segal, *University of Colorado-Colorado Springs*; Ann Rosen Spector, *Rutgers University*; William T. McReynolds, *The University of Tampa*; Kristine Lynn Brady, *California School of Professional Psychology, San Diego*; Debra Hollister, *Valencia Community College*; Gay Melville, *Trident Technical College*; Joseph Lowman, *University of North Carolina at Chapel Hill*; Mitchell Earleywine, *University of Southern California*; Thomas Bradbury, *University of California, Los Angeles*; Frances K. Grossman, *Boston University*; Brad Schmidt, *Ohio State University*; Cooper Holmes, *Emporia State University*; Christopher Layne, *University of Toledo*; Robert D. Coursey, *University of Maryland*; Larry Jamner, *University of California-Irvine*; Kelly Champion, *Gustavus Adolphus College*; D. Growe, *Oakland Community College*; Robert Higgins, *Oakland University*; Mike Connor, *California State University-Long Beach*; James Linder, *California State University-Long Beach*; Paul Rokke, *North Dakota State University*; William G. Iacono, *University of Minnesota*; J. Tate, *Middle Tennessee State University*; Joanne Lindoerfer, *University of Texas*; John Hall, *LaSalle University*; Benjamin Blanding, *Rowan University*; John Suler, *Rider University*; Christine Gayda, *Stockton College*; Herbert Rappaport, *Temple University*; Davis Burdick, *Stockton College*; Michael Zinser, *University of Wisconsin*; Scott Hamilton, *Colorado State University*; Charles Gelso, *University of Maryland*; Donald Strassberg-Carson, *University of Utah*; James Alexander-Carson, *University of Utah*; Melissa Alderfer, *University of Utah*; Jennifer Skeem, *University of Utah*; Gretchen Gimpel, *Utah State University*; L. Dennis Madrid, *University of Southern Colorado*; James Cameron, *University of Southern Colorado*; Bob Coursey, *University of Southern Colorado*; Gordon D. Atlas, *Alfred University*.

Helpful library research for Chapter 18 was provided at the University of Southern California by Bryan Kelly. Special thanks go to Nadine Recker Rayburn for contributing to the revision of the therapy sections of Chapters 7, 10, and 12; and to Elizabeth Kunda for Chapter 16. Thanks also go to Stephanie Corey and Elizabeth Kunda for work on the References. Several chapters benefitted greatly from library research by Jackie Koch at Stony Brook. Historical material was provided by Arthur C. Houts at the University of Memphis.

We signed on with Wiley in 1971 and over the course of the subsequent revisions have enjoyed the skills and dedication of our "Wiley family"—our Editor Tim Vertovec; Developmental Editors Ellen Ford and Beverly Peavler; Marketing Manager Kate Stewart; Editorial Program Assistant and Supplements Project Editor Kristen Babroski; Production Editor Sandra Dumas; Photo Editor Jennifer MacMillan; Illustration Editor Anna Melhorn; Designer Harry Nolan; and the Outside Production Service, Ingrao Associates. One aspect of our textbook that previous users have liked is its readability and its ability to engage the reader in a collaborative quest with the authors for answers to some of the most perplexing problems facing psychology. From time to time, students and faculty colleagues have written us their comments on the book; these communications are always welcome. Readers can e-mail us: gdaviso@rcf.usc.edu, jneale@hargray.com, kring@socrates.berkeley.edu.

For putting up with occasional limited accessibility and mood swings, and for always being there for moral support, our thanks go to the most important people in our lives: Kathleen Chambers, Eve and Asher Davison (GCD), Gail and Sean Neale (JMN), and to Barbara Jean Beck (AMK), to whom this book is dedicated with love and gratitude. Finally, we have maintained the order of authorship for Davison and Neale as it was for the first edition, decided by the toss of a coin, with the addition of Ann Kring as third author.

DECEMBER 2002
Gerald C. Davison, *Los Angeles, CA*
John M. Neale, *Hilton Head, SC*
Ann M. Kring, *Berkeley, CA*

Brief Contents

Contents

4

Clinical Assessment Procedures   80

5

Research Methods in the Study of Abnormal Behavior   111

6

Anxiety Disorders   133

7

Somatoform and Dissociative Disorders   172

8

Psychophysiological Disorders and Health Psychology   197

9

Eating Disorders   245

10

Mood Disorders   267

17

Outcomes and Issues in Psychological Intervention   564

18

Legal and Ethical Issues   607

Focus on Discovery Boxes

1 Introduction: Historical and Scientific Considerations

Slumping in a comfortable leather chair, Ernest H., a thirty-five-year-old city police officer, looked skeptically at his therapist as he struggled to relate a series of problems. His recent inability to maintain an erection when making love to his wife was the immediate reason for his seeking therapy, but after gentle prodding from the therapist, Ernest recounted a host of other difficulties, some of them dating from his childhood but most of them originating during the previous several years.

Ernest's childhood had not been a happy one. His mother, whom he loved dearly, died suddenly when he was only six, and for the next ten years he lived either with his father or with a maternal aunt. His father drank heavily, seldom managing to get through any day without some alcohol. Moreover, the man's moods were extremely variable; he had even spent several months in a state hospital with a diagnosis of manic-depressive psychosis. His father's income was so irregular that he could seldom pay bills on time or afford to live in any but the most run-down neighborhoods. At times Ernest's father was totally incapable of caring for himself, let alone his son. Ernest would then spend weeks, sometimes months, with his aunt in a nearby suburb.

Despite these apparent handicaps, Ernest completed high school and entered the tuition-free city university. He earned his miscellaneous living expenses by waiting tables at a small restaurant. During these college years his psychological problems began to concern him. He often became profoundly depressed for no apparent reason, and these bouts of sadness were sometimes followed by periods of manic elation. His lack of control over these mood swings troubled him greatly, for he had observed this same pattern in his alcoholic father. He also felt an acute self-consciousness with people who he felt had authority over him—his boss, his professors, and even some of his classmates, with whom he compared himself unfavorably. Ernest was especially sensitive about his clothes, which were old and worn compared with those of his peers; their families had more money than his. It was on the opening day of classes in his junior year that he first saw his future wife. When the tall, slender young woman moved to her seat with grace and self-assurance, his were not the only eyes that followed her. Ernest spent the rest of that semester watching her from afar, taking care to sit where he could glance over at her without being conspicuous. Then one day, as they and the other students were leaving class, they bumped into each other quite by accident, and her warmth and charm emboldened him to ask her to join him for some coffee. When she said yes, he almost wished she had not.

Amazingly enough, as he saw it, they soon fell in love, and before the end of his senior year they were married. Ernest could never quite believe that his wife, as intelligent as she was beautiful, really cared for him. As the years wore on, his doubts about himself and about her feelings toward him would continue to grow.

He hoped to enter law school, and both his grades and his scores on the law-school boards made these plans a possibility, but he decided instead to enter the police academy. The reasons that he related to his therapist had to do with doubts about his intellectual abilities as well as his increasing uneasiness in situations in which he felt himself being evaluated. Seminars had become unbearable for Ernest in his last year in college, and he had hopes that the badge and uniform of a police officer would give him the instant recognition and respect that he seemed incapable of earning on his own.

To help him get through the academy, his wife quit college at the end of her junior year, despite Ernest's pleas, and sought a secretarial job. He felt she was far brighter than he and saw no reason why she should sacrifice her potential to help him make his way in life. But at the same time he recognized the fiscal realities and grudgingly accepted her financial support.

The police academy proved to be even more stressful than college. Ernest's mood swings, although less frequent, still troubled him. And like his father, who was now confined to a state mental hospital, he drank to ease his psychological pain. He felt that his instructors considered him a fool when he had difficulty standing up in front of the class to give an answer that he himself knew was correct. But he made it through the physical, intellectual, and social rigors of the academy and was assigned to foot patrol in one of the wealthier sections of the city.

Several years later, when it seemed that life should be getting easier, he found himself in even greater turmoil. Now thirty-two years old, with a fairly secure job that paid reasonably well, he began to think of starting a family. His wife wanted this as well, and it was at this time that his problems with erectile dysfunction began. He thought at first it was the alcohol—he was drinking at least six ounces of bourbon every night except when on the swing shift. Soon, though, he began to wonder whether he was actually avoiding the responsibility of having a child, and later he began to doubt that his wife really found him attractive and desirable. The more understanding and patient she was about his sometimes frantic efforts to consummate sex with her, the less manly he felt he was. He was unable to accept help from his wife, for he did not believe that this was the right way to maintain a sexual relationship. The problems in bed spread to other areas of their lives. The less often they made love, the more suspicious he was of his wife, for she had become even more beautiful and vibrant as she entered her thirties. In addition, she had been promoted to the position of administrative assistant at the law firm where she worked. She would mention—perhaps to taunt him—long, martini-filled lunches with her boss at a posh uptown restaurant.

The impetus for contacting the therapist was an ugly argument with his wife one evening when she came home from work after ten. Ernest had been agitated for several days. To combat his fear that he was losing control, he had consumed almost a full bottle of bourbon each night. By the time his wife walked in the door on that final evening, Ernest was already very drunk, and he attacked her both verbally and physically about her alleged infidelity. In her own anger and fear she questioned his masculinity in striking a woman and taunted him with the disappointments of their lovemaking. Ernest stormed out of the house, spent the night at a local bar, and the next day somehow pulled himself together enough to seek professional help.

Every day of our lives we try to understand other people. Even when their behavior is not as extreme as Ernest's, determining why another person does or feels something is a difficult task. Indeed, we do not always understand why we ourselves feel and behave as we do. Acquiring insight into what we consider normal, expected behavior is difficult enough; understanding human behavior that is beyond the normal range, such as the behavior of the police officer just described, is even more difficult.

This book is concerned with the whole range of abnormality, its description, its causes, and its treatment. We face numerous challenges in this field. Foremost, we must have a tolerance for ambiguity, an ability to be comfortable with tentative, often conflicting information. Then, of course, we must have the endurance to work with that information, to study and research it. As you will see, the human mind remains elusive; we know with certainty much less about our field than we would like. As we approach the study of **psychopathology**, the field concerned with the nature and development of abnormal behavior, thoughts, and feelings, we do well to keep in mind that the subject offers few hard and fast answers. Yet, as will become evident when we discuss our orientation toward scientific inquiry, the study of psychopathology is no less worthwhile because of its ambiguities. The kinds of questions asked, rather than the specific answers to those questions, constitute the essence of the field.

Another challenge we face in studying abnormal psychology is to remain objective. Our subject matter, human behavior, is personal and powerfully affecting, making objectivity difficult but no less necessary. The pervasiveness and disturbing effects of abnormal behavior intrude on our own lives. Who has not experienced irrational thoughts, fantasies, and feelings? Who has not felt profound sadness, even depression, that is more extreme than circumstances can explain? Many have known someone, a friend or perhaps a relative, whose behavior was upsetting and impossible to fathom, and realize how frustrating and frightening it is to try to understand and help a person suffering psychological difficulties. Even if you have had no personal experience with the extremes of abnormal behavior, you have probably been affected by reports in the news of terrifying actions of a person described as mentally disturbed who is found to have had a history of mental instability or even to have been confined at some time in a mental hospital.

Our closeness to the subject matter adds to its intrinsic fascination; undergraduate courses in abnormal psychology are among the most popular in psychology departments and indeed in the entire college curriculum. Our feeling of familiarity with the subject matter encourages us to study abnormal psychology, but it has one distinct disadvantage. All of us bring to our study preconceived notions of what the subject matter is. We have developed certain ways of thinking and talking about behavior, certain words and concepts that somehow seem to fit. For example, we may believe that a useful way to study fear is to focus on the immediate experience of fear, known as a phenomenological approach. This is one way of viewing fear, but it is not the only way.

As behavioral scientists we have to grapple with the difference between what we may feel is the appropriate way to talk about human behavior and experience and what may be a more productive way of defining it in order to study and learn about it. When most people would speak of a "feeling of terror," for example, scientists studying fear might be more inclined to use a phrase such as "fear response of great magnitude." In doing so we would not merely be playing verbal games. The concepts and verbal labels we use to study abnormal behavior scientifically must be free of the subjective feelings of appropriateness ordinarily attached to certain human phenomena. As you read this book and try to understand the mental disorders it discusses, we may be asking you to adopt frames of reference different from those to which you are accustomed, and indeed different from those we ourselves use when we are not wearing our professional hats.

The case study with which this chapter began is open to a wide range of interpretations. No doubt you have some ideas about how Ernest's problems developed, what his primary difficulties are, and perhaps even how you might try to help him. We know of no greater intellectual or emotional challenge than deciding both how to conceptualize the life of a person with psychological problems and how best to treat him or her. In Chapter 2 we will refer again to the case of Ernest H. to illustrate how clinicians from different theoretical orientations might describe him and try to help him.

Now we turn to a discussion of what we mean by the term abnormal behavior. Then we look briefly at how our view of abnormality has evolved through history to the more scientific perspectives of today.

What Is Abnormal Behavior?

One of the more difficult challenges facing those in the field of abnormal psychology is to define **abnormal behavior**. Here we consider several characteristics that have been proposed as components of abnormal behavior. We will see that no single one is adequate, although each has merit and captures some part of what might be the full definition. Consequently, abnormality is usually determined based on the presence of several characteristics at one time. Our best definition of abnormal behavior takes into account the characteristics of statistical infrequency, violation of norms, personal distress, disability or dysfunction, and unexpectedness.

Statistical Infrequency

One aspect of abnormal behavior is that it is infrequent. For example, episodes of depression and mania such as those Ernest experienced occur in only about 1 percent of the population. The **normal curve**, or bell-shaped curve, places the majority of people in the middle as far as any particular characteristic is concerned; very few people fall at either extreme. An assertion that a person is normal implies that he or she does not deviate much from the average in a particular trait or behavior pattern.

Statistical infrequency is used explicitly in diagnosing mental retardation. Figure 1.1 shows the normal distribution of intelligence quotient (IQ) measures in the population. Though a number of criteria are used to diagnose mental retardation, low intelligence is a principal one (see p. 498). When an individual's IQ is below 70, his or her intellectual functioning is considered sufficiently subnormal to be designated as mental retardation.

Although some infrequent behaviors or characteristics of people do strike us as abnormal, in some instances the relationship breaks down. Having great athletic ability is infrequent, but few would regard it as part of the field of abnormal psychology. Only certain infrequent behaviors, such as experiencing hallucinations or deep depression, fall into the domain considered in this book. Unfortunately, the statistical component gives us little guidance in determining which infrequent behaviors psychopathologists should study.

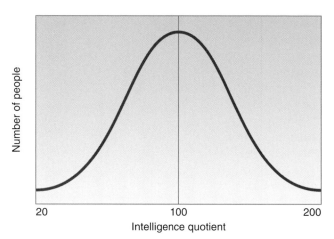

Figure 1.1   The distribution of intelligence among adults, illustrating a normal, or bell-shaped curve.

Violation of Norms

Another characteristic to consider when determining abnormality is whether the behavior violates social norms or threatens or makes anxious those observing it. Ernest's verbal and physical attacks on his wife illustrate this criterion. The antisocial behavior of the psychopath also fits the definition, as do the obsessive-compulsive person's complex rituals and the psychotic patient's conversations with imaginary voices. Yet this component also is at once too broad and too narrow. Criminals and prostitutes violate social norms but are not usually studied within the domain of abnormal psychology; and the highly anxious person, who is generally regarded as a central character in the field of abnormal psychology, typically does not violate social norms and would not be bothersome to many lay observers.

In addition, cultural diversity can affect how people view social norms—what is the norm in one culture may be abnormal in another. This subtle issue is addressed throughout the book (see especially Chapter 4, pp. 105–107).

Personal Distress

Another characteristic of some forms of abnormality is personal suffering; that is, behavior is abnormal if it creates great distress and torment in the person experiencing it. Ernest's self-consciousness and distress about being evaluated illustrate this criterion. Personal distress clearly fits many of the forms of abnormality considered in this book—people experiencing anxiety disorders and depression truly suffer greatly. But some disorders do not necessarily involve distress. The psychopath, for example, treats others coldheartedly and may continually violate the law without experiencing any guilt,

Personal distress such as that shown in this photo, is also part of the definition of abnormal behavior, but unlike grief, which is an expected response to losing a loved one, the distress most relevant to psychopathology is not expected given the situation in which it occurs.

remorse, or anxiety whatsoever. And not all forms of distress—for example, hunger or the pain of childbirth—seem to belong to the field.

Disability or Behavioral Dysfunction

Disability, that is, whether the individual is impaired in some important area of life (e.g., work or personal relationships) because of the abnormality, can also be a component of abnormal behavior. The disruption of Ernest's marital relationship fits this criterion. Substance-use disorders are also defined in part by the social or occupational disability (e.g., poor work performance, serious arguments with one's spouse) created by substance abuse. Similarly, a phobia can produce both distress and disability, for example, if a severe fear of flying prevents someone from taking a job promotion. Like suffering, though, disability applies to some, but not all, disorders. For example, transvestism (cross-dressing for sexual pleasure), which is currently diagnosed as a mental disorder if it distresses the person, is not necessarily a disability. Most transvestites are married, lead conventional lives, and usually cross-dress in private. Other characteristics that might in some circumstances be considered disabilities—such as being short if you want to be a professional basketball player—do not fall within the domain of abnormal psychology. As with distress, we do not have a rule that tells us which disabilities belong and which do not.

Unexpectedness

We have just described how not all distress or disability falls into the domain of abnormal psychology. Distress and disability are often considered abnormal when they are unexpected responses to environmental stressors (Wakefield, 1992). For example, an anxiety disorder is diagnosed when the anxiety is unexpected and out of proportion to the situation, as when a person who is well-off worries constantly about his or her financial situation. Hunger, on the other hand, is an expected response to not eating and thus would be excluded as a state of distress that is relevant to abnormal behavior. Ernest was experiencing some life stress, but many people do so without developing psychological problems.

Abnormal behavior frequently produces disability or dysfunction. But some diagnoses, such as transvestitism, are not clearly disabilities. Shown here is Thailand's Miss Transvestite.

We have considered here several key characteristics of a definition of abnormal behavior. (See Focus on Discovery 1.1 for a controversial perspective on defining abnormality.) Again, none by itself yields a fully satisfactory definition, but together they offer a useful framework for beginning to define abnormality.

Keep in mind too that what we present in a text such as this are human problems that are currently considered abnormal. The disorders we discuss will undoubtedly change

Focus on Discovery 1.1

Wakefield's Harmful Dysfunction Concept

In an influential and widely discussed paper, Wakefield (1992) proposed that mental disorders can be defined as **harmful dysfunctions**. It is important to note that this definition has two parts: a value judgment—this is the "harmful" part of the definition—and an objective, scientific component—the "dysfunction" part.

Mental disorders are defined, in part, by Wakefield as behaviors that are harmful. Clearly, a judgment that a behavior is harmful requires some standard and this standard is likely to depend on sociocultural values. Dysfunctions are said to occur when an internal mechanism is unable to perform the function for which it was designed by evolution. By grounding this part of the definition in evolutionary theory, Wakefield hoped to provide an objective, scientific component to the definition of mental disorder.

In medicine, dysfunctions can often be identified in a rather straightforward manner. For example, clogged arteries impede blood flow and give rise to cardiovascular disease. Arteries evolved to carry blood, and clogging is therefore a failure of arteries to perform their natural function. (Cardiovascular disease is also harmful and so fits both of Wakefield's criteria.) The critical question is whether dysfunction is so easily and objectively defined in the field of mental disorders.

Numerous critics have argued that it is not (e.g., Houts, 2001; Kirmayer & Young, 1999; Lilienfeld & Marino, 1999).

One difficulty is that with mental disorders we do not know exactly what the dysfunctions are. The mental or biological mechanisms that are not functioning properly are largely unknown. Wakefield (1999) has acknowledged this point, in part, referring to plausible dysfunctions rather than proven ones. We indeed have some hypotheses about possible dysfunctional mechanisms (for example, depression results from excessive self blame; schizophrenia is due to excess dopamine activity), but the dysfunctions that may be related to mental disorders are certainly not of the same scientific status as those of medicine. And we also have the problem of deciding what is plausible and what is not. Therefore, we have a situation in which we judge a behavior or set of behaviors to be harmful, do not know the cause, and then decide it is a mental disorder because we believe there must be a malfunction of some internal mechanism (that is, a dysfunction is present). Contrary to Wakefield's contention, the concept of dysfunction is an hypothesis and does not provide an objective, scientific definition of mental disorder.

with time. Because the field is continually evolving, it is not possible to offer a simple definition of abnormality that captures it in its entirety. The characteristics presented constitute a partial definition, but they are not equally applicable to every diagnosis.

History of Psychopathology

As psychopathologists we are interested in the causes of deviant behavior. The search for causes has gone on for a considerable period of time.

Before the age of scientific inquiry, all good and bad manifestations of power beyond the control of humankind—eclipses, earthquakes, storms, fire, serious and disabling diseases, the passing of the seasons—were regarded as supernatural. Behavior seemingly outside individual control was subject to similar interpretation. Many early philosophers, theologians, and physicians who studied the troubled mind believed that deviancy reflected the displeasure of the gods or possession by demons.

Early Demonology

The doctrine that an evil being, such as the devil, may dwell within a person and control his or her mind and body is called **demonology**. Examples of demonological thinking are found in the records of the early Chinese, Egyptians, Babylonians, and Greeks. Among the Hebrews deviancy was attributed to possession of the person by bad spirits, after God in his wrath had withdrawn protection. Christ is reported to have cured a man with an unclean spirit by casting out the devils from within him and hurling them onto a herd of swine (Mark 5:8–13).

Following from the belief that abnormal behavior was caused by possession, its treatment often involved **exorcism**, the casting out of evil spirits by ritualistic chanting or torture. Exorcism typically took the form of elaborate rites of prayer, noisemaking, forcing the afflicted to drink terrible-tasting brews, and on occasion more extreme measures, such as flogging and starvation, to render the body uninhabitable to devils.

Somatogenesis

In the fifth century B.C., Hippocrates (460?–377? B.C.), often regarded as the father of modern medicine, separated medicine from religion, magic, and superstition. He rejected the prevailing Greek belief that the gods sent serious physical diseases and mental disturbances as punishment and insisted instead that such illnesses had natural causes and hence should be treated like other, more common maladies, such as colds and constipation. Hippocrates regarded the brain as the organ of consciousness, of intellectual life, and emotion; thus he thought that deviant thinking and behavior were indications of some kind of brain pathology. Hippocrates is often considered one of the very earliest proponents of **somatogenesis**—the notion that something wrong

Painting of Christ driving evil spirits out of a possessed man.

with the soma, or physical body, disturbs thought and action. **Psychogenesis**, in contrast, is the belief that a disturbance has psychological origins.

Hippocrates classified mental disorders into three categories: mania, melancholia, and phrenitis, or brain fever. Through his teachings the phenomena of abnormal behavior became more clearly the province of physicians rather than of priests. The treatments Hippocrates suggested were quite different from exorcistic tortures. For melancholia, for example, he prescribed tranquillity, sobriety, care in choosing food and drink, and abstinence from sexual activity. Such a regimen was assumed to have a healthful effect on the brain and the body. Because Hippocrates believed in natural rather than supernatural causes, he depended on his own keen observations and made a valuable contribution as a clinician. He also left behind remarkably detailed records describing many of the symptoms now recognized in epilepsy, alcoholic delusion, stroke, and paranoia.

Hippocrates believed that normal brain functioning, and therefore mental health, depended on a delicate balance among four humors, or fluids of the body, namely, blood, black bile, yellow bile, and phlegm. An imbalance produced disorders. If a person was sluggish and dull, for example, the body supposedly contained a preponderance of phlegm. A preponderance of black bile was the explanation for melancholia; too much yellow bile explained irritability and anxiousness; and too much blood, changeable temperament.

Hippocrates' humoral physiology, of course, did not withstand later scientific scrutiny. However, his basic premise—that human behavior is markedly affected by bodily structures or substances and that abnormal behavior is produced by some kind of physical imbalance or even damage—did foreshadow aspects of contemporary thought. In the next seven centuries, Hippocrates' naturalistic approach to disorder was generally accepted by other Greeks as well as by the Romans, who adopted the medicine of the Greeks after their city became the seat of power in the ancient European world.

The Dark Ages and Demonology

In a massive generalization historians have often suggested that the death of Galen (A.D. 130–200), the second-century Greek who is regarded as the last major physician of the classical era, marked the beginning of the Dark Ages for western European medicine and for the treatment and investigation of abnormal behavior. Over several centuries of decay, Greek and Roman civilization ceased to be. The churches gained in influence, and the papacy was declared independent of the state. Christian monasteries, through their missionary and educational work, replaced physicians as healers and as authorities on mental disorder.[1]

The Greek physician Hippocrates held a somatogenic view of abnormal behavior, considering psychopathology a disease of the brain.

---

[1] The generalization we have just offered applies to Western civilization. The teachings of Galen continued to be influential in the Islamic world. For example, the Persian physician al-Razi (865–925) established a unit for the treatment of the mentally ill in Baghdad and was an early practitioner of psychotherapy.

The monasteries cared for and nursed the sick; a few were repositories for the classic Greek medical manuscripts, even though they may not have made use of the knowledge within these works. When monks cared for the mentally disordered, they prayed over them and touched them with relics or they concocted fantastic potions for them to drink in the waning phase of the moon. The families of the deranged might take them to shrines. Many of the mentally ill roamed the countryside, becoming more and more bedraggled and losing more and more of their faculties.

The Persecution of Witches   During the thirteenth and the following few centuries, a populace that was already suffering from social unrest and recurrent famines and plagues turned to demonology to explain these disasters. People in Europe become obsessed with the devil. Witchcraft, now viewed as instigated by Satan, was seen as a heresy and a denial of God. Then, as today, faced with inexplicable and frightening occurrences, people tended to seize on whatever explanation was available. The times conspired to heap enormous blame on those regarded as witches, and these unfortunates were persecuted with great zeal.

In the dunking test, if the woman did not drown, she was thought to be in league with the devil, the ultimate no-win situation.

In 1484, Pope Innocent VIII exhorted the clergy of Europe to leave no stone unturned in the search for witches. He sent two Dominican monks to northern Germany as inquisitors. Two years later they issued a comprehensive and explicit manual, *Malleus Maleficarum* ("the witches' hammer"), to guide the witch hunts. This legal and theological document came to be regarded by Catholics and Protestants alike as a textbook on witchcraft. Those accused of witchcraft should be tortured if they did not confess; those convicted and penitent were to be imprisoned for life; and those convicted and unrepentant were to be handed over to the law for execution. The manual specified that a person's sudden loss of reason was a symptom of demonic possession and that burning was the usual method of driving out the supposed demon. Although records of the period are not reliable, over the next several centuries it is thought that hundreds of thousands of women, men, and children were accused, tortured, and put to death.

Witchcraft and Mental Illness   For some time, modern-day investigators believed that the mentally ill of the later Middle Ages were considered witches (Zilboorg & Henry, 1941). In their confessions the accused sometimes reported having had intercourse with the devil and having flown to sabbats, the secret meetings of their cults. These reports have been interpreted by some writers as delusions or hallucinations and thus are taken to indicate that some of the so-called witches were psychotic.

More detailed examination of this historical period, however, indicates that most of the accused were not mentally ill. Careful analyses of the witch hunts reveal that although some accused witches were mentally disturbed, many more sane than insane people were tried. The delusion-like confessions were typically obtained during brutal torture; words were put on the tongues of the tortured by their accusers and by the beliefs of the times. Indeed, in England, where torture was not allowed, the confessions did not usually contain descriptions indicative of delusions or hallucinations (Schoeneman, 1977).

Evaluations of other sources of information also indicate that witchcraft was not the primary interpretation of mental illness. From the thirteenth century on, as the cities of Europe grew larger, hospitals began to come under secular jurisdiction. Municipal authorities, gaining in power, tended to supplement or take over some of the activities of the church, one of these being the care of the ill. The foundation deed for the Holy Trinity Hospital in Salisbury, England, dating from the mid-fourteenth century, specified the purposes of the hospital, among them that the "mad are kept safe until they are restored of reason." English laws during this period allowed both the dangerously insane and the incompetent to be confined in a hospital. Notably, the people who were confined were not described as being possessed (Allderidge, 1979).

Beginning in the thirteenth century, lunacy trials to determine a person's sanity were held in England. The trials were conducted under the Crown's right to protect the mentally impaired, and a judgment of insanity allowed the Crown to become guardian of the lunatic's estate (Neugebauer, 1979). The defendant's orientation, memory, intellect, daily life, and habits were at issue in the trial. Explanations for strange behavior typically linked it to physical illness or injury or to some emotional shock. In all the cases that Neugebauer examined, only one referred to demonological possession. The preponderance of evidence thus indicates that this explanation of mental disturbance was not as dominant during the Middle Ages as was once thought.

Development of Asylums

Until the end of the Crusades in the fifteenth century there were very few mental hospitals in Europe, although there were many hospitals for lepers. In the twelfth century, England and Scotland had 220 leprosy hospitals for a population of a million and a half. After the principal Crusades had been waged, leprosy gradually disappeared from Europe, probably because with the end of the wars came a break with the eastern sources of the infection. With leprosy no longer of such great social concern and many hospitals available, attention seems to have turned to the mad.

Confinement of the mentally ill began in earnest in the fifteenth and sixteenth centuries. Leprosariums were converted to **asylums**, refuges established for the confinement and care of the mentally ill. Many of these asylums took in a mixed lot of disturbed people and beggars. Beggars were regarded as a great social problem at the time; in sixteenth-century Paris the population of fewer than 100,000 included 30,000 beggars (Foucault, 1965). These asylums had no specific regimen for their inmates other than to get them to work, but during the same period hospitals geared more specifically for the confinement of the mentally ill also emerged.

Bethlehem and Other Early Asylums   The Priory of St. Mary of Bethlehem was founded in 1243. By 1403 it housed six mentally ill men, and in 1547, Henry VIII handed it over to the city of London, thereafter to be a hospital devoted solely to the confinement of the mentally ill. The conditions in Bethlehem were deplorable. Over the years the word bedlam, a contraction and popular name for this hospital, became a descriptive term for a place or scene of wild uproar and confusion. Bethlehem eventually became one of London's great tourist attractions, by the eighteenth century rivaling both Westminster Abbey and the Tower of London. Even as late as the nineteenth century, viewing the violent patients and their antics was considered entertainment, and tickets of admission to Bedlam were sold. Similarly, in the Lunatics Tower constructed in Vienna in 1784, patients were confined in the spaces between inner square rooms and the outer walls, where they could be viewed by passersby. The first mental hospital in what would become the United States was founded in Williamsburg, Virginia, in 1773.

It should not be assumed that the inclusion of abnormal behavior within the domain of hospitals and medicine necessarily led to more humane and effective treatment. Medical treatments were often crude and painful. Benjamin

A tour of St. Mary's of Bethlehem (Bedlam) provides amusement for these two upper-class women in Hogarth's eighteenth-century painting.

Rush (1745–1813), who began practicing medicine in Philadelphia in 1769 and was deeply involved in his country's struggle for independence, is considered the father of American psychiatry. He believed that mental disorder was caused by an excess of blood in the brain. Consequently, his favored treatment was to draw from disordered individuals great quantities of blood (Farina, 1976)!

Rush entertained another hypothesis, that many "lunatics" could be cured by being frightened. In one recommended procedure the physician was to convince the patient of his or her impending death. A New England doctor of the nineteenth century implemented this prescription in an ingenious manner. "On his premises stood a tank of water, into which a patient, packed into a coffin-like box pierced with holes, was lowered.... He was kept under water until the bubbles of air ceased to rise, after which he was taken out, rubbed, and revived—if he had not already passed beyond reviving!" (Deutsch, 1949, p. 82).

Pinel's Reforms   Philippe Pinel (1745–1826) has often been considered a primary figure in the movement for humanitarian treatment of the mentally ill in asylums. In 1793, while the French Revolution raged, he was put in charge of a large asylum in Paris known as La Bicêtre. A historian described the conditions at this particular hospital:

> [The patients were] shackled to the walls of their cells, by iron collars which held them flat against the wall and permitted little movement.... They could not lie down at night, as a rule.... Oftentimes there was a hoop of iron around the waist of the patient and in addition...chains on both the hands and the feet.... These chains [were] sufficiently long so that the patient could feed himself out of a bowl, the food usually being a mushy gruel—bread soaked in a weak soup. Since little was known about dietetics, [no attention] was paid to the type of diet given the patients. They were presumed to be animals...and not to care whether the food was good or bad. (Selling, 1940, p. 54)

Pinel's freeing of the patients at La Bicêtre is often considered to mark the beginning of more humanitarian treatment of people with mental illness.

Many texts assert that Pinel removed the chains of the people imprisoned in La Bicêtre, an event that even became memorialized in some famous paintings. Pinel is said to have begun to treat the inmates as sick human beings rather than as beasts. Many who had been completely unmanageable became calm and much easier to handle. Formerly considered dangerous, they strolled through the hospital and grounds with no inclination to create disturbances or to harm anyone. Light and airy rooms replaced dungeons. Some patients who had been incarcerated for years were apparently restored to health and eventually discharged from the hospital.

Historical research, however, indicates that Pinel did not actually release the patients from their chains. That action was actually taken by a former patient, Jean-Baptiste Pussin, who had become an orderly at the hospital. In fact, Pinel was not even present when the patients were released (Weiner, 1994). Several years later, though, Pinel did praise the efforts of the orderly and began to follow the same practices.

Consistent with the egalitarianism of the new French Republic, Pinel came to believe that the mental patients in his care were essentially normal people who should be approached with compassion and understanding and treated with dignity as individual human beings. He surmised that if their reason had left them because of severe personal and social problems, it might be restored to them through comforting counsel and purposeful activity.

For all the good Pinel did for people with mental illness, however, he was not a complete paragon of enlightenment and egalitarianism. The more humanitarian treatment he reserved for the upper classes; patients of the lower classes were still subjected to terror and coercion as a means of control. Straitjackets replaced the shackles that had formally been used.

Moral Treatment   For a time following the humanitarian changes in La Bicêtre, the hospitals established in Europe and the United States were relatively small and privately supported. A prominent merchant and Quaker, William Tuke (1732–1822), shocked by the conditions at York Asylum in England, proposed to the Society of Friends that it found its own institution. In 1796, York Retreat was established on a country estate. It provided mentally ill patients with a quiet and religious atmosphere in which to live, work, and rest. Patients discussed their difficulties with attendants, worked in the garden, and took walks through the countryside.

In the United States the Friends' Asylum, founded in 1817 in Pennsylvania, and the Hartford Retreat, established in 1824 in Connecticut, were patterned after the York Retreat. Other U.S. hospitals were influenced by the sympathetic and attentive treatment provided by Pinel and Tuke. In accordance with this approach, which became known as **moral treatment**, patients had close contact with attendants, who talked and read to them and encouraged them to engage in purposeful activity; residents led lives as normally as possible and in general took responsibility for themselves within the constraints of their disorders.

Despite these seemingly positive features, two less favorable findings emerged from a review of detailed case records of the York Retreat from 1880 to 1884 (Renvoise & Beveridge, 1989). First, drugs were the most common treatment and included alcohol, cannabis, opium, and chloral hydrate (knockout drops). Second, the outcomes were not very favorable; fewer than one-third of the patients were discharged as improved or recovered.

Moral treatment was largely abandoned in the latter part of the nineteenth century. Ironically, the efforts of Dorothea Dix (1802–1887), a crusader for improved conditions for people with mental illness who fought to have hospitals created for their care, helped effect this change. Dix, a Boston schoolteacher, taught a Sunday-school class at the local prison and was shocked at the deplorable conditions in which the inmates lived. Her interest spread to the conditions of mental hospitals and to the mentally ill people of the time who had nowhere to go for treatment. Dix campaigned vigorously to improve the lot of people with mental illness; she personally helped see that thirty-two state hospitals were built. These large, public hospitals took in the many patients whom the private ones could not accommodate. Unfortunately, the staffs of these new hospitals were unable to provide the individual attention that was a hallmark of moral treatment (Bockhoven, 1963). Moreover, the hospitals came to be administered by physicians, who were interested in the biological aspects of illness and in the physical, rather than the psychological, well-being of mental patients. The money that once paid the salaries of personal attendants now paid for equipment and laboratories. See Focus on Discovery 1.2 for an examination of the conditions in today's mental institutions.

In the nineteenth century, Dorothea Dix played a major role in establishing more mental hospitals in the United States.

The Beginning of Contemporary Thought

Recall that in the West, the death of Galen and the decline of Greco-Roman civilization temporarily ended inquiries into the nature of both physical and mental illness. Not until the late Middle Ages did any new facts begin to emerge. These facts were discovered thanks to an emerging empirical approach to medical science, which gathered knowledge by direct observation. One development that fostered progress was the discovery by the Flemish anatomist and physician Vesalius (1514–1564) that Galen's presentation of human anatomy was incorrect. Galen had presumed that human physiology mirrored that of the apes he studied. It took more than a thousand years for autopsy studies of humans—not allowed during his time—to begin to prove that Galen was wrong. Further progress came from the efforts of the English physician Thomas Sydenham (1624–1689). Sydenham was particularly successful in advocating an empirical approach to classification and diagnosis that subsequently influenced those interested in mental disorders.

Galen was a Greek physician, who followed Hippocrate's ideas, and is regarded as the last major physician of the classical era.

The Mental Hospital Today

Each year over two million Americans are hospitalized for mental disorders. In the 1970s concerns about the restrictive nature of confinement in a mental hospital led to the deinstitutionalization of a large number of mental hospital patients. Budget cuts in the 1980s and 1990s caused this trend to continue. But the problems of the chronic patient, who cannot be deinstitutionalized, have yet to be handled adequately (as we will discuss in more detail in Chapter 18). Treatment in public mental institutions is primarily custodial in nature. Patients are kept alive in a protected environment, but they receive little treatment; their existence is monotonous and sedentary for the most part.

Mental hospitals in the United States today are usually funded either by the federal government or by the state. (In fact, the term state hospital is taken to mean a mental hospital run by the state.) Despite their staggering costs they are often old, grim, and somewhat removed from major metropolitan centers. Many Veterans Administration hospitals and general medical hospitals also contain psychiatric wards.

In addition, there are private mental hospitals. Sheppard and Enoch Pratt near Baltimore, Maryland, and McLean Hospital, in Belmont, Massachusetts, are two of the most famous. The physical facilities and professional care in private hospitals tend to be superior to those of state hospitals for one reason: the private hospitals have more money. The costs to patients in these private institutions can exceed $1,000 per day and yet may not include individual therapy sessions with a member of the professional staff! Although many patients have medical insurance, usually with a ninety-day limit, such hospitals are clearly beyond the means of most citizens.

A somewhat specialized mental hospital, sometimes called a prison hospital, is reserved for people who have been arrested and judged unable to stand trial and for those who have been acquitted of a crime by reason of insanity (see p. 608). Although these patients

have not been sent to prison, armed guards and tight security regiment their lives. Treatment of some kind is supposed to take place during their incarceration.

Even in the best hospitals patients usually have precious little contact with psychiatrists or clinical psychologists, a situation confirmed by the careful observations of Gordon Paul and his co-workers.

Most dormitory rooms at state mental hospitals are bleak and unstimulating.

An Early System of Classification   One of those impressed by Sydenham's approach was a German physician, Wilhelm Griesinger, who insisted that any diagnosis of mental disorder specify a biological cause, a clear return to the somatogenic views first espoused by Hippocrates. A textbook of psychiatry, written by Griesinger's well-known follower Emil Kraepelin (1856–1926) and first published in 1883, furnished a classification system in an attempt to establish the biological nature of mental illnesses.

Kraepelin discerned among mental disorders a tendency for a certain group of symptoms, called a **syndrome**, to appear together regularly enough to be regarded as having an underlying physical cause, much as a particular medical disease and its syndrome may be attributed to a biological dysfunction. He regarded each mental illness as distinct from all others, having its own genesis, symptoms, course, and outcome. Even though cures had not been worked out, at least the course of the disease could be predicted.

Kraepelin proposed two major groups of severe mental diseases: dementia praecox, an early term for schizophrenia, and manic-depressive psychosis. He postulated a chemical imbalance as the cause of schizophrenia and an irregularity in metabolism as the explanation of manic-depressive psychosis. Kraepelin's scheme for classifying these and other mental illnesses became the basis for the present diagnostic categories, which are described more fully in Chapter 3.

These investigators found that most patients had no contact with staff for 80 to 90 percent of their waking hours and that the clinical staff spent less than one-fourth of their working time in contact with patients (Paul, 1987, 1988). Most of a patient's days and evenings are spent either alone or in the company of other patients and of aides, individuals who may not have very extensive training. As with imprisonment, the overwhelming feeling is of helplessness and depersonalization. Patients sit for endless hours in hallways waiting for dining halls to open, for medication to be dispensed, and for consultations with psychologists, social workers, and vocational counselors to begin. Except for the most severely disturbed, patients do have access to the various facilities of a hospital, ranging from woodworking shops to swimming pools, from gymnasiums to basket-weaving shops.

Most hospitals require patients to attend group therapy—here, a general term indicating only that at least two patients are supposed to relate to each other and to a group leader in a room for a specific period of time. Some patients have a few sessions alone with a professional therapist. For the most part, however, traditional hospital treatment over the past forty years has been oriented toward dispensing drugs rather than offering psychotherapy. The institutional setting itself is used as a way to provide supportive care, to try to ensure that patients take their medication, and to protect and look after patients whose conditions make it virtually impossible for them to care for themselves or that render them an unreasonable burden or threat to others (Paul & Menditto, 1992).

One nagging problem is that institutionalization is difficult to reverse once people have resided in mental hospitals for more than a year. We recall asking a patient who had improved markedly over the previous several months why he was reluctant to be discharged. "Doc," he said earnestly, "it's a jungle out there." Although we cannot entirely disagree with his view, there are at least a few advantages to living on the outside; yet this man—a veteran and chronic patient with a clinical folder more than two feet thick—had become so accustomed to the protected environment of various Veterans Administration hospitals that the prospect of leaving was as frightening to him as the prospect of entering a mental hospital is to those who have never lived in one.

A treatment that may offer some promise is **milieu therapy**, in which the entire hospital becomes a "therapeutic community" (e.g., M. Jones, 1953). All its ongoing activities and all its personnel become part of the treatment program. Milieu therapy appears to be a return to the moral practices of the nineteenth century. Social interaction and group activities are encouraged so that through group pressure the patients are directed toward normal functioning. Patients are treated as responsible human beings rather than as custodial cases (Paul, 1969). They are expected to participate in their own readjustment as well as in the readjustment of fellow patients. Open wards allow them considerable freedom. There is some evidence for the efficacy of milieu therapy (e.g., Fairweather, 1964; Greenblatt et al., 1965), the most convincing from a milestone project by Paul and Lentz (1977).

In this ambitious study Paul and Lentz demonstrated encouraging improvement in chronic, hard-core patients through both milieu therapy and a learning-based therapy. In the latter, patients were able to earn rewards for making their beds; observing social conventions, such as saying good morning; combing their hair; and attending classes in which they learned skills needed for living outside the hospital; as well as for socializing with other patients. Described in more detail on pages 342–343, this learning-based therapy rewards patients for behaving in a particular way by giving them tokens that can be exchanged for privileges or other items they desire. On a number of measures of the effectiveness of the therapies, the learning program was more successful than milieu therapy; both treatments were much superior to the routine hospital management of another group in an older Illinois state hospital. Since mental hospitals will be needed for the foreseeable future, especially by people who demonstrate time and again that they have difficulty functioning on the outside, this work is of particular importance. It suggests specific ways in which chronic patients can be helped to cope better not only within the hospital, but after discharge as well.

An Illustrative Case: General Paresis and Syphilis Though the workings of the nervous system were understood somewhat by the mid-1800s, not enough was known to reveal all the expected abnormalities in structure that might underlie various mental disorders. Degenerative changes in the brain cells associated with senile and presenile psychoses and some structural pathologies that accompany mental retardation were identified, however. Perhaps the most striking medical success was the discovery of the full nature and origin of syphilis, a venereal disease that had been recognized for several centuries.

The story of this discovery provides a good illustration of how an empirical approach, the basis for contemporary science, works. Since 1798 it was known that a number of mental patients manifested a syndrome characterized by a steady deterioration of both physical and mental abilities and that these patients suffered multiple impairments, including delusions of grandeur and progressive paralysis. Soon after these symptoms were recognized, it was realized that these patients never recovered. In 1825 this deterioration in mental and physical health was designated a disease, **general paresis**. Although it was established in 1857 that some patients with paresis had earlier had syphilis, there were many competing theories of the origin of paresis. For example, in attempting to account for the high rate of the disorder among sailors, some supposed that seawater might be the cause. And Griesinger, in trying to explain the higher incidence among men, speculated that liquor, tobacco, and coffee might be implicated.

In the 1860s and 1870s, Louis Pasteur established the **germ theory of disease**, which set forth the view that disease is caused by infection of the body by minute organisms. This theory laid the groundwork for demonstrating the relation between syphilis and general paresis. In 1897, after Richard von Krafft-Ebing inoculated paretic patients with matter from syphilitic sores, the patients did not develop syphilis, indicating that they had been infected earlier. Finally, in 1905, the specific microorganism that causes syphilis was discovered. A causal link had been established between infection, destruction of certain areas of the brain, and a form of psychopathology. If one type of psychopathology had a biological cause, so could others. Somatogenesis gained credibility, and the search for more biological causes was off and running.

Psychogenesis The search for somatogenic causes dominated the field of abnormal psychology until well into the twentieth century, no doubt partly because of the stunning discoveries made about general paresis. But in the late eighteenth and throughout the nineteenth century, mental illnesses were considered by other investigators to have an entirely different origin. Various psychogenic points of view, which attributed mental disorders to psychological malfunctions, were fashionable in France and Austria.

Mesmer's procedure for transmitting animal magnetism was generally considered a form of hypnosis.

The French psychiatrist Jean Charcot lectures on hysteria in this famous painting. Charcot was an important figure in reviving interest in psychogenesis.

Mesmer and Charcot During the eighteenth century many people in western Europe were subject to hysterical states; they suffered from physical incapacities, such as blindness or paralysis, for which no physical cause could be found (see p. 174). Franz Anton Mesmer (1734–1815), an Austrian physician practicing in Vienna and Paris in the late eighteenth century, believed that hysterical disorders were caused by a particular distribution of a universal magnetic fluid in the body. Moreover, he felt that one person could influence the fluid of another to bring about a change in the other's behavior.

Mesmer conducted meetings cloaked in mystery and mysticism, at which afflicted patients sat around a covered baquet, or tub, with iron rods protruding through the cover from bottles underneath that contained various chemicals. Mesmer would enter a room, take various rods from the tub, and touch afflicted parts of his patients' bodies. The rods were believed to transmit animal magnetism and adjust the distribution of the universal magnetic fluid, thereby removing the hysterical disorder. Whatever we may think of what seems today to be a questionable theoretical explanation and procedure, Mesmer apparently helped many people overcome their hysterical problems.

You may wonder about our discussing Mesmer's work under the rubric of psychogenic causes, since Mesmer regarded the hysterical disorders as strictly physical. Because of the setting in which Mesmer worked with his patients, however, he is generally considered one of the earlier practitioners of modern-day hypnosis. The word *mesmerize* is an older term for *hypnotize*. (The phenomenon itself was known to the ancients of probably every culture, part of the sorcery and magic of conjurers, fakirs, and faith healers.)

Although Mesmer was regarded as a quack by his contemporaries, the study of hypnosis gradually became respectable. A great Parisian neurologist, Jean Martin Charcot (1825–1893), also studied hysterical states, including anesthesia (loss of sensation), paralysis, blindness, deafness, convulsive attacks, and gaps in memory. Charcot initially espoused a somatogenic point of view. One day, however, some of his enterprising students hypnotized a normal woman and suggested to her certain hysterical symptoms. Charcot was deceived into believing that she was an actual hysterical patient. When the students showed him how readily they could remove the symptoms by waking the woman, Charcot changed his mind about hysteria and became interested in nonphysiological interpretations of these very puzzling phenomena.

Breuer and the Cathartic Method   In nineteenth century Vienna, a physician named Josef Breuer (1842–1925) treated a young woman who had become bedridden with a number of hysterical symptoms. Her legs and right arm and side were paralyzed, her sight and hearing were impaired, and she often had difficulty speaking. She also sometimes went into a dreamlike state, or "absence," during which she mumbled to herself, seemingly preoccupied with troubling thoughts. During one treatment session Breuer hypnotized Anna O. and repeated some of her mumbled words. He succeeded in getting her to talk more freely and ultimately with considerable emotion about some very upsetting past events. Frequently, on awakening from these hypnotic sessions she felt much better. Breuer found that the relief and cure of symptoms seemed to last longer if, under hypnosis, Anna O. was able to recall the precipitating event for the symptom and if her original emotion was expressed. Reliving an earlier emotional catastrophe and the release of the emotional tension produced by previously forgotten thoughts about the event were called catharsis. Breuer's method became known as the **cathartic method**. In 1895 one of his colleagues joined him in the publication of *Studies in Hysteria*, a book considered a milestone in abnormal psychology. In the next chapter we examine the thinking of Breuer's collaborator, Sigmund Freud.[2]

Focus on Discovery 1.3 describes the education and training of professionals who study and treat mental disorders.

Josef Breuer, the Austrian physician and physiologist, collaborated with Freud in the early development of psychoanalysis. He treated only Anna O. by the cathartic method he originated. Becoming alarmed by what would later be called her transference and his own countertransference, he described his procedures to a colleague and turned her over to him.

Science: A Human Enterprise

In space exploration highly sophisticated satellites have been sent aloft to make observations. It is possible, however, that certain phenomena are missed because our instruments do not have sensing devices capable of detecting them. Consider the discussion surrounding an announcement made on August 7, 1996, by the National Aeronautics and Space Administration (NASA). NASA announced that signs that life once existed on Mars may have been found in a piece of Martian rock. The rock, it is believed, was catapulted into space by an asteroid about 16 million years ago and was drawn into Earth's gravity about 13,000 years ago. Found in Antarctica in 1984, this rock has been the subject of study and speculation by chemists and space scientists. Does it contain signs of Martian microbes from 3.6 million years ago? Some scientists believe it does, whereas others disagree.

Though controversy reigns about the Martian rock, of relevance to us here is the question of how one can decide whether there are indeed signs that life once existed on the now-barren planet. How can we be certain that our own understanding of what is alive matches what may have once lived on Mars? Said a NASA astrophysicist, "Everything we know about life we learned from Earth" (cited in Cole, 1996, p. A1). Another scientist put it this way: "We're work-

Martian rock found in Antarctica in 1984 and believed by some to contain evidence of primitive life on Mars.

---

[2] Anna O., the young woman treated by Breuer with the cathartic method, or "talking cure," has become one of the best-known clinical cases in all psychotherapeutic literature. Indeed, the report of this case and four others in 1895 formed the basis of Freud's important later contributions. But historical investigations by Ellenberger (1972) cast serious doubt on the accuracy of Breuer's reporting. Anna O—in reality Bertha Pappenheim, member of a well-to-do Viennese family—was apparently helped only temporarily by Breuer's talking cure. Carl Jung, Freud's renowned colleague, is quoted as saying that during a conference in 1925, Freud told him that Anna O. had never been cured. Hospital records discovered by Ellenberger confirmed that Anna O. continued to rely on morphine to ease the "hysterical" problems that Breuer is reputed to have removed by catharsis. In fact, evidence suggests that some of her problems were biological, not psychological.

The Mental Health Professions

The training of **clinicians**, the various professionals authorized to provide psychological services, takes different forms. Here, we discuss several types of clinicians, the training they receive, and a few related issues.

To be a **clinical psychologist** (the specialty of the authors of this textbook) requires a Ph.D. or Psy.D. degree, which entails four to seven years of graduate study. Training for the Ph.D. in clinical psychology is similar to that in other psychological specialties, such as developmental or physiological psychology. It requires a heavy emphasis on research, statistics, and the empirically based study of human and animal behavior. As in other fields of psychology, the Ph.D. is basically a research degree, and candidates are required to write a dissertation on a specialized topic. But candidates in clinical psychology learn skills in two additional areas, which distinguishes them from other Ph.D. candidates in psychology. First, they learn techniques of assessment and **diagnosis** of mental disorders; that is, they learn the skills necessary to determine that a patient's symptoms or problems indicate a particular disorder. Second, they learn how to practice **psychotherapy**, a primarily verbal means of helping troubled individuals change their thoughts, feelings, and behavior to reduce distress and to achieve greater life satisfaction. Students take courses in which they master specific techniques under close professional supervision; then, during an intensive internship, they gradually assume increasing responsibility for the care of patients.

Other clinical graduate programs are more focused on practice than are the traditional Ph.D. programs. One of these is **counseling psychology**. Although counseling psychologists originally dealt mostly with vocational issues, such programs now can be quite similar to those in clinical psychology. There is also the relatively new degree of Psy.D. (doctor of psychology). The curriculum is similar to that required of Ph.D. students, but with less emphasis on research and more on clinical training. The thinking behind this approach is that clinical psychology has advanced to a level of knowledge and certainty that justifies—even requires—intensive training in specific techniques of assessment and therapeutic intervention rather than combining practice with research.

A **psychiatrist** holds an M.D. degree and has had postgraduate training, called a residency, in which he or she has received supervision in the practice of diagnosis, psychotherapy, and pharmacotherapy (administering psychoactive drugs). By virtue of the medical degree, and in contrast with psychologists, psychiatrists can also continue functioning as physicians—giving physical examinations, diagnosing medical problems, and the like. Most often, however, the only aspect of medical practice in which psychiatrists engage is prescribing **psychoactive drugs**, chemical compounds that can influence how people feel and think.

There has recently been a lively and sometimes acrimonious debate concerning the merits of allowing clinical psychologists with suitable training to prescribe psychoactive drugs. Predictably, such a move is opposed by psychiatrists, for it would represent a clear invasion of their professional turf. It is also opposed by many psychologists, who view it as an ill-advised dilution of the behavioral science focus of psychology. Profits are an issue, but so is the question of whether a non-M.D. can learn enough about biochemistry and physiology to monitor the effects of drugs and protect patients from adverse side effects and drug interactions. This debate will undoubtedly continue for some time before any resolution is reached.

A **psychoanalyst** has received specialized training at a psychoanalytic institute. The program usually involves several years of clinical training as well as the in-depth psychoanalysis of the trainee. Although Sigmund Freud held that psychoanalysts do not need medical training, until recently most U.S. psychoanalytic institutes required of their graduates an M.D. and a psychiatric residency. Nowadays, one need not even have a doctoral degree in psychology to gain admission. It can take up to ten years of graduate work to become a psychoanalyst.

A **social worker** obtains an M.S.W. (master of social work) degree.

A highly diverse group of people can be called **psychopathologists**. These people conduct research into the nature and development of the various disorders that their therapist colleagues try to diagnose and treat. Psychopathologists may come from any number of disciplines; some are clinical psychologists, but the educational backgrounds of others range from biochemistry to developmental psychology. What unites them is their commitment to the study of how abnormal behavior develops. Since we still have much to learn about psychopathology, the diversity of backgrounds and interests is an advantage, for it is too soon to be certain in which area major advances will be made.

ing with a sample of one: life on Earth. That's like trying to learn about fruit by studying only apples. We have to look at a lot of apples and oranges" (cited in Cole, 1996, p. A29).

We can look for life on another planet only with the instruments we have available, and the design of these instruments is determined not just by technology but by our preconceptions of what life is. Tests that are conducted on material from another part of the solar system rest on assumptions about the nature of living matter that may not match what might have evolved elsewhere.

This discussion of space exploration is one way of pointing out that scientific observation is a human endeavor that reflects not only the strengths of human ingenuity and scholarship, but also our intrinsic inability to know fully what the nature of our universe is. Scientists are able to design instruments to make only the kinds of observations about which they have some initial idea. They realize that certain observations are not being made because their knowledge about the nature of the universe is limited.

Subjectivity in Science: The Role of Paradigms

Science, then, is bound by the limitations imposed on scientific inquiry by the current state of knowledge. It is also bound by the scientist's own limitations. We now return to the point with which we began this chapter—the challenge of remaining objective when trying to understand and study abnormal behavior. Our view is that every effort should be made to study abnormal behavior according to scientific principles. But science is not a completely objective and certain enterprise. Rather, as suggested by philosopher of science Thomas Kuhn (1962), subjective factors as well as limitations in our perspective on the universe enter into the conduct of scientific inquiry.

Central to any application of scientific principles, in Kuhn's view, is the notion of **paradigm**, a conceptual framework or approach within which a scientist works. A paradigm, according to Kuhn, is a set of basic assumptions that outline the particular universe of scientific inquiry, specifying the kinds of concepts that will be regarded as legitimate as well as the methods that may be used to collect and interpret data.

A paradigm has profound implications for how scientists operate at any given time, for "[people] whose research is based on shared paradigms are committed to the same rules and standards for scientific practice" (Kuhn, 1962, p. 11). Paradigms specify what problems scientists will investigate and how they will go about the investigation. Paradigms are an intrinsic part of a science, serving the vital function of indicating the rules to be followed. In perceptual terms a paradigm may be likened to a general perspective or approach, a tendency to see certain factors and not to see others.

In addition to injecting inevitable biases into the definition and collection of data, a paradigm may also affect the interpretation of facts. In other words, the meaning or import given to data may depend to a considerable extent on a paradigm. We will describe the major paradigms of abnormal psychology in the next chapter, but for now we would like to give you an idea of how they operate.[3]

An Example of Paradigms in Abnormal Psychology

Two psychologists, Langer and Abelson (1974), were interested in how theoretical orientations or paradigms might affect how trained clinicians view the adjustment of a person, so they designed an experiment to examine this issue. The experiment investigated the effects of two paradigms on clinical judgments.

As we will discuss more fully in the next chapter, behavior therapy stems from the behaviorism-learning branch of psychology, which is concerned with the observation of overt behavior and views behavior as the product of certain kinds of learning. Behavior therapists believe that abnormal behavior is acquired according to the same learning principles by which normal behavior is acquired, and they tend to focus on overt behavior.

In contrast, more traditionally trained clinicians are apt to look for an inner, perhaps hidden, and often nonobvious conflict that is causing disturbed behavior. They tend to view behavior as a means of inferring what is going on in the patient's mind. Often these inferences assume that the patient is unaware of some of these mental processes.

Langer and Abelson reasoned that because they were trained to focus on observable behavior, behavior therapists might be less swayed by being told that a person was ill than would traditionally trained clinicians, who would be more likely to see overtly normal behavior as masking hidden or unconscious problems. To test this supposition they conceived the following experiment. A group of behavior therapists and a group of traditional clinicians with some training in psychoanalysis (see p. 31) were shown a videotape of an interview between two men. Before viewing this videotape, half the participants in each group were told that the interviewee was a job applicant, the other half that

---

[3] O'Donohue (1993) has criticized Kuhn's use of the concept of paradigm, noting that he was inconsistent in its definition. The complexities of this argument are beyond the scope of this book. Suffice it to say that we find it useful to organize our thinking about abnormal behavior around the paradigm concept. We use the term to refer to the general perspectives that constrain the way scientists collect and interpret information in their efforts to understand the world.

he was a patient. The traditional clinicians who were told that the interviewee was a patient were expected to rate him as more disturbed than those who considered him a job applicant. The ratings of the two groups of behavior therapists were expected to be less affected by the labels and thus to be rather similar.

The videotape shown to all the clinicians depicted a bearded professor interviewing a young man in his mid-twenties. The interviewee had been recruited through a newspaper advertisement that offered ten dollars to someone who had recently applied for a new job and was willing to be interviewed and videotaped. The fifteen-minute segment chosen from the original interview contained a rambling, autobiographical monologue by the young man in which he described a number of past jobs and dwelt on his conflicts with bureaucrats. His manner was considered by Langer and Abelson to be intense but uncertain; they felt that he could be regarded either as sincere and struggling or as confused and troubled.

A questionnaire measured the clinicians' impressions about the mental health of the interviewee. When the interviewee was identified as a job applicant there were no differences in the adjustment ratings given by the traditional clinicians and those given by the behavior therapists. But the patient label, as expected, produced sharp differences (Figure 1.2). When the interviewee was identified as a patient, the traditional clinicians rated him relatively disturbed—significantly more so than did the traditional clinicians who viewed the man as a job applicant. In contrast, the behavior therapists rated the "ill" interviewee as relatively well-adjusted; in fact, their ratings were about the same as those of the behavior therapists who thought the man was a job applicant. Qualitative evaluations obtained from the clinicians supported their ratings. Whereas the behavior therapists described the man as "realistic," "sincere," and "responsible," regardless of label, the traditional clinicians who viewed him as a patient used phrases such as "tight, defensive person," "conflict over homosexuality," and "impulsivity shows through his rigidity."

Why, in this particular experiment, did the behavior therapists appear to be unbiased? Langer and Abelson explain it this way. The behavioral approach encourages clinicians to concentrate on overt or manifest behavior and to be skeptical about illness that is not readily apparent. Those with such an orientation had the advantage in this particular study because, however the interviewee rambled, his behavior on balance was not overtly disturbed. In contrast, the traditional therapists had been trained to look beyond what was most obvious in a client. Therefore, they apparently paid too much attention to the negative ramblings about bureaucrats and inferred that something was basically wrong with the man.

Langer and Abelson properly alert readers to the limitations of their experiment, reminding them that a different study—perhaps using an interviewee who is obviously disturbed—might put behavior therapists at a disadvantage. The purpose of the experiment and of this discussion of it is not to pit one orientation against another, but rather to illustrate how a paradigm can affect perception, causing us to attend to certain details and to overlook others.

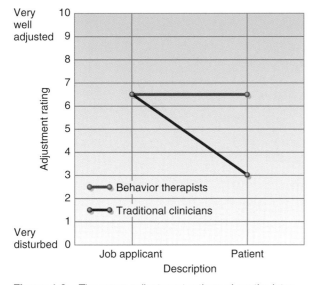

Figure 1.2   The mean adjustment ratings given the interviewee, depending on the investigators' description of him and the diagnosticians' training. Notice that the ratings of the behavior therapists were not influenced by how the interviewee was described. Adapted from Langer and Abelson (1974). Copyright © 1974 by the APA. Reprinted by permission.

Summary

● The study of psychopathology is a search for the reasons people behave, think, and feel in unexpected, sometimes bizarre, and typically self-defeating ways.

● In evaluating whether a behavior is abnormal, psychologists consider several different characteristics: statistical infrequency, violation of societal norms, personal distress, disability or behavioral dysfunction, and unexpectedness. Each characteristic tells something about what can be considered abnormal, but none by itself provides a fully satisfactory definition.

● Since the beginning of scientific inquiry into abnormal behavior, two major points of view have vied for attention: the somatogenic, which assumes that every mental aberration is caused by a physical malfunction; and the psychogenic, which assumes that the person's body is intact and that difficulties are to be explained in psychological terms.

● The somatogenic viewpoint originated in the writings of Hippocrates. After the fall of Greco-Roman civilization, it became less prominent, but it reemerged in the eighteenth and nineteenth centuries through the writings of such people as Kraepelin.

● The psychogenic viewpoint is akin to early demonology, which posited that an evil being could dwell within a person and control his or her mind and body. Its more modern version emerged in the nineteenth century from the work of Charcot and the seminal writings of Breuer and Freud.

● Scientific inquiry is a special way in which human beings acquire knowledge about their world. In a very important sense, people may see only what they are prepared to see; thus, certain phenomena may go undetected because scientists can discover only things about which they already have some general idea.

● A paradigm is a conceptual framework or general perspective. Because the paradigm within which scientists and clinicians work helps to shape what they investigate and find, understanding paradigms helps us to appreciate subjective influences that may affect their work.

Key Terms

abnormal behavior	diagnosis	normal curve	psychopathologists
asylums	exorcism	paradigm	psychopathology
cathartic method	general paresis	psychiatrist	psychotherapy
clinical psychologist	germ theory (of disease)	psychoactive drugs	social worker
clinicians	harmful dysfunctions	psychoanalyst	somatogenesis
counseling psychologists	milieu therapy	psychogenesis	syndrome
demonology	moral treatment		

2 Current Paradigms in Psychopathology and Therapy

Chapter 1 discussed the nature of abnormality—its history and how it has been defined. This chapter considers current paradigms of abnormal behavior and treatment. A paradigm, again, is a set of basic assumptions, a general perspective, that defines how to conceptualize and study a subject, how to gather and interpret relevant data, even how to think about a particular subject. This chapter presents five paradigms of abnormal psychology: biological, psychoanalytic, humanistic and existential, learning, and cognitive.

Current thinking about abnormal behavior tends to be multifaceted. The work of clinicians and researchers is informed by an awareness of the strengths and limitations of the various paradigms. For this reason current views of abnormal behavior and its treatment tend to integrate several paradigms. At the end of this chapter we describe another paradigm—diathesis–stress—which provides the basis for an integrative approach.

Many people go about the study of abnormal psychology without explicitly considering the nature of the paradigm they have adopted. As this chapter will indicate, and as we saw in Langer and Abelson's study in Chapter 1, however, the choice of a paradigm has some very important consequences for the way in which abnormal behavior is defined, investigated, and treated. Our discussion of paradigms will lay the groundwork for the examination of the major categories of disorders and of intervention that makes up the rest of the book.

The Biological Paradigm

The **biological paradigm** of abnormal behavior is a continuation of the somatogenic hypothesis described in Chapter 1. This broad perspective holds that mental disorders are caused by aberrant biological processes. This paradigm has often been referred to as the **medical model** or **disease model**.

The study of abnormal behavior is historically linked to medicine. Many early as well as contemporary workers have used the model of physical illness as the basis for understanding deviant behavior. Within the field of abnormal behavior the terminology of medicine is pervasive.

As we described earlier, when Louis Pasteur discovered the relation between bacteria and disease and soon thereafter postulated viruses, the germ theory of disease provided a new explanation of pathology. External symptoms were assumed to be produced through infection of the body by minute organisms and viruses. For a time, the germ theory was the paradigm of medicine, but it soon became apparent that this theory could not account for all diseases. Diabetes, for example, a malfunction of the insulin-secreting cells of the pancreas, cannot be attributed to infection. Nor does it have a single cause. Heart disease is another example. Many factors—genetic makeup, smoking, obesity, life stress, and perhaps even a person's personality (see p. 427 causes of heart disease. Medical illnesses can differ widely from one another in their causes. However, they all share one characteristic: some biological process is disrupted or not functioning normally. That is why we have chosen to call this the biological paradigm.

Contemporary Approaches to the Biological Paradigm

There is considerable literature, both research and theory based, dealing with biological factors relevant to psychopathology. Heredity probably predisposes a person to have an increased risk of developing schizophrenia (see Chapter 11); depression may result from chemical imbalances within the brain (Chapter 10); anxiety disorders may stem from a defect within the autonomic nervous system that causes a person to be too easily aroused (Chapter 6); dementia can be traced to impairments in structures of the brain (Chapter 16). In each case a type of psychopathology is viewed as caused by the disturbance of some biological process. Those working with the biological paradigm assume that answers to puzzles of psychopathology will be found within the body. In this section, we look at two areas of research within this paradigm in which the data are particularly interesting—behavior genetics and biochemistry.

Behavior Genetics   When the ovum, the female reproductive cell, is joined by the male's spermatozoon, a zygote, or fertilized egg, is produced. It has forty-six chromosomes, the number characteristic of a human being. Each chromosome is made up of thousands of **genes**, the carriers of the genetic information (DNA) passed from parents to child.

Behavior genetics is the study of individual differences in behavior that are attributable in part to differences in genetic makeup. The total genetic makeup of an individual, consisting of inherited genes, is referred to as the **genotype**. An individual's genotype is his or her unobservable genetic constitution. In contrast, the totality of observable, behavioral characteristics, such as level of anxiety, is referred to as the **phenotype**. The genotype is fixed at birth, but it should not be viewed as a static entity. Genes controlling various features of development switch off and on at specific times, for example, to control various aspects of physical development.

The phenotype changes over time and is generally viewed as the product of an interaction between the genotype and the environment. For example, an individual may be

Behavior genetics studies the degree to which characteristics, such as physical resemblance or psychopathology, are shared by family members because of shared genes.

born with the capacity for high intellectual achievement, but whether he or she develops this genetically given potential depends on such environmental factors as upbringing and education. Hence any measure of intelligence is best viewed as an index of the phenotype.

It is critical to recognize that various clinical syndromes are disorders of the phenotype, not of the genotype. Thus it is not correct to speak of the direct inheritance of schizophrenia or anxiety disorders; at most, only the genotypes for these disorders can be inherited. Whether these genotypes will eventually engender the phenotypic behavior disorder will depend on environment and experience; a predisposition, also known as a **diathesis**, may be inherited, but not the disorder itself.

The study of behavior genetics has relied on four basic methods to uncover whether a genetic predisposition for psychopathology is inherited—comparison of members of a family, comparison of pairs of twins, the investigation of adoptees, and linkage analysis.

The **family method** can be used to study a genetic predisposition among members of a family because the average number of genes shared by two blood relatives is known. Children receive a random sample of half their genes from one parent and half from the other, so on average siblings and parents and children are identical in 50 percent of their genetic background. People who share 50 percent of their genes with a given individual are called first-degree relatives of that person. Relatives not as closely related share fewer genes. For example, nephews and nieces share 25 percent of the genetic makeup of an uncle, and are called second-degree relatives. If a predisposition for a mental disorder can be inherited, a study of the family should reveal a relationship between the number of shared genes and the prevalence of the disorder in relatives.

The starting point in such investigations is the collection of a sample of individuals who bear the diagnosis in question. These people are referred to as **index cases**, or **probands**. Then relatives are studied to determine the frequency with which the same diagnosis might be applied to them. If a genetic predisposition to the disorder being studied is present, first-degree relatives of the index cases should have the disorder at a rate higher than that found in the general population. This is the case with schizophrenia: about 10 percent of the first-degree relatives of index cases with schizophrenia can be diagnosed as having this disorder, compared with about 1 percent of the general population.

In the **twin method** both **monozygotic (MZ) twins** and **dizygotic (DZ)** twins are compared. MZ, or identical, twins develop from a single fertilized egg and are genetically the same. DZ, or fraternal, pairs develop from separate eggs and are on average only 50 percent alike genetically, no more alike than are any two siblings. MZ twins are always the same sex, but DZ twins can be either the same sex or opposite in sex. Twin studies begin with diagnosed cases and then search for the presence of the disorder in the other twin. When the twins are similar diagnostically they are said to be concordant. To the extent that a predisposition for a mental disorder can be inherited, **concordance** for the disorder should be greater in genetically identical MZ pairs than in DZ pairs. When the MZ concordance rate is higher than the DZ rate, the characteristic being studied is said to be heritable. We will see in later chapters that the concordance for many forms of psychopathology is higher in MZ twins than in DZ twins.

Although the methodology of family and twin studies is clear, the data they yield are not always easy to interpret. Let us assume that children of agoraphobic parents—people suffering from a cluster of fears centering on being in open spaces and leaving home—are themselves more likely than average to be agoraphobic. Does this mean that a predisposition for this anxiety disorder is genetically transmitted? Not necessarily. The greater number of agoraphobics could reflect the child-rearing practices of the phobic parents as well as the effects of the children's imitating adult behavior.[1] In other words, the data show that agoraphobia runs in families, but not necessarily that a genetic predisposition is involved.

The ability to offer a genetic interpretation of data from twin studies hinges on what is called the equal environment assumption. Because psychopathology is a phenotypic

---

[1] Note that these are possibilities, not proven facts. Theorists who look to the environment as a cause of psychopathology must eventually gather data to support their claims.

characteristic, concordance among twins for psychopathology is a result of the operation of both genetic and environmental factors. For whatever diagnosis is being studied, the *equal environment assumption* is that the environmental factors that are partial causes of concordance are equally influential for both MZ pairs and DZ pairs. This does *not* mean that the environments of MZ and DZ twins are equal in all respects; the assumption of equality applies only to factors that are plausible environmental causes of psychopathology. For example, the equal environment assumption would assert that MZ pairs and DZ pairs have equivalent numbers of stressful life experiences. In general, the equal environment assumption seems to be reasonable, although it is clearly in need of further study (Kendler, 1993).

The **adoptees method** studies children who were adopted and reared completely apart from their biological parents. Though infrequent, this situation has the benefit of eliminating the influence of being raised by disordered parents. If a high frequency of agoraphobia were found in children reared apart from their parents who also had agoraphobia, we would have convincing support for the theory that a genetic predisposition figures in the disorder. (The study of MZ twins reared completely apart would also be valuable, but this situation occurs so rarely that there is almost no research using this method to study psychopathology. We will see in Chapter 13, however, that research involving separated twins does exist in the study of the inheritance of personality traits.)

A fourth method in behavior genetics, **linkage analysis**, goes beyond merely trying to show whether a disorder has a genetic component; it tries to specify the particular gene involved. The method typically studies families in which a disorder is heavily concentrated and collects diagnostic information and blood samples from affected individuals and their relatives. The blood samples are used to study the inheritance pattern of characteristics whose genetics are fully understood, referred to as *genetic markers*. Eye color, for example, is known to be controlled by a gene in a specific location on a specific chromosome. If the occurrence of a form of psychopathology among relatives goes along with the occurrence of another characteristic whose genetics are known (the genetic marker), it is concluded that the gene predisposing to the psychopathology is on the same chromosome and in a similar location on that chromosome (that is, it is linked) as the gene controlling the other characteristic. We will see several examples of linkage analysis in subsequent chapters, especially when we discuss mood disorders (Chapter 10) and schizophrenia (Chapter 11). The greatest success of the method thus far has been in identifying specific genes on several chromosomes that are extremely important in Alzheimer's disease (see Chapter 16).

Biochemistry in the Nervous System   The nervous system is comprised of billions of neurons. Although neurons differ in some respects, each **neuron** has four major parts: (1) the *cell body*; (2) several *dendrites*, the short and thick extensions; (3) one or more *axons* of varying lengths, but usually only one long and thin axon that extends a considerable distance from the cell body; and (4) *terminal buttons* on the many end branches of the axon (Figure 2.1). When a neuron is appropriately stimulated at its cell body or through its dendrites, a **nerve impulse**, which is a change in the electric potential of the cell, travels down the axon to the terminal endings. Between the terminal endings of the sending axon and the cell membrane of the receiving neuron there is a small gap, the **synapse** (Figure 2.2).

For a nerve impulse to pass from one neuron to another and for communication to occur, the impulse must have a way of bridging the synaptic gap. The terminal buttons of each axon contain synaptic vesicles, small structures that are filled with **neurotransmitters**, chemical substances that allow a nerve impulse to cross the synapse. Nerve impulses cause the synaptic vesicles to release molecules of their transmitter substances, which flood the synapse and diffuse toward the receiving, or postsynaptic, neuron. The cell membrane of the postsynaptic cell con-

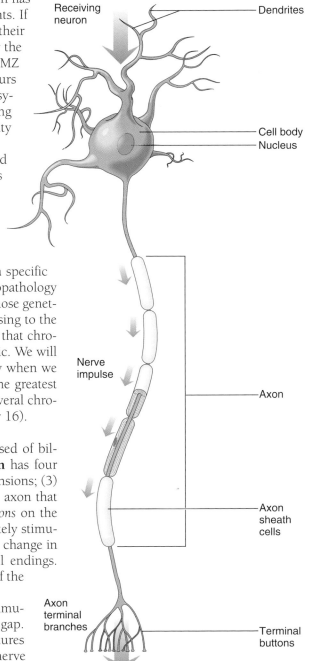

Figure 2.1   The neuron, the basic unit of the nervous system.

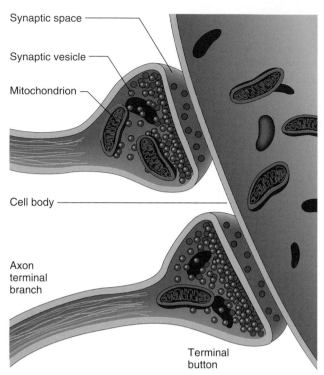

Synaptic space

Synaptic vesicle

Mitochondrion

Cell body

Axon
terminal
branch

Terminal
button

Figure 2.2 A synapse, showing the terminal buttons of two axon branches in close contact with a very small portion of the cell body of another neuron.

tains proteins, called receptor sites, that are configured so that specific neurotransmitters can fit into them. When a neurotransmitter fits into a receptor site, a message can be sent to the postsynaptic cell. What actually happens to the postsynaptic neuron depends on integrating thousands of similar messages. Sometimes these messages are excitatory, leading to the creation of a nerve impulse in the postsynaptic cell; at other times the messages can be inhibitory, making the postsynaptic cell less likely to fire.

Once a presynaptic neuron (the sending neuron) has released its neurotransmitter, the last step is for the synapse to be returned to its normal state. Not all of the released neurotransmitter has found its way to postsynaptic receptors. Some of what remains in the synapse is broken down by enzymes, and some is pumped back into the presynaptic cell through a process called **reuptake**.

Several key neurotransmitters have been implicated in psychopathology. Norepinephrine is a neurotransmitter of the peripheral sympathetic nervous system, where it is involved in producing states of high arousal and thus may be involved in the anxiety disorders. Both serotonin and dopamine are neurotransmitters in the brain; serotonin may be involved in depression and dopamine in schizophrenia. Another important brain transmitter is gamma-aminobutyric acid (GABA), which inhibits some nerve impulses and may be involved in the anxiety disorders.

Theories linking neurotransmitters to psychopathology sometimes have proposed that a given disorder is caused by either too much or too little of a particular transmitter (e.g., mania results from too much norepinephrine, anxiety disorders result from too little GABA). Neurotransmitters are synthesized in the neuron through a series of metabolic steps, beginning with an amino acid. Each reaction along the way to producing an actual transmitter is catalyzed by an enzyme, speeding up the metabolic process. Too much or too little of a particular transmitter could result from an error in these metabolic pathways. Similar disturbances in the amounts of specific transmitters could result from alterations in the usual processes by which transmitters are deactivated after being released into the synapse. For example, a failure to pump leftover neurotransmitter back into the presynaptic cell (reuptake) would leave excess transmitter in the synapse. Then, when a new nerve impulse caused more neurotransmitter to be released into the synapse, the postsynaptic neuron would, in a sense, get a double dose of neurotransmitter, making it more likely for a new nerve impulse to be created.

Finally, contemporary research has focused to a large extent on the possibility that the receptors are at fault in some psychopathologies. If the receptors on the postsynaptic neuron were too numerous or too easily excited, the result would be akin to having too much transmitter released. There would simply be more sites available with which the neurotransmitter could interact, increasing the chances that the postsynaptic neuron would be stimulated. The delusions and hallucinations of schizophrenia may result from an overabundance of dopamine receptors.

Biological Approaches to Treatment

An important implication of the biological paradigm is that prevention or treatment of mental disorders should be possible through alteration of bodily functioning. Certainly if a deficiency in a particular biochemical substance is found to underlie or contribute to some problem, it makes sense to attempt to correct the imbalance by providing appropriate doses of the deficient chemical. In such cases a clear connection exists between viewing a disorder as a biological defect and attempting to correct the fault through a biological intervention.

However, most biological interventions in common use have not been derived from knowledge of what causes a given disorder. Nonetheless, the use of psychoactive drugs has been increasing; in 1985 they were prescribed at about 33 million physician visits, and in 1994 at almost 46 million (Pincus et al., 1998). Tranquilizers, such as Valium, can be effective in reducing the tension associated with some anxiety disorders, perhaps by stimulating GABA neurons to inhibit other neural systems that create the physical symptoms of anxiety. Antidepressants, such as Prozac, increase neural transmission in neurons that use serotonin as a neurotransmitter by inhibiting the reuptake of serotonin. Antipsychotic drugs, such as Thorazine, used in the treatment of schizophrenia, reduce the activity of neurons that use dopamine as a neurotransmitter by blocking their receptors. Stimulants are often employed in treating children with attention-deficit disorder; they increase the levels of several neurotransmitters that help children pay attention.

It should be noted that a person can hold a biological theory about the nature of a mental problem yet recommend psychological intervention. Recall from Chapter 1 that Hippocrates proposed nonsomatic therapies—rest for melancholia, for example—to deal with mental disorders that he considered somatic in origin. Contemporary workers also appreciate that nonbiological interventions can have beneficial effects on the soma. For example, preventing a person from performing a compulsive ritual, which is an effective and widely used behavioral treatment for obsessive-compulsive disorder, has measurable effects on brain activity (see p. 162).

Evaluating the Biological Paradigm

Our discussion of each paradigm will conclude with an evaluation section. For the most part these sections will focus on etiology—the factors that contribute to the development of a disorder—rather than on treatment. Treatments will be evaluated in the chapters dealing with specific disorders as well as in Chapter 17.

Over the past two decades biological researchers have made great progress in elucidating brain–behavior relationships. Biologically based research on both causes and treatment of psychopathology is proceeding at a rapid rate, as we will see when we discuss specific psychopathologies in later chapters. Although we view these developments in a positive light, we also want to caution against reductionism, a position taken by some biologically oriented researchers.

Reductionism refers to the view that whatever is being studied can and should be reduced to its most basic elements or constituents. In the case of mental disorders the position proposes reducing complex mental and emotional responses to simple biology. Using this logic, the argument could be taken even further to propose that biology be reduced to atomic physics. In its extreme form reductionism asserts that psychology and psychopathology will ultimately be nothing more than biology.

Although reductionism is an influential viewpoint among biological psychiatrists, in philosophical circles it has been severely criticized. Once basic elements, such as individual nerve cells, are organized into more complex structures or systems, such as neural pathways or circuits, the properties of these systems cannot be deduced from the properties of the constituents. The whole is greater than the sum of its parts. A good example is provided by the geological theory of plate tectonics. The earth's outer shell is made up of about a dozen large plates and several smaller ones. Movement of the plates at their boundaries is what causes most earthquakes. Although the earth's plates are made up of rock and the rock of atoms, tectonic movement cannot be accounted for at all by our knowledge of atoms.

Valenstein (1998), a noted physiological psychologist, has offered another example.

> [Consider] the story of aliens who land on earth some time in the future when there is no longer any life on this planet. When a library full of books is discovered, the aliens, who do not know what these objects are, give them to their scientists to study. The anatomists report that the specimens are a roughly rectangular block of fibrous material covered ventrally [front] and dorsally [back] with two coarse, fibrous, encapsulated laminae [thin plates] approximately three millimeters thick. Between these lie several hundred white lamellae [very thin plates or layers], all fastened at one end and mobile at the other. On closer inspection, these are found to contain a

*large number of black surface markings arranged in linear groupings in a highly complex man-
ner. Meanwhile, the alien chemists blend some books into a homogenate [uniform mixture in
which particles are reduced to small, uniform size and distributed evenly throughout] and cen-
trifuge out the black contaminants. The chemists report that the objects have a cellulose structure with a [particular] molecular configuration....*

*The point of the story is not...the same as the blind men and the elephant, in which each
man grasps a different part of the truth. What the story really illustrates is that there is an
appropriate level at which to study a phenomenon, and a reductionist approach may miss the
whole point, or at least, the most important point. (p. 140)*

Certain phenomena, then, emerge only at certain levels of analysis and will be missed by
investigators who focus only at the molecular level. In the field of abnormal psychology,
problems such as delusional beliefs, dysfunctional attitudes, and catastrophizing cognitions may well be impossible to explain biologically, even with a detailed understanding
of the behavior of individual neurons (Turkheimer, 1998).

The Psychoanalytic Paradigm

The central assumption of the **psychoanalytic** or **psychodynamic paradigm**, originally
developed by Sigmund Freud (1856–1939), is that psychopathology results from unconscious conflicts in the individual. We will spend considerable time looking at Freud's significant impact in the development of this paradigm; however, the focus of the paradigm
has shifted through the years, and we will examine those changes as well.

Classical Psychoanalytic Theory

Classical psychoanalytic theory refers to the original views of Freud. His theories encompassed both the structure of the mind itself and the development and dynamics of personality.

Sigmund Freud was the founder of the psychoanalytic paradigm, both proposing a
theory of the causes of mental disorder and
devising a new method of therapy.

Structure of the Mind   Freud divided the mind, or the psyche, into three principal parts:
id, ego, and superego. These are metaphors for specific functions or energies. According to
Freud, the **id** is present at birth and is the part of the mind that accounts for all the energy
needed to run the psyche. It comprises the basic urges for food, water, elimination, warmth,
affection, and sex. Trained as a neurologist, Freud saw the source of all the id's energy as
biological. Only later, as the infant develops, is this energy, which Freud called **libido**, converted into psychic energy, all of it **unconscious**, below the level of awareness.

The id seeks immediate gratification, operating on what Freud called the **pleasure
principle**. When the id is not satisfied, tension is produced, and the id strives to eliminate
this tension as quickly as possible. For example, the infant feels hunger, an aversive drive,
and is impelled to move about, sucking, to reduce the tension arising from the unsatisfied
drive. Another means of obtaining gratification is **primary process** thinking, generating
images—in essence, fantasies—of what is desired. The infant who wants mother's milk
imagines sucking at the mother's breast and thereby obtains some short-term satisfaction
of the hunger drive through a wish-fulfilling fantasy. In the not-so-long term, of course,
primary process thinking alone can be fatal. This is where the ego comes in.

The next aspect of the psyche to develop is the **ego**. Unlike the id, the ego is primarily conscious and begins to develop from the id during the second six months of life.
Whereas the id resorts to fantasy if necessary, the task of the ego is to deal with reality.
The ego does not employ primary process thinking, for fantasy will not keep the organism alive. Through its planning and decision-making functions, called **secondary
process** thinking, the ego realizes that operating on the pleasure principle at all times, as
the id would like to do, is not the most effective way of maintaining life. The ego thus
operates on the **reality principle** as it mediates between the demands of reality and the
immediate gratification desired by the id.

The ego, however, derives all its energy from the id and may be likened to a horseback rider who receives energy from the horse he or she is riding. Whereas a horseback rider directs the horse with his or her own energy, not depending on that of the horse for thinking, planning, and moving, the ego derives *all* its energies from the id, yet must also direct what it is entirely dependent on for energy.

The final part of the psyche to emerge is the **superego**, which operates roughly as the conscience and develops throughout childhood. Freud believed that the superego develops from the ego much as the ego develops from the id. As children discover that many of their impulses, such as biting or bed-wetting, are not acceptable to their parents, they begin to incorporate, or **introject**, parental values as their own in order to enjoy parental approval and to avoid disapproval.

The behavior of the human being, as conceptualized by Freud, is thus a complex interplay of three parts of the psyche, all vying for the achievement of goals that cannot always be reconciled. The interplay of these forces is referred to as the *psychodynamics* of the personality. Theorists who follow some of Freud's ideas are thus also referred to as psychodynamic theorists.

Freud was drawn into studying the mind by his work with Breuer on hypnosis and hysteria (see p. 15). The apparently powerful role played by factors of which patients seemed unaware led Freud to postulate that much of human behavior is determined by forces that are inaccessible to awareness. The id's instincts as well as many of the superego's activities are not known to the conscious mind. The ego is primarily conscious, for it is the metaphor for the psychic systems that have to do with thinking and planning. But the ego, too, has important unconscious aspects that protect it from anxiety—the defense mechanisms (which will be discussed shortly). Freud considered most of the important determinants of behavior to be unconscious.

Stages of Psychosexual Development   Freud conceived of the personality as developing through a series of four distinct **psychosexual stages**. At each stage a different part of the body is the most sensitive to sexual excitation and therefore the most capable of providing libidinal satisfaction to the id. The **oral stage** is the first stage of psychosexual development. From birth to about eighteen months the demands of the infant's id are satisfied primarily by feeding and the sucking and biting associated with it. As a result, the body parts involved with this stage are the lips, mouth, gums, and tongue. From about eighteen months to three years of age, the child's enjoyment shifts to the anus. During this **anal stage** the child's main source of libidinous pleasure comes from passing and retaining feces. The **phallic stage** extends from age three to age five or six, and maximum gratification of the id now occurs through genital stimulation. Between the ages of six and twelve the child is in a **latency period**. During these years the id impulses do not play a major role in motivating behavior. The final and adult stage is the **genital stage**, during which heterosexual interests predominate.

During each stage the growing person must resolve the conflicts between what the id wants and what the environment will provide. How this is accomplished determines basic personality traits that last throughout the person's life. For example, a person who in the anal stage experiences either excessive or deficient amounts of gratification, depending on the toilet-training regimen, develops a **fixation** and is likely to regress to this stage when stressed. Such a person might develop obsessive-compulsive disorder and become stingy and obsessively clean.

Perhaps the most important crisis of development occurs during the phallic stage, around age four. Then, Freud asserted, the child is overcome with sexual desire for the parent of the opposite sex; at the same time the child views the parent of the same sex as a rival and fears retaliation. The threat of dire punishment from the parent of the same sex may cause the child to *repress* the entire conflict, pushing these sexual and aggressive urges into the unconscious. This desire and repression (discussed in the next section) are referred to as the **Oedipus complex** for the male and the **Electra complex** for the female. The dilemma is usually resolved through increased identification with the parent of the same sex and through the adoption of society's moral values, which forbid the child to

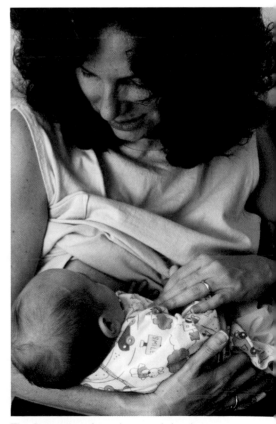

The first stage of psychosexual development is the oral stage, during which libidinal pleasure is obtained from feeding.

desire his or her parent. Through the learning of these moral values the superego develops. According to Freud, resolving the Oedipus complex or the Electra complex is extremely important to the child's ongoing sexual development; failure to do so may lead the child to feel guilty about sexual desires, to fear intimacy, or to develop other difficulties in romantic relationships.

Neurotic Anxiety   When one's life is in jeopardy, one feels **objective anxiety**, or realistic anxiety, the ego's reaction, according to Freud, to danger in the external world. The person whose personality has not developed fully, perhaps because he or she is fixated at one or another stage, may experience **neurotic anxiety**, a feeling of fear that is unrealistic and not connected to any external threat. Freud initially viewed neurotic anxiety as stemming from the blockage or repression of unconscious impulses; a person afraid of small spaces, for example, experiences this neurotic anxiety because he or she has repressed the need for closeness.

Later, Freud came to view neurotic anxiety quite differently, not as stemming from a *lack of expression* of unconscious impulses, but arising from *fear of the disastrous consequences* likely to ensue should a previously punished id impulse be expressed. The boy afraid of closed spaces is really afraid of expressing his desire for sex and intimacy, a desire that was perhaps mocked or thwarted in his childhood. The girl afraid of dirt who cleans obsessively is actually afraid of her childhood fascination with her messy feces, perhaps as a result of parents who were overly strict and disapproving or disgusted when she was toilet training.

Perhaps because Freud's earlier views held that repression of id impulses would create neurotic anxiety, we often hear the charge that Freudians preach as much gratification of impulses as possible, lest a person become neurotic. But this is not the case. Being unaware of conflicts lies at the core of neurotic anxiety, rather than simply being reluctant, unwilling, or unable to reduce the demands of the id. A celibate Catholic priest and nun, for example, are not considered candidates for neurosis provided that they consciously acknowledge their sexual or aggressive tendencies. Such individuals do not have to act on these felt needs to avoid neurotic anxiety. They must only remain aware of these needs whenever the needs vie for expression.

Defense Mechanisms: Coping with Anxiety   According to Freud and elaborated by his daughter Anna (A. Freud, 1966), herself a famous psychoanalyst, the discomfort experienced by the anxious ego can be reduced in several ways. Objective anxiety, rooted in reality, can often be handled by removing or avoiding the danger in the external world or by dealing with it in a rational way. Neurotic anxiety may be handled through an unconscious distortion of reality by means of a defense mechanism.

A **defense mechanism** is a strategy, unconsciously utilized, to protect the ego from anxiety. Perhaps the most important is **repression**, which pushes impulses and thoughts unacceptable to the ego into the unconscious. Repression not only prevents awareness but also keeps buried desires from growing up (Wachtel, 1977). Because they remain repressed, these infantile memories cannot be corrected by adult experience and therefore they retain their original intensity. **Denial** is another important defense mechanism; it entails disavowing a negative experience, such as being raped, and pushing it into the unconscious. **Projection** attributes to external agents characteristics or desires that are possessed by an individual and yet are unacceptable to conscious awareness. For example, a hostile woman may unconsciously find it aversive to regard herself as angry at others and may project her angry feelings onto them; thus she sees others as angry with her. Other defense mechanisms are **displacement**, redirecting emotional responses from a perhaps dangerous object to a substitute, for instance, yelling at one's spouse instead

Too much or too little gratification during one of the psychosexual stages may lead to regression to this stage during stress.

Table 2.1   Selected Ego Defense Mechanisms

Defense Mechanism	Definition	Example
Repression	Keeping unacceptable impulses or wishes from conscious awareness	A professor starting a lecture she has dreaded giving says, "In conclusion…"
Denial	Keeping negative events from conscious awareness	A survivor of incest in childhood cannot recall the incident(s) as an adult.
Projection	Attributing to someone else one's own thoughts or feelings	Someone who hates members of a racial group believes that it is they who dislike him.
Displacement	Deflecting feelings from their original target to someone else	A child gets mad at a sibling but then acts angrily toward her friend.
Rationalization	Offering socially acceptable explanations that are not the real reasons for behavior	A parent berates a child out of anger and impatience, then indicates that she did so to "build character."
Reaction formation	Unacceptable wishes or impulses are transformed into their opposite	A person with sexual feelings toward children leads a campaign against child sexual abuse.
Sublimation	Aggressive or sexual impulses are diverted into prosocial behaviors	Someone who has aggressive feelings toward his father becomes a surgeon.

of at one's boss; **reaction formation**, converting one feeling, such as hate, into its opposite, in this case, love; **regression**, retreating to the behavioral patterns of an earlier age; **rationalization**, inventing a reason for an unreasonable action or attitude; and **sublimation**, converting sexual or aggressive impulses into socially valued behaviors, especially creative activity. (Defense mechanisms are summarized in Table 2.1).

All these defense mechanisms allow the ego to discharge some id energy while not facing frankly the true nature of the motivation. Because defense mechanisms are more readily observed than are other symptoms of a disordered personality, they very often make people aware of their troubled natures and thus provide the impetus for consulting a therapist. It should be noted that contemporary psychoanalytic theorists consider some use of defense mechanisms to be adaptive and healthy. A period of denial after the death of a loved one can help in adjusting to the loss. Sublimation of sexual impulses into hard work or creativity can be adaptive in coping with those impulses when sexual activity is not a feasible alternative. For the most part, however, psychoanalytic scholars believe that defense mechanisms stunt a person's interactions with others and with their own work.

Relationship of Psychoanalytic Concepts to Psychopathology   Freud believed that the various forms of psychopathology resulted from the presence of strong drives or id instincts, which set the stage for the development of unconscious conflicts linked to a particular psychosexual stage. For example, he proposed that phobias, irrational fears and avoidances of harmless objects or situations, were caused by an unresolved Oedipal conflict, with the fear of the father displaced onto some other object or situation. Similarly, obsessive-compulsive disorder was traced to the anal stage, with the urge to soil or to be aggressive transformed by reaction formation into compulsive cleanliness.

In his early writings and lectures Freud postulated that the environmental cause of his patients' hysterical problems was sexual abuse in childhood, typically rape by the father. But in 1897, in a letter to his colleague Wilhelm Fleiss, he indicated that he had come to believe that many of his patients' accounts were fantasies (Masson, 1984). This change had a profound impact on the development of psychoanalysis, for it directed the search for the causes of psychopathology away from the environment and toward the patient and his or her fantasies. Furthermore, the emphasis on fantasy was crucial to Freud's conception of the Oedipal conflict, a cornerstone of psychoanalytic thought. So important was this emphasis on fantasy that in a letter to Jeffrey Masson, a well-known critic of psychoanalysis, Anna Freud wrote that without it there would have been no psychoanalysis.

Neo-Freudian Psychodynamic Perspectives

The significance of Freud's theories and clinical work was widely recognized by his contemporaries. Several of them, including Carl Jung and Alfred Adler, met with Freud periodically to discuss psychoanalytic theory and therapy. As often happens when a brilliant leader attracts brilliant followers and colleagues, disagreements arose about many general issues, such as the relative importance of id versus ego and of biological instinctual drives versus sociocultural determinants; the significance of the earliest years of life in contrast with adult experiences; whether sexual urges are at the core of motives and actions that are themselves not obviously sexual; the relative importance of unconscious processes versus conscious ones; and the reflexlike nature of id impulses versus the purposive behavior governed primarily by conscious ego deliberations.

To elaborate on some of these themes we outline the major ideas of Jung and Adler, theorists who adapted Freud's ideas in forging approaches of their own. Others who adapted and modified Freud's theories are discussed in Chapter 13 (the object-relations theorists) and later in this chapter when we discuss contemporary psychodynamic therapies. All continued to embrace Freud's emphasis on human behavior as influenced strongly by unconscious forces within the psyche.

Carl Jung was the founder of analytical psychology, a blending of Freudian and humanistic concepts.

Jung and Analytical Psychology   Carl Gustav Jung (1875–1961), a Swiss psychiatrist originally considered Freud's heir apparent, broke with Freud on many issues in 1914, after a seven-year period of intense correspondence. Jung proposed ideas radically different from Freud's, ultimately establishing **analytical psychology**, a blend of Freudian psychology and humanistic psychology (see p. 37). The similarity of Jung's theory to humanistic theories arises from Jung's de-emphasis of the importance of biological drives as the main determinants of behavior and the use of the concept of self-realization, a state of fulfillment that occurs when a person balances and gives expression to all the positive and creative aspects of his or her personality.

Jung hypothesized that in addition to our personal unconscious, which Freud stressed, our **collective unconscious** contains information from the social history of humankind. The collective unconscious is the repository of all the experiences people have had over the centuries and, unlike Freud's unconscious, contains positive and creative forces rather than exclusively sexual and aggressive ones. In addition, Jung asserted that each of us has masculine and feminine traits that can be blended and that people's spiritual and religious needs are as basic as their libidinal needs. Jung also catalogued various personality types; perhaps most important among them are extraversion (an orientation toward the external world) versus introversion (an orientation toward the inner, subjective world). This personality dimension continues to be regarded as very important, and we will encounter it again in our discussion of the personality disorders in Chapter 13.

Jung also wrote at length on religious symbolism and the meaning of life and as a consequence became popular among mystics, novelists, and poets. Finally, whereas Freud regarded current and future behavior as determined primarily by the past, Jung focused on purposiveness, decision making, and goal setting. To understand people, according to Jung, one has to appreciate their dreams and aspirations, not just the effects of their past experiences, as important as those may be (Jung, 1935).

Alfred Adler was the founder of individual psychology and well known for his notion of the inferiority complex.

Adler and Individual Psychology   Alfred Adler (1870–1937), also an early adherent of Freud's theories, came to be even less dependent on Freud's views of instincts than was Jung, and Freud remained quite bitter toward Adler after their relationship ended. Adler, who had been a sickly child in Vienna and had had to strive mightily to overcome feelings of inferiority, emphasized striving for superiority, but not in an antisocial sense. Indeed, he regarded people as inextricably tied to their society because he believed that fulfillment was found in doing things for the social good. Like Jung, he stressed the importance of working toward goals, and, also like Jung, much of his theorizing anticipated later developments in humanistic therapy (Adler, 1930).

One central element in Adler's work was his focus on the individual's phenomenology, or **individual psychology**, as the key to understanding that person. Adler worked to help patients change their illogical, mistaken ideas and expectations in the belief that to feel and behave better, one has first to think more rationally, an approach that anticipated contemporary developments in cognitive behavior therapy (p. 54). Finally, Adler's interest in growth and in the prevention of problems and the betterment of society influenced the development of child guidance centers and parent education.

Psychoanalytic Therapy

Since Freud's time, the body of psychoanalytic thinking has changed in important ways, but all treatments purporting to be psychoanalytic have some basic tenets in common. (See Focus on Discovery 2.1 for a discussion of what psychotherapy is.) Classical psychoanalysis is based on Freud's second theory of neurotic anxiety, that such anxiety is the reaction of the ego when a previously punished and repressed id impulse presses for expression. The unconscious part of the ego, encountering a situation that reminds it of a repressed conflict from childhood—one usually having to do with sexual or aggressive impulses—is overcome by debilitating tension. Psychoanalytic therapy is an insight therapy. It attempts to remove the earlier repression and help the patient face the childhood conflict, gain insight into it, and resolve it in the light of adult reality. The repression, occurring so long ago, has prevented the ego from growing in an adult fashion; the lifting of the repression is supposed to enable this relearning to take place.

The essence of psychoanalysis has been captured by Paul Wachtel (1977) in the metaphor of the woolly mammoth. Some of these gigantic creatures, frozen alive eons ago, have been recovered so perfectly preserved that their meat could be eaten. Neurotic problems were considered by Freud to be the encapsulated residue of conflicts from long ago. Present adult problems are merely reflections or expressions of these frozen intrapsychic conflicts.

Some wooly mammoths were frozen during an ice age and perfectly preserved. Wachtel sees repression as similar—neurotic conflicts are buried in the unconscious and thus not responsive to adult reality.

> *The patient's neurosis is seen as deriving most essentially from his continuing and unsuccessful efforts to deal with internalized residues of his past [the "woolly mammoth"] which, by virtue of being isolated from his adaptive and integrated ego, continue to make primitive demands wholly unresponsive to reality. It is therefore maintained that a fully successful treatment must create conditions whereby these anachronistic inclinations can be experienced consciously and integrated into the ego, so that they can be controlled and modified.*
> (Wachtel, 1977, p. 36)

Analysts employ a number of techniques in their efforts to lift repressions. Perhaps the best known is **free association**. The patient reclines on a couch, facing away from the analyst, and is encouraged to give free rein to his or her thoughts, verbalizing whatever comes to mind without the censoring done in everyday life. It is assumed that the patient can gradually learn this skill and that defenses built up over many years can eventually be bypassed. But blocks to free association often do arise; the patient may suddenly become silent or change the topic. These **resistances** are carefully noted by the analyst because they are assumed to signal that a sensitive or ego-threatening area has been encountered. These sensitive areas are precisely what the analyst will want to probe further.

Dream analysis is another analytic technique. Psychoanalytic theory holds that in sleep, ego defenses are relaxed, allowing normally repressed material to enter the sleeper's consciousness. Since this material is extremely threatening, it usually cannot be allowed into consciousness in its actual form; rather, the repressed material is disguised, and dreams

What Is Psychotherapy?

Shorn of its theoretical complexities, any **psychotherapy** is a social interaction in which a trained professional tries to help another person, the client or patient, behave and feel differently. The therapist follows procedures that are to a greater or lesser extent prescribed by a certain theory or school of thought. The basic assumption is that particular kinds of verbal and nonverbal exchanges in a trusting relationship can achieve goals such as reducing anxiety and eliminating self-defeating or dangerous behavior.

Basic as this definition may seem, there is little general agreement about what really constitutes psychotherapy. A person's next-door neighbor might utter the same words of comfort as a clinical psychologist, but should we regard this as psychotherapy? In what way is psychotherapy different from such nonprofessional reassurance? Is the distinction made on the straightforward basis of whether the dispenser of reassurance has a particular academic degree or license? Does it relate to whether the giver of information has a theory that dictates or at least guides what he or she says? Does it depend on how sound the basic assumptions of the theory are? These are difficult questions, and as in other areas of abnormal psychology, there is less than complete agreement among professionals.

It is important to note that the people who seek or are sent for *professional* help have probably tried nonprofessional avenues to feeling better and have failed to obtain relief. Before most individuals go to a therapist, they have confided in friends or in a spouse, perhaps spoken to the family doctor, consulted with a member of the clergy, or maybe tried several of the vast number of self-help books and programs that are so popular. For most people in psychological distress, one or more of these options provide enough relief, and they seek no further help. But for others such attempts fall short, and these individuals are left feeling helpless, often hopeless. These are the people who go to mental health clinics, university counseling centers, and the private offices of independent practitioners.

London (1964, 1986) categorized psychotherapies as **insight therapies** or **action** (behavioral) **therapies**. Insight therapies, such as psychoanalysis, assume that behavior, emotions, and thoughts become disordered because people do not adequately understand what motivates them, especially when their needs and drives conflict. Insight therapies try to help people discover the true reasons they behave, feel, and think as they do. The premise is that greater awareness of motivations will yield greater control over and subsequent improvement in thought, emotion, and behavior.

Of course, insight is not exclusive to the insight therapies, nor is action unique to behavior therapy. As we will see, the action therapies bring insight to the individual as well, and the newer cognitive therapies can be seen as a blend of insight and behavioral therapies. It is a matter of emphasis, a matter of focus. In the behavioral therapies the focus is on changing behavior; insight is often a peripheral benefit. The cognitive therapies place greater emphasis on certain kinds of insights, as we shall see later in this chapter. In the insight therapies the focus is less on changing people's behavior directly than on enhancing their understanding of their motives, fears, and conflicts. To facilitate such insights, therapists of different theoretical persuasions have employed a variety of techniques, ranging from the free association of psychoanalysis to the reflection of feelings practiced in client-centered therapy.

Theories and psychotherapies are great in number. There are scores, perhaps hundreds, each with its enthusiastic supporters. We present in this chapter a close look at the more prominent theories and methods of intervention. Our intent is to provide enough detail about the major approaches to allow a grasp of the basic issues and an overall perspective on the therapeutic enterprise. We hope, too, to provide the reader with the means to evaluate critically new therapies that arise or at the very least to know what questions to ask in order to evaluate them effectively.

take on heavily symbolic content. For example, a woman concerned about aggressive sexual advances from men may dream of being attacked by savages who throw spears at her; the spears are considered phallic symbols, substituting for an explicit sexual advance.

Another key component of psychoanalytic therapy, often regarded as essential to a cure, is the analysis of transference. **Transference** refers to the patient's responses to his or her analyst that are not in keeping with the analyst–patient relationship but seem instead to reflect attitudes and ways of behaving toward important people in the patient's past. For example, a patient may feel that the analyst is generally bored by what he or she is saying and as a result the patient might struggle to be entertaining. Analysts encourage the development of transference by intentionally remaining shadowy figures, sitting behind their patients and divulging little of their personal lives or feelings during a session. Through careful observation and analysis of these transferred attitudes, analysts can gain insight into the childhood origin of repressed conflicts. It is precisely when analysts notice transference developing that they take hope that an important repressed conflict is getting closer to the surface. In the example here, the analyst might find that the patient was made to feel boring and unimportant as a child and could only gain the parental attention he or she craved through humor. (See Table 2.2 for a summary of psychoanalytic therapy techniques and Focus on Discovery 2.2 for an example of transference.)

Excerpt from a Psychoanalytic Session—An Illustration of Transference

Patient: (a fifty-year-old male business executive): I really don't feel like talking today.

Analyst: (Remains silent for several minutes, then) Perhaps you'd like to talk about why you don't feel like talking.

Patient: There you go again, making demands on me, insisting I do what I just don't feel up to doing. (Pause) Do I always have to talk here, when I don't feel like it? (Voice becomes angry and petulant) Can't you just get off my back? You don't really give a damn how I feel, do you?

Analyst: I wonder why you feel I don't care.

Patient: Because you're always pressuring me to do what I feel I can't do.

This excerpt must be viewed in context. The patient had been in therapy for about a year, complaining of depression and anxiety.

Although extremely successful in the eyes of his family and associates, he felt weak and incompetent. Through many sessions of free association and dream analysis, the analyst had begun to suspect that the patient's feelings of failure stemmed from his childhood experiences with an extremely punitive and critical father, a man even more successful than the client, who seemed never to be satisfied with his son's efforts. The exchange quoted here was later interpreted by the analyst as an expression of resentment by the patient of his *father's* pressures on him. The patient's tone of voice (petulant), as well as his overreaction to the analyst's gentle suggestion that he talk about his feelings of not wanting to talk, indicated that the patient was angry not at his analyst, but at his father. The therapist viewed the expression of such feelings—that is, the patient's transferring the feelings from his father to his analyst—as significant, and built on this inference in subsequent sessions to help the patient reevaluate his childhood fears of letting his father down and of expressing anger toward him.

Countertransference refers to the feelings of the analyst toward the patient. Analysts must be aware of their own needs and feelings so they can see the patient clearly, without distortion. For this reason, a training analysis, in which the trainee is psychoanalyzed, is typically part of psychoanalytic training. The challenge that countertransference poses is illustrated by the following discussion of therapy with depressed patients:

> Depressed patients bring their hopelessness and despair into therapy, and the therapist may be affected. If the depression improves slowly, or not at all, the therapist may feel guilty, angry, and/or helpless. After seeing several severely depressed patients in a day, the therapist may feel quite drained and eventually may become unwilling to work in the future with similar patients. Suicidal patients can evoke particularly difficult countertransferences. (Jacobson & McKinney, 1982, p. 215)

As previously repressed material begins to appear in therapy, **interpretation** comes into play. In this technique, the analyst points out to the patient the meaning of certain behav-

---

Table 2.2   Major Techniques of Psychoanalysis

Technique	Description
Free association	The patient tries to say whatever comes to mind without the censoring that usually occurs.
Dream analysis	Based on the assumption that defenses are relaxed during sleep, the symbolic meaning of the content of dreams provides clues regarding repressed conflicts.
Interpretation	The analyst points out to the patient the real meaning of certain of his or her behaviors.
Analysis of Transference	By remaining a shadowy figure, the analyst encourages the patient to respond to him or her in ways that the patient has previously responded to other important figures, especially his parents.

iors. A principal focus of interpretation is defense mechanisms, which, as we have seen, are the ego's unconscious tools for warding off a confrontation with anxiety. For instance, a man who appears to have trouble with intimacy may look out the window and change the subject whenever anything touches on closeness during the course of a session. The analyst will attempt at some point to interpret the patient's behavior, pointing out its defensive nature in the hope of stimulating the patient to acknowledge that he is in fact avoiding the topic.

Modifications in Psychoanalytic Therapy   As happens with all paradigms, changes in the original ideas about the best way to do therapy have occurred over time. One innovation in psychoanalytic therapy was to apply it to groups of people rather than only to individuals. Some analytic groups focus on the psychodynamics of individuals in the group, using typical techniques such as free association, interpretation, and dream analysis (Wolf & Kutash, 1990). Others conceive of the group itself as having a collective set of psychodynamics, manifested by such things as group transference to the therapist. Within psychoanalytic circles there has been some controversy about whether the group approach can possibly work. The key issue is whether the group format will dilute the transference to the therapist and thus make the therapy ineffective.

Other current analytic therapies include ego analysis, brief psychodynamic therapy, and interpersonal psychodynamic therapy.

Ego Analysis   After Freud's death a group of practitioners generally referred to as ego analysts introduced some important modifications to psychoanalytic theory. The major figures in this loosely formed movement include Karen Horney (1942), Anna Freud (1946), Erik Erikson (1950), David Rapaport (1951), and Heinz Hartmann (1958).

Although Freud did not ignore the interactions of the organism with the environment, his view was essentially a push model, in which people are driven by intrapsychic urges. Those who subscribe to **ego analysis** place greater emphasis on a person's ability to control the environment and to select the time and the means for satisfying certain instinctual drives. Their basic contention is that the individual is as much ego as id. In addition, they focus more on the individual's current living conditions than did Freud, although they sometimes advocate delving deeply into the historical causes of an individual's behavior. Generally, they employ most of the psychoanalytic techniques we have just described, but with far less emphasis on transference.

An important assumption for the ego analysts is that there is a set of ego functions (for example, cognition and perception); these functions are primarily conscious, capable of controlling both id instincts and the external environment, and, significantly, do not depend on the id for their energy. Ego analysts assume that these ego functions and capabilities are present at birth and then develop through experience. Underemphasized by Freud, ego functions have energies and gratifications of their own, usually separate from the reduction of id impulses. And, whereas Freud viewed society as essentially a negative inhibition against the unfettered gratification of libidinal impulses, the ego analysts hold that an individual's social interactions can provide their own special kind of gratification.

Brief Psychodynamic Therapy   Although many laypeople assume that patients usually spend many months, even years, in psychodynamic psychotherapy, most courses of therapy last fewer than ten sessions (Garfield, 1978). Actually, Freud originally conceived of psychoanalysis as a relatively short-term process. He thought that the analyst should focus on specific problems, make it clear to the patient that therapy would not exceed a certain number of sessions, and structure sessions in a directive fashion. Freud thus envisioned a more active and briefer psychoanalysis than what eventually developed.

The early pioneers in modern time-limited psychotherapy, called **brief therapy**, were the psychoanalysts Ferenczi (1952) and Alexander and French (1946). Among the many reasons for the short duration of therapy is that people today are less likely to consider the ambitious examination of the past as the best way to deal with today's realities—the essence of classical psychoanalytic treatment. Indeed, most patients expect therapy to be fairly short term and targeted to specific problems in their everyday lives. These expectations contributed to the design of briefer forms of dynamic therapy.

Insurance companies have also played a role both in shortening the duration of treatment and in encouraging analytically oriented workers to adapt their ideas to brief therapy. Insurance companies have become increasingly reluctant to cover more than a limited number of psychotherapy sessions, say, twenty-five, in a given calendar year and have set limits as well on reimbursement amounts (see p. 568 for further discussion of managed care).

Another factor contributing to the growth of brief therapy came from the challenges faced by mental health professionals in responding to psychological emergencies (Koss & Shiang, 1994). Cases of shell shock during World War II led to Grinker and Spiegel's (1944) classic short-term analytic treatment of what is now called posttraumatic stress disorder (p. 163). A related contribution came from Lindemann's (1944) crisis intervention with the survivors of the famous Cocoanut Grove nightclub fire in 1943.

All these factors, combined with the growing acceptability of psychotherapy in the population at large, have set the stage for a stronger focus on time-limited psychodynamic therapy. Brief therapies share several common elements (Koss & Shiang, 1994):

- Assessment tends to be rapid and early.
- The therapist takes a more active role than a traditional psychoanalyst.
- It is made clear right away that therapy will be limited and that improvement is expected within a small number of sessions, from six to twenty-five.
- Goals are concrete and focused on the amelioration of the patient's worst symptoms, on helping the patient understand what is going on in his or her life, and on enabling the patient to cope better in the future.
- Interpretations are directed more toward present life circumstances and patient behavior than on the historical significance of feelings.
- Development of transference is not encouraged, but some positive transference to the therapist is fostered to encourage the patient to follow the therapist's suggestions and advice.
- There is a general understanding that psychotherapy does not cure, but that it can help troubled individuals learn to deal better with life's inevitable stressors.

Interpersonal Psychodynamic Therapy   A variant of brief psychodynamic therapy, often referred to as interpersonal therapy, is found in a group of therapies that emphasize the interactions between a patient and his or her social environment. A pioneer in the development of this approach was the American psychiatrist Harry Stack Sullivan. Sometimes called a neo-Freudian, Sullivan held that the basic difficulty of patients is misperceptions of reality stemming from disorganization in the interpersonal relationships of childhood, primarily the relationship between child and parents.

Sullivan departed from Freud by conceiving of the analyst as a "participant observer" in the therapy process. In contrast with the classical or even ego-analytical view of the therapist as a blank screen for transference, Sullivan argued that the therapist, like the scientist, is inevitably a part of the process he or she is studying; an analyst does not see patients without at the same time affecting them.

A contemporary example of an interpersonal therapy is the **Interpersonal Therapy** (**IPT**) of Klerman and Weissman (Klerman et al., 1984). IPT concentrates on the patient's current interpersonal difficulties and on discussing with the patient—even teaching the patient directly—better ways of relating to others.

Although IPT incorporates some psychodynamic ideas, it is distinct, especially from traditional forms of psychoanalysis. IPT diverges from traditional psychoanalysis in particular in the role of the therapist, which is that of an active patient advocate rather than of a neutral blank screen (Frank & Spanier, 1995; Weissman, 1995). In *Mastering Depression: The Patient's Guide to Therapy*, the following section appears in the description of IPT:

Gerald Klerman and Myrna Weissman husband and wife team who developed interpersonal therapy.

The IPT therapist will not: 1) Interpret your dreams; 2) Have treatment go on indefinitely; 3) Delve into your early childhood; 4) Encourage you to free associate; 5) Make you feel very dependent on the treatment or the therapist. (Weissman, 1995, pp. 11–12)

The techniques an IPT therapist uses combine empathic listening and suggestions for behavioral changes as well as how to implement them. For example, the therapist might explore with the patient the complexities of present-day problems, with an emphasis on the patient's relationships with others. Then the therapist might encourage the patient to make specific behavioral changes, sometimes facilitating these shifts by practicing new behaviors in the consulting room (role-playing). IPT is discussed again in Chapter 10 as an effective therapy for depression.

Evaluating the Psychoanalytic Paradigm

Perhaps no investigator of human behavior has been so honored and so criticized as Freud. Freud's influence on psychoanalytic views of mental disorder has been great, but as we have seen, his theories have been criticized. One of the main criticisms applies to other psychoanalytic theories as well: because they are based on anecdotal evidence gathered during therapy sessions, these theories are not grounded in objectivity and therefore are not scientific. Unlike those who work within the biological paradigm and those who work within the learning and cognitive paradigms discussed later, Freud conducted no formal research on the causes and treatments of abnormal behavior; rather he believed that the information obtained from therapy sessions was enough to validate his theory and demonstrate the effectiveness of the therapy. In Chapter 5 (pp. 116–117) we will discuss the limitations of such data.

Furthermore, Freud's patients were not merely a small sample; they were largely affluent, educated, and Viennese. It is easy to believe that a theory of personality development or structure of the mind based on such a restricted group of troubled individuals might not be generally applicable.

The case reports used by Freud (and his followers) can also be assailed on the grounds of the reliability of Freud's perceptions in those therapy sessions and his ability to recall them accurately, since he did not take careful notes. In addition, Freud's own interest in certain topics, such as patients' possible early sexual experiences, might have affected their accounts, causing them to focus on certain experiences and overlook others based not on their own sense of what was of key importance in their lives, but on Freud's emerging views.

It is also important to keep in mind that psychodynamic concepts, such as id, ego, and the unconscious, though meant to be used as metaphors to describe psychic functions, sometimes were described as though they had an existence of their own and power to act and think. For example, Freud spoke of "immediate and unheeding satisfaction of the instincts, such as the id demands.... The id knows no solicitude about ensuring survival" (1937).

Even with these substantial criticisms, however, Freud's contribution remains enormous and continues to have an important impact on the field of abnormal psychology. Freud's influence is most evident in the following four commonly held assumptions:

1. *Childhood experiences help shape adult personality.* Although acknowledging the role of genetics, contemporary clinicians and researchers still view childhood experiences as crucial. They seldom focus on the psychosexual stages about which Freud wrote but emphasize problematic parent–child relationships in general and how they can influence later adult relationships in negative ways.

2. *There are unconscious influences on behavior.* In Focus 7.2 (p. 181) we review research showing that people can be unaware of the causes of their behavior. However, most current researchers do not think of *an* unconscious or view it as a repository of id instincts.

3. *People use defense mechanisms to control anxiety or stress.* There is a great deal of research on coping with stress (some of it is reviewed in Chapter 8), and defense mechanisms

are included in an appendix of DSM-IV-TR (the fourth edition of the catalogue of mental disorders published by the American Psychiatric Association and reviewed in the next chapter). But contemporary research focuses mostly on *consciously* adopted coping strategies, for example, deliberately trying not to think about some traumatic event. It has yet to be demonstrated whether any unconscious method of coping (even repression) actually plays an important role in controlling anxiety.

4. *The causes and purposes of human behavior are not always obvious.* Freud and his followers sensitized generations of clinicians and psychopathologists to the nonobviousness of the causes and purposes of human behavior. Psychoanalysis cautions us against taking everything at face value. A person expressing disdain for another, for example, may actually like the other person very much yet be fearful of admitting positive feelings. This tendency to look under the surface, to find hidden meanings in behavior, is perhaps the best known legacy of Freud.

Again, although there are many legitimate concerns about the validity and usefulness of Freud's work, it would be a serious mistake to minimize his importance in psychopathology or, for that matter, in the intellectual history of Western civilization. His work has elicited the kind of critical reaction that helps advance knowledge. He was instrumental in getting people to consider nonbiological explanations for disordered behavior, and his descriptions of abnormal behavior were often extremely perceptive. It is impossible to acquire a good grasp of the field of abnormal psychology without some familiarity with Freud's writings.

Humanistic and Existential Paradigms

Humanistic and existential therapies, like psychoanalytic therapies, are insight focused, based on the assumption that disordered behavior results from a lack of insight and can best be treated by increasing the individual's awareness of motivations and needs. But there are useful contrasts between psychoanalysis and its offshoots on the one hand and humanistic and existential approaches on the other.

The psychoanalytic paradigm assumes that human nature, the id, is something in need of restraint, that effective socialization requires the ego to mediate between the environment and the basically antisocial—or, at best, asocial—impulses stemming from biological urges. Psychoanalysis is also a deterministic view of behavior, proposing that all behavior is caused by pressures from the id as well as the mediating influences of the ego and superego. In contrast, humanistic and existential paradigms place greater emphasis on the person's freedom of choice, regarding free will as the person's most important characteristic. Yet free will is a double-edged sword, for it not only offers fulfillment and pleasure, but also threatens acute pain and suffering. It is an innately provided gift that *must* be used and that requires special courage to use. Not everyone can meet this challenge; those who cannot are regarded as candidates for client-centered, existential, and Gestalt therapies.

Humanistic and existential paradigms, also referred to as experiential or phenomenological, seldom focus on how psychological problems develop. Their main influence is on intervention, and so our discussion deals primarily with therapy.

Carl Rogers' Client-Centered Therapy

Carl Rogers was an American psychologist whose theorizing about psychotherapy grew slowly out of years of intensive clinical experience. After teaching at the university level in the 1940s and 1950s, he helped organize the Center for Studies of the Person in La Jolla, California. Rogers's **client-centered therapy** is based on several assumptions about human nature and the means by which we can try to understand it (Ford & Urban, 1963; Rogers, 1951, 1961).

Carl Rogers, a humanistic therapist, proposed that the key ingredient in therapy is the attitude and style of the therapist rather than specific techniques.

- People can be understood only from the vantage point of their own perceptions and feelings, that is, from their phenomenological world. To understand individuals, we must look at the way they experience events rather than at the events themselves, for each person's phenomenological world is the major determinant of behavior and makes that person unique.

- Healthy people are aware of their behavior. In this sense Rogers' system is similar to psychoanalysis and ego analysis, for it emphasizes the desirability of being aware of motives.

- Healthy people are innately good and effective; they become ineffective and disturbed only when faulty learning intervenes.

- Healthy people are purposive and goal directed. They do not respond passively to the influence of their environment or to their inner drives. They are self-directed. In this assumption Rogers is closer to ego analysis than to orthodox Freudian psychoanalysis.

- Therapists should not attempt to manipulate events for the individual; rather, they should create conditions that will facilitate independent decision making by the client. When people are not concerned with the evaluations, demands, and preferences of others, their lives are guided by an innate tendency for **self-actualization**.

Rogers' Therapeutic Intervention   Consistent with his view of what people are like, Rogers avoided imposing goals on the client during therapy. According to Rogers, the client is to take the lead and direct the course of the conversation and of the session. The therapist's job is to create conditions so that during their hour together the client can return once again to his or her basic nature and judge which course of life is intrinsically gratifying. Because of his very positive view of people, Rogers assumed that their decisions would not only make them happy with themselves but also turn them into good, civilized people. The road to these good decisions is not easy, however.

According to Rogers and other humanistic and existential therapists, people must take responsibility for themselves, even when they are troubled. It is often difficult for a therapist to refrain from giving advice, from taking charge of a client's life, especially when the client appears incapable of making his or her own decisions. But Rogerians hold steadfastly to the rule that an individual's innate capacity for growth and self-direction will assert itself provided that the therapeutic atmosphere is warm, attentive, and receptive, and especially if the therapist totally accepts the person for who he or she is, providing what he called **unconditional positive regard**.

Other people set what Rogers called "conditions of worth"—"I will love you if...." In contrast, unconditional positive regard is reflected in the client-centered therapist's valuing clients as they are, even if he or she does not approve of their behavior. People have value merely for being people, and the therapist must care deeply for and respect a client for the simple reason that he or she is another human being engaged in the struggle of growing and being alive.

Although client-centered therapy is not technique oriented, one strategy is central to this approach, namely, empathy. Because empathy is so important to Rogerian therapy and because it is important as well in all other kinds of therapy (not to mention ordinary social intercourse), let us examine it more closely. There is more to empathy than meets the eye.

Empathy   We find it useful to distinguish two types of empathy, following Egan (1975).

Primary empathy refers to the therapist's understanding, accepting, and communicating to the client what the client is thinking or feeling. That is, the therapist conveys primary empathy by restating the client's thoughts and feelings, pretty much in the client's own words.

Advanced empathy entails an inference by the therapist of the thoughts and feelings that lie behind what the client is saying, thoughts and feelings of which the client may only be dimly, if at all, aware. Advanced empathy essentially involves an interpretation by the therapist of the meaning of what the client is thinking and feeling. In our view, advanced empathy represents theory building on the part of the therapist. After considering over a number of sessions what the client has been saying and how he or she has been saying it, the therapist generates a hypothesis about what may be the true source of distress and yet remains hidden from the client.[2]

The following example illustrates the difference between primary and advanced empathy:

> **Client:** I don't know what's going on. I study hard, but I just don't get good marks. I think I study as hard as anyone else, but all of my efforts seem to go down the drain. I don't know what else I can do.
>
> **Counselor A:** You feel frustrated because even when you try hard you fail [primary empathy].
>
> **Counselor B:** It's depressing to put in as much effort as those who pass and still fail. It gets you down and maybe even makes you feel a little sorry for yourself [advanced empathy]. (Egan, 1975, p. 135)

Bear in mind that therapists operating within the client-centered framework assume that the client views things in an unproductive way, as evidenced by the psychological distress that has brought the client into therapy. At the primary empathic level, the therapist accepts this view, understands it, and communicates to the client that it is appreciated. But at the advanced or interpretive level, the therapist offers something new, a perspective that he or she hopes is better and more productive and implies new modes of action. Advanced empathizing builds on the information provided over a number of sessions in which the therapist concentrated on making primary-level empathic statements.

The client-centered therapist, operating within a phenomenological perspective, *must* have as the goal the movement of a client from his or her present phenomenological world to another one, hence the importance of the advanced-empathy stage. Since people's emotions and actions are determined by how they construe themselves and their surroundings—by their phenomenology—those who are dysfunctional or otherwise dissatisfied with their present mode of living are in need of a *new* phenomenology. From the very outset, then, client-centered therapy—and all other phenomenological therapies—concentrates on clients' adopting frameworks different from what they had when they began treatment. Merely to reflect back to clients their current phenomenology cannot in itself bring therapeutic change. A new phenomenology must be acquired.

Existential Therapy

Humanism and existentialism have much in common, but the humanistic work of Americans such as Rogers can be contrasted with the more European existential approach that derives from the writings of such philosophers as Sartre, Kierkegaard, and Heidegger and psychiatrists like Binswanger and Boss of Switzerland and Frankl of Austria, whose logotherapy and views on depression are discussed later (p. 275). In an influential book on existential psychotherapy, Stanford University psychiatrist Irvin Yalom portrayed well the differences between these approaches.

> *The existential tradition in Europe has always emphasized human limitations and the tragic dimensions of existence. Perhaps it has done so because Europeans have had a greater familiarity with geographic and ethnic confinement, with war, death, and uncertain existence. The United States (and the humanistic psychology it spawned) bathed in a Zeitgeist of expansiveness, optimism, limitless horizons, and pragmatism.... The European focus is on limits, on facing and taking into oneself the anxiety of uncertainty and non-being. The humanistic psycholo-*

---

[2] Whether an advanced-empathy statement by the therapist should be regarded as accurate is another question. These interpretations by client-centered therapists can never be known for sure to be true. Rather, like scientific theories and insights into the past, they may be more or less useful.

gists, on the other hand, speak less of limits and contingency than of development of potential, less of acceptance than of awareness, less of anxiety than of peak experiences and oceanic one-ness, less of life meaning than of self-realization [and self-actualization], less of apartness and basic aloneness than of I-thou and encounter. (1980, p. 19)

The existential point of view, like humanism, emphasizes personal growth. Yet, as indicated, there are some important distinctions between the two. Humanism, exemplified by Rogers' views, stresses the goodness of human nature. It holds that if unfettered by groundless fears and societal restrictions, human beings will develop normally, even exceptionally, much as a flower will sprout from a seed if given enough light, air, and water. Existentialism is gloomier; it contains a strain of darkness. Although it embraces free will and responsibility, existentialism stresses the anxiety that is inevitable in making important choices, the existential choices on which existence depends, such as staying or not staying with a spouse, with a job, or even with this world. Hamlet's famous soliloquy beginning, "To be, or not to be, that is the question" (act III, scene 1), is a classic existential statement. To be truly alive is to confront the anxiety that comes with existential choices.

To avoid choices, to pretend that they do not have to be made, may protect people from anxiety, but it also deprives them of living a life with meaning and is at the core of psychopathology. Thus, whereas the humanistic message is upbeat, almost ecstatic, the existential is tinged with sadness and anxiety, but not despair, unless the exercise of free will and the assumption of responsibility that accompanies it are avoided.

The Goals of Existential Therapy

So oftentimes it happens that we live our lives in chains, and we never even know we have the key. (Jack Tempchin & Robb Strandlund, "Already Gone," 1973, 1975)

Based on this view of human existence, therapists operating within an existential framework encourage patients to confront their anxieties concerning choices about how they will live, what they will value, how they will relate to others. Therapists support their clients in examining what is really meaningful in life. According to this view, sometimes the most important and most courageous choice one can make will occasion extreme discomfort. Life is not easy for those who would be true to themselves.

At some point during therapy the client must begin to *behave differently*, both toward the therapist and toward the outside world, in order to change his or her own existential condition. Hence, although the existential view is highly subjective, it strongly emphasizes behavior, in particular *relating to others* in an open, honest, spontaneous, and loving manner. At the same time, it emphasizes that each of us is ultimately and basically alone; the paradox of life is that we are inherently separate from others, that we came into the world alone and must create our own existence in the world alone.

In the existential view, people create their existence anew at each moment. The potential for disorder as well as for growth is ever present. Individuals must be encouraged to accept the responsibility for their own existence and to realize that within certain limits, they can redefine themselves at any moment and behave and feel differently within their own social environment.

The existential writers are vague about what therapeutic techniques will help the client grow. A reliance on technique may even be seen as an objectifying process in which the therapist acts on the client as though he or she were a thing to be manipulated (Prochaska, 1984). The existential approach is best understood as a general attitude taken by certain therapists toward human nature rather than as a set of therapeutic techniques.

Gestalt Therapy

A therapy that has both humanistic and existential elements, **Gestalt therapy** derives from the work of Frederich S. (Fritz) Perls. Like Rogers, Perls held that people have an innate goodness and that this basic nature should be allowed to express itself.

Psychological problems originate in frustrations and denials of this inborn virtue. Gestalt therapists, along with other humanistic therapists, emphasize the creative and expressive aspects of people, rather than the problematic and distorted features on which psychoanalysts often seem to concentrate.

A central goal of Gestalt therapy is to help patients understand and accept their needs, desires, and fears and to enhance their awareness of how they block themselves from reaching their goals and satisfying their needs. A basic assumption is that all of us bring our needs and wants to any situation. We do not merely perceive situations as they are; instead, we engage our social environment by projecting our needs, fears, or desires onto what is out there. Thus, if I am talking to a stranger, I do not merely react to the person as that person exists; I react to the stranger in the context of my needs. Sometimes unfinished business with a significant person from the past can affect how we deal with someone in the present.

Frederich (Fritz) Perls (1893–1970), the colorful founder of Gestalt therapy.

Gestalt Therapy Techniques   Gestalt therapists focus on what a client is doing in the consulting room here and now, without delving into the past, for the most important event in the client's life is what is happening at this moment. In Gestalt therapy all that exists is the now. If the past is bothersome, it is brought into the present. Questions of why are discouraged because searching after causes in the past is considered an attempt to escape responsibility for making choices in the present, a familiar existential theme. Clients are exhorted, cajoled, sometimes even coerced into awareness of what is happening now.

Gestalt therapy is noted for its emphasis on techniques, in contrast to their paucity in the humanistic and existential therapies discussed so far. We describe here a small sample of current Gestalt practices.

- *I-language.* To help patients bear responsibility for their present and future lives, the therapist instructs them to change "it" language into "I" language.

  Therapist: What do you hear in your voice?
  Patient: My voice sounds like it is crying.
  Therapist: Can you take responsibility for that by saying, I am crying? (Levitsky & Perls, 1970, p. 142)

  This simple change in language, besides encouraging the patient to assume responsibility for his or her feelings and behavior, reduces the patient's sense of being alienated from aspects of his or her very being. It helps the patient see the self as active rather than passive, as an open and searching person rather than as someone whose behavior is determined entirely by external events.

- *The empty chair.* In the empty-chair technique, a client projects and then talks to the projection of a feeling or to a person, object, or situation. For example, if a patient is crying, the Gestalt therapist might ask the patient to regard the tears as being in an empty chair opposite him or her and to speak *to* the tears. This tactic often seems to help people confront their feelings. In contrast, to ask a person to talk instead *about* his or her tears is assumed to encourage the person to establish an even greater distance from his or her feelings—which Gestalt therapists assert interferes with psychological well-being. A variation of the empty chair is the two-chair technique, wherein the patient moves to the chair that he or she has been talking to and responds as if he were the person or feeling in the empty chair.

- *Projection of feelings.* Gestalt therapists working with groups sometimes have people pair off, close their eyes, and imagine the face of an individual to whom they have a strong emotional attachment. They are encouraged to concentrate on the feelings they have about that person. Then all open their eyes and look at their partner. After a few moments they are instructed to close their eyes again and think of something neutral, such as an arithmetic problem. They then open their eyes again and look a second time at their partner. Finally, they are asked whether there was an important

In the empty-chair technique the client projects a person, object, or situation onto an empty chair and then talks to it instead of about it.

difference in the way they felt about their partner in the two situations. This exercise is designed to exaggerate what is assumed to be inevitable in all our social interactions, namely, the intrusion of our feelings into whatever is happening at any particular moment.

- *Attending to nonverbal cues.* All therapists pay attention to nonverbal and paralinguistic cues given by the client. Nonverbal cues are body movements, facial expressions, gestures, and the like; paralinguistic cues are tone of voice, speed with which words are spoken, and other audible components of speech beyond its content. People can negate with their hands or their eyes what they are saying with the larynx. Perls placed special emphasis on these nonlinguistic signals, closely observing them to determine what clients might really be feeling. "What we say is mostly lies or bullshit. But the voice is there, the gesture, the posture, the facial expression, the psychosomatic language" (Perls, 1969, p. 54).

- *The use of metaphor.* During the therapy session Gestalt therapists often create unusual scenarios to externalize—to make more vivid and understandable—a problem they believe a client is having. The following scene occurred in a session we observed:

A husband and wife sat together on a sofa, bickering about the woman's mother. The husband seemed very angry with his mother-in-law, and the therapist surmised that she was getting in the way of his relationship with his wife. The therapist wanted to demonstrate to the couple how frustrating this must be for both of them, and he also wished to goad both of them to do something about it. Without warning, he rose from his chair and wedged himself between the couple. Not a word was said. The husband looked puzzled, then hurt, and gradually became angry at the therapist. He asked him to move so that he could sit next to his wife again. The therapist shook his head. When the husband repeated his request, the therapist removed his jacket and placed it over the wife's head so that the husband could not even see her. A long silence followed, during which the husband grew more and more agitated. The wife meanwhile was sitting quietly, covered by the therapist's coat. Suddenly the husband stood up, walked past the therapist, and angrily removed the coat; then he pushed the therapist off the sofa. The therapist exploded in good-natured laughter. "I wondered how long it would take you to do something!" he roared.

This staged scene drove several points home in a way that mere words might not have. The husband, having been trained already by the therapist to get in better touch with his feelings and to express them without fear or embarrassment, reported tearfully that he had felt cut off from his wife by the therapist, in much the same way that he felt alienated from her by her mother. The mother was intruding, and he was not doing anything about it. He did not trust himself to assert his needs and to take action to satisfy them. The fact that he was able to remove the coat and the therapist as well made him wonder whether he might not behave similarly toward his mother-in-law. As he spoke, his wife began to sob; she confided to her husband that all along she had been wanting him to take charge of the problem with her mother. So far so good. But then the therapist turned to the woman and asked her why she had not removed the coat herself! The husband grinned as the therapist gently chided the wife for being unduly passive about her marital problems. By the end of the session, the clients, although emotionally drained, felt in better contact with each other and expressed their resolve to work together actively to alter their relationship with her mother.

Gestalt therapy forcefully conveys the existential message that a person is not a prisoner of the past, that he or she can at any time make the existential choice to be different, and that the therapist will not tolerate stagnation. No doubt this optimistic view helps many people change. Perls' emphasis on responsibility is not to be confused with commitment or obligation to others. Even as a therapist Perls did not present himself as a person who assumed responsibility for others, and he did not urge this on his patients either. The individual has the responsibility to take care of himself or herself, to meet his or her *own* needs as they arise. This apparent egocentrism may be troubling for people with a social conscience and for those who have in the past made commitments to others. Perls believed that such commitments should never be made (Prochaska, 1984).

Table 2.3   Comparison of Humanistic and Existential Therapies

Common to All	Rogerian	Existential	Gestalt
Insight focused Emphasize free will and responsibility Take a phenomenological approach Emphasize personal growth	People are innately good and effective and become disturbed only when faulty learning intervenes. In therapy, goals are not imposed and the therapist totally accepts the client (unconditional positive regard). Empathy is the main therapeutic strategy, both primary empathy—restating the client's thoughts and feelings—and advanced empathy—an interpretation of what lies behind what the client has been saying.	The patient is encouraged to face the anxiety that making choices entails. Therapy techniques are avoided There is a focus on relating to others genuinely.	People are innately good and effective but can lose awareness of their needs and desires. Therapy focuses on the here and now, not on the past. Many techniques (e.g., I-language, empty-chair) are used to make the patient more aware of needs, desires, and fears so that they can be incorporated into his or her personality.

A comparison of the three humanistic and existential therapies we have discussed is presented in Table 2.3.

Evaluating the Humanistic and Existential Paradigms

We have seen that Rogers and the existential therapists focus on the client's phenomenology. But how can the therapist ever know that he or she is truly understanding a patient's world as it appears to the patient? The validity of the inferences made by therapists about the client's phenomenology is an important and unsolved issue.

That people are innately good and, if faulty learning does not interfere, will make choices that are personally fulfilling, is also an assumption that can be questioned. Other social philosophers (for example, Thomas Hobbes) have taken a decidedly less optimistic view of human nature.

Gestalt therapy conveys the message that people are not prisoners of their past, that change is possible. But if the person does not know how to behave differently, considerable damage could be done. For example, if a socially inhibited person has not learned to talk assertively to others, it may do little good to make him or her more aware of this nonassertiveness and encourage greater assertiveness. Lacking the necessary skills, the person may be doomed to fail.

Rogers should be credited with originating the field of psychotherapy research. He insisted that therapy outcomes be empirically evaluated and pioneered the use of tape recordings so that therapists' behavior could be related to therapeutic outcomes. The major prediction of Rogerian therapy, of course, is that therapists' empathy should relate to outcomes. The data are inconsistent (Greenberg, Elliott, & Lietaer, 1994). However, it probably makes sense to continue to emphasize empathy in the training of therapists, as this quality is likely to make it easier for clients to reveal highly personal and sometimes unpleasant facts about themselves.

Learning Paradigms

Psychologists operating in the **learning** (or behavioral) **paradigm** view abnormal behavior as responses learned in the same ways in which other human behavior is learned. Very early in the twentieth century, psychology was dominated not by learning but by structuralism, which held that the proper subject of study was mental functioning. The goal

John B. Watson, American psychologist, was the major figure in establishing behaviorism, defining psychology as the study of observable behavior rather than as an investigation of subjective experience.

of psychology, then a very new discipline, was to learn more about what went on in the mind by analyzing its elementary constituents. Through painstaking **introspection**, self-observation, and reporting about mental processes, psychologists hoped to discover the structure of consciousness.

The Rise of Behaviorism

After some years many, in the field began to lose faith in this approach. The problem was that different laboratories were yielding conflicting data. This dissatisfaction was brought to a head by John B. Watson (1878–1958), who in 1913 revolutionized psychology with his views.

> *Psychology as the behaviorist views it is a purely objective experimental branch of natural science. Its theoretical goal is the prediction and control of behavior. Introspection forms no essential part of its methods, nor is the scientific value of its data dependent upon the readiness with which they lend themselves to interpretation in terms of consciousness. (p. 158)*

To replace introspection Watson looked to the experimental procedures of the psychologists who were investigating learning in animals. Because of his efforts, the dominant focus of psychology switched from thinking to learning. **Behaviorism** can be defined as an approach that focuses on the study of observable behavior rather than on consciousness. We will look at three types of learning that have attracted the research efforts of psychologists: classical conditioning, operant conditioning, and modeling.

Classical Conditioning   One type of learning, **classical conditioning**, was discovered quite by accident by the Russian physiologist and Nobel laureate Ivan Pavlov (1849–1936) at the turn of the twentieth century. In Pavlov's studies of the digestive system, a dog was given meat powder to make it salivate. Before long, Pavlov's laboratory assistants became aware that the dog began salivating when it saw the person who fed it. As the experiment continued, the dog began to salivate even earlier, when it heard the footsteps of its feeder. Pavlov was intrigued by these findings and decided to study the dog's reactions systematically. In the first of many experiments, a bell was rung behind the dog and then the meat powder was placed in its mouth. After this procedure had been repeated a number of times, the dog began salivating as soon as it heard the bell and before it received the meat powder.

In this experiment, because the meat powder automatically elicits salivation with no prior learning, the powder is termed an **unconditioned stimulus (UCS)** and the response of salivation an **unconditioned response (UCR)**. When the offering of meat powder is preceded several times by a neutral stimulus, the ringing of a bell, the sound of the bell alone (the **conditioned stimulus, CS**) is able to elicit the salivary response (the **conditioned response, CR**) (see Figure 2.3). The CR usually differs somewhat from the UCR (e.g., Rescorla, 1988), but these subtleties are beyond the needs of this book. As the number of paired presentations of the bell and the meat powder increases, the number of salivations elicited by the bell alone increases. **Extinction** refers to what happens to the CR when the repeated soundings of the bell are later *not* followed by meat powder; fewer and fewer salivations are elicited, and the CR gradually disappears.

It was discovered that classical conditioning could even instill pathological fear. A famous experiment, questionable from an ethical point of view, was conducted by John Watson and Rosalie Rayner (1920). They introduced a white rat to an eleven-month-old boy, Little Albert, who indicated no fear of the animal and appeared to want to play with it. Whenever the boy reached for the rat, the experimenter made a loud noise (the UCS) by striking a steel bar behind Albert's head, causing him great fright (the UCR). After five such experiences Albert became very frightened (the CR) by the sight of the white rat, even when the steel bar was not struck. The fear initially associated with the loud noise had come

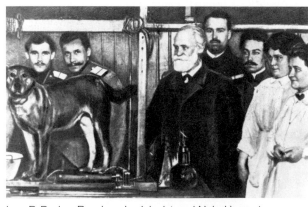

Ivan P. Pavlov, Russian physiologist and Nobel laureate, was responsible for extensive research and theory in classical conditioning. His influence is still very strong in Russian psychology.

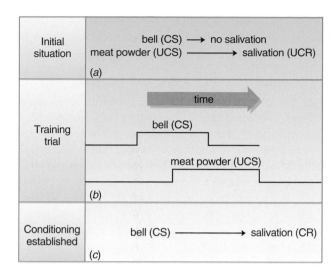

Figure 2.3   The process of classical conditioning. (*a*) Before learning, the meat powder (UCS) elicits salivation (UCR), but the bell (CS) does not. (*b*) A training or learning trial consists of presentations of the CS, followed closely by the UCS. (*c*) Classical conditioning has been accomplished when the previously neutral bell elicits salivation (CR).

to be elicited by the previously neutral stimulus, the white rat (now the CS). This study suggests the possible relationship between classical conditioning and the development of certain emotional disorders, in this instance a phobia.

Operant Conditioning   A second principal type of learning derives primarily from the work of Edward Thorndike (1874–1949), begun in the 1890s. Rather than investigate the association between stimuli, as Pavlov did, Thorndike was interested in the effect of consequences on behavior. He had observed that caged alley cats, in their efforts to escape, would accidentally hit the latch that freed them. Recaged again and again, they would soon come to touch the latch immediately and purposefully. Thorndike formulated what was to become an extremely important principle, the **law of effect**: behavior that is followed by consequences satisfying to the organism will be repeated, and behavior that is followed by noxious or unpleasant consequences will be discouraged. Thus the behavior or response that has consequences serves as an instrument, encouraging or discouraging its own repetition. Learning that focuses on consequences was first called **instrumental learning**.

Important changes in these ideas were made by B. F. Skinner (1904–1990). Skinner introduced the concept of **operant conditioning**, so called because it applies to behavior that operates on the environment. He reformulated the law of effect by shifting the focus from the linking of stimuli and responses—S–R connections—to the relationships between responses and their consequences or contingencies. The distinction is subtle, but it reflects Skinner's contention that stimuli do not so much get connected to responses as they become the occasions for responses to occur, if in the past they have been reinforced. Skinner introduced the concept of **discriminative stimulus** to refer to external events that in effect tell an organism that if it performs a certain behavior, a certain consequence will follow.

Renaming Thorndike's "law of effect" the "principle of reinforcement," Skinner distinguished two types of reinforcement. **Positive reinforcement** refers to the strengthening of a tendency to respond by virtue of the presentation of a pleasant event, called a positive reinforcer. For example, a water-deprived pigeon will tend to repeat behaviors (operants) that are followed by the availability of water. **Negative reinforcement** also strengthens a response, but it does so via the *removal* of an aversive event, such as the cessation of electric shock. Extrapolating his extensive work with pigeons to complex human behavior (his book *Walden Two* is one of the bet-

B. F. Skinner was responsible for the study of operant behavior and the extension of this approach to education, psychotherapy, and society as a whole.

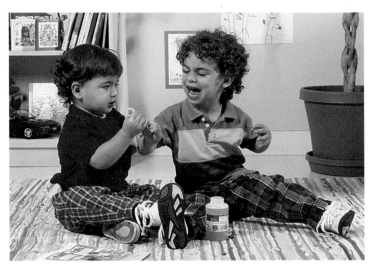

Aggressive responses in children are often rewarded, which makes them more likely to occur in the future.

The Skinner box is often used in studies of operant conditioning to demonstrate how a response can be shaped by rewarding it.

ter known utopian novels, describing an ideal society governed by his principles of reinforcement), Skinner argued that freedom of choice is a myth and that all behavior is determined by the reinforcers provided by the environment.

The goal of the Skinnerians (Skinner, 1953), like that of their mentor, Watson, is the prediction and control of behavior. These experimenters hope that by analyzing behavior in terms of observable responses and reinforcement, they will be able to determine when certain behavior will occur. The information gathered should then help indicate how behavior is acquired, maintained, changed, and eliminated.

The Skinnerian approach avoids abstract terms and concepts. For example, references to needs, motivation, and wants are conspicuously absent in Skinnerian writings. To provide an entirely satisfactory account of human behavior, Skinner believed that psychology must restrict its attention to directly observable stimuli and responses and to the effects of reinforcement. Psychologists who hold this view do not, as human beings, deny the existence of inner states of mind and emotion. Rather, they urge that investigators not employ such mediators in trying to develop a science of behavior.

In a prototypical operant-conditioning experiment, a hungry rat might be placed in a box, known as a Skinner box, that has a lever located at one end. The rat will explore its new environment and by chance come close to the lever. The experimenter may then drop a food pellet into the receptacle located near the lever. After a few such rewards the animal will come to spend more and more time in the area around the lever. But now the experimenter may drop a pellet into the receptacle only when the rat happens to touch the lever. After capitalizing on a few chance touches, the rat begins to touch the lever frequently. With lever touching well established, the experimenter can make the criterion for reward more stringent—the animal must now actually press the lever. Thus the desired operant behavior, lever pressing, is gradually achieved by **shaping**, that is, by rewarding a series of responses, called **successive approximations**, that more and more closely resemble the desired response. The number of lever presses increases as soon as they become the criterion for the release of pellets and decreases, or extinguishes, when the pellet is no longer dropped into the receptacle after a lever press.

As an example of how operant conditioning can produce abnormal behavior, let us consider a key feature of conduct disorder (p. 484), a high frequency of aggressive behavior. Aggression is often rewarded, as when one child beats up another to secure the possession of a toy (getting the toy is the reinforcer). Parents may also unwittingly reinforce aggression by giving in when the child becomes angry or threatens violence to achieve some goal, such as staying up late to watch TV.

Modeling   In real life, learning often goes on even in the absence of reinforcers. We all learn by watching and imitating others, a process called **modeling**. Experimental work has demonstrated that witnessing someone perform certain activities can increase or decrease diverse kinds of behavior, such as sharing, aggression, and fear. For example, Bandura and Menlove (1968) used a modeling treatment to reduce fear of dogs in children. After witnessing a fearless model engage in various activities with a dog, initially fearful children showed a decided increase in their willingness to approach and handle a dog. Similarly, modeling may explain the acquisition of abnormal behavior. Children of parents with phobias or substance-abuse problems may acquire similar behavior patterns, in part through observation.

Mediational Learning Paradigms

Among the learning paradigms, modeling illustrates what is clearly an important issue, namely, the role of mediators in learning and behavior. Consider what happens in the typical modeling experiment. A person watches another do something and immediately shows a change in behavior. No overt responding is necessary for the learning to take place, nor does the observer need to be reinforced. Something is learned before the person makes any observable response. Similar outcomes led some learning theorists of the 1930s and 1940s to infer mediators of various kinds to explain overt behavior.

In the most general terms, a **mediational theory of learning** holds that an environmental stimulus does not initiate an overt response directly; rather, it does so through some intervening process, or **mediator**, such as fear or thinking. The mediator is conceptualized as an internal response. Without divorcing themselves from behaviorism, mediational learning theorists adopt the paradigmatic position that under certain conditions it is both legitimate and important to go beyond observables.

Consider the mediational learning analysis of anxiety developed by O. Hobart Mowrer (1939) and Neal Miller (1948). In a typical experiment rats were shocked repeatedly in the presence of a neutral stimulus, such as the sound of a buzzer. The shock (UCS) produced a UCR of pain, fear, and flight. After several pairings the fear that was naturally produced by the shock came to be produced by the buzzer. The shock could eventually be omitted, and the animal would continue to react fearfully to the previously neutral stimulus (CS). In addition, it was shown that the rat could learn new responses to escape from or avoid the CS (e.g., Miller, 1948). The question became how to conceptualize the finding that animals would learn to *avoid* a harmless event. Mowrer (1947) and others suggested that in this, a typical **avoidance conditioning** experiment, two bits of learning were taking place (Figure 2.4): (1) the animal, by means of classical conditioning, learned to fear the CS; and (2) the animal, by means of operant conditioning, learned an overt behavior to remove itself from the CS and thus to reduce the mediating fear response. This came to be known as two-factor theory.

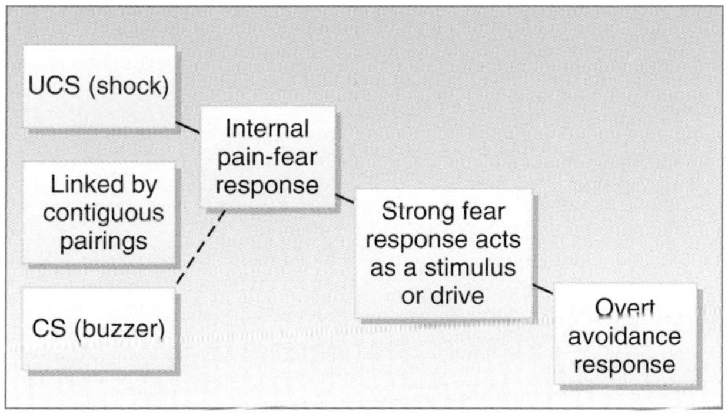

Figure 2.4   Schematic representation of Mowrer's account of avoidance learning. The dashed line indicates that the subject is learning to fear the buzzer, and the solid line that the subject is learning to avoid the shock.

The essential features of this theorizing are that fear or anxiety can be conceived of both as an internal response, which can be learned as observable responses are learned, and as an internal drive, which can motivate avoidance behavior. Anxiety then becomes amenable to the same kind of experimental analysis employed in the investigation of observable behavior. For instance, if we know that repetition of an overt response without reinforcement leads to the extinction of the response, we can predict that repeated evocation of a fear response while withholding the expected pain or punishment will reduce the fear. This is no trivial prediction, and, as we will soon see, treatments based on such reasoning have helped to reduce many irrational fears.

Behavior Therapy

A new way of treating psychopathology, called **behavior therapy**, emerged in the 1950s. In its initial form this therapy applied procedures based on classical and operant conditioning to alter clinical problems. Sometimes the term **behavior modification** is used as well, and therapists who employ operant conditioning as a means of treatment often prefer that term. Although there has been considerable ferment over how to define the field (e.g., Fishman, Rodgers, & Franks, 1988; Mahoney, 1993), behavior therapy today is characterized more by its epistemological stance—its search for rigorous standards of proof—than by allegiance to any particular set of concepts. Behavior therapy is an attempt to change abnormal behavior, thoughts, and feelings by applying in a clinical context the methods used and the discoveries made by experimental psychologists in their study of both normal and abnormal behavior.

Exactly when behavior therapy first began to be developed is difficult to know, but it did not begin when some social scientist woke up one morning and proclaimed that from this day forward people with psychological problems should be treated with techniques suggested by experimental findings. Rather, over a number of years people in the clinical field began to formulate a new set of assumptions about dealing with the problems they were encountering. Although there are areas of overlap, we have found it helpful to distinguish three theoretical approaches in behavior therapy—counterconditioning and exposure, operant conditioning, and modeling. Cognitive behavior therapy is often considered a fourth aspect of behavior therapy, but we will discuss it separately in the section on the cognitive paradigm because of its focus on people's thought processes.

Counterconditioning and Exposure   Because learning paradigms assume that behavior is the result of learning, treatment often involves relearning a new, more adaptive response. **Counterconditioning** is relearning achieved by eliciting a new response in the presence of a particular stimulus. A response (R_1) to a given stimulus (S) can be eliminated by eliciting a new response (R_2) in the presence of that stimulus, as diagrammed in Figure 2.5. For example, in an early and now famous demonstration, Mary Cover Jones successfully treated a young boy's fear of rabbits by feeding him in the presence of a rabbit. The animal was at first kept several feet away and then gradually moved closer on successive occasions. In this way the fear (R_1) produced by the rabbit (S) was replaced by the stronger positive feelings evoked by eating (R_2).

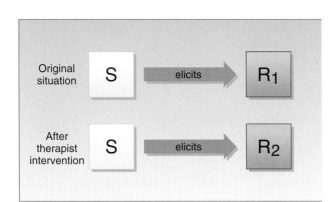

Figure 2.5   Schematic diagram of counterconditioning, whereby an original response (R_1) to a given stimulus (S) is eliminated by evoking a new response (R_2) to the same stimulus.

The **counterconditioning** principle is behind an important behavior therapy technique, **systematic desensitization**, developed by Joseph Wolpe (1958). A person who suffers from anxiety works with the therapist to compile a list of feared situations, starting with those that arouse minimal anxiety and progressing to those that are the most frightening. The person is also taught to relax deeply. Step-by-step, while relaxed, the person imagines the graded series of anxiety-provoking situations. The relaxation tends to inhibit any anxiety that might otherwise be elicited by the imagined scenes. The fearful person becomes able to tolerate increasingly more difficult imagined situations as he or she climbs the hierarchy over a number of therapy sessions.

The thirty-five-year-old substitute mail carrier who consulted us had dropped out of college sixteen years earlier because of crippling fears of being criticized. His disability had taken the form of extreme tension when faced with tests and speaking up in class. When we saw him he was debilitated by fears of criticism in general and of evaluations of his mail sorting in particular. As a consequence, his everyday activities were severely constricted, and though highly intelligent, he had apparently settled for an occupation that did not promise self-fulfillment.

After the client agreed that a reduction in his unrealistic fears would be beneficial, he was taught over several sessions to relax all the muscles of his body while in a reclining chair. We then created for him a list of anxiety-provoking scenes.

You are saying "Good morning" to your boss.
You are standing in front of your sorting bin in the post office, and your supervisor asks why you are so slow.
You are only halfway through your route, and it is already 2:00 p.m.

As you are delivering Mrs. Mackenzie's mail, she opens her screen door and complains about how late you are.
Your wife criticizes you for bringing home the wrong kind of bread.
The officer at the bridge toll gate appears impatient as you fumble in your pocket for the correct change.

These and other scenes were arranged in an anxiety hierarchy, from least to most fear evoking. Desensitization proper began with the client instructed first to relax deeply as he had been taught. Then he was to imagine the easiest item, remaining as relaxed as possible. When he had learned to confront this image without becoming anxious, he went on to the next scene, and so on. After ten sessions the man was able to imagine the most distressing scene in the hierarchy without feeling anxious, and gradually his tension in real life became markedly less (see Focus on Discovery 2.3).[3]

_____

[3] Unreferenced case reports such as this have been drawn from our own clinical files. Identifying features have been altered to protect the confidentiality of the individual.

Virtual Reality as a Psychotherapeutic Tool

A recent technological innovation in psychotherapy is the virtual reality (VR) device (Rizzo et al., 1998). These complex computer-driven apparatuses permit one to create realistic simulations of a wide variety of situations. The user wears a device mounted on his or her head that creates a very realistic depiction of a situation. Because the VR device allows the person to actually interact with the stimulus, it enhances the person's capacity to become immersed in make-believe situations so that feelings and behavior are triggered in ways similar to what would happen in real life. Of course, it has been recognized for many, many years that theater, film, and television ultimately rely for their popularity on the fact that people respond to them in ways that resemble—sometimes surprisingly well—their reactions to reality. What is new in VR is the ability, with high-speed computers, to make the person a part of the simulation by allowing his or her reactions to the simulation to affect what happens next. Important as well, of course, is the dramatic three-dimensional aspect of VR.

Researchers have experimented with VR in treating psychopathology. For example, VR techniques have been used successfully in the treatment of several phobias, including fear of heights (acrophobia), fear of flying (Muehlberger et al., 2001), fear of driving, and fear of spiders (Wiederhold & Wiederhold, 1998, 2000). VR is being applied to more complex problems as well, such as social-skills deficits (Muscott & Gifford, 1994), cognitive impairments (Rizzo et al., 1998; Schultheis & Rizzo, 2001), and attention-deficit hyperactivity disorder (Rizzo et al., 2000). What all these new applications have in common are realistic interactions between the person being tested or treated and a simulated environment that is three-dimensional and truer to life than having someone imagine something, talk about something, or fill out a questionnaire.

The first published case report (Rothbaum et al., 1995a) and controlled study (Rothbaum et al., 1995b) of the successful use of VR involved treating an anxiety disorder, fear of heights. The therapy consisted of five sessions of less than an hour's duration each over a period of three weeks. Exposures involved the person's being encouraged to look out and down from each of several virtual floors in an ascending glass elevator. The VR display showed views from the same elevator in a high-rise (forty-nine-floor) hotel that had been used to assess the client's fear before the treatment. The client's self-reported distress and avoidance of heights decreased markedly as a result of the VR treatment. Similar success was reported by the same clinical research group in the case of a woman who was fearful of flying (Rothbaum et al., 1996).

There are several potential advantages to employing VR for certain psychotherapeutic purposes—we say "potential" because research still needs to be done to compare VR-based interventions with more conventional ones. The VR process is less time-consuming and more controllable than is, for example, taking a person with a fear of heights to the top of a building and encouraging him or her to remain there, perhaps relaxing at the same time to control or countercondition the fear. Virtual reality devices may also produce images that are more realistic than what patients could generate themselves during systematic desensitization, and their use would certainly make sense for fearful individuals who are unable to create realistic images. Evidence abounds that VR does generate very realistic experiences for people (e.g., Hodges et al., cited in Rothbaum et al., 1995b).

The technology of VR continues to advance at a rapid pace. With improvements in both hardware and software, we can expect the realism and complexity of VR to improve in ways that are hard to predict. Some futurists go so far as to warn that VR could lead to social alienation, multiple identities, even virtual worlds—including virtual sex—indistinguishable from the real world (Wiederhold & Wiederhold, 1998). Lest these predictions seem preposterous, consider that just a generation ago e-mail was restricted to a relatively small number of academicians and scientists, that it did not carry images, that the World Wide Web was unknown, and that most people had no idea how to use a computer.

Of course VR will not be appropriate or even necessary for many therapeutic purposes, and some people suffer from "cybersickness" after wearing head-mounted displays for any length of time. Certain therapeutic tasks are likely better approached without the application of this complex, sophisticated technology (Rizzo et al., 1998). Both the potential and the limits of virtual reality technology will be a subject of active research in the coming years.

Virtual reality goggles allow a person to experience life-like images. This may be useful in having patients more realistically confront what they fear.

Wolpe hypothesized that counterconditioning underlies the efficacy of desensitization: a state or response antagonistic to anxiety is substituted for anxiety as the person is exposed gradually to stronger and stronger doses of what he or she fears. Some experiments (e.g., Davison, 1968b) support the idea that counterconditioning underlies the efficacy of the technique, but a number of other explanations are possible. Most contemporary theorists attach importance to exposure per se to what the person fears; relaxation is then considered merely a useful way to encourage a frightened individual to con-

Joseph Wolpe, one of the pioneers in behavior therapy, is known particularly for systematic desensitization, a widely applied behavioral technique.

front what he or she fears (Wilson & Davison, 1971). This technique is useful in reducing a wide variety of fears.

Another type of counterconditioning, **aversive conditioning**, also played an important historical role in the development of behavior therapy. In aversive conditioning, a stimulus attractive to the patient is paired with an unpleasant event, such as a drug that produces nausea or a painful electric shock applied to the hand, in the hope of endowing it with negative properties. For example, a problem drinker who wishes to stop drinking might be asked to smell alcohol while he or she is being made nauseous by a drug. Aversive techniques have been employed to reduce smoking and drug use and the socially inappropriate attraction that objects have for some people, such as the sexual arousal that children produce in pedophiles.

Aversion therapy has been controversial for ethical reasons. A great outcry has been raised about inflicting pain and discomfort on people, even when they ask for it. For example, in its early days aversion therapy was used to try to change the sexual orientation of homosexuals. Gay liberation organizations accused behavior therapists of impeding the acceptance of homosexuality as a legitimate lifestyle. (We explore this issue further in Chapter 18.) Currently, aversion therapy is rarely used as the only treatment for a particular problem. For example, in treating a problem drinker, the aversion treatment may help to temporarily reduce the problem behavior while the client is taught new ways of coping with stress.

Operant Conditioning   Several behavioral procedures derive from operant conditioning. Much of this work has been done with children (See Chapter 15). Problem behavior is analyzed to determine its function, in other words, what is reinforcing it. Generally, problem behavior is thought to be motivated by four possible consequences: attention-seeking, escape from tasks, the generation of sensory reinforcement (such as results from the hand flapping often seen in children with autistic disorder), and gaining access to tangible items or other reinforcers (Carr, 1994). Treatment typically consists of altering the consequences of the problem behavior. For example, if it was established that the problem was motivated by attention seeking, the treatment might be to ignore it. Alternatively, the problem could be followed by **time-out**, a procedure wherein the person is banished for a period of time to a dreary location where positive reinforcers are not available.

Making positive reinforcers contingent on behavior is used to increase the frequency of desirable behavior. For example, a socially withdrawn child could be reinforced for playing with others. Similarly, positive reinforcement has been used to help children with autistic disorder develop language, to remediate learning disabilities, and to help children with mental retardation develop necessary living skills. Other problems treated with these methods include bed-wetting, aggression, hyperactivity, tantrums, and social withdrawal (Kazdin, 1994).

The Token Economy   An early example of work within the operant tradition is the **token economy**, a procedure in which tokens (such as poker chips or stickers) are given for desired behavior and can later be exchanged for desirable items and activities. On the basis of research that Staats and Staats (1963) conducted with children, Ayllon and Azrin (1968) set aside an entire ward of a mental hospital for a series of experiments in which rewards were provided for activities such as making beds and combing hair and were not given when behavior was withdrawn or bizarre. The forty-five female patients, who averaged sixteen years of hospitalization, were systematically rewarded for their ward work and self-care with plastic tokens that could later be exchanged for special privileges, such as listening to records, going to the movies, renting a private room, or enjoying extra visits to the canteen. The life of each patient was as much as possible controlled by this regimen.

Ayllon and Azrin were able to demonstrate the effect of contingencies on the behavior of their ward patients. Figure 2.6 illustrates how the token economy affected grooming and chores. Theirs and subsequent studies (e.g., Menditto, Valdes, & Beck, 1994) attest to the positive impact of token-economy programs in directing staff attention to rewarding self-

Time-out is an operant procedure wherein the consequence for misbehavior is removal to an environment with no positive reinforcers.

care and recreational behaviors and on the acquisition of social skills, in contrast to the more typical situation in which patients get attention more when they are acting maladaptively and sometimes dangerously (Kopelowicz & Liberman, 1998). These experiments have demonstrated how even markedly regressed adult hospital patients can be significantly affected by systematic manipulation of reinforcement contingencies. An elaboration and expansion of the token economy conducted by Gordon Paul and his associates is described in more detail in Focus 11.3.

Modeling   Modeling has also been used in behavior therapy. Bandura, Blanchard, and Ritter (1969) were able to help people reduce their phobic fear of nonpoisonous snakes by having them view both live and filmed encounters in which people gradually approached and successfully handled snakes. Fears of surgery and dental work have been treated in a similar manner (Melamed & Siegel, 1975). Modeling is also part of the treatment for children with autistic disorder, helping them develop complex skills. Films have been used to help sexually inhibited people overcome their discomfort with sexuality (McMullen & Rosen, 1979). Focus on Discovery 2.4 illustrates the use of modeling to encourage assertiveness.

In an analogous fashion, some behavior therapists use **role-playing** in the consulting room. They demonstrate to patients patterns of behaving that might prove more effective than those in which the patients usually engage and then have the patients practice them. Lazarus (1971), in his **behavior rehearsal** procedures, demonstrates exemplary ways of handling a situation and then encourages patients to imitate them during the therapy session. For example, a student who does not know how to ask a professor for an extension on a term paper might watch the therapist portray a potentially effective way of making the request. The clinician would then help the student practice the new skill in a role-playing situation. Similar procedures have helped patients with schizophrenia acquire skills to allow them to deal more effectively with social situations (Marder et al., 1996).

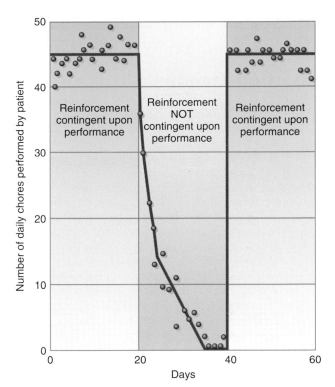

Figure 2.6   Patients on a ward spent more time grooming themselves and doing chores when they received tokens than they did when they were given no reward. Adapted from Ayllon and Azrin (1965).

Evaluating Learning Paradigms

The learning paradigm of abnormal behavior is in much the same position as the biological paradigm. Just as many pertinent biological malfunctions have not been uncovered, abnormality has seldom been convincingly traced to particular learning experiences. Consider how difficult it would be, for example, to show that depression results from a particular reinforcement history. A person would have to be observed continually over a period of years while his or her behavior was recorded and occurrences of reinforcement noted. If identical twins reared by their natural parents developed schizophrenia later in life, the clinician holding a learning view might assert that they had similar reinforcement histories; whereas if fraternal twins were raised at home and only one became schizophrenic, the learning explanation would be that their reinforcement histories were different. Such explanations are as circular and as unsatisfactory as some psychoanalytic inferences of unconscious processes, a practice deplored by behaviorists.

Although adopting a learning explanation of abnormal behavior has clearly led to many treatment innovations, the fact that a treatment based on learning principles is effective in changing behavior does not show that the behavior was itself learned in a similar way. For example, if the mood of depressed persons is elevated by providing them with rewards for increased activity, this cannot be considered evidence that the depression and apathy were initially produced by an absence of rewards (Rimland, 1964).

How is the observation of a model translated into changes in overt behavior? In their original writings on modeling, Bandura and Walters (1963) asserted that an observer could somehow learn new behavior by watching others. Given the emphasis that much of experimental psychology places on learning through doing, this attention to learning without

Assertion Training

"Children should be seen and not heard." "Keep a stiff upper lip." "He's the strong silent type." Our society does not generally value the open expression of beliefs and feelings, and yet people often pay an emotional price for concealing their thoughts and suppressing their feelings. People's wants and needs may not be met if they shy away from stating them clearly. Poor communication between sexual partners is one of the major factors contributing to an unsatisfying sexual relationship, for example. Therapists of all persuasions spend a good deal of time encouraging clients to discover what their desires and needs are and then to take responsibility for meeting them. If patients have trouble expressing their feelings and wishes to others, **assertion training**, conducted individually or in groups, may be able to help them.

Andrew Salter, in his book *Conditioned Reflex Therapy* (1949), was the first behavior therapist to set assertiveness as a positive goal for people. Using Pavlovian classical-conditioning terms, Salter wrote that much human psychological suffering is caused by an excess of cortical inhibition; therefore, greater excitation is warranted. He encouraged socially inhibited people to express their feelings to others in an open, spontaneous way. They should do so verbally, telling people when they are happy or sad, angry or resolute, as well as nonverbally, with smiles and frowns, what Salter called facial talk. They should also contradict people with whom they disagree, with appropriate feeling; use the pronoun I as often as possible; express agreement with those who praise them; and improvise, that is, respond intuitively in the moment without ruminating. In helping patients assert themselves, behavior therapists, whether they acknowledge it or not, are doing therapeutic work

with goals similar to those of humanistic therapists, who also regard expression of positive and negative feelings as a necessary component of effective living.

How are we to define assertion? Might it not be inconsiderate to put ourselves forward and express our beliefs and feelings to others? What if we hurt someone else's feelings in doing so? Much effort has gone into articulating the differences between assertive behavior and aggressive behavior. The following useful distinction was made some years ago by Lange and Jakubowski (1976):

> [Assertion involves] expressing thoughts, feelings, and beliefs in direct, honest, and appropriate ways which respect the rights of other people. In contrast, aggression involves self-expression which is characterized by violating others' rights and demeaning others in an attempt to achieve one's own objectives. (pp. 38–39)

Assertion training is actually a set of techniques having in common the goal of enhancing assertiveness, or what Lazarus (1971) calls "emotional freedom." Because people may be unassertive for any number of reasons, the specific therapy procedures used depend on the reasons believed to be causing the individual's unassertiveness. Goldfried and Davison (1994) suggested several possible causes of unassertiveness—one or more of which may be found in a given individual—as well as related therapy techniques.

- The patient may not know what to say. Some unassertive people

doing was important. But it left out the processes that could be operating. A moment's reflection on the typical modeling experiment suggests the direction that theory and research have taken in recent years. The observer, a child, sits in a chair and watches a film of another child making a number of movements, such as hitting a large, inflated plastic doll in a highly stereotyped manner, and hears the child in the film uttering peculiar sounds. An hour later the youngster is given the opportunity to imitate what was earlier seen and heard. The child is able to do so, as common sense and folk wisdom would predict.

How can we understand what happened? Since the child did not do anything of interest in any motoric way while watching the film, except perhaps fidget in the chair, it would not be fruitful to look at overt behavior for a clue. Obviously, the child's cognitive processes were engaged, including the ability to remember later on what had happened. Data such as these led some behavioral researchers and clinicians to include cognitive variables in their analyses of psychopathology and therapy.

The Cognitive Paradigm

> *There is nothing either good or bad, but thinking makes it so. (Hamlet, act II, scene 2)*
> *The mind is its own place, and in itself*
> *Can make a Heav'n of Hell, a Hell of Heav'n. (Paradise Lost, line 247)*

Cognition is a term that groups together the mental processes of perceiving, recognizing, conceiving, judging, and reasoning. The **cognitive paradigm** focuses on how peo-

lack information on what to say in situations that call for expressiveness. The therapist should supply this information.

- Patients may not know how to behave assertively. They may not assume the tone and volume of voice, the fluency of speech, the facial expression and eye contact, and the body posture necessary for assertiveness. Modeling and role-playing can help these people acquire the signals of firmness and directness.

- Patients may fear that something terrible will happen if they assert themselves. Systematic desensitization may reduce this anticipatory anxiety. Or assertiveness may be blocked by negative self-statements, such as "If I assert myself and am rejected, that would be a catastrophe" (Schwartz & Gottman, 1976). These people may profit from rational-emotive behavior therapy.

- The patient may not feel that it is proper or right to be assertive. The value systems of some people preclude or discourage assertiveness. For example, some of the problems of a Catholic nun undergoing therapy seemed to relate to her unassertiveness, but through discussion it became clear that she would violate her vows were she more expressive and outspoken. By mutual agreement assertion training was not undertaken; instead, therapy focused on helping her work within her chosen profession in ways that were more personally satisfying and yet not more assertive.

Assertion training may begin with conversations in which the therapist tries to get the person to distinguish between assertiveness and aggression. For people who are submissive, even making a reasonable request or refusing a presumptuous one may cause them to feel that they are being hostile. Therapists next usually give patients sample situations that require that they stand up for their rights, their time, and their energies; the situations are such that if the patients are unable to handle them, they feel put-upon.

> You have been studying very hard for weeks, taking no time off at all for relaxation. But now a new film, which will play for only a few days, interests you and you have decided to take a few hours and go late this evening to see it. On the way to an afternoon class, your very good friend tells you that she has free tickets to a concert this evening and asks you to go with her. How do you say no?

Behavior rehearsal is a useful technique in assertion training (Lazarus, 1971). The therapist discusses and models appropriate assertiveness and then has the patient role-play situations. Improvement is rewarded by praise from the therapist or from other members of an assertion-training group. Graded homework assignments, such as asking the mechanic to explain the latest bill for repairs, and, later on, telling a relative that his or her constant criticisms are resented, are given as soon as the client has acquired some degree of assertiveness through session work.

Assertion training raises several ethical issues. To encourage assertiveness in people who, like the nun mentioned earlier, believe that self-denial is a greater good than self-expression would violate their value systems and could generate an unfavorable ripple effect in other areas of their lives. Drawing a distinction between assertion and aggression is also an ethical issue. Behavior considered assertive by one person may be seen by another as aggressive. If we adopt the distinction made by Lange and Jakubowski that assertion respects the rights of others whereas aggression does not, we still have to make a judgment about what the rights of others are. Thus assertion training touches on moral aspects of social living—namely, the definition of other people's rights and the proper means of standing up for one's own rights.

ple (and animals as well) structure their experiences, how they make sense of them, and how they relate their current experiences to past ones that have been stored in memory.

The Basics of Cognitive Theory

At any given moment we are bombarded by far more stimuli than we can possibly respond to. How do we filter this overwhelming input, put it into words or images, form hypotheses, and arrive at a perception of what is out there?

Cognitive psychologists consider the learning process much more complex than the passive formation of new stimulus–response associations. Even classical conditioning is viewed by cognitive psychologists as an active process by which organisms learn about relationships among events rather than as an automatic stamping in of associations between stimuli (Rescorla, 1988). Moreover, cognitive psychologists regard the learner as an active interpreter of a situation, with the learner's past knowledge imposing a perceptual funnel on the experience. The learner fits new information into an organized network of already accumulated knowledge, often referred to as a **schema**, or cognitive set (Neisser, 1976). New information may fit the schema; if not, the learner reorganizes the schema to fit the information or construes the information in such a way as to fit the schema. The cognitive approach may remind you of our earlier discussions of paradigms in science in Chapter 1; scientific paradigms are similar in function to a cognitive schema, for they act as filters to our experience of the world.

Although learning paradigms initially avoided cognitive concepts, contemporary experimental psychology is very much concerned with cognition. The following situation illustrates how a schema may alter the way in which information is processed and remembered.

> *The man stood before the mirror and combed his hair. He checked his face carefully for any places he might have missed shaving and then put on the conservative tie he had decided to wear. At breakfast, he studied the newspaper carefully and, over coffee, discussed the possibility of buying a new washing machine with his wife. Then he made several phone calls. As he was leaving the house he thought about the fact that his children would probably want to go to that private camp again this summer. When the car didn't start, he got out, slammed the door and walked down to the bus stop in a very angry mood. Now he would be late. (Bransford & Johnson, 1973, p. 415)*

Now read the excerpt again, but add the word "unemployed" before the word "man." Now read it a third time, substituting "stockbroker" for "man." Notice how differently you understand the passage. Ask yourself what parts of the newspaper these men read. If you were asked on a questionnaire to recall this information and you no longer had access to the excerpt, you might answer "the want ads" for the unemployed man and "the financial pages" for the stockbroker. Since the passage does not specify which part of the paper was read, these answers are wrong, but in each instance the error would have been a meaningful, predictable one.

Cognitive explanations are now appearing more and more often in the search for the causes of abnormality and for new methods of intervention. A widely held view of depression, for example, places the blame on a particular cognitive set, namely, the individual's overriding sense of hopelessness (see p. 277). Many people who are depressed believe that they have no important effect on their surroundings regardless of what they do. Their destiny seems to them to be out of their hands, and they expect their future to be negative. If depression does develop from a sense of hopelessness, this fact could have implications for how clinicians treat the disorder. Cognitive theorizing will be included in discussions of most of the disorders presented in subsequent chapters.

Cognitive Behavior Therapy

The behavioral therapies discussed earlier pay relatively little attention to the thinking and reasoning processes of the client. In contrast, **cognitive behavior therapy** (**CBT**) incorporates theory and research on cognitive processes. Although we present it here as part of the cognitive paradigm, it has in fact become a blend of the cognitive and learning paradigms. Cognitive behavior therapists pay attention to private events—thoughts, perceptions, judgments, self-statements, and even tacit (unconscious) assumptions—and have studied and manipulated these processes in their attempts to understand and modify overt and covert disturbed behavior. **Cognitive restructuring** is a general term for changing a pattern of thought that is presumed to be causing a disturbed emotion or behavior. This restructuring is implemented in several ways by cognitive behavior therapists.

Aaron Beck developed a cognitive theory of depression and a cognitive therapy for the cognitive biases of depressed people.

Beck's Cognitive Therapy   The psychiatrist Aaron Beck is one of the leading cognitive behavior therapists. He developed a cognitive therapy for depression based on the idea that depressed mood is caused by distortions in the way people perceive life experiences (Beck, 1976; Salkovskis, 1996). For example, a depressed person may focus exclusively on negative happenings and ignore positive ones. Beck's therapy, which we examine in detail in Chapter 10, tries to persuade patients to change their opinions of themselves and the way in which they interpret life events. When a depressed person expresses feelings that nothing ever goes right, for example, the therapist offers counterexamples, pointing out how the client has overlooked favorable happenings. The general goal of Beck's therapy is to provide patients with experiences, both inside and outside the consulting room, that will alter their negative schemas, enabling them to have hope rather than despair.

Ellis's Rational-Emotive Behavior Therapy   Albert Ellis is another leading cognitive behavior therapist. His principal thesis is that sustained emotional reactions are caused by internal sentences that people repeat to themselves and these self-statements reflect some-times unspoken assumptions—**irrational beliefs**—about what is necessary to lead a meaningful life. In Ellis's rational-emotive therapy (RET), now renamed **rational-emotive behavior therapy** (REBT) (Ellis, 1993a, 1995), the aim is to eliminate self-defeating beliefs. Anxious persons, for example, may create their own problems by making unreal-istic demands on themselves or others, such as, "I must win the love of everyone." Or a depressed person may say several times a day, "What a worthless jerk I am." Ellis propos-es that people interpret what is happening around them, that sometimes these interpreta-tions can cause emotional turmoil, and that a therapist's attention should be focused on these beliefs rather than on historical causes or, indeed, on overt behavior (Ellis, 1962, 1984).

Ellis used to list a number of irrational beliefs that people can harbor. One very com-mon notion was that they must be thoroughly competent in everything they do. Ellis sug-gested that many people actually believe this untenable assumption and evaluate every event within this context. Thus if a person makes an error, it becomes a catastrophe because it violates the deeply held conviction that he or she must be perfect. It sometimes comes as a shock to clients to realize that they actually believe such strictures and as a consequence run their lives so that it is virtually impossible to live comfortably or productively.

More recently, Ellis (1991; Kendall et al., 1995) has shifted from a cataloguing of spe-cific beliefs to the more general concept of "demandingness," that is, the musts or shoulds that people impose on themselves and on others. Thus, instead of wanting something to be a certain way, feeling disappointed, and then perhaps engaging in some behavior that might bring about the desired outcome, the person *demands* that it be so. It is this unre-alistic, unproductive demand, Ellis hypothesizes, that creates the kind of emotional dis-tress and behavioral dysfunction that bring people to therapists.

Albert Ellis, a cognitive behavior therapist and founder of rational-emotive behavior therapy, has focused on the role of irrational beliefs as causes of abnormal behavior.

Clinical Implementation of REBT   After becoming familiar with the client's problems, the therapist presents the basic theory of rational-emotive behavior therapy so that the client can understand and accept it.[4] The following transcript is from a session with a young man who had inordinate fears about speaking in front of groups. The therapist guides the client to view his inferiority complex in terms of the unreasonable things he may be telling him-self. The therapist's thoughts during the interview are indicated in italics.

Client: My primary difficulty is that I become very uptight when I have to speak in front of a group of people. I guess it's just my own inferiority complex.

Therapist: *[I don't want to get sidetracked at this point by talking about that conceptualiza-tion of his problem. I'll just try to finesse it and make a smooth transition to something else.)* I don't know if I would call it an inferiority complex but I do believe that people can, in a sense, bring on their own upset and anxiety in certain kinds of situations. When you're in a particular situation, your anxiety is often not the result of the situation itself, but rather the way in which you interpret the situation—what you tell yourself about the situation. For example, look at this pen. Does this pen make you nervous?

Client: No.

Therapist: Why not?

Client: It's just an object. It's just a pen.

Therapist: It can't hurt you?

Client: No....

Therapist: It's really not the object that creates emotional upset in people, but rather what you think about the object. *[Hopefully, this Socratic-like dialogue will eventually bring him to the conclusion that self-statements can mediate emotional arousal.]* Now this holds true for...situations where emotional upset is caused by what a person tells himself about

---

[4] As indicated earlier in this chapter when we discussed empathy statements in client-centered therapy, the useful-ness of an interpretation does not depend on its being true. Neither does the usefulness of REBT. Ellis's views may be only partially correct or even entirely wrong, yet it may be helpful for a client to act as if they were true.

the situation. Take, for example, two people who are about to attend the same social gathering. Both of them may know exactly the same number of people at the party, but one person can be optimistic and relaxed about the situation, whereas the other one can be worried about how he will appear, and consequently be very anxious. *[I'll try to get him to verbalize the basic assumption that attitude or perception is most important here.]* So, when these two people walk into the place where the party is given, are their emotional reactions at all associated with the physical arrangements at the party?

Client: No, obviously not.

Therapist: What determines their reactions, then?

Client: They obviously have different attitudes toward the party.

Therapist: Exactly, and their attitudes—the ways in which they approach the situation—greatly influence their emotional reactions. (Goldfried & Davison, 1994, pp. 163–165)

Having persuaded the client that his or her emotional problems will benefit from rational examination, the therapist proceeds to teach the person to substitute for irrational self-statements an internal dialogue meant to ease the emotional turmoil. At the present time therapists who implement Ellis's ideas differ greatly on how they persuade clients to change their self-talk. Some therapists, like Ellis himself, argue with clients, cajoling and teasing them, sometimes in very blunt language. Others, believing that social influence should be more subtle and that individuals should participate more in changing themselves, encourage clients to discuss their own irrational thinking and then gently lead them to discover more rational ways of regarding the world (Goldfried & Davison, 1994).

Once a client verbalizes a different belief or self-statement during a therapy session, it must be made part of everyday thinking. Ellis and his followers provide patients with homework assignments designed to afford opportunities for the client to experiment with the new self-talk and to experience the positive consequences of viewing life in less catastrophic ways. Ellis emphasizes the importance of getting the patient to behave differently, both to test out new beliefs and to learn to cope with life's disappointments.

Behavior Therapy and CBT in Groups   Many of the behavioral and cognitive behavior therapies we have described have been used with groups as well as with individuals. For example, the deep muscle relaxation of systematic desensitization can be efficiently taught to a group of people; and with a group of people with the same fear, the same hierarchy can be presented to everyone simultaneously, thus saving the therapist's time. Group desensitization has been used effectively to treat the same kinds of fears that have been treated with individual desensitization (e.g., Wright, 1976). Social skills and assertion skills have also been taught to groups of people. For example, depressed people have learned methods of interacting with others that are likely to bring them more reinforcement from others (e.g., Teri & Lewinsohn, 1986). The cognitive behavior therapies of both Beck and Ellis have also been used in groups to treat such problems as panic disorder, social phobia, and obsessive-compulsive disorder (Albano et al., 1995; Kobak, Rock, & Greist, 1995; Neron, Lacroix, & Chaput, 1995).

Evaluating the Cognitive Paradigm

Some criticisms of the cognitive paradigm should be noted. The concepts on which it is based (e.g., schema) are somewhat slippery and not always well-defined. Furthermore, cognitive explanations of psychopathology do not always explain much. That a depressed person has a negative schema tells us that the person thinks gloomy thoughts. But such a pattern of thinking is actually part of the diagnosis of depression. What is distinctive in the cognitive paradigm is that the thoughts are given causal status; that is, the thoughts are regarded as causing the other features of the disorder, such as sadness. Left unanswered is the question of where the negative schema came from in the first place. Cognitive explanations of psychopathology tend to focus more on current determinants of a disorder and less on its historical antecedents.

Is the cognitive point of view basically different and separate from the learning paradigm? Much of what we have just said suggests that it is. But the growing field of cognitive behavior therapy gives us pause, for its workers study the complex interplay of beliefs, expectations, perceptions, and attitudes on the one hand and overt behavior on the other. For example, Albert Bandura (1977), a leading cognitive-behavioral theorist, argues that different therapies produce improvement by increasing people's sense of **self-efficacy**, a belief that they can achieve desired goals. But, at the same time, he argues that changing behavior through behavioral techniques is the most powerful way to enhance self-efficacy. Therapists such as Ellis, in contrast, emphasize direct alteration of cognitions through argument, persuasion, Socratic dialogue, and the like to bring about improvements in emotion and behavior. Complicating matters still further, Ellis and his followers also place considerable importance on homework assignments that require clients to behave in ways in which they have been unable to behave because they have been hindered by negative thoughts. Ellis even renamed his therapy rational-emotive *behavior* therapy to highlight the importance of overt behavior. Therapists identified with cognitive behavior therapy work at both the cognitive and behavioral levels, and most of those who use cognitive concepts and try to change beliefs with verbal means also use behavioral procedures to alter behavior directly.

This issue is reflected in the terminology used to refer to people such as Beck and Ellis. Are they *cognitive therapists* or *cognitive behavior therapists*? For the most part we will use the latter term because it denotes both that the therapist regards cognitions as major determinants of emotion and behavior and that he or she maintains the focus on overt behavior that has always characterized behavior therapy. Nonetheless, it is important for the reader to know that Beck, even though he assigns many behavioral tasks as part of his therapy, is usually referred to as the founder of cognitive therapy (CT), and that Ellis's rational-emotive therapy (RET) used to be spoken of as something separate from behavior therapy. Table 2.4 compares the basic assumptions of the psychoanalytic and a blended cognitive-behavioral paradigm.

Table 2.4   Comparison of Psychoanalytic and Cognitive-Behavioral Paradigms

Psychoanalytic	Cognitive-Behavioral
We don't always say what we mean.	We usually say what we mean, or at least we are able to quite readily.
We don't always even know what we mean.	We usually know what we mean.
We can have strongly inconsistent feelings about things, conflicting desires and fears.	We do have strongly inconsistent feelings, but such conflicts are not emphasized.
What lies on the surface is not (always) the most important aspect of ourselves. In fact, it seldom is.	What lies on the surface is usually the most important aspect of ourselves. Yet looking for controlling variables can take behaviorists into the realm of underlying causes.
Our earliest life experiences are pivotal, especially with our parents and parent figures.	Current factors in one's life are at least as important as past experiences.
We can come to fear our own desires and experience conflict about expressing them.	Fear of our own desires is emphasized far less.
We often/always desire or fear what is nonnormative, unconventional, bizarre, taboo.	People's wishes and fears are much more prosaic. There is little presumption of taboo concerns.
"The truth shall set you free." Insight into one's actual motivations has, in itself, curative properties. It facilitates control over our fears and desires.	Insight, greater awareness of the causes of one's behavior, can be helpful, but the strongest controlling variables are to be found in the environment. But, the more cognitively oriented the behaviorist, the closer he or she comes to insight theorists, such as psychoanalysts.
Sexual gratification is not the key; rather, awareness of one's desires and wishes and fears is. Celibates are not candidates for mental disorder if they remain aware of their wishes and fears. Fulfillment of sexual desires is not necessary for mental health (though Freud originally tilted in the direction that it was).	The satisfaction of primary needs such as sex, thirst, and hunger are very important, but the role of sex is emphasized far less.

Consequences of Adopting a Paradigm

The student of abnormal behavior who adopts a particular paradigm necessarily makes a prior decision concerning what kinds of data will be collected and how they will be interpreted. Thus he or she may very well ignore possibilities and overlook other information in advancing what seems to be the most probable explanation. For example, a behaviorist is prone to attribute the high prevalence of schizophrenia in lower-class groups to the paucity of social rewards that these people have received, the assumption being that normal development requires a certain amount and patterning of reinforcement. A biologically oriented theorist will be quick to remind the behaviorist of the many deprived people who do *not* develop schizophrenia. The behaviorist will undoubtedly counter with the argument that those who do not develop schizophrenia had different reinforcement histories. The biologically oriented theorist will reply that such *post hoc*, or after-the-fact, statements can always be made.

Our biological theorist may suggest that certain biochemical factors that predispose both to schizophrenia and to deficiencies in the intellectual skills necessary to maintain occupational status account for the observed correlation between social class and schizophrenia. The behaviorist will be entirely justified in reminding the biological theorist that these alleged factors have yet to be found, to which the biological theorist might rightfully answer, "Yes, but I'm placing my bets that they are there, and if I adopt your behavioral paradigm, I may not look for them." To which the behaviorist may with justification reply, "Yes, but *your* assumption regarding biochemical factors makes it less likely that you will look for and uncover the subtle reinforcement factors that in all probability account for both the presence and the absence of schizophrenia."

The fact that our two colleagues are in a sense correct and in another sense incorrect is both exasperating and exciting. They are both correct in asserting that certain data are more likely to be found through work done within a particular paradigm. But they are incorrect to become unduly agitated that each and every scientist is not assuming that one and the same factor will ultimately be found crucial in the development of all mental disorders. Abnormal behavior is much too diverse to be explained or treated adequately by any one of the current paradigms. It is probably advantageous that psychologists do *not* agree on which paradigm is the best. We know far too little to make hard-and-fast decisions on the exclusive superiority of any one paradigm, and there is enough important work to go around. We will see, too, that often a plausible way of looking at the data is to assume multiple causation. A particular disorder may very well develop through an interaction of biological defects and environmental factors, a view we turn to next.

Diathesis–Stress: An Integrative Paradigm

A paradigm more general than the ones we have discussed so far, called **diathesis–stress**, links biological, psychological, and environmental factors. It is not limited to one particular school of thought, such as learning, cognitive, or psychodynamic. This paradigm focuses on the interaction between a predisposition toward disease—the diathesis—and environmental, or life, disturbances—the stress. Diathesis refers most precisely to a constitutional predisposition toward illness, but the term may be extended to any characteristic or set of characteristics of a person that increases his or her chance of developing a disorder.

In the realm of biology, for example, a number of disorders considered in later chapters appear to have a genetically transmitted diathesis. That is, having a close relative with the disorder and therefore sharing to some degree his or her genetic endowment increases a person's risk for the disorder. Although the precise nature of these genetic diatheses is currently unknown (for example, we don't know exactly what is inherited that makes one person more likely than another to develop schizophrenia), it is clear that a genetic predisposition is an important component of many psychopathologies. Other biological diatheses include oxygen deprivation at birth, poor nutrition, and a maternal viral infection or smoking during pregnancy. Each of these conditions may lead to changes in the brain that predispose toward psychopathology.

In the psychological realm, a diathesis for depression may be the cognitive set already mentioned, the chronic feeling of hopelessness sometimes found in depressed people. Or, taking a psychodynamic view, an extreme sense of dependency on others, perhaps because of frustrations during one of the psychosexual stages, could also be a diathesis for depression. Other psychological diatheses include the ability to be easily hypnotized, which may be a diathesis for dissociative identity disorder (formerly called multiple personality disorder), and an intense fear of becoming fat, which predisposes toward eating disorders.

These psychological diatheses can arise for a variety of reasons. Some, such as hypnotizability, are personality characteristics that are probably in part genetically determined. Others, such as a sense of hopelessness, may result from childhood experiences with harshly critical parents. Sexual or physical abuse during childhood produces psychological changes that seem to predispose people to develop a number of different disorders. Sociocultural influences also play an important role; for instance, cultural standards of what is beautiful may lead to an intense fear of being fat and thus predispose some people to eating disorders. The diathesis–stress paradigm is integrative because it draws on all these diverse sources of information about the causes of diatheses. In later chapters we will see that concepts from the major paradigms we have already discussed are differentially applicable to different disorders. For example, a genetically determined biological diathesis plays a major role in schizophrenia. Cognitive diatheses, in contrast, are more influential in the anxiety disorders and depression. A diathesis–stress paradigm allows us to draw on concepts from many sources and to make more or less use of them depending on the disorder being considered.

Possessing the diathesis for a disorder increases a person's risk of developing it but does not by any means guarantee that a disorder will develop. The stress part of diathesis–stress is meant to account for how a diathesis may be translated into an actual disorder. In this context stress generally refers to some noxious or unpleasant environmental stimulus that triggers psychopathology. Psychological stressors include major traumatic events (e.g., becoming unemployed, divorce, death of a spouse) as well as more mundane happenings, which many of us experience (e.g., being stuck in traffic). By including these environmental events, the diathesis–stress model goes beyond the major paradigms we have already discussed.

The key point of the diathesis–stress model is that both diathesis and stress are necessary in the development of disorders (see Figure 2.7). Some people, for example, have inherited a biological predisposition that places them at high risk for schizophrenia (see Chapter 11); given a certain amount of stress, they stand a good chance of developing schizophrenia. Other people, those at low genetic risk, are not likely to develop schizophrenia, regardless of how difficult their lives are.

Another major feature of the diathesis–stress paradigm is that psychopathology is unlikely to result from the impact of any single factor. A genetically transmitted diathesis may be necessary for some disorders, but it is embedded in a network of other factors that also contribute to disorder. These factors could include genetically transmitted diatheses for other personality characteristics; childhood experiences that shape personality, the development of behavioral competencies, and coping strategies; stressors encountered in adulthood; cultural influences; and numerous other factors.

Finally, we should note that within this framework the data gathered by researchers holding different paradigms are not incompatible with one another. For example, stress may be needed to activate a predisposition toward a biochemical imbalance. Some of the differences between the paradigms also appear to be more linguistic than substantive. A cognitive theorist may propose that maladaptive cognitions cause depression, whereas a biological theorist may speak of the underactivity of a certain neural pathway. The two positions are not contradictory, but merely reflect different levels of description, just as we could describe a table as pieces of wood in a particular configuration or as a collection of atoms.

Stressors that may activate a diathesis range from minor, such as having a flat tire, to major, such as the aftermath of a hurricane.

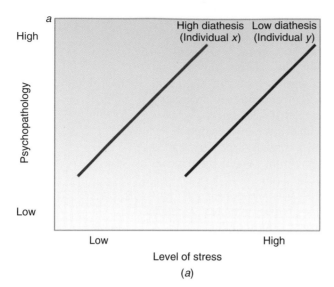

Figure 2.7 Three depictions of diathesis–stress models. (a) An individual with a large dose of the diathesis requires only a moderate amount of stress to develop psychopathology, whereas an individual with a small dose of the diathesis requires a large amount of stress to precipitate a breakdown. (b) The diathesis is dichotomous; stress level has no effect on those without the diathesis. (c) The diathesis is continuous; increasing stress increases psychopathology for all people with at least a minimal amount of the diathesis. After Monroe and Simons (1991).

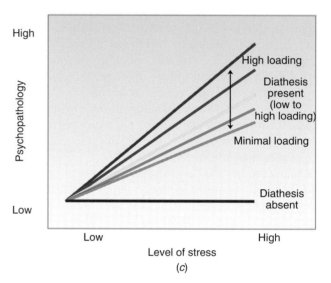

Different Perspectives on a Clinical Problem

To provide a concrete example of how it is possible to conceptualize a clinical case using different paradigms, we now return to the case of the police officer Ernest H. with which this book began. The information provided there is open to a number of interpretations, depending on the paradigm adopted. If you hold a biological point of view, you are attentive to the similarity between the man's alternately manic and depressed states and the cyclical mood swings of his father. You are probably aware of the research (to be reviewed in Chapter 10) that suggests a genetic factor in mood disorders. You do not discount environmental contributions to Ernest's problems, but you hypothesize that some inherited, probably biochemical, defect predisposes him to break down under stress. After all, not everyone who experiences a difficult childhood and adolescence develops the kinds of problems Ernest H. has. For treatment you may prescribe lithium carbonate, a drug that is generally helpful in reducing the magnitude of mood swings in manic-depression.

A psychoanalytic point of view casts Ernest H. in yet another light. Believing that events in early childhood are of great importance in later patterns of adjustment, you may hypothesize that Ernest is still grieving for his mother and has blamed his father for her early death. Such strong anger at the father has been repressed, but Ernest has not been able to regard him as a competent, worthwhile adult and to identify with him. For treatment you may choose dream analysis and free association to help Ernest lift his repressions and deal openly and consciously with his hitherto buried anger toward his father.

Now suppose that you are committed to a behavioral or cognitive-behavioral perspective, which encourages you to analyze human behavior in terms of reinforcement patterns as well as cognitive variables. You may focus on Ernest's self-consciousness at college, which seems related to the fact that compared with his fellow students, he grew up with few advantages. Economic insecurity and hardship may have made him unduly sensitive to criticism and rejection. Moreover, he regards his wife as warm and charming, pointing up his own perceived lack of social skills. Alcohol has been his escape from such tensions. But heavy drinking, coupled with persistent doubt about his own worth as a human being, has interfered with sexual functioning, worsening an already deteriorating marital relationship and further undermining his confidence. As a behavior therapist, you may employ systematic desensitization. You teach Ernest to relax deeply as he imagines a hierarchy of situations in which he is being evaluated by others. Or you may decide on rational-emotive behavior therapy to convince Ernest that he need not obtain universal approval for every undertaking. Or, given Ernest's deficiency in social skills, you may choose behavior rehearsal to teach him how to function effectively in social situations in which he has had little experience. You might follow more than one of these strategies.

Eclecticism in Psychotherapy: Practice Makes Imperfect

A final word is needed about paradigms and the activities of therapists. From our presentation of treatment approaches, it may appear that they are practices of separate, nonoverlapping schools of therapy. You may have the impression that a behavior therapist would never listen to a client's report of a dream, nor would a psychoanalyst be caught dead prescribing assertion training to a patient. Such suppositions could not be further from the truth. Most therapists subscribe to **eclecticism**, employing ideas and therapeutic techniques from a variety of schools (Garfield & Kurtz, 1976).

Therapists often behave in ways that are not entirely consistent with the theories they hold. For years practicing behavior therapists have listened empathically to clients, trying to make out their perspectives on events, on the assumption that this understanding would help them plan a better program for changing troublesome behavior. Behavioral theories do not prescribe such a procedure, but on the basis of clinical experience, and perhaps through their own humanity, behavior therapists have realized that empathic listening helps them establish rapport, determine what is really bothering the client, and plan a sensible therapy program.

By the same token, Freud himself is said to have been more directive and done far more to change immediate behavior than would be concluded from his writings alone. And psychoanalysts today pay more attention to overt behavior and the relief of symptoms than early analytic theory would prescribe. Some contemporary writers, such as Paul Wachtel (see p. 598), have even proposed that analysts should employ behavior therapy techniques, openly acknowledging that behavior therapy has something to offer in the alleviation of behavior pathology.

Treatment is a complex and ultimately highly individual process, and these are weighty issues. In Chapter 17 we will return to these and other issues and will give them the attention they need and deserve. The reader should be aware of this complexity at the beginning, however, in order better to appreciate the intricacies and realities of psychotherapy.

Summary

● Several major paradigms, or perspectives, are current in the study of psychopathology and therapy. The choice of a paradigm has important consequences for the way in which abnormal behavior is defined, investigated, and treated.

● The biological paradigm assumes that psychopathology is caused by a biological defect. Two biological factors relevant to psychopathology are genetics and neurochemistry. Biological therapies attempt to rectify the specific biological defects underlying disorders or to alleviate symptoms of disorders, often using drugs to do so.

● The psychoanalytic, or psychodynamic, paradigm derives from the work of Sigmund Freud. It focuses on repressions and other unconscious processes that are traceable to early-childhood conflicts. The psychoanalytic paradigm has generally searched the unconscious and the early life of the patient for the causes of abnormality, although present-day ego analysts place greater emphasis on conscious ego functions. Therapeutic interventions based on psychoanalytic theory usually attempt to lift repressions so that the patient can examine the infantile and unfounded nature of his or her fears.

● Humanistic and existential therapies are insight oriented, like psychoanalysis, and regard freedom to choose and personal responsibility as key human characteristics. Rogers' client-centered therapy entails complete acceptance of the client; therapists also use empathy, restating the client's thoughts and feelings, and sometimes offer new perspectives on the client's problem. Existential therapies emphasize personal growth and confronting the anxieties that are part of the choices we have to make in life. Perls' Gestalt therapy tries to help patients better understand and accept their needs, desires, and fears.

● Behavioral, or learning, paradigms suggest that aberrant behavior has developed through classical conditioning, operant conditioning, or modeling. Investigators in this tradition share a commitment to examine carefully all situations affecting behavior as well as to define concepts carefully. Behavior therapists try to apply learning principles to alter overt behavior, thought, and emotion. Less attention is paid to the historical causes of abnormal behavior than to what maintains it, such as the reward and punishment contingencies that encourage problematic response patterns.

● Cognitive theorists have argued that certain schemas and irrational interpretations are major factors in abnormality. In both practice and theory, the cognitive paradigm has usually blended with the behavioral in an approach to intervention that is referred to as cognitive-behavioral. Cognitive behavior therapists such as Beck and Ellis focus on altering patients' negative schemas and interpretations.

● Because each paradigm seems to have something to offer to our understanding of mental disorders, there has recently been a movement to develop more integrative paradigms. The diathesis–stress paradigm, which integrates several points of view, assumes that people are predisposed to react adversely to environmental stressors. The diathesis may be biological or psychological and may be caused by early-childhood experiences, genetically determined personality traits, or sociocultural influences.

● Paralleling the current interest in integrative paradigms, most clinicians today are eclectic in their approach to intervention, employing techniques that are outside their paradigm but that seem useful in dealing with the complexities of human psychological problems.

Key Terms

action therapies
adoptees method
advanced empathy
anal stage
analytical psychology
assertion training
aversive conditioning
avoidance conditioning
behavior genetics
behaviorism
behavior modification
behavior rehearsal
behavior therapy
biological paradigm
brief therapy
classical conditioning
client-centered therapy
cognition
cognitive behavior therapy (CBT)
cognitive paradigm
cognitive restructuring
collective unconscious
concordance
conditioned response (CR)
conditioned stimulus (CS)
counterconditioning
countertransference
defense mechanism
denial
diathesis

diathesis–stress
discriminative stimulus
displacement
dizygotic (DZ) twins
dream analysis
eclecticism
ego
ego analysis
Electra complex
extinction
family method
fixation
free association
genes
genital stage
genotype
Gestalt therapy
humanistic and existential therapies
id
index cases (probands)
individual psychology
insight therapies
instrumental learning
Interpersonal Therapy (IPT)
interpretation
introject
introspection
irrational beliefs
latency period

law of effect
learning paradigm
libido
linkage analysis
mediational theory of learning
mediator
medical (disease) model
modeling
monozygotic (MZ) twins
negative reinforcement
nerve impulse
neuron
neurotic anxiety
neurotransmitters
objective (realistic) anxiety
Oedipus complex
operant conditioning
oral stage
phallic stage
phenotype
pleasure principle
positive reinforcement
primary empathy
primary process
projection
psychoanalytic (psychodynamic) paradigm
psychodynamics
psychosexual stages

psychotherapy
rational-emotive behavior therapy (REBT)
rationalization
reaction formation
reality principle
regression
repression
resistance
reuptake
role-playing
schema
secondary process
self-actualization
self-efficacy
shaping
sublimation
successive approximations
superego
synapse
systematic desensitization
time-out
token economy
transference
twin method
unconditional positive regard
unconditioned response (UCR)
unconditioned stimulus (UCS)
unconscious

3 Classification and Diagnosis

Diagnosis is a critical aspect of the field of abnormal psychology. It is essential for professionals to be able to communicate accurately with one another about the types of cases they are treating or studying. Furthermore, to find the causes or best treatments for a disorder, it must first be classified correctly. For example, if one research group has found a successful treatment for depression but has defined it in a manner not followed by other researchers, the finding is not likely to be replicated by another group of investigators. Only in recent years, however, has diagnosis been accorded the attention it deserves.

To beginning students of abnormal psychology, diagnosis can seem tedious because it sometimes relies on fine distinctions. For example, anxiety in social situations—being extremely tense around others—is a symptom of both schizotypal and avoidant personality disorders. In a person with schizotypal personality disorder, however, the anxiety does not decrease as the individual becomes more familiar with people, whereas in a person with avoidant personality disorder exposure does tend to reduce social anxiety. This fine distinction could certainly be viewed as hairsplitting. However, as we will discuss thoroughly later in the chapter, the decisive factor is whether the distinction is useful.

In this chapter we focus on the official diagnostic system widely employed by mental health professionals, the *Diagnostic and Statistical Manual of Mental Disorders*, now in its fourth edition, commonly referred to as **DSM-IV-TR**. The DSM is published by the American Psychiatric Association and has an interesting history.

A Brief History of Classification

By the end of the nineteenth century medicine had progressed far beyond its practice during the Middle Ages, when bloodletting was at least part of the treatment of virtually all physical problems. Gradually people recognized that different illnesses required different treatments. Diagnostic procedures were improved, diseases classified, and applicable remedies administered. Impressed by the successes that new diagnostic procedures had achieved in the field of medicine, investigators of abnormal behavior also sought to develop classification schemes. Advances in other sciences, such as botany and chemistry, had followed the development of classification systems, reinforcing hope that similar efforts in the field of abnormal behavior might bring progress. Unfortunately, progress in classifying mental disorders was not to be easily gained.

Early Efforts at Classification

During the nineteenth century and into the twentieth as well, there was great inconsistency in the classification of abnormal behavior. By the end of the nineteenth century the diversity of classifications was recognized as a serious problem that impeded communication among people in the field, and several attempts were made to produce a system of classification that would be widely adopted. For example, in the United Kingdom in 1882 the Statistical Committee of the Royal Medico-Psychological Association produced a classification scheme. Even though it was revised several times, however, it was never adopted by its members. In Paris in 1889 the Congress of Mental Science adopted a single classification system, but it was never widely used. In the United States the Association of Medical Superintendents of American Institutions for the Insane, a forerunner of the American Psychiatric Association, adopted a somewhat revised version of the British system in 1886. Then, in 1913, this group accepted a new classification, which incorporated some of Emil Kraepelin's ideas (p. 12). Again, consistency was lacking. The New York State Commission on Lunacy, for example, insisted on retaining its own system (Kendell, 1975).

Development of the WHO and DSM Systems

More recent efforts at achieving uniformity of classification have not been totally successful either. In 1939 the World Health Organization (WHO) added mental disorders to the International List of Causes of Death (ICD). In 1948 the list was expanded to become the International Statistical Classification of Diseases, Injuries, and Causes of Death, a comprehensive listing of all diseases, including a classification of abnormal behavior. Although this nomenclature was unanimously adopted at a WHO conference, the mental disorders section was not widely accepted. Even though American psychiatrists had played a prominent role in the WHO effort, the American Psychiatric Association published its own Diagnostic and Statistical Manual (DSM) in 1952.

In 1969 the WHO published a new classification system, which was more widely accepted. A second version of the American Psychiatric Association's DSM, DSM-II (1968), was similar to the WHO system, and in the United Kingdom a glossary of definitions was produced to accompany the WHO system (General Register Office, 1968). But true consensus still eluded the field. The WHO classifications were simply a listing of diagnostic categories; the actual behavior or symptoms that were the bases for the diagnoses were not specified. DSM-II and the British Glossary of Mental Disorders provided some of this crucial information but did not specify the same symptoms for a given disorder. Thus actual diagnostic practices still varied widely. In 1980 the American Psychiatric Association published an extensively revised diagnostic manual, DSM-III. A somewhat revised version, DSM-III-R, appeared in 1987.

In 1988 the American Psychiatric Association appointed a task force to begin work on DSM-IV. Working groups, which included many psychologists, were established to review sections of DSM-III-R, prepare literature reviews, analyze previously collected data, and collect new data if needed. An important change in the process for this edition of the DSM was the adoption of a conservative approach to making changes in the diagnostic criteria—the reasons for changes in diagnoses would be explicitly stated and clearly supported by data. In previous versions of the DSM, the reasons for diagnostic changes had not always been explicit.

DSM-IV was published in 1994. In June 2000, a "text revision," DSM-IV-TR, was published . Almost no changes were made to the diagnostic categories and criteria. What were changed were some discussions bearing on issues such as prevalence rates, course, and etiology, based on recently published research. As in the previous editions of this textbook, our examination of these factors is based on our own analysis of the literature and not on the

DSM. In this chapter we present the major DSM-IV-TR categories in brief summary. We then evaluate classification in general and the DSM in particular. In the next chapter we consider the assessment procedures that provide the data on which diagnostic decisions are based.

The Diagnostic System of the American Psychiatric Association (DSM-IV-TR)

Several major innovations distinguish the third edition and subsequent versions of the DSM. One of these changes is the use of **multiaxial classification**, whereby each individual is rated on five separate dimensions, or axes (Table 3.1). In this section we briefly discuss these five axes and then describe the major diagnostic categories.

Five Dimensions of Classification

The five axes of DSM-IV are:

> Axis I. All diagnostic categories except personality disorders and mental retardation.
>
> Axis II. Personality disorders and mental retardation.
>
> Axis III. General medical conditions.
>
> Axis IV. Psychosocial and environmental problems.
>
> Axis V. Current level of functioning.

The multiaxial system, by requiring judgments on each of the five axes, forces the diagnostician to consider a broad range of information.

Axis I includes all diagnostic categories except the personality disorders and mental retardation, which make up Axis II. Thus Axes I and II comprise the classification of abnormal behavior. A detailed presentation of Axes I and II appears inside the front cover of the book. Axes I and II are separated to ensure that the presence of long-term disturbances, as occur in the personality disorders and mental retardation, are not overlooked. Most people consult a mental health professional for an Axis I condition, such as depression or an anxiety disorder. But prior to the onset of their Axis I condition, they may have had an Axis II condition, such as dependent personality disorder. The separation of Axes I and II is meant to encourage clinicians to be attentive to this possibility. The presence of an Axis II disorder along with an Axis I disorder generally means that the person's problems will be more difficult to treat.

The inclusion in the DSM of Axes III, IV, and V indicates that factors other than a person's symptoms should be considered in an assessment so that the person's overall life situation can be better understood. On Axis III the clinician indicates any general medical conditions believed to be relevant to the mental disorder in question. For example, the existence of a heart condition in a person who was also diagnosed with depression would have important implications for treatment; some antidepressant drugs could worsen the heart condition. Axis IV codes psychosocial and environmental problems that the person has been experiencing and that may be contributing to the disorder. These include occupational problems, economic problems, interpersonal difficulties with family members, and a variety of problems in other life areas, which may influence psychological functioning. Finally, on Axis V, the clinician indicates the person's current level of adaptive functioning, using the Global Assessment of Functioning (GAF) scale. Life areas considered are social relationships, occupational functioning, and use of leisure time. These ratings of current functioning are meant to provide an assessment of how much the person needs treatment.

Diagnostic Categories

In this section we provide a brief description of the major diagnostic categories of Axes I and II. Before presenting the diagnoses we should note that for many of them, the DSM

Table 3.1 DSM-IV-TR Multiaxial Classification System

Axis I

Disorders Usually First Diagnosed in Infancy, Childhood, or Adolescence

Delirium, Dementia, Amnestic and Other Cognitive Disorders

Substance-related Disorders

Schizophrenia and Other Psychotic Disorders

Mood Disorders

Anxiety Disorders

Somatoform Disorders

Factitious Disorders

Dissociative Disorders

Sexual and Gender Identity Disorders

Eating Disorders

Sleep Disorders

Impulse Control Disorders Not Elsewhere Classified

Adjustment Disorders

Axis II

Mental Retardation

Personality Disorders

Axis III

General Medical Conditions

Axis IV
Psychosocial and Environmental Problems

Check:

____ Problems with primary support group.
Specify:

____ Problems related to the social environment.
Specify:

____ Educational problem.
Specify:

____ Occupational problem.
Specify:

____ Housing problem.
Specify:

____ Economic problem.
Specify:

____ Problems with access to health care services.
Specify:

____ Problems related to interaction with the legal system/crime.
Specify:

____ Other psychosocial and environmental problems.
Specify:

Axis V
Global Assessment of Functioning Scale (GAF Scale)

Consider psychological, social, and occupational functioning on a hypothetical continuum of mental health/illness. Do not include impairment in functioning due to physical (or environmental) limitations.

CODE

100	Superior functioning in a wide range of activities, life's problems never seem to get out of hand, is sought out by others
91	because of his many positive qualities. No symptoms.
90	Absent or minimal symptoms (e.g., mild anxiety before an exam), good functioning in all areas, interested and involved in a wide range of activities, socially effective, generally satisfied with life, no more than everyday problems or concerns (e.g.,
81	an occasional argument with family members).
80	If symptoms are present, they are transient and expectable reactions to psychosocial stressors (e.g., difficulty concentrating after family argument); no more than slight impairment in social, occupational, or school functioning (e.g., temporarily
71	falling behind in school work).
70	Some mild symptoms (e.g., depressed mood and mild insomnia) OR some difficulty in social, occupational, or school functioning (e.g., occasional truancy, or theft within the household), but generally functioning pretty well, has some meaningful inter-
61	personal relationships.
60	Moderate symptoms (e.g., flat affect and circumstantial speech, occasional panic attacks) OR moderate difficulty in social, occupational, or school functioning (e.g., no friends,
51	unable to keep a job).
50	Serious symptoms (e.g., suicidal ideation, severe obsessional rituals, frequent shoplifting) OR any serious impairment in social, occupational, or school functioning (e.g., no friends,
41	unable to keep a job).
40	Some impairment in reality testing or communication (e.g., speech is at times illogical, obscure, or irrelevant) OR major impairment in several areas, such as work or school, family relations, judgment, thinking, or mood (e.g., depressed man avoids friends, neglects family, and is unable to work; child frequently beats up younger children, is defiant at home, and
31	is failing at school).
30	Behavior is considerably influenced by delusions or hallucinations OR serious impairment in communication or judgment (e.g., sometimes incoherent, acts grossly inappropriately, suicidal preoccupation) OR inability to function in almost all
21	areas (e.g., stays in bed all day; no job, home, or friends).
20	Some danger of hurting self or others (e.g., suicide attempts without clear expectation of death, frequently violent, manic excitement) OR occasionally fails to maintain minimal personal hygiene (e.g., smears feces) OR gross impairment in
11	communication (e.g., largely incoherent or mute).
10	Persistent danger of severely hurting self or others (e.g., recurrent violence) OR persistent inability to maintain minimal personal
1	hygiene OR serious suicidal act with clear expectation of death.
0	Inadequate information.

Note: Reprinted with permission from the DSM-IV, 1994, American Psychiatric Association.

includes a provision for indicating that the disorder is due to a medical condition or substance abuse. For example, depression resulting from an endocrine gland dysfunction would be diagnosed in the depression section of the DSM but listed as caused by a medical problem. Clinicians must therefore be sensitive not only to the symptoms of their patients but also to possible medical causes of their patients' condition. It should also be noted that beginning with DSM-III, there has been a dramatic expansion of the number of diagnostic categories. Eating disorders, some anxiety disorders (for example, posttraumatic stress disorder), several personality disorders (for example, schizotypal personality disorder), and many of the disorders of childhood were all added in DSM-III or subsequent editions. Focus on Discovery 3.1 describes some diagnoses and axes that are not regarded as well-enough established to be included in DSM-IV-TR, but are in need of further study.

Disorders Usually First Diagnosed in Infancy, Childhood, or Adolescence
Within this broad-ranging category are the intellectual, emotional, and physical disorders that usually begin in infancy, childhood, or adolescence.

- The child with *separation anxiety disorder* has excessive anxiety about being away from home or parents.
- Children with *conduct disorder* repeatedly violate social norms and rules.
- Individuals with *attention-deficit/hyperactivity disorder* have difficulty sustaining attention and are unable to control their activity when the situation calls for it.
- Individuals with *mental retardation* (listed on Axis II) show subnormal intellectual functioning and deficits in adaptive functioning.
- The *pervasive developmental disorders* include *autistic disorder*, a severe condition in which the individual has problems in acquiring communication skills and shows deficits in relating to other people.
- *Learning disorders* refer to delays in the acquisition of speech, reading, arithmetic, and writing skills.

These disorders are discussed in Chapter 15.

Substance-Related Disorders   A substance-related disorder is diagnosed when the ingestion of some substance—alcohol, opiates, cocaine, amphetamines, and so on—has changed behavior enough to impair social or occupational functioning. The individual may become unable to control or discontinue ingestion of the substance and may develop withdrawal symptoms if he or she stops using it. These substances may also cause or contribute to the development of other Axis I disorders, such as those of mood or anxiety. These disorders are examined in Chapter 12.

Schizophrenia   For individuals with schizophrenia, contact with reality is faulty. Their language and communication are disordered, and they may shift from one subject to another in ways that make them difficult to understand. They commonly experience delusions, such as believing that thoughts that are not their own have been placed in their heads. In addition, they are sometimes plagued by hallucinations, in particular, hearing voices that come from outside themselves. Their emotions are blunted, flattened, or inappropriate, and their social relationships and ability to work have markedly deteriorated. This serious mental disorder is discussed in Chapter 11.

Mood Disorders   As the name implies, these diagnoses are applied to people whose moods are extremely high or low.

- In *major depressive disorder* the person is deeply sad and discouraged and is also likely to lose weight and energy and to have suicidal thoughts and feelings of self-reproach.
- The person with mania may be described as exceedingly euphoric, irritable, more active than usual, distractible, and possessed of unrealistically high self-esteem.

Alcohol is the most frequently abused substance.

Issues and Possible Categories in Need of Further Study

One of DSM-IV-TR's appendixes is entitled "Criteria Sets and Axes Provided for Further Study." It contains several proposals for new categories that the DSM-IV task force considers promising but not sufficiently established by data to merit inclusion in DSM-IV. By listing and describing these categories of disorders, the DSM task force hopes to encourage professionals to consider whether a future DSM should contain any of these syndromes or axes as official ways of classifying mental disorders.

Possible New Syndromes

Here is a sampling of the more than two dozen categories mentioned as meriting further study.

Caffeine Withdrawal As with withdrawal from other addicting substances, significant distress or impairment in occupational or social functioning must result from not drinking accustomed levels of beverages containing caffeine. Symptoms include headache, fatigue, anxiety, depression, nausea, and impaired thinking. Inclusion of caffeine withdrawal as a new category would certainly swell the ranks of the mentally disordered.

Premenstrual Dysphoric Disorder Written about a good deal in the press and criticized by people at both ends of the political spectrum, this proposed syndrome is marked by depression, anxiety, anger, mood swings, and decreased interest in activities usually engaged in with pleasure, when occurring a week or so before menstruation for most months in a given year. The symptoms are so severe as to interfere with social or occupational functioning. This category is to be dis-

tinguished from premenstrual syndrome, which is experienced by many more women and is not nearly as debilitating.

Feminists may be pleased or displeased with this possible new category. On the plus side, inclusion might alert people to the hormonal bases of monthly mood changes linked to the menstrual cycle and thereby foster more tolerance and less blame. On the minus side, listing such mood changes in a manual of mental disorders would seem to convey the message that women who experience these psychological changes are mentally disordered.

Mixed Anxiety-Depressive Disorder For a time during the development of DSM-IV it seemed that this disorder would be formally listed, for clinicians have for many years sometimes found it difficult to decide whether to diagnose a person as having primarily a depressive disorder or primarily an anxiety disorder. Depressed mood must have lasted for at least a month and been accompanied by at least four of the following symptoms: concentration or memory problems, disturbances of sleep, fatigue or low energy, irritability, worry, crying easily, hypervigilance, anticipating the worst, pessimism about the future, or feelings of low self-esteem. The person must not be diagnosable as having a major depressive disorder, dysthymic disorder, panic disorder, or generalized anxiety disorder. We will return to this proposed category in Chapter 6.

Passive-Aggressive Personality Disorder (Negativistic Personality Disorder) This personality disorder was present in DSM-III and DSM-III-R but was moved to the appendix in DSM-IV. Not attributable to depression, symptoms include resenting, resisting, and opposing demands and expectations by means of passive activities, such as late-

---

- *Bipolar disorder* is diagnosed if the person experiences episodes of mania or of both mania and depression.

The mood disorders are surveyed in Chapter 10.

Anxiety Disorders Anxiety disorders have some form of irrational or overblown fear as the central disturbance.

- Individuals with a *phobia* fear an object or situation so intensely that they must avoid it, even though they know that their fear is unwarranted and unreasonable and disrupts their lives.

- In *panic disorder* the person is subject to sudden attacks of intense apprehension, so upsetting that he or she is likely to tremble and shake, feel dizzy, and have trouble breathing. Panic disorder may be accompanied by agoraphobia, when the person is also fearful of leaving familiar surroundings.

- In people diagnosed with *generalized anxiety disorder*, fear and apprehension are pervasive, persistent, and uncontrollable. They worry constantly, feel generally on edge, and are easily tired.

- A person with *obsessive-compulsive disorder* is subject to persistent obsessions or compulsions. An obsession is a recurrent thought, idea, or image that uncontrollably dominates a person's consciousness. A compulsion is an urge to perform a stereo-

ness, procrastination, forgetfulness, and intentional inefficiency. The inference is that the person is angry or resentful and is expressing these feelings by not doing certain things rather than by more direct expression, such as assertiveness or aggressiveness. Such people often feel mistreated, cheated, or underappreciated.

Depressive Personality Disorder   In lay terms this personality disorder would be applied to people whose general lifestyle is characterized by gloominess, lack of cheer, and a tendency to worry a lot. This traitlike, long-term disorder may be a precursor to a full-blown major depressive disorder. The DSM admits that it is very difficult to distinguish between depressive personality disorder and the main depressive disorders. Another disorder listed in this appendix is minor depressive disorder, which may be distinguishable only by virtue of its not being as long-standing as depressive personality disorder.

Proposed Axes in Need of Further Study

Professionals are being encouraged to consider whether a future axis should include defense mechanisms (equated by DSM with coping styles), defined as "automatic psychological processes that protect the individual against anxiety and from the awareness of internal or external dangers or stressors" (DSM-IV-TR, 2000, p. 807). Defense mechanisms are divided into groups called defense levels and are measured by a proposed Defensive Functioning Scale. Some of these coping mechanisms derive from psychoanalytic theory.

There are seven defense levels, each with a set of defense mechanisms. The levels range from "High adaptive level" to "Level of defensive dysregulation." The following examples are among the proposed levels and mechanisms.

High Adaptive Level   This most adaptive, healthy defense level contains coping efforts that are realistic ways of handling stress and are conducive to achieving a good balance among conflicting motives. Examples are:

anticipation—experiencing emotional reactions before a stressful event occurs and considering realistic, alternative courses of action; for example, carefully planning for an upcoming meeting with an employer who is unhappy with your performance

sublimation—dealing with a stress by channeling negative feelings into socially acceptable behaviors; for example, working out at a gym

Disavowal Level   This middle level is characterized by defenses that keep troubling stressors or ideas out of conscious awareness.

denial—refusing to acknowledge a degree of discomfort or threat that is obvious to an observer; for example, maintaining that your marriage is fine despite the obvious and repeated conflicts noticed by your friends

projection—falsely attributing to another person one's own unacceptable feelings or thoughts; for example, believing that your professor is angry with you, rather than the reverse

Level of Defensive Dysregulation   This lowest level is marked by a failure to deal with stress, leading to a break with reality.

psychotic denial—denial that is so extreme as to be marked by a gross impairment in reality testing; for example, maintaining that the results of three biopsies showing a cancerous growth are wrong

The reliability of the defense mechanisms axis has been studied. After training, two clinicians rated a series of patients. Unfortunately, reliability was not very good (Perry et al., 1998). Perhaps reliability would improve if a better method were developed for the assessment of defense mechanisms, as happened when structured interviews began to be used to make DSM diagnoses.

typed act with the usually impossible purpose of warding off an impending feared situation. Attempts to resist a compulsion create so much tension that the individual usually yields to it.

- Experiencing anxiety and emotional numbness in the aftermath of a very traumatic event is called *posttraumatic stress disorder*. Individuals have painful, intrusive recollections by day and bad dreams at night. They find it difficult to concentrate and feel detached from others and from ongoing affairs.
- *Acute stress disorder* is similar to posttraumatic stress disorder, but the symptoms do not last as long.

The anxiety disorders are reviewed in Chapter 6.

Somatoform Disorders   The physical symptoms of somatoform disorders have no known physiological cause but seem to serve a psychological purpose.

- Persons with *somatization disorder* have a long history of multiple physical complaints for which they have taken medicine or consulted doctors.
- In *conversion disorder* the person reports the loss of motor or sensory function, such as a paralysis, an anesthesia (loss of sensation), or blindness.
- Individuals with *pain disorder* suffer from severe and prolonged pain.
- *Hypochondriasis* is the misinterpretation of minor physical sensations as serious illness.

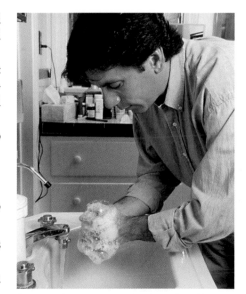

Extreme fear of contamination triggering abnormally frequent hand-washing is common in obsessive-compulsive disorder.

- People with *body dysmorphic disorder* are preoccupied with an imagined defect in their appearance.

These disorders are covered in Chapter 7.

Dissociative Disorders   Psychological dissociation is a sudden alteration in consciousness that affects memory and identity.

- Persons with *dissociative amnesia* may forget their entire past or lose memory for a particular time period.
- With *dissociative fugue* the individual suddenly and unexpectedly travels to a new locale, starts a new life, and is amnesic for his or her previous identity.
- The person with *dissociative identity disorder* (formerly called multiple personality disorder) possesses two or more distinct personalities, each complex and dominant one at a time.
- *Depersonalization disorder* is a severe and disruptive feeling of self-estrangement or unreality.

These rare disorders are examined in Chapter 7.

Sexual and Gender Identity Disorders   The sexual disorders section of DSM-IV-TR lists three principal subcategories.

- In *paraphilias* the sources of sexual gratification—as in exhibitionism, voyeurism, sadism, and masochism—are unconventional.
- Persons with *sexual dysfunctions* are unable to complete the usual sexual response cycle. Inability to maintain an erection, premature ejaculation, and inhibition of orgasms are examples of these problems.
- People with gender *identity disorder* feel extreme discomfort with their anatomical sex and identify themselves as members of the opposite sex.

These disorders are studied in Chapter 14.

Sleep Disorders   Two major subcategories of sleep disorders are distinguished in DSM-IV-TR.

- In the *dyssomnias*, sleep is disturbed in amount (e.g., the person is not able to maintain sleep or sleeps too much), quality (the person does not feel rested after sleep), or timing (e.g., the person experiences inability to sleep during conventional sleep times).
- In the *parasomnias*, an unusual event occurs during sleep (e.g., nightmares, sleepwalking).

These disorders are discussed in Chapter 16.

Eating Disorders   Eating disorders fall into two major categories.

- In *anorexia nervosa* the person avoids eating and becomes emaciated, usually because of an intense fear of becoming fat.
- In *bulimia nervosa* there are frequent episodes of binge eating coupled with compensatory activities such as self-induced vomiting and heavy use of laxatives.

These disorders are discussed in Chapter 9.

Factitious Disorder   A diagnosis of *factitious disorder* is applied to people who intentionally produce or complain of physical or psychological symptoms, apparently because of a psychological need to assume the role of a sick person. This disorder is discussed in Chapter 7.

Adjustment Disorders   An adjustment disorder involves the development of emotional or behavioral symptoms following the occurrence of a major life stressor. However, the symptoms that ensue do not meet diagnostic criteria for any other Axis I diagnosis.

Impulse Control Disorder   Impulse control disorders include a number of conditions in which the person's behavior is inappropriate and seemingly out of control.

- In *intermittent explosive disorder* the person has episodes of violent behavior that result in destruction of property or injury to another person.
- In *kleptomania* the person steals repeatedly, but not for the monetary value of the object or for the use of the object.
- In *pyromania* the person purposefully sets fires and derives pleasure from doing so.
- In *pathological gambling* the person is preoccupied with gambling, is unable to stop, and gambles as a way to escape from problems.
- *Trichotillomania* is diagnosed when the person cannot resist the urge to pluck out his or her hair, often resulting in significant hair loss.

Impulse control disorders include a number of conditions in which the person's behavior is out of control. Pathological gambling is an example.

Personality Disorders   Listed on Axis II, personality disorders are defined as enduring, inflexible, and maladaptive patterns of behavior and inner experience. Examples include:

- In *schizoid personality disorder* the person is aloof, has few friends, and is indifferent to praise and criticism.
- The individual with a *narcissistic personality disorder* has an overblown sense of self-importance, fantasizes about great successes, requires constant attention, and is likely to exploit others.
- *Antisocial personality disorder* surfaces as conduct disorder before the person reaches age fifteen and is manifested in truancy, running away from home, delinquency, and general belligerence. In adulthood the person is indifferent about holding a job, being a responsible partner or parent, planning for the future or even for tomorrow, and staying on the right side of the law. People with antisocial personality disorder—also called psychopathy—do not feel guilt or shame for transgressing social mores.

Chapter 13 covers the personality disorders.

Other Conditions That May Be a Focus of Clinical Attention   This all-encompassing category comprises conditions that are not regarded as mental disorders per se but still may be a focus of professional attention or treatment. This category seems to exist so that anyone entering the mental health system can be categorized, even in the absence of a formally designated mental disorder.

If an individual's medical illness appears to be caused in part or exacerbated by a psychological condition, the diagnosis is *psychological factors affecting physical condition*. Referred to previously as a psychophysiological or psychosomatic disorder, this condition is reviewed in detail in Chapter 8. Among the other diagnoses in this category are the following:

- Academic problem (e.g., underachievement)
- Antisocial behavior (e.g., in professional thieves)
- Malingering (faking physical or psychological symptoms to achieve a goal, such as avoiding work)
- Relational problem (e.g., poor relationship with sibling or spouse)
- Occupational problem (e.g., dissatisfaction with work)
- Physical or sexual abuse
- Bereavement
- Noncompliance with treatment (e.g., refusing medication)

The frequency of Alzheimer's disease, which severely impairs cognitive functioning, increases with advanced age.

- Religious or spiritual problem (e.g., questioning one's faith)
- Phase-of-life problem (difficulties created by a life transition, such as beginning school)

In this context it is interesting to recall our discussion of the difficulties of defining mental disorder (pp. 3–6). Should these life difficulties really be included in a listing of mental disorders? Are mental health professionals qualified, for example, to "treat" religious doubt? Many of these conditions will not be covered in this book, although malingering is discussed in Chapter 7, therapy for marital problems in Chapters 10 and 17, and physical and sexual abuse in Chapters 7 and 14.

Delirium, Dementia, Amnestic, and Other Cognitive Disorders This category covers disorders in which cognition is seriously disturbed.

- *Delirium* is a clouding of consciousness, wandering attention, and an incoherent stream of thought. It may be caused by several medical conditions such as malnutrition as well as by substance abuse.
- *Dementia*, a deterioration of mental capacities, especially memory, is associated with Alzheimer's disease, stroke, and several other medical conditions as well as with substance abuse.
- *Amnestic syndrome* is an impairment in memory when there is no delirium or dementia.

Delirium and dementia are discussed in detail in Chapter 16 because they are often associated with aging.

Now that we have briefly described the DSM's diagnostic categories and its axes, we return to the case of Ernest H. with which the book began. Table 3.2 shows how Ernest's diagnosis would look. On Axis I, Ernest is diagnosed with alcohol dependence, which has also created a problem with sexual arousal. His current problems with his marriage are noted, as is his prior history of bipolar disorder. In addition, Ernest is diagnosed on Axis II as having avoidant personality disorder. His feelings of inferiority, his self-consciousness when around others, and his avoidance of activities because of fear of criticism are the basis of this diagnosis. He has no general medical condition relevant to his problems, so he has no diagnosis on Axis III. His problems with his marriage are noted on Axis IV, and his current level of functioning is rated at 55 on the GAF scale (indicating a moderate level of impairment). Though alcohol may be Ernest's most immediate problem, the multiaxial diagnosis gives clinicians a fairly full picture of the complex of problems that will need to be addressed in treatment.

Issues in the Classification of Abnormal Behavior

Our review of the major diagnostic categories of abnormal behavior was brief because the diagnoses will be examined in more detail throughout this text. On the basis of this overview, however, we will examine here the usefulness of the current diagnostic system. Among those who are critical of the DSM, one group asserts that classification per se is

---

Table 3.2 DSM-IV-TR Multiaxial Diagnosis of Ernest H.

Axis I	Alcohol Dependence
	Alcohol-Induced Sexual Problem, with Impaired Arousal
	Bipolar I Disorder, Most Recent Episode Manic, in Full Remission
	Partner Relational Problem
Axis II	Avoidant Personality Disorder
Axis III	None
Axis IV	Problem with Primary Support Group
Axis V	GAF = 55

irrelevant to the field of abnormal behavior, and a second group finds specific deficiencies in the manner in which diagnoses are made in the DSM.

General Criticisms of Classification

Some critics of diagnosis argue that to classify someone as depressed or anxious results in a loss of information about that person, thereby reducing some of the uniqueness of the individual being studied. In evaluating this claim, recall our earlier discussions of paradigms and their effect on how we glean information about our world. It appears to be in the nature of humankind to categorize whenever we perceive and think about anything. Those who argue against classification per se therefore overlook the inevitability of classification and categorization in human thought.

Consider the simple example of casting dice. Any of the numbers one through six may come up on a given toss of a single die. Let us suppose, however, that we classify each outcome as odd or even. Whenever a one, three, or five comes up on a roll, we call out "odd," and whenever a two, four, or six appears, we say "even." A person listening to our calls will not know whether the call "odd" refers to a one, a three, or a five or whether "even" refers to a two, a four, or a six. In classification, some information must inevitably be lost.

What matters is whether the information lost is *relevant*, which in turn depends on the purposes of the classification system. Any classification is designed to group together objects sharing a common property and to ignore differences in the objects that are not relevant to the purposes at hand. If our intention is merely to count odd and even rolls, it is irrelevant whether a die comes up one, three, or five, or two, four, or six. In judging abnormal behavior, however, we cannot so easily decide what is wheat and what is chaff, for the relevant and irrelevant dimensions of abnormal behavior are uncertain. Thus when we do classify, we may be grouping people together on rather trivial bases while ignoring their extremely important differences.

Classification may also have negative effects on a person. Consider how your life might be changed after being diagnosed as having schizophrenia. You might become guarded and suspicious lest someone recognize your disorder. Or you might be chronically on edge, fearing the onset of another episode. The fact that you are a "former mental patient" could have a stigmatizing effect. Friends and loved ones might treat you differently, and employment might be difficult to obtain.

There is little doubt that diagnosis can have such negative consequences. It is clear from the existing research that the general public holds a very negative view of mental patients and that patients and their families believe that such stigmatizing effects are common (Rabkin, 1974; Wahl & Harrman, 1989). We must recognize and be on guard against the possible social stigma of a diagnosis.

The Value of Classification and Diagnosis

Assuming that various types of abnormal behavior do differ from one another, classifying them is essential, for these differences may constitute keys to the causes and treatments of various deviant behaviors. For example, mental retardation is sometimes caused by phenylketonuria. A deficiency in the metabolism of the protein phenylalanine results in the release of incomplete metabolites that injure the brain (see p. 503). A diet drastically reduced in phenylalanine prevents some of this injury. As Mendels (1970) noted, however, "had we taken 100, or even 1,000, people with mental deficiency and placed them all on the phenylalanine-free diet, the response would have been insignificant and the diet would have been discarded as a treatment. It was first necessary to recognize a subtype of mental deficiency [retardation], phenylketonuria, and then subject the value of a phenylalanine-free diet to investigation in this specific population, for whom it has been shown to have value in preventing the development of mental deficiency" (p. 35).

Forming categories may thus further knowledge, for once a category is formed, additional information may be ascertained about it. Even though the category is only an asserted, and not a proved, entity, it may still be heuristically[1] useful in that it facilitates the acquisition of new information. Only after a diagnostic category has been formed can people who fit its definition be studied in the hope of uncovering factors responsible for the development of their problems and of devising treatments that may help them. For example, only a few decades ago, bipolar disorder (episodes of both mania and depression) was not typically distinguished from depression. If this distinction had not subsequently been made, it is unlikely that lithium would have been recognized as an effective treatment, as it is today.

Specific Criticisms of Diagnosis

In addition to the general criticisms just described, more specific criticisms of psychiatric classification are commonly made. The principal ones concern whether discrete diagnostic categories are justifiable and whether the diagnostic categories are reliable and valid. These criticisms were frequently leveled at DSM-I and DSM-II. At the close of this section we will see how subsequent editions of the DSM have come to grips with them.

Discrete Entity versus Continuum   The DSM represents a **categorical classification**, a yes–no approach to classification. Does the patient have schizophrenia or not? It may be argued that this type of classification, because it postulates discrete diagnostic entities, does not allow continuity between normal and abnormal behavior to be taken into consideration. Those who advance the continuity argument hold that abnormal and normal behavior differ only in intensity or degree, not in kind; therefore, discrete diagnostic categories foster a false impression of discontinuity.

In contrast, in **dimensional classification** the entities or objects being classified must be ranked on a quantitative dimension (e.g., a 1-to-10 scale of anxiety, where 1 represents minimal and 10 extreme). Classification would be accomplished by assessing patients on the relevant dimensions and perhaps plotting the location of the patient in a system of coordinates defined by his or her score on each dimension. (See Figure 3.1 for an illustration of the difference between dimensional and categorical classification.) A dimensional system can subsume a categorical system by specifying a cutting point, or threshold, on one of the quantitative dimensions. This capability is a potential advantage of the dimensional approach.

Clearly, a dimensional system can be applied to most of the symptoms that constitute the diagnoses of the DSM. Anxiety, depression, and the many personality traits that are included in the personality disorders are found in different people to varying degrees and thus do not seem to fit well with the DSM categorical model. In fact, early indications are that DSM-V, scheduled to be published at the end of the decade, will become more dimensional than categorical.

The choice between a categorical and a dimensional system of classification, however, is not as simple as it might seem initially. Consider hypertension (high blood pressure), a topic discussed at length in Chapter 8. Blood-pressure measurements form a continuum, which clearly fits a dimensional approach; yet it has proved useful to categorize certain people as having high blood pressure in order to research its causes and possible treatments. A similar situation could exist for the DSM categories. Even though anxiety clearly exists in differing degrees in different people and thus is a dimensional variable, it could prove useful to create a diagnostic category for those people whose anxiety is extreme. There is a certain inevitable arbi-

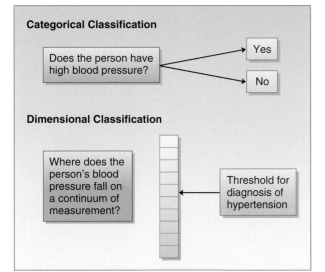

Figure 3.1 Categorical versus dimensional classification.

Categorical Classification

Does the person have high blood pressure? → Yes / No

Dimensional Classification

Where does the person's blood pressure fall on a continuum of measurement? ← Threshold for diagnosis of hypertension

---

[1] *Heuristic* is a central word and concept in science. It comes from the Greek *heuriskein*, "to discover," or "to find," and is defined in *Webster's* as serving to guide, discover, or reveal, and more specifically as valuable for stimulating or conducting empirical research. The frequent use of this word and its derivatives underlines the importance scientists place on ideas in generating new knowledge.

trariness to such a categorization (where exactly should the cutoff be?), but it could be fruitful nonetheless.

It is also possible that a variable that on the surface appears dimensional actually represents an underlying categorical, or off–on, process. This is a complex argument, but some of its flavor can be appreciated by considering a hypothetical single-gene cause for hypertension. Blood pressure might result from a complex interplay between the gene (off or on) and a variety of environmental influences—diet, weight, smoking, stress, and so on. Observed blood pressure is a dimensional variable, but hypertension might result principally from the operation of the single off–on gene, which is a categorical variable. Given that we can observe only the surface variable, how can we tell whether there might be an underlying categorical process? Although well beyond the scope of this book, complex mathematical procedures have been developed to test such questions (e.g., Meehl, 1986), and they have been used to evaluate whether a dimensional or categorical approach is most applicable to several diagnoses (Tykra et al., 1995). We will return to this issue in our discussion of personality disorders in Chapter 13.

Reliability: The Cornerstone of a Diagnostic System

The extent to which a classification system, or a test or measurement of any kind, produces the same scientific observation each time it is applied is the measure of its **reliability**. An example of an unreliable measure would be a flexible, elastic-like ruler whose length changed every time it was used. This flawed ruler would yield different values for the height of the same object every time the object was measured. In contrast, a reliable measure, such as a standard wooden ruler, produces consistent results.

Interrater reliability refers to the extent to which two judges agree about an event. For example, suppose you wanted to know whether a child suspected of having attention deficit/hyperactivity disorder did indeed have difficulty paying attention and staying seated in the classroom. You could decide to observe the child during a day at school. To determine whether the observational data were reliable you would want to have at least two people watch the child and make independent judgments about the level of attention and activity. The extent to which the raters agreed would be an index of interrater reliability (see Figure 3.2 for an illustration).

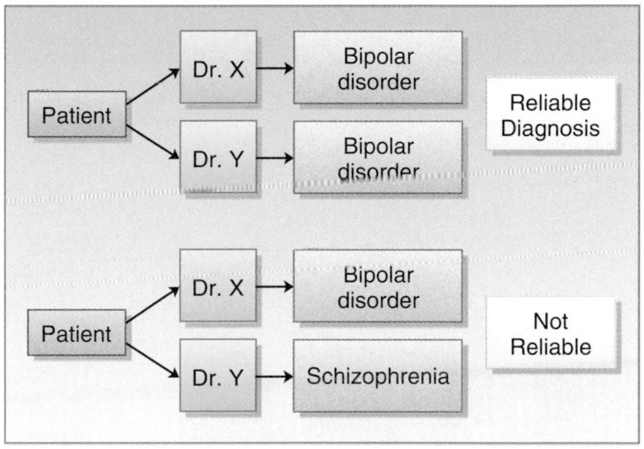

Figure 3.2 Interrater reliability. In this example, the diagnosis of the first patient is reliable—both clinicians diagnose bipolar disorder—whereas the diagnosis of the second is not reliable.

Reliability is a primary criterion for judging any classification system. For a classification system to be useful, those applying it must be able to agree on what is and what is not an instance of a particular category.[2] A person diagnosed as having an anxiety disorder by one clinician should be given the same diagnosis by another clinician as well. After all, if someone is not diagnosed correctly, he or she may not receive the best treatment available. Prior to DSM-III, reliability for DSM diagnoses was not acceptable, mainly because the criteria for making a diagnosis were not presented clearly and methods of assessing a patient's symptoms were not standardized (Ward et al., 1962). As we will soon see, reliability for most current diagnostic categories is good.

How Valid Are Diagnostic Categories?

Validity is a complex topic. There are several types of validity, which we will describe in Chapter 4. Here we discuss the type of validity that is most important for diagnosis— **construct validity**. The diagnoses of DSM are referred to as constructs because they are inferred, not proven, entities. A diagnosis of schizophrenia, for instance, does not have the same status as a diagnosis of diabetes. In the case of diabetes, we know the symptoms, the biological malfunction that produces them, and some of the causes. For schiz-

---

[2] These two components of reliability—agreeing on who is a member of a class and who is not—are termed *sensitivity* and *specificity*. Sensitivity refers to agreement regarding the presence of a specific diagnosis; specificity refers to agreement concerning the absence of a diagnosis.

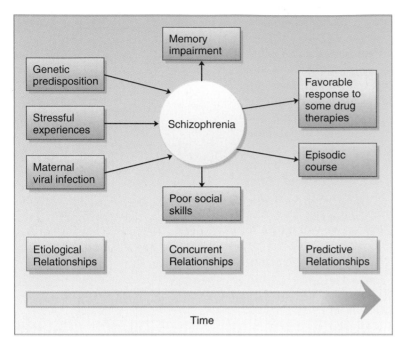

Figure 3.3   Construct validity. Some lawful relationships of the construct of schizophrenia.

ophrenia, we have a proposed set of symptoms but only very tentative information regarding mechanisms that may produce the symptoms.

Construct validity is determined by evaluating the extent to which accurate statements and predictions can be made about a category once it has been formed. In other words, to what extent does the construct enter into a network of lawful relationships? Some of these relationships may be about possible causes of the disorder, for example, a genetic predisposition or a biochemical imbalance. Others could be about characteristics of the disorder that are not symptoms but occur frequently, for example, poor social skills in people with schizophrenia. Other relationships could refer to predictions about the course of the disorder or the probable response to particular treatments. The greater the number and strength of relationships into which a diagnosis enters, the greater the construct validity (see Figure 3.3).

We have organized this book around the major DSM diagnostic categories because we believe that they indeed possess some construct validity. Certain categories have greater validity than others, however, and we will discuss these differences in the chapters on each of the major diagnostic categories.

The DSM and Criticisms of Diagnosis

As we have mentioned, the diagnoses in DSM-II were not very reliable. Beginning with DSM-III and DSM-III-R an effort was made to create more reliable and valid diagnostic categories. Major improvements include the following:

1. The characteristics and symptoms of each diagnostic category in Axes I and II are now described much more extensively than they were in DSM-II. For each disorder there is a description of essential features, then of associated features, such as laboratory findings (e.g., enlarged ventricles in schizophrenia) and results from physical exams (e.g., electrolyte imbalances in people who have eating disorders). Next are statements drawn from the research literature about age of onset, course, prevalence and sex ratio, familial pattern, and differential diagnosis (i.e., how to distinguish one diagnosis from another that is symptomatically similar to it).

2. Much more attention is now paid to how the symptoms of a given disorder may differ depending on the culture in which it appears. For example, it is known that the core symptoms of both schizophrenia (e.g., delusions and hallucinations) and depression (e.g., depressed mood and loss of interest or pleasure in activities) are similar cross-culturally (Draguns, 1989). However, guilt is a frequent symptom of depression in Western society but an infrequent symptom in Japan and Iran. Similarly, depression in Latinos is more likely to involve somatic complaints, such as headaches or "nerves." (Focus on Discovery 3.2 describes further efforts by the DSM to be more sensitive to the effects of culture.)

3. Specific diagnostic criteria—the symptoms and other facts that must be present to justify the diagnosis—are spelled out more precisely, and the clinical symptoms that constitute a diagnosis are defined in a glossary. Table 3.3 compares the descriptions of a manic episode given in DSM-II with the diagnostic criteria given in DSM-IV-TR. The bases for making diagnoses are decidedly more detailed and concrete in DSM-IV-TR.

The core symptoms of depression appear to be similar cross-culturally. However, guilt is less frequent in Japan than in Western cultures.

The improved explicitness of the DSM criteria has reduced the descriptive inadequacies that were the major source of diagnostic unreliability and thus has led to improved reliability. Another factor in improved reliability is the use of standardized, reliably scored interviews for collecting the information needed for a diagnosis. (We will describe such

Table 3.3 Description of Manic Disorder in DSM-II versus DSM-IV-TR

DSM-II (1968, p. 36)

Manic-depressive illness, manic type. This disorder consists exclusively of manic episodes. These episodes are characterized by excessive elation, irritability, talkativeness, flight of ideas, and accelerated speech and motor activity. Brief periods of depression sometimes occur, but they are never true depressive episodes.

DSM-IV-TR (2000, p. 362)

Diagnostic Criteria for a Manic Episode

A. A distinct period of abnormally and persistently elevated, expansive, or irritable mood, lasting at least 1 week (or any duration if hospitalization is necessary).

B. During the period of mood disturbance, three (or more) of the following symptoms have persisted (four if the mood is only irritable) and have been present to a significant degree:

   (1) inflated self-esteem or grandiosity

   (2) decreased need for sleep (e.g., feels rested after only three hours of sleep)

   (3) more talkative than usual or pressure to keep talking

   (4) flight of ideas or subjective experience that thoughts are racing

   (5) distractibility (i.e., attention too easily drawn to unimportant or irrelevant external stimuli)

   (6) increase in goal-directed activity (either socially, at work or school, or sexually) or psychomotor agitation

   (7) excessive involvement in pleasurable activities that have a high potential for painful consequences (e.g., engaging in unrestrained buying sprees, sexual indiscretions, or foolish business investments)

C. The symptoms do not meet criteria for a Mixed Episode.

D. The mood disturbance is sufficiently severe to cause marked impairment in occupational functioning or in usual social activities or relationships with others, or to necessitate hospitalization to prevent harm to self or others, or there are psychotic features.

E. The symptoms are not due to the direct physiological effects of a substance (e.g., a drug of abuse, a medication, or other treatment) or a general medical condition (e.g., hyperthyroidism).

Note: DSM-IV-TR material reprinted with permission from the DSM-IV-TR, 2000, American Psychiatric Association.

interviews in the next chapter.) Results of an extensive evaluation of the reliability of DSM-III-R are shown in Table 3.4. The reliabilities vary but are quite acceptable for most of the major categories. The relatively low figures for anxiety disorders are higher in other studies that used an assessment interview specifically tailored for them (DiNardo et al., 1993). Although the data are not all in yet, the reliability of DSM-IV diagnoses look comparable to those shown in the table (e.g., Zanarini et al., 2000).

Thus far we have described the DSM in positive terms. The attainment of adequate diagnostic reliability is a considerable achievement, but a number of problems remain.

1. The discrete entity versus continuum issue, discussed earlier, has not been satisfactorily resolved.

2. It is unclear whether the rules for making diagnostic decisions are ideal. Examining Table 3.3, we see that for patients to be diagnosed as suffering from mania they must have three symptoms from a list of seven, or four if their mood is irritable. But why require three symptoms rather than two or five (see Finn, 1982)? Just as there is a degree of arbitrariness about the point at which a person is diagnosed as having high blood pressure, so there is an element of arbitrariness to the DSM's diagnostic rules.

3. The reliability of Axes I and II may not always be as high in everyday usage, for diagnosticians may not adhere as precisely to the criteria as do those whose work is being scrutinized in formal research studies.

Table 3.4 Reliability of Selected DSM Diagnoses

Diagnosis	Kappa
Bipolar disorder	.84
Major depression	.64
Schizophrenia	.65
Alcohol abuse	.75
Anorexia nervosa	.75
Bulimia nervosa	.86
Panic disorder	.58
Social phobia	.47

Source: Williams et al., 1992.

Note: The numbers here are a statistic called kappa, which measures the proportion of agreement over and above what would be expected by chance. Generally, kappas over .70 are considered good.

Focus on Discovery 3.2

Ethnic and Cultural Considerations in DSM-IV-TR

Previous editions of the DSM were criticized for their lack of attention to cultural and ethnic variations in psychopathology. DSM-IV-TR attempts to enhance its cultural sensitivity in three ways: (1) by including in the main body of the manual a discussion of cultural and ethnic factors for each disorder; (2) by providing in the appendix a general framework for evaluating the role of culture and ethnicity; and (3) by describing culture-bound syndromes in an appendix.

Among the cultural issues of which clinicians need to be aware are language differences between the therapist and the patient and the way in which the patient's culture talks about emotional distress. Many cultures, for example, describe grief or anxiety in physical terms—"I am sick in my heart" or "My heart is heavy"—rather than in psychological

A therapist must be mindful of the role of cultural differences in the ways in which patients describe their problems.

terms. Individuals also vary in the degree to which they identify with their cultural or ethnic group. Some value assimilation into the majority culture, whereas others wish to maintain close ties to their ethnic background. In general, clinicians are advised to be constantly mindful of how culture and ethnicity influence diagnosis and treatment, a topic discussed in the next chapter.

The DSM also describes "locality-specific patterns of aberrant behavior and troubling experience that may or may not be linked to a particular DSM-IV diagnostic category" (DSM-IV-TR, 2000, p. 898). The following are some examples that may occur in clinical practices in North America.

amok—a dissociative episode in which there is a period of brooding followed by a violent and sometimes homicidal outburst. The episode tends to be triggered by an insult and is found primarily among men. Persecutory delusions are often present as well. The term is Malaysian and is defined by the dictionary as a murderous frenzy. The reader has probably encountered the phrase "run amok."

brain fag—originally used in West Africa, this term refers to a condition reported by high school and university students in response to academic pressures. Symptoms include fatigue, tightness in the head and neck, and blurring of vision. This syndrome resembles certain anxiety, depressive, and somatoform disorders.

dhat—a term used in India to refer to severe anxiety and hypochondriasis linked to the discharge of semen.

ghost sickness—extreme preoccupation with death and those who have died; found among certain Native American tribes.

koro—reported also in south and east Asia, an episode of intense anxiety about the possibility that the penis or nipples will recede into the body, possibly leading to death.

4. Although the improved reliability of the DSM may lead to more validity, there is no guarantee that it will. The diagnoses made according to the DSM criteria may not reveal anything useful about the patients.

5. Subjective factors still play a role in evaluations made according to DSM-IV-TR. Consider again the criteria for manic syndrome in Table 3.3. What exactly does it mean to say that the elevated mood must be abnormally and persistently elevated? Or, what level of involvement in pleasurable activities with high potential for painful consequences is excessive? Such judgments set the stage for the insertion of cultural biases as well as the clinician's own personal ideas of what the average person should be doing at a given stage of life.

6. Not all the DSM classification changes seem positive. Should a problem such as difficulty in learning arithmetic or reading be considered a psychiatric disorder? By expanding its coverage the DSM seems to have made too many childhood problems into psychiatric disorders, without good justification for doing so.

In sum, although the DSM is continually improving, it is far from perfect. Throughout this book, as we present the literature on various disorders, we will have further opportunities to describe both the strengths and the weaknesses of the DSM-IV-TR and to consider how it may deal with some of the problems that still exist. What is most heartening about the DSM is that its attempts to be explicit about the rules for diagnosis make it easier to detect problems in the diagnostic system. We can expect more changes and refinements over the next several years.

Summary

- Diagnosis is a critical aspect of the field of abnormal psychology. Having an agreed-on system of classification makes it possible for clinicians to communicate effectively with one another and facilitates the search for causes and treatments of the various psychopathologies.

- The Diagnostic and Statistical Manual of Mental Disorders (DSM), published by the American Psychiatric Association, is an official classification scheme widely used by mental health professionals. A revision of the fourth edition of the manual, referred to as DSM-IV-TR, was published in 2000.

- A novel feature of the current DSM is its multiaxial organization. Every time a diagnosis is made, the clinician must describe the patient's condition according to each of five axes, or dimensions. A multiaxial diagnosis is believed to provide a more multidimensional and useful description of the patient's mental disorder.

- In the multiaxial organization of DSM, Axes I and II make up the mental disorders per se; Axis III lists any physical disorders believed to bear on the mental disorder in question; Axis IV is used to indicate the psychosocial and environmental problems that the person has been experiencing; and Axis V rates the person's current level of adaptive functioning.

- Some critics of the DSM argue against classification in general. They point out that to classify someone results in a loss of information about that person. Classification may also result in stigmatization and other negative effects for the individual diagnosed.

- Specific shortcomings of the DSM have also been identified. One important criticism concerns whether the categorical classification system used in DSM is justifiable. Such a system uses a yes-no approach to diagnosis and does not allow for continuity between normal and abnormal behavior; in contrast, a dimensional classification system places behavior on a continuum. The issue of categorical versus dimensional classification remains unresolved.

- Another important specific criticism concerns the reliability and validity of the DSM diagnostic categories. Because recent versions of the DSM are more concrete and descriptive than earlier ones, interrater reliability has been improved—that is, independent diagnosticians are now likely to agree on the diagnosis of a particular case. However, construct validity—how well the diagnosis relates to other aspects of the disorder, such as prognosis and response to treatment—remains an open question.

Key Terms

categorical classification
construct validity

*Diagnostic and Statistical Manual of
Mental Disorders (DSM-IV-TR)*

dimensional classification
interrater reliability

multiaxial classification
reliability

4 Clinical Assessment Procedures

This book began with an account of a police officer who had bipolar disorder as well as drinking and marital problems, and the preceding chapter ended with a diagnosis of this man. Yet a DSM diagnosis is only a starting point. Many other questions remain to be answered. Why does Ernest behave as he does? Do his mood swings and violent outbursts constitute a true disorder? Why does he doubt his wife's love for him? What can be done to resolve his marital conflicts? Is his difficulty maintaining an erection caused by physical factors, or psychological factors, or both? Has he performed up to his intellectual potential in school and in his career? What type of treatment would be helpful to him? What obstacles might interfere with treatment? Can his marriage be saved? Should it be saved? These are the types of questions that mental health professionals address before therapy begins and as it unfolds, and a clinical assessment helps them find answers.

All clinical assessment procedures are more or less formal ways of finding out what is wrong with a person, what may have caused a problem or problems, and what steps can be taken to improve the individual's condition. Some of these procedures are also used to evaluate the effects of therapeutic interventions.

In this chapter we describe and discuss the most widely used psychological and biological assessment techniques—and some that are still in the early development phase. We conclude with a look at an important issue that affects all approaches to assessment, that is, the question of whether, in the long run, feelings, thoughts, and behavior are consistent or variable. We also discuss a sometimes neglected aspect of assessment, the role of cultural diversity and clinician bias. We begin our discussion with two concepts that play a key role in assessment: reliability and validity.

Reliability and Validity in Assessment

The concepts of reliability and validity are extremely complex. There are several kinds of each, and an entire subfield of psychology—psychometrics—exists primarily for their study. We provide here a general overview, which supplements our brief discussion in Chapter 3.

Reliability

In the most general sense reliability refers to consistency of measurement. There are several types of reliability, some of which we discuss here.

- **Interrater reliability**, discussed in the preceding chapter, refers to the degree to which two independent observers or judges agree. To take an example from baseball, the third-base umpire may or may not agree with the home-plate umpire as to whether a line drive down the left-field line is fair or foul.

- **Test-retest reliability** measures the extent to which people being observed twice or taking the same test twice, perhaps several weeks or months apart, score in generally the same way. This kind of reliability makes sense only when the theory assumes that people will not change appreciably between testings on the variable being measured; a prime example of a situation in which this type of reliability makes sense is in evaluating intelligence tests (see p. 90).

- Sometimes psychologists use two forms of a test rather than giving the same test twice, perhaps when there is concern that people will remember their answers from the first test taking and aim merely to be consistent. This approach enables the tester to determine **alternate-form reliability**, the extent to which scores on the two forms of the test are consistent.

- Finally, **internal consistency reliability** assesses whether the items on a test are related to one another. For example, with an anxiety questionnaire containing twenty items we would expect the items to be interrelated, or to correlate with one another, if they truly tap anxiety. A person who reports a dry mouth in a threatening situation would be expected to report increases in muscle tension as well.

In each of these types of reliability, a correlation, a measure of how closely two variables are related (see p. 118), is calculated between raters or sets of items. The higher the correlation, the better the reliability.

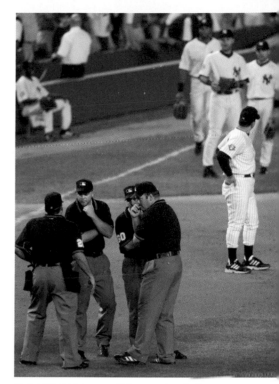

Reliability is an essential property of all assessment procedures. One means of determining reliability is to find if different judges agree, as happens when two umpires witness the same event in a baseball game.

Validity

Validity is a complex concept, generally related to whether a measure fulfills its intended purpose. For example, if a questionnaire is proposed to be able to measure a person's hostility, does it in fact do so? Before we describe several types of validity, it is important to note that validity is related to reliability—unreliable measures will not have good validity. Because an unreliable measure does not yield consistent results (recall our example on p. 75 of trying to measure with a ruler whose length is constantly changing), an unreliable measure will not relate very strongly to other measures. For example, an unreliable measure of coping is not likely to relate well to how a person adjusts to a stressful life experience. Reliability, however, does not guarantee validity. Height can be measured very reliably, but height would not be a valid measure of anxiety.

Content validity refers to whether a measure adequately samples the domain of interest. For example, later in this chapter we will describe an interview that is often used to make an Axis I diagnosis. It has excellent content validity because it contains questions about all the symptoms that are involved in Axis I diagnoses. As another example, consider a measure of life stress that we will examine in more detail in Chapter 8 (see p. 201). It consists of a list of forty-three life experiences. Respondents indicate which of these experiences—for example, losing one's job—they have had in some time period, for example, the past year. Content validity is less certain here. If you read the experiences in Table 8.2 (p. 201), you will likely think of stressors that are not on the list (e.g., the serious illness of someone close to you).

Criterion validity is evaluated by determining whether a measure is associated in an expected way with some other measure (the criterion). Sometimes these relationships are concurrent (both variables are measured at the same point in time) and the resulting validity is sometimes referred to as **concurrent validity**. For example, we will describe later a measure of the distorted thoughts that are believed to play an important role in depression (see p. 96). Criterion validity for this test could be established by showing that it is actually related to depression—that is, depressed people score higher on the test than do nondepressed people. Alternatively, criterion validity can be assessed by evaluating the ability of the measure to predict some other variable that is measured at some point in the future, often referred to as predictive validity. For example, IQ tests were originally developed to predict future school performance. Similarly, a measure of distorted thinking could be used to predict the development of episodes of depression in the future.

Construct validity is a more complex concept. It is relevant when we want to interpret a test as a measure of some characteristic or construct that is not simply defined (Cronbach & Meehl, 1955). A construct is an inferred attribute, such as anxiousness or distorted cognition, that a measure is trying to assess. Consider an anxiety-proneness questionnaire as an example. The construct validity question is whether the variation we observe between people on our self-report test of anxiety proneness is really due to individual differences in anxiety proneness. Just because we call our test a measure of anxiety proneness and the items seem to be about the tendency to become anxious ("I find that I become anxious in many situations."), it is not certain that the test is a valid measure of anxiety proneness. People's responses to a questionnaire are determined by more variables than simply the construct being measured. For example, people vary in their willingness to admit to undesirable characteristics such as anxiety proneness; thus, scores on the questionnaire will be partly determined by this characteristic as well as by anxiety proneness itself.

Construct validity is evaluated by looking at a wide variety of data from multiple sources. For example, people diagnosed as having an anxiety disorder and people without such a diagnosis could be compared on their scores on our self-report measure of anxiety proneness. The self-report measure would achieve some construct validity if the people with anxiety disorders scored higher than the controls. Similarly, the self-report measure could be related to other measures that are thought to reflect anxiety, such as observations of fidgeting, trembling, or excessive sweating. When the self-report measure is associated with the observational one, its construct validity is increased. Studies may also examine change on the self-report measure. For example, if the measure is construct valid, we would expect scores of patients with anxiety disorders to become lower after a course of a therapy that is known to be effective in reducing anxiety.

More broadly, construct validity is related to theory. For example, we might hypothesize that being prone to anxiety is caused by certain childhood experiences. We could then obtain further evidence for the construct validity of our questionnaire by showing that it relates to these childhood experiences. At the same time, we would have also gathered support for our theory of anxiety proneness. Thus, construct validation is an important part of the process of theory testing.

Psychological Assessment

One purpose of psychological assessment techniques is to gather data needed for a diagnosis. But there are also several other important uses of the methods we will be describing here. For example, assessment methods are often used to identify targets for therapeutic intervention. And repeated assessments are very useful in monitoring the effects of treatment over time. We will see that beyond the basic interview, which is used in various guises almost universally, many of the assessment techniques stem from the paradigms presented in Chapter 2. We discuss here clinical interviews, psychological tests, many of which are psychodynamic in nature, and behavioral and cognitive assessment techniques. Although we present these methods individually, a complete psychological assessment of a person will often use several of them. The data from the various methods complement each other and provide a more complete picture of the individual (Meyer et al., 2001).

Clinical Interviews

Most of us have probably been interviewed at one time or another, although the conversation may have been so informal that we did not regard it as an interview. To the layperson the word *interview* connotes a formal, highly structured conversation, but we find it useful to construe the term as any interpersonal encounter, conversational in style, in which one person, the interviewer, uses language as the principal means of finding out about another, the interviewee. Thus a Gallup pollster who asks a college student for whom he or she will vote in an upcoming presidential election is interviewing with the restricted goal of learning which candidate the student prefers. A clinical psychologist who asks a patient about the circumstances of his or her most recent hospitalization is similarly conducting an interview.

Characteristics of Clinical Interviews   One way in which a **clinical interview** is perhaps different from a casual conversation and from a poll is the attention the interviewer pays to how the respondent answers questions—or does not answer them. For example, if a client is recounting marital conflicts, the clinician will generally be attentive to any emotion accompanying the comments. If the person does not seem upset about a difficult situation, the answers will probably be understood differently from how they would be interpreted if the person were crying or agitated while relating the story.

The paradigm within which an interviewer operates influences the type of information sought, how it is obtained, and how it is interpreted. A psychoanalytically trained clinician can be expected to inquire about the person's childhood history. He or she is also likely to remain skeptical of verbal reports because the analytic paradigm holds that the most significant aspects of a disturbed person's developmental history are repressed into the unconscious. How the data are interpreted is influenced by the paradigm. By the same token, the behaviorally oriented clinician is likely to focus on current environmental conditions that can be related to changes in the person's behavior—for example, the circumstances under which the person becomes anxious. Thus the clinical interview does not follow one prescribed course but varies with the paradigm adopted by the interviewer. Like scientists, clinical interviewers in some measure find only the information for which they are looking.

Great skill is necessary to carry out good clinical interviews, for they are usually conducted with people who are under considerable stress. Clinicians, regardless of their theoretical orientation, recognize the importance of establishing rapport with the client. The interviewer must obtain the trust of the person; it is naive to assume that a client will easily reveal information to another, even to an authority figure with the title "Doctor." Even a client who sincerely, perhaps desperately, wants to recount intensely personal problems to a professional may not be able to do so without assistance. Psychodynamic clinicians assume that people entering therapy usually are not even aware of what is truly bothering them. Behavioral clinicians, although they concentrate more on what can be observed, also appreciate the difficulties people have in sorting out the factors responsible for their distress. (Recall the Langer and Abelson study, p. 17.)

Most clinicians empathize with their clients in an effort to draw them out, to encourage them to elaborate on their concerns, and to examine different facets of a problem. Humanistic therapists employ specific empathy techniques (see p.39) to accomplish these goals. A simple summary statement of what the client has been saying can help sustain the momentum of talk about painful and possibly embarrassing events and feelings, and an accepting attitude toward personal disclosures dispels the fear that revealing "secrets of the heart" (London, 1964) to another human being will have disastrous consequences.

The interview can be a source of considerable information to the clinician. Its importance in abnormal psychology and psychiatry is unquestionable. Whether the information gleaned can always be depended on is not so clear, however. Clinicians often tend to overlook situational factors of the interview that may exert strong influences on what the patient says or does. Consider for a moment how a teenager is likely to respond to the question, "How often have you used illegal drugs?" when it is asked by a young, informally dressed psychologist and again when it is asked by a sixty-year-old psychologist in a business suit.

Interviews vary in the degree to which they are structured. In practice, most clinicians probably operate from only the vaguest outlines. Exactly how information is collected is left largely up to the particular interviewer and depends, too, on the responsiveness and responses of the interviewee. Through years of clinical experience and both teaching and learning from students and colleagues, each clinician develops ways of asking questions with which he or she is comfortable and that seem to draw out the information that will be of maximum benefit to the client. Thus, to the extent that an interview is unstructured, the interviewer must rely on intuition and general experience. As a consequence, reliability for clinical interviews is probably low; that is, two interviewers may well reach different conclusions about the same patient. And because the overwhelming majority of clinical interviews are conducted within confidential relationships, it has not been possible to establish either their reliability or their validity through systematic research.

We need to look at the broader picture here, however, to avoid a judgment that may be too harsh. Both reliability and validity may indeed be low for a single clinical interview that is conducted in an unstructured fashion. But clinicians usually do more than one interview with a given patient, and hence a self-corrective process is probably at work. The clinician may regard as valid what a patient said in the first interview, but then at the sixth may recognize it to have been incorrect or only partially correct.

Structured interviews are widely used to make reliable diagnoses.

Structured Interviews   At times mental health professionals need to collect standardized information, particularly for making diagnostic judgments based on the DSM. To meet that need, investigators have developed structured interviews, such as the Structured Clinical Interview (SCID) for Axis I of DSM-IV (Spitzer, Gibbon, & Williams, 1996), which assists researchers and clinicians in making diagnostic decisions. A **structured interview** is one in which the questions are set out in a prescribed fashion for the interviewer.

The SCID is a branching interview, that is, the client's response to one question determines the next question that is asked. It also contains detailed instructions to the interviewer concerning when and how to probe in detail and when to go on to questions about another diagnosis. Most symptoms are rated on a three-point scale of severity, with instructions in the interview schedule for directly translating the symptom ratings into diagnoses. The initial questions pertaining to obsessive-compulsive disorder (discussed in Chapter 6) are presented in Figure 4.1. The interviewer begins by asking about obsessions. If the responses elicit a rating of 1 (absent), the interviewer turns to questions about compulsions. If the patient's responses again elicit a rating of 1, the interviewer is instructed to go to the question for posttraumatic stress disorder. On the other hand, if positive responses (2 or 3) are elicited about obsessive-compulsive disorder, the interviewer continues with further questions about that problem. The use of structured interviews such as the SCID is a major factor in the improvement of diagnostic reliability that we described in Chapter 3.

Structured interviews have also been developed for diagnosing personality disorders and for more specific disorders, such as the anxiety disorders and for diagnosing disorders of childhood (DiNardo et al., 1993; Shaffer et al., 2000). With adequate training, interrater reliability for structured interviews is generally good (Blanchard & Brown, 1998).

Psychological Tests

Psychological tests further structure the process of assessment. The same test is administered to many people at different times, and the responses collected are analyzed to indicate how certain kinds of people tend to respond. Statistical norms for the test can thereby be established as soon as sufficient data have been collected. This process is called **standardization**. The responses of a particular person can then be compared with the statistical norms. We will examine the three basic types of psychological tests: self-report personality inventories, projective personality tests, and tests of intelligence.

Personality Inventories   In a **personality inventory**, the person is asked to complete a self-report questionnaire indicating whether statements assessing habitual tendencies apply to him or her. Perhaps the best known of these tests is the **Minnesota Multiphasic Personality Inventory (MMPI)**, developed in the early 1940s by Hathaway and McKinley

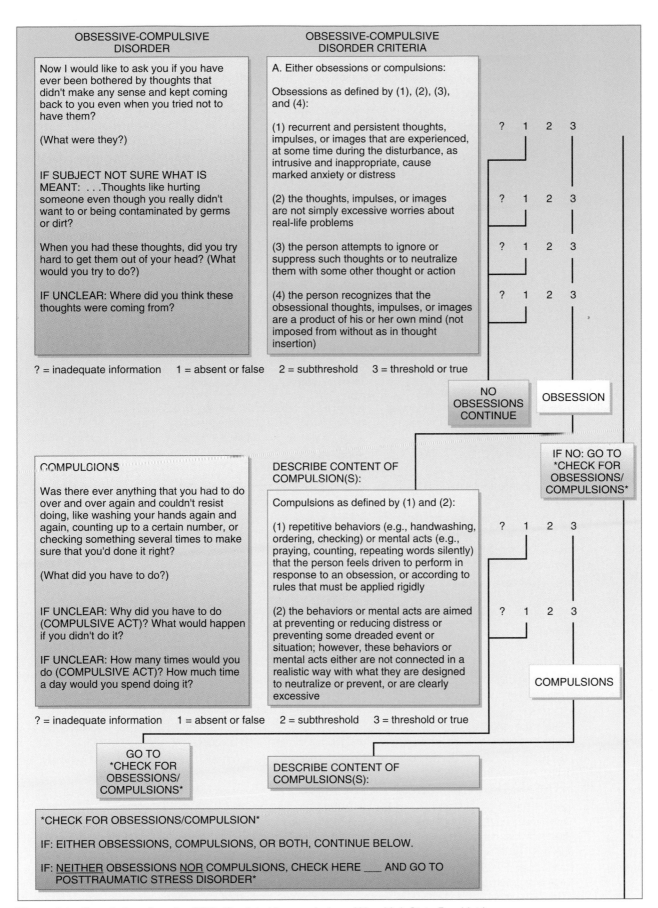

Figure 4.1 Sample item from the SCID. Reprinted by permission of New York State Psychiatric Institute Biometrics Research Division. Copyright © 1996 by the Board of Trustees of the Leland Stanford Junior University. Reprinted by permission of Stanford University Press.

(1943) and revised in 1989 (Butcher et al., 1989). Intended to serve as an inexpensive means of detecting psychopathology, the MMPI is called multiphasic because it was designed to detect a number of psychological problems. Over the years the MMPI has been widely used to screen large groups of people for whom clinical interviews are not feasible.

In developing the test, the investigators relied on factual information. First, many clinicians provided statements that they considered indicative of various mental problems. Second, these items were rated as self-descriptive or not by patients already diagnosed as having particular disorders and by a large group of individuals considered normal. Items that discriminated among the patients were retained; that is, items were selected if patients in one clinical group responded to them more often in a certain way than did those in other groups.

With additional refinements, sets of these items were established as scales for determining whether a respondent should be diagnosed in a particular way. If an individual answered a large number of the items in a scale in the same way as had a certain diagnostic group, his or her behavior was expected to resemble that of the particular diagnostic group. The ten scales are described and illustrated in Table 4.1.

Table 4.1 Typical Clinical Interpretations of Items Similar to Those on the MMPI-2

Scale	Sample Item	Interpretation
? (cannot say)	This is merely the number of items left unanswered or marked both true and false.	A high score indicates evasiveness, reading difficulties, or other problems that could invalidate the results of the test. A very high score could also suggest severe depression or obsessional tendencies.
L (Lie)	I approve of every person I meet. (True)	Person is trying to look good, to present self as someone with an ideal personality.
F (Infrequency)	Everything tastes sweet. (True)	Person is trying to look abnormal, perhaps to ensure getting special attention from the clinician.
K (Correction)	Things couldn't be going any better for me. (True)	Person is guarded, defensive in taking the test, wishes to avoid appearing incompetent or poorly adjusted.
1. Hs (Hypochondriasis)	I am seldom aware of tingling feelings in my body. (False)	Person is overly sensitive to and concerned about bodily sensations as signs of possible physical illness.
2. D (Depression)	Life usually feels worthwhile to me. (False)	Person is discouraged, pessimistic, sad, self-deprecating, feeling inadequate.
3. Hy (Hysteria)	My muscles often twitch for no apparent reason. (True)	Person has somatic complaints unlikely to be due to physical problems; also tends to be demanding and histrionic.
4. Pd (Psychopathy)	I don't care about what people think of me. (True)	Person expresses little concern for social mores, is irresponsible, has only superficial relationships.
5. Mf (Masculinity–Femininity)	I like taking care of plants and flowers. (True, female)	Person shows non-traditional gender characteristics, e.g., men with high scores tend to be artistic and sensitive; women with high scores tend to be rebellious and assertive.
6. Pa (Paranoia)	If they were not afraid of being caught, most people would lie and cheat. (True)	Person tends to misinterpret the motives of others, is suspicious and jealous, vengeful and brooding.
7. Pt (Psychasthenia)	I am not as competent as most other people I know. (True)	Person is overanxious, full of self-doubts, moralistic, and generally obsessive-compulsive.
8. Sc (Schizophrenia)	I sometimes smell things others don't sense. (True)	Person has bizarre sensory experiences and beliefs, is socially reclusive.
9. Ma (Hypomania)	Sometimes I have a strong impulse to do something that others will find appalling. (True)	Person has overly ambitious aspirations and can be hyperactive, impatient, and irritable.
10. Si (Social Introversion)	Rather than spend time alone, I prefer to be around other people. (False)	Person is very modest and shy, preferring solitary activities.

Note: The first four scales assess the validity of the test; the numbered scales are the clinical or content scales.

Source: Hathaway and McKinley (1943); revised by Butcher et al. (1989).

The revised MMPI-2 (Butcher et al., 1989) has several noteworthy changes designed to improve its validity and acceptability. The original sample of sixty years ago lacked representation of racial minorities, including African Americans and Native Americans; its standardization sample was restricted to white men and women—essentially to Minnesotans. The new version was standardized using a sample that was much larger and more representative of 1980 U.S. census figures. Several items containing allusions to sexual adjustment, bowel and bladder functions, and excessive religiosity were removed because they were judged in some testing contexts to be needlessly intrusive and objectionable. Sexist wording was eliminated, along with outmoded idioms. Several new scales deal with substance abuse, Type A behavior (see p. 215), and marital problems.

Aside from these differences, MMPI-2 is otherwise quite similar to the original, having the same format, yielding the same scale scores and profiles (Ben-Porath & Butcher, 1989; Graham, 1988), and in general providing continuity with the vast literature already existing on the original MMPI (Graham, 1990). An extensive research literature shows that the MMPI is reliable and has adequate criterion validity when it is related to diagnoses and to ratings made by spouses or clinicians (Ganellan, 1996; Graham, 1988; Vacha-Hasse et al., 2001).

Like many other personality inventories, the MMPI can now be administered by computer, and there are several commercial MMPI services that score the test and provide narratives about the respondent. Of course, the validity and usefulness of the printouts are only as good as the program, which in turn is only as good as the competency and experience of the psychologist who wrote it. Figure 4.2 shows a hypothetical profile. Such pro-

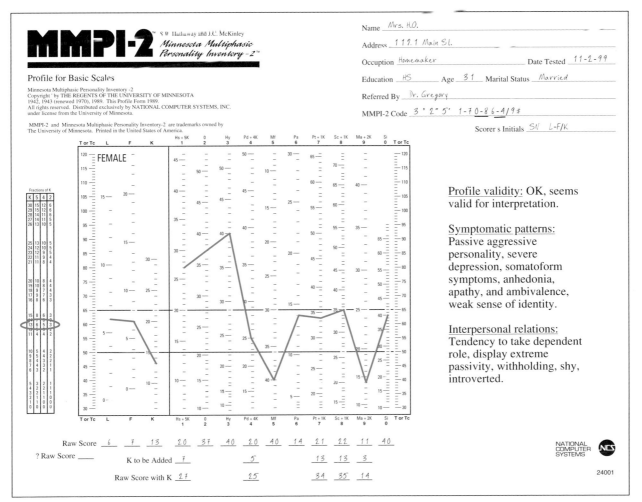

Figure 4.2 Hypothetical MMPI-2 profile.

files can be used in conjunction with a therapist's evaluation to help diagnose a client, assess personality functioning and coping style, and identify likely obstacles to treatment.

We may well wonder whether answers that would designate a person as normal might not be easy to fake. For example, a superficial knowledge of contemporary abnormal psychology would alert even a seriously disturbed person that in order to be regarded as normal, he or she must not admit to worrying a great deal about hearing voices emanating from toaster ovens. There is evidence that these tests can be "psyched out." In most testing circumstances, however, people do not want to falsify their responses, for they want to be helped.

Moreover, as shown in Table 4.1, the test designers have included as part of the MMPI several so-called validity scales designed to detect deliberately faked responses. In one of these, the lie scale, a series of statements sets a trap for the person who is trying to look too good. An item on the lie scale might be, "I read the newspaper editorials every night." The assumption is that few people would be able to endorse such a statement honestly. Individuals who endorse a large number of the statements in the lie scale might well be attempting to present themselves in a particularly good light. High scores on the F scale also discriminate between people trying to fake psychopathology and real patients (Bagby et al., 2002). The scores on other scales of people with high scores on the lie or F scale are generally viewed with more than the usual skepticism. Being aware of these validity scales, however, does allow people to effectively fake a normal profile (Baer & Sekirnjak, 1997; Walters & Clopton, 2000). Focus on Discovery 4.1 discusses other issues surrounding the validity of self-report questionnaires.

Projective Personality Tests   A **projective test** is a psychological assessment device in which a set of standard stimuli—inkblots or drawings—ambiguous enough to allow variation in responses is presented to the individual. The assumption is that because the stimulus materials are unstructured, the patient's responses will be determined primarily by unconscious processes and will reveal his or her true attitudes, motivations, and modes of behavior. This notion is referred to as the **projective hypothesis**. If a patient reports seeing eyes in an ambiguous inkblot, for example, the projective hypothesis might be that the patient tends toward paranoia.

The **Rorschach Inkblot Test** is perhaps the best-known projective technique. In the Rorschach test, a person is shown ten inkblots, one at a time, and asked to tell what the

In the Rorschach test the client is shown a series of inkblots and is asked what the blots look like.

Underreporting of Stigmatized Behaviors

A survey of self-reported drug use, sexual behavior, and violence highlights the importance of the setting in establishing the validity of what people will tell about their actions and attitudes (Turner et al., 1998). Findings from paper-and-pencil questionnaires were compared with results from a novel self-report method—boys and young men (ages fifteen to nineteen) listened by themselves through headphones to questions probing risky, often stigmatized behavioral practices and then indicated whether they had engaged in those behaviors by pressing keys on a computer keyboard labeled Yes and No.

Comparisons with a matched control group responding to the same items on a paper-and-pencil questionnaire consistently showed that the computer respondents admitted much more often to having engaged in a range of high-risk behaviors. For example, they were almost fourteen times more likely to report having sexual intercourse with an intravenous drug user (2.8% versus 0.2%), more than twice as

likely to have been paid for sex (3.8% versus 1.6%), and almost twice as likely to have used cocaine (6.0% versus 3.3%). (One can safely assume that the differences would have been even greater if the boys had been interviewed by an adult researcher facing them across a table, another method that has been used to collect such survey data.) No differences showed up on questions directed at nonstigmatized or legal behaviors such as having sexual intercourse with a female in the preceding year (47.8% for computer users versus 49.6% for paper-and-pencil questionnaires) or drinking alcohol in the past year (69.2% versus 65.9%).

If these findings show nothing else, they suggest strongly that the frequencies of problematic behavior as determined by questionnaire or interview studies may be gross underestimates and that social problems such as needle sharing and unsafe sex may be considerably more serious than most people believe.

blots look like. Half the inkblots are in black, white, and shades of gray, two also have red splotches, and three are in pastel colors.

The **Thematic Apperception Test (TAT)** is another well-known projective test. In this test a person is shown a series of black-and-white pictures one by one and asked to tell a story related to each. For example, a patient seeing a picture of a prepubescent girl looking at fashionably attired mannequins in a store window may tell a story that contains angry references to the girl's parents. The clinician may, through the projective hypothesis, infer that the patient harbors resentment toward his or her parents.

As you might guess, projective techniques are derived from the psychoanalytic paradigm. The use of projective tests assumes that the respondent would be either unable or unwilling to express his or her true feelings if asked directly. Psychoanalytically oriented clinicians often favor such tests, a tendency that is consistent with the psychoanalytic assumption that people defend against unpleasant thoughts and feelings by repressing them into the unconscious. Thus, to bypass the defense mechanism of repression and get to the basic causes of distress, the real purposes of a test are best left unclear. Indeed, this *has* to be the case, for psychoanalytic theory asserts that the factors of greatest importance are unconscious.

The use of the projective hypothesis is not limited to formal tests. A psychoanalytically oriented colleague of ours uses it to form hypotheses about the client during the very first meeting. He sees clients in an office that contains a wide variety and large number of places to sit. When he brings a person into this office for the first time, he makes it a point not to tell the client where to sit. The therapist's belief is that he can learn something useful about the new client from the choice of seating. Being less psychoanalytic in approach, we rejected this tactic outright—until one day one of us had a new client who entered the office and before being shown where to sit, strode resolutely to the author's desk chair! As it turned out, this person was highly resistant to being in therapy and made continual efforts to dominate and control the early sessions.

Our discussion of projective tests has focused on how they were conceptualized and used originally—as a stimulus to fantasy that was assumed to bypass ego defenses. The content of the person's responses was viewed as *symbolic* of internal dynamics; for example, a man might be judged to have homosexual interests on the basis of his seeing buttocks in the Rorschach inkblots (Chapman & Chapman, 1969).

Other uses of the Rorschach test, however, concentrate more on the *form* of the person's responses (Exner, 1978). The test is considered more as a perceptual-cognitive task,

During a ride in the country with his two children, Hermann Rorschach (1884–1922), Swiss psychiatrist, noticed that what they saw in the clouds reflected their personalities. From this observation came the famous inkblot test.

and the person's responses are viewed as a sample of how he or she perceptually and cognitively organizes real-life situations (Exner, 1986). For example, Erdberg and Exner (1984) concluded from the research literature that respondents who express a great deal of human movement in their Rorschach responses (e.g., "The man is running to catch a plane.") tend to use inner resources when coping with their needs, whereas those whose Rorschach responses involve color ("The red spot is a kidney.") are more likely to seek interaction with the environment. Rorschach suggested this approach in his original manual, *Psychodiagnostics: A Diagnostic Test Based on Perception* (1921), but he died only eight months after publishing his ten inkblots and his immediate followers devised other methods of interpreting the test.

The Exner scoring system for the Rorschach test yields scores or indexes that can then be validated by relating them to what they are supposed to predict, for example, the schizophrenia index to schizophrenia or the depression index to depression. The system also has norms, although the sample on which they are based was rather small and did not represent minorities well. Though many, perhaps most, clinical practitioners still rely on the projective hypothesis in analyzing Rorschach responses, Exner's work has attracted a good deal of attention from academic researchers. Regarding its reliability and validity, this work has enthusiastic supporters as well as equally harsh critics (e.g., Garb, Florio, & Grove, 1998; Hunsley & Bailey, 1999; Wood et al., 2000). Perhaps trying to make a blanket statement about the validity of the Exner system for scoring the Rorschach is not the right approach. It may have more validity in some cases than in others. For example, it appears to have considerable validity in identifying people with schizophrenia and people who are at risk for developing schizophrenia (Viglione, 1999). The utility of the Rorschach in this case can most likely be attributed to the fact that a person's responses on the test are highly related to the communication disturbances that are an important symptom of schizophrenia. However, even in this case it is unclear whether the Rorschach provides information that could not be obtained more simply—for example, through an interview.

Intelligence Tests   Alfred Binet, a French psychologist, originally constructed mental tests to help the Parisian school board predict which children were in need of special schooling. Intelligence testing has since developed into one of the largest psychological industries. An **intelligence test**, often referred as an IQ test, is a standardized means of assessing a person's current mental ability. Individually administered tests, such as the Wechsler Adult Intelligence Scale (WAIS), the Wechsler Intelligence Scale for Children (WISC), and the Stanford–Binet are all based on the assumption that a detailed sample of an individual's current intellectual functioning can predict how well he or she will perform in school.

Intelligence tests are also used in other ways:

- in conjunction with achievement tests, to diagnose learning disabilities and to identify areas of strengths and weaknesses for academic planning;
- to help determine whether a person is mentally retarded;
- to identify intellectually gifted children so that appropriate instruction can be provided them in school;
- as part of neuropsychological evaluations, for example, periodically testing a person believed to be suffering from a degenerative dementia so that deterioration of mental ability can be followed over time.

A Spanish-language version of the WAIS has been available for over thirty years (Wechsler, 1968) and can be useful in assessing the intellectual functioning of people from Hispanic cultures (Gomez, Piedmont, & Fleming, 1992; Lopez & Romero, 1988; Lopez & Taussig, 1991).

IQ tests tap several functions asserted to constitute intelligence, including language skills, abstract thinking, nonverbal reasoning, visual-spatial skills, attention and concentration, and speed of processing. Scores on most IQ tests are standardized so that 100 is the mean and 15 or 16 is the standard deviation (a measure of how scores are dispersed

The French psychologist Alfred Binet developed the first IQ test to predict how well children would do in school.

above and below the average). Approximately 65 percent of the population receives scores between 85 and 115. Those with a score below 70 are two standard deviations below the mean of the population and are considered to have "significant subaverage general intellectual functioning." Those with scores above 130 (two standard deviations above the mean) are considered "intellectually gifted." Approximately 2.5 percent of the population falls at each of these extremes. In Chapter 15 we discuss people whose IQ falls at the low end of the distribution.

IQ tests are highly reliable (e.g., Carnivez & Walkins, 1998) and have good criterion validity. For example, they distinguish between individuals who are intellectually gifted and individuals with mental retardation and between people with different occupations or levels of educational attainment (Reynolds et al., 1997). They also predict educational attainment and occupational success (Hanson, Hunsley, & Parker, 1988). Though the correlations between IQ scores and school performance are statistically significant (p. 119), IQ tests explain only a small part of the differences in people's school performance; much more is unexplained by IQ test scores than is explained.

Regarding construct validity, it is important to keep in mind that IQ tests measure only what psychologists consider intelligence. The tasks and items on IQ tests were, after all, invented by psychologists—they did not come down to us inscribed on stone tablets. In addition, factors other than what we think of as pure intelligence play an important role in how people will do in school, such as family and personal circumstances, motivation to do well, levels of performance anxiety, and difficulty of the curriculum. Another factor relevant to IQ test performance is called stereotype threat. It suggests that the social stigma of poor intellectual performance borne by some groups (e.g., African Americans do poorly on IQ tests, women perform more poorly than men on mathematics tests) actually interferes with their performance on these tests. In one study demonstrating this phenomenon, groups of men and women were given a difficult mathematics test. In one condition the participants were told that men scored higher than women on the test they were going to take, while in the other condition they were told there were no gender differences in performance on the test. Only when the test was described as yielding gender differences did the women perform more poorly than men (Spencer, Steele, & Quinn, 1999).

Interest has also focused on "emotional intelligence," reflected in such abilities as delaying gratification and being sensitive to the needs of others (Goleman, 1995). This aspect of human functioning may be as important to future success as the strictly intellectual achievements measured by traditional IQ tests. Some important cross-cultural issues in IQ testing are considered later in this chapter (p. 105).

Behavioral and Cognitive Assessment

Traditional assessment concentrates on measuring underlying personality structures and traits, such as obsessiveness, paranoia, coldness, aggressiveness, intelligence, and so on. Behavioral and cognitively oriented clinicians, on the other hand, are guided by a system that leads them to assess four sets of variables, sometimes referred to by the acronym SORC (Kanfer & Phillips, 1970).

- S stands for stimuli, the environmental situations that precede the problem. For instance, the clinician will try to ascertain which situations tend to elicit anxiety.

- O stands for organismic, referring to both physiological and psychological factors assumed to be operating "under the skin." Perhaps the client's fatigue is caused in part by excessive use of alcohol or by a cognitive tendency toward self-deprecation manifested in such statements as "I never do anything right, so what's the point in trying?" This is the area that traditional assessment focuses on.

- R refers to overt responses. These probably receive the most attention from behavioral clinicians, who must determine what behavior is problematic, as well as the behavior's frequency, intensity, and form. For example, a client might say that he or she is forgetful and procrastinates. Does the person mean that he or she does not return phone calls, arrives late for appointments, or both?

- Finally, C refers to consequent variables, events that appear to be reinforcing or punishing the behavior in question. When the client avoids a feared situation, does his or her spouse offer sympathy and excuses, thereby unwittingly keeping the person from facing up to his or her fears?

A behaviorally oriented clinician attempts to specify SORC factors for a particular client. As might be expected, O variables are underplayed by Skinnerians, who focus more on observable stimuli and responses, and C variables receive less attention from cognitively oriented behavior therapists than do O variables because these therapists' paradigm does not emphasize reinforcement.

The information necessary for a behavioral or cognitive assessment is gathered by several methods, including direct observation of behavior in real life as well as in contrived settings, interviews and self-report measures, and various other methods of cognitive assessment (Bellack & Hersen, 1998). We turn to these now.

Direct Observation of Behavior   It is not surprising that behavior therapists have paid considerable attention to careful observation of overt behavior in a variety of settings, but it should not be assumed that they simply go out and observe. Like other scientists, they try to fit events into a framework consistent with their points of view. The following excerpt from a case report by Gerald Patterson and his colleagues (1969), describing an interaction between a boy named Kevin and his mother, father, and sister Freida, serves as the first part of an example.

> Kevin goes up to father's chair and stands alongside it. Father puts his arms around Kevin's shoulders. Kevin says to mother as Freida looks at Kevin, "Can I go out and play after supper?" Mother does not reply. Kevin raises his voice and repeats the question. Mother says, "You don't have to yell; I can hear you." Father says, "How many times have I told you not to yell at your mother?" Kevin scratches a bruise on his arm while mother tells Freida to get started on the dishes, which Freida does. Kevin continues to rub and scratch his arm while mother and daughter are working at the kitchen sink. (p. 21)

This informal description could probably be provided by any observer. But in formal **behavioral observation**, the observer divides the uninterrupted sequence of behavior into various parts and applies terms that make sense within a learning framework.

> Kevin begins the exchange by asking a routine question in a normal tone of voice. This ordinary behavior, however, is not reinforced by the mother's attention; for she does not reply. Because she does not reply, the normal behavior of Kevin ceases and he yells his question. The mother expresses disapproval—punishing her son—by telling him that he does not have to yell. And this punishment is supported by the father's reminding Kevin that he should not yell at his mother.

This behavioral rendition emphasizes the consequences of ignoring a child's question. At some point, the behavior therapist will undoubtedly advise the parents to attend to Kevin's requests when expressed in an ordinary tone of voice, lest he begin yelling. This example indicates an important aspect of behavioral assessment, its link to intervention (O'Brien & Hayes, 1995). The behavioral clinician's way of conceptualizing a situation typically implies a way to try to change it.

It is difficult to observe most behavior as it actually takes place, and little control can be exercised over where and when it may occur. For this reason, many therapists contrive artificial situations in their consulting rooms or in a laboratory so that they can observe how a client or a family acts under certain conditions. For example, Barkley (1981) had a mother and her

Behavioral assessment often involves direct observation of behavior, as in this case, where the observer is behind a one-way mirror.

hyperactive child spend time together in a laboratory living room, complete with sofas and television set. The mother was given a list of tasks for the child to complete, such as picking up toys or doing arithmetic problems. Observers behind a one-way mirror watched the proceedings and reliably coded the child's reactions to the mother's efforts to control as well as the mother's reactions to the child's compliant or noncompliant responses. These behavioral assessment procedures yielded data that could be used to measure the effects of treatment.

Most of the research just described was conducted within an operant framework, but observational techniques can also be applied within a framework that makes use of mediators. Recall from Chapter 2 (p. 46) that mediational theory holds that an environmental stimulus does not initiate an overt response directly but instead works through an intervening process, or mediator, such as anxiety. An example comes from the work of Gordon Paul (1966) in assessing the anxiety of public speakers. He decided to count the frequency of behaviors indicative of this emotional state. One of his principal measures, the Timed Behavioral Checklist for Performance Anxiety, is shown in Figure 4.3. Participants were asked to deliver a speech before a group. Some members of the group had been trained to reliably rate the participant's behavior every thirty seconds and to record the presence or absence of twenty specific behaviors. By summing the scores, Paul arrived at a behavioral index of anxiety. This study provides one example of how observations of overt behavior have been used to infer the presence of an internal state.

Behavior Observed	Behavior Observed								
	1	2	3	4	5	6	7	8	Σ
1. Paces									
2. Sways									
3. Shuffles feet									
4. Knees tremble									
5. Extraneous arm and hand movement (swings, scratches, toys, etc.)									
6. Arms rigid									
7. Hands restrained (in pockets, behind back, clasped)									
8. Hand tremors									
9. No eye contact									
10. Face muscles tense (drawn, tics, grimaces)									
11. Face "deadpan"									
12. Face pale									
13. Face flushed (blushes)									
14. Moistens lips									
15. Swallows									
16. Clears throat									
17. Breathes heavily									
18. Perspires (face, hands, armpits)									
19. Voice quivers									
20. Speech blocks or stammers									

Figure 4.3   Paul's (1966) Timed Behavioral Checklist for Performance Anxiety.

Self-monitoring generally leads to increases in desirable behaviors and decreases in undesirable ones. Here the person is monitoring smoking and entering information into a palm-top computer.

Self-Observation   In Paul's study, people other than the public speaker made the observations. For several years, behavior therapists and researchers have also asked individuals to observe their own behavior and to keep track of various categories of response. This approach is called **self-monitoring**. Self-monitoring has been used to collect a wide variety of data of interest to both clinicians and researchers, including moods, stressful experiences, coping behaviors, and thoughts (Hurlburt, 1979; Stone et al., 1998).

An example of self-observation is a procedure called **ecological momentary assessment**, or **EMA** (Stone & Shiffman, 1994). EMA involves the collection of data in real time as opposed to the more usual methods of having people reflect back over some time period and report on recently experienced thoughts, moods, or stressors. The methods for implementing EMA range from having people complete diaries at specified times during the day (perhaps signaled by a wristwatch that beeps at those times) to supplying them with palm-top computers that not only signal when reports are to be made but also allow them to enter their responses directly into the computer (Stone & Shiffman, 1994).

The main reason for using EMA is that the retrospective recall of moods, thoughts, or experiences may be inaccurate. Consider, for example, how difficult it would be for you to recall accurately the exact thoughts you had at the time you encountered a stressor. Memory researchers have shown not only that simple forgetting leads to inaccurate retrospective recall, but also that recalled information can be biased. For example, a report of a person's mood for a whole day is overly influenced by moods the person has experienced most recently (Strongman & Russell, 1986).

Given these problems in retrospective recall, some theories in the field of abnormal psychology can best be tested using EMA. For example, current theories of both anxiety disorders and depression propose that emotional reactions to a stressor are determined by thoughts that the stressor elicits. It is unlikely, however, that these thoughts can be recalled accurately in retrospect. Consider also a prominent theory in the health psychology field that proposes that the response to a stressor depends on appraising or evaluating it, attempting to cope with it, and then reappraising it (Lazarus & Folkman, 1984). It isn't at all likely that this process could be captured by retrospective recall.

EMA may also be useful in clinical settings, revealing information that traditional assessment procedures might miss. For example, Hurlburt (1997) describes a case of a man with severe attacks of anxiety. In clinical interviews, the patient reported that his life was going very well, that he loved his wife and children, and that his work was both financially and personally rewarding. No cause of the anxiety attacks could be discerned. The man was asked to record his thoughts as he went about his daily routine. Surprisingly, about a third of his thoughts were concerned with annoyance with his children (e.g., "He left the record player on again").

> Once the high frequency of annoyance thoughts was pointed out to him, he…accepted that he was in fact often annoyed with his children. However, he believed that anger at his children was sinful and felt unfit as a father for having such thoughts and feelings…. [He] entered into brief therapy that focused on the normality of being annoyed by one's children and on the important distinction between being annoyed and acting out aggressively. Almost immediately, his anxiety attacks disappeared. (p. 944)

Although some research indicates that self-monitoring or EMA can provide accurate measurement of such behavior, considerable research indicates that behavior may be altered by the very fact that it is being self-monitored—that is, the self-consciousness required for self-monitoring affects the behavior (Haynes & Horn, 1982). The phenomenon wherein behavior changes because it is being observed is called **reactivity**. In general, desirable behavior, such as engaging in social conversation, often increases in frequency when self-monitored (Nelson, Lipinski, & Black, 1976), whereas behavior the person wishes to reduce, such as cigarette smoking, diminishes (McFall & Hammen, 1971). Such findings suggest that therapeutic interventions can take advantage of the reactivity that is a natural by-product of self-monitoring. Smoking, anxiety, depression, and health problems have all undergone beneficial changes in self-monitoring studies (Febbraro & Clum, 1998).

Interviews and Self-Report Inventories   For all their interest in direct observation of behavior, behavioral clinicians still rely very heavily on the interview to assess the needs of their clients (Sarwer & Sayers, 1998). Within a trusting relationship, the behavior therapist's job is to determine, by skillful questioning and careful observation of the client's emotional reactions during the interview, the SORC factors that help him or her conceptualize the client's problem.

Behavior therapists also make use of self-report inventories. As we will see later, some of these questionnaires are similar to the personality tests we have already described. But others have a greater situational focus than traditional questionnaires. For example, McFall and Lillesand (1971) employed a Conflict Resolution Inventory containing thirty-five items that focused on the ability of the respondent to refuse unreasonable requests. Each item described a specific situation in which a person was asked for something unreasonable. For example, "You are in the thick of studying for exams when a person you know slightly comes into your room and says, 'I'm tired of studying. Mind if I come in and take a break for a while?'" Students were asked to indicate the likelihood that they would refuse such a request and how comfortable they would be in doing so. Concurrent validity for this self-report inventory was established by showing that it correlated with a variety of direct observational data on social skills (Frisch & Higgins, 1986). This and similar inventories, described in the next section, can be used by clinicians and have helped behavioral researchers measure the outcome of clinical interventions as well.

Specialized Approaches to Cognitive Assessment   As with all kinds of assessment, a key feature of contemporary approaches in cognitive assessment is that the development of methods is determined primarily by theory and data as well as by the purposes of the assessment. For example, much research on depression is concerned with cognition—the things people consciously and sometimes unconsciously tell themselves as well as the underlying assumptions or attitudes that can be inferred from their behavior and verbal reports. One cognitive theory (Beck, 1967), which we will examine in greater detail in Chapter 10, holds that depression is caused primarily by negative ideas people have about themselves, their world, and their future. For example, people may believe that they are not worth much and that things are never going to get better.

The most widely employed cognitive assessment methods are self-report questionnaires that tap a wide range of cognitions, such as fear of negative evaluation, a tendency to think irrationally, and a tendency to make negative inferences about life experiences. "When someone criticizes you in class, what thoughts go through your mind?" is a question a client might be asked in an interview or on a paper-and-pencil inventory. When patients are asked about their thoughts in interviews and self-report inventories, they have to reflect backward in time and provide a retrospective and rather general report of their thoughts in certain situations.

Cognitive assessment focuses on the person's perception of a situation, realizing that the same event can be perceived differently. For example, moving could be regarded as very stressful or seen in a positive light.

One self-report questionnaire used by cognitive investigators and therapists is the Dysfunctional Attitude Scale (DAS). The DAS contains items such as "People will probably think less of me if I make a mistake" (Weissman & Beck, 1978). Supporting construct validity, researchers have shown that they can differentiate between depressed and nondepressed people on the basis of their scores on this scale and that scores decrease (that is, improve) after interventions that relieve depression. Furthermore, the DAS relates to other aspects of cognition in ways consistent with Beck's theory. For example, it correlates with another self-report instrument called the Cognitive Bias Questionnaire (Krantz & Hammen, 1979), which measures the ways in which depressed patients distort information. An accumulating body of data is helping to establish both the validity and the reliability of these questionnaires (Glass & Arnkoff, 1997).

As mentioned, people's responses to inventories and to questions asked by interviewers about their thoughts in past situations may well be different from what they would report were they able to do so in the immediate circumstance. Researchers have been working on ways to enable people to tap into their immediate and ongoing thought processes when confronted with particular circumstances (Parks & Hollon, 1988). Can we show, for example, that a socially anxious person does in fact, as Albert Ellis would predict, view criticism from others as catastrophic, whereas someone who is not socially insecure does not?

The Articulated Thoughts in Simulated Situations (ATSS) method of Davison and his associates (Davison, Robins, & Johnson, 1983) is one way to assess immediate thoughts in specific situations. In this procedure, a person pretends that he or she is a participant in a situation, such as listening to a teaching assistant criticize a term paper. Presented on audiotape, the scene pauses every ten or fifteen seconds. During the ensuing thirty seconds of silence, the participant talks aloud about whatever is going through his or her mind in reaction to the words just heard. One taped scene in which the participant overhears two pretend acquaintances criticizing him or her includes the following segments.

> **First acquaintance:** He certainly did make a fool of himself over what he said about religion. I just find that kind of opinion very closed-minded and unaware. You have to be blind to the facts of the universe to believe that. [Thirty-second pause for subject's response.]
> **Second acquaintance:** What really bugs me is the way he expresses himself. He never seems to stop and think, but just blurts out the first thing that comes into his head. [Thirty-second pause.]

Participants readily become involved in the pretend situations, regarding them as credible and realistic. Furthermore, the responses of participants can be reliably coded (Davison et al., 1983). One result that has emerged from studies conducted thus far is that socially anxious therapy patients articulate thoughts of greater irrationality (e.g., "Oh God, I wish I were dead. I'm so embarrassed.") than do nonanxious controls (Bates, Campbell, & Burgess, 1990; Davison & Zighelboim, 1987). In a study that directly compared ATSS data with overt behavior (Davison, Haaga, et al., 1991), thoughts of positive self-efficacy were found to be inversely related to behaviorally indexed speech anxiety; that is, the more anxiously subjects behaved on a timed behavioral checklist measure of public-speaking anxiety, the less capable they felt they were while articulating thoughts in a stressful, simulated speech-giving situation. These and related findings (cf. Davison, Navarre, & Vogel, 1995; Davison, Vogel, & Coffman, 1997) indicate that this method ferrets out people's thinking about both inherently bothersome and "objectively" innocuous situations.

Other cognitive assessment methods have also proved useful. In thought listing, for example, the person writes down his or her thoughts prior to or following an event of interest, such as entering a room to talk to a stranger, as a way to determine the cognitive components of social anxiety (Cacioppo, von Hippel, & Ernst, 1997). Open-ended techniques, such as the ATSS and thought listing, may be preferable when investigators know relatively little and want to get general ideas about the cognitive terrain. More

Table 4.2 Major Psychological Assessment Methods

Interviews	Clinical interviews	Conversational technique in which the clinician attempts to learn about the patient's problems. Content of the interview varies depending on the paradigm of the interviewer.
	Structured interviews	Questions to be asked are spelled out in detail in a booklet; most often used for gathering information to make a diagnosis.
Psychological tests	Personality tests	Self-report questionnaires, used to assess either a broad range of characteristics, as in the MMPI, or a single characteristic, such as dysfunctional attitudes. Behaviorally oriented questionnaires tend to have a situational focus.
	Projective personality tests	Ambiguous stimuli, such as inkblots (Rorschach test), are presented and responses are thought to be determined by unconscious processes.
	Intelligence tests	Assessments of current mental functioning. Used to predict school performance and diagnose mental retardation.
Direct observation		Used by behavioral clinicians to identify SORC factors. Also used to assess cognition, as in the Articulated Thoughts in Simulated Situations technique.
Self-observation		Individuals monitor and keep records of their own behavior; as in ecological momentary assessment.

focused techniques, such as questionnaires, may be better—and are certainly more easily scored—when investigators have more prior knowledge about the cognitions of interest. So far the various cognitive assessment techniques correlate poorly with one another (Clark, 1988, 1997), an important challenge to researchers and clinicians alike.

The psychological assessments we have described are summarized in Table 4.2.

Biological Assessment

For many years researchers and clinicians have attempted to observe directly or make inferences about the functioning of the brain and other parts of the nervous system in their efforts to understand both normal and abnormal psychological functioning (see Focus on Discovery 4.2). Recall from Chapters 2 and 3 that throughout history people interested in psychopathology have assumed, quite reasonably, that some malfunctions of the psyche are likely to be due to or at least reflected in malfunctions of the soma. We turn now to contemporary work in biological assessment.

Brain Imaging: "Seeing" the Brain

Because many behavioral problems can be brought on by brain abnormalities, neurological tests, such as checking the reflexes, examining the retina for any indication of blood-vessel damage, and evaluating motor coordination and perception, have been used for many years to diagnose brain dysfunction. More recently, devices have become available that allow clinicians and researchers a much more direct look at both the structure and functioning of the brain.

Computerized axial tomography, the **CT** or **CAT** scan, helps to assess structural brain abnormalities (and is able to image other parts of the body for medical purposes). A moving beam of X rays passes into a horizontal cross section of the patient's brain, scanning it through 360 degrees; the moving X-ray detector on the other side measures the amount of radioactivity that penetrates, thus detecting subtle differences in tissue density. A computer uses the information to construct a two-dimensional, detailed image of the cross section, giving it optimal contrasts. Then the patient's head is moved, and the

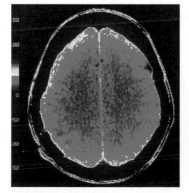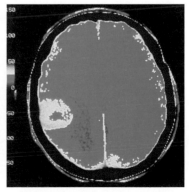

These two CT scans show a horizontal slice through the brain. The one on the left is normal; the one on the right has a tumor on the left side.

Structure and Function of the Human Brain

The brain is located within the protective coating of the skull and is enveloped with three layers of nonneural tissue, membranes referred to as **meninges**. Viewed from the top, the brain is divided by a midline fissure into two mirror-image **cerebral hemispheres**; together they constitute most of the cerebrum. The major connection between the two hemispheres is a band of nerve fibers called the **corpus callosum**. Figure 4.a shows the surface of one of the cerebral hemispheres. The upper, side, and some of the lower surfaces of the hemispheres form the **cerebral cortex**. The cortex consists of six layers of tightly packed neuron cell bodies with many short, unsheathed interconnecting processes. These neurons, estimated to number 10 to 15 billion, make up a thin outer covering, the so-called gray matter of the brain. The cortex is vastly convoluted; the ridges are called **gyri**, and the depressions between them **sulci**, or fissures. Deep fissures divide the cerebral hemispheres into several distinct areas called lobes. The **frontal lobe** lies in front of the central sulcus; the **parietal lobe** is behind it and above the lateral sulcus; the **temporal lobe** is located below the lateral sulcus; and the **occipital lobe** lies behind the parietal and temporal lobes. Different functions tend to be localized in particular areas of the lobes: vision in the occipital; discrimination of sounds in the temporal; reasoning and other higher mental processes plus the regulation of fine voluntary movement in the frontal; initiation of movements of the skeletal musculature in a band in front of the central sulcus; receipt of sensations of touch, pressure, pain, temperature, and body position from skin, muscles, tendons, and joints in a band behind the central sulcus.

The two hemispheres of the brain have different functions. The left hemisphere, which generally controls the right half of the body by a crossing over of motor and sensory fibers, is responsible for speech and, according to some neuropsychologists, for analytical thinking in right-handed people and in a fair number of left-handed people as well. The right hemisphere controls the left side of the body, discerns spatial relations and patterns, and is involved in emotion and intuition. But analytical thinking cannot be located exclusively in the left hemisphere or intuitive and even creative thinking in the right; the two hemispheres communicate with each other constantly via the corpus callosum. Localization of apparently different modes of thought is probably not as clear-cut as some people would believe.

If the brain is sliced in half, separating the two cerebral hemispheres (see Figure 4.b), additional important features can be seen. The gray matter of the cerebral cortex does not extend throughout the interior of the brain. Much of the interior is **white matter**, made up of large tracts or bundles of myelinated (sheathed) fibers that connect cell bodies in the cortex with those in the spinal cord and in other centers lower in the brain. These centers are pockets of gray matter, referred to as **nuclei**. The nuclei serve both as way stations, connecting tracts from the cortex with other ascending and descending tracts, and as integrating motor and sensory control centers. Some cortical cells project their long fibers or axons to motor neurons in the spinal cord, but others project them only as far as these clusters of interconnecting neuron cell bodies. Four masses are deep within each hemisphere, called collectively the basal ganglia. Also deep within the brain are cavities called **ventricles**, which are continuous with the central canal of the spinal cord and are filled with cerebrospinal fluid.

Figure 4.b depicts four important functional areas or structures.

1. The **diencephalon**, connected in front with the hemispheres and behind with the midbrain, contains the **thalamus** and the **hypothalamus**, which consist of groups of nuclei. The thalamus is a

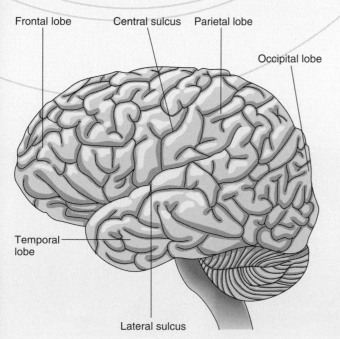

Frontal lobe   Central sulcus   Parietal lobe

Occipital lobe

Temporal lobe

Lateral sulcus

Figure 4.a   Surface of the left cerebral hemisphere, indicating the lobes and the two principal fissures of the cortex.

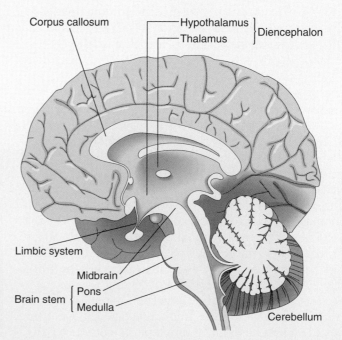

Corpus callosum   Hypothalamus ⎫ Diencephalon
                   Thalamus   ⎭

Limbic system

Midbrain
Brain stem ⎱ Pons
           ⎰ Medulla

Cerebellum

Figure 4.b   Slice of brain through the medial plane, showing the internal structures.

relay station for all sensory pathways except the olfactory. The nuclei making up the thalamus receive nearly all impulses arriving from the different sensory areas of the body before passing them on to the cerebrum, where they are interpreted as conscious sensations. The hypothalamus is the highest center of integration for many visceral processes. Its nuclei regulate metabolism, temperature, perspiration, blood pressure, sleeping, and appetite.

2. The **midbrain** is a mass of nerve-fiber tracts connecting the cerebral cortex with the pons, the medulla oblongata, the cerebellum, and the spinal cord.

3. The **brain stem** comprises the *pons* and the *medulla oblongata* and functions primarily as a neural relay station. The *pons* contains tracts that connect the cerebellum with the spinal cord and with motor areas of the cerebrum. The **medulla oblongata** serves as the main line of traffic for tracts ascending from the spinal cord and descending from the higher centers of the brain. At the bottom of the medulla many of the motor fibers cross to the opposite side. The medulla also contains nuclei that maintain the regular life rhythms of the heartbeat, of the rising and falling diaphragm, and of the constricting and dilating blood vessels. In the core of the brain stem is the **reticular formation**, sometimes called the reticular activating system because of the important role it plays in arousal and in the maintenance of alertness. The tracts of the pons and medulla send in fibers to connect with the profusely interconnected cells of the reticular formation, which in turn send fibers to the cortex, the basal ganglia, the hypothalamus, the septal area, and the cerebellum.

4. The **cerebellum**, like the cerebrum, consists primarily of two deeply convoluted hemispheres with an exterior cortex of gray matter and an interior of white tracts. The cerebellum receives sensory nerves from the vestibular apparatus of the ear and from muscles, tendons, and joints. The information received and integrated relates to balance and posture and equilibrium and to the smooth coordination of the body when in motion.

5. A fifth important part of the brain is the **limbic system**, which comprises structures continuous with one another in the lower cerebrum and developed earlier than the mammalian cerebral cortex. The limbic system controls the visceral and physical expressions of emotion—quickened heartbeat and respiration, trembling, sweating, and alterations in facial expressions—and the expression of appetitive and other primary drives, namely, hunger, thirst, mating, defense, attack, and flight. Important structures in the limbic system are the cingulate gyrus, stretching about the corpus callosum; the septal area, which is anterior to the thalamus; the long, tubelike hippocampus, which stretches from the septal area into the temporal lobe; and the amygdala (one of the basal ganglia), which is embedded in the tip of the temporal lobe.

machine scans another cross section of the brain. The resulting images can show the enlargement of ventricles, which signals degeneration of tissue and the locations of tumors and blood clots (see photo on p. 97).

Newer computer-based devices for seeing the living brain include **magnetic resonance imaging**, also known as **MRI**, which is superior to the CT scan because it produces pictures of higher quality and does not rely on even the small amount of radiation required by a CT scan. In MRI the person is placed inside a large, circular magnet, which causes the hydrogen atoms in the body to move. When the magnetic force is turned off, the atoms return to their original positions and thereby produce an electromagnetic signal. These signals are then read by the computer and translated into pictures of brain tissue. The implications of this technique are enormous. For example, it has allowed physicians to locate and remove delicate brain tumors that would have been considered inoperable without such sophisticated methods of viewing brain structures.

More recently, a modification called **fMRI (functional MRI)**, has been developed that allows researchers to take MRI pictures so quickly that metabolic changes can be measured, providing a picture of the brain at work rather than of its structure alone. Using this technique, studies have found less activation in the frontal lobes of patients with schizophrenia than in the frontal lobes of normal people as they performed a cognitive task (e.g., Yurgelon-Todd et al., 1996).

Positron emission tomography, the **PET scan**, a more expensive and invasive procedure, allows measurement of both brain structure and brain function. A substance used by the brain is labeled with a short-lived radioactive isotope and injected into the bloodstream. The radioactive molecules of the substance emit a particle called a positron, which quickly collides with an electron. A pair of high-energy

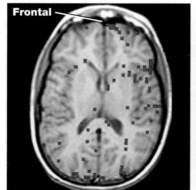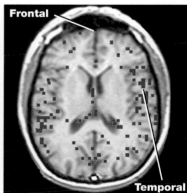

Functional magnetic resonance images (fMRI) of a schizophrenic patient (right) and a healthy individual (left). The red squares represent activation of the brain during a verbal task compared to baseline. The patient shows less frontal and more temporal activation. (Yurgelun-Todd et al., 1996)

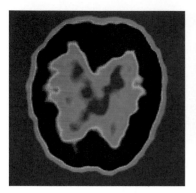 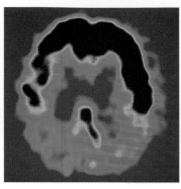

The PET scan on the left shows a normal brain; the one on the right shows the brain of a patient with Alzheimer's disease.

light particles shoot out from the skull in opposite directions and are detected by the scanner. The computer analyzes millions of such recordings and converts them into a picture of the functioning brain. The images are in color; fuzzy spots of lighter and warmer colors are areas in which metabolic rates for the substance are higher.

Visual images of the working brain can indicate sites of epileptic seizures, brain cancers, strokes, and trauma from head injuries, as well as the distribution of psychoactive drugs in the brain. The PET scanner is also being used to study possible abnormal biological processes that underlie disorders, such as the failure of the frontal cortex of patients with schizophrenia to become activated while they attempt to perform a cognitive task.

Neurochemical Assessment

It might seem that assessing the amount of a particular neurotransmitter or the quantity of its receptors in the brain would be straightforward. But it is not. Only recently has PET scanning allowed an assessment of receptors in a living brain. Most of the research on neurochemical theories of psychopathology—of increasing importance in recent years—has relied on indirect assessments.

In postmortem studies, the brains of deceased patients are removed and the amount of specific neurotransmitters in particular brain areas can then be directly measured. Different brain areas can be infused with substances that bind to receptors, and the amount of binding can then be quantified; more binding indicates more receptors. In Chapter 11 we will discuss how this method has been used to study the dopamine theory of schizophrenia.

Another common method of neurochemical assessment involves analyzing the metabolites of neurotransmitters that have been broken down by enzymes. A **metabolite**, typically an acid, is produced when a neurotransmitter is deactivated. For example, the major metabolite of dopamine is homovanillic acid; of serotonin, 5-hydroxyindoleacetic acid. The metabolites can be detected in urine, blood, and cerebrospinal fluid (the fluid in the spinal column and in the brain's ventricles). A high level of a particular metabolite indicates a high level of a transmitter, and a low level indicates a low level of the transmitter. We will see in Chapter 10 that people with depression have low levels of the main metabolite of serotonin—a fact that has played an important role in the serotonin theory of depression.

Neuropsychological Assessment

It is important at this point to note a distinction between neurologists and neuropsychologists, even though both specialists are concerned with the study of the central nervous system. A **neurologist** is a physician who specializes in medical diseases that affect the nervous system, such as muscular dystrophy, cerebral palsy, or Alzheimer's disease. A **neuropsychologist** is a psychologist who studies how dysfunctions of the brain affect the way we think, feel, and behave. As the term implies, a neuropsychologist is trained as a psychologist and as such is interested in thought, emotion, and behavior, but with a focus on how abnormalities of the brain affect behavior in deleterious ways. Both kinds of specialists contribute much to each other as they work in different ways, often collaboratively, to learn how the nervous system functions and how to ameliorate problems caused by disease or injury to the brain.

The preceding section explained how imaging and neurochemical techniques provide startling pictures of and insights into internal organs and permit the gathering of information about living tissue, including the brain. Clinicians and researchers in many disciplines are currently using these techniques both to discover previously undetectable tumors and other brain problems and to conduct inquiries into the neural and chemical bases of thought, emotion, and behavior. It is a very lively and exciting area of research and application. Indeed, one might reasonably assume that neurologists and physicians, with the help of such procedures and technological devices as PET, CT, and MRI scans, could observe the brain and its functions more or less directly and thus assess all brain abnormalities. Results, however, are not strong enough for these methods to be used in diagnosing psychopathology. Moreover, many brain abnormalities and injuries involve alterations in structure so subtle or slight in extent that they have thus far eluded direct physical examination.

Neuropsychologists have developed tests—called **neuropsychological tests**—to assess behavioral disturbances caused by brain dysfunctions. The tests are often used in conjunction with the brain scanning techniques just described. The evidence indicates that these tests have some validity in both detecting brain damage and in localizing it in specific areas of the brain (Garb & Schramke, 1996). Neuropsychological tests are based on the idea that different psychological functions (e.g., motor speed, memory, language) are localized in different areas of the brain. Thus, finding a deficit on a particular test can provide clues about where in the brain some damage may exist.

One neuropsychological test is Reitan's modification of a battery or group of tests previously developed by Halstead. The concept of using a battery of tests, each tapping a different function, is critical, for only by studying a person's pattern of performance can an investigator adequately judge whether the person is brain damaged and where the damage is located. The following are four of the tests included in the Halstead–Reitan battery.

1. **Tactile Performance Test—Time.** While blindfolded, the patient tries to fit variously shaped blocks into spaces of a form board, first using the preferred hand, then the other, and finally both.

2. **Tactile Performance Test—Memory.** After completing the timed test, the participant is asked to draw the form board from memory, showing the blocks in their proper location. Both this and the timed test are sensitive to damage in the right parietal lobe.

3. **Speech Sounds Perception Test.** Participants listen to a series of nonsense words, each comprising two consonants with a long e sound in the middle. They then select the "word" they heard from a set of alternatives. This test measures left-hemisphere function, especially temporal and parietal areas.

Neuropsychological tests assess various performance deficits in the hope of detecting a specific area of brain malfunction. Shown here is the Tactile Performance Test.

Extensive research has demonstrated that the battery is valid for detecting brain damage resulting from a variety of conditions, such as tumors, stroke, and head injury. Furthermore, this battery of tests can play an important role in making difficult diagnostic decisions, for example, discriminating dementia due to depression from dementia due to a degenerative brain disease (Reed & Reed, 1997).

The Luria–Nebraska battery (Golden, Hammeke, & Purisch, 1978), based on the work of the Russian psychologist Aleksandr Luria (1902–1977), is also in widespread use (Moses & Purisch, 1997). A battery of 269 items makes up eleven sections to determine basic and complex motor skills, rhythm and pitch abilities, tactile and kinesthetic skills, verbal and spatial skills, receptive speech ability, expressive speech ability, writing, reading, arithmetic skills, memory, and intellectual processes. The pattern of scores on these sections, as well as on the 32 items found to be the most discriminating and indicative of overall impairment, helps reveal damage to the frontal, temporal, sensorimotor, or parietal-occipital area of the right or left hemisphere.

The Luria–Nebraska battery can be administered in two and a half hours, and research demonstrates that this test can be scored in a highly reliable manner (e.g.,

Kashden & Franzen, 1996). It also has an alternate form. Criterion validity has been established by findings such as a correct classification rate of over 86 percent when used with a sample of neurological patients and controls (Moses et al., 1992). The Luria–Nebraska is also believed to pick up effects of brain damage that are not (yet) detectable by neurological examination or imaging assessment. A particular advantage of the Luria–Nebraska tests is that one can control for educational level so that a less-educated person will not receive a lower score solely because of limited educational experience (Brickman et al., 1984). Finally, a version (Golden, 1981) for children ages eight to twelve has been found useful in diagnosing brain damage and in evaluating the educational strengths and weaknesses of children (Sweet et al., 1986).

Psychophysiological Assessment

The discipline of **psychophysiology** is concerned with the bodily changes that accompany psychological events or that are associated with a person's psychological characteristics (Grings & Dawson, 1978). Experimenters have used measures such as heart rate, tension in the muscles, blood flow in various parts of the body, and brain waves to study physiological changes when people are afraid, depressed, asleep, imagining, solving problems, and so on. Like the brain-imaging methods we have already discussed, the assessments we describe here are not sensitive enough to be used for diagnosis. They can, however, provide important information. For example, in using exposure to treat a patient with an anxiety disorder, it would be useful to know the extent to which the patient shows physiological arousal when exposed to the stimuli that create anxiety. Patients who show higher levels of physiological arousal may be experiencing higher levels of fear, which predict more benefit from the therapy (Foa et al., 1995).

The activities of the autonomic nervous system (see Focus on Discovery 4.3) are frequently assessed by electrical and chemical measurements in attempts to understand the nature of emotion. One important measure is heart rate. Each heartbeat generates changes in electrical potential, which can be recorded by an electrocardiograph or on a suitably tuned polygraph and graphically depicted in an **electrocardiogram (EKG)**. Electrodes are usually placed on the chest and lead to an instrument for measuring electric currents. The deflections of this instrument may be seen as waves on a computer screen, or a pen recorder may register the waves on a continuously moving roll of graph paper. Both types of recordings are called electrocardiograms.

A second measure of autonomic nervous system activity is **electrodermal responding**, or skin conductance. Anxiety, fear, anger, and other emotions increase activity in the sympathetic nervous system, which then boosts sweat-gland activity. Increased sweat-gland activity increases the electrical conductance of the skin. Conductance is typically measured by determining the current that flows through the skin when a known small voltage derived from an external source is passed between two electrodes on the hand. This current shows a pronounced increase after activation of the sweat glands. Since the sweat glands are activated by the sympathetic nervous system, increased sweat-gland activity indicates sympathetic autonomic excitation and is often taken as a measure of emotional arousal. These measures are widely used in research in psychopathology.

Advances in technology allow researchers to track changes in physiological processes such as blood pressure in vivo, as people go about their normal business. Participants wear a portable device that automatically records blood pressure many times during the day. Combining these measures with self-reports

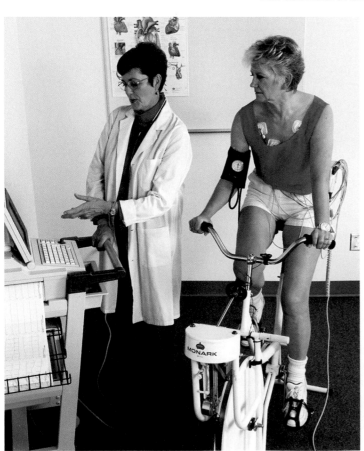

In psychophysiological assessment, physical changes in the body are measured. The electrocardiograph is one such assessment.

Table 4.3 Biological Assessment Methods

Brain imaging	CT and MRI scans reveal the structure of the brain. PET and fMRI are used to study brain function.
Neurochemical assessment	Includes postmortem analysis of neurotransmitters and receptors, assays of metabolites of neurotransmitters, and PET scans of receptors.
Neuropsychological assessment	Behavioral tests such as the Halstead–Reitan and Luria–Nebraska assess abilities such as motor speed, memory, and spatial ability. Deficits on particular tests help localize an area of brain dysfunction.
Psychophysiological assessment	Includes measures of electrical activity in the autonomic nervous system, such as skin conductance, or in the central nervous system, such as the EEG.

recorded by the participants in specially designed diaries, researchers have been able to study how people's changing moods affect blood pressure—data of great interest to psychologically oriented researchers in hypertension (Kamarck et al., 1998; see Chapter 8).

Brain activity can be measured by an **electroencephalogram**, or **EEG**. Electrodes placed on the scalp record electrical activity in the underlying brain area. Abnormal patterns of electrical activity can indicate epilepsy or help in locating brain lesions or tumors.

As with the brain-imaging techniques reviewed earlier, a more complete picture of a human being is obtained when physiological functioning is assessed while the person is engaging in some form of behavior or cognitive activity. If experimenters are interested in psychophysiological responding in patients with obsessive-compulsive disorder, for example, they would likely study the patients while presenting stimuli, such as dirt, that would elicit the problematic behaviors.

The biological assessment methods we have described are summarized in Table 4.3.

A Cautionary Note

A cautionary note regarding biological assessment methods is in order here. Inasmuch as psychophysiology employs highly sophisticated electronic machinery and many psychologists aspire to be as scientific as possible, researchers sometimes believe uncritically in these apparently objective assessment devices without appreciating their real limitations and complications. Many of the measurements do not differentiate clearly among emotional states. Skin conductance, for example, increases not only with anxiety but also with other emotions—among them, happiness.

Neither is there a one-to-one relationship between a score on a given neuropsychological test or a finding on a PET or CAT scan on the one hand and psychological dysfunction on the other. This is especially so with chronic brain damage known or suspected to have been present for some years before the assessment is conducted. The reasons for these sometimes loose relationships have to do with such factors as how the person has, over time, reacted to and coped with the losses brought about by the brain damage. And the success of efforts to cope have, in turn, to do with the social environment in which the individual has lived, for example, how understanding parents and associates have been or how well the school system has provided for the special educational needs of the individual. Therefore, in addition to the imperfect nature of the biological assessment instruments themselves and our incomplete understanding of how the brain actually functions, researchers must consider these experiential factors that operate over time to contribute to the clinical picture.

A final caution is reflected in the simple yet often unappreciated fact that in attempting to understand the neurocognitive consequences of any brain-injuring event, one must understand the abilities that the patient has brought to that event (Boll, 1985). This

Focus on Discovery 4.3

The Autonomic Nervous System

The mammalian nervous system can be divided into two relatively separate functional parts: the **somatic** (or voluntary) **nervous system** and the **autonomic** (or involuntary) **nervous system (ANS)**. Because the autonomic nervous system is especially important in the study of emotional behavior, it will be useful to review its principal characteristics.

Skeletal muscles, such as those that move our limbs, are innervated, or stimulated, by the voluntary nervous system. Much of our behavior, however, is dependent on a nervous system that operates generally without our awareness and has traditionally been viewed as beyond voluntary control, hence the term *autonomic*. However,

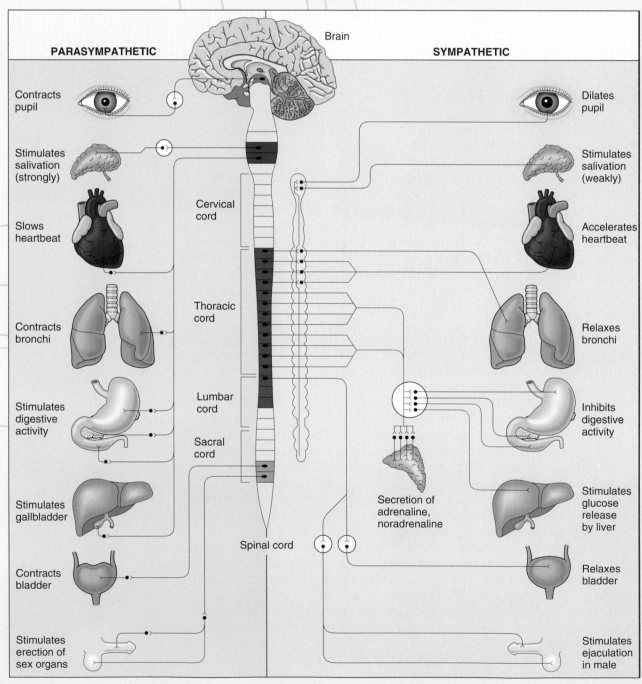

PARASYMPATHETIC

Contracts pupil

Stimulates salivation (strongly)

Slows heartbeat

Contracts bronchi

Stimulates digestive activity

Stimulates gallbladder

Contracts bladder

Stimulates erection of sex organs

Brain

Cervical cord

Thoracic cord

Lumbar cord

Sacral cord

Spinal cord

SYMPATHETIC

Dilates pupil

Stimulates salivation (weakly)

Accelerates heartbeat

Relaxes bronchi

Inhibits digestive activity

Secretion of adrenaline, noradrenaline

Stimulates glucose release by liver

Relaxes bladder

Stimulates ejaculation in male

Figure 4.c   The autonomic nervous system.

research on biofeedback has shown that the ANS is under greater voluntary control than previously believed (see p. 233).

The autonomic nervous system innervates the endocrine glands, the heart, and the smooth muscles that are found in the walls of the blood vessels, stomach, intestines, kidneys, and other organs. This nervous system is itself divided into two parts, the **sympathetic nervous system** and the **parasympathetic nervous system** (Figure 4.c), which work sometimes in opposition to each other, sometimes in unison. The sympathetic portion of the ANS, when energized, accelerates the heartbeat, dilates the pupils, inhibits intestinal activity, increases electrodermal activity, and initiates other smooth-muscle and glandular responses that prepare the organism for sudden activity and stress. Some physiologists view the sympathetic nervous system as primarily excitatory and view the other division, the parasympathetic, as responsible for maintenance functions and more quiescent behavior, such as deceleration of the heartbeat, constriction of the pupils, and acceleration of intestinal contractions. Division of activities is not quite so clear-cut, however, for it is the parasympathetic system that increases blood flow to the genitals during sexual excitement.

straightforward truth brings to mind the story of the man who, recovering from an accident that has broken all the fingers in both hands, earnestly asks the surgeon whether he will be able to play the piano when his wounds heal. "Yes, I'm sure you will," says the doctor reassuringly. "That's wonderful," exclaims the man, "I've always wanted to be able to play the piano."

Cultural Diversity and Clinical Assessment

Studies of the influences of culture on psychopathology and its assessment have proliferated in recent years. As you read about some of this research, it is critical to keep in mind that there are typically more differences within cultural groups than there are between them. Remembering this important point can help avoid the dangers of stereotyping members of a culture.

We should also note that the reliability and validity of various forms of psychological assessment have been questioned on the grounds that their content and scoring procedures reflect the culture of white European Americans and so may not accurately assess people from other cultures. In this section we discuss problems of cultural bias and what can be done about them.

Cultural Bias in Assessment

The issue of cultural bias in assessment is not simple, nor is it clear that such biases make the assessment instruments useless. Studies of bias in testing have demonstrated that mainstream procedures, such as the Wechsler Intelligence Scale for Children—Revised, have equivalent predictive validity for minority and nonminority children (Sattler, 1992); IQ tests predict academic achievement equally well for both groups. Indexes derived from the Exner system of scoring the Rorschach are also similar in African Americans and whites (Meyer, 2002). MMPI profiles are very similar for Caucasians and African Americans (Arbisi, Ben-Porath, & McNulty, 2002; Munley et al., 2001) and relate equally well to clinician ratings among African Americans and Caucasians (McNulty et al., 1997). Among Asians, however, particularly those who have not been fully assimilated into American culture, scores on most MMPI scales are higher than those of Caucasians (Tsai & Pike, 2000). This is unlikely to be due to higher levels of emotional disturbance among Asians.

In addition, cultural biases work in different ways—they may cause clinicians to over- or underestimate psychological problems in members of other cultures (Lopez, 1989, 1996). African American children are overrepresented in special-education classes, which may be a result of subtle biases in the tests used to determine such placement (Artiles & Trent, 1994). Yet take the example of an Asian American man who is very emotionally withdrawn. Should the clinician consider that lower levels of emotional expressiveness in men are viewed more positively in Asian cultures than in Euro-American culture? A clinician who too quickly attributes the behavior to a cultural difference rather

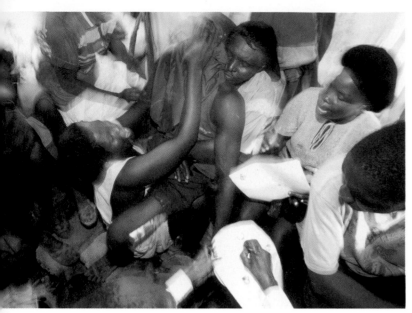

Assessment must take the person's cultural background into account. Believing in possession by spirits is common in some cultures and thus should not always be taken to mean that the believer is psychotic.

than to a psychological disorder risks overlooking an emotional problem that he or she would be likely to diagnose if the patient were a white male. Again, the effect of cultural bias in clinical assessment works both ways (Lopez, 1989).

How do such biases come about? Cultural differences are many, and they may affect assessment in various ways. Language differences, cultural views of competition, differing religious and spiritual beliefs, the alienation or timidity of members of minority cultures when being assessed by clinicians of the Euro-American culture—all these factors can play a role. Spanish-speaking people being assessed by English-speaking clinicians may be poorly served by translators (Sabin, 1975). Clinicians who encounter clients claiming to be surrounded by spirits might view this belief as a sign of schizophrenia. Yet in Puerto Rican cultures such a belief is common; therefore, believing that one is surrounded by spirits should probably not be taken as a sign of schizophrenia in a Puerto Rican person (Rogler & Hollingshead, 1985). Native Americans, taught by their culture to cooperate with others, are less likely to warm to the task of taking an aptitude test, which is by nature highly individualistic and competitive (O'Conner, 1989).

Although it is important to be aware of the potential of cultural differences to bias clinical assessment, it is not clear that attempting to include cultural differences in one's assessment work necessarily contributes to a helpful diagnosis. Consider the results of a survey of mental health practitioners in California (Lopez & Hernandez, 1986). One clinician reported attaching less psychopathological significance to the hallucinations of an African American woman because he believed that hallucinations were more prevalent among African Americans. This clinician minimized the seriousness of the woman's problems by attributing them to a subcultural norm. As a result, he did not consider a diagnosis of schizophrenia, a decision that may not have been in the woman's best interests.

Cultural biases affect not only who is diagnosed, but also how the person is diagnosed. One study found that clinicians were more likely to diagnose a patient as having schizophrenia if the case summary referred to the person as African American than if the person was described as white (Blake, 1973). A hospital-based study found that African American patients were overdiagnosed as having schizophrenia and underdiagnosed as having a mood disorder (Simon et al., 1973). Another study found that, based on identical symptoms, lower-class African American patients were more likely to be diagnosed as alcoholic than were white, middle-class patients, which, given the symptoms exhibited, was a disservice to the white patients (Luepnitz, Randolph, & Gutsch, 1982).

Cultural differences cannot be avoided. And the cultural biases that can creep into clinical assessment do not necessarily yield to efforts to compensate for them. There is no simple answer. DSM-IV-TR's inclusion of cultural factors in the discussion of every category of disorder may well sensitize clinicians to the issue, a necessary first step. When practitioners were surveyed, they overwhelmingly reported taking culture into account in their clinical work (Lopez, 1994), so it appears that the problem, if not the solution, is clearly in focus.

Strategies for Avoiding Cultural Bias in Assessment

Clinicians can—and do—use various methods to minimize the negative effects of cultural biases when assessing patients. Sattler (1982) makes some helpful suggestions that can guide clinicians in the selection and interpretation of tests and other assessment data. First, clinicians should make efforts to learn about the culture of the person being assessed. This knowledge might come from reading, consultation with colleagues, and direct discussion with the client. Second, it is essential for clinicians to determine the client's preferred language and to consider testing in more than one language.

Assessment procedures can also be modified to ensure that the person truly understands the requirements of the task. For example, suppose that a Native American child performed poorly on a test measuring psychomotor speed. The examiner's hunch is that the child did not understand the importance of working quickly and was overconcerned with accuracy instead. The test could be administered again after a more thorough explanation of the importance of working quickly without worrying about mistakes. If the child's performance improves, the examiner has gained an important understanding of him or her and avoids diagnosing psychomotor-speed deficits when test-taking strategy is more at issue.

Finally, when the examiner and client have different ethnic backgrounds, the examiner may need to make an extra effort to establish a rapport that will result in the person's best performance. For example, when testing a shy, Hispanic preschooler, one of the authors was unable to obtain a verbal response to test questions. However, the boy was overheard talking in an animated and articulate manner to his mother in the waiting room, leading to a judgment that the test results did not represent a valid assessment of the child's language skills. When testing was repeated in the child's own home with his mother present, advanced verbal abilities were observed.

Cultural differences can lead to different results on an aptitude or IQ test. For example, Native American children may lack interest in the individualistic, competitive nature of IQ tests because of the cooperative, group-oriented values instilled by their culture.

As Lopez (1994) points out, however, "the distance between cultural responsiveness and cultural stereotyping can be short" (p. 123). To minimize such problems, clinicians are encouraged to be particularly tentative about drawing conclusions with minority patients. Rather, they are advised to make hypotheses about the influence of culture on a particular client, entertain alternative hypotheses, and then test those hypotheses.

In a case from our files, a young man was suspected of having schizophrenia. One prominent symptom he reported was hearing voices. However, he claimed that he heard voices only while meditating and that within his (Buddhist) culture this experience was normative. To test this hypothesis the examiner (with the permission of the client) contacted the family's religious leader. The Buddhist priest indicated that the symptom reported by this young man was very unusual, and it turned out that the religious community to which he belonged was quite concerned about his increasingly bizarre behavior. Thus, the hypothesis that his symptom should be attributed to cultural factors was refuted, and an error of failing to detect psychopathology was avoided.

The Consistency and Variability of Behavior

In this last section we address a critical question that is relevant in any form of clinical assessment: Are people consistent or variable over time? In other words, do we possess personality traits that operate in the same way in a variety of situations, or do we behave differently depending on the situation? This question has prompted much debate and research, and it is of concern in any careful consideration of how to assess people and their problems in clinical settings.

Trait theorists believe that human beings can be described as having a certain amount of a characteristic, such as stinginess or obsessiveness, or, in DSM terms, as having a particular disorder. The assumption is that their thoughts, feelings, and behavior in a variety of situations can be predicted reasonably well by the degree to which they possess a particular characteristic. This paradigmatic position implies that people will behave fairly consistently in a variety of situations—a highly aggressive person, for example, will be more aggressive than someone low in aggression at home, at work, and at play.

After reviewing the evidence bearing on this question, Walter Mischel, in his classic book *Personality and Assessment* (1968), argued that except for IQ, personality traits are

The work of the prominent psychologist Walter Mischel stimulated the current debate concerning whether traits or situations are the most powerful determinants of behavior.

not very important determinants of behavior. He concluded that the behavior of people is often not very consistent from situation to situation.

Not surprisingly, Mischel's attack on trait theory elicited a heated debate in the literature. For example, the psychodynamic theorist Paul Wachtel (1977) pointed out that the studies Mischel cited were generally done with nonpatients, whose behavior is probably more flexible than that of patients. A hallmark of mental disorder may be rigidity and inflexibility, which is another way of saying that behavior is consistent in a variety of situations. Certainly the personality disorders, discussed in Chapter 13, can be seen as extreme instances of traits that are inflexible and maladaptive. By studying basically normal people, Mischel may have reached a conclusion that does not apply to people with these disorders.

Wachtel suggested also that differing perceptions can cause people to experience similar situations differently or can render objectively different situations equivalent in their eyes. For example, a person who might be described as paranoid sees threats in routine and innocuous situations. Having one's credit card purchase checked for approval may be seen by an overly suspicious person as questioning his or her integrity and by a truly paranoid person as part of a sinister plot to humiliate and persecute him or her.

Insensitivity to circumstances is not the person's problem; rather, this person perceives most, if not all, situations as containing threats. In addition, people can *elicit* certain kinds of reactions from their surroundings. The paranoid individual may not only perceive people as threatening, but may make them so by attacking them first. In effect, he or she transforms innocuous situations into dangerous ones. As a result, the paranoid person's behavior varies little.

Wachtel also proposed that a personality disposition can affect the kinds of situations an individual selects or constructs for himself or herself. A generally optimistic person, for example, may seek out situations that confirm his or her positive outlook, which in turn strengthens the trait tendency to find or to construct similar sanguine situations in the future. There is a constantly reciprocating interaction, then, with personality traits influencing what situations the person is in and the situations in turn influencing personality. "Consistency over extended periods of time…may be the product of extended histories of choosing situations conducive to one's attitudes, traits, and dispositions" (Snyder, 1983, p. 510).

In the course of the debate touched off by Mischel's important book, other psychologists suggested that his original position was too extreme. Jack Block (1971) challenged Mischel's conclusions regarding the inconsistency of behavior. In examining the studies Mischel used to support his claim, Block found that most of them had serious flaws. Seymore Epstein (1979) also criticized the studies used by Mischel to buttress the situationist position. Those studies, noted Epstein, looked only at small bits of behavior, a strategy as inappropriate as measuring IQ by looking at a person's score on a single test item. More appropriate is an *averaging* of behavior from a range of situations. In the studies he conducted, Epstein collected and averaged data on a number of occasions and was able to demonstrate marked consistency in behavior.

The original views of the famous psychologist and personality theorist Gordon Allport (1937) on the importance of global traits in understanding complex human behavior are now enjoying a revival of interest as more data are collected supporting the importance of personality dispositions (Funder, 1991). For example, we will see in Chapter 13, that much ongoing work is attempting to describe personality disorders using a model that represents personality as consisting of five major traits.

In support of Mischel's concerns, Bandura (1986) proposed that the heavy reliance of trait theorists on self-report questionnaires colors their conclusions because people may selectively perceive themselves as consistent and respond accordingly on these questionnaires. The questionnaires probe for typical behavior in poorly specified situations, for example, "Do you tend to lose your temper when you get angry?" On the other hand, if people are observed in a variety of different situations, their actual behavior will be much more diverse and sensitive to environmental differences—a conclusion that can be drawn from a vast literature in social and personality psychology.

An intriguing possibility is that a belief in traits conveys predictability and perhaps gives an illusion of control. If Joe is a good guy, then we can rely on him no matter what; and if Dick is a jerk, then that, too, can be relied on and planned around, even if we wish he were a different sort of person. Western culture also fosters a trait orientation to understanding behavior. Most of us grew up with the idea that people can be characterized as nice, good-humored, rotten, and so forth. It may also be the case that most people value consistency in behavior even when that consistency leads us to conclude that little good is to be expected from a given individual.

Bandura (1986) further asserted that Epstein and other trait theorists neglect the functionality of performing behavior X in situation Y, that is, whether it pays off to act a certain way in a particular situation. As a social learning theorist, Bandura focuses more than do trait theorists on the situational determinants of behavior, especially the reinforcements anticipated by the individual. "Aggressive acts by delinquents towards parish priests and rival gang members will correlate poorly, however much averaging one does" (p. 10).

Mischel has provided data to support this notion, coming up with "if…then" statements about children in a camp setting. For example, Henry exhibits aggressive behavior if warned by adults not to, but he complies when threatened by peers. Thus, there is an interaction between a tendency (trait) to be aggressive and the situations in which such behavior does or does not occur. The consequences of expressing a particular tendency, such as aggressiveness, play an important role in determining whether that trait becomes manifest in a given situation (Shoda, Mischel, & Wright, 1994).

Of course, some situations call forth the same behavior from virtually all individuals; a situationist perspective can thus sometimes lead to a traitlike prediction. For example, most people at a beach on a hot summer day are likely to wear few clothes and to swim; and most people in a library are likely to read and to speak only in hushed tones. All well and good, but a complete analysis of behavior would have to include a prediction of whether a given individual would read at the beach, daydream about the beach while sitting in a library, or even be in such a situation at all (Anastasi, 1990)! What is emerging from the sometimes contentious literature on traits versus behavioral variability is an appreciation for how personality factors interact with different environments, a paradigmatic perspective that overlaps considerably with the diathesis–stress viewpoint that marks our own study of psychopathology.

Summary

- Clinicians rely on several modes of psychological and biological assessment in trying to find out how best to describe a patient, search for the reasons the patient is troubled, and design effective preventive or remedial treatments. Regardless of what assessment method is used, it inevitably reflects the paradigm of the clinician.

- In gathering assessment information, clinicians and researchers must be concerned with both reliability and validity. Reliability refers to whether measurements are consistent and replicable; and validity, to whether assessments are tapping into what they are meant to measure. Assessment procedures vary greatly in their reliability and validity.

- Psychological assessments include clinical interviews, psychological tests, and behavioral and cognitive assessments.

- Clinical interviews are structured or relatively unstructured conversations in which the clinician probes the patient for information about his or her problems.

- Psychological tests are standardized procedures designed to assess personality or measure performance. Personality assessments range from empirically derived self-report questionnaires, such as the Minnesota Multiphasic Personality Inventory, to projective tests in which the patient interprets ambiguous stimuli, such as the Rorschach Test. Intelligence tests, such as the Wechsler Adult Intelligence Scale, evaluate a person's intellectual ability and predict how well he or she will perform academically.

- Whereas traditional assessment seeks to understand people in terms of general traits or personality structure, behavioral and cognitive assessment is concerned more with how people act, feel, and think in particular situations. Approaches include direct observation of behavior; interviews and self-report measures that are situational in their focus; and specialized, think-aloud cognitive assessment procedures that attempt to uncover beliefs, attitudes, and thinking patterns related to specific situations.

- Biological assessments include computer-controlled imaging techniques, such as CT scans and PET scans—that enable us to see various structures and access functions of the living brain; neurochemical assays that allow clinicians to make inferences about levels of neurotransmitters; neuropsychological tests, such as the Halstead–Reitan, which seek to identify brain defects based on variations in responses to psychological tests; and psychophysiological measurements, such as heart rate and skin conductance, which are associated with certain psychological events or characteristics.

● Cultural and racial factors play a role in clinical assessment. Assessment techniques developed on the basis of research with white populations may be inaccurate when used with non-white clients, for example. Clinicians can have biases when evaluating minority patients, which can lead to minimizing or exaggerating a patient's psy-

chopathology. Clinicians use various methods to guard against the negative effects of cultural biases in assessment.

● Whether human behavior is stable across situations is highly controversial. This issue has been of both theoretical and practical interest to psychologists for years. The answers are far from in, but it appears that behavior across situations is probably more variable than was once thought by traditional personality theorists and also more stable than is believed by many of those working in the learning paradigm.

Key Terms

alternate-form reliability
autonomic nervous system (ANS)
behavioral observation
brain stem
cerebellum
cerebral cortex
cerebral hemispheres
clinical interview
construct validity
content validity
corpus callosum
criterion validity
CT or CAT scan
diencephalon
ecological momentary assessment (EMA)

electrocardiogram (EKG)
electrodermal responding
electroencephalogram (EEG)test-retest reliability
frontal lobe
functional magnetic resonance imaging (fMRI)
gyri
hypothalamus
intelligence test
internal consistency reliability
limbic system
magnetic resonance imaging (MRI)
medulla oblongata
meninges

metabolite
midbrain
Minnesota Multiphasic Personality Inventory (MMPI)
neurologist
neuropsychological tests
neuropsychologist
nuclei
occipital lobe
parasympathetic nervous system
parietal lobe
personality inventory
PET scan
pons
psychological tests
psychophysiology

projective test
projective hypothesis
reactivity (of behavior)
reticular formation
Rorschach Inkblot Test
self-monitoring
somatic nervous system
standardization
structured interview
sulci
sympathetic nervous system
temporal lobe
thalamus
Thematic Apperception Test (TAT)
ventricles
white matter

5 Research Methods in the Study of Abnormal Behavior

G iven the different ways of conceptualizing and treating abnormal behavior and the problems in its classification and assessment, it follows that there is also less than total agreement about how abnormal behavior ought to be studied and what are the facts of the field. Yet it is precisely because facts about mental disorders are hard to come by that we believe it is important to pursue them using the scientific research methods that are applied in contemporary psychopathology. This chapter discusses these methods and should provide a sense of the strengths and limitations of each. We hope, too, that the reader will gain respect for the information these methods have made available and the discoveries they have made possible.

Science and Scientific Methods

In current practice **science** is the pursuit of systematized knowledge through observation. Thus the term, which comes from the Latin *scire*, "to know," refers both to a method of systematic acquisition and evaluation of information and to a goal, the development of general theories that explain the information. At its core, science is a way of knowing. It is always important for scientific observations and explanations to be testable (open to systematic probes) and reliable. In this section, we look briefly at the criteria of testability and reliability and in more depth at the key role theory plays. In the next section, we examine the major research methods used in studying abnormal psychology.

Testability and Replicability

A scientific approach requires first that propositions and ideas be stated in a clear and precise way. Only then can scientific claims be exposed to systematic probes and tests, any one of which could negate the scientist's expectations about what will be found. Statements, theories, and assertions, regardless of how plausible they may seem, must be testable in the public arena and subject to disproof. The attitude of the scientist must be a doubting one. It is not enough to assert, for example, that traumatic experiences during childhood may cause psychological maladjustment in adulthood. This is no more than a possibility or proposition. According to a scientific point of view, such a hypothesis must be amenable to systematic testing that could show it to be false.

Closely related to testability is the need for each observation that contributes to a scientific body of knowledge to be replicable, or reliable. We have discussed the importance of reliability as it relates to diagnosis and assessment. It is equally important in the research process. Whatever is observed must be replicable, that is, it must occur under prescribed circumstances not once but repeatedly. An event must be reproducible under the circumstances stated, anywhere, anytime. If the event cannot be reproduced, scientists become wary of the legitimacy of the original observation.

The Role of Theory

A **theory** is a set of propositions meant to explain a class of phenomena. A primary goal of science is to advance theories to account for data, often by proposing cause–effect relationships. The results of empirical research allow the adequacy of theories to be evaluated. Theories themselves can also play an important role in guiding research by suggesting that certain additional data be collected. More specifically, a theory permits the generation of *hypotheses*—expectations about what should occur if a theory is true. These hypotheses must then be tested in research. For example, suppose you want to test a classical-conditioning theory of phobias. As a researcher you begin by developing a specific hypothesis based on the theory. For example, if the classical-conditioning theory is valid, people with phobias should be more likely than those in the general population to have had traumatic experiences with the situations they fear, such as flying. By collecting data on the frequency of traumatic experiences with phobic stimuli among people with phobias and comparing this information with corresponding data from people without phobias, you could determine whether your hypothesis was confirmed, supporting the theory, or disconfirmed, invalidating the theory.

The generation of a theory is perhaps the most challenging part of the scientific enterprise—and one of the least understood. It is sometimes asserted, for example, that a scientist formulates a theory simply by considering data that have been previously collected and then deciding, in a rather straightforward fashion, that a given way of thinking about the data is the most economical and useful.

Although some theory building follows this course, not all does. Aspects too seldom mentioned are the *creativity* of the act and the *excitement* of finding a novel way to conceptualize things. A theory sometimes seems to leap from the scientist's head in a wonderful moment of insight. New ideas suddenly occur, and connections previously overlooked are suddenly grasped. What formerly seemed obscure or meaningless makes a new kind of sense within the framework of the new theory (see Focus on Discovery 5.1).

Theories are *constructions* of scientists. In formulating a theory, scientists must often make use of theoretical concepts, unobservable states or processes that are inferred from observable data. Repression is a theoretical concept, as is the mediating fear response discussed in Chapter 2. Theoretical concepts are inferred from observable data. For example, behaviorists infer a mediating fear response based on the avoidance of a situation. Similarly, an analyst might infer the presence of a repressed conflict from a patient's continual avoidance of discussing his or her relationship with authority figures.

Several advantages can be gained by using theoretical terms. Theoretical concepts often allow us to characterize relationships across space and time. An example from early physics shows how a theoretical term may account for a spatial relationship. It had been observed that when a magnet was placed close to iron filings, some of the filings moved toward the magnet. How does one piece of metal influence another over the spatial distance? The inferred concept of magnetic fields proved useful in accounting for this phenomenon. Similarly, in abnormal psychology we may want to bridge temporal gaps with

Chaos Theory and Limits on Understanding and Prediction

...the Butterfly Effect—the notion that a butterfly stirring the air today in Peking can transform storm systems next month in New York. (Gleick, 1987, p. 8)

This quotation captures the essence of chaos theory, a position that suggests that major events (such as a storm system) may be affected by unexpected and seemingly trivial events (the air turbulence created by a flying butterfly). The chaos theory perspective argues against the ability of scientists to predict with any confidence the long-term outcomes of apparently tiny changes in events (Gleick, 1987). (In our view, chaos theory is more a paradigm than a theory.) The world is almost unfathomably complex, and we are inherently limited in what we can predict and explain. We have all experienced frustration, even annoyance, with weather reports—it is a standing joke to blame the meteorologist for favorable forecasts that turn out to be wrong. But an appreciation of the many factors that enter into the development or movement of a storm system justifies a little more tolerance of the limitations of these prognosticators.

In the human sciences it seems especially appropriate to view our task in terms of chaos theory (e.g., Duke, 1994; Gregerson & Sailer, 1993), or, as some would term it more broadly, complexity studies (Mahoney, 1991; Mahoney & Moes, 1997). Even if we knew all the variables controlling behavior—and no one would claim that we do—our ability to predict would be limited by many unexpected and uncontrollable factors that are likely to affect a person over a period of time. People do not behave in a social vacuum any more than they can survive in a physical one. We interact with others all the time, and so many factors are constantly operating on these other individuals that it becomes very risky indeed to predict the social environment in which a given individual can find himself or herself. Consequently, simple cause–effect statements are exceedingly difficult to construct with confidence.

As we review the theories and evidence about the causes of abnormal behavior and how to prevent or treat its occurrence, we will often

Chaos theory suggests that a major storm, such as hurricane Andrew, can be influenced by seemingly trivial events, such as air's being disturbed by a flying butterfly thousands of miles away.

encounter the complexities and shortcomings of efforts to explain and predict. Our discussions of intervention in particular should be informed by the chaos perspective. Therapists have limited contact with and control over their patients, even their hospitalized patients, all of whom live their lives moment to moment in exquisitely complex interaction with others who themselves are affected on a moment-to-moment basis by hundreds of factors that are nigh impossible to anticipate, let alone to influence. This is not an embracing of chaos as a goal—we are not scientific nihilists; rather, we want to counsel a modicum of humility, even awe, in an enterprise that would presume to try to understand the vagaries of the human condition, especially when things go awry.

theoretical concepts. If a child has had a particularly frightening experience and his or her behavior changes for a lengthy period of time, we need to explain how the earlier event exerted an influence over subsequent behavior. The unobservable and inferred concept of acquired fear has been very helpful in this regard.

Theoretical concepts can also summarize already observed relationships. We may observe that people who are taking an examination, who expect a momentary electric shock, or who are arguing with a companion all have sweaty palms, trembling hands, and a fast heartbeat. If we ask them how they feel, they all report that they are tense. These relationships can be depicted as shown in Figure 5.1a. We could also say that all the situations have made these individuals anxious and that anxiety has in turn caused the reported tension, the sweaty palms, the faster heartbeat, and the trembling hands. Figure 5.1b shows anxiety as a theoretical concept explaining what has been observed. The first figure is much more complex than the second, in which the theoretical concept of anxiety becomes a mediator of the relationships. Other things being equal, the simplest possible relationship is typically preferred in science.

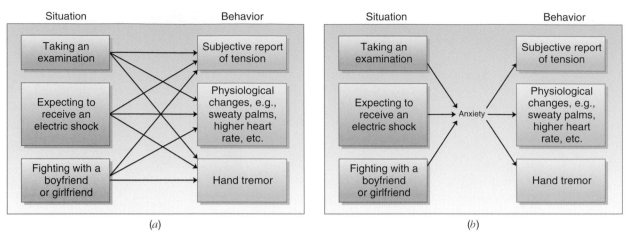

Figure 5.1 An illustration of the advantages of using anxiety as a theoretical concept. The arrows in (b) are fewer and more readily understood. After Miller (1959).

With these advantages in mind we must consider the criteria to be applied in judging the legitimacy of a theoretical concept. One earlier school of thought, operationism, proposed that each concept take as its meaning a single observable and measurable operation. In this way each theoretical concept would be nothing more than one particular measurable event. For example, anxiety might be identified as nothing more than scoring above 50 on a particular anxiety questionnaire.

It soon became clear that this approach deprived theoretical concepts of their greatest advantage. If each theoretical concept is operationalized in only one way, its generality is lost. If the theoretical concept of learning, for instance, is identified as a single operation or effect that can be measured, such as how often a rat presses a bar, other behavior, such as a child's performing arithmetic problems or a college student's studying this book, cannot also be called learning, and attempts to relate the different phenomena to one another might be discouraged.

The early operationist point of view quickly gave way to the more flexible position that a theoretical concept can be defined by *sets* of operations, or effects. In this way the concept can be linked to several different measurements, each of which taps a different facet of the concept. For example, in Figure 5.1b a subjective report of tension, physiological changes, and hand trembling form a set of operations defining anxiety. Theoretical concepts are better defined by sets of operations than by a single operation.

The Research Methods of Abnormal Psychology

All scientific research entails the collection of observable data. Sometimes research remains at a purely descriptive level. For example, there is a large descriptive literature concerning the typical symptoms of people who have been diagnosed as having particular disorders. But often researchers observe several events and try to determine how they are associated or related. For example, symptoms can be related to other characteristics, such as gender or social class. We know that eating disorders are more common in women than in men. But science demands more than descriptions of relationships. We often want to understand the *causes* of the relationships we have observed. For example, we want to know *why* eating disorders are found more often in women than in men. (Discussed more fully in Chapter 9, the answer may lie in social pressures for women to be thin.)

In this section we describe the most commonly used research methods in the study of abnormal behavior: the case study; epidemiological research; the correlational method; and various types of experiments. The methods vary in the degree to which they permit the collection of adequate descriptive data and the extent to which they allow researchers to infer causal relationships.

The Case Study

The most familiar and time-honored method of observing others is to study them one at a time and record detailed information about them. As we did in Chapter 1 with Ernest, clinicians prepare a **case study** by collecting historical and biographical information on a single individual, often including experiences in therapy. A comprehensive case study would cover family history and background, medical history, educational background, jobs held, marital history, and details concerning development, adjustment, personality, the life course, and the current situation. Important to bear in mind, though, is the role of the clinician's paradigm in determining the kinds of information actually collected and reported in a case study. To take but one example, case studies written by psychoanalytically oriented clinicians contain more information about the client's early childhood and conflicts with parents than do reports made by behaviorally oriented practitioners.

Case studies from practicing clinicians may lack the degree of control and objectivity of research using other methods, but these descriptive accounts have played an important role in the study of abnormal behavior. Specifically, the case study has been used:

1. to provide a detailed description of a rare or unusual phenomenon and of important, often novel, methods or procedures of interviewing, diagnosis, and treatment;
2. to disconfirm allegedly universal aspects of a particular theoretical proposition;
3. to generate hypotheses that can be tested through controlled research (Davison & Lazarus, 1994).

Providing Detailed Description   Because it deals with a single individual, the case study can include much more detail than is typically included with other research methods. In a famous case history of multiple personality reported in 1954, two psychiatrists, Thigpen and Cleckley, described a patient, Eve White, who assumed at various times three very distinct personalities. Their description of the case required an entire book, *The Three Faces of Eve*. The following brief summary emphasizes the moments in which new personalities emerged and what the separate selves knew of one another.

Eve White had been seen in psychotherapy for several months because she was experiencing severe headaches accompanied by blackouts. Her therapist, Dr. Thigpen, described her as a retiring and gently conventional figure. One day during the course of an interview, however, she changed abruptly and in a surprising way.

> *As if seized by sudden pain, she put both hands to her head. After a tense moment of silence, both hands dropped. There was a quick, reckless smile, and, in a bright voice that sparkled, she said, "Hi there, Doc!" The demure and constrained posture of Eve White had melted into buoyant repose.... This new and apparently carefree girl spoke casually of Eve White and her problems, always using she or her in every reference, always respecting the strict bounds of a separate identity. ...When asked her name, she immediately replied, "Oh, I'm Eve Black."* (Thigpen & Cleckley, p. 137)

After this rather startling revelation, Eve was observed over a period of fourteen months in a series of interviews that ran to almost a hundred hours. A very important part of Eve White's therapy was to help her learn about Eve Black, her other, infectiously exuberant self, who added seductive and expensive clothing to her wardrobe and lived unremembered episodes of her life. During this period a third personality, Jane, emerged while Eve White was recollecting an early incident in which she had been painfully scalded by water from a wash pot.

Jane, who from then on knew all that happened to the two Eves, although they did not know of her existence, was "far more mature, more vivid, more boldly capable, and more interesting than Eve White." Jane also developed a deep and revering affection for the first Eve, who was considered somewhat a ninny by Eve Black. Jane knew nothing of Eve White's earlier life except what she learned through Eve's memories.

Some eleven months later, in a calamitous session with all three personalities present at different times, Eve Black emerged and reminisced for a moment about the many good times she had had in the past but then remarked that she did not seem to have real fun anymore. She began to sob, the only time Dr. Thigpen had seen her in tears. She told him that she wanted him to have her red dress to remember her by. All expression left her face and her eyes closed. Eve White opened them. When Jane was summoned a few minutes later, she soon realized that there was no longer any Eve White either and began to remember a terrifying event from childhood. "No, no!...Oh no, Mother...I can't...Don't make me do it," she cried. Jane, who earlier had known nothing of Eve's childhood, was five years old and at her grandmother's funeral. Her mother was holding her high off the floor and above the coffin and saying that she must touch her grandmother's face. As she felt her hand leave the clammy cheek, the young woman screamed so piercingly that Dr. Cleckley, Dr. Thigpen's associate, came running from his office across the hall.

The two physicians were not certain who confronted them. In the searing intensity of the remembered moment a new personality had been welded. Their transformed patient did not at first feel herself as apart, and as sharply distinct a person, as had the two Eves and Jane, although she knew a great deal about all of them. When her initial bewilderment lessened, she tended to identify herself with Jane. But the identification was not sure or complete, and she mourned the absence of the two Eves as though they were lost sisters. This new person decided to call herself Mrs. Evelyn White.

The case of Eve White, Eve Black, Jane, and eventually Evelyn constitutes a valuable classic in the literature because it is one of only a few detailed accounts of a rare phenomenon, multiple personality, now known as dissociative identity disorder. This intriguing and controversial topic is discussed in Chapter 7. In addition to illustrating the phenomenon itself, the original report of Thigpen and Cleckley provides valuable details about the interview procedures they followed and how the treatment progressed in this one case of multiple personality.

Chris Sizemore was the subject of the famous "three faces of Eve" case. She subsequently claimed to have had twenty-one separate personalities.

However, the validity of the information gathered in a case study is sometimes questionable. Indeed, the real Eve, a woman named Chris Sizemore, wrote a book that challenged Thigpen and Cleckley's account of her case (Sizemore & Pittillo, 1977). She claimed that following her period of therapy with them, her personality continued to fragment. In all, twenty-one separate and distinct strangers inhabited her body at one time or another. And, contrary to Thigpen and Cleckley's report, Sizemore maintains that nine of the personalities existed before Eve Black ever appeared. One set of personalities—they usually came in threes—would weaken and fade, to be replaced by others. Eventually her personality changes were so constant and numerous that she might become her three persons in rapid switches resembling the flipping of television channels. The debilitating round-robin of transformations and the fierce battle for dominance among her selves filled her entire life. After resolving what she hoped was her last trio, by realizing finally that her alternate personalities were true aspects of herself rather than strangers from without, Chris Sizemore decided to reveal her story as a means of dealing with the ordeals of her past.

The Case Study as Evidence   Case histories can provide especially telling instances that negate an assumed universal relationship or law. Consider, for example, the proposition that episodes of depression are always preceded by an increase in life stress. Finding even a single case in which this is not true would negate the theory or at least force it to be changed to assert that only *some* episodes of depression are triggered by stress.

The case study fares less well in providing evidence *in favor of* a particular theory or proposition. Case studies do not provide the means for ruling out alternative hypotheses. To illustrate this problem, let us consider a clinician who has developed a new treatment for depression, tries it out on a client, and observes that the depression lifts after ten weeks of the therapy. Although it would be tempting to conclude that the therapy worked, such a conclusion cannot legitimately be drawn because any of several other factors could have produced the change. A stressful situation in the patient's life may have resolved itself, or perhaps episodes of depression are naturally time limited (and most are). Thus several plausible rival hypotheses could account for the clinical improvement. The data yielded by the case study do not allow us to determine the true cause of the change.

Generating Hypotheses   Although the case study may not play much of a role in confirming hypotheses, it does play a unique and important role in generating them.

Through exposure to the life histories of a great number of patients, clinicians gain experience in understanding and interpreting them. Eventually they may notice similarities of circumstances and outcomes and formulate important hypotheses that could not have been uncovered in a more controlled investigation. For example, in his clinical work with disturbed children Kanner (1943) noticed that some showed a similar constellation of symptoms, including failure to develop language and extreme isolation from other people. He therefore proposed a new diagnosis—infantile autism—which was subsequently confirmed by larger-scale research and eventually found its way into the DSM (see Chapter 15).

To sum up, the case study is an excellent way of examining the behavior of a single individual in great detail and of generating hypotheses that can later be evaluated by controlled research.[1] It is useful in clinical settings, where the focus is on just one person. Some investigators in the fields of clinical and personality psychology argue that the essence of psychological studies is the unique characteristics of an individual (e.g., Allport, 1961). The case history is an ideal method of study in such an individualistic context. But when general, universal laws are sought to explain phenomena, the case study is of limited use. Information collected on a single person may not reveal principles characteristic of people in general. Furthermore, the case study is unable to provide satisfactory evidence concerning cause–effect relationships.

Although the information yielded by a case study does not fare well as a source of evidence, it is an important source of hypotheses.

Epidemiological Research

Epidemiology is the study of the frequency and distribution of a disorder in a population. In epidemiological research, data are gathered about the rates of a disorder and its possible correlates in a large sample or population. This information can then be used to give a general picture of a disorder, how many people it affects, whether it is more common in men than in women, and whether its occurrence varies according to social and cultural factors.

Epidemiological research focuses on determining three features of a disorder:

1. Prevalence—the proportion of a population that has the disorder at a given point or period in time
2. Incidence—the number of new cases of the disorder that occur in some period, usually a year
3. Risk factors—conditions or variables that, if present, increase the likelihood of developing the disorder

Knowing the prevalence rates of various mental disorders is important for many reasons, including planning health care facilities and allocating money for the study of disorders. A significant, large-scale, national survey used structured interviews to collect information on the prevalence of several diagnoses (Kessler et al., 1994). Some data from this study are displayed in Table 5.1. The table presents what are called **lifetime prevalence rates**, the proportion of the sample that had ever experienced a disorder up to the time of the interview. From the table we can see that major depression and alcoholism have much higher lifetime prevalences than do manic episodes or panic disorder. We will be using the Kessler data throughout this book.

Knowledge about risk factors may give clues to the causes of the disorder being studied. For example, depression is about twice as common in women as in men. Thus, gender is a risk factor for depression. In Chapter 10, we will see that knowledge

Table 5.1 Lifetime Prevalence Rates of Selected Diagnoses (%)

	Male	Female	Total
Major depressive episode	12.7	21.3	17.1
Manic episode	1.6	1.7	1.6
Dysthymia	4.8	8.0	6.4
Panic disorder	2.0	5.0	3.5
Agoraphobia without panic	3.5	7.0	5.3
Social phobia	11.1	15.5	13.3
Simple phobia	6.7	15.7	11.3
Generalized anxiety disorder	3.6	6.6	5.1
Alcohol dependence	20.1	8.2	14.1
Antisocial personality disorder	5.8	1.2	3.5

Source: From data collected in the National Comorbidity Survey (Kessler et al., 1994).

---

[1] Groups, both large and small, can also be the focus of case studies.

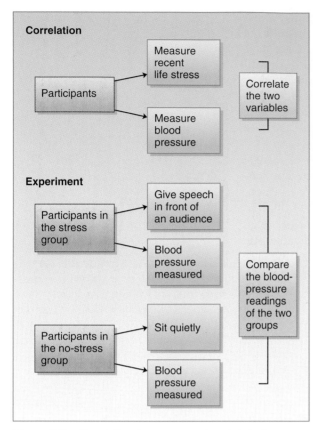

Correlation

Participants → Measure recent life stress

Participants → Measure blood pressure

Correlate the two variables

Experiment

Participants in the stress group → Give speech in front of an audience → Blood pressure measured

Participants in the no-stress group → Sit quietly → Blood pressure measured

Compare the blood-pressure readings of the two groups

Figure 5.2 Correlational versus experimental studies.

Table 5.2 Data for Determining a Correlation

Individuals	Height	Weight (pounds)
John	5'10"	170
Asher	5'10"	140
Eve	5'4"	112
Gail	5'3"	105
Jerry	5'10"	177
Gayla	5'2"	100
Steve	5'8"	145
Margy	5'5"	128
Gert	5'6"	143
Sean	5'10"	140
Kathleen	5'4"	116

Note: For these figures r = + .88

of this risk factor has led to a theory of depression that suggests that it is due to a particular style of coping with stress that is more common in women than in men. The results of epidemiological research may thus provide hypotheses that can be more thoroughly investigated using other research methods.

The Correlational Method

A great deal of research in psychopathology relies on the **correlational method**, which establishes whether there is a relationship between or among two or more variables. The correlational method is often employed in epidemiological research as well as in other studies that use smaller samples.

In correlational research the variables being studied are measured as they exist in nature. This feature distinguishes the method from experimental research (discussed in detail on pp. 121–129), in which variables are actually manipulated and controlled by the researcher.

To illustrate this difference, consider that the possible role of stress in a disorder such as hypertension can be addressed with either a correlational or an experimental design. In a correlational study, we might measure stress levels by having people fill out a questionnaire or interviewing them about their recent stressful experiences. Stress would then be correlated with blood-pressure measurements collected from these same people. In an experimental study, in contrast, the experimenter would create or manipulate stress in the laboratory; for example, while their blood pressure was being monitored, some participants might be asked to give a speech to an audience about the aspect of their personal appearance they find least appealing (see Figure 5.2).

Numerous examples of correlation can be drawn from everyday life. Education correlates with income; the greater the educational level attained, the greater the earning power. Height tends to be positively correlated with weight; taller people are usually heavier.

Correlational studies, then, address questions of the form "Are variable X and variable Y associated in some way so that they vary together (co-relate)?" In other words, questions are asked concerning relationships; for example, "Is schizophrenia related to social class?" or "Are scores obtained on college examinations related to anxiety about taking tests?"

Measuring Correlation The first step in determining a correlation is to obtain pairs of observations of the variables in question, such as height and weight, on each member of a group of participants (Table 5.2). Once such pairs of measurements are obtained, the strength of the relationship between the two sets of observations can be computed to determine the **correlation coefficient**, denoted by the symbol r. This statistic may take any value between −1.00 and +1.00 and measures both the magnitude and the direction of a relationship. The higher the absolute value of r, the larger or stronger the relationship between the two variables. An r of either +1.00 or −1.00 indicates the highest possible, or perfect, relationship, whereas an r of .00 indicates that the variables are unrelated. If the sign of r is positive, the two variables are said to be positively related; in other words, as the values for variable X increase, those for variable Y also tend to increase. The correlation between height and weight, based on the data in Table 5.2, is +.88, indicating a very strong positive relationship; as height increases, so does weight. Conversely, when the sign of r is negative, variables are said to be negatively related; as scores on one variable increase, those for the other tend to decrease. For example, the number of hours spent watching television is negatively correlated with grade point average.

Plotting a relationship graphically often helps make it clearer. Figure 5.3 presents what are called scatter diagrams of positive and negative correlations as well as unrelated variables. In the diagrams, each point corresponds to two values determined for a given person, the value of variable X and that of variable Y. In perfect relationships all the points fall on a straight line; if we know the value of only one of the variables for an individual, we can state with certainty the value of the other variable. Similarly, when the correlation is relatively large, there is only a small degree of scatter about the line of perfect correlation. The values tend to scatter increasingly and become dispersed as the correlations become lower. When the correlation reaches .00, knowledge of a person's score on one variable tells us nothing about his or her score on the other.

Statistical Significance Thus far we have established that the magnitude of a correlation coefficient tells us the strength of a relationship between two variables. But scientists demand a more rigorous evaluation of the importance of correlations and use the concept of **statistical significance** for this purpose. A statistically significant correlation is one that is not likely to have occurred by chance and that scientists will therefore take seriously.

Traditionally in psychological research a correlation is considered statistically significant if the likelihood or probability that it is a chance finding is 5 or less in 100. This level of significance is called the .05 level, commonly written as $p \leq .05$ (the p stands for probability). In general, as the size of the correlation coefficient increases, the result is more and more likely to be statistically significant. For example, a correlation of .80 is more likely than a correlation of .40 to be significant. Whether a correlation attains statistical significance also depends on the number of observations made. The greater the number of observations, the smaller r (the correlation) needs to be in order to reach statistical significance. For example, a correlation of $r = .30$ is statistically significant when the number of observations is large—say, 300—but is not significant if only 20 observations were made. Thus, if the alcohol consumption of 10 depressed and 10 nondepressed

In some epidemiological research, interviewers go to homes in a community, conducting interviews to determine the rate of different disorders..

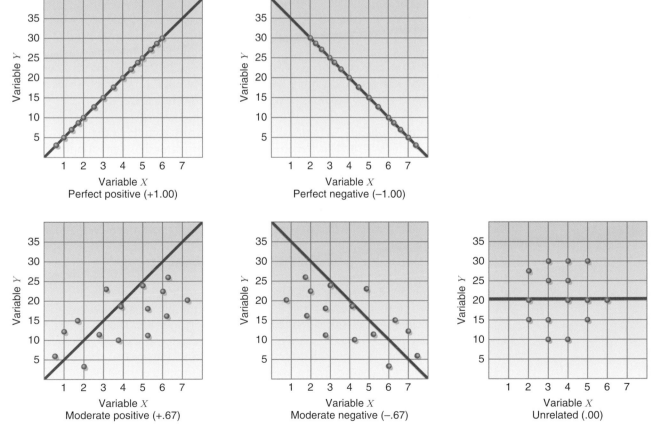

Figure 5.3 Scatter diagrams showing various degrees of correlational relationship.

Table 5.3 Data for a Correlational Study

Participant Number	Diagnosis	Stress Score
1	1	65
2	1	72
3	2	40
4	1	86
5	2	72
6	2	21
7	1	65
8	2	40
9	1	37
10	2	28

Note: Diagnosis—having an anxiety disorder or not, with having an anxiety disorder designated as 1 and not as 2—is correlated with an assessment of recent life stress on a 0–100 scale. Higher scores indicate greater recent stress. As in previous examples, to make the point clearly, we present a smaller sample of cases than would be used in an actual research study. Notice that diagnosis is associated with recent life stress. Patients with an anxiety disorder tend to have higher stress scores than people without an anxiety disorder.

men was studied and the correlation between depression and drinking was found to be .32, the correlation would not be statistically significant. However, the same correlation would be significant if two groups of 150 men were studied.

Applications to Psychopathology The correlational method is widely used in the field of abnormal psychology. Whenever we compare people given one diagnosis with those given another or with normal people, the study is correlational. For example, two diagnostic groups may be compared to see how much stress members of each experienced before the onset of their disorders. Or people with and people without an anxiety disorder may be compared on their physiological reactivity to a stressor administered in the laboratory.

When the correlational method is used in research on psychopathology, one of the variables is typically diagnosis, for example, having an anxiety disorder or not. To calculate a correlation between this variable and another one, diagnosis is quantified so that, for example, having an anxiety disorder is designated by a score of 1 and not having a disorder by 2. (Which numbers are actually used is arbitrary.) The diagnosis variable can then be correlated with another variable, such as the amount of stress that has been recently experienced. An illustration of the data from such a hypothetical study is presented in Table 5.3.

Often such investigations are not recognized as correlational, perhaps because participants sometimes come to a laboratory for testing. But the logic of such studies is correlational; the correlation between two variables—having an anxiety disorder or not and scores on the measure of stress—is what is being examined. Variables such as having an anxiety disorder or not are called **classificatory variables**. The anxiety disorders were already present and were simply measured by the researcher. Other examples of classificatory variables are age, sex, social class, and body build. These variables are naturally occurring patterns and are not manipulated by the researcher, an important requirement for the experimental method discussed later. Thus, most research on the causes of psychopathology is correlational.

Problems of Causality The correlational method, although often employed in abnormal psychology, has a critical drawback: It does not allow determination of cause–effect relationships. A sizable correlation between two variables tells us only that they are related or tend to co-vary with each other, but we do not really know which is cause and which is effect or if either variable is actually the cause of the other.

The Directionality Problem When two variables are correlated, how can we tell which is the cause and which is the effect? For example, a correlation has been found between the diagnosis of schizophrenia and social class; lower-class people are more frequently diagnosed as having schizophrenia than are middle- and upper-class people. One possible explanation is that the stresses of living in the lowest social class cause an increase in the prevalence of schizophrenia. But a second and perhaps equally plausible hypothesis has been advanced. It may be that the disorganized behavior patterns of individuals with schizophrenia cause them to perform poorly in their educational and occupational endeavors and thus to become impoverished. The **directionality problem**, as it is sometimes called, is present in most correlational research designs—hence the often-cited dictum "Correlation does not imply causation."

Although correlation does not imply causation, determining whether two variables correlate may allow for the disconfirmation of certain causal hypotheses. That is, causation *does* imply correlation. For example, if an investigator has asserted that cigarette smoking causes lung cancer, he or she implies that lung cancer and smoking are correlated. Studies of these two variables must show this positive correlation or the theory will be disconfirmed.

One way of overcoming the directionality problem is based on the idea that causes must precede effects. According to this idea, studies investigating the hypothesized causes of psychopathology could use a longitudinal design in which the hypothesized causes are studied before a disorder has developed. In this way the hypothesized cause could be measured before the effect. The most desirable way of collecting information about the development of schizophrenia, for example, would be to select a large sample of babies and follow them for the twenty to forty-five years that are the period of risk for the onset of schizophrenia. But such a method would be prohibitively expensive, for only about one individual in a hundred eventually develops schizophrenia. The yield of data from such a simple longitudinal study would be small indeed.

The **high-risk method** overcomes this problem; with this approach, only individuals with greater than average risk of developing schizophrenia in adulthood would be selected for study. Most current research using this methodology studies individuals who have a parent diagnosed with schizophrenia (having a parent with schizophrenia increases a person's risk for developing schizophrenia). The high-risk method is also used to study several other disorders, and we will examine these findings in subsequent chapters.

The Third-Variable Problem Another drawback to interpreting correlational findings is called the **third-variable problem**; the correlation may have been produced by a third, unforeseen factor. Consider the following example, which points out an obvious third variable.

> *One regularly finds a high positive correlation between the number of churches in a city and the number of crimes committed in that city. That is, the more churches a city has, the more crimes are committed in it. Does this mean that religion fosters crime, or does it mean that crime fosters religion? It means neither. The relationship is due to a particular third variable—population. The higher the population of a particular community, the greater...the number of churches and...the frequency of criminal activity. (Neale & Liebert, 1980, p. 109)*

Psychopathology research offers numerous examples of third variables. Biochemical differences between patients with schizophrenia and normal people have frequently been reported. These differences could reflect different diets or the fact that the patients are taking medication for their condition; the differences do not reveal anything telling about the nature of schizophrenia. Are there any solutions to the third-variable problem? In general, the answer is yes, although the solutions are only partially satisfactory and do not permit unambiguous causal inferences to be made from correlational data.

We have already noted that facts about the causes of abnormal behavior are hard to come by. The issues we have just discussed are major reasons for this state of affairs. The psychopathologist is forced to make heavy use of the correlational method because diagnosis, a classificatory variable, is best suited to this strategy. But the relationships discovered between diagnosis and other variables are then clouded by the third-variable and directionality problems.

The Experiment

The search for factors causing the associations and relationships revealed by correlational research takes us to experimental methods. The **experiment** is generally considered the most powerful tool for determining causal relationships between events. It involves the random assignment of participants to the different conditions being investigated, the manipulation of an independent variable, and the measurement of a dependent variable. In the field of psychopathology the experiment is most often used to evaluate the effects of therapies.

As an introduction to the basic components of experimental research, let us consider here the major aspects of the design and results of a study of how expressing emotions about past traumatic events is related to health (Pennebaker, Kiecolt-Glaser, & Glaser, 1988). In this experiment, fifty undergraduates participated in a six-week study, one part of which required them to come to a laboratory for four consecutive days. On each of the four days, half the students wrote a short essay about a past traumatic event. They were instructed as follows:

> *During each of the four writing days, I want you to write about the most traumatic and upsetting experiences of your entire life. You can write on different topics each day or on the same*

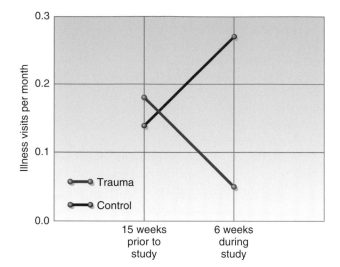

Figure 5.4 Health-center illness visits for the periods before and during the experiment. Visits for students who wrote about past traumas went down while visits for those who wrote about mundane events actually rose. After Pennebaker et al. (1987).

topic for all four days. The important thing is that you write about your deepest thoughts and feelings. Ideally, whatever you write about should deal with an event or experience that you have not talked with others about in detail.

The remaining students also came to the laboratory each day but wrote essays describing such things as their daily activities, a recent social event, the shoes they were wearing, and their plans for the rest of the day.

Information about how often the participating undergraduates used the university health center was available for the fifteen-week period before the study began and for the six weeks after it had begun. These data are shown in Figure 5.4. Members of the two groups had visited the health center about equally prior to the experiment. After writing the essays, however, the number of visits declined for students who wrote about traumas and increased for the remaining students. (This increase may have been due to seasonal variation in rates of visits to the health center. The second measure of number of visits was taken in February, just before midterm exams.) From these data the investigators concluded that expressing emotions has a beneficial effect on health.

Basic Features of Experimental Design   The foregoing example illustrates many of the basic features of an experiment.

1. The researcher typically begins with an **experimental hypothesis**, what he or she assumes will happen when a particular variable is manipulated. Pennebaker and his colleagues hypothesized that expressing emotion about a past upsetting event would improve health.
2. The investigator chooses an **independent variable** that can be manipulated, that is, some factor that will be under the control of the experimenter. In the case of the Pennebaker study, some students wrote about past traumatic events and others about mundane happenings.
3. Participants are assigned to the two conditions by **random assignment** so that each participant has an equal chance of being in each condition.
4. The researcher arranges for the measurement of a **dependent variable**, which is expected to depend on or vary with manipulations of the independent variable. The dependent variable in this study was the number of visits to the health center.
5. When differences between groups are found, the researcher is said to have produced an **experimental effect**.

To evaluate the importance of an experimental effect, as with correlations, researchers determine statistical significance. To illustrate, consider a hypothetical study of the effectiveness of cognitive therapy in reducing depression among twenty depressed patients. (In the realm of actual research, twenty patients would be regarded as a very small sample; we present a small number of cases so the example is easier to follow.) The independent variable is cognitive therapy versus no treatment; ten patients are randomly assigned to receive cognitive therapy and ten are randomly assigned to a no treatment control group. The dependent variable is scores on a standardized measure of the severity of depression, assessed after twelve weeks of treatment or no treatment; higher scores reflect more severe depression.

Data for each of the hypothetical patients in each group are presented in Table 5.4. Note that the average scores of the two groups differ considerably (8.3 for the cognitive-therapy group and 21.7 for the no-treatment group). This difference between groups, also called between-group variance, is the experimental effect; it has been caused by the independent variable. Note also from the table that the scores of individual participants within each group vary considerably; this is called within-group variance. For example, within the cognitive-therapy group, most participants have low scores, but participant number 7 has a high score (18). Cognitive therapy did not seem to be of much help to this individual, but we don't know why. (This issue of treated patients doing less well than controls will be discussed in Chapter 17 when we analyze research in psychotherapy.) Similarly, most people in the no-treatment group have high scores, but participant number 17 has a low score (6). The cause of this within-group variability is unknown.

Statistical significance is tested by dividing the between-group variance (the difference between the average scores of the two groups—in this example 21.7 − 8.3 = 13.4) by a measure of the within-group variance. When the average difference *between* the two groups is large relative to the within-group variance, the result is more likely to be statistically significant. From a statistical analysis of the results of this hypothetical experiment, we would conclude that cognitive therapy decreases depression more than does no treatment at all.

Table 5.4 Results of a Hypothetical Study Comparing Cognitive Therapy to No Treatment for Depression

	Cognitive Therapy		No Treatment
Participant 1	8	Participant 11	22
Participant 2	6	Participant 12	14
Participant 3	12	Participant 13	26
Participant 4	4	Participant 14	28
Participant 5	3	Participant 15	19
Participant 6	6	Participant 16	27
Participant 7	18	Participant 17	6
Participant 8	14	Participant 18	32
Participant 9	7	Participant 19	21
Participant 10	5	Participant 20	23
Group Average	8.3		21.7

Note: Scores for each participant after treatment are shown. Low scores indicate less depression following treatment.

Internal Validity   An important feature of any experimental design is the inclusion of at least one **control group** that does not receive the experimental treatment (the independent variable). A control group is necessary if the effects in an experiment are to be attributed to the manipulation of the independent variable. In the Pennebaker study, the control group wrote about mundane happenings. In the cognitive-therapy example, the control group received no treatment. The data from a control group provide a standard against which the effects of an independent variable can be assessed.

To illustrate this point with another example, consider a study of the effectiveness of a particular therapy in reducing anxiety. Let us assume that persons with high anxiety undergo therapy to remedy their condition. Note that there is no control group in this hypothetical study, so it is not an experiment. At the end of six months the patients are reassessed, and it is found that their anxiety has lessened compared with what it was at the beginning of the study.

Unfortunately, because there is no control group against which to compare the improvement, no valid conclusions can be drawn from such an investigation. The improvement in anxiety from the beginning of the treatment to the end could have been brought about by several factors in addition to or instead of the treatment employed. For example, environmental events, such as the resolution of a difficult financial situation occurring within the six months, could have produced the improvement. Or it may be that people with high anxiety come to feel less tense with just the passage of time.

Variables such as a change in one's life situation or the passage of time are often called **confounds**. Their effects are intermixed with those of the independent variable, and like the third variables in correlational studies, they make the results difficult or impossible to interpret. These confounds and others described in this chapter are widespread in research on the effects of psychotherapy, as is documented often throughout this book. Studies in which the effect obtained cannot be attributed with confidence to the independent variable are called internally invalid studies. In contrast, research has **internal validity** when the effect can be confidently attributed to the manipulation of the independent variable.

In the example just outlined, internal validity could be improved by the inclusion of a control group. Such a group might consist of individuals with high levels of anxiety who do not receive the therapeutic treatment. Changes in anxiety of these control participants would constitute a standard against which the effects of the independent variable could be assessed. If a change in anxiety is brought about by particular environmental events, quite beyond any therapeutic intervention, the experimental group receiving the treatment and the control group receiving no treatment are equally likely to be affected. On the other hand, if after six months the anxiety level of the treated group has lessened more than that of the untreated control group, we can be relatively confident that this difference is attributable to the treatment.

The inclusion of a control group does not always ensure internal validity, however. Consider yet another study of therapy, the treatment of two hospital wards of psychiatric patients. An investigator may decide to select one ward to receive an experimental treatment and another ward as a control. When the researcher later compares the frequencies of deviant behavior in these two groups, he or she will want to attribute any differences between them to the fact that patients in one ward received treatment and those in the other did not. But the researcher cannot legitimately draw this inference, for there is a competing hypothesis that cannot be disproved.

Even before treatment, the patients who happened to receive therapy might have had a lower level of deviant behavior than the patients who became the control group. The principle of experimental design disregarded in this defective study is that of random assignment. To randomly assign participants in a two-group experiment the researchers could, for example, toss a coin for each participant. If the coin turned up heads, the participant would be assigned to one group; if tails to the other group. This procedure minimizes the likelihood that differences between the groups after treatment will reflect pretreatment differences in the samples rather than true experimental effects.

Furthermore, using a control group and random assignment handles the type of confounds we described in our earlier example of treatment for high anxiety. When groups are formed by random assignment, confounds such as the resolution of a stressful life situation are equally likely to occur in both the treated group and the control group. There is no reason to believe that life stress would be resolved more often in one group than the other. Random assignment was employed in the Pennebaker experiment described earlier.

The Placebo Effect   Experimental research on the effects of therapy—psychological or biological—should include a consideration of the **placebo effect**. This term refers to an improvement in physical or psychological condition that is attributable to a patient's expectations of help rather than to any specific active ingredient in a treatment.[2] J. D. Frank (1978) related placebo effects to faith healing in prescientific or nonscientific societies. For centuries, suffering human beings have made pilgrimages to sanctified places and ingested sometimes foul-smelling concoctions in the belief that these efforts would improve their condition. Sometimes they did.

---

[2] When patients improve in a therapy study, the improvement can result from the operation of three sets of variables: (1) the specific effects of the treatment; (2) the placebo effect; (3) such factors as an illness running its course, changes in the patient's life, or *regression to the mean*. Regression to the mean refers to the fact that extreme symptoms, such as those patients typically report when they seek treatment, tend to return toward an average level when they are later reassessed. Thus, when patients improve following the administration of a treatment that has no specific value, some of the improvement may result from the placebo effect, but the improvement can also result from the operation of other factors.

Many people dismiss placebo reactions as not real or as second-best to benefits of actual treatments. After all, if a person has a tension headache, what possible benefit can he or she hope to get from a pill that is totally devoid of chemical action or direct physiological effect? The fact is, however, that the effects of placebos are sometimes significant and even long lasting (e.g., Walsh et al., 2002). Furthermore, placebo effects may be the cause of a common finding in treatment research: When a new treatment is first introduced, its effects are more favorable than those that emerge a number of years later. The initial enthusiasm for a treatment may increase its placebo value. The placebo effect is commonly found and universally accepted in drug research. For example, it has been estimated that among depressed patients who respond favorably to antidepressant medication, many are actually showing a placebo response (Kirsch, 2000; Stewart et al., 1998).

The effects of pilgrimages to shrines, such as Fatima, may be placebo effects.

It is not a simple matter, however, to extend the findings of research on chemical placebos directly to research on psychological placebos. In psychotherapy the mere expectation of being helped can be an active ingredient. Why? If the theory adopted by the therapist holds that positive expectancy of improvement is an active ingredient, then improvement arising from the expectancy would by definition not be considered a placebo effect. Lambert, Shapiro, and Bergin (1986) argued that "placebo factors" should be replaced with the concept of "common factors" in the study of the effects of psychotherapy. They defined common factors as

> those dimensions of the treatment setting...that are not specific to a particular technique. Those factors that are common to most therapies (such as expectation for improvement, persuasion, warmth and attention, understanding, encouragement, etc.) should not be viewed as theoretically inert nor as trivial; they are central to psychological treatments and play an active role in patient improvement. (p. 163)

Because of the importance of the placebo effect, research on the effects of psychotherapy often uses what are called **placebo control groups** instead of no-treatment control groups. Patients in such groups typically have regular contact with a therapist and receive support and encouragement, but they do not receive what is regarded as the active ingredient in the kind of therapy under study (for example, gradual exposure to a feared situation in a behavioral treatment of a phobia).

When the placebo control group design is used, patients are randomly assigned to either the treatment or the placebo group; to reduce the possibility of bias, neither the researchers nor the patients are allowed to know to which group any specific individual is assigned. Because neither the researchers nor the patients are aware of who has been placed in the treatment and placebo control groups, the design is referred to as a **double-blind procedure**.

Research on psychotherapy reveals that patients in placebo control groups generally improve more than patients in no-treatment groups—though often not as much as patients in treatment groups (Lambert et al., 1986). Most psychotherapies, because they offer support and encouragement, may share a common factor that contributes to improvement. The issue of common factors is important in the movement toward psychotherapy integration, a topic examined in Chapter 17.

The place of placebo control groups in psychotherapy research is an often-debated and complex topic. A study that compares a particular therapy to no treatment at all and finds that therapy brings about more improvement does suggest that being treated is better than receiving no treatment. This is not a trivial finding. But a given therapy usually tries to create improvement in a particular way—by removing the person's defenses, by facilitating the individual's way to self-actualization, by enhancing responsible choices, by extinguishing fears, and so forth. To determine whether these processes are at work and are effective, a study needs a control group of patients who are instilled with expectancies of help, who believe that something worthwhile and beneficial is being done for them.

But using a placebo control group involves several problems. First, it raises ethical issues, for effective treatment is being withheld from some patients as it is with a no-treatment control group. Second, a double-blind placebo control group study can be difficult to implement. For example, medications used in treating psychopathology typically produce side effects that are not produced by placebos. Therefore, both researchers and patients may come to know who is getting the active treatment and who is getting the placebo (Salamone, 2000). Finally, informed consent is an issue. Potential participants in research must be informed about the details of the study in which they are being asked to participate (see p. 639). In a placebo control group study, participants must be told that they have some chance of being assigned to the placebo condition. What does this knowledge do to the possibility of experiencing a placebo effect?

Problems such as these have led some researchers to suggest that placebo and no-treatment control groups be abandoned (e.g., Rothman & Michels, 1994). Instead of comparing a group receiving a new treatment with a placebo control group, the experimental group could be compared with a group receiving the currently accepted standard treatment in the field. This approach is being increasingly used in psychotherapy research, as will be seen throughout this book.

External Validity The extent to which the results of any particular piece of research can be generalized beyond the immediate experiment is the measure of **external validity**. If investigators have demonstrated that a particular treatment helps a particular group of patients, they will undoubtedly want to conclude that this treatment will be effective in ministering to other similar patients, at other times, and in other places. For example, Pennebaker and his colleagues would hope that their findings would generalize to other instances of emotional expression (e.g., confiding to a close friend), to other situations, and to people other than those who actually participated in the experiment.

Determining the external validity or generalizability of the results of a psychological experiment is extremely difficult. For example, merely knowing that one is a participant in a psychological experiment often alters behavior, and thus results that are produced in the laboratory may not automatically be produced in the natural environment. Furthermore, in many instances results obtained from investigations with laboratory animals, such as rats, have been generalized to human beings (see the following discussion of analogues). Such generalizations are risky indeed, since there are enormous differences between *Homo sapiens* and *Rattus norvegicus*. Researchers must be alert to the extent to which they claim generalization for findings, for there is no entirely adequate way of dealing with the questions of external validity. The best that can be done is to perform similar studies in new settings with new participants so that the limitations, or the generality, of a finding can be determined. This issue will be revisited in Chapter 17.

Analogue Experiments The experimental method is judged to be the most telling way to determine cause–effect relationships. The efficacy of treatments for psychopathology is usually evaluated by the experimental method, which has proved a powerful tool for determining whether a therapy reduces suffering. As mentioned earlier, however, this method has been little used by those seeking the causes of abnormal behavior. Why?

Suppose that a researcher has hypothesized that a child's emotionally charged, overdependent relationship with his or her mother causes generalized anxiety disorder. An experimental test of this hypothesis would require assigning infants randomly to either of two groups of mothers! The mothers in one group would undergo an extensive training program to ensure that they would be able to create a highly emotional atmosphere and foster overdependence in children. The mothers in the second group would be trained not to create such a relationship with the children under their care. The researcher would then wait until the participants in each group reached adulthood and determine how many of them had developed generalized anxiety disorder.

Obviously such an experimental design contains insurmountable practical problems. But practical issues are hardly the principal ones that must concern us. Consider the ethics of such an experiment. Would the potential scientific gain of proving that an overdependent relationship with a person's mother brings on generalized anxiety disorder outweigh the suffering that would surely be imposed on some of the participants? In almost any person's view, it would not. (Ethical issues are considered in detail in Chapter 18.)

In an effort to take advantage of the power of the experimental method, research on the causes of abnormal behavior has sometimes taken the format of an **analogue experiment**. Investigators attempt to bring a related phenomenon, that is, an analogue, into the laboratory for more intensive study. Because a true experiment is now being conducted, results with good internal validity can be obtained. However, the problem of external validity may be accentuated because the actual phenomenon in which the researchers are interested is not being studied.

In one type of analogue study, behavior is rendered temporarily abnormal through experimental manipulations. For example, lactate infusion can elicit a panic attack, hypnotic suggestion can produce blindness similar to that seen in conversion disorder, and threats to self-esteem can make research participants anxious or sad. If experience similar or even identical to psychopathology can be experimentally induced by any one of these manipulations, the same process existing in the natural environment might well be a cause of the disorder one is interested in studying.

The key to interpreting such studies lies in the validity of the independent variable as a reflection of some experience one might actually have in real life and of the dependent variable as an analogue of a clinical problem. Is a stressor encountered in the laboratory fundamentally similar to one that occurs in the natural environment? Are transient increases in anxiety or depression reasonable analogues of their clinical counterparts? Results of such experiments must be interpreted with great caution and generalized with care, although they can provide valuable information about the origins of psychopathology.

In another type of analogue study, participants are selected because they are considered similar to patients who have certain diagnoses. A large amount of research, for example, has been conducted with college students selected for study because they scored high on a questionnaire measure of anxiety or depression. The question is whether these somewhat anxious or depressed students, who do not have a clinical disorder, are adequate analogues for those with an anxiety disorder or major depression. Some research bearing on this issue is discussed in Chapter 10.

Whether an experiment is regarded as an analogue depends not on the experiment itself, but on the use to which it is put. We can very readily study avoidance behavior in a white rat. The data collected from such studies are not analogue data if we limit our discussion to the behavior of rats. They become analogue data only when we draw implications from them and apply them to other domains, such as anxiety in human beings.

Some of the animal experiments we have already examined are analogue in nature. For example, in Chapter 2 we described research on avoidance learning in rats that was very influential in formulating theories of anxiety in humans. It is important to keep in mind that we are arguing by analogy when we attempt to relate fear reactions of white rats to anxiety in people. At the same time, however, we do not agree with those who regard such analogue research as totally and intrinsically worthless for the study of human behavior. Although human beings and other mammals differ on many important dimensions, it does not follow that principles of behavior derived from animal research are necessarily irrelevant to human behavior.

Harlow's famous analogue research examined the effects of early separation from the mother on infant monkeys. Even a cloth surrogate mother is better than isolation for preventing subsequent emotional distress and depression.

Single-Subject Experimental Research

We have been discussing experimental research as it is conducted on groups of participants, but experiments do not always have to be conducted on groups. In **single-subject experimental designs** *a few* participants are studied one at a time and experience a manipulated variable. The data from the small group of participants are typically presented individually for each person.

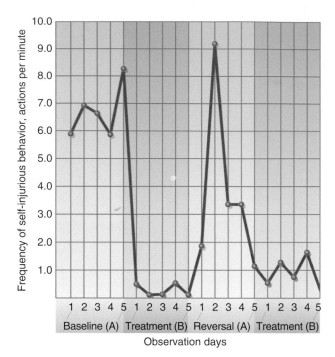

Figure 5.5 Effects of a treatment for self-injurious behavior in an experiment with an ABAB single-subject design. Note the rapid shifts in frequency of problem behavior as treatment is introduced (B), withdrawn (A), and finally reinstated (B). Adapted from Tate and Baroff (1966).

The strategy of relying on a single person appears to violate many of the principles of research design that we have discussed. As with the case study, there is no control group to act as a check on a single subject. Moreover, generalization is difficult because the findings may relate to a unique aspect of the one individual whose behavior has been explored. Hence the study of a single individual would appear unlikely to yield any findings that could possess the slightest degree of internal or external validity. Nevertheless, the experimental study of a single subject can be an effective research technique for certain purposes (Hersen & Barlow, 1976).

A method developed by Tate and Baroff (1966) for reducing the self-injurious behavior of a nine-year-old boy, Sam, serves as an example. The child engaged in a wide range of self-injurious behavior, such as banging his head against the floors and walls, slapping his face with his hands, and kicking himself. Despite his self-injurious behavior, Sam was not entirely antisocial. In fact, he obviously enjoyed contact with other people and would cling to them, wrap his arms around them, and sit on their laps. This affectionate behavior gave the investigators the idea for an experimental treatment.[3]

The study ran for twenty days. For a period of time on each of the first five days, the frequency of Sam's self-injurious actions was observed and recorded. Then, on each of the next five days, the two adult experimenters accompanied Sam on a short walk around the campus, during which they talked to him and held his hands continuously. The adults responded to each of Sam's self-injurious actions by immediately jerking their hands away from him and not touching him again until three seconds after such activity had ceased. The frequency of the self-injurious acts was again recorded. During the next part of the experiment, the experimenters reverted to the procedures of the first five days; there were no walks, and Sam's self-afflicting behavior was again merely observed. Then for the last five days the experimenters reinstated their experimental procedure. The dramatic changes in undesirable behavior induced by reinforcement contingencies is shown in Figure 5.5.

The design of such experiments, usually referred to as a **reversal design** or **ABAB** design, requires that some aspect of the participant's behavior be carefully measured in a specific sequence:

1. During an initial time period, the baseline (A)
2. During a period when a treatment is introduced (B)
3. During a reinstatement of the conditions that prevailed in the baseline period (A)
4. Finally, during a reintroduction of the experimental manipulation (B)

If behavior in the experimental period is different from that in the baseline period, reverses when the experimentally manipulated conditions are reversed, and re-reverses when the treatment is again introduced, there is little doubt that the manipulation, rather than chance or uncontrolled factors, has produced the change.

The reversal technique cannot always be employed, however, for the initial state of a participant may not be recoverable, as when treatment aims to produce enduring change, the goal of all therapeutic interventions. Moreover, in studies of therapeutic procedures, reinstating the original condition of the patient would generally be considered an unethical practice. Most therapists would be extremely unwilling to act in any way that might

---

[3] The use of the adjective *experimental* in this context prompts us to distinguish between two different meanings of the word. As applied to the research methods that have been discussed, the adjective refers to the manipulation of a variable that allows us to draw conclusions about a cause–effect relationship. Here, however, the word refers to a treatment whose effects are unknown or only poorly understood. Thus, an experimental drug is one about which we know relatively little; however, such a drug might well be used in a correlational design or reported in a case study.

bring back the very behavior for which a client has sought help merely to prove that a particular treatment was indeed the effective agent in changing the behavior. Fortunately, other single-subject experimental designs avoid these problems.

As indicated earlier, even though an experiment with a single participant can demonstrate an effect, generalization is usually not possible. The fact that a treatment works for a single subject does not necessarily imply that it will be effective for others. If the search for more widely applicable treatment is the major focus of an investigation, the single-subject design has a serious drawback. However, it may help investigators to decide whether large-scale research with groups is warranted.

Mixed Designs

Experimental and correlational research techniques can be combined in what is called a **mixed design**. Participants from two or more discrete and typically nonoverlapping populations are assigned to each experimental condition. The two different types of populations, for example, patients with either schizophrenia or a phobia, constitute a classificatory variable; that is, the variables schizophrenia and phobia were neither manipulated nor created by the investigator, and they can only be correlated with the manipulated conditions, which are true experimental variables.

As an example of how a mixed design is applied, consider an investigation of the effectiveness of three types of therapy (the experimental variable) on patients divided into two groups on the basis of the severity of their illnesses (the classificatory or correlational variable). The question is whether the effectiveness of the treatments varies with the severity of illness. The hypothetical outcome of such a study is presented in Figure 5.6. Figure 5.6a illustrates the unfortunate conclusions that would be drawn were the patients not divided into those with severe and those with less severe illnesses. When all patients are grouped together, treatment 3 produces the greatest amount of improvement. Therefore, if no information about differential characteristics of the patients were available, treatment 3 would be preferred. When the severity of the patients' difficulties is considered, however, treatment 3 is no longer the therapy of choice for any of the patients. Rather, as seen in Figure 5.6b, treatment 1 would be selected for those with less severe illness and treatment 2 for patients with more severe illness. Thus, a mixed design can identify which treatment applies best to which group of patients.

In interpreting the results of mixed designs we must be continually aware of the fact that one of the variables (severity of illness in our example) is not manipulated but is instead a classificatory or correlational variable. Therefore, the problems we have previously noted in interpreting correlations, especially the possible operation of third variables, arise in interpreting the results of mixed designs as well.

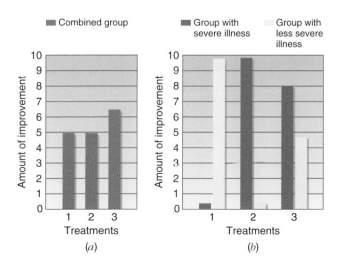

Figure 5.6 Effects of three treatments on patients whose symptoms vary in degree of severity. (a) When the severity of the illness is not known and the patients are grouped together, treatment number 3 appears to be the best. (b) The same data as in (a) are reanalyzed, dividing patients by severity. Now treatment 3 is no longer best for any patients.

Meta-analysis and the Effects of Psychotherapy

Thus far in this chapter we have described the basic research methods of abnormal psychology and their strengths and weaknesses. In doing so we have discussed individual studies. But scientific knowledge is based on integrating a body of evidence, not on merely considering individual studies one at a time. It is thus important to consider how a researcher goes about drawing conclusions from a series of investigations.

A simple way of drawing general conclusions is to read individual studies, mull them over, and decide what they mean overall. The disadvantage with this approach is that the researcher's biases and subjective impressions can play a significant role in determining what conclusion is drawn. It is fairly common for two scientists to read the same studies and reach very different conclusions.

Meta-analysis was developed as a partial solution to this problem. Devised by Smith, Glass, and Miller (1980), meta-analysis has played an important role in recent years in the evaluation of the effects of psychotherapy. The first step in a meta-analysis is a thorough literature search, usually by computer, so that all relevant studies are identified. Because these studies have typically reported their findings in different formats and used different statistical tests, meta-analysis then puts all the results into a common format, using a statistic called the *effect size*. The effect size offers a way of standardizing the differences in improvement between a therapy group and a control group (or between groups receiving two different types of therapy) so that the results of many different studies can be averaged.

The basis of comparison need not be type of therapy. One can compare on dimensions such as types of patients and settings in which therapy was administered (recall that this type of study is using a mixed design). The independent variables, in other words, can be any factors considered influential in the outcome of an intervention.

In their original and oft-cited report, Smith et al. (1980) meta-analyzed 475 psychotherapy outcome studies involving more than 25,000 patients and 1,700 effect sizes and came to two conclusions that have attracted considerable attention and created some controversy. First, they concluded that a wide range of therapies produce more improvement than does no treatment. Specifically, treated patients were found to be better off than almost 80 percent of untreated patients. Subsequent meta-analyses by other authors have confirmed these early findings (Lambert & Bergin, 1994). Second, Smith et al. contended that effect sizes across diverse modes of intervention do not differ from one another; that is, different therapies are equally effective.

In a subsequent meta-analysis, Lambert et al. (1986) went beyond the findings of Smith et al. (1980) and reached further conclusions.

1. Many psychotherapeutic interventions are more effective than a number of placebo control groups. By the same token, what Lambert et al. call "common factors" (see p. 600)—namely, warmth, trust, and encouragement—may themselves effect significant and even lasting improvement in a broad range of anxiety and mood disorders.
2. The positive effects of psychotherapy tend to be maintained for many months following termination. Lambert et al. (1986) based this conclusion on a meta-analysis of sixty-seven outcome stud-

ies by Nicholson and Berman (1983), mostly behavioral in nature, with patients other than those diagnosed as having a psychosis, a brain disorder, an antisocial personality, or substance dependence. This finding is obviously important to the client and to the individual therapist (who hopes that patients will continue to do well once they stop coming for regular sessions). It is important as well to psychotherapy researchers, who often have to undertake expensive and arduous follow-up measures to convince their colleagues that the effects of a given treatment are enduring.
3. There is considerable variability among participants in a given treatment condition, so, although treatment group X may on average show significant improvement, the group is likely also to include patients who get worse. This deterioration effect is discussed in greater detail in Focus 17.1.
4. Meta-analytic studies comparing insight therapy with cognitive and behavioral interventions show a slight but consistent advantage to the latter, although there is criticism by proponents of insight therapy that behavioral and cognitive therapies focus on milder disorders.

Meta-analysis has been criticized by a number of psychotherapy researchers. The central problem is the quality control of studies that are included in a meta-analysis. Therapy studies differ in their internal and external validity as judged by particular researchers. By giving equal weight to all studies, the meta-analyses of Smith et al. created a situation in which a poorly controlled outcome study (such as one that did not make clear what the therapists actually did in each session) received as much attention as a well-controlled one (such as a study in which therapists used a manual that specified what they did with each research participant). When Smith et al. attempted to address this problem by comparing effect sizes of good versus poor studies and found no differences, they were further criticized for the criteria they employed in separating the good from the not so good (Rachman & Wilson, 1980)! O'Leary and Wilson (1987) considered other critiques as well and concluded that the ultimate problem is that someone has to make a judgment of good versus poor quality in psychotherapy research and that others can find fault with that judgment.

This seems an insoluble problem, one that has existed for years in reviews of therapy-outcome research. At times a scholar has no choice but to make his or her own judgment about the validity of a piece of research and to decide whether or not to ignore it. Perhaps Mintz (1983) was correct in saying that the move toward meta-analysis in this field has at least sensitized us to the subjectivity that is inherent in passing judgment on research and has also encouraged greater explicitness in the criteria used to accept or to reject the findings of a given outcome study. Moreover, meta-analysis has uncovered deficiencies in some published research, for example, inadequate reporting of means and standard deviations and the collection of outcome data by persons who were aware of the treatment condition to which subjects were assigned (Shapiro & Shapiro, 1983). A long-term beneficial effect of meta-analysis may be an improvement in research practices and a tightening of publication standards (Kazdin, 1986).

Table 5.5 Research Methods in Abnormal Psychology

Method	Description	Evaluation
Case study	Collection of detailed historical, biographical, and sometimes treatment information on a single individual	Excellent source of hypotheses but cannot determine causal relationships because cannot rule out alternative hypotheses
Epidemiology	Study of the frequency and distribution of a disorder in a population; determines incidence, prevalence, and risk factors	Knowledge of risk factors provides clues regarding causes of disorders
Correlation	Study of the relationship between two or more variables; variables are measured as they exist in nature	Cannot determine causality because of the directionality and third-variable problems; used extensively in research on the causes of psychopathology because diagnosis is a correlational or classificatory variable
Experiment		
With groups of participants	Includes a manipulated independent variable, a dependent variable, at least one control group, and random assignment	Most powerful method for determining causal relationships, used mainly in studies of the effectiveness of therapies
With single subjects	Includes a manipulated variable and contrasts behavior during the time the manipulation is occurring with behavior during a period when the manipulation is not occurring (as in the ABAB design)	Can demonstrate causal relationships, although generalization can be a problem
Mixed design	Includes both an experimental (manipulated) variable and a classificatory (correlational) variable	Able to demonstrate that an experimental variable (e.g., a type of therapy) has different effects depending on the classificatory variable (e.g., severity of illness)

Our survey of the major research methods of abnormal psychology is now complete. A summary of them appears in Table 5.5. It should be apparent that there is no perfect method that will easily reveal the secrets of psychopathology and therapy. Our task in subsequent chapters will be to attempt to synthesize the information yielded by investigations conducted with varying methodologies and to apply these results to advance knowledge. Focus 5.2 discusses how scientists synthesize information using a method called meta-analysis.

Summary

- Science represents an agreed-upon problem-solving enterprise, with specific procedures for gathering and interpreting data to build a systematic body of knowledge.

- The scientific approach requires that propositions and ideas be clearly and precisely stated, be testable, and be replicable. Scientific theories propose explanations for observed data, which can then be tested, and also guide research by suggesting additional studies.

- The scientific research methods most commonly used in the study of abnormal behavior are case studies, epidemiological research, correlational studies, and various types of experiments.

- Clinical case studies serve unique and important functions in psychopathology. They are used to provide detailed descriptions of rare or unusual phenomena or novel methods or procedures; to disconfirm certain aspects of particular theoretical propositions; and to generate hypotheses that can be tested through controlled research. However, the data case studies yield may not be valid, and they are of limited value in providing evidence to favor a theory.

- Epidemiological research gathers information about the prevalence and incidence of disorders in populations and about risk factors that increase the probability of developing a disorder.

- Correlational methods are the most important means of conducting research on the causes of abnormal behavior, for diagnoses are classificatory and not experimentally manipulated variables. In correlational studies, statistical procedures allow us to determine the extent to which two or more variables correlate, or co-vary. In general, conclusions drawn from correlational studies cannot legitimately be interpreted in cause-effect terms, although there is great temptation to do so. The directionality and third-variable problems are the sources of this difficulty.

- The experimental method entails the manipulation of independent variables and the careful measurement of their effects on dependent variables. An experiment begins with a hypothesis to be tested. Generally, participants are randomly assigned to one of at least two groups: an experimental group, which experiences the manipulation of the independent variable; and a control group, which does not. As long as all necessary conditions are met, if differences between the experimental and control groups are observed on the dependent variable, researchers can conclude that the independent variable had an effect. When the experimental effect can be confidently attributed to the manipulation of the independent variable, the experiment has internal validity.

● Placebo control groups are often used in psychotherapy research. Patients in such groups receive support and encouragement, but not what is hypothesized to be the active ingredient in the kind of therapy under study.

● The external validity of research findings—whether they can be generalized to situations and people not studied within the experiment—can be assessed only by performing similar experiments in the actual domain of interest.

● Single-subject experimental designs (the reversal or ABAB design) that expose one person to different treatments over a period of time

can provide internally valid results, although the generality of conclusions is typically limited.

● Mixed designs are combinations of experimental and correlational methods. For example, two different kinds of patients (the classificatory variable) may be exposed to various treatments (the experimental variable).

● Because scientific knowledge is based on a body of evidence, meta-analysis has become an important tool for reaching general conclusions from a group of research studies. It entails putting the result of statistical comparisons into a common format—the effect size—so the results of many studies can be averaged.

● A science is only as good as its methodology. Students of abnormal psychology must appreciate the strengths and limitations of the research methods of the field if they are to adequately evaluate the research and theories that form the subject matter of the remainder of this book.

Key Terms

analogue experiment
case study
classificatory variables
confounds
control group
correlation coefficient
correlational method
dependent variable
directionality problem

double-blind procedure
epidemiology
experiment
experimental effect
experimental hypothesis
external validity
high-risk method
incidence
independent variable

internal validity
lifetime prevalence rates
meta-analysis
mixed design
placebo control groups
placebo effect
prevalence
random assignment

reversal (ABAB) designs
risk factors
science
single-subject experimental
   design
statistical significance
theory
third-variable problem

6 Anxiety Disorders

*H*ow would you like to be a tame, somewhat shy and unaggressive little boy of nine, somewhat shorter and thinner than average, and find yourself put three times a week, every Monday, Wednesday, and Friday, as regularly and inexorably as the sun sets and the sky darkens and the globe turns black and dead and spooky with no warm promise that anyone anywhere ever will awaken again, into the somber, iron custody of someone named Forgione, older, broader, and much larger than yourself, a dreadful, powerful, broad-shouldered man who is hairy, hard-muscled, and barrel-chested and wears immaculate tight white or navy-blue T-shirts that seem as firm and unpitying as the figure of flesh and bone they encase like a mold, whose ferocious, dark eyes you never had courage enough to meet and whose assistant's name you did not ask or were not able to remember, and who did not seem to like you or approve of you? He could do whatever he wanted to you. He could do whatever he wanted to me. (Heller, 1966, p. 236)

This excerpt from Joseph Heller's second novel, *Something Happened*, portrays the helplessness of a terrified nine-year-old boy who has to interact every other school day with a burly gym teacher. As described by his equally fearful father, the youngster has an overwhelming anxiety about his gym class, a situation into which he is forced and from which he cannot escape, a situation that makes demands on him that he feels utterly unable to meet. Once again a gifted novelist captures the phenomenology—the direct experience—of an important human emotion in a way that speaks vividly to each of us.

There is perhaps no other single topic in abnormal psychology that touches so many of us as **anxiety**, that unpleasant feeling of fear and apprehension. This emotional state can occur in many psychopathologies and is a principal aspect of the disorders considered in this chapter. Anxiety also plays an important role in the study of the psychology of normal people, for very few of us go through even a week of our lives without experiencing some measure of what we would all agree is the emotion called anxiety or fear. But the briefer periods of anxiety that beset the normal individual are hardly comparable in intensity or duration, nor are they as debilitating, as those suffered by someone with an anxiety disorder.

The disorders considered in this chapter and the next were for a considerable period regarded as forms of **neuroses**, a large group of disorders characterized by unrealistic anxiety and other associated problems. They were conceptualized through Freud's clinical work with his patients, and thus the diagnostic category of neurosis was inextricably bound with psychoanalytic theory. In DSM-II the behavior encompassed by the different types of neuroses varied widely—the fear and avoidance of phobia, the irresistible urge to perform certain acts over and over again found in obsessive-compulsive disorder, the paralyses and other "neurological" symptoms of conversion disorder. How could such diverse problems be grouped into a single category? Although the observed symptoms differ, all neurotic conditions were assumed, according to the psychoanalytic theory of neuroses, to reflect an underlying problem with repressed id impulses.

Over the years many psychopathologists questioned the viability of the concept of neuroses because it had become so inclusive as to be meaningless as a diagnostic category. Further, no data supported the assumption that all patients labeled neurotic shared some common problem or set of symptoms.[1] Beginning in DSM-III and continuing in DSM-IV-TR, the old categories of neuroses are distributed among several new, more distinct diagnostic classes: anxiety disorders, the topic of this chapter, and somatoform disorders and dissociative disorders, both of which are covered in Chapter 7.

Anxiety disorders are diagnosed when subjectively experienced feelings of anxiety are clearly present. DSM-IV-TR proposes six principal categories: phobias, panic disorder, generalized anxiety disorder, obsessive-compulsive disorder, posttraumatic stress disorder, and acute stress disorder. Often someone with one anxiety disorder meets the diagnostic criteria for another disorder as well, a situation known as **comorbidity**. Comorbidity among anxiety disorders arises for two reasons.

1. Symptoms of the various anxiety disorders are not entirely disorder–specific; for example, somatic signs of anxiety (e.g., perspiration, fast heart rate) are among the diagnostic criteria for panic disorder, phobias, and posttraumatic stress disorder.
2. The etiological factors that give rise to various anxiety disorders may be applicable to more than one disorder; for example, believing that you can't control the stressors you encounter has been proposed as relevant to both phobias and generalized anxiety disorder. And physical or sexual abuse during childhood may increase a person's risk for developing several of the disorders. Comorbidity could reflect the operation of common mechanisms such as these.

As yet, theories of anxiety disorders tend to focus exclusively on a single disorder. The development of theories that take comorbidity into account is a challenge for the future.

We turn now to an examination of the defining characteristics, theories of etiology, and therapies for each of the anxiety disorders. Table 6.1 provides a brief summary of the disorders we will be discussing.

Phobias

DSM-IV-TR Criteria for Phobia

- Excessive, unreasonable, persistent fear triggered by objects or situations
- Exposure to the trigger leads to intense anxiety
- The person recognizes the fear is unrealistic
- The object or situation is avoided or endured with intense anxiety

Psychopathologists define a **phobia** as a disrupting, fear-mediated avoidance that is out of proportion to the danger posed by a particular object or situation and is recognized by the sufferer as groundless. Examples are extreme fear of heights, closed spaces, snakes, or spiders—provided that there is no objective danger—accompanied by sufficient distress to disrupt one's life.

---

[1] In many ways the term *neurosis* serves as a nice counter to another broad-based term, *psychosis*, which is also part of our everyday vocabulary and was prominent in DSM-II. Certain diagnoses in DSM-IV-TR—schizophrenic and paranoid disorders and some mood disorders—are recognized as psychoses although they are not generally grouped as such. Individuals with a psychosis typically suffer extreme mental unrest and have lost contact with reality. Their hallucinations and delusions—false perceptions and misguided beliefs that are a jumble of distortions and impossibilities but are firmly accepted by the individual—so engulf them that they are often unable to meet even the most ordinary demands of life.

Table 6.1 Summary of Major Anxiety Disorders

Disorder	Description
Phobia	Fear and avoidance of objects or situations that do not present any real danger
Panic disorder	Recurrent panic attacks involving a sudden onset of physiological symptoms, such as dizziness, rapid heart rate, and trembling, accompanied by terror and feelings of impending doom; sometimes accompanied by agoraphobia, a fear of being in public places
Generalized anxiety disorder	Persistent, uncontrollable worry, often about minor things
Obsessive-compulsive disorder	The experience of uncontrollable thoughts, impulses, or images—obsessions—and repetitive behaviors or mental acts—compulsions
Posttraumatic stress disorder	Aftermath of a traumatic experience in which the person experiences increased arousal, avoidance of stimuli associated with the event, and anxiety caused by recalling the event
Acute stress disorder	Symptoms are the same as those of posttraumatic stress disorder, but last for four weeks or less

Many specific fears do not cause enough hardship to compel an individual to seek treatment. For example, if a person with an intense fear of snakes lives in a metropolitan area, he or she will probably have little direct contact with the feared object and may therefore not believe that anything is seriously wrong. The term phobia usually implies that the person suffers intense distress and social or occupational impairment because of the anxiety.

Over the years complex terms have been formulated to name these unwarranted avoidance patterns. In each instance the suffix phobia is preceded by a Greek word for the feared object or situation. The suffix is derived from the name of the Greek god Phobos, who frightened his enemies. Some of the more familiar terms are *claustrophobia*, fear of closed spaces; *agoraphobia*, fear of public places; and *acrophobia*, fear of heights. More exotic fears have also been given Greek-derived names, for example, *ergasiophobia*, fear of writing; *pnigophobia*, fear of choking; *taphephobia*, fear of being buried alive; *Anglophobia*, fear of England; *musophobia*, fear of mice; and *hellenologophobia*, fear of pseudoscientific terms (McNally, 1997). Such authoritative terms all too often convey the impression that we understand how a particular problem originated or even how to treat it merely because we have an authoritative-sounding name for it. Nothing could be further from the truth. As with so much in the field of abnormal psychology, there are more theories and jargon pertaining to phobias than there are firm findings.

Psychologists tend to focus on different aspects of phobias depending on the paradigm they have adopted. Psychoanalysts focus on the content of the phobia. They see great significance in the phobic object as a symbol of an important unconscious fear. In a celebrated case reported by Freud, a boy he called Little Hans was afraid of encountering horses if he went outside. Freud paid particular attention to Hans's reference to the "black things around horses' mouths and the things in front of their eyes." The horse was regarded as representing the father, who had a mustache and wore eyeglasses. Freud theorized that fear of the father had become transformed into fear of horses, which Hans then avoided. Countless other such examples might be cited. The principal point is that psychoanalysts believe that the content of phobias has important symbolic value. Behaviorists,

Fear and avoidance of heights is classified as a specific phobia. Other specific phobias include fears of animals, injections, and enclosed spaces

A crowd is likely to be very distressing to a person with agoraphobia, who typically is often afraid of having a panic attack in a public place.

What is feared in a phobia varies cross-culturally. In China, Pa-leng is a fear that loss of body heat will be life threatening.

on the other hand, tend to ignore the content of the phobia and focus instead on its function. For them, fear of snakes and fear of heights are equivalent in the means by which they are acquired, in how they might be reduced, and so on.

With this in mind, let us look now at two types of phobias: specific phobias and social phobias.

Specific Phobias

Specific phobias are unwarranted fears caused by the presence or anticipation of a specific object or situation. DSM-IV-TR subdivides these phobias according to the source of the fear: blood, injuries and injections, situations (e.g., planes, elevators, enclosed spaces), animals, and the natural environment (e.g., heights, water). These phobias are often comorbid with one another (Kendler et al., 2001). Lifetime prevalence is about 7 percent for men and 16 percent for women (Kessler et al., 1994).

What is feared in a phobia can also vary cross-culturally. For example, in China, *Pa-leng* is a fear of the cold in which the person worries that loss of body heat may be life threatening. This fear appears to be related to the Chinese philosophy of yin and yang; yin refers to the cold, windy, energy-sapping aspects of life.

Another example is a Japanese syndrome called *taijin-kyofu-sho*, fear of other people. This is not a social phobia (discussed in the next section); rather, it is an extreme fear of embarrassing others, for example, by blushing in their presence, glancing at their genital areas, or making odd faces. It is believed that this phobia arises from elements of traditional Japanese culture, which encourages extreme concern for the feelings of others while discouraging the direct communication of feelings (McNally, 1997). Thus, beliefs that are prevalent in a culture seem to be able to channel what people come to fear.

Social Phobias

A **social phobia** is a persistent, irrational fear generally linked to the presence of other people. It can be extremely debilitating, so much so that suicide rates among people with this disorder are substantially higher than for those with the other anxiety disorders (Schneier et al., 1992). Indeed, the term "social anxiety disorder" has recently been proposed as a more appropriate term because the pervasiveness of the problem and its negative consequences for people who have it are a good deal greater than for the other phobias (Liebowitz et al., 2000).

The individual with a social phobia usually tries to avoid situations in which he or she might be evaluated and reveal signs of anxiousness or behave in an embarrassing way. Fears concerning excessive sweating or blushing are common. Speaking or performing in public, eating in public, using public lavatories, or virtually any other activity that might be carried out in the presence of others can elicit extreme anxiety, even a full-blown panic attack. Socially phobic people often work in occupations or professions far below their talents or intelligence because their extreme social sensitivity—exceeding by far what we would think of as shyness—exacts too high an emotional cost. Better to resign oneself to a lower-paying job than deal every day with other people in what could be a more rewarding line of work.

Social phobias can be either generalized or specific, depending on the range of situations that are feared and avoided. People with the generalized type have an earlier age of onset, more comorbidity with other disorders, such as depression and alcohol abuse, and more severe impairment (Mannuzza et al., 1995; Wittchen, Stein, & Kessler, 1999). Social anxiety disorder tends to be chronic if the person is not successfully treated.

Social phobias are fairly common, with a lifetime prevalence of 11 percent in men and 15 percent in women (Kessler

Social phobias typically begin in adolescence and interfere with developing friendships with peers.

et al., 1994; Magee et al., 1996). They have a high comorbidity rate with other disorders and often occur in conjunction with generalized anxiety disorder, specific phobias, panic disorder, avoidant personality disorder, mood disorders, and alcohol abuse (Crum & Pratt, 2001; Jansen et al., 1994; Kessler et al., 1999; Lecrubier & Weiller, 1997). As might be expected, onset generally takes place during adolescence, when social awareness and interaction with others are assuming much more importance in a person's life, but as we discuss later (p. 146), such fears are sometimes found in children as well. Like specific phobias, social phobias vary somewhat cross-culturally. For example, as we have noted, in Japan fear of giving offense to others is very important, whereas in the United States fear of being negatively evaluated by others is more common.

Etiology of Phobias

As is true for virtually all the disorders discussed in this book, proposals about the causes of phobias have been made by adherents of the psychoanalytic, behavioral, cognitive, and biological paradigms. We turn now to the ideas of each of these paradigms.

Psychoanalytic Theories   Freud was the first to attempt to account systematically for the development of phobic behavior. According to Freud, phobias are a defense against the anxiety produced by repressed id impulses. This anxiety is displaced from the feared id impulse and moved to an object or situation that has some symbolic connection to it. These objects or situations—for example, elevators or closed spaces—then become the phobic stimuli. By avoiding them the person is able to avoid dealing with repressed conflicts. As discussed in Chapter 2 (p. 28), the phobia is the ego's way of warding off a confrontation with the real problem, a repressed childhood conflict. For example, Freud thought that Little Hans, mentioned earlier, had not successfully resolved the Oedipal conflict, so that his intense fear of his father was displaced onto horses and he became phobic about leaving his home.

According to another psychoanalytic theory of phobias, proposed by Arieti (1979), what is repressed is a particular interpersonal problem of childhood rather than an id impulse. Arieti theorized that as children, people with phobias first lived through a period of innocence during which they trusted the people around them to protect them from danger. Later they came to fear that adults, usually parents, were not reliable. They could not live with this mistrust, or generalized fear of others. To be able to trust people again, they unconsciously transformed this fear of others into a fear of impersonal objects or situations. The phobia surfaces when, in adulthood, the person undergoes some sort of stress. As with most psychoanalytic theorizing, evidence in support of these views is restricted for the most part to conclusions drawn from clinical case reports.

Behavioral Theories   Behavioral theories focus on learning as the way in which phobias are acquired. Several types of learning may be involved.

Avoidance Conditioning   The main behavioral account of phobias is that such reactions are learned avoidance responses. Historically, Watson and Rayner's (1920) demonstration of the apparent conditioning of a fear or phobia in Little Albert (see p. 44) is considered the model of how a phobia may be acquired. The avoidance-conditioning formulation is based on the two-factor theory originally proposed by Mowrer (1947) and holds that phobias develop from two related sets of learning (see p. 47).

1. Via classical conditioning a person can learn to fear a neutral stimulus (the CS) if it is paired with an intrinsically painful or frightening event (the UCS).

2. The person can learn to reduce this conditioned fear by escaping from or avoiding the CS. This second kind of

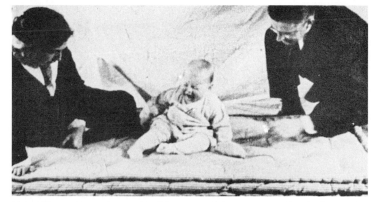

Little Albert, shown here with Watson and Rayner, was classically conditioned to develop a fear of a white rat.

learning is assumed to be operant conditioning; the response is maintained by its reinforcing consequence of reducing fear.

An important issue exists in the application of the avoidance-conditioning model to phobias. The fact that Little Albert's fear was acquired through conditioning cannot be taken as evidence that *all* fears and phobias are acquired by this means. Rather, the evidence demonstrates only the possibility that *some* fears may be acquired in this particular way. Furthermore, attempts to replicate Watson and Rayner's experiment have for the most part not been successful (e.g., English, 1929). Very little experimental evidence supports the contention that human beings can be classically conditioned to develop a durable fear of neutral stimuli even when such stimuli are paired repeatedly with primary aversive stimuli, such as electric shock (e.g., Davison, 1968b; Dawson, Schell, & Banis, 1986).

To be sure, ethical considerations have restrained most researchers from employing highly aversive stimuli with human beings, but considerable evidence indicates that fear is extinguished rather quickly when the CS is presented a few times without the reinforcement of moderate levels of shock (Bridger & Mandel, 1965; Wickens, Allen, & Hill, 1963). The problem may be that a strong unconditioned physiological fear response is not being elicited in the laboratory, and such a response is critical to establishing conditioned fear (Forsyth & Eifert, 1998).

Outside the laboratory, the evidence for the avoidance-conditioning theory is also mixed. Some clinical phobias fit the avoidance-conditioning model rather well. A phobia of a specific object or situation has sometimes been reported to have developed after a particularly painful experience with that object. Some people become intensely afraid of heights after a bad fall; others develop a phobia of driving after experiencing a panic attack in their car (Munjack, 1984); and people with social phobias sometimes report traumatic social experiences (Stenberger et al., 1995). Other data indicate, however, that many people with phobias cannot recall any traumatic event with the object or situation they fear. This is true especially for social phobia (Kendler, Myers, & Prescott, 2002). Can this problem with the avoidance-conditioning model be solved?

Perhaps the apparent absence of a UCS is not critical because the key to fear conditioning is the UCR (Forsyth & Eifert, 1998). That is, someone who experiences an intense episode of physiological arousal (a UCR), for some reason of which he or she is unaware, may wrongly conclude that an innocuous situation has caused the arousal and fear and may thus develop a phobia. But if the situation the person is in is not traumatic, there is no apparent UCS. A case of ours illustrates this possibility.

A thirty-six-year-old man was in treatment for severe anxiety that was directly linked to a number of severe stressors he had encountered recently. In the early stages of treatment he had to fly out of town on business. During the plane trip he experienced an episode of intense physiological arousal. He wasn't thinking about the stressors he had recently encountered and didn't have any explanation for why his arousal level had suddenly escalated. He concluded that the cause was the plane trip. Although he had flown many times before with little or no anxiety, he was unable to get on his return flight and had to return home by bus.

Another possible solution to the puzzle of phobias developing without exposure to an aversive UCS involves modeling.

Modeling   In addition to learning to fear something as a result of an unpleasant experience with it, fears may be learned through imitating the reactions of others. Thus, some phobias may be acquired by modeling, not through an unpleasant experience with the object or situation that is feared. As previously noted (see p. 46), a wide range of behavior, including emotional responses, may be learned by witnessing a model. The learning of fear by observing others is generally referred to as **vicarious learning**.

In one study, Bandura and Rosenthal (1966) arranged for participants to watch another person, the model (a confederate of the experimenter), in an aversive-conditioning situation. The model was hooked up to an impressive-looking array of electrical apparatuses. On hearing a buzzer, the model withdrew his hand rapidly from the arm of the chair and feigned pain. The physiological responses of the participants witnessing this behavior were recorded. After the participants had watched the model "suffer" a number of times, they showed an increased frequency of emotional responses when the buzzer sounded. The participants began to react emotionally to a harmless stimulus even though they had had no direct contact with a noxious event.

Vicarious learning can also be accomplished through verbal instructions; that is, phobic reactions can be learned through another's description of what might happen as well as through observation of another's fear. As an example from everyday life, a parent may repeatedly warn his or her child not to engage in some activity lest dire consequences ensue.

Prepared Learning Another issue that is not addressed by the original avoidance-learning model is that people tend to fear only certain objects and events, such as spiders, snakes, and heights, but not others, such as lambs (Marks, 1969). The fact that certain neutral stimuli, called *prepared stimuli*, are more likely than others to become classically conditioned stimuli may account for this tendency. For example, rats readily learn to associate taste with nausea but not with shock when the two are paired (Garcia, McGowan, & Green, 1972). Some fears may well reflect classical conditioning, but only to stimuli to which an organism is physiologically prepared to be sensitive (Seligman, 1971). Conditioning experiments that show quick extinction of fear may have used CSs that the organism was not prepared to associate with UCSs.

Partial support for this line of reasoning comes from studies that have used different types of stimuli as the CS (Öhman, Erixon, & Loftberg, 1975). During conditioning, electric shock was paired with slides of houses, faces, and snakes, and participants acquired a CR to the slides. During extinction, the CR to the slides of houses or faces quickly diminished, whereas those to the snakes remained strong.

Prepared learning is also relevant to learning fear by modeling. Cook and Mineka (1989) studied four groups of rhesus monkeys, each of which saw a different videotape. The tapes were created by splicing, so that a monkey exhibiting intense fear appeared to be responding to different stimuli: a toy snake, a toy crocodile, flowers, or a toy rabbit. Only the monkeys exposed to the tapes showing the toy snake or toy crocodile acquired fear of the object shown, again demonstrating that not every stimulus is capable of becoming a source of acquired fear.

Diathesis Is Needed A final question to be discussed is why some people who have traumatic experiences do not develop enduring fears. For example, 50 percent of people with a severe fear of dogs reported a prior traumatic experience, yet so did 50 percent of people who were not afraid of dogs (DiNardo et al., 1988). The difference between these groups was that the phobic group focused on and became anxious about the possible occurrence of similar events in the future. Thus, a cognitive diathesis—believing that similar traumatic experiences will occur in the future—may be important in developing a phobia. Another possible psychological diathesis is a history of not being able to control the environment (Mineka & Zinbarg, 1996).

In sum, the data we have reviewed suggest that some phobias may be learned through avoidance conditioning. But avoidance conditioning should not be regarded as a totally validated theory. For example, as mentioned, many people with phobias do not report either direct exposure to a traumatic event or exposure to fearful models (Merckelbach et al., 1989). Furthermore, the avoidance conditioning model has difficulty handling the comorbidity among the various phobias.

Social-Skills Deficits in Social Phobias We turn next to a behavioral model of social phobia that considers inappropriate behavior or a lack of social skills to be the cause of social anxiety. According to this view, the individual has not learned how to behave so that he or she feels comfortable with others, or the person repeatedly commits faux pas, is awkward and socially inept, and is often criticized by social companions.

Mineka's research has shown that when monkeys observe another monkey display fear of a snake, they also acquire the fear. Observational learning may therefore play a role in the etiology of phobias.

DiNardo's study showed that after a traumatic experience with a dog, those who developed a persistent fear of dogs were anxious about having similiar experiences in the future.

Support for this model comes from findings that socially anxious people are indeed rated as being low in social skills (Twentyman & McFall, 1975) and that the timing and placement of their responses in a social interaction, such as saying "thank you" at the right time, are impaired (Fischetti, Curran, & Wessberg, 1977).

Note how this social skills deficit perspective relates to the avoidance conditioning theory reviewed above. A person lacking in social skills is likely to *create* situations with others that are aversive. For example, not knowing how to respond politely yet assertively to the demands of another can offend, leading to awkward interpersonal situations and even tense conflicts. Being punished by others can be expected to make a person more fearful of interacting with them.

Cognitive Theories   Cognitive views of anxiety in general and of phobias in particular focus on how people's thought processes can serve as a diathesis and on how thoughts can maintain a phobia. Anxiety is related to being more likely to attend to negative stimuli, to interpret ambiguous information as threatening, and to believe that negative events are more likely to occur in the future (Heinrichs & Hoffman, 2000; Turk et al., 2001). The key issue in this theory is whether these cognitions cause anxiety or whether anxiety causes these cognitions. Although some experimental evidence indicates that the way stimuli are interpreted can create anxiety in the laboratory (Matthews & Mackintosh, 2000), it is unknown whether cognitive biases precede the development of actual anxiety disorders.

Studies of socially anxious people have investigated cognitive factors related to social phobias. Socially anxious people are more concerned about evaluation than are people who are not socially anxious (Goldfried, Padawer, & Robins, 1984), are more aware of the image they present to others (Bates, 1990), and tend to view themselves negatively even when they have actually performed well in a social interaction (Wallace & Alden, 1997). The study by Davison and Zighelboim (1987) discussed in Chapter 4 provides further evidence for these conclusions. The Articulated Thoughts in Simulated Situations method was used to compare the thoughts of two groups of participants as they role-played participation in both a neutral situation and one in which they were being sharply criticized. One group comprised volunteers from an introductory psychology course; the other group consisted of undergraduates referred from the student counseling center and identified by their therapists as shy, withdrawn, and socially anxious. The thoughts articulated by the socially anxious students in both stressful and neutral situations were more negative than were those of the control subjects. Some of the thoughts expressed by socially anxious students as they imagined themselves being criticized included "I've been rejected by these people," "There is no place to turn to now," "I think I am boring when I talk to people," "I often think I should not talk at all."

Cognitive theories of phobias are also relevant to other features of these disorders—the persistence of the fears and the fact that the fears actually seem irrational to the person experiencing them. These phenomena may occur because fear is elicited through early automatic processes that are not available to conscious awareness. After this initial processing the stimulus is avoided, so it is not processed fully enough to allow the fear to extinguish (Amir, Foa, & Coles, 1998).

In one study, partially testing this notion, people with high levels of fear of either snakes or spiders were presented with pictures of varying content, some expected to elicit fear (snakes and spiders) and some not (flowers and mushrooms). Each picture was followed thirty milliseconds later with another patterned stimulus so that the content of the pictures could not be consciously recognized. Nevertheless, people high in fear of snakes showed increased skin conductance to the snake slides, and those high in fear of spiders showed increased skin conductance to the spider slides, indicating that phobic fears may be elicited by stimuli that are not available to consciousness and may therefore appear irrational (Öhman & Soares, 1994).

Predisposing Biological Factors   The theories we have just described look largely to the environment for the cause and maintenance of phobias. But why do some people acquire unrealistic fears when others do not, given similar opportunities for learning? Perhaps those who are adversely affected by stress have a biological malfunction (a diathesis) that somehow predisposes them to develop a phobia following a particular stressful event. Research in two areas seems promising: the autonomic nervous system and genetic factors.

Autonomic Nervous System   As we mentioned earlier, people with social phobia often fear they will blush or sweat heavily in public. Since both sweating and blushing are controlled by the autonomic nervous system, overactivity of the autonomic nervous system becomes a candidate for a diathesis. However, most of the evidence does not find that individuals with phobias differ much from controls on various measures of autonomic activity, even when in situations such as public speaking in which we would have expected to find differences. It may be that *fear* of blushing or sweating is as important as *actual* blushing or sweating. For example, a recent study assessed blushing during three different stress tasks in three groups of people: those with social phobia who reported that they blushed a lot, those with social phobia who did not report excessive blushing, and controls. Participants with social phobia self-reported more blushing during each of the three stress tests, but they actually blushed more than the controls during only one of the three tests (watching a videotape of themselves singing a children's song). The people with social phobia who had earlier reported blushing did not actually blush more than the people with social phobia who did not report blushing (Gerlach et al., 2001). Therefore, while autonomic overactivity (as reflected in blushing) is of some relevance to social phobia, the fear of the consequences of autonomic activity may be more important.

Genetic Factors   Several studies have examined whether a genetic factor is involved in phobias. Blood-and-injection phobia is strongly familial; 64 percent of patients with blood-and-injection phobia have at least one first-degree relative with the same disorder, whereas the disorder's prevalence in the general population is only 3 to 4 percent (Ost, 1992). Similarly, for both social and specific phobias, prevalence is higher than average in first-degree relatives of patients, and twin studies show higher concordance for MZ than DZ pairs (Hettema, M. Neale, & Kendler, 2001).

Related to these findings is the work of Jerome Kagan on the trait of inhibition or shyness (Kagan & Snidman, 1997). Some infants as young as four months become agitated and cry when they are shown toys or other stimuli. This behavior pattern, which may be inherited, may set the stage for the later development of phobias. In one study, for example, inhibited children were greater than five times more likely than uninhibited children to develop a phobia later (Biederman et al., 1990).

The data we have described do not unequivocally implicate genetic factors. Although close relatives share genes, they also have considerable opportunity to observe and influence one another. The fact that a son and his father are both afraid of heights may indicate a genetic component, the son's direct imitation of the father's behavior, or both. Although there is some reason to believe that genetic factors may be involved in the etiology of phobias, there has as yet been no clear-cut demonstration of the extent to which they may be important.

Therapies for Phobias

Now that we have reviewed theories about the causes of phobias, we describe the principal therapies for them. The treatment sections of Chapter 2 were meant to furnish a context for understanding the discussions of therapy here and in subsequent chapters. An in-depth evaluation of therapy is reserved for Chapter 17.

Most people suffer, sometimes quietly, with their phobias and do not seek treatment (Magee et al., 1996). In fact, many people who could be diagnosed by a clinician as having a phobia do not regard themselves as having a problem that merits attention. A decision to seek treatment often arises when a change in the person's life situation requires exposure that had for years been avoided or minimized.

A thirty-five-year-old industrial engineer consulted us for treatment of his fear of flying when a promotion required him to travel frequently. This professional recognition was a result of his having worked with distinction for several years in his firm at a job that kept him at his desk. Family trips were always by car or train, and those close to him worked around his debilitating fear of getting on an airplane. Imagine his mixed feelings at being informed that his excellence was to be rewarded by the promotion! His ambition and self-respect—and encouragement from family and friends—goaded him into seeking assistance.

Psychoanalytic Approaches   Just as psychoanalytic theory has many variations, so, too, does psychoanalytic therapy. In general, however, all psychoanalytic treatments of phobias attempt to uncover the repressed conflicts that are assumed to underlie the extreme fear and avoidance characteristic of these disorders. Because the phobia itself is regarded as symptomatic of underlying conflicts, it is usually not dealt with directly. Indeed, direct attempts to reduce phobic avoidance are contraindicated because the phobia is assumed to protect the person from repressed conflicts that are too painful to confront.

In various combinations the analyst uses the techniques developed within the psychoanalytic tradition to help lift the repression. During free association (see p. 31) the analyst listens carefully to what the patient mentions in connection with any references to the phobia. The analyst also attempts to discover clues to the repressed origins of the phobia in the manifest content of dreams. Exactly what the analyst believes these repressed origins are depends on the particular psychoanalytic theory held. An orthodox analyst will look for conflicts related to sex or aggression, whereas an analyst holding to Arieti's interpersonal theory will encourage patients to examine their generalized fear of other people.

Contemporary ego analysts focus less on historical insights and more on encouraging the patient to confront the phobia. However, they also view the phobia as an outgrowth of an earlier problem. Alexander and French, in their classic book *Psychoanalytic Therapy* (1946), wrote of the "corrective emotional experience" in therapy, by which they meant the patient's confrontation with what is so desperately feared. They observed that "Freud himself came to the conclusion that in the treatment of some cases, phobias for example, a time arrives when the analyst must encourage the patient to engage in those activities he avoided in the past" (p. 39). Wachtel (1977) even more boldly recommended that analysts employ the fear-reduction techniques of behavior therapists, such as systematic desensitization. (A more detailed discussion of Wachtel's proposals to blend psychoanalysis and behavior therapy is found in Chapter 17.)

Many analytically oriented clinicians recognize the importance of exposure to what is feared, although they usually tend to regard any subsequent improvement as merely symptomatic and not as a resolution of the underlying conflict that was assumed to have produced the phobia (Wolitzky & Eagle, 1990).

Behavioral Approaches   Systematic desensitization (see p. 48) was the first major behavioral treatment to be widely used in treating phobias (Wolpe, 1958). The individual with a phobia imagines a series of increasingly frightening scenes while in a state of deep relaxation. Clinical and experimental evidence indicates that this technique is effective in eliminating, or at least reducing, phobias (Barlow, Raffa, & Cohen, 2002).

In addition, many behavior therapists have come to recognize the critical importance of exposure to real-life phobic situations, sometimes during the period in which a patient is being desensitized in imagination and sometimes instead of the imagery-based procedure (Craske, Rapee, & Barlow, 1992). Most contemporary clinical researchers regard such in vivo exposure as superior to techniques using imagination, not a surprising finding given that imaginary stimuli are by definition not the real thing!

At the same time it is important to note that desensitization in imagination is peculiarly appropriate when it is not possible or practical to expose fearful people in vivo to what they are afraid of. For example, if a therapist wants to provide gradual exposures to authority figures in the patient's life, perhaps even to the patient's deceased father, it is useful to be able to rely on imaginal exposures as "stand-ins" for the real thing and to know that, based on controlled research in Wolpe's original procedure, exposure to imaginary situations bring about significant reductions in anxiety.

Flooding is a therapeutic technique in which the client is exposed to the source of the phobia at full intensity. The extreme discomfort that is an inevitable part of this procedure has until recently tended to discourage therapists from employing it, except perhaps as a last resort when graduated exposure has not worked. When we examine therapy for obsessive-compulsive disorder and posttraumatic stress disorder, we will see more extensive use of flooding techniques.

Blood-and-injection phobias have only recently, in DSM-IV-TR, been distinguished from other kinds of severe fears and avoidances because of the distinctive reactions that people with these phobias have to the usual behavioral approach of relaxation paired with exposure (Page, 1994). Relaxation tends to make matters worse for people with a blood-and-injection phobia. Why? Consider that after the initial fright, associated with dramatic increases in heart rate and blood pressure, a patient with blood-and-injection phobia often experiences a sudden drop in blood pressure and heart rate and then usually faints (McGrady & Bernal, 1986). By trying to relax, patients with these phobias may well contribute to the tendency to faint, increasing their already high levels of fear and avoidance of the entire situation, as well as their embarrassment (Ost, 1992). The upshot of clinical research and observation is that patients with blood-and-injection phobias are now encouraged to tense their muscles instead of relaxing them when confronting the fearsome situation (Hellstrom, Fellenius, & Ost, 1996; Ost, Fellenius, & Sterner, 1991).

Learning social skills can help people with social phobias who may not know what to do or say in social situations. Some behavior therapists encourage patients to role-play or rehearse interpersonal encounters in the consulting room or in small therapy groups (Heimberg & Juster, 1994; Heimberg et al., 1993; Marks, 1995; Mattick & Andrews, 1994). Several studies attest to the effectiveness of such an approach (e.g., Heimberg et al., 1989; Turk, Hope, & Heimberg, 2001; Turner, Beidel, & Cooley-Quille, 1995). As pointed out by Herbert (1995), such practices may also expose the timorous person, even when there is no social-skills deficit, to anxiety-provoking cues, such as being observed by others, so that through real-life exposure extinction of fear takes place (Hope, Heimberg, & Bruch, 1995). This is one of many examples of how a particular therapeutic technique can work for more than one reason.

Modeling is yet another technique that uses exposure to feared situations. In modeling therapy, fearful clients are exposed to filmed or live demonstrations of other people interacting fearlessly with the phobic object, for example, handling nonpoisonous snakes or petting friendly dogs. Showing socially anxious people how they might better interact with others is an integral part of the social-skills training just mentioned in those patients whose social anxieties are, at least in part, due to their not knowing what to do in various social situations.

Behavior therapists who favor operant techniques ignore the fear assumed to underlie phobias and attend instead to the overt avoidance of phobic objects and to the approach behavior that must replace it. They treat approach to the feared situation like any other operant and shape it according to the principle of successive approximations. Real-life exposures to the phobic object are gradually achieved, and the client is rewarded for even minimal successes in moving closer to it. Note that exposure is an inevitable aspect of any operant shaping of approach behaviors.

Many behavior therapists attend both to fear and to avoidance, using techniques such as desensitization to reduce fear and operant shaping to encourage approach (Lazarus, Davison, & Polefka, 1965). In the initial stages of treatment, when fear and avoidance are both very great, the therapist concentrates on reducing the fear through relaxation training and graded exposures to the phobic situation. As therapy progresses, fear becomes less of an issue and avoidance more. An individual with a phobia has often settled into an existence in which other people cater to his or her incapacities and thus in a way reinforce the person for having the phobia (psychoanalysts call this phenomenon *secondary gain*). As the person's anxieties diminish, he or she is able to approach what

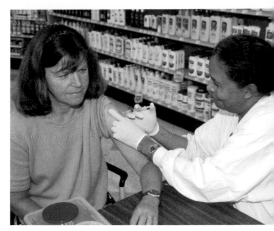

Blood-and-injection phobias are different from other specific phobias. Patients with this type of phobia are encouraged not to relax, but to tense their muscles when they encounter the feared situation.

In the most frequent treatment for phobias, patients are exposed to what they fear most; here, an enclosed space.

used to be terrifying. This overt behavior can then be positively reinforced—and avoidance discouraged—by relatives and friends as well as by the therapist.

Cognitive Approaches   Cognitive treatments for specific phobias have been viewed with skepticism because of a central defining characteristic of phobias: the phobic fear is recognized by the individual as excessive or unreasonable. If the person already acknowledges that the fear is of something harmless, of what use can it be to alter the person's thoughts about it? Indeed, there is no evidence that eliminating irrational beliefs alone, without exposure to the fearsome situations, reduces phobic avoidance (Turner et al., 1992; Williams & Rappoport, 1983).

In contrast, with social phobias such cognitive methods—sometimes combined with social-skills training—are more promising. People with social phobias benefit from treatment strategies based on both Beck and Ellis. That is, they may be persuaded by the therapist to more accurately appraise people's reactions to them (a frown from my teacher may have less to do with disapproval of me than with something the teacher is preoccupied with that has nothing to do with me) and to rely less on approval from others for maintaining a sense of self-worth (just because I have been criticized does not mean that I am a worthless nonentity). With the recognition in recent years that many people with social phobias have adequate social skills but are inhibited by self-defeating thoughts from showing them, there has been increasing emphasis on cognitive approaches. When combined with exposure to fearsome situations, especially in a group therapy context, cognitive approaches have been found to be more effective than any other treatment (Turk et al., 2001).

Even so, statistically significant differences between a treatment group undergoing, for example, cognitive behavior therapy and a control group does not mean that all or even most of the treated patients end up with no social anxiety at all. On the contrary—and this generalization applies to all the therapies judged effective—many patients do not respond at all or achieve only a partial reduction of their anxiety as a result of the treatment (DeRubeis & Crits-Christoph, 1998). Having said this, treatment gains are significant and clinically meaningful for most patients who go through a treatment that exposes them, under comforting and controlled conditions, to interpersonal situations while also encouraging them to alter their negative ways of thinking about their performance.

All the behavioral and cognitive therapies for phobias have a recurrent theme, namely, the need for the patient to begin facing what has been deemed too fearsome, too terrifying to face. Although psychoanalysts believe that the fear resides in the buried past and therefore delay direct confrontation, eventually they too encourage it (e.g., Zane, 1984). Freud stated: "One can hardly ever master a phobia if one waits until the patient lets the analysis influence him to give it up. One succeeds only when one can induce them to go about alone and to struggle with their anxiety while they make the attempt" (Freud, 1919, p. 400). Thus all these therapies reflect a time-honored bit of folk wisdom, one that tells us that we must face up to what we fear. As an ancient Chinese proverb puts it, "Go straight to the heart of danger, for there you will find safety."

Biological Approaches   Drugs that reduce anxiety are referred to as sedatives, tranquilizers, or **anxiolytics** (the suffix *lytic* comes from the Greek word meaning "to loosen or dissolve"). Barbiturates were the first major category of drugs used to treat anxiety disorders, but because they are highly addicting and present great risk of a lethal overdose (cf. p. 374), they were supplanted in the 1950s by two other classes of drugs, propanediols (e.g., Miltown) and benzodiazepines (e.g., Valium and Xanax). The latter are widely used today and, as we will see, are of demonstrated benefit with some anxiety disorders. However, they are not used much with the specific phobias. Furthermore, although the risk of lethal overdose is not as great as with barbiturates, benzodiazepines are physically addicting and produce a severe withdrawal syndrome (Schweizer et al., 1990).

In recent years, drugs originally developed to treat depression (antidepressants) have become popular in treating many of the anxiety disorders, phobias included. One class of these drugs, the monoamine oxidase (MAO) inhibitors, fared better in one study treating social phobia than did a benzodiazepine (Gelernter et al., 1991), and in another study was as effective as cognitive behavior therapy at a twelve-week follow-up (Heimberg et al., 1998). But MAO inhibitors, such as phenelzine (Nardil), can lead to weight gain, insomnia, sexual dysfunction, and hypertension. The more recently available selective serotonin reuptake inhibitors (SSRIs), such as fluoxetine (Prozac), were also originally developed to treat depression. They also have shown some promise in reducing both specific and social phobia in double-blind studies (Benjamin et al., 2000; Van Ameringen et al., 2001). The key problem in treating phobias and other anxiety disorders with drugs, however, is that the drugs may be difficult to discontinue, and relapse is common if patients stop taking them (Herbert, 1995). See Focus on Discovery 6.1 for a discussion of childhood fears and phobias.[2]

Panic Disorder

In **panic disorder** a person suffers a sudden and often inexplicable attack of a host of jarring symptoms—labored breathing, heart palpitations, nausea, chest pain, feelings of choking and smothering; dizziness, sweating, and trembling; and intense apprehension, terror, and feelings of impending doom. **Depersonalization**, a feeling of being outside one's body, and **derealization**, a feeling of the world's not being real, as well as fears of losing control, of going crazy, or even of dying may beset and overwhelm the patient.

Panic attacks may occur frequently, perhaps once weekly or more often; usually last for minutes, rarely for hours; and are sometimes linked to specific situations, such as driving a car. When strongly associated with situational triggers, they are referred to as *cued panic attacks*. When a relationship between a stimulus and an attack is present but not as strong, attacks are referred to as situationally predisposed attacks. Panic attacks can also occur in seemingly benign states, such as relaxation, in sleep, and in unexpected situations; in these cases they are referred to as *uncued attacks*. Recurrent uncued attacks and worry about having attacks in the future are required for the diagnosis of panic disorder, but panic attacks themselves occur fairly often—among 3 to 5% of the general population in any given year—in people who do not meet the criteria for panic disorder (Norton, Cox, & Malan, 1992). The exclusive presence of cued attacks most likely reflects the presence of a phobia.

The lifetime prevalence of panic disorder is about 2 percent for men and more than 5 percent for women (Kessler et al., 1994). It typically begins in adolescence, and its onset is associated with stressful life experiences (Pollard, Pollard, & Corn, 1989). The prevalence of panic disorder varies cross-culturally. For example, in Africa it was diagnosed in about 1 percent of men and 6 percent of women (Hollifield et al., 1990). However, in Taiwan the prevalence of panic disorder is quite low, perhaps because of a stigma about reporting a mental problem (Weissman et al., 1997). Disorders that bear some relationship to panic disorder occur in other cultures also. Among the Eskimo of west Greenland, for example, kayakangst occurs in seal hunters who are alone at sea. Attacks involve intense fear, disorientation, and concerns about drowning. *Ataque de nervios* was originally identified in Puerto Rico and involves physical symptoms and fears of going crazy in the aftermath of severe stress.

In DSM-IV-TR panic disorder is diagnosed as with or without agoraphobia. **Agoraphobia** (from the Greek *agora*, meaning "marketplace") is a cluster of fears centering on public places

DSM-IV-TR Criteria for Panic Disorder

- Recurrent unexpected panic attacks
- At least 1 month of concern regarding the occurrence of further attacks or worry about the consequences of having an attack, or behavioral changes because of the attacks

Disorders similar to panic attacks occur cross-culturally. Among the Eskimo, kayak-angst is defined by intense fear in lone hunters.

---

[2] Some of the drugs that are effective for certain anxiety disorders are classified as antidepressants. This seems an anomaly, but it highlights two issues: (1) depression may be an important component of the anxiety disorders, and (2) it may be useful to categorize drugs such as Prozac as anxiolytics and not merely as antidepressants.

Childhood Fears and Social Withdrawal

Most children experience fears and worries as part of the normal course of development. A classic report by Jersild and Holmes (1935) indicated that children between the ages of two and six average about five fears, and similar findings have been reported by later investigators (e.g., Lapouse & Monk, 1959). Common fears, most of which are outgrown, include fear of the dark and of imaginary creatures (in children under five) and fear of being separated from parents (in children under ten). In general, as with adults, fears and phobias are reported more often for girls than for boys (Lichenstein & Annas, 2000), though this sex difference may be due at least in part to social pressures against boys' admitting that they are afraid of things. For fears and worries to be classified as disorders, children's functioning must be impaired; unlike adults, however, children need not regard their fear as excessive or unreasonable, because children sometimes lack the insight to make such judgments. Using this definition, about 10 to 15 percent of children and adolescents have an anxiety disorder, making these the most common disorders of childhood (Cohen et al., 1993). Although most unrealistic childhood fears dissipate over time, it is also the case that most anxious adults can trace their problems back to childhood.

The seriousness of some childhood anxiety problems should therefore not be underestimated. Not only do they suffer, as do adults, from the aversiveness of being anxious—simply put, it doesn't feel good to be highly anxious—but they may also lose out on mastering developmental tasks at various stages of their young lives. To be specific, a child who is painfully shy and who finds interacting with peers virtually intolerable is unlikely to learn how to interact with other people. This behavioral deficit will persist as the child grows into adolescence and will form the unfortunate foundation of still further "social retardation." Whether the adolescent begins working after high school or enters college, his or her relationships with others are unlikely to be rewarding. A likely result is that the worst fear—people will dislike and reject me—will be based in large measure on reality because the person's awkward, even off-putting behavior toward others produces rejecting and avoiding responses, confirming the person's core fear. As mentioned in our discussion of social phobia, people who were very socially anxious as children tend to have particularly debilitating social anxieties as adults and are more difficult to treat.

School Phobia

One childhood fear, **school phobia**, sometimes called *school refusal*, has serious academic and social consequences for the youngster and can be extremely disabling. Two types of school phobia have been identified. In the more com-

mon type, which is associated with separation anxiety, children worry constantly that some harm will befall their parents or themselves when they are away from their parents; when at home, they shadow one or both of their parents and often try to join them in bed.

Since the beginning of school is often the first circumstance that requires lengthy and frequent separations of children from their parents, separation anxiety is often a principal cause of school phobia. One study found that 75 percent of children who have school refusal caused by separation anxiety have mothers who also avoided school in childhood (Last & Strauss, 1990). It has been hypothesized that the child's refusal or extreme reluctance to go to school stems from some difficulty in the mother–child relationship. Perhaps the mother communicates her own separation anxieties and unwittingly reinforces the child's dependent and avoidant behavior.

The second major type of school refusal is that associated with a true phobia of school—either a fear specifically related to school or a more general social phobia. Children with this type of phobia generally begin refusing to go to school later in life and have more severe and pervasive avoidance of school. Their fear is more likely to be related to specific aspects of the school environment, such as worries about academic failure or discomfort with peers.

Experts agree that if it is untreated (or if it doesn't dissipate without professional intervention), school phobia in childhood can have long-term negative consequences as the person grows into adolescence and adulthood. The child with a school phobia can grow up to be a seriously dependent and fearful person.

School phobia is most commonly associated with separation anxiety disorder, an intense fear of being away from parents or other attachment figures.

Social Phobia

Most classrooms have in attendance at least one or two children who are extremely quiet and shy. Often these children will play only with family members or familiar peers, avoiding strangers both young and old. Their shyness may prevent them from acquiring skills and participating in a variety of activities enjoyed by most of their age-mates, for they avoid playgrounds and games played by neighborhood children. Although some youngsters who are shy may simply be slow to warm up, withdrawn children never do, even after prolonged exposure to new people. Extremely shy children may refuse to speak at all in unfamiliar social circumstances; this condition is called **selective mutism**. In crowded rooms they cling and whisper to their parents, hide behind the furniture, cower in corners, and may even have tantrums. At home they ask their parents endless questions about situations that worry them. Withdrawn children usually have warm and satisfying relationships with family members and family friends, and they show a desire for affection and acceptance.

Because the point at which shyness or withdrawal becomes a problem varies, few reliable statistics have been compiled on the frequency of this disorder. One estimate is that 1 percent of children and adolescents can be diagnosed with social phobia (Kashani & Orvaschel, 1990); it is more of a problem with adolescents, who are of an age when concern about the opinions of others can be acute.

Some children exhibit intense anxiety in specific social situations, showing social phobia similar to that of adults (see p. 136). When such children were asked to keep daily diaries of anxiety-producing events, they reported experiencing anxiety three times more frequently than did children in a normal control group, with concerns about such activities as reading aloud before a group, writing on the board, and performing in front of others. When faced with these events they reported crying, avoidance, and somatic complaints such as shakiness and nausea (Beidel, 1991).

Theories of the etiology of social phobia in children are generally similar to theories of social phobia in adults. For example, research has shown that children with anxiety disorders overestimate the danger in many situations and underestimate their ability to cope with them (Boegels & Zigterman, 2000). The anxiety created by these cognitions then interferes with social interaction, causing the child to avoid social situations and thus not to get much practice at social skills. Another suggestion is that withdrawn children may simply not have the social know-how that facilitates interaction with their age-mates. The finding that isolated children make fewer attempts to make friends and are less imaginative in their play may indicate a deficiency in social skills. Finally, isolated children may have become so because they have in the past spent most of their time with adults; these children interact more freely with adults than with other children (Scarlett, 1980).

Treatment of Childhood Fears and Phobias

How are childhood fears overcome? Many simply dissipate with time and maturation. For the most part, treatment of such fears is similar to that employed with adults, with suitable modifications to accommodate the different abilities and circumstances of childhood.

Perhaps the most widespread means of helping children overcome fears, employed by millions of parents, is to expose them gradually to the feared object, often while acting simultaneously to inhibit their anxiety. If a little girl fears strangers, a parent takes her by the hand and walks her slowly toward the new person. Mary Cover Jones (see p. 48) was the first psychologist to explain this bit of folk wisdom as a counterconditioning procedure.

Contemporary therapists generally agree that exposure is the most effective way of eliminating baseless fear and avoidance. Modeling has also proved effective, both in laboratory studies (e.g., Bandura, Grusec, & Menlove, 1967) and in countless clinical treatments (Barrios & O'Dell, 1989). For example, the therapist may have another child, one the fearful child is likely to imitate, demonstrate fearless behavior. In one innovative study youngsters were helped by viewing films in which other isolated children gradually engaged in and came to enjoy play with their peers (O'Connor, 1969). Another group of researchers paired undergraduate volunteers with socially isolated children on the playground during recess (Allen et al., 1976). The goal was to help start group games that would include the target child and give in vivo feedback to the child about which behaviors promoted or inhibited positive interactions with other children. By the end of the six-month program the volunteers were standing on the sidelines observing the children playing with their peers.

Offering rewards for moving closer to a feared object or situation can also be encouraging to a fearful child. Both modeling and operant treatments involve exposure to what is feared. When the fear and avoidance of a child with school phobia are very great and of long duration, they may require desensitization through direct, graduated exposure plus operant shaping.

In a case already mentioned (Lazarus, Davison, & Polefka, 1965), the therapist began by walking to school with nine-year-old Paul, all the while comforting the boy and, in general, trying to make him feel better as he approached the anxiety-provoking school building. The boy was then exposed more and more to school with lessening contact with the therapist. On successive days Paul first entered the school yard and then returned home; next, he entered an empty classroom after school; then he attended the opening morning exercises and left. Later he sat at a desk and spent time in school, first with the therapist beside him, then with the therapist out of sight but still nearby. In the last steps, when anxiety seemed to have diminished, the therapist provided reinforcement for Paul in the form of promises to play the guitar for him at night, comic books, and tokens that would eventually earn him a baseball glove.

A focus on the child's cognitive capacities is also to be found in therapy with fearful children. Cognitive behavior therapists analyze the child's biased thinking and catastrophizing assumptions in an attempt to relieve unwarranted anxiety. For example, if the child concludes that no one cares for her on the basis of not being invited to the birthday party of one of her classmates, a strategy based on Beck's theorizing would encourage the patient to consider reasons for this exclusion that are not based on no one liking her. A strategy based more on Ellis would encourage the youngster to resist the notion that her self-worth is entirely dependent on whether she gets invited to parties. Admittedly, both approaches, especially Ellis's, are fraught with difficulty, but emerging evidence indicates that such strategies can be helpful to many fearful and socially avoidant children (Kendall, Chu, Pimentel, & Choudbury, 2000).

As with adults, some new situations may be threatening because children lack the knowledge and skills to deal with them. Thus a child's fear of the water may very well be based on a reasonable judgment that danger lurks there because he or she cannot swim. Some shy children lack specific social skills needed for peer interaction. Skills such as asking questions (Ladd, 1981), giving compliments, and starting conversations with age-mates (Michelson et al., 1983) can be taught in small groups or in pairs, with interactions videotaped so the child and coach can observe and modify the new behaviors.

Treatment-outcome studies suggest that time-limited treatment of children's phobias can be very effective (Ollendick & King, 1998). For example, Hampe et al. (1973) treated sixty-seven phobic children for eight weeks, using either a behavioral or an insight-oriented therapy. Sixty percent of the treated children were free of their phobia at the end of the eight-week period and did not experience a relapse or additional emotional problems during the two-year follow-up period. Eighty percent of the sample (those just mentioned plus others who sought further treatment elsewhere) were free of symptoms after two years, with only 7 percent continuing to experience a severe phobia. The authors concluded that although many childhood phobias cease without intervention, treatment greatly hastens recovery. Similarly positive results have been reported by Kendall (1994) and by Barrett, Dadds, and Rapee (1996) in therapies that were more cognitive in nature than the earlier work, entailing instructions to children to talk to themselves in self-reassuring ways and involving the parents in rewarding coping efforts by their children (Kendall, Chu, Pimentel, & Choudbury, 2000). But exposure to feared situations continued as the mainstay of treatment.

In agoraphobia, a person is afraid of being in shopping malls, crowds, and the like, and can become housebound.

and being unable to escape or find help should one become incapacitated by anxiety. Fears of shopping, crowds, and traveling are often present. Many patients with agoraphobia are unable to leave the house or do so only with great distress. Patients who have panic disorder typically avoid the situations in which a panic attack could be dangerous or embarrassing. If the avoidance becomes widespread, panic with agoraphobia is the result. (When agoraphobia occurs in the absence of a diagnosable panic disorder, the person typically has experienced panic symptoms, but not full-blown attacks. So in both cases the agoraphobia is linked to a fear of having an attack.) Panic disorder with agoraphobia and agoraphobia without a history of panic disorder are both much more common among women than among men.

More than 80 percent of patients diagnosed as having one of the other anxiety disorders also experience panic attacks, although not with the frequency that justifies a diagnosis of panic disorder (Barlow et al., 1985). Coexistence of panic disorder and major depression is also common (Johnson & Lydiard, 1998), as is comorbidity between panic disorder and generalized anxiety disorder, phobias (Brown et al., 2001), alcoholism, and personality disorders (Johnson, Weissman, & Klerman, 1990), especially avoidant, dependent, and histrionic personality disorders (see Chapter 13 for a discussion of these and other personality disorders). As with many of the disorders discussed in this book, comorbidity is associated with greater severity and poor outcomes, probably because there are simply more problems to address (Newman et al., 1998).

Etiology of Panic Disorder

Both biological and psychological theories have been proposed to explain panic disorder.

Biological Theories   In a minority of cases, physical sensations caused by an illness lead some people to develop panic disorder. For example, mitral valve prolapse syndrome causes heart palpitations, and inner ear disease causes dizziness that some people construe as terrifying, leading to the development of panic disorder (Asmundson, Larsen, & Stein, 1998; Hamada et al., 1998).

Panic disorder runs in families and has greater concordance in MZ (identical twin) pairs than in DZ (fraternal twins). Thus, a genetic diathesis may be involved (Hettema, Neale, & Kendler, 2001).

Noradrenergic Activity   Another biological theory suggests that panic is caused by overactivity in the noradrenergic system (neurons that use norepinephrine as a neurotransmitter). One version of this theory focuses on a nucleus in the pons called the locus ceruleus. Stimulation of the locus ceruleus causes monkeys to have what appears to be a panic attack, suggesting that naturally occurring attacks might be based on noradrenergic overactivation (Redmond, 1977). Subsequent research with humans has found that yohimbine, a drug that stimulates activity in the locus ceruleus, can elicit panic attacks in patients with panic disorder (Charney et al., 1987). However, more recent research is not consistent with this position. Importantly, drugs that block firing in the locus ceruleus have not been found to be very effective in treating panic attacks (McNally, 1994).

Another idea about noradrenergic overactivity is that it results from a problem in gamma-aminobutryic (GABA) neurons that generally inhibit noradrenergic activity (see p. 24). Consistent with this line of thinking, a PET study found fewer GABA-receptor binding sites in patients with panic disorder than in controls (Malizia et al, 1998), and GABA levels are low in the occipital cortex of panic disorder patients (Goddard et al., 2001). Thus, although no definitive conclusions can be drawn, noradrenergic overactivation remains an area of active research.

Creating Panic Attacks Experimentally   Another line of biological inquiry has focused on experimental manipulations that can induce panic attacks. One approach proposes that panic attacks are linked to hyperventilation, or overbreathing (Ley, 1987). Hyperventilation may activate the autonomic nervous system, thus leading to the familiar somatic aspects of a panic episode. Based on the finding that breathing air containing higher than usual amounts of carbon dioxide (CO_2) can generate a panic attack in a laboratory setting, oversensitive CO_2 receptors have been proposed as a mechanism that could stimulate hyperventilation and then a panic attack (Gorman et al., 1988; Klein, 1993). However, more recent research, which monitored patients with panic disorder in their natural environments, found that hyperventilation occurred in only one of twenty-four attacks (Garssen, Buikhuisen, & Van Dyck, 1996). Therefore this line of biological inquiry has not panned out.

The data indicating that various biological challenges (e.g., carbon dioxide, hyperventilation) can induce panic also show that they do so only in those who have already been diagnosed with the disorder or those who are high in fear of their own bodily sensations (Zinbarg et al., 2001). This could be taken to mean that these stimuli activate some kind of biological abnormality or diathesis in patients with the disorder. However, the physiological responses of people with panic disorder to these biological challenges are very similar to those of people without the disorder (Gorman et al., 2000). Only the self-reported levels of fear induced by the challenge differentiate the two groups (Margraf, Ehlers, & Roth, 1986). Therefore the results may indicate that it is the psychological reaction to the challenge that is central, a possibility that underlies a well-validated treatment for this disorder, as we will see.

Psychological Theories   The principal psychological theory of the agoraphobia that often accompanies panic disorder is the fear-of-fear hypothesis (e.g., Goldstein & Chambless, 1978), which suggests that agoraphobia is not a fear of public places per se, but a fear of having a panic attack in public.

Classical conditioning and a distinction between anxiety and panic form the basis of one recent theory of the panic attacks themselves (Bouton, Mineka, & Barlow, 2001). Panic, as we have already described, is a state of extreme fear and strong autonomic arousal. Anxiety is seen as a state of apprehension and worry. The main point of the theory is that panic attacks become classically conditioned to internal bodily sensations of anxiety. The theory is supported by studies (see p. 94) in which people with panic disorder kept records of their attacks and what preceded them. Anxiety and physical sensations were frequently reported. As we described earlier, panic attacks are not uncommon. Why do some people go on to develop panic disorder while others are able to dismiss the attack? One possibility is that those who will develop the disorder view the attacks as uncontrollable and unpredictable and perceive the attack as particularly intense. This could provide a very strong UCS and thus increase conditioning. Another possibility is that panic disorder develops in people who are generally high in anxiety.

A second theory of panic attacks also focuses on the early signs of an attack but emphasizes the catastrophic misinterpretation of these stimuli (Clark, 1996). Panic attacks develop when a person notices some bodily sensation and interprets it as a sign of impending doom. These thoughts lead to further anxiety and more physical sensations, so a vicious circle is created.

In an important test of this hypothesis, Telch and Harrington (1992) studied college students with no history of panic attacks who were divided into two groups (high and low scorers) based on their scores on a test called the Anxiety Sensitivity Index, which measures the extent to which people respond fearfully to their bodily sensations. (Sample items from the questionnaire are shown in Table 6.2.) All participants experienced two trials. In one trial they breathed room air, and in the other they breathed air with a higher-than-usual concentration of carbon dioxide. Half the participants in each group were told that the carbon dioxide would be relaxing, and half were told that it would produce symptoms of high arousal. The frequency of panic attacks in each group is shown in Table 6.3. Note that panic attacks did not occur in participants when they breathed room

Table 6.2 Sample Items from the Anxiety Sensitivity Index

Unusual body sensations scare me.

When I notice that my heart is beating rapidly, I worry that I might have a heart attack.

It scares me when I feel faint.

It scares me when I feel "shaky" (trembling).

Source: Peterson & Reiss, 1987.

Note: People respond to each item on a 0 (very little) to 4 (very much) scale.

Table 6.3 Frequency of Panic Attacks as a Function of Breathing Room Air versus Breathing Air with Carbon Dioxide, Fear of Bodily Sensations, and Expectations

Inhale	High Fear of Bodily Sensations		Low Fear of Bodily Sensations	
	Expect Relaxation	Expect Arousal	Expect Relaxation	Expect Arousal
Room air	0	0	0	0
Carbon dioxide	52	17	5	5

air, confirming previous findings. Also, the data show that the frequency of panic attacks was higher in participants who were high in fear of their own bodily sensations. Finally, and most important, the frequency of panic attacks was strikingly high in participants who feared their bodily sensations, breathed air containing a high concentration of carbon dioxide, and did not expect it to be arousing. This result is exactly what the theory predicts: unexplained physiological arousal in someone who is fearful of such sensations leads to panic attacks. Furthermore, scores on the Anxiety Sensitivity Index have been shown to be heritable, so this measure may be the source of the genetic diathesis for panic disorder (Stein, King, & Livesley, 1999).

Another study bearing on this theory of panic disorder followed recruits as they went through the stressful experience of basic training (Schmidt, Lerew, & Jackson, 1997). The Anxiety Sensitivity Index was administered, and clinical assessments then determined who developed panic attacks during the course of basic training. Consistent with the theory, high scores on the Anxiety Sensitivity Index predicted the development of panic attacks.

The concept of control is also relevant to panic. Patients with the disorder have an extreme fear of losing control, which would happen if they had an attack in public. The importance of control was clearly demonstrated in a study by Sanderson, Rapee, and Barlow (1989), which was a conceptual replication of an earlier analogue study by Geer, Davison, and Gatchel (1970). Patients with panic disorder breathed carbon dioxide and were told that when a light turned on they could turn a dial to reduce the concentration of carbon dioxide. For half the participants the light was on continuously, whereas for the remainder it never came on. Turning the dial actually had no effect on carbon dioxide levels, so the study evaluated the effects of *perceived* control on reactions to the challenge. Eighty percent of the group with no control had a panic attack, compared with only 20 percent of the group who thought they could control carbon dioxide levels. Note that in addition to clearly demonstrating the importance of perceived control in panic disorder, the data again show that it is not the biological challenge per se that elicits panic; rather, a person's psychological reaction is crucial.

Therapies for Panic Disorder and Agoraphobia

Therapies for panic disorder include both biological and psychological approaches. Some are quite similar to the treatments discussed for phobias.

Biological Treatments   Because panic sufferers usually consult with physicians before they see a psychologist or psychiatrist, psychoactive medications are typically the first and sometimes the only kind of treatment people get. The vigorous marketing of antipanic drugs in the media is probably also a factor. Several drugs have shown some success as biological treatments for panic disorder. They include antidepressants (both selective serotonin reuptake inhibitors, such as Prozac, and tricyclic antidepressants such as Tofranil) and benzodiazepines (such as Alprazolam or Xanax) (Roy-Byrne & Cowley, 1998). Evidence for the effectiveness of Alprazolam is particularly compelling, as it was obtained in a large-scale, multinational study (Ballenger et al., 1998).

On the negative side, when the drugs are administered by patients' family physicians instead of in research studies such as those cited, effectiveness drops off, mostly because of insufficient doses or a course of treatment that was not long enough (Roy-Byrne et al., 2001). Moreover, as many as half of patients with panic disorder who are given tricyclics drop out of treatment because of side effects such as jitteriness and weight gain and more serious side effects such as elevated heart rate and blood pressure (Taylor et al., 1990). Furthermore, the benzodiazepines are addicting, and they produce both cognitive and motor side effects, such as memory lapses and difficulty driving. In their efforts to reduce anxiety many patients use anxiolytics or alcohol on their own; the use and abuse of drugs is common in anxiety-ridden people. Even if it is effective, drug treatment must be continued indefinitely, for symptoms almost always return if it is stopped (Fyer, Sandberg, & Klein, 1991). Finally, Barlow's panic control treatment appears to be superior to currently available drug treatments, especially when long-term follow-up is done, as detailed in the following section.

Psychological Treatments   Exposure-based treatments are often useful in reducing agoraphobia (or, in DSM-IV-TR terms, panic disorder with agoraphobia), and these gains are largely maintained for many years after therapy has ended (Fava et al., 1995). Some studies find that the effects of exposure are enhanced when patients are encouraged to relax during the in vivo experiences (e.g., Michelson, Marchione, & Greenwald, 1989), but other studies do not show added benefit from relaxation (e.g., Ost, Hellstrom, & Westling, 1989).

Married patients whose problem is primarily or solely agoraphobia have benefited from family-oriented therapies that involve the nonphobic spouse, who is encouraged to stop catering to his or her partner's avoidance of leaving the home. Barlow's clinical research program found that successful in vivo exposure treatment, in which the person with agoraphobia is encouraged to venture little by little from "safe" domains, is enhanced when the spouse is involved (Cerny et al., 1987). Contrary to the belief that the nonphobic spouse somehow needs the other to be dependent on him or her (Milton & Hafner, 1979), marital satisfaction tends to improve as the fearful spouse becomes bolder (Craske et al., 1992; Himadi et al., 1986). Thus, although it is understandable that a spouse might become overly solicitous, perhaps from reasonable concern for his or her partner's well-being, perhaps from an inner need to have a spouse who is weak and dependent, the outcome data suggest that relationships improve when the spouse with agoraphobia becomes less fearful (Craske & Barlow, 2001).

Treating agoraphobia with exposure does not always reduce panic attacks (Michelson, Mavissakalian, & Marchione, 1985). Thus, psychological treatment of panic disorder has taken a different direction in recent years, focusing on the finding mentioned earlier that some patients become unduly alarmed by noticing and overreacting to innocuous sensations from their bodies. One well-validated therapy developed by Barlow and his associates and referred to as panic control therapy (PCT) has three principal components:

1. Relaxation training.
2. A combination of Ellis- and Beck-type cognitive-behavioral interventions.
3. The most novel part, exposure to the internal cues that trigger panic (Barlow, 1988; Barlow & Craske, 1994; Craske & Barlow, 2001).

Let us examine the third component in more detail, because it is really quite innovative. The therapist persuades the client to practice in the consulting room behaviors that can elicit feelings associated with panic. For example, a person whose panic attacks begin with hyperventilation is asked to breathe fast for three minutes; someone who gets dizzy might be requested to spin in a chair for several minutes. When sensations such as dizziness, dry mouth, light-headedness, increased heart rate, and other signs of panic begin, the client (1) experiences them under safe conditions and (2) applies previously learned cognitive and relaxation coping tactics (which can include breathing from the diaphragm rather than hyperventilating).

With practice and encouragement or persuasion from the therapist, the client learns to reinterpret internal sensations from being signals of loss of control and panic to cues that are intrinsically harmless and can be controlled with certain skills. The intentional creation of these physical sensations by the client, coupled with success in coping with them, reduces their unpredictability and changes their meaning for the client (Craske, Maidenberg, & Bystritsky, 1995).

Two-year follow-ups have shown that therapeutic gains from this cognitive and exposure therapy have been maintained to a significant degree and are superior to gains resulting from the use of alprazolam (Xanax) (Craske, Brown, & Barlow, 1991), though many patients are not panic free (Brown & Barlow, 1995). Recently the Multisite Comparative Study for the Treatment of Panic Disorder began publishing its findings comparing PCT, imipramine, a placebo, a combination of PCT and imipramine, PCT plus placebo, and imipramine plus placebo (Barlow, Gorman, Shear, & Woods, 2000). All treatments were conducted once a week for three months, followed by six months of maintenance for those who had improved during the three months of weekly treatment. Finally, six months later, there was a follow-up assessment. Among the results published so far:

- Both PCT and imipramine were superior to the placebo immediately posttreatment.
- PCT combined with imipramine was no better than PCT plus placebo immediately posttreatment.
- PCT combined with imipramine was no more effective than either PCT or imipramine alone immediately posttreatment.
- After the six months of maintenance therapy, all treatments were more effective than placebo.
- At the six-month follow-up, those treated with PCT alone were better off than those whose PCT treatment had also included either placebo or imipramine. Put differently, many patients who had taken the drug relapsed.

In general, across numerous studies, more than half of panic-disordered patients treated with PCT are free of panic at the end of treatment and almost two-thirds are "cured" at six- to twelve-month follow-up (Telch et al., 1995). These are impressive statistics, especially the follow-up findings, particularly when compared with drug treatment. A similar cognitive-behavioral treatment independently developed by Clark (1989; Salkovskis & Clark, 1991) has also shown beneficial effects on panic disorder (Clark, Watson, & Mineka, 1994).

Generalized Anxiety Disorder

The patient, a twenty-four-year-old mechanic, had been referred for psychotherapy by his physician, whom he had consulted because of dizziness and difficulties in falling asleep. He was quite visibly distressed during the entire initial interview, gulping before he spoke, sweating, and continually fidgeting in his chair. His repeated requests for water to slake a seemingly unquenchable thirst were another indication of his extreme nervousness. Although he first related his physical concerns, a more general picture of pervasive anxiety soon emerged. He reported that he nearly always felt tense. He seemed to worry about anything and everything. He was apprehensive of disasters that could befall him as he worked and interacted with other people. He reported a long history of difficulties in interpersonal relationships, which had led to his being fired from several jobs. As he put it, "I really like people and try to get along with them, but it seems like I fly off the handle too easily. Little things they do upset me too much. I just can't cope unless everything is going exactly right."

"Worry is interest on a debt that never comes due." David Mamet, "The Spanish Prisoner"

The individual with **generalized anxiety disorder (GAD)** is persistently anxious, often about minor items. Most of us worry from time to time. But patients with GAD worry chronically. They spend a great deal of time worrying about a wide range of topics and describe their worrying as uncontrollable (Ruscio, Borkovec, & Ruscio, 2001). The most frequent worries of patients with GAD concern their health and daily hassles, such as being late for appointments or having too much work to do. GAD is not diagnosed if the worries are confined to concerns driven by another Axis I disorder, for example, the worrying about contamination by a person with obsessive-compulsive disorder. The uncontrollable nature of the worries associated with GAD has been confirmed by both self-reports and laboratory data (Becker et al., 1998; Craske et al., 1989). Other features of GAD include difficulty concentrating, tiring easily, restlessness, irritability, and a high level of muscle tension.

Although patients with generalized anxiety disorder do not typically seek psychological treatment, the lifetime prevalence of the disorder is fairly high; it occurs in about 5 percent of the general population (Wittchen & Hoyer, 2001). GAD typically begins in the person's midteens, though many people who have generalized anxiety disorder report having had the problem all their lives (Barlow et al., 1986). Stressful life events appear to play some role in its onset (Blazer, Hughes, & George, 1987). It is twice as common in women as in men, and it has a high level of comorbidity with other anxiety disorders and with mood disorders (Brown et al., 2001). It is difficult to treat generalized anxiety disorder successfully. In one five-year follow-up study, only 18 percent of patients had achieved a full remission of their symptoms (Woodman et al., 1999), though the outlook is likely to improve as clinicians make greater use of the cognitive-behavioral treatments described below.

Etiology of Generalized Anxiety Disorder

The etiology of generalized anxiety disorder includes psychoanalytic, cognitive-behavioral, and biological perspectives.

Psychoanalytic View   Psychoanalytic theory regards the source of generalized anxiety as an unconscious conflict between the ego and id impulses. The impulses, usually sexual or aggressive in nature, are struggling for expression, but the ego cannot allow their expression because it unconsciously fears that punishment will follow. Since the source of the anxiety is unconscious, the person experiences apprehension and distress without knowing why. The true source of anxiety—namely, desires associated with previously punished id impulses that are striving for expression—is ever present. In a sense, there is no way to evade anxiety; if the person escapes the id he or she is no longer alive. Thus, the person feels anxiety nearly all the time. The patient with a phobia may be regarded as more fortunate since, according to psychoanalytic theory, his or her anxiety is displaced onto a specific object or situation, which can then be avoided. The person with generalized anxiety disorder has not developed this type of defense and thus is constantly anxious.

Cognitive-Behavioral Views   The main idea of of cognitive-behavioral theories of GAD is that it results from distorted cognitive processes. People with GAD often misperceive benign events, such as crossing the street, as involving threats, and their cognitions focus on anticipated future disasters (Beck et al., 1987; Ingram & Kendall, 1987; Kendall & Ingram, 1989). The attention of patients with GAD is easily drawn to threat stimuli (Mogg, Millar, & Bradley, 2000; Thayer et al., 2000). Furthermore, patients with GAD are more inclined to interpret ambiguous stimuli as threatening and to rate ominous events as more likely to occur to them (Butler & Mathews, 1983). The heightened sensitivity of GAD patients to threatening stimuli occurs even when the stimuli cannot be consciously perceived (Bradley et al., 1995).

Another cognitive view has been proposed by Borkovec and his colleagues (e.g., Borkovec & Newman, 1998; Borkovec, Roemer, & Kinyon, 1995). Their focus is on the main symptom of GAD, worry. From a punishment perspective one might wonder why anyone would worry a lot, since worry is thought to be a negative state that should discourage its repetition. Borkovec and his colleagues have marshaled evidence that worry is actually negatively reinforcing; it distracts patients from negative emotions and is thereby strengthened by this favorable outcome for the person.

The key to understanding this position is to realize that worry does not produce much emotional arousal. For example, it does not produce the physiological changes that usually accompany emotion, and it actually blocks the processing of emotional stimuli.

DSM-IV-TR Criteria for GAD

- Excessive anxiety and worry
- The worry is difficult to control
- The patient experiences three or more of the following: restlessness, easily fatigued, difficulty concentrating, irritability, muscle tension, sleep disturbance

Therefore, by worrying, people with GAD are avoiding aversive images. And as a consequence their anxiety about these images does not extinguish. What are the anxiety-evoking images that patients with GAD are avoiding? One possibility comes from data showing that people with GAD report more past trauma involving death, injury, or illness. Yet these are not the topics they worry about; worry may distract patients with GAD from the distressing images of these past traumas.

Biological Perspectives   Some studies indicate that GAD may have a genetic component. GAD is frequently found in relatives of people with the disorder, and there is higher concordance among MZ than DZ twins. But the extent of a genetic component appears to be modest, at best (Hettema, M. Neale, & Kendler, 2000).

The most prevalent neurobiological model for generalized anxiety is based on knowledge of the operation of the benzodiazepines, a group of drugs that are often effective in treating anxiety. Researchers have discovered a receptor in the brain for benzodiazepines that is linked to the inhibitory neurotransmitter gamma-aminobutyric acid (GABA). In normal fear reactions, neurons throughout the brain fire and create the experience of anxiety. This neural firing also stimulates the GABA system, which inhibits this activity and thus reduces anxiety. GAD may result from some defect in the GABA system so that anxiety is not brought under control. The benzodiazepines may reduce anxiety by enhancing the release of GABA. Similarly, drugs that block or inhibit the GABA system lead to increases in anxiety (Insell, 1986). Much remains to be learned, but this approach seems destined to enhance our understanding of anxiety.

Therapies for Generalized Anxiety Disorder

As mentioned, GAD is difficult to treat successfully. Therapies include psychoanalytic, behavioral, cognitive, and biological approaches.

Psychoanalytic Approaches   Because they view generalized anxiety disorder as stemming from repressed conflicts, most psychoanalysts work to help patients confront the true sources of their conflicts. Treatment is much the same as that for phobias.

One uncontrolled study employed a psychodynamic intervention that focused on interpersonal conflicts from the patient's past and present life and encouraged more adaptive ways of dealing with others in the here-and-now, akin to what cognitive behavior therapists call social problem-solving (cf. p. 582). Outcomes from this intervention were quite encouraging and merit closer study with better experimental controls, such as no treatment and contrasting control groups (Crits-Christoph et al., 1996).

Behavioral Approaches   Behavioral clinicians approach generalized anxiety in various ways. If the therapist construes the anxiety as a set of responses to identifiable situations, what appears to be free-floating anxiety can be reformulated into one or more phobias or cued anxieties. For example, a behavior therapist may determine that the generally anxious client seems more specifically afraid of criticizing and of being criticized by others. The anxiety appears free-floating only because the client spends so many hours with other human beings. Systematic desensitization becomes a possible treatment. Of course, from a DSM point of view, such a patient would not qualify for a GAD diagnosis. The behavior therapist would have *reformulated* what initially appeared to be GAD into some sort of phobia.

However, it can be difficult to find specific causes of the anxiety suffered by such patients. This difficulty has led behavioral clinicians to prescribe more generalized treatment, such as intensive relaxation training, in the hope that learning to relax when beginning to feel tense as they go about their lives will keep anxiety from spiraling out of control (Barlow et al., 1984; Borkovec & Mathews, 1988; Ost, 1987b). Patients are taught to relax away low-level tensions, responding to incipient anxiety with relaxation rather than with alarm (Goldfried, 1971; Suinn & Richardson, 1971). Recently, this strategy has been found very effective in alleviating GAD (e.g., Borkovec & Roemer, 1994; Borkovec & Whisman, 1996; see also reviews by DeRubeis & Crits-Christoph, 1998; Borkovec & Ruscio, in press).

Cognitive Approaches   If a feeling of helplessness seems to underlie the pervasive anxiety, the cognitively oriented behavior therapist will help the client acquire whatever skills might engender a sense of competence. The skills, including assertiveness, may be taught by verbal instructions, modeling, or operant shaping—and very likely some judicious combination of the three (Goldfried & Davison, 1994).

Not surprisingly, cognitive techniques have also been employed in the treatment of chronic worrying, a central component of GAD. Worry, after all, is a cognitive event—ruminating about feared outcomes. Borkovec's approach (e.g., Borkovec & Costello, 1993) combines elements of Wolpe and Beck, that is, he encourages graduated exposure to worrisome situations while the patient tries to apply both relaxation skills and a logical analysis of things (e.g., how likely is it that something truly awful is going to happen?).

In contrast, Barlow and his associates favor extended and *exaggerated* exposure to the source of one's overly anxious concern (Brown, O'Leary, & Barlow, 2001). For example, a person worried about why his or her spouse is late coming home from a business trip would be encouraged to imagine the worst possible outcome—that the plane has crashed. The patient is asked to imagine this extreme and very unlikely outcome for half an hour or more and then to consider as many alternative explanations as possible for the tardiness, such as difficulties getting a cab or being caught in heavy traffic from the airport. It is assumed that two processes operate here to reduce the patient's worry:

1. Because the patient remains in a fearsome situation, anxiety is believed to extinguish.
2. By considering the unlikelihood of the worst fears imagined, the patient alters his or her cognitive reactions to his or her spouse's not showing up when expected.

In other words, the patient learns to think about less catastrophic reasons for a particular event.

This strategy of Barlow's is reminiscent of the blow-up technique developed years ago by Arnold Lazarus (1971). He described an application of this technique in the following clinical vignette:

> *[This patient had a] tendency to keep checking the men's room at a theatre or movie for a possible outbreak of fire. Typically, at intermission, or before taking his seat in the movie, he would visit the men's room, smoke a cigarette, and then go inside the theatre. Soon he would feel a mounting panic. He would ask himself, "I wonder whether I accidentally started a fire in the men's room?" He would leave his seat and rush back to the men's room and carefully check to be sure that no fire had in fact broken out. When back at his seat again he would feel that he may have failed to detect the fire, and he would soon develop an overwhelming urge to rush back and make doubly sure....*
>
> *I...gave him the following instructions: "When the urge to check comes over you, do not leave your seat. Instead, I want you to imagine that a fire has indeed broken out. First, picture the toilet paper and then the toilet seats catching fire and spreading to the doors, then going along the floor, so that eventually the entire men's room is ablaze. Then, as you sit in your seat, imagine the crackling flames spreading outside the men's room into the lobby. The carpets quickly catch fire and soon the entire movie house or theatre is a roaring inferno. This blaze is like no other. It cannot be stopped. Still sitting in your seat, imagine the entire neighborhood on fire. Firemen battle the blaze unsuccessfully as all neighboring areas catch fire until the entire city is devoured. And still the flames keep spreading. One city after another is demolished in this voracious chain reaction until the entire country is ablaze. The flames even spread across the oceans until the entire world is on fire. Eventually the whole universe is one raging inferno." (Lazarus, 1971, p. 231)*

This particular patient[3] was reported by Lazarus to have found the exercise very useful as he became amused by the outrageous fantasy, thinking it ridiculous. Soon thereafter he was no longer being bothered by intrusive worrisome thoughts.

---

[3] It should be noted that Lazarus regarded this patient as having obsessive-compulsive disorder, but we discuss it here as illustrative of worry in GAD. There would seem to be some overlap between the intrusive ruminations experienced by a person with obsessive-compulsive disorder and the uncontrollable worrying that is a defining characteristic of GAD.

Outcome data from controlled clinical trials so far are inconsistent in demonstrating that the various cognitive-behavioral approaches are superior either to placebo treatments or to alternative therapies such as Rogerian therapy (Barlow et al., 1998; Borkovec, Newman, Pincus, & Lytle, in press; Brown et al., 2001). Of particular note—with the striking exception of studies by Borkovec and Costello (1993) and Borkovec et al. (in press)—is the finding that not many patients in the various therapies evaluated show what is called high end-state functioning, that is, levels of anxiety or worry that are so minimal as to resemble those of people not diagnosed as having GAD. In other words, many GAD patients, although they show improvement, continue to struggle with many symptoms of anxiety (e.g., Stanley et al., 1996).[4]

When compared with benzodiazepine treatment, however, cognitive-behavior therapy appears to be superior; indeed, when it was combined with the drug treatment, the results were poorer than when it was used alone (Power et al., 1990). Moreover, several studies of cognitive-behavioral therapy with GAD find that improvement is associated with patients' coming to rely less on psychoactive drugs, like the minor tranquilizer Valium. This is indirect but very persuasive evidence for the effectiveness of the cognitive-behavioral intervention (Brown et al., 2001).

Biological Approaches   Anxiolytics, such as those mentioned for the treatment of phobias and panic disorder, are probably the most widespread treatment for generalized anxiety disorder. Drugs, especially the benzodiazepines, such as Valium and Xanax, as well as buspirone (BuSpar), are often used because of the disorder's pervasiveness. Once the drugs take effect, they continue to work for several hours in whatever situations are encountered. A number of double-blind studies confirm that these drugs benefit GAD patients more than do placebos (Apter & Allen, 1999). Other studies show some effectiveness from certain antidepressants, both the tricyclics and the SSRIs (Pollack et al., 2001; Roy-Byrne & Cowley, 1998).

Unfortunately, many of these drugs have undesirable side effects, ranging from drowsiness, memory loss, and depression to physical addiction and damage to bodily organs. In addition, when a patient withdraws from these drugs, the gains achieved in treatment are usually lost (Barlow, 1988). Perhaps these losses occur because the person (rightfully) attributes the improvement to an external agent, the medication, rather than to internal changes and his or her own coping efforts (Davison & Valins, 1969). Thus, the person continues to believe that the anxiety and the worrisome possibilities remain uncontrollable.

Obsessive-Compulsive Disorder

Bernice was forty-six when she entered treatment. This was the fourth time she had been in outpatient therapy, and she had previously been hospitalized twice. Her obsessive-compulsive disorder had begun twelve years earlier, shortly after the death of her father. Since then it had waxed and waned and currently was as severe as it had ever been.

Bernice was obsessed with a fear of contamination, a fear she vaguely linked to her father's death from pneumonia. Although she reported that she was afraid of nearly everything, because germs could be anywhere, she was particularly upset by touching wood, "scratchy objects," mail, canned goods, and "silver flecks." By silver flecks Bernice meant silver embossing on a greeting card, eyeglass frames, shiny appliances, and silverware. She was unable to state why these particular objects were sources of possible contamination.

To try to reduce her discomfort Bernice engaged in a variety of compulsive rituals that took up almost all her waking hours. In the morning she spent 3 to 4 hours in the bathroom, washing and rewashing herself. Between baths she scraped away the outside layer of her bar of soap so that it would be totally free of germs. Mealtimes also lasted for hours, as Bernice performed her rituals—eating three bites of food at a time, chewing each mouthful 300 times. These steps were meant magically to decontaminate her food. Even Bernice's husband was some-

---

[4] Is the glass half full or half empty? Although our critical evaluation of CBT for GAD highlights its limitations, the considerable improvement that most patients derive from these treatments should not be overlooked.

times involved in these mealtime ceremonies, shaking a teakettle and frozen vegetables over her head to remove the germs. Bernice's rituals and fear of contamination had reduced her life to doing almost nothing else. She would not leave the house, do housework, or even talk on the telephone.

Most of us have unwanted thoughts from time to time, and most of us have urges now and then to behave in certain ways that would be embarrassing or even dangerous. But few of us have what is called **obsessive-compulsive disorder (OCD)**, an anxiety disorder in which the mind is flooded with persistent and uncontrollable thoughts and the individual is compelled to repeat certain acts again and again, causing significant distress and interference with everyday functioning.

Obsessive-compulsive disorder has a lifetime prevalence of about 2.5 percent and affects women slightly more than men (Karno & Golding, 1991; Karno et al., 1988; Stein et al., 1997). It appears to have a bimodal age of onset, that is, beginning either before age ten or in late adolescence or early adulthood (Conceicao do Rosario-Campos et al., 2001). It has even been reported to occur in children as young as two (Rapoport, Swedo, & Leonard, 1992). Among later onset cases, OCD often begins following some stressful event, such as pregnancy, childbirth, family conflict, or difficulties at work (Kringlen, 1970).

Early onset is more common among men and is associated with checking compulsions; later onset is more frequent among women and is linked with cleaning compulsions (Noshirvani et al., 1991). During an episode of depression, patients occasionally develop obsessive-compulsive disorder, and significant depression is often found in obsessive-compulsive patients (Karno et al., 1988; Rachman & Hodgson, 1980). Obsessive-compulsive disorder also shows comorbidity with other anxiety disorders, particularly with panic and phobias (Austin et al., 1990), and with various personality disorders (Baer et al., 1990; Mavissikalian, Hammen, & Jones, 1990).

Obsessions are intrusive and recurring thoughts, impulses, and images that come unbidden to the mind, are uncontrollable, and usually though not always appear irrational to the individual experiencing them. Whereas many of us may have similar fleeting experiences, the obsessive individual, like in the Bernice case above, has them with such force and frequency that they interfere with normal functioning. Clinically, the most frequent obsessions concern fears of contamination, fears of expressing some sexual or aggressive impulse, and hypochondriacal fears of bodily dysfunction (Jenike, Baer, & Minichiello, 1986). Obsessions may also take the form of extreme doubting, procrastination, and indecision.

In some ways obsessive thinking is similar to the worrying that defines generalized anxiety disorder. It is full of "what ifs"—excessive ruminative concerns about the possibility that unlikely negative events will occur. The distinction typically drawn is that the OCD sufferers experience their concerns as "ego alien" or "ego dystonic"; that is they regard these thoughts almost as thrust upon them from the outside and not making very much sense. In contrast, the person with GAD is able to construct a logical argument that makes sense of the worry. After all, if my child is late coming home from school, it is possible that she's been kidnapped. Alternatively, if obsessive thinking is strongly believed by the person to be justified (as is true in about 5 percent of the cases), and if compulsive behavior is not present, it is possible that one is dealing with delusional disorder and perhaps even schizophrenia (see Chapter 11 for details on these psychotic disorders) (Eisen et al., 1998).

A **compulsion** is a repetitive behavior or mental act that the person feels driven to perform in order to reduce the distress caused by obsessive thoughts or to prevent some calamity from occurring. The activity is not realistically connected with its apparent purpose or is clearly excessive. Bernice did not need to chew each morsel of food 300 times, for example. An individual who continually repeats some action fears dire consequences if the act is not performed. The sheer frequency with which an act, overt or mental, is repeated may be staggering. Commonly reported compulsions include the following:

- Pursuing cleanliness and orderliness, sometimes through elaborate ceremonies that take hours and even most of the day.

DSM-IV-TR Criteria for OCD

- Obsessions, recurrent and persistent thoughts, impulses, or urges that cause anxiety
- Compulsions—repetitive behaviors and mental acts that the person performs to relieve distress

- Avoiding particular objects, such as staying away from anything brown.
- Performing repetitive, magical, protective practices, such as counting, saying certain numbers, or touching a talisman or a particular part of the body.
- Checking, going back seven or eight times to verify that already performed acts were actually carried out, for example, that lights, gas jets, or faucets were turned off, windows fastened, doors locked.
- Performing a particular act, such as eating extremely slowly.

We often hear people described as compulsive gamblers, compulsive eaters, and compulsive drinkers. Even though individuals may report an irresistible urge to gamble, eat, and drink, such behavior is not clinically regarded as a compulsion because it is often engaged in with pleasure. A true compulsion is often viewed by the person as somehow foreign to his or her personality (ego dystonic). Stern and Cobb (1978) found that 78 percent of a sample of compulsive individuals viewed their rituals as "rather silly or absurd" even though they were unable to stop them.

A frequent consequence of obsessive-compulsive disorder is a negative effect on the individual's relations with other people, especially family members. People saddled with the irresistible need to wash their hands every ten minutes, or touch every doorknob they pass, or count every tile in a bathroom floor are likely to cause concern and even resentment in spouses, children, friends, or co-workers. And the antagonistic feelings experienced by these significant others are likely to be tinged with guilt, for at some level they understand that the person cannot really help doing these senseless things.

The undesirable effects on others can, in turn, be expected to have additional negative consequences, engendering feelings of depression and generalized anxiety in the obsessive-compulsive person and setting the stage for even further deterioration of personal relationships. For such reasons family therapists (Hafner, 1982; Hafner et al., 1981) have suggested that obsessive-compulsive disorder is sometimes embedded in marital distress and actually substitutes for overt marital conflict. This speculative hypothesis cautions therapists to consider couples treatment (p. 293) as well as individual therapies.

This famous scene from Macbeth illustrates a compulsion involving hand washing.

Etiology of Obsessive-Compulsive Disorder

We now turn to psychoanalytic, behavioral, cognitive, and biological views of the etiology of obsessive-compulsive disorder.

Psychoanalytic Theory In psychoanalytic theory, obsessions and compulsions are viewed as similar, resulting from instinctual forces, sexual or aggressive, that are not under control because of overly harsh toilet training. The person is thus fixated at the anal stage. The symptoms observed represent the outcome of the struggle between the id and the defense mechanisms; sometimes the aggressive instincts of the id predominate, sometimes the defense mechanisms. For example, when obsessive thoughts of killing intrude, the forces of the id are dominant. More often, however, the observed symptoms reflect the partially successful operation of one of the defense mechanisms. For example, an individual fixated at the anal stage may, by reaction formation, resist the urge to soil and become compulsively neat, clean, and orderly.

Alfred Adler (1931) viewed obsessive-compulsive disorder as a result of feelings of incompetence. He believed that when children are kept from developing a sense of competence by doting or excessively dominating parents, they develop an inferiority complex and may unconsciously adopt compulsive rituals in order to carve out a domain in which they exert control and can feel proficient. Adler proposed that the compulsive act allows a person mastery of *something*, even if only the positioning of writing implements on a desk.

Behavioral and Cognitive Theories Behavioral accounts of compulsions consider them learned behaviors reinforced by fear reduction (Meyer & Chesser, 1970). For example, compulsive hand washing is viewed as an operant escape-response that reduces an obsessional preoccupation with and fear of contamination by dirt or germs. Similarly, compulsive checking may reduce anxiety about whatever disaster the patient anticipates if the checking ritual is not completed. Anxiety as measured by self-reports (Hodgson & Rachman, 1972) and psychophysiological responses (Carr, 1971) can indeed be reduced by such compulsive behavior. Within this framework, compulsive acts occur very frequently because the stimuli that elicit anxiety are hard to become aware of. For example, it is hard to know when germs are present and when they have been eliminated by some cleaning ritual (Mineka & Zimbarg, 1996).

Another idea about compulsive checking is that it results from a memory deficit. An inability to remember accurately some action (such as turning off the stove) or to distinguish between an actual behavior and an imagined behavior ("Maybe I just thought I turned off the stove") could cause someone to check repeatedly. Most studies, however, have found that patients with OCD do not show memory deficits. For example, one study compared patients with OCD, panic disorder, and normals on a test of general information. There were no differences among the groups in number of correct responses. Patients with OCD, however, were less confident in their answers than were the normals (Dar et al., 2000). Therefore, if memory is relevant to OCD, it appears to be a matter of confidence in one's memories rather than the memories themselves.

How can we account for obsessive thoughts? The obsessions of patients with obsessive-compulsive disorder usually make them anxious (Rabavilas & Boulougouris, 1974), much as do the somewhat similar intrusive thoughts of normal people about stressful stimuli, such as a scary movie (Horowitz, 1975). As noted earlier, most people occasionally experience unwanted ideas that are similar in content to obsessions (Rachman & deSilva, 1978). These unpleasant thoughts increase when people are subjected to stress (Parkinson & Rachman, 1981). Normal individuals can tolerate or dismiss these cognitions. But for individuals with obsessive-compulsive disorder, the thoughts may be particularly vivid and elicit great concern. The development of OCD may also be fostered by believing that thinking about a potentially unpleasant event makes it more likely that the event will actually occur (Rachman, 1997). Persons with obsessive-compulsive disorder have also been shown to have trouble ignoring stimuli, which could contribute to their difficulties (Clayton, Richards, & Edwards, 1999).

People with obsessive-compulsive disorder may try actively to suppress these intrusive thoughts, but often with unfortunate consequences. Wegner et al. (1987, 1991) studied what happens when people are asked to suppress a thought. Two groups of college students were asked either to think about a white bear or not to think about one. One group thought about the white bear and then was told not to; the other group did the reverse. Thoughts were measured by having participants voice their thoughts and also by having them ring a bell every time they thought about a white bear.

Two findings are of particular note. First, attempts to not think about a white bear were not fully successful. Second, the students who first inhibited thoughts of a white bear had more subsequent thoughts about it once the inhibition condition was over. Trying to inhibit a thought may therefore have the paradoxical effect of inducing preoccupation with it. Furthermore, attempts to suppress unpleasant thoughts are typically associated with intense emotional states, resulting in a strong link between the suppressed thought and the emotion. After many attempts at suppression a strong emotion may lead to the return of the thought, accompanied by an increase in negative mood (Wenzlaff, Wegner, & Klein, 1991). The result would be an increase in anxiety.

Cognitive accounts of OCD are similar to Adler's, discussed earlier. It has been hypothesized that OCD (at least the compulsive behavior) is driven by an unreasonable need to feel competent, even perfect, lest one feel worthless (McFall & Wollersheim, 1979). The world is a threatening place, and if one feels limited in one's ability to cope with the perceived dangerousness, then magical rituals may become the only way to achieve some sense of control and competence. Another cognitive theory emphasizes underlying assumptions (similar to Ellis's, cf. p. 55) such as the belief that one should be able to prevent harm to others and that one should be able to control one's thoughts (Salkovskis, 1985).

Biological Factors Encephalitis, head injuries, and brain tumors have all been associated with the development of obsessive-compulsive disorder (Jenike, 1986). Interest has focused on two areas of the brain that could be affected by such trauma, the frontal lobes and the basal ganglia, a set of subcortical nuclei including the caudate, putamen, globus pallidus, and amygdala (see Figure 6.1). PET scan studies have shown increased activation in the frontal lobes of OCD patients, perhaps a reflection of their overconcern with their own thoughts. The focus on the basal ganglia, a system linked to the control of motor behavior, is due to its relevance to compulsions as well as to the relationship between OCD and Tourette's syndrome. Tourette's syndrome is marked by both motor and vocal tics and has been linked to basal ganglia dysfunction. Patients with Tourette's often have OCD as well (Sheppard et al., 1999).

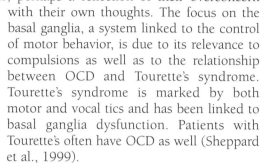

Thalamus

Globus
pallidus
(medial)

Caudate
nucleus

Putamen
(lateral)

Amygdala

Figure 6.1 The basal ganglia.

Providing support for the importance of both brain regions mentioned, Rauch et al. (1994) stimulated OCD symptoms by presenting patients with stimuli specially selected for them, such as a glove contaminated with garbage or an unlocked door. Blood flow in the brain increased in the frontal area and to some of the basal ganglia. Patients with OCD have also been found to have a smaller putamen than controls (Rosenberg et al., 1997).

Research on neurochemical factors has focused on serotonin. As we describe later, antidepressants that inhibit the reuptake of serotonin have proved to be useful therapies for OCD (e.g., Pigott et al., 1990). The usual interpretation of this finding would be that because the drugs facilitate synaptic transmission in serotonin neurons, OCD is related to low levels of serotonin or a reduced number of receptors. However, tests of these ideas have not yielded the expected results. For example, research with drugs that stimulate the serotonin receptor indicates that they can exacerbate the symptoms of OCD instead of reducing them (Bastani, Nash, & Meltzer, 1990; Hollander et al., 1992).

One possible explanation is that OCD is caused by a neurotransmitter system that is coupled to serotonin; when affected by antidepressants, the serotonin system causes changes in this other system, which is the real location of the therapeutic effect (Barr et al., 1994). Both dopamine and acetylcholine have been proposed as transmitters that are coupled to serotonin and play the more important role in OCD (Rauch & Jenike, 1993).

There is some evidence for a genetic contribution to OCD. High rates of anxiety disorders occur among the first-degree relatives of patients with OCD (McKeon & Murray, 1987). The prevalence of OCD is also higher in first-degree relatives of OCD cases than in control relatives (Nestadt et al., 2000). Thus, it is likely that biological factors predispose some people to this disorder.

Therapies for Obsessive-Compulsive Disorder

Obsessive-compulsive disorder is one of the most difficult psychological problems to treat. For example, a forty-year follow-up study showed that only 20 percent of patients had recovered completely (Skoog & Skoog, 1999). The major therapeutic schools have had different impacts on this difficult disorder. But, regardless of treatment modality, OCD patients are seldom cured. Although a variety of interventions can result in significant improvement, obsessive-compulsive tendencies usually persist to some degree, albeit under greater control and with less obtrusiveness into the conduct of patients' lives (White & Cole, 1990).

Psychoanalytic Therapy Psychoanalytic treatment for obsessions and compulsions resembles that for phobias and generalized anxiety, namely, lifting repression and allowing the patient to confront what he or she truly fears. Because the intrusive thoughts and compulsive behavior protect the ego from the repressed conflict, however, they are difficult targets for therapeutic intervention, and psychoanalytic and related psychodynamic procedures have not been effective in treating this disorder (Esman, 1989).

Such shortcomings have prompted some analytic clinicians to take a more active, behavioral approach to these disorders and to use analytic understanding more as a way to increase compliance with behavioral procedures (Jenike, 1990). One psychoanalytic view hypothesizes that the indecision one sees in most obsessive-compulsive patients derives from a need for guaranteed correctness before any action can be taken (Salzman, 1985). Patients therefore must learn to tolerate the uncertainty and anxiety that all people feel as they confront the reality that nothing is certain or absolutely controllable in life. The ultimate focus of the treatment remains insight into the unconscious determinants of the symptoms.

Behavioral Approaches: Exposure and Ritual Prevention (ERP)   The most widely used and generally accepted behavioral approach to compulsive rituals, pioneered in England by Victor Meyer (1966), combines exposure with response prevention (ERP) (Rachman & Hodgson, 1980). This approach has recently been renamed exposure and *ritual* prevention to highlight the almost magical belief by OCD sufferers that their compulsive behavior will prevent awful things from happening. In this method (sometimes called flooding) the person exposes himself or herself to situations that elicit the compulsive act—such as touching a dirty dish—and then refrains from performing the accustomed ritual—hand washing. The assumption is that the ritual is negatively reinforcing because it reduces the anxiety that is aroused by some environmental stimulus or event, such as dust on a chair. Preventing the person from performing the ritual will expose him or her to the anxiety-provoking stimulus, thereby allowing the anxiety to extinguish. Sometimes this exposure and ritual prevention are done in imagination, especially when it is not feasible to do them in vivo, for example, when a person believes that he will burn in hell if he fails to perform a particular ritual.

Controlled research (e.g., Duggan, Marks, & Richards, 1993; Foa, Steketee, & Ozarow, 1985; Stanley & Turner, 1995) suggests that this treatment is at least partially effective for more than half of patients with OCD, including children and adolescents (Franklin & Foa, 1998; March, 1995). In Meyer's original sample of fifteen patients, only two had relapsed at a five-year follow-up (Meyer & Levy, 1973). In one recent study by Edna Foa and her associates, 86 percent of patients who completed the treatment were judged to have improved to a clinically significant degree (Franklin, Abramovitz, Kozak, Levitt, & Foa, 2000). If depression is part of the clinical picture, as it is for almost half of people with OCD, this very demanding behavioral treatment is much less effective (Abramovitz, Franklin, Street, Kozak, & Foa, 2000). This is not surprising, given the degree of effort and commitment demanded of patients undergoing ERP treatment.

Sometimes control over obsessive-compulsive rituals is possible only in a hospital. In fact, in the first report of ERP, Meyer (1966) created a controlled environment at Middlesex Hospital in London to treat OCD. Staff members were specially trained to restrict the patient's opportunities for engaging in ritualistic acts. Generalization of the treatment to the home required the involvement of family members. Preparing them for this work was no mean task, requiring skills and care beyond whatever specific behavioral technique was being employed. There is some preliminary evidence that involving the family in ERP adds to treatment effectiveness (Mehta, 1990). It is common clinical practice—and, in our opinion, just common sense—to enlist the help and support of family members in this kind of treatment regimen (Foa & Franklin, 2001).

In the short term, refraining from performing one's ritual is arduous and extremely unpleasant for clients. (If the reader wants to get some idea of what it is like to resist performing a compulsive ritual, try delaying one or two minutes before scratching an itch.) It typically involves exposures lasting upwards of ninety minutes for fifteen to twenty sessions within a three-week period, with instructions to practice between sessions as well. Whereas Meyer's treatment often involved physical coercion lest a ritual be performed, contemporary practices, which are usually conducted in outpatient settings rather than in hospitals, emphasize encouragement and support from the therapist and significant others (Foa & Franklin, 2001). Sometimes real-life exposure is supplemented with imaginal exposure, as in Meyer's treatment, but it is unclear whether this adds to the effectiveness of in vivo exposure (DeAraujo, Ito, Marks, & Deale, 1995). Up to 25 percent of patients refuse treatment (Foa et al., 1985). Refusal to enter treatment and dropping out are generally recognized problems for many interventions for OCD (Jenike & Rauch, 1994). Patients with OCD tend to procrastinate, to fear changes, and to be overly concerned about others controlling them—characteristics that can be expected to create special problems for manipulative approaches such as behavior therapy.

Rational Emotive Behavior Therapy   Some evidence supports the efficacy of rational-emotive behavior therapy in reducing OCD (e.g., Emmelkamp & Beens, 1991). The idea is to help patients give up the belief that things absolutely have to be the way they want them to be or that any action they take must absolutely lead to a perfect outcome. (Note the similarity to one of the psychoanalytic approaches just mentioned.) Cognitive therapy based on Beck may also be useful (Van Oppen et al., 1995). In this approach, patients are encouraged to test their fears that something awful will happen if they do not perform their compulsive rituals. Clearly, an inherent part of any such cognitive therapy is exposure and response (or ritual) prevention, for to evaluate whether not performing a compulsive ritual will have catastrophic consequences, the patient has to refrain from performing that ritual.[5]

Biological Treatment   Drugs that increase serotonin levels, such as the SSRIs and some tricyclics, are the biological treatments most often given to patients with obsessive-compulsive disorder. Both classes of drugs have yielded some beneficial results, though it is noteworthy that a review of pharmacological treatment by two psychiatrists underscores the importance of ERP as a first-line approach (Rauch & Jenike, 1998).[6] Some studies found tricyclic antidepressants less effective than ERP (Balkom et al., 1994), and one study of antidepressants showed improvement in compulsive rituals only in those OCD patients who were also depressed (Marks et al., 1980). In another study, the benefits of a tricyclic antidepressant on OCD were found to be short-lived; withdrawal from this drug led to a 90 percent relapse rate, much higher than that found with response prevention (Pato et al., 1988). All in all, the picture is uncertain with regard to the effectiveness of tricyclic antidepressants.

Research has shown that serotonin reuptake inhibitors, such as fluoxetine (Prozac), produce more improvement in patients with OCD than do placebos or tricyclics (Kronig et al., 1999). However, treatment gains are modest, and symptoms return if the drugs are discontinued (Franklin & Foa, 1998; McDougle et al., 1994). Staying on the drug does reduce the risk of relapse (Koran et al., 2002). It is not clear whether the drugs work specifically on OCD or on its associated depression (Barr et al., 1994; Tollefson et al., 1994). All antidepressant drugs have side effects that discourage some people from staying on them; examples include nausea, insomnia, agitation, interference with sexual functioning, and even some negative effects on the heart and circulatory system (Rauch & Jenike, 1998).

Technological improvements in measuring various aspects of brain activity (see pp. 97–100) have encouraged researchers to look for brain changes from therapeutic inter-

---

[5] Persuading a patient with OCD that nothing horrible will happen if rituals are not performed—a cognitive-change effort—is a typical part of ERP (Foa & Kozak, 1996). As recently noted by Franklin and Foa (1998), therapists conducting ERP often encourage discussions with the patient that involve such questions as "During the last few days you have successfully stopped retracing your driving routes to check whether or not you've hit somebody. Do you think you have become a reckless driver?" (p. 353). It appears to be very difficult to disentangle the role of exposure and response prevention from the role of cognitive change.

[6] Why do we term this noteworthy? Unfortunately, psychiatrists, who are M.D.'s, more often than not push the use of psychoactive drugs over the application of psychological procedures—a manifestation of the professional turf battles between psychiatry and psychology.

ventions. One notable study compared fluoxetine (Prozac) with in vivo exposure plus response prevention and found that improvement in OCD produced by both treatments was associated with the same changes in brain function, namely, reduced metabolic activity in the right caudate nucleus, overactivity of which has been linked to OCD (Baxter et al., 1992). Only those patients who improved clinically showed this change in brain activity as measured by PET scans. Such findings suggest that markedly different therapies may work for similar reasons, as they are different ways of affecting the same factors in the brain. We should note that in the Baxter et al. study, the drug patients were still on medication during the posttreatment PET scan, whereas the behavior-therapy patients were not and could not be, in any meaningful sense, in treatment, that is, undergoing active response prevention for the rituals.

The desperation of mental health workers, surpassed only by that of the patients, explains the occasional use of psychosurgery in treating obsessions and compulsions. The procedure in current use, cingulatomy, involves destroying two to three centimeters of white matter in the cingulum, an area near the corpus callosum. Although some clinical improvement has been reported and the treatment gains have been maintained (Dougherty et al., 2002; Irle et al., 1998), this intervention is rightfully viewed as a treatment of very last resort given its permanence as well as the risks of psychosurgery and the poor understanding of how it works.

Posttraumatic Stress Disorder

A twenty-seven-year-old singer was referred by a friend for evaluation. Eight months before, her boyfriend had been stabbed to death during a mugging from which she escaped unharmed. After a period of mourning she appeared to return to her usual self. She helped the police in their investigation and was generally considered an ideal witness. Nevertheless, shortly after the arrest of a man accused of the murder, the patient began to have recurrent nightmares and vivid memories of the night of the crime. In the dreams she frequently saw blood and imagined herself being pursued by ominous, cloaked figures. During the day, especially when walking somewhere alone, she often drifted off in daydreams, so that she forgot where she was going. Her friends noted that she began to startle easily and seemed to be preoccupied. She left her change or groceries at the store, or when waited on could not remember what she had come to buy. She began to sleep restlessly, and her work suffered because of poor concentration. She gradually withdrew from her friends and began to avoid work. She felt considerable guilt about her boyfriend's murder, although exactly why was not clear. (Spitzer et al., 1981, p. 17)

Posttraumatic stress disorder (PTSD), introduced as a diagnosis in DSM-III, entails an extreme response to a severe stressor, including increased anxiety, avoidance of stimuli associated with the trauma, and a numbing of emotional responses. Although people have known for many years that the stresses of combat could produce powerful and adverse effects on soldiers, it was the aftermath of the Vietnam War that spurred the acceptance of the new diagnosis.

Like other disorders in the DSM, PTSD is defined by a cluster of symptoms. But unlike the definitions of other psychological disorders, the definition of PTSD includes part of its presumed etiology, namely, a traumatic event or events that the person has directly experienced or witnessed involving actual or threatened death, or serious injury, or a threat to the physical integrity of self or others. The event must have created intense fear, horror, or a sense of helplessness.

In previous editions of the DSM the traumatic event was defined as "outside the range of human experience." This definition was too restrictive, as it would have ruled out the diagnosis of PTSD following such events as an automobile accident or the death of a loved one. The current broadened definition may also be too restrictive, because it focuses on the event's objective characteristics rather than on its subjective meaning (King et al., 1995).

There is a difference between posttraumatic stress disorder and **acute stress disorder**, a diagnosis which first appeared in DSM-IV. Nearly everyone who encounters a trau-

DSM-IV-TR Criteria for PTSD

- Exposure to a traumatic event causing extreme fear
- The event is re-experienced
- The person avoids stimuli associated with the trauma and has a numbing of responsiveness
- Hyperarousal symptoms such as an exaggerated startle response
- Duration of symptoms is more than one month

Unlike most other diagnoses, PTSD includes part of its cause, a traumatic event, in its definition. Rescue workers, such as this fireman who was at the World Trade Center in the aftermath of the 9/11 terrorist attack, could be vulnerable to PTSD.

ma experiences stress, sometimes to a considerable degree. This is normal. If the stressor causes significant impairment in social or occupational functioning that lasts for less than one month, an acute stress disorder is diagnosed. The number of people who develop an acute stress disorder varies with the type of trauma they have experienced. Following rape, the figure is extremely high—over 90 percent (Rothbaum et al., 1992). Less severe traumas, such as exposure to a mass shooting or being in a motor vehicle accident, yield much lower figures, for example, 13 percent for motor vehicle accident victims (Bryant & Harvey, 1998; Classen et al., 1998). Although some people get over their acute stress disorder, a significant number develop PTSD (Brewin et al., 1999). PTSD, then, may be considered as lying at the highest end of adverse reactions to stress (Ruscio, Ruscio & Keane, 2002).

The inclusion in the DSM of severe stress as a significant causal factor of PTSD was meant to reflect a formal recognition that the cause of PTSD is primarily the event, not the person. Instead of implicitly concluding that the person would be all right were he or she made of sterner stuff, the importance of the traumatizing circumstances is formally acknowledged in this definition (Haley, 1978). But many people encounter traumatic life events and do not develop PTSD. For example, in one study only 25 percent of people who experienced a traumatic event leading to physical injury subsequently developed PTSD (Shalev et al., 1996); thus the event itself cannot be the sole cause of PTSD. Current research has moved in the direction of searching for factors that distinguish between people who do and people who do not develop PTSD after experiencing severe stress.

The symptoms for PTSD are grouped into three major categories. The diagnosis requires that symptoms in each category last longer than one month.

1. **Reexperiencing the traumatic event.** The individual frequently recalls the event and experiences nightmares about it. Intense emotional upset is produced by stimuli that symbolize the event (e.g., thunder, reminding a veteran of the battlefield) or on anniversaries of some specific experience (e.g., the day a woman was sexually assaulted). In a laboratory confirmation of this symptom, the Stroop test was administered to Vietnam veterans with and without PTSD (McNally et al., 1990). In this test the participant sees a set of words printed in different colors and must name the color of each word as rapidly as possible and not simply say the word. Interference, measured as a slowing of response time, occurs because of the content of some words. Words from several different categories—neutral (e.g., "input"), positive (e.g., "love"), obsessive-compulsive disorder (e.g., "germs"), and PTSD (e.g., "bodybags")—were used in this study. Veterans with PTSD were slower than veterans without PTSD only on the PTSD words. The same effect has been documented for rape victims (Foa et al., 1991). Similarly, patients with PTSD show better recall for words related to their trauma (Vrana, Roodman, & Beckhan, 1995).

    The importance of reexperiencing cannot be underestimated, for it is the likely source of the other categories of symptoms. Some theories of PTSD make reexperiencing the central feature by attributing the disorder to an inability to successfully integrate the traumatic event into an existing schema (the person's general beliefs about the world) (e.g., Foa, Zinbarg, & Rothbaum, 1992; Horowitz, 1986).

2. **Avoidance of stimuli associated with the event or numbing of responsiveness.** The person tries to avoid thinking about the trauma or encountering stimuli that will bring it to mind; there may be amnesia for the event. Numbing refers to decreased interest in others, a sense of estrangement, and an inability to feel positive emotions. These symptoms seem almost contradictory to those in item 1. In PTSD there is in fact fluctuation; the person goes back and forth between reexperiencing and numbing.

3. **Symptoms of increased arousal.** These symptoms include difficulties falling or staying asleep, difficulty concentrating, hypervigilance, and an exaggerated startle response. Laboratory studies have confirmed these clinical symptoms by documenting the heightened physiological reactivity of PTSD patients to combat imagery (e.g., Orr et al., 1995) and their high-magnitude startle responses (Shalev et al., 2001).

Other problems often associated with PTSD are other anxiety disorders, depression, anger, guilt, substance abuse (self-medication to ease the distress), marital problems, poor physical health, sexual dysfunction, and occupational impairment (Bremner et al., 1996; Jacobsen, Southwick, & Kosten, 2001; Zatzick et al., 1997). Suicidal thoughts and plans are common, as are incidents of explosive violence and stress-related psychophysiological problems, such as low back pain, headaches, and gastrointestinal disorders (Hobfoll et al., 1991).

According to the DSM, children can suffer from PTSD, most often in response to witnessing domestic violence or being physically abused (Silva et al., 2000). The clinical picture of PTSD in children appears to be different from what it is in adults. Sleep disorders with nightmares about monsters are common, as are behavioral changes. For example, a previously outgoing youngster may become quiet and withdrawn or a previously quiet youngster may become loud and aggressive. Some traumatized children begin to think that they will not live until adulthood. Some children lose already acquired developmental skills, such as speech or toilet habits. Finally, young children have much more difficulty talking about their upset than do adults, which is especially important to remember in cases of possible physical or sexual abuse.

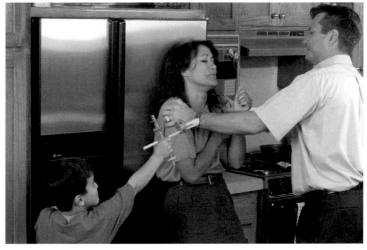

Children can develop PTSD, often after witnessing domestic violence.

PTSD has a prevalence rate of from 1 to 3 percent in the general U.S. population (Helzer, Robins, & McEvoy, 1987), representing over two million people. Even greater numbers have a subsyndromal form of PTSD, in which the person has symptoms of PTSD not severe or numerous enough to warrant the diagnosis but serious enough to cause considerable distress and impairment (Stein et al., 1997). The rate of PTSD was found to be very high (22 percent) among a southwestern Native American tribe (Robin et al., 1997). Given exposure to a traumatic event, the overall prevalence of PTSD rises to 9 percent (Breslau et al., 1998). Prevalences vary depending on the severity of the trauma experienced; it is about 3 percent among civilians who have been exposed to a physical attack, 20 percent among people wounded in Vietnam, and about 50 percent among rape victims and people who were POWs in either World War II or the Korean War (Engdahl et al., 1997; Rothbaum et al., 1992). Based on a telephone survey, it was determined that 7 percent of the adults living south of 110th Street in New York City (well north of the World Trade Center) reported symptoms that would warrant a diagnosis of PTSD following the terrorist attacks of September 11, 2001. This percentage was much higher among those who lived closer to the disaster site in lower Manhattan (Galea et al., 2002). The most frequent trauma that precipitates PTSD is the loss of a loved one, accounting for about a third of all cases (Breslau et al., 1998).

Etiology of Posttraumatic Stress Disorder

Research and theory on the causes of PTSD focus on risk factors for the disorder as well as on psychological and biological factors.

Risk Factors   There are several risk factors for PTSD. Given exposure to a traumatic event, predictors of PTSD include perceived threat to life, being female, early separation from parents, family history of a disorder, previous exposure to traumas, and a preexisting disorder (an anxiety disorder or depression) (Breslau et al., 1997, 1999; Ehlers, Malou, & Bryant, 1998; Nishith, Mechanic, & Resick, 2000; Stein, 1997). Having high intelligence seems to be a protective factor, perhaps because it is associated with having better coping skills (Macklin et al., 1998). The prevalence of PTSD also increases with the severity of the traumatic event; for example, the greater the exposure to combat, the greater the risk. With a high degree of combat exposure, the rates of PTSD are the same in veterans who have family members with other disorders and those who do not. Among those with a family history of disorder, even low combat exposure produces a high rate of PTSD (Foy et al., 1987).

Dissociative symptoms (including depersonalization, derealization, amnesia, and out-of-body experiences) at the time of the trauma also increase the probability of developing PTSD, as does trying to push memories of the trauma out of one's mind (Ehlers, Mayou, & Bryant, 1998). Dissociation may play a role in maintaining the disorder, as it keeps the patient from confronting memories of the trauma. A compelling study of dissociation assessed rape survivors within two weeks of the assault. While the women talked about either the rape or neutral topics, psychophysiological measures and self-reports of stress were taken. The women were divided into two groups based on their scores on a measure of dissociation during the rape (e.g., "Did you feel numb?" "Did you have moments of losing track of what was going on?"). Women with high dissociation scores were much more likely to have PTSD symptoms than were low scorers. Furthermore, high scorers had a dissociation between their subjective stress ratings and their physiological responses. Although they reported high levels of stress when they were talking about being raped, they showed less physiological arousal than did the women with low dissociation scores.

Development of PTSD is also associated with a tendency to take personal responsibility for failures and to cope with stress by focusing on emotions ("I wish I could change how I feel") rather than on the problems themselves (Mikhliner & Solomon, 1988; Solomon, Mikulincev, & Flum, 1988). In general, coping with the trauma by trying to avoid thinking about it is related to developing PTSD (Sharkansky et al., 2000). A strong sense of commitment and purpose differentiated Gulf War veterans who did not develop PTSD from those who did (Sutker et al., 1995). A high level of social support may lessen the risk for the disorder (King et al., 1999; Taft et al., 1999). Access to social support also lessened the risk for PTSD in children who had experienced the trauma associated with hurricane Andrew (Vernberg et al., 1996).

Psychological Theories   Learning theorists assume that PTSD arises from a classical conditioning of fear (Fairbank & Brown, 1987; Keane, Zimering, & Caddell, 1985). A woman who has been raped, for example, may come to fear walking in a certain neighborhood (the CS) because of having been assaulted there (the UCS). Based on this classically conditioned fear, avoidances are built up, and they are negatively reinforced by the reduction of fear that comes from not being in the presence of the CS. PTSD is a prime example of the two-factor theory of avoidance learning proposed years ago by Mowrer (1947; see p. 47). There is a developing body of evidence in support of this view (Orr et al., 2000) and of related cognitive-behavioral theories that emphasize the loss of control and predictability felt by people with PTSD (Chemtob et al., 1988; Foa & Kozak, 1986).

A psychodynamic theory proposed by Horowitz (1986, 1990) posits that memories of the traumatic event occur constantly in the person's mind and are so painful that they are either consciously suppressed (by distraction, for example) or repressed. The person is believed to engage in a kind of internal struggle to integrate the trauma into his or her existing beliefs about himself or herself and the world to make some sense out of it.

Biological Theories   Research on twins and families shows a possible genetic diathesis for PTSD (Hettema, Neale, & Kendler, 2001). Furthermore, the trauma may activate the noradrenergic system, raising levels of norepinephrine and thereby making the person startle and express emotion more readily than is normal. Consistent with this view is the finding that levels of norepinephrine were higher in PTSD patients than among controls (Geracioti et al., 2001). In addition, stimulating the noradrenergic system induced a panic attack in 70 percent and flashbacks in 40 percent of PTSD patients; none of the control participants had such experiences (Southwick et al., 1993). Finally, there is evidence for increased sensitivity of noradrenergic receptors in patients with PTSD (Bremner et al., 1998).

Therapies for Posttraumatic Stress Disorder

As with the other anxiety disorders reviewed so far, treatment of PTSD—regardless of the therapist's theoretical orientation—involves exposure to fear-provoking stimuli. But in the case of PTSD, defined as an anxiety reaction to a known traumatic event, the exposure is to the original fear-provoking occurrence or, more often, to verbal descriptions or images of that occurrence. In one way or another, the traumatized person is encouraged to confront what triggered the initial trauma in order to gain mastery over it and to extinguish the considerable anxiety associated with the horrific event. As recently pointed out by Keane and Barlow (2002), this general strategy can be traced back to Pierre Janet and Sigmund Freud and has taken a number of forms over the past century.

Critical Incident Stress Debriefing   There is a growing area of specialization—sometimes called traumatology, sometimes grief counseling, sometimes debriefing—made up of various kinds of mental health professionals (psychologists, psychiatrists, social workers, and counselors with minimal professional training). Though their techniques differ, a common theme is the long-held belief that it is best to intervene with as many survivors as possible within 24 to 72 hours after a traumatic event, well before PTSD has a chance to develop, encouraging them to review in detail what has just happened and to express as strongly as they can their feelings about the horrific events (Bell, 1995). Also common among these workers is their practice of going as soon as possible to disaster sites—sometimes invited by local authorities (as in the aftermath of the World Trade Center attack), sometimes not—and offering (critics say imposing) their interventions on survivors and their families. Intervening in this way when people are in the acute phase of a posttrauma period is typically referred to as crisis intervention or critical incident stress debriefing (CISD) (Mitchell & Bray, 1990).

This overall approach has become quite controversial. According to many experts, studies of the therapeutic outcomes of CISD and related procedures fail to provide support for their effectiveness, and a good deal of recent research suggests that they may even do more harm than good (e.g., Mayou et al., 2000). The basic criticism is that, immediately following a disaster, people are best served by the social support usually available to them in their families and communities and that the coercion, even if subtle and well-intentioned, to be ministered to by strangers is not helpful and may even be intrusive and harmful (Gist, in press). The harm could come because right after a trauma, some distancing may be more beneficial to people than being encouraged or coerced to deal with memories that they may not be ready to confront.

It is important to recall that the majority of people who have experienced a trauma do not go on to develop PTSD. To be sure, many if not most suffer acute stress disorder, mentioned earlier, whereby they experience extreme negative emotions and disruption of their lives. Whether people in these immediate posttrauma circumstances should be "debriefed" or otherwise therapized by people they do not know is, to many authorities, very doubtful. Indeed, whether this should even be called a disorder at all is debatable, since disasters like hurricanes, floods, brutal rapes, and acts of war are basically UCSs, unconditioned stimuli that evoke certain reactions on an unlearned, automatic basis in all people.

Other critics of CISD espouse the existential position that suffering is a normal part of life and that, after a disaster, one should not avoid the pain and grief but rather should use the traumatic event as an opportunity to confront life's inevitable crises and find meaning in them, to emerge after a period of time with a stronger sense of what is important in life (see Focus Box 10.2 on Viktor Frankl's logotherapy, which he developed out of his concentration camp experiences during World War II). These critical opinions have even begun to appear in the mass media as a counterweight to the widely held view that it is best to intervene as quickly as possible with as many survivors as possible in the aftermath of a disaster, even when assistance is not requested. An example is an article in the *Wall Street Journal* article by Satel and Sommers, October 15, 2001, in reaction to the intervention in the aftermath of the World Trade Center attack.

War-Time Approaches   During World War II "combat-exhausted" soldiers were often treated by narcosynthesis (Grinker & Spiegel, 1944), a procedure that might be considered a drug-assisted catharsis à la Breuer. A soldier was sedated with an intravenous injection of sodium Pentothal, enough to cause extreme drowsiness. The therapist then stated in a matter-of-fact voice that the soldier was on the battlefield, in the front lines. If

Natural disasters, such as this earthquake in Taipei, can trigger PTSD.

necessary and possible, the therapist mentioned circumstances of the particular battle. The patient usually began to recall, often with intense emotion, frightening events that had perhaps been forgotten. Many times the actual trauma was relived and even acted out by the patient. As the patient gradually returned to the waking state, the therapist continued to encourage discussion of the terrifying events in the hope that the patient would realize that they were in the past and no longer a threat. In this fashion a synthesis, or coming together, of the past horror with the patient's present life was sought (Cameron & Magaret, 1951).

The Veterans Administration, which had served veterans of World War II as well as those of the Korean War, was not prepared at first to address the psychological plight of Vietnam veterans. First, many had left the service with "bad paper," that is, with less than honorable discharges. Offenses for which a soldier could receive an undesirable discharge included alcoholism and drug addiction (Kidder, 1978); it seems likely that some of these veterans were suffering from the trauma of combat. Not until 1979, six years after the truce was signed with North Vietnam, were these sorts of dishonorable discharges upgraded as a result of assistance by the American Civil Liberties Union and the veterans made eligible for treatment through the Veterans Administration (M. Beck, 1979). As mentioned at the beginning of this section, PTSD as a formal diagnosis appeared as a clearly articulated and formal diagnosis in 1980 with the appearance of DSM-III. It seems likely that the politics of the Vietnam War played a role in this official recognition of PTSD.

As early as 1971, however, psychiatrist Robert Jay Lifton was approached by antiwar veterans from the New York–New Haven area to work with them in forming rap groups. Initiated by the veterans themselves, these groups had a twofold purpose: a therapeutic goal of healing themselves and a political goal of forcing the American public to begin to understand the human costs of the war (Lifton, 1976). The rap groups spread outward from New York City until 1979 when Congress approved a $25-million package establishing Operation Outreach, a network of ninety-one storefront counseling centers for psychologically distressed Vietnam veterans. In 1981 funding was extended for three additional years.

The rap groups focused on the residual guilt and rage felt by the veterans—guilt over what their status as soldiers had called on them to do in fighting a guerrilla war in which enemy and ally were often indistinguishable from one another, and rage at being placed in the predicament of risking their lives in a cause to which they and their country were not fully committed. Discussion extended as well to present-life concerns, such as relationships with women and feelings about masculinity, in particular the macho view of physical violence. Antidepressant medication was also used, but with equivocal results (Lerer et al., 1987).

In the rap groups—and in the more conventional group-therapy sessions in the 172 Veterans Administration hospitals across the United States—at least two factors probably helped veterans. For perhaps the first time they could partake of the company of returned comrades in arms and feel the mutual support of others who had shared their war experiences. They were also able finally to begin confronting, in often emotional discussions, the combat events whose traumatic effects had been suppressed and therefore not examined. As people have known for many, many years, in order for individuals to come to terms with fearsome happenings, to loose themselves from the hold that events can have over them, they must in effect return to the events and expose themselves fully.

Cognitive and Behavioral Approaches   Controlled research on the treatment of PTSD has accelerated in recent years as more attention has been focused on the aftermath of such traumas as natural disasters, rape, child abuse, and especially combat. Recent work in cognitive behavior therapy provides some findings based on studies that employed careful assessment, details of treatment, and appropriate control groups. (Interventions for the PTSD aftermath of child abuse and rape are described in Chapter 14.)

As should be familiar to the reader by now, the basic principle of exposure-based behavior therapy is that fears are best reduced or eliminated by having the person confront in some fashion whatever he or she most ardently wishes to avoid. A growing body of evidence indicates that structured exposure to trauma-related events, sometimes in imagination, as in systematic desensitization, contributes something beyond the benefits of medication, social support, or being in a safe therapeutic environment (Foa & Meadows, 1997; Keane, 1995; Marks, Lovell, Noshirvani, Livanou, & Thraser, 1998).

As mentioned earlier, the diagnosis of PTSD involves reference to what triggered the problem, and we usually know what that event was. So the decision is a tactical one, that is, how to expose the frightened patient to what is fearsome. Many techniques have been employed. In one well-designed study, for example, Terence Keane and his associates compared a no-treatment control group with an imaginal flooding condition in which patients visualized fearsome, trauma-related scenes for extended periods of time. The researchers found significantly greater reductions in depression, anxiety, reexperiencing of the trauma, startle reactions, and irritability in Vietnam veterans with PTSD in the imaginal procedure (Keane et al., 1989). Conducting such exposure therapy is difficult for both patient and therapist, however, as it requires detailed review of the traumatizing events. As pointed out by Keane et al. (1992), patients may become temporarily worse in the initial stages of therapy, and therapists themselves may become upset when they hear about the horrifying events that their patients experienced.

The new technology of virtual reality (p. 49) has begun to be applied to PTSD to provide exposures more dramatic and more vivid than some patients may be capable of or willing to generate in their imaginations. One study using VR technology showed the therapeutic benefits of having traumatized Vietnam veterans take a VR helicopter trip replete with the sounds of battle (Rothbaum et al., 1999).

How does exposure work? We have already discussed the possibility that it leads to the extinction of the fear response. But it may also change the *meaning* that stimuli have for people. This cognitive view has been elaborated by Edna Foa and her colleagues in a number of studies and theoretical papers. They emphasize the corrective aspects of exposure to what is feared:

> *Exposure promotes symptom reduction by allowing patients to realize that, contrary to their mistaken ideas: (a) being in objectively safe situations that remind one of the trauma is not dangerous; (b) remembering the trauma is not equivalent to experiencing it again; (c) anxiety does not remain indefinitely in the presence of feared situations or memories, but rather it decreases even without avoidance of escape; and (d) experiencing anxiety/PTSD symptoms does not lead to loss of control. (Foa & Meadows, 1997, p. 462)*

However exposure works, there is no doubt about its effectiveness in reducing the effects of trauma, including that arising from sexual assault (p. 458).

In 1989, Shapiro (1989) began to promulgate an approach to treating trauma called Eye Movement Desensitization and Reprocessing (EMDR). EMDR is purported to be extremely rapid—often requiring only one or two sessions—and more effective than the standard exposure procedures just reviewed.[7] In this procedure, the patient imagines a situation related to his or her problem, such as the sight of a horrible automobile accident. Keeping the image in mind, the patient follows with his or her eyes the therapist's fingers as the therapist moves them back and forth about a foot in front of the patient. This process continues for a minute or so or until the patient reports that the aversiveness of the image has been reduced. Then the therapist has the patient verbalize whatever negative thoughts are going through his or her mind, again while following the moving target with his or her eyes. Finally, the therapist encourages the patient to think a more positive thought, such as "I can deal with this," and this thought, too, is held in mind as the patient follows the therapist's moving fingers.

A great deal of controversy surrounds this technique (or techniques, since the specifics of the therapy have been changing since it was initially proposed), and opinions are polarized in ways not often found in science. On the one hand are EMDR proponents

---

[7] Recently the claims of dramatic efficacy have extended to other disorders, including attention-deficit hyperactivity disorder (p. 478), dissociative disorders (p. 185), panic disorder, public-speaking fears, test anxiety, and specific phobias (EMDR Institute 1995, 1997; and as reviewed by Lohr et al., 1998).

who argue that combining eye movements with thoughts about the feared event promotes rapid deconditioning or reprocessing (cognitive restructuring) of the aversive stimulus (e.g., Shapiro, 1995, 1999). On the other hand are studies that show that eye movements do not add anything to what may be happening as a result of exposure itself (e.g., Cahill, Carrigan, Frueh, 1999; Devilly, Spence, & Rapee, 1998; Hazlett-Stevens, Lytle, & Borkovec, 1996, cited in Lohr et al., 1998; Renfrey & Spates, 1994) and that the claims of effectiveness rest on experiments that have major methodological shortcomings (cf. Lohr, Tolin, & Lilienfeld, 1998; Resick & Calhoun, 2001; Rosen, 1999; Tolin et al., 1996). In addition, the theorizing surrounding EMDR has been criticized as inconsistent with what is known about both the psychology and the neuroscientific foundations of learning and brain function (e.g., Keane, 1998; Lohr et al., 1998). However the many questions surrounding EMDR are resolved, no one disputes the important role played by exposure to memories or images of traumatic events. The well-established role of exposure to aversive stimuli is probably the key ingredient in whatever efficacy EMDR has.

Another cognitive-behavioral approach conceptualizes PTSD more generally as an extreme stress reaction and therefore as amenable to the kind of multifaceted approach to stress management described in Chapter 8 (p. 237), which entails relaxation, rational-emotive therapy, and training in problem solving. Among the problems addressed within this broader framework is the anger felt by many patients with PTSD, especially those who have seen combat. Assertion training and couples therapy are often warranted to help patients deal with their anger more appropriately (Keane et al., 1992).

Psychoanalytic Approaches   Horowitz's (1988, 1990) psychodynamic approach has much in common with the aforementioned treatment, for he encourages patients to discuss the trauma and otherwise expose themselves to the events that led to the PTSD. But Horowitz emphasizes the manner in which the trauma interacts with a patient's pretrauma personality, and the treatment he proposes also has much in common with other psychoanalytic approaches, including discussions of defenses and analysis of transference reactions by the patient. This complex therapy awaits empirical verification. The few controlled studies conducted thus far lend a small degree of empirical support to its effectiveness (Foa & Meadows, 1997).

Biological Approaches   Finally, a range of psychoactive drugs have been used with PTSD patients, including antidepressants and tranquilizers (a summary of drugs used in treating all the anxiety disorders can be found in Table 6.4). Sometimes medication is used to deal with conditions comorbid with PTSD, such as depression; improvement in the depression can contribute to improvement in PTSD regardless of how the PTSD itself is treated (by a psychological intervention of the kinds just described, for example [Marshall et al., 1994]). Some modest successes have been reported for antidepressants, especially the serotonin reuptake inhibitors (Brady et al., 2000).

Whatever the specific mode of intervention, experts in PTSD agree that social support is critical. Sometimes finding ways to lend support to others can help the giver as well as the receiver (Hobfoll et al., 1991). Belonging to a religious group; having family, friends, or fellow traumatized individuals listen nonjudgmentally to one's fears and rec-

Table 6.4 Summary of Drugs Used to Treat Anxiety Disorders

Drug Category	Generic Name	Trade Name	Uses
Benzodiazepines	Diazepam, alprazolam	Valium, Xanax	GAD, PTSD
Monoamine oxidase inhibitors	Phenelzine	Nardil	Social phobia
Selective serotonin reuptake inhibitors	Fluoxetine, sertraline	Prozac, Zoloft	Social phobia, panic disorder, OCD, PTSD
Tricyclic antidepressants	Imipramine, clomipramine	Tofranil, Anafranil	Panic disorder, GAD, OCD, PTSD
Buspirone		BuSpar	GAD, panic disorder, OCD

ollections of the trauma; and finding other ways of engendering the belief that one belongs and that others wish to try to help ease the pain may even spell the difference between posttraumatic stress and posttraumatic stress disorder.

Summary

- People with anxiety disorders feel an overwhelming apprehension that seems unwarranted. DSM-IV-TR lists six principal diagnoses: phobic disorders, panic disorder, generalized anxiety disorder, obsessive-compulsive disorder, posttraumatic stress disorder, and acute stress disorder.

- Phobias are intense, unreasonable fears that disrupt the life of an otherwise normal person. They are relatively common. Social phobia is fear of social situations in which the person may be scrutinized by other people. Specific phobias include fears of animals, heights, enclosed spaces, and blood and injections.

- The psychoanalytic view of phobias is that they are a defense against repressed conflicts. Behavioral theorists have several ideas of how phobias are acquired—through classical conditioning, the pairing of an innocuous object or situation with a traumatic event; through operant conditioning, whereby a person is rewarded for avoidance; through modeling, imitating the fear and avoidance of others; and through cognition, by making a catastrophe of a social mishap that could be construed in a less negative fashion. But not all people who have such experiences develop a phobia. It may be that a genetically transmitted physiological diathesis predisposes certain people to acquire phobias.

- A patient with panic disorder has sudden, inexplicable, and periodic attacks of intense anxiety. Panic attacks sometimes lead to fear and avoidance of being outside one's home, known as agoraphobia.

- Panic disorder runs in families, suggesting a genetic diathesis. Psychological theories of panic attacks have posited that the attacks are classically conditioned to internal bodily sensations or that such sensations are misinterpreted, giving rise to panic attacks.

- In generalized anxiety disorder, sometimes called free-floating anxiety, the individual is beset with virtually constant tension, apprehension, and worry.

- Psychoanalytic theory regards the source of generalized anxiety disorder as an unconscious conflict between the ego and id impulses. Cognitive-behavioral theories hold that the disorder results from distorted cognitive processes. Biological approaches focus on the neurotransmitter GABA, which may be deficient in those with the disorder.

- People with obsessive-compulsive disorder have intrusive, unwanted thoughts and feel pressured to engage in stereotyped rituals lest they be overcome by frightening levels of anxiety. This disorder can become disabling, interfering not only with the life of the person who experiences the difficulties but also with the lives of those close to that person.

- Psychoanalytic theory on the etiology of obsessive-compulsive disorder posits strong id impulses that are under faulty and inadequate ego control. In behavioral accounts, compulsions are considered learned avoidance responses, while obsessions may be related to stress and an attempt to inhibit these unwanted thoughts. There is evidence for a genetic contribution to the disorder, indicating that biological factors likely predispose some people to develop it.

- Posttraumatic stress disorder is diagnosed in some people who have experienced a traumatic event that would evoke extreme distress in most individuals. It is marked by symptoms such as reexperiencing the trauma, increased arousal, and emotional numbing.

- Research and theory on the causes of posttraumatic stress disorder focus on risk factors—such as perceived threat to life, family history of a disorder, and previous exposure to traumas—along with psychological and biological factors.

- Psychoanalytic treatment of anxiety disorders tries to lift repression so that childhood conflicts can be resolved; direct alleviation of the manifest problems is discouraged.

- In contrast, behavior therapists employ a range of procedures, directed at the current sources of anxiety, such as systematic desensitization and modeling, to encourage exposure to what is feared.

- Perhaps the most widely employed treatments are anxiolytic drugs dispensed by medical practitioners. Drugs are subject to abuse, however, and discontinuing them usually leads to relapse. Their long-term use may have untoward and still inadequately understood side effects.

Key Terms

acute stress disorder	compulsion	obsessions	school phobia
agoraphobia	depersonalization	obsessive-compulsive disorder	selective mutism
anxiety	derealization	(OCD)	social phobia
anxiety disorders	flooding	panic disorder	specific phobias
anxiolytics	generalized anxiety disorder	phobia	vicarious learning
autonomic lability	(GAD)	posttraumatic stress disorder	
comorbidity	neuroses	(PTSD)	

Social Phobia

This case report is based on a patient who was seen for training purposes in a graduate class in intervention and has been used by the author for teaching purposes. A few personal details have been altered. The contract with the patient was that she would be seen for one semester by the therapist and that the focus would be on what she called her "panic attacks." The patient was not charged for the sessions, and she signed an informed consent form, with enthusiasm, it might be added, because she hoped that the record kept of her treatment might help other people in the future. Because of the very focused and time-limited nature of the treatment, very little information was collected on her past history. What little of her background came to light during the sessions will be integrated into our account of the therapy.

Presenting Clinical Picture

Ling was a 39-year-old mother of two, a second-generation Chinese American living in a large metropolitan area in southern California. A social worker referred the patient to a training clinic run by a clinical psychology Ph.D. program for treatment of her "panic attacks." This therapist, who had been seeing the patient for ten months, described Ling as a full-time high school drama teacher and part-time actress who had been complaining of what she and the referring therapist both called "panic attacks." These were episodes of extreme anxiety marked by elevated heart rate, perspiration, and what the patient called "mind-fucking" cognitions. The social worker also described the patient as suffering from low self-esteem and a high need for approval.

Conceptualization and Treatment

Before even meeting the patient, a question in the mind of the therapist was whether her "panic attacks" were cued or uncued and whether they were a part of what the *DSM-IV-TR* calls panic disorder. Recurrent uncued attacks and worry about having attacks in the future are required for the diagnosis of panic disorder, but panic attacks themselves occur fairly often –among 3 to 5 percent of the general population in any given year – in people who do not meet the criteria for panic disorder (Norton, Cox, & Malan, 1992). The exclusive presence of cued attacks most likely reflects the presence of a phobia. It was this line of reasoning that the therapist decided to pursue in assessing the patient, that is, that her "panic attacks" represented an extreme anxiety response to life events that could be specified.

The first question, then, was whether the therapist should embark on a therapy program drawn from the work of Barlow and his associates on panic disorder (Craske & Barlow, 2001). According to this strategy, the therapist eschews a search for environmental triggers in favor of teaching the panic-disordered person not to catastrophize about internal sensations and to control them with relaxation and other anxiety-reduction techniques. Or should the therapist instead try to find some situations in which the patient experienced these "panic attacks," consistent with the behaviorist assumption that unrealistic anxiety is usually triggered by identifiable environmental antecedents? In a meeting with the referring therapist prior to seeing the patient himself, the present therapist embarked on a line of questioning that ultimately led to a reformulation of the problem as something other than panic disorder.

Believing that the patient's so-called "panic attacks" might be triggered in social situations, the therapist engaged the social worker in a discussion that centered on when these attacks occurred and when they were particularly severe. What emerged was that, indeed, they occurred almost entirely when Ling was being evaluated or criticized, as often happened during auditions for acting roles and in dealings with her husband, who was critical of some of her behavior at home. Ling had a long history of sensitivity to criticism, dating back to childhood experiences with a hypercritical mother. This prompted the therapist to ask whether criticism could be an important cue for Ling's "panic attacks": Does she react with this extreme anxiety when she perceives she might not do well in auditions? Are there situations not relating to auditions in which she experiences the anxiety? Answers by the social worker and, later in the session, by the patient herself, yielded support for the hypothesis that criticism, or social evaluation, might be a powerful cue for sometimes extreme bouts of anxiety, and that these high levels of anxiety were being labeled as panic attacks by both the social worker and the patient.

After talking with the referring therapist for about half an hour, a first session was held with the patient. Ling readily engaged the therapeutic situation with energy and intelligence. She presented as an attractive, intelligent, and articulate person who was strongly motivated to work to reduce her "panic attacks." She showed considerable emotional lability in this session tearful one moment, reflective and composed the next.

As a follow-up to the briefing with the social worker, the first line of questioning focused on determining if specific situations could be in fact be linked to her feelings of intense anxiety. Some excerpts from the first session will illustrate:

Therapist: Are there things that trigger greater or lesser degrees of anxiety? For instance, I understand that you feel anxious during auditions.

Patient: Auditions or any other kind of situation when people might criticize me.

Therapist: Would you describe yourself as sensitive to criticism? Can a negative remark stay with you for hours, even a day or two?

Patient: Definitely. I have always been that way since I was a child. My mother was very critical…. I can hear her nagging….

Therapist: Can you recall a recent situation that was very troubling? One in which you were very anxious about criticism?

Patient: Yeah, a few months ago I auditioned for a part in a television commercial. When I got there I heard that everything had gone wrong that day. There were technical problems and [problems also with] the house they chose for the location. I got very anxious and worried about doing a good job so everyone would feel better. I could feel my heart pounding and my hands were sweating.

From this and subsequent conversations in the first few sessions, the therapist began to discuss with the patient the possibility of viewing her primary problem as one involving what *DSM-IV-TR* calls "social phobia," but one that was rather specific to social situations involving evaluation or criticism. "Panic attacks," especially in the sense of uncued bouts of extremely high anxiety, did not seem as useful a way to construe the patient's predicament as anxiety reactions to a range of specific and specifiable situations. The patient found the therapist's use of the descriptor "thin-skinned" very apt to refer to her sensitivity to criticism. She reported many childhood experiences with a nagging mother. She also tended to blame herself for anything around her going awry. For example, if technicians at a shoot were unhappy, she would see it as her fault and her responsibility to make things right. Critical—but also neutral—reactions from people to her presence or to her actions were perceived as signs of rejection and even danger.

In response to direct questions, Ling also expressed certainty that the "panics" she experienced never occurred out of the blue, and by the end of the second session she began referring to them as anxiety feelings rather than as panicky feelings. Furthermore, as she began to see some orderly relationships between her anxieties and specifiable events in her environment, she derived reassurance that she was not, as she had been fearing, losing her mind (a not infrequent associated symptom of people who suffer high levels of anxiety that seem to come out of nowhere). The lack of evidence for panic disorder marked by recurrent uncued panic attacks, cou-

pled with an emerging picture of a woman who had for years been extremely concerned about pleasing others and very fearful of being criticized by them, gave further support to the reformulation of the patient's difficulties as centering around high levels of social evaluative anxiety.

The therapist explained to the patient that high levels of nervous tension punctuated by extreme anxiety ("panic attacks") in response to social evaluation were understandable, given that she was an actress often going to auditions. As the therapist learned in succeeding sessions, auditions and acting in general provide a very thin schedule of positive reinforcement and a very concentrated schedule of punishment. At the same time, he agreed with the patient's judgment that her anxiety reactions were much greater than the situations warranted and that they were probably interfering with her ability to perform as well as she was capable of.

Designing an Intervention Based on the Reformulation

One of the procedures enjoying empirical support in the treatment of anxiety is Wolpe's systematic desensitization (Wolpe, 1958). Because the therapist considered systematic desensitization as a strong possibility for treatment, he inquired into past experiences that the patient might have had with relaxation training. She reported that she had done Hatha Yoga and considered herself fairly proficient at achieving a state of relaxation when she put her mind to it in a peaceful environment. This boded well for her learning progressive relaxation that would be applied in desensitization. Her background as an actor suggested to the therapist that she would have no trouble in the imaginal role-playing that is intrinsic to desensitization (whereby an imagined event has to be the functional equivalent of an actual one).

During the second session, additional questioning provided further evidence in support of the hypothesis that her principal problem was extreme social evaluative anxiety or social phobia. The context of the following exchange was pursuing an allusion by the patient to fear of the unknown:

Therapist: Does the fear of the unknown have anything to do with not knowing what to do, a fear of harm that might befall you?

Patient: I'm aware of something physiologically that happens to me, the excessive sweating, the adrenaline flowing, and I don't know why that happens. I think it comes down to "they won't like who or what I am." I don't know what any other actors' insides are like, but I can't imagine spending the rest of my life feeling what I have over the past year. I always compare myself to other people. I look around and see that they all seem fine and I'm about to pass out. I am dying inside from the anticipation. One way I judge the appropriateness of how I feel is to see how others are feeling.

"People-pleasing" and sensitivity to criticism usually go hand in hand with assertiveness problems (Goldfried & Davison, 1994;

Lazarus, 1971). Ling was no exception. She readily agreed that she had great difficulty expressing her needs and disagreeing with others. Whether there would be time for dealing with her nonassertiveness was doubtful, but the therapist harbored the belief that reducing her concern about the opinions of others would likely have a beneficial effect on her nonassertiveness.[1]

At the end of the second session, the therapist asked Ling to gather data for their collaborative project as an important first step in an effort to reduce her interpersonal anxiety. She was asked to write down situations or events where she found herself getting more anxious "than you believe the event warrants." Feelings of anxiety, therefore, were construed for her as useful tools for treatment, cues that would help in the design of a therapy that would target her excessive anxiety in reaction to a range of specific situations.

By this point, the therapist was considering also a cognitive intervention based on Ellis (1962, 1993). Because rational-emotive behavior therapy focuses on internal monologues and (sometimes unverbalized) assumptions that reflect an overly demanding, perfectionistic attitude toward the self and/or the environment, the therapist began to ask the patient to consider what goes through her mind when she becomes anxious. Therefore, in addition to the self-monitoring of external events that seemed to trigger unwarranted anxiety, Ling was asked to try to take notice of what she was thinking about while she was feeling inappropriate anxiety. The therapist was thus laying the groundwork for a cognitive therapeutic approach to complement desensitization. The following exchange illustrates how this self-monitoring assessment was presented to the patient:

Therapist: What someone says or does is the external situation, so write that down [in the coming week as soon as possible after it happens]. But an important part is also what you bring to the situation. It's very important and useful to know what the thoughts are when you feel anxious. Start from your anxious feelings and use them as a signal to gather data. Include your "self-statements" or things you say to yourself.

Patient: Subtext. In acting we call it subtext. [2]

The therapist emphasized the distinction between useful and maladaptive anxiety so that Ling would not be concerned that she would "lose her edge" in behaving under the pressure of acting auditions. In other words, the goal of the therapy would not be to render her unconcerned about the quality of her performance, unable to "get up for" an acting challenge; rather it would be to teach her ways to avoid the debilitatingly high degrees of anxiety that had been preventing her from performing at her best and that had been making her role as an aspiring actress little better than a living hell. This theme was discussed again toward the end of treatment, when she was beginning to feel a good deal less anxious generally and in social evaluative situations in particular.

To drive the point home, the therapist described the inverted-U function in experimental psychology, whereby optimal performance is at a point of moderate arousal; too little arousal can contribute to a lackadaisical performance while too much can interfere with the expression of talents and skills that the person possesses. This metaphor seemed to make a great deal of sense to Ling and helped her adopt not only a realistic view of therapy but an adaptive one as well.

Thus, in collaboration with the patient, the therapist generated the hypothesis that a reduction in sometimes high levels of performance anxiety and sensitivity to criticism would be of material benefit. In the interests of making maximum use of the limited time available, the therapist presented to the patient a two-pronged approach: systematic rational restructuring, an imagery-based strategy for implementing Ellis's rational-emotive behavior therapy and Beck's cognitive therapy (see Goldfried & Davison, 1976, 1994, Chapter 8); and taped systematic desensitization, Wolpe's imagery-based method for reducing anxiety (Wolpe, 1958) adapted for audiotaped presentation (Goldfried & Davison, 1976, 1994, Chapter 6). They would be combined on audiotape in order to accommodate the time restriction (an academic semester).

The cognitive component would be directed at altering cognitions in a manner that would lessen the patient's catastrophizing and absolutist attitudes towards acting and other situations in which she could be unfavorably evaluated/criticized. The desensitization component would aim to break the links between specifiable anxiety-provoking situations and what might be noncognitively mediated autonomic reactions that had been classically conditioned to inherently innocuous situations or situations of less than monumental import. While there are empirical data attesting to the efficacy as well as clinical effectiveness of both strategies, the *combination* of the cognitive and desensitization components was new in the therapist's practice and, to his knowledge, not previously (or since) reported on.

Using the information gathered between sessions by the patient, the therapist worked with her over several sessions to cre-

---

[1] Nonassertive patients always pose a process problem for the therapist, namely, a concern that such patients will agree with interpretations and other statements of the therapist when, in fact, they don't. It is always good practice to make an extra effort by pointing out the importance of their expressing their needs and disagreements openly in session. This not only facilitates the treatment but also provides an opportunity for the patient to experiment with being more assertive. In this therapy, we watched for opportunities for the patient to disagree with us and were gratified to have found some. For example, during the relaxation training, Ling brought up problems she was occasionally having with at-home practice sessions that did not result in her feeling more relaxed after listening to a tape than she was beforehand. Also, there were many occasions when she expressed a difference of opinion about the therapist's interpretation of an event. Another sign that the patient was prepared to tell the therapist things she believed he would rather not hear was a comment in the twelfth session when she reported that listening to the desensitization tape the previous week had been "boring" and that she had experienced resistance within herself about working with the tape on a daily basis, as had been prescribed. The therapist construed her boredom as a positive sign, to wit, that the hierarchy items were becoming easier for her to cope with. But the point here is that Ling basically told the therapist that she was bored with some of what he was having her do—a statement unlikely to be made by a patient whose highest priority is to please the therapist.

---

[2] Notice how the patient immediately grasped the importance of a person's ongoing dialogue with herself. The therapist made clear on this and other occasions the connections and similarities between what was going on in their therapy together and what an actor is familiar with and uses to enhance her work.

ate a 19-item anxiety hierarchy that represented her anxiety disorder. A sampling of these items will illustrate this central aspect of the therapy. The numbers in parentheses represent the patient's rating of the aversiveness of the item on a 100-point subjective rating scale, where a rating of 1 indicates that the situation would evoke or has evoked no anxiety at all in real life, and 100 indicates that the situation is or would be as anxiety-provoking as she could imagine anything being. The fact that some of the ratings appear very precise (e.g., 59 instead of 60) is a result of items sometimes clustering within a general range and of the need to rank-order them. *Note:* While the construction of an anxiety hierarchy is usually seen as an aspect of treatment, it is in fact as much a part of the clinical assessment, for it involves the fine-grain specification of the patient's anxiety-related clinical problems.

> At school, you are having a production meeting for the musical. You've done your work, and other people are reporting being on schedule, too. (15, easiest item)
>
> Arriving for the shooting of the industrial [a training film], you are parking your car on the street near the house where the shoot is going to be. (30)
>
> As you enter the house for the shooting of the industrial, the casting director asks you who you are. You tell her who you are. (40)
>
> At home, you are putting on your make-up as you get ready to leave for the production company audition. (48)
>
> You've just arrived at the production company audition, and you're scoping out the competition. (59)
>
> You're walking down a long hall in heels on your way to the production company audition room. (62)
>
> At the reading for the play, you're a few beats late with your first entrance. (65)
>
> At the industrial shoot, the director is yelling at you to get together with the continuity director and clean up the dialogue. (68)
>
> You're sitting around your dining room table with Kathy, Marion, and your daughter. You, Marion, and your daughter are smoking. Your husband comes in, quickly turns on his heel, goes into the kitchen, and bangs around some to show his displeasure. (80)
>
> At the reading for the play, you're making an entrance and realize that you didn't turn the page and you now have to find your place in the script. (92)
>
> At the industrial shoot, you're working with the continuity director to clean up the dialogue, and she is having you repeat each sentence often until you get it correct. (95, most difficult item)

It should be noted that the nature of the hierarchy itself is constructive in nature. That is, we have never viewed a specific anxiety hierarchy as the only or best one for a given patient at a given time. Furthermore, knowing that a person is, as here, exceedingly sensi-

tive to criticism does not in itself dictate those situations to which she will be desensitized or otherwise taught to cope with. An anxiety hierarchy or any other group of situations in a patient's life is, in our view, best seen as a sampling from an infinite number of situations that could be represented. We put the matter thusly many years ago in a discussion of desensitization:

> [We view themes pursued in therapy] as a conceptualization *of the therapist. We have long ago stopped asking ourselves whether we have "truly" isolated a basic anxiety dimension of our clients. Rather, we ask ourselves how best to construe a person's difficulty so as to maximize his gains. In other words, rather than looking for the "real hierarchy," we look for the* most useful hierarchy. *This has important implications, not the least of which is the freedom to attempt to reconceptualize various client problems in terms amenable to desensitization. . . . The clinician must ask himself what the implications are likely to be should a particular desensitization actually succeed. For instance, will a person depressed about her lack of meaningful social contacts be happier if her inhibitions about talking to people are reduced by desensitization [in contrast to suggesting she find different people to associate with, for example, and/or trying to change her relationship with her husband, etc.]? Looked at in this way, the clinician would seem to have both greater freedom and greater challenge in isolating anxiety dimensions (Goldfried & Davison, 1976, 1994, p. 115).*

Recall that the therapist was also planning a cognitive intervention based on Ellis and Beck (primarily Ellis, with his focus on patients learning to decastrophize about negative events). Because rational-emotive behavior therapy focuses on internal monologues and (sometimes unverbalized) assumptions that reflect an overly demanding, perfectionistic attitude toward the self and/or the environment, the therapist began to ask the patient to consider what goes through her mind when she becomes anxious. This kind of discussion took place at various times during the first few sessions.

The anxiety hierarchy constructed with Ling was used in an imagery-based procedure that combined systematic desensitization and the cognitive approach of Albert Ellis. The desensitization component entailed instructing the patient to relax away even the slightest degree of tension elicited by a given aversive image. Relaxation was thereby seen as a coping response to anxiety per the self-control desensitization strategy originally proposed by Goldfried (1971).[3] The cognitive component involved first providing the patient with and then later encouraging her to develop on her own, self- statements that reflected a less demanding, less absolutistic view of her interactions with others. For example, to deal with the item, "You're phoning your friend Jane to borrow an outfit for the production com-

---

[3] There are many ways to conceptualize the mechanisms underlying the effectiveness of systematic desensitization. If the effects derive from counterconditioning (cf. Davison, 1968; Wolpe, 1958), then relaxation is viewed as a response that is substituted for anxiety. As implemented here, we focused on the coping aspects of relaxation as suggested by Goldfried (1971), but the strategy we followed would also satisfy the procedural requirements of counterconditioning.

pany audition," the therapist asked her to cope cognitively with the tension by saying silently to herself, "While it would be nice for the outfit to be great and for the audition to go well, it's not a catastrophe if things don't go perfectly." The patient imagined each item twice, the first time using relaxation to lessen her anxiety, the second time using a coping self-statement to control her tensions.

An aspect worth noting is the degree of choice that this combined treatment was designed to give her. That is, we proposed to her that one of the most frightening and daunting consequences of being exquisitely sensitive to negative evaluation—especially when one's life is full of such challenges, as hers was because of her acting—was that one felt tugged and pulled and dominated by external events. Learning ways to cope with such anxiety should lessen the feeling that one is helpless. Also, inherent to cognitive therapy, as with humanistic and existential therapies, is the core assumption that people do not react so much to what the world serves up to them; rather, they can learn to choose to construe the world in a particular way (within practical and sensible limits, of course). The therapy, then, was aimed at increasing the range of choices she might have. Significantly, this discussion in the fourth session led to the patient crying, a reaction she said arose from feeling the relevance of the choice issue and allowing herself to have some hope that she could achieve more freedom in her emotional life than had been the case for many years.

The combined desensitization-REBT therapy in imagination was carried out across five sessions, with the therapist presenting items serially to the patient in groups of between two and four in session and making a tape of these presentations. This exercise occupied no more than half of a given session, with the patient instructed to practice with the tape daily between sessions. There was always discussion of the patient's experiences with each tape at the beginning of the following session, and then time was available to talk about related issues.

A number of events took place during the therapy that indicated that our particular construction of the patient's problems and the intervention based on it were proving useful. The importance of attending to the patient's self-talk was underscored in the fourth session, when she came in with a report of an audition that week having gone well because she had tried not to "beat up on myself" as she usually did when things were not going as well as they "should." She found herself realizing that she would be unlikely to get the part because she looked too young for it. She thought as well that her race might make her less attractive to the producers than would a Caucasian actress. With this pressure removed, albeit with some obvious resentment about the racial issue, she was able to relax and ended up auditioning very well. This experience, unplanned by the therapist, gave her insight into the role of self-talk and of not taking a "musturbatory" attitude towards a challenge. It also confirmed the therapist's developing belief that a cognitive approach would be useful as part of the therapeutic intervention.

Practicing relaxation with audiotapes was also facilitated by the patient's developing ability to refrain from demanding perfection of herself. She reported in the seventh session that she was able not to worry about how well she was doing with the practice and as a consequence was able to see it as less of a challenge to be perfect and more as something to enjoy, focusing on the process and not the desired outcome.

In the ninth session, she reported a good audition and attributed it to two factors: she knew beforehand that she had the part, and she saw that it was someone else's role that was to be decided on during the audition, not hers.

During the thirteenth session, she recounted being able to deal with some stressors in a less agitated way than usual and made the following comment:

Patient: The good side of all this [dealing with stressful situations] is that I feel so good about situations that come up that before would have made me very nervous and very anxious that haven't. I've had very quick clarity on the ability to put it into perspective and judge what my role is. . . . I'm not getting emotional and I know I couldn't have done that last year. . . . I was at a party where everyone was singing. One of the songs was an audition song of mine and everyone stopped singing because I was singing so well. When they stopped, I could feel my anxiety just go right up, but I was able to continue singing and bring it down again.

In the fifteenth session, Ling commented that the hierarchy items she had worked with the preceding week seemed "silly" to get upset by. These were items that she had earlier ranked as moderately anxiety provoking.

In the second-last session, Ling said she was on her way to an audition and was, to her pleasure, looking forward to it as an occasion to apply her newly learned relaxation and cognitive restructuring skills.

While the therapeutic contract called for a time-limited therapy focused on her "panic attacks," other themes were developed and discussed to some degree during the 17 sessions of treatment. Each of these themes could well have occupied our time, and each of them could have been construed as relevant to the "panic attacks." One was problems the patient and her husband were having with the one of the patient's daughters, a 17-year-old suffering from an eating disorder. This naturally added to the stress that the patient had sought help for. Also a source of concern were conflicts with her husband, which seemed to be centered around his overbearing attitude toward family finances. Coupled with this was a lack of assertiveness in the patient, something she herself traced to her traditional Chinese upbringing, constraints and limitations that she chafed under as a coequal breadwinner in the marriage.

These are issues which, as noted, were discussed from time to time and would, under ordinary circumstances, have demanded greater attention in our therapy. The unease that the therapist experienced in paying little concentrated attention to these problems was alleviated by the knowledge that the patient was maintaining therapeutic contact with the referring social worker, who, it should be mentioned, watched the videotapes made of the treatment and conferred periodically with us.

The last session, the seventeenth, took place five months after the initial consultation and included the referring therapist in a review of the course of the treatment. The social worker, who had seen Ling several times during the course of our therapy with her, confirmed that her general anxiety level had decreased and that her ability to deal with stressful situations had improved greatly. The audition that Ling had gone to immediately following the preceding session, along with a second one that week, had both gone very well. As she put it: "I just nailed both those auditions. I feel the anxiety creeping up and I use it for the auditions. It's just not unmanageable..."

At this wrap-up, the therapist encouraged Ling to practice with the relaxation tapes about once a week and also with the last couple of desensitization-REBT tapes (which dealt with the most difficult hierarchy items) in order to keep these newly acquired cognitive skills fresh and available to apply to the stressors in any person's life. "It's like staying in good physical condition. . . . It takes repetition and drill," the therapist observed. Ling would begin seeing her social worker therapist once again to work in particular on her marital stress, and the plan was for her to phone us for a two-month followup session.

Follow-up

This session in fact took place. Ling was continuing to have good auditions and was even getting some paid acting jobs. She commented jokingly that on one voice-over she was doing, she was feeling so relaxed that the director told her to "put more of an edge on it." She had no trouble doing so. Her home situation continued to pose major challenges—her daughter's bulimia and ongoing conflicts with her husband—but she expressed confidence that, with the continuing help of her social worker therapist, she would be able to cope adequately. In general, she saw herself as less of a pawn and more of an assertive person with legitimate rights and the means to achieve them.

A second follow-up session five months later constituted a seven-month follow-up. At this meeting the gains already noted seemed to be holding. She was continuing to audition and to get jobs, and was planning to leave her teaching job in order to focus more on her acting career. She described her marriage in very positive terms and was having less frequent sessions with the social worker. At the end of the session, she was reminded that slip-ups were inevitable and that she would be well advised to see them as temporary and a part of normal daily life.

A letter 18 months later and a phone call two years after that, or about three years after termination, confirmed that things continued to be going well. She asserted that her social evaluative anxiety was gone. This had given her, she said, a sense of self-empowerment that was having generalized positive effects in her life.

Discussion

This case study illustrates the manner in which a presenting complaint of panic attacks was reformulated into a theme of social evaluative anxiety. This construction of the patient's problem led to a two-pronged approach: systematic desensitization and rational-emotive behavior therapy, combined in a novel imaginal therapeutic procedure that was conducted largely via audiotapes made over several consulting sessions and used in daily at-home practice by the patient. In this procedure, relaxation and positive self-statements were applied by the patient as self-control ways to ease tension in a range of social evaluative situations, most especially auditions for this part-time actress. As with most people who commit to psychotherapy, this patient had other problems as well, among them a bulimic daughter, problems of nonassertiveness, and a marriage that showed some signs of strain. The time-limited nature of the therapy reported here precluded dealing fully with these issues, but the stress occasioned by them seemed to benefit from the anxiety-reduction procedure as much as did the interpersonal performance anxiety that was the target for intervention. A followup of almost three years suggested that the treatment gains were being maintained and that the patient was succeeding in coping well with life's inevitable stressors.

Social Phobia

As mentoned earlier, Ling meets the criteria for the DSM-IV-TR diagnosis of social phobia, which is defined as a persistent, irrational fear generally linked to the presence of other people (Turk, Heimberg, & Hope, 2001). It is sometimes referred to as social anxiety disorder, a term we think is more appropriate since many people with these sensitivities do not avoid social evaluative situations. The reasons are twofold: Either they have no choice but to deal with other people or; as in Ling's case, they have compelling reasons to not want to avoid these situations (in her case, she wanted to get acting jobs).

Social phobia can be extremely debilitating. The individual usually tries to avoid a particular situation in which he or she might be evaluated and reveal signs of anxiousness or behave in an embarrassing way. Speaking or performing in public, eating in public, using public lavatories, or virtually any other activity that might be carried out in the presence of others can elicit extreme anxiety. It is not surprising that such a problem would cause particular hardship for a person who, like Ling, works in a field that requires performances in front of highly critical people.

Social phobias can be either generalized or specific, depending on the range of situations that are feared and avoided. People with the generalized type have an earlier age of onset, more comorbidity with other disorders, such as depression and alcohol abuse, and more severe impairment (Mannuzza et al., 1995; Wittchen, Stein, & Kessler, 1999). In many instances depression and substance abuse are consequences of the phobia. The former because the constriction in one's interactions with other people can create a very unrewarding life; the latter because of efforts to self-medicate, to get some relief, albeit temporary, from the stress of everyday life and from the loss of self-esteem that is often associated with being extremely nervous and fearful around others.

Social phobias are fairly common, with a lifetime prevalence of 11 percent in men and 15 percent in women (Kessler et al., 1994; Magee et al., 1996). They have a high comorbidity rate with other disorders and often occur in conjunction with generalized anxiety disorder, specific phobias, panic disorder, avoidant personality disorder, and mood disorders (Jansen et al., 1994; Kessler et al., 1999; Lecrubier & Weiller, 1997). As might be expected, onset is generally during adolescence, when social awareness and interaction with others are assuming particular importance in a person's life. Such fears are sometimes found in children as well, however. As is the case with specific phobias, for example, fear of animals like dogs and snakes, social phobias vary somewhat cross-culturally. For example, in Japan fear of giving offense to others is very important, whereas in the United States fear of being negatively evaluated by others is more common.

Etiology of Phobias   As is true for virtually all the disorders discussed in this book, proposals about the causes of phobias, including social phobias, have been made by adherents of the psychoanalytic, behavioral, cognitive, and biological paradigms.

Psychoanalytic Theories   Freud was the first to attempt to account systematically for the development of phobic behavior. According to Freud, phobias are a defense against the anxiety produced by repressed id impulses. This anxiety is displaced from the feared id impulse to an object or situation that has some symbolic connection to it. These objects or situations—for example, elevators or closed spaces—then become the phobic stimuli. The phobia is the ego's way of warding off a confrontation with the real problem, a repressed childhood conflict. In one of his classic cases, Little Hans, who was afraid of horses, had not, Freud proposed, successfully resolved his oedipal conflict, so that his intense fear of his father was displaced onto horses.

Behavioral Theories   Behavioral theories focus on learning as the way in which phobias are acquired. Several types of learning may be involved.

The main behavioral account of phobias is that such reactions are *learned avoidance responses*. Historically, Watson and Rayner's (1920) demonstration of the apparent conditioning of a fear or phobia in Little Albert is considered the model of how a phobia may be acquired. The avoidance-conditioning formulation is based on the two-factor theory originally proposed by Mowrer (1947) and based primarily on laboratory experiments with rats. Two-factor theory holds that phobias develop from two related sets of learning:

1. Via classical conditioning a person can learn to fear a neutral stimulus (the CS) if it is paired with an intrinsically painful or frightening event (the UCS).
2. The person can learn to reduce this conditioned fear by escaping from or avoiding the CS. This second kind of learning is assumed to be operant conditioning; the response is maintained by its reinforcing consequence of reducing fear.

Outside the laboratory, the evidence for the avoidance-conditioning theory is mixed. Some clinical phobias fit the avoidance-conditioning model rather well. A phobia of a specific object or situation has sometimes been reported to have developed after a particularly painful experience with that object. Some people become intensely afraid of heights after a bad fall; others develop a phobia of driving after experiencing a panic attack in their car (Munjack, 1984); and people with social phobias often report traumatic social experiences (Stenberger et al., 1995). Other clinical reports suggest that phobias may develop without a prior frightening experience. Many individuals with severe fears of snakes, germs, airplanes, and heights tell clinicians that they have had no particularly unpleasant experiences with any of these objects or situations (Ost, 1987a). Can this problem with the avoidance-conditioning model be solved? One attempt to do so involves modeling.

In addition to learning to fear something as a result of an unpleasant experience with it, fears may be *learned through imitating the reactions of others*. Thus, some phobias may be acquired by modeling, not through an unpleasant experience with the object or situation that is feared. A wide range of behavior, including emotional responses, may be learned by witnessing a model (e.g., Bandura & Rosenthal, 1966). The learning of fear by observing others is generally referred to as vicarious learning.

An issue that is not addressed by the original avoidance-learning model is that people tend to fear only certain objects and events, such as spiders, snakes, and heights, but not others, such as lambs (Marks, 1969). *Prepared learning* refers to the fact that certain neutral stimuli, called prepared stimuli, are more likely than others to become classically conditioned stimuli. For example, rats readily learn to associate taste with nausea but not with shock when the two are paired (Chambers & Bernstein, in press; Garcia, McGowan, & Green, 1972).

Some fears may well reflect classical conditioning, but only to stimuli to which an organism is physiologically prepared to be sensitive (Seligman, 1971). Conditioning experiments that show quick extinction of fear may have used CSs that the organism was not prepared to associate with UCSs. Prepared learning is also relevant to learning fear by modeling. Cook and Mineka (1989) studied four groups of rhesus monkeys, each of which saw a different videotape. The tapes were created by splicing, so that a monkey exhibiting intense fear appeared to be responding to different stimuli: a toy snake, a toy crocodile, flowers, or a toy rabbit. Only the monkeys exposed to the tapes showing the toy snake or toy crocodile acquired fear of the object shown, again demonstrating that not every stimulus is capable of becoming a source of acquired fear.

Diathesis-Stress   But why do some people who have traumatic experiences not develop enduring fears? For example, 50 percent of people with a severe fear of dogs reported a prior traumatic experience, yet so did 50 percent of people who were not afraid of dogs (DiNardo et al., 1988). The difference between these groups was that the phobic group focused on and became anxious about the possible occurrence of similar events in the future. Thus, a cognitive diathesis—believing that similar traumatic experiences will occur in the future—may be important in developing a phobia. Another possible psychological diathesis is a history of not being able to control the environment (Mineka & Zinbarg, 1996).

In sum, the data we have reviewed suggest that some phobias are learned through avoidance conditioning. But avoidance conditioning should not be regarded as a totally validated theory. For example, many people with phobias do not report either direct exposure to a traumatic event or exposure to fearful models (Merckelbach et al., 1989). With respect to Ling, it may be that her Asian background and her having had what she described as a hypercritical mother contributed to her extreme social evaluative anxiety.

Social-Skills Deficits in Social Phobias So far we have discussed theory and research that relate to phobias in general. Social phobia, however, may require conceptualizations that go beyond research that has been conducted primarily with rats and nonhuman primates.

Inappropriate behavior or a lack of social skills may have a lot to do with the development of social anxiety. According to this view, the individual has not learned how to behave so that he or she feels comfortable with others, or the person repeatedly commits faux pas, is awkward and socially inept, and is often criticized by social companions. Put another way, a person lacking in social skills may actually *contribute to* the creation of punishing interpersonal situations. Support for this model comes from findings that socially anxious people are indeed rated as being low in social skills (Twentyman & McFall, 1975) and that the timing and placement of their responses in a social interaction, such as saying thank you at the right time, are impaired (Fischetti, Curran, & Wessberg, 1977).

Note how this social skills deficit perspective relates to the avoidance conditioning theory reviewed above. A person lacking in social skills is likely to *create* situations with others that are aversive. For example, not knowing how to respond politely, yet assertively, to the demands of another can offend, leading to awkward interpersonal situations and even tense conflicts. Being punished by others can be expected to make a person more fearful of interacting with them.

From what we have seen of Ling, it is doubtful that social skills deficits are relevant. When not blocked by debilitating anxiety, Ling showed herself to be very effective in dealing with others in social situations. It appears from the case material that Ling knew what to do in social situations and how to do it.

Cognitive Theories Cognitive views of anxiety in general and of phobias in particular focus on how people's thought processes can serve as a diathesis (see preceding discussion of diathesis-stress) and on how thoughts can maintain a phobia. Anxiety is related to being more likely to attend to negative stimuli, to interpreting ambiguous information as threatening, and to believing that negative events are more likely to occur in the future (Turk et al., 2001). This perspective appears to apply well to Ling, who focused on the negative, construed even innocuous situations as fearsome, and expected that if anything could go wrong, it probably would.

Studies of socially anxious people are also relevant to ideas about the cognitive factors related to social phobias. Socially anxious people are more concerned about evaluation than are people who are not socially anxious (Goldfried, Padawer, & Robins, 1984), are more aware of the image they present to others (Bates, 1990), and tend to view themselves negatively even when they have actually performed well in a social interaction (Wallace & Alden, 1997). A study by Davison and Zighelboim (1987) provides further evidence for these conclusions. This experiment used the Articulated Thoughts in Simulated Situations method (Davison, Robins, & Johnson, 1983; Davison, Vogel, & Coffman, 1997) to compare the thoughts of two groups of participants as they role-played participation in both a neutral situation and one in which they were being sharply criticized. One group comprised volunteers from an introductory psychology course; the other group consisted of undergraduates referred from the student counseling center and identified by their therapists as shy, withdrawn, and socially anxious. The thoughts articulated by the socially anxious students in both stressful and neutral situations were more negative than were those of the control subjects. Some of the thoughts expressed by socially anxious students as they imagined being criticized included: "I've been rejected by these people," "There is no place to turn to now," "I think I am boring when I talk to people," "I often think I should not talk at all."

Predisposing Biological Factors In addition to the psychological diatheses mentioned above, investigators have studied biological predispositions/diatheses for the development of phobias. Why do some people acquire unrealistic fears when others do not, given similar experiences? After all, the criticism and evaluation to which Ling was subjected as an actress and a wife are probably no worse than what most people experience without developing "panic attacks." Perhaps those who are adversely affected by stress have a biological malfunction (a diathesis) that somehow predisposes them to develop a phobia following a particular stressful event. Research in two areas seems promising: the autonomic nervous system and genetic factors.

Regarding the autonomic nervous system, people with social phobia often fear they will blush or sweat heavily in public. Since both sweating and blushing are controlled by the autonomic nervous system (ANS), overactivity of this system could be a diathesis. However, most of the evidence does not find that individuals with phobias differ much from controls on various measures of autonomic activity, even when in situations such as public speaking, in which we would have expected to find differences. It may be that fear of blushing or sweating is as important as actual blushing or sweating. For example, a recent study assessed blushing during three different stress tasks in three groups of people: those with social phobia who reported that they blushed a lot, those with social phobia who did not report excessive blushing, and controls. Participants with social phobia self-reported more blushing during each of the three stress tests, but they actually blushed more than the controls during only one of the three tests (watching a videotape of themselves singing a children's song). The people with social phobia who had earlier reported blushing did not actually blush more than the people with social phobia who did not report blushing (Gerlach et al., 2001). Therefore, while autonomic overactivity (as reflected in blushing) is of some relevance to social phobia, the fear of the consequences of autonomic activity may be more important.

With respect to genetic factors, several studies have examined their relevance to phobias. Blood-and-injection phobia is strongly familial. Sixty-four percent of patients with blood-and-injection phobia have at least one first-degree relative with the same disorder, whereas the disorder's prevalence in the general population is only 3 to 4 percent (Ost, 1992). Similarly, for both social and specific phobias, prevalence is higher than average in first-degree relatives of patients, and twin studies show higher concordance for MZ than DZ pairs (Hettema, Neale, & Kendler, 2001).

Related to these findings is the work of Jerome Kagan on the trait of inhibition or shyness (Kagan et al., 1999). Some infants as young as four months become agitated and cry when they are shown toys or other stimuli. This behavior pattern, which may be inherited, can set the stage for the later development of phobias. In one study, for example, inhibited children were more than five times more likely than uninhibited children to develop a phobia later in life (Biederman et al., 1990).

The data we have described do not unequivocally implicate genetic factors, however. Although close relatives share genes, they also have considerable opportunity to observe and influence one another. The fact that a son and his father are both afraid of heights may indicate a genetic component, the son's direct imitation of the father's behavior, or both. Although there is some reason to believe that genetic factors may be involved in the etiology of phobias, there has as yet been no clear-cut demonstration of the extent to which they may be important.

Treatment of Phobias

Psychoanalytic Approaches Just as psychoanalytic theory has many derivations, so too, does psychoanalytic therapy. In general, however, all psychoanalytic treatments of phobias attempt to uncover the repressed conflicts that are assumed to underlie the extreme fear and avoidance characteristic of these disorders. Because the phobia itself is regarded as symptomatic of underlying conflicts, it is usually not dealt with directly. Indeed, direct attempts to reduce phobic avoidance are contraindicated because the phobia is assumed to protect the person from repressed conflicts that are too painful to confront.

In various combinations the analyst uses the techniques developed within the psychoanalytic tradition to help lift the repression. During free association, which has the patient say whatever comes to mind, without censoring, the analyst listens carefully to what the patient mentions in connection with any references to the phobia. The analyst also attempts to discover clues to the repressed origins of the phobia in the manifest content of dreams. Exactly what the analyst believes these repressed origins are depends on the particular psychoanalytic theory held. An orthodox analyst will look for conflicts related to sex or aggression, whereas an analyst holding to Arieti's interpersonal theory (Arieti, 1979) will encourage patients to examine their generalized fear of other people.

Contemporary ego analysts focus less on historical insights and more on encouraging the patient to confront the phobia. However, they continue to view the phobia as an outgrowth of an earlier problem. Alexander and French, in their classic book *Psychoanalytic Therapy* (1946), wrote of the "corrective emotional experience" in therapy, by which they meant the patient's confrontation with what is so desperately feared. They observed that "Freud himself came to the conclusion that in the treatment of some cases, phobias for example, a time arrives when the analyst must encourage the patient to engage in those activities he avoided in the past" (p. 39). Wachtel (1977) even more boldly recommended that analysts employ the fear-reduction techniques of behavior therapists, such as systematic desensitization.

Behavioral Approaches Systematic desensitization was the first major behavioral treatment to be widely used in treating phobias (Wolpe, 1958). The individual with a phobia imagines a series of increasingly frightening scenes while in a state of deep relaxation. Clinical and experimental evidence indicates that this technique is effective in eliminating, or at least reducing, phobias (Barlow, Raffa, & Cohen, 2002). Many behavior therapists, however, have come to recognize the critical importance of exposure to real-life phobic situations, sometimes during the period in which a patient is being desensitized in imagination, and sometimes instead of the imagery-based procedure (Craske, Rapee, & Barlow, 1992). Most contemporary clinical researchers regard such in vivo exposure as superior to techniques using imagination. This is not a surprising finding given that imaginary stimuli are by definition not the real thing! However, when complex fears like those experienced by Ling are involved, there is a major advantage to using imagery—it is more readily controlled, and any kind of situation can be constructed for the patient.

Learning social skills can help people with social phobias who may not know what to do or say in social situations. Some behavior therapists encourage patients to role-play or rehearse interpersonal encounters in the consulting room or in small therapy groups (Heimberg & Juster, 1994; Heimberg et al., 1993; Marks, 1995; Mattick & Andrews, 1994). Several studies attest to the effectiveness of such an approach (e.g., Heimberg et al., 1989; Turner, Beidel, & Cooley-Quille, 1995). As pointed out by Herbert (1995), such practices may also expose the timorous person, even when there is no social-skills deficit, to anxiety-provoking cues, such as being observed by others, so that through real-life exposure extinction of fear takes place (Hope, Heimberg, & Bruch, 1995). This illustrates how a particular therapeutic technique can work for more than one reason.

Modeling is another technique that uses exposure to feared situations. In modeling therapy, fearful clients are exposed to filmed or live demonstrations of other people interacting fearlessly with the phobic object, for example, handling snakes or petting dogs. Flooding is a therapeutic technique in which the client is exposed to the source of the phobia at full intensity. The extreme discomfort that is an inevitable part of this procedure has until recently tended to discourage therapists from employing it, except perhaps as a last resort when graduated exposure has not worked.

Behavior therapists who favor operant techniques downplay the importance of the fear assumed to underlie phobias and attend instead to the overt avoidance of phobic objects and to the approach behavior that must replace it. They treat approach to the feared situation as any other operant and shape it according to the principle of successive approximations. Real-life exposures to the phobic object are gradually achieved, and the client is rewarded for even minimal successes in moving closer to it. Note that exposure is an inevitable aspect of any operant shaping of approach behaviors.

Cognitive Approaches Cognitive treatments for specific phobias like extreme fear of closed spaces (claustrophobia) or of heights (acrophobia) have been viewed with skepticism because of a central defining characteristic of phobias: the individual recognizes the phobic fear as excessive or unreasonable. If the person already acknowledges that the fear is of something harmless, of what use can it be to alter the person's thoughts about it? Indeed, there is no evidence that eliminating irrational beliefs alone, without exposure to the fearsome situations, reduces phobic avoidance (Turner et al., 1992; Williams & Rappoport, 1983).

With social phobias, on the other hand, such cognitive methods—sometimes combined with social skills training—are more promising. People with social phobias benefit from treatment strategies based on both Beck and Ellis. That is, they may be persuaded by the therapist to more accurately appraise people's reactions to them (a frown from my teacher may have less to do with disapproval of me than with something the teacher is preoccupied with that has nothing to do with me) and to rely less on approval from others for maintaining a sense of self-worth (just because I have been criticized does not mean that I am a worthless nonentity). With the recognition in recent years that many people with social phobias have adequate social skills but are inhibited by self-defeating thoughts from showing them, there has been increasing emphasis on cognitive approaches (Turk, Heimberg, & Hope, 2001).

All the behavioral and cognitive therapies for phobias have a recurrent theme, namely, the need for the patient to begin facing what has been deemed too fearsome, too terrifying to face. We saw this in Ling's case,[4] where imaginal exposure was paired with relaxation in a variant of Wolpe's systematic desensitization which was combined with cognitive restructuring—a variant of Beck and Ellis. Even Freud, on whose writings many psychoanalysts have over the years based their caution against exposing patients to what they phobically avoid, stated: "One can hardly ever master a phobia if one waits until the patient lets the analysis [uncovering the repressed origins of the fear] influence him to give it up. One suc-

ceeds only when one can induce them to go about alone and to struggle with their anxiety while they make the attempt" (Freud, 1919, p. 400). Thus, all these therapies reflect a time-honored bit of folk wisdom, one that tells us that we must face up to what we fear. As an ancient Chinese proverb puts it, "Go straight to the heart of danger, for there you will find safety."

Biological Approaches As is the case with all other psychological disorders, increasing attention is being paid to the possible utility of psychoactive medications in alleviating the fear and avoidance that are the hallmark of phobias. Drugs that reduce anxiety are referred to as sedatives, tranquilizers, or anxiolytics (the suffix "-lytic" comes from the Greek word meaning to loosen or dissolve). Barbiturates were the first major category of drugs used to treat anxiety disorders, but, because they are highly addicting and present great risk of a lethal overdose, they were supplanted in the 1950s by two other classes of drugs, propanediols (e.g., Miltown) and benzodiazepines (e.g., Valium and Xanax). The latter are widely used today and are of demonstrated benefit with some anxiety disorders. However, they are not used much with the specific phobias. Furthermore, although the risk of lethal overdose is not as great as with barbiturates, benzodiazepines are addicting and produce a severe withdrawal syndrome (Schweizer et al., 1990).

In recent years, drugs originally developed to treat depression (antidepressants) have become popular in treating many of the anxiety disorders, phobias included. One class of these drugs, the monoamine oxidase (MAO) inhibitors, fared better in treating social phobia than did a benzodiazepine (Gelernter et al., 1991), and in another study was as effective as cognitive-behavior therapy at a 12-week followup (Heimberg et al., 1998). But MAO inhibitors, such as phenelzine (Nardil), can lead to weight gain, insomnia, sexual dysfunction, and hypertension. The more recently available selective serotonin reuptake inhibitors (SSRIs), such as fluoxetine (Prozac), were also originally developed to treat depression. They also have shown some promise in reducing both specific and social phobia in double-blind studies (Benjamin et al., 2000; Van Ameringen et al., 2001). The key problem in treating phobias and other anxiety disorders with drugs, however, is that the drugs may be difficult to discontinue and relapse is common if patients stop taking them (Herbert, 1995).

Asian Americans and Psychological Intervention

As mentioned in our discussion of the African American lawyer with hypertension (Chapter 5), cultural diversity is important to highly heterogeneous countries, such as the United States and Canada, and it is of importance to other countries as well. Despite our increasing understanding of biological factors in the nature of mental illness and how to prevent and treat many disorders, social circumstances are ignored only at great risk. Because of Ling's ethnicity, we close this case study with a consideration of some diversity issues in psychotherapy.

It is generally assumed that patients do better with therapists who are similar to them in cultural and ethnic background.

---

[4] It should be noted that Ling actually engaged in little avoidance behavior. Because of her strong motivation to succeed as an actress and a teacher, she valiantly thrust herself into situations that she knew would cause her anxiety, sometimes very high anxiety (cf. her "panic attacks"). From our perspective, however, viewing her problems as phobic in nature is appropriate because confronting her demons triggered the kind of anxiety that would probably have led to avoidance in someone lacking the fervent desire to act and/or teach. As mentioned earlier, sometimes social phobia is referred to as social anxiety disorder, presumably to cover people like Ling, who, though terribly stressed by certain situations, nonetheless often engage them, paying a high emotional price to be sure.

Therapists of similar background, perhaps even of the same gender, will better know the life circumstance of those in need, and, most important, will be more acceptable to them. In psychoanalytic terms, similarity between patient and therapist may strengthen the therapeutic alliance.

Extensive research on modeling provides some justification for these assumptions. Participants in studies of learning through observation are found to acquire information more readily from models who are perceived as credible and relevant to them; similarity of age and background are important determinants of credibility and relevance (Rosenthal & Bandura, 1978). Yet it has not been demonstrated that better outcomes are achieved when patient and therapist are similar in race or ethnicity (Beutler, Machado, & Neufeldt, 1994). The jury is out on this question. Because Ling's therapist was a male Caucasian, the successful outcome offers no support for the contention that therapy between a patient and a therapist is disadvantaged if they are not of the same race.

A caveat is in order. Any discussion of racial factors in psychological intervention runs the risk of stereotyping because the literature contains primarily generalizations that experts make about the way a *group* of people react to psychological assistance. People from minority groups are, however, individuals who can differ as much from each other as their racial group differs from another racial group. Nonetheless, a consideration of group characteristics is important and is part of a developing specialty called minority mental health.

Because this patient was Chinese American, some general comments on therapy with Asian Americans are offered here. But first it is important to bear in mind that Asians living in the United States and Canada, as well as other parts of the world, comprise more than two dozen distinct subgroups (e.g., Filipino, Chinese, Japanese, Vietnamese) and differ on such dimensions as how well they speak English, whether they immigrated or came as refugees from war or terrorism in their homeland, and how much they identify with their native land (or that of their parents if they were born in the United States) (Yoshioka et al., 1981, as cited in Sue & Sue, 1992). In general, Asians show a greater tendency than whites to be ashamed of emotional suffering, to experience greater reluctance to seek out professional help, and to be relatively unassertive (according to U.S. standards). It is therefore prudent for therapists working with Asian patients to at least entertain the hypothesis that these general characteristics may be present.

The stereotype of Asian Americans as invariably being highly educated, earning good salaries, and being emotionally well-adjusted is belied by the facts. The discrimination suffered by Asians in the United States and in many other countries is as severe as that endured by other racial and ethnic minority groups (Sue & Sue, 1999). In the United States, for example, over 100,000 Japanese Americans were imprisoned in concentration camps for several years during World War II without any evidence that they posed a security threat. More subtle but nonetheless hurtful discrimination is found in everyday occurrences in more recent times. For example, after the skating competition between Michelle Kwan and Tara Lipinski in the 1998 Olympics, MSNBC reported "American beats

Kwan" (Sue & Sue, 1999, p. 260). The irony, of course, is that while Michelle Kwan's family tree originates in China, Tara Lipinski's originates in eastern Europe. Very few Americans lack foreign lineage. Recall that Ling suspected that her failure to get a particular part might have been due to her race. It's never easy to know such things for certain, but the very fact that the possibility exists—whether in reality or only in the person's mind—is bound to take a psychological toll.

Many suggestions have been made for how to conduct psychotherapy with Asian Americans. Sue and Sue (1999) advise therapists to be sensitive to the personal losses that many Asian refugees have suffered and, especially in light of the great importance that family connections have for them, to the likelihood that they are very stressed from these losses. Another way to put this is to appreciate the role of posttraumatic stress in Asian Americans who have come to the United States as refugees. Therapists should also be aware that Asian Americans have a tendency to "somaticize"—to experience and to talk about stress in physical terms, such as headaches and fatigue, rather than to view their stress in psychological terms, which they often see as equivalent to being crazy or inferior (Nguyen, 1985). Their values are also different from the Western values of the majority culture in the United States. For example—and allowing for considerable individual variation—Asians respect structure and formality in interpersonal relationships, whereas a Western therapist is likely to favor informality and a less authoritarian attitude. Respect for authority may take the form of agreeing readily to what the therapist does and proposes—and perhaps, rather than discussing differences openly, just not showing up for the next session. The acceptability of psychotherapy as a way to handle stress is likely to be much lower among Asian Americans, who tend to see emotional duress as something to be handled on one's own and through willpower (Kinzie, 1985). Asian Americans may also consider some areas off-limits for discussion with a therapist—for example, the nature of the marital relationship, and especially sex.

Asian Americans born in the United States are often caught between two cultures. One form of a resolution is to identify vigorously with majority values and denigrate anything Asian, a kind of racial self-hate. One finds this in other groups that have been discriminated against, for example, African Americans and Jews. Others, torn by conflicting loyalties, experience poorly expressed rage at a discriminatory Western culture but at the same time question aspects of their Asian background. Finally, the therapist may have to be more directive and active than he or she otherwise might be, given the preference of many Asian Americans for a structured approach over a reflective one (Atkinson, Maruyama, & Matsui, 1978; Iwamasa, 1993).

Where does Ling fit in here? Like many offspring of immigrants, she had largely acculturated to the dominant U.S. culture. And it is not possible to interpret with confidence characteristics that are typically attributed to Asian cultures, in particular nonassertiveness and respect for authority. Put differently, and as a rephrase of an old commercial that stated that one didn't have to be Jewish to enjoy so-and-so's rye bread, one doesn't have to be from an Asian culture to suffer from lack of assertiveness or to have a great respect for authority. It could be that, had the therapy not been time-limited and contractually restricted to Ling's "panic attacks," more would have been learned about the influence of her cultural background on her presenting problems. The only thing we can and should do, however, is to note the *possible* role of culture in the present case and leave it at that.

7 Somatoform and Dissociative Disorders

A twenty-seven-year-old male was brought to a hospital emergency room after being picked up by the police for lying down in the middle of a busy intersection. He said that he wanted to die and was very depressed. He had no memory of any events prior to being picked up by the police. He didn't know his name nor anything about his life history.

Several neurological tests were administered and revealed no abnormality. After six days in the hospital, hypnosis was begun. Over the first three hypnotic sessions, details of the patient's past life emerged but not his name nor the events that led up to his hospitalization. During the fourth and fifth sessions, the remaining details came forth. The man had just come to town, looking for work. Two men had noticed his toolbox, approached him, and asked if he wanted a job. All three then had left in a pickup truck, and, after smoking some marijuana, the patient had been forced, at gunpoint, to have sex with the other men. (Kaszniak et al., 1988)

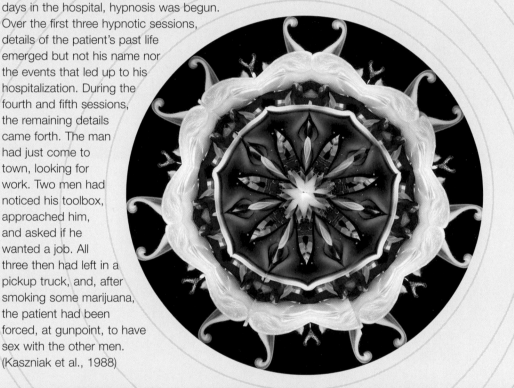

S omatoform and dissociative disorders, our focus for this chapter, are related to anxiety disorders. In early versions of the DSM, all these disorders were subsumed under the heading of neuroses because anxiety was considered the predominant underlying factor in each case. Starting with DSM-III, classification came to be based on observable behavior, not on presumed etiology. In the anxiety disorders, signs of anxiety are obvious, but anxiety is not necessarily observable in the somatoform and dissociative disorders. In **somatoform disorders**, the individual complains of bodily symptoms that suggest a physical defect or dysfunction—sometimes rather dramatic in nature—but for which no physiological basis can be found. In **dissociative disorders**, the individual experiences disruptions of consciousness, memory, and identity, as illustrated in the opening case. The onset of both classes of disorders is typically related to some stressful experience, and these disorders sometimes co-occur. We will examine the somatoform and dissociative disorders in this chapter, focusing in more depth on those disorders about which more is known. As before, we will look at symptoms, etiology, and therapies throughout the discussion.

Somatoform Disorders

As noted in Chapter 1, *soma* means "body." In somatoform disorders psychological problems take a physical form. The physical symptoms of somatoform disorders, which have no known physiological explanation and are not under voluntary control, are thought to be linked to psychological factors, presumably anxiety, and are therefore assumed to be psychologically caused. In this section we look at two somatoform disorders in depth: conversion disorder and somatization disorder. But first we consider briefly three DSM-IV-TR categories of somatoform disorders about which less information is available: pain disorder, body dysmorphic disorder, and hypochondriasis. (A summary of the somatoform disorders appears in Table 7.1.)

Pain Disorder, Body Dysmorphic Disorder, and Hyponchondriasis

In **pain disorder** the person experiences pain that causes significant distress and impairment; psychological factors are viewed as playing an important role in the onset, maintenance, and severity of the pain. The patient may be unable to work and may become dependent on painkillers or tranquilizers. The pain may have a temporal relation to some conflict or stress, or it may allow the individual to avoid some unpleasant activity and to secure attention and sympathy not otherwise available. Accurate diagnosis is difficult because the subjective experience of pain is always a psychologically influenced phenomenon; that is, pain is not a simple sensory experience, as are vision and hearing. Therefore, deciding when a pain becomes a somatoform pain is difficult. Some differentiation may be achieved, however, in the way in which pain is described by patients with somatoform disorder compared with descriptions by patients whose pain is clearly linked to a physical problem. Patients with physically based pain localize it more specifically, give more detailed sensory descriptions of their pain, and link their pain more clearly to situations that increase or decrease it (Adler et al., 1997). (Therapies for managing pain are discussed in Chapter 8, pp. 237–243.)

With **body dysmorphic disorder** a person is preoccupied with an imagined or exaggerated defect in appearance, frequently in the face—for example, facial wrinkles, excess facial hair, or the shape or size of the nose. Women tend also to focus on the skin, hips, breasts, and legs, whereas men are more inclined to believe they are too short, that their penises are too small, or that they have too much body hair (Perugi et al., 1997). Some patients with the disorder may compulsively spend hours each day checking on their defect, looking at themselves in mirrors. Others take steps to avoid being reminded of the defect by eliminating mirrors from their homes or camouflaging the perceived defect, for example, by wearing very loose clothing (Albertini & Phillips, 1999). Some even become housebound to keep other people from seeing their imagined defect. These concerns are distressing and sometimes lead to suicide; consultations with plastic surgeons are frequent and some patients even perform surgery on themselves. Unfortunately, plastic surgery does little to allay patients' concerns (Veale, 2000). Body dysmorphic disorder occurs mostly among women, typically begins in late adolescence, and is frequently comorbid with depression, social phobia, and personality disorders (Phillips & McElroy, 2000; Veale et al., 1996).

Table 7.1 Summary of Somatoform Disorders

Disorder	Description
Pain disorder	Psychological factors play a significant role in the onset and maintenance of pain
Body dysmorphic disorder	Preoccupation with imagined or exaggerated defects in physical appearance
Hypochondriasis	Preoccupation with fears of having a serious illness
Conversion disorder	Sensory or motor symptoms without any physiological cause
Somatization disorder	Recurrent, multiple physical complaints that have no biological basis

Body dysmorphic disorder.

As with pain disorder, subjective factors and matters of taste play a role. When, for example, does one's vanity become a body dysmorphic disorder? A survey of college students (Fitts et al., 1989) found that 70 percent of the students indicated at least some dissatisfaction with their appearance, with a higher figure for women than for men. Determining when these perceived defects become psychological disorders is difficult indeed. How much distress does the condition have to produce? Social and cultural factors surely play a role in how a person determines whether he or she is attractive, as they do with the eating disorders discussed in Chapter 9.

Although there are systematic studies of body dysmorphic disorder, it is unclear whether its status as a specific diagnosis is warranted. For example, because of their excessive preoccupation with appearance and frequent checking on their looks, some cases might be diagnosed with obsessive-compulsive disorder; others might have an eating disorder (distorted body image is an important feature of eating disorders) (Jolanta & Tomasz, 2000; McKay, Neziroglu, & Yarayura-Tobias, 1997). In other cases the belief concerning the defect is so unrelated to reality as to suggest a delusional disorder (Hollander, Cohen, & Simeon, 1993). Preoccupation with imagined defects in physical appearance may therefore not be a disorder itself, but a symptom that can occur in several disorders.

Hypochondriasis is a somatoform disorder in which individuals are preoccupied with fears of having a serious disease which persist despite medical reassurance to the contrary. The disorder typically begins in early adulthood, and tends to have a chronic course. In one study over 60 percent of diagnosed cases still had the disorder when followed up four to five years later (Barsky et al., 1998). Patients with this little-used diagnosis are frequent consumers of medical services; not surprisingly, they view their physicians as incompetent and uncaring (Pershing et al., 2000). The theory is that they overreact to ordinary physical sensations and minor abnormalities—such as irregular heartbeat, sweating, occasional coughing, a sore spot, stomachache—as evidence for their beliefs. Consistent with this idea, when asked to give a possible reason for a physical sensation, such as feeling one's heart is pounding, people with high scores on a measure of hypochondriasis were more likely than others to attribute the feeling to an illness (MacLeod, Haynes, & Sensky, 1998). Similarly, patients with hypochondriasis make catastrophic interpretations of symptoms, such as believing that a red blotch on the skin is a sign of skin cancer (Rief, Hiller, & Margraf, 1998).

Hypochondriasis often co-occurs with anxiety and mood disorders, which has led some researchers to think that it is not a discrete disorder but a symptom of other disorders (Noyes, 1999). Hypochondriasis is not well differentiated from somatization disorder (see below), which is also characterized by a long history of complaints of medical illnesses (Noyes et al., 1994).

We turn now to a discussion of conversion disorder and somatization disorder and then to theories of etiology and therapies.

Conversion Disorder

> ### DSM-IV-TR Criteria for Conversion Disorder
>
> - One or more symptoms affecting motor or sensory functioning and suggesting a neurological or medical condition
> - Symptoms are related to conflict or stress
> - Symptoms are not intentionally produced and cannot be explained by a medical condition

In **conversion disorder**, sensory or motor symptoms, such as a sudden loss of vision or paralysis, suggest an illness related to neurological damage of some sort, though the bodily organs and nervous system are found to be fine. Individuals may experience partial or complete paralysis of arms or legs; seizures and coordination disturbances; a sensation of prickling, tingling, or creeping on the skin; insensitivity to pain; or the loss or impairment of sensations, called **anesthesias**, although they are physiologically normal people. Vision may be seriously impaired; the person may become partially or completely blind or have tunnel vision, in which the visual field is constricted as it would be if the person were peering through a tube. *Aphonia*, loss of the voice and all but whispered speech, and *anosmia*, loss or impairment of the sense of smell, are other conversion symptoms.

The psychological nature of conversion symptoms is also demonstrated by the fact that they appear suddenly in stressful situations, often allowing the individual to avoid some activity or responsibility or to receive badly wanted attention. The term conversion originally derived from Freud, who thought that the energy of a repressed instinct was diverted into sensory-motor channels and interfered with normal functioning. Thus anxiety and psychological conflict were believed to be converted into physical symptoms. Some people with conversion disorders may seem complacent, even serene, and are not particularly eager to part with their symptoms, nor do they connect their symptoms with whatever stressful situation they are in.

Hysteria, the term originally used to describe what are now known as conversion disorders, has a long history dating back to the earliest writings on abnormal behavior. Hippocrates considered it an affliction limited solely to women and brought on by the wandering of the uterus through the body. (The Greek word *hystera* means "womb.") Presumably the wandering uterus symbolized the longing of the body for the production of a child.

Conversion symptoms usually develop in adolescence or early adulthood, typically after the occurrence of some life stress. An episode may end abruptly, but sooner or later the disorder is likely to return, either in its original form or with a symptom of a different nature and site. Prevalence of conversion disorder is less than 1 percent, and more women than men are given the diagnosis (Faravelli et al., 1997; Singh & Lee, 1997). During both world wars, however, a large number of males developed conversion-like difficulties in combat (Ziegler, Imboden, & Meyer, 1960). Conversion disorder is also frequently comorbid with other Axis I diagnoses, for example, depression and substance abuse, and with personality disorders, notably borderline and histrionic personality disorders (Binzer, Anderson, & Kullgren, 1996; Rechlin, Loew, & Jorashky, 1997).

In making diagnoses it is important to distinguish a conversion paralysis or sensory dysfunction from similar problems that have a true neurological basis (see Figure 7.1). Sometimes this task is easy, as when the paralysis does not make anatomical sense. A classic example is "glove anesthesia," a rare syndrome in which the individual experiences little or no sensation in the part of the hand that would be covered by a glove (see Figure 7.1). For years this was the textbook illustration of anatomical nonsense because the nerves here run continuously from the hand up the arm. Yet even in this case it now appears that misdiagnosis can occur. A more recently recognized disease, carpal tunnel syndrome, can produce symptoms similar to those of glove anesthesia. Nerves in the wrist run through a tunnel formed by the wrist bones and membranes. The tunnel can become swollen and may pinch the nerves, leading to tingling, numbness, and pain in the hand. Nowadays, we see a good deal more of carpal tunnel syndrome in people who sit at computer keyboards for many hours a day.

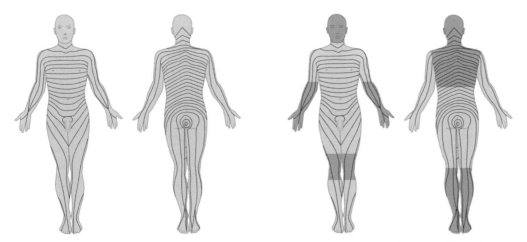

Figure 7.1 Hysterical anesthesias can be distinguished from neurological dysfunctions. The patterns of neural innervation are shown on the left. Typical areas of anesthesia in hysterical patients are superimposed on the right. The hysterical anesthesias do not make anatomical sense. Adapted from an original painting by Frank H. Netter, M.D. From *The CIBA Collection of Medical Illustrations*, copyright © by CIBA Pharmaceutical Company, Division of CIBA-GEIGY Corporation.

Malingering and Factitious Disorder

One diagnostic problem with conversion disorder is distinguishing it from **malingering**, listed in DSM-IV-TR as a condition that may be a focus of clinical attention (see p. 71). In malingering, an individual fakes an incapacity in order to avoid a responsibility, such as work or military duty, or to achieve some goal, such as being awarded a large insurance settlement. Malingering is diagnosed when the conversion-like symptoms are under voluntary control, which is not thought to be the case in true conversion disorders.

In trying to discriminate conversion reactions from malingering, clinicians may attempt to determine whether the symptoms have been consciously or unconsciously adopted. This means of resolving the issue is dubious, for it is difficult, if not impossible, to know with any degree of certainty whether behavior is consciously or unconsciously motivated. One aspect of behavior that can sometimes help distinguish the two disorders is known as **la belle indifférence**, which is characterized by a relative lack of concern or a blasé attitude toward the symptoms that is out of keeping with their severity and supposedly long-term consequences. Patients with conversion disorder sometimes demonstrate this behavior; they also appear willing and eager to talk endlessly and dramatically about their symptoms, but often without the concern one might expect. In contrast, malingerers are likely to be more guarded and cautious, perhaps because they consider interviews a challenge or threat to the success of the lie. But this distinction is not foolproof, for only about one-third of people with conversion disorders show la belle indifférence (Stephens & Kamp, 1962). Furthermore, a stoic attitude is sometimes found among patients with verified medical diseases.

Also related to the disorders we have been discussing is another DSM category, **factitious disorder**. In this disorder the person intentionally produces physical symptoms (or sometimes psychological ones). Patients may make up symptoms, for example, reporting acute pain, or may inflict injuries on themselves. In contrast to malingering, with factitious disorder the symptoms are less obviously linked to a recognizable goal; the motivation for adopting the physical or psycho-

Kathleen Bush is taken into custody, charged with child abuse and fraud for deliberately causing her child's illnesses.

logical symptoms is much less clear. The individual, for some unknown reason, wants to assume the role of patient.

Factitious disorder may also involve a parent creating physical illnesses in a child; in this case it is called factitious disorder by proxy or Munchausen syndrome by proxy. In one extreme case a seven-year-old girl was hospitalized over 150 times and experienced 40 surgeries at a cost of over $2 million. Her mother caused her illnesses by using drugs and even contaminating her feeding tube with fecal material (*Time*, 1996). The motivation in a case such as this appears to be the need to be regarded as an excellent parent and tireless in seeing to the child's needs.

Since the majority of paralyses, analgesias, and sensory failures do have biological causes, true neurological problems may indeed sometimes be misdiagnosed as conversion disorders. Studies conducted during the 1960s indicated that on follow-up many patients diagnosed with conversion disorder may have been misdiagnosed. One of these studies found that nine years after diagnosis, an alarming number—60 percent—of these individuals had either died or developed symptoms of physical disease! A high proportion had diseases of the central nervous system (Slater & Glithero, 1965). Fortunately, with technological advances in detecting brain disease (such as the MRI), the percentage of apparent conversion-disorder patients who subsequently develop a neurological problem now seems to be much lower (Moene et al., 2000). (See Focus on Discovery 7.1 for other diagnostic issues with this disorder.)

Somatization Disorder

In 1859 the French physician Pierre Briquet described a syndrome that first bore his name, Briquet's syndrome, and now in DSM-IV-TR is referred to as **somatization disorder**.

Recurrent, multiple somatic complaints for which medical attention is sought but that have no apparent physical cause are the basis for this disorder. To meet diagnostic criteria, the person must have all the following:

1. Four pain symptoms in different locations (e.g., head, back, joint)
2. Two gastrointestinal symptoms (e.g., diarrhea, nausea)
3. One sexual symptom other than pain (e.g., indifference to sex, erectile dysfunction)
4. One pseudoneurological symptom (e.g., those of conversion disorder)

These symptoms, which are more pervasive than the complaints in hypochondriasis, usually cause impairment, particularly regarding work. DSM-IV-TR notes that the specific symptoms of the disorder may vary across cultures. For example, burning hands or the experience of ants crawling under the skin are more frequent in Asia and Africa than in North America. Furthermore, the disorder is thought to be most frequent in cultures that de-emphasize the overt display of emotion (Ford, 1995).

Somatization disorder and conversion disorder share many of the same symptoms, and both diagnoses may be applicable to the same patient (e.g., Ford & Folks, 1985). Visits to physicians, sometimes to several simultaneously, are frequent, as is the use of medication. Hospitalization and even surgery are common (Guze, 1967). Menstrual difficulties and sexual indifference are frequent (Swartz et al., 1986). Patients typically express their complaints in a histrionic, exaggerated fashion or as part of a long and complicated medical history. Many believe that they have been ailing all their lives. Comorbidity is high with anxiety disorders, mood disorders, substance abuse, and a number of personality disorders (Golding, Smith, & Kashner, 1991, Kirmayer, Robbins, & Paris, 1994).

The lifetime prevalence of somatization disorder is estimated at less than 0.5 percent of the U.S. population; it is more frequent among women, especially African American and Hispanic women (Escobar et al., 1987), and among patients who are in medical treatment. Prevalence is higher in some countries in South America and in Puerto Rico (Tomasson, Kent, & Coryell, 1991).

Interpreting these cultural differences is not straightforward (Kirmayer & Young, 1998). From a western European perspective, for example, it is sometimes suggested that a physical presentation of a psychological problem is somehow primitive or unsophisticated. But this dualistic distinction between physical and psychological reflects a medical tradition that is not universally accepted (for example, in Chinese medicine). It is more reasonable to view a person's culture as providing a concept of what distress is and how it should be communicated.

Somatization disorder typically begins in early adulthood (Cloninger et al., 1986). It may not be as stable as the DSM implies, though, for in one recent study only one-third of patients with somatization disorder still met diagnostic criteria when reassessed twelve months later (Simon & Gureje, 1999). Anxiety and depression are frequently reported, as are a host of behavioral and interpersonal problems, such as truancy, poor work records, and marital difficulties. Somatization disorder also seems to run in families; it is found in about 20 percent of the first-degree relatives of index cases, that is, individuals diagnosed as having somatization disorder (Guze, 1993). The following case illustrates one woman's complaints.

DSM-IV-TR Criteria for Somatization Disorder

- History of many physical complaints over several years
- Four pain symptoms, 2 gastrointestinal, 1 sexual, and 1 pseudoneurological
- Symptoms are not due to a medical condition or are excessive given a medical condition the person may be experiencing

---

Alice was referred to the psychological clinic by her physician, Joyce Williams. Dr. Williams had been Alice's physician for about six months and in that time period had seen her twenty-three times. Alice had dwelt on a number of rather vague complaints—general aches and pains, bouts of nausea, fatigue, irregular menstruation, and dizziness. But various tests—complete blood workups, X rays, spinal taps, and so on—had not revealed any pathology.

On meeting her therapist Alice immediately let him know that she was a somewhat reluctant client: "I'm here only because I trust Dr. Williams and she urged me to come. I'm physically sick and don't see how a psychologist is going to help." But when Alice was asked to describe the history of her physical problems, she quickly warmed to the task. According to Alice, she had always been sick. As a child she had had episodes of high fever, frequent respiratory infections, convulsions, and her first two operations, an appendectomy and a tonsillectomy.

As she continued her somewhat loosely organized chronological account of her medical history, Alice's descriptions of her problems became more and more colorful (and probably exaggerated as well): "Yes, when I was in my early twenties I had some problems with vomiting. For weeks at a time I'd vomit up everything I ate. I'd even vomit up liquids, even water. Just the sight of food would make me vomit. The smell of food cooking was absolutely unbearable. I must have been vomiting every ten minutes." During her twenties Alice had gone from one physician to another. She saw several gynecologists for her menstrual irregularity and dyspareunia (pain during intercourse) and had undergone dilation and curettage (scraping the lining of the uterus). She had been referred to neurologists for her

headaches, dizziness, and fainting spells, and they had performed EEGs, spinal taps, and even a CT scan. Other physicians had ordered X rays to look for the possible causes of her abdominal pain and EKGs for her chest pains. Rectal and gallbladder surgery had also been performed.

When the interview finally shifted away from Alice's medical history, it became apparent that she was highly anxious in many situations, particularly those in which she thought she might be evaluated by other people. Indeed, some of her physical complaints could be regarded as consequences of anxiety. Furthermore, her marriage was shaky, and she and her husband were considering divorce. Their marital problems seemed to be linked to sexual difficulties stemming from Alice's dyspareunia and her general indifference toward sex.

Etiology of Somatoform Disorders

Much of the theorizing in the area of somatoform disorders has been directed solely toward understanding hysteria as originally conceptualized by Freud. Consequently, it has focused on explanations of conversion disorder. Later in this section, we examine psychoanalytic views of conversion disorder and then look at what behavioral, cognitive, and biological theorists have to offer. First, we briefly discuss ideas about the etiology of somatization disorder.

Etiology of Somatization Disorder   It has been proposed that patients with somatization disorder are more sensitive to physical sensations, overattend to them, or interpret them catastrophically (Kirmayer et al., 1994; Rief et al., 1998). Another possibility is that they have stronger physical sensations than other people (Rief & Auer, 2001). A behavioral view of somatization disorder holds that the various aches and pains, discomforts, and dysfunctions are the manifestation of unrealistic anxiety in bodily systems. Consistent with this idea that high anxiety is involved, patients with somatization disorder have high levels of cortisol, an indication that they are under stress (Rief et al., 1998). Perhaps the extreme tension of an individual localizes in stomach muscles, resulting in feelings of nausea or in vomiting. Once normal functioning is disrupted, the maladaptive pattern may strengthen because of the attention it receives or the excuses it provides.

Psychoanalytic Theory of Conversion Disorder   Conversion disorder occupies a central place in psychoanalytic theory, for in the course of treating these cases Freud developed many of the major concepts of psychoanalysis. Conversion disorder offered him a clear opportunity to explore the concept of the unconscious. Consider for a moment how you might try to make sense of a patient's report that she awakened one morning with a paralyzed left arm. Your first reaction might be to give her a series of neurological tests to assess possible biological causes of the paralysis. Let us assume that these tests are negative; no evidence of neurological disorder is present. You are now faced with choosing whether to believe or doubt the patient's communication. On the one hand, she might be lying; she may know that her arm is not paralyzed but has decided to fake paralysis to achieve some end. This would be an example of malingering. But what if you believe the patient? Now you are almost forced to consider that unconscious processes are operating. On a conscious level the patient is telling the truth; she believes and reports that her arm is paralyzed. Only on a level that is not conscious does she know that her arm is actually normal.

In *Studies in Hysteria* (1895/1982), Breuer and Freud proposed that a conversion disorder is caused when a person experiences an event that creates great emotional arousal, but the affect is not expressed and the memory of the event is cut off from conscious experience. The specific conversion symptoms were said to be causally related to the traumatic event that preceded them.

Anna O. (see p. 15), for example, while watching at the bedside of her seriously ill father, had dropped off into a waking dream with her right arm over the back of her chair. She saw a black snake emerge from the wall and come toward her sick father to bite him. She tried to ward it away, but her right arm had gone to sleep. When she looked at her hand, her fingers turned into little snakes with death's heads. The next day a bent branch recalled her hallucination of the snake, and at once her right arm became rigidly extended. After that her arm responded in the same way whenever some object revived her hallucination. Later, when Anna O. fell into her "absences" and took to her own bed, the contracture of her right arm became chronic and extended to paralysis and anesthesia of her right side.

In his later writings Freud hypothesized that conversion disorder in women is rooted in an early, unresolved Electra complex. The young female child becomes sexually attached to her father, and if her parents' responses to these feelings are harsh and disapproving, these early impulses are repressed. The result is both a preoccupation with sex and at the same time an avoidance of it. At a later period of the person's life, sexual excitement or some happenstance reawakens these repressed impulses, creating anxiety. The anxiety is then transformed or converted into physical symptoms. Thus the primary gain from conversion disorder is the avoidance of the unresolved Electra conflict and the previously repressed id impulses. Freud pointed out that there could also be a secondary gain or reinforcement from the symptoms; they might allow the patient to avoid or escape from some currently unpleasant life situation or to obtain attention from others.

A more contemporary psychodynamic interpretation of one form of conversion disorder, hysterical blindness, is based on experimental studies of hysterically blind people whose behavior on visual tests showed that they were influenced by the stimuli even though they explicitly denied seeing them (Sackeim, Nordlie, & Gur, 1979).

Two studies involved cases of teenaged women. The first case, described by Theodor and Mandelcorn (1973), concerned a sixteen-year-old who had experienced a sudden loss of peripheral vision and reported that her visual field had become tubular and constricted (tunnel vision). Although a variety of neurological tests had proved negative, the authors wanted to be certain that they were not dealing with a neurological problem, so they arranged a special visual test. A bright, oval target was presented either in the center or in the periphery of the patient's visual field. On each trial there was a time interval bounded by the sounding of a buzzer. A target was illuminated or not during the intervals, and the young woman's task was to report whether a target was present.

When the target was presented in the center of the visual field, the patient always correctly identified it. This outcome was expected since she had not reported any loss of central vision. For the peripheral showings of the target, however, the young woman was correct only 30 percent of the time. A person would be expected to be correct 50 percent of the time by chance alone if she were truly blind in her periphery. Therefore, she had performed significantly more poorly than would a person who was indeed blind! The clinicians reasoned that she must have been in some sense aware of the illuminated stimulus and that she wanted, either consciously or unconsciously, to preserve her blindness by performing poorly on the test.

Sackeim et al. also reviewed a seemingly contradictory case reported by Grosz and Zimmerman (1970) in which a hysterically near-blind adolescent girl showed almost perfect visual performance. Fifteen-year-old Celia's initial symptom was a sudden loss of sight in both eyes, followed thereafter by slight improvement to severe blurring of vision. Celia claimed not to be able to read small or large print. She had set high standards for herself and did very well at school. Her busy parents, continually rushing off to their own many activities, professed concern about their four children's education but often left Celia responsible for the three younger children. When Celia's vision deteriorated, her parents became obliged to read her studies to her. Testing revealed that Celia could readily identify objects of various sizes and shapes and count fingers at a distance of fifteen feet. When three triangles were projected on three display windows of a console, two of the triangles inverted, one of them upright, in 599 trials of 600 she pressed the switch under the upright triangle, the correct response, which then turned off a buzzer for five seconds. We shall return to Celia later in this chapter.

Sackeim et al. proposed a two-stage defensive reaction to account for these conflicting findings:

1. Perceptual representations of visual stimuli are blocked from awareness, and on this basis people report themselves blind.
2. Information is nonetheless extracted from the perceptual representations.

If patients feel that they must deny being privy to this information, they perform more poorly than they would by chance on perceptual tasks. If patients do not need to deny having such information, they perform the task well but still maintain that they are blind. Whether hysterically blind people unconsciously need to deny receiving perceptual information is viewed as dependent on personality factors and motivation.

Are the people who claim that they are blind and yet on another level respond to visual stimuli being truthful? Sackeim and his colleagues reported that some patients with lesions in the visual cortex, rather than damage to the eye, said that they were blind yet performed well on visual tasks. Such patients have vision (sometimes called blindsight), but they do not know that they can see. So it is possible for people to claim truthfully that they cannot see and at the same time give evidence that they can. On a more general level a dissociation between awareness and behavior has been reported in many perceptual and cognitive studies (see Focus on Discovery 7.2).

In a laboratory setting Sackeim and his colleagues tested their assumption that motivation has a bearing on whether an individual will dissociate behavior from awareness. They hypnotized two susceptible participants, gave each a suggestion of total blindness, and then tested them on a visual discrimination task.[1] One was given instructions designed to motivate her to maintain her blindness; she was expected to deny her perceptions and perform more poorly than she would by chance alone on the visual task. The other person was not explicitly urged to maintain her blindness and was expected to do better than expected by chance on the task. A third person was asked to simulate the behavior of someone who had been hypnotized and given a suggestion of total blindness.

The results agreed with the predictions. The participant highly motivated to maintain blindness indeed performed more poorly than she would be expected to by chance, and the less motivated participant performed perfectly, even while reporting that she was blind. The simulator performed at a chance level for the most part; in a postexperimental interview she stated that she had deliberately tried to simulate chance performance. Bryant and McConkey (1989) provide further support of these findings. Over a large number of sessions they tested a man with hysterical blindness, giving different motivational instructions in some sessions. Again, motivation was found to influence performance.

As proposed in the psychodynamic view of Sackeim and his colleagues, verbal reports and behavior apparently can be unconsciously separated from one another. Hysterically blind persons are able to say that they cannot see and yet at the same time can be influenced by visual stimuli. The way in which they show signs of being able to see may depend on how much they need to be considered blind.

Behavioral Theory of Conversion Disorder A behavioral account of the development of conversion disorder was proposed by Ullmann and Krasner (1975). They view

---

[1] Hypnotic susceptibility refers to whether a person will be a good hypnotic subject, that is, able to experience the suggestions of the hypnotist. This characteristic is most often assessed with the Stanford Hypnotic Susceptibility Scales (Weitzenhoffer & Hilgard, 1959), in which people are given a hypnotic induction and then asked to undertake a number of tasks. For example, the hypnotist may suggest that the person's hand is so heavy that it cannot be raised and then ask the person to try to raise it. The good hypnotic subject will not raise his or her arm or will have great difficulty doing so.

Focus on Discovery 7.2

Cognitive Factors: Awareness, the Unconscious, and Behavior

We are unaware of much that goes on in our minds as we perceive and encode stimuli from our environment. Much of the working of the mind proceeds outside consciousness. We can find a good deal of support for this idea in studies of cognitive psychologists. Consider these examples.

- In one study, people listened to a human voice played into one ear while tone sequences were played in the other ear (Wilson, 1975). The participants, who had been told to attend only to the ear to which the voice was played, reported having heard no tones. Furthermore, in a memory task they showed no evidence of having heard the tones. But another measure revealed a startling result. When asked to rate how much they liked a series of tone sequences, the participants preferred the ones that had been presented earlier to new, unfamiliar sequences. It is known that familiarity affects judgments of tone stimuli similar to those Wilson used; familiar sequences are liked better than unfamiliar ones. Some aspects of the tone sequences must have been absorbed, even though participants said that they had not heard them and demonstrated that they did not recognize them. At some level the unattended tones had become familiar.

- In another study, participants were presented with different shapes for one millisecond (one-thousandth of a second) (Kunst-Wilson & Zajonc, 1980). Later they showed virtually no ability to recognize the shapes they had seen, but when they rated how much they liked the shapes, they preferred the ones they had "seen" to other ones.

- Another study used a more naturalistic dependent variable—ratings of people's faces (Bornstein, Leone, & Galley, 1987). Students participated with two confederates of the experimenter. They were asked to read ten poems and as a group decide on the gen-

der of the author of each poem. By prior arrangement, the two confederates disagreed on seven of the ten, putting the participant in the role of tiebreaker. Prior to judging the poems, half the participants viewed, for four milliseconds, five presentations of a slide of one of the confederates. The other half saw a slide of the second confederate. (Pilot data had already shown that exposures such as these could not be discriminated from blank flashes of light.) As in the studies previously discussed, subliminal exposure was expected to increase liking for the confederate whose photograph had been viewed and hence change behavior to favor that confederate. Consistent with the prior work, participants were more likely to agree with the confederate to whose slide they had been subliminally exposed.

These experiments—a small sampling of current research making a similar point—are related to the psychoanalytic concept of the unconscious. Contemporary investigators, many of whom would identify themselves as cognitive psychologists, have begun to corroborate Freud's view that some human behavior is determined by unconscious processes. But the modern cognitive perspective understands the unconscious processes in a different way. Freud postulated the existence of *the* unconscious, a repository of instinctual energy and repressed conflicts and impulses. Contemporary researchers reject the notions of an energy reservoir and of repression, holding more simply that we are not aware of everything going on around us nor of some of our cognitive processes. At the same time these stimuli and processes of which we are unaware can affect behavior powerfully. This recent research suggests that understanding the causes of human behavior will be a difficult task. It will not be sufficient merely to ask someone, "Why did you do that?"

A child participates in a dichotic listening experiment. Although he attends to information presented to only one ear, the information reaching the unattended ear can affect behavior.

conversion disorder as malingering. The person adopts the symptom to secure some end. In their opinion the person with a conversion disorder attempts to behave according to his or her conception of how a person with a disease affecting the motor or sensory abilities would act. This theory raises two questions: (1) Are people capable of such behavior? (2) Under what conditions would such behavior be most likely to occur?

Considerable evidence indicates that the answer to the first question is yes; people can adopt patterns of behavior that match many of the classic conversion symptoms. For example, paralyses, analgesias, and blindness, as we have seen, can be induced in people under hypnosis.

As a partial answer to the second question Ullmann and Krasner specify two conditions that increase the likelihood that motor and sensory disabilities will be imitated. First, the individual must have some experience with the role to be adopted; he or she may have had similar physical problems or may have observed them in others. Second, the enactment of a role must be rewarded; an individual will assume a disability only if it can be expected either to reduce stress or to reap other positive consequences.

Although this behavioral interpretation might seem to make sense, the literature does not support it completely. Grosz and Zimmerman's patient Celia, for example, did not act in accordance with Ullmann and Krasner's theory. The very intelligent Celia performed perfectly in the visual discrimination task while still claiming severely blurred vision. Such a pattern of behavior seems a rather clumsy enactment of a role. If you wanted to convince someone that you could not see, would you always correctly identify the upright triangle?

Celia's actions seem more consistent with the theorizing offered by Sackeim and his co-workers. On the level of conscious awareness Celia probably saw only blurred images, as she claimed. But during the test the triangles were distinguished on an unconscious level, and she could pick out the upright one wherever it appeared. It is interesting to note that Celia's visual problems gained her crucial attention and help from her parents, which is in the nature of conversion disorder as well as of malingering. Three years after the onset of her visual difficulties Celia suddenly and dramatically recovered clear sight while on a cross-country trip with her parents. Earlier in the summer Celia had graduated from high school with grades well above average. The need to receive reinforcement for poor vision had perhaps passed, and her eyesight returned.

Social and Cultural Factors in Conversion Disorder   A possible role for social and cultural factors is suggested by the apparent decrease in the incidence of conversion disorder over the last century. Although Charcot and Freud seemed to have had an abundance of female patients with this sort of difficulty, contemporary clinicians rarely see anyone with such problems. Several hypotheses have been proposed to explain this apparent decrease. For example, therapists with a psychoanalytic bent point out that in the second half of the nineteenth century, when the incidence of conversion reactions was apparently high in France and Austria, repressive sexual attitudes may have contributed to the increased prevalence of the disorder. The decrease in the incidence of conversion reactions, then, may be attributed to a general relaxing of sexual mores and to the greater psychological and medical sophistication of twentieth-century culture, which is more tolerant of anxiety than it is of dysfunctions that do not make physiological sense.

Support for the role of social and cultural factors also comes from studies showing that conversion disorder is more common among people from rural areas and people of lower socioeconomic status (Binzer et al., 1996; Folks, Ford, & Regan, 1984); these individuals may be less knowledgeable about medical and psychological concepts. Further evidence derives from studies showing that the diagnosis of hysteria has declined in industrialized societies, for example, England (Hare, 1969), but has

Some psychoanalysts believe that the high frequency of conversion disorder in eighteenth-century Europe was due to the repressive sexual attitudes of the time.

remained more common in undeveloped countries, for example, Libya (Pu et al., 1986). These data, although consistent, are difficult to interpret. They could mean that increasing sophistication about medical diseases leads to decreased prevalence of conversion disorder. Alternatively, diagnostic practices may vary from country to country, producing the different rates. A cross-national study conducted by diagnosticians trained to follow the same procedures is needed.

Biological Factors in Conversion Disorder   Although genetic factors have been proposed as being important in the development of conversion disorder, research does not support this proposal. Slater (1961) investigated concordance rates in twelve identical and twelve fraternal pairs of twins. Probands of each pair had been diagnosed as having the disorder, but none of the co-twins in either of the two groups manifested a conversion reaction. Torgerson (1986) reported the results of a twin study of somatoform disorders that included ten cases of conversion disorder, twelve of somatization disorder, and seven of pain disorder. No co-twin had the same diagnosis as his or her proband! Even the overall concordance for somatoform disorders was no higher in the identical twins than in the fraternal twins. Genetic factors, then, from the studies done so far, seem to be of no importance.

Some studies have shown that conversion symptoms are more likely to occur on the left side than on the right side of the body (Binzer et al., 1996). This would be an interesting finding because left-side body functions are typically controlled by the right hemisphere of the brain. The right hemisphere is also thought to be more strongly involved than the left in negative emotional states. However, in the largest study conducted on this issue, no difference was observed in the frequency of symptoms on the right versus the left side of the body (Roelofs et al., 2000).

Another interesting biological difference has been reported between a patient with conversion disorder, who had complete loss of sensation below the elbow of his right arm, and another person, who was instructed to fake the same symptom during testing (Lorenz, Kunze, & Bromm, 1998). Various stimuli were administered to the left and right thumbs of both participants, and the electrical response of the brain to the stimuli was recorded. As expected, the brain responses indicating that a stimulus had been encountered were normal in both participants when either the right or the left thumb was stimulated. However, when the right thumb was stimulated, the brain of the person who was faking the symptom, but not of the patient, also showed another response, which reflects more of a cognitive and less of a sensory response to stimuli. This response, according to the authors' interpretation, meant that the person who was faking the symptom was actively trying to withhold a response to the stimuli. The authors believe that the data show that in conversion disorder there is an inability to use sensory information to direct behavior.

Taken together, these findings indicate that biological factors in conversion disorder should be pursued further.

Therapies for Somatoform Disorders

Because somatoform disorders are rarer than other problems that mental health professionals see, little controlled research exists on the relative efficacy of different treatments. Case reports and clinical speculation are for now the principal sources of information on how to help people with these puzzling disorders. For example, there is nothing approaching controlled research on the treatment of conversion disorder. Case studies suggest that it is usually not a good idea to try to convince the patient that his or her conversion symptoms are related to psychological factors. Clinical lore advises a gentle, supportive approach along with rewarding the patient for any degree of improvement (Simon, 1998).

People with somatoform disorders make many more visits to physicians than to psychiatrists or psychologists, for they define their problems in physical terms. These patients interpret a referral from their physician to a psychologist or psychiatrist as an indication that the doctor thinks the illness is all "in their head"; therefore, they resent referrals to "shrinks." They try the patience of their physicians, who often prescribe one drug or medical treatment after another in the hope of remedying the somatic complaint.

The talking cure into which psychoanalysis developed was based on the assumption that a massive repression had forced psychic energy to be transformed or converted into puzzling anesthesias or paralyses. The catharsis as the patient faced up to the infantile origins of the repression was assumed to help, and even today free association and other efforts to lift repression are commonly used to treat somatoform disorders. Traditional long-term psychoanalysis and psychoanalytically oriented psychotherapy have not been demonstrated to be particularly useful with conversion disorder, however, except perhaps to reduce the patient's concern about the disabling problems (Simon, 1998). On the other hand, recent evidence suggests that short-term psychodynamic treatment may be effective in alleviating the symptoms of somatoform disorders (Junkert-Tress, 2001).

When working with people with somatoform disorders, clinicians must be mindful that such patients often suffer from anxiety and depression (Simon & Fullerton, 2001). Indeed, the reader will recall from Chapter 6 and will see in Chapter 10 that concern about physical health is common among people with anxiety or depression. It should therefore come as no surprise that treating the anxiety or the depression often reduces somatoform concerns (Noyes et al., 1986; Smith, 1992).

Recently there has been interest in comorbidity between obsessive-compulsive disorder and certain somatoform disorders, such as hypochondriasis and body dysmorphic disorder (e.g., Bienvenu et al, 2000; Corovre & Gleaves, 2001; Fallon et al., 2000; Neziroglu et al, 2000). Accordingly the treatment of choice for obsessive-compulsive disorder—exposure and response prevention (ERP, see p. 161)—may also be effective for these somatoform disorders. A controlled study in which exposure plus response prevention was compared with cognitive therapy found that both were more effective in reducing hypochondriacal symptoms than a control condition in which patients were on a waiting list for treatment. (Visser & Bouman, 2001).

Behavior therapists have applied to somatoform disorders a wide range of techniques intended to make it worthwhile for the patient to give up the symptoms. A case reported by Liebson (1967) provides an example. A man had relinquished his job because of pain and weakness in the legs and attacks of giddiness. Liebson helped the patient return to full-time work by persuading his family to refrain from reinforcing him for his idleness and by arranging for the man to receive a pay increase if he succeeded in getting to work. A reinforcement approach attempts to provide the patient with greater incentives for improvement than for remaining incapacitated.

Another important consideration with any such operant tactic, as noted by Walen, Hauserman, and Lavin (1977), is for the therapist to take measures to ensure that the patient does not lose face when parting with the disorder. The therapist should appreciate the possibility that the patient may feel humiliated at becoming better through treatment that does not deal with the medical (physical) problem.

Therapies for Somatization Disorder   Cognitive and behavioral clinicians believe that the high levels of anxiety associated with somatization disorder are triggered by specific situations. Alice, the woman described earlier, revealed that she was extremely anxious about her shaky marriage and about situations in which other people might judge her. Techniques such as exposure or any of the cognitive therapies could address her fears, the reduction of which might help lessen somatic complaints. But it is likely that more treatment would be needed, for a person who has been "sick" for a period of time has grown accustomed to weakness and dependency, to avoiding everyday challenges rather than facing them as an adult.

Chances are that the people who live with Alice have adjusted to her infirmity and are even unwittingly reinforcing her for her avoidance of normal adult responsibilities. Family therapy might help Alice and the members of her family change the web of relationships in order to support her movement toward greater autonomy. Assertion training and social-skills training—for example, coaching Alice in effective ways to approach and talk to people, to maintain eye contact, to give compliments, to accept criticism, to make requests—could be useful in helping her acquire, or reacquire, means of relating to others and meeting challenges that do not begin with the premise "I am a poor, weak, sick person."

In a widely accepted approach to somatization disorder, the physician does not dispute the validity of the physical complaints, but minimizes the use of diagnostic tests and medications, maintaining contacts with the patient regardless of whether the patient is complaining of illness or not (Monson & Smith, 1983). In a study of this approach, it was found that patients showed significant improvement in their medical condition and made less frequent use of health care services (Rost, Kashner, & Smith, 1994). Also of possible use is directing the patient's attention to sources of anxiety and depression that may underlie unexplained somatic symptoms rather than allowing them to focus overly on minor and benign aches and pains. Techniques such as relaxation training and various forms of cognitive therapy have proved useful (e.g., Payne & Blanchard, 1995; Simon, 1998). Biofeedback, which entails gaining control over physiological processes (a method described in greater detail in Chapter 8) has turned out to be effective in reducing catastrophizing cognitions in patients suffering from somatoform disorder—even more so than relaxation training (Nanke & Rief, 2000).

Therapies for Hypochondriasis   In general, cognitive-behavioral approaches have proved effective in reducing hypochondriacal concerns (e.g., Bach, 2000; Fernandez, Rodriguez & Fernandez, 2001). Research has shown that hypochondriacal patients show a cognitive bias in the direction of seeing threat when health issues arise (Smeets et al., 2000). Cognitive-behavioral therapy can be aimed at restructuring such pessimistic thinking. In addition, treatment may entail such strategies as pointing out the patient's selective attention to bodily symptoms and discouraging the patient from seeking medical reassurance that he or she is not ill (e.g., Salkovskis & Warwick, 1986; Visser & Bouman, 1992; Warwick & Salkovskis, 2001).

Therapies for Pain   According to current thinking, it is usually fruitless to make a sharp distinction between psychogenic pain and pain caused by actual medical factors, such as injury to muscle tissue. It is typically assumed that pain always has both components. Effective treatments tend to have the following ingredients:

- Validating that the pain is real, and not just in the patient's head
- Relaxation training
- Rewarding the person for behaving in ways inconsistent with the pain (toughing it out)

These methods are described in greater detail in the chapter on psychophysiological disorders (see p. 237). A recent controlled outcome study reported that a variant of short-term psychodynamic therapy, called psychodynamic body therapy, was effective in reducing patients' pain and maintaining these gains over the long-term (Monsen & Monsen, 2000). There is also evidence from a number of double-blind experiments that low doses of some antidepressant drugs, most especially imipramine (Tofranil), are superior to a placebo in reducing chronic pain and distress (Arnold & Keck, 2000; Fishbain, 2000; Phillip & Fickinger, 1993.) Interestingly, these antidepressants reduce pain even when, in the low dosages given, they don't alleviate the associated depression (Simon, 1998). Some authors note that the strong placebo response that is typical in such pharmacotherapy studies suggests that a major part of the improvement may be the result of self-monitoring and the attention and education the patient receives from the clinician (Fallon & Feinstein, 2001).

In general it seems advisable to shift the focus away from what the patient cannot do because of illness and instead to teach the patient how to deal with stress, to encourage greater activity, and to enhance a sense of control, despite the physical limitations or discomfort the patient is experiencing.

Dissociative Disorders

In this section we examine four dissociative disorders: dissociative amnesia, dissociative fugue, dissociative identity disorder (formerly known as multiple personality disorder), and depersonalization disorder, all of which are characterized by changes in a person's

Table 7.2 Summary of the Dissociative Disorders

Disorder	Description
Dissociative amnesia	Memory loss following a stressful experience
Dissociative fugue	Memory loss accompanied by leaving home and establishing a new identity
Depersonalization disorder	Experience of the self is altered
Dissociative identity disorder	At least two distinct ego states—alters—that act independently of each other

sense of identity, memory, or consciousness. (The dissociative disorders are summarized in Table 7.2.) Individuals with these disorders may be unable to recall important personal events or may temporarily forget their identity or even assume a new identity. They may even wander far from their usual surroundings.

Few high-quality data concerning the prevalence of the dissociative disorders are available. Perhaps the best study to date found prevalences of 7.0 percent, 2.4 percent, and 0.2 percent for amnesia, depersonalization, and fugue, respectively (Ross, 1991). We will describe this study more fully when considering multiple personality disorder.

Dissociative Amnesia

The person with **dissociative amnesia** is unable to recall important personal information, usually after some stressful episode, as was the situation in the chapter-opening case. The information is not permanently lost, but it cannot be retrieved during the episode of amnesia. The holes in memory are too extensive to be explained by ordinary forgetfulness.

Most often the memory loss involves all events during a limited period of time following some traumatic experience, such as witnessing the death of a loved one. More rarely the amnesia is for only selected events during a circumscribed period of distress, is continuous from a traumatic event to the present, or is total, covering the person's entire life (Coons & Milstein, 1992). During the period of amnesia the person's behavior is otherwise unremarkable, except that the memory loss may bring some disorientation and purposeless wandering. With total amnesia the patient does not recognize relatives and friends, but retains the ability to talk, read, and reason and also retains talents and previously acquired knowledge of the world and how to function in it. The amnesic episode may last several hours or as long as several years. It usually disappears as suddenly as it came on, with complete recovery and only a small chance of recurrence.

Memory loss is also common in many brain disorders, as well as in substance abuse, but amnesia and memory loss caused by a brain disease or substance abuse can be fairly easily distinguished. In degenerative brain disorders memory fails more slowly over time, is not linked to life stress, and is accompanied by other cognitive deficits, such as the inability to learn new information. Memory loss following a brain injury caused by some trauma (e.g., an automobile accident) or substance abuse can be easily linked to the trauma or the substance being abused.

In *Spellbound*, Gregory Peck played a man with amnesia. Dissociative amnesia is typically triggered by a stressful event.

Dissociative Fugue

In **dissociative fugue** (from the Latin *fugere*, "to flee") the memory loss is more extensive than in dissociative amnesia. The person not only becomes totally amnesic but suddenly leaves home and work and assumes a new identity. Sometimes the person takes a new name, a new home, a new job, and even a new set of personality characteristics. The person may even succeed in establishing a fairly complex social life. More often, however, the new life does not crystallize to this extent, and the fugue is of briefer duration. It consists for the most part of limited, but apparently purposeful, travel, during which social contacts are minimal or absent.

Fugues typically occur after a person has experienced some severe stress, such as marital quarrels, personal rejections, financial or occupational difficulties, war service, or a natural disaster. Recovery, although it takes varying amounts of time, is usually complete; the individual does not recollect what took place during the flight from his or her usual haunts.

Depersonalization Disorder

Depersonalization disorder, in which the person's perception or experience of the self is disconcertingly and disruptively altered, is also included in DSM-IV-TR as a dissociative disorder. Its inclusion is controversial, however, because depersonalization disorder involves no disturbance of memory, which is typical of the other dissociative disorders. In a depersonalization episode, which is typically triggered by stress, individuals rather suddenly lose their sense of self. They have unusual sensory experiences; for example, their limbs may seem drastically changed in size or their voices may sound strange to them. They may have the impression that they are outside their bodies, viewing themselves from a distance. Sometimes they feel mechanical, as though they and others are robots, or they move as though in a world that has lost its reality. Similar episodes sometimes occur in several other disorders: schizophrenia (see Chapter 11), panic attacks and posttraumatic stress disorder (Chapter 6), and borderline personality disorder (Chapter 13) (Maldonado, Butler, & Spiegel, 1998).

Depersonalization disorder usually begins in adolescence and has a chronic course, that is, it lasts a long time. Comorbid personality disorders are frequent, as are anxiety disorders and depression (Simeon et al., 1997). The following case illustrates the symptoms as well as the fact that childhood trauma is often reported.

> Mrs. A was a 43-year-old woman who was living with her mother and son and worked at a clerical job. She had felt depersonalized as far back as she could remember. "It's as if the real me is taken out and put on a shelf or stored somewhere inside of me. Whatever makes me me is not there. It is like an opaque curtain...like going through the motions and having to exert discipline to keep the unit together." She had suffered several episodes of depersonalization annually and found them extremely distressing. She had experienced panic attacks for 1 year when she was 35 and had been diagnosed with self-defeating personality disorder. Her childhood trauma history included nightly genital fondling and frequent enemas by her mother from earliest memory to age 10. (Simeon et al., 1997, p. 1109)

Dissociative Identity Disorder

Consider what it would be like to have dissociative identity disorder, as did Chris Sizemore, the woman with the famous three faces of Eve (see p. 115). People tell you about things you have done that seem out of character, events of which you have no memory. You have been waking up each morning with the remains of a cup of tea by your bedside—and you do not like tea. How can you explain these happenings? If you think about seeking treatment, do you not worry whether the psychiatrist or psychologist will believe you? Perhaps the clinician will think you psychotic.

We all have days when we are not quite ourselves. This is assumed to be normal and is not what is meant by multiple personality. According to DSM-IV-TR, a proper diagnosis of **dissociative identity disorder (DID)** requires that a person have at least two separate ego states, or alters—different modes of being and feeling and acting that exist independently of each other and that come forth and are in control at different times. Sometimes there is one primary personality, and treatment is typically sought by the primary alter. There are typically two to four alters at the time a diagnosis is made, but over the course of treatment several more often emerge. Gaps in memory are also common and are produced because at least one alter has no contact with the others; that is, alter A has no memory for what alter B is like or even any knowledge of having an alternate state of being. The existence of different alters must also be chronic (long lasting) and

DSM-IV-TR Criteria for Dissociative Identity Disorder

- Presence of 2 or more personalities or identities
- At least 2 of the alters recurrently take control of behavior
- Inability to recall important personal information

severe (causing considerable disruption in one's life); it cannot be a temporary change resulting from the ingestion of a drug, for example.

Each alter may be quite complex, with its own behavior patterns, memories, and relationships; each determines the nature and acts of the individual when it is in command. Usually the personalities are quite different, even opposites of one another. They may have different handedness, wear glasses with different prescriptions, and have allergies to different substances. The original and subordinate alters are all aware of lost periods of time, and the voices of the others may sometimes echo into an alter's consciousness, even though the alter does not know to whom these voices belong. (See Focus on Discovery 7.3.)

Dissociative identity disorder usually begins in childhood, but it is rarely diagnosed until adulthood. It is more extensive than other dissociative disorders, and recovery may be less complete. It is much more common in women than in men. The presence of other diagnoses—in particular, depression, borderline personality disorder, and somatization disorder—is frequent (Boonn & Draijer, 1993). DID is commonly accompanied by headaches, substance abuse, phobias, hallucinations, suicide attempts, sexual dysfunction, and self-abusive behavior, as well as by other dissociative symptoms such as amnesia and depersonalization (Scroppo et al., 1998).

Cases of dissociative identity disorder are sometimes mislabeled in the popular press as schizophrenia. This latter diagnostic category, discussed in greater detail in Chapter 11, derives part of its name from the Greek root *schizo*, which means "splitting away from," hence the confusion. A split in the personality, wherein two or more fairly separate and coherent systems of being exist alternately in the same person, is quite different from any of the recognized symptoms of schizophrenia.

Controversies in the Diagnosis of DID   Although DID is formally recognized as a diagnosis by its being listed in DSM-IV-TR, its inclusion is a matter of some controversy. For example, in a survey of board-certified psychiatrists only one-third reported that they had no reservations about the presence of DID in the DSM (Pope et al., 1999).

DID was first mentioned in the nineteenth century. In a review of the literature, Sutcliffe and Jones (1962) identified a total of seventy-seven cases, most of which had been reported in the period between 1890 and 1920. After that, reports of DID declined until the 1970s, when they increased markedly, not only in the United States but also in nonwestern cultures such as Japan (Uchinuma & Sekine, 2000). More formal data on the prevalence of DID were collected on samples of adults in Winnipeg, Canada, and in Sivas, Turkey (Akyuez et al., 1999; Ross, 1991). Prevalence was 1.3 percent in the Canadian study and 0.4 percent in the Turkish one. Although these prevalence figures may not seem high, they are; prevalence was earlier thought to be about one in one million.

What has caused the reemergence of the DID diagnosis in the past thirty or so years? One possible explanation for the increase is that in DSM-III, which was published in 1980, the diagnostic criteria for DID were spelled out clearly for the first time, causing more cases to be recognized (Putnam, 1996). But it is also possible that more people began to adopt the role of a patient with DID, or that clinicians had always seen a similar number of cases but chose to report them only when interest in DID grew. Alternatively, the earlier decline in the number of diagnoses of DID may have resulted from the increasing popularity of the concept of schizophrenia; cases of DID may have been mistakenly diagnosed as cases of schizophrenia (Rosenbaum, 1980). However, the symptoms of the two disorders are actually not very similar; although the voices of the alters may be experienced as auditory hallucinations, patients with DID do not show the thought disorder and behavioral disorganization of schizophrenia. Another diagnostic issue is that DSM-III-R did not require that the alters be amnesic for one another, raising the possibility that the diagnosis could be applied to people with high levels of variability in their behavior, as occurs with some personality disorders (Kihlstrom & Tataryn, 1991). Although DSM-IV restored the amnesia component to the diagnosis, we do not yet know what effect this will have on how often DID is diagnosed.

The film version of *Sybil* depicted this famous case of dissociative identity disorder. The title role was played by Sally Field.

Focus on Discovery 7.3

Classification of Conversion Disorder and Dissociative Disorders

Now that both conversion disorder and the dissociative disorders have been described, we return to the manner in which they have been separately classified in DSM-IV-TR—conversion as a somatoform disorder because it involves physical symptoms and the dissociative disorders as a distinct category because they involve disruptions in consciousness. John Kihlstrom, a leading researcher in the field, has argued that this separation is a mistake. He believes that both disorders are disruptions in the normal controlling functions of consciousness. In the dissociative disorders there is a dissociation between explicit and implicit memory. *Explicit memory* refers to a person's conscious recall of some experience and is what is disrupted in dissociative disorders. *Implicit memory* refers to behavioral changes elicited by an event that cannot be consciously recalled. Kihlstrom (1994) cites numerous examples of patients with dissociative disorders whose implicit memory remains intact. One woman, for example, became amnesic after being victimized by a practical joke. Although she had no explicit memory of the event, she nonetheless became terrified when passing the location of the incident (implicit memory). The dissociation of explicit and implicit memory is the core of the dissociative disorders.

Kihlstrom argues that the same basic disruption of consciousness is found in conversion disorder, in this case affecting perception. As in the dissociative disorders, stimuli that are not consciously seen, heard, or felt nevertheless affect behavior. (Recall our description of several cases of hysterical blindness that clearly make this point.) So, we might consider conversion disorder as a disruption in explicit perception affecting the sensory and motor systems. Empirical support for Kihlstrom's idea comes from research showing that dissociative symptoms are common in patients with conversion disorder (Roelofs et al., 2002).

As we noted in Chapter 3, beginning with DSM-III the classification of abnormal behavior became behavioral, or symptom based. Kihlstrom's position on conversion and the dissociative disorders illustrates that other principles of classification can be applied to the field. Classification on the basis of what function or mechanism is dysfunctional may be preferable to a behaviorally based system; a behaviorally based system could be misleading in separating disorders with different symptoms that are caused by similar dysfunctions.

Another factor of possible relevance to the increase in DID diagnoses was the 1973 publication of *Sybil*, which presented a dramatic case with sixteen personalities (Schreiber, 1973). This case attracted a great deal of attention and spawned much interest in the disorder.[2] Some critics have hypothesized that this heightened interest led some therapists to suggest strongly to clients that they had DID, sometimes using hypnosis to probe for alters. It is notable that in the post-Sybil era, the number of alters in each case has risen dramatically, from two or three in the past to more than twelve (Goff & Simms, 1993).

The case of Eve White was at one time the most carefully documented report of DID in the clinical literature. But many other cases have been described. One account appeared in 1976 in the *Journal of Abnormal Psychology*. "The Three Faces of Evelyn" is a detailed history by Robert F. Jeans, the psychiatrist who treated the patient. The therapeutic outcome was an integration, or fusion, of several of the patient's personalities, not the elimination of all but one of them. Most contemporary workers regard the alters as important aspects of the whole person, hence the commonly accepted therapeutic goal of trying to fuse them into a single personality (Ross, 1989).

Jeans provides the following background on his patient. He was consulted in December 1965 by a Gina Rinaldi, referred to him by her friends. Gina, single and thirty-one years old, lived with another single woman and was at the time working successfully as a writer at a large educational publishing firm. She was considered an efficient, businesslike, and productive person, but her friends had observed that she was becoming forgetful and sometimes acted out of character. The youngest of nine siblings, Gina reported that she had been sleepwalking since her early teens; her present roommate had told her that she sometimes screamed in her sleep.

Gina described her mother, then aged seventy-four, as the most domineering woman she had ever known. She reported that as a child she had been a quite fearful and obedient daughter. At age twenty-six Gina got braces for her teeth, and at age twenty-eight she had an "affair," her first, with a former Jesuit

---

[2] The Sybil case has been subject to some controversy, for it has been claimed that her alters were created during therapy by a therapist who gave substance to Sybil's different emotional states by giving them names (Rieger, 1998).

priest, although it was apparently not sexual in nature. Then she became involved with T. C., a married man who assured her he would get a divorce and marry her. She indicated that she had been faithful to him since the start of their relationship. However, T. C. did not come through with his promised divorce, stopped seeing Gina regularly, and generally fell out of her favor. Partly on the basis of analysis of one of her dreams, Jeans concluded that Gina was uncomfortable about being a woman, particularly when a close, sexual relationship with a man might be expected of her.

After several sessions with Gina, Jeans began to notice a second personality emerging. Mary Sunshine, as she came to be called by Jeans and Gina, was quite different from Gina. She seemed to be more childlike, more traditionally feminine, ebullient, and seductive. Gina felt that she walked like a coal miner, but Mary certainly did not. Some quite concrete incidents indicated Mary's existence. Sometimes Gina found in the sink cups that had had hot chocolate in them—neither Gina nor her roommate liked hot chocolate. There were large withdrawals from Gina's bank account that she could not remember making. One evening while watching television Gina realized that she was crying and remarked to herself that it was stupid to feel sad about the particular program she was viewing. She even discovered herself ordering a sewing machine on the telephone, although she disliked sewing; some weeks later she arrived at her therapy session wearing a new dress, which Mary had sewn. At work, Gina reported, people were finding her more pleasant to be with, and her colleagues took to consulting her on how to encourage people to work better with one another. All these phenomena were entirely alien to Gina. Jeans and Gina came to realize that sometimes Gina was transformed into Mary.

Then one day T. C. showed up again. Gina was filled with scorn and derision for him, yet she heard herself greeting him warmly with the words, "Gee, I missed you so much! It's good to see you!" (Apparently the psychoanalytically oriented therapy was softening the hitherto impermeable boundaries between the separate ego states of Gina and Mary.) Gina was also surprised to hear T. C. reply on this occasion, "All you ever wanted was to please me. You've done nothing but cater to my every whim,

nothing but make me happy." Mary must have been active in the earlier relationship that Gina had had with this man.

More and more often Jeans witnessed Gina turning into Mary in the consulting room. T. C. accompanied Gina to a session during which her posture and demeanor became more relaxed, her tone of voice warmer. When T. C. explained that he really cared for her, Gina, or rather, Mary, said warmly, "Of course, T., I know you do." At another session Mary was upset and, as Jeans put it, chewed off Gina's fingernails. Then the two of them started having conversations with each other in front of Jeans.

A year after the start of therapy an apparent synthesis of Gina and Mary began to emerge. At first it seemed that Gina had taken over entirely, but then Jeans noticed that Gina was not as serious as before, particularly about "getting the job done," that is, working extremely hard on the therapy. Jeans, probably believing that Mary wanted to converse with him, encouraged Gina to have a conversation with Mary. The following is that conversation:

> I was lying in bed trying to go to sleep. Someone started to cry about T. C. I was sure that it was Mary. I started to talk to her. The person told me that she didn't have a name. Later she said that Mary called her Evelyn.... I was suspicious at first that it was Mary pretending to be Evelyn. I changed my mind, however, because the person I talked to had too much sense to be Mary. She said that she realized that T. C. was unreliable but she still loved him and was very lonely. She agreed that it would be best to find a reliable man. She told me that she comes out once a day for a very short time to get used to the world. She promised that she will come out to see you [Jeans] sometime when she is stronger. (Jeans, 1976, pp. 254–255)

Throughout January, Evelyn appeared more and more often, and Jeans felt that his patient was improving rapidly. Within a few months she seemed to be Evelyn all the time; soon thereafter this woman married a physician. Now, years later, she has had no recurrences of the other personalities.

Etiology of Dissociative Disorders

The term *dissociative disorders* refers to the mechanism, dissociation, that is thought to cause them. Historically, the concept comes from the writings of Pierre Janet, the French neurologist. The basic idea is that consciousness is usually a unified experience, including cognition, emotion, and motivation. But under stress, memories of a trauma may be stored in such a way that they are not later accessible to awareness when the person has returned to a more normal state (Kihlstrom, Tataryn, & Holt, 1993). A possible outcome is amnesia or fugue.

The behavioral view of dissociative disorders is somewhat similar to these earlier speculations. Behavioral theorists generally consider dissociation as an avoidance response that protects the person from stressful events and memories of these events. Because the person does not consciously confront these painful memories, the fear they elicit has no opportunity to extinguish.

A problem with any theory, be it psychoanalytic or behavioral, that holds that traumatic memories are forgotten or dissociated because of their aversiveness is that research on both animals and humans shows that high levels of stress usually enhance rather than impair memory (Shobe & Kihlstrom, 1997). This is certainly what one finds in posttraumatic stress disorder, when the person is sometimes overwhelmed by recurrent, intrusive images of past traumatic events. A response to this criticism, however, is that dissociative disorders are quite rare relative to the frequency with which people experience trauma. In other words, it may well be the case, as Shobe and Kilhstrom (1997) have argued, that the usual response to trauma is enhanced memory, but we are not talking about *usual* ways of responding when it comes to dissociative disorders.

Etiology of DID   There are two major theories of DID. One assumes that DID begins in childhood as a result of severe physical or sexual abuse. The abuse causes dissociation and the formation of alters as a way of escaping the trauma (Gleaves, 1996). There is indeed empirical evidence that child abuse is associated with the development of dissociative symptoms (Chu et al., 2000). Since not everyone who experiences child abuse develops DID, it is further proposed that a diathesis is present among those who do develop DID. One idea is that being high in hypnotizability facilitates the development of alters through self-hypnosis (Bliss, 1983). Another proposed diathesis is that people who develop DID are very prone to engage in fantasy (Lynn et al., 1988).

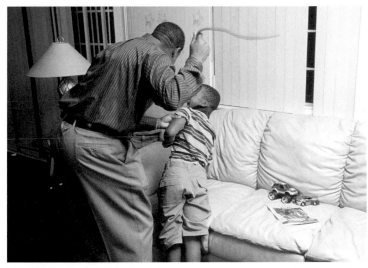
Physical or sexual abuse in childhood is regarded as a major cause of dissociative disorders.

The other theory considers DID to be learned social role enactment. The alters appear in adulthood, typically due to suggestions by a therapist (Lilienfeld et al., 1999; Spanos, 1994). DID is not viewed as a conscious deception (or malingering) in this theory; the issue is not whether DID is real or not but how it developed and is maintained.

Spanos (1994) was a leading advocate of the idea that DID is basically a role-play. He pointed out, for example, that a small number of clinicians contribute most of the diagnoses of DID. For example, a survey conducted in Switzerland found that 66 percent of the diagnoses of DID were made by fewer than 10 percent of the psychiatrists who responded (Modestin, 1992). Perhaps these clinicians have very liberal criteria for making the diagnosis. Alternatively, though, cases of DID may be referred to clinicians who have acquired a reputation for specializing in this condition (Gleaves, 1996). Therefore, the data are inconclusive.

Another source of information on this issue comes from role-playing studies. One of these was conducted in the 1980s after the trial of a serial murderer in California who came to be known as the Hillside Strangler (Spanos, Weekes, & Bertrand, 1985). The accused murderer, Ken Bianchi, unsuccessfully pled not guilty by reason of insanity (see p. 608), claiming that the murders had been committed by his alter, Steve. In the study, undergraduate students were told that they would play the role of an accused murderer and that despite much evidence of guilt, a plea of not guilty had been entered. They were also told that they were to participate in a simulated psychiatric interview that might involve hypnosis. Then the students were taken to another room and introduced to the psychiatrist, actually an experimental assistant. After a number of standard questions, the interview diverged for students assigned to one of three experimental conditions. In the most important of these, the Bianchi condition, students were given a rudimentary hypnotic induction and were then instructed to let a second personality come forward, just as had happened when Bianchi had been hypnotized.

After the experimental manipulations, the possible existence of a second personality was probed directly by the "psychiatrist." In addition, students were asked questions about the facts of the murders. Finally, in a second session, those who had acknowledged the presence of another personality were asked to take two personality tests twice—once each for their two personalities. Eighty-one percent of the students in the Bianchi condition adopted a new name, and many of these admitted guilt for the murders. Even the personality test scores of the two personalities differed considerably.

Ken Bianchi, the Hillside Strangler, attempted an insanity defense for his serial killings, but the court decided that he had merely tried to fake a multiple personality.

Clearly, then, when the situation demands, people can adopt a second personality. Spanos et al. suggest that some people who present as multiple personalities may have a rich fantasy life and considerable practice imagining that they are other people. They adopt the DID role when given suggestions by a therapist or when, like Bianchi, they find themselves in a situation in which there are inducements and cues to behave as though a previous bad act had been committed by another personality. We should remember, however, that this demonstration illustrates only that such role-playing is possible; it in no way demonstrates that cases of multiple personality have such origins. Furthermore, the impact of such role-playing studies depends on how compelling the role-play is as an analogue of DID. Critics have pointed out that DID is a complex disorder involving many symptoms, including auditory hallucinations, time loss, and depersonalization. None of these symptoms has been produced in role-playing studies (Gleaves, 1996).

Critical evidence regarding the two theories is whether people actually develop DID in childhood before entering therapy and whether it is associated with abuse. When patients with DID enter therapy, they are usually unaware of their alters. But as therapy progresses, alters emerge, and patients report that their alters did begin in childhood. Typically, however, there has been no corroborating evidence for this, and we have previously cautioned about the uncritical acceptance of self-reports. The situation is similar regarding physical or sexual abuse: very high rates have been reported (e.g., Ross et al., 1990), but they have not been corroborated (Focus on Discovery 7.4.).

One study, however, has come close to providing clearer data regarding both childhood onset and abuse in cases of DID, although it has been criticized by proponents of the role-enactment theory (Lilienfeld et al., 1999). The study, which was conducted over a period of two decades, examined 150 convicted murderers in detail (Lewis et al., 1997). Fourteen cases of DID were found. That the study was conducted on convicted murderers is important because in this situation adopting the role of a person with DID involves an obvious payoff. But the evidence indicated that 12 of the 14 cases had long-standing DID symptoms that preceded their incarceration: 8 had experienced trances during childhood, 9 had had auditory hallucinations, and 10 had had imaginary companions (which is a frequent report among DID patients). Each of these symptoms was corroborated by at least three outside sources (e.g., interviews with family members, teachers, parole officers). Furthermore, several cases showed distinctly different handwriting styles well before committing their crimes (see Figure 7.2).

Also important in this study was the documentation of physical or sexual abuse during childhood for 11 cases. Again, this was confirmed by outside sources and physical evidence such as scars. Indeed, the authors noted that "The term 'abuse' does not do justice to the quality of maltreatment these individuals endured. A more accurate term would be 'torture'!" For example, one boy was set on fire, another was circumcised by his father at age 3, and another was forced to sit on a hot stove. These data, then, lend support to the proposition that DID does begin in childhood and that it is related to extreme stress. (For further discussion of DID and the insanity defense, see p. 620.)

Therapies for Dissociative Disorders

Dissociative disorders suggest, perhaps better than any other disorders, the possible relevance of psychoanalytic theorizing. In three dissociative disorders—amnesia, fugue, and dissociative identity disorder—people behave in ways that very assuredly indicate that they cannot access forgotten earlier parts of their lives. And since these people may at the same time be unaware of having forgotten something, the hypothesis that they have repressed or dissociated massive portions of their lives is compelling (MacGregor, 1996).

Consequently, psychoanalytic treatment is perhaps more widespread as a choice of treatment for dissociative disorders than for any other psychological problems. The goal of lifting repressions is the order of the day, pursued via the use of basic psychoanalytic techniques.

Because dissociative disorders are widely believed to arise from traumatic events that the person is trying to block from consciousness, there are links between therapies for

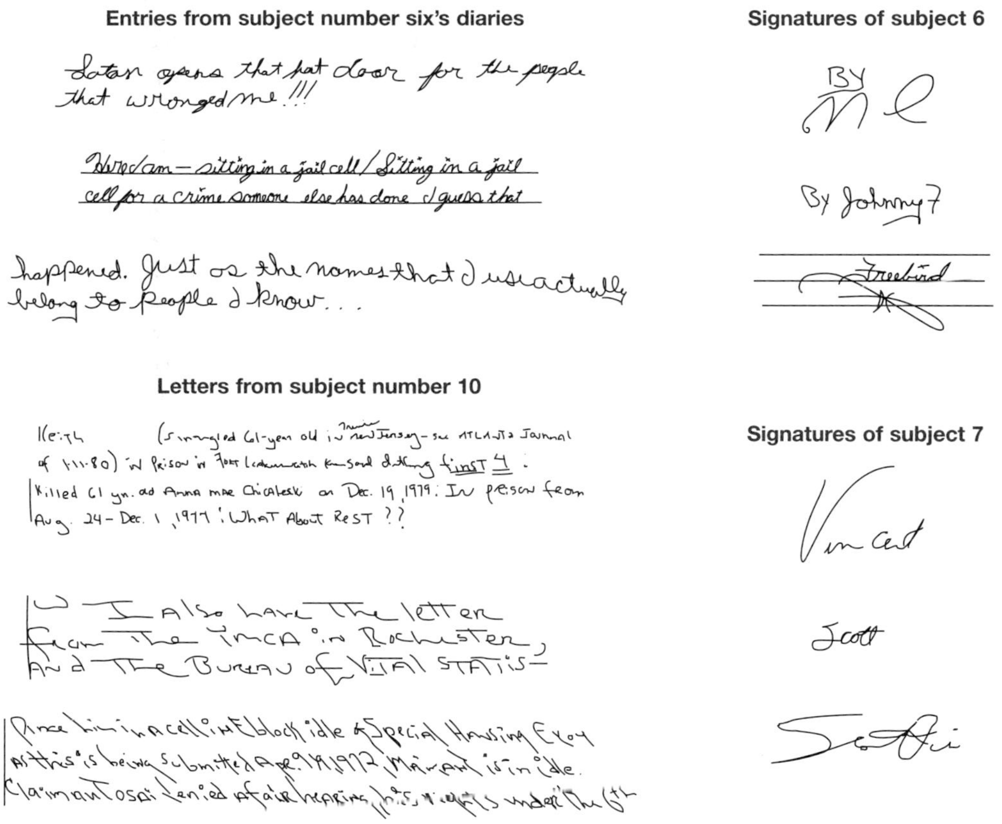

Entries from subject number six's diaries

Satan opens that hat door for the people that wronged me!!!

Here I am — sitting in a jail cell / Sitting in a jail cell for a crime someone else has done. I guess that

happened. Just as the names that I use actually belong to people I know . . .

Letters from subject number 10

Signatures of subject 6

Signatures of subject 7

Figure 7.2 Handwriting samples from DID cases. From Lewis et al., 1997.

these disorders and therapies for posttraumatic stress disorder. Indeed, PTSD is the most commonly diagnosed comorbid disorder with DID (Loewenstein, 1991). It is therefore no surprise that some mental health specialists propose strategies for these problems that are reminiscent of treatments for PTSD, such as encouraging the patients to think back to the traumatic events that are believed to have triggered the problem and to view them in a context of safety, support, and an expectation that they can come to terms with the horrible things that happened to them. The hypothesized link between DID and trauma has led some therapists to argue for incorporation of the controversial Eye Movement Desensitization and Reprocessing therapy (EMDR, see Chapter 6) into the treatment of clients with dissociative identity disorder (Fine & Berkowitz, 2001; Twombly, 2000).

As discussed in Chapter 1, psychoanalysis had its beginnings in hypnosis, with Mesmer's work in the late eighteenth century and Charcot's work in the nineteenth century. Through the years practitioners have continued to use hypnosis with patients diagnosed with dissociative disorders as a means of helping them gain access to hidden portions of the personality—to a lost identity or to a set of events precipitating or flowing from a trauma.

As mentioned earlier, DID patients are unusually hypnotizable, and it is believed that their hypnotizability is used by them (unconsciously) to cope with stress by entering a dissociative, trancelike state in an effort to ward off terrifying memories of traumatic events (Butler et al., 1996). For these reasons hypnosis is commonly used in the treatment of DID (Putnam, 1993). The general idea is that the recovery of repressed painful memories will be facilitated by recreating the state into which the patient presumably entered during the original abuse, a hypothesis consistent with research on state-dependent learning (Bower, 1981; Eich, 1995). Typically the person is hypnotized (sometimes with the aid of drugs such as sodium Amytal) and encouraged to go back in his or her mind to events in childhood—a technique called age regression which, unfortunately, has little scientific support. The hope is that accessing these traumatic memories will allow the adult to realize that the dangers from childhood are not now present and that

Repressed Memories of Child Sexual Abuse

We have seen in this chapter that a history of abuse in childhood is thought to be an important cause of DID, and in later chapters we will learn that sexual abuse is considered to play a role in several other disorders. Until recently child sexual abuse in childhood (CSA) was thought to be a relatively rare occurrence. Now it is estimated that between 15 and 30 percent of women experienced CSA (Finkelhor, 1993). Although the data on the frequency of childhood sexual abuse have been derived from the retrospective reports of patients and thus could be distorted, most researchers assume that the reports are fairly accurate.

In this box we focus on the special instance of recovered memories of sexual abuse. In these cases the patient had no memory of abuse until it came to mind, typically during psychotherapy. Few issues are more hotly debated in psychology and in the courts than whether these recovered memories are valid. Memory researchers caution against a blanket acceptance of memories of sexual or physical abuse recovered during therapy (Loftus, 1997; Payne et al., 1997). It is important to raise these questions; good science requires it, and it is key for court cases when recovered memories may play a major role in convicting a parent or other person of sexual abuse (Pope, 1995).

Recovered memories of CSA have assumed great importance in a series of recent court cases (Earleywine & Gann, 1995). In a typical scenario a woman accuses one or both of her parents of having abused her during childhood and brings charges against them. Courts in several states allow plaintiffs to sue for damages within three years of the time they remember the abuse (Wakefield & Underwager, 1994). These cases depend on memories of childhood abuse that were recovered in adulthood, often during psychotherapy, and were apparently repressed for many years. In the most scientifically accurate study of memories of sexual abuse, Williams (1995) was able to interview women whose abuse years earlier had been verified. Fully 38 percent of these women were unable to recall the abuse when they were asked about it almost two decades later.

Williams's data notwithstanding, is it justifiable to assume that recovered memories are invariably accurate reports of repressed memories? This is a question of enormous legal as well as scientific importance. Studies have been conducted on women who have reported a history of sexual abuse. The women were asked whether there ever was a time when they could not remember the abuse. Based on these data the frequency of "repression" ranges from 18 to 59 percent (Loftus, 1993). But a simple failure to remember does not mean that repression has occurred. Women could actively try to keep these thoughts out of mind because they are distressing. Or the abuse could have happened before the time of their earliest memories (generally around age three or four). Nor has it been scientifically demonstrated that children repress or even forget traumatic events. As already mentioned, one of the hallmarks of posttraumatic stress disorder is frequent reliv-

ing of the trauma in one's memory. Numerous studies have shown that far from repressing negative events, children recall them quite vividly (Earleywine & Gann, 1995).

In some cases allegedly recovered memories may have no basis in fact, but if not, where do they come from? Elizabeth Loftus (1993), a leading researcher and commentator on this issue, suggests several possibilities.

1. **Popular writings.** *The Courage to Heal* (Bass & Davis, 1994) is a guide for victims of CSA and widely known in the recovered-memory movement. It repeatedly suggests to readers that they were probably abused and offers as symptoms of abuse low self-esteem, feeling different from others, substance abuse, sexual dysfunction, and depression. The problem with this interpretation is that symptoms such as these can result from many causal factors, not only from sexual abuse in childhood.

2. **Therapists' suggestions.** By their own accounts some therapists—those who genuinely believe that many adult disorders result from abuse—directly suggest to their clients that childhood sexual abuse is likely, sometimes with the assistance of hypnotic age regression (itself a procedure with no established scientific validity). It is important to bear in mind, however, that one of the defining characteristics of hypnosis is heightened suggestibility. If a therapist believes strongly that sexual abuse has been repressed, it is possible that memories recovered during hypnosis were planted there by the therapist (Loftus, 1997; Loftus & Ketchum, 1994).

3. **Research on memory.** Memory does not function as a tape recorder, and cognitive psychologists have shown that it is possible for people to firmly believe that an event occurred even if it did not. For example, Neisser and Harsch (1991) studied people's memories of where they were when they heard about the Challenger explosion on January 28, 1986. Participants were interviewed the day after the disaster and again two years later. Despite reporting vivid memories, none of the later accounts was entirely accurate, and many were way off the mark. Similarly, an extensive series of studies has shown that it is common to confuse memories of actual happenings with memories of events that have only been imagined (Johnson & Raye, 1981). This last point is clearly relevant to our earlier discussion of the possible role of therapists in planting memories.

Studies of memory show that considerable distortions can exist, even when recalling a major event such as the explosion of the Challenger.

There is little doubt that childhood sexual abuse exists and that it may be much more frequent than any of us would like to believe (Finkelhor, 1993). But we must be wary of accepting reports of abuse uncritically. Social scientists, lawyers, and the courts share a heavy responsibility in deciding whether a given recovered memory is a reflection of an actual (and criminal) event. Erring in either direction creates an injustice for either the accused or the accuser.

The Selective Nature of Publishing Case Studies

To illustrate the problem inherent to case studies we offer this personal observation. While working in a mental hospital some years ago, one of the authors encountered on the ward a man suffering from partial amnesia. He did not recognize members of his family when they came to visit him, but he could still recall most other events in his life. Many efforts were made to restore his memory, ranging from hypnotic suggestions to drug therapy. Both sodium Amytal and Methedrine, a powerful stimulant, were administered, Methedrine intravenously. It was hoped that Methedrine would energize his nervous system and dislodge the blocks to memory, much as a drain cleaner is used to open a clogged drain. In all these attempts the patient was cooperative and even eager for a positive outcome, but none of them worked. The unsuccessful treatment was never written up for publication. There is a strong editorial bias against publishing reports of failed clinical treatments, as indeed there is against publishing inconclusive results of experiments. This, a general problem for psychology and psychiatry, is a particular detriment when, as for dissociative disorders, there is little in the way of controlled research.

his or her current life need not be governed by these ghosts from the past (or, to use Wachtel's metaphor, woolly mammoths, cf. p. 31) (Grinker & Spiegel, 1944; Loewenstein, 1991; Maldonado & Spiegel, 1994). However, it has recently been cautioned that the use of recovered memory treatment may be harmful and could result in a worsening of symptoms in DID patients (Fetkewicz, Sharma, & Merskey, 2000; Powell & Gee, 2000).

It is ironic that family-based interventions are not as often discussed in the DID treatment literature as individual therapy, for DID is widely believed to result from problematic family relationships, specifically, physical and/or sexual abuse in the patient's childhood (Simon, 1998). There have been some proposals to remedy this omission (e.g., Chiappa, 1994).

As DID is often comorbid with anxiety and depression, it is not surprising that case studies suggest that improvement in a DID patient's anxiety and depression is sometimes effected through psychoactive drugs such as tranquilizers and antidepressants. This treatment has no effect on the dissociative identity disorder itself, however (Simon, 1998) (Focus on Discovery 7.5).

There seems to be widespread agreement on several principles in the treatment of dissociative identity disorder, whatever the clinician's orientation (Bowers et al., 1971; Caddy, 1985; Kluft, 1985, 1999; Ross, 1989).

1. The goal is integration of the several personalities.
2. Each alter has to be helped to understand that he or she is part of one person and that the alters are self-generated.
3. The therapist should use the alters' names only for convenience, not as a way to confirm the existence of separate, autonomous personalities who do not share overall responsibility for the actions of the whole person.
4. All alters should be treated with fairness and empathy.
5. The therapist should encourage empathy and cooperation among personalities.
6. Gentleness and supportiveness are needed in consideration of the childhood trauma that may have given rise to the alters.

The goal of any approach to DID should be to convince the person that splitting into different personalities is no longer necessary to deal with traumas, either those in the past that triggered the original dissociation or those in the present or yet to be confronted in the future. In addition, assuming that DID and the other dissociative disorders are in some measure an escape response to high levels of stress, treatment can be enhanced by teaching the patient to cope better with present-day challenges.

Because of the rarity of DID and because it has often been misdiagnosed, there are no controlled outcome studies. Nearly all the well-reported outcome data come from the clinical observations of one highly experienced therapist, Richard Kluft (e.g., 1984a, 2000). Over a ten-year period Kluft had contact with 171 cases. Of these, 83, or 68 percent, achieved integration of their alters that was stable for at least three months (33 remained stable for almost two and a half years). The greater the number of personalities, the longer the treatment lasted (Putnam et al., 1986); in general, therapy took almost two years and upwards of 500 hours per patient. In a more recent follow-up, Kluft reported that 103, or 84 percent of the original 123 patients, had achieved stable integration of their multiple personalities and another 10 percent were at least functioning better (Kluft, 1994). Sometimes complete integration of personalities cannot be achieved, and the most realistic outcome is some manner of "conflict-free collaboration" among the person's various personalities (Kluft, 1988, p. 578). Positive findings have been reported more recently by Ellason and Ross (1997). A recent ten-year follow-up study found that out of 12 patients, 6 ultimately achieved full integration of their several personality states (Coons & Bowman, 2001).

Summary

- In somatoform disorder, there are physical symptoms for which no biological basis can be found. Anxiety is assumed to play a role in these disorders, but it is not expressed overtly; instead, it is transformed into physical symptoms.

- The two principal types of somatoform disorders are conversion disorder and somatization disorder. Other types about which less is known are pain disorder, body dysmorphic disorder, and hypochondriasis.

- The sensory and motor dysfunctions of conversion disorder suggest neurological impairments, but ones that do not always make anatomical sense. The symptoms do, however, seem to serve some psychological purpose; for example, they may arise suddenly in stressful situations, allowing the individual to avoid some activity or responsibility.

- In somatization disorder, multiple physical complaints, not adequately explained by physical disorder or injury, eventuate in frequent visits to physicians, hospitalization, and even unnecessary surgery.

- Theory concerning the etiology of somatoform disorders is speculative and focuses primarily on conversion disorder. Psychoanalytic theory proposes that in conversion disorder, repressed impulses are converted into physical symptoms. In contrast, behavioral theories focus on the conscious and deliberate adoption of the symptoms as a means of obtaining a desired goal. Social and cultural factors may play a role in the disorder as well.

- In therapies for somatoform disorders, analysts try to help the client face up to the repressed impulses, and behavioral treatments attempt to reduce anxiety and reinforce behavior that will allow the patient to relinquish the symptoms.

- Dissociative disorders are disruptions of consciousness, memory, and identity. An inability to recall important personal information, usually after some traumatic experience, is diagnosed as dissociative amnesia. In dissociative fugue, the person moves away, assumes a new identity, and is amnesic for his or her previous life. In depersonalization disorder the person's perception of the self is altered; he or she may experience being outside the body or perceive changes in the size of body parts. The person with dissociative identity disorder has two or more distinct and fully developed personalities, each with unique memories, behavior patterns, and relationships.

- Psychoanalytic theory regards dissociative disorders as instances of massive repression of some undesirable event or aspect of the self. In dissociative identity disorder, the role of abuse in childhood and a high level of hypnotizability are emerging as important. Behavioral theories consider dissociative reactions escape responses motivated by high levels of anxiety.

- Psychoanalytic treatment is perhaps more widespread as a choice for dissociative disorders than for any other psychological treatment. Both analytic and behavioral clinicians focus their treatment efforts on understanding the anxiety associated with the forgotten memories that underlie the disorders.

Key Terms

anesthesias	dissociative disorders	factitious disorder	malingering
body dysmorphic disorder	dissociative fugue	hypochondriasis	pain disorder
conversion disorder	dissociative identity disorder	hysteria	somatization disorder
depersonalization disorder	(DID)somatoform disorders	la belle indifférence	
dissociative amnesia			

Dissociative Identity Disorder: Multiple Personality

The instructor in Paula's human sexuality course suggested that she talk to a psychologist. Several factors contributed to his concern. Although Paula was a good student, her behavior in class had been rather odd on occasion. Every now and then, it seemed as though she came to class "high." She participated actively in the discussions, but she did not seem to be familiar with the readings or previous lecture material. Her scores on the first two exams had been As, but she failed to appear for the third. When he asked her where she had been, Paula maintained with apparent sincerity that she couldn't recall. Finally, she had handed in an essay assignment that described in rather vague, but sufficiently believable, terms the abusive, incestuous relationship that her father had forced upon her from the age of 5 until well after she was married and had had her first child. All of this led her professor to believe that Paula needed help. Fortunately, she was inclined to agree with him because there were a number of things that were bothering her. She made an appointment to talk to Dr. Harpin, a clinical psychologist at the student health center.

Paula Stewart was 38 years old, divorced, and the mother of a son 18 years of age and a daughter 15. She was about 90 pounds overweight, but in other ways her appearance was unremarkable. For the past five years, Paula had been taking courses at the university and working part-time at a variety of secretarial positions on campus. She and her daughter lived together in a small, rural community located about 20 miles from the university—the same town in which Paula had been born. Her son had moved away from home after dropping out of high school. Paula's mother and father still lived in their home just down the street from Paula's.

Over a series of sessions, Dr. Harpin noticed that Paula's behavior was often erratic. Her moods vacillated frequently and quickly from anger and irritability to severe depression. When she was depressed, her movements became agitated, and she mentioned that she experienced sleep difficulties. She threatened suicide frequently and had, on several occasions, made some attempts to harm herself. In addition to these emotional difficulties, Paula frequently complained of severe headaches, dizziness, and breathing problems.

It also seemed that Paula abused alcohol, although the circumstances were not clear. This situation was a source of distress and considerable confusion for Paula. She had found empty beer cans and whiskey bottles in the back seat of her car, but she denied drinking alcoholic beverages of any kind. Once every two or three weeks, she would wake up in the morning with terrible headaches as though she were hung over. Dr. Harpin believed that her confusion and other memory problems could be explained by her alcohol consumption.

Paula's relationships with other people were unpredictable. She would explode with little provocation and often argued that no one understood how serious her problems were. On occasion, she threatened to kill other people, particularly an older man, Cal, who lived nearby. Paula's relationship with Cal was puzzling to both of them. They had known each other since she was an adolescent. Although he was 15 years older than she and had been married to another woman for more than 20 years, Cal had persistently shown a romantic interest in Paula. He would frequently come to her house saying that she had called. More often than not, this made Paula furious. She maintained that she was not at all interested in him and would never encourage such behavior. At other times, however, she insisted that he was the only person who understood and cared for her.

Paula's father was still alive, but she did not spend any time with him. In fact, he behaved as though she didn't exist. She was able to recall and discuss some aspects of the incestuous relationship her father had forced upon her in previous years, but her memory was sketchy, and she preferred not to discuss him.

Throughout the first year of treatment, Paula's memory problems became increasingly severe. The notes she wrote during classes were often incomplete, as though she had suddenly stopped listening in the middle of a number of lectures. She sometimes complained that she lost parts of days. On one occasion, for example, she told Dr. Harpin that she had gone home with a severe headache in the middle of the afternoon and then couldn't remember anything until she awakened the following morning. Another time she was eating lunch, only to find herself hours later driving her car. Her daughter asked her about a loud argument Paula had had with her mother on the phone, and she couldn't remember even talking to her mother that day. These unexplained experiences were extremely frustrating to Paula, but the therapist continued to believe that they were induced by alcohol.

One day, Dr. Harpin received a message from his secretary saying that a woman named Sherry had called. She had identified herself as a friend of Paula's and had said that she would like to discuss the case. Before responding directly to this request, Dr. Harpin decided to check with Paula to find out more about this friend and determine whether she would consent to this consultation. Paula denied knowing anyone named Sherry, so Dr. Harpin did not return the original call. It did strike him as odd, however, that someone knew that he was Paula's therapist.

Two weeks after receiving this call, Dr. Harpin decided to use hypnosis in an attempt to explore the frequent gaps in Paula's memory. They had used hypnosis on one previous occasion as an aid to the process of applied relaxation, and it was clear that Paula was easily hypnotized. Unfortunately, it didn't help with the memory problem; Paula couldn't remember anything else about the time she had lost.

Upon waking out of a trance, Paula complained of a splitting headache. She gazed slowly about the room as though she were lost. Dr. Harpin was puzzled. "Do you know where you are?" he asked. She said she didn't know, so he asked if she knew who he was. Rather than providing a quick answer, she glanced around the room. She noticed his professional license hanging on the wall, read his name, and finally replied, "Yes. You're Dr. Harpin, the one who's working with Paula." This switch to her use of the third person struck Dr. Harpin as being odd and roused further curiosity about her state of mind.

"How do you feel?"
"Okay."
"Do you still have a headache?"
"No. I don't have a headache."

The way she emphasized the word "I" was unusual, so Dr. Harpin said, "You make it sound like somebody else has a headache." He was completely unprepared for her response:

"Yes. Paula does."

Pausing for a moment to collect his wits, Dr. Harpin—who was simultaneously confused and fascinated by this startling exchange—decided to pursue the identity issue further.

"If Paula has a headache, but you don't, what's your name?"
"Why should I tell you? I don't think I can trust you."
"Why not? Don't you want to talk to me?"
"Why should I? You wouldn't talk to me when I called last week!"

Dr. Harpin finally remembered the call from Sherry, who had wanted to talk to him about Paula's case. He asked the woman, once again, what her name was, and she said, "Sherry." After they talked for a couple of minutes, Dr. Harpin said, "I'd like to talk to Paula now."

"Oh, she's boring."
"That doesn't matter. She's my client, and I want to talk to her to see how she feels."
"Will you talk to me again?"
"Yes."
"Why should I believe you? You wouldn't talk to me before."
"Now I know who you are. Please let me talk to Paula."

At that point, she closed her eyes and waited quietly for a few moments. When her eyes opened, Paula was back and her headache was gone, but she could not remember anything about the last half hour. Dr. Harpin was stunned and incredulous. Although he was aware of the literature on multiple personality and a few well-known cases, he could not believe what Paula had said.

When Paula appeared for their next appointment, she still could not remember anything that had happened and seemed just as she had before this remarkable incident. Dr. Harpin decided to attempt to discuss with Paula a traumatic incident that had happened a number of years ago. Paula had frequently mentioned a day when she was 15 years old. She couldn't remember the details, but it was

clearly a source of considerable distress for her and seemed to involve her father.

Dr. Harpin asked Paula to describe what she could remember about the day: where they were living at the time, what time of year it was, who was home, and so on. Paula filled in the details slowly and as best she could. Her father had grabbed her, hit her across the face, and dragged her toward the bedroom. No matter how hard she tried, she couldn't remember anything else. Paula said that she was getting a headache. Dr. Harpin suggested that she lean back in the chair and breathe slowly. She paused for a moment and closed her eyes. In a few moments, she opened her eyes and said, "She can't remember. She wasn't there. I was!" Sherry was back.

Paula's appearance had changed suddenly. She had been very tense, clutching the arms of the chair and sitting upright. She also had had an annoying, hacking cough. Now she eased down in the chair, folded her arms, and crossed her legs in front of her. The cough was completely gone. Sherry explained why Paula couldn't remember the incident with her father. As Sherry put it, when Paula was dragged into the bedroom, she "decided to take off," leaving Sherry to experience the pain and humiliation of the ensuing rape. Dr. Harpin translated this to mean that Paula had experienced a dissociative episode. The incident was so extremely traumatic that she had completely separated the experience and its memory from the rest of her consciousness.

After discussing the rape in some detail, Dr. Harpin decided to find out as much as he could about Sherry. She provided only sketchy information, admitting that she was in her thirties but denying that she had a last name. Sherry's attitude toward Paula was contemptuous. She was angry because Paula had so frequently left Sherry to experience painful sexual encounters. They discussed numerous incidents dating from Paula's adolescence to the present, but none of Sherry's memories traced back prior to the incident with Paula's father. Since that time, Sherry was apparently aware of everything that Paula had done. Paula, on the other hand, was completely oblivious to Sherry's existence.

Toward the end of this conversation, Dr. Harpin asked whether it was Sherry or Paula who had been responsible for the beer bottles Paula found in her car. Sherry said, "Oh, we did that." Intrigued by the plural pronoun, Dr. Harpin asked whom she meant to describe, and the patient said, "Oh, Janet and I."

"Who's Janet?"
"You don't want to talk to her. She's always angry. You know how adolescents are."

By this point, Dr. Harpin knew that Sherry found it easier than Paula to switch back and forth among these personalities, so he encouraged her to try. Sherry agreed, somewhat reluctantly, and soon there was another dramatic change in Paula's appearance. She fidgeted in her chair, pulled at her hair, and began to bounce her leg continuously. She was reluctant to talk, but adopted a coy, somewhat flirtatious manner. She claimed to be 15 years old.

Several sessions later, Sherry presented Dr. Harpin with a request. She said that she and Janet were extremely concerned about Caroline, who was presumably only 5 years old and had been crying a lot lately. Sherry and Janet wanted Dr. Harpin to talk to Caroline. He agreed to try. Sherry closed her eyes and effortlessly transformed her posture and mannerisms to those of a little girl. She pulled her legs up onto the chair and folded them under her body. Holding her hand in a fist clenched close to the side of her mouth almost as if she were sucking her thumb, she turned sideways in the chair and peered at Dr. Harpin bashfully out of the corner of her eye. She seemed to be rather frightened.

"Will you talk to me, Caroline?" Dr. Harpin began.

After an extended pause, Caroline asked, "What's your name? I don't know you." Her voice seemed higher and weaker than it had been moments before.

"I'm Dr. Harpin."
"Do you know my mommy and daddy?"
"No. But I'm a friend of Sherry's. She asked me to talk to you. Do you know Sherry?"
"Yes. She watches me. She takes care of me."
"Do you know Janet?"
"She's big. She has fun!"
"Do you know her very well?"
"Not really. She gets mad easy."
"Sherry told me that you've been feeling sad. Why is that?"
"I'm a bad girl."
"Why do you think you're bad?"
"Mommy told me I'm bad. That's why she has to punish me."
"I don't think you're a bad girl."
"Yes I am. If I'm not bad, why would they punish me?"
"What do they punish you for?"
"I don't know. They just do. They hurt me. Once I pinched my brother when he took my toy puppy. Then they took my puppy away, and they won't give it back! Grandpa gave it to me. He's good to me."

At their next session, Dr. Harpin asked Paula if she remembered ever having a stuffed puppy when she was a child. A fond smile of recognition followed several moments' reflection. She had indeed had such a toy. He asked if she knew what had happened to it. She insisted that she had no idea. It had been almost 30 years since she remembered seeing it, but she agreed to look around in the attic of her mother's house.

Much to everyone's surprise, Paula was able to find the puppy, which was known as Jingles because of the sound made by a small bell sewn into its tail. Unfortunately, it became the source of considerable aggravation for Paula. The first day she found it, she left it in the living room before she went to bed. When she woke up in the morning, Jingles was in bed with her. This happened two nights in a row. On the third night, she locked the puppy in her car, which was kept in the garage, and went to bed. Once again, the puppy was in bed with her when she woke up in the morning. She was annoyed and also a bit frightened by this strange turn of events. In subsequent sessions, Sherry provided the following explanation for what had happened. Caroline would wake up in the middle of the night crying, wanting to hold her stuffed animal. In an effort to console

her, Sherry would then retrieve Jingles from the living room or garage. Of course, Paula would not remember what had happened.

Thus far there were four names: Paula, Sherry, Janet, and Caroline. The clinical picture was as fascinating as it was unbelievable. Dr. Harpin felt that he needed help as much as his client. In his 15 years of clinical experience, he had never seen a case that resembled Paula's in any way. It fit closely with some of the published cases of multiple personality, but he had never really believed that this sort of thing happened, except in fiction. Surely it was the product of the therapist's imagination, or the client's manipulative strategy, he had believed. He sought advice from colleagues and a plan for the treatment of this complex set of problems. His contacts with Paula continued to deal largely with day-to-day crises.

He asked Paula if she had read any of the well-known books or watched any of the popular films dealing with multiple personality. She had not. Since she was not familiar with other examples of this phenomenon, it seemed unlikely that she had simply invented the alter personalities as a way of attracting attention or convincing others of the severity of her problems. In an attempt to help Paula—who was not aware of the alters—understand the problems that she faced, Dr. Harpin asked her to read *The Three Faces of Eve*, the book upon which the famous film was based. She reacted with interest and disbelief. What did it have to do with her situation? She was still completely unable to remember those times when she spoke as if she were Sherry, Janet, or Caroline. Later, however, there were times when Sherry discussed the book with Dr. Harpin, and Janet was also reading it. To make matters more confusing, they all seemed to be reading at a different pace. Paula might be two-thirds of the way through the book, but Janet—an adolescent who did not read as quickly—was aware of only the first part of the book.

Dr. Harpin also used videotape to help Paula understand the problem. With her consent, he recorded her behavior during a sequence of three therapy sessions. She alternated among the various personalities several times during the course of these tapes. Paula was then asked to view the tapes and discuss her reactions to her own behavior. Again, she was surprised, interested, and puzzled, showing no signs of previous awareness of this behavior. She would often ask, "Did *I* say that?" or "Who am I? *What* am I?"

Another unusual set of circumstances led to the identification of still another personality, Heather. Paula had complained on numerous occasions that a loaded shotgun, which belonged to her father, kept appearing at her house. She had no use for guns, and their presence upset her, so she would take the gun back to her father's house. Several days later, she would find it again at her house. Her parents and daughter adamantly denied knowing anything about the gun. Recognizing that Paula was frequently unaware of things that she did as the other personalities, Dr. Harpin discussed the gun with Sherry and Janet. Both denied any knowledge of these incidents. Janet said, "I know you think it's me, but it's not!" Finally, Sherry suggested that it might be someone else. "You mean there might be others?" Dr. Harpin asked. Sherry acknowledged the possibility, but said that she was not aware of any others.

At the beginning of the next session, Dr. Harpin decided to use hypnosis in an effort to see if he could identify more alters. While Paula was in the trance, he asked if anyone else, with whom he had not yet spoken, was able to hear what he was saying. This was when Heather emerged. She was presumably 23. It was she who had been bringing the gun to Paula's house, and it was she who had been calling Cal. Heather told Dr. Harpin that she was in love with Cal. If she couldn't marry him, she wanted to kill herself. This was the first alter with whom Sherry did not have co-consciousness, and her existence explained several important inconsistencies in Paula's behavior and gaps in her memory.

Heather's affection for Cal illustrates another important characteristic of the multiple personality phenomenon. There were important, and occasionally radical, differences among Paula, Sherry, and the other alters in terms of tastes and preferences as well as mannerisms and abilities. Heather loved Cal (she couldn't live without him), but the others hated him. In fact, Paula's most remarkable reaction to videotapes of her own behavior centered around one conversation with Heather. Paula insisted that it was not she. "I would *never* say those things!" she said. Paula's attitude toward her parents was also at odds with those of some of the alters, and this inconsistency undoubtedly explained some of the erratic shifts in her behavior and relationship with other people. Sherry didn't like Paula's children and was inconsiderate in her behavior toward them. She frequently promised them things to keep them quiet and then failed to honor her commitments.

Social History

Paula grew up in a small rural community. She had one older brother. Her mother was an outspoken, dominant woman who maintained firm control of the family. Both parents were strict disciplinarians. The parents of Paula's mother lived nearby. This grandfather was the only sympathetic adult figure throughout Paula's childhood. It was he who gave her the stuffed puppy, Jingles, which became such an important source of comfort to her until her parents took it away. When Paula was upset, her grandfather was the only person who was able to console her and stop her crying (although she never dared to tell him about the things that her father forced her to do).

Paula's father was a shy, withdrawn, unaffectionate man who did not have many friends. For the first few years of her life, he ignored her completely. Then, when she was 5 years old, he began to demonstrate physical affection. He would hug and kiss her roughly, and when no one else was around, he would fondle her genitals. Paula didn't know how to respond. His touches weren't pleasant or enjoyable, but she would accept whatever affection he was willing to provide.

When she was 15, their sexual encounters started to become violent. The pretense of affection and love was obviously dissolved; he wanted to hurt her. In one incident, which Paula and Dr. Harpin had discussed repeatedly, her father dragged her into his bedroom by her hair and tied her to the bed. After slapping her repeatedly, he forced her to have intercourse with him. The incest and physical abuse continued until she was 20 years old.

Paula's mother was a strict disciplinarian who often punished Paula by putting her hands in scalding hot water or locking her in a dark closet for hours on end. Mrs. Stewart did not realize—or seem to care—that her husband was abusing Paula sexually. If she did know, she may have been afraid to intervene. Mr. Stewart may also have abused his wife as well as his daughter, but Paula could not remember witnessing any violence between her parents.

Perhaps in an effort to tear herself away from this abusive family, Paula pursued relationships with other men at an early age. Many of these men were older than she, including teachers and neighbors. The longest relationship of this sort was with Cal, the owner of a small construction business. Paula was 16 and Cal was 31 when they started seeing each other. Although he took advantage of Paula sexually, Cal was a more sympathetic person than her father. He did listen to her, and he seemed to care for her. On numerous occasions, Cal promised that he would marry her. For Paula, he was a "rescuer," someone who offered a way out of her pathological family situation. Unfortunately, he didn't come through. He married another woman but continued to pursue Paula's affection and sexual favors. She continued to oblige, in spite of the strong feelings of anger and betrayal that she harbored.

A few incidents that occurred while Paula was in high school were probably precursors of the memory problems and dissociative experiences that she later encountered as an adult. They suggest that the problem of alter personalities began during adolescence, although it was not discovered until many years later. People sometimes told Paula about things that she had done, things that she could not remember doing. Most of these involved promiscuous behavior. Paula was particularly upset by a rumor that went around the school when she was a sophomore. Several other girls claimed that Paula had been seen in a car with three men. They were parked in a remote picnic area outside of town, and Paula presumably had intercourse with all of them. She couldn't remember a thing, but she also didn't know where she had been that night.

After graduating from high school, Paula enrolled in the university's school of education, but she dropped out after one year. For the next few years, she worked at various clerical jobs, while living either at home with her parents or in apartments that she rented nearby. She was married briefly, gave birth to her children, and was then divorced. Paula decided to return to the university many years later, after her son left home.

Conceptualization and Treatment

Dr. Harpin's initial diagnostic impression, before the emergence of the alter personalities, was that Paula fit the *DSM-IV-TR* criteria for both dysthymia (a long-lasting form of depression that is not sufficiently severe to meet the criteria for major depressive disorder) and borderline personality disorder. Throughout the first year of treatment, his approach to the problem was focused primarily on the management of frequent, specific crises. These included numerous transient suicidal threats, fights with her mother and daughter, confusion and anger over her relationship—or lack of a relationship—with Cal, difficulties in her school work and with professors teaching her classes, and a variety of incidents involving her employers. When immediate problems of this sort were not pressing, Paula usually wanted to talk about the way her father had abused her. Her focus was on both the anger and the guilt that she felt about these incidents. She wondered whether in some way she hadn't encouraged his sexual advances.

After the appearance of the alter personalities, Dr. Harpin's initial hypothesis was that Paula was malingering, that is, feigning a dramatic set of symptoms in an effort to gain some benefit from him or her family. This explanation was attractive for several reasons, including his skepticism regarding the existence of a phenomenon such as multiple personality. Nevertheless, he eventually abandoned this view. One problem was the apparent absence of information that would have been necessary for Paula to fake this disorder. She had not read or seen any of the popular descriptions of multiple personality, and it was therefore unlikely that she would be able to create or imitate the problem in such a believable, detailed fashion. The other problem was the lack of a clear motive. She was not, for example, facing criminal charges that might be avoided by the existence of a severe form of mental illness. Nor was she able to avoid personal or family responsibilities by the onset of these conditions, because she continued to go to school, work, and take care of her daughter after the emergence of the alters. The only thing she might stand to gain was increased attention from Dr. Harpin. It seemed unlikely that this would explain the problem, since he had already been spending an inordinate amount of time and energy on the case as a result of the previous suicidal gestures, and he had repeatedly conveyed to Paula his concern for her numerous problems.

It eventually became clear that Paula was experiencing a genuine disruption of consciousness that was usually precipitated by stressful experiences. Faced with an extremely threatening or unpleasant circumstance, Paula would often dissociate— entirely blot out (or repress) her awareness of that event. This pattern of cognitive activity could apparently be traced to the violent abuse that she received from her father during adolescence. By her own description, when these events began, Paula would usually "leave" the situation and Sherry would be left to face her father. The turbulent nature of these years and the concentration of abuse during this time might account for the fact that the ages of most of the alters seemed to cluster between 15 and 23. Over time, the extent of this fragmentation of conscious experience became more severe, and her control over changes in her patterns of awareness eroded progressively.

One approach to the resolution of these dissociative episodes might involve the recall and exploration of previous traumatic experiences that seemed to be responsible for particular splits in Paula's consciousness. Perhaps the most salient of these episodes was the rape scene involving Paula's father. The existence of Sherry suggested that the split could be traced to about this period of time, and it was an incident that Sherry mentioned repeatedly. Previous accounts of multiple personality suggest that the patient's disturbance in consciousness might improve if the repression of such memories can be lifted. Unfortunately, this approach did not seem to be useful in Paula's case. She and Dr. Harpin spent many hours discussing this incident—from the perspectives of both Paula and Sherry—but it only seemed to make things worse.

A different approach was needed. Dr. Harpin had two principal goals in mind during the next several months of treatment: to discourage further fragmentation of Paula's conscious experience and to facilitate the integration of information across the divisions of conscious experience. In other words, without encouraging or crystallizing the existence of separate personalities, Dr. Harpin wanted to help Paula recognize the nature of the problem and the way her behavior patterns changed in association with loss of memory for these incidents. This was done, in part, by having her read and discuss *The Three Faces of Eve* and allowing her to view videotapes of her own behavior. Dr. Harpin's hope was that the videotapes might jog Paula's memory and begin to break down the barriers that had been erected to prevent the exchange of information between the subdivisions of her conscious working memory.

10-Year Follow-up

Paula remained in treatment with Dr. Harpin for several years during which they were able to establish a strong working relationship. Paula trusted Dr. Harpin, and, based on their extended discussions, she eventually accepted his diagnosis of her problem. Treatment continued to follow an interpersonal, problem-solving approach, in which Paula was encouraged to learn and use new, nondissociative coping skills to deal with stressful events. Emphasis was placed on the identification of strong feelings and the recognition of logical connections between these feelings and specific life events.

Paula's relationship with Cal, the older businessman, illustrates the utility of this approach. Their disagreements, and the confusion associated with their on-and-off affair, had been a source of considerable anxiety and anger for many years. Although it had originally seemed that Cal might rescue Paula from her terrible family situation, he had betrayed her by marrying another woman. Many people experience this type of bitter disappointment; most find a way to resolve their strong, ambivalent feelings and move on to other relationships. Unfortunately, for more than 20 years, Paula had responded to her encounters with Cal using dissociative responses. She continued the romance through one of her alters, Heather. Switching between Paula and Heather, she would alternately threaten to kill Cal and then herself. After many extended discussions of this situation with Dr. Harpin, Paula was finally able to recognize that this situation provided one of the consistent triggers for her dissociative episodes. She confronted Cal and ended their relationship. Shortly after this success, Heather stopped appearing. That particular alter had apparently been integrated with Paula, the host personality.

Paula's relationship with her children had been another source of considerable stress over the years. Arguments with them, and with her mother over her role as a parent, may also have served as a stimulus for dissociative responses. Her son and daughter, now young adults, remained angry for many legitimate reasons. They had been left alone frequently and inconsistently while they were growing up. They had also been bitterly disappointed on numerous occasions when Paula had failed to honor promises that she made to them. Previous attempts to discuss these feelings had been fruitless, in large part because Paula did not recognize her dissociative disorder as the root of the problem with these relationships. Paula had to accept responsibility for her own inconsistent and occasionally harmful parenting behaviors. The children also had to understand her disorder. Many sessions were devoted to discussions of these issues and to face-to-face meetings between Paula and her daughter (her son lived too far away to be included in this process). This aspect of Paula's family situation improved a great deal.

As treatment progressed, Dr. Harpin made an effort to avoid, whenever possible, speaking directly to the alters. For example, he sometimes received phone calls from Sherry, usually to report something inappropriate that Paula had done. Whenever the caller identified herself as one of the alters, Dr. Harpin would ask to speak to Paula. He also began to discourage their appearance in sessions. Over a period of several months, some of the alters stopped making appearances and seemed no longer to influence Paula's behavior. When asked about them, Paula and Sherry (the alter who had been most aware of the others) would reply, "Oh, she's not around anymore."

As the number of alters decreased, Dr. Harpin also noticed a shift in Sherry's attitude toward Paula. She had originally been contemptuous and hostile, but she gradually became compassionate and protective. Dr. Harpin sometimes felt that Sherry had become something like a surrogate therapist. Paula became increasingly aware of Sherry's attitudes and feelings, which were sometimes more adaptive or appropriate than Paula's because they were informed by a more complete understanding of her experience (Janet's being more fragmented by dissociative experiences). Some of the tangible distinctions between these personalities also seemed to fade. For example, the voices in which Paula and Sherry spoke had always been easy to distinguish. Paula was usually distressed when she called, and her voice was often agitated and shrill. Over time, it became softer and more stable in tone. Their accents and vocabularies had also been different (with Sherry using a more prominent rural dialect).

Discussion

The complex and puzzling nature of multiple personality disorder (MPD) is illustrated in the controversy surrounding its name. Most descriptions of this syndrome have emphasized the diagnostic importance of several alter personalities. One unfortunate consequence of this approach has been a tendency toward public sensationalism and a preoccupation with counting the exact number of alters exhibited by any patient. These estimates have occasionally reached preposterous numbers, with some clinicians claiming to see patients who have hundreds of personalities. The dissociative disorders committee for *DSM-IV-TR* (APA, 1994) felt strongly that a different approach should be encouraged. The chairperson of that committee, David Spiegel, explained that "there is a widespread misunderstanding of the essential psychopathology in this dissociative disorder, which is failure of integration of various aspects of identity, memory, and consciousness. The problem is not having *more than one personality*; it is having less than one personality" (cited in Hacking, 1995 p. 18). For this reason, MPD is called Dissociative Identity Disorder (DID) in *DSM-IV-TR*.

Multiple personality disorder is probably a rare phenomenon. Prior to 1980, fewer than two or three hundred cases had been reported in the professional literature (Fahy, 1988). This number is incredibly small compared to the millions of patients who suffer from disorders such as schizophrenia and depression at any point in time. Some investigators have suggested that MPD appears more frequently than previously assumed (e.g., Ross, 1997), but these claims have been disputed (e.g., Lilienfeld et al., 1999). One small but careful study suggests that the prevalence of MPD in the general population is much less than 1 percent (Akyuez et al., 1999).

Multiple personality disorder has attracted considerable attention, partly because a few dramatic cases have received widespread publicity through popular books and films. These include *The Three Faces of Eve* (Thigpen & Cleckley, 1957) and *Sybil* (Schreiber, 1973). Sybil was one of the most famous cases in psychiatry during the twentieth century; interest surrounding the book and the film fueled an enormous increase in interest in this fascinating phenomenon throughout the 1970s and 1980s. The authenticity of the Sybil case has been seriously questioned, however. Some critics contend that the therapist influenced this patient to adopt alternate personalities by employing different names to identify her varying mood states (Acocella, 1999; Rieber, 1999). Unfortunately, for many years, case studies such as these were our best source of information about the disorder. A few investigators have managed to identify samples of patients with MPD for the purpose of research. Their descriptions have made significant contributions to the base of knowledge that is now available regarding this enigmatic disorder.

Among the cases of MPD that have been reported, a few patterns stand out. First, most cases of MPD are women, with the ratio of women to men being at least five to one. Most MPD patients are first assigned that diagnosis in their late twenties or early thirties. Many of these people have already received mental health services while receiving a different diagnosis, often some type of mood disorder, substance use disorder, schizophrenia, or borderline personality disorder (Putnam, 1989; Ross, 1997a).

DSM-IV-TR lists the following diagnostic criteria for Dissociative Identity Disorder:

A. The subject exhibits two or more distinct identities or personality states (each with its own relatively enduring pattern of perceiving, relating to, and thinking about the environment and self)

B. At least two of these identities or personality states recurrently take control of the person's behavior.

C. The subject is unable to recall important personal information that is too extensive to be explained by ordinary forgetfulness

D. The disorder is not due to the direct physiological effects of a substance (such as blackouts or chaotic behavior during alcohol intoxication)

The manual also notes that the transition between different personalities is usually sudden and often beyond voluntary control.

Memory disturbances are perhaps the most important feature of this disorder (Dorahy, 2001; Eich et al., 1997). Most people behave differently, or may seem to be somewhat different people, as a function of the environmental stimuli with which they are confronted, but the changes are seldom as dramatic or complete as those seen in cases of multiple personality. Furthermore, very few people forget what they have done or who they are whenever they alter their pattern of behavior. In multiple personality disorder, the original personality is presumably unaware of the existence of the alters. It is not unusual for the person to express concern about large chunks of time that seem to be missing or unaccounted for. The alter personalities may, or may not, be aware of one another or "co-conscious." At any given moment only one personality is controlling the person's behavior and interacting with the environment, but other personalities may simultaneously perceive, and subsequently remember, events that are taking place. Of course, the inability to recall personal information is based almost exclusively on self-report. There is a serious need for the development of more objective measures of memory impairment in MPD (Allen & Iacono, 2001).

The boundaries of this diagnostic category are difficult to define (Dell, 2001; Spiegel, 2001). Some clinicians have argued that it should be considered broadly, while others would prefer that the term be applied only to severe or classic cases. Putnam (1993), author of the most authoritative book on MPD (Putnam, 1989), has recommended that clinicians make a diagnosis of MPD only after they have: (1) witnessed a switch between two alter personality states, (2) met a given alter personality on at least three separate occasions, so that they can evaluate the degree of uniqueness and stability of the alter personality state, and (3) established that the patient has amnesias, either by witnessing amnesic behavior or by the patient's report.

Because the disorder is rare and clinicians are not routinely familiar with its manifestations, some patients have probably been misdiagnosed as suffering from other disorders, most notably schizophrenia and borderline personality disorder. Several diagnostic signs might alert a clinician to suspect that a patient may be experiencing multiple personality (Greaves, 1980). These include:

1. Reports of time distortions or time lapses
2. Reports of being told of behavioral episodes by others that are not remembered by the patient
3. Reports of notable changes in the patient's behavior by a reliable observer, during which time the patient may call him—or herself by different names or refer to him—or herself in the third person
4. Elicitability of other personalities through hypnosis
5. The use of the word "we" in the course of an interview in which the word seems to take on a collective meaning rather than an editorial "we"
6. The discovery of writing, drawings, or other productions or objects among the patient's personal belongings that he or she does not recognize and cannot account for
7. A history of severe headaches, particularly when accompanied by blackouts, seizures, dreams, visions, or deep sleep

Paula exhibited almost all of the signs included on this list. Time lapses and headaches were a frequent source of concern when she began treatment at the student health center. She had been told about incidents that she could not remember as far back as high school. Her children and at least one professor had noticed marked changes in her behavior that were not easily explained by environmental circumstances. It should be emphasized, of course, that none of these problems, alone or in combination, cannot be considered sufficient evidence to diagnose multiple personality disorder if the patient does not also meet other specific diagnostic criteria such as those listed in *DSM-IV-TR*.

Etiological Considerations

A variety of hypotheses have been proposed to account for the development of multiple personality. One simple explanation is that the patient produces the symptoms voluntarily, or plays the role of multiple personality, in an effort to attract attention or avoid responsibility. The intentional production of false symptoms is called *malingering*. A few widely publicized criminal trials in which the defendant claimed innocence by reason of insanity have indicated that the syndrome can be faked rather convincingly (Brown et al., 1999; James, 1998).

The best known example of malingering involves the case of Kenneth Bianchi, also known as the Hillside Strangler. Several experienced clinicians interviewed Bianchi after he was arrested. With the aid of hypnosis, they discovered an alter personality, Steve, who proudly claimed responsibility for several brutal rape-murders. The prosecution called Martin Orne, a psychiatrist at the University of Pennsylvania, as an expert witness to examine Bianchi. Orne raised serious questions about the case by indicating that the defendant was probably faking hypnosis during the interviews and by demonstrating that Bianchi's symptoms changed dramatically as a result of subtle suggestions (Orne, Dinges, & Orne, 1984). He proposed that the defendant was faking symptoms of multiple personality in an attempt to avoid the death penalty. The court found Orne's skepticism persuasive, and Bianchi was eventually convicted of murder. These circumstances are clearly rather extreme; very few patients have such an obvious motive for feigning a psychological disorder. Although the Bianchi case should not be taken to mean that all patients who exhibit signs of multiple personality are malingering or faking, it does indicate that therapists should be cautious in evaluating the evidence for any diagnostic decision, particularly when the disorder is as difficult to define and evaluate as multiple personality.

The sociocognitive model holds that multiple personality disorder is a product of the therapist's influence on the client (Lilienfeld et al., 1999; Spanos, 1996). This is not to say that the patient is faking the disorder, but rather that MPD patients respond to cues that are provided during the course of assessment and treatment. Clinicians have frequently noted, for example, that patients with multiple personality disorder are easily hypnotized and that the alter personalities are often "discovered" during hypnosis, a process that is capable of inducing phenomena such as amnesia, one important symptom of dissociative disorders. According to this view, some therapists may provide their patients with information and suggestions about multiple personality, subtly and unconsciously encouraging them to behave in ways that are consistent with these expectations, and rewarding them with extra attention and care when they adopt the role. In this regard it is interesting to note that, while the vast majority of clinicians work an entire career without seeing a single case of multiple personality, a small handful of therapists claim to have treated large numbers of multiple personality patients (Modestin, 1992). This radically disproportionate distribution of cases is consistent with the hypothesis that some clinicians find (and perhaps encourage the development of) symptoms in which they are particularly interested.

Are all patients with MPD simply trying to please their therapists or responding to subtle suggestions? The sociocognitive model may explain some cases, but it does not provide a convincing explanation for many others. The model has a number of serious limitations (Gleaves et al., 2001). In many cases, important symptoms have been observed before the patient enters treatment. In Paula's case, the phone call from Sherry (which was the first clear-cut evidence of an independent alter personality) occurred before the use of hypnosis. Furthermore, most therapists are not looking for multiple personality disorder. Dr. Harpin, for example, had never seen a case of this sort before treating Paula. He went out of his way to consider other explanations of her behavior before considering the diagnosis of multiple personality disorder.

If MPD is, in fact, a genuine psychological phenomenon involving a disturbance in consciousness and loss of volitional control, how can we account for its development? Current etiological hypotheses focus on two primary considerations: (1) the impact of repeated, overwhelming trauma during childhood—especially sexual abuse, and (2) individual differences in the ability to enter trancelike states (Forrest, 2001).

One influential model, proposed by Putnam (1989), starts with the proposition that the behavior of all human infants (less than 12 months old) is organized in a series of discrete behavioral states, which are characterized by marked contrasts in emotion and behavior. As the child matures, these states become more integrated. Transitions among them become less abrupt and increasingly subject to voluntary control. Failure to accomplish this integration can set the stage for MPD. Putnam also assumes that children are able to enter dissociative states spontaneously. Some children may find this process easier than others. Those who are adept at it can presumably escape into trances as a way of protecting themselves from the psychological impact of intense trauma. This mechanism allows the child to contain painful memories and emotions outside normal conscious awareness. Alter personalities become stronger, more elaborate, and solidified as the child repeatedly enters particular dissociative states. The child eventually loses control of the process and is unable to stop it or recognize that it is happening. MPD is the final product of these tragic events.

The credibility of Putnam's developmental model rests on a number of assumptions. Perhaps most important is the presumed connection between repeated traumatic events during childhood, particularly sexual abuse, and the subsequent onset of dissociative symptoms. Does the repetition of severe trauma lead inevitably to dissociative disorders? Are patients with MPD always victims of prior sexual abuse? Are patients' memories always authentic? The answers to these questions are open to question (Hacking, 1995; Hornstein & Putnam, 1996; Lewis et al., 1997). Evidence regarding MPD is particularly difficult to evaluate because it is based largely on individual cases. Since the 1970s, most published cases have involved patients who reported being sexually abused as children. Paula is one example. The frequency of such reports has persuaded many clinicians that repeated sexual abuse is a necessary and sufficient condition in the etiology of MPD. But how do we know that the patients' memories are accurate? This is an extremely controversial issue. Efforts to confirm patients' memories of prior abuse meet with mixed results; some can be confirmed while others cannot (Kluft, 1995; Yeager & Lewis, 1997). Cautious skepticism seems to be warranted with regard to the etiological link between abuse and MPD.

Treatment

Most efforts to treat patients with multiple personality disorder have focused on two principal strategies: Stabilize the most functional or competent personality or integrate the disparate personalities into one. The former approach was employed initially by Thigpen and Cleckley (1957) in treating the patient described in *The Three Faces of Eve*. Follow-up reports on this case, which described the subsequent emergence of numerous additional personalities, illustrate the difficulties and possible futility of this method.

Most experts agree that integration is presently the treatment of choice (Kluft, 1999; Putnam, 1989). Dr. Harpin employed a number of techniques in trying to help Paula fuse the various alters. The first step involves facilitating recognition by the patient of the existence of alter personalities. One approach might be to use videotapes of the alter behavior in an effort to help the patient recognize radical changes that are otherwise unknown. It may also be important to help patients understand the general nature of the problem as it has appeared in others' lives so that they can gain perspective on their own dilemma. This was the goal that Dr. Harpin had in mind when he asked Paula to read *The Three Faces of Eve*. Fusion may eventually be accomplished if the main personality comes to share the memories and emotions of the alters. Finally, the most important step involves learning to react to conflict and stress in an adaptive fashion rather than engaging in the avoidance behaviors associated with dissociative states (Fine, 1999).

While working toward the process of integration, it is also important that the therapist avoid further fragmentation of the patient's behavior or personality. Unfortunately, this is a difficult caveat to heed. The existence of independent personalities of such different tastes and styles is fascinating, and the therapist is easily tempted to explore and discuss every exotic detail of the patient's experience. Extended and persistent questioning of this sort may encourage additional dissociative experiences and impede integration. The use of separate names to describe and address alter personalities may also serve to stabilize and condone their existence. Finally, although hypnosis can be a useful tool in attempting to facilitate the patient's recall of forgotten events, it can also lead to the emergence of additional personalities. None of these problems is easy to avoid. They all suggest that therapists who are confronted with patients exhibiting symptoms of multiple personality disorder must be extremely cautious in planning their interventions. They must attend to the unique features of the patient's dissociative experience without ignoring other potentially crucial aspects of the person's problem (Ross, 1997b). The outcome of treatment for MPD is sometimes very positive. Many patients respond well to extensive and prolonged psychological treatment (Maldonado et al., 2002). In that respect, Paula may also be a typical case. Optimistic impressions about the prognosis for this disorder are based largely on clinical impressions because we do not have data from long-term outcome studies with this disorder. One two-year follow-up study of 54 patients found that many were substantially improved (Ellason & Ross, 1997). Unfortunately, randomized clinical trials comparing the efficacy of treatments and placebo programs have not been conducted. The effective ingredients of therapy have not been identified. Treatment research in this area is well behind that in most other areas of mental health services.

8 Psychophysiological Disorders and Health Psychology

Mark Howard was thirty-eight. After earning an M.B.A. he had joined the marketing division of a large conglomerate and had worked his way up the corporate ladder. His talent and long hours of work had recently culminated in a promotion to head of his division. The promotion left him with mixed feelings. On the one hand, it was what he had been working so hard to achieve; but on the other hand, he had never been comfortable giving orders to others and he especially dreaded the staff meetings he would have to run.

Soon after the promotion, during a routine checkup, Mark's physician discovered that Mark's blood pressure had moved into the borderline hypertension range, around 150 over 100. Before implementing any treatment the physician asked Mark to wear an ambulatory monitor for a few days so that his blood pressure could be assessed as he went about his usual routine. The device was programmed to take blood pressure readings twenty times a day.

On the first day of monitoring Mark had a staff meeting scheduled for ten o'clock. While he was laying out the marketing plans for a new product, the cuff inflated to take his blood pressure. A couple of minutes later he checked the reading and became visibly pale. It was 195 over 140—not a borderline reading, but seriously high blood pressure. The next day he resigned his managerial role and returned to a less prestigious but, he hoped, less stressful position.

Psychophysiological disorders, such as asthma, hypertension, headache, and gastritis, are characterized by genuine physical symptoms that are caused or can be worsened by psychological factors. The term *psychophysiological disorders* is preferred today to a term that was formerly used and is perhaps better known, **psychosomatic disorders**. Nevertheless, the term *psychosomatic* connotes quite well the principal feature of these disorders: that the psyche, or mind, is having an untoward effect on the soma, or body.

In contrast to many of the disorders described in Chapter 7 (e.g., hypochondriasis, somatization disorder, and conversion disorder), psychophysiological disorders are diseases involving damage to the body (see Table 8.1). That such disorders are viewed as being related to psychological factors does not make the afflictions imaginary. People can just as readily die from psychologically produced high blood pressure or asthma as from similar diseases produced by infection or physical injury.

Psychophysiological disorders as such do not appear in DSM-IV-TR, as they did in some earlier versions of the DSM. Rather, these disorders show up via the presence of **psychological factors affecting medical condition**, and this diagnosis is coded in the broad section that comprises "other conditions that may be a focus of clinical attention." The implication of this placement is that psychophysiological disorders are not a form of mental disorder. Nonetheless, we consider them here in some detail because of their historical link to the field of psychopathology and because we believe they remain relevant to the concerns of this book.

The new approach to diagnosis is also broader in scope. Formerly, psychophysiological disorders were generally thought to include only some diseases (the classic psychosomatic diseases, such as ulcers, headaches, asthma, and hypertension). The new diagnosis is applicable to any disease, as it is now thought that any disease can be influenced by psychological factors, such as stress. Furthermore, the diagnosis includes cases in which the psychological or behavioral factor influences the course or treatment of a disorder, not just cases in which it influences the onset, again broadening the definition. For example, a person with hypertension may continue to drink alcohol even though he or she knows that alcohol increases blood pressure, or a patient may fail to take prescribed medication regularly. The psychological or behavioral factors involved include Axis I and II diagnoses; personality traits; coping styles, such as holding anger in rather than expressing it; and lifestyle factors, such as failing to exercise regularly.

What is the evidence for the view that any illness may be in part stress related? For years it has been known that various physical diseases can be produced in laboratory animals through exposure to severe stressors. Usually the diseases produced in such studies have been the classic psychophysiological disorders, such as ulcers. However, studies have indicated that a broader range of diseases may be related to stress. Sklar and Anisman (1979), for example, induced tumors in mice and then studied the impact of stress—uncontrollable electric shocks—on growth of the tumors. In animals exposed to electric shock the tumors grew more rapidly, and these animals died earlier. Similarly, a twenty-year follow-up of veterans of the Vietnam War revealed unusually high rates of

Table 8.1 Comparing Psychophysiological and Conversion Disorders

Type of Disorder	Organic Bodily Damage	Bodily Function Affected
Conversion	No	Voluntary
Psychophysiological	Yes	Involuntary

a broad range of diseases involving the circulatory, respiratory, digestive, musculoskeletal, endocrine, and nervous systems (Boscarino, 1997). The stress of war was thought to be a factor at least in the severity of the diseases, if not in their onset.

The many demonstrations of the pervasive role of psychological factors in health form the basis for the fields of **behavioral medicine** and **health psychology**. Since the 1970s these fields have dealt with the role of psychological factors in all facets of health and illness. Beyond examining the role that stress can play in the onset or severity of illness, researchers in these fields study psychological treatments (e.g., biofeedback for headache) and the health care system itself (e.g., how better to deliver services to underserved populations) (Appel et al., 1997; Stone, 1982).

Prevention is also a major focus of health psychology. As the twentieth century progressed and infectious diseases were brought under better control, people were dying more often from such illnesses as cardiovascular disease. The causes of cardiovascular disease involve behavior—people's lifestyles—such as smoking, eating too much, and excessive alcohol use. Thus, it is believed that many cases of cardiovascular disease can be prevented by changing unhealthy lifestyles. Health psychologists are at the forefront of these preventative efforts, some of which we describe later in this chapter.

Health psychology and behavioral medicine are not restricted to a set of techniques or to particular principles of changing behavior. Clinicians in the field employ a wide variety of procedures—from contingency management, to stress reduction, to cognitive-behavioral approaches—all of which share the goal of altering bad living habits, distressed psychological states, and aberrant physiological processes in order to bring about health benefits.

We begin our consideration of psychophysiological disorders and health psychology by reviewing general findings on the relationship between stress and health, as well as theories about how stress can produce illness. Then we turn to an in-depth examination of three disorders—cardiovascular disease, asthma, and acquired immunodeficiency syndrome or AIDS. Finally, we consider psychological interventions.

Stress and Health

To understand the role of stress, we must first be able to define and measure it. Neither task is simple.

Defining the Concept of Stress

In earlier chapters, the term **stress** was used to refer to some environmental condition that triggers psychopathology. Here we examine the term more closely and consider the difficulties in its definition.

In 1936, Hans Selye, a physician, introduced the **general adaptation syndrome (GAS)**, a description of the biological response to sustained and unrelenting physical stress. There are three phases of the model, as shown in Figure 8.1.

1. During the first phase, the alarm reaction, the autonomic nervous system is activated by the stress. If the stress is too powerful, gastrointestinal ulcers form, the adrenal glands become enlarged, and the thymus undergoes atrophy (wasting away).

2. During the second phase, resistance, the organism adapts to the stress through available coping mechanisms.

3. If the stressor persists or the organism is unable to respond effectively, the third phase, a stage of exhaustion follows, and the organism dies or suffers irreversible damage (Selye, 1950).

Selye's concept of stress eventually found its way into the psychological literature, but with substantial changes in its definition. Some researchers

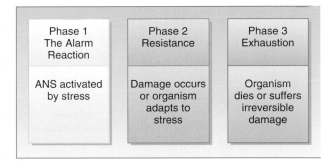

Figure 8.1 Selye's general adaptation syndrome.

According to Richard Lazarus, how a life event is appraised is an important determinant of whether it causes stress. An exam, for example, may be viewed as a challenge or as an event that is extremely stressful.

followed Selye's lead and continued to consider stress a response to environmental conditions, defined on the basis of such diverse criteria as emotional upset, deterioration of performance, or physiological changes such as increased skin conductance or increases in the levels of certain hormones. The problem with these response-based definitions of stress is that the criteria are not clear-cut. Physiological changes in the body can occur in response to a number of stimuli that we would not consider stressful (for example, anticipating a pleasurable event).

Other researchers looked on stress as a stimulus, often referred to as a **stressor**, rather than a response, and identified it with a long list of environmental conditions, such as electric shock, boredom, uncontrollable stimuli, catastrophic life events, daily hassles, and sleep deprivation. Stimuli that are considered stressors can be major (the death of a loved one), minor (daily hassles, such as being stuck in traffic), acute (failing an exam), or chronic (a persistently unpleasant work environment). For the most part they are experiences that people regard as unpleasant.

Like response-based definitions, stimulus-based definitions present problems. Stipulating exactly what constitutes a stressor is difficult. It is not merely negativity, for marriage, generally a positive event, is regarded as a stressor because it requires adaptation. Furthermore, people vary widely in how they respond to life's challenges. A given event does not elicit the same amount of stress in everyone. For example, a family that has lost its home in a flood but has money enough to rebuild and a strong network of friends nearby will experience less hardship from this event than will a family that has neither adequate money to rebuild nor a social network to provide support.

Coping and Stress

Some people believe that it is not possible to define objectively what events or situations qualify as psychological stressors (e.g., Lazarus, 1966). They emphasize the cognitive aspects of stress, that is, they believe that how we perceive or appraise the environment determines whether a stressor is present. When a person determines that the demands of a situation exceed his or her resources, the person experiences stress. A final exam may be merely challenging to one student, yet highly stressful to another who does not feel equipped to take it (whether his or her fears are realistic or not).

Relevant to individual differences in responding to stressful situations is the concept of **coping**, or how people try to deal with a problem or handle the typically negative emotions it produces. Even among those who appraise a situation as stressful, the effects of the stress may vary depending on how the individual copes with the event. Lazarus and his colleagues have identified two broad dimensions of coping (Lazarus & Folkman, 1984).

- *Problem-focused coping* involves taking direct action to solve the problem or seeking information that will be relevant to the solution. An example is developing a study schedule to pace assignments over a semester and thereby reduce end-of-semester pressure.

- *Emotion-focused coping* refers to efforts to reduce the negative emotional reactions to stress, for example, by distracting oneself from the problem, relaxing, or seeking comfort from others.

Coping researchers also refer to *avoidance coping*, a type of coping that involves aspects of both problem-focused and emotion-focused coping (e.g., Carver & Scheier, 1999). The essence of avoidance coping is either attempting to avoid admitting that there is a problem to deal with (e.g., distraction, denial) or neglecting to do anything about the problem (e.g., giving up).

The role of positive emotions in coping is an area of current interest to researchers (e.g., Folkman & Moskowitz, 2000).

Coping can focus on solving the problem itself or on regulating the negative emotions it has created. Seeking comfort or social support from others is an example of emotion-focused coping.

Positive emotions can and do co-occur with negative emotions during stressful situations, and they can provide some benefit. For example, positive emotions can "undo" some of the ill effects of negative emotions, particularly the physiological effects (Fredrickson & Levenson, 1998). In one study, individuals who expressed genuine smiling and laughter when talking about their relationship with a spouse who had died six months earlier had fewer grief-related symptoms and better relationships with others two years after the loss (Bonanno & Keltner, 1997; Keltner & Bonanno, 1997). Another study found that individuals who were able to find positive meaning, such as spiritual growth or an appreciation of life, following a traumatic event were able to respond to a laboratory stressor in a more adaptive fashion (Epel, McEwen, & Ickovics, 1998).

Effective coping often varies with the situation. Distraction may be an effective way of dealing with the emotional upset produced by impending surgery, for example, but it would be a poor way to handle the upset that could be produced by the discovery of a lump on the breast (Lazarus & Folkman, 1984). Similarly, continuing efforts to seek a solution to a problem that is unsolvable lead to increases in frustration, rather than providing any psychological benefit (Terry & Hynes, 1998). Evidence indicates, however, that in general, escape/avoidance coping (such as wishing that the situation would go away or be over with) is the least effective method of coping with many life problems (Roesch & Weiner, 2001).

Efforts to Measure Stress

Given the difficulty of defining stress with precision, it is not surprising that measuring stress is difficult as well. Research on the effects of stress on human health has sought to measure the amount of life stress a person has experienced and then to correlate this measurement with illness. Various scales have been developed to measure life stress. Here we examine two: the Social Readjustment Rating Scale and the Assessment of Daily Experience.

The Social Readjustment Rating Scale   In the 1960s two researchers, Holmes and Rahe (1967), gave a list of life events to a large group of people and asked them to rate each item according to its intensity and the amount of time they thought they would need to adjust to it. Marriage was arbitrarily assigned a stress value of 500; all other items were then evaluated using this reference point. For example, an event twice as stressful as marriage would be assigned a value of 1,000, and an event one-fifth as stressful as marriage would be assigned a value of 100. The average ratings assigned to the events by the respondents in Holmes and Rahe's study are shown in Table 8.2.

From this study the Social Readjustment Rating Scale (SRRS) emerged. A respondent checks off the life events experienced during the time period in question. Ratings are then totaled for all the events actually experienced to produce a Life Change Unit (LCU) score, a weighted sum of events. The LCU score has been related to several different illnesses, for example, heart attacks (Rahe & Lind, 1971), fractures (Tollefson, 1972), onset of leukemia (Wold, 1968), and colds and fevers (Holmes & Holmes, 1970).

Table 8.2 Social Readjustment Rating Scale

Rank	Life Event	Mean Value
1	Death of spouse	100
2	Divorce	73
3	Marital separation	65
4	Jail term	63
5	Death of close family member	63
6	Personal injury or illness	53
7	Marriage	50[a]
8	Fired from work	47
9	Marital reconciliation	45
10	Retirement	45
11	Change in health of family member	44
12	Pregnancy	40
13	Sex difficulties	39
14	New family member	39
15	Business readjustment	39
16	Change in financial state	38
17	Death of close friend	37
18	Change to different line of work	36
19	Change in number of arguments with spouse	35
20	Mortgage over $10,000[b]	31
21	Foreclosure of mortgage or loan	30
22	Change in responsibilities at work	29
23	Child leaving home	29
24	Trouble with in-laws	29
25	Outstanding personal achievement	28
26	Spouse begins or stops work	26
27	Begin or end school	26
28	Change in living conditions	25
29	Revision of personal habits	24
30	Trouble with boss	23
31	Change in work hours or conditions	20
32	Change in residence	20
33	Change in schools	20
34	Change in recreation	19
35	Change in church activities	19
36	Change in social activities	18
37	Mortgage or loan less than $10,000[b]	17
38	Change in sleeping habits	16
39	Change in number of family get-togethers	15
40	Change in eating habits	15
41	Vacation	13
42	Christmas	12
43	Minor violations of the law	11

Source: From Holmes and Rahe, 1967.

[a] Marriage was arbitrarily assigned a stress value of 500; no event was found to be any more than twice as stressful. Here the values are reduced proportionally and range up to 100.

[b] In the mid-1960s, a mortgage like this was considered very large.

Experiencing major life events such as marriage (*left*) or starting school (*right*) statistically increases risk for illness. Research on the effects of these major stressors assesses them with the Social Readjustment Rating Scale.

These results demonstrate a correlational relationship between psychological stress and physical illness, but they do not mean that stress causes or contributes to illness. For example, illness itself could cause a high life-change score, as when chronic absenteeism caused by an illness brings dismissal from a job. In addition, reports of stressful events in such studies could be contaminated by knowledge of subsequently occurring illnesses; that is, someone who has experienced many illnesses may try very hard to recall recent stressors to explain these illnesses. Many studies have used a retrospective method, asking participants to recall both the illnesses and the stressful life events that they experienced over some past time period. As previously mentioned, retrospective reports are subject to considerable distortion and forgetting. In addition, self-reports of illness may not yield a true reflection of disease. For example, what people can say about a past illness may be different from what the illness actually was like.

Finally, the SRRS has been criticized because it contains items that are both the outcomes of stress and the antecedents of stress, with no attempt to separate the two. For example, the item "change in financial status" could be the result of losing a job or could precipitate additional stressful events. Moreover, the SRRS was developed over thirty-five years ago, rendering some of the original ratings of stressful life events potentially out of sync with the times. Two recent studies have given the forty-three original events on the SRRS to community residents and found that indeed a number of the ratings changed compared to the original ratings from the 1960s, with some items being rated as less stressful (e.g., changing jobs), and others being rated as more stressful (e.g., change in financial status) (Miller & Rahe, 1997; Scully, Tosi, & Banning, 2000).

These problems, together with the fact that it often takes many years for stress to contribute to illness, indicate that research on stress and health must be longitudinal so that the biases of retrospective reporting are minimized and so that changes in stress can be shown to precede changes in health.

Assessment of Daily Experience   Problems with the SRRS led Stone and Neale (1982) to develop a new assessment instrument, the Assessment of Daily Experience (ADE). Rather than relying on retrospective reports, the ADE allows individuals to record and rate their daily experiences in prospective investigations. A day was used as the unit of analysis because a thorough characterization of this period should be possible without major retrospective-recall bias. Although the events reported on a day will generally be less severe than those reported over a longer time period, there is now direct evidence that these minor events are related to illness (Jandorf et al., 1986). Part of the ADE is shown in Figure 8.2.

With an assessment of daily experiences in hand, Stone, Reed, and Neale (1987) began a study of the relationship between daily life experiences and health. The goal was to examine the relationship between undesirable and desirable daily events and the onset of episodes of respiratory illness. Respiratory illness was selected as the criterion variable because it occurs with sufficient frequency to allow it to be analyzed as a distinct outcome.

After reviewing the participants' data, the researchers identified thirty who had experienced episodes of infectious illness during the assessment period. Next, the daily frequency of undesirable and desirable events that occurred from one to ten days before the start of an episode was examined. For each person a set of control days, without an episode, was also selected. The control days matched the others for day of the week to control for the higher frequency of desirable and lower frequency of undesirable events typically reported on weekends. The means of desirable events for the days preceding the start of respiratory illness episodes is shown in Figure 8.3; parallel data for undesirable events are shown in Figure 8.4. It was expected that several days before the onset of the illness episode there would be a decrease in desirable events and an increase in undesirable events relative to control days. The results indeed showed that for desirable events there were significant decreases three and four days prior to the onset of respiratory infection; for undesirable events, there were significant increases at four and five days before the onset of the illness.

WORK RELATED ACTIVITIES

Concerning Boss, Supervisor, Upper Management, etc.

▶ Praised for a job well done ☐ ○ ○ △ 01
▶ Criticism for job performance, lateness, etc. ☐ ○ ○ △ 02

Concerning Co-workers, Employees, Supervisees, and/or Clients

▶ Positive emotional interactions and/or happenings with co-workers, employees, supervisees, and/or clients (work related events which were fulfilling, etc.) ☐ ○ ○ △ 03

▶ Negative emotional interactions and/or happenings with co-workers, employees, supervisees, and/or clients (work related events which were frustrating, irritating, etc.) ☐ ○ ○ △ 04

▶ Firing or disciplining (by Target) ☐ ○ ○ △ 05

▶ Socializing with staff, co-workers, employees, supervisees, and/or clients ☐ ○ ○ △ 06

General Happenings Concerning Target at Work

▶ Promotion, raise ☐ ○ ○ △ 07
▶ Fired, quit, resigned ☐ ○ ○ △ 08
▶ Some change in job (different from the above, i.e., new assignment, new boss, etc.) ☐ ○ ○ △ 09
▶ Under a lot of pressure at work (impending deadlines, heavy workload, etc.) ☐ ○ ○ △ 10

Figure 8.2 Sample page from the Assessment of Daily Experience scale (Stone & Neale, 1982). Respondents indicate whether an event occurred by circling the arrows to the left of the list of events. If an event has occurred, it is then rated on the dimensions of desirability, change, meaningfulness, and control using the enclosed spaces to the right.

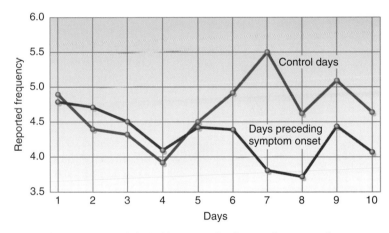

Figure 8.3 Number of desirable events for the ten days preceding an episode of respiratory infection. After Stone, Reed, and Neale (1987).

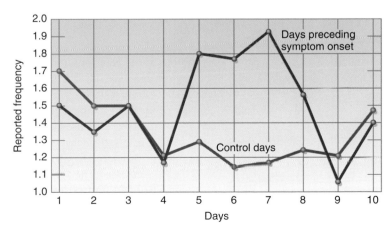

Figure 8.4 Number of undesirable events in the ten days preceding an episode of respiratory infection. After Stone, Reed, and Neale (1987).

These results, which have been replicated (Evans & Edgerton, 1990), were the first to show a relationship between life events and health with both variables measured in a daily, prospective design. Most sources of confounding in prior life-events studies were avoided in this study, and we can now come much closer to asserting that negative life events play a causal role in increasing vulnerability to episodes of infectious illness.

One of the strongest and most interesting aspects of the pattern of events preceding symptom episodes is that there was a peak in undesirable events and a trough in desirable ones several days prior to onset, yet the two days just before onset had average rates of desirable and undesirable events. Thus, speculation that the results were caused by some bias, such as individuals' feeling poorly prior to flagrant symptom onset and thus influencing perception of events, is unlikely to be the case, as most potential biases would produce a change in the frequency of events on days just prior to the onset of symptoms.

Assessing Coping

We have already mentioned the importance of coping. Coping is most often measured by questionnaires, which list a series of coping activities and ask respondents to indicate how much they used each to handle a recent stressor. An example of one such measure, the COPE, is presented in Table 8.3.

As with the effects of stressors, the best way to examine coping is by means of longitudinal study, which can demonstrate that particular ways of coping with stress precede the outcomes in which the researcher is interested. Breast cancer has been investigated in this way. The diagnosis of breast cancer, which strikes about one woman in nine and is the second most deadly cancer (behind lung cancer), is a major stressor on many levels. It is a life-threatening illness; surgical interventions are often disfiguring and thus have serious implications for psychological well-being; and both radiation therapy and chemotherapy have very unpleasant side effects.

Carver et al. (1993) selected women who had just been diagnosed with breast cancer and assessed how they were coping at several times during the following year. Women who accepted their diagnosis and retained a sense of humor had lower levels of distress. Avoidant coping methods, such as denial and behavioral disengagement (see Table 8.3), were related to higher levels of distress. This negative effect of denial on adjustment to breast cancer has been replicated (Heim, Valach, & Schaffner, 1997). Another longitudinal study of several types of cancer found that avoidant coping ("I try not to think about it") predicted greater progression of the disease at a one year follow-up (Epping-Jordan, Compas, & Howell, 1994). These data show that it is not merely the presence of stress that produces physical and emotional effects. How the person reacts to the stressor is crucial as well. In the case of cancer, reducing stress by ignoring the problem is not a good idea.

Social Support as a Moderator of the Stress–Illness Link

Although we can demonstrate that life events are related to the onset of illness, important questions remain. We have already noted that the same life experience apparently can have different effects on different people. This situation raises the possibility that other variables moderate or change the general stress–illness relationship. We have described one significant moderator, coping, and we have seen that the use of avoidant coping increases the likelihood of both emotional and physical effects of stress. Another important factor that can lessen the effects of stress is social support.

There are various types of social support. **Structural social support** refers to a person's basic network of social relationships, for example, marital status and number of friends. **Functional social support** is concerned more with the *quality* of a person's relationships, for example, whether the person believes he or she has friends to call on in a time of need (Cohen & Wills, 1985).

Structural support is a well-established predictor of mortality. People with few friends or relatives tend to have a higher mortality rate than those with a higher level of

Daily hassles such as being stuck in traffic can be emotionally upsetting and also increase risk for illness.

Stone and his colleagues have found that changes in the frequency of daily life events precede the onset of episodes of respiratory infection. The mechanism may be a stress-induced lowering of secretory IgA.

structural support (Kaplan et al., 1994). In one study, people with more diverse social networks were found to be less likely to develop a cold following exposure to a virus (Cohen et al., 1997). Higher levels of functional support have been found to be related to lower rates of atherosclerosis (clogging of the arteries) (Seeman & Syme, 1989), to the ability of women to adjust to chronic rheumatoid arthritis (Goodenow, Reisine, & Grady, 1990), and to less distress among women following surgery for breast cancer (Alferi et al., 2001).

How does social support exert its beneficial effects? One possibility is that people who have higher levels of social support perform positive health behaviors more frequently—for example, eating a healthy diet, not smoking, and moderating alcohol intake. Alternatively, social support (or lack of it) could have a direct effect on biological processes (e.g., Uchino, Cacioppo, & Kiecolt-Glaser, 1996). For example, low levels of social support are related to an increase in negative emotions (Kessler & McLeod, 1985; see also our earlier discussion of PTSD on p. 166), which may affect some hormone levels and the immune system (Cohen et al., 1997; Kiecolt-Glaser et al., 1984).

In recent years social support has been studied in the laboratory, where cause and effect can be more readily established than is possible in the naturalistic studies already described. In one such study college-aged women were assigned to high- or low-stress conditions and experienced them with or without a close friend. In one part of the study, stress was created by having the experimenter behave coldly and impersonally as she told participants to improve their performance on a challenging task. For each woman in the social-support condition, a close friend "silently cheered her on" and sat close to her, placing a hand on her wrist. The dependent variable was blood pressure, measured while participants performed the task. As expected, high stress led to higher blood-pressure levels. But, as Figure 8.5 shows, the high-stress condition produced its effects on blood pressure primarily in those women who experienced the stress alone (Kamarck, Annunziato, & Amateau, 1995). Social support was thus shown to have a causal effect on a physiological process. Further laboratory research indicated that such results were produced only when the support came from a friend, and not when it came from a stranger (Christenfeld et al., 1997). However, subsequent research showed that support from a female stranger can in fact produce the blood pressure benefits for both men and women, but support from a male stranger has no effect (Glynn, Christenfeld, & Gerin, 1999). Perhaps the presence of either a friend or female companion can lead someone to appraise a stressful situation as less threatening.

A possible biological mechanism for the stress-reducing effects of social support is suggested by some research with animals. A hormone called oxytocin is released during social interaction. Oxytocin decreases activity of the sympathetic nervous system, promotes relaxation, and may thereby lessen the physiological effects of a stressor (Carter, DeVries, & Getz, 1995; Uvnas-Moberg, 1997, 1999). Although oxytocin is released during stress for both male and female animals, evidence suggests that this response is even greater among females (Jezova et al., 1996). Studies with humans indicate that oxytocin suppresses the release of glucocorticoids, such as cortisol, suggesting that oxytocin may protect against stress in humans as well (Chiodera et al., 1991; Taylor et al., 1999).

Table 8.3 Scales and Sample Items from the COPE

Active Coping

I've been concentrating my efforts on doing something about the situation I'm in.

Suppression of Competing Activities

I've been putting aside other activities in order to concentrate on this.

Planning

I've been trying to come up with a strategy about what to do.

Restraint

I've been making sure not to make matters worse by acting too soon.

Use of Social Support

I've been getting sympathy and understanding from someone.

Positive Reframing

I've been looking for something good in what is happening.

Religion

I've been putting my trust in God.

Acceptance

I've been accepting the reality of the fact that it happened.

Denial

I've been refusing to believe that it has happened.

Behavioral Disengagement

I've been giving up the attempt to cope.

Use of Humor

I've been making jokes about it.

Self-Distraction

I've been going to movies, watching TV, or reading, to think about it less.

Source: From Carver et al., 1993.

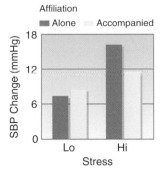
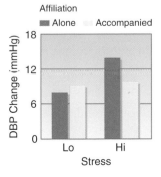

Figure 8.5 Results of a laboratory study of the effects of social support on blood pressure. Stress led to increased blood pressure, but the increase was less pronounced among people who experienced the stressor with a friend. From Kamarck et al. (1995).

Not all research has found that social support has positive effects. With very severe stressors the person may be so overwhelmed that support does no good. This point was well made in a study of social support and breast cancer, in which social support did not lead to reduced distress or less physical impairment (Bolger et al., 1996). A more recent study also showed that being involved in a social support group was not linked to lower mortality among women with advanced breast cancer (Goodwin et al., 2001).

Theories of the Stress–Illness Link

In considering the etiology of psychophysiological disorders, we are confronted with three questions.

1. Why does stress produce illness in only some people who are exposed to it?
2. Why does stress sometimes cause an illness and not a psychological disorder?
3. When stress produces a psychophysiological disorder, what determines which one of the many disorders will be produced?

Although answers to these questions have been sought by biologically as well as psychologically oriented researchers, theories in this domain are invariably diathesis–stress in nature. They differ primarily in whether the diathesis is described in psychological or biological terms.

Before reviewing some theories that describe how stress causes or exacerbates physical illness, it is important to note that much of the research in the field has attempted to link stress to *self-reports* of illness. The problem with this approach is that self-reports may not accurately reflect physical illness, as we have already noted. For example, Watson and Pennebaker (1989), after an extensive review of the literature, concluded that an apparent association between negative emotional states and health was actually only a relationship between negative emotions and illness *reporting*. Similarly, Stone and Costa (1990) noted that neuroticism predicted reports of higher numbers of somatic complaints of all kinds (recall our discussion of hypochondriasis and somatization disorder) but did not predict "hard endpoints," such as death or verified coronary artery disease. Because of such problems, our discussion focuses mainly on research that includes more than self-reports of illness.

In addition, the effects of stress may be indirect—that is, stress may lead to health changes that are not directly due to biological or psychological variables but are due to changes in health behavior. High stress may result in increased smoking, disrupted sleep, increased alcohol consumption, and altered diet (the opposite of what we saw with social support). These behavioral changes may then increase risk for illness. For example, low socioeconomic status (often thought of as a stressor) has been shown to be related to greater mortality from several diseases. In this case, the relationship between low socioeconomic status and death is accounted for by increased rates of negative health behaviors, such as smoking and alcohol use (Lynch et al., 1996). The stress–illness association is real but may be mediated indirectly through changes in health behaviors rather than by some direct biological effect of the stress.

Stress may indirectly increase risk for illness by causing lifestyle changes such as increased consumption of alcohol.

Biological Theories

A biological response to stress is a healthy and regular part of responding to stress. It is only when the biological stress response is continuously activated, or when counter-regulatory processes do not bring the body's systems back to their pre-stress levels within a reasonable amount of time that physiological damage can occur.

Biological approaches attribute particular psychophysiological disorders to specific organ weaknesses, to overactivity of particular organ systems in responding to stress, to the effects of exposure to stress hormones, or to changes in the immune system that are caused by stress.

Somatic-Weakness Theory   Genetic factors, prior illnesses, diet, and the like may disrupt a particular organ system, which may then become weak and vulnerable to stress. According to the **somatic-weakness theory**, the connection between stress and a particular psychophysiological disorder is a weakness in a specific bodily organ. For instance, a congenitally weak respiratory system might predispose the individual to asthma.

Specific-Reaction Theory   People have been found to have their own individual patterns of autonomic response to stress. The heart rate of one individual may increase, whereas another person may react with an increased respiration rate but with no change in heart rate (Lacey, 1967). According to the **specific-reaction theory**, individuals respond to stress in their own idiosyncratic ways, and the bodily system that is the most responsive becomes a likely candidate for the locus of a subsequent psychophysiological disorder. For example, someone reacting to stress with elevated blood pressure may be more susceptible to essential hypertension. Later in this chapter, when we consider specific psychophysiological disorders, evidence in support of both the somatic-weakness theory and the specific-reaction theory will be presented.

Prolonged Exposure to Stress Hormones   A more recent theory attempts to deal with the fact that the biological changes that stress produces are adaptive in the short run, for example, mobilizing energy resources in preparation for physical activity, but harmful over time (McEwen, 1998). The major biological responses to stress involve activation of the sympathetic nervous system and the hypothalamic-pituitary-adrenal axis (HPA). Under conditions of stress, catecholamines such as epinephrine are released from nerves and from the adrenal medulla and lead to secretion of corticotropin from the pituitary. Corticotropin then leads to the release of cortisol from the cortex of the adrenal gland (see Figure 8.6).

The key to this theory is that the body pays a price if it must constantly adapt to stress. This continued need for the body to adapt is referred to as **allostatic load**. For example, the body may be exposed to high levels of stress hormones such as cortisol and become susceptible to disease because of altered immune system functioning. Furthermore, high levels of cortisol can have direct effects on the brain—for example, by killing cells in the hippocampus, which regulates the secretion of cortisol. The result may be that, over time, the person becomes even more susceptible to the effects of stress.

Individuals can manifest allostatic load in different ways according to this theorizing (McEwen & Seeman, 1999). Some people may have high levels of stress hormones because they experience frequent stress. Other people may have some difficulty in adapting to stress, whether due to a genetically predisposed biological stress reaction that is slow to adapt, to behavioral responses that are learned over time and that interfere with adaptation (such as poor diet, limited exercise, smoking, or excessive alcohol consumption), or to some combination of the two. Still others may have trouble "shutting down" the biological stress response; for example, they may exhibit an unusually high level of cortisol secretion even after the stress has abated. Finally, some individuals may have a weakened biological stress response, reflected by low levels of cortisol release in response to stress which in turn causes other areas of the immune system to respond on overdrive.

To illustrate just one way in which stress can interfere with our biological stress response system, consider an example involving public speaking. Most people react to the stress of public speaking with an increase in cortisol secretion. After repeated exposure to such a stress

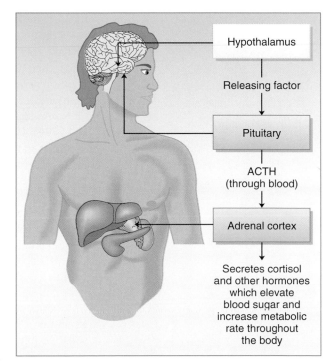

Figure 8.6   The HPA axis.

(i.e., many public speaking experiences), most people adapt to the stress, and the amount of cortisol secreted declines. However, about 10 percent of people show no adaptation and even increase their secretion of cortisol (Kirschbaum et al., 1995). According to McEwen's theory, these are the individuals at risk for disease. In a study measuring the presumed effects of allostatic load on the body (e.g., elevated blood pressure, cholesterol levels, and cortisol secretion), McEwen and colleagues found that higher allostatic load effects predicted greater risk for cardiovascular disease two and a half years later (Seeman et al., 1997).

Stress and the Immune System On a general level, stressors have multiple effects on various systems of the body—the autonomic nervous system, hormone levels, and brain activity. One major area of current interest is the immune system, which is an important consideration in infectious diseases, cancer, and allergies as well as in autoimmune diseases, such as rheumatoid arthritis, in which the immune system attacks the body. A wide range of stressors have been found to produce changes in the immune system—medical-school examinations, depression and bereavement, marital discord and divorce, job loss, caring for a relative with Alzheimer's disease, and the Three Mile Island nuclear disaster, among others (Cohen & Herbert, 1996). Whether such immune-system changes lead to more negative clinical outcomes, such as early death from cancer or the onset of arthritis, is yet to be determined. That is, it is not yet certain that the changes in the immune system that follow stress are great enough to actually increase risk for disease.

The area of research that comes closest to documenting a role for stress and immune-system changes in actual illness is the study of infectious diseases. To illustrate, we discuss two aspects of the immune system—secretory immunity and cytokines—in some detail.

Secretory Immunity The secretory component of the immune system exists in the tears, saliva, gastrointestinal, vaginal, nasal, and bronchial secretions that bathe the mucosal surfaces of the body. A substance found in these secretions, called secretory immunoglobulin A, or sIgA, contains antibodies that serve as the body's first line of defense against invading viruses and bacteria. They prevent the virus or bacterium from binding to mucosal tissues.

A study by Stone and his colleagues (Stone, Cox et al., 1987) showed that changes in the number of sIgA antibodies were linked to changes in mood. Throughout an eight-week study period a group of dental students came to the laboratory three times a week to have their saliva collected and a brief psychological assessment conducted. On days when the students experienced relatively high levels of negative mood, fewer antibodies were present than on days when the students had low levels of negative mood. Similarly, antibody level was higher on days with higher levels of positive mood.

Importantly, the link between sIgA and mood has been replicated (Stone, Neale et al., 1994). Prior research (e.g., Stone & Neale, 1984) had shown that daily events affect mood. It is therefore quite possible that daily events affect fluctuations in mood, which in turn suppress synthesis of the secretory sIgA antibodies. The process could operate as follows. An increase in undesirable life events coupled with a decrease in desirable life events produces increased negative mood, which in turn depresses antibody levels in secretory sIgA. If during this period a person is exposed to a virus, he or she will be at increased risk for infection (see Figure 8.7).

Several studies have confirmed the relationship between stress and respiratory infection. In each of them, volunteers took nasal drops containing a mild cold virus and also completed a battery of measures concerning recent stress. The advantage of this method was that exposure to the virus was an experimental variable under the investigators' control. Researchers found that stress was clearly linked to developing a cold (Cohen, Tyrell, & Smith, 1991; Stone et al., 1992). The stressors most often implicated were interpersonal problems and work difficulties (Cohen et al., 1998). These findings illustrate the complex interplay between psychological and biological variables in the etiology of psychophysiological disorders.

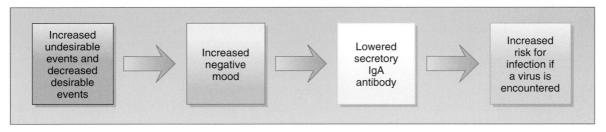

Figure 8.7   Mechanism through which stress could increase risk for viral infection.

Cytokines   When the body detects a foreign substance, such as bacteria, one line of defense that the immune system employs is the activation of cells called macrophages. Activation of macrophages in turn stimulates the release of substances called cytokines. Release of cytokines helps to initiate the body's response to infection, such as fatigue, fever, and activation of the HPA axis. Two cytokines that have been studied with respect to stress and illness are interleukin-1 (IL-1) and interleukin-6 (IL-6). Evidence indicates that stress can trigger this set of immune system responses; thus, when a person is under stress, IL-1 or IL-6 may be released, as if the body were fighting off an infection (e.g., Maier & Watkins, 1998). A laboratory study by Cohen and colleagues demonstrated that higher stress prior to an influenza viral challenge was associated with greater release of IL-6 and more flu-like symptoms, suggesting that the cytokines might be an important mediator between stress and illness (Cohen, Doyle, & Skoner, 1999).

Psychological Theories

Psychological theories try to account for the development of various psychophysiological disorders by considering such factors as unconscious emotional states, personality traits, cognitive appraisals, and specific styles of coping with stress.

Psychoanalytic Theories   Psychoanalytic theories propose that specific conflicts and their associated negative emotional states give rise to psychophysiological disorders. Of the psychoanalytic theorists who have studied psychophysiological disorders, Franz Alexander has had the greatest impact. In his view each of the various psychophysiological disorders is the product of unconscious emotional states specific to that disorder. For example, undischarged hostile impulses are viewed as creating the chronic emotional state responsible for essential hypertension.

> *The damming up of hostile impulses will continue and will consequently increase in intensity. This will induce the development of stronger defensive measures in order to keep pent-up aggressions in check. Because of the marked degree of their inhibitions, these patients are less effective in their occupational activities and for that reason tend to fail in competition with others…envy is stimulated and hostile feelings toward more successful, less inhibited competitors are further intensified. (Alexander, 1950, p. 150)*

Alexander formulated this theory of unexpressed-anger, or **anger-in theory**, on the basis of his observations of patients undergoing psychoanalysis. His hypothesis continues to be pursued in present-day studies of the psychological factors in essential hypertension, as discussed shortly.

Cognitive and Behavioral Factors   Physical threats obviously create stress. But humans perceive more than merely physical threats. We experience regrets about the past and worries about the future. All these perceptions can stimulate sympathetic-system activity and the secretion of stress hormones. But negative emotions, such as resentment, regret, and worry, cannot be fought or escaped as readily as can external threats, nor do they easily pass. They may keep the body's biological systems aroused and the body in a continual state of emergency, sometimes for far longer than it can bear, as suggested by

McEwen's theory (p. 207). The high level of cognition made possible in humans through evolution also creates the potential for distressed thoughts, which can bring about bodily changes that persist longer than they were meant to. Our higher mental capacities, it is theorized, subject our bodies to physical storms that they were not built to withstand.

In our general discussion of stress, we saw that the appraisal of a potential stressor is central to how it affects the person. People who continually appraise life experiences as exceeding their resources may be chronically stressed and at risk for the development of a psychophysiological disorder. How people cope with stress may also be relevant. We will shortly describe some findings that show that how people cope with anger is related to hypertension. Personality traits are also implicated in several disorders, most notably cardiovascular disease. People who chronically experience high levels of negative emotions are at high risk for the development of heart problems.

We turn now to a detailed review of three disorders that have attracted much attention from researchers—cardiovascular disorders, asthma, and acquired immunodeficiency syndrome (AIDS). We then discuss issues of gender, socioeconomic status, and ethnicity that are related to health.

Cardiovascular Disorders

Cardiovascular disorders are diseases involving the heart and blood-circulation system. Cardiovascular disease accounts for almost half the deaths in the United States each year, is the one of the leading killers of men and women from all ethnicities, and affects over 60 million Americans (American Heart Association, 2002). In 1999, the estimated costs associated with cardiovascular diseases, including health care and reductions in productivity, amounted to $286.5 billion dollars (American Heart Association, 1999).

In this section we focus on two forms of cardiovascular disease that appear to be adversely affected by stress—hypertension and coronary heart disease. Of the cardiovascular diseases, coronary heart disease causes the greatest number of deaths. It is generally agreed that many of the deaths resulting from cardiovascular diseases could be prevented or delayed by dealing with one or more of the known risk factors, many of which are behavioral in nature.

Essential Hypertension

Hypertension, commonly called high blood pressure, disposes people to atherosclerosis (clogging of the arteries), heart attacks, and strokes; it can also cause death through kidney failure. Yet no more than 10 percent of all cases in the United States are attributable to an identifiable physical cause. Hypertension without an evident biological cause is called **essential hypertension** (or sometimes primary hypertension). According to recent estimates, varying degrees of hypertension are found in about 20 percent of the adult population of the United States; it is twice as frequent in African Americans as in whites. As many as 10 percent of American college students have hypertension; most of them are unaware of their illness. Unless people have their blood pressure checked, they may go for years without knowing that they are hypertensive. Thus this disease is known as the silent killer.

Blood pressure is measured by two numbers; one represents systolic pressure, and the other represents diastolic pressure. The systolic measure is the amount of arterial pressure when the ventricles contract and the heart is pumping; the diastolic measure is the degree of arterial pressure when the ventricles relax and the heart is resting. A normal blood pressure in a young adult is 120 (systolic) over 80 (diastolic) (Figure 8.8).

Essential hypertension is viewed as a heterogeneous condition brought on by many possible disturbances in the various systems of the body that are responsible for regulating blood pressure. Genes play a substantial role in blood pressure; other risk factors for hypertension include

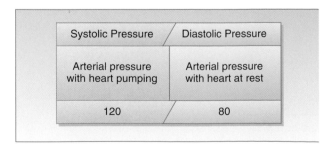

Systolic Pressure	Diastolic Pressure
Arterial pressure with heart pumping	Arterial pressure with heart at rest
120	80

Figure 8.8   Normal young-adult blood pressure.

obesity, excessive intake of alcohol, and salt consumption. Blood pressure may be elevated by increased cardiac output (the amount of blood leaving the left ventricle of the heart), by increased resistance to the passage of blood through the arteries (vasoconstriction), or by both. The physiological mechanisms that regulate blood pressure interact in an extremely complex manner. Activation of the sympathetic nervous system is a key factor, but hormones, salt metabolism, and central nervous system mechanisms are all involved. Many of these physiological mechanisms can be affected by psychological stress. Current thinking is that over the long term, frequent elevations in blood pressure eventually lead the arterial walls to thicken, resulting in sustained hypertension (National Heart, Lung, and Blood Institute, 1998).

Psychological Stress and Blood-Pressure Increase   Various stressful conditions have been examined to determine their role in the etiology of essential hypertension. Stressful interviews, natural disasters such as earthquakes, and job stress have all been found to produce short-term elevations in blood pressure (e.g., Niedhammer et al., 1998).

It is also relatively easy to produce increased blood pressure in the laboratory. The induction of various emotional states, such as anger, fear, and sadness, increases blood pressure (Cacioppo et al., 1993). Similarly, challenging tasks, such as mental arithmetic, mirror drawing, putting a hand in ice water (the cold pressor test), and giving a speech in front of an audience, all lead to increased blood pressure (e.g., Manuck, Kaplan, & Clarkson, 1993; Tuomisto, 1997). A classic series of studies by Obrist and his colleagues (e.g., 1978) used a reaction-time task in which participants were told they would receive an electric shock if they did not respond quickly enough. Good performance led to a monetary bonus. The reaction-time task yielded significant increases in both heart rate and systolic blood pressure.

For ethical reasons no experimental work has been done with human beings to determine whether short-term increases in blood pressure will develop into prolonged hypertension and actual structural changes in the cardiovascular system. In research done on animals, sustained hypertension has proved elusive. In many studies using electric shock as a stressor, blood pressure increased during the period when the animal was stressed but returned to normal when the stressor was removed. Studies that have used more natural stressors, such as competing with other animals for food (Peters, 1977), have proved somewhat more successful in producing long-term blood-pressure elevations. But the overall picture indicates that some predisposing factor or factors, such as the activation of the sympathetic nervous system by anger, are required if stress is to bring on essential hypertension.

Although the results from these laboratory studies are interesting, ultimately we must understand blood-pressure increases in people's natural environments. Therefore, researchers have also undertaken studies of ambulatory blood pressure, wherein participants wear a blood-pressure cuff that takes readings as they go about their daily lives. Many of these studies have asked participants about their emotional state at the time a blood-pressure reading is taken. The general finding has been that both positive and negative emotional states are associated with higher blood pressure (e.g., Jacob et al., 1999; Kamarck et al., 1998). There is also some indication that of various negative emotions, anger is most strongly linked to elevated blood pressure (e.g., Faber & Burns, 1994; Schwartz, Warren, & Pickering, 1994).

Other ambulatory monitoring studies have examined environmental conditions associated with blood pressure. For example, a series of studies examined the effects of stress on blood pressure among paramedics (Shapiro, Jamner, & Goldstein, 1993). In one of these analyses ambulance calls were divided

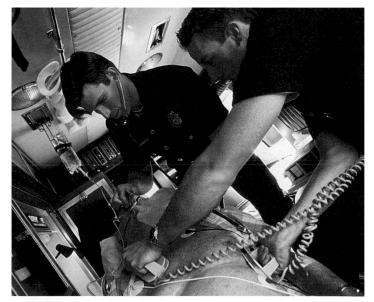

High-stress ambulance calls, as when the victim had to be revived, led to greater blood pressure increases than low-stress calls in the Shapiro, Jamner, and Goldstein study.

into high- and low-stress types. As expected, the high-stress calls were associated with higher blood pressure. Even more interesting were the results when the paramedics were divided into groups using personality-test measures of anger and defensiveness. The groups did not differ in blood pressure during the low-stress calls. However, on the high-stress calls, paramedics high in anger and defensiveness had higher blood pressure. In another study, participants rated job strain each time blood-pressure readings were taken (Kamarck et al., 1998). Blood pressure was lower at times when participants felt in control of their work environment—for example, when they felt they could exercise choice over what they were working on. Still another ambulatory blood pressure study found that for women, the combination of job strain and family responsibilities was associated with increases in systolic and diastolic blood pressure (Brisson et al., 1999).

In the ambulatory monitoring studies just described, the overall amount of blood-pressure increase associated with emotional states or environmental conditions was rather small. But it was also consistently found that a subset of participants had large increases, suggesting that only people who have some predisposition, or diathesis, will experience large blood-pressure increases that over time may lead to sustained hypertension. We turn next to these possible diatheses.

Predisposing Factors   Some people and animals are genetically predisposed to hypertension. Research with animals has identified several powerful diatheses—rearing in social isolation (Henry, Ely, & Stephens, 1972), a high level of emotional behavior (Farris, Yeakel, & Medoff, 1945), and sensitivity to salt (Friedman & Dahl, 1975). In the salt study, the researchers worked with two strains of rats bred to be either sensitive or insensitive to the impact of salt in their diet. The sensitive rats developed hypertension and died on a high-salt diet. These salt-sensitive rats were also likely to show sustained blood-pressure elevations when placed in an experimentally created conflict situation.

Anger as Predisposing Factor   As mentioned earlier, being easily angered could be a psychological diathesis. It should be noted that anger per se is not bad for our cardiovascular health; rather, it is excessive or inappropriate anger that is linked to ill health (Mayne, 2001). What is less clear about the anger variable is which aspect is most important: becoming angry easily, becoming angry and not expressing it, or having a cynical or suspicious attitude toward others. Recent research has not totally resolved this issue, but the data suggest that being easily angered may be the most important variable (e.g., Raikkonen et al., 1999).

Complicating the picture further, anger may function differently in men and women. Stereotypes about gender and anger suggest that men are more prone to anger than women, but the empirical research does not support this popular belief (Kring, 2000). Rather, men's and women's expression and experience of anger differ depending on the situation. With respect to cardiovascular health, expressing anger has been related to increased blood-pressure reactivity in men, whereas suppressing anger has been linked to higher blood-pressure reactivity in women (Burns & Katkin, 1993; Faber & Burns, 1996; Shapiro, Goldstein, & Jamner, 1995).

Sex differences have also been found in the relationship between the trait of becoming angry easily and ambulatory blood pressure. Among men, but not among women, high trait anger is related to higher blood pressure (Guyll & Contrada, 1998). We return to this issue in our discussion of myocardial infarction.

Cardiovascular Reactivity as a Predisposing Factor   In the past decade or so there has been a great deal of interest in cardiovascular reactivity as a biological predisposition to hypertension (and coronary heart disease as well; see p. 217). Cardiovascular reactivity refers to the extent to which blood pressure and heart rate increase in response to stress. The general research strategy is to assess cardiovascular reactivity to a laboratory stressor (or, even better, a battery of stressors) among people who are not currently hypertensive and then to follow up the participants some years later to determine whether the reactivity measure (usually the amount of change from a baseline condition to the stressor) predicts blood pressure. Two important points must be demonstrated to ensure the success of this approach:

1. Reactivity must be reliable if it is going to have predictive power. That is, someone who is high in reactivity must be consistently high. Indications are that reactivity is reliable if it is measured in response to a battery of laboratory stressors (e.g., Kamarck et al., 1992).

2. The laboratory measure of reactivity must actually relate to what the person's cardiovascular system does during day-to-day activities. Because of what is called white-coat hypertension, a person's blood pressure may be high at the clinic or laboratory but normal elsewhere. Though the literature on this issue is somewhat conflicting (see Gerin et al., 1994; Swain & Suls, 1996), studies that have compared laboratory reactivity with reactivity to stressors in the natural environment have shown some relationship in at least some people (Matthews et al., 1992).

What are the results of the studies that have tried to predict blood pressure from reactivity? Again, there is some variability, but those from a well-conducted study are positive (Light et al., 1992). Cardiovascular measures were taken while participants performed a reaction time task in which they were threatened with shock if their responses were slow. A follow-up ten to fifteen years later included both office-based measures of cardiovascular functioning and a day of ambulatory monitoring. Each of the cardiovascular-reactivity measures taken years earlier (heart rate and systolic and diastolic blood pressure) predicted later blood pressure; heart-rate reactivity was the strongest predictor. Importantly, these reactivity measures predicted subsequent blood pressure over and above the contribution of standard clinical predictors such as family history of hypertension. These are very impressive findings.

Further support for the importance of reactivity comes from high-risk research comparing individuals with and without a positive family history for hypertension (e.g., Adler & Ditto, 1998; Lovallo & Al'Absi, 1998). People with such a history show greater blood-pressure reactivity to various stressors. Coupled with research showing the heritability of hypertension, these findings suggest that blood-pressure reactivity is a good candidate for a genetically transmitted diathesis. Furthermore, reactivity is related to other known risk factors for hypertension, such as low social class and race (Gump, Matthews, & Raikkonen, 1999; Jackson et al., 1999).

In spite of these findings, evidence that reactivity actually predicts hypertension in humans is limited at this time. (Bear in mind that the findings just described concern levels of blood pressure but not the actual disease of hypertension.) One study entailed a four-year follow-up of 508 Finnish men whose blood-pressure reactivity had been assessed as they anticipated a bicycle exercise test (Everson et al., 1996). Men whose systolic blood pressure increased by 30 points or more were almost four times more likely to have developed hypertension four years later. One limitation of this study is that reactivity was assessed in an unusual situation. Thus, we can't be sure that the results would generalize to the more usual tests that have been used to assess reactivity.

Furthering our knowledge in this area may require a more fine-grained analysis of blood-pressure reactivity. For example, as we have previously mentioned, increased blood pressure could result from either increases in cardiac output or increases in resistance in the arteries. Thus, two people may show the same amount of blood-pressure increase, but the increases could reflect totally different mechanisms (Manuck et al., 1993). Furthermore, a variable such as cardiac output can be increased by sympathetic nervous system activation or by decreased activation in the parasympathetic system. Knowing which factor has yielded heightened cardiac output might relate to the accuracy of prediction (Miller, 1994). Similarly, the laboratory stressors that produce blood-pressure changes vary widely, from physical challenges, such as exposure to cold, to more cognitive ones, such as trying to solve difficult arithmetic problems. The type of stressor has implications for the mechanism through which reactivity is produced (e.g., mental arithmetic produces small but significant increases in cardiac output, whereas mirror tracing strongly increases peripheral resistance) and therefore may also be an important variable to consider (Sundin et al., 1995).

Research is currently proceeding along these lines and has been facilitated by the development of technology (termed *impedance cardiography*) that allows more detailed measurement of the mechanisms that produce blood-pressure increases. Finally, work has also begun on the mechanisms that return blood pressure to normal after a stressor has been encountered. For example, preliminary support has been found for the idea that more sustained blood-pressure increases may result from a failure of some bodily systems to counteract activity in the sympathetic nervous system (Markovitz et al., 1998). People whose blood pressure takes longer to return to normal may be more likely to develop hypertension. Thus, distinguishing between *reactivity* (how the body responds to stress) and *recovery* (how quickly the body returns to its resting state following stress) is an important area for research on hypertension (Gerin et al., 2000).

Coronary Heart Disease

Coronary heart disease (CHD) takes two principal forms, angina pectoris and myocardial infarction, or heart attack.

Characteristics of the Disease   The symptoms of **angina pectoris** are periodic chest pains, usually located behind the sternum and frequently radiating into the back and sometimes the left shoulder and arm. The major cause of these severe attacks of pain is an insufficient supply of oxygen to the heart (called ischemia), which in turn is due to coronary atherosclerosis, a narrowing or plugging of the coronary arteries by deposits of cholesterol, a fatty material, or to constriction of the blood vessels. In many patients with coronary artery disease, episodes of ischemia do not result in the report of pain. These are called episodes of silent ischemia. Both angina and episodes of silent ischemia are precipitated by physical or emotional exertion and are commonly relieved by rest or medication. Serious physical damage to heart muscle rarely results from an angina or ischemia attack, for blood flow is reduced but not cut off. If, however, the narrowing of one or more coronary arteries progresses to the point of producing a total blockage, a myocardial infarction, or heart attack, is likely to occur.

Myocardial infarction is a much more serious disorder and is the leading cause of death in the United States today. Like angina pectoris, it is caused by an insufficient supply of oxygen to the heart. But unlike angina, a heart attack usually results in permanent damage to the heart.

Several factors increase risk for CHD; the risk generally increases with the number and severity of these factors.

age

sex (males are at greater risk)

cigarette smoking

elevated blood pressure

elevated serum cholesterol

an increase in the size of the left ventricle of the heart

obesity

long-standing pattern of physical inactivity

excessive use of alcohol

diabetes

Stress and Myocardial Infarction   In the short term, physical exertion can trigger a myocardial infarction, as can episodes of anger (Mittleman et al., 1997). Acute stress is another factor—the frequency of myocardial infarction, for example, increased among residents of Tel Aviv on the day of an Iraqi missile attack (NHLBI, 1998). More chronic stressors, such as marital conflict and financial worries, are also relevant. One of the most studied stressors is job strain (Karasek, 1979), an employment situation in which the person experiences a high level of demand—too much work and too little time in which to do it—coupled with little authority to make decisions and lack of opportunity to make full use of his or her skills on the job.

Many studies have found that a high level of job strain is associated with increased risk for myocardial infarction (Schall, Landsbergis, & Baker, 1994). In one study, over 10,000 British civil servants were assessed for the degree of control they could exercise on their jobs. They were then followed for about five years to determine the incidence of CHD. Replicating earlier studies, more CHD was found at follow-up among workers in lower-status jobs (e.g., clerical work). This result, in turn, was related to these workers' reports of having little control on the job (Marmot et al., 1997). In a large-scale study conducted in Finland, a high level of job demands was related to the progression of atherosclerosis (Lynch et al., 1997a) and to cardiovascular disease mortality and morbidity (Lynch et al., 1997b).

Diatheses for Coronary Heart Disease   The traditional risk factors reviewed above leave at least half the instances of coronary heart disease unexplained (Jenkins, 1976). Indeed, people used to pay less attention to contributing causes, such as obesity, poor exercise habits, consumption of fatty foods, and smoking, than they do now, yet in earlier decades the incidence of CHD and related cardiovascular diseases was much lower. Furthermore, in the Midwest, where people's diets are very high in saturated fats and smoking rates are especially high, the incidence of coronary heart disease is low compared with that in more industrialized parts of the United States. Conversely, anyone who has visited Paris is aware of the heavy smoking and the fat-rich diets of the French population, yet CHD is relatively low there. Why?

Psychological Diatheses   The search for predispositions for coronary heart disease has begun to focus on psychological factors. Contemporary evidence linking CHD to psychological variables stems from investigations pioneered many years ago by two cardiologists, Meyer Friedman and Ray Rosenman (Friedman, 1969; Rosenman et al., 1975). In 1958 they identified a behavior pattern called **Type A behavior pattern**. As assessed by a structured interview, the Type A individual has an intense and competitive drive for achievement and advancement, an exaggerated sense of the urgency of passing time and of the need to hurry, and considerable aggressiveness and hostility toward others.

One characteristic of the Type A personality is feeling under time pressure and consequently trying to do several things at once.

Initial evidence supporting the idea that the Type A pattern predicts coronary heart disease came from the classic Western Collaborative Group Study (WCGS) (Rosenman et al., 1975). In this double-blind, prospective investigation, 3,154 men aged thirty-nine to fifty-nine were followed over a period of eight and a half years. Individuals who had been identified as Type A by interview were more than twice as likely to develop CHD as were Type B men, characterized by a less driven and less hostile way of life. Traditional risk factors, such as high levels of cholesterol, were also found to be related to CHD, but even when these factors were controlled for, Type A individuals were still twice as likely to develop CHD.

More recent research, however, has not supported the predictive utility of Type A behavior. For example, in several studies Type A failed to predict either mortality or myocardial infarction (Eaker et al., 1992; Orth-Gomer & Unden, 1990; Shekelle et al., 1983). Other research has not found a relationship between Type A and coronary artery disease (Williams, 1987).

There are several reasons for these conflicting results. One is that later investigators used different methods of assessing Type A (e.g., questionnaires) that may not have adequately measured it. Second, it became apparent that not all aspects of the Type A concept were truly related to CHD. For example, in an analysis of the interview data from the WCGS done by Matthews and her colleagues (1977), only seven of the whole set of items discriminated between Type A individuals who developed CHD and those who did not.

In further analyses of the WCGS data, anger and hostility emerged as the major predictors of CHD (Hecker et al., 1988). A more recent longitudinal study also found that dif-

The expression of anger has been linked to coronary heart disease.

ficulty controlling one's anger is related to higher rates of CHD (Kawachi et al., 1996). And anger and hostility are related to several other variables that play a role in CHD. For example, high levels of anger and hostility are related to greater blood-pressure reactivity to stress, to higher levels of cholesterol, to abnormal deposits of calcium on the walls of coronary arteries, to cigarette smoking and alcohol use, and to greater activation of platelets, which play a major role in the formation of blockages in the coronary arteries (Fredrickson et al., 2000; Iribarren et al., 2000; Weidner et al., 1989). However, more subtle distinctions in the anger construct may be differentially related to CHD risk for men and women. For example, Siegman and colleagues found that indirect expressions of antagonism were associated with CHD risk for women whereas overt expressions of anger were related to CHD risk for men (Siegman et al., 2000).

Other findings (e.g., Almada, 1991; Williams et al., 1986) suggest that cynicism (an approach to life that involves hostility) is a major factor within the Type A complex. The amount of coronary-artery blockage and coronary death were especially high in Type A participants who had earlier endorsed MMPI items reflecting a cynical or hostile attitude (for example, "Most people will use somewhat unfair means to gain profit or advantage, rather than lose it"). An earlier follow-up study of medical students who had been healthy when they took the MMPI twenty-five years earlier found a higher rate of CHD and death in those whose answers had indicated cynicism toward others (Barefoot, Dahlstrom, & Williams, 1983). More recently, cynicism was found to predict atherosclerosis, myocardial infarctions, and death from CHD in the large Finnish study mentioned earlier (Everson et al., 1997; Kamarck et al., 1997).

Additional findings concerning cynicism support a possible role for it in CHD. Cynicism is higher among men than among women and higher among African Americans than among whites (Barefoot et al., 1991); it is also related to avoidance of seeking social support, a high rate of marital separation, high levels of suppressed anger, greater consumption of alcohol, and obesity (Houston & Vavak, 1991; Miller et al., 1995)—all known to be risk factors for CHD.

What is not yet clear is the best way to conceptualize these results. A significant problem is the vague terminology that has been used (anger, hostility, cynicism) and the lack of agreement among measures used to assess these concepts. For example, one study followed a large sample of men for two years, using ultrasound to assess the progression of atherosclerosis (Julkunen et al., 1994). Three components of anger and hostility were assessed:

- *Cognitive*—negative beliefs about others
- *Affective*—impatience and irritability
- *Experience*—whether anger is expressed or not

These measures did not correlate well, indicating that even though the terms sound similar they cannot be readily substituted for one another. The affective component did not predict the progression of atherosclerosis, but the other two did. Furthermore, what was termed *experience* really dealt with the expression of anger, not the experience of anger, so the experience component was mislabeled. Thus, self-reported anger expression, not the experience of anger, was predictive of atherosclerosis. Another study found that men who had experienced myocardial ischemia had more facial expressions of anger, but not more reported hostility, than men who did not experience ischemia (Rosenberg et al. 2001). These studies illustrate the complexity of trying to determine whether anger is related to coronary heart disease. Another important issue is identifying the origin of excessive anger and hostility. Research is just beginning on this topic, but indications are that it may lie in a high level of family conflict (Matthews et al., 1996).

Although interest in anger and hostility remains high, research has begun to examine the relationship between other negative emotions—particularly anxiety and depression—and CHD. For example, anxiety has been shown to be related to the onset of CHD in humans (Kawachi et al., 1994; Kubansky & Kawachi, 2000). Animal research also demonstrates that inducing anxiety in animals with atherosclerosis can precipitate a heart attack (Carpeggio & Skinner, 1991). With regard to depression, it has been found that depressed patients have high rates of death from cardiovascular disease. Similarly, cardiac patients who also have a depressive disorder are over five times more likely than others to die within six months of a heart attack (Glassman & Shapiro, 1998).

Plausible biological mechanisms for these relationships have been proposed. Anxiety, for example, is associated with activation of the sympathetic nervous system, which can lead to both hypertension and atherosclerosis. Research has also shown that depression is linked to a greater tendency for platelets to aggregate and thus produce obstructions in the arteries. Furthermore, depression is often associated with increases in steroidal hormones, which increase blood pressure and damage cells in arteries (Musselman, Evans, & Nemeroff, 1998).

An important caveat is worth noting as well. Not all studies find that anxiety and depression predict mortality following CHD (e.g., Lane et al., 2001; Matthews et al., 1998). Although the reasons for inconsistencies in results are myriad, the same measurement problems described above for anger are relevant for the assessment and measurement of depression and anxiety. A number of different measures of anxiety and depression are available, and failures to replicate findings linking depression and anxiety to cardiac health may reflect differences in measurement. More generally, a number of questions remain to be addressed in additional research. For example, must one have a diagnosed mood or anxiety disorder to be at risk for CHD, or is having mood or anxiety symptoms sufficient? How severe must the symptoms be? Another set of questions concerns behavior. For example, do depressed individuals who have had a heart attack eat poorly, exercise less, smoke more, or engage in other unhealthful behaviors and thereby increase their risk for CHD?

Tying together this interest in CHD and negative emotions—anger, anxiety, and depression—is the newly proposed Type D personality (Denollet, 2000; Denollet & Brutsaert, 1997). Type D is defined by high scores on negative affectivity (a tendency to experience high levels of anxiety, anger, and depression) plus inhibition in the expression of these emotions. In a six-to-ten-year follow-up of patients who had earlier had a myocardial infarction, 52 percent of Type D patients experienced another heart problem, compared with only 12 percent of non–Type Ds. Other investigators are beginning to replicate and extend these results. For example, a study from Norway found that negative affectivity predicted mortality from heart disease (Murberg, Bru, & Aarsland, 2001). Another study found that inhibition of the expression of negative emotions was a better predictor of blood pressure reactivity among men than either hostility or limited social support (Habra, Linden, & Anderson, 2001). Whether Type D will replace Type A as a psychological risk factor remains to be seen.

Biological Diatheses   Like research on hypertension, research on biological predispositions for myocardial infarction has focused on reactivity. Excessive changes in heart rate and the consequent alterations in the force with which blood is pumped through the arteries may injure them, increasing risk for a myocardial infarction. Heart-rate reactivity has been related to CHD in several research contexts. A series of experimental studies investigated monkeys who were on a special diet designed to promote atherosclerosis. On the basis of a stress test, the animals were divided into high versus low heart-rate reactors. Subsequently, the high heart-rate reactors developed twice as much atherosclerosis as did the low reactors (Kaplan, Manuck et al., 1993). In another investigation by the same group, stress was experimentally created by changing the monkeys' living groups every three months. The type of monkeys in this study form hierarchically ordered social groups, with some animals dominant and others submissive. Thus, changing living groups stresses the animals because they are continually forced to reestablish a dominance hierarchy. In an earlier study, this manipulation had been found to promote atherosclerosis in dominant monkeys. This time some animals were given drugs to reduce the sympathetic activation that the stress was expected to produce. Animals treated with the drugs did not show an increase in atherosclerosis.

In studies of humans, heart-rate reactivity and ischemia elicited by laboratory stressors have predicted the development of CHD and the occurrence of cardiac events (Jiang et al., 1996; Keys et al., 1971). Thus, cardiovascular reactivity is a plausible candidate for a biological diathesis, and as we have already seen, it is associated with the psychological diathesis of anger and hostility.

Interest is also growing in another possible biological factor—heart-rate variability, which is thought to provide an index of activation of the parasympathetic division of the autonomic nervous system. Parasympathetic activation can reduce excess sympathetic activity and also protects the heart from fibrillating (a state in which the muscles in the ventricles no longer contract in a coordinated manner, so that no blood is pumped out of the heart). In patients who had experienced a heart attack, higher heart-rate variability was indeed predictive of a lower death rate (NHLBI, 1998).

Asthma

During his childhood Tom had frequent asthma attacks. His asthma was triggered principally by pollen, so that each year he went through a particularly bad period that included several trips to the emergency room of a local hospital. He seemed to get more than his share of colds, which frequently developed into bronchitis. As he reached his teenage years the attacks of asthma mysteriously vanished, and he was symptom free for the next twenty years. But at age thirty-four the attacks returned with a vengeance following a bout of pneumonia. In contrast to his childhood attacks, emotional stress now appeared to be the major precipitant. This hypothesis was confirmed when his physician asked Tom to keep a diary for two weeks in which he recorded how he had been feeling and what had been going on before each attack. He had four attacks over the period, three preceded by unpleasant interactions with his boss at work and one by an argument with his wife over an impending visit by her parents.

Asthma afflicts about 100 million people worldwide and 15 million people in the United States. In 2000, the economic costs of asthma in the United States, including both medical expenditures and lost productivity, amounted to $14.5 billion (NHLBI, 2001). In contrast to the situation with many other diseases, the prevalence of asthma has been on the rise; it increased 74 percent from 1984 to 1994 (National Center for Health Statistics, 1994). The reason for this increase is unknown, but air pollution is a possible factor. Indeed, emergency room visits for asthma declined considerably in urban Atlanta during the 1996 Olympic games, when automobile traffic was severely restricted (Friedman et al., 2001).

Of the 15 million Americans with asthma, one-third are children. Death of children due to asthma-related difficulties increased 78 percent between 1978 and 1993. During childhood, asthma is more common among boys. By age fifteen it becomes more prevalent in women and remains so until after age forty-five, when men again predominate (NHLBI, 1998).

Characteristics of Asthma

In an asthma attack, the air passages in the lungs, which are hypersensitive, become narrowed, causing breathing (particularly exhalation) to be extremely labored and wheezy. This narrowing can be triggered by viral infections, allergens, pollution, smoke, exercise, cold, and emotional states. In addition, an inflammation of lung tissue is mediated by the immune system, resulting in an increase in mucus secretion and edema (accumulation of fluid in the tissues) (Moran, 1991). The major structures of the respiratory system are shown in Figure 8.9.

Asthma attacks occur intermittently, sometimes almost daily and sometimes separated by weeks or months, and vary in severity. For unknown reasons, attacks are most fre-

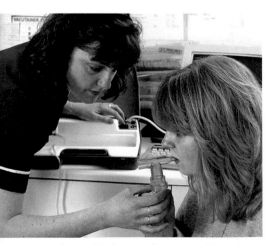

Asthma attacks are often treated by using a nebulizer to spray a fine mist of a bronchodilator into the bronchial tubes.

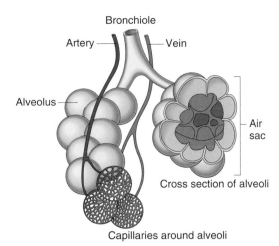

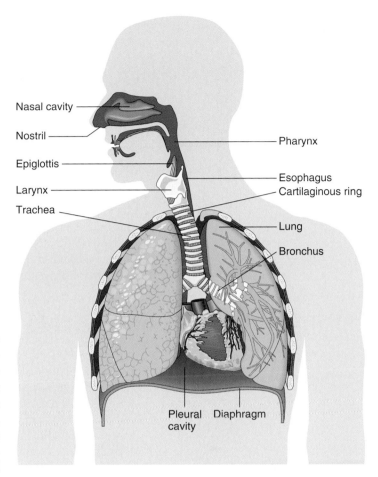

Figure 8.9   Major structures of the respiratory system—trachea, lungs, bronchi, bronchioles, and alveoli—and the ancillary organs. In asthma, the air passages, especially the bronchioles, become constricted and fluid and mucus build up in the lungs.

quent in early morning hours. The frequency of attacks may increase seasonally, when certain pollens are present. The airways are not continuously blocked; rather, the respiratory system returns to normal or near normal either spontaneously or after treatment, thus allowing asthma to be differentiated from chronic respiratory problems such as emphysema (Creer, 1982).

For individuals with exercise-induced asthma, the attacks follow strenuous exercise. Although some athletes are debilitated by the attacks, others are able to perform at the highest level despite their asthma. An example is Jackie Joyner-Kersee, a six-time Olympic medalist in track and field.

Most often, asthma attacks begin suddenly. The asthmatic individual has a sense of tightness in the chest, wheezes, coughs, and expectorates sputum. A severe attack is a frightening experience and may cause a panic attack (Carr, 1998, 1999), which exacerbates the asthma. The person has immense difficulty getting air into and out of the lungs and feels as though he or she is suffocating; the raspy, harsh noise of the gasping, wheezing, and coughing compounds the terror. The person may become exhausted by the exertion and fall asleep as soon as breathing is more normal.

The person with asthma takes a longer time than normal to exhale, and whistling sounds, referred to as rales, can be detected throughout the chest. Symptoms may last an hour or may continue for several hours or sometimes even for days. Between attacks no abnormal signs may be detected when the individual is breathing normally, but forced, heavy expiration often allows the rales to be heard through a stethoscope.

Etiology of Asthma

The importance of psychological factors in the development of asthma is a topic of debate. Some believe that emotions are always implicated. Others have divided the various possible causes into three categories: allergic, infective, and psychological (Rees, 1964). In addition to these three classes of causal agents there are environmental causes, such as caffeine and exercise. When asthma is caused primarily by allergens, the cells in the respiratory tract are especially sensitive to one or more substances or allergens, such as pollen, molds, fur, cockroaches, air pollution, smoke, and dust mites, which bring on an attack. Other environmental toxins, such as secondhand smoke, can trigger asthma attacks. Respiratory infections, most often acute bronchitis, can also make the respiratory system vulnerable to asthma, which seems to have happened in the case at the beginning of this section.

Olympic medalist Jackie Joyner-Kersee suffers from exercise-induced asthma.

Table 8.4 Relative Importance (%) of Allergic, Infective, and Psychological Factors in the Etiology of Asthma

Causal Factors	Dominant	Subsidiary	Unimportant
Allergic	23	13	64
Infective	38	30	32
Psychological	37	33	30

Source: From Rees, 1964.

Anxiety, tension produced by frustration, anger, depression, and anticipated pleasurable excitement are all examples of psychological factors that may disturb the functioning of the respiratory system and thus bring on an asthma attack.

A classic study of 388 asthmatic children in Cardiff, Wales, found that the children could be divided into groups according to the causes of their attacks (Rees, 1964). As shown in Table 8.4, psychological factors were considered a dominant cause in only 37 percent of the cases, and in 30 percent of the cases psychological variables were regarded as totally unimportant—a finding that strongly suggests that asthma is not always psychosomatic.

This study also showed that the different causes of asthma varied in importance depending on the age of the individual. For asthmatic individuals younger than five years of age, the infective factors predominated. From ages six to sixteen the infective factors still predominated, but psychological variables increased in importance. In the range from ages sixteen to sixty-five, psychological factors decreased in importance until about the thirty-fifth year, thereafter becoming more consequential again.

Psychological Factors in Asthma   Even when asthma is originally induced by an infection or allergy, psychological stress can precipitate attacks. Asthma patients report that many attacks are precipitated by emotions such as anxiety (Rumbak et al., 1993).

Because of the link between the autonomic nervous system (ANS) and the constriction and dilation of the airways, and the connection between the ANS and emotions, most research has focused on heightened emotional experience. Research has generally found higher levels of negative emotional expression and experience in people with asthma. Their facial reactions to laboratory stressors are more intense, and they are rated as more hostile and helpless during interviews, as well as more maladjusted. Their self-reports on personality tests also reveal high levels of negative emotions (Lehrer, Isenberg, & Hochron, 1993; Mrazek, Schuman, & Klinnert, 1998).

Emotional arousal has also been found to be directly related to reports of asthma symptoms and peak expiratory flow, a measure of airway obstruction wherein a person takes a deep breath and then exhales as hard as possible into a device that measures the force of the air expelled. Smyth and his colleagues (1999) studied people with asthma over a period of several days. Five times each day they were signaled to complete a measure of peak flow and record in a diary any asthma symptoms they were experiencing as well as their levels of stress and the mood they were in. Reports of higher levels of stress and negative emotions were related to lower peak flow and more reports of asthma symptoms.

In interpreting these data it is probably fair to say that some of this heightened negative emotional experience is a reaction to having a chronic disease. But some research also shows that emotional arousal precedes an asthma attack, indicating that emotion does play a role in precipitating attacks (Hyland, 1990).

Role of the Family   One source of psychological stress associated with asthma is parent–child interaction. One investigation looked at 150 pregnant women who had asthma (Klinnert, Mrazek, & Mrazek, 1994). The investigators intended to study the mothers' offspring who were at genetic risk and assess parental characteristics as well. The parents were interviewed three weeks after the child's birth to determine their attitudes toward the infant, their sensitivity to the infant, their strategy for sharing parenting duties, and the presence of any emotional disturbances. The amount of stress experienced by the mother in the past year was also assessed. The children were closely monitored over the next three years, and the frequency of asthma was then related to the parental characteristics noted earlier. Results showed a high rate of asthma among those children whose mothers had high levels of stress and whose families were rated as having problems (see Figure 8.10).

Not all research, however, has found that parent–child relationships figure in asthma (Eiser et al., 1991; Sawyer et al., 2001). Gauthier and his co-workers (1977, 1978)

studied young asthmatic children and their mothers through a battery of questionnaires and interviews and by making observations in the home. Most of the children and their mothers were well-adjusted. The children's levels of development were normal for their age, and they were independent and successful at coping with their surroundings.

The research we have reviewed is thus not completely consistent regarding the role that the home life of people with asthma plays in their illness. Even if we allow that family relationships are consequential in asthma, we cannot always tell whether the various familial variables are causal or maintaining agents. Although certain negative emotional factors in the home may be important in eliciting early asthmatic attacks in some children, in others the illness may originally develop for nonfamilial reasons, and then the children's parents may unwittingly reward various symptoms of the syndrome. For example, parents may cater to asthmatic children and treat them specially because of the asthma. Given how debilitating and frightening asthma episodes can be, it is not surprising that some parents may be a bit overprotective of children with this condition.

Physiological Predisposition   In the Cardiff study mentioned earlier, Rees found that 86 percent of the asthmatic individuals had had a respiratory infection before asthma developed, compared with only 30 percent of the control group. One interpretation of these results could be that infection weakens the lungs, making that organ vulnerable to stress.

Individuals whose asthma is primarily allergic may have an inherited hypersensitivity of the respiratory mucosa, which then overresponds to usually harmless substances such as dust and pollen. That asthma runs in families is consistent with genetic transmission of a diathesis (Konig & Godfrey, 1973). Recent studies are narrowing in on how genes may interact with environmental factors to produce asthma (e.g., Cookson & Moffatt, 1997, 2000). There is also some indication that people with asthma have a less than normally responsive sympathetic nervous system (Mathe & Knapp, 1971; Miklich et al., 1973). Activation of the sympathetic nervous system is known to reduce the intensity of an asthmatic attack. Finally, two studies have found that asthmatic persons, but not people without asthma, respond to gory films with bronchoconstriction (reviewed by Lehrer et al., 1993), suggesting that their respiratory systems respond to stress in a way that may induce an asthma attack.

A diathesis–stress explanation once again seems to fit the data on a psychophysiological disorder. Once the respiratory system is predisposed to asthma, any number of psychological stressors can interact with the diathesis to produce the disease.

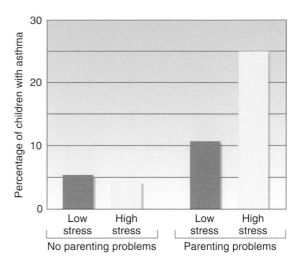

Figure 8.10   The effects of parenting problems and prior stress on the frequency of asthma in their children. Children whose mothers had been under a high level of stress and were raised in families with parenting problems had high rates of asthma. From Klinnert, Mrazek, and Mrazek (1994).

AIDS: A Challenge for the Behavioral Sciences

AIDS (acquired immunodeficiency syndrome) is a major public health threat. This invariably fatal illness has three unique, interrelated characteristics that make it appropriate for discussion in an abnormal psychology textbook: (1) it can arise from behavior that is apparently irrational and certainly self-defeating; (2) it is not presently curable or preventable by medical means; and (3) it can be prevented by psychological means.

Scope of the Problem

First identified in 1981, AIDS has emerged as the most serious infectious epidemic of modern times. In the United States, AIDS was originally proclaimed a disease of gay men. But it never really was a "gay disease," and there are indications that the disease is increasing among heterosexuals, both men and women. In Africa and parts of Latin America, AIDS is found primarily among heterosexuals, and throughout the world infected women are giving birth to babies who are HIV positive, that is, who are infected with the human immunodeficiency virus that causes AIDS. Even in parts of the world where AIDS is not yet a significant health problem, it is likely to become one. The following statistics give some sense of the scope of the problem (CDC, 2001; Kalichman, 1995; Maugh, 1998, 1999a; San Francisco Department of Health, 2002; UNAIDS, 2000).

- Since the start of the epidemic more than 21 million people have died worldwide.
- More than 40 million people worldwide are now living with HIV.
- There were 3 million deaths from HIV/AIDS in 2001.
- Worldwide, women now account for 48 percent of people infected with HIV.
- Nearly 95 percent of people with HIV live in developing countries.
- In seven countries in Africa, one in five adults is infected. In South Africa, nearly 20 percent of the population is infected, up from 13 percent in 2000.
- Incidence is rising sharply in Asia, especially in India and China; most of these new cases result from heterosexual activity.
- Drug abuse is the principal cause of AIDS in Ukraine, Spain, and Vietnam.
- Each year about 40,000 Americans become HIV positive; in recent years about 40 percent of these have been African Americans.
- In 1994, 55,000 Americans died of AIDS-related illnesses—almost as many as died during the entire Vietnam War. Sharp declines were noted in subsequent years, down to 17,000 in 1998, a function primarily of the success of new drug combinations for controlling the spread of infection in the body. Nevertheless, as of December 2000, the total number of deaths in the United States from AIDS was more than 448,000.
- In the United States, African American and Hispanic women are seventeen times more likely than white women to become infected.
- In the United States, AIDS is the fifth leading cause of death among all adults ages twenty-five to forty-four, a remarkable statistic given that it wasn't even included as a cause of death just over 20 years ago.
- In the mid 1980s, there were more than 8,000 new infections a year in San Francisco alone. Transmission rates declined to 500 new infections in 1997. However, HIV rates are rising again as the number of new infections in San Francisco was over 1,000 in 2001.

Description of the Disease

Although the medical complexities of AIDS are beyond the scope of this book, it is important to understand a few fundamentals. AIDS is a disease in which the body's immune system is severely compromised by HIV, putting the individual at high risk for fatal diseases, such as Kaposi's sarcoma, rare forms of lymph cancer, and a wide range of dangerous fungal, viral, and bacterial infections. The term *opportunistic* is often used to describe these illnesses because they are seldom found in people with healthy immune systems. We can say that these diseases take advantage of the opportunity afforded by a weakened immune system (Kalichman, 1996). Strictly speaking, people do not die of AIDS as much as they die of fatal infectious and other diseases to which AIDS makes them vulnerable.

Medical authorities suspect AIDS when an otherwise healthy person presents with an illness that he or she would not likely have with a properly functioning immune system. People who have had an organ transplant, for example, are at risk for such opportunistic diseases because they are given drugs to suppress the immune system so that the body will not reject the new organ. In a sense, an AIDS patient presents similarly without having taken anti–rejection, immunosuppressant medication. The big difference, of course, is that a transplant patient is kept in an antiseptic, intensive-care hospital environment while his or her immune system is being artificially—and temporarily—compromised.

Spread of the Disease

The AIDS crisis has been exacerbated because many untested HIV-positive people feel healthy and are unaware of their illness. HIV-positive individuals can infect others and contribute to what some have called a ticking time bomb in the health of the human race.

Efforts to control transmission of HIV are hindered because the most widely employed tests for HIV detect antibodies to infection and these antibodies do not appear in most people until several months following infection (McCutchan, 1990). Thus, even if an antibody test is negative, a person recently exposed to an infected individual may have HIV. Newer tests may make possible direct and earlier measurement of the concentration of HIV in the blood.

HIV is most often transmitted from one person to another through risky sexual practices, regardless of sexual orientation. HIV is present only in blood, semen, and vaginal secretions and can be transmitted only when infected liquids get into the bloodstream. AIDS cannot be caught through casual social contact or even by living with a person who has AIDS or is HIV positive, provided that reasonable care is taken to avoid contact with the infected person's blood. Unprotected receptive anal intercourse is the riskiest of sexual practices (Kingsley et al., 1987). Considerably less risky but still chancy is vaginal intercourse without a condom. Unprotected oral-genital contact and insertion of fingers or hands into the anus or vagina probably also present risks. The other category of risky behavior occurs among intravenous drug users; sharing unsterilized needles can introduce HIV-carrying blood into the bloodstream of another. Finally, infants born to HIV-positive mothers are at risk, for the virus can cross the placental barrier and infect the developing fetus. The virus can also be transmitted through breast-feeding.

Risk is elevated in people who abuse drugs, including drugs that are not injected, perhaps because the effects of drugs can compromise a person's ability or willingness to consider the consequences of his or her behavior. It is also possible that certain drugs, such as cocaine and amyl nitrite, intensify the sexual experience and thereby lead to rougher and lengthier sexual episodes, which in turn may increase the chances of damaging rectal or vaginal membranes. Another possible mechanism is a risk-taking disposition, for which frequent drug use is a marker; that is, engaging in unprotected sex may be another sign of a tendency to take risks (Chesney, Barrett, & Stall, 1998). Whatever the reasons, ample evidence shows that risky sex is associated with the frequent use of many kinds of drugs, including alcohol.

Preventing the spread of AIDS is turning out to be more difficult than people originally expected. In the 1980s, when prevention efforts focused on encouraging the use of condoms during every sexual contact, new cases of HIV dropped in many large cities, from an annual infection rate among gay men of around 10 percent or more to 1 or 2 percent. But data from the Centers for Disease Control indicated that younger gay men are engaging in more unprotected penetrative sexual behaviors than are older gay men (Boxall, 1995).

Why might this be happening? Perhaps young gay men do not see as many of their age cohort infected as do older gay men, and so they don't consider AIDS as much of a threat for themselves as it is for others. It has also been suggested that in the 1990s some people sensed that a medical cure for AIDS was just around the corner, so that engaging in unsafe sex might no longer seem so life threatening. Indeed, with the introduction of new drugs in the mid-1990s, the hope for cure became ever more intense. After the Food and Drug Administration permitted direct marketing of AIDS medicines to consumers in 1997, ads from drug companies began to appear that portrayed healthy, active, robust, and happy men engaging in all sorts of activities and sports even with HIV/AIDS, perhaps suggesting that these drugs can cure AIDS. While these ads may have portrayed some small percentage of HIV positive men, their relevance for women seems doubtful. Moreover, most men suffer-

"If he doesn't have a condom, you just have to take a deep breath and tell him to go get one."

It's not the easiest thing in the world to say.

But these days, you have to. If you're dating someone who doesn't like condoms, talk before having sex. Explain how you feel. Offer to help during the awkward moments. And if this doesn't work, ask yourself, is it worth the risk?

For more information on condoms and AIDS, call 1-800-342-AIDS. Deaf access: 1-800-AIDS-TTY (1-800-243-7889).

AMERICA RESPONDS TO AIDS

U.S. DEPARTMENT OF HEALTH AND HUMAN SERVICES / PUBLIC HEALTH SERVICE/Centers for Disease Control   CDC

Encouraging assertiveness in sex is a key component to AIDS prevention efforts. This advertisement emphasizes the importance of insisting on condom use.

ing from HIV/AIDS are not as the ads suggested. More importantly, these drugs can neither cure AIDS nor reduce its transmission. The FDA has since ordered that such ads be discontinued. Thus, even with the promising advances of the past few years, safer sex has to become a lifelong commitment—and for all people, not just for gay men. Among the many support groups are groups for HIV-negative gay men to provide encouragement for hewing to the safer-sex line (Boxall, 1995).

Prevention of the Disease

Despite promising advances in drug treatment (e.g., AZT and saquinavir), there is widespread agreement that by far the best strategy is prevention through behavioral changes. For example, scientists generally agree that needle exchange programs or the free distribution of needles and syringes reduces needle sharing and thereby the spread of infectious diseases associated with intravenous drug use (Gibson et al., 2001; Yoast, Williams, Deitchman, & Champion, 2001). The primary focus in preventing sexually transmitted AIDS is on changing sexual practices. One can eliminate the possibility of exposure by being in a monogamous relationship with a partner who tests negative for HIV. However, monogamous relationships are rare among young people and are not invariably found among married people or those in other committed relationships.

Furthermore, rationality does not always prevail in a committed relationship. In a study of gay male couples who had been in their relationship at least six months (the average length was almost four years), Appleby, Miller, and Rothspan (1999) found that engaging in risky sex symbolized trust, love, and commitment, whereas safer sex was seen negatively by partners and could threaten the closeness of a committed relationship. Further, suggestions by a partner that safer sex should be practiced were viewed with suspicion, as a sign of infidelity. There is no reason to expect the views of heterosexual couples to be any different.

This rationalizing of risk poses health hazards because HIV tests can produce false negatives and because a relationship, homosexual or heterosexual, that one partner believes is monogamous may not be (Peplau & Cochran, 1988). In Appleby et al.'s sample, 62 percent of the men in committed male-male relationships reported having had sex with someone else at some time during the relationship, and 84 percent of these reported that their partner knew. In some instances the unfaithful partner in an ostensibly monogamous relationship had unprotected sex with someone else, did not tell his partner, and later had unprotected sex with the partner.

Thus, although advocating monogamous relationships remains a prevalent approach in the public health arena, prevention is best directed at encouraging sexually active people to use condoms, which are about 90 percent effective in preventing HIV infection. Avoiding sex after using alcohol or drugs is also prudent because, as noted, use of these substances increases the tendency to engage in risky sex (Stall et al., 1986). The safest strategy is to use condoms in a monogamous relationship.

Prevention efforts also include advising people to explore the pleasures of low-risk sex, such as mutual masturbation and frottage (body rubbing without insertion of the penis into the vagina, mouth, or anus of the partner). For the most part this advice holds for same- or opposite-sex partners. Prevention for intravenous drug users should include, in addition to these measures, the use of new or sterilized needles, though the best precaution would be to get off drugs altogether.

Ironically, in cities in which AIDS is less of a problem than it is in such centers as New York and San Francisco, high-risk behavior is much more common. Perhaps there is a (mistaken) sense of personal invulnerability when there is not an epidemic in one's immediate vicinity (St. Lawrence et al., 1988). This certainly seems to be the case for young heterosexuals, both male and female, among whom infection has spread particularly fast through unprotected sex (CDC, 1994). These young people apparently continue to view AIDS as limited mostly to gays and drug users; they may also wish to distance themselves from a disease that bears the social stigma of those whom it affects most at the present time.

In African American and Hispanic populations, high-risk sexual behavior has not changed as much among heterosexuals as it has among gay men and lesbians (Maugh, 1998). Adolescents in general see AIDS as less of a personal threat than do people in their twenties and older (Strunin & Hingson, 1987). These facts pose a serious problem because the most prudent judgment for people to make—regardless of sexual orientation—when they consider having sexual relations, especially with a new partner, is that their partner could be HIV positive.

How can changes be brought about, especially in generations of sexually active people for whom the pill (at least for heterosexuals) marked a welcome release from the need to use condoms? Also daunting is the challenge of changing the attitudes and practices of adults for whom the 1960s ushered in a period of sexual liberation, restrained by the danger of herpes and other venereal diseases but not by the certainty of dying. Social psychological and behavior-therapy theory and research suggest strategies that can form the basis of effective preventive interventions (Chernoff, 1998; Kalichman, 1995; Kelly, 1995).

- Provide accurate information about HIV transmission. Such information is readily available online or in pamphlets from the Centers for Disease Control and from local AIDS organizations as well as from commercially available guides in question-and-answer format.

- Explain clearly what the person's risks are (e.g., people with many sexual partners are at higher risk, regardless of sexual orientation; sharing needles with other intravenous drug users is very risky).

- Identify cues to high-risk situations (e.g., drinking alcohol in a sexually provocative situation is associated with higher-risk sexual behavior).

- Provide instruction in condom use (and, as appropriate, needle cleaning and exchanging), including "eroticizing" the use of condoms (suggesting ways in which a condom can be experienced as sexually exciting). Also, emphasize that using condoms confers upon individuals a degree of behavioral control over their health.

- Explain in detail how certain changes in behavior reduce risk (e.g., that a condom usually prevents semen from entering a partner's vagina, anus, or mouth).

- Provide social-skills training that includes sexual assertiveness skills (e.g., resisting pressure to have sex or insisting that safer sex be practiced) and other communication skills that can help preserve relationships while reducing risk of infection with HIV.

- Work at the community level to enhance large-scale social support for making safer sex normative, that is, expected, creating a "We're all in this together" atmosphere.

A review by Chernoff (1998) revealed that interventions implementing these principles often but do not always lead to increases in sexual assertiveness, reductions in unprotected anal intercourse, and increased use of condoms in gay and bisexual men (Kelly et al., 1989, 1990; Roffman et al., 1998), low-income minority women (Auerbach, Wypijewska, & Brodie, 1995), African American gay and bisexual men (Peterson et al., 1996), Mexican American gay and bisexual men (Zimmerman et al., 1997), female prostitutes (Bhave et al., 1995), substance abusers (Kotranski et al., 1998), and mentally ill adults (Susser et al., 1998). School-based efforts to get young adolescents (in middle or junior high school) to forgo sexual activity or to use condoms if they are sexually active have not been at all successful (e.g., Siegel et al., 1995). Somewhat greater success has been achieved with high school (Smith & Katner, 1995) and college students (Reeder, Pryor, & Harsh, 1997). Only mixed success has been reported in discouraging intravenous drug use to reduce HIV exposure (Auerbach, Wypijewska, & Brodie, 1994).

An especially noteworthy study involved over 3,700 heterosexual men and women at the highest risk for HIV infection in thirty-seven sexually transmitted disease (STD) clinics across the United States (NIMH Multisite HIV Prevention Trial Group, 1998). In this, the largest HIV-prevention study ever conducted, three-quarters of the participants were African American and the rest were Latino; most were unemployed and single. All met one or more of the following high-risk criteria: having sex with multiple partners, being infected with an STD, having sex with someone known to have multiple partners, having sex with an intravenous drug user, and having sex with someone known to be HIV positive. A four-week behavioral intervention applying several of the principles mentioned here, compared with a one-session information-only control group, led to significantly more reduction in unprotected sex, with some indications also of fewer cases of STDs over a twelve-month period following the intervention. In addition, the estimated cost per person in the behavioral condition was less than $300, which is equivalent to the cost of about one week of treatment with the newest AIDS drugs (protease inhibitors).

A limitation of most of the research just reviewed, however, is that little of it assesses behavioral change over the long term, and not much is known about the ultimate effects of such interventions on preventing AIDS, which, after all, is the raison d'être for this work. However, the results, except for those for young adolescents, have thus far been encouraging.

A Cautionary Note on the Role of Knowledge about AIDS in AIDS Prevention

The most widely adopted strategy in AIDS prevention is the provision of accurate information about the nature of the disease, how it is transmitted, and how one can reduce one's risk by changing one's behavior. Shouldn't it be enough just to tell people what's what, especially if a given course of action is very dangerous to them? After all, if we don't know how to reach a certain destination, don't we all consult a map or ask someone who we believe might be able to provide directions?

As the song goes in Gershwin's *Porgy and Bess*, it ain't necessarily so. Consider something we will be examining in the chapter on substance abuse (Chapter 12). We have known with a fair degree of certainty since the early 1960s that cigarette smoking is dangerous to health. Indeed, we can remember from the 1950s, when our friends (and we!) were experimenting with cigarettes, that they were often referred to as "coffin nails." People who smoke cigarettes in the new millennium are not stupid and are seldom ignorant of the scientific facts. It's obvious even to the casual observer of human behavior that knowing that something is bad for us is far from a guarantee that we will refrain from partaking of it.

The strong emphasis in prevention programs on educational messages about HIV rests on the assumption that people are rational beings and that they will usually act in their own best interests. This assumption—central to the Western worldview, which values knowledge and enlightenment—has been challenged by two social psychologists, Helweg-Larsen and Collins (1997). They reviewed studies showing that knowledge about the mode of transmission of HIV and ways to prevent its transmission is by no means a guarantee that people will protect themselves. Indeed, many surveys indicate that knowledge about HIV transmission and preventive behaviors is quite high among people who engage in high-risk behavior, including intravenous drug users (Calsyn et al., 1992), heterosexual adolescents (DiClemente et al., 1990), and gay men (Aspinwall et al., 1991).

What we know about AIDS-prevention programs, all of which seek to increase knowledge about the disease and how to avoid it, is that they are far from completely effective. Why? One thing to consider is that when people are in a heightened state of autonomic arousal, especially sexual arousal, they are not exactly paragons of rational thinking. In fact, Masters and Johnson (see our discussion of them in Chapter 14) based their entire treatment of sexual dysfunction on the need for people not to take the "spectator role," which refers to adopting an observing, intellectual perspective on what is happening. Thinking too much, analyzing things, making deliberate and careful decisions—these tend to interfere with sexual enjoyment. It is reasonable to assume that when people are imbibing alcohol or injecting illicit drugs, such as heroin, they are similarly not operating on an entirely rational level.

The focus on providing information about HIV transmission can overlook how people *feel* about the knowledge they have (Petty & Cacioppo, 1986). For example, adolescents can understand that a condom will markedly reduce HIV risk and yet avoid using one because it is a reminder of disease, hardly something one wants to have in mind in sexual situations. Or, they might believe that their immune systems are strong enough to repel HIV. (As we will see in the discussion of smoking prevention and cessation in young people [p. 405], a sense of immortality or at least diminished vulnerability is not uncommon in youth.)

Helweg-Larsen and Collins (1997) discuss ways in which knowledge can actually be a *hindrance*; that is, under some conditions knowledge may have negative consequences. For example, "AIDS information saturation" is a state of irritation of being overwhelmed by a constant barrage of warnings about HIV and exhortations to refrain from high-risk behaviors. In one study, college students judged to be affected by this information overload reported weaker intentions to engage in safer sexual behavior than did students who did not feel overwhelmed by information (Berrenberg et al., 1993, as cited in Helweg-Larsen & Collins, 1997). Repeatedly telling people what they already know can apparently make them less likely to act on that knowledge. Furthermore, as mentioned earlier in the discussion of the Appleby et al. study, introducing condoms into an existing, ostensibly monogamous relationship can engender suspicion and lack of trust.

Another consideration often overlooked in public education campaigns against HIV involves the skills needed to act on knowledge. For example, a young man or woman may understand the benefits of using condoms but may be embarrassed about purchasing them. The ability to purchase condoms from vending machines should lessen this embarrassment. Indeed, there are examples of successful prevention efforts that go beyond providing information. For example, as part of a broad-based program designed to prevent HIV infection among urban women, Hobfoll and colleagues (1994) provided women with a "condom credit card" that allowed them to receive free condoms and spermicide from a local pharmacy for a year. In another program targeting urban women, investigators provided not only information and education about risk, but also training in condom use, assertiveness training, peer support, group support in developing problem-solving skills, and help with identifying triggers for risky sexual behavior. Women who received this intervention increased their use of condoms from 26 percent of the time to 56 percent of the time, and they developed better and more effective sexual communication and negotiation skills and behavior (Kelly et al., 1997).

Gender and Health

At every age from birth to eighty-five and older, more men die than women. Men are more than twice as likely to die in automobile accidents and of homicides, cirrhosis, heart disease, lung disease, lung cancer, and suicide. Women, however, have higher rates of *morbidity*—general poor health or the incidence of several specific diseases. For example, women have higher rates of diabetes, anemia, gastrointestinal problems, systemic lupus erythematosus, and rheumatoid arthritis; they report more visits to physicians, use more prescription drugs, and account for two-thirds of all surgical procedures performed in the United States. And in recent years, women's mortality advantage has been decreasing. For example, the death rate from cardiovascular disease declined among men in the late twentieth century but stayed about the same in women (Rodin & Ickovics, 1990); death from cardiovascular disease is more common among African American women than white women (Casper et al., 2000).

What are some of the possible reasons for the differences in mortality and morbidity rates in men and women? From a biological vantage point it might be that women have some mechanism that protects them from some life-threatening diseases. Data from epidemiological and observational studies have suggested that estrogen may offer protection from cardiovascular disease, for example. Based on this evidence, many women began hormone replacement therapy following menopause in an attempt to reduce the risk of cardiovascular disease. However, with respect to one type of cardiovascular disease, data from the first (and, to date only) randomized clinical trial of hormone replacement therapy for postmenopausal women, called the Heart and Estrogen/Progestin Replacement Study (HERS), failed to find a reduced risk for CHD among women receiving hormone replacement therapy (Hulley et al., 1998). Additional studies need to be conducted to ascertain what, if any, protective effects estrogen may have for reducing the risk of CHD among women.

From a psychological viewpoint, some evidence suggests that women are less likely than men to be Type A personalities and are also less hostile than men (Waldron, 1976; Weidner & Collins, 1993). Eisler and Blalock (1991) hypothesize that the Type A pattern is part and parcel of a rigid commitment to the traditional masculine gender role, which emphasizes achievement, mastery, competitiveness, not asking for help or emotional support, an excessive need for control, and the tendency to become angry and to express anger when frustrated. They link these attributes to the tendency for men to be more prone to coronary problems and other stress-related health risks, such as hypertension (Harrison, Chin, & Ficarrotto, 1989).

Increasing evidence, however, indicates that anger is not necessarily more commonly experienced and expressed by men (e.g., Kring, 2000; Lavoie et al., 2001). Moreover, increased hostility and both the suppression and expression of anger are associated with risk factors for CHD among women (Matthews et al., 1998; Rutledge et al., 2001). In addition, anxiety and depression are more common among women than men (see Chapters 6 and 10) and are also linked to cardiovascular disease. Thus, many questions remain about the role of these psychological variables in differences between the mortality from cardiovascular disease in men and women.

Another question concerns why the gap between mortality rates in men and women is decreasing. In the early twentieth century most deaths were due to epidemics and infection, but now most deaths result from diseases that are affected by lifestyle. One possibility, then, is that lifestyle differences between men and women account for the sex difference in mortality and that these lifestyle differences are decreasing. Men smoke more than women and consume more alcohol. These differences are likely contributors to men's higher mortality from cardiovascular disease and lung cancer. In recent years, however, women have begun to smoke and drink more, and these changes have been paralleled by increases in lung cancer and the failure of the mortality rate for cardiovascular disease to decrease among women (Rodin & Ickovics, 1990).

Other explanations focus on the identification and treatment of disease in women. For example, even though cardiovascular disease is the number one killer of women, there is still a widespread belief that men should be more concerned with heart disease than women. In addition, women are less likely to be referred to a cardiovascular rehabilitation program following a heart attack, perhaps contributing to their persistent rates of mortality (Abbey & Stewart, 2000).

There are several possible explanations for the difference in morbidity of men and women. First, because women live longer than men, they may be more likely to experience several diseases that are associated with aging. Second, women may be more attentive to their health than are men and thus may be more likely to visit physicians and be diagnosed. Third, women are exposed to more stress than men and they rate stress as having a greater impact on them, particularly as it concerns major life events (Davis, Matthews & Twamley, 1999). Fourth, physicians tend to treat women's health concerns and complaints less seriously than men's concerns (e.g., Weisman & Teitelbaum, 1985). Finally, evidence indicates that women's morbidity differs depending on sociodemographic variables, such as income, education, and ethnicity. For example, having more education and a higher income are associated with fewer risk factors for cardiovascular disease, including obesity, smoking, hypertension, and reduced amounts of exercise. In the United States, women unfortunately tend to have lower income than men. However, even after controlling for differences in income level and education, a recent study found that Mexican American and African American women still had a greater likelihood of having more risk factors for CHD than men (Winkleby et al., 1999).

The gathering of scientific data on how best to minimize women's risk for a number of illnesses has likely been compromised by the tendency to exclude women from research studies. Women have been understudied in research on health and stress (Rodin & Ickovics, 1990; Taylor et al., 2000). Not only have women been excluded from studies, but much research has assumed that men and women respond similarly to stress and thus may have similar stress-related health problems. Taylor and her colleagues have called this assumption into question and propose that women may respond differently to stress, both behaviorally and biologically (Taylor et al., 2000). Future studies need to include equal samples of men and women, to consider that men and women may respond to stress differently, and to focus on the special health concerns of women. The Women's Health Initiative represents a promising step in this direction. Beginning in 1992, it is a fifteen-year study of an ethnically diverse sample of more than 200,000 women. One part of the project is evaluating preventive interventions such as a low-fat diet and hormone-replacement therapy for osteoporosis, coronary heart disease, and cancer. Other parts of the investigation include examining why women with low socioeconomic status are at high risk for various diseases and studying psychosocial factors such as life stress and personality that increase risk for these diseases (Matthews et al., 1997; WHI study group, 1998).

Socioeconomic Status, Ethnicity, and Health

Low socioeconomic status (SES) is associated with higher rates of health problems and mortality from all causes. A number of explanations have been proposed for the correlation between SES and poor health and mortality, but many of these are still in need of empirical support. Recent research attempts to chart the pathways between health and SES, encompassing economic, societal, relationship, individual, and biological factors. For example, one pathway to poor health among individuals in lower social classes has to do with environmental factors that reinforce poor health behaviors. Poorer neighborhoods often have high numbers of liquor stores, grocery stores offering fewer healthy food choices, and fewer opportunities for exercise at health clubs. Given these environmental constraints, it is perhaps not surprising to learn that people in lower social classes are more likely than people in higher classes to engage in behaviors that increase risk for disease, such as smoking, eating a high-fat diet, and drinking more alcohol (Lantz et al., 1998).

Other pathways include limited access to health services and greater exposure to stressors. Recall our earlier discussion of allostatic load, the bodily effects of repeated and chronic stress. In a longitudinal study, Singer and Ryff (1999) found that the most economically disadvantaged individuals had the highest allostatic load. These investigators also found that, regardless of SES, individuals who reported having poor relationships with parents or negative relationships with spouses had a higher allostatic load than individuals with positive parental and spousal relationships. Not surprisingly, the combined effect of lower SES and negative relationships had the highest effect on allostatic load. These findings indicate that lower SES is a likely source of chronic stress that impacts the body. Moreover, these findings illustrate the complicated relationship between individual, social, and economic factors and health.

Certainly discrimination and prejudice are likely sources of chronic stress, and these abhorrent social conditions continue to affect people of color as well as people from lower social classes. Since people of color are found in high numbers among the lower social classes, ethnicity has also been a feature of research into the relationship of SES to health. Consider, for example, that the mortality rate for African Americans is nearly two times as high as it is for whites in the United States (Williams, 1999). Why might this be? The reasons are complex and not completely understood. Some research suggests that certain risk factors for disease are more common in people of color. For example, risk factors for cardiovascular disease (such as smoking, obesity, hypertension, and reduced exercise) are higher among women from ethnic minorities than among white women. This finding holds even when members of the two groups are comparable in socioeconomic status (Winkleby et al., 1998). The increased prevalence of some of these risk factors shows up in studies of children as young as six to nine years of age. For example, African American and Mexican American girls in this age range have higher body-mass indexes and higher fat intake than do non-Hispanic white girls (Winkleby et al., 1999). Other studies have found that increased stress associated with discrimination is linked to cardiovascular reactivity among African American women (Guyll, Matthews, & Bromberger, 2001). Consideration of social class at multiple levels, including the individual, family, and neighborhood, is also important. For example, lower family SES and neighborhood SES were found to be associated with greater cardiovascular reactivity for African American children and adolescents, but only lower family SES was associated with greater cardiovascular reactivity among white children and adolescents (Gump et al., 1999). In sum, both social class and ethnicity are clearly very important factors in health.

Ethnicity is also a variable of importance in how people cope with cancer. The race of a person with cancer is associated with detection of illness, adherence to treatment regimens, survival, and quality of life. These relationships were examined in a review by Meyerowitz et al. (1998). Among the many findings based on data from the National Cancer Institute:

- African Americans have the highest rates of cancer overall, as a result of very high rates of lung and prostate cancer among men.
- Although African American women have lower breast cancer rates than do white women, their mortality rates five years after diagnosis are the same because their survival rates are lower.
- Latinos have low rates of cancer in general, but high rates of cervical cancer. Asian Americans have low rates for all cancers except stomach cancer.

These and other findings are illustrative of ethnic differences in the incidence and outcomes of cancer. What might account for these differences? The answers appear to lie less with racial and biological factors than with social and psychological factors such as access to and willingness to seek out medical care (e.g., Bach et al., 2002).[1]

As one might expect, the ability to afford skilled health care is not uniformly found across ethnic and socioeconomic lines. Based on their review, Meyerowitz et al. argue that ethnicity may affect detection of illness, survival, and quality of life by virtue of socioeconomic status and knowledge about and attitudes toward the detection and treatment of cancer. For example, African Americans who are poor are not likely to have health insurance and therefore have less access to health care than do those who come from the middle classes; they tend to have less information on steps to take to detect the illness (e.g., breast self-examination), and then, if a potential problem is detected, they may delay seeing a physician for financial reasons (though in general African American women are more likely than white women to get Pap smears and just as likely to have mammogram screenings). Cultural beliefs about cancer are also relevant. For example, thinking that chiropractic is an effective treatment or believing that cancer is spread through the air are predictors of advanced-stage breast cancer (Lannin et al., 1998).

When it comes to quality of life after cancer treatment, research is much more difficult because cultural and other factors enter into how a person gauges his or her quality of life. Such factors also influence whether impending death is seen as a catastrophic event or as an event that is accepted fatalistically and that provides an opportunity to live a meaningful and even joyous life in the time remaining.[2] Whether a person views his or her life as good, indeed even as worth living, varies from group to group, from person to

---

[1] Of course, biological factors, including genetic factors, have to be taken into consideration, and some of these variables may be linked to race. As Meyerowitz et al. (1998) point out, for example, African American women have a higher incidence of a particularly lethal type of tumor than do white women (Stanford & Greenberg, 1989). However, there is mounting evidence that when biological differences exist in the incidence of illness, they are sometimes a function of (mediated by) behavioral variables (Anderson, Kiecolt-Glaser, & Glaser, 1994). For example, as Asians living in the United States have adopted the eating habits of Americans, their previously low cancer rates have risen to levels comparable to those of non-Hispanic whites (Whittemore et al., 1990). Thus, being Japanese per se appears not to be important; rather, it is the diet (and perhaps also the general lifestyle) that affects rates of illness.

[2] In the late 1980s, a patient of one of us reported that he had just been diagnosed as HIV positive. After several weeks of desperation, regret, and depression, he decided that rather than wait to die, he was going to live. This is what he did, and no doubt thanks to the new drugs available in the past few years, he is not only still alive but working hard and making a good deal of money.

person. Across ethnic groups, it seems that people of color are more accepting of death as a part of life, and that the notion of fighting cancer fits less well into their worldview, than is the case for white people (Mathews et al., 1994; Meyerowitz et al., 1998). For people who don't see dying as something to be avoided at all costs, the quality of life is likely to be higher if they are afflicted with a terminal illness.

Therapies for Psychophysiological Disorders

Since psychophysiological disorders are true physical dysfunctions, sound psychotherapeutic practice calls for close consultation with a physician. Whether high blood pressure is biologically caused or, as in essential hypertension, linked to psychological stress, a number of medications can reduce it. Asthma attacks can also be alleviated by medications, taken either by inhalation or injection, that dilate the bronchial tubes. The help drugs provide in ameliorating the damage and discomfort in the particular bodily systems cannot be underestimated. They are frequently lifesaving. Mental health and medical professionals recognize, however, that most drug interventions treat only the symptoms; they do not address the fact that the person is reacting emotionally to psychological stress. Although the evidence suggests that the predisposition for breakdown of a particular organ is inherited, or at least somatically based, the importance of how a person responds psychologically nevertheless indicates that psychotherapeutic interventions are necessary.

Therapists of all persuasions agree that reducing anxiety, depression, or anger is the best way to alleviate suffering from psychophysiological disorders. The particular disorder—essential hypertension, coronary heart disease, or asthma—is considered to be adversely affected, if not actually caused, by these emotions.

Psychoanalytically oriented therapists employ techniques such as free association and dream analysis, as they do with other patients experiencing anxiety, to help people confront the infantile origins of their fears. Ego analysts, such as Franz Alexander, believe that emotional states underlie the several disorders. Thus they encourage patients with essential hypertension, viewed as laboring under a burden of undischarged anger, to assert themselves and thereby release their anger.

Behavioral and cognitive therapists employ their usual range of procedures for reducing anxiety and anger—systematic desensitization, in vivo exposure, rational-emotive therapy, and assertion training—depending on the source of tension. For example, relaxation training has been used successfully to help asthmatic children exhale more fully (Lehrer et al., 1994; Smyth et al., 1998). Behavior rehearsal and shaping may help people learn to react in difficult situations with less emotional upset.

We turn now to an examination of several areas in which clinicians in the fields of behavioral medicine and health psychology have brought psychological perspectives and interventions to bear on the problem of helping people deal with medical illnesses.

Treating Hypertension and Reducing CHD Risk

Before the advent of effective drugs for treating hypertension in the late 1950s, advice from physicians was basically to "take it easy," lose weight, and restrict salt intake—all reasonably helpful measures. It is noteworthy that simple verbal reassurance was also considered important and was even demonstrated to be helpful in an early study by Reiser et al. (1950), in which non-psychiatrically trained internists (physicians specializing in internal medicine, which includes the diagnosis and treatment of hypertension) provided what we today call non-specific supportive psychotherapy. Clinically significant reductions in blood pressure were observed after two years of regular albeit not frequent contact.

The advent of effective drugs to lower blood pressure shifted the direction of treatment strongly toward their use from the 1960s onward. But over time the undesirable side effects of these medications—drowsiness, light-headedness, and in men, erectile difficulties—as well as the growth of behavioral approaches to treatment led many investigators to explore nonpharmacological treatments for borderline essential hypertension.

(Those with more severe hypertension usually have to take drugs to control its deleterious long-term effects [Shapiro, 2001].)

Successful nonpharmacological efforts have been directed at weight reduction, restriction of salt intake, giving up cigarettes, aerobic exercise, and reduction in alcohol consumption. Weight reduction also ameliorates sleep apnea, a sleep disorder discussed more fully in Chapter 16 (p. 547); this is important because blood pressure can be raised to harmful levels when the person's breathing is obstructed during sleep. Losing weight, reducing salt intake, and exercising regularly can also help reduce harmful levels of cholesterol.

Two of three Americans over the age of sixty have high blood pressure, and more than half of them take costly and sometimes risky hypertensive medication (risky because all drugs pose particularly serious risks to older people). As just mentioned, the importance of losing weight and reducing salt intake has been recognized for many years as useful in keeping blood pressure under control, but until recently there was little optimism that diet and weight loss could play a positive role in older adults, who often have had undesirable dietary habits for a lifetime.

A 1998 report from TONE, the controlled Trial of Nonpharmacologic Interventions in the Elderly (Whelton et al., 1998), indicated for the first time that significant benefits can be achieved by people between the ages of sixty and eighty who are obese and who are taking blood-pressure medication. Specifically, half the overweight people in the study who reduced their salt intake by 25 percent and lost as little as eight pounds over the course of three months were able to come off their antihypertensive medications and maintain normal blood pressure. The ability to maintain normal blood pressure was achieved by 31 percent of the patients who reduced their salt intake, 36 percent of those who lost weight, and more than half of those who reduced both their salt intake and their weight. Furthermore, these results—the dietary and weight changes as well as the maintenance of normal blood pressure without medication—lasted for more than three years.

Regular exercise is another avenue for reducing blood pressure that is available to everyone at little or no cost (Shapiro, 2001). Research has shown that increasing exercise through so-called lifestyle activities—for example, walking up stairs rather than using an elevator, and walking short distances rather than driving—yields as much benefit as a structured program of aerobic exercise (e.g., Dunn et al., 1999). Other research (Dengel, Galecki et al., 1998; Dengel, Hagberg et al., 1998) indicates that people with essential hypertension, as well as those whose blood pressure is within the normal range, should adopt regular exercise habits, such as walking briskly most every day for about half an hour or engaging in other aerobic exercise that raises the heart and respiration rates. Most people can engage in such activity without even checking with their physician if the activity is not so strenuous that it prevents them from carrying on a conversation at the same time. In fact, the research suggests that people with high blood pressure and no other health complications should try exercise for about a year before turning to drugs to lower their blood pressure. For those already taking antihypertension drugs, a regular and not necessarily strenuous exercise regimen can sometimes reduce or even eliminate dependence on medication. Decreases of 10 points in both systolic and diastolic blood pressure—a significant figure—can be achieved by most people after just a few weeks. All these beneficial results may be mediated by the favorable effects that exercise has on stress, weight, and blood cholesterol. And if the sense of well-being that accompanies regular exercise and weight loss generalizes to the adoption of other health-enhancing habits, such as stopping smoking and avoiding drinking to excess, the positive effects on blood pressure will be all the stronger and more enduring.

Another psychological approach has been to teach hypertensive individuals to lower sympathetic nervous system arousal, primarily via training in muscle relaxation, occasionally supplemented by biofeedback (Blanchard, 1994). Results have been mixed (Kaufmann et al., 1988), and it is unclear how enduring the effects of relaxation treatment are (Patel et al., 1985). The success of this approach probably depends ultimately on whether the person maintains the acquired skill to relax, and that in turn depends on whether the person remains motivated to practice that skill.

Exercise, such as walking briskly, can help to reduce blood pressure.

DeQuattro and Davison (Lee et al., 1987) found that intensive relaxation, conducted in weekly sessions over two months and using at-home practice with audiotaped instructions, significantly reduced blood pressure immediately following treatment in borderline hypertensive people, more so than did a control condition that included state-of-the-art medical advice and instructions concerning diet, weight loss, and other known risk factors. (The relaxation group also received the same medical information as the control participants.) Furthermore, these effects were stronger among hypertensive people previously found to have high sympathetic arousal than among those with lower arousal levels. This result supports the hypothesis of Esler et al. (1977) that there is a subset of hypertensive individuals with relatively high resting levels of sympathetic arousal who may be especially well suited for sympathetic-dampening therapies, such as relaxation.

Evidence suggesting the importance of cognitive change as well as the role of anger was reported by Davison, et al. (1991). Borderline hypertensive patients who achieved significant reductions in anger as expressed in their articulated thoughts (see p. 96) showed decreases in blood pressure—as their articulated thoughts became less angry, their blood pressure became lower. This finding is consistent with research linking anger with hypertension.

The recognition that cognition is probably a factor in hypertension has led to increased interest in cognitive-behavioral approaches to lower blood pressure. A study from Nigeria, for example, reports that adding rational-emotive therapy to blood pressure–lowering medication led to significantly greater reductions in systolic blood pressure than did drugs alone (Oluwatelure, 1997).

Exercising regularly can also reduce mortality from cardiovascular disease (Blumenthal et al., 2002; Wannamethee, Shaper, & Walker, 1998). A recent study compared a stress-management intervention with an exercise intervention for men who had a history of CHD (Blumenthal et al., 2002). Patients were randomly assigned to either a weekly stress-management group, an aerobic exercise group, or a no treatment group. The interventions lasted for four months. These men were followed up five years after the intervention, and the findings revealed that the men who received stress-management training or exercise were significantly less likely to have had another cardiac problem than the men who did not receive treatment.

Although the results just reviewed are promising, many studies have failed to find significant and enduring effects from relaxation training and other stress-management procedures (Johnston et al., 1993). One reason for negative findings may be that participants are inadequately trained in relaxation as well as inadequately motivated to apply it in their everyday lives. Another reason may relate to the Davison et al. findings just described: relaxation may work best or even only with people whose sympathetic nervous system arousal levels are particularly high, and these elevated levels may indicate high stress. Consistent with this hypothesis are results from a study that found strong effects from relaxation in hypertensive elderly African American men (Schneider et al., 1995). These participants came from poor neighborhoods where life was difficult. Perhaps these high-stress living conditions create hypertension that is more related to stress than is the hypertension studied in most research, which typically involves participants who are white and better off financially. In any case, continued research in this vein appears useful and promising (Johnston, 1997).

Focus on Discovery 8.1 describes a major effort to prevent cardiovascular disease.

Biofeedback

All learning depends on feedback, that is, knowledge of the consequences of our actions guides our behavior. So the notion that feedback affects what we think, feel, and do is not at all remarkable. What is noteworthy about what is called **biofeedback** is that people can acquire control over behaviors commonly regarded as not being under voluntary control, such as heart rate and skin temperature, if the means are created to provide them with feedback about such behavior. Thus, to teach a person to raise her skin temperature, we need to be able to let her know whether her skin temperature is increasing, feedback that is normally not available to the person (Gatchel, 2001).

Community Psychology—Preventing Cardiovascular Diseases

Up to this point, most of our discussions of therapy have focused on situations in which professionals make themselves available to clients in offices, clinics, or hospitals. This type of service delivery, referred to as the waiting mode (Rappaport & Chinsky, 1974), is characteristic of traditional therapy, whether inpatient or outpatient. **Community psychology**, in contrast, operates in the seeking mode; community psychologists, rather than waiting for people to initiate contact, seek out problems, or even potential problems. In addition, community psychologists often focus on prevention, in contrast to the more usual situation of trying to reduce the severity or duration of an already existing problem. Here we describe a program aimed at the prevention of cardiovascular disease.

Using Mass Media to Reduce Cardiovascular Disease

The risk of premature cardiovascular diseases is increased by the lifestyle of an affluent, industrialized society—little need for physical exertion and plenty of high-calorie foods rich in fat. One way to try to change harmful lifestyles is to use the mass media to inform people of what they can do to reduce their risks for such illnesses (Altman & Goodman, 2001).

A group of researchers in the Stanford Heart Disease Prevention Program, led by Nathan Maccoby (Maccoby & Altman, 1988), a psychologist noted for his work in communications, undertook such a task. For the Three Communities Project, they chose a media campaign and a direct, intensive, instructional program.

Three towns in northern California were the subjects of their investigation. Watsonville and Gilroy were the two experimental towns, and Tracy was the control town. For two years both experimental towns were bombarded by a mass-media campaign to inform citizens about cardiovascular diseases. The campaign consisted of television and radio spots, weekly newspaper columns, and newspaper advertisements and stories urging people to stop smoking, exercise more, and eat foods low in cholesterol. Posters in buses and in stores conveyed briefly and graphically such vital information as the desirability of eating fewer eggs, since yolks are rich in cholesterol. In addition, a sample of Watsonville residents at high risk for heart disease received intensive instruction in group sessions and individual home counseling over a ten-week period. The researchers wanted to examine whether information (e.g., how to select and prepare foods low in fat and cholesterol) and exhortations to alter lifestyle delivered face-to-face might add to whatever positive benefits derived from the mass-media campaign.

The control town, Tracy, had media services that were quite different from those of the two experimental towns. Tracy is separated from Watsonville and Gilroy by a range of low mountains and therefore, at the time, had entirely separate local television stations. The inhabitants of Tracy were not, of course, imprisoned in their hometown for the duration of the two-year study, but for the most part they did not receive through their media the messages that were conveyed to the citizens of the two experimental towns. Because all three towns had a sizable Spanish-speaking population, all media messages were in Spanish as well as in English.

The findings revealed that citizens of Watsonville and Gilroy significantly increased their knowledge of cardiovascular risk factors; people in the control town did not gain in such knowledge. Egg consumption was reduced more in Watsonville and Gilroy than in Tracy, and clinically significant decreases in blood pressure were observed in the two experimental towns, in contrast with small increases in the control town. The high-risk residents of Watsonville who participated in the special intensive-instruction program reaped even greater benefits in lower egg consumption and blood pressure. Finally, the researchers considered the townspeople's overall measure of risk, a weighted aver-

A visit to the commercial exhibit area of any psychological or psychiatric convention will reveal a plentiful display of complex biofeedback apparatuses that provide such information. By using sensitive instrumentation, biofeedback gives prompt and exact information, otherwise unavailable, on muscle activity, brain waves, skin temperature, heart rate, blood pressure, and other bodily functions. As already suggested, it is assumed—and has been frequently demonstrated (Gatchel, 2001)—that a person can achieve greater voluntary control over these phenomena, most of which were once considered under involuntary control. The key is that the person know immediately, through an auditory or visual signal, whether the somatic activity of interest is increasing or decreasing.

Because anxiety has generally been viewed as a state involving the autonomic (involuntary) nervous system, and because psychophysiological disorders often afflict organs innervated by this system, researchers and clinicians have been intrigued by biofeedback. For a time, biofeedback was virtually synonymous with behavioral medicine.

In a series of classic studies at Harvard Medical School, Shapiro, Tursky, and Schwartz (1970; Schwartz, 1973) demonstrated that human volunteers could achieve significant short-term changes in blood pressure and heart rate. They found that some people could even be trained to increase their heart rate while decreasing their blood pressure.

age of the several known physical risk factors—high blood levels of cholesterol, smoking cigarettes, and not exercising enough. They found highly significant drops in risk in the people in the experimental towns, an important result, since we know from previous research that elevated risk scores predict reasonably well the incidence of heart disease over a twelve-year period.

These positive findings led to a more ambitious and larger-scale program called the Stanford Five City Project, which extended face-to-face instructional programs to a variety of community settings, such as schools, community colleges, hospitals, and work sites, and involved many more people across a broader age range. An important goal was to embed the educational programs in existing community organizations so that any beneficial effects might persist well after the researchers had left the scene (Altman, Flora, & Farquhar, 1986). Dependent measures included actual illness and death from cardiovascular diseases. Begun in 1978 and continuing well into the 1990s, results support the efficacy of the interventions in significantly reducing several risk factors, including cigarette smoking, elevated cholesterol levels, low levels of physical activity, and high blood pressure (Farquhar, 1991; Farquhar, Fortmann, Flora, Taylor, et al., 1990; Jackson et al., 1991; Maccoby & Altman, 1988; Schooler, Flora, & Farquhar, 1993).

A community psychology approach to stress management focuses on the environment rather than on the person. To reduce stress, an office can be redesigned with partitions to provide some privacy for employees.

The work of the Stanford group and similar projects in Finland (Tuomilehto et al., 1986) and South Africa (Farquhar, Fortmann, Flora, & Maccoby, 1990) are important as community psychology efforts for they demonstrate that people can learn from properly designed and delivered mass media and other large-scale educational programs how to reduce their overall risk for cardiovascular diseases. The multiyear span of these studies is considerable and highly unusual as far as experiments in psychology are concerned. But in terms of the serious health problems that can develop through certain long-standing detrimental behavior patterns, five or ten or more years is not a very long time at all.

There is great potential for such community-based programs to reduce the incidence and seriousness of many medical illnesses beyond what is achievable by strictly medical practices, for it is increasingly accepted that people's physical health is primarily in their own hands and that changing lifestyle practices is often the best means of reducing the risk of illness (Bandura, 1986). However, such efforts are up against a formidable counterforce, namely, the vigorous promotion of unhealthy food, alcohol, and other negative lifestyle factors, which is much more prevalent than the promotion of healthful changes in behavior (Altman & Goodman, 2001).

Achievement of this fine-grained control lent impetus to biofeedback work with human beings and awakened hope that certain clinical disorders might be alleviated in this new way.

Research using biofeedback to treat patients with essential hypertension has been somewhat encouraging, but results have not been certain enough to establish biofeedback as a standard treatment for the disease (Blanchard, 1994). Moreover, several investigators believe that relaxation training, which is often given along with biofeedback, does more than the biofeedback to reduce blood pressure (Emmelkamp, 1986; Reed, Katkin, & Goldband, 1986).

Tension headaches, believed to be caused by excessive and persistent tension in the frontalis muscles of the forehead and in the muscles of the neck, have also been handled within this framework; the standard treatment entails feedback of tension in the frontalis muscles. Although such biofeedback has indeed been shown to be effective (e.g., Birbaumer, 1977), some studies suggest that cognitive factors may play a role. For example, in a classic study, Holroyd et al. (1984) found that *believing* that one was reducing frontalis tension via biofeedback was associated with reductions in tension headaches, whether or not such reductions were actually being achieved. Enhanced feelings of self-efficacy and internal control appear to have inherent stress-reducing properties, a theme encountered in the discussion of control and anxiety in Chapter 6. Biofeedback may strengthen the sense of control, thus reducing general anxiety levels and ultimately reducing tension headaches (Bandura, 1997). Other studies (e.g., Blanchard et al., 1982) suggest that relaxation per se is the critical variable. Similar conclusions have recently been drawn about biofeedback in the treatment of migraine headache (Compas et al., 1997), although biofeedback may confer some specific benefits above and beyond the benefits of relaxation (Scharff, Marcus, & Masek, 2000).

There is overall little evidence that biofeedback has any specific effects other than distraction, relaxation, and instilling a beneficial sense of control. In addition, clinicians must remain mindful of the complexities of human problems. A person with high blood pressure, for example, might have to alter a tense, driven lifestyle before he or she can significantly reduce blood pressure through biofeedback. It is unwise, and a sign of naive clinical practice, to assume that one technique focused on a specific malfunction or problem will invariably cure the patient.

Reducing Anger and Hostility, Depression, and Social Isolation

Reducing anger and hostility has been a focus of behavioral medicine interventions for many years, especially in hypertension and heart disease. The reason is straightforward: Excessive anger and hostility, as explained earlier in this chapter, have been implicated as risk factors in these illnesses. This relationship was highlighted in research on the Type A behavior pattern. These studies generally involved men who had suffered a myocardial infarction (heart attack), and the focus was on reducing the likelihood that they would have a second one. One of the most comprehensive of these studies was the Recurrent Coronary Prevention Project (Friedman et al., 1982), which served as a model for later research.

In this study participants practiced talking more slowly and listening to others more closely. They attempted to reduce the demands placed on them so they could relax more and, in general, take a less time-pressured and less hostile approach to everyday challenges. In addition to the behavioral changes, participants were encouraged to ease up on the demanding beliefs identified as common among Type A's—the tendency to perceive events as direct personal threats and to believe that the intensity of Type A behavior is essential to success.

This study found that Type A behavior can be changed. After three years of treatment, men who had received Type A counseling had cut their risk of a second heart attack almost in half. Their risk was 7.2 percent annually, compared with 13.2 percent for Type A men who received only cardiological counseling (Friedman et al., 1984; Friedman & Ulmer, 1984; Powell et al., 1984; Thoresen et al., 1985). Reductions in hostility may have been particularly significant, consistent with its increasing importance in Type A research and in psychophysiological disorders generally (Haaga, 1987b).

In recent years, focus has shifted away from Type A to other psychological targets, most especially to hostility (Williams, 2001) and to the desirability of teaching people to, in general, lead more healthful and less stress-laden lives. Attention to anger and hostility has been expanded to include depression and social isolation, also discovered to be risk factors in cardiovascular disease as well as other illnesses. A noteworthy effort to address these issues is a six-session workshop package called the LifeSkills system (V. P. Williams & R. B. Williams, 1997). The components of this treatment package include a number of tried-and-true interventions, such as learning to control negative thinking (cf. Beck and Ellis), communicating clearly with others, empathizing with others, using problem-solving techniques, asserting oneself, and finding ways to increase positive events in one's life. Early reports suggest that this workshop package lessens depression, anger and hostility, and social isolation (Williams, 2001). (See Focus on Discovery 8.2 for a discussion of coping with cancer.)

Stress Management

Stress management is a set of techniques for helping people who are seldom labeled as patients (e.g., hospital personnel, factory workers, students) to cope with the challenges that life poses for all of us. The increasing recognition of the role of stress in a variety of medical illnesses, including diseases affected by immune-system dysfunction, has added impetus to stress management as a strategy for reducing stress-related deficits in the functioning of the immune system (Zakowski, Hall, & Baum, 1992). Stress management has also been used successfully for several other diseases, including tension headaches, cancer, hypertension, coronary artery and heart disease, and, as discussed later, chronic pain (Antoni et al., 2000; Smith, 2000). In recent years stress management has also found its way into high schools, where the pressure for many high-achieving students to excel and gain admission to the top colleges has become worrisome to both parents and teachers (Kelleher, Mathews, & Ritsch, 2002).

Stress management encompasses a variety of techniques, and more than one is typically used in any given instance (Davison & Thompson, 1988; Lehrer & Woolfolk, 1993; Steptoe, 1997).

- *Arousal reduction.* In arousal reduction the person is trained in muscle relaxation, sometimes assisted by biofeedback. Although the evidence is unclear as to the need to use the complex instrumentation required for proper biofeedback, there is confirmation that teaching people to relax deeply and to apply these skills to real-life stressors can be helpful in lowering their stress levels. There is also evidence that the immune function can be improved by relaxation training (Jasnoski & Kugler, 1987; Kiecolt-Glaser et al., 1985), although enduring benefits are doubtful unless relaxation is practiced regularly over a long period of time (Davison & Thompson, 1988; Goldfried & Davison, 1994; Zakowski et al., 1992). Because stress itself can be seen as a reaction to situations perceived by the person as unpredictable, uncontrollable, or both, relaxation training may confer its benefits by virtue of enhancing the individual's sense of self-efficacy, the belief that one is not merely a pawn at the mercy of uncontrollable forces that are not always benign (Bandura, 1997).

- *Cognitive restructuring.* Included under cognitive restructuring are approaches such as those of Albert Ellis (1962) and Aaron Beck (1976). The focus is on altering people's belief systems and improving the clarity of their logical interpretations of experience on the assumption that people's intellectual capacities can affect how they feel and behave. Providing information to reduce uncertainty and enhance people's sense of control, a theme from Chapter 6, has also been helpful in reducing stress. Promising findings have been reported for various stress-related problems, including genital herpes lesions (McLarnon & Kaloupek, 1988) and recovery from surgery (Johnston & Voegele, 1993).

- *Behavioral-skills training.* Because it is natural to feel overwhelmed if one lacks the skills to execute a challenging task, stress management often includes instruction and practice in necessary skills as well as in general issues such as time management and effective prioritizing. Included also under this rubric is training in assertion skills, expressing likes and dislikes without encroaching on the rights of others (see p. 52).

- *Environmental-change approaches.* Whereas the other individual strategies aim at helping the person deal with a particular environment, one can also take the position that sometimes the environment is the problem and that change is best directed at altering it. One kind of environmental approach draws on research mentioned earlier in this chapter (p. 204) on the positive role of social support on health. If social support helps keep people healthy or helps them cope with illnesses, then it is reasonable to assume that enhancing such support can contribute to better functioning. Another kind of environmental change involves the workplace. Altering management practices or providing greater privacy and fewer interruptions can reduce the stress-producing characteristics of the world in which people work and live for a significant portion of their waking hours (Murphy et al., 1995).

The Management of Pain

Like anxiety, pain can be adaptive. People with a congenital inability to feel pain are at an extreme disadvantage, indeed, are at serious risk for injury. Our concern here is with pain that is maladaptive, pain that is out of proportion to the situation and unduly

Coping with Cancer

A growing body of evidence indicates that interventions that alleviate anxiety and depression and foster a fighting spirit can help people cope with cancer (Stolbach et al., 1988; Smith, 2000; Telch & Telch, 1986). (Focus on Discovery 8.3 describes such work with children.) A nonpassive attitude may even enhance the capacity to survive cancer (Greer, Morris, & Pettigale, 1979).

An optimistic, upbeat attitude is important in combating illness, including illnesses as serious as cancer (Carver et al., 1993) and HIV-positive status (Taylor et al., 1992). The mechanism by which an optimistic attitude helps people with life-threatening illnesses may be its link to adaptive coping. Optimistic people—for instance, people with high levels of self-efficacy (Bandura, 1997)—may be more likely to engage in risk-reducing health behaviors such as avoiding risky sex or engaging in prescribed regular exercise following coronary-bypass surgery (Scheier & Carver, 1987).

Psychological Interventions to Help People Cope

A startling report from researchers at Stanford Medical School indicated that the quality of life and even the survival time of patients with terminal cancer might be improved by psychosocial interventions. Patients with metastatic breast cancer participated in weekly supportive group therapy, where they offered understanding and comfort to each other, openly discussed death and dying, expressed their feelings, and encouraged each other to live life as fully as possible in the face of death. They also came to have improved communication with family and learned self-hypnosis techniques to control pain and reduce fatigue, anxiety, and depression (Spiegel, Bloom, & Yalom, 1981). A ten-year follow-up found that this one-year supportive-group intervention actually prolonged survival time. Compared with control-group patients, the group-therapy patients lived twice as long (Spiegel, 1990; Spiegel et al., 1989). *

Speculating about these survival findings—which were not expected and were not a discussion topic for the group therapy—Spiegel and his associates suggested that perhaps the therapy helped patients better comply with medical treatment or improved their appetite and diet by enhancing their mood. Ability to control pain might also have helped them be more physically active. And, consistent with research reviewed earlier on how stress affects the immune system, the therapy might have improved immune function by reducing stress, with social support a key factor (House, Landis, & Umberson, 1988; Levy et al., 1990). Unfortunately, the Stanford group's promising findings on longer survival have not been replicated

by some independent research teams, although the supportive group therapy does seem to improve mood (e.g., Goodwin et al., 2001).

Problem-solving therapy (PST) has shown its value in helping cancer patients cope with the myriad life challenges facing them, from daily hassles to dealing with isolation and depression (Nezu et al., 1997). An important component of PST (and of other approaches that can help cancer patients) is the enhanced sense of control that the patient learns to exercise. It would seem that such control is particularly important for people with a life-threatening illness who are experiencing the side effects of treatment. PST has also been shown to be helpful for caregivers, who have to cope with the patient's many cancer-related problems, such as fatigue and hair loss (Bucher et al.,1999).

The stressfulness of a cancer diagnosis and its treatment makes relevant the kind of stress-management approaches described earlier. Found to be helpful in reducing anxiety both prior to and following various cancer treatments is clear information about the procedures themselves, including what the patient will likely experience during and following them, as well as training in relaxation and hypnosis (Wallace, Priestman, Dunn, & Priestman, 1993). One kind of information that is especially important is that fatigue is a *natural* accompaniment to many treatments for cancer, especially radiation and chemotherapy. Recognizing that fatigue is a normal side effect from treatment can spare the patient and family from concluding that there is a problem with depression (Andersen, Golden-Kreutz, and DiLillo, 2001), although, to be sure, cancer patients can be prone to bouts of depression as well. Another side effect is conditioned food aversions induced by association of the food with nausea from chemotherapy or radiation (see Chambers & Bernstein, 1995; recall earlier discussion on p. 139). These aversions can lead to weight loss as well as to a general sense that one's quality of life has suffered (Andersen et al., 2001).

A concern for men is prostate cancer. The prostate is a small gland surrounding the urethra, the tube that carries urine from the bladder through the penis and outside the body. It is usually surgically excised if cancer is discovered in it. However, since this type of cancer grows slowly, some older men elect not to have the surgery because it is likely that they will die from other causes before the prostate cancer is advanced enough to kill them and, more important, because removal of the prostate often has two very negative side effects, marked diminution or loss of erectile capacity and loss of full urinary control. Recent research examining quality-of-life issues in men who have had prostatectomy surgery has found that post-surgery patients rate their quality of life quite high, especially when they are instructed in the use of erectile aids, such as rigid implants (Perez et al., 1997). With the recent availability of Viagra, a medication that can restore erectile function (see p. 473), the prospects are even better for good psychological adjustment following this kind of surgery.

Interventions to Encourage Prevention

Psychological interventions in a community psychology model also focus on preventing cancer by encouraging healthy behaviors and discouraging unhealthy ones. For example, research programs to help people stop smoking are discussed in Chapter 12. Other interventions are aimed at getting women to perform breast self-examination (BSE). The main hurdle to BSE is that examination significantly raises the

---

* When surprising, even startling, findings are published in professional journals, the editor sometimes includes an accompanying comment. With the Spiegel et al. (1989) report, mindful that the results might be regarded as unbelievable, the editor took pains to comment favorably on the methodology and statistical analyses and to suggest that readers adopt an open-minded attitude toward the report, indicating that "the measures described by Spiegel et al. are at least life-enhancing, in stark contrast to the life impoverishment suffered by many terminally ill patients subjected to the vile diets, costly placebos, and exhausting introspections recommended by the more lunatic fringe among alternative practitioners. Other groups should pursue this intellectually honest approach to the psychosocial management of cancer" (Editorial, *The Lancet* October 14, 1989).

probability of an aversive consequence, that is, finding a lump. Logically, it is better to take this risk than not, but the fact is that the fear of learning something unpleasant is a major deterrent to doing the exam (Mahoney, 1977) and many high-risk women (those with first-degree relatives who had breast cancer) do not have regular mammograms (Vogel et al., 1990).

In an effort to develop ways to help women perform BSE regularly, Meyerowitz and Chaiken (1987) compared two pamphlets on BSE. One contained persuasive arguments to conduct BSE while emphasizing the negative consequences of not performing BSE; the other emphasized the positive consequences of performing BSE. Both pamphlets contained factual information about breast cancer and instructions about how to do BSE. In the following examples, words in parentheses were included in the positive condition, those in brackets in the negative.

> By [not] doing BSE now, you (can)[will not] learn what your normal healthy breasts feel like so that you will be (better)[ill] prepared to notice any small, abnormal changes that might occur as you get older.

> Research shows that women who (do) [not do] BSE have (an increased)[a decreased] chance of finding a tumor in the early, more treatable stage of the disease. (p. 504)

The groups given the different pamphlets did not differ in their attitudes toward BSE immediately after reading the pamphlets. However, four months later, women who had received the negatively framed information were more likely to have engaged in BSE. This effect may have occurred because those who do not engage in regular BSE take an ignorance-is-bliss attitude, but the pamphlet's making the possible negative consequences of not doing BSE more salient made doing the exam more acceptable. This finding is particularly important because most pamphlets intended to help women do BSE stress the positive rather than the negative.

Peter Salovey extended this work by asking whether messages of the kind that Meyerowitz and Chaiken found effective in encouraging BSE—sometimes referred to as "loss frame" communications—might under certain circumstances be less effective than messages that emphasize the benefits of a certain behavior (referred to as "gain frame" messages). The results from two experiments suggest that loss-frame communications are superior when people are being encouraged in detection health behaviors and gain-frame communications are better when people are being encouraged in preventive health behaviors (Rothman & Salovey, 1997).

What is the difference? BSE and mammography are detection behaviors. The person lacks information about whether she has an illness and has to decide whether to engage in behavior that could provide information on her status, in this case, whether she might have breast cancer. This was what Meyerowitz and Chaiken studied. In contrast, a person going to the beach has a choice about putting on sunscreen with a protection factor of 15 or greater, the strength recommended to reduce the chances of getting skin cancer down the line. Such

behavior is preventive in nature, that is, it is designed to have a direct effect on reducing the chances of getting skin cancer.

In a study by Banks, Salovey et al. (1995), the findings of Meyerowitz and Chaiken were replicated. Women told of the risks arising from not taking a mammography exam—the loss-frame approach—were more likely to have a mammogram than were women told of the benefits of doing so. In a later study by Detweiler and Salovey (1999), sunbathers at a beach who were told of the benefits of using sunscreen—a gain-frame communication—were more likely to use sunscreen after reading a communication that emphasized the benefits of such preventive health behavior than were those who read something that focused on the risks of not using sunscreen.

The implications of these studies are important. If one wants to foster healthful detection behaviors, one should emphasize the risks associated with not taking a certain action that could detect a problem. On the other hand, if one wants to foster health-enhancing preventive behaviors, it is best to emphasize the benefits that arise from doing something that can forestall a problem.

The tendency to believe that ignorance is bliss, that not knowing will somehow prevent cancer from occurring, is clearly irrational. Research by Lerman and her colleagues (Lerman & Glanz, 1997) highlights the importance of these nonrational factors in determining whether people engage in practices to promote health and avoid illness. Women who believe that they are at high risk for ovarian cancer—because of family history of an illness that is known to have inherited components—often have the paradoxical response of reducing their adherence to health-promoting practices (Lerman & Schwartz, 1993). Similar findings have been reported for breast-cancer screening (Lerman et al., 1993; Miller, Shoda, & Hurley, 1996).

The distress caused by perceptions of high risk can clearly interfere with rational coping, and one means of reducing this distress seems to be minimizing the perceived danger—a strategy of self-deception that can calm nerves in the short run but that can contribute to serious, long-term negative consequences. Psychological treatment in the form of, for example, breast-cancer risk counseling can reduce these cognitive distortions and enhance health-promoting behaviors by suggesting, for example, that the knowledge that a first-degree relative has breast cancer can serve as an opportunity to take steps to protect one's own health rather than as a sign of unavoidable impending catastrophe (Lerman et al., 1996).

Finally, consider the following. A breast-cancer susceptibility gene, BRCA1, was recently discovered, allowing women to learn if they are at high risk for one form of breast cancer. Yet Lerman et al. (1997) found that more than 40 percent of study participants declined to learn their genetic status. A subsequent study found considerable stress among high-risk women (those who were relatives of women who had earlier tested positive for the gene), confirming how anxiety-provoking such genetic testing can be (Tercyak et al., 2001). As more and more is learned about genetic susceptibilities to disease, people are going to be facing increasingly difficult choices about whether to obtain that information. The ethical implications are profound.

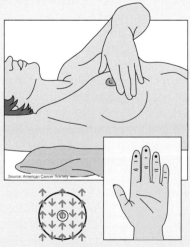

Encouraging women to perform breast self-examination (BSE) can lead to earlier detection of cancer and better treatment outcomes. Shown here is an advertisement from the American Cancer Society demonstrating how to perform BSE

restricts a person's capacity for meaningful and productive living (Davison & Darke, 1991; Morley, 1997).

We know enough about pain to appreciate the fact that there is no one-to-one relationship between a stimulus that is capable of triggering the experience of pain, referred to as *nociceptive stimulation*, and the actual sensation of pain. Soldiers in combat can be wounded by a bullet and yet be so involved in their efforts to survive and inflict harm on the enemy that they do not feel any pain until later. This well-known fact tells us something important about pain even as it hints at ways of controlling it: if one is distracted from a nociceptive stimulus, one may not experience pain, or at least not as much of it, as when one attends to the stimulation (Turk, 2001).

The importance of distraction in controlling pain, both acute and chronic, is consistent with research in experimental cognitive psychology. Each person has only a limited supply of attentional resources, and attention to one channel of input blocks the processing of input in other channels (Cioffi, 1991; Eccleston, 1995; Kahneman, 1973). This human limitation can be seen as a positive benefit when it comes to the experience of pain. In addition to distraction, other factors that reduce pain are lowered anxiety, feelings of optimism and control (Geer et al., 1970), and a sense that what one is engaged in has meaning and purpose (Gatchel, Baum, & Krantz, 1989).

Here are two examples of the use of distraction and refocused attention for controlling pain.

> [A] patient may be taught to construct a vivid mental image which includes features from a number of sensory dimensions, e.g., cutting a lemon and squeezing a drop of the juice onto the tongue. The elaborated sensory features of the image compete with the painful stimulus and reduces its impact.[3] Alternatively the patient may be encouraged to alter the focus of their attention to the pain without switching attention directly away from the pain. In this instance, the subject may be asked to focus on the sensory qualities of the pain and transform it to a less threatening quality. For example, a young man with a severe "shooting" pain was able to reinterpret the sensory quality into an image which included him shooting at goal in a soccer match. As a result of this transformation, the impact of the pain was greatly reduced although its shooting quality remained. (Morley, 1997, p. 236)

Psychologists have contributed to our understanding of both acute and chronic pain. Acute pain is linked to nociception. Chronic pain can evolve from acute pain and refers to pain that is experienced after the time for healing has passed, when there is little reason to assume that nociception is still present. Whatever the specific psychological techniques employed to help alleviate a person's pain, information is always provided as to the nature of pain itself and the reasons the person is experiencing it, including the fact that being in a negative mood can make the pain worse (Morley, 1997).

Acute Pain The importance of a sense of personal control in dealing with acute pain is readily seen in situations in which patients are allowed to administer their own painkillers (with a preset upper limit). This is known as PCA, patient-controlled analgesia. Patients who control the administration of the medication experience greater relief from pain and even use less analgesic medication than do patients who have to ask a nurse for pain medication, which is the more common hospital situation (Morley, 1998; White, 1986).

It is significant that PCA reduces pain even though it requires focusing on the pain, a finding that goes against the well-documented benefits of distraction. Apparently the positive effects of control outweigh the negative consequences of focusing on the pain. Considerable research attests to the beneficial effects of a sense of control: less pain is experienced, mood is better (and thereby pain is less), and people engage in more normal daily activities, all of which enhance a stronger sense of well-being and further reductions in pain (Bandura, 1997).

---

[3] Presumably the patient could do this with an actual lemon, but sometimes it is easier to rely on imagery, sometimes enhanced via a hypnotic induction.

Furthermore, relying on a nurse to administer pain medication also requires the patient to attend to the pain, perhaps even more than when the patient administers the drug. With nurse-administered analgesia the patient learns to wait until the pain is substantial before requesting medication; after making the request, the patient then usually waits until the nurse has time to fulfill it. This system obviously does not enhance distraction from the pain!

Chronic Pain   Chronic pain is the lot of millions of Americans, accounting for billions of dollars of lost work time and incalculable personal and familial suffering (Turk, 2001). Traditional medical treatments seldom help with this kind of pain. To understand chronic pain it is useful to distinguish between pain per se—that is, the perception of nociceptive stimulation (as in acute pain)—and suffering and pain behaviors. Suffering refers to the emotional response to nociception and can be present even in the absence of pain, as when a loved one leaves a person. Pain behaviors refer to observable behaviors associated with pain or suffering; examples include moaning, clenching teeth, irritability, and avoidance of activity (Turk, Wack, & Kerns, 1985).

The treatment of chronic pain focuses on suffering and pain behaviors rather than on whether the person is actually experiencing pain. Patients usually have to be guided to the adoption of realistic goals; a pain-free existence may not be possible. The emphasis is on toughing it out, working through the pain rather than allowing oneself to be incapacitated by it. If handled properly, the result is often increased activity and function, which can sometimes even reduce the actual experience of pain.

A well-researched example of chronic pain is lower back pain caused by severe muscle spasms. Initially the person is unable to engage in activity any more vigorous than getting in and out of bed. In the acute phase this is sensible behavior. As the spasms ease, and if no other damage has occurred, such as to the disks between the vertebrae, the patient is advised to begin moving more normally, stretching, and eventually attempting exercises to strengthen the muscles that went into spasm. Of course, care must be taken not to push patients beyond what their bodies can actually handle.

In their classic work on pain, Fordyce and his colleagues (Fordyce, 1994; Fordyce et al., 1986) have shown the superiority of a behavioral over a traditional medical program for management of back pain. In the traditional program patients exercised and otherwise moved about only until they felt pain; in the behavioral management program patients were encouraged to exercise at a predetermined intensity for a predetermined period of time, even if they experienced pain. Low-back-pain patients have also been given relaxation training and encouraged to relabel their pain as numbness or tickling (Rybstein-Blinchik, 1979), a cognitive-restructuring procedure. The implicit message seems to be that traditional medical practice has underestimated the capabilities of chronic-pain patients (Keefe & Gil, 1986). A frequent outcome of these studies is that increased activity improves muscle tone, which can reduce nociception over time and even reduce the likelihood of future recurrences of muscle spasms (Frost et al., 1998).

In a review of studies on the treatment of chronic pain, Blanchard (1994) concluded that both strictly behavioral (operant conditioning) and cognitive-behavioral approaches are important for effective treatment. There is also some evidence that biofeedback of muscle tension can be effective in alleviating chronic back pain by helping sufferers relax muscles in the lower back and thereby reduce nociception from sensory pain nerves around the spinal column (Flor & Birbaumer, 1993). Of course, pain may be experienced less if the relaxation associated with this kind of biofeedback calms the person down and improves his or her mood. Focus on Discovery 8.3 discusses pain management and other behavioral medicine issues with children.

Our review of several therapeutic approaches to dealing with psychophysiological disorders, many of which can be subsumed under the rubric of behavioral medicine, illustrates the complex relationships between the soma and the psyche, the body and the mind. We come full circle to how we began this chapter, namely, an appreciation of the inseparability of bodily and mental processes.

Behavioral Pediatrics

Russo and Varni (1982) proposed a normal person–abnormal situation (NPAS) model as a way of conceptualizing *behavioral pediatrics*, a branch of behavioral medicine concerned with the psychological aspects of childhood medical problems. An acutely or chronically ill child may have psychological problems only because he or she has been placed by illness in a complex and stressful predicament. Many sick children suffer considerable pain and sometimes defacement and have to spend long periods of time in a hospital, away from parents, siblings, and the comforting surroundings of their homes and neighborhoods. Such absences can in and of themselves interfere with normal social development, making life even more difficult for the children when they are able to rejoin their peers.

Behavioral pediatrics is an interdisciplinary effort that combines behavior therapy and pediatrics to manage disease in children. It is concerned with parent–child, school–child, and medical team–child relations (Varni, La Greca, & Spirito, 2000). Some specific examples will convey the scope and aims of this field (Kellerman & Varni, 1982).

In recent years many forms of childhood cancer, such as acute lymphoblastic leukemia, have become treatable; some types can be treated so effectively that they go into remission and the children are alive five years after the onset of cancer. With such improvements, however, come new problems of a psychological nature for both patients and families as they learn to live with the disease and its treatment.

Concealing from a youngster the true nature of his or her illness and how life threatening it is increases rather than decreases anxiety (e.g., Spinetta, 1980). Open communication with the child is advocated. Research advises maintaining the child in his or her regular school as much as possible (Katz, 1980; Varni et al., 1993). Because cancer and its treatment can bring physical disfigurement, such as hair loss, the child should be taught to handle the teasing that often awaits any youngster who looks different; assertion training and learning to ignore the hurtful remarks can be helpful.

Childhood Pain

Imagine that you are tied down to a table for a painful medical procedure; that you are told little if anything about its purpose, its nature, or how long it will take, and you are assured that it "won't hurt a bit." You have no control over the situation. You cannot reason with your tormentors—which is how you view these people, two of whom are your parents, who have complete power over you and who claim they are just trying to help. You have no choice about when to have the procedures done. When it is all over, those around you underestimate the pain you are feeling and as a result you don't get adequate help coping with the pain and with the horrible memories of what happened. You are assured that it won't happen again, but a month later the same thing takes place.

This is not a sadistic or far-fetched scenario. Rather, it describes what thousands of children go through every day while they are being treated in hospitals and doctors' offices. Since the 1970s psychologists have been developing and evaluating a variety of procedures for easing the pain of children in medical settings.

Why go to the trouble of easing the pain associated with medical illness and its treatment? The main reason is, of course, a non-empirical one, namely, as a society we do not like to inflict pain unnecessar-

ily on others. This is so self-evident to us that we seldom realize that it is a moral judgment we are making; it is not inscribed on stone tablets that people's lives should be as free of pain as possible. Indeed, pain is often not treated as aggressively as it can be, often from a concern that patients, even terminally ill ones, may become addicted to the medications that can ease their pain (we will encounter this issue in Chapter 12 in our discussion of marijuana for seriously ill patients).

But there are also several empirical reasons for trying to reduce people's—especially children's—pain: (1) doing so makes it easier for medical professionals to administer pain-producing diagnostic tests and treatment procedures; (2) less pain actually shortens a patient's treatment and speeds recovery; and (3) in the case of children, minimizing pain creates a more positive developmental history, that is, how pain is managed in childhood can have a major effect on the person's life, including, but not restricted to, how the individual deals with medical challenges later on.

There are several issues of special importance in studying pain in children (Chen, Bush, & Zeltzer, 1997).

- Children often lack the cognitive abilities to understand the purposes of the painful medical procedures they are forced to undergo, to understand the information given them by the adults around them, and to appreciate that (usually) the pain they are being subjected to is limited in duration.

- It is more difficult to assess how much pain children are experiencing than it is to make that assessment for adults. Sometimes parents and medical personnel underestimate the amount of pain and extreme discomfort children feel (Mann, Jacobsen, & Redd, 1992), with the result that their complaints are discounted or minimized (Ross, Bush, & Crummette, 1991), and treatment to manage pain is often less vigorous than it is with adults (Schecter, Allen, & Hanson, 1986). An example of a pictorial scale found useful in helping young children communicate how much pain they are in is portrayed in Figure 8a. With preschool children, this determination relies more on inferences from behavior, such as playing less than usual or being agitated.

- The need for psychological attention to pain does not end when a pain-producing medical procedure is completed. Since we know that anxiety increases the experience of pain (Al-Absi & Rokke, 1991), debriefing is recommended to minimize traumatic recollections, negative expectations, and associated anticipatory anxiety for future painful procedures.

- Looking at pain experiences as possibly traumatic, it should come as no surprise that uncontrollable and extremely painful medical procedures can have long-lasting negative consequences, in particular, an avoidance of medical situations generally (Maddux et al., 1986).

Chronic arthritic pain in the joints is a serious problem for people with hemophilia, whose blood lacks a critical clotting factor. Varni (1981) successfully treated such pain through hypnotic imagery techniques, teaching his patients both to relax and to increase blood flow to the affected joint. A higher surface temperature about the joint diminishes the need for pain medications, many of which have the undesirable side effect of inhibiting platelet aggregation, thus worsen-

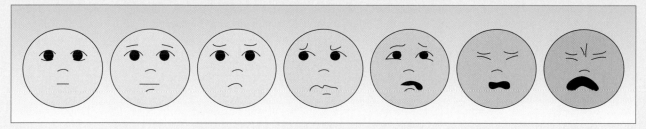

Figure 8a   Faces scale for assessing the experience of pain in children. From Bieri et al. (1989)

ing an already bad blood-clotting condition. Varni's subsequent work in pain management for children with rheumatoid arthritis exemplifies the kind of research-based behavioral medicine that is having a positive impact on helping children and their families cope with serious medical illnesses (Varni & Bernstein, 1991; Varni et al., 2000; Walco, Varni, & Ilowite, 1992).

Pain accompanies both the diagnosis and the treatment of childhood cancer. A child with leukemia must undergo frequent and regular bone-marrow aspiration. The doctor inserts a long needle into the middle of the thigh bone and extracts some marrow. It hurts. And it is not the kind of pain to which a person readily habituates (Katz, Kellerman, & Siegel, 1980). The experience takes a toll on the young patient and on the parents as well. Specialists in behavioral pediatrics have developed multicomponent cognitive-behavioral interventions that include filmed modeling of other children coping with the painful procedure, breathing exercises, positive reinforcement, imagery/distraction, hypnosis, and behavior rehearsal to reduce distress related to painful procedures (Jay et al., 1991; Manne et al., 1994). There is strong evidence for their effectiveness in reducing the pain and trauma of these very stressful procedures in children (Redd & Jacobsen, 2001), and they appear to be more effective than tranquilizing medication (Jay, Elliot, Katz, & Siegel, 1987). These procedures are very upsetting for the parents as well; because their distress usually has a negative impact on their children, cognitive-behavioral interventions have been directed at them as well, with similarly positive effects (Jay & Elliot, 1990).

Though not concerned with cancer-related pain, the following strategy is instructive; it was discovered by a child himself as a way to cope with dental pain.

> *"As soon as I get in the dental chair, I pretend he's the enemy and I'm a secret agent and he's torturing me to get secrets and if I make one sound, I'm telling him secret information, so I never do. I'm going to be a secret agent when I grow up so this is good practice."* Occasionally he got carried away with his fantasy role-playing. One time the dentist asked him to rinse his mouth. Much to the child's own surprise, he snarled, *"I won't tell you a damn thing,"* which momentarily stunned the dentist. (Bandura, 1997, p. 268, quoting from Ross & Ross, 1984)

Children who develop anticipatory anxiety before undergoing painful medical procedures have been helped by viewing films of a coping model (Jay et al., 1982). Systematic desensitization to situations associated with the pain, such as entering the hospital and sitting in the waiting room, can reduce the level of anxiety with which a patient comes to the medical procedure and can thus alleviate the pain. Reducing anxiety can be of more general importance also. An extremely anxious child, for example, may avoid the medical procedure or

may begin to lose weight. Weight loss decreases the chances of surviving cancer (Dewys, Begg, & Lavin et al., 1980).

Treating Psychological Aspects of Medical Illnesses in Children

Children and adolescents with other medical problems have also been helped by behavioral pediatrics. Obesity in children is highly predictive of obesity in adulthood, a major risk factor for such diseases as hypertension, heart disease, and diabetes. Childhood obesity has also been associated with low social competence, behavior problems, and poor self-concept (Banis et al., 1988). Behavioral investigators have been working to help overweight youngsters alter their eating habits, exercise practices, and other aspects of their lifestyles that appear to contribute to the caloric intake and how it is or is not burned off (Epstein, Masek, & Marshall, 1978). For example, obese children, like obese adults, eat faster, take bigger bites, and chew their food less than do age peers of normal weight (Drabman et al., 1979). When their parents are also involved in treatment, weight loss is maintained better (Coates, Killen, & Slinkard, 1982; Epstein et al., 1987). A recent study implicates television viewing as an important factor in childhood obesity, especially among Mexican American and African American youngsters. One possible reason for the excessive TV viewing—upwards of 30 hours a week—is socioeconomic; these children tend more than whites to live in dangerous neighborhoods, and keeping them indoors is one strategy that concerned parents adopt in efforts to protect their loved ones from harm. This situation may be most likely to occur when a parent cannot be available in the midafternoon when the child comes home from school (Anderson et al., 1998).

Therapeutic Compliance

Another topic in behavioral pediatrics (and in behavioral medicine generally) is known as therapeutic compliance. How can we get people to do the things that are necessary to prevent or manage an illness (Varni & Wallander, 1984)? Studies indicate that half of people with a broad range of medical illnesses do not comply with their doctors' instructions—whether it is to take pills as prescribed, use drops to treat serious diseases of the eye, stick with a diet, maintain a certain body weight, or make and keep appointments with health professionals (Morrow, Leirer, & Sheikh, 1988). Juvenile diabetes serves as a good example of the challenge of compliance for both the youngsters and their families. Urine must be tested several times a day to determine glucose (sugar) levels so that food intake and the amount of insulin can be adjusted. Diet poses a major challenge to these youngsters. They must learn to resist candy and other sweets. Their meals need to be timed to coincide with the peak action of an insulin injection so that the insulin does not lower glucose levels abnormally.

Activity and exercise must also become part of the regimen, for they exert their own natural, insulin-like effect of utilizing glucose in the cells (Hobbs, Beck, & Wansley, 1984). With no cure for diabetes in sight, people with this disease need to accept both their condition and the required regulation of some of the most basic of human drives. The complex set of self-care skills that a young person needs to cope with this serious but treatable disease has benefitted from clinical research in behavioral pediatrics, with particularly promising increases in adherence arising from positive reinforcement for following dietary

restrictions and doing regular glucose testing (Epstein et al., 1981). For example, psychologists are beginning to explore the factors associated with the control of blood-sugar levels, including family support, knowledge about the disease, and the importance of considering the patient's developmental level in how the physician can best provide directions and prescriptions (Johnson, 1995). In one study parents of diabetic children were taught relaxation techniques for use with their children; the result was improved control over the children's metabolism and hence the diabetes (Guthrie et al., 1990).

Summary

- Psychophysiological disorders, formerly known as psychosomatic disorders, are physical diseases produced in part by psychological factors, primarily stress. Such disorders usually affect organs innervated by the autonomic nervous system, such as those of the respiratory, cardiovascular, gastrointestinal, and endocrine systems.

- Psychophysiological disorders no longer appear as a diagnostic category in the DSM. Instead, the diagnostician can make a diagnosis of psychological factors affecting a medical condition and then note the condition on Axis III. This change reflects the growing realization that life stress is relevant to all diseases and is not limited to those previously considered psychosomatic.

- In attempting to understand the complex stress-illness relationship, researchers have focused on precisely defining what stress is; on measuring stress using such instruments as the Social Readjustment Rating Scale and the Assessment of Daily Experience; on assessing differences in how people cope with perceived stress; and on moderators of the stress-illness relationship, such as social support.

- Theories of the etiology of psychophysiological disorders are diathesis-stress in nature but differ in whether the diathesis is described in psychological or biological terms. Biological theories attribute particular disorders to specific organ weaknesses, to overactivity of particular organ systems in responding to stress, to the effects of exposure to stress hormones, or to changes in the immune system that are caused by stress. Psychological theories focus more on such factors as unconscious emotional states, personality traits, cognitive appraisals, and specific styles of coping with stress.

- Cardiovascular disorders, which involve the heart and circulatory system, include essential hypertension and coronary heart disease (CHD). While both conditions are complex and multifaceted, their

etiologies appear to include a tendency to respond to stress with increases in blood pressure or heart rate.

- Individuals with asthma tend to have respiratory systems that overrespond to allergens or that have been weakened by prior infection. However, psychological factors such as anxiety, anger, depression, and anticipated excitement may, through inducing emotionality, bring on an asthmatic attack.

- Acquired immunodeficiency syndrome (AIDS) has emerged since its identification in 1981 as the most serious infectious epidemic of modern times. AIDS has psychological elements in that it usually arises from behavior that appears irrational and generally is preventable by psychological means. The primary focus of prevention is to change people's behavior—specifically, to encourage safer sex and to discourage the sharing of needles in intravenous substance abuse..

- Because psychophysiological disorders represent true physical dysfunctions, treatment usually includes medication. The general aim of psychotherapies for these disorders is to reduce anxiety, depression, or anger.

- Researchers in the field of behavioral medicine try to find psychological interventions that can improve patients' physiological state by changing unhealthy behaviors and reducing stress. They have developed ways of helping people relax, smoke less, eat fewer fatty foods, and engage in behaviors that can prevent or alleviate illnesses, such as encouraging breast self-examination and adhering to medical treatment recommendations.

- The emergent field of stress management helps people without diagnosable problems avail themselves of techniques that allow them to cope with the inevitable stress of everyday life and thereby ameliorate the toll that stress can take on the body.

Key Terms

allostatic load
anger-in theory
angina pectoris
asthma
behavioral medicine
biofeedback
cardiovascular disorders

community psychology
coping
coronary heart disease (CHD)
essential hypertension
functional social support
general adaptation syndrome
   (GAS)

health psychology
myocardial infarction
psychological factors affecting
   medical condition
psychophysiological disorders
psychosomatic disorders
somatic-weakness theory

specific-reaction theory
stress
stress management
stressor
structural social support
Type A behavior pattern

Hypertension in an African American Man

John Williams had been complaining to his wife of dizziness, fatigue, and occasional light-headedness that almost caused him to faint one day at the water cooler in the law office where he worked downtown. His boss had been after him for weeks to see a physician, but John had stubbornly refused. He felt angry and frightened when suggestions were made that he see a doctor—angry because he interpreted the suggestion as condescending on his boss's part, and frightened because he had an ineffable feeling that all was not right with him physically.

He was correct about the latter. His first clear knowledge of having hypertension, or high blood pressure, came during a visit to his dentist. Before taking X-rays of his mouth, the dental assistant, as had become routine in the office, wound a black blood pressure cuff around John's right arm, pumped it full of air until the blood stopped flowing, and then slowly released the valve, noting when the first and the last sounds of the pulse could be heard through the stethoscope pressed to the vein in his arm beneath the cuff. Alarmed at the reading—165/110—she took the pressure reading again after doing the X-rays and found it to be almost exactly the same. She tried to smile pleasantly and reassuringly, but found it hard to do, especially when she noticed a worried expression on his face.

He did not ask about the blood pressure reading until he was sitting across from the dentist's desk in the consulting room to discuss treatment plans. How have you been feeling lately, John, was asked by the dentist whom he had known for the past 10 years. Have you been feeling tired, irritable? Any headaches? How has the work been going? Under a lot of pressure? John searched the man's face for some hint of what was going on, but he already sensed that his blood pressure was much too high. Finally, he just asked for the numbers and what they meant, thanked the dentist, and went home.

It took him 30 minutes to reach his condominium in the suburbs. As he turned the key, he wondered how, or whether, he would raise the issue with his wife. Although not a physician himself, he knew what the kind of high blood pressure he seemed to have might mean to a 40-year-old like himself, especially someone who was so driven to succeed professionally and financially. Certainly he would have to slow down and perhaps also take some medication. But what else, he wondered.

Social History

John Williams was the only child of a well-to-do African American family in Atlanta. Born in 1939, he grew up in an upper-middle-class environment. His father was a successful attorney, and his mother was a music teacher in one of the local high schools. Life was sweet in his childhood, as John recalled during one of his therapy sessions with a clinical psychologist. He had many friends in the neighborhood. Even though they were all African American in the segregated part of the city that was his home, he seldom had the feeling of being excluded from anything important. More fortunate than most African Americans, whether in the South or the North, John knew no material wants and was taught during countless dinnertime conversations that there were plenty of opportunities for success available to a youngster like him; he had superior intelligence, an engaging wit, and a degree of ambition that matched that of his hard-working father.

In high school John excelled at everything he attempted. A straight-A student, he was also a varsity athlete in three sports, dated the young women generally regarded by his peers to be the most desirable, and, in his senior year, was elected president of his class. This was the middle 1950s, well before the civil rights struggles and other social activist movements that led to some major legal and social changes in the country, especially in the South. The idea of leaving Georgia for college was tempting, but it created as much anxiety in John's mother as it brought anticipatory pride in his father. Mr. Williams wanted his son to have a college education with "class," as he put it. To be sure, there were first-rate black colleges to which he would apply, such as Howard University in Washington, DC. However, with the encouragement of his guidance counselor and the urging of his father, John also applied to several Ivy League schools. The excitement was considerable in April when the acceptance from Harvard arrived in the mail.

Even though Harvard was located in the "liberal" Northeast, racial discrimination had to be considered. Years later, John told his therapist, a white man with whom he had roomed confided to John that one month before school was to begin their freshman year, he had received a letter from the housing office indicating that they would like to have him room with a Negro student, but that this assignment would be made only if the student had no objection. The student, a Jew from Brooklyn, New York, was outraged because he readily saw the discrimination and prejudice that lay behind the seemingly genteel and considerate inquiry. This incident, and others throughout the four years of friendship between the two young men, was a prototype for many discussions they would have about the pressures on members of minority groups who elected to try to "make it" in society, especially in the elite circles of a private, selective college.

John knew what a "house nigger" was, but it took the handwritten invitation slipped under his door one night to teach him about what he and Matt, his roommate, would call a "club nigger." Fraternities existed at Harvard, but they differed from their Greek-letter counterparts on other campuses in that they were not residential. All undergraduates were affiliated with a house, modeled after the "colleges" of Oxford and Cambridge, in which they lived and took all their meals. The clubs operated outside the house system and were by invitation only. Some of them bore names of winged and sharp-toothed animals such as bats and wolves, others the more familiar Greek initials. It seemed to John that his race would exclude him from these clubs, although he hated himself for even thinking about it. Thinking, he would tell himself, implied that he cared, and to care about the clubs was to accord them a legitimacy and importance he desperately resisted. As he stopped to pick up the engraved envelope, he could feel the blood pound in his ears.

When he looked back on things, this single moment crystallized much of the conflict John felt about his blackness in a white world. He and his race had come far from the days a fair-skinned youngster might hope to "pass" for white. As light as John's complexion was, and as little curliness was to be found in his hair—there was more than one white slave owner in his ancestry—he had grown up proud of the fact that he was African American and feeling that whatever barriers there might be in succeeding in a white society were of less importance than his self-respect and pride. But still, as he lingered over breakfast coffee with Matt the morning the invitation arrived, wasn't it "a gas" that one of the prestigious clubs wanted him as a member?

Not that he got any encouragement from Matt, who viewed his own candidacy for this sort of thing as unlikely an event as John had considered his own. Matt had an uneasy feeling about it all, but he kept it to himself, wondering, for one thing, whether it was not just sour grapes on his own part that this African American man was sought after when he, a Caucasian, was not.

John agonized all day over whether to attend the reception for newly solicited members. He was tempted to phone his parents, but what would he tell them, and how? Was there something to celebrate? Would his father smile quietly to himself as he heard the news, confirming his own good judgment in sending his son to one of the bastions of eastern elitism? Surely John was going to succeed—and in the white world, no less. In the end, John did not phone. He feared at one and the same time that his father would either congratulate him on the invitation or chide him for even considering it. No way to win on that score, he told himself. At some level he knew that it was his own conflict he was wrestling with, not his father's reaction.

The day of his initiation, John awoke with a screaming headache. He took three aspirins—a habit he had gotten into since coming to college—and told himself to stop worrying about the party that evening. Perhaps he need not have worried. The welcome he received seemed genuine. And yet he could not shake the feeling that his new "brothers" were being nicer to him than they were to the other initiates, too nice somehow. His wine glass was never empty, always filled by a brother who, it struck John, smiled a bit too ingratiatingly. In fact, it seemed to him that his new friends must have suffered from aching mouths, so broadly did they smile whenever they talked to him. He tried to reassure himself that the cordiality was real, and maybe it was. The problem, he knew, was that he did not really know, nor could he devise a practical way to find out.

His membership in the club turned out to be a boon to his social standing but an emotional disaster. Headaches and feelings of pressure in the brain were more regularly part of his existence than ever before. He hated himself for even being in the club, yet he prided himself on being the only African American member. He was furious at the fact that so few Jews were members and was also suspicious that there were no other African Americans, but he found the young men in the club congenial and enjoyable to spend time with, and he did experience a thrill whenever he donned the club necktie. His friends from the club were certainly no less bright than his other classmates, no less interested in abstract ideas and "deep" conversations over sherry after dinner. But the clubs were by nature exclusionary, and John was coming to realize that he might be seen as the quintessential Uncle Tom.

His anger at himself and at his brothers grew to an intensity that was frightening. To Matt, in whom he confided his doubts, fears, guilt, and rage, John seemed a tragic figure. There seemed to be no way for him to win. To express his concerns to his club brothers seemed out of the question. But not to do so, at least to one of them, had begun to make the thought of going to the handsome Georgian building for the evening a challenge, almost a dare. He dreaded the possibility of someone making a racist remark. How should he react? He had learned, since coming north, to let it pass, but the muscle tension that mounted in his body told him this was not the best thing for him to do. Once a club member used the word "niggardly," and he felt himself blush. How infantile to react that way, he told himself. And yet, maybe the word was used to taunt him. But how inane to think that. Sure, Uncle Tom, he concluded.

The four years of college passed quickly. As his family and friends expected, John did very well academically and also managed to earn a varsity letter in baseball. His admission to a first-rate law school was a foregone conclusion, although John's problem by this time was his uncertainty as to whether he had been admitted solely on his academic merits or whether the several prestigious schools, like the club, wanted him primarily for his color. And so the conflicts continued through law school. By this time they took the form of John's having to excel to what even his ambitious father regarded to be an unreasonable degree. John just had to prove he was good, indeed, that he was the best.

John became engaged to an African American woman from a prominent family, but the joys of the relationship were dulled by his relentless drive for excellence and perfection. One major change was that his problems with hypertension were now impossible to hide. She insisted that he have a complete physical examination, something he had consciously avoided since entering college. The reading was 130/85, something the doctor called "high normal," sufficient in magnitude to be worrisome in a young man, especially someone in very good physical condition. His fiancée was convinced that John's grim pursuit of straight As, law review, and all the rest were at fault. But she knew little as yet about the reasons that lay behind his near-obsessive push.

John graduated at the top of his law school class. It was now the middle 1960s, and the developing social turmoil surrounding Vietnam and the civil rights movement affected him deeply. On the one hand, he felt that he should be out on the barricades, but his studies and his new job at a top law firm took precedence. He tried to assuage his guilt by donating money to civil rights groups, but it did not seem to help. He had cast his lot with the white world, he told himself, and his wife and his own family back in Atlanta supported that decision. Middle- and upper-middle-class professional African Americans had their role to play, his father continually reminded him, and who could better play that role than John Williams? The sense he had that it was, indeed, a role, turned out to be important in the psychotherapy he began some weeks after the alarmingly high blood pressure reading in the dentist's office.

Conceptualization and Treatment

The choice of a therapist is never an easy matter. For John it presented special difficulties. Though he lived near a large city, there were few African American psychiatrists or psychologists. As he had grown accustomed to doing in most other areas of his life, John decided to work with a white person, in this instance in a very special relationship. He was uncertain whether he could relate openly to a white. His only really close white friend was his old college roommate, Matt, and even then he recalled holding back on the expression of thoughts and emotions having to do with race. Would this same problem arise in a therapeutic relationship? In fact, was race even an issue?

"Well, what do you really want out of life?" asked Dr. Shaw, a distinguished and experienced clinical psychologist. "The same thing everyone else is after," was his reply. "But what is that?" queried the psychologist.

The first couple of sessions were like this: Dr. Shaw trying to get John to examine what he really wanted, and John sparring with him, fending off the probes with generalities about "all other people." In Shaw's mind, John Williams did not want to confront the conflicts of playing a role in the white professional world. He identified with being African American, Shaw believed, but he sensed a falseness about his life. Racial slurs went by without comment. He took pride in the fact that his wife wore her hair straight but, at the same time, castigated himself for feeling this way. He hid from his law office colleagues the fact that he was a member of several civil rights groups and that he considered Martin Luther King to have been somewhat too moderate. But what was he doing about it? King and others had risked personal safety in freedom marches, but John was terrified of being seen in one. What would the people in the firm think of him? Would they want a "radical" in the office?

Dr. Shaw thought to himself during these early sessions that he should pressure his client more, but he realized he was holding back in a way he would not with a white client. Was it his right to suggest to John that he was at the same time proud and ashamed of his racial heritage, that he despised himself for hiding his feelings? Indeed, was it his duty? But how could Shaw be certain, and wouldn't it be terrible if he intimated something to John that was off base? But that, too, was something he worried far less about with his white clients. No therapist is infallible. Yet somehow he believed that with John he had to be more certain about his interpretations.

Dr. Shaw routinely referred clients with medical or psychophysiological problems to an internist. This doctor prescribed some anti-hypertensive medication for John to take daily. But the physician also hoped that this relatively young patient would not come to rely on the drug. In an extended consultation, Shaw and his medical colleague agreed that John's high-pressure life style was a major factor. What they could not agree on was what role the man's race played. Absence of similar problems in three generations of John's family did not support the assumption that the patient had inherited a predisposition for hypertension, although the two men agreed that, for whatever reason, John's particular response to stress was hypertension, more specifically essential hypertension, because physical causes had been ruled out through a complete medical checkup.

A crisis took place in the fifth and final session. For months afterward Dr. Shaw wondered whether he had blundered so badly that his client was driven from therapy.

Dr. Shaw: John, I've been wondering about what you've told me about your college days.

John (a bit suspiciously): What aspect of them?

Dr. Shaw: Well, I guess I was thinking about the club. (Shaw noted to himself that he seldom said "I guess" in such circumstances. Stop pussyfooting, he told himself.)

John (feeling his ears becoming warm): Well, what about the club?

Dr. Shaw: Your feelings of being the only black.

John: Well, I felt really good about it. I used to daydream about what my high school friends would think.

Dr. Shaw: And what would they have thought?

John: They'd have envied me to the utmost. I mean, I must be doing something right to get into one of the Greeks.

Dr. Shaw: Yes, I know you were quite proud about it. . . . But I wonder if you had any other feelings about it.

John (definitely on edge, wary): What do you mean?

Dr. Shaw: Well, lots of times people are conflicted about things that are important to them. Like the nervous bridegroom on the wedding day. He's eager for the honeymoon, but he knows he's giving up something.

John: What do you think I was giving up?

Dr. Shaw: You feel you were giving up something by being in the club?

John: Come on, Doc, don't play games. You know damn well that you think I gave up something. What did I give up?

Dr. Shaw: John, if anything was given up, it was you who gave it up, not I. (That sounded too harsh, he told himself immediately, but maybe it was time to apply more pressure on him. Otherwise he might never move.)

John: I resent what you're implying.

Dr. Shaw: Okay, but can you explore it, just hypothetically?

John (suspicion mounting, almost a feeling of panic setting in): Okay, Shaw, let me think of what I gave up.

At this point there was a lengthy silence. John stared at his feet, Dr. Shaw at his notes, occasionally glancing up at John but not wanting to look at him too much. John began to dwell on the thoughts he had never shared with anyone, not even with his roommate, Matt. Oreo cookie, he called himself, black on the outside and white on the inside. Who needs the damned club? If they were serious about being democratic, I would not be the only African American. Just me, and oh, that Chinese kid, whose family just happened to own half of Hong Kong. Yuh, David and me, the two typical minority members. And they can congratulate themselves for being so damned liberal. And I can congratulate myself for making it in the door. But how would they have reacted if I had dated a white woman? Or worn my hair in an Afro? Or put on a dashiki? Ha! How do you wear a club tie with a dashiki? Even the one overt sign of club membership conflicts with a dashiki! What am I doing with these mothers? How hypocritical can I be?[1]

Dr. Shaw: John, can you share some of your thoughts with me?

John: Doc, I can't do it. You're one of them.

Dr. Shaw: One of whom?

John: Doc, I can't talk to a white man about this. I can't talk to a black man about this. I'm too ashamed, too mixed up (beginning to sob). I can't handle this.

Dr. Shaw: This is hard for you, I know, John. But this is a place you can use to look at those feelings. Try to sort them out. Try to figure out what you really want—

John (interrupting the psychologist): No! It's not for you to tell me what I should be doing. *I'm* the one who has to decide. (long silence again)

Dr. Shaw: John?

John just stares at his feet, jaws clenched, that familiar tightness in his head. My blood pressure must be soaring, he told himself. I can't handle this. If I'm not careful I'll be a psychological success, but I'll die from a stroke. No, that's an exaggeration. Or is it? I'm bullshitting myself so much that I don't even know what I want, or think, or feel . . .

Dr. Shaw: John, perhaps that's enough for today.

John (relieved): Yes, that's right. That's enough . . . for today.

Dr. Shaw: See you next week, same time.

John (knowing he would break the appointment): Yuh. Thanks. I'll see you next week.

Discussion

It has been known for thousands of years that mental and emotional states can affect the functioning of the body. When a person is under emotional strain, there are numerous physiological changes, such as increases in heart rate and in blood pressure; these changes are usually temporary, diminishing when the stressor is removed. But in

---

[1] Dr. Shaw learned later on something of what was going through John's mind during these lengthy silences.

some individuals the changes persist; when this happens over a long period of time, a psychophysiological disorder can result.

In earlier versions of the *DSM*, such disorders were separately listed as one of the mental disorders, but in *DSM-IV-TR*, a diagnostic judgment is called for about the presence of "psychological factors affecting medical condition." Such diagnoses are listed in a general section that comprises "other conditions that may be a focus of clinical attention." In this way, the current *DSM* acknowledges that any medical illness can be influenced by psychological factors while it eschews regarding them as actual mental disorders.

Perhaps you have heard the expression, "Oh, don't worry about that. It's only in your mind." A person suffering from asthma that has some psychogenic components is often seen as someone of weak will or someone with a physical malady that is somehow not genuine. To believe this is to overlook the simple and important fact that many medical illnesses are caused in part or are markedly affected by psychological factors. A disease such as hypertension can be life threatening even when a person's emotions seem to be playing a major role in causing the sustained high blood pressure.

The classic psychophysiological disorders are sometimes grouped in terms of the organ system affected. Some of the major ones are:

1. Skin disorders: Neurodermatitis and hyperhydrosis (dry skin)
2. Respiratory disorders: Bronchial asthma, hyperventilation (breathing very rapidly, often leading to fainting)
3. Cardiovascular disorders: Migraine headache and high blood pressure (hypertension)
4. Gastrointestinal disorders: Ulcerative colitis, heartburn

Psychophysiological disorders are common in highly industrialized societies. One survey (Schwab, Fennell, & Warheit, 1974) found that over 40 percent of Americans had had headaches during the previous year and over 50 percent of Americans had suffered gastrointestinal symptoms such as constipation and diarrhea.

Before we turn to hypertension, let us review briefly the major types of theories that have been advanced about psychophysiological disorders in general. Two basic questions must be addressed in any attempt to understand these problems: (1) Why do only some people exposed to stress develop psychophysiological disorders?, and (2) Given that stress does produce such a disorder, what determines which of them will arise? As with other psychopathologies, both biological and psychological theories have been proposed.

Biological Theories

The *somatic weakness theory* states that a particular organ—for genetic reasons or because of poor diet or earlier illnesses—can be weak and thus vulnerable to stress. For example, a congenitally weak respiratory system might predispose a person to develop asthma under stress. Thus, the connection between stress and a particular psychophysiological disorder is a weakness in a specific bodily organ.

According to the *specific-reaction theory*, individuals respond to stress in their own idiosyncratic ways, and the bodily system that is the most responsive becomes a likely candidate for the locus of a subsequent psychophysiological disorder. For example, someone reacting to stress with elevated blood pressure may be more susceptible to essential hypertension.

A third biological theory attempts to deal with the fact that the biological changes that stress produces are adaptive in the short run, for example, mobilizing energy resources in preparation for physical activity, but that the body pays a price if it must constantly adapt to stress (McEwen, 1998). This can take the form of difficulties "shutting down" the biological stress response, for example, by exhibiting an unusually high level of cortisol secretion even after the stress has abated.

A fourth biological approach entails the study of the body's immune system, which is involved in fighting off infections. Stress can weaken the functioning of the immune system and thereby play a role in such diseases as cancer and allergies as well as autoimmune diseases such as rheumatoid arthritis, in which a person's immune system actually attacks his or her own body. Many stressors produce negative effects on the immune system—examinations, bereavement, divorce, looking after a relative with Alzheimer's disease, and natural disasters (Cohen & Herbert, 1996).

Psychological Theories

Psychoanalysts have for many years viewed psychophysiological disorders as symbolic manifestations of unresolved repressed conflicts. Franz Alexander (1950), for example, proposed that an ulcer can be formed if a person has repressed an unfulfilled childhood longing for parental love; by continually producing acid, the stomach is preparing itself for food, equated symbolically with love. Analytic interpretations of hypertension implicate undischarged hostile impulses, and this line of work will be discussed more fully later.

Cognitive and behavioral factors also have been implicated in psychophysiological disorders. Over millions of years, we have developed autonomic nervous systems that equip us to respond to danger with either fight or flight. In either event, the healthy body prepares itself by increasing the rate of breathing, diverting blood into the muscles, releasing sugar into the bloodstream, and the like. When the danger has passed, this burst of sympathetic nervous system activity subsides. Humankind has developed the dubious distinction, however, of being able to respond in this way to *psychological* dangers, not just to the life-threatening challenges that beset other animals. Indeed, we are able to stir up our autonomic nervous systems by our very thoughts and imaginings, thereby maintaining our bodies in a state of hyperarousal. It is as if we are runners in a 100-yard dash, crouched at the starting line, and tensely ready for the signal "go!" Only no signal comes, and we just stay there, expectant and highly aroused.

We know from personal experience that thoughts cause emotional arousal, and research confirms this (Lazarus & Folkman, 1984). Human beings can stir themselves up with regrets from the past and worries about the future. Our higher mental capacities, then, can subject our bodies to stress without the presence of actual physical danger. Appraisal, one characteristic of our cognitive activity, is of special importance; one person can judge a particular situation as dangerous while another appraises it as challenging and interesting. The autonomic and motoric activity arising from these contrasting cognitions is different.

None of these theories and perspectives enjoys unequivocal support. Some views, such as the psychoanalytic one, are difficult to test. It would seem that a multifactorial point of view should be adopted in attempting to understand these puzzling disorders. Investigators will have to consider both physical diatheses, or predispositions, and highly specific psychological ways of reacting to stress. Thus, one person might have a genetically determined tendency to react to emotional situations with elevated blood pressure and thus be at risk for hypertension; however, she will not develop this disorder if her life does not contain a certain amount of stress. Furthermore, the way she construes an event as stressful will be a function of her psychology. Failing a test, for instance, might be something she has learned to disregard, while a cross look from her boyfriend may be considered a catastrophe. Someone else, on the other hand, might have a constitution that is fortunately not disposed to react in any abnormal way to stress; that is, his blood pressure declines rapidly once a stressor is removed. But his psychology might have him construe as very threatening an event such as failing an examination. He will therefore end up with some sort of emotional problem, such as an anxiety disorder, *but* his organ systems will not be affected as seriously as they might be if he were predisposed. The outcome will be that he will not develop a psychophysiological disorder but, instead, another kind of emotional problem.

Essential Hypertension

We are now ready to consider what is known or hypothesized about the problem from which John Williams suffers. High blood pressure, often referred to as hypertension, is estimated to be involved in a great many deaths in the United States and elsewhere each year, and the problem is showing up in younger and younger age groups. Everyone has blood pressure, of course, because the heart pumps the blood throughout the body under pressure. (If this were not the case, we would all be dead.) If it remains at an elevated level— readings above 140/90 are regarded as high—a strain is placed on the cardiovascular system and, over a period of years, there is an increased risk of stroke or heart attack. Only about 10 to 15 percent of all cases of hypertension in the United States are attributable at this time to an identifiable physical cause; the other 85 to 90 percent are said to have *essential* or *primary hypertension*.

According to recent estimates, varying degrees of hypertension are found in about 20 percent of the adult population of the United States; it is twice as frequent in African Americans as in whites. As many as 10 percent of American college students have hypertension; most of them are unaware of their illness. Unless people have their blood pressure checked, they may go for years without knowing that they are hypertensive. This disease is sometimes referred to as the "silent killer" because (1) over time it is dangerous to one's physical health, and (2) it can be present for years without the person knowing it. Sometimes symptoms do develop, however, as we saw in John Williams's case: fatigue, nervousness, dizziness, heart palpitations, headaches, and, for some people, even a feeling of pressure in the head.

On a physiological level, hypertension is currently viewed as a heterogeneous condition brought on by many possible disturbances in the various systems of the body that are responsible for regulating blood pressure. The mechanisms relevant to the regulation of blood pressure are extremely complex, but there are two basic variables: (1) Increases in blood pressure can be due to increased cardiac output caused by heightened stimulation of the heart by the sympathetic nervous system, kidney malfunction, hormones, salt and water metabolism, as well as central nervous system mechanisms; and (2) increases in blood pressure occur when resistance in the arteries is made greater by narrowing caused by fatty deposits from years of high levels of cholesterol (Weiner, 1977).

Recent evidence points to cardiovascular reactivity as a diathesis for hypertension, that is, the extent to which blood pressure and heart rate increase in response to stress. People differ on this factor, some being very reactive, others less so. More reactive people tend to be more likely to have higher blood pressure over time, though not necessarily hypertension (Light et al., 1992). Of particular relevance to our case, African American children have been found to be higher in blood-pressure reactivity than whites, a fact that may help explain the high incidence of hypertension among blacks (Anderson, McNeilly, & Myers, 1993; Murphy et al., 1995). Many of these controlling physiological mechanisms could be affected by psychological stress, a topic to which we now turn.

We know from various research studies that stress increases blood pressure in the short term. Kasl and Cobb (1970), for example, found that people who knew that their jobs were to be terminated in two months had higher blood pressure during that period as well as two years following the loss of the job than control subjects whose employment remained constant.

With the availability of portable monitoring apparatus, researchers have undertaken studies of ambulatory blood-pressure, wherein participants wear a blood-pressure cuff that takes readings as they go about their daily lives. Many of these studies have asked participants about their emotional state at the time a blood pressure reading is taken. The general finding has been that both positive and negative emotional states are associated with higher blood pressure (e.g., Jacob et al., 1999; Kamarck et al., 1998). There is also some indication that of various negative emotions, anger is most strongly linked to elevated blood pressure (e.g., Faber & Burns, 1996; Schwartz, Warren, & Pickering, 1994).

More directly relevant to John Williams is some classic research by Hokanson and his colleagues (Hokanson & Burgess, 1962; Stone & Hokanson, 1969). In a laboratory setting, college students were given a task but were then made angry by a confederate of the experimenter. Fifty percent of them were given the opportunity to retaliate against their harasser, but the others were not. Results showed that being harassed in this way raised blood pressure, which is not surprising. Of greater interest was the fact that students who could take retaliatory action against the source of their frustration showed larger decreases in their elevated blood pressure than did control subjects, who were denied that opportunity.

Applying these analogue findings to John Williams, we can hypothesize that his habit of inhibiting anger and his resentment of white people played a role in the development of his high blood pressure. An additional finding of Hokanson, however, provides an even more important possibility. Considering only the students who retaliated, blood pressure decreases were found only when they aggressed against a fellow college student, not when their harasser was presented to them as a visiting professor. Expressing resentment and anger to a high-status source of frustration, then, did not reduce blood pressure. In John's case, if he *had* asserted himself more, this might not have helped him *if* he perceived the people angering him as higher in status than himself. This is where issues of race enter, because the therapist would have had to discuss with John his underlying feelings about white people: whether he regarded them as superior, for example. One can appreciate how much more subtle and complex things become when moving from the laboratory study to a real-life case.

Some confirmatory data are closer to actual life circumstances. While there is probably a racial basis to the especially high incidence of hypertension among African Americans, additional causes may be found in social factors, especially having to deal continually with social stress (Neighbors & Jackson, 1996; Sherman, 1994). Harburg et al. (1973) studied two areas of Detroit; one was a poor neighborhood with a high crime rate, much crowding, and many marital breakups, and the other was a middle-class neighborhood. In both, black and white married men had their blood pressure taken several times in their homes, and they were also given a test that posed stressful situations to them and asked how they would respond. One test item, for example, had them imagine that they were seeking a place to rent and that the landlord refused them because of their race or religion. The response categories were: (1) "I'd get angry or mad and show it," (2) "I'd get annoyed and show it," (3)"I'd get annoyed, but would keep it in," (4) "I'd get angry or mad, but would keep it in," (5) "I wouldn't feel angry or annoyed" (p.280).

Results showed that blood pressure was higher among African Americans than among whites. But African Americans living in the poor neighborhood had higher blood pressure than those living in the middle-class area. Thus, while race was one factor, of equal importance was social class and the accompanying stress that comes with living in marginal circumstances. It would seem that high blood pressure among African Americans has a great deal to do with the socially created stress under which they live (Anderson & Armstead, 1995). Furthermore, results from the stressful situation test indicated that for most subjects, holding anger in was related to high blood pressure. Harburg's findings, a reanalysis of them by Gentry, Chesney, Hall, and Harburg (1981) and Gentry, Chesney, Gary, Hall, and Harburg (1982), and a replication by Dimsdale et al. (1986) focus on the role of unexpressed anger, or "anger-in," in the development and maintenance of high blood pressure.

Other research (e.g., Spielberger, Johnson, Russell, Crane, & Worden, 1985) examined the relationship in nonhypertensive subjects between anger and hypertension by correlating blood pressure with scores on the Anger Expression Scale, a 20-item self-report inventory on which subjects respond by indicating how often they react in various ways when they are angry. For example, do they control their temper? Do they keep things in? Do they slam doors, or argue with others? In a study by Johnson (1984, reported in Spielberger et al., 1985), there were strong and positive correlations between blood pressure and the tendency to suppress anger. Suppressed anger, which activates the autonomic nervous system, may over time lead to fixed elevations in blood pressure, that is, high blood pressure. These findings on anger-in and hypertension have also been confirmed in other studies (e.g., Netter & Neuhauser-Mettermich, 1991; Sullivan, Procci et al., 1981; Sullivan, Schoentgen et al., 1981) and are consistent with Alexander's psychoanalytic theorizing mentioned earlier.

John Williams was not stressed by socioeconomic factors, but, like many people, he contributed to his life pressures by his constant striving for perfection, over and above the pressure probably created by the prejudice encountered in his frequent contacts with whites. His blood pressure was apparently increased as well by the tremendous conflicts he experienced as an African American man who felt he was being false to himself, who compromised his beliefs and his ideals in order to succeed in white society.

Remember that the studies discussed so far, except for Harburg's, have at least two major limitations. First, in no instance was true high blood pressure created, only temporary increases in blood pressure. Second, most of the research was analogue in nature; that is, the situations studied were not real life. We must always be mindful when we are extrapolating from "make-believe" to the real world. What we learn from laboratory studies provides fruitful leads and ways of thinking about problems, but matters are still far from proven.

Going back to our general discussion of theories of psychophysiological disorders, we suggested that a diathesis-stress view was the best one to employ. John Williams's life was full of emotionally stressful events. But it was a psychophysiological disorder that he developed, not any of the many other problems that people under duress are subject to, such as mood disorders or anxiety disorders. Furthermore, given that it was a psychophysiological problem, he had essential hypertension, not asthma, hives, or any of the other such disorders. Did he have a somatic weakness in his cardiovascular system, or was his system somehow predisposed to overreact to stress, as in the specific reaction theory? We do not know in John's case. Evidence that should lead us to consider the possibility—although it is unclear what the treatment implications would be—is in research such as a study by Hodapp, Weyer, and Becker (1976). The blood pressure of hypertensive and normals was measured while resting, while viewing slides of landscapes, and while performing a demanding intellectual task (the stressor). All study participants showed blood pressure increases during the stress, but hypertensives maintained that increase even when the stressor was removed. It is as though some people's cardiovascular system is preset to be elevated and to maintain that elevation once it is stressed.

Of course, this study and others like it cannot demonstrate a cause-effect relationship because the hypertensive patients were, in fact, already hypertensive! There are, however, longitudinal data consistent with the idea that heightened blood pressure reactivity may be an important diathesis, consistent with data reviewed earlier showing African American children to be higher on this parameter than white children (Murphy et al., 1995). In one such longitudinal study, Wood et al. (1984) followed up with people who had had their blood pressure monitored during a stress task many years earlier.

Those who had reacted strongly were five times more likely to be hypertensive. Further support for the importance of reactivity comes from high-risk research comparing individuals with and without a positive history for hypertension (e.g., Hastrup, Light, & Obrist, 1982). As anticipated, people with a positive family history showed greater blood pressure reactivity to stress. Coupled with other research showing the heritability of blood pressure reactivity (Matthews & Rakaczky, 1987) and the heritability of hypertension, blood pressure reactivity becomes a good candidate for a genetically transmitted diathesis. There is little doubt that essential hypertension is caused by an interplay between a diathesis and stress.

Issues of Race and Psychotherapy

Cultural diversity is an issue of importance to highly heterogeneous countries like the United States and Canada. Despite our increasing understanding of biological factors in the nature of mental illness and how to prevent and treat many disorders, social circumstances and cultural factors are ignored only at great risk.

Any discussion of racial factors in intervention runs the risk of stereotyping because generalizations are made about the way a *group* of people react to psychological assistance. But no less than whites, people from minority groups are *individuals* who can differ as much from each other as their racial group differs from another racial group. Still, a consideration of group characteristics is important and is part of a developing specialty called minority mental health.

African American clients report higher levels of rapport with African American therapists than with white therapists, prefer African American therapists to white, and report greater satisfaction with them (Atkinson, 1983; 1985). African American clients engage in more self-exploration with counselors of their own race (Jackson, 1973). At the same time, studies suggest that racial differences are *not* insurmountable barriers to understanding between counselor and client (Beutler et al., 1994). Therapists with high levels of empathy are perceived as more helpful by clients, regardless of the racial mix.

African Americans who have not fully accepted the values of white America generally react differently to whites than to other African Americans: With African Americans they are more open and spontaneous, whereas with whites they tend to be more guarded and less talkative (Gibbs, 1980; Ridley, 1984). Also, therapists need to understand that virtually all African Americans have encountered prejudice and racism, and many must often wrestle with their anger and rage at a majority culture that is sometimes insensitive to and unappreciative of the emotional consequences of growing up as a feared, resented, and sometimes hated minority (Hardy & Laszloffy, 1995). On the other hand, as Greene (1985) cautions, therapists' sensitivity to social oppression should not translate into a paternalism that removes personal responsibility and individual empowerment from the African American client. These issues are vividly illustrated in the case of John Williams, both throughout his life and in his brief dealings with his therapist.

Mention has already been made of how being African American might contribute to high blood pressure. John Williams's race also played a role in the therapy he terminated prematurely. Not adequately appreciated in the psychotherapy literature are the social conditions under which African Americans have been living in this country as well as the sometimes subtle, unconscious biases existing in the primarily white investigators who offer the generalizations (Comas-Diaz, 1992).

Complicating the matter still further is the difficulty a white therapist can experience with a black client. It is said that racism entails not only negative stereotypes (e.g., all African Americans are sexually promiscuous) but also positive ones (e.g., they have a natural talent for athletics). The therapist has no easy task to get past these prejudgments, or prejudices, to look at the African American client as he or she would regard a white client, and to consider the person's psychological difficulties in useful ways, placing race in a context that will promote a fruitful assessment and intervention instead of impeding them.

These issues are to be seen in the case of John Williams. Should the therapist have encouraged a more assertive stance toward the prejudices that seemed to be oppressing him? Or should the therapist have promoted an adjustment to the situation, an attitude that he really had things good, that life is imperfect, and perhaps he should just find a way to make the best of it? Did John Williams really wish that he were white—a conclusion some whites reach when African Americans complain of obstacles in their paths to general social acceptance? Should John have declined that seductive invitation to the club at Harvard on the basis that a token African American member was worse than no African American at all? Was his wish to be accepted by his white classmates an unhealthy one, or could it be seen as no less healthy than the wish a white initiate would have? Was John really "Uncle-Tomming" by joining the exclusive group while knowing that true acceptance would ultimately be denied him? Indeed, what evidence did he have that he was not "truly" accepted by his club members? If people were being nice to him, was it because he was African American and they were trying to demonstrate their liberalism and open-mindedness? How was he to know if a display of affection or approval arose from such motivations?

Dr. Shaw was more reluctant to push John than he would have a white client. It has been suggested that some white therapists are overly sympathetic toward their African American clients, lest they seem to be expressing racial prejudice (Adams, 1950; Greene, 1985). In psychoanalytic terms, Shaw was having countertransference problems with Williams; that is, concerns about his own racism and his efforts to overcome it were getting in the way of dealing with his client.

There is, moreover, a general issue in psychotherapy about how much pressure a therapist should place on a client. In one well-known study of group therapy (Yalom & Lieberman, 1971), casualties occurred most often when the group leader was confrontative and authoritative. Clearly, clients can be hurt if their therapists demand more of them than they are capable of giving. On the other hand, the art of therapy requires that therapists encourage movement on the part of their clients that might not occur otherwise. After some hesitation, Dr. Shaw did apply such pressure, but he seemed to misread his client's readiness to explore his conflicts and lost the opportunity to work further with him. By most standards, Dr.

Shaw failed with John Williams, even though he saw him for only five sessions.

Dr. Shaw should have anticipated the difficulties in establishing rapport. Clients in general may need time to feel comfortable with a therapist, to come to trust that this stranger has their best interests at heart and will be able to relate in a nonjudgmental way so that secrets of the heart can be shared (London, 1964). But John, like many African American clients, was suspicious and hostile because of the racial difference itself, as earlier research has shown (Kennedy, 1952; Ridley, 1984; St. Clair, 1951). Will this white person truly be able to empathize with my suffering? Will he or she translate whatever personal prejudices exist into a lack of sympathy, or too much sympathy? Will he or she truly be able to appreciate the tensions I am under? How will he or she judge my desires to be accepted by whites for what I am, my fierce pride in being African American, especially as I succeed in a white world? Will he or she see me as copping out or decide that my inhibition of resentment is adaptive and healthy? Indeed, will and can the therapist help me explore within myself what *I* really want? Must I want only what other African Americans want in order to be a whole person?

The Psychological Treatment of Hypertension

Before the advent of effective drugs for treating hypertension in the late 1950s, advice from physicians was basically to "take it easy," lose weight, get some exercise, and restrict salt intake—all reasonably helpful measures. It is noteworthy that simple verbal reassurance was also considered important and was even demonstrated to be helpful in an early study by Reiser et al. (1950), in which nonpsychiatrically trained internists (physicians specializing in internal medicine, which includes the diagnosis and treatment of hypertension) provided what we today call nonspecific supportive psychotherapy. Clinically significant reductions in blood pressure were observed after two years of regular, albeit not frequent, contact.

The development of effective drugs to lower blood pressure shifted the direction of treatment strongly toward their use from the 1960s onward. But over time the undesirable side effects of these medications—drowsiness, light-headedness, and in men, erectile difficulties—as well as the growth of behavioral approaches to treatment led many investigators to explore nonpharmacological treatments for borderline essential hypertension. (Those with more severe hypertension usually have to take drugs to control its deleterious long-term effects.)

Our focus here is on psychological interventions, but it is important to bear in mind that, since psychophysiological disorders are true medical problems, physicians are often involved in treatment. While there is disagreement about whether drugs alone can be a complete therapy for a disorder like hypertension, the fact of the matter is that there are many pharmacological options available that can lower blood pressure and these have to be considered in any comprehensive approach. Moreover, when there is a medical problem, it is always sound clinical practice to consult with medical professionals even if one is trying to treat the problem by psychological means alone. Regular exercise as well as losing weight through sensible diet continues to be part of any comprehensive approach to controlling high blood pressure (Whelton et al., 1998). But these medical measures also involve psychological change components (Dubbert, 1995).

What kinds of psychological treatments show promise in dealing with essential hypertension? In the most general terms, therapists of various persuasions agree that anxiety, and sometimes anger, must be reduced to lessen the sympathetic nervous system arousal that plays a role in maintaining blood pressure at abnormally high levels. Although there are probably limits to how normal the client can become—over time structural changes occur in the cardiovascular system that render it chronically hyperaroused to some extent—therapy can justifiably be attempted to help the client cope better with pressures and anxiety and thereby reduce blood pressure to a degree.

A psychoanalytically oriented therapist employs techniques such as free association and interpretation in efforts to lift repressions so that the person can examine hitherto repressed conflicts. John might have learned as a young child that to be loved he had to achieve, even if that meant denying himself what he really wanted. Afraid of punishment from his father, he repressed this anger. Operating with the hypothesis that hypertension arises from hostile impulses pressing for discharge, an analyst might encourage the client to recognize and express anger. Hypertension as an illness lends itself well to the hydraulic metaphor of psychoanalysis; siphoning off undischarged energy is expected to reduce the pressure in the psychic apparatus.

Client-centered therapists would focus on John's denial of his inner self, his not marching to the beat of his own drum, his compromising his ideas and deeply felt beliefs in order to meet with favor and acceptance from others (especially his father), or what Carl Rogers called "conditions of worth" (Rogers, 1951). Dr. Shaw was operating in this framework, but we have seen that he did not get further than suggesting to John that he might be acting against his own self.

The transcript provided earlier shows the kind of empathic listening and reflection common in client-centered therapy. Note, however, that Dr. Shaw did not merely reflect back to John what he had just said. A useful distinction should be drawn between what one writer has termed primary accurate empathy and advanced empathy (Egan, 1975); the latter we have elsewhere likened to interpretation (Davison, Neale, & Kring, 2004). Primary empathy is seen in the following exchange.

> **John:** Doc, I can't talk to a white man about this. I can't talk to a black man about this. I'm too ashamed, too mixed up (beginning to sob). I can't handle this.
>
> **Dr. Shaw:** This is hard for you, I know, John. . . .

Dr. Shaw acknowledges that he appreciates how difficult it is for John to be talking about his private thoughts. The hope is that the relationship will be strengthened and that John will be encouraged to continue exploring his feelings. In another part of the session, however, Dr. Shaw goes beyond what John has expressed, restating to him what is implied, what he, Dr. Shaw, believes is going on with John. He makes an *inference*, an interpretation about what is troubling the client in the hope of helping John view himself in a new, better perspective, one that will generate movement, and greater honesty with the self. (Dr. Shaw has asked John how he felt about being the only African American in his club at college.)

> **Dr. Shaw:** [I'd like to know about] your feelings of being the only black.
>
> **John:** Well, I felt really good about it....My high school friends would've envied me to the utmost. . . .
>
> **Dr. Shaw:** Yes, I know you were quite proud about it. . . . But I wonder if you had any other feelings about it.

Advanced empathy can be confrontational, as it certainly was in this instance. Too confrontational, it turned out. From our perspective, Dr. Shaw was on target, but John was too frightened, too angry to consider the interpretation. Therapists, beginning with Freud, have been mindful of the importance of timing. Shaw erred, perhaps because of the impatience he felt with himself for dancing too gingerly around John's problems for fear of sounding like a bigoted white person, or an insensitive therapist who does not truly understand the client's torment.

If John had consulted a behavior therapist, some of the things already mentioned might have happened because contemporary behavior therapists also believe that many clients can benefit from expression of feelings (they call it assertion training, not the discharge of repressed hostility) and from a clearer idea of what is motivating them (they call it behavioral assessment) (Goldfried & Davison, 1994). However, behavior therapists tend to be more concrete and active in prescribing techniques for their clients. For John, there might have been role-playing in the consulting room to help him rehearse with the therapist ways of expressing resentment and disagreement with people.

The therapist, however, would have had to make the ethical judgment of how "activist" John should be: Would an assertive response be called for at the very hint of a racial slur, even at the risk of alienating, say, one of the partners in John's law office? Or would the therapist suggest systematic desensitization to harden John to these racist comments so that they would bother him less and presumably elicit little if any overt response? These are weighty moral questions, inherent to any mode of psychotherapy (Davison, 1991).

Relaxation training and meditation (e.g., Benson, 1975; Patel et al., 1985) have also been used extensively and with some success in efforts to control hypertension (DiTomasso, 1987; Yung & Keltner, 1996). In a clinical trial conducted by DeQuattro and Davison (Lee et al., 1987), intensively practiced relaxation reduced blood pressure in a group of male borderline hypertensives more than did a treatment condition in which participants received state-of-the-art medical advice and instructions concerning diet, weight loss, and other known risk factors (the relaxation group also received this information). Of interest was the additional finding that relaxation was especially effective among those men whose sympathetic arousal was high, supporting an earlier suggestion by Esler et al. (1997) that there is a subset of hypertensives who may be particularly appropriate for sympathetic dampening therapies like relaxation. From the same dataset also emerged the finding that anger and hostility as assessed by a think-aloud cognitive assessment technique called

Articulated Thoughts in Simulated Situations (Davison, Robins, & Johnson, 1983) were reduced significantly more by the relaxation than by the information-only treatment and that this reduction was correlated with drops in blood pressure: The less angry and hostile subjects became in their thinking, the more benefit in blood pressure reduction they achieved from the training in relaxation (Davison, Williams, Nezami, Bice, & DeQuattro, 1991).

There has also been some interest nowadays in biofeedback, a technique that uses a highly sensitive electronic apparatus to inform a person of bodily changes that are usually too subtle to be detected. John might have been taught when his blood pressure had passed a certain level and then been reinforced for bringing it down below that level. Statistically significant changes have been achieved with both normals and hypertensives in laboratory settings (Blanchard, 1990; Blanchard et al., 1996), but what clinical success has been achieved may be due to relaxation per se (McGrady, Nadsady, & Schumann-Brzezinski, 1991). Attention to the person's driven lifestyle also seems to be essential if anything like biofeedback is going to play a significant role in lowering blood pressure.

Given his emotional reticence, the fact that he tended to keep to himself and not even examine on his own the conflicts he felt about what it was taking to succeed as an African American in a white society, it is possible that John Williams would have benefited from an intervention based on Pennybaker's work on writing or talking into a tape recorder about personally relevant emotional experiences (Pennybaker, 1997). A number of studies have shown improvements across a wide range of outcomes—mood, feelings of well-being, frequency of visits to physicians, and even immune function—when people spend just half an hour in the investigator's laboratory for three to five days writing or talking about very important emotional issues that have affected their lives. It is significant that these positive effects occur only via the disclosure that is inherent to the process; participants in such experiments do not interact with or get feedback from anyone else about what they have written or spoken into a tape recorder, and their productions are not even connected to their names. The general instructions that people get in this kind of experiment are as follows (control participants are told to write about superficial topics, such as how they spend their time):

For the next three days, I would like you to write about your deepest thoughts and feelings about an extremely important emotional issue that has affected you and your life. In your writing, I'd like for you to really let go and explore your very deepest emotions and thoughts. You might tie your topic to your relationships with others, including parents, lovers, friends, or relatives to your past, your present, or your future; or to who you have been, who you would like to be, or who you are now. All of your writing will be completely confidential. Don't worry about spelling, sentence structure, or grammar. The only rule is that once you begin writing, continue to do so until your time is up (Pennybaker, 1997, p.162).

How this kind of anonymous self-examination and self-disclosure works is not known. One theory proposed by Pennybaker (1989) suggests that inhibition per se can create or exacerbate stress and that therefore disinhibition of the kind that his writing assignments bring about can be beneficial to both mental and physical health. This is reminiscent of Andrew Salter's (1949) classic book *Conditioned Reflex Therapy*, in which he argued that excess inhibition was detrimental to psychological well-being and that asserting oneself—expressing one's likes and dislikes to others—was helpful for a wide variety of emotional ills. Interestingly, both Pennybaker's research and Salter's earlier theorizing and clinical reports are similar to the tenets of humanistic therapies like the client-centered therapy of Carl Rogers (1951), which regard expression of positive and negative feelings as a necessary component of effective living (Davison & Neale, 1998, p.526).

Another hypothesis derives from learning theory (Bootzin, 1997). Perhaps writing about troubling experiences for hours (as is the case in Pennybaker's experiments) produces extinction of negative feelings through repeated exposure to conditioned aversive stimuli, in much the same way as some theorists believe systematic desensitization works (Wilson & Davison, 1971).

Other work by Pennybaker and his associates examines the linguistic content and structure of what experimental participants write. One analysis showed greater improvement in people whose stories contained relatively high levels of words denoting understanding and insight (e.g., "cause," "reason," "realize") (Pennybaker, Mayne, & Francis, 1997). Such findings suggest that devoting a set amount of time to reflecting on one's important emotional experiences, both positive and negative, *and* expressing those ideas in language may lead to a kind of insight or enhanced self-awareness that can help people place important events in their lives into a meaningful context and thereby attain mental and physical benefits.

9 Eating Disorders

Lynne, twenty-four, was admitted to the psychiatric ward of a general hospital for treatment of anorexia nervosa. Although she didn't really think anything was wrong with her, her parents had consulted with a psychiatrist, and the three of them had confronted her with a choice of admitting herself or being committed involuntarily.

At the time Lynne had only seventy-eight pounds on her five-foot-five-inch frame. She hadn't menstruated for three years and had a variety of medical problems—hypotension (abnormal low blood pressure), irregularities in her heartbeat, and abnormally low levels of potassium and calcium.

Lynne had experienced several episodes of dramatic weight loss, beginning at age eighteen when she was going through the dissolution of her first marriage. But none of the prior episodes had been this severe, and she had not sought treatment before. She had an intense fear of becoming fat, and although she had never really been overweight, she felt that her buttocks and abdomen were far too large. (This belief persisted even when she weighed seventy-eight pounds.) During the periods of weight loss she severely restricted food intake and used laxatives heavily. She had occasionally had episodes of binge eating, typically followed by self-induced vomiting so that she would not gain any weight.

Many cultures are preoccupied with eating. In the United States today, gourmet restaurants abound, as do fast-food eateries, and numerous magazines and television shows are devoted to food preparation. At the same time, many people are overweight. Dieting to lose weight is common, and the desire of many people, especially women, to be thinner has created a multimillion-dollar-a-year business. Given this intense interest in food and eating, it is not surprising that this aspect of human behavior is subject to disorder.

Although clinical descriptions of eating disorders can be traced back many years, these disorders appeared in the DSM for the first time in 1980 as one subcategory of disorders beginning in childhood or adolescence. With the publication of DSM-IV, the eating disorders, anorexia nervosa and bulimia nervosa, became a distinct category, reflecting the increased attention they have received from clinicians and researchers over the past three decades.

Clinical Description

We begin by describing anorexia nervosa and bulimia nervosa. The diagnoses of these two disorders share several clinical features, most important, an intense fear of being overweight. In fact, there are some indications that these may not be distinct diagnoses but may be two variants of a single disorder. For example, co-twins of patients diagnosed with anorexia nervosa are themselves more likely than average to have bulimia nervosa (Walters & Kendler, 1994).

DSM-IV-TR Criteria for Anorexia Nervosa

- Refusal to maintain normal body weight
- Although very underweight, extreme fear of becoming fat
- Body image disturbance
- In postmenarchal women, amenorrhea

Anorexia Nervosa

Lynne, the woman just described, had **anorexia nervosa**. The term *anorexia* refers to loss of appetite, and *nervosa* indicates that the loss is due to emotional reasons. The term is something of a misnomer because most patients with anorexia nervosa actually do not lose their appetite or interest in food. On the contrary, while starving themselves, most patients with the disorder become preoccupied with food; they may read cookbooks constantly and prepare gourmet meals for their families.

Lynne met all four features required for the diagnosi:

1. The person must refuse to maintain a normal body weight; this is usually taken to mean that the person weighs less than 85 percent of what is considered normal for that person's age and height. Weight loss is typically achieved through dieting, although purging (self-induced vomiting, heavy use of laxatives or diuretics) and excessive exercise can also be part of the picture.

2. People with anorexia have an intense fear of gaining weight, and the fear is not reduced by weight loss. They can never be thin enough.

3. Patients with anorexia nervosa have a distorted sense of their body shape. Even when emaciated they maintain that they are overweight or that certain parts of their bodies, particularly the abdomen, buttocks, and thighs, are too fat. To check on their body size, they typically weigh themselves frequently, measure the size of different parts of the body, and gaze critically at their reflections in mirrors. Their self-esteem is closely linked to maintaining thinness.

4. In females, the extreme emaciation causes amenorrhea, the loss of the menstrual period. Of the four diagnostic criteria, amenorrhea seems least important; few differences have been found between women who meet all four criteria and those who meet the other three but not amenorrhea (Garfinkel et al., 1996).

Anorexia nervosa can be a life-threatening condition. It is especially prevalent among young women who are under intense pressure to keep their weight low. Gymnast Christy Henrich died from the condition in 1994.

The distorted body image that accompanies anorexia nervosa has been assessed in several ways, most frequently by a questionnaire such as the Eating Disorders Inventory (Garner, Olmsted, & Polivy, 1983). Some of the items on this questionnaire are presented later in the chapter in Table 9.1 (p. 258). In another type of assessment, patients are shown line drawings of women with varying body weights and asked to pick the one closest to their own and the one that represents their ideal shape (see Figure 9.1). Patients with anorexia nervosa overestimate their own body size and choose a thin figure as their ideal. Despite this distortion in body size, patients with anorexia nervosa are fairly accurate when reporting their actual weight (McCabe, McFarlane, Polivy, & Olmsted, 2001), perhaps because they weigh themselves frequently.

Figure 9.1 In this assessment of body image, respondents indicate their current shape, their ideal shape, and the shape they think is most attractive to the opposite sex. The figure actually rated as most attractive by members of the opposite sex ("Other attractive") is shown in both panels. Ratings of women who scored high on a measure of distorted attitudes toward eating are shown in (a); ratings of women who scored low are shown in (b). The high scorers overestimated their current size and ideally would be very thin. From Zellner, Harner, and Adler (1988).

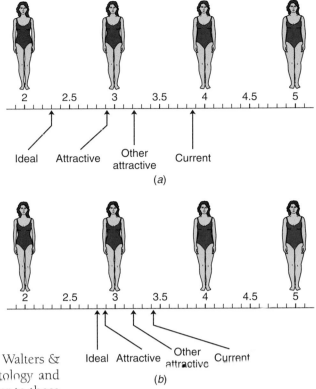

DSM-IV-TR distinguishes two types of anorexia nervosa. In the *restricting type*, weight loss is achieved by severely limiting food intake; in the *binge-eating–purging type*, as illustrated in Lynne's case, the person also regularly engages in binge eating and purging. Numerous differences between these two subtypes support the validity of this distinction. The binging–purging subtype appears to be more psychopathological; patients exhibit more personality disorders, impulsive behavior, stealing, alcohol and drug abuse, social withdrawal, and suicide attempts than do patients with the restricting type of anorexia (e.g., Herzog et al., 2000; Pryor, Wiederman, & McGilley, 1996).

Anorexia nervosa typically begins in the early to middle teenage years, often after an episode of dieting and the occurrence of a life stress. It is at least ten times more frequent in women than in men, with a lifetime prevalence of a little less than 1 percent (Striegel-Moore et al., 1999; Walters & Kendler, 1994). When anorexia nervosa does occur in men, symptomatology and other characteristics, such as reports of family conflict, are generally similar to those reported by women with the disorder (Olivardia et al., 1995). As we discuss more fully later, the gender difference in the prevalence of anorexia most likely reflects the greater cultural emphasis on a thin shape as the ideal over the past several decades.

Patients with anorexia nervosa are frequently diagnosed with depression, obsessive-compulsive disorder, phobias, panic disorder, alcoholism, and various personality disorders (Godart et al., 2000; Ivarsson et al., 2000; Walters & Kendler, 1994). Men with anorexia nervosa are also likely to have a diagnosis of a mood disorder, schizophrenia, or substance dependence (Striegel-Moore et al., 1999). As is often the case, comorbidity declines when community rather than clinical samples are studied because clinical samples usually include people with more serious, multifaceted problems (Welch & Fairburn, 1996).

Anorexia Nervosa and Depression   The strong connection between anorexia nervosa and depression has prompted some researchers to consider the possibility that anorexia causes depression (e.g., through the biochemical changes produced by starvation or the feelings of guilt and shame that accompany it). Anorexia nervosa does not always precede depression, however (Pope & Hudson, 1988). For example, a longitudinal study found that only one of fifty-one adolescents with anorexia had depression prior to the onset of anorexia. Much more common was the development of depression concurrent with or following the onset of anorexia (Ivarsson et al., 2000).

The two disorders could also share a common diathesis or common environmental causes, such as a disturbed family environment or other life stress. Supporting the possibility of a genetic diathesis, studies have shown that relatives of patients with anorexia are at high risk for depression and that the genetic liabilities for anorexia and depression are significantly related (e.g., Hudson et al., 1987; Wade et al., 2000). On the psychological side, research has also found that women with anorexia who are depressed have a depressive attributional style (described more fully in Chapter 10, p. 278). When they experience a stressful life event, they tend to explain the event in ways that create negative emotional states (Metalsky et al., 1997).

Physical Changes in Anorexia Nervosa   Self-starvation and use of laxatives produce numerous undesirable biological consequences in patients with anorexia nervosa.

Despite being thin, women with anorexia believe that parts of their bodies are too fat and spend a lot of time critically examining themselves in front of mirrors.

Blood pressure often falls, heart rate slows, kidney and gastrointestinal problems develop, bone mass declines, the skin dries out, nails become brittle, hormone levels change, and mild anemia may occur. Some patients lose hair from the scalp, and they may develop lanugo, a fine, soft hair, on their bodies. As in Lynne's case, levels of electrolytes, such as potassium and sodium, are altered. These ionized salts, present in various bodily fluids, are essential for the process of neural transmission, and lowered levels can lead to tiredness, weakness, cardiac arrythmias, and even sudden death. EEG abnormalities and neurological impairments are frequent in patients with anorexia (Garner, 1997; Lambe et al., 1997). Structural brain changes, such as enlarged ventricles or sulcal widening, can also occur, but can be reversed (Hoffman et al., 1989; Lambe et al., 1997).

Prognosis   About 70 percent of patients with anorexia eventually recover. However, recovery often takes six or seven years, and relapses are common before a stable pattern of eating and maintenance of weight is achieved (Strober, Freeman, & Morrel, 1997). As we discuss later, changing these patients' distorted views of themselves is very difficult, particularly in cultures that value thinness.

Anorexia nervosa is a life-threatening illness; death rates are ten times higher among patients with the disorder than among the general population and twice as high as among patients with other psychological disorders. Death most often results from physical complications of the illness—for example, congestive heart failure—and from suicide (Herzog et al., 2000; Sullivan, 1995).

Bulimia Nervosa

Jill was the second child born to her parents. Both she and her brother became intensely involved in athletics at an early age, Jill in gymnastics and Tom in Little League baseball. At age four Jill was enrolled in gymnastics school, where she excelled. By the time she was nine her mother had decided that Jill had outstripped the coaching abilities of the local instructors and began driving her to a nationally recognized coach several times a week. Over the next few years, Jill's trophy case swelled and her aspirations for a place on the Olympic team grew. As she reached puberty, though, her thin frame began to fill out, raising concerns about the effects of weight gain on her performance as a gymnast. She began to restrict her intake of food but found that after several days of semistarvation she would lose control and go on an eating binge. This pattern of dieting and binging lasted for several months, and Jill's fear of becoming fat seemed to increase during that time. At age thirteen, she hit on the solution of self-induced vomiting. She quickly fell into a pattern of episodes of binging and vomiting three or four times per week. Although she maintained this pattern in secret for a while, eventually her parents caught on and initiated treatment for her.

Jill's behavior illustrates the features of **bulimia nervosa**. *Bulimia* is from a Greek word meaning "ox hunger." This disorder involves episodes of rapid consumption of a large amount of food, followed by compensatory behavior, such as vomiting, fasting, or excessive exercise, to prevent weight gain. The DSM defines a binge as eating an excessive amount of food within less than two hours. Bulimia nervosa is not diagnosed if the binging and purging occur only in the context of anorexia nervosa and its extreme weight loss; the diagnosis in such a case is anorexia nervosa, binge-eating–purging type. Indeed, one striking difference between anorexia and bulimia is weight loss: patients with anorexia nervosa lose a tremendous amount of weight whereas patients with bulimia nervosa do not.

In bulimia, binges typically occur in secret, may be triggered by stress and the negative emotions it arouses, and continue until the person is uncomfortably full (Grilo, Shiffman, & Carter-Campbell, 1994). Foods that can be rapidly consumed, especially sweets such as ice cream and cake, are usually part of a binge. A recent study found that women with bulimia nervosa were more likely to binge while alone and during the morning or afternoon. In addition, avoiding a craved food on one day was associated with a binge episode the next morning (Waters, Hill, & Waller, 2001). Other studies show that

a binge is likely to occur after a negative social interaction, or at least the perception of a negative social exchange (Steiger et al., 1999).

Although research suggests that patients with bulimia nervosa sometimes ingest enormous quantities of food during binges, often more than what a normal person eats in an entire day, binges are not always as large as the DSM implies, and there is wide variation in the caloric content consumed by individuals with bulimia nervosa during binges (e.g., Rossiter & Agras, 1990). Patients report that they lose control during a binge, even to the point of experiencing something akin to a dissociative state, perhaps losing awareness of what they are doing or feeling that it is not really they who are binging. They are usually ashamed of their binges and try to conceal them.

After the binge is over, disgust, feelings of discomfort, and fear of weight gain lead to the second step of bulimia nervosa, purging to undo the caloric effects of the binge. Patients most often stick fingers down their throats to cause gagging, but after a time many can induce vomiting at will without gagging themselves. Laxative and diuretic abuse (which do little to reduce body weight) as well as fasting and excessive exercise are also used to prevent weight gain.

Although many people binge occasionally and some people also experiment with purging, the DSM diagnosis of bulimia nervosa requires that the episodes of binging and purging occur at least twice a week for three months. Is twice a week a well-established cut-off point? Probably not. Few differences are found between patients who binge twice a week and those who do so less frequently, suggesting that we are dealing with a continuum of severity rather than a sharp distinction (Garfinkel et al., 1995).[1]

Like patients with anorexia nervosa, patients with bulimia nervosa are afraid of gaining weight, and their self-esteem depends heavily on maintaining normal weight. Whereas people without eating disorders typically underreport their weight and say they are taller than they actually are, patients with bulimia nervosa are more accurate in their reports (Doll & Fairburn, 1998; McCabe et al., 2001). Yet patients with bulimia nervosa are also likely to be highly dissatisfied with their bodies. At this point, it remains somewhat unclear if this body dissatisfaction is uniquely related to bulimia nervosa or if it is more strongly linked to comorbid depression or cultural ideas on thinness (Cooper & Hunt, 1998; Keel et al., 2001; Wiederman & Pryer, 2000).

As with anorexia, two subtypes of bulimia nervosa are distinguished: a purging type and a nonpurging type in which the compensatory behaviors are fasting or excessive exercise. Evidence for the validity of this distinction is mixed. In some studies, people diagnosed with nonpurging bulimia were heavier, binged less frequently, and showed less psychopathology than did people with purging-type bulimia (e.g., Mitchell, 1992). But in other research, few differences emerged between the two types (e.g., Tobin & Griffing, 1997).

Bulimia nervosa typically begins in late adolescence or early adulthood. About 90 percent of cases are women, and prevalence among women is thought to be about 1 to 2 percent of the population (Gotesdam & Agras, 1995). Many patients with bulimia nervosa were somewhat overweight before the onset of the disorder, and the binge eating often started during an episode of dieting.

Bulimia nervosa is associated with numerous other diagnoses, notably depression, personality disorders (especially borderline personality disorder, discussed in Chapter 13), anxiety disorders, substance abuse, and conduct disorder (discussed in Chapter 15) (Carroll, Touyz, & Beumont, 1996; Godart et al., 2000; Lilenfeld et al., 1997). Men with bulimia are also likely to be diagnosed with a mood disorder or substance dependence (Striegel-Moore et al., 1999). Suicide rates are much higher among people with bulimia nervosa than in the general population (Favaro & Santonastaso, 1998). Suicide attempts among bulimia nervosa patients are comparable to suicide attempts among patients with major depression and anorexia nervosa (Bulik, Sullivan, & Joyce, 1999).

---

[1] It is research such as this that leads to changes in successive editions of the DSM.

A twin study has found that bulimia and depression are genetically related (Walters et al., 1992).

Physical Changes in Bulimia Nervosa   Like anorexia, bulimia is associated with several physical side effects. Although less common than in anorexia, menstrual irregularities, including amenorrhea, can occur, even though bulimia patients typically have a normal Body Mass Index or BMI (Gendall et al., 2000). (The BMI is calculated by dividing weight in kilograms by height in meters squared and is considered a more valid estimate of body fat than many others [NIH, 1998]. For women, a normal BMI is between 20 and 25). In addition, frequent purging can cause potassium depletion. Heavy use of laxatives induces diarrhea, which can also lead to changes in electrolytes and cause irregularities in the heartbeat. Recurrent vomiting has been linked to menstrual problems and may lead to tearing of tissue in the stomach and throat and to loss of dental enamel as stomach acids eat away at the teeth, which become ragged. The salivary glands may become swollen. Bulimia nervosa, like anorexia, is a serious disorder with many unfortunate physical consequences (Garner, 1997). However, mortality appears to be much less common in bulimia nervosa than in anorexia nervosa (Herzog et al., 2000; Keel & Mitchell, 1997).

Prognosis   Long-term follow-ups of patients with bulimia nervosa reveal that about 70 percent recover, although about 10 percent remain fully symptomatic (Keel et al., 1999; Reas et al., 2000). Intervening soon after a diagnosis is made (i.e., within the first few years) is linked with an even better prognosis (Reas et al., 2000). Patients with bulimia nervosa who binge and vomit more, have comorbid substance abuse, or a history of depression have a poorer prognosis than patients without these factors (Wilson et al., 1999).

Binge Eating Disorder

DSM-IV-TR includes **binge eating disorder** as a diagnosis in need of further study rather than as a formal diagnosis. This disorder includes recurrent binges (two times per week for at least six months), lack of control during the binging episode, and distress about binging, as well as other characteristics, such as rapid eating and eating alone. It is distinguished from anorexia nervosa by the absence of weight loss and from bulimia nervosa by the absence of compensatory behaviors (purging, fasting, or excessive exercise).

Though it did not meet the threshold for inclusion in the current DSM (see Fairburn, Welsh, & Hay, 1993), binge eating disorder has several features that support its validity. It occurs more often in women than in men and is associated with obesity and a history of dieting (Kinzl et al., 1999; Pike et al., 2001). It is linked to impaired work and social functioning, depression, low self-esteem, substance abuse, and dissatisfaction with body shape (Spitzer et al., 1993; Striegel-Moore et al., 1998, 2001). Risk factors for developing binge eating disorder include childhood obesity, critical comments regarding being overweight, low self-concept, depression, and childhood physical or sexual abuse (Fairburn et al., 1998).

Binge eating disorder appears to be more prevalent than either anorexia nervosa or bulimia nervosa, particularly among individuals seeking treatment for weight control. In a community sample it was found in 6 percent of successful dieters (those who had kept their weight off for more than one year) and in 19 percent of unsuccessful dieters (Ferguson & Spitzer, 1995).

One advantage of including this disorder as a diagnosis is that it would apply to many patients who are now given the vague diagnosis of "eating disorder not otherwise specified" because they do not meet criteria for anorexia or bulimia (Spitzer et al., 1993).

Nevertheless, some researchers do not view binge eating disorder as a discrete diagnostic category but rather as a less severe version of bulimia nervosa. The reason is that few differences are found between women with binge eating disorder and the nonpurging form of bulimia nervosa (Hay & Fairburn, 1998; Joiner, Vohs, & Heatherton, 2000;

Striegel-Moore et al., 2001). Making this distinction even more difficult is the fact that the non-purging type of bulimia nervosa is quite rare, so that large sample comparisons are difficult to conduct (Striegel-Moore et al., 2001).

Etiology of Eating Disorders

As with other psychopathologies, a single factor is unlikely to cause an eating disorder. Several areas of current research—genetics, the role of the brain, sociocultural pressures to be thin, personality, the role of the family, and the role of environmental stress—suggest that eating disorders result when several influences converge in a person's life.

Biological Factors

Genetics   Both anorexia nervosa and bulimia nervosa run in families. First-degree relatives of young women with anorexia nervosa are over ten times more likely than average to have the disorder themselves (e.g., Strober et al., 2000). Similar results are found for bulimia nervosa, where first-degree relatives of women with bulimia nervosa are about four times more likely than average to have the disorder (e.g., Kassett et al., 1987; Strober et al., 2000). Although eating disorders are quite rare among men, a recent study found that first-degree relatives of men with anorexia nervosa were at greater risk for having anorexia nervosa (though not bulimia) than relatives of men without anorexia (Strober et al., 2001). Finally, relatives of patients with eating disorders are more likely than average to have symptoms of eating disorders that do not meet the complete criteria for a diagnosis (Lilenfeld et al., 1998; Strober et al., 2000).

Twin studies of eating disorders also suggest a genetic influence. Most studies of both anorexia and bulimia report higher MZ than DZ concordance rates (Fichter & Naegel, 1990; Holland et al., 1988) and genes are of greater influence among twins with eating disorders compared to environmental factors (Wade et al., 2000). Research has also suggested that key features of the eating disorders, such as dissatisfaction with one's body, a strong desire to be thin, binge eating, and preoccupation with weight are heritable (Klump, McGue, & Iacono, 2000; Rutherford et al., 1993). Additional evidence suggests that common genetic factors may account for the relationship between certain personality characteristics, such as negative emotionality, and eating disorders (Klump, McGue, & Iacono, 2002). These data are consistent with the possibility that a genetic diathesis is operating, but adoption studies are also needed. Using the method of genetic linkage analysis (discussed in Chapter 2), a recent study reported evidence for linkage on chromosome 1 among individuals with anorexia (Grice et al., 2002). It will be important to replicate this finding in future studies, but all of these findings suggest that genetics do indeed play a role in eating disorders.

Eating Disorders and the Brain   The hypothalamus is a key brain center in regulating hunger and eating. Research on animals with lesions to the lateral hypothalamus indicates that they lose weight and have no appetite (Hoebel & Teitelbaum, 1966). Thus, it is not surprising that the hypothalamus has been proposed to play a role in anorexia. The level of some hormones regulated by the hypothalamus, such as cortisol, are indeed abnormal in patients with anorexia; rather than causing the disorder, however, these hormonal abnormalities occur as a result of self-starvation, and levels return to normal following weight gain (Doerr et al., 1980; Stöving et al., 1999). Furthermore, the weight loss of animals with hypothalamic lesions does not parallel what we know about anorexia. These animals appear to have no hunger and become indifferent to food, whereas patients with anorexia continue to starve themselves despite being hungry and having an interest in food. Nor does the hypothalamic model account for body-image disturbance or fear of becoming fat. A dysfunctional hypothalamus thus does not seem highly likely as a factor in anorexia nervosa.

Endogenous opioids are substances produced by the body that reduce pain sensations, enhance mood, and suppress appetite, at least among those with low body weight. Opioids are released during starvation and have been viewed as playing a role in both anorexia and bulimia, but in different ways. Starvation among patients with anorexia may increase the levels of endogenous opioids, resulting in a positively reinforcing euphoric state (Marrazzi & Luby, 1986). Furthermore, the excessive exercise seen among some patients would increase opioids and thus be reinforcing (Davis, 1996; Epling & Pierce, 1992). Hardy and Waller (1988) hypothesized that bulimia is mediated by low levels of endogenous opioids, which are thought to promote craving; a euphoric state is then produced by the ingestion of food, thus reinforcing binging.

Some data support the theory that endogenous opioids play a role in eating disorders, at least in bulimia. For example, both Waller et al. (1986) and Brewerton et al. (1992) found low levels of the endogenous opioid beta-endorphin in patients with bulimia. In the Waller study it was also observed that the more severe cases of bulimia had the lowest levels of beta-endorphin. It is important to note, however, that these findings demonstrate that low levels of opioids are seen concurrently with bulimia, not that such levels are seen before the onset of the disorder. Changes in food intake could affect the opioid system rather than the reverse. Indeed, giving an opioid antagonist to obese individuals has been shown to decrease food intake (Drewnowski et al., 1992). Therefore, it is unclear whether the opioid system is directly or indirectly involved in the etiology of bulimia.

Finally, some research has focused on several neurotransmitters related to eating and satiety (feeling full). Animal research has shown that serotonin promotes satiety. Therefore, it could be that the binges of patients with bulimia result from a serotonin deficit that causes them not to feel satiated as they eat. Animal research has also shown that food restriction interferes with serotonin synthesis in the brain. Thus, in patients with anorexia, the severe food intake restrictions could interfere with the serotonin system.

Researchers have examined levels of serotonin and other neurotransmitters or their metabolites in patients with anorexia and bulimia. Several studies have reported low levels of serotonin metabolites in patients with anorexia (e.g., Kaye, Ebert, Raliegh, & Lake, 1984). In addition, patients with anorexia who have not been restored to a healthy weight show a smaller response to serotonin agonists than those patients who have regained a good portion of their weight, again suggesting an underactive serotonin system (Attia et al., 1998; Ferguson et al., 1999; Kaye et al., 2000). Other studies, however, find evidence of increased serotonin metabolites in plasma or cerebrospinal fluid (CSF) in patients with anorexia (Kaye et al., 1991), and so the role of serotonin in anorexia is not entirely clear. The evidence appears to be more consistent in bulimia, with most findings suggesting a decrease in serotonin metabolites (e.g., Carrasco et al., 2000; Jimerson et al., 1992; Kaye et al., 1998). Patients with bulimia also show smaller responses to serotonin agonists (Jimerson et al., 1997; Levitan et al., 1997). Furthermore, when patients who had recovered from bulimia nervosa had their serotonin levels reduced, they showed an increase in cognitions related to eating disorders, such as feeling fat (Smith, Fairburn, & Cowan, 1999).

Other data support the idea that a serotonin deficit might be related to anorexia and bulimia. The antidepressant drugs that are often effective treatments for anorexia and bulimia (discussed later) are known to increase serotonin levels, adding to the possible importance of serotonin. Finally, serotonin could be linked to the comorbid depression often found in anorexia and bulimia and to the impulsive behavior of patients with bulimia nervosa (see the discussion of serotonin, depression, and impulsivity in Chapter 10).

Though we can expect further biochemical research in the future, it is important to keep in mind that much of this work focuses on brain mechanisms relevant to hunger, eating, and satiety and does little to account for other key features of both disorders, in particular, the intense fear of becoming fat. Furthermore, as suggested, it is not clear whether brain changes predate the onset of eating disorders. Social and cultural environments appear to play a role in the faulty perceptions and eating habits of those with eating disorders, and it is to these influences we now turn.

Sociocultural Influences

Throughout history the standards societies have set for the ideal body—especially the ideal female body—have varied greatly. Think of the famous nudes painted by Rubens in the seventeenth century: According to modern standards these women are chubby. In recent times the American cultural ideal has progressed steadily toward increasing thinness. *Playboy* centerfolds became thinner between 1959 and 1978, for example (Garner et al., 1980); and beauty pageant contestants also became thinner through 1988. Some research in the 1990s suggested that this trend might have leveled off (Wiseman et al., 1992). However, a recent study failed to support this idea. The study calculated the BMI of *Playboy* centerfolds from 1985–1997 (Owen & Laurel-Seller, 2000). All but one of the Playboy centerfolds had a BMI of less than 20, which is considered to be a low weight, and almost half of the centerfolds had a BMI of less than 18, which is considered to be severe underweight. Of course, *Playboy* centerfolds are not necessarily the standard to which Western women compare themselves. Still, this study indicates that thin—at least, for women—is still very much "in."

For men, the situation appears somewhat different. In a study parallel to the studies examining *Playboy* centerfolds, Leit, Pope, and Gray (2001) analyzed the BMI of *Playgirl* male centerfolds from 1973–1997. They found that the centerfolds' BMI increased over the period and that their muscularity, assessed using a fat to muscle estimate, increased even more. Nemeroff et al. (1994) analyzed the content of several men's magazines and found that the frequency of articles on weight loss, although lower in men's than in women's magazines, increased during the time period studied. It would probably be incorrect to assume from these data, however, that we are about to witness an explosion of eating disorders in men. It is more plausible that the articles focus attention on the masculine ideal of normal body weight or on increased muscle mass (Mishkind et al., 1986).

Somewhat paradoxically, as cultural standards were moving in the direction of thinness over the later part of the twentieth century, more and more people were becoming overweight. The prevalence of obesity has doubled since 1900. Currently, 20 to 30 percent of Americans are overweight, perhaps because of an abundance of food and a sedentary lifestyle, setting the stage for greater conflict between the cultural ideal and reality.

As society has become more health and fat conscious, dieting to lose weight has become more common; the number of dieters increased from 7 percent of men and 14 percent of women in 1950 to 29 percent of men and 44 percent of women in 1999 (Serdula et al., 1999). The diet industry (books, pills, videos, special foods) is valued at more than $30 billion per year—about what the U.S. government spent on education, training, employment, and social services combined. Finally, liposuction (vacuuming out fat deposits just under the skin) is a very common (and sometimes risky) procedure in plastic surgery (Brownell & Rodin, 1994).

The percentages above indicate that women are more likely than men to be dieters. Dieting to lose weight is especially common among white, upper-socioeconomic status women—the same group with the highest rate of anorexia nervosa. The onset of eating disorders is typically preceded by dieting and other concerns about weight, supporting the idea that social standards stressing the importance of thinness play a role in the development of these disorders (see Focus on Discovery 9.1) (Killen et al., 1994; Stice, 2001).

Cultural standards regarding the ideal feminine shape have changed over time. Even in the 1950s and 1960s, the feminine ideal was considerably heavier than what it became in the 1970s, 1980s, and 1990s.

It is likely that women who either are actually overweight or fear being fat are also dissatisfied with their bodies. Not surprisingly, studies have found both a high BMI and body dissatisfaction to be risk factors for the development of eating disorders (Fairburn et al., 1997; Killen et al., 1996). Body dissatisfaction appears to be on the rise (Garner, 1997), and it is a robust predictor of the development of eating disorders among adolescent girls (Killen et al., 1996). In addition, preoccupation with being thin or feeling pres-

To Diet or Not to Diet?

As dieting has become more common and the diet industry has become a multibillion-dollar-a-year business, the incidence of both eating disorders and obesity has increased. Millions of Americans are overweight. Is there a relationship among these facts? Studies of restrained eaters and patients with eating disorders show that dieting can lead to binging, and very "successful" dieters can become anorexic. Is dieting more dangerous than desirable?

Heredity plays a significant role in obesity. Adoption studies have found that children's weight is more strongly related to the weight of their biological parents than to the weight of their adoptive parents (Price et al., 1987). Similarly, 40 percent of the children of an obese parent will be obese, compared with 7 percent of the children of normal-weight parents. Heredity could produce its effects by regulating metabolic rate or through the hypothalamus and its impact on insulin level or the production of enzymes that make it easier to store fat and gain weight. Dieting may be of little use to people whose obesity is principally genetically caused. Their metabolic rate may simply slow down to help maintain body weight; when the diet is over, the lowered metabolic rate leads to weight gain.

But psychosocial factors are also clearly involved in gaining weight. The prevalence of obesity has doubled over the past few decades; it is unlikely that this dramatic increase could be due to change in genetic makeup (Bandura, 1997). Stress and its associated negative moods can induce eating in some people (Arnow, Kenardy, & Agras, 1992; Heatherton & Baumeister, 1991). And we are all subject to the continuing impact of advertisements, especially those promoting alluring high-fat, high-calorie products such as snack foods, desserts, and meals at fast-food restaurants.

The motivation to achieve thinness is generally tied to several possible goals.

- Being thin increases personal attractiveness, which in turn can produce both psychological benefits (e.g., increased self-esteem) and social benefits (e.g., advancement in the workplace).

- Being thin signifies self-discipline; obesity reflects a lack of self-control and failure.

- Thinness is associated with several health benefits; obesity is associated with health problems. For example, obesity is linked to diabetes, hypertension, cardiovascular disease, and several forms of cancer.

On an empirical level, we have seen at least one potential danger in dieting—it is often a precursor to eating disorders. It is widely known that although many diets achieve weight loss in the short term (for example, one year), the weight is typically regained later (Garner & Wooley, 1991), suggesting that diets don't work in the long term. Weight fluctuation itself could be a health risk (e.g., for cardiovascular disease). Furthermore, the evidence concerning whether weight loss actually yields health benefits is conflicting. For example, the typical weight loss of fifteen pounds may not be sufficient to produce any beneficial effects on health. Finally, it may be that obesity is not the crucial factor that puts people at risk for disease; the distribution of body fat could be more telling. A large concentration of fat around the abdomen is more strongly related to mortality and cardiovascular dis-

ease than is a more even distribution of fat or a concentration of fat below the waist (Garner & Wooley, 1991).

In trying to reconcile the competing positions on dieting, Brownell and Rodin (1994) acknowledge that not all the data are in. Nonetheless, they counter some of the points raised by anti–dieters. They note, for example, that the samples in studies showing the long-term ineffectiveness of dieting typically contained large percentages of binge eaters. Because binge eating is related to a poor prognosis for treating obesity, the data may underestimate the positive effects of dieting. Furthermore, they point to newer studies with more favorable long-term outcomes. In one, participants with an average weight loss of fifty-five pounds maintained 75 percent of the weight loss at a one-year follow-up and 52 percent at two years (Nunn, Newton, & Faucher, 1992). Brownell and Rodin also point out that studies showing an association between weight fluctuation and poor health did not actually study dieting. Therefore, the weight fluctuation that was observed could have been due to other factors, such as alcoholism, stress, or cancer. Finally, they note that returning to pre–diet weight sometime after dieting is not necessarily a bad outcome. Considering a return to baseline as a failure does not take into consideration what the person's weight would have been if no diet had ever been attempted.

Brownell and Rodin suggest that the decision to diet might be more profitably based on individualized risk-to-benefit ratios. Generally these would be expected to become more favorable to dieting in very overweight people. But more individualized applications could also be considered. The benefits of dieting could assume much more importance in someone with a family history of hypertension and cardiovascular disease. Conversely, for someone with a family history of eating disorders, embarking on a diet would have to be viewed as a risky step.

Dieting to lose weight is typically motivated by a desire to become more attractive and to achieve health benefits. Although dieting leads to short-term weight loss, the lost pounds are often regained.

sure to be thin predicts an increase in body dissatisfaction among adolescent girls, which in turn predicts more dieting and feelings of negative emotions. Both of these predict greater eating disorder pathology (Stice, 2001).

The sociocultural ideal of thinness is a likely vehicle through which people learn to fear being or even feeling fat. In addition to creating an undesired physical shape, being fat has negative connotations, such as being unsuccessful and having little self-control. Obese people are viewed by others as less smart and are stereotyped as lonely, shy, and greedy for the affection of others (DeJong & Kleck, 1986).

We have seen that Western culture's thinness standards seem to have changed over the past 40 years or so. However, another sociocultural factor has remained remarkably resilient to change, namely, the objectification of womens' bodies. Womens' bodies are often viewed through a sexual lens; and in effect, women are defined by their bodies. According to objectification theory (Fredrickson & Roberts, 1997), the saturation of objectification messages in Western culture (in television, advertisements, and so forth) has led some women to "self-objectify," which means that they see their own bodies through the eyes of others. Research has shown that self-objectification causes women to feel more shame about their bodies. The emotion of shame is most often elicited in situations where an individual's ideal falls short of a cultural ideal or standard. Thus, women are likely experiencing body shame when they see a mismatch between their ideal self and the cultural (objectified) view of a woman. Research has also shown that both self-objectification and body shame are associated with disordered eating (Fredrickson, et al., 1998; McKinley & Hyde, 1996; Noll & Fredrickson, 1998).

Gender Influences   We have discussed the fact that eating disorders are more common in women than in men. One primary reason for the greater prevalence of eating disorders among women is likely the fact that Western cultural standards reinforce the desirability of being thin for women more than for men. In addition, sociocultural values promote the objectification of womens' bodies, whereas men are esteemed more for their accomplishments. The risk for eating disorders among groups of women who might be expected to be particularly concerned with their weight, for example, models, dancers, and gymnasts, are especially high (Garner et al., 1980).

Cross-Cultural Studies   Eating disorders appear to be more common in industrialized societies, such as the United States, Canada, Japan, Australia, and Europe, than in nonindustrialized nations. In an epidemiological study conducted in Switzerland, the incidence of anorexia nervosa quadrupled from the 1950s to the 1970s (Willi & Grossman, 1983). Similar increases have been found in other countries (Eagles et al., 1995; Hoek et al., 1995). In addition, as cultures undergo social changes associated with adopting the practices of more westernized cultures, the incidence of eating disorders appears to increase (e.g., Abou-Saleh, Younis, & Karim, 1998; Nasser, 1997). Studies have also found that when women from cultures with low prevalence rates of eating disorders move into cultures with higher prevalence rates, prevalence goes up (Nasser, 1986; Yates, 1989).

Presumably, such differences are due to a greater emphasis on thinness and body image in more westernized cultures. Indeed, in some other cultures, higher weight among women is especially valued and considered a sign of fertility and healthiness (Nasser, 1988). The wide variation in the prevalence of eating disorders across cultures provides a window on the importance of culture in establishing realistic versus potentially disordered views of one's body. In a study supporting the notion of cross-cultural differences in body image perception, Ugandan and British college students rated the attractiveness of drawings of nudes ranging from very emaciated to very obese (Furnham & Baguma, 1994). Ugandan students rated the obese females as more attractive than did the British students. As yet, however, because there have been very few cross-cultural epidemiological studies employing similar assessments and diagnostic criteria, it has been difficult to accurately compare prevalence rates of eating disorders across cultures. In one study of 369 adolescent girls in Pakistan, for example, none met diagnostic criteria for

Another indication of our society's preoccupation with thinness is what happened with Miss Universe of 1996, Alicia Machado. When, after winning the title, she gained a few pounds, some people became outraged and suggested she give up her crown.

Standards of beauty vary cross-culturally as shown by Gaugain's painting of Tahitian women.

anorexia nervosa and only one met the criteria for bulimia (Mumford, Whitehouse, & Choudry, 1992). However, other studies have found that eating disorders, or at least milder forms of them, are in fact present in diverse cultures and countries, such as India, the Caribbean island of Curacao, and Spain (Bosch, 2000; Hoek et al., 1998; Srinivasan et al., 1998).

Cross-cultural variation in prevalence of eating disorders thus remains a supposition and a sometimes controversial one. For example, Lee (1994) has described a disorder similar to anorexia nervosa that exists in several nonindustrialized Asian countries (India, Malaysia, the Philippines). This disorder involves severe emaciation, food refusal, and amenorrhea, but not a fear of becoming fat. Is this a cultural variant of anorexia or a different disorder, such as depression? This question is but one of the challenges that face cross-cultural researchers (Lee et al., 2001). Another concerns the role of the individual in relation to family and society in cross-cultural studies of eating disorders.

Ethnic Differences   In the United States, it was reported at one time that the incidence of anorexia was eight times greater in white women than in women of color (Dolan, 1991). More recent studies confirm greater eating disturbances and body dissatisfaction among white women than African American women, but differences in actual eating disorders, particularly bulimia, do not appear to be as great (Wildes, Emery, & Simons, 2001). In addition, the greatest differences between white and African American women in eating disorder pathology appear to be most pronounced in college student samples; fewer differences are observed in either high school or non-clinical community samples (Wildes et al., 2001).

Differences have been observed in some areas, however. Studies show that white teenage girls diet more frequently than do African American teenage girls and are more likely to be dissatisfied with their bodies (Crago et al., 1996; Fitzgibbons et al., 1998; Striegel-Moore et al., 2000). The relationship between BMI and body dissatisfaction also differs by ethnicity. Compared with African American adolescents, white adolescents become more dissatisfied with their bodies as their BMI rises (Striegel-Moore et al., 2000). As already noted, both dieting and body dissatisfaction are related to an increased risk for developing an eating disorder. Indeed, a recent study found that white women with binge eating disorder were more dissatisfied with their bodies than African American women with binge eating disorder, and the white women were more likely to have a history of bulimia nervosa than the African American women (Pike et al., 2001).

Ethnic group membership may not be the only critical variable in observed differences. Social class may also be important (Caldwell, Brownell, & Wilfley, 1997; French et al., 1997). The emphasis on thinness and dieting has now begun to spread beyond white upper- and middle-class women to women of the lower social classes, and the prevalence of eating disorder pathology has increased among these latter groups (e.g., Root, 1990; Striegel-Moore et al., 2000; Story et al., 1995).

Finally, very little is known about the prevalence of eating disorders among Latina or Native American women, and this remains a much-needed research focus.

Psychodynamic Views

There are many psychodynamic theories of eating disorders. Most propose that the core cause is to be found in disturbed parent–child relationships and agree that certain core personality traits, such as low self-esteem and perfectionism, are found among individuals with eating disorders.[2] Psychodynamic theories also propose that the symptoms of an

---

[2] These personality characteristics are not solely the province of psychodynamic theorists; we will see later that cognitive theorists also consider them important.

eating disorder fulfill some need, such as increasing one's sense of personal effectiveness by being successful in maintaining a strict diet or by not growing up sexually by being very thin and thus not achieving the usual female shape (Goodsitt, 1997).

As just suggested, several psychodynamic theories focus on family relationships. One widely held view, proposed by Hilde Bruch (1980), holds that anorexia nervosa is an attempt by children who have been raised to feel ineffectual to gain competence and respect and to ward off feelings of helplessness, ineffectiveness, and powerlessness. This sense of ineffectiveness is believed to be created by a parenting style in which the parents' wishes are imposed on the child without consideration of the child's needs or wishes. For example, parents may arbitrarily decide when the child is hungry or tired, failing to perceive the child's actual state. Children reared in this way do not learn to identify their own internal states and do not become self-reliant. Facing the demands of adolescence, the child seizes on the societal emphasis on thinness and turns dieting into a means of acquiring control and identity. Moreover, negative self-perceptions about weight become the broad lens through which the child sees other aspects of the self, thus contributing to an overall poor self-evaluation.

Another psychodynamic theory, described by Goodsitt (1997), proposes that bulimia nervosa in women stems from a failure to develop an adequate sense of self because of a conflict-ridden mother–daughter relationship. Food becomes a symbol of this failed relationship. The daughter's binging and purging represent the conflict between the need for the mother and the desire to reject her.

Although the evidence in favor of many psychodynamic views is limited, there is some support for these positions from two sources: studies of personality characteristics of patients with eating disorders and studies of the characteristics of their families. It is difficult to reach definitive conclusions in either area, however, because the disorder itself may have resulted in changes in personality or in the patient's family.

Personality and Eating Disorders

We have already seen that neurobiological changes occur as a result of an eating disorder. It is also important to keep in mind that an eating disorder itself can affect personality. A study of semistarvation in male conscientious objectors conducted in the late 1940s supports the idea that the personality of patients with eating disorders, particularly those with anorexia, is affected by their weight loss (Keys et al., 1950). For a period of six weeks the men were given two meals a day, totaling 1,500 calories, to simulate the meals in a concentration camp. On average, they lost 25 percent of their body weight. All the men soon became preoccupied with food. They also reported increased fatigue, poor concentration, lack of sexual interest, irritability, moodiness, and insomnia. Four became depressed, and one developed bipolar disorder. This research shows vividly how severe restriction of food intake can have powerful effects on personality and behavior, which we need to consider when evaluating the personalities of patients with anorexia and bulimia.

In part as a response to the findings just mentioned, some researchers have collected retrospective reports of personality before the onset of an eating disorder. This research describes patients with anorexia as having been perfectionistic, shy, and compliant before the onset of the disorder. The description of patients with bulimia also includes histrionic features, affective instability, and an outgoing social disposition (Vitousek & Manke, 1994). It is important to remember, however, that retrospective reports in which patients and their families recall what the person was like before diagnosis can be inaccurate and biased by awareness of the patient's current problem.

Numerous studies have also measured the current personality of patients with eating disorders, relying on results from established personality questionnaires such as the MMPI. Both patients with anorexia and patients with bulimia are high in neuroticism and anxiety and low in self-esteem. They also score high on a measure of traditionalism, indicating strong endorsement of family and social standards. Some differences emerged between the two groups on the MMPI: patients with anorexia nervosa reported depres-

Table 9.1 Subscales and Illustrative Items from the Eating Disorders Inventory

Drive for thinness	I think about dieting. I feel extremely guilty after overeating. I am preoccupied with the desire to be thinner.
Bulimia	I stuff myself with food. I have gone on eating binges where I have felt that I could not stop. I have the thought of trying to vomit in order to lose weight.
Body dissatisfaction	I think that my thighs are too large. I think that my buttocks are too large. I think that my hips are too big.
Ineffectiveness	I feel inadequate. I have a low opinion of myself. I feel empty inside (emotionally).
Perfectionism	Only outstanding performance is good enough in my family. As a child, I tried hard to avoid disappointing my parents and teachers. I hate being less than best at things.
Interpersonal distrust	I have trouble expressing my emotions to others. I need to keep people at a certain distance (feel uncomfortable if someone tries to get too close).
Interoceptive awareness	I get confused about what emotion I am feeling. I don't know what's going on inside me. I get confused as to whether or not I am hungry.
Maturity fears	I wish that I could return to the security of childhood. I feel that people are happiest when they are children. The demands of adulthood are too great.

Source: From Garner, Olmsted, and Polivy, 1983.

Note: Responses use a six-point scale ranging from always to never.

sion, social isolation, and anxiety, whereas patients with bulimia nervosa exhibited more diffuse and serious psychopathology, scoring higher than the anorexic patients on several of the MMPI scales (Vitousek & Manke, 1994).

The data conflict somewhat as to whether patients with anorexia are high in perfectionism, perhaps because perfectionism is multidimensional and earlier research has not taken this into account. Perfectionism may be self-oriented (setting high standards for oneself), other oriented (setting high standards for others), or socially oriented (trying to conform to the high standards imposed by others). A multinational study found that regardless of subtype, anorexia patients scored higher on self- and other-oriented types of perfectionism than nonpatient controls (Halmi et al., 2000). Researchers have also distinguished between normal perfectionism (striving for success) and neurotic perfectionism (setting impossibly high standards). The poor body image of patients with eating disorders is related to high scores on both forms of perfectionism (Davis, 1997).

Prospective studies examine personality characteristics before an eating disorder is present. In one study, more than 2,000 students in a suburban Minneapolis school district completed a variety of tests for three consecutive years. Among the measures were assessments of personality characteristics as well as an index of the risk for developing an eating disorder based on the Eating Disorders Inventory. During year one of the study, cross-sectional predictors of disordered eating included body dissatisfaction, a measure of interoceptive awareness, which is the extent to which people can distinguish different biological states of their bodies (see Table 9.1 for items that assess interoceptive awareness), and a propensity to experience negative emotions (Leon et al., 1995). At year three, these variables were found to have prospectively predicted disordered eating (Leon et al., 1999).

Data from some studies of the personalities of those with eating disorders are somewhat consistent with psychodynamic theory. Patients with eating disorders have consistently been found to have low self-esteem (e.g., Garner et al., 1983). Furthermore, in line with Bruch's theory, patients with anorexia nervosa tend to be compliant, inhibited, and perfectionistic. The findings by Leon and colleagues that a lack of interoceptive awareness predicts risk for eating disorders confirms Bruch's idea that these people are poor at identifying their own internal states.

Characteristics of Families

Studies of the characteristics of families of patients with eating disorders have yielded variable results. Some of the variation stems, in part, from the different methods used to collect the data and from the sources of the information. For example, self-reports of patients consistently reveal high levels of conflict in the family (e.g., Bulik, Wade, & Kendler, 2000; Hodges, Cochrane, & Brewerton, 1998). However, reports of parents do not necessarily indicate high levels of family problems.

Disturbed family relationships do seem to characterize the families of some patients with eating disorders, with one of the most often observed characteristics being low levels of support. However, these family characteristics could be a result of the eating disorder and not necessarily a cause of it. Moreover, some of these same characteristics of family disturbance have been observed in families with other types of psychopathology, including depression and personality disorders. Thus, these family patterns may not be specific to eating disorder pathology but may be common among families in which a member suffers from psychopathology more generally (e.g., Wonderlich & Swift, 1990).

One study assessed both eating-disordered patients and their parents on tests designed to measure rigidity, closeness, emotional overinvolvement, critical comments, and hostility (Dare et al., 1994). The families showed considerable variation in whether parents were overinvolved with their children; the families were also quite low in conflict (low levels of criticism and hostility). A family study in which assessments were conducted before and after treatment of the patient found that ratings of family functioning improved after treatment (Woodside et al., 1995). Finally, one study examined identical twins discordant for bulimia (i.e., one twin had the disorder; the other didn't). The twin who developed bulimia reported greater family discord than the twin who did not develop the disorder. Because these studies rely on retrospective self-report, it remains unclear whether the family discord was a contributory factor or consequence of the eating disorder.

Patients with eating disorders consistently report that their family life was high in conflict.

To better understand the role of family functioning, it will be necessary to begin to study these families directly by observational measures rather than by reports alone. Although a child's perception of his or her family's characteristics is important, we also need to know how much of reported family disturbance is consistent with controlled scientific observations. In one of the few observational studies conducted thus far, parents of children with eating disorders did not appear to be very different from control parents. The two groups did not differ in the frequency of positive and negative messages given to their children, and the parents of children with eating disorders were more self-disclosing than were the controls. The parents of eating-disordered children did lack some communication skills, however, such as the ability to request clarification of vague statements (van den Broucke, Vandereycken, & Vertommen, 1995). Observational studies such as this, coupled with data on perceived family characteristics, would help determine whether actual or perceived family characteristics are related to eating disorders.

Child Abuse and Eating Disorders

Some studies have indicated that self-reports of childhood sexual abuse are higher than normal among patients with eating disorders, especially those with bulimia nervosa (Deep et al., 1999; Webster & Palmer, 2000). Since, as discussed in Chapter 7, some data indicate that reports of abuse may be created in therapy, it is notable that high rates of sexual abuse have been found among individuals with eating disorders who have not been in treatment as well as those who have (Romans et al. 2001; Wonderlich et al., 1996; Wonderlich et al., 2001). Still, the role of childhood sexual abuse in the etiology of eating disorders remains uncertain. Furthermore, high rates of childhood sexual abuse are found among people in many diagnostic categories, so if it plays some role, it may not be highly specific to eating disorders (Fairburn et al., 1999; Romans et al., 2001).

Research has also found higher rates of childhood physical abuse among patients with eating disorders. These data suggest that future studies should focus on a broad range of abusive experiences. Furthermore, it has been suggested that the presence or absence of abuse may be too general a variable. Abuse at a very early age, involving force, and by a family member may bear a stronger relationship to eating disorders than abuse of any other type (Everill & Waller, 1995).

Cognitive-Behavioral Views

Anorexia Nervosa   Cognitive-behavioral theories of anorexia nervosa include many of the factors detailed above.Fear of fatness and body-image disturbance are hypothesized as the motivating factors that make self-starvation and weight loss powerful reinforcers. Behaviors that achieve or maintain thinness are negatively reinforced by the reduction of anxiety about becoming fat. Furthermore, dieting and weight loss may be positively reinforced by the sense of mastery or self-control they create (Fairburn, Shatran, & Cooper, 1999; Garner, Vitousek, & Pike, 1997). Some theories also include personality and socio-cultural variables in an attempt to explain how fear of fatness and body-image disturbances develop. For example, perfectionism and a sense of personal inadequacy may lead a person to become especially concerned with his or her appearance, making dieting a potent reinforcer. Similarly, seeing portrayals in the media of thinness as an ideal, being overweight, and tending to compare oneself with especially attractive others all contribute to dissatisfaction with one's body (Stormer & Thompson, 1996).

Another important factor in producing a strong drive for thinness and a disturbed body image is criticism from peers and parents about being overweight (Paxton et al., 1991; Thompson et al., 1995). In one study supporting this conclusion, adolescent girls aged ten to fifteen were evaluated twice, with a three-year interval between assessments. Obesity at the first assessment was related to being teased by peers and at the second assessment was linked to dissatisfaction with their bodies. Dissatisfaction was in turn related to symptoms of eating disorder.

It is known that binging frequently results when diets are broken (Polivy & Herman, 1985). Thus, when a lapse occurs in the strict dieting of a person with anorexia nervosa, the lapse is likely to escalate into a binge. The purging following an episode of binge eating can again be seen as motivated by the fear of weight gain that the binge elicited. Patients with anorexia who do not have episodes of binging and purging may have a more intense preoccupation with and fear of weight gain (Schlundt & Johnson, 1990) or may be more able to exercise self-control.

Bulimia Nervosa   Patients with bulimia nervosa are also thought to be overconcerned with weight gain and body appearance; indeed, they judge their self-worth mainly by their weight and shape. They also have low self-esteem, and because weight and shape are somewhat more controllable than are other features of the self, they tend to focus on weight and shape, hoping their efforts in this area will make them feel better generally. They try to follow a pattern of restrictive eating that is very rigid, with strict rules regarding how much to eat, what kinds of food to eat, and when to eat. These strict rules inevitably are broken, and the lapse escalates into a binge. After the binge, feelings of disgust and fear of becoming fat build up, leading to compensatory actions such as vomiting (Fairburn, 1997). Although purging temporarily reduces the anxiety from having eaten too much, this cycle lowers the person's self-esteem, which triggers still more binging and purging, a vicious circle that maintains desired body weight but has serious medical consequences (see Figure 9.2 for a summary of this theory).

Polivy, Herman, and Howard (1980) developed the Restraint Scale (see Table 9.2), a questionnaire measure of concerns about dieting and overeating, to study in the laboratory people who are dieting and have distorted attitudes about eating. These studies are generally conducted under the guise of being taste tests. One such study was described as an assessment of the effects of temperature on taste (Polivy, Heatherton, & Herman, 1988). To achieve a "cold" condition, some partici-

---

Table 9.2 The Restraint Scale Used to Select Participants for Studies of Factors Controlling Eating in Dieters

1. How often are you dieting? Never; rarely; sometimes; often; always.

2. What is the maximum amount of weight (in pounds) you have ever lost within one month? 0–4; 5–9; 10–14; 15–19; 20+.

3. What is your maximum weight gain within a week? 0–1; 1.1–2; 2.1–3; 3.1–5; 5.1+.

4. In a typical week, how much does your weight fluctuate? 0–1; 1.1–2; 2.1–3; 3.1–5; 5.1+.

5. Would a weight fluctuation of 5 pounds affect the way you live your life? Not at all; slightly; moderately; very much.

6. Do you eat sensibly in front of others and splurge alone? Never; rarely; often; always.

7. Do you give too much time and thought to food? Never; rarely; often; always.

8. Do you have feelings of guilt after overeating? Never; rarely; often; always.

9. How conscious are you of what you are eating? Not at all; slightly; moderately; extremely.

10. How many pounds over your desired weight were you at your maximum weight? 0–1; 1–5; 6–10; 11–20; 21+.

Source: From Polivy, Herman, & Howard, 1980.

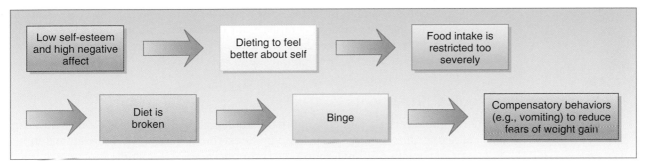

Figure 9.2 Schematic of cognitive-behavioral theory of bulimia nervosa.

pants first drank a fifteen-ounce chocolate milk shake (termed a *preload* by the investigators) and were then given three bowls of ice cream to taste and rate for flavor. Participants were told that once they had completed their ratings, they could eat as much of the ice cream as they wanted. The dependent variable was the amount of ice cream eaten.

In laboratory studies following this general design, people who scored high on the Restraint Scale ate more than nondieters after a fattening preload, even when the preload was only perceived as fattening but was actually low in calories (e.g., Polivy, 1976) and even when the food was relatively unpalatable (Polivy, Herman, & McFarlane, 1994). Thus, people who score high on the Restraint Scale show a pattern similar to that of patients with bulimia nervosa, albeit at a much less intense level.

Several additional conditions have been found to increase further the eating of restrained eaters following a preload, most notably various negative mood states, such as anxiety and depression (e.g., Herman et al., 1987). The increased consumption of restrained eaters is especially pronounced when their self-image is threatened (Heatherton, Herman, & Polivy, 1991) and if they have low self-esteem (Polivy et al., 1988). Finally, when restrained eaters are given false feedback indicating that their weight is high, they respond with increases in negative emotion and increased food consumption (McFarlane, Polivy, & Herman, 1998).

The eating pattern of patients with bulimia is similar to, but more extreme than, the behavior highlighted by Polivy and her colleagues in their studies of restrained eaters. Patients with bulimia nervosa typically binge when they encounter stress and experience negative affect. The binge may therefore function as a means of regulating the negative affect (Stice et al., 1999). Evidence also supports the idea that anxiety is relieved by purging. Patients with bulimia report increased levels of anxiety when they eat a meal and are not allowed to purge (Leitenberg et al., 1984), and these self-reports have been validated by physiological measures, such as skin conductance (e.g., Williamson et al., 1988). Similarly, anxiety levels decline after purging (Jarrell, Johnson, & Williamson, 1986), again supporting the idea that purging is reinforced by anxiety reduction. Given the similarities between people who score high on the Restraint Scale and people with bulimia nervosa, we might expect that the Restraint Scale would predict the development of bulimic symptoms in longitudinal research. Thus far, however, it has failed to do so (e.g., Stice, 1998).

Treatment of Eating Disorders

It is often difficult to get a patient with an eating disorder into treatment because the patient typically denies that he or she has a problem. For this reason, the majority of patients with eating disorders—up to 90 percent of them—are not in treatment (Fairburn et al., 1996).

Hospitalization, sometimes involuntary commitment, is frequently required to treat people with anorexia so that the patient's ingestion of food can be gradually increased and carefully monitored. Weight loss can be so severe that intravenous feeding is necessary to save the patient's life. The medical complications of anorexia, such as electrolyte imbalances, also require treatment. For both anorexia and bulimia, both biological and psychological interventions have been employed.

Biological Treatments

Because bulimia nervosa is often comorbid with depression, it has been treated with various antidepressants. Interest has focused on fluoxetine (Prozac) (e.g., Fluoxetine Bulimia Nervosa Collaborative Study Group, 1992). In one multicenter study, 387 women with bulimia were treated as outpatients for eight weeks. Fluoxetine was shown to be superior to a placebo in reducing binge eating and vomiting; it also decreased depression and lessened distorted attitudes toward food and eating. Findings from most studies, including double-blind studies with placebo controls, confirm the efficacy of a variety of antidepressants in reducing purging and binge eating, even among patients who had not responded to prior psychological treatment (Walsh et al., 2000; Wilson & Fairburn, 1998; Wilson & Pike, 2001).

On the negative side, many more patients drop out of drug-treatment conditions in studies on bulimia than drop out of the kind of cognitive-behavioral interventions described later (e.g., Fairburn, Agras, & Wilson, 1992). In the multicenter fluoxetine study cited, almost one-third of the patients dropped out before the end of the eight-week treatment, primarily because of the side effects of the drug; this figure compares with drop-out rates of under 5 percent with cognitive-behavioral therapy (Agras et al., 1992). Moreover, most patients relapse when various kinds of antidepressant medication are withdrawn (Mitchell & de Zwaan, 1993; Wilson & Pike, 2001), as is the case with most psychoactive drugs. There is some evidence that this tendency to relapse is reduced if antidepressants are given in the context of cognitive-behavioral therapy (Agras et al., 1994).

Drugs have also been used in attempts to treat anorexia nervosa. Unfortunately, they have not been very successful. There has been very limited success with drugs leading to significant weight gain, nor have they changed core features of anorexia, or even added significant benefit to a standard inpatient treatment program (Attia et al., 1998; Johnson, Tsoh, & Varnado, 1996).

Psychological Treatment of Anorexia Nervosa

There is little in the way of controlled research on psychological interventions for anorexia nervosa, but we will present what appear to be the most promising approaches to this life-threatening disorder.

Therapy for anorexia is generally believed to be a two-tiered process. The immediate goal is to help the patient gain weight in order to avoid medical complications and the possibility of death. The patient is often so weak and physiological functioning so disturbed that hospital treatment is medically imperative (in addition to being needed to ensure that the patient ingests some food). Operant-conditioning behavior therapy programs have been somewhat successful in achieving weight gain in the short term (Hsu, 1991). However, the second goal of treatment—long-term maintenance of weight gain—has not yet been reliably achieved by medical, behavioral, or traditional psychodynamic interventions (Wilson, 1995), though fluoxetine (Prozac) may contribute to a maintenance of inpatient weight gain as long as the person remains on the drug (Kaye et al., 1997).

Family therapy is the principal mode of treatment for anorexia, stemming from theories that interactions among members of the patient's family—and remember that most patients are young women living at home or otherwise enmeshed with their families of origin—play a role in the disorder. One influential theorist in this area is Salvador Minuchin.

Minuchin and his colleagues propose that the symptoms of an eating disorder are best understood by considering both the patient and how the symptoms are embedded in a dysfunctional family structure. In this view, often referred to as *family systems theory*, the child is seen as physiologically vulnerable (although the precise nature of this vulnerability is unspecified), and the child's family has several characteristics that promote the development of an eating disorder. Also, the child's eating disorder plays an important role in helping the family avoid other conflicts. Thus the child's symptoms are a substitute for other conflicts within the family.

According to Minuchin et al. (1975) the families of children with eating disorders exhibit the following characteristics.

1. **Enmeshment.** Families have an extreme form of overinvolvement and intimacy in which parents may speak for their children because they believe they know exactly how they feel.
2. **Overprotectiveness.** Family members have an extreme level of concern for one another's welfare.
3. **Rigidity.** Families have a tendency to try to maintain the status quo and avoid dealing effectively with events that require change (e.g., the demand that adolescence creates for increased autonomy).
4. **Lack of conflict resolution.** Families either avoid conflict or are in a state of chronic conflict.

Family therapy such as that shown in this photo is a main form of treatment for anorexia nervosa.

In Minuchin's view, the family member with an eating disorder deflects attention away from underlying conflicts in family relationships. To treat the disorder Minuchin attempts to redefine it as interpersonal rather than individual and to bring the family conflict to the fore. In this way, he theorizes, the symptomatic family member is freed from having to maintain his or her problem, for it no longer deflects attention from the dysfunctional family.

How is this accomplished? The therapist sees the family at a family lunch session, since the conflicts related to anorexia are believed to be most evident at mealtime. These lunch sessions have three major goals:

1. Changing the patient role of the patient with anorexia
2. Redefining the eating problem as an interpersonal problem
3. Preventing the parents from using their child's anorexia as a means of avoiding conflict

One strategy is to instruct each parent to try individually to force the child to eat. The other parent may leave the room. The individual efforts are expected to fail. But through this failure and frustration, the mother and father may now work together to persuade the child to eat. Thus, rather than being a focus of conflict, the child's eating will produce cooperation and increase parental effectiveness in dealing with the child (Rosman, Minuchin, & Liebman, 1975).

Like most other treatments, family therapy has not yet been sufficiently studied for its long-term effects, though studies are currently underway. One report suggested that as many as 86 percent of 50 anorexic daughters treated with their families were still functioning well when assessed at times ranging from three months to four years after treatment (Rosman, Minuchin, & Liebman, 1976). A better-controlled follow-up study of psychodynamically oriented family therapy recently confirmed these earlier findings; patients with early-onset anorexia and a short history of it maintained their gains from family therapy for five years following treatment termination (Eisler et al., 1997). A newer family therapy, based largely on Minuchin's theorizing, was recently developed in England, and preliminary evidence suggests that it is efficacious (Lock & LeGrange, 2001; Lock et al., 2001).

Psychological Treatment of Bulimia Nervosa

The cognitive behavior therapy (CBT) approach of Fairburn (1985; Fairburn, Marcus, & Wilson, 1993) is the best validated and most current standard for the treatment of bulimia.

Television actress Courtney Thorne-Smith has recently spoken out about the pressure to be thin and its relation to eating disorders.

In Fairburn's therapy, the patient is encouraged to question society's standards for physical attractiveness. Patients must also uncover and then change beliefs that encourage them to starve themselves to avoid becoming overweight. They must be helped to see that normal body weight can be maintained without severe dieting and that unrealistic restriction of food intake can often trigger a binge. They are taught that all is not lost with just one bite of high-calorie food and that snacking need not trigger a binge, which will be followed by induced vomiting or taking laxatives that will lead to still lower self-esteem and depression. Altering this all-or-nothing thinking can help patients begin to eat more moderately. They are also taught assertiveness skills (p. 52) to help them cope with unreasonable demands placed on them by others, and they learn as well more satisfying ways of relating to people.

The overall goal of treatment in bulimia nervosa is to develop normal eating patterns. Patients need to learn to eat three meals a day and even some snacks between meals without sliding back into binging and purging. Regular meals control hunger and thereby, it is hoped, the urge to eat enormous amounts of food, the effects of which are counteracted by purging. To help patients develop less extreme beliefs about themselves, the cognitive behavior therapist gently but firmly challenges such irrational beliefs as "No one will respect me if I am a few pounds heavier than I am now" or "Eric loves me only because I weigh 112 pounds and would surely reject me if I ballooned to 120 pounds." A generalized assumption underlying these and related cognitions for female patients might be that a woman has value to a man only if she is a few pounds underweight—a belief that is put forth in the media and advertisements.

One intervention that is sometimes used in the cognitive-behavioral treatment approach has the patient bring small amounts of forbidden food to eat in the session. Relaxation is employed to control the urge to induce vomiting. Unrealistic demands and other cognitive distortions—such as the belief that eating a small amount of high-calorie food means that the patient is an utter failure and doomed never to improve—are continually challenged. (Note the role that Aaron Beck's cognitive therapy plays here: bulimic individuals often engage in all-or-none, black-and-white thinking. Take note also of the influence of Albert Ellis's theorizing about unrealistic assumptions, in this case, that it is a catastrophe if one does not behave perfectly.) The therapist and patient work together to determine events, thoughts, and feelings that trigger an urge to binge and then to learn more adaptive ways to cope with these situations. For example, if the therapist and the patient, usually a young woman, discover that binging often takes place after the patient has been criticized by her boyfriend, therapy could entail any or all of the following:

- Encouraging the patient to assert herself if the criticism is unwarranted
- Teaching her, à la Ellis, that it is not a catastrophe to make a mistake and it is not necessary to be perfect, even if the boyfriend's criticism is valid
- Desensitizing her to social evaluation and encouraging her to question society's standards for ideal weight and the pressures on women to be thin—not an easy task by any means

The outcomes of cognitive-behavioral therapies are rather promising, both in the short term and over time. A recent meta-analysis showed that CBT yielded better results than antidepressant drug treatments (Whittal, Agras, & Gould, 1999), and therapeutic gains were maintained at one year follow-up (Agras et al., 2000) and for as long as 5.8 years (Fairburn et al., 1995). But there are limitations to these positive outcomes, as we shall see.

Findings from a number of studies indicate that CBT often results in less frequent binging and purging, with reductions ranging from 70 to more than 90 percent; extreme dietary restraint is also reduced significantly, and there is improvement in attitudes toward body shape and weight (Compas et al., 1998; Garner et al., 1993; Wilson et al., 1991). However, if we focus on the patients themselves rather than on numbers of binges and purges across patients, we find that at least half of those treated with CBT improve very little (Craighead & Agras, 1991; Wilson, 1995; Wilson & Pike, 1993). And if we look at how patients who do improve significantly are doing at six- and twelve-month follow-ups, we find that only about one-third are maintaining their treatment gains (Fairburn, Peveler, et al., 1993). Clearly, while CBT may be the most effective treatment available, it falls far short of being a cure for bulimia for most patients.

To better understand how it works and how it might be improved, some investigators are conducting what are called component analyses of the CBT therapy package just described. One important aspect that has been examined is the response prevention and exposure component (recall this aspect of the behavioral treatment of obsessive-compulsive disorder, p. 161). This component involves discouraging the patient from purging after eating foods that usually elicit an urge to vomit. Indications are that this is an important component; CBT minus this element does not appear to be as efficacious as the total treatment package (e.g., Fairburn et al., 1995; Wilson et al., 1991). Furthermore, this behavioral homework assignment, which is given to patients early in treatment, may underlie another important research finding, namely that CBT begins to take effect quickly. As recently reviewed by Wilson and Pike (2001), about 70% of the total improvement in frequency of binging and vomiting is evident by the third week of treatment (Wilson et al., 1999; Wilson, Vtousek, & Loeb, 2000). It is likely that these early gains in the core features of bulimia—binging and purging—enhance the patient's self-efficacy and lay the foundation for further and lasting improvement (Bandura, 1977, 1986).

Patients who are successful in overcoming their urge to binge and purge also improve in associated problems such as depression and low self-esteem. This result is not surprising. If a person is able to achieve normal eating patterns after viewing bulimia as an uncontrollable problem, the person can be expected to become less depressed and to feel generally better about himself or herself. One last finding from the empirical CBT literature is that self-help groups that follow a manual based on Fairburn's treatment model and are minimally supervised by a mental health professional can achieve significant benefits (Cooper, Coker, & Fleming, 1994).

Are outcomes better when CBT is combined with antidepressant pharmacotherapy? Adding drug treatment to CBT sometimes does and sometimes does not enhance the effectiveness of CBT, and CBT alone is more effective than any available drug treatment (Compas et al., 1998; Thase, 2000). Adding antidepressant drugs, however, may be useful in alleviating the depression that often occurs with bulimia (Wilson & Fairburn, 1998). Walsh et al. (1997) found that a treatment combining CBT and medication was superior to medication alone. Medication alone was no better than a placebo.

Is CBT superior to other psychological interventions for the treatment of bulimia? Based on research so far, the answer is mostly yes (Wilson & Fairburn, 1998). For example, a comparison of the effects of CBT with those of a psychodynamically oriented supportive therapy showed that CBT was superior (Walsh, Wilson et al., 1997).

In several other studies (e.g., Fairburn et al., 1991; Fairburn, Jones et al., 1993), however, Weissman and Klerman's Interpersonal Therapy (IPT) (p. 35) fared well in comparisons with CBT, though it did not produce results as quickly. The two modes of intervention were equivalent at one-year follow-up in effecting change across all four of the specific aspects of bulimia: binge eating, purging, dietary restraint, and maladaptive attitudes about body shape and weight (Wilson, 1995). This pattern—CBT superior to IPT immediately following treatment but IPT catching up at follow-up—was replicated by Agras and colleagues (2000). (Similar results were achieved by these two treatment approaches in the large outcome study on depression funded by the National Institute of Mental Health; see p. 289.)

The success of IPT suggests that, at least for some patients, disordered eating patterns might be caused by poor interpersonal relationships and associated negative feelings about the self and the world—possibilities that have been emphasized for many years by psychodynamic and family systems therapists such as Minuchin.

Although the outcomes from these two leading psychological treatments, especially the cognitive-behavioral one, appear to be superior to those from other modes of intervention, including drugs, a good deal more remains to be learned about how best to treat bulimia nervosa. Part of the reason at least half of the patients in the controlled studies do not recover may be that significant numbers of the patients in these studies have psychological disorders in addition to eating disorders, such as borderline personality disorder, depression, anxiety, and marital distress (Wilson, 1995). Such patients show less improvement from cognitive-behavioral therapy and from other therapies as well. Gleaves and Eberenz (1994), for example, examined cognitive-behavioral therapy outcomes among 464 women with bulimia in a residential-treatment setting and found that those with a history of multiple therapists or hospitalizations, suicide attempts, and sexual abuse derived significantly less benefit from therapy than did those without such backgrounds. The poor therapeutic outcomes could have resulted because such patients simply have more pervasive and more serious psychopathology. Alternatively, the poor prognosis could result from the patients' failure to engage in the therapy, perhaps because of lack of trust in authority figures owing to earlier sexual abuse. (Therapists are authority figures, and if the patient was abused by a parent, the ensuing distrust and anger may very well be generalized to a therapist. This is particularly a problem for patients with borderline personality disorder, and a therapy designed to address these issues will be discussed in Chapter 13 when we examine Linehan's dialectical behavior therapy.)

Summary

- The two main eating disorders are anorexia nervosa and bulimia nervosa. These disorders share several features, the most important of which is an intense fear of being overweight.
- The symptoms of anorexia nervosa include refusal to maintain normal body weight, an intense fear of being fat, a distorted sense of body shape, and, in women, amenorrhea. Anorexia typically begins in the midteens, is ten times more frequent in women than in men, and is comorbid with several other disorders, notably depression. Its course is not favorable, and it can be life threatening.
- The symptoms of bulimia nervosa include episodes of binge eating followed by purging, fear of being fat, and a distorted body image. Like anorexia, bulimia begins in adolescence, is much more frequent in women than in men, and is comorbid with other diagnoses, such as depression. Prognosis is somewhat more favorable than for anorexia.
- Biological research in the eating disorders has examined both genetics and brain mechanisms. Evidence is consistent with a possible genetic diathesis, though adoption studies have not yet been done. Endogenous opioids and serotonin, both of which play a role in mediating hunger and satiety, have been examined in eating disorders. Low levels of both these brain chemicals have been found in such patients, but evidence that these factors cause eating disorders is limited.
- On a psychological level, several factors play important roles. As cultural standards changed to favor a thinner shape as the ideal for women, the frequency of eating disorders increased. The objectification of women's bodies also exerts pressure for women to see themselves through a sociocultural lens. The prevalence of eating disorders is higher in industrialized countries, where the cultural pressure to be thin is strongest.

- Psychodynamic theories of eating disorders emphasize parent–child relationships and personality characteristics. Bruch's theory, for example, proposes that the parents of children who later develop eating disorders impose their wishes on their children without considering the children's needs. Children reared in this way do not learn to identify their own internal states and become highly dependent on standards imposed by others. Research on characteristics of families with an eating-disordered child has yielded different data depending on how the data were collected, however. Personality research indicates that patients with eating disorders are high in neuroticism and anxiety and low in self-esteem.
- Cognitive-behavioral theories of anorexia nervosa propose that fear of being fat and body-image distortion make weight loss a powerful reinforcer. Among patients with bulimia nervosa, negative affect and stress precipitate binges that create anxiety, which is then relieved by purging.
- Treatment of anorexia often requires hospitalization to reduce the medical complications of the disorder. For bulimia, the main biological treatment is the use of antidepressants. Although somewhat effective, drop-out rates from drug-treatment programs are high and relapse is common when patients stop taking the medication. Drugs have been used to treat anorexia nervosa as well, but with little success.
- Family therapy is the principal mode of psychological treatment from anorexia, whereas a cognitive-behavioral treatment is the best-validated psychological treatment for bulimia. This latter approach focuses on questioning society's standards for physical attractiveness, challenging beliefs that encourage severe food restriction, and developing normal eating patterns. Outcomes are promising, at least in the short term.

Key Terms

anorexia nervosa   binge eating disorder   bulimia nervosa

Eating Disorder: Anorexia Nervosa

Joan was a 38-year-old woman with a good job and family life. She lived with her second husband, Mike; her 16-year-old son, Charlie, from her first marriage; and her husband's 18-year-old daughter from a previous marriage. Joan was employed as a secretary at a university, and Mike was a temporary federal employee. Joan was 5'3" and weighed approximately 125 pounds. Although she was concerned about her weight, her current attitudes and behaviors were much more reasonable than they had been a few years earlier, when she had been diagnosed with anorexia nervosa.

Joan had struggled with a serious eating disorder from the ages of 29 to 34. She was eventually hospitalized for a period of 30 days. The treatment that she received during that hospital stay had finally helped her overcome her eating problems. Four years later, her condition remained much improved. In the following pages, we trace the history of Joan's problems from her childhood and adolescence through their eventual resolution in adulthood.

Social History

Joan was born in a suburb on the outskirts of a large northeastern city. She had one brother, two years younger than she. Her father held various jobs, including that of a supervisor for an aircraft subcontractor. Joan's mother stayed at home while the children were young and then worked part-time for a number of years as a waitress and bookkeeper. Both parents were of average weight.

Joan's early childhood was quite ordinary. She was an above-average student and enjoyed school. She and her brother bickered, but their disagreements did not extend beyond the usual sibling rivalry. Her family lived in a large neighborhood development, filled with lots of children. Joan was somewhat heavy during elementary school. She had high personal standards and strove to be a perfect child. She always did what was right and conformed completely to the wishes of her parents.

When Joan was 14 and entering the ninth grade, tragedy struck her family and forever changed her home life. She and her 12-year-old brother had been left home alone while her parents went to work. Although her brother was too old to require baby-sitting, she was supposed to keep an eye on him. Joan had a friend over, and the two girls were upstairs in her room. Joan heard some loud noise outside and looked out the window. She saw her brother lying dead in the road. He had been run over by a car. Although the feeling became less intense as years passed, Joan continued to feel guilty about her brother's death well into adulthood.

After the accident, Joan's parents changed. They became extremely overprotective, and Joan felt as if she "had a leash on all of the time." From age 14 on, she no longer had a normal childhood. She could not hang out with friends, be away from the house for long periods of time, or go out in cars. Her parents wanted to know where she was and what she was doing, and they set a strict curfew. Joan knew that if she was late her parents would worry, so she always tried to be home early. She made a special effort to do exactly as she was told. Joan did not go out much because she felt the need to stay near her parents so that they would know that she was alive and well.

The rest of high school was unremarkable. Joan received reasonably good grades and got along well with the other students. During the summer after her brother's death, when Joan was 15, she met and began to date a boy who was two years older than she. Joan's parents were initially unhappy with this relationship, in part because Randy owned a car, and they didn't want her to ride around with him. Joan had to meet Randy secretly for the first few months. As her parents got to know him better, they grew to like him, and the young couple no longer had to sneak around. During this time, Joan continued to feel guilty when she was in cars because she was reminded of her brother's death. She frequently stayed home because she knew that her parents would suffer horribly if anything happened to her.

After high school, Joan attended a two-year business school and became engaged to Randy. The couple was married after Joan graduated. She was 19 years old as she began her marriage and her first full-time job, as a secretary in a medical office. Prior to this time, Joan's father had never allowed her to hold even a part-time job. He insisted on providing for all of her needs.

Although this marriage lasted legally for six years, it became clear within nine months that the relationship was in trouble. Joan cared for her husband, but she did not love him. She soon realized that she had used Randy as an escape route from her parents' home. She felt as if she had simply jumped from one dependent relationship into another. When she had been at home, her parents provided everything. Now Randy was taking care of her. Joan worried that she did not know how to take care of herself. In spite of these negative feelings, Joan and Randy tried to make the marriage work. They bought a home one year after their wedding. Two years later, Joan accidentally became pregnant.

Joan gained 80 pounds during the course of her pregnancy. When Charlie was born, she weighed 200 pounds. Over the next few months, Joan found it difficult to lose weight but eventually got down to 140 pounds. Although it was hard for her to adjust to this weight gain, she did not try to change her weight because it felt "safe" to her. Joan and Randy were legally separated two years after Charlie was born. They continued to see each other occasionally and sought marital counseling at various times during the next couple of years. They could not reconcile their differences, however, and Randy eventually moved to another state. The divorce was finalized when Joan was 25 years old.

Shortly after she and Randy were separated, Joan stopped working and went on welfare. With financial help from her father, she managed to keep up the mortgage payments on her house for several months. She and Charlie continued to live on their own, but Joan fell further into debt while she and Randy tried to work things out. She was forced to sell her home when the divorce became final. Although she came to regret the decision, she moved back into her parents' home. Living at home was stressful for Joan. Although she was 25 years old, she felt like a child. Her parents once again took care of Joan, and now they also provided for her son. In this submissive role, Joan started to feel more like Charlie's older sister than his mother.

Joan lost some weight after she and Charlie were involved in a serious car accident, six months after moving back to live with her parents. Charlie was not hurt, but Joan's left hip and leg were broken. She spent a month in the hospital. She was immobile when she came home, and her mother had to take even greater care of her and Charlie. Joan needed repeated surgery on her knee, as well as extensive physical therapy, and she had to relearn how to walk. During her recovery she had little appetite, was nauseated, and did not eat much, but she was not consciously dieting. Joan's weight went down to about 110 pounds, which she considered to be a reasonable weight.

While she was recovering from her injuries, Joan became involved with a man named Jack, whom she met in one of the hospital's rehabilitation programs. She was now 27 years old. In order to escape her parents' overly protective home, she decided to take Charlie and move in with Jack. This move actually created more problems than it solved, in large part because Jack had a serious problem with alcohol. Joan had never been a heavy drinker. In the beginning of their relationship, Joan drank alcohol only during the weekend. After she started living with Jack, drinking became a daily activity. Much of their relationship and socializing revolved around alcohol. On the average weekday, Joan consumed a couple of beers and some wine, or perhaps a glass or two of bourbon. On weekends she drank considerably more. Charlie was increasingly left at day-care centers and with baby-sitters. Joan eventually recognized the destructive nature of this relationship and ended it after a few months. She reluctantly moved back into her parents' home. After leaving Jack, Joan stopped drinking, except occasionally when she was out socializing.

Onset of the Eating Disorder

After breaking up with Jack, Joan lived with her parents for two more years. When she was 29 years old, almost three years after her accident, Joan returned to the hospital for more surgery on her leg. After being discharged, she began the diet that set the stage for five years of serious eating problems and nearly destroyed her life. Joan had gained a few pounds while she was drinking heavily and now weighed 125 pounds. She was concerned that she would start to gain more weight while she was inactive, recovering from surgery.

Joan's diet was strict from the beginning; she measured and weighed all of her food. Within a year, she weighed less than 100 pounds. Her food intake was severely restricted. During the day she consumed only coffee with skim milk and an artificial sweetener. Occasionally, she ate a piece of fruit or a bran muffin. When she and Charlie ate dinner with her parents, Joan took a normal amount of food on her plate but played with it rather than eating it. After dinner, she usually excused herself to go to the bathroom where she took laxatives in an effort to get rid of what little food she had eaten. Joan hardly ate any meats, breads, or starches. She preferred fruits and vegetables because they consist mainly of water and fiber. Although she did not allow herself to eat, Joan still felt hungry; in fact, she was starving most of the time. She thought about food constantly, spent all of her time reading recipe and health books, and cooked elaborate meals for the family.

Although she weighed less than 100 pounds, Joan still felt overweight and believed that she would look better if she lost more weight. She had an overwhelming fear of getting fat, because she believed that gaining weight would mean that she was not perfect. She tried to be a model young adult and struggled to be what she imagined everybody else wanted. She gave little thought to what she would want for herself. It seemed to Joan that everything in her life was out of control and that her weight and body were the only things over which she could be in charge. The demonstration of strict self-control with regard to eating was a source of pride and accomplishment to Joan.

As she lost weight, Joan experienced several of the physical effects that accompany starvation. Her periods stopped; she had problems with her liver; her skin became dry and lost its elasticity; her hair was no longer healthy; and she would often get dizzy when she stood up. At this time, Joan was working as a secretary in a university medical school. Some of her coworkers noticed the drastic change in her appearance and became concerned. An internist in her department recognized her symptoms as those of anorexia nervosa and tried to get Joan to seek help. Joan agreed to attend an eating disorders support group and even went to some outpatient therapy sessions, mostly in an attempt to appease her friends. She also consulted a dietician at the university hospital and worked on an eating plan. There were moments when Joan considered the possibility that her behavior was not normal, but most of the time she viewed her ability to control her weight and appetite as a sign of strength. When she was transferred to a different department within the university, she left therapy and returned to her restrictive dieting.

Joan's parents were also acutely aware of their daughter's abnormal patterns of eating and her excessive weight loss. They were extremely worried about her health. The more they tried to talk to Joan about this issue, the more resistant she became to their pleadings. Arguments about eating became frequent, and the level of tension in the home escalated dramatically.

A year and a half after the onset of her eating disorder, Joan moved with Charlie into an apartment of their own. Her decision was prompted in large part by the aversive nature of her interactions with her parents. She continued to diet and now weighed about 90 pounds. Charlie's diet had also become restricted, in part because there was very little food in the house. Joan could hardly bring herself to go to the grocery store. Once there, she made an effort to behave normally and went through the store putting food into her shopping cart. When it came time to pay, however, she would not actually buy anything. She believed that food was bad and that it was a waste of money. Instead of purchasing anything, she would wander up and down the aisles, eating much of what was in her shopping cart. Her reasoning was that it made no sense to pay for food that could be eaten while you were in the store.

This type of binge eating also happened whenever she did manage to buy something. In one afternoon, she would occasionally eat two dozen donuts, a five-pound box of candy, and some ice cream. After this, Joan took 20 to 30 laxatives to rid herself of the food. At times she made herself vomit by sticking a toothbrush down her throat, but she preferred to take laxatives. Some weeks she did not binge at all, others once or twice. On the days in between binges she ate only a little fruit and drank some liquids.

Joan's eating problems persisted for the next five years. Her weight fluctuated between 90 and 105 pounds during this period. At times she ate more normally, but then she would eat practically nothing for months. She tried therapy, though she was not seriously or consistently committed to changing her behavior. Her life seemed like a roller coaster, as she cycled back and forth between relatively healthy patterns of eating, severe restricting, and bingeing and purging. Most of her diet consisted of liquids such as diet soda, water, and coffee. Occasionally she drank beer, seeking the numbing effect it had on her appetite. She was pleased with her weight, especially when it was very low, but she felt horrible physically. She was weak most of the time, and other people constantly told her that she was too thin. In Joan's mind, however, she was still too heavy.

When she was 32 years old, almost three years after the onset of her eating problems, Joan met Mike at a church group she was attending. They began to date on a regular basis. Mike was different from all of the other men in Joan's past. He genuinely cared about her, and he also liked her son. Her weight was at one of its peaks when they met, somewhere between 100 and 105 pounds, so her eating problems were not immediately obvious to him.

Unfortunately, soon after they began dating, Joan once again began to restrict her eating, and her weight quickly dropped to another low point. Mike noticed the obvious change in her behavior and appearance. His reaction was sympathetic. As their relationship grew stronger, Mike seemed to help Joan feel differently about herself. They talked frequently about her weight and how little she ate. Mike expressed great concern about her health, pleading gently with her to gain weight, but her restrictive patterns of eating persisted in spite of the other psychological benefits that accompanied the development of this relationship.

One year after she started dating Mike, Joan needed major abdominal surgery to remove two cysts from her small intestine. During the operation, the surgeon saw that she had other problems and reconstructed her entire bowel system. When she left the hospital, Joan's weight had fallen to 85 pounds. She ate reasonably well at first, trying to regain her strength. After two months she was feeling better, returned to work, and went back on a restrictive diet. This time, however, Mike and her friends would not let her continue this prolonged pattern of self-imposed starvation.

Treatment

Mike and one of Joan's friends from the medical school sought help for her. Realizing that she would never be free of her problems unless she faced them, Joan agreed to contact an eating disorder specialist. Though it was one of the hardest decisions she ever made, Joan had herself committed to a 30-day stay in a psychiatric ward. She was now 34 years old.

Joan's diet was completely controlled in the hospital. She was started on a 1500-calorie-a-day diet and was required to eat three meals a day in the presence of a staff member. Privileges such as use of the phone, visitors, and outings were made contingent upon eating. Specific goals were set for weight gain, and caloric intake was increased gradually. There were also daily individual therapy sessions in which a staff psychologist explored with Joan how she felt about herself.

At first, hospitalization was difficult for Joan. The amount of food that she was required to eat for breakfast (two pancakes, a bowl of cereal, a glass of milk, one piece of fruit, and a piece of toast) would previously have lasted her for several days. She was initially rebellious, refusing to eat or giving her food away to other patients. She didn't earn any privileges in the first 10 days of her hospital stay. Unaccustomed to eating, she experienced severe constipation, bloating, and indigestion. At times she tried to vomit to get rid of the food, but she was not successful. She eventually accepted the fact that she had no choice and allowed herself to gain 15 pounds. She felt stronger physically but was still troubled. Joan convinced herself that she would lose those extra pounds as soon as she was released from the hospital.

An important turning point in her attitude came during the third week of treatment when Joan received a pass to go home. Outside the hospital, she felt out of control, as if she were too weak to take care of herself. She asked Mike to take her back to the hospital immediately. Safely back in her hospital room, she cried and felt as though she would never get better. This wrenching experience helped Joan recognize that she would, indeed, need to change her eating behavior as well as her attitudes regarding weight control and physical appearance. Somehow, at the end of 30 days, Joan found the strength to leave the hospital. She was frightened at first, but with support from Mike and her family, she was able to maintain a normal pattern of eating. Joan remained in therapy for six more months and was able to gain another 15 pounds.

While she was in the hospital, Joan learned that her own attitudes about eating and her body were the principal problem, and she had become her own worst enemy. She learned that she could control her weight without becoming extremely restrictive in her eating. She began to feel differently about herself and food. Joan could not pinpoint exactly what had happened, but she had become a different person who was no longer preoccupied with dieting and weight control.

Discussion

Anorexia nervosa and bulimia nervosa (discussed in the next chapter) are the two principal eating disorders described in *DSM-IV-TR*. Anorexia nervosa is a condition characterized by extreme weight loss. Ninety to 95 percent of anorexics are female. Current estimates of prevalence vary, but approximately 1 in 100 adolescent girls is affected by this disorder. The course of the disorder can be chronic, and 5 percent of patients with anorexia starve to death (Nielsen, 2001; Steinhausen, 2002). Deaths also occur from physical complications of the illness and from suicide. The *DSM-IV-TR* (p. 589) diagnostic criteria are as follows:

A. Refusal to maintain body weight at or above a minimally normal weight for age and height (e.g., weight loss leading to maintenance of body weight less than 85 percent of that expected; or failure to make expected weight gain during period of growth, leading to body weight less than 85 percent of that expected)

B. Intense fear of gaining weight or becoming fat, even though underweight

C. Disturbance in the way in which one's body weight or shape is experienced, undue influence of body weight or shape on selfevaluation, or denial of the seriousness of the current low body weight

D. In postmenarcheal females, amenorrhea, that is, the absence of at least three consecutive menstrual cycles

The *DSM-IV-TR* specifies two types of anorexia nervosa. Individuals are considered to be the *restricting type* if during the episode of anorexia nervosa they do not regularly engage in eating binges or purge themselves of the food they have eaten during a binge (whether through vomiting or laxative misuse). The *binge-eating/purging* type, which is consistent with Joan's behavior, involves the regular occurrence of binge eating or purging behavior during the episode of anorexia. This approach to subclassification of eating disorders recognizes the frequent appearance of overlapping symptoms. Approximately one-half of patients with anorexia also have bulimic symptoms, and roughly one-third of patients with bulimia have a history of anorexia. The distinction between subtypes of anorexia nervosa should not be taken too literally, however. When anorexia patients are followed over a period of several years, many people who originally fit the description for restricting type have changed over to the binge-eating/purging type (Eddy et al., 2002).

Research has revealed some important differences between the two subtypes of anorexia nervosa. Anorexics who also binge and purge tend to have weighed more before their illness, are more sexually experienced, are more outgoing, tend to have reduced impulse control, are more likely to abuse drugs or steal, and have more variable moods than restrictors (Casper & Troiana, 2001; DaCosta & Halmi, 1992). The presence of bingeing and purging is also thought to be a sign of greater psychological disturbance and an indication of a poorer prognosis (van der Ham, 1997).

Anorexia nervosa is often comorbid with several other disorders, including substance abuse, obsessive compulsive disorder, phobias, panic disorder, and several personality disorders (Walters & Kendler, 1994). The disorder that is most frequently comorbid with anorexia is major depression. These two conditions actually share many of the same symptoms such as insomnia, disturbed sleep, weight loss, constipation, loss of interest in sex, indecisiveness, poor concentration, and social withdrawal. Studies have also shown an increased prevalence of mood disorders in the relatives of patients with anorexia. This relationship has led some researchers to believe that depression causes anorexia nervosa. To examine this relationship, Strober and Katz (1987) conducted a prospective study of adolescents with mood disorders. At the time of follow-up (range of 8 to 48 months), none of the female teens had developed anorexia nervosa. These data suggest that despite similarity of symptoms and diagnostic overlap, anorexia is a separate disorder. It is distinguished from depression by the relentless pursuit of thinness and a more chronic course.

Patients with anorexia are often characterized as being obsessional, conforming, and emotionally reserved. The research evidence supports this impression. It also indicates, however, that many different personality styles are found among those who suffer from anorexia (Thornton & Russell, 1997; Vitousek & Manke, 1994).

Joan met the diagnostic criteria for anorexia nervosa, binge-eating/purging type. She experienced a drastic, self-induced loss of weight, was intensely afraid of becoming fat, could not recognize the true size of her body or the seriousness of her condition, and was no longer menstruating. In addition to her severe restriction of food intake, Joan would also periodically eat large amounts of food and then try to rid herself of the unwanted calories through vomiting and laxatives. Joan also experienced many of the physical and psychological side effects that accompany starvation. These include constipation, hypotension, skin changes, bloating, abdominal pains, dehydration, and laguna (downy hair growth).

It is important to recognize that some of the psychological symptoms of anorexia nervosa are produced by the lack of food and are not necessarily inherent aspects of the anorexic's personality. For example, people who are starving become preoccupied with food and eating. Like Joan, they will often cook for others, read recipe books, and may even develop peculiar food rituals. Obsessive behaviors, such as hoarding, may also appear. There is often an exaggeration of previous personality traits, such as increased irritability, avoidance and social withdrawal, and a narrowing of interests (Kaye, Strober, & Rhodes, 2002).

Etiological Considerations

Various biological factors have been considered in the search for the causes of anorexia nervosa. Some speculation has focused on the possible influence of a dysfunctional hypothalamus, a part of the brain that plays a crucial role in the regulation of feeding behavior (Stoving et al., 1999). Hypothalamic irregularities have been observed among anorexic patients, but it is likely that these problems are the result, rather than the cause, of the eating disorder. Furthermore, a hypothalamic problem would not easily account for the intense fear of being fat that is found in anorexia. It does seem likely that biological factors—including hormones and neurotransmitters that regulate metabolism and mediate perceptions of satiety—are involved in the etiology of anorexia nervosa. The specific nature of these factors and their role in pathways leading to the disorder have not been determined (Ferguson & Pigott, 2000; Halmi, 1996).

Because the onset of anorexia nervosa typically occurs during adolescence, many theories discuss anorexia in terms of maturational problems that are sparked by the physical, emotional, and cognitive changes that occur at this time. Some clinicians view anorexia as the product of resistance to sexual and psychological maturity, or more broadly as trouble with individuation and separation from the family (Shoebridge & Gowers, 2000). The family often plays a role to the extent that parents may set high performance demands and may actively resist attempts by their children to gain independence. Parents of anorexic adolescents have been described as being enmeshed (overly involved in their children's lives), overprotective, and unable to solve problems (Blair, Freeman, & Cull, 1995). Of course, these characteristics may be a response to having a child with a severe eating disorder rather than a reason for the original onset of the child's disorder. Patterns of family interaction may contribute to the development of anorexia among adolescents who also have other predisposing factors, including preoccupation with weight and appearance, body dissatisfaction, and low self-esteem (Leung, 1996).

Joan's case was atypical, in the sense that her eating problems appeared when she was 29 years old. Nevertheless, her family situation did fit the "anorexic profile." After the death of her brother, her parents became overly protective. When she returned to their home after her divorce, she felt as if she were a child again. She seemed to lose her sense of being an independent adult. Joan's parents conscientiously provided for her needs, but by not allowing her to work, they may have contributed to her feelings of ineffectiveness and inadequacy. These aspects of Joan's situation fit the theoretical perspective outlined by Hilde Bruch (1973, 1981), who described anorexia nervosa as the product of fundamental deficits in ego functioning. According to this theory, patients with anorexia suffer from low self-esteem, a sense of personal ineffectiveness, and a lack of trust in their internal states and emotions. Mastery over the body becomes a means of achieving a sense of control.

Cultural attitudes and standards are also thought to play an important role in the development of anorexia nervosa (Bordo, 1997; Simpson, 2002). Culture has a strong influence on standards for what is considered to be the ideal female shape. In Western society, for example, the feminine ideal has shifted from the buxom figure of the early 1900s, to the thin flapper of the 1920s, to the hourglass shape of the 1950s, and more recently, back to a thin body shape. This ideal shape is more than a "look." It takes on additional meaning and comes to symbolize other attributes such as success, beauty, and self-control.

At the same time that contemporary cultural standards have emphasized thinness, women's body weight has been increasing as a result of improved health and nutrition. These circumstances have created a conflict between the ideal shape and a woman's actual shape. The conflict typically leads to prolonged or obsessive dieting, which is often a prelude to the development of anorexia nervosa (Hsu, 1996). As might be expected, given this line of reasoning, the prevalence of anorexia nervosa has increased as the thin feminine ideal took hold, and the prevalence of anorexia nervosa is especially high among women who are under intense pressure to be thin, such as dancers and models. Of course, not all dieting develops into anorexia nervosa. It is hypothesized that sociocultural pressures are part of a larger model of development, which includes other predisposing factors such as problems with autonomy, rapid physical change at puberty, premorbid obesity, personality traits, cognitive style, perceptual disturbances, and interpersonal and familial difficulties (Polivy & Herman, 2002).

The role of sexuality in the development of anorexia is not clear (Ghizzani & Montomoli, 2000; Wiederman, 1996). Although some experienced clinicians have described the disorder as a retreat from maturity, sexual issues are not necessarily the central problem. Rather, the patient with anorexia may be focused more specifically on achieving control of her body and diet. Attempts to examine a possible causal connection between sexual behavior and eating disorders is also made more complicated by the need to consider additional variables, such as personality traits and negative body image.

For some women, sexual abuse is an important factor in the development of an eating disorder. Nevertheless, there does not appear to be a specific relation between eating disorders and exposure to sexual trauma (Wonderlich et al., 1997). It has been estimated that 30 percent of women with eating disorders were sexually abused as children. This figure is similar to some estimates regarding the prevalence of sexual abuse in the general female population. Other studies have found comparable rates of prior sexual abuse among women with eating disorders and women with depression (Vice & Cooper, 1995). Sexual abuse does not explain the development of most cases of anorexia nervosa, but it is one important risk factor for eating disorders as well as other forms of psychological disturbance.

Treatment

Research on anorexia has not identified one form of treatment that is consistently more effective than others. Various forms of psychotherapy are employed by clinicians, with most using cognitive-behavioral therapy or a combination of cognitive-behavioral and psychodynamic techniques (Peterson & Mitchell, 1999).

A number of steps are typically followed in treatment of anorexia nervosa. The first step is often hospitalization. This may be necessary in cases in which weight loss is extreme, suicidal thoughts are present, the patient is still denying her illness, or previous outpatient therapy has been ineffective (Andersen, 1997). Weight restoration must occur before any psychological treatment can begin. This is necessary to alleviate the psychological symptoms of starvation as well as to confront the patient with the body size that she fears. Although there is no single best way to restore weight, the key is to elicit as much cooperation as possible and to be sensitive to the patient's concerns. It is important to work with the patient to set a target weight, usually 90 percent of the average weight for a particular age and height. Behavioral techniques, such as those used with Joan, are often used to facilitate immediate weight gain.

Various types of medication are used to treat patients with eating disorders. Antidepressant drugs are employed most frequently, perhaps because anorexic and bulimic patients are often depressed. Selective serotonin reuptake inhibitors (SSRIs), such as fluoxetine (Prozac), have been beneficial in individual case studies. Research studies indicate that antidepressants are beneficial for many bulimic patients. Unfortunately, controlled outcome studies have not provided support for the efficacy of these drugs in the treatment of anorexia nervosa. No form of medication is better than placebo in supporting long-term weight maintenance, changing distorted attitudes toward eating, or preventing relapse (Attia et al., 2001; Krueger & Kennedy, 2000).

After the person's weight is restored to a normal level, dysfunctional attitudes toward food and body shape can be addressed in psychotherapy. This aspect of treatment can be especially challenging because patients with anorexia are usually not self-referred and most are resistant to treatment. Establishing a connection with the patient and building a therapeutic relationship are particularly important in working with severe cases of anorexia nervosa (Strober, 1997). The therapist's goal is to build a trusting relationship within which other interventions can be employed. Cognitive distortions, superstitious thinking, trouble with expressing emotion, body-image misperceptions, self-esteem, and autonomy are some of the issues that need to be addressed (Cooper , Todd, & Wells, 2002). When the patient is under the age of 16 and is still living at home, family therapy is often recommended.

Joan's treatment followed parts of this approach. During her hospitalization, various behavioral techniques were used to restore her weight to a healthy level. Because Joan was older and living on her own, she was treated individually, rather than in family therapy. Consistent with a cognitive approach, Joan's ways of viewing the world and herself were challenged directly. Cognitive therapy procedures (originally developed by Beck for the treatment of depression) can be applied in the treatment of anorexia nervosa. This process involves several steps: (1) learning to be more aware of thoughts and beliefs; (2) exploring and clarifying the connection between the dysfunctional beliefs and maladaptive behaviors; (3) examining the truth of those beliefs; (4) learning to replace the dysfunctional beliefs with more realistic ones; and (5) eventually changing the underlying assumptions that are creating the dysfunctional beliefs (Kleifield, Wagner, & Halmi, 1996).

The prognosis for patients with anorexia nervosa is mixed. Approximately 50 percent relapse after hospitalization. Five percent die as a direct result of the biological effects of self-imposed starvation. Those who have a relatively good outcome often continue to have difficulties with attitudes toward weight and eating (Eckert et al., 1995). One long-term follow-up study of women who had recovered from anorexia investigated the subjective experience of this process. The women were interviewed 20 years after the onset of their disorder. They reported that "personality strength," "self-confidence," and "being understood" were the most important factors in their sustained health (Hsu, Crisp, & Callender, 1992). Joan had some of these factors working in her favor. She was fortunate to have her husband and close friends as sources of support. She may have also had the advantage of psychological maturity because she was already an adult when she developed her eating disorder. Although she was initially resistant to treatment, she decided to admit herself to the hospital on a voluntary basis and was determined to change her behavior. These factors may have played an important role in her eventual recovery.

10 Mood Disorders

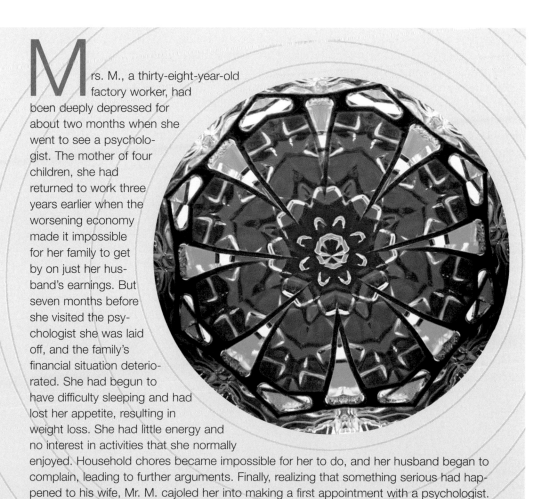

Mrs. M., a thirty-eight-year-old factory worker, had been deeply depressed for about two months when she went to see a psychologist. The mother of four children, she had returned to work three years earlier when the worsening economy made it impossible for her family to get by on just her husband's earnings. But seven months before she visited the psychologist she was laid off, and the family's financial situation deteriorated. She had begun to have difficulty sleeping and had lost her appetite, resulting in weight loss. She had little energy and no interest in activities that she normally enjoyed. Household chores became impossible for her to do, and her husband began to complain, leading to further arguments. Finally, realizing that something serious had happened to his wife, Mr. M. cajoled her into making a first appointment with a psychologist.

In this chapter we discuss the mood disorders. We begin by describing the DSM categories of depression, bipolar disorder, and chronic mood disorders. We then present research on biological and psychological factors relevant to these disorders and discuss their treatment. In the final section we examine suicide.

General Characteristics of Mood Disorders

Mood disorders involve disabling disturbances in emotion—from the sadness of depression to the unrealistic elation and irritability of mania.

Depression—Signs and Symptoms

As illustrated by the case of Mrs. M., **depression** is an emotional state typically marked by great sadness, feelings of worthlessness and guilt, withdrawal from others, and loss of sleep, appetite, sexual desire, and interest and pleasure in usual activities. Just as most of us experience occasional anxiety, so, too, do we experience sadness during the course of our lives, although perhaps not to a degree or with a frequency that warrants the diagnosis of depression. Depression is often associated, or comorbid, with other psychological problems, such as panic attacks, substance abuse, sexual dysfunction, and personality disorders.

Paying attention can be exhausting for people who are depressed. They cannot easily take in what they read and what other people say to them. Conversation may also be a chore; depressed individuals may speak slowly, after long pauses, using few words and a low, monotonous voice. Many prefer to sit alone and remain silent. Others are agitated and cannot sit still. They pace, wring their hands, continually sigh and moan, or complain. When depressed individuals are confronted with a problem, ideas for its solution may not occur to them. Every moment has a great heaviness, and their heads fill and reverberate with self-recriminations. Depressed people may neglect personal hygiene and appearance and make numerous complaints of somatic symptoms with no apparent physical basis (Simon et al., 1999). Utterly dejected and completely without hope and initiative, they may be apprehensive, anxious, and despondent much of the time.

The symptoms and signs of depression vary somewhat across the life span. As we discuss in more detail later (p. 300), depression in children often results in somatic complaints, such as headaches or stomachaches. In older adults, depression is often characterized by distractibility and complaints of memory loss (see Chapter 16). Symptoms of depression exhibit some cross-cultural variation, probably resulting from differences in cultural standards of acceptable behavior. For example, complaints of nerves and headaches are more common in Latino culture, and reports of weakness and fatigue are more common among Asians. Some depression, although recurrent, tends to dissipate with time. But an average untreated episode may stretch on for five months or even longer and may seem to be of even greater duration to patients and their families. And as we discuss later, suicide is a risk. Depression sometimes becomes chronic; in such cases the patient does not completely snap back to an earlier level of functioning between bouts.

Mania—Signs and Symptoms

Mania is an emotional state or mood of intense but unfounded elation or irritability accompanied by hyperactivity, talkativeness, flight of ideas, distractibility, and impractical, grandiose plans. Some people who experience episodic periods of depression also at times suddenly become manic. Although there are clinical reports of individuals who experience mania but not depression, this condition is quite rare in hospital settings.

The person in the throes of a manic episode, which may last from several days to several months, may be readily recognized by his or her loud and incessant stream of remarks, sometimes full of puns, jokes, rhyming, and interjections about nearby objects and happenings that have attracted the speaker's attention. This speech is difficult to interrupt and reveals the manic patient's so-called flight of ideas. Although small bits of talk are coherent, the individual may shift rapidly from topic to topic. The patient's need for activity may cause the person to be annoyingly sociable and intrusive, constantly and sometimes purposelessly busy, and, unfortunately, oblivious to the obvious pitfalls of his or her endeavors. Imprudent sexual behavior can also occur in mania. Any attempt to curb these various excesses can bring quick anger and even rage. Mania usually comes on suddenly over a period of a day or two.

The following description of a case of mania is from our files. The irritability that is often part of this state was not evident in this patient.

Mr. W., a thirty-two-year-old postal worker, had been married for eight years. He and his wife and their two children lived comfortably and happily in a middle-class neighborhood. In retrospect, there appeared to be no warning of what was to happen. One morning, Mr. W. told his wife that he was bursting with energy and ideas, that his job as a mail carrier was unfulfilling, and that he was just wasting his talent. That night he slept little, spending most of the time at a desk, writing furiously. The next morning he left for work at the usual time but returned home at 11:00 A.M, his car filled to overflowing with aquariums and other equipment for tropical fish. He had quit his job, then withdrawn all the money from the family's savings account and spent it on tropical-fish equipment. Mr. W. reported that the previous night he had worked out a way to modify existing equipment so that fish "won't die anymore. We'll be millionaires." After unloading the paraphernalia, Mr. W. set off to canvass the neighborhood for possible buyers, going door-to-door and talking to anyone who would listen.

The following bit of conversation from the period after Mr. W. entered treatment indicates his incorrigible optimism and provocativeness.

Therapist: Well, you seem pretty happy today.

Client: Happy! Happy! You certainly are a master of understatement, you rogue! [Shouting, literally jumping out of his seat.] Why I'm ecstatic. I'm leaving for the West Coast today, on my daughter's bicycle. Only 3,100 miles. That's nothing, you know. I could probably walk, but I want to get there by next week. And along the way I plan to contact a lot of people about investing in my fish equipment. I'll get to know more people that way—you know, Doc, "know" in the biblical sense [leering at the therapist seductively]. Oh, God, how good it feels. It's almost like a nonstop orgasm.

Formal Diagnostic Listings of Mood Disorders

Two of the mood disorders listed in DSM-IV-TR are major depression, also referred to as unipolar depression, and bipolar disorder.

Diagnosis of Depression　　The formal DSM-IV-TR diagnosis of **major depression** requires for at least two weeks either depressed mood or loss of interest and pleasure. In addition, the diagnosis requires the presence of four additional symptoms, such as sleep or appetite disturbances, loss of energy, feelings of worthlessness, suicidal thoughts, and difficulty concentrating.

There is no question that these are the major symptoms of depression. What is controversial, though, is whether a patient with five symptoms and a two-week duration is distinctly different from one who has only three symptoms for ten days. In an evaluation of this issue with a sample of twins, the number of symptoms and the duration of depression were used to predict the likelihood of future episodes and the probability that a cotwin would also be diagnosed as depressed. Even with fewer than five symptoms and a duration of less than two weeks, co-twins were likely also to be diagnosed with depression and patients were likely to have recurrences (Kendler & Gardner, 1998). Further, Gotlib, Lewinsohn, and Seeley (1995) found that individuals with fewer than five symptoms, with so-called subclinical depression, had as many difficulties in psychosocial functioning as did individuals meeting the formal requirements for a diagnosis of depression. It is data like these that might lead to a change of criteria in DSM-V.

DSM-IV-TR Criteria for Depression

- Sad, depressed mood, most of the day, nearly every day for two weeks or loss of interest and pleasure in usual activities, plus at least four of the following:
- Difficulties in sleeping (insomnia); not falling asleep initially; not returning to sleep after awakening in the middle of the night, and early morning awakenings; or, in some patients, a desire to sleep a great deal of the time
- Shift in activity level, becoming either lethargic (psychomotor retardation) or agitated
- Poor appetite and weight loss, or increased appetite and weight gain
- Loss of energy, great fatigue
- Negative self-concept, self-reproach and self-blame; feelings of worthlessness and guilt
- Complaints or evidence of difficulty in concentrating, such as slowed thinking and indecisiveness
- Recurrent thoughts of death or suicide

Major depression is one of the most prevalent of the disorders considered in this book. Lifetime prevalence rates have ranged from 5.2 percent to 17.1 percent in two large-scale studies of Americans (Kessler et al., 1994; Weissman et al., 1996). Reasons for this large discrepancy include use of different interviews for collecting information on symptoms, use of different diagnostic criteria, and differences in the amount of training provided to the interviewers who collected the data. Regardless of these differences in overall prevalence, depression is two to three times more common in women than in men; it occurs more frequently among members of the lower socioeconomic classes and most frequently among young adults. However, depression is also more common than average among Jewish males, and the usual sex difference does not occur between Jewish men and Jewish women (Levav et al., 1997). The prevalence of depression varies considerably cross-culturally. In a major cross-cultural study using the same diagnostic criteria and structured interview in each country, prevalence varied from a low of 1.5 percent in Taiwan to a high of 19 percent in Beirut, Lebanon (Weissman et al., 1996). The reasons for these large differences are not well understood, though the political upheavals in Beirut in the 1970s and 1980s may help account for the high prevalence there. What is more clear, however, is the fact that major depression is one of the world's leading causes of disability (Murray & Lopez, 1996).

The prevalence of depression has increased steadily during the mid to late twentieth century (Klerman, 1988b), and at the same time the age of onset has decreased (the mid-to-late twenties is typical). One possible explanation for this phenomenon lies in the social changes that have occurred over this same period. Today's young people face many challenges, often in the absence of support structures—such as a tightly knit extended family, traditional customs, or religion—that were a more central part of society in the past. Yet, life was hardly easy for earlier generations, which renders this explanation a bit suspect.

Depression tends to be a recurrent disorder. About 80 percent experience another episode, and the average number of episodes, which typically last for three to five months, is about four (Judd, 1997). Even among those who improve sufficiently so that they are no longer diagnosable, subclinical depression can remain for years (Judd et al., 1998). In about 12 percent of cases depression becomes a chronic disorder with a duration of more than two years.

Diagnosis of Bipolar Disorder DSM-IV-TR defines **bipolar I disorder** as involving episodes of mania or mixed episodes that include symptoms of both mania and depression. Most individuals with bipolar I disorder also experience episodes of depression. A formal diagnosis of a manic episode requires the presence of elevated or irritable mood plus three additional symptoms (four if the mood is irritable). Notably, some clinicians do not regard euphoria as a core symptom of mania and report that irritable mood and even depressive features are more common (e.g., Goodwin & Jamison, 1990). As is the case with the other DSM categories, the symptoms must be sufficiently severe to impair social and occupational functioning.

Bipolar disorder occurs less often than major depression, with a lifetime prevalence rate of about 1 percent of the population (Myers et al., 1984). The average age of onset is in the twenties, and it occurs equally often in men and in women. Among women, episodes of depression are more common and episodes of mania less common than among men (Leibenluft, 1996). Like major depression, bipolar disorder tends to recur; over 50 percent of cases have four or more episodes (Goodwin & Jamison, 1990). The severity of the disorder is indicated by the fact that at twelve months after release from hospital, fully 76 percent of patients are rated as impaired and in 52 percent the episode is ongoing (Keck et al., 1998).

Heterogeneity within the Categories

A problem in the classification of mood disorders is their great heterogeneity; people with the same diagnosis can vary greatly from one another. Some bipolar patients, for example, experience the full range of symptoms of both mania and depression almost every day, termed a mixed episode. Other patients have symptoms of only mania or only depression during a clinical episode. Still other patients have episodes of major depression accompanied by **hypomania** (*hypo* comes from the Greek for "under"), a change in behavior and mood that is less extreme than full-blown mania; these patients would meet criteria for bipolar II disorder in DSM-IV-TR. More specifically, episodes of hypomania need only last for about four days and do not markedly impair social or occupational functioning, whereas an episode of mania must last for at least one week and cause marked impairments in social and occupational functioning.

Some depressed patients may be diagnosed as having psychotic features if they are subject to delusions and hallucinations. The presence of delusions appears to be a useful distinction among people with unipolar depression (Johnson, Horvath, & Weissman, 1991); depressed patients with delusions do not generally respond well to the usual drug therapies for depression, but they do respond favorably to these drugs when they are combined with those commonly used to treat other psychotic disorders, such as schizophrenia. Furthermore, depression with psychotic features is more severe than depression without delusions and involves more social impairment and less time between episodes (Coryell et al., 1996).

According to DSM-IV-TR, some patients with depression may have melancholic features. In the DSM, the term *melancholic* refers to a specific pattern of depressive symptoms. Patients with melancholic features find no pleasure in any activity and are unable to feel better even temporarily when something good happens. Their depressed mood is worse in the morning. They awaken about two hours too early, lose appetite and weight, and are either lethargic or extremely agitated. These individuals typically respond well to biological therapies. Studies of the validity of the distinction between depressions with or without melancholic features have yielded mixed results. One study, for example, found that patients with melancholic features had more comorbidity (e.g., with anxiety disorders), more frequent episodes, and more impairment, suggesting it may simply be a more severe type of depression (Kendler, 1997).

Both manic and depressive episodes may be marked by catatonic features, such as motoric immobility or excessive, purposeless activity. Both manic and depressive episodes may also occur within four weeks of childbirth; in this case they are noted to have a postpartum onset.

Finally, DSM-IV-TR states that both bipolar and unipolar disorders can be subdiagnosed as seasonal if there is a regular relationship between an episode and a particular time of the year. Most research has focused on depression that occurs in the winter, and the most prevalent explanation is that it is linked to a decrease in the number of daylight hours. Reduced light does cause decreases in the activity of serotonin neurons of the hypothalamus. These neurons regulate some behaviors, such as sleep, that are part of the syndrome (Schwartz et al., 1997). Therapy for these winter depressions involves exposing the patients to bright white light (Wirz-Justice et al., 1993).

Chronic Mood Disorders

DSM-IV-TR lists two long-lasting, or chronic, disorders in which mood disturbances are predominant. The symptoms of these disorders must have been evident for at least two years but are not considered to be sufficient in number or to interfere enough with social or occupational functioning to warrant a diagnosis of a major depressive or manic episode.

In **cyclothymic disorder**, the person has frequent periods of depressed mood and hypomania. These periods may be mixed with, may alternate with, or may be separated by periods of normal mood lasting as long as two months. People with cyclothymic disorder may have paired sets of symptoms in their periods of depression and hypomania. During depression they feel inadequate; during hypomania their self-esteem is inflated. They withdraw from people, then seek them out in an uninhibited fashion. They sleep too much and then too little. Depressed cyclothymic patients have trouble concentrating,

Self-portrait by Paul Gauguin. He is but one of the many artists and writers who apparently suffered from a mood disorder.

> **DSM-IV-TR Criteria for a Manic Episode**
>
> - Elevated or irritable mood for at least one week, plus three of the following (four if mood is irritable):
> - Increase in activity level at work, socially, or sexually
> - Unusual talkativeness; rapid speech
> - Flights of ideas or subjective impression that thoughts are racing
> - Less than usual amount of sleep needed
> - Inflated self-esteem; belief that one has special talents, powers, and abilities
> - Distractibility; attention easily diverted
> - Excessive involvement in pleasurable activities that are likely to have undesirable consequences, such as reckless spending

Seasonal depression is one of the subtypes of major depressive disorder. This woman is having light therapy, which is an effective treatment for patients whose seasonal depression occurs during the winter.

and their verbal productivity decreases. During hypomania their thinking becomes sharp and creative, and their productivity increases. Patients with cyclothymia may also experience full-blown episodes of mania and depression.

The person with **dysthymic disorder** is chronically depressed. Besides feeling blue and deriving little if any pleasure from usual activities and pastimes, the person experiences several other signs of depression, such as insomnia or sleeping too much; feelings of inadequacy, ineffectiveness, and lack of energy; pessimism; an inability to concentrate and to think clearly; and a desire to avoid the company of others. What distinguishes dysthymia from major depression is the duration, type, and number of symptoms. Patients who meet the DSM-IV-TR criteria for dysthymia have three or more symptoms (instead of the five required for a diagnosis of major depression), including depressed mood but not suicidality, and cannot be without these symptoms for more than two months.

As suggested above, cyclothymia and dysthymia are often considered less severe mood disorders. However, given the chronic and unrelenting presence of symptoms, we must wonder if this assessment is accurate. Indeed, a recent prospective, longitudinal study following patients with depression and dysthymia for five years found that patients with dysthymia had more severe mood symptoms, were more likely to attempt suicide and to be hospitalized, and had more impairments in functioning than patients with depression (Klein et al., 2000).

Mood Disorders and Creativity

In her book *Touched with Fire: Manic-Depressive Illness and the Artistic Temperament* (1992), Kay Jamison, an expert on bipolar disorder and herself a long-time sufferer of this condition, assembled a vast array of data linking mood disorders, especially bipolar disorder, to artistic creativity. Of course, one could list many creative people who do not have mood disorders as well as many people with mood disorders who are not particularly creative. Nevertheless, the list of artists, composers, and writers who experienced mood disorders is impressive and includes Michelangelo, van Gogh, Tchaikovsky, Schumann, Gauguin, Tennyson, Shelley, and Whitman, among others. Perhaps the manic state fosters creativity through its association with elated mood, increased energy, rapid thoughts, and the ability to make connections among ideas that normally would remain unrelated.

In an interesting analysis of the musical compositions of Robert Schumann, Weisberg (1994) showed that Schumann produced more works during periods of hypomania than during periods of depression. However, the works produced during hypomania were not of higher quality than the works produced during periods of depression. Weisberg concluded that changes in mood influence motivation to produce creative works rather than the creative process itself.

Mood Disorders and Emotion

Noted psychologist Kay Redfield Jamison has experienced episodes of both mania and depression and therefore would be regarded as having bipolar disorder. She has written vivid accounts of her experiences.

Given their names, it seems as if mood and emotion ought to be the focus of much research into mood disorders. However, only recently have we begun to learn more about the nature of mood and emotion deficits in both major depressive disorder and bipolar disorder. For example, a number of studies have shown that individuals with depression show fewer positive facial expressions and report experiencing less pleasant emotion in response to pleasant stimuli compared with individuals without depression (Berenbaum & Oltmanns, 1992; Sloan et al., 1997; Sloan, Straus, & Wisner, 2001). Using a psychophysiological method called electrocortical potential, Deldin and colleagues (2001) found that depressed individuals responded less to positive (but not negative) stimuli than did individuals without depression.

One of the puzzles that has recently been a focus of attention is the relationship between anxiety and the mood disorders. In Chapter 6 we saw that anxiety disorders, including panic disorder, agoraphobia, obsessive-compulsive disorder, and posttraumatic stress disorder, all occur frequently with depression. Thus, people can suffer from severe anxiety and clinical depression at the same time. The same phenomenon occurs when anxiety and depression are studied as moods or affects rather than as clinical syndromes; questionnaire measures of anxiety and depression are highly correlated. How, then, can we differentiate anxiety and depression?

One approach to this question conceptualizes it in terms of three broad dimensions of emotion: negative affect, positive affect, and somatic anxiety. Both anxious and depressed people score high on measures of negative affect, which includes distress and negative moods. Anxiety and depression can be distinguished, however, on the next dimension, positive affect, a tendency to experience pleasurable, positive mood states. People who are depressed score lower than do people who are anxious. Finally, anxious people score higher than depressed people on the third dimension of emotion, known as somatic anxiety or anxious arousal, reporting more physical signs, such as sweaty palms and high heart rates (Brown, Chorpita, & Barlow, 1997; Clark, Watson, & Mineka, 1994).

Thus anxiety and depression may be differentiated with the appropriate measures, as shown in Table 10.1. But what about people who score high on negative affect, low on positive affect, and high on somatic anxiety? These individuals may form a diagnostic category called *mixed anxiety-depression*. They do not meet diagnostic criteria for either an anxiety or a mood disorder, but show a mixture of features of both anxiety (worry, anticipating the worst, irritability) and depression (fatigue, hopelessness, low self-esteem). This diagnosis was considered for inclusion in DSM-IV-TR but was eventually classified as a diagnosis in need of further study. Research on it continues, and it is a likely addition to the next DSM.

What about bipolar disorder? Here the picture appears to be more complicated. Although an episode of mania can involve high levels of positive emotions such as euphoria, it can also involve high levels of irritability. Some research has found that patients with bipolar disorder tend to experience very intense negative and positive emotions. Bipolar patients appear to have more intense positive emotional experiences than unipolar patients (e.g., Bagby et al., 1996). However, bipolar patients who experience depression demonstrate increased levels of negative affect, similar to patients with unipolar depression (Lozano & Johnson, 2001).

Table 10.1	Emotion Dimensions in Depression and Anxiety		
	Negative Affect	Positive Affect	Somatic Anxiety
Depression	high	low	low
Anxiety	high	high	high
Mixed Anxiety–Depression	high	low	high

Mood disorders are common among artists and writers. Van Gogh, Tchaikovsky (shown here), and Whitman were all affected.

Psychological Theories of Mood Disorders

Depression has been studied from several perspectives. Here we discuss psychoanalytic views, which emphasize the unconscious conflicts associated with grief and loss; cognitive theories, which focus on the depressed person's self-defeating thought processes; and interpersonal factors, which emphasize the negative ways depressed people interact with others. These theories for the most part describe different diatheses in a general diathesis—stress theory. The role of stressors in precipitating episodes of depression is well established (Kendler, Karkowski, & Prescott, 1999), although their importance seems to lessen as the number of episodes increases (Lewinsohn et al., 1999; Pardoen et al., 1996). The theories we discuss are trying to answer the question, What are the psychological characteristics of people who respond to stress with an episode of a mood disorder? (See Focus on Discovery 10.1 for an existential theory of depression.)

Psychoanalytic Theory of Depression

In his celebrated paper "Mourning and Melancholia," Freud (1917/1950) theorized that the potential for depression is created early in childhood. During the oral period, a child's needs may be insufficiently or oversufficiently gratified, causing the person to become fixated in this stage and dependent on the instinctual gratifications particular to it. With this arrest in psychosexual maturation, this fixation at the oral stage, the person may

An Existential Theory of Depression and Its Treatment

In 1959 a remarkable book, *From Death Camp to Existentialism*, was published by Viktor Frankl, an Austrian psychiatrist who spent three horrible years in Nazi concentration camps during World War II. His wife, brother, and parents, imprisoned with him, all lost their lives. Revised since its initial appearance and retitled *Man's Search for Meaning* (1963), Frankl's book vividly describes the humiliation, suffering, and terror experienced by camp prisoners. Frankl tells how he and others managed to survive psychologically in the brutalizing conditions of the death camps.

Frankl concluded that he was sustained emotionally by having succeeded somehow in finding meaning in his suffering and relating it to his spiritual life. The spirit gives the individual freedom to transcend circumstances, and freedom makes the individual responsible for his or her life. Frankl believed that psychopathology, particularly depression, ensues when a person has no purpose in living. From his concentration camp experiences he developed a psychotherapeutic approach called **logotherapy**, after the Greek word *logos*, "meaning."

The task of logotherapy is to restore meaning to the client's life. This is accomplished first by accepting in an empathic way the subjective experience of the client's suffering, rather than conveying the message that suffering is sick and wrong and should therefore not be regarded as normal. The logotherapist then helps the client make some sense out of his or her suffering by placing it within a larger context, a philosophy of life in which the individual assumes responsibility for his or her existence and for living according to a set of values. As Nietzsche wrote, "He who has a why to live for can bear with almost any how."

It may be useful to relate Frankl's views on depression and its treatment to learned helplessness, for certainly the concentration camp induced helplessness and hopelessness, and profound depression was commonplace. Logotherapy might be an effective way to reverse the helplessness depressed people experience in contemporary society, under less horrific and brutal conditions. By accepting responsibility for their lives and by seeking some meaning even in trying circumstances, they may achieve a sense of control and competence indispensable for forging an acceptable existence.

develop a tendency to be excessively dependent on other people for the maintenance of self-esteem.

From this happenstance of childhood, how can the adult come to suffer from depression? The complex reasoning is based on an analysis of bereavement. Freud hypothesized that after the loss of a loved one, whether by death or, most commonly for a child, separation or withdrawal of affection, the mourner first introjects, or incorporates, the lost person; he or she identifies with the lost one, perhaps in a fruitless attempt to undo the loss. Because, Freud asserted, we unconsciously harbor negative feelings toward those we love, the mourner then becomes the object of his or her own hate and anger. In addition, the mourner resents being deserted and feels guilt for real or imagined sins against the lost person.

According to the theory, the mourner's anger toward the lost one continues to be directed inward, developing into an ongoing process of self-blame, self-abuse, and depression. Overly dependent individuals are believed to be particularly susceptible to this process. This theory is the basis for the widespread psychodynamic view of depression as anger turned against oneself.

Although some research has been generated by psychoanalytic points of view, the little information available does not give strong support to the theory. On the positive side, some depressed people are high in dependency and prone to become depressed following a rejection (Nietzel & Harris, 1990). Some researchers have analyzed dreams and projective tests of depressed individuals, reasoning that they should be means of expressing unconscious needs and fears. But Beck and Ward (1961) analyzed the dreams of depressed people and found themes of loss and failure, not of anger and hostility. Furthermore, if depression comes from anger turned inward, we would expect depressed people to express little hostility toward others. Yet depressed individuals often express intense anger and hostility toward others (Weissman, Klerman, & Paykel, 1971).

Although Freud cloaked his clinical impressions in theoretical terms that have been rejected by many contemporary writers, we must appreciate that some of his basic suppositions have a continuing influence. For instance, cognitive research (discussed next) has found that depressed patients often hold irrational beliefs, such as, "it is a dire necessity that I be universally loved and approved of." This might be connected to Freud's idea that one becomes depressed following the loss of a loved one. Similarly, a large body of evidence indicates that depression is precipitated by stressful life events, and these often involve losses, for example, a divorce or job termination (e.g., Brown & Harris, 1978).

Cognitive Theories of Depression

Discussions of the role of cognition in anxiety in Chapter 6 and of Ellis's concept of irrational beliefs in Chapter 2 and elsewhere indicate that cognitive processes play a decisive role in emotional behavior. In some theories of depression, as in some theories of anxiety, thoughts and beliefs are regarded as major factors in causing or influencing the emotional state. Because cognitive theories of depression are those pursued most actively in controlled studies, we now discuss two of them in some detail: Beck's schema theory and the helplessness/hopelessness theory.

Beck's Theory of Depression   The most important contemporary theory that regards thought processes as causative factors in depression is that of Aaron Beck (1967, 1987). His central thesis is that depressed individuals feel as they do because their thinking is biased toward negative interpretations. Figure 10.1 illustrates the interactions among the three levels of cognitive activity that Beck believes underlie depression.

According to Beck, in childhood and adolescence depressed individuals acquired a negative schema—a tendency to see the world negatively—through loss of a parent, an unrelenting succession of tragedies, the social rejection of peers, the criticisms of teachers, or the depressive attitude of a parent. (Our later discussion of depression in children will indicate that the acquisition of negative schemata early in life can sometimes lead to depression before adulthood.) All of us have schemata of many kinds; by these perceptual sets, these miniparadigms, we order our lives. The negative schemata acquired by depressed persons are activated whenever they encounter new situations that resemble in some way, perhaps only remotely, the conditions in which the schemata were learned. Moreover, the negative schemata of depressed people fuel and are fueled by certain cognitive biases, which lead these people to misperceive reality. Thus an ineptness schema can make depressed individuals expect to fail most of the time, a self-blame schema burdens them with responsibility for all misfortunes, and a negative self-evaluation schema constantly reminds them of their worthlessness.

Negative schemata, together with cognitive biases or distortions, maintain what Beck called the **negative triad**: far-reaching negative views of the self, the world, and the future. The "world" part of Beck's depressive triad refers to the person's judgment that he or she cannot cope with the demands of the environment. It is highly personal—"I cannot possibly cope with all these demands and responsibilities." It is not a concern for global events that do not implicate the self directly—for example, "The world has been going south since the American League adopted the designated hitter rule" (Haaga, Dyck, & Ernst, 1991, p. 218).

The following list describes some of the principal cognitive biases of depressed individuals according to Beck.

- **Arbitrary inference**—a conclusion drawn in the absence of sufficient evidence or of any evidence at all. For example, a man concludes that he is worthless because it is raining the day he is hosting an outdoor party.
- **Selective abstraction**—a conclusion drawn on the basis of but one of many elements in a situation. A worker feels worthless when a product fails to function, even though she is only one of many people who contributed to its production.

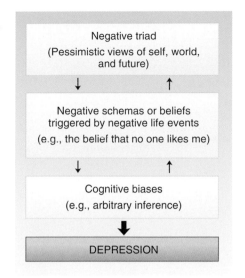

Figure 10.1 The interrelationships among different kinds of cognitions in Beck's theory of depression.

Being rejected by peers may lead to the development of the negative schema that Beck's theory suggests plays a key role in depression.

- **Overgeneralization**—an overall sweeping conclusion drawn on the basis of a single, perhaps trivial, event. A student regards his poor performance in a single class on one particular day as final proof of his worthlessness and stupidity.
- **Magnification and minimization**—exaggerations in evaluating performance. A man, believing that he has completely ruined his car (magnification) when he sees that there is a slight scratch on the rear fender, regards himself as good-for-nothing; a woman believes herself worthless (minimization) in spite of a succession of praise-worthy achievements.

It is important to understand the core of Beck's influential theorizing. Many theorists see people as victims of their passions, creatures whose intellectual capacities can exert little if any control over feelings—Freud's basic position. In Beck's theory the cause–effect relationship operates in the opposite direction. Our emotional reactions are considered primarily a function of how we construe our world. The interpretations of depressed individuals do not mesh well with the way in which most people view the world. Beck sees such people as victims of their own illogical self-judgments.

Evaluation We must consider two key issues in evaluating Beck's theory. The first is whether depressed patients, in contrast to nondepressed individuals, think in the negative ways enumerated by Beck. This point was initially confirmed by Beck's clinical observations (Beck, 1967). Further support comes from a number of sources: self-report questionnaires, laboratory studies of processes such as memory, and the Articulated Thoughts in Simulated Situations method described in Chapter 4 (Dobson & Shaw, 1986; Segal et al., 1995; White et al., 1992).

Perhaps the greatest challenge for cognitive theories of depression is to resolve the second issue—whether the negative beliefs of depressed people follow their depression, or in fact cause the depressed mood. Many studies in experimental psychology have shown that a person's mood can be influenced by how he or she construes events. But manipulating emotion has also been shown to change thinking (e.g., Fredrickson, 1998). Beck and others have found that depression and certain kinds of thinking are correlated, but a specific causal relationship cannot be determined from such data; depression could cause negative thoughts, or negative thoughts could cause depression. The relationship in all likelihood works both ways: depression can make thinking more negative, and negative thinking can probably cause and can certainly worsen depression. In recent years Beck himself has come to this more bidirectional position.

One way to determine if negative thinking causes depression is to study thoughts and depression prospectively, over time. Studies of this type have had mixed results. Stader and Hokanson (1998) followed a sample of people for forty-five days, collecting measures of mood and cognitions each day. Episodes of mild depression were identified, and the investigators then looked at whether these episodes were preceded by an increase in negative cognitions. Although an increase in interpersonal stress and dependency did precede the episodes of depression, negative cognitions did not. In contrast, other longitudinal studies have found negative thinking to precede symptoms of depression. For example, in one study, college students' cognitions and mood were assessed prior to midterm exams, and then their mood was assessed after the exams. The instrument used was the most widely used self-report scale in studies of Beck's theory, the Dysfunctional Attitudes Scale (DAS). Students who scored high on the DAS and also did poorly on the exam showed an increase in depressive symptoms. Students who scored high on the DAS scale but who performed well on the exam did not show the same increase in depressive symptoms (Joiner et al., 1999). These findings suggest that negative thinking in combination with a negative event may precede depression symptoms. Similarly, Lewinsohn and colleagues (2001) found that dysfunctional attitudes in combination with a higher number of negative life events predicted the onset of depression in adolescents.

Recently, researchers have recognized that the DAS is multidimensional, containing subscales that assess different domains of dysfunctional attitudes, for example, a strong need to impress others and a desire to be perfect (Brown et al., 1995). These more specific components of dysfunctional thinking may more successfully predict the subsequent occurrence of depression when they interact with a stressor specific to them, for example, a personal failure in someone who has a strong need to be perfect (Hewitt, Flett, & Ediger, 1996).

Despite some uncertainties, Beck's theory has the advantage of being testable, and it has engendered considerable research on the treatment of depression. As discussed later in this chapter (p. 289), Beck's work has encouraged therapists to focus directly on the thinking of depressed patients in order to change their feelings.

Helplessness/Hopelessness Theories   In this section we discuss the evolution of an influential cognitive theory of depression—actually, three theories—the original helplessness theory; its subsequent, more cognitive, attributional version; and its transformation into the hopelessness theory (see Figure 10.2 for a summary).

Learned Helplessness   The basic premise of the **learned helplessness theory** is that an individual's passivity and sense of being unable to act and to control his or her own life is acquired through unpleasant experiences and traumas that the individual tried unsuccessfully to control, bringing on a sense of helplessness, which leads to depression.

This theory began as a mediational learning theory (cf. p. 46) formulated to explain the behavior of dogs who received inescapable electric shocks. Soon after receiving the first shocks, the dogs seemed to give up and passively accept the painful stimulation. Later, when the shocks could be avoided, these dogs did not acquire the avoidance response as efficiently and effectively as did control animals that had not experienced the inescapable shocks. Rather, most of them lay down in a corner and whined. On the basis of these observations, Seligman (1974) proposed that animals acquire a sense of helplessness when confronted with uncontrollable aversive stimulation. Later, this sense of helplessness impairs their performance in stressful situations that can be controlled.

On the basis of this and other work on the effects of uncontrollable stress, Seligman concluded that learned helplessness in animals could provide a model for at least certain forms of human depression. Like many depressed people, the animals appeared passive in the face of stress, failing to initiate actions that might allow them to cope. They had difficulty eating or retaining what they ate, and they lost weight. Further, one of the neu-

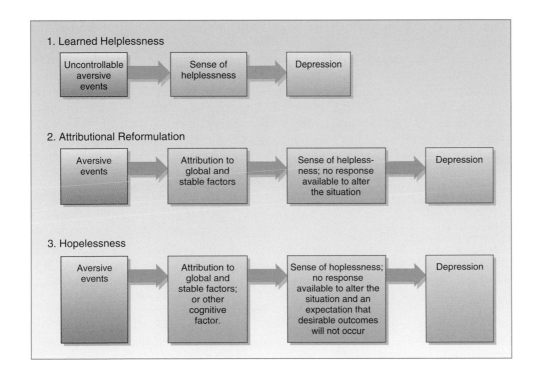

Figure 10.2 The three helplessness theories of depression.

rotransmitter chemicals implicated in depression, norepinephrine, was depleted in Seligman's animals (see p. 24). More recent research with animals has shown that repeated exposure to the environment in which the inescapable shocks were presented prolonged the helplessness effects, perhaps even indefinitely (Maier, 2001).

Attribution and Learned Helplessness   After the original research with animals, investigators began to conduct similar studies with humans. By 1978 several inadequacies of the theory and unexplained aspects of depression had become apparent. For example, many depressed people hold themselves responsible for their failures. But if they regard themselves as helpless, how can they blame themselves? To deal with these and other problems, a revised version of the learned helplessness model was proposed by Abramson, Seligman, and Teasdale (1978).

The essence of the revised theory lies in the concept of **attribution**—the explanation a person has for his or her behavior (Weiner et al., 1971)—and in this way it blends cognitive and learning elements. Given a situation in which the individual has experienced failure, he or she will try to attribute the failure to some cause. Table 10.2 applies the Abramson, Seligman, and Teasdale formulation to various ways in which a college student might attribute a low score on the mathematics portion of the Graduate Record Examination (GRE). The formulation is based on answers to three questions.

1. Are the reasons for failure believed to be internal (personal) or external (environmentally caused)?
2. Is the problem believed to be stable or unstable?
3. How global or specific is the inability to succeed perceived to be?

People become depressed, the theory suggests, when they attribute negative life events to stable and global causes. Whether self-esteem also collapses depends on whether they blame the bad outcome on their own inadequacies. The individual prone to depression is thought to show a depressive attributional style, a tendency to attribute bad outcomes to personal, global, stable faults of character. When persons with this style (a diathesis) have unhappy, adverse experiences (stressors), they become depressed (Peterson & Seligman, 1984).

Some research gives direct support to the reformulated theory. Seligman and his colleagues (1979) devised the Attributional Style Questionnaire and, as the theory predicted, found that mildly depressed college students did indeed more often attribute failure to personal, global, and stable inadequacies than did nondepressed students. Metalsky, Halberstadt, and Abramson (1987) conducted a study with college students taking a course in introductory psychology. Early in the semester the students completed the Attributional-Style Questionnaire and a questionnaire pertaining to their grade aspirations. A checklist was used to collect mood information twice before the midterm exam, right after receipt of the exam grades, and again two days later. According to the revised helplessness theory, a tendency to attribute negative events to global and stable inadequacies, as determined by the Attributional-Style Questionnaire, should predict more depressed mood in those students who received a poor grade, defined in this study as a failure to match aspirations.

Table 10.2   Attributional Schema of Depression: Why I Failed My GRE Math Exam

| Degree | Internal (Personal) | | External (Environmental) | |
	Stable	Unstable	Stable	Unstable
Global	I lack intelligence.	I am exhausted.	These tests are all unfair	It's an unlucky day, Friday the 13th
Specific	I lack mathematical ability.	I am fed up with math.	The math tests are unfair.	My math test was numbered "13."

The results differed depending on which of the post–exam mood assessments was considered. The outcome of the exam was the major determinant of students' initial mood changes; those who did poorly became more depressed. However, two days later, students who had made unstable and specific attributions on the Attributional-Style Questionnaire had recovered, but the stable, global students were still mildly depressed. Following a suggestion by Weiner (1986), Metalsky et al. proposed that a negative event elicits an immediate emotional response that occurs before any attributions are made. Subsequently, causal interpretations are sought, and a pattern of global, stable attributions makes the initial depressive response last longer.

Hopelessness Theory   The latest version of the theory (Abramson, Metalsky, & Alloy, 1989) has moved even further away from the original formulation. Some forms of depression (hopelessness depressions) are now regarded as caused by a state of hopelessness, an expectation that desirable outcomes will not occur or that undesirable ones will occur and that the person has no responses available to change this situation. (The latter part of the definition of *hopelessness*, of course, refers to helplessness, the central concept of earlier versions of the theory.) As in the attributional reformulation, negative life events (stressors) are seen as interacting with diatheses to yield a state of hopelessness.

One diathesis is the attributional pattern already described—attributing negative events to stable and global factors. However, the hopelessness theory now considers the possibility that there are other diatheses—low self-esteem[1] and a tendency to infer that negative life events will have severe negative consequences.

Metalsky and his colleagues (1993) conducted the first test of the hopelessness theory in a study similar to his earlier one. Two new features were the direct measurement of hopelessness and the newly proposed diathesis, low self-esteem. As in the earlier study, attributing poor grades to global and stable factors led to more persistent depressed mood. This pattern was found only among students whose self-esteem was low and was mediated by an increase in feelings of hopelessness, thus supporting the theory. A similar study conducted with children in the sixth and seventh grades yielded almost identical results (Robinson, Garber, & Hillsman, 1995). Lewinsohn and his colleagues (1994) also found that depressive attributional style and low self-esteem predicted the onset of depression in adolescents.

The Temple-Wisconsin Cognitive Vulnerability to Depression (CVD) study was designed to prospectively investigate whether college students with the hypothesized cognitive diathesis would develop major depressive disorder. In the CVD study, a high- and low-risk group were defined based on their scores on measures of attributional style and dysfunctional attitudes. The high-risk group scored in the upper 25 percent of the distributions for both measures; the low-risk group scored in the bottom 25 percent of the distributions. Findings from this study provided tentative support for the hopelessness theory: students in the high-risk group were more likely to develop major depressive disorder two and one-half years after the study began than were students in the low-risk group (e.g., Alloy et al., 1999). Unfortunately, though, both the Dysfunctional Attitudes Scale, a measure most often used to test Beck's theory, *and* the Attributional-Style Questionnaire, the measure used in tests of helplessness/hopelessness theories, were used to define the high-risk group. Thus, we do not know whether this finding supports the hopelessness theory, Beck's theory, or both.

An advantage of the hopelessness theory is that it can deal directly with the comorbidity of depression and anxiety disorders. Accounting for this pattern poses a major challenge for many theories, for they deal with only a single diagnosis. Alloy et al. (1990) pointed out several important features of this comorbidity. First, cases of anxiety without depression are relatively common, but depression without anxiety is rare (Kessler et al., 1996). Second, longitudinal studies reveal that anxiety diagnoses typically precede

---

[1] Low self-esteem is a reasonable diathesis, but other evidence suggests that unstable self-esteem may be more important. People whose self-esteem is very reactive to life events appear to be vulnerable to depression (Roberts & Gotlib, 1997).

depression (e.g., Kessler et al., 1997; Rohde, Lewinsohn, & Seeley, 1991). On the basis of a good deal of prior evidence (e.g., Bowlby, 1980; Mandler, 1972), Alloy and her colleagues proposed that an expectation of helplessness creates anxiety. When the expectation of helplessness becomes certain, a syndrome with elements of both depression and anxiety ensues. Finally, if the perceived probability of the occurrence of negative events becomes certain, hopelessness develops. Additional support for these ideas has continued to accumulate in recent years (Mineka, Watson, & Clark, 1998).

Issues in the Helplessness/Hopelessness Theories   Although these theories are promising, there are some problems worth noting.

1. Which type of depression is being modeled? In his original paper Seligman attempted to document the similarity between learned helplessness and what used to be called reactive depression, depression thought to be brought on by stressful life events. Yet, current research does not support the validity of a reactive type of depression. Abramson et al. (1989) now talk about a hopelessness depression, referring both to the presumed cause of the depression and to a set of symptoms that do not exactly match the DSM criteria. Only future research will tell whether these proposals are more than circular statements (hopelessness depression is caused by hopelessness).

Research on the helplessness/hopelessness theory has often studied college students with high BDI scores. These students may not provide a good analogue for clinical depression.

2. Do college-student populations provide good analogues? Although some research on the theories has been done with clinical populations or has tried to predict the onset of clinical depression, many studies have examined college students selected on the basis of scores on the Beck Depression Inventory (BDI) or have simply tried to predict increases in BDI scores. However, this inventory was not designed to diagnose depression, only to assess its severity in a clinically diagnosed group. Accumulating evidence indicates that selecting subjects solely on the basis of elevated BDI scores does not yield a group of people who can serve as a good analogue for those with clinical depression (Coyne, 1994). High scorers may not be clinically depressed (Santor & Coyne, 2001). Further, Hammen (1980) found that high scorers had markedly lower scores when retested just two to three weeks later.

3. Are attributions relevant? At issue here is the underlying assumption that people actively attempt to explain their own behavior to themselves and that the attributions they make have subsequent effects on their behavior. Some research indicates, however, that making attributions is not a process in which everyone engages (Hanusa & Schulz, 1977). Furthermore, in a series of experiments discussed in Chapter 7, Nisbett and Wilson (1977) showed that people are frequently unaware of the causes of their behavior.[2]

Even if we allow that attributions are relevant and powerful determinants of behavior, we should note that many findings in support of the learned helplessness theory have been obtained by giving individuals the Attributional Style Questionnaire or by determining how they explain laboratory-induced successes or failures. When depressed persons were asked about the five most stressful events of their lives, however, their attributions did not differ from those supplied by nondepressed people (Hammen & Cochran, 1981).

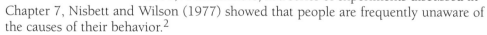

[2] The attribution literature makes the basic assumption that people *care* about what causes their behavior. This central idea is the brainchild of psychologists whose business is to explain behavior. It may be that psychologists have projected their own need to explain behavior onto other people! Laypeople may simply not reflect on why they act and feel as they do to the same extent that psychologists do.

4. One key assumption of the helplessness/hopelessness theories is that the depressive attributional style is a persistent part of the makeup of depressed people; that is, the depressive attributional style must already be in place when the person encounters some stressor. However, some research shows that the depressive attributional style disappears following an episode of depression (Hamilton & Abramson, 1983).

Despite their problems, the helplessness/hopelessness theories have clearly stimulated a great deal of research and theorizing about depression and seem destined to do so for many years to come.

Interpersonal Theory of Depression

In this section we discuss relationships between the depressed person and others. Some of the data we present may be relevant to the etiology of depression and some to its course.

In Chapter 8 we discussed the role of social support in health. This concept has also been applied to research on depression. Depressed individuals tend to have sparse social networks and to regard them as providing little support (Keltner & Kring, 1998). Reduced social support may lessen an individual's ability to handle negative life events and make him or her vulnerable to depression (e.g., Billings, Cronkite, & Moos, 1983).

This deficiency in social support is likely due to the fact that depressed people elicit negative reactions from others (Coyne, 1976). This feature of depression has been studied in a variety of ways, ranging from conducting telephone conversations with depressed patients, to listening to audiotapes of depressed patients, to participating in face-to-face interactions. Data show that the behavior of depressed people elicits rejection. For example, the roommates of depressed college students rated social contacts with them as low in enjoyment and reported high levels of aggression toward them; mildly depressed college students were likely to be rejected by their roommates (Joiner, Alfano, & Metalsky, 1992).

Not surprisingly given these findings, depression and marital or family discord frequently co-occur, and the interactions of depressed people and their spouses are characterized by hostility on both sides (Biglan, Hops, & Sherman, 1988; Kowalik & Gotlib, 1987). Critical comments of spouses of depressed people are a significant predictor of recurrence of depression (Hooley & Teasdale, 1989). Couples in which one of the partners has a mood disorder report less marital satisfaction than do couples in which neither partner has a history of mood disorder (Beach, Sandeen, & O'Leary, 1990; Beach, Smith, & Fincham, 1994).

What is it about the depressed person that elicits these negative reactions? Several studies have demonstrated that the nonverbal behavior of depressed people may play an important role. For example, others may find aversive such things as the following: very slow speech, with silences and hesitations; negative self-disclosures; more negative affect; poor maintenance of eye contact; and fewer positive facial expressions as well as more negative facial expressions (Field, 1995; Gotlib, 1982; Gotlib & Robinson, 1982; Gottman & Krokoff, 1989; Smith, Vivian, & O'Leary, 1990).

More recent research has explored the idea that constant seeking of reassurance is particularly onerous to others (Joiner, 1995; Joiner & Metalsky, 1995). Perhaps as a result of being reared in a cold and rejecting environment (Carnelly, Pietromonaco, & Jaffe, 1994), depressed people seek reassurance that others truly care, but even when reassured, they are only temporarily satisfied. Their negative self-concept causes them to doubt the truth of the positive feedback they have received, and their constant efforts to be reassured come to irritate others. Later, they actually seek out negative feedback, which, in a sense, validates their negative self-concept. Rejection ultimately occurs because of the depressed person's inconsistent behavior. Data collected by Joiner and Metalsky on mildly depressed college students have shown that this inconsistent pattern in seeking reassurance predicts increases in depressed mood. Furthermore, cadets at the U.S. Air Force training academy who scored high on a measure of reassurance–seeking were more likely than others to score high on a depression measure administered five weeks later (Joiner & Schmidt, 1998).

Also of importance in interpersonal theories of depression is the fact that interpersonal relationships are bi-directional. Thus, while depressed individuals may certainly elicit negative reactions from those with whom they interact, the reactions of those interactants are likely have a negative reciprocal impact on depressed individuals. Indeed, the social worlds of depressed people are more complex, more difficult to manage, and more effortful than those of people without depression (Coyne, 1999).

Do any of the interpersonal characteristics of depressed people precede the onset of depression, suggesting a causal relationship? Some research using the high-risk method suggests that the answer is yes. For example, the behavior of elementary-school-age children of depressed parents was rated negatively by both peers and teachers (Weintraub, Liebert, & Neale, 1975; Weintraub, Prinz, & Neale, 1978); low social competence predicted the onset of depression among elementary-school-age children (Cole et al., 1990); poor interpersonal problem-solving skills predicted increases in depression among adolescents (Davila et al., 1995); and marital discord predicted the onset of depression in a community sample (Whisman & Bruce, 1999). Thus interpersonal difficulties and deficits may be a cause of depression as well as a consequence of it. In short, interpersonal behavior clearly plays a major role in depression.

Psychological Theories of Bipolar Disorder

As with unipolar depression, life stress seems important in precipitating mood swings in bipolar disorder (Johnson & Miller, 1997; Malkoff-Schwartz et al., 1998). Other findings regarding depressive episodes in bipolar disorder are also similar to findings for unipolar (or major) depression. In a prospective study of bipolar patients, Johnson and colleagues (1999) found that social support predicted a more rapid recovery as well as a decrease in depressive symptoms but not manic symptoms. In a study of cognitive factors, both attributional style and dysfunctional attitudes in combination with negative life events predicted an increase in depression symptoms among bipolar patients (Reilly-Harrington et al., 1999). Interestingly, attributional style and dysfunctional attitudes in combination with negative life events also predicted an increase in manic symptoms, suggesting that the cognitive theories of depression may also be relevant for bipolar disorder.

The manic phase of the disorder is seen by some as a defense against a debilitating psychological state. The specific negative state that is being avoided varies from theory to theory. One of our own cases illustrates why many theorists have concluded that the manic state serves a protective function.

A forty-two-year-old man was experiencing his third manic episode. During each episode he had exhibited the classic pattern of manic symptoms, and much of his manic behavior centered on a grandiose delusion that he was the world's greatest businessman. "Did you know that I've already bought twenty companies today?" he stated at the beginning of a therapy session. "Not even Bill Gates has anything on me." From sessions between episodes it was apparent that success in business was indeed a central concern to the patient. But he was far from successful. His parents had lent him money to start several companies, but each had gone bankrupt. He was obsessed with matching the business successes of his wealthy father, but as the years passed his opportunities to do so were slipping away. It seemed, therefore, that his manic grandiosity was protecting him from a confrontation with his lack of business success—a realization that would likely have plunged him into a deep depression.

Clinical experience with manic patients as well as studies of their personalities when they are in remission indicate that they appear relatively well-adjusted between episodes. But if mania is a defense, it must be a defense against something, suggesting that the apparently good adjustment of manic people between episodes may not accurately reflect their true state. In an attempt to bypass what may be defensive responding, Winters and Neale (1985) used a specially developed test to examine the notion that manic individuals, even when between episodes, have low self-esteem.

Bipolar patients in remission, unipolar depressive patients, and normal people were given two tests: a self-esteem inventory and a specially constructed memory test. The second test was meant to be a subtle measure of the manic patients' expected low self-esteem. In the memory test, participants first read a paragraph describing a series of events, some of which had a positive outcome, others a negative outcome. They were then given a test that appeared to measure their recall of each story. Some items actually assessed recall of facts, but others forced the participants to go beyond the information and draw inferences. For example, one story concerned a man who was currently out of work. The reason for his unemployment was not stated directly, but the story was constructed to allow either of two inferences to be drawn. Participants could infer either that the man was unemployed through no fault of his own but because the economy was poor, or that the man's poor work record kept him unemployed. People with low self-esteem were expected to make the second inference.

The results agreed exactly with expectation. On the paper-and-pencil measure of self-esteem, both manic and nonpatient participants scored higher than did those with depression. But on the memory test the patients with mania performed similarly to the depressed participants; both groups drew the inferences that revealed low self-esteem. Thus the researchers concluded that the self-esteem of manic individuals may be very low. A recent study came to a similar conclusion (Lyon, Startup, & Bentall, 1999).

Biological Theories of Mood Disorders

Since biological processes are known to have considerable effects on moods, it is not surprising that investigators have sought biological causes for depression and mania. Furthermore, disturbed biological processes must be part of the causal chain if a predisposition for a mood disorder can be genetically transmitted, and evidence that a predisposition for a mood disorder is heritable would provide some support for the view that the disorder has a biological basis. The effectiveness of drug therapies which increase the levels of certain neurotransmitters in the treatment of mood disorders also suggests that biological factors are important. In this section we look at research in the areas of genetics, neurochemistry, and the neuroendocrine system. There is also a growing literature on structural abnormalities of the brains of patients with mood disorders. Because these brain abnormalities are similar to those found in schizophrenia, we discuss them in the next chapter (p. 335).

The Genetic Data

Research on genetic factors in bipolar disorder and unipolar depression has used the family, twin, and adoption methods discussed in Chapter 2. About 10 to 25 percent of the first-degree relatives of bipolar patients have experienced an episode of mood disorder (Gershon, 1990). The risk is higher among the relatives of patients with early onset of the disorder. These figures are greater than those for the general population. Curiously, among the first-degree relatives of bipolar probands, there are more cases of unipolar depression than of bipolar disorder. Averaging across eighteen family studies of bipolar disorder, the risk estimates for the first-degree relatives of bipolar patients are 6.45 percent for bipolar disorder and 10 percent for unipolar depression (Kelsoe, 1997). Overall, the concordance rate for bipolar disorder in identical twins is about 70 percent and in fraternal twins about 25 percent (Kelsoe, 1997). These data plus the results of adoption studies (e.g., Wender et al., 1986) support the notion that bipolar disorder has a heritable component.

The information available on unipolar depression indicates that genetic factors, although influential, are less decisive than in bipolar disorder. For example, in one study the relatives of depressed individuals were at only slightly higher than normal risk (Kendler et al., 1993). Furthermore, their risk for unipolar depression is less than the risk among relatives of bipolar probands (Andreasen et al., 1987). Early onset of depression, the presence of delusions, and comorbidity with an anxiety disorder or alcoholism confer greater risk on relatives (Goldstein et al., 1994; Lyons et al., 1998). Twin studies of unipolar depression consistently report higher concordances in monozygotic than in dizygotic twins, with some suggestion that genetics may play a stronger role in women than in men (Bierut et al., 1999; McGuffin et al., 1996; Silberg et al., 1999). Several small-scale adoption studies have also supported the idea that unipolar depression has a modest heritable component (Cadoret, 1978; Wender et al., 1986).

Linkage analysis, described in Chapter 2 (p. 23), has also been applied to mood disorders. In a widely reported linkage study of the Old Order Amish, Egeland and her colleagues (1987) found evidence favoring the hypothesis that bipolar disorder results from a dominant gene on the eleventh chromosome. However, several attempts to replicate the Egeland study failed, leading many to conclude that the eleventh chromosome may not be involved in bipolar disorder (e.g., Kelsoe, 1997; Smyth et al., 1996). Research on linkage continues and has broadened to focus on other genes on other chromosomes, especially chromosomes 18 and 21.

Neurochemistry and Mood Disorders

Over the past several decades researchers have sought to understand the role played by neurotransmitters in mood disorders. Two neurotransmitters have been most studied: norepinephrine and serotonin. The theory involving norepinephrine is most relevant to bipolar disorder and, in the most general terms, posits that a low level of norepinephrine leads to depression and a high level to mania. The serotonin theory suggests that a low level of serotonin produces depression.

The actions of drugs used to treat depression provided the clues on which both theories are based. In the 1950s two groups of drugs, tricyclics and monoamine oxidase inhibitors, were found effective in relieving depression. **Tricyclic drugs** (e.g., imipramine, trade name Tofranil) are a group of antidepressant medications so named because their molecular structure is characterized by three fused rings. They prevent some of the reuptake of both norepinephrine and serotonin by the presynaptic neuron after it has fired, leaving more of the neurotransmitter in the synapse so that transmission of the next nerve impulse is made easier (see Figure 10.3). **Monoamine oxidase (MAO) inhibitors** (e.g., tranylcypromine, trade name Parnate) are a group of antidepressant drugs that keep the enzyme monoamine oxidase from deactivating neurotransmitters, thus increasing the levels of both serotonin and norepinephrine in the synapse; this action produces the same facilitating effect described for tricyclics, presumably compensating for the abnormally low levels of these neurotransmitters in depressed people. These drug actions suggest that depression and mania are related to serotonin and norepinephrine. Newer antidepressant drugs, called selective serotonin reuptake inhibitors, or SSRIs (e.g., fluoxetine, Prozac), act more selectively than the older drugs, specifically inhibiting the reuptake of serotonin. Because these drugs are effective in treating unipolar depression, a stronger link has been shown between low levels of serotonin and depression.

Two main approaches have been used to evaluate the theories further. The first measures metabolites of these neurotransmitters, the by-products of the breakdown of serotonin and norepinephrine as they are found in urine, blood serum, and cerebrospinal fluid. The problem with such measurements is that they are not direct reflections of levels of either serotonin or norepinephrine in the brain; metabolites measured in this way could reflect neurotransmitters anywhere in the body. Indeed, the majority of the neurons that use serotonin are found in the intestines, and norepinephrine is also an important neurotransmitter in the peripheral nervous system.

A second strategy is to investigate the behavioral effects of drugs other than the antidepressants that are known either to increase or to decrease the brain levels of serotonin and norepinephrine. A drug raising the level of serotonin should alleviate depression; one reducing it should deepen depression or induce it in nondepressed individuals. Similarly, a drug that increases norepinephrine might induce a manic episode. This strategy also has its problems, however. Most drugs have multiple effects, making it difficult to choose one that accomplishes a specific purpose without complicating side effects.

These problems notwithstanding, what can be said of the validity of theories that implicate low levels of norepinephrine or serotonin in depression and high levels of norepinephrine in mania? First, a series of studies conducted by Bunney and Murphy and their colleagues at the National Institute of Mental Health monitored closely the urinary levels of norepinephrine in a group of bipolar patients as they cycled through stages of depression, mania, and normalcy. Urinary levels of norepinephrine decreased as patients became depressed (Bunney et al., 1970) and increased during mania, confirming the hypothesis that low levels of norepinephrine are associated with depression and high levels with mania (Bunney, Goodwin, & Murphy, 1972). A problem in interpreting these data is that such changes could result from increases in activity level, because increased motor activity in mania can increase norepinephrine activity. Nonetheless, there is evidence that increasing norepinephrine levels can precipitate a manic episode in bipolar patients (Altshuler et al., 1995).

Another avenue of research involves the principal metabolite of norepinephrine, 3-methoxy-4-hydroxyphenyl glycol (MHPG). Low levels of norepinephrine should be reflected in low levels of MHPG. As expected, depressed bipolar patients have generally been shown to have low levels of urinary MHPG (e.g., Muscettola et al., 1984); further, MHPG levels are higher during a manic than during a depressed episode and higher in manic patients than in nondepressed people (Goodwin & Jamison, 1990). As with studies that directly measured norepinephrine, however, the MHPG results could reflect differences in activity levels.

Studies of serotonin have examined its major metabolite, 5-hydroxyindoleacetic acid (5-HIAA). A fairly consistent body of data indicates that 5-HIAA levels are low in the cerebrospinal fluid of depressed patients. Studies also show that ingestion of L-tryptophan, from which serotonin is subsequently produced, is somewhat effective as a treatment for depression, especially when used in combination with other drugs (Coppen et al., 1972; Mendels et al., 1975). Furthermore, a drug that suppresses serotonin synthesis reduces the therapeutic effect of drugs that usually lessen depression (Shopsin, Friedman, & Gershon, 1976). Delgado et al. (1990) used a special diet to reduce the level of serotonin in remitted depressed patients by lowering the level of its precursor, tryptophan. They found that 67 percent of patients experienced a return of their symptoms. When patients resumed their normal diet, a gradual remission followed. Similar results have been found in patients with seasonal depression (Lam et al., 1996). Another study used this same tryptophan-depletion strategy in nondepressed participants who had either a positive or a negative family history of depression. Again, as predicted by the low-serotonin theory, those with a positive family history experienced an increase in depressed mood (Benkelfat et al., 1994).

We have indicated that effective antidepressants increase levels of norepinephrine and serotonin and that knowledge of this action formed a keystone of the norepinephrine and serotonin theories of depression. It now appears that the explanation of why these drugs work is not as straightforward as it seemed at first. The therapeutic effects of tricyclics and MAO inhibitors do not depend solely on an increase in levels of neurotransmitters. The earlier findings were correct—tricyclics and MAO inhibitors do indeed increase levels of norepinephrine and serotonin when they are first taken—but after several days the neurotransmitters return to their earlier levels. This information is crucial because it does not fit with data on how much time must pass before antidepressants become effective. Both tricyclics and MAO inhibitors take from seven to fourteen days to relieve depression! By that time the neurotransmitter level has already returned to its previous state. It would seem, then, that a simple increase in norepinephrine or serotonin is not a sufficient explanation for why the drugs alleviate depression.

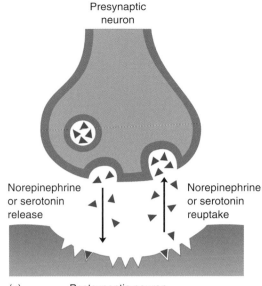

Presynaptic neuron

Norepinephrine or serotonin release

Norepinephrine or serotonin reuptake

(a)   Postsynaptic neuron

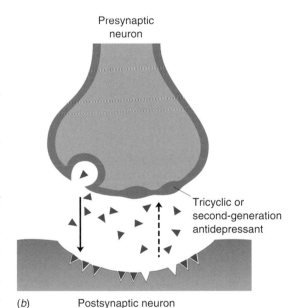

Presynaptic neuron

Tricyclic or second-generation antidepressant

(b)   Postsynaptic neuron

Figure 10.3 (a) When a neuron releases norepinephrine or serotonin from its endings, a pumplike reuptake mechanism immediately begins to recapture some of the neurotransmitter molecules before they are received by the postsynaptic (receptor) neuron. (b) Tricyclic drugs block this reuptake process, enabling more norepinephrine or serotonin to reach, and thus fire, the postsynaptic (receptor) neuron. Serotonin reuptake inhibitors act more selectively on serotonin. Adapted from Snyder (1986) p. 106.

Researchers are now focusing more on the postsynaptic effects of antidepressants and are thus developing theories of depression that implicate postsynaptic mechanisms. For example, one line of research is examining whether antidepressants alter the chemical messengers that a postsynaptic receptor sends into the postsynaptic neuron (Duman, Heninger, & Nestler, 1997; Shelton, Mainer, & Sulser, 1996). These effects in chemical transmission are sometimes termed downstream events, and they are believed to alter the sensitivity of serotonin and norepinephrine postsynaptic receptors (e.g., Shelton, 2000). No definitive answers are as yet available.

Research on bipolar disorder is also moving away from the older norepinephrine theory. One of the major reasons for this shift is that lithium, the most widely used and effective treatment for bipolar disorder, is useful in treating both the manic and the depressive episodes of the disorder, suggesting that it acts by affecting some neurochemical that can either increase or decrease neural activity. One area of current research is focusing on G-proteins (guanine nucleotide-binding proteins), which are found in postsynaptic cell membranes and play an important role in modulating activity in the postsynaptic cell. High levels of G-proteins have been found in patients with mania and low levels in patients with depression (Avisson et al., 1997, 1999), suggesting that the therapeutic effects of lithium may result from its ability to regulate G-proteins (Manji et al., 1995).

Other research in bipolar disorder focuses on disturbances in the ways in which serotonin regulates a particular dopamine pathway involving the ventral tegmental area (VTA) of the brain (e.g., Depue & Zald, 1993; Winters, Scott, & Beavers, 2000). This particular dopamine pathway is implicated in reward motivation and behavior; as is discussed later, patients with bipolar disorder may have trouble regulating reward-related emotions and behaviors.

The Neuroendocrine System

The hypothalamic-pituitary-adrenocortical axis may also play a role in depression (see Figure 8.6, p. 207). The limbic area of the brain is closely linked to emotion and also affects the hypothalamus. The hypothalamus in turn controls various endocrine glands and thus the levels of hormones they secrete. Hormones secreted by the hypothalamus also affect the pituitary gland and the hormones it produces. Because of its relevance to the so-called vegetative symptoms of depression, such as disturbances in appetite and sleep, the hypothalamic-pituitary-adrenocortical axis is thought to be overactive in depression.

Various findings support this proposition. Levels of cortisol (an adrenocortical hormone) are high in depressed patients, perhaps because of oversecretion of thyrotropin-releasing hormone by the hypothalamus (Garbutt et al., 1994). The excess secretion of cortisol in depressed persons also causes enlargement of their adrenal glands (Rubun et al., 1995). Continued excesses of cortisol have been linked to damage to the hippocampus, and studies have found that some patients with depression manifest hippocampal abnormalities (e.g., Duman, Heninger, & Nestler, 1997; Sheline et al., 1996). These high levels of cortisol have even led to the development of a biological test for depression—the dexamethasone suppression test (DST). Dexamethasone suppresses cortisol secretion. When given dexamethasone during an overnight test, some depressed patients, especially those with delusional depression, do not experience cortisol suppression (Nelson & Davis, 1997). The interpretation is that the failure of dexamethasone to suppress cortisol reflects overactivity in the hypothalamic-pituitary-adrenocortical axis of depressed patients. The failure to show suppression normalizes when the depressive episode ends, indicating that it might be a nonspecific response to stress.

Research on a disease called Cushing's syndrome also has linked high levels of cortisol to depression. Abnormal growths on the adrenal cortex lead to oversecretion of cortisol and an ensuing depression. The oversecretion of cortisol in depression may also be associated with the neurotransmitter theories discussed earlier. High levels of cortisol may lower the density of serotonin receptors (Roy et al., 1987) and impair the function of noradrenergic receptors (Price et al., 1986). Finally, the hypothalamic-pituitary-thyroid axis is of possible relevance to bipolar disorder. Disorders of thyroid function are often seen in bipolar patients (Lipowski et al., 1994), and thyroid hormones can induce mania in these patients (Goodwin & Jamison, 1990).

All these data lend some support to theories that mood disorders have biological causes (see Table 10.3 for a summary of the major biological positions). Does this mean that psychological theories are irrelevant or useless? Not in the least. To assert that behavioral disorders have a basis in biological processes is to state the obvious. No psychogenic theorist would deny that behavior is mediated by some kind of bodily changes. The biological and psychological theories may well be describing the same phenomena, but in different terms (such as learned helplessness versus low serotonin). They should be thought of as complementary, not incompatible.

Table 10.3 Summary of Biological Hypotheses about Unipolar Depression and Bipolar Disorder	
Unipolar depression	Genetic diathesis; low serotonin or serotonin-receptor dysfunction; high levels of cortisol
Bipolar disorder	Genetic diathesis; low serotonin or low norepinephrine in depressed phase; high norepinephrine in manic phase; may also be linked to G-proteins; dopamine pathways associated with reward behavior

An Integrated Theory of Bipolar Disorder

Some investigators have hypothesized that bipolar disorder reflects a disturbance in a motivational system called the behavioral activation system or BAS (e.g., Depue, Collins, & Luciano, 1996; Johnson & Roberts, 1995). Behaviorally, the BAS facilitates our ability to approach and obtain rewards in the environment, and it has been linked with positive emotional states, personality characteristics such as extraversion, increased energy, and decreased need for sleep. Biologically, the BAS is believed to be linked to neural pathways in the brain involving the neurotransmitter dopamine, which is often implicated in reward behaviors (e.g., Depue & Collins, 1999). Researchers have demonstrated that responses on a self-report measure of BAS sensitivity are associated with hypomania symptoms among college students and mania symptoms among bipolar patients (Meyer, Johnson, & Carver, 1999; Meyer, Johnson, & Winters, 2001). In addition, a study by Johnson and colleagues found that a particular kind of life event predicted an increase in mania symptoms in bipolar patients over a two-year period (Johnson et al., 2000). Specifically, life events that had to do with attaining goals or rewards, such as gaining acceptance to graduate school or obtaining a new job, predicted an increase in mania symptoms. Other positive life events, however, were unrelated to changes in mania symptoms, and goal attainment events were unrelated to changes in depression symptoms. Thus, the BAS and its behavioral manifestations, including goal attainment, are associated with the manic symptoms of bipolar disorder.

Therapies for Mood Disorders

Most episodes of depression lift after a few months, although the time may seem immeasurably longer to the depressed individual and to those close to him or her. That most depressions are self-limiting is fortunate. However, depression is too widespread and too incapacitating, both to the depressed person and to those around him or her, simply to wait for the disorder to go away untreated. Bouts of depression tend to recur, and as we will see in the last section of this chapter, suicide is a risk for people who are depressed. Thus it is important to treat depression as well as bipolar disorder. Current therapies are both psychological and biological; singly or in combination, they are somewhat effective.

Psychological Therapies for Depression

Psychodynamic Therapies   Because depression is considered to be derived from a repressed sense of loss and from anger unconsciously turned inward, psychoanalytic treatment tries to help the patient achieve insight into the repressed conflict and often encourages outward release of the hostility supposedly directed inward. In the most general terms the goal of psychoanalytic therapy is to uncover latent motivations for the patient's depression. A person may, for example, blame himself or herself for his or her parents' lack of affection but repress this belief because of the anger and pain it causes. The therapist must first guide the patient to confront the fact that he or she feels this way and then help the patient realize that the guilt is unfounded. The recovery of memories of stressful circumstances of the patient's childhood, at which time feelings of inadequacy and loss may have developed, should also bring relief.

Research on the effectiveness of dynamic psychotherapy in alleviating depression is sparse (Craighead, Evans, & Robins, 1992; Klerman, 1988a) and characterized by mixed results, in part owing to the high degree of variability among approaches that come under the rubric of psychodynamic or psychoanalytic psychotherapy. A report from the American Psychiatric Association concludes that there are no controlled data attesting to the efficacy of long-term psychodynamic psychotherapy or psychoanalysis in treating depression (American Psychiatric Association, 1993). However, a recent review of depression treatment outcome studies concludes that the efficacy of *short-term* psychodynamic treatment is comparable to the efficacy of cognitive-behavioral therapy (Leichsenring, 2001).

One of the reasons for this favorable conclusion comes from a well-known large-scale study, the Treatment of Depression Collaborative Research Program (Elkin et al., 1989, described in more detail in the following section on cognitive and behavior therapies). Findings from this study suggest that a form of psychodynamic therapy that concentrates on present-day interactions between the depressed person and the social environment—Klerman and Weissman's interpersonal therapy, or IPT (Klerman et al., 1984)—is particularly effective for alleviating unipolar depression as well as for maintaining treatment gains (Frank et al., 1990; Gillies, 2001). IPT's effectiveness has also been reported for the treatment of postpartum depression (Weissman et al., 2000). In addition, there is evidence that the treatment may be effective in a group format (Stuart et al., 1998).

The core of the therapy is to help the depressed patient examine the ways in which his or her current interpersonal behavior might interfere with obtaining pleasure from relationships. For example, the patient might be taught how to improve communication with others to meet his or her needs better and to have more satisfying social interactions and support. This psychodynamic therapy is not as much intrapsychic as it is interpersonal. It emphasizes better understanding of the interpersonal problems assumed to give rise to depression and aims at improving relationships with others. As such, the focus is on better communication, reality testing, developing effective social skills, and meeting present social-role requirements. The focus is on the patient's current life, not on an exploration of past, often repressed causes of present-day problems. Actual techniques include somewhat nondirective discussion of interpersonal problems, exploration of and encouragement to express unacknowledged negative feelings, improvement of both verbal and nonverbal communications, problem solving, and suggesting new and more satisfying modes of behavior.

Cognitive and Behavior Therapies   In keeping with their cognitive theory of depression, that the profound sadness and shattered self-esteem of depressed individuals are caused by negative schemas and errors in their thinking, Beck and his associates devised a cognitive therapy aimed at altering maladaptive thought patterns. The therapist tries to persuade the depressed person to change his or her opinions of events and of the self. When a client states that he or she is worthless because "Nothing goes right; everything I try to do ends in a disaster," the therapist offers examples contrary to this overgeneralization, such as citing abilities that the client is either overlooking or discounting. The therapist also instructs the patient to monitor private monologues and to identify all patterns of thought that contribute to depression. The therapist then teaches the patient to think through negative prevailing beliefs to understand how they prevent making more realistic and positive assumptions.

Although developed independently of Ellis's rational-emotive method described in Chapter 2, Beck's analyses are similar to it in some ways. For example, Beck suggests that depressed people are likely to consider themselves totally inept and incompetent if they make a mistake. This schema is similar to one of Ellis's irrational beliefs, that the individual must be competent in all things in order to be a worthwhile person.

Beck also includes behavioral components in his treatment of depression. Particularly when patients are severely depressed, Beck encourages them to do things, such as get out of bed in the morning or go for a walk. He gives his patients activity assignments to provide them with successful experiences and allow them to think well of themselves. But the overall emphasis is on cognitive restructuring, on persuading the person to think differently. If a change in overt behavior will help in achieving that goal, fine. Behavioral change by itself, however, cannot be expected to alleviate depression in any significant way, according to Beck.

Over the past nearly three decades, considerable research has been conducted on Beck's therapy, beginning with a widely cited study by Rush et al. (1977), which indicated that cognitive therapy was more successful than the tricyclic imipramine (Tofranil) in alleviating unipolar depression. This finding was questioned, however. The unusually low improvement rate found for the drug in this clinical trial suggests that these patients might have been poorly suited for pharmacotherapy and that therefore this was not a fair comparison. Nonetheless, the efficacy of Beck's therapy in this study and in a twelve-month follow-up (Kovacs et al., 1981) encouraged many other researchers to conduct additional evaluations, which confirmed its efficacy (e.g., Hollon et al., 1989; Simons et al., 1985). In addition, data show that Beck's therapy has a prophylactic effect in preventing subsequent bouts of depression (Evans et al., 1993; Hollon, DeRubeis, & Seligman, 1993). We turn now to an examination of a widely cited study comparing Beck's therapy with interpersonal therapy and with an antidepressant drug.

The NIMH Treatment of Depression Collaborative Research Program   In 1977 the National Institute of Mental Health (NIMH) undertook a large, complex, and expensive three-site study of Beck's cognitive therapy (CT), comparing it with interpersonal psychotherapy (IPT) and pharmacotherapy (Elkin et al., 1985). Called the Treatment of Depression Collaborative Research Program (TDCRP), this was the first multisite coordinated study initiated by the NIMH in the field of psychotherapy (the NIMH had earlier fruitfully conducted such research in pharmacology). Because it is a widely cited and controversial study, and because it illustrates a number of issues in therapy research, we will describe it in some detail.

Three criteria were employed in selecting a psychotherapy to compare with Beck's. The therapy had to have been developed for treating depression, it had to be explicit and standardized enough to allow for instructing other therapists (preferably using a manual), and it had to have empirically shown some efficacy with depressed patients. Further, there should be little overlap with Beck's cognitive therapy. The NIMH team selected Klerman and Weissman's interpersonal psychotherapy, which we described earlier.

A pharmacological therapy, imipramine (Tofranil), a well-tested tricyclic drug widely regarded at the time as a standard therapy for depression, was used as a reference against which to evaluate the two psychotherapies. Dosages were adjusted according to predetermined guidelines that were flexible enough to allow for some clinical judgment of the psychiatrist in the context of clinical management, that is, in a warm, supportive atmosphere (Fawcett et al., 1987). Elkin et al. (1985) regarded this almost as a drug-plus-supportive-therapy condition, supportive referring to the nature of the doctor–patient relationship, not to the application of any explicit psychotherapeutic techniques.

A fourth and final condition was a placebo–clinical management group against which to judge the efficacy of imipramine. It was also conceived of as a partial control for the two psychotherapies because of the presence of strong support and encouragement. In a double-blind design similar to that used in the imipramine condition, patients in this group received a placebo that they believed might be an effective antidepressant medication; they were also given direct advice when considered necessary. As placebo conditions go, this was a very strong one, because it included much more psychological support and even intervention than do most placebo control groups in both the psychotherapy and the pharmacotherapy literatures. Clinical management—support and advice—was common to both this and the imipramine group.

All treatments lasted sixteen weeks, with slight differences in numbers of sessions, depending on the treatment manuals. For example, cognitive-therapy patients received twelve sessions during the first eight weeks, followed by weekly sessions during the second half of the study. These twenty sessions exceeded the sixteen for interpersonal therapy, which, however, could number as many as twenty at the therapist's discretion. Throughout all therapies, patients were closely monitored, and professional safeguards were employed to minimize risk. For example, researchers excluded imminently suicidal patients and maintained close and regular contact during the study. These considerations were particularly important in the placebo condition.

A wide range and large number of assessments were made at pre- and posttreatment of the sixty participants in each of the four conditions, as well as three times during treatment and again at six-, twelve-, and eighteen-month follow-ups. Measures included some that might provide answers to questions about processes of change. For example, do interpersonal-therapy patients learn to relate better to others during therapy, and if so, is this improvement correlated with clinical outcome? Do cognitive-therapy patients manifest less cognitive distortion during the later sessions than at the beginning of treatment, and if so, is this shift associated with better clinical outcome? Other assessment instruments tapped the perspectives of the patient, the therapist, an independent clinical evaluator blind to treatment condition, and, whenever possible, a significant other from the patient's life, for example, a spouse. Three domains of change were assessed: depressive symptomatology, overall symptomatology and life functioning, and functioning related to particular treatment approaches (e.g., the Dysfunctional Attitudes Scale to assess cognitive change).

Analyses of the data suggest variations among research sites, between those who completed treatment and the total sample (including dropouts), and among assessments with different perspectives (e.g., patient versus clinical-evaluator judgments). Some of the complex findings thus far published are summarized here (Elkin et al., 1986, 1989, 1996; Imber et al., 1990; Shea et al., 1990, 1992).

- At termination and without distinguishing patients according to severity of depression, there were no significant differences in reduction of depression or improvement in overall functioning between cognitive therapy (CT) and interpersonal therapy (IPT) or between either of them and imipramine plus clinical management. In general, the three active treatments achieved significant and equivalent degrees of success and were for the most part superior to the placebo group. The placebo-plus-clinical-management patients did show significant improvement, however. (Note: Several other controlled studies have found cognitive therapy superior to other treatments and to placebo conditions, see Persons, Thase, & Crits-Christoph, 1996. There are inconsistencies in the psychotherapy outcome literature!)

- Imipramine was faster than the other treatments in reducing depressive symptoms during treatment. By the end of sixteen weeks of therapy, however, the two psychotherapies had caught up with the drug.

- On some measures the less severely depressed placebo patients were doing as well at termination as the less depressed people in the three active treatment conditions.

- Severely depressed patients in the placebo condition did not fare as well as did those in the three active treatments.

- There was some evidence that IPT was more effective than CT with the more severely depressed patients, most notably in terms of recovery rates.

- There was some evidence that particular treatments effected change in expected domains. For example, IPT patients showed more improvements in social functioning than imipramine or CT patients, and CT reduced certain types of dysfunctional attitudes more than did the other treatments.

- For IPT and pharmacotherapy, but not for CT, patients diagnosed with personality disorders (see Chapter 13) were more likely to have residual depressive symptoms after therapy than those without these Axis II diagnoses.

At the eighteen-month follow-up, the active treatment conditions did not differ significantly, and of those patients across the four conditions who had markedly improved immediately at the end of treatment, only between 20 and 30 percent remained completely without depression. However, interesting treatment differences emerged at the eighteen-month follow-up in patients' ratings of the effects of treatment on their life adjustment. Patients in IPT reported greater satisfaction with treatment, and patients in both IPT and CBT reported significantly greater effects of treatment on their capacity to establish and maintain interpersonal relationships and to recognize and understand sources of their depression than did patients in imipramine or placebo conditions (Blatt et al., 2000).

Particular controversy swirls around the relative effectiveness of the imipramine condition versus the two psychosocial therapies. Recent reanalyses of the TDCRP data confirm the original finding that at least in the short term, imipramine was superior to CT across a wide range of measures (Elkin et al., 1995; Klein & Ross, 1993). Yet Jacobson and Hollon (1996) have pointed out that the TDCRP study is the only one that shows such superiority of pharmacotherapy over CT for even severely depressed patients. They point out also that differences between imipramine and both of the psychotherapy groups were not consistent across the three treatment sites. For example, at one site CT did as well with severely depressed patients as did imipramine, and at another site IPT did as well with these patients as did the drug. Finally, Jacobson and Hollon also noted that 33 percent of the imipramine patients dropped out before completing treatment; of those remaining, half had not recovered when treatment ended, and of those who did recover, half had relapsed within months after medication was withdrawn, far more than people in the CT condition.

Complex situation! To make matters even more complex, Donald Klein (1996), a renowned drug researcher, as well as some of the TDCRP investigators themselves (Elkin et al., 1996), read the very same data and came to the opposite conclusion, namely, that imipramine in this study was significantly more effective for severe depression than was either cognitive or interpersonal therapy. Furthermore, Klein has questioned the adequacy of the imipramine condition itself because of the number of dropouts and notes that imipramine treatment for depression is not synonymous with pharmacotherapy for depression. The newer selective serotonin reuptake inhibitors, such as Prozac (p. 298), have fewer side effects and may well be more effective than tricyclics such as imipramine. To make matters even more complicated, more recent research indicates that both CT and IPT are at least as effective as drugs even with severely depressed individuals (p. 289).

Much remains to be learned about effecting even short-term improvement in depressed patients. Even less is known about how to maintain over the long haul any benefits that are evident right after treatment ends. Certainly there is little in the many findings from this milestone study of comparative outcome that can gladden the hearts of proponents of any of the interventions.

Mindfulness-Based Cognitive Therapy   A recent adaptation of cognitive therapy called mindfulness-based cognitive therapy (MBCT) focuses on relapse prevention following successful treatment for depression (Segal et al., 1996; Segal et al., 2001; Teasdale et al., 1995). This therapy is based on the assumption that vulnerability to relapse and recurrence of depression arise from repeated associations between depressed mood and patterns of negative, self-devaluative, hopeless thinking during episodes of major depression. As a result, if individuals who have recovered from major depression become sad or discouraged, they begin to think in ways similar to how they thought when they were really depressed. These reactivated patterns of thinking in turn maintain and intensify a mildly depressed state (Teasdale, 1988, 1997). In this way, in people with a history of major depression, states of mild depression are more likely to escalate, which effectively increases the risk of further onsets of episodes of major depression.

The goal of MBCT is to teach individuals to recognize when they become depressed and to try to adopt what can be called a "decentered" perspective, viewing their thoughts merely as "mental events" rather than as core aspects of the self or as accurate reflections of reality. Examples include such self-statements as "Thoughts are not facts" and "I am not my thoughts" (Teasdale et al., 2000, p. 616). In other words, they are taught to develop a detached, decentered relationship to their depression-related thoughts and feelings. This perspective, it is believed, can prevent the escalation of negative thinking patterns that may actually cause depression (Teasdale, 1997; Teasdale et al., 1995).

Because of its newness, data on the effectiveness of MBCT are scarce. A recent multisite study (Teasdale et al., 2000) compared relapse rates of formerly depressed patients randomly assigned to MBCT or to "treatment as usual" (e.g., patients were instructed to seek help from their family doctor or other sources, as they normally would). Results of this study showed that MBCT was more effective than the control condition in reducing the risk of depression relapse/recurrence for patients with three or more previous episodes of depression.

Social-Skills Training   Since a key feature of depression is a lack of satisfying experiences with other people, behavioral treatments have focused on helping patients improve social interactions. This treatment approach developed independently of research on interpersonal aspects of depression (discussed on p. 281) but is quite consistent with it. A recent review concluded that treatments based on social-skills training are effective in alleviating depression (Segrin, 2000).

Although there are cognitive components in these approaches—for example, encouraging the depressed patient not to evaluate his or her performance too harshly—evidence supports the effectiveness of a focus on enhancing overt social behaviors by such techniques as assertion and social-skills training (Hersen et al., 1984; Lewinsohn & Gotlib, 1995). Also, as we describe in the discussion of couples therapy (see Focus on Discovery 10.2), improvement in the kinds of interpersonal conflicts found in a distressed marriage or other intimate relationship alleviates depression (Beach et al., 1994; Jacobson, Holzworth-Munroe, & Schmaling, 1989).

Behavioral Activation Therapy   The relatively novel behavioral activation (BA) therapy (Jacobson & Gortner, 2000; Jacobson et al., 2001; Martell, Addis, & Jacobson, 2001) is related to social-skills training in its distinctly behavioral approach to treating depression. It evolved from the empirical findings of a component analysis study (Gortner et al., 1998; Jacobson et al., 1996), which investigated the effective ingredients or mechanisms underlying Beck's traditional cognitive-behavioral therapy described earlier. Results from this study suggested that the behavioral activation component of Beck's therapy performed as well as the full package in the treatment of depression and the prevention of relapse over a two-year follow-up period. These results challenged the notion that clients must directly confront and modify negative core schemas and other negative thinking in order to alleviate depression and suggested instead that activating clients, having them engage in rewarding activities, may be not only necessary but also sufficient.

Indeed, inactivity, withdrawal, and inertia are commonly observed behaviors among depressed individuals. They are most frequently seen as symptoms of depression and are therefore considered to be part of what defines the disorder. From a behavioral activation perspective, however, the function of these behaviors in the context of an individual's life is crucial. Proponents of BA contend that much of the behavior of depressed people serves an avoidance function as the individuals try to cope with environments characterized by low levels of positive reinforcement or high levels of aversiveness. Consequently, behavioral activation seeks to engage the patient in behaviors and activities that will be positively reinforcing and will help disrupt the spiral of depression.

Couples and Family therapy

Couples, married and unmarried, straight and gay, often have conflicts that bring them to therapists. As mentioned in the text, depression is often part of the clinical picture in one or both partners. Sometimes other problems are present. We turn now to a discussion of couples and family therapy. Research on effectiveness is reviewed in Chapter 17 (p. 592).

The Normality of Conflict

There is almost universal agreement among couples therapists and researchers, regardless of theoretical orientation, that conflict is inevitable in a marriage or in any other long-term relationship. The aura of the honeymoon passes when the couple makes unromantic decisions about where to live, where to seek employment, how to budget money, what kinds of meals to prepare and the sharing of that responsibility, when to visit in-laws, if and when to have children, and whether to experiment with novel sexual techniques. Today, in addition, couples have the changed nature of gender roles to negotiate. For example, if both spouses work, will their place of residence be determined by the husband's employment or by the wife's? These sources of conflict must be handled by any two people living together, whether they are married or not, whether they are of the opposite sex or not. Authorities agree that it is how couples deal with such inherent conflicts that determines the quality and duration of their cohabitation relationship (e.g., Schwartz & Schwartz, 1980).

A strategy some couples adopt, deliberately or unconsciously, is to avoid acknowledging disagreements and conflicts. Because they believe in the reality of the fairy-tale ending, "And they lived happily ever after," any sign that their relationship is not going smoothly is threatening and must be ignored. Such patterns may keep peace in the short term but usually at the expense of serious dysfunction in the long term (Gottman & Krokoff, 1989). Dissatisfaction and resentment develop and begin to take their toll as time goes by. Because the partners do not quarrel, they may appear to be a perfect couple to observers, but without opening the lines of communication they may drift apart emotionally. Conversely, whereas disagreement and even the expression of anger are related to unhappiness in couples in the short term, they actually are predictive of more satisfaction over time (Gottman & Krokoff, 1989).

From Individual to Conjoint Therapy

The terms *family therapy* and *couples therapy* do not denote a set procedure. They tell us that therapeutic focus is on at least two people in a relationship, but they leave undefined such issues as how the therapist views the nature and causes of the problem, what techniques are chosen to alleviate it, how often clients are seen, and whether their children and even grandparents are included.

Couples and family therapy share some theoretical frameworks with individual therapy. Psychoanalytic marital therapists, for example, focus on how a person seeks or avoids a partner who resembles, to his or her unconscious, the opposite-sexed parent (Segraves, 1990). Frustrated and unsatisfied by his love-seeking attempts as a child, the adult man may unconsciously seek maternal nurturance from his wife and make excessive, even infantile, demands of her. Much of the discussion in this kind of couples therapy centers on the conflicts he is having with his wife and, presumably, the repressed striving for maternal love that underlies his immature ways of relating to her. These unconscious forces are plumbed, with the wife assisting and possibly revealing some of her own unresolved yearnings for her father. Transference is explored, but in analytic couples therapy it is the transference between the two partners rather than between the client and the therapist that is usually the focus. The overall goal is to help each partner see the other as he or she actually is rather than as a symbolic parent (Fitzgerald, 1973). Sometimes, each partner is seen separately by different therapists (Martin & Bird, 1953), sometimes separately by the same therapist (Greene, 1960), or conjointly by the same therapist (Ackerman, 1966).

Ellis's rational-emotive behavior therapy has been applied to family conflict. Again, the perspective is primarily individualistic or intrapsychic. The therapist assumes that something going on within one or both of the partners is causing the distress in the relationship. The wife, for example, may harbor the irrational belief that her husband must constantly adore her, that his devotion must never falter. She is likely then to overreact when at a social gathering he enjoys himself away from her side, talking to other men and women.

With this as background to the shift from individual to conjoint therapies, we describe now some of the details of conjoint therapy. Some methods are common to all couples and family therapies, whereas others differ according to theoretical orientation.

Approaches to Couples and Family Therapy

The Mental Research Institute Tradition   As an overall approach, couples and family therapy is generally said to have begun in the 1950s at the Mental Research Institute (MRI) in Palo Alto, California. The MRI people targeted for intervention faulty communication patterns, conflict-ridden relationships, and inflexibility. Members of the family were shown how their behavior affected their relations with others. They were then persuaded to make specific changes, such as making their needs and dislikes more clearly known to others. Few family therapists who identify themselves with the MRI approach are concerned with past history. Their focus is on how current problems are being maintained and how they might be changed. Whatever the clinical problem, the family therapist takes a family systems approach, a general view of etiology and treatment that focuses on the complex interrelationships within families. The legacy of the MRI group is less a body of techniques than a general way of thinking about the complexities and constant interactive patterns in couples and family conflict.

Cognitive-Behavioral Approaches   Distressed couples do not react very positively toward each other, and this antagonism is usually evident in the very first session. It is not uncommon for one partner to feel coerced into attending conjoint therapy, even for an initial session. In a pioneering treatise on behavioral marital therapy, Jacobson and Margolin (1979) recommended attending to this problem of antagonism as a first step in helping partners improve their marriage. One strategy is the "caring days" idea of Richard Stuart (1976), which applies an operant strategy to couples conflict. The husband, for example, is cajoled into agreeing to devote himself to doing nice things for his wife all day on a given day, without expecting anything in return. The agreement is that the wife will do the same for him the next day. If successful, this strategy accomplishes at least two important things: first, it breaks the cycle of distance, suspicion, and aversive control of each other, and second, it shows the giving partner that he or she is able to affect the spouse in a positive way. This enhanced sense of positive control is achieved simply by pleasing the partner.

The giving can later be more reciprocal; each partner may agree to please the other in certain specific ways, in anticipation of the partner's reciprocating. For example, one partner may agree to prepare dinner on Tuesdays, and on that day the other contracts to stop at the supermarket on the way home from work and do the weekly shopping. The improved atmosphere that develops as a consequence of each partner's doing nice things for the other and having nice things done for him or her in return helps each become motivated to please the other person on future occasions.

Behavioral couples therapists generally adopt Thibaut and Kelley's (1959) exchange theory of interaction. According to this view of human relationships, people value others if they receive a high ratio of benefits to costs, that is, if they see themselves getting at least as much from the other person as they give. Furthermore, people are assumed to be more disposed to continue a given relationship if other alternatives are less attractive to them, promising fewer benefits and costing more. Therapists therefore try to encourage a mutual dispensing of rewards by partner A and partner B.

Behavioral marital or couples therapy has in common with other approaches, such as the MRI approach, a focus on enhancing communication skills between the partners. But the emphasis is more on increasing the ability of each partner to please the other; the core assumption is that "the relative rates of pleasant and unpleasant interactions determine the subjective quality of the relationship" (Wood & Jacobson, 1985). Indeed, behavioral couples therapists consider this more than an assumption, for they can point to data supporting the view that distressed couples differ from nondistressed couples in that they report lower frequencies of positive exchanges and higher frequencies of unsatisfying exchanges. Also, as Camper et al. (1988) found, spouses in distressed marriages view negative behavior on the part of their partners as global and stable—"There is nothing I can do to please him, and it's never going to change"—whereas they construe positive behavior as less so—"Well, he was happy with me today, but it's not going to last." Distressed couples also tend to get upset by immediate and recent negative events, like the weather's being bad when an outdoor project was scheduled, whereas nondistressed couples are better able to overlook such minor annoyances (Margolin, 1981; Wood & Jacobson, 1985).

Thus behavioral couples therapy concentrates on increasing positive exchanges in the hope not only of enhancing short-term satisfaction, but also of laying a foundation for long-term trust and positive feelings, qualities that are characteristic of nondistressed relationships. Cognitive change is also seen as important, for couples often need training in problem solving and encouragement to acknowledge when positive changes are occurring. Distressed couples often perceive inaccurately the ratio of positive to negative exchanges, tending to overlook the former and fixate on the latter (Gottman et al., 1976).

Behavioral couples therapists have become increasingly interested in cognitive components of relationships and relationship distress, a reflection of the cognitive trend in behavior therapy as a whole (Baucom, Epstein, & Rankin, 1995; Wheeler, Christenson, & Jacobson, 2001). The interest in cognition in couples therapy can also be traced to the influence of attribution theory in social psychology (the study of how people explain the reasons for their own and others' behavior) and the overlap between marital distress and depression (see p. 281). As a result of adding this cognitive component and broadening its treatment strategies, many people now refer to behavioral marital therapy as cognitive-behavioral marital therapy (CBMT). One focus in CBMT is on each person's attributions, for example, whether one partner decides that the other is responsible or blameworthy for an event that was actually not under anyone's control.

Integrative Behavioral Couples Therapy Integrative behavioral couples therapy (IBCT) was developed by Andrew Christensen and Neil S. Jacobson (Christensen, Jacobson, & Babcock, 1995). IBCT uses reinforcement principles as well as behavioral exchange and communication training strategies as just described, but it incorporates the Rogerian notion of acceptance and provides a series of procedures designed to foster acceptance in couples (Cordova & Jacobson, 1993). (Focus on Discovery 17.4, p. 306, contains more details on acceptance.)

The assumption of IBCT is that traditional behavior therapy for couples focuses on superficial variables rather than on trying to uncover the major controlling variables. For example, traditional behavior therapists might focus on discrete observable behavior, such as lack of sex or frequent arguments, rather than on a partner's feeling that he or she is not loved or valued by the other partner. This latter consideration would be the focus in IBCT. This shift in therapeutic attention is not new to psychoanalytically oriented couples therapists nor to the humanistically oriented approach described next.

Emotionally Focused Therapy The approach to conjoint treatment known as emotionally focused therapy (EFT) (Alexander, Holtzworth-Munroe, & Jameson, 1994; Johnson & Greenberg, 1987, 1988, 1995) contains psychodynamic elements, but its humanistic emphasis on feelings strikes us as more salient. This therapy integrates components from attachment theory, which has been used to conceptualize adult romantic relationships (see also Bartholomew & Horowitz, 1991) and which focuses on the "innate adaptive needs for protection, security, and connectedness with significant others" (Johnson & Greenberg, 1995, p. 124). From this vantage point, relationship distress occurs when the attachment needs have not been met and the relationship does not provide a secure base for one or both partners. The overall goal of treatment is for couples to maintain emotional engagement and be accessible and responsive to each other's needs.

General Features of All Couples Therapy

In all forms of couples therapy each partner is trained to listen empathically to the other and to state clearly to the partner what he or she understands is being said and what feelings underlie those remarks. One way to improve communication is to distinguish between the intent of a remark and its impact. Partner A, for example, may wish to be helpful by asking whether partner B would like him or her to get something from the store, but this question may have a negative impact if partner B would prefer partner A to stay home and help with a project. Partner A's intent, then, would be positive, but the question would affect partner B negatively.

Research has shown that the communications of distressed and happy couples may not differ so much in intent as in impact. In one study Gottman and his colleagues (1976) found that both types of couples made the same number of positive statements to partners, but distressed spouses reported having *heard* fewer positive statements. Gottman proposed a technique for clarifying intent when two partners are in a heated argument. One partner calls, "Stop action," and asks the other to indicate what he or she believes the first is trying to say. The feedback indicates immediately whether remarks are having the intended impact.

An interaction pattern known as the demand-withdraw cycle is widely regarded as particularly destructive for couples. First described by MRI people (Watzlawick, Beavin, & Jackson, 1967) and a contemporary research focus of others (Christensen & Pasch, 1993; Christensen & Shenk, 1991), the demand-withdraw pattern is characterized by one partner's attempting to discuss a problem and the other's avoiding or withdrawing from such efforts. This withdrawal generates more demands from the first spouse, who tries harder and harder to engage the other, only to be met with more avoidance. And so the cycle escalates. Christensen and Heavey (1990) suggest that there are sex differences in this pattern; women tend to assume the demanding role whereas men usually withdraw. This pattern is found in couples that have a conflict surrounding closeness; the person demanding change may be trying to generate closeness, and the person avoiding the interaction may be struggling to seek or maintain autonomy (Christensen, 1987). The roles may also vary depending on who is seeking change and who prefers the relationship to remain as it is (Christensen & Pasch, 1993). Knowing who typically plays which role in a couple may benefit the couples therapist when planning intervention strategies to break this destructive cycle.

Couples and family therapy have for years made creative use of videotape equipment. A couple can be given a problem to solve during part of a therapy session, such as where to go on vacation, and can be videotaped while they attempt to solve it. The ways in which they push forward their own wishes—or fail to—and the ways in which they accommodate the other's wishes—or fail to—are but one aspect of their communication patterns that a therapist can come to understand from later viewing the tape, often with the couple watching also. Patterns of communication and miscommunication can be readily discerned using this tool. The partners can agree to try out new ways of negotiating and new ways of dealing with conflictual issues (Margolin & Fernandez, 1985).

A common practice among family therapists is to give couples specific homework assignments to practice new patterns of interaction that they have learned during sessions and begin the important process of generalizing change from the consulting room to their everyday lives. Couples may be asked to practice paraphrasing each other's sentences for a specified time period, such as a half hour after dinner, as part of an active listening assignment. In essence, couples are taught Rogerian empathy skills. They may also be instructed to practice a new parenting skill with their children. Some therapists ask couples to tape-record their assignment so that the therapist can review their progress during the next therapy session.

General Issues and Special Considerations

The severity and nature of marital dysfunction treated by therapists is not all the same, as Margolin and Fernandez (1985) have pointed out.

One couple may seek professional assistance when there is merely dissatisfaction in the relationship, but another may wait until the crisis is so great that one or both partners have already consulted a divorce lawyer. Thus there are different stages of marital distress (Duck, 1984; Weiss & Cerreto, 1980), and different therapeutic approaches may be used, depending on the point at which the therapist judges the couple is. For example, a couple married for five years and on the verge of divorce, with some threat of physical violence, needs a more directive and more intensive approach than a couple who after ten years of reasonable contentment find themselves drifting apart.

An important issue is deciding who the patient is. The term *identified patient* is often used when more than one family member is being seen by a therapist, especially when parents consult a therapist because of problems their child is having. Also, treatment proceeds best when family members agree on what problem is to be addressed. Difficulties also arise when one partner wants to end the relationship and the other wants to save it. Finally, couples therapy varies depending on whether children are involved.

Family therapy is further complicated when sexual or nonsexual physical abuse is present. The therapist must consider what effect saving the relationship may have on the abused spouse and possibly on the abused children, for when there is spousal abuse there is a high likelihood of child abuse also. Regardless of who is the identified patient, the therapist must be sensitive to the needs of all those whose lives are affected by the relationship (Kadis & McClendon, 1995).

Other ethical considerations in family therapy include how to deal with the disclosure of secrets by one spouse when the other spouse is not present. Some therapists handle this at the outset of treatment by telling the couple that nothing that is told to the therapist by one of the partners will be kept secret from the other. Other therapists feel that this policy may keep them from obtaining valuable information (Kadis & McClendon, 1995).

An interesting line of research has focused on individual problems in one of the partners and how such problems respond to conjoint therapy versus an intervention targeted to the individual problem. Noting that depression in at least one of the partners is often a part of a distressed couple's relationship and that relapse into depression is more likely if the formerly depressed partner is in a troubled marriage (Hooley & Teasdale, 1989), researchers at Stony Brook (Beach & O'Leary, 1986; O'Leary & Beach, 1990) and at the University of Washington (Jacobson et al., 1989, 1991) have studied behavioral marital therapy (BMT) as a treatment for depression. The findings indicate that Beck's individualized cognitive therapy for the depressed partner is no more effective than BMT in alleviating depression and that cognitive therapy is not as effective as BMT in enhancing marital satisfaction. In other words, someone who is depressed and is also in a troubled relationship can be helped as much by a systems-oriented approach to the relationship as by an individualized intervention—with the advantage of also deriving benefit for relationship problems. This research highlights both the interpersonal nature of depression— a theme examined earlier in this chapter (p. 281)—and the role of depression in a distressed intimate relationship. Moreover, the finding that individualized cognitive therapy does not improve a marriage in the same way that improvement in a marriage lifts depression points up both the limits of a nonsystems individualized therapy, such as cognitive therapy, as well as the strengths of a systems approach, such as BMT.

Psychological Therapies for Bipolar Disorder

Psychological therapies also show promise in dealing with many of the interpersonal, cognitive, and emotional problems of bipolar patients. For example, preliminary evidence suggests that cognitive-behavioral intervention targeted at the thoughts and interpersonal behaviors that go awry during wide mood swings appears to be effective, though additional controlled trials are still needed (Basco & Rush, 1996; Scott, 2001; Patelis-Siotis et al., 2001; Fava et al., 2001).

A small but significant number of empirical studies attest to the positive role that careful education about bipolar disorder and its treatment can have on improving adherence to medication such as lithium, which is helpful in reducing the mood swings of this disorder and thereby bringing more stability into the patient's life (Craighead et al., 1998; Peet & Harvey, 1991; Van Gent, 2000). Obviously, an effective drug is beneficial only to the extent that it is taken as prescribed. One of the problems in getting bipolar patients to take their medication regularly is that they often lack insight into the inappropriate and self-destructive nature of their behavior.[3] In addition to improving adherence to a drug regimen, though, education about the illness is likely to increase social support from family and friends and to lead overall to a less emotionally charged atmosphere for the patient, and this can reasonably be expected to lessen stress on the patient (Craighead et al., 1998; Bland & Harrison, 2000).

As with patients with schizophrenia, when bipolar patients return from hospital to family settings characterized by high levels of hostility and overinvolvement (called "expressed emotion," see p. 348), they relapse more quickly than when the emotional climate in the home is less charged (Miklowitz et al., 1996). This points up the need for interventions aimed at the family and not merely at the patient. Research indicates that educating the family about the nature of the disorder, the desirability of working to reduce stress at home, and the need to continue medication to help maintain improvement in the discharged bipolar patient are somewhat effective (Glick et al., 1991; Wang et al., 2000).

A therapy approach called family-focused treatment (FFT) is a time-limited outpatient psychosocial treatment for bipolar disorder and their families. It consists of educating the family about the illness, working to enhance communication in the family, and training in problem-solving skills (Miklowitz, 2001; Miklowitz & Goldstein, 1997). Recent studies suggest that the addition of this kind of family-oriented treatment to pharmacotherapy leads to more positive outcomes of bipolar disorder than medication alone (e.g., Rea et al., 2000; Miklowitz et al., 2000).

A problem-solving therapy, called interpersonal and social rhythm therapy, which helps the patient deal better with life events that trigger stress and manic episodes, has also received some empirical support (Craighead & Miklowitz, 2000; Frank et al., 2000b). The approach is based on a chronobiological model of bipolar disorder. According to this view, individuals suffering from the disorder have a genetic predisposition to circadian rhythm and sleep-wake cycle abnormalities. These disturbances may be responsible, in part, for the manifestations of the illness. Both negative and positive life events may disrupt patients' social rhythms. This disruption, in turn, disturbs circadian rhythms and sleep-wake cycles and leads to the development of bipolar symptoms.

Interpersonal and social rhythm therapy is administered together with medications and combines the basic principles of interpersonal psychotherapy with behavioral techniques. Its goal is to help patients regularize their daily routines, diminish interpersonal problems, and adhere to medication regimens. The patient is taught to appreciate how manic episodes interfere with relationships with others and how to deal with everyday challenges without allowing moods to sink into depressive despair or to escalate to levels that create embarrassment and even self-destructive behavior. Reality-based thinking and behavior are taught and encouraged, including acceptance of the reality that the

---

[3] As will be seen in the next chapter, this is also a common problem in patients with schizophrenia.

patient has a chronic disorder that is probably lifelong and that requires proper medication and attention to altering behavior and thought (Frank et al., 1994).[4]

Final Comment on Psychological Therapies

Determining the best therapy for each individual can be a challenge. For instance, a woman who is disheartened because of the way she is treated by men might be better advised by a feminist therapist, who will encourage her to resist continued subjugation by an overbearing spouse or boss, than by an equally well-intentioned cognitive therapist, who might try to teach her that the treatment she receives from her husband or supervisor is not all that bad. A central question in this context is whether the therapist should help the client alter his or her life situation or find a way to adapt to it. Indeed, the very fact that a person is depressed may indicate that he or she is ready for a change in social and personal relations with others. (See p. 641 for further discussion of ethical issues in the selection of therapy goals.)

Biological Therapies of Mood Disorders

A variety of biological therapies are used to treat depression and mania. The two most common are electroconvulsive shock and drugs.

Electroconvulsive Therapy   Perhaps the most dramatic, and controversial, treatment for severe depression is **electroconvulsive therapy (ECT)**. ECT was originated by two Italian physicians, Cerletti and Bini, in the early twentieth century. Cerletti was interested in epilepsy and was seeking a means by which its seizures could be experimentally induced. The solution became apparent to him during a visit to a slaughterhouse, where he saw seizures and unconsciousness induced in animals by electric shocks administered to the head. Shortly thereafter he found that by applying electric shocks to the sides of the human head, he could produce full epileptic seizures. Then, in Rome in 1938, he used the technique on a patient with schizophrenia.

In the decades that followed, ECT was administered to patients with both schizophrenia and severe depression, usually in hospital settings. For the most part its use today is restricted to profoundly depressed individuals. ECT entails the deliberate induction of a seizure and momentary unconsciousness by passing a current between 70 and 130 volts through the patient's brain. Electrodes were formerly placed on each side of the forehead, allowing the current to pass through both hemispheres, a method known as **bilateral ECT**. Today, **unilateral ECT**, in which the current passes through the nondominant (right) cerebral hemisphere only, is more commonly used. In the past the patient was usually awake until the current triggered the seizure, and the electric shock often created frightening contortions of the body, sometimes even causing bone fractures. Now the patient is given a short-acting anesthetic and an injection of a strong muscle relaxant before the current is applied. The convulsive spasms of the body muscles are barely perceptible to onlookers, and the patient awakens a few minutes later remembering nothing about the treatment. The mechanism through which ECT works is unknown. It generally reduces metabolic activity and blood circulation to the brain and may thus inhibit some aberrant brain activity.

Inducing a seizure is still a drastic procedure. Why should anyone in his or her right but depressed mind agree to undergo such radical therapy? How could a parent or a spouse con-

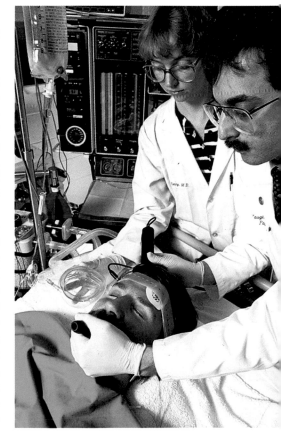

Electroconvulsive therapy (ECT) is an effective treatment for severe depression. Using unilateral shock, anesthetics, and muscle relaxants has reduced its undesirable side effects.

---

[4] Education and acceptance are increasingly included as part of psychological therapies these days. We see this trend here with bipolar disorder, in the next chapter with schizophrenia, and we will see it in Chapter 13 with borderline personality disorder. As more and more is learned—or hypothesized—about biological components of human psychological makeup, emphasis grows on helping patients and their families learn about and accept what cannot be changed or controlled without constant vigilance and treatment. In medicine, this is the situation with diabetes. Given the limits of today's knowledge, people who have the disease will have it for the rest of their lives. Careful monitoring of food intake as well as medications, such as insulin injections, are necessary to sustain life. That's the hand the person was dealt, and this is what we can do about it short of a cure.

sent to such treatment for a patient judged legally incapable of giving consent? The answer is simple. Although we don't know why, ECT may be the optimal treatment for severe depression (Klerman, 1988a). Most professionals acknowledge the risks involved—confusion and memory loss that can be prolonged. However, **unilateral ECT** to the right hemisphere is as clinically effective as bilateral ECT and produces fewer cognitive side effects (Sackeim et al., 2000). A long-term follow-up study of patients treated with ECT during adolescence showed an absence of lasting memory impairment (Cohen et al., 2000). In addition, some evidence suggests that the cognitive side effects of ECT can be minimized when thyroid hormone is used as part of the treatment (Tremont & Stern, 2000). In any case, clinicians typically resort to ECT only when the depression is unremitting and after less drastic treatments have been tried and found wanting. In considering any treatment that has negative side effects, the person making the decision must be aware of the consequences of not providing any treatment at all. Given that suicide is a real possibility among depressed people and given a moral stance that values the preservation of life, the use of ECT, at least after other treatments have failed, is regarded by many as defensible and responsible.

Drug Therapy   Drugs are the most commonly used treatments—biological or otherwise—for mood disorders. They do not work for all people, however, and side effects are sometimes serious (see Table 10.4).

Drug Therapies for Depression   In our earlier discussion of biological research on depression we mentioned three major categories of antidepressant drugs:

1. Tricyclics, such as imipramine (Tofranil) and amitriptyline (Elavil)
2. Selective serotonin reuptake inhibitors (SSRIs), such as fluoxetine (Prozac) and sertraline (Zoloft)
3. Monoamine oxidase (MAO) inhibitors, such as tranylcypromine (Parnate)

These medications have been established as effective in a number of double-blind studies, with improvement rates of 50 to 70 percent among patients who complete a course of treatment (Depression Guideline Panel, 1993; Nemeroff & Schatzberg, 1998). Although early indications were that the SSRIs were clinically more effective than either tricyclics or MAO inhibitors, it now appears that the clinical effectiveness of all three classes of drugs is about the same. The SSRIs do, however, have the advantage of producing fewer side effects (Enserink, 1999), and nowadays it is these drugs that are most often prescribed. The MAO inhibitors have by far the most serious side effects and thus are the least used.

Although antidepressant drugs were established as effective in carefully controlled research, a question has been raised about their use in general practice. Primary care physicians account for about half of all antidepressant prescriptions, and critics have suggested that in these cases patients may receive too short a course of treatment and doses that are too small. To address this issue, Simon and his colleagues (2001) studied antidepressant treatment by both physicians and psychiatrists at an HMO. Unfortunately,

Table 10.4 Drugs for Treating Mood Disorders

Category	Generic Name	Trade Name	Side Effects
Tricyclic antidepressants	Imipramine Amitriptyline	Tofranil Elavil	Heart attack, stroke, hypotension, blurred vision, anxiety, tiredness, dry mouth, constipation, gastric disorders, erectile failure, weight gain
MAO inhibitors	Tranylcypromine	Parnate	Possibly fatal hypertension, dry mouth, dizziness, nausea, headaches
Selective serotonin reuptake inhibitors	Fluoxetine	Prozac	Nervousness, fatigue, gastrointestinal complaints, dizziness, headaches, insomnia
Lithium	Lithium	Lithium	Tremors, gastric distress, lack of coordination, dizziness, cardiac arrhythmia, blurred vision, fatigue, death

only about half of the patients received an adequate regimen of drug therapy, regardless of which type of practitioner treated them.

Although the various antidepressants hasten a patient's recovery from an episode of depression, relapse is still common after the drugs are withdrawn (Reimherr et al., 2001). Continuing to take imipramine after remission is of value in preventing recurrence—provided that maintenance doses are as high as the effective treatment doses (instead of lower, as is usually the case) and that the patient was involved during the drug therapy in a psychological treatment (Frank et al., 1990).

Indeed, antidepressant medication can be and often is used in combination with some kind of psychotherapy. If, for example, a person's depression is, at least in part, caused by lack of personal satisfaction because of problems or deficits in social skills, it is probably essential for the drug treatment to be supplemented by attention to those behavioral deficits (Klerman, 1988a, 1990).

Although the research literature provides few answers on the merits of combined treatment (Persons et al., 1996), a recent study by Frank et al. (2000a) evaluated the combination of interpersonal therapy (IPT) and antidepressant medication by comparing two groups of women with recurrent depression. The first group received a combination of IPT and pharmacotherapy from the outset of treatment. The comparison group received IPT alone first, and only those who did not respond to IPT alone were offered the combination treatment. The researchers found that the remission rate in the "sequential group" was 79 percent, significantly greater than the 66 percent observed in the group that received combination treatment from the outset.

Even if a chemical agent manages to alleviate a bout of depression only temporarily, that benefit in itself should not be underestimated, given the potential for suicide in depression and given the extreme anguish and suffering borne by the individual and usually by his or her family as well. The judicious use of a drug may make unnecessary an avenue of intervention and control that many regard as very much a last resort, namely, being placed in a mental hospital.

Indeed, some studies suggest that antidepressants should always be used for severely depressed patients. Others, however, suggest that cognitive or interpersonal therapy is just as effective (DeRubeis et al., 1999; Jarrett et al., 1999), with the added benefit that there are no drug-produced side effects and there is no relapse when medication is withdrawn (Hollon et al., 1992; Persons et al., 1996).

Drug Therapy for Bipolar Disorder People with the mood swings of bipolar disorder are often helped by carefully monitored dosages of the element lithium, taken in a salt form, **lithium carbonate**. Up to 80 percent of bipolar patients experience at least some benefit from taking this drug (Prien & Potter, 1993). Lithium is effective for bipolar patients when they are depressed as well as when they are manic, and it is much more effective for bipolar patients than for unipolar patients—another bit of evidence that these two mood disorders are basically different from each other.

Because the effects of lithium occur gradually, therapy typically begins with both lithium and an antipsychotic, such as Haldol, which has an immediate calming effect. Several hypotheses concerning how lithium works are being pursued (recall our earlier discussion of the effects of lithium on G-proteins, p. 286). However, conclusive evidence is not yet available.

Because of possibly serious, even fatal, side effects, lithium has to be prescribed and used very carefully. Patients taking lithium must have regular blood tests to ensure that the serum levels of lithium are not too high. When levels get too high, lithium toxicity can result. Signs of lithium toxicity range from mild, including things like tremor, nausea, blurred vision, vertigo, and confusion, to quite severe, including cardiac dysrhythmias, seizures, coma, and even death. Although it has great value in the elimination of a manic episode and forestalling future episodes if it is taken regularly, discontinuation of lithium actually increases a person's risk for recurrence (Suppes et al., 1991). Thus it is recommended that lithium be used continually (Bowden et al., 2000). But many patients discontinue treatment after release from the hospital (Maj et al., 1998).

Two drugs originally used to control seizures offer promise in helping patients with bipolar disorder. Carbamazapine (Tegretol) and divalproex sodium (Depakote) are both effective treatments and are tolerated by some patients who are unable to withstand lithium's side effects (Small et al., 1991). However, neither has been established as preventing future episodes, and a recent study found that Depakote was no more effective than placebo in this regard (Bowden et al., 2000).

Treatment combining antidepressants and mood stabilizers, such as lithium, has been found to be effective for some bipolar patients, but current knowledge does not allow confident selection of the bipolar patients who might benefit from this combination (Sachs & Thase, 2000). In addition, there is evidence that treatment with antidepressants may actually worsen the course of bipolar disorder for some patients (Ghaemi et al., 2000).

Although lithium is the treatment of choice for bipolar disorder (Keck & McElroy, 1998), the psychological aspects of the disorder also need to be considered, if only, as discussed earlier, to encourage the person to continue taking the medication (Goodwin & Jamison, 1990). A friend of one of the authors put it this way (paraphrased): "Lithium cuts out the highs as well as the lows. I don't miss the lows, but I gotta admit that there were some aspects of the highs that I do miss. It took me a while to accept that I had to give up those highs. Wanting to keep my job and my marriage helped!" A drug alone does not address this kind of concern.

Depression in Childhood and Adolescence

Before ending our discussion of the mood disorders, we turn our attention to childhood and adolescence. Considering our typical image of children as happy-go-lucky, it is distressing to observe that major depression and dysthymia occur in children and adolescents as well as in adults. DSM-IV-TR diagnoses mood disorders in children using the adult criteria, while allowing for age-specific features such as irritability and aggressive behavior instead of or in addition to depressed mood.

Symptoms and Prevalence of Childhood and Adolescent Depression

There are similarities and differences in the symptomatology of children and adults with major depression (Garber & Flynn, 2001). Children and adolescents ages seven to seventeen resemble adults in depressed mood, inability to experience pleasure, fatigue, concentration problems, and suicidal ideation. Symptoms that differ are higher rates of suicide attempts and guilt among children and adolescents, and more frequent waking up early in the morning, loss of appetite, weight loss, and early morning depression among adults.

As in adults, depression in children is recurrent. Longitudinal studies have demonstrated that both children and adolescents with major depression are likely to continue to exhibit significant depressive symptoms when assessed even four to eight years later (Garber et al., 1988; Hammen et al., 1990).

Estimates of the prevalence of childhood depression vary depending on the age of the child, the country being studied, the type of samples (community based or clinic referred), the diagnostic criteria, and the methods used to make the assessment (e.g., clinical interviews, questionnaires, reports from parents or teachers [Kazdin, 1989; Nottelmann & Jensen, 1995]). Sometimes depression—often called *masked depression*—is inferred from behaviors such as acting aggressively or misbehaving that would not, in adults, be viewed as reflecting an underlying depression.[5]

---

[5] The reader may consider it problematic to infer depression from behaviors that do not seem depressive in nature. For this reason "masked depression" is an unpopular diagnosis with many clinicians and researchers, for it implies acceptance of the psychoanalytic defense mechanism of reaction formation (recall p. 29), whereby a repressed impulse is said to be converted into its opposite. On the other hand, it is possible that, as already noted, depression is expressed very differently in children than in adults, so that a behavior such as aggression may in fact be a direct sign of childhood depression. The issue is a thorny one.

In general, depression occurs in less than 1 percent of preschoolers (Kashani & Carlson, 1987; Kashani, Hoalcomb, & Orvaschel, 1986) and in 2 to 3 percent of school-age children (Cohen et al., 1993; Costello et al., 1988). In adolescents, rates of depression are comparable to those of adults, with particularly high rates (7 to 13 percent) for girls (Angold & Rutter, 1992; Kashani et al., 1987). This greater prevalence among adolescent young women, almost 2:1 as compared to young men, is the same as that found among adults. Interestingly, this gender difference does not occur before age twelve; depression is found more often among boys during the early years (Anderson et al., 1987).

One problem complicating the diagnosis of depression in children is frequent comorbidity with other disorders (Hammen & Compas, 1994). Up to 70 percent of depressed children also have an anxiety disorder or significant anxiety symptoms (Anderson et al., 1987; Brady & Kendall, 1992; Kovacs, 1990). Recent research indicates that depression and anxiety can be distinguished in children and adolescents in much the same way it can be among adults (cf. page 273): low levels of positive affect appear to be specific to children with depression, whereas high levels of negative affect are seen in both anxiety and depression (Joiner & Lonigan, 2000). Depression is also common in children with conduct disorder and attention-deficit disorder (Fleming & Offord, 1990; Kashani et al., 1987; Rohde et al., 1991). Youngsters with both depression and another disorder have been found to experience more severe depression and to take longer to recover (Keller et al., 1988; Kovacs et al., 1984).

Etiology of Depression in Childhood and Adolescence

What causes a young person to become depressed? As with adults, evidence suggests that genetic factors play a role (Puig-Antich et al., 1989; Klein, Lewinsohn, Seeley, & Rhode, 2001; Tsuang & Faraone, 1990). Indeed, the genetic data on adults reviewed earlier in this chapter naturally apply to children and adolescents, since genetic influences are present from birth. They may not be expressed right away, however.

Studies of depression in children have focused also on family and other relationships as sources of stress that might interact with a biological diathesis. Having a mother who is depressed increases the chances of being depressed as a child or adolescent; less is known about the influence of fathers (Kaslow, Deering, & Racusin, 1994) or the reasons for these linkages. We know that depression in either or both spouses is often associated with marital conflict; we should expect, therefore, that depression will have negative effects on the children in a household, and it does (Hammen, 1997).

Depressed children and their parents have been shown to interact with each other in negative ways, for example, showing less warmth and more hostility toward each other than is the case with nondepressed children and their parents (Biglan et al., 1988; Chiariello & Orvaschel, 1995). Children and adolescents experiencing major depression also have poor social skills and impaired relationships with siblings and friends (Lewinsohn et al., 1994; Puig-Antich et al., 1993). These behavioral patterns are likely to be both a cause and a consequence of depression. Depressed youngsters have fewer and less satisfying contacts with their peers, who often reject them because they are not enjoyable to be around (Kennedy, Spence, & Hensley, 1989). These negative interactions in turn aggravate the negative self-image and sense of worth that the depressed youngster already has (Coyne, 1976). Frequent criticism from parents may be especially harmful to the child's sense of competency and self-worth (Cole & Turner, 1993; Stark et al., 1996).

Consistent with both Beck's theory (1967) and the learned helplessness theory of depression (Abramson et al., 1988), cognitive distortions and negative attributional styles are associated with depression in children and adolescents in ways similar to what has been found with adults (e.g., Garber, Weiss, & Shanley, 1993; Gotlib et al., 1993; Kaslow et al., 1992). For example, cognitive research with depressed children indicates that their outlooks (schemata) are more negative than are those of nondepressed children and resemble those of depressed adults (Prieto, Cole, & Tageson, 1992). Such findings provide a possibly useful connection between childhood depression and Beck's theory and research on

Focus on Discovery 10.3

Depression in Adolescents: The Appearance of Gender Differences

Depression occurs about twice as often in women as in men. Research involving patients in treatment as well as surveys of community residents consistently yield a female–male ratio of 2 to 1. This gender difference does not appear in preadolescent children, however; not until midadolescence does this gender difference emerge consistently (Hankin et al., 1998). Understanding its cause and its timing may yield some further clues to the etiology of depression. After reviewing evidence concerning gender differences in depression, Nolen-Hoeksema and Girgus (1994) concluded that girls are more likely than boys to have certain risk factors for depression even before adolescence, but it is only when these risk factors interact with the challenges of adolescence that the gender differences in depression emerge.

What are these risk factors? Nolen-Hoeksema and Girgus discussed three possibilities.

1. Girls are less assertive than boys and score lower than boys on questionnaires that assess leadership abilities.
2. Girls are more likely than boys to engage in what is called *ruminative coping*. They focus their attention on their depressive symptoms (e.g., "What if I don't get over this?" "What does it mean that I feel this way?"). Supporting the importance of ruminative coping, an eighteen-month longitudinal study has shown that this coping style predicts the onset of episodes of depression and is associated with more

The gender difference in depression does not emerge until adolescence. At that time, young women encounter many stressors and tend to ruminate about the resulting negative feelings.

severe depressive symptoms (Just & Alloy, 1997). Boys and men, in contrast, tend to distract themselves from such introspection by engaging in some physical activity or watching television.
3. Girls are less likely than boys to be physically and verbally aggressive and are less dominant in group interactions.

When adolescence begins, girls are faced with a number of stressors. As their secondary sex characteristics develop, they may dislike their weight gain and loss of their thin figure. They also find their physical appearance to be the focus of interest and often disapproving conversation from their male (and female) peers. At the same time, their risk of physical and sexual abuse increases, as do conflicts with parents over issues of independence and gender-appropriate behavior. These stressors, coupled with the risk factors that may result in less effective coping, may be the keys to understanding why women become depressed more frequently than men.

The implications for treatment are clear according to this view. Depressed women—and men—should be encouraged to increase active coping rather than dwelling excessively on their moods and searching for causes of depression. Problem-solving skills and assertiveness should be nurtured. In a preventive vein, Nolen-Hoeksema suggests that parents and other caretakers encourage girls to adopt active behavior in response to negative moods.

depressed adults. Accumulating evidence indicates that experiences in the home, primarily the manner in which parents deal with their children, cause the cognitions and thoughts that can lead to depression (Stark et al., 1996) (see Focus on Discovery 10.3). However, some research indicates that cognitive distortions in children may be a reflection of depression rather than a cause (Cole et al., 1998). Additional research that incorporates knowledge about children's normal cognitive development will prove beneficial for discerning the role of cognitive factors in childhood depression (e.g., Cole, Jacquez, & Maschman, 2001). For example, it will be important to further investigate how schemata, attitudes, and self-worth develop during the course of childhood and adolescence.

Treatment of Childhood and Adolescent Depression

Therapy with depressed children and adolescents has been studied far less than therapy with adults (Hammen, 1997; Kaslow & Racusin, 1990). One reason suggested for this relative neglect is that depressed young people don't attract as much adult attention as those who act out, such as the youngsters with conduct disorder described later (p. 484) (Kaslow & Thompson, 1998).

Research on the safety and efficacy of pharmacotherapy for childhood and adolescent depression has lagged behind research with adults (Emslie & Mayes, 2001). A recent double-blind study found that fluoxetine reduced symptoms more than a placebo, but complete remission of symptoms was rare (Emslie et al., 1997). In general, evidence suggests that the selective serotonin reuptake inhibitors are superior to tricyclic antidepressants (Emslie et al., 2000; Lynch et al., 2001; Wagner & Ambrosini, 2001). However, other studies have shown that antidepressant drugs are no better than placebos in children and adolescents (e.g., Geller et al., 1992; Keller et al., 2001).

Most psychosocial interventions are modeled after clinical research with adults. For example, interpersonal therapy has been modified for use with depressed adolescents, focusing on issues of concern to adolescents, such as peer pressure, the stress inherent in the transition from childhood to adulthood, and the conflict between dependency on parents (and parental figures, like teachers) and the drive to be independent (Moreau et al., 1992; Mufson et al., 1994). Cognitive-behavioral interventions in school settings appear to be effective and are associated with more rapid reduction of symptoms than family or supportive therapy (Curry, 2001). About 63 percent of depressed adolescents treated with CBT show significant improvement at the end of treatment (Lewinsohn & Clarke, 1999). However, a recent study indicated that this favorable outcome does not hold up during post-treatment follow-up (Birmaher, 2000).

A cognitive-behavioral group intervention involving instruction in coping with depression was found to be effective with depressed adolescents, particularly when parents were involved in treatment (Clarke et al., 1992; Lewinsohn et al., 1990). Fifth and sixth graders showed improvement in depression after a small-group role-playing intervention that concentrated on instructions in social skills and social problem solving in stressful situations (Butler et al., 1980). Social-skills training can be expected to help depressed young people by providing them with the behavioral and verbal means to gain access to pleasant, reinforcing environments, such as making friends and getting along with peers (Stark, Reynolds, & Kaslow, 1987). Findings from Stark et al. (1996) indicate that some depressed children know how to relate appropriately to others but are apparently inhibited from doing so by negative thoughts and physiological arousal, suggesting that cognitive interventions and, for some, such procedures as relaxation training could also be useful. Overall, treatments that include social-skills training, problem solving, and cognitive techniques similar to those employed successfully with adults are effective (Kaslow & Thompson, 1998).

Treatment of depressed children and adolescents may be best accomplished with a broad-spectrum approach that involves not only the child or adolescent but also the family and the school (Hammen, 1997; Stark et al., 1996, 1998). Therapy might well have to focus on a depressed parent in addition to the depressed child. Depressed parents probably communicate to their children their own pessimistic views of themselves and the world, and children are influenced strongly by the ideas of their parents.

The proposal to include the family and school environments is based on the hypothesis that for young people more than for adults, environmental stressors can be more important than cognitive biases, expectations, and attributions (Cole & Turner, 1993). This approach also points up the importance of teaching the young person ways to cope with interpersonal stress via more effective overt behavior—for example, interacting more effectively with others and being appropriately assertive with overbearing peers—so that the person has alternatives other than the polar extremes of anger or withdrawal. The involvement of the family has only recently been recognized as important when dealing with younger people who are depressed (Kaslow & Thompson, 1998).

A case report by Braswell and Kendall (1988) illustrates cognitive-behavioral therapy with a depressed fifteen-year-old girl.

When initially seen, Sharon was extremely dysphoric, experienced recurrent suicidal ideation, and displayed a number of vegetative signs of depression…. [After being] placed on antidepressant medication…she was introduced to a cognitive-behavioral approach to depression…. She was able to understand how her mood was affected by her thoughts and behavior and was able to engage in behavioral planning to increase the occurrence of pleasure and mastery-oriented events. Sharon manifested extremely high standards for evaluating her performance in a number of areas, and it became clear that her parents also ascribed to these standards, so that family therapy sessions were held to encourage Sharon and her parents to reevaluate their standards.

Sharon had difficulty with the notion of changing her standards and noted that when she was not depressed she actually valued her perfectionism. At that point she resisted the therapy because she perceived it as trying to change something she valued in herself. With this in mind, we began to explore and identify those situations or domains in which her perfectionism worked for her and when and how it might work against her. She became increasingly comfortable with this perspective and decided she wanted to continue to set high standards regarding her performance in mathematical coursework (which was a clear area of strength), but she did not need to be so demanding of herself regarding art or physical education. (p. 194)

Suicide

Suicide was not condemned in Western thought until the fourth century, when Saint Augustine proclaimed it a crime because it violated the Sixth Commandment, "Thou shalt not kill." Saint Thomas Aquinas elaborated on this view in the thirteenth century, declaring suicide a mortal sin because it usurped God's power over life and death. So although neither the Old Testament nor the New Testament explicitly forbids suicide, the Western world came to regard it as a crime and a sin (Shneidman, 1973).

The irony is that the Christian injunctions against suicide, deriving from a profound respect for life, contributed to persecution of those who attempted to or actually did take their own lives. As late as 1823, anyone in London who committed suicide was buried with a stake pounded through the heart, and not until 1961 did suicide cease to be a criminal offense in the United Kingdom. In the United States today, some states categorize suicide attempts as misdemeanors, although these offenses are seldom prosecuted. Most states have laws that make it a crime to encourage or advise suicide (Shneidman, 1987).

Suicide is discussed in this chapter because many depressed persons and persons with bipolar disorder have suicidal thoughts and sometimes make genuine attempts to take their own lives. It is believed that more than half of those who try to kill themselves are depressed and despondent at the time of the act (Henriksson et al., 1993), and it is estimated that as many as 15 percent of people who have been diagnosed with major depression ultimately commit suicide (Maris et al., 1992).[6] A significant number of people who are not depressed, however, make suicidal attempts, some with success—most notably people diagnosed with borderline personality disorder (p. 414) (Linehan, 1997). The suicide rate for male alcoholics is greater than that for the general population of men, and it becomes extremely high in alcoholic men who are also depressed (Linehan, 1997). Up to 13 percent of individuals with schizophrenia commit suicide (Roy, 1982). Our focus here is on issues and factors in suicide that transcend specific diagnoses.

Facts about Suicide

Suicide is a complex and multifaceted act (Berman & Jobes, 1996; Brown et al., 2000; Hoyert et al. 2001; Moscicki, 1995). No single theory can hope to explain it. Some facts about suicide are listed here; see Focus on Discovery 10.4 for myths about suicide.

- According to statistics, every twenty minutes someone in the United States kills himself or herself. This figure, translating into about 31,000 suicides a year, is probably a gross underestimate. The overall suicide rate in the United States is about 12 per 100,000. It rises in old age; between the ages of seventy-five and eighty-four the rate reaches 24 per 100,000.

---

[6] It seems worth pointing out that suicidal thoughts or attempts are one of the characteristics of major depression listed in the DSM. Thus the very definition of depression usually includes suicidality. By the same token, when people with schizophrenia or substance-abuse problems commit suicide, they are often diagnosed as also depressed (Roy, 1982; Roy & Linnoila, 1986). It should thus not be surprising that suicidal thoughts are widespread among mentally ill persons, given that self-destructive behavior is indicated as a feature of several mental disorders.

Table 10.5 Comparison of Suicide Attempters and Completers

Characteristics	Attempters	Completers
Gender	Majority female	Majority male
Age	Predominantly young	Risk increases with age
Method	Low lethality (pills, cutting)	More violent (gun, jumping)
Common diagnoses	Dysthymic disorder	Major mood disorder
	Borderline personality disorder	Alcoholism
	Schizophrenia	
Dominant emotion	Depression with anger	Depression with hopelessness
Motivation	Change in situation	Death
	Cry for help	
Hospital course	Quick recovery from dysphoria	
Attitude toward attempt	Relief to have survived	
	Promises not to repeat	

Source: Adapted from Fremouw et al., 1990, p. 24. Reprinted by permission of Simon and Schuster International.

- The ratio of attempted to completed suicides in the United States may be as high as 200 to 1, which means that there may be as many as six million attempts per year.
- About half of those who commit suicide have made at least one previous attempt, but most attempters never make another attempt. Most do not really intend to die, especially children and adolescents. Some differences between attempters and completers are shown in Table 10.5.
- Men are four to five times more likely than women to kill themselves, although the ratio may be diminishing as women are becoming a higher-risk group.
- Three times as many women as men attempt to kill themselves but do not die.
- Being divorced or widowed increases suicide risk by four or five times and may be a risk factor that becomes more influential with age. The importance of marital status may also be one aspect of the role of lack of social support in suicidal risk.
- Suicide incidence in the United States is highest during the spring and summer.
- Suicide is found at all social and economic levels but is especially common among psychiatrists, physicians, lawyers, and psychologists, even more so if they are women. Also at higher risk are law enforcement officers, musicians, and dentists.
- No other kind of death leaves friends and relatives with such long-lasting feelings of distress, shame, guilt, puzzlement, and general disturbance. These survivors are themselves victims, having an especially high mortality rate in the year following the suicide of the loved one.
- Guns are by far the most common means of committing suicide in the United States, accounting for about 60 percent of all suicides. The availability of firearms in U.S. homes increases suicide risk independent of other known risk factors. Men usually choose to shoot or hang themselves; women are more likely to use sleeping pills, a less lethal method, which may account for their lower rate of completed suicide.

Suicide involving violent death, such as jumping off a building, is more common among men than among women.

Focus on Discovery 10.4

Some Myths about Suicide

There are many prevalent misconceptions about suicide (Fremouw et al., 1990; Pokorny, 1968; Shneidman, 1973). It is as important to be familiar with them as it is to know the facts.

1. *People who discuss suicide will not commit the act.* Up to three-quarters of those who take their own lives have communicated their intention beforehand, perhaps as a cry for help, perhaps to taunt.

2. *Suicide is committed without warning.* The falseness of this belief is shown by the preceding statement. The person usually gives many warnings, such as saying that the world would be better off without him or her or making unexpected and inexplicable gifts to others, often of his or her most valued possessions.

3. *Only people of a certain class commit suicide.* Suicide is neither the curse of the poor nor the disease of the rich. People in all socioeconomic classes commit suicide.

4. *Membership in a particular religious group is a good predictor that a person will not consider suicide.* It is mistakenly thought that the strong Catholic prohibition against suicide makes the risk that Catholics will take their lives much lower. This belief is not supported by the evidence, perhaps because an individual's formal religious identification is not always an accurate index of true beliefs.

5. *The motives for suicide are easily established.* The truth is that we do not fully understand why people commit suicide. For example, that a severe reverse in finances precedes a suicide does not mean that it adequately explains the suicide.

6. *All who commit suicide are depressed.* This fallacy may account for the fact that signs of impending suicide are often overlooked because the person does not act despondently. Many people who take their lives are not depressed; some people appear calm and at peace with themselves.

7. *A person with a terminal physical illness is unlikely to commit suicide.* A person's awareness of impending death does not preclude suicide. Perhaps the wish to end their own suffering or that of their loved ones impels many to choose the time of their death.

8. *To commit suicide is psychotic.* Although most suicidal persons are very unhappy, most do appear to be in touch with reality.

9. *Suicide is influenced by cosmic factors such as sunspots and phases of the moon.* No evidence confirms this belief.

10. *Improvement in emotional state means lessened risk of suicide.* Often people, especially those who are depressed, commit suicide after their spirits begin to rise and their energy level improves.

11. *Suicide is a lonely event.* Although the debate whether to commit suicide is waged within the individual's head, deep immersion in a frustrating, hurtful relationship with another person—a spouse, a child, a lover, a colleague—may be a principal cause.

12. *Suicidal people clearly want to die.* Most people who commit suicide appear to be ambivalent about their own deaths; others suffer from depression or alcoholism, the alleviation of which would reduce the suicidal desire. For many people the suicidal crisis passes, and they are grateful for having been prevented from self-destruction.

13. *Thinking about suicide is rare.* Lifetime prevalence estimates from various studies suggest that among nonclinical populations, suicidal ideation runs from 40 percent to as high as 80 percent; that is, these percentages of people have thought about committing suicide at least once in their lives.

14. *Asking a person, especially a depressed person, about suicide will push him or her over the edge and cause a suicidal act that would not otherwise have occurred.* One of the first things clinicians learn in their training is to inquire about suicide in a deeply troubled patient. Asking about it can give the person permission to talk about what he or she might harbor as a terrible, shameful secret, which could otherwise lead to further isolation and depression.

15. *People who attempt suicide by a low-lethal means are not serious about killing themselves.* This statement confuses lethality with intent. Some people are not well-informed about pill dosages or human anatomy. An attempt unlikely to have led to death may nonetheless have been engaged in by someone who really wanted to self-destruct.

• Suicide ranks ninth as a cause of death among American adults in general. It ranks third after accidents and homicides among all those aged fifteen to twenty-four (13.3 per 100,000) and second among whites in this age group. It is the fifth leading cause of death in children between the ages of five and fourteen, behind accidents, cancer, homicide, and congenital abnormalities (the suicide rate being 0.9 per 100,000, which comes to about 330 per year).[7] It is estimated that each year upwards of 10,000 American college students attempt to kill themselves and as many as 20 percent consider suicide at least once during their college years.

• Overall, suicide rates for white and Native American youths are more than twice

---

[7] On the one hand, it is shocking that suicide claims so many children between the ages of five and fourteen in the United States. On the other hand, in percentage terms, suicides in this age range account for only 4 percent of deaths. In contrast, accidents, the leading cause of death, account for about 40 percent of deaths. Also to be borne in mind is that the overall death rate for youngsters this age is quite low.

those for African American youths. However, in the inner cities the rates among young African American men are twice as high as those among young white men (a situation similar to the higher incidence of violence and homicide among young urban African Americans). The highest rates of suicide in the United States are for white males over age fifty. For African Americans suicide is most frequent among those aged fifteen to twenty-four.

- The rates of suicide for adolescents and children in the United States are increasing dramatically. As many as 3,000 young people between the ages of fifteen and nineteen are believed to kill themselves each year, and attempts are made by children as young as six years old. But the rates are far below those of adults. As with adults, thinking about suicide occurs much more often than making an actual attempt; one estimate is that suicidal ideation occurs at least once among 40 percent of children and adolescents.

- Gay and lesbian adolescents are at higher risk for suicide than heterosexual adolescents.

- Rape survivors are at increased risk for suicide, and they are especially more likely to consider it seriously.

- Physical illness, for example, AIDS or multiple sclerosis, is a contributing factor in as many as half of all suicides (see the later discussion of physician-assisted suicide for the terminally ill, p. 314).

- Hungary has the highest rate of suicide in the world. The Czech Republic, Finland, Austria, and Switzerland also have high incidences. The countries with the lowest rates are Greece, Mexico, the Netherlands, and the United Kingdom. The United States is in the middle range.

- Suicide rates rise during depression years, remain stable during years of prosperity, and decrease during war years.

Perspectives on Suicide

In imagining a suicide we usually think of a person deliberately performing a dramatic act explicitly chosen to end life almost immediately—the woman sitting in a car in a garage with the motor running, the man with the gun next to his temple, the child with the bottle of a parent's sleeping pills. But suicidologists also regard people as suicidal when they act in less obvious self-destructive ways that can cause serious injury or death after a prolonged period of time, such as a diabetic patient who neglects taking insulin or adhering to a dietary regimen or an individual with alcoholism who continues to drink and does not seek help despite awareness of the damage being done to his or her body. Sometimes termed *subintentioned death*, these apparent suicides complicate still further the task of understanding and gathering statistics on suicide (Shneidman, 1973).

Ideas about the nature and causes of suicide can be found in many places (Shneidman, 1987). Letters and diaries can provide insights into the phenomenology of people who commit suicide. Novelists, such as Herman Melville and Leo Tolstoy, have provided insights on suicide, as have writers who have killed themselves, such as Virginia Woolf and Sylvia Plath. Many philosophers have written searchingly on the topic, including Descartes, Voltaire, Kant, Heidegger, and Camus.

Studies of suicide notes from ordinary people have found that those who follow through with suicide often leave specific, detailed instructions and that their notes show evidence of more anguish and hostility than do simulated suicide notes written by individuals who were not thinking about suicide but who were matched demographically and asked to write a suicide note as if they were planning to kill themselves (Ogilvie et al., 1983; Shneidman & Farberow, 1970). Lacking in real suicide notes is the kind of general and philosophical content that characterizes those written by simulators; "Be sure to pay the electric bill" would more likely appear in a real suicide note than "Be good to others" (Baumeister, 1990).

Many motives for suicide have been suggested (Mintz, 1968): aggression turned inward; retaliation achieved by inducing guilt in others; efforts to force love from others; efforts to make amends for perceived past wrongs; efforts to rid oneself of unacceptable

Writers who killed themselves, such as Sylvia Plath, have provided insights about the causes of suicide.

The suicide of Nirvana's lead singer, Kurt Cobain, triggered an increase in suicide among teenagers.

feelings, such as sexual attraction to members of one's own sex; the desire for reincarnation; the desire to rejoin a dead loved one; and the desire or need to escape from stress, deformity, pain, or emotional vacuum. Many contemporary mental health professionals regard suicide in general as an individual's attempt at problem solving, conducted under considerable stress and marked by consideration of a very narrow range of alternatives of which self-annihilation appears the most viable (Linehan & Shearin, 1988).

A theory about suicide based on work in social and personality psychology holds that some suicides arise from a strong desire to escape from aversive self-awareness, that is, from the painful awareness of shortcomings and lack of success that the person attributes to himself or herself (Baumeister, 1990). This awareness is assumed to produce severe emotional suffering, perhaps depression. Unrealistically high expectations—and therefore the probability of failing to meet these expectations—play a central role in this perspective on suicide. Of particular importance is a discrepancy between high expectations for intimacy and a reality that falls short, for example, when someone's expectations for closeness are dashed by a loved one who cannot possibly deliver what the person needs (Stephens, 1985). Oblivion through death can appear more tolerable than a continuation of the painful awareness of one's deficiencies. There is considerable research in support of this hypothesis (Baumeister, 1990).

Media reports of suicide may spark an increase in suicides. This disturbing possibility was discussed by Bandura (1986), who reviewed research by Phillips (1974, 1977, 1985) showing several relationships:

1. Suicides rose by 12 percent in the month following Marilyn Monroe's death.
2. Publicized accounts of self-inflicted deaths of people who are not famous also are followed by significant increases in suicide, suggesting that it is the publicity rather than the fame of the person who committed suicide that is important.
3. Publicized accounts of murder-suicides are followed by increases in automobile and plane crashes in which the driver and others are killed.
4. Media reports of natural deaths of famous people are not followed by increases in suicide, suggesting that it is not grief per se that is the influential factor.

We turn now to several other perspectives on suicide, each of which attempts to shed light on this disturbing aspect of humankind.

Freud's Psychoanalytic Theory   Basically, Freud viewed suicide as murder, an extension of his theory of depression. When a person loses someone whom he or she has ambivalently loved and hated, and introjects that person, aggression is directed inward. If these feelings are strong enough, the person will commit suicide.

Durkheim's Sociological Theory   Emile Durkheim (1897, 1951), a renowned sociologist, analyzed the records of suicide for various countries and historical periods and concluded that self-annihilation could be understood in sociological terms. He distinguished three different kinds of suicide. **Egoistic suicide** is committed by people who have few ties to family, society, or community. These people feel alienated from others, cut off from the social supports that are important to keep them functioning adaptively as social beings.

Altruistic suicide   is viewed as a response to societal demands. Some people who commit suicide feel very much a part of a group and sacrifice themselves for what they take to be the good of society. The self-immolations of Buddhist monks and nuns to protest the fighting during the Vietnam War fits into this category. Some altruistic suicides, such as the hara-kiri of the Japanese, are required as the only honorable recourse in certain circumstances.

Finally, **anomic suicide** may be triggered by a sudden change in a person's relation to society. A successful executive who suffers severe financial reverses may experience *anomie*, a sense of disorientation, because what he or she believed to be a normal way of living is no longer possible. Here are two illustrations.

Anomie can pervade a society in disequilibrium, making suicide more likely. An example of anomic suicide occurred among a rural Brazilian tribe, the Guarani Indians. Their suicide rate in 1995 was 160 per 100,000, markedly higher than it had been a year earlier and dramatically higher than the U.S. rate of about 12 per 100,000. The reason may be found in a sudden change in their living conditions. The Guarani had recently lost most of their ancestral lands to industrialization. Communities that had lived by hunting and fishing were now crowded onto reservations too small to support that way of life. Nearby cities tempted the Guarani with consumer goods that they desired and yet could ill afford on their low wages. Because hunting, farming, and family life had religious significance, their demise significantly affected religious life. Life lost its meaning for many of the Guarani (Long, 1995).

Another example of anomic suicide involves natural disasters. Our earlier discussion of posttraumatic stress disorder (p. 164) alerted us to the serious emotional aftermath of such events. Natural disasters give rise to an increase in suicides. Krug et al. (1998) found that suicide rates increase by more than 62 percent in the year following an earthquake, by 14 percent in the four years following a flood, and by 31 percent in the two years after a hurricane. Possible reasons include the obvious—the stress of seeing loved ones and friends killed or hurt and the loss of property

The high suicide rate of the Guarani Indians, who were forced onto crowded reservations, illustrates Durkheim's concept of anomic suicide.

and income. Less obvious, but probably very important also, are the disruption in everyday routines and the loss of social support associated with damage from natural disasters. Depression and general hopelessness are likely exacerbated by less access to familiar stores, bars, clubhouses, and churches—places where many people enjoy social contacts and support in the face of everyday stressors. How much more they must feel the loss of these social supports when experiencing stress following a severe disaster.

If history is any guide, we may see an increase in suicide in the New York City area as a result of the terrorist attack on the World Trade Center. Indeed, the wife of a man who was killed in the attack on September 11, 2001 committed suicide not long after the disaster, with indications that she was horribly distraught after her husband's death (New York Times, December 13, 2001).

As with all sociological theorizing Durkheim's hypotheses have difficulty accounting for the differences among individuals in a given society in their reactions to the same demands and conditions. Not all those who unexpectedly lose their money commit suicide, for example. It appears that Durkheim was aware of this problem, for he suggested that individual temperament would interact with any of the social pressures that he found causative.

Shneidman's Approach to Suicide   Shneidman's psychological approach to suicide is summarized in Table 10.6, which lists the ten most frequent characteristics of suicide, not all of them found in each and every case. His view regards suicide as a conscious effort to seek a solution to a problem that is causing intense suffering. To the sufferer, this solution ends consciousness and unendurable pain—what Melville in *Moby Dick* termed an "insufferable anguish." All hope and sense of constructive action are gone.

Still—and this is of central importance in prevention—most people who contemplate or actually commit suicide are ambivalent. "The prototypical suicidal state is one in which an individual cuts his or her throat, cries for help at the same time, and is genuine in both of these acts.... Individuals would be happy not to do it, if they didn't have to" (Shneidman, 1987, p. 170). There is a narrowing of the perceived range of options; when not in a highly perturbed suicidal state, the person is capable of seeing more choices for dealing with stress. People planning suicide usually communicate their intention, sometimes as a cry for help, sometimes as a withdrawal from others, a search for inviolacy. Typical behaviors include giving away treasured possessions and putting financial affairs in order.

Table 10.6   The Ten Commonalities of Suicide
I. The common purpose of suicide is to seek a solution.
II. The common goal of suicide is the cessation of consciousness.
III. The common stimulus in suicide is intolerable psychological pain.
IV. The common stressor in suicide is frustrated psychological needs.
V. The common emotion in suicide is hopelessness–helplessness.
VI. The common cognitive state in suicide is ambivalence.
VII. The common perceptual state in suicide is constriction.
VIII. The common action in suicide is egression.
IX. The common interpersonal act in suicide is communication of intention.
X. The common consistency in suicide is with lifelong coping patterns.

Source: From Shneidman, 1985, p. 167.

While acknowledging that perhaps 90 percent of suicides could be given a DSM diagnosis, Shneidman (1987) reminds us that the vast majority of people with schizophrenia and mood disorders do not commit suicide. He suggests that the perturbation of mind that he posits as a key feature in a person who commits suicide is not a mental illness.

Neurochemistry and Suicide   Just as low levels of serotonin appear to be related to depression, research has also established a connection among serotonin, suicide, and impulsivity. Low levels of serotonin's major metabolite, 5-HIAA, have been found in people in several diagnostic categories—depression, schizophrenia, and various personality disorders—who committed suicide (see Brown & Goodwin, 1986; van Praag, Plutchik, & Apter, 1990). Postmortem studies of the brains of people who committed suicide have revealed increased binding by serotonin receptors (presumably a response to a decreased level of serotonin) (Turecki et al., 1999). The link between low 5-HIAA levels and suicide is especially compelling in cases of violent and impulsive suicide (Roy, 1994; Traskman et al., 1981; Winchel, Stanley, & Stanley, 1990). Finally, 5-HIAA levels are negatively correlated with questionnaire measures of aggression and impulsivity (Brown & Goodwin, 1986). Other research has found that depressed patients who had an abnormal dexamethasone suppression test response had very high rates of suicide several years later (Coryell & Schlesser, 2001).

Prediction of Suicide from Psychological Tests

It would be of considerable theoretical and practical value to be able to predict suicide on the basis of psychological tests, and several efforts have been made to do so. Significant correlations have been found between suicide intent and hopelessness. Especially noteworthy are Aaron Beck's findings, based on prospective data, that hopelessness is a strong predictor of suicide (Beck, 1986b; Beck et al., 1985, 1990), even stronger than depression (Beck, Kovacs, & Weissman, 1975). The expectation that at some point in the future things will be no better than they are right now—which, to be sure, is part of the phenomenon of depression but can be found among nondepressed people as well—seems to be more instrumental than depression per se in propelling a person to take his or her life.

Another self-report instrument is Marsha Linehan's Reasons for Living (RFL) Inventory (Ivanoff et al., 1994; Linehan, 1985; Linehan et al., 1983). Clusters of items tap what is important to the individual, such as responsibility to family and concerns about children. The approach is different from, and possibly more useful than, scales that focus only on negativism and pessimism, because knowing what there is in a person's life that prevents him or her from committing suicide has both assessment and intervention value. This instrument can discriminate between suicidal and nonsuicidal individuals and can help the clinician with intervention by identifying reasons the person has for not wanting to die (Malone et al., 2000).

Another factor that has been studied is life satisfaction. A recent prospective study in Finland found a significant relationship between a questionnaire measure of life satisfaction and suicidal behavior up to twenty years later. People who expressed relatively high levels of dissatisfaction with their lives at the beginning of the study were significantly more likely to have attempted or committed suicide years later. For example, men with the highest levels of life dissatisfaction were twenty-five times more likely to commit suicide ten years later than men with the lowest levels. Of particular note, in our view, is that the questionnaire was done by mail and contained only four items: how interesting or boring their lives were, how happy or unhappy they were, how easy or difficult their lives were, and how lonely they felt (Koivumaa-Honkanen et al., 2001).

Another avenue of research has focused on the cognitive characteristics of people who attempt suicide. It has been suggested that suicidal individuals are more rigid in their approach to problems (e.g., Neuringer, 1964) and less flexible in their thinking (Levenson, 1972). Constricted thinking could account for the apparent inability to consider solutions to life's problems other than taking one's own life (Linehan et al., 1987).

Research confirms the hypothesis that people who attempt suicide are more rigid than others, lending support to the clinical observations of Shneidman and others that people who attempt suicide seem almost myopically incapable of thinking of alternative solutions to problems and might therefore tend to settle on suicide as the only way out.

Related to the idea that those who attempt suicide differ in cognitive characteristics, a recent study examined neuropsychological deficits in a group of currently depressed patients. The patients were divided into three groups: (1) those who had never attempted suicide; (2) those whose suicide attempts did not cause serious injury or damage, characterized as low-lethal attempts; and (3) those whose suicide attempts nearly caused death, characterized as high-lethal (e.g., an overdose resulting in a coma). Depressed persons with a history of high-lethal suicide attempts had more executive functioning deficits (e.g., difficulties making plans, solving problems, making decisions) than the other two groups, even after controlling for severity of depression, age, and overall intellectual functioning (Keilp et al., 2001). One potential problem with interpreting these findings is that the suicide attempt itself could have caused the deficits in executive functioning; thus, these deficits may not necessarily be a good predictor of who might commit suicide. However, patients with high-lethal suicide attempts did not have deficits in other areas of cognitive functioning.

It has proved difficult to predict suicide based on the kind of trait approach that characterizes these research efforts. As we saw in Chapter 4, behavior is influenced a great deal by the environment, and the environment includes stressful events that themselves can be difficult to predict. We can seldom know, for example, whether a given individual is going to lose employment, experience serious marital problems, suffer the loss of a loved one, or be involved in a serious accident (recall our earlier discussion of chaos theory in Chapter 5, p. 113). In addition, it is hard from a strictly statistical point of view to predict with accuracy an infrequent event such as suicide, even with a highly reliable test (Fremouw et al., 1990; Roy, 1995).

Preventing Suicide

Treating the Underlying Mental Disorder   One way to look at the prevention of suicide is to bear in mind that most people who attempt to kill themselves are suffering from a treatable mental disorder such as depression, schizophrenia, substance abuse, or borderline personality disorder. Thus, when someone following Beck's cognitive approach successfully lessens a patient's depression, that patient's prior suicidal risk is reduced; likewise for the dialectical behavior therapy of Marsha Linehan (1993b), whose therapy with borderline patients is described in Chapter 13 (p. 429).

The view that efforts to prevent suicide should focus on the underlying psychological disorder is held by many experts in the field (e.g., Moscicki, 1995). However, no controlled studies have demonstrated that either psychological or pharmacological treatments that reduce depression have a beneficial impact on suicide (Linehan, 1997). The absence of such a positive effect casts doubt on the strategy of treating a disorder presumed to underlie suicidality.[8]

Treating Suicidality Directly   Another tradition in suicide prevention downplays mental disorder and concentrates instead on the particular characteristics of suicidal people that transcend mental disorders. One of the best-known approaches of this nature is that of Edwin Shneidman, a pioneer in the study of suicide and its prevention. We have already reviewed some of his thinking on suicide. His general strategy of suicide prevention (1985, 1987) is threefold.

---

[8] There is an irony here that Linehan (1997) has pointed out. Most studies that compare, say, treatment X and treatment Y for depression, intentionally *exclude* potential participants who are suicidal. Perhaps investigators are concerned about legal liability should a depressed and suicidal person kill himself or herself in the course of a controlled study. By playing it safe—a defensible position for professionals to take, given the realistic threat of a lawsuit from surviving family members—researchers are reducing the chances of gaining scientifically based information on how to reduce suicidal risk.

1. Reduce the intense psychological pain and suffering
2. Lift the blinders, that is, expand the constricted view by helping the individual see options other than the extremes of continued suffering or nothingness
3. Encourage the person to pull back even a little from the self-destructive act

He cites the example of a wealthy college student who was single, pregnant, and suicidal, with a clearly formed plan. The only solution she could think of besides suicide was never to have become pregnant, even to be virginal again.

> I took out a sheet of paper and began to widen her blinders. I said something like, "Now, let's see: You could have an abortion here locally." She responded, "I couldn't do that." I continued, "You could go away and have an abortion." "I couldn't do that." "You could bring the baby to term and keep the baby." "I couldn't do that." "You could have the baby and adopt it out." Further options were similarly dismissed. When I said, "You can always commit suicide, but there is obviously no need to do that today," there was no response. "Now," I said, "let's look at this list and rank them in order of your preference, keeping in mind that none of them is optimal." (Shneidman, 1987, p. 171)

Shneidman reports that just drawing up the list had a calming effect. The student's lethality—her drive to kill herself very soon—receded, and she was able to rank the list even though she found something wrong with each item. But an important goal had been achieved: she had been pulled back from the brink and was in a frame of mind to consider courses of action other than dying or being a virgin again. "We were then simply 'haggling' about life, a perfectly viable solution" (p. 171).

Based on clinical reports from practitioners and on what little controlled research has been done, Rudd, Joiner, and Rajab (2001) have recently suggested several core ingredients of suicide prevention:

1. Problem solving, usually within a cognitive-behavioral framework that also includes assertion training and other instruction in social skills.
2. Instruction in controlling emotions, especially anger, as well as tolerating distress.
3. Establishment of a strong and empathic therapeutic relationship, instilling trust and hope, even if that means encouraging the suicidal person to be very dependent on the therapist for a period of time.

Suicide Prevention Centers   Many **suicide prevention centers** are modeled after the Los Angeles Suicide Prevention Center, founded in 1958 by Farberow and Shneidman. There are at present more than two hundred such centers in the United States, and there are many abroad as well (Lester, 1995).

Staffed largely by nonprofessionals under the supervision of psychologists or psychiatrists, these centers attempt to provide twenty-four-hour consultation to people in suicidal crises. Usually the initial contact is made by telephone. The center's phone number is well publicized in the community. Workers rely heavily on demographic factors to assess risk (Shneidman, Farberow, & Litman, 1970). They have before them a checklist to guide their questioning of each caller. For example, a caller would be regarded as a lethal risk if he were male, middle-aged, divorced and living alone, and had a history of previous suicide attempts. Usually the more detailed and concrete the suicide plan, the higher the risk. The worker tries to assess the likelihood that the caller will make a serious suicide attempt and, most important, tries to establish personal contact and dissuade the caller from suicide. Staffers are taught above all to view the suicidal person's situation as he or she sees it, and not to convey in any way that the patient is a fool or is crazy to have settled on suicide as a solution to his or her woes. This empathy for suicidal people is sometimes referred to as "tuning in."

Such community facilities are potentially valuable because people who attempt suicide usually give warnings—cries for help—before taking their lives. Ambivalence about living or dying is the hallmark of the suicidal state (Shneidman, 1976). Usually, pleas are

Community mental health centers often provide a twenty-four-hour-a-day hotline for people who are considering suicide.

directed first to relatives and friends, but many people contemplating suicide are isolated from these sources of emotional support. A hot-line service may save the lives of such individuals.

Victims of suicide include survivors, especially if they are among the unfortunate 25 percent who were speaking to or in the presence of the person when the act was committed (Andress & Corey, 1978). Sometimes these survivors are therapists or hospital emergency room personnel. All are subject to strong feelings of guilt and self-recrimination, second-guessing what they might have done to prevent the suicide. Even dispassionate analysis does not invariably allay the guilt and anger. Grieving tends to last much longer than when deaths are not self-inflicted. For these many reasons, peer support groups exist to help survivors cope with the aftermath of a suicide. They provide social support, opportunities to ventilate feelings, constructive information, and referrals to professionals if that seems advisable (Fremouw et al., 1990).

It is exceedingly difficult to do controlled research on suicide, and outcome studies have yielded inconsistent results. A meta-analysis of five studies on the effectiveness of suicide prevention centers failed to demonstrate that rates decline after the implementation of services (Dew et al., 1987). A similarly negative finding was reported from Canada (Leenaars & Lester, 1995). However, another study found that suicide rates declined in the years following the establishment of suicide prevention centers in several cities (Lester, 1991). These inconclusive findings are consistent with the paucity of data on suicide prevention by other means. The most promising approach to suicide prevention appears to be a cognitive-behavioral one that emphasizes social problem solving (Linehan et al., 1991; Salkovskis, Atha, & Storer, 1990). The despair and utter hopelessness of the suicidal person may make him or her see suicide as the only solution, the only exit from an unbearable existence. The therapist encourages consideration of other ways to change the distressed state by construing problems as soluble and then generating life-affirming strategies for dealing with them.

Once again, we are left with conflicting and inconclusive evidence. Human lives are precious, however, and since many people who contact prevention centers weather a suicidal crisis successfully, these efforts will continue.

Clinical and Ethical Issues in Dealing with Suicide

Professional organizations such as the American Psychiatric Association, the National Association of Social Workers, and the American Psychological Association all charge their members to protect people from harming themselves even if doing so requires breaking the confidentiality of the therapist–patient relationship. The suicide of a therapist's patient is frequently grounds for a malpractice lawsuit, and the therapist is likely to lose such a suit if the patient's agents can prove that there was negligence in making adequate assessments and in taking reasonable precautions according to generally accepted standards of care for suicide prevention (Fremouw et al., 1990; Roy, 1995).

It is not easy to agree about what constitutes reasonable care, however, particularly when the patient is not hospitalized and therefore not under surveillance and potential restraint. Clinicians must work out their own ethic regarding a person's right to end his or her life. What steps is the professional willing to take to prevent a suicide? Confinement in a hospital? Or, as is more common today, sedation administered against the patient's wishes and strong enough that the person is virtually incapable of taking any action at all? And for how long should extraordinary measures be taken? Clinicians realize that most suicidal crises pass; the suicidal person is likely to be grateful afterward for having been prevented from committing suicide when it seemed the only course. But to what extreme is the professional prepared to go in the interim to prevent a suicide attempt? In Focus on Discovery 10.5 we discuss some controversial views on this ethical dilemma.

Physician-Assisted Suicide   Physician-assisted suicide has for a number of years been a highly charged issue. It came to the fore in the early 1990s when a Michigan physician,

Jack Kevorkian, a Michigan physician, assisted many patients in taking their own lives. The controversy stimulated by his actions focused attention on the moral issues surrounding suicide.

Jack Kevorkian, helped a fifty-four-year-old Oregonian woman in the early stages of Alzheimer's disease, a degenerative and fatal brain disease, to commit suicide. Not yet seriously disabled, she was helped by Kevorkian to press a button on a machine designed by him to inject a drug that induced unconsciousness and a lethal dose of potassium chloride that stopped her heart (Egan, 1990). Death was painless. For almost ten years Kevorkian played an active role in assisting upwards of a hundred terminally ill people in taking their lives. At the same time, with steadfast intent he provoked a searching and emotional discussion about the conditions under which a physician may take the life of a dying patient—an issue made all the more heated by widespread knowledge that health professionals every day pull the plug on patients who are brain dead but who are being kept physically alive by sophisticated medical apparatus.[9] Kevorkian was brought to trial several times but was not convicted of murder or professional misconduct until the spring of 1999, when he was found guilty of murder and sentenced to prison.

Passionate arguments pro and con continue. Right-to-life advocates claim that especially in this era of managed health care, patients will be pressured, albeit subtly, to ask to have their suffering lives terminated in order to spare their families the high costs of medical care. There is also the fear that physicians will lean in this direction, perhaps pressured by insurance companies that want to save money on expensive terminal medical care, and will influence the patient and his or her family to end the person's life. Among powerful groups opposing assisted suicide are the American Medical Association and the Catholic Church. In contrast, Kevorkian's supporters and others, such as the American Civil Liberties Union, believe that terminally ill people should have the right to end their suffering. Many of these supporters have for years objected to the intrusion of the state on what they regard as a person's inalienable right to make such life or death decisions.

In 1997, Oregon became the first state to have a law—the Death with Dignity Act, originally approved by voters in 1994 and reaffirmed by an even greater margin in 1997—that made physician-assisted suicide legal. This law permits a patient diagnosed by two physicians as having less than six months to live to seek a doctor's prescription for a lethal dose of barbiturates. But the law also requires that the prescribing physician determine that the patient is not suffering from depression or another mental illness[10] and that there be a waiting period of fifteen days before the prescription can be filled.

Since the law went into effect, there have been two interesting developments. First, there has *not* been an increase in such suicides, as had been feared by those who opposed the law as a "slippery slope" that would lead to euthanasia of old and sick people. Simply put, droves of terminally ill patients in Oregon have not begun asking their doctors to prescribe for them drugs that they could use themselves to commit suicide. Second, there has been an increase in the use of morphine to ease the pain of terminally ill patients. This in contrast to the unfortunate practice that is prevalent in other parts of the United States, wherein physicians very often undermedicate for pain. The result of this practice is that patients must endure the unendurable rather than live out their last months or days in relative peace. Indeed, a landmark 1994 study in New York found that nearly 90 percent of physicians caring for cancer patients reported knowingly prescribing too little pain medication (Jackson & Murphy,

---

[9] Decisions not to resuscitate terminally ill patients are made every day in hospitals. One informal estimate is that more than half the deaths in hospitals follow a decision to limit or withhold access to the kinds of life-sustaining equipment currently available. Furthermore, a report published in the *New England Journal of Medicine* in 1998 indicates that, over the course of their careers, close to 20 percent of physicians in the United States have been asked by terminally ill patients to help them die, and of this number, about 15 percent have written at least one prescription to hasten death and about 5 percent have administered at least one lethal injection. Physician-assisted suicide, whether legal or not, occurs with some frequency (Meier et al., 1998). Many people do not consider this practice euthanasia or suicide. Rather than ending life, "they see it as a desire to end dying, to pass gently into the night without tubes running down the nose and a ventilator insistently inflating lungs that have grown weary from the insult" (*Newsweek*, 1991, p. 44). Major legal, religious, and ethical issues whirl around decisions about ending dying among the terminally ill. Is this physician-assisted suicide?

[10] Take note that there is no requirement that the physician be a psychiatrist. In our experience, laws often fail to specify that a physician be required to demonstrate his or her competency to make judgments on mental disorders. Is this any different from a psychologist's making a diagnosis of an illness such as diabetes or tuberculosis?

Focus on Discovery 10.5

An Argument against Coercive Suicide Prevention

In bold and controversial publications on coercive suicide prevention Thomas Szasz (1986, 1999) argues that it is both impractical and immoral to prevent a person from committing suicide. It is impractical because we cannot really force people to live if they are intent on committing suicide unless—and this is when morality becomes an issue—we are prepared not only to commit them but to enslave them via heavy medication or even physical restraints. Even then, hospitalized patients do manage to take their own lives. Indeed, there is suggestive evidence that involuntary hospitalization may actually *increase* the chance of suicidal people killing themselves (Motto, 1976). Szasz asserted further that mental health professionals, in their understandable desire to help their patients, open themselves up to legal liability because, by taking it upon themselves to try to prevent suicide, they assume responsibility for something for which they cannot be responsible. In effect, they are promising more than they can deliver.

Further, Szasz argued that health professionals should not assume such responsibility—even if it were practical to do so—because people, including those seriously disturbed, should be accorded freedom to make choices. He allows one exception for what he calls impulsive suicide, when people are temporarily agitated, perhaps truly deranged, and need to be protected for a short while from their uncontrollable impulses. (Presumably he would broaden this protective stance in the case of children and adolescents, whose problem-solving abilities are not as well developed as those of adults and who therefore need extra social and professional support to protect themselves from impulsive acts.) He draws an analogy with patients coming out of general anesthesia, when it is common medical practice to strap them down lest their flailing about involuntarily lead to unintended and preventable harm. But there are limits here as well, including, in our own view, how we can know when we are dealing with an impulsive act rather than an act that the person has been thinking about and planning for a period of time.

Szasz is not against advising a person not to commit suicide or otherwise treating problems, such as depression, that might have a good deal to do with self-destructive thinking. It is forcible prevention against which he rails. Indeed, he believes that if professionals exclude coercive suicide prevention from their intervention options, they will be able to be more empathic with their patients and perhaps more helpful. He also suggests a psychiatric will, in which a patient, when not feeling suicidal, agrees ahead of time about how to be treated if later on he or she wishes to commit suicide. If the patient opts for coercive prevention in this will, then it would be all right. This strategy brings to mind the instructions Ulysses gave to his sailors before they were to pass by the coast of the Sirens, sea nymphs whose song compelled hapless mariners to commit suicide by throwing themselves into the sea.

He filled the ears of his people with wax, and suffered them to bind him with cords firmly to the mast. As they approached the Sirens' island, the sea was calm, and over the waters came the notes of music so ravishing and attractive that Ulysses struggled to get loose, and by cries and signs to his people begged to be released; but they, obedient to his previous orders, sprang forward and bound him still faster. They held on their course, and the music grew fainter till it ceased to be heard, when with joy Ulysses gave his companions the signal to unseal their ears, and they relieved him from his bonds. (Bulfinch's Mythology, 1979, p. 243)

Like the other arguments involving freedom and responsibility that Szasz has made over the years (see Chapter 18, p. 612, for a discussion of his seminal writings on mental illness and legal responsibility for crimes), his analysis is radical but worthy of serious consideration. In our view the principal omission in his thesis is that many, if not most, people who somehow weather suicidal crises, including those forcibly prevented from killing themselves, are grateful afterward for another chance at life. It may be that if we were to follow Szasz's urgings, we would miss opportunities to save savable lives. Szasz's rejoinder might be that one of the strongest predictors of a suicide attempt is a prior attempt. In other words, many people tend to try more than once to kill themselves. Therefore we would be repeatedly challenged to decide how drastically we were prepared to limit freedom (and sometimes degrade the person by restraints of one kind or another) in the hope of forestalling what may be inevitable. There are no easy answers here, but it is important to raise the questions.

Ulysses & his Companions after his return from the Shades, escaping the Sirens, & passing between the Rocks Scylla & Charybdis.

The song of the Sirens was resisted by Ulysses, who was lashed to the mast of his ship to prevent his suicide. According to Szasz's views, this would be an acceptable instance of voluntary, coercive suicide prevention.

1998; Rubin, 1998). Because of the Oregon law, physicians have not had to worry that prescribing morphine or other strong pain medication in doses sufficient to reduce the sometimes excruciating pain of diseases such as terminal cancer would expose them to charges of murder or medical malpractice for hastening the death of a terminally ill patient.

In 2001, Attorney General John Ashcroft attempted to block Oregon's Death with Dignity Act, declaring that assisted suicide is not an appropriate practice for physicians. The state of Oregon responded by filing suit (*State of Oregon v. Attorney General John Ashcroft*), and in April 2002, a Federal judge ruled that a federal agency cannot overstep powers relegated to the states without specific authority from Congress, thus leaving the Oregon law in place for now.

Concluding Comment

Cases such as that of Jack Kevorkian are unusual. For the most part mental health workers try to prevent suicide, and in that context they should not hesitate to inquire directly whether a client has thought of suicide. Above all, the clinician treating a suicidal person must be prepared to devote more energy and time than usual even for psychotic patients. Late-night phone calls and visits to the patient's home may be frequent. The therapist should realize that he or she is likely to become a singularly important figure in the suicidal person's life and should be prepared both for the extreme dependency of the patient and for the hostility and resentment that sometimes greet efforts to help. Table 10.7 contains general guidelines for dealing with suicidal patients.

Table 10.7   Guidelines for Treating Suicidal Clients

General Procedures

1. Talk about suicide openly and matter-of-factly.
2. Avoid pejorative explanations of suicidal behavior or motives.
3. Present a problem-solving theory of suicidal behavior, and maintain the stance that suicide is a maladaptive and/or ineffective solution.
4. Involve significant others, including other therapists.
5. Schedule sessions frequently enough, and maintain session discipline such that at least some therapy time is devoted to long-term treatment goals.
6. Stay aware of the multitude of variables impinging on patients, and avoid omnipotent taking or accepting of responsibility for patient's suicidal behaviors.
7. Maintain professional consultation with a colleague.
8. Maintain occasional contact with persons who reject therapy.

Pre–Crisis Planning Procedures

9. Anticipate and plan for crisis situations.
10. Continually assess the risk of suicide and parasuicide.
11. Be accessible.
12. Use local emergency/crisis/suicide services.
13. Give the patient a crisis card: telephone numbers of therapist, police, emergency, hospital, significant others.
14. Keep telephone numbers and addresses of patients and their significant others with you.
15. Make a short-term antisuicide contract, and keep it up to date.
16. Contact the patient's physician regarding the risks of overprescribing medications.
17. Do not force the patient to resort to suicidal talk or ideation in order to get your attention.
18. Express your caring openly; provide noncontingent warmth and attention.
19. Clarify and reinforce nonsuicidal responses to problems.
20. Identify to the patient likely therapist responses to the patient's suicidal behaviors (e.g., if the patient dies, the therapist will be sad, but will continue on with life).
21. Ensure that the patient has realistic expectations about the responses of others to future suicidal behaviors.

Source: Linehan, 1981, in H. Glazer and J. Clarkin (Eds.), *Depression, Behavioral and Directive Interpretation Strategies* (pp. 229–294), New York: Garland. Copyright © 1981 by Garland.

Summary

- Mood disorders involve disabling disturbances in emotion. DSM-IV-TR lists two principal kinds of mood disorders: major depression and bipolar disorder.

- In major, or unipolar, depression, a person experiences profound sadness as well as related problems such as sleep and appetite disturbances and loss of energy and self-esteem.

- Bipolar I disorder may include depression but also is characterized by mania. With mania, mood is elevated or irritable and the person becomes extremely active, talkative, and distractible. The person with bipolar I disorder may have episodes of mania alone, episodes of mania and of depression, or mixed episodes, in which both manic and depressive symptoms occur together.

- DSM-IV-TR also lists two chronic mood disorders—cyclothymia and dysthymia—in which symptoms are not considered sufficient to warrant a diagnosis of major depression or bipolar disorder. In cyclothymia, the person has frequent periods of depressed mood and hypomania, a change in behavior and mood that is less extreme than full-blown mania. In dysthymia the person is chronically depressed.

- Psychological theories of depression have been couched in psychoanalytic, cognitive, and interpersonal terms. Psychoanalytic formulations stress fixation at the oral stage (leading to a high level of dependency) and unconscious identification with a lost loved one whose desertion of the individual has resulted in anger turned inward. Beck's cognitive theory ascribes causal significance to negative schemas and cognitive biases and distortions. According to helplessness/hopelessness theory, early experiences in inescapable, hurtful situations instill a sense of hopelessness that can evolve into depression. Such individuals are likely to attribute failures to their own general and persistent inadequacies and faults. Interpersonal theory focuses on the problems depressed people have in relating to others and the negative responses they elicit from others.

- Psychological theories applied to the depressive phase of bipolar disorder are similar to those proposed for unipolar depression. The manic phase of bipolar disorder is considered a defense against a debilitating psychological state, such as low self-esteem.

- Biological theories suggest that there may be an inherited predisposition for mood disorders, particularly for bipolar disorder. Early neurochemical theories related depression to low levels of serotonin and bipolar disorder to norepinephrine (high in mania and low in depression). Recent research has focused on the postsynaptic receptors rather than on the amount of various transmitters. Overactivity of the hypothalamic-pituitary-adrenal axis is also found among depressive patients, indicating that the endocrine system may also influence mood disorders.

- Several psychological therapies are effective for depression. Psychoanalytic treatment tries to give the patient insight into childhood loss and inadequacy and later self-blame. The aim of Beck's cognitive therapy is to uncover negative and illogical patterns of thinking and to teach more realistic ways of viewing events, the self, and adversity. Interpersonal therapy, which focuses on the depressed patient's social interactions, can also be effective. Psychological therapies show promise in treating bipolar patients as well.

- Biological treatments are often used in conjunction with psychological treatment. Electroconvulsive shock and several antidepressant drugs (tricyclics, selective serotonin reuptake inhibitors, and MAO inhibitors) have proved their worth in lifting depression. Patients may avoid the excesses of manic and depressive periods through careful administration of lithium carbonate.

- DSM-IV-TR diagnoses of mood disorders in children use the adult criteria but allow for age-specific features such as irritability and aggressive behavior instead of or in addition to depressed mood.

- The self-annihilatory tendencies of suicide are not restricted to those who are depressed. A good deal of information can be applied to help prevent suicide, although no single theory is likely to account for the wide variety of motives and situations behind it. Most perspectives on suicide regard it as usually an act of desperation to end an existence that the person feels is unendurable.

- Most large communities have suicide prevention centers, and most therapists at one time or another have to deal with patients in suicidal crisis. Suicidal persons need to have their fears and concerns understood but not judged; clinicians must gradually and patiently point out to them that there are alternatives to self-destruction to be explored.

Key Terms

altruistic suicide
anomic suicide
attribution
bilateral ECT
bipolar I disorder
cyclothymic disorder
depression

dysthymic disorder
egoistic suicide
electroconvulsive therapy (ECT)
hypomania
learned helplessness theory
lithium carbonate

logotherapy
major depression
mania
mixed episode
monoamine oxidase (MAO) inhibitors

mood disorders
negative triad
suicide prevention centers
tricyclic drugs
unilateral ECT

Major Depressive Disorder

Janet called the mental health center to ask if someone could help her 5-year-old son, Adam. He had been having trouble sleeping for the past several weeks, and Janet was becoming concerned about his health. Adam refused to go to sleep at his regular bedtime and also woke up at irregular intervals throughout the night. Whenever he woke up, Adam would come downstairs to be with Janet. Her initial reaction had been sympathetic, but as the cycle came to repeat itself night after night, Janet's tolerance grew thin, and she became more argumentative. She found herself engaged in repeated battles that usually ended when she agreed to let him sleep in her room. Janet felt guilty about giving in to a 5-year-old's demands, but it seemed like the only way they would ever get any sleep. The family physician was unable to identify a physical explanation for Adam's problem; he suggested that Janet contact a psychologist. This advice led Janet to inquire about the mental health center's series of parent training groups.

Applicants for the groups were routinely screened during an individual intake interview. The therapist began by asking several questions about Janet and her family. Janet was 30 years old and had been divorced from her husband, David, for a little more than one year. Adam was the youngest of Janet's three children; Jennifer was 10 and Claire was 8. Janet had resumed her college education on a part-time basis when Adam was 2 years old. She had hoped to finish her bachelor's degree at the end of the next semester and enter law school in the fall. Unfortu-nately, she had withdrawn from classes one month prior to her appointment at the mental health center. Her current plans were indefinite. She spent almost all of her time at home with Adam.

Janet and the children lived in a large, comfortable house that she had received as part of her divorce settlement. Finances were a major concern to Janet, but she managed to make ends meet through the combination of student loans, a grant-in-aid from the university, and child-support payments from David. David lived in a nearby town with a younger woman whom he had married shortly after the divorce. He visited Janet and the children once or twice every month and took the children to spend weekends with him once a month.

Having collected the necessary background information, the therapist asked for a description of Adam's sleep difficulties. This discussion covered the sequence of a typical evening's events. It was clear during this discussion that Janet felt com-pletely overwhelmed. At several points during the interview, Janet was on the verge of tears. Her eyes were watery, and her voice broke as they discussed her response to David's occasional visits. The therapist, therefore, suggested that they put off a further analysis of Adam's problems and spend some time discussing Janet's situation in a broader perspective.

Janet's mood had been depressed since her husband had asked for a divorce. She felt sad, discouraged, and lonely. This feel-ing had become even more severe just prior to her withdrawal from classes at the university (one year after David's departure). When David left, she remembered feeling "down in the dumps,"but she could usually cheer herself up by playing with the children or going for a walk. Now she was nearing desperation. She cried frequently and for long periods of time. Nothing seemed to cheer her up. She had lost interest in her friends, and the children seemed to be more of a burden than ever. Her depression was somewhat worse in the morning, when it seemed that she would never be able to make it through the day.

Janet was preoccupied by her divorce from David and spent hours each day brooding about the events that led to their separation. These worries interfered considerably with her ability to concentrate and seemed directly related to her withdrawal from the university. She had been totally unable to study assigned readings or concentrate on lectures. Withdrawing from school precipitated further problems. She was no longer eligible for student aid and would have to begin paying back her loans within a few months. In short, one problem led to another, and her attitude became increasingly pessimistic.

Janet blamed herself for the divorce, although she also har-bored considerable resentment toward David and his new wife. She believed that her return to school had placed additional strain on an already problematic relationship, and she wondered whether she had acted selfishly. The therapist noted that Janet's reasoning about her marriage often seemed vague and illogical. She argued that she had been a poor marital partner and cited several examples of her own misconduct. These included events and circumstances that struck the therapist as being very common and perhaps expected differences between men and women. For example, Janet spent more money than he did on clothes, did not share his enthusiasm for sports, and frequently tried to engage David in discussions about his personal habits that annoyed her and the imperfections of their relationship. Of course, one could easily argue that David had not been sufficiently concerned about his own appearance (spending too *little* effort on his own wardrobe), that he had been too preoccu-pied with sports, and that he had avoided her sincere efforts to work on their marital difficulties. But Janet blamed herself. Rather than viewing these things as simple differences in their interests and per-sonalities, Janet saw them as evidence of her own failures. She blew these matters totally out of proportion until they appeared to her to be terrible sins. Janet also generalized from her marriage to other relationships in her life. If her first marriage had failed, how could she ever expect to develop a satisfactory relationship with another man? Furthermore, Janet had begun to question her value as a friend and parent. The collapse of her marriage seemed to affect the manner in which she viewed all of her social relationships.

The future looked bleak from her current perspective, but she had not given up all hope. Her interest in solving Adam's problem, for example, was an encouraging sign. Although she was not optimistic about the chances of success, she was willing to try to become a more effective parent.

Social History

Janet was reserved socially when she was a child. She tended to have one or two special friends with whom she spent much of her time outside of school, but she felt awkward and self-conscious in larger groups of children. Although her friends were important to her and she enjoyed spending time with them, Janet waited for them to contact her. She did not initiate activities and hesitated to express her own preferences when they were trying to decide what to do. In retrospect, Janet attributed this lack of assertiveness to her fear that her friends would abandon her or ridicule her interests. She was also self-conscious about her weight. She was not obese, but she tended to be a bit plump and was therefore afraid that the others would tease her if she drew attention to herself.

This friendship pattern persisted throughout high school. She was interested in boys and dated intermittently until her junior year in high school, when she began to date one boy on a regular basis. Janet was certain that she was in love with him and soon lost all contact with the few girlfriends with whom she had been close. She and her boyfriend spent all of their time together. Janet remembered that the other kids teased them about acting as if they were married. This criticism troubled Janet, even though she fully expected that they would be married shortly after they graduated from high school.

Her marriage plans did not work out, however. She and her boyfriend broke up during Janet's first year in college. Janet met David a few weeks afterward, and they were married the following summer. Janet later wondered whether she had rushed into her relationship with David primarily to avoid the vacuum created by her previous boyfriend's sudden exit. Whatever her motivation might have been, her marriage was followed shortly by her first pregnancy, which precipitated her withdrawal from the university. For the next seven years, Janet was occupied as a full-time mother and housekeeper.

When Adam was two years old and able to attend a day-care center, Janet decided to resume her college education. Her relationship with David became increasingly strained. They had even less time than usual to spend with each other. David resented his increased household responsibilities. Janet was no longer able to prepare meals for the family every night of the week, so David had to learn to cook. He also had to share the cleaning and drive the children to many of their lessons and social activities. A more balanced and stable relationship would have been able to withstand the stress associated with these changes, but Janet and David were unable to adjust. Instead of working to improve their communications, they bickered continuously. The final blow came when David met another woman to whom he was attracted and who offered him an alternative to the escalating hostility with Janet. He asked for a divorce and moved to an apartment.

Janet was shaken by David's departure, in spite of the fact that they had not been happy together. Fortunately, she did have a few friends to whom she could turn for support. The most important one was a neighbor who had children of approximately the same ages as Janet's daughters. There were also two couples with whom she and David had socialized. They were all helpful for the first few weeks, but she quickly lost contact with the couples. It was awkward to get together as a threesome, and Janet had never been close enough with the women to preserve their relationships on an individual basis. That left the neighbor as her sole adviser and confidante, the only person with whom Janet felt she could discuss her feelings openly.

For the next few months, Janet was able to continue her studies. With the children's help she managed the household chores and kept up with her work. She even found time for some brief social activities. She agreed to go out on two blind dates arranged by people with whom she and David had been friends. These were generally unpleasant encounters; one of her dates was boring and unattractive, and the other was obnoxiously aggressive. After the latter experience, she discontinued the minimal efforts she had made to develop new friendships.

As time wore on, Janet found herself brooding more and more about the divorce. She was gaining weight, and the children began to comment on her appearance. To make matters worse, Claire became sick just prior to Janet's midterm exams. The added worry of Claire's health and her concern about missed classes and lost studying time contributed substantially to a decline in Janet's mood. She finally realized that she would have to withdraw from her classes to avoid receiving failing grades.

By this point, one month prior to her appointment at the mental health center, she had lost interest in most of her previous activities. Even casual reading had come to be a tedious chore. She did not have any hobbies because she never had enough time. She also found that her best friend, the neighbor, was becoming markedly aloof. When Janet called, she seldom talked for more than a few minutes before finding an excuse to hang up. Their contacts gradually diminished to an occasional wave across the street or a quick, polite conversation when they picked up their children from school. It seemed that her friend had grown tired of Janet's company.

This was Janet's situation when she contacted the mental health center. Her mood was depressed and anxious. She was preoccupied with financial concerns and her lack of social relationships. Adam's sleeping problem, which had begun about one week after she withdrew from her classes, was the last straw. She felt that she could no longer control her difficult situation and recognized that she needed help.

Conceptualization and Treatment

The therapist and Janet discussed her overall situation and agreed that Adam was only a small part of the problem. They decided to work together on an individual basis instead of having Janet join the parent training group.

Janet's depression was clearly precipitated by her divorce, which had a drastic impact on many areas of her life. Increased financial burdens were clearly part of this picture, but interpersonal relationships were even more meaningful. Although the marriage had been far from ideal in terms of meeting Janet's needs, her relationship with David had been one important part of the way in which Janet thought about herself. She had lost one of her most important roles (as a wife). The therapist believed that an enduring improvement in her mood would depend on her success in developing new relationships and expanded roles for herself. And she would eventually need to learn parenting skills that would allow her to perform her maternal role more successfully. In other words, the therapist adopted a problem-solving approach to Janet's situation. He was particularly concerned about the passive and ruminative way in which she had begun to respond to the circumstances in her life. The therapist decided to encourage her to engage more actively with her environment while also teaching her to perform specific behaviors more effectively.

As an initial step, the therapist asked Janet to list all of the activities that she enjoyed. He wanted to shift attention away from the unpleasant factors with which Janet was currently preoccupied. Most of the activities Janet mentioned were things that she had not done for several months or years. For example, prior to her return to school, her favorite pastime had been riding horses. She said that she would like to begin riding again, but she felt that it was prohibitively expensive and time consuming. With considerable prodding from the therapist, Janet also listed a few other activities. These included talking with a friend over a cup of coffee, listening to music late at night after the children were asleep, and going for walks in the woods behind her home. In some cases, Janet indicated that these activities used to be pleasant, but she did not think that they would be enjoyable at the present time.

Despite Janet's ambivalence, the therapist encouraged her to pick one activity that she would try at least twice before their next meeting. A short walk in the woods seemed like the most practical alternative, considering that Adam might interrupt listening to music and she did not want to call Susan. The therapist also asked Janet to call the campus riding club to inquire about their activities.

At the same time that the therapist encouraged Janet to increase her activity level, he also began to concentrate on an assessment of her interactions with other people. For several sessions, they covered topics such as selecting situations in which Janet might be likely to meet people with whom she would be interested in developing a friendship, initiating a conversation, maintaining a conversation by asking the other person a series of consecutive questions, and other elementary issues. Having identified areas that were problematic for Janet, they discussed solutions and actually practiced, or role-played, various social interactions.

During the first few weeks of treatment, Janet's mood seemed to be improving. Perhaps most important was her luck in finding a part-time job at a local riding stable. She learned of the opening when she called to ask about the campus riding club. They were looking for someone who would feed and exercise the horses every morning. The wages were low, but she was allowed to ride as long as she wanted each day without charge. Furthermore, the schedule allowed her to finish before the girls returned from school. The money also helped her return Adam to the day-care center on a part-time basis. Janet still felt depressed when she was at home, but she loved to ride and it helped to know that she would go to work in the morning.

An unfortunate sequence of events led to a serious setback shortly after it seemed that Janet's mood was beginning to improve. Her financial aid had been discontinued, and she could no longer cover her monthly mortgage payments. Within several weeks, she received a notice from the bank threatening to foreclose her mortgage and sell her house. Her appearance was noticeably changed when she arrived for her next appointment. She was apathetic and lethargic. She cried through most of the session, and her outlook had grown distinctly more pessimistic. The therapist was particularly alarmed by an incident that Janet described as happening the previous day. She had been filling her car with gas when a mechanic at the service station mentioned that her muffler sounded like it was cracked. He told her that she should get it fixed right away because of the dangerous exhaust fumes. In his words, "that's a good way to kill yourself." The thought of suicide had not occurred to Janet prior to this comment, but she found that she could not get it out of her mind. She was frightened by the idea and tried to distract herself by watching television. The thoughts continued to intrude despite these efforts.

The therapist immediately discussed several changes in the treatment plan with Janet. He arranged for her to consult a psychiatrist, who prescribed fluoxetine (Prozac), an antidepressant drug. She also agreed to increase the frequency of her appointments at the clinic to three times a week. These changes were primarily motivated by the onset of suicidal ideation. More drastic action, such as hospitalization or calling relatives for additional support, did not seem to be necessary because her thoughts were not particularly lethal. For example, she said that she did not want to die, even though she was thinking quite a lot about death. The idea frightened her, and she did not have a specific plan arranged by which she would accomplish her own death. Nevertheless, the obvious deterioration in her condition warranted a more intense treatment program.

The next month proved to be a difficult one for Janet, but she was able to persevere. Three weeks after she began taking the medication, her mood seemed to brighten. The suicidal ideation disappeared, she became more talkative, and she resumed most of her normal activities. The people who owned the riding stable were understanding and held Janet's new job for her until she was able to return. The financial crisis was solved, at least temporarily, when her father agreed to provide her with substantial assistance. In fact, he expressed surprise and some dismay that she had never asked him for help in the past or even told him that she was in financial trouble. The problem-solving and social skills program progressed well after Janet began taking medication. Within several weeks, she was able to reestablish her friendship with Susan. She was able to meet a few people at the riding stable, and her social network seemed to be widening.

After Janet's mood had improved, the issue of Adam's sleeping problem was addressed. The therapist explained that Janet needed to set firm limits on Adam's manipulative behavior. Her inconsistency in dealing with his demands, coupled with the attention that he received during the bedtime scene, could be thought of as leading to intermittent reinforcement of his inappropriate behavior. Janet and the therapist worked out a simple set of responses that she would follow whenever he got up and came downstairs. She would offer him a drink, take him back to his room, tuck him in bed, and leave immediately. Ten days after the procedure was implemented, Adam began sleeping through the night without interruption. This rapid success enhanced Janet's sense of control over her situation. Her enthusiasm led her to enroll in the parent training program for which she had originally applied. She continued to improve her relationship with her children.

Janet's individual therapy sessions were discontinued nine months after her first appointment. At that point, she was planning to return to school, was still working part-time at the riding stable, and had started to date one of the men she met at work. Her children were all healthy, and she had managed to keep their house. She continued to take antidepressant medication.

Discussion

A sad or dysphoric mood is obviously the most prominent feature of clinical depression. Depressed patients describe themselves as feeling discouraged, hopeless, and apathetic. This dejected emotional state is usually accompanied by a variety of unpleasant thoughts that may include suicidal ideation. Beck (1967) has described these cognitive features of depression as the *depressive triad*: a negative view of the self, the world, and the future. Depressed people see themselves as inadequate and unworthy. They are often filled with guilt and remorse over apparently ordinary and trivial events. These patients hold a similarly dim view of their environment. Everyday experiences and social interactions are interpreted in the most critical fashion. The future seems bleak and empty. In fact, some extremely depressed patients find it impossible to imagine any future at all.

Clinical depression is identified by changes in several important areas in the person's life. In addition to a prominent and relatively persistent dysphoric mood, *DSM-IV-TR* (p. 356) lists several features for major depressive episodes. Specifically, at least five of the following symptoms must have been present for at least two weeks if the patient is to meet the criteria for this diagnostic category:

1. Depressed mood most of the day, nearly everyday, as indicated either by subjective report (e.g., feels sad or empty) or observation made by others (e.g., appears tearful)

2. Markedly diminished interest or pleasure in all, or almost all, activities most of the day, nearly every day (as indicated either by subjective account or observation by others)

3. Significant weight loss when not dieting or weight gain (for example, a change of more than 5 percent of body weight in a month), or decrease or increase in appetite nearly every day

4. Insomnia or hypersomnia (prolonged sleep) nearly every day

5. Psychomotor agitation or retardation nearly every day (observable by others, not merely subjective feelings of restlessness or being slowed down)

6. Fatigue or loss of energy nearly every day

7. Feelings of worthlessness or excessive or inappropriate guilt (which may be delusional) nearly every day (not merely self-reproach or guilt about being sick)

8. Diminished ability to think or concentrate, or indecisiveness, nearly every day (either by subjective account or as observed by others)

9. Recurrent thoughts of death (not just fear of dying), recurrent suicidal ideation without a specific plan, or a suicide attempt or a specific plan for committing suicide

Janet clearly fit these criteria. Her mood had been markedly depressed since her separation from David. She had gained considerable weight—25 pounds in nine months. Her concentration was severely impaired, as evidenced by her inability to study and her loss of interest in almost everything. Excessive and inappropriate guilt was clearly a prominent feature of her constant brooding about the divorce. Although she did not actually attempt to harm herself, she experienced a distressing period of ruminative suicidal ideation. Sleep impairment may also have been a problem, but it was difficult to evaluate in the context of Adam's behavior. Prior to her first visit at the clinic, Janet had been sleeping less than her usual number of hours per night, and she reported considerable fatigue. It was difficult to know whether she would have been able to sleep if Adam had not been so demanding of her attention throughout the night.

Most therapists agree that it is important to recognize the difference between clinical depression and other states of unhappiness and disappointment. Consider, for example, people who are mourning the loss of a friend or relative. *DSM-IV-TR* suggests that a diagnosis of major depressive episode should be made only if bereavement persists for more than two months (assuming that the person meets the diagnostic criteria for this condition). Is this a qualitative or a quantitative distinction? Are patients who might be considered clinically depressed simply more unhappy than their peers, or are these phenomena completely distinct? This is one of the most interesting and difficult questions facing investigators in the field of mood disorders. The present diagnostic system handles the problem by including an intermediate category, dysthymia, that lies between major depressive disorder and normal mood. This category includes patients who exhibit chronic depressed symptoms that are not of sufficient severity to meet the criteria for major mood disorder.

Etiological Considerations

Several psychological models have been proposed to account for the development of major depression. Each model focuses on somewhat different features of depressive disorders (e.g., interpersonal relations, inactivity, or self-deprecating thoughts), but most share an interest in the role of negative or stressful events in the precipitation of major depression.

Freud's explanation for the development of depression began with a comparison between depression and bereavement (Freud, 1917, 1925).[1] The two conditions are similar. Both involve a deject-

---

[1] Freud pointed out that his account was intended to apply to only a subset of depressed patients and that biological factors were probably more important in other cases.

ed mood, a loss of interest in the outside world, and an inhibition of activity. One principal feature distinguishes between the person who is depressed and the person who is mourning: a disturbance of self-regard. Depressed people chastise themselves, saying that they are worthless, morally depraved, and worthy of punishment. Freud noted the disparity between such extreme negative views and the more benign opinions of other people who do not hold the depressed person in such contempt. In other words, the depressed person's view does not seem to be an accurate self-perception. Freud went on to argue that depressed people are not *really* complaining about themselves but are, in fact, expressing hostile feelings that pertain to someone else. Depression is therefore the manifestation of a process in which anger is turned inward and directed against the self instead of against its original object.

Why would some people direct hostility against themselves? Freud argued that the foundation for this problem is laid in early childhood. For various reasons, people who are prone to depression have formed dependent interpersonal relationships. This dependency fosters frustration and hostility. Because these negative feelings might threaten the relationship if they are expressed openly, they are denied awareness. Problems then arise when the relationship is ended, for whatever reason. The depressed person's ego presumably identifies with the lost loved one. The intense hostility that had been felt for that person is now turned against the self, or *introjected*. Following this model, treatment would consist of an attempt to make the client aware of these unconscious, hostile impulses. Their more direct expression would presumably eliminate the depression.

At least one aspect of this model seems consistent with Janet's situation. She had, in fact, formed a series of intense, dependent relationships with men, beginning in high school. One might argue that her depression was precipitated by the loss incurred during her separation and divorce from David. She resented the separation deeply. Her guilt might be seen as a criticism of David's behavior. Other aspects of Janet's behavior, however, are inconsistent with Freud's model. Although Janet was critical of herself, she was also quite vocal in David's presence. They fought openly several times, both before and after the divorce, and he was fully aware of Janet's anger and resentment. It therefore seems unlikely that Janet's depression was a simple manifestation of misdirected hostility. It is also unlikely that her depression would be relieved by simply encouraging her to express her feelings more openly.

More recent attempts to explain the development of depression in psychological terms have borrowed and extended various aspects of Freud's psychoanalytic model. One important consideration involves his observation that the onset of depression is often preceded by a dependent personality style and then precipitated by the loss of an important relationship. Personality factors and relational distress may help to explain the fact that women are twice as likely as men to develop major depression.[2] Dependent people base their self-esteem on acceptance and approval by others. Some authors have suggested that, throughout their social development,

women are frequently taught to think this way about themselves (Gilligan, 1982; Notman & Nadelson, 1995). Stereotypes of female roles include descriptions of personality traits such as being passive, dependent, and emotional (while men are presumably more often encouraged to be aggressive, autonomous, and rational). An extension of this hypothesis holds that women are more likely than men to define themselves in terms of their relationships with other people. Women would then presumably be more distressed by marital difficulties and divorce. In Janet's case, the loss of her relationship with David was certainly an important consideration in the onset of her depression. Her sense of self-worth was severely threatened by the divorce, in spite of the fact that her marriage had been far from ideal.

Stressful life events play a causal role in the etiology of depression (see Kessler, 1997; Monroe et al., 1999). One classic study has received considerable attention because it led to the development of a model that begins to explain the relationship between environmental conditions and the onset of depression. Brown and Harris (1978) found an increased incidence of stressful events in the lives of depressed women, but only with regard to a particular subset of such events—those that were severe and involved long-term consequences for the woman's well-being. Divorce and marital separation were prominent among these events, which also included events such as illness, loss of a job, and many other types of personal adversity. The impact of a stressful event apparently depends on the meaning that the event has for the person. Severe events that occur in the context of ongoing difficulties (such as a chronically distressed marriage) and events that occur in areas of a woman's life to which she is particularly committed (such as a child's health or the development of a career) are most likely to lead to the onset of depression (Brown, 1993; Brown, Bifulco, & Harris, 1987).

The association between stressful life events and depression is apparently bidirectional. Stress may cause depression, but depression also causes stress. In comparison to women who are not depressed and women with medical disorders, depressed women generate higher levels of stress, especially in interpersonal relationships such as marriage (Hammen, 2002). This result indicates the operation of a dynamic process. Stressors that are not related to the person's own behavior may precipitate the onset of a depressed mood. The depressed person may then engage in maladaptive ways of coping with the immediate situation, and these dysfunctional behaviors may lead to even higher levels of stress.

Several of these concepts are consistent with Janet's situation. She had clearly experienced a high level of stress in the months before she entered therapy. The divorce from David is one obvious example. Her difficulties with the children may be another instance. When Claire's illness eventually forced her to withdraw from the university, there were important long-term consequences for her graduation and subsequent plans to enter law school.

Stressful life events are likely to precipitate depression, particularly in the absence of adequate social support. The manner in which these experiences combine to take their effect, however, is currently a matter of dispute and speculation. It is important to remember that most people experience stressful events at one time or another, but most people do not become seriously depressed.

---

[2] Specific epidemiological evidence regarding the prevalence of unipolar and bipolar mood disorders is presented in Chapter 8 (p. 129).

What factors make some people more psychologically vulnerable? Do people who are prone to depression respond differently than others to the problems of everyday life? Are they less likely than other people to establish or maintain a protective social support network? These questions have been addressed by other etiological models.

Like Freud, social learning theorists (Coyne, 1999; Joiner, Coyne, & Blalock, 1999) have also emphasized the importance of interpersonal relationships and social skills (cf. narcissism and dependence) in the development and maintenance of depression. This model provides an interesting account of the way in which depressed people respond to stressful life events and the effect that these responses have on other people who constitute their social support systems. Other people respond empathically and are initially attentive when the depressed person talks about depressing experiences, yet, the long-range result of this process is usually negative. The depressed person's few remaining friends eventually become tired of this behavior and begin to avoid further interactions. Whatever sources of social support may have been available are eventually driven away. One important factor in this regard is a deficit in social skills. Depressed people may be ineffective in their interactions with other people. An important aspect of treatment would therefore be to identify specific skills in which the person is deficient and to teach the person more effective ways of interacting with others.

Several aspects of this model are consistent with the present case. After her separation from David, Janet had become isolated. Her long discussions with her neighbor had eventually soured their relationship and eliminated one of her last sources of social support. When Janet and her therapist discussed things that she might do to meet new friends, she seemed lost. The few attempts that she had made, such as her blind dates, had gone badly, and she did not know where else to begin.

Another consideration in social learning views of depression involves the way in which people respond to the onset of a depressed mood. Some people try to distract themselves from negative emotions by becoming involved in some activity. Others respond in a more passive fashion and tend to ruminate about the sources of their distress. Nolen-Hoeksema (1990, 2000) proposed that people who respond in a passive, ruminative way will experience longer and more severe periods of depression. She also suggested that this factor may account for gender differences in the prevalence of depression because women are more likely than men to employ this response style. Janet's behavior following her divorce fits nicely with Nolen-Hoeksema's conceptual framework. Although Janet initially tried to cope actively with her various problems, she soon relinquished most of her efforts to find new friends or to keep up with her studies. She frequently found herself brooding about the divorce and the hopeless nature of her circumstances. Her therapist encouraged Janet to engage more frequently in pleasant activities in an effort to break this cycle of passive, ruminative behavior.

In addition to the social and behavioral aspects of depression, it is also important to consider the way in which depressed people perceive or interpret events in their environment. What do they think about themselves and things that happen in their world? More specifically, how do they explain the experience of negative events? Beck (1987)[3] has proposed that certain negative cognitive patterns play a prominent role in people who are prone to the development of depression. The hopelessness theory of depression presents a similar view (Abramson, Metalsky, & Alloy, 1989; Alloy et al., 1999).[4] According to this theory, the perceived occurrence of negative life events may lead to the development of hopelessness, which in turn causes the onset of symptoms of depression. Two cognitive elements define the state of hopelessness: (1) the expectation that highly desired outcomes will not occur or that highly aversive outcomes will occur, and (2) the belief that the person cannot do anything (is helpless) to change the likelihood that these events will occur.

The crucial link in this causal chain occurs between the perception of negative life events and the appearance of hopelessness. Why do some people become hopeless after such experiences while others do not? The theory holds that the likelihood of developing hopelessness will depend on the person's inferences regarding three factors: the cause of the event, the consequences of the event, and the implications of the event with regard to the self. For example, hopeless depression is likely to occur if the person views a negative event as being important and also attributes the event to factors that are enduring (stable) and likely to affect many outcomes (global). The theory also recognizes that the perceived consequences of the negative event may be as important as inferred causes. If the person views the negative consequences of the event as important, persistent, and wide-ranging, depression will be more likely to develop than if the consequences are viewed as unimportant, short-lived, or limited in scope. The third and final consideration involves negative inferences about the self. Depression is a more likely outcome if the person interprets a negative event to mean that she or he is a less able, worthy, or desirable person.

Depressed people do express an inordinately high proportion of negative statements about themselves and how they relate to the world. Janet's verbal behavior provided several clear examples of the negative schemas that Beck has described, and her interpretation of the events leading up to and surrounding her divorce fit nicely with the hopelessness theory. She believed that the disintegration of her marriage was her own fault rather than David's; she argued that her failure in that relationship was characteristic of her interactions with all other men rather than specific to one person; and she maintained that she would never be able to change this pattern of behavior.

Noone doubts that depressed people express negative thoughts. The difficult question, and one that is currently a matter of considerable controversy, is whether cognitive events play a central, formative role in the development of depression. Are they antecedents or consequences of emotional changes? Cognitive theorists have reported a considerable amount of empirical evidence in support of their position (e.g., Gotlib & Neubauer, 2000). For example, one longitudinal study

---

[3] Specific epidemiological evidence regarding the prevalence of unipolar and bipolar mood disorders is presented in Chapter 8 (p. 129).

[4] This is a revision of the helplessness model of depression that was originally proposed by Seligman (1975) and subsequently revised by Abramson, Seligman, and Teasdale (1978).

of college students found that those who displayed negative cognitive styles at the beginning of the freshman year were much more likely than a comparison group subsequently to develop a major depressive disorder (Alloy, Abramson, & Francis, 1999).

Treatment

Janet's treatment involved a combination of psychotherapy and antidepressant medication. Following the social learning/interpersonal model, her therapist focused on increasing Janet's activity level and helping her learn new social skills. By encouraging activities such as riding, the therapist hoped to interrupt and reverse the ongoing, interactive process in which social isolation, rumination, and inactivity led to increased depression, depression led to further withdrawal, and so on. Through the development of new response patterns, particularly those involving interpersonal communication and parenting skills, he hoped to enable Janet to deal more effectively with future stressful events. Increased social activity and more effective communication would also lead to a more supportive social network that might help reduce the impact of stressful events.

The therapy that Janet received was, in many respects, quite similar to another psychological approach to treating depression that is known as interpersonal psychotherapy, or IPT (Frank, 1996; Klerman, Weissman, Rounsaville, & Chevron, 1984). The focus of IPT is the connection between depressive symptoms and current interpersonal problems. Relatively little attention is paid to long-standing personality problems or developmental issues. The treatment takes a practical, problem-solving approach to resolving the sorts of daily conflicts in close relationships that can exacerbate and maintain depression. Deficits in social skills are addressed in an active and supportive fashion. The depressed person is also encouraged to pursue new activities that might take the place of relationships or occupational roles that have been lost. Therapy sessions often include nondirective discussions of social difficulties and unexpressed or unacknowledged negative emotions as well as role-playing to practice specific social skills.

Antidepressant medication was introduced when the risk of suicide became apparent. Janet's suicidal ideation was not extremely lethal. She had not planned a particular method by which she might end her life, and she reported that the idea of harming herself was frightening. The risk would have been much greater if she did have more specific plans and if she had really wanted to die. Nevertheless, her morbid ruminations marked a clear deterioration in her condition that called for more intensive treatment. Three general classes of drugs are useful in the treatment of depression: tricyclics (TCAs), monoamine oxidase (MAO) inhibitors, and selective serotonin reuptake inhibitors (SSRIs). Improvements in the patient's mood and other specific affective symptoms are typically evident after two to four weeks of drug treatment. Their continued administration also reduces the probability of symptomatic relapse.

Janet was given fluoxetine (Prozac), which is from the third type of antidepressant medications. Selective serotonin reuptake inhibitors (SSRIs) were developed in the 1980s and now account for most prescriptions written for antidepressant medication (Hirschfeld, 2001). Additional examples of SSRIs include fluvoxamine (Luvox),

sertraline (Zoloft), and paroxetine (Paxil). The SSRIs inhibit the reuptake of serotonin into the presynaptic nerve ending and therefore increase the amount of serotonin available in the synaptic cleft. SSRIs have fewer side effects (such as weight gain, constipation, and drowsiness) than TCAs or MAO inhibitors; they are easier to take (one pill a day instead of experimenting for weeks to find the proper dosage); and they are less dangerous if the patient takes an overdose. This does not mean, of course, that they are without side effects of their own. Some patients experience nausea, headaches, fatigue, and restlessness, although these symptoms are usually mild and transient. Controlled outcome studies indicate that Prozac and other SSRIs are at least as effective as traditional forms of antidepressant medication (Kroenke et al., 2001; Masand & Gupta, 1999).

How do the effects of medication and psychotherapy compare in the treatment of depression? Research studies indicate that both forms of treatment can be effective. One ambitious outcome study known as the Treatment of Depression Collaborative Research Program (TDCRP) compared the efficacy of two types of psychotherapy—cognitive and interpersonal therapy—with antidepressant medication over 16 weeks of treatment (Elkin, 1994; Shea & Elkin, 1996). Unipolar depressed outpatients were randomly assigned to one of four treatment groups: interpersonal therapy, cognitive therapy, medication (a tricyclic antidepressant), or placebo plus "clinical management" (extensive support and encouragement).

The results of this study were generally quite positive over the short run. All three types of active treatment were superior to the placebo plus clinical management condition in terms of their ability to reduce depression and improve overall levels of functioning. Patients improved somewhat more rapidly if they were receiving medication, but the rate of improvement in both psychotherapy groups caught up to the drug condition by the end of treatment. Cognitive and interpersonal therapy were equivalent to antidepressant medication in terms of their ability to treat less severely disturbed patients. People who were more severely depressed responded best to medication. Furthermore, within the severely depressed patients, interpersonal therapy was more effective than cognitive therapy (Klein & Ross, 1993).

Follow-up evaluations conducted 18 months after the completion of treatment were less encouraging than the original outcome data, however. By that point, patients in the three active treatment groups were no longer functioning at a higher level than those who received only the placebo and clinical management. Less than 30 percent of the patients who were considered markedly improved at the end of treatment were still nondepressed at follow-up. This aspect of the study's results points to the need for continued efforts to improve currently available treatment methods. Several years after the initial treatment program was conducted, results from the TDCRP are still being debated, particularly as they apply to the value of cognitive-behavior therapy in the treatment of depression (Elkin et al., 1996, Jacobson & Hollon, 1996).

One obvious disadvantage associated with both medication and psychotherapy is the extended delay involved in achieving therapeutic effects. In the face of a serious suicidal threat, for example, the therapist may not be able to wait several weeks for a change in the patient's adjustment. There are also many patients who do not respond positively to medication or psychosocial treatment approaches. Another form of intervention that may be tried with depressed patients, particularly if they exhibit profound motor retardation and have failed to respond positively to antidepressant medication, is electroconvulsive therapy (ECT). In the standard ECT procedure, a brief seizure is induced by passing an electrical current between two electrodes that have been placed over the patient's temples. A full course of treatment generally involves the induction of six to eight seizures spaced at 48-hour intervals. The procedure was first introduced as a treatment for schizophrenia, but it soon became apparent that it was most effective with depressed patients. Many studies have supported this conclusion (Krystal & Coffey, 1997; Stevens et al., 1996).

Much of the controversy surrounding ECT is based on misconceptions concerning the procedure and its effects. Although it is often referred to as "shock therapy," ECT does not involve the perception of an electrical current. In fact, a shortacting anesthetic is administered prior to the seizure so that the patient is not conscious when the current is applied. Many of the deleterious side effects of ECT have been eliminated by modifications in the treatment procedure, such as the use of muscle relaxants to avoid bone fractures during the seizure. The extent and severity of memory loss can be greatly reduced by the use of unilateral electrode placement. If both electrodes are placed over the nondominant hemisphere of the patient's brain, the patient can experience less verbal memory impairment, but the treatment may be less effective in terms of its antidepressant results (Calev et al., 1995; Royal College of Psychiatrists, 1989). There is, of course, the serious question of permanent changes in brain structure and function. Some critics of ECT have argued that it produces irreversible neurological impairment. Proponents of ECT maintain that the evidence for this conclusion is inadequate (Devanand et al., 1994). Most of the objections to the use of ECT are based on misconceptions. The evidence supporting its therapeutic efficacy seems to justify the continued use of ECT with some severely depressed patients who have not responded to less intrusive forms of treatment.

11

Schizophrenia

All of a sudden things weren't going so well. I began to lose control of my life and, most of all, myself. I couldn't concentrate on my schoolwork, I couldn't sleep, and when I did sleep, I had dreams about dying. I was afraid to go to class, imagined that people were talking about me, and on top of that I heard voices. I called my mother in Pittsburgh and asked for her advice. She told me to move off campus into an apartment with my sister.

After I moved in with my sister, things got worse. I was afraid to go outside and when I looked out of the window, it seemed that everyone outside was yelling, "Kill her, kill her." My sister forced me to go to school. I would go out of the house until I knew she had gone to work; then I would return home. Things continued to get worse. I imagined that I had a foul body odor and I sometimes took up to six showers a day. I recall going to the grocery store one day, and I imagined that the people in the store were saying, "Get saved, Jesus is the answer." Things worsened—I couldn't remember a thing. I had a notebook full of reminders telling me what to do on that particular day. I couldn't remember my schoolwork, and I would study from 6:00 P.M. until 4:00 A.M. but never had the courage to go to class on the following day. I tried to tell my sister about it, but she didn't understand. She suggested that I see a psychiatrist, but I was afraid to go out of the house to see him.

One day I decided that I couldn't take this trauma anymore, so I took an overdose of thirty-five Darvon pills. At the same moment, a voice inside me said, "What did you do that for? Now you won't go to heaven." At that instant I realized that I didn't really want to die. I wanted to live, and I was afraid. I got on the phone and called the psychiatrist whom my sister had recommended. I told him I had taken an overdose of Darvon and that I was afraid. He told me to take a taxi to the hospital. When I arrived at the hospital, I began vomiting, but I didn't pass out. Somehow, I just couldn't accept the fact that I was really going to see a psychiatrist. I thought that psychiatrists were only for crazy people, and I definitely didn't think I was crazy. As a result, I did not admit myself right away. As a matter of fact I left the hospital and ended up meeting my sister on the way home. She told me to turn right back around because I was definitely going to be admitted. We then called my mother, and she said she would fly down the following day. (O'Neil, 1984, pp. 109–110)

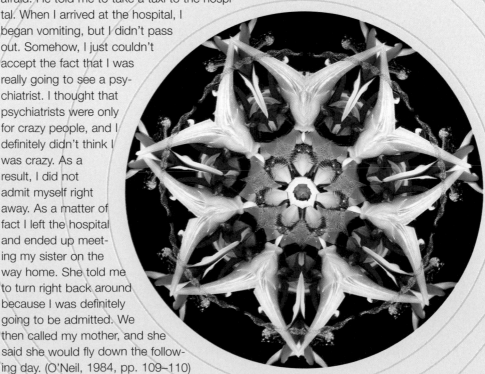

The young woman described in this case study was diagnosed as having schizophrenia. Although the diagnosis of schizophrenia has existed now for over a century and the disorder has spawned more research than any other, we are far from understanding this serious mental disorder.

Schizophrenia is a psychotic disorder characterized by major disturbances in thought, emotion, and behavior—disordered thinking, in which ideas are not logically related; faulty perception and attention; flat or inappropriate affect; and bizarre disturbances in motor activity. Patients with schizophrenia withdraw from people and reality, often into a fantasy life of delusions and hallucinations.

Schizophrenia is one of the most severe psychopathologies we will describe in this book. Its lifetime prevalence is slightly less than one percent and it affects men and women about equally. Although it sometimes begins in childhood, it usually appears in late adolescence or early adulthood, somewhat earlier for men than for women. Age of onset appears to have been decreasing over the last decades (DiMaggio et al., 2001). People with schizophrenia typically have a number of acute episodes of their symptoms; between episodes they often have less severe but still very debilitating symptoms. Comorbid substance abuse is a major problem for patients with schizophrenia, occurring in about 50 percent of them (Kosten & Ziedonis, 1997).

In this chapter we first describe the clinical features of schizophrenia and then consider the history of the concept and how it has changed over the years. Finally, we examine research on the etiology of schizophrenia and therapies for the disorder.

Clinical Symptoms of Schizophrenia

The symptoms of patients with schizophrenia involve disturbances in several major areas—thought, perception, and attention; motor behavior; affect or emotion; and life functioning. The range of problems of people diagnosed as schizophrenic is extensive, although patients typically have only some of these problems at any given time. The DSM determines for the diagnostician how many problems must be present and in what degree to justify the diagnosis (p.326). The duration of the disorder is also important in diagnosis.

Unlike most of the diagnostic categories we have considered, *no essential symptom must be present for a diagnosis of schizophrenia*. Thus patients with schizophrenia can differ from one another more than do patients with other disorders. The heterogeneity of schizophrenia suggests that it may be appropriate to subdivide patients into types that manifest particular constellations of problems, and we examine several recognized types later in this chapter. But first we present the main symptoms of schizophrenia in three categories: positive, negative, and disorganized. We also describe some symptoms that do not fit neatly into these three categories.

Positive Symptoms

Positive symptoms comprise excesses and distortions, such as hallucinations and delusions. They are what define, for the most part, an acute episode of schizophrenia.

Delusions   No doubt all of us at one time or another have been concerned because we believed that others thought ill of us. Some of the time this belief may be justified. After all, who is universally loved? Consider, though, the anguish that would be caused if you were firmly convinced that many people did not like you—indeed, that they disliked you so much that they were plotting against you. Imagine that your persecutors have sophisticated listening devices that allow them to tune in on your most private conversations and gather evidence in a plot to discredit you. Those around you, including your loved ones, are unable to reassure you that these people are not spying on you. Even your closest friends are gradually joining forces with your tormentors and becoming members of the persecuting community. You are naturally quite anxious or angry about your situation, and you begin your own counteractions against the imagined persecutors. You carefully check any new room you enter for listening devices. When you meet people for the first time, you question them at great length to determine whether they are part of the plot against you.

Such **delusions**, beliefs held contrary to reality, are common positive symptoms of schizophrenia. Persecutory delusions such as those just related were found in 65 percent of a large, cross-national sample (Sartorius, Shapiro, & Jablonsky, 1974). Delusions may take several other forms as well. Some of these were described by the German psychiatrist Kurt Schneider (1959). The following descriptions of these delusions are drawn from Mellor (1970).

- The patient may believe that thoughts that are not his or her own have been placed in his or her mind by an external source.

  A twenty-nine-year-old housewife said, "I look out of the window and I think the garden looks nice and the grass looks cool, but the thoughts of Eamonn Andrews come into my mind. There are no other thoughts there, only his. He treats my mind like a screen and flashes his thoughts on it like you flash a picture." (p. 17)

- Patients may believe that their thoughts are broadcast or transmitted, so that others know what they are thinking.

  A twenty-one-year-old student [found that] "As I think, my thoughts leave my head on a type of mental ticker-tape. Everyone around has only to pass the tape through their mind and they know my thoughts." (p. 17)

- Patients may think their thoughts are being stolen from them, suddenly and unexpectedly, by an external force.

  A twenty-two-year-old woman [described such an experience]. "I am thinking about my mother, and suddenly my thoughts are sucked out of my mind by a phrenological vacuum extractor, and there is nothing in my mind, it is empty." (pp. 16–17)

- Some patients believe that their feelings or behaviors are controlled by an external force.

  A twenty-nine-year-old shorthand typist described her [simplest] actions as follows: "When I reach my hand for the comb it is my hand and arm which move, and my fingers pick up the pen, but I don't control them. I sit there watching them move, and they are quite independent, what they do is nothing to do with me. I am just a puppet who is manipulated by cosmic strings. When the strings are pulled my body moves and I cannot prevent it." (p. 17)

Although delusions are found among more than half of people with schizophrenia, they are also found among patients with other diagnoses, notably, mania, delusional depression, and delusional disorder. The delusions of patients with schizophrenia, however, are often more bizarre than are those of patients in these other diagnostic categories; that is, the delusions of patients with schizophrenia are highly implausible, as shown by the delusions just described (Junginger, Barker, & Coe, 1992).

Hallucinations and Other Disorders of Perception   Patients with schizophrenia frequently report that the world seems somehow different or even unreal to them. A patient may mention changes in how his or her body feels, or the patient's body may become so depersonalized that it feels as though it is a machine. As described in the case beginning this chapter, some people report difficulties in attending to what is happening around them.

I can't concentrate on television because I can't watch the screen and listen to what is being said at the same time. I can't seem to take in two things like this at the same time especially when one of them means watching and the other means listening. On the other hand I seem to be

always taking in too much at the one time, and then I can't handle it and can't make sense of it.
(McGhie & Chapman, 1961, p. 106)

The most dramatic distortions of perception are **hallucinations**, sensory experiences in the absence of any stimulation from the environment. They are most often auditory rather than visual; 74 percent of one sample reported having auditory hallucinations (Sartorius et al., 1974). Like delusions, hallucinations can be very frightening experiences.

Some hallucinations are thought to be particularly important diagnostically because they occur more often in patients with schizophrenia than in other psychotic patients. These types of hallucinations include the following (taken from Mellor, 1970):

- Some patients with schizophrenia report hearing their own thoughts spoken by another voice.

  [The] thirty-two-year-old housewife complained of a man's voice speaking in an intense whisper from a point about two feet above her head. The voice would repeat almost all the patient's goal-directed thinking—even the most banal thoughts. The patient would think, "I must put the kettle on," and after a pause of not more than one second the voice would say, "I must put the kettle on." It would often say the opposite, "Don't put the kettle on." (p. 16)

- Some patients claim that they hear voices arguing.

  A twenty-four-year-old male patient reported hearing voices coming from the nurse's office. One voice, deep in pitch and roughly spoken, repeatedly said, "G. T. is a bloody paradox," and another higher in pitch said, "He is that, he should be locked up." A female voice occasionally interrupted, saying, "He is not, he is a lovely man." (p. 16)

- Some patients hear voices commenting on their behavior.

  A forty-one-year-old housewife heard a voice coming from a house across the road. The voice went on incessantly in a flat monotone describing everything she was doing with an admixture of critical comments. "She is peeling potatoes, got hold of the peeler, she does not want that potato, she is putting it back, because she thinks it has a knobble like a penis, she has a dirty mind, she is peeling potatoes, now she is washing them." (p. 16)

Negative Symptoms

The **negative symptoms** of schizophrenia consist of behavioral deficits, such as avolition, alogia, anhedonia, flat affect, and asociality, all of which are described here. These symptoms tend to endure beyond an acute episode and have profound effects on the lives of patients with schizophrenia. They are also important prognostically; the presence of many negative symptoms is a strong predictor of a poor quality of life (e.g., occupational impairment, few friends) two years following hospitalization (Ho et al., 1998).

When assessing negative symptoms it is important to distinguish among those that are truly symptoms of schizophrenia and those that are due to some other factor (Carpenter, Heinrichs, & Wagman, 1988). For example, flat affect (a lack of emotional expressiveness) can be a side effect of antipsychotic medication. Observing patients over extended time periods is probably the only way to address this issue.

Avolition   Apathy or **avolition** refers to a lack of energy and a seeming absence of interest in or an inability to persist in what are usually routine activities. Patients may become inattentive to grooming and personal hygiene, with uncombed hair, dirty nails, unbrushed teeth, and disheveled clothes. They have difficulty persisting at work, school, or household chores and may spend much of their time sitting around doing nothing.

Alogia   A negative thought disorder, **alogia** can take several forms. In poverty of speech, the sheer amount of speech is greatly reduced. In poverty of content of speech, the amount of discourse is adequate, but it conveys little information and tends to be vague and repetitive. The following excerpt illustrates poverty of content of speech.

Interviewer: O.K. Why is it, do you think, that people believe in God?

Patient: Well, first of all because, He is the person that is their personal savior. He walks with me and talks with me. And uh, the understanding that I have, a lot of peoples, they don't really know their personal self. Because they ain't, they all, just don't know their personal self. They don't know that He uh, seems to like me, a lot of them don't understand that He walks and talks with them. And uh, show 'em their way to go. I understand also that, every man and every lady, is not just pointed in the same direction. Some are pointed different. They go in their different ways. The way that Jesus Christ wanted 'em to go. Myself. I am pointed in the ways of uh, knowing right from wrong, and doing it, I can't do any more, or not less than that. (American Psychiatric Association, 1987, pp. 403–404)

Anhedonia An inability to experience pleasure is called **anhedonia**. It is manifested as a lack of interest in recreational activities, failure to develop close relationships with other people, and lack of interest in sex. Patients are aware of this symptom and report that what are usually considered pleasurable activities are not enjoyable for them.

Flat Affect In patients with **flat affect** virtually no stimulus can elicit an emotional response. The patient may stare vacantly, the muscles of the face flaccid, the eyes lifeless. When spoken to, the patient answers in a flat and toneless voice. Flat affect was found in 66 percent of a large sample of patients with schizophrenia (Sartorius et al., 1974).

The concept of flat affect refers only to the outward expression of emotion and not to the patient's inner experience, which may not be impoverished at all. In a study by Kring and Neale (1996), patients with schizophrenia and normal participants watched excerpts from films while their facial reactions and skin conductance were recorded. After each film clip participants self-reported on the moods the films had elicited. As expected, the patients were much less facially expressive than were the normal people, but they reported about the same amount of emotion and were even more physiologically aroused.

Asociality Some patients with schizophrenia have severe impairments in social relationships, referred to as **asociality**. They have few friends, poor social skills, and little interest in being with other people. Indeed, as will be seen later, these manifestations of schizophrenia are often the first to appear, beginning in childhood before the onset of more psychotic symptoms.

Disorganized Symptoms

Disorganized symptoms include disorganized speech and bizarre behavior.

Disorganized speech Also known as formal **thought disorder, disorganized speech** refers to problems in organizing ideas and in speaking so that a listener can understand.

Interviewer: Have you been nervous or tense lately?

Patient: No, I got a head of lettuce.

Interviewer: You got a head of lettuce? I don't understand.

Patient: Well, it's just a head of lettuce.

Interviewer: Tell me about lettuce. What do you mean?

Patient: Well…lettuce is a transformation of a dead cougar that suffered a relapse on the lion's toe. And he swallowed the lion and something happened. The…see, the…Gloria and Tommy, they're two heads and they're not whales. But they escaped with herds of vomit, and things like that.

Interviewer: Who are Tommy and Gloria?

Patient: Uh,…there's Joe DiMaggio, Tommy Henrich, Bill Dickey, Phil Rizzuto, John Esclavera, Del Crandell, Ted Williams, Mickey Mantle, Roy Mantle, Ray Mantle, Bob Chance…

Interviewer: Who are they? Who are those people?

Patient: Dead people...they want to be fucked...by this outlaw.

Interviewer: What does all that mean?

Patient: Well, you see, I have to leave the hospital. I'm supposed to have an operation on my legs, you know. And it comes to be pretty sickly that I don't want to keep my legs. That's why I wish I could have an operation.

Interviewer: You want to have your legs taken off?

Patient: It's possible, you know.

Interviewer: Why would you want to do that?

Patient: I didn't have any legs to begin with. So I would imagine that if I was a fast runner, I'd be scared to be a wife, because I had a splinter inside of my head of lettuce. (Neale & Oltmanns, 1980, pp. 103–104)

This excerpt illustrates the **incoherence** sometimes found in the conversation of individuals with schizophrenia. Although the patient may make repeated references to central ideas or a theme, the images and fragments of thought are not connected, it is difficult to understand exactly what the patient is trying to tell the interviewer.

Speech may also be disordered by what are called **loose associations**, or **derailment**, in which case the patient may be more successful in communicating with a listener but has difficulty sticking to one topic. He or she seems to drift off on a train of associations evoked by an idea from the past. Patients have themselves provided descriptions of this state.

> My thoughts get all jumbled up. I start thinking or talking about something but I never get there. Instead, I wander off in the wrong direction and get caught up with all sorts of different things that may be connected with things I want to say but in a way I can't explain. People listening to me get more lost than I do. My trouble is that I've got too many thoughts. You might think about something, let's say that ashtray and just think, oh yes, that's for putting my cigarette in, but I would think of it and then I would think of a dozen different things connected with it at the same time. (McGhie & Chapman, 1961, p. 108)

Disturbances in speech were at one time regarded as the principal clinical symptom of schizophrenia, and they remain one of the criteria for the diagnosis. But evidence indicates that the speech of many patients with schizophrenia is not disorganized, and the presence of disorganized speech does not discriminate well between schizophrenia and other psychoses, such as some mood disorders (Andreasen, 1979). For example, patients in a manic episode exhibit loose associations as much as do patients with schizophrenia.

Bizarre Behavior   **Bizarre** behavior takes many forms. Patients may fly into inexplicable rages or bouts of agitation, dress in unusual clothes, act in a childlike or silly manner, hoard food, collect garbage, or engage in sexually inappropriate behavior such as masturbating in public. They seem to lose the ability to organize their behavior and make it conform to community standards. They also have difficulty performing the tasks of everyday living.

Other Symptoms

Several other symptoms of schizophrenia do not fit neatly into the categories we have just presented. Two important symptoms of this kind are catatonia and inappropriate affect.

Catatonia   Several motor abnormalities define catatonia. Patients may gesture repeatedly, using peculiar and sometimes complex sequences of finger, hand, and arm movements, which often seem to be purposeful. Some patients manifest an unusual increase in their overall level of activity, including much excitement, wild flailing of the limbs, and great expenditure of energy similar to that seen in mania. At the other end of the spectrum is **catatonic immobility**: patients adopt unusual postures and maintain them for very long periods of time. A patient may stand on one leg, with the other tucked up

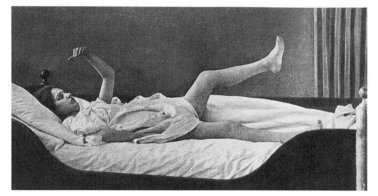

An 1894 photo showing a woman with catatonic schizophrenia. She held this unusual posture for long periods of time.

toward the buttocks, and remain in this position virtually all day. Catatonic patients may also have **waxy flexibility**—another person can move the patient's limbs into strange positions that the patient will then maintain for long periods of time.

Inappropriate Affect   Some people with schizophrenia have **inappropriate affect**. The emotional responses of these individuals are out of context—a patient may laugh on hearing that his or her mother just died or become enraged when asked a simple question about how a new garment fits. These patients are likely to shift rapidly from one emotional state to another for no discernible reason. Although this symptom is quite rare, when it does appear it is of considerable diagnostic importance because it is relatively specific to schizophrenia.

Taken together, these symptoms of schizophrenia have a profound effect on patients' lives as well as the lives of their families and friends. Their delusions and hallucinations may cause considerable distress, both to themselves and others, which is compounded by the fact that their hopes and dreams have been shattered. Their cognitive impairments and avolition make stable employment difficult, leading to impoverishment and often homelessness. Their strange behavior and social-skills deficits lead to loss of friends, a solitary existence, and sometimes ridicule and persecution from others. Substance-abuse rates are high (Fowler et al., 1998), perhaps reflecting an attempt to achieve some relief from negative emotions (Blanchard et al., 1999). Little wonder, then, that the suicide rate among patients with schizophrenia is high.

History of the Concept of Schizophrenia

We turn now to a review of the history of the concept of schizophrenia and how ideas about this disorder have changed over time.

Emil Kraepelin (1856–1926), German psychiatrist, articulated descriptions of dementia praecox that have proved remarkably durable in the light of contemporary research.

Early Desriptions

The concept of schizophrenia was initially formulated by two European psychiatrists, Emil Kraepelin and Eugen Bleuler. Kraepelin first presented his notion of **dementia praecox**, the early term for schizophrenia, in 1898. He differentiated two major groups of psychoses that he asserted were endogenous, or internally caused: manic-depressive illness and dementia praecox. Dementia praecox included several diagnostic concepts—dementia paranoides, catatonia, and hebephrenia—that had been regarded as distinct entities by clinicians in the previous few decades. Although these disorders were symptomatically diverse, Kraepelin believed that they shared a common core and his term *dementia praecox* reflected what he believed was that core—an early onset (praecox) and a deteriorating course marked by a progressive intellectual deterioration (dementia). The dementia in dementia praecox is not the same as the dementias we discuss in the chapter on aging (Chapter 16). The latter are defined principally by severe memory impairments, whereas Kraepelin's term referred to a general "mental enfeeblement."

The view of the next major figure, Eugen Bleuler, represented both a specific attempt to define the core of the disorder and a move away from Kraepelin's emphasis on age of onset and on course in the definition. Bleuler broke with Kraepelin on two major points: he believed that the disorder did not necessarily have an early onset, and he believed that it did not inevitably progress toward dementia. Thus the label *dementia praecox* was no longer appropriate, and in 1908 Bleuler proposed his own term, *schizophrenia*, from the Greek words schizein, meaning "to split," and *phren*, meaning "mind," to capture what he viewed as the essential nature of the condition.

With age of onset and deteriorating course no longer considered defining features of the disorder, Bleuler faced a conceptual problem. Since the symptoms of schizophrenia could vary widely among patients, he had to provide some justification for putting them into a single diagnostic category. Bleuler therefore needed to specify a common denominator, or essential property, that would link the various disturbances. The metaphorical concept that he adopted for this purpose was the "breaking of associative threads."

For Bleuler, associative threads joined not only words but thoughts. Thus, goal-directed, efficient thinking and communication were possible only when these hypothetical structures were intact. The notion that associative threads were disrupted in patients with schizophrenia could then account for other problems. Bleuler viewed attentional difficulties, for example, as resulting from a loss of purposeful direction in thought, in turn causing passive responses to objects and people in the immediate surroundings. In a similar vein, he viewed *blocking*, an apparently total loss of a train of thought, as a complete disruption of the person's associative threads.

Although Kraepelin recognized that a small percentage of patients who originally manifested symptoms of dementia praecox did not deteriorate, he preferred to limit this diagnostic category to patients who had a poor prognosis. Bleuler's work, in contrast, led to a broader concept of schizophrenia. He diagnosed some patients with a good prognosis as schizophrenic, and he also included in his concept of schizophrenia many patients who would have received different diagnoses from other clinicians.

Eugen Bleuler (1857–1939), Swiss psychiatrist, contributed to our conceptions of schizophrenia and coined the term.

The Broadened U.S. Concept

Bleuler had a great influence on the concept of schizophrenia as it developed in the United States. Over the first part of the twentieth century the breadth of the diagnosis was extended considerably. At the New York State Psychiatric Institute, for example, about 20 percent of the patients were diagnosed as schizophrenic in the 1930s. The numbers increased through the 1940s and in 1952 peaked at a remarkable 80 percent. In contrast, the concept of schizophrenia prevalent in Europe remained narrower. The percentage of patients diagnosed as schizophrenic at the Maudsley Hospital in London, for example, stayed relatively constant, at 20 percent, for a forty-year period (Kuriansky, Deming, & Gurland, 1974).

The reasons for the increase in the frequency of diagnoses of schizophrenia in the United States are easily discerned. Several prominent figures in U.S. psychiatry expanded Bleuler's already broad concept of schizophrenia even more. For example, in 1933, Kasanin described nine patients who had been diagnosed with dementia praecox. For all of them the onset of the disorder had been sudden and recovery relatively rapid. Noting that theirs could be said to be a combination of both schizophrenic and affective symptoms, Kasanin suggested the term *schizoaffective psychosis* to describe the disturbances of these patients. This diagnosis subsequently became part of the U.S. concept of schizophrenia and was listed in DSM-I (1952) and DSM-II (1968).

The concept of schizophrenia was further broadened by three additional diagnostic practices.

1. U.S. clinicians tended to diagnose schizophrenia whenever delusions or hallucinations were present. Because these symptoms, particularly delusions, occur also in mood disorders, many patients with a DSM-II diagnosis of schizophrenia may actually have had a mood disorder (Cooper et al., 1972).

2. Patients whom we would now diagnose as having a personality disorder (notably schizotypal, schizoid, borderline, and paranoid personality disorders, discussed in Chapter 13), were diagnosed as schizophrenic according to DSM-II criteria.

3. Patients with an acute onset of schizophrenic symptoms and a rapid recovery were diagnosed as having schizophrenia.

The DSM-IV-TR Diagnosis

Beginning in DSM-III (American Psychiatric Association, 1980) and continuing in DSM-IV (American Psychiatric Association, 1994) and DSM-IV-TR (American Psychiatric

Association, 2000), the U.S. concept of schizophrenia shifted considerably from the former broad definition to a new definition, which narrows the range of patients diagnosed as schizophrenic in five ways.

1. The diagnostic criteria are presented in explicit and considerable detail.
2. Patients with symptoms of a mood disorder are specifically excluded. Schizophrenia, schizoaffective type, is now listed as schizoaffective disorder in a separate section as one of the psychotic disorders. Schizoaffective disorder comprises a mixture of symptoms of schizophrenia and mood disorders.
3. DSM-IV-TR requires at least six months of disturbance for the diagnosis. The six-month period must include at least one month of an acute episode or active phase, defined by the presence of at least two of the following: delusions, hallucinations, disorganized speech, grossly disorganized or catatonic behavior, and negative symptoms. (Only one of these symptoms is required if the delusions are bizarre or if the hallucinations consist of voices commenting or arguing.) The remaining time required for the diagnosis can occur either before the active phase or after the active phase. Problems during these phases include social withdrawal, impaired role functioning, blunted or inappropriate affect, lack of initiative, vague and circumstantial speech, impairment in hygiene and grooming, odd beliefs or magical thinking, and unusual perceptual experiences. These criteria eliminate patients who have a brief psychotic episode, often stress related, and then recover quickly. DSM-II's acute schizophrenic episode is now diagnosed as either schizophreniform disorder or brief psychotic disorder, which are also listed in a new section in DSM-IV-TR. The symptoms of schizophreniform disorder are the same as those of schizophrenia but last only from one to six months. Brief psychotic disorder lasts from one day to one month and is often brought on by extreme stress, such as bereavement.
4. Some of what DSM-II regarded as mild forms of schizophrenia are now diagnosed as personality disorders, for example, schizotypal personality disorder.
5. DSM-IV-TR differentiates between paranoid schizophrenia, to be discussed shortly, and **delusional disorder**. A person with delusional disorder is troubled by persistent persecutory delusions or by delusional jealousy, the unfounded conviction that a spouse or lover is unfaithful. Other delusions include delusions of being followed, delusions of *erotomania* (believing that one is loved by some other person, usually a complete stranger with a higher social status), and *somatic delusions* (believing that some internal organ is malfunctioning). Unlike the person with paranoid schizophrenia, the person with delusional disorder does not have disorganized speech or hallucinations, and his or her delusions are less bizarre. Delusional disorder is quite rare and typically begins later in life than does schizophrenia. In most family studies it appears to be related to schizophrenia, perhaps genetically (Kendler & Diehl, 1993).

Are the DSM-IV-TR diagnostic criteria applicable across cultures? Data bearing on this question were collected in a World Health Organization study of both industrialized and developing countries (Jablonsky et al., 1994). The symptomatic criteria held up well cross-culturally. However, patients in developing countries have a more acute onset and a more favorable course than those in industrialized societies. The cause of this intriguing finding is unknown (Susser & Wanderling, 1994).

Categories of Schizophrenia in DSM-IV-TR

Earlier we mentioned that the heterogeneity of schizophrenic symptoms gave rise to proposals concerning subtypes of the disorder. Three types of schizophrenic disorders included in DSM-IV-TR—disorganized, catatonic, and paranoid—were initially proposed by Kraepelin many years ago. The present descriptions of Kraepelin's original types demonstrate the great diversity of behavior that relates to the diagnosis of schizophrenia.

Disorganized Schizophrenia   Kraepelin's hebephrenic form of schizophrenia is called **disorganized schizophrenia** in DSM-IV-TR. Speech is disorganized and difficult for a listener to follow. The patient may speak incoherently, stringing together similar-sounding words and even inventing new words, often accompanied by silliness or laughter. He or she may have flat affect or experience constant shifts of emotion, breaking into inexplicable fits of laughter and crying. The patient's behavior is generally disorganized and not goal directed; for example, he or she may tie a ribbon around a big toe or move incessantly, pointing at objects for no apparent reason. The patient sometimes deteriorates to the point of incontinence, voiding anywhere and at any time, and completely neglects his or her appearance, never bathing, brushing teeth, or combing hair.

Catatonic Schizophrenia   The most obvious symptoms of **catatonic schizophrenia** are the catatonic symptoms described earlier. Patients typically alternate between catatonic immobility and wild excitement, but one of these symptoms may predominate. These patients resist instructions and suggestions and often echo (repeat back) the speech of others. The onset of catatonic reactions may be more sudden than the onset of other forms of schizophrenia, although the person is likely to have previously shown some apathy and withdrawal from reality. The limbs of the person with catatonic immobility may become stiff and swollen; in spite of apparent obliviousness, he or she may later be able to report all that occurred during the stupor. In the excited state the catatonic person may shout and talk continuously and incoherently, all the while pacing with great agitation.

Catatonic schizophrenia is seldom seen today, perhaps because drug therapy works effectively on these bizarre motor processes. Alternatively, Boyle (1991) has argued that the apparent high prevalence of catatonia during the early part of the century reflected misdiagnosis. Specifically, she details similarities between encephalitis lethargica (sleeping sickness) and catatonic schizophrenia and suggests that many cases of the former were misdiagnosed as the latter. This idea was portrayed in the film *Awakenings*, which was based on the writings of Oliver Saks.

Paranoid Schizophrenia   The diagnosis **paranoid schizophrenia** is assigned to a substantial number of recently admitted patients to mental hospitals. The key to this diagnosis is the presence of prominent delusions. Delusions of persecution are most common, but patients may experience **grandiose delusions**, in which they have an exaggerated sense of their own importance, power, knowledge, or identity. Some patients are plagued by **delusional jealousy**, the unsubstantiated belief that their sexual partner is unfaithful. The other delusions described earlier, such as being persecuted or spied on, may also be evident. Vivid auditory hallucinations may accompany the delusions. Patients with paranoid schizophrenia often develop **ideas of reference**; they incorporate unimportant events within a delusional framework and read personal significance into the trivial activities of others. For instance, they think that overheard segments of conversations are about them, that the frequent appearance of a person on a street where they customarily walk means that they are being watched, and that what they see on television or read in magazines somehow refers to them. Individuals with paranoid schizophrenia are agitated, argumentative, angry, and sometimes violent. They are emotionally responsive, although they may be somewhat stilted, formal, and intense with others. They are also more alert and verbal than are patients with other types of schizophrenia. Their language, although filled with references to delusions, is not disorganized. When patients with schizophrenia get into legal trouble – an issue we deal with in Chapter 18— it is usually those of this paranoid subtype.

Evaluation of the Subtypes   Although these subtypes form the basis of current diagnostic systems, their usefulness is often questioned. Because diagnosing types of schizophrenia is extremely difficult, diagnostic reliability is dramatically reduced. Furthermore, these subtypes have little predictive validity; that is, the diagnosis of one over another form of schizophrenia provides little information that is helpful either in treating or in predicting the course of the problems. There is also considerable overlap among the

Table 11.1 Summary of the Major Symptom Dimensions in Schizophrenia

Positive Symptoms	Negative Symptoms	Disorganization
Delusions, hallucinations	Avolition (apathy), alogia (poverty of speech and poverty of content of speech), anhedonia, flat affect, asociality	Bizarre behavior, disorganized speech

types. For example, patients with all forms of schizophrenia may have delusions. Kraepelin's system of subtyping has thus not proved to be a useful way of dealing with the variability in schizophrenic behavior.

Several additional subtypes are also included in DSM-IV-TR. The diagnosis of **undifferentiated schizophrenia** applies to patients who meet the diagnostic criteria for schizophrenia but not for any of the three subtypes. The diagnosis of **residual schizophrenia** is used when the patient no longer meets the full criteria for schizophrenia but still shows some signs of the illness.

In spite of the problems with current subtyping systems, interest in differentiating types of schizophrenia continues. A system that is currently attracting attention distinguishes among positive, negative, and disorganized symptoms, which we described earlier (p. 319). About thirty years ago, symptoms were divided into positive and negative ones (Crow, 1980; Strauss, Carpenter, & Bartko, 1974). Subsequently, the original category of positive symptoms was divided into two catergories—positive (hallucinations and delusions) and disorganized (disorganized speech and bizarre behavior); see Table 11.1 (Lenzenwenger, Dworkin, & Wethington, 1991). Although this system of symptom categorization suggests that it is possible to talk about types of schizophrenia, subsequent research has indicated that most patients with schizophrenia show mixed symptoms (e.g., Andreasen et al., 1990) and that very few patients fit into the pure types.

Nevertheless, a distinction among types of symptoms and types of patients continues to be used in research on the etiology of schizophrenia. We present evidence relevant to the validity of this distinction in the discussion of the possible roles of genetics, dopamine, and brain pathology in the etiology of schizophrenia.

Etiology of Schizophrenia

We have described how patients with schizophrenia differ from normal people in thought, speech, perception, and imagination. What can explain the scattering and disconnection of their thoughts, their inappropriate emotions or lack of emotion, their misguided delusions and bewildering hallucinations? Broad theoretical perspectives, such as psychoanalysis, have not had much of an impact on research in schizophrenia. We thus focus here on major areas of etiological research. For a different approach to schizophrenia, **labeling theory**, see Focus on Discovery 11.1.

The Genetic Data

What would you do if you wanted to find an individual who had a very good chance of being diagnosed one day as schizophrenic and you could not consider any behavior patterns or other symptoms? Indeed, imagine that you could not even meet the person. This problem, suggested by Paul Meehl (1962), has one solution with a close-to-even chance of picking a person who is potentially schizophrenic: find an individual who has an identical twin with schizophrenia.

A convincing body of literature indicates that a predisposition for schizophrenia is transmitted genetically. The family, twin, and adoption methods employed in this research, as in other behavior-genetics research projects, have led researchers to conclude that a pre-

Focus on Discovery 11.1

Labeling Theory

In a radical departure from the traditional conceptualization of schizophrenia, Scheff (1966), a sociologist, argues that the disorder is a learned social role. This position, also known as **labeling theory**, is essentially unconcerned with etiology. According to Scheff, the crucial factor in schizophrenia is the act of assigning a diagnostic label to the individual. Presumably this label influences the manner in which the person will continue to behave, based on stereotypic notions of mental illness, and at the same time determines the reactions of other people to the individual's behavior. The social role, therefore, is the disorder, and it is determined by the labeling process. Without the diagnosis, Scheff argues, deviant behavior—or, to use his term, residual rule breaking—would not become stabilized. It would presumably be both transient and relatively inconsequential.

By residual rules, Scheff means the rules that are left over after all the formal and obvious ones, about stealing and violence and fairness, have been laid down. The examples are endless. "Do not stand still staring vacantly in the middle of a busy sidewalk." "Do not talk to the neon beer sign in the delicatessen window." "Do not spit on the piano." Scheff believes that one-time violations of residual rules are fairly common. Normal people, through poor judgment or bad luck, may be caught violating a rule and may then be diagnosed as mentally ill. Once so judged, these people are likely to accept this social role and find it difficult to rejoin society. They will be denied employment, and other people will know about their pasts. In the hospital they will receive attention and sympathy and be free of all responsibilities. So, once hospitalized, they actually perceive themselves as mentally ill and settle into acting as they are expected to—crazy.

Scheff's theory has some intuitive appeal. Most people who have worked for any amount of time at a psychiatric facility have witnessed abuses of the diagnostic process. Patients are sometimes assigned labels that are poorly justified.

The theory has a number of serious problems, however, indicating that it is at most of secondary importance to our understanding of schizophrenia. First, Scheff refers to deviance as residual rule breaking, and in his description it is indeed merely that. However, calling schizophrenia residual rule breaking trivializes a serious problem. Second, very little evidence indicates that unlabeled norm violations are indeed transient, as Scheff implies. Third, information regarding the detrimental effects of the social stigma associated with mental illness is inconclusive (Gove, 1970).

An important correlate of the labeling position is the notion of cultural relativism, according to which definitions of abnormality vary across cultures because of differences in social norms and rules. As an example, proponents of labeling theory might argue that the visions of a shaman are the same as the hallucinations of a person diagnosed as schizophrenic but that cultural differences allow a favorable response to shamans.

This and several other questions were addressed by Murphy (1976) in a report of her investigations of Eskimo and Yoruba. Contrary to the labeling view, both cultures have a concept of being crazy that is quite similar to our definition of schizophrenia. The Eskimo's *nuthkavihak* includes talking to oneself, refusing to talk, delusional beliefs, and bizarre behavior. The Yoruba's *were* encompasses similar symptoms. Notably, both cultures also have shamans but draw a clear distinction between their behavior and that of crazy people.

A final perspective on labeling theory is found in an anecdote related by colleagues of Paul Meehl, the famous schizophrenia theorist. Meehl was giving a lecture on genetics and schizophrenia when someone in the audience interrupted him to point out that he thought that patients with schizophrenia behaved in a crazy way because others had labeled them schizophrenic. Meehl had the following reaction:

> I just stood there and didn't know what to say. I was thinking of a patient I had seen on a ward who kept his finger up his ass "to keep his thoughts from running out," while with his other hand he tried to tear out his hair because it really "belonged to his father." And here was this man telling me that he was doing these things because someone had called him a schizophrenic. What could I say to him? (Kimble, Garmezy, & Zigler, 1980, p. 453)

In sum, the labeling position does not have much support. The view that schizophrenia is role taking reinforced by the attitudes of diagnosticians and mental hospital staff is without substantiating evidence.

Some writers have held that the visions of shamans are the same as the hallucinations of people with schizophrenia. Murphy's research, however, finds that the behavior of shamans is clearly distinguished from psychopathology.

disposition to schizophrenia is inherited. It should be noted that many genetic studies of schizophrenia were conducted when the definition of schizophrenia was considerably broader then it is now. However, genetic investigators collected extensive descriptive data on their samples, allowing the samples to be rediagnosed later using newer diagnostic criteria. Reanalyses using DSM-III criteria have substantiated the conclusions reached earlier (e.g., Kendler & Gruenberg, 1984).

Table 11.2 Summary of Major European Family and Twin Studies of the Genetics of Schizophrenia	
Relation to Proband	Percentage with Schizophrenia
Spouse	1.00
Grandchildren	2.84
Nieces/nephews	2.65
Children	9.35
Siblings	7.30
DZ twins	12.08
MZ twins	44.30

Source: After Gottesman, McGuffin, and Farmer, 1987.

Family Studies   Table 11.2 presents a summary of the risk for schizophrenia in various relatives of index cases with schizophrenia. (In evaluating the figures, bear in mind that the risk for schizophrenia in the general population is a little less than 1 percent.) Quite clearly, relatives of patients with schizophrenia are at increased risk, and the risk increases as the genetic relationship between proband and relative becomes closer.

More recent data confirm what is shown in Table 11.2 (Kendler, Larkowski-Shannon, & Walsh, 1996). Furthermore, patients who have schizophrenia in their family histories have more negative symptoms than those whose families are free of schizophrenia (Malaspina et al., 2000), suggesting that negative symptoms may have a stronger genetic component. The relatives of patients with schizophrenia are also at increased risk for other disorders (e.g., schizotypal personality disorder) that are thought to be less severe forms of schizophrenia (Kendler, Neale, & Walsh, 1995).

The data gathered by the family method thus support the notion that a predisposition for schizophrenia can be transmitted genetically. Yet relatives of a schizophrenic index case share not only genes but also common experiences. The behavior of a parent with schizophrenia could be very disturbing to a developing child. Therefore, the influence of the environment cannot be discounted as a rival explanation for the higher morbidity risks.

Twin Studies   Concordance rates for MZ and DZ twins are also given in Table 11.2. Concordance for identical twins (44.3 percent), although greater than that for fraternal twins (12.08 percent), is still much less than 100 percent. Similar results have been obtained in more recent studies (e.g., Cannon et al., 1998; Cardno et al., 1999). The less-than-100-percent concordance in MZ twins is important: If genetic transmission alone accounted for schizophrenia and one twin had schizophrenia, the other twin would also have schizophrenia because MZ twins are genetically identical. Consistent with a genetic interpretation of these data, concordance among MZ twins does increase when the proband is more severely ill (Gottesman & Shields, 1972).

As with family studies, of course, there is a critical problem in interpreting the results of twin studies. A common deviant environment rather than common genetic factors could account for some portion of the concordance rates. By common environment here we mean not only similar child-rearing practices, but also a more similar intrauterine environment, for MZ twins are more likely than DZ twins to share a single blood supply.

A clever analysis supporting a genetic interpretation of the high concordance rates found for identical twins was performed by Fischer (1971). She reasoned that if these rates indeed reflected a genetic effect, the children of even the discordant, or nonschizophrenic, identical co-twins of patients with schizophrenia should be at high risk for the disorder. These nonschizophrenic MZ twins would presumably

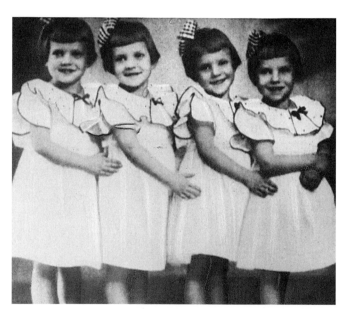

Childhood photograph of the Genain quadruplets. Each of the girls developed schizophrenia later in life.

have the genotype for schizophrenia, even though it was not expressed behaviorally, and thus might pass along an increased risk for the disorder to their children. In agreement with this line of reasoning, the rate of schizophrenia and schizophrenic-like psychoses in the children of nonschizophrenic MZ co-twins of patients with schizophrenia was 9.4 percent. The rate among the children of the patients with schizophrenia themselves was only slightly and nonsignificantly higher, 12.3 percent. Both rates are substantially higher than the 1 percent prevalence found in an unselected population and lend further support to the importance of genetic factors in schizophrenia.

Dworkin and his colleagues reevaluated the major twin studies according to the positive–negative symptom distinction discussed earlier (at the time of this analysis the positive symptom category included disorganized symptoms) (Dworkin & Lenzenweger, 1984; Dworkin, Lenzenweger, & Moldin, 1987). Ratings of positive and negative symptoms were compiled from published case histories of the twins and compared for probands of concordant and discordant pairs. No differences emerged for positive symptoms, but probands from concordant pairs were higher in negative symptoms than were probands from discordant pairs. Like the family data we described earlier, these data suggest that negative symptoms have a stronger genetic component than do positive ones.

Adoption Studies   The study of children whose mothers had schizophrenia but who were reared from early infancy by nonschizophrenic adoptive parents has provided more conclusive information on the role of genes in schizophrenia by eliminating the possible effects of a deviant environment. Heston (1966) was able to follow up forty-seven people born between 1915 and 1945 to women with schizophrenia in a state mental hospital. The infants were separated from their mothers at birth and raised by foster or adoptive parents. Fifty control participants were selected from the same foundling homes that had placed the children of the women with schizophrenia.

The follow-up assessment, conducted in 1964, consisted of an interview, the MMPI, an IQ test, social class ratings, and so on. A dossier on each participant was rated independently by two psychiatrists, and a third evaluation was made by Heston. Ratings were made on a 0 to 100 scale of overall disability, and whenever possible, diagnoses were offered. Overall, the control participants were rated as less disabled than the children of mothers with schizophrenia. Thirty-one of the forty-seven children of mothers with schizophrenia (66 percent), but only nine of the fifty controls (18 percent), were given a DSM diagnosis. None of the controls was diagnosed as schizophrenic, but 16.6 percent (five) of the offspring of women with schizophrenia were so diagnosed.[1] Children of women with schizophrenia were also more likely to be diagnosed as mentally defective, psychopathic, and neurotic (Table 11.3). They had been involved more frequently in criminal activity, had spent more time in penal institutions, and had more often been discharged from the armed services for psychiatric reasons. Children reared without contact with their so-called pathogenic mothers were also more likely to become schizophrenic than were controls. Heston's study provides strong support for the importance of genetic factors in the development of schizophrenia.

A study similar to Heston's was carried out in Denmark under Kety's direction (Kety et al., 1976, 1994). The starting point for the investigation was a culling of the records of children who had been adopted at a young age. All adoptees who had later been admitted to a psychiatric facility and diagnosed as schizophrenic were selected as the index cases. From the remaining cases the investigators chose a control group of people who had no psychiatric history and who were matched to the index group on such variables as sex and age. Both the adoptive and the biological parents and the siblings and half-siblings of the two groups were then identified, and a search was made to determine who among them had a psychiatric history. As might be expected if genetic factors figure in schizophrenia, the biological relatives of the index cases were diagnosed as schizophrenic more often than were members of the general population; the adoptive relatives were not.

Evaluation of the Genetic Data   The data indicate that genetic factors play an important role in the development of schizophrenia. Early twin and family studies were criticized because they did not separate the effects of genes and environment. However, more recent studies of children of parents with schizophrenia who were reared in foster and

Table 11.3 Characteristics of Participants Separated from Their Mothers in Early Infancy

Assessment	Offspring of Schizophrenic Mothers	Control Offspring
Number of participants	47	50
Mean age at follow-up	35.8	36.3
Overall ratings of disability (low score indicates more pathology)	65.2	80.1
Number diagnosed schizophrenic	5	0
Number diagnosed mentally defective	4	0
Number diagnosed psychopathic	9	2
Number diagnosed neurotic	13	7

Source: From Heston, 1966.

---

[1] The figure of 16.6 percent was *age corrected*. By this process raw data are corrected to take into account the age of the participants. If a person in Heston's sample was twenty-four years old at the time of the assessment, he or she might still develop schizophrenia at some point later in life. The age-correction procedure attempts to account for this possibility.

adoptive homes, plus the follow-up of relatives of adopted children who developed schizophrenia, have virtually removed the potential confounding influence of the environment.

Despite this evidence, we cannot conclude that schizophrenia is a disorder completely determined by genetic transmission, for we must always keep in mind the distinction between phenotype and genotype (see p. 21). Like other mental disorders, schizophrenia is defined by behavior; it is a phenotype, and thus reflects the influence of both genes and environment. The diathesis–stress model introduced in Chapter 2 seems appropriate for guiding theory and research into the etiology of schizophrenia. Genetic factors can only be predisposers for schizophrenia. Some kind of stress is required to render this predisposition an observable pathology.

The genetic research in schizophrenia has some further limitations as well. First, it has not been possible to specify exactly how a predisposition for schizophrenia is transmitted. It does not appear that the predisposition is transmitted by a single gene; several multi- or polygenic models remain viable. The results of linkage analysis (see p. 23), in which family pedigrees are studied to try to determine on which chromosome the schizophrenia gene or genes is located, have also been contradictory. The most consistent finding has been linkage to chromosome 8 (Kendler et al., 2000). However, such results have a history of not being replicated (DeLisi et al., 2002), possibly because the success of the method requires that the predisposition be transmitted by a single gene or small set of genes and this assumption may be faulty. It is also possible that schizophrenia is genetically heterogeneous, that is, the genetic diathesis may vary from case to case. Bear in mind that the category "schizophrenia" is certainly symptomatically heterogeneous.

Second, the nature of the inherited diathesis remains unknown. What exactly is inherited that puts some people at risk for schizophrenia? One way of addressing this question is to study relatives of patients with schizophrenia. Although not necessarily disordered, these individuals, who are genetically at risk for schizophrenia, may reveal signs of the genetic predisposition. A major area of research is the study of how well the eyes track a moving target, such as a pendulum. Patients with schizophrenia do poorly on this task, as do about 50 percent of their first-degree relatives (Holzman, 1985). The importance of eye tracking is supported by data showing that it is influenced by genetic factors (Iacono et al., 1992). Deficient eye tracking may reflect a problem in several areas of the brain, including the frontal and temporal lobes as well as the cerebellum (Chen et al., 1999). We will soon see that these brain areas are thought to be very important in schizophrenia.

Despite the problems and loose ends in the genetic data, these data represent an impressive body of evidence. The strong positive correlation between genetic relatedness and the prevalence of schizophrenia remains one of the strongest links in the chain of information about the causes of schizophrenia.

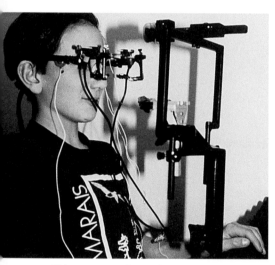

This apparatus is used to assess a person's ability to track a moving target. This ability is impaired in both patients with schizophrenia and their relatives, suggesting that eye tracking is a genetic marker for the disorder.

Biochemical Factors

The demonstrated role of genetic factors in schizophrenia suggests that biochemicals should be investigated, for it is through body chemistry and biological processes that heredity may have an effect. Present research is examining several different neurotransmitters, such as norepinephrine and serotonin. Here we review one of the best researched factors, dopamine.

Dopamine Activity   The theory that schizophrenia is related to excess activity of the neurotransmitter dopamine is based principally on the knowledge that drugs effective in treating schizophrenia reduce dopamine activity. Researchers noted that antipsychotic drugs (see p. 344), in addition to being useful in treating some symptoms of schizophrenia, produce side effects resembling the symptoms of Parkinson's disease. Parkinsonism is known to be caused in part by low levels of dopamine in a particular nerve tract of the brain. It was subsequently confirmed that because of their structural similarities to the dopamine molecule, molecules of antipsychotic drugs fit into and thereby block postsynaptic dopamine receptors. The dopamine receptors that are blocked by antipsychotics are called D2 receptors. (As with other neurotransmitters, there are several subclasses of dopamine receptors that differ in the specifics of how they signal the postsynaptic neuron.) From this knowledge about the action of the drugs that help patients with schizophrenia, it was but a short inductive leap to view schizophrenia as resulting from excess activity in dopamine nerve tracts.

Further indirect support for the **dopamine theory** of schizophrenia came from the literature on amphetamine psychosis. Amphetamines can produce a state that closely resembles paranoid schizophrenia, and they can exacerbate the symptomatology of patients with schizophrenia (Angrist, Lee, & Gershon, 1974). The amphetamines cause the release of catecholamines, including norepinephrine and dopamine, into the synaptic cleft and prevent their inactivation. We can be relatively confident that the psychosis-inducing effects of amphetamines are a result of increasing dopamine rather than of increasing norepinephrine, because antipsychotics are antidotes to amphetamine psychosis.

Based on the data just reviewed, researchers at first assumed that schizophrenia was caused by an excess of dopamine. But as other studies progressed, this assumption did not gain support. For example, the major metabolite of dopamine, homovanillic acid (HVA), was not found in greater amounts in patients with schizophrenia (Bowers, 1974).

Such data, plus improved technologies for studying neurochemical variables in humans, led researchers to propose excess or oversensitive dopamine receptors, rather than a high level of dopamine, as factors in schizophrenia. Research on the antipsychotics' mode of action suggests that the dopamine receptors are a more likely locus of disorder than the level of dopamine itself. Some postmortem studies of brains of schizophrenic patients, as well as PET scans of schizophrenic patients, have revealed that dopamine receptors are greater in number or are hypersensitive in some people with schizophrenia (Goldsmith, Shapiro, & Joyce, 1997; Hietala et al., 1994; Tune et al., 1993; Wong et al., 1986). Having too many dopamine receptors would be functionally akin to having too much dopamine itself. The reason is that when dopamine (or any neurotransmitter) is released into the synapse, only some of it actually interacts with postsynaptic receptors. Having more receptors gives a greater opportunity for the dopamine that is released to stimulate a receptor.

Excess dopamine receptors may not be responsible for all the symptoms of schizophrenia; they appear to be related mainly to positive symptoms. (As with the genetic literature, this work was done before positive symptoms were divided into two categories.) Some studies have shown, for example, that amphetamines do not worsen the symptoms of all patients (e.g., Kornetsky, 1976); one study has reported that symptoms actually *diminish* after an amphetamine has been administered (van Kammen et al., 1977). Furthermore, antipsychotics have been shown to ameliorate only some of the symptoms of schizophrenia. It turns out that these divergent results are related to the positive–negative symptom distinction noted earlier. Amphetamines worsen positive symptoms and lessen negative ones. Antipsychotics lessen positive symptoms but have little or no effect on negative symptoms.

Subsequent developments in the dopamine theory (e.g., Davis et al., 1991) have expanded its scope. The key change involves the recognition of differences among the neural pathways that use dopamine as a transmitter. The excess dopamine activity that is thought to be most relevant to schizophrenia is localized in the mesolimbic pathway (see Figure 11.1), and the therapeutic effects of antipsychotics on positive symptoms occur by blocking dopamine receptors in this neural system and thereby lowering activity.

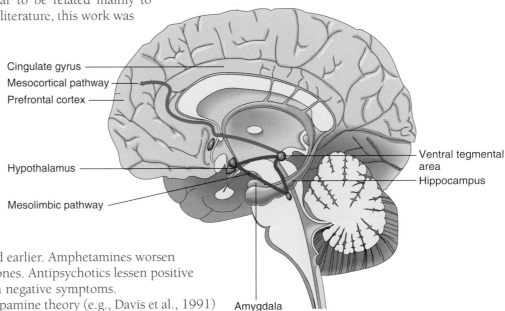

Figure 11.1 The brain and schizophrenia. The mesocortical pathway begins in the ventral tegmental area and projects to the prefrontal cortex. The mesolimbic pathway also begins in the ventral tegmental area, but projects to the hypothalamus, amygdala, hippocampus, and nucleus accumbens.

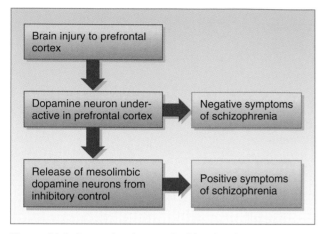

Figure 11.2 Dopamine theory of schizophrenia.

The mesocortical pathway is another dopamine system. It begins in the same brain region as the mesolimbic pathway, but projects to the prefrontal cortex. The prefrontal cortex also projects to limbic areas that are innervated by dopamine. The dopamine neurons in the prefrontal cortex may be underactive and thus fail to exert inhibitory control over the dopamine neurons in the limbic area, with the result that there is overactivity in the mesolimbic dopamine system. Because the prefrontal cortex is thought to be especially relevant to the negative symptoms of schizophrenia, the underactivity of the dopamine neurons in this part of the brain may also be the cause of the negative symptoms of schizophrenia (see Figure 11.2). This proposal has the advantage of allowing the simultaneous presence of positive and negative symptoms in the same patient with schizophrenia. Furthermore, because antipsychotics do not have major effects on the dopamine neurons in the prefrontal cortex, we would expect them to be relatively ineffective as treatments for negative symptoms, and they are. When we examine research on structural abnormalities in the brains of patients with schizophrenia, we will see some close connections between these two domains.

Evaluation of the Biochemical Data   Despite the positive evidence we have reviewed, the dopamine theory does not appear to be a complete theory of schizophrenia. For example, it takes several weeks for antipsychotics to gradually lessen positive symptoms of schizophrenia, although they begin blocking dopamine receptors rapidly (Davis, 1978). This disjunction between the behavioral and pharmacological effects of antipsychotics is difficult to understand within the context of the theory. One possibility is that although antipsychotics do indeed block D2 receptors, their ultimate therapeutic effect may result from the effect this blockade has on other brain areas and other neurotransmitter systems (Cohen et al., 1997).

It is also puzzling that to be therapeutically effective, antipsychotics must reduce dopamine levels or receptor activity to *below normal*, producing Parkinsonian side effects. According to the theory, reducing dopamine levels or receptor activity to normal should be sufficient for a therapeutic effect.

Furthermore, as we describe later, newer drugs used in treating schizophrenia implicate other neurotransmitters, such as serotonin, in the disorder. Dopamine neurons generally modulate the activity of other neural systems; for example, in the prefrontal cortex they regulate GABA neurons. Thus, it is not surprising that GABA transmission is disrupted in the prefrontal cortex of patients with schizophrenia (Volk et al., 2000). Similarly, serotonin neurons regulate dopamine neurons in the mesolimbic pathway. Thus dopamine may be only one piece in a much more complicated jigsaw puzzle.

Glutamate, a transmitter that is widespread in the human brain, may also play a role (Carlsson et al., 1999). Low levels of glutamate have been found in cerebrospinal fluid of patients with schizophrenia (Faustman et al., 1999), and postmortem studies have revealed low levels of the enzyme needed to produce glutamate (Tsai et al., 1995). The street drug PCP (p. 380) can induce a psychotic state, including both positive and negative symptoms, in normal people, and it produces this effect by interfering with one of glutamate's receptors (O'Donnell & Grace, 1998). Furthermore, a decrease in glutamate inputs from either the prefrontal cortex or the hippocampus (both of these brain areas are implicated in schizophrenia) to the corpus striatum (a temporal-lobe structure) could result in increased dopamine activity (O'Donnell & Grace, 1998).

In sum, although dopamine remains the most actively researched biochemical variable, it is not likely to provide a complete explanation of the biochemistry of schizophrenia. Schizophrenia is a disorder with widespread symptoms covering perception, cognition, motor activity, and social behavior. It is unlikely that a single neurotransmitter could account for all of them. Biochemically oriented schizophrenia researchers are starting to cast a broader biochemical net, moving away from an almost exclusive emphasis on dopamine. Glutamate and serotonin may well be at the forefront of these inquiries, perhaps in conjunction with dopamine activity.

The Brain and Schizophrenia

The search for a brain abnormality that causes schizophrenia began as early as the syndrome was identified, but studies did not yield the same findings. Interest gradually waned over the years. In the last two decades, however, spurred by a number of technological advances, the field has reawakened and yielded some promising evidence. Some patients with schizophrenia have been found to have observable brain pathology.

Postmortem analyses of the brains of patients with schizophrenia are one source of evidence. Such studies consistently reveal abnormalities in some areas of the brains of patients with schizophrenia, although the specific problems reported vary from study to study, and there are many contradictory findings. The most consistent finding is of enlarged ventricles, which implies a loss of brain cells. Moderately consistent findings indicate structural problems in subcortical temporal-limbic areas, such as the hippocampus and the basal ganglia, and in the prefrontal and temporal cortex (Dwork, 1997; Heckers, 1997).

Even more impressive are the images obtained in CT scan and MRI studies (p. 97). Researchers were quick to apply these new tools to brains of living patients with schizophrenia. Thus far, these images of living brain tissue have most consistently revealed that some patients, especially males (Nopoulos, Flaum, & Andreasen, 1997), have enlarged ventricles.[2] Research also shows a reduction in cortical gray matter in both the temporal and frontal regions (Gur et al., 2000) and reduced volume in basal ganglia (e.g., the caudate nucleus) and limbic structures (Chua & McKenna, 1995; Gur & Pearlson, 1993; Keshavan et al., 1998; Lim et al., 1998; Velakoulis et al., 1999).

Further evidence concerning large ventricles comes from two MRI studies of pairs of MZ twins who were discordant for schizophrenia (McNeil, Cantor-Graae, & Weinberger, 2000; Suddath et al., 1990). In both studies the ill twin had larger ventricles than the well twin, and in one of the studies most of the twins with schizophrenia could be identified by simple visual inspection of the scan. Because the twins were genetically identical, these data suggest that the origin of these brain abnormalities may not be genetic.

Large ventricles in patients with schizophrenia are correlated with impaired performance on neuropsychological tests, poor adjustment prior to the onset of the disorder, and poor response to drug treatment (Andreasen et al., 1982; Weinberger et al., 1980). The extent to which the ventricles are enlarged, however, is modest, and many patients do not differ from normal people in this respect. Furthermore, enlarged ventricles are not specific to schizophrenia, as they are also evident in the CT scans of patients with other psychoses, such as mania (Rieder et al., 1983) (see Focus on Discovery 11.2).

A variety of data suggest that the prefrontal cortex is of particular importance in schizophrenia.

- The prefrontal cortex is known to play a role in behaviors such as speech, decision-making, and willed action, which are disrupted in schizophrenia.
- MRI studies have shown reductions in gray matter in the prefrontal cortex (Buchanan et al., 1998).
- In a type of functional imaging in which glucose metabolism is studied in various brain regions while patients perform psychological tests, patients with schizophrenia have shown low metabolic rates in the prefrontal cortex (Buchsbaum et al., 1984). Glucose metabolism in the prefrontal cortex has also been studied while patients are performing neuropsychological tests of prefrontal function. Because the tests place demands on the prefrontal cortex, glucose metabolism

---

[2] This difference between male and female schizophrenic patients prompts us to mention that there are other gender effects as well. For example, men with schizophrenia have an earlier age of onset and are more likely to express negative symptoms and to have a more deteriorating course than are women with schizophrenia (Haas et al., 1990).

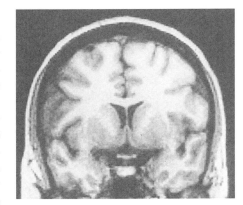

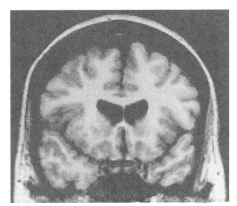

MRI of the brains of a woman with schizophrenia (*bottom*) and a normal woman (*top*). Enlarged ventricles (see dark spaces at center of photos) are one of the best-validated biological features of schizophrenia.

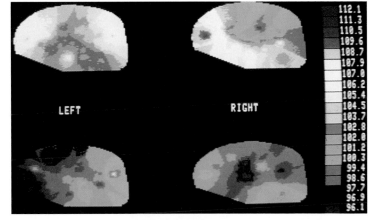

Differences in regional cerebral blood flow between schizophrenics (*bottom*) and normal (*top*) individuals for each hemisphere. The values shown were scored as the percentage change in cerebral blood flow from a control task to the Wisconsin Card Sort, which was expected to activate the prefrontal cortex. The normal participants showed greater prefrontal cortical activation as indexed by the "hotter" color of this brain region. *Source*: Weinberger, Berman, and Illowsky, 1988.

Mood Disorders and Schizophrenia

As we have mentioned, enlarged ventricles are not specific to schizophrenia; other psychotic patients, notably those with mood disorders, show ventricular enlargement almost as great as that seen in schizophrenia (Elkis et al., 1995). Similarly, increased density of dopamine receptors has been reported among psychotic patients with bipolar disorder (Pearlson et al., 1995). Maternal exposure to an influenza virus during the second trimester of pregnancy also increases the risk for mood disorders (Machon, Mednick, & Huttunen, 1997). The phenothiazines, used most often to treat schizophrenia, are also effective with patients with mania and with patients with psychotic depression.

Finally, the twin literature reports a set of identical triplets, two with bipolar disorder and one with schizophrenia.

These data suggest that the diagnostic categories of schizophrenia and psychotic mood disorders may not be totally separate entities. They share some common symptoms (notably delusions) and some possible etiological factors (increased dopamine activity), and they respond similarly to biological treatments. An important implication is that researchers would be well served to focus some of their efforts on psychotic symptoms across diagnostic groups rather than only on the diagnosis of schizophrenia.

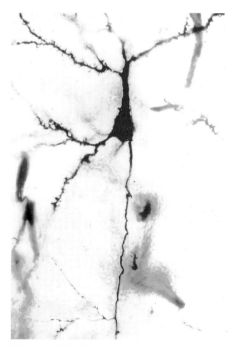

Figure 11.3 Micrograph of a neuron. The bumps on the dendrites are dendritic spines, which receive inputs from other neurons. Fewer dendritic spines may impair connections among neurons and may be a factor in schizophrenia.

normally goes up as energy is used. Patients with schizophrenia, especially those with prominent negative symptoms, do poorly on the tests and also fail to show activation in the prefrontal region (Potkin et al., 2002; Weinberger, Berman, & Illowsky, 1988). Failure to show frontal activation has also been found using the more recently developed fMRI (Barch et al., 2001).

Frontal hypoactivation is less pronounced in the nonschizophrenic twin of discordant MZ pairs, again suggesting that this brain dysfunction may not have a genetic origin (Torrey et al., 1994).[3] Failure to show frontal activation is related to the severity of negative symptoms (O'Donnell & Grace, 1998) and thus parallels the work on dopamine underactivity in the frontal cortex already discussed.

Despite the reduced volume of the gray matter in the temporal and frontal cortexes, the number of neurons in these areas does not appear to be reduced. More detailed studies indicate that what is lost in these areas may be what are called dendritic spines (Goldman-Rakic & Selemon, 1997; McGlashan & Hoffman, 2000). Dendritic spines are small projections on the shafts of dendrites where nerve impulses are received from other neurons (see Figure 11.3). The loss of these dendritic spines would mean that communication among neurons would be disrupted, resulting in what some have termed a "disconnection syndrome." One possible result of the failure of neural systems to communicate could be the speech and behavioral disorganization seen in schizophrenia.

A possible cause of some of these brain abnormalities is damage during gestation or birth. Many studies have shown high rates of delivery complications in patients with schizophrenia; such complications could have resulted in a reduced supply of oxygen to the brain, resulting in loss of cortical gray matter (Cannon et al., 2002). These obstetrical complications do not raise the rate of schizophrenia in everyone who experiences them; rather, the risk for schizophrenia is increased in those who experience complications and have a genetic diathesis (Cannon & Mednick, 1993).

Although the data are not entirely consistent (Westergaard et al., 1999), another possibility is that a virus invades the brain and damages it during fetal development (Mednick, Huttonen, & Machon, 1994; Mednick et al., 1988). During a five-week period in 1957 Helsinki experienced an epidemic of influenza virus. Researchers examined rates of schizophrenia among adults who had likely been exposed during their mothers'

---

[3] The Torrey et al. study of discordant MZ twins consistently found that the well twin was indistinguishable from normal participants on both structural and functional measures of the brain. The authors viewed this finding as evidence that these abnormalities are not genetically determined. However, the small number of participants in the study makes it difficult to statistically differentiate between groups. Furthermore, a large body of evidence has found neuropsychological impairments in the first-degree relatives of people with schizophrenia (e.g., Cannon et al., 1994). Therefore, it would be unwise to conclude that genes play no role in the brain dysfunction of schizophrenia.

pregnancies. People who had been exposed to the virus during the second trimester of pregnancy had much higher rates than those who had been exposed in either of the other trimesters or in nonexposed control adults. This finding is intriguing because we know that cortical development is in a critical stage of growth during the second trimester.

If, as the findings we have just reviewed suggest, the brains of people with schizophrenia are damaged early in their development, why does the disorder begin many years later, in adolescence or early adulthood? Weinberger (1987) proposed one answer to this question. He hypothesized that the brain injury interacts with normal brain development and that the prefrontal cortex is a brain structure that matures late, typically in adolescence. Thus an injury to this area may not show itself in the person's behavior until the period of development when the prefrontal cortex begins to play a larger role in behavior. Notably, dopamine activity also peaks in adolescence, which may further set the stage for the onset of schizophrenic symptoms.

Alternatively, the development of symptoms in adolescence could reflect a loss of synapses due to an overactive pruning mechanism. Pruning refers to the elimination of synaptic connections and is a normal part of brain development in which synapses are reduced to about 60 percent of their maximum. Pruning occurs at different rates in different areas of the brain. It is mostly complete in sensory areas by about two years of age but does not stop in the frontal cortex until mid-adolescence. If pruning was too extensive, the result would be a loss of communication among neurons (McGlashan & Hoffman, 2000).

Further work on the relationship of the brain and schizophrenia is proceeding at a rapid rate. Recognizing that the symptoms of schizophrenia implicate many areas of the brain, the research has moved away from trying to find some highly specific "lesion" and is beginning to examine neural systems and the way different areas of the brain interact with one another. This work is beginning to call attention to the possible role of a wider range of brain structures (e.g., the thalamus, cerebellum) in schizophrenia (Byne et al., 2002; Gilbert et al., 2001)

Psychological Stress and Schizophrenia

We have discussed several possible biological diatheses for schizophrenia, but more than a diathesis is required to produce schizophrenia. Psychological stress plays a key role by interacting with a biological vulnerability to produce this illness. Data show that, as with many of the disorders we have discussed, increases in life stress increase the likelihood of a relapse (Hirsch et al., 1996; Ventura et al., 1989). Furthermore, individuals with schizophrenia appear to be very reactive to the stressors we all encounter in daily living. Groups of psychotic patients (92 percent with schizophrenia), their first-degree relatives, and controls participated in a six-day ecological momentary assessment study (see p. 94) in which they recorded stress and mood several times each day. Stress led to greater decreases in positive moods in both patients and their relatives compared with controls. Stress also led to greater increases in negative moods in the patients compared with both relatives and controls (Myin-Gremeys et al., 2001). Thus, patients with schizophrenia are particularly vulnerable to daily stress. When we review therapies for schizophrenia, we shall see how these findings have guided the development of interventions for this syndrome.

We turn now to the role of life stress in the actual development of schizophrenia. Two stressors that have played an important part in research in this area are social class and the family.

Social Class and Schizophrenia   For many years we have known that the highest rates of schizophrenia are found in central city areas inhabited by people in the lowest socioeconomic classes (e.g., Harvey et al., 1996; Hollingshead & Redlich, 1958; Srole et al., 1962). The relationship between social class and schizophrenia does not show a continuous progression of higher rates of schizophrenia as the social class becomes lower. Rather, there is a decidedly sharp difference between the number of people with schizophrenia in the lowest social class and the number in other social classes. In the classic ten-year Hollingshead and Redlich study of social class and mental illness in New Haven,

The prevalence of schizophrenia is highest among people in the lowest social class.

Connecticut, the rate of schizophrenia was found to be twice as high in the lowest social class as in the next lowest class. These findings have been confirmed cross-culturally by similar community studies carried out in countries such as Denmark, Norway, and the United Kingdom (Kohn, 1968).

The correlations between social class and schizophrenia are consistent, but they are difficult to interpret in causal terms. Some people believe that stressors associated with being in a low social class may cause or contribute to the development of schizophrenia—the **sociogenic hypothesis**. The degrading treatment a person receives from others, the low level of education, and the lack of rewards and opportunity taken together may make membership in the lowest social class such a stressful experience that an individual—at least one who is predisposed—develops schizophrenia. Alternatively, the stressors encountered by those in the lowest social class could be biological; for example, we know that children of mothers whose nutrition during pregnancy was poor are at increased risk for schizophrenia (Susser et al., 1996).

Another explanation of the correlation between schizophrenia and low social class is the **social-selection theory**, which reverses the direction of causality between social class and schizophrenia. During the course of their developing psychosis, people with schizophrenia may drift into the poverty-ridden areas of the city. The growing cognitive and motivational problems besetting these individuals may so impair their earning capabilities that they cannot afford to live elsewhere. Or, they may choose to move to areas where little social pressure will be brought to bear on them and where they can escape intense social relationships.

One possible way of resolving the conflict between these opposing theories would be to study the social mobility of schizophrenic people. However, results have been inconsistent (e.g., Dunham 1965: Turner & Wagonfeld, 1967). Kohn (1968) suggested another way of examining this question: Are the fathers of patients with schizophrenia also from the lowest social class? If they are, this could be considered evidence in favor of the sociogenic hypothesis that lower-class status is conducive to schizophrenia, for class would be shown to precede schizophrenia. If the fathers are from a higher social class, the social-selection hypothesis would be the better explanation. Turner and Wagonfeld (1967) conducted such a study and found evidence for the social-selection hypothesis. Of twenty-six patients in the lowest social class, only four had fathers in the lowest class.

A study in Israel evaluated the two theories by investigating both social class and ethnic background (Dohrenwend et al., 1992). The rates of schizophrenia were examined in Israeli Jews of European ethnic background and in more recent immigrants to Israel from North Africa and the Middle East. The latter group experiences considerable racial prejudice and discrimination. The sociogenic hypothesis would predict that because they experience high levels of stress in all social classes, the members of the disadvantaged ethnic group should have consistently higher rates of schizophrenia in all social classes. However, this pattern did not emerge, supporting the social-selection theory.

In sum, the data are more supportive of the social selection than of the sociogenic theory. But we should not conclude that the social environment plays no role in schizophrenia. For example, the prevalence of schizophrenia among Africans from the Caribbean who remain in their native country is much lower than among those who have emigrated to London (Bhugra et al., 1996). This difference could well be caused by the stress associated with trying to assimilate into a new culture.

The Family and Schizophrenia   Early theorists regarded family relationships, especially those between a mother and her son, as crucial in the development of schizophrenia. At one time the view was so prevalent that the term **schizophrenogenic mother** was coined for the supposedly cold and dominant, conflict-inducing parent who was said to produce schizophrenia in her offspring (Fromm-Reichmann, 1948). These mothers were characterized as rejecting, overprotective, self-sacrificing, impervious to the feelings of others, rigid and moralistic about sex, and fearful of intimacy.

Controlled studies evaluating the schizophrenogenic-mother theory have not yielded supporting data. Studies of families of individuals with schizophrenia have, however, revealed that they differ in some ways from normal families, for example, by showing vague patterns of communication and high levels of conflict. It is plausible, though, that the conflict and unclear communication are a response to having a young family member with schizophrenia.

Some findings do suggest that the faulty communications of parents may play a role in the etiology of schizophrenia. One type of communication deviance that has been studied is illustrated in the following example. Note how the father not only ignores his daughter's concern but ridicules her choice of words.

> **Daughter** (complainingly): Nobody will listen to me. Everybody is trying to still me.
>
> **Mother:** Nobody wants to kill you.
>
> **Father:** If you're going to associate with intellectual people, you're going to have to remember that still is a noun and not a verb. (Wynne & Singer, 1963, p. 195)

In an important study of communication deviance, adolescents with behavior problems were studied along with their families. A five-year follow-up revealed that a number of the young people had developed schizophrenia or schizophrenia-related disorders. The investigators were then able to relate these disorders discovered at follow-up to any deviance in the communications of parents that had been evident five years earlier (Goldstein & Rodnick, 1975). Communication deviance in the families was indeed found to predict the later onset of schizophrenia in their offspring, supporting its significance (Norton, 1982). However, it does not appear that communication deviance is a specific etiological factor for schizophrenia, since parents of manic patients are equally high on this variable (Miklowitz, 1985).

Further evidence favoring some role for the family comes from a substantial adoption study by Tienari and his colleagues (1994) in Finland. A large sample of adopted offspring of mothers with schizophrenia is being studied along with a control group of adopted children. Extensive data were collected on various aspects of family life in the adoptive families, and these family data were related to the adjustment of the children. The families were categorized into levels of maladjustment based on material from clinical interviews as well as psychological tests. More serious psychopathology was found among the adoptees reared in a disturbed family environment. Furthermore, among children reared in a disturbed family environment, those having a biological parent with schizophrenia showed a greater increase in psychopathology than did the control participants. Although it is tempting to conclude that both a genetic predisposition and a noxious family environment are necessary to increase risk for psychopathology, a problem in interpretation remains: The disturbed family environment could be a response to a disturbed child. Thus we can only tentatively say that an etiological role for the family has been established.

A series of studies initiated in London indicate that the family can have an important impact on the adjustment of patients after they leave the hospital. Brown and his colleagues (1966) conducted a nine-month follow-up study of a sample of patients with schizophrenia who returned to live with their families after being discharged from the hospital. Interviews were conducted with parents or spouses before discharge and rated for the number of critical comments made about the patient and for expressions of hostility toward or emotional overinvolvement with him or her. The following statement is an example of a critical comment made by a father remarking on his daughter's behavior. The father is expressing the idea that his daughter is deliberately symptomatic to avoid housework. "My view is that Maria acts this way so my wife doesn't give her any responsibilities around the house" (Weissman et al., 1998). On the basis of this variable, called **expressed emotion** (EE), families were divided into two groups: those revealing a great deal of expressed emotion, called high-EE families, and those revealing little, called low-EE families. At the end of the follow-up period 10 percent of the patients returning to low-EE homes had relapsed. In marked contrast, in the same period, 58 percent of the patients returning to high-EE homes had gone back to the hospital!

This research, which has since been replicated (see Butzlaff & Hooley, 1998, for a meta-analysis), indicates that the environment to which patients are discharged has great bearing on how soon they are rehospitalized. It has also been found that negative symptoms of schizophrenia are most likely to elicit critical comments, as in the example presented in the previous paragraph, and that relatives who make the most critical comments tend to view patients as being able to control their symptoms (Lopez et al., 1999; Weissman et al., 1998).

What is not yet clear is exactly how to interpret the effects of EE. Is EE causal, or do these critical comments reflect a reaction to the patients' behavior? For example, if the condition of a patient with schizophrenia begins to deteriorate, family concern and involvement may be increased. Indeed, bizarre or dangerous behavior by the patient might seem to warrant limit-setting and other familial efforts that could increase the level of expressed emotion.

Research indicates that both interpretations of the operation of EE may be correct (Rosenfarb et al., 1994). Recently discharged schizophrenic patients and their high- or low-EE families were observed as they engaged in a discussion of a family problem. Two key findings emerged.

1. The expression of unusual thoughts by the patients ("If that kid bites you, you'll get rabies") elicited higher levels of critical comments by family members who had previously been characterized as high in EE.
2. In high-EE families critical comments by family members led to increased expression of unusual thoughts by the patients.

Thus this study found a bidirectional relationship: critical comments by members of high-EE families elicited more unusual thoughts by patients; and unusual thoughts expressed by the patients led to increased critical comments in high-EE families.

How does stress, such as a high level of EE, increase the symptoms of schizophrenia and precipitate relapses? One answer to this question relates the effects of stress on the hypothalamic-pituitary-adrenal (HPA) axis (see p. 207) to the dopamine theory (Walker & DiForio, 1997). Stress is known to activate the HPA axis, causing cortisol to be secreted. In turn, cortisol is known to increase dopamine activity and may thereby increase the symptoms of schizophrenia. Furthermore, heightened dopamine activity itself can increase HPA activation, which may make a person overly sensitive to stress. Thus the theory suggests that there is a bidirectional relationship between HPA activation and dopamine activity.

Another possibility is that stress may increase substance abuse. Patients report, for example, that alcohol reduces their anxiety, apathy, sleep difficulties, and anhedonia (Noorsdy et al., 1991). However, the irony is that drugs of abuse stimulate dopamine systems in the brain and may thereby increase the positive symptoms of the disorder.

The theory and research on expressed emotion in families form the basis of very promising interventions that help patients with schizophrenia remain outside of institutional settings (see p. 348).

Developmental Studies of Schizophrenia

What are people who develop schizophrenia like before their symptoms begin, typically in adolescence or early adulthood? An early method of answering this question was to construct developmental histories by examining the childhood records of those who had later become schizophrenic. Such research revealed that individuals who became schizophrenic were different from their contemporaries even before any serious problems were noted in their behavior.

In the 1960s, Albee and Lane and their colleagues repeatedly found that children who later developed schizophrenia had lower IQs than did members of various control groups, usually comprising siblings and neighborhood peers (Albee, Lane, & Reuter, 1964; Lane & Albee, 1965). Investigations of the social behavior of preschizophrenic patients yielded some interesting findings as well. For example, teachers described preschizophrenic boys as disagreeable in childhood and preschizophrenic girls as passive (Watt, 1974; Watt et al., 1970). Both men and women with schizophrenia were described as delinquent and withdrawn in childhood (Berry, 1967).

Researchers have also examined home movies taken before the onset of schizophrenia, just as part of normal family life (Walker, Davis, & Savoie, 1994; Walker et al., 1993). Compared with their siblings who did not later become schizophrenic, preschizophrenic children showed poorer motor skills and more expressions of negative affect.

As intriguing as these findings are, the major limitation of such developmental research is that the data were not originally collected with the intention of describing preschizophrenic patients or of predicting the development of schizophrenia from childhood behavior. More specific information is required if developmental histories are to provide clear evidence regarding etiology.

The high-risk method, described in Chapter 5, can yield this information. The first such study of schizophrenia was begun in the 1960s by Sarnoff Mednick and Fini Schulsinger (Mednick & Schulsinger, 1968). They chose Denmark because the Danish registries of all people make it possible to keep track of them for long periods of time. Mednick and Schulsinger selected as their high-risk subjects 207 young people whose mothers had chronic schizophrenia. The researchers decided that the mother should be the parent with the disorder because paternity is not always easy to determine. Then, 104 low-risk subjects, individuals whose mothers did not have schizophrenia, were matched to the high-risk subjects on variables such as sex, age, father's occupation, rural or urban residence, years of education, and institutional upbringing versus rearing by the family.

In 1972 the now-grown men and women were followed up with a number of measures, including a diagnostic battery. Fifteen of the high-risk subjects were diagnosed as schizophrenic; none of the control men and women was so diagnosed. Looking back to the information collected on the subjects when they were children, the investigators found that several circumstances predicted the later onset of schizophrenia.

These data, albeit from a small study, suggest that the etiology of schizophrenia may differ for positive- and negative-symptom patients. In one analysis of the data, the patients with schizophrenia were divided into two groups, those with predominantly positive and those with predominantly negative symptoms (Cannon, Mednick, & Parnas, 1990). Variables predicting schizophrenia were different for the two groups. Negative-symptom schizophrenia was preceded by a history of pregnancy and birth complications and by a failure to show electrodermal responses to simple stimuli. Positive-symptom schizophrenia was preceded by a history of family instability, such as separation from parents and placement in foster homes or institutions for periods of time.

In the wake of Mednick and Schulsinger's pioneering study several other high-risk investigations were undertaken, some of which have also yielded information concerning the possible causes of adult psychopathology. The New York High-Risk Study found that a composite measure of attentional dysfunction predicted behavioral disturbance at follow-up (Cornblatt & Erlenmeyer-Kimling, 1985). Furthermore, low IQ was a characteristic of the first high-risk children to be hospitalized (Erlenmeyer-Kimling & Cornblatt, 1987). In an Israeli study, poor neurobehavioral functioning (poor concentration, poor verbal ability, lack of motor control and coordination) predicted schizophrenia-like outcomes, as did earlier interpersonal problems (Marcus et al., 1987). As participants in other high-risk studies mature, we will gain further glimpses into the development of this debilitating disorder.

Sarnoff Mednick, a psychologist at the University of Southern California, pioneered the use of the high-risk method for studying schizophrenia. He has also contributed to the hypothesis that a maternal viral infection is implicated in this disorder.

Therapies for Schizophrenia

The puzzling, often frightening array of symptoms displayed by people with schizophrenia makes treatment difficult. The history of psychopathology, reviewed in Chapter 1, is in many respects a history of humankind's efforts, often brutal and unenlightened, to deal with schizophrenia, arguably the most serious of the disorders described in this book. Although some of the profoundly disturbed people confined centuries ago in foul asy-

A Classic Behavior Therapy Project with Hospitalized Schizophrenic Patients

Although the trend over the past forty years has been to have people with schizophrenia spend as little time as possible in a mental hospital, even with advances in psychoactive medication there are still hundreds of thousands of people living in institutional settings, some of them for many years. As described in Chapter 2 (p. 47), behavior therapists introduced an innovation known as the token economy into hospital settings in the 1960s. The most comprehensive and impressive of these efforts was reported by Gordon Paul and Robert Lentz (1977). Because this project was a milestone in the treatment of schizophrenia and an exemplar of comparative therapy research, we describe it here in some detail.

The long-term, regressed, and chronic schizophrenic patients in the program were the most severely debilitated institutionalized adults ever studied systematically. Some of these patients screamed for long periods, some were mute; many were incontinent, a few assaultive. Most of them no longer used silverware, and some buried their faces in their food. The patients were matched for age, sex, socioeconomic background, symptoms, and length of hospitalization and then assigned to one of three wards—social learning (behavioral—basically a token economy), milieu therapy, and routine hospital management. Each ward had twenty-eight residents. The two treatment wards shared ambitious objectives: to teach self-care, housekeeping, communication, and vocational skills; to reduce symptomatic behavior; and to release patients to the community.

- **Social-learning ward.** Located in a new mental health center, the social-learning ward operated on a token economy that embraced all aspects of the residents' lives. Tokens were a necessity, for they purchased meals as well as small luxuries. Residents' appearance had to pass muster in eleven specific ways each morning to earn a token.

Well-made beds, good behavior at mealtime, classroom participation, and socializing during free periods were other means of earning tokens. Residents learned through modeling, shaping, prompting, and instructions. They were also taught to communicate better with one another, and they participated in problem-solving groups. In addition to living by the rules of the token economy, individuals received behavioral treatments tailored to their needs, for example, assertion training to deal with a specific interpersonal conflict they might be having with a staff member. Residents were kept busy 85 percent of their waking hours learning to behave better.

- **Milieu-therapy ward.** The milieu therapy ward in the new center operated according to the principles of Jones's (1953) therapeutic community, an approach reminiscent of Pinel's moral treatment of the late eighteenth century (p. 10). These residents, too, were kept busy 85 percent of their waking hours. Both individually and as a group they were expected to act responsibly and to participate in decisions about how the ward was to function. In general, they were treated more as normal individuals than as incompetent mental patients. Staff members impressed on the residents their positive expectations and praised them for doing well. When patients behaved symptomatically, staff members stayed with them, making clear the expectation that they would soon behave more appropriately.

- **Routine hospital management.** These patients continued their accustomed hospital existence in an older state institution, receiving custodial care and heavy antipsychotic medication. Except for the 5 percent of their waking hours occupied by occasional activity, and recreational, occupational, and individual and group therapies, these people were on their own.

lums may have suffered from problems as prosaic as syphilis (see p. 13), there seems little doubt that many, if examined now, would carry a diagnosis of schizophrenia. Today we know a good deal about the nature and etiology of schizophrenia; but although we can treat its symptoms somewhat effectively, a cure remains elusive.

With the notable exception of an intensive behavior-therapy project described in Focus on Discovery 11.3, for the most part research indicates that hospital care does little to effect meaningful, enduring changes in the majority of mentally disordered patients (we described mental hospitals in Chapter 1, p. 12). The overwhelming body of evidence shows rehospitalization rates of 40 to 50 percent after one year and upwards of 75 percent after two years (Paul & Menditto, 1992). Studies specifically designed to follow patients with schizophrenia after discharge from the hospital show generally poor outcomes as well (Robinson et al., 1999).

A major problem with any kind of treatment for schizophrenia is that many patients with schizophrenia lack insight into their impaired condition and refuse any treatment at all (Amador et al., 1994). As they don't believe they have an illness, they don't see the need for professional intervention, particularly when it includes hospitalization or drugs. This is especially true for those with paranoid schizophrenia, who may regard any therapy as a threatening intrusion from hostile outside forces. Family members therefore face a major challenge in getting their relatives into treatment, which is one reason they sometimes turn to involuntary hospitalization via civil commitment as a last resort.

Before the program began, the staffs of the two treatment wards were carefully trained to adhere to detailed instructions in therapy manuals; regular observations confirmed that they were implementing the principles of a social-learning or a milieu-therapy program. Over the four and a half years of hospitalization and the one and a half years of follow-up, the patients were carefully evaluated at regular six-month intervals by structured interviews and by meticulous, direct, behavioral observations.

The results? Both the social-learning and the milieu therapy reduced positive and negative symptoms, with the social-learning ward achieving better results than the milieu ward on a number of measures. The residents also acquired self-care, housekeeping, social, and vocational skills. The behavior of members of these two groups within the institution was superior to that of the residents of the hospital ward, and by the end of treatment more of them had been discharged—over 10 percent of the social-learning patients left the center for independent living; 7 percent of the milieu patients achieved this goal; and none of the hospital-treatment patients did.

An interesting finding emerged concerning medication use. About 90 percent of the patients in all three groups were receiving antipsychotic drugs at the outset of the study. Over time, use among the routine-hospital-management group increased to 100 percent. In contrast, the percentage dropped to 18 percent in the milieu group and 11 percent in the social-learning ward. This is a remarkable finding in itself, for the medical staff had assumed that these chronic patients absolutely needed their medication or they would be too difficult for the staff to manage. In addition, many patients from all three groups were discharged to community placements, such as boarding homes and halfway houses, where there was supervision but also considerably less restraint than they had experienced while hospitalized. Members of the social-learning group did significantly better at remaining in these community residences than did patients in the other two groups.

Considering how poorly these patients were functioning before this treatment project, these results are extraordinary. That the social-learning program was superior to the milieu program is also significant, for milieu treatment is used in many mental hospitals. As implemented by Paul's team of clinicians, it provided patients with as much attention as those on the social-learning ward received. This equal amount of attention would appear to control well for the placebo effect of the social-learning therapy.

These results, though, should not be accepted as confirming the usefulness of token economies per se, for the social-learning therapy contained elements that went beyond operant conditioning of overt motor behavior. Staff provided information to residents about appropriate behavior and attempted verbally to clarify misconceptions. Paul (personal communication, 1981) relegated the token economy to a secondary, although not trivial, role. He saw it as a useful device for getting the attention of severely regressed patients in the initial stages of treatment. The token economy created the opportunity for his patients to acquire new information, or, in Paul's informal phrase, to "get good things into their heads."

Paul and Lentz never claimed that any one of these patients was cured. Although they were able to live outside the hospital, most continued to manifest many signs of mental disorder, and few of them had gainful employment or participated in the social activities that most people take for granted. The outcome, though, is not to be underestimated: chronic mental patients, those typically shut away on back wards and forgotten by society, can be resocialized and taught self-care. They can learn to behave normally enough to be discharged from mental institutions. This is a major achievement in mental health care. Reports published since the Paul and Lentz study support the effectiveness of social-learning programs (see reviews by Mueser & Liberman, 1995, and Paul & Menditto, 1992; Paul, Stuve, & Cross, 1997). (For a discussion of the aftercare aspects of the Paul–Lentz project, see Focus on Discovery 11.5, p. 354.)

Before we examine the range of therapies for schizophrenia, it is important to point out that the appropriateness of a given therapy depends on the stage of illness that the patient is in. That is, when a patient is in an acutely psychotic phase of the illness, social-skills training or the other psychological interventions described later will not likely be successful because the patient is too distracted, too disabled to concentrate on what the therapist is saying. In such a phase some sort of psychoactive medication is going to be necessary. Once the person becomes less psychotic, a psychological intervention can begin to have a beneficial impact, and the dosage of the medication can be reduced as the patient learns ways to reduce the stress that precipitated the episode (Kopelowicz, Liberman, & Zarate, 2002).

Biological Treatments

Shock and Psychosurgery   The general warehousing of patients in mental hospitals earlier in the twentieth century, coupled with the shortage of professional staff, created a climate that allowed, perhaps even subtly encouraged, experimentation with radical biological interventions. In the early 1930s the practice of inducing a coma with large dosages of insulin was introduced by Sakel (1938), who claimed that up to three-quarters of the patients with schizophrenia whom he treated showed significant improvement. Later find-

Scene from *One Flew over the Cuckoo's Nest*. The character on whom Jack Nicholson is sitting was lobotomized in the film.

ings by others were less encouraging, and insulin-coma therapy—which presented serious risks to health, including irreversible coma and death—was gradually abandoned. As discussed in Chapter 10, electroconvulsive therapy (ECT) was also used after its development in 1938 by Cerletti and Bini; it, too, proved to be only minimally effective.

In 1935, Moñiz, a Portuguese psychiatrist, introduced the **prefrontal lobotomy**, a surgical procedure that destroys the tracts connecting the frontal lobes to lower centers of the brain. His initial reports claimed high rates of success (Moñiz, 1936), and for twenty years thereafter thousands of mental patients—not only those diagnosed with schizophrenia—underwent variations of psychosurgery. The procedure was used especially for those whose behavior was violent. Many patients did indeed quiet down and could even be discharged from hospitals. During the 1950s, however, this intervention fell into disrepute for several reasons. After surgery many patients became dull and listless and suffered serious losses in their cognitive capacities—for example, becoming unable to carry on a coherent conversation with another person—which is not surprising given the destruction of parts of their brains believed responsible for thought. The principal reason for its abandonment, however, was the introduction of drugs that seemed to reduce the behavioral and emotional excesses of many patients.

Drug Therapies   Without question the most important development in the treatment of schizophrenia was the advent in the 1950s of several medications collectively referred to as **antipsychotic drugs**, also referred to as *neuroleptics* because they produce side effects similar to the symptoms of a neurological disease.

Traditional Antipsychotic Drugs   One of the more frequently prescribed antipsychotic drugs, *phenothiazine*, was first produced by a German chemist in the late nineteenth century. Not until the discovery of the antihistamines, which have a phenothiazine nucleus, in the 1940s, did phenothiazines receive much attention.

Reaching beyond their use to treat the common cold and asthma, the French surgeon Laborit pioneered the use of antihistamines to reduce surgical shock. He noticed that they made his patients somewhat sleepy and less fearful about the impending operation. Laborit's work encouraged pharmaceutical companies to reexamine antihistamines in light of their tranquilizing effects. Shortly thereafter a French chemist, Charpentier, prepared a new phenothiazine derivative, which he called *chlorpromazine*. This drug proved very effective in calming patients with schizophrenia. As already mentioned, phenothiazines derive their therapeutic properties by blocking dopamine receptors in the brain, thus reducing the influence of dopamine on thought, emotion, and behavior.

Chlorpromazine (trade name Thorazine) was first used therapeutically in the United States in 1954 and rapidly became the preferred treatment for schizophrenia. By 1970 more than 85 percent of all patients in state mental hospitals were receiving chlorpromazine or another phenothiazine. Other antipsychotics that have been used for years to treat schizophrenia include the *butyrophenones* (e.g., haloperidol, Haldol) and the *thioxanthenes* (e.g., thiothixene, Navane). Both types seem generally as effective as the phenothiazines and work in similar ways. These classes of drugs can reduce the positive symptoms of schizophrenia but have little or no effect on the negative symptoms.

Although the antipsychotics reduce positive symptoms of schizophrenia so that many patients can be released from the hospital, they are not a cure. Furthermore, about 30 percent of patients with schizophrenia do not respond favorably to the antipsychotics just discussed, although some of these patients may respond to newer antipsychotic drugs (e.g., clozapine), which will be discussed later. Because of the side effects of the whole range of antipsychotic drugs, about half the patients who take them quit after one year and up to three-quarters quit after two years (*Harvard Mental Health Letter*, 1995). For this reason patients are frequently treated with long-lasting antipsychotics (e.g., fluphenazine decanoate, Prolixin), which are injected every two to six weeks.

Other drugs are used adjunctively—that is, along with antipsychotics—to treat depression or anxiety or to stabilize mood. These adjunctive medications include lithium, antidepressants, anticonvulsants, and tranquilizers. Antidepressants are also used with schizophrenic patients who become depressed after a psychotic episode (Hogarty et al., 1994; Siris et al., 1994).

Patients who respond positively to the antipsychotics are kept on so-called *maintenance doses* of the drug, just enough to continue the therapeutic effect. They take their medication and return to the hospital or clinic on occasion for adjustment of the dose level. Released patients who are maintained on medication may make only marginal adjustment to the community, however. For example, they may be unable to live unsupervised or to hold down the kind of job for which they would otherwise be qualified. Their social relationships are likely to be sparse. And again, although the antipsychotics keep positive symptoms from returning, they have little effect on negative symptoms such as flat affect. Reinstitutionalization is frequent. The antipsychotics have significantly reduced long-term institutionalization, but they also initiated the revolving-door pattern of admission, discharge, and readmission seen in some patients.

A promising procedure for reducing rehospitalization rates may now be available, however. In a study reported by Herz et al. (2000), patients were randomly assigned to maintenance treatment as usual (medication and supportive group therapy) or a new treatment involving the following components:

1. Educating patients about relapse and recognizing early signs of relapse.
2. Monitoring early signs of relapse by staff.
3. Weekly supportive group or individual therapy.
4. Family educational sessions.
5. Quick intervention, involving both increased doses of medication and crisis oriented problem-solving therapy, when early signs of relapse were detected.

Importantly, staff were able to accurately recognize early signs of relapse and implement procedures to deal with it. Over 18 months, the experimental treatment cut relapse rates in half and reduced rehospitalization rates by about 44%.

Side Effects of Traditional Antipsychotics   Commonly reported side effects of the antipsychotics include dizziness, blurred vision, restlessness, and sexual dysfunction. In addition, a group of particularly disturbing side effects, termed *extrapyramidal side effects*, stem from dysfunctions of the nerve tracts that descend from the brain to spinal motor neurons. Extrapyramidal side effects resemble the symptoms of Parkinson's disease. People taking antipsychotics usually develop tremors of the fingers, a shuffling gait, and drooling. Other side effects include *dystonia*, a state of muscular rigidity, and *dyskinesia*, an abnormal motion of voluntary and involuntary muscles, producing chewing movements as well as other movements of the lips, fingers, and legs; together they cause arching of the back and a twisted posture of the neck and body. *Akasthesia* is an inability to remain still; people pace constantly and fidget. These perturbing symptoms can be treated by drugs used with patients who have Parkinson's disease.

In a muscular disturbance of older patients with schizophrenia, called *tardive dyskinesia*, the mouth muscles involuntarily make sucking, lip-smacking, and chin-wagging motions. In more severe cases the whole body can be subject to involuntary motor movements. This syndrome affects about 10 to 20 percent of patients treated with antipsychotics for a long period of time and is not responsive to any known treatment (Sweet et al., 1995). Finally, a side effect called *neuroleptic malignant syndrome* occurs in about 1 percent of cases. In this condition, which can sometimes be fatal, severe muscular rigidity develops, accompanied by fever. The heart races, blood pressure increases, and the patient may lapse into a coma.

Because of these serious side effects, some clinicians believe it is unwise to take high doses of antipsychotics for extended periods of time. Current clinical practice calls for treating patients with the smallest possible doses of drugs. The clinician is put in a bind by this situation: if medication is reduced, the chance of relapse increases; but if medication is continued, serious and untreatable side effects may develop.

Newer Drug Therapies In the decades following the introduction of the traditional antipsychotic drugs, there appeared to be little interest in developing new drugs to treat schizophrenia. This situation has changed markedly in recent years, with the introduction of *clozapine* (Clozaril), which can produce therapeutic gains in patients with schizophrenia who do not respond well to traditional antipsychotics (Kane et al., 1988) and has produced greater therapeutic gains in reducing positive symptoms than traditional antipsychotics (Rosenheck et al., 1999; Wahlbeck et al., 1999). Patients who take clozapine are also less likely to drop out of treatment (Kane et al., 2001). In addition, Clozapine produces fewer motor side effects than do traditional antipsychotics. Furthermore, maintenance of discharged patients on clozapine reduces relapse rates (Conley et al., 1999). Although the precise biochemical mechanism of the therapeutic effects of clozapine is not yet known, we do know that it has a major impact on serotonin receptors.

Clozapine does have serious side effects, however. It can impair the functioning of the immune system in a small percentage of patients (about 1 percent) by lowering numbers of white blood cells, making patients vulnerable to infection and even death. For this reason, patients taking clozapine have to be carefully monitored. It also can produce seizures and other side effects, such as dizziness, fatigue, drooling, and weight gain (Meltzer, Cola, & Way, 1993).

The success of clozapine stimulated drug companies to begin a more earnest search for other drugs that might be more effective than traditional antipsychotics. Two results of this search are *olanzapine* (Zyprexa) and *risperidone* (Risperdal). Both have the advantage of producing fewer motor side effects than traditional antipsychotics; perhaps, because of the reduced rate of side effects, patients are somewhat less likely to discontinue treatment (Dolder et al., 2002). The newer drugs appear to be as effective as traditional antipsychotics in reducing positive symptoms (Conley & Mahmoud, 2001), perhaps even better (Sanger et al., 1999). They also appear to be superior to traditional drugs in reducing rehospitalization rates (Csernansky et al., 2002).

A psychological approach to the study of risperidone examines fundamental aspects of cognition, such as attention and memory, that are known to be deficient in many patients with schizophrenia (e.g., Green, 1993) and are associated with poor social adaptation (Green, 1996). Evidence is emerging that risperidone improves short-term memory—involved in, for example, remembering a phone number long enough to be able to dial it—more than other antipsychotic drugs, apparently by reducing the activity of serotonin-sensitive receptors in the frontal cortex (Green et al., 1997). Research has also shown that improvements in memory are correlated with improvements in learning social skills in psychosocial rehabilitation programs (Green, 1996; Marder et al., 1999). Risperidone may thus make possible more thoroughgoing changes in schizophrenia and its behavioral consequences than do drugs that do not have these cognitive effects.

Evaluation of Drug Therapies Antipsychotic drugs are an indispensable part of treatment for schizophrenia and will undoubtedly continue to be an important component. They are surely preferable to the straitjackets formerly used to restrain patients. Furthermore, the recent success of clozapine, olanzapine, and risperidone has stimulated a continued effort to find new and more effective drug therapies for schizophrenia. Many other drugs are currently being evaluated, so that we may be on the verge of a new era in the treatment of schizophrenia. See Table 11.4 for a summary of major drugs used to treat schizophrenia.

Table 11.4 Summary of Major Drugs Used in Treating Schizophrenia

Drug Category	Generic Name	Trade Name
Phenothiazine	Chlorpromazine	Thorazine
	Fluphenazine decanoate	Prolixin
Butyrophenone	Haloperidol	Haldol
Thioxanthene	Thiothixene	Navane
Tricyclic dibenzodiazepine	Clozapine	Clozaril
Thienbenzodiazepine	Olanzapine	Zyprexa
Benzisoxazole	Risperidone	Risperdal

And yet, our growing knowledge of biological diatheses for schizophrenia and the continuing improvement in antipsychotic medications, as just seen, should not lead to a neglect of the importance of psychosocial factors in both the causes of and the efforts to control schizophrenia. The case has recently been put clearly by two psychiatrists in a review of empirically supported psychological treatments for schizophrenia. Their sentiments are useful to keep in mind as we turn to such interventions:

> For veteran practitioners who have long considered only biological treatments as effective in protecting schizophrenic individuals from stress-induced relapse and disability...evidence [on reducing expressed emotion in families, reviewed later] that supports the protective value of psychosocial treatments...may serve as an antidote to the insidious biological reductionism that often characterizes the field of schizophrenia research and treatment.... It is essential to view treatments of schizophrenia in their biopsychosocial matrix—leaving out any of the three components...will diminish the impact and efficacy of treatment. (Kopelowicz & Liberman, 1998, p. 192)

Psychological Treatments

It is increasingly understood by mental health professionals as well as patients and families that the cognitive impairments inherent in schizophrenia are likely to limit the degree to which patients with this illness can profit from psychological interventions (Bowen et al., 1994). Add to this the accumulating evidence that whatever the biological diathesis for schizophrenia, it is likely to persist throughout the person's life as a vulnerability (Neuchterlein et al., 1994), and you have a situation that might discourage clinicians from even trying to implement psychosocial treatments. But as we have just seen, as promising as many of the newer antipsychotic drugs are, a neglect of the psychological and social aspect of schizophrenia compromises efforts to deal with people and their families who are struggling with this illness. We turn now to a consideration of various psychological treatments of schizophrenia as we come to appreciate both their limitations and their strengths.

Psychodynamic Therapies   Freud did little, either in his clinical practice or through his writings, to adapt psychoanalysis to the treatment of patients with schizophrenia. He believed that they were incapable of establishing the close interpersonal relationship essential for analysis. It was Harry Stack Sullivan, an American psychiatrist, who pioneered the use of psychotherapy with schizophrenic hospital patients. Sullivan established a ward at the Sheppard and Enoch Pratt Hospital in Towson, Maryland, in 1923 and developed a psychoanalytic treatment reported to be markedly successful.

Sullivan held that schizophrenia reflects a return to early childhood forms of communication. The fragile ego of the individual with schizophrenia, unable to handle the extreme stress of interpersonal challenges, regresses. Therapy therefore requires the patient to learn adult forms of communication and to achieve insight into the role the past has played in current problems. Sullivan advised the very gradual, nonthreatening development of a trusting relationship. For example, he recommended that the therapist sit somewhat to the side of the patient in order not to force eye contact, which he considered too frightening in the early stages of treatment. After many sessions, and with the establishment of greater trust and support, the analyst begins to encourage the patient to examine his or her interpersonal relationships.

A similar ego-analytic approach was proposed by Frieda Fromm-Reichmann (1889–1957), a German psychiatrist who emigrated to the United States and worked for a period of time with Sullivan at Chestnut Lodge, a private mental hospital in Rockville, Maryland. Fromm-Reichmann was sensitive to the symbolic and unconscious meaning of behavior, attributing the aloofness of patients with schizophrenia to a wish to avoid the rebuffs suffered in childhood and thereafter judged inevitable. She treated them with great patience and optimism, making it clear that they need not take her into their world or give up their sickness until they were completely ready to do so. Along with Sullivan, Fromm-Reichmann (1952) helped establish a variant of psychoanalysis as a major treatment for schizophrenia.

The overall evaluation of analytically oriented psychotherapy with such patients justifies little enthusiasm, however (Katz & Gunderson, 1990; Stanton et al., 1984). Although great claims of success were made for the analyses done by Sullivan and Fromm-Reichmann, a close consideration of the patients they saw indicates that many were only mildly disturbed and might not even have been diagnosed as schizophrenic by the strict DSM-IV-TR criteria for the disorder.

Furthermore, the problems patients with schizophrenia have just thinking clearly about things may well make such therapy harmful, at least during the more acute phase of a psychotic episode (Mueser & Berenbaum, 1990). Results from a long-term follow-up of patients bearing a diagnosis of schizophrenia and discharged after treatment between 1963 and 1976 at the New York State Psychiatric Institute showed analytic approaches to be largely unsuccessful with these patients (Stone, 1986). Such treatment may in itself be too intrusive and too intense for some patients with schizophrenia to handle.

More recent psychosocial interventions take a more active, present-focused, and reality-oriented turn as therapists try to help patients and their families deal more directly with the everyday problems they face in coping with this disruptive and debilitating illness. Inherent to this work is the assumption that a good deal of the stress experienced by people with schizophrenia is due to their difficulties in negotiating everyday social challenges, including the pressures that arise in their families when they return home after hospitalization. We turn now to these newer and more effective approaches.

Social-Skills Training   Social-skills training is designed to teach people with schizophrenia how to succeed in a wide variety of interpersonal situations—discussing their medications with their psychiatrist, ordering meals in a restaurant, filling out job applications and learning to interview for jobs (sometimes called vocational rehabilitation), saying no to offers to buy drugs on the street, learning about safer sex, reading bus schedules—behaviors that most of us take for granted and give little thought to in our daily lives. For people with schizophrenia, these life skills are not to be taken for granted; such individuals need to work hard to acquire or reacquire them. Doing so enables the person to partake more of the positive things that are available outside of institutional settings, enhancing their quality of life (Heinssen, Liberman, & Kopelowicz, 2000; Liberman, Eckman, Kopelowicz, & Stolar, 2000).

In an early demonstration of social-skills training, Bellack, Hersen, and Turner (1976) contrived social situations for three chronic schizophrenic patients and then observed whether they behaved appropriately. For instance, a patient was told to pretend that he had just returned home from a weekend trip to find that his lawn had been mowed. As he gets out of the car, his next-door neighbor approaches him and says that he has cut the patient's grass because he was already cutting his own. The patient must then respond to the situation. As expected, patients were initially not very good at making a socially appropriate response, which in this instance might have been some sort of thank-you. Training followed. The therapist encouraged the patients to respond, commenting helpfully on their efforts. If necessary, the therapist also modeled appropriate behavior so that the patients could observe and then try to imitate it.

This combination of role-playing, modeling, and positive reinforcement effected significant improvement in all three patients. There was even generalization to social situations that had not been worked on during the training. This study and others conducted with larger groups of patients indicate that severely disturbed patients can be taught new social behavior that helps them function better—fewer relapses, better social functioning, and higher quality of life (Kopelowicz et al., 2002). Some of the studies are noteworthy (e.g., Lieberman et al., 1998; Marder et al., 1996) in demonstrating benefits over a period of two years following treatment. Social-skills training nowadays is usually a component of treatments for schizophrenia that go beyond the use of medications alone, including family therapies for lowering expressed emotion. We turn to that work now.

Family Therapy and Reducing Expressed Emotion   Many patients with schizophrenia who are discharged from mental hospitals go home to their families of origin.

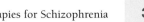

Earlier we discussed research showing that high levels of expressed emotion (EE; including being hostile, hypercritical, and overprotective within the family) have been linked to relapse and rehospitalization (p. 339). Based on this finding, a number of family interventions have been developed. Though they differ in length, setting, and specific techniques, these therapies have several features in common beyond the overall purpose of calming things down for the patient by calming things down for the family.

- *Education about schizophrenia, specifically the biological vulnerability that predisposes some people to the illness, cognitive problems inherent to schizophrenia, its symptoms, and signs of impending relapse.* High-EE families are typically not well informed about schizophrenia, and acquisition of some basic knowledge is intended to help reduce the tendency of family members to be overly critical of the relative with schizophrenia. Knowing, for example, that biology has a lot to do with having schizophrenia and that the illness involves problems thinking clearly and rationally might help the family be more accepting and understanding of the patient's inappropriate or ineffectual actions. Therapists encourage family members to lower their expectations of their schizophrenic kin as a way to reduce their criticism. Therapists make clear to family and patient alike that schizophrenia is primarily a biochemical illness and that proper medication and the kind of therapy they are receiving can reduce stress on the patient and prevent deterioration.

- *Information about and monitoring of the effects of antipsychotic medication.* Therapists impress on both the family and the patient the importance of the patient's taking his or her antipsychotic medication, becoming better informed about the side effects of the medication, and taking initiative and responsibility for seeking medical consultation rather than just discontinuing the drugs.

- *Avoidance of blaming—specifically, encouragement of family members to blame neither themselves nor the patient for the illness and for the difficulties all are having in coping with it.*

- *Improving communication and problem-solving skills within the family.* Therapists focus on teaching the family ways to express both positive and negative feelings in a constructive, empathic, nondemanding manner rather than in a finger-pointing, critical, or overprotective way. They focus as well on defusing tense personal conflicts by teaching family members ways to work together to solve everyday problems.

- *Encouraging patients as well as their families to expand their social contacts, especially their support networks.*

- *Instilling a degree of hope that things can improve, including the hope that the patient may not have to return to the hospital.*

Programs employ various techniques to implement these several strategies. Examples include identifying stressors that could cause relapse, training in communication and problem solving, and having high-EE family members watch videotapes of interactions of low-EE families (Penn & Mueser, 1996). Compared with standard treatments (usually just medication), family therapy plus medication has typically lowered relapse over periods of one to two years. This positive finding is evident particularly in studies in which the treatment lasted for at least nine months (Falloon et al., 1982, 1985; Hogarty et al., 1986, 1991; Kopelowicz & Liberman, 1998; McFarlane et al., 1995; Penn & Mueser, 1996).

Cognitive-Behavioral Therapy   We turn next to several new cognitive-behavioral approaches in the treatment of schizophrenia. It was once assumed that it was futile to try to alter the cognitive distortions, including delusions, of patients with schizophrenia. Now, however, a developing clinical and experimental literature demonstrates that the maladaptive beliefs of some patients can in fact be changed with cognitive-behavioral interventions (Garety, Fowler, & Kuipers, 2000).

Personal Therapy   As encouraging as the family EE-lowering studies were, most patients were still returning to the hospital, and the clinical outcomes of those who managed to remain in the community left a lot to be desired (Hogarty et al., 1997a). What more could be done for discharged patients with schizophrenia to increase their chances of being able to remain longer outside the hospital, whether or not they could do so within their family of origin? This question led to the following efforts by one of the groups that had published positive, though limited, findings on lowering EE (Hogarty et al., 1995, 1997a, 1997b).

What Hogarty et al. call "personal therapy" is a broad-spectrum cognitive-behavioral approach to the multiplicity of problems of patients with schizophrenia who have been discharged from the hospital. This individualistic therapy is conducted both one-on-one and in small groups (workshops). A key element in this approach, based on the finding in EE research that a reduction in emotional reactions by family members leads to less relapse following hospital discharge, is teaching the patient how to recognize inappropriate affect. If ignored, inappropriate affect can build up and lead to cognitive distortions and inappropriate social behavior. Patients are taught also to notice small signs of relapse, such as social withdrawal or inappropriate threats against others, and they learn skills to reduce these problems. Such behaviors, if left unchecked, will likely interfere with the patients' efforts to live by conventional social rules, including keeping a job and making and maintaining social contacts. The therapy also includes some rational-emotive behavior therapy to help patients avoid turning life's inevitable frustrations and challenges into catastrophes and thus to help them lower their stress levels.

In addition, patients are often taught muscle-relaxation techniques as an aid to learning to detect the gradual buildup of anxiety or anger and then to apply the relaxation skills in order to control these emotions better.[4] The operating assumption is that emotional dysregulation is part of the biological diathesis in schizophrenia (we will encounter emotional dysregulation again when we discuss borderline personality disorder in Chapter 13) and a factor that patients must learn to live and cope with rather than eliminate (or cure) altogether. But there is also a strong focus on teaching specific social skills as well as on encouraging patients to continue to take their antipsychotic medication in a maintenance mode, that is, in a dose that is typically lower than what is necessary in the earliest, acute, and most florid phase of the illness.

Hogarty's individual therapy also includes non-behavioral elements, especially warm and empathic acceptance of the patient's emotional and cognitive turmoil along with realistic but optimistic expectations that life can be better. In general, patients are taught that they have emotional vulnerabilities to stress, that their thinking is not always as clear as it should be, that they have to continue with their medication, and that they can learn a variety of skills to make the most of the hand that nature has dealt them. This is not a short-term treatment; it can extend over three years of weekly to biweekly therapy contacts.

Note that the focus of much of this therapy is on the patient, not on the family. Whereas the focus in the family studies was on reducing the high EE of the patient's family—an environmental change from the point of view of the patient—the goal of personal therapy is teaching internal coping skills to the patient, new ways of thinking about

---

[4] Personal note. While one of us was on his clinical internship in 1965, he worked individually with one of the patients on the ward who had a schizophrenia diagnosis. This patient was extremely anxious much of the time, and the medications he was being given were not calming him down more than just a little. Fresh from completing his dissertation on systematic desensitization, your author decided to try some relaxation training with the patient. After a couple of sessions, the patient seemed to derive some degree of temporary benefit, though the sessions had to be kept very short because he had problems concentrating on the instructions. Your author then discussed the treatment with one of his supervisors. Trying to be supportive of these efforts, yet obviously concerned, the supervisor expressed surprise that the relaxation sessions had gone as well as they had. The supervisor believed that "all hell would break loose" if the patient's defenses were lowered by the relaxation training. In other words, the patient's anxiety was seen by the supervisor as holding in check a seething cauldron of primordial libidinal forces that the fragile ego was not equipped to deal with. Lowering defenses by relaxation training would, he feared, expose the patient to feelings and thoughts that he would not be able to handle. The supervisor's concerns might have been well placed for other patients, but, fortunately in the present instance, the training in relaxation, slow and limited as it turned out to be, helped the patient cope better with his anxieties and made it easier for him to discuss areas of sensitivity in his life. Among other things, this clinical vignette underscores again the role that theories and paradigms have in how a clinician conceptualizes a case and how he or she tries to intervene. It obviously made an impact on your author, for he remembers it clearly almost forty years later.

and controlling his or her own affective reactions to whatever challenges are presented by his or her environment.

Finally, important in this therapy is what Hogarty et al. call "criticism management and conflict resolution." This phrase refers to learning how to deal with negative feedback from others and how to resolve the interpersonal conflicts that are an inevitable part of dealing with others. Teaching patients social problem-solving skills—how to deal with the inevitable challenges that everyone faces in dealing with others—is part of this element of the therapy (D'Zurilla & Goldfried, 1971). Indications are that this form of intervention can help many people with schizophrenia stay out of the hospital and function better, with the most favorable outcomes achieved by those who can live with their family of origin (Hogarty et al., 1997a, 1997b).

Reattribution Therapy   We have just reviewed work by Hogarty et al. that includes attempts to apply rational-emotive behavior therapy to help patients with schizophrenia catastrophize less when things don't go their way. There is also evidence that some patients can be encouraged to test out their delusional beliefs in much the same way as normal people do. Through collaborative discussions (and in the context of other modes of interventions, including antipsychotic drugs), some patients have been helped to attach a nonpsychotic meaning to paranoid symptoms and thereby reduce their intensity and aversive nature, similar to what is done in Beck's cognitive therapy for depression and Barlow's approach to panic disorder (Beck & Rector, 2000; Drury et al., 1996; Haddock et al., 1998). With the caveat that this rather intellectual approach is probably suitable for only a minority of patients with schizophrenia, here is an early example of the approach from one of our own cases.

A man had been diagnosed as paranoid schizophrenic, primarily because of his complaints of "pressure points" on his forehead and other parts of his body. He believed that these pressure points were signals from outside forces helping him to make decisions. These paranoid delusions had been resistant to drug treatment and other psychotherapeutic approaches. The therapist, in examining the man's case history, hypothesized that the patient became very anxious and tense when he had to make a decision, that his anxiety took the form of muscular tension in certain bodily parts, and that the patient misconstrued the tension as pressure points, signals from helpful spirits. Both patient and therapist agreed to explore the possibility that the pressure points were in fact part of a tension reaction to specific situations. For this purpose the therapist decided to teach the man deep-muscle relaxation, with the hope that relaxation would enable him to control his tensions, including the pressure points.

But it was also important to have the man question his delusional system. So in the first session the therapist asked the patient to extend his right arm, clench his fist, and bend his wrist downward so as to bring the fist toward the inside of the forearm. The intent was to produce a feeling of tension in his forearm; this is precisely what happened, and the man noted that the feeling was quite similar to his pressure points.

Extensive relaxation training enabled the client to begin to control his anxiety in various situations within the hospital and at the same time to reduce the intensity of the pressure points. As he gained control over his feelings, he gradually came to refer to his pressure points as "sensations," and his conversation in general began to lose its earlier paranoid flavor.

The relaxation training apparently allowed the patient to test a nonparanoid hypothesis about his pressure points, to see it confirmed, and thereby to shake off a belief about these sensations that had contributed to his paranoia. (Davison, 1966)

Attending to Basic Cognitive Functions   In recent years researchers have been attending to fundamental aspects of cognition that are disordered in schizophrenia in an attempt to improve these functions and thereby favorably affect behavior. This approach concentrates on trying to normalize such fundamental cognitive functions as attention and memory, which are known to be deficient in many patients with schizophrenia (e.g., Green, 1993) and are associated with poor social adaptation (Green, 1996; Green, Kern, Braff, & Mintz, 2000).

Efforts are underway at the Clinical Research Center for Schizophrenia and Psychiatric Rehabilitation at UCLA, under the leadership of research psychiatrist Robert Paul Liberman, to enhance through psychological means basic cognitive functions such as verbal learning ability. Another goal is to construct intervention strategies that make maximum use of those cognitive functions that remain relatively intact in schizophrenia, such as the ability to understand and remember what is presented in a picture. For example, photographs relevant to learning a necessary social skill are being employed in addition to the usual verbal means of teaching such skills (Kopelowicz & Liberman, 1998; Kopelowicz et al., 2002).

The assumption—yet to be borne out—is that improvement in these cognitive functions will lead to increased clinical improvement (Liberman & Green, 1992). Recall from our discussion of drug therapy that positive clinical outcomes from risperidone are associated with improvements in certain kinds of memory (Green et al., 1997), lending support to the more general notion that paying attention to fundamental cognitive processes—the kind that nonclinical cognitive psychologists study—holds promise for improving the social and emotional lives of people with schizophrenia.

Case Management

After deinstitutionalization began in the 1960s, many patients with schizophrenia no longer resided in mental hospitals and thus had to fend for themselves in securing needed services. Lacking the centralized hospital as the site where most services were delivered, the mental health system became more complex. In 1977, fearing that many patients were not accessing services, the National Institute of Mental Health (NIMH) established a program giving grants to states to help patients cope with the mental health system. Out of this program, a new mental health specialty, the case manager, was created.

Initially, case managers were basically brokers of services; because they were familiar with the system, they were able to get patients into contact with providers of whatever services the patients required. As the years passed, different models of case management developed. The major innovation was the recognition that case managers often needed to provide direct clinical services and that services might best be delivered by a team rather than brokered out. The Assertive Community Treatment model (Stein & Test, 1980) and the Intensive Case Management model (Surles et al., 1992) both entail a multidisciplinary team that provides services in the community ranging from medication, treatment for substance abuse, help in dealing with stressors patients face regularly (such as managing money), psychotherapy, vocational training, and assistance to patients in obtaining housing and employment. Case managers are the "glue" that holds together and coordinates the range of medical and psychological services that are necessary to keep patients with schizophrenia functioning outside of institutions and with some degree of independence and peace of mind (Kopelowicz et al., 2002).

Indications are that this more intensive treatment is superior to less intensive methods in reducing time spent in the hospital, improving housing stability, and ameliorating symptoms (Mueser, 1998). However, more intensive case management has not shown positive effects in other domains, such as time spent in jail or social functioning. The actual procedures that come under the rubric of case management vary a great deal from study to study. The services provided by a case management team will have positive effects only to the extent that those services are appropriate and effective.

General Trends in Treatment

Only a generation ago many, if not most, mental health professionals and laypeople believed the primary culprit in the etiology of schizophrenia was the child's psychological environment—most especially, the family. As we have seen throughout this chapter, the thinking now is that biological factors predispose a person to develop schizophrenia and that stressors, principally of a psychological nature, trigger the illness in a predisposed individual and interfere with that person's adaptation to community living. The most promising contemporary approaches to treatment make good use of this increased understanding and emphasize the importance of both pharmacological and psychosocial interventions.

- Families and patients can be given realistic and scientifically sound information about schizophrenia as a disability that can be controlled but that is probably life-

Therapy in the Real World for Patients with Schizophrenia

We have described the best available therapeutic approaches to schizophrenia. We have seen that they are both biological and psychosocial in nature, and many published reports attest to the positive impact they make on many patients with schizophrenia. However, there is often a gap between what is available in an ideal world and what the experiences of people actually are, especially when they do not live near large metropolitan centers where most of the research is conducted and where most of the state-of-the-art psychosocial treatments are obtainable.

This issue was highlighted in an article by Lehman et al. (1998) in the *Schizophrenia Bulletin*, a quarterly periodical published by the Division of Clinical and Treatment Research of the National Institute of Mental Health. (NIMH is the principal source of federal funds for supporting research into mental disorders, their prevention, and their treatment.) Data were collected by interviewing over 700 patients and by reviewing their medical records. As expected, almost 90 percent had been prescribed antipsychotic drugs, but of these patients only 62 percent received a dose in the recommended range. About 15 percent got too little, and the remainder too much. Further, although over 90 percent of patients were prescribed maintenance doses of drugs, only 29 percent of these received a dose in the recommended range; of the 71 percent who did not receive a recommended dose, about half were getting too much and half too little. African Americans were much more likely to be prescribed maintenance doses that were too high.

Psychosocial treatments were also examined, but these were more difficult to evaluate because records or patient reports did not allow the researchers to know whether the treatment was one of those considered effective (such as family-EE intervention or social-skills training). Just in terms of whether any psychosocial treatments at all were prescribed for these patients, the data show that some sort of individual or group therapy was provided for over 90 percent of inpatients. But for patients who had regular contact with their families, family treatment of some sort was prescribed for only about 40 percent. For unemployed patients, vocational rehabilitation (teaching job skills) was prescribed for only about 30 percent.

Conclusion? Many patients with schizophrenia are not getting anything near optimal therapy.

long. They learn that, as with many other chronic disabilities, medication is necessary to help maintain control and allow the patient to perform daily activities. What is not necessary, and is even counterproductive, is the guilt of family members, especially parents, who may have been led to believe that something in the patient's child-rearing initiated the problem. Considerable effort is devoted in many treatment programs to dispelling this sense of culpability while encouraging a focus on the biological diathesis and the associated need for medication.

- Medication is only part of the whole treatment picture. Family-oriented treatment aims to reduce the stress experienced by the patient after discharge from the hospital by reducing hostility, overinvolvement, intrusiveness, and criticality in the family (EE). Evidence is also emerging on the importance of cognitive-behavioral interventions that teach patients with schizophrenia how to notice and control their own stress reactions before they snowball and lead to emotional dysregulation and disruptive behaviors.

- It is increasingly recognized that early intervention is important and useful in affecting the course of schizophrenia over time. That is, getting patients onto the right medications and providing support and information to the family and appropriate psychotherapy to the patient can reduce the severity of relapses in the future (Drury et al., 1996). It is also important to teach patients social skills and more reality-based thinking so that they can control their emotions and function more normally outside the hospital and probably reduce the EE encountered both inside and outside the home. Families affected by schizophrenia are encouraged to join support groups and formal organizations, such as the Alliance for the Mentally Ill, to reduce the isolation and stigma associated with having a family member who has schizophenia (Greenberg et al., 1988).

- Though the kind of integrated treatment we have been describing is promising, the sad fact is that it is not widely available or accessible to most patients and their families. The reasons for this are unclear (Baucom et al., 1998; Dixon et al., 1997) (see Focus on Discovery 11.4 for a recent study on this issue). It seems likely, however, that one factor is the increasing popularity and use of psychoactive medications, a trend that, although helpful to many, too narrowly defines schizophrenia as a medical disease that is relatively uninfluenced by social context.

Halfway Houses and Aftercare

Some people function too well to remain in a mental hospital and yet do not function independently enough to live on their own or even within their own families. For such individuals there are halfway houses; Fairweather's "community lodge" is a classic example (Fairweather et al., 1969). These are protected living units, typically located in large, formerly private residences. Here patients discharged from a mental hospital live, take their meals, and gradually return to ordinary community life by holding a part-time job or going to school. As part of what is called vocational rehabilitation, these former hospital patients learn marketable skills that can help them secure employment and thereby increase their chances of remaining in the community. Living arrangements may be relatively unstructured; some houses set up money-making enterprises that help train and support the residents.

Depending on how well funded the halfway house is, the staff may include psychiatrists or clinical psychologists. The most important staff members are paraprofessionals, often undergraduate psychology majors or graduate students in clinical psychology or social work who live in the house and act both as administrators and as friends to the residents. Group meetings, at which residents talk out their frustrations and learn to relate to others in honest and constructive ways, are often part of the routine. More than 100 programs modeled after Fairweather's pioneering efforts have been founded across the United States and have helped thousands of patients, most of them with schizophrenia, make enough of a social adaptation to be able to remain out of the hospital. Integrating therapy with gainful employment is increasingly recognized as important in keeping people with schizophrenia (and also mental retardation; see Chapter 15) out of institutional settings (Kopelowicz & Liberman, 1998; Kopelowicz et al., 2002).

The need in the United States for effective halfway houses for former mental patients cannot be underestimated, especially in light of deinstitutionalization efforts that have seen tens of thousands of patients discharged from mental hospitals. Although civil rights issues are very important in shielding mental patients from ill-advised and even harmful detention—a topic discussed in depth in Chapter 18—discharge has all too often led to shabbily dressed former patients left to fend for themselves in the streets (see p. 635) or being rehospitalized in what has been called the revolving-door syndrome. Discharge is a desirable goal, but ex-patients usually need follow-up community-based services, and these are scarce.

A model of what aftercare can be is part of the Paul and Lentz (1977) comparative treatment study discussed in Focus on Discovery 11.3. When patients were discharged from any of the three wards of the program—social learning, milieu therapy, or routine hospital management—they usually went to live in nearby boarding homes. These homes, often converted motels, were staffed by workers who had been trained by the Paul–Lentz project to treat the ex-patients according to social-learning principles. The workers, some of whom had B.A. degrees, attended to the specific problems of the ex-patients, using rewards, including tokens, to encourage more independence and normal functioning. They positively reinforced appropriate behavior of the residents and did not attend much to bizarre behavior.

Because assessment was careful and ongoing, the staff knew at all times how a particular patient was doing. Paul's mental-health-center project—and this is of paramount importance—acted as consultant to these community boarding homes in order to help their staffs work with the ex-patients as effectively as possible. Some boarding homes for ex-mental patients are supported financially by the state as part of the mental-health system, but only rarely have the procedures followed in these homes been carefully planned and monitored by professional mental health staff.

In spite of many practical problems, such as staff layoffs, the results were as positive as those of the social-learning inpatient program. The ex-patients derived significant benefits from the aftercare; more than 90 percent of the patients discharged from the social-learning ward were able to remain continuously in the community residences during the year-and-a-half follow-up period, and some remained for as long as four years more. The revolving-door syndrome in this instance was halted. Finally, in a finding rather critical in these days of diminishing public funds, the social-learning program—the mental-health-center treatment combined with the aftercare—was much less expensive than the institutional care such patients usually receive.

Aftercare programs are likely to pay increasing attention to preparing patients to obtain and retain employment for which they can qualify. The U.S. government has begun to recognize the importance of employment by allowing people with mental disabilities such as those with schizophrenia to continue receiving Social Security benefits for up to two years while they are earning money from (low-level) jobs that can increase their chances of living independently or at least outside a mental hospital. This welcome change in policy (from one that terminated such benefits once the person began earning money) represents a recognition of the harmful effects of not working and not being able to live in a reasonably independent manner. Coupled with the Americans with Disabilities Act, which requires special consideration to people with a wide range of disabilities to maintain them in their jobs, the trend seems to be to do whatever is necessary to assist people in working and living in as autonomous a manner as their physical and mental condition will allow (Kopelowicz & Liberman, 1998).

Ongoing Issues in the Care of Patients with Schizophrenia

As patients with schizophrenia grow older, they are less likely to be living with their families. The transition to living arrangements outside the parents' home is fraught with risk. Aftercare is one of society's thorniest social problems; we describe it in more detail in Focus on Discovery 11.5. Though only about 5 to 15 percent of homeless people in the United States are mentally ill, many people with schizophrenia are among those without residences. The downward spiral in functioning is difficult to reverse. Social Security benefits are available to those with schizophrenia, but many do not receive all the benefits to which they are entitled because of inadequately staffed federal and state bureaucracies. And many patients with schizophrenia have lost contact with their posthospital treatment programs.

Obtaining employment poses a major challenge because of bias against those who have been in mental hospitals. Although the Americans with Disabilities Act of 1990 prohibits employers from asking applicants if they have a history of serious mental illness, former mental hospital patients still have a difficult time obtaining regular employment because of negative biases and fear on the part of employers. Also a factor is how much leeway employers are willing to give former mental patients, whose thinking, emotions, and behavior are usually unconventional to some degree.

There are some positive signs, however. Twenty or thirty years after first developing symptoms of schizophrenia, about half of patients with schizophrenia are able to look after themselves and participate meaningfully in society at large. Some continue to take medications, but many do not and yet still function well enough to stay out of the hospital (*Harvard Mental Health Letter*, 1995). The United States Department of Housing and Urban Development has recently begun providing rent subsidies to former mental patients to help them live in their own apartments, where they are occasionally checked on by mental health workers.

Preventing substance abuse among patients with schizophrenia is largely an unmet challenge. The lifetime prevalence rate for substance abuse among people with schizophrenia is an astounding 50 percent (Kosten & Ziedonis, 1997); the rate is even higher among the homeless mentally ill population. Programs for treating substance abuse usually exclude people who are seriously mentally ill, and programs for treating people who are seriously mentally ill usually exclude substance abusers. In both instances the reason is that the comorbid condition is considered disruptive to the treatment (Mueser, Bellack, & Blanchard, 1992). Additional problems arise because patients with schizophrenia who are substance abusers often do not continue to take their antipsychotic medication and, as a result, lose ground in their efforts to lead a more normal life.

Summary

- The symptoms of schizophrenia involve disturbances in several major areas, including thought, perception, attention; motor behavior; affect; and life functioning.

- Symptoms are typically divided into positive, negative, and disorganized types. Positive symptoms include excesses and distortions, such as delusions and hallucinations. Negative symptoms refer to behavioral deficits, such as flat affect, avolition, alogia, and anhedonia. Disorganized symptoms include disorganized speech and bizarre behavior. Other symptoms include catatonia and inappropriate affect.

- DSM-IV-TR includes several subtypes of schizophrenia, including disorganized, catatonic, and paranoid. These subtypes are based on the prominence of particular symptoms (e.g., delusions in the paranoid subtype) and reflect the variations in behavior found among people diagnosed with schizophrenia. However, there is considerable overlap among the subtypes, and they have little predictive validity.

- The data on genetic transmission of schizophrenia are impressive. Most importantly, adoption studies show a strong relationship between having a schizophrenic parent and the likelihood of developing the disorder, typically in early adulthood.

- The genetic predisposition to develop schizophrenia may have biochemical correlates. It appears that increased sensitivity of dopamine receptors in the limbic area of the brain is related to the positive symptoms of schizophrenia. The negative symptoms may be due to dopamine underactivity in the prefrontal cortex. Other neurotransmitters, such as serotonin, may also be involved.

- The brains of patients with schizophrenia, especially those with negative symptoms, have enlarged lateral ventricles and prefrontal atrophies, as well as reduced metabolism and structural abnormalities in the frontal and limbic areas. Some of these structural abnormalities could result from maternal viral infection during the second trimester of pregnancy or from damage sustained during a difficult birth.

- The diagnosis of schizophrenia is most frequently applied to members of the lowest social class, apparently because of downward social mobility created by the disorder. In addition, vague communications and conflicts are evident in the family life of patients with schizophrenia and probably contribute to their disorder. High levels of expressed emotion in families, as well as increases in general life stress, have been shown to be an important determinant of relapse.

- Antipsychotic drugs, especially the phenothiazines, have been widely used to treat schizophrenia since the 1950s. Newer medications such as clozapine and risperidone are also effective and produce fewer side effects. Drugs alone are not a completely effective treatment, though, as patients with schizophrenia need to be taught or retaught ways of dealing with the challenges of everyday life. Furthermore, most antipsychotic drugs have serious side effects, such as tardive dyskinesia, especially after long-term use, and many patients with schizophrenia do not benefit from them.

- Psychoanalytic theory assumes that schizophrenia represents a retreat from the pain of childhood rejection and mistreatment, and the analyst attempts to offer the patient a safe haven in which to explore repressed traumas. The efficacy of analytic treatments has not been supported by evidence, however. In contrast, family therapy aimed at reducing high levels of expressed emotion has been shown to be valu-

able in preventing relapse. In addition, social-skills training and various cognitive-behavioral therapies have helped patients to meet the inevitable stresses of family and community living or to lead more ordered and constructive lives within an institution. Recent efforts to change the thinking of people with schizophrenia are showing promise as well.

- The most promising approaches to treatment today emphasize the importance of both pharmacological and psychosocial interventions. Unfortunately, such integrated treatments are not widely available.

Key Terms

alogia	delusional jealousy	grandiose delusions	prefrontal lobotomy
anhedonia	delusions	hallucinations	residual schizophrenia
antipsychotic drugs	dementia praecox	ideas of reference	schizophrenia
asociality	derailment	inappropriate affect	schizophrenogenic mother
avolition	disorganized speech	labeling theory	social-selection theory
bizarre	disorganized schizophrenia	loose associations	sociogenic hypothesis
catatonia	disorganized symptoms	negative symptoms	thought disorder
catatonic immobility	dopamine theory	paranoid schizophrenia	undifferentiated schizophrenia
catatonic schizophrenia	expressed emotion (EE)	positive symptoms	waxy flexibility
delusional disorder	flat affect		

Schizophrenia: Paranoid Type

Bill McClary made his first appointment at the mental health center reluctantly. He was 25 years old, single, and unemployed. His sister, Colleen, with whom he had been living for 18 months, had repeatedly encouraged him to seek professional help. She was concerned about his peculiar behavior and social isolation. He spent most of his time daydreaming, often talked to himself, and occasionally said things that made little sense. Bill acknowledged that he ought to keep more regular hours and assume more responsibility, but he insisted that he did not need psychological treatment. The appointment was finally made in an effort to please his sister and mollify her husband, who was worried about Bill's influence on their three young children.

During the first interview, Bill spoke quietly and frequently hesitated. The therapist noted that Bill occasionally blinked and shook his head as though he was trying to clear his thoughts or return his concentration to the topic at hand. When the therapist commented on this unusual twitch, Bill apologized politely but denied that it held any significance. He was friendly yet shy and clearly ill at ease. The discussion centered on Bill's daily activities and his rather unsuccessful efforts to fit into the routine of Colleen's family. Bill assured the therapist that his problems would be solved if he could stop daydreaming. He also expressed a desire to become better organized.

Bill continued to be guarded throughout the early therapy sessions. After several weeks, he began to discuss his social contacts and mentioned a concern about sexual orientation. Despite his lack of close friends, Bill had had some limited and fleeting sexual experiences. These had been both heterosexual and homosexual in nature. He was worried about the possible meaning and consequences of his encounters with other males. This topic occupied the next several weeks of therapy.

Bill's "daydreaming" was also pursued in greater detail. It was a source of considerable concern to him, and it interfered significantly with his daily activities. This experience was difficult to define. At frequent, though irregular, intervals throughout the day, Bill found himself distracted by intrusive and repetitive thoughts. The thoughts were simple and most often alien to his own value system. For example, he might suddenly think to himself, "Damn God." Recognizing the unacceptable nature of the thought, Bill then felt compelled to repeat a sequence of self-statements that he had designed to correct the initial intrusive thought. He called these thoughts and his corrective incantations "scruples." These self-statements accounted for the observation that Bill frequently mumbled to himself. He also admitted that his unusual blinking and head shaking were associated with the experience of intrusive thoughts.

Six months after Bill began attending the clinic regularly, the therapist received a call from Bill's brother-in-law, Roger. Roger said that he and Bill had recently talked extensively about some of Bill's unusual ideas, and Roger wanted to know how he should respond. The therapist was, in fact, unaware of any such ideas. Instead of asking Roger to betray Bill's confidence any further, the therapist decided to ask Bill about these ideas at their next therapy session. It was only at this point that the therapist finally became aware of Bill's extensive delusional belief system.

For reasons that will become obvious, Bill was initially reluctant to talk about the ideas to which his brother-in-law had referred. Nevertheless, he provided the following account of his beliefs and their development. Shortly after moving to his sister's home, Bill realized that something strange was happening. He noticed that people were taking special interest in him and often felt that they were talking about him behind his back. These puzzling circumstances persisted for several weeks during which Bill became increasingly anxious and suspicious. The pieces of the puzzle finally fell in place late one night as Bill sat in front of the television. In a flash of insight, Bill suddenly came to believe that a group of conspirators had secretly produced and distributed a documentary film about his homosexual experiences. Several of his high school friends and a few distant relatives had presumably used hidden cameras and microphones to record each of his sexual encounters with other men. Bill believed that the film had grossed over $50 million at the box office and that this money had been sent to the Irish Republican Army to buy arms and ammunition. He therefore held himself responsible for the deaths of dozens of people who had died as the result of several recent bombings in Ireland. This notion struck the therapist and Bill's brother-in-law as being quite preposterous, but Bill's conviction was genuine. He was visibly moved as he described his guilt concerning the bombings. He was also afraid that serious consequences would follow his confession. Bill believed that the conspirators had agreed to kill him if he ever found out about the movie. This imagined threat had prevented Bill from confiding in anyone prior to this time. It was clear that he now feared for his life.

Bill's fear was exacerbated by the voices that he had been hearing for the past several weeks. He frequently heard male voices discussing his sexual behavior and arguing about what action should be taken to punish him. They were not voices of people with whom Bill was personally familiar, but they were always males and they were always talking about Bill. For example, one night when Bill was sitting alone in his bedroom at Colleen's home, he thought he overheard a conversation in the next room. It was a heated argument in which one voice kept repeating "He's a goddamned faggot and we've got to kill him!" Two other voices seemed to be asking questions about what he had done and were arguing against the use of such violence. Bill was, of course, terrified by this experience and sat motionless in his room as the debate continued. When Roger tapped on his door to ask if he was all right, Bill was certain that they were coming to take him away. Realizing that it was Roger and that he had not been part of the conversation, Bill asked him who was in the next room. Roger pointed out that two of the children were sleeping in the next room. When Bill went to check, he found the children asleep in their beds. These voices appeared at frequent but unpredictable intervals almost every day. It was not clear whether or not they had first appeared before the development of Bill's delusional beliefs.

The details of the delusional system were quite elaborate and represented a complex web of imaginary events and reality. For example, the title of the secret film was supposedly *Honor Thy Father*, and Bill said his name in the film was Gay Talese. *Honor Thy Father* was, in fact, a popular novel that was written by Gay Talese and published several years prior to the development of Bill's delusion. The actual novel was about organized crime, but Bill denied any knowledge of this "other book with the same title." According to Bill's belief system, the film's title alluded to Bill's disrespect for his own father and his own name in the film was a reference to his reputation as a "gay tease." He also maintained that his own picture had been on the cover of *Time* magazine within the past year with the name Gay Talese printed at the bottom.

An interesting array of evidence was marshaled in support of this delusion. For example, Bill pointed to the fact that he had happened to meet his cousin accidentally on a subway in Brooklyn two years earlier. Why, Bill asked, would his cousin have been on the same train if he were not making a secret film about Bill's private life? In Bill's mind, the cousin was clearly part of a continuous surveillance that had been carefully arranged by the conspirators. The fact that Bill came from a very large family and that such coincidences were bound to happen did not impress him as a counterargument. Bill also pointed to an incident involving the elevator operator at his mother's apartment building as further evidence for the existence of the film. He remembered stepping onto the elevator one morning and having the operator give him a puzzled, prolonged glance. The man asked him if they knew each other. Bill replied that they did not. Bill's explanation for this mundane occurrence was that the man recognized Bill because he had obviously seen the film recently; he insisted that no other explanation made sense. Once again, coincidence was absolutely impossible. His delusional system had become so pervasive and intricately woven that it was no longer open to logical refutation. He was totally preoccupied with the plot and simultaneously so frightened that he did not want to discuss it with anyone. Thus, he had lived in private

fear, brooding about the conspiracy and helpless to prevent the conspirators from spreading knowledge of his shameful sexual behavior.

Social History

Bill was the youngest of four children. He grew up in New York City where his father worked as a firefighter. Both of his parents were first-generation Irish Americans. Many of their relatives were still living in Ireland. Both parents came from large families. Bill's childhood memories were filled with stories about the family's Irish heritage.

Bill was always much closer to his mother than to his father, whom he remembered as being harsh and distant. When his parents fought, which they did frequently, Bill often found himself caught in the middle. Neither parent seemed to make a serious effort to improve their relationship. Bill later learned that his father had carried on an extended affair with another woman. His mother depended on her own mother, who lived in the same neighborhood, for advice and support and would frequently take Bill with her to stay at her parents' apartment after particularly heated arguments. Bill grew to hate his father, but his enmity was tempered by guilt. He had learned that children were supposed to respect their parents and that, in particular, a son should emulate and revere his father. Mr. McClary became gravely ill when Bill was 12 years old, and Bill remembered wishing that his father would die. His wish came true. Years later, Bill looked back on this sequence of events with considerable ambivalence and regret.

Bill could not remember having any close friends as a child. Most of his social contacts were with cousins, nephews, and nieces. He did not enjoy their company or the games that other children played. He remembered himself as a clumsy, effeminate child who preferred to be alone or with his mother instead of with other boys.

He was a good student and finished near the top of his class in high school. His mother and the rest of the family seemed certain that he would go on to college, but Bill could not decide on a course of study. The prospect of selecting a profession struck Bill as an ominous task. How could he be sure that he wanted to do the same thing for the rest of his life? He decided that he needed more time to ponder the matter and took a job as a bank clerk after graduating from high school.

Bill moved to a small efficiency apartment and seemed to perform adequately at the bank. His superiors noted that he was reliable, though somewhat eccentric. He was described as quiet and polite; his reserved manner bordered on being socially withdrawn. He did not associate with any of the other employees and rarely spoke to them beyond the usual exchange of social pleasantries. Although he was not in danger of losing his job, Bill's chances for advancement were remote. This realization did not perturb Bill because he did not aspire to promotion in the banking profession. It was only a way of forestalling a serious career decision. After two years at the bank, Bill resigned. He had decided that the job did not afford him enough time to think about his future.

He was soon able to find a position as an elevator operator. Here, he reasoned, was a job that provided time for thought. Over the next several months, he gradually became more aloof and disorganized. He was frequently late to work and seemed unconcerned about the reprimands that he began receiving. Residents at the apartment house described him as peculiar. His appearance was always neat and clean, but he seemed preoccupied most of the time. On occasion he seemed to mumble to himself, and he often forgot floor numbers to which he had been directed. These problems continued to mount until he was fired after working for one year at this job.

During the first year after finishing high school, while working at the bank, Bill had his first sexual experience. A man in his middle forties who often did business at the bank invited Bill to his apartment for a drink, and they became intimate. The experience was moderately enjoyable but primarily anxiety provoking. Bill decided not to see this man again. Over the next two years, Bill experienced sexual relationships with a small number of other men as well as with a few women. In each case, it was Bill's partner who took the initiative. Only one relationship lasted more than a few days. He became friends with a woman named Patty who was about his own age, divorced, and the mother of a 3-year-old daughter. Bill enjoyed being with Patty and her daughter and occasionally spent evenings at their apartment watching television and drinking wine. Despite their occasional sexual encounters, this relationship never developed beyond the casual stage at which it began.

After he was fired from the job as an elevator operator, Bill moved back into his mother's apartment. He later recalled that they made each other anxious. Rarely leaving the apartment, Bill sat around the apartment daydreaming in front of the television. When his mother returned from work, she would clean, cook, and coax him unsuccessfully to enroll in various kinds of job-training programs. His social isolation was a constant cause of concern for her. She was not aware of his bisexual interests and encouraged him to call women that she met at work and through friends. The tension eventually became too great for both of them, and Bill decided to move in with Colleen, her husband, and their three young children.

Conceptualization and Treatment

Bill's adjustment problems were obviously extensive. He had experienced serious difficulties in the development of social and occupational roles. From a diagnostic viewpoint, Bill's initial symptoms pointed to schizotypal personality disorder. In other words, before his delusional beliefs and hallucinations became manifest, he exhibited a series of peculiar characteristics in the absence of floridly psychotic symptoms. These included several of the classic signs outlined by Meehl (1964): anhedonia (the inability to experience pleasure), interpersonal aversiveness, and ambivalence. Bill seldom, if ever, had any fun. Even his sexual experiences were described in a detached, intellectual manner. He might indicate, for example, that he had performed well or that his partner seemed satisfied, but he never said things like, "It was terrific," or "I was really excited!" He strongly preferred to be alone. When Colleen and Roger had parties, Bill became anxious and withdrew to his room, explaining that he felt ill.

Bill's ambivalence toward other people was evident in his relationship with his therapist. He never missed an appointment; in fact, he was always early and seemed to look forward to the visits. Despite this apparent dependence, he seemed to distrust the therapist and was often guarded in his response to questions. He seemed to want to confide in the therapist and was simultaneously fearful of the imagined consequences. Bill's pattern of cognitive distraction was somewhat difficult to interpret. His "scruples" were, in some ways, similar to obsessive thoughts, but they also bore a resemblance to one of Schneider's (1959) first-rank symptoms of schizophrenia—thought insertion. Considering this constellation of problems, it was clear that Bill was in need of treatment, but it was not immediately obvious that he was psychotic. The therapist decided to address Bill's problems from a cognitive-behavioral perspective. The ambiguity surrounding his cognitive impairment seemed to warrant a delay regarding biological interventions such as medication.

The beginning therapy sessions were among the most difficult. Bill was tense, reserved, and more than a bit suspicious. Therapy had been his sister's idea, not his own. The therapist adopted a passive, nondirective manner and concentrated on the difficult goal of establishing a trusting relationship with Bill. In the absence of such an atmosphere, it would be impossible to work toward more specific behavioral changes.

Many of the early sessions were spent discussing Bill's concerns about homosexuality. The therapist listened to Bill's thoughts and concerns and shared various bits of information about sexuality and homosexual behavior in particular. As might be expected, Bill was afraid that homosexual behavior per se was a direct manifestation of psychological disturbance. He also wondered about his motivation to perform sexual acts with other men and expressed some vague hypotheses about this being a reflection of his desire to have a closer relationship with his father. The therapist assured Bill that the gender of one's sexual partner was less important than the quality of the sexual relationship. In fact, the therapist was most concerned about Bill's apparent failure to enjoy sexual activity and his inability to establish lasting relationships. Instead of trying to eliminate the possibility of future homosexual encounters or to impose an arbitrary decision based on prevailing sexual norms, the therapist tried to (1) help Bill explore his own concerns about the topic, (2) provide him with information that he did not have, and (3) help him develop skills that would improve his social and sexual relationships, whether they involved men or women.

As their relationship became more secure, the therapist adopted a more active, directive role. Specific problems were identified, and an attempt was made to deal with each sequentially. The first area of concern was Bill's daily schedule. The therapist enlisted Colleen's support. Together with Bill they instituted a sequence of contingencies designed to integrate his activities with those of the family. For example, Colleen called Bill once for breakfast at 7:30

A.M. If he missed eating with everyone else, Colleen went on with other activities and did not make him a late brunch as she had done prior to this arrangement. In general, the therapist taught Colleen to reinforce appropriate behavior and to ignore inappropriate behavior as much as possible. Over the initial weeks, Bill did begin to keep more regular hours.

After several weeks of work, this home-based program began to produce positive changes. Bill was following a schedule closer to that of the rest of the family and was more helpful around the house. At this point, the therapist decided to address two problems that were somewhat more difficult: Bill's annoying habit of mumbling to himself and his lack of social contacts with peers. Careful interviews with Bill and his sister served as a base for a functional assessment of the self-talk. This behavior seemed to occur most frequently when Bill was alone or thought he was alone. He was usually able to control his scruples in the presence of others; if he was particularly disturbed by a distracting thought, he most often excused himself and retired to his room. Colleen's response was usually to remind Bill that he was mumbling and occasionally to scold him if he was talking loudly. Given the functional value of Bill's scruples in reducing his anxiety about irreverent thoughts, it seemed unlikely that the self-talk was being maintained by this social reinforcement.

The therapist decided to try a stimulus control procedure. Bill was instructed to select one place in the house in which he could daydream and talk to himself. Whenever he felt the urge to daydream or repeat his scruples, he was to go to this specific spot before engaging in these behaviors. It was hoped that this procedure would severely restrict the environmental stimuli that were associated with these asocial behaviors and thereby reduce their frequency. Bill and the therapist selected the laundry room as his daydreaming room because it was relatively secluded from the rest of the house. His bedroom was ruled out because the therapist did not want it to become a stimulus for behaviors that would interfere with sleeping. Colleen was encouraged to prompt Bill whenever she noticed him engaging in self-talk outside of the laundry room. The program seemed to have modest, positive results, but it did not eliminate self-talk entirely.

Interpersonal behaviors were also addressed from a behavioral perspective. Since moving to his sister's home, Bill had not met any people his own age and had discontinued seeing his friends in New York City. Several avenues were pursued. He was encouraged to call his old friends and, in particular, to renew his friendship with Patty. The therapist spent several sessions with Bill rehearsing telephone calls and practicing conversations that might take place. Although Bill was generally aware of what things he should say, he was anxious about social contacts. This form of behavioral rehearsal was seen as a way of exposing him gradually to the anxiety-provoking stimuli. He was also given weekly homework assignments involving social contacts at home. The therapist discussed possible sources of friends, including a tavern not far from Colleen's home and occasional parties that Colleen and Roger had for their friends. This aspect of the treatment program was modestly effective. Bill called Patty several times and arranged to stay with his mother for a

weekend so that he could visit with Patty and her daughter. Although he was somewhat anxious at first, the visit was successful and seemed to lift Bill's spirits. He was more animated during the following therapy session and seemed almost optimistic about changing his current situation.

It was during one of their visits to the neighborhood tavern that Bill first mentioned the imagined movie to Roger. When the therapist learned of these ideas, and the auditory hallucinations, he modified the treatment plan. He had initially rejected the idea of antipsychotic medication because there was no clear-cut evidence of schizophrenia. Now that psychotic symptoms had appeared, an appointment was arranged with a psychiatrist who agreed with the diagnosis and prescribed risperidone (Risperdal), one of the atypical (or "second-generation") antipsychotic drugs. Because Bill's behavior was not considered dangerous and his sister was able to supervise his activities closely, hospitalization was not necessary. All of the other aspects of the program were continued.

Bill's response to the medication was positive but not dramatic. The most obvious effect was on his self-talk, which was reduced considerably over a four-week period. Bill attributed this change to the virtual disappearance of the annoying, intrusive thoughts. His delusions remained intact, however, despite the therapist's attempt to encourage a rational consideration of the evidence. The following example illustrates the impregnable quality of delusional thinking as well as the naivete of the therapist.

One of Bill's ideas was that his picture had been on the cover of *Time* magazine. This seemed like a simple idea to test, and Bill expressed a willingness to try. Together they narrowed the range of dates to the last eight months. The therapist then asked Bill to visit the public library before their next session and check all issues of *Time* during this period. Of course, Bill did not find his picture. Nevertheless, his conviction was even stronger than before. He had convinced himself that the conspirators had seen him on his way to the library, beaten him there, and switched magazine covers before he could discover the original. Undaunted, the therapist recommended two more public libraries for the next week. As might have been expected, Bill did not find his picture at either library but remained convinced that the cover had appeared. Every effort to introduce contradictory evidence was met by this same stubborn resistance.

Over the next several weeks, Bill became somewhat less adamant about his beliefs. He conceded that there was a *chance* that he had imagined the whole thing. It seemed to him that the plot probably did exist and that the movie was, in all likelihood, still playing around the country, but he was willing to admit that the evidence for this belief was less than overwhelming. Although his suspicions remained, the fear of observation and the threat of death were less immediate, and he was able to concentrate more fully on the other aspects of the treatment program. Hospitalization did not become necessary, and he was able to continue living with Colleen's family. Despite important improvements, it was clear that Bill would continue to need a special supportive environment, and it seemed unlikely that he would assume normal occupational and social roles, at least not in the near future.

Discussion

The diagnostic hallmarks of schizophrenia are hallucinations, delusions, and disturbances in affect and thought. *DSM-IV-TR* (p. 312) requires the following to support a diagnosis of schizophrenia:

A. **Characteristic Symptoms:** Two (or more) of the following, each present for a significant portion of time during a one-month period (or less if successfully treated):
1. Delusions
2. Hallucinations
3. Disorganized speech
4. Grossly disorganized or catatonic behavior
5. Negative symptoms, such as affective flattening, alogia, or avolition

   Note: Only one of these symptoms is required if delusions are bizarre or hallucinations consist of a voice keeping up a running commentary on the person's behavior or thoughts, or two or more voices conversing with each other.

B. **Social/Occupational Dysfunction:** For a significant portion of the time since the onset of the disturbance, one or more major areas of functioning such as work, interpersonal relations, or self-care are markedly below the level achieved prior to the onset.

C. **Duration:** Continuous signs of the disturbance persist for at least six months. This six-month period must include at least one month of symptoms that meet Criterion A (active phase symptoms) and may include periods of prodromal or residual symptoms. During these prodromal or residual periods, the signs of the disturbance may be manifested by only negative symptoms or two or more symptoms listed in Criterion A present in an attenuated form (such as odd beliefs, unusual perceptual experiences).

Bill clearly fit the diagnostic criteria for schizophrenia. Prior to the expression of his complex, delusional belief system, he exhibited several of the characteristics of a prodromal phase. He had been socially isolated since moving to his sister's home. Although he did interact with his sister and her family, he made no effort to stay in touch with the few friends he had known in New York City, nor did he attempt to meet new friends in the neighborhood. In fact, he had never been particularly active socially, even during his childhood. His occupational performance had deteriorated long before he was fired from his job as an elevator operator. Several neighbors had complained about his peculiar behavior. For example, one of Colleen's friends once called to tell her that she had been watching Bill as he walked home from the grocery store. He was carrying a bag of groceries, clearly mumbling to himself, and moving in a strange pattern. He would take two or three steps forward, then one to the side onto the grass next to the sidewalk. At this point, Bill would hop once on his left foot, take one step forward, and then step back onto the sidewalk and continue the sequence. Thinking that this behavior seemed similar to games that children commonly play, Colleen asked Bill about his walk home. He told her that each of these movements possessed a particular meaning and that he followed this pattern to correct scruples that were being placed in his head as he returned from the store. This explanation, and his other comments about his scruples, would be considered an example of magical thinking. Overall, Bill's delusional beliefs and auditory hallucinations can be seen as an extension of the deterioration that began much earlier.

Schizophrenia is a relatively common disorder, affecting approximately 1 to 2 percent of the population (Jones & Cannon, 1998; Keith, Regier, & Rae, 1991). It is found equally in men and women. Onset usually occurs during adolescence or early adulthood, but somewhat later for women than for men. The prognosis is mixed. When Emil Kraepelin first defined the disorder (originally known as *dementia praecox*), he emphasized its chronic deteriorating course. Many patients do, in fact, show a gradual decline in social and occupational functioning and continue to exhibit psychotic symptoms either continuously or intermittently throughout their lives. However, a substantial number of patients seem to recover without signs of residual impairment. Much of the most informative data pertaining to prognosis have come from the World Health Organization's International Pilot Study of Schizophrenia (Leff, Sartorius, Jablensky, Korten, & Ernberg, 1992). Compared to people with other mental disorders, such as mood disorders, schizophrenics tended to have a worse outcome five years after being hospitalized. There was substantial overlap between the groups, however, and considerable variability within the schizophrenic patients. The results of this study and several others indicate that roughly 60 percent of schizophrenic patients follow a chronic pattern and approximately 25 percent recover within five or six years after the initial onset of the disorder (Heiden & Haefner, 2000).

Although people with schizophrenia share some important common characteristics, they are also an extremely heterogeneous group. This feature was emphasized in the title of Eugen Bleuler's classic monograph, *Dementia Praecox or the Group of Schizophrenias* (1911/1950). Kraepelin and Bleuler both outlined subtypes of schizophrenia, including catatonic, paranoid, hebephrenic, and simple types. Each of these subtypes was defined in terms of a few characteristic symptoms. *Catatonic* patients were identified by their bizarre motor movements and the unusual postures they would assume. Their motor behavior might include either a rigid posture with total immobility or undirected, maniclike excitement. *Paranoid* patients were those who expressed delusions of persecution and reference. The primary features of *hebephrenia* were taken to be inappropriate affect and florid symptomatology (e.g., bizarre delusions and hallucinations). *Simple* schizophrenia was a category originally proposed by Bleuler to describe patients without the more obvious symptoms such as hallucinations and delusions. The latter category has been eliminated from the schizophrenic disorders in *DSM-IV-TR* and is now listed as Schizoid Personality Disorder. Bill would clearly be included in the paranoid subcategory of schizophrenic disorders.

Symptomatically defined subgroups possess a certain intuitive appeal, but they have not proved to be particularly useful in other respects (Kendler et al., 1994). One major problem has been a lack of reliability in assigning patients to subcategories. Because of problems in identifying the general category of schizophrenia, it is not surprising that the subtypes present further difficulties. Inconsistency is another drawback; patients who exhibit a particular set of prominent symptoms at one point in time may exhibit another set of features during a later episode. The symptomatically defined subgroups have also not been shown to possess either etiological or predictive validity. For example, a specific treatment that is more or less effective with catatonic patients in comparison with hebephrenics has not been found.

Another system for subdividing schizophrenic patients is based on the use of three symptom dimensions: psychotic symptoms, negative symptoms, and disorganization (Andreasen et al., 1995; O'Leary et al., 2000). Psychotic symptoms include hallucinations and delusions. Negative symptoms include blunted or restricted affect, social withdrawal, and poverty of speech. Verbal communication problems, such as disorganized speech, and bizarre behavior are included in the third symptom dimension, which is called disorganization. The distinctions among psychotic, negative, and disorganized symptom dimensions have generated a considerable amount of interest and research.

Etiological Considerations

Genetic factors are clearly involved in the transmission of schizophrenia (Tsuang, Stone, & Faraone, 1999). The most persuasive data supporting this conclusion come from twin studies and investigations following various adoption methods. Twin studies depend on the following reasoning: Monozygotic (MZ) twins develop from a single zygote, which separates during an early stage of growth and forms two distinct but genetically identical embryos. In the case of dizygotic (DZ) twins, two separate eggs are fertilized by two sperm cells, and both develop simultaneously. Thus, DZ twins share only, on average, 50 percent of their genes, the same as siblings who do not share the same prenatal period. Based on the assumption that both forms of twins share similar environments, MZ twins should manifest a higher concordance rate (i.e., more often resemble each other) for traits that are genetically determined. This is, in fact, the pattern that has now been reported for schizophrenia, over a large number of studies (Gottesman, 1991). For example, one study conducted in Finland reported a concordance rate of 46 percent for MZ twins and only 9 percent among DZ twins (Cannon et al., 1998). This substantial difference between MZ and DZ concordance indicates the influence of genetic factors. On the other hand, the absence of 100 percent concordance among the MZ twins also indicates that genetic factors do not account for all of the variance. The development of the disorder must therefore depend on an interaction between a genetically determined predisposition and various environmental events. This general view is known as a *diathesis-stress model* and is the most widely accepted notion regarding the etiology of schizophrenia.

We do not know how genetic factors interact with environmental events to produce schizophrenia. This problem is enormously complex because the environmental events in question might take any of several different forms. Some investigators have focused on factors such as nutritional deficiencies or viral infections. One hypothesis suggests that prenatal infections increase vulnerability to schizophrenia by disrupting brain development in the fetus (e.g., Brown & Susser, 2002; Susser et al., 1996).

Another approach to environmental events and vulnerability to schizophrenia has focused on interpersonal relations within the family. Adverse family circumstances during childhood may increase the probability of subsequently developing schizophrenia among people who are genetically predisposed toward the disorder (Schiffman et al., 2001).

In addition to questions about the *causes* of the disorder, a considerable amount of research has also stressed the family's influence on the *course* of the disorder. These studies follow the progress of patients who have already been treated for schizophrenia, and they are concerned with *expressed emotion* (EE), or the extent to which at least one family member is extremely critical of the patient and his or her behavior. The patients are typically followed for several months after discharge from the hospital, and the outcome variable is the percentage of patients who return to the hospital for further treatment. Relapse rates are much higher for patients who returned to high EE homes (Butzlaff & Hooley, 1998).

Several studies have confirmed the robust predictive relation between expressed emotion and relapse rates, and they have also shown that this effect is not unique to schizophrenia (Hooley & Gotlib, 2000; Wearden et al., 2000). Depressed patients, for example, are also more likely to relapse if they are living with high EE family members. It has been shown that the critical attitudes of family members, which are reflected in high EE ratings, are often expressed during direct interactions with their depressed and schizophrenic family members. High EE relatives are more likely to direct negative verbal and nonverbal messages to the patients, and in some cases this aversive pattern may escalate rapidly. Many questions remain to be answered about this phenomenon, which is clearly an important factor in the course of these disorders. For example, it is not clear why some relatives develop critical attitudes in the first place, and the process that explains the association between relatives' attitudes and patients' adjustment has not been defined.

The data regarding expressed emotion are consistent with Bill's experience. Bill remembered that when he and his mother were living together, they made each other anxious. His descriptions of her behavior indicate that her emotional involvement was excessive, given that he was an adult and capable of greater independence; she was always worried about his job, or his friends, or what he was doing with his time. Her constant intrusions and coaxing finally led him to seek refuge with his sister's family. The supportive environment provided by Colleen and her family and their willingness to tolerate many of Bill's idiosyncrasies were undoubtedly helpful in allowing Bill to remain outside of a hospital during his psychotic episode.

One final area of investigation is relevant to Bill's case. A considerable body of evidence indicates that schizophrenia and social class are inversely related; a disproportionately large percentage of schizophrenics fall into the lowest social class on the basis of occupational and income ratings (Cohen, 1993; Eaton & Harrison, 2001). There are two competing explanations for this phenomenon. Some investigators have taken these data to indicate that the increased stresses associated with life in low-income homes are causally related to the development of schizophrenia. This is known as the social causation hypothesis. An equally reasonable explanation holds that schizophrenics drift into the lowest social classes as a result of the problems associated with the onset of the disorder. In other words, schizophrenia may lead to educational failure and unemployment, not the other way around. Both explanations have received some empirical support (e.g., Castle, Scott, Wessely, & Murray, 1993; Dohrenwend et al., 1992). Bill was clearly an example of the drift hypothesis. He was raised in a middle-income family and had been expected to go on to college in preparation for a professional career. His indecision at the end of high school led him to delay college enrollment. After his job at the bank, Bill moved to an unskilled position as a elevator operator and eventually became unemployed. His occupational decline was related to his growing preoccupation with unusual ideas and increased interference with his cognitive functions.

Treatment

There are several important variables to consider in selecting a treatment for acute schizophrenic disturbance. Antipsychotic drugs have become the principal form of intervention since their introduction in the 1950s (Bradford, Stroup, & Lieberman, 2002; Kane, 2001). A large number of carefully controlled studies have demonstrated that these drugs have a beneficial effect for many patients with schizophrenia. They lead to an improvement in symptoms during acute psychotic episodes. Antipsychotic medications also reduce the probability of symptom relapse if they are taken on a maintenance basis after the patient has recovered from an episode. Unfortunately, some patients, perhaps as many as 25 percent, do not respond positively to antipsychotic medication.

Antipsychotic medication seems to have a specific effect on many psychotic symptoms, such as hallucinations and disorganized speech. In Bill's case, medication did have a positive effect. The administration of antipsychotic medication was associated with an improvement in his most dramatic symptoms.

Despite these positive effects, there are also several limitations and some problems associated with the use of antipsychotic drugs. One problem, which was evident in Bill's case, is that medication is only a partial solution. Once the most dramatic symptoms have improved, most patients continue to suffer from role impairments that are not the direct product of hallucinations and delusions. In short, medication can sometimes relieve perceptual aberrations, but it does not remove deficiencies in social and occupational skills.

Another problem arises with treatment-refractory patients. Approximately 10 to 20 percent of schizophrenic patients do not benefit from typical forms of antipsychotic medication (Kane, 1996). Others who respond initially will relapse repeatedly during maintenance drug treatment. Therefore, pharmaceutical companies have continued to develop new forms of medication. Clozapine (Clozaril)

and risperidone (Risperdal) are examples of the so-called second generation of antipsychotic drugs. They are also known as *atypical antipsychotic* drugs because they produce fewer adverse side effects and seem to have a different pharmacological mode of action than more traditional antipsychotic drugs. Controlled studies of clozapine and risperidone have found significant improvement in approximately 30 percent of patients who were previously considered "treatment resistant" (Chakos et al., 2001; Kapur & Remington, 2001). The availability of these new forms of medication offers new hope for many patients and their families.

A final problem has been the development of long-term side effects, most notably a serious, involuntary movement disorder known as *tardive dyskinesia* (Latimer, 1995). The most obvious signs of tardive dyskinesia include trembling of the extremities, lip smacking, and protrusions of the tongue. These symptoms can be disconcerting to both patients and those with whom they interact. Fortunately, atypical antipsychotic are much less likely to lead to the development of motor side effects such as tardive dyskinesia (Kapur & Remington, 2001).

Psychosocial treatment programs are also beneficial for patients with schizophrenia (Bustillo et al., 2001). Perhaps most important is the use of family-based programs in conjunction with maintenance medication. Several studies have evaluated treatment programs designed to help patients with families that are rated high in expressed emotion (Falloon et al., 1999; Schooler et al., 1997). In addition to antipsychotic medication, treatment typically includes two principal components. First, the therapist provides family members with information about schizophrenia, on the assumption that some hostility and criticism result from failure to understand the nature of the patient's problems. Second, the therapist focuses on enhancing the family's ability to cope with stressful experiences by working on problem-solving and communication skills. Results with this type of family intervention have been very encouraging.

In Bill's case, his sister's family would not have been considered high in expressed emotion. Direct intervention focused on family patterns of communication was therefore unnecessary. The therapist did, however, spend time talking with Colleen and Roger about Bill's situation in an effort to help them cope with his idiosyncratic behavior. Bill's therapist also directed his attention to the development of social skills. These efforts met with mixed success. Social skills programs are often useful with schizophrenics who are being treated on an outpatient basis (Bellack, Mueser, Gingerich, & Agresta, 1997; Heinssen, Liberman, & Kopelowicz, 2000).

There is also some reason to be cautious about the use of direct, active psychological approaches to the treatment of patients who are socially withdrawn and exhibiting other negative symptoms (e.g., Kopelowicz, Liberman, Mintz, & Zarate, 1997). Directive programs that successfully increase the level of social interaction among chronic schizophrenic patients may also have adverse effects on other areas of the patient's adjustment. Patients with severe, persistent negative symptoms and those who are not on medication may not be able to cope with the increase in stress that is associated with an active, directive form of social intervention. This phenomenon may have been evident in Bill's case. He was not receiving medication until after the therapist became aware of his extensive delusional system. His response to the behavioral program seemed to be more positive after the introduction of antipsychotic medication. Prior to that point, the role-playing that was attempted during sessions and the homework assignments during the week actually seemed to increase his level of anxiety.

12 Substance-Related Disorders

Alice was fifty-four years old when her family finally persuaded her to check into an alcohol rehabilitation clinic. She had taken a bad fall down her bedroom steps while drunk, and it may have been this event that finally got her to admit that something was wrong. Her drinking had been out of control for several years. She began each day with a drink, continued through the morning, and was totally intoxicated by the afternoon. She seldom had any memory for events after noon of any day. Since early adulthood she had drunk regularly, but rarely during the day and never to the point of drunkenness. The sudden death of her husband in an automobile accident two years earlier had triggered a quick increase in her drinking, and within six months she had slipped into a pattern of severe alcohol abuse. She had little desire to go out of her house and had cut back on social activities with family and friends. Repeated efforts by her family to get her to curtail her intake of alcohol had only led to angry confrontations.

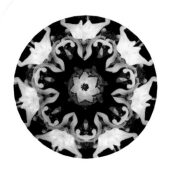

Table 12.1   Percentage of U.S. Population Reporting Drug Use in the Past Month (1999)

Substance	Percentage Reporting Use
Alcohol	47.3
Cigarettes	25.8
Marijuana	5.0
Non-medical psychotherapeutics	1.8
Cocaine	0.7
Hallucinogens	0.4
Crack	0.2
Heroin	0.1

Source: Substance Abuse and Mental Health Services Administration, 2000. Non-medical psychotherapeutics includes pain relievers, stimulants, sedatives, and tranquilizers

DSM-IV-TR Criteria for Substance Dependence

Three or more of the following:

- Tolerance
- Withdrawal
- Substance taken for a longer time or greater amount than intended
- Desire or efforts to reduce or control use
- Much time spent in activities to obtain the substance
- Social, recreational, or occupational activities given up or reduced
- Use continued despite knowing that psychological or physical problems are worsened by it

From prehistoric times humankind has used various substances in the hope of reducing physical pain or altering states of consciousness. Almost all peoples have discovered some intoxicant that affects the central nervous system, relieving physical and mental anguish or producing euphoria. Despite the often devastating consequences of taking such substances into the body, their initial effects are usually pleasing, a factor that is perhaps at the root of substance abuse.

The United States is a drug culture. Americans use drugs to wake up (coffee or tea) and stay alert throughout the day (cigarettes, soft drinks), as a way to relax (alcohol), and to reduce pain (aspirin). The widespread availability and frequent use of various drugs sets the stage for the potential abuse of drugs, the topic of this chapter.

People who abuse drugs pay a high personal cost for so doing—close personal relationships are often destroyed, and work performance impaired. Drug use is associated with risky behaviors that are adverse to health, such as failing to use condoms and sharing needles. The cost of drug abuse to U.S. society—including premature death of abusers, treating abusers, crime, and the medical illnesses that drug abuse often creates—was estimated to be $246 billion in 1992 (National Institute on Drug Abuse [NIDA], 1998).

In 1999, nearly 15 million people in the United States reported having used an illicit drug in the prior month. In addition, 105 million Americans over the age of 12 reported alcohol use of some kind, and 45 million Americans reported at least one episode of binge drinking (defined as having five or more drinks) in the last 30 days (SAMHSA, 2000). Recent data on the frequency of use of several drugs, legal and illegal, are presented in Table 12.1. These figures do not represent the frequency of abuse (figures on abuse are presented in the discussion of individual drugs) but simply provide an indication of the pervasiveness of drug use in the United States.

Drug use by youth is considerable. By the eighth grade, nearly 40 percent of adolescents have tried an illicit drug; by the time they reach high school graduation, over half have tried at least one (Johnston, O'Malley, & Bachman, 2001b). After steady declines in the use of many illicit drugs in the late 1980s and early 1990s, use appears to be once again increasing, perhaps reflecting a shift in generational beliefs about the risks associated with drug use (Johnston et al., 2001a).

The pathological use of substances falls into two categories: substance abuse and substance dependence. **Substance dependence** is characterized by DSM-IV-TR as the presence of many problems related to taking the substance. These include using more of the substance than intended, trying unsuccessfully to stop, having physical or psychological problems made worse by the drug, and experiencing problems at work or with friends.

Substance dependence is diagnosed as being accompanied by physiological dependence (also called addiction) if either tolerance or withdrawal is present. **Tolerance** is indicated by either (a) larger doses of the substance being needed to produce the desired effect or (b) the effects of the drug becoming markedly less if the usual amount is taken. **Withdrawal** symptoms, negative physical and psychological effects, develop when the person stops taking the substance or reduces the amount. The person may also use the substance to relieve or avoid withdrawal symptoms. Some investigators argue that withdrawal should be mandatory for the diagnosis of substance dependence (Langenbucher et al., 2000). In general, being physically dependent on a drug is associated with more severe problems (Schuckit et al., 1999).

For the less serious diagnosis of **substance abuse** the person must experience problems such as failure to meet obligations at work or within the family. Use of the substance may also expose the person to physical dangers as in driving while intoxicated. Social relationships may be strained, and legal problems are frequent.

The DSM-IV-TR section on substance-related disorders includes several other diagnoses. Substance intoxication is diagnosed when the ingestion of a substance affects the central nervous system and produces maladaptive cognitive and behavioral effects. If a person who is addicted to a drug is denied it and then experiences withdrawal, that person receives a diagnosis of both substance dependence and substance withdrawal. An example of substance withdrawal is alcohol withdrawal delirium, commonly known as the DTs (delirium tremens). Furthermore, drugs can cause dementia and the symptoms of other Axis I disorders.

We turn now to an overview of the major substance-related disorders, those involving alcohol, nicotine and cigarette smoking, marijuana, sedatives and stimulants, and the hallucinogens. We will then look at etiological factors suspected in substance abuse and dependence and conclude with an examination of the treatments available for these serious disorders.

DSM-IV-TR Criteria for Substance Abuse

- Maladaptive use of a substance shown by 1 of the following:
- Failure to meet obligations
- Repeated use in situations where it is physically dangerous
- Repeated substance-related legal problems
- Continued use despite problems caused by the substance

Alcohol Abuse and Dependence

The term *alcoholic* is familiar to most people, yet it does not have a precise meaning. To some it implies a person slumped against a building, to others an abusive husband or co-worker, and to still others a man or woman sneaking drinks during the day. All these images are to some extent accurate, yet none provides a full or useful definition. DSM-IV-TR distinguishes between alcohol dependence and alcohol abuse. This distinction is not always made in the research literature. The term abuse is often used to refer to both aspects of the excessive and harmful use of alcohol.

People who are dependent on alcohol generally have more severe symptoms of the disorder, such as tolerance or withdrawal (Schuckit et al., 1998). The effects of the abrupt withdrawal of alcohol in a chronic, heavy user may be rather dramatic because the body has become accustomed to the drug. Subjectively, the person is often anxious, depressed, weak, restless, and unable to sleep. Tremors of the muscles, especially of the small musculatures of the fingers, face, eyelids, lips, and tongue, may be marked, and pulse, blood pressure, and temperature are elevated.

In relatively rare cases a person who has been drinking heavily for a number of years may also experience **delirium tremens (DTs)** when the level of alcohol in the blood drops suddenly. The person becomes delirious as well as tremulous and has hallucinations that are primarily visual but may be tactile as well. Unpleasant and very active creatures—snakes, cockroaches, spiders, and the like—may appear to be crawling up the wall or over the person's body or they may fill the room. Feverish, disoriented, and terrified, the person may claw frantically at his or her skin to get rid of the vermin or may cower in the corner to escape an advancing army of fantastic animals. The delirium and physiological paroxysms caused by withdrawal of alcohol indicate that the person is addicted.

Increased tolerance is evident following heavy drinking over a period of years. Some can drink a quart of bourbon a day without showing signs of drunkenness (Mello & Mendelson, 1970). Moreover, levels of alcohol in the blood of such people are unexpectedly low after what is usually viewed as excessive drinking, suggesting that the body adapts to the drug and becomes able to process it more efficiently.

Although changes in the liver enzymes that metabolize alcohol can account to a small extent for tolerance, most researchers now believe that the central nervous system is implicated. Some research suggests that tolerance results from changes in the number or sensitivity of GABA or glutamate receptors (Tsai et al., 1998; see p. 24, 334). Withdrawal may result because some neural pathways increase their activation to compensate for alcohol's inhibitory effects in the brain.

An etching displaying the vivid portrayal of delirium tremens in a scene in a play.

People who are alcohol dependent may need to drink daily and are unable to stop or cut down despite repeated efforts to abstain completely or to restrict drinking to certain periods of the day. They may go on occasional binges, remaining intoxicated for two, three, or more days. They may suffer blackouts for the events that took place during a bout of intoxication; their craving may be so overpowering that they are forced to ingest alcohol in a nonbeverage form, such as hair tonic. Such drinking, of course, often causes social and occupational difficulties, quarrels with family or friends, sometimes violence when intoxicated, frequent absences from work, possibly loss of job, and arrests for intoxication or traffic accidents.

Polysubstance abuse involves the use of multiple drugs. Alcohol and nicotine are a frequent combination, although most people who smoke and drink in social situations do not become substance abusers.

As indicated earlier, people who abuse alcohol experience negative social and occupational effects from the drug. However, unlike those who are alcohol dependent, they do not show tolerance, withdrawal, or a compulsive pattern of abuse.

Both alcohol abuse and dependence are often part of **polydrug abuse**, using or abusing more than one drug at a time. It is estimated, for example, that 80 to 85 percent of alcohol abusers are smokers. In addition, alcohol serves as a cue for smoking; smoking is twice as frequent in situations where a person is also drinking (Shiffman et al., 1994). This very high level of comorbidity may occur because alcohol and nicotine are cross-tolerant; that is, nicotine can induce tolerance for the rewarding effects of alcohol and vice versa. Thus consumption of both drugs may be increased to maintain their rewarding effects.

Polydrug abuse can create serious health problems because the effects of some drugs when taken together are synergistic—their effects combine to produce an especially strong reaction. For example, mixing alcohol and barbiturates is a common means of suicide, intentional and accidental. Alcohol is also believed to contribute to deaths from heroin, for it can reduce the amount of the narcotic needed to make a dose lethal.

Prevalence of Alcohol Abuse and Comorbidity with Other Disorders

The prevalence of alcohol abuse and dependence in the United States varies according to such factors as gender, age, region, ethnicity, and education level.

In the large U.S. epidemiological study described on page 117, lifetime prevalence rates for alcohol dependence defined by DSM criteria were greater than 20 percent for men and just over 8 percent for women (Kessler et al., 1994). Rates of problem drinking among young women are approaching those of men, although heavy drinking is still more prevalent among men. The prevalence of alcohol dependence declines for both men and women with advancing age, both because of early death among long-term abusers and because many have managed to stop drinking (Wilsnack & Wilsnack, 1995; Vaillant, 1996). Some data suggest that women develop alcohol-related health problems, such as heart disease, stomach and liver disease, more quickly than men even though men consume more alcohol (Lewis et al., 1996; York & Welte, 1994).

Alcohol use is especially frequent among college-aged adults. An example is binge drinking, defined as having five drinks in a short period of time, like within an hour. In recent surveys, just under half of college men reported an episode of binge drinking during the prior two weeks compared with around a third of women (Johnston et al., 2001c; SAMHSA, 2000). Binge drinking even occurs with high frequency among high school students. In a recent survey, for example, 30 percent of twelfth graders reported binging in the previous two weeks (Johnston et al., 2001b; National Institute on Alcohol Abuse and Alcoholism [NIAAA], 1997). Generally speaking, the prevalence of binge drinking is highest among individuals ages eighteen to twenty-five, with a peak prevalence at age twenty-one (SAMHSA, 2000).

Within the college population, binge drinking is often associated with sorority and fraternity life. One recent study found that sorority and fraternity members reported drinking more often than college athletes; those students who were involved in both Greek life and college athletics reported drinking the most and were more likely to engage in binge drinking (Meilman, Leichliter, & Presley, 1999). Other evidence suggests that although being affiliated with a sorority or fraternity is indeed associated with heavier drinking during college, it is not associated with continued heavy drinking after college (Sher, Bartholow, & Shivani, 2000).

Researchers have also found regional differences in problematic drinking within the United States. For example women in rural areas of the southern United States are less likely to drink to excess than women in other areas of the country.

The prevalence of alcohol problems differs by ethnicity and education level as well. White adolescents and adults are more likely to misuse alcohol than African American adolescents and adults. The rates of alcohol abuse or dependence among whites and Latinos are highest in those aged eighteen to twenty-nine. For African Americans, the highest rate is among thirty- to forty-four-year-olds. However, the gap between whites and blacks narrows considerably among individuals who drop out of high school (Barr et al., 1993; Paschall, Flewelling, & Faulkner, 2000). Dropping out of high school is associated with greater drug use in general, among both white and African American individuals (Obot & Anthony, 1999, 2000).

Alcohol abuse is common in some Native American tribes and is associated with 40 percent of deaths and with virtually all crimes committed by Native Americans (Yetman, 1994). Native American youth have higher rates of alcohol abuse than other ethnic groups. It is important to note, however, that over half of the population in some Native American communities completely abstain from alcohol (Weisner, 1984).

Problem drinking is comorbid with several personality disorders, mood disorders, other drug use, schizophrenia, and anxiety disorders; it is also a factor in 25 percent of all suicides (Kessler et al., 1997; Morgenstren et al., 1997; Skinstad & Swain, 2001). According to the Substance Abuse and Mental Health Services Administration, as many as 37 percent of people suffering from alcohol dependence also have at least one other mental disorder (SAMHSA, 1997).

Course of the Disorder

At one time the life histories of alcohol abusers were thought to have a common, downhill progression. On the basis of an extensive survey of 2,000 members of Alcoholics Anonymous, Jellinek (1952) described the male alcohol abuser as passing through four stages, beginning with social drinking and progressing to a stage at which the person lives only to drink. One message from this stage model is that the alcoholic follows an inevitable decline, with no possibility of returning to an earlier stage.

Although Jellinek's description has been widely cited, the available evidence does not always corroborate it. The histories of some alcohol-dependent people do indeed show a progression from alcohol abuse to alcohol dependence (Langenbucher & Chung, 1995); however, data reveal considerable fluctuations in the drinking patterns of many drinkers, from heavy drinking for some periods of time to abstinence or lighter drinking at others (Shuckit et al., 2001; Shuckit, Tip, & Smith, 1997; Vaillant, 1996). Furthermore, patterns of maladaptive use of alcohol are more variable than Jellinek implied. Heavy use of the drug may be restricted to weekends, or long periods of abstinence may be interspersed with binges of continual drinking for several weeks (Robins et al., 1988).

In addition, the great majority of people who meet criteria for alcohol abuse do not go on to develop alcohol dependence (Hasin et al., 1997; Shuckit, 1998; Shuckit & Smith, 1996; Shuckit et al., 2001). For example, one recent prospective study found that only 3.5 percent of persons meeting alcohol abuse criteria had developed alcohol dependence five years later, a number not significantly greater than the 2.5 percent of the population who developed alcohol dependence for the first time over the same five-year period (Shuckit et al., 2001). And prospective studies also indicate that almost one third of individuals dependent on alcohol and over half of individuals meeting criteria for alcohol abuse fail to show any alcohol-related problems one to five years later, refuting the idea of an inevitable decline (Hasin et al., 1997; Shuckit et al., 2001).

Evidence also indicates that Jellinek's account does not apply to women. Difficulties with alcohol usually begin at a later age in women than in men and sometimes after an inordinately stressful experience, such as a serious family crisis, as in Alice's case at the beginning of this chapter. For women the time interval between the onset of heavy drinking and alcohol abuse is briefer than it is for men (Mezzich et al., 1994). Women with drinking problems tend more than men to be steady drinkers and to drink alone. They also seek treatment sooner after the development of alcohol-related problems (Shuckit et al., 1998). Put simply, there is no single pattern of alcohol abuse.

Costs of Alcohol Abuse and Dependence

Although most people who have a drinking problem do not seek professional help, people who abuse alcohol constitute a large proportion of new admissions to mental and general hospitals. Expenditures on health care for problem drinkers have been estimated to be over $26 billion annually (National Institute on Alcohol Abuse and Alchoholism [NIAA], 2001). As mentioned in Chapter 10, the suicide rate of alcohol abusers is much higher than that of the general population.

Alcohol-related traffic fatalities present a serious problem (Alonso-Zaldivar, 1999). The highest-risk drivers are young men. Through vigorous efforts of law enforcement and educational campaigns such as those waged by MADD (Mothers Against Drunk Driving),

Alcohol is often implicated in vehicular accidents. The driver of this New York subway train, which derailed, killing five and injuring over one hundred people, was intoxicated.

the situation has improved in recent years. Deaths from drinking-related driving declined from over 22,000 a year in 1994 to over 15,000 a year in 1999; and between 1982 and 1999, alcohol-related fatalities declined from 57 percent to 38 percent of traffic fatalities (U.S. National Highway Transportation & Safety Administration, 2002). Even so, nearly four out of every ten traffic fatalities in 1999 were alcohol related. Associated costs include as much as $45 billion in loss of earnings and productivity, as well as the direct costs.

Alcohol may also be a factor in airplane crashes, boating accidents, industrial accidents, and mishaps in the home. Alcohol presents law-enforcement problems as well. About one-third of all arrests in the United States are for public drunkenness. Homicide is an alcohol-related crime—it is believed that over half of all murders are committed under its influence—as are rape, assault, and family violence (Murdoch, Pihl, & Ross, 1990).

The overall cost of problem drinking in the United States—from absenteeism to damaged health—was estimated in 1998 at more than $185 billion. The human costs, in terms of broken lives and losses to society, are incalculable.

Short-Term Effects of Alcohol

How does alcohol produce its short-term effects? After being swallowed and reaching the stomach, alcohol begins to be metabolized by enzymes. Most of it goes into the small intestines and from there is absorbed into the blood. It is then broken down, primarily in the liver, which can metabolize about one ounce of 100-proof (50% alcohol) whiskey per hour. Quantities in excess of this amount remain in the bloodstream. Whereas absorption of alcohol can be very rapid, removal is always slow.

The effects of alcohol vary with the level of concentration of the drug in the bloodstream, which in turn depends on the amount ingested in a particular period of time, the presence of food in the stomach to retain the alcohol and reduce its absorption rate, the size of the individual's body, and the efficiency of the liver. Two ounces of alcohol will thus have different effects on a 180-pound man who has just eaten than on a 110-pound woman with an empty stomach. However, women achieve higher blood alcohol concentrations even after adjustment for differences in body weight, perhaps due to differences in body water content between men and women.

Because drinking alcoholic beverages is accepted in most societies, alcohol is rarely regarded as a drug, especially by those who drink. But it is indeed a drug, and it has what is referred to as a biphasic effect. The initial effect of alcohol is stimulating; the drinker experiences an expansive feeling of sociability and well-being as his or her blood-alcohol level rises. But after the blood-alcohol level peaks and begins to decline, alcohol acts as a depressant, and the person may experience increases in negative emotions. Large amounts of alcohol interfere with complex thought processes; motor coordination, balance, speech, and vision are also impaired. At this stage of intoxication some individuals become depressed and withdrawn. Alcohol is also capable of blunting pain and, in larger doses, of inducing sedation, sleep, and even death.

Alcohol produces its effects through its interactions with several neural systems in the brain. It stimulates GABA receptors, which may account for its ability to reduce tension. (GABA is a major inhibitory neurotransmitter; the benzodiazepines, such as Valium, have an effect on the GABA receptor similar to that of alcohol.) Alcohol also increases levels of serotonin and dopamine, and these effects may be the source of its ability to produce pleasurable effects. Finally, alcohol inhibits glutamate receptors, which may cause the cognitive effects of alcohol intoxication, such as slurred speech and memory loss (U.S. Department of Health and Human Services, 1994).

There are many beliefs about the effects of alcohol. It is thought to reduce anxiety, increase sociability, relax inhibitions, and so on. But it appears that some of the short-term effects of ingesting small amounts of alcohol are as strongly related to the drinker's expectations about the effects of the drug as they are to its chemical action on the body. For example, alcohol is commonly thought to stimulate aggression and increase sexual responsiveness. Research has shown, however, that these reactions may not be caused by alcohol itself but by the drinker's *beliefs* about alcohol's effects. In now classic experiments demonstrating these points, participants are told that they are consuming a quantity of alcohol when they are actually given an alcohol-free beverage with its taste disguised. They subsequently become more aggressive (Lang et al., 1975) and report increased sexual arousal (Wilson & Lawson, 1976). People who actually drink alcohol also report increased sexual arousal, even though alcohol makes them less aroused physiologically (Farkas & Rosen, 1976). Once again, cognitions have a demonstrably powerful effect on behavior. Data suggest a reciprocal relationship between beliefs or expectancies and alcohol use: positive expectancies predict alcohol use, and alcohol use helps to maintain and expand positive expectancies (e.g., Sher et al. 1996). We shall see later that beliefs about the effects of drugs are importantly related to their abuse.

Long-Term Effects of Prolonged Alcohol Abuse

The possible long-term effects of prolonged drinking are vividly illustrated in the following case history, which is a good example of the course of the disorder, the toll it takes on family relationships, and the difficulty of quitting drinking.

At the time of his first admission to a state hospital at the age of twenty-four, the patient, an unmarried and unemployed laborer, already had a long history of antisocial behavior, promiscuity and addiction to alcohol and other drugs.... There had been eight brief admissions to private sanatoria for alcoholics, a number of arrests for public intoxication and drunken driving, and two jail terms for assault.

The patient had been born into a wealthy and respected family in a small town. The patient's father, a successful and popular businessman, drank excessively and his death at the age of fifty-seven was partly due to alcoholism. The mother also drank to excess. The parents exercised little control over the patient as a child, and he was cared for by nursemaids. His father taught him to pour drinks for guests of the family when he was very young and he reported that he began to drain the glasses at parties in his home before he was six; by the time he was twelve he drank almost a pint of liquor every weekend and by seventeen was drinking up to three bottles every day. His father provided him with money to buy liquor and shielded him from punishment for drunken driving and other consequences of his drinking.

The patient was expelled from high school his freshman year for striking a teacher. He then attended a private school until the eleventh grade, when he changed the date on his birth certificate and joined the Army paratroops. After discharge, he was unemployed for six months; he drank heavily and needed repeated care at a sanatorium. When a job was obtained for him

he quit within a month. On his third arrest for drunken driving he was jailed. His father bailed him out with the warning that no more money would be forthcoming. The patient left town and worked as an unskilled laborer—he had never acquired any useful skills—but returned home when his father died. During the next few years he was jailed for intoxication, for blackening his mother's eyes when he found a male friend visiting her, and for violating probation by getting drunk. He assaulted and badly hurt a prison guard in an escape attempt and was sentenced to two additional years in prison. When released, he began to use a variety of stimulant, sedative and narcotic drugs as well as alcohol. (Rosen, Fox, & Gregory, 1972, p. 312)

Chronic drinking creates severe biological damage in addition to psychological deterioration. Almost every tissue and organ of the body is adversely affected by prolonged consumption of alcohol. Malnutrition may be severe. Because alcohol provides calories—a pint of 80-proof spirits supplies about half a day's caloric requirements—heavy drinkers often reduce their intake of food. But the calories provided by alcohol are empty; they do not supply the nutrients essential for health. Alcohol also contributes directly to malnutrition by impairing the digestion of food and absorption of vitamins. In older chronic alcohol abusers, a deficiency of B-complex vitamins can cause amnestic syndrome, a severe loss of memory for both recent and long-past events. These memory gaps are often filled in by reporting imaginary events that are highly improbable (confabulation).

Prolonged alcohol use plus reduction in the intake of proteins contribute to the development of cirrhosis of the liver, a disease in which some liver cells become engorged with fat and protein, impeding their function; some cells die, triggering an inflammatory process. When scar tissue develops, blood flow is obstructed. Cirrhosis ranks seventh among causes of death in the United States, with between 10,000 and 24,000 cirrhosis deaths per year caused by prolonged alcohol use (NIAA,1998).

Other common physiological changes include damage to the endocrine glands and pancreas, heart failure, erectile dysfunction, hypertension, stroke, and capillary hemorrhages, which are responsible for the swelling and redness in the face, and especially the nose, of chronic alcohol abusers. Prolonged use of alcohol appears to destroy brain cells; a five-year longitudinal study found significant loss of gray matter from the temporal lobes (Pfefferbaum et al., 1998). Chronic heavy drinking is associated with damage to many areas of the brain, many of which are implicated in memory functions. Despite sex differences in the prevalence of problem drinking, damage to the brain associated with chronic and heavy drinking does not spare either gender. In fact, some evidence suggests that women develop liver and neurological damage with less alcohol intake over a shorter period of time (Lancaster, 1994). Even shorter-term abuse may affect cognitive performance: alcohol-abusing college students show impairment on neuropsychological tests (Sher et al., 1997). Alcohol also reduces the effectiveness of the immune system, resulting in increased susceptibility to infection and cancer. For example, women's risk of breast cancer increases steadily with the amount they drink (Smith-Warner et al., 1998).

Heavy alcohol consumption during pregnancy is the leading known cause of mental retardation. The growth of the fetus is slowed, and cranial, facial, and limb anomalies are produced. The condition is known as **fetal alcohol syndrome**. Even moderate drinking can produce less severe but undesirable effects on the fetus, leading the National Institute on Alcohol Abuse and Alcoholism to counsel total abstention during pregnancy as the safest course (*Alcohol, Drug Abuse and Mental Health Administration News*, 1980).

Although it is appropriate and accurate to concentrate on the deleterious effects of alcohol, tantalizing evidence suggests positive health benefits for some people. Light drinking (fewer than three drinks a day), especially of red wine, has been related to decreased risk for coronary heart disease and stroke (Sacco et al., 1999; Theobald et al.,

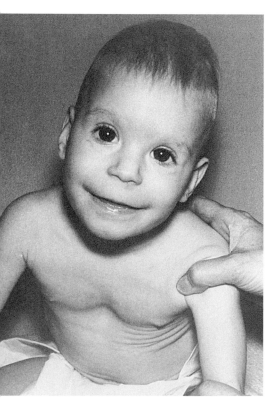

Heavy drinking during pregnancy causes fetal alcohol syndrome. These children have facial abnormalities as well as mental retardation.

2000). Not all researchers, however, accept this finding at face value. Some people who abstain may do so for health reasons, for example, because of hypertension. Comparing these less healthy abstainers to light drinkers could result in misleading conclusions. If alcohol does have a beneficial effect, it could be either physiological (e.g., acetate, a metabolite of alcohol, increases coronary blood flow) or psychological (a less-driven lifestyle and decreased levels of hostility).

Research on this topic was stimulated by the so-called French paradox—despite diets rich in saturated fats, the French have relatively low cholesterol levels. Some hypothesize that consumption of low to moderate amounts of red wine may lower cholesterol levels. Indirect evidence for this hypothesis has recently been found in an animal study, where researchers discovered that pigment substances in red wine called polyphenols interfered with the synthesis of a peptide called endothelin-1, which is believed to contribute to atherosclerosis (Corder et al., 2001). Of course, the French lifestyle has other characteristics that may result in lower risk of heart disease: the French eat more fresh foods and get more daily exercise than Americans, for example, by walking instead of driving to work.

The psychological, biological, and social consequences of prolonged consumption of alcohol are extremely serious. Because the alcohol abuser's own functioning is so severely disrupted, the people with whom he or she interacts are also deeply affected and hurt.

Nicotine and Cigarette Smoking

Not long after Columbus's first commerce with Native Americans, sailors and merchants began to imitate the Native Americans' smoking of rolled leaves of tobacco and experienced, as they did, an increasing craving for it. When not smoked, tobacco was—and is—chewed or ground into small pieces and inhaled as snuff.

Nicotine is the addicting agent of tobacco. It stimulates nicotinic receptors in the brain. The neural pathways that become activated stimulate the dopamine neurons in the mesolimbic area that seem to be involved in producing the reinforcing effects of most drugs (Stein et al., 1998). Some idea of the addictive qualities of tobacco can be appreciated by considering how much people have sacrificed to maintain their supplies. In sixteenth-century England, for example, tobacco was exchanged for silver ounce for ounce. Poor people squandered their meager resources for their several daily pipefuls. Even the public tortures and executions engineered as punishment by Sultan Murad IV of Turkey during the seventeenth century could not dissuade those of his subjects who were addicted to the weed (Brecher, 1972).

Prevalence and Health Consequences of Smoking

The threat to health posed by smoking has been documented convincingly by the Surgeon General of the United States in a series of reports since 1964. It is estimated that more than 430,000 American tobacco users die prematurely each year (Schultz, 1991). Cigarette smoking is responsible in some way for one of every six deaths in the United States, killing more than 1,100 people each day. It remains the single most preventable cause of premature death in the United States as well as other parts of the world. Tobacco kills more Americans each year than AIDS, car accidents, cocaine, crack, heroin, homicide, and suicide combined. Lung cancer kills more people than any other cancer, and smoking is probably the cause of as many as 87 percent of lung cancers. The health risks of smoking are significantly less for cigar and pipe smokers because they seldom inhale the smoke into their lungs; however, these smokers increase their risk for cancers of the mouth.

Among the other medical problems associated with, and almost certainly caused or exacerbated by, long-term cigarette smoking are emphysema, cancer of the larynx and of the esophagus, and a number of cardiovascular diseases. The most probable harmful components in the smoke from burning tobacco are nicotine, carbon monoxide, and tar;

the latter consists primarily of certain hydrocarbons, many of which are known carcinogens (Jaffe, 1985). Health risks from smoking decline dramatically over a period of five to ten years after quitting, to levels only slightly above those of nonsmokers, although the destruction of lung tissue is not reversible (Jaffe, 1985).

Reports from the Surgeon General (USDHHS, 1989, 1990a), the Centers for Disease Control (Cimons, 1992), and the Substance Abuse and Mental Health Services Administration (SAMSHA, 1999), as well as other publications (Cherner, 1990; Jansen, Glynn, & Howard, 1996; Johnston et al., 2001a; Tye, 1991; Youth Risk Behavior Survey, 1997) draw several conclusions from more than forty years of focused efforts by the federal government to discourage cigarette smoking.

- The prevalence of habitual smoking among American adults decreased from a little over 40 percent in 1965 to about 25 percent in 1997, a hefty 25 percent decrease; almost half of all living adults who ever smoked quit. But 57 million Americans still smoke, and smoking rates are higher still in Asia and South America. In the United States, the rate of quitting from 1987 to the present more than doubled the rate of quitting between 1965 and 1985.

- Rates of smoking have, however, been increasing among teenagers since 1992 and have now reached a level equal to that found in 1977, at least among white adolescents (Johnston et al., 2001a). Smoking also increased among college students beginning in 1995, though it began to level off in 1999. In 1999, an analysis by the Centers for Disease Control indicated that nearly 35 percent of high school students had reported smoking cigarettes at least one time in the prior 30 days, up from 28 percent in 1991; 17 percent of high school students were classified as frequent smokers in 1999, up from 13 percent in 1991. Prevalence rates of smoking are greater for white and Hispanic adolescents than for African American adolescents, but the prevalence rate among African American youth has gone up alarmingly since the early 1990s following years of decline.

- Prevalence remains high among Native Americans, blue-collar workers, and less educated individuals. Prevalence is lowest among college graduates and those over the age of seventy-five.

- Prevalence has declined much less among women than among men

- People begin to smoke primarily in childhood and adolescence; the age at which smoking begins is decreasing, especially among young women.

- Of the more than 1,000 children and adolescents who begin smoking every day, 750 will die prematurely from a preventable, smoking-related disease.

Research demonstrates the significance of race in nicotine addiction, as well as the intricate interplay among behavioral, social, and biological factors (Carballo et al., 1998; Leischow, Ranger-Moore, & Lawrence, 2000). It has been known for years that African American cigarette smokers are less likely to quit and are more likely, if they continue to smoke, to get lung cancer. Why? It turns out that they retain nicotine in their blood longer than do whites, that is, they metabolize it more slowly. It has also been found that African Americans draw in much more nicotine per cigarette smoked because they take more puffs and inhale more deeply. They thus become more strongly addicted to nicotine and would therefore have more difficulty quitting even if they smoked fewer cigarettes than whites. One possibility for this behavioral difference is that blacks more often prefer menthol-treated cigarettes than do whites, and the effect of menthol is to cool the smoke and otherwise reduce the irritation in the mouth and throat that is a natural consequence of smoking. These palliative effects may encourage the smoker to, as it were, get more out of each cigarette by drawing on it more often and by taking the smoke more deeply into the lungs. Furthermore, a serious consequence of this behavioral pattern is that the smoker takes in more of the cancer-causing components of smoke; this would help account for the higher lung-cancer rates among African American smokers than among white smokers.

Mortality rates also differ between whites and African Americans, with the latter more likely to die from lung-related or cardiovascular illness associated with smoking.

Parental smoking greatly increases the chances that children will themselves begin to smoke.

Indeed, the 1998 Surgeon's General Report on ethnic minorities and tobacco use indicated that the health burdens associated with smoking are greatest among African Americans. At a broader societal level, African Americans are more likely to live in poverty and less likely to have health insurance than whites and thus are likely to have less access to health care and treatment programs for smoking cessation.

Recent research has found that Chinese Americans metabolize less nicotine from cigarettes than either white or Latino smokers (Benowitz et al., 2002). In general, lung cancer rates are lower among Asians than whites or Latinos. The relatively lower metabolism of nicotine among Chinese Americans may help explain why lung cancer rates are lower in this group.

As with alcohol, the socioeconomic cost of smoking is staggering. Each year smokers compile over 80 million lost days of work and 145 million days of disability, considerably more than do their nonsmoking peers. This loss of productivity coupled with the health care costs associated with smoking runs to more than $65 billion annually in the United States. Or, looking at it another way, this figure amounts to $178 million a day—enough money to feed 19,000 children for a year or to build a major urban teaching hospital.

Emerging data that cigarette smoking contributes to erectile problems in men—not surprising, given that nicotine constricts blood vessels—gave rise in 1998 to several televised public-service announcements aimed at creating some second thoughts about how sexy smoking is. One ad shows a well-dressed young man looking with interest at an attractive woman at a fancy cocktail party. He lights up a cigarette, and when she looks over in his direction, the cigarette goes limp. She shakes her head and walks away (Morain, 1998).

Cigarettes are not the only form of nicotine that is hazardous to health. Smokeless tobacco is particularly popular among younger men, with prevalence estimates around 9 percent for men aged eighteen to twenty-four (USDHHS, 1996). Interestingly, use of smokeless tobacco is higher among Native American young women than women of any ethnicity and most men of other ethnicities. The image of the major league baseball player spitting out tobacco juice from a wad of chewing tobacco bulging in his cheeks is almost an American archetype. Because of its popularity among athletes, the NCAA banned the use of chewing tobacco during practice and competition in its collegiate sports. So far, compliance with this rule, implemented in 1995, appears to be fairly good, with estimates of around 77 percent of schools complying (Chakravorty et al., 2000).

WARNING: SMOKING CAUSES IMPOTENCE

California's Tobacco Education Media Campaign parodies tobacco ads to illustrate potential health effects of smoking and to attack pro-tobacco influences.

Consequences of Secondhand Smoke

As we have known for many years, the health hazards of smoking are not restricted to those who smoke. The smoke coming from the burning end of a cigarette, so-called **secondhand smoke**, or environmental tobacco smoke (ETS), contains higher concentrations of ammonia, carbon monoxide, nicotine, and tar than does the smoke actually inhaled by the smoker. Environmental tobacco smoke is blamed for more than 50,000 deaths a year in the United States.[1] In 1993 the Environmental Protection Agency classified ETS as a hazard on a par with asbestos and radon. Effects include the following:

- Nonsmokers can suffer lung damage, possibly permanent, from extended exposure to cigarette smoke. Those living with smokers are at greatest risk. Precancerous lung abnormalities have been observed in those living with smokers. In addition, most non-

[1] To get some perspective on this statistic, U.S. fatalities from the entire Vietnam War totaled about 58,000.

Parental smoking greatly increases the chances that children will begin to smoke. Moreover children of mothers who smoke are at increased risk for respiratory infections, bronchitis, and inner ear infections.

smokers greatly dislike the smell of smoke from burning tobacco, and some have allergic reactions to it.

- Nonsmokers are at greater risk for developing cardiovascular disease.
- Babies of women who smoke during pregnancy are more likely to be born prematurely, to have lower birth weights, and to have birth defects.
- Children of smokers are more likely to have upper-respiratory infections, bronchitis, and inner ear infections than are their peers whose parents do not smoke.

In recent years various local governments have passed ordinances regulating cigarette smoking in public places and work settings. Smoking is banned in many supermarkets, buses, hospitals, and government buildings and on all domestic U.S. airline flights. Restaurants must often post signs indicating whether they have an area for nonsmokers, and many restaurants, like those in California, ban smoking altogether. In California, workplaces with more than fifty employees must either ban smoking on the premises or restrict it to designated areas, and smoking is also banned in all bars. Many nonsmokers express enthusiastic approval of such measures, but pressure from smokers and from the tobacco industry sometimes defeats efforts to enact laws. Some smokers object strongly to what they view as undue infringement on their rights.

Marijuana

Marijuana consists of the dried and crushed leaves and flowering tops of the hemp plant, *Cannabis sativa*. It is most often smoked, but it may be chewed, prepared as a tea, or eaten in baked goods. **Hashish**, much stronger than marijuana, is produced by removing and drying the resin exudate of the tops of high-quality cannabis plants.

Originally the hemp plant was extensively cultivated in the United States not for smoking but for its fibers, which were used in the manufacture of cloth and rope. By the nineteenth century the medicinal properties of cannabis resin had been noted, and it was marketed by several drug companies as a treatment for rheumatism, gout, depression, cholera, and neuralgia. It was also smoked for pleasure, though little seen in the United States until 1920. At that time, the passage of the Eighteenth Amendment prohibiting the sale of alcohol prompted some people to begin smoking marijuana brought across the border from Mexico. Unfavorable reports in the press attributing crimes to marijuana use led to the enactment of a federal law against the sale of the drug in 1937. Today marijuana use is illegal in most countries, many of them bound by a United Nations treaty prohibiting its sale (Goodwin & Guze, 1984).

Prevalence of Marijuana Use

The use of marijuana peaked in 1979, then declined for the next decade, rose between 1991 and 1997, and has shown little change since then (see Figure 12.1 for data on youth from 1985 to 2000) (Kozel & Adams, 1986; Marijuana Research Findings, 1980; Johnston et al., 2001a; NIDA, 1998). About 6 percent of high school seniors reported smoking marijuana daily in the year 2000 (Johnston et al., 2001b). Although the prevalence rates are higher for men than women, the data suggest that use by women increased more rapidly in the 1990s (Greenfield & O'Leary, 1999).

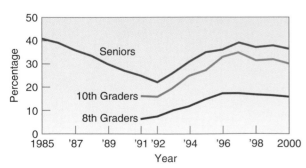

Figure 12.1 Trends in adolescents' annual use of marijuana.

The Stepping-Stone Theory—From Marijuana to Hard Drugs

A concern prevalent for some time is expressed in the so-called stepping-stone theory of marijuana use. According to this view, marijuana is dangerous not only in itself but also because it is a first step that can lead young people to become addicted to other drugs, such as heroin. In the late 1960s, when information on the harmfulness of marijuana was scant, the issue was basically political and generational. People in their teens and college years believed that the older generation, lacking scientific data to discourage marijuana use, had concocted the stepping-stone theory, which itself lacked empirical support, to justify harsh legal penalties for the use and sale of marijuana. Since there was little doubt that hard drugs were very harmful, marijuana was said to be so too because it was a first step to a lifetime of abusing these drugs.

Studies done since that time have established several specific dangers from using marijuana, as described in the text. But is marijuana a stepping-stone to more serious substance abuse? The question may not be so difficult to answer. First of all, there is little evidence to suggest that this theory applies to African Americans at all. Furthermore, about 40 percent of regular marijuana users do not go on to use such drugs as heroin and cocaine (Stephens, Roffman, & Simpson, 1993). So if by *stepping stone* we mean that escalation to a more serious drug is inevitable, then marijuana is not a stepping-stone. On the other hand, we do know that many, but far from all, who abuse heroin and cocaine began their drug experimentation with marijuana. At least in the United States, users of marijuana are more likely than nonusers to experiment later with heroin and cocaine (Kandel, 1984; Miller & Volk, 1996). Moreover, the single best predictor of cocaine use in adulthood is heavy use of marijuana during adolescence (Kandel, Murphy, & Karus, 1985; Kozel & Adams, 1986).

Most people who use marijuana do not go on to use other drugs, such as heroin, but many heroin abusers did begin their drug use with marijuana.

Better than a stepping-stone theory might be a network theory. Network implies a complex set of relationships in which cause and effect are virtually impossible to isolate but some degree of association among many variables is acknowledged. Some regular users of heroin and cocaine, for example, turn to marijuana as a safer substitute, or lesser evil (Sussman et al., 1996). Marijuana is part of the picture, but only one of many contributing factors to involvement in harmful substance use.

Effects of Marijuana

Like most other drugs marijuana has its risks. Generally, the more we learn about a drug, the less benign it turns out to be, and marijuana is no exception (see Focus on Discovery 12.1).

Psychological Effects   The intoxicating effects of marijuana, like those of most drugs, depend in part on its potency and the size of the dose. Smokers of marijuana find it makes them feel relaxed and sociable. Large doses have been reported to bring rapid shifts in emotion, to dull attention, to fragment thoughts, and to impair memory. Time seems to move more slowly. Extremely heavy doses have sometimes been found to induce hallucinations and other effects similar to those of LSD, including extreme panic, sometimes arising from the belief that the frightening experience will never end. Dosage can be difficult to regulate because it may take up to half an hour after smoking marijuana for its effects to appear; many users thus get much higher than intended. People with psychological problems are generally believed to be at highest risk for negative reactions to marijuana or any psychoactive drug, perhaps because the lack of control is especially frightening to them.

The major active chemical in marijuana has been isolated and named delta-9-tetrahydrocannabinol (THC). The amount of THC in marijuana is variable, but in general marijuana is more potent now than it was two decades ago (Zimmer & Morgan, 1995).

Early recreational use of hashish in a fashionable apartment in New York City. An 1876 issue of the Illustrated Police News carried this picture with the title "Secret Dissipation of New York Belles: Interior of a Hasheesh Hell on Fifth Avenue."

In the late 1980s cannabis receptors were discovered in the brain; shortly thereafter it was found that the body produces its own cannabis-like substance, anandamide, named for the Sanskrit word for bliss (Sussman et al., 1996).

An abundance of scientific evidence indicates that marijuana interferes with a wide range of cognitive functions. Laboratory studies conducted for the most part in the late 1960s found that a number of tests—substituting symbols for numbers, reaction-time tests, repeating series of digits forward and backward, arithmetic calculations, reading comprehension and speech tests—revealed intellectual impairment in those under the influence of marijuana (*Marijuana Research Findings*, 1980). Of special significance are findings that show loss of short-term memory. It appears that the many high school students who use marijuana regularly may be seriously hindering their learning.

Several studies have demonstrated that being high on marijuana impairs complex psychomotor skills necessary for driving. Highway fatality and driver-arrest figures indicate that marijuana plays a role in a significant proportion of accidents and arrests (Brookoff et al., 1994). Marijuana has similarly been found to impair manipulation of flight simulators. Some performance decrements measurable after smoking one or two marijuana cigarettes containing 2 percent THC can persist for up to eight hours after a person believes he or she is no longer high, creating the very real danger that people will attempt to drive or fly when they are not functioning adequately.

Does chronic use of marijuana affect intellectual functioning even when the person is not using the drug? Studies of memory and problem solving conducted in Egypt and India in the late 1970s indicated some deterioration in users compared with nonusers (Soueif, 1976; Wig & Varma, 1977). A more recent U.S. study found memory impairment but not a general intellectual inefficiency (Millsaps, Azrin, & Mittenberg, 1994). It is impossible to know whether these problems existed before heavy drug use.

Somatic Effects   The short-term somatic effects of marijuana include bloodshot and itchy eyes, dry mouth and throat, increased appetite, reduced pressure within the eye, and somewhat raised blood pressure.

There is no evidence that smoking marijuana has untoward effects on a normal heart. The drug apparently poses a danger to people with already abnormal heart functioning, however, for it elevates heart rate, sometimes dramatically. As a report from the National Institute on Drug Abuse suggests, this effect may be of particular concern as present smokers grow older. The relatively healthy thirty-year-old marijuana users of today are the fifty-year-olds of tomorrow, with a statistically greater chance of having a cardiovascular system impaired for other reasons, such as atherosclerosis. If they are still using the drug then, their hearts will be more vulnerable to its effects. It is also possible that long-term use of marijuana, like the chronic use of tobacco, may be harmful in ways that cannot be predicted from the short-term effects studied so far.

We do know that the long-term use of marijuana seriously impairs lung structure and function (Grinspoon & Bakalar, 1995). Even though marijuana users smoke far fewer cigarettes than do tobacco smokers, most inhale marijuana smoke more deeply and retain it in their lungs for much longer periods of time. Since marijuana has some of the same carcinogens found in tobacco cigarettes, its harmful effects are much greater than would be expected were only the absolute number of cigarettes or pipefuls considered. For example, one marijuana cigarette smoked in the typical way is the equivalent of five tobacco cigarettes in carbon monoxide intake, four in tar intake, and ten in terms of damage to cells lining the airways (Sussman et al., 1996).

How does marijuana affect the brain? In the early 1990s, researchers identified two cannabinoid brain receptors, called CB1 and CB2 (Matsuda et al., 1990; Munro et al., 1993). CB1 receptors are found throughout the body and the brain, with a particularly high number in the hippocampus, an important region of the brain for a number of learning and memory abilities. Based on accumulating evidence, researchers have concluded that the well-documented short-term memory problems associated with marijuana use are linked to the effects of marijuana on these receptors in the hippocampus (e.g., Sullivan, 2000).

In addition, a recent PET study found that smoking marijuana was associated with increased blood flow to regions in the brain often associated with emotion, including limbic structures and the anterior cingulate gyrus. Decreased blood flow was observed in regions of the temporal lobe that have been associated with auditory attention, and participants in this study who were high on marijuana performed poorly on a dichotic listening task (O'Leary et al., 2000). These findings might help explain some of the psychological effects associated with marijuana use, including changes in emotion and attentional capabilities.

Is marijuana addictive? Contrary to widespread earlier belief, it may be. The development of tolerance began to be suspected when U.S. service personnel returned from Vietnam accustomed to concentrations of THC that would be toxic to domestic users. Controlled observations have confirmed that habitual use of marijuana does produce tolerance (Compton, Dewey, & Martin, 1990; Nowlan & Cohen, 1977). Whether long-term users experience physical withdrawal when accustomed amounts of marijuana are not available is less clear (Johnson, 1991).

The question of physical addiction to marijuana is complicated by what is termed *sensitization*. A person addicted to heroin needs greater and greater amounts to achieve the same effects. In contrast, experienced smokers need only a few hits or puffs to become high from a marijuana cigarette, whereas less experienced users puff many times to reach a similar state of intoxication.

Therapeutic Effects   In a seeming irony, therapeutic uses of marijuana came to light just as the negative effects of regular and heavy usage of the drug were being uncovered. In the 1970s several double-blind studies (e.g., Salan, Zinberg, & Frei, 1975) showed that THC and related drugs can reduce the nausea and loss of appetite that accompany chemotherapy for some cancer patients. Later findings confirmed this result (Grinspoon & Bakalar, 1995). Marijuana often appears to reduce nausea when other antinausea agents fail. Marijuana is also a treatment for the discomfort of AIDS (Sussman et al., 1996).

In addition to these clinical observations, confirming data have been reported from laboratories using animal models. For example, the active ingredient of marijuana, THC, has been demonstrated to relieve pain by blocking pain signals from injuries or inflammation (as in arthritis) and thereby preventing them from reaching the brain. The analgesic effects have been shown with both injections of THC and by direct application to an affected area (Attias et al., 1997; Meng et al., 1997; Richardson, Kilo, & Hargreaves, 1997; Simone, Daughters, & Li, 1997).

In 1998, the potential benefits of smoking marijuana were confirmed in a report by a panel of experts to the National Institutes of Health (NIH); the report suggested that these benefits be taken more seriously by medical researchers and clinicians (Ad Hoc Advisory Group of Experts, 1998). The NIH agreed to fund research on the subject, including research on whether the benefits from taking THC in pill form are comparable to what patients report from smoking marijuana. (Most people report more beneficial effects from smoking than from swallowing THC in capsule form; this may be due to compounds in marijuana leaves that are separate from THC.) The report warned, however, that undesirable effects from smoking marijuana, such as suppression of immune function, had to be considered, especially with people whose immune system is already compromised, as with AIDS.

Positive findings were again confirmed by a committee of the Institute of Medicine, a branch of the National Academy of Sciences, in 1999 (Institute of Medicine, 1999). The report of this committee recommended that patients with "debilitating symptoms" or terminal illnesses be allowed to smoke marijuana under close medical supervision for up to six months; the rationale for smoking was based on the just-mentioned findings that

Demonstrators in New York advocate the legalization of marijuana for medical purposes.

THC swallowed by mouth does not provide the same level of relief. But the Institute of Medicine report also emphasized the dangers of smoking per se and urged the development of alternative delivery systems, such as inhalers.

The recommendations of medical experts represent sharp disagreement with the federal government. A controversial law, Proposition 215, passed in California in 1996, made it legal for physicians to recommend marijuana to help AIDS patients and other seriously ill individuals cope with pain and relieve nausea from medications used in treating their illnesses. Federal authorities took issue with the California law, and the U.S. Supreme Court ruled in May 2001 that federal law prohibits the dispensing of marijuana for those medical purposes. Interestingly, the ruling did not expressly forbid the use of the drug to alleviate pain and nausea. Voters in eight other states have approved laws similar to California's, making it likely that the debate on this issue will continue for years to come.

Sedatives and Stimulants

Addiction to drugs was disapproved of but tolerated in the United States until 1914, when the Harrison Narcotics Act made the unauthorized use of various drugs illegal and those addicted to them criminals. One of the concerns at that time was the opiate drugs, which fall under the category of sedatives. In this section, we discuss both sedatives and stimulants.

Sedatives

The major **sedatives**, often called downers, slow the activities of the body and reduce its responsiveness. This group of drugs includes the opiates—opium and its derivatives morphine, heroin, and codeine—and the synthetic barbiturates and tranquilizers, such as secobarbital (Seconal) and diazepam (Valium).

Opiates   The **opiates** are a group of addictive sedatives that in moderate doses relieve pain and induce sleep. Foremost among them is **opium**, originally the principal drug of illegal international traffic and known to the people of the Sumerian civilization dating as far back as 7000 B.C. They gave the poppy that supplied this drug the name by which it is still known, meaning "the plant of joy."

In 1806 the alkaloid **morphine**, named after Morpheus, the Greek god of dreams, was separated from raw opium. This bitter-tasting powder proved to be a powerful sedative and pain reliever. Before its addictive properties were noted, it was commonly used in patent medicines. In the middle of the nineteenth century, when the hypodermic needle was introduced in the United States, morphine began to be injected directly into the veins to relieve pain. Many soldiers wounded in battle and those suffering from dysentery during the Civil War were treated with morphine and returned home addicted to the drug.

Concerned about administering a drug that could disturb the later lives of patients, scientists began studying morphine. In 1874 they found that morphine could be converted into another powerful pain-relieving drug, which they named **heroin**. Used initially as a cure for morphine addiction, heroin was substituted for morphine in cough syrups and other patent medicines. So many maladies were treated with heroin that it came to be known as G.O.M., or "God's own medicine" (Brecher, 1972). However, heroin proved to be even more addictive and more potent than morphine, acting more quickly and with greater intensity. In 1909, President Theodore Roosevelt called for an international investigation of opium and the other opiates. Today, heroin is most often injected, though it can also be smoked, snorted, or taken orally.

More recently, prescription pain medications, including hydrocodone and oxycodone have become opiates of abuse (NDIC, 2001).

An opium poppy. Opium is harvested by slitting the seed capsule, which allows the raw opium to seep out.

Prevalence of Opiate Abuse   Heroin is today the most abused of the opiates. In spite of enormous difficulties in gathering data, the considered opinion is that there are more than a million heroin addicts in the United States (NIDA, 2000). For years dependence has been many times higher among physicians and nurses than in any other group with a comparable educational background. This problem is believed to arise from a combination of the relative availability of opiates in medical settings and the stresses under which people often work in such environments (Jaffe, 1985).

Heroin used to be confined to poor neighborhoods and the inner city. In the early 1990s, it became the cool drug for middle- and upper-middle-class college students and young professionals, and it is beginning to vie with cocaine for popularity among these groups. The number of new users of heroin has been steadily increasing since 1992 (NIDA, 1997). Among seniors in high school the prevalence rose from 1 percent to 1.6 percent in the year 2000 (Johnston et al., 2001b). Furthermore, the number of people seen in emergency rooms after injecting or snorting heroin more than doubled, rising from 35,898 in 1991 to 73,846 in 1998 (NIDA, 2000). Drug rehabilitation centers have seen commensurate increases in heroin users (Corwin, 1996).

Heroin was synthesized from opium in 1874 and was soon being added to a variety of medicines that could be purchased without prescription. This ad shows a teething remedy containing heroin. It probably worked.

Some of the increases in drug casualties are due to the nature of the heroin now available. In the early 1980s, the heroin sold in southern California, for example, was in powder form that was less than 5 percent pure. By the mid 1990s, heroin ranged from 25 to 50 percent pure and was being sold in a gummy form that is difficult to dilute, or step down, making it more likely for users, especially the less experienced, to overdose (Corwin, 1996). New forms of heroin that need not be injected are believed to be responsible for the increased use by high school students.

From 1990 to 1997, reports of hydrocodone abuse increased by 173 percent in the United States, and reports of oxycodone abuse increased 43 percent in just one year, from 1997 to 1998 (NIDA, 1999). Trade names for oxycodone include Percodan, Tylox, and OxyContin. Prescriptions for OxyContin jumped 1800 percent between 1996 and 2000 (DEA, 2001), and the illicit supply seems to come largely from prescriptions that are forged, stolen, or diverted to dealers on the black market. As prescribed, OxyContin comes in a pill format with polymer coating. Unfortunately the pills can easily be dissolved into a form that can then be injected or snorted by abusers. Legitimate sales of a 40 milligram OxyContin pill range from $.50 to $1.00, but they sell on the street for $25.00 to $40.00 per pill. Abuse of OxyContin appears to be more prevalent in rural areas, but it is rapidly spreading to larger metropolitan areas (DEA, 2001; *New York Times Magazine*, 2001). Because OxyContin's effects are so similar to those of heroin, health professionals are concerned that individuals dependent on OxyContin who can no longer afford its hefty street price will turn to the less expensive heroin.

Psychological and Physical Effects   Opium and its derivatives morphine and heroin produce euphoria, drowsiness, reverie, and sometimes a lack of coordination. Heroin and OxyContin have an additional initial effect—the rush, a feeling of warm, suffusing ecstasy immediately following an intravenous injection. The user sheds worries and fears and has great self-confidence for four to six hours, but then experiences letdown, bordering on stupor.

Opiates produce their effects by stimulating neural receptors of the body's own opioid system. Heroin, for example, is converted into morphine in the brain and then binds to opioid receptors. The body produces opioids, called endorphins and enkephalins, and opium and its derivatives fit into their receptors and stimulate them. Opioid receptors are located throughout the brain, and some evidence points to the linkage between these receptors and the dopamine system as being responsible for opiates' pleasurable effects. However, evidence from animal studies suggests that opiates may achieve their pleasurable effects via their action in the area of the brain called the nucleus accumbens, perhaps independent from the dopamine system (Koob et al., 1999).

Opiates are clearly addicting in the physiological sense, for users show both increased tolerance of the drugs and withdrawal symptoms when they are unable to obtain another dose. Reactions to not having a dose of heroin may begin within eight hours of the last injection, at least after high tolerance has built up. During the next few hours the individual typically has muscle pain, sneezes, sweats, becomes tearful, and yawns a great deal. The symptoms resemble those of influenza. Within thirty-six hours the withdrawal symptoms become more severe. There may be uncontrollable muscle twitching, cramps, chills alternating with excessive flushing and sweating, and a rise in heart rate and blood pressure. The addicted person is unable to sleep, vomits, and has diarrhea. These symptoms typically persist for about seventy-two hours and then diminish gradually over a five- to ten-day period.

Opiates present a serious set of problems for the abuser. In a twenty-four-year follow-up of 500 heroin addicts, about 28 percent had died by age forty; half of these deaths were from homicide, suicide, or accident, and one-third were from overdose (Hser, Anglin, & Powers, 1993). Several deaths caused by OxyContin overdose have also been reported. For example, 19 OxyContin-related deaths occurred in Pike County, Kentucky during the year 2000 (NDIC, 2001). Equally serious are the social consequences of using an illegal drug. The drug and obtaining it become the center of the abuser's existence, governing all activities and social relationships. The high cost of the drugs—addicts must often spend upwards of $200 per day for their opiates—means that they must either have great wealth or acquire money through illegal activities, such as theft, prostitution, or selling drugs. The correlation between opiate addiction and criminal activities is thus rather high, undoubtedly contributing to the popular notion that drug addiction per se causes crime.

An additional problem now associated with intravenous drug use is exposure, through sharing needles, to the human immunodeficiency virus (HIV) and AIDS (see p. 221). Notably, there is good consensus among scientists that needle exchange programs and the free distribution of needles and syringes reduce needle sharing and the infectious diseases associated with intravenous drug use (Gibson et al., 2001; Yoast et al., 2001). Contrary to popular rhetoric, such programs in combination with methadone treatment (discussed later in this chapter) do not lead to an increase in either initial or continued use of drugs.

Synthetic Sedatives   A major type of sedative, **barbiturates** were synthesized as aids for sleeping and relaxation. The first barbiturate was produced in 1903, and since then hundreds of derivatives of barbituric acid have been made. These drugs were initially considered highly desirable and were prescribed frequently. In the 1940s a campaign was mounted against them because they were discovered to be addicting, and physicians began to prescribe barbiturates less frequently. Use steadily declined from 1975 to the early 1990s; however, use of these drugs appears to be once again on the rise (Johnston et al., 2001c).

Other types of synthetic sedatives are also part of this upward trend. Benzodiazepines, such as Valium, are commonly used and abused. Ketamine, an anesthetic used for both animals and humans, is used particularly as part of the club scene.

In the United States sedatives are manufactured in vast quantities—enough, it is estimated, to supply each man, woman, and child with fifty pills per year. Many are shipped legally to Mexico and then brought back into the United States and trafficked illegally. Many polydrug abusers choose a barbiturate or other sedative as one of their drugs, sometimes to come down from a stimulant or to reduce withdrawal effects.

Sedatives relax the muscles, reduce anxiety, and in small doses produce a mildly euphoric state. Like alcohol, they are thought to produce these psychological effects by stimulating the GABA system.[2] With excessive doses, however, speech becomes slurred and gait unsteady. Judgment, concentration, and ability to work may be extremely impaired. The user loses emotional control and may become irritable and combative before falling into a deep sleep. Very large doses can be fatal because the diaphragm muscles relax to such an extent that the individual suffocates. As indicated in Chapter 10,

---

[2] Methaqualone, a sedative sold under the trade names Quaalude and Sopor, is similar in effect to barbiturates and has become a popular street drug. Besides being addictive it brings other dangers—internal bleeding, coma, and even death from overdose.

sedatives are frequently chosen as a means of suicide. However, many users accidentally kill themselves by drinking alcohol, which magnifies the depressant effects of sedatives. Prolonged excessive use can damage the brain, and personality deteriorates.

Increased tolerance follows prolonged use of sedatives. The withdrawal reactions after abrupt termination are particularly severe and long lasting and can cause sudden death. The delirium, convulsions, and other symptoms resemble the symptoms that follow abrupt withdrawal of alcohol.

Stimulants

Stimulants, or uppers, such as cocaine, act on the brain and the sympathetic nervous system to increase alertness and motor activity. The amphetamines, such as Benzedrine, are synthetic stimulants; cocaine is a natural stimulant extracted from the coca leaf. Focus on Discovery 12.2 discusses a less risky and more prevalent stimulant, caffeine.

Amphetamines   Seeking a treatment for asthma, the Chinese American pharmacologist Chen studied ancient Chinese descriptions of drugs. He found a desert shrub called mahuang commended again and again as an effective remedy. After systematic effort Chen was able to isolate an alkaloid from this plant belonging to the genus *Ephedra*, and ephedrine did indeed prove highly successful in treating asthma. But relying on the shrub for the drug was not viewed as efficient, and so efforts to develop a synthetic substitute began. **Amphetamines** were the result of these efforts (Snyder, 1974).

The first amphetamine, Benzedrine, was synthesized in 1927. Almost as soon as it became commercially available in the early 1930s as an inhalant to relieve stuffy noses, the public discovered its stimulating effects. Physicians thereafter prescribed it and the other amphetamines soon synthesized to control mild depression and appetite. During World War II soldiers on both sides were supplied with the drugs to ward off fatigue; today amphetamines are often used to treat hyperactive children (see p. 483).

Amphetamines, such as Benzedrine, Dexedrine, and Methedrine, produce their effects by causing the release of norepinephrine and dopamine and blocking the reuptake of these neurotransmitters. They are taken orally or intravenously and can be addicting. Wakefulness is heightened, intestinal functions are inhibited, and appetite is reduced— hence their use in dieting. The heart rate quickens, and blood vessels in the skin and mucous membranes constrict. The individual becomes alert, euphoric, and outgoing and is possessed with seemingly boundless energy and self-confidence. Larger doses can make a person nervous, agitated, and confused, subjecting him or her to palpitations, headaches, dizziness, and sleeplessness. Sometimes the heavy user becomes so suspicious and hostile that he or she can be dangerous to others. Large doses taken over a period of time can induce a state quite similar to paranoid schizophrenia, including its delusions.

Tolerance to amphetamines develops rapidly so that more and more of the drug is required to produce the stimulating effect. One study demonstrated tolerance effects in as quick as six days of repeated use (Comer et al., 2001). As tolerance increases the user may stop taking pills and inject Methedrine, the strongest of the amphetamines, directly into the veins. The so-called speed freaks give themselves repeated injections of the drug and maintain intense and euphoric activity for a few days, without eating or sleeping (a run), after which, exhausted and depressed, they sleep, or crash, for several days. Then the cycle starts again. After several repetitions of this pattern, the physical and social functioning of the individual deteriorates considerably. Behavior is erratic and hostile, and the speed freak may become a danger to him- or herself and to others.

Amphetamine use in the workplace has increased. Under time pressure to produce— the saying of the nineties was "do more with less"—many white-collar workers turned to speed to stay awake, be more productive, and in general feel more energized, even euphoric. In some instances supervisors encouraged use, even supplying the drug to an already motivated employee. Although this may work in the short run, over time extreme irritability sets in and the person may take more and more of the addicting substance to combat the angry feelings. Sometimes the individual uses alcohol in the evening to wind

Our Tastiest Addiction—Caffeine

What may be the world's most popular drug is seldom viewed as a drug at all, and yet it has strong effects, produces tolerance in people, and even subjects habitual users to withdrawal (Hughes et al., 1991). Users and nonusers alike joke about it, and most readers of this book have probably had some this very day. We are, of course, referring to caffeine, a substance found in coffee, tea, cocoa, cola and other soft drinks, some cold remedies, and some diet pills.

Two cups of coffee, containing between 150 and 300 milligrams of caffeine, affect most people within half an hour. Metabolism, body temperature, and blood pressure all increase; urine production goes up, as most of us will attest; there may be hand tremors, appetite can diminish, and, most familiar of all, sleepiness is warded off. Panic disorder can be exacerbated by caffeine, not surprising in light of the heightened sympathetic nervous system arousal occasioned by the drug. Extremely large doses of caffeine can cause headache, diarrhea, nervousness, severe agitation, even convulsions and death. Death, though, is virtually impossible unless the individual grossly

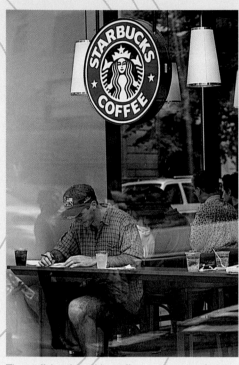

The caffeine found in coffee, tea, and soft drinks is probably the world's favorite drug.

overuses tablets containing caffeine, because the drug is excreted by the kidneys without any appreciable accumulation.

Although it has long been recognized that drinkers of very large amounts of regular coffee daily can experience withdrawal symptoms when consumption ceases, people who drink no more than two cups of regular coffee a day can suffer from clinically significant headaches, fatigue, and anxiety if caffeine is withdrawn from their daily diet (Silverman et al., 1992), and these symptoms can markedly interfere with social and occupational functioning. These findings are disturbing because more than three-quarters of Americans consume a little more than two cups of regular coffee a day (Roan, 1992). And although parents usually deny their children access to coffee and tea, they often do allow them to imbibe caffeine-laden cola drinks, hot chocolate, and cocoa, and to eat chocolate candy and chocolate and coffee ice cream. Thus our addiction to caffeine can begin to develop as early as six months of age, the form of it changing as we move from childhood to adulthood.

down. The emotional and physical costs are steep as the addict's personal relationships begin to deteriorate along with his or her job performance.

Methamphetamine Abuse of a derivative of amphetamine called **methamphetamine** skyrocketed in the 1990s. Some estimates indicate that as many as 4.7 million people in the United States have tried methamphetamine at some point (Anglin et al., 2000). Additionally, methamphetamine-related deaths nearly tripled between the years 1991 and 1994.

Hospital admissions for methamphetamine intoxication have also increased dramatically. From 1992 to 1993, admissions for methamphetamine use across 42 states increased 43 percent (Greenblatt, Gfroerer, & Melnick, 1995). In 1994 and 1995, 35 percent of admissions to California drug treatment centers were for methamphetamine abuse, compared with 27 percent for heroin and 24 percent for cocaine. The problem was, until recently, more serious in California than elsewhere in the United States because of the high concentration there of clandestine laboratories that manufacture this easily made and inexpensive drug. However, abuse is now becoming more widespread in the midwestern and southwestern United States.

Men tend to abuse methamphetamine more often than women in contrast with other forms of amphetamine use, where few gender differences occur. Abuse among both male and female adolescents has almost doubled since 1992, however (Oetting et al., 2000). Although white males are the typical meth abusers, recent data suggest that use among Hispanic and Native Americans is on the rise (Oetting et al., 2000).

Like other amphetamines, methamphetamine can be taken orally or intravenously. It can also be taken intranasally (i.e., snorting). In a clear crystal form, the drug is often referred to as "crystal meth" or "ice." Craving for methamphetamine is particularly strong, often lasting several years after use of the drug is discontinued. Craving is also a reliable predictor of later use (Hartz, Fredrick-Osborne, & Galloway, 2001).

Several studies done with animals have indicated that chronic use of methamphetamine causes damage to the brain, affecting both dopamine and serotonin systems (Frost & Cadet, 2000). Recent neuroimaging studies with humans have found similar effects in the brain, particularly in the dopamine system. Volkow and colleagues (2001) reported that methamphetamine abusers who were currently clean of the substance, some for as long as eleven months, had a significant reduction in a dopamine transporter. In fact, in three of the patients studied, the reduction in dopamine reuptake was similar to that seen in less severe stages of Parkinson's disease. Moreover, the methamphetamine abusers performed more slowly than a comparison group on several motor tasks, a finding similar to that seen with Parkinson's patients. Other studies have documented the cognitive deficits associated with chronic methamphetamine use as well (e.g., Simon et al., 2000). Not surprisingly, use of methamphetamine by pregnant women can have severe consequences for the developing fetus. In short, the deleterious effects of methamphetamine are many and serious.

Chemicals for manufacturing methamphetamine are readily available, though recent laws, such as the Methamphetamine Control Act of 1996, have been passed to try to cut off the supply. When supplies of ephedrine became low, pseudoephedrine, a common substance in many over-the-counter decongestants, was substituted, but these substances are now also better regulated. Some chemicals used to make methamphetamine are highly volatile and dangerous to breathe. The hazardous chemicals cause damage ranging from eye irritation and nausea to coma and death. They also create risks for fire and explosions.

Cocaine Cocaine, as mentioned, comes from the coco shrub. The natives of the Andean uplands, to which the coca shrubs are native, chew the leaves. Europeans, introduced to coca by the Spanish conquistadors, chose instead to brew the leaves in beverages. The alkaloid **cocaine** was extracted from the leaves of the coca plant in the mid-1800s and has been used since then as a local anesthetic.

In 1884, while still a young neurologist, Sigmund Freud began using cocaine to combat his depression. Convinced of its wondrous effects, he prescribed it to a friend who had a painful disease. Freud published one of the first papers on the drug, "Song of Praise," which was an enthusiastic endorsement of the exhilarating effects he had experienced. Freud subsequently lost his enthusiasm for cocaine after nursing a physician friend to whom he had recommended the drug through a night-long psychotic state brought on by it. Perhaps the most famous fictional cocaine addict was Sherlock Holmes.

In addition to reducing pain, cocaine has other effects. It acts rapidly on the brain, blocking the reuptake of dopamine in mesolimbic areas that are thought to yield pleasurable states; the result is that dopamine is left in the synapse and thereby facilitates neural transmission and resultant positive feelings. Self-reports of the pleasure induced by cocaine are strongly related to the extent cocaine has blocked dopamine reuptake (Volkow et al., 1997). Cocaine increases sexual desire and produces feelings of self-confidence, well-being, and indefatigability. An overdose may bring on chills, nausea, and insomnia, as well as a paranoid breakdown and terrifying hallucinations of insects crawling beneath the skin. Chronic use can lead to changes in personality, which include heightened irritability, impaired social relationships, paranoid thinking, and disturbances in eating and sleeping (Scientific Perspectives on Cocaine Abuse, 1987). Ceasing cocaine use appears to cause a severe withdrawal syndrome. Cocaine can take hold of people with as much tenacity as do the other addictive drugs. As with alcohol, developing fetuses are markedly and negatively affected in the womb by the mother's use of cocaine during pregnancy, and many babies are born addicted to the drug.

Cocaine is a vasoconstrictor, causing the blood vessels to narrow. As users take larger and larger doses of the purer forms of cocaine now available, they are more often rushed to emergency rooms and may die of an overdose, often from a heart attack (Kozel, Crider, & Adams, 1982). Cocaine also increases a person's risk for stroke and causes cognitive impairments, such as difficulty paying attention and remembering. Because of its

A coca plant. The leaves contain about 1 percent cocaine.

Cocaine can be smoked, swallowed, injected, or snorted as shown here.

strong vasoconstricting properties, cocaine poses special dangers in pregnancy, for the blood supply to the developing fetus may be compromised.

Cocaine can be sniffed (snorted), smoked in pipes or cigarettes, swallowed, or even injected into the veins; some heroin addicts mix the two drugs. In the 1970s cocaine users in the United States began to separate, or free, a component of cocaine by heating it with ether. When purified by this chemical process the cocaine base—or freebase—produces very powerful effects because it is absorbed so rapidly. It is usually smoked in a water pipe or sprinkled on a tobacco or marijuana cigarette. It is rapidly absorbed into the lungs and carried to the brain in a few seconds, where it induces an intense two-minute high, followed by restlessness and discomfort. Some freebase smokers go on marathon binges lasting up to four days (Goodwin & Guze, 1984). The freebasing process is hazardous, however, because ether is flammable. Comedian Richard Pryor nearly died from the burns he suffered when the ether he was using ignited.

In the mid-1980s a new form of freebase, called crack, appeared on the streets. The presence of crack brought about an increase in freebasing and in casualties. Because it was available in small, relatively inexpensive doses ($10 for about 100 milligrams versus the $100 per gram that users formerly had to pay to obtain cocaine), younger and less affluent buyers began to experiment with the drug and to become addicted (Kozel & Adams, 1986).

Cocaine use in general soared in the 1970s and 1980s, increasing by more than 260 percent between 1974 and 1985. Men use cocaine and crack more often than women. Although the use of cocaine dramatically decreased in the late 1980s and early 1990s, it began to rise again in the mid-1990s, particularly among high school and college students and young adults in general. Since then, the frequency of use of crack has not shown much of a decline among college students and young adults, but use among high school students finally began to decline in the late 1990s (Johnston et al., 2001b). It appears that intensive efforts toward educating people about the pernicious effects of crack have begun to pay off, as rates of crack use have not risen in most US cities since 1996.

LSD and Other Hallucinogens

In 1943 a Swiss chemist, Albert Hofmann, recorded a description of an illness he had seemingly contracted.

> Last Friday…I had to interrupt my laboratory work…I was seized with a feeling of great restlessness and mild dizziness. At home, I lay down and sank into a not unpleasant delirium, which was characterized by extremely exciting fantasies. In a semiconscious state with my eyes closed…fantastic visions of extraordinary realness and with an intense kaleidoscopic play of colors assaulted me. (Cited in Cashman, 1966, p. 31)

Earlier in the day Hofmann had manufactured a few milligrams of d-lysergic acid diethylamide, a drug that he had first synthesized in 1938. Reasoning that he might have unknowingly ingested some and that this was the cause of his unusual experience, he deliberately took a dose and confirmed his hypothesis.

After Hofmann's experiences with **LSD** in 1943, the drug was referred to as psychotomimetic because it was thought to produce effects similar to the symptoms of a psychosis. Then the term psychedelic, from the Greek words for "soul" and "to make manifest," was applied to emphasize the subjectively experienced expansions of consciousness reported by users of LSD and often referred to by them as a trip. The term in current use for LSD is **hallucinogen**, which describes one of the main effects of such drugs, producing hallucinations. Unlike hallucinations in schizophrenia, however, these are usually recognized by the person as being caused by the drug.

The following description is of the general effects of LSD, but it also applies to the other hallucinogens.

> Synesthesias, the overflow from one sensory modality to another, may occur. Colors are heard

and sounds may be seen. Subjective time is also seriously altered, so that clock time seems to pass extremely slowly. The loss of boundaries [between one's sense of self and one's environment] and the fear of fragmentation create a need for a structuring or supporting environment; and in the sense that they create a need for experienced companions and an explanatory system, these drugs are "cultogenic." During the "trip," thoughts and memories can vividly emerge under self-guidance or unexpectedly, to the user's distress. Mood may be labile, shifting from depression to gaiety, from elation to fear. Tension and anxiety may mount and reach panic proportions. After about 4 to 5 hours, if a major panic episode does not occur, there may be a sense of detachment and the conviction that one is magically in control.... The user may be greatly impressed with the drug experience and feel a greater sensitivity for art, music, human feelings, and the harmony of the universe. (Jaffe, 1985, p. 564)

The effects of hallucinogens depend on a number of psychological variables in addition to the dose itself. A person's set—that is, attitudes, expectancies, and motivations with regard to taking drugs—is widely held to be an important determinant of his or her reactions to hallucinogens. The setting in which the drug is experienced is also important.

Among the most prominent dangers of taking LSD is the possibility of experiencing a bad trip, which can sometimes develop into a full-blown panic attack and is far more likely to occur if some aspect of taking the drug creates anxiety. Often the specific fear is of going crazy. These panics are usually short-lived and subside as the drug is metabolized. A minority of people, however, go into a psychotic state that can require hospitalization and extended treatment.

Flashbacks, a recurrence of psychedelic experiences after the physiological effects of the drug have worn off, also sometimes occur, most frequently in times of stress, illness, or fatigue (Kaplan & Sadock, 1991). Flashbacks are not believed to be caused by drug-produced physical changes in the nervous system, in part because only 15 to 30 percent of users of hallucinogenic drugs are estimated ever to have flashbacks (e.g., Stanton & Bardoni, 1972). Moreover, there is no independent evidence of measurable neurological changes in these drug users. Flashbacks seem to have a force of their own; they may come to haunt people weeks and months after they have taken the drug and are very upsetting for those who experience them.

Four other important hallucinogens are mescaline, psilocybin, and two similar synthetic compounds, MDA (methylenedioxyamphetamine) and MDMA (methylenedioxymethamphetamine). Each of these substances is structurally similar to several neurotransmitters, but their effects are thought to be due to stimulating serotonin receptors.

- In 1896 **mescaline**, an alkaloid and the active ingredient of peyote, was isolated from small, disklike growths of the top of the peyote cactus. The drug has been used for centuries in the religious rites of Indian peoples living in the Southwest and northern Mexico.

- **Psilocybin** is a crystalline powder that Hofmann isolated from the mushroom Psilocybe mexicana in 1958. The early Aztec and Mexican cultures called the sacred mushrooms "God's flesh," and the Indians of Mexico still use them in their worship.

- **MDMA** was first synthesized in the early 1900s, and it was used as an appetite suppressant for World War I soldiers. Chemical precursors to MDMA are found in several commonly used spices, such as nutmeg, dill, saffron, and sassafras. Not until the 1970s were the psychoactive properties of MDMA reported in the scientific literature.

- **MDA** was first synthesized in 1910, but it was not until the 1960s that its psychedelic properties came to the attention of the drug-using, consciousness-expanding generation of the times.

Mescaline, obtained from the peyote cactus, is used in religious rites of Native American people of the American Southwest and northern Mexico.

In the 1960s, Timothy Leary was one of the leading proponents of the use of hallucinogens to expand consciousness.

During the 1950s, LSD, mescaline, and psilocybin were given in research settings to study what were thought to be psychotic experiences. In 1960, Timothy Leary and Richard Alpert of Harvard University began an investigation of the effects of psilocybin on institutionalized prisoners. The early results, although subject to several confounds, were encouraging: released prisoners who had taken psilocybin proved less likely to be rearrested. At the same time the investigators started taking trips themselves and soon had gathered around them a group of people interested in experimenting with psychedelic drugs. By 1962 their activities had attracted the attention of law-enforcement agencies. As the investigation continued, the situation became a scandal, culminating in Leary's and Alpert's departures from Harvard.[3] The affair seemed to give tremendous impetus to the use of the hallucinogens, particularly since the manufacture of LSD and the extraction of mescaline and psilocybin were relatively easy and inexpensive. In 1966 the use of these substances was banned by Congress. Since then, little research has been done on their effects in humans.

The use of LSD and other hallucinogens peaked in the 1960s; by the 1980s only 1 or 2 percent of people could be classified as regular users. Even those who used hallucinogens did not indulge more than once or twice every two weeks (NIDA, 1982, 1983a). LSD use increased somewhat in the early 1990s (NIDA, 1998), but it seems to be once again on the decline among high school and college students as well as young adults (Johnston et al., 2001b,c). There is no evidence of withdrawal symptoms during abstinence, but tolerance appears to develop rapidly (McKim, 1991).

A new hallucinogen-like substance, **Ecstasy**, became illegal in 1985. Ecstasy includes both MDA and MDMA, which were mentioned earlier. It is chemically similar to mescaline and the amphetamines and is the psychoactive agent in nutmeg. Ecstasy contains compounds from both the hallucinogen and amphetamine families, but its effects are sufficiently different from either that some have suggested it be in its own category called the "entactogens" (e.g., Morgan, 2000). Today it is popular on college campuses. In addition, use of Ecstasy increased precipitously in 1998 among high school students, and it is now used more often than cocaine in this group (Johnston et al., 2001b). Prevalence rates of Ecstasy use for 2000 among high school seniors, college students, and young adults were 8, 9, and 7 percent, respectively (Johnston et al., 2001b, 2001c).

Ecstasy acts primarily by activating the serotonin system via the serotonin transporter, contributing both to the release and subsequent reuptake of serotonin (e.g., Huether et al., 1997; Liechti et al., 2000; Morgan, 2000). It was believed at one time that the use of Ecstasy was relatively harmless, but accumulating scientific evidence suggests that it may have neurotoxic effects on the serotonin system (e.g., De Souza et al., 1990; Gerra et al., 2000). It is difficult to say if these toxic effects are directly due to drug use, since no studies in humans to date have assessed serotonin functioning both before and after the initiation of Ecstasy use. Studies with animals, however, have shown that a single dose of Ecstasy causes serotonin depletion, and prolonged use can damage serotonin axons and nerve terminals (Harkin et al., 2001; Morgan, 2000). Evidence of this alteration has been observed in monkeys several years after use of the drug was discontinued (Hatzidimitriou et al., 1999). Other studies show that more extensive use of Ecstasy is associated with some impairments in learning and memory (e.g., Verkes et al., 2001) and that these impairments are correlated with serotonin reductions (e.g., Renemen et al., 2000). It is important to note, though, that many studies examining the cognitive effects of Ecstasy use have not been able to attribute cognitive impairments solely to Ecstasy, since many users have used other drugs concurrently with or prior to using Ecstasy. For example, one study found that users of both marijuana and Ecstasy had impairments in

---

[3] Like many of the old-timers in the psychedelic drug revolution, Alpert went on to espouse an Eastern meditation philosophy that urged people to forsake drugs and work instead on creating their own meaningful trips without the aid of chemical agents. Known as Baba Ram Dass, he has lectured and written eloquently about the possibility of cultivating expanded states of consciousness. Those who would devote the necessary time and energy to meditation techniques will be open to such experiences, according to Ram Dass. Most recently Ram Dass seems to have rediscovered his Jewish roots and is exploring the possibilities of integrating Judaism with the teachings of Eastern mystics.

Focus on Discovery 12.3

Nitrous Oxide—Not a Laughing Matter

Nitrous oxide is a colorless gas that has been available since the nineteenth century. Within seconds it induces light-headedness and a state of euphoria in most people; for some, important insights seem to flood the mind. Clinical reports and some controlled research (e.g., Devine et al., 1974) confirm that this gaseous mixture raises pain thresholds, perhaps by an induction of positive feelings that dull sensations that would normally be experienced as noxious. Many people find otherwise mundane events and thoughts irresistibly funny, hence the nickname "laughing gas."

Perhaps readers of this book have had nitrous oxide at a dentist's office to facilitate relaxation and otherwise make a potentially uncomfortable and intimidating dental procedure more palatable (and to make it easier for the dentist to work on the patient). A major advantage of nitrous oxide over other analgesics and relaxants is that the patient can return to the normal waking state within minutes of breathing enriched oxygen or normal air. An additional advantage is that patients can be taught to control how deep they go by taking a few breaths of regular air through the mouth (the gas is administered through a small mask that covers only the nose; otherwise the dentist could not work on the person's teeth). The health professional can easily make continuing adjustments based on experienced judgment of the patient's level of intoxication.

Nitrous oxide has been used recreationally since it first became available, although it has been illegal for many years in most states except as administered by appropriate health professionals. As with the other mind-altering drugs examined in this chapter, illegality has not prevented unsupervised use. Sometimes called hippie crack, nitrous oxide balloons are often supplemented with the use of Ecstasy and other designer drugs in a psychedelic atmosphere of bright laser lights and loud dance music (i.e., raves). Illicit use of nitrous oxide is not a priority for police, perhaps because there is no evidence that it is physically addicting. And because nitrous oxide is legally available for refilling aerosol canisters and souping up race-car engines, its use is not (yet) associated with crime, as is the use of heroin and cocaine. Nor does nitrous oxide directly provoke violent behavior, as does phencyclidine (PCP). It does, however, carry serious risk.

An important difference between the way in which dentists use nitrous oxide and the way in which it is used casually is that in the dental office the air mixture is seldom more than 80 percent nitrous oxide (the rest is oxygen). This mixture allows for the safe and effective use of the gas. Such was not the case for three men who were found dead in the closed cab of a pickup truck in the early morning hours of March 6, 1992. They had apparently been asphyxiated from the nitrous oxide in an eighty-pound industrial-sized canister that was lying across their laps. Evidence at the scene suggested that they had been filling balloons with the gas and, perhaps inadvertently, allowed the gas to escape freely into the sealed cab. With little air from outside, the men had been breathing pure nitrous oxide and their own exhaled carbon dioxide—and very little oxygen. They were not the first victims. In 1988 four young adults met a similar death in a dental storage room in Cedar City, Utah. And in Birmingham, Alabama, a party host was charged with manslaughter in 1990 for allegedly giving the gas to a teenager, who died after inhaling it. In September 1999, an MIT student died from asphyxiation after using a plastic bag placed over his head to inhale nitrous oxide.

Some of this material was taken from two *Los Angeles Times* articles: Connelly (1992) and Romero (1992).

---

memory, word fluency, and dexterity that were comparable to the impairments observed in users of marijuana alone (Croft et al., 2001).

Users report that the drug enhances intimacy and insight, improves interpersonal relationships, elevates mood and self-confidence, and promotes aesthetic awareness. It can also cause muscle tension, rapid eye movements, jaw-clenching, nausea, faintness, chills or sweating, and anxiety, depression, depersonalization, and confusion. Some evidence suggests that the subjective and physiological effects of Ecstasy, both pleasurable and adverse, may be stronger for women than men (Liechti et al., 2000). The Drug Enforcement Administration considers the use of Ecstasy and other so-called club drugs unsafe and a serious threat to health. Several deaths have been reported from accidental overdose (Climko et al., 1987) (see Focus on Discovery 12.3 on **nitrous oxide**).

A drug not easy to classify is PCP, phencyclidine, often called angel dust. Developed as a tranquilizer for horses and other large animals, it generally causes serious negative reactions, including severe paranoia and violence. Coma and death are also possible. PCP affects multiple neurotransmitters in the brain, and chronic use is associated with a variety of neuropsychological deficits. However, like most drug abusers, abusers of PCP are likely to have used other drugs either prior to or concurrently with PCP, so it is difficult to sort out whether the neuropsychological impairment is due solely to PCP, other drugs, or to the combination. Use of PCP increased in the early to mid-1990s but appears to be on the decline.

Etiology of Substance Abuse and Dependence

In considering the causes of substance abuse and dependence disorders, we must recognize that becoming substance dependent is generally a developmental process. The person must first have a positive attitude toward the substance, then begin to experiment with using it, then begin using it regularly, then use it heavily, and finally abuse or become physically dependent on it (see Figure 12.2). The general idea is that after prolonged heavy use the person becomes ensnared by the biological processes of tolerance and withdrawal.

Researchers have only recently begun to consider the nature of this process (Stice, Barrera, & Chassin, 1998). It appears that what variables contribute to substance dependence may depend on what point in the process is being considered. For example, developing a positive attitude toward smoking and beginning to experiment with tobacco are strongly related to smoking by other family members (Robinson et al., 1997). In contrast, becoming a regular smoker is more strongly related to smoking by peers and being able to acquire cigarettes readily (Robinson et al., 1997; Wang et al., 1997).

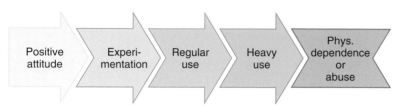

Figure 12.2 The process of becoming a drug abuser.

More generally, adopting a developmental approach to understanding substance abuse etiology requires the study of persons across time, beginning at the earliest sign of substance use. Studies of the trajectories of substance-related problems among adolescents are becoming more frequent, and the findings suggest, not surprisingly, that different adolescents follow different trajectories (e.g., Jackson, Sher, & Wood, 2000; Wills et al., 1999). For example, one study identified two typical trajectories toward alcohol abuse in adolescence: (1) a group that began drinking early in adolescence and continued to increase their drinking throughout high school and (2) a group that started drinking a lesser amount, and increased drinking at two peak points, one in middle school and another later in high school. Boys were more likely to follow the trajectory of the first group; girls were more likely to follow the trajectory of the second group, with even steeper trajectories in drinking than the boys (Li, Duncan, & Hops, 2001). Early deviant behavior predicted membership in the first group; peer encouragement predicted later drinking for both groups.

Although applicable in many cases, a developmental approach does not account for all cases of substance abuse or dependence. For example, there are documented cases in which heavy use of tobacco or heroin did not result in addiction. Furthermore, we must remember that we are not talking about an inevitable progression through stages. Some people have periods of heavy use of a substance, for example, alcohol, and then return to moderate use. Nevertheless, most research has examined variables related to initial use and its subsequent escalation. In the following sections, we discuss sociocultural, psychological, and biological variables related to substance abuse. It is important to keep in mind that these factors are likely to be differentially related to different substances. A genetic diathesis, for example, may play some role in alcoholism but be irrelevant to hallucinogen abuse.

Sociocultural Variables

Sociocultural variables play a widely varying role in drug abuse. From the effects of peers and parents to the influence of the media and what is considered acceptable behavior in a particular culture, the social world can affect people's interest in and access to drugs.

At the broadest level, for example, we can look at great cross-national variation in alcohol consumption. The data in Figure 12.3, from a large-scale longitudinal study, illustrate that there are commonalities in the alcohol consumption of various countries. First, over the study period (1950–1980) alcohol consumption rose greatly in each country studied. Second, variations in consumption across locations decreased with the passage of time, although large differences remained. Similarly, a recent cross-national study of alcohol and drug use among high school students that included 36 countries worldwide found that alcohol was the most common substance used across countries, despite great variation in the proportions of students who consumed alcohol, ranging from 32 percent in Zimbabwe to 99 percent in Wales (Smart & Ogborne, 2000). In all but two of the countries studied, marijuana was the next most commonly used drug. In those countries where marijuana was used most often (that is, more than 15 percent of high school students who had ever used marijuana), there were also higher rates of use of amphetamines, Ecstasy, and cocaine. Other research has found striking cross-national differences in alcohol consumption, some of them greater than those shown in Figure 12.3. For example, the highest consumption rates have typically been found in wine-drinking societies, such as those of France, Spain, and Italy, where drinking alcohol regularly is widely accepted (deLint, 1978). Cultural attitudes and patterns of drinking thus influence the likelihood of drinking heavily and therefore of abusing alcohol.

Ready availability of the substance is also a factor. For example, in the wine-drinking cultures just mentioned, wine is present in many social settings, even in university cafeterias. And rates of alcohol abuse are high among bartenders and liquor store owners, people for whom alcohol is readily available (Fillmore & Caetano, 1980). With regard to smoking, if cigarettes are perceived as being easy to get and affordable, the rate of smoking increases (Robinson et al., 1997).

Family variables are important sociocultural influences as well. For example, if both parents smoke, a child is four times more likely to do so than if no other family member smokes. Similarly, exposure to alcohol use by parents increases children's likelihood of drinking (Hawkins et al., 1997) Acculturation into American society may interact with family variables for people of different cultural and ethnic backgrounds. For example, a study of middle school Hispanic students in New York found that children who spoke English with their parents were more likely to smoke marijuana than children who spoke Spanish (Epstein, Botvin, & Diaz, 2001). Psychiatric, marital, or legal problems in the family are also related to drug abuse, and a lack of emotional support from parents is linked to increased use of cigarettes, cannabis, and alcohol (Cadoret et al., 1995a; Wills, DuHamel, & Vaccaro, 1995). Finally, longitudinal studies have shown that a lack of parental monitoring leads to increased association with drug-abusing peers and subsequent higher use of drugs (Chassin et al., 1996; Thomas et al., 2000).

The social milieu in which a person operates can also affect substance abuse. Having friends who smoke predicts smoking (Killen et al., 1997). In longitudinal studies, peer-group identification in the seventh grade predicted smoking in the eighth (Sussman et al., 1994), and in a three-year study it predicted increased drug use in general (Chassin et al., 1996). Peer influences are also important in promoting alcohol and marijuana use (Hussong et al., 2001; Stice et al., 1998; Wills & Cleary, 1999). Although peer influence is important in the decisions adolescents make about using substances, those who have a high sense of self-efficacy (Bandura, 1997) are influenced less by their peers. Adolescents with this quality agree with statements like "I can imagine refusing to use tobacco with students my age and still have them like me" (Stacy et al., 1992, p. 166).

These findings support the idea that social networks influence an individual's drug or alcohol behavior. However, other evidence indicates that individuals who are inclined to abuse substances may actually select social networks that conform to their own drinking or drug use patterns. Thus, two broad explanations for how the social environment

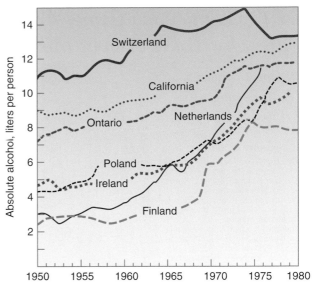

Figure 12.3 Annual consumption of alcoholic beverages among people aged fifteen years and over in countries from 1950 to 1980. After Mäkelä et al., 1981.

Alcoholism is higher in countries in which alcohol use is heavy, such as vinicultural societies. Everyone is drinking wine in this French bar.

F.T.C. Charges Joe Camel Ad Illegally Takes Aim at Minors

Internal Documents of R. J. Reynolds Are Cited by Agency

By JOHN M. BRODER

WASHINGTON, May 28 — In another blow to an industry under siege, the Federal Trade Commission charged today that the R. J. Reynolds Tobacco Company illegally aimed its Joe Camel advertising campaign at minors.

The agency asserted in an administrative complaint that the company violated Federal fair trade practice laws by promoting a lethal and addictive product to children and adolescents who could not legally purchase or use it.

This is the first time that the commission has accused the tobacco industry of peddling its products to minors. The complaint will be supported, agency officials said, by extensive citations from internal company documents.

The Government says it believes that R. J. Reynolds papers will prove that the company deliberately designed its cartoon-based advertising campaign in the mid-1980's to increase its shrinking market share among young smokers.

The complaint amounts to a civil indictment of a company commission official

Linda Rosier for The New York Times

Advertising is an important sociocultural variable in stimulating drug use. The Joe Camel campaign greatly increased Camel's share of the market among elementary and high school students.

is related to substance abuse are posited: a social influence model and a social selection model. A longitudinal study of over 1,200 adults designed to test which model best accounted for drinking behavior found support for both the social influence and social selection models (Bullers, Cooper, & Russell, 2001). An individual's social network predicted individual drinking, but individual drinking also predicted subsequent social network drinking. In fact, the social selection effects were stronger, indicating that individuals often choose social networks with drinking patterns similar to their own. No doubt the selected networks then support or reinforce their drinking. Similar results have been found for adolescents (Kandal, 1985; Farrell & Danish, 1993).

Another variable to be considered is the media. We are bombarded with TV commercials in which beer is associated with athletic-looking males, bikini-clad women, and good times. Billboards equate cigarettes with excitement, relaxation, or being in style. Supporting the role of advertising in promoting alcohol use is an analysis of consumption in seventeen countries between 1970 and 1983. Those countries that banned ads for spirits had 16 percent less consumption than those that did not (Saffer, 1991).

A particularly pernicious example of the role of the media was the Joe Camel campaign for Camel cigarettes. With the number of smokers declining, the tobacco industry's profitability depends on recruiting new smokers to replace those who are quitting. The obvious target—elementary and high school students. Camel launched its campaign in 1988 with the Joe Camel character modeled after James Bond or the character played by Don Johnson in the television program *Miami Vice*, a popular show of the time. Prior to the campaign, in the period from 1976 to 1988, Camels were the preferred brand of less than 0.5 percent of seventh through twelfth graders. By 1991 Camel's share of this illegal market had increased to 33 percent (DiFranza et al., 1991)!

In March 1992, the surgeon general as well as the American Medical Association (AMA) asked R. J. Reynolds, the manufacturer of Camel cigarettes, to drop Joe Camel from its ads because of this apparent appeal to youngsters. Billboard companies and print media were also requested to stop running the ads. The response from R. J. Reynolds? "We have no reason to believe that this campaign is causing anyone to begin smoking. If we thought it was causing young people to smoke, we'd pull it" (spokesperson for the company, quoted in Horovitz, 1992). The evidence indicates, however, that advertising does influence smoking. In a longitudinal study of nonsmoking adolescents, those who had a favorite cigarette ad were twice as likely subsequently to begin smoking or to be willing to do so (Pierce et al., 1998).

The days of Joe Camel and other cartoon characters that appeal to young people are over. On March 13, 1996, the Liggett Group, manufacturers of cigarettes, agreed to stop using such advertising tools and to take other steps to discourage smoking among minors. These actions were part of a settlement in a class action lawsuit against the U.S. cigarette industry that charged companies with manipulating nicotine levels to keep smokers addicted.

Psychological Variables

We examine next three classes of psychological variables. The first class comprises primarily the effects of alcohol on mood, the situations in which a tension-reducing effect occurs, and the role of cognition in this process. The second concerns beliefs about the prevalence with which the drug is used and health risks associated with that drug. The third includes the personality traits that may make it more likely for some people to use drugs heavily.

Mood Alteration   It is generally assumed that one of the principal psychological motives for using drugs is to alter mood. Drug use is therefore reinforcing, either by enhancing positive mood states or by diminishing negative ones. Things are more complex, however.

Most of the early research in this area focused on the tension-reducing properties of alcohol; more recent research has looked at the tension-reducing properties of nicotine. Early animal experiments (Conger, 1951) showed that alcohol impairs avoidance learning, which is usually regarded as being mediated by anxiety. Some later experiments with humans (e.g., Sher & Levenson, 1982) also indicated that alcohol reduces tension in people who are not yet alcohol abusers, but some conflicting findings emerged as well (e.g., Thyer & Curtis, 1984). For example, if alcohol reduces tension, it ought to have an effect on negative emotions associated with anxious or threatening situations. However, research assessing emotional responding in intoxicated people has found that alcohol lessens overall responding for both positive and negative emotions but does not have a selective effect on negative emotions in response to threatening cues (Curtin et al., 1997; 1998; Stritzke, Patrick, & Lang, 1995). Studies of the tension-reducing properties of nicotine have also yielded mixed findings, with some studies showing that nicotine reduces tension (e.g., Pomerleau & Pomerleau, 1987) and others failing to find tension reduction following nicotine ingestion (e.g., Jarvik et al., 1989).

Subsequent research to examine the reasons for these inconsistent results has focused on the situation in which alcohol or nicotine is consumed—specifically, a situation in which distraction is present. Findings indicate that alcohol may produce its tension-reducing effect by altering cognition and perception (Curtin et al., 1997, 1998; Steele & Josephs, 1988, 1990). Alcohol impairs cognitive processing and narrows attention to the most immediately available cues, resulting in what Steele and Josephs term "alcohol myopia"—the intoxicated person has less cognitive capacity to distribute between ongoing activity and worry. If a distracting activity is available, attention will be diverted to it rather than given to worrisome thoughts, with a resultant decrease in anxiety. The benefits of distraction have also been documented for nicotine. Specifically, smokers who smoked in the presence of a distracting activity realized a reduction in anxiety, whereas smokers who smoked without a distracting activity did not experience a reduction in anxiety (Kassel & Shiffman, 1997; Kassel & Unrod, 2000). However, in some situations alcohol and nicotine may increase tension, for example, when no distractors are present and an intoxicated person therefore focuses all his or her limited processing capacity on unpleasant thoughts as when an unhappy person drinks alone. In this case the discouraged person broods and can become even more depressed while drinking, a situation reflected in the expression "crying in one's beer."

Another situational variable that influences the tension-reducing effects of alcohol and nicotine is the temporal relationship between consumption and stress, that is, whether alcohol or nicotine consumption precedes or follows stress. The notion most people have about alcohol and tension reduction is that an increase in tension (e.g., because of a bad day at the office) leads to increased consumption to reduce the effects of the earlier stressor. Empirical support for this idea comes from studies showing that increases in life stress precede relapses in recovered alcoholics (e.g., Brown et al., 1990). However, experimental research on the tension-reducing properties of alcohol has typically reversed the order of the two variables, having subjects drink and then encounter a stressor. One study compared alcohol's effects in both orders (stress–alcohol versus alcohol–stress) and found tension reduction only in the alcohol–stress sequence (Sayette & Wilson, 1991). Similarly, a recent longitudinal study assessing the temporal relationship between stress and drinking did not find greater alcohol consumption following reports of greater life stress. Rather, greater alcohol consumption predicted later reductions in health and financial stress for women and later reductions in health stress for men (Brennan, Schutte, & Moos, 1999). Based on these results, alcohol may not be a potent tension reducer in many life situations when it is consumed after stress has already occurred.

With respect to smoking, some have argued that smoking causes increases in stress and tension (e.g., Parrott, 1999), whereas others have argued that stress causes increases in smoking (e.g., Gilbert & McClernon, 2000; Kassel, 2000). A recent longitudinal study of adolescent smokers found that increases in negative affect and negative life events were associated with increases in smoking. There was no evidence that increases in smoking caused increases in negative affect (Wills, Sandy, & Yaeger, 2002). These findings suggest that smoking may be used as a way to cope with negative affect and stress, even though smoking is not a healthy or beneficial manner of coping (Wills & Cleary, 1995).

If it is true that alcohol does not reduce stress when consumed after the fact, why do so many people who drink believe that it helps them unwind? Returning to a concept introduced earlier in this chapter (p. 363), it may be that people use alcohol after stress not because it reduces distress directly but because they *expect* it to reduce their tension. In support of this idea, studies have shown that people who expect alcohol to reduce stress and anxiety are those likely to be frequent users (Rather et al., 1992; Sher et al., 1991; Tran, Haaga, & Chambless, 1997). Furthermore, positive expectancies about alcohol and drinking appear to influence each other. The expectation that drinking will reduce anxiety increases drinking, which in turn makes the positive expectancies even stronger (Smith et al., 1995). Other research has shown that positive expectancies about a drug's effects predict increased drug use in general (Stacy, Newcomb, & Bentler, 1991).

Research has also looked for factors within the person that would make the tension-reducing effects of alcohol especially reinforcing. Some research has found that people for whom alcohol produces a very strong reduction in tension score high on the Anxiety Sensitivity Index (see p. 149) (Conrod, Pihl, & Vassileva, 1998; Stewart et al., 1997). This is consistent with the finding that alcohol abuse is comorbid with PTSD and indicates that alcohol may be particularly reinforcing for people who have anxiety problems.

Tension reduction is only one aspect of the possible effects of drugs on mood. Some people may use drugs to reduce negative affect, whereas others use drugs when they are bored or underaroused to increase positive affect (Cooper et al., 1995). In both cases drug use could reflect a failure of other means of coping with emotional states. But in the former case, a high level of negative affect plus expecting drugs to reduce tension lead to increased drug use, whereas in the latter case a high need for stimulation plus expectancies that drugs will promote increased positive affect lead to increased substance use. This line of reasoning has been confirmed among alcohol and cocaine abusers (Ball, Carroll, & Rounsaville, 1994; Cooper et al., 1995; Hussong et al., 2001).

Beliefs About Risks and Prevalence   Two other psychological variables related to drug use are the extent to which a person believes a drug is harmful and the perceived prevalence of use by others. For example, use of marijuana peaked in 1978, when almost 11 percent of high school seniors reported daily use. At that time only 12 percent of seniors believed there was risk associated with occasional use, and 35 percent believed there was risk with regular use. Compare this with 1985, when daily use had plummeted to 5 percent; 25 percent of high school seniors believed marijuana was harmful if used occasionally, and 70 percent believed it was harmful if used on a regular basis (Kozel & Adams, 1986). This twofold increase in perceived risk indicates that as beliefs change, so does behavior. The dramatic increase in marijuana use in the 1990s was mainly among those adolescents who considered marijuana harmless (USDHHS, 1994). Similarly, many smokers do not believe that they are at increased risk for cancer or cardiovascular disease (Ayanian & Cleary, 1999). Furthermore, alcohol and tobacco are used more frequently among people who overestimate the frequency with which these substances are used by others (Jackson, 1997).

There are also ethnic differences in beliefs about the risks associated with substance use. Analyzing data from the 1996 and 1997 National Household Surveys on Drug Abuse (SAMHSA, 1997a, 1997b), Ma and Shive (2000) found that whites reported less perceived risk associated with alcohol, cigarettes, marijuana, and cocaine than did African Americans and Hispanics. Not surprisingly, actual use of these substances was higher among whites than either African Americans or Hispanics in 1996 and 1997, consistent with the notion that the lower the perceived risk, the greater the usage.

Personality and Drug Use   Neither sociocultural factors nor mood-alteration theories can completely account for individual differences in drug use. Not all members of a particular culture or subculture are heavy users, nor do all who experience stress increase drug usage. Personality variables attempt to explain why certain people are drawn to substance abuse.

High levels of negative affect and an enduring desire for arousal and increased positive affect are two personality traits that have been studied in this context. In one study demonstrating these points, kindergarten children were rated by their teachers on several personality traits and were followed up several years later. Anxiety (e.g., worries about things, fear of new situations) and novelty seeking (e.g., being restless, fidgety) predicted the onset of getting drunk, using drugs, and smoking. Depression is related to the initiation of smoking (Killen et al., 1997).

An association has been found between drug use in general and antisocial personality disorder (Ball et al., 1994). Drug abuse may be part of the thrill-seeking behavior of the psychopath, to be discussed in Chapter 13. Furthermore, alcohol use is comorbid with several personality disorders, most notably antisocial personality disorder for men and borderline personality disorder for women (Morgenstern et al., 1997). Rebelliousness and high levels of aggression are also related to substance abuse (Anderrson, Magnusson, & Wennberg, 1997; Masse & Trembley, 1997). In addition, we might expect opiates and tranquilizers to be used by anxious individuals to reduce their distress.

Attention deficit/hyperactivity disorder (ADHD) in childhood, which is highly correlated with antisocial behavior, is also related to drug abuse, probably for reasons similar to those noted for antisocial personalities. For example, in a prospective study spanning more than ten years, ADHD was an important predictor of later alcohol abuse (Hechtman, Weiss, & Perlman, 1984). ADHD has been associated also with tobacco and cannabis use (Wills, et al., 1995) and with cocaine abuse (Ball et al., 1994) as well.

Biological Variables

Most of the research on biological factors in substance abuse has addressed the possibility that there is a genetic predisposition for problem drinking and the abuse of other drugs.

Evidence for a genetic predisposition for alcohol abuse is found in studies in which animals have been bred that greatly prefer alcohol to other beverages (Li et al., 1981). Data also indicate that problem drinking in human beings runs in families, suggesting a genetic component (but consistent also with social influence factors). Several studies have shown that relatives and children of problem drinkers have higher than expected rates of alcohol abuse or dependence (e.g., Chassin et al., 1999). Furthermore, family studies show that the relatives of substance abusers are at increased risk for abusing many substances, not just the one that was the basis for selecting the proband (Bierut et al., 1998; Merilcangas et al., 1998). Further evidence for a genetic diathesis comes from twin studies. Such studies have revealed greater concordance in identical twins than in fraternal twins for alcohol abuse (e.g., McGue, Pickens, & Svikis, 1992), caffeine use (Kendler & Prescott, 1999), smoking (True et al., 1993), heavy use or abuse of cannabis (Kendler & Prescott, 1998), and drug abuse in general (Tsuang et al., 1998).

The ability to tolerate alcohol may be what is inherited as a diathesis for alcohol abuse or dependence (Goodwin, 1979). To become a problem drinker, a person first has to be able to drink a lot; in other words, the person must be able to tolerate large quantities of alcohol. Some ethnic groups, such as Asians, may have a low rate of alcohol abuse because of physiological intolerance, which is caused by an inherited deficiency in an enzyme that metabolizes alcohol. About three-quarters of Asians experience unpleasant effects from small quantities of alcohol. Noxious effects of the drug may thus protect a person from alcohol abuse.

This hypothesis focuses on short-term effects, possibly on how alcohol is metabolized or on how the central nervous system responds to alcohol. Animal research indicates that genetic components are at work in both these processes (Schuckit, 1983). Corroborating this notion are findings from research using the high-risk method. These studies have compared young, nonalcoholic adults with a first-degree alcohol-abusing relative to similar individuals without a positive family history for the disorder. Two variables were able to predict the development of alcohol abuse in men in a ten-year follow-up (Schuckit, 1994; Schuckit & Smith, 1996): (1) self-report of a low level of intoxication after a dose of alcohol and (2) less body sway (a measure of steadiness while standing) after drinking. Both findings indicate that alcohol abuse is more likely to occur in those in whom alcohol has little effect. Notably, these variables predict alcohol abuse among men with and without an alcohol-abusing father.[4]

The smaller response to alcohol in men who later became alcohol abusers may at first seem puzzling, but it fits with the notion that you have to drink a lot to become a problem drinker. A small response to alcohol may set the stage for heavier than normal drinking. The size of the response to alcohol is also related to our earlier discussion of alcohol's biphasic effects (p. 363). In Shuckitt and colleagues' follow-up studies, the largest differences between sons of problem drinkers and controls occurred when their blood levels of alcohol were declining. Therefore, sons of alcohol abusers may experience fewer of the negative, depressing effects of alcohol. Other research indicates that sons of alcohol abusers experience greater effects of alcohol, for example, more tension reduction, as their blood-alcohol levels are on the rise. Thus, these genetically predisposed individuals receive more reinforcement and less punishment from the drug (Newlin & Thomson, 1990).

What about women? Studies examining genetic factors for women who abuse alcohol are fewer and more equivocal, with some studies finding evidence for a genetic component and others failing to find evidence in favor of a strong genetic component (e.g., Kendler et al., 1994; McGue, Pickens, & Svikis, 1992). However, recent though preliminary data from the Collaborative Study on the Genetics of Alcoholism suggest that a low level of intoxication after alcohol and body sway may also distinguish women with a positive family history of alcohol dependence from women with a negative family history (Schuckit et al., 2000).

Exciting research has recently emerged on the mechanism through which genetics plays a role in smoking. Like most drugs, nicotine appears to derive its reinforcing properties by stimulating dopamine release and inhibiting its reuptake. Furthermore, individuals who are more sensitive to the effects of nicotine are likely to become regular smokers (Pomerleau et al. 1993). Research has examined a link between a gene that regulates the reuptake of dopamine and smoking. One form of this gene has been related to being less likely to begin smoking (Lerman et al., 1999) and to being more likely to have quit (Sabo et al., 1999). One explanation for these results may be that people who have this particular form of this gene experience less reinforcement from nicotine, making it less likely that they will start smoking and enabling them to quit more easily if they do.

Having reviewed the nature and possible causes of the several kinds of substance-related disorders, we turn now to their treatment and prevention.

Therapy for Alcohol Abuse and Dependence

The havoc created by problem drinking, both for the drinker and for his or her family, friends, employer, and community, makes this problem a serious public health issue in the United States and many other countries. Consequently, a great deal of research and clinical effort has gone into the design and evaluation of various treatments.

The treatment of alcohol abuse is difficult not only because of the addictive nature of the drug but also because many other psychological problems are likely to be present. Alcohol abusers often experience depression, anxiety, and severe disruptions in their social and occupational functioning. As indicated elsewhere, the risk of suicide is also very high. Although some of these problems may have preceded and even contributed to the abuse of alcohol, by the time an abuser is treated it is seldom possible to know what is cause and

---

[4] Interestingly, like the children of alcoholics, Native Americans do not report intense effects from a dose of alcohol. These data, therefore, contradict the idea that the problems Native Americans have with alcohol result from some kind of heightened sensitivity to the drug (Garcia-Andrade, Wall, & Ehlers, 1997).

what is effect. What is certain is that the person's life is usually a shambles, and any treatment that has any hope of success has to address more than merely the excessive drinking.

Interventions for problem drinking are both biological and psychological. Whatever the kind of intervention, the first step is for the person to admit the problem and decide to do something about it.

Admitting the Problem

To admit that one has a serious drinking problem may sound straightforward to someone who has never drunk too much or has never known someone who did. However, substance abusers of all kinds are adept at denying that they have a problem and may react angrily to any suggestion that they do. Moreover, because patterns of problem drinking are highly variable—someone physically dependent on alcohol, for example, does not always drink uncontrollably—the need for intervention is not always recognized by friends or even by health professionals.

Enabling the drinker to take the first step to betterment—what has been called the contemplation stage (Prochaska, DiClimente, & Norcross, 1992)—can be achieved through questions that get at the issue somewhat indirectly.

> *Do you sometimes feel uncomfortable when alcohol is not available?*
> *Do you drink more heavily than usual when you are under pressure?*
> *Are you in more of a hurry to get to the first drink than you used to be?*
> *Do you sometimes feel guilty about your drinking?*
> *Are you annoyed when people talk about your drinking?*
> *When drinking socially, do you try to sneak in some extra drinks?*
> *Are you constantly making rules for yourself about what and when to drink?* (Harvard Mental Health Letter, 1996c, pp. 1–2)

Once the alcohol abuser recognizes that he or she has a problem, many approaches to treatment are available.

Traditional Hospital Treatment

Public and private hospitals worldwide have for many years provided retreats for alcohol abusers, sanctums where individuals can dry out and avail themselves of a variety of individual and group therapies. Withdrawal from alcohol, **detoxification**, can be difficult, both physically and psychologically, and usually takes about one month. Tranquilizers are sometimes given to ease the anxiety and general discomfort of withdrawal. Because many alcohol abusers misuse tranquilizers, some clinics try a gradual tapering off without tranquilizers rather than a sudden cutoff of alcohol. This non-drug-assisted withdrawal works for most problem drinkers (Wartenburg et al., 1990). To help get through withdrawal, dependent drinkers also need carbohydrate solutions, B vitamins, and, sometimes, anticonvulsants. Many addicts have to go through the detoxification process multiple times. Unfortunately, multiple previous detoxifications are associated with less responsive treatment (Malcolm et al., 2000), reflecting perhaps a particularly serious addiction problem. In recent years, the population served in detoxification centers has changed demographically: There have been large increases in admissions of women, African Americans, and Hispanics, as well as a decline in the mean age at admission and an increase in unemployed patients (McCarty et al., 2000).

The number of for-profit hospitals treating alcohol abuse has increased dramatically over the past thirty years, in part because such treatment is covered in large measure by both private insurance companies and the federal government (Holder et al., 1991). Annual costs run in the billions. Because inpatient treatment is much more expensive than outpatient treatment, its cost-effectiveness has been questioned. Is it worth the expense? Apparently not, at least in many cases. The therapeutic results of hospital treatment are not superior to those of outpatient treatment (Mundle et al., 2001; Soyka et al., 2001). In addition, short stays (less than eight days) in detoxification hospitalizations may be as effective as longer stays (Foster et al., 2000). Some data even suggest that home detoxification may be a viable alternative to day hospital or inpatient treatment for selected groups of patients (Allan et al., 2000). However, an analysis of treatment for alcohol dependence concludes that an inpatient approach is probably necessary for people with few sources of social support who are living in environments that encourage the abuse of alcohol, especially individuals with serious psychological problems in addition to their substance abuse (Finney & Moos, 1998).

Biological Treatments

Biological treatments are best viewed as adjunctive, that is, they may offer some benefit when combined with a psychological intervention. However, there are currently few data on therapy involving both the combination of medication with psychotherapy or the combinations of different medications (Myrick et al., 2001). Moreover, such basic issues as the optimal dosing strategy and duration of treatment are unknown for the most common medication treatments for alcohol dependence (Kranzler, 2000).

Some problem drinkers who are in treatment, inpatient or outpatient, take disulfiram, or **Antabuse**, a drug that discourages drinking by causing violent vomiting if alcohol is ingested. It blocks the metabolism of alcohol so that noxious by-products are created. As one can imagine, adherence to an Antabuse regimen can be a problem. The drinker must already be strongly committed to change. If an alcohol abuser is able or willing to take the drug every morning as prescribed, one would assume that the chances are good that drinking will lessen because of the negative consequences of imbibing (Sisson & Azrin, 1989). However, in a large, multicenter study with placebo controls, Antabuse was not shown to have any specific benefit, and drop-out rates were as high as 80 percent (Fuller, 1988; Fuller et al., 1986). Antabuse can also cause serious side effects, such as inflammation of nerve tissue (Moss, 1990).

The Food and Drug Administration has approved the opiate antagonists naltrexone and naloxone (discussed below in the section on treatment for illicit drug use), which block the activity of endorphins that are stimulated by alcohol, thus reducing the craving for it. Evidence is mixed regarding whether these drugs are more effective than a placebo in reducing drinking when they are the only treatment (Krystal et al., 2001). But they do appear to add to overall treatment effectiveness when combined with cognitive-behavioral therapy (Streeton & Whelan, 2001; Volpicelli et al., 1995, 1997; Ward et al., 1998). As with most other drug treatments we have discussed, the benefits of naltrexone and naloxone continue only for as long as the person continues to take them, and long-lasting compliance with the treatment is difficult to achieve (Johnson & Ait-Daoud, 2000; O'Malley et al., 1996).

The serotonin agonist buspirone is of some therapeutic value in the treatment of alcohol dependence (Kranzler et al., 1994). Clonidine, which reduces noradrenergic activity in the brain, also has some value in reducing withdrawal effects from several drugs, including alcohol, opiates, and nicotine (Baumgartner & Rowen, 1987).

Acamprosate, which has been in regular use in Europe for fourteen years under the brand name Campral, is currently under review by the FDA. Although its action is not completely understood, researchers believe that it impacts the glutamate and GABA neurotransmitter systems and thereby reduces the cravings associated with withdrawal. A recent review of data from all published double-blind, placebo-controlled clinical trials of acamprosate among alcohol dependent outpatients suggests that it is highly effective (Mason, 2001). A meta-analysis comparing the effectiveness of acamprosate and naltrexone found them equally effective (Kranzler & Van Kirk, 2001).

Though not specifically targeted to excessive drinking, certain psychoactive drugs are used to treat problems associated with drinking. Thus, antidepressants may be used for depression and antianxiety medications for anxiety. By bringing about improvement in emotional problems which are often associated with problem drinking, these drugs can have a beneficial impact on alcohol dependence and abuse. For example, fluoxetine (Prozac) has produced improvement in depression and reduced drinking among alcohol abusers who are also depressed (Cornelius et al., 1997). Indeed, some researchers suggest that the superior safety and tolerability of selective serotonin reuptake inhibitors (SSRIs) should make them a first-line alternative to traditional pharmacotherapy for alcoholism (Thas et al., 2001).

It should be noted that the use of drugs to treat alcohol-abusing patients carries some risk. Liver function is often impaired in the patient, and therefore the metabolism of the prescribed drug in the liver can be adversely affected, leading to undesirable side effects (Klerman et al., 1994). There is also the more general question of whether treating a substance-abuse problem by giving another drug is necessarily a prudent strategy if one believes that some people come to rely on drugs in part because they are looking for a chemical solution to problems in their lives.

Alcoholics Anonymous

The largest and most widely known self-help group in the world is Alcoholics Anonymous (AA), founded in 1935 by two recovering alcoholics. It currently has about 70,000 chapters and membership numbering more than two million people in the United States and more than a hundred other countries throughout the world. Each AA chapter runs regular and frequent meetings at which newcomers rise to announce that they are alcoholics, and older, sober members give testimonials relating the stories of their problem drinking and indicating how their lives are better now. The group provides emotional support, understanding, and close counseling for the problem drinker as well as a social life to relieve isolation. Members are urged to call on one another around-the-clock when they need companionship and encouragement not to relapse into drink. About 70 percent of Americans who have ever been treated for alcohol abuse have attended at least one AA meeting. Programs modeled after AA are available for other substance abusers, for example, Cocaine Anonymous and Marijuana Anonymous. There are even similar twelve-step programs called Overeaters Anonymous and Gamblers Anonymous.

The belief is instilled in each AA member that alcohol abuse is a disease that can never be cured, and that continuing vigilance is necessary to resist taking even a single drink lest uncontrollable drinking begin all over again. The basic tenet of AA was vividly articulated in the classic film *Lost Weekend*, for which Ray Milland won an Oscar for best actor. In a scene in which he is confronted with his denial of the seriousness of his drinking problem, his brother remonstrates, "Don't you ever learn that with you it's like stepping off a roof and expecting to fall just one floor?" And later in the film, the comment is made that "One's too many. A hundred's not enough."

The spiritual aspect of AA is apparent in the twelve steps of AA shown in Table 12.2, and there is evidence that belief in this philosophy is linked with achieving abstinence (Fiorentine & Hillhouse, 2000; Tonigan et al., 2000).

Two related self-help groups have developed from AA. The relatives of problem drinkers meet in Alanon Family Groups for mutual support in dealing with their family members and in realizing that it is exceedingly difficult to make them change their ways. Similarly, Alateen is for the children of alcohol abusers, who require support and understanding to help them overcome the sense that they are in some way responsible for their parents' problems and responsible also for changing them.

Other self-help groups do not have the religious overtones of AA, relying instead on social support, reassurance, encouragement, and suggestions for leading a life without alcohol. One such approach, termed *Rational Recovery*, focuses on the individual regaining self-reliance rather than reliance on a higher

Table 12.2   Twelve Suggested Steps of Alcoholics Anonymous
1. We admitted we were powerless over alcohol—that our lives had become unmanageable.
2. Came to believe that a power greater than ourselves could restore us to sanity.
3. Made a decision to turn our will and our lives over to the care of God as we understood Him.
4. Made a searching and fearless moral inventory of ourselves.
5. Admitted to God, to ourselves, and to another human being the exact nature of our wrongs.
6. Were entirely ready to have God remove all these defects of character.
7. Humbly asked Him to remove our shortcomings.
8. Made a list of all persons we had harmed, and became willing to make amends to them all.
9. Made direct amends to such people wherever possible, except when to do so would injure them or others.
10. Continued to take personal inventory and, when we were wrong, promptly admitted it.
11. Sought through prayer and meditation to improve our conscious contact with God as we understood Him, praying only for knowledge of His will for us and the power to carry that out.
12. Having had a spiritual awakening as the result of these steps, we tried to carry this message to alcoholics and to practice these principles in all our affairs.

Source: The Twelve Steps and Twelve Traditions. Copyright © 1952 by Alcoholics Anonymous World Services, Inc. Reprinted with permission of Alcoholics Anonymous World Services, Inc.

Alcoholics Anonymous is the largest self-help group in the world. At their regular meetings, newcomers rise to announce their addiction and receive advice and support from others.

power (Trimpey, Velton, & Dain, 1993). This treatment approach also contains many tenets found in Ellis's rational-emotive behavior therapy (discussed in Chapter 17).

Claims made by AA about the effectiveness of its treatment have begun to be subjected to scientific scrutiny. Significant benefit from AA has been demonstrated (Ouimette, Finney, & Moos, 1997). However, AA has high drop-out rates, and the dropouts are not always factored into the results. In addition, there is only limited long-term follow-up of AA clients. Results from the best controlled study to date are mixed (Walsh & Hingson, 1991). However, a recent long-term follow-up study indicated that participation in AA was very effective (Timko et al., 2001). There have been no controlled studies testing the efficacy of Rational Recovery, though two findings from preliminary studies suggest that it may be effective (Schmidt, Carns, & Chandler, 2001).

It does appear that many people who choose AA and stay with it for more than three months—a select group, to be sure—remain abstinent for at least a few years (Emrick et al., 1993). The needs of people who are helped by AA seem to be met by the fellowship, support, and religious overtones of AA. For them it becomes a way of life; members often attend meetings regularly for many years, as often as four times a week, even when they are out of town. Such frequent attendance is associated with significant psychosocial improvement (Tonigan, 2001).

Preliminary evidence shows that frequent AA attenders differ from nonfrequent attenders in having histories of greater lifetime drug use, more arrests and treatment experiences, earlier age of initial alcohol use, and perceived helpfulness of twelve-step programs (Brown et al., 2001). Among low-income alcoholics, it was found that African-Americans and people with concurrent illicit drug problems do not prefer AA-type programs (Kingree, 2001). These findings can guide clinicians in making referrals to twelve-step groups or alternative treatment programs.

Couples and Family Therapy

Alcohol severely disrupts the lives of problem drinkers. For this reason, many have fairly solitary existences, and this lack of social support no doubt exacerbates their drinking problem. An additional problem for those who do remain married or in other close relationships is that problem drinkers often physically or sexually abuse members of their families (O'Farrell & Murphy, 1995)

This intertwining of alcohol abuse and family conflict—the cause–effect relationship goes both ways (O'Farrell, 1993)—has led to the use of various kinds of couples and family therapy to help the drinker abstain or control his or her excessive drinking. Behaviorally oriented marital or couples therapy (O'Farrell & Fals-Stewart, 2000) has been found to achieve some reductions in problem drinking as well as some improvement in couples' distress generally (e.g., McCrady & Epstein, 1995). In addition, couples therapy is associated with reduced domestic violence (O'Farrell & Fals-Stewart, 2000; O'Farrell et al., 2000). One focus of this therapy is involving the spouse in helping the drinker take his or her Antabuse on a regular basis. Couples therapy is also a part of Nathan Azrin's community-reinforcement approach, discussed later.

The importance of a partner's support in the problem drinker's effort to deal with life's inevitable stresses is not to be underestimated. But also not to be underestimated is the difficulty of maintaining moderate drinking or abstinence at one- and two-year follow-ups regardless of the mode of marital intervention and its short-term positive effects (Alexander et al., 1994; Baucom et al., 1998). It is thus interesting to note that one-year follow-up data show that the gains associated with the behaviorally oriented therapy discussed above are maintained (FalsStewart et al., 2000).

Cognitive and Behavioral Treatments

Behavioral and cognitive-behavioral researchers have been studying the treatment of alcohol abuse for many years—indeed, one of the earliest articles on behavior therapy concerned aversion therapy as a treatment for alcoholism (Kantorovich, 1930). In general, cognitive and behavioral therapies represent the most effective psychological treatments for alcohol abuse (Finney & Moos, 1998).

Aversion Therapy   In aversion therapy a problem drinker is shocked or made nauseous while looking at, reaching for, or beginning to drink alcohol. In one procedure, called **covert sensitization** (Cautela, 1966), the problem drinker is instructed to imagine being made violently and disgustingly sick by his or her drinking.

Despite some evidence that aversion therapy may slightly enhance the effectiveness of inpatient treatment (Smith, Frawley, & Polissar, 1991), some well-known behavior therapists discourage its use because it lacks empirical support and causes great discomfort (e.g., Wilson, 1991). Aversion therapy, if used at all, seems best implemented in the context of broadly based programs that attend to the patient's particular life circumstances, for example, marital conflict, social fears, and other factors often associated with problem drinking (Tucker, Vuchinich, & Downey, 1992).

Contingency Management and the Community-Reinforcement Approach
Contingency-management therapy (a term often used interchangeably with operant conditioning) for alcohol abuse involves teaching patients and those close to them to reinforce behaviors inconsistent with drinking—for example, taking Antabuse and avoiding situations that were associated with drinking in the past. It is based on the belief that environmental contingencies can play an important role in encouraging or discouraging drinking. This therapy also includes teaching job-hunting and social skills, as well as assertiveness training for refusing drinks. For socially isolated individuals, assistance and encouragement are provided to establish contacts with other people who are not associated with drinking. As noted earlier, this approach also includes couples therapy. Other effective contingency based treatments include providing reinforcers for sobriety, such as opportunities to win prizes (Petry et al., 2000) and abstinence-contingent partial support for housing, food, recreational activities, and access to supportive therapy (Gruber et al., 2000). Often referred to as the community-reinforcement approach, contingency-management therapy has generated very promising results (Azrin et al., 1982; Baucom et al., 1998; Sisson & Azrin, 1989; Smith & Meyers, 2000). A review of the literature shows that it is consistently found to be one of the most efficacious and cost-effective intervention treatments available (Smith et al., 2001).

A strategy sometimes termed *behavioral self-control training* (Tucker et al., 1992) builds on the work just described. This approach emphasizes patient control and includes one or more of the following:

Nathan Azrin, one of the first behavior therapists to apply operant conditioning principles to problem behaviors.

- Stimulus control, whereby patients narrow the situations in which they allow themselves to drink; for example, with others on a special occasion.
- Modification of the topography of drinking; for example, having only mixed drinks and taking small sips rather than gulps.
- Reinforcing abstinence; for example, allowing oneself a nonalcoholic treat if one resists the urge to drink.

A central issue not formally addressed by advocates of behavioral self-control training is getting the person to abide by restrictions and conditions that, if implemented, will reduce or eliminate drinking (see p. 588 on the limits of self-control in a behavioral paradigm). In other words, the challenge with such therapies seems not so much to discover the means necessary to control drinking as to get the alcohol abuser to employ these tools without constant external supervision and control. In any event, there is evidence for the general effectiveness of this approach (Hester & Miller, 1989).

Moderation in Drinking   Until recently it was generally believed that alcohol abusers had to abstain completely if they were to be cured, for they were assumed to have no control over imbibing once they had taken that first drink. Although this continues to be the belief of Alcoholics Anonymous, research mentioned earlier, indicating that drinkers' beliefs about themselves and alcohol may be as important as the physiological addiction

Mark and Linda Sobell introduced controlled drinking approaches to treatment of alcohol abuse.

to the drug itself (p. 363), has called this assumption into question. Considering the difficulty in society of avoiding alcohol altogether, it may even be preferable to teach the problem drinker, at least the person who does not abuse alcohol in an extreme fashion, to imbibe with moderation. A drinker's self-esteem will certainly benefit from being able to control a problem and from feeling in charge of his or her life.

The term **controlled drinking** was introduced into the domain of alcohol treatment by the Sobells (Sobell & Sobell, 1993). It refers to a pattern of alcohol consumption that is moderate, avoiding the extremes of total abstinence and inebriation. Findings of one well-known treatment program suggested that at least some alcohol abusers can learn to control their drinking and improve other aspects of their lives as well (Sobell & Sobell, 1976). Problem drinkers attempting to control their drinking were given shocks when they chose straight liquor rather than mixed drinks, gulped their drinks down too fast, or took large swallows rather than sips. They also received problem-solving and assertiveness training, watched videotapes of themselves inebriated, and identified the situations that precipitated their drinking so that they could settle on a less self-destructive course of action. Their improvement was greater than that of alcohol abusers who tried for total abstinence and were given shocks for any drinking at all.

Controlled-drinking treatment programs were further developed to teach patients to respond adaptively to situations in which they might otherwise drink excessively. They learn various social skills to help them resist pressures to drink; they receive assertiveness, relaxation, and stress-management training, sometimes including biofeedback and meditation; and they are encouraged to exercise and maintain a healthy diet.

Patients are also taught—or more precisely, are encouraged to believe—that a lapse will not inevitably precipitate a total relapse and should be regarded as a learning experience rather than as a sign that the battle is lost, a marked contrast from the AA perspective (Marlatt & Gordon, 1985). This noncatastrophizing approach to relapse after therapy—falling off the wagon—is important because the overwhelming majority of problem drinkers who become abstinent do experience a relapse over a four-year period (Polich, Armor, & Braiker, 1980). In this therapy, alcohol abusers examine sources of stress in their work, family, and relationships so that they can become active and responsible in anticipating and resisting situations that might tempt excessive drinking (Marlatt, 1983; Sobell, Toneatto, & Sobell, 1990). And when they do lapse, as mentioned, they are encouraged not to see it as a sign that they are going to return to their earlier alcoholic state.

The Sobells' current approach to teaching moderation to problem drinkers has evolved even further. Termed *guided self-change*, this outpatient approach emphasizes personal responsibility and control. The basic assumption is that people have more potential control over their immoderate drinking than they typically believe and that heightened awareness of the costs of drinking to excess as well as of the benefits of abstaining or cutting down can be of material help. Problem drinkers also typically overestimate how heavily other people drink. Providing accurate information on the drinking patterns of others—social comparison—is part of this treatment approach. Patients are encouraged to view themselves as basically healthy people who have been making unwise, often self-destructive choices about how to deal with life's inevitable stresses, rather than as victims of an addictive disease.

In guided self-change, the therapist is empathic and supportive while he or she makes salient to the problem drinker the negative aspects of excessive drinking that the person may have been overlooking. For example, most problem drinkers don't calculate the expense of drinking to excess (the cost of drinking at home can easily run to more than $2,000 a year, and the cost of drinking in a bar or restaurant is double or triple that amount) or the amount of weight gain attributable to alcohol. They also seldom try to identify seemingly minor behavioral changes that can help them drink less, such as finding a new route home that does not take them by a bar they have been frequenting. Sometimes getting the person to delay twenty minutes before taking a second or third drink can help him or her reflect on the costs versus the benefits of drinking to excess. Evidence supports the effectiveness of this approach in helping problem drinkers moderate their intake and otherwise improve their lives (Sobell & Sobell, 1993).

The principles of controlled drinking have also been adopted by self-help groups such as Moderation Management (MM) (Nowinski, 1999). However, MM's approach to moderation states clearly that it is not intended for persons who are alcohol dependent (physically addicted). In addition, it recommends a period of abstinence prior to any attempts at moderation. Qualitative data indicate that MM involvement is often precipitated by a conscious rejection of the twelve-step philosophy of AA and many other professional treatment programs (Klaw & Humphreys, 2000).

Whether abstinence or controlled drinking should be the goal of treatment is controversial. This issue pits influential forces, such as AA, that uphold abstinence as the only proper goal for problem drinkers, against more recent researchers, such as the Sobells and those adopting their general approach, who have shown that moderation can work for many patients, including those with severe drinking problems. If the therapeutic means of achieving the goal of moderate drinking are available—and research strongly suggests that they are—then controlled drinking may be a more realistic goal even for an addicted person. Controlled drinking is currently much more widely accepted in Canada and Europe than it is in the United States.

Clinical Considerations in Treating Alcohol Abuse

Many attempts to treat problem drinking are impeded by the therapist's often unstated assumption that all people who drink to excess do so for the same reasons. From what we have examined thus far in this chapter, we know that this assumption is incorrect.

A comprehensive clinical assessment considers what place drinking occupies in the person's life (Tucker et al., 1992). A woman in a desperately unhappy marriage, with time on her hands now that her children are in school, may seek the numbing effects of alcohol to help pass the time and avoid facing life's dilemmas. Making the taste of alcohol unpleasant for this patient by pairing it with shock or an emetic seems neither sensible nor adequate. The therapist should concentrate on the marital and family problems and try to reduce the psychological pain that permeates the patient's existence. She will also need help in tolerating the withdrawal symptoms that come with reduced consumption. Without alcohol as a reliable anesthetic, she will need to mobilize other resources to confront her hitherto-avoided problems. Social-skills training and finding rewarding activities outside the home may help her do so.

We have seen that problem drinking is sometimes associated with other mental disorders, in particular with anxiety disorders, mood disorders, and psychopathy. Therapists of all orientations have to recognize that depression is often comorbid with alcohol abuse and that suicide is also a risk. The clinician must therefore conduct a broad-spectrum assessment of the patient's problem, for if heavy drinking stems from the desperation of deep depression, a regimen of Antabuse or any other treatment focused on alcohol alone is unlikely to be of lasting value.

Alcohol researchers have been aware for some time that different treatment approaches are most likely appropriate for different kinds of drinkers (Mattson et al., 1994). The issue is which factors in the drinkers are important to align with which factors in treatment. Client–treatment matching, or what in the psychotherapy literature is coming to be known as *aptitude-treatment interaction* (ATI), has been cited by the Institute of Medicine (1990a) as a critical issue in the development of better interventions for problem drinking. A large-scale effort to address the question was Project MATCH, a multisite clinical trial designed to test the hypothesis that certain kinds of treatments are good matches for certain kinds of problem drinkers. This widely cited study is described in Focus on Discovery 12.4.

Researchers have so far directed little attention to treating polydrug abuse. It is known, for example, that up to 90 percent of problem drinkers also smoke cigarettes regularly and thus are probably addicted to both alcohol and nicotine. But few attempts have been made to treat the nicotine dependence along with the alcohol problem, probably because it is regarded as too stressful to try to give up two addictions at the same time. However, research shows that this assumption is incorrect (Hunt et al., 1994). Adding a

Focus on Discovery 12.4

Matching Patient to Treatment—Project MATCH

For many years both practitioners and researchers have understood the importance of employing treatments that are suitable for particular patients. This notion goes beyond the question of the kind of therapy best suited for a particular kind of problem (which we address in the therapy sections of Chapters 6 through 16). Rather, what is called aptitude-treatment interaction (ATI) focuses on characteristics of patients with a particular disorder that might make them more suitable for one generally effective treatment than for another.

To see how ATI comes into play, consider the technique of systematic desensitization, which relies on the ability to imagine oneself in a fearsome situation and to become anxious from this image. The procedure requires that an image stand in the place of the actual event. If patients cannot conjure up an image that makes them anxious, then there is no point in going through a time-consuming procedure that has as its aim imagining a frightening situation without becoming anxious!

The question of matching patient to treatment was tested in Project MATCH, a large, eight-year, multisite study on alcohol abuse (Project MATCH Research Group, 1997). This study has become controversial in professional circles because of its failure to find what it was looking for, namely, a way to match particular kinds of alcoholic patients with specific interventions.

Ten matching variables, among them severity of alcohol dependency, severity of cognitive impairment, motivation to change, severity of psychological disturbance (referred to as "psychiatric severity"), support from one's social milieu for drinking, and sociopathic tendencies, were chosen because they had been found in previous research to be associated with outcome of intervention. There were three treatments.

- The twelve-step facilitation treatment (TSF) was designed to convert patients to the AA view of alcoholism as an incurable but manageable disease and to encourage their involvement in AA.
- The motivational-enhancement therapy (MET), based on William Miller's approach (Miller et al., 1992), attempted to mobilize the person's own resources to reduce drinking. Part of this intervention involved highlighting for the person the ways in which current maladaptive behavior was interfering with his or her valued goals.
- A cognitive-behavioral coping-skills therapy (CBT) presented to patients the idea that drinking is functionally related to problems in a person's life; this treatment taught patients skills for coping with situations that trigger drinking or for preventing relapse.

Some of the predicted interactions were that drinkers under heavy pressure to stop would do best with the twelve-step facilitation therapy; those with psychological problems would do best with the cognitive therapy; and those with low motivation to change would do best with the motivational-enhancement therapy.

All treatments were carefully administered in individual sessions by trained therapists over a twelve-week period, following treatment manuals prepared for this study. Exclusionary criteria were used in selecting patients; they could not be dependent on other drugs and otherwise had to have pretty stable lives. As in other efficacy studies (cf. p. 123), internal validity was quite good, but external validity—the generalizability of the findings to therapy as actually practiced—was apparently low.

The principal dependent (outcome) measures were percentage of days abstinent and drinks per drinking day during a one-year post-treatment assessment period. Figure 12.a portrays the main results of this study. Significant within-group improvement was observed—all treatments were very helpful on average, consistent with a subsequent study by Ouimette et al. (1997). But, as noted at the outset of this discussion, interactions between treatments and matching variables—the main purpose of the study—were not found except for psychiatric severity: Patients in better psychological shape had more abstinent days after the twelve-step facilitation program than did patients in the cognitive-behavioral condition, although patients in worse psychological

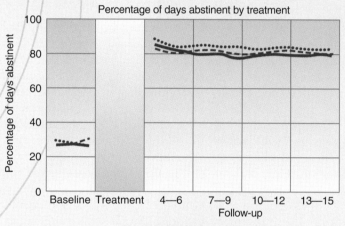

Percentage of days abstinent by treatment

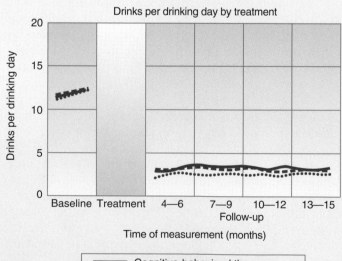

Drinks per drinking day by treatment

— Cognitive-behavioral therapy
---- Motivational-enhancement therapy
······· Twelve-step facilitation

Figure 12.a Monthly percentage of days abstinent and drinks per drinking day (DDD) for baseline (averaged over 3 months prior to treatment) and for each month of the posttreatment period (months 1–15).

condition did not fare differently across the three treatments. However, this one significant finding did not hold up at the one-year follow-up (Fuller & Allen, 2000). The researchers concluded that:

> The lack of other robust matching effects suggests that, aside from psychiatric severity, providers need not take [the] client characteristics [that were studied] into account when triaging clients to one or the other of these three individually administered treatment approaches, despite their different treatment philosophies. (Project MATCH Research Group, 1997, p. 7)

There is a long way to go before statements can be made with confidence about the kinds of patients who will benefit from particular generally effective treatments.

smoking-cessation program to an alcohol-treatment program did not affect the success of the alcohol treatment and did lead some participants to quit smoking.

Even with the many treatment programs available, it has been estimated that no more than 10 percent of people with drinking problems are ever in professional treatment and that upwards of 40 percent cure themselves. How does such recovery take place? Among the apparent factors are a new marriage, new job, religious or spiritual experience or conversion, a near-fatal auto accident while driving drunk, and being shaken by a serious illness. It is not known, however, why some people can stop drinking after a serious crisis while others react by seeking the solace of the bottle or other chemical substance.

It is doubtful that a single event, even a dramatic one, can bring about the kind of profound changes necessary to wean a person from an addiction. It is more probable that successful abstinence or controlled drinking, whether resulting from treatment or not, relies on a confluence of many life events and forces that can support the recovering alcoholic's efforts to lead a life without substance abuse. Whatever combination of factors helps problem drinkers become abstinent or controlled drinkers, a key element is social support for their efforts from family, friends, work, or self-help groups such as AA (McCrady, 1985).

Therapy for the Use of Illicit Drugs

Some factors involved in treatment for alcohol abuse are relevant also to treatment for addiction to illegal drugs. We focus here on issues and data that have special relevance for those who abuse illicit drugs.

People turn to drugs for many reasons, and even though in most instances drug use becomes controlled primarily by a physical addiction, the entire pattern of an addict's existence is bound to be affected by the drug and must therefore be addressed in any treatment. One of the chief difficulties of maintaining abstinence is the negative influence of many stimuli on the recovering addict.

Central to the treatment of people who use addicting drugs, such as heroin and cocaine, is detoxification—withdrawal from the drug itself. Heroin-withdrawal reactions range from relatively mild bouts of anxiety, nausea, and restlessness for several days to more severe and frightening bouts of delirium and panic anxiety, depending primarily on the purity of the heroin that the individual has been using. Someone high on amphetamines can be brought down by appropriate dosages of one of the phenothiazines, a class of drugs used to treat schizophrenia (see p. 344), although it is important to remember that the person may also have been using other drugs in conjunction with amphetamines. Withdrawal reactions from barbiturates are especially severe, even life threatening; they begin about twenty-four hours after the last dose and peak two or three days later. They usually abate by the end of the first week but may last for a month if large doses were taken. Withdrawal from barbiturates is best undertaken gradually, not cold turkey (a term that derives from the goosebumps that occur during withdrawal, making the person's skin resemble that of a plucked turkey), and should take place under close medical supervision.

Detoxification is the first way in which therapists try to help an addict or drug abuser, and it may be the easiest part of the rehabilitation process. Enabling the drug user to function without drugs after detoxification has been achieved is an arduous task that promises more disappointment and sadness than success for both helper and client. A variety of approaches to this task are available, including both biological and psychological treatments.

Biological Treatments

Two widely used drug-therapy programs for heroin addiction involve the administration of **heroin substitutes**, drugs chemically similar to heroin that can replace the body's craving for it, or **heroin antagonists**, drugs that prevent the user from experiencing the heroin high. The first category includes **methadone**, levomethadyl acetate, and bupreophine, synthetic narcotics designed to take the place of heroin. Since these drugs are themselves addicting, successful treatment essentially converts the heroin addict into someone who is addicted to a different substance. This conversion occurs because these synthetic narcotics are **cross-dependent** with heroin; that is, by acting on the same central nervous system receptors, they become a substitute for the original dependency. Of course, methadone used as described here is legal, whereas heroin is not! Abrupt discontinuation of methadone results in its own pattern of withdrawal reactions. Because these reactions are less severe than those of heroin, methadone has potential therapeutic properties for weaning the addict altogether from drug dependence (Strain et al., 1999).

For treatment with heroin substitutes, the addict usually goes to a drug treatment clinic and swallows the drug in the presence of a staff member, once a day for methadone and three times a week for levomethadyl acetate and bupreophine. In some cases, the addict receives treatment instead through weekly visits to a primary care physician; there is some evidence that methadone maintenance carried out in this way is as effective as treatment in narcotic treatment programs (Fiellin et al., 2001). Some users in treatment regimens are able to hold jobs, commit no crimes, and refrain from using other illicit drugs (Eissenberg et al., 1997; Sees et al., 2000; Schottenfeld et al., 2000), but many users are unable to do so (Condelli et al., 1991). The effectiveness of methadone treatment is improved if a high (80–100 milligram) dose is used as opposed to the more typical 40–50 milligram dose (Strain et al., 1999) and if it is combined with regular psychological counseling (Ball & Ross, 1991). Drug treatment experts generally believe that such biological intervention is best conducted in the context of a supportive social interaction and not merely as a medical encounter (Lilly et al., 2000).

Preexisting behavioral patterns and life circumstances play a role in how the individual will react to methadone treatment. Since methadone does not provide a euphoric high, many addicts will return to heroin if it becomes available to them. In addition, many people drop out of methadone programs in part because of side effects, such as insomnia, constipation, excessive sweating, and diminished sexual functioning. It has recently been found that the older the addict, the better the likelihood that he or she will remain with the treatment regimen (Friedmann et al., 2001).

Especially in this era of AIDS and the transmission of the human immunodeficiency virus through shared needles (p. 224), treatment with methadone has a big advantage because methadone can be swallowed. Moreover, methadone programs may reduce the frequency of risky sexual behaviors: Some evidence suggests that methadone patients have fewer sexual partners as well as fewer high-risk sexual partners and exhibit greater use of condoms than nonmethadone patients (Lollis et al., 2000; Sorensen & Copeland, 2000). Overall, a report from the Council on Scientific Affairs on methadone maintenance therapy confirms that it reduces heroin use and associated problems in a cost-effective manner without negative public health impacts (Yoast et al., 2001).

In treatment with the opiate antagonists cyclazocine and naloxone, addicts are first gradually weaned from heroin. They then receive increasing dosages of one of these drugs, which prevent them from experiencing any high should they later take heroin. These drugs have great affinity for the receptors to which opiates usually bind; their mol-

Methadone is a synthetic narcotic substitute. Former heroin addicts come to clinics each day and swallow their dose.

ecules occupy the receptors without stimulating them, and heroin molecules have no place to go and therefore do not have their usual effect on the user. As with methadone, however, addicts must make frequent and regular visits to a clinic, which requires motivation and responsibility on their part. In addition, addicts do not lose the craving for heroin for some time. Thus, patient compliance with therapy involving opiate antagonists is very poor, and the overall outcomes are only fair (Ginzburg, 1986; Goldstein, 1994). Both clinical effectiveness and treatment compliance can be increased by adding a contingency management component to the therapy (Carroll et al., 2001). Giving addicts vouchers that they can exchange for food and clothing in return for taking naltrexone and having drug-free urine samples markedly improves effectiveness.

The search is now on for drugs that will ease the symptoms of withdrawal and perhaps also attack the physical basis of cocaine addiction. Research findings are mixed. For example, two similarly conducted double-blind experiments compared the tricyclic antidepressant desipramine (Norpramine) with a placebo. In the first study, cocaine abusers who used Norpramine did not show decreased use of cocaine at the end of eight weeks of treatment (Kosten et al., 1992). In the second study, cocaine use was significantly greater in Norpramine users than in placebo patients at three- and six-month follow-ups after a twelve-week treatment period (Arndt et al., 1992). Similarly, while imipramine (Tofranil) helped alleviate depression in cocaine abusers who were depressed, it did not help the patients achieve abstinence from cocaine (Nunes et al., 1998). However, desipramine fared better in another study, which will be discussed shortly (Carroll, Rounsaville, & Gordon, 1994).

Clonidine, an antihypertensive medication, may ease withdrawal from a variety of addicting drugs, including cocaine (Baumgartner & Rowen, 1987). Bromocriptine also shows some promise in reducing craving, perhaps by reversing the depletion of dopamine that is believed to underlie cocaine's addicting properties (Dackis & Gold, 1985; Moss, 1990).

Psychological Treatments

Drug abuse is sometimes treated in the consulting rooms of psychiatrists, psychologists, and other mental health workers. Several kinds of psychotherapy are applied to drug-use disorders, as they are to other human maladjustments, often in combination with biological treatments aimed at reducing the physical dependence.

In the first direct comparison in a controlled study, the desipramine and a cognitive-behavioral treatment were found to be somewhat effective in reducing cocaine use as well as in improving abusers' family, social, and general psychological functioning. In a twelve-week study by Carroll and his co-workers (Carroll, Rounsaville, & Gordon, 1994; Carroll et al., 1995), desipramine was better than a placebo in patients with a low degree of dependence on cocaine, whereas the cognitive treatment was better in patients with a high degree of dependence. This finding illustrates the significance of the psychological aspects of substance abuse.

In Carroll's study, patients receiving cognitive treatment learned how to avoid high-risk situations (e.g., being around people using cocaine), recognize the lure of the drug for them, and develop alternatives to using cocaine (e.g., recreational activities with nonusers). Cocaine abusers in this study also learned strategies for coping with the craving and for resisting the tendency to regard a slip as a catastrophe ("relapse prevention training," per Marlatt & Gordon, 1985). The more depressed the patient, the more favorable the outcome from both the antidepressant drug and the cognitive therapy. Overall, the results for the psychosocial treatment were superior to those for the antidepressant drug in reducing cocaine use, and this pattern was maintained at a one-year follow-up (Carroll, Rounsaville, & Nich, 1994). The authors of the study take pains to point out that different treatments are probably necessary for different kinds of patients, a theme that is increasingly evident in the therapy literature.

A more recent study testing the effectiveness of cognitive-behavioral treatment for illicit substance abuse in a community setting found that there was no difference in out-

Group therapy in residential settings is frequently used to treat heroin addiction.

comes between CBT and standard substance-abuse counseling (Morgenstern et al., 2001). Thus, disseminating CBT to community settings may not necessarily improve outcomes.

A more operant type of program has shown some promise. Modeled after the token economy employed in hospital settings (p. 50), vouchers are provided for not using cocaine or heroine (verified by urine samples). The tokens are exchangeable for things that the person would like to have more of (Dallery et al., 2001; Katz et al., 2001; Silverman et al., 1996). Some evidence exists also for the effectiveness of treatment programs that follow a psychodynamic approach combined with methadone (Woody et al., 1990).

Self-help residential homes or communes are the most widespread psychological approach to dealing with heroin addiction and other drug abuse. Modeled after Synanon, a therapeutic community of former drug addicts founded in 1958 by Charles Dederich in Santa Monica, California, these residences are designed to restructure radically the addict's outlook on life so that illicit drugs no longer have a place. Daytop Village, Phoenix House, Odyssey House, and other drug-rehabilitation homes share the following features:

- Separation of addicts from previous social contacts, on the assumption that these relationships have been instrumental in fostering the addictive lifestyle.
- A comprehensive environment in which drugs are not available and continuing support is offered to ease the transition from regular drug use to a drug-free existence.
- The presence of charismatic role models, former addicts who appear to be meeting life's challenges without drugs.
- Direct, often brutal confrontation in group therapy,[5] in which addicts are goaded into accepting responsibility for their problems and for their drug habits and are urged to take charge of their lives.
- A setting in which addicts are respected as human beings rather than stigmatized as failures or criminals.

There are several obstacles to evaluating the efficacy of residential drug-treatment programs. Since entrance is voluntary, only a small minority of dependent users enter such settings. Furthermore, because the drop-out rate is high, those who remain cannot be regarded as representative of the population of people addicted to illicit drugs; their motivation to go straight is probably much stronger than that of the average addict. Any improvement participants in these programs make may reflect their uncommonly strong desire to rid themselves of the habit more than the specific qualities of the treatment program. Such self-regulating residential communities do, however, appear to help a large number of those who remain in them for a year or so (Institute of Medicine, 1990b; Jaffe, 1985).

A final cautionary note. As successful as all these efforts are, the fact remains that most people who participate in the various individual and group programs do not achieve abstinence by the end of formal contact with the treatment, and of those who do, the majority fail to remain abstinent. The abuse of opiates and other illicit drugs remains a serious societal and health problem that resists even the most intensive therapeutic efforts.

---

[5] In 1966 one of us visited a Synanon community in San Francisco and learned about the origin of the name. The confrontational group meetings were called "seminars." One of the early residents was unfamiliar with that word and mispronounced it as "synanon." Another personal observation was how articulate, persuasive, and smooth many of the residents in leadership positions were. One of our more cynical friends opined that they were really psychopaths, capable of selling anything they wanted to. We were never able to verify or disconfirm this hypothesis.

Treatment of Cigarette Smoking

As we mentioned earlier, numerous laws today prohibit smoking in restaurants, trains, airplanes, and public buildings. These laws are part of a social context that provides more incentive and support to stop smoking than existed in 1964, when the Surgeon General first warned of the serious health hazards associated with cigarette smoking. It is estimated that 2.1 million smoking-related deaths have been postponed or avoided between 1986 and 2000 owing to the publicity from the Surgeon General's reports and associated programs to discourage the habit (Foreyt, 1990). Furthermore, smokers who quit before age fifty reduce their risk of dying in the following fifteen years by half, as compared with those who continue to smoke (USDHHS, 1998).

Of the more than 40 million smokers who have quit since 1964, it is believed that 90 percent did so without professional help (National Cancer Institute, 1977; USDHHS, 1982, 1989). Each year more than 30 percent of cigarette smokers try to quit with minimal outside assistance, but fewer than 10 percent succeed even in the short run (Fiore et al., 1990). Research is ongoing on smokers' use of self-help methods outside the framework of formal smoking-cessation programs (DiClemente, 1993; Orleans et al., 1991).

Some smokers attend smoking clinics or consult with professionals for specialized smoking-reduction programs. The American Cancer Society, the American Lung Association, and the Church of the Seventh Day Adventists have been especially active in offering programs to help large groups of people stop smoking. Even so, it is estimated that only about half of those who go through smoking-cessation programs succeed in abstaining by the time the program is over; only about 20 percent of those who have succeeded in the short term actually remain nonsmoking after a year. The greatest success overall is found among smokers who are better educated, older, or have acute health problems (USDHHS, 1998).

Laws that have banned smoking in many places have probably increased the frequency of quitting.

Psychological Treatments

Although short-term results of psychological treatments are often very encouraging—some programs (e.g., Etringer, Gregory, & Lando, 1984) have reported as many as 95 percent of smokers abstinent by the end of treatment—longer-term results are far less positive. Regardless of how well things look when an intervention ends, most smokers return to smoking within a year (DiClemente, 1993), and they do so especially quickly if they have been heavy smokers (USDHHS, 1998). This evidence does not belie the fact that a substantial minority of smokers can be helped; as with other efforts to change behavior, though, the task is not easy.

Many techniques have been tried. The idea behind some of them is to make smoking unpleasant, even nauseating. For a while in the 1970s there was considerable interest in rapid-smoking treatment, in which a smoker sits in a poorly ventilated room and puffs much faster than normal, perhaps as often as every six seconds (e.g., Lando, 1977). Newer variations include rapid puffing (rapid smoking without inhaling), focused smoking (smoking for a long period of time but at a normal rate), and smoke holding (retaining smoke in the mouth for several minutes but without inhaling). Although such treatments reduce smoking and foster abstinence more than no-treatment control conditions, they usually do not differ from each other or from other credible interventions, showing high rates of relapse at follow-ups of several months to a year (Schwartz, 1987; Sobell et al., 1990).

Cognitively oriented investigators have tried to encourage more control in people who smoke with treatments that have them develop and utilize various coping skills, such as relaxation and positive self-talk, when confronted with tempting situations—for example, following a meal or sitting down to read a book. Results are not very promising, however (Hill, Rigdon, & Johnson, 1993; Smith et al., 2001).

As reviewed by Compas et al. (1998), scheduled smoking shows real promise. The strategy is to reduce nicotine intake gradually over a period of a few weeks by getting the smoker to agree to increase the time intervals between cigarettes. For example, during the first week of treatment, a pack-a-day smoker would be put on a schedule allowing only ten cigarettes per day; during the second week only five cigarettes are allowed; and during the third week, the person would taper off to zero. These cigarettes have to be smoked on a schedule provided by the treatment team, not when the smoker feels an intense craving. In this way, smoking cigarettes is controlled by the passage of time rather than by urges, mood states, or situations. Breaking this link—assuming the smoker is able to stay with the agreed-upon schedule—has led to 44 percent abstinence after one year, a very impressive outcome (Cinciripini et al., 1994).

Probably the most widespread intervention is advice or direction from a physician to stop smoking. Each year millions of smokers are given this counsel—because of hypertension, heart disease, lung disease, diabetes, or on general grounds of preserving or improving health. Indeed, by age 65, most smokers have managed to quit (USDHHS, 1998).[6] There is some evidence that a physician's advice can get some people to stop smoking, at least for a while, especially when the patients also chew nicotine gum (Law & Tang, 1995; Russell et al., 1983). But much more needs to be learned about the nature of the advice, the manner in which it is given, its timing, and other factors that must surely play a role in determining whether an addicted individual is prepared and able to alter his or her behavior primarily on a physician's say-so (USDHHS, 1998).

By age 18 about two-thirds of cigarette smokers regret having started smoking, one-half have already made an attempt to quit, and nearly 40% show interest in obtaining treatment for their dependence (Henningfield et al., 2000). Unfortunately, treatment in young people has not kept pace with the emerging need for treatment. A new school-based program called Project EX includes training in coping skills and a psychoeducational component about the harmful effects of smoking. Emerging data on the program's effectiveness are promising (Sussman et al., 2001).

Smoking reduction rather than cessation programs offer an alternative intervention for smokers who are not interested in quitting but wish to reduce the number of cigarettes they smoke. Currently there are no data on whether reduced smoking will reduce smoking risks. However, it appears that attempts at reduction do not undermine the probability of not smoking at all in the future. On the contrary, it appears that reduction promotes future cessation (Hughes, 2000).

As with other addictions, psychological factors may make it difficult for smokers to quit. As these factors can vary significantly among addicts, one treatment package cannot be expected to help all smokers. People have trouble quitting for many different reasons, and diverse methods need to be developed to help them. Yet in their zeal to make an impact on the smoking problem, clinicians have until recently put smokers in standardized programs. Future efforts will no doubt require careful attention to the diverse psychological factors that cause people to continue to smoke even when they know that it is unhealthful for them to do so. A focus on the addicting nature of nicotine also merits attention, a topic to which we turn next.

Biological Treatments

Reducing a smoker's craving for nicotine by providing it in a different way is one biological approach to treatment. Attention to nicotine dependence is clearly important because the more cigarettes smoked daily, the less successful any quitting attempt is. Nicotine may be supplied in gum, patches, or inhalers. The idea is to help smokers endure the nicotine withdrawal that accompanies any effort to stop smoking. Hughes (1995) points out that although nicotine replacement alleviates withdrawal symptoms—which justifies its use in gum and in the nicotine patches to be described next (Hughes et al., 1990)— the severity of withdrawal is only minimally related to success in stopping smoking

---

[6] This encouraging statistic should be viewed in the context of the fact that a good many smokers die before they reach age sixty-five.

(Hughes & Hatsukami, 1992). Thus the logic of employing nicotine replacement to help people stop smoking appears a bit shaky.

Gum containing nicotine has been available in the United States since 1984 by doctor's prescription and more recently became available over the counter. The nicotine in gum is absorbed much more slowly and steadily than that in tobacco. The long-term goal is for the former smoker to be able to cut back on the use of the gum as well, eventually eliminating reliance on nicotine altogether.

This treatment involves some controversy, however. Ex-smokers can become dependent on the gum. Moreover, in doses that deliver an amount of nicotine equivalent to smoking one cigarette an hour, the gum causes cardiovascular changes, such as increased blood pressure, that can be dangerous to people with cardiovascular diseases. Nevertheless, some experts believe that even prolonged, continued use of the gum is healthier than obtaining nicotine by smoking, because at least the poisons in the smoke are avoided (deWit & Zacny, 2000). The best results are obtained when the gum is combined with a behaviorally oriented treatment (Hughes, 1995; Killen et al., 1990), although one well-controlled study showed no additional benefit from the gum over a behavioral intervention that emphasized educational information and environmental changes, such as the removal of ashtrays from home and work settings (Hill et al., 1995).

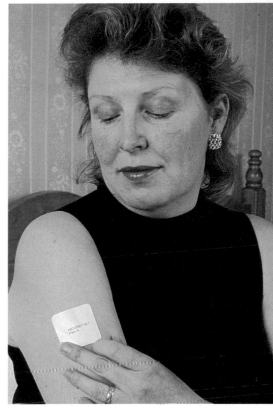

Nicotine patches are now available over the counter to help relieve withdrawal symptoms.

Nicotine patches first became available in December 1991 with a doctor's prescription and in 1996 over the counter. A polyethylene patch taped to the arm serves as a transdermal (through the skin) nicotine delivery system that slowly and steadily releases the drug into the bloodstream and thence to the brain. An advantage of the patch over nicotine gum is that the person need only apply the patch each day and not remove it, making compliance easier. A program of treatment usually lasts ten to twelve weeks, with smaller and smaller patches used as treatment progresses. A drawback is that a person who continues smoking while wearing the patch risks increasing the amount of nicotine in the body to dangerous levels.

Evidence suggests that the nicotine patch is superior to the use of a placebo patch in terms of abstinence as well as subjective craving (see Hughes, 1995). However, as with nicotine gum, the patch is not a panacea. Abstinence rates are less than 40 percent immediately following the termination of treatment, and at nine-month follow-ups differences between the drug and a placebo disappear. The manufacturers state that the patch is to be used only as part of a psychological smoking-cessation program and then for not more than three months at a time.

The newest nicotine replacement therapy involves an inhaler. The user inhales the nicotine through a plastic tube shaped like a cigarette holder; unlike gum or patches, this method of nicotine delivery has some resemblance to smoking as the person handles the device and inhales. In a comparison of these inhalers with placebo inhalers that did not actually contain nicotine, one-year abstinence rates were 28 percent for the treatment group and 18 percent for the placebo group (Hjalmarson et al., 1997).

Based on research showing that attempting to quit smoking can precipitate an episode of depression in someone who has previously been depressed, interest has also focused on the possible role of antidepressants in aiding smoking cessation. Thus far, the evidence shows that antidepressants that have strong effects on dopamine (and not on serotonin) do have some benefit, regardless of whether the person has a history of depression (Hall et al., 1998; Hurt, Sachs, & Glover, 1997). Patients are typically given an amount of the antidepressant that is less than would be used to treat depression. They take the drug for some period of time before trying to stop smoking and then continue taking the antidepressant for some amount of time (e.g., seven weeks) as they try to give up smoking. One study combined brief counseling with either buproprion (an antidepressant sold under the names of Wellbutrin and Zyban) or a placebo and found one-year abstinence rates of 23 percent in the treated group and 12 percent in the placebo group (Hurt et al., 1997). Combining buproprion and nicotine patches has yielded a twelve-month abstinence rate of 35 percent, an impressive (albeit far from perfect) figure (Jorenby et al., 1999). Other promising non-nicotine pharmacotherapy for smoking cessation has included the anti-hypertensive drug clonidine and silver acetate (Benowitz & Peng, 2000), as well as glucose tablets (West, 2001).

Relapse Prevention

Mark Twain quipped that stopping smoking was easy—he'd done it hundreds of times! Most smokers relapse within a year of stopping, regardless of the means used to stop. In a pattern we have already seen, people who smoked the most—and are presumably more addicted to nicotine—relapse more often and more quickly than moderate or light smokers. Frequent slips, younger age, nicotine dependence, low self-efficacy, weight concerns, and previous quitting attempts are all predictors of relapse (Ockene at al., 2000).

What factors contribute to success? Data (and common sense) tell us that ex-smokers who do not live with a smoker do better at follow-up than do those who do live with a smoker (McIntyre-Kingsolver, Lichtenstein, & Mermelstein, 1986). So-called booster or maintenance sessions help, but in a very real sense they represent a continuation of treatment; when they stop, relapse is the rule (Brandon, Zelman, & Baker, 1987). Intensive interventions, such as a telephone counseling (Brandon et al., 2000), improve maintenance of cessation; however, they reach relatively few smokers. Brief relapse prevention interventions during medical visits are cost-effective and could potentially reach most smokers but are not consistently delivered (Ockene et al., 2000). On a positive note, there is considerably more social support for not smoking than there was just ten years ago, at least in the United States. Perhaps as time goes on, societal sanctions against smoking will help those who have succeeded in quitting remain abstinent. (It is certainly more difficult to find a place to light up nowadays.)

One specific approach to the relapse problem is to focus on the cognitions of ex-smokers (Baer & Lichtenstein, 1988). Using the articulated thoughts paradigm (Davison et al., 1983; see p. 96), Haaga (1989) found that recent ex-smokers who tended to think of smoking without prompting relapsed more readily three months later. However, if they learned some effective ways of countering these smoking-related thoughts, such as distracting themselves, their abstinence was better months later. Using a questionnaire measure, Haaga found that ex-smokers' self-efficacy in their most difficult challenge situation—for example, having coffee and dessert following a pleasant dinner—was a good predictor of abstinence a year later (Haaga, 1990). These and related studies indicate that the prediction of maintenance or relapse in smoking cessation is enhanced by measuring the cognitions of ex-smokers. Such information may help therapists design programs that will improve the ability of a person to remain a nonsmoker (Compas et al., 1998).

Prevention of Substance Abuse

From all that is known about the etiology of substance abuse, discouraging people from beginning to abuse drugs makes the most sense. It is difficult—often impossible—for people to loose themselves from substances that create both psychological and physical dependency. We turn our attention next to prevention efforts in the realm of alcohol abuse, illicit drug abuse, and cigarette smoking.

Many prevention efforts have been aimed at adolescents because substance abuse in adulthood often follows experimentation in the teens and earlier. Programs, usually conducted in schools, have been directed at enhancing the young adolescent's self-esteem, teaching social skills, and encouraging the young person to say no to peer pressure. The results are mixed (Hansen, 1993; Jansen et al., 1996). Self-esteem enhancement, sometimes called affective education, has not demonstrated its effectiveness. In contrast, social-skills training and resistance training (learning to say no) have shown some positive results, particularly with girls. A highly publicized program, Project DARE (Drug Abuse Resistance Education), which combines affective education and resistance training and is delivered by police officers in fifth- and sixth-grade classrooms, has shown disappointing results (Clayton, Catterello, & Walden, 1991; Ringwalt, Ennett, & Holt, 1991).

Other preventive efforts, yet to be adequately evaluated, include the following:

- Parental involvement in school programs for their children.
- Warning labels on containers of alcoholic beverages (mandated by law in 1989).

- Informing consumers that drinking alcohol during pregnancy can cause birth defects in the fetus and that alcohol impairs driving a car and operating machinery.
- Cautionary announcements in the media about stiff legal penalties for driving under the influence and exhortations to arrange for designated drivers before imbibing at social occasions.
- Testing for alcohol and drugs in the workplace.

In recent years we have seen well-known sports and entertainment figures urge audiences not to experiment with illicit drugs, especially cocaine. The message in the 1960s and the 1970s was often that certain drugs—especially the hallucinogens—would help people realize their potential or at least provide an escape from the humdrum and the stressful. In the 1990s, however, the message became that mind-altering drugs interfere with psychological functioning and the achievement of one's personal best and that, above all, these drugs are harmful to the body and can cause unexpected death. Timothy Leary's 1970s mantra "Turn on, tune in, drop out" was replaced with "Just say no."

Also better appreciated are the relationships among drug-usage patterns. As mentioned earlier, it now appears that marijuana may be one factor—although not the only causal factor (Institute of Medicine, 1999)—in subsequent, more serious drug abuse, a hypothesis that in the 1960s was ridiculed by young people for whom marijuana was as much a form of political and social protest as a mind-altering excursion (recall Focus on Discovery 12.1, p. 369).

Developing ways of discouraging young people from experimenting with tobacco has become a top priority among health researchers and politicians, with encouragement from the Surgeon General and funding from the National Cancer Institute, one of the National Institutes of Health. Why? Because half of adult smokers began their habit before the age of fifteen, and nearly all before the age of nineteen (USDHHS, 1998).

The measures that hold promise for persuading young people to resist smoking may be useful also in dissuading them from trying illicit drugs and alcohol. Many people apparently do fear disastrous consequences later in life and try to cut down on cigarettes, yet both young and old smokers seem able to discount the possibility that they are at higher risk for coronary heart disease or lung cancer—the "It won't happen to me" syndrome. Although heavy smokers are eleven times more likely than nonsmokers to develop lung cancer, many heavy smokers do live long and healthy lives. In addition, it is the nature of young people to have a limited time perspective. Teenagers would seem to be more concerned with next Saturday evening's festivities or Friday's math exam than with their life situation at age sixty.

Statewide comprehensive tobacco control programs, which include increasing taxes on cigarettes, restricting tobacco advertising, conducting public education campaigns, and creating smoke-free environments, appear to be an effective strategy for reducing teenage smoking (Wakefield & Chaloupka, 2000). In addition, recent years have seen scores of school-based programs aimed at preventing young people from starting to use tobacco. By and large such programs have succeeded in delaying the onset of smoking (Sussman et al., 1995). These programs share some common components, not all of them shown to be effective (Evans, 2001; Hansen, 1992; Sussman, 1996):

1. **Peer-pressure resistance training.** Students learn about the nature of peer pressure and ways to say no. For example, specially prepared films portray teenagers resisting appeals from friends to try smoking (Evans et al., 1981), not an easy matter for young people for whom peer approval and acceptance are acutely important. Sixth graders who learned assertive refusal skills smoked less two years later than a control group that received only attention and information about the harmful effects of smoking (Luepker & Perry, 1991; Schinke & Gilchrist, 1985). Refusal-skills training is much more effective for girls than for boys (Graham et al., 1990). Overall, studies suggest that programs based on peer-pressure resistance training are effective in reducing the onset and level of tobacco use, as well as drug use, in young people (Lantz et al., 2000; Tobler et al., 2000).

2. **Correction of normative expectations.** Many young people believe that cigarette smoking is more prevalent (and by implication, more okay) than it actually is. Changing beliefs about the prevalence of smoking has been shown to be an effective

strategy, perhaps because of the sensitivity young people have to what others their age do and believe. (Recall this social-comparison aspect of the Sobells' treatment of alcohol abuse, p. 394.) Establishing that it is not standard behavior to smoke cigarettes (or drink alcohol or use marijuana) appears to be significantly more effective than resistance training (Hansen & Graham, 1991).

3. **Inoculation against mass-media messages.** Some prevention programs try to counter the positive images of smokers that have been put forth in the media, for example, the Joe Camel ads mentioned earlier. For several years television and radio have not carried cigarette ads, and print ads have had to contain explicit warnings about the dangers of smoking. Some researchers argue that sophisticated mass media campaigns, similar to the ones that have made tobacco a profitable consumer product, can be successful in discouraging smoking (Lantz et al., 2000). Combating tobacco advertising with anti-smoking messages may be a crucial tool in smoking prevention efforts, since teenagers' receptivity to tobacco marketing is strongly related to whether or not they will actually smoke (Unger et al., 2001).

4. **Information about parental and other adult influences.** Since it is known that parental smoking is strongly correlated with and most probably contributes to smoking by their children, some programs point out this fact and argue that this aspect of one's parents' behavior does not have to be imitated.

5. **Peer leadership.** Most smoking and other drug-prevention programs involve peers of recognized status to enhance the impact of the anti-use messages being conveyed.

6. **Affective education, self-image enhancement.** Several programs focus on the idea that intrapsychic factors, such as poor self-image and inability to cope with stress, underlie the onset of smoking in young people. However, there are indications that such programs may actually increase drug use, perhaps because their focus on drugs as a poor way to resolve self-esteem issues unintentionally suggests drug experimentation as a way to deal with life stress.

7. **Other components.** Additional features of preventive programs include information about the harmful effects of smoking or of drug use (a common element in adult smoking-cessation programs but not demonstrated to be effective with young people) and producing a public commitment not to smoke, such as making a commitment on videotape. Attention to other risk factors is also important because smoking prevalence is higher among children who are depressed or are having family or school problems (USDHHS, 1998).

Beginning in August 1995 the Clinton administration, and especially the Food and Drug Administration (FDA), began to focus public attention on the addictive nature of nicotine and in particular on the need to discourage young people from taking up the habit. Cigarettes were described as "nicotine-delivery systems," despite denials from the heads of major tobacco companies that nicotine is addictive.[7] A year later President Clinton took action to give the FDA regulatory control over tobacco products, suggesting that since nicotine is a drug, and an addicting one at that, its promotion and sale should be under the purview of the FDA.

On August 14, 1998, a federal appeals court ruled that the FDA does not have authority to regulate nicotine as a drug or cigarettes as nicotine-delivery systems, which was a serious setback to the Clinton administration's efforts to curb tobacco use (Rubin, 1998). In March 2000 the U.S. Supreme Court upheld the appeals court ruling, thereby preventing the FDA from exercising control over the production and sale of tobacco products. It remains to be seen whether any future governmental regulations will have the intended effect or whether, as some people predict, young people will only see the use of tobacco as more cool because the adult establishment makes it more difficult for them to obtain and use the product (Stolberg, 1996a).

---

[7] In March 1997, Liggett broke ranks with the other cigarette companies and finally admitted that nicotine is addictive. In the following couple of years the other cigarette manufacturers followed suit.

Summary

- Using substances to alter mood and consciousness is a human characteristic, and so too is the tendency to abuse them. DSM-IV-TR distinguishes between substance dependence and substance abuse. Dependence refers to a compulsive pattern of substance use and consequent serious psychological and physical impairments. It can involve physiological dependence, or addiction, when tolerance and withdrawal are present. In the less serious disorder, substance abuse, drug use leads to failure to meet obligations and to interpersonal and legal problems.

- Major substance-related disorders include maladaptive use of alcohol, nicotine, marijuana, sedatives and stimulants, and the hallucinogens. Alcohol and nicotine can, of course, be legally obtained. Some sedatives and stimulants can be used with a physician's prescription, although their unauthorized use is illegal. Still other drugs, such as heroin and cocaine, are illegal in any context.

- Alcohol has a variety of short-term and long-term effects on human beings, ranging from poor judgment and impaired motor coordination and their dire consequences to addiction, which makes an ordinary, productive life impossible and is extremely difficult to overcome. Chronic long-term drinking creates severe biological damage, especially to the liever, as well as psychological deterioration.

- Nicotine, especially when taken into the body via the inhaled smoke from a cigarette, has worked its addictive power on humankind for centuries; and despite somberly phrased warnings from public-health officials, it continues in widespread use. Medical problems associated with long-term cigarette smoking include lung cancer, emphysema, cancer of the larynx and esophagus, and cardiovascular disease. Moreover, the health hazards of smoking are not restricted to those who smoke, for secondhand (environmental) smoke can also cause lung damage and other problems.

- Recent trends indicate that marijuana use declined in the 1980s, increased in the 1990s, and has leveled off since then. When used regularly, marijuana can damage the lungs and cardiovascular system and lead to cognitive impairments. Constituents of marijuana may also adversely affect fetal development, heart function in people who already have coronary problems, and pulmonary function. Further, marijuana appears to be addicting. Ironically, just as the possible dangers of marijuana began to be uncovered, it was found to ease the nausea of cancer patients undergoing chemotherapy.

- Sedatives are addictive drugs that slow the activities of the body and, in moderate doses, are used to relieve pain and induce sleep. One class is the opiates, which include opium, morphine, and heroin. Heroin has been a focus of concern because usage is up and stronger varieties have become available. Another group is the synthetic barbiturates and tranquilizers. Barbiturates have for some time been implicated in both intentional and accidental suicides; they are particularly lethal when taken with alcohol.

- Stimulants, which include amphetamines and cocaine, act on the brain and the sympathetic nervous system to increase alertness and motor activity. All are addictive, and crack cocaine and methamphetamine, a derivative of amphetamine, are especially so. The number of methamphetamine abusers has skyrocketed in recent years.

- The hallucinogens—LSD, mescaline, and psilocybin—alter or expand consciousness. Their use reflects humankind's desire not only to escape from unpleasant realities but also to explore inner space. Use of the hallucinogen-like drug Ecstasy has dramatically risen, and it is considered a serious threat to health.

- Several factors are related to the etiology of substance abuse and dependence. Social attitudes and culture can play a role. Sociocultural variables, such as attitudes toward the substance, peer pressure, and how the substance is portrayed by the media, are all related to how frequently a substance is used. Many substances are used to alter mood (for example, to reduce tension or increase positive affect), and people with certain personality traits, such as those high in negative affect or psychopathy, are especially likely to use drugs. Cognitive variables, such as the expectation that the drug will yield positive effects, are also important. Finally, biological factors, most notably a genetic predisposition or diathesis, appear to play a role in the use of some substances, particularly alcohol.

- Therapies of all kinds have been used to help people refrain from the use of both legal drugs (e.g., alcohol and nicotine) and illegal drugs (e.g., heroin and cocaine). Biological treatments have attempted to release users from their physiological dependency. Some benefits have been observed for treatments using such drugs as clonidine, naltrexone, and methadone. Recently, nicotine replacement via gum, patches, or inhalers has met with some success in reducing cigarette smoking. None of these somatic approaches appears to lead to enduring change however, unless accompanied by psychological treatments with such goals as helping patients resist pressures to indulge, cope with normal life stress, control emotions without relying on chemicals, and make use of social supports, such as Alcoholics Anonymous.

- Health professionals recognize that substance dependence and abuse are multifaceted problems, requiring a broad range of interventions, and that different people use and abuse drugs for different reasons, making it necessary to assess carefully those factors of particular importance for a given individual. Since it is far easier never to begin using drugs than to stop using them, considerable effort has been expended in recent years to prevent substance abuse by implementing educational and social programs to equip young people to develop their lives without a reliance on drugs.

Key Terms

amphetamines	delirium tremens	hashish	MDA	nitrous oxide	sedatives
Antabuse	(DTs)	heroin	MDMA	opiates	stimulants
barbiturates	detoxification	heroin antagonists	mescaline	opium	substance abuse
clonidine	Ecstasy	heroin substitutes	methadone	oxycodone	substance
cocaine	fetal alcohol	hydrocodone	methamphetamine	polydrug abuse	dependence
controlled drinking	syndrome	LSD	morphine	psilocybin	tolerance
covert sensitization	flashback	marijuana	nicotine	secondhand smoke	withdrawal
cross-dependent	hallucinogen				

Alcohol Dependence

Dr. Lawton received a phone call from Grace Patterson. Her husband, Barry, had a history of heavy drinking, and it had escalated recently. Dr. Lawton suggested that she try to talk to Barry about her concerns. He emphasized that she should pick a time when Barry had not been drinking. She should tell him that she had spoken to a psychologist who had agreed to see Barry for an evaluation. After the evaluation, the psychologist would be able to give them some advice about what they might do.

Grace called again several weeks later. She had spoken to Barry, and he refused to entertain the possibility of coming in for an evaluation. Grace was at a loss regarding what to do next, so Dr. Lawton scheduled an appointment to see her alone. The main topic of the session was how Grace could change how she behaved toward Barry in the hope of motivating him to enter treatment. She was instructed to explain calmly to him the negative consequences of his drinking and to indicate how concerned she was about it. Grace and Dr. Lawton identified several recent incidents and rehearsed how she could respond. For example, several weeks ago Barry and Grace had dinner plans with another couple, but by late afternoon Barry was too drunk to go out. Grace had to call the other couple and make an excuse about canceling the dinner. That evening Grace and Barry had a huge argument about Barry's drinking. Whenever Barry was really drunk, it was impossible to have a reasoned conversation with him, especially about his drinking. In the future Grace was to wait until the next morning and then express her concerns about the drinking and how this pattern might cause them to lose some good friends. The problem was ruining their marriage.

About a month later, Grace called Dr. Lawton to say that there had been no change in Barry's drinking. She described several occasions in which she had explained to Barry that his drinking was having destructive effects on their lives. Although Grace was discouraged, Dr. Lawton persuaded her to continue the plan. Three weeks later Grace called to make an appointment for both her and Barry to come in for an evaluation. She told Dr. Lawton that she and Barry had had a terrible fight the previous evening; Barry had raised his hand to hit her but held back at the last second. This incident apparently alarmed Barry as much as it frightened Grace, and it led him to finally agree to see Dr. Lawton.

Dr. Lawton greeted Barry and Grace in the waiting room and invited them into his office. One primary goal of the initial session was to avoid scaring Barry out of therapy. At this initial meeting Dr. Lawton explained that he understood Barry's reluctance to come in. He told him that the purpose of this session was to gather information about Barry's drinking habits and any problems that alcohol might be causing. Furthermore, toward the end of the session, if Barry wanted to, they could discuss treatment options.

Barry was indeed drinking heavily on a daily basis, beginning after work and continuing into the evening. On weekends, he typically started to drink around noon and was quite intoxicated by dinner time. He recognized that his drinking was out of control and that it was indeed having adverse effects on both him and his wife. Barry and Grace had begun arguing frequently. On several occasions, Barry had broken dinnerware and punched holes in walls. The couple now saw friends infrequently. Barry's high blood pressure certainly wasn't being helped by the alcohol. Toward the end of the session, when the issue of treatment was raised, Barry indicated that he knew he should cut back on his drinking but that he did not really want to stop entirely. He knew that abstinence was usually the goal of alcohol treatment programs like AA, and he did not want to become totally abstinent. At this point, Dr. Lawton pointed out that some treatments are focused on making changes that lead to moderate drinking. Barry seemed interested in this possibility. The session ended with Barry agreeing to consider entering treatment.

A week later Barry called and scheduled another appointment.

Social History

This history is based on information gathered from Barry while he was in treatment as well as from Grace.

Barry's childhood was rather uneventful. His father was an electrical engineer, and his mother worked part time in a local library once Barry and his older brother, James, were in school. Barry's mother and father were very light drinkers—an occasional beer or glass of wine. Barry recalled that his older brother was closer to their father than Barry. James shared his father's interest in electronic projects, and the two of them often worked together. Barry, in contrast, had little interest and even less aptitude for electronics. He was more interested in reading, particularly history.

Barry achieved excellent grades in both elementary and high school. In high school, he was also on the wrestling team. He began drinking in high school, typically at house parties on weekends. He recalled that he found drinking relaxing and that it reduced the anxiety he sometimes felt in social situations. He remembered that his anxieties were greatest when around women; he often felt tongue tied and was unable to sustain conversations.

He graduated from high school and went to a small college where he majored in history and education. His goal was to become a high school history teacher. His drinking increased somewhat in college, both in amount and frequency. His drinking was no longer confined to weekends, and he typically drank six or more beers at a sitting. As he had said about his drinking in high school, he said that he drank mostly to relax. He maintained a decent GPA but recalled that his anxieties around women persisted. He met his future wife at the college. They were both taking an art history class. Barry was immediately attracted to Grace and she to him. Grace's social and conversational skills put Barry at ease, and they began seeing each other regularly. They planned to marry at the end of college.

After college Barry took a job teaching high school history, and Grace found work at a jewelry store. They lived in an apartment for two years, saving toward the down payment on a house. Because he aspired to become head of the history department or perhaps get into administration, Barry enrolled in an evening M.A. program at a local university. Barry recalled that these were very happy times. He and Grace were deeply in love.

He was drinking regularly now. A couple of scotches before dinner on weekdays and the usual scotches plus wine with dinner on the weekends. Grace joined her husband in a scotch before dinner, but only one. Barry remembered that when he and Grace went out for dinner with friends, he would wolf down two drinks before dinner while everyone else had only one. And when they were at a party, Barry would generally drink considerably more than anyone else. He claimed he needed the alcohol to feel at ease in social situations.

This drinking pattern continued for several years. During this time, Barry received his M.A., and he and Grace had a child, Richard. The couple indeed bought a small house, and life continued smoothly for the most part. Four years later the position of head of the history department opened, and Barry applied for the post. He wasn't selected and was both crushed and very angry. His drinking began to increase. He would secretly freshen up his scotch when Grace was out of the room, so he was probably having three or four instead of his usual two. After a while Grace noticed that they were buying their scotch more often than usual and began to suspect that Barry was drinking heavily. When she confronted him, Barry angrily denied it and changed his drinking pattern.

Now he began drinking on the way home from work. He would stop at a liquor store, buy a half pint of brandy, and drink it on the way home. He was careful to vary the liquor stores he stopped at and took back routes home to reduce the chance of being stopped by a police officer. Before getting home, he stowed the empty bottle in the trunk of his car, freshened his breath, and was ready to greet Grace and start in on the scotch. He began to fall asleep (pass out?) regularly after dinner. His after work drinking led him to give up his afternoon racquet ball games, and he no longer was able to engage in any activities after dinner. He started "forgetting" appointments he had made. For example, friends might call to invite Barry and Grace to a movie or dinner. But the next day Barry had no memory of the call. The number of calls from friends began to decrease. During this period Grace was becoming increasingly upset. She was having less and less interaction with Barry and their friends, and she was coming to believe that Barry must be drinking secretly.

After several months Grace became fairly certain that Barry must be drinking outside the home. One day, she checked his trunk and found a dozen brandy bottles. Beside herself with anger and anxiety, she confronted Barry, and an ugly argument ensued—the first of many. Barry became even more secretive about his drinking, now throwing the empties away before arriving home, but his drinking did not decrease. He realized his drinking was out of control and made several attempts to cut back. Unfortunately, his resolve typically lasted only a day or two.

Treatment

During the first session, Dr. Lawton and Barry discussed treatment options in more detail. Barry was adamant that he wanted to cut down rather than aim for abstinence. Dr. Lawton told him that while he thought abstinence was a better goal, he was willing to help Barry reduce his consumption. Dr. Lawton indicated that, in order to regain control of drinking, a month of abstinence would be necessary. While Barry showed signs of increased tolerance for alcohol he had not experienced withdrawal symptoms; therefore, quitting "cold turkey" appeared to be a safe procedure. Barry agreed to this period of abstinence, albeit reluctantly. They also discussed the positive and negative consequences of Barry's drinking. Somewhat surprisingly, Barry was hard pressed to come up with much in the way of positives. He said that alcohol had allowed him to cope with stress in the past, but now it had just become a habit, a way of filling time. Their discussion of negative consequences produced a long list—marital problems, loss of friends, giving up activities, and the fact that Barry's high blood pressure was undoubtedly adversely affected by alcohol. Dr. Lawton also provided Barry with normative information about the amounts people typically drank. Barry was surprised at how much he deviated from average.

Both Grace and Barry were present for the next session. They discussed ways for Barry to cope with abstinence. Dr. Lawton pointed out that urges to drink would pass with time, especially if Barry could engage in some alternative activities. Barry was taught to think past the urge and to focus on the longer term consequences of heavy drinking. In therapy sessions, he practiced how to imagine longer-term consequences of getting drunk such as DWI, ruining his marriage, and losing friends. Together, they planned a number of activities to engage Barry in the hours after work. Barry decided to help out with the wrestling team at school and also return to playing racquetball. If neither of these activities was possible on a given day, Barry was to stay later at work and grade papers or revise lectures. If he was having difficulty controlling his urges, he was to call Grace. Barry agreed to have Grace remove all alcohol from their home, and the couple came up with a list of activities that they could engage in to fill the time that Barry would have typically spent drunk or "asleep." Essentially these involved social activities like going to the movies with friends, renting a film to watch at home, playing bridge, and going out for dinner.

Over the next several weeks, Barry met with Dr. Lawton twice a week, with Grace present at some of the sessions. Barry was able to maintain abstinence and followed through on the plan to become involved in alternative activities. He reported that he experienced cravings, mostly after work and in the evening, but that they were not too severe. The cravings were nothing like those he had experienced when he had quit smoking several years previously. He described them as rather vague hungers, "like when you're sort of hungry but don't know what you really want." During these sessions Barry was also taught deep muscle relaxation as a way to cope with the negative affect that he reported experiencing as an accompaniment to urges to drink.

Once the abstinence period was over, alcohol was reintroduced to the home. Barry agreed to have no more than two drinks per day. And they had to be carefully measured drinks in contrast to his earlier practice of just filling a highball glass with scotch. He also agreed to drink only when in Grace's company. Drinks were now to be sipped, and a 20-minute waiting period had to elapse between drinks. Barry reported that he was enjoying the activities in which he was now engaging, especially the racquetball and renewing old friendships.

The moderate drinking pattern seemed well established in about a month, so the frequency of sessions was reduced. Over the next months, Barry and Dr. Lawton continued to discuss Barry's efforts to cope with urges. They also began to discuss the possibility of relapse. Dr. Lawton distinguished between a *lapse*—drinking too much on a single day—and *relapse*—returning completely to his old pattern. Dr. Lawton pointed out that while lapses would likely occur, a lapse would not mean that all of Barry's progress had been lost. Dr. Lawton and Barry also discussed the need for continuing treatment and attending meetings of a local group of recovering alcohol abusers. The group was somewhat similar to Alcoholics Anonymous but with fewer religious overtones and less emphasis on abstinence as the only solution to alcohol abuse. Barry agreed to attend meetings and treatment was terminated.

Follow-up

Three years later, Dr. Lawton received another call from Grace, who told him that Barry had returned to heavy drinking. She and Barry had discussed returning to treatment, but Barry was reluc-

tant, saying that it clearly hadn't worked the first time. Dr. Lawton suggested that she try to get Barry to call him. Barry called several days later and reiterated his belief that treatment had failed. Barry said that he had started drinking heavily when he had again been passed over for a promotion and then had just slipped back into his old pattern. Dr. Lawton pointed out that maintaining moderate drinking for several years was not really a failure. Furthermore, Dr. Lawton told Barry that he believed that treatment could again help but that they would need to attend more carefully to maintaining treatment gains this time. Sensing Barry's continuing reluctance to return to treatment, Dr. Lawton told him that because his drinking had only been out of control for a short time, a period of abstinence would be all that would not be necessary this time. Barry agreed to come for a session with Grace.

Grace was the first to speak. Tearfully, she explained that Barry was drinking heavily again. Barry sat quietly, head down, as Grace related what had been happening recently. Grace indicated that she wasn't sure she could get through another prolonged episode of the problems that always seemed to occur when Barry was drinking. Divorce had become an option she was considering. Barry didn't disagree with anything Grace said. He wanted to try treatment again and would make an effort to stay sober.

Treatment was similar to the earlier one, but there was no period of abstinence. Barry was quickly able to reestablish a pattern of moderate drinking. In addition, a good deal of time was spent discussing Barry's reaction about being passed over for promotion. Barry's view of this event was that it was a catastrophe and proved how worthless he was. Dr. Lawton worked with Barry to try to get him to see it as unfortunate but not a complete disaster. During these meetings, Barry told Dr. Lawton that after therapy had terminated he had not followed through with the suggestion to attend group meetings. As with the first therapy, the last sessions were spent discussing maintenance of the gains that had been achieved. Barry insisted that he would attend group meetings this time, and Dr. Lawton agreed to continue to see him once a month. Barry was also told to call Dr. Lawton and schedule a meeting if he drank heavily for more than two days in a row.

Barry continued to see Dr. Lawton for the next six months. Although he had a couple of lapses, for the most part he maintained moderate drinking and attended group meetings regularly. But then he began to cancel appointments and missed several without calling. At the end of a year, Dr. Lawton closed the case.

Two years later, Grace called to say the old pattern had returned. This time, Barry was unwilling even to call Dr. Lawton. Grace indicated she was initiating a divorce proceeding. She felt depressed and wanted to schedule some therapy sessions. These sessions dealt mostly with her feelings about Barry. Grace did not seem to be clinically depressed, but she was indeed experiencing considerable distress. Barry continued to drink heavily, and Grace finally ordered him out of the house. Shortly thereafter, Barry had a major heart attack and died. Therapy with Grace continued for several months, focusing on her distress and guilt over Barry's death.

Discussion

According to *DSM-IV-TR*, the maladaptive use of various substances falls into two categories: substance dependence and substance abuse. Alcohol dependence is diagnosed if the person meets three of the following criteria:

- Withdrawal symptoms, negative psychological and physical effects, appear if the person stops drinking.
- Tolerance develops. The person needs to drink more and more alcohol to produce the desired effect.
- The person uses more alcohol than intended or uses it for a longer time then intended.
- The person recognizes that alcohol consumption is excessive and may have unsuccessfully tried to cut down or stop.
- Much time is spent trying to obtain alcohol or recover from its effects.
- Alcohol use continues despite psychological or physical problems caused by it.
- Participation in many activities (work, recreation, social) is reduced because of the drug.

Alcohol dependence can be diagnosed as being accompanied with physiological dependence if either tolerance or withdrawal is present. The concept of physiological dependence refers to what many people mean when they use the term addiction. Some researchers believe that the *DSM-IV-TR* concept of dependence is too liberal and that it should be reserved for those people who show clear withdrawal symptoms (Langerbucher et al., 2000).

Alcohol abuse, a less serious diagnosis, is diagnosed if one of the following is present:

- Failure to fulfill major obligations, for example, absences from work.
- Exposure to physical dangers, such as driving while intoxicated.
- Legal problems such as disorderly conduct or DWI.
- Persistent social problems such as arguments with spouse.

Barry clearly met the criteria for alcohol dependence. He had developed tolerance, recognized that he was drinking too much, had unsuccessfully tried to cut back, gave up activities that he had previously enjoyed, and continued to drink despite knowing that it was creating serious marital problems and contributing to his high blood pressure.

Lifetime prevalence rates for alcohol dependence are about 20 percent for men and 8 percent for women (Kessler et al.,

1994), making it one of the most prevalent *DSM-IV-TR* diagnoses. The path to the development of alcohol problems is somewhat variable. Some people, like Barry, progress steadily from moderate use to heavy use and then to abuse and dependence. But for many others the pattern is less regular. For example, some people become alcohol abusers during a time of stress and then return to light drinking when the stress has resolved (Langenbucher & Chung, 1995; Vaillant, 1996). Once a person becomes dependent, however, the disorder is often chronic. For example, in one study two-thirds of alcoholic men with alcohol dependence were still dependent when they were reassessed five years later (Schuckit et al., 2001).

Etiological Considerations

A genetic diathesis may well be present for alcohol abuse and dependence. Research clearly shows that problem drinking runs in families, with higher than expected rates among relatives (Chassin et al., 1999). Twin studies showing higher concordance in MZ than DZ pairs and adoption studies demonstrating high rates of problem drinking among people who were adopted and not raised by their alcoholic parents add further support to the importance of genetics (Cadoret et al., 1995; McGue, Pickens, & Svikis, 1992). Barry did not have a clear family history of problem drinking. Neither his parents nor his brother drank heavily, but he did recall an uncle who always seemed to be drunk at family gatherings.

The ability to tolerate alcohol may be what is inherited as a diathesis (Goodwin, 1979). This idea has been pursued in research studying young nonalcoholic adults who have an alcohol-abusing parent and similar individuals who do not have a positive family history for the disorder. Two variables, measured in young adulthood, were found to predict the onset of alcohol abuse 10 years later: (1) self-report of a low level of intoxication after a dose of alcohol and (2) less body sway, a measure of steadiness while standing, after drinking (Schuckit, 1994; Schuckit & Smith, 1996). The largest difference between the two groups occurred when their blood alcohol levels were declining. While this small response to alcohol in people who later became abusers may at first seem puzzling, it fits with the idea that you have to drink a lot to later become a problem drinker. During the period when blood alcohol levels are declining, alcohol acts as a depressant and often produces unpleasant emotions. Future alcohol abusers may, then, experience fewer of these punishing side-effects, setting the stage for heavier drinking. Furthermore, other research shows that sons of alcoholics experience more positive effects of alcohol on their mood when their blood alcohol levels are on the rise, making alcohol more positively reinforcing for them (Newlin & Thompson, 1990).

The principal psychological theory regarding alcohol abuse is that it is used to alter mood. Alcohol use might therefore be reinforcing, either by reducing negative emotions or by enhancing positive ones. Heavy alcohol use is then seen as a way of regulating mood and may reflect a failure of other means of coping with emotional states. Note that the theory is focusing on a variable that might lead someone to drink heavily but does not attempt to deal with questions concerning how heavy drinking might later lead to abuse or dependence. This tension-reduction idea does fit the clinical information we presented on Barry. He began heavy drinking when faced with major disappointments in life.

Much of the work in this area has focused on the tension-reducing properties of alcohol. Alcohol use does seem to be related to other negative moods such as sadness and hostility, but there are fewer data on them (Hussong et al., 2000). Early animal experiments showed that alcohol impaired avoidance learning, presumably because it made the animals less fearful of shock (Conger, 1951). Later laboratory research with humans also demonstrated that alcohol reduced tension among people who were not heavy drinkers (e.g., Sher & Levenson, 1982). Similarly, research in which people recorded their moods and drinking on a daily basis has shown that nervousness predicts increased use of alcohol (Swendsen et al., 2000).

Some inconsistent results also emerged in this literature. Both laboratory and naturalistic studies have sometimes found no tension-reducing effect of alcohol (e.g., Thyer & Curtis, 1984). In attempting to account for these discrepancies, subsequent research examined alcohol's tension-reducing effects more closely. One variable to emerge is the situation in which alcohol is consumed.

Alcohol may produce its tension-reducing effects by altering cognition and perception. Alcohol impairs cognitive processing and narrows attention to immediately available cues, resulting in what Steele and Josephs (1988) call alcohol myopia—the intoxicated person has less cognitive processing capacity to distribute between ongoing activity and worry. If a distracting activity is available, the intoxicated person will focus on it instead of worrying about whatever stress he or she is trying to deal with. But alcohol can also increase negative moods if no distractors are present; in this case, the intoxicated person focuses his or her limited cognitive capacity only on the unpleasant source of worry and feels even worse.

Another approach to the inconsistent findings has been to propose that the tension-reducing effects of alcohol are found only among some people. The relationship between alcohol use and negative moods has been found to be stronger among males, people who lack alternative ways of coping with stress, and those who expect alcohol to alleviate their negative moods (Cooper et al., 1995; Kusher, Abram, & Borechardt, 2000). Similarly, the relationship is stronger among people with less intimate and supportive social relationships (Hussong et al., 2001).

Treatment

Many people with drinking problems do not believe they have a problem and therefore are unwilling to enter treatment. Therefore, as with Barry, initial treatment efforts are often focused on motivating the person to change. Drawing on work by Miller and his colleagues (e.g., Miller et al., 1992), this is what Dr. Lawton tried to accomplish by having Grace point out the negative consequences of Barry's drinking and later drawing up a list of the negative consequences of drinking during treatment. As recommended by the Sobells (Sobell & Sobell, 1976), providing Barry with feedback about how far his drinking departed from national norms was also part of this process.

Once the person has decided to enter treatment, many options are available. Public and private hospitals provide detoxification, supervised withdrawal from alcohol, and a variety of group and individual therapies. In general, however, hospital treatment does not appear to be superior to outpatient therapy, except for people with few sources of social support and other psychological problems (Finney & Moos, 1998; Holder et al., 1991).

Self help groups figure prominently in treatment. The best known of these is Alcoholics Anonymous. An AA chapter runs regular meetings at which new members rise to announce they are alcoholics, and older members relate stories about their problem drinking and how their lives have improved since giving up alcohol. The group provides emotional support, understanding, and a social life to relieve isolation. There is a heavy religious emphasis; one of the 12 steps is: "Make a decision to turn our will and our lives over to the care of God, as we understood him." Members are encouraged to call on one another when they need companionship or encouragement not to relapse. AA promotes the idea that alcoholism is a disease that never can be cured. Complete abstinence is necessary because it is believed that a single drink can trigger a complete relapse. Evidence shows that AA can be an effective treatment (Emrick et al., 1993; Ouimette, Finney, & Moos, 1997). However, the dropout rates are high.

After his treatment with Dr. Lawton, Barry was encouraged to join a local group that had many features of AA but without the religious overtones and without the emphasis on abstinence. Many similar groups (such as Rational Recovery) now exist throughout the country.

The treatment Barry received drew on the work of the Sobells (1976). The Sobells initiated moderate drinking as a treatment goal and demonstrated the effectiveness of such an approach. The Sobells teach patients to respond adaptively to situations in which they might otherwise drink excessively. Social skills, relaxation, and assertiveness training (especially regarding how to refuse a drink) can be parts of the treatment. Feedback is also provided about the drinking patterns of others—alcoholics often overestimate how much others drink—and the negative aspects of drinking are made salient. Other strategies include increasing exercise, reducing the presence of cues for drinking (for example, taking a new route home that does go by a bar), sipping rather than gulping drinks, and not imposing a delay between drinks. Relapse prevention, pioneered by Marlatt (1985), is also part of the package. As was done with Barry, a distinction is drawn between a lapse and a relapse. Patients are encouraged to believe that a lapse does not signal a total relapse. A lapse should be regarded as a learning experience, not as a sign that the battle has been lost.

This case did not have a happy ending. Barry's fatal heart attack was probably related to his high blood pressure, which was worsened by his chronic alcohol abuse. Stress also plays a role in raising blood pressure, and Barry certainly experienced a lot of it, related both to his job and his marriage.

13 Personality Disorders

Mary was twenty-six years old at the time of her first admission to a psychiatric hospital. She had been in outpatient treatment with a psychologist for several months when her persistent thoughts of suicide and preoccupation with inflicting pain on herself (by cutting or burning) led her therapist to conclude that she could no longer be managed as an outpatient.

Mary's first experience with some form of psychological therapy occurred when she was an adolescent. Her grades had declined sharply in the eleventh grade, and her parents suspected she was using drugs. She began to miss curfews and even failed to come home at all on a few occasions. She was frequently truant. Family therapy was undertaken, and it seemed to go well at first. Mary was enthusiastic about her therapist and asked for additional, private sessions with him.

During the family sessions her parents' fears were confirmed as Mary revealed an extensive history of drug use, including "everything I can get my hands on." She had been promiscuous and had prostituted herself several times to get drug money. Her relationships with her peers were changeable, to say the least. The pattern was a constant parade of new friends, at first thought to be the greatest ever, but who soon disappointed Mary somehow and were cast aside, often in a very unpleasant way. Except for the one person with whom she was currently enamored, Mary had no friends. She reported that she stayed away from others for fear that they would harm her in some way.

After several weeks of therapy Mary's parents noticed that her relationship with the therapist had cooled appreciably. The sessions were marked by Mary's angry and abusive outbursts toward the therapist. After several more weeks had passed, Mary refused to attend any more sessions. In a subsequent conversation with the therapist, Mary's father learned that she had behaved seductively toward him during their private sessions and that her changed attitude coincided with the rejection of her advances, despite the therapist's attempt to mix firmness with warmth and empathy.

Mary managed to graduate from high school and enrolled in a local community college, but the old patterns returned. Poor grades, cutting classes, continuing drug use, and lack of interest in her studies finally led her to quit in the middle of the first semester of her second year. After leaving school Mary held a series of clerical jobs. Most of them didn't last long, as her relationships with co-workers paralleled her relationships with her peers in high school. When Mary started a new job she would find someone she really liked, but something would come between them and the relationship would end angrily. She was frequently suspicious of her co-workers and reported that she often heard them talking about her, plotting how to prevent her from getting ahead on the job. She was quick to find hidden meanings in their behavior, as when she interpreted being the last person asked to sign a birthday card to mean that she was the least liked person in the office. She indicated that she "received vibrations" from others and could tell when they really didn't like her even in the absence of any direct evidence.

Mary's behavior includes many characteristic symptoms of several personality disorders, in particular, borderline personality disorder. Her frequent mood swings, with periods of depression and extreme irritability, led her to seek therapy several times. But after initial enthusiasm, her relationship with her therapist always deteriorated, resulting in premature termination of therapy. The therapist she was seeing just before her hospitalization was her sixth.

Personality disorders are a heterogeneous group of disorders, coded on Axis II of the DSM and regarded as long-standing, pervasive, and inflexible patterns of behavior and inner experience that deviate from the expectations of a person's culture and that impair social and occupational functioning. Some, but not all, can cause emotional distress.

As we examine the personality disorders, some may seem to fit people we know, not to mention ourselves! This seems a good time to remind readers about the medical student syndrome, so called because medical students (and psychology students) have a tendency to see themselves or their families and friends in descriptions of disorders they study. However, although the symptoms of the personality disorders come close to describing characteristics that we all possess from time to time and in varying degrees, an actual personality disorder is defined by the *extremes* of several traits and by the rather inflexible and maladaptive way these traits are expressed.

The personality each of us develops over the years reflects a persistent means of dealing with life's challenges, a certain style of relating to other people. One person is overly dependent; another is challenging and aggressive; another is shy and avoids social contact; and still another is concerned more with appearance and bolstering his or her vulnerable ego than with relating honestly and on a deep level with others. These individuals would not be diagnosed as having personality disorders unless the patterns of behavior were long-standing, pervasive, and dysfunctional. For example, on entering a crowded room and shortly thereafter hearing a loud burst of laughter, you might feel that you are the target of some joke and that people are talking about you. Such concerns become symptoms of paranoid personality disorder only if they occur frequently and intensely and prevent the development of close personal relationships.

One final prefatory comment. In addition to being viewed as clinical syndromes in their own right, personality disorders are often comorbid with an Axis I disorder. Personality disorders can serve as a *context* for Axis I problems, shaping them in different ways (Millon, 1996). For example, a person diagnosed with an anxiety disorder on Axis I and obsessive-compulsive personality disorder on Axis II will express anxiety in ways such as perfectionism and indecision. An analogy might be viewing the same photograph through different-colored lenses or listening to the same song played on a piano versus hearing it performed by a full orchestra. As Millon put it,

> [Different personality disorders] will…evoke contrasting ways of perceiving and coping with [an individual's Axis I disorder]. For these and other reasons, we believe that clinicians should be oriented to the "context of personality" when they deal with…all forms of psychiatric [Axis I] disorders. (1996, p. vii)

In this chapter we look first at how personality disorders are classified in the DSM and then at the problems associated with classification. Then we turn to the personality disorders themselves, theory and research on their etiology, and therapies for dealing with them. The extent of our coverage of the specific personality disorders varies depending on how much is known about them; for example, there are very few empirical data about histrionic personality disorder but a vast literature on antisocial personality disorder.

Classifying Personality Disorders: Clusters, Categories, and Problems

The idea that personality can be disordered goes back at least to the time of Hippocrates and his humoral theory, which we discussed in Chapter 1. Personality disorders were listed in the early DSMs, but the diagnoses were very unreliable. As with other diagnoses, the publication of DSM-III began a trend toward improved reliability (Coolidge & Segal, 1998).

Beginning with DSM-III, personality disorders were placed on a separate axis, Axis II, to ensure that diagnosticians would pay attention to their possible presence. Although a diagnostic interview sometimes points directly to the presence of a personality disorder, more often a person arrives at a clinic with an Axis I disorder (such as panic disorder), which, quite naturally, is the primary focus of attention. Placing the personality disorders on Axis II is meant to guide the clinician to consider whether a personality disorder is also present.

As we have mentioned, diagnoses of personality disorders used to have little reliability. One clinician might diagnose a flamboyant patient as narcissistic whereas another might consider him or her psychopathic. These low reliabilities have been improved because of two developments.

1. The publication of specific diagnostic criteria in DSM-III and succeeding editions
2. The development of structured interviews specially designed for assessing personality disorders

Data now indicate that good reliability can be achieved, even across cultures (Loranger et al., 1987; Widiger et al., 1988). Interrater reliabilities from a recent study of the DSM-IV diagnostic criteria are presented in Table 13.1 (Zanarini et al., 2000a); the figures compare favorably with reliability figures for Axis I disorders (Chapter 3, p. 77). Thus, by using structured interviews, reliable diagnoses of personality disorders can be achieved. Interviews with people who know the patient well are sometimes part of the diagnostic workup and improve the accuracy of diagnosis (Bernstein et al., 1997).

Because personality disorders are defined as being more stable over time than some episodic Axis I disorders (e.g., depression), test-retest reliability—a comparison of whether patients receive the same diagnosis when they are assessed twice with some time interval separating the two assessments—is also an important factor in their evaluation. A summary of test-retest reliability is also given in Table 13.1 (Zimmerman, 1994). Note the wide variability of the figures. Antisocial personality disorder has a high test-retest reliability, indicating that it is a stable diagnosis—a patient given the diagnosis at one time is very likely to receive the same diagnosis when evaluated later. The figures for schizotypal and dependent personality disorders, on the other hand, are very low, indicating that the symptoms of people with these latter two diagnoses are not stable over time. Thus it appears that many of the personality disorders are not as enduring as the DSM asserts.

Another major problem with the category of personality disorders is comorbidity with both Axis I disorders and with other personality disorders. It is often difficult to diagnose a single, specific personality disorder because many disordered people exhibit a wide range of traits that make several diagnoses applicable. In the case opening this chapter, Mary met the diagnostic criteria not only for borderline personality disorder but also for paranoid personality disorder, and she came close to meeting the criteria for schizotypal disorder as well. (Descriptions of the diagnostic criteria for these disorders are found below.) One study found that 55 percent of patients with borderline personality disorder also met the diag-

Table 13.1 Interrater and Test-Retest Reliability for the Personality Disorders

Diagnosis	Interrater Reliability	Test-Retest Reliability
Paranoid	.86	.57
Schizoid	.69	—
Schizotypal	.91	.11
Borderline	.90	.56
Histrionic	.83	.40
Narcissistic	.88	.32
Antisocial	.97	.84
Dependent	.87	.15
Avoidant	.79	.41
Obsessive-compulsive	.85	.52

Source: Figures for interrater reliability are from the Zanarini et al. (2000) study and reflect the amount of agreement above chance. Test-retest figures are rates of agreement from Zimmerman's (1994) summary of longer (generally more than a year) studies.

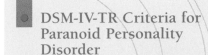

nostic criteria for schizotypal personality disorder, 47 percent for antisocial personality disorder, and 57 percent for histrionic personality disorder (Widiger, Frances, & Trull, 1987). Such data are particularly discouraging when we try to interpret the results of research that compares patients who have a specific personality disorder with some control group. If, for example, we find that people with borderline disorder differ from normal people, is what we have learned specific to borderline personality disorder or related to personality disorders in general or perhaps even applicable to an Axis I diagnosis?

Although some decrease in comorbidity occurred with the publication of DSM-IV (Blais, Hilsenroth, & Castlebury, 1997), the data still suggest that the categorical diagnostic system of the DSM may not be ideal for classifying personality disorders. The personality traits that constitute the data for classification form a continuum; that is, most of the relevant characteristics are present in varying degrees in most people. When people with a personality disorder take a general personality inventory, what is revealed is a personality with a structure similar to that of normal people, but more extreme (Livesley & Schroeder, 1993). Thus, the personality disorders can be construed as the extremes of characteristics we all possess. A dimensional approach to classification of personality disorders (see Chapter 3, p. 74), then, may be more appropriate. A dimensional system was in fact considered for inclusion in both DSM-III-R and DSM-IV, but consensus could not be reached on which dimensions to include. An effort to develop a dimensional classification system is described later (Focus on Discovery 13.1, p. 426).

Despite problems with the diagnosis of personality disorders, we should not dismiss the utility of trying to make such diagnoses. These disorders are prevalent, and they cause severe impairment in peoples' lives. Some of the problems with diagnosis stem from the fact that the personality disorders have been the subject of serious research for a much shorter time than have most of the other diagnoses considered in this book. As research continues, the diagnostic categories will most likely be refined, perhaps with a dimensional system, and many of these problems may be solved.

Personality disorders are grouped into three clusters in DSM-IV-TR:

1. Individuals in cluster A (paranoid, schizoid, and schizotypal) are odd or eccentric
2. Those in cluster B (antisocial, borderline, histrionic, and narcissistic) are dramatic, emotional, or erratic
3. Those in cluster C (avoidant, dependent, and obsessive-compulsive) are anxious or fearful

Although the empirical evidence on the validity of these clusters is mixed, they form a useful organizational framework for this chapter.

Odd/Eccentric Cluster

The odd/eccentric cluster comprises three diagnoses—paranoid, schizoid, and schizotypal personality disorders. The symptoms of these disorders bear some similarity to the symptoms of schizophrenia, especially to the less severe symptoms of its prodromal and residual phases.

Paranoid Personality Disorder

The individual with **paranoid personality** disorder is suspicious of others. People with this diagnosis expect to be mistreated or exploited by others and thus are secretive and continually on the lookout for possible signs of trickery and abuse. They are often hostile and react angrily to perceived insults. Such individuals are reluctant to confide in others and tend to blame them and hold grudges even when they themselves are at fault. They are extremely jealous and may unjustifiably question the fidelity of a spouse or lover.

Patients with paranoid personality disorder are preoccupied with unjustified doubts about the loyalty or trustworthiness of others. They may read hidden negative or threat-

DSM-IV-TR Criteria for Paranoid Personality Disorder

Presence of four or more of the following and not occurring exclusively during a course of schizophrenia, psychotic depression, or as part of a pervasive developmental disorder; also not due to a general medical condition:

- Pervasive suspiciousness of being harmed, deceived, or exploited
- Unwarranted doubts about the loyalty or trustworthiness of friends or associates
- Reluctance to confide in others because of preceding criterion
- Hidden meanings read into the innocuous actions of others
- Grudges for perceived wrongs
- Angry reactions to perceived attacks on character or reputation
- Akin to first two criteria, unwarranted suspiciousness of the fidelity of spouse or other sexual partner

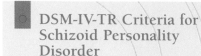

DSM-IV-TR Criteria for Schizoid Personality Disorder

Presence of four or more of the following and not occurring exclusively during a course of schizophrenia, psychotic depression, or as part of a pervasive developmental disorder; also not due to a general medical condition:

- Lack of desire or enjoyment of close relationships
- Almost exclusive preference for solitude
- Little interest in sex with others
- Few if any pleasures
- Lack of friends
- Indifference to praise or criticism from others
- Flat affect, emotional detachment

DSM-IV-TR Criteria for Schizotypal Personality Disorder

Presence of five or more of the following and not occurring exclusively during a course of schizophrenia, psychotic depression, or as part of a pervasive developmental disorder:

- Ideas of reference
- Peculiar beliefs or magical thinking, e.g., belief in extrasensory perception
- Unusual perceptions, e.g., distorted beliefs about one's body
- Peculiar patterns of speech
- Extreme suspiciousness, paranoia
- Inappropriate affect
- Odd behavior or appearance
- Lack of close friends
- Extreme discomfort and sometimes extreme anxiety around other people

ening messages into events; for example, the individual may believe that a neighbor's dog deliberately barks in the early morning to disturb him or her. This diagnosis is different from schizophrenia, paranoid type, because other symptoms of schizophrenia, such as hallucinations, are not present and there is less impairment in social and occupational functioning. Also absent is the cognitive disorganization that is characteristic of schizophrenia. It differs from delusional disorder because full-blown delusions are not present.

Paranoid personality disorder occurs most frequently in men and co-occurs most frequently with schizotypal, borderline, and avoidant personality disorders (Bernstein, 1993; Morey, 1988). Its prevalence is about 2 percent (Torgersen, Kringlen, & Cramer, 2001).

Schizoid Personality Disorder

Patients with **schizoid personality** disorder do not desire or enjoy social relationships and usually have no close friends. They appear dull, bland, and aloof and have no warm, tender feelings for other people. They rarely report strong emotions, are not interested in sex, and experience few pleasurable activities. Indifferent to praise, criticism, and the sentiments of others, individuals with this disorder are loners and pursue solitary interests. The prevalence of schizoid personality disorder is reported to be less than 2 percent. It is slightly less common among women than among men (Torgersen, Kringlen, & Cramer, 2001).

Comorbidity is highest for schizotypal, avoidant, and paranoid personality disorders, most likely because of the similar diagnostic criteria in the four categories. The diagnostic criteria for schizoid personality disorder are also similar to some of the symptoms of the prodromal (prior to illness) and residual (following the illness) phases of schizophrenia.

Schizotypal Personality Disorder

The concept of the **schizotypal personality** grew out of Danish studies of the adopted children of schizophrenic parents (Kety et al., 1968). Although some of these children developed full-blown schizophrenia as adults, an even larger number developed what seemed to be an attenuated form of schizophrenia. The diagnostic criteria for schizotypal personality disorder were devised by Spitzer, Endicott, and Gibbon (1979) to describe these individuals. These criteria were incorporated in DSM-III and were narrowed somewhat in DSM-III-R and DSM-IV-TR.

Patients with schizotypal personality disorder usually have the interpersonal difficulties of the schizoid personality and excessive social anxiety that do not diminish as they get to know others. Several additional, more eccentric symptoms occur in schizotypal personality disorder. These symptoms are essentially those that define the prodromal and residual phases of schizophrenia.

Patients with schizotypal personality disorder may have odd beliefs or magical thinking—superstitiousness, beliefs that they are clairvoyant and telepathic—and recurrent illusions—they may sense the presence of a force or a person not actually there. In their speech, they may use words in an unusual and unclear fashion, for example, "not a very talkable person." Their behavior and appearance may also be eccentric; they may talk to themselves or wear dirty and disheveled clothing, for example. Also common are ideas of reference (the belief that events have a particular and unusual meaning for the person), suspiciousness, and paranoid ideation. Affect appears to be constricted and flat. In a study of the relative importance of these symptoms for diagnosis, Widiger et al. (1987) found that paranoid ideation, ideas of reference, and illusions were most telling. The prevalence of schizotypal personality disorder is estimated at less than 1 percent (Torgersen, Kringlen, & Cramer, 2001).

A significant problem in the diagnosis of schizotypal personality disorder is its comorbidity with other personality disorders. Morey (1988) found that 33 percent of people diagnosed with schizotypal personality according to DSM-III-R criteria also met the diagnostic criteria for borderline personality disorder, 33 percent for narcissistic personality disorder, 59 percent for avoidant personality disorder, 59 percent for paranoid personality disorder, and 44 percent for schizoid personality disorder. Clearly these comorbidity figures are unsatisfactory if we want to consider schizotypal personality disorder a discrete diagnostic entity.

Etiology of the Odd/Eccentric Cluster

What causes the odd, sometimes paranoid thinking, bizarre behavior, and interpersonal difficulties that appear in this cluster of personality disorders? The search for causes has been guided by the idea that these disorders are genetically linked to schizophrenia, perhaps as less severe variants of this Axis I disorder. The evidence for this idea varies depending on which of the odd/eccentric disorders is considered.

- Family studies have consistently shown that the relatives of patients with schizophrenia are at increased risk for schizotypal personality disorder (Nigg & Goldsmith, 1994). However, increased rates of schizotypal personality disorder have also been found in the first-degree relatives of patients with unipolar depression, suggesting that schizotypal personality disorder is not related just to schizophrenia (Squires-Wheeler et al., 1993).

- Family studies of paranoid personality disorder for the most part find higher than average rates in the relatives of patients with schizophrenia or delusional disorder (Bernstein, Useda, & Siever, 1993).

- No clear pattern has emerged from behavior-genetic research on schizoid personality disorder, although a family study found that the prevalence of schizoid personality disorder was elevated among the relatives of people with schizotypal personality disorder (Battaglia et al., 1995).

Thus, family studies provide at least some evidence that personality disorders of the odd/eccentric cluster are related to schizophrenia. For schizotypal personality disorder there is also further evidence on this point. Such patients have deficits in cognitive and neuropsychological functioning that are similar to those seen in schizophrenia (Cadenhead et al., 1999; Chen et al., 1998; Roitman et al., 2000). Furthermore, and again paralleling findings from schizophrenia research, patients with schizotypal personality disorder have enlarged ventricles and less temporal lobe gray matter (Dickey et al., 1999; Downhill et al., 2001).

Dramatic/Erratic Cluster

The diagnoses in the dramatic/erratic cluster—borderline, histrionic, narcissistic, and antisocial personality disorders—include patients with a wide variety of symptoms, ranging from highly variable behavior to inflated self-esteem, exaggerated emotional displays, and antisocial behavior.

Borderline Personality Disorder

Borderline personality disorder (BPD) was adopted by the DSM as an official diagnosis in 1980. The core features of this disorder are impulsivity and instability in relationships and mood (Sanislow, Grilo, & McGlashan, 2000). For example, attitudes and feelings toward other people may vary considerably and inexplicably over short periods of time. Emotions are erratic and can shift abruptly, particularly from passionate idealization to contemptuous anger. Patients with borderline personality disorder are argumentative, irritable, sarcastic, quick to take offense, and altogether very hard to live with. Their unpredictable and impulsive behavior, which may include gambling, spending, indiscriminate sexual activity, substance abuse, and eating sprees, is potentially self-damaging.

These individuals have not developed a clear and coherent sense of self and remain uncertain about their values, loyalties, and career choices. They cannot bear to be alone, have fears of abandonment, and demand attention. Subject to chronic feelings of depres-

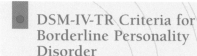

DSM-IV-TR Criteria for Borderline Personality Disorder

Presence of five or more of the following:

- Frantic efforts to avoid abandonment, both real and imagined
- Instability and extreme intensity in interpersonal relationships, marked by splitting, that is, idealizing others in one moment and reviling them the next
- Unstable sense of self
- Impulsive behavior, including reckless spending and sexual promiscuity
- Recurrent suicidal (gestures as well as genuine attempts) and self-mutilating behavior
- Extreme emotional lability
- Chronic feelings of emptiness
- Extreme problems controlling anger
- Paranoid thinking and dissociative symptoms triggered by stress

sion and emptiness, they often attempt suicide and engage in self-mutilating behavior, such as slicing into their legs with a razor blade. Transient psychotic and dissociative symptoms may appear during periods of high stress.[1]

Clinicians and researchers have used the term borderline personality for some time, but they have given it many meanings. Originally the term implied that the patient was on the borderline between neurosis and schizophrenia. The DSM concept of borderline personality no longer has this connotation. The current conceptualization of borderline personality derives from two main sources. After reviewing the available research literature and interview studies of individuals diagnosed as borderline personalities, Gunderson, Kolb, and Austin (1981) proposed a set of specific diagnostic criteria similar to those that ultimately appeared in DSM-III. The second source of the diagnostic criteria was a study of the relatives of patients with schizophrenia done by Spitzer et al. (1979). As discussed earlier, some of these relatives had schizotypal personality disorder. But Spitzer et al. also identified another syndrome in the relatives, and the characteristics of this syndrome came to identify borderline personality disorder.

Borderline personality disorder typically begins in adolescence or early adulthood, has a prevalence of about 1 percent, and is more common in women than in men (Swartz et al., 1990; Torgersen, Kringlen, & Cramer, 2001). Prognosis is not favorable: in a seven-year follow-up, about 50 percent of a sample still had the disorder (Links, Heslegraves, & van Reeken, 1998). Borderline patients are likely to have an Axis I mood disorder (Zanarini et al., 1998), and their parents are more likely than average to have mood disorders (Shachnow et al., 1997). Comorbidity is also found with substance abuse, PTSD, and eating disorders, as well as with personality disorders from the odd/eccentric cluster (Skodol, Oldham, & Gallaher, 1999; Trull et al., 2000; Zanarini et al., 1998).

A good sense of this disorder can be obtained from a colorful account written by Jonathan Kellerman, a clinical psychologist turned successful mystery writer.

> The borderline patient is a therapist's nightmare…because borderlines never really get better. The best you can do is help them coast, without getting sucked into their pathology…. They're the chronically depressed, the determinedly addictive, the compulsively divorced, living from one emotional disaster to the next. Bed hoppers, stomach pumpers, freeway jumpers, and sad-eyed bench-sitters with arms stitched up like footballs and psychic wounds that can never be sutured. Their egos are as fragile as spun sugar, their psyches irretrievably fragmented, like a jigsaw puzzle with crucial pieces missing. They play roles with alacrity, excel at being anyone but themselves, crave intimacy but repel it when they find it. Some of them gravitate toward stage or screen; others do their acting in more subtle ways….
>
> Borderlines go from therapist to therapist, hoping to find a magic bullet for the crushing feelings of emptiness. They turn to chemical bullets, gobble tranquilizers and antidepressants, alcohol and cocaine. Embrace gurus and heaven-hucksters, any charismatic creep promising a quick fix of the pain. And they end up taking temporary vacations in psychiatric wards and prison cells, emerge looking good, raising everyone's hopes. Until the next letdown, real or imagined, the next excursion into self damage.
>
> What they don't do is change. (Kellerman, 1989, pp. 113–114)[2]

Etiology of Borderline Personality Disorder There are several views concerning the causes of borderline personality disorder. We discuss biological research, object-relations theory, and Linehan's diathesis–stress theory.

Biological Factors Borderline personality disorder runs in families, suggesting that it may have a genetic component (Baron et al., 1985). Borderline patients are also high in neuroticism, a trait known to be heritable (Nigg & Goldsmith, 1994).

---

[1] Patients with both borderline and schizotypal personality disorders would probably have been diagnosed as schizophrenic using DSM-II criteria. Designating the behavior of these people as the criteria for these two personality disorders is one way in which DSM-III-R and DSM-IV narrowed the schizophrenia diagnosis (see Chapter 11).

[2] Fortunately Linehan's research on new treatments for BPD, reviewed below (p. 429), indicate a more positive outlook than expressed here by Kellerman.

Some data suggest impaired frontal lobe functioning, which is often thought to play a role in impulsive behavior. For example, patients with borderline personality disorder perform poorly on neurological tests of frontal-lobe functioning, and they show low levels of glucose metabolism in the frontal lobes (Goyer et al., 1994). In a similar vein, patients with borderline personality disorder show increased activation of the amygdala, a brain structure regarded as very important in regulating emotion (Herpetz et al., 2001a). The increased activation of the amygdala may well be relevant to the intense emotions seen in borderline patients.

Consistent with the idea that low levels of the neurotransmitter serotonin are associated with impulsivity, when borderline patients were administered a drug to activate serotonin systems in the brain, they showed a smaller response than controls (Soloff et al., 2000). This may indicate that the serotonin system is difficult to activate in borderline patients. Thus biological research on borderline personality disorder has yielded some promising leads concerning their impulsive behavior.

Object-Relations Theory Object-relations theory, an important variant of psychoanalytic theory, is concerned with the way children incorporate (or introject) the values and images of important people, such as their parents. In other words, the focus is on the manner in which children identify with people to whom they have strong emotional attachments. These introjected people (object representations) become part of the person's ego, but they can come into conflict with the wishes, goals, and ideals of the developing adult—for example, when a college-age woman who has adopted her mother's notion of the proper role of a woman in society finds herself drawn to the more modern ideals of feminism.

Object-relations theorists hypothesize that people react to their world through the perspectives of important people from their past, primarily their parents or primary caregivers. Sometimes these perspectives conflict with the person's own wishes and interests. The leading object-relations theorist is Otto Kernberg, who has written extensively about borderline personality.

Kernberg (1985) proposes that adverse childhood experiences—for example, having parents who provide love and attention inconsistently, perhaps praising achievements but unable to offer emotional support and warmth—cause children to develop insecure egos, a major feature of borderline personality disorder.

Although people with borderline personality disorder have weak egos and need constant reassuring, they retain the capacity to test reality. However, while these patients are in touch with reality, they frequently engage in a defense mechanism called splitting—dichotomizing objects into all good or all bad and failing to integrate positive and negative aspects of another person or the self into a whole. This tendency causes extreme difficulty in regulating emotions because the borderline patient sees the world, including himself or herself, in black-and-white terms. Somehow this defense protects the patient's weak ego from intolerable anxiety.

A number of studies have yielded data relevant to Kernberg's theory. As expected, patients with borderline personality disorder report a low level of care by their mothers (Zanarini et al., 2000b). They view their families as emotionally unexpressive, low in cohesion, and high in conflict. They also frequently report childhood sexual and physical abuse (Zanarini et al., 1997), which has been verified in some studies (Johnson et al., 1999), and have often experienced separation from parents during childhood (Reich & Zanarini, 2001).

What is less clear about these data is whether these experiences are specific to borderline personality disorder. For example, it has been found that low levels of family support and high levels of conflict are reported by personality disordered patients in general (Klonsky et al., 2000). Similarly, experiencing verbal abuse during childhood is associated with borderline, narcissistic, paranoid, and obsessive-compulsive personality disorders (Johnson et al., 2001). Some research has, however, differentiated patients with borderline personality disorder from patients with other Axis II disorders. For example, patients with borderline personality disorder have reported more difficulty with separation and verbal and emotional abuse than other Axis II patients (Reich & Zanarini, 2001;

Otto Kernberg, one of the leading object-relations theorists, has been very influential in the study of borderline personality disorder.

Zanarini et al., 2000b). In summary, it is clear that patients with borderline personality disorder report having had adverse experiences during childhood, but it is not yet clear whether any of these experiences are specific to them.

Linehan's Diathesis–Stress Theory   Linehan proposes that borderline personality disorder develops when people with a biological diathesis (possibly genetic) of difficulty controlling their emotions are raised in a family environment that is invalidating. That is, a diathesis for what she calls emotional dysregulation can interact with experiences that invalidate the developing child—leading to the development of borderline personality.

An invalidating environment is one in which the person's wants and feelings are discounted and disrespected; efforts to communicate one's feelings are disregarded or even punished. An extreme form of invalidation is child abuse, sexual and nonsexual: Daddy says he loves me and yet he is hurting me and threatening to hurt me even more if I tell. A recent example of our own—somewhat humorous if looked at a certain way—illustrates invalidation between a husband and a wife.

> **Wife:** Honey, could you help me with something for a minute?
> **Husband:** Sure, but I have to go to the bathroom first.
> **Wife:** No, you don't.

The two main hypothesized factors—dysregulation and invalidation—interact with each other in a dynamic fashion (see Figure 13.1). For example, the emotionally dysregulated child makes enormous demands on his or her family. The exasperated parents ignore or even punish the child's outbursts. This response can lead to the youngster's suppressing his or her emotions, only to have them build up to an explosion, which then gets the attention of the parents. The result is that the parents can end up reinforcing the very behaviors that they find aversive. Many other patterns are possible, of course, but what they have in common is a constant back-and-forth, a vicious circle, between the diathesis of dysregulation and the stress of invalidation.

A key piece of evidence concerning Linehan's theory concerns childhood physical and sexual abuse. Such abuse is believed to be more frequent among people with borderline personality disorder than among people diagnosed with most other disorders (Herman et al., 1989; Wagner, Linehan, & Wasson, 1989), though not all the evidence supports this belief (Paris, 2000). One exception to the possibility that abuse in childhood is associated more with BPD than other disorders is to be found in dissociative identity disorder, in which we also find very high rates of childhood abuse. Given the frequency of dissociative symptoms in borderline personality, we can speculate that the two disorders may be related and that dissociation in both disorders is caused by the extreme stress of child abuse. Indeed, a recent study found that the relationship between child abuse and borderline symptoms was mediated by a tendency to engage in dissociation (Ross et al., 1998).

As Linehan herself has cautioned, most aspects of her theory of etiology remain to be investigated. For example, self-reports by borderline patients that they suffered invalidating experiences as children are subject to the same kinds of questions as any retrospective self-report from a patient in therapy. Considering how sensitive such patients are to invalidating experiences as adults, it is conceivable that their recollections of such past events are colored by their current psychological turmoil.

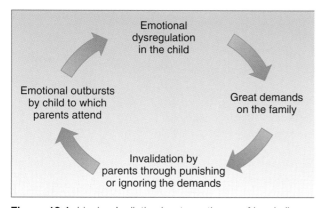

Figure 13.1 Linehan's diathesis–stress theory of borderline personality disorder.

Histrionic Personality Disorder

The diagnosis of **histrionic personality**, formerly called hysterical personality, is applied to people who are overly dramatic and attention seeking. They often use features of their physical appearance, such as unusual clothes, makeup, or hair color, to draw attention to themselves. These individuals, although displaying emotion extravagantly, are thought to be emotionally shallow. They are self-centered, overly concerned with their physical attractiveness, and uncomfortable when not the center of attention. They can be inappropriately sexually provocative and seductive and are easily influenced by others. Their speech is often impressionistic and lacking in detail. For example, they may state a strong opinion yet be unable to give any supporting information.

This diagnosis has a prevalence of about 2 percent and is more common among women than among men (Torgersen, Kringlen, & Cramer, 2001). Histrionic personality disorder is more prevalent among separated and divorced people, and it is associated with depression and poor physical health (Nestadt et al., 1990). Comorbidity with borderline personality disorder is high.

Etiology of Histrionic Personality Disorder   Little research has been conducted on histrionic personality disorder. Psychoanalytic theory predominates and proposes that emotionality and seductiveness were encouraged by parental seductiveness, especially father to daughter. Patients with this disorder are thought to have been raised in a family environment in which parents talked about sex as something dirty yet behaved as though it was exciting and desirable. This upbringing may explain the preoccupation with sex, coupled with a fear of actually behaving sexually. The exaggerated displays of emotion on the part of histrionic persons are seen as symptoms of such underlying conflicts, and their need to be the center of attention is seen as a way of defending against their true feelings of low self-esteem (Apt & Hurlbert, 1994; Stone, 1993).

Narcissistic Personality Disorder

People with a **narcissistic personality** disorder have a grandiose view of their own uniqueness and abilities; they are preoccupied with fantasies of great success. To say that they are self-centered is an understatement. They require almost constant attention and excessive admiration and believe they can be understood only by special or high-status people. Their interpersonal relationships are disturbed by their lack of empathy, by feelings of envy and arrogance, and by taking advantage of others as well as by their feelings of entitlement—they expect others to do special, not-to-be-reciprocated favors for them. Constantly seeking attention and adulation, narcissistic personalities are extremely sensitive to criticism and deeply fearful of failure. Sometimes they seek out others whom they can idealize because they are disappointed in themselves, but they generally do not allow anyone to be genuinely close to them. Their personal relationships are few and shallow; when people inevitably fall short of their unrealistic expectations, people with narcissistic personality disorder (like those with borderline personality disorder) become angry and rejecting. The inner lives of these people are similarly impoverished because, despite their self-aggrandizement, they actually think very little of themselves. Most of these characteristics, with the exception of lack of empathy and extreme reactions to criticism, have been validated in empirical studies as aspects of narcissistic personality disorder (Ronningstan & Gunderson, 1990). The prevalence of this disorder is less than 1 percent. It most often co-occurs with borderline personality disorder (Morey, 1988).

Etiology of Narcissistic Personality Disorder   The diagnosis of narcissistic personality disorder is rooted in modern psychoanalytic writings. Many psychoanalytically oriented clinicians have regarded it as a product of our times and our system of values. On the surface the person with this disorder has a remarkable sense of self-importance, complete self-absorption, and fantasies of limitless success, but, it is theorized, these characteristics mask a very fragile self-esteem.

At the center of contemporary interest in narcissism is Heinz Kohut, whose two books, *The Analysis of the Self* (1971) and *The Restoration of the Self* (1977), have established a variant of psychoanalysis known as self-psychology. According to Kohut, the self emerges early in life as a bipolar structure with an immature grandiosity at one pole and a dependent overidealization of other people at the other. A failure to develop healthy

---

DSM-IV-TR Criteria for Histrionic Personality Disorder

Presence of five or more of the following

- Strong need to be the center of attention
- Inappropriately sexually seductive behavior
- Rapidly shifting expression of emotions
- Use of physical appearance to draw attention to self
- Speech excessively impressionistic, passionately held opinions lacking in detail
- Exaggerated, theatrical emotional expression
- Overly suggestible
- Misreads relationships as being more intimate than they actually are

DSM-IV-TR Criteria for Narcissistic Personality Disorder

Presence of five or more of the following:

- Grandiose view of one's importance, arrogance
- Preoccupation with one's success, brilliance, beauty
- Extreme need for admiration
- Strong sense of entitlement
- Tendency to exploit others
- Envy of others

Narcissistic personality disorder draws its name from Narcissus of Greek mythology. He fell in love with his own reflection, was consumed by his own desire, and was transformed into a flower.

self-esteem occurs when parents do not respond with approval to their children's displays of competency; that is, the child is not valued for his or her own self-worth but is valued as a means to foster the parents' self-esteem.

When parents respond to a child with respect, warmth, and empathy, they endow the youngster with a normal sense of self-worth, a healthy self-esteem. But when parents further their own needs rather than directly approve of their children, the result, according to Kohut, may be a narcissistic personality.

> A little girl comes home from school, eager to tell her mother about some great successes. But this mother, instead of listening with pride, deflects the conversation from the child to herself [and] begins to talk about her own successes which overshadow those of her little daughter. (Kohut & Wolf, 1978, p. 418)

Children neglected in this way do not develop an internalized, healthy self-esteem and have trouble accepting their own shortcomings. They develop into narcissistic personalities, striving to bolster their sense of self through unending quests for love and approval from others.

Antisocial Personality Disorder and Psychopathy

In current usage the terms antisocial personality disorder and psychopathy (sometimes referred to as sociopathy) are often used interchangeably. Antisocial behavior, such as breaking laws, is an important component of both terms. There are important differences between the two, however.

Characteristics of Antisocial Personality Disorder   The DSM-IV-TR concept of **antisocial personality** disorder (APD) involves two major components.

1. The presence of a conduct disorder (described in Chapter 15) before the age of fifteen. Truancy, running away from home, frequent lying, theft, arson, and deliberate destruction of property are major symptoms of conduct disorder.
2. The continuation of this pattern of antisocial behavior in adulthood.

Thus, the DSM diagnosis involves not only certain patterns of antisocial behavior but patterns that began in childhood. Upwards of 60 percent of children with conduct disorder later develop antisocial personality disorder (Myers, Stewart, & Brown, 1998). Research shows, however, that there are few differences between those who meet the adult criteria for APD and were conduct disordered in childhood and those who meet the adult criteria but did not have conduct disorder (Langbehn & Cadoret, 2001). Requiring that APD begin in childhood may not, therefore, be a justifiable part of the DSM diagnosis.

The adult with antisocial personality disorder shows irresponsible and antisocial behavior by working only inconsistently, breaking laws, being irritable and physically aggressive, defaulting on debts, and being reckless. He or she is impulsive and fails to plan ahead. Like patients with narcissistic personality disorder, those with APD show little regard for truth and may experience little remorse for their misdeeds.

It is estimated that about 3 percent of adult American men and 1 percent of women in the United States are antisocial personalities (Robins et al., 1984). Rates are much higher among younger than among older adults, and the disorder is more common among people of low socioeconomic status. Antisocial personality disorder is comorbid with a number of other diagnoses, most notably substance abuse.

Characteristics of Psychopathy   The concept of **psychopathy** is closely linked to the writings of Hervey Cleckley and his classic book *The Mask of Sanity* (1976). On the basis of his vast clinical experience Cleckley formulated a set of criteria by which to recognize the disorder. Unlike the DSM criteria for antisocial personality disorder, Cleckley's criteria for psychopathy refer less to antisocial behavior per se and more to the psychopathic individual's thoughts and feelings.

DSM-IV-TR Criteria for Antisocial Personality Disorder

Pervasive pattern of disregard for the rights of others since the age of 15 and at least three of the characteristics 1 through 7 plus 8 through 10:

1. Repeated law-breaking
2. Deceitfulness, lying
3. Impulsivity
4. Irritableness and aggressiveness
5. Reckless disregard for own safety and that of others
6. Irresponsibility as seen in unreliable employment history or not meeting financial obligations
7. Lack of remorse
8. Age at least 18
9. Evidence of conduct disorder before the age of 15
10. Antisocial behavior not occurring exclusively during episodes of schizophrenia or mania

One of the key characteristics of psychopathy is poverty of emotions, both positive and negative. Psychopathic people have no sense of shame, and even their seemingly positive feelings for others are merely an act. The psychopath is superficially charming and manipulates others for personal gain. The lack of anxiety may make it impossible for psychopaths to learn from their mistakes, and the lack of positive emotions leads them to behave irresponsibly and often cruelly toward others. Another key point in Cleckley's description is that the antisocial behavior of the psychopath is performed impulsively, as much for thrills as for something like financial gain.

Most researchers diagnose psychopathy using a checklist developed by Hare and his associates (Hare et al., 1990). The checklist identifies two major clusters of psychopathic behaviors. The first, referred to as emotional detachment and similar to narcissistic personality disorder, describes a selfish, remorseless individual with inflated self-esteem who exploits others. The second characterizes an antisocial lifestyle marked by impulsivity and irresponsibility.[3] Based on the Hare checklist, psychopathy occurs more among men than among women (Salekin, Rogers, & Sewell, 1997). Among Axis I diagnoses, psychopathy is frequently comorbid with abuse of alcohol and other drugs (Smith & Newman, 1990).

A version of the Hare checklist has been developed for use with children, relying on ratings by mothers to make diagnoses (Lynam, 1997). This instrument has revealed that psychopathic children are similar to psychopathic adults—they are impulsive and severely delinquent and show little remorse for sometimes very cruel acts.

Controversies with Diagnoses of Antisocial Personality Disorder and Psychopathy   We have seen that these two diagnoses—antisocial personality disorder and psychopathy—are related, but they are by no means identical. A recent study found that only about 20 percent of people with antisocial personality disorder scored high on the Hare checklist (Rutherford, Cacciola, & Alterman, 1999). Several issues have been identified regarding which diagnosis is preferable.

Hare, Hart, and Harpur (1991) have criticized the DSM diagnosis of antisocial personality disorder because it requires accurate reports of events that took place many years earlier by people who are habitual liars (recall the onset-in-childhood criterion). Furthermore, many researchers believe that a diagnostic concept in the field of psychopathology should not be synonymous with criminality. But 75 to 80 percent of convicted felons meet the criteria for antisocial personality disorder. In contrast, only 15 to 25 percent of convicted felons meet the criteria for psychopathy (Hart & Hare, 1989). Moreover, lack of remorse, a hallmark of psychopathy, is but one of seven criteria for the DSM's antisocial personality diagnosis, and only three of these seven criteria need to be present to make the diagnosis. Therefore, the person diagnosed with APD by the DSM may not have the lack of remorse that is intrinsic to the concept of psychopathy.

As we review the research in this area, it is important to keep in mind that it has been conducted on individuals diagnosed in different ways—some as antisocial personalities and some as psychopaths—which makes integrating these findings somewhat difficult.

The Case of Dan   Before considering current research on psychopathy, we will examine an excerpt from a case history. This case history was compiled by a psychologist, Elton McNeil (1967), a personal friend of the subject's. This case illustrates the classic characteristics of the psychopath but is unusual in that the person described was neither a criminal nor in psychiatric treatment at the time the data for the study were collected. This is an important point, for the majority of psychopaths who are the subjects of research studies have broken the law and been caught for doing so. Only rarely do we have the opportunity to examine in detail the behavior of an individual who fits the diagnostic definition, yet has managed not to break the law or at least has not been convicted of a crime.

---

[3] Unfortunately, the Hare checklist does not include items to assess an absence of anxiety, a key feature of psychopathy according to Cleckley (Schmidt & Newman, 1999). Furthermore, some research indicates that the content of the checklist may be better summarized by three clusters than two. Essentially, the first cluster may be better divided into two—one dealing with interpersonal features and the other emotional ones (Cooke & Mitchie, 2001).

Dan was a wealthy actor and disc jockey who lived in an expensive house in an exclusive suburb and generally played his role as a "character" to the hilt. One evening, when he and McNeil were out for dinner, Dan made a great fuss over the condition of the shrimp de Johnge he had ordered. McNeil thought that Dan had deliberately contrived the whole scene for the effect it might produce, and he said to his companion:

"I have a sneaking suspicion this whole scene came about just because you weren't really hungry." Dan laughed loudly in agreement and said, "What the hell, they'll be on their toes next time." "Was that the only reason for this display?"

"No," he replied, "I wanted to show you how gutless the rest of the world is. If you shove a little they all jump. Next time I come in, they'll be all over me to make sure everything is exactly as I want it. That's the only way they can tell the difference between class and plain ordinary. When I travel I go first class."

"Yes, but how do you feel about you as a person— as a fellow human being?"

"Who cares?" he laughed. "If they were on top they would do the same to me. The more you walk on them, the more they like it. It's like royalty in the old days. It makes them nervous if everyone is equal to everyone else. Watch. When we leave I'll put my arm around that waitress, ask her if she still loves me, pat her on the fanny, and she'll be ready to roll over any time I wiggle my little finger." (McNeil, 1967, p. 85)

Another incident occurred when a friend of Dan's committed suicide. Most of the other friends whom Dan and McNeil had in common were concerned and called McNeil to see whether he could provide any information about why the man had taken his life. Dan did not. Later, when McNeil mentioned the suicide to Dan, all he could say was, "That's the way the ball bounces." In his public behavior, however, Dan's attitude toward the incident appeared quite different. He was the one who collected money and presented it personally to the widow. In keeping with his character, however, Dan remarked that the widow had a sexy body that really interested him.

These two incidents convey the flavor of Dan's behavior. McNeil had witnessed a long succession of similar events, which led him to conclude:

[The incidents] painted a grisly picture of lifelong abuse of people for Dan's amusement and profit. He was adept at office politics and told me casually of an unbelievable set of deceptive ways to deal with the opposition. Character assassination, rumor mongering, modest blackmail, seduction, and barefaced lying were the least of his talents. He was a jackal in the entertainment jungle, a jackal who feasted on the bodies of those he had slaughtered professionally. (p. 91)

In his conversations with Dan, McNeil was also able to inquire into Dan's life history. One early and potentially important event was related by Dan.

I can remember the first time in my life when I began to suspect I was a little different from most people. When I was in high school my best friend got leukemia and died and I went to his funeral. Everybody else was crying and feeling sorry for themselves and as they were praying to get him into heaven I suddenly realized that I wasn't feeling anything at all. He was a nice guy but what the hell. That night I thought about it some more and found that I wouldn't miss my mother and father if they died and that I wasn't too nuts about my brothers and sisters for that matter. I figured there wasn't anybody I really cared for but, then, I didn't need any of them anyway so I rolled over and went to sleep. (p. 87)

An extreme callousness toward others clearly marks Dan's behavior. A person may be otherwise quite rational and show no loss of contact with reality and yet behave in a habitually and exceedingly unethical manner. The final excerpt illustrated Dan's complete lack of feeling for others, a characteristic that will later be shown to have considerable relevance in explaining the behavior of the psychopath.

Research and Theory on the Etiology of Antisocial Personality Disorder and Psychopathy We now turn to research and theory on the etiology of antisocial personality disorder and psychopathy. We examine genetics as well as the psychological factors that operate in the family and in emotions. A final section on response modulation and impulsivity ties together several of the individual research domains. Note again, however, that most research has been conducted on psychopathic individuals who have already been convicted as criminals. Thus the available literature may not allow generalization to the behavior of psychopaths who elude arrest.

The Role of the Family Since much psychopathic behavior violates social norms, many investigators have focused on the primary agent of socialization, the family, in their search for the explanation of such behavior. McCord and McCord (1964) concluded, on the basis of a review of the literature, that lack of affection and severe parental rejection were the primary causes of psychopathic behavior. Several other studies have related psychopathic behavior to parents' inconsistencies in disciplining their children and in teaching them responsibility toward others, to physical abuse, and to parental loss (Marshall & Cooke, 1999; Johnson et al., 1999). Furthermore, the fathers of psychopaths are likely to be antisocial in their behavior.

Self-reported data on early rearing must, however, be interpreted cautiously, as they were gathered by means of retrospective reports—individual recollections of past events. We have seen (see p. 94) that information obtained in this way cannot be accepted uncritically. When people are asked to recollect early events in the life of someone now known to be psychopathic, their knowledge of the person's adult status may well affect what they remember or report about childhood events. They may be more likely to recall deviant incidents, whereas more typical or normal events that do not fit with the person's current behavior may be overlooked. Moreover, it is risky to trust the retrospective reports of psychopaths themselves because lying is a key feature of this disorder.

The problems of retrospective data can be avoided by conducting a follow-up study in adulthood of individuals who as children were seen at child-guidance clinics. In one such study detailed records had been kept on the children, including the type of problem that had brought them to the clinic and considerable information relating to the family (Robins, 1966). Ninety percent of an initial sample of 584 cases were located thirty years after their referral to the clinic.[4] In addition, 100 control participants who had lived in the geographic area served by the clinic but who had not been referred to it were also interviewed in adulthood.

By interviewing the now-adult people in the two samples, the investigators were able to diagnose and describe any maladjustments of these individuals. They then related the adult problems to the characteristics that these people had had as children to find out which characteristics predicted psychopathic behavior in adulthood. Robins's summary brings to mind the category of conduct disorder, mentioned earlier in relation to APD and discussed at length in Chapter 15.

> If one wishes to choose the most likely candidate for a later diagnosis of [psychopathy] from among children appearing in a child guidance clinic, the best choice appears to be a boy referred for theft or aggression who has shown a diversity of antisocial behavior in many episodes, at least one of which could be grounds for Juvenile Court appearance, and whose antisocial behavior involves him with strangers and organizations as well as with teachers and parents.... More than half of the boys appearing at the clinic [with these characteristics were later] diagnosed sociopathic [a term often used instead of psychopathic] personality. Such boys had a history of truancy, theft, staying out late, and refusing to obey parents. They lied gratuitously, and showed little guilt over their behavior. They were generally irresponsible about being where they were supposed to be or taking care of money. (p. 157)

In addition to these characteristics, several aspects of family life were found to be consequential. Both inconsistent discipline and no discipline at all predicted psychopathic behavior in adulthood, as did antisocial behavior of the father.

Two important limitations to this research should be noted: (1) the harsh or inconsistent disciplinary practices of parents could be reactions to trying to raise a child who is displaying antisocial behavior rather than factors contributing to the child's behavior; (2) many individuals who come from what appear to be similarly disturbed social backgrounds do not become psychopaths or develop any other behavior disorders. This second point is important. Adults may have no problems whatsoever in spite of an inconsistent and otherwise problematic upbringing. Thus, although family experience is probably a significant factor in the development of psychopathic behavior, it is not the sole factor. As we have seen in earlier chapters, a diathesis also is required.

---

[4] It should be appreciated that tracking down this large a percentage of individuals thirty years after their contact with the clinic is an incredible feat.

Genetic Correlates of APD Research suggests that both criminality and antisocial personality disorder have heritable components, but behavior-genetics research has not been conducted on the concept of psychopathy developed by Cleckley and Hare.

Adoption studies and twin studies, including those of twins reared apart, indicate that genetic factors play a significant role in the likelihood that a person will commit a criminal act (Gottesman & Goldsmith, 1994; Grove et al., 1990; Mednick, Gabrielli, & Hutchings, 1984). For antisocial personality disorder, twin studies show higher concordance for MZ than for DZ pairs (Lyons et al., 1995); and adoption studies reveal higher than normal prevalence of antisocial behavior in adopted children of biological parents with antisocial personality disorder and substance abuse (Cadoret et al., 1995b; Ge et al., 1996).

Both twin and adoption studies also show that the environment plays a substantial role in antisocial personality disorder. For example, in the Cadoret adoption study just mentioned, an adverse environment in the adoptive home (such as marital problems and substance abuse) was related to the development of antisocial personality disorder, whether or not the adoptive parents had antisocial personality disorder. Furthermore, high levels of conflict and negativity and low levels of parental warmth predicted antisocial behavior in a twin study by Reiss et al. (1995).

Adoption research has also shown that some of the characteristics of adoptive families that are related to antisocial behavior in their children appear to be reactions to a "difficult" child (Ge et al., 1996). That is, the genetically influenced antisocial behavior of the child leads to environmental factors such as harsh discipline and lack of warmth, which, in turn, exacerbate the child's antisocial tendencies.

Emotion and Psychopathy In defining the psychopathic syndrome, Cleckley pointed out the inability of such persons to profit from experience or even from punishment; they seem to be unable to avoid the negative consequences of social misbehavior. Many are chronic lawbreakers despite their experiences with jail sentences. They seem immune to the anxiety or pangs of conscience that help keep most of us from breaking the law or lying to or injuring others, and they have difficulty curbing their impulses. In the terminology of learning theory, psychopaths have not been well socialized because they were unresponsive to punishments for their antisocial behavior. They presumably do not experience conditioned fear responses when they encounter situations in which the conditioned fear response would normally serve to inhibit antisocial behavior.

In a classic study based on Cleckley's clinical observations, Lykken (1957) tested the idea that psychopaths have few inhibitions about committing antisocial acts because they experience so little anxiety. He performed several tests to determine whether psychopaths do indeed have low levels of anxiety. One of the most important tests involved avoidance learning, which is generally assumed to be mediated by anxiety. Lykken studied the ability of psychopaths and controls to avoid shock. Supporting the idea that psychopaths are indeed low in anxiety, they were poorer than controls at avoiding the shocks.

Studies of the activity of the autonomic nervous system are also consistent with the idea that psychopaths respond less anxiously to fear-eliciting stimuli. In resting situations psychopaths have lower than normal levels of skin conductance, and their skin conductance is less reactive when they are confronted with intense or aversive stimuli or when they anticipate an aversive stimulus (Harpur & Hare, 1990; Herpertz et al., 2001b; Raine et al., 2000). One possible interpretation of these findings is that psychopaths are readily able to ignore stimuli that do not interest them (Hare, 1978). This idea has also been confirmed in subsequent research (Ogloff & Wong, 1990). Further research by Hare and his associates has confirmed that in both their behavior and their biological response (Jutai & Hare, 1983), psychopaths are particularly adept at ignoring certain stimuli and instead focusing their attention on what interests them (Forth & Hare, 1989).

Research using other methods of assessing emotion has also confirmed Lykken's original result. One of these methods involves the measurement of the eye-blink component of the startle response, currently considered the best nonverbal indicator of whether a person is in a positive or negative emotional state. The magnitude of the startle response varies depending on the emotional state a subject is in when a noise occurs. A negative emotional state, like fear, causes the startle reflex to increase, whereas a positive emotional state causes it to decrease. Consistent with research using other methods to assess emotion, psychopaths do not show increased startle while they are viewing stimuli designed to elicit negative emotions (Levenston et al., 2000).

Another startle-response study was conducted on four groups of penitentiary inmates selected with the Hare checklist: nonpsychopaths (low on both antisocial behavior and emotional detachment), detached white-collar offenders (high only on emotional detachment), antisocial offenders (high only on antisocial behavior), and psychopaths (high on both components). Participants were first exposed to a baseline condition in which a simple visual cue was presented, sometimes with a blast of loud noise. Next they experienced a situation in which they again saw the visual cue and were told that when it disappeared the loud noise would occur.

During the second phase of the study marked differences emerged among the groups in the magnitude of their startle responses. Both the psychopaths and the detached offenders showed much smaller increases in their startle responses, indicating that less fear had been aroused. The pattern of results is important because it suggests that it is the emotional deficits of psychopaths, not their antisocial behavior, that is linked to emotional detachment (Patrick, 1994).

The research we have described thus far has been based on the idea that punishment does not arouse strong emotions in psychopaths and thus is not available to inhibit antisocial behavior. But some researchers do not believe that punishment is the critical agent of socialization. Instead, they think that empathy, being in tune with the emotional reactions of others, is more important. For example, empathizing with the distress that callous treatment might cause in someone else could inhibit such behavior. Based on this line of reasoning, it is possible that some features of psychopathy arise from a lack of empathy.

This idea has been tested by monitoring the skin conductance of psychopathic and nonpsychopathic men as they viewed slides of varying content. Three types of slides were used: threatening (e.g., gun, shark), neutral (e.g., book), and distress (e.g., a crying person). No differences were found between the two groups in their responses to the first two types of slides, but the psychopaths were less responsive to the distress slides (Blair et al., 1997). Thus, the psychopaths indeed appeared to show less empathy for the distress of others (see Figure 13.2).

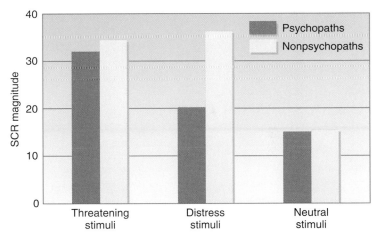

Figure 13.2 Skin-conductance response (SCR) of psychopathic and nonpsychopathic men to three types of stimuli. The psychopathic men showed less responsiveness to the distress stimuli, indicating a deficit in empathy (Blair et al., 1997).

Response Modulation, Impulsivity, and Psychopathy   An important addition to our current thinking about the causes of psychopathy might be the inclusion of a factor that would stimulate or push for antisocial behavior. Similarities between aspects of psychopathy and the behavior of animals who have had parts of their brains destroyed— including the septum, hippocampus, and prefrontal cortex—have led some researchers to propose that a key element of psychopathy is heightened impulsivity (Gorenstein & Newman, 1980). For example, these lesioned animals show deficits in avoidance learning as well as impulsive responding to immediate rewards. The idea that a key feature of psychopathy is impulsivity is supported by studies showing that they have impaired performance on neuropsychological tests of frontal functioning and reduced gray matter in the frontal lobes (Dinn & Harris, 2000; Raine et al., 2000). (Recall that the frontal lobes are thought to play a major role in inhibiting impulsivity.)

Impulsivity shows up when psychopaths are presented with a task designed to test their ability to modify their responses depending on success or failure (Patterson & Newman, 1993). In one study demonstrating this phenomenon, participants viewed playing cards on a computer-generated video display (Newman, Patterson, & Kosson,

The card guessing used by Newman, Patterson, and Kosson to demonstrate psychopaths' impulsivity.

1987). If a face card appeared, the participant won five cents; if a nonface card appeared, he or she lost five cents. After each trial the participant had the opportunity to continue or end the game. The probability of losing was controlled by the experimenter and started at 10 percent. Thereafter the probability of losing increased by 10 percent for every ten cards played until it reached 100 percent. Psychopaths continued to play the game much longer than nonpsychopaths. Nine of twelve psychopaths never quit even though they had lost money on nineteen of the last twenty trials. They were unable to alter their maladaptive responses even though they were being punished.

The same game was played again with one procedural variation—a five-second waiting period was imposed after feedback, thus delaying the decision about whether to play again. This manipulation dramatically reduced the number of trials for which psychopaths played the game. Enforcing a delay may therefore force psychopaths to reflect on the negative feedback they have received and thus behave less impulsively.

The insensitivity to contextual information shown by psychopaths in the first condition described appears to be a general feature of the disorder; it occurs even in situations that do not involve threat of punishment (Newman, Schmitt, & Voss, 1997). In addition to being related to impulsivity, because social interactions are heavily dependent on context, lack of sensitivity to contextual cues might well relate to psychopaths' insensitivity to other people.

The studies we have reviewed show that psychopaths do not react as most of us do. In particular, they have little anxiety, so anxiety can have little deterrent effect on their antisocial behavior. Their callous treatment of others may also be linked to their lack of empathy. Because psychopaths are deficient in using contextual information and in planning, they behave impulsively. These are possible reasons for the psychopath's misconduct without regret and thrill seeking without regard for society's rules.

Anxious/Fearful Cluster

This cluster comprises three personality disorders.

- Avoidant personality disorder applies to people who are fearful in social situations
- Dependent personality disorder refers to those who lack self-reliance and are overly dependent on others
- Obsessive-compulsive personality disorder applies to those who have a perfectionistic approach to life

DSM-IV-TR Criteria for Avoidant Personality Disorder

Presence of at least four of the following:

- Avoidance of interpersonal contacts because of fears of criticism or rejection
- Unwillingness to get involved with others unless certain of being liked
- Restraint in intimate relationships for fear of being shamed or ridiculed
- Preoccupation about being criticized or rejected
- Feelings of inadequacy
- Feelings of inferiority
- Extreme reluctance to try new things for fear of being embarrassed

Avoidant Personality Disorder

The diagnosis of **avoidant personality** disorder applies to people who are very fearful of the possibility of criticism, rejection, or disapproval and are therefore reluctant to enter into relationships unless they are sure they will be liked. They may even avoid employment that entails a lot of interpersonal contact. In social situations they are restrained because of an extreme fear of saying something foolish or of being embarrassed by blushing or other signs of anxiety. They believe they are incompetent and inferior to others and are reluctant to take risks or try new activities.

The prevalence of avoidant personality disorder is about 5 percent (Torgersen, Kringlen, & Cramer, 2001), and it is comorbid with dependent personality disorder (Trull, Widiger, & Frances, 1987) and borderline personality disorder (Morey, 1988). Avoidant personality is also comorbid with the Axis I diagnoses of depression and generalized social phobia (Alpert et al., 1997). The comorbidity with generalized social phobia is likely due to the great similarity between the diagnostic criteria for these two disorders; avoidant personality disorder may actually be a more chronic variant of generalized social phobia (Alden et al., 2002).

Both avoidant personality disorder and social phobia are related to a syndrome that occurs in Japan, called *taijin kyoufu* (*taijin* means "interpersonal" and *kyoufu* means "fear"). Like patients with avoidant personality disorder and social phobia, those with *taijin kyoufu* are overly sensitive and avoid interpersonal contact. But what they fear is somewhat different from the usual fears of those with the DSM diagnoses. Patients with *taijin kyoufu* tend to be anxious or ashamed about how they affect or appear to others, for example, fearing that they are ugly or have body odor (Ono et al., 1996).

Dependent Personality Disorder

The core feature of **dependent personality** disorder is a lack of both self-confidence and a sense of autonomy. Patients with dependent personality disorder view themselves as weak and other people as powerful. They also have an intense need to be taken care of, which often leads them to feel uncomfortable when alone. They subordinate their own needs to ensure that they do not break up the protective relationships they have established. When a close relationship ends, they urgently seek another relationship to replace the old one.

The DSM criteria also include some features that do not appear to be well supported by the research literature. These diagnostic criteria generally portray people with dependent personality disorder as being very passive (e.g., having difficulty initiating projects or doing things on their own, not being able to disagree with others, allowing others to make decisions for them). Research indicates, however, that these passive traits do not prevent dependent people from doing what is necessary to maintain a close relationship. This could involve being very deferential and passive, but it could also entail taking active steps to preserve a relationship (Bornstein, 1997).

The prevalence of dependent personality disorder is about 1.5 percent (Torgersen, Kringlen, & Cramer, 2001); higher figures are found in India and Japan, perhaps because these societies encourage dependent behavior. It occurs more frequently among women than among men, perhaps because of different childhood socialization experiences of men and women (Corbitt & Widiger, 1995; Weissman, 1993). Dependent personality disorder co-occurs frequently with borderline, schizoid, histrionic, schizotypal, and avoidant personality disorders as well as with the Axis I diagnoses of bipolar disorder, depression, anxiety disorders, and bulimia.

Obsessive-Compulsive Personality Disorder

The **obsessive-compulsive personality** is a perfectionist, preoccupied with details, rules, schedules, and the like. These people often pay so much attention to detail that they may never finish projects. They are work rather than pleasure oriented and have inordinate difficulty making decisions (lest they err) and allocating time (lest they focus on the wrong thing). Their interpersonal relationships are often poor because they are stubborn and demand that everything be done their way. "Control freak" is a popular term for these individuals. They are generally serious, rigid, formal, and inflexible, especially regarding moral issues. They are unable to discard worn-out and useless objects, even those with no sentimental value, and are likely to be miserly and stingy.

Obsessive-compulsive personality disorder is quite different from obsessive-compulsive disorder in that it does not include the obsessions and compulsions that define the latter. While the use of the two similar terms suggests that the two disorders are related, the relationship does not appear to be very strong. Although obsessive-compulsive personality disorder is found more frequently among patients with OCD than among patients with panic disorder or depression (Diaferia et al., 1997), it is found in only a minority of OCD cases (Baer & Jenike, 1992). Obsessive-compulsive personality disorder is most highly comorbid with avoidant personality disorder and has a prevalence of about 2 percent (Lassano, del Buoeno, & Latapano, 1993; Torgersen, Kringlen, & Cramer, 2001).

See Focus on Discovery 13.1 for a comparison of the DSM-IV-TR discrete entity approach to diagnosing personality disorders and a dimensional approach.

DSM-IV-TR Criteria for Dependent Personality Disorder

Presence of at least five of the following:

- Difficulty making decisions without excessive advice and reassurance from others
- Need for others to take responsibility for most major areas of life
- Difficulty disagreeing with others for fear of losing their support
- Difficulty doing things on own because of lack of self-confidence
- Doing unpleasant things as a way to obtain the approval and support of others
- Feelings of helplessness when alone because of lack of confidence in ability to handle things without the intervention of others
- Urgently seeking of new relationship when present one ends
- Preoccupation with fears of having to take care of self

DSM-IV-TR Criteria for Obsessive-Compulsive Personality Disorder

Presence of at least four of the following:

- Preoccupation with rules and details to the extent that the major point of an activity is lost
- Extreme perfectionism to the degree that projects are seldom completed
- Excessive devotion to work to the exclusion of leisure and friendships
- Inflexibility about morals
- Difficulty discarding worthless items
- Reluctance to delegate unless others conform to one's standards
- Miserliness
- Rigidity and stubbornness

A Dimensional Approach to Personality Disorders

A promising dimensional approach to personality disorders considers that they represent extremes of personality traits that are found in everyone. Although literally hundreds of traits could be considered, much contemporary research in personality focuses on a conception of personality called the five-factor model (McCrae & Costa, 1990). The five factors, or major dimensions, of personality are neuroticism, extraversion/introversion, openness to experience, agreeableness/antagonism, and conscientiousness. The accompanying table presents questionnaire items that assess each of these dimensions. By reading the table carefully you can acquire a sense of what each dimension means.

Widiger and Costa (1994) summarized the results of several studies linking these personality traits to schizoid, borderline, and avoidant personality disorders. Patients with schizoid personality disorder and those with avoidant personality disorder are high in introversion. Thus the five-factor model would predict that these two disorders would be hard to differentiate, and this has indeed been found to be true. There is some differentiation between the two disorders, however, on the neuroticism dimension; patients with avoidant personality disorder are higher than those with schizoid personality disorder. Rather than forcing each patient into a discrete category and encountering problems in distinguishing between these two disorders, the dimensional approach would simply describe patients on their levels of neuroticism and introversion.

Borderline personality disorder is most strongly related to neuroticism and antagonism. Because high scores on neuroticism are found in many personality disorders and Axis I disorders as well, it is not surprising that borderline personality is comorbid with numerous personality disorders and Axis I conditions. Borderline patients also score high on antagonism, which allows them to be discriminated from patients with avoidant personality disorder. High scores on antagonism are also found in patients with paranoid and antisocial disorders, so comorbidity with these disorders would be expected. Again, the dimensional approach doesn't force patients into discrete categories, but simply describes their scores on the five factors.

It does not appear, however, that the five-factor model will be the final answer to providing a dimensional system for the personality disorders. In an empirical study in which patients with personality disorders completed a questionnaire assessing the five factors, the profiles of the various personality disorders turned out to be rather similar to one another (Morey et al., 2000). Proponents of the five-factor model have responded to this difficulty by claiming that to achieve differentiation among the different personality disorders,

the five factors need to be broken down into their "facets." (Lynam & Widiger, 2001). Each of the five factors has six facets or components; for example, the extraversion factor includes warmth, gregariousness, assertiveness, activity, excitement seeking, and positive emotions. The idea is that differentiating among the personality disorders will require a more complicated description of their personalities.

Thus, the five-factor model is certainly not a total solution to the problem of classifying personality disorders. The model loses elegance if thirty facets need to be considered. And even using the thirty facets, research has not found the personality disorders to be easily differentiated (Morey et al., 2002). But the important point is that a dimensional model has several distinct advantages. First and foremost, it handles the comorbidity problem, because comorbidity is a difficulty only in a categorical classification system like the DSM. A dimensional system also forges a link between normal and abnormal personality so that the findings on personality development in general become relevant to the personality disorders. The five-factor model is not the only system for describing personality; other models are currently under consideration (e.g., Livesley, Jang, & Vernon, 1998). However, the trend in all this research is clear—dimensional approaches to the personality disorders offer some distinct advantages.

Sample Items from the Revised NEO Personality Inventory Assessing the Five-Factor Model

Neuroticism	I am not a worrier (–)
	I am not easily frightened (–)
	I rarely feel fearful or anxious (–)
	I often feel tense or jittery (+)
Extroversion/introversion	I really like most people I meet (+)
	I don't get much pleasure from chatting with people (–)
	I'm known as a warm and friendly person (+)
	Many people think of me as somewhat cold and distant (–)
Openness to experience	I have a very active imagination (+)
	I try to keep my thoughts directed along realistic lines and avoid flights of fancy (–)
	I have an active fantasy life (+)
	I don't like to waste my time daydreaming (–)
Agreeableness/antagonism	I tend to be cynical and skeptical of others' intentions (–)
	I believe that other people are well intentioned (+)
	I believe that most people will take advantage of you if you let them (–)
	I think most people I deal with are honest and trustworthy (+)
Conscientiousness	I am known for my prudence and common sense (+)
	I don't take civic duties like voting very seriously (–)
	I keep myself informed and usually make intelligent decisions (+)
	I often come into situations without being prepared (–)

Source: Costa and McCrae, 1992.

Note: Agreeing with an item marked with a + increases one's score on that factor; agreeing with an item marked – decreases it.

Etiology of the Anxious/Fearful Cluster

Few data exist on the causes of the personality disorders in this cluster. Speculation has focused on parent–child relationships. For example, it has been argued that dependent personality disorder results from an overprotective and authoritarian parenting style that prevents the development of feelings of self-efficacy (Bornstein, 1997).

Dependent personality disorder could also be a reflection of what are referred to as attachment problems (Livesley, Schroeder, & Jackson, 1990). Attachment has been studied by developmental psychologists and is regarded as important for personality development. The basic idea is that the young infant becomes attached to an adult and uses the adult as a secure base from which to explore and pursue other goals. Separation from the adult leads to anger and distress. As development proceeds, the child becomes less dependent on the attachment figure for security. It is possible that the abnormal attachment behaviors seen in dependent personalities reflect a failure in the usual developmental process arising from a disruption in the early parent–child relationship caused by death, neglect, rejection, or overprotectiveness. Persons with dependent personality disorder engage in a number of tactics, originally established to maintain their relationship with their parents, to keep their relationships with other people at any cost—for example, always agreeing with them (Stone, 1993).

Much like the fears and phobias discussed in Chapter 6, avoidant personality disorder may reflect the influence of an environment in which the child is taught to fear people and situations that most of us regard as harmless. For example, one of the child's parents may have similar fears, which are transmitted by modeling. Alternatively, the fact that avoidant personality disorder runs in families may indicate a role for a genetic diathesis (Tillfors et al., 2001).

Obsessive-compulsive personality traits were originally viewed by Freud as caused by fixation at the anal stage of psychosexual development. More contemporary psychodynamic theories emphasize a fear of loss of control, which is handled by overcompensation. For example, the man who is a compulsive workaholic may fear that his life will fall apart if he allows himself to relax and have fun.[5]

Children normally go through a phase in which separation from a parent is distressing. People with dependent personality disorder may be experiencing a similar phenomenon in their adult relationships.

Therapies for Personality Disorders

It is important to bear in mind that a therapist working with personality disordered patients is typically also concerned with Axis I disorders. Indeed, most patients with personality disorders enter treatment because of an Axis I disorder rather than a personality disorder. For example, a person with antisocial personality disorder is likely to have substance-abuse problems; a person with avoidant personality disorder may seek treatment for a social phobia; and a patient with obsessive-compulsive personality disorder may be seen for depression. In this connection, it can be mentioned that patients with Axis I disorders *and* personality disorders usually do not improve as much from various forms of psychotherapy as do patients with Axis I diagnoses alone (Reich & Vasile, 1993; Crits-Christoph & Barber, 2002). The reason seems pretty clear: people with diagnoses on both axes are more seriously disturbed than are those with only Axis I diagnoses and therefore may require therapy that is both more intensive (because of the long-standing nature of personality disorders) and more extensive (that is, focused on a broad range of psychological problems).

Psychoactive drugs are often used to treat the various personality disorders (Koenigsberg, Woo-Ming, & Siever, 2002). The choice of drug is determined by the Axis

---

[5] DSM-IV proposed diagnostic criteria for two additional personality disorders that were not formal diagnoses, but "categories in need of further study." The most controversial of these was self-defeating personality disorder; the other was sadistic personality disorder. These two diagnoses were dropped entirely from DSM-IV-TR. Passive-aggressive personality disorder, which was previously a formal diagnosis, was demoted in DSM-IV to a category in need of further study.

I problem that the personality disorder resembles. For example, patients with avoidant personality disorder can be prescribed tranquilizers, such as the benzodiazepine Xanax, in hopes of reducing their social anxieties and phobias. When depression is present in an Axis II disorder, antidepressant medication, such as fluoxetine (Prozac) can be helpful. Given the connections noted earlier between schizophrenia and schizotypal personality disorder, it is not surprising that antipsychotic drugs like risperidone have shown some effectiveness with schizotypal personality disorder (Koenigsberg et al., 2001).

Psychodynamic therapists aim to alter the patient's present-day views of the childhood problems assumed to underlie a personality disorder. For example, they may guide an obsessive-compulsive personality to the realization that the childhood quest to win the love of his or her parents by being perfect need not be carried into adulthood—that he or she does not need to be perfect to win the approval of others, that it is possible to take risks and make mistakes without being abandoned by those whose love and caring are sought.

Behavioral and cognitive therapists, in keeping with their attention to situations rather than to traits, have had little to say until recently about specific treatments for the personality disorders designated by the DSM (Howes & Vallis, 1996). These therapists tend to analyze the individual problems that taken together reflect a personality disorder. For example, a person diagnosed as having a paranoid or an avoidant personality is extremely sensitive to criticism. This sensitivity may be treated by behavioral rehearsal (social-skills training), systematic desensitization, or rational-emotive behavior therapy (Renneberg et al., 1990). The paranoid personality's argumentativeness and hostility when disagreeing with other people pushes others away and provokes counterattacks from them. The behavior therapist may help the paranoid individual learn less antagonizing ways of disagreeing with other people. Social-skills training in a support group might be suggested to encourage avoidant personalities to be more assertive with other people; one controlled study confirmed that this is a promising strategy (Alden, 1989). Such an approach, perhaps combined with rational-emotive behavior therapy, may help these patients cope when efforts to reach out do not succeed, as is bound to happen at times (Millon, 1996; Turkat & Maisto, 1985).

In looking at cognitive therapy for personality disorders, Beck and his associates (1990) apply the same kind of analysis as that found promising in the treatment of depression (cf. pp. 54, 289). Each disorder is analyzed in terms of logical errors and dysfunctional schemata. For example, cognitive therapy with an obsessive-compulsive personality entails first persuading the patient to accept the essence of the cognitive model, that feelings and behaviors are primarily a function of thoughts. Errors in logic are then explored, such as when the patient concludes that he or she cannot do anything right because of failing in one particular endeavor (an example of overgeneralization). The therapist also looks for dysfunctional assumptions or schemata that might underlie the person's thoughts and feelings, for example, the belief that it is critical for every decision to be correct (adherents of Ellis's methods would also take this step). Beck's approach to personality disorders represents a combination of a variety of behavioral and cognitive-behavioral techniques, all designed to address the particular, long-standing, and pervasive difficulties presented by patients.

Therapy for the Borderline Personality

Whatever the intervention modality, one thing is certain: few patients pose a greater challenge to treatment than do those with borderline personality disorder. The problems that borderline personalities have with other people are replicated in the consulting room.

For the borderline patient, trust is inordinately difficult to create and sustain, thus handicapping the therapeutic relationship. The patient alternately idealizes and vilifies the therapist, demanding special attention and consideration one moment—such as therapy sessions at odd hours and countless phone calls during periods of particular crisis — and refusing to keep appointments the next, imploring for understanding and support, but insisting that certain topics are off-limits.

Suicide is always a serious risk, but it is often difficult for the therapist to judge whether a frantic phone call at 2:00 A.M. is a call for help or a manipulative gesture designed to see how special the patient is to the therapist and to what lengths the therapist will go to meet the patient's needs at the moment. As happened in the case presented at the beginning of this chapter, hospitalization is often necessary when the behavior of the patient becomes unmanageable on an outpatient basis or when the threat of suicide cannot be handled without the greater supervision possible only in the controlled setting of a mental hospital.

Seeing such patients is so stressful that it is common practice for therapists to have regular consultations with another therapist, sometimes for support and advice, sometimes for professional help in dealing with their own emotions as they try to cope with the extraordinary challenges of helping borderline patients. (In psychoanalytic terms, these feelings of the therapist are called countertransference, discussed on p. 32.) In her own cognitive-behavioral approach to therapy with borderlines (discussed later), Linehan makes this kind of ongoing consultation an integral part of the treatment.

A number of drugs have been tried in the pharmacotherapy of borderline personality disorder, most notably antidepressants and antipsychotic medications. There is some evidence that fluoxetine (Prozac) decreases some of the aggressiveness and depression often found in BPD patients (Coccaro & Kavoussi, 1995), and that lithium can reduce some of the irritability, anger, and suicidality (Links et al., 1990). Antipsychotics show some modest effects on borderline patients' anxiety, suicidality, and psychotic symptoms (Bendetti et al., 1998; Gitlin, 1993; Koenigsberg et al., 2002). Because such patients often abuse drugs and are suicide risks, extreme caution must be used in any drug-therapy regimen (Waldenger & Frank, 1989).

Object-Relations Psychotherapy   As noted earlier, object-relations theory focuses on how children identify with people to whom they have strong emotional attachments. Earlier in the chapter we described the views of the object-relations theorist Otto Kernberg on the borderline personality.

As noted earlier, Kernberg (1985) operates from the basic assumption that borderline personalities have weak egos and therefore inordinate difficulty tolerating the probing that occurs in psychoanalytic treatment. Kernberg's modified analytic treatment has the overall goal of strengthening the patient's weak ego so that he or she does not fall prey to splitting, or dichotomizing (Kernberg et al., 1989). Splitting is regarded as resulting from an inability to form complex ideas (object representations) that do not fit a simple good–bad dichotomy. For example, the patient may see the therapist as a godlike genius only to be crushed and furious when the therapist later mentions that the patient is behind in therapy payments; in an instant the therapist becomes evil and incompetent. The techniques employed are basically interpretive—that is, the therapist points out how the patient is allowing his or her emotions and behavior to be regulated by such defenses as splitting.

But Kernberg's approach is more directive than that of most analysts. In addition to interpreting defensive behavior, he gives the patient concrete suggestions for behaving more adaptively, and he will hospitalize a patient whose behavior becomes dangerous to him- or herself or others. Kernberg's opinion that such patients are inappropriate for classical psychoanalysis because of their weak egos is consistent with a long-term study conducted at the world-famous analytically oriented Menninger Clinic (Stone, 1987).

Dialectical Behavior Therapy   An approach that combines client-centered empathy and acceptance with cognitive-behavioral problem solving and social-skills training was introduced by Marsha Linehan (1987). What she calls **dialectical behavior therapy (DBT)** has three overall goals for borderline individuals.

1. Teach them to modulate and control their extreme emotionality and behaviors
2. Teach them to tolerate feeling distressed
3. Help them learn to trust their own thoughts and emotions

Why does Linehan use the word dialectical in describing her therapy? The concept of dialectics comes from the German philosopher Hegel (1770–1831). For our purposes it

Marsha Linehan created dialectical behavior therapy, which combines cognitive behavior therapy with Zen and Rogerian notions of acceptance.

is enough to know that dialectics refers to a worldview that holds that reality is an out-come of a constant tension between opposites. Any event—called the thesis—tends to generate a force in opposition to it—its antithesis. The tension between the opposites is resolved by the creation of a new event—the synthesis. For example, John loves Mary (thesis). But he finds in her some qualities that annoy him, creating in him some doubt as to whether he truly loves her (antithesis). John then comes to realize that he can love Mary in spite of her faults, perhaps even because of them (synthesis). This synthesis can then split into another pair of dialectical opposites, with a new synthesis eventually emerging that can reconcile them. And so on and on.

Linehan uses the term dialectic to describe the seemingly paradoxical stance that the therapist must take with a borderline patient—accepting the patient as he or she is and yet helping him or her to change. Linehan also uses the term to refer to the borderline patient's realization that he or she need not split the world into black and white, but can achieve a synthesis of apparent opposites. For example, instead of a friend being either all bad (thesis) or all good (antithesis), the friend can be a person with both kinds of qual-ities (synthesis). In a sense, one goal of DBT is to teach the patient to adopt a dialectical view of the world, an understanding that life is constantly changing and that things are not really all bad or all good.

DBT centers on the therapist's full acceptance of borderline personalities with all their contradictions and acting out, empathically validating their (distorted) beliefs with a matter-of-fact attitude toward their suicidal and other dysfunctional behavior. The cog-nitive-behavioral aspect of the treatment, conducted both individually and in groups, involves helping patients learn to solve problems, to acquire more effective and socially acceptable ways of handling their daily living problems and controlling their emotions. Work is also done on improving their interpersonal skills and controlling their anger and anxieties. After many months of intensive treatment, limits are set on their behavior, con-sistent with what Kernberg advocates. Basically, DBT is cognitive behavior therapy with-in the paradoxical context of validating and accepting the person for who he or she is. In Linehan's words:

> Stylistically, DBT blends a matter-of-fact, somewhat irreverent, and at times outrageous attitude about current and previous parasuicidal and other dysfunctional behaviors with therapist warmth [and] flexibility.… [A] focus…on active problem-solving [is] balanced by a correspond-ing emphasis on validating the patient's current emotional, cognitive, and behavioral responses just as they are. (1993b, p. 19)

For a closer look at the dialectic between acceptance and change, see Focus on Discovery 13.2.

Linehan and her associates published the results of the first randomized, controlled study of a psychological intervention for borderline personality disorder (Linehan et al., 1991). Patients were randomly assigned either to dialectical behavior therapy or to treat-ment as usual, meaning any therapy available in the community (Seattle, Washington). At the end of one year of treatment and again six and twelve months later, patients in the two groups were compared on a variety of measures (Linehan, Heard, & Armstrong, 1993). The findings immediately after treatment revealed highly significant superiority of DBT on measures of intentional self-injurious behavior, including suicide attempts; drop-ping out of treatment; and inpatient hospital days. There were, however, no differences in self-reported depression and hopelessness between the two treatment groups.

At the follow-ups the superiority of DBT was maintained. Additionally, DBT patients had better work histories, reported less anger, and were judged as overall better adjust-ed than the comparison therapy patients. *But* most patients were still quite miserable at a one-year follow-up, underscoring the extreme difficulty of treating such patients.

A similarly designed study with BPD women who were also drug dependent found less substance abuse following dialectical behavior therapy as compared to treatment as usual in the community (Linehan et al., 1999).

As a result of these and other studies (recently reviewed by Koerner & Linehan, 2000) and a book and manual on dialectical behavior therapy (Linehan, 1993a, 1993b),

Focus on Discovery 13.2

Acceptance in Dialetical Behavior Therapy

Marsha Linehan's (1987, 1993a, 1993b) notion of acceptance within the framework of her dialectical behavior therapy is subtle and not easy to understand; hence some elaboration is warranted. Linehan argues that a therapist working with a borderline personality has to adopt what to the Western mind is an inconsistent posture. The therapist must be clear with the patient about limits and work for change while at the same time accepting the person as client-centered therapists would, which means accepting the real possibility that no changes are going to occur.

Linehan's reasoning is that the borderline personality is so exquisitely sensitive to rejection and criticism as well as so emotionally unstable that even gentle encouragement to behave or think differently can lead to high levels of emotional arousal and subsequent misinterpretation of suggestions as a serious rebuke. The therapist who a moment earlier was revered is now vilified and spurned. Thus, while observing limits—"I would be very sad if you killed yourself so I hope very much that you won't"—the therapist must convey to the borderline patient that he or she is fully accepted even while threatening suicide and making everyone else's life, including the therapist's, miserable!

This complete acceptance of the patient does not mean that the therapist approves of everything the patient is doing, only that the therapist accepts the situation for what it is. Indeed, argues Linehan, the therapist must truly accept the patient as he or she is; acceptance

should not be in the service of change, an indirect way of encouraging the patient to behave differently. Linehan's concept of acceptance is not a means to an end. "Acceptance can transform but if you accept in order to transform, it is not acceptance. It is like loving. Love seeks no reward but when given freely comes back a hundredfold. He who loses his life finds it. He who accepts, changes" (M. M. Linehan, personal communication, November 16, 1992). For a more instrumental view of acceptance as a way of encouraging change see page 594.

Full and thoroughgoing acceptance does not, in Linehan's view, preclude change. She proposes that it is the refusal to accept that prevents change. She might put it this way when talking to her patients:

> If you hate the color purple, move into a house that is painted purple, and then refuse to rush out and buy paint to repaint it. The person who immediately accepts that the house is painted purple—without excess ado or distortion or denial or outrage at the fact of the color or one's own preferences—will probably get it repainted the quickest. (personal communication, September 18, 1992)[*]

---

[*] A similar approach to treatment that combines acceptance and change is the Acceptance and Commitment Therapy of Steven Hayes (Hayes, Strosahl, & Wilson, 1999). The focus is on encouraging patients to accept, not run away from, negative feelings and thoughts, much like what one finds in Gestalt therapy (p. 41).

there is widespread interest in this approach to borderline personality disorder, and many outcome studies are in progress around the world to evaluate its effectiveness.

From Disorder to Style: A Comment on Goals

The traits that characterize the personality disorders are probably too ingrained to change thoroughly. Instead, the therapist—regardless of theoretical orientation—may find it more realistic to change a disorder into a style, a problem into a general and adaptive but particular way of approaching life (Millon, 1996).

> If all goes well, avoidant personality disorder becomes avoidant personality style: discreet, reserved, sensitive to what others think, comfortable with familiar routines; close to family and a few friends but not gregarious. Dependent personality disorder becomes dependent personality style: polite, agreeable, and thoughtful; respectful of authority and the opinions of others, strongly committed to friends and romantic partners, disliking solitude and preferring teamwork in a subordinate role. Obsessive personality disorder becomes obsessive personality style: thrifty, cautious, orderly, morally principled, proud of doing jobs right, and careful to weigh all alternatives before making decisions. (Harvard Mental Health Letter, 1996b, p. 3)

Therapy for Psychopathy

Most experts of varying theoretical persuasions have for many years asserted that it is pointless to try to alter the callous and remorseless nature of psychopaths (Cleckley, 1976; Gacono et al., 2001; McCord & McCord, 1964; Palmer, 1984). In those few instances when behavioral change is observed—as with social-skills training in prison—the apparent therapeutic gains vanish when the person is released (Corrigan, 1991). A plausible reason is that the psychopath just plays along with the therapist is order to derive some benefits, a manifestation of the manipulativeness that characterizes these people.

It may be that people with the classic symptoms listed by Cleckley are by their very natures incapable of benefiting from any form of psychotherapy. In fact, it is unlikely that psychopaths would even want to be in therapy! The primary reason for their unsuitability for psychotherapy is that they are unable and unmotivated to form any sort of trusting, honest relationship with a therapist. People who lie almost without knowing it, who care little for the feelings of others and understand their own even less, who appear not to realize that what they are doing is morally wrong, who lack any motivation to obey society's laws and mores, and who, living only for the present, have no concern for the future are, all in all, extremely poor candidates for therapy.

One clinician experienced in working with psychopaths has suggested three general principles for therapists working with these patients.

> First, the therapist must be continually vigilant with regard to manipulation on the part of the patient. Second, he must assume, until proven otherwise, that information given him by the patient contains distortions and fabrications. Third, he must recognize that a working alliance develops, if ever, exceedingly late in any therapeutic relationship with a psychopath. (Lion, 1978, p. 286)

These pessimistic views have recently been challenged in a comprehensive meta-analysis of forty-two studies on psychosocial treatment of psychopaths (Salekin, 2002). Although they had many methodological problems, seventeen studies involving eighty-eight psychopathic individuals found psychoanalytic psychotherapy very helpful in such domains as better interpersonal relationships, increases in capacity for feeling remorse and empathy, less lying, being released from probation, and holding down a job. Similar positive therapeutic effects were found in five studies employing cognitive behavioral techniques involving 246 psychopaths. The younger the patient, the better the beneficial effects of therapy. To be at all effective, treatment had to be quite intensive, that is, four times a week for at least a year—a very heavy dose of psychosocial treatment whatever one's theoretical orientation.

These are remarkably positive findings given the widely held belief that psychopathy is basically untreatable. And yet, as optimistic as Salekin is about current and future treatment efforts for psychopaths, we find noteworthy his cautionary comment at the end of his article: "…research needs to make some attempt to determine whether clients are 'faking good' in treatment studies or whether the changes are genuine" (p. 107).

Many psychopaths spend time in prison for committing crimes, and the discouraging results of imprisonment as rehabilitation may be traced at least in part to the extreme difficulty of modifying psychopathic behavior. As criminologists have stated repeatedly, our prison system seems to operate more as a school for crime than as a place where criminals, and psychopaths, can be rehabilitated.

An interesting argument in favor of incarceration is that psychopaths often settle down in middle age and thereafter (Craft, 1969). Whether through biological changes, eventual insight into their self-defeating natures, or simply becoming worn out and unable to continue in their finagling, often violent ways, many psychopaths grow less disruptive as they approach age forty. Prison therefore protects society from the antisocial behavior of active psychopaths, with release considered more plausible when the prisoner enters a stage of life in which the excesses of the disorder are less in evidence.

Summary

● Coded on Axis II in DSM-IV-TR, personality disorders are defined as enduring patterns of behavior and inner experience that disrupt social and occupational functioning. They are usually codiagnosed with such Axis I disorders as depression and anxiety disorders. These diagnoses overlap considerably, and it is usual for a person to meet diagnostic criteria for more than one. This high comorbidity, coupled with the fact that personality disorders are seen as the extremes of continuously distributed personality traits, has led to proposals to develop a dimensional rather than a categorical means of classifying these disorders.

- Personality disorders are grouped into three clusters in DSM-IV-TR: odd/eccentric, dramatic/erratic, and anxious/fearful.

- Specific diagnoses in the odd/eccentric cluster include paranoid, schizoid, and schizotypal. These disorders are usually considered to be less severe variants of schizophrenia. Behavior genetic research gives some support to this assumption, especially for schizotypal personality disorder.

- The dramatic/erratic cluster includes borderline, histrionic, narcissistic, and antisocial personality disorders. The major symptom of borderline personality disorder is unstable, highly changeable emotions and behavior; of histrionic personality disorder, exaggerated emotional displays; and of narcissistic personality disorder, highly inflated self-esteem. Antisocial personality disorder and psychopathy overlap a great deal but are not exactly equivalent. The diagnosis of antisocial personality focuses on antisocial behavior, whereas that of psychopathy emphasizes emotional deficits, such as a lack of fear, regret, guilt, or shame.

- Theories of the etiology of borderline, histrionic, and narcissistic disorders focus on early parent-child relationships. For example, the object-relations theorist Kernberg and the self-psychologist Kohut have detailed proposals concerning borderline and narcissistic personality disorders, focusing on the child developing an insecure ego because of inconsistent love and attention from the parents. Linehan's cognitive-behavioral theory of borderline personality disorder proposes an interaction between a deficit in emotional regulation and an invalidating family environment.

- Genetic studies suggest that a predisposition to antisocial personality disorder is inherited. As to the etiology of psychopathy, research indicates that psychopaths tend to have fathers who were antisocial and that discipline during their childhoods was absent or inconsistent. However, the core problem of the psychopath may be that impending punishment creates no inhibitions about committing antisocial acts. A lack of empathy may also be a factor in the psychopath's callous treatment of others.

- The anxious/fearful cluster includes avoidant, dependent, and obsessive-compulsive personality disorders. The major symptom of avoidant personality disorder is fear of rejection or criticism; of dependent personality disorder, low self-confidence; and of obsessive-compulsive personality disorder, a perfectionistic, detail-oriented style.

- Theories of etiology for the anxious/fearful cluster focus on early experience. Avoidant personality disorder may result from the transmission of fear from parent to child via modeling. Dependent personality may be caused by disruptions of the parent-child relationship (e.g., through separation or loss) that lead the person to fear losing other relationships in adulthood.

- Although psychodynamic, behavioral and cognitive, and pharmacological treatments all are used for personality disorders, little is known about their effectiveness. Some promising evidence is emerging, however, for the utility of dialectical behavior therapy for borderline personality disorder. This approach combines client-centered acceptance with a cognitive-behavioral focus on making specific changes in thought, emotion, and behavior. Recent research suggests that even psychopathy, often considered virtually untreatable, may respond to intensive psychological treatment.

Key Terms

antisocial personality	dialectical behavior therapy	obsessive-compulsive personality	psychopathy
avoidant personality	(DBT)	paranoid personality	schizoid personality
borderline personality	histrionic personality	personality disorders	schizotypal personality
dependent personality	narcissistic personality		

Borderline Personality Disorder

Alice Siegel was 22 years old when she reluctantly agreed to interrupt her college education in midsemester and admit herself for the eighth time to a psychiatric hospital. Her psychologist, Dr. Swenson, and her psychiatrist, Dr. Smythe, believed that neither psychotherapy nor medication was currently effective in helping her control her symptoms and that continued outpatient treatment would be too risky. Of most concern was that Alice was experiencing brief episodes in which she felt that her body was not real. This feeling terrified her. She sometimes reacted to it by cutting herself with a knife in order to feel pain, thereby feeling real. During the first part of the admission interview at the hospital, Alice angrily denied that she had done anything self-destructive. She did not sustain this anger, however, and was soon in tears as she recounted her fears that she would fail her midterm examinations and be expelled from college. The admitting psychiatrist also noted that, at times, Alice behaved in a flirtatious manner, asking inappropriately personal questions such as whether any of the psychiatrist's girlfriends were in the hospital.

On arrival at the inpatient psychiatric unit, Alice once again became quite angry. She protested loudly, using obscene and abusive language when the nurse-in-charge searched her luggage for illegal drugs and sharp objects (a routine procedure with which Alice was well acquainted). These impulsive outbursts of anger had become quite characteristic for Alice over the past several years. She would often express anger at an intensity level that was out of proportion to the situation. When she became this angry, she would typically do or say something that she later regretted, such as verbally abusing a close friend or breaking a prized possession. In spite of the negative consequences of these actions and the ensuing guilt and regret on Alice's part, she was unable to stop herself from periodically losing control of her anger.

That same day, Alice filed a "three-day notice," a written statement expressing an intention to leave the hospital within 72 hours. Dr. Swenson told Alice that if she did not agree to remain in the hospital voluntarily, he would initiate legal proceedings for her involuntary commitment on the ground that she was a threat to herself. Two days later, Alice retracted the three-day notice, and her anger seemed to subside.

Over the next two weeks, Alice appeared to be getting along rather well. Despite some complaints of feeling depressed, she was always well dressed and groomed, in contrast to many of the other patients. Except for occasional episodes when she became verbally abusive and slammed doors, Alice appeared and acted like a staff member. Indeed, Alice began to adopt a "therapist" role with the other patients, listening intently to their problems and suggesting solutions. She would often serve as a spokesperson for the more disgruntled patients, expressing their concerns and complaints to the administrators of the treatment unit. With the help of her therapist, Alice also

wrote a contract stating that she would not actually hurt herself and that she would notify staff members if she began to have thoughts of doing so. Given that her safety was no longer an issue, she was allowed a number of passes off the unit with other patients and friends.

Alice became particularly attached to several staff members and arranged one-to-one talks with them as often as possible. She used these talks to complain about alleged incompetence and lack of professionalism among other staff members. She would also point out, in an ingratiating way, that the person to whom she was talking was one of the few who knew her well enough to be of any help to her. These talks were replete with flattering compliments from Alice as to how understanding and helpful she found that particular staff person. These overtures made it difficult for certain of these selected staff members to confront Alice on issues such as violations of rules of the treatment unit. For instance, when Alice returned late from a pass off grounds, it was often overlooked. If she was confronted, especially by someone with whom she felt she had a special relationship, she would feel betrayed and, as if an emotional switch had flipped, lash out angrily and accuse that person of being "just like the rest of them."

By the end of the third week of hospitalization, Alice no longer appeared to be in acute distress, and discussions were begun concerning her discharge from the hospital. At about this time, Alice began to drop hints in her therapy sessions with Dr. Swenson that she had been withholding some kind of secret. Dr. Swenson confronted this issue in therapy and encouraged her to be more open and direct if there was something about which she was especially concerned. Alice then revealed that since her second day in the hospital, she had been receiving illegal street drugs from two friends who visited her. Besides occasionally using the drugs herself, Alice had been giving them to other patients on the unit. This situation was quickly brought to the attention of all the other patients on the unit in a meeting called by Dr. Swenson. During the meeting, Alice protested that the other patients had forced her to bring them drugs and that she actually had no choice in the matter. Dr. Swenson didn't believe Alice's explanation and instead thought that Alice had found it intolerable to be denied approval and found it impossible to say no.

Soon after this incident came to light, Alice experienced another episode of feeling as if she were unreal and cut herself a number of times across her wrists with a soda can she had broken in half. The cuts were deep enough to draw blood but were not life threatening. In contrast to previous incidents, she did not try to keep this hidden and several staff members therefore concluded that Alice was exaggerating the severity of her problems so she could remain in the hospital longer. The members of Alice's treatment team then met to decide the best course of action with regard to the dilemma.

Not everyone agreed about Alice's motivation for cutting herself. Alice was undoubtedly self-destructive and possibly suicidal. Therefore, she needed further hospitalization. But she had been sabotaging the treatment of other patients and could not be trusted to refrain from doing so again. With the members of her treatment team split on the question of whether or not Alice should be allowed to remain in the hospital, designing a coherent treatment program would prove difficult at best.

Social History

Alice was the older of two daughters born to a suburban middle-class family. She was 2 years old at the time her sister, Jane, was born. Alice's mother and father divorced four years later, leaving the children in the custody of the mother. Financial problems were paramount at that time, as Alice's father provided little in the way of subsequent child support. He remarried soon afterward and was generally unavailable to his original family. He never remembered the children on birthdays or holidays. When Alice was 7 years old, her mother began working as a waitress in a neighborhood restaurant. Neighbors would check in on Alice and Jane after school, but the children were left largely unattended until their mother returned home from work in the evening. Thus, at a very early age Alice was forced into a caretaker role for her younger sister. Over the next few years Alice took on a number of household responsibilities that were more appropriate for an adult or much older child (e.g., babysitting, regular meal preparation, shopping). Alice voiced no complaints about the situation and did not present any behavioral problems at home or in school. However, she remained distressed about the absence of her father. Had she somehow had something to do with the divorce? How much better would her life have been if only her father were with her?

When Alice was 13 years old, her mother married a man she had been dating for about three months. The man, Arthur Siegel, had a 16-year-old son named Michael who joined the household on a somewhat sporadic basis. Michael had been moving back and forth between his mother's and father's houses since their divorce four years earlier. His mother had legal custody but was unable to manage his more abusive and aggressive behaviors, so she frequently sent him to live with his father for several weeks or months. Because she still entertained the fantasy that her mother and father would remarry, Alice resented the intrusion of these new people into her house and was quite upset when her mother changed her and her children's last name to Siegel. She also resented the loss of some of her caretaking responsibilities, which were now shared with her mother and stepfather.

The first indications of any behavioral or emotional problems with Alice occurred shortly after the marriage. She was doing very well academically in the seventh grade when she began to skip classes. Her grades fell precipitously over the course of a semester, and she began spending time with peers who were experimenting with alcohol and street drugs. Alice became a frequent user of these drugs, even though she experienced some frightening symptoms after taking them (e.g., vivid visual hallucinations and strong feelings of paranoia). By the end of the eighth grade, Alice's grades were so poor and her school attendance so erratic that it was recommended that she be evaluated by a psychologist and possibly held back for a year. The family arranged for such an assessment, and Alice was given a fairly extensive battery of intelligence, achievement, and projective tests. She was found to be extremely intelligent, with an IQ of 130. Projective test results (Rorschach, Thematic Apperception Test) were interpreted as reflecting a significant degree of underlying anger, which was believed to be contributing to Alice's behavioral problems. Of more concern was that Alice gave a number of bizarre and confused responses on the projective tests. For example, when people report what they "see" in the famous Rorschach inkblots, it is usually easy for the tester to share the client's perception. Several of Alice's responses, however, just didn't match any discernible features of the inkblots. This type of response is usually seen in more serious disorders such as schizophrenia. The psychologist, although having no knowledge of Alice's home life, suspected that her problems may have been a reflection of her difficulties at home and recommended family therapy at a local community mental health center.

Several months later Alice and her mother and sister had their first appointment with a social worker at the mental health center. Mr. Siegel was distrustful of the prospect of therapy and refused to attend, stating, "No shrink is going to mess with my head!" In the ensuing therapy, the social worker first took a detailed family history. She noticed that Alice appeared very guarded and was reluctant to share any feelings about or perceptions of the events of her life. The next phase of family therapy was more educational in nature, consisting of teaching Mrs. Siegel more effective methods of discipline and helping Alice to see the importance of attending school on a regular basis.

Family therapy ended after three months with only marginal success. Although Mrs. Siegel had been a highly motivated client and diligently followed the therapist's suggestions, Alice had remained a reluctant participant in the therapy and was unwilling to open up. One very serious problem Alice had been experiencing had not even been brought to light; she was being sexually abused by her older stepbrother, Michael. The abuse had started soon after her mother's marriage to Mr. Siegel. Michael had told Alice that it was important for her to learn about sex and, after having sexual intercourse with her, threatened that if she ever told anyone he would tell all her friends that she was a "slut." This pattern of abuse continued on numerous occasions whenever Michael was living with his father. Even though Alice found these encounters aversive, she felt unable to refuse participation or to let anyone know what was occurring. At the time Mr. and Mrs. Siegel divorced, when Alice was 15 years old, these instances of sexual abuse were the extent of Alice's sexual experience. She was left feeling depressed and guilty, with a very low opinion of herself.

When Alice began high school, she continued her association with the same peer group she had known in junior high. They all regularly abused drugs. Alice had her first experiences of feeling unreal and dissociated from her surroundings while under the influence of drugs. She felt as though she were ghostlike, that she was transparent and could pass through objects or people.

Alice also began a pattern of promiscuous sexual activity. As happened when she was being abused by her stepbrother, she felt guilty for engaging in sex but was unable to turn down sexual advances, from either men or women. She was particularly vulnerable when under the influence of drugs and would, under some circumstances, participate in various sadomasochistic sexual activities. For example, Alice was sometimes physically abused (e.g., struck in the face with a fist) by her sexual partners while having sex. She didn't protest and, after a while, came to expect such violence. On some occasions, Alice's sexual partners would ask her to inflict some kind of pain on them during sexual activity, for example, biting during fellatio or digging her nails into her partner's buttocks. Even though these activities left Alice with a sense of shame and guilt, she felt unable either to set limits on her peers, to leave her particular peer group, or to avoid those whose sexual activities were most troubling to her.

By the time Alice was 16 years old, she rarely, if ever, wanted to spend time alone. She was often bored and depressed, particularly if she had no plans for spending time with anyone else. An important incident occurred at about this time. One night while cruising in a car with friends, a siren and flashing lights appeared. The police stopped the car because it had been stolen by one of her friends. Street drugs were also found in the car. Alice claimed that she had not known that the car was stolen. The judge who subsequently heard the case was provided with information concerning Alice's recent history at home and school. He was quite concerned with what appeared to be a progressive deterioration in Alice's academic performance and social functioning. Because previous outpatient treatment had failed, he recommended inpatient treatment as a means of helping her gain some control over her impulses and preventing future legal and psychological problems. Alice was being offered a choice between being prosecuted as an accessory to car theft and for possession of illegal substances or signing into a mental hospital. Reluctantly, she chose the hospitalization.

During her first hospitalization, Alice's mood swings seemed to intensify. She vacillated between outbursts of anger and feelings of emptiness and depression. She showed signs of depression, such as lack of appetite and insomnia. Antidepressant medication was tried for several weeks and found to be ineffective. Alice spent most of her time with a male patient in the hospital. To any observer, their relationship would not have seemed to have a romantic component. They watched TV together, ate together, and played various games that were available on the ward. After only a couple of meetings with him, Alice had revealed the most intimate details of her life. There was no physical contact or romantic talk. Nonetheless, Alice idealized the man and had fantasies of marrying him. When he was discharged from the hospital and severed the relationship, Alice had her first nondrug-induced episode of feeling unreal (derealization) and subsequently cut herself with a kitchen knife in order to feel real. She began making suicide threats over the telephone to the former patient, saying that if he did not take her back she would kill herself. She was given a short trial of an antipsychotic medication, which proved as ineffective as the antidepressants had been.

While in the hospital, Alice started individual psychotherapy, which was continued after discharge from the hospital. The therapy was psychodynamically oriented and focused on helping Alice to establish a trusting relationship with a caring adult (her therapist). The therapist also attempted to help Alice understand the intrapsychic conflicts that had started very early in her life. For example, the therapist hypothesized that her biological parents' divorce, and Alice's idea that she was somehow responsible for it, led to her fear of being abandoned by people who were important to her. One of the therapist's goals was to show Alice that he would still be available (i.e., not leave her) regardless of how she behaved. It was hoped that this would help Alice to feel more secure in her interpersonal relationships.

Despite these therapy sessions, which she thought were helpful, Alice continued to experience the problems that had developed over the past several years, including drug abuse, promiscuity, depression, feelings of boredom, episodes of intense anger, suicide threats, derealization, and self-injurious behavior (cutting herself). Several hospitalizations were required when Alice's threats and/or self-injurious behavior became particularly intense or frequent. These were usually precipitated by stressful interpersonal events, such as breaking up with a boyfriend or discussing emotionally charged issues in psychotherapy (e.g., her past sexual abuse). Most of the hospitalizations were relatively brief (one to two weeks), and Alice was able to leave after the precipitating crisis had been resolved. She received a number of diagnoses during these hospitalizations, including brief psychotic disorder, major depressive episode, atypical anxiety disorder, adjustment disorder with mixed emotional features, substance use disorder, adjustment disorder with mixed disturbances of emotion and conduct, and borderline personality disorder.

During one of these hospitalizations, Alice decided that she wanted to change therapists, and, after careful consideration, her treatment team decided to grant her request. When Alice was 19 years old, she was introduced to Dr. Swenson, a psychologist, and she began individual behaviorally oriented psychotherapy with him.

Conceptualization and Treatment

Dr. Swenson's approach was somewhat different from that of Alice's previous therapist. It was more focused and more directive, concentrating on helping Alice solve specific problems and to behave in ways that would be more personally rewarding. At the same time, Dr. Swenson did not try to force change on Alice. He was empathic and accepting, and gave Alice the opportunity to identify areas that she wanted to work on. Over a number of sessions Alice and Dr. Swenson identified several problem areas: (1) lack of direction or goals, (2) feelings of depression, (3) poor impulse control, and (4) excessive and poorly controlled anger. Specific interventions were designed for each of these areas. Concerning the first problem, Alice had done so poorly in her schoolwork and was so far behind that going back to high school to graduate was not realistic. Alice therefore decided to study to take an examination for a General Equivalency Diploma, which would then allow her to pursue further education or job training. Alice passed the exam after studying for approximately four months. This success enhanced her self-esteem because she had never before maintained the self-discipline necessary to accomplish any but the most short-term goals.

Because antidepressants had not helped Alice in the past, her depression was treated with cognitive therapy along the lines elaborated by Beck and his colleagues (see Beck, 1967; Beck et al., 1979). The therapy is based on the assumption that a person's thoughts can influence her mood. In order to help Alice become more aware of the thoughts that might make her more vulnerable to depression, she was asked to keep a written record of her mood three times daily. Next to her mood, she wrote down what she was thinking, particularly those thoughts that involved predictions about how a given situation might turn out. Through this exercise, Alice came to realize that she often made negative predictions about how events would turn out and subsequently felt sad and depressed.

In order to learn to restructure or "talk back" to these negative thoughts, Alice was given another exercise. When faced with an anxiety-provoking situation, Alice was asked to write three different scenarios for the situation: (1) a worst-case scenario in which everything that could go wrong did go wrong, (2) a best-case scenario in which events turned out just as she wanted, and (3) a scenario that she believed, after appropriate reflection, was most likely to occur. The actual outcome was then compared with the three different predicted outcomes. More often than not, the actual events were markedly different from either the best- or worst-case predictions. With time, this exercise helped Alice control some of her more negative thoughts and replace them with more adaptive and realistic ways of thinking that were based on her own experiences.

An example of the use of cognitive therapy had to do with Alice's difficulties keeping a job. She held numerous part-time jobs that usually lasted for one or two months before she quit or was fired for not showing up to work. Alice typically believed that other people at work (particularly her supervisors) did not like her to begin with and were looking for excuses to fire her. After the smallest of negative interactions with someone at work, Alice assumed that she was about to be fired. She then stopped showing up to work and created a self-fulfilling prophecy. Through monitoring her mood, Alice came to see that the predominant emotion she experienced in these situations was fear—fear that she would be rejected by either her coworkers or supervisors. In order to prevent that, she typically rejected them first. After Alice obtained a part-time job in a supermarket, her therapist had her write out the three scenarios mentioned, prior to her actually starting work. The scenarios Alice produced were as follows:

[worst case] *I'll show up to work and nobody will like me. Nobody will show me how to do my job, and they will probably make fun of me because I'm new there. I'll probably quit after one day.*

[best case] *This will be a job that I can finally do well. It will be the kind of work I have always wanted, and I'll be promoted quickly and earn a high salary. Everyone at work will like me.*

[most likely] *I'm new at work, but everyone else was new at one time too. Some people may like me, and some may not, but that's the way it is with everyone. Some conflict with other people is inevitable. I can still do my job even if everyone does not like me. One bad day at work does not mean I have to quit.*

Alice was instructed to rehearse mentally the "most likely" scenario daily, especially when she felt like quitting. This helped her to keep the part-time job in the supermarket for 18 months, which was substantially longer than she had kept previous jobs.

Alice had a number of problems with impulsivity, chiefly drug abuse, self-mutilation, promiscuity, and anger. Swenson convinced Alice to join Narcotics Anonymous (NA), a nonprofessional self-help group for drug addicts based on the same principles as Alcoholics Anonymous. Whenever Alice had an impulse to use drugs, she was to use a technique called time delay. This involves a commitment not to use drugs for at least 15 minutes and during that time to engage in an alternative activity. This alternative activity could be telephoning another member of NA and asking for help in controlling the impulse to use drugs. A similar approach was taken with Alice's self-mutilation behaviors; she was instructed to telephone Dr. Swenson or go to a hospital emergency room if she thought she could not control the impulse on her own. Since Alice's problems with anger concerned the impulsive manner in which she acted it out, this too was handled with similar procedures. Dr. Swenson attempted to help Alice see anger not as a negative emotion, but as a positive emotion that becomes destructive only when it is too intense. He then taught Alice time-delay procedures to help her wait before expressing anger. During the waiting period, the intensity of the emotion declined, and she had an opportunity to think over different ways of dealing with the situation, possibly resulting in a more appropriate expression of anger.

Alice made noticeable progress over the first few months of therapy with Dr. Swenson, showing a marked decline in her symptoms. She felt optimistic for the first time in a long while. However, this optimism soon deteriorated in the face of conflicts at home. For example, Alice did not want to help maintain the household, either financially or by doing work around the house. She insisted that it was her mother's responsibility to take care of her. She also wanted her boyfriends to be able to spend the night with her, which her mother would not allow. Alice's mother then asked her to move out of the house, but Alice refused. Instead, she threatened suicide, superficially cut her wrists with a razor blade, and had to be rehospitalized. Alice followed this same pattern over the next few years, making apparent gains in therapy for a month or so and then falling back in the face of interpersonal conflict. Each time her problems returned they seemed increasingly stressful for Alice, because she usually came to believe during her periods of relative stability that her problems had been "cured."

When Alice was 22 years old, she decided to attend college on a full-time basis while living at home. Dr. Swenson was opposed to this because Alice had not shown enough psychological stability to complete even a semester of college, let alone a degree program. Alice went to college anyway and soon became sexually involved with another student. As with previous relationships, Alice idealized this boyfriend and became quite dependent on him. She had to be the sole focus of his attention and couldn't tolerate the times when they were apart. After an argument in which Alice smashed plates and glasses on the floor, her boyfriend left her. Alice once again became suicidal and self-destructive. This episode led to the hospitalization described at the beginning of this chapter.

Alice's treatment team at the hospital noted that none of the therapeutic interventions attempted with Alice (e.g., medication, insight-oriented psychotherapy, behavior therapy) had had any lasting impact. Alice had a poor employment history and showed little evidence that she would be able to support herself independently in the foreseeable future. It was also feared that she might continue to deteriorate, perhaps winding up in a state hospital on a long-term basis. It was decided that Dr. Swenson needed help in working with Alice, especially because those symptoms tended to worsen after dealing with difficult issues in therapy. She was referred to a day-treatment program at a local hospital, where she would have regular access to staff members who could provide therapy and support, while living outside the hospital and possibly working part-time at an entry-level unskilled job. The treatment team realized that it would require a great deal of work to convince Alice to accept these recommendations because accepting them would be an admission that she was more seriously disturbed than she cared to admit. Even if she did follow the recommendations, Alice's prognosis was guarded.

Discussion

As an Axis II diagnosis in *DSM-IV-TR*, borderline personality describes a set of inflexible and maladaptive traits that characterize a person's long-term functioning. A person with borderline personality disorder reveals instability in relationships, behavior, mood, and self-image (Blair, Hilsenroth, & Castlebury, 1997; Sanislow, Grilo, & McGlashen, 2000). For example, attitudes and feelings toward other people may vary considerably and inexplicably over short periods of time. Emotions are also erratic and can shift abruptly, particularly to anger. People with borderline personalities are argumentative, irritable, and sarcastic. Their unpredictable and impulsive behavior, such as suicide attempts, gambling, spending, sex, and eating sprees, is potentially self-damaging. These individuals have not developed a clear and coherent sense of self and remain uncertain about their values, loyalties, and choice of career. They cannot bear to be alone, and they have fears of abandonment. They tend to have a series of intense one-on-one relationships that are usually stormy and transient, alternating between idealization (the other person is perfect and can do no wrong) and devaluation (the other person is horrible, worthless). Subject to chronic feelings of depression and emptiness, they make manipulative attempts at suicide. Paranoid ideation and dissociative symptoms may appear during periods of high stress. Alice's interpersonal relationships were both intense and unstable. She was very impulsive, couldn't control her anger, and had an unstable self-image. She clearly met the diagnostic criteria for borderline personality disorder.

A voluminous literature on patients diagnosed as borderlines has been published over the last few decades. Although this category was not included in the first or second edition of the *DSM*, it was still widely used in certain areas of the country. Originally, the diagnosis implied that the person was on the borderline between neurosis and psychosis. The term no longer has this connotation.

The current conception of borderline personality derived from two sources. Based on a review of the literature and their own clinical experience, Gunderson and his colleagues published a set of diagnostic criteria similar to those that eventually appeared in the *DSM* (Gunderson, Kolb, & Austin, 1981). The second source was a study of the relatives of patients with schizophrenia. Some of these relatives had schizotypal personality disorder (described earlier in Chapter 18); other relatives showed a set of characteristics that came to be the diagnostic criteria for borderline personality disorder (Spitzer, Endicott, & Gibbon, 1979).

Borderline personality disorder has a lifetime prevalence of 1 to 2 percent and may be somewhat more prevalent in women than in men (Maier et al., 1992; Swartz et al., 1990). The disorder typically begins in adolescence (McGlashan, 1983). People with borderline personalities are very likely to have an Axis I mood disorder (Manos, Vasilopoulou, & Sotiriou, 1987), and there is a high rate of completed suicide (Paris, 1990). On several occasions Alice met the diagnostic criteria for an episode of major depression with depressed mood, suicidal thoughts, insomnia, poor appetite, and feelings of self-reproach and guilt.

As to comorbidity with other Axis I diagnoses, many of those with borderline personality disorder also meet the diagnostic criteria for posttraumatic stress disorder, eating disorders, and substance abuse (Gunderson & Sabo, 1993; Skodol, Oldham, & Gallagher, 1999; Zanarini et al., 1998). In Chapter 18, we described the extensive comorbidity among the personality disorders. Borderline personality disorder is in much the same position as the other personality disorders. It has high levels of comorbidity with several other personality disorders, including antisocial, histrionic, narcissistic, and schizotypal (Becker et al., 2000; Skodol, Oldham, & Gallagher, 1999).

Both environmental and biological variables have been studied in an attempt to discover the etiology of borderline personality disorder, and a diathesis-stress theory appears promising (e.g., Linehan, 1993). The main stressors appear to lie in family relations. Patients with borderline personality disorder report that their families were low in support and closeness and high in conflict (Klonsky et al., 2000). As with Alice's case, they also report high levels of physical and sexual abuse (Silk et al., 1995), which have been validated in one report (Johnson et al., 1999); patients with borderline personality disorder have often experienced separation from parents during childhood (Paris, Zweig, & Giudzer, 1994). Linehan (1993) proposes that the key factor is what she calls an invalidating environment. In an invalidating environment, a person's needs and feelings are disrespected, and efforts to communicate feelings are ignored or punished.

As to a diathesis, borderline personality disorder runs in families, suggesting it may have a genetic component (Baron et al., 1985). One of the characteristics that may be inherited is neuroticism, a tendency to easily become anxious. Borderline patients are high in neuroticism; this trait is a key feature of borderline personality disorder and is known to be heritable (Morey & Zanarini, 2000; Nigg & Goldsmith, 1994). Also of possible relevance, particularly to the impulsivity and emotional dysregulation of patients with borderline personality disorder, is reduced activity of the neurotransmitter serotonin (Hollander et al., 1994). A diathesis-stress theory may thus provide a way of conceptualizing borderline personality disorder, with childhood experiences providing the stressors and an inherited component, perhaps involving serotonin, the diathesis (Zanarini & Frankenburg, 1997).

Treatment

A number of drugs have been tried in the pharmacotherapy of borderline personality disorder, most notably antidepressants and antipsychotics. However, until recently, most of the available data came from uncontrolled clinical trials. The results from better controlled studies are inconsistent. One research group found that antipsychotics were useful but later failed to replicate this finding and instead determined that an antidepressant (a monoamine oxidase inhibitor) was of some benefit (Soloff et al., 1993).

Object Relations Psychotherapy.   Object relations theory, a branch of psychoanalytic theory, deals with the nature and development of mental representations of the self and others. It includes not only the representations themselves but also the fantasies and emotions attached to these representations and how these variables mediate interpersonal functioning. The object relations of borderlines are often described as malevolent. Analyses of borderline patients' responses to projective tests indicate that they view other people as capricious and destructive for no reason (e.g., Nigg et al., 1992). This theory has been particularly important in the field of personality disorders. The leading contemporary object relations theorist is Otto Kernberg, who has written extensively about the borderline personality.

Kernberg (1985) operates from the basic assumption that borderline personalities have weak egos and therefore experience inordinate difficulty tolerating the regression (probing of childhood conflicts) that occurs in psychoanalytic treatment. The weak ego fears being flooded by primitive primary process thinking of the id. Kernberg's modified analytic treatment has the overall goal of strengthening the patient's weak ego. Therapy involves analysis of a principal defense of the borderline person, namely, splitting, or dichotomizing into all good or all bad and not integrating positive and negative aspects of a person into a whole. Splitting is the result of an inability to form complex object representations that do not fit a simple good/bad dichotomy. That is, the person with borderline personality disorder does not see people as fairly complex and capable of both good and bad behavior. This causes extreme difficulty in regulating emotions because the person sees the world in black-and-white terms. Other people and even the self are either all good or all bad; there is no middle ground. We saw many examples of this in Alice, as when she idolized her boyfriend but could then turn on a dime and hate him.

Kernberg's approach is more directive than that of most analysts: He gives the patient concrete suggestions for behaving more adaptively and will hospitalize a patient whose behavior becomes dangerous to either the self or others. His opinion that such patients are inappropriate for classical psychoanalysis is consistent with a long-term study conducted at the world-famous analytically oriented Menninger Clinic (Stone, 1987).

Dialectical Behavior Therapy.   An approach to treating borderline personality disorder that combines client-centered empathy with behavioral problem solving was suggested by Marsha Linehan (1993). What she calls dialectical behavior therapy (DBT) centers on the therapist's full acceptance of people with borderline personalities with all their contradictions and acting out, empathically validating their (distorted) beliefs with a matter-of-fact attitude toward their suicidal and other dysfunctional behavior. This total acceptance is necessary, argues Linehan, because the patient is extremely sensitive to criticism and rejection and will pull away from therapy if any hint of a possible rejection is perceived. This acceptance is a dialectical (or polar opposite) of the goal of bringing about change in the patient.

The behavioral aspect of the treatment involves helping patients learn to solve problems, that is, to acquire more effective and social-

ly acceptable ways of handling their daily living problems and controlling their emotions. Work is also done on improving their interpersonal skills and in controlling their anxieties. After many months of intensive treatment, limits are set on their behavior. This is consistent with what Kernberg advocates.

Linehan and her associates have reported the results of the first randomized, controlled study of a psychological intervention of borderline personality disorder (Linehan et al., 1991). Patients were randomly assigned either to dialectical behavior therapy or to treatment-as-usual, meaning any therapy available in the community (Seattle, Washington). At the end of one year of treatment and again six and twelve months later, patients in the two groups were compared on a variety of measures (Linehan, Heard, & Armstrong, 1992). Findings immediately after treatment revealed the significant superiority of DBT on the following measures: intentional self-injurious behavior, including suicide attempts, fewer dropouts from treatment, and fewer inpatient hospital days. At the follow-ups, superiority was maintained and, in addition, DBT patients reported less anger and were judged as overall better adjusted than the comparison therapy patients.

This study has generated a great deal of interest in this approach to borderline personality disorder. Workshops and seminars have been offered around the country, and the therapy is becoming rather widely used. Criticism has also begun to emerge (e.g., Scheel, 2000). The number of patients with borderline personality disorder in Linehan's study was small (22), and after treatment, the therapy and control groups did not differ on a number of important variables—depression, suicidal thoughts, overall life satisfaction, and work performance. Clearly, larger scale studies will be needed before dialectical behavior therapy can be regarded as more than just promising.

Alice's therapists faced a common dilemma encountered with borderline patients: Should treatment be aimed at structural intrapsychic change or simply better adaptation to the environment (see Gordon & Beresin, 1983)? Waldinger and Gunderson (1984) found in a retrospective study that relatively few borderline patients complete the process of intensive psychotherapy, often terminating when an impasse in therapy occurs. When Alice decided to change therapists, a decision had to be made as to whether or not she was seeking change in order to avoid working through a difficult impasse in therapy. It was determined that this may have been the case, but that she was unlikely to remain in therapy if her request was not granted.

Although Alice's treatment seemed largely unsuccessful, it should not be assumed that all borderlines are equally impaired. For example, McGlashan (1986) has reported on a 15-year follow-up of patients in several diagnostic groups. As a group, patients with borderline personality disorder fared considerably better than those with schizotypal personality disorder. Indeed, there is a great deal of heterogeneity within the domain of borderline personality disorder. Many patients can be maintained in outpatient psychotherapy without ever being admitted to a hospital, and the outcome of therapy is not invariably negative. One of the major differences between hospitalized and nonhospitalized borderlines is that the latter group is involved in significantly fewer incidents of self-mutilation (Koenigsberg, 1982). Clearly, not all borderline patients are as self-destructive as Alice. Nevertheless, they present a daunting challenge to anyone who treats them.

14 Sexual and Gender Identity Disorders

William V. is a twenty-eight-year-old computer programmer who currently lives alone. He grew up in a rural area within a conservative family with strong religious values. He has two younger brothers and an older sister. William began to masturbate at age fifteen; his first masturbatory experience took place while he watched his sister urinate in an outdoor toilet. Despite considerable feelings of guilt, he continued to masturbate two or three times a week while having voyeuristic fantasies....

On a summer evening at about 11:30 P.M. William was arrested for climbing a ladder and peeping into the bedroom of a suburban home. Just before this incident he had been drinking heavily at a cocktail lounge featuring a topless dancer.... Feeling lonely and depressed [after leaving the bar], he had begun to drive slowly through a nearby suburban neighborhood, where he noticed a lighted upstairs window. With little premeditation, he had parked his car, erected a ladder he found lying near the house, and climbed up to peep. The householders, who were alerted by the sounds, called the police, and William was arrested. Although this was his first arrest, William had committed similar acts on two previous occasions....

[In therapy] William described a lonely and insecure life.... Six months before the arrest, he had been rejected in a long-term relationship.... As an unassertive and timid individual, he had responded by withdrawing from social relationships and increasing his use of alcohol. His voyeuristic fantasies, which were present to begin with, became progressively more urgent as William's self-esteem deteriorated. His arrest had come as a great personal shock, although he recognized that his behavior was both irrational and self-destructive. (Rosen & Rosen, 1981, pp. 452–453. Reprinted by permission of McGraw-Hill Book Company.)

Sexuality is one of the most personal—and generally private—areas of an individual's life. Each of us is a sexual being with preferences and fantasies that may surprise or even shock us from time to time. These are part of normal sexual functioning.

But when our fantasies or desires begin to affect us or others in unwanted or harmful ways, as with William's peeping, they begin to qualify as abnormal. This chapter considers the full range of human sexual thoughts, feelings, and actions that are generally regarded as abnormal and dysfunctional and are listed in DSM-IV-TR as **sexual and gender identity disorders** (Table 14.1).

Our study of these disorders is divided into three major sections. First we examine theory and research in gender identity disorder, a diagnosis used to describe people who believe they are of the opposite sex. Next we consider the paraphilias, in which people are attracted to unusual sexual activities or objects. We include some critical discussion of homosexuality. Though no longer listed as a sexual disorder in the DSM, the history of controversy regarding the status of homosexuality warrants our consideration. Present also in this section is rape, which, although not a diagnostic listing in DSM-IV-TR, merits examination in an abnormal psychology textbook. The third major section of the chapter addresses sexual dysfunctions, disruptions in normal sexual functioning found in many people who are in otherwise reasonably sound psychological health.

Gender Identity Disorder

"Are you a boy or a girl?" "Are you a man or a woman?" For virtually all people—even those with serious mental disorders such as schizophrenia—the answer to such questions is immediate and obvious. And others would also agree unequivocally with the answer. Our sense of ourselves as male or female, our **gender identity**, is so deeply ingrained from earliest childhood that whatever stress is suffered at one time or another, the vast majority of people are certain beyond a doubt of their gender. In contrast, sexual identity or **sexual orientation** is the preference we have for the sex of a partner. For example, a man may be attracted to men—a matter of sexual orientation—without believing he is a woman—a matter of gender identity.

Characteristics of Gender Identity Disorder

People with gender identity disorder (GID), sometimes referred to as **transsexualism**, feel deep within themselves, usually from early childhood, that they are of the opposite sex. They have an aversion to same-sex clothing and activities. The evidence of their anatomy—normal genitals and the usual secondary sex characteristics, such as beard growth for men and developed breasts for women—does not persuade them that they are what others see them to be. A man can look at himself in a mirror, see the body of a biological man, and yet personally experience that body as belonging to a woman. He may try to pass as a member of the opposite sex and may even want to surgically alter his body to bring it in line with his gender identity. Typically when a female transsexual feels sexual attraction to another woman, she views the appeal as heterosexual in nature and also wants the other woman to be attracted to her *as a man*. The situation is analogous for most men who believe themselves to be really women (Carroll, 2000).

When gender identity disorder begins in childhood it is associated with a number of cross-gender behaviors, such as dressing in opposite-sex clothes, preferring opposite-sex playmates, and engaging in play that would usually be considered more typical of the opposite sex (e.g., a boy's playing with Barbie dolls). Gender identity disorder in a child is usually recognized by parents when the child is between two and four years old (Green & Blanchard, 1995). Based on rates of clinic referrals, it appears to be about six times more frequent in boys than in girls (Zucker, Bradley, & Sanikhani, 1997). Most children with gender identity disorder do not grow up to be disordered in adulthood, however, even without professional intervention (Zucker et al., 1984), although many demonstrate a homosexual orientation (Coates & Person, 1985; Green, 1985).

Excluded from GID are people with schizophrenia who on very rare occasions claim to be of the other sex (Manderson & Kumar, 2001), as well as hermaphrodites, so-called intersexed individuals, who have both male and female reproductive organs. GID is also

Table 14.1 Sexual and Gender Identity Disorders

A. Gender Identity Disorder

B. Paraphilias
1. Fetishism
2. Transvestic fetishism
3. Pedophilia
4. Exhibitionism
5. Voyeurism
6. Frotteurism
7. Sexual masochism
8. Sexual sadism
9. Paraphilias not otherwise specified (e.g., coprophilia, necrophilia)

C. Sexual Dysfunctions
1. Sexual desire disorders
   a. Hypoactive sexual desire disorder
   b. Sexual aversion disorder
2. Sexual arousal disorders
   a. Female sexual arousal disorder
   b. Male erectile disorder
3. Orgasmic disorders
   a. Female orgasmic disorder (inhibited female orgasm)
   b. Male orgasmic disorder (inhibited male orgasm)
   c. Premature ejaculation
4. Sexual pain disorders
   a. Dyspareunia
   b. Vaginismus

Source: From DSM-IV-TR, 2000.

DSM-IV-TR Criteria for Gender Identity Disorder

- Strong and persistent identification with the opposite sex
- In children, presence of four or more of the following:
  A. Repeatedly stated desire to be or insistence that she or he is the other sex
  B. Preference for wearing opposite sex clothes
  C. Preference for cross-sex roles in play or persistent fantasies of being of the opposite sex
  D. Preference for stereotypical play of the opposite sex
  E. Preference for playmates of the opposite sex
- In adolescents and adults, such symptoms as desire to be the opposite sex, passing as member of the opposite sex, desire to be treated as a member of the opposite sex, conviction that his or her emotions are typical of the opposite sex
- Persistent discomfort with one's biological sex or a sense of alienation from the gender roles of that sex
  A. In children, manifested by any of the following: In boys, finding penis disgusting and convinced that it will disappear with time; dislike of stereotyped boys' play activities. In girls, rejection of urinating while sitting; belief that they will grow a penis; aversion to developing breasts and menstruating; aversion to conventional female clothing
  B. In adolescents and adults, manifested by any of the following: Strong desire to get rid of secondary sex characteristics via hormones and/or surgery; belief that he or she was born the wrong sex
- Not concurrent with a physical intersex condition
- Causes marked distress or impairment in social or occupational functioning

differentiated from transvestic fetishism, which is one of the paraphilias discussed later in this chapter. Although they often dress in clothing typical of the opposite sex, transvestites do not identify themselves as of the opposite sex.

Predictably, those with GID often arouse the disapproval of others and often experience discrimination in employment when they choose to cross-dress. Disapproving attitudes in Western societies go back hundreds of years. For example, the *Malleus Maleficarum* (witches' hammer, cf. p. 8) was the DSM of the fifteenth and sixteenth centuries and, among other things, invoked God in regarding as witches people who took on the persona of the opposite sex (Carroll, 2000). The prescribed "treatment" was, of course, burning at the stake. But in some societies transsexuals have long been accorded high status. For example, in some Native American cultures the berdache are considered a third gender, neither male nor female, and are not at all viewed in a negative light.

Cross-dressing is less of a problem for women with GID because contemporary fashions have for many years allowed women to wear clothing very similar to that worn by men. People with gender identity disorder generally experience anxiety and depression, not surprising in light of their psychological predicament and the contemptuous attitudes most people have toward them. The prevalence rates for GID are slight, one in about 30,000 for men and one in 100,000 to 150,000 in women (American Psychiatric Association, 1994). It is much more prevalent in children than in adults (Zucker & Bradley, 1995).

Causes of Gender Identity Disorder

The categorization of boys and girls as having their own masculine and feminine ways is so heavily laden with value judgments and stereotyping that considering cross-gender behavioral patterns in children to be abnormal may seem unjustified. In fact, it has been recently argued that GID in childhood should be dropped from the DSM altogether because, as just mentioned, most children who experience some discomfort in their socially prescribed gender role (like boys who dislike rough-and-tumble play) tend not to be uncomfortable about their biological sex and do not grow up to be transsexuals (Barlett, Vasey, Bukowski, 2000).

Biological Factors Setting aside these issues, some data suggest tentatively that these patterns can come from a physical disturbance (also see Focus on Discovery 14.1 for a discussion of nature versus nurture in gender identity). Specifically, evidence indicates that gender identity is influenced by hormones. A study demonstrating this point was conducted on the members of an extended family in the Dominican Republic (Imperato-McGinley et al., 1974). The participants in this study were unable to produce a hormone that is responsible for shaping the penis and scrotum in males during fetal development. They were born with very small penises and scrotums that looked like labial folds. Two-thirds were raised as girls, but when they reached puberty and their testosterone levels increased, their sex organs changed. The penis enlarged, and the testicles descended into the scrotum. Seventeen of eighteen participants then developed a male gender identity.

Other research shows that human and other primate offspring of mothers who have taken sex hormones during pregnancy frequently behave like members of the opposite sex and have anatomical abnormalities. For example, girls whose mothers took synthetic progestins, which are precursors to male sex hormones, to prevent uterine bleeding during pregnancy were found to be tomboyish (e.g., climbing trees, playing with guns) during their preschool years (Ehrhardt & Money, 1967). Young boys whose mothers ingested female hormones when pregnant were found to be less athletic as young children and to engage less in rough-and-tumble play than their male peers (Yalom, Green, & Fisk, 1973). Although such children were not necessarily abnormal in their gender identity, the mother's ingestion of prenatal sex hormones did apparently give them higher than usual levels of cross-gender interests and behavior.

Levels of sex hormones have also been studied in adults with gender identity disorder. In a review of several such investigations, Gladue (1985) found few if any differences in hormone levels among men with GID, male heterosexuals, and male homosexuals. A

Focus on Discovery 14.1

Joan/John: Nature versus Nurture in Gender Identity

In 1965, Linda Thiessen gave birth to twin boys. Seven months later, she noticed that the boys' foreskins were closing, making urination difficult. Her pediatrician recommended circumcision to correct the problem. However, because of either an equipment problem or an error by the surgeon, the penis of John, one of the twins, was destroyed. Although the Thiessens consulted with several physicians, none held out much hope of surgically reconstructing John's penis.

In December 1966, the Thiessens happened to see a television program on which John Money, a well-known sex researcher at Johns Hopkins University, described the successful use of sex-change surgery for transsexuals. The Thiessens contacted Money, who responded optimistically about what could be done for John at Johns Hopkins. Shortly thereafter, the Thiessens went to Baltimore to meet with Money, who proposed that turning John into Joan was the best option. The plan entailed castration, construction of female genitals, later treatment with sex hormones, and relating to the child as a girl. After several months of soul-searching and consultations with many professionals, the surgery was performed and John became Joan.

Several years later Money began to discuss the case with other health professionals, describing it as a total success and using it to buttress his theory that gender identity is determined by the environment. Over subsequent years, he wrote several follow-ups, again claiming success. The facts reveal otherwise. Two researchers who managed to find Joan several years later conducted interviews with her and her parents and discovered a picture very different from the one Money had painted, one that suggests that there is a strong biological influence on gender identity.

Despite having been instructed to encourage feminine behavior in Joan, her parents reported that Joan behaved in a very boyish way. At age two she ripped off her first dress; during her preschool years her play activities were clearly masculine. The same pattern continued into her elementary-school years. At age eleven it was time to begin treatment with female hormones to promote the development of breasts and other feminine characteristics. Vaginal surgery was also recommended to construct a more feminine vagina than the rudimentary one that had been created during the original surgery. Although she reluctantly began taking estrogen, Joan steadfastly held out against the surgery.

By age 14, Joan decided to stop living as a girl. She adopted male attire, began to urinate standing up, and enrolled in a technical high school. Given Joan's refusal to have the surgery and a life that was filled with considerable distress, Joan's physicians finally recommended that she be told the whole story. She immediately decided to do everything possible to reverse the earlier treatments and changed her name back to John. She took male hormones, had her breasts removed, and had an artificial penis constructed. At age twenty-one, John had another operation to improve his artificial penis, and at age 25 he married a woman.

Clearly, this case demonstrates a strong biological underpinning for gender identity; despite not having a penis, being encouraged to behave in a feminine way, and developing breasts as a result of taking estrogen, John never developed a female gender identity (Colapinto, 1997).

more recent study found equivocal results: some women with GID had elevated levels of male hormones, but others did not (Bosinski et al., 1997). Even when differences are found, however, they are difficult to interpret because many people with GID use sex hormones in an effort to alter their bodies in the direction of the sex to which they believe they belong. Even though a researcher may study only transsexuals who have not taken such exogenous hormones for a few months, relatively little is known at present about the long-term effects of earlier hormonal treatment.

The available data, then, do not clearly support an explanation of adult transsexualism solely in terms of hormones (Carroll, 2000). Even less conclusive is the research on possible chromosomal abnormalities, and efforts to find differences in brain structure between transsexuals and control subjects have likewise been negative (Emory et al., 1991).

Social and Psychological Factors   What about the possible role of the environment? Many, perhaps most, young children engage in cross-gender behavior now and then. In some homes such behavior may receive too much attention and reinforcement from parents and other relatives. Interviews with the parents of children who show signs of GID frequently reveal that they did not discourage, and in many instances clearly encouraged, cross-dressing behavior in their atypical children. This holds true especially for feminine boys. Many mothers, aunts, and grandmothers found it cute when the boys dressed in the mother's old dresses and high-heeled shoes, and very often they instructed the youngsters on how to apply makeup. Family albums typically contain photographs of the young boys attired in women's clothing. Such reactions on the part of the family to an atypical child probably contribute in a major way to the conflict between his or her anatomical sex and the acquired gender identity (Green, 1974, 1987; Zuckerman & Green, 1993). A factor

Although dressing up is normal in childhood, most transsexuals trace their gender-identity disturbance to childhood and report dressing in gender-inappropriate clothes.

that may contribute to this pattern of parental behavior is the attractiveness of the child. Boys with GID have been rated as more attractive than control children, and girls with GID as less attractive (Fridell et al., 1996; Zucker et al., 1993). In addition, male patients with GID report having had a distant relationship with their fathers; females report a history of physical or sexual abuse (Bradley & Zucker, 1997).

A novel hypothesis is that stereotypically feminine behavior in boys is encouraged by mothers who, prior to the child's birth, wanted very much to have a girl. This hypothesis was not, however, confirmed in a study by Zucker et al. (1994). Mothers whose sons did not have a childhood feminine identity reported that they had had the same level of interest in having a girl as mothers whose sons did manifest a feminine identification.

Investigators working in this field are very much aware of the culture-relative aspects of masculinity and femininity and of the difference between enjoying activities more typical of the opposite sex and actually believing that one *is* of the opposite sex. The vast majority of little boys engage in varying amounts of traditional feminine play, and little girls in varying amounts of traditional masculine play, with no identity conflicts whatsoever (Green, 1976). This is not to say that feminine boys are not subject to considerable stress. Our society has a low tolerance for boys who engage in activities more typical of girls, whereas girls can play games and dress in a manner more typical of boys and still conform to acceptable standards of behavior for girls (Williams, Goodman, & Green, 1985). In any event, gender identity disorder in both childhood and adulthood is far less prevalent than would be indicated by the numbers of little boys who play with dolls and little girls who engage in contact sports.

Therapies for Gender Identity Disorder

We turn now to the interventions available to help people with gender identity disorder. These interventions are of two main types. One attempts to alter the body to suit the person's psychology; the other is designed to alter the psychology to match the person's body.

Body Alterations A person with GID who enters a program that entails alteration of the body is generally required to undergo six to twelve months of psychotherapy and living as the desired gender (Harry Benjamin International Gender Dysphoria Association, 1998). The therapy typically focuses not only on the anxiety and depression that the person has likely been experiencing but also on various options available to the person for altering his or her body. For example, some people with GID may choose to have only cosmetic surgery; a male-to-female transsexual may have electrolysis to remove facial hair and surgery to reduce the size of the chin and Adam's apple. Many transsexuals also take hormones to bring their bodies physically closer to their beliefs about their gender. For example, female hormones will promote breast growth and soften the skin of male-to-female transsexuals (Schaefer, Wheeler, & Futterweit, 1997). Many people with gender identity disorder go no further than using such methods, but some take the additional step of having sex-reassignment surgery.

Sex-reassignment surgery is an operation in which the existing genitalia are altered to make them more similar to those of the opposite sex. The first sex-reassignment operation took place in Europe in 1930, but the surgery that attracted worldwide attention was performed on an ex-soldier, Christine (originally George) Jorgensen, in Copenhagen, Denmark, in 1952.

For male-to-female reassignment surgery, the male genitalia are almost entirely removed, with some of the tissue retained to form an artificial vagina. At least a year before the operation, female hormones are given to begin the process of changing the body. Most male-to-female transsexuals have to undergo extensive and costly electrolysis to remove facial and body hair and receive training to raise the pitch of their voices, as the female hormones prescribed do not make hair distribution and the voice less masculine. Some male-to-female transsexuals also have plastic surgery to attain a more feminine appearance. At the same time, the sex-change patient begins to live as a female member of society in order to experience as fully as possible what it is like. The genital surgery itself is usually not done until a one- or two-year trial period has been completed. Conventional heterosexual intercourse is possible for male-to-female transsexuals, although pregnancy is out of the question since only the external genitalia are altered.

The female-to-male reassignment process is more difficult in some ways and less difficult in others. On the one hand, the surgically constructed penis is small and not capable of normal erection; artificial supports are therefore needed for conventional sexual intercourse. An operation extends the urethra into the newly constructed penis to allow the person the social comfort of being able to use public urinals. On the other hand, less cosmetic follow-up is needed than for male-to-female transsexuals because the male hormones prescribed to women seeking sexual reassignment drastically alter fat distribution and stimulate the growth of facial and body hair. The relatively greater ease of the cosmetic female-to-male change may be due in part to society's lesser focus on the physical attributes of men. A small, soft-spoken man with a relatively high-pitched voice may be more acceptable to society than a deep-voiced woman of large stature. Nevertheless, sex-reassignment surgery is an option much more frequently exercised by men than by women.

How beneficial is sex-reassignment surgery? Over the years controversy has existed over its benefits, and the quality of the research itself is fairly low (Carroll, 2000). One of the first and most controversial outcome studies (Meyer & Reter, 1979) found no advantage to the individual "in terms of social rehabilitation" (p. 1015). The findings of this study led to the termination of the Johns Hopkins University School of Medicine sex-reassignment program, the largest such program in the United States. However, other researchers criticized the Meyer Reter findings. A review of twenty years of research indicated an overall improvement in social-adaptation rates as a result of sex-reassignment surgery, with female-to-male transsexuals showing somewhat greater success than male-to-female transsexuals (Abramovitz, 1986).

A subsequent review by Green and Fleming (1990) of reasonably controlled outcome studies published between 1979 and 1989 with at least a one-year follow-up drew even more favorable conclusions. Of 130 female-to-male surgeries, about 97 percent could be judged satisfactory; of 220 male-to-female surgeries, 87 percent were satisfactory. Preoperative factors that seemed to predict favorable postsurgery adjustment were (1) reasonable emotional stability, (2) successful adaptation in the new role for at least one year before the surgery, (3) adequate understanding of the actual limitations and consequences of the surgery, and (4) psychotherapy in the context of an established gender-identity program. The authors caution, however, that satisfactory ratings meant only that the patients reported that they did not regret having had the surgery. Such patient reports may be an overly generous criterion for favorable outcome, especially since they follow the investment of considerable time, money, and energy in an outcome that is, for the most part, irreversible. A more recent report from the University of Pennsylvania indicated that sexual responsiveness and sexual satisfaction increase dramatically in both male-to-female and female-to-male transsexuals, with an overall high level of satisfaction with the results of the surgery (Lief & Hubschman, 1993). Finally, an even more recent long-term study found that young men who had undergone sex reassignment were no longer gender dysphoric, had no regrets about the procedures, and were otherwise functioning better than men who had been denied the hormonal treatment and surgery (Smith, van Goozen, & Cohen-Kettenis, 2001).

Sex-reassignment programs continue in many medical-psychological settings. It is estimated that each year in the United States more than 1,000 transsexuals are surgically altered to the opposite sex. Given that people who go to great lengths to have this surgery claim that their future happiness depends on the change, should this surgery be evaluated in terms of how happy such people are afterward? If so, it can probably be said that most GID patients who have crossed over anatomically are generally better off, although some are not. But if a surgically altered transsexual becomes dismally unhappy, is the surgery to be indicted as antitherapeutic? Consider this: people who undergo these procedures often cut their ties to former friends and family members and to many aspects of their previous lives—"Was it I who played tailback on the football team?" Considerable stress is the lot of those who divorce themselves from the past, for the past contributes to

Author and historian James Morris (in a 1960 picture), after sex-reassignment surgery, became Jan Morris (in a 1974 photograph).

our sense of ourselves as people, as much as do the present and the future. A person who has sex-reassignment surgery confronts challenges few others have occasion to face, and this adjustment may well have to be made without the social support of family and friends.

Experienced therapists, whatever their theoretical persuasion, are wary of a client who says, "If only..." The variations are legion: "If only I were not so fat,..." "If only I were not so nervous,..." "If only I had not left school before graduating...." Following each "if only" clause is some statement indicating that life would be far better, even wonderful...if only. Most of the time the hopes expressed are an illusion. Things are seldom so simple. People who focus on the discrepancy between their gender identity and biological makeup tend to blame present dissatisfactions on the horrible trick nature has played on them. But these people usually find that sex reassignment falls short of solving life's problems. It may handle this one set of them, but it usually leaves untouched other difficulties to which all human beings are subject, such as conflicts at work, with intimates, and even within oneself. Indeed, many transsexuals decide against the surgery after the mandatory one-year period of living as the other gender, for they come to realize that their dissatisfactions with their lives are not going to be solved by changing the external aspects of their biological sex (Carroll, 2000).

Alterations of Gender Identity   Is sex reassignment the only option? Surgery and associated hormone administration used to be considered the only viable treatment for gender identity disorder because psychological attempts to shift gender identity had consistently failed. Gender identity was assumed to be too deep-seated to alter. A small number of apparently successful procedures for altering gender identity through behavior therapy have been reported, however.

In one case the patient was a seventeen-year-old male who wanted to change his gender identity rather than—the choice of most transsexuals—change his anatomy to fit his feminine gender identity (Barlow, Reynolds, & Agras, 1973). The treatment involved shaping various specific behaviors, such as mannerisms and interpersonal behavior—how to talk to young women, for instance—but it also included attention to cognitive components, such as fantasies. One technique paired slides of women with slides of men, the idea being that the sexual arousal from the latter might be transferred, or classically conditioned to, the former. This positive approach to changing the arousal properties of images and fantasies was complemented by aversion therapy to reduce the attractiveness of men. After half a year of intensive treatment the young man was thinking of himself as a man, not as a woman, and was finding women sexually attractive. At a five-year follow-up these changes were still present (Barlow, Abel, & Blanchard, 1979).

Two additional cases treated in the same way were reported by Barlow et al. Two men in their mid twenties were on route to sex-reassignment surgery but had second thoughts. The behavioral retraining succeeded in altering their gender identity but not their attraction to men; that is, their sexual orientation remained homosexual.

This work demonstrates that cross-gender identity may be amenable to change. But as the researchers point out, their clients might have been different from others with GID because they consented to participate in a therapy program aimed at changing gender identity. Most transsexuals refuse such treatment. For them, physically altering their bodies is the only legitimate goal. But if the surgical option did not exist, would more professional energy be expended on developing psychological procedures for altering gender identity? And if those procedures involved teaching men to be more traditionally masculine and women more traditionally feminine, would that be desirable or ethically defensible? And consider a recent article by Marks, Green, and Mataix-Cols (2000) that reported fluctuations in gender identity over a period of years, with some men losing all of their gender dysphoria without formal therapy of any kind. Such findings make one wonder whether any kind of gender identity change efforts *or* sex reassignment surgery should even be performed.

These are but some of the ethical conundrums associated with treating disorders of gender identity. Ethical issues are part and parcel of any therapeutic effort, especially when pressures are brought to bear on people to feel uncomfortable with the way they are. We address some of the ethical issues in the treatment of homosexuality later in this chapter (p. 461) and in the final chapter of the book (p. 644).

The Paraphilias

In DSM-IV-TR the **paraphilias** are a group of disorders involving sexual attraction to unusual objects or sexual activities that are unusual in nature. In other words, there is a deviation (*para*) in what the person is attracted to (*philia*). The fantasies, urges, or behaviors must last at least six months and cause significant distress or impairment. A person can have the behaviors, fantasies, and urges that a person with a paraphilia has (such as exhibiting the genitals to an unsuspecting stranger or fantasizing about doing so) but not be diagnosed with a paraphilia if the fantasies or behaviors are not recurrent or if he or she is not markedly distressed by them. Indeed, surveys have shown that many people occasionally fantasize about some of the activities we will be describing. For example, 50 percent of men report voyeuristic fantasies of peeping at unsuspecting naked women (Hanson & Harris, 1997).

As you might suspect, the DSM diagnostic criterion requiring distress or impairment has created some debate because many people with the behavioral features of a paraphilia are neither distressed nor impaired (Hudson & Ward, 1997). For example, someone who has repeatedly had sex with young children but is not distressed or impaired cannot be diagnosed as having pedophilia according to the DSM criteria. Therefore, many researchers as well as clinicians ignore the distress and disability parts of the DSM definition (Maletsky, 2002).

People often exhibit more than one paraphilia, and such patterns can be aspects of other mental disorders, such as schizophrenia, depression, or one of the personality disorders. Accurate prevalence statistics are not available for most of the paraphilias. When responding to a community survey, many people with paraphilias may choose not to reveal their deviance. Similarly, statistics on arrests are likely to be underestimates because many crimes go unreported and some paraphilias (e.g., voyeurism) involve an unsuspecting victim. The data do indicate, though, that most people with paraphilias, whatever their sexual orientation, are male; even with masochism and pedophilia, which do occur in noticeable numbers of women, men vastly outnumber women. As some persons with paraphilias seek nonconsenting partners or otherwise violate people's rights in offensive ways (as we shall see in exhibitionism), these disorders often have legal consequences.

Fetishism

Fetishism involves a reliance on an inanimate object for sexual arousal. The person with fetishism, almost always a male, has recurrent and intense sexual urges toward nonliving objects, called fetishes (e.g., women's shoes), and the presence of the fetish is strongly preferred or even necessary for sexual arousal to occur.

Feet and shoes, sheer stockings, rubber products such as raincoats, gloves, toilet articles, fur garments, and especially underpants are common sources of arousal for fetishists. Some can carry on their fetishism by themselves in secret by fondling, kissing, smelling, sucking, placing in their rectum, or merely gazing at the adored object as they masturbate. Others need their partner to don the fetish as a stimulant for intercourse. Fetishists sometimes become interested in acquiring a collection of the desired objects, and they may commit burglary week after week to add to their hoard.

The attraction felt by the fetishist toward the object has a compulsive quality; it is experienced as involuntary and irresistible. It is the degree of the erotic focalization—the exclusive and very special status the object occupies as a sexual stimulant—that distinguishes fetishisms from the ordinary attraction that, for example, high heels and blue jeans may hold for heterosexual men in Western cultures. The boot fetishist must see or touch a boot to become aroused, and when the fetish is present, the arousal is overwhelmingly strong.

The disorder usually begins by adolescence, although the fetish may have acquired special significance even earlier, during childhood. Fetishists often have other paraphilias, such as pedophilia, sadism, and masochism (Mason, 1997).

Transvestic Fetishism

When a man is sexually aroused by dressing in women's clothing, although he still regards himself as a man, the term **transvestic fetishism**, or transvestism, applies. The extent of transvestism varies from wearing women's underwear under conventional clothing to full cross-dressing. Some transvestites may enjoy appearing socially as women; some female impersonators become performers in nightclubs, catering to the delight that many sexually conventional people take in observing skilled cross-dressing. Unless the cross-dressing is associated with sexual arousal, however, these impersonators are not considered transvestic. Transvestism should not be confused with the cross-dressing associated with gender identity disorder or with the cross-dressing preferences of some homosexuals.

Transvestic fetishism usually begins with partial cross-dressing in childhood or adolescence. Transvestites are heterosexual, always males, and by and large cross-dress episodically rather than on a regular basis. They tend to be otherwise masculine in appearance, demeanor, and sexual preference. Many are married and lead otherwise conventional lives. Cross-dressing usually takes place in private and in secret and is known to few members of the family. This is one of the paraphilias for which the DSM distress and disability criteria do not seem to apply at all.

The urge to cross-dress may become more frequent over time and sometimes is accompanied by gender dysphoria—discomfort with one's anatomical sex, but not to the extent that is found in GID. Transvestism is comorbid with other paraphilias, notably masochism (Zucker & Blanchard, 1997).

Pedophilia and Incest

According to the DSM, **pedophiles** (*pedos*, Greek for "child") are adults who derive sexual gratification through physical and often sexual contact with prepubertal children unrelated to them. DSM-IV-TR requires that the offender be at least sixteen years old and at least five years older than the child. Research does not appear to support the DSM's statement that all pedophiles prefer prepubescent children; some of them victimize postpubescent children who are younger than the legal age to consent to having sex with an adult (Marshall, 1997).

Pedophilia occurs more frequently in men than in women. It is often comorbid with mood and anxiety disorders, substance abuse, and other paraphilias (Raymond et al., 1999). The pedophile can be heterosexual or homosexual. In recent years, the Internet has played an increasing role in pedophilia; pedophiles use the Internet to acquire child pornography and to contact potential victims (Durkin, 1997).

Violence is seldom a part of the molestation—although it can be, as occasionally comes to people's attention through lurid stories in the media. But even if most pedophiles do not physically injure their victims, some intentionally frighten the child by, for example, killing a pet and threatening further harm if the youngster tells his or her parents. Sometimes the pedophile is content to stroke the child's hair, but he may also manipulate the child's genitalia, encourage the child to manipulate his, and, less often, attempt intromission. The molestations may be repeated over a period of weeks, months, or years if they are not discovered by other adults or if the child does not protest.

A minority of pedophiles, who might also be classified as sexual sadists or antisocial (psychopathic) personalities, inflict serious bodily harm on the object of their passion. They may even murder them. These individuals, whether psychopathic or not, are perhaps best viewed as child rapists and are fundamentally different from pedophiles by virtue of their wish to hurt the child physically at least as much as to obtain sexual gratification (Groth, Hobson, & Guy, 1982).

DSM-IV-TR Criteria for Transvestic Fetishism

- Recurrent, intense, and occurring over a period of at least six months in a heterosexual male, sexually arousing fantasies, urges, or behaviors involving cross-dressing
- Causes marked distress or impairment in social or occupational functioning
- Can be associated with a degree of gender dysphoria (discomfort with person's gender identity)

DSM-IV-TR Criteria for Pedophilia

- Recurrent, intense, and occurring over a period of at least six months, sexually arousing fantasies, urges, or behaviors involving sexual contact with a prepubescent child
- Person has acted on these urges, or the urges and fantasies cause marked distress or interpersonal problems
- Person is at least 16 years old and 5 years older than the child

Incest refers to sexual relations between close relatives for whom marriage is forbidden. It is most common between brother and sister. The next most common form, which is considered more pathological, is between father and daughter.

The taboo against incest seems virtually universal in human societies (Ford & Beach, 1951), with a notable exception in the marriages of Egyptian pharaohs to their sisters or other females of their immediate families. In Egypt it was believed that the royal blood should not be contaminated by that of outsiders. The incest taboo makes sense according to present-day scientific knowledge. The offspring from a father-daughter or a brother-sister union have a greater probability of inheriting a pair of recessive genes, one from each parent. For the most part, recessive genes have negative biological effects, such as serious birth defects. The incest taboo, then, has adaptive evolutionary significance.

There is evidence that the structure of families in which incest occurs is unusually patriarchal and traditional, especially with respect to the subservient position of women relative to men (Alexander & Lupfer, 1987). Parents in these families also tend to neglect and remain emotionally distant from their children (Madonna, Van Scoyk, & Jones, 1991). Furthermore, it is believed that incest is more prevalent when the mother is absent or disabled (Finkelhor, 1979), as mothers otherwise usually protect their daughters from intrafamilial sexual abuse.

Incest is listed in DSM-IV-TR as a subtype of pedophilia. Two major distinctions are drawn between incest and pedophilia. First, incest is by definition between members of the same family. Second, incest victims tend to be older than the victims of a pedophile's desires. It is more often the case that a father becomes interested in his daughter when she begins to mature physically, whereas the pedophile is usually interested in the youngster precisely because he or she is sexually immature. Data from penile plethysmography studies (see Figure 14.1 for an explanation of these measures) confirm that men who molest children unrelated to them are sexually aroused by photographs of nude children, whereas men who molest children within their families show greater penile arousal to adult heterosexual cues (Marshall, Barbaree, & Christophe, 1986).

Men who are otherwise conventional in their sexual interests and behavior can be sexually aroused by pedophilic stimuli. In a study using both self-report and penile plethysmographic measures, one-quarter of people drawn from a community sample showed or reported pedophilic arousal (Hall et al., 1995). The investigators found that this arousal was correlated with conventional arousal, that is, the more aroused the people were to adult heterosexual pictures, the more aroused they were to the pedophilic pictures. Although this finding might be disturbing to us, it highlights the importance of the distinction made by the DSM and by health professionals in general between fantasy and behavior.

It is sometimes alleged that child pornography is a critical ingredient in motivating child molestation in some people, but a recent clinical study of eleven male pedophiles indicates that such materials may not even be necessary. These men were arousable by media materials widely available, such as television ads and clothing catalogs picturing young children in underwear. In other words, rather than using explicitly pornographic materials, these men appeared to construct in their minds their own sexually stimulating material from sources generally viewed as innocuous (Howitt, 1995).

As in most paraphilias, a strong subjective attraction impels the behavior. According to Gebhard and his colleagues (1965), pedophiles generally know the children they molest; they are neighbors or friends of the family. Alcohol use and stress increase the likelihood of molesting a child. Recent evidence also suggests that child molesters have sexual fantasies about children when their mood is negative, perhaps as a way to cope with their dysphoria; however, it appears also that having the pedophilic fantasy enhances the negative affect. Perhaps this downward spiral leads at some point to the person's acting on the impulse to molest a child (Looman, 1995). Data also suggest that pedophiles are low in social maturity, self-esteem, impulse control, and social skills (Kalichman, 1991; Overholser & Beck, 1986). Most older heterosexual pedophiles are or have been married.

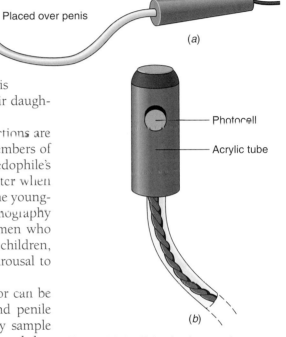

Placed over penis

(a)

Photocell

Acrylic tube

(b)

Figure 14.1 Behavioral researchers use two genital devices for measuring sexual arousal. Both are sensitive indicators of vasocongestion of the genitalia, that is, the flooding of the veins with blood, a key physiological process in sexual arousal; both provide specific measurements of sexual excitement (e.g., Geer, Morokoff, & Greenwood, 1974; Howes, 1998; Lalumiére & Quinsey, 1994). (a) For men, the penile plethysmograph measures changes in the circumference of the penis by means of a strain gauge, consisting of a very thin rubber tube filled with mercury. As the penis is engorged with blood, the tube stretches, changing its electrical resistance, which can then be measured by a suitably configured polygraph. (b) For women, sexual arousal can be measured by a vaginal plethysmograph, such as the device invented by Sintchak and Geer (1975). Shaped like a menstrual tampon, this apparatus can be inserted into the vagina to provide direct measurement of the increased blood flow characteristic of female sexual arousal.

Up to half of all child molestations, including those that take place within the family, are committed by adolescent males (Becker, Kaplan, et al., 1986; Morenz & Becker, 1995). About 50 percent of adult offenders began their illegal behavior in their early teens. These juveniles have typically experienced a chaotic and negative family life. Their homes often lack structure and positive support (Blaske et al., 1989). Many of these teenagers were themselves sexually abused as children (Worling, 1995). Those who engage in child molestation are more socially isolated and have poorer social skills than peers who are in trouble with the law for nonsexual crimes (Awad & Saunders, 1989). Academic problems are also common (Becker & Hunter, 1997). In general, these young males (females are much less often found among the ranks of sex offenders) are what one would call juvenile delinquents, in frequent trouble with the police for a wide variety of lawbreaking. Not surprisingly, conduct disorder and substance abuse are frequent comorbid diagnoses made of these young men. Somewhat more surprisingly, depression and anxiety disorders are also common features (Becker et al., 1991; Galli et al., 1999); perhaps behind their calloused exploitation of young children, these people are profoundly unhappy with their lives.

Because overt physical force is seldom used in incest or pedophilia, the child molester often denies that he is actually forcing himself on his victim. But it is disingenuous to assume that there is no coercion. The adolescent or adult takes advantage of the naiveté of the victim and of the imbalanced power relationship that exists between an adult and a child (e.g., the scoutmaster and one of the boys in his troop, the camp counselor and one of the children in his cabin, and as we have seen the past few years, the priest and an altar boy). Sometimes the molester rationalizes that he is doing something good for the child, despite the betrayal of trust that is inherent in **child sexual abuse** and despite the serious negative psychological consequences that can befall the abused child some years later (Focus on Discovery 14.2).

Both incest and pedophilia occur much more often than was formerly assumed. A study of 796 college students found that an astounding 19 percent of the women and 8.6 percent of the men reported that they had been sexually abused as children. Of the abused women, 28 percent had had incestuous relations; of the men, 23 percent had (Finkelhor, 1979). More recent survey data confirm these findings (Siegel et al., 1987). When states pass more effective legislation on reporting molestation, such as requiring health care professionals and teachers to report child abuse if they suspect it, confirmed cases increase 50 to 500 percent.

Voyeurism

Now and then a man may by chance happen to see a nude woman without her knowing he is watching her. If his sex life is primarily conventional, his act is voyeuristic, but he would not generally be considered a voyeur. Similarly, voyeuristic fantasies are quite common in men but do not by themselves warrant a diagnosis (Hanson & Harris, 1997). **Voyeurism** involves a marked preference for obtaining sexual gratification by watching others in a state of undress or having sexual relations. For some men, voyeurism is the only sexual activity in which they engage; for others, it is preferred but not absolutely essential for sexual arousal (Kaplan & Kreuger, 1997). As in the case of William at the beginning of this chapter, the looking, often called peeping, is what helps the individual become sexually aroused and is sometimes essential for arousal. The voyeur's orgasm is achieved by masturbation, either while watching or later, remembering what he saw. Sometimes the voyeur fantasizes about having sexual contact with the observed person, but it remains a fantasy; in voyeurism, there is seldom contact between the observer and the observed.

A true voyeur, almost always a man, does not find it particularly exciting to watch a woman who is undressing for his special benefit. The element of risk seems important, for the voyeur is excited by the anticipation of how the woman would react if she knew he was watching. Some voyeurs derive special pleasure from secretly observing couples having sexual relations. As with all categories of behavior that are against the law, fre-

DSM-IV-TR Criteria for Voyeurism

- Recurrent, intense, and occurring over a period of at least six months, sexually arousing fantasies, urges, or behaviors involving the observation of unsuspecting others who are naked or engaged in sexual activity
- Person has acted on these urges, or the urges and fantasies cause marked distress or interpersonal problems

quencies of occurrence are difficult to assess since the majority of all illegal activities go unnoticed by the police. Indeed, voyeurs are most often charged with loitering rather than with peeping itself (Kaplan & Kreuger, 1997).

Voyeurism typically begins in adolescence. It is thought that voyeurs are fearful of more direct sexual encounters with others, perhaps because they are not very socially skilled. Their peeping serves as a substitute gratification and possibly gives them a sense of power over those watched. Voyeurs often have other paraphilias, but they do not seem to be otherwise disturbed.

After all restrictions against the sale of pornographic materials to adults had been lifted in Denmark in the 1960s, one of the few observed effects of this liberalization was a significant reduction in peeping, at least as reported to the police (Kutchinsky, 1970). It may be that the increased availability of completely frank pictorial and written material, typically used in masturbation, partially satisfied the needs that had made voyeurs of some men in the absence of other outlets. Perhaps the ready availability of pornography on the Internet will have a similar, but more global, effect.

Exhibitionism

Exhibitionism is a recurrent, marked preference for obtaining sexual gratification by exposing one's genitals to an unwilling stranger, sometimes a child. It typically begins in adolescence (Murphy, 1997). As with voyeurism there is seldom an attempt to have actual contact with the stranger. However, some exhibitionists do get arrested for other crimes involving contact with a victim (Sugarman et al., 1994). Sexual arousal comes from fantasizing that one is exposing himself or from actually doing so, and the exhibitionist masturbates either while fantasizing or even during the actual exposure. In most cases there is a desire to shock or embarrass the observer.

Voyeurism and exhibitionism together account for a majority of all sexual offenses that come to the attention of the police. The frequency of exhibitionism is much greater among men, who are often arrested for what is legally termed indecent exposure. Other paraphilias are very common in exhibitionists, notably voyeurism and frotteurism (see next section) (Freund, 1990).

The urge to expose seems overwhelming and virtually uncontrollable to the exhibitionist, or flasher, and is apparently triggered by anxiety and restlessness as well as by sexual arousal. One exhibitionist persisted in his practices even after suffering a spinal cord injury that left him without sensation or movement from the waist down (DeFazio et al., 1987). Because of the compulsive nature of the urge, the exposures may be repeated rather frequently and even in the same place and at the same time of day. Apparently exhibitionists are so strongly driven that at the time of the act, they are usually oblivious to the social and legal consequences of what they are doing (Stevenson & Jones, 1972). In the desperation and tension of the moment, they may experience headaches and palpitations and have a sense of unreality (also called derealization). Afterward they flee in trembling and remorse (Bond & Hutchinson, 1960). Generally, exhibitionists are immature in their approaches to the opposite sex and have difficulty in interpersonal relationships. Over half of all exhibitionists are married, but their sexual relationships with their spouses are not satisfactory (Mohr, Turner, & Jerry, 1964).

The penile plethysmograph was used in a study of male exhibitionists in an effort to determine whether they were sexually aroused by stimuli that do not arouse nonexhibitionists (Fedora, Reddon, & Yeudall, 1986). Compared with normal people and with sex offenders who had committed violent assaults, the exhibitionists showed significantly greater arousal in response to slides of fully clothed women in nonsexual situations, such as riding on an escalator or sitting in a park, but they showed similar levels of sexual interest in response to erotic and sexually explicit slides. These results are consistent with the hypothesis that exhibitionists misread cues in the courtship phase of sexual contact, in the sense that they construe certain situations as sexual that are judged nonerotic by nonexhibitionists.

> **DSM-IV-TR Criteria for Exhibitionism**
>
> - Recurrent, intense, and occurring over a period of at least six months, sexually arousing fantasies, urges, or behaviors involving showing one's genitals to an unsuspecting stranger
> - Person has acted on these urges, or the urges and fantasies cause marked distress or interpersonal problems

Focus on Discovery 14.2

Child Sexual Abuse: Effects on the Child and Modes of Intervention

Pedophilia and incest are forms of child sexual abuse (CSA) and should be distinguished from nonsexual child abuse. Both sexual and nonsexual abuse can have very negative consequences, and sometimes children suffer both forms of abuse. Nonsexual child abuse may include neglecting the child's physical and mental welfare, for example, punishing the child unfairly; belittling the child; intentionally withholding suitable shelter, food, and medical care; and striking or otherwise inflicting physical pain and injury. Parents often engage in nonsexual abuse of their children when no sexual abuse is involved. Both types of abuse are reportable offenses, that is, such professionals as psychologists and teachers are required by law to report them to the police or child protective agencies.

Effects on the Child

The effects of CSA short term are variable. Almost half of children who are exposed to CSA do not appear to experience adverse effects (Kuehnle, 1998). Among the majority who are negatively affected, problems include anxiety, depression, low self-esteem, and conduct disorder.

Several factors likely contribute to how CSA affects a child. One is the nature of the abuse itself. Consider, for example, the probable differences in consequences between a case involving the repeated raping of a seven-year-old girl by her father over a long period of time, sometimes years, and that of a twelve-year-old boy who has a sexual relationship with an older woman. Sometimes the aftermath of CSA is posttraumatic stress disorder. Indeed, DSM-IV-TR lists sexual assault as one of the stressors that can be traumatic. A high level of self-blame and lack of a supportive family environment increase the chances that the CSA will produce negative reactions (Kuehnle, 1998). No doubt the stress is increased by threats the perpetrator often makes if the child were to tell another adult, for example, killing the child's pet.

Regarding long-term effects, the picture is complex. We have seen in previous chapters that a history of CSA is found among patients in many diagnostic categories—notably, dissociative identity disorder, eating disorders, and borderline personality disorder. It has also been proposed that CSA is related to the development of depression (Culter & Nolen-Hoeksema, 1991), and we will see later in this chapter that it is related to sexual dysfunctions. Other long-term problems include substance abuse, deep distrust of others, and self-mutilation (Litrownik & Castillo-Cañez, 2001). Among these clinically disordered adults, CSA probably served as but one of many factors that combined to produce a clinical disorder. We suggest this possibility because studies of the relationship between CSA *alone* and adjustment in the general population do not find a strong relationship between the two variables (Rind, Tromovitch, & Bauserman, 1998).[*]

The Issue of Betrayal

A molester is usually not a stranger. He may be an uncle, a brother, a teacher, a coach, a neighbor, or even a cleric. This fact is very difficult to discuss with a child, difficult also to confront for ourselves, but the child molester is often a male adult whom the child knows and probably also trusts.

The betrayal of this trust makes the crime more abhorrent than it would be if no prior relationship existed between molester and child. This type of betrayal is also experienced by adults and children who are sexually abused by clergy or others in what can be called ministe-

rial relationships. These offenders include choir directors, religious school teachers, lay ministers, church camp counselors, and seminary faculty and administrators.

The year 2002 saw hundreds of Catholic clergy, some of them bishops, being accused of having molested children many years earlier. (Actually, the first complaints occurred as long ago as the early 1980s.) In most instances these molestations involved boys but in some instances girls and women were also involved. As with childhood incest, molestation or sexual harassment by a religious authority figure violates trust and respect. The victim, whatever his or her age, cannot give meaningful consent even if inclined to do so. The power differential is just too great. Self-blame is likely to be strong in the victim because the offender is part of the person's religion. If the priest or minister or rabbi is doing this, how can it be wrong? Is the cleric not a representative of God? The consequences can be as severe as those found among incest survivors—self-hate, guilt, rage, betrayal, depression, anxiety, and, because religion is involved, a crisis of faith.

When a person is approached sexually by a physician or psychotherapist, he or she is also particularly vulnerable and dependent; the situation is very similar to that a child is in with a parent. Also, because of the offender's special status, the abused person is often disbelieved, leading to considerable reluctance to speak up. As we have seen in news reports over the past several years, sometimes it takes as many as thirty or more years before a person abused as a child musters the courage to speak out. Special legal and ethical problems arise when, during psychotherapy, so-called "recovered memories" come to light. These issues are discussed later in Chapter 18 (p. 646).

---

[*] When the Rind et al. article appeared (it was actually a review of other people's research), it led to an uproar in the press and even in the U.S. Congress. The American Psychological Association (APA), in one of whose journals the paper was published, was accused of condoning the sexual abuse of children because it had published the article. Three years later, in 2001, a brouhaha arose when a manuscript critical of APA's handling of the Rind controversy was rejected in an unusual way by one of APA's leading publications, the *American Psychologist*. This triggered heated discussion on several APA listservs as to whether undue political correctness biased the editor against publishing the paper. These debates led to the ultimate publication of the paper (Lilienfeld, 2002) along with a series of articles critical as well as supportive of what had happened with the Lilienfeld critique of APA. In our view, the negative reactions to the Rind et al. article itself arose from a serious misunderstanding of the meaning of the results. Just because many childhood victims of CSA do not show psychological scars from having been abused, it does not mean that the sexual abuse of children is acceptable. Even if *no* victims of CSA showed any negative effects immediately or years later—and no one was making this claim anyway—it would be entirely consistent to condemn the commission of CSA and to hold perpetrators morally and legally responsible. The distinction between "is" and "ought" is unfortunately not always appreciated when emotionally laden issues like CSA are at stake. Simply stated, the APA and other organizations hold that CSA is wrong, period, whether it leads to negative emotional sequelae or not. Furthermore, the Rind et al. findings are readily interpreted in a way that is self-affirming: The fact that many CSA victims are not permanently affected reflects the ability of people—even as children—to cope with very stressful events and, somehow, to get past negative experiences. This is not to endorse CSA as a way to make people stronger! It is only to say that the fact that many, perhaps most, people somehow survive such bad experiences with a minimum of psychological harm is a testament to the strength of the human spirit.

Prevention

An important goal of any prevention program is to reduce the incidence, prevalence, and severity of a particular problem. For CSA, prevention efforts have focused on elementary schools. Content varies from program to program, but common elements include teaching children to recognize inappropriate adult behavior, resist inducements, leave the situation quickly, and report the incident to an appropriate adult (Wolfe, 1990). Children are taught to say no in a firm, assertive way when an adult talks to or touches them in a manner that makes them feel uncomfortable. Instructors may use comic books, films, and descriptions of risky situations to try to teach about the nature of sexual abuse and how children can protect themselves.

Evaluations of school programs tend to support the notion that they increase awareness of sexual abuse among children, but less is known about whether the children are able to translate what they have learned into overt behavior and whether such changes reduce the problem (Wolfe, 1990). At the very least these programs legitimize discussion of the problem at home (Wurtele & Miller-Perrin, 1987) and might therefore achieve one important goal, namely, to increase the reporting of the crime by encouraging and empowering children to tell their parents or guardians that an adult has made a sexual overture to them.

Dealing with the Problem

When they suspect that something is awry, parents must learn to raise the issue with their children; many adults are uncomfortable doing so. Physicians also need to be sensitized to signs of sexual abuse. As mentioned earlier, licensed health professionals and teachers are required in most states to report sexual abuse (as well as nonsexual child abuse) to child protection agencies or the police when they become aware of it. In California, licensed psychologists must take a day-long course on the subject to ensure that they are at least minimally knowledgeable about it and aware of their legal responsibilities to report child sexual abuse.

For a child, reporting sexual abuse can be extremely difficult. We tend to forget how helpless and dependent a youngster feels, and it is difficult to imagine how frightening it would be to tell one's parents that one had been fondled by a brother or grandfather. Even more threatening are advances from the father, for the child is likely to be torn by allegiance to and love for his or her father on the one hand, and by fear and revulsion on the other, coupled with the knowledge that what is happening is wrong. And when, as sometimes is the case, the mother suspects what is happening to her child and yet allows it to continue, the child's complaints to the mother can be met with lack of support, disbelief, and even hostility. This situation can lead to what is called secondary victimization, psychological damage that results from being punished for reporting the abuse. We will encounter this problem again in our discussion of rape (p. 456).

The vast majority of cases of sexual abuse do not leave any physical evidence, such as torn vaginal tissue. Furthermore, there is no behavioral pattern, such as anxiety, depression, or increased sexual activity, that unequivocally indicates that abuse has occurred (Kuehnle, 1998). Therefore, the primary data regarding CSA must come from the child's self-report. The problem is that leading questions may be needed to facilitate disclosure, but at the same time these leading questions may lead to some false reports. Great skill is required in questioning a child about possible sexual abuse to ensure that the report is accurate, to avoid biasing the youngster one way or the other, and to minimize the stress that is inevitable in recounting a disturbing experience, especially if a decision is made to prosecute. Some jurisdictions use innovative procedures that can reduce the stress on the child while protecting the rights of the accused adult, for example, videotaped testimony, closed-courtroom trials, closed-circuit televised testimony, and special assistants and coaching sessions to explain courtroom etiquette and what to expect (Wolfe, 1990).

Having the child play with anatomically correct dolls can be useful in getting at the truth, but it should be but one part of an assessment, because many nonabused children portray such dolls having sexual intercourse (Jampole & Weber, 1987). All things considered, it is little wonder that many, perhaps most, occurrences of child molestation within families go unreported and become a developing adult's terrible secret that can lower self-esteem, distort what could otherwise be positive relationships, and even in some instances contribute to serious mental disorders.

Parents go through their own crisis when they become aware that someone has been molesting their child. If incest is involved, it is a true family crisis; and if it is the father, then there is often conflict about what to do, for he is frequently the dominant figure in the family and is feared as well as loved. Shame and guilt abound within the home, and the family may well be struggling with other serious problems, such as alcoholism in one or both parents. Decisions have to be made about how to protect the youngster from further sexual abuse or vindictive threats or actions from a frightened, angry perpetrator. The incest victim's mother is in a particularly difficult situation, sometimes torn between her partner and her child, sometimes facing financial uncertainty should the father leave the home or be arrested. It is impossible to know what percentage of incest cases are not reported to the police, but it is safe to say that it is sizable, perhaps the great majority (Finkelhor, 1983). Pedophilic offenses, when the perpetrator is not a member of the family, are more frequently reported to police and prosecuted in court.

Parents also need help in knowing how to respond to the child's allegations. A parent's strong emotional reaction, although understandable, is likely to make the child feel worse, yet the complaints must be taken seriously. It is important to remember that children construe things differently than adults, and although molestation of any kind is serious, pre-school-age children may not understand the exact nature of what has been done to them. Still, they must be protected and sometimes treated for physical injuries.

After the immediate crisis is past, many children may need continued professional attention (Litrownik & Castillo-Cañez, 2001). Like adult survivors of rape—and in a very real sense molested children are often rape victims—posttraumatic stress disorder can be a consequence. Many interventions are similar to those used for PTSD in adults; the emphasis is on exposure to memories of the trauma through discussion in a safe and supportive therapeutic atmosphere (Johnson, 1987). Also important is learning that healthy human sexuality is not about power and fear, that it can be a bolstering part of one's personality as one continues to mature (McCarthy, 1986). Inhibitions about bodily contact can be addressed in group therapy settings via structured, nonsexual hand-holding and back rubs (Wolfe, 1990). As with rape, it is important to externalize the blame for what happened, changing the individual's attribution of responsibility from an "I was bad" self-concept to "He/she was bad." Intervention varies with the person's age—a fourteen-year-old does not need dolls to recount what was done, and a three-year-old is not an appropriate candidate for group therapy. As yet there has been no controlled research on these various and complex interventions, but clinical reports are encouraging.

DSM-IV-TR Criteria for Frotteurism

- Recurrent, intense, and occurring over a period of at least six months, sexually arousing fantasies, urges, or behaviors involving touching and rubbing up against a nonconsenting person
- Person has acted on these urges, or the urges and fantasies cause marked distress or interpersonal problems

DSM-IV-TR Criteria for Sexual Masochism

- Recurrent, intense, and occurring over a period of at least six months, sexually arousing fantasies, urges, or behaviors involving the act (not the fantasy) of being humiliated or beaten
- Causes marked distress or impairment in social or occupational functioning

DSM-IV-TR Criteria for Sexual Sadism

- Recurrent, intense, and occurring over a period of at least six months, sexually arousing fantasies, urges, or behaviors involving acts (not the fantasy) in which the humiliation or physical suffering of the other is sexually arousing
- Causes marked distress or impairment in social or occupational functioning or the person has acted on these urges with a nonconsenting other

Frotteurism

Frotteurism involves the sexually oriented touching of an unsuspecting person. The frotteur may rub his penis against a woman's thighs or buttocks or fondle her breasts or genitals. These attacks typically occur in places, such as a crowded bus or sidewalk, that provide an easy means of escape. Frotteurism has not been studied very extensively. It appears to begin in adolescence and typically occurs along with other paraphilias (Krueger & Kaplan, 1997).

Sexual Sadism and Sexual Masochism

A marked preference for obtaining or increasing sexual gratification by inflicting pain or psychological suffering (such as humiliation) on another is the key characteristic of **sexual sadism**. A marked preference for obtaining or increasing sexual gratification through subjecting oneself to pain or humiliation is the key characteristic of **sexual masochism**.

Both these disorders are found in heterosexual and homosexual relationships. Some sadists and masochists are women; surveys have found that 20 to 30 percent of the members of sadomasochistic clubs are female (Moser & Levitt, 1987). Alcoholism is common among sadists (Allnut et al., 1996). The disorders seem to begin by early adulthood, and most sadists and masochists are relatively comfortable with their unconventional sexual practices (Spengler, 1977). The majority of sadists and masochists lead otherwise conventional lives, and there is some evidence that they are above average in income and educational status (Moser & Levitt, 1987; Spengler, 1977).

The majority of sadists establish relationships with masochists to derive mutual sexual gratification. From 5 to 10 percent of the population has engaged in some form of sadomasochistic activity, such as blindfolding one's partner, but few do so regularly, and even fewer prefer such activities during sex (Baumeister & Butler, 1997). The sadist may derive full orgasmic pleasure by inflicting pain on his or her partner, and the masochist may be completely gratified by being subjected to pain. For other partners the sadistic and masochistic practices, such as spanking, are a prelude to or aspect of sexual intercourse.

Although a great many people are switchable—that is, able to take both dominant and submissive roles—masochists outnumber sadists. For this reason bondage-and-discipline services may constitute a considerable portion of the business of a house of prostitution. The manifestations of sexual masochism are varied. Examples include restraint (physical bondage), blindfolding (sensory bondage), spanking, whipping, electric shocks, cutting, humiliation (e.g., being urinated or defecated on, being forced to wear a collar and bark like a dog, or being put on display naked), and taking the role of slave and submitting to orders and commands. The term infantilism refers to a desire to be treated like a helpless infant and clothed in diapers. One particularly dangerous form of masochism, called hypoxyphilia, involves sexual arousal by oxygen deprivation, which can be achieved using a noose, a plastic bag, chest compression, or a chemical that produces a temporary decrease in brain oxygenation by peripheral vasodilation (American Psychiatric Association, 1994).

The shared activities of a sadist and a masochist are heavily scripted (Gagnon & Simon, 1977); that is, they are embedded in a story with agreed-upon rules and procedures. In fact, the loss of control that masochists seem to desire is partly illusory since they have typically established clear rules about what activities they want to engage in. Pain, humiliation and domination, or both take place as part of a story that the two participants agree to act out together. The activities of the sadist and masochist assume for both parties a certain fictional meaning that heightens sexual arousal. The masochist, for example, may be a mischievous child who must be punished by a discipline-minded teacher or a slave from ancient times, recently sold to a powerful sultan. Themes of submission–domination appear to be as important as the infliction of physical pain.

Occasionally, sadists murder and mutilate; and some are among sex offenders who are imprisoned for torturing victims, mostly strangers, and deriving sexual satisfaction from doing so (Dietz, Hazelwood, & Warren, 1990). When sadists commit acts of aggression against people, the pattern of their offenses differs from that of nonsadistic sex offenders; sadistic offenders seem more often to impersonate police officers, commit serial murders, tie up their victims, and conceal corpses (Gratzer & Bradford, 1995).

Etiology of the Paraphilias

Of the many theories and hypotheses about the etiology of the paraphilias, the principal ones come from psychodynamic and behavioral perspectives; others are from the biological perspective.

Psychodynamic Perspectives   The paraphilias are viewed by psychodynamic theorists as defensive in nature, guarding the ego from dealing with repressed fears and memories and representing fixations at pregenital stages of psychosexual development. The person with a paraphilia is seen as someone who is fearful of conventional heterosexual relationships, even of heterosocial relationships that do not involve sex. His (less often, her) social and sexual development is immature, stunted, and inadequate for both social and heterosexual intercourse with the adult world (Lanyon, 1986).[1]

For example, the fetishist and the pedophile are viewed as men whose castration anxiety makes heterosexual sex with adult women too threatening. Castration anxiety leads the exhibitionist to reassure himself of his masculinity by showing his manhood (his genitals) to others (usually girls and women); it results in the sadist dominating others.

The voyeur prefers to spy on unaware women rather than to have direct contact with them. If the woman whom the voyeur is watching should become aware of him, he might conclude that she has some interest in him; because of his insecurity as a man and a lover, that would be extremely threatening and therefore less sexually arousing to him. It may be, then, that a man engages in voyeurism not because the risk of being discovered is titillating; rather, undiscovered peeping, because it protects the voyeur from a possible relationship with a woman, may be the least frightening way for him to have some kind of contact with her.

Behavioral and Cognitive Perspectives   Some theorists operating within a behavioral paradigm hold the view that the paraphilias arise from classical conditioning that by chance has linked sexual arousal with classes of stimuli deemed by the culture to be inappropriate. Though seldom acknowledged in the behavior therapy literature, this theory was first put forward in the famous Kinsey reports on sexual behavior in American men and women (Kinsey, Pomeroy, & Martin, 1948; Kinsey et al., 1953). For example, a young man may masturbate to pictures or images of women dressed in black leather boots. According to this theory, repetitions of these experiences make boots sexually arousing. Similar proposals have been made for transvestism, pedophilia, voyeurism, and exhibitionism. Although there is some minor support from clinical case studies (e.g., McGuire, Carlisle, & Young, 1965) and controlled experimentation (e.g., Rachman, 1966), this orgasm-conditioning hypothesis has very little empirical support (O'Donohue & Plaud, 1994). However, as described later, some innovative therapeutic strategies have been developed based on this etiological speculation.

Most current behavioral and cognitive theories of the paraphilias are multidimensional and propose that a paraphilia results when a number of factors impinge on an individual. The childhood histories of individuals with paraphilias reveal that often they were subjected to physical and sexual abuse and grew up in a family in which the parent–child relationship was disturbed (Mason, 1997; Murphy, 1997). These early experiences may well contribute to the low level of social skill, low self-esteem, loneliness, and lack of intimate relationships often seen among those with paraphilias (Kaplan & Kreuger, 1997; Marshall, Serran, & Cortoni, 2000). Paraphilias such as exhibiting or peeping may thus be activities that substitute for more conventional relationships and sexual activity. On the other hand, the fact that many pedophiles and exhibitionists have conventional social-sexual relationships indicates that the issue is more complex than a simple absence of nondeviant sexual outlets (Langevin & Lang, 1987; Maletsky, 2000). Furthermore, the widely accepted belief that sexual abuse in childhood predisposes people to paraphilic behavior in adulthood needs to be qualified by research showing that fewer than a third of adult sex offenders were sexually abused when they were below the age of eighteen (Maletzky, 1993).

---

[1] It is interesting to note that psychoanalytic views of sexual problems often implicate nonsexual factors such as those just mentioned, whereas analytic theorizing about nonsexual disorders usually implicates sexual urges.

Table 14.2 Examples of Distortions, Assumptions, and Justifications in Sexual Paraphilias

Category	Pedophilia	Exhibitionism	Rape
Misattributing blame	"She started it by being too cuddly." "She would always run around half-dressed."	"She kept looking at me like she was expecting it." "The way she was dressed, she was asking for it."	"She was saying no, but her body said yes." "I was always drinking when I did it."
Minimizing or denying sexual intent	"I was just teaching her about sex… better from her father than someone else."	"I was just looking for a place to pee." "My pants just slipped down."	"I was just trying to teach her a lesson; she deserved it."
Debasing the victim	"She'd had sex before with her boyfriend." "She always lies."	"She was just a slut anyway."	"The way she came on to me at the party, she deserved it." "She never fought back; she must have liked it."
Minimizing consequences	"She's always been real friendly to me, even afterward." "She was messed up even before it happened."	"I never touched her, so I couldn't have hurt her." "She smiled, so she must have liked it."	"She'd had sex with hundreds of guys before. It was no big deal."
Deflecting censure	"This happened years ago. Why can't everyone forget about it?"	"It's not like I raped anyone."	"I only did it once."
Justifying the cause	"If I wasn't molested as a kid, I'd never have done this."	"If I knew how to get dates, I wouldn't have to expose."	"If my girlfriend gave me what I want, I wouldn't be forced to rape."

Source: Maletzky, B. M. (2002). The paraphilias research and treatment. In P. E. Nathan and J. M. Gorman (Eds.), A Guide to Treatments that Work (pp. 525-558). New York: Oxford University Press.

Distorted parent–child relationships may also create hostility or a general negative attitude and lack of empathy toward women, which may increase the chances of victimizing a woman. Alcohol and negative affect often are triggers of incidents of pedophilia, voyeurism, and exhibitionism. This is consistent with what we know about the disinhibiting effects of alcohol (see Chapter 12). Deviant sexual activity, like alcohol use, may be a means of escaping from negative affect (Baumeister & Butler, 1997).

Cognitive distortions also play a role in the paraphilias. For example, a voyeur may believe that a woman who left her blinds up while undressing really wanted someone to look at her (Kaplan & Kreuger, 1997). A pedophile may believe that children really want to have sex with adults (Marshall, 1997). Table 14.2 contains examples of the kinds of unwarranted beliefs that may be associated with pedophilia and exhibitionism. Rape, a topic dealt with late in this chapter, is also included in the table.

Hypotheses that focus on cognitions sometimes sound psychoanalytic in nature. For example, some clinicians of a cognitive-behavioral perspective and some of a psychodynamic persuasion regard transvestism as a beleaguered male's refuge from responsibilities he sees himself saddled with solely by virtue of being a man. Women's clothing, then, is believed to have a particular meaning for the male transvestite beyond any sexual arousal he experiences by donning it. Perhaps less rigid gender roles will alter the meaning that women's clothes have for such men.

From an operant conditioning perspective, many paraphilias are considered an outcome of inadequate social skills or reinforcement of unconventionality by parents or relatives. For example, case histories of transvestites often refer to childhood incidents in which the little boy was praised and fussed over for looking cute in his mother's dresses.

Biological Perspectives As the overwhelming majority of people with paraphilias are male, there has been speculation that androgen, the principal male hormone, plays a role. Because the human fetus begins as a female, with maleness emerging from later hormonal influences, perhaps something can go wrong during fetal development. Findings of hormonal differences between normal people and people with paraphilias are inconclusive, however. As to differences in the brain, a dysfunction in the temporal lobe may be relevant to a minority of cases of sadism and exhibitionism (Mason, 1997; Murphy, 1997). If biology turns out to be important, it most likely will be but one factor in a complex network of causes that includes experience as a major, if not the major, player (Meyer, 1995).

Therapies for the Paraphilias

Because most paraphilias are illegal, many people diagnosed with them are imprisoned and their treatment is ordered by the court. Outcomes for incarcerated adult sex offenders are highly variable; published success rates range from more than 90 percent to as low as 30 percent (Marshall et al., 1991). Juvenile sex offenders have also been the focus of some research, as most offenders begin in adolescence. The results, as with the findings on adults, are quite variable (Becker & Hunter, 1997). Published data are hard to interpret for several reasons. Experimental designs are not the rule here; ethical considerations have led most researchers to conclude that control groups should not be used. Some programs select the most problematic prisoners for treatment, whereas others treat those with the most promising prognoses, for example, first offenders. Some programs do not have follow-up sessions after release, whereas others do. Recidivism increases as the years go by, especially when two years have passed since termination of treatment (Maletzky, 2002).

As we have seen with substance abusers, sex offenders often lack motivation to try to change their illegal behavior. Undermining their motivation for treatment are such factors as denial of the problem, minimization of the seriousness of their problem, a belief that their victims will not be credible witnesses, and the confidence that they can control their behavior without professional assistance. Some blame the victim—even a child— for being overly seductive. For these reasons (see Table 14.2) such people are frequently judged to be inappropriate for treatment programs (Dougher, 1988); when they do become involved, they frequently drop out (Knopp, 1984). There are several methods to enhance their motivation to commit to treatment (Miller & Rollnick, 1991):

1. The therapist can empathize with the offender's reluctance to admit that he is an offender, thereby reducing the defensiveness and hostility
2. The therapist can point out to the offender the treatments that might help him control his behavior better and emphasize the negative consequences of refusing treatment (e.g., transfer to a less attractive incarceration setting if the person is already in custody) and of offending again (e.g., stiffer legal penalties)
3. Having elaborated on the possible benefits of treatment, the therapist can implement a paradoxical intervention (see p. 586) by expressing doubt that the person is motivated to enter into or continue in treatment, thereby challenging him to prove wrong the therapist whom he has been resisting
4. The therapist can explain that there will be a psychophysiological assessment of the patient's sexual arousal, the implication being that this can reveal the patient's sexual proclivities without his admitting to them (Garland & Dougher, 1991)

With the foregoing as background, we now describe psychoanalytic, behavioral, cognitive, and biological treatments for the paraphilias. A final section considers legal efforts to protect the public from sex offenders.

Psychoanalytic Therapy   A prevalent psychoanalytic view of the paraphilias is that they arise from a character disorder, an older term for personality disorder, and that they are therefore exceedingly difficult to treat with any reasonable expectation of success. This perspective is probably also held by the courts and by the lay public (Lanyon, 1986). Although psychoanalytic views have had an impact on views of causation, they have made few contributions to effective therapy for these disorders.

Behavioral Techniques   Behavior therapists have been less interested in presumed deep-seated personality defects among people with paraphilias and have focused more on the particular pattern of unconventional sexuality. Consequently, they have tried to develop therapeutic procedures for changing only the sexual aspect of the individual's makeup. Some successes have been achieved, especially when a variety of techniques are used in a broad-spectrum, multifaceted treatment (Becker, 1990; Maletzky, 2002; Marshall et al., 1991).

In the earliest years of behavior therapy, paraphilias were narrowly viewed as attractions to inappropriate objects and activities. Looking to experimental psychology for ways to reduce these attractions, researchers fixed on aversion therapy. Thus a boot fetishist would be given shock (on the hands or feet) or an emetic (a drug that produces nausea) when looking at a boot, a transvestite when cross-dressing, a pedophile when gazing at a photograph of a nude child, and so on. A variation based on imagery is covert sensitization, whereby the person *imagines* situations he finds inappropriately arousing and imagines also feeling sick or ashamed for feeling and acting this way (Cautela, 1966). Although aversion therapy may not completely eliminate the attraction, in some cases it provides the patient with a greater measure of control over the overt behavior (McConaghy, 1990, 1994). Another method is called satiation; the man masturbates for a long time, typically after ejaculating, while fantasizing out loud about his deviant activity. There is reason to believe that both aversion therapy and satiation, especially when combined with other types of psychological interventions, such as social-skills training, can have some beneficial effects on pedophilia, transvestism, exhibitionism, and fetishism (Brownell, Hayes, & Barlow, 1977; Laws & Marshall, 1991; Marks & Gelder, 1967; Marks, Gelder, & Bancroft, 1970; Marshall & Barbaree, 1990).

Orgasmic reorientation has been employed to help the patient learn to become more aroused by conventional sexual stimuli. In this procedure patients (again, most of whom are men) are confronted with a conventionally arousing stimulus, such as a photograph of a woman, while they are responding sexually for other, undesirable reasons. In the first clinical demonstration of this technique, Davison (1968a) instructed a young man troubled by sadistic fantasies to masturbate at home in the following manner:

> When assured of privacy in his dormitory room…he was first to obtain an erection by whatever means possible—undoubtedly with a sadistic fantasy, as he indicated. He was then to begin to masturbate while looking at a picture of a sexy, nude woman (the target sexual stimulus)…. If he began losing his erection, he was to switch back to his sadistic fantasy until he could begin masturbating effectively again. Concentrating again on the…picture, he was to continue masturbating, using the fantasy only to regain the erection. As orgasm was approaching, he was at all costs to focus on the…picture. (p. 84)

The client was able to follow these instructions, and over a period of weeks began to find conventional pictures, ideas, and images sexually arousing. However, the therapist had to complement the orgasmic procedure with some covert sensitization for the sadistic fantasies. The follow-up after a year and a half found the client capable of conventional arousal, although he apparently reverted at will to his sadistic fantasies every now and again. This dubious outcome has been reported for other instances of orgasmic reorientation. Behavior therapists continue to explore its possibilities, despite no clear evidence of its effectiveness (Laws & Marshall, 1991).

In addition to the arousal-based procedures just described, several other techniques are in widespread use. Social-skills training is often used because many individuals with paraphilias have social-skills deficits. Another technique, alternative behavioral completion, entails imagining a typical deviant activity but changing its ending.

> As you drive home one night you notice an attractive woman driver on your right in a van. She can see right into your car. You slow down and drive parallel with her as you begin to get aroused. You want to rub your penis and take it out to show her. However, the urge this time is weaker and you drive past her quickly without exposing. You feel good about yourself for being able to exert control. (Maletzky, 1997, p. 57)

Cognitive Treatment   Cognitive procedures are often used to counter the distorted thinking of individuals with paraphilias. Table 14.2 (p. 450) contains examples of cognitive distortions that would be targets for modification. For example, an exhibitionist might claim that the girls he exposes himself to are too young to be harmed by it. The therapist would counter this distortion by pointing out that the younger the victim the worse the harm will be (Maletzky, 1997). Training in empathy toward others is another cognitive technique; teaching the patient to consider how his behavior would affect someone else may lessen the sex offender's tendency to engage in such activities. Relapse prevention, modeled after the work on substance abuse described in Chapter 12, is also an important component of many treatment programs.

In general, cognitive and behavioral approaches have become more sophisticated and broader in scope since the 1960s, when the paraphilias were addressed almost exclusively in terms of sexual attraction that had been classically conditioned to inappropriate environmental stimuli. In many instances therapy is modeled on the approach of Masters and Johnson (1970; cf. p. 468), under the assumption that some paraphilias develop or are maintained by unsatisfactory sexual relationships with consenting adults (Marshall & Barbaree, 1990). Overall, both institution-based and outpatient programs that follow a cognitive-behavioral model with sex offenders reduce recidivism more than what would be expected were no treatment at all attempted (Maletzky, 2002). These outcomes are much better for child molesters than for rapists. Although sex offenders generally evoke disgust and fear more than genuine interest from people, society often overlooks the fact that efforts to treat such people, even if only minimally effective, are not only cost-effective but stand the chance of protecting others when the person is released from prison (Prentky & Burgess, 1990).

Biological Treatment   A variety of biological interventions have been tried on sex offenders. Castration, or removal of the testes, was used a great deal in western Europe two generations ago, with some apparent effectiveness in reducing the incidence of paraphilic behavior (e.g., Langeluddeke, 1963). However, those operated on were a heterogeneous group; among them were homosexuals involved in noncoercive sex with other adults (Marshall et al., 1991). It is unclear how many were offenders whose crimes harmed innocent others—that is, child molesters and rapists. The lack of clarity of outcome, coupled with major ethical concerns, has led to infrequent use of castration today, although there are trends to use chemical means, as described next.

Biological efforts to control illegal and socially disapproved paraphilic behavior among sex offenders have more recently involved the use of drugs. Treatment has employed medroxyprogesterone acetate (MPA, trade name Depo-Provera), which lowers testosterone levels in men. By reducing the frequency of erections and ejaculations, use of this drug presumably inhibits sexual arousal (to both conventional and unconventional stimuli) and consequent disapproved behavior. Cyproterone acetate, which also lowers testosterone levels, has also been used to produce similar effects (Hall, 1995).

Results so far are mixed. An early study by Berlin and Meinecke (1981) found that after periods of MPA administration ranging from five to twenty years, seventeen of twenty sex offenders did not engage in paraphilic behaviors; however, when the drug was discontinued, most reverted to such behavior. More recent findings are more positive in reducing recidivism (Prentky, 1997). However, if these sexual appetite suppressants have to be taken indefinitely, many ethical issues are raised, particularly as these drugs may have serious side effects with long-term use, such as infertility and diabetes (Gunn, 1993). Another problem is the high drop-out rate among participants in these programs. Fluoxetine (Prozac) has recently been tried, with uncertain outcomes, because of its occasional effectiveness in treating obsessions and compulsions, the rationale being that paraphilias are constituted of irresistible thoughts and urges similar to OCD (Kafka, 1995).

Megan's Law   The variable outcomes of efforts to rehabilitate sex offenders, which often result in the release from prison of rapists and child molesters who commit these crimes again, have led to public pressure to forbid such offenders from returning to the locales where they were arrested. A further trend is exemplified in recent laws that allow police to publicize the whereabouts of registered sex offenders if they are considered to be a potential danger. These laws also permit citizens to use police computers to determine whether such individuals are living in their neighborhoods.

Referred to by some as Megan's law, this statute and others like it across the United States arose from public outrage at the brutal murder of a second grader in New Jersey who was kidnapped while walking home from school. The person convicted of this crime was a twice-convicted child molester. The law applies to sex offenders who have harmed either adults or children (Ingram, 1996). Tracking offenders is facilitated by a national computer network created by President Clinton in August 1996, which allows police to monitor these people anywhere in the United States (Kempster, 1996).

An unintended consequence of Megan's law is that people who were arrested many years ago for consensual gay sex have been contacted by police departments to demand that they register as sex offenders so that their presence in their community can be known—even though the laws under which these people were originally arrested are no longer on the books, and even though the current concern is to protect people from sexual predators, not from people involved long ago in consensual homosexual sex with another adult. It should come as no surprise that these laws are being challenged by civil rights groups.

We have mentioned rape several times in our discussion of the paraphilias, especially in connection with pedophilia and incest; yet forced sexual contact occurs far more often between adults than between an adult and a child. We turn now to an examination of the important topic of rape.

Rape

In legal terms, rape falls into two categories—forced and statutory. **Forced rape** is sexual intercourse with an unwilling partner. **Statutory rape** refers to sexual intercourse with a minor, someone under the age of consent. The age of consent is decided by state statutes and is typically eighteen, although in recent years people have suggested lowering the age. It is assumed that a person younger than the age of consent should not be held responsible for her sexual activity. A charge of statutory rape can be made even if the person says that she entered into the situation knowingly and willingly. Thus statutory rape need not involve force, only sex with a minor that was reported to the police. We focus in this section on forced rape.

The Crime

The specifics of rape cases vary widely. Some rapes are planned, and some are thought to be more impulsive, spur-of-the moment crimes. Up to 70 percent of rapes are associated with intoxication (Marshall & Barbaree, 1990). Some rapes seem motivated by a desire to control the other person. Others are more clearly sexually motivated, although many rapists experience erectile failure or fail to reach organism (Groth & Burgess, 1977; Hudson & Ward, 1997). In what is sometimes termed sadistic rape, the rapist severely injures the victim, for example, by inserting foreign objects into her vagina or pulling and burning her breasts; some rapists also murder their victims. Little wonder, then, that rape is considered as much an act of violence, aggression, and domination as an act of sex. In many jurisdictions the definition of rape includes forced oral and anal entry as well as vaginal penetration. Although men can be victims of sexual assault—especially by other men in prison—our discussion focuses on women because rape is primarily an act committed by men against women.

Many feminist groups object to the classification of rape as a sexual crime at all, lest this terminology mask the basically assaultive and typically brutal nature of the act and create an atmosphere in which the sexual motives of the victim are questioned. Although a person who is beaten and robbed without being sexually abused is hardly suspected of secretly wanting to be attacked, by cruel irony a woman who has been raped must often prove her moral purity to husband, friends, police—even to herself. What did she do that might have contributed to the incident? After all, she must have done something, especially if the rapist is not a complete stranger. There are indications that such attitudes are being replaced by more enlightened views.

Rape occurs also on dates, called **acquaintance rape**, or **date rape**. Rapes of this kind outnumber rapes by strangers by as much as three to one (Kilpatrick & Best, 1990). Date-rape victims especially tend to be blamed for the rape and tend to blame themselves more than do women who are raped by strangers—after all, date-rape victims associated willingly with the men who raped them. This viewpoint has been strongly challenged, however, for it overlooks the right of the weaker party, usually the woman, to say no at any time. Willingness to have dinner, even to embrace and kiss, is not tantamount to consenting to anything more intimate.

A recent development with regard to date rape is the use of the tranquilizer Rohypnol. This drug is odorless and tasteless and can be easily slipped into a drink; if ingested, it causes the person to pass out and have little if any memory of what happens. Men have used Rohypnol to enable them to rape women when on a date and without having to apply physical force. In

This famous scene from Gone with the Wind illustrates one of the myths about rape—that despite initial resistance women like to be "taken."

August 1996 a federal law was passed making it possible to add up to twenty years to a sentence for conviction of rape or other violent crimes if Rohypnol had been used. What is particularly significant is that this is the first U.S. law that makes the use of a drug in a criminal offense grounds for increasing the penalty for that crime (Associated Press, 1996).

As many as 25 percent of American women will be raped during their lifetimes (Kilpatrick & Best, 1990), most often by someone they know (Hudson & Ward, 1997), and it is likely that more than 80 percent of sexual assaults are not reported. If we consider coerced sexual activity that stops short of rape, findings show that as many as 75 percent of female college students have been subjected to some type of unwanted sexual activity (Koss, 1985).

The Victim, the Attack, and the Aftermath

A prevalent belief is that all women who are raped are young and attractive. This is a myth. Although many victims do fit this description, many others do not. Age and physical appearance are no barriers to some rapists; they may choose children as young as one year old or women in their eighties.

Rape victims are usually traumatized by the attack, both physically and mentally (Calhoun, Atkeson, & Resick, 1982; Resick, 1993; Resick et al., 1986; Rothbaum et al., 1992). Two weeks after a rape, 94% of women suffer from acute stress disorder (cf. p. 164), and nine months later, 42% suffer from full-blown PTSD (Rothbaum & Foa, 1993).

In the minutes or seconds preceding rape, the woman begins to recognize her dangerous situation but can scarcely believe what is about to happen to her. During the assault she is first and foremost in great fear for her life. The physical violation of her body and the ripping away of her freedom of choice are enraging, but the victim also usually feels her vulnerability in not being able to fight off her typically stronger attacker. Moreover, the attacker usually has the element of surprise and sometimes a weapon to intimidate and coerce. Resistance is seriously compromised by terror.

For weeks or months following the rape many victims feel extremely tense and deeply humiliated. They feel guilt that they were unable to fight harder and may have angry thoughts of revenge. Many have nightmares about the rape. Depression and loss of self-esteem are common. Some victims of rape develop phobias about being outdoors or indoors or in the dark, depending on where the rape took place. They may also fear being alone or in crowds or having anyone behind them. Unfortunately, some of these reactions are exacerbated by insensitivity on the part of police and even friends and loved ones, some of whom may question the victim's complicity in what happened (more on this later). Sometimes an unwanted pregnancy results from a rape, and justifiable concern about sexually transmitted diseases, including AIDS (p. 222), adds to the trauma of the attack. For good reason DSM-IV-TR mentions rape as one of the traumas that can give rise to posttraumatic stress disorder (p. 165).

Many women who have been raped subsequently develop a negative attitude toward sex and experience difficulty in their relationships with their husbands or lovers (Becker, Skinner, et al., 1986). So certain are Calhoun and Atkeson (1991), two experienced clinical researchers on rape, that sexual problems are a frequent long-term consequence of untreated rape trauma, that they urge clinicians to consider the possibility that rape or sexual assault has occurred in women who come to therapy for many of the sexual dysfunctions discussed later in this chapter. For some women, even though frequency of sex and of orgasms may not be diminished, satisfaction with sex can be reduced for years (Feldman-Summers, Gordon, & Mengler, 1979).

Without intervention, symptoms of anxiety and depression—and in some cases, full-blown PTSD—can persist in some women for many years following an assault (Calhoun & Atkeson, 1991; Resick, 1993). Suicidal risk is also high for many rape survivors (Cohen & Roth, 1987; Kilpatrick, Edmunds, & Seymour, 1992; Kilpatrick et al., 1985), as is substance abuse (Burnam et al., 1988), which might have begun as an attempt to self-medicate to reduce anxiety and general dysphoria. Moreover, consistent with research on the effects of stress on physical health, rape survivors can experience a variety of somatic problems, and their use of medical services tends to increase (Phelps, Wallace, & Waigant, 1989).

The nature and duration of what some call rape trauma syndrome (Burgess & Holmstrom, 1974) depend a great deal on the person's life both prior to and following the attack. Factors that can mitigate the negative aftermath of rape include a supportive spouse and friends as well as the kind of crisis intervention described later (Atkeson et al., 1982; Ruch & Leon, 1983). Research is inconclusive, however, as to whether the negative emotional consequences of rape correlate with the violence of the assault, the setting, or the familiarity of the rapist (Resick, 1993). These complexities led Calhoun and Atkeson (1991) to conclude that the aftermath is more a function of how the person appraises the events than of the circumstances themselves. Again we see the apparent importance of how people construe events.

Many jurisdictions allow the very existence of rape trauma syndrome in a victim, which may include depression, anxiety, and sleep disturbances, to be admitted as evidence supporting an allegation of rape. The existence of the syndrome (which is equivalent to acute stress disorder and posttraumatic stress disorder) may also explain behavior on the part of the victim that might otherwise be considered an indication of consent, for example, delays in reporting the crime, memory loss, and making inconsistent statements (Block, 1990).

The Rapist

As documented some years ago in a classic book on the politics of rape, the fact that men with their generally superior strength can usually overpower women buttresses the view that rape has served in the past and still serves to control and intimidate women (Brownmiller, 1975). Nonetheless, the sexual component per se appears to be an essential component in most rapes (Seto & Barbaree, 2000).

Rape in Wartime The Crusaders raped their way across Europe on their holy pilgrimages in the eleventh through the thirteenth centuries; the Germans raped as they rampaged through Belgium in World War I; U.S. forces raped Vietnamese women and girls as they searched and destroyed; and Iraqi soldiers raped and brutalized women as they occupied Kuwait in 1990. Brownmiller contends that rape is actually *expected* in war. In her view, being in the armed forces encourages a perverse sense of masculine superiority and creates a climate in which rape is acceptable (Brownmiller, 1975).

In June 1996 a United Nations tribunal announced the indictment of eight Bosnian Serb soldiers and police for the rape of Muslim women during the Bosnian war in 1992–1993. These rapes were ordered by their commanders; they were not sexual/aggressive acts perpetrated by individual soldiers. Rather, they had a specific military purpose: The fact that virginity in unmarried women is extremely important among Muslims, their being raped destroyed their honor and integrity and was designed to demoralize them (and their society generally) in addition to instilling fear (Bell-Fialkoff, 1996).

In March 1998, for the first time in history, a soldier was found guilty of rape as a war crime (Associated Press, 1998). What is noteworthy about this action against a Serbian military man is that it is the first time sexual assault has been treated separately as a war crime. Previously, as in the Nuremberg trials that judged Nazi war crimes during World War II, rape was not mentioned specifically. Rape during war will now occupy the attention of the international community, making it less likely that it will be tacitly condoned or regarded as an inevitable part of one nation or group waging war against another (Simons, 1996).

Rape victims of the war in Bosnia. Rape occurs frequently during war but only recently has sexual assault been considered a war crime.

Who Is the Rapist?   Is the rapist primarily the psychopath who seeks the thrill of dominating and humiliating a woman through intimidation and often brutal assault? Is he an ordinarily unassertive man with a fragile ego who, feeling inadequate after disappointment and rejection in work or love, takes out his frustrations on an unwilling stranger? Is he an otherwise respectable, even honored, man in authority who takes advantage of his position of power over a woman? Is he a teenager, provoked by a seductive and apparently available young woman who, it turns out, was not as interested as he in sexual intimacy? Is he a college student whose inhibitions against expressing anger have been dissolved by alcohol? The best answer is that the rapist is any and all these men, often operating under a combination of several of these circumstances.

What many rapists probably have in common is unusually high hostility toward women, arising from beliefs of having been betrayed, deceived, or demeaned by them or from exposure to parental violence and physical or sexual abuse during childhood (Duke & Durham, 1990; Malamuth et al., 1993). Reports from rapists indicate that the urge to rape is heightened by feelings of loneliness, anger, humiliation, inadequacy, and rejection (McKibben, Proulx, & Lusignan, 1994). Some rapists also seem to have problems distinguishing friendliness from seductiveness and in accurately reading cues from a woman indicating that she wants intimacies to cease (Malamuth & Brown, 1994). They often lack social skills, have low self-esteem, and have little empathy for their victims (Hudson & Ward, 1997).

From a sociological perspective, the more a society accepts interpersonal violence as a way to handle conflict and solve problems, the higher the frequency of rape (Sanday, 1981). It seems worth noting that in a controlled experiment, male college students who stated that they regarded rape as unacceptable were aroused by video portrayals of rape if the woman was depicted as having an orgasm during the assault (Malamuth & Check, 1983). This research suggests that rape may be encouraged by pornography that depicts women enjoying coerced sexual relations.

Therapy for Rapists and Rape Victims

Unlike most of the disorders discussed in this book, rape has the dubious distinction of presenting two different challenges to the mental health professional: treating the man who has committed the act and treating the woman who has been the victim.

Therapy for Rapists   Therapy programs for incarcerated rapists are typically multidimensional in nature and are evaluated by following men after release from prison to determine recidivism rates. Among the components of these programs are cognitive techniques aimed at rapists' distorted beliefs and inappropriate attitudes toward women (such as the belief that women want to be raped—see Table 14.2), attempts to increase empathy with their victims, anger management, techniques to improve self-esteem, and efforts to reduce substance abuse. These methods are often implemented in confrontational group-therapy sessions that attempt to goad the rapist into taking responsibility for his aggressive behavior. As with the paraphilias, this psychologically based therapy is sometimes supplemented with the use of biological treatments to reduce the rapist's sex drive. Although these programs typically have not had adequate control groups, meta-analyses have led to the conclusion that cognitive therapy and the biological interventions may lower recidivism somewhat, especially among men who complete treatment programs (Hall, 1995; Hanson & Bussiere, 1998; Maletsky, 2002).

Therapy for Rape Victims   Efforts to counsel rape victims have expanded considerably in recent years. Rape crisis centers and telephone hot lines have been established throughout the United States and other countries. Some are associated with hospitals and clinics; others operate on their own. Staffed both by professionals and by female volunteers who may themselves have been rape victims, these centers offer support and advice within a crisis-intervention framework. They focus on normalizing the victim's emotional reactions—"Everyone goes through this emotional turmoil after an assault"—encouraging her to talk about her feelings, and helping her meet immediate needs, such as arranging for child care or improving the security arrangements in her home. In short, the goal is to help the victim solve problems and cope with the immediate aftermath of the traumatic event (Calhoun & Atkeson, 1991; Sorenson & Brown, 1990). Discouraging self-blame is also important (Frazier, 1990), especially when the rapist was someone the woman knew (Stewart et al., 1987).

Rape counselors urge the woman not to withdraw or become inactive. Women from the crisis center often accompany the rape victim to the hospital and to the police station, where they help her with the legal procedures and with recounting the events of the attack. They may later arrange for examinations for pregnancy and venereal diseases and for professional therapy if necessary. The possibility of HIV infection also has to be addressed. Empathic companions from the crisis center help the victim begin to express her feelings about the ordeal, and they urge her to continue venting with her own relatives and friends. If the attacker or attackers have been apprehended, women from the center support the victim in her decision to go through with prosecuting the rapist. They attend both her meetings with the district attorney and the trial itself.

If the victim sees a mental health professional, attention is typically focused on the woman's ongoing relationships, which may be disrupted or negatively affected by the rape. Friends and family, especially spouses and lovers, will need help handling their own emotional turmoil so that they can provide the kind of nonjudgmental support that rape victims need.

Much of the therapy for rape has a great deal in common with the treatment of PTSD (cf. page 169). The victim is asked to relive the fearsome events of the attack by discussing them with the therapist, perhaps also imagining them in vivid detail.

Rape counselors support a victim's decision to prosecute the rapist and provide therapy similar to that used in treating PTSD.

Such repeated exposure to the trauma is designed to extinguish the fear (or, in psycho-analytic terms, work it through) (Calhoun & Atkeson, 1991; Resick & Calhoun, 2001; Rothbaum & Foa, 1992). As is the case with other kinds of anxieties, it is no easy task to encourage the person to reflect on her fears, because denial and avoidance are the typical coping methods used by rape victims—for the most part unsuccessfully. Depression can be addressed by helping the woman reevaluate her role in the rape, as many victims tend to see themselves as at least partially responsible. A little-researched topic is the anger and rage many victims have toward their assailants; women are often afraid of expressing or are socialized not to express such feelings (Calhoun & Atkeson, 1991).

A cognitive-behavioral intervention that is beginning to be empirically validated is the cognitive processing therapy of Patricia Resick (1992; Resick & Schnicke, 1992; Resick et al., 2002). This therapy combines the exposure to memories of the trauma that is found in other anxiety-reduction interventions with the kind of cognitive restructuring found in the work of Ellis and Beck. For example, the rape victim is encouraged to dispute any tendency to attribute the blame to herself and to consider fully those aspects of the attack that were beyond her control.

Social attitudes and support systems encourage the victim to report rape and pursue the prosecution of the alleged rapist, but the legal situation is still problematic. Interviews with half a million women indicated three reasons for reluctance to report rape:

1. Considering the rape a private matter
2. Fearing reprisals from the rapist or his family or friends
3. Believing that the police would be inefficient, ineffective, or insensitive (Wright, 1991)

Estimates are that only a very small percentage of rapists are ultimately convicted of their crimes. Furthermore, there is no denying that going to trial is very stressful. Any familiarity of the victim with her assailant makes conviction of the man more difficult to achieve, and the victim's role in her own assault is almost always examined by defense attorneys. Finally, even though many rapists rape hundreds of times, they are only occasionally imprisoned for an offense.

Before closing the discussion of the paraphilias, we present in Focus on Discovery 14.3 a brief discussion of a sexual variation that used to be considered abnormal—homosexuality.

Sexual Dysfunctions

Robert S. was a highly intelligent and accomplished twenty-five-year-old graduate student in physics at a leading East Coast university who consulted us for what he called "sexual diffidence." He was engaged to a young woman whom he said he loved very much and with whom he felt compatible in every conceivable way except in bed. There, try as he might, and with apparent understanding from his fiancée, he found himself interested very little either in initiating sexual contact or in responding to it when initiated by her. Both parties believed for the two years of their friendship and later engagement that academic pressures on the man lay at the root of the problem, but an early discussion with the therapist revealed that the client had had little interest in sex—either with men or with women—for as far back as he could remember, and that his desire for sex did not increase when pressures from other obligations lessened. He asserted that he found his fiancée very attractive and appealing, but, as with other young women he had known, his feelings were not passionate.

He had masturbated very infrequently in adolescence and did not begin dating until late in college, though he had had many female acquaintances. His general approach to life, including sex, was analytical and intellectual, and he described his problems in a very dispassionate and detached way to the therapist. He freely admitted that he would not have contacted a therapist at all were it not for the quietly stated wishes of his fiancée, who worried that his lack of interest in sex would interfere with their future marital relationship.

After a few individual sessions the therapist asked the young man to invite his fiancée to a therapy session, which the client readily agreed to do. During a conjoint session the couple appeared to be very much in love and looking forward to a life together, though the woman expressed concern about her fiancé's lack of interest in her sexually.

Having discussed the unconventional patterns of sexual behavior of a small minority of the population, we turn now to sexual problems that interfere with conventional sexual enjoyment during the course of many people's lives. Our concern here is with **sexual dysfunctions**, the range of sexual problems that are usually considered to represent inhibitions in the normal sexual response cycle.

What is defined as normal and desirable in human sexual behavior varies with time and place. The contemporary view that inhibitions of sexual expression underlie abnormality can be contrasted with views held during the nineteenth and early twentieth centuries in the Western world, when *excess* was regarded as the culprit. A recent feminist analysis of female sexual dysfunction argues that the DSM pays too little attention to the relational components of human sexuality, especially for women. The proposal is that there be a more women-centered definition that includes "discontent or dissatisfaction with any emotional, physical, or relational aspect of sexual experience" (Tiefer, Hall, & Tavris, 2002, pp. 228–229). We must keep these varying temporal and cultural norms in mind as we study human sexual dysfunctions.

Psychological problems have consequences not only for the people who experience them but also for those with whom they are involved. This aspect of human emotional problems is especially important in our consideration of sexual dysfunctions, which usually occur in the context of intimate personal relationships. A marriage is likely to suffer if one of the partners fears or is repelled by sex. And most of us, for better or for worse, base part of our self-concept on our sexuality. Do we please the people we love, do we gratify ourselves, or, more simply, are we able to enjoy the fulfillment and relaxation that can come from a pleasurable sexual experience? Sexual dysfunctions can be so severe that tenderness itself is lost, let alone the more intense satisfaction of sexual activity.

We look first at the human sexual response cycle as it normally functions. With that as context, we examine the several sexual dysfunctions. Then we discuss etiologies and therapies for these problems.

Sexual Dysfunctions and the Human Sexual Response Cycle

As indicated in Table 14.1 (p. 435), DSM-IV-TR divides sexual dysfunctions into four principal categories: sexual desire disorders, sexual arousal disorders, orgasmic disorders, and sexual pain disorders. The difficulty should be persistent and recurrent, a clinical judgment acknowledged in the DSM to entail a degree of subjectivity. The disturbance should also cause marked distress or interpersonal problems. This requirement is new in the DSM and allows the person's own reactions to, say, having no interest in sex play a role in whether he or she should be diagnosed. A diagnosis of sexual dysfunction is not made if the disorder is believed to be due entirely to a medical illness (such as advanced diabetes, which can cause erectile problems in men) or if it is due to another Axis I disorder (such as major depression).

Most contemporary conceptualizations of the sexual response cycle are a distillation of proposals by Masters and Johnson (1966) and Kaplan (1974). The work of Masters and Johnson almost forty years ago signaled a revolution in the nature and intensity of research in and clinical attention to human sexuality. These researchers extended the earlier interview-based breakthroughs of the Kinsey group (Kinsey et al., 1948, 1953) by making direct observations and physiological measurements of people masturbating and having sexual intercourse. Four phases in the human sexual response cycle are typically identified; they are considered quite similar in men and women.

1. **Appetitive.** Introduced by Kaplan (1974), this stage refers to sexual interest or desire, often associated with sexually arousing fantasies.[2]

The pioneering work of the sex therapists William H. Masters and Virginia Johnson helped launch a candid and scientific appraisal of human sexuality.

---

[2] Masters and Johnson omitted this stage because, we believe, they used well-functioning volunteers in their landmark laboratory work; the issue of desire or readiness to be sexual did not arise. This is a good example of how the nature of knowledge-gathering techniques—in this case, the kinds of people studied—constrains the kinds of information obtained.

Focus on Discovery 14.3

Some Comments on Homosexuality

Although homosexuality does not appear in DSM-IV-TR as a clearly definable category, we believe that sufficient controversy remains about these patterns of emotion and behavior—among both laypeople and health professionals—to warrant consideration of the topic. A historical overview will provide perspective on some of the many issues surrounding the ways in which we view those whose sexual preferences include or are restricted to members of their own sex.

Homosexuality and the DSM

Until 1973, **homosexuality**, sexual desire or activity directed toward a member of one's own sex, was listed in the DSM as one of the sexual deviations. In 1973 the Nomenclature Committee of the American Psychiatric Association, under pressure from many professionals and from gay activist groups, recommended to the general membership the elimination of the category "homosexuality" and the substitution of "sexual orientation disturbance." This new diagnosis was to be applied to gay men and women who are "disturbed by, in conflict with, or wish to change their sexual orientation." The members of the psychiatric association voted on the issue, and the change was approved, but not without vehement protests from several renowned psychiatrists who remained convinced that homosexuality reflects a fixation at an early stage of psychosexual development and is therefore inherently abnormal.

The controversy continued among mental health professionals, but as DSM-III was being developed during the late 1970s it became increasingly clear that the new nomenclature would maintain the tolerant stance toward homosexuality that had become evident in 1973. The new DSM-III category **ego-dystonic homosexuality** referred to a person who is homosexually aroused, finds this arousal a persistent source of distress, and wishes to become heterosexual. DSM-III, in our view, thereby took an inconsistent position: a homosexual is abnormal if he or she has been persuaded by a prejudiced society that his or her sexual orientation is inherently deviant; at the same time, according to DSM-III, homosexuality is not in itself abnormal!

In the years following publication of DSM-III in 1980, very little use was made by mental health professionals of the diagnosis of ego-dystonic homosexuality. Was this because homosexual men and women in therapy were no longer asking for sexual reorientation? Did the greater tolerance of homosexuality—despite the AIDS crisis (p. 222) and the erroneous allegation that AIDS was a problem of gay men and maybe even God's punishment for their sins—enable gay men and women to seek therapy for problems unrelated to their sexual orientation? Perhaps some gay people, as gay activists had been urging for twenty years, were no longer willing to tolerate the prejudice against their sexual orientation and were seeking assistance in resisting societal biases. Perhaps clinicians began to focus more on such problems as anxiety and depression in their gay clients without seeing these problems as necessarily connected with a wish to become heterosexual. It is impossible to establish the exact reasons, but it is clear that by the time the American Psychiatric Association was ready in 1987 to publish DSM-III-R, it had decided that even the watered-down diagnosis of ego-dystonic homosexuality should not be included. Instead, the catchall category of "sexual disorder not otherwise specified" referred to "persistent and marked distress about one's sexual orientation" (p. 296); this category is also included in DSM-IV and DSM-IV-TR. DSM-III-R and DSM-IV contain no specific mention of homosexuality as a disorder in its own right. It is noteworthy that the new category does not specify a sexual orientation. Although the door is still open for a diagnosis of ego-dystonic homosexuality, the psychiatric nosology now appears to allow as well for ego-dystonic heterosexuality. Our own expectation is that neither diagnosis is going to be made very often.

Homophobia: A Defense against Latent Homosexuality?

One of the arguments gay activists have made over the years is that antagonism toward homosexuality reflects not a rational analysis, but an irrational fear of or aversion to homosexuality—what has been called **homophobia**. Some writers have alleged that homophobia is an unconscious defensive reaction against a person's unacknowledged homosexual interests or inclinations, a sort of reaction formation.

That homophobic men may be defending against their own homosexuality has been a psychoanalytic hypothesis for many years (e.g., West, 1977). An ingenious experiment lends support to this hitherto theoretical and political position. Adams, Wright, and Lohr (1996) demonstrated that homophobia may be related to unacknowledged (repressed?) homosexual inclinations (latent homosexuality). Undergraduate, male, heterosexual college students, categorized as either homophobic or nonhomophobic via a questionnaire, viewed videotapes explicitly depicting heterosexual, male homosexual, and lesbian acts. Sexual arousal was assessed with a penile plethysmograph and by self-report. The plethysmograph findings showed that, whereas both groups of participants were sexually aroused by the heterosexual and lesbian videos (a common finding among heterosexual men), only the homophobic men were sexually aroused by the male homosexual portrayals, although to a much lesser extent than they were aroused by the heterosexual and lesbian videos. The self-reports of sexual arousal indicated no differences between the two groups, which is consistent with the notion that homophobic men deny their homosexual interests.

In DSM-II, homosexuality was listed as one of several sexual deviations. In subsequent editions of the DSM, homosexuality was gradually dropped as a mental disorder, in part due to pressure from gay rights groups.

2. **Excitement.** Masters and Johnson's original first stage, a subjective experience of sexual pleasure associated with physiological changes brought about by increased blood flow to the genitalia and, in women, also to the breasts. This tumescence, the flow of blood into tissues, shows up in men as erection of the penis and in women as enlargement of the breasts and changes in the vagina, such as increased lubrication.

3. **Orgasm.** In this phase sexual pleasure peaks in ways that have fascinated poets and the rest of us ordinary people for thousands of years. In men, ejaculation feels inevitable and indeed almost always occurs (in rare instances some men can have an orgasm without ejaculating, and vice versa). In women, the walls of the outer third of the vagina contract. In both sexes there is general muscle tension and involuntary pelvic thrusting.

4. **Resolution.** This last of Masters and Johnson's stages refers to the relaxation and sense of well-being that usually follow an orgasm. In men there is an associated refractory period, during which further erection and arousal are not possible, but for varying periods of time across individuals and even within the same person across occasions. Women are often able to respond again with sexual excitement almost immediately, a capability that permits multiple orgasms.

It is important to note that this rendition of the human sexual response cycle is a construct—a creation, a way of conceptualizing into different stages what is really a continuous set of thoughts, feelings, behaviors, and biological reactions. This four-stage view is one of many conceivable ways to organize and discuss the relevant body of information (Gagnon, 1977; Kuhn, 1962). We are about to see how the DSM uses this scheme to describe sexual dysfunctions.

Descriptions and Etiology of Sexual Dysfunctions

The prevalence of occasional disturbances in sexual functioning is quite high. Table 14.3 presents data from a survey of over 3,000 men and women who were asked whether they had experienced various symptoms of sexual dysfunction in the past twelve months (Laumann, Paik, & Rosen, 1999). The overall prevalence was 43 percent for women and 31 percent for men. Because these symptoms are so prevalent, people should not assume they need treatment if they sometimes experience one or more of the problems described in this section. In the diagnostic criteria for each sexual dysfunction the phrase "persistent or recurrent" is used to underscore the fact that a problem must be serious indeed for the diagnosis to be made. In addition, there is a fair amount of comorbidity among the sexual dysfunctions. For example, almost half of both men and women diagnosed with hypoactive sexual disorder (low sexual desire) also have at least one other dysfunction (Segraves & Segraves, 1991). As we review the various disorders, their interconnectedness will become evident.

Sexual Desire Disorders DSM-IV-TR distinguishes two kinds of sexual desire disorders. **Hypoactive sexual desire disorder** refers to deficient or absent sexual fantasies and urges; **sexual aversion disorder** represents a more extreme form of the disorder, in which the person actively avoids nearly all genital contact with another. Twenty to thirty percent of the general adult population, more often women than men, may have hypoactive sexual desire disorder (Laumann et al., 1994), although accurate estimates are difficult to obtain because of the inevitable problem of getting people to report accurately on something as personal as a sexual dysfunction. Among people seeking treatment for sexual dysfunctions, more than half complain of low desire; and among these people it is often comorbid with an orgasmic disorder. Hypoactive sexual desire increased in clinical samples for both men and women from the 1970s to the 1990s (Beck, 1995).

Of all the DSM-IV-TR diagnoses, the sexual desire disorders, often colloquially referred to as low sex drive (as illustrated in the case that opened this section), seem the most problematic. How frequently should a person want sex? And with what intensity or urgency? The reason a person goes to a clinician in the first place and ends up with this diagnosis is probably that someone else is dissatisfied with that person's interest in sex.

DSM-IV-TR Criteria for Hypoactive Sexual Desire Disorder

- Persistently deficient or absent sexual fantasies and desires
- Causes marked distress or interpersonal problems
- Not due to another Axis I disorder (except another sexual dysfunction) or to the direct physiological effects of a drug or a general medical illness

DSM-IV-TR Criteria for Sexual Aversion Disorder

- Persistent avoidance of (almost) all sexual contact
- Causes marked distress or interpersonal problems
- Not due to another Axis I disorder (except another sexual dysfunction)

The hypoactive desire category appeared for the first time in DSM-III in 1980, under the title of "inhibited sexual desire,"[3] and may owe its existence to the high expectations some people have about being sexual. It is striking that entire books—for example, Leiblum and Rosen (1988)—have been written about a disorder that twenty-five years ago was hardly mentioned in professional sexology circles. Data attest to the significance of subjective factors in the extent to which a person believes he or she has a low sex drive; for example, hypoactive sexual desire disorder was reported more often by American men than by British (Hawton et al., 1986) or German men (Arentewicz & Schmidt, 1983).

We know little about the causes of either hypoactive sexual desire or sexual aversion disorder. Because women with the disorder show normal sexual responses to sexual stimuli in laboratory studies, it does not appear that they are incapable of becoming fully aroused (Kaplan, 1997). Among the causes of low sex drive in people seen clinically are religious orthodoxy, trying to have sex with a partner of the nonpreferred sex, fear of loss of control, fear of pregnancy, depression, side effects from such medications as antihypertensives and tranquilizers, and lack of attraction resulting from such factors as poor personal hygiene in the partner (LoPiccolo & Friedman, 1988). Having another sexual dysfunction, such as erectile disorder in a man, is also likely to be a contributing factor, for losing one's erection during a sexual encounter can be expected over time to make the whole idea of initiating sex unappealing for both parties (Bach et al., 2001).

Relationship factors may also be part of the picture as women with sexual desire disorder report that their communication with their husbands is poor and that they are unhappy with the way conflicts are resolved (Stuart et al., 1987). Other possible causes include a past history of sexual trauma, such as rape or childhood sexual abuse (Stuart & Greer, 1984), and fears of contracting sexually transmitted diseases, such as AIDS (Katz et al., 1989). Two empirical studies indicate that anger is a major factor in reducing sexual desire in both men and women, though it has a smaller role for women (Beck & Bozman, 1995; Bozman & Beck, 1991). Sexual desire is lower when people complain of high levels of everyday stress (Morokoff & Gilliland, 1993). There are also data pointing to the importance of testosterone levels in men—the lower the levels, the lower the sexual desire (Bancroft, 1988).

Sexual Arousal Disorders   Some people have little or no trouble experiencing sexual desire but do have difficulty attaining or maintaining sexual arousal, the next stage of the sexual response cycle described by Masters and Johnson. The two subcategories of arousal disorders are **female sexual arousal disorder** and **male erectile disorder**. The former used to be called frigidity, and the latter, impotence.

Replacement of the words impotence and frigidity by the phrase sexual arousal disorder can be considered an advance. Impotence implies that the man is not potent, in control, or truly masculine, and supports the macho conception of masculinity that many people today challenge. Frigidity implies that the woman is emotionally cold, distant, unsympathetic, and unfeeling. Both terms are derogatory.

The diagnosis of arousal disorder is made for a woman when there is consistently inadequate vaginal lubrication for comfortable completion of intercourse and for a man when there is persistent failure to attain or maintain an erection through completion of the sexual activity. The prevalence rate for female arousal disorder is about 20 percent (Laumann et al., 1994). For male erectile disorder prevalence is estimated at between 3 and 9 percent (e.g., Ard, 1977; Frank, Anderson, & Rubenstein, 1978) and increases

Table 14.3   Self-Reported Rates of Experiencing Various Sexual Problems in the Past Twelve Months

Problem	Men	Women
Lacked interest in sex	13–17%	27–32%
Unable to achieve orgasm	7–9%	22–28%
Climax too early	28–32%	NA
Sex not pleasurable	6–8%	17–24%
Trouble maintaining/achieving erection	11–18%	NA
Trouble lubricating	NA	18–27%
Pain during sex	NA	8–15%

Source: After Loumann et al., 1999.
Note: The ranges reflect the fact that rates vary according to age.

DSM-IV-TR Criteria for Female Sexual Arousal Disorder

- Persistent inability to attain or maintain sexual excitement (lubrication and swelling of the genitalia) adequate for completion of sexual activity
- Causes marked distress or interpersonal problems
- Not due to another Axis I disorder (except another sexual dysfunction) or to the direct physiological effects of a drug or a general medical illness

DSM-IV-TR Criteria for Male Erectile Disorder

- Persistent inability to attain or maintain an erection adequate for completion of sexual activity
- Causes marked distress or interpersonal problems
- Not due to another Axis I disorder (except another sexual dysfunction) or to the direct physiological effects of a drug or a general medical illness

---

[3] The DSM-III term *inhibited* was deemed by those who produced DSM-III-R to suggest psychodynamic causality. In DSM-III-R, DSM-IV, and DSM-IV-TR preference was given to the more descriptive term *hypoactive* (Lief, 1988).

greatly in older adults (Feldman et al., 1994; Kinsey et al., 1948). Arousal problems account for about half the complaints of men and women who seek help with sexual dysfunctions (Frank, Anderson, & Kupfer, 1976; Renshaw, 1988).

In addition to the fear of performance and the spectator role (observing the sexual interaction rather than just "going with the flow") discussed later as general causes of sexual dysfunctions, some specific causes are believed to underlie female arousal problems. A woman may not have learned adequately what she finds sexually arousing and may even lack knowledge about her own anatomy. She may be shy about communicating her needs and in addition may find the behavior of her partner unstimulating and even aversive. Marital conflict appears to be another factor, as do several medical problems (such as estrogen deficiency and diabetes) and some drugs (such as medication taken for hypertension) (Fenel, 1997).

Helen Singer Kaplan (1974) outlined a wide range of erectile problems for men. Some get an erection easily but lose it as they enter the woman's vagina. Others are flaccid when intercourse is imminent but maintain an erection easily during oral sex. Some men are erect when the partner dominates the situation, others when they themselves are in control. An obvious aspect of the problem is that it is in fact obvious. A woman can usually go through the motions of lovemaking whether aroused or not, but sexual intercourse is stalemated if the man is not erect. A great deal is at stake for both the man and his partner if the penis becomes flaccid when it "should" be erect.

As many as two-thirds of erectile problems have some biological basis, usually combined with psychological factors. In general, any disease, drug, or hormonal imbalance that can affect the nerve pathways or blood supply to the penis can contribute to erectile problems; examples are certain drugs, such as Thorazine, Prozac, and some antihypertensive medications, and illnesses, such as diabetes, kidney problems, and chronic alcoholism. As indicated, though, somatic factors usually interact with psychological factors to produce and maintain erectile difficulties. For example, anxiety and depression are common among men with erectile disorder (Araujo et al., 1998; Schiavi, 1997). Once the disorder has begun, fears of sexual failure arise and could certainly inhibit subsequent sexual responding (Rowland, Cooper, & Slob, 1996).

Orgasmic Disorders   Three kinds of orgasmic disorders are described in DSM-IV-TR, one found in women and two in men.

Female Orgasmic Disorder   Formerly called inhibited female orgasm, **female orgasmic disorder** refers to absence of orgasm after a period of normal sexual excitement. The published prevalence rates for female orgasmic disorder vary widely. One review of this literature found prevalences ranging from 5 to 20 percent (Spector & Carey, 1990). A more recent study, which involved interviewing a large sample of women, found a prevalence of 24 percent (Laumann et al., 1994). Whatever the true prevalence rate, this is the problem that most often brings women into therapy (Kaplan, 1974; Spector & Carey, 1990). Failure to achieve orgasm is not only a problem for women; it is also an important aspect of sex for their partners, who may come to believe they are unskilled or insensitive lovers, or that their partner no longer cares for them (both of which possibilities may in fact be true). This last point probably accounts for the fact that up to 60 percent of women report faking an orgasm on occasion (McConaghy, 1993).

There is an important distinction between problems a woman may have in becoming sexually aroused and those she may have in reaching an orgasm. Although as many as 10 percent of adult women have never experienced an orgasm (Anderson, 1983), far fewer are believed to remain unaroused during sexual activity. Indeed, laboratory research has shown that women with orgasmic disorder are as responsive to erotic stimuli as are control women (Meston & Gorzalka, 1996).

Numerous reasons have been put forward to explain the problem. Perhaps many women, unlike men, have to learn to become orgasmic; that is, the capacity to have an orgasm may not be innate in females as it is in males. In men, ejaculation, which almost always is accompanied by orgasm, is necessary for reproduction and can be understood

DSM-IV-TR Criteria for Female Orgasmic Disorder

- Persistent delay in or absence of orgasm following a normal period of sexual arousal Consideration given to woman's age, sexual experience, and adequacy of sexual stimulation she receives
- Causes marked distress or interpersonal problems
- Not due to another Axis I disorder (except another sexual dysfunction) or to the direct physiological effects of a drug or a general medical illness

as an inborn trait that has evolutionary advantage (propagating the species). Survey findings indicate that women who masturbated little or not at all before they began to have intercourse were much more likely to be nonorgasmic than were those who had masturbated to orgasm before becoming sexually active with a partner (Hite, 1976; Hoon & Hoon, 1978; Kinsey et al., 1953). These are, of course, correlational data; some third factor may be responsible both for infrequent masturbation and for diminished ability to have orgasms. Lack of sexual knowledge also appears to play a role according to clinical data; many nonorgasmic women, as well as those who experience little excitement during sexual stimulation, are unaware of their own genital anatomy and therefore have trouble knowing what their needs are and communicating them to a partner. Chronic use of alcohol may be a somatic factor in orgasmic dysfunction in women (Wilsnak, 1984).

Another factor is that women have different thresholds for orgasm. Although some have orgasms quickly and without much clitoral stimulation, others seem to need intense and prolonged stimulation during foreplay or intercourse. Because a man may conclude that he and his penis are inadequate if the female asks for or herself provides manual stimulation of her clitoris during intercourse, the reaction of a woman's partner can contribute to the problem.

Yet another factor may be fear of losing control. The French have an expression for orgasm, *la petite mort*, "the little death." Some women fear that they will scream uncontrollably, make fools of themselves, or faint. A related source of inhibition is a belief, perhaps poorly articulated, that to let go and allow the body to take over from the conscious, controlling mind is somehow unseemly.

The state of a relationship is important as well. Although some women can enjoy making love to a person they are angry with, or even despise, most hold back under such circumstances. The nonsexual feelings each partner has for the other play a role.

Male Orgasmic Disorder and Premature Ejaculation   Male orgasmic disorder and premature ejaculation are the two orgasmic disorders of men in DSM-IV-TR. **Male orgasmic disorder**, or difficulty in ejaculating, is relatively rare, occurring in 4 to 10 percent of patients in treatment (Spector & Carey, 1990). Causes that have been put forth include fear of impregnating a female partner, withholding love, expressing hostility, and, as with female orgasmic problems, fear of letting go. In some instances the problem may be traced to a physical source, such as spinal cord injury or certain tranquilizers (Pryor, 2002).

Premature ejaculation is probably the most prevalent sexual dysfunction among males; it is a problem for as many as 40 percent of men at some time in their lives (Laumann et al., 1994; St. Lawrence & Madakasira, 1992). Sometimes premature ejaculation occurs even before the penis enters the vagina, but it more usually occurs within a few seconds of intromission. Premature ejaculation is generally associated with considerable anxiety.

There is some laboratory-based evidence that men who have such problems are more sexually responsive to tactile stimulation than men who don't have this problem (Rowland et al., 1996). Perhaps, then, their penises are very sensitive, causing them to ejaculate more quickly. Men with premature ejaculation also have longer periods of abstinence from climactic sex than do men who are not premature ejaculators (Spiess, Geer, & O'Donohue, 1984). Learning has also been proposed as a factor. For example, a man may acquire the tendency to ejaculate quickly as a result of having hurried sex because of not being in a private place and fearing detection (Metz et al., 1997).

Concern about ejaculating too soon may be a natural result of an overemphasis on intercourse in sexual behavior among heterosexuals. The problem for couples who prize conventional sexual intercourse above all other sexual activities is that because the man's erection is slowly lost after an ejaculation, his partner may be deprived of her own orgasm. If sexual activity stops when the penis is no longer hard, ejaculation may indeed be premature. But if, as sex therapists advise, couples expand their repertoire of activities to include techniques not requiring an engorged penis, such as oral or manual manipulation, gratification of the partner is possible after the man has climaxed. When the exclusive focus on penile-vaginal or penile-anal intercourse is removed, a couple's anxieties about sex usually diminish sufficiently to permit greater ejaculatory control in the male

DSM-IV-TR Criteria for Male Orgasmic Disorder

- Persistent delay in or absence of orgasm following a normal period of sexual arousal. Consideration given to man's age and adequacy of sexual stimulation he receives
- Causes marked distress or interpersonal problems
- Not due to another Axis I disorder (except another sexual dysfunction) or to the direct physiological effects of a drug or a general medical illness

DSM-IV-TR Criteria for Premature Ejaculation

- Persistent ejaculation after minimal stimulation and before the man wishes it. Consideration given to factors that affect the duration of excitement phase, such as the man's age, novelty of the situation or the partner, and recent frequency of sexual contacts
- Causes marked distress or interpersonal problems
- Not due exclusively to the direct effects of a drug

DSM-IV-TR Criteria for Dyspareunia

- Recurrent genital pain associated with sexual intercourse
- Causes marked distress or interpersonal problems
- Not caused exclusively by vaginismus or lack of vaginal lubrication or due to another Axis I disorder (except another sexual dysfunction) or to the direct physiological effects of a drug or a general medical illness

DSM-IV-TR Criteria for Vaginismus

- Recurrent spasm of the outer third of the vagina such that conventional sexual intercourse is not possible
- Causes marked distress or interpersonal problems
- Not due to another Axis I disorder or to the direct physiological effects of a general medical illness

and sexual intercourse of longer duration. It will be interesting to observe whether shifts in sexual expectations and practices alter the concept of premature ejaculation.

Sexual Pain Disorders   Two pain disorders associated with sex are listed in the DSM: dyspareunia and vaginismus. **Dyspareunia** is diagnosed when there is persistent or recurrent pain during sexual intercourse. It is rarely diagnosed in men. Some women report that the pain starts at entry, whereas others report pain only after penetration (Meana et al., 1997). Not surprisingly, women with dyspareunia show normal levels of sexual arousal to films of oral sex, but their arousal declines when they watch a depiction of intercourse (Wouda et al., 1998). In women, the diagnosis of dyspareunia should not be made when the pain is believed to be due to lack of vaginal lubrication (when presumably female sexual arousal disorder would be diagnosed); nor should it be made when it is judged to be a function of the second pain disorder, vaginismus.

Vaginismus is marked by involuntary spasms of the outer third of the vagina to a degree that makes intercourse impossible. It can appear also in response to penetration by a finger as well as during gynecological examinations. Despite not being able to have intercourse, women with vaginismus have normal sexual arousal and have orgasms from manual or oral stimulation that does not involve penetration.

Prevalence rates for dyspareunia in women range from 8 percent (Schover, 1981) to 15 percent (Laumann et al., 1994). It is generally accepted that the disorder is far less often found in men, perhaps in as few as 1 percent (Bancroft, 1989). Estimates for vaginismus range from 12 to 17 percent of women seeking sex therapy (Rosen & Leiblum, 1995), and it is a very common complaint seen by gynecologists (Leiblum, 1997).

Genital pain associated with intercourse is usually caused by a medical problem, such as an infection of the vagina, bladder, or uterus or of the glans of the penis (McCormick, 1999; Meana et al., 1997). Depressive symptoms, anxiety, and marital problems are also associated with dyspareunia (Meana et al., 1998). One theory regarding the source of vaginismus supposes that the woman wishes, perhaps unconsciously, to deny herself, her partner, or both the pleasures of sexual intimacy. As plausible as this idea may seem, no evidence supports it. However, fear of pregnancy, anxiety, relationship problems, and negative attitudes toward sex in general may play a role in vaginismus (e.g., Reissing, Binik, & Khalife, 1999; Tugrul & Kabacki, 1997). Negative attitudes often are traceable to molestation in childhood or to rape (LoPiccolo & Stock, 1987). Masters and Johnson found that for a number of the couples they treated, the man's inability to maintain an erection preceded the development of vaginismus in his partner. For some women, then, the sexual problems of their partners may be so anxiety provoking as to result in the development of this disorder.

General Theories of Sexual Dysfunctions

Having reviewed descriptions of the sexual dysfunctions and some of the causes believed to underlie each, we turn now to a consideration of general theoretical perspectives.

At one time, sexual dysfunctions were generally viewed as a result of moral degeneracy. Excessive masturbation in childhood was widely believed to lead to sexual problems in adulthood. Von Krafft-Ebing (1902) and Havelock Ellis (1910) postulated that early masturbation damaged the sexual organs and exhausted a finite reservoir of sexual energy, resulting in lessened abilities to function sexually in adulthood. Even in adulthood excessive sexual activity was thought to underlie such problems as erectile failure. The general Victorian view was that sexual appetite was basically dangerous and therefore had to be restrained. To discourage handling of the genitals by children, metal mittens were promoted; and to distract adults from too much sex, outdoor exercise and a bland diet were recommended. In fact, Kellogg's Corn Flakes and graham crackers were developed as foods that would lessen sexual interest. They didn't.

Psychoanalytic views have assumed that sexual dysfunctions are symptoms of underlying repressed conflicts. The analyst focuses on the symbolic meaning of the symptom both to understand its etiology and to guide treatment. Since sexual dysfunctions bring discomfort and psychological pain to the individual and to his or her partner, and since unimpaired sexuality is inherently pleasurable, the theme of repressed anger and aggression competing with the gratification of sexual needs pervades psychoanalytic writings. Thus a man who ejaculates so quickly that he frustrates his female partner may be expressing repressed hostility toward women, who remind him unconsciously of his mother. A woman with vaginismus may be expressing her hostility toward men, perhaps as a result of childhood sexual abuse or more directly because of her husband's overbearing manner.

Many contemporary psychoanalysts supplement their therapy with cognitive-behavioral techniques (LoPiccolo, 1977). The spirit of rapprochement has also affected cognitive-behavioral approaches to the treatment of sexual dysfunctions, as these therapists are coming to appreciate the role of psychodynamic themes in what used to be straightforward behavioral treatments (cf. p. 472).

The most comprehensive account of the etiology of human sexual dysfunctions was offered by Masters and Johnson in their widely acclaimed book *Human Sexual Inadequacy* (1970), based on case studies from their practice. We will first examine their suggestions and then consider subsequent modifications and extensions of their ideas.

The Theoretical Model of Masters and Johnson   Masters and Johnson (1970) used a two-tier model of current and historical causes to conceptualize the etiology of human sexual inadequacy (Figure 14.2).

Current Causes   The current or proximal causes can be distilled down to two: fears about performance and the adoption of a spectator role. **Fear of performance** refers to being overly concerned with how one is "performing" during sex. The **spectator role**

In the early twentieth century, corn flakes were promoted as part of a bland diet to reduce sexual desire.

refers to being an observer rather than a participant in a sexual experience. Both involve a pattern of behavior in which the individual's focus on and concern for sexual performance impedes his or her natural sexual responses.

We have no conclusive evidence, however, that these factors are the causal agents in sexual dysfunctions. The reason is the directionality problem, discussed first in Chapter 5 and again in many places throughout this book. Researchers have consistently shown

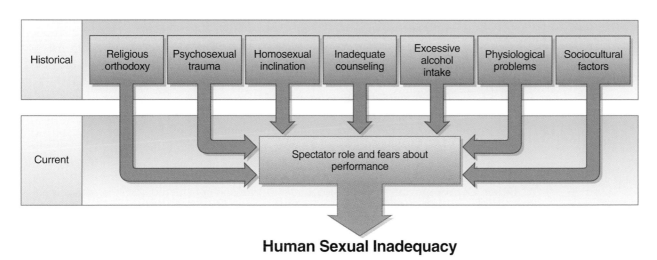

Human Sexual Inadequacy

Figure 14.2 Historical and current causes of human sexual inadequacies, according to Masters and Johnson.

that performance fears do exist in people with sexual dysfunctions, but the data do not show that the fear preceded and caused the dysfunction. Someone with an erectile dysfunction caused by diabetes, for example, may well become fearful that he will not attain or maintain an erection in a sexual encounter. The anxiety may function here as a factor that is maintaining the disorder, not one that caused it in the first place.

Historical Causes   In the Masters and Johnson model, the current, or proximal, reasons for sexual dysfunctions were hypothesized to have one or more historical antecedents.

- **Religious orthodoxy.** Some conservative religious upbringing looks askance at sexuality for the sake of pleasure, particularly outside marriage. Masters and Johnson found that many of their sexually dysfunctional patients had negative views of sexuality as a consequence. One female patient, for example, had been taught as she was growing up not to look at herself naked in the mirror and that intercourse was reserved for marriage and then only to be endured for purposes of having children.
- **Psychosexual trauma.** Some dysfunctions can be traced to rape or other degrading encounters. One male patient of Masters and Johnson had been told by a prostitute that he would never be able to "get the job done" with other women if he didn't "get it done here and now with a pro."
- **Homosexual inclination.** Sexual enjoyment is understandably less if a person with homosexual inclinations tries to engage in heterosexual sex.
- **Inadequate counseling.** This phrase is a euphemism for comments made by professionals that are incorrect and destructive, such as a health care worker's telling a healthy sixty-five-year-old man to forget about sex, or a cleric's saying that erectile dysfunction is God's punishment for sins.
- **Excessive intake of alcohol.** As Shakespeare wrote in Macbeth, "It provokes the desire but it takes away the performance" (act II, scene 3). If an inebriated man cannot achieve or maintain an erection, he may begin to fear that his erectile problem will recur rather than attribute the problem to alcohol. Because he becomes preoccupied with the possibility of not maintaining an erection, he begins to assume the spectator role. Empathy from his partner may then be misinterpreted as condescension and as a threat to his masculinity and overall sexual attractiveness. The relationship suffers, and the originally alcohol-induced erectile problem becomes pervasive and serious.
- **Biological causes.** Masters and Johnson alerted us back in 1970 to somatic factors contributing to sexual dysfunction. Now even more is known about such factors; we have considered this information in our discussions of the individual dysfunctions. In general, biological factors include diseases of the vascular (blood vessel) system such as atherosclerosis (p. 214); diseases that affect the nervous system such as diabetes, multiple sclerosis, and spinal cord injury; low levels of testosterone or estrogen; as just noted above, heavy alcohol use (though the negative effect may be mediated by the disruption in interpersonal relationships that alcohol abuse often brings about); certain medications, such as antihypertensive drugs and especially the SSRI antidepressant drugs like Prozac and Zoloft; and heavy cigarette smoking (Bach, Wincze, & Barlow, 2001).
- **Sociocultural factors.** Expectations and concerns differ between women and men and as a function of social class. For example, men have the blessing, even demand, of society to develop sexual expressiveness and to take the initiative. Despite the changes that have resulted from the feminist movement of the past thirty-plus years, it remains questionable whether this holds true for women.

Other Contemporary Views   Masters and Johnson considered sexual dysfunctions as problems in and of themselves that could be treated directly, rather than as symptoms of other intrapsychic or nonsexual interpersonal difficulties. The couples whose treatment formed the basis of their book *Human Sexual Inadequacy* (1970) had marriages that, in spite of sexual problems, were marked by caring and closeness. But as the Masters and Johnson therapy techniques became widespread and as the social milieu changed so as to make more people feel comfortable seeking help, sex therapists began to see people whose relationships were seriously impaired. In such situations, by the time a therapist is consulted, it is impossible to know whether the hostility between the two people caused the sexual problem or vice versa.

The working assumption of most contemporary sex therapists is that sexually dysfunctional couples have both sexual and interpersonal problems (Rosen & Leiblum, 1995). It is unrealistic to expect a satisfying sexual encounter when, for example, the man is angry with the woman for spending more and more time outside the home, or the woman resents the man's insensitive dealings with their children. Such negative thoughts and emotions can intrude into the sexual situation and thereby inhibit whatever arousal and pleasure might otherwise be found (Bach et al., 2001).

Many other causes of sexual dysfunction have been identified. As mentioned earlier, people who have sexual problems are often found to lack knowledge and skill (LoPiccolo & Hogan, 1979). Their partners may have deficiencies, for example, the husbands of nonorgasmic women are often reported to be awkward lovers (Kaplan, 1974; LoPiccolo, 1977). Simply caring for the partner may not be enough to establish a mutually satisfying sexual relationship. In fact, Kaplan (1974) suggested that inhibiting anxiety can arise when one partner wants too much to please the other; he or she may feel in the spotlight, resulting in a kind of performance anxiety. Another proposed cause of sexual dysfunction is what has been called response anxiety—anxiety about not being aroused (Apfelbaum, 1989).

Poor communication between partners also contributes to sexual dysfunction. For any number of reasons—embarrassment, distrust, dislike, resentment, depression, to name but a few—one lover may not inform the other of his or her preferences, likes, and dislikes and then may misinterpret the failure of the partner to anticipate or mind-read as a sign of not really caring. Although communication about sexual matters is frequently inadequate in distressed marriages and is therefore addressed in couples therapy (see p. 293), it can also be poor in people who are otherwise compatible. Open discussions of sex by partners, among friends, in the media, and even in professional training programs are, after all, relatively recent phenomena.

Concerns about contracting a venereal disease have probably long been a distractor and hence an inhibitor of deriving pleasure from sex with a partner. The spread of acquired immunodeficiency syndrome among sexually active individuals is no doubt now yet another reason behind many sexual dysfunctions.

Masters and Johnson emphasized the interpersonal nature of sexual dysfunction. In recent years more attention has been paid to *individual* factors (Bach et al., 2001). For example, people who are depressed are twice as likely as nondepressed individuals to have a sexual dysfunction (62 versus 26%) (Angst, 1998). And people with a panic disorder, fearful of physical sensations like rapid heart rate and sweating, are also at risk for sexual dysfunction (Sbrocco, Weisberg, Barlow, & Carter, 1997).

In considering these hypothesized etiological factors, it is important to keep two things in mind. First, many people have unsatisfying episodes in their sex lives, perhaps after a bruising argument with their partner or when preoccupied with problems at work. Usually these periods pass, and the sexual relationship returns to normal. Second, many people who have past histories or present lives that include one or more of the pathogenic factors discussed do not develop persistent sexual dysfunctions. Although to date there is little real understanding of this phenomenon, there is speculation that other variables, such as an unusually supportive network of friends or a particularly understanding sexual partner, must be operating in these people's present lives to mitigate the effects of the pathogenic factors.

Therapies for Sexual Dysfunctions

The pioneering work of Masters and Johnson (1970) in the treatment of sexual dysfunctions is described in Focus on Discovery 14.4. Over the past thirty-plus years therapists and researchers have elaborated on this early report and devised new procedures for the clinicians who seek to improve the lives of sexually dysfunctional patients. We will describe several strategies and procedures that extend the Masters and Johnson work. A therapist may choose only one technique for a given case, but the complex and multi-

Masters and Johnson's Therapy for Sexual Dysfunctions

In 1970 the publication of Masters and Johnson's *Human Sexual Inadequacy* generated an excitement in the mental health community that is seldom encountered. This book reported on the highly successful results of a therapy program carried out with close to 800 sexually dysfunctional people. Each couple had traveled to St. Louis and spent two weeks attending the Reproductive Biology Research Foundation for intensive therapy during the day and doing sexual homework in a motel at night. Away from home, couples were free of domestic distractions and able to make their stay a sort of second honeymoon.

Many of the Masters and Johnson techniques have now been used by therapists for some time, and, although some reports have found success rates comparable to those in the original report, others have not (McConaghy, 1997; Segraves & Althof, 1998). The likely reason for these findings is that as sex therapy became popularized, clinicians began to see more difficult cases, especially those in which the marital relationship itself had deteriorated.

Masters and Johnson virtually created the sex-therapy movement, and their work therefore deserves a detailed description. With some variations, such as not using a dual-sex therapy team or meeting weekly instead of daily, their approach is still followed by many practitioners conducting therapy for sexual dysfunctions.

The overall aim of Masters and Johnson was to reduce or eliminate fears of performance and to take the participants out of the maladaptive spectator role. They hoped that these steps would enable the couple to enjoy sex freely and spontaneously.

Each day the couple met with a dual-sex therapy team, under the assumption that men best understand men and women best understand women. For the first several days the experiences of all couples were the same, regardless of their specific problem. An important stipulation in those early days was that sexual activity between the two partners was expressly forbidden. A complete social and sexual history was obtained during the first two days, and physical examinations were conducted to determine whether there were biological factors that needed specific medical attention.

The assessment interviews placed considerable focus on the so-called **sexual value system**, the ideas of each partner about what was acceptable and needed in a sexual relationship. Sometimes the sexual value system of one or both partners had to be changed before sexual functioning could improve. For example, if one partner regarded sexuality as ugly and unacceptable, even the most powerful therapy would not be likely to help that person and the partner enjoy sex.

On the third day the therapists began to offer interpretations about why problems had arisen and why they were continuing. In all cases the emphasis was on the problems in the relationship, not on individual difficulties of either partner. A basic premise of the Masters and Johnson therapy was that "there is no such thing as an uninvolved partner in any marriage in which there is some form of sexual inadequacy" (1970, p. 2). Whatever the problem, the couple was encouraged to see it as their mutual responsibility. At this time the clients were introduced to the idea of the spectator role. They were told, for example, that a male with erectile problems—and often his partner as well—usually worries about how well or poorly he is doing rather than participating freely and that this pattern of observing the state of the erection, although totally understandable in context, blocks his natural responses and greatly interferes with sexual enjoyment.

At the end of the third day an all-important assignment was given to the couple, namely, to engage in **sensate focus**. The couple was instructed to choose a time when both partners felt "a natural sense of warmth, unit compatibility…or even a shared sense of gamesmanship" (Masters & Johnson, 1970, p. 71). They were to undress and give each other pleasure by touching each other's bodies. The co-therapists appointed one marital partner to do the first pleasuring, or giving; the partner who was "getting" was simply to be allowed to enjoy being touched. The one being touched was not required to feel a sexual response and was responsible for immediately telling the partner if something became distracting or uncomfortable. Then the roles were to be switched. Attempts at intercourse were still forbidden. To Masters and Johnson this approach was a way of breaking up the fran-

faceted nature of sexual dysfunctions usually demands several. These approaches are suitable for homosexual as well as heterosexual sex.

Anxiety Reduction   Well before the publication of the Masters and Johnson therapy program, behavior therapists appreciated that their sexually dysfunctional clients needed gradual and systematic exposure to anxiety-provoking aspects of the sexual situation. Wolpe's systematic desensitization and in vivo desensitization (desensitization by real-life encounters) have been employed with some success (Anderson, 1983; Hogan, 1978; Wolpe, 1958), especially when combined with skills training. For example, a woman with vaginismus might first be trained in relaxation and then practice inserting her fingers or dilators into her vagina, starting with small insertions and working up to larger ones (Leiblum, 1997). In vivo desensitization would appear to be the principal technique of the Masters and Johnson program, although additional components probably contribute to its overall effectiveness.

Directed Masturbation   We have previously mentioned that women with orgasmic disorder frequently lack knowledge of their own sexual anatomy. Directed masturbation,

tic groping common among these couples. The sensate-focus assignment usually promoted contact where none had existed for years, constituting a first step toward gradually reestablishing sexual intimacy.

Although sensate focus might uncover deep, hidden animosities, most of the time partners began to realize that encounters in bed could be intimate and pleasurable without necessarily being a prelude to sexual intercourse. On the second evening the partner being pleasured was instructed to give specific encouragement and direction by placing his or her hand on the hand of the giving partner in order to regulate pressure and rate of stroking. The touching of genitals and breasts was now allowed. Still, however, there was no mention of orgasm, and the prohibition on intercourse remained in effect. The partners were shown diagrams if they were ignorant of or uncertain about basic female and male anatomy, as they often were. After this second day of sensate focusing, treatment branched out according to the specific problem or problems of the couple. To illustrate the process, we will outline the therapy for female orgasmic disorder.

After the sensate-focus exercises made the couple more comfortable with each other in bed, the woman was encouraged to focus on maximizing her own sexual stimulation without trying to have an orgasm. As a result, her own sexual excitement usually increased. The therapists gave her partner explicit instructions about generally effective means of manually stroking the female genital area, although ultimate decisions were to be made by the female partner, who was encouraged to make her wishes clear to the man moment by moment. In the treatment of this dysfunction, as in the treatment of others, it was emphasized that at this stage having orgasms was not the focus of interaction between partners.

After the woman began to enjoy being pleasured by manual stimulation, the next step was to move the source of sensate pleasure from the man's hand on her body to his penis inside her vagina. She was told to place herself on top of the man, gently insert the penis, and simply tune in to her feelings. When she felt inclined, she could begin slowly to move her pelvis. She was encouraged to regard the penis as something for her to play with, something that could provide her with pleasure. The male could also begin to thrust slowly. At all times, however, the woman was to decide what should happen next and when. When the couple was able to maintain this containment for minutes at a time,

without the man thrusting forcefully toward orgasm, a major change had usually taken place in their sexual interactions: For perhaps the first time the woman was allowed to feel and think sexually, and indeed selfishly, about her own pleasure. In their subsequent encounters most couples began to have mutually satisfying intercourse.

Clinicians had to be extremely sensitive in presenting these various treatment procedures to a couple whose problems may have stretched back many years. Sometimes the couple discussed sex for the very first time at the Masters and Johnson clinic. The calm and open manner of the therapists put the couple at ease, encouraging in them both a commitment to follow certain instructions and a more open attitude toward sex and the activities in which people may engage together when making love. Although behavioral prescriptions were specific, the therapists could never lose sight of the atmosphere that had to be maintained in the consulting room and, it was hoped, transferred over to the privacy of the bedroom, where much of the actual therapy took place. As in other forms of behavior therapy, there was a strong emphasis on technique, but interpersonal factors set the stage for behavior to change.

A caveat about sensate focus is in order. As LoPiccolo (1992a) pointed out, more and more people are aware that not getting an erection from sensate focus is at the same time expected and not expected! That is, although the instruction from the therapist is not to feel sexual, even a moderately knowledgeable man knows that at some point he is supposed to get an erection from this nonsexual situation (which, after all, is not really nonsexual at all, involving as it does two nude people who care for each other enough to be spending time and money to feel more sexual toward each other). Thus, rather than reducing performance anxiety and the spectator role, sensate focus may create in some men what can be called metaperformance anxiety, taking the form of self-statements such as, "Okay, I don't have any pressure to get an erection and have intercourse. Right. So now ten minutes have passed, there's no pressure to perform, but I don't have an erection yet. When am I going to get an erection? And if I do, will I be able to maintain it long enough to insert it?" The sensate-focus stage of treatment, and indeed other aspects of Masters and Johnson's sex therapy, have elements of a very subtle approach to intervention known as paradoxical therapy, which we discuss in Chapter 17 (p. 586).

devised by Lopiccolo and Lobitz (1972), is a multistep therapy that supplements the Masters and Johnson program. The first step is for the woman to carefully examine her nude body, including her genitals, and identify various areas with the aid of diagrams. Next, she is instructed to touch her genitals and locate areas that produce pleasure. With this accomplished, she then increases the intensity of masturbation using erotic fantasies. If orgasm has not been achieved by this time, she is instructed to buy a vibrator and taught how to use it in her masturbation. Finally, her partner enters the picture, first watching his mate masturbate, then doing for her what she has been doing for herself, and finally having intercourse in a position that allows him to stimulate the woman's genitals manually or with a vibrator. Directed masturbation appears to add significantly to the effectiveness of treatment of orgasmic disorder (O'Donohue, Dopke, & Swingen, 1997) and is helpful also in the treatment of sexual desire disorder (Renshaw, 2001).

Procedures to Change Attitudes and Thoughts   In what are called **sensory-awareness procedures**, clients are encouraged to tune in to the pleasant sensations that accompany even incipient sexual arousal. The sensate-focus exercises described in Focus on

Discovery 14.4, for example, are a way of opening the individual to truly sensual and sexual feelings. Rational-emotive behavior therapy tries to substitute less self-demanding thoughts for "musturbation," the "I must" thoughts that often cause problems for people with sexual dysfunctions. A therapist might try to reduce the pressure a man with erectile dysfunction feels by challenging his belief that intercourse is the only true form of sexual activity. Kaplan (1997) recommends several procedures to try to increase the attractiveness of sex. She has clients engage in erotic fantasies and gives them courtship and dating assignments, such as getting away for a weekend.

Skills and Communication Training   To improve sexual skills and communication, therapists assign written materials and show clients explicit videotapes and films demonstrating sexual techniques (McMullen & Rosen, 1979). Of particular importance for a range of sexual dysfunctions is encouraging partners to communicate their likes and dislikes to each other (Hawton, Catalan, & Fagg, 1992; Rosen, Leiblum, & Spector, 1994). Taken together, skills and communication training also expose patients to anxiety-provoking material—such as seeing one's partner naked—which allows for a desensitizing effect. Telling a partner one's preferences in sex is often made more difficult by tensions that go beyond the sexual relationship, which leads us to the next strategy.

Couples Therapy   Sexual dysfunctions are often embedded in a distressed marital or other close relationship, and troubled couples usually need special training in nonsexual-communication skills (Rosen, 2000). As noted earlier, recent writings on sex therapy emphasize the need for a systems perspective, that is, for the therapist to appreciate that a sexual problem is embedded in a complex network of relationship factors (Wylie, 1997). Sometimes a therapy that focuses on nonsexual issues, such as difficulties with in-laws or with child rearing, is necessary and appropriate—either in addition to or instead of a Masters and Johnson type of sex therapy.

Psychodynamic Techniques and Perspectives   A man may not at first admit that he cannot have an erection, in which case the therapist must listen for clues in what he says. A woman may be reluctant to initiate sexual encounters because, although she may not verbalize it to the therapist, she considers such assertiveness unseemly and inappropriate to her traditional female role. In such instances the general psychodynamic view that clients are often unable to express clearly to their therapists what truly bothers them can help in proper assessment and planning for behavioral treatment (Kaplan, 1974). No doubt elements of psychodynamic therapy are to be found in the actual practices of sex therapists, even if they are usually not made explicit by these workers when discussing their techniques in journals or with colleagues. Our earlier discussion of eclecticism in therapy (p. 61) may serve as a reminder of the complexity of the therapeutic enterprise.

Medical and Physical Procedures   As more discoveries are made about biological factors in sexual dysfunctions, it becomes increasingly important for therapists to consider whether underlying somatic problems are contributing to the dysfunction (LoPiccolo, 1992b; Rosen & Leiblum, 1995). Consideration of possible somatic factors is especially important for the disorders of dyspareunia and complete erectile dysfunction. Dyspareunia can be ameliorated in postmenopausal women by estrogen treatments, which can reduce the thinning of vaginal tissue and improve vaginal lubrication (Masters, Johnson, & Kolodny, 1988; Walling, Anderson, & Johnson, 1990). When depression is part of the clinical picture along with severely diminished sex drive, antidepressant drugs can be helpful. Tranquilizers are also used as an adjunct to anxiety-reduction techniques. However, a complicating factor is that some of these psychoactive drugs themselves interfere with sexual responsiveness.

A number of medical procedures have been used to treat erectile dysfunction. Since the advent of Viagra, described below, their use has been declining. For example, a semirigid silicone rod can be implanted in a chronically flaccid penis, or a device can be implanted in the penis that can be stiffened with fluid from a reservoir and a small pump that is implanted in the scrotum. However, long-term follow-ups of men who have had such operations indicate that poor sexual functioning continues in many cases (Tiefer, Pedersen, &

Melman, 1988). If the psychological components of the problem are not addressed, men with rod implants may continue to have sexual problems, but with a penis that is never flaccid. (With a rod, sexual interest and arousal are not necessary for intercourse, and this situation is usually not favorable for long-term psychological adjustment.) Vascular surgery involves correction of problems with blood inflow via arteries or outflow via veins in the penis. Results are mixed at best (Melman & Rossman, 1989), but the possibility exists for restoration of normal functioning because, unlike the case with implants, erection will occur only with desire and arousal (Wincze & Carey, 1991).

A nonsurgical intervention entails the use of a cylinder attached to a vacuum pump. The penis is placed in the cylinder; when air is pumped out, blood is drawn into the penis, producing an erection. When the penis is erect, the cylinder is removed and an elastic band is put around its base to trap the blood and maintain the erection. This device is one of the treatments that has been recommended as effective by the American Urological Association (Skolnick, 1998).

"YOU WANT A RAISE, BREWSTER? HOW ABOUT A VIAGRA PILL?"

Several drugs have been successfully used in the treatment of sexual dysfunctions. One group of drugs (including alprostadil and paparevine hydrochloride) has to be injected into the penis; it dilates the arteries and thus produces an erection, even in the absence of sexual stimulation (Fallon, 1995). Not surprisingly, many men do not find this approach palatable (Rosen, 2000). Antidepressants have had mixed results with treating erectile dysfunction, as have testosterone injections; however, antidepressants have produced some good results with treating premature ejaculation (Evanoff & Newton, 1997, Haensel et al., 1998; Rakic et al., 1997; Strassberg et al., 1999).

The aforementioned medical interventions are being largely supplanted by Viagra (sildenafil). It was approved by the FDA in March 1998 and in its first three months was prescribed over 3 million times; it is even being sold illegally over the Internet. Viagra relaxes smooth muscles and thereby allows blood to flow into the penis during sexual stimulation, creating an erection. It is taken one hour before sex, and its effects last about four hours, thus allowing an erection to be maintained for a substantial time period. It is important to note that Viagra does not cause an erection in the absence of sexual stimulation; this means that the psychological dimension of erectile dysfunction must be attended to if this drug is to be effective (Rosen, 2000). While promising, research reports indicate that between 16 and 44% of men do not derive much benefit from the drug (Bach et al., 2001). Viagra also produces side effects such as headaches and indigestion. Moreover, it may be dangerous for men with cardiovascular disease, and this is a concern since many men who use Viagra are older adults and therefore more likely to have hypertension and coronary artery disease. Medical research into similar drugs for women has been underway for the past several years (Leiblum & Rosen, 2000).

In all instances of medical intervention, consideration of psychosocial factors remains important, for sexual dysfunctions are almost always embedded in a complex set of interpersonal and intrapsychic conflicts. The current trend toward viewing sexual dysfunctions as medical or biological problems may divert the attention of therapists and patients from the inherently interpersonal nature of these problems, giving rise to a quick-fix mentality that is probably ill-advised (Rosen & Leiblum, 1995).

Summary

- Gender identity disorder (GID) involves the deep and persistent conviction of the individual that his or her anatomic sexual makeup and psychological sense of self as male or female are discrepant. Thus, a man with GID is physically male but considers himself a woman and desires to live as a woman.

- Hormonal causes (for example, too much male hormone in a woman) have been considered for GID, but the data are equivocal. Another theory proposes that child-rearing practices may have encouraged the young child to believe that he or she was of the opposite sex.
- For a time, the only kind of help available to individuals with GID

was sex-reassignment surgery to bring certain bodily features into line with their gender identity. Now, however, there is some evidence that behavior therapy can help bring gender identity into line with anatomy in some cases.

- In the paraphilias, unusual imagery and acts are persistent and necessary for sexual excitement or gratification. The principal paraphilias are fetishism, reliance on inanimate objects for sexual arousal; transvestic fetishism, sometimes called transvestism, the practice of dressing in the clothing of the opposite sex, usually for the purpose of sexual arousal but without the gender identity confusion of a person with GID; pedophilia and incest, marked preferences for sexual contact with minors and, in the case of incest, for members of one's own family; voyeurism, a marked preference for watching others undressed or in sexual situations; exhibitionism, obtaining sexual gratification by exposing oneself to unwilling strangers; frotteurism, obtaining sexual contact by rubbing against or fondling women in public places; sexual sadism, a reliance on inflicting pain and humiliation on another person to obtain or increase sexual gratification; and sexual masochism, obtaining or enhancing sexual gratification through being subjected to pain, usually from a sadist.

- Psychoanalytic theories about the etiology of the paraphilias generally hold that they are defensive in nature, protecting the person from repressed conflicts and representing fixations at immature stages of psychosexual development. According to this perspective, the person with a paraphilia is basically fearful of conventional heterosexual relationships. Behavioral and cognitive theorists focus more directly on the sexual behavior itself. One view is that a fetishistic attraction to objects, such as boots, arises from accidental classical conditioning of sexual arousal. Another behavioral hypothesis posits deficiencies in social skills that make it difficult for the person to interact normally with other adults. Cognitive distortions appear to be involved, as voyeurs may claim that the women they viewed wanted to be seen in sexually compromising situations. Efforts have also been made to detect hormonal anomalies in people with paraphilias, but the findings are inconclusive.

- The most promising treatments for the paraphilias are multidimensional, entailing several behavioral and cognitive components. One procedure is reducing the arousal to the stimulus that is involved in the paraphilia by pairing it with painful or otherwise negative events. Another, orgasmic reorientation, tries to increase arousal to conventional sexual stimuli by associating them with high levels of sexual arousal via masturbation. Cognitive methods focus on the cognitive distortions of the person with a paraphilia; social-skills training and empathy training are also used frequently.

- Rape, although it is not separately diagnosed in DSM-IV-TR, is a pattern of behavior that results in considerable social and psychological trauma for the victim. The inclusion of rape in a discussion of human sexuality is a matter of some controversy, as many theorists regard rape as an act of aggression and violence rather than of sex.

- Few emotional problems are of greater interest to people than the sexual dysfunctions. These disruptions in the normal sexual response cycle are often caused by inhibitions, and they rob many people of sexual enjoyment. The DSM categorizes these disturbances in four groups: sexual desire disorders, sexual arousal disorders, orgasmic disorders, and sexual pain disorders. The disorders can vary in severity, chronicity, and pervasiveness, occurring generally or only with certain partners and in particular situations.

- Although biological factors must be considered, especially for dyspareunia and erectile failure, the etiology of the disorders usually lies in a combination of unfavorable attitudes, unpleasant or even traumatic early experiences, fears of performance, assumption of a spectator role, relationship problems, and lack of specific knowledge and skills. Sex-role stereotypes may play a part in some dysfunctions—a man who has trouble maintaining his erection is often called impotent, with the implication that he is not much of a man; and a woman who does not regularly have orgasms is often termed frigid, with the implication that she is generally cold and unresponsive. The problems of women in particular appear to be linked to cultural prejudices against their sexuality.

- Several therapists have devised effective interventions for sexual dysfunctions, many of them cognitive and behavioral in nature, often blended with psychodynamic perspectives and techniques. Direct sex therapy, aimed at reversing old habits and teaching new skills, was propelled into public consciousness by the Masters and Johnson work. Their method hinges on gradual, nonthreatening exposure to increasingly intimate sexual encounters and the sanctioning of sexuality by credible and sensitive therapists. Other means applied by sex therapists include educating patients in sexual anatomy and physiology; reducing anxiety; teaching communication skills; and working to change patients' attitudes and thoughts about sex and their own sexuality. Couples therapy is sometimes appropriate as well. Biological treatments such as Viagra may also be used, especially when the sexual dysfunction is primarily physical rather than psychological in nature, as in many cases of erectile dysfunction.

Key Terms

acquaintance (date) rape	frotteurism	pedophiles	sexual masochism
child sexual abuse	gender identity	premature ejaculation	sexual sadism
dyspareunia	homophobia	sensate focus	sexual value system
ego-dystonic homosexuality	homosexuality	sensory-awareness procedures	spectator role
exhibitionism	hypoactive sexual desire disorder	sex-reassignment surgery	statutory rape
fear of performance	incest	sexual and gender identity disorders	transsexualism
female orgasmic disorder	male erectile disorder	sexual aversion disorder	transvestic fetishism
female sexual arousal disorder	male orgasmic disorder	sexual dysfunctions	vaginismus
fetishism	orgasmic reorientation		voyeurism
forced rape			

Gender Identity Disorder: Transsexualism

Chris Morton was a 21-year-old senior in college. In most respects, she was an exceptionally well-adjusted student, successful academically and active socially. Her problem involved a conflict in gender identity—a problem so fundamental that it is difficult to decide whether to refer to Chris as he or she, although Chris used the masculine pronoun. We have somewhat arbitrarily decided to use the feminine pronoun in relating this case because it may be less confusing to the reader. And in many respects this is a confusing case. It calls into question one of the most fundamental, and seemingly irrefutable, distinctions that most of us make—the distinction between men and women.

Chris's physical anatomy was that of a woman. But this distinction was not made easily on the basis of overt, physical appearance. She was tall and slender: 5'8" inches and about 130 pounds. Her hips were narrow and her breasts, which she wrapped with an Ace bandage under her clothes, were small. Chris's face was similarly androgynous; her skin had a soft, smooth appearance, but her features were not particularly delicate or feminine. Her hair was cut short, and she wore men's clothes. A typical outfit included Levi's and a man's shirt with a knit tie and a sweater vest. She wore men's underwear and men's shoes, often Oxfords or penny loafers. She also wore a man's ring on her right hand and a man's wrist watch. Her appearance was generally neat and preppy. At first glance, it was not clear whether Chris was a man or a woman. Listening to Chris's voice did not provide any more useful clues because it was neither deep nor high pitched. Many people assumed that she was a man; others were left wondering.

On the basis of her own attitudes and behaviors, Chris considered herself to be like men. Like other transsexuals, she described herself as being a man trapped in a woman's body. She did not consider herself to be confused about her gender identity. From a biological point of view, Chris recognized that she was not a man. She knew that she had breasts and a vagina. She menstruated. But there was more to it than physical anatomy. In every other way possible, and for as long as she could remember, Chris had always felt more male than female. When she tried to explain this feeling to others, she would say, "You can think what you want—and I know that most people don't want to believe this—but if you spend time with me, talk to me, you will see what I mean. You'll know that I am not a woman." The details of this subjective perception, the experiences that served as support for Chris's belief, lie at the core of our notions of what is feminine and what is masculine.

Chris felt a sense of camaraderie in the presence of men. She wasn't sexually attracted to them, and it never would have occurred to her to flirt with them. She wanted to be buddies with them—to swap stories about adventures and compare notes on sexual exploits with women. They were her friends. In her behavior toward women, Chris was often characteristically masculine and excessively polite; she liked to hold doors for women, to pull out their chairs when they sat down to eat, to stand up when they entered a room. This is, of course, not to say that these behaviors are innately masculine, for they are learned as part of our upbringing. Chris felt more comfortable behaving this way because it made her feel masculine, and she said it seemed natural.

People responded in a variety of ways when meeting Chris for the first time. Most assumed that she was a man, but others took her to be a woman. Chris usually corrected people if they happened to address her as a woman. For example, if an instructor used a feminine pronoun when addressing or describing Chris during an initial meeting, she would quickly say "he" or "his." In situations that might arouse curiosity or attract attention, Chris tried to adopt exaggerated male postures or vocal patterns to overcome the observer's sense of ambiguity. One example occurred when she walked into a small seminar for the first time. Chris sauntered across the room, sat down so her legs crossed with one heel on the other knee, and then slouched down in the chair, adopting a characteristically masculine posture. When answering the phone, she usually tried to lower the pitch of her voice.

Chris was sexually attracted to women and, consistent with her male gender identity (her conviction that she was more like men than women), she considered herself to be heterosexual. In fact, she had had two long-term, intimate relationships, and both were with other women. Her present lover, Lynn, was a 26-year-old bisexual who treated Chris as a man and considered their relationship to be heterosexual. Lynn said that when they first met, she thought that Chris was a woman and she was attracted to her as a woman. But as their relationship developed, Lynn came to think of Chris as a man. Part of this impression could be traced to physical behaviors. Lynn agreed that making love with Chris was more like making love with a man than a woman. Although this impression was difficult to describe in words, it seemed to revolve around the way Chris held her and touched her. Perhaps more important were the emotional and intellectual qualities that Lynn noticed. Chris cried about different things than Lynn cried about and seemed unable to empathize with many of Lynn's experiences—experiences that seemed characteristically feminine. She was surprised, for example, at Chris's apparent inability to empathize with her discomfort during menstruation. And Lynn was often surprised by Chris's questions. Once when they were making love, Chris asked Lynn what it felt like to have something inside her vagina. It was a sensation Chris had never experienced (and never wanted to experience).

Chris's parents had known about her gender identity conflict since her senior year in high school. This was a difficult issue for them to address, but they both assured Chris that their love for her was more important than their concern about the problems she would face as a transsexual. Their reactions were also very different. Chris's mother accepted the problem and made every effort to provide emotional support for Chris. Her father, on the other hand, seemed to deal with the issue at a more intellectual level and continued to believe that it was merely a phase that she was going through. Both were opposed to her interest in physical treatment procedures that might permanently alter her appearance.

Although Chris's life was going well in most respects, she wanted to do something about her body to make it more compatible with her masculine gender identity. Several options seemed reasonable. First, she wanted to have her breasts removed. She also wanted to begin taking male hormones so that her voice would deepen and she would grow facial hair. Finally, she wanted to have surgery to remove her uterus and ovaries, primarily because their continued presence might conflict with the consumption of testosterone. Although she would also have preferred to have a penis, she did not want to go through genital surgery because it would not leave her with a functional male organ. Furthermore, the possibility of "mutilating" her existing organs and losing her capacity for orgasm through clitoral stimulation frightened her.

One interesting feature of Chris's masculine identity was revealed in her discussion of the advantages and disadvantages of the physical procedures involved in changing her body. Lynn mentioned, for example, the possible traumatic consequences of losing the capacity to bear children. What if Chris decided in a few years that she had been mistaken and now wanted to raise a family? The idea was totally foreign to Chris! It was a concern that never would have occurred to her. For Chris, the justification for the change was primarily cosmetic. Her concern involved plans for the future. "Right now I can pass for a young man. That's okay when I'm 21, but what happens when I'm 40 and still look like I'm 20 because I don't have facial hair? I can't date 20-year-old women all my life. I wouldn't be happy."

During her senior year in college, Chris made an appointment to see a psychologist at the student health center on campus. She wanted to talk about her desire to take male hormones and alter her body surgically. Although she had thought about the decision for a long time and discussed it with several other people, she wanted to get the opinion of a mental health professional.

Social History

Chris was the oldest of four children. She had one brother, who was one year younger than she, and two younger sisters.

Chris said that she had always felt like a boy. Other people viewed her as a typical "tomboy," but Chris recognized the difference. When she was very young, she and her brother and their father played together all the time. Sports were a central activity in the family, especially basketball. Mr. Morton spent numerous hours teaching Chris and her brother to dribble and shoot baskets on their driveway.

These were pleasant memories for Chris, but she also remembered feeling excluded from this group as she and her brother grew older. For example, at that time, Little League rules prohibited girls from participating, and Chris found that she was generally discouraged from playing with boys in the organized games that became more common when they were 9 or 10 years old. She and her brother both played on organized youth teams, and their father served as a coach for both of them. But Chris had to play on girls' teams and she didn't think that was fair, either for her or to the other girls. She remembered thinking to herself that, although she was always the best player on the girls' team, she would have been only an average player on a boys' team, and that was where she felt she belonged. When she got to high school, she finally quit the team, in spite of the fact that she was one of the best players, because she didn't want her name or picture to appear in the paper as being part of a girls' team.

Although Chris spent a great deal of time with her father and brother, she also had a good relationship with her mother, whom she remembers as being a source of emotional support and sympathy in difficult times. Her mother was not athletically inclined, so she didn't participate in the activities of Mr. Morton and the children, but she and Chris did spend time talking and shopping together. On the other hand, Chris was never interested in many of the other activities that some girls share with their mothers, like cooking.

She also wasn't interested in playing with toys that many other girls preferred. She and Rick shared most of their favorite toys, including slot cars, toy soldiers, and baseball cards. She and a friend did play with Barbie dolls for a while, but they only did so when combining them with G.I. Joes and weaving them into mock wars and sexual adventures.

When she started school and began meeting other children in public situations, Chris began to confront and think about issues that are taken for granted by virtually everyone else. How many children, for example, ever think twice about which bathroom to use? As early as the first and second grade Chris could remember feeling uncomfortable about using the girls' room. In the first grade, she attended a parochial school in which the girls were required to wear uniforms. She wore the dress and had her hair long and in a pony tail, but that changed as soon as she reached the second grade. After their parents arranged for Chris and Rick to transfer to a public school, Chris cut her hair very short and began wearing slacks and shirts that made her indistinguishable from the boys.

Similar issues centered around locker rooms. When Chris was 9 years old, her mother arranged for her and Rick to take swimming lessons at a public pool. Chris developed a crush on a cute girl in her class. She remembered feeling ashamed and embarrassed at being in the same locker room with the other girls and being seen in a girl's swimming suit.

Chris's sex play as a child involved little girls rather than little boys. When she was 9 years old, Chris spent long hours "making out" with an 11-year-old neighbor girl, who also experimented sexually with many of the young boys in their neighborhood. Thus, even at this fairly young age, Chris was sexually attracted to girls rather than boys. She had numerous opportunities to play sex games with young boys, who occasionally asked Chris to "mess around," but she wasn't interested. Girls were more attractive and interesting.

By the time she reached junior high school, Chris had begun systematically to avoid using her given name, Christine. She also came to dislike Chris, because although it is a name that is used by both men and women, she thought of it as being more feminine. She came instead to be known by her nickname, "Morty," which sounded more masculine to her.

Adolescence presented a difficult turning point for Chris. The separation of the sexes became more obvious. All of the girls wanted to wear dresses and date boys. Chris wanted to wear pants and date girls. The situation became even more frustrating in high school as her body began to change in obvious ways. The onset of menstruation was awkward, and the development of her breasts presented an even more difficult situation because their presence could be noticed by other people. As soon as her breasts began to enlarge, Chris began binding them tightly with a skin-colored belt that would not show through her shirt. The belt often left bruises on her chest. When she had to change clothes for gym class, she always had to find an isolated locker, away from the other girls, so that no one would see her taking off the belt. Nevertheless, the discomfort and pain associated with this procedure were preferable to the embarrassment of having other people realize that she was developing a woman's body.

Chris continued to have a lot of friends and to be active in academic and extracurricular activities in spite of her discomfort with gender-specific roles and behaviors. In fact, she was so popular and well respected by the other students that she was elected president of her freshman class in high school. Although she dressed in masculine clothes, everyone knew that she was a girl because she was forced to take the girls' gym class at school. Many of the social activities in which Chris and her friends engaged centered on roller skating in the evening and on weekends. Large numbers of teenagers from their own school and several others in the city gathered there to skate to rock music, eat pizza, and have a good time. Because she was a good athlete and enjoyed physical activity, these were pleasant times for Chris. There were awkward moments, however, such as when the disc jockey would announce "girls only" or "boys only." In either case, Chris would leave the rink; she didn't want to be seen with the girls and wasn't allowed to be with the boys.

Chris's parents separated and were eventually divorced when she was a sophomore in high school. Because their parents had concealed the fact that they were not getting along, the news came as a shock to all of the children. In retrospect, Chris said that she should have known that something was going on because her parents had been spending so much time together talking quietly in their room; her parents had usually been content to go their separate ways. There were, of course, hard feelings on both sides, but the arrangements for the separation were made to minimize the children's involvement in the dispute. They continued to live with their mother and visited their father on weekends.

When Chris was 17, she finally decided to have a talk with her mother about her discomfort with femininity. She told her mother that she wanted to be a boy. Her mother's reply was, "I know you do. I was also a tomboy when I was your age, but you'll grow out of it." Her mother tolerated her masculine dress but didn't seem to comprehend the depth of Chris's feelings.

Chris's best friends in high school were three boys who spent most of their time together. They were the liberal intellectuals of the class. These boys accepted Chris as one of their group without being concerned about her gender. One of her friends later told her, "I never really thought of you as a girl. I guess it wasn't important. You were just Morty." She did attract some attention, however, from other children and teachers. She wore men's pants and shirts, and sometimes ties and sport coats. Chris and her friends were also good dancers and spent a lot of time on weekends at a local club. They were the life of the party. When they arrived, everyone else started dancing and having fun.

Sex presented an extremely frustrating dilemma for Chris. She was attracted to girls, as were all of her male friends. When the boys talked—in the usual crude adolescent way—about girls they knew, Chris wanted to join in. But all of her friends knew that she was a girl. She was particularly attracted to one girl, Jennifer, who had moved to their school the previous year. Jennifer was bright, attractive, and engaging. Her appearance and manners were quite feminine. She spent a lot of time with Chris and her friends, but she was going with a boy who was the captain of the basketball team. Chris and Jennifer began to spend more and more time together as the school year wore on. They talked on the phone every night for at least an hour and were virtually inseparable on weekends.

During their junior year, Jennifer's boyfriend moved away to go to college. The relationship began to deteriorate, but Jennifer didn't know how to break things off. Chris became her principal source of emotional support during these difficult months. Chris became very fond of Jennifer and recognized that she was sexually attracted to her but feared that she might destroy their relationship if she mentioned these feelings to Jennifer.

This all changed rather abruptly one Saturday evening. They went to see a movie together, and, as they were sitting next to each other in the darkened theater, Jennifer became conscious of the strong emotional attraction that she felt toward Chris. She sat wishing that Chris would put her hand on her leg or put her arm around her. Jennifer explained these feelings to Chris as they drove home after the film was over, and Chris, in turn, made an effort to explain her feelings for Jennifer. They continued the discussion inside Jennifer's house, and eventually retired to Jennifer's bedroom where they spent the rest of the night talking and making love.

Their physical relationship—which both Chris and Jennifer considered to be heterosexual in nature—was an exceptionally pleasant experience for both of them. It was not without its awkward moments, however. For example, Chris would not let Jennifer touch her breasts or genitals for the first six months after they began having sex. She touched Jennifer with her mouth and hands, but did not let Jennifer reciprocate beyond holding and kissing. In fact, Chris always kept her pants on throughout their love making. This hesitation or resistance was primarily due to Chris's sense that she was in the wrong body. If she allowed Jennifer to touch her, they would both be reminded that she had a woman's body. This was frustrating for both of them, but especially for Jennifer, who by this point was not concerned about whether Chris was a man or a woman. She was simply in love with Chris as a person and wanted a complete, reciprocal relationship. Chris was also frustrated because she continued to feel—in spite of

Jennifer's frequent protests to the contrary—that she could not satisfy Jennifer in the way that Jennifer most wanted because she did not have a penis. Their relationship gradually extended to allow more open physical reciprocity, primarily as a result of Jennifer's gentle insistence. Chris found that she enjoyed being stimulated manually and orally by Jennifer and had no trouble reaching orgasm.

Chris and Jennifer were able to continue their intimate relationship without interference from their parents because their parents viewed Chris as a girl and never considered the possibility that she and Jennifer were lovers. They frequently spent nights together at Jennifer's house without arousing any serious suspicion. Jennifer's mother occasionally made comments and asked questions about Chris's masculine wardrobe and manners, but she was totally oblivious to the complexities of Chris's behavior and to the nature of her daughter's involvement.

Despite Jennifer's obvious affection for Chris, their relationship created problems as Jennifer became increasingly sensitive to the reactions of other people. Part of the problem centered on gossip that spread quickly through their school, despite attempts by Chris and Jennifer to conceal the fact that they were dating. Other students had always been reasonably tolerant of Chris's masculine behavior, but their criticism became more overt when a close friend, in whom they had confided, let it become known that Chris and Jennifer were dating each other. That seemed to step beyond most other students' limit for acceptable behavior.

Their sexual relationship ended during Chris's freshman year at college. Jennifer's mother discovered some intimate love letters that Chris had written to Jennifer, who was also in college. She was furious! She threatened to discontinue financial support for Jennifer's education and refused to let her be in their home as long as Jennifer continued to see Chris. The pressure was simply too much. Chris and Jennifer continued to be good friends, but the romantic side of their relationship had to be abandoned. Jennifer dated two or three men afterwards and was eventually married.

After breaking up with Jennifer, Chris met and dated a few other women before starting her relationship with Lynn. One of these encounters is particularly interesting, because it also provides some insight into Chris's sexual orientation and gender identity. One of her male friends from high school, Robert, was also a freshman at the university. They continued to spend a lot of time together and eventually talked openly about Chris's "story" and the fact that Robert was gay. Both admitted considerable interest regarding sexual response in bodies of the opposite sex—responses that neither had had the opportunity to observe. In order to satisfy their curiosity, they decided to have sex with each other. Chris later described it as a pleasant experience, but one that felt uncomfortable. They engaged in mutual masturbation, but Chris did not allow him to penetrate her vagina with his penis. Chris had never experienced a sexual encounter with a male before, and her principal interest was in observing Robert's behavior. She wanted to watch him become aroused and reach orgasm. She had always sensed that her own sexual behavior was more like that of a man than a woman, and this would give her a chance to decide. She ended the evening convinced more than ever that her own behavior was masculine and that she was not sexually attracted to men.

Chris strongly preferred monogamous relationships. This was in part a matter of convenience, because it was obviously very difficult for her to get to know someone with sufficient intimacy to begin a sexual relationship. It was also a matter of choice. She did not understand, for example, how some people—particularly males—could be so promiscuous.

During her sophomore year in college, Chris stumbled across some literature on transsexualism. This was the first time that she realized that other people experienced the same feelings that she had and that the condition had a formal label. In addition to the comfort that she was not alone in this dilemma, she also obtained some useful information. For example, she learned that many transsexual females use Ace bandages, rather than belts, to bind their breasts. She felt much more comfortable after the change. She also learned about the possibilities of hormonal treatments and various surgical procedures that might be used to alter the appearance of her body. Recognition of these alternatives led Chris to pursue extensive reading at the university library. Having decided that she would like to change the appearance of her body, she made an appointment at the student health center.

Conceptualization and Treatment

When Chris came to see a psychologist at the student health center, she did not indicate that she wanted to change her behavior. Extended consultation with a mental health professional is generally considered to be a prerequisite for the other procedures that might be used to alter her appearance. Chris sincerely wanted to learn as much as possible about her feelings and motivations for change before embarking upon a difficult set of procedures that carried some possibility for health hazards. She knew, for example, that the hormone treatments might lead to the development of acne and that the hair on the top of her head might begin to thin out. Although she felt strongly about her masculine gender identity, she was willing to consider the possibility that she needed psychological treatment rather than the sex change procedure.

Chris's exceptional social adjustment was an important consideration in the evaluation of her condition. She was clearly functioning at a high level; her grades were good, and she had lots of friends—many of whom knew her only as a man—and she was satisfied with her current sexual relationship, which was based on her masculine identity. Even if procedures were available to alter her gender identity and convince Chris to act and feel like a woman, it did not seem likely that she could be any better adjusted. And, in all probability, she would have been miserable. Therefore, the psychologist decided that she would not try to persuade her that her problem regarding gender identity was the manifestation of more deeply ingrained psychopathology. She played a supportive role as Chris made her own decision about the pending medical procedures.

15-Year Followup

In the following pages, we describe many important experiences that Chris has had since this case was originally written. Chris is now living as a man. This successful transition leads us to use the masculine pronoun, "he," when referring to Chris in this update.

Chris attended psychotherapy on a regular basis for approximately two years. As Chris had hoped, the psychologist referred him to an endocrinologist (a physician who specializes in disorders of the hormonal system) after the first year of psychotherapy. The doctor asked Chris to complete a battery of psychological tests and a psychiatric evaluation prior to beginning hormone therapy. The doctor wanted this information so that he could be certain that transsexualism was the correct diagnosis.

The psychological test profile and psychiatrist's report indicated that Chris was an intelligent person who was able to evaluate the external world objectively. There was no evidence of psychotic thinking. The endocrinologist therefore granted Chris's request for hormone therapy. Chris was 22 years old and in his first year of graduate school. He can recall with vivid detail the first injection of a synthetic male hormone he received at the medical center. The prescription was Depo-Testosterone 300mg (1-1/2cc) every three weeks. He looked at his face in the mirror and wondered how he might change physically and emotionally. Would he be satisfied with the results? What if he didn't feel "like himself?"

The first major physical change came two months later with the cessation of the menstrual period. There would be no more obvious monthly reminders that he was physically female. The other changes were more gradual. His voice deepened and cracked just like the voices of pubescent boys. His fat distribution changed, especially around the hips and thighs. He became more muscular and his breast tissue shrank so he no longer had to wear the Ace bandage to conceal his breasts. It would take at least five years for the torso bruising (from the bandaging) to disappear completely. Chris grew more hair on his arms, legs, stomach, and chest. The hair on his face took longer to grow. In the beginning, he shaved every four to five days. He now shaves every other day and sports a handsome mustache and goatee.

Chris had not anticipated a change in his feelings about sex. He had always seemed to have a normal sex drive. Nevertheless, his sex drive skyrocketed during the first two years of hormone therapy. He felt as though he was experiencing puberty all over again. His "first puberty" was spent daydreaming of kissing girls and holding hands. Now he could understand the urges adolescent boys feel for sex. It was often difficult to think of anything other than sex and how to get it. Fortunately, his age and maturity afforded him some control over such impulses. Chris developed sexual relationships with three women during graduate school. He noticed his orgasms were more intense. He was becoming much more comfortable with his own body and could even enjoy masturbating.

Chris could no longer hide the physical changes from his family. People were asking questions about his voice, and the hair on his legs was quite noticeable. Chris enlisted the help of his father and stepmother, who agreed to explain his transsexualism to most of his relatives. But he wanted personally to discuss the situation with his brother and sisters. To Chris's surprise and great relief, not one family member rejected or ridiculed him. Some did not understand his psychosexual disorder, but all professed their love as well as admiration for his courage in pursuing his dream. He had always enjoyed a great deal of support from his friends. Now, with his family's blessing, he no longer had to pretend to be a woman in any aspect of his life. He would now be known as a man.

Chris received a master's degree and landed his first professional job in the crisis department of a major metropolitan hospital. He was initially anxious about being discovered as a transsexual because he was living near the area where he grew up. Fortunately, this never happened. Over the next two years, he grew to trust several colleagues and eventually told them his story. His colleagues readily accepted his situation—although his male work friends often joked that he was "turned the wrong way" in the restroom stalls.

Many transsexuals resort to creative means to pass for the gender they wish to be. Chris frequently had to think fast on his feet to escape awkward situations. He demonstrated considerable ingenuity when he decided it was time to have the gender changed on his driver's license. This is normally a formal process that requires a court order and official documents, which he did not possess. He devised another approach. He began by renewing his current license, allowing his old information to be transferred to the new one. His gender was listed as "F" for female. A few days later, he returned to the same license branch and nonchalantly explained that someone must have made an honest error in recording his gender. He noted that it was a common mistake. Sometimes people would just look at the name "Chris," assume the person was female, and record it as such. The clerk apologized profusely and immediately issued a new license. He said it was obvious "just by looking" that Chris was male.

Chris was functioning as a male at work and with his friends. At 25 years of age, it was time to consider officially changing his name and gender. Chris hired an attorney to help guide him through the legal system. Chris asked his psychologist, physician, employer, and friends to write letters of endorsement to the court attesting to his stature as an upstanding citizen in the community who was living and functioning as a man. Several months later, after a five-minute hearing, the judge lowered his gavel and declared Christine to be now Christopher and legally male. This was done without any surgeries to remove organs (uterus, ovaries, breasts) or to add them (creation of a penis and scrotum).

To date, Chris has opted to forgo surgical interventions. He accepts his body, even though he is not entirely satisfied with it. He wishes that he had been born with a penis, but he does not need one to live, function, and be accepted as male. He will need medication for the rest of his life, although he now requires less testosterone to maintain his outward appearance. He does acknowledge some concern about the medication because the long-term effects of hormone use for female-to-male transsexuals have not been studied extensively. If Chris were to stop the injections for several months, the menstrual cycle would resume, body fat would redistribute, and his facial hair would be lost. His voice would retain its low pitch. Once the vocal cords thicken as the result of male hormones, they will remain so unless surgically altered. Chris has no plans to stop the medication.

Important developments have also taken place in Chris's social life. He had always loved Jennifer, his high school sweetheart, despite his involvement in other romantic relationships. Jennifer was married, but Chris never lost hope of renewing his relationship with her. As luck would have it, they became reacquainted while working on their high school five-year reunion committee. Their friendship picked up where it left off. Jennifer confided to Chris that she was unhappy in her marriage and was contemplating divorce. Chris hoped that their renewed friendship would evolve into something more intimate, but he did not want to be the cause of Jennifer's divorce. Jennifer believed that she would have been divorced eventually regardless of her relationship with Chris.

Jennifer was introduced to Chris's circle of friends and was invited to their social events. Jennifer began to spend occasional nights at Chris's apartment, although they slept separately. After a few months, their relationship became sexual. Sex was now more satisfying to them than it had been before, perhaps because Chris was more comfortable with his own body. In spite of the excitement and happiness that they found in their new romance, Chris and Jennifer felt uneasy having an illicit affair. One year after they became reacquainted, Jennifer filed for divorce and moved into an apartment near Chris. Soon, they moved in together. Chris's dream of marrying his high school sweetheart was going to come true. They had been living together for four years when he proposed to Jennifer.

Now they had lots of planning to do. Could they apply for a marriage license? Who would marry them? Would they need to disclose the fact that Chris was transsexual? They struggled with these and many other issues. Their relationship had faced many obstacles over the years, but could it survive planning a wedding? They were confronted with even more stressful situations during that year. Jennifer graduated from nursing school and took her licensing board examination. Some of Chris's extended family members refused to attend the wedding because of their religious beliefs. In spite of these hurdles, they obtained a wedding license, found a judge, and had a beautiful ceremony.

Chris's life was normal in most ways. He and Jennifer both had successful careers. They bought a house. However, Jennifer felt something was missing. She wanted children. Despite a few reservations about parenthood, they forged ahead with the process of artificial insemination. They chose an anonymous donor who matched Chris's physical characteristics and personality type. Two years later, Jennifer was pregnant . . . with twins!

Chris and Jennifer faced some unique circumstances, above and beyond all the normal anxieties that come with first-time parenthood. Preparing for the births of their son and daughter made them wonder how they would handle Chris's transsexuality. How would they deal with their own nudity? How would they respond to the children's normal curiosity about sex? As it turned out, the most pressing issues during the first year of parenthood were finding time for sleep and keeping enough diapers on hand.

It would have been impractical to expect that the children would never see Chris's body, though he tried his best to be discreet. Jennifer and Chris decided to respond to the children's questions about sexuality with honest, age-appropriate explanations. They learned quickly that all their rehearsed responses could be easily thwarted by their children's brutal honesty. For example, Chris recalled a dinner table conversation in which his 3-year-old son announced that "when I grow up, I want to be a man without a penis, like Daddy." Perhaps the most interesting implication of this bold declaration is the fact that Chris's son viewed him as a man, in spite of his physical anatomy. In fact, neither child ever confused

Chris with a woman. Their daughter sometimes announced proudly to her brother, "Mommy and I are girls, and you and Daddy are boys." To date, Chris only once has explained his genitalia to the children. He said, "Daddy's penis didn't get made all the way. But your penis and vagina were made just fine." Chris knows that the issue will come up again; simple explanations will not always be sufficient.

Chris's transsexuality is with him everyday, but it is no longer the focal point in his life. The issues arise infrequently now. Although the old anxieties of rejection and ridicule can still be evoked from time to time, he accepts himself and lives a full and happy life. Chris does not think of his transsexualism as a disorder from which he can be cured. He views it as a condition that he has learned to integrate and manage.

Discussion

Because the discussion of this case involves a number of subtle and frequently controversial issues, it may be helpful to begin with the definition of some elementary terms. *Gender identity* involves a person's belief or conviction that he or she is a male or a female. The public expression of this belief involves role-specific behaviors associated with masculinity and femininity. *Sexual orientation*, on the other hand, represents the person's preference for male or female sexual partners. In the infinite variety of human behavior, there can be endless combinations of gender identity, gender-role behaviors, and sexual orientations (Kessler & McKenna, 2000; Newman, 2002).

People with gender identity disorders vary considerably with regard to the severity and persistence of their problems. Relatively few children who exhibit gender identity problems continue to experience similar problems as adults (Bradley & Zucker, 1997; Green, 1987). In *DSM-IV-TR*, the term *transsexualism* is used to describe severe gender identity disorder in adults.

Why is gender identity disorder a controversial topic? Perhaps because it raises such difficult questions about the way in which we view ourselves and our world. Perhaps because the attitudes of many transsexuals, as well as the surgical procedures that have been used to help them attain their goals, are inconsistent with popularly held notions about men and women.

Transsexuals raise a larger issue, in an era of wholesale efforts to relax rigid sex roles and give men and women more freedom to behave in ways that have traditionally been labeled "masculine" or "feminine." For, by their insistence on surgery—which gives them the form if not always the function of the sexual apparatus they desire—transsexuals seem to reassert the primacy of genital forms in defining sex and gender. (Restak, 1979, p. 20)

The following discussion focuses on clinical and scientific issues involved in the study of transsexualism rather than its political and social implications.

Descriptions of individuals whose gender identity is inconsistent with their anatomical sex can be traced to antiquity, but the term *transsexualism* was not introduced until 1949 by Caldwell. The disorder began to attract attention in the professional literature through the writings of Harry Benjamin (1953, 1966) and descriptions of famous cases—such as Christine Jorgensen—that appeared in the popular press during the 1950s (Bullough, 1999). The term first appeared in the American Psychiatric Association's official nomenclature with the publication of *DSM-III* (APA, 1980), in which transsexualism was listed with adult forms of sexual disorder under the heading Gender Identity Disorders.

In *DSM-IV-TR*, Gender Identity Disorder is listed in a general section with sexual dysfunctions and paraphilias. There is, of course, an important difference between Gender Identity Disorders and Sexual Disorders. The latter are defined primarily in terms of problems that interfere with the capacity for reciprocal, affectionate sexual activity. Chris's situation illustrates why Gender Identity Disorders are not considered sexual disorders. Although she was uncomfortable with her anatomic sex and wanted to live as a man, she was sexually functional and actively involved in a mutually satisfying relationship.

DSM-IV-TR (pp. 581-582) description of Gender Identity Disorder can apply to children, adolescents, or adults. In fact, most transsexuals report that their discomfort with their anatomic sex began during childhood. The disorder is defined by the following criteria:

A. A strong and persistent cross-gender identification (not merely a desire for any perceived cultural advantages of being the other sex)

   In children, the disturbance is manifested by four (or more) of the following:

   1. Repeatedly stated desire to be, or insistence that he or she is, the other sex

   2. In boys, preference for cross-dressing or simulating female attire; in girls, insistence on wearing only stereotypical masculine clothing

   3. Strong and persistent preferences for cross-sex roles in make-believe play or persistent fantasies of being the other sex

   4. Intense desire to participate in the stereotypical games and pastimes of the other sex

   5. Strong preference for playmates of the other sex

   In adolescents and adults, the disturbance is manifested by symptoms such as a stated desire to be the other sex, frequent passing as the other sex, desire to live or be treated as the other sex, or the conviction that he or she has the typical feelings and reactions of the other sex.

B. Persistent discomfort with his or her sex or sense of inappropriateness in the gender role of that sex

C. The disturbance is not concurrent with a physical intersex condition

D. The disturbance causes clinically significant distress or impairment in social, occupational, or other important areas of functioning

Because discomfort with one's anatomic sex and the desire to be rid of one's own genitals form a central part of this definition, it is important to point out that transsexuals are not the only people who seek sex reassignment surgery. Meyer (1974) described a number of subtypes among those individuals seeking sex change surgery at the Johns Hopkins Sexual Behaviors Consultation Unit. These include self-stigmatized homosexuals who believe that they should be punished, schizoid and psychotic individuals, and sadomasochists who derive sexual pleasure from inflicting and experiencing physical pain.

Disturbances in gender identity should also be distinguished from two related but generally distinct conditions. First, it would be misleading to say that transsexuals are, by definition, delusional. There are, of course, a few transsexuals who are psychotic, but the vast majority are not. They acknowledge the inconsistency between their anatomy and their gender identity. A delusional man might argue, for example, that he is a woman; a transsexual would be more likely to say, "I am not a woman *anatomically*, but I am a woman in almost every other way." Furthermore, unlike delusional patients whose beliefs are completely idiosyncratic, transsexuals are frequently able to convince other people that they are right. In Chris's case, for example, Jennifer and Lynn concurred with the belief that Chris was more like a man than a woman.

Second, there is an important difference between transsexualism and transvestic fetishism, but the two conditions are not mutually exclusive (Zucker & Bradley, 2000). Transvestic fetishism is a disorder in which heterosexual (or bisexual) men dress in women's clothing for the purpose of sexual excitement. The gender identity of transvestic fetishists is typically not inconsistent with their anatomic sex, and many transsexuals do not become sexually excited by cross-dressing. Nevertheless, a substantial proportion of male-to-female transsexuals do become sexually aroused at least occasionally when they dress in women's clothing (Blanchard & Clemmensen, 1988), and some transvestic fetishists do seek sex reassignment surgery (Wise & Meyer, 1980). According to *DSM-IV-TR*, males who meet the criteria for both gender identity disorder and transvestic fetishism should be assigned both diagnoses.

Precise epidemiological data regarding transsexualism are difficult to obtain. Estimates of the prevalence of the disorder are based on the number of people who apply for treatment rather than comprehensive surveys of the general population. We do know that transsexualism is a relatively infrequent problem and that it may be more common among men than women. Early studies reported a male-to-female ratio of approximately three to one, but the proportion of females may be increasing. One study computed prevalence estimates on the basis of the number of patients seeking treatment at the only gender treatment center in the Netherlands. The investigators reported a prevalence of 1 transsexual in every 12,000 males and 1 in 30,000 females (Bakker, van Kesteren, Gooren, & Bezemer, 1993). More recent data suggest that, when narrow diagnostic criteria are employed, the incidence of new cases may be roughly equivalent in men and women (Landen, Walinder, & Lundstrom, 1996).

There appear to be some fairly consistent differences between male and female transsexuals in terms of psychological characteristics. For example, female transsexuals tend to report better relationships with their parents, more stable relationships with sexual partners, and greater satisfaction with their sexual experiences prior to treatment (e.g., Lewins, 2002; Verschoor & Poortinga, 1988).

Many male transsexuals, perhaps as many as half of those seeking treatment, experience additional psychological problems. The most common symptoms are depression, anxiety, and social alienation (Bower, 2001; Zucker & Bradley, 2000). Some exhibit severe personality disorders, but very few are considered psychotic. The level of psychopathology observed in female transsexuals, on the other hand, does not seem to be different from that seen in the general population. Chris may therefore be similar to other female transsexuals. Aside from the issue of gender identity, he was well-adjusted in terms of his mood as well as his social and occupational functioning.

The relationship between transsexualism and homosexuality has been the source of some controversy (Chivers & Bailey, 2000). Some people have argued that transsexuals are simply homosexuals who use their cross-gender identity as a convenient way of escaping cultural and moral sanctions against engaging in sexual behavior with members of their own sex. There are a number of problems with this hypothesis. First, unlike transsexuals, homosexual men and women are not uncomfortable with their own gender identities. Lesbians, for example, are typically proud of their status as women and would be horrified at the suggestion that they want to be men. Second, many transsexuals, like Chris, are not obviously uncomfortable with homosexuals. The suggestion that transsexuals are denying their homosexual inclinations is sometimes supported by the observation that some transsexuals go out of their way to avoid any contact or association with homosexual men or women. However, some of Chris's friends were homosexual men and women. One of his previous lovers, Lynn, was bisexual and had been living with another woman when they met.

Etiological Considerations

It is not clear why some people develop gender identity disorders. In fact, the process by which anyone develops a sense of masculine or feminine identity is a matter of considerable interest and dispute (Gangestad, Bailey, & Martin, 2000). As in other areas of human behavior, alternative explanations invoke the ubiquitous nature/nurture controversy. Is gender identity determined genetically prior to the infant's birth, or is it largely determined by biological or social factors that the individual encounters in his or her environment? Explanations for the development of transsexualism have taken both sides of this argument.

Some investigators and clinicians have emphasized the importance of the parents and family in the etiology of the disorder. Stoller (1985), for example, placed principal emphasis in male transsexualism on the absence (either physical or psychological) of the father and the presence of a close-binding, dominant mother. A different family pattern was identified in cases of female transsexualism. In these families, according to Stoller, the mothers are prone to depression. Rather than providing support and care for their spouses, the fathers are presumably aloof and uninvolved. Thus, the daughter is forced to fill the supportive, masculine role vacated by her father. Other masculine behaviors are also reinforced by the father, but femininity is discouraged.

Chris's experience was not consistent with Stoller's hypothesis. His mother was not depressed while Chris was a child, and he was

not expected to take the place of his father. Chris's parents were not close to each other, but they did not involve the children in their disagreements. His masculine gender identity was clearly fixed several years before his parents' conflict became known to the children. Although he did not spend a great deal of time with his mother, they did have a good relationship; they spoke to each other openly—including several talks about the fact that Chris felt more like a boy than a girl—and cared very much for each other.

Green (1987) proposed a multifaceted model for the development of feminine behavior in boys and masculine behavior in girls. His view places considerable emphasis on learning principles such as modeling and social reinforcement. According to Green, gender identity disturbances are likely to develop when the parent of the opposite sex is dominant and provides the most salient model for the child's social behavior. The same-sexed parent is presumably retiring or unavailable. When the child begins to imitate cross-role behaviors, rather than objecting, the parents provide attention and praise. Peer relations also play a role in Green's model; feminine boys prefer and spend more time with girls while masculine girls spend more time with boys. This combination of parental and peer support enhances the process of identification with the opposite sex. Eventually, this process of socialization becomes an obstacle to any attempt to change the pattern and integrate the child with members of his or her own sex.

In Chris's case, his father certainly provided reinforcement for playing masculine games. Chris spent a great deal of time in rough, competitive play with boys. His father also discouraged open displays of emotion, such as crying. It is difficult to say, however, that the social reinforcement he provided was definitely responsible for Chris's gender identity disorder, particularly since so many other girls are treated in similar ways without becoming transsexual.

Relatively little empirical evidence is available regarding the influence of environmental events in the development of transsexualism. A few research studies have compared people with gender identity disorders and control subjects in terms of their recollections of their parents' behavior. One study found that male-to-female transsexuals remembered their fathers as having been less warm and more rejecting in comparison to the way in which control subjects remembered their fathers (Cohen-Kettenis, & Arrindell, 1990). It is important to note, however, that these data were collected after the people with gender identity disorder were adults and had sought treatment for their condition. It is not clear that the styles of interaction that were reported by these people preceded or contributed to the original development of their problems in gender identity. Interactions between the parents and their transsexual sons and daughters may have been determined, at least in part, by a reaction to the gender identity problems of the children. Prospective data, collected prior to the onset of gender identity problems, have not been reported on this issue.

Case studies provide the basis for much speculation regarding the possible influence of environmental and biological factors in the etiology of transsexualism. For example, Garden and Rothery (1992) described one pair of 13-year-old female monozygotic (MZ) twins who were discordant for gender identity disorder. The authors hypothesized that differences between the girls in terms of their social upbringing were responsible for the discrepancy in their gender identities. Their father had problems with alcohol dependence and played little, if any, role in the family. Their anxious and depressed mother seemed to treat the transsexual twin as a confidante. This pattern is consistent with Stoller's hypothesis. The fact that these genetically identical individuals were discordant for the condition indicates that genetic factors do not account for all of the variance in its etiology. That is, of course, not a particularly surprising result because concordance rates in MZ twins do not approach 100 percent for any form of mental disorder. Analyses based on large samples of MZ and DZ twin pairs indicate that genetic factors make a larger contribution than environmental factors in the development of gender identity disorder (Coolidge, Thede, & Young, 2002).

There is, in fact, good reason to believe that certain aspects of gender identity are influenced by biological as well as environmental factors (Zucker, 2001). Speculation regarding biological considerations has also been fueled by case studies. One example involves the extraordinary experiences of several members of a single extended family in the Dominican Republic (Imperato-McGinley, Guerrero, Gautier, & Peterson, 1974). These individuals are unable to produce dihydrotestosterone, a hormone that is responsible, in the male fetus, for shaping the penis and scrotum. In the absence of this hormone, the children are born with external genitalia that are ambiguous in appearance, including a very small, clitoral-like penis, a scrotum that looks like labial folds, and a blind vaginal pouch. Of the 24 cases described in the initial report, 18 were raised as girls. Then, when they reached puberty, everything changed in response to an increase in testosterone. Each child's "clitoris" enlarged and became a penis—just as it would have in utero if the appropriate hormone had been present—and testicles descended into a scrotum. Their voices deepened and the muscle mass of their bodies increased to produce a masculine appearance. Quite remarkably, 17 of the 18 quickly developed a male gender identity; they consider themselves to be men and are sexually attracted to women.

The cases of the Dominican children suggest that the effects of the postnatal environment may not be as salient as many investigators concerned with transsexualism have suggested. The children were raised as girls, but they were able to alter their gender identities promptly and with considerable success when their anatomy changed. If their interactions with parents, siblings, and peers during childhood were of primary importance, how could this transformation have been accomplished? Strictly environmental views of gender identity have obvious difficulty dealing with this problem. An alternative account, favored by more biologically minded investigators (e.g., Diamond & Sigmundson, 1997), holds that gender identity is one characteristic that may be shaped very early, during the development of the human embryo, by exposure to male hormones.

The latter possibility suggests that Chris's masculine gender identity is, at least in part, the product of a fundamental, biological process. Viewed from a subtle neurological perspective, and regardless of the shape of his external sexual characteristics, this argument would hold that Chris's brain is essentially masculine. Unfortunately, although there is considerable reason to believe that there are reliable group differences between men and women in terms of brain structure and function, there are not valid tests that would be useful in this regard at an individual level. The issue is, therefore, unresolved.

Treatment

There are two obvious solutions to problems that involve gender identity conflict: Change the person's gender identity to match his or her anatomy, or change the anatomy to match the person's gender identity. Various forms of psychotherapy have been used in an attempt to alter the gender identity of transsexual patients, but the success of these interventions has been limited. Some positive results have been reported by Barlow, Abel, and Blanchard (1979), who used behavioral procedures to shape and maintain masculine sex role behaviors in three male transsexual patients. Uncontrolled follow-up reports indicate that behavior therapy can be beneficial for prepubescent boys who exhibit symptoms of gender identity disorder. Rekers, Kilgus, and Rosen (1990) studied a group of 29 boys approximately four years after the end of treatment. Greatest improvement was found among those boys who had been treated at younger ages.

As an alternative to trying to change the transsexual's gender identity, some physicians have used surgical procedures to transform transsexuals' bodies so that they will match their gender identities. Surgical procedures can be used to alter and construct both male and female genitalia. Some of these methods were initially developed for the treatment of problems such as traumatic loss or congenital abnormalities. An artificial penis can be constructed from abdominal tissue that is transplanted and formed into a tube. The goals of such surgery may include cosmetic considerations (i.e., the construction of an organ that resembles a penis) as well as physiological criteria (e.g., passing urine in a standing position, accomplishing intercourse, and sensing stimulation). Although it is not possible to construct a completely functional penis that will become erect in response to sexual stimulation, erection can be achieved through the use of removable implants made of bone, cartilage, or silicone. In the case of female-to-male transsexuals, the labia are fused, but the clitoris is left intact and remains the primary receptor for sexual stimulation. Prostheses can be inserted to resemble testicles in a scrotum.

Surgical procedures for transsexuals can become quite complex and involve several areas of the body in addition to the genitals. Surgery for male-to-female transsexuals may include breast augmentation as well as changing the size of the nose and shaving the larnyx. Surgery for female-to-male transsexuals can involve a series of steps, including removal of the ovaries, Fallopian tubes, uterus, and breast tissue.

The sporadic use of sex change surgery can be traced back to 1882 (see Bullough & Bullough, 1993). Such procedures did not become widely used or attract the attention of the general public until Hamburger, Sturup, and Dahl-Iverson (1953) reported the case of Christine Jorgensen, a male-to-female transsexual who had received surgery in Copenhagen in 1951. This case differed from many of the previous reports in that the patient was treated with large doses of female sex hormones for several months prior to the surgical removal of his penis and the construction of female genitalia. Subsequent to this report, a number of gender identity clinics were established at medical schools in Europe and the United States. One of the best known was begun at the Johns Hopkins University in 1965. Sex-reassignment surgery was performed frequently throughout the 1960s and 1970s. Exact figures are not available regarding the numbers of men and women who have received this radical treatment, but reports suggest that they must number in the thousands.

Clinical impressions regarding the relative success of these procedures have been positive. Case studies suggest that most patients are pleased with the results of the surgery and relieved finally to have the body they desire. Many find that they are able to adjust to life as a member of the opposite sex, and some report adequate sexual functioning and marriage (Smith, van Goozen, & Cohen-Kettenis, 2001). Almost no one reports postsurgical grief over the loss of his sexual organ, although isolated cases have occurred. The most frequent complaints center on requests for further medical and surgical procedures. In the case of male-to-female transsexuals, these requests include improvements in genital appearance and functioning, increased breast size, and inhibition of beard growth. Follow-up reports suggest that at least 80 percent of patients are considered generally satisfied by their surgeons. Interviews with patients who have gone through sex reassignment surgery indicate that most are satisfied with the results. The vast majority report reduced levels of anxiety and depression and believe that they do not have any trouble passing as a member of their newly assumed gender (Bodlund & Kullgren, 1996; Cohen-Kettenis & van Goozen, 1997; Rehman et al., 1999).

Although these results seem rather encouraging, there are some limitations associated with the data that have been used to evaluate the outcome of sex reassignment surgery. Postsurgical adjustment is often assessed in terms of the surgeon's global, subjective impression of the patient's adjustment rather than specific measures of occupational and social functioning made by people who do not know that the patient had received surgery. Appropriate control groups are seldom employed, and follow-up periods are often rather short. It should not be surprising, therefore, that some reports provide a more pessimistic picture of surgical outcome (Lindemalm[VG2C4], Korlin, & Uddenberg, 1986; Meyer & Reter, 1979). These studies demonstrate, for example, that the social and occupational functioning of many transsexuals does not improve following surgery in spite of the fact that the patients are subjectively satisfied with the results of the operation. Partially in response to data of this sort and questions that were raised about the value of surgery, the Gender Identity Clinic at Johns Hopkins stopped providing sex reassignment surgery for transsexuals in 1979. There are, however, many other centers that continue to perform these procedures (Petersen & Dickey, 1995).

Surgery and psychotherapy are not the only options available to people with gender identity disorders. Chris was already well-adjusted in his personal and professional roles without surgery. It seems unlikely that the surgical alteration of his body would lead to an even better adjustment. Like Chris, many transsexuals forego surgery but still cross-dress and live full-time as a member of the opposite gender with the help of hormone therapy. This alternative has become a more reasonable and appealing option as the law and popular opinion have become somewhat more accommodating toward people with gender identity disorders (Green, 1994). People who are considering treatment for gender identity disorders and the mental health professionals who want to help them should consider carefully the many thoughtful recommendations that are included in a set of standards of care for gender identity disorders, written by an international committee of experts on these problems (Levine, 1999).

15 Disorders of Childhood

"Eric. Eric? Eric!!" His teacher's voice and the laughter of his classmates roused the boy from his reverie. Glancing at the book of the girl sitting next to him, he noticed that the class was pages ahead of him. He was supposed to be answering a question about the Declaration of Independence, but he had been lost in thought about what seats he and his father would have for the baseball game they'd be attending that evening. A tall, lanky twelve-year-old, Eric had just begun seventh grade. His history teacher had already warned him about being late to class and not paying attention, but Eric just couldn't seem to get from one class to the next without stopping for drinks of water or to investigate an altercation between classmates. In class, he was rarely prepared to answer when the teacher called on him, and he usually forgot to write down the homework assignment. He already had a reputation among his peers as a "space cadet."

Eric's relief at the sound of the bell was quickly replaced by anxiety as he reached the playground for physical education. Despite his speed and physical strength, Eric was always picked last for baseball teams. His team was up to bat first, and Eric sat down to wait his turn. Absorbed in studying a pile of pebbles at his feet, he failed to notice his team's third out and missed the change of innings. The other team had already come in from the outfield before Eric noticed that his team was out in the field—too late to avoid the irate yells of his P.E. teacher to take his place at third base. Resolved to watch for his chance to field the ball, Eric nonetheless found himself without his glove on when a sharply hit ball rocketed his way; he had taken it off to toss it in the air in the middle of the pitch.

At home, Eric's father told him he had to finish his homework before they could go to the Dodgers game. He had only one page of math problems and was determined to finish them quickly. Thirty minutes later, his father emerged from the shower to find Eric building an elaborate Lego structure on the floor of his room; the math homework was half done. In exasperation, Eric's father left for the game without him.

By bedtime, frustrated and discouraged, Eric was unable to sleep. He often lay awake for what seemed like hours, reviewing the disappointments of the day and berating himself for his failures. On this night, he ruminated about his lack of friends, the frustration of his teachers, and his parents' exhortations to pay attention and "get with the program." Feeling hopeless to do better despite his daily resolve, Eric's thoughts often turned to suicide. Tonight he reviewed his fantasy of wandering out into the street in front of a passing car. Although Eric had never acted on his suicidal thoughts, he frequently replayed in his mind his parents' sorrow and remorse, his classmates' irritation with him, and the concern of his teachers.

Eric's difficulty in focusing his attention is characteristic of attention-deficit/hyperactivity disorder—just one of the disorders found in the DSM-IV-TR section entitled "Disorders Usually First Diagnosed in Infancy, Childhood, or Adolescence." These disorders cover a wide range of difficulties, from an attentional problem such as that suffered by Eric to the sometimes serious intellectual deficits found in mental retardation, the gross and sometimes callous disregard for the rights of others found in conduct disorder, and the language impairment and social and emotional difficulties of autistic disorder. Children typically have access to fewer social, financial, and psychological resources than do adults in dealing with such problems. Thus, whether troubled children receive professional attention at all usually depends on the adults in their lives—parents, teachers, school counselors.

Most psychodynamic, behavioral, cognitive, and biological theories consider childhood experience and development critically important to adult mental health. Most theories also regard children as better able to change than adults and thus as particularly suitable for treatment. Although earlier research devoted little attention to childhood disorders, recent years have brought a dramatic increase in professional interest in the nature, etiology, prevention, and treatment of child psychopathology.

In this chapter we discuss several of the emotional and behavioral disorders that are most likely to arise in childhood and adolescence. Mood and anxiety disorders in these age groups have already been presented (see pp. 300 and 146). We consider now disorders involving attention and socially unacceptable behavior, followed by disorders in which the acquisition of cognitive, language, motor, or social skills is disturbed. These include learning disabilities as well as the most severe of developmental disorders, mental retardation and pervasive developmental disorders (especially autism), which are usually chronic and often persist into adulthood.

Classification of Childhood Disorders

To classify abnormal behavior in children, diagnosticians must first consider what is normal for a particular age. The diagnosis for a child who lies on the floor kicking and screaming when he or she doesn't get his or her way must take into account whether the child is two years old or seven. The field of developmental psychopathology studies disorders of childhood within the context of normal life-span development, enabling us to identify behaviors that are appropriate at one stage but are considered disturbed at another.

Table 15.1 outlines those childhood disorders included in DSM-IV-TR, such as depression, that are subsumed under the criteria used for adults. Most childhood disorders, such as separation anxiety disorder, are unique to children. Still others, such as attention-deficit/hyperactivity disorder (ADHD), have been conceptualized primarily as childhood disorders but may nonetheless continue into adulthood. The DSM description of these disorders specific to children are provided in the DSM tables in the margins.

The more prevalent childhood disorders are often organized in two broader domains, called externalizing and internalizing disorders. **Externalizing disorders** are characterized by more outward-directed behaviors, such as aggressiveness, noncompliance, overactivity, and impulsiveness, and include the DSM-IV-TR categories of ADHD, conduct disorder (CD), and oppositional defiant disorder (ODD). **Internalizing disorders** are characterized by more inward-focused experiences and behaviors such as depression, social withdrawal, and anxiety, and include childhood anxiety and mood disorders. Children and adolescents may exhibit symptoms from both domains, as Eric did.

The Role of Culture in Childhood Problems of Self-Control

The values and mores of a culture play a role in whether a certain pattern of child behavior develops or is considered a problem. One study found that in Thailand, children with internalizing behavior problems, such as fearfulness, were most likely to be seen in clinics, whereas in the United States, those with externalizing behavior problems, such as aggressiveness and hyperactivity, were more commonly seen (Weisz et al., 1987). The researchers attributed these differences to Thailand's widely practiced Buddhism, which disapproves of and discourages aggression.

Child-rearing practices in Thailand reflect parental intolerance of externalizing behaviors, such as disrespect and aggression. The additional finding that internalizing problems were reported more often for adolescents than for children may be due to the fact that Buddhist strictures are especially strong in the teen years, when young men may serve as novices in the temples, an activity that demands strong discipline and self-control.

The underlying assumption of this study is that because externalizing behaviors are actively discouraged in Thai culture and religion, Thai children, virtually by default, are more likely than American children to develop internalizing disorders. Could it be, though, that adults in Thailand have a lower tolerance for externalizing problems? Further research suggests that, compared with Americans, Thai parents and teachers have a higher tolerance for both externalizing and internalizing behaviors. Consistent with Buddhist teachings, adults in Thailand perceive children's problems as transient and likely to change

for the better (Weisz et al., 1988). The finding that Thai children are more likely to be referred for internalizing problems probably reflects the actual higher prevalence of these problems in Thailand, although it may be that Thai parents are too embarrassed to seek help for their children's externalizing behavior because they are reluctant to reveal to outsiders that their children are aggressive or disobedient.

Thai teenagers serving as novices in a Buddhist temple. Buddhist culture may contribute to a reduction in the prevalence of externalizing disorders.

Externalizing and internalizing behaviors are prevalent across many countries, including Switzerland (Steinhausen & Metzke, 1998), Australia (Achenbach et al., 1990), Puerto Rico (Achenbach et al., 1990), Kenya (Weisz et al., 1993), and Greece (MacDonnald et al., 1995). Externalizing behaviors are consistently found more often among boys and internalizing behaviors more often among girls, at least in adolescence, across cultures (Weisz et al., 1987). Focus on Discovery 15.1 discusses the possible role of culture in the prevalence of behavior problems in children.

Table 15.1 Diagnoses That May Be Applied to Children as well as Adults

Substance-related disorders: See Chapter 12

Schizophrenia: See Chapter 11

Mood disorders: See Chapter 10

Anxiety disorders, such as specific phobia, social phobia, obsessive-compulsive disorder, posttraumatic stress disorder, generalized anxiety disorder: See Chapter 6; for aftermath of child sexual abuse, see Chapter 14

Somatoform disorders: See Chapter 7

Dissociative disorders: See Chapter 7

Gender identity disorders: See Chapter 14

Eating disorders, such as anorexia nervosa and bulimia nervosa: See Chapter 9

Parasomnias: Abnormal behavioral or physiological events occurring in association with sleep. For example, nightmare disorder, sleep terror disorder, and sleepwalking disorder.

Source: Adapted from DSM-IV-TR.

Attention-Deficit/Hyperactivity Disorder

One of the externalizing disorders is **attention-deficit/hyperactivity disorder (ADHD)**. The term hyperactive is familiar to most people, especially parents and teachers. The child who is constantly in motion, tapping fingers, jiggling legs, poking others for no apparent reason, talking out of turn, and fidgeting is often called hyperactive. These children also have difficulty concentrating on the task at hand for an appropriate period of time.

What distinguishes the normal range of hyperactive behaviors from a diagnosable disorder? When these behaviors are extreme for a particular developmental period, persistent across different situations, and linked to significant impairments in functioning, the diagnosis of ADHD may be appropriate (NIH Consensus Statement, 1998). The ADHD diagnosis does not properly apply to youngsters who are rambunctious, active, or slightly distractible, for in the early school years children are often so (Whalen, 1983). To use the label simply because a child is more lively and more difficult to control than a parent or teacher would like represents a misuse of the term. The diagnosis of ADHD is reserved for truly extreme and persistent cases.

Children with ADHD seem to have particular difficulty controlling their activity in situations that call for sitting still, such as in the classroom or at mealtimes. When required to be quiet, they appear unable to stop moving or talking. They are disorganized, erratic, tactless, obstinate, and bossy. Their activities and movements seem haphazard. They quickly wear out their shoes and clothing, smash their toys, and exhaust their families and teachers. They are difficult, however, to distinguish from children without ADHD during free play, when there are fewer restrictions placed on behavior. What this indicates is that non-ADHD children can be as rambunctious and "off the wall" as ADHD youngsters when adult constraints are absent.

Many children with ADHD have inordinate difficulty getting along with peers and establishing friendships (Hinshaw & Melnick, 1995; Whalen & Henker, 1985), perhaps because their behavior is often aggressive and generally annoying and intrusive to others. Although these children are usually friendly and talkative, they often miss subtle social cues, such as noticing when playmates are tiring of their constant jiggling. They also frequently misinterpret the wishes and intentions of their peers and make inadvertent social mistakes, such as reacting aggressively because they assume that a neutral action by a peer was meant to be aggressive. (Such cognitive misattributions are also found in some children with conduct disorder.)

A study involving observation of children playing tabletop football demonstrated that children with ADHD, particularly those who are also aggressive, have different social goals than comparison children. The aggressive ADHD children approached the game with sensation-seeking goals, such as making trouble, seeking domination, and showing off, whereas comparison children were more likely to have a goal of playing fair (Melnick & Hinshaw, 1996).

Children with ADHD can know what the socially correct action is in hypothetical situations but be unable to translate this knowledge into appropriate behavior in real-life social interactions (Whalen & Henker, 1985, 1999). Children with ADHD are often singled out very quickly and rejected or neglected by their peers. For example, in a study of previously unacquainted boys at a summer camp, boys with ADHD who exhibited a number of externalizing behaviors, such as overt aggression and noncompliance, were regarded quite negatively by their peers during the first day of camp, and these impressions remained unchanged throughout the six-week camp period (Erhardt & Hinshaw, 1994; Hinshaw et al., 1997).

About 15 to 30 percent of children with ADHD have a learning disability (see p. 492) in math, reading, or spelling (Barkley, DuPaul, & McMurray, 1990; Casey, Rourke, & DelDotto, 1996; Semrud-Clikeman et al., 1992), and about half of ADHD children are placed in special educational programs because of their difficulty in adjusting to a typical classroom environment (Barkley et al., 1990).

DSM-IV TR Criteria for Attention-Deficit/Hyperactivity Disorder

- Either A or B:

  A. Six or more manifestations of inattention present for at least six months to a maladaptive degree and greater than what would be expected, given person's developmental level, for example, careless mistakes, not listening well, not following instructions, easily distracted, forgetful in daily activities

  B. Six or more manifestations of hyperactivity-impulsivity present for at least six months to a maladaptive degree and greater than what would be expected, given person's developmental level, for example, squirming in seat, running about inappropriately (in adults, restlessness), acting as if "driven by a motor," incessant talking

- Some of the above present before age 7
- Present in two or more settings, e.g., at home and at school or work
- Significant impairment in social, academic, or occupational functioning
- Not part of other disorders such as schizophrenia, an anxiety disorder, a mood disorder

Because the symptoms of ADHD are varied, DSM-IV-TR includes three subcategories:

1. Predominantly Inattentive type: Children whose problems are primarily those of poor attention.
2. Predominantly Hyperactive-Impulsive type: Children whose difficulties result primarily from hyperactive-impulsive behavior.
3. Combined type: Children who have both sets of problems.

The combined type comprises the majority of ADHD children. These children are more likely to develop conduct problems and oppositional behavior, to be placed in special classes for behavior-disordered children, and to have difficulties interacting with their peers (Barkley et al., 1990; Faraone et al., 1998). Children with attentional problems but with otherwise developmentally appropriate activity levels appear to have more difficulties with focused attention or speed of information processing (Barkley, Grodzinsky, & DuPaul, 1992), perhaps associated with a problem in frontal or striatal areas of the brain (Tannock, 1998). Accumulating evidence suggests that it may be best to think of two separate disorders, one of inattention and one involving both inattention and hyperactive/impulsive behavior (e.g., Barkley, 1998; Milich, Balentine, & Lynam, in press). However, most of the theory and research on ADHD does not make this distinction. Moreover, it is not clear if some of the observed differences between the combined type and predominantly inattentive type apply to girls with ADHD (e.g., Biederman et al., 1999; Hinshaw, in press; Hinshaw et al., in press).

A difficult differential diagnosis is between ADHD and conduct disorder (CD), which, as we shall see soon, involves gross violation of social norms. An overlap of 30 to 90 percent between the two categories (Hinshaw, 1987) has caused some researchers to assert that the two types of externalizing disorders are actually the same disorder (Quay, 1979). There are some differences, however. ADHD is associated more with off-task behavior in school, cognitive and achievement deficits, and a better long-term prognosis. Children with conduct disorder act out in school and elsewhere and are likely to be much more aggressive and to have antisocial parents. Their home life is also marked by family hostility and low socioeconomic status, and they are much more at risk for delinquency and substance abuse in adolescence (Faraone et al., 1997; Hinshaw, 1987; Jensen, Martin, & Cantwell, 1997).

When these two disorders occur in the same youngster, the worst features of each are manifest. Such children exhibit the most serious antisocial behavior, are most likely to be rejected by their peers, have the worst academic achievement, and have the poorest prognosis (Biederman, Newcorn, & Sprich, 1991; Cadoret & Stewart, 1991; Hinshaw, Lahey, & Hart, 1993; Moffitt, 1990). It has been suggested that children with ADHD and conduct disorder form a distinct category highly likely to progress to the adult psychopathic patterns of antisocial personality disorder (Frick & Ellis, 1999; Lynam, 1998). It may be that ADHD comes first, with the child's aggravating behavior eliciting hostile reactions from peers and adults; then the situation escalates with more extreme attacks and counterattacks, finally resulting in the aggressive behaviors that are characteristic of conduct disorder. Indeed, having ADHD is associated with an earlier age of onset of CD symptoms (Hinshaw et al., 1993).

Internalizing disorders, such as anxiety and depression, also frequently co-occur with ADHD. Recent estimates suggest that as many as 30 percent of children with ADHD may have comorbid internalizing symptoms or disorders (e.g., Jensen et al., 1997; MTA Cooperative Group, 1999b).

The prevalence of ADHD has been difficult to establish because of varied definitions of the disorder over time and differences in the populations sampled. Estimates vary from 2 to 7 percent in the United States (August et al., 1996; Kashani et al., 1989), New Zealand (Fergusson, Horwood, & Lynskey, 1993; McGee et al., 1990), and Germany (Esser, Schmidt, & Woerner, 1990), with somewhat higher rates found in India (Bhatia et al., 1991) and China (Leung et al., 1996). The consensus is that about 3 to 7 percent of school-age children worldwide currently have ADHD (DSM-IV-TR, 2000).

Much evidence indicates that ADHD is more common in boys than in girls, but exact figures depend on whether the sample is taken from clinic referrals or from the general population. Boys are more likely to be referred to clinics because of a higher likelihood of aggressive and antisocial behavior. Until recently, very few carefully controlled studies of girls with ADHD have been conducted. Because so little research has been done with female samples, it is important to document the characteristics, correlates, comorbid disorders, and other social and cognitive deficits in a carefully selected sample of girls with ADHD. Two groups of researchers have recently conducted such studies (Biederman et al., 1999; Hinshaw, in press; Hinshaw et al., in press). Hinshaw and colleagues examined a large and ethnically diverse sample of girls with and without ADHD and reported a number of key findings:

- Girls with ADHD were more likely than comparison girls to have been adopted (see also Simmel, Brooks, Barth, & Hinshaw, 2001).
- Similar to findings with male samples, girls with the combined type had more disruptive behavior symptoms than girls with the inattentive type.
- Girls with the combined type were more likely to have a comorbid diagnosis of conduct disorder or oppositional defiant disorder than girls without ADHD.
- Girls with ADHD were more likely to have elevated anxiety and depression than were comparison girls.
- Girls with the combined type were viewed more negatively by peers than girls with the inattentive type and girls without ADHD; girls with the inattentive type were also viewed more negatively than the comparison girls.
- Girls with ADHD exhibited a number of neuropsychological deficits, particularly in executive functioning (e.g., planning, solving problems), compared with girls without ADHD, replicating other findings (e.g., Castellanos et al., 2000; Klorman et al., 1999).

As suggested earlier, although many preschoolers are considered inattentive and overactive by their parents and teachers, the majority of these youngsters are going through a typical developmental stage that will not become a persistent pattern of ADHD (Campbell, 1990). On the other hand, most children who do develop ADHD exhibit excessive activity and temperamental behavior quite early in life. Their insatiable curiosity and vigorous play make childproofing[1] a necessity to avoid such tragedies as accidental poisoning, tumbling down stairs, and falling out of windows. Although the preschool years are stressful for parents whose children have ADHD, the problems become salient when the children enter school and are suddenly expected to sit in their seats for longer periods of time, complete assignments independently, and negotiate with peers on the playground.

At one time it was thought that ADHD simply went away by adolescence. However, this belief has been challenged by numerous longitudinal studies (e.g., Barkley et al., 2002; Biederman et al., 1996; Claude & Firestone, 1995; Weiss & Hechtman, 1993). Although they do show reduced severity of symptoms in adolescence (Hart et al., 1995), 65 to 80 percent of children with ADHD still meet criteria for the disorder in adolescence and in adulthood. Table 15.2 provides a catalog of behaviors that are found more often among adolescents with ADHD than among adolescents without it. In addition to these fidgety, distractible, impulsive behaviors, adolescents with ADHD are far more likely to drop out of high school and develop antisocial behavior than are their peers. In adulthood, although most are employed and financially independent, these individuals generally reach only a lower socioeconomic level and change jobs more frequently than would normally be expected (Mannuzza et al., 1993; Weiss & Hechtman, 1993). Although most

---

[1] Childproofing refers to implementing safety measures such as using bottle caps that are difficult to open and special locks on kitchen cabinets so that children can't get into them.

adults with a history of ADHD continue to exhibit some symptoms of the disorder, most also learn to adapt to these symptoms, perhaps by finding a niche for themselves in the working world.[2]

Biological Theories of ADHD

The search for causes of ADHD is complicated by the heterogeneity of children given this diagnosis; any factor found to be associated with the syndrome is perhaps linked with only some of those judged to have ADHD.

Genetic Factors   Research suggests that a genetic predisposition toward ADHD may play a role. When parents have ADHD, half of their children are likely to have the disorder (Biederman et al., 1995). Adoption studies (e.g., van den Oord, Boomsma, & Verhulst, 1994) and numerous large-scale twin studies (e.g., Levy et al., 1997; Sherman, Iacono, & McGue, 1997) indicate a genetic component to ADHD, with MZ concordance rates as high as .70 to .80 (Tannock, 1998).

Exactly what is inherited is as yet unknown, but recent studies suggest that brain function and structure differ in children with and without ADHD. Studies have documented that the frontal lobes of children with ADHD are underresponsive to stimulation (Rubia et al., 1999; Tannock, 1998), and cerebral blood flow is reduced (Sieg et al., 1995). Moreover, parts of the brains (frontal lobes, caudate nucleus, globus pallidus) of ADHD children are smaller than normal (Castellanos et al., 1996; Filipek et al., 1997; Hynd et al., 1993). Evidence from other research shows poorer performance of ADHD children on neuropsychological tests of frontal-lobe functioning (such as inhibiting behavioral responses), providing further support for the theory that a basic deficit in this part of the brain may be related to the disorder (Barkley, 1997; Klorman et al., 1999, Nigg, 1999; 2001; Tannock, 1998).

Perinatal and Prenatal Factors   Other biological risk factors for ADHD include a number of perinatal and prenatal complications. Low birth weight, for example, is a quite specific predictor of the development of ADHD (e.g., Breslau et al., 1996; Whitaker et al., 1997). Other complications associated with childbirth, as well as substances ingested by mothers such as tobacco (discussed below) and alcohol are also predictive of ADHD symptoms (Tannock, 1998).

Environmental Toxins   Early theories of ADHD that were quite popular in the 1970s involved the role of environmental toxins in the development of hyperactivity. A biochemical theory of hyperactivity put forth by Feingold (1973) enjoyed much attention in the popular press for many years. He proposed that food additives upset the central nervous systems of hyperactive children, and he prescribed a diet free of them. However, well-controlled studies of the Feingold diet have found that very few ADHD children respond positively to it (Goyette & Conners, 1977). Similarly, the popular view that refined sugar can cause ADHD (Smith, 1975) has not been supported by careful research (Wolraich, Wilson, & White, 1995).

Although some evidence suggests that lead poisoning may be associated to a small degree with symptoms of hyperactivity and attentional problems (Thompson et al.,

Table 15.2 Prevalence of Symptoms and Behaviors in Adolescents with and without ADHD

Symptom	ADHD, %	No ADHD, %
Fidgets	73.2	10.6
Difficulty remaining seated	60.2	3.0
Easily distracted	82.1	15.2
Difficulty waiting turn	48.0	4.5
Blurts out answers	65.0	10.6
Difficulty following instructions	83.7	12.1
Difficulty sustaining attention	79.7	16.7
Shifts from one uncompleted task to another	77.2	16.7
Difficulty playing quietly	39.8	7.6
Talks excessively	43.9	6.1
Interrupts others	65.9	10.6
Doesn't seem to listen	80.5	15.2
Loses things needed for tasks	62.6	12.1
Engages in physically dangerous activities	37.4	3.0

Source: Adapted from Barkley et al., 1990.

---

[2]We are acquainted with a faculty colleague who once described himself to us as an ADHD youngster grown up. Now fifty years of age, he is boundlessly energetic and interested in a wide variety of things. Unfortunately, he has trouble concentrating on any one task long enough to bring it to satisfactory completion, and he tends to blurt out opinions about issues without giving them appropriate thought. In spite of these attentional deficits, he managed to achieve considerable success as a university faculty member.

1989), most children with lead poisoning do not develop ADHD, and most children with ADHD do not show elevated levels of lead in the blood.

Nicotine—specifically, maternal smoking—is an environmental toxin that may play a role in the development of ADHD. Milberger et al. (1996) reported that 22 percent of mothers of children with ADHD reported smoking a pack of cigarettes per day during pregnancy, compared with 8 percent of mothers whose children did not develop ADHD. This effect remained even after controlling for maternal depression and alcohol use (Chabrol et al., 1997). Animal studies indicate that chronic exposure to nicotine increases dopamine release in the brain and causes hyperactivity (Fung & Lau, 1989; Johns et al., 1982). On the basis of these data, Milberger and his associates hypothesize that maternal smoking can affect the dopaminergic system of the developing fetus, resulting in behavioral disinhibition and ADHD.

Smoking cigarettes during pregnancy has recently been linked to increased risk for ADHD.

Psychological Theories of ADHD

The child psychoanalyst Bruno Bettelheim (1973) proposed a diathesis–stress theory of ADHD, suggesting that hyperactivity develops when a predisposition to the disorder is coupled with authoritarian upbringing by parents. If a child with a disposition toward overactivity and moodiness is stressed by a parent who easily becomes impatient and resentful, the child may be unable to cope with the parent's demands for obedience. As the parent becomes more and more negative and disapproving, the parent–child relationship ends up a battleground. With a disruptive and disobedient pattern established, the child cannot handle the demands of school, and his or her behavior is often in conflict with the rules of the classroom.

Learning may figure in ADHD as well. Hyperactivity could be reinforced by the attention it elicits, thereby increasing in frequency or intensity. Or, as Ross and Ross (1982) have suggested, hyperactivity may be modeled on the behavior of parents and siblings. However, such theories have not been supported by research. Neurological and genetic factors have far greater support than psychological factors in the etiology of ADHD.

In any event, the parent–child relationship is at the very least bidirectional and more likely a "complex chain of associations" (Hinshaw et al., 1997). Just as parents of hyperactive children may give them more commands and have negative interactions with them (e.g., Anderson, Hinshaw, & Simmel, 1994; Heller et al., 1996), so hyperactive children have been found to be less compliant and more negative in interactions with their parents (Barkley, Karlsson, & Pollard, 1985; Tallmadge & Barkley, 1983). Certainly, it must be difficult to parent a child who is impulsive, aggressive, noncompliant, and unable to follow instructions. As we will describe shortly, stimulant medication has been shown to reduce hyperactivity and increase compliance in some ADHD children. Significantly, when such medication is used, either alone or in combination with behavioral treatment, the parents' commands, negative behavior, and ineffective parenting also decrease (Barkeley, 1990; Wells, et al. 2000), suggesting that it is, at least in part, the child's behavior that affects the parents negatively rather than the reverse.

It is also important to consider a parent's own history of ADHD. As noted above, there appears to be a substantial genetic component to ADHD. Thus, it is not surprising that many parents of ADHD children have ADHD themselves. In one study that examined couples' parenting practices with their ADHD children, fathers who had a diagnosis of ADHD were less effective parents, suggesting that parental psychopathology may make parenting all the more difficult (Arnold, O'Leary, & Edwards, 1997). Family characteristics and patterns thus may well be correlated with the maintenance or exacerbation of the symptoms and consequences of ADHD; however, there is little evidence to suggest that families cause ADHD (Johnston & Marsh, 2001).

Treatment of ADHD

ADHD is typically treated with medication and behavioral methods based on operant conditioning.

Stimulant Medications   Stimulant medications, in particular methylphenidate, or Ritalin, have been prescribed for ADHD since the early 1960s (Sprague & Gadow, 1976). Other medications prescribed to treat ADHD include amphetamine, or Adderall, and pemoline, or Cylert; however, Ritalin is the most commonly prescribed medication. For the years 1996–2000, 11 million prescriptions of Ritalin were written each year in the United States, and 80 percent of them were for children diagnosed with ADHD (Drug Enforcement Agency, 2000). The prescription of these medications has sometimes continued into adolescence and adulthood in light of the accumulating evidence that the symptoms of ADHD do not usually disappear with the passage of time.

The drugs used to treat ADHD reduce disruptive behavior and improve ability to concentrate. Numerous controlled studies comparing stimulants with placebos in double-blind designs have shown short-term improvements in concentration, goal-directed activity, classroom behavior, and social interactions with parents, teachers, and peers and reductions in aggressiveness and impulsivity in about 75 percent of ADHD children (Spencer et al., 1996; Swanson et al., 1995).

Perhaps the best-designed randomized controlled clinical trial of treatments for ADHD was the Multimodal Treatment of Children with ADHD, or MTA study. The study, conducted at six different sites for fourteen months in nearly 600 children with ADHD, compared three different treatments: (1) medication alone, (2) medication plus intensive behavioral treatment, involving both parents and teachers, and (3) behavioral treatment alone. Children who received these three treatments were then compared with a fourth group, children receiving standard community-based care. Outcomes assessed across the fourteen-month period indicated fewer ADHD symptoms for children receiving medication alone than for children receiving intensive behavioral treatment alone. The combined treatment was slightly superior to the medication alone and showed an advantage in not requiring as high a dosage of Ritalin to reduce ADHD symptoms. In addition, the combined treatment improved positive functioning such as social skills more than the medication alone. The medication alone and combined treatments were superior to community-based care, though the behavioral treatment alone was not (MTA Cooperative Group, 1999a, 1999b).

In secondary analyses undertaken to clarify the key findings from the MTA study, Swanson et al. (2001) reported that the behavioral treatment alone was superior to community-based care at three of the six sites, but not at the other three. In addition, further comparisons of the combined treatment with treatment by medication alone suggested that 20 percent more children who received the combined treatment achieved an excellent treatment response. The combined treatment was also associated with fewer behavioral problems at school, and additional analyses suggest that this effect may be linked to a decrease in negative and ineffective parenting (Hinshaw et al., 2000).

Despite the promising findings on the efficacy of stimulant medications for ADHD, other research indicates that these drugs may not improve academic achievement over the long haul (Weiss & Hechtman, 1993; Whalen and Henker, 1991). Further, stimulant medication has side effects. In addition to transient loss of appetite and sleep problems, a risky side effect of the widespread prescription of stimulants has emerged. *Newsweek* magazine reported in the mid-1990s that children had begun to use Ritalin and other stimulants obtained from their siblings or friends as recreational drugs (Leland, 1995). Its use has also spread among high school and college students not suffering from ADHD but finding that snorting it like cocaine helps them focus better on their schoolwork and ward off fatigue (Tennant, 1999). While these misuses of Ritalin are indeed troubling, it is nonetheless efficacious in the treatment of ADHD and should be considered a critical component of treatment programs.

Psychological Treatment   Other than medication, the most promising treatments of ADHD children involve parent training and changes in classroom management based on operant-conditioning principles. These programs have demonstrated at least short-term success in improving both social and academic behavior. In these treatments, children's behavior is monitored at home and in school, and they are reinforced for behaving appro-

Point systems and star charts, which are common in classrooms, are particularly useful in the treatment of attention-deficit/hyperactivity disorder.

priately, for example, for remaining in their seats and working on assignments. Point systems and star charts are typical components of these programs. Youngsters earn points and younger children earn stars for behaving in certain ways; the children can then spend their earnings for rewards. The focus of these operant programs is on improving academic work, completing household tasks, or learning specific social skills, rather than on reducing signs of hyperactivity, such as running around and jiggling. Accumulating evidence supports the efficacy of parent training programs, although it is unclear whether they improve children's behavior beyond the effects of treatment with medication (Abikoff & Hechtman, 1996; Anastopoulos et al., 1993; MTA Cooperative Group, 1999a, b).

School interventions for children with ADHD include training teachers to understand the unique needs of these children and to apply operant techniques in the classroom (Welsh et al., 1997), peer tutoring in academic skills (DuPaul & Henningson, 1993), and having teachers provide daily reports to parents about in-school behavior, which is followed up with rewards and consequences at home (Kelley, 1990). Research has demonstrated that certain classroom structures can have a favorable impact on children with ADHD. For example, in the ideal classroom environment teachers vary the presentation format and materials used for tasks, keep assignments brief and provide immediate feedback regarding accuracy, have an enthusiastic and task-focused style, provide breaks for physical exercise, use computer-assisted drill programs, and schedule academic work during the morning hours. Such environmental changes are designed to accommodate the limitations imposed by this disorder rather than to change the disorder itself (Pfiffner & Barkley, 1998).

Finally, findings from the just-mentioned MTA study indicate that intensive behavioral interventions can be very helpful to children with ADHD. In that study, some of the children participated in an intensive eight-week summer program that included a number of validated behavioral interventions. At the end of the summer program, children in the combined treatment had very few significant improvements over children in the intensive behavior treatment alone (Pelham et al., 2000). This finding suggests that intensive behavioral intervention may be as effective as Ritalin combined with a less intense operant program.

Conduct Disorder

Conduct Disorder is another major externalizing disorder. The DSM-IV-TR definition of conduct disorder focuses on behaviors that violate the basic rights of others and major societal norms. Nearly all such behavior is also illegal. The types of behavior considered symptomatic of conduct disorder include aggression and cruelty toward people or animals, damaging property, lying, and stealing. Conduct disorder denotes a frequency and severity of acts that go beyond the mischief and pranks common among children and adolescents. Often the behavior is marked by callousness, viciousness, and lack of remorse, making conduct disorder one of the historical criteria for adult antisocial personality disorder (p. 418).

A related but less well understood externalizing category in the DSM is **oppositional defiant disorder** (ODD). There is some debate as to whether ODD is distinct from conduct disorder, a precursor to it, or an earlier and milder manifestation of it (Hinshaw & Lee, in press; Lahey, McBurnett, & Loeber, 2000; Loeber et al., 2000). ODD is diagnosed if a child does not meet the criteria for conduct disorder—most especially, extreme physical aggressiveness—but exhibits such behaviors as losing his or her temper, arguing with adults, repeatedly refusing to comply with requests from adults, deliberately doing things to annoy others, and being angry, spiteful, touchy, or vindictive. The DSM also mentions that such children, most of them boys, seldom see their conflicts with others as their fault; they justify their oppositional behavior by claiming that unreasonable demands are being placed on them. In everyday parlance these children are simply referred to as brats.

Problems commonly comorbid with ODD are ADHD, learning disorders, and communication disorders (p. 493), but ODD is different from ADHD in that the defiant behavior is not thought to arise from attentional deficits or sheer impulsiveness. One way to appreciate the difference is that ODD children are more deliberate in their obstreperousness than ADHD children. Although conduct disorder is three to four times more common among boys than girls, research suggests that boys are only slightly more likely to have ODD, and some studies find no difference in prevalence rates for ODD between boys and girls (Loeber et al., 2000). Because of ODD's somewhat uncertain status, our attention is focused here on the more serious diagnosis of conduct disorder.

Perhaps more than any other childhood disorder, conduct disorder is defined by the impact of the child's behavior on people and surroundings. Schools, parents, peers, and the criminal justice system usually determine which externalizing behaviors constitute unacceptable conduct. Preadolescents and adolescents are often identified as conduct problems by legal authorities, in which case they might be considered juvenile delinquents—a legal, not a psychological, term.

Many children with conduct disorder display other problems as well. We have already noted the high degree of comorbidity between conduct disorder and ADHD. This is true for boys; much less is known about comorbid conduct disorder and ADHD among girls. Substance abuse also commonly co-occurs with conduct problems. The Pittsburgh Youth Study, a longitudinal investigation of conduct problems in boys, found a strong association between substance use and delinquent acts (vanKammen, Loeber, & Stouthamer-Loeber, 1991). For example, among seventh graders who reported having tried marijuana, more than 30 percent had attacked someone with a weapon and 43 percent admitted breaking and entering; fewer than 5 percent of children who reported no substance use had committed these acts. Although some research suggests that conduct disorder precedes substance use problems, other findings suggest that conduct disorder and substance use problems occur concomitantly, with the two conditions exacerbating one another (Loeber et al., 2000). With respect to gender, some evidence indicates that comorbid conduct disorder and substance use portends a more severe outcome for boys than it does girls (Whitmore et al., 1997).

Anxiety and depression, generally viewed as internalizing problems, are common among children with conduct disorder, with comorbidity estimates varying from 15 to 45 percent (Loeber & Keenan, 1994; Loeber et al., 2000). There is some evidence that conduct-disordered boys with comorbid behavioral inhibition are less likely to be delinquent than those with conduct disorder comorbid with social withdrawal (Kerr et al., 1997). Emerging evidence suggests that girls with conduct disorder are at higher risk for developing comorbid disorders, including anxiety, depression, substance abuse, and ADHD, than are boys with conduct disorder, that is, conduct disorder in girls may indicate greater severity of psychopathology (Loeber & Keenan, 1994).

Population-based studies indicate that conduct disorder is fairly common. A review of epidemiological studies reveals prevalence rates ranging from 4 to 16 percent for boys and 1.2 to 9 percent for girls (Loeber et al., 2000). Burglary and violent crimes such as forcible rape and aggravated assault are largely crimes of male adolescents. As shown in Figure 15.1, both the incidence and the prevalence of serious lawbreaking peak sharply at around age seventeen and drop precipitously in young adulthood (Moffitt, 1993).

Conduct disorder is diagnosed among those who are aggressive, steal, lie, and vandalize property.

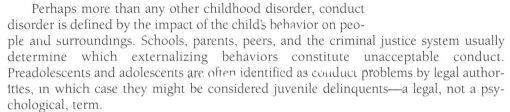

DSM-IV-TR Criteria for Conduct Disorder

- Repetitive and persistent behavior pattern that violates the basic rights of others or conventional social norms as manifested by the presence of three or more of the following in the previous twelve months and at least one of them in the previous six months:

  A. Aggression to people and animals, for example, bullying, initiating physical fights, physically cruel to people or animals, forcing someone into sexual activity

  B. Destruction of property, for example, fire-setting, vandalism

  C. Deceitfulness or theft, for example, breaking into another's house or car, conning, shoplifting

  D. Serious violation of rules, for example, staying out at night before age 13 in defiance of parental rules, truancy before age 13

- Significant impairment in social, academic, or occupational functioning

- If person older than 18, criteria not met for antisocial personality disorder

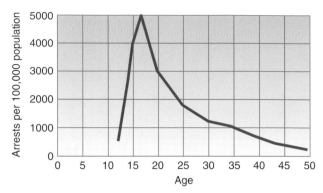

Figure 15.1 Arrest rates across ages for the crimes of homicide, forcible rape, robbery, aggravated assault, and auto theft. From "Criminal Career Research: Its Value for Criminology," by A. Blumstein, J. Cohen, and D. P. Farrington, 1988. *Criminology: 26*, p. 11. Copyright © 1988 by the American Society of Criminology. Adapted by permission.

Although not all these criminal acts are marked by the viciousness and callousness that are often a part of conduct disorder, these data do help illustrate the problem of antisocial behavior in children and adolescents.

The prognosis for children diagnosed as having conduct disorder is mixed. Robins (1978) summarized several longitudinal studies that examined antisocial behavior in a number of cohorts from the 1920s to the 1970s, with follow-ups over as long as thirty years. She concluded that the vast majority of highly antisocial adults had also been highly antisocial as children. However, more than half the children with conduct disorder did not become antisocial adults. These findings have been replicated in more recent studies (Loeber, 1991; Zoccolillo et al., 1992). Thus, conduct problems in childhood do not inevitably lead to antisocial behavior in adulthood, though they certainly are a predisposing factor. Furthermore, a recent longitudinal study indicated that although about half of boys with conduct disorder did not meet full criteria for the diagnosis at a later assessment (one to four years later), almost all of them continued to demonstrate some conduct problems (Lahey et al., 1995).

Moffitt (1993) has theorized that two different courses of conduct problems should be distinguished. Some individuals seem to show a "life-course-persistent" pattern of antisocial behavior, beginning their conduct problems by age three and continuing serious transgressions in adulthood. Others are "adolescence-limited." These people have typical childhoods, engage in high levels of antisocial behavior during adolescence, and return to nonproblematic lifestyles in adulthood. Moffitt proposed that the temporary form of antisocial behavior is the result of a maturity gap between the adolescent's physical maturation and his or her opportunity to assume adult responsibilities and obtain the rewards usually accorded such behavior.

There is some evidence supporting this distinction. For example, children with the life-course-persistent form of conduct disorder do indeed show an early onset of antisocial behavior that persists into and throughout adolescence, and these youngsters have a number of other problems, such as academic underachievement, neuropsychological deficits, and comorbid ADHD (Moffitt & Caspi, 2001). Other evidence supports the notion that children with the life-course-persistent type have more severe neuropsychological deficits and family psychopathology, and these findings have been replicated across cultures (Hinshaw & Lee, 2000).

The original sample from which Moffitt and colleagues made the life-course-persistent and adolescent-limited distinction has now been followed into early adulthood (age 26). Those who were classified as life-course-persistent continue to have the most severe problems, including psychopathology, lower levels of education, partner and child abuse, and violent behavior. However, those classified as adolescent-limited, who were expected to "grow out" of their aggressive and antisocial behavior, have apparently not done so. The men now in their mid twenties continue to have troubles with substance abuse and dependence, impulsivity, crime, and overall mental health (Moffitt et al., in press). Additional follow-ups of this sample will help us learn whether or not these maladaptive patterns get better toward the later twenties or early thirties.

The ability to identify which youths are most likely to persist in their antisocial behavior would be important. Research shows that most boys who are very aggressive at an early age, including but not restricted to those with conduct disorder, do not persist in this aggressive behavior into and beyond adolescence (e.g., Moffitt et al., in press; Nagin & Trembly, 1999). Lahey et al. (1995) found that boys with conduct disorder were

Children with the life-course-persistent type of conduct disorder continue to have trouble with the law into their early 20s and perhaps even longer.

much more likely to persist in their antisocial behavior if they had a parent with antisocial personality disorder or if they had low verbal intelligence. Boys with higher verbal IQs and no antisocial parent apparently had a more transient form of the disorder. In this study, other factors, including socioeconomic status and ethnicity, did not predict which boys would continue to show conduct disorder over time. Other research, however, suggests that the interaction of individual factors, such as temperament, parent psychopathology, and dysfunctional parent-child interactions, with sociocultural factors, such as poverty and low social support, contribute to the greater likelihood of early and persistent aggressive behavior (e.g., Campbell, 2002; DeKlyen & Speltz, 2001; Shaw, Bell, & Gilliom, 2000; Shaw et al., 2001).

Etiological and Risk Factors for Conduct Disorder

Numerous proposals have been put forward for the etiology of conduct disorder, including biological factors, learning and cognitive factors, and sociological variables. Moreover, a good deal of research has highlighted variables that increase the risk for conduct disorder and antisocial/aggressive behavior, including parental psychopathology, parenting practices, and peer influences. The most comprehensive accounts of etiology consider multiple contributors, including biological, psychological, and social (Coie & Dodge, 1998).

Biological Factors   The evidence for genetic influences in conduct disorder is mixed, although heritability may well play a part. For example, a study of over 3,000 twin pairs indicated only modest genetic influence on childhood antisocial behavior; family-environment influences were more significant (Lyons et al., 1995). However, a study of 2,600 twin pairs in Australia found a substantial genetic influence and almost no family-environment influence for childhood symptoms of conduct disorder (Slutske et al., 1997). The authors of the latter study point out that differences in the samples may have accounted for the different findings.

To date, three large-scale adoption studies, in Sweden, Denmark, and the United States, have been conducted, but two of them focused on the heritability of criminal behavior rather than conduct disorder or adult antisocial personality disorder (Simonoff, 2001). These studies indicate that criminal and aggressive behavior is accounted for by both genetic and environmental factors, with a slight edge toward the environmental factors. Interestingly, despite different prevalence rates for boys and girls, the evidence favoring genetic and environmental contributions to conduct disorder and antisocial behavior does not differ for boys and girls.

Distinguishing types of conduct problems may help to clarify findings on heritability of conduct disorder. Evidence from twin studies indicates that aggressive behavior (e.g., cruelty to animals, fighting, destroying property) is clearly heritable, whereas other delinquent behavior (e.g., stealing, running away, truancy) may not be (Edelbrock et al., 1995). Other evidence suggests that when antisocial and aggressive behavior problems begin is related to heritability. For example, aggressive and antisocial behavior that begins in childhood, as in the case of Moffitt's life-course-persistent type, is more heritable than similar behaviors that begin in adolescence (Taylor, Iacono, & McGue, 2000). As Hinshaw and Lee (in press) note, what is likely heritable in conduct disorder are temperamental characteristics that interact with other biological difficulties (e.g., neuropsychological deficits) as well as with a whole host of environmental factors (e.g., parenting, school performance, peer influences) to cause conduct disorder.

Neuropsychological deficits, as suggested above, have been implicated in the childhood profiles of children with conduct disorder (Lynam & Henry, 2001; Moffitt, Lynam, & Sylva, 1994). These deficits include poor verbal skills, difficulty with executive functioning (the ability to anticipate, plan, use self-control, and problem solve), and problems with memory. In addition, children who develop conduct disorder at an earlier age (life-course-persistent type) have been shown to have an IQ score of one standard deviation below age-matched peers without conduct disorder, and this IQ deficit is not apparently attributable to lower socioeconomic status, race, or school failure (Lynam, Moffitt, & Stouthamer-Loeber, 1993; Moffitt & Silva, 1988).

Psychological Factors   An important part of normal child development is the growth of moral awareness, the acquisition of a sense of what is right and wrong and the ability, even desire, to abide by rules and norms. Most people refrain from hurting others not only because it is illegal but because it would make them feel guilty to do otherwise. Children with conduct disorder, like the psychopathic individuals discussed in Chapter 13, often seem to be deficient in this moral awareness, lacking remorse for their wrongdoing and viewing antisocial acts as exciting and rewarding, as central to their very self-concept (Ryall, 1974).

Learning theories that look to both modeling and operant conditioning provide useful explanations of the development and maintenance of conduct problems. Bandura and Walters (1963) were among the first researchers to appreciate the significance of the fact that children can learn aggressiveness from parents who behave aggressively. Indeed, children who are physically abused by parents are likely to be aggressive when they grow up (Coie & Dodge, 1994). Children may also imitate aggressive acts seen from other sources, such as on television (Huesmann & Miller, 1994). Since aggression is an effective, albeit unpleasant, means of achieving a goal, it is likely to be reinforced. Thus, once imitated, aggressive acts will probably be maintained.

This social mimicry may at least partially explain the dramatic surge in delinquent behavior in adolescents who had not previously shown conduct problems. Moffitt (1993) proposed that these adolescents imitate the behavior of persistently antisocial peers because they see them as enjoying high-status possessions and sexual opportunities.

In addition, parenting characteristics such as harsh and inconsistent discipline and lack of monitoring are consistently associated with antisocial behavior in children. Perhaps children who do not experience negative consequences for early signs of misbehavior later develop more serious conduct problems (Coie & Dodge, 1998).

A social-cognitive perspective on aggressive behavior (and, by extension, conduct disorder) comes from the work of Kenneth Dodge and his associates. In one of his early studies (Dodge & Frame, 1982), Dodge found that the cognitive processes of aggressive children had a particular bias; these youngsters interpreted ambiguous acts, such as being bumped in line, as evidence of hostile intent. Such perceptions may lead these children to retaliate aggressively for actions that may not have been intended as provocative. Subsequently, their peers, remembering these aggressive behaviors, may tend to be aggressive more often against them, further angering the already aggressive children and continuing a cycle of rejection and aggression (see Figure 15.2). Dodge has constructed a social-information processing theory of child behavior that focuses on how children process information about their world and how these cognitions markedly affect their behavior (Crick & Dodge, 1994).

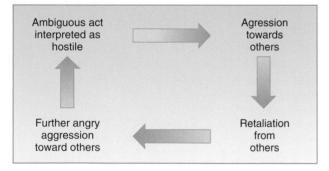

Figure 15.2   Dodge's cognitive theory of aggression. Interpretation of ambiguous acts as hostile is part of a vicious cycle with aggression toward and from others.

Peer Influences   Investigations of how peers influence aggressive and antisocial behavior in children have focused on two broad areas: (1) acceptance or rejection by peers and (2) affiliation with deviant peers. Being rejected by peers has been shown to be causally related to aggressive behavior, particular in combination with ADHD (Hinshaw & Melnick, 1995). Other studies have shown that being rejected by peers can predict later aggressive behavior, even after controlling for prior levels of aggressive behavior (Coie and Dodge, 1998). Associating with other delinquent peers also increases the likelihood of delinquent behavior (Capaldi & Patterson, 1994). One question that remains to be answered is whether delinquent children choose to associate with like-minded peers, thus continuing on their path of antisocial behavior, or if simply being around delinquent peers can influence the beginnings of antisocial behavior.

Sociological Factors   Any discussion of conduct disorder and delinquency must recognize the work of sociologists. Social class and urban living are related to the incidence of delinquency. High unemployment, poor educational facilities, disrupted family life, and a subculture that deems delinquency acceptable have all been found to be contributing factors (Lahey et al., 1999; Loeber & Farrington, 1998). The combination of early antisocial behavior in the child and socioeconomic disadvantage in the family predicts early criminal arrests (Patterson, Crosby, & Vuchinich, 1992).

A study of African American and white youths drawn from the Pittsburgh Youth Study indicates that the commonly found greater severity of delinquent acts among African Americans appears to be linked to their living in poorer neighborhoods, not to their race. Peeples and Loeber (1994) designated neighborhoods as underclass or non-underclass based on factors such as family poverty/welfare, families with no one employed, male joblessness, and nonmarital births. In the total sample—ignoring differences in social class—African American youths were much more likely than white youths to have committed serious delinquent acts (e.g., car theft, breaking and entering, aggravated assault). But African American youths who were not living in underclass neighborhoods did not differ from white youths in serious delinquent behavior. Social factors matter. The strongest correlates of delinquency other than neighborhood were hyperactivity and lack of parental supervision; once these factors were controlled, residence in underclass neighborhoods was significantly related to delinquent behavior, whereas ethnicity was not.

Treatment of Conduct Disorder

The management of conduct disorder poses a formidable challenge to contemporary society. Sociologists and politicians as well as community psychologists, working on the assumption that poor economic conditions create most of the problem, argue for a fairer distribution of income and for job programs and other large-scale efforts to alleviate the material deprivation of people in the lower socioeconomic classes. We emphasize here psychological methods aimed at the particular individuals and their families, rather than such sociological considerations. However, as we will see, working to influence the multiple systems involved in the life of a youngster (family, peers, school, neighborhood) may be critical to the success of treatment efforts.

As mentioned, some young people with conduct disorder are the psychopaths of tomorrow. And like psychopaths, young people who commit violent and antisocial acts with little remorse or emotional involvement are extraordinarily difficult to reach. Incarceration, release, and recidivism are the rule. One of society's most enduring problems is how to deal with people whose social consciences appear grossly underdeveloped. Simply jailing juvenile delinquents will not reduce crime. A longitudinal study demonstrated that punitive discipline, such as juvenile incarceration, leads to lower job stability and more adult crime. Thus, harsh discipline, whether imposed by the state or by the parents, appears to contribute in a major way to further delinquency and criminal activity in adulthood (Laub & Sampson, 1995).

Family Interventions   Some of the most promising approaches to treating conduct disorder involve intervening with the parents or families of the antisocial child. Gerald Patterson and his colleagues have worked for over four decades developing and testing a behavioral program of parental management training (PMT), in which parents are taught to modify their responses to their children so that prosocial rather than antisocial behavior is consistently rewarded. Parents are taught to use techniques such as positive reinforcement when the child exhibits positive behaviors and time-out and loss of privileges for aggressive or antisocial behaviors.

Both parents' and teachers' reports of children's behavior and direct observation of behavior at home and at school support the program's effectiveness (Patterson, 1982). PMT has been shown to alter parent-child interactions, which in turn is associated with a decrease in antisocial and aggressive behavior (Dishion & Andrews, 1995; Dishion, Patterson, & Kavenagh, 1992). PMT has also been shown to improve the behavior of siblings and reduce depression in mothers involved in the program (Kazdin, 1985).

Head Start: A Successful Community-Based Prevention Program

Head Start is a federally funded program whose goal is to prepare children socially and culturally to succeed in the regular school setting by giving them experiences that they may be missing at home. The impetus for the program came during the 1960s, when national attention in the United States was directed to problems of hunger and civil rights.

The core of the Head Start program is community-based preschool education, focusing on the early development of cognitive and social skills. Head Start contracts with professionals in the community to provide children with health and dental services, including vaccinations, hearing and vision testing, medical treatment, and nutrition information (North, 1979). Mental health services are another important component of these programs. Psychologists may identify children with psychological problems and consult with teachers and staff to help make the preschool environment sensitive to psychological issues; for example, they may share knowledge of child development, consult on an individual case, or help staff address parents' concerns (Cohen, Solnit, & Wohlford, 1979). Social workers can serve as advocates for the child's family, linking families with needed social services and encouraging parents to get involved with their children's education (Lazar, 1979).

A comparison of Head Start children with other disadvantaged youngsters who attended either a different preschool or no preschool showed that Head Start children improved significantly more than both control groups on social-cognitive ability and motor impulsivity; the relative improvement was strongest for African American children, particularly those with initial ability below average. Although the Head Start program succeeded in enhancing the functioning of the neediest children, they were still behind their peers in terms of absolute cognitive levels after one year in the program (Lee, Brooks-Gunn, & Schnur, 1988). Other reports confirm the value of Head Start in helping poor youngsters improve their intellectual functioning (e.g., Cronan et al., 1996; Perkins, 1995; Schleifer, 1995).

A study of chronic adolescent offenders by Patterson's group (Bank et al., 1991) found that both parent training and court-provided family treatment reduced rates of criminal offense. However, the parent-training approach, which included teaching parents to monitor their adolescents more closely and use age-appropriate rewards and consequences, led to more rapid improvement. Longer-term follow-ups suggest that the beneficial effects of PMT persist one to three years later (Brestan & Eyberg, 1998; Long et al., 1994). Recently, parent and teacher training approaches have been incorporated into larger community-based programs like Head Start and have been shown to reduce childhood conduct problems and increase positive parenting behaviors (Webster-Stratton, 1998; Webster-Stratton, Reid & Hammond, 2001). See Focus on Discovery 15.2 for more on Head Start.

Multisystemic Treatment   A new and promising treatment for serious juvenile offenders is Henggeler's multisystemic treatment (MST), which has demonstrated reductions in arrests four years following treatment (Borduin et al., 1995). MST involves delivering intensive and comprehensive therapy services in the community, targeting the adolescent, the family, the school, and in some cases the peer group (Figure 15.3). The intervention views the conduct problem as influenced by multiple contexts within the family and between the family and other social systems.

The strategies used by MST therapists are varied, incorporating behavioral, cognitive, family-systems, and case-management techniques. The therapy's uniqueness (and, apparently, its effectiveness; see Henggeler et al., 1998) lies in emphasizing individual and family strengths, identifying the context for the conduct problems, using present-focused and action-oriented interventions, and using interventions that require daily or weekly efforts by family members. Treatment is provided in "ecologically valid" settings, such as the home, school, or local recreational center, to maximize generalization of therapeutic changes.

In comparison with a control group that received an equivalent number of sessions (about twenty-five) of traditional individual therapy in an office setting, adolescents in the multisystemic treatment group showed reduced behavior problems and far fewer arrests over the following four years. For example, whereas more than 70 percent of adolescents receiving traditional therapy were arrested in the four years following treatment, only 22 percent of those completing the multisystemic treatment were arrested. In addi-

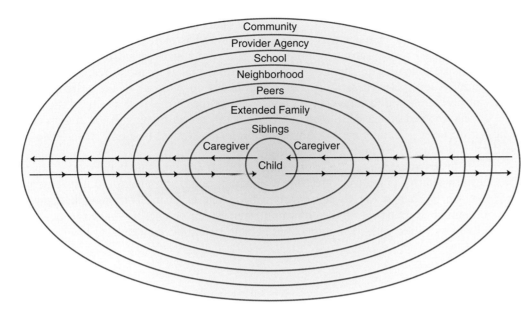

Figure 15.3 Multisystemic Treatment (MST) includes many considerations when developing a child's treatment, including family, school, community, and peers.

tion, assessment of other family members indicated that parents who were involved in multisystemic treatments showed reductions in psychiatric symptomatology, and families showed improved supportiveness and decreased conflict and hostility in videotaped interactions. In contrast, the quality of interactions in the families of the adolescents receiving traditional individual therapy deteriorated following treatment. Even the adolescents in the multisystemic group who dropped out of treatment after about four sessions demonstrated significantly reduced arrest rates compared with adolescents who completed the full course of traditional individual therapy.

Cognitive Approaches   Although research by Patterson's and Henggeler's groups suggests that intervention with parents and families is a critical component of success, such treatment is expensive and time-consuming (though clearly less so than incarceration). Indeed, some families may not be able or willing to become involved in it. Thus, it is noteworthy that other research indicates that individual cognitive therapy with conduct-disordered children can improve their behavior even without the involvement of the family.

For example, teaching children cognitive skills to control their anger shows real promise in helping them reduce their aggressive behavior. In anger-control training, aggressive children are taught self-control in anger-provoking situations. They learn to withstand verbal attacks without responding aggressively by using distracting techniques such as humming a tune, saying calming things to themselves, or turning away. The children then apply these self-control methods while a peer provokes and insults them (Hinshaw, Henker, & Whalen, 1984b; Lochman & Wells, 1996).

Another strategy involves focusing on the deficient moral development of conduct-disordered children. Teaching moral-reasoning skills to groups of behavior-disordered adolescents in school has achieved some degree of success (Arbuthnot & Gordon, 1986). Adolescents who were nominated by their teachers as having behavior problems (such as aggressiveness, stealing, and vandalism) participated for four to five months in weekly groups at school aimed at encouraging higher levels of moral reasoning. Group sessions included discussion of vignettes such as the following:

> Sharon and her best friend, Jill, are shopping in a boutique. Jill finds a blouse she wants but cannot afford. She takes it into a fitting room and puts it on underneath her jacket. She shows it to Sharon and, despite Sharon's protests, leaves the store. Sharon is stopped by a security guard. The manager searches Sharon's bag, but finding nothing, concludes that Jill shoplifted the blouse. The manager asks Sharon for Jill's name, threatening to call both Sharon's parents and the police if she doesn't tell. Sharon's dilemma is whether or not to tell on her best friend.

Members were encouraged to debate the merits of alternative perspectives and the rights and responsibilities of characters in the dilemmas as well as of other people and society. Compared with a control group of nominated students who received no intervention, adolescents participating in the groups showed improvement in moral-reasoning skills and school grades, as well as reductions in tardiness, in referrals to the principal for behavior problems, and in contacts with police or juvenile courts. Follow-ups in the next school year showed increased differences between the two groups, with the adolescents who had received the intervention showing continued advances in moral reasoning and further reductions in behavior problems.

This improvement is impressive, but other research cautions that behavioral changes produced by altering cognitive patterns may yield only short-term gains—improvements that may be lost when the youngsters return to their familiar, "bad" neighborhoods. Environmental contingencies—the communities in which people live—need to be considered when dealing with the complexities of aggression (Guerra & Slaby, 1990).

Learning Disabilities

Several years ago a young man in one of our undergraduate courses showed an unusual pattern of strengths and difficulties. His oral comments in class were exemplary, but his handwriting and spelling were sometimes indecipherable. After the instructor had noted these problems on the student's midterm examination, the undergraduate came to see him and explained that he was dyslexic and that it took him longer to complete the weekly reading assignments and to write papers and exams. The instructor decided to accord him additional time for preparing written work. The student was obviously of superior intelligence and highly motivated to excel. Excel he did, earning an A in the seminar and on graduation being admitted to a leading law school.

Learning disabilities signify inadequate development in a specific area of academic, language, speech, or motor skills that is not due to mental retardation, autism, a demonstrable physical disorder, or deficient educational opportunities. Children with these disorders are usually of average or above-average intelligence but have difficulty learning some specific skill (e.g., arithmetic or reading), and thus their progress in school is impeded.

The term learning disabilities is not used by DSM-IV-TR but is used by most health professionals to group together three disorders that do appear in the DSM: learning disorders, communication disorders, and motor skills disorder. Any of these disorders may apply to a child who fails to develop to the degree expected by his or her intellectual level in a specific academic, language, or motor-skill area. Learning disabilities are often identified and treated within the school system rather than through mental health clinics. Although they are widely believed to be far more common in males than in females, evidence from population-based studies (which avoid the problem of referral biases) indicates that the disorders are only slightly more common in males (e.g., Shaywitz et al., 1990). Though individuals with learning disabilities usually find ways to cope with their problems, their academic and social development is nonetheless affected, sometimes quite seriously. (See Focus on Discovery 15.3 for a discussion of another problem of childhood—enuresis.)

Learning Disorders

DSM-IV-TR divides **learning disorders** into three categories: reading disorder, disorder of written expression, and mathematics disorder. None of these diagnoses is appropriate if the disability can be accounted for by a sensory deficit, such as a visual or auditory problem.

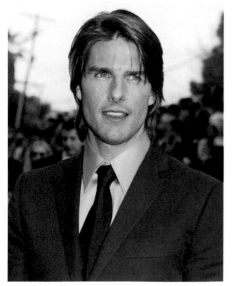
Tom Cruise, accomplished actor, suffered from dyslexia.

- Children with **reading disorder**, better known as **dyslexia**, have significant difficulty with word recognition, reading comprehension, and typically written spelling as well. When reading out loud they omit, add, or distort the pronunciation of words to an extent unusual for their age. In adulthood, problems with reading, comprehension, and written spelling persist (Bruck, 1987). This disorder, present in 5 to 10 percent of school-age children, does not preclude great achievements. For example, it is widely known that Tom Cruise, well-known and accomplished actor, has dyslexia.

- **Disorder of written expression** describes an impairment in the ability to compose the written word (including spelling errors, errors in grammar or punctuation, or very poor handwriting) that is serious enough to interfere significantly with academic achievement or daily activities that require writing skills. Few systematic data have yet been collected on the prevalence of this disorder, which the college student in our case had in addition to his dyslexia.

- Children with **mathematics disorder** may have difficulty rapidly and accurately recalling arithmetic facts, counting objects correctly and quickly, or aligning numbers in columns.

Communication Disorders

Several categories of communication disorders have been distinguished:

- In **expressive language disorder**, the child has difficulty expressing himself or herself in speech. The youngster may seem eager to communicate but have inordinate difficulty finding the right words; for example, he or she may be unable to come up with the word *car* when pointing to a car passing by on the street. By age four, this child speaks only in short phrases. Old words are forgotten when new ones are learned, and the use of grammatical structures is considerably below age level.

- Unlike children who have trouble finding words, youngsters with **phonological disorder** comprehend and are able to use a substantial vocabulary, but their speech is not clear; *blue* comes out *bu*, and *rabbit* sounds like *wabbit*, for example. They have not learned articulation of the later-acquired speech sounds, such as *r, sh, th, f, z, l,* and *ch*. With speech therapy complete recovery occurs in almost all cases, and milder cases may recover spontaneously by age eight.

- A third communication disorder is **stuttering**, a disturbance in verbal fluency that is characterized by one or more of the following speech patterns: frequent repetitions or prolongations of sounds, long pauses between words, substituting easy words for those that are difficult to articulate (e.g., words beginning with certain consonants), and repeating whole words (e.g., saying "go-go-go-go" instead of just a single "go"). Sometimes bodily twitching and eye blinking accompany the verbal dysfluencies. Stuttering can interfere with academic, social, and occupational functioning and can prevent otherwise capable people from fulfilling their potential. It is frequently worse when the person is nervous and often improves or even disappears when the person sings. The stuttering of a friend of ours would disappear almost completely when he performed in plays, even though being on stage was somewhat anxiety provoking for him. He told us that it was much easier to verbalize the words from a script than to speak on his own, consistent with the improvement often seen in stutterers when they read aloud. About three times as many males as females have the problem, which usually shows up at around age five and almost always before the age of ten. The DSM estimates that up to 80 percent of individuals with stuttering difficulties recover, most of them without professional intervention, before the age of sixteen.

A speech therapist works with a child with phonological disorder by having him practice the sounds he finds difficult.

Motor Skills Disorder

In **motor skills disorder**, also referred to as developmental coordination disorder, children show marked impairment in the development of motor coordination that is not explainable by mental retardation or a known physical disorder such as cerebral palsy. The young child may have difficulty tying shoelaces and buttoning shirts and, when older, with building models, playing ball, and printing or handwriting. The diagnosis is made only if the impairment interferes significantly with academic achievement or with the activities of daily living.

Focus on Discovery 15.3

Enuresis

It is well-known that infants have no bladder or bowel control. As they become older, the inevitable toilet training begins. Some children learn toileting at eighteen months, others at thirty months, and so on. When is it no longer normal to be unable to control the bladder? The answer, determined by cultural norms and statistics, is fairly arbitrary.

DSM-IV-TR and other classification systems distinguish among children who wet during sleep—nocturnal enuresis—those who wet while awake—diurnal enuresis—and those who wet both days and nights. Daytime continence is established earlier because bladder control is a much simpler matter when one is awake. When a child falls behind in bladder control, it is usually for the nighttime hours. DSM-IV-TR estimates that at age five, 7 percent of boys and 3 percent of girls are enuretic; at age ten, 3 percent of boys and 2 percent of girls; and at age eighteen, 1 percent of young men and less for young women. In the United States nocturnal enuresis is not diagnosed, according to DSM-IV-TR, until the child is five years old.

Causes of Enuresis

One consistent finding about enuresis is that the likelihood of an enuretic person's having a first-degree relative who also wets is very high, approximately 75 percent (Bakwin, 1973). A recent Danish study provides the first direct genetic link for bed-wetting; a segment of chromosome 13 apparently holds the gene for nocturnal enuresis (Eiberg, Berendt, & Mohr, 1995).

As many as 10 percent of all cases of enuresis are caused by purely medical conditions, such as a urinary tract infection, chronic renal or kidney disease, tumors, diabetes, and seizures (Kolvin, McKeith, & Meadows, 1973; Stansfield, 1973). Because of the substantial incidence of physical causes of enuresis, most professionals refer enuretic patients to physicians before beginning psychological treatment.

Bladder control, the inhibition of a natural reflex until voluntary voiding can take place, is a skill of considerable complexity. Medical evidence regarding activity of the pelvic floor muscles provides support for the idea that children who wet the bed fail to spontaneously contract these muscles at night (Norgaard, 1989a, 1989b).

Some psychological theories consider enuresis a symptom of a more general psychological disorder, such as anxiety. Many investigators argue, however, that such problems as anger and anxiety are a reaction to the embarrassment and guilt of wetting, rather than causes of enuresis. Learning theorists propose that children wet because they have not learned to awaken as a conditioned response to a full bladder or to inhibit sufficiently relaxation of the sphincter muscle that controls urination (Walker, 1995).

Treatment of Enuresis

Home remedies for bed-wetting have run the gamut from restricting fluids to making children sleep on golf balls or hanging the incriminating evidence—wet sheets—out the window (Houts, 1991). Most such strategies are ineffective. Similarly, waiting for the child to grow out of the problem is not satisfactory. Only about 15 percent of enuretic youngsters between ages five and nineteen show spontaneous remission within a year (Forsythe & Redmond, 1974).

The two most widely used treatments prescribed by professionals involve either medication or urine alarm systems. The latter first came on the scene in 1938, when Mowrer and Mowrer introduced the bell and pad. Over the years this treatment has proved markedly successful in reducing or eliminating bed-wetting. It is estimated that 75 percent of enuretic children will learn to stay dry through the night with the help of this remarkably simple device.

A bell and a battery are wired to a pad composed of two metallic foil sheets, the top one perforated, separated by a layer of absorbent cloth (Figure 15.a). The pad is inserted into a pillowcase and placed beneath the child at bedtime. When the first drops of urine, which act as an electrolyte, reach the cloth, the electric circuit is completed between the two

Etiology of Learning Disabilities

Most research on learning disabilities concerns dyslexia, perhaps because it is the most prevalent of this group of disorders. Although studies on mathematics disorder are beginning to emerge, the literature has advanced more slowly in this area.

Etiology of Dyslexia   Past psychological theories focused on perceptual deficits as the basis for dyslexia. One popular hypothesis suggested that children with reading problems perceive letters in reverse order or mirror image, mistaking, for example, a *d* for a *b*. However, more recent findings have not supported this hypothesis (Wolff & Melngailis, 1996); most children make letter reversals when first learning to read, but even dyslexic individuals very rarely make letter reversals after age nine or ten. No relationship has been found between letter confusions at age five or six and subsequent reading ability (Calfee, Fisk, & Piontkowski, 1985), nor does a person need to be able to see to have reading problems—blind people may have difficulty learning to read braille (McGuiness, 1981).

There is fairly good consensus among investigators today that the core deficits comprising dyslexia include problems in visual/auditory and language processes. Evidence from psychological, neuropsychological, and neuroimaging studies supports this con-

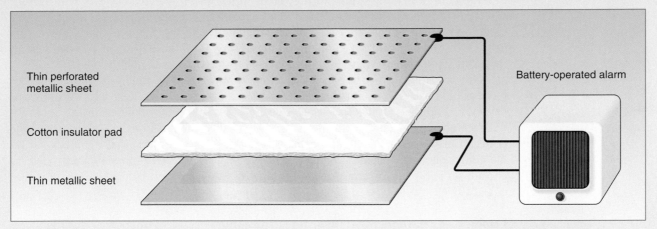

Figure 15.3a   The bell-and-pad apparatus for halting bed-wetting, devised by O. H. Mowrer and W. M. Mowrer.

foil sheets. The completed circuit sets off the bell or alarm, which awakens the child immediately or soon after beginning to wet. The child then typically stops urinating, turns off the device, and goes to the bathroom.

Mowrer and Mowrer (1938) viewed the bell and pad as a classical-conditioning procedure wherein an unconditioned stimulus, the bell, elicits wakefulness in the child, the unconditioned response. The bell is paired with the sensations of a full bladder so that these sensations eventually become a conditioned stimulus that produces the conditioned response of awakening before the bell sounds. Others have questioned the classical-conditioning theory, suggesting, in operant-conditioning terms, that the bell, by waking the child, serves as a punisher and thus reduces the undesirable behavior of wetting (Walker, Milling, & Bonner, 1988). In actual practice the bell usually wakes the child's parents too; their reactions may serve as an additional incentive for the child to remain dry.

Other methods that use an operant-conditioning approach without the help of the urine alarm have not been nearly as successful (Houts, 2000; Houts, Berman, & Abramson, 1994). On the other hand, greater success may be achieved by additions to the basic urine-alarm procedure, such as drinking increasing amounts of fluid on successive nights before bedtime (to get the child used to retaining fluid in the bladder without wetting the bed) and making sure that the child awakens and changes sheets each time the alarm rings (to add another negative consequence to bed-wetting) (Barclay & Houts, 1995; Mellon & Houts, 1998). Newer urine alarms are worn on the body and are more reliable than the original mattress pad.

Pharmacological treatment is another approach. About one-third of enuretic patients who seek professional help are prescribed medications, such as the antidepressant imipramine (Tofranil) and, more recently, desmopressin, which increases absorption of water in the kidneys. Such medications work either by changing the reactivity of the muscles involved in urinating (imipramine) or by concentrating urine in the bladder (desmopressin). Although an immediate positive effect is usually seen, in the vast majority of cases children relapse as soon as the medication is stopped (Houts, 1991), and negative side effects of imipramine (sleep problems, tiredness, stomach aches) can be problematic.

tention. For example, dyslexic children do not perform as well as children without dyslexia on visual tasks that require rapid processing, such as determining how many dots are presented on a screen in a series of presentations (Eden et al., 1995). In addition, research points to one or more problems in language processing that might underlie dyslexia, including perception of speech and analysis of the sounds of spoken language and their relation to printed words (Mann & Brady, 1988). Indeed, a series of longitudinal studies suggests that some early language problems can predict later dyslexia. Certain children are more likely to develop dyslexia: those who have difficulty recognizing rhyme and alliteration at age four (Bradley & Bryant, 1985); those who have problems rapidly naming familiar objects at age five (Scarborough, 1990; Wolf, Bally, & Morris, 1986); and those with delays in learning syntactic rules at age two and a half (Scarborough, 1990).

Studies that use various brain imaging techniques during performance of visual, auditory, and language tasks reveal how differences in activation of particular areas of the brain distinguish dyslexic from nondyslexic individuals. For example, a PET scan study showed that during a test that required children to detect rhymes, the left temporoparietal cortex was activated in the nondyslexic children but not in the dyslexic children. This finding is important because the temporoparietal cortex is related to an aspect of language processing called phonological awareness, which is believed to be critical to the development of reading skills (Rumsey et al., 1992, 1994; Shaywitz & Shaywitz, 1999). A recent study using fMRI also found that compared with nondyslexic children, dyslexic children failed to activate the temporoparietal area during a phonological processing task (Temple et al., 2001). Similar findings using fMRI have been found with adult dyslexics (Horwitz, Rumsey, & Donahue, 1998; Klingberg et al., 2000).

Other evidence, too, suggests that brain abnormalities, possibly heritable, may be responsible for dyslexia. For example, autopsies of the brains of right-handed individuals with childhood dyslexia have revealed microscopic abnormalities in the location, number, and organization of neurons in what is called the posterior language area of the cortex (Galaburda, 1989, 1993). Family and twin studies confirm that there is a heritable component to dyslexia (Pennington, 1995; Raskind, 2001), possibly controlled by chromosome 6 (Cardon et al., 1994; Fisher et al., 1999; Gayan et al., 1999; Grigorenko et al., 1997).

Etiology of Mathematics Disorder   Three subtypes of mathematics disorder have been proposed (Geary, 1993). The first involves a deficit in semantic verbal memory (memory for the meaning of words) and leads to problems with memorizing and retrieving arithmetic facts, even after extensive drilling. This type of math disorder appears to be associated with some dysfunction in the left hemisphere of the brain and often occurs together with a reading disorder.

The second subtype of math disorder involves use of developmentally immature strategies for solving arithmetic problems and frequent errors in solving simple problems. For example, when first-grade children with this subtype are asked to add 3 and 4, they first count to three on their fingers, then count four more. In contrast, children this age with more typical math abilities start by putting out four fingers (without counting them) and then count three more (Geary & Brown, 1991; Geary, Brown, & Samaranayake, 1991). No evidence is yet available on the etiology of this type of disability, which appears to involve a developmental lag and generally improves with age.

Finally, a third and less common subtype of math disorder apparently involves impaired visuospatial skills, resulting in misaligning numbers in columns or making place-value errors (putting decimal points in wrong places). This type of disorder is much less likely to be associated with reading disorders than is the semantic-memory subtype.

Although no studies have been done on the heritability of mathematics disorders, there is evidence of some genetic component to individual variation in math skills. In particular, the type of math disability that involves poor semantic memory is most likely to be heritable. A study of over 250 twin pairs conducted through the Colorado Learning Disabilities Research Center suggested that common genetic factors underlie both reading and math deficits in children with both disorders (Gillis & DeFries, 1991).

Treatment of Learning Disabilities

The anxiety of parents whose otherwise typical child lags behind in reading or cannot speak effectively for his or her age cannot be underestimated. Professional attempts to remedy learning disabilities have been subject to somatic, educational, and psychological fads—from using stimulants and tranquilizers to training the child in motor activities (such as crawling) believed to have been inadequately mastered at a younger age. The hope is that such motor training will reorganize neuronal connections in the brain.

Most treatment for learning disabilities occurs within special-education programs in the public schools (see Focus on Discovery 15.4). Educational approaches include identifying and working with the child's cognitive strengths while circumventing his or her deficits; targeting study skills and organizational strategies; and teaching verbal self-instruction strategies (Culbertson, 1998). Although special-education interventions are extremely common, their effectiveness in improving the academic performance of children with learning disabilities has not been carefully evaluated (Council for Exceptional Children, 1993).

Focus on Discovery 15.4

Immersion and the Education of Disabled Children

In 1975 the United States Congress passed Public Law 94-142, the Education for All Handicapped Children Act. Passage of this law represented substantial gains for the educational rights of children with disabilities and secured their integration into the community. The law guarantees children between the ages of three and twenty-one a free, appropriate public education in "the least restrictive environment" (see p. 629 for further discussion of this important legal principle). Such an environment is one that allows the student with a disability to develop mentally, physically, and socially with the fewest barriers yet provides necessary support. The goals for each child are set forth in an individual educational program (IEP) that is evaluated annually.

Immersion of disabled children received a big push when Public Law 99–457 was passed in 1986. This law extended the earlier statute by requiring that all public schools serve disabled preschoolers by 1991 or lose their federal funding. Both laws apply to all children with exceptional needs, including those with mental retardation, autism, and learning disabilities, as well as children with speech, hearing, motor, or visual impairments, gifted and talented children,[*] and children with serious emotional disturbances that interfere with their school progress.

Immersion has its problems, however. For example, African Americans have been overrepresented among children diagnosed as having mental retardation. Since scores on standardized intelligence tests are central in deciding on such placement, there is some concern that African Americans may be unfairly stigmatized and otherwise disadvantaged by being assigned

Students with disabilities are often mainstreamed—educated together in classrooms with students without disabilities.

to special-education classes, even though the classes are in public schools (Heller, Holtzman, & Messick, 1982). The reasons for the disproportionately large numbers of African Americans in such classes are complex; they include historical patterns of discrimination that can lead to poor economic conditions, disrupted home lives, malnutrition, poor-quality school instruction, and other disadvantages that contribute to low test scores and poor academic performance. Personal biases of teachers and administrators may also play a role in whether a child is placed in a special class.

Generally, programs that are sensitive to the problems inherent in immersion appear likely to yield positive results both for students with and without disabilities (Gottlieb, 1990; Zigler, Hodapp, & Edison, 1990). Typically developing children can learn early in life that there is tremendous diversity among human beings and that a child may be different in some very important ways and yet be worthy of respect and friendship.

---

[*] It may seem odd that gifted and talented children are covered by this law, apparently designed for those with serious disabilities. Surely being uncommonly bright or talented in an area such as music or art is not a disability! True. But parents of such children know that the public schools sometimes do damage to gifted youngsters by not challenging them sufficiently and sometimes by discouraging, even disparaging, their abilities and interests. Such young people also have special educational needs; but it is understandable that when budgets are tight, resources are directed toward those who have mental retardation or are otherwise intellectually or physically compromised.

Several strategies are currently being used to treat learning disabilities, both in school programs and in private tutoring. Traditional linguistic approaches, used primarily in cases of reading and writing difficulties, focus on instruction in listening, speaking, reading, and writing skills in a logical, sequential, and multisensory manner, such as reading out loud under close supervision. In young children, readiness skills, such as letter discrimination, phonetic analysis, and learning letter–sound correspondences, may need to be taught before explicit instruction in reading is attempted. Findings from the National Reading Panel, a comprehensive review of the research on teaching children to read, indicate that phonics instruction was beneficial for children with reading difficulties. Phonics involves instruction in converting sounds to words (National Institute of Child Health and Human Development, 2000). As in the case described at the beginning of this section, individuals with dyslexia often can succeed in college with the aid of instructional supports, such as tape-recorded lectures, tutors, writing editors, and untimed tests (Bruck, 1987). Colleges are required by law to provide special services to help such students, and public schools are now required to provide transitional vocational and career planning for older adolescents with learning disabilities.

In recent years, there has been an exciting development in treating communication disorders (Merzenich et al., 1996; Tallal et al., 1996). Based on previous findings that children with such disorders have difficulty discriminating certain sounds, the researchers developed special computer games and audiotapes that slow speech sounds. After intensive training with these modified speech stimuli for one month, children with severe language disorders were able to improve their language skills by approximately two years, to the point at which they were functioning as typically developing children do. Similar training using unmodified speech stimuli resulted in very little progress.

Based on their promising initial findings, these investigators expanded the treatment, now called Fast ForWord, and conducted a larger study including 500 children from the United States and Canada. Children received daily training for six to eight weeks, and results again indicated that the intervention was effective. Children improved in speech, language, and auditory processing skills by about one and one-half years of ability (Tallal et al., 1998). The researchers speculate that this training method may even help prevent dyslexia, since many reading-disordered children had difficulties understanding language as young children.

Most children with learning disabilities have probably experienced a great deal of frustration and failure, eroding their motivation and confidence. Whatever their design, treatment programs should provide opportunities for children to experience feelings of mastery and self-efficacy. Rewarding small steps can be helpful in increasing the child's motivation, focusing attention on the learning task, and reducing behavioral problems caused by frustration. In addition to targeting academic skills, treatment for children with learning disabilities should include strategies to address the secondary social and emotional adjustment problems they experience. For example, educating children and parents about the disability, addressing their emotional reactions to the disability, and teaching them strategies to adapt are all helpful in improving overall adjustment (Culbertson, 1998).

Mental Retardation

Mental retardation, an Axis II disorder, is defined in DSM-IV-TR as (1) significantly subaverage intellectual functioning along with (2) deficits in adaptive behavior and (3) occurring prior to age eighteen. We first examine traditional criteria and then discuss perspectives from the American Association of Mental Retardation, the principal professional organization devoted to research, education, and application in the field of mental retardation.

Traditional Criteria for Mental Retardation

Intelligence-Test Scores   The first component of the DSM definition requires a judgment of intelligence. As discussed in Chapter 4 (p. 90), approximately two-thirds of the population achieves IQ (intelligent quotient) test scores between 85 and 115. Those with a score below 70 to 75, two standard deviations below the mean of the population, meet the criterion of "significant subaverage general intellectual functioning." Approximately 3 percent of the population falls into this category.

The determination of IQ should be based on tests administered to an individual by a competent, well-trained professional. Interpretation of scores must take into account cultural, linguistic, and sensory or motor limitations that may affect performance. For example, when testing a child with cerebral palsy who has limited use of his or her hands, the examiner might select IQ tests that require verbal responses or simple gestural responses, rather than the traditional intellectual tests, which include a nonverbal or performance component requiring fairly complex and rapid motor movements. Similarly, a child who speaks Farsi at home and English at school cannot be tested in a valid way using only English-language measures (American Association of Mental Retardation [AAMR], 1992).

Adaptive Functioning   Adaptive functioning refers to mastering childhood skills such as toileting and dressing; understanding the concepts of time and money; being able to use

DSM-IV TR Criteria for Mental Retardation

- Significantly below-average intellectual functioning, IQ less than 70
- Deficits in adaptive social functioning in at least two of the following areas: communication, self-care, home living, interpersonal skills, use of community resources, ability to make own decisions, functional academic skills, leisure, work, health, and safety
- Onset before age 18

tools, to shop, and to travel by public transportation; and becoming socially responsive. An adolescent, for example, is expected to be able to apply academic skills, reasoning, and judgment to daily living and to participate in group activities. An adult is expected to be self-supporting and to assume social responsibilities.

Several tests have been constructed to assess adaptive behavior. Best known are the Adaptive Behavior Scale, or ABS (Nihira et al., 1975), and the Vineland Adaptive Behavior Scales (Sparrow, Ballo, & Cicchetti, 1984; see Table 15.3). Although impairments in adaptive functioning have long been included in the definition of mental retardation, only recently have the tests been adequately standardized with firmly established norms. One problem with many assessments of adaptive behavior is that they fail to consider the environment to which the person must adapt. A person who lives in a small rural community where everyone is acquainted may not need skills as complex as those needed by someone who lives in New York City. Youngsters who are competent working at farm chores, walking to school, and shopping at the local store may, when transported to a city, be considered deficient in adaptive behavior if they are not able to ride the subway to school or buy groceries at a store where a foreign language is spoken. By the same token, city children may find themselves at a loss with some of the activities expected of youngsters living on a farm. An effective and valid assessment of adaptive behavior should therefore consider the interaction between the child and the surroundings in which he or she must function.

Table 15.3 Sample Items from the Vineland Adaptive Behavior Scales

Age, Years	Adaptive Ability
2	Says at least fifty recognizable words. Removes front-opening coat, sweater, or shirt without assistance.
5	Tells popular story, fairy tale, lengthy joke, or plot of television program. Ties shoelaces into a bow without assistance.
8	Keeps secrets or confidences for more than one day. Orders own meal in a restaurant.
11	Uses the telephone for all kinds of calls without assistance. Watches television or listens to radio for information about a particular area of interest.
16	Looks after own health. Responds to hints or indirect cues in conversation.

Source: From Sparrow, Ballo, and Cicchetti, 1984.

Age of Onset   A final definitional criterion is that mental retardation be manifest before age eighteen, to rule out classifying as mental retardation any deficits in intelligence and adaptive behavior from injury or illnesses occurring later in life. Children with severe impairments are often diagnosed during infancy. Most children considered mentally retarded, however, are not identified as such until they enter school. These children have no obvious physiological, neurological, or physical manifestations, and their problems become apparent only when they are unable to keep up with their peers in school.

When assessing normal adaptive behavior, the environment must be considered. A person living in a rural community may not need the same skills as those needed by someone living in New York City and vice versa.

Classification of Mental Retardation

Four levels of mental retardation are recognized by DSM-IV-TR, each corresponding to a specific subaverage range on the far left of the normal distribution curve of measured intelligence (recall Figure 1.1, p. 4). Again, the IQ ranges are not the sole basis of diagnosis; deficiencies in adaptive behavior are also a criterion of mental retardation. Some persons falling in the mildly retarded range based on IQ may have no deficits in adaptive behavior and thus would not be considered mentally retarded. In fact, the IQ criterion is usually applied only after deficits in adaptive behavior have been identified. The following is a brief summary of characteristics of people at each level of mental retardation (DSM-IV-TR, 2000; Robinson & Robinson, 1976).

- **Mild Mental Retardation** (50–55 to 70 IQ). About 85 percent of all those who have IQs less than 70 are classified as having mild mental retardation. They are not always distinguishable from normal youngsters before they enter school. By their late teens they can usually learn academic skills at about a sixth-grade level. As adults they are likely to be able to maintain themselves in unskilled jobs or in sheltered workshops, although they may need help with social and financial problems. They may marry and have children.

- **Moderate Mental Retardation** (35–40 to 50–55 IQ). About 10 percent of those with IQs less than 70 are classified as having moderate mental retardation. Brain damage and other pathologies are frequent. People with moderate mental retardation may have physical defects and neurological dysfunctions that hinder fine motor skills, such as grasping and coloring within lines, and gross motor skills, such as running and climbing. They may, with considerable guidance and practice, be able to learn to travel alone in a familiar locality. Many live in institutions, but most live dependently within the family or in supervised group homes.

- **Severe Mental Retardation** (20–25 to 35–40 IQ). Of those people with IQs less than 70, about 3 to 4 percent come under the category of severe mental retardation. These people commonly have congenital physical abnormalities and limited sensorimotor control. Most are institutionalized and require constant aid and supervision. Adults with severe retardation may be friendly but usually can communicate only briefly on a very concrete level. They engage in little independent activity and are often lethargic, for their severe brain damage leaves them relatively passive, and the circumstances of their lives allow them little stimulation. They may be able to perform very simple work under close supervision.

- **Profound Mental Retardation** (below 20–25 IQ). Only 1 to 2 percent of people with mental retardation are classified as having profound mental retardation, requiring total supervision and often nursing care all their lives. Most have severe physical deformities as well as neurological damage and cannot get around on their own. The mortality rate during childhood for people with profound mental retardation is very high.

The Approach of the American Association of Mental Retardation

We turn now to a very different approach to mental retardation, which is being followed by increasing numbers of professionals. In the ninth edition of its classification system, the American Association of Mental Retardation (AAMR, 1992) shifted its focus from identifying severity of disability to determining what remedial steps are necessary to facilitate higher functioning. Professionals are now encouraged to identify an individual's strengths and weaknesses on psychological, physical, and environmental dimensions with a view toward determining the kinds and intensities of supports needed to enhance the person's functioning in different domains. The approach focuses more on what people *can* do than on what they cannot do and directs professional attention to how best to make positive changes in the person's life.

The AAMR approach encourages a more individualized assessment of a person's skills and needs. For example, a survey of over 200 people with severe mental retardation (IQs between 20 and 40) found that these individuals varied greatly in their communication skills, with some communicating only through nonverbal signals that could seldom be interpreted by caregivers and others able to combine symbols (through spoken words, manual signs, or communication boards) to make their needs known (McLean, Brady, & McLean, 1996).

As an example of the AAMR approach to classification, consider Roger, a twenty-four-year-old man with an IQ of 45 who has attended a special program for mentally retarded children since he was six. According to the DSM, he would be considered moderately mentally retarded. Based on this diagnosis he would not be expected to be able to live independently, get around on his own, or progress beyond second grade. The AAMR classification system, however, would emphasize what is needed to maximize Roger's functioning. Thus, a clinician might discover that Roger can use the bus system if he takes a route familiar to him, and thus he might be able to go to a movie by himself from time to time. And although he cannot prepare complicated meals, he might be able to learn to prepare frozen entrées in a microwave oven. The assumption is that by concentrating and building on what he can do, Roger will make more progress.

In the schools, an individualized placement is based on the person's strengths and weaknesses and on the amount of instruction needed. A student who needs considerable one-on-one instruction because of deficient intellectual functioning may be placed in the same classroom with a child who needs intensive instruction because of emotional problems or physical disabilities. Students are identified by the classroom environment they are judged to need. This approach can lessen the stigmatizing effects of being considered retarded and may also encourage a focus on what can be done to improve the student's learning rather than on how to label the child.

Etiology of Mental Retardation

In only 25 percent of the population with mental retardation can the primary cause be identified at this time. Those specific causes that can be identified are typically biological.

No Identifiable Etiology   Persons with mild or moderate mental retardation do not, as far as is known at this time, have an identifiable brain defect. And whereas persons whose mental retardation is associated with identifiable biological impairments are found in much the same percentages throughout all socioeconomic, ethnic, and racial groups, those with mild or moderate mental retardation are overrepresented in the lower socioeconomic classes, suggesting that certain social conditions of deprivation are major factors in retarding their intellectual and behavioral development.

Baumeister, Kupstas, and Klindworth (1991) have suggested several classes of variables that might act in concert to produce milder forms of mental retardation. These include predisposing variables (diatheses), such as undetermined genetic factors, and resource variables, such as educational and health-care resources. Consider two persons with the same biological brain impairment, so subtle as to be undetectable by the neurological methods currently available. One youngster comes from a higher socioeconomic level, the other from a lower level. The first individual's slight deficit could be compensated for by the enriched social and educational environment made possible by the family's financial resources. In contrast, the second individual's deficit might be exaggerated by impoverished circumstances. To show signs of retardation, a socially advantaged person would have to have more extensive damage, which is less responsive to or even impervious to help from an enriched upbringing.

Known Biological Etiology   As just noted, about 25 percent of people have mental retardation for which there is a known biological cause. These individuals create what is referred to as a bump at the far left end of the normal curve, as shown in Figure 15.4. The bump indicates that the prevalence of mental retardation at this point in the curve is greater

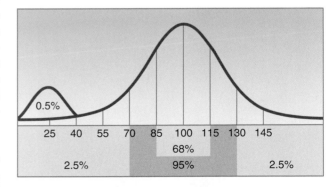

Figure 15.4   Normal curve showing the theoretical distribution of IQ scores. The bump on the left represents the actual frequency of severe and profound retardation with biological causes.

Child with Down syndrome.

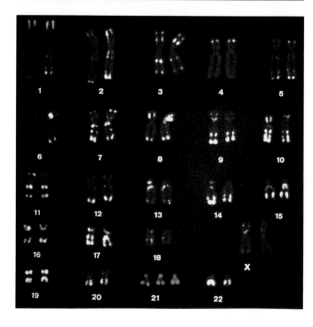

than would be statistically expected. Causes of impairment include genetic factors, infectious diseases, accidents, and environmental hazards.

Genetic or Chromosomal Anomalies   Chromosomal abnormalities occur in just under 5 percent of all recognized pregnancies. The majority of these pregnancies end in spontaneous abortions or miscarriages. In all, about one-half of 1 percent of the babies who are born have a chromosomal abnormality (Smith, Bierman, & Robinson, 1978). A significant proportion of these infants die soon after birth. Of the babies who survive, the majority have **Down syndrome**, or **trisomy 21**. Down syndrome is found in approximately one in 800 to 1,200 live births.

People with Down syndrome have moderate to severe retardation as well as several distinctive physical signs, such as short and stocky stature; oval, upward-slanting eyes; a prolongation of the fold of the upper eyelid over the inner corner of the eye; sparse, fine, straight hair; a wide and flat nasal bridge; square-shaped ears; a large, furrowed tongue, which protrudes because the mouth is small and its roof low; and short, broad hands with stubby fingers.

About 40 percent of children with Down syndrome have heart problems; a small minority may have blockages of the upper intestinal tract; and about one in six dies during the first year. Mortality after age forty is high. At autopsy, brain tissue generally shows deterioration similar to that in Alzheimer's disease (p. 525). Despite having mental retardation, some of these children learn to read, write, and do arithmetic.

Down syndrome is named after the British physician Langdon Down, who first described its clinical signs in 1866. In 1959 the French geneticist Jerome Lejeune and his colleagues identified its genetic basis. Human beings normally possess forty-six chromosomes, inheriting twenty-three from each parent. Individuals with Down syndrome almost always have forty-seven chromosomes instead of forty-six. During maturation of the egg, the two chromosomes of pair 21, the smallest ones, fail to separate. If the egg unites with a sperm, there will be three of chromosome 21—thus the technical term trisomy 21.

Another chromosomal disease that can cause mental retardation is **fragile X syndrome**, in which the X chromosome breaks in two. Fragile X is the second leading cause, after Down syndrome, of mental retardation with a chromosomal basis (Dykens et al., 1988). Physical symptoms associated with fragile X include facial features such as large, underdeveloped ears, a long, thin face, and a broad nasal root. In males, the testicles may be enlarged. Recent studies using DNA testing of individuals with the fragile X genotype have provided evidence for a spectrum of dysfunction in individuals with different forms of fragile X (Hagerman, 1995). Many such individuals exhibit mental retardation and behavior problems. Others have normal IQ but show problems such as learning disabilities, difficulties with frontal-lobe and right-hemisphere tasks, and mood lability. It is believed that some cases of autistic disorder (p. 506) are caused by a form of fragile X. Some individuals with fragile X have very few problems but have been found to have social difficulties, such as shyness or poor eye contact (Dykens et al., 1988).

Recessive-Gene Diseases   Several hundred recessive-gene diseases have been identified, and many of them cause mental retardation. Genetic counseling can help future parents determine whether their backgrounds suggest that they are at risk for carrying certain of these recessive genes. Here we discuss one recessive-gene disease, phenylketonuria.

(Top) The normal complement of chromosomes is 23 pairs; (Bottom) in Down syndrome there is a trisomy of chromosome 21.

In **phenylketonuria (PKU)** the infant, born normal, soon suffers from a deficiency of a liver enzyme, phenylalanine hydroxylase. This enzyme is needed to convert phenylalanine, an amino acid contained in protein, to tyrosine, an amino acid that is essential for the development of such hormones as epinephrine. Because of this enzyme deficiency, phenylalanine and its derivative phenylpyruvic acid are not broken down and instead build up in the body's fluids. This buildup eventually causes irreversible brain damage because the unmetabolized amino acid interferes with the process of myelination, the sheathing of neuron axons, which is essential for the rapid transmittal of impulses and thus of information. The neurons of the frontal lobes, the site of many important mental functions, such as rational decision making, are particularly affected, so mental retardation is profound.

Although PKU is rare, with an incidence of about one in 14,000 live births, it is estimated that one person in seventy is a carrier of the recessive gene. A blood test is available for prospective parents who have reason to suspect that they might be carriers. Pregnant women who carry the recessive gene must monitor their diet closely so that the fetus will not be exposed to toxic levels of phenylalanine (Baumeister & Baumeister, 1995). State laws require testing newborns for PKU. After the newborn with PKU has consumed milk for several days, an excess amount of unconverted phenylalanine can be detected in the blood. If the test is positive, the parents are urged to provide the infant a diet low in phenylalanine.

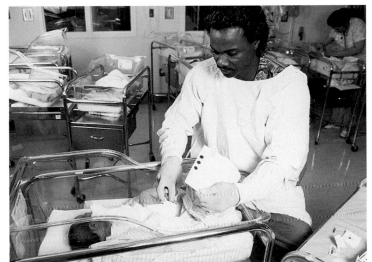

States require that newborns be tested for PKU. If excess phenylalanine is found in the blood, a special diet is recommended for the baby.

Although early guidelines suggested restricting the diets of such children from three months to six years of age (Collaborative Study of Children Treated for Phenylketonuria, 1975), parents are now encouraged to introduce the special diet as early as possible and to maintain it indefinitely. Studies have indicated that children whose dietary restrictions stop at age five to seven begin to show subtle declines in functioning, particularly in IQ, reading, and spelling (Fishler et al., 1987; Legido et al., 1993). Even among children with PKU who maintain the diet, however, deficits in perceptual, memory, and attentional abilities have been observed (e.g., Banich et al., 2000; Huijbregts et al., 2002; Smith, Klim, & Hanley, 2000).

Infectious Diseases   While in utero the fetus is at increased risk of mental retardation resulting from maternal infectious diseases such as rubella (German measles). The consequences of these diseases are most serious during the first trimester of pregnancy, when the fetus has no detectable immunological response, that is, its immune system is not developed enough to ward off infection. Cytomegalovirus, toxoplasmosis, rubella, herpes simplex, and syphilis are all maternal infections that can cause both physical deformities and mental retardation of the fetus. The mother may experience slight or no symptoms from the infection, but the effects on the developing fetus can be devastating. Pregnant women who go to prenatal clinics are given a blood test for syphilis. Women today can also have their blood tested to determine whether they are immune to rubella; nearly 85 percent of American women are. Women who are not immune are advised to be vaccinated at least six months before becoming pregnant. If a fetus contracts rubella from the mother, the child is likely to be born with brain lesions that cause mental retardation.

HIV infection (cf. p. 223) has become a significant cause of mental retardation. When not treated for HIV infection during pregnancy and delivery, an HIV-positive woman is more likely to pass on the virus to the developing fetus, and about half these infected infants develop mental retardation. Some develop normally at first but decline in cognitive and motor functioning as their HIV condition worsens; some remain HIV infected for many years without any impairment in intelligence.

Infectious diseases can also affect a child's developing brain after birth. Encephalitis and meningococcal meningitis may cause irreversible brain damage and even death if

Although lead-based paint is now illegal, it can still be found in older homes. Eating these paint chips can cause lead poisoning and mental retardation.

contracted in infancy or early childhood. These infections in adulthood are usually far less serious, probably because the brain is largely developed by about age six. There are several forms of childhood meningitis, a disease in which the protective membranes of the brain are acutely inflamed and fever is very high. Some children who survive without severe retardation may become mildly to moderately retarded. Other disabling after-effects are deafness, paralysis, and epilepsy.

Accidents   In the United States accidents are the leading cause of severe disability and death in children over one year of age. Falls, near drownings, and automobile accidents are among the most common mishaps in early childhood and may cause varying degrees of head injuries and mental retardation. The institution of laws mandating that children riding in automobiles wear seat belts and that they wear protective helmets when bicycling may play a major role in reducing the incidence of mental retardation in children.

Environmental Hazards   Several environmental pollutants can cause poisoning and mental retardation. One such pollutant is mercury, which may be ingested by eating affected fish. Another is lead, which is found in lead-based paints, smog, and the exhaust from automobiles that burn leaded gasoline. Lead poisoning can cause kidney and brain damage as well as anemia, mental retardation, seizures, and death. Lead-based paint is now prohibited in the United States, but it is still found in older homes, where it may be flaking and may be picked up and eaten by curious tykes.

Prevention and Treatment of Mental Retardation

In the early part of the twentieth century many large institutions were built in the United States to house retarded individuals apart from the rest of the population. Most were no more than warehouses for anyone unfortunate enough to do poorly on newly constructed intelligence tests (Blatt, 1966). The majority of residents were recently arrived immigrants, members of racial minorities, children with physical disabilities, and indigents.

Although conditions have improved somewhat in the United States, children with mental retardation are still warehoused in many parts of the world. For example, in Russia, the old Soviet ideal of "perfect children" continues to encourage parents to give up their disabled children to the care—actually neglect—of state-run institutions (Bennett, 1997).

Prevention of mental retardation depends on understanding its causes. The field of medical genetics is not yet equipped to prevent the more severe genetic causes of mental retardation, but startling advances in genetics may change this situation in the not-too-distant future. When the causes of mental retardation are unknown, prevention is not possible, but treatment to improve the person's ability to live on his or her own is an option. When an impoverished environment is the source of mild retardation, enrichment programs, such as Head Start, can prevent further deficits and sometimes even overcome existing ones.

Residential Treatment   Since the 1960s there have been serious and systematic attempts to educate children with mental retardation as fully as possible. Most people with mental retardation can acquire the competence needed to function effectively in the community. The trend has been to provide these individuals with educational and community services rather than largely custodial care in big mental hospitals.

Since 1975, individuals with mental retardation have had a right to appropriate treatment in the least restrictive setting. Ideally, adults with moderate retardation live in small- to medium-sized homelike residences that are integrated into the community. Medical care is provided, and trained, live-in supervisors and aides attend to the residents' special needs around the clock. Residents are encouraged to participate in the household routines to the best of their abilities. Many adults with mild retardation have jobs and are able to live independently in their own apartments. Others live semi-independently in apartments housing three to four retarded adults, with the aid of a counselor generally provided in the evening. Severely retarded children may live at home or in foster-care homes provided with educational and psychological services. Only people with severe and profound retardation and with physical disabilities tend to remain in institutions (Cunningham & Mueller, 1991).

Behavioral Interventions Based on Operant Conditioning   Whereas programs such as Head Start can help prevent mild mental retardation in disadvantaged children, other early-intervention programs using cognitive and behavioral techniques have been developed to improve the level of functioning of individuals with more serious retardation. Several pilot projects have intervened with children with Down syndrome during infancy and early childhood to attempt to improve their functioning. These programs typically include systematic home- and treatment-center-based instruction in language skills, fine and gross motor skills, self-care, and social development. Specific behavioral objectives are defined; and in an operant fashion, children are taught skills in small, sequential steps (e.g., Clunies-Ross, 1979; Reid, Wilson, & Faw, 1991).

Children with severe mental retardation usually need intensive instruction to be able to feed, toilet, and groom themselves. To teach a severely retarded child a particular routine, the therapist usually begins by analyzing and dividing the targeted behavior, such as eating, into smaller components: pick up spoon, scoop food from plate onto spoon, bring spoon to mouth, remove food with lips, chew and swallow food. Operant-conditioning principles are then applied to teach the child these components of eating. For example, the child may be reinforced for successive approximations to picking up the spoon until he or she is able to do so.

This operant approach, sometimes called **applied behavior analysis**,[3] is also used to reduce inappropriate and self-injurious behavior. Children with severe and profound mental impairment who live in institutions are especially prone to stereotyped behaviors performed in isolation—repetitive, rhythmic, self-stimulatory motions, such as rocking back and forth, swaying, rolling the head—and to aggression against the self or toward other children and staff. These maladaptive movements and injurious actions can often be reduced by reinforcing substitute responses.

Studies of these programs indicate consistent improvements in fine motor skills, acceptance by others, and self-help skills. However, the programs appear to have little effect on gross motor skills and linguistic abilities, and no long-term improvements in IQ or school performance have been demonstrated. It is not yet clear whether the benefits of the programs are greater than what parents can provide in the home without special training (Gibson & Harris, 1988).

The significance of learning self-care and of reducing stereotyped and injurious actions in people with severe or profound retardation must be recognized. Toilet-trained children, for example, are more comfortable, are liked better by the staff and by other children, and can leave the ward for other rooms and leave the building to play on the grounds. Mastering toilet training and learning to feed and dress themselves may even mean that children with mental retardation can live at home. Most people with mental retardation face discrimination from others, based in part on violations of social norms. Being able to act more normally increases their chances of interacting meaningfully with others. Moreover, the self-esteem that comes from learning to take better care of themselves is extremely bolstering.

Cognitive Interventions   Many children with mental retardation fail to use strategies in solving problems, and when they do have strategies, they often do not apply them effectively. **Self-instructional training** teaches these children to guide their problem-solving efforts through speech. Meichenbaum and Goodman (1971) outlined a five-step procedure.

1. The teacher performs the task, speaking instructions aloud to himself or herself while the child watches and listens.
2. The child listens and performs the task while the teacher says instructions to the child.

---

[3] In the behavioral literature on mental retardation, this term is used more frequently than operant conditioning. The two terms refer to the same kinds of assessments and interventions.

3. The child repeats the task while giving himself or herself instructions aloud.
4. The child repeats the task again while whispering the instructions.
5. Finally, the child is ready to perform the task while uttering instructions silently to himself or herself.

Children with more severe retardation use signs rather than speech to guide themselves through the tasks.

Self-instructional training has been employed to teach retarded children self-control and how to pay attention as well as how to master academic tasks. Children with severe retardation can effectively master self-help skills through this technique. For example, Hughes, Hugo, and Blatt (1996) taught high school students with IQs below 40 to make their own buttered toast and clean up after themselves. A teacher would demonstrate and verbalize the steps to solve a problem, such as the toaster's being upside down or unplugged. The young people learned to talk themselves through the steps using simple verbal or signed instructions. For example, when the toaster was presented upside down, the person would be taught to first state the problem ("Won't go in"), state the response ("Turn it"), self-evaluate ("Fixed it"), and self-reinforce ("Good"). They were rewarded with praise and high fives when they verbalized and solved the problem correctly. Several studies have demonstrated that even individuals with severe mental retardation can learn self-instructional approaches to problem solving and then generalize the strategy to new tasks, including taking lunch orders at a cafeteria and performing janitorial duties (Hughes & Agran, 1993).

Computer-assisted instruction is well suited for applications in the field of mental retardation.

Computer-Assisted Instruction Computer-assisted instruction is increasingly found in educational settings of all kinds; it may be especially well suited to the education of individuals with mental retardation. The visual and auditory components of computers maintain the attention of distractible students; the level of the material can be geared to the individual, ensuring successful experiences; and the computer can meet the need for numerous repetitions of material without becoming bored or impatient as a human teacher might. Computer-assisted instruction programs have been shown to be superior to traditional methods for teaching people with mental retardation spelling, money handling, arithmetic, text reading, word recognition, handwriting, and visual discrimination (Conners, Caruso, & Detterman, 1986).

Autistic Disorder

Imagine that you are walking into a special-education classroom for children. You are taking a course on child disabilities, and one of the requirements is to volunteer some time in this class. You notice a child in the room. He is standing in front of the fish tank. As you approach him, you notice his graceful, deft movements, the dreamy, remote look in his eyes. You wonder if he is a visitor to the class or a sibling of one of the students. You start talking to him about the fish. Instead of acknowledging your comment, or even your presence, he begins rocking back and forth while continuing to smile, as if enjoying a private joke. When the teacher enters the room, your first question is about the boy at the fish tank. She tells you that he has autistic disorder.

Characteristics of Autistic Disorder

From the time it was first distinguished, **autistic disorder** has had a somewhat mystical aura. The syndrome was identified in 1943 by a psychiatrist at Harvard, Leo Kanner, who noticed in the course of his clinical work that eleven disturbed children behaved in ways that were not common in children with mental retardation or schizophrenia. He named the syndrome early infantile autism because he observed that "there is from the start an extreme autistic aloneness that, whenever possible, disregards, ignores, shuts out anything that comes to the child from the outside" (Kanner, 1943).

Kanner considered autistic aloneness the most fundamental symptom. He also found that these eleven children had been unable from the beginning of life to relate to people in the ordinary way. They were severely limited in language and had a strong obsessive desire for everything about them to remain exactly the same. Despite its early description by Kanner and others (e.g., Rimland, 1964), the disorder was not accepted into official diagnostic nomenclature until the publication of DSM-III in 1980.

Official acceptance of the diagnosis of autism was delayed by general confusion in the classification of serious disorders that begin in childhood. DSM-II used the diagnosis of childhood schizophrenia for these conditions, implying that autism was simply an early-onset form of adult schizophrenia, but the available evidence indicates that childhood-onset schizophrenia and autism are separate disorders (Frith, 1989; Rutter & Schopler, 1987). Although the social withdrawal and inappropriate affect seen in autistic children may appear similar to the negative symptoms of schizophrenia, autistic children do not exhibit hallucinations and delusions and, above all, do not develop schizophrenia as adults (Wing & Attwood, 1987). Further, people with autism do not have a higher prevalence of schizophrenia in their families, as do children and adults with schizophrenia. Other features associated with autism but not with schizophrenia include a higher male–female ratio (more boys than girls have autism), onset in infancy or very early childhood, and co-occurrence of mental retardation and epileptic seizures.

Autistic disorder begins in early childhood and can be evident in the first months of life. It occurs infrequently in the general population, in two to five infants in 10,000, or 0.05 percent of births. To put this in perspective, recall that the prevalence of schizophrenia is estimated at a little less than 1 percent, almost twenty times greater. Studies show that about four times more boys than girls have autism (Volkmar, Szatmari, & Sparrow, 1993). For reasons still unknown, there has been a very large increase in the incidence of autism over the past 25 years—up close to 300% in California, for example (Maugh, 2002). Autism is found in all socioeconomic classes and in all ethnic and racial groups.

In part to clarify the differentiation of autism from schizophrenia, DSM-III introduced (and DSM-III-R, DSM-IV, and DSM-IV-TR have retained) the term **pervasive developmental disorders**. This term emphasized that autism involves a serious abnormality in the developmental process itself and thus differs from the mental disorders that originate in adulthood. In DSM-IV-TR autistic disorder is but one of several pervasive developmental disorders; the others are Rett's disorder, child disintegrative disorder, and Asperger's disorder.

- Rett's disorder is very rare and found only in girls. Development is entirely normal until the first or second year of life, when the child's head growth decelerates. She loses the ability to use her hands for purposeful movements, instead engaging in stereotyped movements such as hand-wringing or hand washing; walks in an uncoordinated manner; learns only poorly to speak and understand others; and is profoundly retarded. The child does not relate well to others, though this may improve later in life.

- Childhood disintegrative disorder occurs in children who have had normal development in the first two years of life followed by significant loss of social, play, language, and motor skills. Abnormalities in social interaction and communication, and the presence of stereotyped behavior are very similar to those in autism.

- Asperger's disorder is often regarded as a mild form of autism. Social relationships are poor and stereotyped behavior is intense and rigid, but language and intelligence are intact.

Unfortunately, there is very little research on these three categories. In addition, there has been considerable debate concerning the validity of childhood disintegrative disorder and whether it is distinct from autistic disorder (Hendry, 2000). It is also not clear if

DSM-IV TR Criteria for Autistic Disorder

- A total of six or more items from A, B, and C below, with at least two from A and one each from B and C:

  A. Impairment in social interactions as manifested by at least two of the following:
  —Marked impairment in use of nonverbal behaviors such as eye contact, facial expression, body language
  —Deficit in development of peer relationships appropriate to developmental level
  —Lack of spontaneous sharing of things or activities with others
  —Lack of social or emotional reciprocity

  B. Impairment in communication as manifested by at least one of the following:
  —Delay in or total lack of spoken language without attempts to compensate by nonverbal gestures
  —In those who have some speech, marked impairment in ability to initiate or sustain a conversation with another
  —Repetitious or idiosyncratic language
  —Lack of developmentally appropriate play

  C. Repetitive or stereotyped behaviors or interests, manifested by at least one of the following:
  —Abnormal preoccupation with objects or activities
  —Rigid adherence to certain rituals
  —Stereotyped mannerisms
  —Abnormal preoccupation with parts of objects

- Delays or abnormal functioning in at least one of the following areas, beginning before age 3: social interactions, language for communication with others, or imaginative play

- Disturbance not better described as Rett's disorder or childhood disintegrative disorder

Asperger's disorder differs qualitatively from autistic disorder or if it differs only in severity. Because of these limitations, we focus here on autism.

Autism and Mental Retardation   Approximately 80 percent of autistic children score below 70 on standardized intelligence tests. Because a significant number of children with autism also have mental retardation, it is sometimes difficult to differentiate the two disabilities.

There are important differences, however. Although children with mental retardation usually score poorly on all parts of an intelligence test, the scores of children with autism may have a differentiated pattern. Generally, children with autism do worse on tasks requiring abstract thought, symbolism, or sequential logic, all of which may be associated with their language deficits (Carpentieri & Morgan, 1994). They usually obtain better scores on items requiring visual-spatial skills, such as matching designs in block-design tests and putting together disassembled objects (Rutter, 1983). Sometimes they may have isolated skills that reflect great talent, such as the ability to multiply two four-digit numbers rapidly in their heads. They may also have exceptional long-term memory, being able to recall the exact words of a song heard years earlier. Sensorimotor development is the area of greatest relative strength among children with autism. These children, who may show severe and profound deficits in cognitive abilities, can be quite graceful and adept at swinging, climbing, or balancing, whereas children with mental retardation are much more delayed in areas of gross-motor development, such as learning to walk.

Social and Emotional Disturbances   We mentioned earlier that autistic aloneness is a central part of the disorder. In a sense, autistic children do not withdraw from society—they never fully joined it to begin with. Table 15.4 shows how such children have been described by their parents.

Normally infants show signs of attachment, usually to their mothers, as early as three months of age. In children with autism this early attachment is less pronounced. Parents

Table 15.4 Parental Report of Social Relatedness in Autistic Children before Age Six

	Percentages of Responses				
Relatedness Measure	Never	Rarely	Often	Very Often	Almost Always
1. Ignored people	0	4	22	29	45
2. Emotionally distant	0	8	23	19	50
3. Avoided eye contact	2	4	20	16	58
4. No affection or interest when held	11	11	35	26	17
5. Going limp when held	30	33	17	17	2
6. Stiff/rigid when held	33	24	7	18	18
7. Ignored affection	6	30	34	11	19
8. Withdrew from affection	12	33	29	10	15
9. Cuddling when held	26	24	29	10	15
10. Accept/return affection	30	34	26	4	6
11. Looked through people	4	10	22	22	41
12. Seemed not to need mother	12	20	32	8	28
13. Responsive smile to mother	14	30	30	14	12
14. Unaware of mother's absence	17	25	25	14	19

Source: Adapted from F. R. Volkmar, D. J. Cohen, and R. Paul, 1986. "An Evaluation of DSM-III Criteria for Infantile Autism," *Journal of the American Academy of Child Psychiatry, 25,* p. 193. Copyright © 1986 by the American Academy of Child Psychiatry. Adapted by permission.

of autistic children must work harder to make contact and share affection with their babies. Autistic children rarely try to engage their parents in play, and they do not point to, show, or share objects of play with others.

Children with autism appear to have profound social-skills problems. They rarely approach others and may look through or past people or turn their backs on them. For example, one study found that autistic children rarely offered a spontaneous greeting or farewell, either verbally or through smiling, making eye contact, or gesturing, when meeting or departing from an adult (Hobson & Lee, 1998). Few children with autism initiate play with other children, and they are usually unresponsive to any who may approach them. Children with autism do sometimes make eye contact, but their gaze has an unusual quality. Typically developing children gaze to gain someone's attention or to direct the other person's attention to an object; children with autism generally do not (Mirenda, Donnellan, & Yoder, 1983). They just stare.

When play is initiated by someone else, autistic children may be compliant and engage in the selected activity for a period of time. Physical play, such as tickling and wrestling, may not be enjoyable to children with autism. Observations of their spontaneous play in an unstructured setting reveal that children with autism spend much less of their time engaged in symbolic play, such as making a doll drive to the store or pretending that a block is a car, than do either mentally retarded or normal children of comparable mental age (Sigman et al., 1987). Autistic children are more likely to twirl a favorite block continually for hours on end.

Some autistic children appear not to recognize or distinguish one person from another. However, they become preoccupied with and form strong attachments to inanimate objects (e.g., keys, rocks, a wire-mesh basket, light switches, a large blanket) and to mechanical objects (e.g., refrigerators and vacuum cleaners). If the object is something they can carry, they may walk around with it in their hands, thus preventing them from learning to do more useful things.

Recently some researchers have proposed that the autistic child's deficient "theory of mind" represents the core deficit and leads to the kinds of social dysfunctions we have described here (Gopnik, Capps, & Meltzoff, 2000; Sigman, 1994). Theory of mind refers to our understanding that other people have desires, beliefs, intentions, and emotions that may be different from our own. This ability is crucial for social interaction and understanding. Among typically developing children, theory of mind develops between two and one-half and five years of age. In contrast to children whose development follows this path, children with autism seem unable to understand others' perspectives and emotional reactions, leading some theorists to suggest that they lack empathy. Thus, for example, when a parent shows distress or pain, the child with autism withdraws rather than showing concern; this withdrawal may indicate the child's inability to understand and empathize with another's feelings.

Although high-functioning autistic children can learn to understand emotional experiences, they "answer questions about…emotional experiences like normal children answer difficult arithmetic questions" (Sigman, 1994, p. 15), with concentrated cognitive effort. Laboratory studies of children with high-functioning autism have found that although these children may exhibit surface level understanding of others' emotions, they do not fully understand why and how others feel different emotions (Capps et al., 1992, 1999; Rasco & Capps, 2001). For example, when asked to explain why someone might feel angry, a child with autism responded "because he was yelling" (Capps, Losh, & Thurber, 2000; Rasco & Capps, 2001).

Theory of mind problems may indeed be central to autism, but they may not be unique to this disorder. A recent review of theory of mind deficits among children with autism found that these deficits were also found among children who did not have autism but did have mental retardation (Yirmiya, Erel, Shaked, & Solomonica-Levi, 1998).

Communication Deficits   Even before they acquire language, autistic children show deficits in communication. Babbling, a term describing the utterances of infants before they actually begin to use words, is less frequent in infants with autism and conveys less information than it does in other infants (Ricks, 1972). By two years of age, most typically developing children use words to represent objects in their surroundings and construct one- and two-word sentences to express more complex thoughts, such as "Mommy go" or "Me juice." About 50 percent of all autistic children never learn to speak at all (Paul, 1987). The speech of those who do learn includes various peculiarities.

One such feature is **echolalia**, in which the child echoes, usually with remarkable fidelity, what he or she has heard another person say. The teacher may ask an autistic child, "Do you want a cookie?" The child's response may be "Do you want a cookie?" This is immediate echolalia. In delayed echolalia the child may be in a room with the television on and appear to be completely uninterested. Several hours later or even the next day, the child may echo a word or phrase from the television program. Mute autistic children who later acquire some functional speech through training usually first pass through a stage of echolalia.

In the past, most educators and researchers believed that echolalia served no functional purpose. Echolalia may, however, be an attempt to communicate (Prizant, 1983). The child who was offered a cookie may decide later that he or she does want one. The child will approach the teacher and ask, "Do you want a cookie?" Although the child may not know what each individual word means, he or she has learned that the words used earlier by the adult are connected with getting a cookie.

Another language abnormality common in the speech of autistic children is **pronoun reversal**. Children refer to themselves as "he," "she," or "you" or by their own proper names. Pronoun reversal is closely linked to echolalia. Since autistic children often use echolalic speech, they refer to themselves as they have heard others speak of them and misapply pronouns. For example:

> **Parent:** What are you doing, Johnny?
> **Child:** He's here.
> **Parent:** Are you having a good time?
> **Child:** He knows it.

If speech continues to develop more normally, this pronoun reversal might be expected to disappear. In many instances, however, it is highly resistant to change (Tramontana & Stimbert, 1970). Some children have required very extensive training even after they have stopped parroting the phrases of other people.

Neologisms, made-up words or words used in unusual ways, are another characteristic of the speech of autistic children. A two-year-old autistic child might refer to milk as "moyee" and continue to do so well beyond the time when a normal child has learned to say "milk."

Children with autism are very literal in their use of words. If a father provided positive reinforcement by putting the child on his shoulders when he or she learned to say the word yes, then the child might say "yes" to mean that he or she wants to be lifted onto the father's shoulders. Or the child may say, "Do not drop the cat" to mean "no," because his or her mother had used these emphatic words when the child was about to drop the family feline.

These communication deficiencies may be the source of the social deficits in children with autism rather than the other way around. Such a causal relationship is made plausible by the often spontaneous appearance of affectionate and dependent behavior in these children after they have been trained to speak. Even after they learn to speak, however, people with autism often lack verbal spontaneity and are sparse in their verbal expression and not always appropriate in their use of language (Paul, 1987).

Repetitive and Ritualistic Acts   Children with autism can become extremely upset over changes in their daily routines and surroundings. An offer of milk in a different drinking cup or a rearrangement of furniture may make them cry or precipitate a temper tantrum. One child had to be greeted with the set phrase "Good morning, Lily, I am very, very glad to see you." If any word, even one "very," was omitted, or another added, the child would begin to scream (Diamond, Baldwin, & Diamond, 1963).

An obsessional quality pervades the behavior of autistic children in other ways as well. In their play they may continually line up toys or construct intricate patterns with household objects. As they grow older, they may become preoccupied with train schedules, subway routes, and number sequences. Children with autism are also likely to perform a more limited number of behaviors and are less likely to explore new areas or surroundings.

Children with autism are also given to stereotypical behavior, peculiar ritualistic hand movements, and other rhythmic movements, such as endless body rocking, hand flapping, and walking on tiptoe. They spin and twirl string, crayons, sticks, and plates, twiddle their fingers in front of their eyes, and stare at fans and spinning things. These are often described as self-stimulatory activities. They may become preoccupied with manipulating a mechanical object and may become very upset when interrupted.

Prognosis for Autistic Disorder   What happens to such severely disturbed children when they reach adulthood? Kanner (1973) reported on the adult status of nine of the eleven children whom he had described in his original paper on autism. Two developed epileptic seizures; one of these died, and the other was in a state mental hospital. Four others had spent most of their lives in institutions. Of the remaining three, one was still mute but was working on a farm and as an orderly in a nursing home. The other two had made satisfactory recoveries. Although both still lived with their parents and had little social life, they were gainfully employed and had developed some recreational interests.

Other follow-up studies corroborate this generally gloomy picture of adults with autism (e.g., Lotter, 1974; Rutter, 1967; Treffert, McAndrew, & Dreifuerst, 1973). From his review of all published studies, Lotter (1978) concluded that only 5 to 17 percent of autistic children had made a relatively good adjustment in adulthood, leading independent lives but with some residual problems, such as social awkwardness. Most of the others led limited lives, and about half were institutionalized.

Similar outcomes have been found in more recent population-based, follow-up studies (Gillberg, 1991; Nordin & Gilberg, 1998; von Knorring & Hagglof, 1993). Generally, children with higher IQs who learned to speak before age six have the best outcomes, and a few of these function nearly normally in adulthood. Follow-up studies focusing on non–mentally retarded, high-functioning autistic individuals have indicated that most do not require residential care and some are able to attend college and support themselves through employment (Yirmiya & Sigman, 1991). Still, many independently functioning adults with autism continue to show impairment in social relationships (Howlin, Mawhood, & Rutter, 2001). Focus on Discovery 15.5 describes an autistic woman whose adult life is remarkable for its professional distinction blended with autistic social and emotional deficits.

Prior to the passage of the Developmentally Disabled Assistance and Bill of Rights Act in 1975, children with autism were often excluded from educational programs in the public schools. Thus most of the autistic children followed into adulthood had not had the benefit of intensive educational interventions or behavioral programs. Additional follow-up studies are needed to determine whether the prognosis for autism will remain as universally devastating as it was before the training and education of people with autism were taken seriously by society (Howlin & Goode, 1998).

Autistic children frequently engage in stereotyped behavior, such as ritualistic hand movements.

Etiology of Autistic Disorder

The earliest theorizing about the etiology of autism was that it was psychogenic, that is, that psychological factors were responsible for its development. This narrow and faulty perspective has been replaced in recent years by evidence supporting the importance of biological factors, some of them genetic, in the etiology of this puzzling syndrome.

Psychological Bases   Some of the same reasons that led Kanner to believe that autistic children were of average intelligence—their normal appearance and apparently normal physiological functioning—led early theorists to mistakenly discount the importance of biological factors. People may have tacitly assumed that for a biological cause to underlie something as devastating as autism, it would have other obvious signs, such as the physical stigmata of Down syndrome. Thus the early focus was on psychological factors, primarily family influences very early in life.

The Story of a High-Functioning Autistic Woman

Temple Grandin is an autistic woman. She also has a Ph.D. in animal science, runs her own business designing machinery for use with farm animals, and is on the faculty at Colorado State University. Two autobiographical books (Grandin, 1986, 1995) and a profile by neurologist Oliver Sacks (1995) provide a moving and revealing portrait of the perplexities of autism.

Lacking understanding of the complexities and subtleties of human social intercourse, deficient in ability to empathize with others, Grandin sums up her relationship to the nonautistic world saying, "Much of the time I feel like an anthropologist on Mars" (Sacks, 1995, p. 259). Because of her high level of intellectual functioning, the diagnosis of Asperger's syndrome might be applicable. Controversy exists, however, as to whether this should be a separate diagnostic entity or viewed as a less severe form of autism.

Grandin recalls from her childhood sudden impulsive behavior and violent rages, as well as a hyperfocus of attention, "a selectivity so intense that it could create a world of its own, a place of calm and order in the chaos and tumult" (Sacks, 1995, p. 254). She describes "sensations heightened, sometimes to an excruciating degree [and] she speaks of her ears, at the age of 2 or 3, as helpless microphones, transmitting everything, irrespective of relevance, at full, overwhelming volume" (Sacks, 1995, p. 254).

Diagnosed with autism at age three, Grandin had no speech at all, and doctors predicted that institutionalization would be her fate. With the help of a therapeutic nursery school and speech therapy and with the support of her family, she learned to speak by age six and began to make more contact with others. Still, as an adolescent observing other children interact, Grandin "sometimes wondered if they were all telepathic" (Sacks, 1995, p. 272), so mysterious did she find the ability of normal youngsters to understand each other's needs and wishes, to empathize, to communicate.

Visiting her one day at her university, Sacks made several observations that convey the autistic flavor of this uncommon person.

She sat me down [in her office] with little ceremony, no preliminaries, no social niceties, no small talk about my trip or how I liked Colorado. She plunged straight into talking of her work, speaking of her early interests in psychology and animal behavior, how they were connected with self-observation and a sense of her own needs as an autistic person, and how this had joined with the *[highly developed] visualizing and engineering part of her mind to point her towards the special field she had made her own: the design of farms, feedlots, corrals, slaughterhouses—systems of many sorts for animal management.*

She spoke well and clearly, but with a certain unstoppable impetus and fixity. A sentence, a paragraph, once started, had to be completed; nothing left implicit, hanging in the air. (Sacks, 1995, pp. 256–257)

Having traveled all day, missing lunch, feeling hungry and thirsty, Sacks hoped in vain for Grandin to notice his fatigued and needy state and offer him something to drink or suggest they go somewhere for a bite, but after an hour, realizing that this was not going to happen, he asked for some coffee.

Despite being diagnosed with autism in early childhood, Temple Grandin, Ph.D., has had a successful academic career.

Psychoanalytic Theories Although there have been many psychoanalytic proposals on the causes of autistic disorder (e.g., Roser & Buchholz, 1996; Tustin, 1994), the best known was formulated by Bruno Bettelheim (1967), who worked extensively with autistic children. His basic supposition was that autism closely resembles the apathy and hopelessness found among inmates of German concentration camps during World War II and that therefore something extremely damaging must have taken place in early childhood. Bettelheim hypothesized that the young infant has rejecting parents and is able to perceive their negative feelings. The infant finds that his or her own actions have little impact on the parents' unresponsiveness. The child thus comes to believe that he/she can have no impact on the world and then builds the "empty fortress" of autism to protect itself from pain and disappointment. As we shall see, there is no empirical support for Bettelheim's theory.

There was no "I'm sorry, I should have offered you some before," no intermediacy, no social junction. Instead she immediately took me to a coffeepot that was kept brewing in the secretaries' office upstairs. She introduced me to the secretaries in a somewhat brusque manner, giving me the feeling, once again, of someone who had learned, roughly, "how to behave" in such situations without having much personal perception of how other people felt—the nuances, the social subtleties involved. (Sacks, 1995, p. 257)

In her own writings Grandin points out that many autistic people are great fans of *Star Trek*, and especially of Spock and Data, the former a member of the Vulcan race, characterized by a purely intellectual, logical approach that eschews any consideration of the emotional side of life, the latter an android, a highly sophisticated computer housed in human form and, like Spock, lacking in affective experience. (One of the dramatic themes in both characters was, of course, their flirtation with the experience of human emotion, portrayed with particular poignancy by Data. This is a theme in Grandin's life as well.) As Grandin wrote at age forty-seven:

All my life I have been an observer, and I have always felt like someone who watches from the outside. I could not participate in the social interactions of high school life.

Even today, personal relationships are something I don't really understand. I've remained celibate because doing so helps me avoid the many complicated situations that are too difficult for me to handle. [M]en who want to date often don't understand how to relate to a woman. They [and I myself] remind me of Data, the android on Star Trek. In one episode, Data's attempts at dating were a disaster. When he tried to be romantic [by effecting a change in a subroutine of his computer program], he complimented his date by using scientific terminology. Even very able adults with autism have such problems. (1995, pp. 132–133)

Some of the deficiencies of people with autism make them charmingly honest and trustworthy. "Lying," wrote Grandin, "is very anxiety-provoking because it requires rapid interpretations of subtle social cues [of which I am incapable] to determine whether the other person is really being deceived" (Grandin, 1995, p. 135).

Grandin's professional career is impressive. She uses her remarkable powers of visualization and her empathy for farm animals to design machines such as a chute leading cows to slaughter that takes them on a circular route, protecting them from awareness of their fate until the moment of death. She has also designed and built a "squeeze machine," a device that provides comforting hugs without the need for human contact. It has "two heavy, slanting wooden sides, perhaps four by three feet

each, pleasantly upholstered with a thick, soft padding. They [are] joined by hinges to a long, narrow bottom board to create a V-shaped, body-sized trough. There [is] a complex control box at one end, with heavy-duty tubes leading off to another device, in a closet. [An] industrial compressor 'exerts a firm but comfortable pressure on the body, from the shoulders to the knees' " (Sacks, 1995, pp. 262–263). Her explanation of the rationale behind this contraption is that as a little girl she longed to be hugged but was also very fearful of any physical contact with another person. When a favorite, large-bodied aunt hugged her, she felt both overwhelmed and comforted. Terror comingled with pleasure.

She started to have daydreams—she was just five at the time—of a magic machine that could squeeze her powerfully but gently, in a huglike way, and in a way entirely commanded and controlled by her. Years later, as an adolescent, she had seen a picture of a squeeze chute designed to hold or restrain calves and realized that that was it: a little modification to make it suitable for human use, and it could be her magic machine. (Sacks, 1995, p. 263)

After watching her demonstrate the machine and trying it himself, Sacks observed:

It is not just pleasure or relaxation that Temple gets from the machine but, she maintains, a feeling for others. As she lies in her machine, she says, her thoughts often turn to her mother, her favorite aunt, her teachers. She feels their love for her, and hers for them. She feels that the machine opens a door into an otherwise closed emotional world and allows her, almost teaches her, to feel empathy for others. (Sacks, 1995, p. 264)

Sacks has great admiration for Grandin's professional success and for the interesting and productive life she has made for herself, but when it comes to human interactions it is clear that she does not get it. "I was struck by the enormous difference, the gulf, between Temple's immediate, intuitive recognition of animal moods and signs and her extraordinary difficulties understanding human beings, their codes and signals, the way they conduct themselves" (p. 269).

Accounts such as those of Grandin and Sacks can provide insights into ways of adapting to idiosyncrasies, using the sometimes peculiar gifts that one has been given and working around the deficiencies with which one has been saddled. "Autism, while it may be pathologized as a syndrome, must also be seen as a whole mode of being, a deeply different mode or identity, one that needs to be conscious (and proud) of itself," wrote Sacks (p. 277). "At a recent lecture, Temple ended by saying, 'If I could snap my fingers and be nonautistic, I would not—because then I wouldn't be me. Autism is part of who I am'" (p. 291).

Behavioral Theory Like the psychoanalytically oriented theorists, some behavioral theorists have postulated that certain childhood learning experiences cause autism. In an influential article, Ferster (1961) suggested that the inattention of the parents, especially of the mother, prevents establishment of the associations that make human beings social reinforcers. Because the parents have not become reinforcers, they cannot control the child's behavior, and the result is autistic disorder. Again, there is no support for this theory.

Evaluation of Psychological Theories of Autistic Disorder Both Bettelheim and Ferster, as well as others, have stated that parents play the crucial role in the etiology of autism. Many investigators have therefore studied the characteristics of these parents. For a psychogenic theory of a childhood disorder to have any plausibility at all, something very unusual and destructive about the parents' treatment of their children would have to be demonstrated. This has not happened. That is, there is no evidence to support the psychoanalytic or behavioral theories.

Some early clinical writings suggested that parents of autistic children were cold, distant, insensitive, passive, and apathetic. Systematic investigations, however, failed to confirm these clinical impressions. For example, Cox and colleagues (1975) compared the parents of autistic children with those of children with receptive aphasia (a disorder in understanding speech). The two groups did not differ in warmth, emotional demonstrativeness, responsiveness, or sociability. This and other studies (e.g., Cantwell, Baker, & Rutter, 1978) provide no evidence that there is anything remarkable about the parents of autistic children. In fact, such parents raise other normal and healthy siblings.

Of course, when one reflects on what it must be like to have an autistic child, it would be surprising if parents (and siblings) were not negatively affected. However, there is no evidence that the family life of autistic children is characterized by the kind of extreme emotional maltreatment, deprivation, or neglect that could conceivably produce behavior resembling the dramatically pathological symptoms of autism. Nonetheless, over the years a tremendous emotional burden has been placed on parents who were told that they are at fault. Psychogenic theories of autism are thus not only wrong but pernicious as well.

Biological Bases   The very early onset of autism, along with an accumulation of neurological and genetic evidence that we turn to now, strongly implicates a biological basis for this disorder.

Genetic Factors   Genetic studies of autism are difficult to conduct because the disorder is so rare. The family method presents special problems because autistic persons almost never marry. Nonetheless, emerging evidence strongly suggests a genetic basis for autistic disorder. For example, the risk of autism in the siblings of people with the disorder is about seventy-five times greater than it is if the index case does not have autistic disorder (McBride, Anderson, & Shapiro, 1996). Even stronger evidence for genetic transmission of autism comes from twin studies, which have found 60 to 91 percent concordance for autism between identical twins, compared with concordance rates of 0 to 20 percent in fraternal twins (Bailey et al., 1995; LeCouteur et al., 1996; Steffenberg et al., 1989).

A series of studies following twins and families with an autistic member suggests that autism is linked genetically to a broader spectrum of deficits in communicative and social areas (Bailey et al., 1995; Bolton et al., 1994; Folstein & Rutter, 1977a, 1977b). For example, almost all the nonautistic identical twins of autistic adults are unable to live independently or maintain a close and confiding relationship. In addition, most of the nonautistic identical twins evidenced communication deficits, such as language delays or reading impairments, as well as severe social deficits, including no social contacts outside the family, lack of responsiveness to social cues or conventions, and little or no spontaneous affection with caregivers. In contrast, nonidentical twins of autistic children are almost always normal in their social and language development and marry and live independently in adulthood (LeCouteur et al., 1996). Taken together, the evidence from family and twin studies strongly supports a genetic basis for autistic disorder.

Neurological Factors   Early EEG studies of autistic children indicated that many had abnormal brain-wave patterns (e.g., Hutt et al., 1964). Other types of neurological examinations also revealed signs of brain dysfunction in many autistic children (e.g., Campbell et al., 1982; Gillberg & Svendsen, 1983). For example, two studies using magnetic resonance imaging (MRI) have found young autistic men (but not women) to have an overall enlarged brain size relative to people without autism (Piven et al., 1995, 1996).[4]

---

[4] Having an enlarged brain is not necessarily better. The "pruning" of neurons is an important part of brain maturation; older children have fewer neurons than do babies. A larger brain, called macrocephaly, can lead to mental retardation, for example.

Furthermore, sixteen MRI and autopsy studies from nine independent research groups all found abnormalities in the cerebellum of autistic children (Haas et al., 1996), and more recent studies have confirmed this finding (e.g., Hardan et al., 2001). Neurological abnormalities in individuals with autism suggest that in the course of their brain development, cells fail to align properly and do not form the network of connections found in normal brain development.

In adolescence, 30 percent of those who had severe autistic symptoms as children begin having seizures, another sign that a problem in the brain is involved in the disorder. The prevalence of autism in children whose mothers had rubella during the prenatal period is approximately ten times higher than that in the general population of children, and we know that rubella in the mother during pregnancy can harm the developing fetus's brain. A syndrome similar to autism sometimes follows in the aftermath of meningitis (a bacterial disease which causes inflammation of the membrane enveloping the brain), encephalitis (inflammation of the brain), fragile X (see p. 502), and tuberous sclerosis (a hardening of brain tissue), all of which may affect central nervous system functioning. These findings, together with the degree of mental retardation commonly found in autism, seem to strengthen the link between autism and brain damage (Courchesne et al., 1988).

Recent research has begun to study the linkages between neurological abnormalities and the behavioral difficulties associated with autism. For example, one study used fMRI to compare changes in blood flow of different brain areas of adults with and without autism as they processed facial expressions of emotion. In individuals with autism, the areas of the brain associated with the processing of faces (temporal-lobe region) and emotion (amygdala) were not activated during this task (Critchley et al., 2001). Another study found the limited exploration behaviors commonly observed in autism to be correlated with abnormal cerebellum size (Pierce & Courchesne, 2001).

Treatment of Autistic Disorder

Because their isolation is so moving and their symptoms so pronounced, a great deal of attention has been given to trying to improve the condition of children with autism. As with theories of etiology, the earliest efforts were psychological in nature, and some of them have shown considerable promise. More recently, various psychopharmacotherapies have been studied as well, with few positive results. Treatments for autistic children usually try to reduce their unusual behavior and improve their communication and social skills. Sometimes an eagerly sought-after goal for a family is simply to be able to take their autistic child to a restaurant or market without attracting negative attention.

It is worth noting that even though biological theories of the etiology of autism have much more empirical support than psychological theories, it is the psychological interventions that currently show the most promise, not biological ones. A biological defect does not preclude psychological treatment.

Special Problems in Treating Children with Autism   Children with autism have several characteristics that make treating them difficult. For one thing, they do not adjust well to changes in routine, and the very nature and purpose of treatment involves change. For another, their isolation and self-stimulatory movements may interfere with effective teaching. Although the similar behavior of children with other disabilities may intrude on the teacher's efforts, it does not do so with the same frequency and severity.

In addition, it is particularly difficult to find ways to motivate children with autism. To be effective with these children, reinforcers must be explicit, concrete, and highly salient. A widely used method of increasing the range of reinforcers to which autistic children respond is to pair social reinforcement, such as praise, with primary reinforcers, such as a highly desired food (Davison, 1964).

A further problem that often interferes with the learning of children with autism is their overselectivity of attention; when the child's attention becomes focused on one particular aspect of a task or situation, other properties, including relevant ones, may not even be noticed (Lovaas et al., 1971). The overselective nature of these children's attention makes it especially difficult for them to generalize or apply their learning to other areas. For example, the child who has learned several words by watching the instructor's lip movements may not comprehend the same words spoken by another person with less pronounced lip movements.

In spite of these problems, educational programs for children with autism have achieved some positive results, and we turn to these now.

Behavioral Treatment of Children with Autism   Using modeling and operant conditioning, behavior therapists have taught autistic children to talk (Hewett, 1965), modified their echolalic speech (Carr, Schreibman, & Lovaas, 1975), encouraged them to play with other children (Romanczyk et al., 1975), and helped them become more generally responsive to adults (Davison, 1964).

Ivar Lovaas, a behavior therapist, is noted for his operant-conditioning treatment of autistic children.

Ivar Lovaas, a leading clinical researcher at the University of California at Los Angeles, conducted an intensive operant program with very young (under four years old) autistic children (Lovaas, 1987). Therapy encompassed all aspects of the children's lives for more than 40 hours a week over more than two years. Parents were trained extensively so that treatment could continue during almost all the children's waking hours. Nineteen children receiving this intensive treatment were compared with forty control youngsters who received a similar treatment for less than 10 hours per week. All children were rewarded for being less aggressive, more compliant, and more socially appropriate—for example, talking and playing with other children. The goal of the program was to mainstream the children, the assumption being that autistic children, as they improve, benefit more from being with normal peers than from remaining by themselves or with other seriously disturbed children.

The results of this landmark study were dramatic and encouraging. The measured IQ's for the intensive-therapy group averaged 83 in first grade (after about two years in the intensive therapy) compared with about 55 for the control children; twelve of the nineteen reached the normal range, compared with only two (of forty) in the control group. Furthermore, nine of the nineteen in the intensive-therapy group were promoted to second grade in a regular public school, whereas only one of the much larger control group achieved this level of normal functioning. A follow-up of these children four years later indicated that the children's intensive-treatment group maintained their gains in IQ, adaptive behavior, and grade promotions in school (McEachin, Smith, & Lovaas, 1993). Although critics have pointed out weaknesses in the study's methodology and outcome measures (Schopler, Short, & Mesibov, 1989), this ambitious program confirms the benefits of heavy involvement of both professionals and parents in dealing with the extreme challenge of autistic disorder.

There is reason to believe that the education provided by parents is more beneficial to the child than is clinic- or hospital-based treatment. Parents are present in many different situations and thus can help children generalize the gains they make. For example, Koegel and his colleagues (1982) demonstrated that 25 to 30 hours of parent training was as effective as 200 hours of direct clinic treatment in improving the behavior of autistic children. More recently, Koegel's research group has focused on comparing different strategies for behavioral parent training, with interesting discoveries. Rather than teach parents to focus on changing individually targeted problem behaviors in a sequential manner, Koegel, Bimbela, and Schreibman (1996) found that parents could be more effective when taught to focus on increasing their autistic children's general motivation and responsiveness. For example, allowing the child to choose the teaching materials, providing natural reinforcers (e.g., play and social praise) rather than edible reinforcers, and reinforcing attempts to respond as well as correct responses all led to improved family interactions and more positive communication with their autistic children. One of the first interventions that sought to include parents in the treatment process is the TEACHC program, or Treatment and Education of Autistic and related Communication Handicapped Children, developed by Schopler and colleagues at the University of North Carolina (Schopler, 1986). This community-based intervention emphasizes parents and teachers working together in the treatment of autism. Variants of the TEACCH program have been adopted in a number of different countries, including Sweden and Japan.

It must be clearly understood, however, that some autistic and other severely disturbed children can be adequately cared for only in a hospital or in a group home staffed by mental health professionals. Moreover, the circumstances of some families preclude the home care of a seriously disturbed child. That effective treatments can be implemented by parents does not mean that this is the appropriate course for all families.

Psychodynamic Treatment of Children with Autism   Because he viewed attachment difficulties and emotional deprivation as the sources of autism, Bruno Bettelheim (1967, 1974) argued that a warm, loving atmosphere must be created to encourage the child to enter the world. Patience and what Rogerians would call unconditional positive regard were believed to be necessary for the child with autism to begin to trust others and to take chances in establishing relationships. At his Orthogenic School at the University of Chicago, Bettelheim and his colleagues reported many instances of success, but the uncontrolled nature of their observations makes it difficult to evaluate their claims. Furthermore, the accuracy of Bettelheim's reports on the procedures used and the successes achieved with the students at his school have been called into question, casting serious doubt on the validity of his claims (Gardner, 1997; Pollak, 1997).

Drug Treatment of Children with Autism   The most commonly used medication for treating problem behaviors in autistic children is haloperidol (brand name Haldol), an antipsychotic medication frequently used in the treatment of schizophrenia. Some controlled studies have shown that this drug reduces social withdrawal, stereotyped motor behavior, and maladaptive behavior, such as self-mutilation and aggression (Anderson et al., 1989; McBride et al., 1996; Perry et al., 1989). Many autistic children do not respond positively to the drug, however, and it has not shown any positive effects on other aspects of autistic disorder, such as abnormal interpersonal relationships and language impairment (Holm & Varley, 1989). Haloperidol also has potentially serious side effects (Posey & McDougle, 2000). In a recently completed longitudinal study, over 30 percent of autistic children developed drug-related dyskinesias, or jerky muscle disturbances, although most were reversible after the drug was withdrawn (Campbell et al., 1997).

Evidence that autistic children may have elevated blood levels of serotonin (Anderson & Hoshino, 1987) encouraged research on medications that reduce the action of serotonin. In the early 1980s a large, multisite study was conducted in twenty medical centers to examine the effectiveness of fenfluramine, a drug known to lower serotonin levels in rats and monkeys. After an initial flurry of enthusiastic claims that the drug effected dramatic improvement in the behavior and thought processes of autistic children (Ritvo et al., 1983), later studies delivered much more modest findings. Although fenfluramine may have some small positive effects in some autistic children by improving social adjustment, attention span, activity level, and stereotyped behavior, no consistent effect has been shown on cognitive measures such as IQ or language functioning. Reviews concur that the effects of fenfluramine are at best subtle, and the drug certainly does not represent a cure for autism (Leventhal et al., 1993; Rapin, 1997).

Researchers have also studied an opioid receptor antagonist, naltrexone, and found that this drug reduces hyperactivity in autistic children and produces a moderate increment in social interaction initiations (Aman & Langworthy, 2000; Williams et al., 2001; Willemsen-Swinkels, Buitelaar, & van Engeland, 1996). One controlled study suggested mild improvements in initiation of communication as well (Kolmen et al., 1995), but others found no changes in communication or social behavior (Feldman, Kolmen, & Gonzaga, 1999; Willemsen-Swinkels et al., 1995, 1996). The drug does not appear to affect the core symptoms of autism, and some evidence suggests that at some doses it may increase self-injurious behavior (Anderson et al., 1997).

In sum, pharmacological treatment of autism is, at this point, less effective than behavioral interventions.

Summary

- Childhood disorders are often organized into two domains: externalizing disorders and internalizing disorders. Externalizing disorders are characterized by such behaviors as aggressiveness, noncompliance, overactivity, and impulsiveness; they include attention-deficit/hyperactivity disorder, conduct disorder, and oppositional defiant disorder. Internalizing disorders are characterized by such behaviors as depression, social withdrawal, and anxiety and include childhood anxiety and mood disorders.

- Attention-deficit/hyperactivity disorder (ADHD) is a persistent pattern of inattention and/or hyperactivity and impulsivity that is more frequent and more severe than what is typically observed in youngsters of a given age. There is growing evidence for genetic and neurological factors in its etiology. Stimulant drugs, such as Ritalin, and reinforcement for staying on task have some effectiveness in reducing the symptoms of ADHD.

- Conduct disorder is sometimes a precursor to antisocial personality disorder in adulthood, though many children carrying the diagnosis do not progress to that extreme. It is characterized by high and widespread levels of aggression, lying, theft, vandalism, cruelty to other people and to animals, and other acts that violate laws and social norms. Among the apparent etiological and risk factors are a genetic predisposition, inadequate learning of moral awareness, modeling and direct reinforcement of antisocial behavior, negative peer influences, and living in impoverished and crime-ridden areas. The most promising approach to treating young people with conduct disorder involves intensive intervention in multiple systems, including the family, school, and peer systems.

- Learning disorders are diagnosed when a child fails to develop to the degree expected for his or her intellectual level in a specific academic, language, or motor-skill area. These disorders are usually identified and treated within the school system rather than through mental health clinics. There is mounting evidence that the most widely studied of the learning disorders, dyslexia, has genetic and other biological components. The most widespread interventions for dyslexia, however, are educational.

- The traditional diagnostic criteria for mental retardation are subaverage intellectual functioning and deficits in adaptive behavior, with onset before the age of eighteen. Contemporary analyses, however, focus more on the strengths of individuals with mental retardation than on their assignment to a particular level of severity. This shift in emphasis is associated with increased efforts to design psychological and educational interventions that make the most of individuals' abilities.

- The more severe forms of mental retardation have a biological basis, such as the chromosomal trisomy that causes Down syndrome. Certain infectious diseases in the pregnant mother, such as HIV, rubella, and syphilis, as well as illnesses that affect the child directly, such as encephalitis, can stunt cognitive and social development, as can malnutrition, severe falls, and automobile accidents that injure the brain. Environmental factors are considered the principal causes of mild retardation. People with mild retardation are often from lower-class homes, living in an environment of social and educational deprivation.

- Researchers try to prevent mild retardation by giving children at risk through impoverished circumstances special preschool training and social opportunities. Many children with mental retardation who would formerly have been institutionalized are now being educated in the public schools under the provisions of Public Law 94-142. In addition, using applied behavioral analysis, self-instructional training, and modeling, behavior therapists have been able to treat successfully many of the behavioral problems of individuals with mental retardation and to improve their intellectual functioning.

- Autistic disorder, one of the pervasive developmental disorders, begins before the age of two and a half. The major symptoms are a failure to relate to other people; communication problems, consisting of either a failure to learn any language or speech irregularities, such as echolalia and pronoun reversal; and preservation of sameness, an obsessive desire to keep daily routines and surroundings exactly the same.

- Autistic disorder was originally believed to be the result of coldness and aloofness in parents and their rejection of their children, but recent research gives no credence to such notions. Although the specific biological basis of autism has yet to be isolated, a biological cause is suspected for a number of reasons: its onset is very early; family and twin studies give compelling evidence of a genetic predisposition; abnormalities have been found in the brains of autistic children; a syndrome similar to autism can develop following meningitis and encephalitis; and many autistic children have the low intelligence associated with brain dysfunctions.

- The most promising treatments of autism are psychological in nature, involving modeling and operant conditioning procedures. Although the prognosis for autistic children remains poor in general, recent work suggests that intensive behavioral treatment involving the parents as their children's therapists may allow some of these children to participate meaningfully in normal social intercourse. Various drug treatments have been used but have proved less effective than behavioral interventions.

Key Terms

applied behavior analysis
attention-deficit/hyperactivity disorder (ADHD)
autistic disorder
conduct disorder
disorder of written expression
Down syndrome (trisomy 21)
echolalia

enuresis
expressive language disorder
externalizing disorders
fragile X syndrome
internalizing disorders
learning disabilities
learning disorders

mathematics disorder
mild mental retardation
moderate mental retardation
motor skills disorder
oppositional defiant disorder
pervasive developmental disorders
phenylketonuria (PKU)

phonological disorder
profound mental retardation
pronoun reversal
reading disorder (dyslexia)
self-instructional training
severe mental retardation
stuttering

Autistic Disorder

Sam Williams was the second child of John and Carol Williams. The couple had been married for five years when Sam was born; John was a lawyer, and Carol a homemaker. Sam weighed 7 pounds, 11 ounces at birth, which had followed an uncomplicated full-term, pregnancy. Delivered by Caesarean section, he came home six days after the delivery.

His parents reported that Sam's early development seemed quite normal. He was not colicky, and he slept and ate well. During his first two years, there were no childhood illnesses except some mild colds. After Sam's second birthday, however, his parents began to become concerned. He had been somewhat slower than his older sister in achieving some developmental milestones (such as sitting up alone and crawling). Furthermore, his motor development seemed uneven. He would crawl normally for a few days and then not crawl at all for a while. Although he made babbling sounds, he had not developed any speech and did not even seem to understand anything his parents said to him. Simple requests such as, "Come" or, "Do you want a cookie?" elicited no response.

Initially, the Williamses thought that Sam might be deaf. Later they vacillated between this belief and the idea that Sam was being stubborn. They reported many frustrating experiences in which they tried to force him to obey a command or say "Mama" or "Dada." Sometimes Sam would go into a tantrum during one of these situations, yelling, screaming, and throwing himself to the floor. That same year, the Williamses' pediatrician told them that Sam might be mentally retarded.

Toward his third birthday, Sam's parents began to notice him engaging in more and more strange and puzzling behavior. Most obvious were his repetitive hand movements. Many times each day he would suddenly flap his hands for several minutes. (Activities like this are called self-stimulatory behaviors.) Other times he rolled his eyes around in their sockets. He still did not speak, but he made smacking sounds and sometimes he would burst out laughing for no apparent reason. He was walking now and often walked on his toes. Sam had not been toilet trained, although his parents had tried to do so.

Sam's social development was also beginning to concern his parents. Although he would let them hug and touch him, he would not look at them and generally seemed indifferent to their attention. He also did not play at all with his older sister, seeming to prefer being left alone. Even his solitary play was strange. He did not really play with his toys—for example, pretending to drive a toy car into a service station. Instead, he was more likely just to manipulate a toy, such as a car, holding it and repetitively spinning its wheels. The only thing that really seemed to interest him was a ceiling fan in the den. He was content to sit there for as long as permitted, watching intently as the fan spun around and around. Temper tantrums often ensued when the fan was turned off.

At the age of 3, the family's pediatrician recommended a complete physical and neurological examination. Sam was found to be in good health, and the neurological examination revealed nothing remarkable. A psychiatric evaluation was performed several months later. Sam was brought to a treatment facility specializing in behavior disturbances of childhood and was observed for a day. During that time, the psychiatrist was able to see first hand most of the behaviors that Sam's parents had described—hand flapping, toe walking, smacking sounds, and preference for being left alone. When the psychiatrist evaluated Sam, she observed that a loud slapping noise did not elicit a startle response as it does in most children. The only vocalization she could elicit that approximated speech was a repetitive "nah, nah." Sam did, however, obey some simple commands such as "Come" and "Go get a potato chip." The psychiatrist diagnosed Sam as having autistic disorder and recommended placement in a day-treatment setting.

Conceptualization and Treatment

Sam was 4 years old by the time there was an opening for him at the treatment center. He was bused to and from a special school five days a week, spending the remainder of his time at home with his parents and sister. The school provided a comprehensive educational program conducted by specially trained teachers. The program was organized mainly along operant conditioning principles. In addition, Sam's parents attended classes once a week to learn operant conditioning so they could continue the school program at home. The school's personnel conducted another evaluation of Sam, observing him in the school and later at home. Interviews with the parents established that they were both well adjusted and that their marriage was stable. Both parents were, however, experiencing considerable stress from having to cope with Sam on a day-to-day basis and from their feelings that Sam's condition might have been caused by something they had done.

One of the first targets of the training program was eye contact. When working with Sam, his teacher provided small food rewards when Sam spontaneously looked at him. The teacher also began requesting eye contact and again rewarded Sam when he complied. Along with this training, the teacher worked on having Sam obey other simple commands. The teacher would try to select a time when Sam seemed attentive and would then, establishing eye contact, say the command and at the same time show him what was meant (i.e., model the desired behavior). For example, the teacher would say, "Sam, stretch your arms up like this," and then the teacher would lift Sam's arms up and reward him with praise and a small amount of food, such as a grape. This procedure was repeated several times. Once Sam began to become more skilled at following the command, the teacher stopped raising Sam's arms for him and let him do it entirely for himself. These training trials were conducted daily. As the response to a particular command became well established, the command would be made in other situations and by other people. Sam's progress was slow. It often took weeks of training to establish his response to a simple command. After his first year in the school, he did respond reliably to several simple requests such as "Come," "Give it to me," and "Put on your coat."

At the same time that Sam was learning to respond to commands, other aspects of the training program were also being implemented. While Sam was in the classroom, his teacher worked with him on trying to develop skills that would be important in learning, for example, sitting in his seat, maintaining eye contact, and listening and working for longer periods of time. Each activity was rewarded in much the same way as his performance of simple behaviors had been.

As these skills became better established, the teacher also began working on expanding Sam's vocabulary by teaching him the meaning of pictures of common objects. A picture of one object, such as an orange, was placed on a table in front of Sam. Once Sam had looked at the object, the teacher said, "This is an orange. Point to the orange." When Sam pointed to the orange, he was rewarded. If necessary, the teacher would move his hand for him at first. Next another picture, such as a cat, was selected and the same procedure followed again. Then the two pictures were placed in front of Sam and the teacher asked him to point to one of them: "Point to the orange." If Sam pointed correctly, he was rewarded. If he did not, the teacher moved his hand to the correct object. After Sam had correctly pointed to the orange several times in a row, the teacher asked him to point to the cat. With that response established, the teacher switched the position of the pictures and repeated the process. When Sam had begun to point correctly to the orange and the cat, a third picture was introduced and the training procedure was started anew. During one year of training, Sam learned the names of 38 common objects with this procedure.

Sam's speech therapist, whom he saw daily, was also working with him on language skills. Initially, they worked on getting Sam to imitate simple sounds. Sitting across a table from Sam and waiting until Sam was looking (or prompting him to look by holding a piece of food near his mouth), the teacher would say, "Say this, ah," taking care to accentuate the movements required for this sound. At first Sam was rewarded for making any sound. Subsequently, rewards were forthcoming only as Sam's productions approximated more and more closely the required sound. As sounds were mastered, Sam was trained to say simple words in a similar fashion. Over the course of a year, Sam learned a few words—"bye-bye," "no more," and "mine," however, overall, his verbal imitation remained poor.

Having Sam learn to dress and undress himself was another target during the first year. Initially, his teacher helped him through the entire sequence, describing each step as they did it. Next, they would go through the sequence again, but now Sam had to do the last step himself (taking off his shoes, putting on his shoes). More difficult steps (tying shoes) were worked on individually to give Sam more practice on them. Once some progress was being made, this aspect of the treatment was carried out by the parents. They first observed the teacher working with Sam and then discussed the procedure and were shown how to make a chart to record Sam's progress. Over a period of weeks, the number of steps that Sam had to complete by himself was gradually increased, moving from the last toward the first. Sam was rewarded each time he dressed or undressed, usually with a special treat (e.g., a favorite breakfast food). In this case, the training was quite successful. By midyear Sam had mastered dressing and undressing.

Toilet training was another area that Sam's parents and teachers tackled. At home and at school, Sam was rewarded for using the toilet. He was checked every hour to see if his pants were dry. If they were, he was praised and reminded that when he went to the toilet he would get a reward. Shortly thereafter, Sam would be taken to the toilet, where he would remove his pants and sit. If he urinated or defecated, he was given a large reward. If not, he was given a small reward just for sitting. As this training was progressing, Sam was also taught to associate the word "potty" with going to the toilet. Progress was slow at first, and there were many "accidents," which both teachers and parents were instructed to ignore. But Sam soon caught on and began urinating or defecating more and more often when he was taken to the bathroom. Then the parents and teachers began working on having Sam tell them when he had to go. When they checked to see if his pants were dry, they would tell him to let them know, by saying "potty" when he had to go to the toilet. Although there were many ups and downs in Sam's progress, by the end of the year he was having an average of fewer than two accidents per week.

One reason for Sam's relatively slow progress during his first year in the special school was his temper tantrums. These occurred sometimes when he was given a command or when a teacher interrupted something he was doing. Not getting a reward during a training session also led to tantrums. Sam would scream loudly at the top of his voice, throw himself to the ground, and flail away with his arms and legs. Several interventions were tried. It had been observed that Sam's tantrums usually led to getting his own way, particularly at home. For example, a tantrum had often succeeded in getting his parents to keep the ceiling fan on, even when they wanted to turn it off. Thus, ignoring the tantrum was the first approach. Sam's teachers and parents simply let the tantrum play itself out, acting as if it had not happened. The procedure had no apparent effect. Next, "time-out" was tried. Every time a tantrum started, Sam was picked up, carried to a special room, and left there for 10 minutes or until the screaming stopped. This procedure also failed to have much of an effect on the tantrums and screaming, even with several modifications such as lengthening the time-out period.

During the second year of Sam's treatment, many of the first year's programs were continued. The range of commands to which Sam responded was expanded, and his ability to recognize and point to simple objects increased. In his speech therapy he learned to imitate more sounds and some new words ("hello," "cookie," and "book"). His progress in speech therapy, however, remained slow and uneven. He would seem to master some sound or word and then somehow lose it. He was, however, still dressing and undressing himself and going to the toilet reliably.

Feeding skills were one of the first targets for the second-year program. Although his parents had tried to get him to use a knife, fork, and spoon, Sam resisted these attempts and ate with his fingers or by licking the food from his plate. Drinking from a cup was also a problem. Sam still used a baby cup with only a small opening at the top. As in some of the previous programs, this one was implemented by both Sam's teachers and parents and involved a combination of modeling and operant conditioning. Training sessions conducted at mealtime first involved getting Sam to use a spoon. Sam was shown how to hold the spoon; then the teacher picked up the spoon, saying, "Watch me. You push the spoon in like this and then lift it up to your mouth." Sam did not initially imitate, so the teacher had to guide him through the necessary steps: moving his hand and spoon to pick up food, raising his arm until the spoon was at his mouth, telling him to open his mouth, and guiding the spoon in. Praise was provided as each step in the chain was completed. After many repetitions, Sam was required to do the last step by himself. Gradually, more and more of the steps were done by Sam himself. Successes were followed by praise and failures by saying "no" or removing his meal for a short time. When eating with a spoon was well established, the training was expanded to using a fork and drinking from a cup. In several months, Sam was eating and drinking well.

Sam's failure to play with other children was also a major focus during the second year. The first step was to get Sam to play near other children. Most of his playtime was spent alone, even when other children were in the playroom with him. So his teacher watched Sam carefully and rewarded him with small bits of food whenever he was near another child with autistic disorder. A procedure was also used to force Sam to interact with another child. Sam and another child with autistic disorder would be seated next to each other and given the task of stacking some blocks. Each child was, in turn, given a block and prompted to place it on the stack. In addition to praising them individually as they stacked each block, both children were rewarded with praise and food when they had completed their block tower. After repeating this process several times, the program was expanded to include the cooperative completion of simple puzzles. "Sam, put the dog in here. Okay, now, Nancy, put the cat here." Gradually, the prompts were faded out, and the children were simply rewarded for their cooperative play. Although this aspect of therapy progressed well, transferring these skills to the natural play environment proved difficult. Attempts were made to have Sam and another child play together with toys such as a farm set or a small train. The teacher encouraged them to move the objects around, talking to them about what they were doing and rewarding them for following simple commands. Although Sam would usually follow these commands, his play remained solitary, with little eye contact or cooperation with the other child.

Sam's self-stimulatory behavior was a final target of the second year. Sam's hand flapping and eye rolling had already decreased somewhat over the past year, perhaps because more of his day was being filled with constructive activities. Now a specific intervention, to be used by Sam's teachers and his parents, was planned. Whenever Sam began hand flapping, he was stopped and told to hold his hands still, except when told to move them, for five minutes. During the five-minute period, he was told to hold his hands in several different positions for periods of 30 seconds. If he did not follow the command, the teacher or parent moved his hands into the desired position; if he did not maintain the position for 30 seconds, the teacher or parent held his hands still. Food rewards were provided for successful completion of each 30-second period. Gradually, the teachers and parents were able to get Sam to comply without moving his hands for him or holding him. Then they turned to the eye rolling and implemented a similar program, having Sam fix his gaze on certain objects around his environment whenever he began to roll his eyes. Over a period of several months of training, Sam's self-stimulatory behavior decreased by about 50 percent.

At the beginning of his third year in school, Sam, now 7 years old, was tested with an intelligence test and achieved an IQ of 30, a score generally regarded as reflecting severe mental retardation. The language and speech training continued, as did the attempt to reduce the frequency of his self-stimulatory behavior. His tantrums, which had not responded to previous interventions, were becoming worse. In addition to screaming and throwing himself on the floor, he now became violent at times. On several occasions he had either punched, bitten, or kicked his sister. His parents reported that during these tantrums he became so out of control that they feared he might seriously injure someone. Similar episodes occurred in school, usually when an ongoing activity was interrupted or he failed at some task.

Trouble had also emerged on the bus that brought him to and from school. All the children were required to keep their seat belts on, but Sam would not do so and was often out of his seat. Twice in one week the bus driver stopped the bus and tried to get Sam buckled back into his seat. She was bitten once the first time and twice the second. The bus company acted quickly and suspended service for Sam. In an initial attempt to resolve the problem, Sam was put on haloperidol (Haldol), a drug widely used in the treatment of schizophrenia in adults. But after a month of the drug and no apparent effect, it was stopped. In the meantime, Sam's mother had to drive him to and from school. He was beginning to miss days or be late when his mother's schedule conflicted with the school's.

The seriousness of the tantrum problem and the fact that other treatments had not worked led to the implementation of a punishment system. Because Sam's tantrums and violent outbursts were almost invariably preceded by loud screaming, it was decided to try to break up the usual behavior sequence and punish the screaming. Whenever Sam began to scream, a mixture of water and Tabasco sauce was squirted into his mouth. The effect of this procedure, which was used by both his teachers and parents, was dramatic. The first day of the treatment, Sam began screaming six times. His response to the Tabasco mixture was one of shock and some crying, which stopped quickly after he was allowed to rinse out his mouth. For the next three days, he experienced the Tabasco twice each day, went two days with no screams, and then had one screaming episode; thereafter, he neither screamed nor had a severe temper tantrum again for the rest of the year.

Sam's progress in other areas was not so dramatic. He continued to expand his vocabulary slowly, learning to say more words and recognize more and more objects. But his performance remained highly variable from day to day. His self-stimulatory behavior continued, although at a level below that which had been present earlier. He still remained isolated, preferring to be alone rather than with other children.

Discussion

From the time it was first identified, autistic disorder seemed to have a mystical aura about it. The syndrome was first described in 1943 by a psychiatrist at Harvard, Leo Kanner, who noticed that 11 disturbed children behaved in ways that were not common in children with mental retardation or with schizophrenia. He named the syndrome early infantile autism because he observed that there is an extreme autistic aloneness that shuts out anything that comes to the child from the outside. Kanner considered autistic aloneness the most fundamental symptom, but he also found that these 11 children had been unable from the beginning of life to relate to other people, were severely limited in language, and had an obsessive desire that everything about them remain exactly the same. Despite its early description by Kanner and others (e.g., Rimland, 1964), the disorder was not accepted into official diagnostic nomenclature until the publication of *DSM-III* in 1980. In *DSM-IV-TR* autistic disorder is classified as one of the Pervasive Developmental Disorders.

A major feature of autistic disorder is "extreme autistic aloneness," an inability to relate to people or to any situation other than being alone in a crib, which is found from the very beginning of life. Autistic infants are often reported to be "good babies," apparently because they do not place any demands on their parents. They do not coo or fret or demand attention, nor do they reach out or smile or look at their mothers when being fed. When they are picked up or cuddled, they often arch their bodies away from their caretakers instead of molding themselves against the adult as other babies do. Infants with autistic disorder are content to sit quietly in their playpens for hours, never even noticing other people. After infancy they do not form attachments with people but, instead, may become extremely attached to mechanical objects such as refrigerators or vacuum cleaners. Because they avoid all social interaction, they rapidly fall behind their peers in development. Clearly, this feature was very characteristic of Sam. Although he did not actively avoid human contact or develop an attachment with a mechanical object, he was almost totally asocial.

Communication deficits are a second major feature of autism. Even before the period when language is usually acquired, autistic children show deficits in communication. Babbling, a term used to describe the utterances of children before they actually begin to use words, is less frequent in autistic children and conveys less information than it does with other children (Ricks, 1972). The difficulties that older autistic children have with language are equally pronounced. Mutism—complete absence of speech—is prevalent, as was true

with Sam. About 50 percent of all autistic children never learn to speak (Paul, 1987). When they do speak, peculiarities are often found, including echolalia. The child echoes, usually with remarkable fidelity, what he or she has heard another person say. In delayed echolalia, the child may not repeat the sentence or phrase until hours or weeks after hearing it. Another abnormality common in the speech of autistic children is pronoun reversal. The children refer to themselves as "he," "you," or by their own proper names; they seldom use the pronouns "I" or "me" and then only when referring to others. Pronoun reversal is closely linked to echolalia. Since autistic children often use echolalic speech, they will refer to themselves as they have heard others speak of them; pronouns are, of course, misapplied.

Communication deficiencies are clearly one of the most serious problems of children with autistic disorder. The fact that about 75 percent of these children score in the mentally retarded range on IQ tests is undoubtedly a reflection of these deficiencies. Communication problems are also likely contributors to the social deficits of children with autistic disorder.

The ability or inability to speak is often an effective means of predicting the later adjustment of children with autistic disorder, an additional indication of the central role of language. Eisenberg and Kanner (1956) followed up a sample of 80 children with autistic disorder classified according to whether or not they had learned to speak by age 5. Fifty percent of the children who had been able to speak at this age were later rated as showing fair or good adjustment, but only 3 percent of the nonspeaking children were so rated. Other studies have also shown a close link between the acquisition of language and later adjustment (Gillberg, 1991). Based on these findings, we would predict a relatively poor outcome for Sam.

A third major feature of autistic disorder is compulsive and ritualistic activity, such as a fascination with spinning objects, as shown by Sam. Furthermore, children with autistic disorder often become extremely upset over changes in daily routine and their surroundings. An offer of milk in a different drinking cup or a rearrangement of furniture may make them cry or bring on a temper tantrum. Even common greetings must not vary. Sam did not exhibit this symptom.

In addition to the three major signs just described, many children with autistic disorder have problems in eating, often refusing food or eating only one or a few kinds of food. They may also have difficulty walking but be quite proficient at twirling and spinning objects and in performing ritualistic hand movements. Other rhythmic movements, such as endless body rocking, seem to please them. They may also become preoccupied with manipulating a mechanical object and be very upset when interrupted. Often the children have sensory problems. Like Sam, some children with autistic disorder are first diagnosed as being deaf because they never respond to any sound; some even seem to be insensitive to sound or light. Bowel training is frequently delayed, and head banging and other self-injurious behaviors are common (Rutter, 1974).

Finally, other features of the behavior of children with autistic disorder also have an "obsessional" quality, similar to the preservation of sameness. In their play, they may continually line up toys or construct intricate patterns out of household objects. They engage in much less symbolic play (e.g., driving a toy car to a gas station) than either normal or mentally retarded children of the same mental age (Sigman et al., 1987). They may become preoccupied with train schedules, subway routes, or number sequences. Clearly, Sam displayed many of these behaviors.

What happens to such severely disturbed children when they reach adulthood? Kanner (1973) reported the adult status of 9 of the 11 children whom he had described in his original paper. Two developed epileptic seizures; by 1966 one of them had died and the other was in a state mental hospital. Four others had spent most of their lives in institutions. Of the remaining three, one had remained mute but was working on a farm and as an orderly in a nursing home. The last two made at least somewhat satisfactory recoveries. Although both still lived with their parents and had little social life, they were gainfully employed and had some recreational interests. From his review of early follow-up studies, Lotter (1978) concluded that only 5 to 17 percent of autistic children had a relatively good outcome in adulthood. Most of the remaining children had a poor outcome, and 50 percent were institutionalized. More recent studies have reached similar conclusions (e.g., Nordan & Gillberg, 1998).

Etiological Considerations

Several facts make biological accounts of autism very plausible. First, the age of onset is very early. If a psychological stress were to precipitate such disorders, it would indeed have to be a particularly noxious event. Yet the available evidence does not indicate that children with autistic disorder are reared in especially unpleasant environments or that they have suffered some severe trauma. This point was certainly true in Sam's case. Second, a syndrome quite similar to autism may develop in the aftermath of brain diseases such as encephalitis and meningitis. Third, mental subnormality is often associated with some kind of brain dysfunction; about 80 percent of children with autistic disorder have low levels of intelligence.

Various types of neurological examination have also revealed signs of damage in a large percentage of children with autistic disorder (Gillberg & Svendsen, 1983; Steffenburg, 1991). Further evidence supporting the possibility of neurological dysfunction includes studies using magnetic resonance scans of the brain. The most impressive and well-replicated finding to date is that portions of the cerebellum are underdeveloped in children with autistic disorder (Hardan et al., 2001). In adolescence, 30 percent of those who had severe autistic symptoms as children begin having epileptic seizures. Furthermore, the prevalence of autism in children whose mothers had rubella during the prenatal period is approximately 10 times higher than in the general population of children. These findings, plus the degree of mental retardation, would seem to link autism and brain damage.

Genetic studies of autistic disorder are difficult to conduct because the disorder is so rare. In cases where children with autistic disorder have siblings, the rate of autistic disorder in their brothers and sisters is about 2 percent (McBride, Anderson, & Shapiro, 1996). Although this is a small percentage, it represents a *fiftyfold* increase in risk as compared to the morbidity risk in the general population. Further evidence of the importance of genetic factors in autistic disorder is provided by twin studies. In Folstein and Rutter's (1978) study, there was no concordance among the dizygotic twins. But in the 11 pairs of identical twins, one of whom had autistic dis-

order, 4 of the cotwins also had autistic disorder, yielding a concordance rate of 36 percent. Even more striking results have been reported by Steffenberg et al. (1989) and Bailey et al. (1995), with monozygotic concordance rates over 60 percent.

A series of studies using both the family and twin methods suggest that autistic disorder is genetically linked to a broader range of deficits in both the communication and social realms. For example, most of the nonautistic identical twins in Folstein and Rutter's study had language delays or reading impairments. Similarly, family studies reveal delayed language acquisition and social deficits in the nonautistic relatives of index cases with autistic disorder (e.g., Piren et al., 1997). Taken together, the evidence from family and twin studies supports a genetic basis for autistic disorder.

In Sam's case there was no evidence of any neurological abnormality, nor was there any family history of autism. Consistent with Folstein and Rutter's findings, however, Sam's older sister did have a learning disability.

As might be expected, theorists of a psychogenic bent attribute autism to early experiences, especially those shared by the mother and child. In his early papers, Kanner had described the parents of children with autistic disorder as cold, insensitive, meticulous, introverted, distant, and highly intellectual (Kanner & Eisenberg, 1955). He concluded that the children are reared in "emotional refrigeration." Others (e.g., Rimland, 1964; Singer & Wynne, 1963) have also noted the detachment of parents of children with autistic disorder, although in less pejorative terms.

Social learning theorists have also postulated that certain childhood learning experiences cause psychotic childhood disorders. Ferster (1961), in an extremely influential article, suggested that the inattention of the parents, especially of the mother, prevents establishment of the associations that make human beings reinforcers. Because the parents have not become reinforcers, they cannot control the child's behavior.

The theories we have just described led many investigators to study the characteristics of the parents of children with autistic disorder. These studies (e.g., Cox et al., 1975) have *failed* to confirm the earlier clinical impressions. When the parents of children with autistic disorder were compared to those of children with receptive aphasia (a disorder in understanding speech), the two groups did not differ in warmth, emotional demonstrativeness, responsiveness, or sociability. Similarly, DeMyer et al. (1973) did not find that parents of children with autistic disorder were rejecting. Cantwell, Baker, and Rutter (1978) and McAdoo and DeMyer (1978) did not observe parental deviance using standard personality tests. The weight of the evidence is overwhelming: The parents of children with autistic disorder are unremarkable, as was the case with the Williamses.

Even if we were to ignore these findings, the direction of a possible correlation between parental characteristics and autism is not easily determined. The deviant parental behavior that has been reported could easily be a reaction of the child's abnormality rather than the other way around. And if parental behavior causes autism, why is the incidence of similar difficulties so low in siblings? Moreover, although autism is a severe disorder, the parental behavior that has been discussed does not seem likely to be more than mildly damaging. It would seem that only very gross mistreatment, such as keeping the child in a locked closet, could precipitate such severe problems so early in life.

Treatment

Numerous biological therapeutic approaches have been tried with autistic disorder, most commonly the same kinds of medication (e.g., haloperidol) that are used to treat adult patients who have psychotic disorders. Although some improvement is found with this drug (e.g., reducing stereotyped motor behavior, social withdrawal, and aggression), positive effects are not found for language impairment and social deficits (McBride et al., 1996). There has also been some interest in two other drugs—fenfluramine, an amphetamine derivitive, and naltrexone, a drug that blocks the brain's opioid receptors. Both may lead to some improvement, although neither appears to alter the core symptoms of the disorder (Kolmen et al., 1995; Rapin, 1997).

The major psychological treatment for autism is behavior therapy. As we saw in Sam's case, it requires a great expenditure of time and effort. Furthermore, these children have several problems that make teaching them difficult. They have difficulty adjusting to changes in routine, such as substitute teachers. Their self-stimulatory behavior interferes with effective teaching, and finding reinforcers that motivate autistic children can be difficult.

In general, behavior therapists focus on reliably assessed, observable behaviors and manipulate the consequences these behaviors elicit from the environment. As in Sam's case, desirable behaviors (e.g., speech, playing with other children) are rewarded, and undesirable ones (e.g., hand flapping, screaming) are either ignored or punished. The desired behaviors are broken down into smaller elements that are learned first and then assembled into a whole. A good example of this procedure was seen in the procedures used to try to get Sam to speak. Modeling is a frequent adjunct in these operant behavior therapy programs.

Many aspects of autistic disorder can be changed with behavioral programs. Self-care skills, social behavior, and language have all shown improvements in controlled studies (e.g., Koegel et al., 1982). Undesirable behaviors such as self-stimulation and self-injurious behavior have been decreased (Ross & Nelson, 1979).

Ivar Lovaas, a leading clinical researcher at the University of California at Los Angeles, has described an intensive behavior therapy program with very young (under 4 years) children with autistic disorder (Lovaas, 1987). Therapy encompassed all aspects of the children's lives for more than 40 hours a week for more than two years. Parents were trained extensively so that treatment could continue during almost all waking hours of the children's lives. Nineteen youngsters receiving this intensive treatment were compared to 40 control children who received a similar treatment for less than 10 hours per week. All children were rewarded for being less aggressive, more compliant, and more socially appropriate, including talking and playing with other children. The goal of the program was to mainstream the children, the assumption being that autistic children, as they improve, benefit more from being with normal peers rather than remaining by themselves or with other severely disturbed children.

The results were quite dramatic and encouraging for the intensive therapy group. Their measured IQs averaged 83 in first grade (after about two years in the intensive therapy) compared to about 55 for the controls; 12 of the 19 reached the normal range as compared to only 2 (of 40) in the control group. Furthermore, 9 out of the 19 intensives were promoted to second grade in a normal public school, whereas only one of the much larger control group achieved this level of normal functioning. A follow-up of these children four years later showed that they had maintained their gains (McEachin, Smith, & Lovaas, 1993).

This ambitious study confirms the need for heavy involvement of both professionals and parents in dealing with the extreme challenge of autistic disorder. Although such intensive treatment is expensive and time-consuming, the long-term dependence and loss of productive work in less intensively treated children with autistic disorder represent a far greater cost of society than a treatment that enables some of these children to achieve a normal level of functioning.

16 Aging and Psychological Disorders

The patient is a fifty-six-year-old right-handed businessman who had entered the hospital for cervical disk surgery. Because of his busy schedule and his anxiety relating to surgery, he had canceled his admission on two previous occasions. The patient was a fairly heavy social drinker but not to the point of interfering in any way with his business performance. The surgery was uneventful and there were no immediate complications of the procedure. The patient was greatly relieved and seemed to be making a normal recovery until the third postoperative night. During that night he became quite restless and found it difficult to sleep. The next day he was visibly fatigued but otherwise normal. The following night his restlessness became more pronounced, and he became fearful and anxious. As the night progressed, he thought that he saw people hiding in his room, and shortly before dawn he reported to the nurse that he saw some strange little animals running over his bed and up the drapes. At the time of morning rounds, the patient was very anxious and frightened. He was lethargic, distractible, and quite incoherent when he tried to discuss the events of the night before. He knew who he was and where he was but did not know the date or when he had had his surgery. During that day his mental status fluctuated, but by nightfall he had become grossly disoriented and agitated. At this point, psychiatric consultation was obtained.

The consultant's diagnosis was acute postoperative confusional state [delirium]. The cause was probably due to a combination of factors: withdrawal from alcohol, fear of surgery, use of strong analgesics, stress of the operation, pain, and the sleepless nights in an unfamiliar room. The treatment consisted of a reduction in medications for pain, partial illumination of the room at night, and a family member in attendance at all times. These simple changes in conjunction with 50 mg of chlorpromazine (Thorazine) three times daily and 500 mg of chloral hydrate at bedtime reversed his confusional state within two days, and he was able to return home in a week with no residual evidence of abnormal behavior. To date there has been no recurrence of these problems. (Strub & Black, 1981, pp. 89–90)

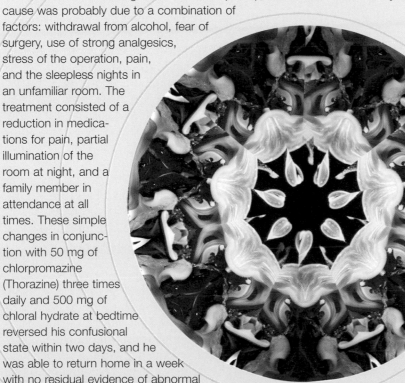

Issues, Concepts, and Methods in the Study of Older Adults

Diversity in Older Adults
Age, Cohort, and Time-of-Measurement Effects
Diagnosing Psychopathology in Later Life
Range of Problems

Old Age and Brain Disorders

Dementia
Delirium

Old Age and Psychological Disorders

Overall Prevalence of Mental Disorders in Late Life
Depression
Anxiety Disorders
Delusional (Paranoid) Disorders
Schizophrenia
Substance-Related Disorders
Hypochondriasis
Sleep Disorders
Suicide
Sexuality and Aging

Treatment and Care of Older Adults

Nursing Homes
Alternative Living Settings
Community-Based Care

Issues Specific to Therapy with Older Adults

Content of Therapy
Process of Therapy

Summary

The more fortunate readers of this book will grow old one day. As you do, physiological changes are inevitable, and there may be many emotional and mental changes as well. Are aged people at higher risk for mental disorders than young people? Are earlier emotional problems, such as anxiety and depression, likely to become worse in old age? Do these emotional problems develop in people who did not have them when younger?

Most segments of society in the United States tend to have certain assumptions about old age. We fear that we will become doddering and befuddled. We worry that our sex lives will become unsatisfying, perhaps even non-existent. This chapter examines such issues and questions and considers whether some therapies are better suited than others to deal with the psychological problems of older adults. We shall consider also whether, as life expectancy extends well into the seventies and beyond, society is devoting enough intellectual and monetary resources to studying aging and helping older adults.

In contrast to the esteem in which they are held in most Asian countries, older adults are generally not treated very well in the United States. The process of growing old, although inevitable for us all, is resented by many, even abhorred. Perhaps this lack of regard for older adults stems from our own deep-seated fear of and misconceptions about growing old. The old person with serious infirmities is an unwelcome reminder that any one of us may one day walk with a less steady gait, see less clearly, taste food less keenly, enjoy sex with less intensity, and fall victim to some of the diseases and maladies that are the lot of many old people.

The psychological and social problems of aging may be especially severe for women. Even with the consciousness-raising of the past three decades, our society does not readily accept in women the wrinkles and sagging that become more and more prominent with advancing years. Although gray hair at the temples and even a bald head are often considered distinguished in a man, signs of aging in women are not valued in U.S. society and in many other countries. The cosmetics and plastic-surgery industries make billions of dollars each year exploiting the fear inculcated in women about looking their age.[1]

Older individuals from minority ethnic groups experience a double jeopardy. African American and Mexican American elders have considerably lower incomes and poorer health, as well as less life satisfaction, than their white counterparts (Dowd & Bengston, 1978; Gerber, 1983). Indeed, according to some observers, societal biases against women contribute to triple jeopardy, with older minority women running the greatest risk of economic dependency and associated problems (Blau, Oser, & Stephens, 1979). According to other experts, however, being female or a member of a minority group or both as one ages confers certain benefits, as explored in Focus on Discovery 16.1.

The physical realities of aging are complicated by **ageism**, which can be defined as discrimination against any person, young or old, based on chronological age. Ageism can be seen when a professor in his or her late sixties is considered too old to continue teaching at a university as well as when a person older than seventy-five is ignored in a social gathering on the assumption that he or she has nothing to contribute to the conversation. Like any prejudice, ageism ignores the diversity among people in favor of employing stereotypes (Gatz & Pearson, 1988).

Mental health professionals have until recently paid little attention to the psychological problems of older adults. Many operate under the popular misconceptions that intellectual deterioration is prevalent and inevitable, that depression among old people is widespread and untreatable, that sex is a lost cause. Although those who provide mental health services are probably not extremely ageist (Gatz & Pearson, 1988), their attitudes and practices merit special attention because of the influence they have on policies that affect the lives of older adults. Since the 1980s many schools and universities that prepare people for the health professions have added research and training in gerontology

Ageism refers to discrimination against someone because of his or her age. In one form of ageism, countermyth, we especially applaud achievements of the elderly, as in former president Bush's parachute jump.

---

[1] The value that American society places on youth seems to be extending to men, with the result that more men have been undergoing plastic surgery in an effort to look younger than their years.

Gender Role Flexibility, Discrimination, and the Transition to Old Age in Women

Older women in U.S. society face many significant threats to their well-being. They are more likely than older men to be widowed or divorced (Moen, 1996); they are more likely to live in poverty (Estes, Gerard, & Clarke, 1985) and to experience a loss in income in old age, often as a result of widowhood, divorce, and inadequate pensions and health insurance (Moen, 1996); and they are more likely to be the victims of crime, particularly domestic violence (Jones, 1987). Older women report higher levels of symptomatic, chronic health problems and impairments in physical activity and mobility than do older men (Herzog, 1989). In addition, they experience the double jeopardy of ageism and sexism—what one writer has termed "the deadly duo" (Markson, 1995).

Despite these disadvantages, it has been observed that on some levels, women adapt more successfully to the aging process than do men. For example, whereas the suicide rate for men rises steadily as they age, the rate for women peaks in middle age—in their fifties—and then slightly yet steadily declines across the rest of their life span (McIntosh, 1995; McIntosh et al., 1994).

There may be mediating factors that help explain women's relative resilience in old age. Some writers have hypothesized that older women may be better equipped than men to cope with the discrimination resulting from ageism that they may encounter, since they have learned to cope with other forms of discrimination, such as sexism, long before they reach old age. Canetto (1992) has observed that men usually come to late life with unrealistic expectations and a limited range of coping strategies. When they reach old age and experience marginalization and discrimination for perhaps the first time, they are unprepared. Indeed, there is evidence to suggest that coping skills learned across the life span play a role in successful aging for oppressed groups in general. Some researchers (Friend, 1991; Turk, Rose, & Gatz, 1996) have noted the coping strengths that lesbians and gay men bring to old age as a result of contending with homophobia and heterosexism throughout their lives. Similarly, others have observed that older adults belonging to minority populations bring coping skills to old age resulting from a lifetime of experience with

racism (e.g., Hill, Colby, & Phelps, 1983, cited in Stoller & Gibson, 1994).

Women may come to old age having filled more roles than men, and they may have more experience in navigating major role changes over the course of their lives (from, for example, maternal and spousal roles to possible career-related roles to postparental, caregiver, and widowhood roles). In contrast, men often remain in a more stable role—the career- or work-dominated role of the provider—up until they reach old age and retirement (Sinnott, 1986). The ability to become involved in multiple social roles in old age is associated with fewer depressive symptoms, greater life satisfaction, and higher levels of perceived self-efficacy in both women and men (Adelmann, 1994; Turk-Charles et al., 1996). In particular, there is evidence that more flexible gender roles may help both women and men to adjust to the aging process and that rigid adherence to traditional gender roles is disadvantageous for both women and men as they grow old.

One survey-based study (E. H. Davison, 1999) investigated how gender role flexibility, perceived sexism, and perceived ageism might affect the subjective well-being of older women. Women aged sixty-five dwelling in the community completed questionnaires designed to measure their subjective well-being, the amount of sexism and ageism they had experienced during their lives, and their gender role flexibility (the degree to which they felt comfortable assuming the traditional roles of both sexes—for example, being a mother of a small child fifty years ago and working outside the home). Both gender role flexibility and perceived discrimination were found to correlate with the women's levels of subjective well-being: gender role flexibility was predictive of higher levels of subjective well-being, and perceived discrimination was predictive of lower subjective well-being. These findings reinforce the notion that gender role flexibility is correlated with (and may contribute to) well-being in older women. Additionally, these data underscore the importance of considering the effects of discrimination on well-being in late life.

This material is based on E. H. Davison (1999).

to their curricula; yet there is still a dearth of professionals committed primarily to serving the needs of older adults (Gatz & Smyer, 1992; Knight, 1996).

In any discussion of the differences between those who are old and those not yet old, the old are usually defined as those over the age of sixty-five. The decision to use this age was set largely by social policies, not because age sixty-five is some critical point at which the physiological and psychological processes of aging suddenly begin. To have some rough demarcation points for better describing the diversity of the older population, gerontologists usually divide people over age sixty-five into three groups: the young-old, those aged sixty-five to seventy-four; the old-old, those aged seventy-five to eighty-four; and the oldest-old, those over age eighty-five. The health of these groups differs in important ways.

Currently in the United States, people 65 and older comprise 12.4 percent (35 million) of the population (U.S. Bureau of the Census, 2000). It is estimated that Americans over age sixty-five will number 52 million by the year 2020, an increase of more than 20 million since the late 1980s (Spencer, 1989). The oldest-old, those above age eighty-five, are expected to grow to at least 24 million by the year 2040, up from 3.8 million in the mid-

1990s. As of 1999, there were 70,000 Americans at least 100 years old; by the year 2050, that number is expected to grow more than tenfold to over 800,000 (U.S. Bureau of the Census, 1999). And as the first generation of baby boomers begins to reach age 65 in 2010, the percent of elderly in the United States will rise dramatically, comprising an estimated 20 percent of the population by the year 2030 (U.S. Bureau of the Census, 2000). Thus it is important to examine what we know about the psychological and neuropsychological issues facing older adults and to expose some of our misconceptions about aging.

In this chapter we review first some general concepts and topics critical to the study of aging. We look next at brain disorders of old age. Then we examine psychological disorders—most of which were discussed earlier—with a particular focus on how these disorders are manifest in old age. Finally, we discuss general issues of treatment and care for older adults.

Issues, Concepts, and Methods in the Study of Older Adults

Theory and research bearing on older adults require an understanding of several rather specialized issues. We turn to these issues now.

Diversity in Older Adults

The word diversity is well suited to the older population. Not only are older people different from one another, but they are more different from one another than are individuals in any other age group. People tend to become less alike as they grow older. That all old people are alike is a prejudice held by many people. A moment's honest reflection may reveal that certain traits come to mind when we hear that a person is age, say, sixty-seven. But to know that a person is sixty-seven years old is actually to know very little about him or her. The many differences among people who are sixty-five and older will become increasingly evident in the course of reading this chapter.

Age, Cohort, and Time-of-Measurement Effects

Chronological age is not as simple a variable in psychological research as it might seem. Because other factors associated with age may be at work, we must be cautious when we attribute differences in age groups solely to the effects of aging. In the field of aging, as in studies of earlier development, including childhood, a distinction is made among three kinds of effects (Table 16.1):

As illustrated by John Glenn's space flight, advancing age need not lead to a curtailment of activities.

- **Age effects** are the consequences of being a given chronological age.
- **Cohort effects** are the consequences of having been born in a given year and having grown up during a particular time period with its own unique pressures, problems, challenges, and opportunities.
- **Time-of-measurement effects** are confounds that arise because events at a particular point in time can have a specific effect on a variable that is being studied over time (Schaie & Hertzog, 1982).

The two major research designs used to assess developmental change, the cross-sectional and the longitudinal, clarify these terms. In **cross-sectional studies** the investigator compares different age groups at the same moment in time on the variable of interest. Suppose that in 1995 we took a poll and found that many interviewees over age eighty spoke with a European accent, whereas those in their forties and fifties did not. Could we conclude that as people grow older, they develop European accents? Hardly! Cross-sectional studies do not examine the same people over time; consequently, they allow us to make statements only about age effects in a particular study or experiment, not about age changes over time.

In **longitudinal studies**, the researcher selects one cohort—say, the graduating class of 2004—and periodically retests it using the same measure over a number of years. This design allows us to trace individual patterns of consistency or change over time—cohort

Table 16.1 Age, Cohort, and Time-of-Measurement Effects

Age Effects	Cohort Effects	Time-of-Measurement Effects
The consequences of being a given chronological age; e.g., becoming old enough to receive Social Security benefits.	The consequences of having been born in a given year and having grown up during a particular time period; e.g., a difference in frugality between those who lived through the Great Depression of the 1930s and the baby boomers born during the late 1940s.	The consequences of the effects that a particular factor can have at a particular time; e.g., people responding in the 1990s to surveys about their sexual behavior were more likely to be frank and open than were people responding to the same questions in the 1950s, because public discussions of sex were much more the norm in the 1990s.

effects—and to analyze how behavior in early life relates to behavior in old age.

However, because each cohort is unique, conclusions drawn from longitudinal studies are restricted to the particular cohort chosen. For example, if members of a cohort studied from 1956 to 1996 are found to decline in sexual activity as they enter their sixties, we cannot conclude that the sexuality of those in a cohort studied from 1996 to 2036 will decline when they reach the same age. Improvements over time in health care and changes in other variables, such as social mores, might enhance the sexual activity of the younger cohort, a time-of-measurement effect.

An additional problem that arises with longitudinal studies is the phenomenon known as attrition, in which participants often drop out as the studies proceed, either due to death or lack of interest, creating a source of bias commonly called **selective mortality**. The least able people are the most likely to drop out from a study; the nonrepresentative people who remain are usually healthier than the general population. Thus findings based on longitudinal studies may be overly optimistic concerning the rate of decline of a variable such as sexual activity over the life span.

Diagnosing Psychopathology in Later Life

The DSM criteria for older adults are basically the same as those for younger adults. The nature and manifestations of mental disorders are usually assumed to be the same in adulthood and old age, even though little research supports this assumption (Gatz, Kasl-Godley, & Karel, 1996; LaRue, Dessonville, & Jarvik, 1985). We often do not know what certain symptoms in older adults mean because we have few specifics about psychopathology in old age (Zarit, Eiler, & Hassinger, 1985). For example, somatic symptoms are generally more prevalent in late life, but these symptoms are also evident in depression in older adults. Are the somatic symptoms of a depressed older adult necessarily a part of depression, or might they (also) reflect physical changes?

Cohort effects refer to the fact that people of the same chronological age may differ considerably depending on when they were born.

Range of Problems

We know that mental health may be tied to the physical and social problems in a person's life. As a group, no other people have more of these problems than the aged. They have them all—physical decline and disabilities, sensory and neurological deficits, loss of loved ones, the cumulative effects of a lifetime of many unfortunate experiences, and social stresses such as ageism. However, it is important to remember that in addition to a lifetime of exposure to losses and to other stressors, older adults have many positive life experiences, many coping mechanisms, and wisdom on which to draw. Moreover, some cultural and ethnic factors appear to mitigate the negative effects of aging, as suggested in Focus on Discovery 16.1. Finally, older adults who belong to groups that provide meaningful, strong roles for them seem to have an easier time adjusting to growing old than do those who are not allowed such input into the family or society (Amoss & Harrell, 1981; Keith, 1982).

Old Age and Brain Disorders

Although the majority of older people do not have brain disorders, these problems account for more admissions and hospital inpatient days than any other condition of geriatric adults (Zarit & Zarit, 1998). We will examine two principal types of brain disorders, dementia and delirium.

Dementia

"...the past is like the rudder of a ship. It keeps you moving through the present, steers you into the future. Without it, without memory, you are unmoored, a wind-tossed boat with no anchor. You learn this by watching someone you love drift away" (Davis, 2002).

Dementia—what laypeople call senility—is a general descriptive term for the deterioration of intellectual abilities to the point that social and occupational functions are impaired. Dementia comes on very slowly over a period of years; subtle cognitive and behavioral deficits can be detected well before the person shows any noticeable impairment (Small et al., 2000). Difficulty remembering things, especially recent events, is the most prominent symptom of dementia. People may leave tasks unfinished because they forget to return to them after an interruption. The person who had started to fill a teapot at the sink leaves the water running; a parent is unable to remember the name of a daughter or son and later may not even recall that he or she has children or recognize them when they come to visit. Hygiene may be poor and appearance slovenly because the person forgets to bathe or how to dress adequately. Patients with dementia also get lost, even in familiar surroundings. The poignant quote above comes from one of Ronald Reagan's daughters.

Judgment may become faulty, and the person may have difficulty comprehending situations and making plans or decisions. People with dementia relinquish their standards and lose control of their impulses; they may use coarse language, tell inappropriate jokes, shoplift, and make sexual advances to strangers. The ability to deal with abstract ideas deteriorates, and disturbances in emotions are common, including symptoms of depression, flatness of affect, and sporadic emotional outbursts. Delusions and hallucinations occur in over 50 percent of patients (Fahrer et al., 2000). Patients with dementia are likely to show language disturbances as well, such as vague patterns of speech. Although the motor system is intact, they may have difficulty carrying out motor activities, such as those involved in brushing the teeth, waving good-bye, or dressing themselves. Despite intact sensory functioning, they may also have trouble recognizing familiar surroundings or naming common objects. Episodes of delirium, a state of great mental confusion (discussed in detail later), may also occur.

The course of dementia may be progressive, static, or remitting, depending on the cause. Many people with progressive dementia eventually become withdrawn and apathetic. In the terminal phase of the illness, the personality loses its sparkle and integrity. Relatives and friends say that the person is just not himself or herself anymore. Social involvement with others keeps narrowing. Finally, the person is oblivious to his or her surroundings.

The prevalence of dementia increases with advancing age. One study found a prevalence of 1 percent in people aged sixty-five to seventy-four, 4 percent in those aged seventy-five to eighty-four, and 10 percent in those over age eighty-four (George et al., 1991). These figures may well be underestimates because they do not include individuals who have died from some causes of dementia (see the following discussion of Alzheimer's disease). The annual incidence, that is, the number of new cases developing in a year, in the United States is more than 5 percent for those over age eighty-five (Gao et al., 1998).

Causes of Dementia   Dementias are typically classified into four types. Alzheimer's disease is the most common; frontal-temporal and frontal-subcortical dementias are defined by the areas of the brain that are most affected, and vascular dementias by their cause—a stroke.

Alzheimer's Disease   More common in women than in men because of women's greater longevity, Alzheimer's disease accounts for about 50 percent of dementia in older people and afflicts over four million Americans.

In **Alzheimer's disease**, initially described by the German neurologist Alois Alzheimer in 1906, the brain tissue irreversibly deteriorates, and death usually occurs ten or twelve years after the onset of symptoms. About 100,000 Americans die each year from this disease. The person may at first have difficulties only in concentration and in memory for newly learned material, and may appear absentminded and irritable, shortcomings that may be overlooked for several years but that eventually interfere with daily living. Indeed, subtle deficits in learning and memory revealed by neuropsychological tests are found in people who will later develop the disease well before the onset of any clinical symptoms (Linn et al., 1995). As the disease develops, the person often blames others for personal failings and may have delusions of being persecuted. Memory continues to deteriorate, and the individual becomes increasingly disoriented and agitated. Depression is common, occurring in up to 30 percent of people with Alzheimer's disease (Strauss & Ogrocki, 1996).

The main physiological change in the brain, evident at autopsy, is an atrophy (wasting away) of the cerebral cortex, first the entorhinal cortex and the hippocampus, and later the frontal, temporal, and parietal lobes. As neurons and synapses are lost, the fissures widen and the ridges become narrower and flatter. The ventricles also become enlarged. **Plaques**—small, round areas comprising the remnants of the lost neurons and ß-amyloid, a waxy protein deposit—are scattered throughout the cortex. Tangled abnormal protein filaments—**neurofibrillary tangles**—accumulate within the cell bodies of neurons. These plaques and tangles are present throughout the cerebral cortex and the hippocampus.

The cerebellum, spinal cord, and motor and sensory areas of the cortex are less affected, which is why Alzheimer's patients do not appear to have anything physically wrong with them until late in the disease process. For some time patients are able to walk

Former president Ronald Reagan has Alzheimer's disease.

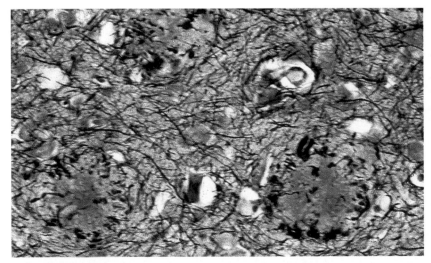
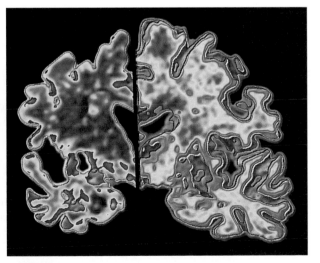

In the photograph on the left of brain tissue from a patient with Alzheimer's disease, the waxy amyloid shows up as areas of dark pink. On the right are computer-generated images of a brain of a patient with Alzheimer's disease and a normal brain. Note that the patient's brain (*left*) has shrunk considerably owing to the loss of nerve cells.

DSM-IV TR Criteria for Dementia

Of the Alzheimers type:

- Multiple cognitive deficits manifested by both A and B:
  A. Memory impairment
  B. One or more of the following: aphasia, apraxia (impairment in doing something even though motor components intact), agnosia, and disturbance in executive functioning
- Significant impairment in social or occupational functioning and represent a major decline from a previous level of functioning
- Gradual onset and continuing cognitive decline
- Above cognitive deficits not due to any of the following:
  A. Other CNS conditions that cause such progressive declines, for example, Parkinson's disease, brain tumor
  B. Systemic conditions known to cause dementia, for example, hypothyroidism, niacin deficiency, syphilis, HIV infection
  C. Substance-induced conditions
- Above cognitive deficits not occurring exclusively during an episode of delirium
- Above cognitive deficits not better accounted for by another Axis I disorder, for example, major depression or schizophrenia

around normally, and their overlearned habits, such as making small talk, remain intact, so that in short encounters strangers may not notice anything amiss.

About 25 percent of patients with Alzheimer's disease also have brain deterioration similar to the deterioration that occurs in Parkinson's disease. Neurons are lost in the nigrostriatal pathway (recall our discussion of this pathway in Chapter 11).

There is some controversy over the relative importance of the amyloid deposits and the neurofibrillary tangles in Alzheimer's disease. Both substances can disrupt brain function. When amyloid builds up in a cell, the cell dies. Neurofibrillary tangles are associated with changes in tau proteins, which are crucial for maintaining the transport of essential components of neural function (such as synaptic vesicles) from the axon to the synaptic terminal. Evidence favoring the importance of amyloid comes from genetic studies and from the fact that amyloid increases very early in the disease (Naslund et al., 2000). However, since an increase in amyloid is found in normal aging as well, it is not unique to Alzheimer's disease. The tangles, in contrast, are more specific to Alzheimer's and thus are likely to be important in its etiology. Furthermore, when amyloid and tangles are correlated with cognitive deficits, tangles show a stronger association (Berg et al., 1998). These substances continue to be the subject of much research.

Although neural pathways using other transmitters (e.g., serotonin, norepinephrine) deteriorate in Alzheimer's (Lawler et al., 1989; Wester et al., 1988), those using acetylcholine (ACh) are of particular importance. There is evidence that anticholinergic drugs (those that reduce ACh) can produce memory impairments in normal people similar to those found in Alzheimer's patients. There are fewer acetylcholine terminals in the brains of patients with Alzheimer's disease (Strong et al., 1991), and levels of the major metabolite of acetylcholine are also low and are associated with greater mental deterioration (Wester et al., 1988).

There is very strong evidence for a genetic basis for Alzheimer's. The risk for Alzheimer's is increased in first-degree relatives of afflicted individuals (Heun et al., 2001), and concordance for MZ twins is greater than that for DZ twins (Bergen, Engedal, & Kringlen, 1997). Among early-onset (before age sixty) cases, which account for less than 5 percent of all cases of Alzheimer's disease, the pattern of inheritance suggests the operation of a single, dominant gene.

Because people with Down syndrome often develop Alzheimer's disease if they survive until middle age, interest focused initially on chromosome 21, which is aberrant in Down syndrome (see p. 502). A gene controlling the protein responsible for the formation of ß-amyloid was found to be on the long arm of chromosome 21, and studies have demonstrated that this gene causes the development of about 5 percent of cases of early-onset Alzheimer's disease. Dominant genes causing a small percentage of early onset cases of Alzheimer's disease have also been found on chromosomes 1 and 14.

Note that we used the verb "cause" in the previous two sentences. Unlike the genetic diatheses we have described in earlier chapters, the presence of these Alzheimer's disease genes does not appear to require activation by a stressor to result in the disease. For example, no person with the gene on chromosome 21 has survived beyond the age of sixty-seven without developing Alzheimer's disease.

The majority of late-onset cases of Alzheimer's disease exhibit a particular form of a gene on chromosome 19 (called the apolipoprotein E 4 allele), which functions more like the genetic diatheses we have considered so often before. Having one E 4 allele increases the risk of Alzheimer's disease to almost 50 percent, and having two alleles brings the risk to above 90 percent (Farlow, 1997). Having a different form of this gene (the E 2 allele) lowers the risk of developing Alzheimer's disease. The E 4 allele is strongly related to Alzheimer's disease among Hispanics in the Caribbean and is the likely cause of the higher rates among first-degree relatives of African Americans with the disease (Green et al., 2002; Romas et al., 2002).

The importance of this gene to the etiology of Alzheimer's disease is further shown by the fact that whites with two of the E 4 alleles show abnormal glucose metabolism in the cortex even before the onset of any symptoms (Reiman et al., 1996). How, exactly, does the gene increase the risk for Alzheimer's disease? The answer is not certain, but the gene appears to be related to the development of both plaques and tangles, and it seems to increase the likelihood that the brain will incur damage from free radicals, which are unstable molecules derived from oxygen that attack proteins and DNA.

Finally, the environment is likely to play a role in most cases of Alzheimer's, as demonstrated by reports of long-lived MZ twins who are discordant for the disorder. The reasoning is the same as for judging the importance of genetic and environmental factors in any disorder—if two people with the same genetic material (i.e., MZ twins) do not both develop a particular disorder, then environmental factors must play a role.

A history of head injury is a risk factor for developing Alzheimer's disease (Gallo & Lebowitz, 1999; Rasmassen et al., 1995). Longitudinal studies have also shown that depression increases the risk for Alzheimer's disease, but appears to do so only for people who were showing mild cognitive impairment at the time the study was begun (Bassuk et al., 1998; Gallo & Lebowitz, 1999).

Some environmental factors appear to offer protection against developing Alzheimer's. Nonsteroidal anti-inflammatory drugs such as ibuprofen appear to reduce the risk of Alzheimer's disease (Gallo & Lebowitz, 1999; Stewart et al., 1997), as does nicotine (Whitehouse, 1997). The class of drugs referred to as statins and used to control cholesterol also seem to be protective (Rockwood et al., 2002). Unfortunately, these protective factors can have undesirable effects—the well-known negative effects of smoking on the cardiovascular system and gastrointestinal and liver problems due to anti-inflammatories and statins.

Having a high level of cognitive ability may also offer protection. This possibility was demonstrated in a study of nuns who had written autobiographies in the weeks preceding their religious vows. These autobiographies were analyzed for their grammatical complexity and idea density, concepts related to general knowledge, vocabulary skills, and other cognitive abilities. Excerpts from two sisters illustrate the differences in linguistic ability that were found.

> *Low linguistic ability:* I was born in Eau Claire, Wis. on May, 24, 1913 and was baptized in St. James church.
>
> *High linguistic ability:* The happiest day of my life so far was my First Communion Day which was in June nineteen hundred and twenty when I was but eight years of age, and four years later I was confirmed by Bishop D. D. (Snowden et al., 1996, p. 530).

Relating this linguistic measure to Alzheimer's disease among sisters who had died, low linguistic ability was found in 90 percent of those who developed Alzheimer's disease many years later and in only 13 percent of those who didn't (Snowden et al., 1996). Similar findings have emerged from studies showing that higher mental ability reduces the risk for Alzheimer's and that continuing to engage in cognitive activities (such as reading a newspaper regularly) reduces risk (Whalley et al., 2001; Wilson et al., 2002).

This research is part of a growing interest in early identification of people at high risk for Alzheimer's, spurred in part by the hope that early intervention might mitigate or even prevent the later development of the disease or at least some of its most damaging features. We are still far from understanding the causes of Alzheimer's disease, but progress is clearly being made.

Frontal-Temporal Dementias   This type of dementia accounts for about 10 percent of cases. It typically begins in a person's late fifties. In addition to the usual cognitive impairments of a dementia, frontal-temporal dementias are marked by extreme behavioral and personality changes. Sometimes patients are very apathetic and unresponsive to their environment; at other times they show an opposite pattern of euphoria, overactivity, and impulsivity (Levy et al., 1996). Unlike Alzheimer's disease, frontal-temporal dementias are not closely linked to loss of cholinergic neurons; serotonin neurons are most affected. There is widespread loss of neurons in the frontal and temporal lobes. Pick's disease is one cause of frontal-temporal dementia. Like Alzheimer's disease, Pick's disease is a degenerative disorder in which neurons are lost. It is also characterized by the presence of Pick bodies, spherical inclusions within neurons. Frontal-temporal dementias have a strong genetic component, although the specifics of the genetics are not as well understood as for Alzheimer's disease (Usman, 1997).

Frontal-Subcortical Dementias   These dementias affect circuits in the brain that run from subcortical areas to the cortex. Because subcortical brain areas are involved in the control of motor movements, both cognition and motor activity are affected. Types of frontal-subcortical dementias include the following:

Michael J. Fox has Parkinson's disease.

- Huntington's chorea is caused by a single dominant gene located on chromosome 4 and is diagnosed principally by neurologists on the basis of genetic testing. Its major behavioral feature is the presence of writhing (choreiform) movements. Perhaps best-known of people with this disease was folk-song writer and singer Woody Guthrie.

- Parkinson's disease is marked by muscle tremors, muscular rigidity, and akinesia (an inability to initiate movement), and can lead to dementia. Muhammad Ali and Michael J. Fox have Parkinson's disease.[2]

- Normal pressure hydrocephalus, an impairment in the circulation of the cerebrospinal fluid that leads to its accumulation in the brain's ventricles ("water on the brain"), can also cause a frontal-subcortical dementia. Pressure builds and creates dementia as well as difficulty standing and walking. The condition is reversible with surgery to restore normal circulation of cerebrospinal fluid.

- Vascular dementia. This is the second most common type, next to Alzheimer's disease. It is diagnosed when a patient with dementia has neurological signs such as weakness in an arm or abnormal reflexes or when brain scans show evidence of cerebrovascular disease. Most commonly, the patient had a series of strokes in which a clot formed, impairing circulation and causing cell death. Genetic factors appear to be of no importance (Bergen et al., 1997), and risk for vascular dementia increases with the same risk factors described for cardiovascular disease in general—for example, a high level of "bad" (LDL) cholesterol (Moroney et al., 1999).

Other Causes of Dementia   A number of infectious diseases can produce irreversible dementia. Encephalitis, a generic term for any inflammation of brain tissue, is caused by viruses that enter the brain either from other parts of the body (such as the sinuses or ears) or from the bites of mosquitoes or ticks. Meningitis, an inflammation of the membranes covering the outer brain, is usually caused by a bacterial infection. The organism that produces the venereal disease syphilis (*Treponema pallidum*) can invade the brain and cause dementia.

HIV and AIDS can also cause irreversible dementia. Although this kind of dementia is so far primarily a problem of younger people, cases have been reported of AIDS-related dementia in older adults (Rosenzweig & Fillit, 1992; Weiler, Mungas, & Pomerantz, 1988). These same authors have cautioned that HIV- and AIDS-related symptoms in older adults may be misdiagnosed as Alzheimer's or as other, more common forms of dementia. There is a need for increased awareness of the growing numbers of HIV and AIDS cases among older adults (Catania et al., 1989). Older adults are one of the most rapidly growing HIV-infected groups in the United States, and they are becoming infected primarily through unprotected sex (Drummond, 1999). HIV-positive older adults are often misdiagnosed or undiagnosed, because their doctors fail to consider the possibility that their patients are sexually active and do not educate them about safer sexual practices. Since the HIV virus proceeds to full-blown AIDS twice as fast in older as in younger adults, early detection is particularly important in this population. In an effort to educate older adults about the risk of HIV infection, the American Association of Retired Persons (AARP) has produced and distributed the AIDS-prevention video *It Could Happen to Me.* However, it is equally important that doctors and other medical health providers educate themselves on this issue.

Finally, head traumas, brain tumors, nutritional deficiencies (especially of B-complex vitamins), kidney or liver failure, and endocrine-gland problems such as hyperthy-

---

[2] Fox's Parkinson's is under fairly good control at the present time.

roidism can result in dementia. Exposure to toxins, such as lead or mercury, as well as chronic use of drugs, including alcohol, are additional causes.

Treatment of Dementia　If the dementia has a reversible cause, appropriate medical treatment (such as correcting a hormonal imbalance) can be beneficial. Despite numerous investigations, no clinically significant treatment has been found that can halt or reverse Alzheimer's disease, although some drugs, as described below, show promise in effecting modest improvement in certain cognitive functions for a short period of time.

Biological Treatments of Alzheimer's Disease　Because Alzheimer's disease involves the death of brain cells that secrete acetylcholine, various studies have attempted to increase the levels of this neurotransmitter. Research using choline (a precursor of the enzyme that catalyzes the reaction that produces acetylcholine) and physostigmine (a drug that prevents the breakdown of acetylcholine) has been disappointing. Tetrahydroaminoacridine (tacrine, brand name Cognex), which inhibits the enzyme that breaks down acetylcholine, produces mild improvement or slows the progression of cognitive decline (Qizilbash et al., 1998). Tacrine cannot be used in high doses, however, because it has severe side effects; for example, it is toxic to the liver. Donepezil (Aricept) is similar to tacrine in its method of action and results but produces fewer side effects (Rogers et al., 1998). Hydergine is another drug approved for use in Alzheimer's disease by the Food and Drug Administration; its effects appear to be very modest at best (Schneider & Olin, 1994).

Long-term strategies focus on slowing the progression of the disease. Operating on the hypothesis that the buildup of ß-amyloid is the crucial factor in Alzheimer's, research is focusing on ways of blocking the creation of amyloid from its precursor protein (Whyte, Bayreuther, & Masters, 1994). Recent findings also indicate that antioxidants, such as vitamin E, may be useful in slowing the progression of the disease (Emilian et al., 2001). Management of other symptoms of Alzheimer's disease includes many of the drugs previously discussed, for example, phenothiazines for paranoia, antidepressants for depression, benzodiazepines for anxiety, and sedatives for sleep difficulties.

Psychosocial Treatments of Alzheimer's Disease for Patients and Their Families Although effective medical treatment for Alzheimer's is not yet available, patients and their families can be helped to deal with the effects of the disease. The general psychological approach is supportive, with the overall goal of minimizing the disruption caused by the patient's behavioral changes. This goal is achieved by allowing the person and the family the opportunity to discuss the illness and its consequences, providing accurate information about it, helping family members care for the patient in the home, and encouraging a realistic rather than a catastrophic attitude in dealing with the many specific issues and challenges that this brain disorder presents (Knight, 1996; Zarit, 1980).

Counseling the person with Alzheimer's is difficult. Because of cognitive losses, psychotherapy provides little long-term benefit for those with severe deterioration. However, some patients seem to enjoy and be reassured by occasional conversations with professionals and with others not directly involved in their lives—in both individual and group settings. Interventions employed with normally functioning older adults, like Butler's life review (described later in this chapter, p. 561), can also be useful for early- to mid-stage Alzheimer's patients, whose cognitive abilities have not markedly deteriorated (Kasl-Godley & Gatz, 2000). In contrast to what we have seen in dealing with virtually all other psychological problems, it may be desirable not to make an effort to get patients to admit to their problems, for their denial may be the most effective coping mechanism available (Zarit, 1980). Little if any controlled research has been done on such interventions with demented older adults.

The cognitive limitations of persons with dementia should always be treated with gentleness. Others should not consider them nonbeings, talking about their disabilities in their presence, making fun of their occasional antics and forgetfulness, discounting their paranoid suspicions about others. Older people, even those with no biological disorder, are often infantilized or ignored by their juniors, a sign of disrespect that demeans not only the older adult but the person showing the discourtesy.

Caring for a relative with Alzheimer's disease is a source of severe stress.

For every individual with a severely disabling dementia like Alzheimer's living in an institution, there are at least two living in the community, usually supported by a spouse, daughter, or other family member. As the care of the older adult with dementia generally falls on family members (especially wives and daughters), psychosocial treatment concerns not only the individual but the family as well. Family caregivers and friends, faced with taxing demands on their time, energies, and emotions, can become depressed. Caregivers need support, encouragement, and opportunities to vent their feelings of guilt and resentment. Some may need permission to take time off or to feel that they will be able to should the pressure become too great (Olshevski, Katz, & Knight, 1999).

Caring for a person with Alzheimer's disease has been shown to be extremely stressful (Anthony-Bergstone, Zarit, & Gatz, 1988; Gwynther & George, 1986; Zarit, Todd, & Zarit, 1986). Two studies (Dura, Stukenberg, & Kiecolt-Glaser, 1991; Schulz & Williamson, 1991) have documented unusually high levels of clinical depression and anxiety in adult children and spouses caring for their parents or spouses with dementia as compared with noncaregiver controls. Other studies have found more physical illness (Haley et al., 1987; Potashnik & Pruchno, 1988) and decreased immune functioning (Kiecolt-Glaser et al., 1991) among such caregivers. In many instances the disorders seem to be attributable to the stresses of caregiving; prior to these challenges the families of caregivers usually did not experience psychological difficulties (Gatz, Bengtson, & Blum, 1990). Factors that increase depression and anxiety among caregivers include the severity of the patient's problem behaviors, perceived unavailability of social support, and concerns about financial resources to handle expenses during the long, debilitating, and often expensive illness. Because the family members are so powerfully affected, it is often recommended that they be given respites from their task. The patient may be hospitalized for a week, a health care worker may take over and give the family an opportunity for a holiday, or the patient may be enrolled at an adult day care center.

Researchers have begun to examine cognitive factors that affect caregivers (e.g., Gatz et al., 1990; Pearlin et al., 1990; Zarit, 1989). For example, it may be less stressful for a caregiver to adopt a fatalistic attitude toward the patient's behavior—"There's nothing I can do to change the situation, so let me just resign myself to it and make the necessary adjustments"—rather than take a more active approach—"How can I get Mom to remember to put her coat on before leaving the house?" The latter attitude is more suitable to dealing with challenges that are amenable to modification (Fiore, Becker, & Coppel, 1983; Folkman & Lazarus, 1985). In a study by Knight, Lutzky, and Olshevski (1992), efforts to help distressed caregivers solve problems and accept responsibility actually increased their stress as measured by cardiovascular reactivity. Knight et al. speculate that problem-solving training may reinforce the view that the caregiver is responsible for the patient's problem behaviors.[3]

Families can be taught, however, to cope better with the stress of having a family member with Alzheimer's and at the same time help their relatives with dementia cope with lost functions. It can help to provide accurate information on the nature of the patient's problems. For example, because people with Alzheimer's have great difficulty placing new information into memory, they can engage in a reasonable conversation but forget a few minutes later what has been discussed. A caregiver may become impatient unless he or she understands that this impairment is to be expected because of the underlying brain damage.

Substituting recognition for recall in daily situations may help some patients and families better manage their lives, at least in the earliest stages of the disease. Families can be taught to ask questions that embed the answer. For example, it is much easier to respond to "Was the person you just spoke to on the phone Harry or Tom?" than to "Who just called?" Labels on drawers, appliances, and rooms may help orient some early stage patients. If the individual has lost the ability to read, pictures instead of verbal labels can

---

[3] This brings to mind our observations in the previous chapter (p. 514) on the pernicious nature of psychogenic theories of psychopathology. Those who are entrusted with the care of children or of older adults with dementia are often subtly encouraged to accept responsibility and hence blame for the predicament of their charges. We do not wish to advocate inaction and neglect, rather only to place a caregiver's responsibilities in proper perspective.

be used. Prominent calendars, clocks, and strategic notes, as well as an automatic dialer on a telephone, may help (Woods, 1994). Based on the empirical literature, however, not too much is to be expected of memory training (Kasl-Godley & Gatz, 2000).

Behavioral approaches have also been employed in an effort to reduce disruptive behavior as well as to alleviate depression in Alzheimer's patients. For example, self-care skills can be improved, verbal outbursts diminished, and depressed mood lifted (by encouraging pleasant activities) with the application of appropriate reinforcement contingencies (Cohen-Mansfield et al., 1996; Kasl-Godley & Gatz, 2000; Teri, 1994).

It is useful for caregivers to understand that patients do not always recognize their limitations and may attempt to engage in activities beyond their abilities, sometimes dangerously so. Although it is not advisable to coddle patients, it is important to set limits in light of their obliviousness to their own problems and impairments. Sometimes, however, the caregiver's reactions to the patient's problems require attention. In one case, the

Providing memory aids is one way of combating memory loss.

daughter-in-law of a woman was offended by the woman's color combinations in clothing and wished to take over responsibility for coordinating her wardrobe, even though the patient was capable of dressing herself in an adequate although not aesthetically pleasing fashion. The caregiver was urged not to impose her standards and taste on the patient and to understand that the patient's ability to dress herself and to take responsibility for her clothes was more important than adherence to conventional appearance (Zarit, 1980).

Some of the tensions between caregiver and patient may well have their roots in aspects of the relationship that predated the onset of the dementia. There is a tendency to consider the most obvious facet of a situation, in this case the cognitive impairments of a sick person, as the cause of all difficulties. Counseling directed toward long-standing problems may be needed.

Perhaps the most wrenching decision is whether to institutionalize the person with dementia. For many people, custodial care (e.g., in-home assistance with bathing, grooming, and dressing) can delay the need for placement in a nursing home. However, at some point the patient's nursing needs may become so onerous and mental state so deteriorated that a nursing home is the only realistic option for the benefit of the person and of the family. The conflicts people face when making this decision are considerable. The counselor can be a source of information about nearby facilities as well as a source of support for making and implementing a decision (Zarit, 1980).

Delirium

The term **delirium** is derived from the Latin words *de*, meaning "from" or "out of" and *lira*, meaning "furrow" or "track." The term implies being off track or deviating from the usual state (Wells & Duncan, 1980). As illustrated in the case that opened this chapter, delirium is typically described as a clouded state of consciousness. The patient, sometimes rather suddenly, has great trouble concentrating and focusing attention and cannot maintain a coherent and directed stream of thought. In the early stages of delirium the person is frequently restless, particularly at night. The sleep-waking cycle becomes disturbed so that the person is drowsy during the day and awake, restless, and agitated during the night. The individual is generally worse during sleepless nights and in the dark. Vivid dreams and nightmares are common.

Delirious patients may be impossible to engage in conversation because of their wandering attention and fragmented thinking. In severe delirium, speech is rambling and incoherent. Bewildered and confused, some delirious individuals may become disoriented for time, place, and sometimes person, that is, they are unclear about what day it is, where they are, and even who they are. They are often so inattentive that they cannot be engaged in conversation. Memory impairment, especially for recent events, is common.

DSM-IV TR Criteria for Delirium

- Disturbance of consciousness (reduced awareness of the environment and attentional difficulties)
- A change in cognition, such as a language disturbance, or a perceptual disturbance not better accounted for by a dementia
- Rapid development, like over the course of a few hours or days, and fluctuation during the course of a day
- Evidence of presence of a medical condition causing it, such as malnutrition

In the course of a twenty-four-hour period, however, delirious people have lucid intervals and become alert and coherent. These daily fluctuations help distinguish delirium from other syndromes, especially Alzheimer's disease.

Perceptual disturbances are frequent in delirium. Individuals mistake the unfamiliar for the familiar; for example, they may state that they are at home instead of in a hospital. Although illusions and hallucinations are common, particularly visual and mixed visual-auditory ones, they are not always present. Delusions have been noted in about 25 percent of delirious older adults (Camus et al., 2000). These delusions tend to be poorly worked out, fleeting, and changeable.

Swings in activity and mood accompany disordered thoughts and perceptions. Delirious people can be erratic, ripping their clothes one moment and sitting lethargically the next. Sometimes the clinical picture in delirium is just a hypoactive (basically lethargic) pattern, which contributes to the difficulty in diagnosing it (Webster & Holroyd, 2000). Delirious patients are, however, usually in great emotional turmoil and may shift rapidly from one emotion to another—depression, anxiety, fright, anger, euphoria, and irritability. Fever, flushed face, dilated pupils, tremors, rapid heartbeat, elevated blood pressure, and incontinence of urine and feces are common. If the delirium proceeds, the person will completely lose touch with reality and may become stuporous (Lipowski, 1980, 1983; Strub & Black, 1981). Although delirium is one of the most frequent biological mental disorders in older adults, it has been neglected in research and, like dementia, is often misdiagnosed (Knight, 1996).

People of any age are subject to delirium, but it is more common in children and older adults. It is particularly common in hospitalized older adults. It is estimated that 15 to 20 percent of all general hospital patients experience delirium, but the figures become much higher for the aged (Meagher, 2001). For example, in one recent study, 46 percent of hip fracture patients experienced delirium (Mercantonio et al., 2001). These figures are much higher than those obtained from a review of hospital charts, indicating that doctors and other hospital personnel often misdiagnose or otherwise miss the problem (Zarit & Zarit, 1998). In certain subgroups of inpatients, such as postoperative older adults (in particular, those who have had orthopedic surgery for hip fracture and those who have undergone heart surgery), the rates of delirium are even higher (Zarit & Zarit, 1998). Older inpatients who develop delirium stay longer in the hospital and have a greater chance of dying (Pompei et al., 1994). Their risk of death continues to be high for up to three years after their discharge (Curyto et al., 2001; McCusker et al., 2001). Rates of delirium in nursing homes also appear to be high. One study found that between 6 and 12 percent of nursing home residents may develop delirium in the course of one year (Katz, Parmalee, & Brubaker, 1991).

Although these rates vary widely, even the lowest figures indicate that delirium is a serious health problem for older adults. The mortality rate for delirium is extremely high; approximately 40 percent of patients die, either from exhaustion or from the condition causing the delirium, such as a drug overdose or malnutrition (Rabins & Folstein, 1982). When fatality rates for dementia and delirium are compared over a one-year period, the rates are higher for delirium than for dementia: 37.5 percent compared with 16 percent.

Although the accurate diagnosis of delirium and its differentiation from conditions that resemble it are critical to the welfare of older persons, the disorder often goes unrecognized. For example, an older woman found in a filthy apartment with no food was believed by a poorly informed physician to have dementia and was given routine custodial care in a nursing home. A professional knowledgeable about delirium learned that she had recently become depressed over the loss of a loved one and had neglected her diet. Once this was recognized, appropriate attention was given to her nutritional deficiencies, and her condition improved such that she was discharged to her own home after one month (Zarit, 1980).

Unfortunately, such neglect of delirium is fairly typical. Cameron et al. (1987) assessed 133 consecutive admissions to an acute medical ward. They found fifteen cases of delirium, only one of which had been detected by the admitting physician. Older adults are frequently misdiagnosed as having an irreversible dementia and therefore considered beyond hope. Long-term institutional care is all too often viewed as the only option even though the person may have a reversible delirium. The older adult who has a cognitive impairment must be examined thoroughly for all possible reversible causes of the disorder, such as drug intoxication, infections, fever, malnutrition, and head trauma, and then treated accordingly.

Knight (1996) offers a useful suggestion for distinguishing delirium from dementia:

> The clinical "feel" of talking with a person with delirium is rather like talking to someone who is acutely intoxicated or in an acute psychotic episode. Whereas the demented patient may not remember the name of the place where she or he is, the delirious patient may believe it is a different sort of place altogether, perhaps mistaking a psychiatric ward for a used car lot… Hallucinations, especially visual hallucinations, are common in delirium, but are rarely seen in demented patients until the very late stages of the disease. (pp. 96–97)

Causes of Delirium   The causes of delirium in older adults can be grouped into several general classes: drug intoxications and drug-withdrawal reactions, metabolic and nutritional imbalances (as in uncontrolled diabetes and thyroid dysfunction), infections or fevers, neurological disorders, and the stress of a change in the person's surroundings (Knight, 1996). As mentioned earlier, delirium may also occur following major surgery, most commonly, hip surgery (Zarit & Zarit, 1998); during withdrawal from psychoactive substances; and following head trauma or seizures. Common physical illnesses that cause delirium in this age group include congestive heart failure, pneumonia, urinary tract infection, cancer, kidney or liver failure, malnutrition, and cerebrovascular accidents or stroke. However, as in the case at the start of this chapter, delirium usually has more than one cause.

Although delirium usually develops swiftly (within a matter of hours or days), the exact mode of onset depends on the underlying cause. Delirium resulting from a toxic reaction or concussion has an abrupt onset; when infection or metabolic disturbance underlies delirium, the onset of symptoms is somewhat more gradual.

Why are older adults especially vulnerable to delirium? Many explanations have been offered: the physical declines of aging, the increased general susceptibility to chronic diseases, the many medications prescribed for older patients, the greater sensitivity to drugs, and vulnerability to stress. One other factor, brain damage, increases the risk of delirium. Older individuals with dementing disorders appear to be the most susceptible to delirium. A retrospective review of 100 hospital admissions of people of all ages who had a diagnosis of delirium revealed that 44 percent of them had delirium superimposed on another brain condition (Purdie, Honigman, & Rosen, 1981).

Treatment of Delirium   Complete recovery from delirium is possible if the syndrome is correctly identified and the underlying cause promptly and effectively treated. It generally takes one to four weeks for the condition to clear; it takes longer in older patients than in younger patients. If the underlying causative condition is not treated, however, the brain can be permanently damaged and the patient may die.

Regarding the high rates of delirium in hospitalized older adults, a recent study examined the efficacy of primary prevention strategies—in other words, the aim was to prevent delirium from beginning. The researchers examined 852 inpatients who were seventy years old or older, some of whom received usual care and some of whom received an intervention designed to prevent onset of delirium. This intervention comprised standardized protocols to address such risk factors for delirium as sleep deprivation, immobility, dehydration, visual and hearing impairment, and cognitive impairment. The patients who received the intervention had significantly lower rates of delirium, and for those who did develop delirium, the durations of the episodes were significantly shorter (Inouye et al., 1999).

One often-neglected aspect of the management of delirium is educating the family of a person with dementia to recognize the symptoms of delirium and know about its reversible nature. This is important because they may interpret the onset of delirium as a new stage of a progressive dementia. For example, a patient with Alzheimer's disease may run a high fever from an infection and begin to hallucinate and otherwise act

Table 16.2 Comparative Features of Dementia and Delirium

Dementia	Delirium
Gradual deterioration of intellectual abilities, especially memory for recent events	Trouble concentrating and staying with a train of thought
Difficulties in everyday problem solving	Restlessness at night, nightmares
Loss of control of impulses, can result in antisocial behavior, e.g., shoplifting or making sexual advances	Rambling speech; appearance of intoxication or psychosis
Periods of depression	Frequent lucid intervals
Problems naming common objects	Hallucinations, sometimes loss of contact with reality
Faulty orientation to time (e.g., day of week), place (e.g., location), and person (e.g., who the self is or others are)	Large swings in mood and activity
Usually progressive and nonreversible	Usually reversible but potentially fatal if cause, e.g., malnutrition, not treated
Prevalence increases with age	Prevalence is high in the very young as well as the old

bizarrely. These new symptoms, superimposed on the intellectual deterioration to which members of the family have become accustomed, may alarm them into concluding that the patient is losing ground fast and irreversibly. They may be rushed into a premature decision to institutionalize the patient. With proper diagnosis and treatment, however, the person can usually return to the earlier state, which, although problematic, can be coped with in the home. Table 16.2 compares the features of dementia and delirium.

Old Age and Psychological Disorders

We tend to attribute all the ups and downs of older adults to their advanced years. The most obvious characteristic of a seventy-five-year-old man is that he is old. If he is cranky, it is because he is old. If he is depressed, it is because he is old. Even when he is happy, it is often assumed to be because of his age. Moreover, the old-age explanation is generally a somatic one, even if this is not made explicit. In other words, some ill-defined physical deterioration is assumed to underlie not only the physical problems of old people but their psychological problems as well.

As we have seen throughout this book, a psychological disorder at any age may have at least a partial physical explanation. This explanation, however, can be misleading, because much psychopathology found in older adults has not been directly linked to the physiological processes of aging. Rather, maladaptive personality traits and inadequate coping skills that the person brings into old age play a role in psychological disturbances, as do health, genetic predisposition, and life stressors.

We look first at the prevalence of mental disorders in late life and then survey a number of them, paying specific attention to their characteristics in older adults.

Overall Prevalence of Mental Disorders in Late Life

Is age itself a contributing factor to emotional and mental malfunction? Do more old people than young people have mental disorders?

Whether mental disorders become more prevalent with age is not entirely clear, partly because of the methodological and conceptual difficulties we have already discussed. An extensive cross-sectional study conducted by the National Institute of Mental Health (NIMH) yielded valuable data on mental disorders in all age groups, including the old (Myers et al., 1984; Regier et al., 1988).

Current prevalence data indicate that persons over age sixty-five have the lowest overall rates of all age groups when the various mental disorders are grouped together. The primary problem of old age was found to be cognitive impairment, not a separate DSM category but an important characteristic of more than one disorder (e.g., depression, dementia, delirium). Rates for mild cognitive impairment were about 14 percent for older men and women; for severe cognitive impairment, rates were 5.5 percent for older men and 4.7 percent for older women. These rates tell us only the overall prevalence of cognitive impairment among elderly people, not whether the causes were reversible or irreversible.

The majority of persons sixty-five years of age and older are free from serious psychopathology, but 10 to 20 percent do have psychological problems severe enough to warrant professional attention (Gatz et al., 1996; Gurland, 1991). Of those with severe mental illness, many are community-dwelling individuals who tend to be poor, have three or more physical illnesses, and receive little assistance from the mental health system beyond medication (Meeks & Murrell, 1997). Currently, the health care system poorly serves the needs of the geriatric mentally ill. More research on the mental disorders in the elderly will, it is assumed, lead to greater knowledge so that assessment and treatment as well as prevention and intervention strategies can be improved (Gallo & Lebowitz, 1999; Jeste et al., 1999). In addition, new methods of training clinicians and specialists need to be implemented to ensure appropriate care for their geriatric patients (Jeste et al., 1999).

Depression

According to NIMH and other data, mood disorders are less prevalent in older adults than in younger adults—under 3 percent compared with as high as 20 percent among younger people (Eaton et al., 1989; Myers et al., 1984; Regier et al., 1988)—but they are estimated to account for nearly half the admissions of older adults to acute psychiatric care (Gurland & Cross, 1982; Wattis, 1990). Most depressed older adults are not experiencing depression for the first time; rather, their depression appears to be a continuation of a condition present earlier in life. For those older adults who do have true late-onset depression, their depression can often be traced to a specific biological cause (Fiske et al., 1998).

Unipolar depression is much more common than bipolar depression among older patients (Post, 1978; Regier et al., 1988). Bipolar disorder after the age of sixty-five is believed to be rare (Jamison, 1979; Shulman, 1993); Regier et al. found very few people aged sixty-five or older who met diagnostic criteria for mania. Our discussion therefore addresses unipolar depression in older adults.

Women have more periods of depression than men for most of their lives, except possibly when they reach old-old age (eighty-five years old and older; Gallo & Lebowitz, 1999; Wolfe, Morrow, & Frederickson, 1996). As many as 40 percent of older individuals who have chronic health problems or are confined in hospitals are depressed (Rapp, Parisi, & Walsh, 1988). Moreover, people with a dementing disorder, such as Alzheimer's, may also be depressed. In addition to the 30 percent of patients with dementia of the Alzheimer's type who are estimated to have a superimposed major depressive disorder, many more have some symptoms of depression that interfere with their lives (Burns, 1991). Other risk factors for depression in late life include widowhood, low education levels, impaired functional status (e.g., serious vision problems, difficulties walking), and heavy alcohol consumption (Gallo & Lebowitz, 1999). Furthermore, whites tend to have higher incidences of depression compared to African Americans and other minorities (Gallo & Lebowitz, 1999).

Characteristics of Depression in Older versus Younger Adults   Worry, feelings of uselessness, sadness, pessimism, fatigue, inability to sleep, and difficulties getting things done are common symptoms of depression in both older (Blazer, 1982) and younger adults. But there are also some differences (Blazer, 1982; Small et al., 1986). Feelings of guilt are less common and somatic complaints are more common in depressed older adults. Furthermore, older depressed patients show greater motor retardation, more weight loss, more of a general physical decline, less hostility, and less suicidal ideation than younger depressed patients (Musetti et al., 1989). The difference in suicidal ideation contrasts with the fact that actual suicide attempts and completed suicides increase as

Although depression is less common among older adults than younger ones, it accounts for a very large proportion of psychiatric hospital admissions among the aged.

men enter old age (see p. 307); such increases are not found in older women. Finally, memory complaints—not necessarily actual memory problems—are more common in older than in younger depressed individuals (O'Connor et al., 1990).

Using standard DSM-IV-TR criteria for depressive disorders may not be entirely appropriate when attempting to diagnose older adults, as adherence to these criteria may lead to underdiagnosis. For example, older adults are less likely to demonstrate impaired social and occupational functioning as a result of their depression because they are less likely to be working than are younger people (Fiske et al., 1998). Some researchers (Fogel & Fretwell, 1985; Newmann et al., 1996) have described a subtype of depression more commonly seen in older adults, called depletion syndrome. This syndrome is characterized chiefly by loss of pleasure, vitality, and appetite as well as hopelessness and somatic symptoms; in contrast to other forms of depression, self-blame, guilt, and dysphoric mood are either absent or are less prominent.

Depression versus Dementia As noted earlier, a number of case histories and research studies have documented that symptoms of older individuals, seemingly of dementia, remit spontaneously or improve when they are treated for depression (LaRue, 1992). Indeed, cases of depression in older adults are often misdiagnosed as a dementing disorder because of the cognitive impairment often found in depressed people. This is an important issue in differential diagnosis because depression is generally reversible whereas dementia usually is not.

Depressed patients may be absentminded, leading their loved ones to suspect dementia. But whereas depressed persons may complain of forgetfulness (Kahn et al., 1975; Raskin & Rae, 1981), those with dementia may forget that they forget! Moreover, depressed patients tend to underestimate their abilities and to be preoccupied with negative feedback (Weingartner & Silverman, 1982). Depressed older adults, although they complain more than nondepressed control patients about memory problems, do not perform more poorly than controls on neuropsychological memory tests (O'Connor et al., 1990); their performance on these tests (recall the earlier discussion of neuropsychological assessment, p. 100) is above average or superior even if they complain about memory deficits (Williams et al., 1987). This discrepancy between memory complaints and actual memory deficits among older adults with depression is found also among younger people and probably reflects self-deprecating evaluations (putting oneself down) in the clinical syndrome of depression.

Another difference between those who are depressed and those who have dementia is that depressed people tend to have more errors of omission; they may not answer a question because it is just too much effort for them or because they expect to make mistakes. People with dementia, on the other hand, tend to make random or confabulatory errors (Spar & LaRue, 1990). (Confabulation refers to filling in gaps in memory with contrived and often improbable stories that the person accepts as true.)

Of course, patients can have both dementia and depression. For example, an Alzheimer's patient can become depressed over his or her growing physical and cognitive limitations (Reifler, Larson, & Hanley, 1982; Teri & Reifler, 1987). And recall also (p. 527) recent research that suggests the opposite cause–effect relationship, that is, that depression increases the risk for Alzheimer's disease (Bassuk et al., 1998).

Causes of Depression in Older Adults Many aged patients in poor physical health are depressed. A survey of 900 older adults living in the community found that 44 percent of people with depressive symptoms were medically ill (Blazer & Williams, 1980). In a study of hospitalized medical patients who were old, about 15 percent were found to be clinically depressed (Reifler, 1994). Older men who have their first onset of depression in late life are likely to have undergone surgery before their episode of depression, to have unusually high rates of chronic illness, and to have had more medical conditions than have other people (Roth & Kay, 1956). Many physicians who care for older medical patients are insensitive to the likelihood of depression coexisting with physical illnesses. More often than not they do not diagnose, and therefore do not treat, the psychological condition (Rapp, Parisi,

& Walsh, 1988; Rapp, Parisi, Wallace, & Walsh, 1988). This oversight can worsen not only the depression but also the medical problem itself (Wolfe et al., 1996).

Physical illness and depression are linked for reasons other than the disheartening aspects of an illness. A genetic diathesis for depression may also play a role. A higher prevalence of depression is found among the relatives of Alzheimer's disease patients who became depressed after the onset of the disease (Strauss & Ogrocki, 1996). Medications prescribed to treat a chronic condition can aggravate a depression that already exists, cause a depression to start, or produce symptoms that resemble the disorder but are not in fact a true depression (Klerman, 1983). The drugs most likely to have these effects are antihypertensive medications; other possibilities include hormones, corticosteroids, and antiparkinsonism medications (Spar & LaRue, 1990). On the other side of the coin, longitudinal and retrospective studies have found that individuals who are depressed may be predisposed to develop physical illness (Vaillant, 1979; Wigdor & Morris, 1977). And because of their discouraged and lethargic state of mind, they may not seek appropriate medical treatment for symptoms they are experiencing, for example, weakness in the limbs, lethargy, or unpredictable bouts of nausea, which could be signals of serious cardiovascular problems.

As we grow older we almost inevitably experience a number of life events that could cause depression. Kraaij and DeWilde (2001) found that negative life events experienced throughout the life span have long-term consequences on well-being and are related to depression in late life. Various other studies have documented higher rates of illness and death among people who are widowed (Clayton, 1973; Parkes & Brown, 1972), and bereavement has been hypothesized to be a common precipitating factor for depressions that hospitalize older patients (Turner & Sternberg, 1978). However, studies have found relatively low rates of depression in bereaved individuals (Musetti et al., 1989), and it has been concluded that the symptoms of depression in such individuals are generally less severe and fewer than those in individuals institutionalized for depression (Bornstein et al., 1973; Gallagher et al., 1982). Few older people, then, appear to develop a disabling depressive illness following an expected loss of a loved one. (It is very disheartening when someone close dies, but as we get older, most of us come to terms with the reality that loved ones are going to pass on.)

As with younger adults, psychological stress plays a role in depression in older adults, but a stressor that might trigger or exacerbate a depressive episode in a younger person may not do so in an older adult (George, 1994). For example, social isolation is not as strongly linked to depression in old age as it is in middle age (Musetti et al., 1989), due perhaps to older people being bothered less when not interacting with others for days at a time (see also discussion of Carstensen's research on social selectivity, 560). The importance of race and socioeconomic factors seems secondary to such variables as medical problems; that is, older adults of a racial minority may have more serious medical problems or poorer health care, and it seems it is these factors, rather than racial prejudice or financial pressures, that contribute most to depression (Blazer, George, & Hughes, 1991). Many people over the age of sixty-five—and of course younger people as well—are challenged by the stress of looking after relatives with disabilities, and several studies have revealed high levels of depression (as well as anxiety) among these caregivers, especially among those caring for relatives with Alzheimer's disease (e.g., Hannappel, Calsyn, & Allen, 1993).

Although retirement has been assumed to have negative consequences, research does not generally support this assumption (Atchley, 1980; George, 1980). Any ill effects of retirement may have more to do with the poor health and low incomes of some retirees and less with retirement per se (Pahkala, 1990). Retirement decisions and experiences throughout retirement tend to be based upon the individual's economic resources, social relationships, and personal resources (Kim & Moen, 2001). Marital status as well as marital quality have been found to be positively related to retirement adjustment. In addition, higher education levels, higher job prestige prior to retirement, and higher levels of self-efficacy and self-esteem also facilitate successful adjustments to retirement (Kim & Moen, 2001). For many older adults, retirement ushers in a satisfying period of life (Wolfe et al., 1996).

Each older person brings to late life a developmental history that makes his or her reactions to common problems unique. Each person's coping skills and personality determine how effectively that individual will respond to new life events (Butler & Lewis, 1982). We would do well to assume that adaptation rather than depression is the common reaction to losses and stress in late life.

Treatment of Depression   Although clinical lore holds that depressions in older patients are more resistant to treatment, we have known for some time that these claims are not substantiated (Small & Jarvik, 1982). Rather, there is considerable evidence that depressed older adults can be helped by both psychological and pharmacological interventions.

Gallagher and Thompson (1982, 1983) compared cognitive, behavioral, and brief psychodynamic psychotherapies for older individuals with depression. All three were found equally effective, and in subsequent studies (Gallagher-Thompson & Thompson, 1995a, 1995b; Gallagher-Thompson et al., 2000; Thompson, Gallagher, & Breckenridge, 1987) about three-quarters of the patients were judged either completely cured or markedly improved. These rates compare very favorably with the outcomes of psychotherapy in younger people with depression. Another notable finding is that untreated control patients did not improve, as younger untreated depressed patients often do, suggesting that older adults are less likely than younger patients to recover without treatment.

Landreville et al. (2001) studied older adults' acceptance of psychological and pharmacological treatments for depression. Cognitive therapy and bibliotherapy (reading assigned books and articles suitable for laypeople and dealing with the person's psychological predicament) were found to be more acceptable than antidepressant medications with individuals who had mild to moderate symptoms. With patients who had severe depression, cognitive therapy was found to be more acceptable than both bibliotherapy and antidepressant medications.

Interpersonal psychotherapy (IPT) has also been used successfully to treat depression in older adults (Gallagher-Thompson et al., 2000; Hinrichsen, 1999). As described earlier (p. 352), IPT is a short-term psychotherapy that addresses themes such as role loss, role transition, and interpersonal disputes, problem areas prominent in the lives of many older adults. Although it is not yet considered a well-established treatment for depression in older adults (Gatz et al., 1998), it has shown great promise with this age group (Hinrichsen, 1999).

Research on the use of drugs to treat depression is not as extensive for older adults as it is for younger adults, but emerging evidence suggests that certain antidepressants can be useful, particularly selective serotonin reuptake inhibitors such as fluoxetine (Prozac) (Hale, 1993). However, the use of antidepressant drugs with older adults is complicated by side effects, such as postural hypotension (a fall in blood pressure when standing up), which causes some patients to become dizzy when they stand up and then to fall. (Falls in older adults are far more serious than they are for younger people. Broken bones take much longer to heal, and certain head injuries can be fatal.) These drugs also pose a risk to the cardiovascular system, with the danger of a heart attack. Moreover, older people generally are at high risk for toxic reactions to medications of all kinds. Worth noting also is a study examining the effects of SSRIs and other antidepressants in older adults (Menting et al., 1996). This clinical trial found that about 76 percent of the SSRI patients experienced at least some side effects, 25 percent dropped out because of side effects, and about 41 percent dropped out overall. These results occurred even though most of the participants were relatively healthy elderly people (Menting et al., 1996). For these reasons, nonpharmacological approaches to depression in older adults are particularly important (Bressler, 1987; Scoggin & McElerath, 1994).

Electroconvulsive therapy (p. 297) is back in favor among many geriatric psychiatrists (Hay, 1991), particularly for patients who had an earlier favorable response to it (Janicak et al., 1993). ECT does, however, carry significant risks, and it should be considered only when other treatments have not been effective or are contraindicated or when a rapid response (such as in the case of an acutely suicidal patient) is needed (Zarit & Zarit, 1998).

Anxiety Disorders

Anxiety disorders are more prevalent than depression among older adults (Gatz et al., 1996; Regier et al., 1988; Scoggin, 1998; Wetherell, 1998). However, less research has been done on them than on depression (Gallo & Lebowitz, 1999).

Anxiety disorders in old age can be a continuation or reemergence from problems earlier in life, or they can develop for the first time in the senior years. Like depression, DSM-defined anxiety disorders appear to be less prevalent among older than among younger adults (Kessler et al., 1994). As nearly all the available data are cross-sectional, however, it is wise to be cautious about this conclusion. Although anxiety disorders may decrease with age, people becoming old in the twenty-first century may experience an upward trend in prevalence.

A further complicating factor in determining prevalence is that, as with younger people and as we just saw with depression, symptoms of anxiety among older adults are more predominant than are diagnosable anxiety disorders, indicating that unwarranted anxiety among seniors is fairly common (Gurian & Miner, 1991). The quality of a person's life can be compromised by symptoms that, although not severe, frequent, or enduring enough to warrant a formal DSM diagnosis, could still justify professional concern and intervention (Fisher & Noll, 1996).

In general, symptoms of anxiety disorders do not differ as people enter old age. However, as in the case of depression, it has been recently noted that diagnostic criteria for anxiety may be insufficient or ill suited for diagnosis of the disorder in older adults, thus rendering current prevalence rates underestimates (Wetherell, 1998).

Causes of Anxiety in Older Adults Causes of anxiety disorders reflect some of the circumstances of getting older (Fisher & Noll, 1996). Anxiety problems are often associated with medical illness (Heidrich, 1993) and can be a reaction to worries about being sick and becoming infirm. Sometimes an older person's anxieties can be a reaction to medication (e.g., antidepressants or antiparkinsonism drugs) or part of the delirium that frequently accompanies medical illness in older patients (Lipowski, 1990). Signs of extreme distress, sometimes aggression, are seen in people who have dementias such as Alzheimer's and probably reflect anxiety arising from confusion and frustration when they are unable to deal with seemingly minor tasks, such as putting on a coat (Fisher et al., 1994, cited in Fisher & Noll, 1996).

Many other medical diseases can create anxiety symptoms that are not properly considered part of an anxiety disorder but that warrant professional attention. Some of these are found in all adults, but most of them are more often found in older adults. Metabolic conditions, such as hypoglycemia and anemia; endocrine disorders, such as hyperthyroidism; cardiovascular conditions, such as angina and congestive heart failure; and excessive caffeine consumption all may cause such symptoms as a faster heart rate, which is also a symptom of anxiety (Fisher & Noll, 1996) or can be construed by the person as a symptom of anxiety (recall our earlier discussion of misattribution in panic disorder, p. 149). Age-related deterioration in the vestibular system (inner-ear control of one's sense of balance) can account for panic symptoms such as severe dizziness (Raj, Corvea, & Dagon, 1993).

Scogin (1998) remarks that posttraumatic stress disorder (PTSD) and acute stress disorder, two anxiety disorders that may be especially relevant to the lives of older adults, have received scant attention from researchers. PTSD can be seen in some older war veterans (Cook, 2001; Wetherell, 1998) and has been observed in older patients following such trauma as major health crises (Scogin, 1998). One study found that even after 50 years since the event, many veterans still are affected by their war experiences (Hunt & Robbins, 2001).

Treatment of Anxiety Anxiety problems in older adults seem to respond to the same kinds of psychological treatments found useful with younger adults (cf. Chapter 6), but controlled research in this area is in its infancy (Stanley, Beck, & Glassco, 1997; Wetherell, Gatz, & Craske, in press). Because the physician usually hears the psycholog-

Anxiety disorders are more prevalent than depression among older adults. Worries about illnesses and becoming incapacitated may play an important role.

ical complaints of older adults—at least for current cohorts of these patients—psychoactive medications are in widespread use (see the later discussion of the abuse of such drugs by older patients). However, potentially dangerous interactions with other drugs that older adults frequently take, along with their increased sensitivity to any drug, make antianxiety medication a risky intervention (Fisher & Noll, 1996; Hersen & Van Hasselt, 1992).

A concluding comment by Fisher and Noll (1996) in their review of anxiety disorders in elderly people could be applied to other psychological disorders as well.

> Although old age naturally presents the challenges of physical and emotional losses that may seem overwhelming to the young, the ability to competently cope with these losses [and challenges] is indeed probably the most remarkable aspect of the relationship between aging and anxiety. Perhaps through the study of the means by which the majority of older adults rise to the challenges associated with aging, researchers will better inform the treatment of anxiety across the lifespan. (p. 323)

Delusional (Paranoid) Disorders

A sixty-six-year-old married woman reluctantly agreed to a clinical evaluation. She [had] a six-week history of bizarre delusions and hallucinations of her husband spraying the house with a fluid that smelled like "burned food." She complained that he sprayed the substance everywhere around the house, including draperies and furniture, although she had never seen him do it. She could smell the substance almost constantly, and it affected her head, chest, and rectum. She also complained that someone in the neighborhood had been throwing bricks and rocks at her house. In addition, she suspected her husband of having affairs with other women, whose footprints she claimed to have seen near home....

Interviews revealed a sullen woman who was extremely hostile toward her husband. She focused on the delusion that he was spraying an unusual substance in an attempt to upset her; other issues in the relationship seemed secondary. She looked very sad at times and would occasionally wipe away a tear; but her predominant affect was extreme hostility and consternation about her husband's alleged behavior. (Varner & Gaitz, 1982, p. 108)

In addition to the distress experienced by the patient, paranoia may have a disturbing and immediate impact on others, often bringing angry reactions and contributing to a decision to institutionalize the older adult (Berger & Zarit, 1978). Paranoid symptomatology is found in many older psychiatric patients (Heston, 1987; Pfeiffer, 1977).

Causes of Delusional Disorder   Paranoia in older patients may be the continuation of a disorder that began earlier in life or it may accompany brain diseases such as delirium and dementia. Paranoia may even serve a function for patients with dementia, filling in the gaps caused by memory loss. Instead of admitting, "I can't remember where I left my keys," they think, "Someone must have come in and taken my keys" (Zarit, 1980).

Paranoid ideation has been linked to sensory losses, in particular to loss of hearing. Some believe that older people with severe paranoid disorders tend to have long-standing hearing loss in both ears (Eastwood et al., 1985; Pearlson & Rabins, 1988; Post, 1980). An older person who is deaf may believe that other people are whispering about him or her so that he or she cannot hear what is being said. The person's paranoid reactions may be an attempt to fill in the blanks caused by sensory loss (Pfeiffer, 1977; see Focus on Discovery 16.2). By explaining bewildering events, delusions are in a sense adaptive and understandable. There is, however, conflicting evidence about this presumed link between hearing problems and delusional disorders. Whereas some researchers report that hearing loss precedes the onset of paranoid symptoms, others report that such sensory losses are not common among people with delusional disorder (Jeste et al., 1988).

Since people who become paranoid also have poor social adjustment, the onset of their symptoms may follow a period in which they have become increasingly isolated (Gurland, 1991). This isolation itself limits the person's opportunities to check his or her suspicions about the world, making it easier for delusions to take hold. The individual builds a pseudocommunity—a private world of his or her own—rather than social relations based on good communication and mutual trust (Cameron, 1959).

Older people are especially vulnerable to all kinds of abuse. Others may talk about them behind their backs, or even to their faces, as though they were not present, and people take advantage of older adults in many ways. The complaint of persecution from an older person that is blithely dismissed as a sign of late-life paranoia may be justified. An older client of one of the authors complained bitterly about being followed by a detective hired by her evil husband. Inquiry revealed that the husband was worried that she was having an affair and had indeed hired someone to follow her! It should always be determined whether suspicions have any bases in reality before they are attributed to paranoia.

Treatment of Delusional Disorder   The treatment of paranoia is much the same for older adults as for younger adults. Although controlled data are lacking, clinicians suggest that a patient, supportive approach is best, with the therapist providing empathic understanding of the person's concerns. Directly challenging the paranoid delusion or attempting to reason the person out of his or her beliefs is seldom effective. By the time the patient sees a health professional, many others—family, friends, the police—have probably tried this approach. Nonjudgmental recognition of the distress caused by the paranoia is more likely to promote a therapeutic relationship with the patient. When the patient trusts and feels safe with the therapist, the delusions can gradually be questioned. The cognitive therapy described earlier for delusions in schizophrenia should be suitable for older adults as well (p. 351).

If an auditory or visual problem is present, a hearing aid or corrective lenses may alleviate some of the paranoid symptoms. If the individual is socially isolated, efforts can be made to increase his or her activities and contacts. Regular supportive therapy may help the patient in reestablishing relations with family members and friends. Positive reinforcement can be provided for appropriate behavior; for example, the therapist may pay special attention to comments by the patient that are not paranoid in nature. Even if these straightforward measures do not relieve paranoia, they may be beneficial in other areas of the person's life.

Studies of therapy outcomes indicate that delusions in older patients can be treated with some success with phenothiazines (Schneider, 1996), although paranoid individuals are generally suspicious of the motives of those who give them drugs. Toxicity from medications must also be considered, given the particular sensitivity of older people to drugs. Institutionalization, best viewed as a last resort, may do little good. In practice, this decision depends more on the level of tolerance in the person's social environment than on the severity and disruptiveness of the paranoid beliefs.

Schizophrenia

As discussed in Chapter 11, the symptoms of schizophrenia include delusions, cognitive impairment, hallucinations, and negative symptoms such as flat affect. The prevalence of schizophrenia in older adults overall is lower than it is in the total population. This difference is attributable to two factors. First, some people with schizophrenia die before they reach old age; individuals with this disorder die at a higher rate than members of the general population (Karon & VandenBos, 1998). Second, many people with schizophrenia evidence a marked reduction, and sometimes a complete remission, of symptoms by the time they reach old age (Zarit & Zarit, 1998). Nevertheless, older adults with schizophrenia tend to be poorer, have lower education levels, and higher unemployment rates (Meeks & Murrell, 1997).

Does schizophrenia ever appear for the first time in old age? Debate on this question has raged for years. Even Kraepelin had doubts that it was always appropriate to use the adjective praecox—meaning early onset—to describe schizophrenia. It is estimated that 90 percent of cases of schizophrenia have onset before the person reaches age sixty. Late-onset schizophrenia, then, is indeed rare, though it does occur (Karon & VandenBos, 1998).

When schizophrenia does appear for the first time in older adults, it is often called **paraphrenia** (Howard, 1993; Roth, 1955). Symptoms differ from those seen in early-

Partial Deafness, Growing Old, and Paranoia

A possible relationship between hearing problems in old age and the development of paranoid thinking was noted many years ago by Emil Kraepelin and has been supported since by some laboratory studies (Cooper et al., 1974). The connection appears to be specific to paranoia, for the relationship between difficulties in hearing and depression in older individuals is not as great. Since, according to some research, hearing losses appear to predate the onset of paranoid delusions, this may be a cause–effect relationship of some importance.

Psychologist Philip Zimbardo and his associates conducted an ingenious experiment to study the relation of poor hearing to paranoia. They reasoned that loss of hearing acuity might set the stage for the development of paranoia if the person does not acknowledge, or is unaware of, the hearing problem (Zimbardo, Andersen, & Kabat, 1981). The scenario goes something like this: "If I have trouble hearing people around me, which makes them seem to be whispering, I may conclude that they are whispering about me and that what they say is unfavorable. I will think this way, however, only if I am unaware of my hearing problem. If I know that I am partially deaf, I will appreciate that I do not hear them well because of my deafness and will not think that they are whispering." For example, a hard-of-hearing grandfather may eventually challenge the light-voiced, gesturing grandchildren he believes are whispering about him; and they will deny that they are. A tense cycle of allegations, denials, and further accusations will isolate the increasingly hostile and suspicious grandfather from the company of his grandchildren.

The experiment done by Zimbardo and his group examined the initial stage of this hypothesized development of paranoia. College students, previously determined to be easily hypnotized and capable of responding to a posthypnotic suggestion of partial deafness, participated in what they believed to be a study of the effects of various hypnotic procedures on creative problem solving. Each student sat in a room with two others who were confederates of the experimenter. The trio were provided a task to perform either cooperatively or by themselves—they were to make up a story concerning a Thematic Apperception Test (TAT) picture. First the word focus was shown on a screen, then the picture was projected. The confederates, as planned, began to joke with each other as they made decisions about the story, inviting the student to join them in the cooperative venture. After the story was completed, the person was left alone to fill out questionnaires, among them MMPI measures of paranoia and a checklist of adjectives to assess mood.

As described so far, there is nothing particularly notable about this experiment. The actual manipulations had taken place earlier, before the TAT picture was presented. Each student had been hypnotized and given one of the following three posthypnotic suggestions.

1. *Induced partial deafness without awareness.* Members of this group were told that when they saw the word focus projected on a screen in the next room, they would have trouble hearing noises and what other people were saying, the others would seem to be whispering, and they would be concerned about not being able to hear. They were also instructed that they would not be aware of this suggestion until an experimenter removed the amnesia by touching their shoulder.

2. *Induced partial deafness with awareness.* Students in the second group, the control group, were given the same partial-deafness suggestion, but they were instructed to remember that their hearing difficulty was by posthypnotic suggestion.

3. *Posthypnotic-suggestion control.* Participants in the third group, controls for the effects of posthypnotic suggestion, were instructed to react to the word focus by experiencing an itchiness in the left earlobe, with amnesia for this suggestion until touched on the shoulder by the experimenter.

onset schizophrenia; paraphrenia typically involves more hallucinations and paranoid delusions (Howard, Almeida, & Levy, 1993; Jeste et al., 1988). Patients tend to be unmarried, live in isolation, have few surviving relatives, experience hearing losses, have a family history of schizophrenia, and belong to the lower socioeconomic classes (Harris & Jeste, 1988; Post, 1987).

In the United States the term paraphrenia has been inconsistently used (Berger & Zarit, 1978; Bridge & Wyatt, 1980; Howard, 1993). Some researchers believe that a number of the older patients diagnosed as having paraphrenia actually have a mood disorder (Cooper, Garside, & Kay, 1976; Kay et al., 1976), for in many with prominent symptoms, cognition and overall functioning are preserved; that is, their lives are not marked by the deterioration and upheaval common in schizophrenia. In a study of patients who appeared to have developed schizophrenia for the first time after age sixty-five, roughly two-thirds actually had dementia or a mood disorder (Leuchter, 1985).

With older adults, biological factors that have little or nothing to do with mental disturbance per se must be considered with special care when making a diagnosis of a mental illness such as paraphrenia. For example, several reversible medical and surgical problems can produce signs and symptoms that mimic schizophrenia (Marengo & Westermeyer, 1996), including hyperthyroidism, hypothyroidism, Addison's disease,

After being given their posthypnotic suggestions, all participants were awakened from the hypnotic state and ushered into the next room, where the experiment proceeded with the TAT picture, as described. It can now be appreciated that participants who had deafness without awareness might perceive the joking of the confederates as directed toward them, for they would have trouble hearing what was being said and would be unlikely to attribute this difficulty to any hearing problem of their own. Those who had deafness with awareness would have the same problem hearing the joking, but they would know that they had a temporary decrement in hearing through hypnotic suggestion. The other control students would have no hearing problems, just itchy earlobes. At the completion of the study all were informed about the purposes of the experiment, and steps were taken to ensure that the posthypnotic suggestions of partial deafness and itchy earlobes had been lifted.

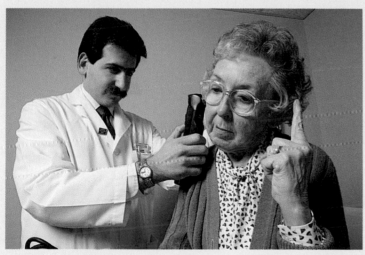

Aging is sometimes accompanied by hearing loss.

The results were fascinating. The experience of being partially deaf without awareness showed up significantly on cognitive, emotional, and behavioral measures. Compared with members of the two control groups, these students scored as more paranoid on the MMPI scales and described themselves as more irritated, agitated, and hostile. The two confederates who were in the same room with these students rated them as more hostile than they rated the control students. (The confederates were not aware to which group a given participant belonged.) When the confederates invited each person to work with them in concocting the TAT story, only one of six students in the deafness-without-awareness group accepted the overture, although most of the control participants agreed. At the end of the study, just before the debriefing, all were asked whether they would like to participate in a future experiment with the same partners; none of the deafness-without-awareness participants responded affirmatively, but most of the control participants did.

The overall reaction of those who had trouble hearing and had no ready explanation for their difficulty other than that others were whispering was suspicion, hostility, agitation, and unwillingness to affiliate with these people. This pattern is similar to what Zimbardo hypothesized to be the earliest stage of the development of some paranoid delusions. The creation of this "analogue incipient paranoia" in the laboratory is consistent with the view that when people's hearing becomes poor in old age, some of them are susceptible to paranoia if, for whatever reasons, they do not acknowledge their deafness. In subsequent research, Zimbardo strengthened these findings by inducing physiological arousal via hypnotic suggestion and then suggesting amnesia for the true source of the arousal. Unexplained arousal was experienced as significantly more distressing than arousal that could be attributed to the hypnosis (Zimbardo, LaBerge, & Butler, 1993). Other studies indicate that if people look to the actions of others to understand the reasons for their unexplained arousal, they become more paranoid than people whose search for the causes of the arousal is guided into other domains, for example, something in the physical environment (Zimbardo, personal communication, September 29, 1992).

Cushing's disease, Parkinson's disease, Alzheimer's disease, and vitamin deficiencies (Jeste, Manley, & Harris, 1991).

For the treatment of schizophrenia in older adults antipsychotic medications, such as the phenothiazines discussed earlier (p. 344), are effective (Jeste et al., 1993), though side effects and interactions with other drugs being taken by the patient can pose a challenge to the prescribing physician. A supportive therapeutic relationship also appears to be helpful and bolstering (Marengo & Westermeyer, 1996). Cognitive behavior therapy (CBT) interventions appear to reduce overall symptoms and reduce the severity of delusions (Dickerson, 2000). However, as we saw in Chapter 11 with schizophrenia in general, a combination of both antipsychotic medications and CBT appears to be the most successful in treating older patients with schizophrenia.

Substance-Related Disorders

Substance abuse is less prevalent in today's cohorts of older adults than among younger adults, but it is a problem nonetheless. One reason for the lower prevalence may be increased mortality among those who have abused drugs in the past or are doing so in their elder years. However, many researchers (e.g., Gomberg & Zucker, 1998; Zarit &

Zarit, 1998) predict that as successive cohorts enter old age, the prevalence of substance abuse and dependence in older adults will begin to rise.

Alcohol Abuse and Dependence   Alcohol abuse is less prevalent in older than in younger cohorts, yet the problem is not trivial. Prevalence rates for DSM-defined alcohol abuse or dependence are 3.1 percent for older men and 0.46 percent for older women (Helzer, Burnam, & McEvoy, 1991; Myers et al., 1984), averaging out to less than 2 percent. This rate is much lower than the rates that have been determined for the general adult population (p. 360).

If older adults who consume at least a dozen drinks a week are included, about 8 percent of older adults are heavy drinkers (Molgaard et al., 1990). Many of the DSM-IV-TR criteria for alcohol dependence and abuse are inapplicable to older adult drinkers; thus adhering to the DSM may lead to underidentification of—and underutilization of treatment services by—older problem drinkers.

From a longitudinal perspective, it appears that heavy drinkers tend to drink less as they enter old age (Fillmore, 1987). More importantly, many alcohol abusers do not survive to old age. The peak years for death from cirrhosis are between fifty-five and sixty-four years of age. Mortality from cardiovascular problems is also higher in heavy drinkers than in those who have not drunk to excess earlier in life (Shaper, 1990).

It might be assumed that problem drinking in an older adult is always a continuation of a pattern established earlier in life, but this is not the case. Many problem drinkers begin having alcohol-related problems after the age of sixty—so-called late-onset alcoholism. Estimates vary widely, but between one-third and one-half of those who have drinking problems in old age began their problem drinking after the age of sixty (Liberto, Oslin, & Ruskin, 1996).

As noted, tolerance for alcohol diminishes with age, in part because the ratio of body water to body mass decreases with time, resulting in higher blood-alcohol concentration per unit of alcohol imbibed (Morse, 1988). In addition, older people metabolize alcohol more slowly. Thus the drug may cause greater changes in brain chemistry and may more readily bring on toxic effects, such as delirium, in older people. Several neuropsychological studies have shown that cognitive deficits associated with alcohol abuse, such as memory problems, are likely to be more pronounced in the aged alcoholic than in younger individuals with comparable drinking histories (Brandt et al., 1983). Although some intellectual functioning is recovered with abstinence, residual effects may remain long after the older person has stopped drinking.

Clinicians may be less likely to look for alcohol abuse in older people than in younger patients and may instead attribute symptoms such as poor motor coordination and impaired memory to a medical problem or to late-life depression. Indeed, alcohol problems often are comorbid with major depression and brain damage (Liberto et al., 1996). Whether there is comorbidity or not, however, if alcohol abuse goes unrecognized, treatment of the patient will be severely compromised. Controlled research on intervention is limited.

Abuse of Illegal Drugs   Although comprehensive figures have been quite difficult to obtain, it seems certain that the current older population abuses illegal drugs less frequently than do other age groups. In the previously cited NIMH survey (Regier et al., 1988), none of those aged sixty-five and older, and only 0.1 percent of those between forty-five and sixty-four years of age, had a drug abuse or dependency disorder, compared with much higher rates for younger age groups. Many experts believe, however, that the abuse of illegal drugs is higher than these formal estimates indicate. Additionally, as successive cohorts of adults enter old age, it is expected that rates of illegal drug use and abuse will rise. (Recall our earlier discussion of cohort effects and the limits of cross-sectional research designs.)

For example, some studies of older narcotics abusers indicate that they began their habit early in life and reduced their drug intake as they grew older (Ball & Chambers, 1970), and it has been assumed that all addicts either stop using or die before reaching old age. However, it now appears that a growing proportion of heroin addicts are aged sixty or older. One study (Pascarelli, 1985) found that people aged sixty and older constituted only 0.005 percent of methadone-program consumers in 1974, but accounted for 2 percent of methadone-program consumers in 1985—a 400 percent increase in a time span of only eleven years. Current data on cocaine and cannabis use in older adults are scarce; however, rates will undoubtedly rise as adults who came of age in the 1960s and 1970s—a period of widespread use of illegal drugs, especially marijuana—reach their later years (See Chapter 12).

Medication Misuse   The misuse of prescription and over-the-counter medicines is a much greater problem than alcohol or illegal drug abuse in the aged population (LaRue et al., 1985). Elderly people have a higher overall rate of legal drug intake than any other group; although they constitute only 13 percent of the population, they consume about one-third of all prescribed medications (Weber, 1996). Older patients use more antianxiety medications than any other age group: rates of benzodiazepine use in community-dwelling older adults have been estimated at 14 to 37 percent; rates in nursing-home residents are thought to be even higher (Wetherell, 1998). Some of this use reflects serious drug abuse.

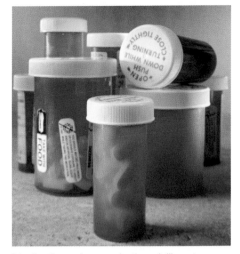

Medication misuse, whether deliberate or inadvertent, can be a serious problem among older patients and can cause delirium.

Although abuse of prescription or legal drugs is often inadvertent, it can be deliberate. Some people may seek drugs to abuse, obtaining medications from a number of sources—for example, by going to more than one physician, filling their prescriptions at different pharmacies, and paying cash instead of using credit cards to reduce the chances that their multiple prescriptions will be discovered (Weber, 1996). One study of 141 well-functioning middle-class older adults living in their own homes found that almost half reported having misused prescription or over-the-counter drugs at least once over a period of six months (Folkman, Bernstein, & Lazarus, 1987).

Older adults may abuse tranquilizers, antidepressants, or sleep aids prescribed years earlier to deal with postoperative pain or the grief and anxiety of losing a loved one. These drugs often create physical as well as psychological dependency (see the later discussion on the treatment of insomnia). However, because older adults tend not to go to work regularly and may sometimes not even be seen in public for days or weeks at a time, they can hide their abuse for years. The slurred speech and memory problems caused by drugs may be attributed by others to old age and dementia (LaRue et al., 1985), another example of how popular stereotypes can interfere with proper diagnosis and treatment. Said one addiction specialist, "They're not like a 25-year-old mixing it up [using drugs and alcohol] to get high.... They're trying to make a lonely, miserable life less miserable" (Weber, 1996, p. A36). A former Valium addict and now a leader of Pills Anonymous groups in California stated the problem this way: "Closet junkies, that's what we call them here. They're at home. They're alone. They're afraid. They're just hiding. Their drug pusher is their doctor" (Weber, 1996, p. A36).

With the growth of health plans that compensate physicians for the number of patients they look after rather than for the time they spend with each, there is less incentive for doctors to take the time to find out what is really bothering an older patient; thus, many just write out a prescription that may reduce the verbal complaints. And because of the lack of adequate time spent with the geriatric patient, the time-pressured physician most likely will not check their records to see what other medications the patient is currently taking. What results is polypharmacy, the prescribing of multiple drugs for an individual patient. Polypharmacy, along with less efficient metabolism of drugs that occurs with aging, produces an increased incidence of adverse drug reactions which cause numerous side affects, toxicity, and allergic reactions. What tends to occur is that the physician ends up prescribing more medications to combat the side effects, thus continuing the vicious cycle. Furthermore, as most psychoactive drugs are tested on younger people, gauging the dosage appropriate for the less efficient kidneys and liver of the older person represents a difficult challenge for the medical practitioner (Gallo & Lebowitz, 1999). Therefore, it is important that the primary care physician of the geriatric patient keep track of all the medications that are being taken, cease the use of any drugs that are not essential, and keep the amount to only the necessary minimum.

Since the current cohort of older adults is not as acculturated as are younger people to seeking help for psychological problems, including drug problems, many make unsupervised efforts to abstain, sometimes going cold turkey. Doing so can be very dangerous, even life-threatening, because withdrawal reactions place great demands on the cardiovascular system. When people now in middle age reach their seventies and beyond, the prevalence of prescription-drug abuse may be even greater, exacerbated by the "take a pill for your ills" mentality they have acquired and by the likely availability of even more medications designed to affect mood and ease discomfort.

Some older addicts end up in places where one doesn't expect to find an older adult.

Her skin itched as if an invisible case of hives were creeping across her flesh. She would shiver, then sweat. She felt suffocated by despair.

She was 65, a doctor's wife, a proud grandma with a purseful of photographs. But there she was, curled in a ball like any other junkie at the…drug treatment center, sobbing as her body withdrew from a diet of painkillers and tranquilizers.

She couldn't believe it had come to this.

People her age, the woman said, "don't associate themselves with the lowlifes [who] sneak into doorways to shoot up. No, they sneak into the bathroom for a pill" (Weber, 1996, p. A1).

Hypochondriasis

Older adults may experience a multitude of physical problems, among them sore feet and backs, poor digestion, constipation, labored breathing, and cold extremities. All are to be taken seriously by health professionals. However, some older adults believe they are ill and complain unendingly about aches and pains for which there are no plausible physical causes.

It has been widely believed that hypochondriasis is especially common in the older population, but the prevalence of hypochondriasis may not be any greater among older adults than among others (Siegler & Costa, 1985). Taken as a group, older adults actually tend to underreport somatic symptoms rather than overreport them and often fail to seek help for serious illnesses (Besdine, 1980), perhaps because of concern for health care costs or a belief—probably true—that aches and pains are an inevitable part of aging and may not reflect a specific medical problem.

Longitudinal survey data indicate that concerns about health do not increase with age but remain fairly stable over the life span. Since actual health problems do increase with age without accompanying increases in concerns about health, such data do not support the idea that people become more hypochondriacal as they get older (Costa et al., 1987). Those older persons who have many physical complaints have long-standing personality traits that predict such complaining (Siegler & Costa, 1985). Their excessive somatic complaints appear to be associated with neuroticism or poor adjustment, which are not associated with age. In addition, the NIMH epidemiological study (Regier et al., 1988) found that only 0.1 percent of those aged sixty-five years or older had somatization disorder, the same rate found in younger age groups.

No controlled studies of the treatment of hypochondriasis in older adults have been done. Clinicians generally agree that reassuring the person that he or she is healthy is generally useless, for these people are not swayed by negative laboratory tests or authoritative pronouncements from official sources. Some tentative evidence suggests that ignoring the somatic complaints and concentrating instead on more positive aspects of existence can be helpful (Goldstein & Birnbom, 1976). "I know that you're feeling bad and that your feet really hurt, but let's take a walk in Palisades Park anyway." Diverting activities may allow these individuals to function in the face of their perceived medical ills and perhaps obtain some satisfaction from life.

Sleep Disorders

Insomnia is a frequent complaint among older adults. One national survey found insomnia in 25 percent of respondents aged sixty-five to seventy-nine, as compared with 14 percent in the eighteen to thirty-four age group; another 20 percent had less serious but still problematic insomnia (Mellinger, Balter, & Uhlenhuth, 1985).

The most common sleep problems experienced by older adults are waking often at night, frequent early-morning awakenings, difficulty falling asleep, and daytime fatigue (Miles & Dement, 1980). These complaints parallel the physiological changes that occur normally as people enter old age (Bootzin, Engle-Friedman, & Hazelwood, 1983). Older adults sleep somewhat less or the same amount of time as do younger adults, but their sleep is also more often spontaneously interrupted; additionally, they take longer to fall back asleep after awakening (Webb & Campbell, 1980). Thus older people generally sleep less in relation to the total time they spend in bed at nighttime; they tend to make up for this loss with daytime naps.

Older adults also spend less absolute time in a phase known as rapid eye movement (REM) sleep, and stage 4 sleep—the deepest stage—is virtually absent. Older men generally experience more disturbances of their sleep than do older women, a difference found to a lesser extent in young adults (Dement, Laughton, & Carskadon, 1981). The sleep problems of older adults must be treated seriously, as the symptoms of chronic insomnia have been found to be associated with higher rates of morbidity and mortality (Neckelmann, 1996).

Causes of Sleep Disorders   In addition to the changes associated with aging, various illnesses, medications, caffeine, stress, anxiety, depression, lack of activity, and poor sleep habits may make insomniacs of older adults. Depressed mood—even in the absence of a full-blown mood disorder— has been shown to be related to sleep disturbances in older adults, especially early-morning awakening (Rodin, McAvay, & Timko, 1988). Since the prevalence of insomnia greatly exceeds the prevalence of depression in old age, however, not all geriatric sleep problems should be attributed to an underlying depression (Morgan, 1992). In men, frequent awakenings can be caused by needing to urinate during the night because of prostate problems.

Pain, particularly that of arthritis, is a principal disrupter of sleep for older adults (Prinz & Raskin, 1978). Sleep problems are also strongly associated with Alzheimer's disease; progressive disruptions of the normal sleep phases occur as the dementia advances (Hoch et al., 1992).

Whatever the cause of insomnia at any age, it is worsened by self-defeating actions such as ruminating over it and counting the number of hours slept and those spent waiting to fall asleep. Sleeping problems can also be worsened by medications that are taken to deal with them.

Sleep apnea is a respiratory disorder in which breathing ceases repeatedly for a period of a few seconds to as long as half a minute as the person sleeps. It seriously disrupts normal sleep and can lead to fatigue, muscle aches, and elevation in blood pressure over a period of time. The disruption in normal breathing is usually due to markedly reduced airflow caused by relaxation-produced obstruction from excess tissue at the back of the throat. These interruptions in breathing can occur upwards of 60 times an hour! It is rare for the person to become aware of the problem unless his or her bed partner complains about snoring, a typical accompaniment to most apnea problems. Sometimes the partner is aware of the person's ceasing to breathe and then loudly gasping for breath. Apneic episodes can be frightening to the observer. Both snoring (which may or may not be linked to obstructive sleep apnea) and sleep apnea increase as people get older (Bliwise et al., 1984). Reliable diagnosis of sleep apnea requires the person to spend a night in a sleep lab, where various parameters of sleep (e.g., eye movements, respiration, muscle tension) are monitored.

Treatment of Sleep Disorders   Over-the-counter medications and prescription drugs are taken by many older people with insomnia. The little bottle of sleeping pills is a familiar companion to the many medications that sit on the night table. Older adults are major consumers of sleep aids; more than 60 percent of users of prescription sleep drugs are over the age of fifty (Mellinger et al., 1985). Yet sleep drugs rapidly lose their effectiveness and

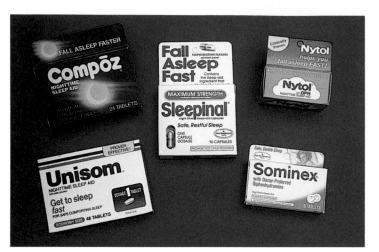

Over-the-counter sleep aids can have serious side effects.

with continuous use may even make sleep light and fragmented. REM rebound sleep, an increase in REM sleep after prolonged reliance on drugs, is fitful (Bootzin et al., 1996). Medications can even bring about what is called a drug-dependent insomnia. These so-called aids can also give people drug hangovers and increase respiratory difficulties, which in older adults is a great hazard, given the increased prevalence of sleep apnea.

There is considerable evidence that tranquilizers are not the appropriate treatment for the patient of any age with chronic insomnia, and particularly not for the older patient with insomnia. Side effects of tranquilizers such as the benzodiazepines (e.g., Valium) include problems in learning new information and serious difficulties in thinking clearly the following day (Ghoneim & Mewaldt, 1990; Schatzberg, 1991). Nonetheless, tranquilizers are prescribed for most nursing home residents, and in many instances they are administered daily even without evidence of a sleep disturbance (Bootzin et al., 1996; Cohen et al., 1983).

Melatonin, a hormone secreted by the pineal gland, plays an important role in regulating sleep and is known to decrease with aging. Thus, it is not surprising that it has been used to treat sleep disorders in older adults and has had some success (Garfinkel et al., 1995).

Jokes have been told for years about taking a little nip of alcohol to help get to sleep. As a central nervous system depressant, alcohol does induce relaxation and drowsiness in most people. But like nearly all other drugs, alcohol has negative effects on what is called the architecture of sleep—the presence of certain stages of sleep, such as rapid eye movement (REM) sleep, which is associated with dreaming. Alcohol markedly reduces REM sleep, resulting in such problems as fatigue and difficulty thinking clearly the next day. It also increases the severity of sleep apnea. Furthermore, since tolerance develops with alcohol use, the person drinks more in an effort to obtain the same effect. People with sleep disturbances, including older adults, sometimes mix alcohol with sedatives or tranquilizers. These combinations—which can lead to unintended death—can be particularly dangerous for older adults because of their greater sensitivity to biochemicals.

Intervention for sleep apnea usually entails the person's wearing a nasal or full-face mask attached to a device that increases airflow, thereby relieving the obstruction at the back of the throat. This treatment is generally quite effective and also virtually eliminates loud snoring, a bonus that can improve interpersonal relations between the patient and his or her bed partner! Surgery is sometimes used to widen the airways at the back of the throat, but evidence for its effectiveness is at this time less certain than for the airflow treatment (Bootzin et al., 1996).

In general, explaining the nature of sleep and the changes that take place as a normal part of the aging process can reduce the worry that older persons have about their sleep patterns, concern that itself can interfere with sleep. The therapist can also reassure patients that going without sleep from time to time is not a calamity; it will not cause irreversible brain damage or mental illness, as some people fear. Worrying less about sleeping usually helps one sleep. As with people of any age, attending to any psychopathological condition underlying the sleep disturbance, such as anxiety or depression, can lead to improvement in sleep.

Some individuals are given relaxation training to help them fall asleep and instructions to help them develop good sleep habits: rising at the same time every day; avoiding activities at bedtime that are inconsistent with falling asleep; and lying down only when sleepy, and, if unable to go to sleep, getting up and going into another room. Regular exercise can also help (Stevenson & Topp, 1990). All these tactics can loosen the grip of insomnia on adults of all ages (Bootzin et al., 1996; Morin & Azrin, 1988).

For years, practitioners have believed that medication was the most effective treatment for sleep problems in older adults; however, recent research into nonpharmacological treatment of sleep disorders in this population has yielded extremely promising results. A study published in the *Journal of the American Medical Association* provides incontrovertible evidence that older adults can benefit greatly from cognitive-behavioral intervention for their sleep difficulties; in fact, these interventions may, in the long run, be superior to drug therapies (Morin et al., 1999). In a controlled, randomized study of seventy-one older adults, one-fourth were assigned to a drug-treatment-only group (they were administered the sleep aid Restoril, one of the benzodiazepines), one-fourth to a behavioral-treatment-only group (ninety-minute sessions once a week for eight weeks), one-fourth to a combination drug-and-behavioral-treatment group, and the remainder to a placebo control group. The behavioral treatment consisted of many of the components just described, for example, education about sleep hygiene, correction of faulty expectations and beliefs about sleep, the teaching and practicing of good sleep habits, and relaxation training.

At the end of the study, the members of all three treatment groups were sleeping much better, and the amount of improvement across the three groups was essentially the same. However, at two-year follow-up, the group that had received the behavioral treatment had largely maintained its gains, whereas the group that had received the sleep medication had not. Most surprising, the group that had received a combination of medication and behavioral treatment did not maintain as much improvement as the group that had received the behavioral treatment alone. The authors of the study suggest that the former group might have attributed improvement to the medication and consequently may not have invested as much time and energy into the behavioral treatment (the issue of attribution of drug-produced improvement is discussed on p. 585).

Suicide

Several factors put people in general at especially high risk for suicide: serious physical illness and functional impairment, psychiatric illness, feelings of hopelessness, social isolation, loss of loved ones, dire financial circumstances, and depression (see Chapter 10). Because these problems are widespread among older adults, it should not be surprising that suicide rates for people over age sixty-five are high, perhaps three times greater than the rate for younger individuals (McIntosh, 1995).

However, an examination of cross-sectional data indicates that the relationship between suicide rates and age is not as straightforward as it initially appears. The suicide rate for men rises from youth and increases in a linear fashion with age, whereas the rate for women peaks in middle age—in their fifties—and then slightly yet steadily declines across the rest of the life span (McIntosh et al., 1994). Older white men are more likely to commit suicide than are members of any other group; the peak ages for committing suicide in this group are from eighty to eighty-four (Conwell, 2001; Gallo & Lebowitz, 1999). Thus, rates of suicide in men increase sharply during old age, and rates for women decline somewhat. Marked increases have also been noted among minority men, most notably, African Americans (Alston et al., 1995). As for older women, studies have shown that those who were victims of physical and/or sexual abuse are more likely to be suicidal or express suicidal ideations (Osgood & Manetta, 2000). Consequently, as more and more people survive longer, the number of suicides in people over age sixty-five could increase.

Older persons are less likely to communicate their intentions to commit suicide than are younger people, and they make fewer attempts. When older people attempt suicide, however, they use more lethal methods and they more often kill themselves (Conwell, 2001; Gallo & Lebowitz, 1999). Once people are past age sixty-five, their attempts rarely fail (Butler & Lewis, 1998). Furthermore, the statistics are probably underestimates; older adults have many opportunities to give up on themselves by neglecting their diet or medications, thus killing themselves in a more passive fashion (this is sometimes called subintentioned suicide).

Butler and Lewis (1998) argued that the suicide of older adults may more often be a rational or philosophical decision than is that of younger people. Consider, for example, the older person who faces the intractable pain of a terminal illness and knows that with each passing day the cost of medical care is using up more and more of the money that might otherwise be left to his or her family. Recall also our earlier discussions of how some older people with Alzheimer's and other debilitating diseases have arranged to take their own lives. The issue of physician-assisted suicide (p. 313) is likely to focus increasing attention on suicide among elderly people.

Intervention to prevent the suicide of an older person is similar to that discussed in Chapter 10. In general, the therapist tries to persuade the person to regard his or her problems in less desperate terms. In many cases, the suicidal individual is suffering from major depression and if they were diagnosed and treated appropriately, it is most probable that their suicidal tendencies would diminish. Studies have tested this hypothesis and have found reduced rates of suicide in the elderly when depression is recognized and treated (Conwell, 2001). Mental health professionals, who are usually younger and healthier, may unwittingly try less hard to prevent an older person's suicide attempt. But as is true of younger people, an older person, once the crisis has passed, is usually grateful to have another chance at life.

Sexuality and Aging

People tend to expect both men and women to lose interest in and capacity for sex once they reach their senior years. Some believe that old people are unable to enjoy anything more passionate than an affectionate hug and a kiss on the cheek. In contrast to the strong sexual value placed on them when young, older women are no longer considered especially sexual (Steuer, 1982). Furthermore, their capacity for sexual arousal is confused by some people with their postmenopausal inability to procreate.

In spite of such beliefs, most older people have considerable sexual interest and capacity (Deacon, Minichiello, & Plummer, 1995; Hodson & Skeen, 1994). This holds true even for many healthy eighty- to one-hundred-year-old individuals, among whom the preferred activities tend to be caressing and masturbation, with some occasions of sexual intercourse (Bretschneider & McCoy, 1988). Our earlier mention of a rapidly growing problem with HIV infection among older adults through unprotected sex (p. 528) confirms their continuing interest in sex.

As we review the data, it is important to bear in mind that sexual interest and activity vary greatly in younger adults; disinterest or infrequent sex on the part of an older person should not be taken as evidence that older people are inherently asexual. The sixty-eight-year-old man who has no sex life may well have had little if any interest at age twenty-eight. Whether the person is twenty-eight or sixty-eight, one of the best predictors of future sexual activity is past sexual enjoyment and frequency (Antonovsky, Sadowsky, & Maoz, 1990; Pedersen, 1998).

Early studies of the frequencies of sexual activity, such as the famous Kinsey reports (Kinsey et al., 1948, 1953) and the Duke Longitudinal Studies (George & Weiler, 1981; Pfeiffer, Verwoerdt, & Wang, 1968, 1969), noted a decline in heterosexual activity, masturbation, and homosexual contact beginning around age thirty and continuing across the life span. The belief that sex necessarily becomes less important to people in their middle years and in old age was not substantiated by later research, however. The second Duke study (George & Weiler, 1981), which covered the years 1968 through 1974, indicated no decline in the sexual activity of people between ages forty-six and seventy-one, and it further indicated that 15 percent of older persons increased their sexual activity as they aged. Other studies have shown that about half of those between the ages of sixty and seventy-one have regular and frequent intercourse (Comfort, 1980; Turner & Adams, 1988). A later study of cognitively unimpaired men living in nursing homes confirmed high levels of sexual interest and, when partners were available, sexual intercourse and other forms of sexual activity (Mulligan & Palguta, 1991).

These facts can be interpreted in several ways. Clearly, older people can be sexually active; even the earlier surveys indicated that. But it is noteworthy that the second Duke study did not reveal the decline found in the first report. The older people surveyed in the second study may have had to contend with less negative stereotyping and may have been healthier—both cohort effects. They may also have been more willing to discuss their sexual interests and activities with researchers because the cultural atmosphere had become more supportive—a time-of-measurement effect. Historical factors and sexual

Contrary to stereotypes, many older people maintain an active interest in sex. Studies indicate that the frequency of sexual activity among those in their seventies is as high as it is among middle-aged people.

attitudes in society at large may affect sexuality among older adults. In one study, from the late 1970s, seventy- and eighty-year-olds reported rates of intercourse similar to those that Kinsey found in forty-year-olds in the 1940s and 1950s (Starr & Weiner, 1981). Perhaps the amount of sexual activity in older adults will continue to rise as today's young grow older, which would be a cohort effect.

Physiological Changes in Sexual Response with Aging   Among the volunteer subjects studied by Masters and Johnson (1966) were a number of older adults. We know a great deal about heterosexual sexuality in older adults both from this physiological research and from later work (Comfort, 1984; O'Donohue; 1987; Segraves & Segraves, 1995; Weg, 1983). Research into nonheterosexual sexuality in older adults, however, is scant. What is true of both sexes is that there are wide individual differences in sexual capacity and behavior among older adults, as indeed is the case for other areas in the lives of seniors. Some of the differences between older and younger adults are discussed next.

Men   Older men take longer to have an erection, even when they are being stimulated in a way they like. They can maintain an erection longer before ejaculating than younger men, however, and the feeling that ejaculation is inevitable may disappear. It is not known whether physiological changes or control learned over the years explains this. During the orgasm phase, contractions are less intense and fewer in number, and less seminal fluid is expelled under less pressure. Once orgasm has occurred, erection is lost more rapidly in older men, and the capacity for another erection cannot be regained as quickly as in younger men. The refractory period actually begins to lengthen in men in their twenties (Rosen & Hall, 1984).

Older men are capable of the same pattern of sexual activity as younger men, the major difference being that things take longer to happen, and when they do happen, there is less urgency. How men and their partners view normal, age-related physiological changes may contribute to sexual dysfunction. If, for example, a man or his partner reacts with alarm to a slow buildup of sexual arousal, the stage is set for performance fears, a principal reason for sexual dysfunction (p. 477). Changes that occur normally with aging are often misinterpreted as evidence that older men are becoming impotent (LoPiccolo, 1991; Sbrocco, Weisberg, & Barlow, 1995), yet older men do not lose their capacity for erection and ejaculation unless physical or emotional illness interferes (Badeau, 1995; Kaiser et al., 1988). The recent advent and consequent widespread popularity of the drug Viagra will no doubt have an impact on levels of sexual activity in older men.

Women   A number of age-related differences have been found in older women, but, again, none justifies the conclusion that older women are incapable of a satisfactory sex life (Morokoff, 1988; Sherwin, 1991). Like younger women, older women are capable of at least as much sexual activity as are men. Some women become orgasmic for the first time in their lives at age eighty. Older women need more time to become sexually aroused, which may dovetail with the slowdown in men's arousal patterns. Vaginal lubrication is slower and reduced because estrogen levels are lower, and there may be vaginal itching and burning. Hormone-replacement therapy can reduce many of these symptoms. Vaginal contractions during orgasm are fewer in number compared with those of younger women. Spastic contractions of the vagina and uterus, rather than the rhythmic ones of orgasm in younger women, can cause discomfort and even pain in the lower abdomen and legs. Estrogen deficiency, which can be corrected, can change skin sensitivity such that caressing the breast and having a penis inside the vagina may not feel as pleasurable as it did when the woman was younger (Morokoff, 1988). Older women return more quickly to a less-aroused state. There is some evidence that these physical changes are not as extensive in women who have been sexually stimulated on a regular basis once or twice a week throughout their sexual lives.

Age-Related Problems   Physical illness can interfere with sex in older people just as it can in younger people. Because older people have more chronic ailments, however, the potential for interference from illness and medications is greater (Badeau, 1995; Mulligan et al., 1988). This is especially the case for men, as any disease that disrupts male hormone balance, the nerve pathways to the pelvic area, or blood supply to the penis can prevent erection. Diabetes is one such disease; it affects men and women similarly in terms of nerve damage and reduction of blood supply to the genitalia, but older women seem to complain less than do older men about its negative effects on their sexuality. It may be that the current cohorts of older women, raised at a time when female sexuality was downplayed and even denigrated, suffer as much from diabetes-related reduction in vaginal lubrication as men do from erectile difficulties, but they do not tell their partners and physicians and may simply use a lubricant to reduce vaginal pain during intercourse (LoPiccolo, 1991).

Tranquilizers and antihypertensive drugs can bring about sexual dysfunction, as can fatigue and excessive drinking and eating (Segraves & Segraves, 1995). Older adults are sometimes challenged as well by having to adjust to disease-related changes in their bodies, such as alterations in the genitalia from treatment of urological cancer (Anderson & Wolf, 1986).

Fears of resuming sexual activities after a heart attack or coronary-bypass surgery have inhibited older adults and their lovers; but for most of them the fears are exaggerated (Friedman, 1978). Heart rate, for example, is frequently higher during such activities as climbing stairs than it is during intercourse. Physicians often fail to provide accurate information to these patients, including the fact that periodically increasing heart rate through aerobic activities such as sexual intercourse can often be helpful in cardiac rehabilitation. The situation for patients with congestive heart failure, in which the heart is unable to maintain an adequate circulation of blood in the tissues of the body or to pump out venous blood returned by the venous circulation, does create for some a risk in intercourse, but less strenuous sexual activity is usually not a problem (Kaiser et al., 1988).

Although women experience fewer physical problems than do men, they are subject to many myths about aging women's sexuality (Deacon et al., 1995; Gatz, Pearson, & Fuentes, 1984). Also, a heterosexual woman's sexual activity typically centers on having a partner and on whether he is well (Caven, 1973). Thus, older women are less sexually active than are older men, perhaps because they lack a partner or because if they are married, their husbands tend to be older and to have significant health problems. Women live longer than men and therefore are more likely to have lost a spouse. Divorced or widowed men tend to remarry women younger than they, sometimes considerably so; older widowers have a remarriage rate seven times that of older widows (U.S. Bureau of the Census, 1986). Obviously, differences in life expectancy are not an issue for older women in nonheterosexual relationships.

Treatment of Sexual Dysfunction   Making the facts of sexuality in old age available to the general public and to the professionals who look after their medical and mental health needs is likely to benefit many older people (Hodson & Skeen, 1994). As with younger adults, a degree of permission-giving is useful—it is okay to have sex and to enjoy it when you are past age sixty-five—especially in light of widespread societal stereotypes of the asexuality of seniors. Physicians have been guilty of telling older patients to forget about sex or of not raising the issue when discussing the patient's adjustment, perhaps because of their own discomfort, lack of knowledge, or ageism (LoPiccolo, 1991). Clinicians need to bear in mind that the current cohort of people over age sixty-five was socialized into sexuality at a time when the open discussion of sex was in no way as prevalent as it has been since the 1960s. Nursing homes are often intolerant of sexuality among their residents; a married couple residing in the same nursing home may not be allowed to share a room (Ballard, 1995; Comfort, 1984; Deacon et al., 1995). The situation for gay and lesbian residents is even worse. In addition, the authors have witnessed nurses in geriatric wards cautioning residents against stimulating themselves in public but failing to provide them with privacy.

Some older people prefer not to be sexually active, but older adults who are experiencing and are troubled by sexual dysfunctions are likely to be good candidates for the type of sex therapy devised by Masters and Johnson (Berman & Lief, 1976) and Kaplan (1991). Providing these people with information about normal age-related changes in sexual functioning is particularly important. As today's older adults acquired their attitudes toward sex at a time when, for example, genital foreplay was not emphasized, and indeed was often discouraged, clinicians have to be tactful about asking an older patient to fondle his or her partner in order to provide the tactile stimulation older people often need to become aroused (LoPiccolo, 1991).

With older adults greater attention must be paid to physical condition than when working with younger adults, including creative and open discussion of sexual techniques and positions that take into consideration physical limitations resulting from such illnesses as arthritis (Deacon et al., 1995; Zeiss, Zeiss, & Dornbrand, 1988).

This focus on sexuality should not blind us to the links between sexual satisfaction and the nonsexual aspects of a relationship between adults, especially if the people are married or in an otherwise committed relationship. As with younger adults, nonsexual distress in a couple can be both a cause and an effect of sexual problems. The situation can be particularly complex with older partners, who must deal with such transitions as retirement and illness. Many couples who have been together for decades encounter distress in their relationship for the first time in their senior years. One particularly daunting challenge arises when one of the partners is cast in the role of caregiver for the other, especially when the ill spouse has a degenerative disorder such as Alzheimer's disease. Communication and problem-solving training (p. 293) may be of value in such cases (Smyer, Zarit, & Qualls, 1990).

Treatment and Care of Older Adults

Older adults sometimes go to mental health centers or seek private psychotherapy through referrals. Yet older people are less likely than younger adults to be referred (Ginsburg & Goldstein, 1974; Knight, 1996; Kucharski, White, & Schratz, 1979). General practitioners, for example, usually fail to detect depression in older patients (Bowers et al., 1990). This situation may be due in part to inadequate geriatric training for medical professionals. The reimbursement system used by many health care providers may pose some problems as well, for it is biased toward inpatient care and pays less for outpatient therapy, especially for mental health services.

Clinicians tend to expect less success in treating older patients than in treating young patients (Knight, 1996; Settin, 1982). In one study, older patients were rated by therapists as having more severe psychopathology, less motivation for treatment, a poorer prognosis, and less insight than younger patients (Karasu, Stein, & Charles, 1979). Yet research does not show that psychotherapy is less successful for older patients (Gallagher-Thompson & Thompson, 1995a, 1995b; Kasl-Godley & Gatz, 2000; Knight, 1996). If older patients are viewed as having limited possibilities for improvement, they may not be treated. On the other hand, a therapist may lack the knowledge necessary to give good treatment to older people, which would keep them from improving.

There is an irony in questioning whether psychotherapy is appropriate for older adults. With increasing years come increasing reflectiveness and a tendency to be philosophical about life (Neugarten, 1977). Running counter to earlier pessimism about the capacity for older people to change, both of these traits augur well for the suitability of older adults for psychotherapeutic interventions, and, indeed, this suitability is borne out by data already reviewed as well as findings that will be described later.

Admissions of older adults to state and county mental hospitals and to psychiatric wards of city hospitals have substantially decreased in recent years owing to changes in national mental health policy. Most older people needing mental health treatment now live in nursing homes or receive community-based care.

Nursing Homes

The prevalent myth regarding nursing homes is that families dump their older relatives into these institutions at the first sign of frailty. However, families usually explore all their

Nursing homes play a major role in the institutional care of the aged. They have often been criticized for the poor care they provide as well as the lack of stimulation in the environment.

alternatives and exhaust their own resources before they institutionalize an older relative. Thus, the decision to institutionalize comes as a last resort, not as a first choice.

Institutionalization can sometimes have a negative impact on family relations, for heated disagreement, anger, and feelings of guilt may arise from discussions of whether to place the parent in a nursing home. One study, however, found that for a large number of families, moving the parent to a nursing home strengthened family ties and brought a renewed closeness between the parent and the child who was the primary caregiver. The care provided by the nursing home alleviated the strain and pressure caused by the multiple physical or mental problems of the parent. In only about 10 percent of the families were relations worsened by the move (Smith & Bengtson, 1979).

Nursing homes are now the major locus for institutional care for older adults with severe chronic illnesses and mental disorders (Gatz & Smyer, 1992; Horgas, Wahl, & Baltes, 1996). Given projected future needs, it does not appear that enough people are being trained to provide mental health services within nursing homes. This is a matter of concern, particularly since few of the nation's approximately 17,000 nursing homes offer counseling as a routine service, and the great majority of patients have diagnosed mental disorders (including dementia). Worse still, recent nursing home reforms aim to exclude from such settings older adults with mental disorders, a step that is likely to place further strains on state and private psychiatric hospitals as well as on general hospitals with psychiatric units (Gatz & Smyer, 1992; Smyer & Gatz, 1995), and it is unlikely that care in these settings will be any better.

Even a good nursing home—and not all of them are run well—may have unintended negative consequences on some residents. This caution is based on a classic study by Blenker (1967). Older adults who went to a family service center were randomly assigned to one of three treatments: intensive, intermediate, and minimal. Intensive treatment involved the services of a nurse and a social worker; intermediate treatment involved somewhat less professional attention; minimal treatment consisted of information and referral to community-based services. One might expect intensive treatment to have been the most effective, but after half a year the death rate of members of the intensive-care group was four times that of people in the minimal-care group! The intermediate-care group was also better off than the intensive-care group; the death rate of its members was "only" twice that of the minimal-care group.

What happened? It turned out that the major factor was being placed in an institution such as a nursing home. A person was much more likely to be institutionalized if a nurse and social worker were intensively involved in planning his or her care, and the excessive death rates were found in institutionalized patients. Since people had been assigned randomly to the three treatments, it is unlikely that the death rates were related to differences existing before treatment began.

What is it about some nursing homes that could contribute to such decline? First, relocation to a new setting is in itself stressful and is believed to play a role in increased mortality (Schultz & Brenner, 1977). Once in the nursing home, the extent and nature of care discourage rehabilitation and even maintenance of whatever self-care skills and autonomous activities the resident may be capable of. For example, a resident able to feed himself or herself, but slowly and with occasional spills, will be assisted or even fed like a child at mealtimes to shorten the time devoted to serving meals and minimize messes on the floor and stains on the patient's clothing. The resident then no longer thinks of himself or herself as able to eat without help, which is likely to lead to still more loss of function and lowered morale. Muscles weaken and deteriorate through disuse. Relatives, anxious to know that they have made the right decision and that their loved one is being well cared for, are pleased by the tidiness and orderliness that are the result of excessive staff involvement in all details of living.

During the late 1980s a series of investigations into lax practices in nursing homes led to a number of governmental reforms. Despite resulting improvements in most nursing homes, there remain serious problems with many of them, confirmed recently in an 18-month review released in March 2002 by the Senate Special Committee on Aging. These deficiencies undermine the belief that residents reliably receive even minimally satisfactory care.

For example, nursing assistants are often inadequately trained, overworked, and underpaid—and it is the nursing assistants, not the professional nursing staff or physicians, who have by far the most contact with nursing home residents. Many nursing assistants do not speak the same language as the residents; they are often high school dropouts and homeless; some work two jobs for as many as eighteen hours a day. Turnover in these positions is high. Despite the best intentions, nursing assistants are presented with an overwhelming set of challenges, owing in part to cutbacks in government funding to nursing homes and a resulting workload that is unreasonably heavy. Sometimes they lack even basic supplies, such as diapers, soap, and toilet paper.

In a study by the California Department of Health Services and the California Advocates for Nursing Home Reform, some residents were reported to have been harmed, sometimes fatally, by errors of omission and of commission by nursing assistants. Consider the following examples from the period from 1997 to 1999 (Pyle, 1999):[4]

- A resident suffocated after dangling over the side of her bed on a roll belt that a nursing assistant had not been taught to attach properly.
- A ninety-two-year-old amputee fell out of her wheelchair and broke her leg because a nursing assistant did not know how to secure her in the chair.
- A dialysis patient died from infection because people on the nursing staff did not wash their hands properly before inserting the tubes into his veins.
- Nursing assistants did not wash their hands between the time they emptied bedpans and the time they handled ice that was placed in residents' drinks.
- An eighty-nine-year-old resident died of dehydration because the nursing home failed to notify her doctor that she was not taking in enough fluid.
- A resident too tall for his bed had to leave his feet dangling over the bed frame, resulting in a raw wound that grew to seven inches in length and was left untreated for weeks.
- Residents suffered from deep bedsores that became infected because they were allowed to lie in bed in their own waste for long periods of time.
- Nursing assistants along with many other health care professionals are frequently untrained in managing behaviorally disruptive residents. This puts the residents' quality of care at risk.

Depression is a particular problem among the residents of nursing homes. The type of intervention employed is usually a drug, and the psychoactive drug prescribed is more likely to be a tranquilizer than an antidepressant—a less agitated, relatively inactive patient is easier to handle. Psychological interventions are virtually unheard of, for staff members either are untrained in their implementation or operate under the widely held assumption that such therapy is inappropriate for an old person. This situation is unfortunate, as interventions such as behavior therapy have been found to be quite effective in reducing unwanted behaviors and improving overall functioning in nursing home residents with dementia; in fact, medication can often be significantly reduced once behavior therapy has been implemented (Mansdorf et al., 1999).

In sum, all the problems of institutionalization are exhibited in bold and exaggerated relief in some nursing homes. Independence is inadvertently, but with sad consequences, discouraged, and both physical and mental deterioration, because they are expected, occur (see Focus on Discovery 16.3).

Alternative Living Settings

Recently, the United States has seen a dramatic rise in assisted living, a viable alternative to placement in nursing homes for many older adults who require assistance of one sort

---

[4] The abuses listed here are shocking and are not representative of the general state of nursing homes nationwide. But these problems have been observed in many nursing homes and continue to demand the attention of government and private citizens.

Loss of Control and Mindlessness in Nursing Homes

Is the loss of control over one's life that results when a person comes to reside in a nursing home actually damaging to the person's physical and mental health? Ellen Langer and Judith Rodin believe that it is. Since we know that a perceived or actual lack of control leads to deterioration in adaptive behavior, at least some of what we regard as signs of dementia—the inactivity of older people and their poor adjustment to changing circumstances—may be caused by loss of control rather than by progressive brain disease (Langer, 1981). Residents of nursing homes, even if they are able to do so, are not permitted to cook, do their laundry, buy groceries, or tend the yard. This diminution in a sense of self-efficacy and control appears to have especially negative effects in these older adults (Langer & Rodin, 1976b; Rodin, 1986).

In our eagerness to help older people we often end up preventing them from making decisions they are able to make. In our concern to protect them from physical harm we arrange environments that require little effort to control, reducing their opportunities to operate independently. And for many occupations we set ages for compulsory retirement, overlooking the large individual differences of old people. These practices, especially in a society that values competence and activity, do much to destroy an older person's belief that he or she is worthwhile.

Langer and Rodin's research indicates that giving older nursing home residents control and responsibility can improve their health. In one study, patients were assigned a particular fifteen-minute period during which the nurse would be on call specifically for them, thus increasing each individual's control over his or her own caretaking. The health of these patients improved more than that of patients in the control group, and they were more sociable (Rodin, 1980).

In another study, Langer and Rodin (1976) told one group of residents that they would be given a variety of decisions to make themselves, instead of the staff's making decisions for them; they were also given plants to take care of. A control group was told how eager the staff was to take care of them; the plants they were given would be looked after by the staff. Although initially matched on variables such as health, these two groups of older residents differed three weeks later on several measures of alertness, happiness, and general well-being. Members of the group given enhanced responsibility—and presumably a sense of greater control—tested higher on these measures. Even more impressive was the finding eighteen months later that only half as many members of the experimental group had died—seven of forty-seven, compared with thirteen of forty-four for the control group. Moreover, the group given responsibilities continued to show better psychological and physical health (Rodin & Langer, 1977).

In a subsequent study, Rodin (1983) found that nursing home residents who were taught coping skills manifested lower stress in self-reports, on physiological measures, and on physicians' judgments of health. Rodin's presumption is that the skills training enhanced both their perceived and their actual control over problems that commonly arise in nursing homes. Other research has generally shown that people who feel in greater control actually do more things that enhance their health, such as complying with medical regimens, losing weight, and engaging in other self-care behaviors (Rodin, 1986).

Increased control is not positive under all circumstances and for all individuals, however, as Rodin concluded after a review of work in diverse areas on control (Rodin, 1986). With increased control comes more responsibility, and some people may convert this into self-blame when such an internal attribution is not warranted, for example, in the case of a dementing illness caused by factors beyond the patient's control. And if the actual environment is not supportive of increased efforts to exert control and assume responsibility, people are likely to feel worse. For example, if nursing home staff discourage independence, a patient's efforts to become less dependent on staff might lead to arguments rather than to encouragement. With this caveat in mind, Rodin concludes that health professionals as well as family members should look for ways to enhance control in older adults, including those in institutional settings such as nursing homes.

Not only may our treatment of old people engender in them a sense of powerlessness, but their repetitious, unchallenging environments—especially the surroundings of those who are hospital patients or live in nursing homes—may encourage a mode of cognitive functioning that Langer terms mindlessness (Langer, 1989). Mindlessness is a kind of automatic information processing that entails little cognitive effort or attention. It is adaptive when people are in situations that recur frequently—for example, tying one's shoes. Attending to such overlearned activities—making the information processing conscious, not mindless—can actually interfere with performance. However, when a situation is novel and requires our attention, we want to operate mindfully.

Older adult patients may be afforded too few opportunities to be thoughtful and to maintain an alert state of mind. Because of the restricted mobility of nursing home residents and hospital patients and because little is demanded of them, their experiences tend to be repetitious and boring. Langer and Rodin's nursing home research may well demonstrate that conscious thinking as well as perceived control are essential in maintaining emotional and physical well-being. Lack of control and mindlessness are probably related, for what is there really to think about when people believe that they have lost control over the events in their lives?

or another. The American Association of Retired Persons (AARP) reports that assisted living is the fastest growing category of housing for older adults in the United States (AARP, 1999). In contrast to nursing homes, assisted-living facilities resemble hotels, with separate rooms and suites for the residents as well as dining rooms and on-site amenities such as beauty and barber shops. The philosophy of assisted living stresses autonomy, independence, dignity, and privacy (AARP, 1999). Assisted living may sometimes go by other names, such as group homes or board-and-care. Many such residences are quite luxurious, with attentive staff, nursing and medical assistance readily available, daily activities, such as bingo and movies, and other services all designed to provide assisted care for older adults too infirm to live on their own but not so infirm as to require a nursing home.[5] However, as with nursing homes, there is a great deal of variability in quality of care.

In addition to assisted-living facilities and nursing homes, continuing care retirement communities (CCRCs) offer a full continuum of care which enables residents to move from one housing option to another depending on their needs (AARP, 2001). CCRCs are a type of facility that combines independent living, assisted living, and nursing homes together by having all the facilities on the same grounds. Therefore, an individual may begin living in independent housing and move to other housing options as they require more assistance with their activities of daily living (ADLs). The cost of living in these communities is quite high. Depending on the specific CCRC, residents may own their own space or it is rented to them. The majority of CCRCs require their potential residents to have a medical examination to assess their current health status.

Community-Based Care

At any given time 95 percent of older persons reside in the community. Many of these individuals are frail and have an urgent need for help with daily living arrangements. Some communities and for-profit agencies are organized to provide various services, such as:

- telephone reassurance, daily phone calls to older persons living alone to check that they are alright;
- home services, such as Meals on Wheels, which bring a hot meal each day to the person's door;
- home visitors; visits from volunteers who cook meals and do household chores;
- shopping help and light repair work by volunteers;
- senior centers, which may also serve hot lunches and provide help with state and federal forms, and also opportunities for socializing;
- sheltered housing, apartments in which several old people may live together semi-independently;
- home visits by health professionals and social workers, who can assess the actual needs of old people and treat them;
- regular social visits from community neighbors;
- adult day services, which provide a variety of health and social services in a daytime group setting.

A range of available services allows a true match with the needs of the older person so that he or she will not have too much or too little help (Evashwick, 2001).

Some research indicates that such community psychology projects can enhance the quality of life of older people and reduce their dependency on institutional care (e.g., Knight, 1983; Nocks et al., 1986). However, current incentives provided in insurance coverage encourage either obtaining more expensive inpatient care or refraining from seeking mental health services altogether (Gatz & Smyer, 1992).

Mere availability of services is not enough. Services must be coordinated, and in most localities they are not. All too often an older person and his or her family are shuffled from one agency to another, getting lost in kafkaesque bureaucracies. Even professionals who have experience with the system often have difficulty working through it to get needed services for their clients. Frustrating rules can interfere with the very goals for which programs were instituted. In California, for example, Medicare does not always pay for rehabilitation services, such as physical therapy after a broken hip has healed. As a consequence, many older people do not regain as much function as they might; thus, they may experience additional physical and emotional deterioration, exacerbations that require more expensive services.

Among community-based services are day-care centers, where older people participate in various activities, such as exercise classes.

---

[5] It is worth noting that nursing homes are usually much more expensive than even upscale assisted care facilities.

Focus on Discovery 16.4

Interdisciplinary Teamwork in Geriatric Health Care

The health problems of older adults—including problems involving their psychological functioning—are often more complex and longer standing (chronic) than are those of younger adults and of children (Birren & Schaie, 2001). Thus the guiding principle that organizes the thinking and the work of gerontological practitioners is interdisciplinary (Zeiss & Steffen, 1996). Although we have sounded this theme before (see especially our discussion of the broad-spectrum treatment of schizophrenia, p. 362), there is a particular need for professionals from several disciplines to work collaboratively in helping older adults deal with psychological difficulties. The diagram in Figure 16.a graphically illustrates interdisciplinary roles in a hospital-based home-care team devoted to serving geriatric patients who are being discharged to live at home with a caregiver (Zeiss & Steffen, 1996).

What this diagram portrays is a complex set of disciplinary responsibilities and resources that operate both separately (the nonoverlapping areas) and collaboratively (the overlapping areas) so that the respective expertise of the several groups of professionals can be brought to bear in a fruitful way to assess, plan, and intervene on behalf of a particular patient. For example, although the medical doctor serves as the primary care physician, the cognitive screening (how well the patient remembers and thinks about things) can be done by the physician, by the psychologist, or by both.

It is no easy matter to assemble or participate in such an interdisciplinary team, for the ethos in graduate training in all these health-related disciplines is still discipline centered, even when the subject matter is not. While overlapping areas in Figure 16.a indicate domains of collaboration, they also show where turf battles can erupt. The care of older adults constitutes an arena in which these tensions are being put aside for the ultimate benefit of the consumer. (There are other examples, of course. In Chapter 8, we discussed how psychologists collaborate with physicians in the new field called behavioral medicine.)Not all geriatric problems require such an approach, but as Zeiss and Steffen (1996) argue, even a seemingly straightforward health problem in an older adult can benefit from an interdisciplinary approach.

They give an example of an eighty-year-old woman with bronchitis. Can she be adequately treated by a physician alone? Maybe not. It may be essential to know that she is a caregiver for a husband with dementia, what other medications she is taking, what her immune status is, and other issues pertinent to her physical and emotional well-being. Social workers, pharmacists, psychologists, psychiatrists, or other team members may be essential in planning not only acute treatment for her bronchitis but also backup care for her demented husband.

It may seem that coordinating the efforts of all these professionals represents an unnecessary expense, but consider what would happen if medication were prescribed for the woman but then not taken by her because its side effects interfered with her ability to care for her infirm husband. Such noncompliance—a serious problem with all medications

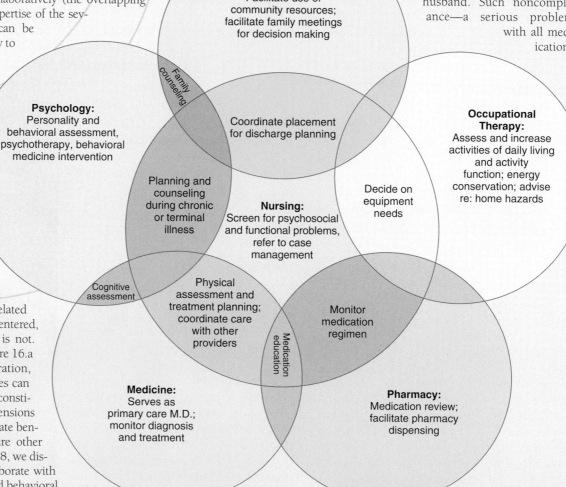

Figure 16.a Geriatric interdisciplinary-team role map. Note both the separate and the overlapping areas of responsibility and expertise. From Zeiss, A. M., & Steffen, A. M. (1996). Interdisciplinary health care teams: The basic unit of geriatric care. In L. L. Carstensen, D. A. Edelstein, & L. Dornbrand (Eds.), *The practical handbook of clinical gerontology.* Thousand Oaks, CA: Sage.

across all ages—would result in a failed medical intervention and possibly a worsening of the patient's medical condition, and this could result in even more expensive intervention down the line, including hospitalization and its associated risks. And while in the hospital, the care of the husband would become an acute and salient problem. Many other complicated and problematic scenarios are possible.

Interdisciplinary teams are committed to the idea that patients will be best served when their care is coordinated and provided by team members who learn from each other, rely on each other, and are willing to challenge each other when appropriate. Interdisciplinary teams require the wise and creative integration of diverse viewpoints and function best when team members value diversity, remain cohesive when viewpoints conflict, and negotiate agreement to which all team members are committed (Zeiss & Steffen, 1996).

One of the main difficulties when it comes to health care for older adults is that the chronic health problems of old people are not appealing to physicians because they seldom diminish. Many, if not most, of the maladies of old people—such as hearing loss; visual impairments; loss of mobility; aches and pains, especially in the feet (Pearson & Gatz, 1982); and a steadily declining cardiovascular system—are unlikely to get better and must somehow be adjusted to. Older persons rely heavily on their relationships with health care providers, but these providers may become impatient with them because, as Zarit (1980) suggested, the illnesses of older people are often incurable and therefore violate a "law" by which most medical professionals live. Furthermore, older people do not always take medication as instructed, and even when they do, adverse drug reactions are not uncommon (Leach & Roy, 1986).

In addition, older people's relations with family members who must look after them are likely to suffer. Ailing older patients are sometimes torn both by feelings of guilt for needing so much from others and by anger toward these younger people whom they have spent so many years looking after and sacrificing for. The sons and daughters also have feelings of guilt and anger (Zarit, 1980). Focus on Discovery 16.4 describes the kind of interdisciplinary team effort that can serve the needs of older adults.

Issues Specific to Therapy with Older Adults

As mentioned throughout this chapter, discussing a group of people who have only chronological age in common runs the risk of overlooking important differences in their backgrounds, developmental histories, and personalities (Smyer et al., 1990). Although adults over age sixty-five do share some physical and psychological characteristics that make them different from younger adults, they are nonetheless individuals, each of whom has lived a long time and experienced unique joys and sorrows. In spite of this uniqueness, there are a few general issues important to consider in the conduct of therapy with older people. They can be divided into issues of content and issues of process (Zarit, 1980).

Content of Therapy

The incidence of brain disorders increases with age, but as we have seen, other mental health problems of older adults are not that different from those experienced earlier in life. Although clinicians should appreciate how physical incapacities and medications may intensify psychological problems, consistency and continuity from earlier decades of the older person's life are also to be noted.

The emotional distress of older adults may be a realistic reaction to problems in living. Medical illnesses can create irreversible difficulties in walking, seeing, and hearing. Finances may be a problem. Therapists treating psychological distress in older adults must bear in mind that much of it is an understandable response to real-life challenges rather than a sign of psychopathology. Professional intervention, however, may still be helpful.

Therapy with older adults must take into account the social contexts in which they live, something that cannot be accomplished merely by reading the professional literature. The therapist who, for example, urges a lonely widower to seek companionship in a neighborhood recreation center for senior citizens may be misguided if the nature of that center does not suit the particular patient (Knight, 1996); such an experience may make the patient feel even lonelier. All social organizations, even those as loosely structured as a senior center, develop their own local mores and practices, or what social scientists have come to call social ecology. Some may be tolerant of physical frailty, others not. Some may be frequented primarily by people who used to be well-paid professionals, others may have primarily former state mental hospital patients as regulars. Mental health care workers need to know and understand the social environments in which their older patients live. We take this need for granted when dealing with younger patients but, Knight points out, often neglect to consider it with older adults.

Older patients often have social needs different from those of younger people. Widespread concern that old people are socially isolated and that they need to be encouraged to interact more with others, as perhaps they did when younger, appears to be ill founded. There is no relationship between level of social activity and psychological well-being among old people (Carstensen, 1996). As we age, our interests shift away from seeking new social interactions to cultivating those few social relationships that really matter to us, such as spending time with family and with close friends and associates.

What some therapists see as psychologically harmful social withdrawal, then, is really social selectivity. When we have less time ahead of us, we tend to place a higher value on emotional intimacy than on learning more about the world. This preference applies not just to older people, but also to younger people who see themselves as having limited time, such as when they are preparing to move far away from those to whom they feel closest (Frederickson & Carstensen, 1990) or if they have AIDS. When we can't see a future without end, we prefer to interact less with casual acquaintances—like those one might meet in a recreation center for older adults—and to be more selective about the people with whom we spend our limited time.

Women may suffer doubly as psychotherapy patients, as not only ageist but also sexist attitudes can negatively influence the direction of psychotherapy (Steuer, 1982). For example, stress in an older couple can increase when the husband retires. A common therapeutic goal is to help the woman accommodate to the husband's loss of status and learn to spend more time with him each day rather than to help the husband make accommodations.

The expectations and values that present-day cohorts of older adults place on marriage can be quite different from those of people in their fifties and younger, at least in Western societies. Most readers of this book probably expect a marriage to provide happiness and personal fulfillment. When these expectations are not met, divorce is often the result. But people who are currently in their seventies and older may have different expectations (Knight, 1996). These people married at a time when stability and commitment were the foundation of a marital union and often took precedence over personal fulfillment.[6]

Death and dying figure prominently in therapy with older patients. They may need help dealing with the fear of facing death or a debilitating illness that requires life support. It may be helpful to counsel some older clients to examine their lives from a philosophical or a religious perspective. These perspectives can help some people transcend the limitations that aging imposes on human existence. When the person is dying, discussions of the meaning of the individual's life can facilitate self-disclosure and enhance his or her sense of well-being and personal growth (see the discussion of life review that follows). The person's loved ones, who will experience the inevitable loss, will also benefit from such discussions.

---

[6] An interesting question, however, concerns the expectations of older adults who have remarried in their sixties or seventies. Do they bring with them their earlier values and expectations about marriage or do they enter their late-life marriage with views more similar to those of younger people?

Process of Therapy

We have already indicated that traditional individual, group, family, and marital therapies are effective with older adults (Gatz et al., 1985). Some clinicians make adaptations in these therapies and focus on here-and-now practical problems. They hold that therapy with older patients needs to be more active and directive, providing information, taking the initiative in seeking out agencies for necessary services, and helping the client and his or her family through the maze of federal and local laws and offices that are in place to help them.

Some characteristics of aging may mean that therapy will proceed differently (Knight, 1996; Light, 1990). For example, certain kinds of thinking simply take longer for many older people. Older people also tend to experience some diminution in the number of things that can be held in mind at any one time. Therapists may thus find that it helps to move with greater deliberation when seeing an older adult. Explanations may have to be more elaborate and conversation more extended. Therapists need to avoid the common tendency, when another person seems not to be following the thread of the conversation, to become nervous and speak louder; this latter reaction can arise from the stereotyped notion that impaired hearing in the older person is causing the communication problem.

In a historical overview of psychotherapy with older adults, Knight, Kelly, and Gatz (1992) discuss life review, proposed by Butler (1963) as a psychotherapeutic approach uniquely suitable for older adults. This approach reflects the influence of Erik Erikson's (1950, 1968) life-span developmental theory, which postulates stages of conflict and growth extending well into the senior years. Life review facilitates what appears to be a natural tendency of older adults to reflect on their lives and to try to make sense of what has happened to them. In Eriksonian terms, it helps the person address the conflict between ego integrity and despair. Ego integrity refers to a process of finding meaning in the way one has led one's life, and despair reflects the discouragement that can come from unreached goals and unmet desires. Life-review methods include having the patient bring in old photographs, travel to a childhood home, and write an autobiography. As one might imagine, people can feel worse as well as better from this kind of therapy; it takes considerable skill on the part of the therapist to guide the patient to a positive view of life and its coming end.

The very process of being in therapy can foster dependency. Older adults, whether institutionalized or living at home with caregivers, often receive much more social reinforcement (attention, praise) for dependent behaviors, such as asking for help or being concerned about the opinion of their therapist, than for instances of independent functioning (Baltes, 1988). The growing specialization of behavioral gerontology (Nemeroff & Karoly, 1991) emphasizes helping older people to enhance their self-esteem by focusing on specific, deceptively minor behaviors, such as controlling their toileting better (Whitehead, Burgio, & Engel, 1985), increasing self-care and mobility (Burgio et al., 1986), and improving their telephone conversational skills as a way to enhance social contacts (Praderas & MacDonald, 1986). A recent development, though hardly a formal therapy, involves teaching older adults computer skills so that they can access the Internet and make the kinds of social contacts that were inconceivable only a few years ago (Cody et al., 1999).

No matter what their theoretical orientation, all therapists must be able to interpret the facial expressions of their patients as an aid to understanding the meaning of what the patients are saying and otherwise to appreciate their phenomenological experience of the world. Research on emotional changes over the life span suggests real potential for error when a therapist younger than the patient is working with an older adult (Knight, 1996). Because of their more varied and more extensive life experiences, older people's emotions can be more complex and subtle than those of younger adults (Schulz, 1982). This sets the stage for younger people to commit more errors when trying to identify emotions in the faces of older adults than they do with

Being able to use a computer and access the Internet is one way older adults can increase their social contacts.

people closer to them in age (Malatesta & Izard, 1984). All this adds to the challenge of therapeutically working with older adults.

Finally, an aspect of psychotherapy, regardless of theoretical orientation, that is highlighted by working with elderly patients is reminiscent of the analytic concept of countertransference. Therapists, usually many years younger than these patients, can be troubled by the patients' problems, for these difficulties can touch on sensitive personal areas of their own, such as unresolved conflicts with their own parents, worries about their own aging process, and a reluctance to deal with issues of death and dying. As Knight, Kelly, and Gatz (1992) speculated, "the perception that therapy is different with older adults is now thought to be due more to the emotional impact on the therapists of working with the elderly than to actual differences in technique, process, or likelihood of success.... [Working with older adults] will challenge therapists intellectually and emotionally to reach a maturity beyond their years" (pp. 540, 546).

Summary

- Until recently, the psychological problems of older people were neglected by mental health professionals. As the proportion of people who live beyond age sixty-five continues to grow, it will become ever more important to learn about the disorders suffered by some older people and the most effective means of preventing or ameliorating them. Although physical deterioration is an obvious aspect of growing old, most emotional distress of older people is psychologically produced.

- Serious brain disorders affect a small minority of older people. Two principal disorders have been distinguished: dementia and delirium.

- In dementia, the person's intellectual functioning declines and memory, abstract thinking, and judgment deteriorate. If the dementia is progressive, as most are, the individual comes to seem like another person altogether and is, in the end, oblivious to his or her surroundings. A variety of diseases can cause this deterioration. The most important is Alzheimer's disease, a progressive, irreversible illness in which cortical cells waste away. Genes probably play some role in the etiology of Alzheimer's disease. A history of head injury and depression are also risk factors.

- In delirium, there is sudden clouding of consciousness and other problems in thinking, feeling, and behaving: fragmented and undirected thought, incoherent speech, inability to sustain attention, hallucinations, illusions, disorientation, lethargy or hyperactivity, and mood swings. The condition is reversible, provided that the underlying cause is self-limiting or adequately treated. Causes include overmedication, infection of brain tissue, high fevers, malnutrition, dehydration, endocrine disorders, head trauma, cerebrovascular problems, and surgery.

- The treatments of dementia and delirium differ widely. If delirium is suspected, there should be a search for the cause—for example, a toxic reaction to medication—so that it can be rectified. Progressive dementia usually cannot be treated, but the person and the family affected by the disease can be counseled on how to make the remaining time manageable and even rewarding. If adequate support is given to caregivers, many patients can be looked after at home. There usually comes a time, however, when the burden of care impels most families to place the person in a nursing home or hospital.

- Older people may experience the entire spectrum of psychological disorders, in many instances brought with them from their earlier years. Data indicate that persons over age sixty-five have the lowest overall rates of all age groups when the various mental disorders are grouped together.

- Depression in older adults is often misdiagnosed as dementia because of the cognitive impairment often found in depressed people. Poor physical health is one common cause of depression in older patients. To treat depression, cognitive, behavioral, and psychodynamic psychotherapies have all been used and found effective.

- Anxiety disorders are more prevalent than depression among older adults and arise from a number of causes, including medical illnesses. These disorders appear to respond to the same kinds of treatments found useful with younger adults.

- Delusional (paranoid) disorder and schizophrenia (sometimes called paraphrenia) may also be seen in older patients. Sometimes they are linked to biological factors. For example, sensory losses, particularly loss of hearing, have been linked with paranoid ideation; and several reversible medical and surgical problems can produce symptoms that mimic schizophrenia. Both delusional disorder and schizophrenia are treated as in younger patients.

- Hypochondriasis; substance abuse, in particular the misuse of medication; sexual dysfunctions; and sleep disorders are other psychological disorders experienced by older people. All are treatable.

- More of the suicide attempts of old people result in death than do those of younger people. Mental health professionals, most of them younger than age sixty-five, may assume that people who are old and debilitated have nothing to live for. This attitude may reflect their own fear of growing old.

- Considerable mythology has surrounded sexuality and aging, the principal assumption being that at the age of sixty-five, sex becomes improper, unsatisfying, and even impossible. Evidence indicates otherwise. Barring serious physical disability, older people are capable of deriving enjoyment from sexual intercourse and other kinds of lovemaking. The principal differences as people age are that it takes longer to become aroused and the orgasm is less intense.

- Nursing homes sometimes do little to encourage residents to maintain or enhance whatever skills and capacities they have. Both physical and mental deterioration may occur. Serious neglect can be found in some nursing homes, despite efforts to correct the deficiencies. An increasingly popular alternative is assisted-living facilities, which resemble hotels but offer various forms of assistance to residents. Most older persons reside in the community. There, such comprehensive services as Meals on Wheels, regular home visits by health professionals, and support for caregivers seem to be beneficial. All intervention should be minimal so that older adults remain as independent as their circumstances permit.

● Many older people can benefit from psychotherapy, but several issues specific to treating older adults need to be kept in mind. The emotional distress of older adults is often realistic in content. They have often experienced irreplaceable losses and face real medical and financial problems; it is unwise always to attribute their complaints to a psychopathological condition. Death is a more immediate issue as well. As for the process of therapy, clinicians should sometimes be active and directive, providing information and seeking out the agencies that give the social services needed by their clients. Therapy should also foster a sense of control, self-efficacy, and hope and should help the older patient create a sense of meaning as he or she approaches the end of life.

Key Terms

age effects	cross-sectional studies	neurofibrillary tangles	selective mortality
ageism	delirium	paraphrenia	sleep apnea
Alzheimer's disease	dementia	plaques	time-of-measurement effects
cohort effects	longitudinal studies		

Depression, Delirium, and Suicidality in an Older Woman Caring for an Alzheimer's Patient

Helen Kay, age 73, had been found at 4:00 A.M. by a city police officer during his routine patrol of the beach near the amusement pier. She was huddled against a wooden piling, an empty pint of whisky in her left hand. He thought at first that she was dead, but she was still breathing, faintly. Hustling her into his car, he took her to the emergency room of the county hospital.

When they arrived, Mrs. Kay was mumbling incoherently to herself and occasionally thrashing around. The physician in charge was tempted to administer a tranquilizer just to quiet her down but wisely refrained from doing so, given her state of apparent alcohol intoxication and the ultrasensitivity many older people have to drugs.

Information gleaned later from acquaintances at the hotel in which she lived provided the following picture of the previous two days. Mrs. Kay failed to show up in the dining room of the retirement hotel for breakfast on a Monday morning. The manager, careful about such incidents among his elderly clientele, sent one of the waiters upstairs to check on her; he returned 30 minutes later to report that Mrs. Kay had opened her door with a frightened look on her face and then proceeded to scream at him: "I did what I could!" The waiter managed to extricate himself to report the situation to his boss, who went to talk to her himself. He had known Mrs. Kay since she took up residence a few months earlier and believed he could deal with her better, which indeed turned out to be the case. She refused to come downstairs to eat, but she did agree to eat the breakfast that was brought upstairs to her.

This incident was not totally unexpected. Over the preceding months Mrs. Kay had occasionally acted peculiarly, her moods shifting from elation one moment to utter lethargy and despondency the next. These mood swings seemed to be related to her shopping trips to a nearby liquor store. She had, in fact, begun to drink heavily by herself in her suite. The staff had come to expect verbal abuse from her within a few hours of her return from the store. On this particular morning, the manager noticed a strong odor of alcohol when he was persuading her to eat some breakfast; he concluded that she had been drinking earlier that morning.

Later that evening Mrs. Kay was herself again, sober and very depressed. Despondency was not unheard of among other residents of the hotel, but Mrs. Kay's sadness had a morbidity and oppressiveness that worried and angered the other guests. For example, at dinner the same day, Mrs. Kay went on and on about her aching back and feet, her poor eyesight, and generally about the woes that God had inflicted on her as punishment. A woman sitting beside her walked only with the aid of a four-pointed cane, was almost completely blind, and was otherwise in poorer physical health as well as more problematic financial circumstances than Mrs. Kay—and exclaimed that to her angrily. Mrs. Kay's reaction was to sulk and brood even more, eventually excusing herself before dessert was served and retreating to her room to drink herself into a stupor once again.

The following morning saw a repeat of her refusal to come down for breakfast, but this time she also refused to open her door to the manager. A tray was left outside her door but remained untouched the rest of the morning. In the early afternoon Mrs. Kay was seen leaving the hotel and heading in the direction of the liquor store. Just before dinnertime, a couple from the hotel saw her walking morosely by herself in the park across the street from the hotel. Occasionally stopping to gaze at the ocean, with a liquor bottle dangling from one hand, she seemed altogether miserable. Their impulse to approach was suppressed by their expectation of verbal abuse from her.

Mrs. Kay did not return to her hotel that evening. Instead, at twilight, she unsteadily negotiated the wooden stairs leading down to the beach and walked along the water's edge until it grew dark. Suddenly chilled by the night ocean breezes, she found her way to the pier and settled herself against a piling to finish her bottle. Hours later she was discovered by the police officer.

Social History

Mrs. Kay had led an interesting and rewarding life. The daughter of a well-to-do family from the Midwest, she had grown up amid the warmth and friendliness of a small town. She was popular with peers and successful in school. Influenced by an English teacher in her junior year of high school, she applied to some private colleges in the East in addition to the nearby state university, where most of her classmates would go. At the end of her senior year she elected to attend Radcliffe.

Her years in Cambridge were pivotal for her. Although subject to the sexism taken for granted in the 1920s, she nonetheless learned to value her own intelligence and drive, deciding—to her family's dismay—that she would forge a career for herself after college instead of immediately marrying the law student who had proposed to her.

But it was not just her ambitiousness that characterized her college years. She found herself subject to occasional profound depressive episodes, some of them serious enough to have her roommates take her to the university health service. She declined to see a psychiatrist or a psychologist, believing in spite of her growing worldliness that "shrinks" were only for crazy people. She believed that she could, and should, deal with her moodiness on her own, and she somehow managed to do this. She excelled at Radcliffe socially and academically and easily obtained a position with a prestigious literary monthly in New York City immediately after graduation. Her law-school boyfriend, Harold Kay, visited her often. After his own graduation, he got a job with a good firm in New York City. Two years later they married.

The marriage was a generally happy one: three children, all of them bright and ultimately successful in their respective careers and lives; two careers, not a common occurrence at that time; considerable income from both their jobs; and reasonably good physical health. Three years after they married, they moved to Los Angeles, where Mr. Kay had received an offer from a noted law firm and Mrs. Kay an editorial position with a leading city newspaper. They enjoyed an active social life, built mostly around their respective professional contacts as well as a country club near their elegant home.

Mr. Kay retired from his lucrative law practice at 72 years of age. He had intended to continue working, slowing his pace only a little as he broke in a new young partner. But a morning cough and increasing forgetfulness thwarted those plans. A cancerous lung had to be removed, regrettably without halting the spread of the disease. His intellectual deterioration, diagnosed as dementia due to Alzheimer's disease, progressed month after month. Mr. Kay became bedridden for the remaining three years of his life.

His wife, as devoted to him as ever, insisted on looking after him at home, against her children's wishes. She withdrew from nearly all her friends and acquaintances, leaving the house only for brief grocery shopping trips when absolutely necessary. She rearranged furniture in their house so that she was seldom more than a few feet from his bedside. Her books, typewriter, and sewing machine were nestled into a corner of the master bedroom, and there was even a hotplate on the dresser so that she could make tea for the two of them without leaving the room. Her depressions were coming upon her more often now and with frightening intensity, accompanied by sleeplessness, poor appetite, and thoughts of suicide. Still, she nursed her ever-deteriorating husband.

Mrs. Kay began to notice her husband becoming less and less responsive to her and to events around him—except for occasional fits of rage when she insisted that he allow her to bathe him. In one horrible moment of insight she confessed to herself that he had no idea who she was or who he was. She had been warned of this aspect of Alzheimer's disease; the brain wastes away inexorably and inevitably, and the worsening memory eventually obliterates the person's sense of identity. She was forced to realize that she was looking after a man whose resemblance to the person she had been married to for over 50 years was becoming more and more remote.

She hated herself for having these thoughts. Who knows what is going on in his mind, she would ask herself. Surely he needs and appreciates my personal care each day and night. Surely he will die if I let him go into a hospital. Family, friends, and Mr. Kay's own physician had been urging that decision on her for months, but she could not bear the image of his being lifted from bed to stretcher, and then to an ambulance, and then into a hospital corridor and, ultimately, into a strange bed in which he would be placed to die.

But that is exactly what happened. She was persuaded to hospitalize him on the basis of medical needs that the physician insisted, almost angrily now, could not be met at home. The dreaded scene of transfer to the hospital took place in a fashion eerily similar to her nightmare fantasy. One day later he died.

Although the death was hardly unanticipated, Mrs. Kay was devastated. At the funeral, she interrupted the minister's eulogy repeatedly with declamations of her responsibility for her husband's death. The other mourners, familiar with the actual circumstances of Mr. Kay's illness, shook their heads in sadness. At the gravesite, she had to be physically restrained from falling on top of the casket as it was lowered into the ground. Even though she insisted that she wanted to return to her home that evening, she was taken by her son to his home. He arranged with his mother in the following weeks to sell his parents' house and have her live with him and his family.

Her welcome into the five-bedroom house of her son was genuine. Mrs. Kay's daughter-in-law was a caring and empathic person. Even though the routine of her household had to be altered to accommodate the presence of another person, she was sincere and generous in her efforts to make her mother-in-law feel at home. But these efforts were largely unnoticed. The woman complained at meals every day of what a burden she was to the family, and no amount of reassurance changed her mind. Ironically, her very act of complaining was the most burdensome aspect of her living with them.

She began, several months after her husband's death, to beseech her son to find her a place where she could live on her own; he reluctantly did so. Consulting with a social service agency, he was referred to several retirement hotels along a pleasant boulevard and across the street from a lush city park overlooking the ocean. There were palm trees and green grass all year round and many other older people living in the neighborhood. Mrs. Kay's good physical health and her favorable financial circumstances made entry into one of the hotels feasible. The social worker assured Mr. Kay that such a move was the best alternative for his mother. An inspection of the hotel by the entire family confirmed all of this. A week later Mrs. Kay moved some of her belongings into a small but comfortable suite on the fourth floor of the Hotel Gregorian. A sign over the entrance read "A Retirement Hotel for the Active Retired."

At first Mrs. Kay did well in her new surroundings. The other residents were mostly widows like herself. A few couples who shared suites were the envy of the single women, even though many of the married folks scarcely seemed to speak to each other in the dining room or on the veranda that faced the ocean boulevard. A few women befriended Mrs. Kay, finding her to be an uncommonly intelligent and worldly woman, which she was. There were many stories to be told about going to college back east, working and living in New York City, traveling with her husband, and, of course, the wonders of children and grandchildren.

A few months after her arrival at the Gregorian, however, her new friends and acquaintances began to notice a change in Mrs.

Kay. She would sometimes come down to breakfast sullen and depressed. Deflecting inquiries about her health, she would eat quietly and then leave as soon as the meal was over, withdrawing to her rooms for most of the day and evening. But even more worrisome were her daily, almost furtive exits in the late afternoon to return 30 minutes later with a small paper bag that seemed to contain a tall bottle. The strong odor of alcohol that one of the residents noted one day when she came to fetch Mrs. Kay for dinner confirmed the growing suspicion that she had begun drinking—heavily, regularly, and by herself.

Never more than a social drinker, Mrs. Kay, during the long illness of her husband, had happened on the numbing effects of alcohol in her frantic efforts to ease her mind during the long vigils at his bedside. For several months she had sampled from his well-supplied liquor cabinet, steadily working her way from the front to the back. When she took up residence in the hotel, she had to learn a new skill—unobtrusively finding a liquor store and buying her own liquor. Unfortunately, she mastered the task readily.

Conceptualization and Treatment

The first therapeutic task was to keep Mrs. Kay from dying. Her bizarre behavior in the emergency room of the hospital to which the police officer had taken her suggested delirium from a reversible malfunction of the brain; it can be caused by such things as over-medication, alcohol intoxication, and malnutrition. The examining physician made this diagnosis because of Mrs. Kay's obvious state of alcohol intoxication and because of her age. Older people are particularly susceptible to delirium states. He also made the judgment that her diet might not have been adequate in recent days or weeks, given her disheveled appearance and the tendency for alcohol abuse and malnourishment to go together. Poor nutrition had no doubt contributed to her delirium.

Her son's name and phone number were listed in her wallet; he arrived at his mother's bedside within a few hours. Blaming himself for his mother's present state, Mr. Kay brooded over his stupidity and callousness at allowing her to leave the safety of his home some months ago. His first impulse was to take her home immediately, but the doctor cautioned him about the danger she was in and the need to restore her to a normal state of brain function through withdrawal from alcohol and a proper diet.

During his anxious hours at the hospital, Mrs. Kay's son tried to gain an understanding of how she could have come so close to drinking herself to death. He reflected on his mother's recurrent depressions throughout her adult life and on the seemingly inordinate responsibility she took for anything bad that happened to her children or to her husband. The depressive episodes she had experienced since her husband's death a few years ago were not new, nor was the blame she heaped on herself for Harold's condition during his final years.

The hospital maintained a social service department, and the following day Mr. Kay and his wife spent an hour with a counselor to discuss the options for his mother. Mr. Kay believed that she needed close surveillance and round-the-clock care, which was not available at the retirement hotel. Surely she should move back with his family

or enter a nursing home. The counselor, however, on the basis of the history Mr. Kay provided about his mother's recent and distant past, believed Mrs. Kay was capable of far more independent functioning than would be possible in either setting. She urged the son to consider not changing her living arrangement but to try to interest her in talking to a therapist on a regular basis while at the same time having a social worker visit her a few times a week to check on how she was doing. Mr. Kay reluctantly agreed to give it a try if his mother would agree to the plan.

Obtaining Mrs. Kay's agreement (in fact, talking about anything at all with her) proved impossible for the next few days. The family did not yet know that her intent had been to get as drunk as possible and then walk as far as she could into the nearby surf and drown herself. When she came to her senses several days later to find herself still alive, she experienced the kind of shame and guilt often felt by people who have made an unsuccessful suicide attempt. (This was not revealed until many weeks later, during a treatment session with her therapist.) After a week's time, however, Mrs. Kay was able to discuss things with the counselor and her son and agreed to the plan. Its appeal for her, however, was that it avoided having to burden her son and his family again by returning to their home. It also did not preclude her attempting again to kill herself at a later date.

Mrs. Kay's return to the Gregorian two weeks later was a happy, almost rambunctious event. The manager had planned a surprise welcome, complete with colored bunting and a large sign reading, "Welcome back, Helen, we all love you." Mrs. Kay's reaction to this outpouring of affection was mixed. She wanted desperately to believe that she was really wanted and loved, yet she felt unworthy to receive such affection from her hotel friends. On balance, her response was positive because, in her own mind, it meant that even though she had left the hotel a suicidal drinker, she was able to come back for another chance at life with her new friends and acquaintances.

A Cognitive-Behavioral Therapy

Mrs. Kay's therapist was a woman in her late forties, recently graduated from a clinical psychology program that offered specialty training in gerontology. Dr. Gardner had received the usual training of a clinical psychologist and had devoted special study to the physical and psychological problems of older people. The initial session was spent getting acquainted, since the psychologist knew of Mrs. Kay's previous aversion to mental health workers. Her warmth and empathy, however, won over Mrs. Kay, who began in the next session to recount her reasons for the suicide attempt.

As the story unfolded, Mrs. Kay said that she initially liked the retirement hotel because she knew she was no longer "bothering" her son's family, and, in a more positive vein, she enjoyed the privacy and increased feeling of independence. The other residents of the hotel, after all, were capable of getting around on their own; no one was blatantly senile (the colloquial term Mrs. Kay used to refer to the memory and interpersonal deficits known more technically as dementia), and they all shared some common experiences that could be discussed at meals and at odd hours in rocking chairs on the attractive veranda that looked out onto the oceanfront park. There was something satisfying about making a reference to the

Great Depression without one's listener believing you were referring to the last time someone felt extremely morose and despondent.

After the initial positive period of a few weeks, however, her guilt about the death of her husband returned. It was only because he had worked so hard all his life that she could now afford to live in these comfortable surroundings. She gave no consideration to her own contributions to the family's estate. If she had not been so selfish and weak, he would not have been hospitalized and allowed to die alone among strangers and without the nurturance that a wife should have been there to provide. What good had she really been to him, not only after he became seriously ill but even during the earlier years of their long marriage? What good was she to anybody? Her son's family found her an unwelcome burden, an ordeal to endure because she was a pitiable old woman who had lost her husband. Finally, what kind of person was she that she could not cope with the loss of her beloved husband? Weren't the other widows at the Gregorian managing on their own without the self-blame and hopelessness that tormented her in her waking hours and also during her fitful sleep?

Mrs. Kay had suffered a great loss. Selling her home and moving in with her son's family led to further feelings that she no longer had control over her life. Reality, then, was providing some reason to feel helpless and depressed. But the conclusions Mrs. Kay drew from the facts seemed exaggerated and distorted, suggesting the viability of a cognitive intervention modeled after Beck's work on the treatment of depression (Beck et al., 1979). Of importance also was the fact that Mrs. Kay had been subject to depression all her adult life, and inquiry into these earlier episodes revealed a similar pattern of illogical self-blame and unjustified self-deprecation.

The following transcript of part of one therapy session illustrates the kinds of discussions Dr. Gardner had with Mrs. Kay over a period of several months:

Dr. Gardner: We were talking last week about why your husband died.

Mrs. Kay (eyes cast downward): Yes, I was to blame for it.

Dr. Gardner: I understand you feel that way, Helen, but let's talk about other aspects of his illness some more. You said he'd had an operation six months earlier to remove a cancerous lung?

Mrs. Kay (sobbing): Yes. . . .The only reason he got cancer was because of me.

Dr. Gardner: What do you mean?

Mrs. Kay: He smoked a lot till he was almost 60. When we first met in Cambridge, he was smoking two packs a day. Camels, no less. Of course, in those days, the 1920s, no one worried about cancer from cigarettes. Still, I never liked it and told him so.

Dr. Gardner: You did? What was his reaction?

Mrs. Kay: He'd pat me on my fanny and tell me I was cute when I got angry. I guess these days you'd call that pretty sexist. (almost smiling)

Dr. Gardner: Yes, I would myself. But then, that was then. Tell me, was it your fault that he had begun smoking in the first place?

Mrs. Kay: Well, not really. . . . Well, I guess not, you see, he'd already been smoking for several years before we met.

Dr. Gardner: Okay, so you were not responsible for his taking up the habit.

Mrs. Kay: I don't see how I could have been. But certainly I could have made him stop.

Dr. Gardner: Tell me.

Mrs. Kay: What do you mean?

Dr. Gardner: Can you tell me how you could have made him stop? How did you fail him in those early parts of your relationship?

Mrs. Kay: Well, I didn't mean to say I failed him or anything. I just . . . well . . . (flustered)

Dr. Gardner: Oh, sorry. I must have misunderstood. I thought I heard you say or, at least imply, that you were responsible for his smoking.

Mrs. Kay: I guess I did. I guess I have felt that way for a long time.

Dr. Gardner: Is it possible that *he* might have been the responsible one? Or is it possible that he was just addicted to the nicotine?

Mrs. Kay: Is that true? Do people get addicted?

Dr. Gardner: Definitely. He might have been able to stop, but only with a lot of effort and pain.

Mrs. Kay: Yes, he tried many times. But it didn't work. He seemed able to do most anything he set out to do, but that smoking was something he never could handle. Or at least the price seemed too high to pay. You know, he'd be unable to sit still those first few days after stopping, his work went to hell, I mean bad, and he became almost like another person. Mr. Hyde, I used to call him, when he was trying to stop. The children, too, they called him that, and it did break the tension a little.

Dr. Gardner: So he tried, but he didn't make it.

Mrs. Kay: No. But he was a good man.

Dr. Gardner: Of course. I agree a person can be good and still fail at things.

Mrs. Kay: Now, doctor, are you making a point about *me*?

Dr. Gardner (smiling): Well, now that you mention it, I guess I am. But I'm saying something else, Helen, I'm. . .

Mrs. Kay: I know, my dear. You're telling me that I'm not to blame for everything that's not right with my life, with my family. But I've always been that way. My daddy always told me to look out for others. Jesus did that, you know.

Dr. Gardner: Yes, it's a nice thing to strive for. But it doesn't mean you have to succeed every time.

Mrs. Kay: No, I suppose not. But listen, we were talking about his death. He didn't want to leave our home. (crying again now) He wanted to stay, with me at his side. I *know* it.

Dr. Gardner: Helen, how do you know that? He hadn't talked to you for weeks.

Mrs. Kay: Yes, poor man. (crying loudly now) He didn't know where he was. He didn't even know me.

Dr. Gardner: Helen, even if he did, do you really think he wanted you to be with him all the time?

Mrs. Kay: Well, now that you ask, we did have some discussions when he was thinking clearly, about his going into a nursing home when it became too much for me and . . . (falls silent)

Dr. Gardner: And what?

Mrs. Kay (composing herself): . . .and he made me promise that when he didn't know me anymore, I would do what the doctors said. And he knew they'd say he should go into a hospital, or something.

Dr. Gardner: Helen, he told you not to sacrifice yourself totally for him.

Mrs. Kay: Yes, dear man. (crying loudly now) He was too good for me.

Dr. Gardner: Tell me, Helen, how do you feel about what he said?

Mrs. Kay: What do you mean?

Dr. Gardner: I mean, well . . . did any of the other women at your hotel go through anything like this? You know, taking care of a sick husband at home and having to let him go after a while.

Mrs. Kay: Yes, there's Mrs. Hancock, a lovely woman. Her husband had gotten senile like my Harold, and she just couldn't take it. She put him in a nursing home, and he seemed okay there. But she had a hard time finding a good one.

Dr. Gardner: Yes, I know, there are some crummy ones around. But good ones, too, and necessary when people need the kind of total care that your husband needed. But besides, it was his cancer, wasn't it? And it was the hospital that you had him admitted to, wasn't it?

Mrs. Kay: Yes, the doctor insisted on it. He said the only way to make him comfortable was to have him in the hospital. The drugs he needed were too powerful and dangerous for me to give to him.

Dr. Gardner: So, it doesn't seem a bad decision.

Mrs. Kay: But then he died the following day, doctor! (sobbing)

Dr. Gardner: Oh, my dear Helen, don't you think he'd have died the following day in your house? What could have happened in the hospital to make him die sooner?

Mrs. Kay: Maybe it was just moving him.

Dr. Gardner (conceding to herself that this was a good point): Yes, maybe, but you can't be sure, and besides, didn't the doctor say his death was inevitable, and that the morphine he planned to begin administering would probably have dulled the pain only a little, that his whole body. . . .

Mrs. Kay: Oh, please don't say that. (crying)

Dr. Gardner (remaining silent for a minute): Helen, I know this is hard to talk about, but you need to face it squarely. You need to look at what happened more objectively. It doesn't seem that anything more could have been done for your husband. You had a wonderful life together, and taking care of him at home gave you time to talk about things with him. But

at the end he was gravely ill, and he might have been made more comfortable in the hospital if it wasn't his time to die soon after he got there.

Mrs. Kay: Yes, I can see that now. I see it. Do you really believe what you're saying?

Dr. Gardner: Helen, I'll not lie to you. You're not a perfect individual—who is?—but you were wonderful to your husband, and you did everything, no, you did *more* than could have been expected. You didn't kill him, Helen. (smiling) You don't have *that* much power!

Mrs. Kay smiling): You're quite the joker, doctor. Yes, I'm going to think about that for a while.

People do not change their minds easily, and Dr. Gardner was under no illusion that she had convinced her client to stop blaming herself for her husband's death. But this discussion helped Mrs. Kay begin to consider other ways to construe what happened. Repeated examination over several sessions of her role in the course of her husband's illness did gradually lead Mrs. Kay to admit to herself that there were some things "even she" could not do, and that she could not reasonably blame herself for her husband's demise.

Because the heavy drinking seemed to be due to her depression, no specific treatment was undertaken for this aspect of her problem. Nevertheless, Mrs. Kay was provided with some factual information on how excessive alcohol consumption could produce a temporary delirium state in an older person. The psychologist also warned her about drug interactions.

There was a total of 30 therapy sessions. Dr. Gardner had assumed at the outset that she would have to have a number of conjoint sessions with the son and his wife as well. She changed her mind when Mrs. Kay showed progress in reconstruing her responsibility for her husband's death and began to view some negative events as caused by factors beyond her control. With Mrs. Kay's permission, the therapist telephoned the son after therapy had been ongoing for one month to assure him that things were proceeding well and to confirm the suitability of Mrs. Kay's remaining in her hotel. The occasional visits by a social worker became less frequent. After six months, Mrs. Kay was reasonably comfortable and taking a more active interest than before in the many social functions available to older people in the surrounding community. She had also stopped drinking.

Follow-up

Mrs. Kay lived at the Gregorian for the remaining 11 years of her life. During that time she experienced several bouts of depression and consulted with a clinical psychologist during one of the more debilitating episodes. She tried social drinking a few times, having a glass of sherry with friends, but, on the advice of her therapist, did her best to refrain even from this occasional drinking because of a concern that she might return to alcohol as a salve for her periods of extreme unhappiness. Her son and his family visited her about once a month, and she derived some enjoyment from her grandchildren. Memories of her late husband provided an admixture of sadness and joy, and she would talk to him at his gravesite a few times a year when her son drove her to the cemetery. She died in her sleep after a bout with the flu one very soggy winter.

Discussion

Growing Old

Older people have for some time been neglected by mental health professionals, but recently more and more training programs have begun to pay systematic attention to the particular physical and psychological challenges people face as they age. The growth in interest perhaps reflects the fact that the proportion of the population that is 65 and older is increasing steadily. This is attributable to many factors, especially decreased infant, childhood, and maternal mortality, as well as improved sanitation and more effective control of infectious diseases.

Currently in the United States, people 65 and older compose 12.4 percent (35 million) of the population (U.S. Bureau of the Census, 2000). It is estimated that Americans over age 65 will number 52 million by the year 2020, an increase of more than 20 million since the late 1980s (Spencer, 1989). The oldest-old cohort, those above age 85, is expected to grow to at least 24 million by the year 2040, up from 3.8 million in the mid-1990s. As of 1999, there were 70,000 Americans at least 100 years old; by the year 2050, that number is expected to grow more than tenfold to over 800,000 (U.S. Bureau of the Census, 1999). And as the first generation of baby boomers begins to reach age 65 in 2010, the percentage of elderly in the United States will rise dramatically, comprising an estimated 20 percent of the population by the year 2030 (U.S. Bureau of the Census, 2000).

The most obvious fact about an older person is his or her age. Physiological aging is an inexorable process, affecting all who make it through 60 or more years of existence. To be sure, certain cosmetic and medical measures can mitigate somewhat the biological effects of growing old, and there is many a 70-year-old in better physical condition than a 50-year-old. But eventually gravity is everyone's worst enemy.

In some measure, it is the way older people react to inevitable and more serious physical changes that affects how psychologically sound they are in their later years. The heavy emphasis on youth in our culture does little to reassure most of us that life is worth living beyond one's forties. The burden may rest especially heavily on women, who are devalued more than men as they grow old. The feminist movement of the 1960s and beyond has helped reduce the stigma of a woman's growing old, but, like other cultural phenomena, changes are slow in coming.

Old people face many real problems: medical care that is expensive and often poorly suited to their needs; economic challenges and sometimes privation; deteriorating health; and loss of friends and loved ones. They seem to have more than their share of problems, but they cope very well as a group. In fact, people over 65 have the lowest overall prevalence of mental disorders among all age groups (Gatz, Kasl-Godley, & Karel, 1996). This includes depression, estimated to be prevalent among only 3 percent of the elderly as compared to the 20 percent estimate in people under age 65 (Anthony & Aboraya, 1992; Eaton et al., 1989; Myers et al., 1984; Regier et al., 1988). These are cross-sectional comparisons, however, and it is possible that those now young and suffering from depression will swell the numbers of depressed older adults as they proceed in life. Indeed, there is some indication that younger cohorts of older adults may be more clinically depressed than older groups. That is, people joining the ranks of older adults today show more signs of clinical depression than cohorts born earlier in the twentieth century (Gatz et al., 1996).

Various studies have documented higher rates of illness and death among people who are widowed (Clayton, 1973; Parkes & Brown, 1972), and bereavement has been hypothesized to be a common precipitating factor for depressions that hospitalize older patients (Turner & Sternberg, 1978). And yet, studies have found relatively low rates of depression in bereaved individuals (Musetti et al., 1989). Few older people, then, appear to develop a disabling depressive illness following an expected loss of a loved one. It is very disheartening when someone close dies, but as we get older, most of us come to terms with the reality that loved ones are going to pass on.

Most of the depressive episodes among older people are recurrences from their earlier years, as was the case with Mrs. Kay, but some show up for the first time in old age (Gurland, 1976; Koenig & Blazer, 1992). Life problems alone would not explain Mrs. Kay's depression; as just mentioned, most older people suffer losses *without* becoming profoundly depressed. The case material reveals a long-standing tendency on her part to blame herself for negative events in her life and the lives of others close to her. She also insisted that she excel without help from others. In terms of Beck's theory of depression, the schema she was operating in was one of self-deprecation and self-blame (Beck, 1967). This cognitive structure led her to construe as her fault unfortunate events such as her husband's chronic cigarette smoking, his contracting lung cancer, and his dying a day after she allowed him to be hospitalized.

The therapy undertaken by the psychologist was aimed at uncovering these unspoken beliefs; examining them openly; considering their validity; and offering other, presumably more realistic ways of regarding certain happenings in her life. This is a very intellectual therapy, relying on the ability and willingness of clients to understand the basic framework and accept it as applying to their own particular circumstances. Dr. Gardner no doubt saw Mrs. Kay as a suitable candidate, considering her keen intelligence and solid educational background. One of the unanswered questions in Beck's approach is whether it is appropriate for people whose abilities and general attitudes toward life do not so readily accommodate a highly intellectual approach.

Be that as it may, more and more research data confirm that older adults who are depressed respond well to a variety of psychotherapeutic interventions (Gallagher-Thompson & Thompson, 1995; Gallagher-Thompson et al., 2000), including the cognitive therapy that Mrs. Kay had. Interpersonal psychotherapy (IPT) has also been used successfully to treat depression in older adults (Gallagher-Thompson et al., 2000; Hinrichsen, 1999). IPT is a short-term psychodynamic psychotherapy that addresses themes such as role loss, role transition, and interpersonal disputes, problem areas prominent in the lives of many older adults. Although it is not yet considered a well-established treatment for depression in older adults (Gatz et al., 1998), it has shown great promise with this age group (Hinrichsen, 1999). A notable finding from these and other studies of therapy for depressed seniors is that untreated control patients did not improve. Younger untreated depressed patients often do improve, suggesting that older adults are less likely than younger patients to recover without treatment.

It is ironic that psychotherapy with older adults has only recently been studied and advocated; the irony comes from the possibility that older people may be *particularly well suited* for psychotherapy because persons in their senior years have a greater tendency to be reflective and introspective (Neugarten, 1977).

Suicide

People at highest risk for suicide are those who are physically ill, feel hopeless, are isolated from others or have lost loved ones, are in dire financial circumstances, and are depressed. Because a combination of these factors is often found among older people, it should come as no surprise that suicide rates are higher for people over 65 than for younger individuals (McIntosh, 1995).

The rate is especially high for white males, increasing steadily into their eighties (Conwell, 1994, 2001). Butler and Lewis (1977) suggest that white males are particularly susceptible to suicide because they suffer an especially great loss in status, having held the greatest power and influence in societies like ours. What about women like Mrs. Kay? Suicide rates increase for white females until the age of 50 but then decrease thereafter. Older women who were victims of physical and/or sexual abuse are more likely to be suicidal or express suicidal ideation (Osgood & Manetta, 2000). Rates for nonwhite men and women in the United States fluctuate throughout the life span, with marked increases for men (Manton, Blazer, & Woodbury, 1987).

One statistic is particularly noteworthy. The ratio of unsuccessful to completed suicides is seven to one for people under 65 but two to one for those who are older. When older people decide to commit suicide, they are more likely to die (McIntosh et al., 1994), perhaps because of a greater resolve, or perhaps because their bodies are more vulnerable to sleeping pills or falls. Older people can also "give up" and passively kill themselves more readily than younger individuals by neglecting their diet or not taking prescribed medications for chronic diseases that are life-threatening. Older persons are also less likely to communicate their intentions to commit suicide than are younger people.

Suicide among older adults may also be the result of a rational and philosophical decision to stop living, such as when an elderly man decides that the intractable pain of his terminal illness is not worth the effort or the financial drain on his or his children's resources. One of the earliest suicides in which Dr. Jack Kevorkian participated was that of a woman in the earliest stages of Alzheimer's disease. She decided, well before she was incapacitated, to end her life because of quality issues. She used the services of Kevorkian, a retired pathologist, who had invented a device that administered intravenously a lethal drug—controlled by a button pushed by the patient. As expected, this "suicide machine" and the fact that a physician actively assisted in a person's death generated considerable publicity and conflicting opinions about its morality (Egan, 1990; Wilkerson, 1990).

Intervention with a suicidal elderly person is similar to what is practiced with younger individuals: counseling to help the person consider nonlethal alternatives to desperate situations. Suicidologists hold that life itself is sacred; they are also mindful of the fact that many people who become suicidal are grateful afterward that they have another chance at life. Even in older people suicidal crises pass, as happened with Mrs. Kay, who did take advantage of a second chance at life. Cognitive therapy seemed to alleviate the depression viewed as the underlying cause of her attempted suicide.

Delirium and Dementia

The problems of older people do not appear as a separate category in the DSM. Notice is taken here and there of the course of particular disorders, but the psychiatric profession has yet to confront aging itself as a major variable in mental and emotional disorders. The sole exception fits the prevalent stereotype that when an old person is unhappy or depressed or paranoid, it is somehow due to physical malfunctions: *DSM-IV-TR* has a separate main section called Delirium, Dementia, and Amnestic and Other Cognitive Disorders, and many of them are linked to diseases found among older people.

Only 5 percent of older adults have diseases of the brain, although these problems account for more admissions and hospital inpatient days than any other condition of geriatric adults (Zarit & Zarit, 1998). One of these syndromes, Delirium, was noted in Mrs. Kay when she was found under the pier by the police officer. The DSM describes delirium as a rapid-onset disorder characterized by difficulties in maintaining and shifting attention; disorganized thinking; and disturbances in perception (e.g., hallucinations), orientation, and memory. In the early stages of delirium, the person is frequently restless, particularly at night. The sleep-waking cycle becomes disturbed so that the person is drowsy during the day and awake, restless, and agitated during the night. The individual is generally worse during sleepless nights and in the dark. Vivid dreams and nightmares are common.

The person's behavior can also be erratic, ranging from thrashing around in bed to being lethargic and sluggish. The former pattern can be particularly dangerous in hospital settings, when the patient may be hooked up to intravenous food and medication; this often leads the staff to strap delirious patients in restraints to protect them from harming themselves. Mood can also fluctuate widely, from anger to euphoria, from irritability to apathy. In the course of a twenty-four-hour period, delirious people have lucid intervals and become alert and coherent. These daily fluctuations help distinguish delirium from other syndromes, especially Alzheimer's disease.

Delirium is usually reversible if the underlying cause is temporary, self-limiting, or adequately treated. Brain tissue may malfunction because of a metabolic disturbance without being destroyed. Although it can happen at any age, delirium is especially frequent among older people, whose body chemistry is sensitive to drug effects (like alcohol, as was the case with Mrs. Kay), drug overdoses, and malnutrition. It is especially a problem during hospitalization: One estimate is that up to half of the hospitalized elderly are likely to become delirious at some time during their stay (Lipowski, 1983). It is important for those who care for older people to understand that delirium, if not treated, can worsen, brain cells can be destroyed, and the person may actually die. (Well over 25 percent actually do die, either from the untreated underlying condition or from exhaustion—see Rabins & Folstein, 1982). The (unspoken) belief that old people do not get better may sometimes lead professionals to misdiagnose and regard a temporary delirium as the first sign of a progressive and irreversible brain disease.

Irreversible brain diseases do exist and are characterized by dementia, a steady and gradual deterioration of intellectual abilities over several years. (Some forms of dementia are reversible, however, depending on the underlying cause.) Memory problems are common, and abstract thinking suffers. The ability to do everyday things like read a newspaper or boil water is compromised. The person becomes unable to attend even to the most basic human needs; becomes incontinent, sometimes unruly; and, in the most fundamental and tragic sense, is no longer the person he or she once was. Unlike delirium, there is often actual destruction of brain cells from such causes as stroke and especially Alzheimer's disease, in which there is an atrophy or wasting away of cortical cells. Death usually follows within 10 to 14 years of onset.[1] In addition to his cancer, Mr. Kay had suffered from Alzheimer's.

A major decision that confronts families is how to care for the person with Alzheimer's disease. In the last few years of her husband's life, Mrs. Kay was faced with the challenge of nursing him at home. She persisted long after many caretakers would have given up and institutionalized the patient. Clinical depression and anxiety are widespread among those who care for their dementing relatives at home (Schulz & Williamson, 1991). Mrs. Kay certainly paid a steep emotional cost by looking after her husband on her own until the very end of his life, and she did not profit from advice and counsel that are becoming more widely available from mental health workers with training in gerontology. For example, she did not have a nurse come regularly to her home, even though she could have easily afforded it. She gave herself no time off, and her own inordinately high standards for herself continued to take their toll after her husband died. She blamed herself so severely for his death that she almost committed suicide.

Unfortunately, her concern about nursing homes was well founded; even in the better ones patients often receive the kind of care that fosters unnecessary dependency and even muscular and

---

[1] Because it is difficult to know with any precision when the person's dementia actually began, the length of time one can live with a progressive dementing disease is hard to estimate

mental deterioration (Rosenblatt & Spiegel, 1988). Geared to maximum levels of custodial care, most nursing homes take a conservative approach. If a person needs a walker to move about alone, better to wheel the patient around in a wheelchair because it is faster and poses less risk of injury; if a person spills food but does manage to eat, better to feed that person because it is more efficient and keeps the place neater. Even with the best intentions, this kind of care does not benefit all residents.

But worse than this misguided care, many nursing homes are poorly run. During the late 1980s, a series of investigations into lax practices in nursing homes led to a number of governmental reforms. Despite resulting improvements in many nursing homes, there remain serious problems, confirmed recently in an 18-month review released in March 2002 by the Senate Special Committee on Aging. These deficiencies undermine the belief that residents reliably receive even minimally satisfactory care.

Mrs. Kay was lucky in many ways. Her son's family cared about her and remained willing to have her live with them. Her physical health was good, and she was therefore not dependent on others for taking care of basic needs such as dressing herself, eating, shopping, and so forth. She also had considerable financial resources, unlike many older people. As a woman, she entered her senior years with a sharp and active mind and a set of interests developed during her own professional career as a journalist. This made her interesting to be around and probably contributed to her popularity in her retirement hotel; the welcome she received when she was discharged from the hospital played no small role in her recovery.

Pessimism has been the rule in caring for the aged. Because they have relatively little time to live—relative, that is, to the mental health professionals whose responsibility it is to look after them—their psychological problems have received less emphasis than those of younger adults. And yet older people suffer from the entire range of psychological disorders—paranoia, anxiety and depression, hypochondriasis, substance abuse, insomnia, psychosis, and sexual dysfunction.

Older people also have a set of problems that are more or less unique. People in their 80s have usually outlived their friends and spouses, and new social contacts are often not as easy to make, as was the case with Mrs. Kay. As mentioned, physical losses can also be a heavy burden especially when the society at large is geared to people whose reflexes are sharper and whose sensorimotor capacities are speedier and more acute. As we have seen, evidence is accumulating that psychological interventions can have a positive impact on older people. What is needed now is a strong social commitment to study the ways people change as they age and to develop appropriate methods to help them adapt and continue growing. Failure to change our thinking and actions about the elderly will prove disadvantageous not only to them but to the older adults of tomorrow—*us*.

17 Outcomes and Issues in Psychological Intervention

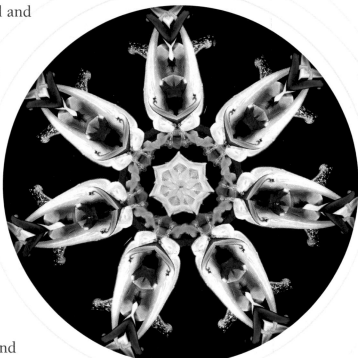

I n Chapter 2 we described in some detail the major approaches to psychological therapeutic intervention, and in Chapters 6 through 16 we reviewed how these approaches have treated various psychopathologies. We turn now to a more general review and critical appraisal of a number of psychological interventions. We discuss the research on their effectiveness and offer as well some general comments that, we hope, will enrich the reader's understanding of the complexities of psychotherapy.

General Issues in Evaluating Psychotherapy Research

We begin with a few general issues that will inform our understanding and appreciation of research in psychotherapy.

The Use of Therapy Manuals in Randomized Clinical Trials

Therapy manuals are detailed guides on how to conduct a particular therapy, stipulating specific procedures to be followed at different stages of treatment. The use of such manuals has become the norm in psychotherapy research (e.g., Chambless & Ollendick, 2001; Nathan & Gorman, 2002; Wilson, 1996). Indeed, it is impossible nowadays to obtain funding to conduct a study of the outcome of psychotherapy without first explicitly defining the independent variables (p. 122) via a manual that the therapists in the study must follow as closely as possible.

The use of therapist manuals began with the earliest randomized clinical trials (RCTs) on Wolpe's technique of systematic desensitization (Davison, 1968b; Lang & Lazovik, 1963; Paul, 1966). In contrast, in earlier psychotherapy research of the 1940s and 1950s, the activity of the therapist was, for the most part, described only in terms of his or her theoretical orientation (psychodynamic, client centered, etc.). But what therapists actually *do* in the consulting room is often difficult to know based on what they *say* they do and on their allegiance to a particular orientation (London, 1964). Specifying via manuals what therapists are to do in a controlled study and then monitoring what they actually do in their sessions with patients has thus been hailed as a significant advance in the scientific study of therapeutic interventions. It allows someone reading a psychotherapy study to know what actually happened to patients in a given experimental condition.

All well and good, but a moment's reflection suggests a problem. Although the use of manuals buys us greater internal validity (p. 123)—results obtained can be attributed with some confidence to the action of the independent variable—what about external validity? Do the results obtained from manual-based studies generalize to the actual practice of psychotherapy outside the constraints of a controlled study? There is perhaps no more important and more hotly debated topic in psychotherapy than this (Beutler, 1999; Goldfried & Davison, 1994; Persons, 1989).

Here's a way to look at the issue. It is an oft-documented fact that most therapists describe themselves as eclectic (e.g., Jensen, Bergin, & Greaves, 1990; Smith, 1982; recall our earlier discussion of "practice makes imperfect," p. 61). This fact suggests that controlled studies of specific techniques (e.g., desensitization) or approaches (e.g., client-centered therapy) are limited in what they can tell us about the nature and outcomes of therapy *as actually practiced* (Lambert & Bergin, 1994). That is, we know that most therapists seldom behave strictly in line with a particular theoretical orientation—whether psychoanalytic, client centered, or behavioral. Therefore, the kinds of controlled studies emphasized in this chapter and earlier in the book are limited in what they can tell us about the effectiveness of the psychotherapy available to patients who are not participants in research studies. This situation is ironic, for it is these randomized clinical trials that provide the evidence used by proponents of particular techniques or general theoretical approaches to support their positions!

TREATMENT MANUALS FOR PRACTITIONERS

Treating *the* Trauma *of* Rape

Cognitive-Behavioral Therapy for PTSD

Edna B. Foa
Barbara Olasov Rothbaum

A treatment manual that guides the therapist in working with a patient.

The Role of the Therapist

A related issue is the therapist. The purpose of using treatment manuals is to minimize the role of the therapist. This is of course not to say that therapists are irrelevant! It is only to say that RCTs and treatment manuals assume that differences among therapists can be minimized with the use of manuals. As pointed out by Teyber et al. (2001), however, there is research showing that there is great variability among therapists even in RCTs. For example, in the well-known NIMH Treatment of Depression Collaborative Research Program (cf. p. 290), therapists trained to use the same manuals varied in how well they implemented the manuals *and* in the results achieved: Some therapists were more successful than others using the same manual (Elkin, 1994; Blatt et al., 1996). In addition, research suggests that, in general, the differences between *therapists* is greater than the differences between *treatments* (Beutler, 1997). What appears necessary is not to allow the focus on treatment variables in RCTs to blind us to the importance of therapist variables—factors like empathy, interpersonal sensitivity, and ability to inspire trust.

Some Limitations of Randomized Clinical Trials

A common characteristic of today's controlled studies is the exclusion of people on various grounds. For example, people may be excluded from a study if they have more problems than the one being studied (the comorbidity issue). In addition, studies rely on people who are willing to participate in a highly structured treatment protocol. In short, the patients who volunteer and are accepted as participants in controlled studies are different from many—and probably from the vast majority of—patients in psychotherapy. This situation may make it risky to generalize from controlled studies to the actual practice of psychotherapy.

Another related attribute of controlled studies is the widespread use of a DSM diagnosis to define patients as homogeneous. For example, the large-scale NIMH RCT of depression that we examined in Chapter 10 (p. 290) followed the DSM criteria in defining people as having major depression and then randomly assigned them to different experimental conditions. But as we have seen many times, people are depressed, anxious, or dependent on alcohol or cigarettes for many different reasons. What is not possible in such studies is an idiographic analysis of a person—that is, an analysis of the unique features of a single case—to determine which factors are most important in making that one person feel, think, and behave in a certain way (Beutler, 1997; Davison, 2000). Note that psychotherapy researchers do not really believe that the people who are diagnosed as, for example, depressed and then randomly assigned to different treatment conditions are depressed for the same reasons (e.g., biased thinking that maintains a schema of ineptness). Rather, for the sake of creating an experiment with as much internal validity as possible, they pretend that this is the case. For this reason, among others, large numbers of participants are needed in psychotherapy research; the differences that are obviously present among people are assumed to "randomize out" with large groups.

Therapy as actually practiced takes a more idiographic approach, that is, it is tailored to the particular needs and characteristics of a particular patient. In terms recently employed by Haaga and Stiles (2000), treatment manuals encourage a *ballistic* approach, that is, a therapy manual is adhered to quite closely with as few adjustments as possible being made in response to what the research participant is doing. In contrast, therapy as conducted in nonresearch settings is more *responsive* to the particular reactions of the patient to what the therapist is doing. When they are working in clinical settings, therapists make continual accommodations that are not constrained by the demands of a scientific study. In contrast, the very essence of treatment manuals is to minimize the tailoring of intervention to individual patients. The problem is that too rigid adherence to a treatment manual can create tension between therapist and patient if the patient senses that his or her particular concerns are not being addressed (Henry et al., 1993). It remains a challenge to researchers and clinicians alike to reconcile the seemingly incompatible needs of these two approaches (Davison, 1998; Fishman, 1999; Howard et al.,

1996). Flexibility and responsiveness in the design and use of treatment manuals has to be balanced against the research requirement that independent variables be clearly defined (Davison, 1998).

In this connection, psychotherapy researchers have recently been distinguishing between efficacy and effectiveness. The **efficacy** of an intervention is what we determine from a controlled RCT, typically conducted in an academic research setting. The **effectiveness** of an intervention refers to what is offered to and received by people in the everyday world. Whereas the elimination of observable, well-defined problems, such as how far a person with agoraphobia can venture from his or her home, is the usual focus of efficacy studies, effectiveness is usually judged by patients themselves on the basis of more global and subjective criteria, such as the level of satisfaction people have with their therapy, how much they believe they have been helped, and whether they believe that the quality of their life has improved (see *Consumer Reports*, 1995; Seligman, 1995, 1996).[1] Moreover, such studies rarely employ treatment manuals and, in general, lack the experimental controls that are inherent to RCTs. Effectiveness studies are beginning to appear in support of certain cognitive-behavioral treatments of anxiety (e.g., Wade, Treat, & Stuart, 1998) and depression (e.g., Persons, Bostrom, & Bertagnoli, 1999). Similar to the issue of treatment manuals, the efficacy-effectiveness distinction is a topic of lively debate in the field.

Troubled people may talk about their problems with friends or seek professional therapy. Therapy is typically sought by those for whom the advice and support of family or friends have not provided relief.

Aligning Practice with Research

One can take a different approach to the disjunction between scientific research and clinical practice. Perhaps it is the practice that needs changing, not the research! That is, rather than trying to make randomized clinical trials or other scientific evaluations of treatment truer to the current activities of clinicians (i.e., improve the external validity or generalizability of the research, see p. 123), it can be argued that it is the normal activities of therapists that should be changed, to bring them more in line with the research (Davison, 1998).

An example of this from our own professional experience can serve as an illustration. In the late 1960s, when we were at the start of our academic-clinical careers, it rarely happened that therapists ever left their offices with their patients to conduct therapy. It was assumed that the sanctity of the consulting room was inviolate, that it was unprofessional to go out in public with the patient as part of the therapy hour. (Of course it *is* frowned upon for clinicians to go out in public with their patients *outside of* therapy!) But then came articles about in vivo desensitization with agoraphobics and other people with phobias that suggested that many fearful patients could be helped by having the therapist accompany the patient in confrontations with what they feared, goading them on and giving reassurance (recall the case report by Lazarus, Davison, & Polefka [1965] with the school phobic child, p. 147). Over the past thirty-plus years it has become much more accepted for therapists to work with patients in settings other than their offices, sometimes in virtual reality labs (cf. p. 49), sometimes in the street or in a supermarket, and so on.

[1] Of course, the criteria applied in efficacy versus effectiveness studies are not mutually exclusive. For example, the satisfaction that a patient with agoraphobia reports after being in treatment is likely to have something to do with whether he or she can leave the home.

The Challenge of Managed Care

No doubt you have heard of managed care. Your own health care is most likely provided to you via an insurance company that attempts to control costs (and maximize profits) by requiring prior approval of the nature and extent of treatment and by reducing the amount of payment provided to hospitals, clinics, and medical and psychological personnel for their services.

Run for the most part by businesspeople rather than by health care providers, managed care organizations (MCOs) may have brought down (or at least slowed the rise of) the costs of care over the past few decades. They have also demanded increased accountability from providers. MCOs look to scientific evidence to warrant what health professionals do with their patients. Surgical, dental, and medical procedures are justified by scientific evidence. Drugs approved by the Food and Drug Administration for use in the United States are judged from controlled research to be safe and effective for particular conditions. More recently, these standards have been applied to assessments and treatments of mental disorders (Chambless & Ollendick, 2001). The scrutiny that physicians and dentists have been accustomed to for many years is now being brought to bear on mental health professionals.

Who can take issue with controlling costs—for we all end up paying for one another's health care expenses one way or the other—and making treatment as scientifically grounded as possible? The picture is not that simple. Managed care is strongly opposed by some mental health professionals on the grounds that it intrudes on the privacy of patients as well as on the independent decision-making of the clinician, who no longer has the freedom to choose how many sessions to have with a patient and what kinds of assessments and treatments to employ because most insurers will cover only certain interventions and impose limits on the number of sessions they will pay for.

Stepped Care

Partly in response to managed care, a strategy that is becoming more widely followed in psychology and psychiatry is something referred to as **stepped care** (Haaga, 2000). It is commonly followed in medicine. Briefly stated, stepped care refers to the practice of beginning one's therapeutic efforts with the least expensive and least intrusive intervention possible and moving on to more expensive and/or more intrusive interventions only if necessary. So, for example, if a patient is suffering from panic attacks, the clinician begins with what the research literature suggests is the least expensive and least intrusive intervention and moves on to more expensive and more intrusive interventions only if the panic attacks have not been alleviated.

Stepped care is consistent with the "doing more with less" mantra of the 90s. Throughout the last decade, business cut back on the number of (lower and middle-level) employees. The U.S. military was downsized. Universities reduced the hiring of tenure-track faculty and began to rely increasingly on outside contract instructors (whose compensation is usually less than that of a graduate assistant for the same work). And managed care has markedly reduced the number of sessions covered for psychotherapy services as well as the compensation that practitioners can expect for a given amount of professional effort (Kent & Hersen, 2000).

Stepped care is consistent with the legal principle of least restrictive alternative. As discussed in greater detail in the next chapter (p. 629), mental health professionals are generally supposed to provide that treatment which restricts the patient's liberty to the least possible degree while remaining workable and effective (*In Re: Tarpley* 556 N.E. 2d, superseded by 581 N.E. 2d 1251 [1991]). It is, for example, unconstitutional to confine a nondangerous mentally ill patient who is capable of surviving on his or her own or with the help of willing and responsible family or friends (*Project Release* v. *Prevost*, 722 F2d 960 [2d Cir. 1983]). More generally, and consistent with the principles of stepped care, treatment should entail as little intrusion as possible.

However, are less expensive and less intense interventions necessarily in the patient's best interests? Maybe not. If a patient is provided the least expensive and least intrusive intervention first and if that intervention does not improve things, the patient may lose heart and drop out of therapy altogether, something that may not have happened if the therapist had employed at the outset the most powerful—and *not the least expensive and intrusive*—intervention available (Wilson et al., 2000). Thus, there are risks associated with beginning with low-intensity treatments across the board.

Indeed, this risk is related to an issue that is not acknowledged sufficiently, namely, the consequences of patients getting *worse* from ineffective treatments, or the so-called deterioration effect. Not only do ineffective treatments not bring about desired change (by definition); they may also have a negative impact on the patient's self-esteem and reduce his or her motivation to continue trying to change. Moreover, the time spent with an ineffective treatment—whether it be inexpensive, unobtrusive, or both—is time that could have been devoted to a more appropriate intervention, albeit a more "stepped-up" one.

With these general observations as background, we turn now to an evaluation of several therapeutic approaches, both the data on their effectiveness and some issues pertaining to them.

Review of Psychoanalytic Therapies

Before evaluating several psychoanalytic psychotherapies, it will be good to review and summarize their core features. Information on the whole range of psychotherapy was presented in greater detail in Chapter 2.

Basic Concepts and Techniques in Classical Psychoanalysis and its Variations

At the heart of classical psychoanalysis is the therapeutic attempt to remove repressions that have prevented the ego from helping the individual grow into a healthy adult. Psychopathology is assumed to develop when people remain unaware of their true motivations and fears. They can be restored to healthy functioning only by becoming conscious of what has been repressed. When people can understand what is motivating their actions, they have a greater number of choices. Where id is, let there ego be, to paraphrase a maxim of psychoanalysis. The ego—the primarily conscious, deliberating, choosing portion of the personality—can better guide the individual in rational, realistic directions if repressions are minimal.

Wachtel's (1977) woolly mammoth (see p. 31) is an apt metaphor for the unresolved, buried conflicts that psychoanalytic theory assumes underlie psychological problems. The proper focus of therapy, then, is not on the presenting problem, such as fears of being rejected, but on unconscious childhood conflicts that exist in the psyche. Only by lifting the repression can the person confront the underlying problem and reevaluate it in the context of his or her adult life.

As described in Chapter 2 (p. 31), psychoanalysts employ a variety of techniques to achieve the goal of insight into repressed conflicts. Among these are free association (in which the patient, reclining on a couch, is encouraged to give free rein to thoughts and feelings and to verbalize whatever comes to mind); the analysis of dreams (in which the therapist guides the patient in remembering and later analyzing his or her dreams, the assumption being that during sleep the ego defenses are lowered, allowing repressed material to come forth, usually in disguised form); and interpretation (whereby the therapist helps the person finally face the emotionally loaded conflict that was previously repressed; at the right time the analyst begins to point out the patient's defenses and the underlying meaning of his or her dreams, feelings, thoughts, and actions).

Of particular importance to psychoanalysts and also to those who have revised Freud's theorizing is the concept of transference. Freud noted that his patients sometimes acted toward him in an emotion-charged and unrealistic way. For example, a patient much older than Freud would behave in a childish manner during a therapy session.

Although these reactions were often positive and loving, they could also be negative and hostile. Since these feelings seemed out of character with the ongoing therapy relationship, Freud assumed that they were relics of attitudes transferred to him from those held in the past toward important people in the patient's childhood, most often parents. That is, Freud felt that patients responded to him as though he were one of the important people in their past. Freud used this transference of attitudes and feelings, which he came to consider an inevitable aspect of psychoanalysis, as a means of explaining to patients the childhood origin of many of their concerns and fears. This revelation and explanation, he believed, tended also to help lift repressions and allow the confrontation of buried impulses. In psychoanalysis, transference is regarded as essential to a complete cure. It is precisely when analysts notice transference developing that they take hope that the important repressed conflict from childhood is getting closer to the surface.

Those who have introduced modifications to classical psychoanalysis to make it more efficient—generally referred to as psychodynamic therapists—are more oriented toward the present than was Freud, but their general views and procedures are quite similar; they emphasize unconscious motivation and the need for patients to understand the hidden reasons for their current feelings and behavior.

Therapists identified as ego analysts focus more than do classical psychoanalysts on people's ability to influence what happens around them. The basic assumption is that the individual is as much ego as id. In addition, ego analysts attend more to the patient's current life than did Freud, although they sometimes follow the classic psychoanalytic strategy of searching for the past causes of a patient's behavior.

Ego analysts emphasize ego functions that are primarily conscious, capable of controlling both id instincts as well as the environment, and that operate on energy of their own, separate from the id. And whereas Freud viewed society essentially as an obstacle to the unrestrained gratification of id impulses, ego analysts assert that an individual's social interactions can provide their own special kind of gratification.

What is called brief therapy, or brief psychodynamic therapy, is similar to ego analysis but focuses more on practical, real-life problems—still within the general framework of psychoanalysis. The therapist tends to be more active than in longer-term psychoanalytic and psychodynamic therapies. The principal features of brief therapies were described in Chapter 2 (p. 34).

A variant of psychodynamic therapy, often referred to as interpersonal therapy (IPT), emphasizes the interactions between a patient and his or her social environment. A pioneer in the development of this approach was the American psychiatrist Harry Stack Sullivan. Sullivan held that the basic difficulty of patients lies in misperceptions of reality stemming from disorganization in the interpersonal relations of childhood, primarily those between child and parents.

Sullivan departed from Freud in his conception of the analyst as a "participant observer" in the therapy process. In contrast with the classical or even ego-analytical view of the therapist as a blank screen for the transference neurosis, Sullivan argued that the therapist, like the scientist, is inevitably a part of the process he or she is studying. An analyst does not see patients without at the same time affecting them.

IPT, especially as practiced today (Klerman et al., 1984), includes strategies from both psychodynamic and cognitive-behavioral therapies. Its focus is on here-and-now problems rather than on childhood or developmental issues, an emphasis in stark contrast to that of traditional psychoanalytic theory. In particular, a therapist practicing IPT is much more active and directive as he or she concentrates on the patient's present-day interactions with others and how to have more satisfying interpersonal relationships.

Evaluation of Classical Psychoanalysis

Some General Conceptual Issues One's paradigm affects one's evaluation of the effectiveness of psychoanalysis, in all its various forms. What are the criteria for improvement? A principal criterion is the lifting of repressions, making the unconscious conscious. But how is that to be demonstrated? Attempts to assess outcome have sometimes relied on projective tests, such as the Rorschach, which in turn rely on the concept of the unconscious (Cook, Blatt, & Ford, 1995). For those who reject the very concept of an unconscious, data from projective tests will not be very convincing.

The central concept of insight has also been questioned. Rather than accept insight as the recognition by the client of some important, externally valid, historical connection or relationship, several writers (e.g., Levy, 1962; London, 1964) have proposed that the development of insight is better understood as a social conversion process, whereby the patient comes to accept the belief system of his or her therapist. Marmor (1962), a noted psychoanalytic scholar, suggested that insight means different things depending on the school of therapy; a patient treated by a proponent of any one of the various schools develops insights along the lines of its particular theoretical predilections. Freudians tend to elicit insights regarding oedipal dilemmas, Sullivanians insights regarding interpersonal relationships, and so forth.

If an insight is part of a social conversion process, do we need to be concerned with its truth? We encountered this question earlier in our examination of cognitive behavior therapy, especially Ellis's rational-emotive behavior therapy (p. 55). Therapists who encourage clients to look at things differently—as do all insight-oriented therapists as well as cognitive behavior therapists—believe that an insight may help the client change, whether or not the insight is true. Furthermore, because of the immense complexity of human lives, it is sometimes impossible to know with any degree of certainty whether an event really happened, and if it did, whether it caused the current problem.

This issue has other ramifications. In our discussion of ethics in therapy in Chapter 18, we examine the proposal that psychotherapy is inherently, ultimately, a moral enterprise. That is, therapists, sometimes unwittingly, convey to clients messages about how to live their lives. Therapists assume the role of secular priest (London, 1964, 1986). In this framework, the usefulness of a given insight depends on whether it helps the client lead a life more consonant with a particular set of shoulds and oughts. Whether a given insight is true or not is irrelevant; indeed, it may be impossible to determine whether it is true at all.

As noted by several leading researchers in analytic therapy (Henry et al., 1994), it is difficult to distinguish between classical psychoanalysis and psychodynamic psychotherapy in practice. It is generally held that most classical psychoanalysts act in a fairly passive way, in contrast to those who practice psychodynamic psychotherapy, especially brief therapy. However, Freud seems to have been a good deal less remote and more directive than the classical analysts who have followed him. In a report of a large psychoanalytic psychotherapy project from the famous Menninger Foundation, a psychoanalytic clinical and research center in Topeka, Kansas, Wallerstein (1989) downplayed clear distinctions between psychoanalysis and forms of treatment based on Freud's thinking but containing greater amounts of direct support and direction from the therapist: "Real treatments *in actual practice* [italics added] are intermingled blends of expressive-interpretive and supportive-stabilizing elements; all treatments (including even pure psychoanalyses) carry many more supportive components than they are usually credited with" (p. 205).

With all these cautions in mind, let us consider the efforts researchers have made to evaluate the efficacy of classical psychoanalytic, ego-analytic, and interpersonal therapies.

Outcomes of Research   As Bachrach et al. (1991) have pointed out, there are only four outcome studies of long-term psychoanalytic treatment. Each of these studies has methodological problems, the most limiting of which is the lack of a no-treatment control group. Although some people argue that the inclusion of a control group may be unethical (Wolitzky, 1995), it is difficult to make a compelling case for any therapy given such an omission.

Perhaps the most ambitious attempt to evaluate the effectiveness of psychoanalysis was the Menninger Foundation Psychotherapy Research Project, which began in the mid-1960s. In this study forty-two patients—mostly whites with anxiety, depression, or both (what used to be referred to as "garden variety neuroses")—were seen in either psychoanalysis or short-term psychodynamic psychotherapy. In both groups about 60 percent of the patients improved. There were no significant differences between the two groups either immediately after treatment or at follow-up of two to three years (Wallerstein, 1986, 1989).

Major reviews of research on classical psychoanalysis suggest the following conclusions (Henry et al., 1994; Luborsky & Spence, 1978):

- Patients with severe psychopathology (e.g., schizophrenia) do not do as well as those with anxiety disorders. This result is understandable in view of Freud's admitted emphasis on neurosis (roughly what are called anxiety disorders today) rather than on psychosis and given also the heavy reliance of psychoanalysis on rationality and verbal abilities.

- The more education a patient has, the better he or she does in analysis, probably because of the heavy emphasis on verbal interaction.

- A key ingredient is the therapist's identifying and interpreting transference reactions—for example, indicating to a male patient that his behavior toward the therapist seems to reflect unresolved conflicts with his mother. It appears, though, that a high frequency of such interpretations is often not helpful either to the patient–therapist relationship or to the outcome of the psychoanalysis.

- There is conflicting evidence as to whether the outcome of psychoanalysis is any better than what would be achieved through the mere passage of time or by engaging other health professionals such as a family doctor (Bergin, 1971). This is not to say that psychoanalysis does no good, only that clear evidence is lacking as to its specific effectiveness. Given the great diversity in the characteristics of both patients and therapists and in the severity of patients' problems, the question is probably too complex to yield a single, scientifically acceptable answer.

Evaluation of Brief Psychodynamic and Interpersonal Therapies

We look first at outcome research—whether a therapy works—and then at research aimed at elucidating the processes by which favorable outcomes might be achieved.

Outcome Research   The picture emerging from outcome studies on brief psychodynamic therapy is inconsistent but generally positive. Koss and Butcher (1986) reached the conclusion that brief therapy is no less effective than time-unlimited psychoanalysis, perhaps because both patient and therapist work harder and focus on goals that are more specific and manageable than a major restructuring of the personality. Two other reviews indicate either no superiority (Crits-Christoph, 1992) or modest superiority (Svartberg & Stiles, 1991), compared with nonpsychotherapeutic interventions such as self-help groups. In their review, Goldfried, Greenberg, and Marmar (1990) concluded that brief psychodynamic therapy is effective in treating stress and bereavement (Marmar & Horowitz, 1988), late-life depression (Thompson, Gallagher, & Breckenridge, 1987), and mood and personality disorders (Marziali, 1984). Other literature reviews have found that brief psychodynamic therapy is useful with job-related distress and a variety of anxiety disorders (Koss & Shiang, 1994), including posttraumatic stress disorder (Horowitz, 1988).

The NIMH Treatment of Depression Collaborative Research Program, described in detail in Chapter 10, provides evidence that Weissman and Klerman's version of interpersonal psychotherapy (IPT) is effective in treating depression in adults, confirming some earlier research (DiMascio et al., 1979). Similar positive results have been reported for depression in adolescents (Mufson et al., 1999). Another well-controlled RCT assessed the maintenance of treatment gains from IPT three years following termination of therapy for depression (Frank et al., 1990). The conclusions point to the potential of IPT to bring about long-term improvement (Frank & Kupfer, 1994). These findings have been replicated with older adults as well (Reynolds et al., 1999). Thus IPT may be successful in relapse prevention in depression, which is always a concern in the arena of psychotherapy effectiveness (Weissman & Markowitz, 2002).

One especially interesting outcome study pitted IPT against cognitive and behavioral therapies in the treatment of bulimia nervosa. IPT was as effective as the other therapies in the treatment of this disorder immediately after treatment (see p. 265) (Fairburn et al., 1991) and had surpassed the other therapies in some assessment areas at a one-year follow-up (Fairburn et al., 1993), with the caveat that only one-third of the patients had maintained their treatment gains. IPT showed these positive effects even with no discussion at all of eating behaviors or body image. Frank and Spanier (1995) suggested that this study may indicate the centrality of interpersonal conflict in a variety of psychological conditions.

As discussed in Chapter 13 (p. 431), psychoanalytically oriented psychotherapy was found to be effective in a number of studies on psychopaths (Salekin, 2002). This is a notable outcome for *any* sort of psychotherapy since psychopaths have been assumed to be unreachable either with drugs or psychosocial interventions.

Process Research   The just-mentioned Fairburn et al. study on bulimia provocatively raises the question of what may be the active ingredients in IPT. Frank and Spanier (1995) summarized the hypothesis in this way: IPT may exert its therapeutic effect by enhancing social support, decreasing adversity, and/or improving the patient's ability to cope with hardship. In this connection, Frank and Spanier related a conversation with the late Daniel Freedman, a leading academic psychiatrist, on the subject of IPT's active ingredient(s). Freedman suggested the possibility that IPT may work through what it does *not* do rather than through what it does. Specifically, the focus on current and future issues may preclude the patient's preoccupation with the past, thereby preventing the individual from ruminating on past events that cannot be changed.

Process research in brief therapy has improved since 1980, with more careful delineation of therapeutic procedures, the use of manuals, and more operational measurement of concepts such as the working alliance between therapist and patient (Hartley & Strupp, 1983; Howard & Orlinsky, 1989). The term **therapeutic** or **working alliance** refers here to rapport and trust and to a sense that the therapist and the patient are working together to achieve mutually agreed-upon goals. A study by Kolden (1991) found that the better this bond, the more favorable the outcome after an average of twenty-five sessions. Reviews of other studies confirm that the stronger the therapeutic relationship, or alliance, the better the outcome (Henry et al., 1994; K. I. Howard et al., 1991; Luborsky, Barber, & Crits-Cristoph, 1990; Luborsky et al., 1988).

There are different views on how a good working alliance works (Henry et al., 1994). It might have a direct therapeutic effect (Henry & Strupp, 1994), or it might make interpretations more effective, thus having an indirect effect. It may also be that a strong working alliance is the result, rather than the cause, of therapeutic change. That is, patients might feel better about their relationship with their therapist if they have improved for other reasons. This seemed to be the case in a study on cognitive therapy of depression (Feeley, DeRubeis, & Gelfand, 1999). However the alliance works, it seems to be an important factor for any therapeutic approach, not only for psychodynamic approaches.

Recent studies of interpretations of the transference relationship suggest that higher frequencies of interpretations may be related to poorer outcome (Henry et al., 1994; this was just noted in our discussion of classical psychoanalysis). Frequent interpretations may get in the way of the therapeutic alliance, perhaps by making the patient feel criticized and defensive if not in agreement with the therapist's views.[2] Although findings such as these arise from correlational studies having certain methodological problems, they do tend to confirm the wisdom of briefer forms of dynamic and cognitive-behavioral therapies, which discourage the development and interpretation of transference.

A well-known psychodynamic psychotherapy research group at Vanderbilt University led by Hans Strupp examined transference and countertransference using a treatment manual (a highly unusual research strategy for investigators interested in psychodynamic

---

[2] Of course, if the patient finds no validity in the therapist's interpretation and disagrees with it, it may be that the interpretation is wrong. At the very least, it is not very useful. As Henry et al. (1994) put it, "high levels of interpretations may make patients feel criticized and cause them to 'shut down.' [W]ith given patients, certain interpretations might be perceived as irrelevant or intrusive and traumatizing" (p. 477).

therapies). They came to address this question because, in an earlier therapy outcome study, they found what they called "negative complementarity" (Strupp, 1980) in some of the treatment sessions, that is, negative, counterproductive responses of therapists to hostility expressed by the patient toward them and associated with poor outcome. And so, they instructed their therapists in ways to identify interactions with their patients that could interfere with progress in therapy, for example, feelings of annoyance or anger on the part of the therapist toward the patient. What they discovered was that, in fact, therapists adhered to the manual to the extent of becoming more aware of countertransference issues, both in their own treatment sessions and when viewing videotaped sessions of other therapists in the study. And they showed more instances of making interpretations of transference and countertransference phenomena during the sessions. So far so good. Unfortunately the therapists showed *more* hostility toward their respective patients (Henry, Schacht, Strupp, Butler, & Binder, 1993) and, in adhering to the manual, often showed poor judgment and behaved in a rather mechanical way.

An example will illustrate this dubious outcome:

> *…a female patient disclosed concerns about her ability to remain sexually faithful in significant heterosexual relationships. Rather than exploring the patient's concerns further, the male therapist immediately began probing to determine whether there was a "pattern" in her selection of men. In the midst of the patient's anxious confusion about this question, the therapist abruptly raised the issue of her feelings for him. Though she denied any feelings for the therapist, he continued to force the issue. After awhile the patient said, "I don't feel I've really opened up much yet," and she switched the conversation away from her sexual concerns.… Although the therapist was attempting to adhere to [the treatment manual] by detecting an interpersonal pattern and then relating it to the therapeutic relationship, his effort was concrete and mechanical and too vague, insensitive, and ill-timed to foster any security in self-exploration on the part of the patient. (Vakoch & Strupp, 2000, p. 207; based on material in Butler & Strupp, 1989).*

In a searching critique of transference, Wachtel (1977) opposed the orthodox psychoanalytic view that a shadowy therapist enables transference to develop. He hypothesized that such unvarying behavior on the part of the therapist frustrates the client, who may be seeking some indication of how the therapist feels about what he or she is doing and saying. Wachtel regarded the sometimes childish reactions assumed to be part of the transference neurosis as, in part, the normal reactions of an adult who is thwarted. The troubled client sees the analyst as a professional person who remains distant and noncommittal in the face of the client's increasing expression of emotion. Thus, rather than an unfolding of the client's personality, transference may actually be in some measure the client's extreme frustration with minimal feedback. Moreover, because the analyst restricts his or her own behavior so severely in the consulting room, the analyst can sample only a limited range of the client's behavior, attitudes, and feelings. Wachtel's blend of psychoanalytic and behavioral viewpoints is further explored in the later discussion of developments toward a rapprochement between these major paradigms (p. 598).

Review of Client-Centered Therapy

Basic Concepts and Techniques of Client-Centered Therapy

Usually regarded as a humanistic psychotherapy, Rogers's client-centered therapy rests on the basic premise that people can be understood only from their own phenomenology—the immediate experience that they have of themselves and their world—and that they become disordered when they fail to attend to their own inner nature and instead guide their behavior according to what others wish. Client-centered therapy emphasizes people's freedom to choose and the responsibility that comes from having that freedom. We are what we make of ourselves, is the credo of Rogerian and other humanistic and existential therapists (sometimes referred to as experiential or phenomenological therapists). The therapist's principal role is to create conditions in therapy that are totally accepting and nonjudgmental, doing so by being empathic rather than directive. The result is that the client gradually comes to understand better his or her own wishes, needs, fears, and aspirations and gains the courage to pursue his or her own goals rather than the goals that others have set for him or her. To march to the beat of one's own drum is the goal of Rogerian and related therapies.

Evaluation of Client-Centered Therapy

Largely because of Rogers's insistence that the outcome and process of therapy be carefully scrutinized and empirically validated, many efforts have been made to evaluate client-centered therapy. Indeed, Rogers is rightfully credited with originating the field of psychotherapy research. He and his students deserve the distinction of removing the mystique and excessive privacy of the consulting room. For example, they pioneered the tape-recording of therapy sessions for subsequent analysis by researchers.

Most research on Rogerian therapy has focused principally on relating outcome to the personal qualities of therapists. Results have been inconsistent, casting doubt on the widely held assumption that positive outcome is strongly related to the therapist's empathy and genuineness (Beutler, Crago, & Arizmendi, 1986; Greenberg, Elliott, & Lietaer, 1994; Lambert, Shapiro, & Bergin, 1986). And yet it probably makes sense to continue emphasizing these qualities in the training of clinicians, as such qualities are likely to help create an atmosphere of trust and safety within which the client can reveal the deep inner workings of the self (Bohart & Greenberg, 1997). It is not justifiable, however, from a research perspective, to assert that these qualities by themselves are sufficient to help clients change.

A meta-analysis of studies on client-centered therapy from 1978 to 1992 revealed only eight that had a control group and concluded that after such intervention clients were better off than about 80 percent of comparable people who had not received any professional therapy (Greenberg et al., 1994). Although not bad, this outcome is no better than that achieved by comparison therapies, such as brief psychodynamic treatment, with people who are not severely disturbed.

In keeping with Rogers's phenomenological approach, self-reports by clients have been the usual measures of the outcome of therapy. The basic data have been the individual's own phenomenological evaluation of and reaction to the self and events in his or her world. The overt behavior believed to follow from these perceptions—that is, how patients actually behave following therapy—has not typically been the primary focus of study by client-centered therapy researchers.

Rogers's emphasis on subjective experience raises epistemological problems, for the therapist must be able to make accurate inferences about what the client is feeling or thinking. Validity is a real issue. Rogers relied on what the client said, yet he also asserted that clients can be unaware of their true feelings; it is this lack of awareness that brings most of them into therapy in the first place. As with psychoanalysis, we must ask how a therapist is to make an inference about internal processes of which a client is seemingly unaware and then by what procedures the usefulness or validity of that inference is to be evaluated.

The exclusive use of self-descriptive measures of outcome in the earliest research on client-centered therapy has been supplemented with more direct assessment of the patient's daily functioning in life, such as the adequate performance of social roles. An associated trend is the use of multiple methods of assessing therapeutic change as investigators have come increasingly to appreciate the complex nature of behavior and the need to assess it along many dimensions (Beutler, 1983; Lambert et al., 1986). For example, self-reports from patients can be supplemented by physiological measures as well as by reports from significant others in the patients' lives (e.g., spouses).

Rogers may be criticized for assuming that self-actualization is the principal human motivation. He inferred this motive from his observation that people seek out situations offering fulfillment, but then he proposed the self-actualization tendency as an explanation of the search for these situations—an example of circular reasoning.

Finally, Rogers assumed both that the psychologically healthy person makes choices to satisfy self-actualizing tendencies and that people are by their very natures good. But some social philosophers have taken a less optimistic view of human nature. The British philosopher Thomas Hobbes, for example, stated that life is "nasty, brutish, and short." How do we explain a person who behaves in a brutish fashion and yet asserts that this behavior is intrinsically gratifying and self-actualizing?

It may be that the problem of extreme unreasonableness was not adequately addressed by Rogers because he and his colleagues concentrated on people who were only mildly disturbed. As a way to help unhappy but not severely disturbed people understand themselves better (and perhaps even to behave differently), client-centered therapy may be appropriate and effective.

Review of Gestalt Therapy

Generally regarded as an existential therapy, Gestalt therapy's literature has much more in the way of case studies and theoretical argumentation than the kind of controlled research characteristic of the client-centered tradition we have just examined and the cognitive-behavioral approach we will examine later. One reason for this difference is that existential therapists tend to see the experimental methodologies of contemporary science as dehumanizing and thus to be avoided. They believe that applying scientific principles to the study of people denies their uniqueness and humanity.

Basic Concepts and Techniques of Gestalt Therapy

Fritz Perls and his Gestalt therapy followers hold, like Rogers, that there is an innate goodness in people and that therapy should serve the goal of enabling them to become aware of their basic needs and desires and to trust their instincts. But whereas the Rogerians shy away from specific techniques, Gestalt therapy is full of what may be the most imaginative and creative techniques on the entire psychotherapy scene—from having people talk to empty chairs to having them assume that they are part of every image in every dream they have. True to their roots in existentialism, Gestalt therapists emphasize that people create their own existence every day, in fact, every minute of their lives. People can change, and the Gestalt therapist, in sometimes very confrontational ways, does not tolerate stagnation. More details about Gestalt therapy, including its techniques, are in Chapter 2 (pp. 41–42).

Evaluation of Gestalt Therapy

A few studies have attempted to examine aspects of Gestalt therapy, in particular, the empty-chair technique. In an analogue study with college undergraduates, Conoley and his colleagues (1983) found that self-rated anger was reduced after a twenty-minute empty-chair exercise. Greenberg and Rice (1981) reported that the technique increases awareness and emotional expression, and Clarke and Greenberg (1986) found it superior to problem solving in helping people make decisions. On the whole, however, there is virtually no controlled research on this and other humanistic and existential approaches (except client-centered therapy).

All therapies are subject to abuse. Gestalt is no exception, and it may indeed present special problems. It is not difficult, even for trainees with a minimum of experience, to induce clients to express strong feelings. Some Gestalt techniques may be so powerful in opening people up that clients can be harmed unintentionally. The forcefulness of Perls's personality and his confrontational style have led some therapists to mimic him without the thoughtfulness, skill, and caring he appeared to possess in unusual abundance. The responsible Gestalt therapist is a professional who keeps the client's interests at the forefront and who understands that the expression of strong emotion for its own sake is seldom enough to ease an individual's suffering. The nature of Gestalt therapy and the fact that a cult has grown up around the memory of Fritz Perls are reasons that practicing Gestalt therapists should strive for an extra measure of caution and humility.

Review of Behavioral and Cognitive Therapies

Behavioral and cognitive therapies attempt to use the investigative methods of experimental psychology to develop and evaluate therapeutic interventions. Many of the principles are drawn from animal research on classical and operant conditioning, but the more recent cognitive trends understandably rely on research and theory with humans. Because the techniques vary greatly, we provide summary details of the several behavioral and cognitive therapies in the separate sections devoted to evaluating each one.

Evaluation of Counterconditioning and Exposure Methods

Clinicians have treated many different anxiety-related problems by systematic desensitization, developed by Joseph Wolpe in the 1950s (p. 48). The technique appears deceptively simple: It involves having a deeply relaxed person imagine a hierarchy of situations that he or she finds unduly fear-provoking in real life. However, as with any therapy for people in emotional distress, its proper application is a complicated affair. The clinician must first determine, by means of a comprehensive behavioral assessment, that the situations eliciting the patient's anxious reactions do not warrant such reactions. If a person is anxious because he or she lacks the skills to deal with a given set of circumstances—for example, if a person is anxious about piloting an airplane because he or she doesn't know how—desensitization is inappropriate. Desensitization is appropriate, however, if a person seems to be inhibited by anxiety from behaving in customary and known ways. Sometimes the technique can be used when the patient does not appear obviously anxious, as when depression is caused by an unfulfilling lifestyle that, in turn, arises from social anxiety (see our later discussion of underlying causes in behavior therapy, p. 588).

As with all the techniques we describe, systematic desensitization is very rarely used exclusively. A person fearful of social interactions might well be given training in conversational and other social skills in addition to desensitization. In the most general sense the applicability of desensitization depends largely on the therapist's ingenuity in discovering the source of the anxiety underlying a patient's problems (Goldfried & Davison, 1994).

Researchers became interested in studying desensitization because clinical reports in the 1950s and early 1960s indicated that the technique was effective. There is a large literature documenting that exposing fearful people to what they are frightened of or uneasy about—whether in imagination as in Wolpe's technique or in real life—usually leads to marked reductions in their unrealistic fears. Whether it is, as Wolpe originally claimed, necessary to associate exposure with a relaxed state is far less certain; it appears more and more likely that relaxation may operate by encouraging the anxious person to expose himself or herself to fearsome events, a sort of safety blanket to embolden the person to face up to what he or she has been avoiding (Wilson & Davison, 1971).

The demonstrated importance of exposure has benefited patients with a wide variety of anxiety disorders, including simple phobias, posttraumatic stress disorder, obsessive-compulsive disorder, panic disorder, and agoraphobia (Chambless & Ollendick, 2001; DeRubeis & Crits-Christoph, 1998). Although most of the research has been done with adults, fearful children have also benefited from exposure-based procedures (Kazdin & Weisz, 1998).

Evaluation of Operant Methods

Operant methods have proved successful with a wide range of behavioral problems in both adults and children. Recall the token-economy work described earlier (p. 50) and especially Paul's classic study with seriously impaired patients in a mental hospital (p. 342). More recently, inroads on the problems of substance abuse have been made by reinforcing behavior that is incompatible with the use of a drug to deal with the stresses of everyday life (Higgins, Budney, & Sigmon, 2001). It can also be noted that Linehan's dialectical behavior therapy (cf. pp. 429 ff) contains important operant elements as part of its complex therapy package for patients with borderline personality disorder. Another example of the successful use of operant conditioning with adult patients is the "behavioral activation" emphasis in the treament of depression (Jacobson et al., 1996; Jacobson, Martell, & Dimidjian, 2001). As described in Chapter 10 (p. 292), behavioral activation entails encouraging the patient to behave differently and to then experience positive outcomes for doing so.

Systematically rewarding desirable behavior and extinguishing undesirable behavior have been particularly successful in the treatment of many childhood problems, as reviewed in some detail in Chapter 15. Perhaps one reason operant-conditioning behavior therapy has been so effective with children is that much of children's behavior is subject to the control of others. Children, after all, tend more than adults to be under continual supervision. At school their behavior is scrutinized by teachers, and at home their parents frequently oversee their play and other social activities. In most instances the behavior therapist works with the parents and teachers in an effort to change the ways in which they reward and punish the children for whom they have responsibility. Before applying operant techniques, the therapist must determine that the problem behavior is, in fact, an operant—that it is under the control of a contingent reinforcer. A child who is crying because of physical pain, for example, should be attended to. It has been shown that altering the reinforcement practices of the adults in a child's life will ultimately change the child's behavior (Kazdin & Weicz, 1998).

The range of childhood problems dealt with through operant conditioning is broad, including bed-wetting, thumb-sucking, nail-biting, aggression, tantrums, hyperactivity, disruptive classroom behavior, poor school performance, language deficiency, extreme social withdrawal, mental retardation, autistic disorder, and asthmatic attacks (Kazdin & Weisz, 1998). Self-mutilation has also been effectively treated with punishment procedures, sometimes involving contingent application of painful electric shock to the hands or feet. Such extreme measures are used only when less drastic interventions are ineffective and when the problem behaviors are health or life threatening (Sandler, 1991; see also p. 643).

Evaluation of Cognitive Behavior Therapy

The core assumption of all cognitive therapies is that the way people construe their world is a major—if not the major—determinant of their feelings and behavior. Our examination of cognitive behavior therapy (CBT) focuses first on Albert Ellis's REBT (p. 55), then on Beck's cognitive therapy (p. 55), and then on a comparison of the two. Finally we offer some general reflections on CBT as a whole.

Ellis's Rational-Emotive Behavior Therapy　The basic premise of REBT is that emotional suffering is due primarily to the often unverbalized assumptions and demands that people carry around with them as they negotiate their way in life. Demanding perfection from oneself and from others is, Ellis hypothesizes, a principle cause of emotional distress. Expecting that one has to be approved of by everyone and for everything one does is another belief that Ellis regards as irrational and that other writers (Goldfried & Davison, 1994) have called unproductive or self-defeating. Therapy along rational-emotive behavioral lines involves the therapist's challenging these assumptions and persuading the patient that living a life without imposing on oneself unattainable demands and goals will be less stressful and more satisfying.

Several conclusions can be offered on the outcome research on REBT (Baucom et al., 1998; Chambless & Ollendick, 2001; Engels, Garnefski, & Diekstra, 1993; Haaga & Davison, 1989; Kendall et al., 1995).

- REBT reduces self-reports of general anxiety, speech anxiety, and test anxiety.
- REBT improves both self-reports and behavior for social anxiety, though it may be less effective than systematic desensitization.
- REBT is inferior to exposure-based treatments for agoraphobia.
- Preliminary evidence suggests that REBT may be useful in treating excessive anger, depression, and, in children, antisocial behavior.
- REBT is useful only as part of more comprehensive behavioral programs for sexual dysfunction.

- As described in Chapter 8, REBT shows promise in reducing the Type A behavior pattern.
- There is some preliminary evidence that REBT may be useful as a preventive measure for untroubled people, that is, to help emotionally healthy people cope better with everyday stress.
- Rational-emotive education, whereby teachers explain to children in classrooms the principles of REBT and how they can be applied to the children's everyday lives, has been used in the hope of forestalling full-blown emotional problems later in life. Evidence suggests that this education can improve self-concept (Cangelosi, Gressard, & Mines, 1980) and reduce test anxiety (Knaus & Bokor, 1975).
- There is some tentative evidence only (e.g., Smith, 1983) that REBT achieves its effects through a reduction in the irrationality of thought.
- The importance of the support REBT gives patients to confront what they fear and to take risks with new, more adaptive behavior should not be underestimated. In other words, analogous to the role that relaxation might play in systematic desensitization, some of the fear-reducing effects of REBT might derive from its encouraging people to expose themselves to what they fear.

As with most other clinical procedures, the relevance of REBT to a given problem depends in part on how the clinician conceptualizes the patient's predicament. Thus, a therapist who is trying to help an overweight person lose pounds might conceptualize eating as a way of reducing anxiety; in turn, the anxiety might be viewed as the result of social distress that is caused by extreme fear of rejection arising from an irrational need to please everyone and never make a mistake. The REBT therapist would direct his or her efforts to the irrational beliefs about pleasing others and being perfect, with the rationale that this will alleviate the patient's distress and ultimately the overeating. Such analysis of underlying causes is discussed later.

Defining Irrationality and the Issue of Ethics in REBT   Like other therapists, Ellis advocates an ethical system; this becomes clear when we try to define irrational or rational thinking. If we say that irrational thinking is what creates psychological distress, the definition is unsatisfyingly circular. If we regard as irrational any thought that is not objective and rigorous, then we would have to conclude that much of the thinking of nondistressed people is irrational, for considerable research indicates that the stories people tell themselves in order to live (Didion, 1979) frequently have illusory elements (e.g., Geer, Davison, & Gatchel, 1970; Taylor & Brown, 1988). It is possible that in order to achieve something unique or outstanding, one sometimes has to harbor beliefs that might be seen as unrealistic by those not committed to a cause. Albert Bandura put it this way:

> *Visionaries and unshakable optimists, whose misbeliefs foster hope and sustain their efforts in endeavors beset with immense obstacles, do not flock to psychotherapists.... Similarly, the efforts of social reformers rest on illusions about the amount of social change their collective actions will accomplish. Although their fondest hopes are likely to be unrealized during their lifetime, nevertheless their concerted efforts achieve some progress and strengthen the perceived efficacy of others to carry on the struggle. For those leading impoverished, oppressed lives, realism can breed despair.... Clearly the relationship between illusion and psychological functioning is a complex one. (1986, p. 516)*

We do not believe that a definition of irrational thinking can be constructed on empirical or scientific grounds. Ultimately, REBT therapists—and their patients—decide that it would be more useful or satisfying or even more noble to think about the world in certain ways. As Ellis has acknowledged (Ellis, 1995), this decision is based on what one believes is functional or ethical, not necessarily on what is strictly objective or rational.

Beck's Cognitive Therapy   Like Ellis, Beck hypothesizes that people in emotional distress operate with assumptions—he calls them schemas—that are impossible to live with, such as believing that one has to be a perfect parent or student. But in contrast to Ellis, Beck focuses a great deal on the lack of objective evidence that depressed and anxious people have for maintaining their maladaptive schemas. Beck engages the patient in a process very much like a scientific investigation, asking such questions as what evidence the patient has for believing that he or she is totally inept and worthless. A principal focus is on cognitive biases, errors in information processing—such as selective abstraction and overgeneralization (cf. p. 276)—that filter experience in a way that contributes to negative beliefs about oneself and the world.

The effectiveness of Beck's cognitive therapy (CT) has been under intensive study for over thirty years (Hollon, Haman, & Brown, 2002). A number of early experiments confirmed the favorable impact it has on depression (Rush et al., 1977; Shaw, 1977; Wilson, Goldin, & Charbonneau-Powis, 1983), and a meta-analysis of outcome studies of diverse therapies for depression concluded that Beck's therapy achieves greater short-term improvement than wait-list controls, drug therapies, noncognitive behavioral treatments, and a heterogeneous group of other psychotherapies (Dobson, 1989). CT may also be better at preventing future episodes than is drug treatment, a consideration of major importance in light of the oft-observed tendency for depressive episodes to recur (Blackburn, Eunson, & Bishop, 1986; Freeman & Reinecke, 1995; Hollon, DeRubeis, & Evans, 1996). Perhaps cognitive-therapy patients acquire some useful cognitive behavior skills that they are able to use following termination of therapy. As seen in Chapter 16, because older patients can be extremely sensitive to medications and can also have medical problems that contraindicate prescribing psychoactive drugs, nonpharmacological interventions are especially appropriate for them. Beck's CT has proven effective also in treating depression in children (Stark et al., 1991) as well as adolescents (Brent et al., 1997).

The great interest in CT led to the widely publicized comparative outcome study sponsored by the National Institute of Mental Health (Elkin et al., 1985), a study that, unlike other studies in the literature, did not find CT superior to a drug therapy (imipramine, trade name Tofranil) but nonetheless supported the utility of Beck's approach to the treatment of depression (recall our in-depth discussion on this milestone study, p. 289). More recently, a large collaborative study has found that cognitive therapy is as good as medications in treating severely depressed patients and that its effects are enduring over a one-year follow-up period (Amsterdam, DeRubeis, O'Reardon, & Young, 2002; Hollon, Shelton, Salomon, & Lovett, 2002). These findings are consistent with a recent mega-analysis (a variant of meta-analysis that pools outcomes across many studies) that found CT as effective as medications in treating severely depressed patients (DeRubeis, Gelfand, Tang, & Simmons, 1999).

Further, a task force of the clinical division of the American Psychological Association has concluded that Beck's cognitive therapy is an effective treatment for panic disorder, generalized anxiety disorder, social phobia, chronic pain, irritable bowel syndrome, and bulimia nervosa, and that it often fares better than medications alone (Chambless et al., 1996).

Data are becoming available that when cognitive therapy works, it does so because—as originally hypothesized by Beck—it helps patients change their cognitions. Predictable changes in cognitions do occur in cognitive therapy (Hollon & Beck, 1994; Hollon et al., 1996)—but they are found as well in successful treatment of depression by drugs (e.g., Rush et al., 1982). Cognitive change may therefore be the *consequence* of change produced by other means (Jacobson et al., 1996). Or, at least with depression (the disorder in which cognitive therapy has been most researched), cognitive change may be the mediator of therapeutic improvement brought about by *any* therapy, including Beck's cognitive therapy, interpersonal therapy, and pharmacotherapy.

Because cognitive therapy involves patients in logical analysis and empirical study of their life situation—a challenging intellectual task—it has been assumed that more intelligent individuals are better suited to this approach (Whisman, 1993). This does not seem to be the case, however (Haaga, Dyck, & Ernst, 1991). Perhaps intelligence is too general a concept, entailing as it does a variety of human cognitive processes, such as memory, reasoning, verbal facility, and quantitative skills. A more focused search for cognitive variables might prove more fruitful (Haaga, Rabois, & Brody, 1999).

An interesting example of more focused research is to be found in a dichotic listening experiment by Bruder et al. (1997). Recall from our discussion of dissociative disorders in Chapter 7 that in a dichotic listening task a person hears sounds in both ears but is instructed to attend only to the sounds in one ear. In the Bruder experiment, it was found that greater accuracy in hearing syllables in the right ear was predictive of a favorable response to CT for depression. Since right-ear accuracy for syllables reflects effective processing of information in the left hemisphere of the brain, and since the left hemisphere is strongly involved in language comprehension, the findings confirm the importance of verbal processing ability in cognitive therapy. That is, the reinterpretation of negative events that is at the core of Beck's cognitive therapy might be done better by people whose left hemisphere functions particularly well as it processes language information.[3]

Some Comparisons between the Therapies of Beck and Ellis   The theories and techniques of Ellis and Beck are widely used by therapists today. With the inevitable changes that inventive clinicians make as they apply the work of others, and with the evolution in the thinking of the theorists themselves, the differences between the two therapies can sometimes be difficult to discern. They do contrast, however, in interesting and important ways (Haaga & Davison, 1991, 1992).

To a parent who became depressed on learning that his or her child had failed a test at school, Ellis would say immediately, in essence, "So what if you are an inadequate parent? It is irrational to demand perfection from yourself and then to become depressed when you fall short." Beck, in contrast, would first examine the evidence for the conclusion. His is a more empirical approach. "What evidence is there for thinking that you are an inadequate parent?" If proof is lacking, this discovery in itself will be therapeutic. Ellis regards his own type of solution as more thoroughgoing. Even if the person is wanting as a parent, the world will not end, for a person does not have to be competent in everything he or she does. Beck will also eventually question with the patient whether one has to be competent in everything to feel good about oneself, but perhaps not until accumulated evidence suggests that the person is in fact an inadequate parent.

The therapist adopting Beck's approach certainly has preconceptions about negative schemas (which are sometimes similar to Ellis's irrational beliefs) and especially about the forms that maladaptive, illogical, or biased thinking takes, such as overgeneralization. But working with a depressed individual is a collaborative, inductive procedure by which patient and therapist attempt to discover, by examining the patient's biased thinking (recall Figure 10.1, p. 275), the particular dysfunctional assumptions underlying the person's negative thoughts. Rational-emotive behavior therapists, in contrast, operate much more deductively; they are confident that a distressed person subscribes to one or more of a predetermined list of irrational beliefs or that they make unrealistic demands of themselves or others, and then they seek out evidence to support their hypotheses.

Beck's therapy and standard rational-emotive practices also differ in style, and this difference appears to be somewhat related to the inductive–deductive dimension. Beck suggests that the therapist should avoid being overly didactic, but Ellis often uses minilectures and didactic speeches. Beck proposes calling negative thoughts "unproductive ideas" to promote rapport. He does not favor adjectives such as irrational or nutty, which might be heard—with supportive humor, it must be pointed out—from Ellis. Finally, in Rogerian fashion, Beck recommends that the therapist begin by acknowledging the patient's frame of reference and asking for an elaboration of it. Having had a chance to present his or her case and feel understood, the person may be more willing to go through the collaborative process of challenging unproductive beliefs. Ellis, on the

---

[3] The fact that this study confirms the importance of brain processes in cognitive therapy does not mean that an important role for genetics has been found. The ability of a person to understand and use language well, along with left-hemisphere advantage as shown here, could arise from any number of factors, genetic or environmental (such as good educational opportunities).

other hand, supposes that quite forceful interventions are necessary to disrupt a well-learned maladaptive pattern of thinking. He will therefore directly confront the patient's irrational beliefs, sometimes within minutes in the first session.

Both approaches have one thing in common, and this factor makes Beck and Ellis soul mates of the humanistic and existential therapies reviewed earlier in this chapter. They both convey the message that people can change their psychological predicaments by thinking differently. They emphasize that how a person construes himself or herself and the world is a major determinant of the kind of person he or she will be—and that people have choice in how they construe things. They assert that people can, sometimes with great effort, choose to think, feel, and behave differently. Unlike behavior therapists who are not cognitive, but like the humanists and existentialists, Beck and Ellis believe that new behavior is important primarily for the evidence it can provide about how the person looks at himself or herself and the world. Thus the focus remains on the cognitive dimension of humankind and on the abiding belief that people's minds can be set free and that their thinking can provide the key to positive psychological change.

Reflections on Cognitive Behavior Therapy   We turn now to some general issues surrounding cognitive behavior therapy. Some are of historical significance, others focus more on the present, and still others concern the future.

CBT: A Return to Psychology's Cognitive Roots   As we indicated earlier in this book (p. 47), behavior therapy initially aligned itself with the study of classical and operant conditioning, under the assumption that principles and procedures derived from conditioning experiments could be applied to lessen psychological suffering. What developed into cognitive behavior therapy (or cognitive therapy) may appear to be a radical and novel departure, given the earlier focus of behavior therapists on conditioning and their de-emphasis or even total avoidance of cognition as a controlling variable in behavior and emotion. But in a historical sense CBT really represents a return to the cognitive foci of the earliest period of experimental psychology (cf. our earlier discussion of the cognitive paradigm, p. 52). Many experimental psychologists have through the years conducted research into cognition—into the mental processes of perceiving, recognizing, conceiving, judging, and reasoning, of problem solving, imagining, and other symbolizing activities. Cognitive behavior therapy has actually caught up with what has been going on for years in experimental psychology.

Restructuring versus Replacing Cognitions   Two distinctions are often drawn in cognitive behavior therapy on the basis of whether a technique is aimed at restructuring cognitions or replacing them (Arnkoff, 1986). Restructuring is found in Beck's and Ellis's approaches to treatment, which assume that cognitive-change efforts should be directed toward changing particular thoughts the patient is having. For example, as we have seen, Ellis holds that troubled patients operate with particular irrational beliefs, such as the need to be approved of by everyone. This belief is the target for REBT—efforts are made to alter this particular cognition. In contrast, a replacement strategy has the therapist assume nothing about the patient's cognitions other than that they are interfering with his or her life. The goal is simply to teach a way of thinking that is believed to be more adaptive than the cognitions with which the patient is operating, whatever they may be. An example is the problem-solving therapy of D'Zurilla and Goldfried (1971). In this approach, the therapist teaches the patient a set of problem-solving strategies that are believed to be generally applicable to a wide range of situations. No effort is expended in determining—as Ellis and Beck do—the nature of the cognitions that the person currently has that are getting him or her into psychological trouble (Haaga et al., 1999).

Early Behavior Therapy's Cognitive Features   Ellis and Beck try to change cognitive processes directly in order to relieve psychological distress. From the beginning, however, behavior therapists have relied heavily on the human being's capacity to symbolize, to process information, to represent the world in words and images. Wolpe's systematic desensitization is a clear example. This technique, believed by Wolpe to rest on conditioning principles, is inherently a cognitive procedure, for the patient *imagines* what is fearful. The most exciting overt behavioral event during a regimen of desensitization is the person's occasional signaling of anxiety by raising an index finger. If anything important is happening, it is surely going on under the skin, and some of this activity is surely cognitive.

The Continuing Importance of Behavior Change in CBT   As behavior therapy goes cognitive, however, it is important to bear in mind that many contemporary researchers continue to believe that behavioral procedures are more powerful than strictly verbal ones in affecting cognitive processes (Bandura, 1977). That is, they favor behavioral techniques while maintaining that it is important to alter a person's beliefs in order to effect an enduring change in behavior and emotion. Bandura suggests that all therapeutic procedures, to the extent that they are effective, work their improvement by giving the person a sense of mastery, of self-efficacy (Bandura, 1997). At the same time he finds that the most effective way to gain a sense of self-efficacy (obviously a cognitive concept) is by changing overt behavior. Whether or not we believe self-efficacy is as important as Bandura does, a distinction can be made between processes that underlie improvement (cognitions, according to Bandura) and procedures that set these processes in motion (new behaviors).

Cognitive behavior therapists continue to be behavioral in their use of performance-based procedures and in their commitment to behavioral change (Dobson & Jackman-Cram, 1996; Jacobson et al., 1996), but they are cognitive in the sense that they believe that cognitive change (e.g., enhanced self-efficacy) is an important mechanism that accounts for the effectiveness of at least some behavioral procedures. Cognition and behavior continually and reciprocally influence each other—new behavior can alter thinking, and new modes of thinking can in turn facilitate new behavior. In addition, the environment influences both thought and action and is influenced by them. This model, termed **triadic reciprocality** by Bandura (1986), highlights the close interrelatedness of thinking, behaving, and the environment.

The Importance of Emotion in CBT   As Salovey and Singer (1991) have pointed out, Bandura's triadic reciprocality underemphasizes emotion. People have many cognitions that are affect-laden, sometimes referred to as "hot cognitions", and these tend to relate to the self (Cantor et al., 1986), to one's dreams and fantasies, fondest hopes, and direst fears, what Singer (1984) called the private personality. "The therapist must be alert to emotions that color the maladaptive cognitions that are traditionally the focus of [cognitive behavioral] treatment. Even though feelings often also arise as a consequence of cognition, it may still be possible to alter maladaptive cognitions by first assessing and then intervening at the level of feelings" (Salovey & Singer, 1991, p. 366). Both clinical observations (Greenberg & Safran, 1984; Westen, 2000) and experimental findings (e.g., Snyder & White, 1982) point to the importance of emotion in personality and suggest that it should be included more systematically in cognitive-behavioral conceptions of disorder and treatment.

The Phenomenological Essence of CBT   All cognitive behavior therapists heed the mental processes of their patients in another way: they pay attention to the world as it is perceived by the patient. It is not what impinges on us from the outside that controls our behavior, the assumption that has guided behavioral psychology for decades. Rather, our feelings and behavior are determined by how we view the world. The Greek philosopher Epictetus stated in the first century: "[People] are disturbed not by things, but by the view they take of them." And Hamlet, in the famous Shakespearean play, put it this way: "There is nothing either good or bad, but thinking makes it so" (*Hamlet*, act II, scene 2). Similarly, a central thesis of experiential therapists, such as Rogers and Perls, is that clients must be understood from their own frame of reference, from their phenomenological world, for it is this experience of the world that controls life and behavior.

From a philosophical point of view, such assumptions on the part of those who would understand people and try to help them are profoundly important. Experimentally minded clinicians and researchers are intrigued by how much cognitive behavior therapy has in common with the experientialists and their attention to the phenomenological world of their patients. To be sure, the techniques used by cognitive behavior therapists are usually quite different from those of the followers of Rogers and Perls. But as students of psychotherapy and of human nature, these surface differences should not blind us to the links between the two approaches. Further discussion of integration among diverse therapeutic modalities is found at the end of this chapter.

Generalization and Maintenance of Treatment Effects in Behavioral and Cognitive Therapies

We turn now to a problem that is common to all treatments but perhaps especially to the behavioral and, to a lesser extent, the cognitive therapies—maintaining whatever gains have been achieved while the patient is in regular contact with the therapist. Insight therapists assume that therapeutic effects are enduring because of the restructuring of the personality. In contrast, looking a good deal to the environment for factors that affect people, behavior therapists wonder how therapeutic changes can be made to last once clients return to their everyday situations, which are often assumed to have been a factor in creating their problems in the first place! This challenge has been addressed in several ways.

Intermittent and Naturalistic Reinforcement Because laboratory findings indicate that intermittent reinforcement—rewarding a response only a portion of the times it appears—makes new behavior more enduring, many operant programs take care to move away from continuous schedules of reinforcement once desired behavior is occurring with satisfactory regularity. For example, if a teacher has succeeded in helping a disruptive child spend more time sitting down by praising the child generously for each arithmetic problem finished while seated, the teacher will gradually reward the child for every other success, and ultimately only infrequently.

Another strategy is to move from artificial reinforcers to those that occur naturally in the social environment. A token program might be maintained only long enough to encourage certain desired behavior, after which the person is weaned to naturally occurring reinforcers, such as praise from peers.

Environmental Modification Another approach to bringing about generalization takes the therapist into the province of community psychology (p. 234). Behavior therapists manipulate surroundings, or attempt to do so, to support changes brought about in treatment. For example, Lovaas and his colleagues (1987; McEachin, Smith, & Lovaas, 1993) found that the gains painstakingly achieved in therapy for autistic children were sustained only when their parents continued to reinforce their good behavior.

Eliminating Secondary Gain Most behavior therapists assign their clients homework tasks to do between sessions. Patients may be asked to listen to audiotapes containing relaxation-training instructions, for example. They sometimes fail to follow through in a consistent fashion, however, complaining of not having enough quiet time at home to listen to the tapes or saying that they forgot about the assignment. Many patients are so resistant to doing on their own what they consciously and rationally agree is in their best interest that therapists sometimes invoke as an explanation the psychoanalytic concept of secondary gain, that the patient derives benefit from his or her problem. For complex and poorly understood reasons people sometimes act as though they unconsciously wish to keep their symptoms. Therapists, whatever their persuasion, may have to examine the client's interpersonal relationships for clues as to why a person who is suffering directly from a problem seems to prefer to hold on to it (see Focus on Discovery 17.1).

Relapse Prevention Marlatt (1985) proposed the "abstinence violation effect" as a focus of concern in relapse prevention. His research on alcoholism sensitized him to the generally negative effects of a slip, as when a former drinker, after a successful period of abstinence, imbibes to a stupor after taking a single drink. Marlatt suggested that the manner in which the person reacts cognitively to the slip determines whether he or she will overcome the setback and stay on the wagon or relapse and resume drinking to excess. The consequences of the slip are hypothesized to be worse if the person attributes it to internal, stable, and global factors believed to be uncontrollable—much as Abramson, Seligman, and Teasdale (1978) theorized about helplessness and depression (see p. 277). An example would be a belief, fostered by Alcoholics Anonymous (p. 391), that the lapse was caused by an uncontrollable disease process that overwhelms the person once a single drink is taken. In contrast, relapse is assumed to be less likely if the individual attributes the slip to causes that are external, unstable, specific, and controllable, such as an unexpectedly stressful life event. In essence, the person is encouraged to distinguish between a lapse and relapse. Cognitive behavior therapists attempt to minimize the abstinence violation effect by encouraging the person to attribute lapses to external, unstable, and specific factors and by teaching strategies for coping with life stressors. In this way it is hoped that gains achieved in therapy will persist once formal contact with the therapist has ended.

Attribution to Self   We have just commented on how people explain their behavior to themselves as a factor in their subsequent actions. A person who has terminated therapy might attribute improvement in behavior to an external cause, such as a drug or the power of the therapist, and therefore lose ground, even relapse, once that attributed factor is no longer present.

In the first experimental demonstration of this effect (Davison & Valins, 1969), college undergraduates were shocked on their fingertips to determine how much pain they could bear. Then they took a "fast-acting vitamin compound" (actually an inert placebo) and were told that they would be able to endure greater amounts of shock. Indeed they were, at least in their own minds. The experimenters had surreptitiously lowered the voltage levels to create this belief. Half the participants were then told that the capsule ingested was only a placebo, the others that its pain-reducing effects would soon wear off. Those who believed that they had taken a placebo attributed to themselves a greater ability to withstand discomfort and endured higher levels of shock on the third test. Those who believed that they had been given a real analgesic drug that was no longer effective were in the third round able to endure only lesser amounts of shock, mirroring the relapses found with most psychoactive drugs.

In an experiment with a similar design, conducted with people who were having trouble falling asleep, Davison, Tsujimoto, and Glaros (1973) obtained comparable results, indicating that real problems may be treated by helping patients attribute improvements to themselves. Individuals attempting to reduce smoking (Chambliss & Murray, 1979; Colletti & Kopel, 1979), lose weight (Jeffrey, 1974), and reduce the frequency of panic attacks (Başoğlu et al., 1994) have similarly benefitted from attributing gains to their own efforts and changes in attitudes rather than to external forces. In a series of non-behavior-therapy outcome studies from the Johns Hopkins Psychotherapy Research Unit, anxious and depressed patients who attributed their gains to a drug did not maintain their improvement as much as did those who construed their changes as arising from their own efforts (Frank, 1976).

What are the implications of attribution research? Since in behavior therapy much improvement seems to be controlled by environmental forces, especially therapy relying on operant manipulation, it might be wise for behavior therapists to help their clients feel more responsible. By encouraging an "I did it" attitude, perhaps by motivating them to practice new skills and to expose themselves to challenging situations, therapists may help their clients depend less on therapy and therapist and better maintain their treatment gains. Insight therapies have always emphasized the desirability of patients' assuming primary responsibility for their improvement. Behavior therapists have begun to realize that they must come to grips with the issue. On a more general level, the question of attributing improvement underscores the importance of cognitive processes in behavior therapy (and in other approaches as well).

Finally, when patients maintain their improvement, it is often assumed that they are continuing to apply after termination of treatment specific skills that they acquired during treatment. A controlled comparative outcome study (an RCT), discussed in Chapter

You're Changed If You Do and Changed If You Don't

Have you ever tried to persuade a friend to do something by asking him or her not to do it? Intuition tells us that this sneaky ploy might be effective when a person is spiteful or doesn't like to be controlled by others. The thinking of such an individual might be: "So, he wants me to continue arriving late, huh? I'll show him—I'll start arriving early!"

Since the publication of *Pragmatics of Human Communication*, a book by Watzlawick, Beavin, and Jackson (1967) on complex communication and interaction, a small but committed number of psychotherapists have been drawn to what have come to be called **paradoxical interventions**. These therapeutic strategies typically involve a request or prescription by the therapist for the patient to continue the problem or to increase its severity or frequency. If a person cannot go to sleep, he or she is asked to remain awake. If a patient cannot stop thinking of a disturbing event, he or she is asked to think of it more often. If a person becomes anxious for no apparent reason, he or she is requested to make himself or herself anxious. Sometimes the request or instruction is embedded in what is called a "positive reframe," for example, praising a depressed client for her ability to tolerate solitude or her willingness to make sacrifices for the benefit of others (Shoham & Rohrbaugh, 1999).

According to Shoham and Rohrbaugh (1999), clinical reports illustrate the effectiveness of paradoxical interventions with a variety of problems including anxiety, depression, insomnia, obsessive-compulsive disorder, headaches, asthma, enuresis, blushing, tics, procrastination, eating disorders, child and adolescent conduct problems, marital and family problems, pain, work and school problems, and psychotic behavior (Frankl,1967; Seltzer, 1986; Shoham-Salomon & Rosenthal, 1987). There is also some controlled research that confirms the clinical reports (e.g., Akillas & Efroan, 1995; Ascher & Turner, 1979).

We examine here some research by Shoham-Salomon and her co-workers. They postulate two mechanisms that could account for the beneficial changes reported clinically for some patients: reactance and increases in self-efficacy. **Reactance** refers to a motivational state aroused when people perceive that their range of freedom is being limited—they make efforts to restore their freedom (Brehm & Brehm, 1981). A reactant person, when asked by the therapist to become more anxious, will see this symptom prescription as an infringement on their freedom and will protect himself or herself from this perceived threat by becoming less anxious.

The second mechanism proposed by Shoham-Salomon, which underlies the response of nonreactant patients to a paradoxical directive, is Bandura's (1986) concept of self-efficacy, the sense that one is capable of performing a desired behavior. In the context of psychotherapy, this entails the person's gaining control over the problem and reducing its intensity or frequency. Bandura's research suggests that self-efficacy is enhanced when people have successful experiences. Thus, when a nonreactant patient follows a paradoxical directive, for example, and increases his or her anxiety, the short-term outcome is not symptom reduction, as with the reactant person, but cognitive change, namely, a belief that he or she is not helpless and can exert some control over the previously uncontrollable problem (even if the control leads to something that is opposite to what the person really wants). The implication is promising: if patients can make themselves worse, then maybe they can make themselves better. What has felt

In the study by Shoham-Salomon and colleagues, some students who had difficulty with procrastination were given the paradoxical directive not to study at certain times.

12 (p. 399), on the treatment of cocaine dependence (Carroll, Rounsaville, Gordon et al., 1994; Carroll, Rounsaville, Nich et al., 1994) found two important instances of generalization at a one-year follow-up: patients treated with the drug desipramine maintained their treatment-produced gains; and patients in the cognitive-behavior-therapy condition not only maintained their improvement but showed signs of even further improvement, or what the authors called "delayed emergence of effects" (Carroll, Rounsaville, Nich et al., 1994, p. 995). That the drug-produced effects were maintained at one-year follow-up is a welcome exception to the general finding of relapse following drug withdrawal. That the cognitive-behavioral treatment gains were actually greater at one-year follow-up prompted the investigators to speculate that CBT had taught patients coping skills that they were able to implement long after formal therapy had ended, something lacking in the drug-therapy group (Focus on Discovery 17.2).

uncontrollable now is more controllable—even if the control is initially in the form of being able to make one's problem *worse*.

Both kinds of individuals are expected to change in positive ways from paradoxical treatment, but for different reasons and at different times. The reactant person is expected to change rather quickly because he or she is defying the therapist's directive. The nonreactant client is expected not to change right away, but the groundwork is laid for later behavioral change via an increase in self-efficacy. This nonreactant person will not improve in the short term, but will construe his or her symptomatic behavior as more controllable and may improve later on.

These predictions were confirmed in two studies of procrastination in college students (a problem we are sure none of the readers of this book have!). The article (from whose title the title of this Focus on Discovery was derived) was published by Shoham-Salomon, Avner, and Neeman (1989). Participants were divided into reactant and nonreactant groups, using procedures that detected spitefulness in tone of voice. The experimenters then had them undergo one of two treatments, each conducted for two weekly sessions.

Paradoxical intervention: The therapist explained that they needed to understand their procrastination problem better and become more aware of it. To this end they were to observe the problem carefully by trying to procrastinate deliberately. Students were instructed to gather all their study materials on their desks but not to study for half an hour, to resist any impulse to study, and to concentrate on procrastinating, for example, by ruminating about the problem as they usually did when procrastination occurred normally. Studying at these times was not permitted. If they succeeded in this unusual observation task for six days, on the seventh day they could either study or not study, as they wished and whenever they wished. At the second therapy session participants discussed this assignment. Those who were able to do it were congratulated and reminded that their not studying had allowed them to better understand their problem and therefore to begin to deal with it. If a student reported having studied more, he or she was not praised; in fact, the therapist voiced skepticism and suggested that the change was probably only temporary. If students had not scheduled procrastination time, the therapist exhorted them to try it again in the coming week.[*] Above all, participants were not encouraged to procrastinate less or study more.

Behavioral intervention: The contrasting intervention was traditionally behavioral; that is, a direct attempt was made to reduce procrastination and increase studying. Students were told that procrastination was a learned habit and that they needed to develop new behaviors incompatible with procrastination. They were directed to select a place in which they could study more effectively and to try to study as much as possible there, the idea being that these new stimulus conditions would become associated with improved study habits. Any reported successes were praised by the therapist.

Results showed that study time as well as self-efficacy were improved via both treatments, but the really interesting results concerned interactions between reactance and treatment modality. Higher reactance was correlated with improvement in study habits (less procrastination) in the paradoxical but not in the behavioral group, as expected. That is, students who were motivated to restore freedom that they viewed as being threatened engaged in behavior that went against the instructions of the therapist—told to study less, they studied more. This contrariness was not found among reactant students in the behavioral condition.

Increases in self-efficacy were correlated with better studying in the behavioral condition, consistent with many findings that show a link between behavioral improvement and self-efficacy (Bandura, 1986). However, this link was not found in the paradoxical-treatment group, for which increases in self-efficacy were associated with lack of behavioral change, as predicted. The findings from this mixed-design study (reactance was a correlational variable embedded in an experimental design; cf. p. 129) were replicated in a second experiment.

Further research with more clinically disturbed patients and with long follow-ups needs to be conducted, and Shoham-Salomon and her colleagues have undertaken such efforts (e.g., with insomnia [Shoham et al., 1995]). But these two analogue experiments provide strong empirical support for the idea that for some people—those who resist efforts by others to control them—telling them not to change their problematic behaviors may be more effective than encouraging them to work directly on making those behavioral changes.

Several important issues are raised by the success of paradoxical interventions. Do some treatments or therapists arouse more reactance in patients than do others? Are changes brought about by paradoxical maneuvers as stable as those effected by less indirect procedures? Does trust in the therapist suffer if the patient comes to realize that the therapist is saying one thing but intending another (Gann & Davison, 1999)? Can the problems that all therapies have with compliance be addressed more effectively by studying therapeutic paradoxes?

---

[*] An interesting problem arises in paradoxical therapy when a reactant patient defies the therapist's directive to exacerbate a problem behavior. One might label this "meta-defiance." If one is not careful, one can get caught in an infinite regress!

Since one purpose of professional intervention is to make the professional helper superfluous, we can expect increasing formal attention to be focused on what it is that patients take away from treatment that can help them maintain and enhance their gains as well as deal with the new challenges that await them in their day-to-day lives (or, as the lyricist-satirist Tom Lehrer put it, as they "go sliding down the razorblade of life").

Some Basic Issues In Cognitive and Behavioral Therapy

We complete our discussion of cognitive and behavioral therapy with a consideration of some general problems and issues. An understanding of what follows will help the reader appreciate both the strengths and limitations of this approach to psychotherapy.

Self-Control—Outside a Behavioral Paradigm?

Operant research and theory seem to assume that the human being is a relatively passive recipient of stimulation from the environment. Given this apparent dependence on the external world, how can we account for behavior that appears to be autonomous, willed, and often contrary to what might be expected in a particular situation? How, for example, do we account for the fact that a person on a diet refrains from eating a luscious piece of chocolate cake even when hungry?

Psychoanalytic writers, including ego analysts, posit some kind of agent within the person. Many ego analysts assert that the ego can operate on its own power, making deliberate decisions for the entire psychic system, including decisions that go against the wishes of the id. Behaviorists, especially Skinner (1953), have objected to this explanation, regarding it as simply a relabeling of the phenomenon. Perhaps the most widely accepted behavioral view of self-control is Skinner's—an individual engages in self-control when he or she arranges the environment so that only certain controlling stimuli are present. A person wishing to lose weight rids the house of fattening foods and avoids passing restaurants when hungry. Behavior remains a function of the surroundings, but the surroundings are controlled by the individual.

Self-control, as illustrated by dieting, is difficult to explain within a behavioral paradigm.

A related behavioral conception of self-control is reflected in Bandura's (1969) explanation of aversive conditioning. Rather than being passively conditioned to feel distaste for stimuli that have been paired with shock, a person learns a skill of aversive self-stimulation, which he or she deliberately applies in real life. According to this view, a person resists a temptation by deliberately recalling the earlier aversive experience of being shocked or nauseated during therapy. The individual is said to create symbolic stimuli that control behavior. This is a variant of Skinner's view of self-control.

A familiar means of exercising self-control, also discussed in the behavior therapy literature, is setting standards for oneself and denying oneself reinforcement unless they are met (Bandura & Perloff, 1967). One such tactic is often employed by the authors of this book—I will not check my e-mail until I have finished writing this page. When a person sets goals, makes a contract with himself or herself about achieving them before enjoying a reward, and then keeps to the contract without obvious external constraints, that person is said to have exercised self-control.

Self-control can be applied with any therapy technique. The only stipulation is that the person must implement the procedure on his or

Internal Behavior and Cognition In Chapter 5 we discussed how the inference of intervening processes and other explanatory fictions is useful in interpreting data and generating fruitful hypotheses. Behavior therapists are sometimes thought to hold only the radical behavioristic positions of Watson and Skinner, that it is not useful or legitimate to make inferences about internal processes of the organism. But behavior therapy, as applied experimental psychology, is legitimately concerned with internal as well as external events, provided that the internal mediators—for example, thoughts and feelings—are securely anchored to observable stimuli or responses. (Recall our earlier discussion of the importance of operationalizing theoretical concepts, p. 114.)

Unconscious Factors and Underlying Causes With the growing interest in cognitive factors, cognitive therapists have begun to focus their assessments and interventions on internal mediators that lie outside the patient's awareness—that is, that are unconscious (Bowers & Meichenbaum, 1984; Mahoney, 1993). Ellis, for example, assumes that people are distressed by one or more beliefs that he designates irrational—even though a patient seldom states the problem in such terms. Based on what the patient says and how the patient says it, and working from rational-emotive theory, Ellis may infer the operation of a belief such as "It is a dire necessity that I be perfect in everything I do." He then persuades the patient to accept the notion that this belief underlies the problems. Therapy is directed at altering that belief, of which the patient may well have been unaware earlier. Although he tends to work more slowly and more induc-

her own, after receiving instructions from the therapist. For example, a patient of one of us who was being desensitized decided to imagine some of the hierarchical scenes while relaxing at home in a warm tub. He felt that he understood the rationale of desensitization well enough and had enough control over the processes of his imagination to meet the procedural requirements of the technique on his own. Consequently, after achieving what he felt to be a state of deep relaxation in the bathtub, he closed his eyes and carried out the scene presentation and termination as he had been taught. When he was with the therapist later, they were able to skip the items to which he had desensitized himself in the tub and proceed more rapidly through the anxiety hierarchy.

Implicit in all concepts of self-control are three criteria:

1. there are few external controls that can explain the behavior;
2. control is difficult enough that the person has to put forth some effort; and
3. the behavior is engaged in with conscious deliberation and choice.

The individual actively decides to exercise self-control either by performing some action or by keeping himself or herself from doing something, such as overeating. The person does not do this automatically and is not forced by someone else to take action.

To illustrate these criteria, let us take the example of a male jogger. If an army sergeant is goading the jogger along, the first criterion is not met; the running is not an instance of self-control even though considerable effort is probably required to maintain it.

If the jogger finds running pleasurable, so that he would rather jog than engage in other activities, the running cannot be considered an instance of self-control. Self-control may be seen in the earliest stages of a jogging regime, when the person may indeed be exerting great effort—he groans as he dons his Nikes, looks at his watch after only a few minutes of running to see how long this torture has been going on, and collapses in relief after half a mile, glad that the ordeal is over. But when the jogger is running because he or she prefers it to other available activities, the effortful criterion is not met.

The third criterion, acting with conscious deliberation and choice, distinguishes self-control from actions people perform in a mindless way. It is probably a good thing that much of our everyday behavior is mindless, for imagine how fatiguing (and boring) it would be to mull over and make specific decisions to do such things as tie our shoelaces. (Indeed, try tying your shoelaces while paying very close attention to what you are doing. Chances are you will have difficulty performing this overlearned skill.) But these very acts would be categorized as instances of self-control if, on a given occasion, we had to decide whether to engage in them. Eating would require self-control if we were on a strict diet and had agreed with our partner, or doctor, or self to reduce caloric intake.

In our opinion, the concept of self-control places a strain on the behavioral paradigm, for people are described as acting independently, putting forth effort, deliberating and choosing. Each of these verbs supposes the person to be an initiator of action, the place where control begins. Ardent behaviorists may counter by asserting with Skinner that the view of the person as an initiator only indicates ignorance of the external forces that ultimately control behavior. Thus the person who denies himself or herself an extra dessert is not really controlling the self; rather, this self-denial is controlled by some subtle reward unappreciated by the observer, or by a distant reinforcer, such as the potential to wear clothes of a smaller size. The flaw in this line of reasoning is that it is purely post hoc (after the fact) and irrefutable. We can always assert that at some later date the reinforcer that sustains the behavior will arrive. Such an explanation should be as unsatisfactory to the behaviorist as the psychoanalyst's post hoc invocation of an unconscious defense mechanism to account for an action.

tively than Ellis, Beck infers similar beliefs, which he calls negative schemas or dysfunctional assumptions.

This is an interesting turn of events for an approach that developed in the 1950s out of a rejection of conceptualizations that relied on the notion of unconscious motivation and thought! Yet it is consistent with decades of research by experimental cognitive psychologists, who infer sets, beliefs, attitudes, and other abstract cognitive concepts of which the person is often unaware (e.g., Bruner, Goodnow, & Austin, 1956). To be sure, appreciation of factors of which a person may be unaware does not make any of the cognitive therapies equivalent to psychoanalysis, but it does demonstrate the wisdom of some of Freud's clinical insights and is reflected in the kinds of rapprochements we explore later in this chapter.

Cognitive behavior therapists, like their analytic counterparts, have come to believe generally that there is more to the patient than immediately meets the eye (Goldfried & Davison, 1976, 1994). Guidano and Liotti (1983) spoke of the "protective belt" behind which one must search for core beliefs, which themselves are generally related to one's idea of oneself, such as a negative self-image. According to Mahoney (1982, 1990), core cognitions may be extremely difficult to change, even when uncovered, because they stem from one's earlier developmental history. And well before the popularity of cognitive behavior therapy, George Kelly distinguished between "core constructs" and "peripheral constructs," the former relating to the person's basic sense of self or identity (Kelly, 1955).

Although changing core beliefs is not a simple matter for either patient or therapist, it is believed by many contemporary researchers to be essential to cognitive therapy if the positive effects of therapy are to be enduring. The subtlety in assessing variables that are not immediately apparent is similar to that of advanced accurate empathy, discussed earlier (p. 39), as illustrated in the following case from Safran et al. (1986).

> A client who failed an exam…accessed the automatic thought: "I can't handle university." At this point the therapist could have challenged this belief or encouraged the client to examine evidence relevant to this belief. Instead she decided to engage in a process of vertical exploration. In response to the therapist's probes a constellation of automatic thoughts emerged that revolved around the client's beliefs that he was not smart enough. The client at this point spontaneously recalled two memories of situations in which he had felt humiliated and worthless because he felt he had "been stupid" at the time. As he recounted these memories he became visibly more emotional. Further exploration revealed that these feelings of intellectual inferiority and associated feelings of worthlessness cut across a number of problem situations for the client. It also emerged that he believed that his value as a person was completely dependent upon his intellectual performance. In this situation had the therapist intervened when the first automatic thought emerged, she may not have accessed the entire chain of self-evaluative cognitions and higher level constructs that underlay the client's distress. (p. 515)

Broad-Spectrum Treatment   In clinical practice, behavior therapists usually employ several procedures at once or sequentially in an attempt to deal with all the important controlling variables; this approach is generally referred to as broad-spectrum behavior therapy (Lazarus, 1971; see Focus on Discovery 17.3). For example, a patient fearful of leaving home might well undergo in vivo desensitization by walking out the door and gradually engaging in activities that take him or her farther from that safe haven. Over the years, however, the person may also have built up a dependent relationship with his or her spouse. As the person becomes bolder in venturing forth, this change in behavior may disrupt the equilibrium of the relationship that the couple has worked out over the years. To attend only to the fear of leaving home would be incomplete (Lazarus, 1965) and might even lead to replacement of the agoraphobia with another difficulty that would serve to keep the person at home—a problem frequently called symptom substitution.

In a related vein, cognitive and behavioral therapists do not invariably focus only on the patient's complaint as stated during the first interview (Goldfried & Davison, 1994). As an illustration, one of us was supervising a clinical graduate student who was desensitizing an undergraduate for test anxiety. The patient made good progress up the hierarchy of imagined situations but was not improving at all in the real world of test taking. The supervisor suggested that the therapist find out whether the patient was studying for the tests. It turned out that he was not! Worry about the health of his mother was markedly interfering with his attempts to study. Thus the goal of making the person nonchalant about taking tests was inappropriate, for he was approaching the tests themselves without adequate preparation. On the basis of additional assessment, the therapy shifted away from desensitization to a discussion of his feelings about his mother's possible impending death.

Relationship Factors   Regardless of theoretical orientation, a good relationship between patient and therapist is important for many reasons. It is doubtful that people will reveal deeply personal information if they do not trust or respect their therapists. Furthermore, since therapy can seldom be imposed on an unwilling client, a therapist must obtain the cooperation of the person if the techniques are to have their desired effect. In desensitization, for example, a patient could readily sabotage the best efforts of the therapist by not imagining a particular scene, by not signaling anxiety appropriately, and by not practicing relaxation. And in virtually all other cognitive and behavior therapy procedures—and in all therapies—clients are able to, and sometimes will, work against the therapist if relationship factors are neglected (Davison, 1973; Patterson & Chamberlain, 1992).

The therapeutic relationship is central to Linehan's dialectical behavior therapy (p. 429). She argues that it is essential to create an atmosphere of acceptance and empathy within which specific cognitive-behavioral techniques can be implemented with patients who have borderline personality disorder. Although behavior therapists seldom use the

A strong relationship between therapist and patient is widely regarded as essential for implementing therapy procedures.

Multimodal Therapy

Multimodal therapy is a variation of cognitive behavior therapy proposed by Rutgers University psychologist Arnold Lazarus (1989, 1997, 2002). Lazarus broke with Wolpe in the late 1960s out of dissatisfaction with what he viewed as undue constraints placed by the behavioral paradigm on assessment and on the design of maximally effective psychotherapeutic interventions.

Lazarus's basic premise is that people are a composite of seven dimensions, according to the acronym BASIC IB: Behavior, Affective processes, Sensations, Images, Cognitions, Interpersonal relationships, and Biological functions. Effective therapy must attend to problems in all or in some subset of these areas, decide the order in which problems should be treated, and then apply to each problem area the techniques that are best suited to it.

If, for example, a patient's duress seems to be triggered by aberrant thought processes, attention should focus on the C, cognition, and

Arnold A. Lazarus, Rutgers psychologist and master clinician, who developed multimodal therapy.

to act in ways that are not reinforced by his or her present environment.

For each patient Lazarus draws up a modality profile, which helps him and the patient see the areas that merit attention. This scheme is similar to (and preceded by several years) the multiaxial system of the DSM in that it is designed to draw attention to domains that are worthy of attention, basically forcing the clinician to focus on particular categories or areas. But the BASIC IB approach goes further in that Lazarus attempts to outline for each of the seven areas a range of procedures that can be effective.

Lazarus's approach as described thus far fits easily into a general cognitive-behavioral framework and is indistinguishable from the broad-spectrum behavior therapy discussed in the text. But he goes on to argue that the decision to use a given technique should be guided not by theoretical approach or school affiliation, but by an open-minded consideration of the data. For example, given what the therapist believes he or she knows about how to change cognitions, what techniques might be used to change the maladaptive beliefs of this particular client? If a technique from Gestalt therapy could be useful, then use it, Lazarus suggests. In this sense Lazarus was one of the early principal figures in the psychotherapy integration movement (discussed later, p. 600).

procedures that clinical and experimental research has suggested are well suited to altering how people think about things should be applied. However, the first B, behavior, might be problematic as well, and although set in motion by an aberrant thought, might require specific attention in and of itself, for example, when a person has learned

---

term therapeutic alliance (recall its importance in psychoanalytic therapies, p. 573), the strongly affective interpersonal bond between therapist and patient is increasingly recognized as a necessary condition for implementing cognitive and behavioral procedures (Goldfried & Davison, 1994).

It is worth noting that transference—minus the psychosexual overtones of psychoanalysis—is a subject of research by experimental cognitive psychologists, who find value in studying how people's present-day interactions are affected by their relationships with significant others (Andersen & Berk, 1998; Chen & Andersen, 1999). There is nothing mysterious about the fact that our perceptions of people in the here and now are colored by our feelings toward others from our past or from other aspects of our current lives. If behavior therapists are to be true to their credo that their clinical interventions derive from basic (nonclinical) research, they should not be as reluctant as they used to be to examine the therapist–patient relationship.

Flesh on the Theoretical Skeleton   A challenge faced by any therapist is moving from a general principle to a concrete clinical intervention. To illustrate, consider an early study in which undergraduates were trained to analyze the behavior of severely disturbed children in operant-conditioning terms (Davison, 1964). The students were encouraged to adopt an operant perspective and assume that the important determinants of the children's behavior were the consequences of that behavior. Armed with M & M candies as reinforcers, these student-therapists attempted to bring the behavior of the severely disturbed children under their control. Eventually, one child appeared to be losing interest in earning the candies. Working within a framework that required an effective reinforcer, the therapist looked around for another incentive. He noticed that each time the child passed a window, she would pause for a moment to look at her reflection. So the therapist obtained a mirror and was subsequently able to make peeking into the mirror the reinforcer for desired behavior; the peeks into the mirror were used in the same functional way as the M & M candies. Thus, although guided by a general principle, the therapist had to rely on improvisation and inventiveness as demanded by the clinical situation.

Devising interventions along behavioral lines requires ingenuity and creativity. As with any therapy, the application of a general principle to a particular case is not a simple matter. Although a given theoretical framework helps guide the clinician's thinking, it is by no means sufficient.

> The clinician in fact approaches his work with a given set, a framework for ordering the complex data that are his domain. But frameworks are insufficient. The clinician, like any other applied scientist, must fill out the theoretical skeleton. Individual cases present problems that always call for knowledge beyond basic psychological principles. (Lazarus & Davison, 1971, p. 203)

The preceding quotation from two behavior therapists is very similar to the following one from two experimental social psychologists.

> In any experiment, the investigator chooses a procedure which he intuitively feels is an empirical realization of his conceptual variable. All experimental procedures are "contrived" in the sense that they are invented. Indeed, it can be said that the art of experimentation rests primarily on the skill of the investigator to judge the procedure which is the most accurate realization of his conceptual variable and has the greatest impact and the most credibility for the subject. (Aronson & Carlsmith, 1968, p. 25)

Behavior therapists face the same kinds of decision-making challenges faced by their experimental colleagues. There are no easy solutions in dealing with human problems.

Review of Couples and Family Therapy

Basic Concepts and Techniques in Couples and Family Therapy

As described earlier (Focus on Discovery 10.3, p. 293), there is great variety within couples and family therapy—from psychoanalytic to Gestalt to behavioral. The techniques employed reflect the particular theoretical orientation of the therapist. A psychoanalytically oriented couples therapist will attend to possible unconscious factors in each person's behavior toward the other, whereas a cognitive-behavioral marital therapist will focus instead on unrealistic demands the partners have of each other and on maladaptive behavioral patterns that are being unwittingly reinforced in the relationship. What all couples and family therapies have in common is the view that conflicts and tensions are inevitable when people live together and that the best way to address these problems is to involve all members of the family unit in therapy. A principal focus is improving communication among family members so that people's needs can be met without sacrificing the needs and wishes of others.

Evaluation of Couples and Family Therapy

A meta-analysis of twenty carefully selected outcome studies meeting stringent methodological standards concluded that overall, couples therapy has beneficial effects for many relationship problems (Hazelrigg, Cooper, & Borduin, 1987). Comprehensive reviews of the

When a problem involves a couple, therapy is most effective if the couple is seen together.

area by Baucom et al. (1998), Baucom, Epstein, and Gordon (2000); Gurman and Kniskern (1978), Gurman, Kniskern, and Pinsoff (1986), Jacobson and Addis (1993), and Lebow and Gurman (1995) have reached the following specific conclusions about outcome and process in couples and family therapy.

- Conjoint therapy for couples problems appears to be more successful than individual therapy with one partner. The state of about 10 percent of patients seen individually for couples problems worsens.

- Behavioral couples therapy (BCT, which focuses on here-and now skills training in communication and increasing positive exchanges between the partners)—has been shown in more than two dozen studies in at least four countries to relieve distress in the relationship and/or increase partner satisfaction (Hahlweg & Markman, 1988). BCT has stronger effects than both no-treatment and placebo-controlled treatments, and these positive outcomes sometimes last for up to a year.

- Adding a cognitive component to BCT (e.g., encouraging empathy) has not been shown to add to the positive outcomes (Baucom, Sayers, & Sher, 1990).

- Positive findings from a small number of studies have been reported for emotion-focused therapy (EFT), an experiential therapy (Greenberg & Johnson, 1988; Johnson & Greenberg, 1985; Johnson, Hunsley, Greenberg, & Schindler, 1999) and for a psychodynamic insight-oriented therapy (Snyder & Wills, 1989). Both approaches focus on encouraging partners to explore their feelings and needs and to share these innermost aspects of themselves with the other. One study found an extremely low divorce rate in couples treated with an insight-oriented couples therapy (Snyder & Wills, 1989; Snyder, Wills, & Grady-Fletcher, 1991). At a four-year follow-up, Snyder's insight couples therapy was found to be superior to BCT in terms of divorce rates and marital satisfaction (Snyder et al., 1991). Another study showed superiority of an experiential therapy over BCT (Johnson & Greenberg, 1985). However, EFT may not produce long-lasting results, especially in couples experiencing serious relationship problems (Goldman & Greenberg, 1992).

- Although statistically significant, the outcomes of couples therapy research are not all clinically significant (Jacobson et al., 1984). For example, across all studies no more than half the treated couples were really happily married at the end of treatment (even if they had improved in a strictly statistical sense). Furthermore, few studies included much in the way of follow-ups, and those that did—and these were mostly behaviorally oriented—found frequent relapse (Alexander, Holtzworth-Munroe, & Jameson, 1994; Jacobson, Schmaling, & Holtzworth-Munroe, 1987) and divorce (Snyder et al., 1991). As Jacobson and Addis have cautioned, these findings should temper premature enthusiasm for the efficacy of conjoint therapies, regardless of their theoretical bases (see Focus on Discovery 17.4 for what Jacobson and his colleague Christensen did with these discouraging findings).

- Although focused on the fearfulness of one partner, Barlow's exposure treatment, which involves encouragement and collaboration by the spouse, has proved effective in reducing agoraphobia (see Chapter 6, p. 151) and has avoided the deterioration in the marital relationship that has sometimes been reported when the agoraphobic partner gets better (Brown & Barlow, 1995; Himadi et al., 1986).

- The results of couples therapy are generally better for younger couples and when no steps have been taken toward divorce. (This finding probably reflects less serious marital problems for such couples.)

- Predictors of poor outcome include what Jacobson and Addis (1993) call "emotional disengagement," manifested by poor communication of feelings and by low frequency of sexual activity. Another sign of a poor prognosis in couples therapy is a relationship marked by rigidly held traditional gender roles, when the wife is oriented to affiliation and relationships and the husband is oriented primarily to work and autonomy (Jacobson, Follette, & Pagel, 1986). Finally, depression in one of the partners does not bode well for couples therapy (even though, as noted, behavioral cou-

Acceptance in Behavioral Couples Therapy

An interesting development in behavioral couples therapy (BCT), a term that seems to be replacing behavioral marital therapy, is a growing appreciation of the importance of acceptance of the partner while trying to encourage and support change. Based on earlier work by Rogers and Ellis and on Linehan's (1993a, 1993b) dialectical behavior therapy (p. 429), Neil Jacobson and Andrew Christensen (Christensen, Jacobson, & Babcock, 1995; Christensen & Jacobson, 2000; Jacobson & Christensen, 1996) argue that behavior therapists have overlooked the importance of the ability of people in a committed relationship to accept their partner while at the same time hoping for and encouraging change.

The notion of acceptance has a time-honored history in clinical psychology and psychiatry, dating back at least to Sigmund Freud. As Christensen and Jacobson indicate, the use of interpretation in psychoanalytic couples therapy (e.g., Scharff, 1995) can lead to greater acceptance of displeasing behavior by attributing it to childhood wounds, thereby fostering sympathy for the partner who is behaving in negative ways.[*] But the concept assumes greater meaning in the work of Carl Rogers, whose client-centered therapy rests on the belief that "conditions of worth" should not be set for others. Rather, we should try to accept them (and ourselves) as worthy people deserving of respect regardless of their (or our) behavior at any point in time. Ellis's rational-emotive behavioral approach also emphasizes acceptance by encouraging people to renounce many of the demands (shoulds) they impose on themselves and on others.

How did Jacobson and Christensen come to the view that acceptance might be an overlooked and essential part of successful couples therapy? In following up the results from an earlier outcome study (Jacobson, 1984), they noticed that after two years, of the two-thirds of couples who had benefited from behavioral couples therapy, one-third

had relapsed (Jacobson et al., 1987). Thus, although the therapy was very effective for almost half the couples, it was not effective for the other half over an extended (two-year) period of time. This led to the question of what might be wrong or missing from behavioral couples therapy.

As just noted (p. 593), predictors of poor outcome from this approach include being married for a long time, emotional disengagement, high severity of distress in the relationship, and rigidly held gender roles. It seemed to Jacobson and Christensen that a factor or theme common to these negative predictors might be low amenability to compromise with and to accommodate to the other person. And since behavioral couples therapy requires compromise—by, for example, trying to meet the partner's wishes in exchange for certain reinforcers—it may not be surprising that the approach works less well for people who cannot readily accommodate to the desires of their partners.

This should not be news to anyone who has tried to mediate in a marital problem or who has been in a distressed marriage. When a couple has been together for many years, there can be an accumulation of anger, hurt, resentment, and betrayal that makes it a challenge even to decide what restaurant to go to on a Friday evening. Good will is gone. Motives are constantly questioned. If a negative interpretation can be placed on a positive behavior, it will be. And if a behavior therapist asks the partners to do something nice for each other, the kind of couple Jacobson and Christensen are talking about will either not budge or, if they do make a specific change, will readily attribute it to the therapist's instruction, for example, "He doesn't really appreciate me for my good work at the office today; he's complimenting me only because Dr. Smith told him to." It is no accident that couples therapy sessions can be extraordinarily taxing for the therapist and unusually boisterous and noisy.

Another factor working against direct attempts to change is reactance, the resistance people can feel when another person is trying to change them (Brehm, 1966; Davison, 1973). Reactance is likely to be especially high when the would-be influencer is held in contempt by

---

[*]At the same time, such historical attributions can be used by the patient as an excuse not to change. Therapists like Fritz Perls (p. 40) were inclined to see such explanations as cop-outs. Behavioral and cognitive therapists take a similar tack.

---

ples therapy can have a positive impact both on a person's depression and on the relationship).

- Brief training in communication skills can enhance future satisfaction with the relationship and even lower divorce rates when compared with no-intervention controls (Markman et al., 1988). Since couples therapy generally works better when people are younger and highly involved with each other, prevention efforts seem particularly sensible and promising.

- Overall, most nonbehavioral approaches, such as the analytic and humanistic approaches, have not been subjected to as much controlled research as have behavioral and systems approaches, a probable reflection of the lesser research emphasis in these paradigms. Johnson and Greenberg (1985) did find superiority of a Gestalt therapy–based couples intervention that focused on uncovering unacknowledged feelings and needs (the emotion-focused therapy mentioned earlier) as compared with the problem-solving component of behavioral couples therapy. As they speculated, it may be important for a couples intervention to work directly on increasing trust and sensitivity to one's own unmet needs and hidden fears as well as the fears the would-be influencee. Since behavior therapy is characterized by open attempts to change people, this type of influence is unlikely to succeed when exchanges are encouraged between two partners who feel little affection and respect for each other.

With all this as context, what is acceptance in Christensen's and Jacobson's terms? It refers to "a letting go of the struggle to change and in some cases even embracing those aspects of a partner which have…been precipitants of conflict…[it] implies that some conflicts cannot be resolved, and it attempts to turn areas of conflict into sources of intimacy and closeness" (Jacobson, 1992, p. 497).** Acceptance does imply change—but the change is in the partner who is giving up efforts to change the other! And, if reactance diminishes with acceptance, as indeed it might (see our earlier discussion of Shoham-Salomon's paradoxical therapy research on p. 586), more change in the partner may come about by giving up on trying to effect change! A specific example of what acceptance might look like is in the following "reframing" exercise:

> …What one partner sees as the other partner's "uptightness" might be the "stability" that first attracted him/her. Or alternatively, what one partner sees as the other's "flakiness" or "irresponsibility" might be the "free-spiritedness" or "rebelliousness" that so attracted him/her in the beginning of their relationship. The…therapist must help the partners notice the positive aspects of what they have come to see as purely negative behavior. And often this behavior is in some way related to a quality one partner once found attractive about the other (Wheeler, Christensen, & Jacobson, 2001, p. 617).†

Jacobson's behavioral roots show, however, in his suggestions about how therapists can bring about change within the context of

---

** Some might say that this is the closest that psychologists come to defining love.

† Of course characteristics that one person found appealing, even sexy, when they were courting another may, twenty years later, be very difficult to see in a positive light. The flakiness of the 19-year old with few family responsibilities may wear a little thin when, years later, there are children and the myriad of other responsibilities that people usually face as they move through the life cycle.

acceptance. He gives the example of a wife who found her husband's unavailability objectionable. (The assumption is that the man's unavailability was not due to such things as seeing other women. Jacobson is certainly attuned to the ethical and political dimensions of psychotherapy [cf. Jacobson, 1983, 1989]). In addition to the traditional goal of helping them improve their intimacy with each other, he encouraged the woman to develop some independent interests so that she would not rely so much on her husband on those occasions when he could not be present.

Is acceptance tantamount to resignation, to accepting a status quo that keeps one or both partners in a destructive relationship, one that perhaps demeans one partner in order to satisfy the selfish demands of the other? Jacobson and Christensen argue that acceptance is actually affirmative, holding out the promise of even greater intimacy. And as suggested here, some behavioral changes that were formerly—and unsuccessfully—worked toward in behavioral couples therapy with direct change attempts might actually be facilitated by embedding such efforts within a context of acceptance. Or, as they recently put it:

> …The purpose of "acceptance work" is not to promote resignation to the relationship as it is.… Rather, it is designed to help couples use their unsolvable problems as vehicles to establish greater closeness and intimacy. For couples who have difficulty changing their behavior, acceptance provides a viable alternative for building a closer relationship. For couples who do benefit from the traditional approach [that directly aims to change problematic behavior], [acceptance-based behavioral couples therapy] can facilitate further progress by providing an alternative way to establish a closer relationship, given that there are problems in every relationship that are impervious to change. Paradoxically, acceptance interventions are also predicted to produce change in addition to acceptance…because at times the pressure to change may be the very factor that prevents it from occurring." (Jacobson, Christensen, Prince, Cordova, & Eldridge, 2000, pp. 351–352.

Preliminary research suggests that this approach is effective in alleviating couples' distress (Christensen & Heavey, 1999; Jacobson et al., 2000).

and needs of one's partner. Behavioral couples therapists are paying increased attention to the affective dimensions of conflict, yet another sign of the move toward rapprochement among contrasting therapeutic orientations (p. 598).

- Despite the growing use of the term "couples" rather than "marital" therapy, practically no research has been done on same-sex or unmarried heterosexual couples.
- Some studies have been conducted on divorce mediation, consultations occurring before a divorce has been obtained. An alternative to the usual adversarial process, mediation is conducted by a third party (a lawyer, counselor, or trained layperson) who strives for neutrality and whose goal is to help the distressed couple reach agreement on child custody and financial arrangements before involving their own lawyers. Mediation can help estranged couples continue functioning as parents even as they move toward divorce. Data indicate that mediation is associated with "(1) a higher rate of pretrial agreements; (2) a higher level of satisfaction with the agreements; (3) major reductions in the amount of litigation after final court orders; (4) an increase in joint custody agreements; and (5)…decrease in public expenses such as custody studies and court costs (Sprenkle and Storm, 1983)" (Gurman et al., 1986, p. 589).

Review of Community Psychology

Basic Concepts and Techniques of Community Psychology

Reaching out to large populations in an attempt to prevent the onset or spread of a physical illness or a mental disorder characterizes community psychology. The means of doing so may involve mass-media campaigns, instructional programs in schools, or other techniques designed to prevent disorder in groups of people. The general strategy is twofold: (1) to reduce environmental factors that put people at risk; and (2) to strengthen protective factors so as to decrease people's vulnerability to (1) (Coie et al., 1993). This strategy constitutes what has come to be called prevention science (Heller, Wyman, & Allen, 2000). As with individual psychotherapy, the theoretical rationales and the techniques used vary greatly.

We have previously described many community psychology programs. Examples include:

- school-based programs for the prevention of cigarette smoking (p. 402);
- the prevention of HIV infection and AIDS through programs aimed at changing sexual practices among sexually active adults and adolescents (see p. 223);
- reducing the risk of cardiovascular disease through mass-media education about improving diet and lifestyle (p. 234);
- the establishment of suicide prevention centers with telephone hot lines, which desperate people can use to weather a suicidal crisis (p. 312);
- efforts through Head Start programs to prevent educational deficits and associated social and economic disadvantages (p. 504).

Evaluation of Community Psychology

It has been suggested that the results of community psychology have been disappointing (Bernstein & Nietzel, 1980; Phares & Trull, 1997), but in recent years many projects have shown their worth (Durlak & Wells, 1997; Heller et al., 2000). And yet some of the problems community psychologists are trying to prevent are not readily amenable to environmental or social manipulation because they have major genetic or biological components that are left untouched by community-based interventions. As we saw in Chapter 11, for example, there is very strong evidence that schizophrenia has some kind of biological diathesis. Although an environmental preventive effort may conceivably reduce the amount of stress that a predisposed individual is subject to in normal daily living, it seems unlikely that any realistic social change will be able to keep stress levels low enough to prevent episodes of schizophrenia from occurring or recurring in high-risk people. Family therapy for reducing expressed emotion (p. 349) is a prototype of what might be necessary on a societal scale to have a positive impact on the recurrence of episodes of schizophrenia.

Evaluation of community-psychology efforts is particularly challenging because the interventions occur in the field, where it is difficult to set up experimental controls and thus harder to draw causal inferences (Linney, 1989). There are many alternative explanations for the effect of a preventive intervention. For example, if a reduction in gang activity follows a school-based intervention aimed at that goal, it may be that a community center, such as the YMCA, or even a single, inspirational teacher had something to do with the observed change. Another concern in the current practice of prevention science is the problem of attrition, or loss of participants (Mrazek & Haggerty, 1994). Those who drop out of an intervention must be monitored in some fashion, for these individuals could be at the highest risk and may constitute the group for which preventive efforts are most appropriate.

Political and Ethical Factors in Community Psychology

The study of community psychology raises an interesting question. In the 1960s and 1970s, there was a shift to community activism in the prevention of mental disorders. Why? The answer is complex.

For many years it was obvious that few people could avail themselves of psychotherapeutic services, which were usually very expensive, in short supply, and geared to so-called YAVIS clients—individuals who are Young, Attractive, Verbal, Intelligent, and Successful (Schofield, 1964). Eysenck (1952) had earlier questioned the effectiveness of most kinds of insight-oriented psychotherapy, finding treated patients' rates of improvement no better than the spontaneous remission rate. Although Eysenck's criticisms were compellingly rebutted by a number of scholars (e.g., Bergin, 1971), the idea took hold among mental health professionals that psychotherapy aimed at changing the individual might not be the best way to alleviate the psychological problems of the majority of people. Focus began to shift from repressions, conflicts, and conditioned anxiety to large-scale social problems, such as poverty, overcrowding, poor education, segregation, the alienation felt in large cities, and the impersonal nature of many aspects of present-day living. Community psychology's emphasis on prevention became especially important in the United States, where a large gap had developed between the need for mental health care and the availability of services (Weissberg, Caplan, & Sivo, 1989).

The shift from intrapsychic to social factors probably also reflected the Zeitgeist, or tenor of the times. The 1960s and early 1970s were a period of tremendous social upheaval and activism. Institutions of all kinds were being challenged. Cities and college campuses erupted in riots, and a range of minority groups, from African Americans to gays, demonstrated against racism and political repression. This social upheaval, which at times seemed to border on revolution, further encouraged looking at social institutions for causes of individual suffering. At the same time, the Kennedy and Johnson administrations (1961–1969) lent the monetary clout of the federal government to a progressive liberalism. John Kennedy's New Frontier and Lyndon Johnson's Great Society programs poured tens of millions of dollars (equivalent to hundreds of millions today) into attempts to better the human condition.

Community psychology has as its goal the change of large systems and groups of people rather than treating individual problems. And it is primarily in the seeking mode; psychologists take the initiative in serving people rather than waiting for individuals in need to come to them. On the face of it, this is a tall order. What do we know about the principles that operate to produce change in societal values and institutions? If the community psychologist hopes to take actions that meet the wishes and needs of the community, how does he or she determine them? Recall from Chapters 3 and 4 the difficulties the psychologist has in assessing the needs of an individual client with whom there is extensive direct contact. How much more difficult, then, to assess the needs of thousands of people!

Community psychologists become social activists to some degree, which raises the danger that these well-meaning professionals may impose values and goals on their clients. What is mental health? Who is to decide how people should live their lives? To what extent do the people being served by community psychologists have a say in how they are to be helped? These are but a few of the nettlesome questions that must continually be posed if community psychology is to act responsibly and effectively. The focus of this field is on large-scale factors. Many people are involved; many lives, then, will be affected by decisions and actions. Questions of values are inherent in any effort to alter the human condition (cf. Focus on Discovery 18.5, p. 644), but they are of special importance when the clients themselves do not seek the intervention.

Psychotherapy Integration

Having reviewed the theory and research on the major psychological interventions, we turn now to the question of whether useful connections can be made among them. We examine first whether contemporary psychoanalysis is compatible with behavior therapy. Then we turn to more general questions about eclecticism and integration in psychotherapy.

Paul Wachtel, an early proponent of integrating psychoanalysis and behavior therapy in both theory and practice.

Psychoanalysis and Behavior Therapy: A Rapprochement?

The question as to whether there is common ground between psychoanalysis and behavior therapy has been discussed for many years. Few professionals are optimistic about a meaningful rapprochement, arguing that these two points of view are incompatible paradigms. But Paul Wachtel, in his work on just such an integration (1977, 1997) offers a scheme that holds considerable promise, at least for establishing a dialogue between psychoanalytically oriented therapists and behavior therapists.

As indicated earlier in this chapter (p. 570), ego analysts place much more emphasis on current ego functioning than did Freud. Sullivan, for example, suggested that patients would feel better about themselves and function more effectively if they focused on problems in their current interpersonal behavior. But it appears that Sullivan was ambivalent about the wisdom of working directly on how people act and feel in the present if doing so meant that they would not recover memories of repressed infantile conflicts. Wachtel, on the other hand, suggests that therapists, including those working within a psychoanalytic paradigm, should help the client change current behavior, not only so that he or she can feel better in the here and now, but, indeed, so that he or she can resolve repressed conflicts from the past.

Wachtel bases his principal position on Horney (1939), Sullivan (1953), and Erikson (1950) and calls it "cyclical psychodynamics" (1982). He believes that people's current behavior maintains repressed problems via the feedback it brings from their present-day interactions with others. Wachtel holds to the psychoanalytic notion that people's problems are set in motion by repressed past events, but he departs from psychoanalysis and from most ego analysts as well by suggesting that people act in ways that maintain these problems.

For example, consider a young man who has repressed his extreme rage at his mother for having mistreated his father years ago, during his childhood. As a youngster, to control this rage, he developed defenses that took the form of overpoliteness and deference to women. Today this solicitude and unassertiveness encourage some women to take advantage of him, but he also misperceives situations in which women are genuinely nice to him. By misinterpreting friendly overtures as condescending insults, he has come to resent women even more and to retreat still further. This young man's present-day submissiveness, originating in his "woolly mammoth" (p. 31)—his buried childhood rage against his mother—is creating personal problems in the present and has revived his repressed rage. It is as though his adult ego is saying, unconsciously, "You see, women, like my mother, really are bitchy. They're not to be trusted. They're hurtful and sadistic." This present-day confirmation of his belief from childhood turns back on the buried conflict and keeps it alive. The cycle continues, with the young man's own behavior and misconceptions confirming the nastiness of women.

Wachtel suggests that therapy should attempt to alter current behavioral patterns both for their own sake, which is the behavior therapist's credo, and for the purpose of uncovering and changing the underlying psychodynamics, which is the focus of psychoanalytic approaches. By pointing out that a direct alteration of behavior may help patients attain a more realistic understanding of their repressed past conflicts, Wachtel hopes to interest his analytic colleagues in the techniques employed by behavior therapists. He would probably give the deferential young man some assertion training (p. 52) in the hope of breaking into the vicious circle by changing his here-and-now relations with women. After repeated disconfirmation of the belief that all women want to take advantage of him, the young man could begin to understand and ultimately let go of the repressed conflict of love–hate with his mother.

Wachtel has some things to say to behavior therapists, too. He holds that behavior therapists can learn much from their analytic colleagues, especially concerning the kinds of problems people tend to develop. For example, psychoanalytic theory tells us that children have strong and usually ambivalent feelings about their parents, some of which are so unpleasant that they are repressed, or at least are difficult to focus on and talk about openly.

To a behavior therapist the deferential young man might initially appear fearful of heterosexual relationships. Taking these fears at face value, the therapist would work to help the client reduce them, perhaps by a combination of desensitization, rational-emotive behavior therapy, and social-skills training. But the behavior therapist would probably fail to explore the possibility, suggested by the psychoanalytic literature, that the young man is basically *angry* with women. His fear of women would be seen as a defensive reaction, a way of minimizing contact with them in order to escape from the threat of his aggressive impulses toward them. Wachtel would advise the behavior therapist to be sensitive to the childhood conflicts on which analysts focus and to question the young man about his relationship with his mother. The patient's reply or manner might give a hint of resentment. The therapist would then see the deferential young man differently and hypothesize that he is not fearful of women but angry with them, because he associates them with a mother who has been the object of both hate and love from early childhood. This additional information would presumably suggest a different behavioral intervention, one aimed at the patient's anger toward women, not his apparent fear of them.

Wachtel also wants behavior therapists to appreciate that reinforcers can be subtle and that a patient may deny that he or she really wants something and may well be unaware of this denial. In other words, therapists should be attuned to unconscious motivation, to the possibility that a person may be motivated or reinforced by a set of events of which he or she is unaware.

Contemporary psychoanalytic thought may help behavior therapists become aware of the *meaning* that a particular intervention has for a patient. Consider one of our own cases, a young woman with whom we decided to do assertion training. As we began to describe role-playing procedures, she stiffened in her chair and then began to sob. To proceed with the training without dealing with her reaction to its description would have been insensitive and poor clinical practice. An awareness of psychoanalytic theory had sensitized us to the possibility that assertion training *symbolized* something to the woman. So we gently encouraged her to talk freely, to free-associate about the idea of assertion training. She recalled a series of incidents from childhood in which her parents had criticized the way she acted with her friends without providing support and constructive suggestions about other ways to behave. Without initially being aware of it herself, the patient was reminded of this pain from the past when we suggested that she learn more assertive ways of dealing with others. We were able to explain to her the current enterprise, assertion training, and to distinguish it from the unhelpful and negative criticisms made in the past. We were able thereby to persuade the young woman to try role-playing. This incident also reflected the patient's unresolved problems with her parents and with authority figures in general.

In a related vein, Wachtel argues that psychoanalysts are more likely than behavior therapists to consider the nonnormative or unusual concerns, wishes, and fears of their patients. Guided by the view that emotional problems derive from the repression of id impulses, they consider psychological difficulties to be reflections of infantile wishes and fears, dark mysteries of primary-process thinking, such as feeling hostility toward a loved one. Behavior therapists tend to have a more straightforward, perhaps more prosaic, view of their patients' problems.

In our view as clinical psychologists who have taught and practiced in a cognitive-behavioral framework for many years, the actual practice of experienced behavioral clinicians often reflects the kind of subtlety that is characteristic of psychodynamic clinicians such as Wachtel. What is unclear to us, and we believe to Wachtel, is the degree to which sophisticated practice can be derived from the theories that constitute contemporary cognitive and behavior therapy. The disjunction between theory and practice lies at the core of Wachtel's critical discussion of behavior therapy and the ways in which psychoanalysis might enrich both behavioral theory and practice. We turn now to some general issues in eclecticism and psychotherapy integration.

Eclecticism and Theoretical Integration in Psychotherapy

Wachtel's efforts at rapprochement between psychoanalysis and behavior therapy are part of a long tradition in the field of psychotherapy (e.g., Dollard & Miller, 1950; Frank,

1971; Goldfried & Davison, 1976; Marmor, 1971). Forty years ago Perry London, in his critical analysis of insight and behavioral therapies, wrote:

> There is a quiet blending of techniques by artful therapists of either school, a blending that takes account of the fact that people are considerably simpler than the Insight schools give them credit for, but that they are also more complicated than the Action [behavior] therapists would like to believe. (London, 1964, p. 39)

Three Types of Psychotherapy Integration   Distinctions have been drawn among three modes of psychotherapy integration (Arkowitz, 1989; Westen, 2000): technical eclecticism, common factorism, and theoretical integration.

In **technical eclecticism**,[4] exemplified in Lazarus's multimodal approach (Focus on Discovery 17.3) and in Beutler's prescriptive psychotherapy (Beutler & Harwood, 1995), the therapist works within a particular theoretical framework, for example, cognitive behavior therapy, but sometimes imports from other orientations techniques deemed effective without subscribing to the theories that spawned them. "Use whatever works" is the operating principle of the technical eclectic, but rationalize the use of a technique from one's own framework. For example, Lazarus sometimes uses the Gestalt empty chair as a method of behavioral rehearsal rather than as a way to help the patient reclaim disowned parts of his or her personality, which is how the technique is conceived in Gestalt therapy.

Common factorism (e.g., Frank, 1961, 1982; Goldfried, 1980, 1991; Schofield, 1964) seeks strategies that all therapy schools might share. For example, informing a patient how he or she affects others is a strategy employed by many different kinds of therapists and believed by many (e.g., Brady et al., 1980) to be an important component of any effective psychotherapy.

The third approach, **theoretical integration**, tries to synthesize not only techniques but theories. Wachtel's efforts to justify and make sense of assertion training within a modified psychoanalytic framework is a prime example of an effort toward theoretical integration. The resulting theory—cyclical psychodynamics—is itself something different because of the blending of psychoanalytic and behavioral elements.

Arguments against Premature Integration

In contemplating efforts at theoretical integration, we have wondered whether a grand, all-encompassing theory or approach is necessarily desirable or even possible. We believe not, and our own use of different paradigms in the study of both psychopathology and intervention aligns us more with the views of Garfield and Bergin.

> A comprehensive conception of how the body works does not demand that every system or organ of the body operate according to the same principles. Thus, our view of how the circulatory system works is quite different from our view of the nervous system. The forces and actions of the human heart operate according to the principles of fluid mechanics, whereas the principles of electrochemistry apply to the transmission of nerve impulses through the neuron; yet these two quite different processes occur in the same human body and are coordinated harmoniously despite their apparently disparate functions.
>
> Similarly, human personality may operate in accordance with a complex interaction of seemingly disparate processes that act together, though each differently and in its own sphere. Thus, it is conceivable that the same individual may suffer at one time from a repressed conflict, a conditioned response, an incongruent self-image, and irrational cognitions; and that each of these dysfunctions may operate in semi-independent systems of psychic action that are amenable

---

[4] As discussed in Chapter 2 (p. 61), eclecticism per se refers to "a largely pragmatic approach in which the therapist uses whatever techniques he or she believes are likely to be effective, with little or no underlying theory to guide these choices" (Arkowitz, 1992, p. 262). This strategy is regarded with skepticism by many mental health professionals, including Lazarus and the authors of this book, for it lacks a rationale for determining which technique to use and under what circumstances. Without theoretical guidelines to help the therapist conceptualize the patient's problem and the processes of therapeutic change, eclecticism is equivalent to chaos. Choices are made on whim, on the basis of what feels right, or for any number of other reasons that make for neither good science nor sound practice.

to rather different interventions, each of which is compatible with the "system" to which it is being applied. Diagnosis and therapy might then become concerned with the locus of the disorder or with which portion or portions of the multisystem psyche is involved. (1986, p. 10)

Indeed, not all those interested in psychotherapy integration agree with the overall notion that the more blurring between conceptual frameworks, the better. A leading critic of theoretical integration is Arnold Lazarus himself, who was trained as a behavior therapist by Wolpe in the late 1950s in South Africa. As just mentioned, Lazarus has for many years advocated what he calls "technical eclecticism," a willingness to use whatever techniques work best for a particular patient or disorder without regard to the theoretical approach from which they are drawn. The technique then is incorporated into the therapist's theoretical framework. This view is elaborated in his own approach to psychotherapy, multimodal therapy (Focus on Discovery 17.3).

Lazarus argues not only that this empirically based eclecticism at the technique level will be of most benefit to the most patients, but that to attempt rapprochement or integration at the theoretical level—for example, seeking a way, as Wachtel does, to blend psychoanalytic and behavioral theory—is fruitless, a waste of time, and impossible. Recent moves toward theoretical integration, instead of facilitating dialogue and rapprochement, are, in Lazarus's view, creating even more chaos. Why? Because, says Lazarus, most theories of psychotherapy are epistemologically incompatible. For example, the definition of a fact in psychoanalysis differs from the definition of a fact in behavior therapy. Different standards of evidence prevail. The argument is that one cannot integrate two theories that do not share the same definition of reality. Our earlier discussion of Kuhn and paradigms in science bears directly on this discussion (cf. p. 17).

Another critique of theoretical integration was put forward in an article entitled "Disappearing Differences Do Not Always Reflect Healthy Integration" (Haaga and Davison, 1991). These authors used Ellis's REBT and Beck's CT to make their point. Over the years Ellis's REBT and Beck's CT have begun to merge. For example, Beck originally focused almost entirely on cognitive biases and how they might distort a person's analysis of a situation. Thus a depressed person who complains that he or she has no friends is encouraged, like a scientist, to determine whether in fact this is true. In contrast, Ellis has always emphasized the belief or assumption under which a person operates, for example, "I must be perfect in everything I do." Now, however, Beck devotes considerable time to talking about "dysfunctional schemas," which can look a great deal like Ellis's "irrational beliefs." And, similar to Beck, Ellis does not ignore social realities, for even when he first began promulgating his REBT approach (Ellis, 1962), he advocated teaching someone without social skills how better to interact with others, with the goal of improving relationships (rather than merely encouraging the person to care little about turning people off).

From an integrative point of view this might be seen as progress, but Haaga and Davison caution that such optimism may be ill-advised. They suggest that we may lose something by blurring such distinctions,[5] especially if integration is not based on research (and they argue that it isn't). If we preserve the uniqueness of these two therapies, we might then be more inclined to construct a more integrative therapy that uses the particular strengths of each.

For example, perhaps for certain people under certain circumstances it is best to focus on changing social realities, whereas other circumstances might call for changing people's interpretations of an unchanging and perhaps unchangeable social reality. Creating this kind of integration requires (1) holding on to at least some of the original distinctions between REBT and CT and, more important, (2) constructing or utilizing a superordinate theory that can subsume both REBT and CT and specify when a particular aspect of one is suitable and when a feature of the other is appropriate. The intricacies of this process

---

[5] A former student of ours used a salad metaphor to describe what is lost if one blurs distinctions between elements that are best combined *without* blending them. Salads are tasty, in part, because it is pleasing to chew a mouthful of spinach, tomatoes, and lettuce. The ingredients are kept separate while one chews and tastes them. The eating experience would be quite different—and not as pleasant—if one were to combine the different vegetables in a blender and then eat the resulting mush (C. J. Getty, personal communication, December 1994).

are beyond our purposes; suffice it to say that science sometimes moves forward more readily when rapprochement among divergent theories is *not* encouraged.

Cultural and Racial Factors in Psychological Intervention

As we close our discussion of intervention, we revisit the issue of cultural diversity that has been addressed many times already throughout this book. Cultural diversity is important to highly heterogeneous countries, such as the United States and Canada, and it is of importance to other countries as well because most of our discussion of psychopathology and intervention is presented within the context and constraints of western European society. Despite our increasing understanding of biological factors in the nature of mental illness and how to prevent and treat many disorders, social circumstances are ignored only at great risk.

It is generally assumed that patients do better with therapists who are similar to them in cultural and ethnic background. Therapists of similar background, perhaps even of the same gender, will better know the life circumstance of those in need, and, most important, will be more acceptable to them. In psychoanalytic terms, similarity between patient and therapist may strengthen the therapeutic alliance.

Extensive research on modeling provides some justification for these assumptions (e.g., Sue et al., 1991). Participants in studies of learning through observation are found to acquire information more readily from models who are perceived as credible and relevant to them; similarity of age and background are important determinants of credibility and relevance (Rosenthal & Bandura, 1978). Yet it has not been demonstrated that better outcomes are achieved when patient and therapist are similar in race or ethnicity (Beutler, Machado, & Neufeldt, 1994). The jury is out on this question. The operating factor may be what is called "cultural competence" and not just ethnic matching. It may be that a therapist who is not a member of the same racial or ethnic group as the patient can still understand the patient well and create a good working alliance if he or she is as familiar with the patient's culture as a matching therapist is likely to be (USDHHS, 2002; Lopez, Kopelowicz, & Canive, 2002).

A caveat. Our discussion of racial factors in intervention runs the risk of stereotyping because we are going to review generalizations that experts make about the way a *group* of people react to psychological assistance. People from minority groups are, however, individuals who can differ as much from each other as their racial or ethnic group differs from another racial or ethnic group. Nonetheless, a consideration of group characteristics is important and is part of a developing specialty called minority mental health.

African Americans and Psychological Intervention

African Americans experience much greater difficulty than whites in feeling comfortable about seeking professional help with their emotional problems (Hays, 1996). They report higher levels of rapport with African American therapists than with white therapists, prefer African American therapists to white therapists, and report greater satisfaction with them (Atkinson, 1983, 1985). One study found that African American clients engage in more self-exploration with counselors of their own race (Jackson, 1973). Furthermore, African Americans who have not fully accepted the values of white America generally react differently to whites than to other African Americans. With African Americans they are more open and spontaneous, whereas with whites they tend to be more guarded and less talkative (Gibbs, 1980; Ridley, 1984; Sue & Sue, 2002).

Negative bias on the part of some white therapists could help explain the lower levels of rapport and trust on the part of African American patients. One experiment revealed that white therapists rated case-study information about African American patients as reflecting more pathology than did African American therapists and also considered photographs of the patients less attractive (Atkinson et al., 1996). At the same time, studies suggest that racial differences are not insurmountable barriers to understanding between counselor and client (Beutler et al., 1994). Therapists with considerable empathy are perceived as more helpful by clients, regardless of the racial mix.

Therapists need to accept that virtually all African Americans have encountered prejudice and racism and many must wrestle with their anger and rage at a majority culture that is sometimes insensitive to and unappreciative of the emotional consequences of growing up as a member of a feared, resented, and sometimes hated minority (Clark, Anderson, Clark, & Williams, 1999; Hardy & Laszloffy, 1995; USDHHS, 2002; Vontress & Epp, 1997). And, like members of all the minority groups discussed in this section, African Americans have been subjected to hate crimes, which obviously add to their sense of alienation from the mainstream culture (see Focus on Discovery 18.5, p. 644 for a discussion of hate crimes in the context of homosexuality). On the other hand, as Greene (1985) cautioned, therapists' sensitivity to social oppression should not translate into a paternalism that removes personal responsibility and individual empowerment from African American clients. Indeed, both despite and because of more than two hundred years of discrimination, including slavery until after the U.S. Civil War, African Americans have developed successful coping strategies, many of them deriving from strong religious beliefs (USDHHS, 2002).

African Americans prefer African American therapists and report greater satisfaction with them.

Latinos and Psychological Intervention

The life experiences of Hispanic Americans in the United States vary a great deal depending on the region they originally came from—Mexico, Cuba, Puerto Rico, or Central America. So, as is the case with other minority groups, generalizations are to be made with caution.

Lopez, Lopez, and Fong (1991) found that Mexican Americans reported a clear preference for ethnically similar therapists, especially when the clinical problem related to ethnic concerns (e.g., a woman's feeling pressure from Mexican parents to marry rather than have a career). Less acculturated Latinos have been shown to view ethnically similar counselors as more credible sources of help than Anglo counselors (Ponce & Atkinson, 1989).

Therapy with most Latinos should appreciate their difficulty in expressing psychological concerns. Men in particular may have great trouble expressing weakness and fear, which may be exacerbated by the growing independence of many Latina women as wage earners. The fact that many Latinos do not speak English fluently and therefore require an interpreter with most therapists creates another risk—the interpreter may minimize the patient's problems in order to save face (Marcos, 1979).

As just noted with many African Americans, religion plays a very strong role in most Latin cultures and therefore needs to be considered in any therapeutic approach with Latinos. The religious component can be appreciated in the following comment from a Latina regarding her brother's emotional problems (USDHHS, 2002):

> We all have an invisible doctor that we do not see, no? This doctor is God. Always when we go in search of a medicine, we go to a doctor, but we must keep in mind that this doctor is inspired by God and that he will give us something that will help us. We must also keep in mind that who really does the curing is God, and that God can cure us of anything that we have, material or spiritual (Guarnaccia et al., 1992, p. 206).

Cognitive behavior therapy may be more acceptable than insight-oriented psychotherapy to traditionally oriented Latinos because it aims more at giving advice and guidance and problem solving around issues of immediate importance. The didactic style of cognitive behavior therapy may also serve to demystify the process and render it more educational than psychotherapeutic in nature, thus reducing the possible stigmatizing effects of "having one's head shrunk" (Organista & Munoz, 1996).

However, these considerations would seem to apply generally to lower-income people, regardless of race or ethnicity. What this means with Latinos is that socioeconomic class has to be considered. Consider Cuban-Americans. Because of the circumstances under which many Cubans came to the United States in the 1960s—being from the more privileged strata of Cuban society before Castro came into power in 1959—and given also their economic successes in many parts of the country, especially south Florida, there is no reason to assume that they and other higher income Latinos are any less suitable for insight-oriented therapy than Anglos.

Asian Americans, Pacific Islanders, and Psychological Intervention

Asian Americans and Pacific Islanders comprise more than three dozen distinct subgroups (e.g., Filipino, Chinese, Japanese, Vietnamese, Hawaiian, Samoan). They differ on such dimensions as how well they speak English, whether they immigrated or came as refugees from war or terrorism in their homeland, and how much they identify with their native land (or that of their parents if they were born in the United States) (Yoshioka et al., 1981, as cited in Sue & Sue, 2002). In general, these groups show a greater tendency than whites to be ashamed of emotional suffering, to experience greater reluctance to seek out professional help, and to be relatively unassertive (according to U.S. standards).

Above all, the stereotype of Asian Americans (and to a lesser extent Pacific Islanders) as invariably being highly educated, earning good salaries, and being emotionally well-adjusted is belied by the facts. The discrimination suffered in the United States and in many other countries is as severe as that endured by other racial and ethnic minority groups (Sue & Sue, 2002). In the United States, for example, over 120,000 Japanese Americans—70,000 of them born in the United States (USDHHS, 2002)—were imprisoned in concentration camps and prisons for several years during World War II without any evidence that they posed a security threat. More subtle but nonetheless hurtful discrimination is found in everyday occurrences in more recent times. For example, after the competition between U.S. figure skaters Michelle Kwan and Tara Lipinski in the 1998 Olympics, MSNBC reported "American beats Kwan" (Sue & Sue, 1999, p. 260). The irony, of course, is that while Michelle Kwan's family tree originates in China, Tara Lipinski's originates in eastern Europe. Both skaters were born in the United States. Very few U.S. citizens lack foreign lineage.

There are many implications for how to conduct psychotherapy with Asian Americans and Pacific Islanders. Sue and Sue (2002) advise therapists to be sensitive to the personal losses that many Asian refugees have suffered and, especially in light of the great importance that family connections have for them, to the likelihood that they are very stressed from these losses. Another way to put this is to appreciate the role of posttraumatic stress in Asian Americans who have come to the United States as refugees. Therapists should also be aware that Asian Americans have a tendency to "somaticize"—to experience and to talk about stress in physical terms, such as headaches and fatigue, rather than to view their stress in psychological terms, which is often seen by them as equivalent to being crazy or inferior (Nguyen, 1985). Their values are also different from the Western values of the majority culture in the United States. For example—and allowing for considerable individual variation—Asians respect structure and formality in interpersonal relationships, whereas a Western therapist is likely to favor informality and a less authoritarian attitude. (Quite the opposite holds for many Pacific Islanders such as Hawaiians, whose informality in relating to others is one of the things tourists like about vacationing on the Hawaiian islands.) Respect for authority may take the form of agreeing readily to what the therapist does and proposes—and perhaps, rather than discussing differences openly, just not showing up for the next session. The acceptability of psychotherapy as a way to handle stress is likely to be much lower among Asian Americans, who tend to see emotional duress as something to be handled on one's own and through willpower (Kinzie, 1985). Asian Americans may also consider some areas off-limits for discussion with a therapist, for example, the nature of the marital relationship, and especially sex.

Asian Americans born in the United States are often caught between two cultures. (Pacific Islanders like Hawaiians are, of course, U.S. citizens.) One form of a resolution

Tara Lipinski receiving her gold medal at the 1998 Olympics.

is to identify vigorously with majority values and denigrate anything Asian, a kind of racial self-hate. Others, torn by conflicting loyalties, experience poorly expressed rage at a discriminatory Western culture but at the same time question aspects of their Asian background. Finally, the therapist may have to be more directive and active than he or she otherwise might be, given the preference of many Asian Americans for a structured approach over a reflective one (Atkinson, Maruyama, & Matsui, 1978; Iwamasa, 1993).

American Indians, Alaska Natives, and Psychological Intervention

Like other minorities, American Indians and Alaska Natives (sometimes referred to collectively as Native Americans or First Americans) are a highly heterogeneous group, with more than 500 tribes residing in the United States and many in Canada as well, speaking more than 200 languages, some of them as dissimilar to each other as English is to Chinese (Chafe, 1962; Fleming, 1992). With due regard for individual differences, such as the degree to which the person is assimilated into the majority culture, some generalizations can be made that pertain to therapeutic approaches (Sue & Sue, 2002; Sue, Zane, & Young, 1994).

American Indians and to a lesser but still very significant extent Alaska Natives have experienced severe institutional discrimination for over 300 years. They have been forbidden to speak their own language, driven from the land that their tribes had inhabited for hundreds of years, forbidden to engage in traditional native spiritual practices (in the case of American Indians), forced onto reservations in not very desirable locations without regard for the special sanctity that land has for them, and subjected to other indignities that are bound to have created an inherently stressful environment. In recent years, however, their social and economic conditions have been improving and tribes are achieving more control over their lives (USDHHS, 2002).

Because Native American children are often looked after in the households of various relatives, the pattern of a child's or young adult's moving among different households is not necessarily a sign of trouble. A youngster's avoidance of eye contact is a traditional sign of respect but may be misconstrued by someone unfamiliar with the culture as quite the opposite and regarded as a problem to be remedied (Everett, Proctor, & Cartmell, 1989). As with members of other minority groups, conflicts about identification can be severe—young people can be torn between traditional values and those of the decidedly more privileged majority culture, which may underlie the high rates of truancy, substance abuse, and suicide among Native American young people (Red Horse, 1982). Drug abuse, especially alcoholism, is a widespread problem in some tribes and frequently leads to child abuse, an issue that also needs to be considered when there is family conflict. A value placed on cooperativeness rather than competitiveness can be misinterpreted by a culturally unaware therapist as lack of motivation. The importance of family may make it advisable to conduct treatment in the home with family members present and an integral part of the intervention. Very little controlled research has been conducted on Native Americans in therapy (Sue et al., 1994).

Toward a More Complete Science of Behavior

Regardless of whether the therapist has the same skin color or ethnicity as the client, it is important that the mental health professional be aware of and sensitive to the different value structures and life experiences of the client. The same can be said of the treatment of any client who is different from the therapist in ways that affect attitudes and behavior. The study of ethnic or racial factors in psychological intervention, as well as their role in clinical assessment (p. 105), can be seen in the broader context of the social and scientific importance of including such variables in the study of human behavior. The inclusion of diversity can enhance our scientific understanding of people (Betancourt & Lopez, 1993; Rokeach, 1979). If membership in a particular subculture plays a role, for example, in how readily emotion is expressed, then neglecting culture as a variable may limit our understanding of the role of expressing emotion in psychopathology. And such a constraint may vitiate not only our data-based knowledge but our ability to meet our social responsibilities as well. Culture and values are increasingly recognized as key factors in how a society structures its science and makes its policy. Our sensitivity throughout this book to paradigms in science reflects this understanding. In our final chapter, we further examine the complex interplay between scientific knowledge and the use to which that knowledge is put in affecting people's lives.

Summary

- Research on the effectiveness of various forms of psychotherapy has been conducted for many decades, with sometimes complicated and inconsistent results. The evaluation of the effects of psychotherapy has grown in significance as increased demands for accountability are being imposed by health insurance companies.

- There are differences between the way therapies have been examined in experimental settings and the way they are actually practiced by clinicians. Randomized clinical trials employ treatment manuals that specify what experimenters are to do when applying given therapies to research participants. Although this practice enhances the internal validity of psychotherapy research, the contrast with therapy as practiced—making adjustments depending on the needs of the individual patient—limits the external validity of such research.

- Classical psychoanalysis tries to uncover childhood repressions so that infantile fears of libidinal expression can be examined by the adult ego in the light of present-day realities. Variants include brief psychodynamic therapy, a time-limited therapy that places more emphasis on practical, real-life problems within the general framework of psychoanalysis. Research on psychoanalytic therapies suggests that they can be useful for a variety of anxiety and depressive disorders but not as useful for more serious psychopathology.

- Rogers's client-centered therapy uses empathy and unconditional positive regard to help patients view themselves more accurately and trust their own instincts for self-actualization. Research on client-centered therapy has investigated whether such factors as empathy and genuineness on the part of the therapist are associated with good outcomes. Results are inconsistent. Moreover, Rogers's assumption that people are by nature good and that they have an innate drive to self-actualization does not apply to many disorders.

- The Gestalt therapy of Perls stresses living in the now, and the many techniques he and his followers have introduced are designed to help clients experience their current needs and feel comfortable about satisfying them as they emerge. Gestalt and other humanistic and existential therapies have engendered little research, perhaps because of the objection that research is an objectifying, dehumanizing process.

- The cognitive and behavior therapies attempt to apply the methodologies and principles of experimental psychology to the alleviation of psychological distress. They have been the subject of much research, and evidence attests to the efficacy of counterconditioning, exposure, operant, and cognitive-behavioral interventions in alleviating a wide range of disorders. However, high end-state functioning is often not achieved even by patients whose improvement is significant.

- Cognitive therapies, such as Ellis's rational-emotive behavior therapy and Beck's cognitive therapy, alter the thoughts that are believed to underlie emotional disorders. They reflect the increasing importance of cognition in experimentally based psychological interventions. Self-control presents some interesting challenges to the behavioral paradigm: an active and conscious human being by autonomous and deliberate choice acts independently of environmental influences.

- Of particular importance for the cognitive and behavioral therapies is the generalization of treatment effects once the patient is no longer seeing the therapist regularly. Several procedures hold promise for maintaining any gains achieved during treatment. Of particular importance for techniques that rely heavily on influence from the therapist is how patients explain to themselves why they have improved. Encouraging an internal "I was a major factor in my own improvement" attribution is a way to help people maintain their gains once therapy is over.

- Marital or couples therapy helps distressed couples resolve the conflicts inevitable in any ongoing relationship of two adults living together. Behavioral and some insight-oriented therapies show promise in easing the stress that many couples experience.

- Community psychology aims primarily at the prevention of disorder. It adopts a seeking rather than the traditional waiting mode in helping communities cope with large-scale stressors and other life challenges, such as HIV infection and cardiovascular diseases. Political and ethical issues are intrinsic aspects of any therapeutic effort that aims to help people who have not actually asked for assistance.

- Eclecticism and theoretical integration in psychotherapy represent a trend that reflects growing awareness on the part of many clinicians and researchers of the limitations of their respective theoretical approaches. Psychoanalysis and behavior therapy might inform each other and take advantage of the strengths each can offer to help professionals better understand the human condition and design effective therapeutic interventions. There are risks, however, in integrating diverse theoretical perspectives—for example, glossing over differences that might better be examined and evaluated.

- The cultural and racial backgrounds of patients present a variety of challenges. Specific issues surround the treatment of such diverse groups as African Americans, Latinos, Asian Americans, and Native Americans, including the kinds of problems people in these groups may have and the kinds of sensitivities clinicians should possess in order to deal with them respectfully and effectively.

Key Terms

common factorism	multimodal therapy	stepped care	therapeutic (working) alliance
effectiveness	paradoxical interventions	technical eclecticism	triadic reciprocality
efficacy	reactance	theoretical integration	

18 Legal and Ethical Issues

Amendment 1 *Congress shall make no law respecting an establishment of religion, or prohibiting the free exercise thereof; or abridging the freedom of speech, or of the press; or the right of the people peaceably to assemble, and to petition the Government for a redress of grievances.*

Amendment 4 The right of the people to be secure in their persons, houses, papers, and effects, against unreasonable searches and seizures, shall not be violated....

Amendment 5 No person...shall be compelled in any criminal case to be a witness against himself, nor be deprived of life, liberty, or property, without due process of law....

Amendment 6 In all criminal prosecutions, the accused shall enjoy the right to a speedy and public trial...to be confronted with the witnesses against him; to have compulsory process for obtaining witnesses in his favor, and to have the Assistance of Counsel for his defense.

Amendment 8 Excessive bail shall not be required, nor excessive fines imposed, nor cruel and unusual punishment inflicted.

Amendment 13 ...Neither slavery nor involuntary servitude, except as a punishment for crime whereof the party shall have been duly convicted, shall exist within the United States, or any place subject to their jurisdiction....

Amendment 14 ...No State shall...deprive any person of life, liberty, or property, without due process of law; nor deny to any person within its jurisdiction the equal protection of the laws.

Amendment 15 ...The right of citizens of the United States to vote shall not be denied or abridged by the United States or by any State on account of race, color, or previous condition of servitude.

These eloquent statements describe and protect some of the rights of U.S. citizens and others residing in the United States. Against what are these rights being protected? Be mindful of the circumstances under which most of these statements were issued. After the Constitutional Convention had delineated the powers of government in 1787, the first Congress saw fit in 1789 to amend what had been framed and to set specific limits on the federal government. This was accomplished with what came to be called the Bill of

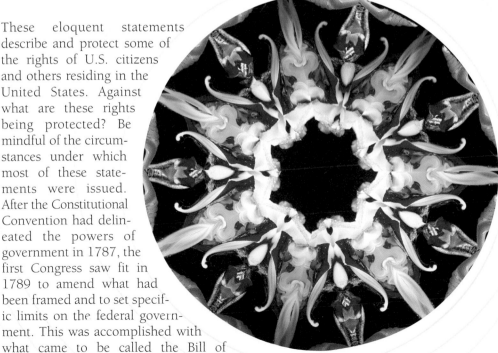

Rights, which are the first ten amendments to the Constitution. Amendments beyond the original ten have been added since that time. The philosophical ideal of the U.S. government is to allow citizens the maximum degree of liberty consistent with preserving order in the community at large.

We open our final chapter in this way because the legal and mental health systems collaborate continually, although often subtly, to deny a substantial proportion of the U.S. population their basic civil rights. With the best of intentions, judges, governing boards of hospitals, bar associations, and professional mental health groups have worked over the years to protect society at large from the actions of people regarded as mentally ill or mentally defective and considered dangerous to themselves or to others. But in so doing they have denied many thousands of people their basic civil rights.

Mentally ill individuals who have broken the law or who are alleged to have done so are subject to **criminal commitment**, a procedure that confines a person in a mental institution either for determination of competency to stand trial or after acquittal by reason of insanity. **Civil commitment** is a set of procedures by which a mentally ill and dangerous person who has not broken a law can be deprived of liberty and incarcerated in a mental hospital. Both commitments in effect remove individuals from the normal processes of the law. In this chapter we look at these legal procedures in depth. Then we turn to an examination of some important ethical issues as they relate to therapy and research.

Criminal Commitment

We examine first the role of psychiatry and psychology in the criminal justice system. Almost as early as the concept of *mens rea*, or "guilty mind," and the rule "No crime without an evil intent" had begun to be accepted in English common law, insanity had to be taken into consideration, for a disordered mind may be regarded as unable to formulate and carry out a criminal purpose (Morse, 1992). In other words, a disordered mind cannot be a guilty mind; and only a guilty mind can engender culpable actions.

At first insanity was not a trial defense, but in England the Crown sometimes granted pardons to people who had been convicted of homicide if they were judged completely and totally mad (A. A. Morris, 1968). By the reign of Edward I (1272–1307) the concept of insanity had begun to be argued in court and could lessen punishment. During the course of the fourteenth century it became the rule of law that a person proved to be wholly and continually mad could be defended against a criminal charge.

In today's courts, judges and lawyers call on psychiatrists and clinical psychologists for assistance in dealing with criminal acts thought to result from the accused person's disordered mental state rather than from free will. Are such emotionally disturbed perpetrators less criminally responsible than those who are not distraught but commit the same crimes? Should such individuals even be brought to trial for transgressions against society's laws? Although efforts to excuse or protect an accused person by invoking the insanity defense or by judging him or her incompetent to stand trial are undoubtedly well-intentioned, invoking these doctrines can often subject those accused to a greater denial of liberties than they would otherwise experience.

The Insanity Defense

The **insanity defense** is the legal argument that a defendant should not be held responsible for an illegal act if it is attributable to mental illness that interferes with rationality or that results from some other excusing circumstance, such as not knowing right from wrong. A staggering amount of material has been written on the insanity defense, even though it is pleaded in less than 1 percent of all cases that reach trial and is rarely successful (N. Morris, 1968; Morse, 1982b; Steadman, 1979; Steadman et al., 1993).

Stone (1975) proposed an intriguing reason for this great interest in finding certain people not guilty by reason of insanity (NGRI). Criminal law rests on the assumption that people have free will and that if they do wrong, they have chosen to do so, are blameworthy, and

Table 18.1   Landmark Cases and Laws Regarding the Insanity Defense

Irresistible impulse	A pathological impulse or drive that the person could not control compelled that person to commit a criminal act.
M'Naghten Rule	The person did not know the nature and quality of the criminal act in which he or she engaged, or, if the person did know it, the person did not know he or she was doing what was wrong.
Durham Rule	The person's criminal act is the product of mental disease or mental defect.
American Law Institute Guidelines	**1.** The person's criminal act is a result of "mental disease or defect" that results in the person's not appreciating the wrongfulness of the act or in the person's inability to behave according to the law (combination of M'Naghten and irresistible impulse).
	2. "[T]he terms 'mental disease or defect' do not include an abnormality manifested only by repeated criminal or otherwise antisocial conduct" (American Law Institute, 1962).
Insanity Defense Reform Act	**1.** The person's criminal act is a result of severe mental illness or defect that prevents the person from understanding the nature of his or her crime.
	2. The burden of proof is shifted from the prosecution to the defense. The defense has to prove that the person is insane.
	3. If the person is judged to have recovered from mental illness, then instead of being released from the prison hospital, the person remains incarcerated for at least as long as he or she would have been imprisoned if he or she had been convicted.
Guilty but Mentally Ill	The person can be found legally guilty of a crime—thus maximizing the chances of incarceration—and the person's mental illness plays a role in how he or she is dealt with. Thus, even a seriously ill person can be held morally and legally responsible, but can then be committed to a prison hospital or other suitable facility for psychiatric treatment rather than to a regular prison for punishment.

should therefore be punished. Stone suggests that the insanity defense strengthens the concept of free will by pointing to the few people who constitute an exception because they do not have it, namely, those judged to be insane. These individuals are assumed to have less responsibility for their actions because of a mental defect, an inability to distinguish between right and wrong, or both. They lack the degree of free will that would justify holding them legally accountable for criminal acts. By exclusion, everyone else has free will! "The insanity defense is in every sense the exception that proves the rule. It allows the courts to treat every other defendant as someone who chose 'between good and evil'" (Stone, 1975, p. 222).

Landmark Cases and Laws   In modern Anglo-American criminal law, several court rulings and established principles bear on the problems of legal responsibility and mental illness. Table 18.1 summarizes these rulings and principles.

Irresistible Impulse   The so-called **irresistible impulse** concept was formulated in 1834 in a case in Ohio. According to this concept, if a pathological impulse or drive that the person could not control compelled that person to commit the criminal act, an insanity defense is legitimate. The irresistible-impulse test was confirmed in two subsequent court cases, *Parsons* v. *State* and *Davis* v. *United States*.[1]

The M'Naghten Rule   The second well-known concept, the **M'Naghten rule**, was formulated in the aftermath of a murder trial in England in 1843. The defendant, Daniel M'Naghten, had set out to kill the British prime minister, Sir Robert Peel, but had mistaken Peel's secretary for Peel. M'Naghten claimed that he had been instructed to kill Lord Peel by the "voice of God." The judges ruled that

> to establish a defense of insanity, it must be clearly proved that, at the time of the committing of the act, the party accused was labouring under such a defect of reason, from disease of the mind, as not to know the nature and quality of the act he was doing; or if he did know it, that he did not know he was doing what was wrong.

---

[1] *Parsons* v. *State*, 2 So. 854, 866-67 (Ala. 1887); *Davis* v. *United States*, 165 U.S. 373, 378 (1897).

By the beginning of the twentieth century this right–wrong test was being used in all the states except New Hampshire and in all federal courts. By the late 1980s it was the sole test in eighteen states and in several others was applied in conjunction with irresistible impulse. However, a committee of the American Psychiatric Association expressed the view that understanding the difference between right and wrong was out of step with modern conceptions of insanity. It was in this context that a third important court decision was made.

The Durham Rule Judge David Bazelon ruled in 1954, in the case of *Durham* v. *United States*,[2] that the "accused is not criminally responsible if his unlawful act was the product of mental disease or mental defect." Bazelon believed that by referring simply to mental illness he would leave the profession of psychiatry free to apply its full knowledge. It would no longer be limited to considering impulses or knowledge of right and wrong.

Bazelon purposely did not incorporate in what would be called the Durham test any particular symptoms of mental disorder that might later become obsolete. The psychiatrist was accorded great liberty to convey to the court his or her own evaluation of the accused's mental condition. Forcing the jury to rely to this extent on expert testimony did not prove workable courtroom practice, however. Since 1972 the Durham test has not been used in any jurisdiction, and Bazelon eventually withdrew his support for it, feeling that it allowed too much leeway to expert witnesses.

American Law Institute Guidelines In 1962 the American Law Institute (ALI) proposed its own guidelines, which were intended to be more specific and informative to lay jurors than were other tests.

1. A person is not responsible for criminal conduct if at the time of such conduct as a result of mental disease or defect he lacks substantial capacity either to appreciate the criminality (wrongfulness) of his conduct or to conform his conduct to the requirements of law.
2. As used in the Article, the terms "mental disease or defect" do not include an abnormality manifested only by repeated criminal or otherwise antisocial conduct. (American Law Institute, 1962, p. 66)

The first ALI guideline combines the M'Naghten rule and the concept of irresistible impulse. The second concerns those who are repeatedly in trouble with the law; they are not to be deemed mentally ill only because they keep committing crimes. Indeed, the phrase "substantial capacity" in the first guideline is designed to limit an insanity defense to those with the most serious mental disorders. The second guideline excludes psychopathy as an excusing condition.

Until 1984 the ALI test was in use in more than half the states and in all federal courts. Some scholars, however, have argued that such words as *substantial* and *appreciate* introduce ambiguities that foster disagreements among expert witnesses as well as jurors as to whether a defendant's state of mind is sufficiently disturbed to justify a verdict of not guilty by reason of insanity (Simon & Aaronson, 1988).

Insanity Defense Reform Act In the 1980s a fifth major effort began in the United States to clarify the legal defense of insanity. It sprang in part from an NGRI (not guilty by reason of insanity) verdict in the highly publicized trial of John Hinckley, Jr. for an assassination attempt against President Ronald Reagan in March 1981. After the NGRI verdict, the court received a flood of mail from citizens outraged that a would-be assassin of a U.S. president had not been held criminally responsible and had only been committed to an indefinite stay in a mental hospital until deemed mentally healthy enough for release. (Hinckley has been incarcerated in St. Elizabeth's Hospital, a public mental

---

[2] *Durham v. United States*, 214 F.2d 862, 876 (D.C. Cir. 1954).

hospital in Washington, D.C., for over 20 years, but can be released whenever his mental health is deemed adequate.)

Because of the publicity surrounding the trial and the public outrage at the NGRI verdict, the insanity defense became a target of vigorous and sometimes vituperative criticism from many quarters. As Judge Parker, who presided at the trial, put it: "For many, the [Hinckley] defense was a clear manifestation of the failure of our criminal justice system to punish individuals who have clearly violated the law" (Simon & Aaronson, 1988, p. vii).

As a consequence of political pressures to get tough on criminals, Congress enacted in October 1984 the Insanity Defense Reform Act, addressing the insanity defense for the first time at the federal level. This new law, which has been adopted in all federal courts, contains several provisions designed to make it more difficult to plead NGRI.

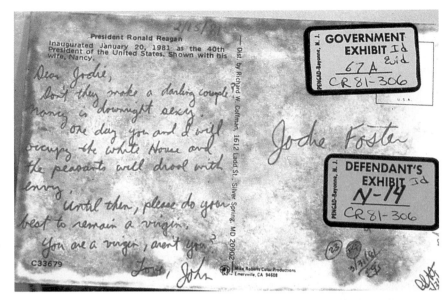

- It eliminates the irresistible impulse component of the ALI rules. This volitional and behavioral aspect of the ALI guidelines had been strongly criticized because one could regard *any* criminal act as arising from an inability to stay within the limits of the law. Such an interpretation would have the unacceptable consequence of excluding all criminals from the usual processes of the criminal justice system.
- It changes the ALI's "lacks substantial capacity...to appreciate" to "unable to appreciate." This alteration in the cognitive component of the law is intended to tighten the grounds for an insanity defense by making more stringent the criterion for impaired judgment.
- The act also stipulates that the mental disease or defect must be "severe," the intent being to exclude insanity defenses on the bases of nonpsychotic disorders, such as antisocial personality disorder. (The ALI guidelines were developed to impose similar restrictions by the use of the word substantial to describe incapacity; this apparently was not considered strong enough in the immediate aftermath of the Hinckley acquittal.) Also abolished by the act were defenses relying on "diminished capacity" or "diminished responsibility," based on such mitigating circumstances as extreme passion or "temporary insanity." Again, the purpose was to make it harder to mount an insanity defense.
- It shifts the burden of proof from the prosecution to the defense. Instead of the prosecution's having to prove that the person was sane beyond a reasonable doubt at the time of the crime (the most stringent criterion, consistent with the constitutional requirement that people are considered innocent until proved guilty), the defense must prove that the defendant was not sane and must do so with "clear and convincing evidence" (a less stringent but still demanding standard of proof). The importance of this shift can be appreciated by keeping in mind that if the prosecution bears the burden of proof beyond a reasonable doubt, then the defense need only introduce a reasonable doubt to defeat the prosecution's efforts to prove sanity. The heavier burden now placed on the defense is, like the other provisions, designed to make it more difficult to relieve a defendant of moral and legal responsibility.[3]

John Hinckley, President Reagan's assailant, wrote this letter to actress Jodie Foster expressing his dream of marrying her and becoming president.

---

[3] According to Simon and Aaronson (1988), this provision arose in large measure from the inability of the prosecution to prove John Hinckley's sanity when he shot Reagan and three others. Several members of the jury testified after the trial to a subcommittee of the Senate Judiciary Committee that the judge's instructions on the burden of proof played a role in their verdict of NGRI. Even before the act, almost half the states required that the defendant must prove insanity, but only one, Arizona, had the "clear and convincing" standard. A majority of the states now place the burden of proof on the defense, albeit with the least exacting of legal standards of proof, "by a preponderance of the evidence."

Thomas S. Szasz and the Case against Forensic Psychiatry and Psychology

Szasz's Polemic

By codifying acts of violence as expressions of mental illness, we neatly rid ourselves of the task of dealing with criminal offenses as more or less rational goal-directed acts, no different in principle from other forms of conduct. (Szasz, 1963, p. 141)

This quotation from one of Thomas Szasz's most widely read books enunciates the basic theme of his argument against the weighty role that his own profession of psychiatry plays in the legal system. (Note that the quote is from 1963. Mental health specialists play an even greater role in the courts today.) We have already mentioned Szasz's distinction between descriptive and ascriptive responsibility: to hold a person criminally responsible is to ascribe legal responsibility for an act for which the person is descriptively responsible. A given social group makes the judgment whether a person who is descriptively responsible for a criminal act will receive criminal punishment. As Szasz points out, being criminally responsible is not an inherent trait that society uncovers. Rather, society at a given time and for a given criminal act decides whether it will hold the perpetrator legally responsible and punish him or her.

Szasz suggests that mental illness began to be used as an explanation for criminal behavior when people acted in a way that was threatening to society. According to Szasz, these excep-

Noted psychiatrist Thomas S. Szasz argues strongly against the use of the insanity defense.

tional cases all involved violence against people of high social rank. In the shooting of an English nobleman in 1724, a man named Arnold was believed to have as little understanding of his murderous act as "a wild beast." Another man, James Hadfield, was deemed deranged for attempting to assassinate King George III as he sat in a box at the Theatre Royal in 1800. And a third person, named Oxford, was regarded as insane for trying to kill Queen Victoria in 1840. The best-known case has already been mentioned, that of Daniel M'Naghten (1843), who killed Sir Robert Peel's private secretary after mistaking him for Peel. In all these cases from English law, which forms the basis for U.S. law, people of low social rank openly attacked their superiors. Szasz offers the provocative notion that "the issue of insanity may have been raised in these trials in order to obscure the social problems which the crimes intended to dramatize" (1963, p. 128).

Other cases in the United States and abroad, such as the assassinations of John and Robert Kennedy, South African prime minister Hendrik Verwoerd, Martin Luther King, Jr., and John Lennon, and the attempted assassinations of Ronald Reagan and Pope John Paul II, may to a degree reflect the social ills of the day. Moreover, events in the former Soviet Union provide examples of the role of politics in criminal and civil commitment. In *A Question of Madness*, the well-known Russian biochemist Zhores Medvedev (1972) told how Soviet psychiatrists collaborated with the state in attempt-

- Finally, the new act responds to what many felt was the most troublesome feature of the existing laws—that the person could be released from commitment after a shorter period of time than would be allowed under an ordinary sentence. According to this act, if the person is judged to have recovered from mental illness, then instead of being released from the prison hospital, he or she can be incarcerated up to the maximum time allowable for the crime.

Guilty but Mentally Ill Over a dozen states have since created what seems to be a compromise verdict—guilty but mentally ill (GBMI). Initially adopted by Michigan in 1975, this principle allows an accused person to be found legally guilty of a crime—thus maximizing the chances of incarceration—but allows for psychiatric judgment on how to deal with the convicted person if he or she is considered to have been mentally ill when the act was committed. Thus, even a seriously ill person can be held morally and legally responsible, but can then be committed to a prison hospital or other suitable facility for psychiatric treatment rather than to a regular prison for punishment.

This trend reflects the uneasiness of the legal and mental health professions in excusing a person who, in Thomas Szasz's terms, is descriptively responsible for a crime—that is, who indisputably committed the act—without being held ascriptively responsible— that is, without having to suffer some sort of negative societal consequence for breaking

ing to muzzle his criticism of the government. They diagnosed him as suffering from paranoid delusions, multiple personality, and other mental ailments that would make it dangerous for him to be at large in society.

Of course Szasz does not claim that all insanity pleas involve some sort of silent conspiracy of the Establishment to cover up social problems, for the vast majority of pleas of insanity are made in far more ordinary cases. Szasz sets forth a polemic much broader in scope. His basic concern is with individual freedom and responsibility for one's actions, which include the right to deviate from prevailing mores and the duty to assume responsibility for one's behavior.* (Recall Szasz's argument that people should not be forcibly prevented from committing suicide; p. 315) Far from advocating that people be held less accountable for antisocial acts, he argues that legal responsibility should be extended to *all*, even to those whose actions are so far beyond the limits of convention that some explain their behavior in terms of mental illness. Szasz's overall lament is that instead of recognizing the deviant as an individual different from those who would judge him or her, but nonetheless worthy of their respect, he or she is first discredited as a responsible human being and then subjected to humiliating punishment defined and disguised as treatment (1963).

Evaluation of Szasz's Position

The Insanity Defense Reform Act of 1984, as well as changes in civil commitment to be described shortly, are consistent with the arguments that Szasz has put forward since the 1960s. These shifts toward holding mentally ill persons accountable for their actions and thereby more deserving of protection of their civil rights are probably due in large measure to Szasz's unrelenting attacks on the liaison between the law and the mental health professions.

However, Szasz has been criticized by those who believe that psychiatry and psychology should have an important role in deciding how to deal with people whose acts, whether criminal or not, seem attrib-

utable to mental illness. The abuses documented by Szasz should not blind us to the fact that—for whatever combination of biological and psychological reasons—some people are at times a danger to others and to themselves and cannot judge and control their behavior in ways that are in line with societal laws and mores. Although Szasz and others object to mental illness as an explanation, it is difficult to deny that there is madness in the world. People do occasionally imagine persecutors, against whom they sometimes act with force. Some people do hallucinate and on this basis may behave in a dangerous fashion. Our concern for the liberties of one individual has always been tempered with our concern for the rights of others.

But does it help a criminal acquitted by reason of insanity to be placed in a prison mental hospital with an indeterminate sentence, pending rehabilitation? The answer cannot be an unqualified yes. Should such a person, then, be treated like any other convicted felon and be sent to a penitentiary? Considering the psychic damage that we know may occur in ordinary prisons, a yes to this question cannot be enthusiastic either. But a prison sentence is more often a finite term of incarceration. If we cannot demonstrate that people are rehabilitated in mental hospitals, perhaps it is just as well to rely on our prisons and on the efforts of penologists to improve these institutions and to find ways of helping inmates alter their behavior so that they will not be antisocial after release.

---

* In a provocative book, *The Abuse Excuse*, Alan Dershowitz, a well-known and high-profile law professor at Harvard University, argues that more and more lawbreakers are trying to avoid responsibility for their criminal acts by invoking one or another hardship in their past history as a reason for their unlawful actions (Dershowitz, 1994b). One such excuse is the so-called adopted child syndrome, which holds that children who are given up by their biological parents for adoption feel such a profound sense of rejection that they should not be blamed for some of their antisocial behavior as adults. One lawyer employed this novel defense in claiming that his client murdered seventeen women, most of them prostitutes, because he had been rejected by his birth parents.

the law (see Focus on Discovery 18.1). This legal modification avoids the following ironical situation:

1. It is determined that a person committed a crime.

2. It is determined that the person is not to be held legally responsible because of insanity at the time of the crime (the NGRI defense).

3. By the time the person is to be criminally committed (or shortly after commitment), he or she is judged to be no longer mentally ill.

4. The person is not incarcerated or the person is released after a confinement shorter than it would have been had he or she been found guilty of (ascriptively responsible for) the crime he or she actually committed.[4]

A GBMI verdict, as mentioned, allows the usual sentence to be imposed but also allows for the person to be treated for mental illness during incarceration, a proposal Szasz made in the 1960s.

Critics of the GBMI verdict argue that it does not benefit mentally ill criminal defendants and does not result in appropriate psychiatric treatment for those convicted

---

[4] Things can go the other way, however, as demonstrated in the case of *Jones v. United States* described shortly.

(Leblanc-Allman, 1998; Paull, 1996; Woodmansee, 1996). A 1997 South Carolina Supreme Court case[5] found that South Carolina's GBMI statute did, to some degree, benefit defendants convicted under it. It mandated that convicted mentally ill people receive mental health evaluations before being placed in the general prison population. However, this particular benefit has not been shown to lead to better treatment in general.

Insanity and Mental Illness   In general, the insanity defense requires applying an abstract principle to specific life situations. As in all aspects of the law, terms can be defined in a number of ways—by defendants, defense lawyers, prosecutors, judges, and jurors—and testimony can be presented in diverse fashion, depending on the skill of the interrogators and the intelligence of the witnesses. Furthermore, because an NGRI defense is based on the accused's mental condition at the time the crime was committed, retrospective, often speculative, judgment on the part of attorneys, judges, jurors, and psychiatrists is required. And disagreement between defense and prosecution psychiatrists and psychologists is the rule.

A final point should be emphasized. There is an important difference between insanity and mental illness or defect. A person can be diagnosed as mentally ill and yet be held responsible for a crime. Insanity is a legal concept, not a psychiatric or psychological concept. This distinction was made vivid by the February 15, 1992, conviction of Jeffrey Dahmer in Milwaukee, Wisconsin. He had been accused of and had admitted to butchering, cannibalizing, and having sex with the corpses of fifteen boys and young men. Dahmer pled guilty but mentally ill, and his sanity was the sole focus of an unusual trial that had jurors listening to conflicting testimony from mental health experts about the defendant's state of mind during the serial killings to which he had confessed. They had to decide whether he had had a mental disease that prevented him from knowing right from wrong or from being able to control his actions (note the blend of the ALI guidelines, M'Naghten, and irresistible impulse). Even though there was no disagreement that he was mentally ill, diagnosable as having some sort of paraphilia, Dahmer was deemed sane and therefore legally responsible for the grisly murders. He was sentenced by the judge to fifteen consecutive life terms (Focus 18.2).

The Case of *Jones v. United States*   To illustrate the predicament that a person can get into by raising insanity as an excusing condition for a criminal act, we consider a celebrated—some would call it infamous—Supreme Court case.[6]

The Case   Michael Jones was arrested, unarmed, on September 19, 1975, for attempting to steal a jacket from a department store in Washington, D.C. He was charged the following day with attempted petty larceny, a misdemeanor punishable by a maximum prison sentence of one year. The court ordered that he be committed to St. Elizabeth's Hospital for a determination of his competency to stand trial (details of competency to stand trial are presented on p. 617).

On March 2, 1976, almost six months after the alleged crime, a hospital psychologist reported to the court that Jones was competent to stand trial, although he had "schizophrenia, paranoid type." The psychologist also reported that the alleged crime resulted from Jones's condition, his paranoid schizophrenia. This comment is noteworthy because the psychologist was not asked to offer an opinion on Jones's state of mind during the crime, only on whether Jones was competent to stand trial. Jones then decided to plead not guilty by reason of insanity. Ten days later, on March 12, the court found him NGRI and formally committed him to St. Elizabeth's Hospital for treatment of his mental disorder.

On May 25, 1976, a customary fifty-day hearing was held to determine whether Jones should remain in the hospital any longer. A psychologist from the hospital testified that Jones still suffered from paranoid schizophrenia and was therefore a danger to him-

---

[5] *South Carolina v. Hornsby*, 484 S.E.2d 869 (S.C. Sup. Ct. 1997).
[6] *Jones v. United States*, 463 U.S. 354 (1983).

Focus on Discovery 18.2

Another Look at Insanity versus Mental Illness

On June 20, 2001, believing that her five children, ranging in age from six months to seven years, were condemned to eternal damnation, thirty-seven-year-old Andrea Yates, who lived with her husband and children in Houston, Texas, systematically drowned each child in a bathtub. As recounted on the CNN website:

> …when the police reached [the] modest brick home on Beachcomber Lane in suburban Houston, they found Andrea drenched with bath-water, her flowery blouse and brown leather sandals soaking wet. She had turned on the bathroom faucet to fill the porcelain tub and moved aside the shaggy mat to give herself traction for kneeling on the floor. It took a bit of work for her to chase down the last of the children; toward the end, she had a scuffle in the family room, sliding around on wet tile.... She dripped watery footprints from the tub to her bedroom, where she straightened the blankets around the kids in their pajamas once she was done with them. She called 911 and then her husband. 'It's time. I finally did it,' she said before telling him to come home and hanging up."

The nation was horrified by her actions, and in the months following the murders, information became known about Ms. Yates' frequent bouts of depression, especially after giving birth, as well as her several suicide attempts and hospitalizations for severe depression.

Eight months later her trial was held. The defense argued that she was mentally ill at the time of the murders—and for many periods of time preceding the events—and that she also could not distinguish right from wrong when she put her children to death. The prosecution argued that she did know right from wrong and should therefore be found guilty. On two things the defense and the prosecution agreed: (1) she had murdered her children; and (2) she was mentally ill at the time of the murder. Where they disagreed was on the crucial question as to whether her mental illness entailed not being able to distinguish right or wrong, the familiar M'Naghten principle of criminal responsibility. (Note: Despite her disturbed state of

Andrea Yates, who drowned her five children, pled NGRI. Although she was suffering from mental illness, her plea was unsuccessful because she was judged capable of knowing right from wrong.

mind during the murders, she had been judged competent to stand trial.)

This trial shows the difficulty of making a successful insanity defense and is a vivid example of the critical difference between mental illness and insanity. No one disagreed that she was severely depressed, probably psychotic, when she killed her five small children. But, as we have seen, mental illness is not the same as legal insanity. Employing the right–wrong principle, the jury deliberated for only three hours and forty minutes on March 12, 2002, and delivered a verdict of guilty. They had rejected the defense's contention that Ms. Yates could not distinguish right from wrong at the time of the crime. On March 15, the jury decided to spare her life and recommended to the presiding judge that she get life in prison, not being eligible for parole for forty years.

The trial and the guilty verdict occasioned impassioned discussion in the media and among millions of people in their everyday lives. How could the jury not have considered her insane? If such a person is not insane, who could be judged to be so? Should the right–wrong M'Naghten principle be dropped from the laws of half the states in the United States? Did not her phoning 911 to report what she had done prove that she knew she had done something very wrong? Did not the careful and systematic way she killed her children reflect a mind that, despite her deep depression and delusional thinking, could formulate a complex plan and execute it successfully? Was she not perhaps so unhappy with her life and angry enough at her husband for leaving her to raise all these children pretty much on her own that she made a rational decision to relieve herself of child-rearing responsibilities and do something very hostile toward her husband? Had she received proper treatment from psychiatrists, especially from the one who had recently taken her off antidepressant medication that had been helping her and had sent her home without adequate follow-up?

These are but some of the questions that the Yates trial has raised and that will no doubt be debated in the months and years to come.

self and to others. A second hearing was held on February 22, 1977, seventeen months after the commission of the crime and Jones's original commitment to St. Elizabeth's for determination of competency. The defendant demanded release since he had already been hospitalized longer than the one-year maximum sentence he would have served had he been found guilty of the theft of the jacket. The court denied the request and returned him to St. Elizabeth's.

The District of Columbia Court of Appeals agreed with the original court. Ultimately, in November 1982, more than seven years after his hospitalization, Jones's appeal to the

Supreme Court was heard. On June 29, 1983, by a five-to-four decision, the Court affirmed the earlier decision: Jones was to remain at St. Elizabeth's. His public defender reported to us several years ago that Jones has spent most of his committed years in St. Elizabeth's, living in the community for a period of time in the late 1980s, but always returning to the hospital (Fulton, personal communication, April 22, 1997).

The Decision of the Supreme Court   The basic question Jones took to the Supreme Court was whether someone "who was committed to a mental hospital upon being acquitted of a criminal offense by reason of insanity must be released because he has been hospitalized for a period longer than he might have served in prison had he been convicted" (*Jones* v. *United States*, p. 700). Having already spent much more time in the prison hospital than he would have served in prison had he been convicted, Jones believed that he should be released. The Supreme Court, however, viewed matters differently (S Rep No. 1170, 84th Cong, 1st Sess 13 [1955], as cited in *Jones* v. *United States*):

> An insanity acquittee is not entitled to his release merely because he has been hospitalized for a period longer than he could have been incarcerated if convicted. The length of a sentence for a particular criminal offense is based on a variety of considerations, including retribution, deterrence, and rehabilitation. However, because an insanity acquittee was not convicted, he may not be punished. *The purpose of his commitment is to treat his mental illness and protect him and society from his potential dangerousness. There simply is no necessary correlation between the length of the acquittee's hypothetical criminal sentence and the length of time necessary for his recovery. (p. 700, emphasis added)*[7]
>
> Where [the] accused has pleaded insanity as a defense to a crime, and the jury has found that the defendant was, in fact, insane at the time the crime was committed, it is just and reasonable…that the insanity, once established, should be presumed to continue and that the accused should automatically be confined for treatment until it can be shown that he has recovered. (p. 705)
>
> And because it is impossible to predict how long it will take for any given individual to recover—or indeed whether he ever will recover—Congress has chosen, as it has with respect to civil commitment, to leave the length of commitment indeterminate, subject to periodic review of the patient's suitability for release. (p. 708)

What Does This Mean?   Essentially, the Supreme Court ruled that since Jones was acquitted, he could not be punished for the crime. The constitutional justification for being punished is that the individual must be blameworthy. Jones's insanity left him legally blameless, for he could not possess *mens rea*, "a guilty mind." This is the logic of the insanity defense. Furthermore, according to the Court, since punishment cannot have any of its intended individual or societal effects on a mentally disturbed person—rehabilitation, deterrence, or retribution—it was irrelevant that Jones was being held longer than a normal prison sentence. Jones would clearly have been better off not to have pleaded insanity!

Critique of the Decision   In this case, the burden of proof was on Jones, the acquittee, to prove that he was no longer mentally ill or dangerous to society, whereas in the normal practice of justice in the United States a person's accusers have the burden of proving him or her guilty. This situation differs as well from civil commitment (see p. 621) in which the government, not the person, bears the burden of proof. Jones was denied this civil right.

The Court was concerned about Jones's illness-produced dangerousness. Jones argued in his petition to the Supreme Court that his theft of the jacket was not dangerous because it was not a violent crime. The Court stated, however, that for there to be violence in a criminal act, the act itself need not be dangerous. It cited a previous decision that a nonviolent theft of an article such as a watch may frequently result in violence

---

[7] At the time, this absence of correlation between the criminal act and the length of incarceration could also work the other way—specifically, "no matter how serious the act committed by the acquittee, he may be released within fifty days of his acquittal if he has recovered" (p. 708).

through the efforts of the criminal to escape, or of the victim to protect his or her property, or of the police to apprehend the fleeing thief.[8]

The dissenting justices of the Court commented that the longer someone such as Jones had to remain in the hospital, the harder it would be for him to demonstrate that he was no longer a dangerous person or mentally ill. Extended institutionalization would likely make it more difficult for him to afford medical experts other than those associated with the hospital and to behave like someone who was not mentally ill.

> The current [use of] psychotropic drugs…may render mental patients docile…,but it does not "cure" them or allow them to demonstrate that they would remain non-violent if they were not drugged…. At petitioner's May 1976 hearing, the Government relied on testimony [from hospital mental health experts] that petitioner was "not always responsive in a positive way to what goes on" and was "not a very active participant in the informal activities on the Ward" to support its contention that he had not recovered. (p. 716, n. 16)

Jones's case is unusual, even kafkaesque. Most NGRI decisions are for crimes considerably more heinous than stealing a jacket. But the Jones case did reach the Supreme Court, and it illustrates some of the reasons that the insanity defense remains a controversial and emotionally charged issue for a society that values the rule of law and civil rights for its citizens.

Competency to Stand Trial

The insanity defense concerns the accused person's mental state *at the time of the crime*. A question that arises before the issue of what kind of defense an accused person offers is whether the person is competent to stand trial *at all*. The U.S. criminal justice system is organized such that the fitness of individuals to stand trial must be decided before it can be determined whether they are responsible for the crime of which they are accused. It is possible for a person to be judged competent to stand trial yet be acquitted by reason of insanity.

The legal standard for being competent to stand trial has not changed since it was articulated by a 1960 U.S. Supreme Court decision:[9] "The test [is] whether [the defendant] has sufficient present ability to consult with his lawyer with a reasonable degree of rational understanding, and whether he has a rational as well as a factual understanding of the proceedings against him."

Far greater numbers of people are committed to prison hospitals after being judged incompetent to stand trial—estimated at between 24,000 and 60,000 a year in the United States—than are tried and acquitted by reason of insanity.

With the 1966 Supreme Court case *Pate* v. *Robinson*[10] as precedent, the defense attorney, prosecutor, or judge may raise the question of mental illness whenever there is reason to believe that the accused person's mental condition might interfere with his or her upcoming trial. Another way to look at competency is that the courts do not want a person to be brought to trial in absentia (" not present")—which is a centuries-old principle of English common law—referring here to the person's mental state, not his or her physical presence. If after examination the person is deemed too mentally ill to participate meaningfully in a trial, the trial is routinely delayed, and the accused person is incarcerated with the hope that means of restoring adequate mental functioning can be found. This is what happened to Jones immediately after his arrest.

If a court fails to order a hearing when there is evidence that raises a reasonable doubt about competency to stand trial, or if it convicts a legally incompetent defendant, there is a violation of due process.[11] Once competency is questioned there must be a preponderance of evidence showing that the defendant is competent to stand trial.[12] As just

[8] *Overholser v. O'Beirne*, 302 F.2d 85, 861 (D.C. Cir. 1961).

[9] *Dusky v. United States*, 362 U.S. 402 (1960).

[10] *Pate v. Robinson*, 383 U.S. 375 (1966).

[11] *United States v. White*, 887 F.2d 705 (6th Cir. 1989); *Wright v. Lockhart*, 914 F.2d 1093, cert. denied, 111 S.Ct. 1089 (1991).

[12] *United States v. Frank*, 956 F.2d 872, cert. denied, 113 S.Ct. 363 (1992); *United States v. Blohm*, 579 F.Supp. 495 (1983).

indicated, the test to be applied is whether the defendant is able to consult adequately with his or her lawyer and whether he or she can understand the proceedings.[13] The court has to consider evidence such as irrational behavior as well as any medical or psychological data that might bear on the defendant's competency.[14] However, analogous to the insanity defense, being deemed mentally ill does not necessarily mean that the person is incompetent to stand trial; a person with schizophrenia, for example, may still understand legal proceedings and be able to assist in his or her defense (Winick, 1996).

Being judged incompetent to stand trial can have severe consequences for the individual. Bail is automatically denied, even if it would be routinely granted had the question of incompetency not been raised. The person is usually kept in a facility for the criminally insane for the pretrial examination. During this period the accused person is supposed to receive treatment to render him or her competent to stand trial.[15] In the meantime, he or she may lose employment and undergo the trauma of being separated from family and friends and from familiar surroundings for months or even years, perhaps making his or her emotional condition even worse and thus making it all the more difficult to show competency to stand trial. Until the 1970s, some people languished in prison hospitals for many years waiting to be found competent to stand trial.

A 1972 Supreme Court case, *Jackson v. Indiana*,[16] forced the states to a speedier determination of incompetency. The case concerned a mentally retarded deaf and mute man who was deemed not only incompetent to stand trial but unlikely ever to become competent. The Court ruled that the length of pretrial confinement must be limited to the time it takes to determine whether treatment during this detainment is likely to render the defendant competent to stand trial. If the defendant is unlikely ever to become competent, the state must after this period either institute civil commitment proceedings or release the defendant. Legislation in most states defines more precisely the minimal requirements for competency to stand trial, ending the latitude that has deprived thousands of people of their rights to due process (Fourteenth Amendment) and a speedy trial (Sixth Amendment). Defendants today cannot be committed for determination of competency for a period longer than the maximum possible sentence they face.[17]

Modern medicine has had an impact on the competency issue. The concept of "synthetic sanity" (Schwitzgebel & Schwitzgebel, 1980) has been used to argue that if a drug, such as Thorazine, temporarily produces a modicum of rationality in an otherwise deranged defendant, the trial may proceed. The likelihood that the defendant will again become incompetent to stand trial if the drug is withdrawn does not disqualify the person from going to court.[18] However, the individual rights of the defendant are to be protected against forced medication, because there is no guarantee that such treatment would render the person competent to stand trial and there is a chance that it might cause harm. A subsequent Supreme Court ruling[19] held that a criminal defendant generally cannot be forced to take psychotropic medication in an effort to render him or her competent to stand trial; one of the justices expressed strong reservations that a drugged defendant could ever get a fair trial. In general, the courts have responded to the existence of powerful psychoactive medications by requiring safeguards against their involuntary use to ensure that the defendant's civil rights are protected, even when a drug might restore legal competency to stand trial.[20]

The implications of the various rulings on synthetic sanity have been debated in the mental health law literature (Gutierrez, 1994; Healy, 1994; Winich, 1994) and remain

---

[13] Frank, 956 F.2d at 872; *Wright v. Lockhart*, 914 F.2d 1093 (8th Cir. 1990).

[14] *United States* v. *Hemsi*, 901 F.2d 293 (2d Cir. 1990); *Balfour v. Haws*, 892 F.2d 556 (7th Cir. 1989).

[15] *United States* v. *Sherman*, 912 F.2d 907 (7th Cir. 1990).

[16] *Jackson v. Indiana*, 406 U.S. 715 (1972).

[17] *United States* v. *DeBellis*, 649 F.2d 1 (1st Cir. 1981); *State v. Moore*, 467 N.W. 2d 201 (Wis. Ct. App. 1991).

[18] *State v. Hampton*, 218 So.2d 311 (La. 1969); *State v. Stacy*, no. 446 (Crim. App., Knoxville, Tenn., August 4, 1977); *United States v. Hayes*, 589 F.2d 811 (1979).

[19] *Riggins v. Nevada*, 504 U.S. 127 (1992)

[20] *United States v. Waddell*, 687 F.Supp. 208 (1988).

uncertain. In September 1999, the controversy appeared on the national scene. A judge ruled that the man who forced his way into the United States House of Representatives and shot two security officers could be made to take a psychoactive drug in an effort to make him competent to stand trial; his stated intention was to gain access to a secret machine that was exerting a malign control over people.

Finally, if the defendant wishes, the effects of the medication must be explained to the jury, lest—if the defendant is pleading NGRI—the jury conclude from the defendant's relatively rational drug-produced demeanor that he or she could not have been insane at the time of the crime.[21] This requirement acknowledges that juries form their judgments of legal responsibility or insanity at least in part on how the defendant appears during the trial. If the defendant appears normal, the jury may be less likely to believe that the crime was an act of a disturbed mental state rather than of free will—even though an insanity defense has to do with the defendant's state of mind during the crime, not his or her psychological state during the trial.

Focus on Discovery 18.3 discusses the unusual challenge posed by dissociative identity disorder in criminal commitments.

Insanity, Mental Retardation, and Capital Punishment

As we have just seen, an accused person's mental state can be taken into consideration to determine whether he or she is competent to stand trial and/or should be held legally responsible for a criminal act. On very rare occasions the sanity or mental capacities of a person also becomes an issue after a conviction. The question is, Should a person convicted of a capital offense and sentenced to be put to death by the state have to be legally sane at the time of the execution? Furthermore, what if the person is deemed so mentally retarded that he may not understand what is about to happen to him?

The question of insanity and capital punishment arose in April 1998 in California in the case of Horace Kelly, a thirty-nine-year-old man who had been found guilty of the brutal 1984 rape and murders of two women and the slaying of an eleven-year-old boy (LaGanga, 1998). Neither the issue of competency to stand trial nor an insanity defense to excuse him from criminal responsibility for the crimes had been raised at the time of his trial, but the man's lawyers argued—twelve years later and just days before his scheduled execution by lethal injection—that Kelly's mental health had deteriorated during his imprisonment on death row to such an extent that one of his defense attorneys referred to him as a "walking vegetable." They made reference to a 1986 Supreme Court ruling stating that it is a violation of the Eighth Amendment (which prohibits cruel and unusual punishment) for an insane individual to be executed, even if the person was duly convicted and sentenced to death as a sane person.

We need to remember that insanity is a legal concept, and not everyone judged to be mentally ill is held to be legally insane. Evidence of mental illness (and possible insanity) during Kelly's imprisonment included psychiatrists' reports of delusions, hallucinations, and inappropriate affect. He was also described by fellow inmates and by guards as hoarding his feces and smearing them on the walls of his prison cell. By 1995, after ten years on death row, one court-appointed psychiatrist concluded that Kelly was legally insane. On the other hand, another psychiatrist reported that when asked what being executed would mean for him, Kelly gave the rational reply that he would not be able to have a family; he was also able to name two of his victims and beat the psychiatrist in several games of tic-tac-toe.

In their effort to delay the execution, Kelly's lawyers argued that the stress on death row is so severe that some convicted felons inevitably go crazy there. Kelly was portrayed as particularly vulnerable, having endured a very troubled childhood, full of sexual and physical abuse from both his parents, his siblings, and strangers. As a child, he was also subject to what his mother called "trances," beginning at age two, with other signs of emotional and mental impairment throughout childhood and adolescence.

---

[21] *State v. Jojola,* 553 F.2d 1296 (N.M. Ct. App. 1976).

Focus on Discovery 18.3

Dissociative Identity Disorder and the Insanity Defense

Imagine that as you are having a cup of coffee one morning you hear pounding at the front door. You hurry to answer and find two police officers staring grimly at you. One of them asks, "Are you Jane Smith?" "Yes," you reply. "Well, ma'am, you are under arrest for grand theft and for the murder of John Doe." The officer then reads you your Miranda rights against self-incrimination, handcuffs you, and takes you to the police station, where you are allowed to call your lawyer.

This would be a scary situation for anybody. What is particularly frightening and puzzling to you and your lawyer is that you have absolutely no recollection of having committed the crime that a detective later describes to you. You are aghast that you cannot account for the time period when the murder was committed—in fact, your memory is startlingly blank for that entire time. And, as if this were not bizarre enough, the detective then shows you a videotape in which you are clearly firing a gun at a bank teller during a holdup. "Is that you in the videotape?" asks the detective. You confer with your lawyer, saying that it certainly looks like you, including the clothes, but you are advised not to admit anything one way or the other.

Let's move forward in time now to your trial some months later. Witnesses have come forward and identified you beyond a reasonable doubt. There is no one you know who can

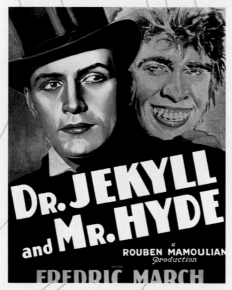

Poster for the classic film about Jekyll and Hyde.

testify that you were somewhere other than at the bank on the afternoon of the robbery and the murder. And it is clear that the jury is going to find you, in Szasz's terms, descriptively responsible for the crimes. But did you murder the teller in the bank? You are able to assert honestly to yourself and to the jury that you did not. And yet even you have been persuaded that the person in the videotape is you, and that that person committed the robbery and the murder.

Because of the strange nature of the case, your lawyer arranged prior to the trial to have you interviewed by a psychiatrist and a clinical psychologist, both of them well-known experts in forensics. Through extensive questioning they have decided that you have dissociative identity disorder (DID, formerly called multiple personality disorder) and that the crimes were committed not by you, Jane Smith, but by your rather violent alter, Laura. Indeed, during one of the interviews, Laura emerged and boasted about the crime, even chuckling over the fact that you, Jane, would be imprisoned for it.

This fictional account is not as far-fetched as you might think (recall the discussion of dissociative identity disorder in Chapter 7). Mental health lawyers have for some time been concerned with such scenarios as they have wrestled with various aspects of the insanity defense. But nearly all the people who successfully use

A federal judge decided in June 1998 and the U.S. Supreme Court concurred in April 1999 to stay (delay) Horace Kelly's execution and allow his lawyers to argue, among other things, that he should not be put to death because he was insane. Among the many riveting questions that this case raises is the ethics of a mental health professional's working to improve a person's psychological condition to the extent that the person can be judged sane enough to be executed. And consider how the issue of synthetic sanity just described affects a death penalty situation: Does a person sentenced to death have the right to refuse psychotropic medication because he or she knows it would improve his or her mental condition enough so that he or she could be executed?

Increasing attention is being paid to this issue of synthetic sanity and the general question of whether it is constitutional to execute criminals who are deemed insane or mentally retarded at the time of their scheduled capital punishment. In February 2002, for example, the Georgia Board of Pardons and Paroles commuted the death sentence of a convicted rapist and murderer on the grounds that he was delusional (note that he had not been found NGRI and that he had been on death row for nearly 16 years). What makes this case significant is that the person had been forced to take psychoactive medication that improved his mental condition enough to meet the federal standard that only a person who is legally sane can be executed (Weinstein, 2002).

A man named Daryl Atkins was sentenced to death in Virginia for a kidnapping and murder he committed in 1996. His IQ is rated at 59, which places him in the range of the moderately retarded. His defense attorney argued that his intellectual limitations render

this defense are diagnosable as having schizophrenia (or more generally, as psychotic), and DID is regarded as a dissociative disorder (and used to be classified as one of the neuroses). Can DID be an excusing condition for a criminal act? Should Jane Smith be held ascriptively responsible for a crime committed by her alter, Laura? The quandary is clearly evident in the title of an article that addresses the DID issue: "Who's on Trial?" (Appelbaum & Greer, 1994).

Consider the widely accepted legal principle that people accused of crimes should be punished only if they are blameworthy. The several court decisions and laws we have reviewed in this chapter all rest on this principle. In reviews of the DID literature and of its forensic implications, Elyn Saks (1992, 1997) of the University of Southern California Law Center argues that DID should be regarded as a special case in mental health law, that a new legal principle should be established, "irresponsibility by virtue of multiple personality disorder." Her argument takes issue with legal practice that would hold a person with DID ascriptively responsible for a crime as long as the personality acting at the time of the crime intended to commit it.

What is intriguing about Saks's argument is that she devotes a major portion of it to defining personhood. What is a person? Is a person the body we inhabit? Well, most of the time our sense of who we are as persons does not conflict with the bodies we have come to know as our own, or rather, as us. But in DID there is a discrepancy. The body that committed the crimes at the bank was Jane Smith. But it was her alter, Laura, who committed the crimes. Saks argues that, peculiar as it may sound, the law should be interested in the body only as a container for the person. It is the person who may or may not be blameworthy, not the body. Nearly all the time they are one and the same, but in the case of DID they are not. In a sense, Laura committed the murder by using Jane's body.

Then is Jane blameworthy? The person Jane did not commit the crime; she did not even know about it. For the judge to sentence Jane,

or more specifically, the body in the courtroom who usually goes by that name, would be unjust, argues Saks, for Jane is descriptively innocent. To be sure, sending Jane to prison would punish Laura, for whenever Laura would emerge, she would find herself imprisoned. But what of Jane? Saks concludes that it is unjust to imprison Jane because she is not blameworthy. Rather, we must find her not guilty by reason of dissociative identity disorder and remand her for treatment of the disorder.

Dissociative identity disorder would not, however, be a justification for a verdict of NGRI if the alter that did not commit the crime was aware of the other alter's criminal intent and did not do anything to prevent the criminal act. Under these circumstances, argues Saks, the first alter would be complicit in the crime and would therefore be somewhat blameworthy. A comparison Saks draws is to Robert Louis Stevenson's fictional character of Dr. Jekyll and Mr. Hyde. Jekyll made the potion that caused the emergence of Mr. Hyde, his alter, with the foreknowledge that Hyde would do evil. So even though Jekyll was not present when Hyde was in charge, he would nonetheless be blameworthy because of his prior knowledge of what Hyde would do—not to mention that he, Jekyll, has concocted the potion that created his alter, Hyde.

Saks is optimistic about the effectiveness of therapy for DID and believes that people like Jane/Laura can be integrated into one personality and then released to rejoin society. Saks goes so far as to argue that people with DID who are judged dangerous but who have not committed a crime should be subject to civil commitment, even though this would be tantamount to preventive detention. In this way, she suggests, future crimes might be avoided.*

---

*It should be recalled that a substantial number of mental health professionals dispute the existence of DID. For them Saks's arguments would not be persuasive.

capital punishment unconstitutional because he lacks understanding of the consequences of his actions and is therefore not as morally culpable for his acts as a person of normal intelligence. Eighteen of the 38 states that allow capital punishment already prohibit the execution of the mentally retarded on eighth amendment grounds against cruel and unusual punishment. The appeal to the U.S. Supreme Court may make this the law of the land (Cloud & Shepherd, 2002).

Civil Commitment

Historically, governments have had a duty to protect their citizens from harm. We take for granted the right and duty of government to set limits on our freedom for the sake of protecting us. Few drivers, for example, question the legitimacy of the state's imposing limits on them by providing traffic signals that often make them stop when they would rather go. Most people comply with the Food and Drug Administration when it bans uncontrolled use of drugs that cause cancer in laboratory animals, although some people feel they have the right to decide for themselves what risks to take with their own bodies. Government has a long-established right as well as an obligation to protect us both from ourselves—the *parens patriae*, "power of the state" —and from others—the police power of the state. Civil commitment is one further exercise of these powers.

In virtually all states a person can be committed to a psychiatric hospital against his or her will if a judgment is made that he or she is (1) mentally ill and (2) a danger to self—that is, unable to provide for the basic physical needs of food, clothing, and shelter—or a danger to others (Perlin, 1994). (There is also something called outpatient commitment, which we will describe later.) At present, dangerousness to others is more often the second criterion, and recent court rulings point to imminent dangerousness as the principal criterion (e.g., the person is right on the verge of committing a violent act).[22] In some states, a finding of imminent dangerousness must be evidenced by a recent overt act, attempt or threat; however, there are some states that do not require an overt act (In re Albright, 836 P.2d 1 [Kan. App. 1992]). Such commitment is supposed to last for only as long as the person remains dangerous.[23]

Specific commitment procedures generally fit into one of two categories, formal or informal. Formal or judicial commitment is by order of a court. It can be requested by any responsible citizen; usually the police, a relative, or a friend seeks the commitment. If the judge believes that there is a good reason to pursue the matter, he or she will order a mental health examination. The person has the right to object to these attempts to "certify" him or her, and a court hearing can be scheduled to allow the person to present evidence against commitment.

Informal, emergency commitment of mentally ill persons can be accomplished without initially involving the courts. For example, if a hospital administrative board believes that a voluntary patient requesting discharge is too disturbed and dangerous to be released, it is able to detain the patient with a temporary, informal commitment order.

Any person acting in an out-of-control, dangerous fashion may be taken immediately to a mental hospital by the police. Perhaps the most common informal commitment procedure is the 2PC, or two physicians' certificate. In most states, two physicians, not necessarily psychiatrists, can sign a certificate that allows a person to be incarcerated for some period of time, ranging from twenty-four hours to as long as twenty days. Detainment beyond this period requires formal judicial commitment.

Civil commitment affects far more people than criminal commitment. It is beyond the scope of this book to examine in detail the variety of state civil commitment laws and regulations; each state has its own, and they are in almost constant flux. Our aim is to present an overview that will provide a basic understanding of the issues and of current directions of change.

Preventive Detention and Problems in the Prediction of Dangerousness

The perception is widespread that mentally ill people account for a significant proportion of the violence that besets contemporary society, but this is not the case (Bonta, Law, & Hanson, 1998; Monahan, 1992). Only about 3 percent of the violence in the United States is clearly linked to mental illness (Swanson et al., 1990). Moreover, about 90 percent of people diagnosed as psychotic (primarily schizophrenic) are not violent (Swanson et al., 1990). Mentally ill persons—even allowing for their relatively small numbers—do not account for a large proportion of violent offenses, especially when compared with substance abusers and people who are in their teens and twenties, are male, and are poor (Mulvey, 1994). Indeed, one recent study suggests that former mental patients who are not substance abusers are no more likely to engage in violence than are non-mentally ill individuals who are not substance abusers. Thus, if substance abuse is not involved, mentally ill people are no more prone to violence than the average person. Also, when former patients do act aggressively, it is usually against family members or friends, and the incidents tend to occur at home (Steadman et al., 1998). By and large, then, the general public is seldom affected by violence from former mental patients.

---

[22] *Suzuki v. Yuen*, 617 F.2d 173 (9th Cir. 1980).

[23] *United States v. DeBellis*, 649 F.2d 1 (1st Cir. 1981).

Yet there is a strong connection in the public mind between violence and mental illness, and this belief is central to society's justification of civil commitment (Monahan & Shah, 1989; Steadman et al., 1998) as well as to the stigma attached to having been a patient in a psychiatric institution (Link et al., 1987; Steadman et al., 1998). And, in fact, there is some evidence that mental disorder may sometimes contribute to violence, enough so as to justify preventive detention. In the Steadman et al. (1998) study just mentioned, for example, substance abuse increased the chances of violent behavior more among discharged mental patients than among nonpatient controls. Let us examine the issues and the evidence.

The Prediction of Dangerousness   Civil commitment is necessarily a form of preventive detention; the prediction is made that a person judged mentally ill may in the future behave in a dangerous manner and should therefore be detained. But the entire U.S. legal and constitutional system is organized to protect people from preventive detention. Thus, unless mental illness comes into the picture, a person can generally be imprisoned only after having been found guilty of committing a crime (or, if accused and not yet convicted, denied bail if the crime was especially heinous and if the person poses a risk of leaving the jurisdiction to avoid trial). Furthermore, ordinary prisoners are routinely released from penitentiaries even though statistics show that most will commit additional crimes.

But what if a person openly threatens to inflict harm on others, such as an individual who for an hour each day stands in the street and shouts threats to people in a nearby apartment house? Does the state have to wait until the person acts on the threats? Usually not. In such a case the civil commitment process can be brought into play if the person is deemed not only an imminent danger to others but mentally ill as well (Perlin, 1994). Most mental health professionals, in agreement with laypeople, would conclude that a person has to be psychotic to behave in this way.

The likelihood of committing a dangerous act is central to civil commitment, but is dangerousness easily predicted? Early studies examining the accuracy of predictions that a person would commit a dangerous act found that mental health professionals were poor at making this judgment (e.g., Kozol, Boucher, & Garofalo, 1972; Monahan, 1973, 1976; Stone, 1975). Some researchers went on to argue that civil commitment for the purposes of preventive detention should be abolished. Monahan (1978), however, carefully scrutinized these studies and concluded that the ability to predict violence had not been adequately assessed. Most of the studies conformed to the following methodological pattern.

- People were institutionalized for mental illness and for being a danger to the community
- While these people were in the hospital, it was again predicted that some of them would be violent if they were released into the community
- After a period of time, these people were released, thus putting together the conditions for a natural experiment
- Checks on the behavior of the released patients over the next several years did not reveal much dangerous behavior

What is wrong with such research? Monahan pointed out that little if any consideration was given to changes that institutionalization itself might have effected. In the studies reviewed, the period of incarceration ranged from several months to fifteen years. Prolonged periods of enforced hospitalization might very well make patients more docile, if for no other reason than that they become that much older. Furthermore, conditions in the open community where the predicted violence would occur can vary widely. Thus we should not expect this kind of prediction to have great validity (Mischel, 1968; recall our discussion in Chapter 4 of the importance of situational control over behavior, p. 107).

Monahan reasoned that prediction of dangerousness is probably far easier and surer in true emergency situations than after extended periods of hospitalization. When an emergency commitment is sought, the person may appear out of control and may be threatening violence. He or she may also have been violent in the past—a good predictor of future violence—and victims and weapons may be on hand. A dangerous outburst seems imminent. In short, violence that requires an emergency commitment is expected almost immediately and in a known situation.

Common sense tells us that predictions of violence in such instances are likely to be very accurate. To test the validity of these expectations, however, we would have to leave alone half the people expected to be immediately violent and later compare their behavior with that of persons hospitalized in similar circumstances. Such an experiment would be ethically irresponsible. When experimental data are impossible to collect, mental health professionals must apply logic and make the most prudent judgments possible.

Reconsideration of earlier research suggests that greater accuracy can be achieved than previously assumed in predicting dangerousness in the longer term (Monahan, 1984; Monahan & Steadman, 1994; Steadman et al., 1998). Violence prediction is most accurate under the following conditions (note the role played by situational factors, sometimes in interaction with personality variables) (e.g., Campbell, Stefan, & Loder, 1994).

- If a person has been repeatedly violent in the recent past, it is reasonable to predict that he or she will be violent in the near future unless there have been major changes in the person's attitudes or environment. Thus, if a violent person is placed in a restrictive environment, such as a prison or high-security psychiatric hospital facility, he or she may well not be violent given the markedly changed environment.

- If violence is in the person's distant past, and if it was a single but very serious act, and if that person has been incarcerated for a period of time, then violence can be expected on release if there is reason to believe that the person's predetention personality and physical abilities have not changed and if the person is going to return to the same environment in which he or she was previously violent.

- Even with no history of violence, violence can be predicted if the person is judged to be on the brink of a violent act, for example, if the person is pointing a loaded gun at an occupied building.

In addition, as stated earlier, the presence of substance abuse significantly raises the rate of violence (Steadman et al., 1998). This finding supports including substance abuse as one of the factors to be considered when attempting to predict violence. (Substance abuse predicts violence also among non-mentally disordered individuals [Gendreau, Little, & Goggin, 1996].)

Violence in discharged mental patients is usually attributable to some of the individuals who do not take their medication as instructed (Monahan, 1992). **Outpatient commitment** is one way of increasing medication compliance. It is an arrangement whereby a patient is allowed to leave the hospital but must live in a halfway house or other supervised setting and report to a mental health agency frequently and regularly. To the extent that outpatient commitment increases compliance with medication regimens and with maintaining regular contact with mental health professionals—and evidence indicates that it does (Munetz et al., 1996)—we can expect violence from formerly hospitalized patients to be reduced. Indeed, support services, such as halfway houses, can markedly reduce the chances that a person who might otherwise be prone to committing a violent act will actually commit one (Dvoskin & Steadman, 1994).

Preventive Detention and Sex Offenders   One example of preventive detention is provided by laws passed in seven states that enable some repeat and dangerous sex offenders to be deemed mentally ill when they are about to be released from prison and then to be civilly committed to a prison hospital for an indefinite period until treatment cures them of their presumed illness. Although this appears to some legal scholars to be unconstitutional—detaining a person for a crime that he or she *may* commit in the future—many argue that it makes sense to keep sexual predators out of society.

Proponents of these laws, usually called sexually violent predator acts, point to rapists and child molesters with long histories of recidivism. Based on past experience and sometimes on comments made by the prisoners themselves (e.g., one man said that the only way to keep him from victimizing children on his release would be to execute him), the probability may be high that such prisoners will harm people after their release. Should they not be prevented from doing so?

In 1997 the Supreme Court ruled that such preventive detention is in fact constitutional.[24] Even though we don't detain other kinds of criminals when they have served their time because of the likelihood that they will be recidivists, if a person is deemed mentally ill and dangerous, he or she can be civilly committed, as we have already discussed (p. 622). This feature of civil commitment laws allows sexual predator laws to stand. However, the Supreme Court decision remains controversial (Dorsett, 1998; Gould, 1998; Pollack, 1998). (For a discussion of therapists' responsibilities to predict dangerousness, see Focus on Discovery 18.4.)

Recent Trends Toward Greater Protection

The United States Constitution is a remarkable document. It lays down the basic duties of elected federal officials and guarantees a set of civil rights. But there is often some distance between the abstract delineation of a civil right and its day-to-day implementation. Moreover, judges must interpret the Constitution as it bears on specific contemporary problems. Since nowhere in this cornerstone of U.S. democracy is there specific mention of committed mental patients, lawyers and judges interpret various sections of the document to justify what they consider necessary in society's treatment of people whose mental health is in question (Table 18.2).

In 1972 voluntary admissions to mental hospitals began to outnumber involuntary admissions. But a great number of people are still admitted and retained against their wishes, and it is impossible to know how many of those who admit themselves voluntarily do so under threat of civil commitment. One early survey (Gilboy & Schmidt, 1971) revealed that 40 percent of patients who had "voluntarily" admitted themselves to a psychiatric hospital in Chicago had actually been threatened with commitment by the police officers who had taken them there. The issue of enforced hospitalization is still very much with us. Even though psychiatrists, psychologists, the courts, and hospital staff are growing more reluctant to commit, tens of thousands of mentally ill patients are in hospitals against their will.

In a democratic society the most grievous wrong that can be suffered by a citizen is loss of liberty. The rights accorded to ordinary citizens, and even to criminals, are gradually being extended to those threatened with civil commitment and to those who have been involuntarily hospitalized. It is no longer assumed that deprivation of liberty for purposes of mental health care is a reason to deny to the individual his or her other rights.

For example, a 1976 federal court decision in Wisconsin, *Lessard* v. *Schmidt*,[25] gives a person threatened with civil commitment the right to timely written notice of the proceeding, opportunity for a hearing with counsel, the right to have the hearing decided by jury, Fifth Amendment protection against self-incrimination, and other similar procedural safeguards already accorded defendants in criminal actions, including being present at any hearing to decide the need for commitment.[26] Such protections are to be provided even under emergency commitment conditions.[27] A 1979 Supreme Court decision, *Addington* v. *Texas*[28], further provides that the state must produce clear and convincing evidence that a person is mentally ill and dangerous before he or she can be involuntarily committed to a psychiatric hospital. In 1980 the Ninth Circuit Court of Appeals ruled that this danger must be imminent.[29] Clearly the intent is to restrict the state's power to curtail individual freedoms because of mental illness. Although protection of the rights

---

[24] *Kansas v. Hendricks*, 117 S.Ct. 2072 (1997).

[25] *Lessard v. Schmidt*, 349 F.Supp. 1078 (E.D. Wisc. 1972), vacated and remanded on other grounds, 94 S.Ct. 713 (1974), reinstated in 413 F.Supp. 1318 (E.D. Wisc. 1976).

[26] *In Re: Lawaetz* 728 F.2d 225 (3d Cir. 1984).

[27] *Doremus v. Farrell*, 407 F.Supp. 509 (1975).

[28] *Addington v. Texas*, 441 U.S. 418 (1979).

[29] *Suzuki v. Yuen*, 617 F.2d at 173.

Table 18.2 Major Issues and Trends in Civil Commitment

Preventive Detention and Predicting Dangerousness

How good are we at knowing how likely it is that a person will do something dangerous either to others or to himself or herself? How good does the prediction have to be to justify a suspension of that individual's civil right of being presumed innocent until proven guilty? An especially difficult issue because as a group, mental patients are no more violent than people not diagnosed with a mental illness.

Recent Trends in Protecting Patients' Rights

Clear evidence required that a person is both mentally ill and dangerous before being committed

Least restrictive treatment and setting necessary to provide therapy and protect the patient and the public

Right to adequate treatment and confinement settings

Right to refuse treatment, even if the best professional judgment is that a given intervention will ultimately enhance the patient's freedom

The Tarasoff Case—The Duty to Warn and to Protect

The client's right to privileged communication—the legal right of a client to require that what goes on in therapy remain confidential—is an important protection, but it is not absolute. Society has long stipulated certain conditions in which confidentiality in a relationship should not be maintained because of the harm that can befall others. A famous California court ruling in 1974[*] described circumstances in which a therapist not only may but *must* breach the sanctity of a client's communication. First, what appear to be the facts in the case:

> In the fall of 1968, Prosenjit Poddar, a graduate student from India studying at the University of California at Berkeley, met Tatiana (Tanya) Tarasoff at a folk dancing class. They saw each other weekly during the fall, and on New Year's Eve she kissed him. Poddar interpreted this act as a sign of formal engagement (as it might have been in India, where he was a member of the Harijam or "untouchable caste"). [But] Tanya told him that she was involved with other men, and indicated that she did not wish to have an intimate relationship with him.
>
> Poddar was depressed as a result of the rebuff, but he saw Tanya a few times during the spring (occasionally tape recording their conversations in an effort to understand why she did not love him). Tanya left for Brazil in the summer, and Poddar at the urging of a friend went to the student health facility where a psychiatrist referred him to a psychologist for psychotherapy. When Tanya returned in October 1969, Poddar discontinued therapy. Based in part on Poddar's stated intention to purchase a gun, the psychologist notified the campus police, both orally and in writing, that Poddar was dangerous and should be taken to a community mental health center for psychiatric commitment.
>
> The campus police interviewed Poddar, who seemed rational and promised to stay away from Tanya. They released him and notified the health service. No further efforts at commitment were made because the supervising psychiatrist apparently decided that such was not needed and, as a matter of confidentiality, requested that the letter to the police as well as certain therapy records be destroyed.
>
> On October 27, Poddar went to Tanya's home armed with a pellet gun and a kitchen knife. She refused to speak to him. He shot her with the pellet gun. She ran from the house, was pursued, caught, and repeatedly and fatally stabbed by him. Poddar was found guilty of voluntary manslaughter rather than first- or second-degree murder. The defense established with the aid of the expert testimony of three psychiatrists that Poddar's diminished mental capacity, paranoid schizophrenia, precluded the malice necessary for first- or second-degree murder. After his prison term, he returned to India, where, according to his own report, he is happily married. (Schwitzgebel & Schwitzgebel, 1980, p. 205)

Under the privileged communication statute of California, the counseling center psychologist properly breached the confidentiality of the professional relationship and took steps to have Poddar civilly committed, for he judged Poddar to be an imminent danger. Poddar had stated that he intended to purchase a gun, and by his other words and actions he had convinced the therapist that he was desperate enough to harm Tarasoff. What the psychologist did not do, and what the court decided he should have done, was to warn the likely victim, Tanya Tarasoff, that her former friend had bought a gun and might use it against her. Such a warning would have been consistent with previous court decisions requiring physicians to warn the public when they are treating people with contagious diseases and requiring mental institutions to warn others when a dangerous patient has escaped (Knapp & Vandecreek, 1982). Or, as stated by the California Supreme Court in *Tarasoff*: "Once a therapist does in fact determine, or under applicable professional standards reasonably should have determined, that a patient poses a serious danger of violence to others, he bears a duty to exercise reasonable care to protect the foreseeable victims of that danger." The *Tarasoff* ruling, now being applied in other states as well,[†] requires clinicians, in deciding when to violate confidentiality, to use the very imperfect skill of predicting dangerousness.

Extending Protection to Foreseeable Victims

A subsequent California court ruling[‡] held by a bare majority that foreseeable victims include those in close relationship to the identifiable victim. In this instance a mother was hurt by a shotgun fired by the dangerous patient, and her seven-year-old son was present when the shooting took place. The boy later sued the psychologists for damages brought on by emotional trauma. Since a young child is likely to be in the company of his or her mother, the court concluded in *Hedlund* that the *Tarasoff* ruling extended to the boy.

Chilling Effect of Tarasoff?

In the years since the *Tarasoff* ruling, health professionals have wondered whether it would have a negative effect, perhaps even a chilling effect, on psychotherapists. If clients are informed of this limitation to the confidentiality of what they say to their therapists, they may become reluctant to express feelings of extreme anger to therapists for fear that therapists will notify the people with whom they are angry. Clients might become less open with their therapists, perhaps derive less benefit from therapy, and even become more likely to inflict harm on others if they have not disclosed their fury as a first step toward controlling it. The welfare of the people whom the *Tarasoff* decision intended to protect might be endangered by the very ruling itself! It is unclear whether these concerns are well-founded.

A survey of more than 1,200 psychologists and psychiatrists in California soon after Tarasoff became law indicated that the court decision was affecting their thinking and practices (Wise, 1978). On the plus side, one-third reported consulting more often with colleagues

---

[*] *Tarasoff v. Regents of the University of California*, 529 P.2d 553 (Cal. 1974), vacated, reheard in bank, and affirmed, 131 Cal. Rptr. 14, 551 P.2d 334 (1976). The 1976 California Supreme Court ruling was by a four-to-three majority.

[†] *White v. United States*, 780 F.2d 97 (D.C. Cir. 1986); *Soutear v. United States*, 646 F.Supp. 524 (1986); *Dunkle v. Food Services East Inc.*, 582 A.2d 1342 (1990); *People v. Clark*, 50 Cal. 3d 583, 789 P.2d 127 (1990).

[‡] *Hedlund v. Superior Court*, 34 Cal.3d 695 (1983).

concerning cases in which violence was an issue. This practice should have a good outcome, since input from other professionals may improve the solitary clinician's decision making, presumably to the benefit of the client. (Consultation can also demonstrate that the clinician took extra steps to adhere to *Tarasoff*, which can reduce legal liability if the patient later harms someone [Monahan, 1993]). On the minus side, about 20 percent of the respondents indicated that they avoided asking their clients questions about violence, an ostrich-like stance that may keep the clinician from obtaining important information and may reduce his or her legal liability should the client harm another person. A substantial number of therapists were keeping less detailed records, again in an effort to reduce legal liability.

Thirty years later, the emerging picture is that *Tarasoff* has not hobbled the practice of psychotherapy. Therapists seem to be managing to balance the rights of others with respect for the confidentiality of their patients (Mangalmurti, 1991). Psychotherapists in other countries are not as yet bound by such rulings. For example, in the United Kingdom, no such duty to warn or to protect has been placed on therapists, but that could change (Kennedy & Jones, 1995).

Extending Protection Further to Potential Victims

A 1983 decision of a federal circuit court in California[§] extended *Tarasoff* still further. The court ruled that Veterans Administration psychiatrists should earlier have warned the murdered lover of an outpatient, Phillip Jablonski, that she was a foreseeable victim, even though the patient had never made an explicit threat against her to the therapists. The reasoning was that Jablonski, having previously raped and otherwise harmed his wife, would likely direct his continuing "violence…against women very close to him" (p. 392).

The court also found the hospital psychiatrists negligent in not obtaining Jablonski's earlier medical records. These records showed a history of harmful violent behavior, which, together with the threats his lover was complaining about, should have moved the hospital to institute emergency civil commitment. The court ruled that the failure to warn was a proximate or immediate cause of the woman's murder. Proper consideration of the medical records, said the judge, would have convinced the psychiatrists that Jablonski was a real danger to others and should be committed.

This broadening of the duty to warn and protect has placed mental health professionals in California in an even more difficult predicament, for the potentially violent patient need not even mention the specific person he or she may harm. It is up to the therapist to deduce who are possible victims, based on what he or she can learn of the patient's

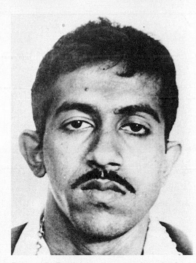

Prosenjit Poddar was convicted of manslaughter in the death of Tatiana Tarasoff. The court ruled that his therapist, who had become convinced Poddar might harm Tarasoff, should have warned her of the impending danger.

past and present circumstances. Ironically, Jablonski's lover realized that she was in danger; she had moved out of the apartment she was sharing with him and had complained to her priest and to the Veterans Administration psychiatrists themselves that she feared for her safety. One of the psychiatrists had even advised her to leave Jablonski, at least while he was being evaluated at the medical center. But "when [she] responded, 'I love him,' [the psychiatrist] did not warn her further because he believed she would not listen to him" (p. 393). The court found this warning "totally unspecific and inadequate under the circumstances" (p. 398).

Extending Protection to Property

Tarasoff was further extended by a Vermont State Supreme Court ruling, *Peck v. Counseling Service of Addison County*,[||] which held that a mental health practitioner has a duty to warn a third party if there is a danger of damage to property. The case involved a twenty-nine-year-old male patient who, after a heated argument with his father, told his therapist that he wanted to get back at his father and indicated that he might do so by burning down his father's barn. He proceeded to do just that. No people or animals were harmed in the fire; the barn housed no animals and was located 130 feet away from the parents' home. The court's conclusion that the therapist had a duty to warn was based on reasoning that arson is a violent act and therefore a lethal threat to people who may be in the vicinity of the fire. This ruling can be seen as an expansion of the Hedlund court decision as well; whereas Hedlund speaks of humans who may be at risk because of possible physical proximity to the endangered victim, Peck speaks of humans who could be harmed via threat to an inanimate object.

Extending Protection to Potential Victims as Yet Unknown

Many courts have augmented the duty to warn and protect to foreseeable victims of child abuse and even to possible victims as yet unknown. In one such case,[#] a medical student underwent a training analysis as one of the requirements to become a psychoanalyst. During the therapy he admitted that he was a pedophile. Later in his training he saw a male child as a patient as part of his psychiatric residency and sexually assaulted the boy. The court decided that the training analyst, who was not just the student's therapist but an instructor in the school, had reason to know that his patient-student "posed a specific threat to a specific group of persons, namely future minor patients, with whom [the student] would necessarily interact as part of his training" (p. 8). Even though, at the time the student revealed his pedophilia he did not have child patients (and

---

[§] *Jablonski by Pahls v. United States*, 712 F.2d 391 (1983).

[||] *Peck v. Counseling Service of Addison County*, 499 A.2d 422 (Vt. 1985).

[#] *Almonte v. New York Medical College*, 851 F. Supp. 34, 40 (D. Conn. 1994) (denying motion for summary judgment).

thus there were no specific people whom the instructor could warn and take steps to protect), the supervisor—as his instructor, not just his therapist—was judged to have sufficient control over the student's professional training and activities (specifically, the power to keep the student from pursuing his interests in working with children) for the *Tarasoff* ruling to be relevant. The court decided that the supervisor could have and therefore should have "redirect[ed the student's] professional development without even compromising the confidentiality of [the student's] disclosures to him" (p. 8). Instead, the supervisor and, by virtue of his faculty status, the medical school in which he worked allowed the patient-student to pursue his interests in child psychiatry, which resulted in the sexual molestation of a child patient.

HIV and Tarasoff

Consider now the situation of a therapist who is treating an HIV-positive patient who has not disclosed his or her seropositive status to a partner and continues to engage in unsafe sex with that person. Where do the therapist's responsibilities lie? Emerging guidelines from professional associations such as the American Psychiatric Association support the therapist's breaking confidentiality as mandated by *Tarasoff* if the therapist is not successful in convincing the patient to disclose his or her status or engage in safer sexual behavior (American Psychiatric Association, 1992). This position is consistent with long-standing professional rules that require physicians to notify others of a patient's infectious disease so as to protect the public. The likelihood that the person is seropositive because of infidelity makes such actions fraught with difficulty for the patient's relationship with loved ones.

A relevant factor may be the mental competence of the patient. Some people who are HIV positive or have AIDS have impairments in their judgment and reasoning processes, which may prevent them from fully understanding the dangers their seropositive status poses to others through unsafe sex or needle sharing. Under such conditions especially, health professionals may have the legal and ethical duty to follow *Tarasoff* (Searight & Pound, 1994). Some states have enacted statutes that impose a duty to warn, whereas other states do not have a duty to warn but instead provide immunity (protection from prosecution or lawsuit) to health care providers if they decide to warn (Gostin & Hodge, 1998). We can expect considerable debate on this issue in years to come.

Tarasoff—Perhaps not as Worrisome as We Thought

As problematic as *Tarasoff* and associated rulings may be for the mental health professions, the situation may not be as worrisome as it originally appeared. When the 1974 *Tarasoff* ruling was reaffirmed in 1976 by the California Supreme Court, the duty to warn was broadened to a duty to protect (see the earlier quotation from the 1976 decision), and it is this seemingly slight change that makes it possible for practitioners to adhere to *Tarasoff* without necessarily breaking confidentiality, that is, without having always to warn a potential victim. As Appelbaum (1985) pointed out, clinicians can undertake such preventive measures as increased frequency of sessions, initiation of or changes in psychotropic medication, and, in general, closer supervision of the patient. He suggested further that if such measures are judged reasonable, the therapist is unlikely to be held liable if the patient does ultimately harm somebody.

One strategy described by Appelbaum involved an eighteen-year-old patient who threatened during a session that he would beat up his landlady for not permitting her son to associate with him. On the basis of other information about the patient, the therapist determined that *Tarasoff* was relevant. He decided to involve the patient in the discussion, explaining his legal responsibility to protect a potential victim but also his reluctance to break therapeutic confidentiality. He presented to the patient the choice between hospitalization (the patient was indeed sometimes psychotic) and warning the landlady. The patient preferred to stay out of the hospital and did not object to the therapist's calling the landlady. When the landlady was called, she told the therapist that the young man had threatened her previously and that she knew how to take care of herself. In other words, she did not take the threats seriously. Appelbaum observed that the patient's threats seemed to be manipulative—he succeeded in once again issuing a verbal threat to his landlady, this time through his psychotherapist. But the psychotherapist succeeded in involving the patient in the decision making as well as preserving trust in the therapeutic relationship.

As anxiety-provoking as *Tarasoff* can be to clinicians, it does not call for therapists to reflexively pick up the phone to call a possible victim whenever a patient expresses a threat. Many other responsible options are available, such as directly asking the patient or relatives whether he or she has previously assaulted someone and taking care to check hospital records of a potentially dangerous patient (Monahan, 1993).

of mentally ill individuals adds tremendously to the burden of both civil courts and state and county mental-hospital staffs, it is a price a free society must pay.

> *Given the record…of legal commitment used to warehouse American citizens, it is…important that the individual feel sure that the [present] mental health system [in particular] cannot be so used and abused…for while the average citizen may have some confidence that if called by the Great Inquisitor in the middle of the night and charged with a given robbery, he may have an alibi or be able to prove his innocence, he may be far less certain of his capacity, under the press of fear, to instantly prove his sanity.* (Stone, 1975, p. 57)

We turn now to a discussion of several issues and trends that revolve around the greater protections being provided to mental patients in recent years: the principle of the least restrictive alternative; the right to treatment; the right to refuse treatment; questions of free will in the law; and, finally, the way in which these several themes conflict in efforts to provide humane mental-health treatment while respecting individual rights. We shall see that competing interests operate to create a complex and continually changing picture.

Least Restrictive Alternative   As noted earlier, civil commitment rests on presumed dangerousness, a condition that may vary depending on the circumstances. A person may be deemed dangerous if living in an apartment by himself or herself, but not dangerous if living in a boarding home and taking prescribed psychoactive drugs every day under medical supervision. The least restrictive alternative to freedom is to be provided when treating disturbed people and protecting them from harming themselves and others. A number of court rulings require that only those mentally ill patients who cannot be adequately looked after in less restrictive homes be confined in hospitals.[30] Thus, commitment is no longer necessarily in an institution. As mentioned earlier, a patient might well be required to reside in a supervised boarding home or in other sheltered quarters under an outpatient commitment arrangement. In general terms, mental health professionals have to provide the treatment that restricts the patient's liberty to the least possible degree while remaining workable.[31] It is unconstitutional to confine a nondangerous mentally ill patient who is capable of surviving on his or her own or with the help of willing and responsible family or friends.[32] Of course, this principle will have meaning only if society provides suitable residences and treatments, which rarely happens.

Least restrictive alternatives were supposed to be created when the deinstitutionalization movement took hold in the 1970s, but since the virtual cessation of federal funding for community mental health centers and other nonhospital placements in the 1980s, U.S. society has been faced with a growing number of people, usually ex–mental hospital patients, who are no longer dangerous and yet in need of more care than is available outside a hospital. Turkheimer and Parry (1992) argue that an awareness of the scarcity of less restrictive alternatives has led to rather perfunctory protection of civil rights (e.g., attorneys may not argue vigorously against commitment) and to commitment of people even when they are not judged dangerous.

Right to Treatment   Another aspect of civil commitment that has come to the attention of the courts is the so-called right to treatment, a principle first articulated by Birnbaum (1960). If a person is deprived of liberty because he or she is mentally ill and is a danger to self or others, is the state not required to provide treatment to alleviate these problems? Is it not unconstitutional (and even indecent) to incarcerate someone without afterward providing the help he or she is supposed to need? This important question has been the subject of several court cases since Birnbaum first articulated the issue.

The right to treatment has gained in legal status since the 1960s and was extended to all civilly committed patients in a landmark 1972 case, *Wyatt v. Stickney*.[33] In that case an Alabama federal court ruled that the only justification for the civil commitment of patients to a state mental hospital is treatment. As stated by Judge Frank Johnson, "to deprive any citizen of his or her liberty upon the altruistic theory that the confinement is for humane and therapeutic reasons and then fail to provide adequate treatment violates the very fundamentals of due process." Committed mental patients "have a constitutional right to receive such individual treatment as will give each of them a realistic opportunity to be cured or to improve his or her mental condition." This ruling, upheld on appeal, is frequently cited as ensuring protection of people confined by civil commitment, at least to the extent that the state cannot simply put them away without meeting minimal standards of care. In fact, when mentally retarded patients (as opposed to those judged to be mentally ill) are released from an institution, health officials are not relieved of their constitutional duty to provide reasonable care and safety as well as appropriate training.[34]

The *Wyatt* ruling was significant, for previously the courts had asserted that it was beyond their competence to pass judgment on the care given to mentally ill patients, and

Civil commitment supposedly requires that the person be dangerous. But in actual practice the decision to commit can be based on a judgment of severe disability, as in the case of some people who are homeless.

---

[30] *Lake v. Cameron*, 267 F. Supp 155 (D.C. Cir. 1967); Lessard, 349 F. Supp. at 1078.

[31] *In Re: Tarpley*, 556 N.E.2d, superseded by 581 N.E.2d 1251 (1991).

[32] *Project Release v. Prevost*, 722 F.2d 960 (2d Cir. 1983).

[33] *Wyatt v. Stickney*, 325 F.Supp. 781 (M.D. Ala. 1971), enforced in 334 F.Supp. 1341 (M.D. Ala. 1971), 344 F.Supp. 373, 379 (M.D. Ala. 1972), aff'd sub nom *Wyatt v. Anderholt*, 503 F.2d 1305 (5th Cir. 1974).

[34] *Thomas S. v. Flaherty*, 902 F.2d 250, cert. denied, 111 S.Ct. 373 (1990).

they had assumed that mental health professionals possessed special and exclusive knowledge about psychopathology and its treatment. Repeated reports of abuses, however, gradually prodded the U.S. judicial system to rule on what goes on within the walls of mental institutions. The *Wyatt* decision set forth very specific requirements—dayrooms of at least forty square feet; curtains or screens for privacy in multipatient bedrooms; bedrooms limited to a maximum of five persons; a comfortable bed; one toilet per eight persons; the right of the patient to wear any clothing he or she wishes, provided it is not deemed dangerous; opportunities to interact with members of the opposite sex; and no physical restraints except in emergency situations. Further, to provide care twenty-four hours a day, seven days a week, there should be, for every 250 patients, at least two psychiatrists, three additional physicians, twelve registered nurses, ninety attendants, four psychologists, and seven social workers. When the *Wyatt* action was taken, Alabama state mental facilities averaged one physician per 2,000 patients, an extreme situation indeed.[35] The Wyatt requirements are still good law, and similar protections have been extended to people with mental retardation.[36]

The trend of the *Wyatt* ruling may have been weakened by a later Supreme Court decision, *Youngberg* v. *Romeo*,[37] regarding the treatment of a mentally retarded boy, Nicholas Romeo, who had been placed in physical restraints on occasion to keep him from hurting himself and others. While maintaining that patients have a right to reasonable care and safety, this 1982 decision deferred to the professional judgment of the mental health professionals responsible for the boy: "courts must show deference to the judgment exercised by a qualified professional…the decision, if made by a professional, is presumptively valid" (pp. 322, 323). This decision thus gives more leeway to mental health professionals than the *Wyatt* ruling did. On the other hand, the 1990 *Thomas S.* v. *Flaherty* decision held that professional judgment is not the final word when it comes to constitutional protections of mentally retarded patients in public mental hospitals. The situation seems to be in flux.

In a celebrated case, *O'Connor* v. *Donaldson*,[38] which eventually went to the Supreme Court in 1975, a civilly committed mental patient sued two state hospital doctors for his release and for monetary damages on the grounds that he had been incarcerated against his will for fourteen years without being treated and without being dangerous to himself or to others. In January 1957, at the age of forty-nine, Kenneth Donaldson was committed to the Florida state hospital at Chattahoochee on petition of his father, who felt that his son was delusional. At a brief court hearing a county judge found that Donaldson had paranoid schizophrenia and committed him for "care, maintenance, and treatment." The Florida statute then in effect allowed for such commitment on the usual grounds of mental illness and dangerousness, the latter defined as inability to manage property and to protect oneself from being taken advantage of by others.

In 1971, Donaldson sued Dr. O'Connor, the hospital superintendent, and Dr. Gumanis, a hospital psychiatrist, for release. Evidence presented at the trial in a U.S. district court in Florida indicated that the hospital staff could have released Donaldson at any time following a determination that he was not a dangerous person. Testimony made it clear that at no time during his hospitalization had Donaldson's conduct posed any real danger to others or to himself. Furthermore, just before his commitment in 1957 he had been earning a living and taking adequate care of himself (and immediately on discharge he secured a job in hotel administration). Nonetheless, O'Connor had repeatedly refused the patient's requests for release, feeling it was his duty to determine whether a committed patient could adapt successfully outside the institution. His judgment was that

---

[35] The underlying assumption is that patients civilly committed to public mental hospitals will receive adequate care, but the evidence for this level of care is weak. Even though the extremely negligent conditions that the *Wyatt* decision remedied in Alabama are seldom found today, it is questionable, argued Morse (1982c), whether forced hospitalization benefits patients. At the very least, however, public mental hospitals can provide shelter, food, protection, and custodial care, which many deinstitutionalized patients lack.

[36] *Feagley* v. *Waddill*, 868 F.2d 1437 (5th Cir. 1989).

[37] *Youngberg* v. *Romeo*, 102 S.Ct. 2452 (1982).

[38] *O'Connor* v. *Donaldson*, 95 S.Ct. 2486 (1975).

Donaldson could not. In deciding the question of dangerousness on the basis of how well the patient could live outside the institution, O'Connor was applying a more restrictive standard than that required by most state laws.

Several responsible people had attempted to obtain Donaldson's release by guaranteeing that they would look after him. In 1963 a halfway house formally requested that Donaldson be released to its care, and between 1964 and 1968 a former college classmate made four separate attempts to have the patient released to his custody. O'Connor refused, saying that the patient could be released only to his parents, who by this time were quite old.

The evidence indicated that Donaldson received only custodial care during his hospitalization. No treatment that could conceivably alleviate or cure his assumed mental illness was undertaken. The milieu therapy that O'Connor claimed Donaldson was undergoing consisted of being kept in a large room with sixty other patients, many of whom were under criminal commitment. Donaldson had been denied privileges to stroll around the hospital grounds or even to discuss his case with Dr. O'Connor. O'Connor also regarded as delusional Donaldson's expressed desire to write a book about his hospital experiences (which Donaldson did after his release; the book sold well).

The original trial and a subsequent appeal concluded that Donaldson was not dangerous and had been denied his constitutional right to treatment, based on the Fifth Amendment. Throughout this litigation Donaldson declared that he was neither dangerous nor mentally ill. But, went his claim, even if he were mentally ill, he should be released because he was not receiving treatment.

The Supreme Court ruled on June 26, 1975, that "a State cannot constitutionally confine…a nondangerous individual who is capable of surviving safely in freedom by himself or with the help of willing and responsible family members or friends." In 1977, Donaldson settled for $20,000 from Dr. Gumanis and from the estate of Dr. O'Connor, who had died during the appeals process.

Kenneth Donaldson, displaying a copy of the Supreme Court opinion stating that nondangerous mental patients cannot be confined against their will under civil commitment.

The Supreme Court decision on *O'Connor v. Donaldson* created a stir when it was issued and has since given mental health professionals pause in detaining patients. Although this decision is often cited as yet another affirmation of the right to treatment, the Supreme Court did not, in fact, rule on the constitutionality of this doctrine. Indeed, Chief Justice Warren E. Burger issued some warnings about the right to treatment.

> *Given the present state of medical knowledge regarding abnormal behavior and its treatment, few things would be more fraught with peril than [for] a State's power to protect the mentally ill [to depend on its ability to provide] such treatment as will give them a realistic opportunity to be cured. Nor can I accept the theory that a State may lawfully confine an individual thought to need treatment and justify that deprivation of liberty solely by providing such treatment. Our concepts of due process would not tolerate such a "trade off." (O'Connor v. Donaldson, pp. 588–589)*

The Donaldson decision did say that a committed patient's status must be periodically reviewed, for the grounds on which a patient was committed cannot be assumed to continue in effect forever. In other words, people can change while in a mental hospital and may no longer require confinement. This position seems straightforward enough, yet it may still be overlooked. For example, a 1986 court decision involved a woman with mental retardation who had spent her entire adult life in a state institution for the retarded after having been committed at age fifteen; during her twenty years of confinement she was never given a hearing to reconsider the grounds for the original commitment.[39]

---

[39] *Clark v. Cohen*, 794 F.2d 79, cert. denied, 479 U.S. 962 (1986).

Right to Refuse Treatment If a committed patient has the right to expect appropriate treatment, since the need for help has resulted in loss of freedom, does he or she have the right to refuse treatment or a particular kind of treatment? The answer is yes, albeit with qualifications. Let us examine this thorny issue.

A state hospital may have adequate staff to provide up-to-date chemotherapy as well as group therapy but lack the professional resources to offer individual therapy. Suppose that a patient refuses the available modalities and insists on individual therapy. Would the patient later be able to sue the hospital for not offering the specific services requested? If the patient has the right to refuse certain forms of treatment, how far should the courts go in ensuring this right, remaining at the same time realistic about the state's ability to provide alternatives? When should the judgment of a professional override the wishes of a patient, especially one who is severely psychotic? Are the patient's best interests always served if he or she can veto the plans of those responsible for care (Stone, 1975; Winick, 1994), especially if refusing to take a therapeutic drug keeps a criminal defendant from being considered competent to stand trial (Winick, 1993) (recall the *Riggins* v. *Nevada* case discussed earlier, p. 618)? Does the right to refuse treatment mean that patients have the freedom to "rot with their rights on" (Appelbaum & Gutheil, 1980)?

The right of committed patients to refuse psychoactive drugs is hotly debated. Although somatic therapies such as electroconvulsive therapy and psychosurgery have for some time been subject to judicial review and control, only recently has close attention been paid to drugs used with patients in mental institutions. Significant legal and ethical issues surround the use of psychoactive medications (and such drugs are often the only kind of treatment a patient in a state hospital receives with any regularity). The side effects of most antipsychotic drugs are often aversive to the patient and are sometimes harmful and irreversible in the long run. Moreover, the drugs do not truly address all of the patient's psychosocial problems (see the discussion of negative symptoms on p. 344), and about one-third of the patients who take psychoactive drugs do not benefit from them.

Some court decisions illustrate the difficult issues that arise when the right to refuse treatment is debated. In a 1979 decision on some cases in which "unjustified polypharmacy" and "force or intimidation" had allegedly been applied without due consideration for the serious negative side effects of drugs, the judge in a New Jersey federal district court concluded that drugs can actually inhibit recovery and that therefore, except in emergencies, even an involuntarily committed patient can refuse to take them, based on the rights of privacy (First Amendment) and due process (Fourteenth Amendment).[40] The judge ordered that advocates be available in each state mental hospital to help patients exercise the right to refuse treatment and that a listing of all the side effects of the drugs that might be given to the patients be posted in each hospital ward. In a reconsideration of this case, however, the judge stated that the opinion of the health professional must take precedence over the right to refuse treatment when patients are a danger to themselves or to others, in other words, in emergency situations.[41]

The question of the right to refuse medication continues to be the subject of lawsuits on behalf of both involuntary and voluntary mental hospital patients. Decisions on behalf of patients judged incompetent are frequently made by the hospital's professional staff. Although there is inconsistency across jurisdictions and the forensic picture is still developing, there is a trend toward granting even involuntarily committed patients certain rights to refuse psychoactive medication, based on the constitutional protections of freedom from physical invasion, freedom of thought, and the right to privacy.[42] In an extension of the least-restrictive-treatment principle, the court in *United States* v. *Charters* ruled that the government cannot force antipsychotic drugs on a person only on the supposition that at some future time he or she might become dangerous. Threat to the public safety has to be clear and imminent to justify the risks and restrictions that such med-

---

[40] *Rennie v. Klein*, Civil Action No. 77-2624, Federal District Court of New Jersey, 14 September 1979.

[41] *Rennie v. Klein*, 720 F.2d 266 (3d Cir. 1983).

[42] *United States v. Charters*, 829 F.2d 479 (1987); *United States v. Watson*, 893 F.2d 970 (1990).

ications pose, and it must be shown that less intrusive intervention will not likely reduce impending danger to others. In other words, forcible medication necessarily restricts liberty in addition to whatever physical risks it could bring; there has to be a very good reason to deprive even a committed mental patient of liberty and privacy via such intrusive measures.

The hands of mental health professionals are not tied, though. For example, it was ruled in a 1987 case that forcing a psychoactive drug on a former mental patient did not violate his constitutional rights because he had been threatening to assassinate the president of the United States, he posed a threat to his own safety, and he could be shown by clear and convincing evidence to be seriously mentally impaired.[43] Decisions of health professionals are, however, subject to judicial review.[44]

Opponents of the right to refuse treatment are concerned that mental hospitals will revert to being warehouses of poorly treated patients. Psychiatrists fear that lawyers and judges will not accept that some people are too mentally deranged to be believed, too mentally disturbed to be able to make sound judgments about their treatment. In a book on what he calls America's mental health crisis, psychiatrist E. Fuller Torrey asserts that upwards of 90 percent of psychotic patients have no insight into their condition. Believing that they do not need any treatment, they subject themselves and their loved ones to sometimes desperate and frightening situations by refusing medication or other modes of therapy, most of which involve hospitalization (Torrey, 1996).

When someone already hospitalized is believed to be too psychotic to give informed consent about a treatment, mental health law sometimes invokes the doctrine of substituted judgment, the decision that the patient would have made if he or she had been able or competent to make a decision.[45] This principle creates as many problems as it solves. Deciding when a patient is competent to refuse treatment is one of the most controversial topics in the mental health law literature (e.g., Appelbaum & Grisso, 1995; Grisso & Appelbaum, 1995; Winick, 1997).

To complicate matters even further, recent research findings indicate that most committed patients, although showing impairment in their ability to think and make decisions, nonetheless demonstrate enough legally relevant abilities to be considered competent to participate in treatment decisions. Specifically, they show an ability to state a choice, to understand relevant information, to understand the nature of the situation they are in, and to think reasonably about the information pertaining to their treatment. This is especially so for depressed patients. Furthermore, patients diagnosed with schizophrenia who initially show major cognitive impairments that can interfere with their capacity to make treatment decisions for themselves usually improve enough after a few weeks of medication to be able to participate in decisions about their future therapy (Appelbaum & Grisso, 1995; Applebaum et al., 1999).

Law, Free Will, and Ethics   Mental health law experts and social scientists construe voluntariness somewhat differently. Social-science paradigms assign less importance to the concept of free will than does the law, which rests utterly on that idea (Morse, 1992). As psychologists familiar with actual practices in mental hospitals, we are sensitive to the subtle coercion that can operate on hospitalized patients, even those who entered voluntarily (Hoge et al., 1997). A hospital patient is subject to strong persuasion and pressure to accept the treatment recommendations of professional staff. Although one could argue that this is as it should be, the fact remains that even a "voluntary" and informed decision to take psychotropic medication or to participate in any other therapy regimen is often (perhaps usually) less than free. The issue thus is more complicated and thorny than mental health law usually considers it to be—and the arguments of the legal profession do not lack for complexity and thorniness!

---

[43] *Dautremont v. Broadlawns Hospital*, 827 F.2d 291 (8th Cir. 1987).

[44] *United States v. Charters*, 863 F.2d 302, cert. denied, 494 U.S. 1016 (1990).

[45] *Guardianship of Weedon*, 565 N.E. 2d 432, 409 Mass. 196 (1991).

We are dealing ultimately with an ethical issue that is sometimes obscured by legal argumentation.

> *The most important force behind the notion of a patient's right to reject therapy is the recognition that the weighing of risks and benefits inherent in a decision to undergo or to defer treatment is value-laden. Personal preferences play a role in determining which risks are unacceptable and which benefits are desirable. For instance, the doctor's decision to treat an objecting patient with psychotropic drugs is a value judgment; it reflects the physician's view that freedom from psychosis outweighs the costs of overriding the patient's wishes and of exposing him or her to side effects. This means, at a minimum, that a physician and patient may not always agree on what constitutes the "best" therapy.... [Furthermore, the argument that the psychiatrist is acting only in the patient's best interests] assumes a general entitlement to intervene in another's best interest. Society, however, does not generally overrule an individual's decisions merely because they are not objectively self-regarding, to say nothing of not being in his or her best interest. People are permitted to engage in all sorts of dangerous activities, from hang-gliding to cigarette smoking. (Clayton, 1988, pp. 19–20)*

Related questions of freedom of choice are discussed later in this chapter in Focus on Discovery 18.5 (p. 644).

Rights to Treatment, to Refuse Treatment, and to Be Treated in the Least Restrictive Setting—Can They Be Reconciled?

We have reviewed several legal principles developed over the years that guide the courts and mental health professionals in meeting their constitutional obligations to civilly committed mental patients. Actions taken to implement one principle may conflict with another, however. The basic question is whether the right to be treated in the least restrictive fashion can be reconciled with both the right to treatment and the right to refuse treatment. A creative proposal was put forth in the 1970s by Paul and Lentz (1977) in their report on social-learning and milieu therapies in institutional settings (see p. 342). They argued that under certain conditions a committed mental patient can and should be coerced into a particular therapy program, even if the patient states that he or she does not wish to participate, and that these conditions would not, as *Rennie* v. *Klein* (cited in footnote 41) requires, have to be emergencies.

Paul and Lentz proposed that some hospital treatments have minimal and others optimal goals and that institutions should have the right and the duty to do whatever is reasonable to move patients toward minimal goals. Achievement of minimal goals—self-care, such as getting up in the morning, bathing, eating meals, and the like; communication with others on the most basic level; and the absence of violence—will allow patients to move into a less restrictive residence. The elimination of symptomatic behavior would also be regarded as a minimal goal if the local community required patients to conform, at least to some extent, to community standards.[46] Paul and Lentz argued further that if empirical evidence indicates that particular treatments do achieve minimal goals—as the social-learning program did in their study—patients might justifiably be forced to participate in them, even if they or their legal guardians do not give consent voluntarily. Protection of their interests would be the responsibility of an institutional review board, a group of professionals and laypeople who would review all therapy and research activities for a given hospital. The board would decide for patients which therapy is likely to achieve minimal goals that would allow them to leave the hospital.

If it is determined that the patient is operating above minimal levels, he or she should have the right to refuse treatments that have optimal goals, such as acquiring vocational skills, obtaining a high school diploma, and other objectives that might enhance the quality of a patient's life. According to Paul and Lentz, these goals are not considered so vital that the patient should be forced to work toward them.

Another approach to the conflict between right to treatment and right to refuse treatment is the so-called **advanced directive**, a legal document modeled after living wills.

---

[46] Many therapists are accused of forcing patients to conform to community standards that are open to question. The basic issue here, however, is not whether mentally ill patients wear clean pants with a belt to hold them up, but whether they wear pants at all.

An advanced directive is composed by people who are legally competent and able to make decisions and specify how they want to be treated in the event that, sometime in the future, they need psychological or medical therapy but are mentally unfit to make decisions bearing on their therapy. The document may state what procedures the person consents to or refuses—for example, whether to have electroconvulsive shock treatment if he or she becomes profoundly depressed and is unresponsive to any available medication or psychological intervention. Or the document may name another person to make such decisions. Many states now have laws that make such documents legally binding.

The use of advanced directives may enable people who are psychologically troubled but still competent to have more power over their future health care. But can such people really know what they will want or need if and when they become legally incompetent in the future? We can expect the debates on this issue of patient autonomy to continue (Winick, 1996).

Deinstitutionalization, Civil Liberties, and Mental Health

The cumulative impact of court rulings such as *Wyatt* v. *Stickney* and *O'Connor* v. *Donaldson* was to put mental health professionals on notice that they must be more careful about keeping people in mental hospitals against their will and that they must attend more to the specific treatment needs of committed patients. Pressure was placed on state governments to upgrade the quality of care in mental institutions. In view of the abuses that have been documented in hospital care, these are surely encouraging trends. But the picture is not all that rosy. For judges to declare that patient care must meet certain minimal standards does not automatically translate into realization of that praiseworthy goal. Money is not in unlimited supply, and the care of mentally ill individuals has not been one of government's high priorities.

Since the 1960s, many states have embarked on a policy of deinstitutionalization, discharging as many patients as possible from mental hospitals and discouraging admissions. Civil commitment is more difficult to achieve now than it was in the fifties and sixties, and committed patients are able, with the help of civil rights–minded lawyers, to refuse much of the treatment made available to them in the hospital. The population of state mental hospitals peaked in the 1950s at almost half a million patients; by the late 1990s the population had dropped to around 70,000. The maxim is now "Treat them in the community," the assumption being that virtually anything is preferable to institutionalization.

But what is this community that former mental hospital patients are supposed to find more helpful to them on discharge? Facilities outside hospitals are not prepared to cope with the influx of these patients. Some promising programs were described in Chapter 11, but these are very much the exception, not the rule. The state of affairs in many large metropolitan areas is an unrelenting social crisis, for hundreds of thousands of chronically ill mental patients have been released without sufficient job training and without community services to help them. It is doubtful, too, that deinstitutionalization has reduced the rate of chronic mental illness. As Gralnick (1987) argued, acutely ill persons are largely neglected because it is difficult to commit them unless they are found to be a danger to themselves and others, a condition that can take years to develop; by that time the problems may have become chronic and more difficult to deal with. The irony is that deinstitutionalization may be contributing to the very problem it was designed to alleviate, chronic mental illness.

Indeed, deinstitutionalization may be a misnomer. *Trans*institutionalization may be more apt, for declines in the census of public mental hospitals have occasioned increases in the presence of mentally ill people in prisons, nursing homes, and the mental health departments of nonpsychiatric hospitals (Cloud, 1999; Kiesler, 1991), and these settings are by and large not equipped to handle the particular needs of mental patients. The oft-mentioned revolving door is seen in the increase in readmission rates from 25 percent before the deinstitutionalization movement to around 80 percent by the 1980s (Paul & Menditto, 1992).

Many patients discharged from mental hospitals are eligible for benefits from the Veterans Administration and for Social Security Disability Insurance, but a large number are not receiving this assistance. Homeless persons do not have fixed addresses and need help in establishing eligibility and residency for the purpose of receiving benefits. A common sight nowadays, especially in larger cities, is people who have been discharged from psychiatric hospitals living in the streets, in train and bus terminals, in abandoned buildings, on subways, and in shelters operated by public agencies, churches, and charitable organizations. It is estimated that there are about 200,000 such people (Cloud, 1999). Their lives are desperate.

> [In a train station at 11:00 P.M.] the attendant goes off duty and women rise from separate niches and head for the bathroom. There they disrobe, and wash their clothes and bodies. Depending on the length of [the] line at the hand dryers, they wait to dry their clothes, put them in their bags or wear them wet. One woman cleans and wraps her ulcerated legs with paper towels every night. The most assertive claim toilet cubicles, line them with newspapers for privacy and warmth and sleep curled around the basin. Once they are taken, the rest sleep along the walls, one on a box directly beneath the hand dryer which she pushes for warm air. One of the women regularly cleans up the floors, sinks and toilets so that no traces of their uncustomary use remain. (Baxter & Hopper, 1981, p. 77)

Those discharged mental patients who are not homeless live marginal and unhealthful lives in nursing homes, jails, and run-down hotels. Although a visible part of the population, their visibility may be diminishing as many other people have been dispossessed from their homes and have lost their jobs. The state of homelessness undoubtedly exacerbates the emotional suffering of former mental patients. Mentally ill persons are an especially defenseless segment of the homeless population.

The relationships between homelessness and mental health were enumerated and analyzed by a committee of the National Academy of Sciences (NAS; Committee on Health Care for Homeless People, 1988, as summarized in Leeper, 1988). The committee estimated that 25 to 40 percent of the homeless population are alcoholics; similar proportions have some form of serious mental illness, usually schizophrenia. Such problems are probably aggravated by their nomadic and dangerous existence; homeless people, especially women, are likely victims of violence and rape, even when living in shelters for the homeless (D'Ercole & Struening, 1990).

Children are also found among the homeless population, a fact the committee termed "a national disgrace"; these youngsters are forced to live their formative years in chaotic and dangerous situations, with parents under severe stress. One committee member noted in an interview that "many children have developmental delays. I've seen two-year-olds who can't walk, six-month-olds who don't cuddle in your arms, and four-year-olds acting like mothers to one-year-olds because their mother isn't giving them the care they need" (Leeper, 1988, p. 8). That these children often drop out of school and suffer from anxiety, depression, and substance abuse and are subject to physical and sexual abuse should come as no surprise.

Do such appalling conditions, still found in the late 1990s, justify reversing the policy of deinstitutionalization? In the view of the NAS committee, no, because in its view the problem lies with the failure of communities to provide suitable living and rehabilitation conditions, a theme sounded often in this book.

There are signs that the pendulum may begin to swing back in the direction of more involuntary hospitalization, even when the person does not pose a real danger to self or to others, but is wandering homeless on the streets and living in squalor. Being "persistently and acutely disabled" is, in some jurisdictions, replacing being a danger to oneself or to others (Shogren, 1994). It remains to be seen how this trend will develop in the light of laws and court rulings that have been making it more and more difficult to keep people institutionalized against their will.

Some people fear that individuals with schizophrenia are increasingly being seen as misfits, drug abusers, and panhan-

Homeless children at a school in Arizona. The school not only provides education but also food and clothing.

dlers rather than as ill people in need of professional care (Gralnick, 1986). They end up more often in jails, shelters, and church basements than in mental wards. A large-scale field study (Teplin, 1984) found that police officers were 20 percent more likely to arrest people if they were showing signs of mental disorder than if they were (merely) committing offenses for which arrest was an option.

Furthermore, any treatment made available to these individuals is likely to be biological and drug based because such treatment is cheaper and more straightforward and does not require the close interpersonal relationship that is intrinsic to any psychotherapy (Gralnick, 1986). Biological factors are emphasized to the exclusion of psychological factors.[47] This focus threatens to interfere with achieving full understanding of serious mental illness, which most workers in the field, as we have seen throughout the book, view as a complex interaction between biological diatheses and environmental stressors. Gralnick recommends that the psychiatric hospital be restored to its previous position as the place of choice to treat and research schizophrenia and that research be more vigorously pursued in aftercare for patients who are discharged.

Ethical Dilemmas in Therapy and Research

In this textbook we have examined a variety of theories and a multitude of data focusing on *what is* and *what is thought to be*. Ethics and values, often embodied in laws, are a different order of discussion. They concern *what ought to be*, having sometimes little to do with what is. It is extremely important to recognize the difference.

Within a given scientific paradigm we are able to examine what we believe is reality. As the study of philosophy and ethics reveals, however, the statements people have made for thousands of years about what *should be* are another matter. The Ten Commandments are such statements. They are prescriptions and proscriptions about human conduct. For example, the Eighth Commandment, Thou shalt not steal, in no way describes human conduct, for stealing is not uncommon. It is, instead, a pronouncement of an ideal to which people should aspire. The integrity of an ethical code that proscribes stealing does not depend on any evidence concerning the percentage of people who steal. Morals and data are two separate realms of discourse.

The legal trends reviewed thus far in this chapter place limits on the activities of mental health professionals. These legal constraints are important, for laws are one of society's strongest means of encouraging all of us to behave in certain ways. Mental health professionals also have professional and ethical constraints. All professional groups promulgate shoulds and should nots, and by guidelines and mandates they limit to some degree what therapists and researchers should do with their patients, clients, and research participants. Courts as well have ruled on some of these questions. Most of the time what we believe is unethical is also illegal, but sometimes existing laws are in conflict with our moral sense of right and wrong. We examine now the ethics of making psychological inquiries and interventions into the lives of other human beings.

Ethical Restraints on Research

Basic to the nature of science is that what can be done will usually be attempted. The most reprehensible ethical insensitivity was evidenced in the brutal experiments conducted by German physicians on concentration camp prisoners during World War II. One experiment, for example, investigated how long people lived when their heads were bashed repeatedly with a heavy stick. Even if important information might be obtained

---

[47] Gralnick is not arguing that major advances are not being made in biological approaches to diagnosis, etiology, and treatment—one would have to be out of contact with reality to believe this. Rather, he is concerned that scientific advances will be coupled to a distancing from the personal plight of people with schizophrenia and lead to a scientifically unjustified and socially questionable neglect of their sad living situations in the era of what he and others regard as misguided deinstitutionalization.

from this kind of experiment, such actions violate our sense of decency and morality. The Nuremberg Trials, conducted by the Allies following the war, brought these and other barbarisms to light and meted out severe punishment to some of the soldiers, physicians, and Nazi officials who had engaged in or contributed to such actions, even when they claimed that they had merely been following orders.

It would be reassuring to be able to say that such gross violations of human decency take place only during incredible and cruel epochs such as the Third Reich, but unfortunately this is not the case. Spurred on by a blind enthusiasm for their work, researchers in the United States and other countries have sometimes dealt with human subjects in reproachable ways.[48]

Henry K. Beecher, a research professor at Harvard Medical School, surveyed medical research since 1945 and found that "many of the patients [used as subjects in experiments] never had the risk satisfactorily explained to them, and...further hundreds have not known that they were the subjects of an experiment although grave consequences have been suffered as the direct result" (1966, p. 1354). One experiment compared penicillin with a placebo as a treatment to prevent rheumatic fever. Even though penicillin had already been acknowledged as the drug of choice for people with a streptococcal respiratory infection in order to protect them from later contracting rheumatic fever, placebos were administered to 109 service personnel without their knowledge or permission. More subjects received penicillin than received the placebo, but three members of the control group contracted serious illnesses—two had rheumatic fever and one acute nephritis, a kidney disease. None of those who had received penicillin contracted such illnesses.

Half a century later, in January 1994, spurred on by Eileen Welsome, a journalist who won a Pulitzer Prize for her investigative reporting on the issue, the United States Energy Department began to publicize numerous experiments conducted in the 1950s through the 1970s that had exposed hundreds of people—usually without their informed consent or prior knowledge—to harmful doses of radiation. Particular concern was expressed because the overwhelming majority were people of low socioeconomic status, members of racial minorities, people with mental retardation, nursing home patients, or prisoners. The scientists, for the most part supported in their research with federal funds, understood that the risks were great even though relatively little was known about the harmful effects of radiation at the time. This is reflected in the fact that "they were doing it to poor and black people. You didn't see them doing it at the Mayo Clinic" (lawyer arguing for compensation for some of the subjects, quoted in Healy, 1994). Some of these experiments involved giving women in the third trimester of pregnancy a radioactive tonic to determine safe levels of exposure and irradiating the testicles of prisoners to find out the degree of radiation that service personnel could endure without negative effects on sperm production. That these experiments took place many years after the Nuremberg Trials is particularly troubling.

Defendants at the Nuremberg trials.

The training of scientists equips them splendidly to pose interesting questions, sometimes even important ones, and to design research that is as free as possible of confounds. They have no special qualifications, however, for deciding whether a particular line of inquiry that involves humankind should be followed. Society needs knowledge, and a scientist has a right in a democracy to seek that knowledge. However, the ordinary citizens employed as participants in experiments must be protected from unnecessary harm, risk, humiliation, and invasion of privacy.[49]

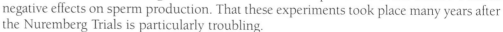

[48] Scientists who conduct research on animals have also sometimes dealt with their subjects in gratuitously harsh fashion. The American Psychological Association has guidelines for handling laboratory animals that are intended to minimize their discomfort and danger. Strict standards have also been promulgated by the National Institutes of Health.

[49] This very statement is an ethical, not an empirical, one.

Several international codes of ethics pertain to the conduct of scientific research—the Nuremberg Code formulated in 1947 in the aftermath of the Nazi war-crime trials, the 1964 Declaration of Helsinki, and statements from the British Medical Research Council. In 1974 the U.S. Department of Health, Education, and Welfare began to issue guidelines and regulations governing scientific research that employs human and animal subjects. In addition, a blue-ribbon panel, the National Commission for the Protection of Human Subjects of Biomedical and Behavioral Research, issued a report in 1978 that arose from hearings and inquiries into restrictions that the U.S. government might impose on research performed with patients in psychiatric institutions, prisoners, and children. These various codes and principles are continually being reevaluated and revised as new challenges are posed to the research community (e.g., Brennan, 1999; Levine, 1999).

For the past thirty years the proposals of behavioral researchers, many of whom conduct experiments related to psychopathology and therapy, have been reviewed for safety and general ethical propriety by institutional review boards in hospitals, universities, and research institutes. Such committees—and this is significant—comprise not only behavioral scientists but also citizens from the community, lawyers, students, and specialists in a variety of disciplines, such as professors of English, history, and comparative religion. They are able to block any research proposal or require questionable aspects to be modified if in their collective judgment the research would put participants at too great a risk. Such committees also now pass judgment on the scientific merits of proposals, the rationale being that it is not ethical to recruit participants for studies that will not yield valid data (Capron, 1999; Rosenthal, 1995). In 2000, universities and other research institutions were required to begin certifying researchers on the basis of special coursework and examinations, to make it less likely that research participants will be put at risk.

Changes in the Declaration of Helsinki are being debated, spurred on by two recent developments in biomedical research. The first is an increase in research sponsored by for-profit organizations such as pharmaceutical companies. Faced with fierce competition and marketplace pressures to maximize profits, such companies may push for research that would not be approved by human subjects committees in nonprofit organizations such as universities. The internationalization of research is a second factor in the possible attenuation of protection of human subjects. Developing countries are particularly eager for partnerships in research and do not always have the same historical commitment to individual informed consent and safety that is prevalent in more industrialized and democratic countries. A danger seen by some is that utilitarian standards—will the research yield generally useful results?—are becoming more important than the focus of the past half century on the rights and safety of individual research participants (Brennan, 1999).

In reaction to some ethical lapses in hospital-based research with mental patients, the National Bioethics Advisory Commission recommends special precautions to ensure that research subjects with mental illness fully understand the risks and benefits of any research they are asked to participate in and that particular care be taken to make certain that they can decline or withdraw from research without feeling coerced. Specifically, instead of simply allowing a guardian or family member to make the decision for the patient, the commission proposes that a health professional who has nothing to do with the particular study make a judgment on whether a given patient can give informed consent. The commission recommends also that, if a guardian is allowed to give consent on behalf of a patient judged incompetent to do so, the guardian's own ability to give consent also be evaluated (Capron, 1999).

Informed Consent

This recent concern about conducting research with mental patients underscores the all-important concept of **informed consent**. Just as committed mental patients are gaining some right to refuse treatment, so may anyone refuse to be a participant in an experiment. The investigator must provide enough information to enable people to judge whether they want to accept any risks inherent in being a participant. Prospective participants must be legally capable of giving consent, and there must be no deceit or coercion in obtaining it. For example, an experimental psychologist might wish to determine whether imagery helps college students associate one word with another. One group of students might be asked to associate pairs of words in their minds by generating a fanciful image connecting the two, such as a cat riding on a bicycle. Current standard operating procedure allows a prospective participant to decide that the experiment is likely to be boring and to decline to participate. Furthermore, if the person begins to participate as a research subject, he or she is free to withdraw from the experiment at any time without fear of penalty.

Paired-associates research such as that just described is relatively innocuous, but what if the experiment poses real risks, such as ingesting a drug, or what if a patient with schizophrenia whose condition has improved by taking a drug is withdrawn from it so that the investigator can assess the effects of "drug washout"? Or what if the prospective participant is a committed mental patient, or a child with mental retardation, unable to understand fully what is being asked? Such a person may not feel free or even be able to refuse participation. Although recent research mentioned earlier (p. 632) shows that even committed patients with schizophrenia may be competent to understand and participate in treatment decisions, the degree of coercion that is part and parcel of being in a hospital setting must not be overlooked.

A further complication is that it is not always easy to demonstrate that a researcher has obtained informed consent. Epstein and Lasagna (1969) found that only one-third of those volunteering for an experiment really understood what the experiment entailed. In a more elaborate study, Stuart (1978) discovered that most college students could not accurately describe a simple experiment, even though it had just been explained to them and they had agreed to participate. A signature on a consent form is no assurance that informed consent has been obtained, which poses a challenge to investigators and members of review panels who are committed to upholding codes of ethics governing participation of human subjects in research.

As suggested earlier (Capron, 1999), such problems are especially pronounced in clinical settings where there is a question of whether patients understand the nature of antipsychotic medication. Irwin et al. (1985) found that although most patients said they understood the benefits and side effects of their drugs, only a quarter of them could actually demonstrate such understanding when queried specifically. The authors concluded that simply reading information to hospitalized patients—especially the more disturbed ones—is no guarantee that they fully comprehend; therefore, informed consent cannot be said to have been obtained. The recent report of the National Bioethics Advisory Commission pointed to many published experiments involving mental patients in which no effort was made to determine whether the research participants had the decision-making capacity to give informed consent (Capron, 1999).

Still, as with the right to refuse treatment, there is recognition that being judged mentally ill—more specifically, being diagnosed with schizophrenia and being hospitalized—does not necessarily mean being incapable of giving informed consent (Appelbaum & Gutheil, 1991; Grisso, 1986). An experiment by Grisso and Applebaum (1991) found that, although patients with schizophrenia on average understood issues relating to treatment involving medication less well than did nonpsychiatric patients, there was a wide range of understanding among the patients; some showed as good understanding as did nonpsychiatric patients.

These results point to the importance of examining each person individually for ability to give informed consent, rather than assuming that a person is unable to do so by virtue of being hospitalized for schizophrenia. Before a mental patient can give informed consent in New York state hospitals, for example, a licensed psychologist or psychiatrist must certify that the person is capable of doing so. Thus, although professional judgment is required, and may therefore be erroneous, there is the real possibility that being judged mentally ill will not *ipso facto* deny a patient the ability to give informed consent.

Confidentiality and Privileged Communication

When an individual consults a physician, psychiatrist, or clinical psychologist, he or she is assured by professional ethics codes that what goes on in the session will remain confidential. **Confidentiality** means that nothing will be revealed to a third party, except only to other professionals and those intimately involved in the treatment, such as a nurse or medical secretary.

A **privileged communication** goes even further. It is communication between parties in a confidential relationship that is protected by law. The recipient of such a communication cannot legally be compelled to disclose it as a witness. The right of privileged communication is a major exception to the access courts have to evidence in judicial proceedings. Society believes that in the long term the interests of people are best served if communications to a spouse and to certain professionals remain off limits to the prying eyes and ears of the police, judges, and prosecutors. The privilege applies to such relationships as those between husband and wife, physician and patient, pastor and penitent, attorney and client, and psychologist and patient. The legal expression is that the patient or client "holds the privilege," which means that only he or she may release the other person to disclose confidential information in a legal proceeding.

There are important limits to a client's right of privileged communication, however. For example, according to the current California psychology licensing law (similar elements are present in other state laws), this right is eliminated for any of the following reasons.

- The client has accused the therapist of malpractice. In such a case, the therapist can divulge information about the therapy in order to defend himself or herself in any legal action initiated by the client.

- The client is less than sixteen years old and the therapist has reason to believe that the child has been a victim of a crime such as child abuse. In fact, the psychologist is required to report to the police or to a child welfare agency within thirty-six hours any suspicion he or she has that the child client has been physically abused, including any suspicion of sexual molestation.

- The client initiated therapy in hopes of evading the law for having committed a crime or for planning to do so.

- The therapist judges that the client is a danger to self or to others and if disclosure of information is necessary to ward off such danger (recall Focus on Discovery 18.3 on *Tarasoff*).

Who Is the Client or Patient?

Is it always clear to the clinician who the client is? In private therapy, when an adult pays a clinician a fee for help with a personal problem that has nothing to do with the legal system, the consulting individual is clearly the client. But an individual may be seen by a clinician for an evaluation of his or her competency to stand trial, or the clinician may be hired by an individual's family to assist in civil commitment proceedings. Perhaps the clinician is employed by a state mental hospital as a regular staff member and sees a particular patient about problems in controlling aggressive impulses.

It should be clear, although it sometimes is not, that in these instances the clinician is serving more than one client. In addition to the patient, he or she serves the family or the state, and it is incumbent on the mental health professional to inform the patient that this is so. This dual allegiance does not necessarily indicate that the patient's own interests will be sacrificed, but it does mean that discussions will not inevitably remain secret and that the clinician may in the future act in a way that displeases or even seriously compromises the interests of the individual.

Choice of Goals

Ideally the client sets the goals for therapy, but in practice it is naive to assume that some are not imposed by the therapist and may even go against the wishes of the client. For example, a school system may want to institute a program that will teach children to "be still, be quiet, be docile" (Winett & Winkler, 1972, p. 499). Many behavior therapists have assumed that young children should be compliant, not only because the teacher can then run a more orderly class but because children are assumed to learn better when they are so. But do we really know that the most efficient and most enjoyable learning takes place when children are forced to remain quietly in their seats? Some advocates of open classrooms believe that curiosity and initiative, even in the youngest elementary-school pupil, are at least as important as the acquisition of academic skills.

As is generally the case in psychology, evidence is less plentiful than are strongly held and vehemently defended opinions. But it is clear that professionals consulted by a school system have to be mindful of their own personal biases with respect to goals and should be prepared to work toward different ones if the parents and school personnel so wish. Any therapist has the option of not working for a client whose goals and proposed means of attaining them are abhorrent in his or her view.

This question of goals is particularly complex in family and couples therapy (Margolin, 1982). If several people are clients simultaneously—inevitable in family treatment—an intervention that benefits one or more individuals may well work to the disadvantage of one or more others. This can happen if one partner in couples therapy really wants to end the relationship, but the other sees the therapy as a way to save it. Because people often do not openly express their real concerns and wishes at the very beginning of therapy, the therapist can already be deeply enmeshed in their lives before learning that the two partners have conflicting goals. For this reason, among others, couples and family therapy is particularly challenging.

Although the plight of people who voluntarily consult therapists is in no way as confining as that of institutionalized patients, there are constraints on their freedom. This issue was addressed by Seymour Halleck (1971), a psychiatrist, who asserts that the neutrality of the therapist is a myth. In his opinion therapists influence their clients in ways that are subtle yet powerful.

> At first glance, a model of psychiatric [or psychological] practice based on the contention that people should just be helped to learn to do the things they want to do seems uncomplicated and desirable. But it is an unobtainable model. Unlike a technician, a psychiatrist [or psychologist] cannot avoid communicating and at times imposing his own values upon his patients. The patient usually has considerable difficulty in finding the way in which he would wish to change his behavior, but as he talks to the psychiatrist his wants and needs become clearer. In the very process of defining his needs in the presence of a figure who is viewed as wise and authoritarian, the patient is profoundly influenced. He ends up wanting some of the things the psychiatrist thinks he should want. (Halleck, 1971, p. 19)

Research supports the contention that clients are indeed influenced by the values of their therapists (e.g., Rosenthal, 1955). A person not only seeks out a therapist who suits his or her taste and meets his or her perceived needs, but also adopts some of the ideals, sometimes even the mannerisms, of the therapist. Most therapists are keenly aware of this modeling phenomenon, which increases the already heavy responsibilities of their professional role. Perry London (1964, 1986), a leading writer on the ethics of therapeutic intervention, suggested that therapists are contemporary society's secular priests, purveyors of values and ethics to help clients live "the good life" (see Focus on Discovery 18.5).

Sometimes the values held by therapists are subtle and difficult to discern. In an interesting examination of ethics in psychoanalysis and in behavior therapy, Paul Wachtel, whose ideas about psychotherapy integration we examined in the preceding chapter, writes of "the ethics of the lonely struggle" that, as a psychoanalyst himself, he sees as an unacknowledged characteristic of the insight therapies. He criticizes both psychoanalysis and the humanistic-existential approaches for an overemphasis on the need for people to change from within rather than being assisted, even directed, in their efforts to change in the manner customary in cognitive behavior therapy. By concentrating on people's gaining their own insights and making behavioral changes pretty much on their own and by discouraging therapists from influencing their patients by directly teaching them new skills, insight-oriented therapists unwittingly teach an ethic of aloneness devoid of social support. He questions whether this is a proper message to convey to patients and to society-at-large. As he puts it, *many [insight] therapists who criticize behavior therapy as an agent of cultural norms are themselves upholding one of the basic tenets of our capitalistic society, when they stress change based solely on autonomous action and deride the need for direct assistance from others.... It is, after all, just as human to be able to turn to others as it is to stand alone. (Wachtel, 1997, pp. 289–290)*

Choice of Techniques

The end does not justify the means. This canon is said to be intrinsic to a free society. For years questions concerning behavioral techniques have been debated among professionals and have been the subject of court rulings. Perhaps because the various insight therapies deemphasize direct efforts to change behavior, they have seldom been scrutinized as has behavior therapy. The very concreteness, specificity, and directiveness of behavioral techniques have called attention to them, as has their alignment with experimental psychology. It is offensive to some to believe that our understanding of human beings could possibly be advanced by employing rats and pigeons as analogues to humans.

Particular concern has been expressed about the ethics of inflicting pain for purposes of therapy. For some people the term behavior therapy conjures up an image of the violent protagonist in Kubrick's classic film *A Clockwork Orange*, eyes propped open with a torturous apparatus, being made nauseous by a drug while scenes of violence flash on a screen. Aversion-therapy programs never reach this level of coercion and drama, but certainly any such procedure entails making the patient uncomfortable, sometimes extremely so. Making patients vomit or cringe with pain from electric shock applied to the extremities are two aversion techniques worthy of their name. Can there be any circumstances that justify therapists' inflicting pain on clients?

Before quickly exclaiming, "No!" consider the following report.

> The patient was a nine-month-old baby who had already been hospitalized three times for treatment of vomiting and chronic rumination (regurgitating food and rechewing it in the mouth). A number of diagnostic tests, including an EEG, plus surgery to remove a cyst on the right kidney, had revealed no biological basis for the problems, and several treatments, including a special diet, had been attempted without success. When referred to Lang and Melamed (1969), two behavior therapists, the child was in critical condition and was being fed by tubes leading from the nose directly into the stomach. The attending physician had stated that the infant's life was in imminent danger if the vomiting could not be halted.
>
> Treatment consisted of delivering a series of one-second-long electric shocks to the infant's calf each time he showed signs of beginning to vomit. Sessions followed feeding and lasted under an hour. After just two sessions, shock was rarely required, for the infant learned quickly to stop vomiting in order to avoid the shock. By the sixth session he was able to fall asleep after eating. Nurses reported that the in-session inhibition of vomiting generalized as the infant progressively reduced his vomiting during the rest of the day and night. About two weeks later the mother began to assume some care of the hospitalized child, and shortly thereafter the patient was discharged with virtually complete elimination of the life-threatening pattern of behavior. Throughout the three weeks of treatment and observation, the child gained weight steadily. One month after discharge the child weighed twenty-one pounds and was rated as fully recovered by the attending physician. Five months later he weighed twenty-six pounds and was regarded as completely normal, both physically and psychologically.

The use of aversion therapy has been subject to an understandably high degree of regulation. An additional reason for administrative and judicial concern is that aversion techniques smack more of research than of standard therapy. The more established a therapeutic procedure, whether medical or psychological, the less likely it is to attract the attention of the courts or other governmental agencies. Paul and Lentz (1977) had a few very assaultive patients in their study of hospital treatment. Their account of administrative problems demonstrates that patients might be subject to more extreme procedures because of restrictions placed on the use of new techniques.

> *Some consideration was given to the contingent use of mild electric shock.... However, early in the explorations of the necessary safeguards and review procedures to be followed before evaluating such methods, the department director telephoned to explain that aversion conditioning was a politically sensitive issue. Therefore, more than the usual proposal, preparation, documentation, and committee reviews would be required—to the extent that approval would probably*

Not Can but Ought: An Opinion on the Treatment of Homosexuality

For many years homosexual individuals have consulted therapists for help in changing from same-sex to opposite-sex partners. But according to several psychologists, the social pressures on these individuals to become heterosexual make it difficult to believe that they acted with free choice (Begelman, 1975; Davison, 1974, 1976, 1991; Silverstein, 1972).

Discrimination, Hate Crimes, and the Desire to Change Sexual Orientation

Although most states have dropped their sodomy laws, which used to be enforced selectively against homosexual acts, some legal pressure against homosexuality remains. A 1986 U.S. Supreme Court decision,[*] still valid, refused to find constitutional protection of the right to privacy for consensual adult homosexual activity and thereby upheld a Georgia law that prohibits oral–genital and anal–genital acts, even in private and between consenting adults.

But legal pressures are not the whole story. Research supports the view that gays and lesbians are discriminated against and that this discrimination takes a particularly heavy toll on their emotional well-being. So-called hate crimes highlight this problem. A hate crime (sometimes referred to as a bias crime) is an assault that is linked to a person's (perceived) membership in a group against which the perpetrator is prejudiced. The ultimate hate crime was, of course, the Holocaust in Germany and other parts of western Europe prior to and during World War II. The Nazis sought out for imprisonment and execution millions of Jews and hundreds of thousands of gypsies, Communists, and homosexuals. The September 11, 2001, attacks on the World Trade Center towers and the Pentagon, and the thwarted effort to attack other targets in Washington, D.C., could probably also be classified as hate crimes. But hate crimes are carried out every day in less organized and less dramatic fashion.

With respect to homosexuals, research shows that as many as 92 percent of gays and lesbians have been subjected to verbal abuse and threats—often from members of their own family—and that as many as 24 percent have been physically attacked because of their sexual orientation (Herek, 1989; Herek et al., 1997). A quarter of gay youth are ejected from their homes when they come out to their families, and as many as half of the homeless young people in New York City are homosexuals. Furthermore, the lifetime risk of suicide and suicidal behaviors is much higher among homosexual men than among heterosexuals (Herrell et al., 1999).

As compared to non–hate crimes, bias crimes and verbal assaults are believed to create more psychological distress, perhaps because they are an attack not just against the person as a physical being but against the person's very identity (Garnets et al., 1990). Furthermore, such crimes may impart to the victim a sense of danger and even loathing of an aspect of the self that could otherwise be a source of pleasure and pride.

In addition to violence from strangers and acquaintances, lesbians and gay men experience "invisibility, isolation, lack of information, lack of role models, negative attitudes from others, lack of family and social support, uninformed or biased helping professionals, religious prohibitions, workplace discriminations, lack of legal supports, and

internalized homophobia" (Fassinger & Richie, 1997, p. 90). Fassinger (1991) concluded that while growing up, most gays and lesbians acquire the same negative attitudes toward gays as heterosexuals do, and this internalized homophobia makes it all the more difficult for them to confront their sexual orientation and to consider it in a positive light.

Antigay attitudes are strong, sometimes virulent, with many people believing that homosexuals are sick and their behavior disgusting (Herek, 1994). These negative attitudes can take the form of open heterosexism—as when people directly insult a gay person with epithets, such as "faggot" or "dyke"—or a more subtle, indirect kind of antihomosexual stance—as when people tell jokes that deride homosexuality without knowing (or caring) if a gay person is present. This prejudice creates what has been termed minority stress, a source of pressure and tension that is a special burden of those in despised or feared minorities (Meyer, 1995) and no doubt is the major factor in the particularly high levels of depression found among gay and lesbian people (Herek et al., 1996).

In light of all this, it is not surprising that gays may seek out sexual reorientation treatment. Being subjected to verbal and physical assault for being gay is not likely to enhance the person's sense of comfort with and acceptance of his or her sexual orientation. It can be argued, therefore, that the expression of a desire to change sexual preference is not truly voluntary.

The Nature of Sexual Conversion Treatments

Questions have also been raised about the kinds of interventions that have been used with gays and lesbians. In the past, efforts to eliminate or reduce homosexuality have taken many nasty forms, including the following medical procedures (as reviewed by Cruz, 1999): psychosurgery (e.g., lobotomy), implanting the testicles of just-deceased heterosexual men into homosexual men, castration or removal or mutilation of the ovaries or clitoris, electroconvulsive therapy and chemicals to induce seizures, and injection of sexual hormones (e.g., androgen for gay men and estrogen for lesbian women). Nonmedical interventions have included bed rest, riding a bicycle to exhaustion, immersion in tubs of roiling water (so-called hydrotherapy), and the vigorous study of mathematics. Less drastic efforts have included the various forms of psychotherapy, such as psychoanalysis and behavior therapy, and especially aversion therapy.

The Availability of Sexual Conversion Treatments

It has been suggested that the mere availability of change-of-orientation programs upholds the prejudice against homosexuality. After all, clinicians develop procedures and study their effects only if they are concerned about the problem that their techniques address. The therapy literature contains much less material on helping homosexual persons develop as individuals without changing their sexual orientation than on how best to discourage homosexual behavior and substitute for it heterosexual patterns. With regard to aversion therapy, which used to be the most widely used behavioral technique (Davison & Wilson, 1973; Henkel & Lewis-Thomé, 1976), one researcher asks, "What are we really saying to our clients when, on the one hand, we assure them that they are not abnormal and on the other hand, present

[*] *Bowers v. Hardwick*, 106 S.Ct. 2841 (1986).

them with an array of techniques, some of them painful, which are aimed at eliminating that set of feelings and behavior that we have just told them is okay?" (Davison, 1976, p. 161).

This viewpoint was affirmed by the American Psychological Association in 1997 and the American Psychiatric Association in 1998. These organizations took the position that efforts to alter sexual preference can not only cause depression and anxiety in patients undergoing the change efforts but can also harm homosexuals who themselves are not in conversion therapy. The reason for the general harm was said to be that the availability of such treatment affirms that homosexuality is a disease (Associated Press, as reported in the *Los Angeles Times*, December 12, 1998, p. A18).

Another way to understand this argument is to consider the availability of operations to alter the facial appearance of Asian women by making their eyes rounder and by narrowing the bridge of the nose—changes designed to approximate Caucasian standards of appearance and beauty. What do the availability of and the desire for this kind of elective cosmetic surgery say about the way Asian facial features are appraised? One critic put it this way:

> [Such efforts are] attempts to escape persisting racial prejudice that correlates their stereotyped genetic physical features...with negative behavioral characteristics.... Medicine is effective in perpetuating these racist notions [by normalizing] not only the negative feelings of Asian American women about their features but also their ultimate decision to undergo cosmetic surgery.... [While most of the Asian American women studied denied that they were conforming to any Western standards of beauty and that they had freely chosen the cosmetic surgery], most agreed...that their decision to alter their features was primarily a result of their awareness that as women they are expected to look their best and that this meant, in a certain sense, less stereotypically Asian.... [Rather than] confront the cultural and institutional structures that are the real cause of the women's feelings of distress, [such surgery] helps to entrench these structures by further confirming the undesirability of "stereotypical" Asian features.... Rather than celebrations of the body, [these surgeries] are mutilations of the body, resulting from a devaluation of the self and induced by historically determined relationships among social groups and between the individual and society. (Kaw, 1993, pp. 75, 83, 77–78, as cited in Cruz, 1999)

Thus, by providing surgery to alter Asian facial features in the direction of Caucasian features, the medical profession unwittingly reinforces the prejudice against such features. Critics of sexual reorientation efforts see in this kind of cosmetic surgery a strengthening of the bias against Asians. They question as well the meaningfulness of assertions that such women are voluntarily seeking such surgery, for such women are hypothesized to be doing so out of the kind of self-hate that, the argument goes, lies behind the stated wish of some homosexuals to alter their sexual orientation in a heterosexual direc-

Gay pride march in New York City. Similar marches occur across the country and may help counteract the impact of negative attitudes of some members of society.

tion. By implication, anticonversionists question the ethical propriety of making such surgery available even when it is requested.

A Proposal to Forsake Sexual Conversion Treatment

For the reasons just described, it has been proposed that therapists not help homosexual clients become heterosexual, even when the clients request such treatment. This radical proposal, probably held by a small yet growing minority of clinicians, has evoked some strong reactions. Gay-activist groups consider this suggestion concrete support for the belief that homosexuality per se is not a mental disorder. They believe also that it will reduce prejudice against homosexuality.

But many psychologists and psychiatrists are concerned about limiting the choices available to people seeking therapy. Why should a therapist decide for potential clients what options should be available? Is it not the responsibility of therapists to satisfy the needs expressed by their clients (Sturgis & Adams, 1978)? A reply to this important criticism is that therapists routinely decide what therapy will be available when they refuse to take as clients people with whose goals they disagree. The request of a patient for a certain kind of treatment has never been sufficient justification for providing that treatment (see Davison, 1978). Therapists do not operate from a position of ethical neutrality (London, 1964).

It has been asserted that continued research will help develop sexual-reorientation programs that are more effective than those already available (Sturgis & Adams, 1978), and that to discourage such work would deprive today's homosexual clients of promising therapies and tomorrow's homosexual clients of improved treatments. The counterargument is that the fact that we *can* do something does not mean that we *should* do it. The proposal to deny sexual-reorientation therapy is philosophical and ethical in nature, not empirical. The decision whether to change sexual orientation will have to be made on moral grounds (Davison, 1978).

The Consequences of Terminating Sexual Conversion Efforts

Will numbers of people be hurt by eliminating the option of sexual reorientation? Some have raised the specter of an upsurge in suicides among homosexual clients if therapists refuse to help them switch. These are very serious concerns, but they overlook the possibility, some would say the fact, that far greater numbers of people have been hurt over the years by the availability of sexual-reorientation programs. As suggested earlier, the existence of these treatments is consistent with societal prejudices and discrimination against homosexuals.

It is noteworthy that since the initial articulation of this proposal (Davison, 1974; Silverstein, 1972), there has been a dramatic reduction in the use of aversion therapy for changing homosexual orientation to heterosexual (Rosen & Beck, 1988) and a sharp decrease also in reports of other procedures for altering homosexuality (Campos &

Hathaway, 1993). Other signs of increased acceptance of homosexuality as a lifestyle are the elimination of ego-dystonic homosexuality from the DSM in 1987 and the establishment within the American Psychological Association of the Division of Lesbian and Gay Psychologists and the Committee on Lesbian and Gay Concerns of the Board of Social and Ethical Responsibility.

The proponents who wish to terminate change-of-orientation programs believe that much good can come of their proposal. Homosexual individuals will be helped to think better of themselves, and greater attention can be directed to the problems they have, rather than to the issue of homosexuality.

It would be nice if an alcoholic homosexual, for example, could be helped to reduce his or her drinking without having his or her sexual orientation questioned. It would be nice if a homosexual fearful of interpersonal relationships, or incompetent in them, could be helped without the therapist assuming that homosexuality lies at the root of the problem. It would be nice if a nonorgasmic or impotent homosexual could be helped as a heterosexual would be rather than [being guided] to change-of-orientation regimens…the hope [is] that therapists will concentrate their efforts on such human problems rather than focusing on the most obvious "maladjustment"—loving members of one's own sex. (Davison, 1978, p. 171)

take about eighteen months. Instead, it was suggested that convulsive shock…be employed since "ECT is an accepted medical treatment." With those alternatives, our choice was to abandon either use of shock. (p. 499)

But should we be concerned only with physical pain? The anguish we suffer when a loved one dies is psychologically painful. It is perhaps more painful than an electric shock of 1,500 microamperes. Who is to say? Since we allow that pain can be psychological, should we forbid a Gestalt therapist from making a patient cry by confronting the patient with feelings that have been avoided for years? Should we forbid a psychoanalyst from guiding a patient to an insight that will likely cause great anguish, all the more so for the conflict's having been repressed for years?

The Ethical and Legal Dimensions of Recovered Memories

In Chapter 7 we examined the scientific controversies raised by so-called recovered memories (p. 194). The growing debate over the validity and reliability of reports of child abuse that surface when adults are in therapy has created considerable ethical and legal concern (Ceci & Hembrooke, 1998). One of the most important of the guidelines issued by the American Psychiatric Association (1993) stipulates that therapists should remain neutral when a patient reports abuse. Because a given symptom—for example, avoidance of sexual contact—may have many possible origins, it is not ethical according to the APA to attribute such symptoms to repressed memories of childhood sexual abuse without corroborating evidence.

A problem with this laudable stance is explored in Focus on Discovery 18.5, which challenges the notion that therapists can maintain neutrality. Furthermore, as mentioned in Chapter 14, some experts on sexual dysfunctions recommend that therapists inquire into possible sexual abuse whenever patients, especially women, report aversions to or disinterest in sex. The basic difficulty, then, is that many therapists are predisposed by their theorizing or by personal biases to believe that sexual abuse lies behind a wide range of psychological disorders. By the same token, therapists who do not believe that traumatic memories are often repressed may overlook childhood sexual abuse when it has taken place.

An incorrect diagnosis of repressed memories of sexual abuse can harm not only the patient but also the persons whom the patient accuses of having molested him or her years earlier. Courts in some jurisdictions have held that in addition to their duty to their patients, therapists may have a duty to those wrongly accused of abuse as a result of revelations during psychotherapy.[50]

---

[50] See, for example, *Montoya v. Bebensee*, 761 P.2d 285 (Colo. Ct. App. 1988); *Peterson v. Walentiny*, No. 93-C-399-K (N.D. Okla., Jan. 6, 1995) (denying motion for summary judgment); but see *Bird v. W.C.W.*, 868 S.W. 2d 767 (Tex.1994). More recent cases include *Card v. Blakeslee*, 937 P.2d 846 (Colo. Ct. App. 1991) and *Althaus v. Cohen*, 710 A2d 1147 (Pa. Super. Ct. 1998).

The statute of limitations has been extended, allowing those who believe they were abused as children to file suit twenty or more years after the abuse purportedly occurred. However, there has been a backlash against these kinds of lawsuits as accused parents and others (e.g., clergy, youth leaders, and other professionals in positions of trust with children and adolescents) have begun to deny such charges vigorously, and some patients have recanted their allegations. This turn of events has resulted in lawsuits being filed against therapists both by the accused parties and by the patients (MacNamara, 1993).

Probably the best known legal incident concerned Gary Romona, a man who claimed that an irresponsible therapist had implanted false memories into his adult daughter's mind. The daughter sued her father for allegedly having molested her when she was a child, but the father sued her therapist for having allegedly planted this erroneous idea into his daughter's mind. The father won a nearly half-million-dollar judgment (Kramer, 1995), at which point the daughter's suit against her father was dismissed. It is estimated that thousands of parents and other third parties have either already filed or plan to file lawsuits against therapists (Lazo, 1995). In addition to possible therapist bias, the concern in these lawsuits is with particular treatments that may increase susceptibility to suggestion, such as hypnosis and sodium amytal (truth serum).

It is not clear, however, whether such lawsuits will be allowed to go forward in the future. In a recent case in California, a parent falsely accused of molesting a child based on repressed memories elicited during therapy was not allowed to sue the therapist. The court ruled that a therapist must be free to act solely in the interests of the client and can be sued only by the client for negligent diagnosis or treatment. A therapist, the court said, is entitled to examine the possibility of past sexual abuse and should not be inhibited by the possibility of a suit by the alleged abuser. "The therapist risks utter professional failure in his or her duty to the patient if possible childhood sexual abuse is ignored," the judge said (Associated Press, February 18, 1999).

With the scientific status of the validity of recovered memories very much in dispute, legal scholars as well as professional associations advise extreme caution in dealing with the issue. The danger of false positives—concluding that there was abuse when there wasn't—is as serious a matter as the danger of false negatives—concluding that there was no abuse when there was.

Concluding Comment

An underlying theme of this book concerns the nature of knowledge. How do we decide that we understand a phenomenon? The rules of science that govern our definition of and search for knowledge require theories that can be tested, studies that can be replicated, and data that are public. But given the complexity of abnormal behavior and the vast areas of ignorance, far more extensive than the domains that have already been mapped by science as it is currently practiced, we have great respect for theoreticians and clinicians, those inventive souls who make suppositions, offer hypotheses, follow hunches—all based on rather flimsy data, but holding some promise that scientific knowledge will be forthcoming (Davison & Lazarus, 1995, 1997).

This final chapter demonstrates again something emphasized at the very beginning of this book, namely, that the behavioral scientists and mental health professionals who conduct research and give treatment are only human beings. They suffer from the same foibles that sometimes plague nonspecialists. They occasionally act with a certainty their evidence does not justify, and they sometimes fail to anticipate the moral and legal consequences of the ways in which they conduct research and apply the tentative findings of their young discipline. When society acts with great certainty on the basis of expert scientific opinion, particularly when that opinion denies to an individual the rights and respect accorded others, it may be well to let Szasz (1963) remind us that Sir Thomas Browne, a distinguished English physician, testified in an English court of law in 1664 that witches did indeed exist, "as everyone knew."

Summary

- Some civil liberties are rather routinely set aside when mental health professionals and the courts judge that mental illness has played a decisive role in determining an individual's behavior. This may occur through criminal or civil commitment.

- Criminal commitment sends a person to a hospital either before a trial for an alleged crime, because the person is deemed incompetent to stand trial, or after an acquittal by reason of insanity.

- Several landmark cases and principles in Anglo-American law address the conditions under which a person who has committed a crime might be excused from legal responsibility for it—that is, not guilty by reason of insanity. These involve the presence of an irresistible impulse, the notion that some people may not be able to distinguish between right and wrong (the M'Naghten rule), and the principle that a person should not be held criminally responsible if his or her unlawful act is the product of mental disease or mental defect (the Durham principle). The Insanity Defense Reform Act of 1984 made it harder for accused criminals to argue insanity as an excusing condition.

- Today, a relatively new verdict—guilty but mentally ill—is in use in a number of states. This emergent legal doctrine reflects an uneasiness in legal and mental health circles about not holding people ascriptively responsible for crimes for which they are descriptively responsible.

- There is an important difference between mental illness and insanity. The latter is a legal concept. A person can be diagnosed as mentally ill and yet be deemed sane enough both to stand trial and to be found guilty of a crime.

- A person who is considered mentally ill and dangerous to self and to others, although he or she has not broken a law, can be civilly committed to an institution or be allowed to live outside of a hospital but only under supervision and with restrictions placed on his or her activities.

- Recent court rulings have provided greater protection to all committed mental patients, particularly those under civil commitment. They have the right to written notification, to counsel, to a jury decision concerning their commitment, and to Fifth Amendment protection against self-incrimination; the right to the least restrictive treatment setting; the right to be treated; and in most circumstances, the right to refuse treatment, particularly any procedure that entails considerable risk. However, there is a trend toward preventive detention when, for example, convicted sexual predators are about to be released from prison with every indication that they will harm others again.

- Ethical issues concerning research include restraints on what kinds of research are allowable and the duty of scientists to obtain informed consent from prospective human subjects.

- In the area of therapy, ethical issues concern the right of clients to confidentiality, the question of who is the client (for example, an individual or the state mental hospital that is paying the clinician), the question of who sets the therapy goals, and the choice of techniques. Diagnosis of sexual abuse in childhood based on so-called recovered memories has also presented ethical problems, as well as legal dilemmas, for therapists.

Key Terms

advanced directive	criminal commitment	irresistible impulse	outpatient commitment
civil commitment	informed consent	M'Naghten rule	privileged communication
confidentiality	insanity defense		

Glossary

abnormal behavior. Patterns of emotion, thought, and action deemed pathological for one or more of the following reasons: infrequent occurrence, violation of norms, personal distress, disability or dysfunction, and unexpectedness.

accurate empathic understanding. In client-centered therapy, an essential quality of the therapist, referring to the ability to see the world through the client's *phenomenology*[1] as well as from perspectives of which the client may be only dimly aware.

acetylcholine. A *neurotransmitter* of the central, *somatomotor*, and *parasympathetic nervous systems* and of the ganglia and the *neuron*–sweat gland junctions of the *sympathetic nervous system.*

acquaintance (date) rape. Forcible sex when the people involved know each other, sometimes occurring on a date.

acute stress disorder. New in DSM-IV, a short-lived anxiety reaction to a traumatic event; if it lasts more than a month, it is diagnosed as *posttraumatic stress disorder.*

addiction. See *substance dependence.*

adoptees method. Research method which studies children who were adopted and reared completely apart from their abnormal parents, thereby eliminating the influence of being raised by disordered parents.

adrenal glands. Two small areas of tissue located just above the kidneys. The inner core of each gland the medulla, secretes *epinephrine* and *norepinephrine*; the outer cortex secretes *cortisol* and other steroid hormones.

adrenaline. A hormone that is secreted by the *adrenal glands*; also called *epinephrine.*

adrenergic system. All the nerve cells for which *epinephrine* and *norepinephrine* are the transmitter substances, as contrasted with the *cholinergic system*, which consists of the nerve cells activated by acetylcholine.

advanced directive. Legal document in which an individual prescribes and proscribes certain courses of action that are to be taken to preserve his or her health or terminate life support. These instructions are prepared before the person becomes incapable of making such decisions.

advanced accurate empathy. A form of *empathy* in which the therapist infers concerns and feelings that lie behind what the client is saying; it represents an *interpretation*. Compare with *primary empathy.*

affect. A subjective feeling or emotional tone often accompanied by bodily expressions noticeable to others.

age effects. The consequences of being a given chronological age. Compare with *cohort effects.*

ageism. Discrimination against someone because of his or her age.

agoraphobia. A cluster of fears centering on being in open spaces and leaving the home. It is often linked to *panic disorder.*

AIDS (acquired immunodeficiency syndrome). A fatal disease transmitted by transfer of the human immunodeficiency virus, usually during sexual relations or by using needles previously infected by an HIV-positive person; it compromises the immune system to such a degree that the person ultimately dies from cancer or from one of any number of infections.

alcoholism. A behavioral disorder in which consumption of alcoholic beverages is excessive and impairs health and social and occupational functioning; a physiological dependence on alcohol. See *substance dependence.*

alkaloid. An organic base found in seed plants, usually in mixture with a number of similar alkaloids. Alkaloids are the active chemicals that give many drugs their medicinal properties and other powerful physiological effects.

alogia. A *negative symptom* in *schizophrenia*, marked by poverty of speech and of speech content.

---

[1]Italicized words or variants of these terms are themselves defined elsewhere in the glossary.

alternate form reliability. See *reliability.*

altruistic suicide. As defined by Durkheim, self-annihilation that the person feels will serve a social purpose, such as the self-immolations practiced by Buddhist monks during the Vietnam War.

Alzheimer's disease. A *dementia* involving a progressive atrophy of cortical tissue and marked by memory impairment, involuntary movements of limbs, occasional convulsions, intellectual deterioration, and psychotic behavior.

ambivalence. The simultaneous holding of strong positive and negative emotional attitudes toward the same situation or person.

American Law Institute guidelines. Rules proposing that *insanity* is a legitimate defense plea if during criminal conduct, an individual could not judge right from wrong or control his or her behavior as required by law. Repetitive criminal acts are disavowed as a sole criterion. Compare *M'Naghten rule* and *irresistible impulse.*

amino acid. One of a large class of organic compounds important as the building blocks of proteins.

amnesia. Total or partial loss of memory that can be associated with a *dissociative disorder*, brain damage, or *hypnosis.*

amniocentesis. A prenatal diagnostic technique in which fluid drawn from the uterus is tested for birth defects, such as *Down syndrome.*

amphetamines. A group of stimulating drugs that produce heightened levels of energy and, in large doses, nervousness, sleeplessness, and paranoid *delusions.*

anal personality. An adult who, when anal retentive, is found by psychoanalytic theory to be stingy and sometimes obsessively clean; when anal expulsive, to be aggressive. Such traits are assumed to be caused by *fixation* through either excessive or inadequate gratification of id impulses during the *anal stage* of *psychosexual* development.

anal stage. In psychoanalytic theory, the second *psychosexual* stage, which occurs during the second year of life when the anus is considered the principal *erogenous zone.*

analgesia. An insensitivity to pain without loss of consciousness, sometimes found in *conversion disorder.*

analogue experiment. An experimental study of a phenomenon different from but related to the actual interests of the investigator.

analysand. A person being *psychoanalyzed.*

analysis of defenses. The study by a *psychoanalyst* of the ways in which a patient avoids troubling topics by the use of *defense mechanisms.*

analyst. See *psychoanalyst.*

analytical psychology. A variation of Freud's *psychoanalysis* introduced by Carl Jung and focusing less on biological drives and more on factors such as self-fulfillment, collective *unconscious*, and religious symbolism.

anesthesia. An impairment or loss of sensation, usually of touch but sometimes of the other senses, that is often part of *conversion disorder.*

anger-in theory. The view that *psychophysiological disorders*, such as *essential hypertension*, arise from a person's not expressing anger or resentment.

angina pectoris. See *coronary heart disease.*

anhedonia. A *negative symptom* in *schizophrenia* in which the individual is unable to feel pleasure.

animal phobia. The fear and avoidance of animals.

anomic suicide. As defined by Durkheim, self-annihilation triggered by a person's inability to cope with sudden and unfavorable change in a social situation.

anorexia nervosa. A disorder in which a person refuses to maintain normal weight, has an intense fear of becoming obese, and feels fat even when emaciated.

anoxia. A deficiency of oxygen reaching the tissues that is severe enough to damage the brain permanently.

Antabuse (trade name for disulfiram). A drug that makes the drinking of alcohol produce nausea and other unpleasant effects.

antidepressant. A drug that alleviates *depression*, usually by energizing the patient and thus elevating mood.

antipsychotic drug. Psychoactive drugs, such as *Thorazine*, that reduce *psychotic* symptoms but have long-term side effects resembling symptoms of neurological *diseases*.

antisocial personality. Also called a psychopath or a sociopath, a person with this disorder is superficially charming and a habitual liar, has no regard for others, shows no remorse after hurting others, has no shame for behaving in an outrageously objectionable manner, is unable to form relationships and take responsibility, and does not learn from punishment.

anxiety. An unpleasant feeling of fear and apprehension accompanied by increased physiological arousal. In learning theory it is considered a drive that mediates between a threatening situation and avoidance behavior. *Anxiety* can be assessed by self-report, by measuring physiological arousal, and by observing overt behavior.

anxiety disorders. Disorders in which fear or tension is overriding and the primary disturbance: *phobic disorders, panic disorder, generalized anxiety disorder, obsessive-compulsive disorder, acute stress disorder,* and *posttraumatic stress disorder.* These disorders form a major category in DSM-IV-TR and cover most of what used to be referred to as the *neuroses.*

anxiety neurosis. DSM-II term for what are now diagnosed as *panic disorder* and *generalized anxiety disorder.*

anxiolytics. Tranquilizers; drugs that reduce *anxiety.*

aphasia. The loss or impairment of the ability to use language because of lesions in the brain: *executive*, difficulties in speaking or writing the words intended; *receptive*, difficulties in understanding written or spoken language.

apnea. Cessation of breathing for short periods of time, sometimes occurring during sleep.

applied behavior analysis. The study of the antecedent conditions and *reinforcement* contingencies that control behavior. See also *operant conditioning.*

aptitude test. A paper-and-pencil assessment of a person's intellectual functioning that is supposed to predict how the person will perform at a later time; well-known examples include the Scholastic Aptitude Test and the Graduate Record Examination.

aptitude-treatment interaction. The suitability of a particular therapeutic intervention to a particular patient characteristic.

arousal. A state of behavioral or physiological activation.

ascriptive responsibility. The social judgment assigned to someone who has committed an illegal act and who is expected by society to be punished for it. Contrast with *descriptive responsibility.*

asociality. A *negative symptom* of *schizophrenia* marked by an inability to form close relationships and to feel intimacy.

Asperger's disorder. Believed to be a mild form of *autism* in which social relationships are poor and stereotyped behavior is intense and rigid, but language and intelligence are intact.

assertion training. *Behavior therapy* procedures that attempt to help a person more easily express thoughts, wishes, beliefs, and legitimate feelings of resentment or approval.

asthma. A *psychophysiological disorder* characterized by narrowing of the airways and increased secretion of mucus, often causing extremely labored and wheezy breathing.

asylums. Refuges established in western Europe in the fifteenth century to confine and provide for the mentally ill; the forerunners of the mental hospital.

attention-deficit/hyperactivity disorder (ADHD). A disorder in children marked by difficulties in focusing adaptively on the task at hand, by inappropriate fidgeting and antisocial behavior, and by excessive non-goal-directed behavior.

attribution. The explanation a person has for his or her behavior.

autistic disorder. In this *pervasive developmental disorder*, the child's world is one of profound aloneness. Speech is often absent, and the child has an obsessive need for everything to remain the same.

automatic thoughts. In Beck's theory, the things people picture or tell themselves as they make their way in life.

autonomic lability. Tendency for the *autonomic nervous system* to be easily aroused.

autonomic nervous system (ANS). The division of the nervous system that regulates involuntary functions; innervates *endocrine glands, smooth muscle,* and *heart muscle*; and initiates the physiological changes that are part of the expression of emotion. See *sympathetic* and *parasympathetic nervous systems.*

aversion therapy. A *behavior therapy* procedure that pairs a noxious stimulus, such as a shock, with situations that are undesirably attractive to make the situations less appealing.

aversive conditioning. Process believed to underlie the effectiveness of *aversion therapy.*

aversive stimulus. A stimulus that elicits pain, fear, or avoidance.

avoidance conditioning. Learning to move away from a stimulus that has previously been paired with an *aversive stimulus* such as electric shock.

avoidance learning. An experimental procedure in which a neutral stimulus is paired with a noxious one so that the organism learns to avoid the previously neutral stimulus.

avoidant personality disorder. Individuals with this disorder have poor self-esteem and thus are extremely sensitive to potential rejection and remain aloof even though they very much desire affiliation and affection.

avolition. A *negative symptom* in *schizophrenia* in which the individual lacks interest and drive.

barbiturates. A class of synthetic *sedative* drugs that are addictive and in large doses can cause death by almost completely relaxing the diaphragm.

baseline. The state of a phenomenon before the *independent variable* is manipulated, providing a standard against which the effects of the variable can be measured.

behavior genetics. The study of individual differences in behavior that are attributable to differences in genetic makeup.

behavior modification. A term sometimes used interchangeably with *behavior therapy.*

behavior rehearsal. A *behavior therapy* technique in which a client practices new behavior in the consulting room, often aided by demonstrations and role-play by the therapist.

behavior therapy. A branch of *psychotherapy* narrowly conceived as the application of *classical* and *operant conditioning* to the alteration of clinical problems, but more broadly conceived as applied experimental psychology in a clinical context.

behavioral assessment. A sampling of ongoing cognitions, feelings, and overt behavior in their situational context. Contrast with *projective test* and *personality inventory.*

behavioral medicine. An interdisciplinary field concerned with integrating knowledge from medicine and behavioral science to understand health and illness and to prevent as well as to treat *psychophysiological disorders* and other illnesses in which a person's psyche plays a role. See also *health psychology.*

behavioral observation. A form of *behavioral assessment* that entails careful observation of a person's overt behavior in a particular situation.

behavioral pediatrics. A branch of *behavioral medicine* concerned with psychological aspects of childhood medical problems.

behaviorism. The school of psychology associated with John B. Watson, who proposed that observable behavior, not consciousness, is the proper subject matter of psychology. Currently, many who consider themselves behaviorists do use *mediational* concepts, provided they are firmly anchored to observables.

bell and pad. A *behavior therapy* technique for eliminating nocturnal *enuresis*; if the child wets, an electric circuit is closed and a bell sounds, waking the child.

bilateral ECT. *Electroconvulsive therapy* in which electrodes are placed on each side of the forehead and an electrical current is passed between them through both hemispheres of the brain.

binge eating disorder. Categorized in DSM-IV-TR as a diagnosis in need of further study; includes recurrent episodes of unrestrained eating.

biofeedback. Procedures that provide an individual immediate information on minute changes in muscle activity, skin temperature, heart rate, blood pressure, and other somatic functions. It is assumed that voluntary control over these bodily processes can be achieved through this knowledge, thereby ameliorating to some extent certain *psychophysiological disorders.*

biological paradigm. A broad theoretical view that holds that mental disorders are caused by some aberrant somatic process or defect.

bipolar I disorder. A term applied to the disorder of people who experience episodes of both *mania* and *depression* or of *mania* alone.

bisexuality. Sexual desire or activity directed toward both men and women.

blocking. A disturbance associated with *thought disorders* in which a train of speech is interrupted by silence before an idea is fully expressed.

body dysmorphic disorder. A *somatoform disorder* marked by preoccupation with an imagined or exaggerated defect in appearance, for example, facial wrinkles or excess facial or body hair.

borderline personality disorder. People with a borderline personality are impulsive and unpredictable, with an uncertain self-image, intense and unstable social relationships, and extreme swings of mood.

brain stem. The part of the brain connecting the spinal cord with the *cerebrum*. It contains the *pons* and *medulla oblongata* and functions as a neural relay station.

brief reactive psychosis. A disorder in which a person has a sudden onset of psychotic symptoms—*incoherence, loose associations, delusions, hallucinations*—immediately after a severely disturbing event; the symptoms last more than a few hours but no more than two weeks. See *schizophreniform disorder*.

brief therapy. Time-limited psychotherapy, usually ego-analytic in orientation and lasting no more than twenty-five sessions.

Briquet's syndrome. See *somatization disorder*.

bulimia nervosa. A disorder characterized by episodic uncontrollable eating binges followed by purging either by vomiting or by taking laxatives.

Cannabis sativa. See *marijuana*.

cardiovascular disorder. A medical problem involving the heart and the blood circulation system, such as *hypertension* or *coronary heart disease*.

case study. The collection of historical or biographical information on a single individual, often including experiences in therapy.

castration. The surgical removal of the *testes*.

castration anxiety. The fear of having the genitals removed or injured.

catatonic immobility. A fixity of posture, sometimes grotesque, maintained for long periods, with accompanying muscular rigidity, trancelike state of consciousness, and *waxy flexibility*.

catatonic schizophrenia. A subtype of *schizophrenia* whose primary symptoms alternate between stuporous immobility and excited agitation.

catecholamines. *Monoamine* compounds, each having a catechol portion. Catecholamines known to be *neurotransmitters* of the central nervous system are *norepinephrine* and *dopamine*; another, *epinephrine*, is principally a hormone.

categorical classification. An approach to assessment in which the basic decision is whether a person is or is not a member of a discrete grouping. Contrast with *dimensional classification*.

cathartic method. A therapeutic procedure introduced by Breuer and developed further by Freud in the late nineteenth century whereby a patient recalls and relives an earlier emotional catastrophe and reexperiences the tension and unhappiness, the goal being to relieve emotional suffering.

central nervous system. The part of the nervous system that in vertebrates consists of the brain and spinal cord, to which all sensory impulses are transmitted and from which motor impulses pass out; it also supervises and coordinates the activities of the entire nervous system.

cerebellum. An area of the hindbrain concerned with balance, posture, and motor coordination.

cerebral atherosclerosis. A chronic disease impairing intellectual and emotional life, caused by a reduction in the brain's blood supply through a buildup of fatty deposits in the arteries.

cerebral contusion. A bruising of neural tissue marked by swelling and hemorrhage and resulting in coma; it may permanently impair intellectual functioning.

cerebral cortex. The thin outer covering of each of the *cerebral hemispheres*; it is highly convoluted and composed of nerve cell bodies which constitute the *gray matter* of the brain.

cerebral hemisphere. Either of the two halves that make up the *cerebrum*.

cerebral hemorrhage. Bleeding onto brain tissue from a ruptured blood vessel.

cerebral thrombosis. The formation of a blood clot in a cerebral artery that blocks circulation in that area of brain tissue and causes paralysis, loss of sensory functions, and possibly death.

cerebrovascular disease. An illness that disrupts blood supply to the brain, such as a *stroke*.

cerebrum. The two-lobed structure extending from the *brain stem* and constituting the anterior (frontal) part of the brain. The largest and most recently developed portion of the brain, it coordinates sensory and motor activities and is the seat of higher cognitive processes.

character disorder. The old term for *personality disorder*.

child sexual abuse. Sexual contact with a minor.

childhood disintegrative disorder. A lifelong developmental disorder characterized by significant loss of social, play, language, and motor skills after the second year of life. Abnormalities in social interaction and communication are similar to *autism*.

chlorpromazine. One of the *phenothiazines*, the generic term for one of the most widely prescribed *antipsychotic drugs*, sold under the name *Thorazine*.

cholinergic system. All the nerve cells for which *acetylcholine* is the transmitter substance, in contrast to the *adrenergic system*.

choreiform. Pertaining to the involuntary, spasmodic, jerking movements of the limbs and head found in *Huntington's chorea* and other brain disorders.

chromosomes. The threadlike bodies within the nucleus of the cell, composed primarily of DNA and bearing the genetic information of the organism.

chronic. Of lengthy duration or recurring frequently, often with progressing seriousness.

chronic brain syndrome. See *senile dementia*.

civil commitment. A procedure whereby a person can be legally certified as mentally ill and hospitalized, even against his or her will.

classical conditioning. A basic form of learning, sometimes referred to as Pavlovian conditioning, in which a neutral stimulus is repeatedly paired with another stimulus (called the *unconditioned stimulus*, UCS) that naturally elicits a certain desired response (called the *unconditioned response*, UCR). After repeated trials the neutral stimulus becomes a *conditioned stimulus* (CS) and evokes the same or a similar response, now called the *conditioned response* (CR).

classificatory variables. The characteristics that people bring with them to scientific investigations, such as sex, age, and mental status; studied by *correlational research* and *mixed designs*.

client-centered therapy. A *humanistic-existential insight therapy*, developed by Carl Rogers, which emphasizes the importance of the therapist's understanding the client's subjective experiences and assisting the client to gain more awareness of current motivations for behavior; the goal is not only to reduce anxieties but also to foster actualization of the client's potential.

clinical interview. General term for conversation between a clinician and a patient that is aimed at determining diagnosis, history, causes for problems, and possible treatment options.

clinical psychologist. An individual who has earned a Ph.D. degree in psychology or a Psy.D. and whose training has included an internship in a mental hospital or clinic.

clinical psychology. The special area of psychology concerned with the study of psychopathology, its diagnosis, causes, prevention, and treatment.

clinician. A health professional authorized to provide services to people suffering from one or more pathologies.

clitoris. The small, heavily innervated structure located above the vaginal opening; the primary site of female responsiveness to sexual stimulation.

clonidine. An antihypertensive drug that shows some promise in helping people wean themselves from *substance dependence*.

cocaine. A pain-reducing, stimulating, and addictive *alkaloid* obtained from coca leaves, which increases mental powers, produces euphoria, heightens sexual desire, and in large doses causes *paranoia* and *hallucinations*.

cognition. The process of knowing; the thinking, judging, reasoning, and planning activities of the human mind; behavior is now often explained as depending on these processes.

cognitive behavior therapy (CBT). *Behavior therapy* which incorporates theory and research on *cognitive* processes such as thoughts, perceptions, judgments, self-statements, and tacit assumptions. A blend of both the cognitive and behavioral paradigms.

cognitive paradigm. General view that people can best be understood by studying how they perceive and structure their experiences.

cognitive restructuring. Any *behavior therapy* procedure that attempts to alter the manner in which a client thinks about life so that he or she changes overt behavior and emotions.

cognitive therapy (CT). A *cognitive restructuring* therapy associated with the psychiatrist Aaron T. Beck, concerned with changing negative *schemata* and certain cognitive biases or distortions that influence a person to construe life in a depressing or otherwise maladaptive way.

cohort effects. The consequences of having been born in a given year and having grown up during a particular time period with its own unique pressures, problems, challenges, and opportunities. To be distinguished from *age effects*.

coitus. Sexual intercourse.

collective unconscious. Jung's concept that every human being has within him or her the wisdom, ideas, and strivings of those who have come before.

communication disorders. Learning disabilities in a child who fails to develop to the degree expected by his or her intellectual level in a specific language skill area. Includes expressive language disorder, phonological disorder, and stuttering.

community mental health. The delivery of services to needy, underserved groups through centers that offer outpatient therapy, short-term inpatient care, day hospitalization, twenty-four-hour emergency services, and consultation and education to other community agencies, such as the police.

community psychology. An approach to therapy that emphasizes prevention and the seeking out of potential difficulties rather than waiting for troubled individuals to initiate consultation. The location for professional activities tends to be in the person's natural surroundings rather than in the therapist's office. See *prevention*.

comorbidity. The co-occurrence of two disorders, as when a person is both depressed and alcoholic.

competency to stand trial. A legal decision as to whether a person can participate meaningfully in his or her own defense.

compulsion. The irresistible impulse to repeat an irrational act over and over again.

concordance. As applied in *behavior genetics*, the similarity in psychiatric diagnosis or in other traits within a pair of twins.

concurrent validity. See *validity*.

concussion. A jarring injury to the brain produced by a blow to the head that usually involves a momentary loss of consciousness followed by transient disorientation and memory loss.

conditioned response (CR). See *classical conditioning*.

conditioned stimulus (CS). See *classical conditioning*.

conduct disorder. Patterns of extreme disobedience in youngsters, including theft, vandalism, lying, and early drug use; may be precursor of *antisocial personality disorder*.

confabulation. Filling in gaps in memory caused by brain dysfunction with made-up and often improbable stories that the person accepts as true.

confidentiality. A principle observed by lawyers, doctors, pastors, psychologists, and psychiatrists that dictates that the goings-on in a professional and private relationship are not divulged to anyone else. See *privileged communication*.

conflict. A state of being torn between competing forces.

confounds. Variables whose effects are so intermixed that they cannot be measured separately, making the design of an *experiment* internally invalid and its results impossible to interpret.

congenital. Existing at or before birth but not acquired through heredity.

conjoint therapy. *Couples* or *family therapy* where partners are seen together and children are seen with their parents and possibly with an extended family.

construct. An entity inferred by a scientist to explain observed phenomena. See also *mediator*.

construct validity. The extent to which scores or ratings on an assessment instrument relate to other variables or behaviors according to some theory or hypothesis.

content validity. See *validity*.

contingency. A close relationship, especially of a causal nature, between two events, one of which regularly follows the other.

control group. Those in an *experiment* for whom the *independent variable* is not manipulated, thus forming a *baseline* against which the effects of the manipulation of the experimental group can be evaluated.

controlled drinking. A pattern of alcohol consumption that is moderate and avoids the extremes of total abstinence and of inebriation.

conversion disorder. A *somatoform disorder* in which sensory or muscular functions are impaired, usually suggesting neurological disease, even though the bodily organs themselves are sound; *anesthesias* and paralyses of limbs are examples.

convulsive therapy. See *electroconvulsive therapy*.

coronary heart disease (CHD). Angina pectoris, chest pains caused by insufficient supply of blood and thus oxygen to the heart; and myocardial infarction, or heart attack, in which the blood and oxygen supply is reduced so much that heart muscles are damaged.

corpus callosum. The large band of nerve fibers connecting the two *cerebral hemispheres*.

correlation. The tendency for two *variables*, such as height and weight, to co-vary.

correlation coefficient. A statistic that measures the degree to which two *variables* are related.

correlational method. The research strategy used to establish whether two or more *variables* are related. Relationships may be positive—as values for one variable increase, those for the other do also—or negative—as values for one variable increase, those for the other decrease.

cortisol. A hormone secreted by the *adrenal* cortices.

co-twin. In *behavior genetics* research using the *twin method*, the member of the pair who is tested later to determine whether he or she has the same diagnosis or trait discovered earlier in the birth partner.

counseling psychologist. A doctoral level mental health professional whose training is similar to that of a *clinical psychologist*, though usually with less emphasis on research and serious *psychopathology*.

counterconditioning. Relearning achieved by eliciting a new response in the presence of a particular stimulus.

countertransference. Feelings that the *psychoanalyst* unconsciously directs to the *analysand*, stemming from his or her own emotional vulnerabilities and unresolved *conflicts*.

couples (marital) therapy. Any professional intervention that treats relationship problems of a couple.

covert sensitization. A form of *aversion therapy* in which the person is told to imagine undesirably attractive situations and activities while unpleasant feelings are being induced by imagery.

criminal commitment. A procedure whereby a person is confined in a mental institution either for determination of *competency to stand trial* or after acquittal by reason of insanity.

criterion validity. See *validity*.

critical period. A stage of early development in which an organism is susceptible to certain influences and during which important irreversible patterns of behavior are acquired.

cross-dependent. Acting on the same receptors, as *methadone* does with *heroin*. See *heroin substitutes*.

cross-sectional studies. Studies in which different age groups are compared at the same time. Compare with *longitudinal studies*.

CT scan. Refers to computerized axial tomography, a method of diagnosis in which X rays are taken from different angles and then analyzed by computer to produce a representation of the part of the body in cross section; often used on the brain.

cultural-familial retardation. A mild backwardness in mental development with no indication of brain pathology but evidence of similar limitation in at least one of the parents or siblings.

cunnilingus. The oral stimulation of female genitalia.

Cushing's syndrome. An endocrine disorder usually affecting young women, produced by oversecretion of *cortisone* and marked by mood swings, irritability, agitation, and physical disfigurement.

cyclical psychodynamics. The reciprocal relations between current behavior and *repressed* conflicts, such that they mutually reinforce each other.

cyclothymic disorder. Chronic swings between elation and depression not severe enough to warrant the diagnosis of *bipolar disorder*.

defense mechanisms. In psychoanalytic theory, reality-distorting strategies unconsciously adopted to protect the *ego* from *anxiety*.

delay of reward gradient. The learning theory term for the finding that rewards and punishments lose their effectiveness the further they are removed in time from the response in question.

delayed echolalia. See *echolalia*.

delirium. A state of great mental confusion in which consciousness is clouded, attention cannot be sustained, and the stream of thought and speech is incoherent. The person is probably disoriented, emotionally erratic, restless or lethargic, and often has *illusions*, *delusions*, and *hallucinations*.

delirium tremens (DTs). One of the *withdrawal* symptoms that sometimes occurs when a period of heavy alcohol consumption is terminated; marked by fever, sweating, trembling, cognitive impairment, and *hallucinations*.

delusional (paranoid) disorder. A disorder in which the individual has persistent persecutory *delusions* or *delusional jealousy* and is very often contentious but has no *thought disorder* or hallucinations.

delusional jealousy. The unfounded conviction that one's mate is unfaithful; the individual may collect small bits of "evidence" to justify the *delusion*.

delusions. Beliefs contrary to reality, firmly held in spite of evidence to the contrary; common in *paranoid disorders*; **of control**, belief that one is being manipulated by some external force such as radar, television, or a creature from outer space; **of grandeur**, belief that one is an especially important or powerful person; **of persecution**, belief that one is being plotted against or oppressed by others.

dementia. Deterioration of mental faculties—memory, judgment, abstract thought, control of impulses, intellectual ability—that impairs social and occupational functioning and eventually changes the personality. See *Alzheimer's disease*.

dementia praecox. An older term for *schizophrenia*, chosen to describe what was believed to be an incurable and progressive deterioration of mental functioning beginning in adolescence.

demographic variable. A varying characteristic that is a vital or social statistic of an individual, sample group, or population, for example, age, sex, *socioeconomic status*, racial origin, education.

demonology. The doctrine that a person's *abnormal behavior* is caused by an autonomous evil spirit.

denial. *Defense mechanism* in which a thought, feeling, or action is disavowed by the person.

dependent personality disorder. Lacking in self-confidence, such people passively allow others to run their lives and make no demands on them so as not to endanger these protective relationships.

dependent variable. In a psychological experiment, the behavior that is measured and is expected to change with manipulation of the *independent variable*.

depersonalization. An alteration in perception of the self in which the individual loses a sense of reality and feels estranged from the self and perhaps separated from the body. It may be a temporary reaction to *stress* and fatigue or part of *panic disorder, depersonalization disorder*, or *schizophrenia*.

depersonalization disorder. A *dissociative disorder* in which the individual feels unreal and estranged from the self and surroundings enough to disrupt functioning. People with this disorder may feel that their extremities have changed in size or that they are watching themselves from a distance.

depression. A disorder marked by great sadness and apprehension, feelings of worthlessness and guilt, withdrawal from others, loss of sleep, appetite, sexual desire, loss of interest and pleasure in usual activities, and either lethargy or agitation. Called *major depression* in DSM-IV-TR and *unipolar depression* by others. It can be an associated symptom of other disorders.

derealization. Loss of the sense that the surroundings are real; present in several psychological disorders, such as *panic disorder, depersonalization disorder*, and *schizophrenia*.

descriptive responsibility. In legal proceedings, the judgment that the accused performed an illegal act. Contrast with *ascriptive responsibility*.

deterioration effect. In abnormal psychology, a harmful outcome from being in psychotherapy.

detoxification. The initial stage in weaning an addicted person from a drug; involves medical supervision of the sometimes painful *withdrawal*.

detumescence. The flow of blood out of the genital area.

diagnosis. The determination that the set of symptoms or problems of a patient indicates a particular disorder.

dialectical behavior therapy. A therapeutic approach to *borderline personality disorder* that combines *client-centered empathy* and acceptance with behavioral problem solving, social-skills training, and limit setting.

diathesis. *Predisposition* toward a disease or abnormality.

diathesis–stress paradigm. As applied in *psychopathology*, a view that assumes that individuals predisposed toward a particular mental disorder will be particularly affected by *stress* and will then manifest *abnormal behavior*.

dichotic listening. An experimental procedure in which a person hears two different taped messages simultaneously through earphones, one in each ear, usually with the instruction to attend to only one of the messages.

diencephalon. The lower area of the forebrain, containing the *thalamus* and *hypothalamus*.

dimensional classification. An approach to assessment according to which a person is placed on a continuum. Contrast with *categorical classification*.

directionality problem. A difficulty that arises in the *correlational method* of research when it is known that two *variables* are related but it is unclear which is causing the other.

discriminative stimulus. An event that informs an organism that if a particular response is made, *reinforcement* will follow.

disease. The medical concept that distinguishes an impairment of the normal state of the organism by its particular group of symptoms and its specific cause.

disease model. See *medical model*.

disorder of written expression. Difficulties writing without errors in spelling, grammar, or punctuation.

disorganized schizophrenia. In this subtype of *schizophrenia* the person has diffuse and *regressive* symptoms; the individual is given to silliness, facial grimaces, and inconsequential rituals and has constantly changeable moods and poor hygiene. There are few significant remissions and eventually considerable deterioration. This form of *schizophrenia* was formerly called *hebephrenia*.

disorganized speech (thought disorder). Speech found in schizophrenics that is marked by problems in the organization of ideas and in speaking so that others can understand.

disorientation. A state of mental confusion with respect to time, place, identity of self, other persons, and objects.

displacement. A *defense mechanism* whereby an emotional response is unconsciously redirected from an object or concept perceived as dangerous to a substitute less threatening to the *ego*.

dissociation. A process whereby a group of mental processes is split off from the mainstream of consciousness, or behavior loses its relationship with the rest of the personality.

dissociative amnesia. A *dissociative disorder* in which the person suddenly becomes unable to recall important personal information to an extent that cannot be explained by ordinary forgetfulness.

dissociative disorders. Disorders in which the normal integration of consciousness, memory, or identity is suddenly and temporarily altered; *dissociative amnesia, dissociative fugue, dissociative identity disorder (multiple personality)*, and *depersonalization disorder* are examples.

dissociative fugue. Disorder in which the person experiences total *amnesia*, moves, and establishes a new identity.

dissociative identity disorder (DID). A rare *dissociative disorder* in which two or more fairly distinct and separate personalities are present within the same individual, each with his or her own memories, relationships, and behavior patterns, with only one of them dominant at any given time. Formerly called multiple personality disorder.

divorce mediation. A form of *couples (marital) therapy* in which a distressed couple is helped to collaborate on issues such as child custody outside the adversarial framework of a formal legal process.

dizygotic (DZ) twins. Birth partners who have developed from separate fertilized eggs and who are only 50 percent alike genetically, no more so than siblings born from different pregnancies; sometimes called fraternal twins.

dominant gene. One of a pair of *genes* that predominates over the other and determines that the trait it fosters will prevail in the *phenotype*.

dopamine. A *catecholamine* that is both a precursor of *norepinephrine* and itself a *neurotransmitter* of the *central nervous system*. Disturbances in certain of its tracts apparently figure in *schizophrenia* and *Parkinson's disease*.

dopamine activity theory. The view that *schizophrenia* arises from an increase in the number of *dopamine* receptors.

double-bind theory. An interpersonal situation in which an individual is confronted over long periods of time by mutually inconsistent messages to which she or he must respond, formerly believed by some theorists to cause *schizophrenia*.

double-blind procedure. A method for reducing the biasing effects of the expectations of research participant and experimenter; neither is allowed to know whether the independent *variable* of the experiment is being applied to the participant.

Down syndrome (trisomy 21). A form of mental retardation generally caused by an extra chromosome. The child's *IQ* is usually less than 50, and the child has distinctive physical characteristics, most notably slanted eyes.

dream analysis. A key psychoanalytic technique in which the unconscious meanings of dream material are uncovered.

drive. A construct explaining the motivation of behavior, or an internal physiological tension impelling an organism to activity.

drug abuse. See *substance abuse*.

drug addiction. See *substance dependence*.

DSM-IV-TR. The current *Diagnostic and Statistical Manual of Mental Disorders* of the American Psychiatric Association.

dualism. Philosophical doctrine, advanced most definitively by Descartes, that a human being is both mental and physical and that these two aspects are separate but interacting. Contrast with *monism*.

Durham decision. A 1954 U.S. court ruling that an accused person is not *ascriptively responsible* if his or her crime is judged attributable to mental disease or defect.

dysfunction. An impairment or disturbance in the functioning of an organ, organ system, behavior, or *cognition*.

dyslexia. A disturbance in the ability to read; it is one of the *learning disorders*.

dyspareunia. Painful or difficult sexual intercourse; the pain or difficulty is usually caused by infection or a physical injury, such as torn ligaments in the pelvic region.

dysthymic disorder. State of *depression* that is long lasting but not severe enough for the diagnosis of *major depression.*

echolalia. The immediate repetition of the words of others, often found in autistic children. In **delayed echolalia** this inappropriate echoing takes place hours or weeks later.

eclecticism. In psychology, the view that more is to be gained by employing concepts and techniques from various theoretical systems than by restricting oneself to a single approach.

ecological momentary assessment (EMA). Form of self-observation involving collection of data in real time (e.g., diaries) regarding thoughts, moods, and stressors.

Ecstasy. A relatively new *hallucinogen* that is chemically similar to *mescaline* and the *amphetamines.*

ego. In psychoanalytic theory, the predominantly conscious part of the personality, responsible for decision making and for dealing with reality.

ego analysis. An important set of modifications of classical *psychoanalysis*, based on a conception of the human being as having a stronger, more autonomous ego with gratifications independent of *id* satisfactions. Sometimes called *ego psychology.*

ego analysts. Those who practice *ego analysis.*

ego-alien. Foreign to the self, such as a *compulsion.*

ego-dystonic homosexuality. According to DSM-III, a disorder of people who are persistently dissatisfied with their *homosexuality* and wish instead to be attracted to members of the opposite sex.

egoistic suicide. As defined by Durkheim, self-annihilation committed because the individual feels extreme alienation from others and from society.

Electra complex. See *Oedipus complex.*

electrocardiogram. A recording of the electrical activity of the heart, made with an electrocardiograph.

electroconvulsive therapy (ECT). A treatment that produces a convulsion by passing electric current through the brain. Though an unpleasant and occasionally dangerous procedure, it can be useful in alleviating profound *depression.*

electrodermal responding. A recording of the minute electrical activity of the sweat glands on the skin, allowing the inference of an emotional state.

electroencephalogram (EEG). A graphic recording of electrical activity of the brain, usually of the *cerebral cortex*, but sometimes of lower areas.

empathy. Awareness and understanding of another's feelings and thoughts. See *primary empathy* and *advanced accurate empathy.*

empty-chair technique. A *Gestalt therapy* procedure for helping the client become more aware of denied feelings; the client talks to important people or to feelings as though they were present and seated in a nearby vacant chair.

encephalitis. Inflammation of brain tissue caused by a number of agents, the most significant being several viruses carried by insects.

encephalitis lethargica. Known as sleeping sickness, a form of encephalitis that occurred early in this century and was characterized by lethargy and prolonged periods of sleeping.

encopresis. A disorder in which, through faulty control of the sphincters, the person repeatedly defecates in his or her clothing after an age at which continence is expected.

encounter group. See *sensitivity training group.*

endocrine gland. Any of a number of ductless glands that release *hormones* directly into the blood or lymph. The secretions of some endocrine glands increase during emotional arousal.

endogenous. Attributable to internal causes.

endorphins. *Opiates* produced within the body; they may have an important role in the processes by which the body builds up *tolerance* to drugs and is distressed by their withdrawal.

enuresis. A disorder in which, through faulty control of the bladder, the person wets repeatedly during the night (nocturnal enuresis) or during the day after an age at which continence is expected.

enzyme. A complex protein produced by the cells to act as a catalyst in regulating metabolic activities.

epidemiology. The study of the frequency and distribution of illness in a population.

epilepsy. An altered state of consciousness accompanied by sudden changes in the usual rhythmical electrical activity of the brain.

epinephrine. A *hormone* (a *catecholamine*) secreted by the medulla of the *adrenal gland*; its effects are similar, but not identical, to those of stimulating the *sympathetic* nerves. It causes an increase in blood pressure, inhibits peristaltic movements, and liberates glucose from the liver. Also called *adrenaline.*

erogenous. Capable of giving sexual pleasure when stimulated.

Eros (libido). Freud's term for the life-integrating instinct or force of the *id*, sometimes equated with sexual drive. Compare *Thanatos.*

essential hypertension. A *psychophysiological disorder* characterized by high blood pressure that cannot be traced to an organic cause. Over the years it causes degeneration of small arteries, enlargement of the heart, and kidney damage.

estrogen. A female sex hormone produced especially in the ovaries that stimulates the development and maintenance of the secondary sex characteristics, such as breast enlargement.

etiological validity. See *validity.*

etiology. All the factors that contribute to the development of an illness or disorder.

eugenics. The field concerned with improving the hereditary qualities of the human race through social control of mating and reproduction.

excitement phase. As applied by Masters and Johnson, the first stage of sexual arousal, which is initiated by any appropriate stimulus.

executive aphasia. See *aphasia.*

executive functioning. The *cognitive* capacity to plan how to do a task, how to devise strategies, and how to monitor one's performance.

exhibitionism. Marked preference for obtaining sexual gratification by exposing one's genitals to an unwilling observer.

existential analysis. See *existential therapy.*

existential therapy. An *insight therapy* that emphasizes choice and responsibility to define the meaning of one's life. In contrast with *humanistic therapy*, it tends to be less cheerful or sanguine in outlook, focusing more on the *anxiety* that is inherent to confronting one's ultimate aloneness in the world.

exogenous. Attributable to external causes.

exorcism. The casting out of evil spirits by ritualistic chanting or torture.

experiment. The most powerful research technique for determining causal relationships, requiring the manipulation of an *independent variable*, the measurement of a *dependent variable*, and the *random assignment* of participants to the several different conditions being investigated.

experimental effect. A statistically significant difference between two groups experiencing different manipulations of the *independent variable.*

experimental hypothesis. What the investigator assumes will happen in a scientific investigation if certain conditions are met or particular variables are manipulated.

expressed emotion (EE). In the literature on *schizophrenia*, the amount of hostility and criticism directed from other people to the patient, usually within a family.

expressive language disorder. Difficulties expressing oneself in speech.

external validity. See *validity.*

extinction. The elimination of a *classically conditioned* response by the omission of the *unconditioned stimulus.* In *operant conditioning*, the elimination of the *conditioned response* by the omission of *reinforcement.*

factitious disorders. Disorders in which the individual's physical or psychological symptoms appear under voluntary control and are adopted merely to assume the role of a sick person. The disorder can also involve a parent producing a disorder in a child and is then called factitious disorder by proxy or Munchausen syndrome.

falsifiability. The extent to which a scientific assertion is amenable to systematic probes, any one of which could negate the scientist's expectations.

familiar. In witchcraft, a supernatural spirit often embodied in an animal and at the service of a person.

family method. A research strategy in *behavior genetics* in which the frequency of a *trait* or of *abnormal behavior* is determined in relatives who have varying percentages of shared genetic background.

family systems approach. A general approach to *etiology* and treatment that focuses on the complex interrelationships within families.

family therapy. A form of *group therapy* in which members of a family are helped to relate better to one another.

fear drive. In the Mowrer–Miller theory, an unpleasant internal state that impels avoidance. The necessity to reduce a fear drive can form the basis for new learning.

fear of performance. Being overly concerned with one's behavior during sexual contact with another, postulated by Masters and Johnson as a major factor in *sexual dysfunction.*

fear response. In the Mowrer–Miller theory, a response to a threatening or noxious situation that is covert and unobservable but that is assumed to function as a stimulus to produce measurable physiological changes in the body and observable overt behavior.

female orgasmic disorder. A recurrent and persistent delay or absence of *orgasm* in a woman during sexual activity adequate in focus, intensity, and duration; in many instances the woman may experience considerable sexual excitement.

female sexual arousal disorder. Formally called frigidity, the inability of a female to reach or maintain the lubrication–swelling stage of sexual excitement or to enjoy a subjective sense of pleasure or excitement during sexual activity.

fetal alcohol syndrome. Retarded growth of the developing fetus and infant; cranial, facial, and limb anomalies; and *mental retardation* caused by heavy consumption of alcohol by the mother during pregnancy.

fetishism. Reliance on an inanimate object for sexual arousal.

first-rank symptoms. In *schizophrenia*, specific *delusions* and *hallucinations* proposed by Schneider as particularly important for its more exact diagnosis.

fixation. In *psychoanalytic* theory, the arrest of *psychosexual* development at a particular stage through too much or too little gratification at that stage.

flashback. An unpredictable recurrence of *psychedelic* experiences from an earlier drug trip.

flat affect. A deviation in emotional response wherein virtually no emotion is expressed whatever the stimulus, emotional expressiveness is blunted, or a lack of expression and muscle tone is noted in the face.

flight of ideas. A symptom of *mania* that involves a rapid shift in conversation from one subject to another with only superficial associative connections.

flooding. A *behavior therapy* procedure in which a fearful person is exposed to what is frightening, in reality or in the imagination, for extended periods of time and without opportunity for escape.

follow-up study. A research procedure whereby individuals observed in an earlier investigation are contacted at a later time for further study.

forced rape. The legal term for rape, forced sexual intercourse or other sexual activity with another person. **Statutory rape** is sexual intercourse between an adult male and someone who is under the age of consent, as fixed by local statute.

forced-choice item. A format of a *personality inventory* in which the response alternatives for each item are equated for *social desirability*.

forensic psychiatry or psychology. The branch of psychiatry or psychology that deals with the legal questions raised by disordered behavior.

fragile X syndrome. Malformation (or even breakage) of the X *chromosome* associated with *moderate mental* retardation. Symptoms include large, underdeveloped ears, a long, thin face, a broad nasal root, and enlarged testicles in males; many individuals show attention deficits and hyperactivity.

free association. A key *psychoanalytic* procedure in which the *analysand* is encouraged to give free rein to his or her thoughts and feelings, verbalizing whatever comes into the mind without monitoring its content. The assumption is that over time, *repressed* material will come forth for examination by the *analysand* and *psychoanalyst*.

freebase. The most potent part of *cocaine*, obtained by heating the drug with ether.

free-floating anxiety. Continual *anxiety* not attributable to any specific situation or reasonable danger. See *generalized anxiety disorder*.

frontal lobe. The forward or upper half of each *cerebral hemisphere*, in front of the central *sulcus*, active in reasoning and other higher mental processes.

fugue. See *dissociative fugue*.

functional magnetic resonance imaging (fMRI). Modification of *magnetic resonance imaging (MRI)* which allows researchers to take pictures of the brain so quickly that metabolic changes can be measured, resulting in a picture of the brain at work rather than its structure alone.

functional social support. The quality of a person's relationships, for example, a good versus a distressed marriage. Contrast with *structural social support*.

gay. A colloquial term for *homosexual*, now often adopted by homosexuals who have openly announced their sexual orientation.

gay liberation. The often militant movement seeking to achieve civil rights for homosexuals and recognition of the normality of *homosexuality*.

gender identity. The deeply ingrained sense a person has of being either a man or a woman.

gender identity disorder. Disorder in which there is a deeply felt incongruence between anatomic sex and the sensed gender; *transsexualism* and gender identity disorder of childhood are examples.

gene. An ultramicroscopic area of the *chromosome*; the gene is the smallest physical unit of the DNA molecule that carries a bit of hereditary information.

general adaptation syndrome (GAS). Hans Selye's model to describe the biological reaction of an organism to sustained and unrelenting *stress*; there are several stages, culminating in death in extreme circumstances.

general paresis. See *neurosyphilis*.

generalized anxiety disorder (GAD). In this *anxiety disorder*, anxiety is so chronic, persistent, and pervasive that it seems *free-floating*. The individual is jittery and strained, distractible, and worried that something bad is about to happen. A pounding heart, fast pulse and breathing, sweating, flushing, muscle aches, a lump in the throat, and an upset gastrointestinal tract are some of the bodily indications of this extreme anxiety.

genital stage. In *psychoanalytic* theory, the final *psychosexual stage*, reached in adulthood, in which *heterosexual* interests predominate.

genotype. An individual's unobservable, genetic constitution; the totality of *genes* possessed by an individual. Compare *phenotype*.

genuineness. In *client-centered therapy*, an essential quality of the therapist, referring to openness and authenticity.

germ theory (of disease). The general view in medicine that disease is caused by infection of the body by minute organisms and viruses.

gerontology. The interdisciplinary study of aging and of the special problems of the elderly.

Gestalt therapy. A *humanistic therapy* developed by Fritz Perls, which encourages clients to satisfy emerging needs so that their innate goodness can be expressed, to increase their awareness of unacknowledged feelings, and to reclaim parts of their personality that have been denied or disowned.

gestation period. The length of time, normally nine months in human beings, during which a fertilized egg develops into an infant ready to be born.

glans. The heavily innervated tip of the penis.

glove anesthesia. A lack of sensation in the part of the arm that would be covered by a glove. One of the *conversion disorders*.

grandiose delusions. Found in *paranoid schizophrenia*, *delusional disorder*, and *mania*, an exaggerated sense of one's importance, power, knowledge, or identity.

Graves' disease. An endocrine disorder resulting from oversecretion of the *hormone* thyroxin, in which metabolic processes are speeded up, producing apprehension, restlessness, and irritability.

gray matter. The neural tissue made up largely of nerve cell bodies that constitutes the cortex covering the *cerebral hemisphere*, the *nuclei* in lower brain areas, columns of the spinal cord, and the ganglia of the *autonomic nervous system*.

grimace. A distorted facial expression, often a symptom of *schizophrenia*.

group therapy. Method of treating psychological disorders whereby several persons are seen simultaneously by a single therapist.

gyrus. A ridge or convolution of the *cerebral cortex*.

habituation. In physiology, a process whereby an organism's response to the same stimulus lessens with repeated presentations.

halfway house. A homelike residence for people who are considered too disturbed to remain in their accustomed surroundings but do not require the total care of a mental institution.

hallucinations. Perceptions in any sensory modality without relevant and adequate external stimuli.

hallucinogen. A drug or chemical whose effects include *hallucinations*. Hallucinogenic drugs such as *LSD*, *psilocybin*, and *mescaline* are often called *psychedelic*.

hashish. The dried resin of the *Cannabis* plant, stronger in its effects than the dried leaves and stems that constitute *marijuana*.

health psychology. A branch of psychology dealing with the role of psychological factors in health and illness. See also *behavioral medicine*.

hebephrenia. See *disorganized schizophrenia*.

helplessness. A *construct* referring to the sense of having no control over important events; considered by many theorists to play a central role in *anxiety* and *depression*. See *learned helplessness theory*.

hermaphrodite. A person with parts of both male and female genitalia.

heroin. An extremely addictive narcotic drug derived from *morphine*.

heroin antagonists. Drugs, such as *naloxone*, that prevent a *heroin* user from experiencing any high.

heroin substitutes. Narcotics, such as *methadone*, that are *cross-dependent* with *heroin* and thus replace it and the body's craving for it.

heterosexual. A person who desires or engages in sexual relations with members of the opposite sex.

high-risk method. A research technique involving the intensive examination of people who have a high probability of later becoming abnormal.

histrionic personality disorder. This person is overly dramatic and given to emotional excess, impatient with minor annoyances, immature, dependent on others, and often sexually seductive without taking responsibility for flirtations; formerly called hysterical personality.

homophobia. Fear of or aversion to *homosexuality*.

homosexuality. Sexual desire or activity directed toward a member of one's own sex.

homovanillic acid. A major metabolite of *dopamine*.

hormone. A chemical substance produced by an *endocrine gland* and released into the blood or lymph for the purpose of controlling the function of a distant organ or organ system. Metabolism, growth, and development of secondary sexual characteristics are among the functions so controlled.

humanistic and existential therapies. A generic term for insight *psychotherapies* that emphasize the individual's subjective experiences, free will, and ever-present ability to decide on a new life course.

humanistic therapy. An *insight therapy* that emphasizes freedom of choice, growth of human potential, the joys of being a human being, and the importance of the patient's *phenomenology*; sometimes called an experiential therapy. See also *existential therapy*.

Huntington's chorea. A fatal *disease* passed on by a single dominant *gene*. Symptoms include spasmodic jerking of the limbs, psychotic behavior, and mental deterioration.

5-hydroxyindoleacetic acid (5-HIAA). The major metabolite of *serotonin*.

hyperactivity. See *attention-deficit/hyperactivity disorder*.

hyperkinesis. See *attention-deficit/hyperactivity disorder*.

hypertension. Abnormally high arterial blood pressure, with or without known organic causes. See *essential hypertension*.

hyperventilation. Very rapid and deep breathing associated with high levels of *anxiety*; causes the level of carbon dioxide in blood to be lowered with possible loss of consciousness.

hypnosis. A trancelike state or behavior resembling sleep, induced by suggestion, characterized primarily by increased suggestibility.

hypoactive sexual desire disorder. The absence of or deficiency in sexual fantasies and urges.

hypochondriasis. A *somatoform disorder* in which the person, misinterpreting rather ordinary physical sensations, is preoccupied with fears of having a serious disease and is not dissuaded by medical opinion. Difficult to distinguish from *somatization disorder*.

hypomania. An above-normal elevation of mood, but not as extreme as *mania*.

hypothalamus. A collection of nuclei and fibers in the lower part of the diencephalon concerned with the regulation of many visceral processes, such as *metabolism*, temperature, and water balance.

hysteria. A disorder known to the ancient Greeks in which a physical incapacity—a paralysis, an *anesthesia*, or an *analgesia*—is not due to a physiological dysfunction, for example, *glove anesthesia*; an older term for *conversion disorder*. In the late nineteenth century *dissociative disorders* were identified as such and considered hysterical states.

hysterical neurosis. The DSM-II category for *dissociative* and *somatoform disorders*.

id. In *psychoanalytic* theory, that part of the personality present at birth, composed of all the energy of the *psyche*, and expressed as biological urges that strive continually for gratification.

ideas of reference. *Delusional* thinking that reads personal significance into seemingly trivial remarks and activities of others and completely unrelated events.

idiographic. In psychology, relating to investigative procedures that consider the unique characteristics of a single person, studying them in depth, as in the *case study*. Contrast with *nomothetic*.

idiot savant. An individual with a rare form of *mental retardation*, extraordinarily talented in one or a few limited areas of intellectual achievement; sometimes called autistic savant.

illusion. A misperception of a real external stimulus, such as hearing the slapping of waves as footsteps.

imipramine. An *antidepressant* drug, one of the *tricyclic* group, trade name Tofranil.

in absentia. Literally, "in one's absence." Courts are concerned that a person be able to participate personally and meaningfully in his or her own trial and not be tried in absentia because of a distracting mental disorder.

in vivo. As applied in psychology, taking place in a real-life situation.

inappropriate affect. Emotional responses that are out of context, such as laughter when hearing sad news.

incest. Sexual relations between close relatives, most often between daughter and father or between brother and sister.

incidence. In *epidemiological* studies of a particular disorder, the rate at which new cases occur in a given place at a given time. Compare with *prevalence*.

incoherence. In *schizophrenia*, an aspect of *thought disorder* wherein verbal expression is marked by disconnectedness, fragmented thoughts, and jumbled phrases.

independent variable. In a psychological *experiment*, the factor, experience, or treatment that is under the control of the experimenter and that is expected to have an effect on participants as assessed by changes in the *dependent variable*.

index case (proband). The person who in a genetic investigation bears the diagnosis or *trait* in which the investigator is interested.

individual psychology. A variation of Freud's *psychoanalysis* introduced by Alfred Adler and focusing less on biological drives and more on such factors as people's conscious beliefs and goals for self-betterment.

infectious disease. An illness caused when a microorganism, such as a bacterium or a virus, invades the body, multiplies, and attacks a specific organ or organ system; pneumonia is an example.

informed consent. The agreement of a person to serve as a research participant or to enter therapy after being told the possible outcomes, both benefits and risks.

inhibited male orgasm. A recurrent and persistent delay or absence of ejaculation after an adequate phase of sexual excitement.

insanity defense. The legal argument that a defendant should not be held *ascriptively responsible* for an illegal act if the conduct is attributable to mental illness.

insight therapy. A general term for any psychotherapy that assumes that people become disordered because they do not adequately understand what motivates them, especially when their needs and drives conflict.

instrumental learning. See *operant conditioning*.

intelligence quotient (IQ). A standardized measure indicating how far an individual's raw score on an *intelligence test* is from the average raw score of his or her chronological age group.

intelligence test. A standardized means of assessing a person's current mental ability, for example, the Stanford–Binet test and the Wechsler Adult Intelligence Scale.

internal consistency reliability. See *reliability*.

internal validity. See *validity*.

interpersonal therapy. A *psychodynamic* psychotherapy that focuses on the patient's interactions with others and that directly teaches how better to relate to others.

interpretation. In *psychoanalysis*, a key procedure in which the *psychoanalyst* points out to the *analysand* where *resistance* exists and what certain dreams and verbalizations reveal about impulses *repressed* in the *unconscious*; more generally, any statement by a therapist that construes the client's problem in a new way.

interrater reliability. See *reliability*.

introjection. In psychoanalytic theory, the *unconscious* incorporation of the values, attitudes, and qualities of another person into the individual's own *ego* structure.

introspection. A procedure whereby trained subjects are asked to report on their conscious experiences. This was the principal method of study in early twentieth-century psychology.

irrational beliefs. Self-defeating assumptions that are assumed by *rational-emotive* therapists to underlie psychological distress.

irresistible impulse. The term used in an 1834 Ohio court ruling on criminal responsibility that determined that an *insanity defense* can be established by proving that the accused had an uncontrollable urge to perform the act.

la belle indifférence. The blasé attitude people with *conversion disorder* have toward their *symptoms*.

labeling theory. The general view that serious *psychopathology*, such as *schizophrenia*, is caused by society's reactions to unusual behavior.

labile. Easily moved or changed, quickly shifting from one emotion to another, or easily aroused.

language disorder. Difficulties understanding spoken language (receptive) or expressing thoughts verbally (expressive).

latency period. In *psychoanalytic* theory, the years between ages six and twelve, during which id impulses play a minor role in motivation.

latent content. In dreams, the presumed true meaning hidden behind the *manifest content*.

law of effect. A principle of learning that holds that behavior is acquired by virtue of its consequences.

learned helplessness theory. The theory that individuals acquire passivity and a sense of being unable to act and to control their lives; this happens through unpleasant experiences and traumas against which their efforts were ineffective; according to Seligman, this brings on *depression*.

learning disabilities. General term for *learning disorders*, *communication disorders*, and *motor skills disorder*.

learning disorders. A set of developmental disorders encompassing *dyslexia*, *mathematics disorder*, and *disorder of written expression* and characterized by failure to develop in a specific academic area to the degree expected by the child's intellectual level. Not diagnosed if the disorder is due to a sensory deficit.

learning (behavioral) paradigm. In abnormal psychology, a set of assumptions that *abnormal behavior* is learned in the same way as other human behavior.

least restrictive alternative. The legal principle according to which a committed mental patient must be treated in a setting that imposes as few restrictions as possible on his or her freedom

lesion. Any localized abnormal structural change in organ or tissue caused by disease or injury.

libido. See *Eros*.

Life Change Unit (LCU) score. A score produced by totaling ratings of the stressfulness of recently experienced life events; high scores are found to be related to the contraction of a number of physical illnesses.

life-span developmental psychology. The study of changes in people as they grow from infancy to old age.

lifetime prevalence rate. The proportion of a sample that has ever had a disorder.

limbic system. The lower parts of the *cerebrum*, made up of primitive cortex; controls visceral and bodily changes associated with emotion and regulates drive-motivated behavior.

linkage analysis. A technique in genetic research whereby occurrence of a disorder in a family is evaluated alongside a known genetic marker.

lithium carbonate. A drug useful in treating both *mania* and *depression* in *bipolar disorder*.

lobotomy. A brain operation in which the nerve pathways between the *frontal lobes* of the brain and lower brain structures are cut in hopes of effecting beneficial behavioral change.

logotherapy. An *existential psychotherapy*, developed by Viktor Frankl, aimed at helping the demoralized client restore meaning to life by placing his or her suffering in a larger spiritual and philosophical context. The individual assumes responsibility for his or her existence and for pursuing a meaningful life.

longitudinal studies. Investigation that collects information on the same individuals repeatedly over time, perhaps over many years, in an effort to determine how phenomena change. Compare with *cross-sectional studies*.

loose associations (derailment). In *schizophrenia*, an aspect of *thought disorder* wherein the patient has difficulty sticking to one topic and drifts off on a train of associations evoked by an idea from the past.

LSD. *d*-lysergic acid diethylamide, a drug synthesized in 1938 and discovered by accident to be a *hallucinogen* in 1943.

Luria–Nebraska test. A battery of *neuropsychological tests* that can detect impairment in different parts of the brain.

magical thinking. The conviction of the individual that his or her thoughts, words, and actions may in some manner cause or prevent outcomes in a way that defies the normal laws of cause and effect.

magnetic resonance imaging (MRI). A technique for measuring the structure (or, in the case of *functional magnetic resonance imaging*, the activity) of the living brain. The person is placed inside a large circular magnet that causes hydrogen atoms to move; the return of the atoms to their original positions when the current to the magnet is turned off is translated by a computer into pictures of brain tissue.

mainstreaming (immersion). A policy of placing children with disabilities in regular classrooms; although special classes are provided as needed, the children share as much as possible in the opportunities and ambience afforded youngsters without disabilities.

maintenance dose. An amount of a drug designed to enable a patient to continue to benefit from a therapeutically effective regimen of medication. It is often less than the dose required to initiate the positive change.

major (unipolar) depression. A disorder of individuals who have experienced episodes of *depression* but not of *mania*.

male erectile disorder. A recurrent and persistent inability to attain or maintain an erection until completion of sexual activity.

male orgasmic disorder. See *inhibited male orgasm*.

malingering. Faking a physical or psychological incapacity in order to avoid a responsibility or gain an end; the goal is readily recognized from the individual's

circumstances. To be distinguished from *conversion disorder*, in which the incapacity is assumed to be beyond voluntary control.

malleus maleficarum ("the witches' hammer"). A manual written by two Dominican monks in the fifteenth century to provide rules for identifying and trying witches.

mammillary body. Either of two small rounded structures located in the *hypothalamus* and consisting of *nuclei*.

mania. An emotional state of intense but unfounded elation evidenced in talkativeness, *flight of ideas*, distractibility, grandiose plans, and spurts of purposeless activity.

manic-depressive illness, manic-depressive psychosis. Originally described by Kraepelin, a *mood disorder* characterized by alternating euphoria and profound sadness or by one of these moods. Called *bipolar disorder* in DSM-IV-TR.

manifest content. The immediately apparent, conscious content of dreams. Compare with *latent content*.

marathon group. A group therapy session run continuously for a day or even longer, typically for *sensitivity training*, the assumption being that defenses can be worn down by the physical and psychological fatigue generated through intensive and continuous group interaction.

marijuana. A drug derived from the dried and ground leaves and stems of the female hemp plant, *Cannabis sativa*.

marital therapy. See *couples therapy*.

masochism. See *sexual masochism*.

mathematics disorder. Difficulties dealing with arithmetic symbols and operations; one of the *learning disorders*.

mediational theory of learning. In psychology, the general view that certain stimuli do not directly initiate an overt response but activate an intervening process, which in turn initiates the response. It explains thinking, drives, emotions, and beliefs in terms of stimulus and response.

mediator. In psychology, an inferred state intervening between the observable stimulus and response, activated by the stimulus and in turn initiating the response; in more general terms, a thought, drive, emotion, or belief. Also called a *construct*.

medical (disease) model. As applied in abnormal psychology, a set of assumptions that conceptualizes *abnormal behavior* as similar to physical diseases.

medulla oblongata. An area in the *brain stem* through which nerve fiber tracts ascend to or descend from higher brain centers.

megalomania. A paranoid *delusion of grandeur* in which an individual believes that he or she is an important person or is carrying out great plans.

melancholia. A vernacular diagnosis of several millennia's standing for profound sadness and *depression*. In *major depression* with melancholia the individual is unable to feel better even momentarily when something good happens, regularly feels worse in the morning and awakens early, and suffers a deepening of other symptoms of *depression*.

meninges. The three layers of nonneural tissue that envelop the brain and spinal cord. They are the dura mater, the arachnoid, and the pia mater.

meningitis. An inflammation of the *meninges* through infection, usually by a bacterium, or through irritation. *Meningococcal*, the epidemic form of the disease, takes the lives of 10 percent of those who contract it and causes cerebral palsy, hearing loss, speech defects, and other forms of permanent brain damage in one of four people who recover.

mental age. The numerical index of an individual's cognitive development determined by standardized *intelligence tests*.

mental retardation. Subnormal intellectual functioning associated with impairment in adaptive behavior and identified at an early age.

meprobamate. Generic term for *Miltown*, an *anxiolytic*, the first introduced and for a time one of the most widely used.

mescaline. A *hallucinogen* and *alkaloid* that is the active ingredient of *peyote*.

mesmerize. The first term for *hypnotize*, after Franz Anton Mesmer, an Austrian physician who in the late eighteenth century treated and cured hysterical or *conversion disorders* with what he considered the animal magnetism emanating from his body and permeating the universe.

meta-analysis. A quantitative method of analyzing and comparing various therapies by standardizing their results.

metabolism. The sum of the intracellular processes by which large molecules are broken down into smaller ones, releasing energy and wastes, and by which small molecules are built up into new living matter by consuming energy.

metacognition. The knowledge people have about the way they know their world, for example, recognizing the usefulness of a map in finding their way in a new city.

methadone. A synthetic addictive *heroin substitute* for treating *heroin* addicts that acts as a substitute for *heroin* by eliminating its effects and the craving for it.

methedrine. A very strong *amphetamine*, sometimes shot directly into the veins.

3-methoxy-4-hydroxyphenylethylene glycol (MHPG). A major metabolite of *norepinephrine*.

midbrain. The middle part of the brain that consists of a mass of nerve fiber tracts connecting the spinal cord and *pons, medulla,* and *cerebellum* to the *cerebral cortex*.

migraine headaches. Extremely debilitating headaches caused by sustained dilation of the extracranial arteries, the temporal artery in particular; the dilated arteries trigger pain-sensitive nerve fibers in the scalp.

mild mental retardation. A limitation in mental development measured on *IQ* tests at between 50–55 and 70; children with such a limitation are considered the educable mentally retarded and are usually placed in special classes.

milieu therapy. A treatment procedure that attempts to make the total environment and all personnel and patients of the hospital a *therapeutic community,* conducive to psychological improvement; the staff conveys to the patients the expectation that they can and will behave more normally and responsibly.

Miltown. The trade name for *meprobamate,* one of the principal *anxiolytics.*

Minnesota Multiphasic Personality Inventory (MMPI). A lengthy *personality inventory* by which individuals are diagnosed through their true–false replies to groups of statements indicating states such as *anxiety, depression, masculinity–femininity,* and *paranoia.*

mixed design. A research strategy in which both *classificatory* and experimental *variables* are used; assigning people from discrete populations to two experimental conditions is an example.

mixed receptive-expressive language disorder. Difficulties producing and understanding spoken language.

M'Naghten rule. An 1843 British court decision stating that an *insanity defense* can be established by proving that the defendant did not know what he or she was doing or did not realize that it was wrong.

modeling. Learning by observing and imitating the behavior of others.

moderate mental retardation. A limitation in mental development measured on *IQ* tests between 35–40 and 50–55; children with this degree of retardation are often institutionalized, and their training is focused on self-care rather than on development of intellectual skills.

mongolism. See *Down syndrome.*

monism. Philosophical doctrine that ultimate reality is a unitary organic whole and that therefore mental and physical are one and the same. Contrast with *dualism.*

monoamine. An organic compound containing nitrogen in one amino group (NH). Some of the known *neurotransmitters* of the central nervous system, called collectively brain amines, are *catecholamines* and indoleamines, which are monoamines.

monoamine oxidase (MAO). An enzyme that deactivates *catecholamines* and indoleamines within the presynaptic neuron, indoleamines in the *synapse.*

monoamine oxidase inhibitors. A group of *antidepressant* drugs that prevent the enzyme *monoamine oxidase* from deactivating *neurotransmitters* of the central nervous system.

monozygotic (MZ) twins. Genetically identical siblings who have developed from a single fertilized egg; sometimes called identical twins.

mood disorders. Disorders in which there are disabling disturbances in emotion.

moral anxiety. In *psychoanalytic* theory, the *ego's* fear of punishment for failure to adhere to the *superego's* standards of proper conduct.

moral treatment. A therapeutic regimen, introduced by Philippe Pinel during the French Revolution, whereby mental patients were released from their restraints and were treated with compassion and dignity rather than with contempt and denigration.

morbidity risk. The probability that an individual will develop a particular disorder.

morphine. An addictive narcotic *alkaloid* extracted from *opium,* used primarily as an analgesic and as a *sedative.*

motor skills disorder. A *learning disability* characterized by marked impairment in the development of motor coordination that is not accounted for by a physical disorder such as cerebral palsy.

mourning work. In Freud's theory of *depression,* the recall by a depressed person of memories associated with a lost one, serving to separate the individual from the deceased.

multiaxial classification. Classification having several dimensions, each of which is employed in categorizing; DSM-IV-TR is an example.

multifactorial. Referring to the operation of several variables influencing in complex fashion the development or maintenance of a phenomenon.

multimodal therapy. A *cognitive-behavioral therapy* introduced by Arnold Lazarus, which employs techniques from diverse approaches in an effort to help people make positive changes in their BASIC IB: behavior, *affects,* sensations, images, *cognitions,* interpersonal relationships, and biological functioning.

multiple personality disorder (MPD). See *dissociative identity disorder* (DID).

mutism. The inability or refusal to speak.

myocardial infarction. Heart attack. See *coronary heart disease.*

narcissistic personality disorder. Extremely selfish and self-centered, people with a narcissistic personality have a grandiose view of their uniqueness, achievements, and talents and an insatiable craving for admiration and approval from others. They are exploitative to achieve their own goals and expect much more from others than they themselves are willing to give.

narcosynthesis. A psychiatric procedure originating during World War II in which a drug was employed to help stressed soldiers recall the battle traumas underlying their disorders.

narcotics. Addictive *sedative* drugs, for example, *morphine* and *heroin,* that in moderate doses relieve pain and induce sleep.

negative reinforcement. The strengthening of a tendency to exhibit desired behavior by rewarding responses in that situation with the removal of an *aversive stimulus.*

negative symptoms. Behavioral deficits in *schizophrenia,* such as *flat affect* and *apathy.*

negative triad. In Beck's theory of *depression,* a person's baleful views of the self, the world, and the future; the triad is in a reciprocal causal relationship with pessimistic assumptions (*schemata*) and cognitive biases such as *selective abstraction.*

neo-Freudian. A person who has contributed to the modification and extension of Freudian theory.

neologism. A word made up by the speaker that is usually meaningless to a listener.

nerve impulse. A change in the electric potential of a *neuron;* a wave of depolarization spreads along the neuron and causes the release of *neurotransmitter.*

neurofibrillary tangles. Abnormal protein filaments present in the cell bodies of brain cells in patients with *Alzheimer's disease.*

neurologist. A physician who studies the nervous system, especially its structure, functions, and abnormalities.

neuron. A single nerve cell.

neuropsychological tests. Psychological tests, such as the *Luria–Nebraska,* that can detect impairment in different parts of the brain.

neuropsychologist. A psychologist concerned with the relationships among *cognition, affect,* and behavior on the one hand, and brain function on the other.

neuroses. Old term for a large group of non-*psychotic* disorders characterized by unrealistic *anxiety* and other associated problems, for example, *phobic* avoidances, *obsessions,* and *compulsions.* See *anxiety disorders.*

neurosyphilis (general paresis). Infection of the *central nervous system* by the spirochete *Treponema pallidum,* which destroys brain tissue; marked by eye disturbances, tremors, and disordered speech as well as severe intellectual deterioration and *psychotic* symptoms.

neurotic anxiety. In *psychoanalytic* theory, a fear of the consequences of expressing previously punished and *repressed id* impulses; more generally, unrealistic fear.

neurotransmitter. A chemical substance important in transferring a nerve impulse from one *neuron* to another; for example, *serotonin* and *norepinephrine.*

nicotine. The principal *alkaloid* of tobacco (an addicting agent).

nitrous oxide. A gas that, when inhaled, produces euphoria and sometimes giddiness.

nomenclature. A system or set of names or designations used in a particular discipline, such as the DSM-IV-TR.

nomothetic. Relating to the universal and to the formulation of general laws that explain a range of phenomena. Contrast with *idiographic.*

norepinephrine. A *catecholamine* that is a *neurotransmitter* of the *central nervous system.* Disturbances in its tracts apparently figure in *depression* and *mania.* It is also a *neurotransmitter* secreted at the nerve endings of the *sympathetic nervous system,* a *hormone* liberated with *epinephrine* in the adrenal medulla and similar to it in action, and a strong vasoconstrictor.

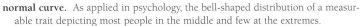

normal curve. As applied in psychology, the bell-shaped distribution of a measurable trait depicting most people in the middle and few at the extremes.

nosology. A systematic classification of diseases.

nucleus. In anatomy, a mass of nerve cell bodies (*gray matter*) within the brain or spinal cord by which descending nerve fibers connect with ascending nerve fibers.

object choice. In the psychology of sex, the type of person or thing selected as a focus for sexual desire or activity.

objective (realistic) anxiety. In *psychoanalytic* theory, the *ego's* reaction to danger in the external world; realistic fear. Contrast with *neurotic anxiety*.

observer drift. The tendency of two raters of behavior to begin to agree with each other, achieving unusually high levels of *reliability*; their way of coding behavior differentiates their scores from those of another pair of raters. This is regarded as a threat to reliable and valid *behavioral assessment*.

obsession. An intrusive and recurring thought that seems irrational and uncontrollable to the person experiencing it.

obsessive-compulsive disorder (OCD). An *anxiety disorder* in which the mind is flooded with persistent and uncontrollable thoughts or the individual is compelled to repeat certain acts again and again, causing significant distress and interference with everyday functioning.

obsessive-compulsive personality disorder. People with an obsessive-compulsive personality have inordinate difficulty making decisions, are overly concerned with details and efficiency, and relate poorly to others because they demand that things be done their way. They are unduly conventional, serious, formal, and stingy with their emotions.

occipital lobe. The posterior area of each *cerebral hemisphere*, situated behind the *parietal lobe* and above the *temporal lobes*, responsible for reception and analysis of visual information and for some visual memory.

Oedipus complex. In Freudian theory, the desire and conflict of the four-year-old male child who wants to possess his mother sexually and to eliminate the father rival. The threat of punishment from the father causes *repression* of these *id* impulses. Girls have a similar sexual desire for the father, which is repressed in analogous fashion and is called the *Electra complex*.

operant behavior. A response that is supposedly voluntary and operates on the environment, modifying it so that a reward or goal is attained.

operant conditioning. The acquisition or elimination of a response as a function of the environmental contingencies of *reward* and *punishment*.

operationism. A school of thought in science that holds that a given concept must be defined in terms of a single set of identifiable and repeatable operations that can be measured.

opiates. A group of addictive *sedatives* that in moderate doses relieve pain and induce sleep.

opium. One of the opiates, the dried, milky juice obtained from the immature fruit of the opium poppy. This addictive *narcotic* produces euphoria and drowsiness and reduces pain.

oppositional defiant disorder. An undercontrolled disorder of children marked by high levels of disobedience to authority but lacking the extremes of *conduct disorder*.

oral stage. In *psychoanalytic* theory, the first *psychosexual stage*, which extends into the second year; during it the mouth is the principal *erogenous* zone.

organismic variable. A physiological or psychological factor assumed to be operating "under the skin"; these variables are a focus of *behavioral assessment*.

orgasm (climax). The involuntary, intensely pleasurable, climactic phase in sexual arousal that lasts a number of seconds and usually involves muscular contractions and ejaculation in the male and similar contractions in the genitalia of the female.

orgasmic reorientation. A *behavior therapy* technique for altering classes of stimuli to which people are sexually attracted; individuals are confronted by a conventionally arousing stimulus while experiencing *orgasm*.

outcome research. Research on the efficacy of *psychotherapy*. Contrast with *process research*.

outpatient commitment. A form of *civil commitment* whereby the person is not institutionalized, rather is allowed to be free in the community but under legal-medical constraints that ensure, for example, that prescribed medication and other measures are taken to maximize the chances of the patient being able to live outside of a mental hospital. Consistent with the principle of *least restrictive alternative*.

overcontrolled (behavior). In reference to childhood disorders, problems that create distress for the child, such as *anxiety* and *social withdrawal*.

pain disorder. A *somatoform disorder* in which the person complains of severe and prolonged pain that is not explainable by organic pathology; it tends to be *stress*-related or permits the patient to avoid an aversive activity or to gain attention and sympathy.

panic disorder. An *anxiety disorder* in which the individual has sudden and inexplicable attacks of jarring symptoms, such as difficulty breathing, heart palpitations, dizziness, trembling, terror, and feelings of impending doom. In DSM-IV-TR, said to occur with or without *agoraphobia*.

paradigm. A set of basic assumptions that outlines the universe of scientific inquiry, specifying both the concepts regarded as legitimate and the methods to be used in collecting and interpreting data.

paradoxical intervention. A therapeutic strategy that asks patients to increase or observe the frequency or intensity of a symptom, for example, having anxious patients make themselves more anxious or note when and how severely they become anxious.

paranoia. The general term for *delusions of persecution*, of *grandiosity*, or both; found in several pathological conditions, *delusional disorders*, *paranoid schizophrenia*, and *paranoid personality disorder*. It can also be produced by large doses of certain drugs, such as *cocaine* or alcohol.

paranoid disorder. See *delusional disorder*.

paranoid personality disorder. The person with this personality expects to be mistreated by others, becomes suspicious, secretive, jealous, and argumentative. He or she will not accept blame and appears cold and unemotional.

paranoid schizophrenia. A type of *schizophrenia* in which the patient has numerous systematized *delusions* as well as *hallucinations* and *ideas of reference*. He or she may also be agitated, angry, argumentative, and sometimes violent.

paraphilias. Sexual attraction to unusual objects and sexual activities unusual in nature.

paraphrenia. A term sometimes used to refer to *schizophrenia* in an older adult.

paraprofessional. In clinical psychology, an individual lacking a doctoral degree but trained to perform certain functions usually reserved for clinicians, for example, a college student trained and supervised by a behavioral therapist to shape the behavior of *autistic* children through contingent reinforcers.

parasympathetic nervous system. The division of the *autonomic nervous system* that is involved with maintenance; it controls many of the internal organs and is active primarily when the organism is not aroused.

paresthesia. *Conversion disorder* marked by a sensation of tingling or creeping on the skin.

parietal lobe. The middle division of each *cerebral hemisphere*, situated behind the central *sulcus* and above the lateral *sulcus*; the receiving center for sensations of the skin and of bodily positions.

Parkinson's disease. A disease characterized by uncontrollable and severe muscle tremors, a stiff gait, a masklike, expressionless face, and withdrawal.

pathology. The anatomical, physiological, and psychological deviations of a disease or disorder; the study of these abnormalities.

PCP. See *phencyclidine*.

Pearson product moment correlation coefficient (*r*). A statistic, ranging in value from -1.00 to +1.00; the most common means of denoting a *correlational* relationship. The sign indicates whether the relationship is positive or negative, and the magnitude indicates the strength of the relationship.

pedophile. Person with a marked preference for obtaining sexual gratification through contact with youngsters defined legally as underage; pedophilia is a *paraphilia*.

penile plethysmograph. A device for detecting blood flow and thus for recording changes in size of the penis.

perseveration. The persistent repetition of words and ideas, often found in *schizophrenia*.

personality disorders. A heterogeneous group of disorders, listed separately on Axis II, regarded as longstanding, inflexible, and maladaptive personality *traits* that impair social and occupational functioning.

personality inventory. A self-report questionnaire by which an examinee indicates whether statements assessing habitual tendencies apply to him or her.

personality structure. See *trait*.

pervasive developmental disorders. Severe childhood problems marked by profound disturbances in social relations and oddities in behavior. *Autistic disorder* is one.

PET scan. Computer-generated picture of the living brain, created by analysis of radioactive particles from isotopes injected into the bloodstream.

peyote. A *hallucinogen* obtained from the root of the peyote cactus; the active ingredient is *mescaline*, an *alkaloid*.

phallic stage. In *psychoanalytic* theory, the third *psychosexual stage*, extending from ages three to six, during which maximal gratification is obtained from genital stimulation.

phencyclidine (PCP). Also known as angel dust, PeaCE Pill, zombie, and by other street names, this very powerful and hazardous drug causes profound disorientation, agitated and often violent behavior, and even seizures, coma, and death.

phenomenology. As applied in psychology, the philosophical view that the phenomena of subjective experience should be studied because behavior is considered to be determined by how people perceive themselves and the world, rather than by objectively described reality.

phenothiazine. The name for a group of drugs that relieve psychotic symptoms; their molecular structure, like that of the *tricyclic drugs*, consists of three fused rings. An example is *chlorpromazine (Thorazine)*.

phenotype. The totality of observable characteristics of a person. Compare with *genotype*.

phenylketonuria (PKU). A genetic disorder that, through a deficiency in a liver enzyme, phenylalanine hydroxylase, causes severe *mental retardation* unless phenylalanine can be largely restricted from the diet.

phobia. An *anxiety disorder* in which there is intense fear and avoidance of specific objects and situations, recognized as irrational by the individual.

phonological disorder. A *learning disability* in which some words sound like baby talk because the person is not able to make certain speech sounds.

physiology. The study of the functions and activities of living cells, tissues, and organs and of the physical and chemical phenomena involved.

placebo. Any inactive therapy or chemical agent, or any attribute or component of such a therapy or chemical, that affects a person's behavior for reasons related to his or her expectation of change.

placebo control group. A group in an experiment which receives contact, support, and encouragement from a therapist, but not the active ingredient in the particular kind of therapy under study.

placebo effect. The action of a drug or psychological treatment that is not attributable to any specific operations of the agent. For example, a *tranquilizer* can reduce *anxiety* both because of its special biochemical action and because the recipient expects relief. See *placebo*.

plaques. Small, round areas composed of remnants of lost *neurons* and beta-amyloid, a waxy protein deposit; present in the brains of patients with *Alzheimer's disease*.

plateau phase. According to Masters and Johnson, the second stage in sexual arousal, during which excitement and tension have reached a stable high level before *orgasm*.

play therapy. The use of play as a means of uncovering what is troubling a child and of establishing *rapport*.

pleasure principle. In *psychoanalytic* theory, the demanding manner by which the *id* operates, seeking immediate gratification of its needs.

plethysmograph. An instrument for determining and registering variations in the amount of blood present or passing through an organ.

polydrug abuse. The misuse of more than one drug at a time, such as drinking heavily and taking *cocaine*.

pons. An area in the *brain stem* containing nerve-fiber tracts that connect the *cerebellum* with the spinal cord and with motor areas of the *cerebrum*.

positive reinforcement. The strengthening of a tendency to behave in a certain situation by presenting a desired reward following previous responses in that situation.

positive spikes. An *EEG* pattern recorded from the *temporal lobe* of the brain, with frequencies of 6 to 8 cycles per second and 14 to 16 cycles per second, often found in impulsive and aggressive people.

positive symptoms. In *schizophrenia*, behavioral excesses, such as *hallucinations* and bizarre behavior. Compare with *negative symptoms*.

posttraumatic stress disorder (PTSD). An *anxiety disorder* in which a particularly stressful event, such as military combat, rape, or a natural disaster, brings in its aftermath intrusive reexperiencings of the trauma, a numbing of responsiveness to the outside world, estrangement from others, a tendency to be easily startled, and nightmares, recurrent dreams, and otherwise disturbed sleep.

poverty of content. Reduced informational content in speech, one of the *negative symptoms* of *schizophrenia*.

poverty of speech. Reduced amount of talking, one of the *negative symptoms* of *schizophrenia*.

predictive validity. See *validity*.

predisposition. An inclination or *diathesis* to respond in a certain way, either inborn or acquired; in abnormal psychology, a factor that lowers the ability to withstand stress and inclines the individual toward *pathology*.

prefrontal lobotomy. A surgical procedure that destroys the tracts connecting the *frontal lobes* to lower centers of the brain; once believed to be an effective treatment for *schizophrenia*.

premature ejaculation. Inability of the male to inhibit his *orgasm* long enough for mutually satisfying sexual relations.

premorbid adjustment. In research on *schizophrenia*, the social and sexual adjustment of the individual before the onset or diagnosis of the symptoms. Patients with good premorbid adjustment are those found to have been relatively normal earlier; those with poor premorbid adjustment had inadequate interpersonal and sexual relations.

preparedness. In *classical conditioning* theory, a biological *predisposition* to associate particular stimuli readily with the *unconditioned stimulus*.

prevalence. In *epidemiological* studies of a disorder, the percentage of a population that has the disorder at a given time. Compare with *incidence*.

prevention. *Primary* prevention comprises efforts in *community psychology* to reduce the incidence of new cases of psychological disorder by such means as altering stressful living conditions and genetic counseling; *secondary* prevention includes efforts to detect disorders early, so that they will not develop into full-blown, perhaps chronic, disabilities; *tertiary* prevention attempts to reduce the long-term consequences of having a disorder, equivalent in most respects to therapy.

primary empathy. A form of *empathy* in which the therapist understands the content and feeling of what the client is saying and expressing from the client's *phenomenological* point of view. Compare with *advanced accurate empathy*.

primary prevention. See *prevention*.

primary process. In *psychoanalytic* theory, one of the *id*'s means of reducing tension, by imagining what it desires.

privileged communication. The communication between parties in a confidential relationship that is protected by statute. A spouse, doctor, lawyer, pastor, psychologist, or psychiatrist cannot be forced, except under unusual circumstances, to disclose such information.

proband. See *index case*.

process research. Research on the mechanisms by which a therapy may bring improvement. Compare with *outcome research*.

profound mental retardation. A limitation in mental development measured on IQ tests at less than 20–25; children with this degree of retardation require total supervision of all their activities.

progestins. Steroid progestational hormones that are the biological precursors of androgens, the male sex *hormones*.

prognosis. A prediction of the likely course and outcome of an illness. Compare with *diagnosis*.

projection. A *defense mechanism* whereby characteristics or desires unacceptable to the *ego* are attributed to someone else.

projective hypothesis. The notion that highly unstructured stimuli, as in the *Rorschach*, are necessary to bypass defenses in order to reveal *unconscious* motives and conflicts.

projective test. A psychological assessment device employing a set of standard but vague stimuli on the assumption that unstructured material will allow *unconscious* motivations and fears to be uncovered. The *Rorschach* series of inkblots is an example.

pronoun reversal. A speech problem in which the child refers to himself or herself as "he," "she," or "you" and uses "I" or "me" in referring to others; often found in the speech of children with *autistic disorder*.

pseudocommunity. An illusory world built up by a *paranoid* person, dominated by false beliefs that are not properly verified and shared by others.

psilocybin. A *psychedelic* drug extracted from the mushroom *Psilocybe mexicana*.

psyche. The soul, spirit, or mind as distinguished from the body. In *psychoanalytic* theory, it is the totality of the *id*, *ego*, and *superego*, including both conscious and *unconscious* components.

psychedelic. A drug that expands consciousness. See also *hallucinogen*.

psychiatrist. A physician (M.D.) who has taken specialized postdoctoral training, called a residency, in the diagnosis, treatment, and prevention of mental disorders.

psychoactive drugs. Chemical compounds having a psychological effect that alters mood or thought process. *Valium* is an example.

psychoanalysis. A term applied primarily to the therapy procedures pioneered by Freud, entailing *free association, dream analysis,* and *working through* the *transference neurosis.* More recently the term has come to encompass the numerous variations on basic Freudian therapy.

psychoanalyst (analyst). A therapist who has taken specialized postdoctoral training in *psychoanalysis* after earning an M.D. or a Ph.D. degree.

psychoanalytic (psychodynamic) paradigm. General view based on *psychoanalysis.*

psychodynamics. In *psychoanalytic* theory, the mental and emotional forces and processes that develop in early childhood and their effects on behavior and mental states.

psychogenesis. Development from psychological origins, as distinguished from somatic origins. Contrast with *somatogenesis.*

psychological autopsy. The analysis of an individual's *suicide* through the examination of his or her letters and through interviews with friends and relatives in the hope of discovering why the person committed suicide.

psychological deficit. The term used to indicate that performance of a pertinent psychological process is below that expected of a normal person.

psychological dependency. The term sometimes applied as the reason for *substance abuse;* a reliance on a drug but not a physiological addiction.

psychological factor influencing a medical condition. A diagnosis in DSM-IV-TR that a physical illness is caused in part or exacerbated by psychological *stress.* See *psychophysiological disorders.*

psychological tests. Standardized procedures designed to measure a person's performance on a particular task or to assess his or her personality.

psychopath. See *antisocial personality.*

psychopathologists. Mental health professionals who conduct research into the nature and development of mental disorders. Their academic backgrounds can differ; some are trained as experimental psychologists, others as psychiatrists, and still others as biochemists.

psychopathology. The field concerned with the nature and development of mental disorders.

psychopathy. See *antisocial personality.*

psychophysiological disorders. Disorders with physical symptoms that may involve actual tissue damage, usually in one organ system, and that are produced in part by continued mobilization of the *autonomic nervous system* under *stress.* Hives and ulcers are examples. Now listed in DSM-IV-TR on Axis I as *psychological factor influencing a medical condition;* on Axis III the specific physical condition is given.

psychophysiology. The discipline concerned with the bodily changes that accompany psychological events.

psychosexual stages. In *psychoanalytic* theory, critical developmental phases that the individual passes through, each stage characterized by the body area providing maximal erotic gratification. The adult personality is formed by the pattern and intensity of instinctual gratification at each stage.

psychosexual trauma. As applied by Masters and Johnson, an earlier frightening or degrading sexual experience that is related to a present *sexual dysfunction.*

psychosis. A severe mental disorder in which thinking and emotion are so impaired that the individual is seriously out of contact with reality.

psychosocial stages of development. In Erik Erikson's theory, phases through which people pass from infancy through old age, each characterized by a particular challenge or crisis.

psychosomatic (disorder). See *psychophysiological disorders.*

psychosurgery. Any surgical technique in which neural pathways in the brain are cut in order to change behavior. See *lobotomy.*

psychotherapy. A primarily verbal means of helping troubled individuals change their thoughts, feelings, and behavior to reduce distress and to achieve greater life satisfaction. See *insight therapy* and *behavior therapy.*

psychotic (delusional) depression. A profound sadness and unjustified feelings of unworthiness, which also include *delusions.*

punishment. In psychological *experiments,* any noxious stimulus imposed on an organism to reduce the probability that it will behave in an undesired way.

random assignment. A method of assigning people to groups in an *experiment* that gives each person an equal chance of being in each group. The procedure helps to ensure that groups are comparable before the experimental manipulation begins.

rape. See *forced rape.*

rapid-smoking treatment. A *behavior therapy* technique for reducing cigarette smoking in which the person is instructed to puff much more quickly than usual in an effort to make the whole experience aversive.

rapport. A close, trusting relationship, believed to be essential for effective *psychotherapy.*

rational-emotive behavior therapy (REBT). New term for *rational-emotive therapy.*

rational-emotive therapy (RET). A *cognitive-restructuring behavior therapy* introduced by Albert Ellis and based on the assumption that much disordered behavior is rooted in absolutistic demands that people make on themselves. The therapy aims to alter the unrealistic goals individuals set for themselves, such as, "I must be universally loved."

rationalization. A *defense mechanism* in which a plausible reason is unconsciously invented by the *ego* to protect itself from confronting the real reason for an action, thought, or emotion.

reactance. Resistance to efforts by another to change the person.

reaction formation. A *defense mechanism* whereby an *unconscious* and unacceptable impulse or feeling that would cause anxiety is converted into its opposite so that it can become conscious and can be expressed.

reactivity (of behavior). The phenomenon whereby behavior is changed by the very fact that it is being observed.

reading disorder. See *dyslexia.*

reality principle. In psychoanalytic theory, the manner in which the *ego* delays gratification and otherwise deals with the environment in a planned, rational fashion.

receptive aphasia. See *aphasia.*

receptor. Proteins embedded in the membrane covering a neural cell that interact with one or more *neurotransmitters.*

recessive gene. A *gene* that must be paired with one identical to it in order to determine a trait in the *phenotype.*

recovery time. The period it takes for a physiological process to return to *baseline* after the body has responded to a stimulus.

refractory phase. The brief period after stimulation of a nerve, muscle, or other irritable element during which it is unresponsive to a second stimulus; or the period after intercourse during which the male cannot have another *orgasm.*

regression. A *defense mechanism* in which *anxiety* is avoided by retreating to the behavior patterns of an earlier *psychosexual stage.*

reinforcement. In *operant conditioning,* increasing the probability that a response will recur either by presenting a contingent positive event or by removing a negative one.

reliability. The extent to which a test, measurement, or classification system produces the same scientific observation each time it is applied. Some specific kinds of reliability include **test-retest,** the relationship between the scores that a person achieves when he or she takes the same test twice; **interrater,** the relationship between the judgments that at least two raters make independently about a phenomenon; **split half,** the relationship between two halves of an assessment instrument that have been determined to be equivalent; **alternate form,** the relationship between scores achieved by people when they complete two versions of a test that are judged to be equivalent; **internal consistency,** degree to which different items of an assessment are related to one another.

repression. A *defense mechanism* whereby impulses and thoughts unacceptable to the *ego* are pushed into the *unconscious.*

residual schizophrenia. Diagnosis given to patients who have had an episode of *schizophrenia* but who presently show no psychotic symptoms, though signs of the disorder do exist.

resistance. During *psychoanalysis,* the defensive tendency of the *unconscious* part of the *ego* to ward off from consciousness particularly threatening *repressed* material.

resistance to extinction. The tendency of a *conditioned response* to persist in the absence of any *reinforcement.*

resolution phase. The last stage in the sexual arousal cycle, during which sexual tensions abate.

response cost. An *operant conditioning punishment* procedure in which the misbehaving person is fined already earned reinforcers.

response deviation. A tendency to answer questionnaire items in an uncommon way, regardless of their content.

response hierarchy. The ordering of a series of responses according to the likelihood of their being elicited by a particular stimulus.

response prevention. A *behavior therapy* technique in which the person is discouraged from making an accustomed response; used primarily with *compulsive rituals*.

response set. The tendency of an individual to respond in a particular way to questions or statements on a test—for example, with a False—regardless of the content of each query or statement.

reticular formation. Network of *nuclei* and fibers in the central core of the *brain stem* that is important in arousing the cortex and maintaining alertness, in processing incoming sensory stimulation, and in adjusting spinal reflexes.

retrospective reports. Recollections by an individual of past events.

Rett's disorder. A very rare disorder found only in girls, with onset in the first or second year of life. Symptoms include decelerated head growth, lost ability to use hands purposefully, uncoordinated walking, poor speech production and comprehension, and poor interpersonal relations. Child may improve later in life, but usually will remain severely or profoundly *mentally retarded*.

reuptake. Process by which released *neurotransmitters* are pumped back into the pre-synaptic cell, making them available for enhancing transmission of *nerve impulses*.

reversal (ABAB) design. An experimental design in which behavior is measured during a baseline period (A), during a period when a treatment is introduced (B), during the reinstatement of the conditions that prevailed in the baseline period (A), and finally during a reintroduction of the treatment (B). It is commonly used in *operant* research to isolate cause–effect relationships.

reward. Any satisfying event or stimulus that, by being contingent on a response, increases the probability that the person will make that response again.

Rh factor. A substance present in the red blood cells of most people. If the Rh factor is present in the blood of a fetus but not in that of the mother, her system produces antibodies that may enter the bloodstream of the fetus and indirectly damage the brain.

right to refuse treatment. A legal principle according to which a committed mental patient may decline to participate in treatment.

right to treatment. A legal principle according to which a committed mental patient must be provided some minimal amount and quality of professional intervention, enough to afford a realistic opportunity for meaningful improvement.

risk factor. A condition or variable that, if present, increases the likelihood of developing a disorder.

role-playing. A technique that teaches people to behave in a certain way by encouraging them to pretend that they are in a particular situation; it helps people acquire complex behaviors in an efficient way. See also *behavior rehearsal*.

Rorschach Inkblot Test. A *projective test* in which the examinee is instructed to interpret a series of ten inkblots reproduced on cards.

rubella (German measles). An infectious disease that, if contracted by the mother during the first three months of pregnancy, has a high risk of causing *mental retardation* and physical deformity in the child.

sadism. See *sexual sadism*.

schema. A mental structure for organizing information about the world.

schizoaffective disorder. Diagnosis applied when a patient has symptoms of both *mood disorder* and either *schizophreniform disorder* or *schizophrenia*.

schizoid personality disorder. The person with a schizoid personality is emotionally aloof, indifferent to the praise, criticism, and feelings of others, and usually a loner with few, if any, close friends and with solitary interests.

schizophrenia. A group of *psychotic* disorders characterized by major disturbances in thought, emotion, and behavior; disordered thinking in which ideas are not logically related; faulty perception and attention; bizarre disturbances in motor activity; flat or inappropriate emotions; and reduced tolerance for *stress* in interpersonal relations. The patient withdraws from people and reality, often into a fantasy life of *delusions* and *hallucinations*. See *schizoaffective disorder*, *schizophreniform disorder*, and *brief reactive psychosis*.

schizophreniform disorder. Diagnosis given to people who have all the symptoms of *schizophrenia*, except that the disorder lasts more than two weeks but less than six months. See *brief reactive psychosis*.

schizophrenogenic mother. A cold, dominant, conflict-inducing mother formerly believed to cause *schizophrenia* in her child.

schizotypal personality disorder. The person with a schizotypal personality is eccentric, has oddities of thought and perception (*magical thinking*, *illusions*, *depersonalization*, *derealization*), speaks digressively and with overelaborations, and is usually socially isolated. Under *stress* he or she may appear *psychotic*.

school phobia. An acute, irrational dread of attending school, usually accompanied by somatic complaints. It is the most common *phobia* of childhood.

science. The pursuit of systematized knowledge through reliable observation.

secondary gain. Benefits that a person unconsciously obtains from a disability.

secondary prevention. See *prevention*.

secondary process. The reality-based decision-making and problem-solving activities of the *ego*. Compare with *primary process*.

secondhand smoke. Also referred to as sidestream smoke, the smoke from the burning end of a cigarette, which contains higher concentrations of ammonia, carbon monoxide, nicotine, and tar than does the smoke inhaled by the smoker.

sedative. A drug that slows bodily activities, especially those of the *central nervous system*; it is used to reduce pain and tension and to induce relaxation and sleep.

selective abstraction. A cognitive bias in Beck's theory of *depression* whereby a person picks out from a complex situation only certain features and ignores aspects that could lead to a different conclusion.

selective mortality. A possible confound in *longitudinal studies*, whereby the less healthy people in a sample are more likely to drop out over time.

selective mutism. A pattern of continuously refusing to speak in almost all social situations, including school, even though the child understands spoken language and is able to speak.

self-actualization. Fulfilling one's potential as an always growing human being; believed by *client-centered therapists* to be the master motive.

self-efficacy. In Bandura's theory, the person's belief that he or she can achieve certain goals.

self-instructional training. A cognitive-behavioral approach that tries to help people improve their overt behavior by changing how they silently talk to themselves.

self-monitoring. In *behavioral assessment*, a procedure whereby the individual observes and reports certain aspects of his or her own behavior, thoughts, or emotions.

self-psychology. Kohut's variant of *psychoanalysis*, in which the focus is on the development of the person's self-worth from acceptance and nurturance by key figures in childhood.

senile plaques. Small areas of tissue degeneration in the brain, made up of granular material and filaments.

sensate focus. A term applied to exercises prescribed at the beginning of the Masters and Johnson sex therapy program; partners are instructed to fondle each other to give pleasure but to refrain from intercourse, thus reducing anxiety about sexual performance.

sensory-awareness procedures. Techniques that help clients tune into their feelings and sensations, as in *sensate-focus* exercises, and to be open to new ways of experiencing and feeling.

separation anxiety disorder. A disorder in which the child feels intense fear and distress when away from someone on whom he or she is very dependent; said to be a significant cause of *school phobia*.

serotonin. An indoleamine that is a *neurotransmitter* of the *central nervous system*. Disturbances in its tracts apparently figure in *depression*.

severe mental retardation. A limitation in mental development measured in *IQ* tests at between 20–25 and 35–40. Individuals often cannot care for themselves, communicate only briefly, and are listless and inactive.

sex-reassignment surgery. An operation removing existing genitalia of a *transsexual* and constructing a substitute for the genitals of the opposite sex.

sexual and gender identity disorders. In DSM-IV-TR, disorders comprising the *paraphilias*, *sexual dysfunctions*, and *gender identity disorders*.

sexual aversion disorder. Avoidance of nearly all genital contact with other people.

sexual dysfunctions. Dysfunctions in which the appetitive or psychophysiological changes of the normal *sexual response cycle* are inhibited.

sexual masochism. A marked preference for obtaining or increasing sexual gratification through subjection to pain or humiliation.

sexual orientation disturbance. An earlier term for DSM-III's *ego-dystonic homosexuality*.

sexual response cycle. The general pattern of sexual physical processes and feelings, building to an *orgasm* by stimulation and made up of five phases: *interest*, *excitement*, *plateau*, *orgasm*, and *resolution*.

sexual sadism. A marked preference for obtaining or increasing sexual gratification by inflicting pain or humiliation on another person.

sexual script. Rules people have for guiding their actions in sexual situations.

sexual value system. As applied by Masters and Johnson, the activities that an individual holds to be acceptable and necessary in a sexual relationship.

shaping. In *operant conditioning*, reinforcing responses that are successively closer approximations to the desired behavior.

shell shock. A term from World War I for what is now referred to as *posttraumatic stress disorder*; it was believed to be due to sudden atmospheric changes from nearby explosions.

significant difference. See *statistical significance*.

single-subject experimental design. A design for an *experiment* conducted with a single subject, for example, the *reversal design* in *operant conditioning* research.

situational determinants. The environmental conditions that precede and follow a particular piece of behavior, a primary focus of *behavioral assessment*.

skeletal (voluntary) muscle. Muscle that clothes the skeleton of the vertebrate, is attached to bone, and is under voluntary control.

Skinner box. A laboratory apparatus in which an animal is placed for an *operant-conditioning experiment*. It contains a lever or other device that the animal must manipulate to obtain a reward or avoid punishment.

sleep apnea. Respiratory disorder in which breathing ceases repeatedly for a period of ten seconds or more hundreds of times throughout the night.

sleeping sickness. See *encephalitis lethargica*.

smooth (involuntary) muscle. Thin sheets of muscle cells associated with *viscera* and walls of blood vessels, performing functions not usually under direct voluntary control.

social desirability. In completion of *personality inventories*, the tendency of the responder to give what he or she considers the socially acceptable answer, whether or not it is accurate.

social phobia. A collection of fears linked to the presence of other people.

social problem solving. A form of *cognitive behavior therapy* that has people construe their psychological difficulties as stemming from soluble problems in living and then teaches them how to generate useful solutions.

social selection theory. An attempt to explain the correlation between social class and *schizophrenia* by proposing that people with schizophrenia move downward in social status.

social worker. A mental health professional who holds a master of social work (M.S.W.) degree.

social-skills training. *Behavior therapy* procedures for teaching socially unknowledgeable individuals how to meet others, talk to them and maintain eye contact, give and receive criticism, offer and accept compliments, make requests and express feelings, and otherwise improve their relations with other people. *Modeling* and *behavior rehearsal* are two such procedures.

socioeconomic status. A relative position in the community as determined by occupation, income, and level of education.

sociogenic hypothesis. Generally, an idea that seeks causes in social conditions, for example, that being in a low social class can cause one to become *schizophrenic*.

sociopath. See *antisocial personality*.

sodomy. Originally, penetration of the male organ into the anus of another male; later broadened in English law to include heterosexual anal intercourse and by some U.S. state statutes to cover unconventional sex in general.

soma. The totality of an organism's physical makeup.

somatic nervous system. That part of the nervous system that controls muscles under voluntary control.

somatic weakness. The vulnerability of a particular organ or organ system to psychological *stress* and thereby to a particular *psychophysiological disorder*.

somatization disorder (Briquet's syndrome). A *somatoform disorder* in which the person continually seeks medical help for recurrent and multiple physical symptoms that have no discoverable physical cause. The medical history is complicated and dramatically presented. Compare with *hypochondriasis*.

somatoform disorders. Disorders in which physical symptoms suggest a physical problem but have no known physiological cause; they are therefore believed to be linked to psychological conflicts and needs but not voluntarily assumed. Examples are *somatization disorder* (Briquet's syndrome), *conversion disorder*, *pain disorder*, *hypochondriasis*.

somatoform pain disorder. A *somatoform disorder* in which the person complains of severe and prolonged pain that is not explainable by organic pathology; it tends to be *stress* related or permits the patient to avoid an aversive activity or to gain attention and sympathy.

somatogenesis. Development from bodily origins, as distinguished from psychological origins. Compare with *psychogenesis*.

SORC. An acronym for the four sets of variables that are the focus of *behavioral assessment*: *situational determinants*, *organismic variables*, (overt) *responses*, and *reinforcement contingencies*.

specific phobia. An unwarranted fear and avoidance of a specific object or circumstance, for example, fear of nonpoisonous snakes or fear of heights.

specific-reaction theory. The hypothesis that an individual develops a given *psychophysiological disorder* because of the innate tendency of the *autonomic nervous system* to respond in a particular way to *stress*, for example, by increasing heart rate or developing tension in the forehead.

spectator role. As applied by Masters and Johnson, a pattern of behavior in which the individual's focus on and concern with sexual performance impedes his or her natural sexual responses.

split-half reliability. See *reliability*.

stability–lability. A dimension of classifying the responsiveness of the *autonomic nervous system*. Labile individuals are those in whom a wide range of stimuli can elicit autonomic *arousal*; stable individuals are less easily aroused.

standardization. The process of constructing an assessment procedure that has norms and meets the various psychometric criteria for *reliability* and *validity*.

state-dependent learning. The phenomenon whereby an organism shows the effects of learning that took place in a special condition, such as while intoxicated, better than in another condition.

state-dependent memory. The phenomenon whereby people are more able to remember an event if they are in the same state as when it occurred. If they are in a greatly different state when they try to remember—happy now, and sad then, for example—memory is poorer.

statistical significance. A result that has a low probability of having occurred by chance alone and is by convention regarded as important.

statutory rape. See *forced rape*.

stepped care. The practice of beginning treatment with the least intrusive intervention possible and moving on to more intensive efforts only if necessary.

stepping-stone theory. The belief that the use of one kind of drug, such as *marijuana*, leads to the use of a more dangerous one, such as *cocaine*.

stimulant. A drug that increases alertness and motor activity and at the same time reduces fatigue, allowing an individual to remain awake for an extended period of time. Examples are *cocaine* and *amphetamines*.

strategic processing. The use of *cognitive* strategies to solve problems; said to be defective in people with *mental retardation*.

stress. State of an organism subjected to a *stressor*; it can take the form of increased *autonomic* activity and in the long term can cause the breakdown of an organ or development of a mental disorder.

stress management. A range of psychological procedures that help people control and reduce their *stress* or *anxiety*.

stressor. An event that occasions *stress* in an organism, for example, loss of a loved one.

stroke. A sudden loss of consciousness and control followed by paralysis; caused when a blood clot obstructs an artery or by hemorrhage into the brain when an artery ruptures.

structural social support. A person's network of social relationships, for example, number of friends. Contrast with *functional social support*.

structured interview. An interview in which the questions are set out in a prescribed fashion for the interviewer. Assists professionals in making diagnostic decisions based upon standardized criteria.

stuttering. One of the communication disorders of childhood, marked by frequent and pronounced verbal dysfluencies, such as repetitions of certain sounds.

subintentioned death. A form of *suicide* that is believed to have been caused in some measure by the person's *unconscious* intentions.

sublimation. *Defense mechanism* entailing the conversion of sexual or aggressive impulses into socially valued behaviors, especially creative activity.

substance abuse. The use of a drug to such an extent that the person is often intoxicated throughout the day and fails in important obligations and in attempts to abstain, but there is no physiological dependence. See *psychological dependency*.

substance dependence. The abuse of a drug sometimes accompanied by a physiological dependence on it, made evident by *tolerance* and *withdrawal* symptoms; also called addiction.

substance-related disorders. Disorders in which drugs such as alcohol and *cocaine* are abused to such an extent that behavior becomes maladaptive; social and occupational functioning are impaired, and control or abstinence becomes impossible. Reliance on the drug may be either psychological, as in *substance abuse*, or physiological, as in *substance dependence*, or addiction.

successive approximations. Responses that closer and closer resemble the desired response in *operant conditioning*. See *shaping*.

suicide. The taking of one's own life intentionally.

suicide prevention centers. Based on the assumption that people are often ambivalent about taking their own lives, these centers are staffed primarily by paraprofessionals who are trained to be *empathic* and to encourage suicidal callers to consider nondestructive ways of dealing with what is bothering them.

sulcus (fissure). A shallow furrow in the *cerebral cortex* separating adjacent convolutions or *gyri*.

superego. In *psychoanalytic* theory, the part of the personality that acts as the conscience and reflects society's moral standards as learned from parents and teachers.

symbolic loss. In *psychoanalytic* theory, the *unconscious* interpretation by the *ego* of an event such as the rebuff of a loved one as a permanent rejection.

sympathetic nervous system. The division of the *autonomic nervous system* that acts on bodily systems—for example, contracting the blood vessels, reducing activity of the intestines, and increasing the heartbeat—to prepare the organism for exertion, emotional *stress*, or extreme cold.

symptom. An observable physiological or psychological manifestation of a disease, often occurring in a patterned group to constitute a *syndrome*.

synapse. A small gap between two *neurons* where the nerve impulse passes from the axon of the first to the dendrites, cell body, or axon of the second.

syndrome. A group or pattern of *symptoms* that tends to occur together in a particular *disease*.

systematic desensitization. A major *behavior therapy* procedure that has a fearful person, while deeply relaxed, imagine a series of progressively more fearsome situations. The two responses of relaxation and fear are incompatible and fear is dispelled. This technique is useful for treating psychological problems in which *anxiety* is the principal difficulty.

systematic rational restructuring. A variant of *rational-emotive therapy* in which the client imagines a series of increasingly *anxiety*-provoking situations while attempting to reduce distress by talking about them to the self in a more realistic, defusing fashion.

systems perspective. A general viewpoint that holds that a phenomenon, for example, a child's conduct problem, is best understood in the broad context in which it occurs, for example, the child's family and school environments.

tachycardia. A racing of the heart, often associated with high levels of *anxiety*.

tardive dyskinesia. A muscular disturbance of older patients who have taken *phenothiazines* for a very long time, marked by involuntary lip smacking and chin wagging.

Taylor Manifest Anxiety Scale. Fifty items drawn from the MMPI, used as a self-report questionnaire to assess *anxiety*.

temporal lobe. A large area of each *cerebral hemisphere* situated below the lateral *sulcus* and in front of the *occipital lobe*; contains primary auditory projection and association areas and general association areas.

tertiary prevention. See *prevention*.

testes. Male reproductive glands or gonads; the site where sperm develop and are stored.

testosterone. Male sex *hormone* secreted by the *testes* that is responsible for the development of sex characteristics, such as enlargement of the testes and growth of facial hair.

test-retest reliability. See *reliability*.

tetrahydrocannabinol (THC). The major active chemical in *marijuana* and *hashish*.

thalamus. A major brain relay station consisting of two egg-shaped lobes located in the *diencephalon*; it receives impulses from all sensory areas except the olfactory and transmits them to the *cerebrum*.

Thanatos. In *psychoanalytic* theory, the death instinct; with *Eros*, the two basic instincts within the *id*.

Thematic Apperception Test (TAT). A *projective test* consisting of a set of black-and-white pictures reproduced on cards, each depicting a potentially emotion-laden situation. The examinee, presented with the cards one at a time, is instructed to make up a story about each situation.

theory. A formally stated and coherent set of propositions that purport to explain a range of phenomena, order them in a logical way, and suggest what additional information might be gleaned under certain conditions.

therapeutic community. A concept in mental health care that views the total environment as contributing to *prevention* or treatment.

thiamine. One of the complex of B *vitamins*.

third-variable problem. The difficulty in the *correlational method* of research whereby the relationship between two *variables* may be attributable to a third factor.

Thorazine. Trade name for *chlorpromazine*, one of the *antipsychotic drugs* and a member of the *phenothiazine* group.

thought disorder. A symptom of *schizophrenia*, evidenced by problems such as *incoherence*, *loose associations*, *poverty of speech*, and *poverty of content* of speech.

thyroid gland. An endocrine structure whose two lobes are located on either side of the windpipe; it secretes thyroxin.

time-of-measurement effects. A possible confound in *longitudinal studies* whereby conditions at a particular point in time can have a specific effect on a *variable* that is being studied over time.

time-out. An *operant conditioning* punishment procedure in which, after bad behavior, the person is temporarily removed from a setting where reinforcers can be obtained and placed in a less desirable setting, for example, in a boring room.

token economy. A *behavior therapy* procedure, based on *operant conditioning* principles, in which institutionalized patients are given scrip rewards, such as poker chips, for socially constructive behavior. The tokens can be exchanged for desirable items and activities such as cigarettes and extra time away from the ward.

tolerance. A physiological process in which greater and greater amounts of an addictive drug are required to produce the same effect. See *substance dependence*.

trait. A somatic characteristic or an enduring psychological *predisposition* to respond in a particular way, distinguishing one individual from another.

tranquilizer. A drug that reduces *anxiety* and agitation, such as *Valium*. See *anxiolytics*.

transference. The venting of the *analysand's* emotions, either positive or negative, by treating the *psychoanalyst* as the symbolic representative of someone important in the past. An example is the analysand's becoming angry with the *psychoanalyst* to release emotions actually felt toward his or her father.

transference neurosis. A crucial phase of *psychoanalysis* during which the *analysand* reacts emotionally toward the *psychoanalyst*, treating the analyst as a parent and reliving childhood experiences in his or her presence. It enables both *psychoanalyst* and *analysand* to examine hitherto *repressed* conflicts in the light of present-day reality.

transsexual. A person who believes he or she is opposite in sex to his or her biological endowment; *sex-reassignment surgery* is frequently desired.

transvestic fetishism. The practice of dressing in the clothing of the opposite sex, for the purpose of sexual arousal.

trauma. A severe physical injury or wound to the body caused by an external force, or a psychological shock having a lasting effect on mental life. *Pl.* traumata.

tremor. An involuntary quivering of voluntary muscle, usually limited to small musculature of particular areas.

triadic reciprocality. The influence of *cognition* and behavior on each other through the relationships among thinking, behavior, and the environment.

tricyclic drugs. A group of *antidepressants* with molecular structures characterized by three fused rings. Tricyclics are known to interfere with the reuptake of *norepinephrine* and *serotonin* by a *neuron* after it has fired.

trisomy. A condition wherein there are three rather than the usual pair of homologous *chromosomes* within the cell nucleus.

tumescence. The flow of blood into the genitals.

tumor (neoplasm). Abnormal growth that when located in the brain can either be malignant and directly destroy brain tissue or be benign and disrupt functioning by increasing intracranial pressure.

twin method. Research strategy in *behavior genetics* in which *concordance* rates of *monozygotic* and *dizygotic* twins are compared.

two-factor theory. Mowrer's theory of *avoidance learning* according to which (1) fear is attached to a neutral stimulus by pairing it with a noxious *unconditioned stimulus*, and (2) a person learns to escape the fear elicited by the *conditioned stimulus*, thereby avoiding the *unconditioned stimulus*. See *fear-drive*.

Type A behavior pattern. One of two contrasting psychological patterns revealed through studies seeking the cause of *coronary heart disease*. Type A people are competitive, rushed, hostile, and overcommitted to their work, and are believed to be at heightened risk for heart disease. Those who meet the other pattern, Type B people, are more relaxed and relatively free of pressure.

unconditional positive regard. According to Rogers, a crucial attitude for the *client-*

centered therapist to adopt toward the client, who needs to feel complete acceptance as a person in order to evaluate the extent to which current behavior contributes to *self-actualization*.

unconditioned response (UCR). See *classical conditioning*.

unconditioned stimulus (UCS). See *classical conditioning*.

unconscious. A state of unawareness without sensation or thought. In *psychoanalytic theory*, it is the part of the personality, in particular the *id* impulses, or *id* energy, of which the *ego* is unaware.

undercontrolled (behavior). In reference to childhood disorders, problem behavior of the child that creates trouble for others, such as disobedience and aggressiveness.

undifferentiated schizophrenia. Diagnosis given for patients whose symptoms do not fit any listed category or meet the criteria for more than one subtype.

unilateral ECT. *Electroconvulsive therapy* in which electrodes are placed on one side of the forehead so that current passes through only one brain hemisphere.

unipolar depression. A term applied to the disorder of individuals who have experienced episodes of *depression* but not of *mania*; referred to as *major depression* in DSM-IV-TR.

vagina. The sheathlike female genital organ that leads from the uterus to the external opening.

vaginal barrel. The passageway of the vaginal canal leading from the external opening to the uterus.

vaginal orgasm. Sexual climax experienced through stimulation of the *vagina*.

vaginal plethysmograph. A device for recording the amount of blood in the walls of the *vagina* and thus for measuring arousal.

vaginismus. Painful, spasmodic contractions of the outer third of the *vaginal barrel*, which make insertion of the penis impossible or extremely difficult.

validity. Different types of validity include **internal**, the extent to which experimental results can be confidently attributed to the manipulation of the *independent variable*; **external**, the extent to which research results may be generalized to other populations and settings. Validity as applied to psychiatric diagnoses includes **concurrent**, the extent to which previously undiscovered features are found among patients with the same diagnosis; **predictive**, the extent to which predictions can be made about the future behavior of patients with the same diagnosis; **etiological**, the extent to which a disorder in a number of patients is found to have the same cause or causes. Validity as applied to psychological and psychiatric measures includes **content validity**, the extent to which a measure adequately samples the domain of interest; **criterion**, the extent to which a measure is associated in an expected way with some other measure (the criterion). See also *construct validity*.

Valium. An *anxiety*-reducing drug, or *anxiolytic*; one of the benzodiazepines.

value self-confrontation. A procedure whereby a person's values and behavior are changed by demonstrating that the values of people he or she wishes to emulate are different from the ones currently held by the person.

variable. A characteristic or aspect in which people, objects, events, or conditions vary.

vasoconstriction. A narrowing of the space within the walls (lumen) of a blood vessel; implicated in diseases such as *hypertension*.

vicarious learning. Learning by observing the reactions of others to stimuli or by listening to what they say.

Vineland Adaptive Behavior Scale. An instrument for assessing how many age-appropriate, socially adaptive behaviors a child engages in.

viscera. The internal organs of the body located in the great cavity of the trunk proper.

vitamins. Various organic substances that are, as far as is known, essential to the nutrition of many animals, acting usually in minute quantities to regulate various *metabolic* processes.

voyeurism. Marked preference for obtaining sexual gratification by watching others in a state of undress or having sexual relations.

vulnerability schema. The schema of people who are socially anxious and who generally think about danger, harm, and unpleasant events that may come to them.

waxy flexibility. An aspect of *catatonic immobility* in which the patient's limbs can be moved into a variety of positions and maintained that way for unusually long periods of time.

white matter. The neural tissue, particularly of the brain and spinal cord, consisting of tracts or bundles of myelinated (sheathed) nerve fibers.

withdrawal. Negative physiological and psychological reactions evidenced when a person suddenly stops taking an addictive drug; cramps, restlessness, and even death are examples. See *substance abuse*.

woolly mammoth. A metaphor for the way in which the *repressed conflicts* of *psychoanalytic* theory are encapsulated in the *unconscious*, making them inaccessible to examination and alteration; thus maintained, the conflicts cause disorders in adulthood.

working through. In *psychoanalysis*, the arduous, time-consuming process through which the *analysand* confronts *repressed conflicts* again and again and faces up to the validity of the *psychoanalyst's interpretations* until problems are satisfactorily solved.

Zeitgeist. The German word for the trends of thought and feeling of culture and taste of a particular time period.

zygote. The fertilized egg cell formed when the male sperm and female ovum unite.

References

Abikoff, H.B. & Hechtman, L. (1996). Multimodal therapy and stimulants in the treatment of children with attention-deficit hyperactivity disorder. In E.D. Hibbs & P.S. Jensen (Eds.), *Psychosocial treatments for child and adolescent disorders: Empirically based strategies for clinical practice* (pp. 341-369). Washington, D.C.: American Psychological Association.

Abramowitz, J.S., Franklin, M.E., Street, G.P., Kozak, M.J. & Foa, E.B. (2000). Effects of comorbid depression on response to treatment for obsessive compulsive disorder. *Behavior Therapy, 31,* 517-528.

Abramson, L.Y., Metalsky, G.I., & Alloy, L.B. (1989). Hopelessness depression: A theory-based subtype of depression. *Psychological Review, 96,* 358-372.

Abramson, L.Y., Seligman, M.E.P., & Teasdale, J.D. (1978). Learned helplessness in humans: Critique and reformulation. *Journal of Abnormal Psychology, 87,* 49-74.

Achenbach, T.M., & Edelbrock, C.S. (1978). The classification of child psychopathology: A review of empirical efforts. *Psychological Bulletin, 85,* 1275-1301.

Achenbach, T.M., Bird, H.R., Canino, G., Phares, V., Gould, M.S. & Rubio-Stipec, M. (1990). Epidemiological comparisons of Puerto Rican and U.S. mainland children: Parent, teacher and self-reports. *Journal of the American Academy of Child and Adolescent Psychiatry, 29,* 84-93.

Achenbach, T.M., Hensley, V.R., Phares, V., & Grayson, D. (1990). Problems and competencies reported by parents of Australian and American children. *Journal of Child Psychology and Psychiatry, 31,* 265-286.

Ackerman, N.W. (1966). *Treating the troubled family.* New York: Basic Books.

Adams, H.E., Wright, L.W., Jr., & Lohr, B.A. (1996). Is homophobia associated with homosexual arousal? *Journal of Abnormal Psychology, 105,* 440-445.

Adams, K.M. (1980). In search of Luria's battery: A false start. *Journal of Consulting and Clinical Psychology, 48,* 511-516.

Adelmann, P.K. (1994). Multiple roles and psychological well-being in a national sample of older adults. *Journal of Gerontology, 49,* S277-S285.

Adler, A. (1929). *Problems of neurosis.* New York: Harper & Row.

Adler, A. (1930). *Guiding the child on the principles of individual psychology.* New York: Greenberg.

Adler, P.S., & Ditto, B. (1998). Psychophysiological effects of interviews about emotional events on offspring of hypertensives and normotensives. *International Journal of Psychophysiolgy, 28,* 263-271.

Adler, R.H., Zamboni, P., Hofer, T., & Hemmeler, W. (1997). How not to miss a somatic needle in a haystack of chronic pain. *Journal of Psychosomatic Research, 42,* 499-505.

Agras, W.S., Rossiter, E.M., Arnow, B., Schneider, J.A., Telch, C.F., Raeburn, S.D., Bruce, B., Perl, M., & Koran, L.M. (1992). Pharmacologic and cognitive-behavioral treatment for bulimia nervosa: A controlled comparison. *American Journal of Psychiatry, 149,* 82-87.

Akbarian, S., Kim, J.J., Potkin, S.G., Hagman, J.O., Tafazzoli, A., et al. (1995). Gene expression for glutamic acid decarboxylase is reduced without loss of neurons in prefrontal cortex of schizophrenics. *Archives of General Psychiatry, 52,* 258-266.

Akillas, E., & Efran, J.S. (1995). Symptom prescription and reframing: Should they be combined? *Cognitive Therapy and Research, 19,* 263-279.

Akyuez, G., Dogan, O., Sar, V., Yargic, L.I., & Tutkun, H. (1999). Frequency of dissociative disorder in the general population in Turkey. *Comprehensive Psychiatry, 40,* 151-159.

Al-Absim, M., & Rokke, P.D. (1991). Can anxiety help us tolerate pain? *Pain, 46,* 43-51.

Albano, A.M., Marten, P.A., Holt, C.S., Heimberg, R.G., et al. (1995). Cognitive-behavioral group treatment for social phobia in adolescents: A preliminary study. *Journal of Nervous and Mental Disease, 183,* 649-656.

Albee, G.W., Lane, E.A., & Reuter, J.M. (1964). Childhood intelligence of future schizophrenics and neighborhood peers. *Journal of Psychology, 58,* 141-144.

Albertini, R.S., & Phillips, K.A. (1999). Thirty-three cases of body dysmorphic disorder in children and adolescents. *Journal of the American Academy of Child and Adolescent Psychiatry, 38,* 453-459.

Alcohol, Drug Abuse, and Mental Health Administration. (1996). *Reports of the Secretary's Task Force on Youth Suicide* (Vols. 1-4). Washington, DC. U.S. Government Printing Office.

Alden, L.E., Laposa, J.M., Taylor, C.T., & Ryder, A.G. (2002). Avoidant personality disorder: Current status and future directions. *Journal of Personality Disorders, 16,* 1-29.

Alden, L.E. (1989). Short-term structured treatment for avoidant personality disorder. *Journal of Consulting and Clinical Psychology, 57,* 756-764.

Alexander, F. (1950). *Psychosomatic medicine.* New York: Norton.

Alexander, F., & French, T.M. (1946). *Psychoanalytic therapy.* New York: Ronald Press.

Alexander, J.F., Holtzworth-Munroe, A., & Jameson, P. (1994). The process and outcome of marital and family therapy: Research review and evaluation. In A.E. Bergin & S.L. Garfield (Eds.), *Handbook of psychotherapy and behavior change* (4th ed., pp. 595-630). New York: Wiley.

Alexander, P.C., & Lupfer, S.L. (1987) Family characteristics and long-term consequences associated with sexual abuse. *Archives of Sexual Behavior, 16,* 235-245.

Allderidge, P. (1979). Hospitals, mad houses, and asylums: Cycles in the care of the insane. *British Journal of Psychiatry, 134,* 321-324

Allen, G.J., Chinsky, J.M., Larsen, S.W., Lockman, J.E., & Selinger, H.V. (1976). *Community psychology and the schools: A behaviorally oriented multilevel preventive approach.* Hillsdale, NJ: Erlbaum.

Allen, M.G. (1976). Twin studies of affective illness. *Archives of General Psychiatry, 33,* 1476-1478.

Allison, R.B. (1984). Difficulties diagnosing the multiple personality syndrome in a death penalty case. *International Journal of Clinical and Experimental Hypnosis, 32,* 102-117.

Allnutt, S.H., Bradford, J.M., Greenberg, D.M., & Curry, S. (1996). Co-morbidity of alcoholism and the paraphilias. *Journal of Forensic Science, 41,* 234-239.

Alloy, L.B., Kelly, K.A., Mineka, S., & Clements, C.M. (1990). Comorbidity in anxiety and depressive disorders: A helplessness/hopelessness perspective. In J.D. Maser & C.R. Cloninger (Eds.), *Comorbidity in anxiety and mood disorders.* Washington, DC: American Psychiatric Press.

Allport, G.W. (1937). *Personality: A psychological interpretation.* New York: Holt, Rinehart & Winston.

Allport, G.W. (1961). *Pattern and growth in personality.* New York: Holt, Rinehart & Winston.

Almada, S.J. (1991). Neuroticism and cynicism and risk of death in middle aged men: The Western Electric study. *Psychosomatic Medicine, 53,* 165-175.

Alonso-Zaldivar, R. (1999, February 23). Alcohol-related road deaths analyzed. *Los Angeles Times,* pp. A12

Alpert, J.E., Uebelacker, L.A., McLean, N.E., Nierenberg, A.A., & et al. (1997). Social phobia, avoidant personality disorder and atypical depression: Co-occurrence and clinical implications. *Psychological Medicine, 27,* 627-633.

Alston, M.H., Rankin, S.H., & Harris, C.A. (1995). Suicide in African American elderly. *Journal of Black Studies, 26,* 31-35.

Altman, D.G., Flora, J.A., & Farquhar, J.W. (1986, August). Institutionalizing community-based health promotion programs. Paper presented at the annual meeting of the American Psychological Association, Washington, DC.

Altshuler, L.L., Post, R.M., Leverich, G.S., Mikalauskas, K., Rusoff, A., & Ackerman, L. (1995). Antidepressant-induced mania and cycle acceleration: A controversy revisited. *American Journal of Psychiatry, 152,* 1130-1138.

Amador, X.F., Flaum, M., Andreasen, N.C., Strauss, D.H., Yale, S.A., et al. (1994). Awareness of illness in schizophrenia and schizoaffective and mood disorder. *Archives of General Psychiatry, 51,* 826-836.

American Association of Mental Retardation. (1992). *Mental retardation: Definition, classification, and systems of support.* Washington, DC: Author.

American Heart Association (2002). *2002 Heart and stroke statistical update.* Dallas, Texas: American Heart Association.

American Law Institute. (1962). *Model penal code: Proposed official draft.* Philadelphia: Author.

American Psychiatric Association (1994). *Diagnostic and statistical manual of mental disorders (DSM-IV)* (4th ed.). Washington, DC: Author.

American Psychiatric Association Board of Trustees. (1993). *Statement on memories of sexual abuse.* Washington, DC: American Psychiatric Association.

American Psychiatric Association. (1992). AIDS policy: Guidelines for outpatient psychiatric services. *American Journal of Psychiatry, 149,* 721.

American Psychiatric Association. (1993). Practice guidelines for major depressive disorder in adults. *American Journal of Psychiatry, 150,* All.

American Psychiatric Association. *Diagnostic and statistical manual of mental disorders (DSM-IV-TR).* First edition, 1952; second edition, 1968; third edition, 1980; revised, 1987. Washington, DC: Author.

Amir, N., Foa, E.B., & Coles, M.E. (1998). Automatic activation and strategic avoidance of threat-relevant information in social phobia. *Journal of Abnormal Psychology, 107,* 285-290.

Amoss, P.T., & Harrell, S. (1981). Introduction: An anthropological perspective on aging. In P.T. Amoss & S. Harrell (Eds.), *Other ways of growing old* (pp. 1-24). Stanford, CA: Stanford University Press.

Amsterdam, J.D., DeRubeis, R.J., O'Reardon, J.P., & Young, P.R. (2002, May). Cognitive therapy vs medications for severe depression: Response to acute treatment. In J. Fawcett (Chair), Cognitive therapy vs. medications for severe depression: Acute response and relapse prevention. Symposium presented at the 155th Annual Meeting of the American Psychiatric Association, Philadelphia.

Anastasi, A. (1990). *Psychological testing* (6th ed.). New York: Macmillan.

Anastopoulos, A.D., Shelton, T., DuPaul, G.J., & Guevremont, D.C. (1993). Parent training for attention deficit hyperactivity disorder: Its impact on parent functioning. *Journal of Abnormal Child Psychology, 20,* 503-520.

Andersen, B.L., Kiecolt-Glaser, J.K., & Glaser, R. (1994). A biobehavioral model of cancer stress and disease course. *American Psychologist, 49,* 389-404.

Andersen, S.M., & Berk, M.S. (1998). The social-cognitive model of transference: Experiencing past relationships in the present. *Current Directions in Psychological Science, 7,* 109-115.

Anderson, B.J., & Wolf, F.M. (1986). Chronic physical illness and sexual behavior: Psychological issues. *Journal of Consulting and Clinical Psychology, 54,* 168-175.

Anderson, B.L. (1992). Psychological interventions for cancer patients to enhance quality of life. *Journal of Consulting and Clinical Psychology, 60,* 552-568.

Anderson, C.A. (1991). How people think about causes: Examination of the typical phenomenal organization of attributions for success and failure. *Social Cognition, 9,* 295-329.

Anderson, G.M., & Hoshino, Y. (1987). Neurochemical studies of autism. In D.J. Cohen, A.M. Donnellan, & R. Paul (Eds.), *Handbook of autism and pervasive developmental disorders* (pp. 166-191). New York: Wiley.

Anderson, J.C., Williams, S., McGee, R., & Silva, A. (1987). DSM-III disorders in pre-adolescent children: Prevalence in a large sample from the general population. *Archives of General Psychiatry, 44,* 69-76.

Anderson, L.T., Campbell, M., Adams, P., Small, A.M., Perry, R., & Shell, J. (1989). The effects of haloperidol on discrimination learning and behavioral symptoms in autistic children. *Journal of Autism and Developmental Disorders, 19,* 227-239.

Anderson, R.E., Crespo, C.J., Bartlett, S.J., Cheskin, L.J., & Pratt, M. (1998). Relationship of physical activity and television watching with body weight and level of fatness among children: Results from the third National Health and Nutrition Examination survey. *Journal of the American Medical Association, 279,* 938-942.

Anderson, S., Hanson, R., Malecha, M., Oftelie, A., Erickson, C., & Clark, J.M. (1997). The effectiveness of naltrexone in treating task attending, aggression, self-injury, and stereotypic mannerisms of six young males with autism or pervasive developmental disorders. *Journal of Developmental and Physical Disabilities, 9,* 211-221.

Andersson, T., Magnusson, D., & Wennberg, P. (1997). Early aggressiveness and hyperactivity as indicators of adult alcohol problems and criminality: A prospective longitudinal study of male subjects. *Studies on Crime and Crime Prevention, 6,* 7-20.

Andreasen, N.C. (1979). Thought, language, and communication disorders: 2. Diagnostic significance. *Archives of General Psychiatry, 36,* 1325-1330.

Andreasen, N.C., & Olsen, S.A. (1982). Negative versus positive schizophrenia. Definition and validation. *Archives of General Psychiatry, 39,* 789-794.

Andreasen, N.C., Flaum, M., Swayze, V.W., Tyrrell, G., & Arndt, S. (1990). Positive and negative symptoms in schizophrenia: A critical reappraisal. *Archives of General Psychiatry, 47,* 615-621.

Andreasen, N.C., Olsen, S.A., Dennert, J.W., & Smith, M.R. (1982). Ventricular enlargement in schizophrenia: Relationship to positive and negative symptoms. *American Journal of Psychiatry, 139,* 297-302.

Andreasen, N.C., Rice, J., Endicott, J., Coryell, W., Grove, W.W., & Reich, T. (1987). Familial rates of affective disorder. *Archives of General Psychiatry, 44,* 461-472.

Andreasen, N.C., Swayze, V.W., Flaum, M., Yates, W.R., et al. (1990). Ventricular enlargement in schizophrenia evaluated with computed tomographic scanning: Effects of gender, age, and stage of illness. *Archives of General Psychiatry, 47,* 1008-1015.

Andress, V.R., & Corey, D.M. (1978). Survivor-victims: Who discovers or witnesses suicide? *Psychological Reports, 42,* 759-764.

Andrews, B., Brewin, C. R., Rose, S., & Kirk, M. (2000). Predicting PTSD symptoms in victims of violent crime: The role of shame, anger, and childhood abuse. *Journal of Abnormal Psychology,* 109, 69-73.

Angold, A., & Rutter, M. (1992). Effects of age and pubertal status on depression in a large clinical sample. *Development and Psychopathology, 4,* 5-28.

Angrist, B., Lee, H.K., & Gershon, S. (1974). The antagonism of amphetamine-induced symptomatology by a neuroleptic. *American Journal of Psychiatry, 131,* 817-819.

Angst, J. (1998). Sexual problems in healthy and depressed persons. *International Clinical Psychopharmacology, 13(Suppl. 6),* S1-S4.

Anthony-Bergstone, C., Zarit, S.H., & Gatz, M. (1988). Symptoms of psychological distress among caregivers of dementia patients. *Psychology and Aging, 3,* 245-248.

Antoni, M.H., Baggett, L., Ironson, G., LaPerriere, A., August, S., Klimas, N., Schneiderman, N., & Fletcher, M.A. (1991). Cognitive-behavioral stress management intervention buffers distress responses and immunologic changes following notification of HIV-1 seropositivity. *Journal of Consulting and Clinical Psychology, 59,* 906-915.

Antoni, M.H., Schneiderman, N., Fletcher, M.A., Goldstein, D.A., Ironson, G., & Laperriere, A. (1990). Psychoneuroimmunology and HIV-1. *Journal of Consulting and Clinical Psychology, 58,* 38-49.

Antonovsky, H., Sadowsky, M., & Maoz, B. (1990). Sexual activity of aging men and women: An Israeli study. *Behavior, Health, and Aging, 1,* 151-161.

Apfelbaum, B. (1989). Retarded ejaculation: A much-misunderstood syndrome. In S.R. Leiblum & R.C. Rosen (Eds.), *Principles and practice of sex therapy: Update for the 1990s* (pp. 168-206). New York: Guilford.

Appel, L.J., Moore, T.J., Obarzanek, E., Vollmer, W.M., Svetkey, L.P., Sacks, F.M., Bray, G.A., Vogt, T.M., Cutler, J.A., Windhauser, M.M., Lin, P-H, Karanja, N., for the DASH Collaborative Research Group. (1997). A clinical trial of the effects of dietary patterns on blood pressure. *New England Journal of Medicine, 336,* 1117-1124.

Appelbaum, P.S. (1985). Tarasoff and the clinician: Problems in fulfilling the duty to protect. *American Journal of Psychiatry, 142,* 425-429.

Appelbaum, P.S., & Greer, A. (1994). Who's on trial? Multiple personalities and the insanity defense. *Hospital and Community Psychiatry, 45,* 965-966.

Appelbaum, P.S., & Grisso, T. (1995). The MacArthur Treatment Competence Study: 1. Mental illness and competence to consent to treatment. *Law and Human Behavior, 19,* 105-126.

Appelbaum, P.S., & Gutheil, T. (1980). The Boston State Hospital case: "Involuntary mind control," the Constitution, and the "right to rot." *American Journal of Psychiatry, 137,* 720-727.

Appelbaum, P.S., & Gutheil, T. (1991). *Clinical handbook of psychiatry and the law.* Baltimore: Williams & Wilkins.

Appelbaum, P.S., Grisso, T., Frank, E., O'Donnel, S., & Kupfer, D. (1999). Capacities of depressed patients to consent to research. *American Journal of Psychiatry, 156,* 1380-1384

Appleby, P.R., Miller, L.C., & Rothspan, S. (1999). The paradox of trust for male couples: When risking is a part of loving. *Personal Relationships, 6,* 81-93.

Apt, C., & Hurlbert, D.H. (1994). The sexual attitudes, behavior, and relationships of women with histrionic personality disorder. *Journal of Sex and Marital Therapy, 20,* 125-133.

Apter, J.T., & Allen, L.A. (1999). Buspirone: Future directions. *Journal of Clinical Psychopharmacology, 19,* 86-93.

Araujo, A.B., Durante, R., Feldman, H.A., Goldstein, I., & McKinley, J.B. (1998). The relationship between depressive symptoms and male erectile dysfunction: Cross-sectional results from the Massachusetts Male Aging Study. *Psychosomatic Medicine, 60,* 458-465.

Arbisi, P.A., Ben-Porath, Y. S., & McNulty, J. (2002). A comparison of MMPI-2 validity in African American and Caucasian psychiatric patients. *Psychological Assessment, 14,* 3-15.

Arbuthnot, J., & Gordon, D.A. (1986). Behavioral and cognitive effects of a moral reasoning development intervention for high-risk behavior disordered adolescents. *Journal of Consulting and Clinical Psychology, 54,* 208-216.

Ard, B.N., Jr. (1977). Sex in lasting marriages: A longitudinal study. *Journal of Sex Research, 13,* 274-285.

Arentewicz, G., & Schmidt, G. (1983). *The treatment of sexual disorders: Concepts and techniques of couple therapy.* New York: Basic Books.

Arieti, S. (1979). New views on the psychodynamics of phobias. *American Journal of Psychotherapy, 33,* 82-95.

Arkowitz, H. (1989). The role of theory in psychotherapy integration. *Journal of Integrative and Eclectic Psychotherapy, 8,* 8-16.

Arkowitz, H. (1992). Integrative theories of therapy. In D. Freedheim (Ed.), *The history of psychotherapy: A century of change.* Washington, DC: American Psychological Association.

Arndt, I.O., Dorozynsky, L., Woody, G.E., McLellan, A.T., & O'Brien, C.P. (1992). Desipramine treatment of cocaine dependence in methadone-maintained patients. *Archives of General Psychiatry, 49,* 888-893.

Arnow, B., Kenardy, J., & Agras, W.S. (1992). Binge eating among the obese. *Journal of Behavioral Medicine, 15,* 155-170.

Arolt, V., Lencer, R., Nolte, A., Muller-Myhsok, B., Purmann, S., et al. (1996). Eye-tracking dysfunction is a putative phenotypic susceptibility marker for schizophrenia and maps to a locus on chromosome 6p in families with multiple occurrence of the disease. *American Journal of Medical Genetics, 67,* 564-579.

Aronson, E. (1972). *The social animal.* San Francisco: Freeman.

Aronson, E., & Carlsmith, J.R. (1968). Experimentation in social psychology. In G. Lindzey & E. Aronson (Eds.), *The handbook of social psychology: Vol 2. Research methods.* Menlo Park, CA: Addison-Wesley.

Artiles, A.J., & Trent, S.C. (1994). Overrepresentation of minority students in special education: A continuing debate. *Journal of Special Education, 27,* 410-437.

Ascher, L.M., & Turner, R.M. (1979). Paradoxical intention and insomnia: An experimental investigation. *Behaviour Research and Therapy, 17,* 408-411.

Asmundson, G.J., Larsen, D.K., & Stein, M.B. (1998). Panic disorder and vestibular disturbance: An overview of empirical findings and clinical implications. *Journal of Psychosomatic Research, 44,* 107-120.

Aspinwall, L.G., Kemeny, M.E., Taylor, S.E., Schneider, S.G., & Dudley, J.P. (1991). Psychological predictors of gay mens' AIDS risk-reduction behavior. *Health Psychology, 10,* 432-444.

Associated Press. (1996, October 5). Congress adds to penalty for using "date-rape" drugs. *Los Angeles Times,* pp. A3.

Associated Press. 1998a. Bill aims to thwart assisted suicides. *Los Angeles Times,* pp. A18.

Associated Press. 1998b. Bosnian Serb admits to raping four women. *Los Angeles Times,* pp. A6.

Atchley, R. (1980). Aging and suicide: Reflection of the quality of life. In S. Haynes & M. Feinleib (Eds.), *Proceedings of the Second Conference on the Epidemiology of Aging.* National Institute of Health, Washington, DC: U.S. Government Printing Office.

Atkeson, B.M., Calhoun, K.S., Resick, P.A., & Ellis, E.M. (1982). Victims of rape: Repeated assessment of depressive symptoms. *Journal of Consulting and Clinical Psychology, 50,* 96-102.

Atkinson, D. (1985). Karl Marx and group therapy. *Counseling and Values, 29,* 183-184.

Atkinson, D.R., & Lowe, S.M. (1995). The role of ethnicity, cultural knowledge, and conventional techniques in counseling and psychotherapy. In J.G. Ponterotto, J.M. Casas, L.A. Suzuki, & C.M. Alexander (Eds.), *Handbook of multicultural counseling* (pp. 387-414). Thousand Oaks, CA: Sage.

Atkinson, D.R., Brown, M.T., Matthews, L.G., Landrum-Brown, J., & Kim, A.U. (1996). African American client skin tone and clinical judgments of African American and European American psychologists. *Professional Psychology: Research and Practice, 27,* 500-505.

Atkinson, D.R., Maruyama, M., & Matsui, S. (1978). The effects of counselor race and counseling approach on Asian Americans' perception of counselor credibility and utility. *Journal of Counseling Psychology, 25,* 76-83.

Attia, E., Haiman, C., Walsh, B.T., & Flater, S.R. (1998). Does fluoxetine augment the inpatient treatment of anorexia nervosa? *American Journal of Psychiatry, 155,* 548-551.

August, G.J., Realmuto, G.M., MacDonald, A.W., Nugent, S.M., & Crosby, R. (1996). Prevalence of ADHD and comorbid disorders among elementary school children screened for disruptive behavior. *Journal of Abnormal Child Psychology, 24,* 555-569.

Austin, J.P., Azia, H., Potter, L., Thelmo, W., Chen, P., Choi, K., Brandys, M., Macchia, R.J., & Rotman, M. (1990). Diminished survival of young Blacks with adenocarcinoma of the prostate. *American Journal of Clinical Oncology, 13,* 465-469.

Author (1994). *AIDS and behavior: An integrated approach.* Washington, DC: National Academy Press.

Author (1995). *Job stress interventions.* Washington, DC: American Psychological Association.

Author (1996). Why Jenifer got sick: The mother of a poster child is accused of causing her daughter's illness. *Time, 147,* 70.

Author (1997). Workshop on the medical utility of marijuana: Report to the Director, National Institutes of Health, by the Ad Hoc Group of Experts.

Author (1998). Expert witnesses in child abuse cases: What can and should be said in court. Washington, DC: American Psychological Association.

Avissar, S., Nechamkin, Y., Barki-Harrington, L., Roitman, G., & Schreiber, G. (1997). Differential G protein measures in mononuclear leucocytes of patients with bipolar mood disorder are state dependent. *Journal of Affective Disorders, 43,* 85-93.

Avissar, S., Schreiber, G., Nechamkin, Y., Nehaus, I., Lam, G., et al. (1999). The effects of seasons and light therapy on G protein levels in mononuclear leukocytes of patients with seasonal, affective disorder. *Archives of General Psychiatry, 56,* 178-184.

Awad, G.A., & Saunders, E. (1989). Adolescent child molesters: Clinical observations. *Child Psychiatry and Human Development, 19,* 195-206.

Ayanian, J.Z., & Cleary, P.D. (1999). Perceived risks of heart disease and cancer among cigarete smokers. *JAMA, 281,* 1019-1021.

Ayllon, T., & Azrin, N.H. (1968). *The token economy: A motivational system for therapy and rehabilitation.* New York: Appleton-Century-Crofts.

Azrin, N.H., Sisson, R.W., Meyers, R., & Godley, M. (1982). Alcoholism treatment by disulfiram and community reinforcement therapy. *Journal of Behaviour Therapy and Experimental Psychiatry, 13,* 105-112.

Azrin, N.H., Sneed, T.J., & Foxx, R.M. (1973). Dry bed: A rapid method of eliminating bedwetting (enuresis) of the retarded. *Behaviour Research and Therapy, 11,* 427-434.

Bach, A.K., Wincze, J.P., & Barlow, D.H. (2001). Sexual dysfunction. In D.H. Barlow (Eds.), *Clinical Handbook of Psychological Disorders* (pp. 562-608). New York: Guilford Press.

Bach, G.R. (1966). The marathon group: Intensive practice of intimate interactions. *Psychological Reports, 181,* 995-1002.

Bachrach, H., Galatzer-Levy, R., Skolnikoff, A., & Waldron, S. (1991). On the efficacy of psychoanalysis. *Journal of the American Psychoanalytic Association, 39,* 871-916.

Badeau, D. (1995). Illness, disability and sex in aging. *Sexuality and Disability, 13,* 219-237.

Badian, N.A. (1983). Dyscalculia and nonverbal disorders of learning. In H.R. Myklebust (Ed.), *Progress in learning disabilities* (Vol. 5). New York: Grune & Stratton.

Baer, J.S., & Lichtenstein, E. (1988). Cognitive assessment. In D.M. Donovan & G.A. Marlatt (Eds.), *Assessment of addictive behaviors* (pp. 189-213). New York: Guilford.

Baer, L., & Jenike, M.A. (1992). Personality disorders in obsessive-compulsive disorder. *Psychiatric Clinics of North America, 15,* 803-812.

Baer, L., Jenike, M.A., Ricciardi, J.N., Holland, A.D., Seymour, R.J., et al. (1990). Standardized assessment of personality disorders in obsessive compulsive disorder. *Archives of General Psychiatry, 47,* 826-831.

Baer, R.A., & Sekirnjak, G. (1997). Detection of underreporting on the MMPI-II in a clinical population. Effects of information about validity scales. *Journal of Personality Assessment, 69,* 555-567.

Bagby, M.R., Nicholson, R.A., Bacchionchi, J.R. et al. (2002). The predictive capacity of the MMPI-2 and PAI validity scales and indexes to detect coached and uncoached feigning. *Journal of Personality Assessment, 78,* 69-86.

Bailey, A., LeCouteur, A., Gottesman, I., Bolton, P., Simonoff, E., Yuzda, E., & Rutter, M. (1995). Autism as a strongly genetic disorder: Evidence from a British twin study. *Psychological Medicine, 25,* 63-77.

Baker, T., & Brandon, T.H. (1988). Behavioral treatment strategies. In A report of the Surgeon General: The health consequences of smoking: Nicotine *addiction.* Rockville, MD: U.S. Department of Health and Human Services.

Bakwin, H. (1973). The genetics of enuresis. In J. Kolvin, R.C. MacKeith, & S.R. Meadow (Eds.), *Enuresis and encopresis.* Philadelphia: Lippincott.

Ball, J.C., & Chambers, C.D. (Eds.). (1970). *The epidemiology of opiate addiction in the United States.* Springfield, IL: Charles C. Thomas.

Ball, J.C., & Ross, A. (1991). *The effectiveness of methadone maintenance treatment.* New York: Springer-Verlag.

Ball, S.A., Carroll, K.M., & Rounsaville, B.T. (1994). Sensation seeking, substance abuse, and psychopathology in treatment-seeking and community cocaine abusers. *Journal of Consulting and Clinical Psychology, 62,* 1053-1057.

Ballard, E.L. (1995). Attitudes, myths, and realities: Helping family and professional caregivers cope with sexuality in the Alzheimer's patient. *Sexuality and Disability, 13,* 255-270.

Ballenger, J.C., Burrows, G.O., DuPont, R.L., Lesser, M., Noyes, R.C., Pecknold, J.C., Rifkin, A., & Swinson, R.P. (1988). Alprazolam in panic disorder and agoraphobia, results from multicenter trial. *Archives of General Psychiatry, 45,* 413-421.

Ball-Rokeach, S.J., Rokeach, M., & Grube, J.W. (1984). *The great American values test.* New York: Free Press.

Baltes, M.M. (1988). The etiology and maintenance of dependency in the elderly: Three phases of operant research. *Behavior Therapy, 19,* 301-319.

Bancroft, J.H. (1988). Sexual desire and the brain. *Sexual and Marital Therapy, 3,* 11-29.

Bancroft, J.H. (1989). *Human sexuality and its problems (2nd ed.).* Edinburgh: Churchill Livingston.

Bandura, A. (1969). *Principles of behavior modification.* New York: Holt, Rinehart & Winston.

Bandura, A. (1977). Self-efficacy: Toward a unifying theory of behavioral change. *Psychological Review, 84,* 191-215.

Bandura, A. (1982). The psychology of chance encounters. *American Psychologist, 37,* 747-755.

Bandura, A. (1986). *Social foundations of thought and action: A social cognitive theory.* Englewood Cliffs, NJ: Prentice-Hall.

Bandura, A. (1997). *Self-efficacy: The exercise of control.* New York: Freeman.

Bandura, A., & Menlove, F.L. (1968). Factors determining vicarious extinction of avoidance behavior through symbolic modeling. *Journal of Personality and Social Psychology, 8,* 99-108.

Bandura, A., & Perloff, B. (1967). Relative efficacy of self-monitored and externally imposed reinforcement systems. *Journal of Personality and Social Psychology, 7,* 111-116.

Bandura, A., & Rosenthal, T.L. (1966). Vicarious classical conditioning as a function of arousal level. *Journal of Personality and Social Psychology, 3,* 54-62.

Bandura, A., & Walters, R.H. (1963). *Social learning and personality development.* New York: Holt, Rinehart & Winston.

Bandura, A., Blanchard, E.B., & Ritter, B. (1969). Relative efficacy of desensitization and modeling approaches for inducing behavioral, affective, and attitudinal changes. *Journal of Personality and Social Psychology, 13,* 173-199.

Bandura, A., Grusec, J.E., & Menlove, F.L. (1967). Vicarious extinction of avoidance behavior. *Journal of Personality and Social Psychology, 5,* 16-23.

Bandura, A., Jeffrey, R.W., & Bachicha, D.L. (1974). Analysis of memory codes and cumulative rehearsal in observational learning. *Journal of Research in Personality, 7,* 295-305.

Banis, H.T., Varni, J.W., Wallander, J.L., Korsch, B.M., Jay, S.M., Adler, R., Garcia-Temple, E., & Negrete, V. (1988). Psychological and social adjustment of obese children and their families. *Child: Care, Health, and Development, 14,* 157-173.

Bank, L., Marlowe, J.H., Reid, J.B., Patterson, G.R., & Weinrott, M.R. (1991). A comparative evaluation of parent-training interventions for families of chronic delinquents. *Journal of Abnormal Child Psychology, 19,* 15-33.

Banks, S.M., Salovey, P., Greener, S., Rothman, A.J., et al. (1995). The effects of message framing on mammography utilization. *Health Psychology, 14,* 178-184.

Barbaree, H.E., & Seto, M.C. (1997). Pedophilia: Assessment and treatment. In D.R. Laws & W. O'Donohue (Eds.), *Sexual deviance* (pp. 175-193). NY: Guilford Press.

Barbaree, H.E., Marshall, W.L., Yates, E., & Lightfoot, L. (1983). Alcohol intoxication and deviant sexual arousal in male social drinkers. *Behaviour Research and Therapy, 21,* 365-373.

Barbarin, O.A., & Soler, R.E. (1993). Behavioral, emotional, and academic adjustment in a national probability sample of African-American children: Effects of age, gender, and family structure. *Journal of Black Psychology, 19,* 423-446.

Barch, D.M., Carter, C.S., Braver, T.S. et al. (2001). Selective deficits in prefrontal cortex function in medication-naïve patients with schizophrenia. *Archives of General Psychiatry, 58,* 280-288.

Barclay, D.R., & Houts, A.C. (1995). Childhood enuresis. In C. Schaefer (Ed.), *Clinical handbook of sleep disorders in children* (pp. 223-252). Northvale, NJ: Jason Aronson.

Barefoot, J.C., Dahlstrom, G., & Williams, R.B. (1983). Hostility, CHD incidence, and total mortality: A 25-year follow-up study of 255 physicians. *Psychosomatic Medicine, 45,* 59-63.

Barefoot, J.C., Peterson, B.L., Dahlstrom, W.G., Siegler, I.C., Anderson, N.B., et al. (1991). Hostility patterns and health implications: Correlates of Cook-Medley hostility scale scores in a national survey. *Health Psychology, 10,* 18-24.

Barkley, R.A. (1981). *Hyperactive children: A handbook for diagnosis and treatment.* New York: Guilford.

Barkley, R.A. (1990). *Attention-deficit hyperactivity disorder: A handbook for diagnosis and treatment.* New York: Guilford.

Barkley, R.A. (1997). Behavioral inhibition, sustained attention, and executive function: Constructing a unifying theory of ADHD. *Psychological Bulletin, 121,* 65-94.

Barkley, R.A. (1998). *Attention-deficit hyperactivity disorder: A handbook for diagnosis and treatment* (2nd ed.). New York, NY: Guilford Press.

Barkley, R.A., DuPaul, G.J., & McMurray, M.B. (1990). A comprehensive evaluation of attention deficit disorder with and without hyperactivity defined by research criteria. *Journal of Consulting and Clinical Psychology, 58,* 775-789.

Barkley, R.A., Fischer, M., Edelbrock, C.S., & Smallish, L. (1990). The adolescent outcome of hyperactive children diagnosed by research criteria: 1. An 8 year prospective follow-up study. *Journal of the American Academy of Child and Adolescent Psychiatry, 29,* 546-557.

Barkley, R.A., Grodzinsky, G., & DuPaul, G.J. (1992). Frontal lobe functions in attention deficit disorder with and without hyperactivity: A review and research report. *Journal of Abnormal Child Psychology, 20,* 163-188.

Barkley, R.A., Karlsson, J., & Pollard, S. (1985). Effects of age on the mother-child interactions of hyperactive children. *Journal of Abnormal Child Psychology, 13,* 631-638.

Barkowski, J.G. & Varnhagen, C.K. (1984). Transfer of learning strategies: Contrast of self-instructional and traditional learning formats with EMR children. *American Journal of Mental Deficiency, 88,* 369-379.

Barlow, D.H. (1988). *Anxiety and its disorders: The nature and treatment of anxiety and panic.* New York: Guilford.

Barlow, D.H. (1999). NIMH Collaborative Trial on the Treatment of Panic Disorder. Paper presented at the annual convention of the Association for Advancement of Behavior Therapy, Toronto.

Barlow, D.H., Abel, G.G., & Blanchard, E.B. (1979). Gender identity change in transsexuals. *Archives of General Psychiatry, 36,* 1001-1007.

Barlow, D.H., Blanchard, E.B., Vermilyea, J.A., Vermilyea, B.B., & DiNardo, P.A. (1986). Generalized anxiety and generalized anxiety disorder: Description and reconceptualization. *American Journal of Psychiatry, 143,* 40-44.

Barlow, D.H., Cohen, A.B., Waddell, M.T., Vermilyea, B.B., Klosko, J.S., Blanchard, E.B., & DiNardo, P.A. (1984). Panic and generalized anxiety disorders: Nature and treatment. *Behavior Therapy, 15,* 431-449.

Barlow, D.H., Craske, M.G., Cerny, J.A., & Klosko, J.S. (1989). Behavioral treatment of panic disorder. *Behavior Therapy, 26,* 261-282.

Barlow, D.H., Esler, J.L., & Vitali, A.E. (1998). Psychosocial treatments for panic disorders, phobias, and generalized anxiety disorder. In P.E. Nathan & J.M. Gorman (Eds.), *A guide to treatments that work* (pp. 288-318). New York: Oxford University Press.

Barlow, D.H., Gorman, J.M., Shear, M.K., & Woods, S.W. (2000). Cognitive-behavioral therapy, imipramine, or their combination for panic disorder: A randomized controlled trial. *Journal of the American Medical Association, 283*, 2529-2536.

Barlow, D.H., Reynolds, E.J., & Agras, W.S. (1973). Gender identity change in a transsexual. *Archives of General Psychiatry, 29*, 569-576.

Barlow, D.H., Vermilyea, J., Blanchard, E., Vermilyea, B., DiNardo, P., & Cerny, J. (1985). The phenomenon of panic. *Journal of Abnormal Psychology, 94*, 320-328.

Baron, M., Risch, N., Levitt, M., & Gruen, R. (1985). Familial transmission of schizotypal and borderline personality disorders. *American Journal of Psychiatry, 142*, 927-934.

Barr, L.C., Goodman, W.K., McDougle, C.J., Delgado, P.I., Heninger, G.R., et al. (1994). Tryptophan depletion in patients with obsessive-compulsive disorder who respond to serotonin reuptake blockers. *Archives of General Psychiatry, 51*, 309-317.

Barrios, B.A., & O'Dell, S.I. (1989). Fears and anxieties. In E.J. Mash & R.A. Barkley (Eds.), *Treatment of childhood disorders*. New York: Guilford.

Barsky, A.J., Brener, J., Coeytaux, R.R., & Cleary, P.D. (1995). Accurate awareness of heartbeat in hypochondriacal and non-hypochondriacal patients. *Journal of Psychosomatic Research, 39*, 489-497.

Barsky, A.J., Fama, J.M., Bailey, E.D., & Ahern, D.K. (1998). A prospective 4- to 5-year study of DSM-III-R hypochondriasis. *Archives of General Psychiatry, 55*, 737-744.

Bartholomew, K., & Horowitz, L.M. (1991). Attachment styles among young adults: A test of a four-category model. *Journal of Personality and Social Psychology, 61*, 226-244.

Bartlett, F. (1932). *Remembering*. Cambridge: Cambridge University Press.

Bartlett, J. (1992). *Familiar quotations: A collection of passages, phrases and proverbs traced to their sources in ancient and modern literature*. Boston: Little, Brown and Company.

Bartlett, J.G. (1993). *The Johns Hopkins Hospital guide to medical care of patients with HIV infection*. Baltimore: Williams & Wilkins.

Bartzokis, G., Liberman, R.P., & Hierholzer, R. (1990). Behavior therapy in groups. In I.L. Kutash & A. Wolf (Eds.), *The group psychotherapist's handbook: Contemporary theory and technique*. New York: Columbia University Press.

Basco, M.R., & Rush, A.J. (1996). *Cognitive-behavioral therapy for bipolar disorder*. New York: Guilford.

Basoglu, M., Marks, I.M., Kilic, C., Brewin, C.R., & Swinson, R.P. (1994). Alprazolam and exposure for panic disorder with agoraphobia: Attribution of improvement to medication predicts subsequent relapse. *British Journal of Psychiatry, 164*, 652-659.

Bass, E., & Davis, L. (1994). *The courage to heal: A guide for women survivors of child sexual abuse*. New York: Harper Collins.

Bassuk, S.S., Berkman, L.F., & Wypij, D. (1998). Depressive symptomatology and incident cognitive decline in an elderly community sample. *Archives of General Psychiatry, 55*, 1073-1081.

Bastani, B., Nash, J.F., & Meltzer, H.Y. (1990). Prolactin and cortisol responses to MK-212, a serotonin agonist, in obsessive compulsive disorder. *Archives of General Psychiatry, 47*, 833-839.

Bates, G.W. (1990). Social anxiety and self-presentation: Conversational behaviours and articulated thoughts of heterosexually anxious males. Unpublished doctoral dissertation, University of Melbourne, Australia.

Bates, G.W., Campbell, T.M., & Burgess, P.M. (1990). Assessment of articulated thoughts in social anxiety: Modification of the ATSS procedure. *British Journal of Clinical Psychology, 29*, 91-98.

Battaglia, M., Bernardeschi, L., Franchini, L., Bellodi, L., & et al. (1995). A family study of schizotypal disorder. *Schizophrenia Bulletin, 21*, 33-45.

Baucom, D.H., Epstein, N., & Coop Gordon, K. (2000). Marital therapy: Theory, practice, and empirical status. In C.R. Snyder & R.E. Ingram (Eds.), *Handbook of Psychological Change: Psychotherapy processes & practices for the 21st century* (pp. 280-308). New York: John Wiley & Sons, Inc.

Baucom, D., Epstein, N., & Rankin, L. (1995). Integrative couple therapy. In N.S. Jacobson & A.S. Gurman (Eds.), *Clinical handbook of couple therapy* (pp. 65-90). New York: Guilford.

Baucom, D.H., & Hoffman, J.A. (1986). The effectiveness of marital therapy: Current status and application to the clinical setting. In N.S. Jacobson & A.S. Gurman (Eds.), *Clinical handbook of marital therapy* (pp. 597-620). New York: Guilford.

Baucom, D.H., Epstein, N., Sayers, S.L., & Sher, T.G. (1989). The role of cognitions in marital relationships: Definitional, methodological, and conceptual issues. *Journal of Consulting and Clinical Psychology, 57*, 31-38.

Baucom, D.H., Sayers, S.L., & Sher, T.G. (1990). Supplementing behavioral marital therapy with cognitive restructuring and emotional expressiveness training: An outcome investigation. *Journal of Consulting and Clinical Psychology, 58*, 636-645.

Baumeister, A.A., & Baumeister, A.A. (1995). Mental retardation. In M. Hersen, & R.T. Ammerman (Eds.), *Advanced abnormal child psychology* (pp. 283-303). Hillsdale, NJ: Lawrence Erlbaum Associates.

Baumeister, A.A., Kupstas, F.D., & Klindworth, L.M. (1991). The new morbidity: A national plan of action. *American Behavioral Scientist, 34*, 468-500.

Baumeister, R.F. (1990). Suicide as escape from self. *Psychological Review, 97*, 90-113.

Baumeister, R.F., & Butler, J.L. (1997). Sexual masochism: Deviance without pathology. In D.R. Laws & W. O'Donohue (Eds.), *Sexual deviance* (pp. 225-239). NY: Guilford Press.

Baumgartner, G.R., & Rowen, R.C. (1987). Clonidine vs. chlordiazepoxide in the management of acute alcohol withdrawal. *Archives of Internal Medicine, 147*, 1223-1226.

Baxter, E., & Hopper, K. (1981). *Private lives/public places: Homeless adults on the streets of New York City*. New York: Community Service Society.

Baxter, L.R., Schwartz, J.M., Bergman, K.S., Szuba, M.P., Guze, B.H., Mazziotta, J.C., Alazraki, A., Selin, C.E., Ferng, H., Munford, P., & Phelps, M.E. (1992). Caudate glucose metabolic rate changes with both drug and behavior therapy for obsessive-compulsive disorder. *Archives of General Psychiatry, 49*, 681-689.

Beach, S.R.H., & O'Leary, K.D. (1986). The treatment of depression occurring in the context of marital discord. *Behavior Therapy, 17*, 43-49.

Beach, S.R.H., Sandeen, E.F., & O'Leary, K.D. (1990). *Depression in marriage*. New York: Guilford.

Beck, A.T., Butler, A.C., Brown, G.K. et al. (2001). Dysfunctional beliefs discriminate personality disorders. *Behaviour Research and Therapy, 39*, 1213-1225.

Beck, A.T. & Rector, N.A. (2000). Cognitive therapy of schizophrenia: A new therapy for the new millennium. *American Journal of Psychotherapy, 54*, 291-300.

Beck, A.T. (1967). *Depression: Clinical, experimental and theoretical aspects*. New York: Harper & Row.

Beck, A.T. (1976). *Cognitive therapy and the emotional disorders*. New York: International Universities Press.

Beck, A.T. (1986a). Cognitive therapy: A sign of retrogression or progress. *The Behavior Therapist, 9*, 2-3.

Beck, A.T. (1986b). Hopelessness as a predictor of eventual suicide. In J.J. Mann & M. Stanley (Eds.), *Psychobiology of suicidal behavior*. New York: New York Academy of Sciences.

Beck, A.T. (1987). Cognitive models of depression. *Journal of Cognitive Psychotherapy: An International Quarterly, 1*, 5-37.

Beck, A.T., Brown, G., Berchick, R.J., Stewart, B.L., & Steer, R.A. (1990). Relationship between hopelessness and ultimate suicide: A replication with psychiatric outpatients. *American Journal of Psychiatry, 147*, 190-195.

Beck, A.T., Brown, G., Steer, R.A., Eidelson, J.I., & Riskind, J.H. (1987). Differentiating anxiety and depression: A test of the cognitive-content-specificity hypothesis. *Journal of Abnormal Psychology, 96*, 179-183.

Beck, A.T., Kovacs, M., & Weissman, A. (1975). Hopelessness and suicidal behavior: An overview. *Journal of the American Medical Association, 234*, 1146-1149.

Beck, A.T., Kovacs, M., & Weissman, A. (1979). Assessment of suicidal ideation: The Scale for Suicide Ideation. *Journal of Consulting and Clinical Psychology, 47*, 343-352.

Beck, A.T., Schuyler, D., & Herman, I. (1974). Development of suicidal intent scales. In A.T. Beck, H.L.P. Resnik, & D.J. Lettieri (Eds.), *The prediction of suicide*. Bowie, MD: Charles Press.

Beck, A.T., Steer, R.A., Kovacs, M., & Garrison, B. (1985). Hopelessness and eventual suicide: A 10-year prospective study of patients hospitalized with suicidal ideation. *American Journal of Psychiatry, 142*, 559-563.

Beck, J.G. (1995). Hypoactive sexual desire disorder: An overview. *Journal of Consulting and Clinical Psychology, 63*, 919-927.

Beck, J.G., & Bozman, A. (1995). Gender differences in sexual desire: The effects of anger and anxiety. *Archives of Sexual Behavior, 24*, 595-612.

Beck, M. (1979, November 12). Viet vets fight back. *Newsweek*, 44-49.

Becker, E.S., Rinck, M., Roth, W.T., & Margraf, J. (1998). Don't worry and beware of white bears: Thought suppression in anxiety patients. *Journal of Anxiety Disorders, 12,* 39-55.

Becker, J.V. (1990). Treating adolescent sexual offenders. *Professional Psychology: Research and Practice, 21,* 362-365.

Becker, J.V., & Hunter, J.A. (1999). Understanding and treating child and adolescent sexual offenders. In T.H. Ollendick & R.J. Prinz (Eds.), *Advances in clinical child psychology* (pp. 177-196). New York: Plenum Press.

Becker, J.V., Kaplan, M.S., Cunningham-Rathner, J., & Kavoussi, R.J. (1986). Characteristics of adolescent incest sexual perpetrators: Preliminary findings. *Journal of Family Violence, 1,* 85-97.

Becker, J.V., Kaplan, M.S., Tenke, C.E., & Tartaglini, A. (1991). The incidence of depressive symptomatology in juvenile sex offenders with a history of abuse. *Child Abuse and Neglect, 15,* 531-536.

Becker, J.V., Skinner, L.J., Abel, G.G., & Cichon, J. (1986). Level of postassault sexual functioning in rape and incest victims. *Archives of Sexual Behavior, 15,* 37-49.

Bedell, J.R., Archer, R.P., & Marlow, H.A. (1980). A description and evaluation of a problem-solving skills training program. In D. Upper & S.M. Ross (Eds.), *Behavioral group therapy: An annual review* (pp. 3-35). Champaign, IL: Research Press.

Bednar, R.L., & Kaul, T.J. (1994). Experiential group research: Can the canon fire? In A.E. Bergin & S.L. Garfield (Eds.), *Handbook of psychotherapy and behavior change* (4th ed.). New York: Wiley.

Beecher, H.K. (1966). Ethics and clinical research. *New England Journal of Medicine, 274,* 1354-1360.

Begelman, D.A. (1975). Ethical and legal issues of behavior modification. In M. Hersen, R. Eisler, & P.M. Miller (Eds.), *Progress in behavior modification.* New York: Academic Press.

Beidel, D.C. (1991). Social phobia and overanxious disorder in school-age children. *Journal of the American Academy of Child and Adolescent Psychiatry, 30,* 545-552.

Bell, J.E. (1961). *Family group therapy.* Washington, DC: U.S. Department of Health, Education, and Welfare.

Bellack, A.S., & Hersen, M. (1998). *Behavioral assessment: A practical handbook* (4th ed.). Boston: Allyn and Bacon.

Bellack, A.S., & Mueser, K.T. (1993). Psychosocial treatments for schizophrenia. *Schizophrenia Bulletin, 19,* 317-336.

Bellack, A.S., Hersen, M., & Turner, S.M. (1976). Generalization effects of social skills training in chronic schizophrenics: An experimental analysis. *Behavior Research and Therapy, 14,* 391-398.

Bellack, A.S., Morrison, R.L., & Mueser, K.T. (1989). Social problem solving in schizophrenia. *Schizophrenia Bulletin, 15,* 101-116.

Bendetti, F., Sforzini, L., Colombo, C., Marrei, C., & Smeraldi, E. (1999). Low-dose clozapine in acute and continuation treatment of borderline personality disorder. *Journal of Clinical Psychiatry, 59,* 103-107.

Benes, F.M., McSparren, J., Bird, T.D., SanGiovanni, J.P., Vincent, S.L., et al. (1991). Deficits in small interneurons in prefrontal and cingulate cortices of schizophrenic and schizoaffective patients. *Archives of General Psychiatry, 48,* 986-1001.

Benjamin, J., Ben-Zion, I.K., Karbofsky, E., & Dannon, P. (2000). Double-blind-placebo-controlled pilot study of paroxetine for specific phobia. *Psychopharmacology, 149,* 194-196.

Benkelfat, C., Ellenbogen, M.A., Dean, P., Palmour, R.M., & Young, S.N. (1994b). Mood-lowering effect of tryptophan depletion: Enhanced susceptibility in young men at genetic risk for major affective disorders. *Archives of General Psychiatry, 51,* 687-700.

Bennett, C.C., Anderson, L.S., Cooper, S., Hassol, L., Klein, D.C., & Rosenblum, G. (Eds.). (1966). Community psychology: A report of the Boston *Conference on the education of psychologists for community mental health.* Boston: Boston University Press.

Bennett, I. (1960). *Delinquent and neurotic children.* London: Tavistock.

Bennett, V. (1997, February 22). Russia's forgotten children. *Los Angeles Times,* pp. A1, A10.

Ben-Porath, Y.S., & Butcher, J.N. (1989). The comparability of MMPI and MMPI-2 scales and profiles. *Psychological Assessment, 1,* 345-347.

Ben-Tovim, M.V., & Crisp, A.H. (1979). Personality and mental state within anorexia nervosa. *Journal of Psychosomatic Research, 23,* 321-325.

Berg, L., McKeel, D.W., Miller, J.P., Storandt, M., Rubin, E.H., et al. (1998). Clinicopathologic studies in cognitively healthy aging and Alzheimer disease. *Archives of Neurology, 55,* 326-335.

Bergem, A.L., Engedal, K., & Kringlen, E. (1997). The role of heredity in late-onset Alzheimer's disease and vascular dementia: A twin study. *Archives of General Psychiatry, 54,* 264-270.

Berger, K.S., & Zarit, S.H. (1978). Late life paranoid states: Assessment and treatment. *American Journal of Orthopsychiatry, 48,* 528-537.

Bergin, A.E. (1971). The evaluation of therapeutic outcomes. In A.E. Bergin & S.L. Garfield (Eds.), *Handbook of psychotherapy and behavior change: An empirical analysis.* New York: Wiley.

Bergin, A.E., & Garfield, S.L. (Eds.). (1994). *Handbook of psychotherapy and behavior change* (4th ed.). New York: Wiley.

Bergin, A.E., & Lambert, M.J. (1978). The evaluation of therapeutic outcomes. In S.L. Garfield & A.E. Bergin (Eds.), *Handbook of psychotherapy and behavior change: An empirical analysis* (2nd ed.). New York: Wiley.

Berlin, F.S., & Meinecke, C.F. (1981). Treatment of sex offenders with antiandrogenic medication: Conceptualization, review of treatment modalities, and preliminary findings. *American Journal of Psychiatry, 138,* 601-607.

Berman, A.L., & Jobes, D.A. (1996). *Adolescent suicide: Assessment and intervention.* Washington, DC: American Psychological Association.

Berman, E.M., & Lief, H.I. (1976). Sex and the aging process. In W.W. Oaks, G.A. Melchiode, & I. Ficher (Eds.), *Sex and the life cycle.* New York: Grune & Stratton.

Berman, J.S., & Norton, N.C. (1985). Does professional training make a therapist more effective? *Psychological Bulletin, 98,* 401-407.

Bernstein, D. (1993). Paranoid personality disorder: A review of the literature and recommendations for DSM-IV. *Journal of Personality Disorders, 7,* 53-62.

Bernstein, D.A., & Nietzel, M.T. (1980). *Introduction to clinical psychology.* New York: McGraw-Hill.

Bernstein, D.P., Kasapis, C., Bergman, A., Weld, E., Mitropoulou, V., & et al. (1997). Assessing Axis II disorders by informant interview. *Journal of Personality Disorders, 11,* 158-167.

Bernstein, D.P., Useda, D., & Siever, L.J. (1993). Paranoid personality disorder: Review of the literature and recommendations for DSM-IV. *Journal of Personality Disorders, 7,* 53-62.

Berrenberg, J.L., Dougherty, K.L., Erikson, M.S., Loew, J.L., Pacot, D.M., & Rousseau, C.N.S. (1993). Saturation in AIDS education: Can we still make a difference? Paper presented at the annual meeting of the Rocky Mountain and Western Psychological Associations, Phoenix, AZ,

Berrettini, W.H., Goldin, L.R., Gelernter, J., Geiman, P.Z., Gershon, E., et al. (1990). X-chromosome markers and manic-depressive illness: Rejection of linkage to Xq28 in nine bipolar pedigrees. *Archives of General Psychiatry, 47,* 366-373.

Berry, J.C. (1967). Antecedents of schizophrenia, impulsive character and alcoholism in males. Paper presented at the 75th Annual Convention of the American Psychological Association, Washington, DC.

Besdine, R.W. (1980). Geriatric medicine: An overview. In C. Eisodorfer (Ed.), *Annual review of gerontology and geriatrics.* New York: Springer.

Betancourt, H., & Lopez, S. (1993). The study of culture, ethnicity, and race in American psychology. *American Psychologist, 48,* 629-637.

Bettelheim, B. (1967). *The empty fortress.* New York: Free Press.

Bettelheim, B. (1973). Bringing up children. *Ladies Home Journal, 90,* 28.

Bettelheim, B. (1974). *A home for the heart.* New York: Knopf.

Beutler, L.E. (1979). Toward specific psychological therapies for specific conditions. *Journal of Consulting and Clinical Psychology, 47,* 882-897.

Beutler, L.E. (1983). *Eclectic psychotherapy: A systematic approach.* New York: Pergamon.

Beutler, L.E. (1991). Have all won and must all have prizes? Revisiting Luborsky et al.'s verdict. *Journal of Consulting and Clinical Psychology, 59,* 226-232.

Beutler, L.E. (1997). The psychotherapist as a neglected variable in psychotherapy: An illustration by reference to the role of therapist experience and training. *Clinical Psychology: Science and Practice, 4,* 44-52.

Beutler, L.E., & Davison, E.H. (1995). What standards should we use? In S.C. Hayes, V.M. Follette, R.M. Dawes, & K.E. Grady (Eds.), *Scientific standards of psychological practice: Issues and recommendations* (pp. 11-24). Reno, NV: Context Press.

Beutler, L.E., & Harwood, T.M. (1995). Prescriptive psychotherapies. *Applied and Preventive Psychology, 4,* 89-100.

Beutler, L.E., Crago, M., & Arizmendi, T.G. (1986). Therapist variables in psychotherapy process and outcome. In S.L. Garfield & A.E. Bergin (Eds.), *Handbook of psychotherapy and behavior change* (3rd ed.). New York: Wiley.

Beutler, L.E., Machado, P.P.P., & Neufeldt, S.A. (1994). Therapist variables. In A.E. Bergin & S.L. Garfield (Eds.), *Handbook of psychotherapy and behavior change* (4th ed., pp. 229-269). New York: Wiley.

Beutler, L.E., Scogin, F., Kirkish, P., Schretlen, D., Corbishley, A., Hamblin, D., Meredith, K., Potter, R., Bamford, C.R., & Levenson, A.I. (1987). Group cognitive therapy and alprazolam in the treatment of depression in older adults. *Journal of Consulting and Clinical Psychology, 55*, 550-556.

Bhatia, M.S., Nigam, V.R., Bohra, N., & Malik, S.C. (1991). Attention deficit disorder with hyperactivity among pediatric outpatients. *Journal of Child Psychology and Psychiatry, 32*, 297-306.

Bhave, G., Lindan, C.P., Hudes, E.S., Desai, S., Wagle, I., Tripathi, S.P., & Mandel, J.S. (1995). Impact of an intervention on HIV, sexually transmitted diseases, and condom use among sex workers in Bombay, India. *AIDS, 9*, S21-S30.

Biederman, J., Faraone, S., Mick, E., Spencer, T., Wilens, T., Kiely, K., Guite, J., Ablon, J.S., Reed, E., & Warbuton, R. (1995). High risk for attention deficit hyperactivity disorder among children of parents with childhood onset of the disorder: A pilot study. *American Journal of Psychiatry, 152*, 431-435.

Biederman, J., Faraone, S., Milberger, S., Curtis, S., Chen, L., Marrs, A., Ouellette, C., Moore, P., & Spencer, T. (1996). Predictors of persistence and remission of ADHD into adolescence: Results from a four-year prospective follow-up study. *Journal of the American Academy of Child and Adolescent Psychiatry, 35*, 343-351.

Biederman, J., Newcorn, J., & Sprich, S. (1991). Comorbidity of attention deficit hyperactivity disorder with conduct, depressive, and other disorders. *American Journal of Psychiatry, 148*, 564-577.

Biederman, J., Rosenbaum, J., Hirshfeld, D., Faraone, S., Bolduc, E., et al. (1990). Psychiatric correlates of behavioral inhibition in young children of parents with and without psychiatric disorders. *Archives of General Psychiatry, 47*, 21-26.

Bieri, D., Reeve, R.A., & Champion, C.E. (1989). The Faces Pain Scale for the self-assessment of the severity of the pain experience by children: Development, initial validation, and preliminary investigation for ratio scale properties. *Pain, 41*, 139-150.

Bierut, L.J., Dinwiddie, S.H., Begleiter, H., Crowe, R.R., Hesselbrock, V., et al (1998). Familial transmission of substance dependence: Alcohol, marijuana, cocaine, and habitual smoking: A report from the Collaborative Study on the Genetics of Alcoholism. *Archives of General Psychiatry, 55*, 982-994.

Bierut, L.J., Heath, A.C., Bucholz, K.K., Dinwiddie, S.H., Madden, P.A.F., & et al. (1999). Major depressive disorder in a community-based twin sample: Are there different genetic contributions for men and women? *Archives of General Psychiatry, 56*, 557-564.

Billings, A.G. (1979). Conflict resolution in distressed and nondistressed married couples. *Journal of Consulting and Clinical Psychology, 47*, 368-376.

Billings, A.G., Cronkite, R.C., & Moos, R.H. (1983). Social-environmental factors in unipolar depression: Comparisons of depressed patients and nondepressed controls. *Journal of Abnormal Psychology, 92*, 119-133.

Binzer, M., Andersen, P.M., & Kullgren, G. (1997). Clinical characteristics of patients with motor disability due to conversion disorder: A prospective control group study. *Journal of Neurology, Neurosurgery, and Psychiatry, 63*, 83-88.

Bion, W. (1959). *Experiences in groups*. New York: Basic Books.

Birbaumer, H. (1977). Biofeedback training: A critical review of its clinical applications and some possible future directions. *European Journal of Behavioral Analysis and Modification, 4*, 235-251.

Birnbaum, M. (1960). The right to treatment. *American Bar Association Journal, 46*, 499-505.

Birren, J.E. & Schaie, K.W. (Eds.) (2001). *Handbook of the psychology of aging* (5th ed.). San Diego, CA: Academic Press.

Birren, J.E., & Schaie, K.W. (Eds). (1996). *Handbook of the psychology of aging* (4th ed.). San Diego, CA: Academic Press.

Blair, R.J.D., Jones, L., Clark, F., & Smith, M. (1997). The psychopathic individual: A lack of responsiveness to distress cues? *Psychophysiology, 34*, 192-198.

Blais, M.A., Hilsenroth, M.J., & Castlebury, F.D. (1997). Content validity of the newly revised Diagnostic and Statistical Manual of Mental Disorders-IV (DSM-IV) narcissistic personality disorder (NPD) and borderline personality disorder (BPD) criteria sets. *Comprehensive Psychiatry, 38*, 31-37.

Blake, W. (1973). The influence of race on diagnosis. *Smith College Studies in Social Work, 43*, 184-192.

Blanchard, E.B. (1994). Behavioral medicine and health psychology. In A.E. Bergin & S.L. Garfield (Eds.), *Handbook of psychotherapy and behavior change* (4th ed., pp. 701-733). New York: Wiley.

Blanchard, E.B., Andrasik, F., Neff, D.F., Arena, J.G., Ashles, T.A., Jurish, S.E., Pallmeyer, T.P., Saunders, N.L., & Teders, S.J. (1982). Biofeedback and relaxation training with three kinds of headache: Treatment effects and their prediction. *Journal of Consulting and Clinical Psychology, 50*, 562-575.

Blanchard, J.J., & Brown, S.B. (1998). Structured diagnostic interviews. In C.R. Reynolds (Ed.), *Comprehensive clinical psychology, vol 3, assessment* (pp. 97-130). New York: Elsevier.

Blanchard, J.J., Squires, D., Henry, T., Horan, W.P., Bogenschutz, M., et al. (1999). Examining an affect regulation model of substance abuse in schizophrenia: The role of traits and coping. *Journal of Nervous and Mental Disease, 187*, 72-79.

Blaske, D.M., Borduin, C.M., Hengeler, S.W., & Mann, B.J. (1989). Individual, family, and peer characteristics of adolescent sex offenders and assaultive offenders. *Developmental Psychology, 25*, 846-855.

Blatt, B. (1966). The preparation of special educational personnel. *Review of Educational Research, 36*, 151-161.

Blau, Z.S., Oser, G.T., & Stephens, R.C. (1979). Aging, social class, and ethnicity: A comparison of Anglo, Black, and Mexican-American Texans. *Pacific Sociological Review, 22*, 501-525.

Blazer, D.G. (1982). *Depression in late life*. St. Louis: Mosby.

Blazer, D.G., & Williams, C.D. (1980). Epidemiology of dysphoria and depression in the elderly population. *American Journal of Psychiatry, 137*, 439-444.

Blazer, D.G., Bachar, J.R., & Manton, K.G. (1986). Suicide in late life: Review and commentary. *Journal of the American Geriatrics Society, 34*, 519-525.

Blazer, D.G., George, L.K., & Hughes, D. (1991). The epidemiology of anxiety: An age comparison. In C. Salzman & B.D. Lebovitz (Eds.), *Anxiety in the elderly*. New York: Springer.

Blazer, D.G., Hughes, D., & George, L.K. (1987). Stressful life events and the onset of a generalized anxiety syndrome. *American Journal of Psychiatry, 144*, 1178-1183.

Blazer, D.G., Kessler, R.C., & McGonagle, K.A (1994). The prevalence and distribution of major depression in a national community sample: The National Comorbidity Survey. *American Journal of Psychiatry, 151*, 979-986.

Blenker, M. (1967). Environmental change and the aging individual. *Gerontologist, 7*, 101-105.

Bliss, E.L. (1980). Multiple personalities: A report of 14 cases with implications for schizophrenia and hysteria. *Archives of General Psychiatry, 37*, 1388-1397.

Bliss, E.L. (1983). Multiple personalities, related disorders, and hypnosis. *American Journal of Clinical Hypnosis, 26*, 114-123.

Bliwise, D., Carskadon, M., Carey, E., & Dement, W. (1984). Longitudinal development of sleep-related respiratory disturbance in adult humans. *Journal of Gerontology, 39*, 290-293.

Block, A.P. (1990). Rape trauma syndrome as scientific expert testimony. *Archives of Sexual Behavior, 19*, 309-323.

Block, J. (1971). *Lives through time*. Berkeley, CA: Bancroft Books.

Bloomfield, H.H. (1973). Assertive training in an outpatient group of chronic schizophrenics: A preliminary report. *Behavior Therapy, 4*, 277-281.

Blumstein, A., & Cohen, J. (1987). Characterizing criminal careers. *Science, 237*, 985-991.

Bockhoven, J. (1963). *Moral treatment in American psychiatry*. New York: Springer.

Boegels, S.M. & Zigterman, D. (2000). Dysfunctional cognitions in children with social phobia, separation anxiety disorder, and generalized anxiety disorder. *Journal of Abnormal Child Psychology, 28*, 205-211.

Bohart, A.C., & Greenberg, L.S. (1997) (Eds.), *Empathy reconsidered: New directions in psychotherapy*. Washington, DC: American Psychological Association.

Bolger, N., Foster, M., Vinokur, A.D., & Ng, R. (1996). Close relationships and adjustment to a life crisis: The case of breast cancer. *Journal of Personality and Social Psychology, 70*, 283-294.

Boll, T.J. (1985). Developing issues in clinical neuropsychology. *Journal of Clinical and Experimental Neuropsychology, 7*, 473-485.

Bolton, P., MacDonald, H., Pickles, A., Rios, P., Goode, S., Crowson, M., Bailey, A., & Rutter, M. (1994). A case-control family history study of autism. *Journal of Child Psychology and Psychiatry, 35*, 877-900.

Bondolfi, G., Dufour, H., Patris, M., May, J.P., Baumann, P., & the Risperidone Study Group. (1998). Respiridone versus clozapine in treatment-resistant chronic schizophrenia: A randomized,double-blind study. *American Journal of Psychiatry, 155*, 499-504.

Bonta, J., Law, M., & Hanson, K. (1998). The prediction of criminal and violent recidivism among mentally disordered offenders. *Psychological Bulletin, 123*, 123-142.

Boon, S., & Draijer, N. (1993). *Multiple personality disorder in the Netherlands.* Amsterdam: Swets & Zeitlinger.

Boon, S., & Draijer, N. (1993). Multiple personality disorder in the Netherlands: A clinical investigation of 71 cases. *American Journal of Psychiatry, 150*, 489-494.

Bootzin, R.R., & Engle-Friedman, M. (1987). Sleep disturbances. In L.L. Carstensen & B.A. Edelstein (Eds.), *Handbook of clinical gerontology.* New York: Pergamon.

Bootzin, R.R., Engle-Friedman, M., & Hazelwood, L. (1983). Sleep disorders and the elderly. In P.M. Lewinsohn & L. Teri (Eds.), *Clinical geropsychology: New directions in assessment and treatment.* New York: Pergamon.

Borduin, C.M., Mann, B.J., Cone, L.T., Henggeler, S.W., Fucci, B.R., Blaske, D.M., & Williams, R.A. (1995). Multisystemic treatment of serious juvenile offenders: Long-term prevention of criminality and violence. *Journal of Consulting and Clinical Psychology, 63*, 569-578.

Borkovec, T.D., & Costello, E. (1993). Efficacy of applied relaxation and cognitive behavioral therapy in the treatment of generalized anxiety disorder. *Journal of Consulting and Clinical Psychology, 61*, 611-619.

Borkovec, T.D., & Inz, J. (1990). The nature of worry in generalized anxiety disorder: A predominance of thought activity. *Behaviour Research and Therapy, 28*, 153-158.

Borkovec, T.D., & Mathews, A. (1988). Treatment of nonphobic anxiety disorders: A comparison of nondirective, cognitive and coping desensitization therapy. *Journal of Consulting and Clinical Psychology, 56*, 877-884.

Borkovec, T.D., & Newman, M.G. (1998). Worry and generalized anxiety disorder. In P. Salkovskis (Ed.), *Comprehensive clinical psychology.* Oxford: Elsevier.

Borkovec, T.D., & Roemer, L. (1994). Generalized anxiety disorder. In M. Hersen & R.T. Ammerman (Eds.), *Handbook of prescriptive treatments for adults* (pp. 261-281). New York: Plenum.

Borkovec, T.D., & Whisman, M.A. (1996). Psychosocial treatment for generalized anxiety disorder. In M. Mavissakalian & R.E. Prien (Eds.), *Long-term treatment of anxiety disorders* (pp. 171-199). Washington, DC: American Psychiatric Association.

Borkovec, T.D., Roemer, L., & Kinyon, J. (1995). Disclosure and worry: Opposite sides of the emotional processing coin. In J.W. Pennebaker (Ed.), *Emotion, disclosure, and health.* Washington, DC: American Psychological Association.

Bornstein, P.E., Clayton, P.J., Halikas, J.A., & Robins, E. (1973). The depression of widowhood after thirteen months. *British Journal of Psychiatry, 122*, 561-566.

Bornstein, R.F. (1997). Dependent personality disorder in the DSM-IV and beyond. *Clinical Psychology: Science and Practice, 4*, 175-187.

Bornstein, R.F., Leone, D.R., & Galley, D.J. (1987). The generalizability of subliminal mere exposure effects: Influence of stimuli perceived without awareness on social behavior. *Journal of Personality and Social Psychology, 53*, 1070-1079.

Boscarino, J.A. (1997). Diseases among men 20 years after exposure to severe stress: Implications for clinical research and care. *Psychosomatic Medicine, 59*, 605-614.

Bosinski, H.A., Peter, M., Bonatz, G., Arndt, R., Heidenreich, M., et al. (1997). A higher rate of hyperadrenergic disorders in female-to-male transsexuals. *Psychoneuroendocrinology, 22*, 361-380.

Botvin, G.J., & Tortu, S. (1988). Peer relationships, social competence, and substance abuse prevention: Implications for the family. *Journal of Chemical Dependency Treatment, 1*, 245-273.

Bouchard, T.J., Lykken, D.T., McGue, M., Segal, N.L., & Tellegen, A. (1990). Sources of human psychological differences: The Minnesota Study of Twins Reared Apart. *Science, 250*, 223-228.

Boudreaux, R. (1996, September 29). HIV now haunts streets of former Soviet model city. *Los Angeles Times*, pp. A1, A14.

Bouton, M.E., Mineka, S., & Barlow, D.H. (2001). A modern learning theory perspective on the etiology of panic disorder. *Psychological Review, 108*, 4-32.

Bowden, C.L., Calabrese, J.R., McElroy, S.L. et al. (2000). A randomized, placebo-controlled 12-month trial of divalproex and lithium in treatment of patients with bipolar I disorder. *Archives of General Psychiatry, 57*, 481-489.

Bowen, L., Wallace, C.J., Glynn, S.M., Nuechterlein, K.H., Lutzger, J.R., & Kuehnel, T.G. (1994). Schizophrenics' cognitive functioning and performance in interpersonal interactions and skills training procedures. *Journal of Psychiatric Research, 28*, 289-301.

Bower, G.H. (1981). Mood and memory. *American Psychologist, 36*, 129-141.

Bowers, J., Jorm, A.F., Henderson, S., & Harris, P. (1990). General practitioners'

detection of depression and dementia in elderly patients. *The Medical Journal of Australia, 153*, 192-196.

Bowers, K.S., & Meichenbaum, D. (Eds.). (1984). *The unconscious reconsidered.* New York: Praeger.

Bowers, M.B., Jr. (1974). Central dopamine turnover in schizophrenic syndromes. *Archives of General Psychiatry, 31*, 50-54.

Bowers, M.K., Brecher-Marer, S., Newton, B.W., Piotrowski, Z., Spyer, T.C., Taylor, W.S., & Watkins, J.G. (1971). Therapy of multiple personality. *International Journal of Clinical and Experimental Hypnosis, 19*, 57-65.

Bowlby, J. (1980). *Attachment and loss: Sadness and depression.* New York: Basic Books.

Boxall, B. (1995, September 3). Young gays stray from safer sex, new data shows. *Los Angeles Times*, pp. A1, A24.

Boyle, M. (1991). *Schizophrenia: A scientific delusion?* New York: Routledge.

Bozman, A., & Beck, J.G. (1991). Covariation of sexual desire and sexual arousal: The effects of anger and anxiety. *Archives of Sexual Behavior, 20*, 47-60.

Bradley, B.P., Mogg, K., Millar, N., & White, J. (1995). Selective processing of negative information: Effects of clinical anxiety, concurrent depression, and awareness. *Journal of Abnormal Psychology, 104*, 532-536.

Bradley, L., & Bryant, P.E. (1985). *Rhyme and reason in reading and spelling.* Ann Arbor: University of Michigan Press.

Brady, E., & Kendall, P. (1992). Comorbidity of anxiety and depression in children and adolescents. *Psychological Bulletin, 111*, 244-255.

Brady, J.P., Davison, G.C., DeWald, P.A., Egan, G., Fadiman, J., Frank, J.D., Gill, M.M., Hoffman, I., Kempler, W., Lazarus, A.A., Raimy, V., Rotter, J.B., & Strupp, H.H. (1980). Some views on effective principles of psychotherapy. *Cognitive Therapy and Research, 4*, 269-306.

Brady, K., Pearlstein, T., Asnis, G. et al. (2000). Efficacy and safety of sertraline treatment of posttraumatic stress disorder. *JAMA, 283*, 1837-1844.

Brandon, Y.H., Zelman, D.C., and Baker, T.B. (1987). Effects of maintenance sessions on smoking relapse: Delaying the inevitable? *Journal of Consulting and Clinical Psychology, 55*, 780-782.

Brandt, J., Buffers, N., Ryan, C., & Bayog, R. (1983). Cognitive loss and recovery in chronic alcohol abusers. *Archives of General Psychiatry, 40*, 435-442.

Bransford, J.D., & Johnson, M.K. (1973). Considerations of some problems of comprehension. In W.G. Chase (Ed.), *Visual information processing.* New York: Academic Press.

Braswell, L., & Kendall, P.C. (1988). Cognitive-behavioral methods with children. In K.S. Dobson (Ed.), *Handbook of cognitive-behavioral therapies.* New York: Guilford.

Bray, N.W., & Turner, L.A. (1987). Production anomalies (not strategic deficiencies) in mentally deficient individuals. *Intelligence, 11*, 49-60.

Brecher, E.M., & the Editors of Consumer Reports. (1972). *Licit and illicit drugs.* Mount Vernon, NY: Consumers Union.

Brehm, J.W. (1966). *A theory of psychological reactance.* New York: Academic Press.

Brehm, S.S., & Brehm, J.W. (1981). *Psychological reactance: A theory of freedom and control.* New York: Academic Press.

Breier, A., Schreiber, J.L., Dyer, J., & Pickar, D. (1991). National Institute of Mental Health longitudinal study of chronic schizophrenia: Prognosis and predictors of outcome. *Archives of General Psychiatry, 48*, 239-246.

Bremner, J.D., Innis, R.B., Ng, C.K., Staib, L.H., Salomon, R.A., et al. (1997). Positron emission tomography measurement of cerebral metabolic correlates of yohimbine administration in combat-related posttraumatic stress disorder. *Archives of General Psychiatry, 54*, 246-256.

Bremner, J.D., Southwick, S.M., Darnell, A., & Charney, D.S. (1996). Chronic posttraumatic stress disorder in Vietnam combat veterans: Course of illness and substance abuse. *American Journal of Psychiatry, 153*, 369-375.

Brent, D.A., Holder, D., Kolko, D., Birmaher, B., Baugher, M., et al. (1997). A clinical psychotherapy trial for adolescent depression comparing cognitive, family, and supportive therapy. *Archives of General Psychiatry, 54*, 877-885.

Breslau, N., Chilcoat, H.D., Kessler, R.C., & Davis, G.C. (1999). Previous exposure to trauma and PTSD effects of subsequent trauma: Results from the Detroit area survey of trauma. *American Journal of Psychiatry, 156*, 902-907.

Breslau, N., Davis, G.C., Andreski, P., Peterson, E.L., & Schultz, L.R. (1997). Sex differences in posttraumatic stress disorder. *Archives of General Psychiatry, 54*, 1044-1048.

Breslau, N., Holmes, J.P., Carlson, D.C., Pelton, G.H., et al. (1998). Trauma and posttraumatic stress disorder in the community: The 1996 Detroit area survey of trauma. *Archives of General Psychiatry, 55*, 626-632.

Bretschneider, J.G., & McCoy, N.L. (1988). Sexual interest and behavior in healthy 80 to 102-year-olds. *Archives of Sexual Behavior, 17*, 109-129.

Brettle, R.P., & Leen, L.S. (1991). The natural history of HIV and AIDS in women. *AIDS, 5*, 1283-1292.

Breuer, J., & Freud, S. (1982). *Studies in hysteria.* (J. Strachey, Trans. and Ed., with the collaboration of A. Freud). New York: Basic Books. (Original work published 1895.)

Brewerton, T.D., Lydiard, B.R., Laraia, M.T., Shook, J.E., & Ballenger, J.C. (1992). CSF Beta-endorphin and dynorphin in bulimia nervosa. *American Journal of Psychiatry, 149,* 1086-1090.

Brewin, C.R., Andrews, B., Rose, S., & Kirk, M. (1999). Acute stress disorder and posttraumatic stress disorder in victims of violent crime. *American Journal of Psychiatry, 156*, 360-366.

Brickman, A.S., McManus, M., Grapentine, W.L., & Alessi, N. (1984). Neuropsychological assessment of seriously delinquent adolescents. *Journal of the American Academy of Child Psychiatry, 23*, 453-457.

Bridge, T.B., & Wyatt, R.J. (1980). Paraphrenia: Paranoid states of late life. 2. American research. *Journal of the American Geriatrics Society, 28*, 205-210.

Bridger, W.H., & Mandel, I.J. (1965). Abolition of the PRE by instructions in GSR conditioning. *Journal of Experimental Psychology, 69*, 476-482.

Brody, N. (1985). The validity of tests of intelligence. In B.B. Wolman (Ed.), *Handbook of intelligence* (pp. 353-389). New York: Wiley.

Brookoff, D., Cook, C.S., Williams, C., & Mann, C.S. (1994). Testing reckless drivers for cocaine and marijuana. *The New England Journal of Medicine, 331*, 518-522.

Brown, G.L., & Goodwin, F.K. (1986). Cerebrospinal fluid correlates of suicide attempts and aggression. *Annals of the New York Academy of Science, 487*, 175-188.

Brown, G.P., Hammen, C.L., Craske, M.G,, & Wickens, T.D. (1995). Dimensions of dysfunctional attitudes as vulnerabilities to depressive symptoms. *Journal of Abnormal Psychology, 104*, 431-435.

Brown, G.W., & Birley, J.L.T. (1968). Crises and life changes and the onset of schizophrenia. *Journal of Health and Social Behavior, 9*, 203-214.

Brown, G.W., & Harris, T.O. (1978). *Social origins of depression.* London: Tavistock.

Brown, G.W., Bone, M., Dalison, B., & Wing, J.K. (1966). *Schizophrenia and social care.* London: Oxford University Press.

Brown, S.A., Vik, P.W., McQuaid, J.R., Patterson, T.L., Irwin, M.R., et al. (1990). Severity of psychosocial stress and outcome of alcoholism treatment. *Journal of Abnormal Psychology, 99*, 344-348.

Brown, T.A., Campbell, L.A., Lehman, C.L. et al. (2001). Current and lifetime comorbidity of the DSM-IV anxiety and mood disorders in a large clinical sample. *Journal of Abnormal Psychology, 110*, 585-599.

Brown, T.A., & Barlow, D.H. (1995). Long-term outcome in cognitive-behavioral treatment of panic disorder: Clinical predictors and alternative strategies for assessment. *Journal of Consulting and Clinical Psychology, 63*, 754-765.

Brown, T.A., O'Leary, T.A., & Barlow, D.H. (2001). Generalized anxiety disorder. In D.H. Barlow (Ed.), *Clinical Handbook of Psychological Disorders* (pp. 154-208). New York, NY: Guilford Press.

Brownell, K.D., & Rodin, J. (1994). The dieting maelstrom: Is it possible or advisable to lose weight? *American Psychologist, 49*, 781-791.

Brownell, K.D., & Wadden, T.A. (1992). Etiology and treatment of obesity: Toward understanding a serious, prevalent, and refractory disorder. *Journal of Consulting and Clinical Psychology, 60*, 505-517.

Brownell, K.D., Stunkard, A.J., & Albaum, J.M. (1980). Evaluation and modification of exercise patterns in the natural environment. *American Journal of Psychiatry, 137*, 1540-1545.

Brownmiller, S. (1975). *Against our will: Men, women and rape.* New York: Simon & Schuster.

Bruch, H. (1980). Preconditions for the development of anorexia nervosa. *American Journal of Psychoanalysis, 40*, 169-172.

Bruck, M. (1987). The adult outcomes of children with learning disabilities. *Annals of Dyslexia, 37*, 252-263.

Bruder, G.E., Stewart, J.W., Mercier, M.A., Agosti, V., Leite, P., Donovan, S., & Quitkin, F.M. (1997). Outcome of cognitive-behavioral therapy for depression: Relation to hemispheric dominance for verbal processing. *Journal of Abnormal Psychology, 106*, 138-144.

Bryant, R.A. (1995). Autobiographical memory across personalities in dissociative identity disorder. *Journal of Abnormal Psychology, 4*, 625-632.

Bryant, R.A., & Harvey, A.G. (1998). Relationship between acute stress disorder and posttraumatic stress disorder following mild traumatic brain injury. *American Journal of Psychiatry, 155*, 625-629.

Bryant, R.A., & McConkey, K.M. (1989). Visual conversion disorder: A case analysis of the influence of visual information. *Journal of Abnormal Psychology, 98*, 326-329.

Buchanan, A., Reed, A., & Weseley, S., et al. (1993). Acting on delusions . II: The phenomenological correlates of acting on delusions. *British Journal of Psychiatry, 163*, 77-81.

Buchanan, R.W., Breier, A., Kirkpatrick, B., Ball, P., & Carpenter, W.T. (1998). Positive and negative symptom response to clozapine in schizophrenic patients with and without the deficit syndrome. *American Journal of Psychiatry, 155*, 751-760.

Buchanan, R.W., Vladar, K., Barta, P.E., & Pearlson, G.D. (1998). Structural evaluation of the prefrontal cortex in schizophrenia. *American Journal of Psychiatry, 155*, 1049-1055.

Bucher, J.A., Houts, P.S., Nezu, C.M., & Nezu, A.M. (1999). Improving problem-solving skills of family caregivers through group education. *Journal of Psychosocial Oncology, 16*, 73-84.

Buchsbaum, M.S., Kessler, R., King, A., Johnson, J., & Cappelletti, J. (1984). Simultaneous cerebral glucography with positron emission tomography and topographic electroencephalography. In G. Pfurtscheller, E.J. Jonkman, & F.H. Lopes da Silva (Eds.), *Brain ischemia. Quantitative EEG and imaging techniques.* Amsterdam: Elsevier.

Buckley, P.F., Buchanan, R.W., Schulz, S.C., & Tamminga, C.A. (1996). Catching up on schizophrenia: The Fifth International Congress on Schizophrenia Research, Warm Springs, VA, April 8-12, 1995. *Archives of General Psychiatry, 53*, 456-462.

Bulfinch, T. (1979). *Bulfinch's mythology.* New York: Avenel Books.

Bulik, C.M., Sullivan, P.F., Fear, J.L., & Joyce, P.R. (1997). Eating disorders and antecedent anxiety disorders: A controlled study. *Acta Psychiatrica Scandanavica, 96*, 101-107.

Bunney, W.E., Goodwin, F.K., & Murphy, D.L. (1972). The "Switch Process" in manic-depressive illness. *Archives of General Psychiatry, 27*, 312-317.

Bunney, W.E., Murphy, D.L., Goodwin, F.K., & Borge, G.F. (1970). The switch process from depression to mania: Relationship to drugs, which alter brain amines. *Lancet, 1*, 1022.

Burgess, A.W., & Holmstrom, L.L. (1974). *Rape: Victim of crisis.* Bowie, MD: Robert J. Brady Company.

Burgio, L.D., Burgio, K.L., Engel, B.T., & Tice, L.M. (1986). Increasing distance and independence of ambulation in elderly nursing home residents. *Journal of Applied Behavior Analysis, 19*, 357-366.

Burns, A. (1991). Affective symptoms in Alzheimer's disease. *International Journal of Geriatric Psychiatry, 6*, 371-376.

Buss, A.H. (1966). *Psychopathology.* New York: Wiley.

Butcher, J.N., Dahlstrom, W.G., Graham, J.R., Tellegen, A., & Kraemer, B. (1989). *Minnesota Multiphasic Personality Inventory-2: Manual for administration and scoring.* Minneapolis: University of Minnesota Press.

Butler, G., & Mathews, A. (1983). Cognitive processes in anxiety. *Advances in Behaviour Research and Therapy, 5*, 51-62.

Butler, L., Miezitis, S., Friedman, R., & Cole, I.D. (1980). The effect of two school-based intervention programs on depressive symptoms. *American Educational Research Journal, 17*, 111-119.

Butler, L.D., Duran, R.E.F., Jasiukaitis, P., Koopman, C., & Spiegel, D. (1996). Hypnotizability and traumatic experience: A diathesis-stress model of dissociative symptomatology. *American Journal of Psychiatry, 153*, 42-63.

Butler, R.N. (1963). The life review: An interpretation of reminiscence in the aged. *Psychiatry, 119*, 721-728.

Butler, R.N., Lewis, M.I., & Sunderland, T. (1998). *Aging and mental health: positive psychosocial and biomedical approaches.* 5th ed. Boston : Allyn & Bacon.

Butler, R.N., Lewis, M.I., & Sunderland, T. (1998). *Aging and mental health: positive psychosocial and biomedical approaches.* 5th ed. Boston : Allyn & Bacon.

Butterfield, E.C., & Belmont, J.M. (1977). Assessing and improving the cognitive functions of mentally retarded people. In I. Bialer & M. Sternlicht (Eds.), *The psychology of mental retardation: Issues and approaches.* New York: Psychological Dimensions.

Butzlaff, R.L., & Hooley, J.M. (1998). Expressed emotion and psychiatric relapse: A meta-analysis. *Archives of General Psychiatry, 55,* 547-553.

Byne, W., Buchsbaum, M.S., Mattiace, L.A. et al. (2002). Postmortem assessment of thalamic nuclear volume in subjects with schizophrenia. *American Journal of Psychiatry, 159,* 59-65.

Caccioppo, J.T., Glass, C.R., & Merluzzi, T.V. (1979). Self-statements and self-evaluations: A cognitive-response analysis of heterosexual social anxiety. *Cognitive Therapy and Research, 3,* 249-262.

Caccioppo, J.T., Klein, D.J., Bernston, G.G., & Hatfield, E. (1998). The psychophysiology of emotion. In M. Lewis & E. Haviland (Eds.), *Handbook of emotions* (pp. 119-142). New York: Guilford.

Caccioppo, J.T., von Hippel, W., & Ernst, J.M. (1997). Mapping cognitive structures and processes through verbal content: The thought-listing technique. *Journal of Consulting and Clinical Psychology, 65,* 928-940.

Caddy, G.R. (1983). Alcohol use and abuse. In B. Tabakoff, P.B. Sutker, & C.L. Randell (Eds.), *Medical and social aspects of alcohol use.* New York: Plenum.

Caddy, G.R. (1985). Cognitive behavior therapy in the treatment of multiple personality. *Behavior Modification, 9,* 267-292.

Cadenhead, K.S., Perry, W., Shafer, K., & Braff, D.L. (1999). Cognitive functions in schizotypal personality disorder. *Schizophrenia Research, 37,* 123-132.

Cadoret, R.J. (1978). Evidence for genetic inheritance of primary affective disorder in adoptees. *American Journal of Psychiatry, 135,* 463-466.

Cadoret, R.J., & Stewart, M.A. (1991). An adoption study of attention deficit/aggression and their relationship to adult antisocial personality. *Archives of General Psychiatry, 47,* 73-82.

Cadoret, R.J., Yates, W.R., Troughton, E., Woodworth, G., & Stewart, M.A. (1995a). Adoption study demonstrating two genetic pathways to drug abuse. *Archives of General Psychiatry, 52,* 42-52.

Cadoret, R.J., Yates, W.R., Troughton, E., Woodworth, G., & Stewart, M.A. (1995b). Genetic-environment interaction in the genesis of aggressivity and conduct disorders. *Archives of General Psychiatry, 52,* 916-924.

Cahill, S.P., Carrigan, M.H., & Frueh, B.C. (1999). Does EMDR work? And if so, why?: A critical review of controlled outcome and dismantling research. *Journal of Anxiety Disorders, 13,* 5-33.

Caldwell, M.B., Brownell, K.D., & Wilfley, D. (1997). Relationship of weight, body dissatisfaction, and self-esteem in African American and white female dieters. *International Journal of Eating Disorders, 22,* 127-130.

Calfee, R.C., Fisk, L., & Piontkowski, D. (1975). "On-off" tests of cognitive skills in reading acquisition. In M.P. Douglass (Ed.), *Claremont Reading Conference 39th Yearbook 1975.* Claremont, CA: Claremont Graduate School.

Calhoun, J.B. (1970). Space and the strategy of life. *Ekistics, 29,* 425-437.

Calhoun, K.S., Atkeson, B.M., & Resick, P.A. (1982). A longitudinal examination of fear reactions in victims of rape. *Journal of Counseling Psychology, 29,* 655-661.

Calsyn, D.A., Saxon, A.J., Freeman, G., & Whitaker, S. (1992). Ineffectiveness of AIDS education and HIV antibody testing in reducing high-risk behaviors among injection drug users. *American Journal of Public Health, 82,* 573-575.

Cameron, D.J., Thomas, R.I., Mulvhill, M., & Bronheim, H. (1987). Delirium: A test of the Diagnostic and Statistical Manual III criteria on medical inpatients. *Journal of the American Geriatrics Society, 35,* 1007-1010.

Cameron, N. (1959). The paranoid pseudocommunity revisited. *American Journal of Sociology, 65,* 52-58.

Cameron, N., & Magaret, A. (1951). *Behavior pathology.* Boston: Houghton Mifflin.

Campbell, J., Stefan, S., & Loder, A. (1994). Putting violence in context. *Hospital and Community Psychiatry, 45,* 633.

Campbell, M., Anderson, L.T., Small, A.M., Adams, P., Gonzales, N.M., & Ernst, M. (1993). Naltrexone in autistic children: Behavioral symptoms and attentional learning. *Journal of the American Academy of Child and Adolescent Psychiatry, 32,* 1283-1291.

Campbell, M., Armenteros, J.L., Malone, R.P., Adams, P.B., Eisenberg, Z.W., & Overall, J.E. (1997). Neuroleptic-related dyskinesias in autistic children: A prospective, longitudinal study. *Journal of the American Academy of Child and Adolescent Psychiatry, 36,* 835-843.

Campbell, M., Rosenbloom, S., Perry, R., George, A.E., Kercheff, I.I., Anderson, L., Small, A.M., & Jennings, S.J. (1982). Computerized axial tomography in young autistic children. *American Journal of Psychiatry, 139,* 510-512.

Campbell, S.B. (1990). *Behavioral problems in preschoolers: Clinical and developmental issues.* New York: Guilford.

Campbell, S.B. (2002). *Behavioral problems in preschool children: Clinical and developmental issues* (2nd ed.). New York: Guilford.

Camper, P.M., Jacobson, N.S., Holtzworth-Munroe, A., & Schmaling, K.B. (1988). Causal attributions for interactional behaviors in married couples. *Cognitive Therapy and Research, 12,* 195-209.

Campos, P.E., & Hathaway, B.E. (1993). Behavioral research on gay issues 20 years after Davison's ethical challenge. *The Behavior Therapist, 16,* 193-197.

Camus, V., Burtin, B., Simeone, I., et al. (2000). Factor analysis supports the evidence of existing hyperactive and hypoactive subtypes of delirium. *International Journal of Geriatric Psychiatry, 15,* 313-316.

Canetto, S.S. (1992). Gender and suicide in the elderly. *Suicide and Life-Threatening Behavior, 22,* 80-97.

Cangelosi, A., Gressard, C.F., & Mines, R. A. (1980). The effects of a rational thinking group on self-concepts in adolescents. *The School Counselor, 27,* 357-361.

Canivez, G.L., & Watkins, M.W. (1998). Long-term stability of the Wechsler Intelligence Scale for Children (3rd ed.). *Psychological Asessment, 10,* 285-291.

Cannon, D.S., Baker, T.B., Gino, A., & Nathan, P.E. (1986). Alcohol-aversion therapy: Relation between strength of aversion and abstinence. *Journal of Consulting and Clinical Psychology, 54,* 825-830.

Cannon, T.D., van Erp, T.G., Rosso, I.M. et al. (2002). Fetal Hypoxia abs structural brain abnormalities in schizophrenic patients, their siblings, and controls. *Archives of General Psychiatry, 59,* 35-42.

Cannon, T.D., & Mednick, S.A. (1993). The schizophrenia high-risk project in Copenhagen: Three decades of progress. *Acta Psychiatrica Scandanavica,* 33-47.

Cannon, T.D., Kaprio, J., Lonnqvist, J., Huttunen, M., & Koskenvuo, M. (1998). The genetic epidemiology of schizophrenia in a Finnish twin cohort: A population-based modeling study. *Archives of General Psychiatry, 55,* 67-74.

Cannon, T.D., Mednick, S.A., & Parnas, J. (1990). Antecedents of predominantly negative and predominantly positive-symptom schizophrenia in a high-risk population. *Archives of General Psychiatry, 47,* 622-632.

Cannon, T.D., Zorilla, L.E., Shtasel, D., Gur, R.E., Gur, R.C., et al. (1994). Neuropsychological functioning in siblings discordant for schizophrenia and healthy volunteers. *Archives of General Psychiatry, 51,* 651-661.

Cantor, N., Markus, H., Niedenthal, P., & Nurius, P. (1986). On motivation and the self-concept. In R.M. Sorrentino & E.T. Higgins (Eds.), *Handbook of motivation and cognition: Foundations of social behavior* (pp. 96-121). New York: Guilford.

Cantos, A.L., Neidig, P.H., & O'Leary, K.D. (1994). Injuries of women and men in a treatment program for domestic violence. *Journal of Family Violence, 9,* 113-124.

Cantwell, D.P., Baker, L., & Rutter, M. (1978). Family factors. In M. Rutter & E. Schopler (Eds.), *Autism: A reappraisal of concepts and treatment.* New York: Plenum.

Caplan, G. (1964). *Principles of preventive psychiatry.* New York: Basic Books.

Caplan, M., Weissberg, R.P., Grober, J.S., Sivo, P.J., et al. (1992). Social competence promotion with inner-city and suburban young adolescents: Effects on social adjustment and alcohol use. *Journal of Consulting and Clinical Psychology, 66,* 56-63.

Capron, A.M. (1999). Ethical and human rights issues in research on mental disorders that may affect decision-making capacity. *The New England Journal of Medicine, 340,* 1430-1434.

Cardno, A.G., Marshall, E.J., Coid, B., Macdonald, A.M., Ribchester, T.R., et al. (1999). Heritability estimates for psychotic disorders: The Maudsley Twin Psychosis Series. *Archives of General Psychiatry, 56,* 162-170.

Cardon, L.R., Smith, S.D., Fulker, D.W., Kimberling, W.J., Pennington, B.F., & DeFries, J.C. (1994). Quantitative trait locus for reading disability on chromosome 6. *Science, 266,* 276-279.

Carlsson, A., Hanson, L.O., Waters, N., & Carlsson, M.L. (1999). A glutamatergic deficency model of schizophrenia. *British Journal of Psychiatry, 174,* 2-6.

Carnelly, K.B., Pietomonaco, P.R., & Jaffe, K. (1994). Depression, working models of others and relationship functioning. *Journal of Personality and Social Psychology, 66,* 127-141.

Carone, B.J., Harrow, M., & Westermeyer, J.F. (1991). Posthospital course and outcome in schizophrenia. *Archives of General Psychiatry, 48,* 247-253.

Carpeggiani, C., & Skinner, J.E. (1991). Coronary flow and mental stress: Experimental findings. *Circulation, 83,* 90-93.

Carpenter, W.T., Heinrichs, D.W., & Wagman, A.M.I. (1988). Deficit and nondeficit forms of schizophrenia: The concept. *American Journal of Psychiatry, 145,* 578-583.

Carpentieri, S.C. & Morgan, S.B. (1994). Brief report: A comparison of patterns of cognitive functioning of autistic and nonautistic retarded children on the Stanford-Binet (4th ed.). *Journal of Autism and Developmental Disorders, 24,* 215-223.

Carpentieri, S.C. & Morgan, S.B. (1996). Adaptive and intellectual functioning in autism. *Journal of Autism and Developmental Disorders, 26,* 611-620.

Carr, A.T. (1971). Compulsive neurosis: Two psychophysiological studies. *Bulletin of the British Psychological Society, 24,* 256-257.

Carr, E.G., Schreibman, L., & Lovaas, O.I. (1975). Control of echolalic speech in psychotic children. *Journal of Abnormal Child Psychology, 3,* 331-351.

Carr, R.E. (1998). Panic disorder and asthma: Causes, effects, and research implications. *Journal of Psychosomatic Research, 44,* 43-52.

Carr, R.E. (1999). Panic disorder and asthma. *Journal of Asthma, 36,* 143-152.

Carrasco, J.L., Dyaz-Marsa, M., Hollander, E., Cesar, J., & Saiz-Ruiz, J. (2000). Decreased monoamine oxidase activity in female bulimia. *European Neuropsychopharmacology, 10,* 113-117.

Carroll, B.J. (1982). The dexamethasone suppression test for melancholia. *British Journal of Psychiatry, 140,* 292-304.

Carroll, J.M., Touyz, S.M., & Beumont, P.J. (1996). Specific comorbidity between bulimia nervosa and personality disorders. *International Journal of Eating Disorders, 19,* 159-170.

Carroll, K.M., Ball, S.A., Nich, C. et al. (2001). Targeting behavioral therapies to enhance naltrexone treatment of opioid dependence: Efficacy of contingency management and significant other involvement. *Archives of General Psychiatry, 58,* 755-761.

Carroll, K.M. (1996). Relapse prevention as a psychosocial treatment: A review of controlled clinical trials. *Experimental and Clinical Psychopharmacology, 4,* 46-54.

Carroll, K.M., Rounsaville, B.J., Gordon, L.T., Nich, C., Jatlow, P., Bisighini, R.M., & Gawin, F.H. (1994). Psychotherapy and pharmacotherapy for ambulatory cocaine abusers. *Archives of General Psychiatry, 51,* 177-187.

Carroll, K.M., Rounsaville, B.J., Nich, C., Gordon, L.T., & Gawin, F. (1995). Integrating psychotherapy and pharmacotherapy for cocaine dependence: Results from a randomized clinical trial. In L.S. Onken, J.D. Blaine, & J.J. Boren (Eds.), *Integrating behavioral therapies with medications in the treatment of drug dependence* (pp. 19-36). Rockville, MD: National Institute on Drug Abuse.

Carroll, K.M., Rounsaville, B.J., Nich, C., Gordon, L.T., Wirtz, P.W., & Gawin, F. (1994). One-year follow-up of psychotherapy and pharmacotherapy for cocaine dependence. *Archives of General Psychiatry, 51,* 989-997.

Carroll, R.A. (2000). Assessment and treatment of gender dysphoria. In S. R. Lieblum & R. C. Rosen (Eds.), *Principles and practice of sex therapy* (pp.368-397). New York: Guilford Press.

Carstensen, L.L. (1996). Evidence for a life-span theory of socioemotional selectivity. *Current Directions in Psychological Science, 4,* 151-156.

Carver, C.S., & Scheier, M.F. (1999). Stress, coping, and self-regulatory processes. In L.A. Pervin & O.P. John (Eds.), *Handbook of Personality* (2nd ed., pp.553-575). New York: Guildford Press.

Carver, C.S., Pozo, C., Harris, S.D., Noriega, V., Scheier, M., Robinson, D., Ketcham, A., Moffat, F.L., & Clark, K. (1993). How coping mediates the effect of optimism on distress: A study of women with early stage breast cancer. *Journal of Personality and Social Psychology, 65,* 375-390.

Casey, J.E., Rourke, B.P., & Del Dotto, J.E. (1996). Learning disabilities in children with attention deficit disorder with and without hyperactivity. *Child Neuropsychology, 2,* 83-98.

Cashman, J.A. (1966). *The LSD story.* Greenwich, CT: Fawcett.

Casper, M.L., Barnett, E., Halverson, J.A., Elmes, G.A., Braham, V.E., Majeed, Z.A., Boom, A.S., & Stanley, S. (2000). *Women and heart disease: An atlas of recial and ethnic disparities in mortality* (2nd ed.). Office for Social and Environmental Health Research, West Virginia University, and the National Center for Chronic Disease Prevention and Health Promotion, Centers for Disease Control and Prevention, Atlanta, GA.

Casriel, D. (1971). The dynamics of Synanon. In R.W. Siroka, E.K. Siroka, & G.A. Schloss (Eds.), *Sensitivity training and group encounter.* New York: Grosset & Dunlap.

Castellanos, F.X., Giedd, J.N., Marsh, W.L., Hamburger, S.D., Vaituzis, A.C., Dickstein, D.P., Sarfatti, S.E., Vauss, Y.C., Snell, J.W., Lange, N., Kaysen, D., Krain, A.L., Ritchie, G.F., Rajapaske, J.C., & Rapoport, J.L. (1996). Quantitative brain magnetic resonance imaging in attention-deficit/hyperactivity disorder. *Archives of General Psychiatry, 53,* 607-616.

Castle, D.J., & Murray, R.M. (1993). The epidemiology of late-onset schizophrenia. *Schizophrenia Bulletin, 19,* 691-700.

Catania, J.A., Turner, H., Kegeles, S.M., Stall, R., et al. (1989). Older Americans and AIDS: Transmission risks and primary prevention research needs. *Gerontologist, 29,* 373-381.

Cautela, J.R. (1966). Treatment of compulsive behavior by covert sensitization. *Psychological Record, 16,* 33-41.

Caven, R.S. (1973). Speculations on innovations to conventional marriage in old age. *The Gerontologist, 13,* 409-411.

Centers for Disease Control. (1994). *HIV/AIDS surveillance report.* Atlanta: Centers for Disease Control.

Cerny, J.A., Barlow, D.H., Craske, M.G., & Himadi, W.G. (1987). Couples treatment of agoraphobia: A two year follow-up. *Behavior Therapy, 18,* 401-415.

Chafe, W. (1962). Estimates regarding the present speakers of North American Indian languages. *International Journal of American Linguistics, 28,* 162-171.

Chambers, K.C., & Bernstein, I.L. (1995). Conditioned flavor aversions. In R.L. Doty (Ed.), *Handbook of olfaction and gustation* (pp. 745-773). New York: Marcel Dekker.

Chambless, D.L., & Ollendick, T.H. (2001). Empirically supported psychological interventions: controversies and evidence. *Annual Review* of *Psychology, 52,* 685-716.

Chambless, D.L., Sanderson, W.C., Shoham, V., Johnson, S.B., Pope, K.S., Crits-Christoph, P., Baker, M., Johnson, B., Woody, S.R., Sue, S., Beutler, L.E., Williams, D.A., & McCurry, S. (1996). An update on empirically validated therapies. *The Clinical Psychologist, 49,* 5-18.

Chambliss, C.A., & Murray, E.J. (1979). Efficacy attribution, locus of control, and weight loss. *Cognitive Therapy and Research, 3,* 349-353.

Chaney, E.F., O'Leary, M.R., & Marlatt G A (1978). Skills training with alcoholics. *Journal of Consulting and Clinical Psychology, 46,* 1092-1104.

Chapman, L.J., & Chapman, J.P. (1969). Illusory correlation as an obstacle to the use of valid psychodiagnostic signs. *Journal of Abnormal Psychology, 74,* 271-287.

Charney, D.S., Woods, S.W., Goodman, W.K., & Heninger, G.R. (1987). Neurobiological mechanisms of panic anxiety: Biochemical and behavioral correlates of yohimbine-induced panic attacks. *American Journal of Psychiatry, 144,* 1030-1036.

Chassin, L., Curran, P.J., Hussong, A.M., & Colder, C. R. (1996). The relation of parent alcoholism to adolescent substance abuse: A longitudinal follow-up. *Journal of Abnormal Psychology, 105,* 70-80.

Chassin, L., Pitts, S.C., DeLucia, C., & Todd, M. (1999). A longitudinal study of children of alcoholics: Predicting young adult substance use disorders, anxiety, and depression. *Journal of Abnormal Psychology, 108,* 106-119.

Chemtob, C., Roitblat, H.C., Hamada, R.S., Carlson, J.G., & Twentyman, C.T. (1988). A cognitive action theory of posttraumatic stress disorder. *Journal of Anxiety Disorders, 2,* 253-275.

Chen, E., Bush, J.P., & Zeltzer, L. (1997). Psychologic issues in pediatric pain management. *Current Review of Pain, 1,* 153-164.

Chen, S., & Andersen, S.M. (1999). Relationships from the past in the present: Significant-other representations and transference in interpersonal life. In M.P. Zanna (Ed.), *Advances in experimental social psychology.* San Diego: Academic Press.

Chen, W.J., Liu, S.K., Chang, C.-G., Lien, Y.-J., et al. (1998). Sustained attention deficit and schizotypal personality features in nonpsychotic relatives of schizophrenic patients. *American Journal of Psychoatry, 155,* 1214-1220.

Chen, Y., Levy, D.L., Nakayama, K., Matthysse, S., et al. (1999). Dependence of impaired eye tracking on velocity discrimination in schizophrenia. *Archives of General Psychiatry, 56,* 155-161.

Cherner, J. (1990). *A smoke-free America.* New York: Smokefree Educational Services.

Chernoff, R.A. (1998). *The short- and long-term behavioral outcomes of HIV prevention interventions: A critical evaluation.* Unpublished manuscript. University of Southern California.

Chernoff, R.A., & Davison, G. C. (1997, August). *Values and their relationship to HIV/AIDS risk behavior.* Paper presented at the annual convention of the American Psychological Association, Chicago.

Chesney, M.A., & Folkman, S. (1994). Psychological impact of HIV disease and implications for intervention. *Psychiatric Clinics of North America, 17,* 163-182.

Chesney, M.A., Barrett, D.C., & Stall, R. (1998). Histories of substance use and risk behavior: Precursors to HIV seroconversion in homosexual men. *American Journal of Public Health, 88,* 113-116.

Chiappa, F. (1994). Effective management of family and individual interventions in the treatment of dissociative disorders. *Dissociation, 7,* 185-190.

Chiariello, M.A., & Orvaschel, H. (1995). Patterns of parent-child communication: Relationship to depression. *Clinical Psychology Review, 15,* 395-407.

Chow, T.W., Miller, B.L., Hayashi, V.N., & Geschwind, D.H. (1999). Inheritance of frontotemporal dementia. *Archives of Neurology, 56,* 817-822.

Christenfeld, N., Gerin, W., Linden, W., Sanders, M., Mathur, J.D., et al. (1998). Social support effects on cardiovascular reactivity: Is a stranger as effective as a friend? *Psychosomatic Medicine, 59,* 388-398.

Christensen, A., & Heavey, C.L. (1990). Gender and social structure in the demand/withdraw pattern of marital interaction. *Journal of Personality and Social Psychology, 59,* 73-81.

Christensen, A., & Jacobson, N.S. (2000). *Reconcilable differences.* New York: Guilford Press.

Christensen, A., & Jacobson, N.S. (1993). Who or what can do psychotherapy? *Psychological Science, 5,* 8-14.

Christensen, A., & Shenk, J.L. (1991). Communication, distress, and psychological distance in nondistressed, clinic, and divorcing couples. *Journal of Consulting and Clinical Psychology, 59,* 458-463.

Christensen, A., Jacobson, N.S., & Babcock, J.C. (1995). Integrative behavioral couple therapy. In N.S. Jacobson, & A.S. Gurman (Eds.), *Clinical handbook of couples therapy* (pp. 31-64). New York: Guilford Press.

Christensen, A., Jacobson, N.S., & Babcock, J.C. (1995). Integrative behavioral couples therapy. In N.S. Jacobson & A.S. Gurman (Eds.), *Clinical handbook of couples therapy* (pp. 31-64). New York: Guilford.

Christie, A.B. (1982). Changing patterns in mental illness in the elderly. *British Journal of Psychiatry, 140,* 154-159.

Chu, J.A., Frey, L.M., Ganzel, B.L., & Matthews, J.A. (1999). Memories of childhood abuse: Dissociation, amnesia, and corroboration. *American Journal of Psychiatry, 156,* 749-755.

Chua, S.T., & McKenna, P.T. (1995). Schizophrenia—a brain disease? *British Journal of Psychiatry, 166,* 563-582.

Cimons, M. (1992, May 22). Record number of Americans stop smoking. *Los Angeles Times,* pp. A4.

Cimons, M. (1995, December 16). Smoking, illegal drug use still rising among teens, national survey shows. *Los Angeles Times,* pp. A25.

Cimons, M. (1996, March 19). Firm adjusted nicotine in cigarettes, affidavits say. *Los Angeles Times,* pp. A1, A13.

Cimons, M. (1998, April 3). Study finds sharp rise in teenage tobacco use. *Los Angeles Times,* pp. A1, A26.

Cimons, M. (1999, May 21). Marijuana studies to be aided by likely policy reversal. *Los Angeles Times,* pp. A15.

Cinciripini, P.M., Lapitsky, L., Seay, S., Wallfisch, A., Kitchens, K., & Van Vunakis, H. (1995). The effect of smoking schedules on cessation outcome: Can we improve on common methods of gradual and abrupt nicotine withdrawal? *Journal of Consulting and Clinical Psychology, 63,* 388-399.

Cinciripini, P.M., Lapitsky, L.G., Wallfisch, A., Mace, R., Nezami, E., & Van Vunakis, H. (1994). An evaluation of a multicomponent treatment program involving scheduled smoking and relapse prevention procedures: Initial findings. *Addictive Behaviors, 19,* 13-22.

Cioffi, D. (1991). Beyond attentional strategies: A cognitive-perceptual model of somatic interpretation. *Psychological Bulletin, 109,* 25-41.

Clark, D.M. (1996). Panic disorder: From theory to therapy. In P.M. Salkovskis (Ed.), *Frontiers of cognitive therapy.* (pp. 318-344). NY: Guilford.

Clark, D.A. (1997). Twenty years of cognitive assessment: Current status and future directions. *Journal of Consulting and Clinical Psychology, 65,* 996-1000.

Clark, D.F. (1988). The validity of measures of cognition: A review of the literature. *Cognitive Therapy and Research, 12,* 1-20.

Clark, D.M. (1989). Anxiety states: Panic and generalized anxiety. In K. Hawton, P. Salkovskis, J. Kirk, & D.M. Clark (Eds.), *Cognitive behavior therapy for psychiatric problems: A practical guide.* Oxford, U.K. Oxford University Press.

Clark, D.M., Salkovskis, P.M., Hackmann, A., Middleton, H., Anastasiades, P., & Gelder, M. (1994). A comparison of cognitive therapy, applied relaxation, and imipramine in the treatment of panic disorder. *British Journal of Psychiatry, 164,* 759-769.

Clark, L.A., Watson, D., & Mineka, S. (1994). Temperament, personality, and the mood and anxiety disorders. *Journal of Abnormal Psychology, 103,* 92-102.

Clark, R., Anderson, N. B., Clark, V. R., & Williams, D. R. (1999). Racism as a stressor for African Americans. *American Psychologist, 54,* 805-816.

Clark, R.F., & Goate, A.M. (1993). Molecular genetics of Alzheimer's disease. *Archives of Neurology, 50,* 1164-1172.

Clarke, G., Hops, H., Lewinsohn, P.M., Andrews, J., Seeley, J.R., & Williams, J. (1992). Cognitive-behavioral group treatment of adolescent depression: Prediction of outcome. *Behavior Therapy, 23,* 341-354.

Clarke, K., & Greenberg, L. (1986). Differential effects of the gestalt two chair intervention and problem solving in resolving decisional conflict. *Journal of Counseling Psychology, 33,* 48-53.

Clarkin, J.F., Marziali, E., & Munroe-Blum, H. (Eds.). (1992). *Borderline personality disorder: Clinical and empirical perspectives.* New York: Guilford.

Clary, M. (1998, May 8). Teen-driven ad campaign puts heat on big tobacco. *Los Angeles Times,* pp. A1, A25.

Classen, C., Koopman, C., Hales, R., & Spiegel, D. (1998). Acute stress disorder as a predictor of posttraumatic stress disorder. *American Journal of Psychiatry, 155,* 620-624.

Claude, D., & Firestone, P. (1995). The development of ADHD boys: A 12-year follow-up. *Canadian Journal of Behavioral Science, 27,* 226-249.

Clausen, J.A., & Kohn, M.L. (1959). Relation of schizophrenia to the social structure of a small city. In B. Pasamanick (Ed.), *Epidemiology of mental disorder.* Washington, DC: American Association for the Advancement of Science.

Clayton, E.W. (1988). From Rogers to Rivers: The rights of the mentally ill to refuse medications. *American Journal of Law and Medicine, 13,* 7-52.

Clayton, I.C., Richards, J.C., & Edwards, C.J. (1999). Selective attention in obsessive-compulsive disorder. *Journal of Abnormal Psychology, 108,* 171-175.

Clayton, P.J. (1973). The clinical morbidity of the first year of bereavement: A review. *Comparative Psychiatry, 14,* 151-157.

Clayton, R.R., Catterello, A., & Walden, K.P. (1991). Sensation seeking as a potential mediating variable for school-based prevention intervention: A two-year follow-up of DARE. *Health Communication, 3,* 229-239.

Cleckley, H. (1976). *The mask of sanity* (5th ed.). St. Louis: Mosby.

Climko, R.P., Roehrich, H., Sweeney, D.R., & Al-Razi, J. (1987). Ecstasy: A review of MDMA and MDA. *International Journal of Psychiatry in Medicine, 16,* 359-372.

Clomipramine Collaborative Study Group. (1991). Clomipramine in the treatment of patients with obsessive-compulsive disorder. *Archives of General Psychiatry, 48,* 730-738.

Cloninger, R.C., Martin, R.L., Guze, S.B., & Clayton, P.L. (1986). A prospective follow-up and family study of somatization in men and women. *American Journal of Psychiatry, 143,* 713-714.

Cloud, J. (1999, June 7). Mental health reform: What it would really take. *Time Magazine,* 54-56.

Clunies-Ross, G.G. (1979). Accelerating the development of Down's syndrome infants and young children. *The Journal of Special Education, 13,* 169-177.

Coates, S., & Person, E.S. (1985). Extreme boyhood femininity: Isolated behavior or pervasive disorder? *Journal of the American Academy of Child Psychiatry, 24,* 702-709.

Cocarro, E.F., & Kavousi, R.J. (1997). Fluoxetine and impulsive aggressive behavior in personality-disordered subjects. *Archives of General Psychiatry, 54,* 1081-1088.

Coccaro, E.F., & Kavoussi, R.J. (1995, May 20-25). *Fluoxetine in aggression in personality disorders* [New Research Abstracts]. Presented at the American Psychiatric Association 148th annual meeting, Miami.

Cody, M., Wendt, P., Dunn, D., Ott, J., Pierson, J., & Pratt, L. (1997) *Friendship formation and community development on the Internet.* International Communication Association Meeting, Montreal, May.

Cody, M.J., Dunn, D., Hoppin, S., & Wendt, P. (1999). Silver surfers: Training and evaluating Internet use among older adult learners. *Communication Education, 48,* 269-286.

Cohen, D., Eisdorfer, C., Prinz, P., Breen, A., Davis, M., & Gadsby, A. (1983). Sleep disturbances in the institutionalized aged. *Journal of the American Geriatrics Society, 31,* 79-82.

Cohen, D.J., Solnit, A.J., & Wohlford, P. (1979). Mental health services in Head Start. In E. Zigler & J. Valentine (Eds.), *Project Head Start.* New York: Free Press.

Cohen, L.J., & Roth, S. (1987). The psychological aftermath of rape: Long-term effects and individual differences in recovery. *Journal of Social and Clinical Psychology, 5,* 525-534.

Cohen, P., Cohen, J., Kasen, S., Velez, C.N., Hartmark, C., Johnson, J., Rojas, M., Brook, J., & Streuning, E.L. (1993). An epidemiological study of disorders in late childhood and adolescence: 1. Age and gender-specific prevalence. *Journal of Child Psychology and Psychiatry, 34,* 851-867.

Cohen, R.M., Nordahl, T.E., Semple, W.E., Andreason, P., et al. (1997). The brain metabolic patterns of clozapine and fluphenazine-treated patients with schizophrenia during a continuous performance task. *Archives of General Psychiatry, 54,* 481-486.

Cohen, S., & Herbert, T.B. (1996). Health psychology: Psychological factors and physical disease from the perspective of human psychoneuroimmunology. In J.T. Spence, J.M. Darley, & D.J. Foss (Eds.), *Annual review of psychology* (pp. 123-142). Stanford, CA: Stanford University Press.

Cohen, S., & Wills, T.A. (1985). Stress, social support, and the buffering process. *Psychological Bulletin, 98,* 310-357.

Cohen, S., Doyle, W.J., Skoner, D.P., Rabin, B.S., & Gwaltney, J.M. (1997). Social ties and susceptibility to the common cold. *JAMA, 277,* 1940-1945.

Cohen, S., Frank, E., Doyle, W.J., Rabin, B.S., et al. (1998). Types of stressors that increase susceptibility to the common cold in healthy adults. *Health Psychology, 17,* 214-223.

Cohen, S., Tyrell, D.A.J., & Smith, A.P. (1991). Psychological stress and susceptibility to the common cold. *New England Journal of Medicine, 325,* 606-612.

Cohen-Mansfield, J., Werner, P., Culpepper, W.J., III, Wolfson, M.A., & Bicket, E. (1996). Wandering and aggression. In L.L. Carstensen, B.A. Edelstein, & L. Dombrand (Eds.), *The practical handbook of clinical gerontology* (pp. 274-397). Thousand Oaks, CA: Sage Publications.

Colapinto, J. (1997). The true story of Joan/John. *Rolling Stone,* 55-tt.

Cole, D., & Turner, J., Jr. (1993). Models of cognitive mediation and moderation in child depression. *Journal of Abnormal Psychology, 102,* 271-281.

Cole, D.A., Martin, J.M., Powers, B., & Truglio, R. (1990). Modeling causal relations between academic and social competence and depression: A multitrait-multimethod longitudinal study of children. *Journal of Abnormal Psychology, 105,* 258-270.

Cole, J., Watt, N., West, S., Hawkins, J., Asarnow, J., Markman, H., Ramey, S., Shure, M., & Long, B. (1993). The science of prevention: A conceptual framework and some directions for a national research program. *American Psychologist, 48,* 1013-1022.

Cole, J.D. (1988). Where are those new anti-depressants they promised us? *Archives of General Psychiatry, 45,* 193-194.

Cole, K.C. (1996, November 22). Trying to solve the riddle of the rock. *Los Angeles Times,* pp. A1, A29.

Collaborative study of children treated for phenylketonuria, preliminary report 8. (1975, February). R. Koch, principal investigator. Presented at the Eleventh General Medicine Conference, Stateline, NV.

Colletti, G., & Kopel, S.A. (1979). Maintaining behavior change: An investigation of three maintenance strategies and the relationship of self-attribution to the long-term reduction of cigarette smoking. *Journal of Consulting and Clinical Psychology, 47,* 614-617.

Collins, L.F., Maxwell, A.E., & Cameron, C. (1962). A factor analysis of some child psychiatric clinic data. *Journal of Mental Science, 108,* 274-285.

Combs, G., Jr., & Ludwig, A.M. (1982). Dissociative disorders. In J.H. Greist, J.W. Jefferson, & R.L. Spitzer (Eds.), *Treatment of mental disorders.* New York: Oxford University Press.

Comfort, A. (1980). Sexuality in later life. In J.E. Birren & R.B. Sloane (Eds.), *Handbook of mental health and aging.* Englewood Cliffs, NJ: Prentice-Hall.

Comfort, A. (1984). Sexuality and the elderly. In J.P. Abrahams & V. Crooks (Eds.), *Geriatric mental health.* Orlando, FL: Grune & Stratton.

Committee on Government Operations. (1985). *The federal response to the homeless crisis.* Washington, DC: U.S. Government Printing Office.

Committee on Health Care for Homeless People. (1988). *Homelessness, health, and human needs.* Washington, DC: National Academic Press.

Compas, B.E., Ey, S., & Grant, K.E. (1993). Taxonomy, assessment and diagnosis of depression during adolescence. *Psychological Bulletin, 144,* 323-344.

Compas, B.E., Haaga, D.A.F., Keefe, F.J., Leitenberg, H., & Williams, D.A. (1998). Sampling of empirically supported psychological treatments from health psychology: Smoking, chronic pain, cancer, and bulimia nervosa. *Journal of Consulting and Clinical Psychology, 66,* 89-112.

Compton, D.R., Dewey, W.L., & Martin, B.R. (1990). Cannabis dependence and tolerance production. *Advances in Alcohol and Substance Abuse, 9,* 129-147.

Conceicao do Rosario-Campos, M., Leckman, J. F., Mercadante, M. T. et al. (2001). Adults with early-onset obsessive-compulsive disorder. *American Journal of Psychiatry, 158,* 1899-1903.

Condelli, W.S., Fairbank, J.A., Dennis, M.L., & Rachal, J.V. (1991). Cocaine use by clients in methadone programs: Significance, scope, and behavioral interventions. *Journal of Substance Abuse Treatment, 8,* 203-212.

Conger, J.J. (1951). The effects of alcohol on conflict behavior in the albino rat. *Quarterly Journal of Studies on Alcohol, 12,* 129.

Conley, R.R. & Mahmoud, R. (2001). A randomized double-blind study of risperidone and olanzapine in the treatment of schizophrenia or schizoaffective disorder. *American Journal of Psychiatry, 158,* 765-774.

Conley, R.R., Love, R.C., Kelly, D.L., & Bartko, J.J. (1999). Rehospitalization rates of patients recently discharged on a regimen of risperidone or clozapine. *American Journal of Psychiatry, 156,* 863-868.

Conley, R.R., Tamminga, C.A., Bartko, J.J., Richardson, C., Peszke, M., et al. (1998). Olanzapine compared with chlorpromazine in treatment-resistant schizophrenia. *American Journal of Psychiatry, 155,* 914-920.

Connelly, M. (1992, March 7). 3 found dead after inhaling laughing gas. *Los Angeles Times,* pp. A1, A23.

Conners, C.K. (1969). A teacher rating scale for use in drug studies with children. *American Journal of Psychiatry, 126,* 884-888.

Conners, F.A., Caruso, D.R., & Detterman, D.K. (1986). Computer-assisted instruction for the mentally retarded. In N.R. Ellis & N.W. Bray (Eds.), *International review of research in mental retardation* (Vol. 14). New York: Academic Press.

Conoley, C.W., Conoley, J.C., McConnell, J.A., & Kimzey, C.E. (1983). The effect of the ABCs of rational emotive therapy and the empty-chair technique of Gestalt therapy on anger reduction. *Psychotherapy: Theory, Research, and Practice, 20,* 112-117.

Conrod, P.J., Pihl, R.O., & Vassileva, J. (1998). Differential sensitivity to alcohol reinforcement in groups of men at risk for distinct alcoholic syndromes. *Alcoholism: Clinical and Experimental Research, 22,* 585-597.

Consumer Reports. (1995, November). Mental health. Does therapy help? *Consumer Reports,* pp. 734-739.

Conwell, Y. (1994). Suicide in elderly patients. In L.S. Schneider, C.F. Reynolds, III, B.D. Lebowitz, & A.J. Friedhoff (Eds.), *Diagnosis and treatment of depression in late life* (pp. 397-418). Washington, DC: American Psychiatric Press.

Conwell, Y. (2001). Suicide in later life: a review and recommendations for prevention. *Suicide and Life-Threatening Behavior, 31,* 32-47.

Cook, B., Blatt, S.J., & Ford, R.Q. (1995). The prediction of therapeutic response to long-term intensive treatment of seriously disturbed young adult inpatients. *Psychotherapy Research, 5,* 218-230.

Cook, J.M. (2001). Post-traumatic stress disorder in older adults. *PTSD Research Quarterly, 12 (3),* 1-3.

Cook, M., & Mineka, S. (1989). Observational conditioning of fear to fear-relevant versus fear-irrelevant stimuli in rhesus monkeys. *Journal of Abnormal Psychology, 98,* 448-459.

Cooke, D.J. & Michie, C. (2001). Refining the concept of psychopathy: Towards a hierarchical model. *Psychological Assessment, 13,* 171-188.

Coolidge, F.L., & Segal, D.L. (1998). Evolution of personality disorder diagnosis in the Diagnostic and Statistical Manual of Mental Disorders. *Clinical Psychology Review, 18,* 585-589.

Coons, P. M., & Bowman, E.S. (2001). Ten-year follow-up study of patients with dissociative identity disorder. *Journal of Trauma and Dissociation, 2,* 73-89.

Coons, P.M., & Milstein, V. (1992). Psychogenic amnesia: A clinical investigation of 25 cases. *Dissociation: Progress in the Dissociative Disorders, 5,* 73-79.

Cooper, A.F., Garside, R.F., & Kay, D.W.K. (1976). A comparison of deaf and non-deaf patients with paranoid and affective psychoses. *British Journal of Psychiatry, 129,* 532-538.

Cooper, A.F., Kay, D.W.K., Curry, A.R., Garside, R.F., & Roth, M. (1974). Hearing loss in paranoid and affective psychoses of the elderly. *Lancet, 2,* 851-854.

Cooper, J.E., Kendell, R.E., Gurland, B.J., Sharpe, L., Copeland, J.R.M., & Simon, R. (1972). *Psychiatric diagnosis in New York and London.* London: Oxford University Press.

Cooper, M.L., Frone, M.R., Russell, M., & Mudar, P. (1995). Drinking to regulate positive and negative emotion: A motivational model of alcoholism. *Journal of Personality and Social Psychology, 69,* 961-974.

Cooper, P.J., Coker, S., & Fleming, C. (1994). Self-help for bulimia nervosa: A preliminary report. *International Journal of Eating Disorders, 16,* 401-404.

Coppen, A., Prange, A.J., Whybrow, P.C., & Noguera, R. (1972). Abnormalities in indoleamines in affective disorders. *Archives of General Psychiatry, 26,* 474-478.

Corbitt, E.M., & Widiger, T.A. (1995). Sex differences in the personality disorders: An exploration of the data. *Clinical Psychology: Science and Practice, 2,* 225-238.

Cordova, J.V., & Jacobson, N.S. (1993). Couple distress. In D.H. Barlow (Ed.), *Clinical handbook of psychological disorders* (2nd ed., pp. 461-512). New York: Guilford.

Cornblatt, B., & Erlenmeyer-Kimling, L.E. (1985). Global attentional deviance in children at risk for schizophrenia: Specificity and predictive validity. *Journal of Abnormal Psychology, 94,* 470-486.

Cornelius, J.R., Salloum, I.M., Ehler, J.G., Jarrett, P.J., Cornelius, M.D., et al. (1997). Fluoxetine in depressed alcoholics: A double-blind, placebo-controlled trial. *Archives of General Psychiatry, 54,* 700-705.

Cornelius, J.R., Salloum, I.M., Mezzich, J., Cornelius, M.D., Fabrega, H., et al. (1995). Disproportionate suicidability in patients with comorbid major depression and alcoholism. *American Journal of Psychiatry, 152,* 358-364.

Cororve, M.B. & Gleaves, D.H. (2001). Body dysmorphic disorder: A review of conceptualizations, assessment, and treatment strategies. *Clinical Psychology Review, 21,* 949-970.

Corwin, M. (1996). Heroin's new popularity claims unlikely victims. *Los Angeles Times,* pp. A1.

Coryell, W., Winokur, G., Shea, T., Maser, J.W., Endicott, J., & Akiskal, H.S. (1994). The long-term stability of depressive subtypes. *American Journal of Psychiatry, 151,* 199-204.

Costa, P.T., Jr., & McCrae, R.R. (1988). Personality in adulthood: A six-year longitudinal study of self-reports and spouse ratings on the NEO Personality Inventory. *Journal of Personality and Social Psychology, 54,* 853-863.

Costa, P.T., Jr., & McCrae, R.R. (1992). *NEO-PI-R.* Odessa, FL: Psychological Assessment Resources.

Costa, P.T., Jr., Zonderman, A.B., McCrae, R.R., Cornoni-Huntley, J., Locke, B.Z., & Barbano, H.E. (1987). Longitudinal analyses of psychological well-being in a national sample: Stability of mean levels. *Journal of Gerontology, 42,* 50-55.

Costello, E.J., Costello, A.J., Edelbrock, C., Burns, B.J., Dulcan, M.K., Brent, D., & Janiszewski, S. (1988). Psychiatric disorders in pediatric primary care. *Archives of General Psychiatry, 45,* 1107-1116.

Council for Exceptional Children (1993). *Inclusion: What does it mean for children with learning disabilities?* Reston, VA: Division for Learning Disabilities.

Courchesne, E., Yeung-Courchesne, R., Press, G.A., Hesselink, J.R., & Jernigan, T.L. (1988). Hypoplasia of cerebellar vermal lobules VI and VII in autism. *New England Journal of Medicine, 318,* 1349-1354.

Covi, L., Lipman, R.S., Derogatis, L.R., Smith, J.E., & Pattison, J.H. (1974). Drugs and group psychotherapy in neurotic depression. *American Journal of Psychiatry, 131,* 191-197.

Cox, A., Rutter, M., Newman, S., & Bartak, L. (1975). A comparative study of infantile autism and specific developmental language disorders: 2. Parental characteristics. *British Journal of Psychiatry, 126,* 146-159.

Coyne, J.C. (1976). Depression and the response of others. *Journal of Abnormal Psychology, 85,* 186-193.

Coyne, J.C. (1994). Self-reported distress: Analog or ersatz depression? *Psychological Bulletin, 116,* 29-45.

Craft, M.J. (1969). The natural history of psychopathic disorder. *British Journal of Psychiatry, 115,* 39-44.

Craig, M.M., & Glick, S.J. (1963). Ten years' experience with the Glueck social prediction table. *Crime and Delinquency, 9,* 249-261.

Craighead, L.W., & Agras, W.S. (1991). Mechanisms of action in cognitive-behavioral and pharmacological interventions for obesity and bulimia nervosa. *Journal of Consulting and Clinical Psychology, 59,* 115-125.

Craighead, W.E., Evans, D.D., & Robins, C.J. (1992). Unipolar depression. In S.M. Turner, K.S. Calhoun, & H.E. Adams (Eds.), *Handbook of clinical behavior therapy* (2nd ed., pp. 99-116). New York: Wiley.

Craske, M.G. & Barlow, D.H. (2001). Panic disorder and agoraphobia. In D.H. Barlow (Ed.), *Clinical Handbook of Psychological Disorders* (pp. 1-59). New York, NY: Guilford Press.

Craske, M.G., Brown, A.T., & Barlow, D.H. (1991). Behavioral treatment of panic disorder: A two-year follow-up. *Behavior Therapy, 22,* 289-304.

Craske, M.G., Maidenberg, E., & Bystritsky, A. (1995). Brief cognitive-behavioral versus nondirective therapy for panic disorder. *Journal of Behavior Therapy & Experimental Psychiatry, 26,* 113-120.

Craske, M.G., Rapee, R.M., & Barlow, D.H. (1992). Cognitive-behavioral treatment of panic disorder, agoraphobia, and generalized anxiety disorder. In S.M. Turner, K.S. Calhoun, & H.E. Adams (Eds.), *Handbook of clinical behavior therapy* (2nd ed., pp. 39-65). New York: Wiley.

Craske, M.G., Rapee, R.M., Jackel, L., & Barlow, D.H. (1989). Quantitative dimensions of worry in DSM-III-R generalized anxiety disorder subjects and non-anxious controls. *Behaviour Research and Therapy, 27,* 397-402.

Creer, T.L. (1982). Asthma. *Journal of Consulting and Clinical Psychology, 50,* 912-921.

Creer, T.L., Renna, C.M., & Chai, H. (1982). The application of behavioral techniques to childhood asthma. In D.C. Russo & J.W. Varni (Eds.), *Behavioral pediatrics: Research and practice.* New York: Plenum.

Crick, N.R., & Dodge, K.A. (1994). A review and reformulation of social information-processing mechanisms in children's social adjustment. *Psychological Bulletin, 115,* 74-101.

Critis-Christoph, P., Connolly, M.B., Azarian, K., Crits-Christoph, K., & Shapell, S. (1996). An open trial of brief supportive-expressive psychotherapy in the treatment of generalized anxiety disorder. *Psychotherapy, 33,* 418-430.

Crits-Christoph, P. (1992). The efficacy of brief dynamic psychotherapy. *American Journal of Psychiatry, 149,* 151-158.

Crits-Christoph, P., & Barber, J.P. (2002). Psychological treatments for personality disorders. In P.E. Nathan & J.M. Gorman (Eds.), *A guide to treatments that work.* New York: Oxford University Press.

Cronan, T.A., Cruz, S.G., Arriaga, R.I., & Sarkin, A.J. (1996). The effects of a community-based literacy program on young children's language and conceptual development. *American Journal of Community Psychology, 24,* 251-272.

Cronbach, L.J., & Meehl, P.E. (1955). Construct validity in psychological tests. *Psychological Bulletin, 52,* 281-302.

Crow, T.J. (1980). Molecular pathology of schizophrenia: More than one disease process? *British Medical Journal, 280,* 784-788.

Crowe, R.R., Noyes, R., Pauls, D.I., & Slyman, D.J. (1983). A family study of panic disorder. *Archives of General Psychiatry, 40,* 1065-1069.

Crum, R.M. & Pratt, L.A. (2001). Risk of heavy drinking and alcohol use disorders in social phobia: A prospective analysis. *American Journal of Psychiatry, 158,* 1693-700.

Cruz, D.B. (1999). Controlling desires: Sexual orientation conversion and the limits of knowledge and law. *Southern California Law Review, 72,* 1297-1400.

Csernansky, J.G., Mahmoud, R., & Brenner, R. (2002). A comparison of risperidone and haloperidol for the prevention of relapse in patients with schizophrenia. *The New England Journal of Medicine, 356,* 16-22.

Csikszentmihalyi, M., & Figurski, T.J. (1982). Self-awareness and aversive experience in everyday life. *Journal of Personality, 50,* 15-28.

Culbertson, J.L. (1998). Learning disabilities. In Ollendick, T.H. & Hersen, M. (Eds.), *Handbook of child psychopathology* (3rd ed.). New York: Plenum Press.

Culter, S.E., & Nolen-Hoeksema, S. (1991). Accounting for sex differences in depression through female victimization: Childhood sexual abuse. *Sex Roles, 24,* 425-438.

Cummings, E.M., Davies, P.T., & Simpson, K.S. (1994). Marital conflict, gender, and children's appraisals and coping efficacy as mediators of child adjustment. *Journal of Family Psychology, 8,* 141-149.

Cunningham, P.J., & Mueller, C.D. (1991). Individuals with mental retardation in residential facilities: Findings from the 1987 National Medical Expenditure Survey. *American Journal on Mental Retardation, 96,* 109-117.

Curtin, J.J., Lang, A.R., Patrick, C.J., & Strizke, W.G.K. (1998). Alcohol and fear-potiantiated startle: The role of competing cognitive demands in the stress-reducing effects of intoxication. *Journal of Abnormal Psychology, 107,* 547-557.

Curtis, V.A., Bullmore, E.T., Bramer, M.J., Wright, I.C., Williams, S.C.R., et al. (1998). Attenuated frontal activation during a verbal fluency task in patients with schizophrenia. *American Journal of Psychiatry, 155,* 1056-1063.

Curyto, K.J., Johnson, J., TenHave, T. et al. (2001). Survival of hospitalized patients with delirium: A prospective study. *American Journal of Geriatric Psychiatry, 9,* 141-147.

D'Ercole, A., & Struening, E. (1990). Victimization among homeless women: Implications for service delivery. *Journal of Community Psychology, 18,* 141-152.

D'Zurilla, T.J. (1986). *Problem-solving therapy: A social competence approach to clinical intervention.* New York: Springer.

D'Zurilla, T.J. (1990). Problem-solving training for effective stress management and prevention. *Journal of Cognitive Psychotherapy: An International Quarterly, 4,* 327-355.

D'Zurilla, T.J., & Goldfried, M.R. (1971). Problem-solving and behavior modification. *Journal of Abnormal Psychology, 78,* 107-126.

D'Zurilla, T.J., & Sheedy, C.F. (1991). Relation between social problem-solving ability and subsequent level of psychological stress in college students. *Journal of Personality and Social Psychology, 61,* 841-846.

D'Zurilla, T.J., & Sheedy, C.F. (1992). The relation between social problem-solving ability and subsequent level of academic competence in college students. *Cognitive Therapy and Research, 16,* 589-599.

Dackis, C.A., & Gold, M.S. (1985). Pharmacological approaches to cocaine addiction. *Journal of Substance Abuse Treatment, 2,* 139-145.

DaCosta, M., & Halmi, K.A. (1992). Classifications of anorexia nervosa: Question of subtypes. *International Journal of Eating Disorders, 11,* 305-313.

Daneman, E.A. (1961). Imipramine in office management of depressive reactions (a double-blind study). *Diseases of the Nervous System, 22,* 213-217.

Daniolos, P.T., & Holmes, V.F. (1995). HIV public policy and psychiatry: An examination of ethical issues and professional guidelines. *Psychosomatics, 36,* 12-21.

Danner, D.D., Snowdon, D.A., & Friesen, W.V. (2001). Positive emotions in early life and longevity findings from the nun study. *Journal of Personality and Social Psychology, 80,* 804-813.

Dar, R., Rish, S., Hermesh, H. et al. (2000). Realism of confidence in obsessive-compulsive checkers. *Journal of Abnormal Psychology, 109,* 673-678.

Dare, C., LeGrange, D., Eisler, I., & Rutherford, J. (1994). Redefining the psychosomatic family: Family process of 26 eating disordered families. *International Journal of Eating Disorders, 16,* 211-226.

Davies, P.T., & Cummings, E.M. (1994). Marital conflict and child adjustment: An emotional security hypothesis. *Psychological Bulletin, 116,* 387-411.

Davila, J., Hammen, C.L., Burge, D., Paley, B., & Daley, S.E. (1995). Poor interpersonal problem solving as a mechanism of stress generation in depression among adolescent women. *Journal of Abnormal Psychology, 104,* 592-600,

Davis, C. (1996). The interdependence of obsessive-compulsiveness, physical activity, and starvation: A model for anorexia nervosa. In W.F. Epling & W.D. Pierce (Eds.), *Activity nervosa: Theory, research, and treatment* (pp. 209-218). Mahwah, NJ: Erlbaum.

Davis, C. (1997). Normal and neurotic perfectionism in eating disorders: An interactive model. *International Journal of Eating Disorders, 22,* 421-426.

Davis, J.M. (1978). Dopamine theory of schizophrenia: A two-factor theory. In L.C. Wynne, R.L. Cromwell, & S. Matthysse (Eds.), *The nature of schizophrenia.* New York: Wiley.

Davis, K.L., Kahn, R.S., Ko, G., & Davidson, M. (1991). Dopamine and schizophrenia: A review and reconceptualization. *American Journal of Psychiatry, 148,* 1474-1486.

Davison, E.H. (1999). *The interrelationships among subjective well-being, gender role flexibility, perceived sexism, and perceived ageism in older women.* Unpublished dissertation, University of California at Santa Barbara.

Davison, E.H. (1996). *Women and aging.* Unpublished manuscript, University of California at Santa Barbara.

Davison, G.C. (1964). A social learning therapy programme with an autistic child. *Behaviour Research and Therapy, 2,* 146-159.

Davison, G.C. (1966). Differential relaxation and cognitive restructuring in therapy with a "paranoid schizophrenic" or "paranoid state." *Proceedings of the 74th Annual Convention of the American Psychological Association.* Washington, DC: American Psychological Association.

Davison, G.C. (1968a). Elimination of a sadistic fantasy by a client-controlled counterconditioning technique. *Journal of Abnormal Psychology, 73,* 84-90.

Davison, G.C. (1968b). Systematic desensitization as a counterconditioning process. *Journal of Abnormal Psychology, 73,* 91-99.

Davison, G.C. (1973). Counter control in behavior modification. In L.A. Hamerlynck, L.C. Handy, & E.J. Mash (Eds.), *Behavior change: Methodology, concepts and practice.* Champaign, IL: Research Press.

Davison, G.C. (1974). *Homosexuality: The ethical challenge.* Presidential address to the Eighth Annual Convention of the Association for Advancement of Behavior Therapy, Chicago.

Davison, G.C. (1976). Homosexuality: The ethical challenge. *Journal of Consulting and Clinical Psychology, 44,* 157-162.

Davison, G.C. (1978). Not can but ought: The treatment of homosexuality. *Journal of Consulting and Clinical Psychology, 46,* 170-172.

Davison, G.C. (1991). Constructionism and therapy for homosexuality. In J. Gonsiorek & J. Weinrich (Eds.), *Homosexuality: Research findings for public policy.* Newbury Park, CA: Sage.

Davison, G.C., & Darke, L. (1991). Managing pain. In R. Bjork & D. Druckman (Eds.), *In the mind's eye: Understanding the basis of human performance.* Washington, DC: National Academy Press.

Davison, G.C., & Lazarus, A.A. (1995). The dialectics of science and practice. In S.C. Hayes, V.M. Follette, T. Risley, R.D. Dawes, & K. Grady (Eds.), *Scientific standards of psychological practice: Issues and recommendations* (pp. 95-120). Reno, NV: Context Press.

Davison, G.C., & Thompson, R.F. (1988). Stress management. In D. Druckman & J.A. Swets (Eds.), *Enhancing human performance: Issues, theories, and techniques.* Washington, DC: National Academy Press.

Davison, G.C., & Valins, S. (1969). Maintenance of self-attributed and drug-attributed behavior change. *Journal of Personality and Social Psychology, 11,* 25-33.

Davison, G.C., & Wilson, G.T. (1973). Attitudes of behavior therapists toward homosexuality. *Behavior Therapy, 4,* 686-696.

Davison, G.C., & Zighelboim, V. (1987). Irrational beliefs in the articulated thoughts of college students with social anxiety. *Journal of Rational-Emotive Therapy, 5,* 238-254.

Davison, G.C., Feldman, P.M., & Osborn, C.E. (1984). Articulated thoughts, irrational beliefs, and fear of negative evaluation. *Cognitive Therapy and Research, 8,* 349-362.

Davison, G.C., Haaga, D.A., Rosenbaum, J., Dolezal, S.L., & Weinstein, K.A. (1991). Assessment of self-efficacy in articulated thoughts: "States of Mind" analysis and association with speech anxious behavior. *Journal of Cognitive Psychotherapy: An International Quarterly, 5,* 83-92.

Davison, G.C., Navarre, S.G., & Vogel, R.S. (1995). The articulated thoughts in simulated situations paradigm: A think-aloud approach to cognitive assessment. *Current Directions in Psychological Science, 4,* 29-33.

Davison, G.C., Robins, C., & Johnson, M.K. (1983). Articulated thoughts during simulated situations: A paradigm for studying cognition in emotion and behavior. *Cognitive Therapy and Research, 7,* 17-40.

Davison, G.C., Tsujimoto, R.N., & Glaros, A.G. (1973). Attribution and the maintenance of behavior change in falling asleep. *Journal of Abnormal Psychology, 82,* 124-133.

Davison, G.C., Williams, M.E., Nezami, E., Bice, T.L., & DeQuattro, V. (1991). Relaxation, reduction in angry articulated thoughts, and improvements in borderline essential hypertension and heart rate. *Journal of Behavioral Medicine, 14,* 453-468.

Dawes, R.M. (1994). *House of cards: Psychology and psychotherapy built on myth.* New York: Free Press.

Dawson, G., & Lewy, A. (1989). Reciprocal subcortical-cortical influences in autism. In G. Dawson (Ed.), *Autism: Nature, diagnosis, and treatment* (pp. 144-173). New York: Guilford.

Dawson, M.E., Schell, A.M., & Banis, H.T. (1986). Greater resistance to extinction of electrodermal responses conditioned to potentially phobic CSs: A noncognitive process? *Psychophysiology, 23,* 552-561.

Deacon, S., Minichiello, V., & Plummer, D. (1995). Sexuality and older people: Revisiting the assumptions. *Educational Gerontology, 21,* 497-513.

DeAraujo, L.A., Ito, L.M., Marks, I.M., & Deale, A. (1995). Does imaginal exposure to the consequences of not ritualizing enhance live exposure for OCD? A controlled study: I. Main outcome. *British Journal of Psychiatry, 167,* 65-70.

Deep, A.L., Lilenfeld, L.R., Plotnicov, K.H., Pollice, C., & Kaye, W.H. (1999). Sexual abuse in eating disorder subtypes and control women: The role of cormorbid substance dependence in bulimia nervosa. *International Journal of Eating Disorders, 25,* 1-10.

DeJong, W., & Kleck, R.E. (1986). The social psychological effects of overweight. In C.P. Herman, M.P. Zanna, & E.T. Higgins (Eds.), *Physical appearance, stigma, and social behavior.* Hillside, NJ: Erlbaum.

Delgado, P.L., Charney, D.S., Price, L.H., Aghajanian, G.K., Landis, H., et al. (1990). Serotonin function and the mechanism of antidepressant action: Reversal of antidepressant induced remission by rapid depletion of plasma tryptophan. *Archives of General Psychiatry, 47,* 411-418.

deLint, J. (1978). Alcohol consumption and alcohol problems from an epidemiological perspective. *British Journal of Alcohol and Alcoholism, 17,* 109-116.

DeLisi, L.E., Shaw, S.H., Crow, T.J. et al. (2002). A genome-wide scan for linkage to chromosomal regions in 382 sibling pairs with schizophrenia or schizoaffective disorder. *American Journal of Psychiatry, 159,* 803-812.

Dement, W.C., Laughton, E., & Carskadon, M.A. (1981). "White paper" on sleep and aging. *Journal of the American Geriatrics Society, 30*, 25-50.

Denollet, J., & Brutsaert, D.L. (1998). Personality, disease severity, and the risk of long-term cardiac events in patients with a decreased ejection fraction after myocardial infarction. *Circulation, 97*, 167-173.

Depression Guideline Panel. (1997). *Depression in primary care: Detection and diagnosis.* Rockville, MD: U.S. Department of Health and Human Services.

Dershowitz, A. (1994a, May 15). "Abuse Excuse" du jour victimizes many. *Los Angeles Times,* pp. B5.

Dershowitz, A. (1994b). *The abuse excuse and other cop-outs, sob stories, and evasions of responsibility.* Boston: Little Brown.

DeRubeis, R.J., & Crits-Christoph, P. (1998). Empirically supported individual and group psychological treatments for adult mental disorders. *Journal of Consulting and Clinical Psychology, 66*, 37-52.

DeRubeis, R.J., Gelfand, L.A., Tang, T.Z., & Simons, A.D. (1999). Medications versus cognitive behavior therapy for severely depressed outpatients: MegaAnalysis of four randomized comparisons. *American Journal of Psychiatry, 156*, 1007-1013.

DeRubeis, R.J., Hollon, S.D., Evans, M.D., & Bemis, K.M. (1982). Can psychotherapies for depression be discriminated? A systematic investigation of cognitive therapy and interpersonal therapy. *Journal of Consulting and Clinical Psychology, 50*, 744-760.

Detterman, D.K. (1979). Memory in the mentally retarded. In N.R. Ellis (Ed.), *Handbook of mental deficiency, psychological theory and research* (2nd ed.). Hillsdale, NJ: Erlbaum.

Deutsch, A. (1949). *The mentally ill in America.* New York: Columbia University Press.

Devilly, G.J., Spence, S., & Rapee, R. (1998). Statistical and reliable change with eye movement desensitization and reprocessing: Treating trauma within a veteran population. *Behavior Therapy, 29*, 435-455.

Devine, V., Adelson, R., Goldstein, J., Valins, S., & Davison, G.C. (1974). Controlled test of the analgesic and relaxant properties of nitrous oxide. *Journal of Dental Research, 53*, 486-490.

DeVries, H.A. (1975). Physiology of exercise and aging. In D.S. Woodruff & J.E. Birren (Eds.), *Aging: Scientific perspectives and social issues.* New York: Van Nostrand-Reinhold.

Dew, M.A., Bromet, E.J., Brent, D., & Greenhouse, J.B. (1987). A quantitative literature review of the effectiveness of suicide prevention centers. *Journal of Consulting and Clinical Psychology, 55*, 239-244.

Dewys, W.D., Begg, C., & Lavin, P.T. (1980). Prognostic effect of weight loss prior to chemotherapy in cancer patients. *American Journal of Medicine, 69*, 491-497.

Diaferia, P., Bianchi, I., Bianchi, M.L., Cavedini, P., et al. (1997). Relationship between obsessive-compulsive personality disorder and obsessive-compulsive disorder. *Comprehensive Psychiatry, 38*, 38-42.

Diamond, S., Baldwin, R., & Diamond, R. (1963). *Inhibition and choice.* New York: Harper & Row.

Dickerson, F.B. (2000). Cognitive behavioral psychotherapy for schizophrenia: A review of recent empirical studies. *Schizophrenia Research, 43*, 71-90.

Dickey, C.C., McCarley, R.W., Volgmaier, M.M., Niznikiewicz, M.A., Seidman, L.J., et al. (1999). Schizotypal personality disorder and MRI abnormalities of temporal grey matter. *Biological Psychiatry, 45*, 1392-1402.

DiClemente, C.C. (1993). Changing addictive behaviors: A process perspective. *Current Directions in Psychological Science, 2*, 101-106.

DiClemente, R.J., Forrest, K.A., Mickler, S., & Principal Site Investigators. (1990). College students' knowledge and attitudes about AIDS and changes in HIV-preventive behaviors. *AIDS Education and Prevention, 2*, 201-212.

Didion, J. (1979). *The white album.* New York: Simon & Schuster.

Dietz, P.E., Hazelwood, R.R., & Warren, J. (1990). The sexually sadistic criminal and his offenses. *Bulletin of the American Academy of Psychiatry and the Law, 18*, 163-178.

DiFranza, J.R., Richards, J.W., Paulman, P.M., Wolf-Gillespie, N., Fletcher, C., et al. (1991). RJR Nabisco's cartoon camel promotes Camel cigarettes to children. *Journal of the American Medical Association, 266*, 3149-3153.

DiMaggio, C., Martinez, M., Menard, J.-F. (2001). Evidence of a cohort effect for age of onset of schizophrenia. *American Journal of Psychiatry, 158*, 489-492.

DiMascio, A., Weissman, M.M., Prusoff, B.A., Neu, C., Zwilling, M., & Klerman, G.L. (1979). Differential symptom reduction by drugs and psychotherapy in acute depression. *Archives of General Psychiatry, 36*, 1450-1456.

DiNardo, P.A., Guzy, L.T., Jenkins, J.A., Bak, R.M., Tomasi, S.F., & Copland, M. (1988). Etiology and maintenance of dog fears. *Behaviour Research and Therapy, 26*, 241-244.

DiNardo, P.A., O'Brien, G.T., Barlow, D.H., Waddell, M.T., & Blanchard, E.B. (1993). Reliability of the DSM-III-R anxiety disorders categories using the Anxiety Disorders Interview Schedule-Revised (ADIS-R). *Archives of General Psychiatry, 50*, 251-256.

Dinn, W.M. & Harris, C.L. (2000). Neurocognitive function in antisocial personality disorder. *Psychiatry Research, 97*, 173-190.

Dixon, L., Scott, J., Lyles, A., Fahey, A., Skinner, A., & Shore, A. (1997). Adherence to schizophrenia PORT family treatment recommendations. *Schizophrenia Research, 24*, 221.

Dobson, K.S. (1989). A meta-analysis of the efficacy of cognitive therapy for depression. *Journal of Consulting and Clinical Psychology, 57*, 414-419.

Dobson, K.S., & Jackman-Cram, S. (1996). Common change processes in cognitive-behavioral therapies. In K.S. Dobson & K.D. Craig (Eds.), *Advances in cognitive-behavioral therapy* (pp. 63-82). Thousand Oaks, CA: Sage Publications.

Dobson, K.S., & Shaw, B.F. (1986). Cognitive assessment with major depressive disorders. *Cognitive Therapy and Research, 10*, 13-29.

Dodge, K.A., & Coie, J.D. (1987). Social information-processing factors in reactive and proactive aggression in children's peer groups. *Journal of Personality and Social Psychology, 53*, 1146-1158.

Dodge, K.A., & Frame, C.L. (1982). Social cognitive biases and deficits in aggressive boys. *Child Development, 53*, 620-635.

Doerr, P., Fichter, M., Pirke, K.M., & Lund, R. (1980). Relationship between weight gain and hypothalamic-pituitary-adrenal function in patients with anorexia nervosa. *Journal of Steroid Biochemistry, 13*, 529-537.

Dohrenwend, B.P., Levav, P.E., Schwartz, S., Naveh, G., Link, B.G., Skodol, A.E., & Stueve, A. (1992). Socioeconomic status and psychiatric disorders: The causation-selection issue. *Science, 255*, 946-952.

Dolan, B. (1991). Cross-cultural aspects of anorexia and bulimia: A review. *International Journal of Eating Disorders, 10*, 67-78.

Dolder, C.R. Lacro, J.P., Dunn, L.B., & Jeste, D.V. (2002). Antipsychotic medication adherence: Is there a difference between typical and atypical agents? *American Journal of Psychiatry, 159*, 103-108.

Dollard, J., & Miller, N.E. (1950). *Personality and psychotherapy.* New York: McGraw-Hill.

Dougher, M.J. (1988). Clinical assessment of sex offenders. In B.K. Schwartz (Ed.), *A practitioner's guide to treating the incarcerated male sex offender* (pp. 77-84). Washington, DC: U.S. Department of Justice.

Dougherty, D.D., Baer, L., Cosgrove, G.R. et al. (2002). Prospective long-term follow-up opf 44 patients who received cingulotomy for treatment of refractory obsessive-compulsive disorder. *American Journal of Psychiatry, 159*, 269-275.

Dowd, J.J., & Bengston, V.L. (1978). Aging in minority populations: An examination of the double jeopardy hypothesis. *Journal of Gerontology, 33*, 427-436.

Downhill, J.E., Buchsbaum, M.S., Hazlett, E.A. et al. (2001). Temporal lobe volume determined by magnetic resonance imaging in schizotypal personality disorder and schizophrenia. *Schizophrenia Research, 48*, 187-199.

Dowson, J.H. (1992). Associations between self-induced vomiting and personality disorder in patients with a history of anorexia nervosa. *Acta Psychiatrica Scandinavica, 86*, 399-404.

Draguns, J.G. (1989). Normal and abnormal behavior in cross-cultural perspective: Specifying the nature of their relationships. In J.J. Berman (Ed.), *Nebraska symposium on motivation.* Lincoln: University of Nebraska Press.

Drug Enforcement Adinistration (2001). *Working to prevent the diversion and abuse of Oxycontin.* Drug Enforcement Administration, Office of Diversion Control, June 12, 2001.

Drummond, T. (1999, June 7). Never too old: Sexually active seniors are one of the fastest-growing HIV-infected populations in the U.S. *Time, 84H.*

Drury, V., Birchwood, M., Cochrane, R., & Macmillan, R. (1996). Cognitive therapy and recovery from acute psychosis: A controlled trial. *British Journal of Psychiatry, 169*, 593-601.

Dubbert, P. (1995). Behavioral (life style) modification in the prevention and treatment of hypertension. *Clinical Psychology Review, 15*, 187-216.

Duck, S. (1984). A perspective on the repair of personal relationships. In S. Duck (Ed.), *Personal relationships: 5. Repairing personal relationships.* New York: Academic Press.

Duggan, C.E., Marks, I., & Richards, D. (1993). Clinical audit of behavior therapy training of nurses. *Health Trends, 25*, 25-30.

Duggan, C.F., Lee, A.S., & Murray, R.M. (1991). Do different subtypes of hospitalized depressives have different long term outcomes? *Archives of General Psychiatry, 48*, 308-312.

Duke, M.P. (1994). Chaos theory and psychology: Seven propositions. *Genetic, Social, & General Psychology Monographs, 120*, 267-286.

Dunham, H.W. (1965). *Community and schizophrenia: An epidemiological analysis.* Detroit: Wayne State University Press.

Dunn, A.L., Marcus, B.H., Kampert, J.B., Garcia, M.E., et al. (1999). Comparison of lifestyle and structured interventions to increase physical activity and cardiorespiratory fitness. *JAMA, 281*, 327-324.

DuPaul, G.J. & Henningson, P.N. (1993). Peer tutoring effects on the classroom performance of children with attention deficit hyperactivity disorder. *School Psychology Review, 22*, 134-143.

DuPaul, G.J. (1991). Parent and teacher ratings of ADHD symptoms: Psychometric properties in a community-based sample. *Journal of Clinical Child Psychology, 20*, 245-253.

Dura, J.R., Stukenberg, K.W., & Kiecolt-Glaser, J.K. (1991). Anxiety and depressive disorders in adult children caring for demented parents. *Psychology and Aging, 6*, 467-473.

Durkheim, E. (1951). *Suicide.* (J.A. Spaulding & G. Simpson, Trans.). New York: Free Press. (Original work published 1897; 2nd ed., 1930)

Durkin, K.L. (1997). Misuse of the internet by pedophiles: Implications for law enforcement and probation practice. *Federal Probation, 61*, 14-18.

duVerglas, G., Banks, S.R., & Guyer, K.E. (1988). Clinical effects of fenfluramine on children with autism: A review of the research. *Journal of Autism and Developmental Disorders, 18*, 297-308.

Dvoskin, J.A., & Steadman, H.J. (1994). Using intensive case management to reduce violence by mentally ill persons in the community. *Hospital and Community Psychiatry, 45*, 679-684.

Dwork, A.J. (1997). Postmortem studies of the hippocampal formation in schizophrenia. *Schizophrenia Bulletin, 23*, 385-402.

Dworkin, R.H., & Lenzenwenger, M.F. (1984). Symptoms and the genetics of schizophrenia: Implications for diagnosis. *American Journal of Psychiatry, 141*, 1541-1546.

Dworkin, R.H., Lenzenwenger, M.F., & Moldin, S.O. (1987). Genetics and the phenomenology of schizophrenia. In P.D. Harvey and E.F. Walker (Eds.), *Positive and negative symptoms of psychosis.* Hillsdale, NJ: Erlbaum.

Dykens, E., Leckman, J., Paul, R., & Watson, M. (1988). Cognitive, behavioral, and adaptive functioning in fragile X and non-fragile A retarded men. *Journal of Autism and Developmental Disorders, 18*, 41-52.

Dysken, M.W. (1979). Clinical usefulness of sodium amobarbital interviewing. *Archives of General Psychiatry, 36*, 789-794.

Eagles, J.M., Johnston, M.I., Hunter, D., Lobban, M., & Millar, H.R. (1995). Increasing incidence of anorexia nervosa in the female population of northeast Scotland. *American Journal of Psychiatry, 152*, 1266-1271.

Eaker, E.D., Pinsky, J., & Castelli, W.P. (1992). Myocardial infarction and coronary death among women: Psychosocial predictors from a 20 year follow-up of women in the Framingham study. *American Journal of Epidemiology, 135*, 854-864.

Earleywine, M., & Gann, M.K. (1995). Challenging recovered memories in the courtroom. In J. Ziskin (Ed.), *Coping with psychiatric and psychological testimony* (pp. 1100-1134). Los Angeles: Law and Psychology Press.

Eastwood, M.R., Corbin, S., Reed, M., Nobbs, H., & Kedward, M.B. (1985). Acquired hearing loss and psychiatric illness: An estimate of prevalence and co-morbidity in a geriatric setting. *British Journal of Psychiatry, 147*, 552.

Eaton, W.W., Kramer, M., Anthony, J.C., Dryman, A., Shapiro, S., et al. (1989). The incidence of specific DIS/DSM-III mental disorders: Data from the NIMH Epidemiologic Catchment Area Programs. *Acta Psychiatrica Scandinavica, 79*, 163-178.

Eccleston, C. (1995). Chronic pain and distraction: An experimental investigation into the role of sustained and shifting attention in the processing of chronic persistent pain. *Behaviour Research and Therapy, 33*, 391-406.

Eckhardt, C.I., Barbour, K.A., & Stuart, G.L. (1997). Anger and hostility in maritally violent men: Conceptual distinctions, measurement issues, and literature review. *Clinical Psychology Review, 17*, 333-358.

Edelbrock, C., Rende, R., Plomin, T., & Thompson, L.A. (1995). A twin study of competence and problem behavior in childhood and early adolescence. *Journal of Child Psychology and Psychiatry and Allied Disciplines, 36*, 775-789.

Eden, G.F., & Zeffiro, T.A. (1996). PET and fMRI in the detection of task-related brain activity: Implications for the study of brain development. In R.W. Thatcher & G.R. Lyon (Eds.), *Developmental neuroimaging: Mapping the development of brain and behavior* (pp. 77-90). San Diego, CA: Academic Press.

Eden, G.F., Stein, J.F., Wood, H.M., & Wood, F.B. (1995). Temporal and spatial processing in reading disabled and normal children. *Cortex, 31*, 451-468.

Egan, G. (1975). *The skilled helper.* Monterey, CA: Brooks/Cole.

Egan, T. (1990). As memory and music faded, Alzheimer patient met death. *The New York Times, 89*, A1, A16.

Egeland, J.A., Gerhard, D.S., Pauls, D.L., Sussex, J.N., Kidd, K.K., Allen, C.R., Hosterer, A.M., & Housman, D.E. (1987). Bipolar affective disorders linked to DNA markers on chromosome 11. *Nature, 325*, 783-787.

Ehlers, A., Mayou, R.A., & Bryant, B. (1998). Psychological predictors of chronic posttraumatic stress disorder after motor vehicle accidents. *Journal of Abnormal Psychology, 107*, 508-519.

Ehrhardt, A., & Money, J. (1967). Progestin-induced hermaphroditism: IQ and psychosexual identity in a study of ten girls. *Journal of Sex Research, 3*, 83-100.

Eiberg, H., Berendt, I., & Mohr, J. (1995). Assignment of dominant inherited nocturnal enuresis to chromosome 13Q. *Nature Genetics, 10*, 354-356.

Eich, E. (1995). Searching for mood-dependent memory. *Psychological Science, 6*, 67-75.

Eich, E., Macaulay, D., Loewenstein, R.J., & Dihle, P.H. (1997). Memory, identity, and dissociative identity disorder. *Psychological Science, 8*, 417-422.

Eisen, J.L., Phillips, K.A., Baer, L., Beer, D.A., Atala, K.D., & Rasmussen, S.A. (1998). The Brown Assessment of Beliefs Scale: Reliability and validity. *American Journal of Psychiatry, 155*, 102-108.

Eiser, C., Eiser, R.J., Town, C., & Tripp, J. (1991). Discipline strategies and parental perceptions of preschool children with asthma. *British Journal of Medical Psychology, 64*, 45-53.

Eisler, R.M., & Blalock, J.A. (1991). Masculine gender role stress: Implications for the assessment of men. *Clinical Psychology Review, 11*, 45-60.

Eissenberg, T., Bigelow, G.E., Strain, E.C., & Walsh, S.L. (1997). Dose-related efficacy of levomethadyl acetate for treatment of opioid dependence. *JAMA, 277*, 1945-1951.

Elias, M., & Clabby, J.F. (1989). *Social decision making skills: A curriculum for the elementary grades.* Rockville, MD: Aspen Publishers.

Elkin, I. (1994). Treatment of Depression Collaborative Research Program: Where we began and where we are. In A.E. Bergin & S.L. Garfield (Eds.), *Handbook of psychotherapy and behavior change* (4th ed., pp. 114-139). New York: Wiley & Sons.

Elkin, I., Gibbons, R.D., Shea, M.T., & Shaw, B.F. (1996). Science is not a trial (but it can sometimes be a tribulation). *Journal of Consulting and Clinical Psychology, 64*, 92-103.

Elkin, I., Gibbons, R.D., Shea, M.T., Sotsky, S.M., Watkins, J.T., Pilkonis, P.A., & Hedeker, D. (1995). Initial severity and differential treatment outcome in the NIMH Treatment of Depression Collaborative Research Program. *Journal of Consulting and Clinical Psychology, 63*, 841-847.

Elkin, I., Parloff, M.B., Hadley, S.W., & Autry, J.H. (1985). NIMH Treatment of Depression Collaborative Research Program. *Archives of General Psychiatry, 42*, 305-316.

Elkin, I., Shea, M.T., Watkins, J.T., Imber, S.D., Sotsky, S.M., Collins, J.F., Glass, D.R., Pilkonis, P.A., Leber, W.R., Docherty, J.P., Fiester, S.J., & Parloff, M.B. (1989). NIMH Treatment of Depression Collaborative Research Program: 1. General effectiveness of treatments. *Archives of General Psychiatry, 46*, 971-983.

Elkin, I., Shea, T., Imber, S., Pilkonis, P., Sotsky, S., Glass, D., Watkins, J., Leber, W., & Collins, J. (1986). *NIMH Treatment of Depression Collaborative Research Program: Initial outcome findings.* Paper presented to the American Association for the Advancement of Science.

Elkis, H., Friedman, L., Wise, A., & Meltzer, H.T. (1995). Meta-analysis of studies of ventricular enlargement and cortical sulcal prominence in mood disorders. *Archives of General Psychiatry, 52*, 735-746.

Ellason, J.W., & Ross, C.A. (1997). Two-year follow-up of inpatients with dissociative identity disorder. *American Journal of Psychiatry, 154*, 832-839.

Ellenberger, H.F. (1972). The story of "Anna O": A critical review with new data. *Journal of the History of the Behavioral Sciences, 8*, 267-279.

Ellis, A. (1962). *Reason and emotion in psychotherapy*. New York: Lyle Stuart.

Ellis, A. (1984). Rational-emotive therapy. In R.J. Corsini (Ed.), *Current psychotherapies* (3rd ed.). Itasca, IL: Peacock Press.

Ellis, A. (1991). The revised ABC's of rational-emotive therapy (RET). *Journal of Rational-Emotive and Cognitive Behavior Therapy, 9*, 139-172.

Ellis, A. (1993a). Changing rational-emotive therapy (RET) to rational emotive behavior therapy (REBT). *The Behavior Therapist, 16*, 257-258.

Ellis, A. (1993b). Fundamentals of rational-emotive therapy for the 1990s. In W. Dryden & L. Hill (Eds.), *Innovations in rational-emotive therapy*. Newbury Park, CA: Sage.

Ellis, A. (1995). Changing rational-emotive therapy (RET) to rational emotive behavior therapy (REBT). *Journal of Rational-Emotive and Cognitive Behavior Therapy, 13*, 85-89.

Ellis, J.A. & Spanos, N.P. (1994). Cognitive-behavioral interventions for children's distress during bone marrow aspirations and lumbar punctures: A critical review. *Journal of Pain and Symptom Management, 9*, 96-108.

Ellis, N.R., Deacon, J.R., & Wooldridge, P.W. (1985). Structural memory deficits of mentally retarded persons. *American Journal of Mental Deficiency, 89*, 393-402.

Ellis, R.J., Jan, K., Kawas, C., Koller, W.C., Lyons, K.E., et al. (1998). Diagnostic validity of the Questionnaire for Alzheimer's Disease. *Archives of Neurology, 55*, 360-365.

Elmore, A.M., & Tursky, B. (1978). The biofeedback hypothesis: An idea in search of a theory and method. In A.A. Sugerman & R.E. Tarter (Eds.), *Expanding dimensions of consciousness*. New York: Springer.

Elmore, J.L., & Sugerman, A.A. (1975). Precipitation of psychosis during electroshock therapy. *Diseases of the Nervous System, 3*, 115-117.

EMDR Institute (1995). *International EMDR conference: Research and clinical application*. Pacific Grove, CA: Author.

EMDR Institute (1998). Promotional advertisement. *APA Monitor, 28*, 65.

Emery, R.E., & O'Leary, K.D. (1979). *Children's perceptions of marital discord and behavior problems of boys and girls*. Paper presented at the annual meeting of the Association for Advancement of Behavior Therapy, San Francisco.

Emmelkamp, P.M.G. (1986). Behavior therapy with adults. In S.L. Garfield & A.E. Bergin (Eds.), *Handbook of psychotherapy and behavior change* (3rd ed.). New York: Wiley.

Emmelkamp, P.M.G., & Beens, H. (1991). Cognitive therapy with obsessive-compulsive disorder. *Behaviour Research and Therapy, 29*, 293-300.

Emmelkamp, P.M.G., Visser, S., & Hoekstra, R.J. (1988). Cognitive therapy versus exposure in vivo in the treatment of obsessive-compulsives. *Cognitive Therapy and Research, 12*, 103-114.

Emmons, R.A., & Diener, E. (1986). Situation selection as a moderator of response consistency and stability. *Journal of Personality and Social Psychology, 51*, 1013-1019.

Emory, L.E., Williams, D.H., Cole, C.M., Amparo, E.G., & Meyer, W.J. (1991). Anatomic variation of the corpus callosum in persons with gender dysphoria. *Archives of Sexual Behavior, 20*, 409-417.

Emrick, C.D., Tonigan, J.S., Montgomery, H., & Little, L. (1993). Alcoholics Anonymous: What is currently known? In B.S. McCrady & W.R. Miller (Eds.), *Research on Alcoholics Anonymous: Opportunities and alternatives* (pp. 41-76). New Brunswick, NJ: Rutgers Center of Alcohol Studies.

Emslie, G.J., Rush, J., Weinberg, W.A., Kowatch, R.A., Hughes, C.W., et al. (1997). A double-blind randomized, placebo-controlled trial of fluoxetine in children and adolescents with depression. *Archives of General Psychiatry, 54*, 1031-1037.

Engdahl, B., Dikel, T.N., Eberly, R., & Blank, A. (1997). Posttraumatic stress disorder in a community group of former prisoners of war: A normative response to severe trauma. *American Journal of Psychiatry, 154*, 1576-1581.

Engels, G.I., Garnefski, N., & Diekstra, R.F.W. (1993). Efficacy of rational-emotive therapy: A quantitative analysis. *Journal of Consulting and Clinical Psychology, 61*, 1083-1090.

English, H.B. (1929). Three cases of the "conditioned fear response." *Journal of Abnormal and Social Psychology, 34*, 221-225.

Enright, J.B. (1970). An introduction to Gestalt techniques. In J. Fagan & I.L. Shepherd (Eds.), *Gestalt therapy now: Theory, techniques, applications*. Palo Alto, CA: Science & Behavior Books.

Enserink, M. (1999). Drug therapies for depression: From MAO inhibitors to substance. *Science, 284*, 239.

Epling, W.F., & Pierce, W.D. (1992). *Solving the anorexia puzzle*. Toronto, Can.: Hogrefe & Huber.

Epping-Jordan, J.E., Compas, B.E., & Howell, D.C. (1994). Predictors of cancer progression in young adult men and women: Avoidance, intrusive thoughts, and psychological symptoms. *Health Psychology, 13*, 539-547.

Epstein, L.C., & Lasagna, L. (1969). Obtaining informed consent. *Archives of Internal Medicine, 123*, 682-688.

Epstein, L.H., Beck, S., Figneroa, J., Farkas, G., Kazdin, A.E., Danema, D., & Becker, D. (1981). The effects of point economy and parent management on urine glucose and metabolic control in children with insulin dependent diabetes. *Journal of Applied Behavior Analysis, 14*, 365-375.

Epstein, L.H., Masek, B.J., & Marshall, W.R. (1978). A nutritionally based school program for control of eating in obese children. *Behavior Therapy, 9*, 766-788.

Epstein, L.H., Wing, R.R., Thompson, J.K., & Griffen, W. (1980). Attendance and fitness in aerobics exercise: The effects of contract and lottery procedures. *Behavior Modification, 4*, 465-479.

Epstein, S. (1979). The stability of behavior: On predicting most of the people much of the time. *Journal of Personality and Social Psychology, 37*, 1097-1126.

Erdberg, P., & Exner, J.E., Jr. (1984). Rorschach assessment. In G. Goldstein & M. Hersen (Eds.), *Handbook of psychological assessment*. New York: Pergamon.

Erlenmeyer-Kimling, L.E., & Cornblatt, B. (1987). The New York high-risk project: A follow-up report. *Schizophrenia Bulletin, 13*, 451-461.

Ernst, M., Liebenauer, L.L., King, A.C., Fitzgerald, G.A., Cohen, R.M., & Zametkin, A.J. (1994). Reduced brain metabolism in hyperactive girls. *Journal of the American Academy of Child and Adolescent Psychiatry, 33*, 858-868.

Escobar, J.I., Burnam, M.A., Karno, M., Forsythe, A., Golding, J.M., et al. (1987). Somatization in the community. *Archives of General Psychiatry, 44*, 713-720.

Esler, J., Julius, S., Sweifler, A., Randall, O., Harburg, E., Gardiner, H., & DeQuattro, V. (1977). Mild high-renin essential hypertension: A neurogenic human hypertension. *New England Journal of Medicine, 296*, 405-411.

Esman, A. (1989). Psychoanalysis in general psychiatry: Obsessive-compulsive disorder as a paradigm. *Journal of American Psychoanalytical Association, 37*, 319-336.

Esser, G., Schmidt, M.H., & Woerner, W. (1990). Epidemiology and course of psychiatric disorders in school-age children: Results of a longitudinal study. *Journal of Child Psychology and Psychiatry, 31*, 243-263.

Estes, C.L., Gerard, L., & Clarke, A. (1985). Women and the economics of aging. In B.B. Hess & E.W. Markson (Eds.), *Growing old in America: New perspectives on old age* (3rd ed., pp. 546-562). New Brunswick: Transaction Books.

Estes, C.L. (1995). Mental health services for the elderly: Key policy elements. In M. Gatz (Ed.), *Emerging issues in mental health and aging* (pp. 303-327). Washington, DC: American Psychological Association.

Etringer, B.D., Gregory, V.R., & Lando, H.A. (1984). Influence of group cohesion on the behavioral treatment of smoking. *Journal of Consulting and Clinical Psychology, 52*, 1080-1086.

Evanoff, A., & Newton, W.P. (1998). Treatment of premature ejaculation. *Journal of Family Practice, 46*, 280-281.

Evans, M.D., Hollon, S.D., DeRubeis, R.J., Piasecki, J.M., Grove, W.M., et al. (1992). Differential relapse following cognitive therapy, pharmacotherapy, and combined cognitive-pharmacotherapy for depression. *Archives of General Psychiatry, 49*, 802-808.

Evans, P.D., & Edgerton, N. (1990). Life events as predictors of the common cold. *British Journal of Medical Psychology, 64*, 35-44.

Evans, R.I., Rozelle, R.M., Maxwell, S.E., Raines, B.E., Dill, C.A., Guthrie, T.J., Henderson, A.H., & Hin, P.C. (1981). Social modelling films to deter smoking in adolescents: Results of a three-year field investigation. *Journal of Applied Psychology, 66*, 399-414.

Evashwick, C.J. (2001). Definition of the continuum of care. In C.J. Evashwick (Ed.), *The continuum of long-term care* (pp. 3-13). Albany, NY: Delmar.

Everett, F., Proctor, N., & Cartmell, B. (1989). Providing psychological services to American Indian children and families. In D.R. Atkinson, G. Morten, & D.W. Sue (Eds.), *Counseling American minorities* (3rd ed.). Dubuque, IA: W.C. Brown.

Everill, J.T., & Waller, G. (1995). Reported sexual abuse and eating psychopathology: A review of the evidence for a causal link. *International Journal of Eating Disorders, 18*, 1-11.

Everson, S.A., Kaplan, G.A., Goldberg, D.A., & Salonen, J.T. (1996). Anticipatory blood pressure response to exercise predicts future high blood pressure in middle-aged men, *Hypertension, 27*, 1059-1064.

Everson, S.A., Kauhanen, J., Kaplan, G.A., Goldberg, D.E., Julkunen, J., et al.

(1997). Hostility and increased risk of mortality and acute myocardial infarction: The mediating role of behavioral risk factors. *American Journal of Epidemiology, 146*, 142-152.

Exner, J.E. (1978). *The Rorschach: A comprehensive system: Vol. 2. Current research and advanced interpretation.* New York: Wiley.

Exner, J.E., Jr. (1986). *The Rorschach: A comprehensive system: Vol. 1. Basic foundations* (2nd ed.). New York: Wiley.

Eysenck, H.J. (1952). The effects of psychotherapy: An evaluation. *Journal of Consulting Psychology, 16*, 319-324.

Eysenck, H.J. (1975). Crime as destiny. *New Behaviour, 9*, 46-49.

Fairbank, J.A., & Brown, T.A. (1987). Current behavioral approaches to the treatment of posttraumatic stress disorder. *The Behavior Therapist, 3*, 57-64.

Fairbank, J.A., DeGood, D.E., & Jenkins, C.W. (1981). Behavioral treatment of a persistent post-traumatic startle response. *Journal of Behaviour Therapy and Experimental Psychiatry, 12*, 321-324.

Fairburn, C.G. (1985). Cognitive-behavioral treatment for bulimia. In D.M. Garner, & P.E. Garfinkel (Eds.), *Handbook of psychotherapy for anorexia nervosa and bulimia* (pp. 160-192). New York: Guilford.

Fairburn, C.G. (1997). Eating disorders. In D.M. Clark & C.G. Fairburn (Eds.), *Science and practice of cognitive behavior therapy* (pp. 209-243). New York: Oxford.

Fairburn, C.G., Agras, W.S., & Wilson, G.T. (1992). The research on the treatment of bulimia nervosa: Practical and theoretical implications. In G.H. Anderson & S.H. Kennedy (Eds.), *The biology of feast and famine: Relevance to eating disorders.* New York: Academic Press.

Fairburn, C.G., Cooper, Z., Doll, H.A., & Welch, S.L. (1999). Risk factors for anorexia nervosa: Three integrated case-control comparisons. *Archives of General Psychiatry, 56*, 468-478.

Fairburn, C.G., Jones, R., Peveler, R.C., Carr, S.J., Solomon, R.A., O'Connor, M.E., Burton, J., & Hope, R.A. (1991). Three psychological treatments for bulimia nervosa. *Archives of General Psychiatry, 48*, 463-469.

Fairburn, C.G., Jones, R., Peveler, R.C., Hope, R.A., & O'Connor, M.E. (1993). Psychotherapy and bulimia nervosa: The longer-term effects of interpersonal psychotherapy, behavior therapy, and cognitive therapy. *Archives of General Psychiatry, 50*, 419-428.

Fairburn, C.G., Marcus, M.D., & Wilson, G.T. (1993). Cognitive behaviour therapy for binge eating and bulimia nervosa: A comprehensive treatment manual. In C.G. Fairburn & G.T. Wilson (Eds.), *Binge eating: Nature, assessment, and treatment.* New York: Guilford.

Fairburn, C.G., Norman, P.A., Welch, S.L., O'Connor, M.E., Doll, H.A., & Peveler, R.C. (1995). A prospective study of outcome in bulimia nervosa and the long-term effects of three psychological treatments. *Archives of General Psychiatry, 52*, 304-312.

Fairburn, C.G., Peveler, R.C., Jones, R., Hope, R.A., & Doll, H.A. (1993). Predictors of twelve-month outcome in bulimia nervosa and the influence of attitudes to shape and weight. *Journal of Consulting and Clinical Psychology, 61*, 696-698.

Fairburn, C.G., Shafran, R., & Cooper, Z. (1999). A cognitive behavioural theory of anorexia nervosa. *Behaviour Research and Therapy, 37*, 1-13.

Fairburn, C.G., Welch, S.L., & Hay, P.J. (1993). The classification of recurrent overeating: The "binge eating disorder" proposal. *International Journal of Eating Disorders, 13*, 155-159.

Fairburn, C.G., Welch, S.L., Norman, P.A., O'Conner, M.E., & Doll, H.E. (1996). Bias and bulimia nervosa: How typical are clinic cases? *American Journal of Psychiatry, 153*, 386-391.

Fairweather, G.W. (Ed.). (1964). *Social psychology in treating mental illness: An experimental approach.* New York: Wiley.

Fairweather, G.W., Sanders, D.H., Maynard, H., & Cressler, D.L. (1969). *Community life for the mentally ill: An alternative to institutional care.* Chicago: Aldine-Atherton.

Falkner, B., Kusher, H., Oresti, G., & Angelakus, E.T. (1981). Cardiovascular characteristics in adolescents who develop essential hypertension. *Hypertension, 3*, 496-505.

Fallon, B. (1995). Intracavernous injection therapy for male erectile dysfunction. *Urological Clinics of North America, 22*, 833-845.

Fallon, B., Liebowitz, M.R., Salmon, E., Schieier, F.R., Jusino, C., Hollander, E., & Klein, D.F. (1998). Fluoxetine for hypochondriacal patients without major depression. *Journal of Clinical Psychopharmacology, 13*, 438-441.

Falloon, I.R.H., Boyd, J.L., McGill, C.W., Razani, J., Moss, H.B., & Gilderman, A.N.

(1982). Family management in the prevention of exacerbation of schizophrenia: A controlled study. *New England Journal of Medicine, 306*, 1437-1440.

Falloon, I.R.H., Boyd, J.L., McGill, C.W., Williamson, M., Razani, J., Moss, H.B., Gilderman, A.M., & Simpson, G.M. (1985). Family management in the prevention of morbidity of schizophrenia. *Archives of General Psychiatry, 42*, 887-896.

Faraone, S.V., Biederman, J., Chen, W.J., Milberger, S., Warburton, R., & Tsuang, M.T. (1995). Neuropsychological functioning among the nonpsychotic relatives of schizophrenic patients: A diagnostic efficiency analysis. *Journal of Abnormal Psychology, 104*, 286-304.

Faraone, S.V., Biederman, J., Jetton, J G., & Tsuang, M.T. (1997). Attention deficit disorder and conduct disorder: Longitudinal evidence for a family subtype. *Psychological Medicine, 27*, 291-300.

Faraone, S.V., Biederman, J., Weber, W., & Russell, R.L. (1998). Psychiatric, neuropsychological, and psychosocial features of DSM-IV subtypes of attention-deficit/hyperactivity disorder: Results from a clinically referred sample. *Journal of the American Academy of Child and Adolescent Psychiatry, 37*, 185-193.

Farber, N.B., Rubin, E.H., Newcomer, J.W. et al., (2000). Increased neurofibrillary tangle density in subjects with Alzheimer disease and psychosis. *Archives of General Psychiatry, 57*, 1165-1173.

Farina, A. (1976). *Abnormal psychology.* Englewood Cliffs, NJ: Prentice-Hall.

Farkas, G., & Rosen, R.C. (1976). The effects of alcohol on elicited male sexual response. *Studies in Alcohol, 37*, 265-272.

Farlow, M. (1997). Alzheimer's disease: Clinical implications of the apolipoprotein E genotype. *Neurology, 48, Supplement 6*, s30-s34.

Farquhar, J.W. (1991). The Stanford cardiovascular disease prevention programs. *Annals of the New York Academy of Sciences, 623*, 327-331.

Farquhar, J.W., Fortmann, S.P., Flora, J.A., & Maccoby, N. (1990). Methods of communication to influence behaviour. In W Holland, R. Detels, & G. Knox (Eds.), *Oxford textbook of public health* (2nd ed.). New York: Oxford University Press.

Farquhar, J.W., Fortmann, S.P., Flora, J.A., Taylor, B., Haskell, W.L., Williams, P.T., Maccoby, N , & Wood, P.D. (1990). Effects of communitywide education on cardiovascular disease risk factors: The Stanford Five-City Project. *Journal of the American Medical Association, 264*, 359-365.

Farris, E.J., Yeakel, E.H., & Medoff, H. (1945). Development of hypertension in emotional gray Norway rats after air blasting. *American Journal of Physiology, 144*, 331-333.

Fassinger, R.E. (1991). Counseling lesbian women and gay men. *The Counseling Psychologist, 19*, 157-176.

Fassinger, R.E. (1991). The hidden minority: Issues and challenges in working with lesbian women and gay men. *The Counseling Psychologist, 19*, 157-176.

Fassinger, R.E., & Richie, B.S. (1997). Sex matters: Gender and sexual orientation in training for multicultural competency. In D.B. Pope-Davis & H.L.K. Coleman (Eds.), *Multicultural counseling competencies: Assessment, education and training, and supervision* (pp. 83-110). Thousand Oaks, CA: Sage Publications.

Faustman, W.O., Bardgett, M., Faull, K.F., Pfefferman, A., & Cseransky, J.G. (1999). Cerebrospinal fluid glutamate inversely correlates with positive symptom severity in unmedicated male schizophrenic/ schizoaffective patients. *Biological Psychiatry, 45*, 68-75.

Fava, G.A., Zielezny, M., Savron, G., & Grandi, S. (1995). Long-term effects of behavioural treatment for panic disorder with agoraphobia. *British Journal of Psychiatry, 166*, 87-92.

Fava, M., Rosenbaum, J.F., Pava, J.A., McCarthy, M.K., et al. (1993). Anger attacks in unipolar depression. Part I. Clinical correlates and response to fluoxetine treatment. *American Journal of Psychiatry, 150*, 1158-1163.

Favaro, A., & Santonastaso, P. (1997). Suicidality in eating disorders: Clinical and psychological correlates. *Acta Psychiatrica Scandanavica, 95*, 508-514.

Fawcett, J., Epstein, P., Fiester, S.J., Elkin, I., & Autry, J.H. (1987). Clinical Management-Imipramine/placebo administration manual: NIMH Treatment of Depression Collaborative Research Program. *Psychopharmacology Bulletin, 23*, 309-324.

Febbraro, G.A.R., & Clum, G.A. (1998). Meta-analytic investigation of the effectiveness of self-regulatory components in the treatment of adult behavior problems. *Clinical Psychology Review, 18*, 143-161.

Fedora, O., Reddon, J.R., & Yeudall, L.T. (1986). Stimuli eliciting sexual arousal in genital exhibitionists: A possible clinical application. *Archives of Sexual Behavior, 15*, 417-427.

Feeley, M., DeRubeis, R. J., & Gelfand, L. A. (1999). The temporal relation of adherence and alliance to symptom change in cognitive therapy for depression. *Journal of Consulting and Clinical Psychology, 67*, 578-582.

Fein, D., Pennington, B., Markowitz, P., Braverman, M., & Waterhouse, L. (1986). Toward a neuropsychological model of infantile autism: Are the social deficits primary? *Journal of the American Academy of Child Psychiatry, 25*, 198-212.

Feingold, B.F. (1973). *Introduction to clinical allergy.* Springfield, IL: Charles C. Thomas.

Feinsilver, D.B., & Gunderson, J.G. (1972). Psychotherapy for schizophrenics—Is it indicated? *Schizophrenia Bulletin, 1*, 11-23.

Feldman, H.A., Goldstein, I., Hatzichristou, G., Krane, R.J., and McKinlay, J.B. (1994). Impotence and its medical and psychosocial correlates: Results of the Massachusetts male aging study. *Journal of Urology, 151*, 54-61.

Felner, R.D., Farber, S.S., & Primavera, J. (1983). Transition and stressful events: A model for primary prevention. In R.A. Felner, L.A. Jason, J.N. Mortisugu, & S.S. Farber (Eds.), *Preventive psychology: Theory, research, and practice* (pp. 199-229). New York: Pergamon.

Fenigstein, A. (1979). Self-consciousness, self-attention, and social interaction. *Journal of Personality and Social Psychology, 37*, 75-86.

Fenigstein, A., Scheier, M.F., & Buss, A.H. (1975). Public and private self-consciousness: Assessment and theory. *Journal of Consulting and Clinical Psychology, 43*, 522-527.

Fentiman, L.C. (1985). Guilty but mentally ill: The real verdict is guilty. *Boston College Law Review, 26*, 601-653.

Ferenczi, S. (1952). *First contributions to psychoanalysis.* New York: Brunner/Mazel.

Ferguson, K.J., & Spitzer, R.L. (1995). Binge eating disorder in a community-based sample of successful and unsuccessful dieters. *International Journal of Eating Disorders, 18*, 167-172.

Fergusson, D.M., Horwood, L.J., & Lynskey, M.T. (1993). Prevalence and comorbidity of DSM-III-R diagnoses in a birth cohort of 15 year olds. *Journal of the American Academy of Child and Adolescent Psychiatry, 32*, 1127-1134.

Ferster, C.B. (1961). Positive reinforcement and behavioral deficits of autistic children. *Child Development, 32*, 437-456.

Fichter, M.M., & Noegel, R. (1990). Concordance for bulimia nervosa in twins. *International Journal of Eating Disorders, 9*, 425-436.

Filipek, P.A., Semrud-Clikeman, M., Steingard, R.J., Renshaw, P.F., Kennedy, D.N., & Biederman, J. (1997). Volumetric MRI analysis comparing subjects having attention-deficit hyperactivity disorder with normal controls. *Neurology, 48*, 589-601.

Fillmore, K.M. (1987). Prevalence, incidence and chronicity of drinking patterns and problems among men as a function of age: A longitudinal and cohort analysis. *British Journal of Addiction, 82*, 77-83.

Fillmore, K.M., & Caetano, R. (1980, May 22). *Epidemiology of occupational alcoholism.* Paper presented at the National Institute on Alcohol Abuse and Alcoholism's Workshop on Alcoholism in the Workplace, Reston, VA.

Fils-Aime, M.L., Eckardt, M.J., George, D.T., Brown, G.L., Mefford, I., & Linnoila, M. (1996). Early-onset alcoholics have lower cerebrospinal fluid 5-hydroxyindoleacetic acid levels than late-onset alcoholics. *Archives of General Psychiatry, 53*, 211-216.

Finkelhor, D. (1979). *Sexually victimized children.* New York: Free Press.

Finkelhor, D. (1983). Removing the child—Prosecuting the offender in cases of sexual abuse: Evidence from the national reporting system for child abuse and neglect. *Child Abuse and Neglect, 7*, 195-205.

Finkelhor, D. (1993). Epidemiological factors in the clinical identification of child sexual abuse. *Child Abuse and Neglect, 17*, 67-70.

Finkelhor, D., Hotaling, G., Lewis, I.A., & Smith, C. (1990). Sexual abuse in a national survey of adult men and women: Prevalence, characteristics, and risk factors. *Child Abuse and Neglect, 14*, 19-28.

Finn, S.E. (1982). Base rates, utilities, and DSM-III: Shortcomings of fixed-rule systems of psychodiagnosis. *Journal of Abnormal Psychology, 91*, 294-302.

Finney, J.W., & Moos, R.H. (1998). Psychosocial treatments for alcohol use disorders. In P.E. Nathan & J.M. Gorman (Eds.), *A guide to treatments that work* (pp. 156-166). New York: Oxford University Press.

Fiore, J., Becker, J., & Coppel, D.B. (1983). Social network interactions: A buffer or a stress? *American Journal of Community Psychology, 11*, 423-439.

Fiore, M.C., Novotny, T.F., Pierce, J.P., Giovino, G.A., Hatziandreu, E.J., Newcomb, P.A., Surawicz, T.S., & Davis, R.M. (1990). Methods used to quit smoking in the United States: Do cessation programs help? *Journal of the American Medical Association, 263*, 2760-2765.

Fiore, M.C., Smith, S.S., Jorenby, D.E., & Baker, T.B. (1994). The effectiveness of the nicotine patch for smoking cessation: A meta-analysis. *Journal of the American Medical Association, 271*, 1940-1947.

First, M.B., Spitzer, R.L., Gibbon, M., & Williams, J.B. (1995). The Structured Clinical Interview for DSM-IIIR Personality Disorders (SCID-II): Part I: Description. *Journal of Personality Disorders, 9*, 83-91.

Fischer, M. (1971). Psychoses in the offspring of schizophrenic monozygotic twins and their normal co-twins. *British Journal of Psychiatry, 118*, 43-52.

Fischetti, M., Curran, J.P., & Wessberg, H.W. (1977). Sense of timing. *Behavior Modification, 1*, 179-194.

Fisher, J.E., & Noll, J.P. (1996). Anxiety disorders. In L.L. Carstensen, B.A. Edelstein, & L. Dornbrand (Eds.), *The practical handbook of clinical gerontology* (pp. 304-323). Thousand Oaks: Sage.

Fisher, J.E., Goy, E.R., Swingen, D.N., & Szymanski, J. (1994, November). *The functional context of behavioral disturbances in Alzheimer's disease patients.* Paper presented at the annual convention of the Association for Advancement of Behavior Therapy.

Fishler, K., Azen, C.G., Henderson, R., Friedman, E.G., & Koch, R. (1987). Psychoeducational findings among children treated for phenylketonuria. *American Journal of Mental Deficiency, 92*, 65-73.

Fishman, D.B. (1999). *The case for pragmatic psychology.* New York: NYU Press.

Fishman, D.B., Rodgers, F., & Franks, C.M. (Eds.). (1988). *Paradigms in behavior therapy: Present and promise* (pp. 254-293). New York: Springer.

Fiske, A., Kasl-Godley, J. E., & Gatz, M. (1998). Mood disorders in late life. In A. S. Bellack & M. Hersen (Eds.), *Comprehensive clinical psychology:* (Vol. 7, pp. 193-229). New York: Elsevier.

Fitts, S.N., Gibson, P., Redding, C.A., & Deiter, P.J. (1989). Body dysmorphic disorder: Implications for its validity as a DSM-III-R clinical syndrome. *Psychological Reports, 64*, 655-658.

Fitzgerald, R.V. (1973). *Conjoint marital therapy.* New York: Jason Aronson.

Fleming, C.M. (1992). American Indians and Alaska Natives: Changing societies past and present. In M.A. Orlandi, R. Weston, & L.G. Epstein (Eds.), *Cultural competence for evaluators: A guide for alcohol and other drug abuse prevention practitioners working with ethnic/racial communities (OSAP cultural competence series 1)* (pp. 147-171). Rockville, MD: U.S. Department of Health & Human Services.

Fleming, J.E., & Offord, D.R. (1990). Epidemiology of childhood depressive disorders: A critical review. *Journal of the American Academy of Child and Adolescent Psychiatry, 29*, 571-580.

Flor, H., & Birbaumer, N. (1993). Comparison of the efficacy of electromyographic biofeedback, cognitive-behavioral therapy, and conservative medical interventions in the treatment of chronic musculoskeletal pain. *Journal of Consulting and Clinical Psychology, 61*, 653-658.

Fluoxetine Bulimia Nervosa Collaborative Study Group. (1992). Fluoxetine in the treatment of bulimia nervosa: A multicenter, placebo-controlled, double blind trial. *Archives of General Psychiatry, 49*, 139-147.

Foa, E., Riggs, D.S., Marsie, E.D., & Yarczower, M. (1995). The impact of fear activation and anger on the efficacy of exposure treatment for posttraumatic stress disorder. *Behavior Therapy, 26*, 487-499.

Foa, E.B. & Franklin, M.E. (2001). Obsessive-compulsive disorder. In D.H. Barlow (Ed.), *Clinical Handbook of Psychological Disorders* (pp. 209-263). New York, NY: Guilford Press.

Foa, E.B. (1996). Psychological treatment for obsessive-compulsive disorder. In M.R. Mavissakalian & R.F. Prien (Eds.), *Long-term treatments of anxiety disorders* (pp. 285-309). Washington, DC: American Psychiatric Press.

Foa, E.B., & Kozak, M.J. (1986). Emotional processing of fear: Exposure to corrective information. *Psychological Bulletin, 99*, 20-35.

Foa, E.B., Feske, U., Murdock, T. B., Kozak, M.J., & McCarthy, P.R. (1991). Processing of threat-related information in rape victims. *Journal of Abnormal Psychology, 100*, 156-165.

Foa, E.B., Kozak, M.J., Steketee, G.S., & McCarthy, P.R. (1992). Treatment of depressive and obsessive-compulsive symptoms in OCD by imipramine and behavior therapy. *British Journal of Clinical Psychology, 31*, 279-292.

Foa, E.B., Steketee, G.S., & Ozarow, B.J. (1985). Behavior therapy with obsessive-compulsives: From theory to treatment. In M. Mavissakalian, S.M. Turner, & L. Michelson (Eds.), *Obsessive-compulsive disorder: Psychological and pharmacological treatment.* New York: Plenum.

Foa, E.B., Zinbarg, R., & Rothbaum, B.O. (1992). Uncontrollability and unpredictability in post-traumatic stress disorder: An animal model. *Psychological Bulletin, 112,* 218-238.

Fodor, I. (1978). *Phobias in women: Therapeutic approaches. In Helping women change: A guide for professional counseling.* New York: BMA Audio Cassette Program.

Folkman, S., & Lazarus, R.S. (1985). If it changes it must be a process: Study of emotions and coping during 3 stages of college examination. *Journal of Personality and Social Psychology, 48,* 150-170.

Folkman, S., Bernstein, L., & Lazarus, R.S. (1987). Stress processes and the misuse of drugs in older adults. *Psychology and Aging, 2,* 366-374.

Folks, D.G., Ford, C.V., & Regan, W.M. (1984). Conversion symptoms in a general hospital. *Psychosomatics, 25,* 285-295.

Follette, V.M. (1994). Acceptance and commitment in the treatment of incest survivors: A contextual approach. In S.C. Hayes, N.S. Jacobson, V.M. Follette, & M. Dougher (Eds.), *Acceptance and change: Content and context in psychotherapy.* Reno, NV: Context Press.

Folstein, S., & Rutter, M. (1977a). Genetic influences and infantile autism. *Nature, 265,* 726-728.

Folstein, S., & Rutter, M. (1977b). Infantile autism: A genetic study of 21 twin pairs. *Journal of Child Psychology and Psychiatry, 18,* 291-321.

Foong, J., Ridding, M., Cope, H., Mardsen, C.D., & Ron, M.A. (1997). Corticospinal function in conversion disorder. *Journal of Neuropsychiatry and Clinical Neurosciences, 9,* 302-303.

Ford, C.S., & Beach, F.A. (1951). *Patterns of sexual behavior.* New York: Harper.

Ford, C.V. (1995). Dimensions of somatization and hypochondriasis. Special Issue: Malingering and conversion reactions. *Neurological Clinics, 13,* 241-253.

Ford, C.V., & Folks, D.G. (1985). Conversion disorders: An overview. *Psychosomatics, 26,* 371-383.

Ford, D.H., & Urban, H.B. (1963). *Systems of psychotherapy: A comparative study.* New York: Wiley.

Fordyce, W.E. (1994). Pain and suffering: What is the unit? *Quality of Life Research: An International Journal of Quality of Life Aspects of Treatment, Care, and Rehabilitation, 3,* S51-S56.

Fordyce, W.E., Brockway, J.A., Bergman, J.A., & Spengler, D. (1986). Acute back pain: A control-group comparison of behavioral vs. traditional methods. *Journal of Behavioral Medicine, 9,* 127-140.

Forsyth, J.P., & Eifert, G.H. (1998). Reponse intensity in content-specific fear conditioning comparing 20% versus 13% CO2-enriched air as unconditioned stimuli. *Journal of Abnormal Psychology, 107,* 291-304.

Forsythe, W.I., & Redmond, A. (1974). Enuresis and spontaneous cure rate: Study of 1129 enuretics. *Archives of Disease in Childhood, 49,* 259-263.

Forth, A.E., & Hare, R.D. (1989). The contingent negative variation in psychopaths. *Psychophysiology, 26,* 676-682.

Foucault, M. (1965). *Madness and civilization.* New York: Random House.

Foulkes, S.H. (1964). *Therapeutic group analysis.* New York: International Universities Press.

Fowler, I.L., Carr, V.J., Carter, N.T., & Lewin, T.J. (1998). Patterns of current and lifetime substance use in schizophrenia. *Schizophrenia Bulletin, 24,* 443-455.

Foy, D.W., Resnick, H.S., Sipprelle, R.C., & Carroll, E.M. (1987). Premilitary, military, and postmilitary factors in the development of combat-related posttraumatic stress disorder. *The Behavior Therapist, 10,* 3-9.

Frances, A., Pincus, H.A., Widiger, T.A., Davis, W.W., & First, M.B. (1990). DSM-IV: Work in progress. *American Journal of Psychiatry, 147,* 1439-1448.

Frances, R., Franklin, J., & Flavin, D. (1986). Suicide and alcoholism. *Annals of the New York Academy of Science, 287,* 316-326.

Frank, E., & Kupfer, D.J. (1994). Maintenance therapy in depression: In reply. *Archives of General Psychiatry, 51,* 504-505.

Frank, E., & Spanier, C. (1995). Interpersonal psychotherapy for depression: Overview, clinical efficacy, and future directions. *Clinical Psychology: Science and Practice, 2,* 349-369.

Frank, E., Anderson, C., & Kupfer, D.J. (1976). Profiles of couples seeking sex therapy and marital therapy. *American Journal of Psychiatry, 133,* 559-562.

Frank, E., Anderson, C., & Rubenstein, D. (1978). Frequency of sexual dysfunctions in "normal" couples. *New England Journal of Medicine, 299,* 111-115.

Frank, E., Kupfer, D.J., Ehlers, C.L., & Monk, T.H. (1994). Interpersonal and social rhythm therapy for bipolar disorder: Integrating interpersonal and behavioral approaches. *The Behavior Therapist, 17,* 143.

Frank, E., Kupfer, D.J., Perel, J.M., Cornes, C., Jarrett, D.B., et al. (1990). Three-year outcomes for maintenance therapies in recurrent depression. *Archives of General Psychiatry, 47,* 1093-1099.

Frank, E., Kupfer, D.J., Wagner, E.F., McEachran, A.B., & Cornes, C. (1991). Efficacy of interpersonal psychotherapy as a maintenance treatment of recurrent depression: Contributing factors. *Archives of General Psychiatry, 48,* 1053-1059.

Frank, J.D. (1961). *Persuasion and healing.* Baltimore: Johns Hopkins University Press. Second edition, 1973; third edition, 1978.

Frank, J.D. (1971). Therapeutic factors in psychotherapy. *American Journal of Psychotherapy, 25,* 350-361.

Frank, J.D. (1976). Psychotherapy and the sense of mastery. In R.L. Spitzer & D.F. Klein (Eds.), *Evaluation of psychotherapies: Behavioral therapies, drug therapies and their interactions.* Baltimore: Johns Hopkins University Press.

Frank, J.D. (1982). Therapeutic components shared by all psychotherapies. In J.H. Harvey & M.M. Parks (Eds.), *The Master Lecture Series: Vol. 1. Psychotherapy research and behavior change* (pp. 73-122). Washington, DC: American Psychological Association.

Frankenhaeuser, M.U., Lundberg, M., Fredriksson, B., Melin, M., Thomisto, A., et al. (1989). Stress on and off the job as related to sex and occupational status in whitecollar workers. *Journal of Organizational Behavior, 10,* 321-346.

Frankl, V. (1959). *From death camp to existentialism.* Boston: Beacon.

Frankl, V. (1963). *Man's search for meaning.* New York: Washington Square.

Frankl, V. (1967). *Psychotherapy and existentialism.* New York: Simon & Schuster.

Franklin, J.C., Schiele, B.C., Brozerk, J., & Keys, A. (1948). Observations on human behavior in experimental semistarvation and rehabilitation. *Journal of Clinical Psychology, 4,* 28-45.

Franklin, M.E., & Foa, E.B. (1998). Cognitive-behavioral treatments for obsessive-compulsive disorder. In P.E. Nathan & J.M. Gorman (Eds.), *A guide to treatments that work* (pp. 339-357). New York: Oxford University Press.

Franklin, M.E., Abramowitz, J.S., Bux, D.A., Zoellner, L.A., & Fenny, N.C. (2000). *Exposure and ritual prevention with and without concomitant pharmacotherapy in the treatment of OCD.* Manuscript submitted for publication.

Franks, C.M., Wilson, G.T., Kendall, P.C., & Foreyt, J.P. (1990). *Review of behavior therapy: Theory and practice.* New York: Guilford.

Frazier, P.A. (1990). Victim attributions and post-rape trauma. *Journal of Personality and Social Psychology, 59,* 298-304.

Frederickson, B.L., & Carstensen, L.L. (1990). Choosing social partners: How old age and anticipated endings make people more selective. *Psychology and Aging, 5,* 335-347.

Freeman, A., & Reinecke, M.A. (1995). Cognitive therapy. In A.S. Gurman & S.B. Messer (Eds.), *Essential psychotherapies: Theory and practice.* New York: Guilford.

Freeman, V.G., Rathore, S.S., Weinfurt, K.P., Schulman, K.A., & Sulmasy, D.P. (1999). Lying for patients: Physician deception of third party payers. *Archives of Internal Medicine, 159,* 2263-2270.

French, S.A., Story, M., Neumark-Sztainer, D., Downes, B., Resnick, M., et al. (1997). Ethnic differences in psychosocial and health behavior correlates of dieting, purging, and binge eating in a population-based sample of adolescent females. *International Journal of Eating Disorders, 22,* 315-322.

Freud, A. (1946). *The ego and mechanisms of defense.* New York: International Universities Press.

Freud, A. (1966). *The ego and the mechanisms of defense.* New York: International Universities Press.

Freud, S. (1917). *Mourning and melancholia.* In Collected papers (Vol. 4). London: Hogarth and the Institute of Psychoanalysis, 1950.

Freud, S. (1937). Analysis terminable and interminable. *International Journal of Psychoanalysis, 18,* 373-391.

Freud, S. (1955). Lines of advance in psychoanalytic therapy. In *The complete psychological works of Sigmund Freud.* J. Strachey (Ed. and Trans.) London: Hogarth and the Institute of Psychoanalysis. (Original work published 1918)

Freud, S. (1956). Analysis of a phobia in a five-year-old boy. In *Collected works of Sigmund Freud (Vol. 10).* London: Hogarth. (Original work published 1909)

Freund, K. (1990). Courtship disorders. In W.L. Marshall, D.R. Laws, & H.E. Barbaree (Eds.), *Handbook of sexual assault: Issues, theories, and treatment* (pp. 195-207). NY: Plenum Press.

Freund, K., & Kuban, M. (1994). The basis of the abused abuser theory of pedophilia: A further elaboration on an earlier study. *Archives of Sexual Behavior, 23,* 553-563.

Fridell, S.R., Zucker, K.J., Bradley, S.J., & Maing, D.M. (1996). Physical attractiveness of girls with gender identity disorders. *Archives of Sexual Behavior, 25,* 17-31.

Friedman, J.M. (1978). Sexual adjustment of the postcoronary male. In J. LoPiccolo & L. LoPiccolo (Eds.), *Handbook of sex therapy*. New York: Plenum.

Friedman, J.M., & Hogan, D.R. (1985). Sexual dysfunction: Low sexual desire. In D.H. Barlow (Ed.), *Clinical handbook of psychological disorders*. New York: Guilford.

Friedman, M. (1969). *Pathogenesis of coronary artery disease*. New York: McGraw-Hill.

Friedman, M., & Ulmer, D. (1984). *Treating type A behavior and your heart*. New York: Fawcett Crest.

Friedman, M., Thoresen, C.E., Gill, J.J., Powell, L.H., Ulmer, D., Thompson, L., Price, V.A., Rabin, D.D., Breall, W.S., Dixon, T., Levy, R., & Bourg, E. (1984). Alteration of type A behavior and reduction in cardiac recurrences in postmyocardial infarction patients. *American Heart Journal, 108*, 237-248.

Friedman, M., Thoresen, C.E., Gill, J.J., Ulmer, D., Thompson, L., Powell, L., Price, A., Elek, S.R., Rabin, D.D., Breall, W.S., Piaget, G., Dixon, T., Bourg, E., Levy, R., & Tasto, D.I. (1982). Feasibility of altering type A behavior pattern after myocardial infarction. *Circulation, 66*, 83-92.

Friedman, R., & Dahl, L.K. (1975). The effects of chronic conflict on the blood pressure of rats with a genetic susceptibility to experimental hypertension. *Psychosomatic Medicine, 37*, 402-416.

Friend, R.A. (1991). Older lesbian and gay people: A theory of successful aging. *Journal of Homosexuality, 20*, 99-118.

Frisch, M.B., & Higgins, R.L. (1986). Instructional demand effects and the correspondence among role-play, self-report, and naturalistic measures of social skill. *Behavioral Assessment, 8*, 221-236.

Frith, U. (1989). *Autism: Explaining the enigma*. Cambridge, MA: Basil Blackwell.

Fromm-Reichmann, F. (1948). Notes on the development of treatment of schizophrenics by psychoanalytic psychotherapy. *Psychiatry, 11*, 263-273.

Fromm-Reichmann, F. (1952). Some aspects of psychoanalytic therapy with schizophrenics. In E. Brady & F.C. Redlich (Eds.), *Psychotherapy with schizophrenics*. New York: International Universities Press.

Fuller, R.K. (1988). Disulfiram treatment of alcoholism. In R.M. Rose & J.E. Barrett (Eds.), *Alcoholism: Treatment and Outcome*. New York: Raven.

Fuller, R.K., Branchey, L., Brightwell, D.R., Derman, R.M., Emrick, C.D., Iber, F.L., James, K.E., & Lacoursiere, R.B. (1986). Disulfiram treatment of alcoholism: A Veterans Administration cooperative study. *Journal of the American Medical Association, 256*, 1449-1455.

Furnham, A., & Baguma, P. (1994). Cross-cultural differences in the evaluation of male and female body shapes. *International Journal of Eating Disorders, 15*, 81-89.

Fyer, A.J., Sandberg, D., & Klein, D.F. (1991). The pharmacological treatment of panic disorder and agoraphobia. In J.R. Walker, G.R. Norton, & C.A. Ross (Eds.), *Panic disorder and agoraphobia: A comprehensive guide for the practitioner* (pp. 211-251). Belmont, CA: Brooks/Cole.

Gabbay, F.H. (1992). Behavior genetic strategies in the study of emotion. *Psychological Science, 3*, 50-55.

Gacono, C.B., Nieberding, R.J., Owen, A., Rubel, J., & Bodholt, K. (2001). Treating conduct disorder, antisocial, and psychopathic personalities. In J.B. Ashford, B.D. Sales, & W.H. Reid (Eds.), *Treating adult and juvenile offenders with special needs*. Washington, DC: American Psychological Association.

Gagnon, J.H. (1977). *Human sexualities*. Chicago: Scott, Foresman.

Gaines, J. (1974). The founder of Gestalt therapy: A sketch of Fritz Perls. *Psychology Today, 8*, 117-118.

Galaburda, A.M. (1989). Ordinary and extraordinary brain development: Anatomical variation in developmental dyslexia. *Annals of Dyslexia, 39*, 67-80.

Galaburda, A.M. (1993). Neuroanatomical basis of developmental dyslexia. *Neurologic Clinics, 11*, 161-173.

Galanter, M., & Castaneda, R. (1985). Self-destructive behavior in the substance abuser. *Psychiatric Clinics of North America, 8*, 251-261.

Gallagher, D., & Thompson, L.W. (1982). *Elders' maintenance of treatment benefits following individual psychotherapy for depression: Results of a pilot study and preliminary data from an ongoing replication study*. Paper presented at the annual meeting of the American Psychological Association, Washington, DC.

Gallagher, D., & Thompson, L.W. (1983). Cognitive therapy for depression in the elderly. A promising model for treatment and research. In L.D. Breslau & M.R. Haug (Eds.), *Depression and aging: Causes, care and consequences*. New York: Springer.

Gallagher, D., Breckenridge, J.N., Thompson, L.W., Dessonville, C., & Amaral, P.

(1982). Similarities and differences between normal grief and depression in older adults. *Essence, 5*, 127-140.

Gallagher-Thompson, D., & Thompson, L.W. (1995a). Efficacy of psychotherapeutic interventions with older adults. *The Clinical Psychologist, 48*, 24-30.

Gallagher-Thompson, D., & Thompson, L.W. (1995b). Psychotherapy with older adults in theory and practice. In B. Bongar & L.E. Beutler (Eds.), *Comprehensive textbook of psychotherapy: Theory and practice* (pp. 359-379). New York: Oxford University Press.

Gallagher-Thompson, D., McKibbin, C., Koonce-Volwiler, D., Menedez, A., Stewart, D., & Thompson, L.W. (2000). Psychotherapy for older adults. In C.R. Synder & R.E. Ingram (Eds.), *Handbook of Psychological Change* (pp. 614-636). New York: Wiley.

Galli, V., McElroy, S.L., Soutullo, C.A., Kizer, D., Raute, N., et al. (1999). The psychiatric diagnoses of twenty-two adolescents who have sexually molested children. *Comprensive Psychiatry, 40*, 85-88.

Gallo, J.J., & Lebowitz, B.D. (1999). The epidemiology of common late-life mental disorders in the community: Themes for the new century. *Psychiatric Services, 50*, 1158-1166.

Ganellan, R.J. (1996). Comparing the diagnostic efficiency of the MMPI, MCMI-II, and Rorschach: A review. *Journal of Personality Assessment, 67*, 219-243.

Gann, M.K., & Davison, G.C. (1999). *Assessing psychological reactance: Defiant thoughts at the ATSS paradigm*. Unpublished manuscript. University of Southern California.

Gao, S., Hendrie, H.C., Hall, K.S., & Hui, S. (1998). Relationships between sex, age, and the incidence of dementia and Alzheimer's disease: A meta-analysis. *Archives of General Psychiatry, 55*, 809-816.

Garb, H.N. & Schramke, C.J. (1996). Judgment research and neuropsychological assessment: A narrative review and meta-analyses. *Psychological Bulletin, 120*, 140-153.

Garb, H.N., Florio, C.M., & Grove, W.M. (1998). The validity of the Rorschach and the Minnesota Multiphasic Personality Inventory: Results from meta-analyses. *Psychological Science, 5*, 402-404.

Garber, J., Kriss, M.R., Koch, M., & Lindholm, L. (1988). Recurrent depression in adolescents: A follow-up study. *Journal of the American Academy of Child and Adolescent Psychiatry, 27*, 49-54.

Garber, J., Weiss, B., & Shanley, N. (1993). Cognitions, depressive symptoms, and development in adolescents. *Journal of Abnormal Psychology, 102*, 47-57.

Garbutt, J.C., Mayo, J.P., Little, K.Y., Gillette, G.M., Mason, G.A., et al. (1994). Dose-response studies with protirelin. *Archives of General Psychiatry, 51*, 875-883.

Garcia, J., McGowan, B.K., & Green, K.F. (1972). Biological constraints on conditioning. In A.H. Black & W.F. Prokasy (Eds.), *Classical conditioning: 2. Current research and theory*. New York: Appleton-Century-Crofts.

Garcia-Andrade, C., Wall, T.L., & Ehlers, C.L. (1997). The firewater myth and response to alcohol in Mission Indians. *American Journal of Psychiatry, 154*, 983-988.

Gardner, H. (1997, January 19). Review of "The Creation of Dr. B." *Los Angeles Times*, Book Review, pp. 3.

Garety, P.A., Fowler, D., & Kuipers, E. (2000). Cognitive-behavioral therapy for medication-resistant symptoms. *Schizophrenia Bulletin, 26*, 73-86.

Garfield, S.L. (1978). Research on client variables in psychotherapy. In S.L. Garfield & A.E. Bergin (Eds.), *Handbook of psychotherapy and behavior change* (2nd ed.). New York: Wiley.

Garfield, S.L., & Bergin, A.E. (1986). Introduction and historical overview. In S.L. Garfield & A.E. Bergin (Eds.), *Handbook of psychotherapy and behavior change* (3rd ed.). New York: Wiley.

Garfield, S.L., & Kurz, R. (1976). Clinical psychologists in the 1970s. *American Psychologist, 31*, 1-9.

Garfinkel, D., Laudon, M., Nof, D., & Zisapel, N. (1995). Improvement of sleep quality in elderly people by controlled-release melatonin. *Lancet, 346*, 541-543.

Garfinkel, P.E., Goering, E.L., Goldbloom, S.D., Kennedy, S., Kaplan, A.S., & Woodside, D.B. (1996). Should amenorrhea be necessary for the diagnosis of anorexia nervosa? *British Journal of Psychiatry, 168*, 500-506.

Garfinkel, P.E., Kennedy, S.H., & Kaplan, A.S. (1995). Views on classification and diagnosis of eating disorders. *Canadian Journal of Psychiatry, 40*, 445-456.

Garland, R.J., & Dougher, M.J. (1991). Motivational interviewing in the treatment of sex offenders. In W.R. Miller & S. Rollnick (Eds.), *Motivating interviewing: Preparing people to change addictive behavior* (pp. 303-313). New York: Guilford.

Garner, D.M. (1997b). Psychoeducational principles. In D.M. Garner & P.E. Garfinkel (Eds.), *Handbook of treatment for eating disorders* (pp. 145-177). New York: Guilford Press.

Garner, D.M., & Wooley, S.C. (1991). Confronting the failure of behavioral and dietary treatments of obesity. *Clinical Psychology Review, 11*, 729-780.

Garner, D.M., Garfinkel, P.E., Schwartz, D., & Thompson, M. (1980). Cultural expectation of thinness in women. *Psychological Reports, 47*, 483-491.

Garner, D.M., Olmsted, M.P., & Polivy, J. (1981). The Eating Disorder Inventory: A measure of cognitive-behavioral dimensions of anorexia nervosa and bulimia. In P.L. Darby, P.E. Garfinkel, D.M. Garner, & D.V. Coscina (Eds.), *Anorexia nervosa: Recent developments in research*. New York: Liss.

Garner, D.M., Olmsted, M.P., & Polivy, J. (1983). Development and validation of a multi-dimensional eating disorder inventory for anorexia nervosa and bulimia. *International Journal of Eating Disorders, 2*, 15-34.

Garner, D.M., Rockert, W., Davis, R., Garner, M.V., Olmsted, M.P., & Eagle, M. (1993). Comparison between cognitive-behavioral and supportive-expressive therapy for bulimia nervosa. *American Journal of Psychiatry, 150*, 37-46.

Garner, D.M., Vitousek, K.M., & Pike, K.M. (1997). Cognitive-behavioral therapy for anorexia nervosa. In D.M. Garner & P.E. Garfinkel (Eds.), *Handbook of treatment for eating disorders* (pp. 94-144). New York: Guilford Press.

Garnets, L., Herek, G.M., & Levy, B. (1990). Violence and victimization of lesbians and gay men: Mental health conseqences. *Journal of Interpersonal Violence, 5*, 366-383.

Garrison, C.Z., McKeown, R.E., Valois, R.F., & Vincent, M.L. (1993). Aggression, substance use, and suicidal behaviors in high school students. *American Journal of Public Health, 83*, 179-184.

Garssen, B., Buikhuisen, M., & Van Dyck, R. (1996). Hyperventilation and panic attacks. *American Journal of Psychiatry, 153*, 513-518.

Gatchel, R.J., Baum, A., & Krantz, D.S. (1989). *An introduction to health psychology* (2nd ed.). New York: Random House.

Gatz, M., & Pearson, C.G. (1988). Ageism revised and the provision of psychological services. *American Psychologist, 43*, 184-188.

Gatz, M., & Smyer, M.A. (1992). The mental health system and older adults in the 1990s. *American Psychologist, 47*, 741-751.

Gatz, M., Bengtson, V.L., & Blum, M.J. (1990). Caregiving families. In J.E. Birren & K.W. Schaie (Eds.), *Handbook of the psychology of aging* (3rd ed., pp. 404-426). New York: Academic Press.

Gatz, M., Fiske, A., Fox, L. S., Kaskie, B., Kasl-Godley, J. E., McCallum, T. J., & Wetherell, J. L. (1998). Empirically validated psychological treatments for older adults. *Journal of Mental Health and Aging, 4*, 9-46.

Gatz, M., Kasl-Godley, J.E., & Karel, M.J. (1996). Aging and mental disorders. In J.E. Birren & K.W. Schaie (Eds.), *Handbook of the psychology of aging*. San Diego: Academic Press.

Gatz, M., Pearson, C., & Fuentes, M. (1984). Older women and mental health. In A.U. Rickel, M. Gerrard, & I. Iscoe (Eds.), *Social and psychological problems of women: Prevention and crisis intervention*. Washington, DC: Hemisphere.

Gatz, M., Popkin, S.J., Pino, C.D., & VandenBos, G.R. (1985). Psychological interventions with older adults. In J.E. Birren & W.K. Schaie (Eds.), *Handbook of the psychology of aging* (pp. 755-785). New York: Van Nostrand Reinhold.

Gauthier, Y., Fortin, C., Drapeau, P., Breton, J., Gosselin, J., Quintal, L., Weisnagel, J., & Lamarre, A. (1978). Follow-up study of 35 asthmatic preschool children. *Journal of the American Academy of Child Psychiatry, 17*, 679-694.

Gauthier, Y., Fortin, C., Drapeau, P., Breton, J., Gosselin, J., Quintal, L., Weisnagel, J., Tetreault, L., & Pinard, G. (1977). The mother-child relationship and the development of autonomy and self-assertion in young (14-30 months) asthmatic children. *Journal of the American Academy of Child Psychiatry, 16*, 109-131.

Ge, X., Conger, R.D., Cadoret, R.J., Neiderhiser, J.M., Yates, W., et al. (1996). The developmental interface between nature and nurture: A mutual influence model of child antisocial behavior and parent behaviors. *Developmental Psychology, 32*, 574-589.

Geary, D.C. & Brown, S.C. (1991). Cognitive addition: Strategy choice and speed-of-processing differences in gifted, normal, and mathematically disabled children. *Developmental Psychology, 27*, 398-406.

Geary, D.C. (1993). Mathematical disabilities: Cognitive, neuropsychological, and genetic components. *Psychological Bulletin, 114*, 345-362.

Geary, D.C., Brown, S.C., & Samaranayake, V.A. (1991). Cognitive addition: A short longitudinal study of strategy choice and speed-of-processing differences in nor-

mal and mathematically disabled children. *Developmental Psychology, 27*, 787-797.

Gebhard, P.H., Gagnon, J.H., Pomeroy, W.B., & Christenson, C.V. (1965). *Sex offenders*. New York: Harper & Row.

Geer, J.H., Davison, G.C., & Gatchel, R.I. (1970). Reduction of stress in humans through nonveridical perceived control of aversive stimulation. *Journal of Personality and Social Psychology, 16*, 731-738.

Gelernter, C.S., Uhde, T.W., Cimbolic, P., Arnkoff, D.B., Vittone, B.J., et al. (1991). Cognitive behavioral and pharmacological treatments of social phobia: A controlled study. *Archives of General Psychiatry, 18*, 938-945.

Geller, B., Cooper, T.B., Graham, D., Fetner, H., Marstellar, F., & Wells, J. (1992). Pharmacokinetically designed double-blind placebo-controlled study of nortriptyline in 6-to 12-year-olds with major depressive disorder. *Journal of the American Academy of Child and Adolescent Psychiatry, 31*, 34-44.

General Register Office. (1968). *A glossary of mental disorders*. London: Author.

George, L.K. (1980). *Role transitions in later life*. Monterey, CA: Brooks/Cole.

George, L.K. (1994). Social factors and depression in late life. In L.S. Schneider, C.F. Reynolds, III, B.D. Lebowitz, & A.J. Friedhoff (Eds.), *Diagnosis and treatment of depression in late life* (pp. 131-153). Washington, DC: American Psychiatric Press.

George, L.K., & Weiler, S.J. (1981). Sexuality in middle and late life: The effects of age, cohort, and gender. *Archives of General Psychiatry, 38*, 919-923.

George, L.K., Landoman, R., Blazer, D.G., & Anthony, J.C. (1991). Cognitive impairment. In L.N. Robins & D.A. Regier (Eds.), *Psychiatric disorders in America*. New York: Free Press.

Geracioti, T.D., Baker, D.G., Ekhator, N.N. et al. (2001). CSF norepinephrine concentrations in posttraumatic stress disorder. *American Journal of Psychiatry, 158*, 1227-1230.

Gerber, L.M. (1983). Ethnicity still matters: Socio demographic profiles of the ethnic elderly in Ontario. *Canadian Ethnic Studies, 15*, 60-80.

Gergen, K.J. (1982). *Toward transformation in social knowledge*. New York: Plenum.

Gerin, W., Rosolsky, M., Pieper, C., & Pickering, T.G. (1994). A test of generalizability of cardiovascular reactivity using a controlled ambulatory procedure. *Psychosomatic Medicine, 56*, 360-368.

Gerlach, A.L., Wilhelm, F.H., Gruber, K. & Roth, W.T. (2001). Blushing and physiological arousability in social phobia. *Journal of Abnormal Psychology, 110*, 247-258.

Gesten, E.L., & Jason, L.A. (1987). Social and community interventions. *Annual Review of Psychology, 38*, 427-460.

Ghoneim, M.M., & Mewaldt, S.P. (1990). Benzodiazepines and human memory: A review. *Anesthesiology, 72*, 926-938.

Gibbs, J.T. (1980). The interpersonal orientation in mental health consultation: Toward a model of ethnic variations in consultation. *American Journal of Orthopsychiatry, 45*, 430-445.

Gibson, D., & Harris, A. (1988). Aggregated early intervention effects for Down's syndrome persons: Patterning and longevity of benefits. *Journal of Mental Deficiency Research, 32*, 1-17.

Gielen, A.C., Faden, R.R., O'Campo, P., Kass, N., & Anderson, J. (1994). Women's protective sexual behaviors: A test of the health belief model. *AIDS Education and Prevention, 6*, 1-11.

Gilbert, A.R., Rosenberg, D.R., Harenski, K. et al. (2001). Thalamic volumes in patients with first episode schizophrenia. *American Journal of Psychiatry, 158*, 618-624.

Gilboa-Schechtman, E. & Foa, E. B. (2001). Patterns of recovery from trauma: The use of intraindividual analysis. *Journal of Abnormal Psychology, 110*, 392-400.

Gilboy, J.A., & Schmidt, J.R. (1971). "Voluntary" hospitalization of the mentally ill. *Northwestern University Law Review, 66*, 429-439.

Gillberg, C. (1991). Outcome in autism and autistic-like conditions. *Journal of the American Academy of Child and Adolescent Psychiatry, 30*, 375-382.

Gillberg, C., & Svendsen, P. (1983). Childhood psychosis and computed tomographic brain scan findings. *Journal of Autism and Developmental Disorders, 13*, 19-32.

Gillis, J.J. & DeFries, J.C. (1991). Confirmatory factor analysis of reading and mathematics performance measures in the Colorado Reading Project. *Behavior Genetics, 21*, 572-573.

Ginsburg, A.B., & Goldstein, S.G. (1974). Age bias in referral to psychological consultation. *Journal of Gerontology, 29*, 410-415.

Ginzburg, H.M. (1986). Naltrexone: Its clinical utility. In B. Stimmel (Ed.), *Advances in alcohol and substance abuse* (pp. 83-101). New York: Haworth.

Gist, R. (In press). What have they done to my song? Social science, social movements, and the debriefing debates. *Cognitive & Behavioral Practice*.

Gitlin, M.J. (1993). Pharmacotherapy of personality disorders: Conceptual framework and clinical strategies. *Journal of Clinical Psychopharmacology, 13*, 343-353.

Gittelman, R., Abikoff, H., Pollack, E., Klein, D., Katz, F., & Mattes, J. (1980). A controlled trial of behavior modification and methylphenidate in hyperactive children. In C. Whalen & B. Henker (Eds.), *Hyperactive children: The social ecology of identification and treatment* (pp. 221-246). New York: Academic Press.

Gladue, B.A. (1985). Neuroendocrine response to estrogen and sexual orientation. *Science, 230*, 961.

Glantz, L.A. & Lewis, D.A. (2000). Decreased dendritic spine density on prefrontal cortical pyramidal neurons in schizophrenia. *Archives of General Psychiatry, 57*, 65-73.

Glass, C.R., & Arnkoff, D.B. (1997). Questionnaire methods of cognitive self-statement assessment. *Journal of Consulting and Clinical Psychology, 65*, 911-927.

Glassman, A.H., & Shapiro, P.A. (1998). Depression and the course of cardiovascular disease. *American Journal of Psychiatry, 155*, 4-11.

Gleaves, D.H. (1996). The sociocognitive model of dissociative identity disorder: A reexamination of the evidence. *Psychological Bulletin, 120*, 42-59.

Gleaves, D.H., & Eberenz, K.P. (1994). Sexual abuse histories among treatment-resistant bulimia nervosa patients. *International Journal of Eating Disorders, 15*, 227-231.

Gleick, J. (1987). *Chaos: Making a new science*. New York: Penguin Books.

Glick, I.D., Clarkin, J.F., Haas, G.L., Spencer, J.H., & Chen, C.L. (1991). A randomized clinical trial of inpatient family intervention: VI. Mediating variables and outcome. *Family Process, 30*, 85-99.

Goddard, A.W., Mason, G.F., Almai, A. et al. (2001). Reductions in occipital cortex GABA in panic disorder detected with sup-1H-magnetidc resonance spectroscopy. *Archives of General Psychiatry, 58*, 556-561.

Goff, D.C., & Simms, C.A. (1993). Has multiple personality disorder remained consistent over time? A comparison of past and present cases. *Journal of Nervous and Mental Disease, 181*, 595-600.

Goldberg, E.M., & Morrison, S.L. (1963). Schizophrenia and social class. *British Journal of Psychiatry, 109*, 785-802.

Golden, C.J. (1981a). The Luria-Nebraska Children's Battery: Theory and formulation. In G.W. Hynd & J.E. Obrzut (Eds.), *Neuropsychological assessment and the school-age child: Issues and procedures*. New York: Grune & Stratton.

Golden, C.J. (1981b). A standardized version of Luria's neuropsychological tests: A quantitative and qualitative approach to neuropsychological evaluation. In S.B. Filskov & T.J. Boil (Eds.), *Handbook of clinical neuropsychology*. New York: Wiley.

Golden, C.J., Hammeke, T., & Purisch, A. (1978). Diagnostic validity of a standardized neuropsychological battery derived from Luria's neuropsychological tests. *Journal of Consulting and Clinical Psychology, 46*, 1258-1265.

Goldfried, M.R., & Davison, G.C. (1976). *Clinical behavior therapy*. New York: Holt, Rinehart & Winston.

Goldfried, M.R. (1971). Systematic desensitization as training in self-control. *Journal of Consulting and Clinical Psychology, 37*, 228-234.

Goldfried, M.R. (1980). Toward the delineation of therapeutic change principles. *American Psychologist, 35*, 991-999.

Goldfried, M.R. (1991). Research issues in psychotherapy integration. *Journal of Psychotherapy Integration, 1*, 5-25.

Goldfried, M.R., & D'Zurillia, T.J. (1969). A behavioral-analytic model for assessing competence. In C.D. Speilberger (Ed.), *Current topics in clinical and community psychology* (Vol. 1). New York: Academic Press.

Goldfried, M.R., & Davison, G.C. (1994). *Clinical behavior therapy* (expanded edition). New York: Wiley.

Goldfried, M.R., Greenberg, L.S., & Marmar, C. (1990). Individual psychotherapy: Process and outcome. *Annual Review of Psychology, 41*, 659-688.

Goldfried, M.R., Padawer, W., & Robins, C. (1984). Social anxiety and the semantic structure of heterosocial interactions. *Journal of Abnormal Psychology, 93*, 87-97.

Golding, J.M., Smith, G.R., & Kashner, T.M. (1991). Does somatization disorder occur in men? Clinical characteristics of women and men with unexplained somatic symptoms. *Archives of General Psychiatry, 48*, 231-235.

Goldman, A., & Greenberg, L. (1992). Comparison of integrated systemic and emotionally focussed approaches to couples therapy. *Journal of Consulting and Clinical Psychology, 60*, 962-969.

Goldman, L., & Haaga, D.A.F. (1995). Depression and the experience of anger in marital and other relationships. *Journal of Nervous and Mental Disease, 183*, 505-509.

Goldman-Rakic, P. S. & Selemon, L. D. (1997). Functional and anatomical aspects of prefrontal pathology in schizophrenia. *Schizophrenia Bulletin, 23*, 437-458.

Goldmeier, J. (1988). Pets or people: Another research note. *The Gerontologist, 26*, 203-206.

Goldstein, A.J., & Chambless, D.L. (1978). A reanalysis of agoraphobic behavior. *Behavior Therapy, 9*, 47-59.

Goldstein, J.L. (1999). *Snoring can kill*. Pacific Palisades, CA: Caren Publishing Group.

Goldstein, M.J., & Rodnick, E. (1975). The family's contribution to the etiology of schizophrenia: Current status. *Schizophrenia Bulletin, 14*, 48-63.

Goldstein, R.B., Weissman, M.M., Adams, P.B., Horwath, E., Lish, J.D., et al. (1994). Psychiatric disorders in relatives of probands with panic disorder or major depression. *Archives of General Psychiatry, 51*, 383-394.

Goldstein, S.E., & Birnbom, F. (1976). Hypochondriasis and the elderly. *Journal of the American Geriatrics Society, 24*, 150-154.

Goleman, D. (1995). *Emotional intelligence*. New York: Bantam.

Gomberg, E.S.L., & Zucker, R.A. (1998). Substance use and abuse in old age. In I.H. Nordhus, G.R. VandenBos, S. Berg, & P. Fromholt (Eds.), *Clinical geropsychology* (pp. 189-204). Washington, D.C.: American Psychological Association.

Gomez, F.C., Piedmont, R.L., & Fleming, M.Z. (1992). Factor analysis of the Spanish version of the WAIS: The Escala de Inteligencia Wechsler para Adultos (EIWA). *Psychological Assessment, 4*, 317-321.

Goodenow, C., Reisine, S.T., & Grady, K.E. (1989). Quality of social support and associated social and psychological functions in women with rheumatoid arthritis. *Health Psychology, 9*, 266-284.

Goodman, L.A., Koss, M.P., Fitzgerald, L.F., Russo, N.F., et al. (1993). Male violence against women: Current research and future directions. *American Psychologist, 48*, 1054-1058.

Goodman, R., & Stevenson, J. (1989). A twin study of hyperactivity: 2. The aetiological role of genes, family relationships, and perinatal adversity. *Journal of Child Psychology and Psychiatry, 30*, 691-709.

Goodsitt, A. (1997). Eating disorders: A self-psychological perspective. In D.M. Garner & P.E. Garfinkel (Eds.), *Handbook of treatment for eating disorders* (pp. 205-228). New York: Guilford Press.

Goodwin, D.W. (1979). Alcoholism and heredity: A review and hypothesis. *Archives of General Psychiatry, 36*, 57-61.

Goodwin, D.W., & Guze, S.B. (1984). *Psychiatric diagnosis* (3rd ed.). New York: Oxford University Press.

Goodwin, D.W., Schulsinger, F., Hermansen, L., Guze, S.B., & Winokur, G.A. (1973). Alcohol problems in adoptees raised apart from alcoholic biological parents. *Archives of General Psychiatry, 128*, 239-243.

Goodwin, F., & Jamison, K. (1990). *Manic-depressive illness*. New York: Oxford University Press.

Goodwin, P.J., Leszcz, M., Ennis, M., Koopmans, J., Vincent, L., Guther, H., Drysdale, E., Hundleby, M., Chochinov, H.M., Navarro, M., Speca, M., Masterson, J., Dohan, L., Sela, R., Warren, B., Paterson, A., Pritchard, K.I., Arnold, A., Doll, R., O'Reilly, S.E., Quirt, G., Hood, N. Hunter, J. (2001). The effect of group psychosocial support on survival in metastatic breast cancer. *The New England Journal of Medicine, 345*, 1719-1726.

Gorenstein, E.E., & Newman, J.P. (1980). Disinhibitory psychopathology: A new perspective and a model for research. *Psychological Review, 87*, 301-315.

Gorman, J. M., Kent, J., Martinez, J. et al. (2001). Physiological changes during carbon dioxide inhalation in patients with panic disorder, major depression, and premenstrual dysphoric disorder: Evidence for a central fear mechanism. *Archives of General Psychiatry, 58*, 125-132.

Gorman, J.M. (1994). New and experimental pharmacological treatments for panic disorder. In B.E. Wolfe & J.D. Maser (Eds.), *Treatment of panic disorder: A consensus development conference* (pp. 83-90). Washington, DC: American Psychiatric Press.

Gorman, J.M., Fyer, M.R., Goetz, R., Askanazi, J., Leibowitz, M.R., Fyer, A.J., Kinney, J., & Klein, D.F. (1988). Ventilatory physiology of patients with panic disorder. *Archives of General Psychiatry, 45*, 53-60.

Gopnik, A., Capps, L., & Meltzoff, A.N. (2000). Early theories of mind: What the theory can tell us about autism. In S. Baren-Cohen, H. Tager-Flusberg, & D.

Cohen (Eds.), *Understanding Other Minds* (2nd ed., pp. 50-72). Oxford, England: Oxford University Press.

Gostin, L.O., & Hodge, J. G. (1998). Piercing the veil of secrecy in HIV/AIDs and other sexually transmitted diseases: Theories of privacy and disclosure in partner notification. *Duke Journal of Gender Law and Policy, 5,* 9-88.

Gotesdam, K.G., & Agras, W.S. (1995). General population-based epidemiological survey of eating disorders in Norway. *International Journal of Eating Disorders, 18,* 119-126.

Gotlib, I.H. (1982). Self-reinforcement and depression in interpersonal interaction: The role of performance level. *Journal of Abnormal Psychology, 93,* 19-30.

Gotlib, I.H., & Asarnow, R.F. (1979). Interpersonal and impersonal problem-solving skills in mildly and clinically depressed students. *Journal of Consulting and Clinical Psychology, 47,* 86-95.

Gotlib, I.H., & Robinson, L.A. (1982). Responses to depressed individuals: Discrepancies between self-report and observer-rated behavior. *Journal of Abnormal Psychology, 91,* 231-240.

Gotlib, I.H., Lewinsohn, P.M., Seeley, J.R., Rohde, P., & Rednew, J.E. (1993). Negative cognitions and attributional style in depressed adolescents: An examination of stability and specificity. *Journal of Abnormal Psychology, 102,* 607-615.

Gottesman, I., & Shields, J. (1972). *Schizophrenia and genetics: A twin study vantage point*. New York: Academic Press.

Gottesman, I.I., & Goldsmith, H.H. (1994). Developmental psychopathology of antisocial behavior: Inserting genes into its ontogenesis and epigenesis. In C.A. Nelson (Ed.), *Threats to optimal development*. Hillside, NJ: Erlbaum.

Gottesman, I.I., McGuffin, P., & Farmer, A.E. (1987). Clinical genetics as clues to the "real" genetics of schizophrenia. *Schizophrenia Bulletin, 13,* 23-47.

Gottlieb, J. (1990). Mainstreaming and quality education. *American Journal on Mental Retardation, 95,* 16-25.

Gottman, J.M. (1979). *Marital interaction: Experimental investigations*. New York: Academic Press.

Gottman, J.M., & Krokoff, L.J. (1989). Marital interaction and satisfaction: A longitudinal view. *Journal of Consulting and Clinical Psychology, 57,* 47-52.

Gottman, J.M., Notarius, C., Gonso, J., & Markman, H. (1976). *A couple's guide to communication*. Champaign, IL.: Research Press.

Gould, M.S., Wallenstein, S., & Kleinman, M.H. (1990). Time-space clustering of teenage suicide. *American Journal of Epidemiology, 131,* 71-78.

Gove, W.R. (1970). Societal reaction as an explanation of mental illness: An evaluation. *American Sociological Review, 35,* 873-884.

Goyer, P., Andreason, P.J., Semple, W.E., Clayton, A.H., et al. (1994). Positron-emission tomography and personality disorders. *Neuropsychopharmacology, 10,* 21-28.

Goyette, C.H., & Conners, C.K. (1977). *Food additives and hyperkinesis*. Paper presented at the 85th Annual Convention of the American Psychological Association.

Graham, J.R. (1988). *Establishing validity of the revised form of the MMPI*. Symposium presentation at the 96th Annual Convention of the American Psychological Association, Atlanta.

Graham, J.R. (1990). *MMPI-2: Assessing personality and psychopathology*. New York: Oxford University Press.

Graham, J.W., Johnson, C.A., Hansen, W.B., Flay, B.R., & Gee, M. (1990). Drug use prevention programs, gender, and ethnicity: Evaluation of three seventh-grade Project SMART cohorts. *Preventive Medicine, 19,* 305-313.

Graham, P.J., Rutter, M.L., Yule, W., & Pless, I.B. (1967). Childhood asthma: A psychosomatic disorder? Some epidemiological considerations. *British Journal of Preventive Medicine, 21,* 78-85.

Gralnick, A. (1986). Future of the chronic schizophrenic patient: Prediction and recommendation. *American Journal of Psychotherapy, 40,* 419-429.

Gramling, S.E., Clawson, E.P., & McDonald, M.K. (1996). Perceptual and cognitive abnormality model of hypochondriasis: Amplification and physiological reactivity in women. *Psychosomatic Medicine, 58,* 423-431.

Grandin, T. (1986). *Emergence: Labeled autistic*. Novato, CA: Arena Press.

Grandin, T. (1995). *Thinking in pictures*. New York: Doubleday.

Gratzer, T., & Bradford, J.M.W. (1995). Offender and offense characteristics of sexual sadists: A comparative study. *Journal of Forensic Sciences, 40,* 450-455.

Gray, E.B. (1983). *Final report: Collaborative research of community and minority group action to prevent child abuse and neglect: Vol. 3. Public awareness and education using the creative arts*. Chicago: National Committee for Prevention of Child Abuse.

Green, M.F. (1993). Cognitive remediation in schizophrenia. *American Journal of Psychiatry, 150,* 178-187.

Green, M.F. (1996). What are the functional consequences of neurocognitive deficits in schizophrenia? *American Journal of Psychiatry, 153,* 321-330.

Green, M.F., Kern, R.S., Braff, D.L., & Mintz, J. (2000). Neurocognitive deficits and functional outcome in schizophrenia: Are we measuring the "right stuff"? *Schizophrenia Bulletin, 26,* 119-136.

Green, M.F., Marshall, B.D., Wirshing, W.C., Ames, D., Marder, S.R., McGurk, S., Kern, R.S., & Mintz, J. (1997). Does risperidone improve verbal working memory in treatment-resistant schizophrenia? *American Journal of Psychiatry, 154,* 799-804.

Green, R. (1969). Mythological, historical and cross-cultural aspects of transsexualism. In R. Green & J. Money (Eds.), *Transsexualism and sex reassignment*. Baltimore: Johns Hopkins University Press.

Green, R. (1974). *Sexual identity conflict in children and adults*. New York: Basic Books.

Green, R. (1976). One hundred ten feminine and masculine boys: Behavioral contrasts and demographic similarities. *Archives of Sexual Behavior, 5,* 425-446.

Green, R. (1985). Gender identity in childhood and later sexual orientation: Follow-up of 78 males. *American Journal of Psychiatry, 142,* 339-341.

Green, R. (1987). *The "sissy boy syndrome" and the development of homosexuality*. New Haven: Yale University Press.

Green, R. (1992). *Sexual science and the law*. Cambridge, MA: Harvard University Press.

Green, R., & Blanchard, R. (1995). Gender identity disorders. In H.I. Kaplan & B.J. Sadock (Eds.), *Comprehensive textbook of psychiatry* (pp. 1347-1360). Baltimore, MD: Williams & Wilkins.

Green, R., & Fleming, D.T. (1990). Transsexual surgery follow-up: Status in the 1990s. In J. Bancroft, C. Davis, & D. Weinstein (Eds.), *Annual review of sex research* (pp. 163-174).

Green, R., & Money, J. (1969). *Transsexualism and sex reassignment*. Baltimore: Johns Hopkins University Press.

Green, R.C., Cupples, A., Go, R., et al. (2002). Risk of dementia among white and African American relatives of patients with Alzheimer disease. *JAMA, 287,* 329-336.

Greenberg, J. (1996, August 21). Teen drug use has doubled in 4 years, U.S. says. *Los Angeles Times*, pp. A1, A17.

Greenberg, L., Elliott, R., & Lietaer, G. (1994). Research on experiential therapies. In A.E. Bergin & S.L. Garfield (Eds.), *Handbook of psychotherapy and behavior change* (4th ed., pp. 509-539). New York: Wiley.

Greenberg, L., Fine, S.B., Cohen, C., Larson, K., Michaelson-Baily, A., Rubinton, P., & Glick, I.D. (1988). An interdisciplinary psychoeducation program for schizophrenic patients and their families in an acute care setting. *Hospital and Community Psychiatry, 39,* 277-281.

Greenberg, L.S., & Johnson, S.M. (1988). *Emotionally focussed couples therapy*. New York: Guilford.

Greenberg, L.S., & Rice, L.N. (1981). The specific effects of a gestalt intervention. *Psychotherapy: Theory, Research, and Practice, 18,* 31-37.

Greenberg, L.S., & Safran, J. (1984). Integrating affect and cognition: A perspective on the process of therapeutic change. *Cognitive Therapy and Research, 8,* 559-578.

Greenblatt, M., Solomon, M.H., Evans, A.S., & Brooks, G.W. (Eds.). (1965). *Drugs and social therapy in chronic schizophrenia*. Springfield, IL: Charles C. Thomas.

Greene, B.A. (1985). Considerations in the treatment of black patients by white therapists. *Psychotherapy, 22,* 115-122.

Greene, B.L. (1960). Marital disharmony: Concurrent analysis of husband and wife. *Diseases of the Nervous System, 21,* 1-6.

Greer, S., Morris, T., & Pettigale, K.W. (1979). Psychological response to breast cancer: Effect on outcome. *Lancet, 2,* 785-787.

Gregerson, H.B., & Sailer, L. (1993). Chaos theory and its implications for social science. *Human Relations, 46,* 777-802.

Grice, D.E., Halmi, K.A., Fichter, M.M., Strober, M., Woodside, D.B., Treasure, J.T., Kaplan, A.S., Magistretti, P.J., Goldman, D., Bulik, C.M., Kaye, W.H., & Berrettini, W.H. (2002). Evidence for a susceptibility gene for anorexia nervosa on chromosome 1. *American Journal of Human Genetics, 70,* 787-792.

Grifin, M.G., Resick, P.A., & Mechanic, M.B. (1997). Objective assessment of peritraumatic dissociation: Psychophysiological indicators. *American Journal of Psychiatry, 154,* 1081-1088.

Grigorenko, E.L. (1997). Susceptibility for distinct components of developmental dyslexia on chromosomes 6 and 15. *American Journal of Human Genetics, 60*, 27-39.

Grigorenko, E.L., Wood, F.B., Meyer, M.S., Hart, L.A., Speed, W.C., Shuster, A., & Pauls, D.L. (in press). Susceptibility loci for distinct components of developmental dyslexia on chromosome 6 and 15. *American Journal of Human Genetics*.

Grilo, C.M., Shiffman, S., & Carter-Campbell, J.T. (1994). Binge eating antecedents in normal weight nonpurging females: Is there consistency? *International Journal of Eating Disorders, 16*, 239-249.

Grings, W.W., & Dawson, M.E. (1978). *Emotions and bodily responses: A psychophysiological approach*. New York: Academic Press.

Grinker, R.B., & Spiegel, J.P. (1945). *Men under stress*. Philadelphia: Blakiston.

Grinker, R.R., & Spiegel, J.P. (1944). *Management of neuropsychiatric casualties in the zone of combat: Manual of military neuropsychiatry*. Philadelphia: W.B. Saunders.

Grinker, R.R., & Spiegel, J.P. (1979). *War neuroses*. New York: Arno Press.

Grinspoon, L., & Bakalar, J.B. (1995). Marijuana as medicine: A plea for reconsideration. *Journal of the American Medical Association, 273*, 1875-1876.

Grisso, T. (1986). *Evaluating competencies: Forensic assessments and instruments*. New York: Plenum.

Grisso, T., & Appelbaum, P.S. (1991). Mentally ill and non-mentally ill patients' abilities to understand informed consent disclosures for medication: Preliminary data. *Law and Human Behavior, 15*, 377-388.

Grisso, T., & Appelbaum, P.S. (1992). Is it unethical to offer predictions of future violence? *Law and Human Behavior, 16*, 621-633.

Grisso, T., & Appelbaum, P.S. (1995). The MacArthur Treatment Competence Study: 3. Abilities of patients to consent to psychiatric and medical treatments. *Law and Human Behavior, 19*, 149-174.

Gross, M.D. (1984). Effects of sucrose on hyperkinetic children. *Pediatrics, 74*, 876-878.

Grosz, H.J., & Zimmerman, J. (1970). A second detailed case study of functional blindness: Further demonstration of the contribution of objective psychological laboratory data. *Behavior Therapy, 1*, 115-123.

Groth, N.A., & Burgess, A.W. (1977). Sexual dysfunction during rape. *New England Journal of Medicine, 297*, 764-766.

Groth, N.A., Hobson, W.F., & Guy, T.S. (1982). The child molester: Clinical observations. In J. Conte & D.A. Shore (Eds.), *Social work and child sexual abuse*. New York: Haworth.

Grove, W.R., Eckert, E.D., Heston, L., Bouchard, T., et al. (1990). Heritability of substance abuse and antisocial behavior in monozygotic twins reared apart. *Biological Psychiatry, 27*, 1293-1304.

Grych, J.H., & Fincham, F.D. (1990). Marital conflict and children's adjustment: A cognitive-contextual framework. *Psychological Bulletin, 108*, 267-290.

Guarnaccia, P. J., De La Cancela, V., & Carrillo, E. (1989). The multiple meanings of ataques de nervios in the Latino community. *Medical Anthropology, 11*, 47-62.

Guerra, N., & Slaby, R. (1990). Cognitive mediators of aggression in adolescent offenders: 2. Intervention. *Developmental Psychology, 26*, 269-277.

Guidano, V.F., & Liotti, G. (1983). *Cognitive processes and emotional disorders*. New York: Guilford.

Gump, B.S., Matthews, K.A., & Raikkonen, K. (1999). Modeling relationships among socioeconomic status, hostility, cardiovascular reactivity, and left ventricular mass in African American and White children. *Health Psychology, 18*, 140-150.

Gunderson, J.G., Kolb, J.E., & Austin, V. (1981). The diagnostic interview for borderline patients. *American Journal of Psychiatry, 138*, 896-903.

Gunn, J. (1993). Castration is not the answer. *British Medical Journal, 307*, 790-791.

Gur, R.E., Turetsky, B.I., Cowell, P.E. et al. (2000). Temporolimbic volume reductions in schizophrenia. *Archives of General Psychiatry, 57*, 769-776.

Gur, R.E., & Pearlson, G.D. (1993). Neuroimaging in schizophrenia research. *Schizophrenia Bulletin, 19*, 337-353.

Gurian, B., & Miner, J.H. (1991). Clinical presentation of anxiety in the elderly. In C. Salzman & B.D. Lebowitz (Eds.), *Anxiety in the elderly*. New York: Springer.

Gurland, B. (1991). Epidemiology of psychiatric disorders. In J. Sadavoy, L.W. Lazarus, & L.F. Jarvik (Eds.), *Comprehensive review of geriatric psychiatry* (pp. 25-40). Washington, DC: American Psychiatric Press.

Gurland, B.J., & Cross, P.S. (1982). Epidemiology of psychopathology in old age. In L.F. Jarvik & G.W. Small (Eds.), *Psychiatric Clinics of North America*. Philadelphia: Saunders.

Gurman, A.S., & Kniskern, D.P. (1978). Research on marital and family therapy: Progress, perspective, and prospect. In S.L. Garfield & A.E. Bergin (Eds.), *Handbook of psychotherapy and behavior change: An empirical analysis (2nd ed.)*. New York: Wiley.

Gurman, A.S., & Kniskern, D.P. (1981). Family therapy outcome research: Knowns and unknowns. In A.S. Gurman & D.P. Kniskern (Eds.), *Handbook of family therapy*. New York: Brunner/Mazel.

Gurman, A.S., Kniskern, D.P., & Pinsoff, W.M. (1986). Research on the process and outcome of marital and family therapy. In S.L. Garfield & A.E. Bergin (Eds.), *Handbook of psychotherapy and behavior change* (3rd ed.). New York: Wiley.

Gustafson, Y., Berggren, D., Bucht, B., Norberf, A., Hansson, L.I., & Winblad, B. (1988). Acute confusional states in elderly patients treated for femoral neck fracture. *Journal of the American Geriatrics Society, 36*, 525-530.

Guyll, M., & Contrada, R.J. (1998). Trait hostility and ambulatory cardiovascular activity: Responses to social interaction. *Health Psychology, 17*, 30-39.

Guze, S.B. (1967). The diagnosis of hysteria: What are we trying to do? *American Journal of Psychiatry, 124*, 491-498.

Guze, S.B. (1993). Genetics of Briquet's syndrome and somatization disorder: A review of family, adoption, and twin studies. *Annals of Clinical Psychiatry, 5*, 225-230.

Gwynther, L.P., & George, L.K. (1986). Caregivers for dementia patients: Complex determinants of well-being and burden. *The Gerontologist, 26*, 245-247.

Haaga, D.A. (1987a). *Smoking schemata revealed in articulated thoughts predict early relapse from smoking cessation*. Paper presented at the 21st Annual Convention of the Association for Advancement of Behavior Therapy, Boston.

Haaga, D.A. (1987b). Treatment of the type A behavior pattern. *Clinical Psychology Review, 7*, 557-574.

Haaga, D.A. (1988). *Cognitive aspects of the relapse prevention model in the prediction of smoking relapse*. Paper presented at the 22nd Annual Convention of the Association for Advancement of Behavior Therapy, New York.

Haaga, D.A., & Davison, G.C. (1989). Outcome studies of rational-emotive therapy. In M.E. Bernard & R. DiGiuseppe (Eds.), *Inside rational-emotive therapy*. New York: Academic Press.

Haaga, D.A.F. (1989). Articulated thoughts and endorsement procedures for cognitive assessment in the prediction of smoking relapse. *Psychological Assessment: A Journal of Consulting and Clinical Psychology, 1*, 112-117.

Haaga, D.A.F. (1990). Issues in relating self-efficacy to smoking relapse: Importance of an "Achilles' Heel" situation and of prior quitting experience. *Journal of Substance Abuse, 2*, 191-200.

Haaga, D.A.F., & Davison, G.C. (1991). Cognitive change methods. In F.H. Kanfer & A.P. Goldstein (Eds.), *Helping people change: A textbook of methods* (4th ed.). Elmsford, NY: Pergamon.

Haaga, D.A.F., & Davison, G.C. (1992). Disappearing differences do not always reflect healthy integration: An analysis of cognitive therapy and rational-emotive therapy. *Journal of Psychotherapy Integration, 1*, 287-303.

Haaga, D.A.F., DeRubeis, R.J., Stewart, B.L., & Beck, A.T. (1991). Relationship of intelligence with cognitive therapy outcome. *Behaviour Research and Therapy, 29*, 277-281.

Haaga, D.A.F., Dyck, M.J., & Ernst, D. (1991). Empirical status of cognitive theory of depression. *Psychological Bulletin, 110*, 215-236.

Haaga, D.A.F., Rabois, D., & Brody, C. (1999). Cognitive behavior therapy. In M. Hersen & A.S. Bellack (Eds.), *Handbook of comparative treatments for adult disorders* (2nd ed., pp. 8-61). New York: Wiley.

Haas, G.L., Glick, I.D., Clarkin, J.F., Spencer, J.H., & Lewis, A.B. (1990). Gender and schizophrenia outcome: A clinical trial of an outpatient intervention. *Schizophrenia Bulletin, 16*, 277-292.

Haas, R.H., Townsend, J., Courchesne, E., Lincoln, A.J., Schreibman, L., & Yeung-Courchesne, R. (1996). Neurologic abnormalities in infantile autism. *Journal of Child Neurology, 11*, 84-92.

Haddock, G., Tarrier, N., Spaulding, W., Yusupoff, L. K., & McCarthy, E. (1998). Individual cognitive-behavior therapy in the treatment of hallucinations and delusions: A review. *Clinical Psychology Review, 18*, 821-838.

Haensel, S.M., Klem, T.M., Hop, C.J., & Slob, A.K. (1998). Fluoxetine and premature ejaculation: A double-blind, cross-over, placebo-controlled trial. *Journal of Clinical Psychopharmacology, 18*, 72-77.

Hafner, R.J. (1982). Marital interaction in persisting obsessive-compulsive disorders. *Australian and New Zealand Journal of Psychiatry, 16*, 171-178.

Hafner, R.J., Gilchrist, P., Bowling, J., & Kalucy, R. (1981). The treatment of obsessional neurosis in a family setting. *Australian and New Zealand Journal of Psychiatry, 15*, 145-151.

Hagerman, R.J. (1995). Molecular and clinical correlations in Fragile X syndrome. *Mental Retardation and Developmental Disabilities Research Reviews, 1*, 276-280.

Hahlweg, K., & Markman, H.J. (1988). The effectiveness of behavioral marital therapy: Empirical status of behavioral techniques in preventing and alleviating marital distress. *Journal of Consulting and Clinical Psychology, 56*, 440-447.

Hale, A.S. (1993). New antidepressants: Use in high-risk patients. *Journal of Clinical Psychiatry, 54*, 61-70.

Haley, S.A. (1978). Treatment implications of post-combat stress response syndromes for mental health professionals. In C.R. Figley (Ed.), *Stress disorders among Vietnam veterans*. New York: Brunner/Mazel.

Haley, W.E., Levine, E.G., Brown, S.L., Berry, J.W., & Hughes, G.H. (1987). Psychological, social, and health consequences of caring for a relative with senile dementia. *Journal of the American Geriatrics Society, 35*, 405-411.

Hall, C.S., Lindzey, G., Loehlin, J.C., & Manosevitz, M. (1985). *Introduction to theories of personality*. New York: Wiley.

Hall, G.C., Hirschman, R., & Oliver, L.L. (1995). Sexual arousal and arousability to pedophilic stimuli in a community sample of normal men. *Behavior Therapy, 26*, 681-694.

Hall, G.C.N. (1995). Sexual offender recidivism revisited: A meta-analysis of treatment studies. *Journal of Consulting and Clinical Psychology, 63*, 802-809.

Hall, S.M., Munoz, R.F., & Reus, V.I. (1994). Cognitive-behavioral intervention increases abstinence rates for depressive-history smokers. *Journal of Consulting and Clinical Psychology, 62*, 141-146.

Hall, S.M., Munoz, R.F., Reus, V.I., Sees, K.L., Duncan, C., Humfleet, G.L., & Hartz, D.T. (1996). Mood management and nicotine gum in smoking treatment: A therapeutic contract and placebo-controlled study. *Journal of Consulting and Clinical Psychology, 64*, 1003-1009.

Hall, S.M., Reuss, V.I., Munoz, R.F., Sees, K.L., Humfleet, G., et al. (1998). Nortriptyline and cognitive-behavioral therapy in the treatment of cigarette smoking. *Archives of General Psychiatry, 55*, 683-690.

Halleck, S.L. (1971). *The politics of therapy*. New York: Science House.

Hamada, T., Koshino, Y., Misawa, T., Isaki, K., & Geyjo, F. (1998). Mitral valve prolapse and autonomic function in panic disorder. *Acta Psychiatrica Scandanavica, 97*, 139-143.

Hamilton, E.W., & Abramson, L.Y. (1983). Cognitive patterns and major depressive disorder: A longitudinal study in a hospital setting. *Journal of Abnormal Psychology, 92*, 173-184.

Hammen, C.L. (1997). *Depression*. East Sussex, Great Britain: Psychology Press.

Hammen, C.L., & Compas, B.E. (1994). Unmasking unmasked depression in children and adolescents: The problem of comorbidity. *Clinical Psychology Review, 14*, 585-603.

Hammen, C.L. (1980). Depression in college students: Beyond the Beck Depression Inventory. *Journal of Consulting and Clinical Psychology, 48*, 126-128.

Hammen, C.L., & Cochran, S.D. (1981). Cognitive correlates of life stress and depression in college students. *Journal of Abnormal Psychology, 90*, 23-27.

Hampe, E., Noble, H., Miller, L.C., & Barrett, C.L. (1973). Phobic children one and two years posttreatment. *Journal of Abnormal Psychology, 82*, 446-453.

Hankin, B.J., Abramson, L.Y., Moffitt, T.E., Silva, P.A., McGee, R., et al. (1998). Development of depression from preadolescence to young adulthood: Emerging gender differences in a 10-year longitudinal study. *Journal of Abnormal Psychology, 107*, 128-140.

Hannappel, M., Calsyn, R.J., & Allen, G. (1993). Does social support alleviate the depression of caregivers of dementia patients? *Journal of Gerontological Social Work, 20*, 35-51.

Hansen, W.B. (1992). School-based substance abuse prevention: A review of the state of the art in curriculum, 1980-1990. *Health Education Research: Theory and Practice, 7*, 403-430.

Hansen, W.B. (1993). School-based alcohol prevention programs. *Alcohol Health and Research World, 18*, 62-66.

Hansen, W.B., & Graham, J.W. (1991). Preventing alcohol, marijuana, and cigarette use among adolescents: Peer pressure resistance training versus establishing conservative norms. *Preventive Medicine, 20*, 414-430.

Hanson, R.K., & Bussiere, M.T. (1998). Predicting relapse: A meta-analysis of sexual offender recidivism studies. *Journal of Consulting and Clinical Psychology, 66*, 348-362.

Hanson, R.K., & Harris, A.J.R. (1997). Voyeurism: Assessment and treatment. In D.R. Laws & W. O'Donohue (Eds.), *Sexual deviance* (pp. 311-331). NY: Guilford Press.

Hanson, R.K., Hunsely, J., & Parker, K. C. H. (1988). The relationship between WAIS subtest reliability, "g" loadings, and meta-analytically derived validity estimates. *Journal of Clinical Psychology, 44*, 557-563.

Hanusa, B.H., & Schulz, R. (1977). Attributional mediators of learned helplessness. *Journal of Personality and Social Psychology, 35*, 602-611.

Haracz, J.L. (1982). The dopamine hypothesis: An overview of studies with schizophrenic patients. *Schizophrenia Bulletin, 8*, 438-469.

Hardy, B.W., & Waller, D.A. (1988). Bulimia as substance abuse. In W.G. Johnson (Ed.), *Advances in eating disorders*. New York: JAI.

Hardy, J. (1993). Genetic mistakes point the way to Alzheimer's disease. *Journal of NIH Research, 5*, 46-49.

Hardy, K.V., & Laszloffy, T.A. (1995). Therapy with African Americans and the phenomenon of rage. *In Session: Psychotherapy in Practice, 1*, 57-70.

Hare, E. (1969). *Triennial statistical report of the Royal Maudsley and Bethlem Hospitals*. London: Bethlem and Maudsley Hospitals.

Hare, R.D. (1978). Electrodermal and cardiovascular correlates of sociopathy. In R.D. Hare & D. Schalling (Eds.), *Psychopathic behavior: Approaches to research*. New York: Wiley.

Hare, R.D., Harpur, T.J., Hakstian, R.A., Forth, A.E., Hart, S.D., et al. (1990). The revised Psychopathy Checklist: Reliability and factor structure. *Psychological Assessment, 2*, 338-341.

Hare, R.D., Hart, S.D., & Harpur, T.J. (1991). Psychopathy and the DSM-IV criteria for antisocial personality disorder. *Journal of Abnormal Psychology, 100*, 391-398.

Harpur, T.J., & Hare, R.D. (1990). Psychopathy and attention. In J. Enns (Ed.), *The development of attention: Research and theory*. Amsterdam: New Holland.

Harris, M.J., & Jeste, D.V. (1988). Late-onset schizophrenia: A review. *Schizophrenia Bulletin, 14*, 39-55.

Harrison, J., Chin, J., & Ficarrotto, T. (1989). Warning: Masculinity may be dangerous to your health. In M.S. Kimmel & M.A. Messner (Eds.), *Men's lives* (pp. 296-309). New York: Macmillan.

Harry Benjamin International Gender Dysphoria Association. (1998). *The standards of care of gender identity disorders (5th version)*. Dusseldorf: Symposion.

Hart, E.L., Lahey, B.B., Loeber, R., Applegate, B., & Frick, P.J. (1995). Developmental changes in attention-deficit hyperactivity disorder in boys: A four-year longitudinal study. *Journal of Abnormal Child Psychology, 23*, 729-750.

Hart, S.D., & Hare, R.D. (1989). Discriminant validity of the Psychopathy Checklist in a forensic psychiatric population. *Psychological Assessment, 1*, 211-218.

Hartley, D.E., & Strupp, H.H. (1983). The therapeutic alliance: Its relationship to outcome in brief psychotherapy. In J. Masling (Ed.), *Empirical studies of psychoanalytical theories (Vol. 1)*. Hillsdale, NJ: Analytical Press.

Hartmann, H. (1958). *Ego psychology and the problem of adaptation*. New York: International Universities Press.

Harvard Mental Health Letter. (1994a, July). *Borderline personality-Part III, 11*, 1-3.

Harvard Mental Health Letter. (1994b, July). *Borderline personality-Part I and II, Special Supplement, 11*, 1-3.

Harvard Mental Health Letter. (1995, July). *Schizophrenia update-Part II, 12*, 1-5.

Harvard Mental Health Letter. (1996a, August). *Treatment of alcoholism-Part I, 13*, 1-4.

Harvard Mental Health Letter. (1996b, February). *Personality disorders: The anxious cluster-Part I, 12*, 1-3.

Harvard Mental Health Letter. (1996c, March). *Personality disorders: The anxious cluster-Part II, 12*, 1-3.

Hastrup, J.L., Light, K.C., & Obrist, P.A. (1982). Parental hypertension and cardiovascular response to stress in healthy young adults. *Psychophysiology, 19*, 615-622.

Hathaway, S.R., & McKinley, J.C. (1943). *MMPI manual*. New York: Psychological Corporation.

Hawkins, J.D., Graham, J.W., Maguin, E., Abbott, R., et al. (1998). Exploring the effects of age of alcohol use initiation and psychosocial risk factors on subsequent alcohol misuse. *Journal of Studies on Alcohol, 58*, 280-290.

Hawton, K., Catalan, J., & Fagg, J. (1992). Sex therapy for erectile dysfunction: Characteristics of couples, treatment outcome, and prognostic factors. *Archives of Sexual Behavior, 21*, 161-176.

Hawton, K., Catalan, J., Martin, P., & Fagg, J. (1986). Long-term outcome of sex therapy. *Behaviour Research and Therapy, 24*, 665-675.

Hay, D.P. (1991). Electroconvulsive therapy. In J. Sadavoy, L.W. Lazarus, & L.F. Jarvik (Eds.), *Comprehensive review of geriatric psychiatry* (pp. 469-485). Washington, DC: American Psychiatric Press.

Hay, P., & Fairburn, C.G. (1998). The validity of the DSM-IV scheme for classifying eating disorders. *International Journal of Eating Disorders, 23*, 7-15.

Hayashi, K., Toyama, B., & Quay, H.C. (1976). A cross-cultural study concerned with differential behavioral classification: 1. The Behavior Checklist. *Japanese Journal of Criminal Psychology, 2*, 21-28.

Hayes, R.L., Halford, W.K., & Varghese, F.T. (1995). Social skills training with chronic schizophrenic patients: Effects on negative symptoms and community functioning. *Behavior Therapy, 26*, 433-449.

Hayes, S.C., Strosahl, K.D., Wilson, K.G. (1999). *Acceptance and commitment therapy: An experiential approach to behavior change.* New York, NY: Guilford Press.

Hayes, S.C. (1987). A contextual approach to therapeutic change. In N.S. Jacobson (Ed.), *Psychotherapists in clinical practice: Cognitive and behavioral perspectives.* New York: Guilford.

Haynes, S.N., & Horn, W.F. (1982). Reactivity in behavioral observation: A review. *Behavioral Assessment, 4*, 369-385.

Hays, P.A. (1996). Addressing the complexities of culture and gender in counseling. *Journal of Counseling and Development, 74*, 332-338.

Hazelrigg, M.D., Cooper, H.M., & Borduin, C.M. (1987). Evaluating the effectiveness of family therapies: An integrative review and analysis. *Psychological Bulletin, 101*, 428-442.

Healy, M. (1994, January 8). Science of power and weakness. *Los Angeles Times*, pp. A1, A12.

Heatherton, T.F., & Baumeister, R.F. (1991). Binge eating as escape from self-awareness. *Psychological Bulletin, 110*, 86-108.

Heatherton, T.F., Herman, C.P., & Polivy, J. (1991). Effects of physical threat and ego threat on eating behavior. *Journal of Personality and Social Psychology, 60*, 138-143.

Heatherton, T.F., Nichols, P., Mahamedi, F., & Keel, P. (1995). Body weight, dieting, and eating disorder symptoms among college students, 1982 to 1992. *American Journal of Psychiatry, 152*, 1623-1630.

Hechtman, L., Weiss, G., & Perlman, T. (1984). Hyperactives as young adults: Past and current substance abuse and antisocial behavior. *American Journal of Orthopsychiatry, 54*, 415-425.

Hecker, M.H.L., Chesney, M., Black, G.W., & Frautsch, N. (1988). Coronary-prone behavior in the Western Collaborative Group Study. *Psychosomatic Medicine, 50*, 153-164.

Heckers, S. (1997). Neuropathology of schizophrenia: Cortex, basal ganglia, and neurotransmitter-specific projection systems. *Schizophrenia Bulletin, 23*, 403-421.

Heidrich, S.M. (1993). The relationship between physical health and psychological well-being in elderly women: A developmental perspective. *Research in Nursing and Health, 16*, 123-130.

Heim, E., Valach, L., & Schaffner, L. (1997). Coping and psychosocial adaptation: Longitudinal effects over time and stages in breast cancer. *Psychosomatic Medicine, 59*, 408-418.

Heiman, J.R., & Verhulst, J. (1990). Sexual dysfunction and marriage. In F.D. Fincham, & T.N. Bradbury (Eds.), *The psychology of marriage: Basic issues and applications* (pp. 299-322). New York: Guilford.

Heimberg, R.G., & Juster, H.R. (1994). Treatment of social phobia in cognitive-behavioral groups. *Journal of Clinical Psychiatry, 55*, 38-46.

Heimberg, R.G., Liebowitz, M.R., Hope, D.A., Schneir, F.R., Holt, C.S., et al. (1998). Cognitive behavioral group therapy vs phenelzine therapy for social phobia: 12-week outcome. *Archives of General Psychiatry, 55*, 1133-1142.

Heimberg, R.G., Salzman, D.G., Holt, C.S., & Blendell, K. (1993). Cognitive behavioral group treatment for social phobia: Effectiveness at five-year follow-up. *Cognitive Therapy and Research, 17*, 325-339.

Heinrichs, N. & Hofman, S.G. (2001). Information processing in social phobia: A critical review. *Clinical Psychology Review, 21*, 751-770.

Heinssen, R.K., Liberman, R.P., & Kopelowicz, A. (2000). Psychosocial skills training for schizophrenia: Lessons from the laboratory. *Schizophrenia Bulletin, 26*, 21-46.

Heller, J. (1966). *Something happened.* New York: Knopf.

Heller, K., Wyman, M.F., & Allen, S.M. (2000). Future directions for prevention science: from research to adoption. In C.R. Snyder & R.E. Ingram (Eds.), *Handbook of Psychological Change: Psychotherapy processes & practices for the 21st century* (pp. 660-680). New York: John Wiley & Sons, Inc.

Heller, K.A., Holtzman, W.H., & Messick, S. (Eds.). (1982). *Placing children in special education: A strategy for equity.* Washington, DC: National Academy Press.

Hellstrom, K., Fellenius, J., & Ost, I. (1993). One versus five sessions of applied tension in the treatment of blood phobia. *Behaviour Research and Therapy, 34*, 101-112.

Helweg-Larsen, M., & Collins, B.E. (1997). A social psychological perspective on the role of knowledge about AIDS in AIDS prevention. *Current Directions in Psychological Science, 6*, 23-26.

Helzer, J.E., Burnam, A., & McEvoy, L.T. (1991). Alcohol abuse and dependence. In L. Robins & D. Reiger (Eds.), *Psychiatric disorders in America: The Epidemiologic Catchment Area Study* (pp. 9-38). New York: Free Press.

Helzer, J.E., Robins, L.N., & McEvoy, L. (1987). Post-traumatic stress disorder in the general population. *New England Journal of Medicine, 317*, 1630-1634.

Hembree, W.C., Nahas, G.G., & Huang, H.F.S. (1979). Changes in human spermatozoa associated with high dose marihuana smoking. In G.G. Nahas & W.D.M. Paton (Eds.), *Marijuana: Biological effects.* Elmsford, NY: Pergamon.

Henggeler, S.W., Schoenwald, S.D., Borduin, C.M., Rowland, M.D., & Cunningham, P.B. (1998). *Multisystemic treatment of antisocial behavior in children and adolescents.* New York: Guilford Press.

Henkel, H., & Lewis-Thomé, J. (1976). *Verhaltenstherapie bei männlichen Homosexuellen.* Diplomarbeit der Studierenden der Psychologie. University of Marburg, Germany.

Henker, B., & Whalen, C. K. (1999). The child with attention-deficit/hyperactivity disorder in school and peer settings. In H. C. Quay, & A. E. Hogan, *Handbook of disruptive behavior disorders* (pp. 157-178). New York: Kluwer Academic/Plenum.

Henriksson, M.M., Aro, H.M., Marttunen, M.J., Heikkinen, M.E., Isometsa, E.T., Kuoppasalmi, K.I., & Lonnqvist, J.K. (1993). Mental disorders and comorbidity in suicide. *American Journal of Psychiatry, 150*, 935-940.

Henry, J.P., Ely, D.L., & Stephens, P.M. (1972). Changes in catecholamine-controlling enzymes in response to psychosocial activation of defense and alarm reactions. In *Physiology, emotion, and psychosomatic illness.* Ciba Symposium 8. Amsterdam, Netherlands: Associated Scientific Publishers.

Henry, R.M. (1996). Psychodynamic group therapy with adolescents: Exploration of HIV-related risk taking. *International Journal of Group Psychotherapy, 46*, 229-253.

Henry, W. P., Schacht, T.E., Strupp, H.H., Butler, S.F., & Binder, J.L. (1993). Effects of training in time-limited dynamic psychotherapy: Mediators of therapists' responses to training. *Journal of Consulting and Clinical Psychology, 61*, 441-447.

Henry, W.P., & Strupp, H.H. (1994). The therapeutic alliance as interpersonal process. In A. Horvath & L. Greenberg (Eds.), *The working alliance: Theory, research and practice* (pp. 51-84). New York: Guilford.

Henry, W.P., Strupp, H.H., Schacht, T.E., & Gaston, L. (1994). Psychodynamic approaches. In A.E. Bergin & S.L. Garfield (Eds.), *Handbook of psychotherapy and behavior change* (4th ed., pp. 467-508). New York: Wiley.

Herbert, J.D. (1995). An overview of the current status of social phobia. *Applied and Preventive Psychology, 4*, 39-51.

Herek, G.M. (1989). Hate crimes against lesbians and gay men: Issues for research and policy. *American Psychologist, 44*, 948-955.

Herek, G.M. (1994). Assessing heterosexuals' attitudes towards lesbians and gay men: A review of the empirical research with the ATLG scale. In B. Greene & G.M. Herek (Eds.), *Contemporary perspectives on lesbian and gay issues in psychology* (pp. 206-228). Newbury Park, CA: Sage.

Herek, G.M., Gillis, R., Kogan, J.C., & Glunt, E.K. (1996). Hate crime victimization among lesbian, gay, and bisexual adults. *Journal of Interpersonal Violence, 12*, 195-215.

Herman, C.P., & Polivy, J. (1980). Restrained eating. In A. Stunkard (Ed.), *Obesity.* Philadelphia: Sanders.

Herman, C.P., Polivy, J., Lank, C., & Heatherton, T.F. (1987). Anxiety, hunger, and eating. *Journal of Abnormal Psychology, 96*, 264-269.

Herman, J.L., Perry, J.C., & van der Kolk, B.A. (1989). Childhood trauma in borderline personality disorder. *American Journal of Psychiatry, 146*, 490-495.

Herpetz, S.C., Dietrich, T.M., Wenning, B. et al. (2001a). Evidence of abnormal amygdala functioning in borderline personality disorder: A functional MRI study. *Biological Psychiatry, 50*, 292-298.

Herpetz, S.C., Werth, U., Lucas, G. et al. (2001b). Emotion in criminal offenders with psychopathy and borderline personality disorders. *Archives of General Psychiatry, 58*, 737-745.

Herrell, R., Goldberg, J., True, W.R., Ramakrishnan, V., Lyons, M., Eisen, S., & Tsuang, M.T. (1999). Sexual orientation and suicidality: A co-twin control study of adult men. *Archives of General Psychiatry, 56*, 867-874.

Hersen, M., & Barlow, D.H. (1976). *Single case experimental designs: Strategies for studying behavior change.* New York: Pergamon.

Hersen, M., & Van Hasselt, V.B. (1992). Behavioral assessment and treatment of anxiety in older adults. *Clinical Psychology Review, 12*, 619-640.

Hersen, M., Bellack, A.S., Himmelhoch, J.M., & Thase, M.E. (1984). Effects of social skill training, amitriptyline, and psychotherapy in unipolar depressed women. *Behavior Therapy, 15*, 21-40.

Herz, M.I., Lamberti, J.S., Mintz, J. et al. (2000). A program for relapse prevention in schizophrenia: A controlled study. *Archives of General Psychiatry,57*, 277-284.

Herzog, A.R. (1989). Physical and mental health in older women: Selected research issues and data sources. In A.R. Herzog, K.C. Holden, & M.M. Seltzer (Eds.), *Health and economic status of older women: Research issues and data sources* (pp. 35-91). Amityville, NY: Baywood Publishing Co.

Hester, R.K., & Miller, W.R. (1989). Self-control training. In R.K. Hester & W.R. Miller (Eds.), *Handbook of alcoholism treatment approaches: Effective alternatives* (pp. 141-149). New York: Pergamon.

Heston, L.L. (1966). Psychiatric disorders in foster home reared children of schizophrenic mothers. *British Journal of Psychiatry, 112*, 819-825.

Heston, L.L. (1987). The paranoid syndrome after mid-life. In N.E. Miller & G.D. Cohen (Eds.), *Schizophrenia and aging* (pp. 249-257). New York: Guilford.

Hettema, J.M., Neale, M.C., & Kendler, K.S. (2001). A review and meta-analysis of the genetic epidemiology of the anxiety disorders. *American Journal of Psychiatry, 158*, 1568-1578.

Hewitt, P.L., Flett, G.L., & Ediger, E. (1996). Perfectionism and depression: Longitudinal assessment of a specific vulnerability hypothesis. *Journal of Abnormal Psychology, 105*, 276-280.

Heyd, D., & Bloch, S. (1981). The ethics of suicide. In S. Bloch & P. Chodoff (Eds.), *Psychiatric ethics.* New York: Oxford University Press.

Hietala, J., Syvalahti, E., Vuorio, K., Nagren, K., Lehikoinen, P., et al. (1994). Striatal D2 dopamine receptor characteristics in drug-naive schizophrenic patients studied with positive emission tomography. *Archives of General Psychiatry, 51*, 116-123.

Hill, C.E., O'Grady, K.E., & Elkin, I. (1992). Applying the Collaborative Study Psychotherapy Rating Scale to rate therapist adherence to cognitive-behavior therapy, interpersonal therapy, and clinical management. *Journal of Consulting and Clinical Psychology, 60*, 73-79.

Hill, J.H., Liebert, R.M., & Mott, D.E.W. (1968). Vicarious extinction of avoidance behavior through films: An initial test. *Psychological Reports, 12*, 192.

Himadi, W.G., Cerny, J.A., Barlow, D.H., Cohen, S., & O'Brien, G.T. (1986). The relationship of marital adjustment to agoraphobia treatment outcome. *Behaviour Research and Therapy, 24*, 107-115.

Hinrichsen, G. A. (1997). Interpersonal psychotherapy for depressed older adults. *Journal of Geriatric Psychiatry, 30*, 239-257.

Hinrichsen, G. A. (1999). Treating older adults with interpersonal psychotherapy for depression. *Psychotherapy in Practice, 55 (8)*, 949-960.

Hinshaw, S.P. (1987). On the distinction between attentional deficits/hyperactivity and conduct problems/aggression in child psychopathology. *Psychological Bulletin, 101*, 443-463.

Hinshaw, S.P. (1991). Stimulant medication and the treatment of aggression in children with attentional deficits. *Journal of Clinical Child Psychology, 20*, 301-312.

Hinshaw, S.P., Henker, B., & Whalen, C.K. (1984a). Cognitive-behavioral and pharmacologic interventions for hyperactive boys: Comparative and combined effects. *Journal of Consulting and Clinical Psychology, 52*, 739-749.

Hinshaw, S.P., Henker, B., & Whalen, C.K. (1984b). Self-control in hyperactive boys in anger-inducing situations: Effects of cognitive-behavioral training and of methylphenidate. *Journal of Abnormal Child Psychology, 12*, 55-77.

Hirschi, T. (1969). *Causes of delinquency.* Berkeley, CA: University of California Press.

Hite, S. (1976). *The Hite Report: A nationwide study of female sexuality.* New York: Dell.

Ho, B-C., Nopoulos, P., Flaum, M., Arndt, S., & Andreasen, N.C. (1998). Two-year outcome in first-episode schizophrenia: Predictive value of symptoms for quality of life. *American Journal of Psychiatry, 155*, 1196-1201.

Hobbs, S.A., Beck, S.J., & Wansley, R.A. (1984). Pediatric behavioral medicine: Directions in treatment and prevention. In M. Hersen, R.M. Eisler, & P.M. Miller (Eds.), *Progress in behavior modification* (Vol. 16). New York: Academic Press.

Hobfoll, S.E., Spielberger, C.D., Breznitz, S., Figley, C., Folkman, S., Lepper-Green, B., Meichenbaum, D., Milgram, N.A., Sandler, I., Sarason, I., & van der Kolk, B. (1991). War-related stress: Addressing the stress of war and other traumatic events. *American Psychologist, 46*, 848-855.

Hobson, R.P. & Lee, A. (1998). Hello and goodbye: A study of social engagement in autism. *Journal of Autism and Developmental Disorders, 28*, 117-127.

Hodges, E.L., Cochrane, C.E., & Brewerton, T.D. (1998). Family characteristics of binge-eating disorder patients. *International Journal of Eating Disorders, 23*, 145-151.

Hodges, L.F., Rothbaum, B.O., Kooper, R., Opdyke, D., Meyer, T., de Graff, J.J., & Williford, J.S. (1994). *Presence as the defining factor in a VR application: Virtual reality graded exposure in the treatment of acrophobia.* Tech Rep GIT-GVU-94-96, Georgia Institute of Technology.

Hodgson, R.J., & Rachman, S.J. (1972). The effects of contamination and washing on obsessional patients. *Behaviour Research and Therapy, 10*, 111-117.

Hodson, D.S., & Skeen, P. (1994). Sexuality and aging: The hammerlock of myths. *Journal of Applied Gerontology, 13*, 219-235.

Hoebel, B.G., & Teitelbaum, P. (1966). Weight regulation in normal and hypothalamic hyperphagic rats. *Journal of Comparative and Physiological Psychology, 61*, 189-193.

Hogan, D. (1978). The effectiveness of sex therapy: A review of the literature. In J. LoPiccolo & L. LoPiccolo (Eds.), *Handbook of sex therapy.* New York. Plenum.

Hogarty, G.E. (1993). Prevention of relapse in chronic schizophrenic patients. *Journal of Clinical Psychiatry, 54*, 18-23.

Hogarty, G.E., Anderson, C.M., Reiss, D.J., Kornblith, S.J., Greenwald, D.P., et al. (1986). Family psychoeducation, social skills training, and maintenance chemotherapy in the aftercare treatment of schizophrenia: 1. One-year effects of a controlled study on relapse and expressed emotion. *Archives of General Psychiatry, 43*, 633-642.

Hogarty, G.E., Anderson, C.M., Reiss, D.J., Kornblith, S.J., Greenwald, D.P., Ulrich, R.F., Carter, M., & The Environmental-Personal Indicators in the Course of Schizophrenia (EPICS) Research Group. (1991). Family psychoeducation, social skills training, and maintenance chemotherapy in the aftercare treatment of schizophrenia. *Archives of General Psychiatry, 48*, 340-347.

Hogarty, G.F., Greenwald, D., Ulrich, R.F., Kornblith, S.J., DiBarry, A.L., Cooley, S., Carter, M., & Flesher, S. (1997a). Three-year trials of personal therapy among schizophrenic patients living with or independent of family, II: Effects on adjustment of patients. *Archives of General Psychiatry, 154*, 1514-1524.

Hogarty, G.E., Kornblith, S.J., Greenwald, D., DiBarry, A.L., Cooley, S., Ulrich, R.F., Carter, M., & Flesher, S. (1997b). Three-year trials of personal therapy among schizophrenic patients living with or independent of family, I: Description of study and effects on relapse rates. *Archives of General Psychiatry, 154*, 1504-1513.

Hogarty, G.E., Kornblith, S.J., Greenwald, D., DiBarry, A.L., Cooley, S., Flesher, S., Reiss, D., Carter, M., & Ulrich, R. (1995). Personal therapy: A disorder-relevant psychotherapy for schizophrenia. *Schizophrenia Bulletin, 21*, 379-393.

Hogarty, G.E., McEvoy, J.P., Ulrich, R.F., DiBarry, A.L., Bartone, P., et al. (1994). Pharmacotherapy of impaired affect in recovering schizophrenic patients. *Archives of General Psychiatry, 52*, 29-41.

Hoge, S., Lidz, C., Eisenberg, M., Gardner, W., Monahan, J., Mulvey, E., Roth, L., & Bennet, N. (1997). Perceptions of coercion in the admission of voluntary and involuntary psychiatric patients. *International Journal of Law and Psychiatry, 20*, 167-181.

Holden, C. (1972). Nader on mental health centers: A movement that got bogged down. *Science, 177*, 413-415.

Holder, H.D., Longabaugh, R., Miller, W.R., & Rubonis, A.V. (1991). The cost effectiveness of treatment for alcoholism: A first approximation. *Journal of Studies on Alcohol, 52*, 517-540.

Holland, A.J., Hall, A., Murray, R., Russell, G.F.M., & Crisp, A.H. (1984). Anorexia nervosa: A study of 34 twin pairs and one set of triplets. *British Journal of Psychiatry, 145*, 414-419.

Hollander, E., Allen, A., Lopez, R. P. et al. (2001). A preliminary double-blind placebo-controlled trial of divalproex sodium in borderline personality disorder. *Journal of Clinical Psychiatry, 62*, 199-203.

Hollander, E., Cohen, L.J., & Simeon, D. (1993). Body dysmorphic disorder. *Psychiatric Annals, 23*, 359-364.

Hollander, E., DeCaria, C.M., Nitescu, A., Gully, R., Suckow, R.F., et al. (1992). Serotonergic function in obsessive-compulsive disorder: Behavioral and neuroendocrine responses to oral m-chlorophenylpiperazine and fenfluramine in patients and healthy volunteers. *Archives of General Psychiatry, 49,* 21-27.

Hollander, E., Stein, D.J., Decaria, D.M., Cohen, L.J., Saond, J.B., et al. (1994). Serotonergic sensitivity in borderline personality disorder. *American Journal of Psychiatry, 151,* 277-280.

Hollifield, M., Katon, W., Spain, D., & Pule, L. (1990). Anxiety and depression in a village in Lesotho, Africa: A comparison with the United States. *British Journal of Psychiatry, 156,* 343-350.

Hollingshead, A.B., & Redlich, F.C. (1958). *Social class and mental illness: A community study.* New York: Wiley.

Hollon, S. D., Haman, K. L., & Brown, L. L. In I. H. Gotlib (Ed.), *Handbook of Depression* (pp. 383-403). New York: Guilford Press.

Hollon, S.D., Shelton, R.C., Salomon, R.M., & Lovett, M.L. (2002, May). Cognitive therapy vs medications for severe depression: Prevention of recurrence. In J. Fawcett (Chair), *Cognitive therapy vs. medications for severe depression: Acute response and relapse prevention.* Symposium presented at the 155th Annual Meeting of the American Psychiatric Association, Philadelphia.

Hollon, S.D., & Beck, A.T. (1986). Cognitive and cognitive-behavioral therapies. In S.L. Garfield & A.E. Bergin (Eds.), *Handbook of psychotherapy and behavior change* (3rd ed.). New York: Wiley.

Hollon, S.D., & Beck, A.T. (1994). Cognitive and cognitive behavioral therapies. In A.E. Bergin & S.L. Garfield (Eds.), *Handbook of psychotherapy and behavior change* (4th ed., pp. 428-466). New York: Wiley.

Hollon, S.D., & Kendall, P.C. (1980). Cognitive self-statements in depression: Development of an automatic thoughts questionnaire. *Cognitive Therapy and Research, 4,* 383-395.

Hollon, S.D., De Rubeis, R.J., & Evans, M.D. (1996). Cognitive therapy in the treatment and prevention of depression. In P.M. Salkovskis (Ed.), *Frontiers of cognitive therapy* (pp. 293-317). New York: Guilford.

Hollon, S.D., DeRubeis, R.J., & Seligman, M.E.P. (1992). Cognitive therapy and the prevention of depression. *Applied and Preventive Psychology, 1,* 89-95.

Hollon, S.D., DeRubeis, R.J., Evans, M.D., Wiemer, J.J., Garvey, J.G., Grove, W.M., & Tuason, V.B. (1992). Cognitive therapy and pharmacotherapy for depression: Singly and in combination. *Archives of General Psychiatry, 49,* 774-781.

Hollon, S.D., DeRubeis, R.J., Tuason, V.B., Weimer, M.J., Evans, M.D., & Garvey, M.J. (1989). *Cognitive therapy, pharmacotherapy, and combined cognitive-pharmacotherapy in the treatment of depression: 1. Differential outcome.* Unpublished manuscript, Vanderbilt University, Nashville, TN.

Holm, V.A., & Varley, C.K. (1989). Pharmacological treatment of autistic children. In G. Dawson (Ed.), *Autism: Nature, diagnosis, and treatment* (pp. 386-404). New York: Guilford.

Holme, I. (1990). An analysis of randomized trials on cholesterol reduction on total mortality and coronary heart disease risk. *Circulation, 82,* 1916-1924.

Holmes, T.H., & Rahe, R.H. (1967). The social readjustment rating scale. *Journal of Psychosomatic Research, 11,* 213-218.

Holmes, T.S., & Holmes, T.H. (1970). Short-term intrusions into the life style routine. *Journal of Psychosomatic Research, 14,* 121-132.

Holroyd, K., Penzien, D., Hursey, K., Tobin, D., Rogen, L., Holm, J., Marcille, P., Hall, J., & Chila, A. (1984). Change mechanisms in EMG biofeedback training: Cognitive changes underlying improvements in tension headache. *Journal of Consulting and Clinical Psychology, 52,* 1039-1053.

Holtzworth-Munroe, A., Markman, H., O'Leary, K.D., Neidig, P., Leber, D., Heyman, R., Hulbert, D., & Smutzler, N. (1995). The need for marital violence prevention efforts: A behavioral cognitive secondary prevention program for engaged and newly married couples. *Applied and Preventive Psychology, 4,* 77-88.

Holzman, P.S. (1985). Eye movement dysfunctions and psychosis. *Review of Neurobiology, 27,* 179-205.

Hooley, J.M., & Teasdale, J.D. (1989). Predictors of relapse in unipolar depressives: Expressed emotion, marital distress, and perceived criticism. *Journal of Abnormal Psychology, 98,* 229-235.

Hoon, E.F., & Hoon, P.W. (1978). Styles of sexual expression in women: Clinical implications of multivariate analyses. *Archives of Sexual Behavior, 7,* 105-116.

Hope, D.A., Heimberg, R.G., & Bruch, M.A. (1995). Dismantling cognitive-behavioral group therapy for social phobia. *Behaviour Research and Therapy, 33,* 637-650.

Horn, A.S., & Snyder, S.H. (1971). Chlorpromazine and dopamine: Conformational similarities that correlate with the anti-psychotic activity of phenothiazine drugs. *Proceedings of the National Academy of Sciences, 68,* 2325-2328.

Hornblower, M., & Svoboda, W. (1987, November 23). Down and out—but determined: Does a mentally disturbed woman have the right to be homeless? *Time,* 29.

Horney, K. (1939). *New ways in psychoanalysis.* New York: International Universities Press.

Horney, K. (1942). *Self-analysis.* New York: Norton.

Horovitz, B. (1992, March 10). Cigarette ads under fire. *Los Angeles Times,* pp. D1, D6.

Horowitz, M.J. (1975). Intrusive and repetitive thoughts after experimental stress. *Archives of General Psychiatry, 32,* 223-228.

Horowitz, M.J. (1986). *Stress response syndromes.* Northvale, NJ: Aronson.

Horowitz, M.J. (1988). *Introduction to psychodynamics: A new synthesis.* New York: Basic Books.

Horowitz, M.J. (1990). Psychotherapy. In A.S. Bellack & M. Hersen (Eds.), *Handbook of comparative treatments for adult disorders* (pp. 289-301). New York: Wiley.

Horwath, E., Wolk, S.I., Goldstein, R.B., Wickramaratne, P., Sobin, C., et al. (1995). Is the comorbidity between social phobia and panic disorder due to familial cotransmission or other factors? *Archives of General Psychiatry, 52,* 574-581.

Horwitz, L. (1974). *Clinical prediction in psychotherapy.* New York: Jason Aronson.

House, J.S., Landis, K.R., & Umberson, D. (1988). Social relationships and health. *Science, 241,* 540-544.

Houston, B.K., & Vavak, C.R. (1991). Cynical hostility: Developmental factors, psychosocial correlates, and health behaviors. *Health Psychology, 10,* 9-17.

Houts, A.C. (2001). Harmful dysfunction and the search for value neutrality in the definition of mental disorder: Response to Wakefield, part 2. *Behaviour Research and Therapy, 39,* 1099-1132.

Houts, A.C. (1991). Nocturnal enuresis as a biobehavioral problem. *Behavior Therapy, 22,* 133-151.

Houts, A.C., Berman, J., & Abramson, H. (1994). Effectiveness of psychological and pharmacological treatments for nocturnal enuresis. *Journal of Consulting and Clinical Psychology, 62,* 737-745.

Howard, K.I., Moras, K., Brill, P.L., Martinovich, Z., & Lutz, W. (1996). Evaluation of psychotherapy: Efficacy, effectiveness, and patient progress. *American Psychologist, 51,* 1059-1064.

Howard, K.I., Orlinsky, D.E., Saunders, S.M., Bankoff, E., Davidson, C., & O'Mahoney, M. (1991). Northwestern University-University of Chicago Psychotherapy Research Program. In L. Beutler & M. Crago (Eds.), *Psychotherapy research.* Washington, DC: American Psychological Association.

Howard, R. (1993). Late paraphrenia. *International Review of Psychiatry, 5,* 455-460.

Howard, R., Almeida, O.P., & Levy, R. (1993). Schizophrenic symptoms in late paraphrenia. *Psychopathology, 26,* 95-101.

Howard, R., Castle, D., O'Brien, J., Almeida, O., & Levy, R. (1991). Permeable walls, floors, ceilings, and doors: Partition delusions in late paraphrenia. *International Journal of Geriatric Psychiatry, 7,* 719-724.

Howard, R., Castle, D., Wessely, S., & Murray, R. (1993). A comparative study of 470 cases of early-onset and late-onset schizophrenia. *British Journal of Psychiatry, 163,* 352-357.

Howes, J.L., & Vallis, T.M. (1996). Cognitive therapy with nontraditional populations: Application to post-traumatic stress disorder and personality disorders. In K.S. Dobson & K.D. Craig (Eds.), *Advances in cognitive-behavioral therapy* (pp. 237-272). Thousand Oaks, CA: Sage.

Howes, R.J. (1998). Plethysmographic assessment of incarcerated sexual offenders: A comparison with rapists. *Sexual Abuse: A Journal of Research and Treatment, 10,* 183-194.

Howitt, D. (1995). Pornography and the paedophile: Is it criminogenic? *British Journal of Medical Psychology, 68,* 15-27.

Hser, Y., Anglin, M.D., & Powers, K. (1993). A 24-year follow-up of California narcotics addicts. *Archives of General Psychiatry, 50,* 577-584.

Hsu, L.K.G. (1990). *Eating disorders.* New York: Guilford.

Hudson, J.I., Pope, H.G., Yurgelun-Todd, D., Jonas, J.M., & Frankenburg, F.R. (1987). A controlled study of lifetime prevalence of affective and other psychiatric disorders in bulimic patients. *American Journal of Psychiatry, 144,* 1283-1287.

Hudson, S.M., & Ward, T. (1997). Rape: Psychopathology and theory. In D.R. Laws & W. O'Donohue (Eds.), *Sexual deviance* (pp. 332-355). New York: Guilford Press.

Huesmann, L.R., & Miller, L.S. (1994). Long-term effects of repeated exposure to media violence in childhood. In L.R. Huesmann (Ed.), *Aggressive behavior: Current perspectives* (pp. 153-186). New York: Plenum.

Hughes, C. & Agran, M. (1993). Teaching persons with severe disabilities to use self-instruction in community settings: An analysis of applications. *The Journal of the Association for Persons with Severe Handicaps, 18*, 261-274.

Hughes, C., Hugo, K., & Blatt, J. (1996). Self-instructional intervention for teaching generalized problem-solving within a functional task sequence. *American Journal on Mental Retardation, 100*, 565-579.

Hughes, J.R., & Hatsukami, D.K. (1992). The nicotine withdrawal syndrome: A brief review and update. *International Journal of Smoking Cessation, 1*, 21-26.

Hughes, J.R., Higgins, S.T., & Hatsukami, D.K. (1990). Effects of abstinence from tobacco: A critical review. In L.T. Kozlowski, H. Annis, H.D. Cappell, F. Glaser, M. Goodstadt, Y. Israel, H. Kalant, E.M. Sellers, & J. Vingilis (Eds.), *Research advances in alcohol and drug problems*. New York: Plenum.

Hughes, J.R., Higgins, S.T., Bickel, W.K., Hunt, W.K., & Fenwick, J.W. (1991). Caffeine self-adminstration, withdrawal, and adverse effects among coffee drinkers. *Archives of General Psychiatry, 48*, 611-617.

Humphreys, K., & Rappaport, J. (1993). From the community mental health movement to the war on drugs: A study in the definition of social problems. *American Psychologist*, 892-901.

Hunsley in press in 8th   1999,11, 266-277

Hunsley, J., & Bailey, J.M. (1999). The clinical utility of the Rorschach: Unfulfilled promises and an uncertain future. *Psychological Assessment, 11*, 266-277.

Hunt, N. & Robbins, I. (2001). The long-term consequences of war: the experience of World War II. *Aging & Mental Health, 5 (2)*, 183-190.

Hunter, J.E. (1986). Cognitive ability, cognitive aptitudes, job knowledge, and job performance. *Journal of Vocational Behavior, 29*, 340-362.

Hurlburt, R.T. (1979). Random sampling of cognitions and behavior. *Journal of Research on Personality, 13*, 103-111.

Hurlburt, R.T. (1997). Randomly sampling thinking in the natural environment. *Journal of Consulting and Clinical Psychology, 65*, 941-949.

Hurst, J. (1992, March). Blowing smoke. *Los Angeles Times*, pp. A3, A29.

Hurt, R.D., Eberman, K.M., & Croghan, J.T. (1994). Nicotine dependence treatment during inpatient treatment for other addictions: A prospective intervention trial. *Alcohol: Clinical and Experimental Research, 18*, 867-872.

Hurt, R.D., Sachs, D.P.L., & Glover, E.D. (1997). A comparison of sustained release buprioprion versus placebo for treatment of nicotine dependence. *New England Journal of Medicine, 337*, 1195-1202.

Hussian, R.A., & Lawrence, P.S. (1980). Social reinforcement of activity and problem-solving training in the treatment of depressed institutionalized elderly patients. *Cognitive Therapy and Research, 5*, 57-69.

Hutt, C., Hutt, S.J., Lee, D., & Ountsted, C. (1964). Arousal and childhood autism. *Nature, 204*, 908-909.

Hyland, M.E. (1990). The mood-peak flow relationship in adult asthmatics: A pilot study of individual differences and direction of causality. *British Journal of Medical Psychology, 63*, 379-384.

Hynde, G.W., Hern, K.L., Novey, E.S., Eliopulos, D., Marshall, R., Gonzalez, J.J., & Voeller, K.K. (1993). Attention-deficit hyperactivity disorder and asymmetry of the caudate nucleus. *Journal of Child Neurology, 8*, 339-347.

Iacono, W.G., Morean, M., Beiser, M., Fleming, J.A., et al. (1992). Smooth pursuit eye-tracking in first episode psychotic patients and their relatives. *Journal of Abnormal Psychology, 101*, 104-116.

Imber, S.D., Elkin, I., Watkins, J.T., Collins, J.F., Shea, M.T., Leber, W.R., & Glass, D.R. (1990). Mode-specific effects among three treatments for depression. *Journal of Consulting and Clinical Psychology, 58*, 352-359.

Imperato-McGinley, J., Guerrero, L., Gautier, T., & Peterson, R.E. (1974). Steroid 5a-reductase deficiency in man: An inherited form of pseudohermaphroditism. *Science, 186*, 1213-1215.

Ingram, C. (1996, September 26). Bill signed to let police tell of sex offenders' whereabouts. *Los Angeles Times*, pp. A3, A19.

Ingram, R.E., & Kendall, P.C. (1987). The cognitive side of anxiety. *Cognitive Therapy and Research, 11*, 523-536.

Inouye, S.K., Bogardus, S.T., Jr., Charpentier, P.A., Leo-Summers, L., Acampora, D.,

Holford, T.R., & Cooney, L.M., Jr. (1999). A multicomponent intervention to prevent delirium in hospitalized older patients. *New England Journal of Medicine, 340*, 669-676.

Insell, T.R. (1986). The neurobiology of anxiety. In B.F. Shaw, Z.V. Segal, T.M. Wallis, & F.E. Cashman (Eds.), *Anxiety disorders*. New York: Plenum.

Institute of Medicine. (1990a). *Matching. In Broadening the base of treatment for alcohol problems* (pp. 279-302). Washington, DC: National Academy Press.

Institute of Medicine. (1990b). *Treating drug problems*. Washington, DC: National Academy Press.

Institute of Medicine. (1999). *Marijuana and medicine: Assessing the science base*. Washington, DC: National Academy Press.

Insull, W. (Ed.). (1973). *Coronary risk handbook*. New York: American Heart Association.

Irle, E., Exner, C., Thielen, K., Weniger, G., & Ruther, E. (1998). Obsessive-compulsive disorder and ventromedial lesions: Clinical and neuropsychological findings. *American Journal of Psychiatry, 155*, 255-263.

Irwin, M., Lovitz, A., Marder, S.R., Mintz, J., Winslade, W.J., Van Putten, T., & Mills, M.J. (1985). Psychotic patients' understanding of informed consent. *American Journal of Psychiatry, 142*, 1351-1354.

Issidorides, M.R. (1979). Observations in chronic hashish users: Nuclear aberrations in blood and sperm and abnormal acrosomes in spermatozoa. In G.G. Nahas & W.D.M. Paton (Eds.), *Marihuana: Biological effects*. Elmsford, NY: Pergamon.

Ivanoff, A., Jang, S.J., Smyth, N.J., & Linehan, M.M. (1994). Fewer reasons for staying alive when you are thinking of killing yourself: The Brief Reasons for Living Inventory. *Journal of Psychopathology and Behavioral Assessment, 16*, 1-13.

Iwamasa, G.Y. (1993). Asian Americans and cognitive behavioral therapy. *The Behavior Therapist, 16*, 233-235.

Jablonsky, A., Sartorius, N., Cooper, J.E., Anker, A., Korten, A., & Bertelson, A. (1994). Culture and schizophrenia. *British Journal of Psychiatry, 165*, 434-436.

Jackson, A.M. (1973). Psychotherapy: Factors associated with the race of the therapist. *Psychotherapy: Theory, Research, and Practice, 10*, 273-277.

Jackson, C. (1997). Testing a multi-stage model for the adoption of alcohol and tobacco behaviors by children. *Addictive Behaviors, 22*, 1-14.

Jackson, C., Winkleby, M.A., Flora, J.A., & Fortmann, S.P. (1991). Use of educational resources for cardiovascular risk reduction in the Stanford Five-City Project. *American Journal of Preventive Medicine, 7*, 82-88.

Jackson, R.L., & Murphy, K. (1998, June 6). U.S. won't block Oregon suicide law, Reno says. *Los Angeles Times*, pp. A1, A14.

Jackson, R.L., & Weinstein, H. (1996, March 16). Liggett agrees to pay 5 states for tobacco illnesses. *Los Angeles Times*, pp. A1, A15.

Jackson, R.W., Treiber, F.A., Turner, J.R., Davis, H., & Strong, W.B. (1999). Effects of race, sex, and socioeconomic status upon cardiovascular stress responsivity and recovery in youth. *International Journal of Psychophysiology, 31*, 111-119.

Jacob, R.G., Thayer, J.F., Manuck, S.B., Muldoon, M.F., Tamres, L.K., et al. (1999). Ambulatory blood pressure responses and the circumplex model of mood: A 4-day study. *Psychosomatic Medicine, 61*, 319-333.

Jacobs, M., Jacobs, A., Gatz, M., & Schaible, T. (1973). Credibility and desirability of positive and negative structured feedback in groups. *Journal of Consulting and Clinical Psychology, 40*, 244-252.

Jacobsen, L.K., Southwick, S.M., & Kosten, T.R. (2001). Substance use disorders in patients with posttraumatic stress disorder: A review of the literature. *American Journal of Psychiatry, 158*, 1184-1190.

Jacobson, A., & Herald, C. (1990). The relevance of childhood sexual abuse to adult psychiatric inpatient care. *Hospital and Community Psychiatry, 41*, 154-158.

Jacobson, A., & McKinney, W.T. (1982). Affective disorders. In J.H. Griest, J.W. Jefferson, & R.L. Spitzer (Eds.), *Treatment of mental disorders*. New York: Oxford University Press.

Jacobson, E. (1929). *Progressive relaxation*. Chicago: University of Chicago Press.

Jacobson, N.S. (1983). Beyond empiricism: The politics of marital therapy. *American Journal of Family Therapy, 11*, 11-24.

Jacobson, N.S. (1989). The therapist-client relationship in cognitive behavior therapy: Implications for treating depression. *Journal of Cognitive Psychotherapy, 3*, 85-96.

Jacobson, N.S., Christensen, A., Prince, S.E., Cordova, J., & Eldridge, K. (2000). Integrative behavioral couple therapy: an acceptance-based, promising new treatment for couple discord. *Journal of Consulting and Clinical Psychology, 68*, 351-355.

Jacobson, N. S., Martell, C. R., Dimidjian, S. (2001). Behavioral activation treatment for depression: Returning to contextual roots. *Clinical Psychology: Science & Practice, 8,* 255-270.

Jacobson, N.S. (1984). A component analysis of behavioral marital therapy: The relative effectiveness of behavior exchange and problem solving training. *Journal of Consulting and Clinical Psychology, 52,* 295-305.

Jacobson, N.S. (1992). Behavioral couple therapy: A new beginning. *Behavior Therapy, 23,* 493-506.

Jacobson, N.S., & Addis, M.E. (1993). Research on couples and couple therapy: What do we know? Where are we going? *Journal of Consulting and Clinical Psychology, 61,* 85-93.

Jacobson, N.S., & Christensen, A. (1996). *Integrative couple therapy: Promoting acceptance and change.* New York: Norton.

Jacobson, N.S., & Hollon, S.D. (1996). Cognitive-behavior therapy versus pharmacotherapy: Now that the jury's returned its verdict, it's time to present the rest of the evidence. *Journal of Consulting and Clinical Psychology, 64,* 74-80.

Jacobson, N.S., & Margolin, G. (1979). *Marital therapy: Strategies based on social learning.* New York: Brunner/Mazel.

Jacobson, N.S., Dobson, K., Fruzzetti, A.E., Schmaling, K.B., & Salusky, S. (1991). Marital therapy as a treatment for depression. *Journal of Consulting and Clinical Psychology, 59,* 547-557.

Jacobson, N.S., Dobson, K.S., Truax, P.A., Addis, M.E., Koerner, K., Gollan, J.K., Gortner, E., & Prince, S.E. (1996). A component analysis of cognitive-behavioral treatment for depression. *Journal of Consulting and Clinical Psychology, 64,* 295-304.

Jacobson, N.S., Follette, W.C., & Pagel, N. (1986). Predicting who will benefit from behavioral marital therapy. *Journal of Consulting and Clinical Psychology, 54,* 518-522.

Jacobson, N.S., Follette, W.C., Revenstorf, D., Baucom, D.H., Hahlweg, K., & Margolin, G. (1984). Variability of outcome and clinical significance of behavioral marital therapy: A reanalysis of outcome data. *Journal of Consulting and Clinical Psychology, 52,* 497-504.

Jacobson, N.S., Fruzzetti, A.E., Dobson, K., Whisman, M., & Hops, H. (1993). Couple therapy as a treatment for depression. 2: The effects of relationship quality and therapy on depressive relapse. *Journal of Consulting and Clinical Psychology, 61,* 516-519.

Jacobson, N.S., Gottman, J.M., Waltz, J., Rushe, R., Babcock, J., & Holtzworth-Munroe, A. (1994). Affect, verbal content, and psychophysiology in the arguments of couples with a violent husband. *Journal of Consulting and Clinical Psychology, 62,* 982-988.

Jacobson, N.S., Holzworth-Munroe, A., & Schmaling, K.B. (1989). Marital therapy and spouse involvement in the treatment of depression, agoraphobia, and alcoholism. *Journal of Consulting and Clinical Psychology, 57,* 5-10.

Jacobson, N.S., Schmaling, K.B., & Holtzworth-Munroe, A. (1987). Component analysis of behavioral marital therapy: Two-year follow-up and prediction of relapse. *Journal of Marital and Family Therapy, 13,* 187-195.

Jacobson, N.S., Waldron, H., & Moore, D. (1980). Toward a behavioral profile of marital distress. *Journal of Consulting and Clinical Psychology, 48,* 696-703.

Jaffe, J.H. (1985). Drug addiction and drug abuse. In Goodman & Gilman (Eds.), *The pharmacological basis of therapeutic behavior.* New York: Macmillan.

Jamison, K.R. (1979). Manic-depressive illness in the elderly. In O.J. Kaplan (Ed.), *Psychopathology of aging.* New York: Academic Press.

Jamison, K.R. (1992). *Touched with fire: Manic depressive illness and the artistic temperament.* New York: Free Press.

Jampole, L., & Weber, M.K. (1987). An assessment of the behavior of sexually abused and nonsexually abused children with anatomically correct dolls. *Child Abuse and Neglect, 11,* 187-192.

Jandorf, L., Deblinger, E., Neale, J.M., & Stone, A.A. (1986). Daily vs. major life events as predictors of symptom frequency. *Journal of General Psychology, 113,* 205-218.

Janicak, P.G., Davis, J.M., Preskorn, S.H., & Ayd, F.J. (1993). *Principles and practice of psychopharmacological therapy.* Baltimore: Williams & Wilkins.

Janoff-Bulman, R. (1992). *Shattered assumptions: Toward a new psychology of trauma.* New York: Free Press.

Jansen, M.A., Arntz, A., Merckelbach, H., & Mersch, P.P.A. (1994). Personality disorders and features in social phobia and panic disorder. *Journal of Abnormal Psychology, 103,* 391-395.

Jansen, M.A., Glynn, T., & Howard, J. (1996). Prevention of alcohol, tobacco and other drug abuse. *American Behavioral Scientist, 39,* 790-807.

Jarrell, M.P., Johnson, W.G., & Williamson, D.A. (1986). *Insulin and glucose response in the binge purge episode of bulimic women.* Paper presented at the annual convention of the Association for Advancement of Behavior Therapy, Chicago.

Jarrett, R.B., Schaffer, M., McIntire, D., Witt-Browder, A., Kraft, D., & Risser, R.C. (1999). Treatment of atypical depression with cognitive therapy or phenelzine: A double blind, placebo controlled trial. *Archives of General Psychiatry, 56,* 431-437.

Jary, M.L., & Stewart, M.A. (1985). Psychiatric disorder in the parents of adopted children with aggressive conduct disorder. *Neuropsychobiology, 13,* 7-11.

Jasnoski, M.L., & Kugler, J. (1987). Relaxation, imagery, and neuroimmunomodulation. *Annals of the New York Academy of Sciences, 496,* 722-730.

Jay, S.M., Elliott, C.H., Ozolins, M., & Olson, R.A. (1982). *Behavioral management of children's distress during painful medical procedures.* Paper presented at the annual meeting of the American Psychological Association, Washington, DC.

Jay, S.M., Elliott, C.J., Woody, P.D., & Siegel, S. (1991). An investigation of cognitive-behavioral therapy combined with oral Valium for children undergoing painful medical procedures. *Health Psychology, 10,* 317-322.

Jeans, R.F.I. (1976). An independently validated case of multiple personality. *Journal of Abnormal Psychology, 85,* 249-255.

Jeffrey, D.B. (1974). A comparison of the effects of external control and self-control on the modification and maintenance of weight. *Journal of Abnormal Psychology, 83,* 404-410.

Jeffrey, R.W. (1991). Weight management and hypertension. *Annals of Behavioral Medicine, 13,* 18-22.

Jeffrey, R.W., Forster, J.L., & Schmid, T.L. (1989). Worksite health promotion: Feasibility testing of repeated weight control and smoking cessation classes. *American Journal of Health Promotion, 3,* 11-16.

Jellinek, E.M. (1952). Phases of alcohol addiction. *Quarterly Journal of Studies on Alcohol, 13,* 673-684.

Jenike, M.A. (1986). Theories of etiology. In M.A. Jenike, L. Baer, & W.E. Minichiello (Eds.), *Obsessive-compulsive disorders.* Littleton, MA: PSG Publishing.

Jenike, M.A. (1990). Psychotherapy. In A.S. Bellack & M. Hersen (Eds.), *Handbook of comparative treatments for adult disorders* (pp. 245-255). New York: Wiley.

Jenike, M.A., & Rauch, S.L. (1994). Managing the patient with treatment-resistant obsessive-compulsive disorder: Current strategies. *Journal of Clinical Psychiatry, 55,* 11-17.

Jenike, M.A., Baer, L., & Minichiello, W.E. (1986). *Obsessive-compulsive disorders: Theory and management.* Littleton, MA: PSG Publishing.

Jenkins, C.D. (1976). Recent evidence supporting psychologic and social risk factors for coronary disease. *New England Journal of Medicine, 294,* 1033-1038.

Jenkins, J.M., & Smith, M.A. (1991). Marital disharmony and children's behaviour problems: Aspects of a poor marriage that affect children adversely. *Journal of Child Psychology & Psychiatry & Allied Disciplines, 32,* 793-810.

Jensen, J.P., Bergin, A.E., & Greaves, D.W. (1990). The meaning of eclecticism: New survey and analysis of components. *Professional Psychology: Research and Practice, 21,* 124-130.

Jensen, P.S., Martin, D., & Cantwell, D.P. (1997). Comorbidity in ADHD: Implications for research, practice, and DSM-V. *Journal of the American Academy of Child and Adolescent Psychiatry, 27,* 742-747.

Jeste, D.V. et al (1999). Consensus statement on the upcoming crisis in geriatric mental health. *Archives of General Psychiatry, 56,* 848-853.

Jeste, D.V., Harris, M.J., Pearlson, G.D., Rabins, P.V., Lesser, I., Miller, B., Coles, C., & Yassa, R. (1988). Late-onset schizophrenia: Studying clinical validity. *Psychiatric Annals of North America, 11,* 1-13.

Jeste, D.V., Lacro, J.P., Gilbert, P.L., Kline, J., & Kline, N. (1993). Treatment of late-life schizophrenia with neuroleptics. *Schizophrenia Bulletin, 19,* 817-830.

Jeste, D.V., Manley, M., & Harris, M.J. (1991). Psychoses. In J. Sadavoy, L.W. Lazarus, & L.F. Jarvik (Eds.), *Comprehensive review of geriatric psychiatry* (pp. 353-368). Washington, DC: American Psychiatric Press.

Jiang, V., Babyak, M., Krantz, D.S., Waugh, R.A., Coleman, E., et al. (1996). Mental stress-induced myocardial ischemia and cardiac events. *JAMA, 275,* 1651-1656.

Jimerson, D.C., Lesem, M.D., Kate, W.H., & Brewerton, T.D. (1992). Low serotonin and dopamine metabolite concentrations in cerebrospinal fluid from bulimic patients with frequent binge episodes. *Archives of General Psychiatry, 49,* 132-138.

Jimerson, D.C., Wolfe, B.E., Metzger, E.D., Finkelstein, D.M., Cooper, T.B., et al. (1997). Decreased serotonin function in bulimia nervosa. *Archives of General Psychiatry, 54,* 529-536.

Johnson, B.A. (1991). Cannabis. In I.B. Glass (Ed.), *International handbook of addiction behavior.* London: Tavistock/Routledge.

Johnson, C.L., Rifkind, B.M., & Sempos, C.T., et al. (1993). Declining serum total cholesterol levels among U.S. adults. *Journal of the American Medical Association, 269*, 3002-3008.

Johnson, D.R. (1987). The role of the creative arts therapist in the diagnosis and treatment of psychological trauma. *The Arts in Psychotherapy, 14*, 7-13.

Johnson, J.G., Cohen, P., Smailes, E.M. et al. (2001). Childhood verbal abuse and risk for personality disorders during adolescence and early childhood. *Comprehensive Psychiatry, 42*, 16-23.

Johnson, J., Horvath, E., & Weissman, M.M. (1991). The validity of depression with psychotic features based on a community study. *Archives of General Psychiatry, 48*, 1075-1081.

Johnson, J., Weissman, M.M., & Klerman, G.L. (1990). Panic disorder, comorbidity, and suicide attempts. *Archives of General Psychiatry, 47*, 805-808.

Johnson, J.G., Cohen, P., Brown, J., Smailes, E.M., & Bernstein, D.P. (1999). Childhood maltreatment increases risk for personality disorders during early adulthood. *Archives of General Psychiatry, 56*, 600-606.

Johnson, K.W., Anderson, N.B., Bastida, E., Kramer, B.J., Williams, D., & Wong, M. (1995). Macrosocial and environmental influences on minority health. *Health Psychology, 14*, 601-612.

Johnson, L. (1995). *Psychotherapy in the age of accountability*. New York: Norton.

Johnson, M.K., & Raye, C.L. (1981). Reality monitoring. *Psychological Review, 88*, 67-85.

Johnson, M.R., & Lydiard, R.B. (1998). Comorbidity of major depression and panic disorder. *Journal of Clinical Psychology, 54*, 201-210.

Johnson, S.M., Hunsley, J., Greenberg, L., Schindler, D. (1999). Emotionally focused couples therapy: Status and challenges. *Clinical Psychology: Science & Practice , 6*, 67-79.

Johnson, S.L., & Miller, I. (1997). Negative life events and time to recovery from episodes of bipolar disorder. *Journal of Abnormal Psychology, 196*, 449-457.

Johnson, S.M., & Greenberg, L.S. (1985). Differential effects of experiential and problem-solving interventions in resolving marital conflict. *Journal of Consulting and Clinical Psychology, 53*, 175-184.

Johnson, S.M., & Greenberg, L.S. (1987). Emotionally focused marital therapy: An overview. *Psychotherapy, 24*, 552-560.

Johnson, W.G., Tsoh, J.Y., & Varnado, P.J. (1996). Eating disorders: Efficacy of pharmacological and psychological interventions. *Clinical Psychology Review, 16*, 457-478.

Johnston, D.W. (1997). Hypertension. In A. Baum, S. Newman, J. Weinman, R West, & C. McManus (Eds.), *Cambridge handbook of psychology, health and medicine* (pp. 500-501). Cambridge, UK: Cambridge University Press.

Johnston, D.W., Gold, A., Kentish, J., Leach, G., & Robinson, B. (1993). Effect of stress management on blood pressure in mild primary hypertension. *British Medical Journal, 306*, 963-966.

Johnston, H.F., & Fruehling, J.J. (1994). Pharmacotherapy for depression in children and adolescents. In W.M. Reynolds & H.F. Johnston (Eds.), *Handbook of depression in children and adolescents*. New York: Plenum Press.

Johnston, L.D., O'Malley, P.M., & Bachman, J.G. (2001a). *Monitoring the future national results on adolescent drug use: Overview of key findings, 2000*. (NIH Publication No. 01-4923). Bethesda, MD: National Institute on Drug Abuse. (Also available on the Web at www.monitoringthefuture.org.)

Johnston, L.D., O'Malley, P.M., & Bachman, J.G. (2001b). *Monitoring the future national results on adolescent drug use, 1975-2000*. Volume I: Secondary school students (NIH Publication No. 01-4924). Bethesda, MD: National Institute on Drug Abuse, c. 492 pp.

Johnston, L.D., O'Malley, P.M., & Bachman, J.G. (2001c). *Monitoring the future national results on adolescent drug use, 1975-2000*. Volume II: College students and adults ages 19-40 (NIH Publication No. 01-4925). Bethesda, MD: National Institute on Drug Abuse, c. 238 pp.

Johnston, M., & Voegele, C. (1993). Benefits of psychological preparation for surgery: A meta-analysis. *Annals of Behavioral Medicine, 15*, 245-256.

Johnston, M.B., Whitman, T.L., & Johnson, M. (1980). Teaching addition and subtraction to mentally retarded children: A self-instructional program. *Applied Research in Mental Retardation, 1*, 141-160.

Joiner, T.E. (1995). The price of soliciting and receiving negative feedback: Self-verification theory as a vulnerability to depression theory. *Journal of Abnormal Psychology, 104*, 364-372.

Joiner, T.E. (1999). The clustering and contagion of suicide. *Current Directions in Psychological Science, 8*, 89-92.

Joiner, T.E., & Metalsky, G.I. (1995). A prospective test of an integrative interpersonal theory of depression: A naturalistic study of college roommates. *Journal of Personality and Social Psychiatry, 69*, 778-789.

Joiner, T.E., & Schmidt, N.B. (1998). Excessive reassurance-seeking predicts depressive but not anxious reactions to acute stress. *Journal of Abnormal Psychology, 107*, 533-537.

Joiner, T.E., Alfano, M.S., & Metalsky, G.I. (1992). When depression breeds contempt: Reassurance seeking, self-esteem, and rejection of depressed college students by their roommates. *Journal of Abnormal Psychology, 101*, 165-173

Jolanta, J. R. & Tomasz, M. S. (2000). The links between body dysmorphic disorder and eating disorders. *European Psychiatry, 15*, 302-305.

Jones, G.M. (1987). Elderly people and domestic crime: Reflections on ageism, sexism, victimology. *British Journal of Criminology, 27*, 191-201.

Jones, M. (1953). *The therapeutic community*. New York: Basic Books.

Jones, M.C. (1924). A laboratory study of fear: The case of Peter. *Pedagogical Seminary, 31*, 308-315.

Jones, R.T. (1980). Human effects: An overview. In *Marijuana research findings*. Washington, DC: U.S. Government Printing Office.

Jorenby, D.E., Leischow, S.J., Nides, M.A., Rennard, S.I., Johnston, J.A., et al. (1999). A controlled trial of sustained-release buproprion, a nicotine patch, or both for smoking cessation. *New England Journal of Medicine, 340*, 685-691.

Journal of Clinical Psychology, 56, 395-430.

Judd, L.J., Akiskal, H.S., Maser, J.D., Zeller, P.J., Endicott, J., et al. (1998). A prospective 12-year study of subsyndromal and syndromal depressive symptoms in unipolar major depressive disorders. *Archives of Gerneral Psychiatry, 55*, 694-701.

Judd, L.L. (1997). The clinical course of unipolar depressive disorders. *Archives of General Psychiatry, 54*, 989-992.

Julkunen, J.T., Salonen, R., Kaplan, G.A., Chesney, M.A., & Salonen, J.T. (1994). Hostility and the progression of carotid atherosclerosis. *Psychosomatic Medicine, 56*, 519-525.

Jung, C.G. (1935). Fundamental psychological conceptions. In M. Barker & M. Game (Eds.), *A report of five lectures*. London: Institute of Medical Psychology.

Junginger, J., Barker, S., & Coe, D. (1992). Mood theme and bizarreness of delusions in schizophrenia and mood psychosis. *Journal of Abnormal Psychology, 101*, 287-292.

Just, N., & Alloy, L.B. (1997). The response styles theory of depression: Tests and an extension of the theory. *Journal of Abnormal Psychology, 106*, 221-229.

Jutai, J.W., & Hare, R.D. (1983). Psychopathy and selective attention during performance of a complex perceptual-motor task. *Psychophysiology, 20*, 140-151.

Kafka, M. (1995, October). *Hypersexual desire in males: An operational definition and clinical implications for men with paraphilias and paraphilic-related disorders*. Presented at the annual conference of the Association for the Treatment of Sexual Abusers, New Orleans. As cited in Maletzky (2002).

Kagan, J., & Snidman, N. (1991a). Infant predictors of inhibited and uninhibited profiles. *Psychological Science, 2*, 40-44.

Kahana, R.J. (1987). Geriatric psychotherapy: Beyond crisis management. In J. Sadavoy & M. Leszcz (Eds.), *Treating the elderly with psychotherapy*. Madison, CT: International Universities Press.

Kahn, R.L., Zarit, S.H., Hilbert, N.M., & Niederehe, G. (1975). Memory complaint and impairment in the aged: The effect of depression and altered brain function. *Archives of General Psychiatry, 32*, 1569-1573.

Kahneman, D. (1973). *Attention and effort*. Englewood Cliffs, NJ: Prentice-Hall.

Kail (1992). General slowing of information-processing by persons with mental retardation. *American Journal on Mental Retardation, 97*, 333-341.

Kaiser, F.E., Viosca, S.P., Morley, J.E., Mooradian, A.D., Davis, S.S., & Korenman, S.G. (1988). Impotence and aging: Clinical and hormonal factors. *Journal of the American Geriatrics Society, 36*, 511-519.

Kalichman, S.C. (1991). Psychopathology and personality characteristics of criminal sexual offenders as a function of victim age. *Archives of Sexual Behavior, 20*, 187-198.

Kalichman, S.C. (1995). *Understanding AIDS: A guide for mental health professionals*. Washington, DC: American Psychological Association.

Kalichman, S.C. (1996). *Answering your questions about AIDS*. Washington, DC: American Psychological Association.

Kalichman, S.C., Sikkema, K., & Somlai, A. (1995). Assessing persons with human immunodeficiency virus (HIV) infection using the Beck Depression Inventory:

Disease processes and other potential confounds. *Journal of Personality Assessment, 64*, 86-100.

Kamarck, T.M., Shiffman, S.M., Smithline, L., Goodie, J.L., Paty, J.A., et al. (1998). Effects of task strain, social conflict, and emotional activation on ambulatory cardiovascular activity: Daily life consequences of recurring stress in a multiethnic adult sample. *Health Psychology, 17*, 17-29.

Kamarck, T.W., Annunziato, B., & Amateau, L.M. (1995). Affiliations moderate the effects of social threat on stress-related cardiovascular responses: Boundary conditions for a laboratory model of social support. *Psychosomatic Medicine, 57*, 183-194.

Kamarck, T.W., Everson, S.A., Kaplan, G.A., Manuck, S.B., Jennings, J.R., et al. (1997). Exaggerated blood pressure responses during mental stress are associated with enhanced carotid atherosclerosis in middle-aged Finnish men. *Circulation, 96*, 3842-3848.

Kamarck, T.W., Jennings, J.R., Debski, T.T., Glickman-Weiss, E., Johnson, P.S., et al. (1992). Reliable measures of behaviorally-evoked cardiovascular reactivity from a PC-based test battery: Results from student and community samples. *Psychophysiology, 29*, 17-28.

Kammen, D.P. van, Bunney, W.E., Docherty, J.P., Jimerson, J.C., Post, R.M., et al. (1977). Amphetamine induced catecholamine activation in schizophrenia and depression. *Advances in Biochemical Psychopharmacology, 16*, 655-659.

Kandel, D.B., Davies, M., Karus, D., & Yamaguchi, K. (1986). The consequences in young adulthood of adolescent drug involvement. *Archives of General Psychiatry, 43*, 746-754.

Kandel, D.B., Murphy, D., & Karus, D. (1985). *National Institute on Drug Abuse Research Monograph Series 61*. Washington, DC: NIDA.

Kane, J.M., Marder, S.R., Schooler, N.R. et al. (2001). Clozapine and haloperidol in moderately refractory schizophrenia: A 6-month randomized and double-blind comparison. *Archives of General Psychiatry, 58*, 965-972.

Kane, J., Honigfeld, G., Singer, J., Meltzer, H., and the Clozapine Collaborative Study Group. (1988). Clozapine for treatment resistant schizophrenics. *Archives of General Psychiatry, 45*, 789-796.

Kane, J.M., Woerner, M., Weinhold, P., Wegner, J., Kinon, B., & Bernstein, M. (1986). Incidence of tardive dyskinesia: Five-year data from a prospective study. *Psychopharmacology Bulletin, 20*, 387-389.

Kane, R.L., Parsons, D.A., & Goldstein, G. (1983). Statistical relationships and discriminative accuracy of the Halstead-Reitan, Luria-Nebraska, and Wechsler IQ scores in the identification of brain damage. *Journal of Clinical and Experimental Neuropsychology, 7*, 211-223.

Kanfer, F.H., & Busenmeyer, J.R. (1982). The use of problem-solving and decision making in behavior therapy. *Clinical Psychology Review, 2*, 239-266.

Kanfer, F.H., & Phillips, J.S. (1970). *Learning foundations of behavior therapy*. New York: Wiley.

Kanner, L. (1943). Autistic disturbances of affective contact. *Nervous Child, 2*, 217-250.

Kanner, L. (1973). *Childhood psychosis: Initial studies and new insights*. Washington, D.C.: V. H. Winston and Sons.

Kantorovich, N.V. (1930). An attempt at associative-reflex therapy in alcoholism. *Psychological Abstracts, 4*, 493.

Kaplan, H.I., & Sadock, B.J. (1991). *Synopsis of psychiatry: Behavioral sciences, clinical psychiatry*. Baltimore: Williams & Williams.

Kaplan, H.S. (1974). *The new sex therapy*. New York: Brunner/Mazel.

Kaplan, H.S. (1991). Sex therapy with older patients. In W.A. Myers (Ed.), *New techniques in the psychotherapy of older patients* (pp. 21-37). Washington, DC: American Psychiatric Press.

Kaplan, H.S. (1997). Sexual desire disorders (hypoactive sexual desire and sexual aversion). In G.O. Gabbard & S.D. Atkinson (Eds.), *Synopsis of treatments of psychiatric disorders* (2nd ed., pp. 771-780). Washington, DC: American Psychiatric Press.

Kaplan, J.R., Manuck, S.B., Williams, J.K., & Strawn, W. (1993). Psychosocial influences on atherosclerosis: Evidence for effects and mechanisms in nonhuman primates. In J. Blascovich & E.S. Katkin (Eds.), *Cardiovascular reactivity* (pp. 3-26). Washington, DC: American Psychological Association.

Kaplan, M.S., & Kreuger, R.B. (1997). Voyeurism: Psychopathology and theory. In D.R. Laws & W. O'Donohue (Eds.), *Sexual deviance* (pp. 297-310). NY: Guilford Press.

Karasek, R.A. (1979). Job demands, job decision latitude, and mental strain: Implications for job redesign. *Administrative Science, 24*, 285-308.

Karasu, T.B., Stein, S.P., & Charles, E.S. (1979). Age factors in the patient-therapist relationship. *Journal of Nervous and Mental Disease, 167*, 100-104.

Karno, M., & Golding, J.M. (1991). Obsessive-compulsive disorder. In L.N. Robinson & D.A. Regier (Eds.), *Psychiatric disorders in America*. New York: Free Press.

Karno, M.G., Golding, M., Sorensen, S.B., & Burnam, A. (1988). The epidemiology of OCD in five U.S. communities. *Archives of General Psychiatry, 45*, 1094-1099.

Karon, B.P., & VandenBos, G.R. (1998). Schizophrenia and psychosis in elderly populations. In I.H. Nordhus, G.R. VandenBos, S. Berg, & P. Fromholt, (Eds.), *Clinical geropsychology* (pp. 219-227). Washington, D.C.: American Psychological Association.

Kasanin, J. (1933). The acute schizoaffective psychoses. *American Journal of Psychiatry, 13*, 97-123.

Kashani, J.H., & Carlson, G.A. (1987). Seriously depressed preschoolers. *American Journal of Psychiatry, 144*, 348-350.

Kashani, J.H., Beck, N.C., Hoeper, E.W., Fallahi, C., Corcoran, C.M., McAllister, J.A., Rosenberg, T.K., & Reid, J.C. (1987). Psychiatric disorders in a community sample of adolescents. *American Journal of Psychiatry, 144*, 584-589.

Kashani, J.H., Holcomb, W.R., & Orvaschel, H. (1986). Depression and depressive symptoms in preschool children from the general population. *American Journal of Psychiatry, 143*, 1138-1143.

Kashani, J.H., Orvaschel, H., Rosenberg, T.K., & Reid, J.C. (1989). Psychopathology in a community sample of children and adolescents: A developmental perspective. *Journal of the American Academy of Child and Adolescent Psychiatry, 28*, 701-706.

Kasl-Godley, J. & Gatz, M. (2000). Psychosocial intervention for individuals with dementia: An integration of theory, therapy, and a clinical understanding of dementia. *Clinical Psychology, 20* (6), 755-782.

Kasl-Godley, J.E., Gatz, M., & Fiske, A. (1998). Depression and depressive symptoms in old age. In I.H. Nordhus, G.R. VandenBos, S. Berg, & P. Fromholt (Eds.), *Clinical geropsychology* (pp. 211-217). Washington, D.C.: American Psychological Association.

Kasl-Godley, J., & Gatz, M. (1999). *Psychosocial interventions for individuals with dementia: An integration of theory, therapy, and a clinical understanding of dementia*. Unpublished manuscript, University of Southern California.

Kaslow, N.J., & Racusin, G.R. (1990). Childhood depression: Current status and future directions. In A.S. Bellack, M. Hersen, & A.E. Kazdin (Eds.), *International handbook of behavior modification and therapy* (2nd ed.). New York: Plenum.

Kaslow, N.J., & Thompson, M.P. (1998). Applying the criteria for empirically supported treatments to studies of psychosocial interventions for child and adolescent depression. *Journal of Clinical Child Psychology, 27*, 146-155.

Kaslow, N.J., Brown, R.T., & Mee, L. (1994). Cognitive and behavioral correlates of childhood depression: A developmental perspective. In W.M. Reynolds & H.F. Johnston (Eds.), *Handbook of depression in children and adolescents*. New York: Plenum Press.

Kaslow, N.J., Stark, K.D., Printz, B., Livingston, R., & Tsai, Y. (1992). Cognitive Triad Inventory for Children: Development and relationship to depression and anxiety. *Journal of Clinical Child Psychology, 21*, 339-347.

Kasprowicz, A.L., Manuck, S.B., Malkoff, S., & Kranz, D.S. (1990). Individual differences in behaviorally evoked cardiovascular response: Temporal stability and hemodynamic patterning. *Psychophysiology, 27*, 605-619.

Kassett, J.A., Gershon, E.S., Maxwell, M.E., et al. (1989). Psychiatric disorders in the first-degree relatives of probands with bulimia nervosa. *American Journal of Psychiatry, 146*, 1468-1471.

Kaszniak, A.W., Nussbaum, P.D., Berren, M.R., & Santiago, J. (1988). Amnesia as a consequence of male rape: A case report. *Journal of Abnormal Psychology, 97*, 100-104.

Katz, E.R. (1980). Illness impact and social reintegration. In J. Kellerman (Ed.), *Psychological aspects of childhood cancer*. Springfield, IL: Charles C. Thomas.

Katz, E.R., Kellerman, J., & Siegel, S.E. (1980). Behavioral distress in children with leukemia undergoing bone marrow aspirations. *Journal of Consulting and Clinical Psychology, 48*, 356-365.

Katz, E.R., Varni, J.W., Rubenstein, C.L., Blew, A., & Hubert, N. (1992). Teacher, parent, and child evaluative ratings of a school reintegration program for children with newly diagnosed cancer. *Children's Health Care, 21*, 69-75.

Katz, H.M., & Gunderson, J.G. (1990). Individual psychodynamically oriented psychotherapy for schizophrenic patients. In M.I. Herz, S.J. Keith, & J.P. Docherty (Eds.), *Handbook of schizophrenia: Psychosocial treatment of schizophrenia* (pp. 69-90). Amsterdam, The Netherlands: Elsevier Science Publishers.

Katz, R.C., Gipson, M.T., Kearl, A., & Kriskovich, M. (1989). Assessing sexual aversion in college students: The Sexual Aversion Scale. *Journal of Sex and Marital Therapy, 15*, 135-140.

Katzelnick, D.J., Kobak, K.A., Greist, J.H., Jefferson, J.W., Mantle, J.M., & Serlin, R.C. (1995). Sertraline for social phobia: A double-blind, placebo-controlled crossover study. *American Journal of Psychiatry, 152*, 1368-1371.

Kaufmann, P.G., Jacob, R.G., Ewart, C.K., Chesney, M.A., Muenz, L.R., Doub, N., Mercer, W., & HIPP Investigators. (1988). Hypertension intervention pooling project. *Health Psychology, 7*, 209-224.

Kaw, E. (1993). Medicalization of racial features: Asian American women and cosmetic surgery. *Medical Anthropology Quarterly, 7*, 74.

Kawachi, I., Colditz, G.A., Ascherio, A., Rimm, E.B., Giovannucci, E., et al. (1994). Prospective study of phobic anxiety and risk of coronary heart disease in men. *Circulation, 89*, 1992-1997.

Kawachi, I., Sparrow, D., Spiro, A., Vokonas, P., & Weiss, S.T. (1996). A prospective study of anger and coronary heart disease: The normative aging study. *Circulation, 94*, 2090-2094.

Kawas, C., Resnick, S., Morrison, A., Brookmeyer, R., et al. (1997). A prospective study of estrogen replacement therapy (ERT) and the risk of developing Alzheimer's disease: The Baltimore longitudinal study of aging. *Neurology, 48*, 1517-1521.

Kay, D.W.K., Cooper, A.F., Garside, R.F., & Roth, M. (1976). The differentiation of paranoid from affective psychoses by patient's premorbid characteristics. *British Journal of Psychiatry, 129*, 207-215.

Kaye, W.H., Greeno, C.G., Fernstrom, J., Fernstrom, M., Moss, H., et al. (1998). Alterations in serotonin activity and psychiatric symptoms after recovery from bulimia nervosa. *Archives of General Psychiatry, 55*, 927-935.

Kazdin, A.E. (1985). *Treatment of antisocial behavior in children and adolescents.* Homewood, Il.: Dorsey Press.

Kazdin, A.E. (1994). Psychotherapy for children and adolescents. In A.E. Bergin & S.L. Garfield (Eds.), *Handbook of psychotherapy and behavior change* (4th ed., pp. 543-594). New York: Wiley.

Kazdin, A.E., & Kagan, J. (1994). Models of dysfunction in developmental psychopathology. *Clinical Psychology: Science and Practice, 1*, 35-52.

Kazdin, A.E., & Weisz, J.R. (1998). Identifying and developing empirically supported child and adolescent treatments. *Journal of Consulting and Clinical Psychology, 66*, 19-36.

Keane, T.M. (in press). The role of exposure therapy in the psychological treatment of PTSD. *PTSD Clinical Quarterly*.

Keane, T.M., & Wolfe, J. (1990). Co-morbidity in post-traumatic stress disorder: An analysis of community and clinical studies. *Journal of Applied Social Psychology, 20*, 1776-1788.

Keane, T.M., Fairbank, J.A., Caddell, J.M., & Zimering, R.T. (1989). Implosive (flooding) therapy reduces symptoms of PTSD in Vietnam combat veterans. *Behavior Therapy, 20*, 245-260.

Keane, T.M., Fisher, L.M., Krinsley, K.E., & Niles, B.L. (1994). Posttraumatic stress disorder. In M. Hersen & R.T. Ammerman (Eds.), *Handbook of prescriptive treatments for adults* (pp. 237-260). New York: Plenum.

Keane, T.M., Foy, D.W., Nunn, B., & Rychtarik, R.G. (1984). Spouse contracting to increase Antabuse compliance in alcoholic veterans. *Journal of Clinical Psychology, 40*, 340-344.

Keane, T.M., Gerardi, R.J., Quinn, S.J., & Litz, B.T. (1992). Behavioral treatment of post-traumatic stress disorder. In S.M. Turner, K.S. Calhoun, & H.E. Adams (Eds.), *Handbook of clinical behavior therapy* (2nd ed., pp. 87-97). New York: Wiley.

Keane, T.M., Zimering, R.T., & Caddell, J. (1985). A behavioral formulation of post-traumatic stress disorder in Vietnam veterans. *The Behavior Therapist, 8*, 9-12.

Keck, P.E., & McElroy, S.L. (1998). Pharmacological treatment of bipolar disorders. In P.E. Nathan & J.M. Gorman (Eds.), *A guide to treatments that work* (pp. 249-269). New York: Oxford University Press.

Keck, P.E., McElroy, S.L., Strakowski, S.M., West, S.A., Sax, K.W., et al. (1998). 12-month outcome of patients with bipolar disorder following hospitalization for a manic or mixed episode. *American Journal of Psychiatry, 155*, 646-652.

Keefe, F.J., & Gil, K.M. (1986). Behavioral concepts in the analysis of chronic pain syndromes. *Journal of Consulting and Clinical Psychology, 54*, 776-783.

Keefe, R.S., Silverman, J.M., Mohs, R.C., Siever, L.J., et al. (1997). Eye tracking, attention, and schizotypal symptoms in nonpsychotic relatives of patients with schizophrenia. *Archives of General Psychiatry, 54*, 169-176.

Keel, P.K., & Mitchell, J.E. (1997). Outcome in bulimia nervosa. *American Journal of Psychiatry, 154*, 313-321.

Keel, P.K., Mitchell, J.E., Miller, K.B., Davis, T.L., & Crowe, S.J. (1999). Long-term outcome of bulimia nervosa. *Archives of General Psychiatry, 56*, 63-69.

Keith, J. (1982). *Old people as people.* Boston: Little, Brown.

Keller, M.B., Beardslee, W., Lavori, P.W., Wunder, J., Dils, D.L., & Samuelson, H. (1988). Course of major depression in non-referred adolescents: A retrospective study. *Journal of Affective Disorders, 15*, 235-243.

Keller, M.B., Kocsis, J.H., Thase, M.E., Gelenberg, A.J., Rush, J., et al. (1998). Maintenance phase efficacy of sertraline for chronic depression. *JAMA, 280*, 1665-1672.

Keller, M.B., Shapiro, R.W., Lavori, P.W., & Wolpe, N. (1982). Relapse in major depressive disorder: Analysis with the life table. *Archives of General Psychiatry, 39*, 911-915.

Kellerman, J. (1989). *Silent partner.* New York: Bantam Books.

Kellerman, J., & Varni, J.W. (1982). Pediatric hematology/oncology. In D.C. Russo & J.W. Varni (Eds.), *Behavioral pediatrics: Research and practice.* New York: Plenum.

Kelley, M.L. (1990). *School-home notes: Promoting children's classroom success.* New York: Guilford Press.

Kellner, R. (1982). Disorders of impulse control (not elsewhere classified). In J.H Griest, J.W. Jefferson, & R.L. Spitzer (Eds.), *Treatment of mental disorders.* New York: Oxford University Press.

Kelly, G.A. (1955). *The psychology of personal constructs.* New York: Norton.

Kelly, J.A. (1985). Group social skills training. *The Behavior Therapist, 8*, 93-95.

Kelly, J.A. (1995). *Changing HIV risk behavior: Practical strategies.* New York: Guilford.

Kelly, J.A., & St. Lawrence, J.S. (1988a). *The AIDS health crisis: Psychological and social interventions.* New York: Plenum.

Kelly, J.A., & St. Lawrence, J.S. (1988b). AIDS prevention and treatment: Psychology's role in the health crisis. *Clinical Psychology Review, 8*, 255-284.

Kelly, J.A., Murphy, D., Sikkema, K., & Kalichman, S.C. (1993). Psychological interventions are urgently needed to prevent HIV infection: New priorities for behavioral research in the second decade of AIDS. *American Psychologist, 48*, 1023-1034.

Kelly, J.A., St. Lawrence, J.S., Betts, R., Brasfield, T., & Hood, H. (1990). A skills training group intervention model to assist persons in reducing risk behaviors for HIV infection. *AIDS Education and Prevention, 2*, 24-35.

Kelly, J.A., St. Lawrence, J.S., Hood, H., & Brasfield, T. (1989). Behavioral intervention to reduce AIDS risk activities. *Journal of Consulting and Clinical Psychology, 57*, 60-67.

Kempster, N. (1996, August 25). Clinton orders tracking of sex offenders. *Los Angeles Times*, pp. A20.

Kendall, P.C., Haaga, D.A.F., Ellis, A., Bernard, M., DiGiuseppe, R., & Kassinove, H. (1995). Rational-emotive therapy in the 1990s and beyond: Current status, recent revisions, and research questions. *Clinical Psychology Review, 15*, 169-185.

Kendall, P.C. (1990). Cognitive processes and procedures in behavior therapy. In C.M. Franks, G.T. Wilson, P.C. Kendall, & J.P. Foreyt (Eds.), *Review of behavior therapy: Theory and practice* (Vol. 12, pp. 103-137). New York: Guilford.

Kendall, P.C., & Braswell, L. (1985). *Cognitive-behavioral therapy for impulsive children.* New York: Guilford.

Kendall, P.C., & Ingram, R.E. (1989). Cognitive-behavioral perspectives: Theory and research on depression and anxiety. In P.C. Kendall & D. Watson (Eds.), *Anxiety and depression: Distinctive and overlapping features* (pp. 27-54). New York: Academic Press.

Kendell, R.E. (1975). *The role of diagnosis in psychiatry.* London: Blackwell.

Kendler, K.S., Myers, J.M., O'Neill, F.A. et al. (2000). Clinical features of schizophrenia and linkage to chromosomes 5q, 6p, 8p, and 10p in the Irish study of high-density schizophrenia families. *American Journal of Psychiatry, 157*, 402-408.

Kendler, K.S., Myers, J., & Prescott, C.A. (2002). The etiology of phobias: An evaluation of the stress-diathesis model. *Archives of General Psychiatry, 59*, 242-249.

Kendler, K.S., Myers, J., Prescott, C.A., & Neale, M.C. (2001). The genetic epidemiology of irrational fears and phobias in men. *Archives of General Psychiatry, 58,* 257-267.

Kendler, K.S., Pedersen, N., Johnson, L., Neale, M.C., & Mathe, A. (1993). A Swedish pilot twin study of affective illness, including hospital and population-ascertained subsamples. *Archives of General Psychiatry, 50,* 699-706.

Kendler, K.S. (1993). Twin studies of psychiatric illness: Current status and future directions. *Archives of General Psychiatry, 50,* 905-914.

Kendler, K.S. (1997). The diagnostic validity of melancholic major depression in a population-based sample of female twins. *Archives of General Psychiatry, 54,* 299-304.

Kendler, K.S., & Gardner, C.O. (1998). Boundaries of major depression: An evaluation of DSM-IV criteria. *American Journal of Psychiatry, 155,* 172-177.

Kendler, K.S., & Gruenberg, A.M. (1984). Independent analysis of Danish adoption study of schizophrenia. *Archives of General Psychiatry, 41,* 555-562.

Kendler, K.S., & Prescott, C.A. (1998). Cannabis use, abuse, and dependence in a population-based sample of female twins. *American Journnal of Psychiatry, 155,* 1016-1022.

Kendler, K.S., & Prescott, C.A. (1999). Caffeine intake, tolerance, and withdrawal in women: A population-based twin study. *American Journal of Psychiatry, 156,* 223-228.

Kendler, K.S., Karkowski, L.M., & Prescott, C.A. (1999). Causal relationship between stressful life events and the onset of major depression. *American Journal of Psychiatry, 156,* 837-841.

Kendler, K.S., Karkowski-Shuman, L., & Walsh, D. (1996). Age of onset in schizophrenia and risk of illness in relatives. *British Journal of Psychiatry, 169,* 213-218.

Kendler, K.S., Neale, M.C., & Walsh, D. (1995). Evaluating the spectrum concept of schizophrenia in the Roscommon Family Study. *American Journal of Psychiatry, 152,* 749-754.

Kendler, K.S., Neale, M.C., Kessler, R.C., Heath, A.C., & Eaves, L.J. (1992). The genetic epidemiology of phobias in women: The interrelationship of agoraphobia, social phobia, and simple phobia. *Archives of General Psychiatry, 49,* 273-281.

Kennedy, E., Spence, S.H., & Hensley, R. (1989). An examination of the relationship between childhood depression and social competence amongst primary school children. *Journal of Child Psychology and Psychiatry, 30,* 561-573.

Kent, J.S., & Clopton, J.R. (1992). Bulimic women's perceptions of their family relationships. *Journal of Clinical Psychology, 48,* 281-292.

Kernberg, O.F. (1985). *Borderline conditions and pathological narcissism.* Northvale, NJ: Jason Aronson.

Keshavan, M.S., Rosenberg, D., Sweeney, J.A., & Pettegrew, J.W. (1998). Decreased caudate volume in neuroleptic-naive psychotic patients. *American Journal of Psychiatry, 155,* 774-778.

Kessel, N., & Grossman, G. (1961). Suicide in alcoholics. *British Medical Journal, 2,* 1671-1672.

Kessler, R.C., & McLeod, J.D. (1985). Social support and mental health in community samples. In S. Cohen & L. Syme (Eds.), *Social support and health* (pp. 219-240). Orlando, FL: Academic Press.

Kessler, R.C., Crum, R.M., Warner, L.A., Nelson, C.B., et al. (1997). Lifetime co-occurrence of DSM-IIIR alcohol dependence with other psychiatric disorders in the National Comorbidity Study. *Archives of General Psychiatry, 54,* 313-321.

Kessler, R.C., McGonagle, K.A., Zhao, S., Nelson, C.B., Hughes, M., et al. (1994). Lifetime and 12-month prevalence rates of DSM-III-R psychiatric disorders in the United States: Results from the National Comorbidity Survey. *Archives of General Psychiatry, 51,* 8-19.

Kessler, R.C., Wittchen, H.-U., Stein, M., & Walters, E.E. (1999). Lifetime comorbidities between social phobia and mood disorders in the US National Comorbidity Survey. *Psychological Medicine, 29,* 555-567.

Kety, S.S., Rosenthal, D., Wender, P.H., & Schulsinger, F. (1968). The types and prevalence of mental illness in the biological and adoptive families of adopted schizophrenics. In D. Rosenthal & S.S. Kety (Eds.), *The transmission of schizophrenia.* Elmsford, NY: Pergamon.

Kety, S.S., Rosenthal, D., Wender, P.H., & Schulsinger, F. (1975). Mental illness in the adoptive and biological families of adopted individuals who have become schizophrenic. In R.R. Fieve, D. Rosenthal, & H. Brill (Eds.), *Genetic research in psychiatry.* Baltimore: Johns Hopkins University Press.

Kety, S.S., Wender, P.H., Jacobsen, B., Ingraham, L.T., Jansson, L., et al. (1994). Mental illness in the biological and adoptive relatives of schizophrenic adoptees: Replication of the Copenhagen study in the rest of Denmark. *Archives of General Psychiatry, 51,* 442-468.

Keys, A., Brozek, J., Hsu, L.K.G., McConoha, C.E., & Bolton, B. (1950). *The biology of human starvation.* Minneapolis: Univ of Minnesota Press.

Keys, A., Taylor, H.L., et al. (1971). Mortality and coronary heart disease in men studied for 23 years. *Archives of Internal Medicine, 128,* 201-214.

Kidder, T. (1978). Soldiers of misfortune. *The Atlantic Monthly, 241,* 41-52.

Kiecolt-Glaser, J., Dura, J.R., Speicher, C.E., & Trask, O. (1991). Spousal caregivers of dementia victims: Longitudinal changes in immunity and health. *Psychosomatic Medicine, 54,* 345-362.

Kiecolt-Glaser, J., Glaser, R., Strain, E., Stout, J.C., Tarr, K.L., Holliday, J.E., & Speicher, C.E. (1986). Modulation of cellular immunity in medical students. *Journal of Behavioral Medicine, 9,* 5-21.

Kiecolt-Glaser, J.K., Garner, W., Speicher, C.E., Penn, G.M., Holliday, J., & Glaser, R. (1984). Psychosocial modifiers of immunocompetence in medical students. *Psychosomatic Medicine, 46,* 7-14.

Kiecolt-Glaser, J.K., Glaser, R., Williger, D., Stout, J., Messick, G., Sheppard, S., Ricker, D., Romischer, S.C., Briner, W., Bonnell, G., & Donnerberg, R. (1985). Psychosocial enhancement of immunocompetence in a geriatric population. *Health Psychology, 4,* 25-41.

Kiesler, C.A. (1991). Changes in general hospital psychiatric care. *American Psychologist, 46,* 416-421.

Kihlstrom, J.F. (1994). Dissociative and conversion disorders. In D.J. Stein & J.E. Young (Eds.), *Cognitive science and clinical disorders.* San Diego, CA: Academic Press.

Kihlstrom, J.F. (1997). Exhumed memory. In S.J. Lynn, K.M. McConkey, & N.P. Spanos (Eds.), *Truth in memory.* New York: Guilford.

Kihlstrom, J.F., & Tataryn, D. J. (1991). Dissociative disorders. In P.B. Sutker & H.E. Adams (Eds.), *Comprehensive handbook of psychopathology* (2nd ed.). New York: Plenum.

Kihlstrom, J.F., Tataryn, D.J., & Hoyt, I.P. (1993). Dissociative disorders. In P.B. Sutker & H.E. Adams (Eds.), *Comprehensive handbook of psychopathology* (pp. 203-234). New York: Plenum.

Killen, J.D., Fortmann, S.P., Newman, B., & Varady, A. (1990). Evaluation of a treatment approach combining nicotine gum with self-guided behavioral treatments for smoking relapse prevention. *Journal of Consulting and Clinical Psychology, 58,* 85-92.

Killen, J.D., Robinson, T.N., Haydel, K.F., Hayward, C., et al. (1997). Prospective study of risk factors for the initiation of cigarette smoking. *Journal of Consulting and Clinical Psychology, 65,* 1011-1016.

Killen, J.D., Taylor, C.B., Hayward, C., Wilson, D.M., Haydel, K.F., et al. (1994). Pursuit of thinness and onset of eating disorders in a community sample of adolescent girls. *International Journal of Eating Disorders, 16,* 227-238.

Killen, J.D., Taylor, C.B., Telch, M.J., Saylor, K.E., Maron, D.J., & Robinson, T.N. (1986). Self-induced vomiting and laxative and diuretic use among teenagers: Precursors of the binge-purge syndrome. *Journal of the American Medical Association, 255,* 1447-1449.

Kilpatrick, D.G., & Best, C.L. (1990, April). *Sexual assault victims: Data from a random national probability sample.* Paper presented at the annual convention of the Southeastern Psychological Association, Atlanta.

Kilpatrick, D.G., Best, C.L., Veronen, L.J., Amick, A.E., Villeponteaux, L.A., & Ruff, G.A. (1985). Mental health correlates of criminal victimization: A random community survey. *Journal of Consulting and Clinical Psychology, 53,* 866-873.

Kilpatrick, D.G., Edmunds, C.N., & Seymour, A.K. (1992). *Rape in America: A report to the nation.* Arlington,VA: National Victim Center.

Kim, J.E. & Moen, P. (2001). Is retirement good or bad for subjective well-being? *Current Directions in Psychological Science Special Issue, 10* (3), 83-86.

Kimble, G.A., Garmezy, N., & Zigler, E. (1980). *Principles of general psychology.* New York: Wiley.

King, D.W., King, L.A., Foy, D.W., Keane, T.M., & Fairbank, J.A. (1999). Posttraumatic stress disorder in a national sample of female and male Vietnam veterans: Risk factors, war-zone stressors, and resilience-recovery variables. *Journal of Abnormal Psychology, 198,* 164-170.

King, D.W., King, L.A., Gudanowski, D.M., & Vreven, D.L. (1995). Alternative representations of war zone stressors: Relationship to posttraumatic stress disorder in male and female Vietnam veterans. *Journal of Abnormal Psychology, 104,* 184-196.

Kingsley, L.A., Kaslow, R., Rinaldo, C.R., Detre, K., Odaka, N., Van-Raden, M., Detels, R., Polk, B.F., Chmiel, J., Kelsey, S.F., Ostrow, D., & Visscher, B. (1987).

Risk factors for seroconversion to human immunodeficiency virus among male homosexuals. *Lancet, 1*, 345-348.

Kinsey, A.C., Pomeroy, W.B., & Martin, C.E. (1948). *Sexual behavior in the human male*. Philadelphia: Saunders.

Kinsey, A.C., Pomeroy, W.B., Main, C.E., & Gebhard, P.H. (1953). *Sexual behavior in the human female*. Philadelphia: Saunders.

Kinzie, J.D. (1985). Overview of clinical issues in the treatment of Southeast Asian refugees. In T.C. Owan (Ed.), *Southeast Asian mental health treatment, prevention services, training, and research*. Washington, DC: National Institute of Mental Health.

Kinzl, J.F., Traweger, C., Trefalt, E., Mangweth, B., & Biebl, W. (1999). Binge eating disorder in females; A population based investigation. *International Journal og Eating Disorders, 25*, 287-292.

Kipke, M.D., Montgomery, S., & MacKenzie, R.G. (1993). Substance use among youth who attend community-based health clinics. *Journal of Adolescent Health, 14*, 289-294.

Kirmayer, L.J. & Young, A. (1999). Culture and context in the evolutionary concept of mental disorder. *Journal of Abnormal Psychology*, 108, 446-452.

Kirmayer, L.J., & Young, A. (1998). Culture and somatization: Clinical, epidemiological, and ethnographic perspectives. *Psychosomatic Medicine, 60*, 420-430.

Kirmayer, L.J., Robbins, J.M., & Paris, J. (1994). Somatoform disorders: Personality and social matrix of somatic distress. *Journal of Abnormal Psychology, 103*, 125-136.

Kirsch,I. (2000). Are drug and placebo effects in depression additive? *Biological Psychiatry, 47*, 733-735.

Kirschbaum, C., Prussner, J.C., & Stone, A.A. (1995). Persistent high cortisol responses to repeated psychological stress in a subpopulation of healthy men. *Psychosomatic Medicine, 57*, 468-474.

Kivlighan, D.M., & Mullison, D. (1988). Participants' perception of therapeutic factors in group counseling: The role of interpersonal style and stage of group development. *Small Group Development, 19*, 452-468.

Klein, D. (1992, April 1). The empty pot. *Los Angeles Times*, pp. A3, A14.

Klein, D.F. (1993). False suffocation alarms, spontaneous panics, and related conditions: An integrative hypothesis. *Archives of General Psychiatry, 50*, 306-317.

Klein, D.F. (1996). Preventing hung juries about therapy studies. *Journal of Consulting and Clinical Psychology, 64*, 81-87.

Klein, D.F., & Ross, D.C. (1993). Reanalysis of the National Institute of Mental Health Treatment of Depression Collaborative Research Program general effectiveness report. *Neuropsychopharmacology, 8*, 241-251.

Klerman, G.L. (1983). Problems in the definition and diagnosis of depression in the elderly. In M. Hauge & L. Breslau (Eds.), *Depression in the elderly: Causes, care, consequences*. New York: Springer.

Klerman, G.L. (1988a). Depression and related disorders of mood (affective disorders). In A.M. Nicholi, Jr. (Ed.), *The new Harvard guide to psychiatry*. Cambridge, MA: Harvard University Press.

Klerman, G.L. (1988b). The current age of youthful melancholia. *British Journal of Psychiatry, 152*, 4-14.

Klerman, G.L. (1990). Treatment of recurrent unipolar major depressive disorder. *Archives of General Psychiatry, 47*, 1158-1162.

Klerman, G.L., & Weissman, M.M. (Eds.), (1993). *New applications of interpersonal psychotherapy*. Washington, DC: American Psychiatric Press.

Klerman, G.L., Weissman, M.M., Markowitz, J.C., Glick, I., Wilner, P.J., Mason, B., & Shear, M.K. (1994). Medication and psychotherapy. In A.E. Bergin & S.L. Garfield (Eds.), *Handbook of psychotherapy and behavior change* (4th ed., pp. 734-782). New York: Wiley.

Klerman, G.L., Weissman, M.M., Rounsaville, B.J., & Chevron, E.S. (1984). *Interpersonal psychotherapy of depression*. New York: Basic Books.

Klinnert, M.D., Mrazek, P.J., & Mrazek, D.A. (1994). Early asthma onset: The interaction between family stressors and adaptive parenting. *Psychiatry, 57*, 51-61.

Klonsky, E.D., Oltmanns, T.F., Turkheimer, E., & Fieldler, E.R. (2000). Recollections of conflict with parents and family support in the personality disorders. *Journal of Personality Disorders, 14*, 327-338.

Klosko, J.S., Barlow, D.H., Tassinari, R., & Cerny, J.A. (1990) A comparison of alprazolam and behavior therapy in treatment of panic disorder. *Journal of Consulting and Clinical Psychology, 58*, 77-84.

Kluft, R.P. (1984a). An introduction to multiple personality disorder. *Psychiatric Annals, 7*, 19-24.

Kluft, R.P. (1984b). Multiple personality in childhood. *Psychiatric Clinics of North America, 7*, 121-134.

Kluft, R.P. (1984c). Treatment of multiple personality disorder: A study of 33 cases. *Psychiatric Clinics of North America, 7*, 929.

Kluft, R.P. (1985). The treatment of multiple personality disorder (MPD): Current concepts. In F.F. Flach (Ed.), *Directions in psychiatry*. New York: Hatherleigh.

Kluft, R.P. (1988). The dissociative disorders. In R.E. Hales & S.C. Yudofsky (Eds.), *Textbook of psychiatry* (pp. 557-585). Washington, DC: American Psychiatric Press.

Kluft, R.P. (1994). Treatment trajectories in multiple personality disorder. *Dissociation, 7*, 63-75.

Knapp, M.J., Knopman, D.S., Solomon, P.R., et al. (1994). A 30-week randomized controlled trial of high-dose tacrine in patients with Alzheimer's disease. *JAMA, 271*, 985-989.

Knapp, S., & Vandecreek, L. (1982). Tarasoff: Five years later. *Professional Psychology, 13*, 511-516.

Knaus, W., & Bokor, S. (1975). The effect of rational-emotive education lessons on anxiety and self-concept in sixth grade students. *Rational Living, 10*, 7-10.

Knehnle, K. (1998). Child sexual abuse allegations: The scientist-practitioner model. *Behavioral Science and the Law, 16*, 5-20.

Knight, B. (1983). An evaluation of a mobile geriatric team. In M.A. Smyer & M. Gatz (Eds.), *Mental health and aging: Programs and evaluations*. Beverly Hills, CA: Sage.

Knight, B.G., Kelly, M., & Gatz, M. (1992). Psychotherapy and the older adult. In D.K. Freedheim (Ed.), *History of psychotherapy: A century of change* (pp. 528-551). Washington, DC: American Psychological Association.

Knight, B.G. (1996). *Psychotherapy with older adults*. 2nd ed. Thousand Oaks, CA: Sage.

Knight, B.G., Lutzky, S.M., & Olshevski, J.L. (1992). *A randomized comparison of stress reduction training to problem solving training for dementia caregivers: Processes and outcomes*. Unpublished manuscript, University of Southern California, Los Angeles.

Knopp, F.H. (1984). *Retraining adult sex offenders*. New York: Safer Society Press.

Kobak, K.A., Rock, A.L., & Greist, J.H. (1995). Group behavior therapy for obsessive-compulsive disorder. *Journal for Specialists in Group Work, 20*, 26-32.

Koegel, R.L., Bimbela, A., & Schreibman, L. (1996). Collateral effects of parent training on family interactions. *Journal of Autism and Developmental Disorders, 26*, 347-359.

Koegel, R.L., Schreibman, L., Britten, K.R., Burkey, J.C., & O'Neill, R.E. (1982). A comparison of parent training to direct child treatment. In R.L. Koegel, A. Rincover, & A.L. Egel (Eds.), *Educating and understanding autistic children*. San Diego, CA: College-Hill.

Koenig, H.G., & Blazer, D.G. (1992). Mood disorders and suicide. In J.E. Birren, R.B. Sloane, & G.D. Cohen (Eds.), *Handbook of mental health and aging* (pp. 379-407). San Diego: Academic Press.

Koenig, K., & Masters, J. (1965). Experimental treatment of habitual smoking. *Behaviour Research and Therapy, 3*, 235-243.

Koenigsberg, H.W., & Handley, R. (1986). Expressed emotion: From predictive index to clinical construct. *American Journal of Psychiatry, 143*, 1361-1373.

Koenigsberg, H.W., Goodman, M., Reynolds, D., Mitropoulou, V., Trestman, R., Kirrane, R., New, A.S., Anwunah, I., & Siever, L.J. (2001). Risperidone in the treatment of schizotypal personality disorder. *Biological Psychiatry* (abstracts), 56th Annual Meeting Society of Biological Psychiatry, New Orleans.

Koenigsberg, H.W., Woo-Ming, A.M., & Siever, L.J. (2002). Pharmacological treatments for personality disorders. In P.E. Nathan & J.M. Gorman (Eds.), *A guide to treatments that work*. New York: Oxford University Press.

Koerner, K., & Linehan, M.M. (2000). Research on dialectical behavior therapy for patients with borderline personality disorder. *Psychiatric Clinics of North America, 23*, 151-167.

Kohn, M.L. (1968). Social class and schizophrenia: A critical review. In D. Rosenthal & S.S. Kety (Eds.), *The transmission of schizophrenia*. Elmsford, NY: Pergamon.

Kohut, H. (1971). *The analysis of the self*. New York: International Universities Press.

Kohut, H. (1977). *The restoration of the self*. New York: International Universities Press.

Kohut, H., & Wolf, E.S. (1978). The disorders of the self and their treatment: An outline. *International Journal of Psychoanalysis, 59*, 413-425.

Kolden, G.G. (1991). The generic model of psychotherapy: An empirical investigation of patterns of process and outcome relationships. *Psychotherapy Research, 1*, 62-73.

Kolmen, B.K., Feldman, H.E., Handen, B.L., & Janosky, J.E. (1995). Naltrexone in young autistic children: A double-blind, placebo-controlled crossover study. *Journal of the American Academy of Child and Adolescent Psychiatry, 34*, 223-231.

Kolvin I., McKeith, R.C., & Meadows, S.R. (1973). *Bladder control and enuresis.* Philadelphia: Lippincott.

Konig, P., & Godfrey, S. (1973). Prevalence of exercise-induced bronchial liability in families of children with asthma. *Archives of Diseases of Childhood, 48*, 518.

Kopelowicz, A., & Liberman, R.P. (1998) Psychosocial treatments for schizophrenia. In P.E. Nathan, & J.M. Gorman (Eds.), *A guide to treatments that work* (pp. 190-211). New York: Oxford University Press.

Kopelowicz, A., Liberman, R.P., & Zarate, R. (2002). Psychosocial treatments for schizophrenia. In P.E. Nathan & J.M. Gorman (Eds.), *A guide to treatments that work* (pp. 201-229). New York, NY: Oxford University Press.

Koran, L.M., Hackett, E., Rubin, A. et al. (2001).Efficacy of sertreline in the long-term treatment of obsessive-compulsive disorder. *American Journal of Psychiatry, 158*, 88-95.

Korchin, S.J. (1976). *Modern clinical psychology.* New York: Basic Books.

Kornetsky, C. (1976). Hyporesponsivity of chronic schizophrenic patients to dex-troamphetamine. *Archives of General Psychiatry, 33*, 1425-1428.

Koss, M.P. (1985). The hidden rape victim: Personality, attitudinal, and situational characteristics. *Psychology of Women Quarterly, 9*, 193-212.

Koss, M.P., & Butcher, J.N. (1986). Research on brief psychotherapy. In S.L. Garfield & A.E. Bergin (Eds.), *Handbook of psychotherapy and behavior change (3rd ed.).* New York: Wiley.

Koss, M.P., & Shiang, J. (1994). Research on brief psychotherapy. In A.E. Bergin & S.L. Garfield (Eds.), *Handbook of psychotherapy and behavior change* (4th ed., pp. 664-700). New York: Wiley.

Kosten, T.R., Mason, J.W., Giller, E.L., Ostroff, R., & Harkness, I. (1987). Sustained urinary norepinephrine and epinephrine elevation in posttraumatic stress disorder. *Psychoneuroendocrinology, 12*, 13-20.

Kosten, T.R., Morgan, C.M., Falcione, J., & Schottenfeld, R.S. (1992). Pharmacotherapy for cocaine-abusing methadone-maintained patients using amantadine or desipramine. *Archives of General Psychiatry, 49*, 894-898.

Koston, T.R., & Ziedonis, D.M. (1997). Substance abuse and schizophrenia: Editors' introduction. *Schizophrenia Bulletin, 23*, 181-186.

Kotranski, L., Semaan, S., Collier, K., Lauby, J., Halbert, J., & Feighan, K. (1998). Effectiveness of an HIV risk reduction counseling intervention for out-of-treatment drug users. *AIDS Education and Prevention, 10*, 19-33.

Kovacs, M. (1990). Comorbid anxiety disorders in childhood-onset depressions. In J.D. Maser & C.R. Cloninger (Eds.), *Comorbidity of mood and anxiety disorders* (pp. 272-281). Washington, DC: American Psychiatric Press.

Kovacs, M., Feinberg, T.L., Crouse-Novack, M.A., Paulauskas, S.L., & Finkelstein, R. (1984). Depressive disorders in childhood: 1. A longitudinal prospective study of characteristics and recovery. *Archives of General Psychiatry, 41*, 229-237.

Kovacs, M., Rush, A.J., Beck, A.T., & Hollon, S.D. (1981). Depressed outpatients treated with cognitive therapy or pharmacotherapy: A one-year follow-up. *Archives of General Psychiatry, 38*, 33-39.

Kowalik, D.L., & Gotlib, I.H. (1987). Depression and marital interaction: Concordance between intent and perception of communication. *Journal of Abnormal Psychology, 96*, 127-134.

Kowall, N.K., & Beal, M.F. (1988). Cortical somatostatin, neuropeptide Y, and NADPH diphorase neurons: Normal anatomy and alterations in Alzheimer's disease. *Annals of Neurology, 23*, 105-113.

Kozel, N.J., & Adams, E.H. (1986). Epidemiology of drug abuse: An overview. *Science, 234*, 970-974.

Kozel, N.J., Crider, R.A., & Adams, E.H. (1982). National surveillance of cocaine use and related health consequences. *Morbidity and Mortality Weekly Report 31,* 20, 265-273.

Kozol, H., Boucher, R., & Garofalo, R. (1972). The diagnosis and treatment of dangerousness. *Crime and Delinquency, 18*, 37-92.

Kraaij, V. & De Wilde, E.J. (2001). Negative life events and depressive symptoms in the elderly: a life span perspective. *Aging & Mental Health, 5 (1)*, 84-91.

Kraepelin, E. (1981). *Clinical psychiatry.* (A.R. Diefendorf, Trans.). NY: Delmar, Scholars' Facsimiles and Reprints. (Original work published 1883)

Kramer, E.F. (1995). Controversial litigation issue may be shifting our focus away from a more serious problem. *Res Gestae, 12*, 10-22.

Krantz, S., & Hammen, C.L. (1979). Assessment of cognitive bias in depression. *Journal of Abnormal Psychology, 88*, 611-619.

Kranzler, H.R., Burleson, J.A., Del Boca, F.K., Babor, T.F., Korner, P., et al. (1994). Busipirone treatment of anxious alcoholics: A controlled trial. *Archives of General Psychiatry, 51*, 720-731.

Kreuger, R.B., & Kaplan, M.S. (1997). Frotteurism: Assessment and treatment. In D.R. Laws & W. O'Donohue (Eds.), *Sexual deviance* (pp. 131-151). New York: Guilford Press.

Kring, A.M., & Neale, J.M. (1996). Do schizophrenics show a disjunctive relationship among expressive, experiential and physiological components of emotion? *Journal of Abnormal Psychology, 105*, 249-257.

Kringlen, E. (1970). Natural history of obsessional neurosis. *Seminars in Psychiatry, 2*, 403-419.

Kronig, M.H., Apter, J., Asnis, G., Bystritsky, A., Curtis, G., et al. (1999). Placebo-controlled, multicenter study of sertraline treatment for obsessive-compulsive diosorder. *Journal of Clinical Psychopharmacology, 19*, 172-176.

Krug, E.G., Kresnow, M., Peddicord, J.P., Dahlberg, L.L., Powell, K.E., Crosby, A.E., & Annest, J.L. (1998). Suicide after natural disasters. *The New England Journal of Medicine, 338*, 373-378.

Krystal, J.H., Cramer, J.A., Krol, W.F. et al. (2001). Naltrexone in the treatment of alcohol dependence. *The New England Journal of Medicine, 345*, 1734-1739.

Krystal, J.H., Karper, L.P., Seibyl, J.P., Freeman, G.K., Delaney, R., et al. (1995). Subanesthetic effects of the non-competitive NMDA antagonist, ketamine, in humans: Psychotomimetic, perceptual, cognitive, and neuroendocrine effects. *Archives of General Psychiatry, 51*, 199-214.

Krystal, J.H., Kosten, T.R., Southwick, S., Mason, J.W., Perry, B.D., & Giller, E.L. (1989). Neurobiological aspects of PTSD: Review of clinical and preclinical studies. *Behavior Therapy, 20*, 177-198.

Kucharski, L.T., White, R.M., & Schratz, M. (1979). Age bias, referral for psychological assistance and the private physician. *Journal of Gerontology, 34*, 423-428.

Kuhn, T.S. (1962). *The structure of scientific revolutions.* Chicago: University of Chicago Press.

Kuhn, T.S. (1970). *The structure of scientific revolutions.* Chicago: University of Chicago Press.

Kundera, M. (1991). *Immortality.* New York: Grove Press.

Kung, H.-C., Liu, X., & Joun, H.-S. (1998). Risk factors for suicide in Caucasians and African-Americans: A matched case-control study. *Social Psychiatry, 33*, 155-161.

Kunst-Wilson, W.R., & Zajonc, R.B. (1980). Affective discrimination of stimuli that cannot be recognized. *Science, 207*, 557-558.

Kuriansky, J.B., Deming, W.E., & Gurland, B.J. (1974). On trends in the diagnosis of schizophrenia. *American Journal of Psychiatry, 131*, 402-407.

Kutchinsky, B. (1970). *Studies on pornography and sex crimes in Denmark.* Copenhagen: New Social Science Monographs.

Lacey, J.I. (1967). Somatic response patterning and stress: Some revisions of activation theory. In M.H. Appley & R. Trumball (Eds.), *Psychological stress.* New York: McGraw-Hill.

Ladd, G.W. (1981). Effectiveness of a social learning method for enhancing children's social interaction and peer acceptance. *Child Development, 52*, 171-178.

Lahey, B.B., Loeber, R., Hart, E.L., Frick, P.J., Applegate, B., Zhang, Q., Green, S.M., & Russo, M.F. (1995). Four-year longitudinal study of conduct disorder in boys: Patterns and predictors of persistence. *Journal of Abnormal Psychology, 104*, 83-93.

Lahey, B.B., Miller, T.L., Gordon, R.A., & Riley, A.W. (1999). Developmental epidemiology of the disruptive behavior disorders. In H.C. Quay & A. Hogan (Eds.), *Handbook of Disruptive Behavior Disorders* (pp. 23-48). New York: Plenum.

Lahey, B.B., McBurnett, K., & Loeber, R. (2000). Are attention-deficit/hyperactivity disorder and oppositional defiant disorder developmental precursors to conduct disorder? In A.J. Sameroff & M. Lewis, et al. (Eds.), *Handbook of developmental psychopathology* (2nd ed., pp. 431-446). New York: Kluwer Academic/Plenum.

Lahey, B.B., Piacentini, J.C., McBurnett, K., Stone, P., Hartdagen, S., & Hynd, G. (1988). Psychopathology in the parents of children with conduct disorder and hyperactivity. *Journal of the American Academy of Child and Adolescent Psychiatry, 27*, 163-170.

Lalumiere, M.L., & Quinsey, V.L. (1994). The discriminability of rapists from non-sex offenders using phallometric measures. *Criminal Justice and Behavior, 21*, 150-175.

Lam, R.W., Zis, A.P., Grewal, A., Delgado, P.L., Charney, D.S., & Krystal, J.H. (1996). Effects of rapid tryptophan depletion in patients with seasonal affective disorder in remission after light therapy. *Archives of General Psychiatry, 53*, 41-46.

Lambe, E.K., Katzman, D.K., Mikulis, D.J., Kennedy, S.H., & Zipursky, R.B. (1997). Cerebral gray matter volume deficits after weight recovery from anorexia nervosa. *Archives of General Psychiatry, 54*, 537-542.

Lambert, M.J., & Bergin, A.E. (1994). The effectiveness of psychotherapy. In A.E. Bergin & S.L. Garfield (Eds.), *Handbook of psychotherapy and behavior change* (4th ed., pp. 143-189). New York: Wiley.

Lambert, M.J., Bergin, A.E., & Collins, J.L. (1977). Therapist-induced deterioration in psychotherapy. In A.S. Gurman & A.M. Razin (Eds.), *Effective psychotherapy: A handbook of research*. Elmsford, New York: Pergamon.

Lambert, M.J., Shapiro, D.A., & Bergin, A.E. (1986). The effectiveness of psychotherapy. In S.L. Garfield & A.E. Bergin (Eds.), *Handbook of psychotherapy and behavior change* (3rd ed.). New York: Wiley.

Lando, H.A. (1977). Successful treatment of smokers with a broad-spectrum behavioral approach. *Journal of Consulting and Clinical Psychology, 45*, 361-366.

Landreville, P., Landry, J., Baillargeon, L., Guerette, A. & Matteau, E. (2001). Older adults' acceptance of psychological and pharmacological treatments for depression. *Journal of Gerontology: Psychological Sciences, 56B* (5), P285-P291.

Lane, E.A., & Albee, G.W. (1965). Childhood intellectual differences between schizophrenic adults and their siblings. *American Journal of Orthopsychiatry, 35*, 747-753.

Lang, A.R., Goeckner, D.J., Adessor, V.J., & Marlatt, G.A. (1975). Effects of alcohol on aggression in male social drinkers. *Journal of Abnormal Psychology, 84*, 508-518.

Lang, P.J., & Lazovik, A.D. (1963). Experimental desensitization of a phobia. *Journal of Abnormal and Social Psychology, 66*, 519-525.

Lang, P.J., & Melamed, B.G. (1969). Case report: Avoidance conditioning therapy of an infant with chronic ruminative vomiting. *Journal of Abnormal Psychology, 74*, 1-8.

Langbehn, D.R. & Cadoret, R.J. (2001). The adult antisocial syndrome with and without antecedent conduct disorder: Comparisons from an adoption study. *Comprehensive Psychiatry, 42*, 272-282.

Lange, A.J., & Jakubowski, P. (1976). *Responsible assertive behavior*. Champaign, IL: Research Press.

Langeluddeke, A. (1963). *Castration of sexual criminals*. Berlin: de Gruyter.

Langenbucher, J.W., & Chung, T. (1995). Onset and staging of DSM-IV alcohol dependence using mean age and survival hazard methods. *Journal of Abnormal Psychology, 104*, 346-354.

Langer, E.J. (1981). Old age: An artifact? In J. McGaugh & S. Kiesler (Eds.), *Aging: Biology and behavior*. New York: Academic Press.

Langer, E.J. (1989). *Mindfulness*. Reading, MA: Addison-Wesley.

Langer, E.J., & Abelson, R.P. (1974). A patient by any other name...: Clinician group difference in labelling bias. *Journal of Consulting and Clinical Psychology, 42*, 4-9.

Langer, E.J., & Rodin, J. (1976). The effects of choice and enhanced personal responsibility for the aged. *Journal of Personality and Social Psychology, 34*, 191-198.

Langevin, R., & Lang, R.A. (1987). The courtship disorders. In G.D. Wilson (Ed.), *Variant sexuality: Research and theory* (pp. 202-228). London: Croon Helm.

Lannin, D.R., Mathews, H.F., Mitchell, J., Swanson, M.S., et al. (1998). Influence of socioeconomic and racial differences in late-stage presentation of breast cancer. *JAMA, 279*, 1801-1807.

Lantz, P.M., House, J.S., Lepkowski, J.M., Williams, D.R., et al. (1998). Socioeconomic factors, health behaviors, and mortality. *JAMA, 279*, 1703-1708.

Lara, M.E., & Klein, D.N. (in press). *Processes underlying chronicity in depression*.

LaRue, A. (1992). *Aging and neuropsychological assessment*. New York: Plenum.

LaRue, A., Dessonville, C., & Jarvik, L.F. (1985). Aging and mental disorders. In J.E. Birren & K.W. Schaie (Eds.), *Handbook of psychology of aging* (2nd ed.). New York: Van Nostrand-Reinhold.

Lassano, D., del Buono, G., & Latapano, P. (1993). The relationship between obsessive-compulsive personality and obsessive-compulsive disorder: Data obtained by the personality disorder examination. *European Psychiatry, 8*, 219-221.

Last, C.G., & Strauss, C.C. (1990). School refusal in anxiety-disordered children and adolescents. *Journal of the American Academy of Child and Adolescent Psychiatry, 29*, 31-35.

Laub, J.H., & Sampson, R.J. (1995). The long-term effects of punitive discipline. In J. McCord (Ed.), *Coercion and punishment in long-term perspective* (pp. 247-258). Cambridge, MA: Cambridge University Press.

Laumann, E.O., Gagnon, J.H., Michael, R.T., & Michaels, S. (1994). *The social organization of sexuality*. Chicago: University of Chicago Press.

Lavelle, T.L., Metalsky, G.I., & Coyne, J.C. (1979). Learned helplessness, test anxiety, and acknowledgment of contingencies. *Journal of Abnormal Psychology, 88*, 381-387.

Law, M., & Tang, J.L. (1995). An analysis of the effectiveness of interventions intended to help people stop smoking. *Archives of Internal Medicine, 155*, 1933-1941.

Lawler, B.A., Sunderland, T., Mellow, A.M., Hill, J.L., Molchan, S.E., et al. (1989). Hyperresponsivity to the serotonin agonist m-chlorophenylpiperazine in Alzheimer's disease. *Archives of General Psychiatry, 46*, 542-548.

Layne, C. (1986). Painful truths about depressives' cognitions. *Journal of Clinical Psychology, 39*, 848-853.

Lazar, I. (1979). Social services in Head Start. In E. Zigler & J. Valentine (Eds.), *Project Head Start*. New York: Free Press.

Lazarus, A.A. (1961). Group therapy of phobic disorders by systematic desensitization. *Journal of Abnormal and Social Psychology, 63*, 504-510.

Lazarus, A.A. (1965). Behavior therapy, incomplete treatment, and symptom substitution. *Journal of Nervous and Mental Disease, 140*, 80-86.

Lazarus, A.A. (1968a). Behavior therapy in groups. In G.M. Gazda (Ed.), *Basic approaches to group psychotherapy and counseling*. Springfield, IL: Charles C. Thomas.

Lazarus, A.A. (1968b). Learning theory and the treatment of depression. *Behavior Research and Therapy, 6*, 83-89.

Lazarus, A.A (1971). *Behavior therapy and beyond*. New York: McGraw-Hill.

Lazarus, A.A. (1973). Multimodal behavior therapy: Treating the basic ID. *Journal of Nervous and Mental Disease, 156*, 404-411.

Lazarus, A.A. (1989). *The practice of multimodal therapy*. Baltimore: Johns Hopkins University Press.

Lazarus, A.A. (1997). *Brief but comprehensive psychotherapy: The multimodal way*. New York: Springer.

Lazarus, A.A., & Davison, G.C. (1971). Clinical innovation in research and practice. In A.E. Bergin & S.L. Garfield (Eds.), *Handbook of psychotherapy and behavior change: An empirical analysis*. New York: Wiley.

Lazarus, A.A., & Messer, S.B. (1991). Does chaos prevail? An exchange on technical eclecticism and assimilative integration. *Journal of Psychotherapy Integration, 1*, 143-158.

Lazarus, A.A., Davison, G.C., & Polefka, D. (1965). Classical and operant factors in the treatment of school phobia. *Journal of Abnormal Psychology, 70*, 225-229.

Lazarus, R.S. (1966). *Psychological stress and the coping process*. New York: McGraw-Hill.

Lazarus, R.S., & Folkman, S. (1984). *Stress, appraisal, and coping*. New York: Springer.

Lazo, J. (1995). True or false: Expert testimony on repressed memory. *Loyola of Los Angeles Law Review, 28*, 1345-1413.

Le Couteur, A., Bailey, A., Goode, S., Pickles, A., Robertson, S., Gottesman, I., & Rutter, M. (1996). A broader phenotype of autism: The clinical spectrum in twins. *Journal of Child Psychology and Psychiatry and Allied Disciplines, 37*, 785-801.

Leach, S., & Roy, S.S. (1986). Adverse drug reactions: An investigation on an acute geriatric ward. *Age and Ageing, 15*, 241-246.

Lebow, J.L., & Gurman, A.S. (1995). Research assessing couple and family therapy. *Annual Review of Psychology, 46*, 27-57.

Lecrubier, Y., & Weiller, E. (1997). Comorbidities in social phobia. *International Clinical Psychopharmacology, 12*, s17-s21.

Lee, D., DeQuattro, V., Cox, T., Pyter, L., Foti, A., Allen, J., Barndt, R., Azen, S., & Davison, G.C. (1987). Neurohormonal mechanisms and left ventricular hypertrophy: Effects of hygienic therapy. *Journal of Human Hypertension, 1*, 147-151.

Lee, S. (1994). The Diagnostic Interview Schedule and anorexia nervosa in Hong Kong. *Archives of General Psychiatry, 51*, 251-252.

Lee, V.E., Brooks-Gunn, J., & Schnur, E. (1988). Does Head Start work? A 1-year follow-up comparison of disadvantaged children attending Head Start, no preschool, and other preschool programs. *Developmental Psychology, 24*, 210-222.

Leenaars, A.A., & Lester, D. (1995). Impact of suicide prevention centers on suicide in Canada. *Crisis, 16*, 39.

Leeper, P. (1988). Having a place to live is vital to good health. *News Report, 38*, 5-8.

Legido, A., Tonyes, L., Carter, D., Schoemaker, A., DiGeorge, A., & Grover, W.D. (1993). Treatment variables and intellectual outcome in children with classic phenylketonuria: A single-center-based study. *Clinical Pediatrics, 32*, 417-425.

Lehman, A.F., Steinwachs, D.M., & the survey co-investigators from the Schizophrenia Patient Outcomes Research Team (PORT) client survey. (1998). Patterns of usual care for schizophrenia: Initial results from the Schizophrenia Patient Outcomes Research Team (PORT) client survey. *Schizophrenia Bulletin, 24*, 11-20.

Lehrer, P.M., & Woolfolk, R.L. (1993) *Principles and practice of stress management* (2nd ed.). New York: Guilford.

Lehrer, P.M., Hochron, S.M., Mayne, T., Isenberg, S., et al. (1994). Relaxation and music therapies for asthma among patients prestabilized on asthma medication. *Journal of Behavioral Medicine, 17*, 1-24.

Lehrer, P.M., Isenberg, S., & Hochron, S.M. (1993). Asthma and emotion: A review. *Journal of Asthma, 30*, 5-21.

Leibel, R.I., Rosenbaum, M., & Hirsch, J. (1995). Changes in energy expenditure resulting from altered body weight. *The New England Journal of Medicine, 332*, 621-628.

Leibenluft, E. (1996). Women with bipolar illness: Clinical and research issues. *American Journal of Psychiatry, 153*, 163-173.

Leiblum, S.R. (1997). Sexual pain disorders. In G.O. Gabbard & S.D. Atkinson (Eds.), *Synopsis of treatments of psychiatric disorders* (2nd ed., pp. 805-810). Washington,DC: American Psychiatric Press.

Leiblum, S.R., & Rosen, R.C. (Eds.). (1988). *Sexual desire disorders*. New York: Guilford.

Leitenberg, H., Gross, H., Peterson, H., & Rosen, J.C. (1984). Analysis of an anxiety model in the process of change during exposure plus response prevention treatment of bulimia nervosa. *Behavior Therapy, 15*, 3-20.

Lenane, M.C., Swedo, S.E., Leonard, H., Pauls, D.L., Sceery, W., et al. (1990). Psychiatric disorders in first degree relatives of children and adolescents with obsessive compulsive disorder. *Journal of the American Academy of Child and Adolescent Psychiatry, 29*, 407-412.

Lenzenwenger, M.F., Dworkin, R.H., & Wethington, E. (1991). Examining the underlying structure of schizophrenic phenomenology: Evidence for a 3-process model. *Schizophrenia Bulletin, 17*, 515-524.

Leon, G.R., Fulkerson, J.A., Perry, C.L., & Early-Zald, M.B. (1995). Prospective analysis of personality and behavioral vulnerabilities and gender influences in the later development of disordered eating. *Journal of Abnormal Psychology, 104*, 140-149.

Lerer, B., Bleich, A., Kotler, M., Garb, R., Hertzberg, M., & Levin, B. (1987). Posttraumatic stress disorder in Israeli combat veterans. *Archives of General Psychiatry, 44*, 976-981.

Lerman, C., & Glanz, K. (1997). Stress, coping, and health behavior. In K. Glanz, F. Lewis, & B. Rimer (Eds.), *Health behavior and health education: Theory, research and practice*. San Francisco: Jossey-Bass.

Lerman, C., Caporaso, N.E., Audrain, J., Main, D., Bowman, E.D., et al. (1999). Evidence suggesting the role of specific genetic factors in cigarette smoking. *Health Psychology, 18*, 14-20.

Lerman, C., Schwartz, M.D., Lin, T.H., Narod, S., & Lynch, H.T. (1997). The influence of psychological distress on use of genetic testing for cancer risk. *Journal of Consulting and Clinical Psychology, 65*, 414-420.

Lerman, C., Schwartz, M.D., Miller, S.M., Daly, M., Sands, C., & Rimer, B.K. (1996). A randomized trial of breast cancer risk counseling: Interacting effects of counseling, educational level, and coping style. *Health Psychology, 15*, 75-83.

Lerner, H.P. (1983). Contemporary psychoanalytic perpectives on gorge-vomiting: A case illustration. *International Journal of Eating Disorders, 3*, 47-63.

Lesage, A., & Lamontagne, Y. (1985). Paradoxical intention and exposure in vivo in the treatment of psychogenic nausea: Report of two cases. *Behavioral Psychotherapy, 13*, 69-75.

Lester, D. (1991). Do suicide prevention centers prevent suicide? *Homeostasis in Health and Disease, 33*, 190-194.

Leuchter, A.F. (1985). Assessment and treatment of the late-onset psychoses. *Hospital and Community Psychiatry, 36*, 815-818.

Leung, P.W., Luk, S.L., Ho, T.P., Taylor, E., Mak, F.L., & Bacon-Shone, J. (1996). The diagnosis and prevalence of hyperactivity in Chinese schoolboys. *British Journal of Psychiatry, 168*, 486-496.

Levav, I., Kohn, R., Golding, J.M., & Weissman, M.M. (1997). Vulnerability of Jews to major depression. *American Journal of Psychiatry, 154*, 941-947.

Levenson, M. (1972). *Cognitive and perceptual factors in suicidal individuals*. Unpublished doctoral dissertation, University of Kansas, Lawrence.

Levenston, G.K., Patrick, C.J., Bradley, M.M., & Lang, P.J. (2000). The psychopath as observer: Emotion and attention in picture processing. *Journal of Abnormal Psychology, 109*, 373-385.

Leventhal, B.L., Cook, E.H., Morford, M., Ravitz, A.J., Heller, W., & Freedman, D.X. (1993). Clinical and neurochemical effects of fenfluramine in children with autism. *The Journal of Neuropsychiatry and Clinical Neurosciences, 5*, 307-315.

Levin, R.L. (1992). The mechanisms of human female sexual arousal. *Annual Review of Sex Research, 3*, 1-48.

Levine, S.B., & Yost, M.A. (1976). Frequency of sexual dysfunction in a general gynecological clinic: An epidemiological approach. *Archives of Sexual Behavior, 5*, 229-238.

Levitan, R.D., Kaplan, A.S., Joffe, R.T., Levitt, A.J., & Brown, G.M. (1997). Hormonal and subjective responses to intravenous meta-chlorophenylpiperazine in bulimia nervosa. *Archives of General Psychiatry, 54*, 521-528.

Levitsky, A., & Perls, F.S. (1970). The rules and games of Gestalt therapy. In J. Fagan & I.L. Shepherd (Eds.), *Gestalt therapy now: Theory, techniques, applications*. Palo Alto, CA: Science & Behavior Books.

Levy, F., Hay, D.A., McStephen, M., Wood, C., & Waldman, I. (1997). Attention-deficit hyperactivity disorder: A category or a continuum? Genetic analysis of a large-scale twin study. *Journal of the American Academy of Child and Adolescent Psychiatry, 36*, 737-744.

Levy, L.H. (1963) *Psychological interpretation*. New York: Holt, Rinehart & Winston.

Levy, M.L., Miller, B.L., Cummings, J.L., Fairbanks, L.A., & Craig, A. (1996). Alzheimer disease and frontotemporal dementias. *Archives of Neurology, 53*, 687-690.

Levy, S.M., Herberman, R.B., Whiteside, T., Sanzo, K., Lee, J., & Kirkwood, J. (1990). Perceived social support and tumor estrogen/progesterone receptor status as predictors of natural killer cell activity in breast cancer patients. *Psychosomatic Medicine, 52*, 73-85.

Levy-Lehad, E., & Bird, T.D. (1996). Genetic factors in Alzheimer's disease: A review of the recent evidence. *Annals of Neurology, 40*, 829-840.

Lewinsohn, P.M., & Gotlib, I.H. (1995). Behavioral and cognitive treatment of depression. In E.E. Becker & W.R. Leber (Eds.), *Handbook of depression* (pp. 352-375). New York: Guilford Press.

Lewinsohn, P.M., Allen, N.B., Seeley, J.R., & Gotlib, I.H. (1999). First onset versus recurrence of depression: Differential processes of psychosocial risk. *Journal of Abnormal Psychology, 108*, 483-489.

Lewinsohn, P.M., Clarke, G.N., Hops, H., & Andrews, J. (1990). Cognitive-behavioral treatment for depressed adolescents. *Behavior Therapy, 21*, 385-401.

Lewinsohn, P.M., Hops, H., Roberts, R.E., Seeley, J.R., & Andrews, J.A. (1993). Adolescent psychopathology: 1. prevalence and incidence of depression and other DSM-III disorders in high school students. *Journal of Abnormal Psychology, 102*, 133-144.

Lewinsohn, P.M., Mischef, W., Chapion, W., & Barton, R. (1980). Social competence and depression: The role of illusory self-perceptions. *Journal of Abnormal Psychology, 89*, 203-212.

Lewinsohn, P.M., Roberts, R.E., Seeley, J.R., Rohde, P., Gotlib, I.H., & Hops, H. (1994). Adolescent psychopathology: 2. Psychosocial risk factors for depression. *Journal of Abnormal Psychology, 103*, 302-315.

Lewinsohn, P.M., Rohde, P., Fischer, S.A., & Seeley, J.R. (1991). Age and depression: Unique and shared effects. *Psychology and Aging, 6*, 247-260.

Lewinsohn, P.M., Steimetz, J.L., Larsen, D.W., & Franklin, J. (1981). Depression related cognitions: Antecedent or consequences? *Journal of Abnormal Psychology, 90*, 213-219.

Lewinsohn, P.M., Weinstein, M., & Alper, T. (1970). A behavioral approach to the group treatment of depressed persons: A methodological contribution. *Journal of Clinical Psychology, 26*, 525-532.

Lewis, D.O., Yeager, C.A., Swica, Y., Pincus, J.H., & Lewis, M. (1997). Objective documentation of child abuse and dissociation on 12 murderers with dissociative identity disorder. *American Journal of Psychiatry, 154*, 1703-1710.

Ley, R. (1987). Panic disorder: A hyperventilation interpretation. In L. Michelson & L.M. Asher (Eds.), *Anxiety and stress disorders*. New York: Guilford.

Li, T-K., Lumeng, L., McBride, W.J., & Waller, M.B. (1981). Indiana selection studies on alcohol related behaviors. In R.A. McClearn, R.A. Deitrich, & V.G. Erwin (Eds.), *Development of animal models as pharmacogenetic tools*. Washington, DC: U.S. Government Printing Office.

Liberman, R.P. (1972). Reinforcement of social interaction in a group of chronic mental patients. In R. Rubin et al., *Advances in behavior therapy*. New York: Academic Press.

Liberman, R.P. (1994). Psychosocial treatments for schizophrenia. *Psychiatry: Interpersonal and Biological Processes, 57*, 104-114.

Liberman, R.P. (Ed.). (1992). *Handbook of psychiatric rehabilitation*. New York: Macmillan.

Liberman, R.P., DeRisi, W.J., & Mueser, K.T. (1989). *Social skills training for psychiatric patients*. Elmsford, NY: Pergamon.

Liberman, R.P., Eckman, T.A., Kopelowicz, A., & Stolar, D. (2000). *Friendship and intimacy module*. Camarillo, CA: Psychiatric Rehabilitation Consultants, PO Box 2867, Camarillo, CA 93011.

Liberman, R.P., Wallace, C.J., Blackwell, G., Kopelowicz, J.V., et al. (1998). Skills training versus psychosocial occupational therapy for persons with persistent schizophrenia. *American Journal of Psychiatry, 155*, 1087-1091.

Liberto, J.G., Oslin, D.W., & Ruskin, P.E. (1996). Alcoholism in the older population. In L.L. Carstensen, B.A. Edelstein, & L. Dornbrand (Eds.), *The practical handbook of clinical gerontology* (pp. 324-348). Thousand Oaks, CA: Sage.

Lichtenstein, P. & Annas, P. (2000). Heritability and prevalence of specific fears and phobias in childhood. *Journal of Child Psychology & Psychiatry & Allied Disciplines, 41*, 927-937.

Lieberman, M.A., Yalom, J.D., & Miles, M.B. (1973). *Encounter groups: First facts*. New York: Basic Books.

Liebowitz, M.R., Heimberg, R.G., Fresco, D.M., Travers, J., & Stein, M.B. (2000). Social phobia or social anxiety disorder: What's in a name? *Archives of General Psychiatry, 57*, 191-192.

Liebson, I. (1967). Conversion reaction: A learning theory approach. *Behaviour Research and Therapy, 7*, 217-218.

Lief, H.I. (1988). Foreword. In S.R. Leiblum & R.C. Rosen (Eds.), *Sexual desire disorders*. New York: Guilford.

Lief, H.I., & Hubschman, L. (1993). Orgasm in the postoperative transsexual. *Archives of Sexual Behavior, 22*, 145-155.

Lifton, R.J. (1976). Advocacy and corruption in the healing profession. In N.L. Goldman & D.R. Segal (Eds.), *The social psychology of military service*. Beverly Hills, CA: Sage.

Light, E., & Lebowitz, B.D. (Eds.). (1991). *The elderly with chronic mental illness*. New York: Springer.

Light, K.C., Dolan, C.A., Davis, M.R., & Sherwood, A. (1992). Cardiovascular responses to an active coping challenge as predictors of blood pressure patterns 10 to 15 years later. *Psychosomatic Medicine, 54*, 217-230.

Light, L.L. (1990). Interactions between memory and language in old age. In J.E. Birren & K.W. Schaie (Eds.), *Handbook of the psychology of aging* (pp. 275-290). San Diego: Academic Press.

Lilienfeld, L.R., Kaye, W.H., Greeno, C.G., Merikangas, K.R., Plotnicov, K., et al. (1999). Psychiatric disorders in women with bulimia nervosa and their first-degree relatives: Effects of comorbid substance dependence. *International Journal of Eating Disorders, 22*, 253-264.

Lilienfeld, L.R., Kaye, W.H., Greeno, C.G., Merikangas, K.R., Plotnicov, K., et al. (1998). A controlled family study of anorexia nervosa and bulimia nervosa: Psychiatric disorders in first-degree relatives and effects of proband comorbidity. *Archives of General Psychiatry, 55*, 603-610.

Lilienfeld, S.O. & Marino, L. (1999). Essentialism revisited: Evolutionary theory and the concept of mental disorder. *Journal of Abnormal Psychology, 108*, 400-411.

Lilienfeld, S.O., Lynn, S.J., Kirsch, I., Chaves, J.F., et al. (1999). Dissociative identity disorder and the sociogenic model: Recalling lessons from the past. *Psychological Bulletin, 125*, 507-523.

Lim, K.O., Adalsteinssom, E., Spielman, D., Sullivan, E.V., Rosenbloom, M.J., & Pfefferman, A. (1998). Proton magnetic resonance spectroscopic imaging of cortical gray and white matter in schizophrenia. *Archives of General Psychiatry, 55*, 346-353.

Lindemann, E. (1944). Symptomatology and management of acute grief. *American Journal of Psychiatry, 101*, 141-148.

Linehan, M.M. (1985). The reasons for living inventory. In P. Keller & L. Ritt (Eds.), *Innovations in clinical practice: A sourcebook* (pp. 321-330). Sarasota, FL: Professional Resource Exchange.

Linehan, M.M. (1987). Dialectical behavior therapy for borderline personality disorder. *Bulletin of the Menninger Clinic, 51*, 261-276.

Linehan, M.M. (1993a). *Behavioral skills training manual for treating borderline personality disorder*. New York: Guilford Press.

Linehan, M.M. (1993b). *Cognitive behavioral treatment of borderline personality disorder: The dialectics of effective treatment*. New York: Guilford.

Linehan, M.M. (1997). Behavioral treatments of suicidal behaviors: Definitional obfuscation and treatment outcomes. In D.M. Stoff & J.J. Mann (Eds.), *Neurobiology of suicide* (pp. 302-327). New York: Annals of the New York Academy of Sciences.

Linehan, M.M., & Shearin, E.N. (1988). Lethal stress: A social-behavioral model of suicidal behavior. In S. Fisher & J. Reason (Eds.), *Handbook of life stress, cognition, and health*. New York: Wiley.

Linehan, M.M., Armstrong, H.E., Suarez, A., Allmon, D., & Heard, H.L. (1991). Cognitive-behavioral treatment of chronically parasuicidal borderline patients. *Archives of General Psychiatry, 48*, 1060-1064.

Linehan, M.M., Camper, P., Chiles, J.A., Strosahl, K., & Shearin, E.N. (1987). Interpersonal problem-solving and parasuicide. *Cognitive Therapy and Research, 11*, 1-12.

Linehan, M.M., Goodstein, J.L., Nielsen, S.L., & Chiles, J.A. (1983). Reasons for staying alive when you are thinking of killing yourself. *Journal of Consulting and Clinical Psychology, 51*, 276-286.

Linehan, M.M., Heard, H.L., & Armstrong, H.E. (1993). Naturalistic follow-up of a behavioral treatment for chronically parasuicidal borderline patients. *Archives of General Psychiatry, 50*, 971-974.

Linehan, M.M., Heard, H.L., & Armstrong, H.E. (1994). Naturalistic follow-up of a behavioral treatment for chronically parasuicidal borderline patients. *Archives of General Psychiatry, 51*, 422-434.

Linehan, M.M., Schmidt, H., Dimeff, L.A., Craft J.C., Kanter, J., & Comtois, K.A. (1999). Dialectical behavior therapy for patients with borderline personality disorder and drug-dependence. *American Journal on Addictions, 8*, 279-292.

Link, B., Cullen, F., Frank, J., & Wozniak, J. (1987). The social rejection of former mental patients: Understanding why labels matter. *American Journal of Sociology, 92*, 1401-1500.

Links, P., Steiner, M., Boiago, I., & Irwin, D. (1990). Lithium therapy for borderline patients: Preliminary findings. *Journal of Personality Disorders, 4*, 173-181.

Links, P.S., Heslegrave, R., & van Reekum, R. (1998). Prospective follow-up of borderline personality disorder: Prognosis, prediction outcome, and Axis II comorbidity. *Canadian Journal of Psychiatry, 43*, 265-270.

Linn, R.T., Wolf, P.A., Bachman, D.L., Knoefel, J.E., Cobb, J., et al. (1999). The "preclinical phase" of probable Alzheimer's disease: A 13-year prospective study of the Framingham cohort. *Archives of Neurology, 52*, 485-490.

Linney, J.A. (1989). Optimizing research strategies in the schools. In L.A. Bond & B.E. Compas (Eds.), *Primary prevention and promotion in the schools* (pp. 50-76). Newbury Park, CA: Sage.

Lion, J.R. (1978). Outpatient treatment of psychopaths. In W.H. Reid (Ed.), *The psychopath: A comprehensive study of antisocial disorders and behaviors*. New York: Brunner/Mazel.

Lipowski, C.J. (1990). *Acute confusional states*. New York: Oxford University Press.

Lipowski, P., Kerkhofs, M., VanOnderbergen, A., Hubain, P., Copinschi, G., et al. (1994). The 24 hour profiles of cortisol, prolactin, and growth hormone secretion in mania. *Archives of General Psychiatry, 51*, 616-624.

Lipowski, Z.J. (1980). *Delirium: Acute brain failure in man*. Springfield, IL: Charles C. Thomas.

Lipowski, Z.J. (1983). Transient cognitive disorders (delirium and acute confusional states) in the elderly. *American Journal of Psychiatry, 140*, 1426-1436.

Liskow, B. (1982). Substance induced and substance use disorders: Barbiturates and similarly acting sedative hypnotics. In J.H. Greist, J.W. Jefferson, & R.L. Spitzer (Eds.), *Treatment of mental disorders*. New York: Oxford University Press.

Liston, E.H. (1982). Delirium in the aged. In L.E. Jarvik & G.W. Small (Eds.), *Psychiatric clinics of North America*. Philadelphia: Saunders.

Litrownik, A. F., & Castillo-Canez, I. (2000). Childhood maltreatment: Treatment of abuse and incest survivors. In C. R. Snyder & R. E. Ingram (Eds.), *Handbook of Psychological Change* (pp. 520-545). New York: John Wiley & Sons, Inc.

Litwack, T.R. (1985). The prediction of violence. *The Clinical Psychologist, 38*, 87-90.

Livesley, W.J., Jang, K.L., & Vernon, P.A. (1998). Phenotypic and genetic structure of traits in delineating personality disorder. *Archives of General Psychiatry, 55*, 941-948.

Livesley, W.J., Schroeder, M.L., Jackson, D.N., & Jung, K.L. (1994). Categorical distinctions in the study of personality disorder: Implications for classification. *Journal of Abnormal Psychology, 103,* 6-17.

Lobitz, W.C., & Post, R.D. (1979). Parameters of self-reinforcement and depression. *Journal of Abnormal Psychology, 88,* 33-41.

Loeber, R. (1991). Antisocial behavior: More enduring than changeable? *Journal of the American Academy of Child and Adolescent Psychiatry, 30,* 393-397.

Loeber, R., & Keenan, K. (1994). Interaction between conduct disorder and its comorbid conditions: Effects of age and gender. *Clinical Psychology Review, 14,* 497-523.

Loeber, R., Keenan, K., Lahey, B.B., Green, S.M., & Thomas, C. (1993). Evidence for developmentally based diagnoses of oppositional defiant disorder and conduct disorder. *Journal of Abnormal Child Psychology, 21,* 377-410.

Loeber, R., Lahey, B., & Thomas, C. (1991). Diagnostic conundrum of oppositional defiant disorder and conduct disorder. *Journal of Abnormal Psychology, 100,* 379-390.

Loeber, R., Stouthamer-Loeber, M., Van Kammen, W., & Farrington, D.P. (1989). Development of a new measure of self-reported antisocial behavior for young children: Prevalence and reliability. In M. Klein (Ed.), *Cross-national research in self-reported crime and delinquency* (pp. 203-226). Boston: Kluwer-Nijhoff.

Loewenstein, R.J. (1991). Psychogenic amnesia and psychogenic fugue: A comprehensive review. In A. Tasman & S.M. Goldfinger (Eds.), *American Psychiatric Press Review of Psychiatry* (pp. 189-222). Washington, DC: American Psychiatric Press.

Loffin, R.B., & Kenny, P.J. (1998). Training the Hubble space telescope flight team. *IEEE Computer Graphics and Applications,* 31-37.

Loftus, E.F. (1993). The reality of repressed memories. *American Psychologist, 48,* 518-537.

Loftus, E.F. (1997). Memory for a past that never was. *Current Directions in Psychological Science, 6,* 60-62.

Loftus, E.F., & Ketchum, K. (1994). *The myth of repressed memory: False memories and allegations of sexual abuse.* New York: St. Martin's Press.

Lohr, J.M., Tolin, D.F., & Lilienfeld, S.O. (1998). Efficacy of eye movement desensitization and reprocessing: Implications for behavior therapy. *Behavior Therapy, 29,* 123-156.

London, P. (1964). *The modes and morals of psychotherapy.* New York: Holt, Rinehart & Winston.

London, P. (1986). *The modes and morals of psychotherapy* (2nd ed.). New York: Hemisphere.

Loney, J., Langhorne, J.E., Jr., & Paternite, C.E. (1978). An empirical basis for subgrouping the hyperkinetic-minimal brain dysfunction syndrome. *Journal of Abnormal Psychology, 87,* 431-441.

Long, W.R. (1995, November 24). A changing world proves deadly to Brazil Indians. *Los Angeles Times,* pp. A1, A47, A48.

Looman, J. (1995). Sexual fantasies of child molesters. *Canadian Journal of Behavioural Science, 27,* 321-332.

Lopez, S.R., Kopelowicz, A., & Canive, J.M. (2002). Strategies in developing culturally congruent family interventions for schizophrenia: The case of Hispanics in Madrid and Los Angeles. In H.P. Lefley & D.L. Johnson (Eds.), *Family interventions in mental illness: International perspectives* (pp. 61- 90). Westport, CT: Greenwood.

Lopez, S.R. (1989). Patient variable biases in clinical judgment: Conceptual overview and methodological considerations. *Psychological Bulletin, 106,* 184-203.

Lopez, S.R. (1994). Latinos and the expression of psychopathology: A call for direct assessment of cultural influences. In C. Telles & M. Karno (Eds.), *Latino mental health: Current research and policy perspectives.* Los Angeles: UCLA.

Lopez, S.R. (1996). Testing ethnic minority children. In B.B. Wolman (Ed.), *The encyclopedia of psychology, psychiatry, and psychoanalysis.* New York: Henry Holt.

Lopez, S.R., & Hernandez, P. (1986). How culture is considered in evaluations of psychopathology. *Journal of Nervous and Mental Disease, 176,* 598-606.

Lopez, S.R., & Romero, A. (1988). Assessing the intellectual functioning of Spanish-speaking adults: Comparison of the EIWA and the WAIS. *Professional Psychology: Research and Practice, 19,* 263-270.

Lopez, S.R., & Taussig, I.M. (1991). Cognitive-intellectual functioning of Spanish-speaking impaired and nonimpaired elderly: Implications for culturally sensitive assessment. *Psychological Assessment: A Journal of Consulting and Clinical Psychology, 3,* 448-454.

Lopez, S.R., Lopez, A.A., & Fong, K.T. (1991). Mexican Americans' initial prefer-

ences for counselors: The role of ethnic factors. *Journal of Counseling Psychology, 38,* 487-496.

Lopez, S.R., Nelson, K.A., Snyder, K.S., & Mintz, J. (1999). Attributions and affective reactions of family members and course of schizophrenia. *Journal of Abnormal Psychology, 108,* 307-314.

LoPiccolo, J. (1991). Counseling and therapy for sexual problems in the elderly. *Clinics in Geriatric Medicine, 7,* 161-179.

LoPiccolo, J. (1992a). Post-modern sex therapy for erectile failure. In R.C. Rosen & S.R. Leiblum (Eds.), *Erectile failure: Assessment and treatment.* New York: Guilford.

LoPiccolo, J. (1992b). Psychological evaluation of erectile failure. In R. Kirby, C. Carson, & G. Webster (Eds.), *Diagnosis and management of male erectile failure dysfunction.* Oxford: Butterworth-Heinemann.

LoPiccolo, J. (in press). Sex therapy: A post-modern model. In S.J. Lynn & J.P. Garske (Eds.), *Contemporary psychotherapies: Models and methods.* New York: Merrill.

LoPiccolo, J., & Friedman, J. (1988). Broad-spectrum treatment of low sexual desire: Integration of cognitive, behavioral, and systemic therapy. In S. Leiblum & R.C. Rosen (Eds.), *Sexual desire disorders.* New York: Guilford.

LoPiccolo, J., & Friedman, J.M. (1985). Sex therapy: An integrated model. In S.J. Lynn & J.P. Garskee (Eds.), *Contemporary psychotherapies: Models and methods.* New York: Merrill.

LoPiccolo, J., & Hogan, D.R. (1979). Multidimensional treatment of sexual dysfunction. In O.F. Pomerleau & J.P. Brady (Eds.), *Behavioral medicine: Theory and practice.* Baltimore: Williams & Wilkins.

LoPiccolo, J., & Lobitz, W.C. (1972). The role of masturbaton in the treatment of orgasmic dysfunction. *Archives of Sexual Behavior, 2,* 163-171.

LoPiccolo, J., & Stock, W.E. (1987). Sexual function, dysfunction, and counseling in gynecological practice. In Z. Rosenwaks, F. Benjamin, & M.L. Stone (Eds.), *Gynecology.* New York: Macmillan.

Loranger, A.W., Oldham, J., Russakoff, L.M. & Susman, V. (1987). Structured interviews and borderline personality disorder. *Archives of General Psychiatry, 41,* 565-568

Loranger, A.W., Sartorius, N., Andreoli, A., Berger, P., Buchleim, P., et al. (1994). The International Personality Disorders Examination: The World Health Organization/Alcohol, Drug Abuse and Mental Health Administration international pilot study of personality disorders. *Archives of General Psychiatry, 51,* 215-223.

Lorenz, J., Kunze, K., & Bromm, B. (1998). Differentiation of conversive sensory loss and malingering by P300 in a modified oddball task. *NeuroReport, 9,* 187-191.

Lotter, V. (1974). Factors related to outcome in autistic children. *Journal of Autism and Childhood Schizophrenia, 4,* 263-277.

Lotter, V. (1978). Follow-up studies. In M. Rutter & E. Schopler (Eds.), *Autism: A reappraisal of concepts and treatment.* New York: Plenum.

Lovaas, O.I. (1987). Behavioral treatment and normal educational and intellectual functioning in young autistic children. *Journal of Consulting and Clinical Psychology, 55,* 3-9.

Lovaas, O.I., Berberich, J.P., Perloff, B.F., & Schaeffer, B. (1966). Acquisition of imitative speech by schizophrenic children. *Science, 151,* 705-707.

Lovaas, O.I., Freitag, G., Gold, V.J., & Kassoria, I.C. (1965). Experimental studies in childhood schizophrenia: Analysis of self-destructive behavior. *Journal of Applied Behavior Analysis, 6,* 131-166.

Lovaas, O.I., Newsom, C., & Hickman, C. (1987). Self-stimulatory behavior and perceptual reinforcement. *Journal of Applied Behavior Analysis, 20,* 45-68.

Lovallo, W.R., & Al'Absi, M. (1998). Hemodynamics during rest and behavioral stress in normotensive men at high risk for hypertension. *Psychophysiology, 35,* 47-53.

Lovass, O.I., Schreibman, L., Koegel, R., & Rehm, R. (1971). Selective responding by autistic children to multiple sensory input. *Journal of Abnormal Psychology, 77,* 221-222.

Lubin, B. (1983). Group therapy. In I.B. Weiner (Ed.), *Clinical methods in psychology* (2nd ed.). New York: Wiley.

Luborsky, L., & Spence, D.P. (1978). Quantitative research on psychoanalytic therapy. In S.L. Garfield & A.E. Bergin (Eds.), *Handbook of psychotherapy and behavior change: An empirical analysis* (2nd ed.). New York: Wiley.

Luborsky, L., Barber, J.P., & Crits-Christoph, P. (1990). Theory-based research for understanding the process of dynamic psychotherapy. *Journal of Consulting and Clinical Psychology, 58,* 281-287.

Luborsky, L., Crits-Christoph, P., Melon, J., & Auerbach, A. (1988). *Who will benefit from psychotherapy?: Predicting therapeutic outcomes*. New York: Basic Books.

Luecken, L.J., Suarez, E.C., Kuhn, C.M., Barefoot, J.C., Blumenthal, J.A., et al. (1997). Stress in employed women: Impact of marital status and children in the home on neurohormone output and home strain. *Psychosomatic Medicine, 59*, 352-359.

Luepnitz, R.R., Randolph, D.L., & Gutsch, K.U. (1982). Race and socioeconomic status as confounding variables in the accurate diagnosis of alcoholism. *Journal of Clinical Psychology, 38*, 665-669.

Lykken, D.T. (1957). A study of anxiety in the sociopathic personality. *Journal of Abnormal and Social Psychology, 55*, 6-10.

Lynam, D.R. & Widiger, T.A. (2001). Using the five-factor model to represent DSM-IV personality disorders: An expert consensus approach. *Journal of Abnormal Psychology, 110*, 401-412.

Lynam, D.R. (1996). Early identification of chronic offenders: Who is the fledgling psychopath? *Psychological Bulletin, 120*, 209-234.

Lynam, D.R. (1997). Pursuing the psychopath: Capturing the fledgling psychopath in a nomological net. *Journal of Abnormal Psychology, 106*, 425-438.

Lynch, J., Kaplan, G.A., Salonen, R., & Salonen, J.T. (1997). Workplace demands, economic reward, and the progression of atherosclerosis. *Circulation, 96*, 302-307.

Lynch, J., Krause, N., Kaplan, G.A., Tuomilehto, J., & Salonen, J.T. (1997). Workplace conditions, socioeconomic status, and the risk of mortality and acute myocardial infarction. *American Journal of Public Health, 87*, 617-622.

Lynch, J.W., Kaplan, G.A., Cohen, R.D., Tuomilehto, J., & Salonen, J.T. (1996). Do cardiovascular risk factors explain the relation between socioeconomic status, risk of all-cause mortality, cardiovascular mortality, and acute myocardial infarction? *American Journal of Epidemiology, 111*, 931-912.

Lyon, H.M., Startup, M., & Bentall, R.P. (1999). Social cognition and the manic defense: Attribution, selective attention, and self-schema in bipolar affective disorder. *Journal of Abnormal Psychology, 108*, 273-282.

Lyons, M.J., Eisen, S.A., Goldberg, J., True, W., Lin, N., et al. (1998). A registry-based twin study of depression in men. *Archives of General Psychiatry, 55*, 468-472.

Lyons, M.J., True, W.S., Eisen, A., Goldberg, J., Meyer, J.M., et al. (1995). Differential heritability of adult and juvenile antisocial traits. *Archives of General Psychiatry, 52*, 906-915.

Lystad, M.M. (1957). Social mobility among selected groups of schizophrenics. *American Sociological Review, 22*, 288-292.

Maccoby, N., & Altman, D.G. (1988). Disease prevention in communities: The Stanford Heart Disease Prevention Program. In R.H. Price, E.L. Cowen, R.P. Lorion, & J. Ramos-McKay (Eds.), *14 ounces of prevention: A casebook for practitioners* (pp. 165-174). Washington, DC: American Psychological Association.

MacDonald, V.M., Tsiantis, J., Achenbach, T.M., Motti-Stefanidi, F., & Richardson, C. (1995). Competencies and problems reported by parents of Greek and American children, ages 6-11. *European Child and Adolescent Psychiatry, 4*, 1-13.

Mace, C.J., & Trimble, M.R. (1996). Ten-year prognosis of conversion disorder. *British Journal of Psychiatry, 169*, 282-288.

MacGregor, M.W. (1996). Multiple personality disorder: Etiology, treatment, and techniques from a psychodynamic perspective. *Psychoanalytic Psychology, 13*, 389-402.

Machon, R.A., Mednick, S.A., & Huttunen, M.O. (1997). Adult major affective disorder after prenatal exposure to an influenza epidemic. *Archives of General Psychiatry, 54*, 322-328.

Macklin, M.L., Metzger, L.J., Litz, B.T., McNally, R.J., Lasko, N.B., et al. (1998). Lower precombat intelligence is a risk factor for posttraumatic stress disorder. *Journal of Consulting and Clinical Psychology, 66*, 323-326.

MacLeod, A.K., Haynes, C., & Sensky, T. (1998). Attributions about common bodily sensations: Their associations with hyponchondriasis and anxiety. *Psychological Medicine, 28*, 225-228.

MacLeod, C., & Hemsley, D.R. (1985). Visual feedback of vocal intensity in the treatment of hysterical aphonia. *Journal of Behaviour Therapy and Experimental Psychiatry, 4*, 347-353.

MacLeod, C., Mathews, A., & Tata, P. (1986). Attentional bias in emotional disorders. *Journal of Abnormal Psychology, 95*, 15-20.

MacNamara, M. (1993). Fade away: The rise and fall of the repressed memory theory in the courtroom. *California Lawyer, 15*, 36-41.

Maddux, J.E., Roberts, M.C., Sledden, E.A., & Wright, L. (1986). Developmental issues in child health psychology. *American Psychologist, 41*, 25-34.

Madonna, P.G., Van Scoyk, S., & Jones, D.B. (1991). Family interactions within incest and nonincest families. *American Journal of Psychiatry, 148*, 46-49.

Maffei, C., Fossati, A., Agostini, I., Barraco, A., et al. (1997). Interrater reliability and internal consistency of the Structured Clinical Interview for Axis II Personality Disorders (SCID-II), Version 2.0. *Journal of Personality Disorders, 11*, 279-284.

Magee, W.J., Eaton, W.W., Wittchern, H.U., McGonagle, K.A., & Kessler, R.C. (1996). Agoraphobia, simple phobia and social phobia in the National Comorbidity Survey. *Archives of General Psychiatry, 53*, 159-168.

Maher, B.A. (1966). *Principles of psychopathology: An experimental approach*. New York: McGraw-Hill.

Mahoney, L.J. (1977). Early diagnosis of breast cancer: The breast self-examination problem. *Progress in Clinical and Biological Research, 12*, 203-206.

Mahoney, M.J. (1974). *Cognition and behavior modification*. Cambridge, MA: Ballinger.

Mahoney, M.J. (1982). Psychotherapy and human change processes. In *Psychotherapy research and behavior change* (Vol. 1). Washington, DC: American Psychological Association.

Mahoney, M.J. (1989) Scientific psychology and radical behaviorism: Important distinctions based in scientism and objectivism. *American Psychologist, 44*, 1372-1377.

Mahoney, M.J. (1991). *Human change processes: The scientific foundations of psychotherapy*. New York: Basic Books.

Mahoney, M.J. (1993). Theoretical developments in the cognitive psychotherapies. *Journal of Consulting and Clinical Psychology, 7*, 138-157.

Mahoney, M.J., & Moes, A.J. (1997). Complexity and psychotherapy. Promising dialogues and practical issues. In F. Masterpasque & A. Perna (Eds.), *The psychological meaning of chaos: Self-organization in human development and psychotherapy* Washington, DC: American Psychological Association.

Maj, M., Pirozzi, R., Magliono, L., & Bartoli, L. (1998). Long-term outcome of lithium prophylaxis in bipolar disorder: A 5-year prospective study of 402 patients at a lithium clinic. *American Journal of Psychiatry, 155*, 30-35.

Makela, K., Rooms, R., Single, E., Sulkunen, P., Walsh, B., et al. (1981). *John. Alcohol, society, and the state: A comparative study of alcohol control*. Toronto: Addiction Research Foundation.

Maladonado, J.R., Butler, L.D., & Spiegel, D. (1998). Treatments for dissociative disorders. In P.E. Nathan & J.M. Gorman (Eds.), *A guide to treatments that work* (pp. 423-447). NY: Oxford University Press.

Malamuth, N.M., & Brown, L.M. (1994). Sexually aggressive men's perceptions of women's communications: Testing three explanations. *Journal of Personality and Social Psychology, 67*, 699-712.

Malamuth, N.M., & Check, J.V.P. (1983). Sexual arousal to rape depictions: Individual differences. *Journal of Abnormal Psychology, 92*, 55-67.

Malaspina, D., Goetz, R. R., Yale, S. et al. (2000). Relation of familial schizophrenia to negative symptoms but not to the deficit syndrome. *American Journal of Psychiatry,157*, 994-1003.

Malatesta, C.Z., & Izard, C.E. (1984). The facial expression of emotion: Young, middle-aged, and older adult expressions. In C.Z. Malatesta & C.E. Izard (Eds.), *Emotion in adult development* (pp. 253-273). Beverly Hills, CA: Sage.

Maldonado, J.R., & Spiegel, D. (1994). Treatment of post traumatic stress disorder. In S.J. Lynn & R. Rhue (Eds.), *Dissociation: Clinical, theoretical and research perspectives* (pp. 215-241). New York: Guilford Press.

Maldonado, J.R., Butler, L.D., & Spiegel, D. (1998). Treatments for dissociative disorders. In P.E. Nathan & J.M. Gorman (Eds.), *A guide to treatments that work* (pp. 423-446). New York: Oxford University Press.

Maletzky, B.M. (1991). *Treating the sexual offender*. Newbury Park, CA: Sage.

Maletzky, B.M. (1993). Factors associated with success and failure in the behavioral and cognitive treatment of sex offenders. *Annals of Sex Research, 6*, 241-258.

Maletzky, B.M. (1997). Exhibitionism: Assessment and treatment. In D.R. Laws & W. O'Donohue (Eds.), *Sexual deviance* (pp. 40-74). New York: Guilford Press.

Maletzky, B.M. (2000). Exhibitionism. In M. Hersen & M. Biaggio (Eds.), *Effective brief therapy: A clinician's guide* (pp. 235-257). New York: Plenum.

Maletzky, B.M. (2002). The paraphilias: research and treatment. In P.E. Nathan & J.M. Gorman (Eds.), *A guide to treatments that work* (pp. 525-558). New York: Oxford University Press.

Malizia, A.L., Cunningham, V.J., Bell, C.J., Liddle, P.F., et al. (1998). Decreased brain GABAa-benzodiazepine receptor binding in panic disorder: Preliminary results from a quantitative study. *Archives of General Psychiatry, 55,* 715-720.

Malkoff-Schwartz, S., Frank, E., Anderson, B., Sherrill, J.T., Siegel, L., et al. (1998). Stressful life events and social rhythm disruption in the onset of manic and depressive bipolar episodes: A preliminary investigation. *Archives of General Psychiatry, 55,* 702-707.

Mandler, G. (1966). Anxiety. In D.L. Sills (Ed.), *International encyclopedia of the social sciences.* New York: Macmillan.

Mandler, G. (1972). Helplessness: Theory and research in anxiety. In C.D. Spielberger (Ed.), *Anxiety: Current trends in theory and research.* New York: Academic Press.

Manji, H.K., Chen, G., Shimon, H., Hsiao, J.K., Potter, W.Z., & Belmaker, R.H. (1995). Guanine nucleotide-binding proteins in bipolar affective disorder: Effects of long-term lithium treatment. *Archives of General Psychiatry, 52,* 135-144.

Mann, V.A., & Brady, S. (1988). Reading disability: The role of language deficiencies. *Journal of Consulting and Clinical Psychology, 56,* 811-816.

Manne, S., Jacobsen, P.B., & Redd, W.H. (1992). Assessment of acute pediatric pain: Do child self-report, parent ratings, and nurse ratings measure the same phenomenon? *Pain, 48,* 45-52.

Manne, S.L., Bakeman, R., & Jacobsen, P.B. (1994). An analysis of behavioral intervention for children undergoing venipuncture. *Health Psychology, 13,* 556-566.

Mannuzza, S., Klein, R.G., Bonagura, N., Malloy, P., Giampino, T.L., & Addalli, K.A. (1991). Hyperactive boys almost grown up: 5. Replication of psychiatric status. *Archives of General Psychiatry, 48,* 77-83.

Mannuzza, S., Schneier, F.R., Chapman, T.F., Leibowitz, M.R., Klein, D.F., & Fyer, A.J. (1995). Generalized social phobia: Reliability and validity. *Archives of General Psychiatry, 52,* 230-237.

Manos, N., Vasilopoulou, E., & Sotiriou, M. (1987). DSM-III diagnoses of borderline disorder and depression. *Journal of Personality Disorders, 1,* 263-268.

Mansdorf, I.J., Calapai, P., Caselli, L., & Burstein, Y. (1999). Reducing psychotropic medication usage in nursing home residents: The effects of behaviorally oriented psychotherapy. *The Behavior Therapist, 22,* 21-39.

Manton, K.G., Blazer, D.G., & Woodbury, M.A. (1987). Suicide in middle age and later life: Sex and race specific life table and cohort analyses. *Journal of Gerontology, 42,* 219-227.

Manuck, S.B., Kamarck, T.M., Kasprowicz, A.S., & Waldstein, S., R. (1993). Stability and patterning of behaviorally evoked cardiovascular activity. In J. Blascovich & E.S. Katkin (Eds.), *Cardiovascular reactivity* (pp. 111-134). Washington, DC: American Psychological Association.

Manuck, S.B., Kaplan, J.R., & Clarkson, T.B. (1983). Behaviorally induced heart rate reactivity and atherosclerosis in cynomolgus monkeys. *Psychosomatic Medicine, 49,* 95-108.

Manuck, S.B., Kaplan, J.R., Adams, M.R., & Clarkson, T.B. (1989). Behaviorally elicited heart rate reactivity and atherosclerosis in female cynomolgus monkeys (Macaca fascicularis). *Psychosomatic Medicine, 51,* 306-318.

Manuzza, S., Gittelman-Klein, R., Bessler, A., Malloy, P., & LaPadula, M. (1993). Adult outcome of hyperactive boys: Educational achievement, occupational rank, and psychiatric status. *Archives of General Psychiatry, 50,* 565-576.

Marcantonio, E.R., Flacker, J.M., Wright, R.J., & Resnick, N.M. (2001). Reducing delirium after hip fracture: A randomized trial. *Journal of the American Geriatrics Society, 49,* 516-522.

March, J.S. (1995). Cognitive-behavioral psychotherapy for children and adolescents with OCD: A review and recommendations for treatment. *Journal of the American Academy of Child and Adolescent Psychiatry, 34,* 7-18.

Marcos, L.R. (1979). Effects of interpreters on the evaluation of psychopathology in non-English-speaking patients. *American Journal of Psychiatry, 136,* 171-174.

Marcus, J., Hans, S.L., Nagier, S., Auerbach, J.G., Mirsky, A.F., & Aubrey, A. (1987). Review of the NIMH Israeli Kibbutz-City and the Jerusalem infant development study. *Schizophrenia Bulletin, 13,* 425-438.

Marder, S.R., & Meibach, R.C. (1994). Risperidone in the treatment of schizophrenia. *American Journal of Psychiatry, 151,* 825-836.

Marder, S.R., Wirshing, W.C., Glynn, S.M., Wirshing, D.A., Mintz, J., & Liberman, R.P. (1999). Risperidone and haloperidol in maintenance treatment: Interactions with psychosocial treatments. *Schizophrenia Research, 36,* 288.

Marder, S.R., Wirshing, W.C., Mintz, J., McKenzie, J., Johnston, K., et al. (1996). Two-year outcome of social-skills training and group psychotherapy for outpatients with schizophrenia. *American Journal of Psychiatry, 153,* 1585-1592.

Marder, S.R., Wirshing, W.C., VanPutten, T., Mintz, J., McKenzie, R.N., et al. (1994). Fluphenazine vs. placebo supplementation for prodromal signs of relapse in schizophrenia. *Archives of General Psychiatry, 51,* 280-287.

Marengo, J., & Westermeyer, J.F. (1996). Schizophrenia and delusional disorder. In L.L. Carstensen, B.A. Edelstein, & L. Dornbrand (Eds.), *The practical handbook of clinical gerontology* (pp. 255-273). Thousand Oaks, CA: Sage.

Margolin, G. (1981). Behavior exchange in happy and unhappy marriages: A family cycle perspective. *Behavior Therapy, 12,* 329-343.

Margolin, G. (1982). Ethical and legal considerations in marital and family therapy. *American Psychologist, 37,* 788-801.

Margolin, G., & Burman, B. (1993). Wife abuse vs. marital violence: Different terminologies, explanations, and solutions. *Clinical Psychology Review, 13,* 59-73.

Margolin, G., & Fernandez, V. (1985). Marital dysfunction. In M. Hersen & A.S. Bellack (Eds.), *Handbook of clinical behavior therapy with adults.* New York: Plenum.

Margolin, G., & Wampold, B.F. (1981). Sequential analysis of conflict and accord in distressed and non-distressed marital partners. *Journal of Consulting and Clinical Psychology, 49,* 554-567.

Margraf, J., Ehlers, A., & Roth, W.T. (1986). Sodium lactate infusions and panic attacks: A review and critique. *Psychosomatic Medicine, 48,* 23-51.

Marijuana research findings. (1980). Washington, DC: U.S. Government Printing Office.

Maris, R.W., Berman, A.L., Maltsberger, J.T., & Yufit, R.I. (1992). *Assessment and prediction of suicide.* New York: Guilford.

Markman, H.J., Floyd, F.J., Stanley, S.M., & Storaasli, R.D. (1989). Prevention of marital distress: A longitudinal investigation. *Journal of Consulting and Clinical Psychology, 56,* 210-217.

Markman, H.J., Silvern, L., Clements, M., & Kraft-Hanak, S. (1993). Men and women dealing with conflict in heterosexual relationships. *Journal of Social Issues, 49,* 107-125.

Markovitz, J.H., Tucker, D., Sanders, P.W., & Warnock, D.G. (1998). Inverse relationship between urinary cyclic GMP to blood pressure reactivity in the CARDIA study: Vasodilatory regulation of sympathetic vasoconstriction. *Psychosomatic Medicine, 60,* 319-326.

Markowitz, J.C., Rabkin, J., & Perry, S. (1994). Treating depression in HIV-positive patients. *AIDS, 8,* 403-412.

Marks, I., Green, R., & Mataix-Cols, D. (2000). Adult gender identity disorder can remit. *Comprehensive Psychiatry, 41,* 273-275.

Marks, I., Lovell, K., Noshirvani, H., Livanou, M., & Thrasher, S. (1998). Treatment of post-traumatic stress disorder by exposure and/or cognitive restructuring: A controlled study. *Archives of General Psychiatry, 55,* 317-325.

Marks, I., Lovell, K., Noshirvani, H., Livanou, M., & Thrasher, S. (1998). Treatment of post-traumatic stress disorder by exposure and/or cognitive restructuring: A controlled study. *Archives of General Psychiatry, 55,* 317-315.

Marks, I., Lovell, K., Noshirvani, H., Livanou, M., & Thrasher, S. (1998). Treatment of posttraumatic stress disorder by exposure and/or cognitive restructuring. *Archives of General Psychiatry, 55,* 317-325.

Marks, I.M. (1969). *Fears and phobias.* New York: Academic Press.

Marks, I.M. (1995). Advances in behavioral-cognitive therapy of social phobia. *Journal of Clinical Psychiatry, 56,* 25-31.

Marks, I.M., & Gelder, M.G. (1967). Transvestism and fetishism: Clinical and psychological changes during faradic aversion. *British Journal of Psychiatry, 113,* 711-729.

Marks, I.M., Gelder, M.G., & Bancroft, J. (1970). Sexual deviants two years after electrical aversion. *British Journal of Psychiatry, 117,* 73-85.

Marks, I.M., Stern, R.S., Mawson, D., Cobb, J., & Markson, E. W. (1995). Issues affecting older women. In L. A. Bond & S. J. Cutter (Eds.), *Promoting successful and productive aging* (pp. 261-278). Thousand Oaks, CA: Sage Publications.

Marlatt, G.A. (1983). The controlled drinking controversy: A commentary. *American Psychologist, 38,* 1097-1110.

Marlatt, G.A. (1985). Relapse prevention: Theoretical rationale and overview of the model. In G.A. Marlatt & J. Gordon (Eds.), *Relapse prevention: Maintenance strategies in addictive behavior change.* New York: Guilford.

Marlatt, G.A., & Gordon, J.R. (1985). (Eds.), *Relapse prevention: Maintenance strategies in the treatment of addictive behaviors.* New York: Guilford.

Marmar, C., & Horowitz, M.J. (1988). Diagnosis and phase-oriented treatment of post-traumatic stress disorders. In J. Wilson (Ed.), *Human adaptation to extreme stress: From the Holocaust to Vietnam.* New York: Brunner/Mazel.

Marmor, J. (1962). Psychoanalytic therapy as an educational process: Common denominators in the therapeutic approaches of different psychoanalytic schools. In J.H. Masserman (Ed.), *Science and psychoanalysis: Vol. 5. Psychoanalytic education.* New York: Grune & Stratton.

Marmor, J. (1971). Dynamic psychotherapy and behavior therapy: Are they irreconcilable? *Archives of General Psychiatry, 24,* 22-28.

Marmot, M.G., Bosma, H., Hemingway, H., Brunner, E., & Stansfeld, S. (1997). Contribution of job control and other risk factors to social variations in coronary heart disease incidence. *The Lancet, 350,* 235-239.

Marrazzi, M.A., & Luby, E.D. (1986). An auto-addiction model of chronic anorexia nervosa. *International Journal of Eating Disorders, 5,* 191-208.

Marsh, B. (1996, July 7). Meth at work: In virtually every industry, use among employees is on the rise [editorial]. *Los Angeles Times,* pp. D1, D4.

Marshall, R.D., Printz, D., Cardenas, D., Abbate, I., & Liebowitz, M.R. (1995). Adverse events in PTSD patients taking fluoxetine. *American Journal of Psychiatry, 152,* 1238-1239.

Marshall, W.L. (1997). Pedophilia: Psychopathology and theory. In D.R. Laws & W. O'Donohue (Eds.), *Sexual deviance* (pp. 152-174). New York: Guilford Press.

Marshall, W.L., Jones, R., Ward, T., Johnston, P., & Barbaree, H.E. (1991). Treatment outcomes with sex offenders. *Clinical Psychology Review, 11,* 465-485.

Marshall, W.L., Serran, G.A., & Cortoni, F.A. (2000). Childhood attachments, sexual abuse, and their relationship to adult coping in child molesters. *Sexual Abuse: A Journal of Research and Treatment, 12,* 17-26.

Marshall. L.A. & Cooke, D.J. (1999). The childhood experiences of psychopaths: A retrospective study of familial and societal factors. *Journal of Personality Disorders, 13,* 211-225.

Martin, J.E., Dubbert, P.M., & Cushman, W.C. (1991). Controlled trial of aerobic exercise in hypertension. *Circulation, 81,* 1560-1567.

Martin, P.A., & Bird, H.W. (1953). An approach to the psychotherapy of marriage partners. The stereoscopic technique. *Psychiatry, 16,* 123-127.

Maruish, M.E., Sawicki, R.F., Franzen, M.D., & Golden, C.J. (1984). Alpha coefficient reliabilities for the Luria-Nebraska Neuropsychological Battery summary and localization scales by diagnostic category. *The International Journal of Clinical Neuropsychology, 7,* 10-12.

Marziali, E. (1984). Prediction of outcome of brief psychotherapy from therapist interpretive interventions. *Archives of General Psychiatry, 41,* 301-304.

Masling, J. (1960). The influences of situational and interpersonal variables in projective testing. *Psychological Bulletin, 57,* 65-85.

Maslow, A.H. (1968). *Toward a psychology of being.* New York: Van Nostrand-Reinhold.

Mason, F.L. (1997). Fetishism: Psychopathology and theory. In D.R. Laws & W. O'Donohue (Eds.), *Sexual deviance* (pp. 75-91). New York: Guilford Press.

Masse, L.C., & Tremblay, R.E. (1997). Behavior of boys in kindergarten and the course of substance use during adolescence. *Archives of General Psychiatry, 54,* 62-68.

Masson, J.M. (1984). *The assault on truth: Freud's suppression of the seduction theory.* New York: Farrar, Strauss, Giroux.

Masters, W.H., & Johnson, V.E. (1966). *Human sexual response.* Boston: Little, Brown.

Masters, W.H., & Johnson, V.E. (1970). *Human sexual inadequacy.* Boston: Little, Brown.

Masters, W.H., Johnson, V.E., & Kolodny, R.C. (1988). *Human sexuality* (3rd ed.). Boston: Little Brown.

Mathe, A., & Knapp, P. (1971). Emotional and adrenal reactions of stress in bronchial asthma. *Psychosomatic Medicine, 33,* 323-329.

Mathews, A., & MacLeod, C. (1994). Cognitive approaches to emotion and emotional disorders. In L.W. Porter & M.R. Rosenzweig (Eds.), *Annual Review of Psychology* (pp. 25-50). Stanford, CA: Stanford University Press.

Mathews, H.F., Lannin, D.R., & Mitchell, J.P. (1994). Coming to terms with advanced breast cancer: Black women's narratives from eastern North Carolina. *Social Science and Medicine, 38,* 789-800.

Matthews, A. & Mackintosh, B. (2000). Induced emotional interpretation bias and anxiety. *Journal of Abnormal Psychology, 109,* 602-615.

Matthews, K.A. (1982). Psychological perspectives on the type A behavior pattern. *Psychological Bulletin, 91,* 293-323.

Matthews, K.A., & Rakaczky, C.J. (1987). Familial aspects of type A behavior and physiologic reactivity to stress. In T. Dembroski & T. Schmidt (Eds.), *Behavioral factors in coronary heart disease.* Heidelberg: Springer-Verlag.

Matthews, K.A., Glass, D.C., Rosenman, R.H., & Bonner, R.W. (1977). Competitive drive, pattern A, and coronary heart disease: A further analysis of some data from the Western Collaborative Group Study. *Journal of Chronic Diseases, 30,* 489-498.

Matthews, K.A., Meilan, E., Kuller, L.M., Kelsey, S.F., Caggiula, A., et al. (1989). Menopause and risk factors in coronary heart disease. *New England Journal of Medicine, 321,* 641-646.

Matthews, K.A., Owens, J.F., Allen, M.T., & Stoney, C.M. (1992). Do cardiovascular responses to laboratory stress relate to ambulatory blood pressure levels?: Yes, in some of the people, some of the time. *Psychosomatic Medicine, 54,* 686-697.

Matthews, K.A., Shumaker, S.A., Bowen, D.J., Langer, R.D., Hunt, J.R., et al. (1997). Women's healthy initiative: Why now? What is it? What's new? *American Psychologist, 52,* 101-116.

Matthews, K.A., Woodall, K.L., Jacob, T., & Kenyon, K. (1995). Negative family environment as a predictor of boy's future status on measures of hostile attitudes, interview behavior, and anger expression. *Health Psychology, 15,* 30-37.

Mattick, R.P., & Andrews, G. (1994). Social phobia. In M. Hersen & R.T. Ammerman (Eds.), *Handbook of prescriptive treatments for adults* (pp. 157-177). New York: Plenum.

Mattson, M.E., Allen, J.P., Longabaugh, R., Nickless, C.J., Connors, G.J., & Kadden, R.M. (1994). A chronological review of empirical studies matching alcoholic clients to treatment. *Journal of Studies on Alcohol, 55,* 16-29.

Maugh, T.H. II. (1996a, July 10). AIDS forum addresses ways to help women. *Los Angeles Times,* pp. A6.

Maugh, T.H. II. (1996b, July 7). Experts alarmed by HIV spread, hopeful on prevention. *Los Angeles Times,* pp. A6.

Maugh, T.H. II. (1996c, July 4) New AIDS drug therapies could check epidemic. *Los Angeles Times,* pp. A1, A24.

Maugh, T.H. II. (1996d, July 11). New AIDS test may predict disease's course. *Los Angeles Times,* pp. A1, A8.

Maugh, T.H. II. (1998a, February 3). AIDS deaths down 44% in U.S.; new cases drop. *Los Angeles Times,* pp. A1-A11.

Maugh, T.H. II. (1998b, July 5). Simpler therapy is new goal of AIDS research. *Los Angeles Times,* pp. A1, A18.

Maugh, T.H. II. (2002). "Sobering" state report calls autism an epidemic. *Los Angeles Times,* October 18, pp. A1, A25.

Mavissikalian, M., Hammen, M.S., & Jones, B. (1990). DSM-III personality disorders in obsessive-compulsive disorder. *Comprehensive Psychiatry, 31,* 432-437.

Mayne, T.J. (2001). Emotions and health. In T.J. Mayne & G.A. Bonanno (Eds.), *Emotions: Current issues and future directions* (pp. 361-397). New York: Guilford Press.

Mays, D.T., & Franks, C.M. (1980). Getting worse: Psychotherapy or no treatment: The jury should still be out. *Professional Psychology, 11,* 78-92.

McArthur, D.S., & Roberts, G.E. (1982). *Roberts Apperception Test for Children Manual.* Los Angeles: Western Psychological Services.

McBride, P.A., Anderson, G.M., & Shapiro, T. (1996). Autism research: Bringing together approaches to pull apart the disorder. *Archives of General Psychiatry, 53,* 980-983.

McCarthy, B.W. (1986). A cognitive-behavioral approach to understanding and treating sexual trauma. *Journal of Sex and Marital Therapy, 12,* 322-329.

McCollum, V.J.C. (1997). Evolution of the African American family personality: Considerations for family therapy. *Journal of Multicultural Counseling and Development, 25,* 219-229.

McConaghy, N. (1990). Sexual deviation. In A.S. Bellack, M. Hersen, & A.E. Kazdin (Eds.), *International handbook of behavior modification and therapy* (2nd ed., pp. 565-580). New York: Plenum.

McConaghy, N. (1993). *Sexual behavior: Problems and management.* New York: Plenum.

McConaghy, N. (1994). Paraphilias and gender identity disorders. In M. Hersen & R.T. Ammerman (Eds.), *Handbook of prescriptive treatments for adults* (pp. 317-346). New York: Plenum.

McConaghy, N. (1997). Sexual and gender identity disorders. In S.M. Turner & M. Hersen (Eds.), *Adult psychopathology and diagnosis* (pp. 409-464). New York: Wiley.

McConaghy, N. (1998). *Sexual behavior: Problems and management* (2nd ed.). New York: Plenum.

McConaghy, N., Blaszczynski, A., & Kidson, W. (1988). Treatment of sex offenders with imaginal desensitization and/or medroxyprogesterone. *Acta Psychiatrica Scandinavica, 77,* 199-206.

McCord, W., & McCord, J. (1964). *The psychopath: An essay on the criminal mind*. New York: Van Nostrand-Reinhold.

McCormick, N.B. (1999). When pleasure causes pain: Living with interstitial cystitis. *Sexuality and Disability, 17*, 7-18.

McCrady, B.S. (1985). Alcoholism. In D.H. Barlow (Ed.), *Clinical handbook of psychological disorders*. New York: Guilford.

McCrady, B.S., & Epstein, E.E. (1998). Directions for research on alcoholic relationships: Marital- and individual-based models of heterogeneity. *Psychology of Addictive Behaviors, 9*, 157-166.

McCrady, B.S., Noel, N.E., Abrams, D.B., Stout, R.L., Nelson, H.F., & Hay, W.M. (1986). Comparative effectiveness of three types of spouse involvement in outpatient behavioral alcoholism treatment. *Journal of Studies on Alcohol, 47*, 459-467.

McCrady, B.S., Stout, R., Noel, N., Abrams, D., & Nelson, H.F. (1991). Effectiveness of three types of spouse-involved behavioral alcoholism treatment. *British Journal of the Addictions, 86*, 1415-1424.

McCrady, B.S., Stout, R.L., Noel, N.E., Abrams, D.B., & Nelson, H.F. (in press). Comparative effectiveness of three types of spouse-involved behavioral alcoholism treatment: Outcomes 18 months after treatment. *British Journal of Addictions*.

McCrae, R.R., & Costa, P.T., Jr. (1990). *Personality in adulthood*. New York: Guilford.

McCusker, J., Cole, M., & Abrahamowicz, M. (2002). Delirium predicts 12-month mortality. *Archives of Internal Medicine, 162*, 457-463.

McCutchan, J.A. (1990). Virology, immunology, and clinical course of HIV infection. *Journal of Consulting and Clinical Psychology, 58*, 5-12.

McDonald, R. (1980). Clomimpramine and exposure for obsessive-compulsive rituals — I. *British Journal of Psychiatry, 136*, 1-25.

McDougle, C.J., Black, J.E., Malison, R.T., Zimmerman, R.C., Kosten, T.R., et al. (1994). Noradrenergic dysregulation during discontinuation of cocaine use in addicts. *Archives of General Psychiatry, 51*, 713-719.

McDougle, C.J., Goodman, W.K., Leckman, J.F., Lee, N.C., Heninger, G.R., & Price, L.H. (1994). Haloperidal addition in fluvoxamine-refractory obsessive-compulsive disorder: A double-blind, placebo controlled study in patients with and without tics. *Archives of General Psychiatry, 51*, 302-308.

McDougle, C.J., Naylor, S.T., Volkmar, F.R., Heninger, G.R., & Price, L.H. (1996). A double-blind placebo-controlled study of fluvoxamine in adults with autistic disorder. *Archives of General Psychiatry, 53*, 1001-1008.

McEachin, J.J., Smith, T., & Lovaas, O.I. (1993). Long-term outcome for children with autism who received early intensive behavioral treatment. *American Journal on Mental Retardation, 97*, 359-372.

McEwen, B.S. (1998). Protective and damaging effects of stress mediators. *New England Journal of Medicine, 338*, 171-179.

McFall, M.E. & Wollersheim, J.P. (1979). Obsessive-compulsive neurosis: A cognitive-behavioral formulation and approach to treatment. *Cognitive Therapy and Research, 3*, 333-348.

McFall, R.M., & Hammen, C.L. (1971). Motivation, structure, and self-monitoring: Role of nonspecific factors in smoking reduction. *Journal of Consulting and Clinical Psychology, 37*, 80-86.

McFall, R.M., & Lillesand, D.B. (1971). Behavior rehearsal with modeling and coaching in assertion training. *Journal of Abnormal Psychology, 77*, 313-323.

McFarlane, T., Polivy, J., & Herman, C.P. (1998). Effects of false weight feedback on mood, self-evaluation, and food intake in restrained and unrestrained eaters. *Journal of Abnormal Psychology, 107*, 312-318.

McFarlane, W.R., Lukens, E., Link, B., Dushay, R., Deakins, S., Newmark, M., Dunne, E.J., Horen, B., & Toran, J. (1995). Multiple-family groups and psychoeducation in the treatment of schizophrenia. *Archives of General Psychiatry, 52*, 679-687.

McGee, R., & Feehan, M. (1991). Are girls with problems of attention underrecognized? *Journal of Psychopathology and Behavioral Assessment, 13*, 187-198.

McGee, R., & Williams, S. (1988). A longitudinal study of depression in nine-year-old children. *Journal of the American Academy of Child and Adolescent Psychiatry, 27*, 49-54.

McGee, R., Feehan, M., Williams, S., Partridge, F., Silva, P.A., & Kelly, J. (1990). DSM-III disorders in a large sample of adolescents. *Journal of the American Academy of Child and Adolescent Psychiatry, 29*, 611-619.

McGhie, A., & Chapman, I.S. (1961). Disorders of attention and perception in early schizophrenia. *British Journal of Medical Psychology, 34*, 103-116.

McGlashan, T.H. & Hoffman, R.E. (2000). Schizophrenia as a disorder of developmentally reduced synaptic connectivity. *Archives of General Psychiatry,57*, 637-648.

McGlynn, F.D. (1994). Simple phobia. In M. Hersen & R.T. Ammerman (Eds.), *Handbook of prescriptive treatments for adults* (pp. 179-196). New York: Plenum.

McGrady, A.V., & Bernal, G.A.A. (1986). Relaxation-based treatment of stress induced syncope. *Journal of Behavior Therapy and Experimental Psychiatry, 17*, 23-27.

McGue, M., Pickens, R.W., & Svikis, D.S. (1992). Sex and age effects on the inheritance of alcohol problems: A twin study. *Journal of Abnormal Psychology, 101*, 3-17.

McGuffin, P., Katz, R., Watkins, S., & Rutherford, J. (1996). A hospital-based twin registry study of the heritability of DSM-IV unipolar depresson. *Archives of General Psychiatry, 53*, 129-136.

McGuiness, D. (1981). Auditory and motor aspects of language development in males and females. In A. Ansara (Ed.), *Sex differences in dyslexia*. Towson, MD: The Orton Dyslexia Society.

McGuire, J., Nieri, D., Abbott, D., Sheridan, K., et al. (1995). Do Tarasoff principles apply in AIDS-related psychotherapy? Ethical decision making and the role of therapist homophobia and perceived client dangerousness. *Professional Psychology: Research and Practice, 26*, 608-611.

McGuire, R.J., Carlisle, J.M., & Young, B.G. (1965). Sexual deviations as conditioned behaviour: A hypothesis. *Behaviour Research and Therapy, 2*, 185-190.

McIntosh, J.L. (1995). Suicide prevention in the elderly (65-99). In M.M. Silverman & R.W. Maris (Eds.), *Suicide prevention toward the year 2000* (pp. 180-192). New York: Guilford.

McIntosh, J.L., Santos, J.F., Hubbard, R.W., & Overholser, J.C. (1994). *Elder suicide: Research, theory, and treatment*. Washington, DC: American Psychological Association.

McIntyre-Kingsolver, K., Lichtenstein, E., & Mermelstein, R.J. (1986). Spouse training in a multicomponent smoking-cessation program. *Behavior Therapy, 17*, 67-74.

McKay, D., Nezeroglu, F., & Yaryura-Tobias, J.A. (1997). Comparison of clinical characteristics in obsessive-compulsive disorder and body dysmorphic disorder. *Journal of Anxiety Disorders, 11*, 447-454.

McKay, D., Todaro, J., Neiziroglu, F. et al. (1997). Body dysmorphic disorder: A preliminary evaluation of treatment and maintenance using exposure with response prevention. *Behaviour Research and Therapy, 35*, 67-70.

McKeon, P., & Murray, R. (1987). Familial aspects of obsessive-compulsive neurosis. *British Journal of Psychiatry, 151*, 528-534.

McKibben, A., Proulx, J., & Lusignan, R. (1994). Relationships between conflict, affect, and deviant sexual behaviors in rapists and pedophiles. *Behaviour Research and Therapy, 32*, 571-575.

McKim, W.A. (1991). *Drugs and behavior: An introduction to behavioral pharmacology*. Englewood Cliffs, NJ: Prentice-Hall.

McLarnon, L.D., & Kaloupek, D.G. (1988). Psychological investigation of genital herpes recurrence: Prospective assessment and cognitive-behavioral intervention for a chronic physical disorder. *Health Psychology, 7*, 231-249.

McLean, L.K., Brady, N.C., & McLean, J.E. (1996). Reported communication abilities of individuals with severe mental retardation. *American Journal on Mental Retardation, 100*, 580-591.

McMullen, S., & Rosen, R.C. (1979). Self-administered masturbation training in the treatment of primary orgasmic dysfunction. *Journal of Consulting and Clinical Psychology, 47*, 912-918.

McNally, R.J. (1994). *Panic disorder: A critical analysis*. New York: Guilford.

McNally, R.J. (1997). Atypical phobias. In G.C.L. Davey (Ed.), *Phobias: A handbook of theory, research and treatment* (pp. 183-199). Chichester,UK: Wiley.

McNally, R.J., Caspi, S.P., Riemann, B.C., & Zeitlin, S.B. (1990). Selective processing of threat cues in posttraumatic stress disorder. *Journal of Abnormal Psychology, 99*, 398-406.

McNeil, E. (1967). *The quiet furies*. Englewood Cliffs, NJ: Prentice-Hall.

McNeil, T.F., Cantor-Graae, E., & Weinberger, D.R. (2000). Relationship of obstetric complications and differences in size of brain structures in monozygotic twin pairs discordant for schizophrenia. *American Journal of Psychiatry, 157*, 203-212.

McNulty, J.L., Graham, J.R., Ben-Porath, Y.S., & Stein, L.A.R. (1997). Comparative validity of MMPI-II scales of African-American and Caucasian mental health center clients. *Psychological Assessment, 9*, 464-470.

Meador, D.M. & Ellis, N.R. (1987). Automatic and effortful processing by mentally retarded and nonretarded persons. *American Journal of Mental Deficiency, 91*, 613-619.

Meagher, D. J. (2001). Delirium: Optimizing management. *British Medical Journal*, 322, 144-149.

Meana, M., Binik, I., Khalife, S., & Cohen, D. (1998). Affect and marital adjustment in women's ratings of dyspareunic pain. *Canadian Journal of Psychiatry, 43*, 381-385.

Meana, M., Binik, Y.M., Khalife, S., & Cohen, D. (1997). Dyspareunia: Sexual dysfunction or pain syndrome? *Journal of Nervous and Mental Disease, 185*, 561-569.

Mednick, S.A., & Schulsinger, F. (1968). Some premorbid characteristics related to breakdown in children with schizophrenic mothers. In D. Rosenthal & S.S. Kety (Eds.), *The transmission of schizophrenia*. Elmsford, NY: Pergamon.

Mednick, S.A., Gabrielli, W.F., & Hutchings, B. (1984). Genetic influences in criminal convictions: Evidence from an adoption cohort. *Science, 224*, 891-894.

Mednick, S.A., Huttonen, M.O., & Machon, R.A. (1994). Prenatal influenza infections and adult schizophrenia. *Schizophrenia Bulletin, 20*, 263-268.

Mednick, S.A., Machon, R., Hottunen, M.O., & Bonett, D. (1988). Fetal viral infection and adult schizophrenia. *Archives of General Psychiatry, 45*, 189-192.

Medvedev, Z. (1972). *A question of madness*. New York: Knopf.

Meehl, P.E. (1962). Schizotaxia, schizotypy, schizophrenia. *American Psychologist, 17*, 827-838.

Meehl, P.E. (1986). Diagnostic taxa as open concepts: Methodological and statistical questions about reliability and construct validity in the grand strategy of nosological revision. In T. Millon & G.L. Klerman (Eds.), *Contemporary directions in psychopathology*. New York: Wiley.

Meeks, S. & Murrell, S.A. (1997). Mental illness in late life: Socioeconomic conditions, psychiatric symptoms, and adjustment of long term sufferers. *Psychology and Aging, 12*, 296-308.

Mehta, M. (1990). A comparative study of family-based and patients-based behavioural management in obsessive-compulsive disorder. *British Journal of Psychiatry*, 157, 133-135.

Meichenbaum, D.H. (1971). Examination of model characteristics in reducing avoidance behavior. *Journal of Personality and Social Psychology, 17*, 298-307.

Meichenbaum, D.H., & Asarnow, J. (1979). Cognitive-behavioral modification and metacognitive development: Implications for the classroom. In P.C. Kendall & S.D. Hollon (Eds.), *Cognitive-behavioral interventions: Theory, research, and procedures*. New York: Academic Press.

Meier, D.E., Emmons, C.A., Wallenstein, S., Quill, T., Morrison, R.S., & Cassel, C.K. (1998). A national survey of physician-assisted suicide and euthanasia in the United States. *New England Journal of Medicine, 338*, 1193-1201.

Melamed, B.G., & Siegel, L.J. (1975). Reduction of anxiety in children facing hospitalization and surgery by use of filmed modeling. *Journal of Consulting and Clinical Psychology, 43*, 511-521.

Melamed, B.G., Hawes, R.R., Heiby, E., & Glick, J. (1975). Use of filmed modeling to reduce uncooperative behavior of children during dental treatment. *Journal of Dental Research, 54*, 797-801.

Mellinger, G.D., Balter, M.B., & Uhlenhuth, E.H. (1985). Insomnia and its treatment. *Archives of General Psychiatry, 42*, 225-232.

Mello, N.K., & Mendelson, J.H. (1970). Experimentally induced intoxication in alcoholics: A comparison between programmed and spontaneous drinking. *Journal of Pharmacology and Experimental Therapy, 173*, 101.

Mellor, C.S. (1970). First rank symptoms of schizophrenia. *British Journal of Psychiatry, 117*, 15-23.

Melman, A., & Rossman, B. (1989). *Penile vein ligation for corporal incompetence: An evaluation of short and long term results*. Paper presented at the 15th Annual Meeting of the International Academy of Sex Research, Princeton. As cited in Wincze & Carey (1991).

Melnick, S.M. & Hinshaw, S.P. (1996). What they want and what they get: The social goals of boys with ADHD and comparison boys. *Journal of Abnormal Child Psychology, 24*, 169-185.

Meltzer, H.Y. (1998). Suicide in schizophrenia: Risk factors and clozapine treatment. *Journal of Clinical Psychiatry, 59*, 15-20.

Meltzer, H.Y., Cola, P., & Way, L.E. (1993). Cost effectiveness of clozapine in neuroleptic-resistant schizophrenia. *American Journal of Psychiatry, 150*, 1630-1638.

Mendels, J. (1970). *Concepts of depression*. New York: Wiley.

Mendels, J., Stinnett, J.L., Burns, D., & Frazer, A. (1975). Amine precursors and depression. *Archives of General Psychiatry, 32*, 22-30.

Menditto, A.A., Valdes, L.A., & Beck, N.C. (1994). Implementing a comprehensive social-learning program within the forensic psychiatric service of Fulton State Hospital. In P.W. Corrigan & R.P. Liberman (Eds.), *Behavior therapy in psychiatric hospitals* (pp. 61-78). New York: Springer.

Mendlewicz, J., & Rainer, J.D. (1977). Adoption study supporting genetic transmission in manic-depressive illness. *Nature, 268*, 327-329.

Merckelbach, H., de Ruiter, C., van den Hout, M.A., & Hoekstra, R. (1989). Conditioning experiences and phobias. *Behaviour Research and Therapy, 27*, 657-662.

Merikangas, K.R., Stolar, M., Stevens, D.E., Goulet, J., Preisig, M.A., et al. (1998). Familial transmission of substance use disorders. *Archives of General Psychiatry, 55*, 973-981.

Merrill, E.C. & McCauley, C. (1988). Phasic alertness and differences in picture encoding speed. *American Journal of Mental Retardation, 93*, 245-249.

Merrill, E.C. & O'Dekirk, J.M. (1994). Visual selective attention and mental retardation. *Cognitive neuropsychology, 11*, 117-132.

Merzenich, M.M., Jenkins, W.M., Johnson, P., Schreiner, C., Miller, S.L., & Tallal, P. (1996). Temporal processing deficits of language-learning impaired children ameliorated by training. *Science, 271*, 77-81.

Messer, S.B., Sass, L.A., & Woolfolk, R.L. (Eds.). *Hermeneutics and psychological theory: Integrative perspectives on personality, psychotherapy and psychopathology*. New Brunswick, NJ: Rutgers University Press.

Meston, C.M., & Gorzalka, B.B. (1996). Differential effects of sympathetic activation on sexual arousal in sexually dysfunctional and functional women. *Journal of Abnormal Psychology, 105*, 582-591.

Metalsky, G.I., Halberstadt, L.J., & Abramson, L.Y. (1987). Vulnerability and invulnerability to depressive mood reactions: Toward a more powerful test of the diathesis-stress and causal mediation components of the reformulated theory of depression. *Journal of Personality and Social Psychology, 52*, 386-393.

Metalsky, G.I., Joiner, T.E., Hardin, T.S., & Abramson, L.Y. (1993). Depressive reactions to failure in a natural setting: A test of the hopelessness and self-esteem theories of depression. *Journal of Abnormal Psychology, 102*, 101-109.

Metalsky, G.I., Joiner, T.E., Wonderlich, S.A., Beatty, W.W., Staton, R.D., et al (1997). When will bulimics be depressed and when not? The moderating role of attributional style. *Cognitive Therapy and Research, 21*, 61-72.

Metz, M.E., Pryor, J.L., Nesvacil, L.J., Abuzzahab, F., et al. (1997). Premature ejaculation: A psychophysiological review. *Journal of Sex and Marital Therapy, 23*, 3-23.

Meyer, B., Johnson, S.L., & Winters, R. (2001). Responsiveness to threat and incentive in bipolar disorder: Relations of the BIS/BAS scales with symptoms. *Journal of Psychopathology and Behavioral Assessment, 23*, 133-143.

Meyer, G.J. (2002). Exploring possible differences and bias in the Rorschach Comprehensive System. *Journal of Personality Assessment, 78*, 104-129.

Meyer, G.J., Finn, S.J., Eyde, L.D. et al. (2001). Psychological testing and psychological assessment: A review of evidence and issues. *American Psychologist, 56*, 128-165.

Meyer, G.J. (1997). Thinking clearly about reliability: More critical corrections regarding the Rorschach Comprehensive System. *Psychological Assessment, 9*, 495-498.

Meyer, I. (1995). Minority stress and mental health in gay men. *Journal of Health Sciences and Social Behavior, 36*, 38-56.

Meyer, J.J., & Reter, D.J. (1979). Sex reassignment follow-up. *Archives of General Psychiatry, 36*, 1010-1015.

Meyer, J.K. (1995). Paraphilias. In H.I. Kaplan & B.J. Sadock (Eds.), *Comprehensive textbook of psychiatry* (pp. 1334-1347). Baltimore: Williams & Wilkins.

Meyer, V. (1966). Modification of expectations in cases with obsessional rituals. *Behaviour Research and Therapy, 4*, 273-280.

Meyer, V., & Chesser, E.S. (1970). *Behavior therapy in clinical psychiatry*. Baltimore: Penguin.

Meyerowitz, B.E., & Chaiken, S. (1987). The effect of message framing on breast self-examination attitudes, intentions, and behavior. *Journal of Personality and Social Psychology, 52*, 500-510.

Meyerowitz, B.E., Richardson, J., Hudson, S., & Leedham, B. (1998). Ethnicity and cancer outcomes: Behavioral and psychosocial considerations. *Psychological Bulletin, 123*, 47-70.

Mezzich, A.C., Moss, H., Tarter, R.E., Wolfenstein, M., et al. (1994). Gender differences in the pattern and progression of substance use in conduct disordered adolescents. *American Journal on Addiction, 3*, 289-295.

Michelson, L., Mavissakalian, M., & Marchione, K. (1985). Cognitive and behavioral treatments of agoraphobia: Clinical, behavioral, and psychophysiological treatments of agoraphobia. *Journal of Consulting and Clinical Psychology, 53*, 913-925.

Michelson, L., Sugai, D.P., Wood, R.P., & Kazdin, A.E. (1983). *Social skills assessment and training with children: An empirically based handbook.* New York: Plenum.

Mikhliner, M., & Solomon, Z. (1988). Attributional style and post-traumatic stress disorder. *Journal of Abnormal Psychology, 97*, 308-313.

Miklich, D.R., Rewey, H.H., Weiss, J.H., & Kolton, S. (1973). A preliminary investigation of psychophysiological responses to stress among different subgroups of asthmatic children. *Journal of Psychosomatic Research, 17*, 1-8.

Miklowitz, D.J. (1985). *Family interaction and illness outcome in bipolar and schizophrenic patients.* Unpublished Ph.D. thesis, University of California at Los Angeles.

Miklowitz, D.J., Simoneau, T.L., Sachs-Ericsson, N., Warner, R., & Suddath, R. (1996). Family risk indicators in the course of bipolar affective disorder. In E. Mundt et al. (Eds.), *Interpersonal factors in the origin and course of affective disorders* (pp. 204-217). London: Gaskell Press.

Miklulineen, M., & Solomon, Z. (1988). Attributional style and posttraumatic stress disorder. *Journal of Abnormal Psychology, 97*, 308-313.

Milberger, S. (1997, October). *Impact of adversity on functioning and comorbidity of girls with ADHD.* Paper presented at the American Academy of Child and Adolescent Psychiatry, Toronto, Canada.

Milberger, S., Biederman, J., Faraone, S. V., & Chen, L. (1996) Is maternal smoking during pregnancy a risk factor for attention deficit hyperactivity disorder in children? *American Journal of Psychiatry, 153*, 1138-1142.

Miles, L.E., & Dement, W.C. (1980). Sleep and aging. *Sleep, 3*, 119-220.

Miller, A.C., Rathus, J.H., Linehan, M.M., Wetzler, S., & Leigh, E. (1997). Dialectical behavior therapy adapted for suicidal adolescents. *Journal of Practice Psychology and Behavioral Health*, 78-86.

Miller, H.R. (1981). Psychiatric morbidity in elderly surgical patients. *British Journal of Psychiatry, 128*, 17-20.

Miller, N.E. (1948). Studies of fear as an acquirable drive: I. Fear as motivation and fear-reduction as reinforcement in the learning of new responses. *Journal of Experimental Psychology, 38*, 89-101.

Miller, N.E. (1959). Liberalization of basic S-R concepts: Extensions to conflict behavior, motivation, and social learning. In S. Koch (Ed.), *Psychology: A study of a science* (Vol. 2). New York: McGraw-Hill.

Miller, N.S. (1995). History and review of contemporary addiction treatment. *Alcoholism Treatment Quarterly, 12*, 1-22.

Miller, S.B. (1994). Parasympathetic nervous system control of heart rate responses to stress in offspring of hypertensives. *Psychophysiology, 31*, 11-16.

Miller, S.M., Shoda, Y., & Hurley, K. (1996). Applying cognitive-social theory to health-protective behavior: Breast self-examination in cancer screening. *Psychological Bulletin, 119*, 70-94.

Miller, S.O. (1989). Optical differences in cases of multiple personality disorder. *Journal of Nervous and Mental Disease, 177*, 480-487.

Miller, T.Q., & Volk, R.J. (1996). Weekly marijuana use as a risk factor for initial cocaine use.: Results from a six wave national survey. *Journal of Chld and Adolescent Substance Abuse, 5*, 55-78.

Miller, T.Q., Markides, K.S., Chiriboga, D.A., & Ray, L.A. (1995). A test of the psychosocial and health behavior models of hostility: Results from an 11-year follow-up of Mexican Americans. *Psychosomatic Medicine, 57*, 572-581.

Miller, W.R., & Hester, R.K. (1986). Inpatient alcoholism treatment: Who benefits? *American Psychologist, 41*, 794-805.

Miller, W.R., & Hester, R.K. (1986). The effectiveness of alcoholism treatment: What research reveals. In W.R. Miller (Ed.), *Treating addictive behaviors: Processes of change* (pp. 121-174). New York: Guilford.

Miller, W.R., & Rollnick, S.(Eds.). (1991). *Motivational interviewing: Preparing people to change addictive behavior.* New York: Guilford.

Miller, W.R., Zweben, A., DiClemente, C.C., & Rychtarik, R.G. (1992). *Motivational Enhancement Therapy manual: A clinical research guide for therapists treating individuals with alcohol abuse and dependence.* NIAA Project MATCH Monograph, Vol. 2, DHHS Publication No. (ADM) 92-1894.

Millon, T. (1996). *Disorders of personality: DSM-IV and beyond* (2nd ed.). New York: Wiley.

Millsaps, C.L., Azrin, R.L., & Mittenberg, W. (1994). Neuropsychological effects of chronic cannabis use on the memory and intelligence of adolescents. *Journal of Child and Adolescent Substance Abuse, 3*, 47-55.

Milton, F., & Hafner, J. (1979). The outcome of behavior therapy for agoraphobia in relation to marital adjustment. *Archives of General Psychiatry, 36*, 807-811.

Mineka, S. (1992). Evolutionary memories, emotional processing, and the emotional disorders. In D. Medin (Ed.), *The psychology of learning and motivation* (Vol. 28). New York: Academic Press.

Mineka, S., & Zinbarg, R. (1996). Perspectives on anxiety, panic, and fear. In *Nebraska symposium on motivation.* (pp. 135-210). Lincoln: University of Nebraska Press.

Mineka, S., Davidson, M., Cook, M., & Keir, R. (1984). Observational conditioning of snake fear in rhesus monkeys. *Journal of Abnormal Psychology, 93*, 355-372.

Mintz, E. (1967). Time-extended marathon groups. *Psychotherapy, 4*, 65-70.

Mintz, M. (1991). Tobacco roads: Delivering death to the third world. *Progressive, 55*, 24-29.

Mintz, R.S. (1968). Psychotherapy of the suicidal patient. In H.L.P. Resnik (Ed.), *Suicidal behaviors.* Boston: Little, Brown.

Minuchin, S., Baker, L., Rosman, B.L., Lieberman, R., Milman, L., & Todd, T.C. (1975). A conceptual model of psychosomatic illness in children. *Archives of General Psychiatry, 32*, 1031-1038.

Miranda, J., & Persons, J.B. (1988). Dysfunctional thoughts are mood-state dependent. *Journal of Abnormal Psychology, 97*, 237-241.

Miranda, J., Gross, J.J., Persons, J.B., & Hahn, J. (1998). Mood matters: Negative mood induction activates dysfunctional attitudes in women vulnerable to depression. *Cognitive Therapy and Research, 22*, 363-376.

Mirenda, P.L., Donnellan, A.M., & Yoder, D.E. (1983). Gaze behavior: A new look at an old problem. *Journal of Autism and Developmental Disorders, 13*, 397-409.

Mischel, W. (1968). *Personality and assessment.* New York: Wiley.

Mischel, W. (1977). On the future of personality assessment. *American Psychologist, 32*, 246-254.

Mishkind, M.E., Rodin, J., Silberstein, L.R., & Striegel-Moore, R.H. (1986). The embodiment of masculinity: Cultural, psychological, and behavioral dimensions. *American Behavioral Scientist, 29*, 545-562.

Mitchell, J.E. (1992). Subtyping of bulimia nervosa. *International Journal of Eating Disorders, 11*, 327-332.

Mitchell, J.E., & Pyle, R.L. (1985). Characteristics of bulimia. In J.E. Mitchell (Ed.), *Anorexia nervosa and bulimia: Diagnosis and treatment.* Minneapolis: University of Minnesota Press.

Mittleman, M.A., Maclure, M., Sherwood, J.B., Murly, R.P., Tofler, G.A., et al., (1997). Triggering of acute myocardial infarction onset by episodes of anger. *Circulation, 92*, 1720-1725.

Modestin, J. (1987). Quality of interpersonal relationships: The most characteristic DSM-III BPD characteristic. *Comprehensive Psychiatry, 28*, 397-402.

Moen, P. (1996). Gender, age, and the life course. In R. H. Binstock & L. K. George (Eds.), *Handbook of aging and the social sciences* (4th ed., pp. 171-187). San Diego, CA: Academic Press.

Moene, F. C., Landberg, E. H., Hoogduin, K. A. et al. (2000). Organic syndromes diagnosed as conversion disorder: Identification and frequency in a study of 85 patients. *Journal of Psychosomatic Research, 49*, 7-12.

Moffitt, T.E. (1990). Juvenile delinquency and attention deficit disorder: Boys' developmental trajectories from age 13 to 15. *Child Development, 61*, 893-910.

Moffitt, T.E. (1993). Adolescence-limited and life-course-persistent antisocial behavior: A developmental taxonomy. *Psychological Review, 100*, 674-701.

Moffitt, T.E., Lynam, D., & Silva, P.A. (1994). Neuropsychological tests predict persistent male delinquency. *Criminology, 32*, 101-124.

Mogg, K., Millar, N., & Bradley, B. P. (2000). Biases in eye movements to threatening facial expressions in generalized anxiety disorder and depressive disorder. *Journal of Abnormal Psychology, 109*, 695-704.

Mohr, D.C., & Beutler, L.E. (1990). Erectile dysfunction: A review of diagnostic and treatment procedures. *Clinical Psychology Review, 10*, 123-150.

Mohr, J.W., Turner, R.E., & Jerry, M.B. (1964). *Pedophilia and exhibitionism.* Toronto: University of Toronto Press.

Molgaard, C.A., Nakamura, C.M., Stanford, E.P., Peddecord, K.M., & Morton, D.J. (1990). Prevalence of alcohol consumption among older persons. *Journal of Community Health, 15*, 239-251.

Monahan, J. (1973). The psychiatrization of criminal behavior. *Hospital and Community Psychiatry, 24*, 105-107.

Monahan, J. (1976). The prevention of violence. In J. Monahan (Ed.), *Community mental health and the criminal justice system.* Elmsford, NY: Pergamon.

Monahan, J. (1978). Prediction research and the emergency commitment of dangerous mentally ill persons: A reconsideration. *American Journal of Psychiatry, 135,* 198-201.

Monahan, J. (1984). The prediction of violent behavior: Toward a second generation of theory and policy. *American Journal of Psychiatry, 141,* 10-15.

Monahan, J. (1992). Mental disorder and violent behavior: Perceptions and evidence. *American Psychologist, 47,* 511-521.

Monahan, J. (1993). Limiting therapist exposure to Tarasoff liability: Guidelines for risk containment. *American Psychologist, 48,* 242-250.

Monahan, J., & Shah, S. (1989). Dangerousness and commitment of the mentally disordered in the United States. *Schizophrenia Bulletin, 15,* 541-553.

Monahan, J., & Steadman, H. (1994). Toward a rejuvenation of risk assessment research. In J. Monahan & H. Steadman (Eds.), *Violence and mental disorder: Developments in risk assessment.* Chicago: University of Chicago Press.

Moniz, E. (1936). *Tentatives operatoires dans le traitement de cereteines psychoses.* Paris: Mason.

Monroe, S.M., & Simons, A.D. (1991). Diathesis-stress theories in the context of life stress research: Implications for the depressive disorders. *Psychological Bulletin, 110,* 406-425.

Monson, R., & Smith, C.R. (1983). Current concepts in psychiatry: Somatization disorder in primary care. *New England Journal of Medicine, 308,* 1464-1465.

Morain, D. (1998). New state TV ads link smoking to impotence in men. *Los Angeles Times,* pp. A3-A18.

Moran, M. (1991). Psychological factors affecting pulmonary and rheumatological diseases: A review. *Psychosomatics, 32,* 14-23.

Moreau, D., Mufson, L., Weissman, M.M., & Klerman, G.L. (1992). Interpersonal psychotherapy for adolescent depression: Description of modification and preliminary application. *Journal of the Academy of Child and Adolescent Psychiatry, 30,* 642-651.

Morenz, B., & Becker, J.V. (1995). The treatment of youthful sexual offenders. *Applied and Preventive Psychology, 4,* 247-256.

Morey, L.C. & Zanarini, M.C. (2000). Borderline personality: Traits and disorder. *Journal of Abnormal Psychology, 109,* 733-737.

Morey, L.C., Gunderson, J., Quigley, B.D., & Lyons, M. (2000). Dimensions and categories: The "big five" factors and the DSM personality disorders. *Assessment, 7,* 203-216.

Morey, L.C. (1988). Personality disorders in DSM-III and DSM-IIIR: Convergence, coverage, and internal consistency. *American Journal of Psychiatry, 145,* 573-577.

Morey, L.C., Gunderson, J.G., Quigley, B.D., Shea, M.T., Skodol, A.E., McGlashan, T.H., et al. (2002). The representation of borderline, avoidant, obsessive-compulsive, and schizotypal personality disorders by the five-factor model. *Journal of Personality Disorders, 16,* 215-234.

Morgan, C.A., Grillon, C., Southwick, S.M., Davis, M., & Charney, D.S. (1996). Exaggerated acoustic startle reflex in Gulf War veterans with post-traumatic stress disorder. *American Journal of Psychiatry, 153,* 64-68.

Morgan, K. (1992). Sleep, insomnia, and mental health. *Reviews in Clinical Gerontology, 2,* 246-253.

Morgernstern, J., Langenbucher, J., Labouvie, E., & Miller, K.J. (1997). The comorbidity of alcoholism and personality disorders in a clinical population; Prevalence rates and relation to alcohol typology variables. *Journal of Abnormal Psychology, 106,* 74-84.

Morin, C.M., Colecchi, C., Stone, J., Sood, R., & Brink, D. (1999). Behavioral and pharmacological therapies for late-life insomnia: A randomized controlled trial. *Journal of the American Medical Association, 281,* 991-999.

Morin, C.M., & Azrin, N.H. (1988). Behavioral and cognitive treatments of geriatric insomnia. *Journal of Consulting and Clinical Psychology, 56,* 748-753.

Morley, S. (1997). Pain management. In A. Baum, S. Newman, J. Weinman, R. West, & C. McManus (Eds.), *Cambridge handbook of psychology, health and medicine* (pp. 234-237). Cambridge, UK: Cambridge University Press.

Morokoff, P.J. (1988). Sexuality in perimenopausal and postmenopausal women. *Psychology of Women Quarterly, 12,* 489-511.

Morokoff, P.J., & Gilliland, R. (1993). Stress, sexual functioning, and marital satisfaction. *Journal of Sex Research, 30,* 43-53.

Moroney, J.T., Tang, M-X., Berglund, L., Small, S., Merchant, C., et al. (1999). Low-density lipoprotein cholesterol and the risk of dementia with stroke. *JAMA, 282,* 254-260.

Morris, A.A. (1968). Criminal insanity. *Washington Review, 43,* 583-622.

Morris, N. (1966). Impediments to legal reform. *University of Chicago Law Review, 33,* 627-656.

Morris, N. (1968). Psychiatry and the dangerous criminal. *Southern California Law Review, 41,* 514-547.

Morrow, G.R., Leirer, V., & Sheikh, J. (1988). Adherence and medication instructions: Review and recommendations. *Journal of the American Geriatrics Society, 36,* 1147-1160.

Morse, R.M. (1988). Substance abuse among the elderly. *Bulletin of the Menninger Clinic, 52,* 259-268.

Morse, S.J. (1982a, June 23). In defense of the insanity defense. *Los Angeles Times.*

Morse, S.J. (1982b). Failed explanation and criminal responsibility: Experts and the unconscious. *Virginia Law Review, 678,* 971-1084.

Morse, S.J. (1982c). A preference for liberty: The case against involuntary commitment of the mentally disordered. *California Law Review, 70,* 54-106.

Morse, S.J. (1992). The "guilty mind": Mens rea. In D.K. Kagehiro & W.S. Laufer (Eds.), *Handbook of psychology and law* (pp. 207-229). New York: Springer-Verlag.

Morse, S.J. (1996). Blame and danger: An essay on preventive detention. *Boston University Law Review, 76,* 113-155.

Moscicki, E.K. (1995). Epidemiology of suicidal behavior. In M.M. Silverman & R.W. Maris (Eds.), *Suicide prevention: Toward the year 2000* (pp. 22-35). New York: Guilford.

Moser, C., & Levitt, E.E. (1987). An exploratory-descriptive study of a sadomasochistically oriented sample. *The Journal of Sex Research, 23,* 322-337.

Moser, P.W. (1989, January). Double vision: Why do we never match up to our mind's ideal? *Self Magazine,* 51-52.

Moses, J.A. (1983). Luria-Nebraska Neuropsychological battery performance of brain dysfunctional patients with positive or negative findings on current neurological examination. *International Journal of Neuroscience, 22,* 135-146.

Moses, J.A., & Purisch, A.D. (1997). The evolution of the Luria-Nebraska Battery. In G. Goldstein & T. Incagnoli (Eds.), *Contemporary approaches to neuropsychological assessment* (pp. 131-170). New York: Plenum.

Moses, J.A., & Schefft, B.K. (1984). Interrater reliability analyses of the Luria-Nebraska neuropsychological battery. *The International Journal of Clinical Neuropsychology, 7,* 31-38.

Moses, J.A., Schefft, B.A., Wong, J.L., & Berg, R.A. (1992). Interrater reliability analyses of the Luria-Nebraska neuropsychological battery, form II. *Archives of Clinical Neurology, 7,* 251-269.

Mosher, L.R., & Burti, L. (1989). *Community mental health: Principles and practice.* New York: Norton.

Mosher, L.R., Kresky-Wolff, M., Mathews, S., & Menn, A. (1986). Milieu therapy in the 1980s: A comparison of two residential alternatives to hospitalization. *Bulletin of the Menninger Clinic, 50,* 257-268.

Moss, H.B. (1990). Pharmacotherapy. In A.S. Bellack & M. Hersen (Eds.), *Handbook of comparative treatments for adult disorders* (pp. 506-520). New York: Wiley.

Motto, J.A. (1976). Suicide prevention for high-risk persons who refuse treatment. *Suicide: A Quarterly Journal of Life-Threatening Behavior, 6,* 223-230.

Mowrer, O.H. (1939). A stimulus-response analysis of anxiety and its role as a reinforcing agent. *Psychological Review, 46,* 553-565.

Mowrer, O.H. (1947). On the dual nature of learning: A reinterpretation of "conditioning" and "problem-solving." *Harvard Educational Review, 17,* 102-148.

Mowrer, O.H., & Mowrer, W.M. (1938). Enuresis: A method for its study and treatment. *American Journal of Orthopsychiatry, 8,* 436-459.

Mrazek, D.A., Schuman, W.B., & Klinnert, M. (1998). Early asthma onset: Risk of emotional and behavioral difficulties. *Journal of Child Psychology and Psychiatry and Allied Disciplines, 39,* 247-254.

Mrazek, P.J., & Haggerty, R.J. (1994). *Reducing risks for mental disorders: Frontiers for preventive intervention research.* Washington, DC: National Academy Press.

Mueser, K., Bellack, A.S., & Blanchard, J.J. (1992). Co-morbidity of schizophrenia and substance abuse: Implications for treatment. *Journal of Consulting and Clinical Psychology, 60,* 845-856.

Mueser, K.T., & Glynn, S.M. (1995). *Behavioral family therapy for psychiatric disorders.* Boston: Allyn & Bacon.

Mueser, K.T., & Liberman, R.P. (1995). Behavior therapy in practice. In B. Bongar & L.E. Beutler (Eds.), *Comprehensive textbook of psychotherapy: Theory and practice* (pp. 84-110). New York: Oxford University Press.

Mueser, K.T., Bond, G.R., Drake, R.E., & Resnick, S.G. (1998). Models of community care for severe mental illness: A review of research on case management. *Schizophrenia Bulletin, 24,* 37-74.

Mulligan, T., & Palguta, R.F. (1991). Sexual interest, activity, and satisfaction among male nursing home residents. *Archives of Sexual Behavior, 20,* 199-204.

Mulligan, T., Retchin, S.M., Chinchilli, V.M., & Bettinger, C.B. (1988). The role of aging and chronic disease in sexual dysfunction. *Journal of the American Geriatrics Society, 36*, 520-524.

Mulvey, E.P. (1994). Assessing the evidence of a link between mental illness and violence. *Hospital and Community Psychiatry, 45*, 663-668.

Mumford, D.B., Whitehouse, A.M., & Choudry, I.Y. (1992). Survey of eating disorders in English-medium schools in Lahore, Pakistan. *International Journal of Eating Disorders, 11*, 173-184.

Mundle, G., Bruegel, R., Urbaniak, H., Laengle, G., Buchkremer, G., & Mann, K. (2001). Kurz- und mittelfristige Erfolgsraten ambulanter Entwoehnungsbehandlungen fuer alkoholabhaengige Patienten. Eine 6-, 18-, und 36-Monats-Katamnese./Short- and medium-term outcome of outpatient treatment for alcohol dependent patients in Germany – A 6-, 18-, and 36-month follow-up. *Fortschritte der Neurologie Psychiatrie, 69*, 374-378.

Munetz, M.R., Grande, T., Kleist, J., & Peterson, G.A. (1996). The effectiveness of outpatient civil commitment. *Psychiatric Services, 47*, 1251-1253.

Munjack, D.J. (1984). The onset of driving phobias. *Journal of Behavior Therapy and Experimental Psychiatry, 15*, 305-308.

Munley, P. H., Morris, J. R., Murray, D. A., & Baines, T. C. (2001). A comparison of African-American and White American MMPI-2 profiles. *Assessment, 8*, 1-10.

Murdoch, D., Pihl, R.O., & Ross, D. (1990). Alcohol and crimes of violence: Present issues. *International Journal of Addiction, 25*, 1059-1075.

Murphy, J. (1976). Psychiatric labeling in cross-cultural perspective. *Science, 191*, 1019-1028.

Murphy, J.K., Stoney, C.M., Alpert, B.S., & Walker, S.S. (1995). Gender and ethnicity in children's cardiovascular reactivity: 7 years of study. *Health Psychology, 14*, 48-55.

Murphy, W.D. (1997). Exhibitionism: Psychopathology and theory. In D.R. Laws & W. O'Donohue (Eds.), Sexual deviance (pp. 22-39). New York: Guilford Press.

Muscettola, G., Potter, W.Z., Pickar, D., & Goodwin, F.K. (1984). Urinary 3-methoxy-4-hydroxyphenyl glycol and major affective disorders. *Archives of General Psychiatry, 41*, 337-342.

Muse, M. (1986). Stress-related, posttraumatic chronic pain syndrome: Behavioral treatment approach. *Pain, 25*, 389-394.

Musetti, L., Perugi, G., Soriani, A., Rossi, V.M., Cassano, G.B., & Akiskal, H.S. (1989). Depression before after age 65: A re-examination. *British Journal of Psychiatry, 155*, 330-336.

Musselman, D.L., Evans, D.L., & Nemeroff, C.B. (1998). The relationship of depression to cardiovascular disease: Epidemiology, biology, and treatment. *Archives of General Psychiatry, 55*, 580-592.

Myers, J.K., Weissman, M.M., Tischler, G.L., Holzer, C.E., Leaf, P.J., Orvaschel, H.A., Anthony, J.C., Boyd, J.H., Burke, J.E., Kramer, M., & Stoltzman, R. (1984). Six-month prevalence of psychiatric disorders in three communities: 1980-1982. *Archives of General Psychiatry, 41*, 959-967.

Myers, M.G., Stewart, D.G., & Brown, S.A. (1998). Progression from conduct disorder to antisocial personality disorder. *American Journal of Psychiatry, 155*, 479-485.

Myin-Germeys, I., van Os, J., Schwartz, J. E. et al. (2001). Emotional reactivity to daily life stress in schizophrenia. *Archives of General Psychiatry, 58*, 1137-1144.

Nahas, G.G., & Manger, W.M. (1995). Marijuana as medicine: In reply. *Journal of the American Medical Association, 274*, 1837-1838.

Naslund, J., Haroutunian, V., Mohs, R., et al. (2000). Correlation between elevated levels of amyloid B-peptide in the brain and cognitive decline. *JAMA, 283*, 1571-1577.

National Cancer Institute. (1977). *The smoking digest: Progress report on a nation kicking the habit*. Washington, DC: U.S. Department of Health, Education and Welfare.

National Center for Child Abuse and Neglect. (1988). *Study of national incidence and prevalence of child abuse and neglect, 1988*. Washington, DC: U.S. Department of Health and Human Services.

National Center for Health Statistics (1989). *National nursing home survey* (DHHS Publication No. PHS 89-1758, Series 13, No. 97). Washington, DC: U.S. Government Printing Office.

National Drug Intelligence Center (2001). *OxyContin diversion and abuse*. NDIC, Department fo Justice, January 2001, Document ID: 2001-L0424-001. (Also available online at http://www.usdoj.gov/ndic/pubs/651/index.htm.)

National Heart, Lung, and Blood Institute. (1995). *Global initiative for asthma: Strategy for asthma management and prevention*. Bethesda, MD: NIH.

National Heart, Lung and Blood Institute. (1998). *Behavioral research in cardiovascular, lung, and blood health and disease*. Washington, DC: U.S. Department of Health and Human Services.

National Institute of Child Health and Human Development (2000). *Report of the National Reading Panel. Teaching Children to Read: An Evidence-Based Assessment of the Scientific Research Literature on Reading and Its Implications for Reading Instruction* [Online]. Available at http://www.nichd.nih.gov/publications/nrp/smallbook.htm.

National Institute of Mental Health (NIMH) Multisite HIV Prevention Trial Group. (1998). The NIMH multisite HIV prevention trial: Reducing HIV sexual risk behavior. *Science, 280*, 1889-1894.

National Institute of Alcohol Abuse and Alcoholism (1998). *Alcohol Alert No. 42: Alcohol and Liver: Research Update*. Rockville, MD. (Also available online at http://www.niaaa.nih.gov/publications/aa42-text.htm.)

National Institute of Alcohol Abuse and Alcoholism (2001). *Alcohol Alert No. 51: Economic Perspectives in Alcoholism Research*. Rockville, MD. (Also available online at http://www.niaaa.nih.gov/publications/aa51-text.htm.)

National Institute on Drug Abuse. (1979). *National Survey on Drug Abuse*. Washington, DC: Author.

National Institute on Drug Abuse. (1982). *National Survey on Drug Abuse*. Washington, DC: Author.

National Institute on Drug Abuse. (1983a). *National Survey on Drug Abuse: Main Findings 1982* (DHHS Publication No. ADM 83-1263). Washington, DC: U.S. Government Printing Office.

National Institute on Drug Abuse. (1983b). *Population projections, based on the National Survey on Drug Abuse, 1982*. Rockville, MD: Author.

National Institute on Drug Abuse. (1988). *National household survey on drug abuse: Main findings 1985*. Washington, DC: Department of Health and Human Services.

National Institute on Drug Abuse. (1991). *National Household Survey on Drug Abuse: Population Estimates, 1991*. Washington, DC.

National Institute on Drug Abuse. (1995). *National survey results on drug use from the Monitoring the Future study, 1975-1994*. Washington: U.S. Department of Health and Human Services.

National Institute on Drug Abuse. (1996). *National household survey on drug abuse: Population estimates 1995*. Washington: Department of Health and Human Services.

Nauss, D.W. (1996, March 9). Kevorkian found not guilty of aiding two suicides. *Los Angeles Times*, pp. A1, A15.

Nawas, M.M., Fishman, S.T., & Pucel, J.C. (1970). The standardized densensitization program applicable to group and individual treatment. *Behaviour Research and Therapy, 6*, 63-68.

Neale, J.M., & Liebert, R.M. (1986). *Science and behavior: An introduction to methods of research* (3rd ed.). Englewood Cliffs, NJ: Prentice-Hall.

Neale, J.M., & Oltmanns, T. (1980). *Schizophrenia*. New York: Wiley.

Neisser, U. (1976). *Cognition and reality*. San Francisco: Freeman.

Neisser, U., & Harsch, N. (1991). Phantom flashbulbs: False recognitions of hearing the news about Challenger. In E. Winograd & U. Neisser (Eds.), *Affect and accuracy of recall: Studies of "flashbulb" memories*. New York: Cambridge University Press.

Nelson, J.C., & Davis, J.M. (1997). DST studies in psychotic depression: A meta-analysis. *American Journal of Psychiatry, 154*, 1497-1503.

Nelson, R.E., & Craighead, W.E. (1977). Selective recall of positive and negative feedback, self-control behaviors, and depression. *Journal of Abnormal Psychology, 86*, 379-388.

Nelson, R.O., Lipinski, D.P., & Black, J.L. (1976). The reactivity of adult retardates' self-monitoring: A comparison among behaviors of different valences, and a comparison with token reinforcement. *Psychological Record, 26*, 189-201.

Nemeroff, C.B., & Schatzberg, A.F. (1998). Pharmacological treatment of unipolar depression. In P.E. Nathan & J.M. Gorman (Eds.), *A guide to treatments that work* (pp. 212-225). New York: Oxford University Press.

Nemeroff, C.F., Stein, R.I., Diehl, N.S., & Smilack, K.M. (1994). From the Cleavers to the Clintons: Role choices and body orientation as reflected in magazine article content. *International Journal of Eating Disorders, 16*, 167-176.

Nemeroff, C.J., & Karoly, P. (1991). Operant methods. In F.H. Kanfer & A.P. Goldstein (Eds.), *Helping people change: A textbook of methods* (4th ed.). Elmsford, NY: Pergamon.

Nemetz, G.H., Craig, K.D., & Reith, G. (1978). Treatment of female sexual dysfunction through symbolic modeling. *Journal of Consulting and Clinical Psychology, 46*, 62-73.

Neron, S., Lacroix, D., & Chaput, Y. (1995). Group vs. individual cognitive behaviour therapy in panic disorder: An open clinical trial with a six month follow-up. *Canadian Journal of Behavioural Science, 27*, 379-392.

Nestadt, G., Romanoski, A., Chahal, R., Merchant, A., et al. (1990). An epidemiological study of histrionic personality disorder. *Psychological Medicine, 20*, 413-422.

Nestadt, G., Samuals, J., Riddle, M. et al. (2000). A family study of obsessive compulsive disorder. *Archives of General Psychiatry, 57*, 358-363.

Nettelbeck, T. (1985). Inspection time and mild mental retardation. In N.R. Ellis & N.W. Bray (Eds.), *International review of research in mental retardation* (Vol. 13). New York: Academic Press.

Neugarten, B.L. (1977). Personality and aging. In J.E. Birren & K.W. Schaie (Eds.), *Handbook of the psychology of aging* (pp. 626-649). New York: Van Nostrand.

Neugebauer, R. (1979). Mediaeval and early modern theories of mental illness. *Archives of General Psychiatry, 36*, 477-484.

Neuringer, C. (1964). Rigid thinking in suicidal individuals. *Journal of Consulting Psychology, 28*, 54-58.

Newlin, D.B., & Thomson, J.B. (1990). Alcohol challenge with sons of alcoholics: A critical review and analysis. *Psychological Bulletin, 108*, 383-402.

Newman, D.L., Moffitt, T.E., Caspi, A., & Silva, P.A. (1998). Comorbid mental disorders: Implications for treatment and sample selection. *Journal of Abnormal Psychology, 107*, 305-311.

Newman, J.P., Patterson, C.M., & Kosson, D.S. (1987). Response perseveration in psychopaths. *Journal of Abnormal Psychology, 96*, 145-149.

Newman, J.P., Schmitt, W.A., & Voss, W.D. (1997). The impact of motivationally neutral cues on psychopathic individuals: Assessing the generality of the response modulation hypothesis. *Journal of Abnormal Psychology, 196*, 563-575.

Nezu, A.A., Nezu, C.M., Friedman, S.H., Houts, P.S., & Faddis, S. (1997). The Project Genesis: Application of problem-solving therapy to individuals with cancer. *the Behavior Therapist, 20*, 155-158.

Nezu, A.M. (1986). Efficacy of a social problem-solving therapy approach for unipolar depression. *Journal of Consulting and Clinical Psychology, 54*, 196-202.

Nezu, A.M., & Perri, M.G. (1989). Social problem-solving therapy for unipolar depression: An initial dismantling investigation. *Journal of Consulting and Clinical Psychology, 57*, 408-413.

Nezu, A.M., Nezu, C.M., D'Zurilla, T.J., & Rothenberg, J.L. (1996). Problem-solving therapy. In J.S. Kantor (Ed.), *Clinical depression during addiction recovery* (pp. 187-219). New York: Marcel Dekker.

Nguyen, S.D. (1985). Mental health services for refugees and immigrants in Canada. In T.C. Owen (Ed.), *Southeast Asian mental health: Treatment, prevention, services, training, and research* (pp. 261-282). Washington,DC: National Institute of Mental Health.

NIAA. (1997). Youth drinking: Risk factors and consequences. *Alcohol Alert*, 1-7.

Nicholson, R.A., & Berman, J.S. (1983). Is follow-up necessary in evaluating psychotherapy? *Psychological Bulletin, 93*, 261-278.

NIDA. (1998a). *The economic costs of alcohol and drug abuse in the United States.* Rockville, MD: National Clearinghouse for Drug and Alcohol Information.

NIDA. (1998b). *Director's Report to the National Advisory Council on Drug Abuse.* Rockville, MD: Author.

Niedhammer, I., Goldberg, M., Leclerc, A., David, S., et al. (1998). Psychosocial work environment and cardiovascular risk factors in an occupational cohort in France. *Journal of Epidemiology and Community Health, 52*, 93-100.

Nielsen, G.H., Nordhus, I.H., & Kvale, G. (1998). Insomnia in older adults. In I.H. Nordhus, G.R. VandenBos, S. Berg, & P. Fromholt, (Eds.), *Clinical geropsychology* (pp. 167-175). Washington, D.C.: American Psychological Association.

Nietzel, M.T., & Harris, M.J. (1990). Relationship of dependency and achievement/autonomy to depression. *Clinical Psychology Review, 10*, 279-297.

NIH-National Heart, Lung, and Blood Institute (NHBLI) (1998, June). *Clinical guidelines of the identification, evaluation, and treatment of overweight and obese adults.* NHLB accessed; July 25, 2001, *www.nhlbi.nih.gov/guidelines/obesity/ob_home.htm.*

Nigg, J.T., & Goldsmith, H.H. (1994). Genetics of personality disorders: Perspectives from personality and psychopathology research. *Psychological Bulletin, 115*, 346-380.

Nihira, K., Foster, R., Shenhaas, M., & Leland, H. (1975). *AAMD-Adaptive Behavior Scale.* Washington, DC: American Association on Mental Deficiency.

Nisbett, R.E., & Wilson, T.D. (1977). Telling more than we can know: Verbal reports on mental processes. *Psychological Review, 84*, 231-259.

Nishith, P., Mechanic, M. B., & Resick, P. A. (2000). Prior interpersonal trauma: The contribution to current PTSD symptoms on female rape victims. *Journal of Abnormal* Psychology, 109, 20-25.

Nobler, M.S., Sackeim, H.A., Prohovnik, I., Moeller, J.R., Mukherjee, S., et al. (1994). Regional cerebral blood flow in mood disorders, 3. Treatment and clinical response. *Archives of General Psychiatry, 51*, 884-896.

Nocks, B.C., Learner, R.M., Blackman, D., & Brown, T.E. (1986). The effects of a community-based long term care project on nursing home utilization. *The Gerontologist, 26*, 150-157.

Nolen-Hoeksema, S., & Girgus, J.S. (1994). The emergence of gender differences in depression during adolescence. *Psychological Bulletin, 115*, 424-443.

Noorsdy, D.L., Drake, R.E., & Teague, G.B. (1991). Subjective experiences related to alcohol use among schizophrenics. *Journal of Nervous and Mental Disease, 79*, 410-414.

Norgaard, J.P. (1989a). Urodynamics in enuretics: 1. Reservoir function. *Neurourology and Urodynamics, 8*, 199-211.

Norgaard, J.P. (1989b). Urodynamics in enuretics: 2. A pressure/flow study. *Neurourology and Urodynamics, 8*, 213-217.

North, A.F. (1979). Health services in Head Start. In E. Zigler & J. Valentine (Eds.), *Project Head Start.* New York: Free Press.

Norton, G.R., Cox, B.J., & Malan, J. (1992). Non-clinical panickers: A critical review. *Clinical Psychology Review, 12*, 121-139.

Norton, J.P. (1982). *Expressed emotion, affective style, voice tone and communication deviance as predictors of offspring schizophrenia spectrum disorders.* Unpublished doctoral dissertation, University of California at Los Angeles.

Noshirvani, H.F., Homa, F., Kasvikis, Y., Marks, I.M., Tsakiris, F., et al. (1991). Gender-divergent factors in obsessive-compulsive disorder. *British Journal of Psychiatry, 158*, 260-263.

Nottelmann, E.D., & Jensen, P.S. (1995). Comorbidity of disorders in children and adolescents: Developmental perspectives. *Advances in Clinical Child Psychology, 17*, 109-155.

Nowlan, R., & Cohen, S. (1977). Tolerance to marijuana: Heart rate and subjective "high." *Clinical Pharmacology Therapeutics, 22*, 550-556.

Noyes, R. (1999). The relationship of hypochondriasis to anxiety disorders. *General Hospital Psychiatry, 21*, 8-17.

Noyes, R., Holt, C.S., Happel, R.L., Kathol, R.G., & Yagla, S.J. (1997). A family study of hypochondriasis. *Journal of Nervous and Mental Disease, 185*, 223-232.

Noyes, R., Kathol, R.G., Fisher, M.M., Phillips, S.B., & Suezer, M.T. (1994). Psychiatric comorbidity among patients with hypochondriasis. *General Hospital Psychiatry, 16*, 78-87.

Nuechterlein, K.H., Dawson, M.E., Ventura, J., Gitlin, M., Subotnik, K.L., Snyder, K.S., Mintz, J., & Bartzokis, G. (1994). The vulnerability/stress model of schizophrenic relapse. *Acta Psychiatrica Scandinavica, 89*, 58-64.

Nunes, E.V., Quitkin, F.M., Donovan, S.J., Deliyannides, D., et al. (1998). Imipramine treatment of opiate-dependent patients with depressive disorders: A placebo-controlled trial. *Archives of General Psychiatry, 55*, 153-160.

Nunn, R.G., Newton, K.S., & Faucher, P. (1992). 2.5 year follow-up of weight and body mass index values in the weight control for life program. *Addictive Behaviors, 17*, 579-585.

O'Brien, W.H., & Haynes, S.N. (1995). Behavioral assessment. In L.A. Heiden & M. Hersen (Eds.), *Introduction to clinical psychology* (pp. 103-139). New York: Plenum.

O'Conner, M.C. (1989). Aspects of differential performance by minorities on standardized tests: Linguistic and sociocultural factors. In B.R. Gifford (Ed.), *Test policy and test performance: Education, language, and culture* (pp. 129-181). Boston: Kluwer Academic Publishers.

O'Connor, B.P., & Dyce, J.A. (1998). A test of models of personality disorder configuration. *Journal of Abnormal Psychology, 107*, 3-16.

O'Connor, D.W., Pollitt, P.A., Roth, M., Brook, P.B., & Reiss, B.B. (1990). Memory complaints and impairment in normal, depressed, and demented elderly persons identified in a community survey. *Archives of General Psychiatry, 47*, 224-227.

O'Connor, R.D. (1969). Modification of social withdrawal through symbolic modeling. *Journal of Applied Behavior Analysis, 2*, 15-22.

O'Donnell, P., & Grace, A.A. (1998). Dysfunctions in multiple interrelated systems as the neurobiological bases of schizophrenic symptom clusters. *Schizophrenia Bulletin, 24*, 267-283.

O'Donohoe, W. (1993). The spell of Kuhn on psychology: An exegetical elixir. *Philosophical Psychology, 6*, 267-287.

O'Donohue, W. (1987). The sexual behavior and problems of the elderly. In L.L. Carstensen & B.A. Edelstein (Eds.), *Handbook of clinical gerontology*. New York: Pergamon.

O'Donohue, W., & Plaud, J.J. (1994). The conditioning of human sexual arousal. *Archives of Sexual Behavior, 23*, 321-344.

O'Donohue, W., Dopke, C.A., & Swingen, D.N. (1997). Psychotherapy for female sexual dysfunction: A review. *Clinical Psychology Review, 17*, 537-566.

O'Farrell, T.J. (1993). A behavioral marital therapy couples group program for alcoholics and their spouses. In T.J. O'Farrell (Ed.), *Treating alcohol problems: Marital and family interventions* (pp. 170-209). New York: Guilford Press.

O'Leary, K.D., & Wilson, G.T. (1987). *Behavior therapy: Application and outcome*. Englewood Cliffs, NJ: Prentice-Hall.

O'Leary, K.D., Pelham, W.E., Rosenbaum, A., & Price, G.H. (1976). Behavioral treatment of hyperkinetic children: An experimental evaluation of its usefulness. *Clinical Pediatrics, 15*, 510-515.

O'Malley, S.S., Jaffe, A.J., Chang, G., Rode, S., Schottenfeld, R., et al. (1996). Six month follow-up of naltrexone and psychotherapy for alcohol dependence. *Archives of General Psychiatry, 53*, 217-224.

O'Neal, J.M. (1984). First person account: Finding myself and loving it. *Schizophrenia Bulletin, 10*, 109-110.

O'Neil, P.M., & Jarrell, M.P. (1992). Psychological aspects of obesity and dieting. In T.A. Wadden & T.B. Vanltallie (Eds.), *Treatment of the seriously obese patient* (pp. 231-251). New York: Guilford.

Obrist, P.A., Gaebelein, C.J., Teller, E.S., Langer, A.W., Grignolo, A., Light, K.C., & McCubbin, J.A. (1978). The relationship among heart rate, carotid dP/dt, and blood pressure in humans as a function of the type of stress. *Psychophysiology, 15*, 102-115.

Ochitil, H. (1982). Conversion disorder. In J.H. Greist, J.W. Jefferson, & R.L. Spitzer (Eds.), *Treatment of mental disorders*. New York: Oxford University Press.

Offord, D.R., Boyle, M.H., Szatmari, P., Rae-Grant, N.I., Links, P.S., Cadman, D.T., Byles, J.A., Crawford, J.W., Blum, H.M., Byrne, C., Thomas, H., & Woodward, C.A. (1987). Ontario Child Health Study: 2. Six-month prevalence of disorder and rates of service utilization. *Archives of General Psychiatry, 44*, 832-836.

Ogilvie, D.M., Stone, P.J., & Shneidman, E.S. (1983). A computer analysis of suicide notes. In E.S. Shneidman, N. Farberow, & R. Litman (Eds.), *The psychology of suicide* (pp. 249-256). New York: Jason Aronson.

Ogloff, J.R., & Wong, S. (1990). Electrodermal and cardiovascular evidence of a coping response in psychopaths. *Criminal Justice and Behavior, 17*, 231-245.

Öhman, A., & Soares, J.J.F. (1994). "Unconscious anxiety": Phobic responses to masked stimuli. *Journal of Abnormal Psychology, 103*, 231-240.

Öhman, A., Erixon, G., & Loftberg, I. (1975). Phobias and preparedness: Phobic versus neutral pictures as conditional stimuli for human autonomic responses. *Journal of Abnormal Psychology, 84*, 41-45.

Olds, D.L. (1984). *Final report: Prenatal/early infancy project*. Washington, DC: Maternal and Child Health Research, National Institute of Health.

Olivardia, R., Pope, H.G., Mangweth, B., & Hudson, J.I. (1995). Eating disorders in college men. *American Journal of Psychiatry, 152*, 1279-1284.

Olshevski, J.L., Katz, A.D. & Knight, B. (1999). *Stress reduction for caregivers*. Philadelphia, PA: Brunner/Mazel.

Olshevski, J.L., Katz, A.D. & Knight, B. (1999). *Stress reduction for caregivers*. Philadelphia, PA: Brunner/Mazel.

Oltmanns, T.F., Broderick, J.E., & O'Leary, K.D. (1976). *Marital adjustment and the efficacy of behavior therapy with children*. Paper presented at the Association for the Advancement of Behavior Therapy, New York.

Oltmanns, T.F., Neale, J.M., & Davison, G.C. (1995). *Case studies in abnormal psychology* (4th ed.). New York: Wiley.

Ondersma, S.J. & Walker, C.E. (1998). Elimination disorders. In T.H. Ollendick & M. Hersen (Eds.), *Handbook of Child Psychopathology* (3rd ed.) New York: Plenum Press.

Ono, Y., Yoshimura, K., Sueoka, R., Yaumachi, K., et al. (1996). Avoidant personality disorder and taijin kyoufu: Sociocultural implications of the WHO/ADAMHA International Study of Personality Disorders in Japan. *Acta Psychiatrica Scandanavica, 93*, 172-176.

Organista, K.C., & Munoz, R.F. (1996). Cognitive behavioral therapy with Latinos. *Cognitive and Behavioral Practice, 3*, 255-270.

Orleans, C.T., Schoenbach, V.J., Wagner, E.H., Quade, D., Salmon, M.A., Pearson, D.C., Fiedler, J., Porter, C.Q., & Kaplan, B.H. (1991). Self-help quit smoking interventions: Effects of self-help materials, social support instructions, and tele-phone counseling. *Journal of Consulting and Clinical Psychology, 59*, 439-448.

Orne, M.T., Dinges, D.F., & Orne, E.C. (1984). The differential diagnosis of multiple personality in the forensic court. *International Journal of Clinical and Experimental Hypnosis, 32*, 118-169.

Orr, S.P., Metzger, L.J., Lasko, N.B. et al. (2000). De novo conditioning in trauma-exposed individuals with and without posttraumatic stress disorder. *Journal of Abnormal Psychology, 109*, 290-298.

Orr, S.P., Lasko, N.B., Shalev, A.Y., & Pitman, R.K. (1995). Physiological responses to loud tones in Vietnam veterans with post-traumatic stress disorder. *Journal of Abnormal Psychology, 104*, 75-82.

Orth-Gomer, K., & Unden, A.L. (1990). Type A behavior, social support, and coronary risk: Interaction and significance for mortality in cardiac patients. *Psychosomatic Medicine, 52*, 59-72.

Osgood, N.J. & Manetta, A.A. (2000). Abuse and suicidal issues in older women. *OMEGA, 42 (1)*, 71-81.

Ost, L-G. (1987b). Applied relaxation: Description of a coping technique and review of controlled studies. *Behaviour Research and Therapy, 25*, 397-409.

Ost, L-G. (1992). Blood and injection phobia: Background and cognitive, physiological, and behavioral correlates. *Journal of Abnormal Psychology, 101*, 68-74.

Ost, L-G., Fellenius, J., & Sterner, U. (1991). Applied tension, exposure in vivo, and tension-only in the treatment of blood phobia. *Behaviour Research and Therapy, 29*, 561-574.

Ost, L-G., Hellstrom, K., & Westling, B.E. (1989). *Applied relaxation, exposure in vivo, and cognitive methods in the treatment of agoraphobia*. Paper presented at the meeting of the Association for Advancement of Behavior Therapy.

Ouimette, P.C., Finney, J.W., & Moos, R.H. (1997). Twelve-step and cognitive-behavioral treatment for substance abuse: A comparison of treatment effectiveness. *Journal of Consulting and Clinical Psychology, 65*, 230-240.

Overholser, J.C., & Beck, S. (1986). Multimethod assessment of rapists, child molesters, and three control groups on behavioral and psychological measures. *Journal of Consulting and Clinical Psychology, 54*, 682-687.

Owen, P.P., & Laurel-Seller, E. (2000). Weight and shape ideals: Thin is dangerously in. *Journal of Applied Social Psychology, 54*, 682-687.

Page, A.C. (1994). Blood-injection phobia. *Clinical Psychology Review, 14*, 443-461.

Pahkala, K. (1990). Social and environmental factors and atypical depression in old age. *International Journal of Geriatric Psychiatry, 5*, 99-113.

Palmer, T. (1984). Treatment and the role of classification: Review of basics. *Crime and Delinquency, 30*, 245-267.

Pardoen, D., Bauwens, F., Dramaix, M., Tracy, A., Genevrois, C., et al. (1996). Life events and primary affective disorders: A one year prospective study. *British Journal of Psychiatry, 169*, 160-166.

Paris, J. (2000). Childhood precursors of borderline personality disorder. *Psychiatric Clinics of North America, 23*, 77-88.

Paris, J., Zweig, F.M., & Guzder, J. (1994). Psychological risk factors for borderline personality disorder in female patients. *Comprehensive Psychiatry, 35*, 301-305.

Parker, K.C.H., Hanson, R.K., & Hunsley, J. (1988). MMPI, Rorschach, and WAIS: A meta-analytic comparison of reliability, stability, and validity. *Psychological Bulletin, 103*, 367-373.

Parker, S.R., Mellins, R.B., & Sogn, D.D. (1989). Asthma education: A national strategy. *American Journal of Respiratory Disease, 140*, 848-853.

Parkes, C.M., & Brown, R.J. (1972). Health after bereavement: A controlled study of young Boston widowers. *Psychosomatic Medicine, 34*, 49-461.

Parkinson, L., & Rachman, S. (1981). Intrusive thoughts: The effects of an uncontrived stress. *Advances in Behavior Research and Therapy, 3*, 111-118.

Parks, C.V., Jr., & Hollon, S.D. (1988). Cognitive assessment. In A.S. Bellack & M. Hersen (Eds.), *Behavioral assessment* (3rd ed.). Elmsford, NY: Pergamon.

Parvathy, S., Davies, P., Haroutunian, V., et al. (2001). Correlation between abx-40-, abx-42-, and abx43-containing amyloid plaques and cognitive decline. *Archives of Neurology, 58*, 2034-2039.

Patel, C., Marmot, M.G., Terry, D.J., Carruthers, M., Hunt, B., & Patel, M. (1985). Trial of relaxation in reducing coronary risk: Four year follow-up. *British Medical Journal, 290*, 1103-1106.

Pato, M.T., Zohar-Kadouch, R., Zohar, J., & Murphy, D.L. (1988). Return of symptoms after discontinuation of clomipramine and patients with obsessive-compulsive disorder. *American Journal of Psychiatry, 145*, 1521-1525.

Paton, A. (1995). *Education in the virtual factory*. Paper presented at The Spring VR WORLD '95 Conference, San Jose, CA.

Patrick, C.J. (1994). Emotion and psychopathy: Some startling new insights. *Psychophysiology, 31*, 319-330.

Patrick, M., Hobson, R.P., Castle, D., Howard, R., et al. (1994). Personality disorder and the mental representation of early social experience. *Development and Psychopathology, 6*, 375-388.

Patterson, C.M., & Newman, J.P. (1993). Reflectivity and learning from aversive events: Toward a psychological mechanism for the syndromes of disinhibition. *Psychological Review, 100*, 716-736.

Patterson, G.R. (1982). *Coercive family process*. Eugene, OR: Castilia.

Patterson, G., & Chamberlain, P. (1992). A functional analysis of resistance (a neobehavioral perspective). In H. Arkowitz (Ed.), *Why people don't change: New perspectives in resistance and noncompliance*. New York: Guilford.

Patterson, G.R. (1974). A basis for identifying stimuli which control behaviors in natural settings. *Child Development, 45*, 900-911.

Patterson, G.R., Crosby, L., & Vuchinich, S. (1992). Predicting risk for early police arrest. *Journal of Quantitative Criminology, 8*, 335-355.

Patterson, G.R., Ray, R.S., Shaw, D.A., & Cobb, J.A. (1969). *Manual for coding of family interactions*. New York: ASIS/NAPS, Microfiche Publications.

Paul, G.L. (1966). *Insight vs. desensitization in psychotherapy*. Stanford, CA: Stanford University Press.

Paul, G.L. (1969). Chronic mental patient: Current status–future directions. *Psychological Bulletin, 71*, 81-94.

Paul, G.L., & Lentz, R.J. (1977). *Psychosocial treatment of chronic mental patients: Milieu versus social learning programs*. Cambridge, MA: Harvard University Press.

Paul, G.L., & Menditto, A.A. (1992). Effectiveness of inpatient treatment programs for mentally ill adults in public psychiatric facilities. Applied and Preventive Psychology: *Current Scientific Perspectives, 1*, 41-63.

Paul, G.L., & Shannon, D.T. (1966). Treatment of anxiety through systematic desensitization in therapy groups. *Journal of Abnormal Psychology, 71*, 124-135.

Paul, G.L., Stuve, P., & Cross, J.V. (in press). Real-world inpatient programs: Shedding some light. *Applied and Preventive Psychology*.

Paul, G.L., Stuve, P., & Menditto, A.A. (in press). Social-learning program (with token economy) for adult psychiatric inpatients. *The Clinical Psychologist*.

Paul, R. (1987). Communication. In D.J. Cohen, A.M. Donnellan, & R. Paul (Eds.), *Handbook of autism and pervasive developmental disorders* (pp. 61-84). New York: Wiley.

Paxton, S.J., Schutz, H.K., Wertheim, E.H., & Muir, S.L. (1999). Friendship clique and peer influences on body image concerns, dietary restraint, extreme weight-loss behaviors, and binge eating in adolescent girls. *Journal of Abnormal Psychology, 108*, 255-264.

Payne, A., & Blanchard, E.B. (1995). A controlled comparison of cognitive therapy and self-help support groups in the treatment of irritable bowel syndrome. *Journal of Consulting and Clinical Psychology, 63*, 779-786.

Payne, D.G., Neuschatz, J.S., Lampinen, J.M., & Lynn, S.J. (1997). Compelling memory illusions: The qualitative characteristics of false memories. *Current Directions in Psychological Science, 6*, 56-60.

Pearlin, L.I., Mullan, J.T., Semple, S.J., & Skaff, M.M. (1990). Caregiving and the stress process: An overview of concepts and their measures. *The Gerontologist, 30*, 583-594.

Pearlson, G.D., & Rabins, P.V. (1988). The late-onset psychoses: Possible risk factors. *Psychiatric Clinics of North America, 11*, 15-32.

Pearlson, G.D., Wong, D.F., Tune, L.E., Ross, C.A., Chase, G.A., et al. (1995). In vivo D2 dopamine receptor density in psychotic and non-psychotic patients with bipolar disorder. *Archives of General Psychiatry, 52*, 471-477.

Pearson, C., & Gatz, M. (1982). Health and mental health in older adults: First steps in the study of a pedestrian complaint. *Rehabilitation Psychology, 27*, 37-50.

Pedersen, J.B. (1998). Sexuality and aging. In I.H. Nordhus, G.R. VandenBos, S. Berg, & P. Fromholt, (Eds.), *Clinical geropsychology* (pp. 141-145). Washington, D.C.: American Psychological Association.

Pedro-Carroll, J.L., & Cowen, E.L. (1985). The children of divorce intervention program: An investigation of the efficacy of a school-based prevention program. *Journal of Consulting and Clinical Psychology, 53*, 603-611.

Pedro-Carroll, J.L., Cowen, E.L., Hightower, A.D., & Guare, J.C. (1986). Preventive intervention with latency-aged children of divorce: A replication study. *American Journal of Community Psychology, 14*, 277-290.

Peeples, F. & Loeber, R. (1994). Do individual factors and neighborhood context explain ethnic differences in juvenile delinquency? *Journal of Quantitative Criminology, 10*, 141-157.

Peet, M., & Harvey, N.S. (1991). Lithium maintenance: I. A standard education programme for patients. *British Journal of Psychiatry, 158*, 197-200.

Pelham, W.E., Carlson, C., Sams, S.E., Vallano, G., Dixon, M.J., & Hoza, B. (1993). Separate and combined effects of methylphenidate and behavior modification on boys with attention deficit/hyperactivity disorder in the classroom. *Journal of Consulting and Clinical Psychology, 61*, 506-515.

Pelham, W.E., McBurnett, K., Harper, G.W., Milich, R., Murphy, D.A, Clinton, J., & Thiele, C. (1990). Methylphenidate and baseball playing in ADHD children: Who's on first? *Journal of Consulting and Clinical Psychology, 58*, 130-133.

Penn, D.L., & Mueser, K.T. (1996). Research update on the psychosocial treatment of schizophrenia. *American Journal of Psychiatry, 153*, 607-617.

Pennebaker, J.W., Kiecolt-Glaser, J.K., & Glaser, R. (1988). Disclosure of traumas and immune function: Health implications for psychotherapy. *Journal of Consulting and Clinical Psychology, 56*, 239-245.

Pennebaker, J.W. (1990). *Opening up: The healing power of confiding in others*. New York: William Morrow & Co.

Pennington, B.F. (1995). Genetics of learning disabilities. *Journal of Child Neurology, 10*, S69-S77.

Pentoney, P. (1966). Value change in psychotherapy. *Human Relations, 19*, 39-46.

Peplau, L.A., & Cochran, S.D. (1988). Value orientations in the intimate relationships of gay men. In J. De Cecco (Ed.), *Gay relationships* (pp. 195-216). New York: Harrington Park Press.

Perez, M.A., Meyerowitz, B.E., Lieskovsky, G., Skinner, D.G., Reynolds, B., & Skinner, E.C. (1997). Quality of life and sexuality following radical prostatectomy in patients with prostate cancer who use or do not use erectile aids. *Urology, 50*, 740-746.

Perkins, D.D. (1995). Speaking truth to power: Empowerment ideology as social intervention and policy. *American Journal of Community Psychology, 23*, 765-794.

Perley, M.J, & Guze, S.B. (1962). Hysteria: The stability and usefulness of clinical criteria. *New England Journal of Medicine, 266*, 421-426.

Perlin, M.L. (1994). *Law and mental disability*. Charlottesville, The Michie Company.

Perls, F.S. (1947). *Ego, hunger, and aggression*. New York: Vintage.

Perls, F.S. (1969). *Gestalt therapy verbatim*. Moab, UT: Real People Press.

Perls, F.S. (1970). Four lectures. In J. Fagan & I.L. Shepherd (Eds.), *Gestalt therapy now: Therapy, techniques, applications*. Palo Alto, CA: Science & Behavior Books.

Perls, F.S., Hefferline, R.F., & Goodman, P. (1951). *Gestalt therapy: Excitement and growth in the human personality*. New York: Julian Press.

Perry, J.C., Hoglend, P., Shear, K., Vaillant, G.E., Horowitz, M., et al. (1998). Field trial of a diagnostic axis for defense mechanisms for DSM-IV. *Journal of Personality Disorders, 12*, 56-68.

Perry, R., Campbell, M., Adams, P., Lynch, N., Spencer, E.K., Curren, E.L., and Overall, J.E. (1989). Long-term efficacy of haloperidol in autistic children: Continuous versus discontinuous administration. *Journal of the American Academy of Child and Adolescent Psychiatry, 28*, 87-92.

Persing, J.S., Stuart, S.P., Noyes, R., & Happel, R. L. (2000). Hypochondrisis: The patient's perspective. *International Journal of Psychiatry in Medicine, 30*, 329-342.

Persons, J. (1989). *Cognitive therapy in practice: A case formulation approach*. New York: Norton.

Persons, J. B., Bostrom, A., Bertagnolli, A. (1999). Results of randomized controlled trials of cognitive therapy for depression generalize to private practice. *Cognitive Therapy Research, 23*, 535-548.

Persons, J.B., & Miranda, J. (1992). Cognitive theories of vulnerability to depression: Reconciling negative evidence. *Cognitive Therapy and Research, 16*, 185-202.

Persons, J.B., Thase, M.E., & Crits-Christoph, P. (1996). The role of psychotherapy in the treatment of depression: Review of two practice guidelines. *Archives of General Psychiatry, 53*, 283-290.

Perugi, G., Akiskal, H.S., Giannotti, D., Frare, F., et al. (1997). Gender-related differences in body dysmorphic disorder. *Journal of Nervous and Mental Disease, 185*, 578-582.

Peters, M. (1977). Hypertension and the nature of stress. *Science, 198*, 80.

Peterson, C., & Seligman, M.E.P. (1984). Causal explanations as a risk factor for depression: Theory and evidence. *Psychological Review, 91*, 347-374.

Peterson, D. (1995). The reflective educator. *American Psychologist, 50*, 975-984.

Peterson, J.L., Coates, T.J., Catania, J., Hauck, W.W., Acree, M., Daigle, D., Hillard, B., Middleton, L., & Hearst, N. (1996). Evaluation of an HIV risk reduction intervention among African-American homosexual and bisexual men. *AIDS, 10,* 319-325.

Petty, R.E., & Cacioppo, J.T. (1986). *Communication and persuasion: Central and peripheral routes to attitude change.* New York: Springer-Verlag.

Pfefferman, A., Sullivan, E.V., Rosenbloom, M.J., Mathalon, D.H., & Lim, K.O. (1998). A controlled study of cortical grey matter and ventricular changes in alcoholic men over a 5-year interval. *Archives of General Psychiatry, 55,* 905-912.

Pfeiffer, E. (1977). Psychopathology and social pathology. In J.E. Birren & K.W. Schaie (Eds.), *Handbook of psychology and aging.* New York: Van Nostrand-Reinhold.

Pfeiffer, E., Verwoerdt, A., & Wang, H.H. (1969). The natural history of sexual behavior in a biologically advantaged group of aged individuals. *Journal of Gerontology, 24,* 193-198.

Pfeiffer, E., Verwoerdt, A., & Wang, H.S. (1968). Sexual behavior in aged men and women: 1. Observations on 254 community volunteers. *Archives of General Psychiatry, 19,* 753-758.

Phares, E.J., & Trull, T.J. (1997). *Clinical psychology.* Pacific Grove, CA: Brooks/Cole.

Phelps, L., Wallace, D., & Waigant, A. (1989, August). *Impact of sexual assault: Post assault behavior and health status.* Paper presented at the annual convention of the American Psychological Association, New Orleans. As cited in Calhoun & Atkeson (1991).

Philips, K.A. & McElroy, S.L. (2000). Personality disorders and traits in patients with body dysmorphic disorder. *Comprehensive Psychiatry, 41,* 229-236.

Philips, K.A., McElroy, S.L., Dwight, M. M. et al. (2001). Delusionality and response to open-label fluvoxamine in body dysmorphic disorder. *Journal of Clinical Psychiatry, 62,* 87-91.

Phillip, M., & Fickinger, M. (1993). Psychotropic drugs in the management of chronic pain syndromes. *Pharmacopsychiatry, 26,* 221-234.

Phillips, D.P. (1974). The influence of suggestion on suicide: Substantive and theoretical implications of the Werther effect. *American Sociological Review, 39,* 340-354.

Phillips, D.P. (1977). Motor vehicle fatalities increase just after publicized suicide stories. *Science, 196,* 1464-1465.

Phillips, D.P. (1985). The found experiment: A new technique for assessing impact of mass media violence on real-world aggressive behavior. In G. Comstock (Ed)., *Public communication and behavior* (Vol. 1). New York: Academic Press.

Phillips, K.A., McElroy, S.L., Keck, P.E., Pope, H.G., & Hudson, J.L. (1993). Body dysmorphic disorder: 30 cases of imagined ugliness. *American Journal of Psychiatry, 150,* 302-308.

Pierce, J.P., Choi, W.S., Gilpin, E.A., Farkas, A.J., & Berry, C.C. (1998). Tobacco ads, promotional items linked with teen smoking. *JAMA, 279,* 511-515.

Pigott, T.A., Pato, M.T., Bernstein, S.E., Grover, G.N., Hill, J.L., et al. (1990). Controlled comparison of clomipramine and fluoxetine in the treatment of obsessive-compulsive disorder. *Archives of General Psychiatry, 47,* 926-932.

Pilowsky, I. (1970). Primary and secondary hypochondriasis. *Acta Psychiatrica Scandinavica, 46,* 273-285.

Pinel, P. (1962). *A treatise on insanity, 1801.* English (D.D. Davis, Trans.). New York: Hafner.

Pinkston, E., & Linsk, N. (1984). Behavioral family intervention with the impaired elderly. *The Gerontologist, 24,* 576-583.

Piper, W.E., Azim, F.A., Joyce, S.A., McCallum, M., Nixon, G., & Segal, P.S. (1991). Quality of object relations vs. interpersonal functioning as predictors of alliance and outcome. *Archives of General Psychiatry, 48,* 946-953.

Piran, N., Kennedy, S., Garfinkel, P.E., & Owens, M. (1985). Affective disturbance in eating disorders. *Journal of Nervous and Mental Disease, 173,* 395-400.

Pirsig, R.M. (1974). *Zen and the art of motorcycle maintenance: An inquiry into values.* New York: Morrow.

Pitman, R.K., Orr, S.P., Forgue, D.F., Altman, B., deJong, J.B., et al. (1990). Psychophysiologic responses to combat imagery of Vietnam veterans with post-traumatic stress disorder vs. other anxiety disorders. *Journal of Abnormal Psychology, 99,* 49-54.

Piven, J., Arndt, S., Bailey, J., & Andreasen, N. (1996). Regional brain enlargement in autism: A magnetic resonance imaging study. *Journal of the American Academy of Child and Adolescent Psychiatry, 35,* 530-536.

Piven, J., Arndt, S., Bailey, J., Havercamp, S., Andreasen, N.C., & Palmer, P. (1995). An MRI study of brain size in autism. *American Journal of Psychiatry, 152,* 1145-1149.

Pliner, P., & Haddock, G. (1996). Perfectionism in weight-concerned and unconcerned women: An experimental approach. *International Journal of Eating Disorders, 19,* 381-389.

Plotkin, D.A., Mintz, J., & Jarvik, L.F. (1985). Subjective memory complaints in geriatric depression. *American Journal of Psychiatry, 142,* 1103-1105.

Pokorny, A.D. (1968). Myths about suicide. In H.L.P. Resnik (Ed.), *Suicidal behaviors.* Boston: Little, Brown.

Polich, J.M., Armor, D.J., & Braiker, H.B. (1980). Patterns of alcoholism over four years. *Journal of Studies on Alcohol, 41,* 397-415.

Polivy, J. (1976). Perception of calories and regulation of intake in restrained and unrestrained eaters. *Addictive Behaviors, 1,* 237-244.

Polivy, J., & Herman, C.P. (1985). Dieting and binging: A causal analysis. *American Psychologist, 40,* 193-201.

Polivy, J., Heatherton, T.F., & Herman, C.P. (1988). Self-esteem, restraint and eating behavior. *Journal of Abnormal Psychology, 97,* 354-356.

Polivy, J., Herman, C.P., & Howard, K. (1980). The Restraint Scale. In A. Stunkard (Ed.), *Obesity.* Philadelphia: Saunders.

Polivy, J., Herman, C.P., & McFarlane, T. (1994). Effects of anxiety on eating: Does palatability moderate distress-induced overeating in dieters? *Journal of Abnormal Psychology, 103,* 505-510.

Pollack, M.H., Zainelli, R., Goddard, A. et al. (2001). Paroxetine in the treatment of generalized anxiety disorder: Results of a placebo-controlled, flexible dosage trial. *Journal of Clinical Psychiatry, 62,* 350-357.

Pollak, M.H. (1994). Heart rate reactivity to laboratory tests and in two daily life settings. *Psychosomatic Medicine, 56,* 271-276.

Pollak, R. (1997). *The creation of Dr. B.* New York: Simon & Schuster.

Pollard, C.A., Pollard, H.J., & Corn, K.J. (1989). Panic onset and major events in the lives of agoraphobics: A test of contiguity. *Journal of Abnormal Psychology, 98,* 318-321.

Polusny, M.A., & Follette, V.M. (1995). Long-term correlates of child sexual abuse: Theory and review of the empirical literature. *Applied and Preventive Psychology, 4,* 143-166.

Ponce, F., & Atkinson, D. (1989). Mexican-Americans and acculturation, counselor ethnicity, counseling style, and perceived counselor credibility. *Journal of Counseling Psychology, 36,* 203-208.

Pope, H.G., & Hudson, J.I. (1988). Is bulimia a heterogeneous disorder? Lessons from the history of medicine. *International Journal of Eating Disorders, 7,* 155-166.

Pope, H.G., Oliva, P.S., Hudson, J.I., Bodkin, J.A., & Gruber, A.J. (1999). Attitudes toward DSM-IV dissociative disorders among board-certified American psychiatrists. *American Journal of Psychiatry, 156,* 321-323.

Pope, K.S. (1995). What psychologists better know about recovered memories, research, lawsuits, and the pivotal experiment: A review of "The Myth of Repressed Memory: False Memories and Allegations of Sexual Abuse," by Elizabeth Loftus and Katherine Ketcham. *Clinical Psychology: Science and Practice, 2,* 304-315.

Posner, M.I. (1992). Attention as a cognitive and neural system. *Current Directions in Psychological Science, 1,* 11-14.

Post, F. (1978). The functional psychosis. In A.D. Isaacs & F. Post (Eds.), *Studies in geriatric psychiatry.* Chichester, England: Wiley.

Post, F. (1980). Paranoid, schizophrenia-like and schizophrenic states in the aged. In J.E. Birren & R.B. Sloane (Eds.), *Handbook of mental health and aging.* Englewood Cliffs, NJ: Prentice-Hall.

Post, F. (1987). Paranoid and schizophrenic disorders among the aging. In L.L. Carstensen & B.A. Edelstein (Eds.), *Handbook of clinical gerontology.* New York: Pergamon.

Poster, D.S., Penta, J.S., Bruno, S., & Macdonald, J.S. (1981). Delta 9-tetrahydrocannabinol in clinical oncology. *Journal of the American Medical Association, 245,* 2047-2051.

Potashnik, S., & Pruchno, R. (1988, November). *Spouse caregivers: Physical and mental health in perspective.* Paper presented at the meeting of the Gerontological Society of America, San Francisco.

Potkin, S.G., Alva, G., Fleming, K. et al. (2002). A PET study of the pathophysiology of negative symptoms in schizophrenia. *American Journal of Psychiatry, 159,* 227-237.

Powell, L.H., Friedman, M., Thoresen, C.E., Gill, J.J., & Ulmer, D.K. (1984). Can the type A behavior pattern be altered after myocardial infarction? A second year report from the Recurrent Coronary Prevention Project. *Psychosomatic Medicine, 46,* 293-313.

Power, K.G., Simpson, R.J., Swanson, V., Wallace, I.A., Feistner, A.T.C., & Sharp, D. (1990). A controlled comparison of cognitive-behaviour therapy, diazepam, and placebo, alone and in combination, for the treatment of generalized anxiety disorder. *Journal of Anxiety Disorders, 4,* 267-292.

Praderas, K., & MacDonald, M.L. (1986). Telephone conversational skills training with socially isolated impaired nursing home residents. *Journal of Applied Behavior Analysis, 19,* 337-348.

Premack, D. (1959). Toward empirical behavior laws: 1. Positive reinforcement. *Psychological Review, 66,* 219-233.

Prentky, R.A. (1997). Arousal reduction in sexual offenders: A review of antiandrogen interventions *Sexual Abuse: A Journal of Research and Treatment, 9,* 335-347.

Prescott, C.A., & Kendler, K.S. (1999). Genetic and environmental contributions to alcohol abuse and dependence in a population-based sample of male twins. *American Journal of Psychiatry, 156,* 34-40.

Pressman, B., & Sheps, A. (1994). Treating wife abuse: An integrated model. *International Journal of Group Psychotherapy, 44,* 477-498.

Price, L.H., Charney, D.S., Rubin, A.L., & Heninger, G.R. (1986). Alpha-2 adrenergic receptor function in depression. *Archives of General Psychiatry, 43,* 849-860.

Price, R.A., Cadoret, R.J., Stunkard, A.J., & Troughton, E. (1987). Genetic contributions to human fatness: An adoption study. *American Journal of Psychiatry, 144,* 1003-1008.

Prien, R.F., & Potter, W.Z. (1993). Maintenance treatment for mood disorders. In D.L. Dunner (Ed.), *Current psychiatric therapy.* Philadelphia: Saunders.

Prieto, S.L., Cole D.A., & Tageson, C.W. (1992) Depressive self-schemas in clinic and nonclinic children. *Cognitive Therapy and Research, 16,* 521-534.

Prinz, P., & Raskind, M. (1978). Aging and sleep disorders. In R. Williams & R. Karacan (Eds.), *Sleep disorders: Diagnosis and treatment.* New York: Wiley.

Prizant, B.M. (1983). Language acquisition and communicative behavior in autism: Toward an understanding of the "whole" of it. *Journal of Speech and Hearing Disorders, 48,* 296-307.

Prochaska, J.O. (1984). *Systems of psychotherapy* (2nd ed.). Homewood, IL: Dorsey Press.

Project Match Research Group. (1997). Matching alcoholism treatments to client heterogeneity: Project MATCH posttreatment drinking outcomes. *Journal of Studies on Alcohol, 58,* 7-29.

Pryor, J.P. (2002). Orgasmic and ejaculatory dysfunction. *Sexual & Relationship Therapy, 17,* 87-95.

Pryor, T., Wiederman, M.W., & McGilley, B. (1996). Clinical correlates of anorexia subtypes. *International Journal of Eating Disorders, 19,* 371-379.

Pu, T., Mohamed, E., Imam, K., & El-Roey, A.M. (1986). One hundred cases of hysteria in eastern Libya. *British Journal of Psychiatry, 148,* 606-609.

Puig-Antich, J., Goetz, D., Davies, M., Kaplan, T., Davies, S., Ostrow, L., Asnis, L., Twomey, J., Iyengar, S., & Ryan, N.D. (1989). A controlled family history study of prepubertal major depressive disorder. *Archives of General Psychiatry, 46,* 406-418.

Puig-Antich, J., Kaufman, J., Ryan, N.D., Williamson, D.E., Dahl, R.E., Lukens, E., Todak, G., Ambrosini, P., Rabinovich, H., & Nelson, B. (1993). The psychosocial functioning and family environment of depressed adolescents. *American Academy of Child and Adolescent Psychiatry, 32,* 244-253.

Puig-Antich, J., Perel, J.M., Lupatkin, W., Chambers, W.J., Tabrizi, M.A., King, J., Goetz, R., Davies, M., & Stiller, R.L. (1987). Imipramine in prepubertal major depressive disorders. *Archives of General Psychiatry, 44,* 81-89.

Purcell, K., & Weiss, J.H. (1970). Asthma. In C.G. Costello (Ed.), *Symptoms of psychopathology: A handbook.* New York: Wiley.

Purdie, F.R., Honigman, T.B., & Rosen, P. (1981). Acute organic brain syndrome: A view of 100 cases. *Annals of Emergency Medicine, 10,* 455-461.

Putnam, F.W. (1993). Dissociative disorders in children: Behavioral profiles and problems. *Child Abuse and Neglect, 17,* 39-45.

Putnam, F.W. (1996). A brief history of multiple personality disorder. *Child and Adolescent Psychiatric Clinics of North America, 5,* 263-271.

Putnam, F.W., Guroff, J.J., Silberman, E.K., Barban, L., & Post, R.M. (1986). The clinical phenomenology of multiple personality disorder: Review of 100 recent cases. *Journal of Clinical Psychiatry, 47,* 285-293.

Putnam, F.W., Post, R.M., & Guroff, J.J. (1983). *100 cases of multiple personality dis-*

order. Paper presented at the annual meeting of the American Psychiatric Association, New York.

Putnam, F.W., Zahn, T.P., & Post, R.M. (1990). Differential autonomic nervous system activity in multiple personality disorder. *Psychiatry Research, 31,* 251-260.

Pyle, A. (1999, May 28). Seeking a remedy for nursing homes' ills. *Los Angeles Times,* pp. A1-A30.

Qizilbash, N., Whitehead, A., Higgins, J., Wilcock, G., Schneider, L., et al. (1998). Cholinesterase inhibition for Alzheimer disease: A meta-analysis of Tacrine trials. *JAMA, 280,* 1777-1782.

Quay, H.C. (1979). Classification In H.C. Quay & J.S. Werry (Eds.), *Psychopathological disorders of childhood* (2nd ed.). New York: Wiley.

Quay, H.C., & Parskeuopoulos, I.N. (1972, August). *Dimensions of problem behavior in elementary school children in Greece, Iran, and Finland.* Paper presented at the 20th International Congress of Psychology, Tokyo.

Rabavilas, A., & Boulougouris, J. (1974). Physiological accompaniments of ruminations, flooding and thought-stopping in obsessional patients. *Behaviour Research and Therapy, 12,* 239-244.

Rabins, P.V., & Folstein, M.F. (1982). Delirium and dementia: Diagnostic criteria and fatality rates. *British Journal of Psychiatry, 140,* 149-153.

Rabkin, J.G. (1974). Public attitudes toward mental illness: A review of the literature. *Schizophrenia Bulletin,* 9-33.

Rachman, S. & deSilva, P. (1978). Abnormal and normal obsessions. *Behaviour Research and Therapy, 16,* 233-248.

Rachman, S. (1997). A cognitive theory of obsessions. *Behaviour Research and Therapy, 35,* 793-802.

Rachman, S.J. (1966). Sexual fetishism: An experimental analogue. *Psychological Record, 16,* 293-296.

Rachman, S.J., & Hodgson, R.J. (1980) *Obsessions and compulsions.* Englewood Cliffs, NJ: Prentice-Hall.

Rachman, S.J., & Wilson, G.T. (1980). *The effects of psychological therapy* (2nd ed.) Elmsford, NY: Pergamon.

Rahe, R.H., & Lind, E. (1971). Psychosocial factors and sudden cardiac death: A pilot study. *Journal of Psychosomatic Research, 15,* 19-24.

Raikkonen, K., Matthews, K.A., Flory, J.D., & Owens, J.F. (1999). Effects of hostility on ambulatory blood pressure and mood during daily living. *Health Psychology, 18,* 44-53.

Raine, A., Lencz, T., Bihrle, S. et al. (2000). Reduced prefrontal gray matter and reduced autonomic activity in antisocial personality disorder. *Archives of General Psychiatry, 57,* 119-127.

Raj, B.A., Corvea, M.H., & Dagon, E.M. (1993). The clinical characteristics of panic disorder in the elderly: A retrospective study. *Journal of Clinical Psychiatry, 54,* 150-155.

Rajkowska, G., Selemon, L.D., & Goldman-Rakic, P.S. (1998). Neuronal and glial soma size in the prefrontal cortex: A postmortem morphometric study of schizophrenia and Huntington disease. *Archives of General Psychiatry, 55,* 215-224.

Rakic, Z., Starcevic, V., Starcevic, V.P., & Marinkovic, J. (1997). Testerone treatment in men with erectile disorder and low levels of total testosterone in serum. *Archives of Sexual Behavior, 26,* 495-504.

Ralph, J.A., & Mineka, S. (1998). Attributional style and self-esteem: The prediction of emotional distress following a midterm exam. *Journal of Abnormal Psychology, 107,* 203-215.

Ramsey, J.M., Andreason, P., Zametkin, A.J., Aquino, T., King, A.C., Hamburger, S.D., Pikus, A., Rapoport, J.L., & Cohen, R.M. (1992). Failure to activate the left tempoparietal cortex in dyslexia: An oxygen 15 positron emission tomographic study. *Archives of Neurology, 49,* 527-534.

Ramsey, J.M., Zametkin, A.J., Andreason, P., Hanahan, A.P., Hamburger, S.D., Aquino, T., King, A.C., Pikus, A., & Cohen, R.M. (1994). Normal activation of frontotemporal language cortex in dyslexia, as measured with oxygen 15 positron emission tomography. *Archives of Neurology, 51,* 27-38.

Rapaport, D. (1951). *The organization and pathology of thought.* New York: Columbia University Press.

Rapoport, J.L., Swedo, S.E., & Leonard, H.L. (1992). Childhood obsessive compulsive disorder. *Journal of Clinical Psychiatry, 53*(4, Suppl.), 11-16.

Rapp, S.R., Parisi, S.A., & Walsh, D.A. (1988). Psychological dysfunction and physical health among elderly medical inpatients. *Journal of Consulting and Clinical Psychology, 56,* 851-855.

Rapp, S.R., Parisi, S.A., Walsh, D.A., & Wallace, C.E. (1988). Detecting depression in elderly medical impatients. *Journal of Consulting and Clinical Psychology, 56,* 509-513.

Rappaport, J. (1977). *Community psychology: Values, research, and action.* New York: Holt, Rinehart & Winston.

Rappaport, J., & Chinsky, J.M. (1974). Models for delivery of service from a historical and conceptual perspective. *Professional Psychology, 5,* 42-50.

Raskin, F., & Rae, D.S. (1981). Psychiatric symptoms in the elderly. *Psychopharmacology Bulletin, 17,* 96-99.

Rasmussen, D.X., Brandt, J., Martin, D.B., & Folstein, M.F. (1995). Head injury as a risk factor in Alzheimer's disease. *Brain Injury, 9,* 213-219.

Rather, B.C., Goldman, M.S., Roehrich,L., & Brannick, M. (1992). Empirical modeling of an alcohol expectancy memory network using multidimensional scaling. *Journal of Abnormal Psychology, 101,* 174-183.

Rauch, S.L., & Jenike, M.A. (1993). Neurobiological models of obsessive-compulsive disorder. *Psychosomatics, 34,* 20-30.

Rauch, S.L., Jenike, M.A., Alpert, N.M., Baer, L., Breiter, H.C.R., et al. (1994). Regional cerebral blood flow measured during symptom provocation in obsessive-compulsive disorder using oxygen-15 labeled carbon dioxide and positron emission tomography. *Archives of General Psychiatry, 51,* 62-70.

Raymond, N.C., Coleman, E., Ohlerking, F., Christenson, G.A., & Miner, M. (1999). Psychiatric comorbidity in pedophilic sex offenders. *American Journal of Psychiatry, 156,* 786-788.

Rechlin, T., Loew, T.H., & Joraschky, P. (1997). Pseudoseizure "status." *Journal of Psychosomatic Research, 42,* 495-498.

Red Horse, Y. (1982). A cultural network model: Perspectives for adolescent services and paraprofessional training. In S. Manson (Ed.), *New directions in prevention among American Indians and Alaskan Native communities.* Portland: Oregon Health Sciences University.

Redmond, D.E. (1977). Alterations in the function of the nucleus locus coeruleus. In I. Hanin & E. Usdin (Eds.), *Animal models in psychiatry and neurology.* New York: Pergamon.

Reed, J.C., & Reed, H.B.C. (1997). The Halstead-Reitan Neuropsychological Battery. In G. Goldstein & T. Incagnoli (Eds.), *Contemporary approaches to neuropsychological assessment* (pp. 93-130). New York: Plenum.

Reed, S.D., Katkin, E.S., & Goldband, S. (1986). Biofeedback and behavioral medicine. In F.H. Kanfer & A.P. Goldstein (Eds.), *Helping people change: A textbook of methods* (3rd ed.). Elmsford, NY: Pergamon.

Reeder, G.D., Pryor, J.B., & Harsh, I. (1997). Activity and similarity in safer sex workshops led by peer educators. *AIDS Education and Prevention, 9,* 77-89.

Rees, L. (1964). The importance of psychological, allergic and infective factors in childhood asthma. *Journal of Psychosomatic Research, 7,* 253-262.

Regier, D.A., Boyd, J.H., Burke, J.D., Jr., Rae, D.S., Myers, J.K., Kramer, M., Robins, L.N., George, L.K., Karno, M., & Locke, B.Z. (1988). One-month prevalence of mental disorders in the United States. *Archives of General Psychiatry, 45,* 977-986.

Regier, R. (1998). *Manufacturing MPD: The case of Sybil.* Unpublished manuscript.

Reich, D. & Zanarini, M. C. (2001). Developmental aspects of borderline personality disorder. *Harvard Review of Psychiatry, 9,* 294-301.

Reich, J. (1990). Comparison of males and females with DSM-III dependent personality disorder. *Psychiatry Research, 33,* 207-214.

Reid, D.H., Wilson, P.G., & Faw, G.D. (1991). Teaching self-help skills. In J.L. Matson & J.A. Mulick (Eds.), *Handbook of mental retardation.* New York: Pergamon Press.

Reifler, B.V. (1994). Depression: Diagnosis and comorbidity. In L.S. Schneider, C.F. Reynolds, III, B.D. Lebowitz, & A.J. Friedhoff (Eds.), *Diagnosis and treatment of depression in late life* (pp. 55-59). Washington, DC: American Psychiatric Press.

Reifler, B.V., Larson, E., & Hanley, R. (1982). Coexistence of cognitive impairment and depression in geriatric outpatients. *American Journal of Psychiatry, 139,* 623-626.

Reiman, E.M., Caselli, R.J., Yun, L., Chen, K., Bandy, D., et al. (1996). Preclinical evidence of Alzheimer's disease in persons homozygous for the e4 allele for apolipoprotein E. *New England Journal of Medicine, 334,* 752-756.

Reiss, D., Heatherington, E.M., Plomin, R., Howe, G.W., Simmens, S.J., et al. (1995). Genetic questions for environmental studies: Differential parenting and psychopathology in adolescence. *Archives of General Psychiatry, 52,* 925-936.

Reiss, I.L., & Leik, R.K. (1989). Evaluating strategies to avoid AIDS: Number of partners vs. use of condoms. *The Journal of Sex Research, 26,* 411-433.

Reissing, E.D., Binik, Y.M., & Khalife, S. (1999). Does vaginismus exist? A critical review of the literature. *Journal of Nervous and Mental Disease, 187,* 261-274.

Rekers, G.A., & Lovaas, O.I. (1974). Behavioral treatment of deviant sex role behaviors in a male child. *Journal of Applied Behavioral Analysis, 7,* 173-190.

Renneberg, B., Goldstein, A.J., Phillips, D., & Chambless, D.L. (1990). Intensive behavioral group treatment of avoidant personality disorder. *Behavior Therapy, 21,* 363-377.

Renshaw, D. C. (2001). Women coping with a partner's sexual avoidance. *Family Journal—Counseling & Therapy for Couples & Families, 9,* 11-16.

Renshaw, D.C. (1988). Profile of 2376 patients treated at Loyola Sex Clinic between 1972 and 1987. *Sexual and Marital Therapy, 3,* 111-117.

Renvoize, E.B., & Beveridge, A.W. (1989). Mental illness and the late Victorians: A study of patients admitted to three asylums in York, 1880-1884. *Psychological Medicine, 19,* 19-28.

Reppucci, N.D., & Haugaard, J.J. (1989). Prevention of child sexual abuse: Myth or reality. *American Psychologist, 44,* 1266-1275.

Reppucci, N.D., Jones, L.M., & Cook, S.L. (1994). Involving parents in child sexual abuse prevention programs. *Journal of Child and Family Studies, 3,* 137-142.

Rescorla, R.A. (1988). Pavlovian conditioning: It's not what you think it is. *American Psychologist, 43,* 151-160.

Resick, P.A., & Calhoun, K.S. (2001). Posttraumatic stress disorder. In D. H. Barlow (Eds.), *Clinical handbook of psychological disorders* (pp. 60-113). New York: Guilford Press.

Resick, P.A., Nishith, P., Weaver, T.L., Astin, M.C., & Feuer, C.A. (in press). A comparison of cognitive processing therapy, prolonged exposure and a waiting condition for the treatment of posttraumatic stress disorder in female rape victims. *Journal of Consulting and Clinical Psychology.*

Resick, P.A. & Calhoun, K.S. (2001). Posttraumatic stress disorder. In D.H. Barlow (Ed.), *Clinical Handbook of Psychological Disorders* (pp. 60-113). New York, NY: Guilford Press.

Resick, P.A. (1992). Cognitive treatment of crime-related post-traumatic stress disorder. In R. Peters, R. McMahon, & V. Quinsey (Eds.), *Aggression and violence throughout the life span* (pp. 171-191). Newbury Park, CA: Sage.

Resick, P.A. (1993). The psychological impact of rape. *Journal of Interpersonal Violence, 8,* 223-255.

Resick, P.A., & Schnicke, M.K. (1992). Cognitive processing therapy for sexual assault victims. *Journal of Consulting and Clinical Psychology, 60,* 748-756.

Resick, P.A., Nishith, P., Weaver, T.L., Astin, M.C., & Feuer, C.A. (2000). *A comparison of cognitive processing therapy, prolonged exposure and a waiting condition for treatment of posttraumatic stress disorder in female rape victims.* Manuscript submitted for publication.

Resick, P.A., Veronen, L.J., Calhoun, K.S., Kilpatrick, D.G., & Atkeson, B.M. (1986). Assessment of fear reactions in sexual assault victims: A factor-analytic study of the Veronen-Kilpatrick Modified Fear Survey. *Behavioral Assessment, 8,* 271-283.

Reynolds, C.R., Chastain, R.L., Kaufman, A.S., & McLean, J.E. (1997). Demographic characteristics and IQ among adults: Analysis of the WAIS-R standardization sample as a function of the stratification variables. *Journal of School Psychology, 25,* 323-342.

Riccardo, N., & Leeds, J. (1997, February 24). Megan's law calling up old, minor offenses. *Los Angeles Times,* pp. A1, A16.

Richardson, J.L., Dwyer, K.M., McGuigan, K., Hansen, W.B., Dent, C.W., Johnson, C.A., Sussman, S.Y., Brannon, B., & Flay, B. (1989). Substance use among eighth grade students who take care of themselves after school. *Pediatrics, 84,* 556-566.

Richman, D.D. (1996). HIV therapeutics. *Science, 272,* 1886-1888.

Richters, J.E., Arnold, L.E., Jensen, P.S., Abikoff, H. (1995). NIMH collaborative multisite multimodal treatment study of children with ADHD: I. Background and rationale. *Journal of the American Academy of Child and Adolescent Psychiatry, 34,* 987-1000.

Ricks, D.M. (1972). *The beginning of vocal communication in infants and autistic children.* Unpublished doctoral dissertation, University of London.

Ridley, C.R. (1984). Clinical treatment of the nondisclosing black client. *American Psychologist, 39,* 1234-1244.

Rieder, R.O., Mann, L.S., Weinberger, D.R., van Kammen, D.P., & Post, R.M. (1983). Computer tomographic scans in patients with schizophrenia, schizoaffective, and bipolar affective disorder. *Archives of General Psychiatry, 40,* 735-739.

Rief, W., Hiller, W., & Margraf, J. (1998). Cognitive aspects of hypochondriasis and somatization syndrome. *Journal of Abnormal Psychology, 107,* 587-596.

Rief, W., Shaw, R., & Fichter, M.M. (1998). Elevated levels of psychophysiological arousal and cortisol in patients with somatization syndrome. *Psychosomatic Medicine, 60,* 198-203.

Riesmann, F. (1990). Restructuring help: A human services paradigm for the 1990s. *American Journal of Community Psychology, 18,* 221-231.

Riggs, D. et al. (1991). *Post-traumatic stress disorder following rape and nonsexual assault: A predictive model.* Unpublished manuscript.

Rimland, B. (1964). *Infantile autism.* New York: Appleton-Century-Crofts.

Rind, B., Tromovitch, P., & Bauserman, R. (1998). A meta-analytic examination of assumed properties of child sexual abuse using college students. *Psychological Bulletin, 124,* 22-53.

Ringwalt, C., Ennett, S.T., & Holt, K.D. (1991). An outcome evaluation of Project DARE (Drug Abuse Resistance Education). *Health Education Research, 6,* 327-337.

Ritter, B. (1968). The group treatment of children's snake phobias, using vicarious and contact desensitization procedures. *Behaviour Research and Therapy, 6,* 1-6.

Rittig, S., Knudsen, U.B., Norgaard, J.P., Pedersen, E.B., & Djurhuus, J.C. (1989). Abnormal diurnal rhythm of plasma vasopressin and urinary output in patients with enuresis. *American Journal of Physiology, 256,* 664-671.

Ritvo, E.R., Freeman, B.J., Geller, E., & Yuwiler, A. (1983). Effects of fenfluramine on 14 outpatients with the syndrome of autism. *Journal of the American Academy of Child Psychiatry, 22,* 549-558.

Rizzo, A.A., Buckwalter, J.G., Neumann, U., Kesselman, C., & Thiebaux, M. (1998). Basic issues in the application of virtual reality for the assessment and rehabilitation of cognitive impairments and functional disabilities. *CyberPsychology and Behavior, 1,* 59-78.

Roan, S. (1992, October 15). Giving up coffee tied to withdrawal symptoms. *Los Angeles Times,* pp. A26.

Roberts, J.E., & Kassel, J.D. (1997). Labile self-esteem, life stress, and depressive symptoms: Prospective data and a model of vulnerability. *Cognitive Therapy and Research, 21,* 569-589.

Roberts, M.C., Wurtele, S.K., Boone, R.R., Ginther, L.J., & Elkins, P.D. (1981). Reduction of medical fears by use of modeling: A preventive application in a general population of children. *Journal of Pediatric Psychology, 6,* 293-300.

Robin, R.W., Chester, B., Rasmussen, J.K., Jaranson, J.M., & Goldman, D. (1997). Prevalence and characteristics of trauma and posttraumatic stress disorder in a Southwestern American Indian community. *American Journal of Psychiatry, 154,* 1582-1588.

Robins, L.N. (1966). *Deviant children grown up.* Baltimore: Williams & Wilkins.

Robins, L.N. (1978). Sturdy childhood predictors of adult antisocial behavior: Replications from longitudinal studies. *Psychological Medicine, 8,* 611-622.

Robins, L.N., & Regier, D. (1991). *Psychiatric disorders in America.* New York: Free Press.

Robins, L.N., Helzer, J.E., Przybec, T.R., & Regier, D.A. (1988). Alcohol disorders in the community: A report from the Epidemiologic Catchment Area. In R.M. Rose & J.E. Barrett (Eds.), *Alcoholism: Origins and outcome.* NY: Raven.

Robinson, D., Woerner, M.G., Alvir, J., Bilder, R., Goldman, R., et al. (1999). Predictors of relapse following response from a first episode of schizophrenia or schizoaffective disorder. *Archives of General Psychiatry, 56,* 241-247.

Robinson, L.A., Klesges, R.C., Zbikowski, S.M., & Glaser, R. (1997). Predictors of risk for different stages of adolescent smoking in a biracial sample. *Journal of Consulting and Clinical Psychology, 65,* 653-662.

Robinson, N.M., & Robinson, H.B. (1976). *The mentally retarded child* (2nd ed.). New York: McGraw-Hill.

Robinson, N.S., Garber, J., & Hillsman, R. (1995). Cognitions and stress: Direct and moderating effects on depression versus externalizing symptoms during the junior high school transition. *Journal of Abnormal Psychology, 104,* 453-463.

Rockwood, K., Kirkland, S., Hogan, D. B. et al. (2002). Use of lipid-lowering agents, indication bias, and the risk of dementia in community-dwelling elderly people. *Archives of Neurology, 59,* 223-227.

Rodin, J. (1980). Managing the stress of aging: The control of control and coping. In H. Ursin & S. Levine (Eds.), *Coping and health.* New York: Academic Press.

Rodin, J. (1983). Behavioral medicine: Beneficial effects of self-control training in aging. *International Review of Applied Psychology, 32,* 153-181.

Rodin, J. (1986). Aging and health: Effects of the sense of control. *Science, 233,* 1271-1276.

Rodin, J., & Ickovics, J.R. (1990). Women's health: Review and research agenda as we approach the 21st century. *American Psychologist, 45,* 1018-1034.

Rodin, J., & Langer, E.J. (1977). Long-term effects of a control-relevant intervention with the institutionalized aged. *Journal of Personality and Social Psychology, 35,* 897-902.

Rodin, J., McAvay, G., & Timko, C. (1988). A longitudinal study of depressed mood and sleep disturbances in elderly adults. *Journal of Gerontology: Psychological Sciences, 43,* 45-53.

Roelofs, K., Hoogduin, K.A.L., Keijsers, G.P.J. et al. (2002). Hypnotic susceptibility in patients with conversion disorder. *Journal of Abnormal Psychology, 111,* 390-395.

Roelofs, K., Naering, G.W., Moene, F.C. & Hoogduin, C.A. (2000). The question of lateralization in conversion disorder. *Journal of Psychosomatic Research, 49,* 21-25.

Roesch, R., & Golding, S.L. (1980). *Competency to stand trial.* Urbana: University of Illinois Press.

Roffman, R.A., Stephens, R.S., Curtin, L., Gordon, J.R., Craver, J.N., Stern, M., Beadnell, B., & Downey, L. (1998). Relapse prevention as an intervention model for HIV risk reduction in gay and bisexual men. *AIDS Education and Prevention, 10,* 1-18.

Rogers, C.R. (1942). *Counseling and psychotherapy: New concepts in practice.* Boston: Houghton Mifflin.

Rogers, C.R. (1951). *Client-centered therapy.* Boston: Houghton Mifflin.

Rogers, C.R. (1961). *On becoming a person: A therapist's view of psychotherapy.* Boston: Houghton Mifflin.

Rogers, C.R. (1970). *Carl Rogers on encounter groups.* New York: Harper & Row.

Rogers, S.L., Doody, R.S., Mohs, R.C., Friedhoff, L.T., & the Donepezil Study Group. (1998). Donepezil improves cognition and global function in Alzheimer disease. *Archives of Internal Medicine, 158,* 1021-1031.

Rogler, L.H., & Hollingshead, A.B. (1985). *Trapped: Families and schizophrenia* (3rd ed.). Maplewood, NJ: Waterfront Press.

Rohde, P., Lewinsohn, P.M., & Seeley, J.R. (1991). Comorbidity of unipolar depression: 2. Comorbidity with other mental disorders in adolescents and adults. *Journal of Abnormal Psychology, 54,* 653-660.

Roitman, S.E., Mitropoulou, V., Keefe, R.S. et al. (2000). Visuospatial working memory in schizotypal personality disorder patients. *Schizophrenia Research, 41,* 447-455.

Rokeach, M. (1973). *The nature of human values.* New York: Free Press.

Rokeach, M. (1979). *Some unresolved issues in theories of beliefs, attitudes, and values.* Proceedings of the Nebraska Symposium on Motivation. Lincoln: University of Nebraska Press.

Romanczyk, R.G., Diament, C., Goren, E.R., Trundeff, G., & Harris, S.L. (1975). Increasing isolate and social play in severely disturbed children: Intervention and postintervention effectiveness. *Journal of Autism and Childhood Schizophrenia, 43,* 730-739.

Romas, S.N., Santyana, V., Williamson, J. et al. (2002). Familial Alzheimer disease among Caribbean Hispanics. *Archives of Neurology, 59,* 87-91.

Romero, D. (1992, March 7). Two drugs crash the party scene. *Los Angeles Times,* pp. A1, A22-23.

Ronningstam, E., & Gunderson, J.G. (1990). Identifying criteria for narcissistic personality disorder. *American Journal of Psychiatry, 147,* 918-922.

Root, M.P. (1990). Disordered eating in women of color. *Sex Roles, 22,* 525-536.

Rooth, F.G. (1973). Exhibitionism, sexual violence, and pedophilia. *British Journal of Psychiatry, 122,* 705-710.

Rorsman, B., Hagnell, O., & Lanke, J. (1986). Prevalence and incidence of senile and multi-infarct dementia in the Lundby Study: A comparison between time periods 1947-1957 and 1957-1972. *Neuropsychobiology, 15,* 122-129.

Rorty, M., Yager, J., & Rossotto, E. (1994). Childhood sexual, physical, and psychological abuse in bulimia nervosa. *American Journal of Psychiatry, 151,* 1122-1126.

Rose, D.T., Abramson, L.Y., Hodulik, C.J., Halberstadt, L., & Gaye, L. (1994). Heterogeneity of cognitive style among depressed inpatients. *Journal of Abnormal Psychology, 103,* 419-429.

Rose, J. (1996). Anger management: A group treatment program for people with mental retardation. *Journal of Developmental and Physical Disabilities, 8,* 133-149.

Rose, S.D. (1986). Group methods. In F.H. Kanfer & A.P. Goldstein (Eds.), *Helping people change: A textbook of methods* (3rd ed.). Elmsford, NY: Pergamon.

Rosen, E., Fox, R., & Gregory, I. (1972). *Abnormal psychology* (2nd ed.). Philadelphia: Saunders.

Rosen, G.M. (1999). Treatment fidelity and research on Eye Movement Desensitization and Reprocessing (EMDR). *Journal of Anxiety Disorders, 13,* 173-184.

Rosen, R.C. (2000). Medical and psychological interventions for erectile dysfunction: Toward a combined treatment approach. In S. R. Lieblum & R. C. Rosen (Eds.), *principles and practice of sex therapy* (pp.276-304). New York: Guilford Press.

Rosen, R. C., & Leiblum, S. R. (2000). Introduction: Sex therapy in the age of Viagra. In S. R. Lieblum & R. C. Rosen (Eds.), *Principles and practice of sex therapy* (pp.1-13). New York: Guilford Press.

Rosen, R.C., & Beck, J.G. (1988). *Patterns of sexual arousal: Psychophysiological processes and clinical applications.* New York: Guilford.

Rosen, R.C., & Hall, E. (1984). *Sexuality.* New York: Random House.

Rosen, R.C., & Leiblum, S.R. (1995). Treatment of sexual disorders in the 1990s: An integrated approach. *Journal of Consulting and Clinical Psychology, 63,* 877-890.

Rosen, R.C., & Rosen, L. (1981). *Human sexuality.* New York: Knopf.

Rosen, R.C., Leiblum, S.R., & Spector, I. (1994). Psychologically based treatment for male erectile disorder: A cognitive-interpersonal model. *Journal of Sex and Marital Therapy, 20,* 67-85.

Rosenbaum, M. (1980). The role of the term schizophrenia in the decline of diagnoses of multiple personality. *Archives of General Psychiatry, 37,* 1383-1385.

Rosenberg, D.R., Keshavan, M.S., O'Hearn, K.M., Seymour, A.B., Birmaher, B., et al. (1997). Frontostriatal measurement in treatment-naive children with obsessive-compulsive disorder. *Archives of General Psychiatry, 54,* 824-830.

Rosenberg, M.S., & Reppucci, N.D. (1985). Primary prevention of child abuse. *Journal of Consulting and Clinical Psychology, 53,* 576-585.

Rosenblatt, R.A. (1998, October 27). Alzheimer's focus shifts to delay, not cure. *Los Angeles Times,* pp. A1-A16.

Rosenfarb, I.S., Goldstein, M.J., Mintz, J., & Neuchterlein, K.H. (1994). Expressed emotion and subclinical psychopathology observable within transactions between schizophrenics and their family members. *Journal of Abnormal Psychology, 104,* 259-267.

Rosenheck, R., Cramer, J., Allan, E., Erdos, J., Frisman, J., et al. (1999). Cost-effectivness of clozapine in patients with high and low levels of hospital use. *Archives of General Psychiatry, 56,* 565-572.

Rosenman, R.H., Brand, R.J., Jenkins, C.D., Friedman, M., Straus, R., & Wurm, M. (1975). Coronary heart disease in the Western Collaborative Group Study: Final follow-up experience of 8 years. *Journal of the American Medical Association, 233,* 872-877.

Rosenthal, D. (1955). Changes in some moral values following psychotherapy. *Journal of Consulting Psychology, 19,* 431-436.

Rosenthal, N.E., Carpenter, C.J., James, S.P., Parry, B.L., Rogers, S.L.B., & Wehr, T.A. (1986). Seasonal affective disorder in children and adolescents. *American Journal of Psychiatry, 143,* 356-358.

Rosenthal, T.L., & Bandura, A. (1978). Psychological modeling: Theory and practice. In S.L. Garfield & A.E. Bergin (Eds.), *Handbook of psychotherapy and behavior change: An empirical analysis* (2nd ed.). New York: Wiley.

Rosenzweig, R., & Fillit, H. (1992). Probable heterosexual transmission of AIDS in an aged woman. *Journal of the American Geriatric Society, 40,* 1261-1264.

Roser, K. & Buchholz, E.S. (1996). Autism from an intersubjective perspective. *Psychoanalytic Review, 83,* 305-323.

Rosman, B.L., Minuchin, S., & Liebman, R. (1975). Family lunch session: An introduction to family therapy in anorexia nervosa. *American Journal of Orthopsychiatry, 45,* 846-852.

Rosman, B.L., Minuchin, S., & Liebman, R. (1976). Input and outcome of family therapy of anorexia nervosa. In J.L. Claghorn (Ed.), *Successful psychotherapy.* New York: Brunner/Mazel.

Ross, C.A. (1989). *Multiple personality disorder: Diagnosis, clinical features, and treatment.* New York: Wiley.

Ross, C.A. (1991). Epidemiology of multiple personality disorder and dissociation. *Psychiatric Clinics of North America, 14,* 503-517.

Ross, D.M., & Ross, S.A. (1982). *Hyperactivity: Research, theory, and action.* New York: Wiley.

Ross, D.M., & Ross, S.A. (1984). Childhood pain: The school-aged child's view. *Pain, 20,* 179-191.

Ross, R.S., Bush, J.P., & Crummette, B.D. (1991). Factors affecting nurses' decisions to administer PRN analgesia medication to children after surgery: An analogue investigation. *Journal of Pediatric Psychology, 16,* 151-167.

Rossiter, E.M., & Agras, W.S. (1990). An empirical test of the DSM-IIIR definition of binge. *International Journal of Eating Disorders, 9,* 513-518.

Rosso, I.M., Cannon, T.D., Huttunen, T. et al. (2000). Obstetric risk factors for early-onset schizophrenia in a Finnish birth cohort. *American Journal of Psychiatry, 157,* 801-807.

Rost, K., Kashner, T.M., & Smith, G.R. (1994). Effectiveness of psychiatic intervention with somatization disorder patients: Improved outcomes at reduced costs. *General Hospital Psychiatry, 16,* 381-387.

Roth, D., & Rehm, L.P. (1980). Relationships among self-monitoring processes, memory, and depression. *Cognitive Therapy and Research, 4,* 149-157.

Roth, M. (1955). The natural history of mental disorder in old age. *Journal of Mental Science, 99,* 439-450.

Roth, M., & Kay, D.W.K. (1956). Affective disorder arising in the senium: 2. Physical disability as an etiological factor. *Journal of Mental Science, 102,* 141-150.

Rothbaum, B.O., Foa, E.B. (1993). Subtypes of posttraumatic stress disorder and duration of symptoms. In J.R.T. Davidson & E.B. Foa (Eds.), *Post-traumatic stress disorder: DSM-IV and beyond* (pp. 23-35). Washington, DC: American Psychiatric Press.

Rothbaum, B. O., Hodges, L., Alarcon, R., Ready, D., Shahar, F., Graap, K., Pair, J., Hebert, P., Gotz, D., Will, B., & Baltzell, D. (1999). Virtual reality exposure therapy for PTSD Vietnam veterans: A case study. *Journal of Traumatic Stress, 12(2),* 263-271.

Rothbaum, B.O., Hodges, L., Alarcon, R., Ready, D., Shahar, F., Graap, K., Pair, J., Hebert, P., Gotz, D., Will, B., & Baltzell, D. (1999). Virtual reality exposure therapy for PTSD Vietnam veterans: A case study. *Journal of Traumatic Stress, 12(2),* 263-271.

Rothbaum, B.O., & Foa, E.B. (1992). Exposure therapy for rape victims with post-traumatic stress disorder. *The Behavior Therapist, 15,* 219-222.

Rothbaum, B.O., Foa, E.B., Murdock, T., Riggs, D.S., & Walsh, W. (1992). A prospective examination of post-traumatic stress disorder in rape victims. *Journal of Traumatic Stress, 5,* 455-475.

Rothbaum, B.O., Hodges, L., Watson, B.A., Kessler, G.D., et al. (1996). Virtual reality exposure therapy in the treatment of fear of flying: A case report. *Behaviour Research and Therapy, 34,* 477-481.

Rothbaum, B.O., Hodges, L.F., Kooper, R., Opdyke, D., Williford, J.S., & North, M. (1995a). The efficacy of virtual reality graded exposure in the treatment of acrophobia. *American Journal of Psychiatry, 152,* 626-628.

Rothbaum, B.O., Hodges, L.F., Kooper, R., Opdyke, D., Williford, J.S., & North, M. (1995b). Virtual reality graded exposure in the treatment of acrophobia. A case report. *Behavior Therapy, 26,* 547-554.

Rothman, A.J., & Salovey, P. (1997). Shaping perceptions to motivate healthy behavior: The role of message framing. *Psychological Bulletin, 121,* 3-19.

Rothman, K.J., & Michels, K.B. (1994). The continuing unethical use of placebo controls. *New England Journal of Medicine, 331,* 394-397.

Rounsaville, B.J., Chevron, E.S., & Weissman, M.M. (1984). Specification of techniques in interpersonal psychotherapy. In J.B.W. Williams & R.L. Spitzer (Eds.), *Psychotherapy research: Where are we and where should we go?* New York: Guilford.

Rovner, B.W., Kafonek, S., Filipp, L., Lucas, M.J., & Folstein, M.F. (1986). Prevalence of mental illness in a community nursing home. *American Journal of Psychiatry, 143,* 1446-1449.

Rowland, D.L., Cooper, S.E., & Slob, A.K. (1996). Genital and psychoaffective responses to erotic stimulation in sexually functional and dysfunctional men. *Journal of Abnormal Psychology, 105,* 194-203.

Roy, A. (1982). Suicide in chronic schizophrenia. *British Journal of Psychiatry, 141,* 171-180.

Roy, A. (1994). Recent biologic studies on suicide. *Suicide and Life Threatening Behaviors, 24,* 10-24.

Roy, A. (1995). Suicide. In H.I. Kaplan & B.J. Sadock (Eds.), *Comprehensive textbook of psychiatry* (pp. 1739-1752). Baltimore: Williams & Wilkins.

Roy, A., & Linnoila, M. (1986). Alcoholism and suicide. *Suicide and Life Threatening Behaviors, 16,* 244-259.

Roy, A., Everett, D., Pickar, D., & Paul, S.M. (1987). Platelet tritiated imipramine binding and serotonin uptake in depressed patients. *Archives of General Psychiatry, 44,* 320-327.

Roy, A., Segal, N., Centerwall, B., & Robinette, D. (1991). Suicide in twins. *Archives of General Psychiatry, 48,* 29-36.

Roy-Byrne, P.P., Katon, W. Cowley, D.S., & Russo, J. (2001). A randomized effectiveness trial of collaborative care for patients with panic disorder in primary care. *Archives of General Psychiatry, 58,* 869-876.

Roy-Byrne, P.P., & Cowley, D.S. (1998). Pharmacological treatment of panic, generalized anxiety, and phobic disorders. In P.E. Nathan & J.M. Gorman (Eds.), *A guide to treatments that work* (pp. 319-338). New York: Oxford University Press.

Ruberman, W., Weinblatt, E., Goldberg, J.D., & Chaudhary, B.S. (1984). Psychosocial influences on mortality after myocardial infarction. *New England Journal of Medicine, 311*, 552-559.

Rubia, K., Overmeyer, S., Taylor, E., Brammer, M., Williams, S.C.R., et al. (1999). Hypofrontality in attention deficit hyperactivity disorder during higher-order motor control: A study with functional MRI. *American Journal of Psychiatry, 156*, 891-896.

Rubin, A.J. (1998a, August 15). Court rules FDA cannot regulate tobacco as a drug. *Los Angeles Times*, pp. A1-A10.

Rubin, A.J. (1998b, September 15). Fight ensues to block undoing of doctor-assisted suicide law. *Los Angeles Times*, pp. A5

Rubin, P., Holm, S., Madsen, R.L., Friberg, L., et al. (1993). Regional cerebral blood flow in newly diagnosed schizophrenic and schizophreniform disorders. *Psychiatry Research, 53*, 57-75.

Rubin, R.T., Phillips, J.J., Sadow, T.F., & McCracken, J.T. (1995). Adrenal gland volume in major depression: Increase during the depressive episode and decrease with successful treatment. *Archives of General Psychiatry, 52*, 213-218.

Ruch, L.O., & Leon, J.J. (1983). Sexual assault trauma and trauma change. *Women and Health, 8*, 5-21.

Rumbak, M.J., Kelso, T.M., Arheart, K.L., & Self, T.H. (1993). Perception of anxiety as a contributing factor in asthma: Indigent versus non-indigent. *Journal of Asthma, 30*, 165-169.

Ruscio, A.M., Borkovec, T.D., & Ruscio, J. (2000). A taxometric investigation of the latent structure of worry. *Journal of Abnormal Psychology, 110*, 413-422.

Ruscio, A.M., Ruscio, J., & Keane, T.M. (2001). The latent structure of posttraumatic stress disorder: A taxometric investigation of reaction to extreme stress. *Journal of Abnormal Psychology, 111*, 290-301.

Rush, A.J., Beck, A.T., Kovacs, M., & Hollon, S.D. (1977). Comparative efficacy of cognitive therapy and pharmacotherapy in the treatment of depressed outpatients. *Cognitive Therapy and Research, 1*, 17-39.

Rush, A.J., Beck, A.T., Kovacs, M., Weissenberger, J., & Hollon, S.D. (1982). Comparison of the effects of cognitive therapy on hopelessness and self-concept. *American Journal of Psychiatry, 139*, 862-866.

Russell, M.A.H., Feyerabend, C., & Cole, P.V. (1976). Plasma nicotine levels after cigarette smoking and chewing nicotine gum. *British Medical Journal, 290*, 1043-1046.

Russo, D.C., & Varni, J.W. (1982). Behavioral pediatrics. In D.C. Russo & J.W. Varni (Eds.), *Behavioral pediatrics: Research and practice*. New York: Plenum.

Rutherford, J., & Noegel, R. (1993). Genetic influences on eating attitudes in a normal female twin population. *Psychological Medicine, 23*, 425-436.

Rutherford, M.J., Cacciola, J.S., & Alterman, A.I. (1999). Antisocial personality disorder and psychopathy in cocaine-dependent women. *American Journal of Psychiatry, 156*, 849-856.

Rutter, M. (1967). Psychotic disorders in early childhood. In A.J. Cooper (Ed.), Recent developments in schizophrenia [Special publication]. *British Journal of Psychiatry*.

Rutter, M. (1971). Parent-child separation: Psychological effects on the children. *Journal of Child Psychology and Psychiatry, 12*, 233-260.

Rutter, M. (1988). Stress, coping, and development: Some issues and some questions. In N. Garmezy, R. Norman, & M. Rutter (Eds.) *Stress, coping, and development in children* (pp. 1-41). Baltimore, MD: Johns Hopkins University Press.

Rutter, M. (1996). Stress research: Accomplishments and tasks ahead. In R.J. Haggerty, & L.R. Sherrod, (Eds.), *Stress, risk, and resilience in children and adolescents: Processes, mechanisms, and interventions* (pp. 354-385). New York: Cambridge University Press.

Rutter, M., & Schopler, E. (1987). Autism and pervasive developmental disorders: Concepts and diagnostic issues. *Journal of Autism and Developmental Disorders, 17*, 159-186.

Ryall, R. (1974). Delinquency: The problem for treatment. *Social Work Today, 15*, 98-104.

Ryan, W. (1971). *Blaming the victim*. New York: Random House.

Rybstein-Blinchik, E. (1979). Effects of different cognitive strategies on chronic pain experience. *Journal of Behavioral Medicine, 2*, 93-101.

Sabin, J.E. (1975). Translating despair. *American Journal of Psychiatry, 132*, 197-199.

Sabol, S.Z., Nelson, M.L., Fisher, C., Gunzerath, L., Brody, C.L., et al. (1999). A genetic association for cigarette smoking behavior. *Health Psychology, 18*, 7-13.

Sacco, R.L., Elkind, M., Boden-Albala, B., Lin, I., Kargman, D.E., et al. (1999). The protective effect of moderate alcohol consumption on ischemic stroke. *JAMA, 281*, 53-60.

Sachs, J.S. (1983). Negative factors in brief psychotherapy: An empirical assessment. *Journal of Consulting and Clinical Psychology, 51*, 557-564.

Sackeim, H.A., Prudic, J., Devenand, D.P. et al. (2000). A prospective, randomized, double-blind comparison of bilateral and right unilateral electroconvulsive shock therapy at different stimulus intensities.. *Archives of General Psychiatry, 57*, 425-434.

Sackeim, H.A., Nordlie, J.W., & Gur, R.C. (1979). A model of hysterical and hypnotic blindness: Cognition, motivation and awareness. *Journal of Abnormal Psychology, 88*, 474-489.

Sacks, O. (1985). *The man who mistook his wife for a hat and other clinical tales*. New York: Harper & Row.

Sacks, O. (1995). *An anthropologist on Mars*. New York: Knopf.

Saffer, H. (1991). Alcohol advertising bans and alcohol abuse: An international perspective. *Journal of Health Economics, 10*, 65-79.

Safran, J.D., Vallis, T.M., Segal, Z.V., & Shaw, B.F. (1986). Assessment of core cognitive processes in cognitive therapy. *Cognitive Therapy and Research, 10*, 509-526.

Sager, C.J. (1990). Foreword. In I.L. Kutash & A. Wolf (Eds.), *The group psychotherapist's handbook: Contemporary theory and technique*. New York: Columbia University Press.

Sakel, M. (1938). The pharmacological shock treatment of schizophrenia. *Nervous and Mental Disease Monograph*, 62.

Saks, E.R. (1997). *Jekyll on trial: Multiple personality disorder and criminal law*. New York: New York University Press.

Salamone, J.D. (2000). A critique of recent studies on placebo effects of antidepressants: Importance of research on active placebos. *Psychopharmacology, 152*, 1-6

Salan, S.E., Zinberg, N.E., & Frei, E. (1975). Antiemetic effect of delta-9-THC in patients receiving cancer chemotherapy. *New England Journal of Medicine, 293*, 795-797.

Salekin, R.T. (2002). Psychopathy and therapeutic pessimism: Clinical lore or clinical reality? *Clinical Psychology Review, 22*, 79-112.

Salekin, R.T., Rogers, R., & Sewell, K.W. (1997). Construct validity of psychopathy in a female offender sample: A multitrait-multimethod evaluation. *Journal of Abnormal Psychology, 106*, 576-585.

Salkovskis, P., & Warwick, H.M. (1986). Morbid preoccupations, health anxiety, and reassurance: A cognitive-behavioural approach to hypochondriasis. *Behaviour Research and Therapy, 24*, 597-602.

Salkovskis, P.M. (1985). Obsessional compulsive problems: A cognitive-behavioral analysis. *Behaviour Research and Therapy, 23*, 571-583.

Salkovskis, P.M., & Clark, D.M. (1991). Cognitive therapy for panic disorder. *Journal of Cognitive Psychotherapy, 5*, 215-226.

Salkovskis, P.M., Atha, C., & Storer, D. (1990). Cognitive-behavioral problem-solving in the treatment of patients who repeatedly attempt suicide: A controlled trial. *British Journal of Psychiatry, 157*, 871-876.

Salovey, P., & Singer, J.A. (1991). Cognitive behavior modification. In F.H. Kanfer & A.P. Goldstein (Eds.), *Helping people change: A textbook of methods* (4th ed.). Elmsford, NY: Pergamon.

Salter, A. (1949). *Conditioned reflex therapy*. New York: Farrar, Strauss.

Salzman, L. (1980). *Psychotherapy of the obsessive personality*. New York: Jason Aronson.

Salzman, L. (1985). Psychotherapeutic management of obsessive-compulsive patients. *American Journal of Psychotherapy, 39*, 323-330.

Sanday, P.R. (1981). The socio-cultural context of rape: A cross-cultural study. *The Journal of Social Issues, 37*, 5-27.

Sanderson, W.C., Rapee, R.M., & Barlow, D.H. (1989). The influence of an illusion of control on panic attacks induced via inhalation of 5.5% carbon dioxide-enriched air. *Archives of General Psychiatry, 46*, 157-162.

Sanger, T.M., Lieberman, J.A., Tohen, M., Grundy, S., et al. (1999). Olanzapine versus haloperidol in first-episode psychosis. *American Journal of Psychiatry, 156*, 79-87.

Sanislow, C.A., Grilo, C.M., & McGlashan, T.H. (2000). Factor analysis of the DSM-III-R borderline personality disorder criteria in psychiatric inpatients. *American Journal of Psychiatry, 157*, 1629-1633.

Sano, M., Ernesto, C., Thomas, R.G., Klauber, M.R., Schafer, K., Grundman, M.,

Woodbury, P., Growdon, J., Cotman, C.W., Pfeiffer, E., Schneider, L.S., Thai, L. J., for the Members of the Alzheimer's Disease Cooperative Study. (1997). A controlled trial of selegiline, alpha-tocopherol, or both as treatment for Alzheimer's disease. *New England Journal of Medicine, 336,* 1216-1222.

Sartorius, N., Shapiro, R., & Jablonsky, A. (1974). The international pilot study of schizophrenia. *Schizophrenia Bulletin, 2,* 21-35.

Sarwer, D.B., & Sayers, S.L. (1998). Behavioral interviewing. In A.S. Bellack & M. Hersen (Eds.), *Behavioral assessment: A practical handbook* (pp. 63-103). Boston: Allyn and Bacon.

Satava, R.M. (1996). Medical virtual reality: The current status of the future. In S.J. Weghorst, H.B. Sieburg, & K.S. Morgan (Eds.), *Proceedings of the Medical Meets Virtual Reality Conference* (pp. 100-106). Amsterdam: IOS Press.

Savage, D.G. (1996, December 11). High court debates sexual predator law. *Los Angeles Times,* pp. A26.

Savage, D.G., & Dolan, M. (1996, December 12). Sex predator law faces high court challenge. *Los Angeles Times,* pp. A1, A22.

Sayette, M.A., & Wilson, G.T. (1991). Intoxication and exposure to stress: Effects of temporal patterning. *Journal of Abnormal Psychology, 100,* 56-62.

Sbrocco, T., Weisberg, R. B., Barlow, D. H., & Carter, M. M. (1997). The conceptual relationship between panic disorder and male erectile dysfunction. *Journal of Sex and Marital Therapy, 23,* 212-220.

Sbrocco, T., Weisberg, R.B., & Barlow, D.H. (1995). Sexual dysfunction in the older adult: Assessment of psychosocial factors. *Sexuality and Disability, 13,* 201-218.

Scarborough, H.S. (1990). Very early language deficits in dyslexic children. *Child Development, 61,* 128-174.

Scarlett, W. (1980). Social isolation from age-mates among nursery school children. *Journal of Child Psychology and Psychiatry, 21,* 231-240.

Schaefer, L.C., Wheeler, C.C., & Futterweit, W. (1997). Gender identity disorders (transsexualism). In G.O. Gabbard & S.D. Atkinson (Eds.), *Synopsis of treatments of psychiatric disorders* (2nd ed., pp. 843-858). Washington, DC: American Psychiatric Press.

Schaie, K.W., & Hertzog, C. (1982). Longitudinal methods. In B.B. Wolman (Ed.), *Handbook of developmental psychology.* Englewood Cliffs, NJ: Prentice-Hall.

Schall, P.L., Landsbergis, P.A., & Baker, D. (1994). Job strain and cardiovascular disease. *Annual Review of Public Health, 15,* 381-411.

Scharff, J.S. (1995). Psychoanalytic marital therapy. In N.S. Jacobson & A.S. Gurman (Eds.), *Clinical handbook of couple therapy.* New York: Guilford.

Schatzberg, A.F. (1991). Overview of anxiety disorders: Prevalence, biology, course, and treatment. *Journal of Clinical Psychiatry, 52,* 5-9.

Schecter, N.L., Allen, D.A., & Hanson, K. (1986). Status of pediatric pain control: A comparison of hospital analgesic usage in children and adults. *Pediatrics, 77,* 11-15.

Scheerer, M., Rothman, E., & Goldstein, K. (1945). A case of "idiot savant": An experimental study of personality organization. *Psychological Monographs, 58* (Whole No. 269).

Scheff, T.J. (1966). *Being mentally ill: A sociological theory.* Chicago: Aldine.

Schiavi, R.C. (1997). Male erectile disorder. In G.O. Gabbard & S.D. Atkinson (Eds.), *Synopsis of treatments of psychiatric disorders* (2nd ed., pp. 781-788). Washington, DC: American Psychiatric Press.

Schinke, S.P., & Gilchrist, L.D. (1985). Preventing substance abuse with children and adolescents. *Journal of Consulting and Clinical Psychology, 53,* 596-602.

Schleifer, M. (1995). Should we change our views about early childhood education? *Alberta Journal of Educational Research, 41,* 355-359.

Schlundt, D.G., & Johnson, W.G. (1990). *Eating disorders: Assessment and treatment.* Needham Heights, MA: Allyn & Bacon.

Schmidt, N.B., Lerew, D.R., & Jackson, R.J. (1997). The role of anxiety sensitivity in the pathogenesis of panic: Prospective evaluation of spontaneous panic attacks during acute stress. *Journal of Abnormal Psychology, 106,* 355-364.

Schmitt, W.A., & Newman, J.P. (1999). Are all psychopathic individuals low-anxious? *Journal of Abnormal Psychology, 108,* 353-358.

Schnall, P.L., Landsbergis, P.A., & Baker, D. (1994). Job strain and cardiovascular disease. *Annual Review of Public Health, 15,* 381-411.

Schneider, J. (1996). Geriatric psychopharmacology. In L.L. Carstensen, B.A. Edelstein, & L. Dornbrand (Eds.), *The practical handbook of clinical gerontology* (pp. 481-542). Thousand Oaks, CA: Sage.

Schneider, J.A., O'Leary, A., & Agras, W.S. (1987). The role of perceived self-efficacy in recovery from bulimia: A preliminary examination. *Behaviour Research and Therapy, 25,* 429-432.

Schneider, K. (1959). *Clinical psychopathology.* New York: Grune & Stratton.

Schneider, L.S., & Olin, J.T. (1994). Overview of clinical trials of Hydergine in dementia. *Archives of Neurology, 51,* 787-796.

Schneider, N.G. (1987). Nicotine gum in smoking cessation: Rationale, efficacy, and proper use. *Comprehensive Therapy, 13,* 32-37.

Schneider, R.A., Staggers, F., Alexander, C.N., Sheppard, W., Rainforth, M., Kondwani, K., Smith, S., & King, C.G. (1995). A randomized controlled trial of stress reduction for hypertension in older African Americans. *Hypertension, 26,* 820-827.

Schneier, F.R., Johnson, J., Horning, C.D., Liebowitz, M.R., & Weissman, M.M. (1992). Social phobia: Comorbidity and morbidity in an epidemiologic sample. *Archives of General Psychiatry, 49,* 282-288.

Schoenbach, V., Kaplan, B.H., Fredman, L., & Kleinaum, D.G. (1986). Social ties and mortality in Evans County, Georgia. *American Journal of Epidemiology, 123,* 577-591.

Schoeneman, T.J. (1977). The role of mental illness in the European witch-hunts of the sixteenth and seventeenth centuries: An assessment. *Journal of the History of the Behavioral Sciences, 13,* 337-351.

Schofield, W. (1964). *Psychotherapy: The purchase of friendship.* Englewood Cliffs, NJ: Prentice-Hall.

Schooler, C., Flora, J.A., & Farquhar, J.W. (1993). Moving toward synergy: Media supplementation in the Stanford Five-City Project. *Communication Research, 26,* 587-610.

Schooler, N.R., Keith, S.J., Severe, J.B., Matthews, S.M., Bellack, A.S., et al. (1997). Relapse and rehospitalization during maintenance treatment of schizophrenia: The effects of dose reduction and family treatment. *Archives of General Psychiatry, 54,* 453-464.

Schopler, E., Short, B., & Mesibov, G.B. (1989). Comments. *Journal of Consulting and Clinical Psychology, 157,* 162-167.

Schottenfeld, R.S., Pakes, J., O'Conner, P., et al. (2000). Thrice-weekly versus daily buprenorphine maintenance. *Biological Psychiatry, 47,* 1072-1079.

Schover, L.R. (1981). Unpublished research. As cited in Spector & Carey (1990).

Schreiber, F.L. (1973). *Sybil.* Chicago: Regnery.

Schuckit, M.A. (1983). The genetics of alcoholism. In B. Tabakoff, P.B. Sulker, & C.L. Randall (Eds.), *Medical and social aspects of alcohol use.* New York: Plenum.

Schuckit, M.A. (1994). Low level of response to alcohol as a predictor of future alcoholism. *American Journal of Psychiatry, 151,* 184-189.

Schuckit, M.A., & Smith, T.L. (1996). An 8-year follow-up of 450 sons of alcoholic and control subjects. *Archives of General Psychiatry, 53,* 202-210.

Schuckit, M.A., Daeppen, J.-B., Danko, G.P., Tripp, M.L., Smith, T.L., & et al. (1999). Clinical implications for four drugs of the DSM-IV distinction between substance with and without a physiological component. *American Journal of Psychiatry, 156,* 41-49.

Schuckit, M.A., Smith, T.L., Daeppen, J.-B., Eng, M., Li, T.-K., et al. (1998). Clinical relevance of the distinction between alcohol dependence with and without a physiological component. *American Journal of Psychiatry, 155,* 733-740.

Schultz, J. (1991). Smoking-attributable mortality and years of potential life lost: U.S., 1988. *Morbidity and Mortality Weekly Report, 40,* 63-71.

Schultz, R., & Brenner, G. (1977). Relocation of the aged: A review and theoretical analysis. *Journal of Gerontology, 32,* 323-333.

Schulz, R. (1982). Emotionality and aging: A theoretical and empirical analysis. *Journal of Gerontology, 37,* 42-51.

Schulz, R., & Williamson, G.M. (1991). A 2-year longitudinal study of depression among Alzheimer's caregivers. *Psychology and Aging, 6,* 569-578.

Schwartz, G.E. (1973). Biofeedback as therapy: Some theoretical and practical issues. *American Psychologist, 28,* 666-673.

Schwartz, M.S. (1946). *The economic and spatial mobility of paranoid schizophrenics.* Unpublished master's thesis, University of Chicago.

Schwartz, P.J., Murphy, D.L., Wehr, T.A., Garcia-Borreguero, D., Oren, D.A., et al. (1997). Effects of Meta-chlorphenylpiperazine infusions in patients with seasonal affective disorder and healthy control subjects. *Archives of General Psychiatry, 54,* 375-385.

Schwartz, R., & Schwartz, L.J. (1980). *Becoming a couple.* Englewood Cliffs, NJ: Prentice-Hall.

Schwartz, R.M., & Gottman, J.M. (1976). Toward a task analysis of assertive behavior. *Journal of Consulting and Clinical Psychology, 44,* 910-920.

Schwartz, S.H., & Inbar-Saban, N. (1988). Value self-confrontation as a method to aid in weight loss. *Journal of Personality and Social Psychology, 54,* 396-404.

Schwarz, J.R. (1981). *The Hillside Strangler: A murderer's mind.* New York: New American Library.

Schweizer, E., Rickels, K., Case, G., & Greenblatt, D.J. (1990). Long-term therapeutic use of benzodiazapines: Effects of gradual taper. *Archives of General Psychiatry, 47,* 908-915.

Schwitzgebel, R.L., & Schwitzgebel, R.K. (1980). *Law and psychological practice.* New York: Wiley.

Scientific perspectives on cocaine abuse. (1987). *Pharmacologist, 29,* 20-27.

Scoggin, F., & McElreath, L. (1994). Efficacy of psychosocial treatments for geriatric depression: A quantitative review. *Journal of Consulting and Clinical Psychology, 62,* 69-74.

Scogin, F. (1998). Anxiety in old age. In I.H. Nordhus, G.R. VandenBos, S. Berg, & P. Fromholt, (Eds.), *Clinical geropsychology* (pp. 205-209). Washington, D.C.: American Psychological Association.

Scroppo, J.C., Drob, S.L., Weinberger, J.L., & Eagle, P. (1998). Identifying dissociative identity disorder: A self-report and projective study. *Journal of Abnormal Psychology, 107,* 272-284.

Searight, H.R., & Pound, P. (1994). The HIV-positive psychiatric patient and the duty to protect: Ethical and legal issues. *International Journal of Psychiatry in Medicine, 24,* 259-270.

Seeman, P., & Nizik, H.B. (1990). Dopamine receptors and transporters in Parkinson's disease and schizophrenia. *Federation of Associated Society of Experimental Biology, 4,* 2737-2744.

Seeman, T.E., & Syme, S.L. (1987). Social networks and coronary artery disease: A comparison of the structure and function of social relations as predictors of disease. *Psychosomatic Medicine, 49,* 381-406.

Sees, K. L., Delucchi, K. L., Masson, C. et al. (2000). Methadone maintenance vs 180-day psychosocially enriched detoxification for treatment of opioid dependence. *JAMA, 283,* 578-589.

Segal, Z.V., Williams, J. M., & Teasdale, J. D. (2001). *Mindfulness-based cognitive therapy for depression.* New York: Guilford.

Segal, Z.V., & Shaw, B.F. (1988). Cognitive assessment: Issues and methods. In K.S. Dobson (Ed.), *Handbook of cognitive behavioral therapies* (pp. 39-81). New York: Guilford.

Segal, Z.V., Gemar, M., Truchon, C., Guirguis, M., & Horowitz, L.M. (1995). A priming methodology for studying self-representation in major depressive disorder. *Journal of Abnormal Psychology, 104,* 205-213.

Segraves, K.B., & Segraves, R.T. (1991). Hypoactive sexual desire disorder: Prevalence and comorbidity in 906 subjects. *Journal of Sex and Marital Therapy, 17,* 55-58.

Segraves, R.T. (1990). Theoretical orientations in the treatment of marital discord. In F.D. Fincham & T.N. Bradbury (Eds.), *The psychology of marriage: Basic issues and applications* (pp. 281-298). New York: Guilford.

Segraves, R.T., & Althof, S. (1998). Psychotherapy and pharmacotherapy of sexual dysfunctions. In P.E. Nathan & J.M. Gorman (Eds.), *A guide to treatments that work.* NY: Oxford.

Segraves, R.T., & Segraves, K.B. (1995). Human sexuality and aging. *Journal of Sex Education and Therapy, 21,* 88-102.

Selemon, L.D., Rajkowska, G., & Goldman-Rakic, P.S. (1995). Abnormally high neuronal density in the schizophrenic cortex: A morphometric analysis of prefrontal area 9 and occipital area 17. *Archives of General Psychiatry, 52,* 805-818.

Seligman, L. (1990). *Selecting effective treatments: A comprehensive, systematic guide to treating adult mental disorders.* San Francisco: Jossey-Bass.

Seligman, M.E.P. (1971). Phobias and preparedness. *Behavior Therapy, 2,* 307-320.

Seligman, M.E.P. (1974). Depression and learned helplessness. In R.J. Friedman & M.M. Katz (Eds.), *The psychology of depression: Contemporary theory and research.* Washington, DC: Winston-Wiley.

Seligman, M.E.P. (1995). The effectiveness of psychotherapy: The Consumer Reports study. *American Psychologist, 50,* 965-974.

Seligman, M.E.P. (1996). Science as an ally of practice. *American Psychologist, 51,* 1072-1079.

Seligman, M.E.P., & Binik, U. (1977). The safety signal hypothesis. In H. Davis & H. Horowitz (Eds.), *Operant-Pavlovian interaction.* Hillsdale, NJ: Erlbaum.

Seligman, M.E.P., Abramson, L.V., Semmel, A., & Von Beyer, C. (1979). Depressive attributional style. *Journal of Abnormal Psychology, 88,* 242-247.

Selling, L.S. (1940). *Men against madness.* New York: Greenberg.

Seltzer, L.F. (1986). *Paradoxical strategies in psychotherapy: A comprehensive overview and guidebook.* New York: Wiley.

Selye, H. (1950). *The physiology and pathology of exposure to stress.* Montreal: Acta.

Semrud-Clikeman, M., Biederman, J., Sprich-Buckminster, S., Lehman, B.K., Faraone, S.V., & Norman, D. (1992). Comorbidity between ADDH and learning disability: A review and report in a clinically referred sample. *Journal of the American Academy of Child and Adolescent Psychiatry, 31,* 439-448.

Serdula, M.K., Mokdad, A.H., Williamson, D.F., Galuska, D.A., et al. (1999). Prevalence of attempting weight loss and strategies for controlling weight. *JAMA, 282,* 1353-1358.

Seto, M.C., & Barbaree, H.E. (2000). Paraphilias. In V.B. Van Hasselt & M. Hersen (Eds.), *Aggression and violence: An introductory text* (pp. 198-213). Needham Heights, MA: Allyn & Bacon.

Settin, J.M. (1982). Clinical judgment in geropsychology practice. *Psychotherapy: Theory, Research and Practice, 19,* 397-404.

Shachnow, J., Clarkin, J., DiPalma, C.-S., Thurston, F., et al. (1997). Biparental psychopathology and borderline personality disorder. *Psychiatry—Interpersonal and Biological Processes, 60,* 171-181.

Shader, R.I., & DiMascio, A. (1970). *Psychotropic drug side-effects: Clinical and theoretical perspectives.* Baltimore: Williams & Wilkins.

Shaffer, D., Fisher, P. Lucas, C. P. et al. (2000). NIMH Diagnostic Interview for Children Version IV (NIMH DISC-IV): Description, differences from previous versions, and reliability of some common diagnoses. *Journal of the American Academy of Child & Adolescent Psychiatry, 39,* 28-38.

Shalev, A.Y., Peri, T., Brandes, D. et al. (2000). Auditory startle response in trauma survivors with posttraumatic stress disorder: A prospective study. *American Journal of Psychiatry, 157,* 255-261.

Shalev, A.Y., Peri, T., Canetti, L., & Schreiber, S. (1996). Predictors of post-traumatic stress disorder in injured trauma survivors: A prospective study. *American Journal of Psychiatry, 153,* 219-225.

Shalev, A.Y., Sahar, T., Freedman, S., Peri, T., Glick, N., Brandes, D., et al. (1998). A prospective study of heart rate response following trauma and the subsequent development of posttraumatic stress disorder. *Archives of General Psychiatry, 55,* 553-560.

Sham, P.C., Jones, P., Russell, A., Gilvarry, K., Bebbington, P., et al. (1994). Age of onset, sex and familial psychiatric morbidity in schizophrenia. *British Journal of Psychiatry, 165,* 466-473.

Shaper, A.G. (1990). Alcohol and mortality: A review of prospective studies. *British Journal of Addiction, 85,* 837-847.

Shapiro, D., Goldstein, I.B., & Jamner, L.D. (1995). Effects of anger and hostility, defensiveness, gender and family history of hypertension on cardiovascular reactivity. *Psychophysiology, 32,* 425-435.

Shapiro, D., Jamner, L.D., & Goldstein, I.B. (1993). Ambulatory stress psychophysiology: The study of "compensatory and defensive counterforces" and conflict in a natural setting. *Psychosomatic Medicine, 55,* 309-323.

Shapiro, D., Tursky, B., & Schwartz, G.E. (1970). Control of blood pressure in man by operant conditioning. *Circulation Research, 26,* 127-132.

Shapiro, D.A., Barkham, M., Rees, A., Hardy, G., Reynolds, S., & Startup, M. (1994). Effects of treatment duration and severity of depression on the effectiveness of cognitive-behavioral and psychodynamic-interpersonal psychotherapy. *Journal of Consulting and Clinical Psychology, 62,* 522-534.

Shapiro, F. (1999). Eye Movement Desensitization and Reprocessing (EMDR) and the anxiety disorders: Clinical and research implications of an integrated psychotherapy treatment. *Journal of Anxiety Disorders, 13,* 35-67.

Sharkansky, E.J., King, D.W., King, L.A. et al. (2000). Coping with Gulf War combat stress: Mediating and moderating effects. *Journal of Abnormal Psychology 109,* 188-197.

Shaw, B.F. (1977). Comparison of cognitive therapy and behavior therapy in the treatment of depression. *Journal of Consulting and Clinical Psychology, 45,* 543-551.

Shaw, B.F. (1984). Specification of the training and evaluation of cognitive therapists for outcome studies. In J.B.W. Williams & R.L. Spitzer (Eds.), *Psychotherapy research: Where are we and where should we go?* New York: Guilford.

Shaywitz, S.E., Shaywitz, B.A., Fletcher, J.M., & Escobar, M.D. (1990). Prevalence of reading disability in boys and girls. *Journal of the American Medical Association, 264,* 998-1002.

Shea, M.T., Elkin, I., Imber, S.D., Sotsky, S.M., Watkins, J.T., Collins, J.F., Beckham, E., Glass, D.R., Dolan, R.T., & Parloff, M.B. (1992). Course of depressive symptoms over follow-up: Findings from the National Institute of Mental Health Treatment of Depression Collaborative Research Program. *Archives of General Psychiatry, 49,* 782-787.

Shea, M.T., Pilkonis, P.A., Beckham, E., Collins, J.F., Elkin, I., Sotsky, S.M., & Docherty, J.P. (1990). Personality disorders and treatment outcome in the NIMH Treatment of Depression Collaborative Research Program. *American Journal of Psychiatry, 147*, 711-718.

Shekelle, R.B., Honey, S.B., Neaton, J., Billings, J., Borlani, N., Gerace, T., Jacobs, D., Lasser, N., & Stander, J. (1983). Type A behavior pattern and coronary death in MRFIT. *American Heart Association Cardiovascular Disease Newsletter, 33*, 34.

Sheppard, D.M., Bradshaw, J.L., Purcell, R., & Pantelis, C. (1999). Tourette's and comorbid syndromes: Obsessive-compulsive and attention deficit hyperactivity disorder. A common etiology? *Clinical Psychology Review, 19*, 531-552.

Sher, K.J., & Levenson, R.W. (1982). Risk for alcoholism and individual differences in the stress-response-dampening effects of alcohol. *Journal of Abnormal Psychology, 91*, 350-367.

Sher, K.J., & Otto, R. (1983). Cognitive deficits in compulsive checkers: An exploratory study. *Behaviour Research and Therapy, 21*, 357-363.

Sher, K.J., Martin, E.D., Wood, P.K., & Rutledge, P.C., . (1997). Alcohol use disorders and neuropsychological functioning in first year undergraduates. *Experimental and Clinical Psychopharmacology, 5*, 304-315.

Sher, K.J., Walitzer, K.S., Wood, P.K., & Brent, E.F. (1991). Characteristics of children of alcoholics: Putative risk factors, substance use and abuse, and psychopathology. *Journal of Abnormal Psychology, 100*, 427-448.

Sherman, D.K., Iacono, W.G., & McGue, M.K. (1997). Attention-deficit hyperactivity disorder dimensions: A twin study of inattention and impulsivity-hyperactivity. *Journal of the American Academy of Child and Adolescent Psychiatry, 36*, 745-753.

Sherwin, B.B. (1991). The psychoendocrinology of aging and female sexuality. *Annual Review of Sex Research, 2*, 181-198.

Shiffman, S., Fischer, L.A., Paty, J.A., Gnys, M., et al. (1994). Drinking and smoking: A field study of their association. *Annals of Behavioral Medicine, 16*, 203-209.

Shneidman, E.S. (1973). Suicide. In *Encyclopedia Britannica*. Chicago: Encyclopedia Britannica.

Shneidman, E.S. (1976). A psychological theory of suicide. *Psychiatric Annals, 6*, 51-66.

Shneidman, E.S. (1985). *Definition of suicide*. New York: Wiley.

Shneidman, E.S. (1987). A psychological approach to suicide. In G.R. VandenBos & B.K. Bryant (Eds.), *Cataclysms, crises, and catastrophes: Psychology in action*. Washington, DC: American Psychological Association.

Shneidman, E.S., & Farberow, N.L. (1970). A psychological approach to the study of suicide notes. In E.S. Shneidman, N.L. Farberow, & R.E. Litman (Eds.), *The psychology of suicide*. New York: Jason Aronson.

Shneidman, E.S., Farberow, N.L., & Litman, R.E. (Eds.). (1970). *The psychology of suicide*. New York: Jason Aronson.

Shobe, K.K., & Kihlstrom, J.F. (1997). Is traumatic memory special? *Current Directions in Psychological Science, 6*, 70-74.

Shoda, Y., Mischel, W., & Wright, J.C. (1994). Intraindividual stability in the organization and patterning of behavior: Incorporating psychological situations into the idiographic analysis of personality. *Journal of Personality and Social Psychology, 67*, 674-687.

Shogren, E. (1994, August 18). Treatment against their will. *Los Angeles Times*, pp. A1, A16.

Shoham, V. & Rohrbaugh, M.J. (1999). Paradoxical interventions. In W.E. Craighead & C. Nemeroff (Eds.), *Encyclopedia of Psychology and Neuroscience*. New York: John Wiley & Sons.

Shoham, V., Rohrbaugh, M., & Patterson, J. (1995). Problem- and solution-focused couple therapies: The MRI and Milwaukee models. In N.S. Jacobson & A.S. Gurman (Eds.), *Clinical handbook of couple therapy* (pp. 142-163). New York: Guilford.

Shoham,V., Bootzin, R.R., Rohrbaugh, M., & Urry, H. (1995). Paradoxical versus relaxation treatment for insomnia: The moderating role of practice. *Sleep Research, 25a*, 365.

Shoham-Salomon, V., & Rosenthal, R. (1987). Paradoxical interventions: A meta-analysis. *Journal of Consulting and Clinical Psychology, 55*, 22-27.

Shoham-Salomon, V., Avner, R., & Neeman, R. (1989). You're changed if you do and changed if you don't: Mechanisms underlying paradoxical interventions. *Journal of Consulting and Clinical Psychology, 57*, 590-598.

Shontz, F.C., & Green, P. (1992). Trends in research on the Rorschach: Review and recommendations. *Applied and Preventive Psychology, 1*, 149-156.

Shopsin, B., Friedman, E., & Gershon, S. (1976). Parachlorophenylalanine reversal of tranylcypromine effects in depressed patients. *Archives of General Psychiatry, 33*, 811-819.

Shulman, K.I. (1993). Mania in the elderly. *International Review of Psychiatry, 5*, 445-453.

Shure, M., & Spivack, G. (1988). Interpersonal cognitive problem-solving. In R. Price, E. Cowen, R. Lorion, & X. Ramos-McKay (Eds.), *14 ounces of prevention* (pp. 111-122). Washington, DC: American Psychological Association.

Sieg, K.G., Gaffney, G.R., Preston, D.F., & Hellings, J.A. (1995). SPECT brain imaging abnormalities in attention deficit hyperactivity disorder. *Clinical Nuclear Medicine, 20*, 55-60.

Siegel, D., DiClemente, R., Durbin, M., Krasnovsky, F., & Saliba, P. (1995). Change in junior high school students' AIDS-related knowledge, misconceptions, attitudes, and HIV-preventive behaviors: Effects of a school-based intervention. *AIDS Education and Prevention, 7*, 534-543.

Siegel, J.M., Sorenson, S.B., Golding, J.M., Burnam, M.A., & Stein, J.A. (1987). The prevalence of childhood sexual assault: The Los Angeles Epidemiological Catchment Area Project. *American Journal of Epidemiology, 126*, 1141-1153.

Siegel, R.K. (1982). Cocaine smoking. *Journal of Psychoactive Drugs, 14*, 277-359.

Siegler, I.C., & Costa, P.T., Jr. (1985). Health behavior relationships. In J.E. Birren & K.W. Schaie (Eds.), *Handbook of the psychology of aging* (2nd ed.). New York: Van Nostrand-Reinhold.

Siever, L.J., Rotter, M., Losonczy, M., Guo, S.-L., et al. (1997). Lateral ventricular enlargement in schizotypal personality disorder. *Psychiatry Research, 57*, 109-118.

Sifton, D.W. (1988). *PDR drug interactions and side effects index*. Oradell, NJ: Medical Economics.

Sigman, M. (1994). What are the core deficits in autism? In S.H. Broman, & J. Grafman (Eds.), *Atypical cognitive deficits in developmental disorders: Implications for brain function* (pp. 139-157). Hillsdale, NJ: Lawrence Erlbaum Associates.

Sigman, M., Ungerer, J.A., Mundy, P., & Sherman, T. (1987). Cognition in autistic children. In D.J. Cohen, A.M. Donnellan, & R. Paul (Eds.), *Handbook of autism and pervasive developmental disorders* (pp. 103-120). New York: Wiley.

Silberg, J., Pickles, A., Rutter, M., Hewitt, J., Simonoff, E., et al. (1999). The influence of genetic factors and life stress on depression among adolescent girls. *Archives of General Psychiatry, 56*, 225-233.

Silberg, J., Rutter, M., Meyer, J., Maes, H., Hewitt, J., Simonoff, E., Pickles, A., Loeber, R., & Eaves, L. (1996). Genetic and environmental influences on the covariation between hyperactivity and conduct disturbance in juvenile twins. *Journal of Child Psychology and Psychiatry, 37*, 803-816.

Silva, R.R., Alpert, M., Munoz, D.M. et al. (2000). Stress and vulnerability to post-traumatic stress disorder in children and adolescents. *American journal of Psychiatry, 157*, 1229-1235.

Silverman, J.M., Li, G., Zaccario, M.L., Smith, C., Schmeidler, J., et al. (1994). Patterns of risk in first-degree relatives with Alzheimer's disease. *Archives of General Psychiatry, 51*, 568-576.

Silverman, K., Evans, S.M., Strain, E.C., & Griffiths, R.R. (1992). Withdrawal syndrome after the double-blind cessation of caffeine consumption. *New England Journal of Medicine, 327*, 1109-1114.

Silverman, K., Higgins, S.T., Brooner, R.K., Montoya, I.D., Cone, E.J., Schuster, C.R., & Preston, K.I. (1996). Sustained cocaine abstinence in methadone maintenance patients through voucher-based reinforcement therapy. *Archives of General Psychiatry, 53*, 409-413.

Silverstein, B., Feld, S., & Kozlowski, L.T. (1980). The availability of low-nicotine cigarettes as a cause of cigarette smoking among teenage females. *Journal of Health and Social Behavior, 21*, 383-388.

Silverstein, C. (1972). *Behavior modification and the gay community*. Paper presented at the annual convention of the Association for Advancement of Behavior Therapy, New York.

Simeon, D., Gross, S., Guralnik, O., Stein, D.J., Schmeidler, J., & Hollander, E. (1997). Feeling unreal: 30 cases of DSM-III-R depersonalization disorder. *American Journal of Psychiatry, 154*, 1107-1112.

Simon, G.E., Von Korff, M., Rutter, C.M., & Peterson, D.A. (2001). Treatment process and outcomes for managed care patients receiving new antidepressant prescriptions from psychiatrists and primary care physicians. *Archives of General Psychiatry, 58*, 395-401.

Simon, G.E. (1998). Management of somatoform and factitious disorders. In P.E.

Nathan & J.M. Gorman (Eds.), *A guide to treatments that work* (pp. 408-422). New York: Oxford University Press.

Simon, G.E., & Gureje, O. (1999). Stability of somatization disorder and somatization symptoms among primary care patients. *Archives of General Psychiatry, 56,* 90-95.

Simon, G.E., VonKorff, M., Piccinelli, M., Fullerton, C., & Ormel, J. (1999). An international study of the relation between somatic symptoms and depression. *New England Journal of Medicine, 341,* 1329-1335.

Simon, R.J., & Aaronson, D.E. (1988). *The insanity defense: A critical assessment of law and policy in the post-Hinckley era.* New York: Praeger.

Simons, A.D., Garfield, S.L., & Murphy, G.E. (1984). The process of change in cognitive therapy and pharmacotherapy for depression: Changes in mood and cognition. *Archives of General Psychiatry, 41,* 45-51.

Simons, A.D., Lustman, P.J., Wetzel, R.D., & Murphy, G.E. (1985). Predicting response to cognitive therapy of depression: The role of learned resourcefulness. *Cognitive Therapy and Research, 9,* 79-89.

Simons, A.D., Murphy, G.E., Levine, J.L., & Wetzel, R.D. (1985). Sustained improvement one year after cognitive and/or pharmacotherapy of depression. *Archives of General Psychiatry, 43,* 43-48.

Simons, M. (1996, June 28). For first time, court defines rape as war crime. *New York Times,* 1.

Sinclair, J.J., Larzelere, R.E., Paine, M., Jones, P., et al. (1995). Outcome of group treatment for sexually abused adolescent females living in a group home setting: Preliminary findings. *Journal of Interpersonal Violence, 10,* 533-542.

Singer, J.L. (1984). The private personality. *Personality and Social Psychology Bulletin, 10,* 7-30.

Singer, R., & Ryff, C.D. (1999). Hierarchies of life histories and associated health risks. In N.E. Alder, M. Marmot, B.E., McEwen, & J. Stewart (Eds.), *Socioeconomic status and health in industrial nations: social, psychological, ad biological pathways* (pp. 96-115). New York: New York Academy of Sciences.

Sinnott, J.D. (1986). *Sex roles and aging: Theory and research from a systems perspective.* Basel, Switzerland: Karger.

Sintchak, G.H., & Geer, J.H. (1975). A vaginal plethysmograph system. *Psychophysiology, 12,* 113-115.

Siris, S.G., Bermanzohn, P.C., Mason, S.E., & Shuwall, M.A. (1994). Maintenance imipramine therapy for secondary depression in schizophrenia: A controlled trial. *Archives of General Psychiatry, 51,* 109-115.

Sisson, R.W., & Azrin, N.H. (1989). The community-reinforcement approach. In R.K. Hester & W.R. Miller (Eds.), *Handbook of alcoholism treatment approaches: Effective alternatives* (pp. 242-258). New York: Pergamon.

Sizemore, C.C., & Pittillo, E.S. (1977). *I'm Eve.* Garden City, NY: Doubleday.

Sizemore, J.P. (1995). Alabama's confidentiality quagmire: Psychotherapists, AIDS, mandatory reporting, and Tarasoff. *Law and Psychology Review, 19,* 241-257.

Skinner, B.F. (1953). *Science and human behavior.* New York: Macmillan.

Sklar, L.A., & Anisman, H. (1979). Stress and coping factors influence tumor growth. *Science, 205,* 513-515.

Skodol, A.E., Gallaher, P.E., & Oldham, J.M. (1997). Excessive dependency and depression: Is the relationship specific? *Journal of Nervous and Mental Disease, 184,* 165-171.

Skodol, A.E., Oldham, J.M., & Gallaher, P.E. (1999). Axis II comorbidity of substance use disorders among patients referred for treatment of personality disorders. *American Journal of Psychiatry, 156,* 733-738.

Skolnick, A.S. (1998). Guidelines for treating erectile dysfunction issued. *JAMA, 277,* 24-26.

Skoog, G., & Skoog, I. (1999). A 40-year follow-up of patients with obsessive-compulsive disorder. *Archives of General Psychiatry, 56,* 121-130.

Slater, E. (1961). The thirty-fifth Maudsley lecture: Hysteria 311. *Journal of Mental Science, 107,* 358-381.

Slater, E., & Glithero, E. (1965). A follow-up of patients diagnosed as suffering from hysteria. *Journal of Psychosomatic Research, 9,* 9-13.

Slavson, S.R. (1950). *Analytic group psychotherapy with children, adolescents and adults.* New York: Columbia University Press.

Sloane, R.B. (1980). Organic brain syndrome. In J.E. Birren & R.B. Sloane (Eds.), *Handbook of mental health and aging.* Englewood Cliffs, NJ: Prentice-Hall.

Slutske, W.S., Heath, A.C., Dinwiddie, S.H., Madden, P.A.F., Bucholz, K.K., Dunne, M.P., Stathan, D.J., & Martin, N.G. (1997). Modeling genetic and environmental influences in the etiology of conduct disorder: A study of 2,682 adult twin pairs. *Journal of Abnormal Psychology, 106,* 266-279.

Small, B.J., Fratiglioni, L., Viitanen, M. et al. (2000). The course of cognitive impairment in preclinical Alzheimer disease. *Archives of Neurology , 57,* 839-844.

Small, G.W., & Jarvik, L.F. (1982). The dementia syndrome. *Lancet,* 1443-1446.

Small, G.W., Komanduri, R., Gitlin, M., & Jarvik, L.F. (1986). The influence of age on guilt expression in major depression. *International Journal of Geriatric Psychiatry, 1,* 121-126.

Small, J.C., Klapper, M.H., Milstein, V., Kellans, J.J., Miller, M.J., et al. (1991). Carbamazapine compared with lithium in the treatment of mania. *Archives of General Psychiatry, 48,* 915-921.

Smith, D. (1982) Trends in counseling and psychotherapy. *American Psychologist, 37,* 802-809.

Smith, D.W., Bierman, E.L., & Robinson, N.M. (1978). *The biologic ages of man: From conception through old age.* Philadelphia: Saunders.

Smith, G. (1992). The epidemiology and treatment of depression when it coincides with somatoform disorders, somatization, or panic. *General Hospital Psychiatry, 14,* 265-272.

Smith, G.T., Goldman, M.S., Greenbaum, P.E., & Christiansen, B.A. (1995). Expectancy for social facilitation from drinking: The divergent paths of high expectancy and low expectancy adolescents. *Journal of Abnormal Psychology, 104,* 32-40.

Smith, J., Frawley, P.J., & Polissar, L. (1991). Six- and twelve-month abstinence rates in inpatient alcoholics treated with aversion therapy compared with matched inpatients from a treatment registry. *Alcoholism: Clinical and Experimental Research, 15,* 862-870.

Smith, K.A., Fairburn, C.G., & Cowen, P.J. (1999). Symptomatic relapse in bulimia nervosa following acute tryptophan depletion. *Archives of General Psychiatry, 56,* 171-176.

Smith, K.F., & Bengston, V.L. (1979). Positive consequences of institutionalization: Solidarity between elderly parents and their middle aged children. *The Gerontologist, 5,* 438-447.

Smith, M.U., & Katner, H.P. (1995). Quasi-experimental evaluations of three AIDS prevention activities for maintaining knowledge, improving attitudes, and changing risk behaviors of high school seniors. *AIDS Education and Prevention, 7,* 391-402.

Smith, S.S., & Newman, J.P. (1990). Alcohol and drug dependence in psychopathic and nonpsychopathic criminal offenders. *Journal of Abnormal Psychology, 99,* 430-439.

Smith, T., Snyder, C.R., & Perkins, S.C. (1983). Self-serving function of hypochondriacal complaints: Physical symptoms as self-handicapping strategies. *Journal of Personality and Social Psychology, 44,* 787-797.

Smith, T.W. (1983). Change in irrational beliefs and the outcome of rational-emotive psychotherapy. *Journal of Consulting and Clinical Psychology, 51,* 156-157.

Smith-Warner, S.A., Spiegelman, D., Yaun, S.-S., van den Brandt, P.A., Folsom, A.R., et al. (1998). Alcohol increases risk for breast cancer. *JAMA, 279,* 535-540.

Smolowe, J. (1996, Fall). Older, longer. *Time, 148 (Special Issue),* 76-80.

Smyer, M.A., & Gatz, M. (1995). The public policy context of mental health care for older adults. *The Clinical Psychologist, 48,* 31-36.

Smyer, M.A., Zarit, S.H., & Qualls, S.H. (1990). Psychological interventions with the aging individual. In J.E. Birren & K.W. Schaie (Eds.), *Handbook of the psychology of aging* (3rd ed., pp. 375-403). New York: Academic Press.

Smyth, C., Kalsi, G., Brynjofsson, J., O'Neill, J., Curtis, D., et al. (1996). Further tests for linkage of bipolar affective disorder to the tyrosine hydroxylase gene of chromosome 11p15 in a new series of multiplex British affective disorder pedigrees. *American Journal of Psychiatry, 153,* 271-274.

Smyth, J.M., Soefer, M.H., Hurewitz, A., & Stone, A.A. (1998). The effect of tape-recorded relaxation training on well-being, symptoms, and peak expiratory flow in adult asthmatics: A pilot study. *Psychology and Health, 14,* 487-501.

Smyth, J.M., Soefer, M.H., Kliment, A., & Stone, A.A. (1999). Daily psychosocial factors predict levels and diurnal cycles of asthma symptomatology and peak flow. *Journal of Behavioral Medicine, 22,* 179-193.

Snowdon, D.A., Kemper, S.J., Mortimer, J.A., Greiner, L.H., et al. (1996). Linguistic ability in early life and cognitive function and Alzheimer's disease in late life: Findings from the nun study. *JAMA, 275,* 528-534.

Snyder, D.K., & Wills, R.M. (1989). Behavioral versus insight-oriented marital therapy: Effects of individual and interspousal functioning. *Journal of Consulting and Clinical Psychology, 57,* 39-46.

Snyder, D.K., Wills, R.M., & Grady-Fletcher, A. (1991). Long-term effectiveness of behavioral versus insight-oriented marital therapy: A 4-year follow-up study. *Journal of Consulting and Clinical Psychology, 59,* 138-141.

Snyder, M. (1983). The influence of individuals on situations: Implications for understanding the links between personality and social behavior. *Journal of Personality, 51,* 497-516.

Snyder, M., & White, E. (1982). Moods and memories: Elation, depression, and remembering the events of one's life. *Journal of Personality, 50,* 149-167.

Snyder, S.H. (1974). *Madness and the brain.* New York: McGraw-Hill.

Sobell, L.C., Toneatto, A., & Sobell, M.B. (1990). Behavior therapy. In A.S. Bellack & M. Hersen (Eds.), *Handbook of comparative treatments for adult disorders* (pp. 479-505). New York: Wiley.

Sobell, M.B., & Sobell, L.C. (1976). Second-year treatment outcome of alcoholics treated by individualized behavior therapy: Results. *Behaviour Research and Therapy, 14,* 195-215.

Sobell, M.B., & Sobell, L.C. (1993). *Problem drinkers: Guided self-change treatment.* New York: Guilford.

Society of Behavioral Medicine. (1989). *Bylaws of the Society of Behavioral Medicine.* Washington, DC: Author.

Soloff, P. H., Meltzer, C. C., Greer, P. J. et al. (2000). A fenfluramine-activated FDG-PET study of borderline personality disorder. *Biological Psychiatry, 47,* 540-547.

Solomon, Z., Mikulincev, M., & Flum, H. (1988). Negative life events, coping response, and combat-related psychopathology: A prospective study. *Journal of Abnormal Psychology, 97,* 302-307.

Sorenson, S.B., & Brown, V.B. (1990). Interpersonal violence and crisis intervention on the college campus. *New Directions for Student Services, 49,* 57-66.

Soueif, M.I. (1976). Some determinants of psychological deficits associated with chronic cannabis consumption. *Bulletin of Narcotics, 28,* 25-42.

Southwick, S.M., Krystal, J.H., Morgan, C.A., Johnson, D., Nagy, L.M., et al. (1993). Abnormal noradrenergic function in posttraumatic stress disorder. *Archives of General Psychiatry, 50,* 266-274.

Spacapan, S., & Oskamp, S. (1989). Introduction to the social psychology of aging. In S. Spacapan & S. Oskamp (Eds.), *The social psychology of aging* (pp. 9-24). Newbury Park, CA: Sage.

Spanos, N.P. (1994). Multiple identity enactments and multiple personality disorder: A sociocognitive perspective. *Psychological Bulletin, 116,* 143-165.

Spanos, N.P., Weekes, J.R., & Bertrand, L.D. (1985). Multiple personality: A social psychological perspective. *Journal of Abnormal Psychology, 94,* 362-376.

Spar, J.E., & LaRue, A. (1990). *Geriatric psychiatry.* Washington, DC: American Psychiatric Press.

Sparrow, S.S., Ballo, D.A., & Cicchetti, D.V. (1984). *Vineland Adaptive Behavior Scales.* Circle Pines, MI: American Guidance Service.

Spector, I.P., & Carey, M.P. (1990). Incidence and prevalence of the sexual dysfunctions: A critical review of the empirical literature. *Archives of Sexual Behavior, 19,* 389-408.

Spencer, G. (1989). *Projections of the population of the United States, by age, sex, and race: 1988 to 2080.* Washington, DC: U.S. Department of Commerce.

Spencer, S.J., Steele, C.M., & Quinn, D.M. (1999). Stereotype threat and women's math performance. *Journal of Experimental Social Psychology, 35,* 4-28.

Spencer, T., Biederman, J., Wilens, T., Harding, M., O'Donnell, D., & Griffin, S. (1996). Pharmacotherapy of attention-deficit hyperactivity disorder across the life cycle. *Journal of the American Academy of Child and Adolescent Psychiatry, 35,* 409-432.

Spengler, A. (1977). Manifest sadomasochism of males: Results of an empirical study. *Archives of Sexual Behavior, 6,* 441-456.

Spiegel, D. (1990). Can psychotherapy prolong cancer survival? *Psychosomatics, 31,* 361-366.

Spiegel, D., Bloom, J.R., & Yalom, I. (1981). Group support for patients with metastatic cancer: A randomized prospective outcome study. *Archives of General Psychiatry, 38,* 527-534.

Spiegel, D., Bloom, J.R., Kraemer, H.C., & Gottheil, E. (1989). Effect of psychosocial treatment on survival of patients with metastatic breast cancer. *Lancet, 2,* 888-891.

Spiers, P.A. (1982). The Luria-Nebraska Neuropsychological Battery revisited: A theory in practice or just practicing? *Journal of Consulting and Clinical Psychology, 50,* 301-306.

Spiess, W.F.J., Geer, J.H., & O'Donohue, W.T. (1984). Premature ejaculation: Investigation of factors in ejaculatory latency. *Journal of Abnormal Psychology, 93,* 242-245.

Spinetta, J.J. (1980). Disease-related communication: How to tell. In J. Kellerman (Ed.), *Psychological aspects of childhood cancer.* Springfield, IL: Charles C. Thomas.

Spitzer, R.L., Endicott, J., & Gibbon, M. (1979). Crossing the border into borderline personality and borderline schizophrenia. *Archives of General Psychiatry, 36,* 17-24.

Spitzer, R.L., Gibbon, M., & Williams, J.B.W. (1986). *Structured clinical interview of DSM-IV Axis I disorders.* New York: N.Y. State Psychiatric Institute, Biometrics Research Department.

Spitzer, R.L., Skodol, A.E., Gibbon, M., & Williams, J.B.W. (1981). *DSM-III casebook.* Washington, DC: American Psychiatric Press.

Spitzer, R.M., Stunkard, A., Yanovski, S., Marcus, M.D., Wadden, T., et al. (1993). Binge eating disorders should be included in DSM-IV. *International Journal of Eating Disorders, 13,* 161-169.

Sprague, R.L., & Gadow, K.D. (1976). The role of the teacher in drug treatment. *School Review, 85,* 109-140.

Sprenkle, D.H., & Storm, C.L. (1983). Divorce therapy outcome research: A substantive and methodological review. *Journal of Marital and Family Therapy, 9,* 239-258.

Spunt, B., Goldstein, P., Brownstein, H., & Fendrich, M. (1994). The role of marijuana in homicide. *International Journal of the Addictions, 29,* 195-213.

Squires-Wheeler, E., Skodal, A., Agamo, O.M., Bassett, A.S., et al. (1993). Personality features and disorder in the subjects in the New York High-Risk Project. *Journal of Psychiatric Research, 27,* 379-393.

Srole, L., Langner, T.S., Michael, S.T., Opler, M.K., & Rennie, T.A.C. (1962). *Mental health in the metropolis: The midtown Manhattan study.* New York: McGraw-Hill.

St. Lawrence, J., Jefferson, K.W., Banks, P.G., Cline, T.R., et al. (1994). Cognitive-behavioral group intervention to assist substance-dependent adolescents in lowering HIV infection. *AIDS Education and Prevention, 6,* 425-435.

St. Lawrence, J.S., & Madakasira, S. (1992). Evaluation and treatment of premature ejaculation: A critical review. *International Journal of Psychiatry in Medicine, 22,* 77-97.

Staats, A.W., & Staats, C.K. (1963). *Complex human behavior.* New York: Holt, Rinehart & Winston.

Stacy, A.W., Newcomb, M.D., & Bentler, P.M. (1991). Cognitive motivation and drug use: A 9-year longitudinal study. *Journal of Abnormal Psychology, 100,* 502-515.

Stacy, A.W., Sussman, S., Dent, C.W., Burton, D., & Flay, B.R. (1992). Moderators of peer social influence in adolescent smoking. *Personality and Social Psychology Bulletin, 18,* 163-172.

Stader, S.R., & Hokanson, J.E. (1998). Psychosocial antecedents of depressive symptoms: An evaluation using daily experiences methodology. *Journal of Abnormal Psychology, 107,* 17-26.

Stall, R.D., McKusick, L., Wiley, J., Coates, T., & Ostrow, D. (1986). Alcohol and drug use during sexual activity and compliance with safe sex guidelines for AIDS: The AIDS Behavioral Research Project. *Health Education Quarterly, 13,* 359-371.

Stanford, J.L., & Greenberg, R.S. (1989). Breast cancer incidence in young women by estrogen receptor status and race. *American Journal of Public Health, 79,* 71-73.

Stanley, M.A., & Turner, S.M. (1995). Current status of pharmacological and behavioral treatment of obsessive-compulsive disorder. *Behavior Therapy, 26,* 163-186.

Stanley, M.A., Beck, J.G., & Glassco, J.D. (1997). Treatment of generalized anxiety disorder in older adults: A preliminary comparison of cognitive-behavioral and supportive approaches. *Behavior Therapy, 27,* 565-581.

Stansfield, J.M. (1973). Enuresis and urinary tract infection. In I. Kolvin, R.C. MacKeith, & S.R. Meadow (Eds.), *Bladder control and enuresis* (pp. 102-103). London: William Heinemann.

Stanton, A.H., Gunderson, J.G., Knapp, P.H., Frank, A.E., Vanicelli, M.L., Schnitzer, R., & R. Rosenthal, (1984). Effects of psychotherapy in schizophrenia. *Schizophrenia Bulletin, 10,* 520-563.

Stanton, M.D., & Bardoni, A. (1972). Drug flashbacks: Reported frequency in a military population. *American Journal of Psychiatry, 129,* 751-755.

Stark, K., Rouse, L., & Livingston, R. (1991). Treatment of depression during childhood and adolescence: cognitive-behavioral procedures for the individual and family. In P. C. Kendall (Ed.), *Child and adolescent therapy* (pp.165-206). New York: Guilford.

Stark, K.D., Kaslow, N.J., & Reynolds, W.M. (1987). A comparison of the relative efficacy of self-control therapy and a behavioral problem-solving therapy for depression in children. *Journal of Abnormal Child Psychology, 15*, 91-113.

Stark, K.D., Linn, J.D., MacGuire, M., & Kaslow, N.J. (in press). The social functioning of depressed and anxious children: Social skills, social knowledge, automatic thoughts, and physical arousal. *Journal of Clinical Child Psychology.*

Stark, K.D., Napolitano, S., Swearer, S., Schmidt, K., Jaramillo, D., & Hoyle, J. (1996). Issues in the treatment of depressed children. *Applied and Preventive Psychology, 5*, 59-83.

Stark, K.D., Schmidt, K., Joiner, T.E., & Lux, M.G. (1996). Cognitive triad: Relationship to depressive symptoms, parents' cognitive triad, and perceived parental messages. *Journal of Abnormal Child Psychology, 24*, 615-631.

Stark, K.D., Swearer, S., Sommer, D., Hickey, B.B., Napolitano, S., Kurowski, C., & Dempsey, M. (1998). School-based group treatment for depressive disorders in children. In T.R. Kratochwill & K.C. Stoiber (Eds.), *Handbook of group intervention for children and families* (pp. 68-99). Boston: Allyn & Bacon.

Starr, B.D., & Weiner, M.B. (1981). *The Starr-Weiner report on sex and sexuality in the mature years.* New York: Stein & Day.

Steadman, H.J. (1979). *Beating a rap: Defendants found incompetent to stand trial.* Chicago: University of Chicago Press.

Steadman, H.J., McGreevy, M.A., Morrissey, J.P., Callahan, L.A., Robbins, P.C., & Cirincione, C. (1993). *Before and after Hinckley: Evaluating insanity defense reform.* New York: Guilford.

Steadman, H.J., Mulvey, E.P., Monahan, J., Robbins, P.C., Appelbaum, P.S., Grisso, T., Roth, L.H., & Silver, E. (1998). Violence by people discharged from acute psychiatric inpatient facilities and by others in the same neighborhoods. *Archives of General Psychiatry, 55*, 393-401.

Steele, C.M., & Josephs, R.A. (1988). Drinking your troubles away: 2. An attention-allocation model of alcohol's effects on psychological stress. *Journal of Abnormal Psychology, 97*, 196-205.

Stein, E.A., Pankiewicz, J., Harsch, H.H., Cho, J.-K., Fuller, S.A., et al. (1998). Nicotine-induced limbic cortical activation in the human brain: A functional MRI study. *American Journal of Psychiatry, 155*, 1009-1015.

Stein, L.I., & Test, M.A. (1980). Alternative to mental hospital treatment: I. Conceptual model, treatment program, and clinical evaluation. *Archives of General Psychiatry, 37*, 392-397.

Stein, M.B., Chartier, M.J., Hazen, A.L., Kozak, M.V., Tancer, M.E., et al. (1998). A direct-interview family study of generalized social phobia. *American Journal of Psychiatry, 155*, 90-97.

Stein, M.B., Forde, D.R., Anderson, G., & Walker, J.R. (1997). Obsessive-compulsive disorder in the community: An epidemiologic survey with clinical reappraisal. *American Journal of Psychiatry, 154*, 1120-1126.

Stein, M.B., Fyer, A.J., Davidson, J.R.T., Pollack, M.H., & Wiita, B. (1999). Fluvoxamine treatment of social phobia (social anxiety disorder): A double-blind, placebo-controlled study. *American Journal of Psychiatry, 156*, 756-760.

Stein, M.B., Jang, K.L., & Livesley, W.J. (1999). Heritability of anxiety sensitivity: A twin study. *American Journal of Psychiatry, 156*, 246-251.

Stein, M.B., Walker, J.R., Hazen, A.L., & Forde, D.R. (1997). Full and partial post-traumatic stress disorder: Findings from a community survey. *American Journal of Psychiatry, 154*, 1114-1119.

Steinhausen, H.C. & Metzke, C.W. (1998). Youth self-report of behavioral and emotional problems in a Swiss epidemiological study. *Journal of Youth and Adolescence, 27*, 429-441.

Stephens, B.J. (1985). Suicidal women and their relationships with husbands, boyfriends, and lovers. *Suicide and Life-Threatening Behavior, 15*, 77-89.

Stephens, J.H., & Kamp, M. (1962). On some aspects of hysteria: A clinical study. *Journal of Nervous and Mental Disease, 134*, 305-315.

Stephens, R.S., Roffman, R.A., & Simpson, E.E. (1993). Adult marijuana users seeking treatment. *Journal of Consulting and Clinical Psychology, 61*, 1100-1104.

Steptoe, A. (1997). Stress management. In A. Baum, S. Newman, J. Weinman, R. West, & C. McManus (Eds.), *Cambridge encyclopedia of psychology, health and medicine* (pp. 262-264). Cambridge, UK: Cambridge University Press.

Stern, R.S., & Cobb, J.P. (1978). Phenomenology of obsessive-compulsive neurosis. *British Journal of Psychiatry, 132*, 233-234.

Sternberger, R.T., Turner, S.M., Beidel, D.C., & Calhoun, K.S. (1995). Social phobia: An analysis of possible developmental pathways. *Journal of Abnormal Psychology, 104*, 526-531.

Stets, J.E., & Straus, M.A. (1989). The marriage license as a hitting license: A comparison of assaults in dating, cohabiting, and married couples. *Journal of Family Violence, 4*, 161-180.

Steuer, J.L. (1982). Psychotherapy with older women: Ageism and sexism in traditional practice. *Psychotherapy: Theory, research and practice, 19*, 429-436.

Stevenson, J., & Jones, I.H. (1972). Behavior therapy technique for exhibitionism: A preliminary report. *Archives of General Psychiatry, 27*, 839-841.

Stevenson, J.S., & Topp, R. (1990). Effects of moderate and low intensity long-term exercise by older adults. *Research in Nursing and Health, 13*, 209-213.

Stewart, B.D., Hughes, C., Frank, E., Anderson, B., Kendall, K., & West, D. (1987). Profiles of immediate and delayed treatment seekers. *Journal of Nervous and Mental Disease, 175*, 90-94.

Stewart, J.W., Quitkin, F.M., McGrath, P.J., Amsterdam, J., Fava, M., et al. (1998). Use of pattern analysis to predict differential relapse of remitted patients with major depression during 1 year of treatment with flouxetine or placebo. *Archives of General Psychiatry, 55*, 334-345.

Stewart, W.F., Kawas, C., Corrada, M., & Metter, J.E. (1997). Risk of Alzheimer's disease and duration of NSAID use. *Neurology, 48*, 626-632.

Stice, E. (1998). Relations of restraint and negative affect to bulimic pathology: A longitudinal test of three competing models. *International Journal of Eating Disorders, 23*, 243-260.

Stice, E., Barrera, M., & Chasin, L. (1998). Prospective differential prediction of adolescent alcohol use and problem use: Examining the mechanisms of effect. *Journal of Abnormal Psychology, 107*, 616-628.

Stice, E., Killen, J.D., Hayward, C., & Taylor, C.B. (1998). Age of onset for binge eating and purging during late adolescence: A 4-year survival analysis. *Journal of Abnormal Psychology, 107*, 671-675.

Stinson, F.S., & DeBakey, S.F. (1992). Alcohol-related mortality in the United States 1979-1988. *British Journal of Addiction, 87*, 777-783.

Stolbach, L.L., Brandt, U.C., Borysenko, J.Z., Benson, H., Maurer, S.N., Lesserman, J., Albright, T.E., & Albright, N.L. (1988, April). *Benefits of a mind/body group program for cancer patients.* Paper presented at the annual meeting of the Society for Behavioral Medicine, Boston.

Stolberg, A.L., & Garrison, K.M. (1985). Evaluating a primary prevention program for children of divorce. *American Journal of Community Psychology, 13*, 111-124.

Stolberg, S. (1996a, August 24). Clinton imposes wide crackdown on tobacco firms. *Los Angeles Times*, pp. A1, A10.

Stolberg, S. (1996b, October 1). Ending life on their own terms. *Los Angeles Times*, pp. A1, A14.

Stoller, E.P., & Gibson, R.C. (1994). *Worlds of difference: Inequality in the aging experience.* Thousand Oaks, CA: Pine Forge Press.

Stoller, F.H. (1968). Accelerated interaction: A time-limited approach based on the brief intensive group. *International Journal of Group Psychotherapy, 18*, 220-235.

Stom, M., French, S.A., Resnick, M.D., & Blum, R.W. (1995). Ethnic/racial and socioeconomic differences in dieting behaviors and body image perceptions in adolescents. *International Journal of Eating Disorders, 18*, 173-179.

Stone, A.A. (1975). *Mental health and law: A system in transition.* Rockville, MD: National Institute of Mental Health.

Stone, A.A., & Neale, J.M. (1982). Development of a methodology for assessing daily experiences. In A. Baum and J. Singer (Eds.), *Environment and health.* Hillsdale, NJ: Erlbaum.

Stone, A.A., & Neale, J.M. (1984). The effects of "severe" daily events on mood. *Journal of Personality and Social Psychology, 46*, 137-144.

Stone, A.A., & Shiffman, S. (1994). Ecological momentary assessment (EMA) in behavioral medicine. *Annals of Behavioral Medicine, 16*, 199-202.

Stone, A.A., Bovbjerg, D.H., Neale, J.M., Napoli, A., Valdimarsdottir, H., et al. (1992). Development of common cold symptoms following experimental rhinovirus infection is related to prior stressful life events. *Behavioral Medicine, 18*, 115-120.

Stone, A.A., Cox, D.S., Valdimarsdottir, H., Jandorf, L., & Neale, J.M. (1987). Evidence that secretory IgA antibody is associated with daily mood. *Journal of Personality and Social Psychology, 52*, 988-993.

Stone, A.A., Reed, B.R., & Neale, J.M. (1987). Changes in daily event frequency precede episodes of physical symptoms. *Journal of Human Stress, 13*, 70-74.

Stone, A.A., Schwartz, J., Neale, J.M., Shiffman, S., Marco, C.A., et al. (1998). A comparison of coping assessed by Ecological Momentary Assessment and retrospective recall. *Journal of Personality and Social Psychology, 74*, 1670-1680.

Stone, G. (1982). Health Psychology, a new journal for a new field. *Health Psychology, 1,* 1-6.

Stone, M.H. (1986). Exploratory psychotherapy in schizophrenia-spectrum patients: A reevaluation in the light of long-term follow-up of schizophrenic and borderline patients. *Bulletin of the Menninger Clinic, 50,* 287-306.

Stone, M.H. (1987). Psychotherapy of borderline patients in light of long-term follow-up. *Bulletin of the Menninger Clinic, 51,* 231-247.

Stone, M.H. (1993). *Abnormalities of personality. Within and beyond the realm of treatment.* New York: Norton.

Stone, S.V., & Costa, P.T. (1990). Disease-prone personality or distress-prone personality? The role of neuroticism in coronary heart disease. In H.S. Friedman (Ed.), *Personality and disease.* New York: Wiley.

Stormer, S.M., & Thompson, J.K. (1996). Explanations of body image disturbance: A test of maturational status, negative verbal commentary, and sociological hypotheses. *International Journal of Eating Disorders, 19,* 193-202.

Story, M., French, S.A., Resnick, M.D., & Blum, R.W. (1995). Ethnic/racial and socioeconomic differences in dieting behaviors and body image perceptions in adolescents. *International Journal of Eating Disorders, 18,* 173-179.

Storzbach, D.M., & Corrigan, P.W. (1996). Cognitive rehabilitation for schizophrenia. In P.W. Corrigan & S.C. Yudofsky (Eds.), *Cognitive rehabilitation for neuropsychiatric disorders* (pp.311-327). Washington, DC: American Psychiatric Press.

Strain, E.C., Bigelow, G.E., Liebson, I.A., & Stitzer, M.L. (1999). Moderate- vs high-dose methadone in the treatment of opioid dependence: A randomized trial. *JAMA, 281,* 1000-1005.

Strain, E.C., Bigelow, G.E., Liebson, I.A., & Stitzer, M.L. (1999). Moderate- vs low-dose methadone in the treatment of opioid dependence. *JAMA, 281,* 1000-1005.

Strassberg, D.S., de Gouveia Brazao, C.A., Rowland, D.L., Tan, P., & Slob, A.K. (1999). Clomipramine in the treatment of rapid (premature) ejaculation. *Journal of Sex and Marital Therapy, 25,* 89-101.

Strauss, J.S., Carpenter, W.T., & Bartko, J.J. (1974). The diagnosis and understanding of schizophrenia: Part 3. Speculations on the processes that underlie schizophrenic signs and symptoms. *Schizophrenia Bulletin, 1,* 61-69.

Strauss, M.E., & Ogrocki, P.K. (1996). Confirmation of an association between family history of affective disorder and the depressive syndrome in Alzheimer's disease. *American Journal of Psychiatry, 153,* 1340-1342.

Striegel-Moore, R.H., Wilson, G.T., Wilfley, D.E., Elder, K.A., & Brownell, K.D. (1998). Binge eating in an obese community sample. *International Journal of Eating Disorders, 23,* 27-36.

Stringer, A.Y., & Josef, N.C. (1983). Methylphenidate in the treatment of aggression in two patients with antisocial personality disorder. *American Journal of Psychiatry, 140,* 1365-1366.

Strober, M., Freeman, R., & Morrell, W. (1997). The long-term course of severe anorexia nervosa in adolescents: Survival analysis of recovery, relapse, and outcome predictors over 10-15 years in a prospective study. *International Journal of Eating Disorders, 22,* 339-360.

Strober, M., Lampert, C., Morrell, W., Burroughs, J., & Jacobs, C. (1990). A controlled family study of anorexia nervosa: Evidence of family aggregation and lack of shared transmission with affective disorders. *International Journal of Eating Disorders, 9,* 239-253.

Strober, M., Morrell, B., Burroughs, J., Salkin, B., & Jacobs, C. (1985). A controlled family study of anorexia nervosa. *Journal of Psychiatric Research, 19,* 239-246.

Strober, M., Salkin, B., Burroughs, J., & Morrell, W. (1982). Validity of the bulimia-restrictor distinction in anorexia nervosa. *Journal of Nervous and Mental Disease, 170,* 345-351.

Strong, R., Huang, J.S., Huang, S.S., Chung, H.D., Hale, C., et al. (1991). Degeneration of the cholinergic innervation of the locus ceruleus in Alzheimer's disease. *Brain Research, 542,* 23-28.

Strongman, K.T., & Russell, P.N. (1986). Salience of emotion in recall. *Bulletin of the Psychonomic Society, 24,* 25-27.

Strub, R.L., & Black, F.W. (1981). *Organic brain syndromes: An introduction to neurobehavioral disorders.* Philadelphia: F.A. Davis.

Strunin, L., & Hingson, R. (1987). Acquired immunodeficiency syndrome: Knowledge, beliefs, attitudes, and behaviors. *Pediatrics, 79,* 825-828.

Strupp, H.H. (1989). Psychotherapy: Can the practitioner learn from the researcher? *American Psychologist, 44,* 717-724.

Strupp, H.H., Hadley, S.W., & Gomes-Schwartz, B. (1977). *Psychotherapy for better or worse: An analysis of the problem of negative effects.* New York: Jason Aronson.

Stuart, F.M., Hammond, D.C., & Pett, M.A. (1987). Inhibited sexual desire in women. *Archives of Sexual Behavior, 16,* 91-106.

Stuart, I.R., & Greer, J.G. (Eds.). (1984). *Victims of sexual aggression: Treatment of children, women and men.* New York: Van Nostrand-Reinhold.

Stuart, R.B. (1976). An operant interpersonal program for couples. In D.H.L. Olson (Ed.), *Treating relationships.* Lake Mills, IA: Graphic Publishing.

Stuart, R.B. (1978). Protection of the right to informed consent to participate in research. *Behavior Therapy, 9,* 73-82.

Sturgis, E.T., & Adams, H.E. (1978). The right to treatment: Issues in the treatment of homosexuality. *Journal of Consulting and Clinical Psychology, 46,* 165-169.

Substance Abuse and Mental Health Services Administration (1998). *Substance abuse among older adults. Treatment Improvement Protocol (TIP) Series #26.* Rockville, MD: U.S. Department of Health and Human Services.

Suddath, R.L., Christison, G.W., Torrey, E.F., Cassonova, M.F., Weinberger, D.R. et al. (1990). Anatomical abnormalities in the brains of monozygotic twins discordant for schizophrenia. *New England Journal of Medicine, 322,* 789-793.

Sue, D.W. & Sue, D. (2002). *Counseling the Culturally Diverse: Theory and Practice* (4th ed.). New York: Wiley.

Sue, D.W., & Sue, D. (1999). *Counseling the culturally different* (3rd ed.). NY: Wiley.

Sue, S., Fujino, D. C., Hu, L., & Takeuchi, D. T. (1991). Community mental health services for ethnic minority groups: A test of the cultural responsiveness hypothesis. *Journal of Consulting and Clinical Psychology, 59,* 533-540.

Sue, S., Zane, N., & Young, K. (1994). Research on psychotherapy with culturally diverse populations. In A.E. Bergin & S.L. Garfield (Eds.), *Handbook of psychotherapy and behavior change* (4th ed., pp. 783-820). New York: Wiley.

Sugarman, P., Dumughn, C., Saad, K., Hinder, S., & Bluglass, S. (1994). Dangerousness in exhibitionists. *Journal of Forensic Psychiatry, 5,* 287-296.

Suinn, R.M., & Richardson, R. (1971). Anxiety management training: A nonspecific behavior therapy program for anxiety control. *Behavior Therapy, 2,* 498-510.

Sullivan, H.S. (1953). *The interpersonal theory of psychiatry.* New York: Norton.

Sullivan, P.F. (1995). Mortality in anorexia nervosa. *American Journal of Psychiatry, 152,* 1073-1075.

Sultenfuss, J., & Geczy, B., Jr. (1996). Group therapy on state hospital chronic wards: Some guidelines. *International Journal of Group Psychotherapy, 46,* 163-176.

Sundin, O., _hman, A., Palm, T., & Strom, G. (1995). Cardiovascular reactivity, Type A behavior, and coronary heart disease: Comparisions between myocardial infarction patients and controls during laboratory-induced stress. *Psychophysiology, 32,* 28-35.

Suppes, T., Baldessarini, R.J., Faedda, G.L., & Tohen, M. (1991). Risk of recurrence following discontinuation of lithium treatment in bipolar disorder. *Archives of General Psychiatry, 48,* 1082-1087.

Surles, R.C., Blanch, A.K., Shern, D.L., & Donahue, S.A. (1992). Case management as a strategy for systems change. *Health Affairs, 11,* 151-163.

Susser, E., & Wanderling, J. (1994). Epidemiology of nonaffective acute remitting psychosis versus schizophrenia: Sex and sociocultural setting. *Archives of General Psychiatry, 51,* 294-301.

Susser, E., Neugebauer, R., Hoek, H.W., Brown, A.S., Lin, S., et al. (1996). Schizophrenia after prenatal famine: Further evidence. *Archives of General Psychiatry, 53,* 25-31.

Susser, E., Valencia, E., Berkman, A., Sohler, N., Conover, S., Torres, J., Betne, P., Felix, A., & Miller, S. (1998). Human immunodeficiency virus sexual risk reduction in homeless men with mental illness. *Archives of General Psychiatry, 55,* 266-272.

Sussman, S. (1996). Development of a school-based drug abuse prevention curriculum for high-risk youth. *Journal of Psychoactive Drugs, 28,* 169-182.

Sussman, S., Dent, C.W., McAdams, L., Stacy, A.W., Burton, D., & Flay, B.R. (1994). Group self-identification and adolescent cigarette smoking: A 1-year prospective study. *Journal of Abnormal Psychology, 103,* 576-580.

Sussman, S., Dent, C.W., Simon, T.R., Stacy, A.W., Galaif, E.R., Moss, M.A., Craig, S., & Johnson, C.A. (1995). Immediate impact of social influence-oriented substance abuse prevention curricula in traditional and continuation high schools. *Drugs and Society, 8,* 65-81.

Sussman, S., Stacy, A.W., Dent, C.W., Simon, T.R., & Johnson, C.A. (1996). Marijuana use: Current issues and new research directions. *The Journal of Drug Issues, 26,* 695-733.

Sutcliffe, J.P., & Jones, J. (1962). Personal identity, multiple personality, and hypnosis. *International Journal of Clinical and Experimental Hypnosis, 10,* 231-269.

Sutker, P.B., Davis, J.M., Uddo, M., & Ditta, A. (1995). Warzone stress, personal resources, and post-traumatic stress disorder in Persian Gulf War returnees. *Journal of Abnormal Psychology, 104*, 444-453.

Svartberg, M., & Stiles, T.C. (1991). Comparative effects of short-term psychodynamic psychotherapy: A meta-analysis. *Journal of Consulting and Clinical Psychology, 59*, 704-714.

Swain, A., & Suls, J. (1996). Reproducibility of blood pressure and heart rate reactivity: A meta-analysis. *Psychophysiology, 33*, 162-174.

Swan, N. (1994). Marijuana, other drug use among teens continues to rise. *NIDA Notes, 10*, 8-9.

Swann, W.B., Jr. (1996). *Self-traps: The elusive quest for higher self-esteem*. New York: W.H. Freeman.

Swanson, J., McBurnett, K., Christian, D.L., & Wigal, T. (1995). Stimulant medications and the treatment of children with ADHD. In T.H. Ollendick & R.J. Prinz (Eds.), *Advances in clinical child psychology* (Vol 17, pp. 265-322). New York: Plenum.

Swanson, J.W., Holzer, C.E., Ganju, V.K., & Jono, R.T. (1990). Violence and psychiatric disorder in the community: Evidence from the Epidemiological Catchment Area surveys. *Hospital and Community Psychiatry, 41*, 761-770.

Swartz, M., Blazer, D., George, L., & Landerman, R. (1986). Somatization disorder in a community population. *American Journal of Psychiatry, 143*, 1403-1408.

Swartz, M., Blazer, D., George, L., & Winfield, I. (1990). Estimating the prevalence of borderline personality in the community. *Journal of Personality Disorders, 4*, 257-272.

Sweet, J.J., Carr, M.A., Rossini, E., & Kasper, C. (1986). Relationship between the Luria-Nebraska Neuropsychological Battery and the WISC-R: Further examination using Kaufman's factors. *International Journal of Clinical Neuropsychology, 8*, 177-180.

Sweet, R.A., Mulsant, B.H., Gupta, B., Rifai, A.H., Pasternak, R.E., et al. (1995). Duration of neuroleptic treatment and prevalence of tardive dyskinesia in late life. *Archives of General Psychiatry, 52*, 478-486.

Sweeting, H.W. (1995). Family life and health in adolescence. *Social Science and Medicine, 40*, 163-175.

Syndulko, K. (1978). Electrocortical investigations of sociopathy. In R.D. Hare & D. Schalling (Eds.), *Psychopathic behaviour: Approaches to research*. New York: Wiley.

Szasz, T.S. (1963). *Law, liberty, and psychiatry*. New York: Macmillan.

Szasz, T.S. (1986). The case against suicide prevention. *American Psychologist, 41*, 806-812.

Szasz, T.S. (1999). *Fatal freedom: The ethics and politics of suicide*. Westport, CT: Praeger.

Szasz, T.S. (Ed.). (1974). *The age of madness: The history of involuntary hospitalization*. New York: Jason Aronson.

Szatmari, P., Offord, D.R., & Boyle, M.H. (1989). Ontario child health study: Prevalence of attention deficit disorder with hyperactivity. *Journal of Child Psychology and Psychiatry, 30*, 219-230.

Taft, C.T., Stern, A.S., King, L.A., & King, D.W. (1999). Modeling physical health and functional health status: The role of combat exposure, posttraumatic stress disorder, and personal resource attributes. *Journal of Traumatic Stress, 12*, 3-23.

Tallal, P., Miller, S.L., Bedi, G., Byma, G., Wang, X., Nagarajan, S.S., Schreiner, C., Jenkins, W.M., & Merzenich, M.M. (1996). Language comprehension in language-learning impaired children improved with acoustically modified speech. *Science, 271*, 81-84.

Tallmadge, J., & Barkley, R.A. (1983). The interactions of hyperactive and normal boys with their mothers and fathers. *Journal of Abnormal Child Psychology, 11*, 565-579.

Tannock, R. (1998). Attention deficit hyperactivity disorder: Advances in cognitive, neurobiological, and genetic research. *Journal of Child Psychology and Psychiatry, 39*, 65-100.

Tarrier, (1998). Randomised control trial of intensive cognitive behaviour therapy for patients with chronic schizophrenia. *British Medical Journal, 317*, 303-307.

Task Force on Promotion and Dissemination of Psychological Procedures. (1995). Training in and dissemination of empirically-validated psychological treatments: Report and recommendations. *The Clinical Psychologist, 48*, 3-23.

Tate, B.G., & Baroff, G.S. (1966). Aversive control of self-injurious behavior in a psychotic boy. *Behaviour Research and Therapy, 4*, 281-287.

Taylor, C.B. (1983). DSM-III and behavioral assessment. *Behavioral Assessment, 5*, 5-14.

Taylor, C.B., Hayward, C., King, R., et al. (1990). Cardiovascular and symptomatic reduction effects of alprazolam and imipramine in patients with panic disorder: Results of a double-blind, placebo-controlled trial. *Journal of Clinical Psychopharmacology, 10*, 112-118.

Taylor, C.B., Ironson, G., & Burnett, K. (1990). Adult medical disorders. In A.S. Bellak, M. Hersen, & A.E. Kazdin (Eds.), *International handbook of behavior modification and therapy*. New York: Plenum.

Taylor, S.E., & Brown, J.D. (1988). Illusion and well-being: A social psychological perspective on mental health. *Psychological Bulletin, 103*, 193-210.

Taylor, S.E., Kemeny, M.E., Aspinwall, L.G, Schneider, S.G., Rodriguez, R., & Herbert, M. (1992). Optimism, coping, psychological distress, and high-risk sexual behavior among men at risk for acquired immunodeficiency syndrome (AIDS). *Journal of Personality and Social Psychology, 63*, 460-473.

Telch, C.F., & Telch, M.J. (1986). Group coping skills instruction and supportive group therapy for cancer patients: A comparison of strategies. *Journal of Consulting and Clinical Psychology, 54*, 802-808.

Telch, M.J., & Harrington, P.J. (unpublished manuscript). *Anxiety sensitivity and expectedness of arousal in mediating affective response to 35% carbon dioxide inhalation.*

Telch, M.J., Schmidt, N.B., Jaimez, T.L., Jacquin, K.M., & Harrington, P.J. (1995). Impact of cognitive-behavioral treatment on quality of life in panic disorder patients. *Journal of Consulting and Clinical Psychology, 63*, 823-830.

Teplin, L.A. (1984). Criminalizing mental disorder: The comparative arrest rate of the mentally ill. *American Psychologist, 29*, 794-803.

Tercyak, K.P., Lerman, C., Peshkin, B.N., Hughes, C., Main, D., Isaacs, C.N., Schwartz, M.D. (2001). Effects of coping style and BRCA1 and BRCA2 test results on anxiety among women participating in genetic counseling and testing for breast and ovarian cancer risk. *Health Psychology Special Issue, 20*, 217-222.

Teri, L. (1994). Behavioral treatment of depression in patients with dementia. *Alzheimer's Disease and Associated Disorders, 8*, 66-74.

Teri, L., & Lewinsohn, P.M. (1986). Individual and group treatment of unipolar depression: Comparison of treatment outcome and identification of predictors of successful treatment outcome. *Behavior Therapy, 17*, 215-228.

Teri, L., & Logsdon, R.G. (1992). The future of psychotherapy with older adults. *Psychotherapy, 29*, 81-87.

Teri, L., & Reifler, B.V. (1987). Depression and dementia. In L.L. Carstensen & B.A. Edelstein (Eds.), *Handbook of clinical gerontology*. New York: Pergamon.

Terman, L.M. (1995). *Genetic studies of genius*. Stanford, CA: Stanford University Press.

Terman, M., Terman, J.S., & Ross, D.C. (1998). A controlled trial of timed bright light and negative air ionization for treatment of winter depression. *Archives of General Psychiatry, 55*, 875-882.

Terry, D.J., & Hynes, G.J. (1998). Adjustment to a low-control situation: Reexamining the role of coping responses. *Journal of Personality and Social Psychology, 74*, 1078-1092.

Test, M.A. (1992). Training in community living. In R.P. Liberman (Ed.), *Handbook of psychiatric rehabilitation* (pp. 153-170). New York: Macmillan.

Teyber, E., & McClure, F. (2000). Therapist variables. In C. R. Snyder & R. E. Ingram (Eds.), *Handbook of psychological change: Psychotherapy processes & practices for the 21st century* (pp. 62-87). New York: John Wiley & Sons, Inc.

Thayer, J.F., Friedman, B.H., Borkovec, T.D. et al. (2000). Phasic heart period reactions to cued threat and nonthreat stimuli in generalized anxiety disorder. *Psychophysiology, 37*, 361-368.

The MTA Cooperative Group (1999). A 14-month randomized clinical trial of treatment strategies for attention-deficit/hyperactivity disorder. *Archives of General Psychiatry, 56*, 1073-1086.

Theodor, L.H., & Mandelcorn, M.S. (1973). Hysterical blindness: A case report using a psychophysical technique. *Journal of Abnormal Psychology, 82*, 552-553.

Thibaut, J.W., & Kelley, H.H. (1959). *The social psychology of groups*. New York: Wiley.

Thigpen, C.H., & Cleckley, H. (1954). *The three faces of Eve*. Kingsport, TN: Kingsport Press.

Thomas, S., Gilliam, A., & Iwrey, C. (1989). Knowledge about AIDS and reported risk behaviors among black college students. *Journal of American College Health, 31*, 61-66.

Thompson, G.O.B., Raab, G.M., Hepburn, W.S., Hunter, R., Fulton, M., & Laxen, D.P.H. (1989). Blood-lead levels and children's behaviour: Results from the Edinburgh lead study. *Journal of Child Psychology and Psychiatry, 30*, 515-528.

Thompson, L.W., Gallagher, D., & Breckenridge, J.S. (1987). Comparative effectiveness of psychotherapies for depressed elders. *Journal of Consulting and Clinical Psychology, 55*, 385-390.

Thoresen, C.E., Friedman, M., Powell, L.H., Gill, J.J., & Ulmer, D.K. (1985). Altering the type A behavior pattern in postinfarction patients. *Journal of Cardiopulmonary Rehabilitation, 5*, 258-266.

Thyer, B.A., & Curtis, G.C. (1984). The effects of ethanol on phobic anxiety. *Behaviour Research and Therapy, 22*, 599-610.

Tiefer, L., Hall, M., and Tavris, C. (2002). Beyond dysfunction: A new view of women's sexual problems. *Journal of Sex & Marital Therapy, 28*, 225-232.

Tiefer, L., Pedersen, B., & Melman, A. (1988). Psychosocial follow-up of penile prosthesis implant with patients and partners. *Journal of Sex and Marital Therapy, 14*, 184-201.

Tienari, P. (1991). Interaction between genetic vulnerability and family environment: The Finnish adoptive family study of schizophrenia. *Acta Psychiatrica Scandinavica, 84*, 460-465.

Tillfors, M., Furmark, T., Ekselius, L., & Fredrikson, M. (2001). Social phobia and avoidant personality disorder as related to parental history of social anxiety: A general population study. *Behaviour Research and Therapy, 39*, 289-298.

Tillich, P. (1952). *The courage to be.* New Haven, CT: Yale University Press.

Tobin, D.L., Griffing, A., & Griffing, S. (1997). An examination of subtype criteria for bulimia nervosa. *International Journal of Eating Disorders, 22*, 179-186.

Tollefson, D.J. (1972). *The relationship between the occurrence of fractures and life crisis events.* Unpublished Master of Nursing thesis, University of Washington, Seattle.

Tollefson, G.D., Beasley, C.M., Tamura, R.N., Tran, P.V., & Potvin, J.H. (1997). Blind, controlled, long-term study of the comparative incidence of treatment-emergent tardive dyskinesia with olanzapine or haloperidol. *American Journal of Psychiatry, 154*, 1248-1254.

Tollefson, G.D., Rampey, A.H., Jr., Potvin, J.H., Jenike, M.A., Rush, A.J., et al. (1994). A multicenter investigation of fixed-dose fluoxetine in the treatment of obsessive-compulsive disorder. *Archives of General Psychiatry, 51*, 552-558.

Tollefson, G.D., Sanger, T., Lu, L., & Thieme, M.E. (1998). Depressive signs and symptoms in schizophrenia: A prospective trial of olanzapine and haloperidol. *Archives of General Psychiatry, 55*, 250-258.

Tomasson, K., Kent, D., & Coryell, W. (1991). Somatization and conversion disorders: Comorbidity and demographics at presentation. *Acta Psychiatrica Scandinavica, 84*, 288-293.

Tondo, L., Baldessarini, R.J., Hennen, J., & Floris, G. (1998). Lithium maintainance treatment of depression and mania in bipolar I disorders. *American Journal of Psychiatry, 155*, 647-652.

Torgersen, S. (1983). Genetic factors in anxiety disorders. *Archives of General Psychiatry, 40*, 1085-1089.

Torgersen, S. (1986). Genetics of somatoform disorder. *Archives of General Psychiatry, 43*, 502-505.

Torgersen, S., Kringlen, E., & Cramer, V. (2001). The prevalence of personality disorders in a community sample. *Archives of General Psychiatry, 58*, 590-596.

Torrey, E.F. (1996). *Out of the shadows: Confronting America's mental health crisis.* New York: Wiley.

Torrey, E.F., Taylor, E., Bowler, A., & Gottesman, I. (1994). *Schizophrenia and manic depressive disorder: The biological roots of mental illness as revealed by the landmark study of identical twins.* New York: Basic Books.

Tramontana, J., & Stimbert, V. (1970). Some techniques of behavior modification with an autistic child. *Psychological Reports, 27*, 498-515.

Tran, G.Q., Haaga, D.A.F., & Chambless, D.L. (1997). Expecting that alcohol will reduce social anxiety moderates the relation between social anxiety and alcohol consumption. *Cognitive Therapy and Research, 21*, 535-553.

Traskman, L., Asberg, M., Bertilsson, L., & Sjostrand, L. (1981). Monoamine metabolites in CSF and suicidal behavior. *Archives of General Psychiatry, 38*, 631-639.

Treffert, D.A., McAndrew, J.B., & Dreifuerst, P. (1973). An inpatient treatment program and outcome for 57 autistic and schizophrenic children. *Journal of Autism and Childhood Schizophrenia, 3*, 138-153.

Trickett, P.K., & Putnam, F.W. (1993). Impact of child sexual abuse on females: Toward a developmental, psychobiological integration. *Psychological Science, 4*, 81-87.

True, W.R., Xiam, H., Scherrer, J.F., Madden, P., Bucholz, K.K., et al. (1999). Common genetic vulnerability for nicotine and alcohol dependence in men. *Archives of General Psychiatry, 56*, 655-662.

Trull, T. J., Sher, K. J., Minks-Brown, C. et al. (2000). Borderline personality disorder and substance use disorders: A review and integration. *Clinical Psychology Review, 20*, 235-253.

Trull, T.J., Widiger, T.A., & Frances, A. (1987). Covariation of criteria for avoidant, schizoid, and dependent personality disorders. *American Journal of Psychiatry, 144*, 767-771.

Tsai, D. C. & Pike, P. L. (2000). Effects of acculturation on the MMPI-2 scores of Asian American students. *Journal of Personality Assessment, 74*, 216-230.

Tsai, G., Parssani, L.A., Slusher, B.S., Carter, R., Baer, L., et al. (1995). Abnormal excitatory neurotransmitter metabolism in schizophrenic brains. *Archives of General Psychiatry, 52*, 829-836.

Tsoi, W.F. (1990). Developmental profile of 200 male and 100 female transsexuals in Singapore. *Archives of Sexual Behavior, 19*, 595-605.

Tsuang, M.T., & Faraone, S.V. (1990). *The genetics of mood disorders.* Baltimore: Johns Hopkins University Press.

Tsuang, M.T., Lyons, M.J., Meyer, J.M., Doyle, T., Eisen, S.A., et al. (1998). Co-occurrence of abuse of different drugs in men: The role of drug-specific and shared vulnerabilities. *Archives of General Psychiatry, 55*, 967-972.

Tucker, J.A., Vuchinich, R.E., & Downey, K.K. (1992). Substance abuse. In S.M. Turner, K.S. Calhoun, & H.E. Adams (Eds.), *Handbook of clinical behavior therapy* (pp. 203-223). New York: Wiley.

Tugrul, C., & Kabacki, E. (1997). Vaginismus and its correlates. *Sexual and Marital Therapy, 12*, 23-34.

Tune, L.E., Wong, D.F., Pearlson, G.D., Strauss, M.E., Young, T., et al. (1993). Dopamine D2 receptor density estimates in schizophrenia: A positron-emission tomography study with "C-methylspiperone." *Psychiatry Research, 49*, 219-237.

Tuomilehto, J., Geboers, J., Salonen, J.T., Nissinen, A., Kuulasman, K., & Puska, P. (1986). Decline in cardiovascular mortality in North Karelia and other parts of Finland. *British Medical Journal, 293*, 1068-1071.

Tuomisto, M.T. (1997). Intra-arterial blood pressure and heart rate reactivity to behavioral stress in normotensive, borderline, and mild hypertensive men. *Health Psychology, 16*, 554-565.

Turecki, G., Briere, R., Dewar, K., Antonetti, T., Seguin, M., et al. (1999). Prediction of level of serotonin 2A receptor binding by serotonin receptor 2A genetic variation in postmortem brain sample from subjects who did or did not commit suicide. *American Journal of Psychiatry, 156*, 1456-1458.

Turk, C.L., Heimberg, R.G., & Hope, D.A. (2001). Social anxiety disorder. In D.H. Barlow (Ed.), *Clinical Handbook of Psychological Disorders* (pp. 114-153). New York, NY: Guilford Press.

Turk, C.L., Heimberg, R.G., & Hope, D.A. (2001). Social anxiety disorder. In D.H. Barlow (Ed.), *Clinical Handbook of Psychological Disorders* (pp. 114-153). New York, NY: Guilford Press.

Turk, C.L., Lerner, J., Heimberg, R.G., & Rapee, R.M. (2001). An integrated cognitive-behavioral model of social anxiety. In S.G. Hofmann & P.M. DiBartolo (Eds.), *From social anxiety to social phobia: Multiple perspectives* (pp.281-303). Needham Heights, MA: Allyn & Bacon.

Turk, D.C. (1996). Cognitive factors in chronic pain and disability. In K.S. Dobson & K.D. Craig (Eds.), *Advances in cognitive-behavioral therapy* (pp. 83-115). Thousand Oaks, CA: Sage.

Turk, D.C., Meichenbaum, D.H., & Genest, M. (1983). *Pain and behavioral medicine: A cognitive behavioral perspective.* New York: Guilford.

Turk, D.C., Wack, J.T., & Kerns, R.D. (1985). An empirical examination of the "pain behavior" construct. *Journal of Behavioral Medicine, 8*, 119-130.

Turkat, I.D., & Maisto, S.A. (1985). Personality disorders: Application of the experimental method to the formulation and modification of personality disorders. In D.H. Barlow (Ed.), *Clinical handbook of psychological disorders.* New York: Guilford.

Turk-Charles, S., Rose, T., & Gatz, M. (1996). The significance of gender in the treatment of older adults. In L.L. Carstensen, B.A. Edelstein, & L. Dornbrand (Eds.), *The practical handbook of clinical gerontology* (pp. 107-128). Thousand Oaks, CA: Sage.

Turkewitz, H., & O'Leary, K.D. (1977). *A comparison of communication and behavioral marital therapy.* Paper presented at the Eleventh Annual Convention of the Association for Advancement of Behavior Therapy, Atlanta.

Turkheimer, E. (1998). Heritability and biological explanation. *Psychological Review, 105*, 782-791.

Turkheimer, E., & Parry, C.D. (1992). Why the gap? Practice and policy in civil commitment hearings. *American Psychologist, 47*, 646-655.

Turner, B.F., & Adams, C.G. (1988). Reported change in preferred sexual activity. *The Journal of Sex Research, 25*, 289-303.

Turner, C.F., Ku, S.M., Rogers, L.D., Lindberg, J.H., & Pleck, F.L. (1998). Adolescent sexual behavior, drug use, and violence: Increased reporting with computer survey technology. *Science, 280*, 867-873.

Turner, J.A., Deyo, R.A., Loeser, J.D., Von Korff, M., & Fordyce, W.E. (1994). The importance of placebo effects in pain treatment and research. *JAMA, 271*, 1609-1614.

Turner, L.A., Althof, S.E., Levine, S.B., Risen, C.B., Bodner, D.R., Kursh, E.D., & Resnick, M.I. (1989). Self-injection of papaverine and phentolamine in the treatment of psychogenic impotence. *Journal of Sex and Marital Therapy, 15*, 163-176.

Turner, R.J., & Sternberg, M.P. (1978). Psychosocial factors in elderly patients admitted to a psychiatric hospital. *Age and Aging, 7*, 171-177.

Turner, R.J., & Wagonfeld, M.O. (1967). Occupational mobility and schizophrenia. *American Sociological Review, 32*, 104-113.

Turner, R.M. (1993). Dynamic-cognitive-behavior therapy. In T. Giles (Ed.), *Handbook of effective psychotherapy* (pp. 437-454). New York: Plenum.

Turner, R.M. (1994). Borderline, narcissistic, and histrionic personality disorders. In M. Hersen & R.T. Ammerman (Eds.), *Handbook of prescriptive treatments for adults* (pp. 393-420). New York: Plenum.

Turner, S.M., Beidel, D.C., & Cooley-Quille, M.R. (1995). Two-year follow-up of social phobics treated with Social Effectiveness Therapy. *Behaviour Research and Therapy, 33*, 553-555.

Turner, S.M., Beidel, D.C., & Townsley, R.M. (1992). Behavioral treatment of social phobia. In S.M. Turner, K.S. Calhoun, & H.E. Adams (Eds.), *Handbook of clinical behavior therapy* (2nd ed., pp. 13-37). New York: Wiley.

Tuschen, B., & Bent, H. (1995). Intensive brief inpatient treatment of bulimia nervosa. In K.D. Brownell & C.G. Fairburn (Eds.), *Eating disorders and obesity: A comprehensive handbook*. New York: Guilford.

Tustin, F. (1990). *Autistic states in children* (revised edition). London and New York: Tavistock/Routledge.

Tustin, F. (1994). Autistic children who are assessed as not brain-damaged. *Association of Child Psychotherapists, 20*, 103-131.

Tustin, F. (1995). *Autism and childhood psychosis*. London: Karnac Books.

Twentyman, C.T., & McFall, R.M. (1975). Behavioral training of social skills in shy males. *Journal of Consulting and Clinical Psychology, 43*, 384-395.

Tye, J. (1991). *Stop teenage addiction to tobacco*. Springfield, MA: Stop Teen Addiction to Tobacco.

Tykra, A.R., Cannon, T.D., Haslam, N., Mednick, S.A, Schulsinger, F., et al. (1995). The latent structure of schizotypy. I. Premorbid indicators of a taxon of individuals at risk for schizophrenia spectrum disorders. *Journal of Abnormal Psychology, 104*, 173-184.

U.S. Bureau of the Census (1999). *Current population reports, special studies*. Washington, DC: U.S. Government Printing Office.

U.S. Bureau of the Census. (1986). *Statistical brief*. Washington, DC: U.S. Government Printing Office.

U.S. Department of Health and Human Services (1991). *Health United States: 1990*. Washington, DC. U.S. Government Printing Office.

U.S. Department of Health and Human Services, National Center for Health Statistics. (1990a, August 30). *Monthly vital statistics*.

U.S. Department of Health and Human Services. (1982). Prevention in adulthood: Self-motivated quitting. In *Cancer: The health consequences of smoking, a report of the Surgeon General*. Washington, DC: U.S. Government Printing Office.

U.S. Department of Health and Human Services. (1989). *Reducing the health consequences of smoking: 25 years of progress. A report of the surgeon general, Executive summary* (DHHS Publication No. CDC 89-8411). Washington, DC: U.S. Government Printing Office.

U.S. Department of Health and Human Services. (1990b). *The health benefits of smoking cessation: A report of the surgeon general*. Alexandria, VA: Author.

U.S. Department of Health and Human Services. (1993). *Eighth special report to the U.S. Congress on alcohol and health*. Alexandria, VA: Author.

U.S. Department of Health and Human Services. (1994). *National survey results on drug use from the Monitoring the Future Study, 1975-1993*. Rockville, MD: National Institute on Drug Abuse.

U.S. Department of Health and Human Services. (1997). *Alcohol and health*. Washington, DC: NIH.

U.S. Department of Health and Human Services. (2002). *Supplement to Mental Health: A Report of the Surgeon General* (SMA-01-3613). Retrieved July 2, 2002, from http://www.mentalhealth.org/Publications/allpubs/SMA-01-3613/sma-01-3613.pdf.

Uchinuma,Y. & Sekine, Y. (2000). Dissociative identity disorder (DID) in Japan: A forensic case report and the recent increase in reports of DID. *International Journal of Psychiatry in Clinical Practice, 4*, 155-160.

Ullmann, L., & Krasner, L. (1975). *A psychological approach to abnormal behavior* (2nd ed.). Englewood Cliffs, NJ: Prentice-Hall.

Upper, D., & Ross, S.M. (Eds.). (1980). *Behavioral group therapy 1980: An annual review*. Champaign, IL: Research Press.

USDHHS. (1998). *NHLBLI report of the task force on Behavioral Research in Cardiovascular, Lung, and Blood Health and Disease*. Washington, D.C.: U.S. Government Printing Office.

Usman, M.A. (1997). Frontotemporal dementias. In P.D. Nussbaum (Ed.), *Handbook of neuropsychology and aging* (pp. 159-176). NY: Plenum.

Vacha-Haase, T., Kogan, L.R., Tani, C.R. & Woodall, R.A. (2001). Reliability generalization: Exploring variation of reliability coefficients of MMPI clinical scale scores. *Educational and Psychological Measurement, 61*, 45-49.

Vaillant, G.E. (1979). Natural history of male psychologic health: Effects of mental health on physical health. *New England Journal of Medicine, 301*, 1249-1254.

Vaillant, G.E. (1996). A long-term follow-up of male alcohol abuse. *Archives of General Psychiatry, 53*, 243-250.

Vakoch, D.A., & Strupp, H.H. (2000). Psychodynamic approaches to psychotherapy: Philosophical and theoretical foundations of effective practice. In C.R. Snyder & R.E. Ingram (Eds.), *Handbook of Psychological Change: Psychotherapy processes & practices for the 21st century* (pp. 200-216). New York: John Wiley & Sons, Inc.

Valdes, M., Garcia, L., Treserra, J., et al. (1989). Psychogenic pain and depressive disorders: An empirical study. *Journal of Affective Disorders, 16*, 21-25.

Van Amerigen, M.A., Lane, R.M., Walker, J.R. et al. (2001). Sertreline treatment of generalized social phobia: A 20-week, double-blind, placebo-controlled study. *American Journal of Psychiatry, 158*, 275-281.

van den Broucke, S., Vandereycken, W., & Vertommen, H. (1995). Marital communication in eating disorders: A controlled observational study. *International Journal of Eating Disorders, 17*, 1-23.

Van den Oord, E.J., Boomsma, D.I., & Verhulst, F.C. (1994). A study of problem behaviors in 10- to 15-year-old biologically related and unrelated international adoptees. *Behavior Genetics, 24*, 193-205.

van Egeren, L.F., & Madarasmi, S. (1987). A computerized diary for ambulatory blood pressure monitoring. In N. Schneiderman (Ed.), *Handbook on methods and measurements in cardiovascular behavioral medicine*. New York: Plenum.

van Praag, H., Plutchik, R., & Apter, A. (Eds.), (1990). *Violence and suicidality*. New York: Brunner/Mazel.

van Reekum, R., Conway, C.A., Gansler, D., & White, R. (1993). Neurobehavioral study of borderline personality disorder. *Journal of Psychiatry and Neuroscience, 18*, 121-129.

van Vliet, I.M., den Boer, J.A., & Westernberg, H. (1994). Psychopharmacological treatment of social phobia: A double-blind placebo-controlled study with fluvoxamine. *Psychopharmacology, 115*, 128-134.

vanKammen, D.P., Bunney, W.E., Docherty, J.P., Jimerson, D.C., Post, R.M., Sivis, S., Ebart, M., & Gillin, J.C. (1977). Amphetamine-induced catecholamine activation in schizophrenia and depression. *Advances in Biochemical Psychopharmacology, 16*, 655-659.

vanKammen, D.P., Hommer, D.W., & Malas, K.L. (1987). Effects of pimozide on positive and negative symptoms in schizophrenic patients: Are negative symptoms state dependent? *Neuropsychobiology, 18*, 113-117.

vanKammen, W.B., Loeber, R., & Stouthamer-Loeber, M. (1991). Substance use and its relationship to conduct problems and delinquency in young boys. *Journal of Youth and Adolescence, 20*, 399-413.

Vanzi, M. (1996, August 31). Drug castration bill passes, goes to Gov. Wilson. *Los Angeles Times*, pp. A1, A26.

Vardaris, R.M., Weisz, D.J., Fazel, A., & Rawitch, A.B. (1976). Chronic administration of delta-9-tetrahydrocannabinol to pregnant rats: Studies of pup behavior and placental transfer. *Pharmacology and Biochemistry of Behavior, 4*, 249-254.

Varner, R.V., & Gaitz, C.M. (1982). Schizophrenic and paranoid disorders in the aged. In L.F. Jarvik & G.W. Small (Eds.), *Psychiatric Clinics of North America*. Philadelphia: Saunders.

Varni, J.M., Katz, E.R., Colegrove, R., & Dolgin, M. (1993). The impact of social skills training on the adjustment of children with newly diagnosed cancer. *Journal of Pediatric Psychology, 18*, 751-767.

Varni, J.W. (1981). Self-regulation techniques in the management of chronic arthritic pain in hemophilia. *Behavior Therapy, 12*, 185-194.

Varni, J.W., & Bernstein, B.H. (1991). Evaluation and management of pain in children with rheumatoid diseases. *Pediatric Rheumatology, 17*, 985-1000.

Varni, J.W., & Dietrich, S.L. (1981). Behavioral pediatrics: Towards a reconceptualization. *Behavioral Medicine Update, 3*, 5-7.

Varni, J.W., & Wallander, J.L. (1984). Adherence to health-related regimens in pediatric chronic disorders. *Clinical Psychology Review, 4*, 585-596.

Varni, J.W., Blount, R.L., Waldron, S.A., & Smith, A.J. (1997). Management of pain and distress. In M.C. Roberts (Ed.), *Handbook of pediatric psychology*. New York: Guilford..

Veale, D. (2000). Outcome of cosmetic surgery and "DIY" surgery in patients with body dysmorphic disorder. *Psychiatric Bulletin, 24*, 218-221.

Veale, D., Boocock, A., Gournay, K. et al. (1996). Body dysmorphic disorder: A cognitive-behavioral model and pilot randomized controlled trial. *Behaviour Research and Therapy, 34*, 717-729.

Veale, D., Boocook, A., Gournay, K., & Dryden, W. (1996). Body dysmorphic disorder: A survey of fifty cases. *British Journal of Psychiatry, 169*, 196-201.

Velakoulis, D., Pantelis, C., McGorry, P.D., Dudgeon, P., Brewer, W., et al. (1999). Hippocampal volume in first-epiode psychoses and chronic schizophrenia: A high-resolution magnetic resonance imaging study. *Archives of General Psychiatry, 56*, 133-141.

Ventura, J., Neuchterlein, K.H., Lukoff, D., & Hardesty, J.D. (1989). A prospective study of stressful life events and schizophrenic relapse. *Journal of Abnormal Psychology, 98*, 407-411.

Verdoux, H., Geddes, J.R., Takei, N., Lawrie, S.M., Bovet, P., et al. (1997). Obstetric complications and age at onset in schizophrenia: An international collaborative meta-analysis of individual patient data. *American Journal of Psychiatry, 154*, 1220-1227

Vernberg, E.M., LaGreca, A.M., Silverman, W.K., & Prinstein, M.J. (1996). Prediction of post-traumatic stress symptoms in children after hurricane Andrew. *Journal of Abnormal Psychology, 105*, 237-249.

Viglione in press in 8th   1999, 11, 251-265

Viglione, D.J. (1999). A review of recent research addesssing the utility of the Rorschach. *Psychological Assessment, 11*, 251-265.

Vinogradov, S., & Yalom, I. (1989). *Group therapy*. Washington, DC: American Psychiatric Press.

Visser, S., & Bouman, T.K. (1992). Cognitive-behavioural approaches to the treatment of hypochondriasis: Six single-case crossover studies. *Behaviour Research and Therapy, 30*, 301-306.

Vitale, J.E. & Newman, J.P. (2001). Response preservation in female psychopaths. *Journal of Abnormal Psychology, 110*, 644-647.

Vitousek, K., & Manke, F. (1994). Personality variables and disorders in anorexia nervosa and bulimia nervosa. *Journal of Abnormal Psychology, 103*, 137-147.

Vogel, V.G., Graves, D.S., Vernon, S.W., Lord, J.A., Winn, R.J., & Peters, G.N. (1990). Mammographic screening of women with increased risk of breast cancer. *Cancer, 66*, 1613-1620.

Voglmaier, M.M., Seidman, L.J., Salisbury, D., & McCarley, R.W. (1997). Neuropsychological dysfunction in schizotypal personality disorder: A profile analysis. *Biological Psychiatry, 41*, 530-540.

Vogt, T.M., Mullooly, J.P., Ernst, D., Pope, C.R., & Hollis, J.F. (1992). Social networks as predictors of ischemic heart disease, stroke, and hypertension. *Journal of Clinical Epidemiology, 45*, 659-666.

Volk, D.W., Austin, M.C., Pierri, J.N. et al. (2000). Decreased glutamic acid decarboxylase67 messenger RNA expression in a subset of prefrontal cortical γ-aminobutyric acid neurons in subjects with schizophrenia. *Archives of General Psychiatry,57*, 237-248.

Volkmar, F.R., Szatmari, P., & Sparrow, S.S. (1993). Sex differences in pervasive developmental disorders. *Journal of Autism and Developmental Disorders, 23*, 579-591.

Volkow, N.D., Wang, G.J., Fischman, M.W., & Foltin, R.W. (1997). Relationship between subjective effects of cocaine and dopamine transporter occupancy. *Nature, 386*, 827-830.

Volpicelli, J.R., Rhines, K.C., Rhines, J.S., Volpicelli, L.A., et al. (1997). Naltrexone and alcohol dependence: Role of subject compliance. *Archives of General Psychiatry, 54*, 737-743.

Volpicelli, J.R., Watson, N.T., King, A.C., Shermen, C.E., & O'Brien, C.P. (1995). Effects of naltrexone on alcohol "high" in alcoholics. *American Journal of Psychiatry, 152*, 613-617.

Von Knorring, A.L. & Hagglof, B. (1993). Autism in northern Sweden: A population-based follow-up study: Psychopathology. *European Child and Adolescent Psychiatry, 2*, 91-97.

von Krafft-Ebing, R. (1902). *Psychopathia sexualis*. Brooklyn, NY: Physicians and Surgeons Books.

vonStrauss, E., Viitanen, M., De Ronchi, D., Winblad, B., & Fratiglioni, L. (1999). Aging and the occurrence of dementia: Findings from a population-based cohort with a large sample of nonagenarians. *Archives of Neurology, 56*, 587-592.

Vontress, C.E., & Epp, L.R. (1997). Historical hostility in the African American client: Implications for counseling. *Journal of Multicultural Counseling and Development, 25*, 170-184.

Vrana, S.R., Roodham, A., & Beckham, J.C. (1995). Selective processing of trauma-relevant words in posttraumatic stress disorder. *Journal of Anxiety Disorders, 9*, 515-530.

Vygotsky, L.S. (1978). *Mind in society: The development of higher psychological processes* (M. Cole, V. John-Steiner, S. Scribner, & E. Souberman, Eds. and Trans.). Cambridge, MA: Harvard University Press.

Wachtel, E.F., & Wachtel, P.L. (1986). *Family dynamics in individual psychotherapy: A guide to clinical strategies*. New York: Guilford.

Wachtel, P.L. (1977). *Psychoanalysis and behavior therapy: Toward an integration*. New York: Basic Books.

Wachtel, P.L. (1997). *Psychoanalysis, behavior therapy and the relational world*. Washington, DC: American Psychological Association.

Wade, W.A., Treat, T.A., & Stuart, G.A. (1998). Transporting an empirically supported treatment for panic disorder to a service clinic setting: a benchmarking strategy. *Journal of Consulting and Clinical Psychology, 66*, 231-239.

Wagner, A.W., & Linehan, M.M. (1997). The relationship between childhood sexual abuse and suicidal behaviors in borderline patients. In M. Zanarini (Ed.), *The role of sexual abuse in the etiology of borderline personality disorder*. Washington, DC: American Psychiatric Association.

Wahl, O.F. & Harrman, C.R. (1989). Family views of stigma. *Schizophrenia Bulletin, 15*, 131-139.

Wahlbeck, K., Cheine, M., Essali, A., & Adams, C. (1999). Evidence of clozapine's effectiveness in schizophrenia: A systemic review and meta-analysis of randomized trials. *American Journal of Psychiatry, 156*, 990-999.

Wakefield, H., & Underwager, R. (1994). *Return of the furies: An investigation into recovered memory therapy*. Chicago: Open Court Publishing.

Wakefield, J. (1992). Disorder as dysfunction: A conceptual critique of DSM-III-R's definition of mental disorder. *Psychological Review, 99*, 232-247.

Wakefield, J.C. (1999. Philosophy of science and the progressiveness of DSM's theory-neutral nosology: Response to Follette and Houts, Part 1. *Behaviour Research and Therapy, 37*, 963-969.

Walco, G.A., Varni, J.W., & Ilowite, N.T. (1992). Cognitive-behavioral pain management in children with juvenile rheumatoid arthritis. *Pediatrics, 89*, 1075-1079.

Waldenger, R.J., & Frank, A.E. (1989). Clinicians' experiences in combining medication and psychotherapy in the treatment of borderline patients. *Hospital and Community Psychiatry, 40*, 712-718.

Waldron, I. (1976). Why do women live longer than men? *Journal of Human Stress, 2*, 1-13.

Walen, S., Hauserman, N.M., & Lavin, P.J. (1977). *Clinical guide to behavior therapy*. Baltimore: Williams & Wilkins.

Walitzer, K.S., & Connors, G.J. (1994). Psychoactive substance use disorders. In M. Hersen & R.T. Ammerman (Eds.), *Handbook of prescriptive treatments for adults* (pp. 53-71). New York: Plenum.

Walker, C.E. (1995). Elimination disorders: Enuresis and encopresis. In P. Magrab (Ed.), *Psychological management of pediatric problems* (Vol 1, pp. 129-189). Baltimore, MD: University Park Press.

Walker, C.E., Milling, L.S., & Bonner, B.L. (1988). Incontinence disorders: Enuresis and encopresis. In D.K. Routh (Ed.), *Handbook of pediatric psychology* (pp. 363-397). New York: Guilford Press.

Walker, E.F., & DiForio, D. (1997). Schizophrenia: A neural diathesis-stress model. *Psychological Review, 104*, 667-685.

Walker, E.F., Davis, D.M., & Savoie, T.D. (1994). Neuromotor precursors of schizophrenia. *Schizophrenia Bulletin, 20*, 441-451.

Walker, E.F., Grimes, K.E., Davis, D.M., & Adina, J. (1993). Childhood precursors of schizophrenia: Facial expressions of emotion. *American Journal of Psychiatry, 150,* 1654-1660.

Walker, J.L., Lahey, B.B., Russo, M.F., Frick, P.J., Christ, M.A.G., McBurnett, K., Loeber, R., Stouthamer-Loeber, M., & Green, S.M. (1991). Anxiety, inhibition, and conduct disorder in children: 1. Relations to social impairment. *Journal of the American Academy of Child and Adolescent Psychiatry, 30,* 187-191.

Wallace, C.J., & Liberman, R.P. (1985). Social skills training for patients with schizophrenia: A controlled clinical trial. *Psychiatric Research, 15,* 239-247.

Wallace, C.J., Boone, S.E., Donahoe, C.P., & Foy, D.W. (1985). The chronically mentally disabled: Independent living skills training. In D.H. Barlow (Ed.), *Clinical handbook of psychological disorders.* New York: Guilford.

Wallace, S.T., & Alden, L.E. (1997). Social phobia and positive social events: The price of success. *Journal of Abnormal Psychology, 106,* 416-424.

Waller, D.A., Kiser, S., Hardy, B.W., Fuchs, I., & Feigenbaum, L.P. (1986). Eating behavior and plasma beta-endorphin in bulimia. *American Journal of Clinical Nutrition, 4,* 20-23.

Wallerstein, R.S. (1986). *Forty-two lives in treatment: A study of psychoanalysis and psychotherapy.* New York: Guilford.

Wallerstein, R.S. (1989). The Psychotherapy Research Project of the Menninger Foundation: An overview. *Journal of Consulting and Clinical Psychology, 57,* 195-205.

Walling, M., Anderson, B.L., & Johnson, S.R. (1990). Hormonal replacement therapy for postmenopausal women: A review of sexual outcomes and related gynecologic effects. *Archives of Sexual Behavior, 19,* 119-137.

Walsh, B.T., Seidman, S.N., Sysko, R., & Gould, M. (2002). Placebo response in studies of major depression: Variable, substantial, and growing. *JAMA, 287,* 1840-1847.

Walsh, B.T., Wilson, G.T., Loeb, K.L., Devlin, M.J., et al. (1997). Medication and psychotherapy in the treatment of bulimia nervosa. *American Journal of Psychiatry, 154,* 523-531.

Walsh, D.C., Hingson, R.W., et al (1991). A randomized trial of treatment options for alcohol abusing workers. *New England Journal of Medicine, 325,* 775-782.

Walsh, T.B., Agras, S.W., Devlin, M.J. et al. (2000). Fluoxetine for bulimia nervosa ,following poor response to psychotherapy. *American Journal of Psychiatry, 157,* 1332-1334.

Walters, E., & Kendler, K.S. (1994). Anorexia nervosa and anorexia-like symptoms in a population based twin sample. *American Journal of Psychiatry, 152,* 62-71.

Walters, E.E., Neale, M.C., Eaves, L.J., Lindon, J., & Heath, A.C. (1992). Bulimia nervosa and major depression: A study of common genetic and environmental factors. *Psychological Medicine, 22,* 617-622.

Walters, G.L. & Clopton, J.R. (2000). Effect of symptom information and validity scale information on the malingering of depression on the MMPI-2. *Journal of Personality Assessment, 75,* 183-199.

Wang, M.Q., Fitzhugh, E.C., Eddy, J.M., Fu, Q., et al. (1997). Social influences on adolescents' smoking progress: A longitudinal analysis. *American Journal of Health Behavior, 21,* 111-117.

Wannamethee, S.G., Shaper, A.G., & Walker, M. (1998). Changes in physical activity, mortality, and incidence of coronary heart disease in older men. *The Lancet, 351,* 1603-1608.

Ward, C.H., Beck, A.T., Mendelson, M., Mock, E., & Erbaugh, J.K. (1962). The psychiatric nomenclature: Reasons for diagnostic disagreement. *Archives of General Psychiatry, 7,* 198-205.

Warren, C.A.B. (1982). *The court as last resort: Mental illness and the law.* Chicago: University of Chicago Press.

Warren, J. (1998, May 27). Officials suggest ways to distribute medical marijuana. *Los Angeles Times,* pp. A3-A22.

Wartenberg, A.A., Nirenberg, T.D., Liepman, M.R., Silvia, L.Y., Begin, A.M., & Monti, P.M. (1990). Detoxification of alcoholics: Improving care by symptom-triggered sedation. *Alcoholism: Clinical and Experimental Research, 14,* 71-75.

Waskow, I.E. (1984). Specification of the technique variable in the NIMH Treatment of Depression Collaborative Research Program. In J.B.W. Williams & R.L. Spitzer (Eds.), *Psychotherapy research: Where are we and where should we go?* New York: Guilford.

Watson, D., & Pennebaker, J.W. (1989). Health complaints, stress, and distress: Exploring the central role of negative affectivity. *Psychological Review, 96,* 234-254.

Watson, J.B. (1913). Psychology as the behaviorist views it. *Psychological Review, 20,* 158-177.

Watson, J.B., & Rayner, R. (1920). Conditioned emotional reactions. *Journal of Experimental Psychology, 3,* 1-14.

Watt, N.F. (1974). Childhood and adolescent roots of schizophrenia. In D. Ricks, A. Thomas, & M. Roll (Eds.), *Life history research in psychopathology* (Vol. 3). Minneapolis: University of Minnesota Press.

Watt, N.F., Stolorow, R.D., Lubensky, A.W., & McClelland, D.C. (1970). School adjustment and behavior of children hospitalized for schizophrenia as adults. *American Journal of Orthopsychiatry, 40,* 637-657.

Wattis, J.P. (1990). Diagnostic issues in depression in old age. *International Clinical Psychopharmacology, 5,* 1-6.

Watzlawick, P., Beavin, J., & Jackson, D.D. (1967). *Pragmatics of human communication: A study of interactional patterns, pathologies, and paradoxes.* New York: Norton.

Weaver, T.L., & Clum, G.A. (1993). Early family environments and traumatic experiences associated with borderline personality disorder. *Journal of Consulting and Clinical Psychology, 61,* 1068-1075.

Webb, W.B., & Campbell, S.S. (1980). Awakenings and the return to sleep in an older population. *Sleep, 3,* 41-66.

Weber, T. (1996, December 2). Tarnishing the golden years with addiction. *Los Angeles Times,* pp. A1, A37.

Webster, R. & Holroyd, S. (2000). Prevalence of psychotic symptoms in delirium. *Psychosomatics, 41,*519-522.

Wechsler Intelligence Scale for Children (3rd ed.) (1991). San Antonio. The Psychological Corporation.

Wechsler, D. (1968). *Escala de Inteligencia Wechsler para Adultos.* New York: Psychological Corporation.

Wechsler, H., Davenport, A., Dowdell, G., Moeykens, B., & Castillo, S. (1994). Health and behavioral consequences of binge drinking in college: A national survey of students at 140 campuses. *Journal of the American Medical Association, 272,* 1672-1677.

Weg, R.B. (Ed.). (1983). *Sexuality in the later years: Roles and behavior.* New York: Academic Press.

Wegner, D.M., Schneider, D.J., Carter, S.R., & White, T.L. (1987). Paradoxical effects of thought suppression. *Journal of Personality and Social Psychology, 53,* 5-13.

Wegner, D.M., Schneider, D.J., Knutson, B., & McMahon, S.R. (1991). Polluting the stream of consciousness: The effect of thought suppression on the mind's environment. *Cognitive Therapy and Research, 15,* 141-152.

Weidner, G., & Collins, R.L. (1993). Gender, coping, and health. In H.W. Krohne (Ed.), *Attention and avoidance.* New York: Springer-Verlag.

Weidner, G., & Griffin, K.W. (1995). Psychological aspects of cholesterol-lowering. *Cardiovascular Risk Factors, 5,* 1-7.

Weidner, G., Connor, S.L., Hollis, J.F., & Connor, W.E. (1992). Improvements in hostility and depression in relation to dietary change and cholesterol lowering. *Annals of Internal Medicine, 117,* 820-823.

Weidner, G., Friend, R., Ficarroto, T.J., & Mendell, N.R. (1989). Hostility and cardiovascular reactivity to stress in women and men. *Psychosomatic Medicine, 51,* 36-45.

Weikel, D. (1996, April 7). Meth labs: How young lives are put in peril. *Los Angeles Times,* pp. A1, A18.

Weiler, P.G., Mungas, D., & Pomerantz, S. (1988). AIDS as a cause of dementia in the elderly. *Journal of the American Geriatrics Society, 36,* 139-141.

Weinberger, D.R. (1987). Implications of normal brain development for the pathogenesis of schizophrenia. *Archives of General Psychiatry, 44,* 660-669.

Weinberger, D.R., Berman, K.F., & Illowsky, B.P. (1988). Physiological dysfunction of dorsolateral prefrontal cortex in schizophrenia: 3. A new cohort and evidence for a monoaminergic mechanism. *Archives of General Psychiatry, 45,* 609-615.

Weinberger, D.R., Cannon-Spoor, H.E., Potkin, S.G., & Wyatt, R.J. (1980). Poor premorbid adjustment and CT scan abnormalities in chronic schizophrenia. *American Journal of Psychiatry, 137,* 1410-1413.

Weinberger, D.R., Wagner, R.L., & Wyatt, R.J. (1983). Neuropathological studies of schizophrenia: A selective review. *Schizophrenia Bulletin, 9,* 193-212.

Weiner, B. (1986). *An attributional theory of motivation and emotion.* Unpublished manuscript, University of California at Los Angeles.

Weiner, B., Frieze, L., Kukla, A., Reed, L., Rest, S., & Rosenbaum, R.M. (1971). *Perceiving the causes of success and failure.* New York: General Learning Press.

Weiner, D. B. (1994). Le geste de Pinel: The history of psychiatric myth. In M.S. Micale & R. Porter (Eds.) , *Discovering the history of psychiatry*. NY: Oxford.

Weiner, H. (1977). *Psychobiology and human disease*. New York: Elsevier.

Weingartner, H., & Silberman, E. (1982). Models of cognitive impairment: Cognitive changes in depression. *Psychopharmacology Bulletin, 18*, 27-42.

Weinstein, H. (1996, March 7). Assisted deaths ruled legal: 9th Circuit lifts ban of doctor-aided suicide. *Los Angeles Times*, pp. A1, A16.

Weinstein, H. (1998, May 8). Big tobacco settles Minnesota lawsuit for $6.6 billion. *Los Angeles Times*, pp. A1-A12.

Weinstein, H. (2002, February 19). Killer's Sentence of Death Debated. *Los Angeles Times*, pp. A1, A14.

Weinstein, H., & Groves, M. (1996, March 14). Tobacco firm agrees to settle a health suit. *Los Angeles Times*, pp. A1, A12.

Weintraub, S., Liebert, D.E., & Neale, J.M. (1975). Teacher ratings of children vulnerable to psychopathology. *American Journal of Orthopsychiatry, 45*, 838-845.

Weintraub, S., Prinz, R., & Neale, J.M. (1978). Peer evaluations of the competence of children vulnerable to psychopathology. *Journal of Abnormal Child Psychology, 6*, 461-473.

Weintraub, S., Winters, K.C., & Neale, J.M. (1986). Competence and vulnerability in children with an affectively disordered parent. In M. Rutter, C.E. Izard, & P.B. Read (Eds.), *Depression in young people: Development and clinical perspectives*. New York: Guilford.

Weisman, A.G., Nuechterlein, K.H., Goldstein, M.J., & Snyder, K.S. (1998). Expressed emotion, attributions, and schizophrenia symptom dimensions. *Journal of Abnormal Psychology, 107*, 355-359.

Weiss, B., Weisz, J.R., & Bromfield, R. (1986). Performance of retarded and nonretarded persons on information-processing tasks: Further tests of the similar structure hypothesis. *Psychological Bulletin, 100*, 157-175.

Weiss, G. & Hechtman, L. (1993). *Hyperactive children grown up* (2nd ed.). New York: Guilford Press.

Weiss, G. (1983). Long-term outcome: Findings, concepts, and practical implications. In M. Rutter (Ed.), *Developmental neuropsychiatry*. New York: Guilford.

Weiss, G., & Hechtman, L. (1986). *Hyperactive children grown up*. New York: Guilford.

Weiss, R.L., & Cerreto, M.C. (1980). The Marital Status Inventory: Development of a measure of dissolution potential. *American Journal of Family Therapy, 8*, 80-85.

Weissberg, R.P., Caplan, M.Z., & Sivo, P.J. (1989). A new conceptual framework for establishing school-based social competence promotion programs. In L.A. Bond, & B.E. Compas (Eds.), *Primary prevention and promotion in the schools* (Vol. 12, pp. 255-296). Newbury Park, CA: Sage Publications.

Weissberg, R.P., Caplan, M., & Harwood, R.L. (1991). Promoting competent young people in competence-enhancing environments: A systems-based perspective on primary prevention. *Journal of Consulting and Clinical Psychology, 59*, 830-841.

Weissberg, R.P., Gesten, E.L., Rapkin, B.D., Cowen, E.L., Davidson, E., deApodaca, R.F., & McKim, B.J. (1981). Evaluation of a social-problem-solving training program for suburban and inner-city third-grade children. *Journal of Consulting and Clinical Psychology, 49*, 251-261.

Weissman, A.N., & Beck, A.T. (1978). *Development and validation of the Dysfunctional Attitude Scale: A preliminary investigation*. Paper presented at the annual meeting of the American Educational Research Association, Toronto.

Weissman, M.M., & Markowitz, J.C., (2002). Interpersonal psychotherapy for depression. In I.H. Gotlib (Ed.), *Handbook of Depression* (pp. 404-421). New York: Guilford Press.

Weissman, M.M. (1993). The epidemiology of personality disorders: A 1990 update. *Journal of Personality Disorders, 7*, 44-61.

Weissman, M.M. (1995). *Mastering depression: A patient's guide to interpersonal psychotherapy*. New York: Graywind.

Weissman, M.M., & Markowitz, J.C. (1994). Interpersonal psychotherapy: Current status. *Archives of General Psychiatry, 51*, 599-605.

Weissman, M.M., Bland, R.C., Canino, G.J., Faravelli, C., Greenwald, S., et al. (1996). Cross-national epidemiology of major depression and bipolar disorder. *JAMA, 276*, 293-299.

Weissman, M.M., Bland, R.C., Canino, G.J., Faravelli, C., Grenwald, S., et al. (1997). The cross-national epidemiology of panic disorder. *Archives of General Psychiatry, 54*, 305-312.

Weissman, M.M., Klerman, G.L., & Paykel, E.S. (1971). Clinical evaluation of hostility in depression. *American Journal of Psychiatry, 128*, 261-266.

Weissman, M.M., Prusoff, B.A., DiMascio, A., New, C., Goklaney, M., & Klerman, G.L. (1979). The efficacy of drugs and psychotherapy in the treatment of acute depressive episodes. *American Journal of Psychiatry, 36*, 555-558.

Weisz, J.R., Suwanlert, S.C., Wanchai, W., & Bernadette, R. (1987). Over- and undercontrolled referral problems among children and adolescents from Thailand and the United States: The wat and wai of cultural differences. *Journal of Consulting and Clinical Psychology, 55*, 719-726.

Weisz, J.R., & Weiss, B. (1991). Studying the "referability" of child clinical problems. *Journal of Consulting and Clinical Psychology, 59*, 266-273.

Weisz, J.R., & Yeates, K.D. (1981). Cognitive development in retarded and nonretarded persons: Piagetian tests of the similar structure hypothesis. *Psychological Bulletin, 90*, 153-178.

Weisz, J.R., Sigman, M., Weiss, B., & Mosk, J. (1993). Parent reports of behavioral and emotional problems among children in Kenya, Thailand and the United States. *Child Development, 64*, 98-109.

Weitzenhoffer, A.M., & Hilgard, E.R. (1959). *Stanford hypnotic susceptibility scale, Forms A and B*. Palo Alto, CA: Consulting Psychologists Press.

Wells, C.E., & Duncan, G.W. (1980). *Neurology for psychiatrists*. Philadelphia: F.A. Davis.

Welsh, R., Burcham, B., DeMoss, K., Martin, C., & Milich, R. (1997). *Attention deficit hyperactivity disorder diagnosis and management: A training program for teachers*. Franfurt: Kentucky Department of Education.

Wender, P.H., Kety, S.S., Rosenthal, D., Schulsinger, F., Ortmann, J., & Lunde, I. (1986). Psychiatric disorders in the biological and adoptive families of adopted individuals with affective disorders. *Archives of General Psychiatry, 43*, 923-929.

Wenzlaff, R.M., Wegner, D.M., & Klein, S.B. (1991). The role of thought suppression in the bonding of thought and affect. *Journal of Personality and Social Psychology, 60*, 500-508.

West, D.J. (1977). *Homosexuality re-rexamined*. Minneapolis: University of Minnesota Press.

Westen, D. (2000). Integrative psychotherapy: Integrating psychodynamic and cognitive-behavioral therapy and technique. In C. R. Snyder & R. E. Ingram (Eds.), *Handbook of psychological change: Psychotherapy processes & practices for the 21st century* (pp. 217-242). New York: John Wiley & Sons, Inc.

Wester, P., Eriksson, S., Forsell, A., Puu, G., & Adolfsson, R. (1988). Monoamine metabolite concentrations and cholinesterase activities in cerebrospinal fluid of progressive dementia patients: Relation to clinical parameters. *Acta Neurologica Scandinavica, 77*, 12-21.

Wetherell, J.L. (1998). Treatment of anxiety in older adults. *Psychotherapy, 35*, 444-458.

Wetherell, J.L. (in press). Treatment of anxiety in older adults. *Psychotherapy*.

Wetherell, J.L., Gatz, M., & Craske, M.G. (in press). Treatment of generalized anxiety disorder in older adults. *Journal of Consulting and Clinical Psychology*.

Whalen, C.K. & Henker, B. (1992). The social profile of attention-deficit hyperactivity disorder: Five fundamental facts. *Child and Adolescent Psychiatric Clinics of North America, 1*, 395-409.

Whalen, C.K. (1983). Hyperactivity, learning problems, and the attention deficit disorders. In T.H. Ollendick & M. Hersen (Eds.), *Handbook of child psychopathology*. New York: Plenum.

Whalen, C.K., & Henker, B. (1985). The social worlds of hyperactive (ADDH) children. *Clinical Psychology Review, 5*, 447-478.

Whalen, C.K., & Henker, B. (1991). Therapies for hyperactive children: Comparisons, combinations, and compromises. *Journal of Consulting and Clinical Psychology, 59*, 126-137.

Whalen, C.K., Henker, B., Hinshaw, S.P., Heller, T., & Huber-Dressler, A. (1991). Messages of medication: Effects of actual versus informed medication status on hyperactive boys' expectancies and self-evaluations. *Journal of Consulting and Clinical Psychology, 59*, 602-606.

Whalley, L.J., Starr, J.M., Athawes, R. et al. (2000). Childhood mental ability and dementia. *Neurology, 55*, 1455-1459.

Wheeler, J.C., Christenson, A., & Jacobson, N.S. (2001). Couple distress. In D.H. Barlow (Ed.), *Clinical handbook of psychological disorders* (3rd ed.). New York: Guilford Press.

Whelton, P.K., Appel, L.J., Espeland, M.A., Applegate, W.B., Ettinger, W.H., Kostis, J.B., Kumanyika, S., Lacy, C.R., Johnson, K.C., Folmar, S., Cutler, J.A. for the TONE Collaborative Research Group. (1998). Sodium reduction and weight loss in the treatment of hypertension in older persons: A randomized controlled trial of nonpharmacologic interventions in the elderly (TONE). *Journal of the American Medical Association, 279*, 839-846

Whisman, M.A. (1993). Mediators and moderators of change in cognitive therapy of depression. *Psychological Bulletin, 114*, 248-265.

White, J., Davison, G.C., Haaga, D.A.F., & White, K. (1992). Articulated thoughts and cognitive distortion in depressed and nondepressed psychiatric patients. *Journal of Nervous and Mental Disease, 180*, 77-81.

White, K., & Cole, J.O. (1990). Pharmacotherapy. In A.S. Bellack & M. Hersen (Eds.), *Handbook of comparative treatments for adult disorders* (pp. 266-284). New York: Wiley.

White, P.F. (1986). Patient-controlled analgesia: A new approach to the management of postoperative pain. *Seminars in Anesthesia, 4*, 255-266.

Whitehead, W.E., Burgio, K.L., & Engel, B.T. (1985). Biofeedback treatment of fecal incontinence in geriatric patients. *Journal of the American Geriatrics Society, 33*, 320-324.

Whitehouse, P.J. (1997). Genesis of Alzheimer's disease. *Neurology, 48, Supplement 7*, s2-s6.

Whitford, R., & Parr, V. (1995). Use of rational emotive behavior therapy with juvenile sex offenders. *Journal of Rational-Emotive and Cognitive Behavior Therapy, 13*, 273-282.

Whitman, T.L. (1990). Self-regulation and mental retardation. *American Journal on Mental Retardation, 94*, 347-362.

Whittal, M.L., Agras, S.W., & Gould, R.A. (1999). Bulimia nervosa: A meta-analysis of psychosocial anf pharmacological treatments. *Behavior Therapy, 30*, 117-135.

Whittemore, A., Wu-Williams, A., Lee, M., Zheng, S., Gallagher, R., Jiao, D.A., Zhou, L., Wang, X., Chen, K., Jung, D., Teh, C.Z., Ling, C., Xu, J.Y., Paffenberger, R., & Henderson, B.E. (1990). Diet, physical activity and colorectal cancer among Chinese in North America and the People's Republic of China. *Journal of the National Cancer Institute, 82*, 915-926.

Whyte, S., Bayreuther, K., & Masters, C.L. (1994). Rational therapeutic strategies for Alzheimer's disease. In D.B. Calne (Ed.), *Neurodegenerative diseases*. Philadelphia: Saunders.

Wickens, D.D., Allen, C.K., & Hill, F.A. (1963). Effects of instruction on extinction of the conditioned GSR. *Journal of Experimental Psychology, 66*, 235-240.

Wicks-Nelson, R., & Israel, A.C. (1997). *Behavior disorders of childhood*. Upper Saddle River, NJ: Prentice-Hall.

Widiger, T.A., & Costa, P.T., Jr. (1994). Personality and personality disorders. *Journal of Abnormal Psychology, 95*, 43-51.

Widiger, T.A., Frances, A., & Trull, T.J. (1987). A psychometric analysis of the social-interpersonal and cognitive-perceptual items for schizotypal personality disorder. *Archives of General Psychiatry, 44*, 741-745.

Widiger, T.A., Frances, A., Spitzer, R.L., & Williams, J.B.W. (1988). The DSM-III personality disorders: An overview. *American Journal of Psychiatry, 145*, 786-795.

Wiederhold, B.K., & Wiederhold, M.D. (1998). A review of virtual reality as a psychotherapeutic tool. *CyberPsychology and Behavior, 1*, 45-52.

Wig, N.N., & Varma, V.K. (1977). Patterns of long-term heavy cannabis use in North India and its effects on cognitive functions. A preliminary report. *Drug and Alcohol Dependence, 2*, 211-219.

Wigdor, B., & Morris, G. (1977). A comparison of twenty-year medical histories of individuals with depressive and paranoid states. *Journal of Gerontology, 32*, 160-163.

Willemsen-Swinkels, S.H.N., Buitelaar, J.K., & van Engeland, H. (1996). The effects of chronic naltrexone treatment in young autistic children: A double-blind placebo-controlled crossover study. *Biological Psychiatry, 39*, 1023-1031.

Willemsen-Swinkels, S.H.N., Buitelaar, J.K., Weijnen, F.G., & van Engeland, H. (1995). Placebo-controlled acute dosage naltrexone study in young autistic children. *Psychiatry Research, 58*, 203-215.

Willi, J., & Grossman, S. (1983). Epidemiology of anorexia nervosa in a defined region of Switzerland. *American Journal of Psychiatry, 140*, 564-567.

Williams, C.J. (1999, May 27). In Kosovo, rape seen as awful as death. *Los Angeles Times*, pp. A1, A18.

Williams, H., & McNicol, K.N. (1969). Prevalence, natural history and relationship of wheezy bronchitis and asthma in children: An epidemiological study. *British Medical Journal, 4*, 321-325.

Williams, J.B.W., Gibbon, M., First, M.B., Spitzer, R.L., Davies, M., et al. (1992). The Structured Clinical Interview for DSM-III-R (SCID): 2. Multisite test-retest reliability. *Archives of General Psychiatry, 49*, 630-636.

Williams, J.M., Little, M.M., Scates, S., & Blackman, N. (1987). Memory complaints and abilities among depressed older adults. *Journal of Consulting and Clinical Psychology, 55*, 595-598.

Williams, L.M. (1995). Recall of childhood trauma: A prospective study of women's memories of child sexual abuse. *Journal of Consulting and Clinical Psychology, 62*, 1167-1176.

Williams, M.E., Davison, G.C., Nezami, E., & DeQuattro, V. (1992). Cognitions of type A and type B individuals in response to social criticism. *Cognitive Therapy and Research, 16*, 19-30.

Williams, R.B. (1987). Psychological factors in coronary artery disease: Epidemiological evidence. *Circulation, 76*, 117-123.

Williams, S.L., & Rappoport, A. (1983). Cognitive treatment in the natural environment for agoraphobics. *Behavior Therapy, 14*, 299-313.

Williamson, D.A., Goreczny, A.J., Davis, C.J., Ruggiero, L., & MacKenzie, S.L. (1988). Psychophysiological analysis of the anxiety model of bulimia nervosa. *Behavior Therapy, 19*, 1-9.

Wills, T.A., & Cleary, S.D. (1999). Peer and adolescent substance use among 6th-9th graders: Latent growth analysis of influence versus selection mechanisms. *Health Psychology, 18*, 453-463.

Wills, T.A., DuHamel, K., & Vaccaro, D. (1995). Activity and mood temperament as predictors of adolescent substance use: Test of a self-regulation model. *Journal of Personality and Social Psychology, 68*, 901-916.

Wilsnak, S.C. (1984). Drinking, sexuality, and sexual dysfunction in women. In S.C. Wilsnak & L.J. Beckman (Eds.), *Alcohol problems in women: Antecedents, consequences, and intervention* (pp. 189-227). New York: Guilford.

Wilson, G.T. (in press). Manual-based treatment and clinical practice. *Clinical Psychology: Science and Practice.*

Wilson, G.T. (1991). Chemical aversion conditioning in the treatment of alcoholism: Further comments. *Behaviour Research and Therapy, 29*, 405-420.

Wilson, G.T. (1995). Empirically validated treatments as a basis for clinical practice: Problems and prospects. In S.C. Hayes, V.M. Follette, R.M. Dawes, & K.E. Grady (Eds.), *Scientific standards of psychological practice: Issues and recommendations*. Reno, NV: Context Press.

Wilson, G.T. (1996). Manual-based treatments: The clinical application of research findings. *Behaviour Research and Therapy, 34*, 295-314.

Wilson, G.T., & Davison, G.C. (1971). Processes of fear reduction in systematic desensitization. Animal studies. *Psychological Bulletin, 76*, 1-14.

Wilson, G.T., & Lawson, D.M. (1976). The effects of alcohol on sexual arousal in women. *Journal of Abnormal Psychology, 85*, 489-497.

Wilson, G.T., & Pike, K.M. (1993). Eating disorders. In D.H. Barlow (Ed.), *Clinical handbook of psychological disorders* (pp. 278-317). New York: Guilford.

Wilson, G.T., Eldredge, K.L., Smith, D., & Niles, B. (1991). Cognitive-behavioural treatment with and without response prevention for bulimia. *Behaviour Research and Therapy, 29*, 575-583.

Wilson, R.S., Mendes de Leon, C., Barnes, L. et al. (2002). Participation in cognitively stimulation activities and risk of incident Alzheimer's disease. *JAMA, 287*, 742-748.

Wilson, T.D., Goldin, J.C., & Charbonneau-Powis, M. (1983). Comparative efficacy of behavioral and cognitive treatments of depression. *Cognitive Therapy and Research, 7*, 111-124.

Wilson, W.R. (1975). *Unobtrusive induction of positive attitudes*. Unpublished doctoral dissertation, University of Michigan.

Winchel, R.M., Stanley, B., & Stanley, M. (1990). Biochemical aspects of suicide. In S.J. Blumenthal & D.J. Kupfer (Eds.), *Suicide over the life cycle: Risk factors, assessment and treatment of suicidal patterns* (pp. 97-126). Washington, DC: American Psychiatric Press.

Wincze, J.P., & Carey, M.P. (1991). *Sexual dysfunction: A guide for assessment and treatment*. New York: Guilford.

Winett, R.A., & Winkler, R.C. (1972). Current behavior modification in the classroom: Be still, be quiet, be docile. *Journal of Applied Behavior Analysis, 5*, 499-504.

Wing, L., & Attwood, A. (1987). Syndromes of autism and atypical development. In D.J. Cohen, A.M. Donnellan, & R. Paul (Eds.), *Handbook of autism and pervasive developmental disorders* (pp. 3-19). New York: Wiley.

Winick, B.J. (1993). Psychotropic medication in the criminal trial process: The constitutional and therapeutic implications of Riggins v. Nevada. *New York Law School Journal of Human Rights, 10*, 637-709.

Winick, B.J. (1994). The right to refuse mental health treatment: A therapeutic jurisprudence analysis. *International Journal of Law and Psychiatry, 17*, 99-117.

Winick, B.J. (1996a). Advance directive instruments for those with mental illness es. *University of Miami Law Review, 51*, 57-78.

Winick, B.J. (1996b). The MacArthur Treatment Competence Study: Legal and therapeutic implications. *Psychology, Public Policy, and Law, 2*, 137-166.

Winick, B.J. (1997) *The right to refuse mental health treatment.* Washington, DC: American Psychological Association.

Winick, C. (1962). Maturing out of narcotic addiction. *Bulletin on Narcotics, 14*, 1-7.

Winkleby, M.A., Kraemer, H.C., Ahn, D.K., & Varady, A.N. (1998). Ethnic and socioeconomic differences in cardiovascular disease risk factors. *JAMA, 280*, 356-362.

Winkleby, M.A., Robinson, T.N., Sundquist, J., & Kraemer, H.C. (1999). Ethnic variation in cardiovascular disease risk factors among children and young adults. *JAMA, 281*, 1006-1013.

Winters, K.C., & Neale, J.M. (1985). Mania and low self-esteem. *Journal of Abnormal Psychology, 94*, 282-290.

Wirshing, D.A., Marshall, B.D., Green, M.F., Mintz, J., et al. (1999). Risperidone in treatment-refractory schizophrenia. *American Journal of Psychiatry, 156*, 1374-1379.

Wischik, C. (1994). Molecular neuropathology of Alzheimer's disease. In C.L.A. Katona (Ed.), *Dementia disorders: Advances and prospects.* London: Chapman and Hall.

Wiseman, C.V., Gray, J.J., Mosimann, J.E., & Arhens, A.H. (1992). Cultural expectations of thinness in women: An update. *International Journal of Eating Disorders, 11*, 85-89.

Wittchen, H.-U. & Hoyer, J. (2001). Generalized anxiety disorder: Nature and course. *Journal of Clinical Psychiatry, 62*, 15-19.

Wittchen, H.-U., Stein, M.B., & Kessler, R.C. (1999). Social fears and social phobia in a community sample of adolescents and young adults: Prevalence, risk factors, and co-morbidity. *Psychological Medicine, 29*, 309-323.

Wold, D.A. (1968). *The adjustment of siblings to childhood leukemia.* Unpublished medical thesis, University of Washington, Seattle.

Wolf, A. (1949). The psychoanalysis of group. *American Journal of Psychotherapy, 3*, 16-50.

Wolf, A., & Kutash, I.L. (1990). Psychoanalysis in groups. In I.L. Kutash & A. Wolf (Eds.), *The group psychotherapist's handbook: Contemporary theory and technique.* New York: Columbia University Press.

Wolf, M., Bally, H., & Morris, R. (1986). Automaticity, retrieval processes, and reading: A longitudinal study in average and impaired readers. *Child Development, 57*, 988-1000.

Wolfe, D.A., Reppucci, N.D., & Hart, S. (1995). Child abuse prevention: Knowledge and priorities. *Journal of Clinical Child Psychology, 24*, 5-22.

Wolfe, J.L. (1995). Rational emotive behavior therapy women's groups: A twenty year retrospective. *Journal of Rational-Emotive and Cognitive Behavior Therapy, 13*, 153-170.

Wolfe, R., Morrow, J., & Frederickson, B.L. (1996). Mood disorders in older adults. In L.L. Carstensen, B.A. Edelstein, & L. Dornbrand (Eds.), *The practical handbook of clinical gerontology* (pp. 274-303). Thousand Oaks, CA: Sage.

Wolfe, V.V. (1990). Sexual abuse of children. In A.S. Bellack, M. Hersen, & A.E. Kazdin (Eds.), *International handbook of behavior modification and therapy* (2nd ed., pp. 707-729). New York: Plenum.

Wolff, P. H., & Melngailis, I. (1996). Reversing letters and reading transformed text in dyslexia: A reassessment. *Reading and Writing, 8*, 341-355.

Wolitzky, D. (1995). Traditional psychoanalytic psychotherapy. In A.S. Gurman & S.B. Messer (Eds.), *Essential psychotherapies: Theory and practice.* New York: Guilford.

Wolitzky, D.L., & Eagle, M.N. (1990). Psychotherapy. In A.S. Bellack & M. Hersen (Eds.), *Handbook of comparative treatments for adult disorders* (pp. 123-143). New York: Wiley.

Wolpe, J. (1958). *Psychotherapy by reciprocal inhibition.* Stanford, CA: Stanford University Press.

Wolraich, M., Milich, R., Stumbo, P., & Schultz, F. (1985). The effects of sucrose ingestion on the behavior of hyperactive boys. *Pediatrics, 106*, 675-682.

Wolraich, M.L., Wilson, D.B., & White, J.W. (1995). The effect of sugar on behavior or cognition in children: A meta-analysis. *Journal of the American Medical Association, 274*, 1617-1621.

Wong, A.H.C., Smith, M., & Boon, H.S. (1998). Herbal remedies in psychiatric practice *Archives of General Psychiatry, 55*, 1033-1044.

Wong, D.F., Wagner, H.N., Tune, L.E., Dannals, R.F., Pearlson, G.D., Links, J.M., et al. (1986). Positron emission tomography reveals elevated D2 dopamine receptors in drug-naive schizophrenics. *Science, 234*, 1558-1562.

Wong, N. (1995). Group psychotherapy, combined individual and group psychotherapy, and psychodrama. In H.I. Kaplan & B.J. Sadock (Eds.), *Comprehensive textbook of psychiatry* (pp. 1821-1838). Baltimore: Williams & Wilkins.

Wood, J.M., Lilienfeld, S.O., Garb, H.N., & Nezworski, M.T. (2000). The Rorschach test in clinical diagnosis: A critical review, with a backward look at Garfield.

Wood, J.M., Nezworski, M.T., & Stejskal, W.J. (1996). The Comprehensive System for the Rorschach: A critical examination. *Psychological Science, 7*, 3-10.

Wood, J.M., Nezworski, M.T., & Stejskal, W.J. (1997). The reliability of the Comprehensive System for the Rorschach: A comment on Meyer (1997). *Psychological Assessment, 9*, 490-494.

Wood, L.F., & Jacobson, N.S. (1985). Marital distress. In D.H. Barlow (Ed.), *Clinical handbook of psychological disorders.* New York: Guilford.

Woodman, C.L., Noyes, R., Black, D.W., Schlosser, S., & Yagla, S.J. (1999). A 5-year follow-up study of generalized anxiety disorder and panic disorder. *Journal of Nervous and Mental Disease, 187*, 3-9.

Woodmansee, Mark A. (1996). The guilty but mentally ill verdict: Political expediency at the expense of moral principle. *Notre Dame Journal of Law, Ethics and Public Policy, 10*, 341-387.

Woods, B. (1994). Management of memory impairment in older people with dementia. *International Review of Psychiatry, 6*, 153-161.

Woodside, D.B., Shekter-Wolfson, L.F., Garfinkel, P.E., & Olmsted, M.P. (1995). Family interactions in bulimia nervosa: Study design, comparisons to established population norms and changes over the course of an intensive day hospital treatment program. *International Journal of Eating Disorders, 17*, 105-115.

Woody, G.E., Luborsky, L., McLellan, A.T., & O'Brien, C.P. (1990). Corrections and revised analyses for psychotherapy in methadone maintenance programs. *Archives of General Psychiatry, 47*, 788-789.

Woody, G.M., McLellan, T., Luborsky, L., & O'Brien, C.P. (1995). Psychotherapy in community methadone programs: A validation study. *American Journal of Psychiatry, 152*, 1302-1308.

World Health Organization. (1948). *Manual of the international statistical classification of diseases, injuries, and causes of death.* Geneva: Author.

World Health Organization. (1993). *1992 world health statistics annual.* Geneva: Author.

Worling, J.R. (1995). Sexual abuse histories of adolescent male sex offenders: Differences on the basis of the age and gender of their victims. *Journal of Abnormal Psychology, 104*, 610-613.

Wortman, C.B., & Brehm, J.W. (1975). Responses to uncontrollable outcomes: An integration of the reactance theory and the learned helplessness model. In L. Berkowitz (Ed.), *Advances in social psychology.* New York: Academic Press.

Wouda, J.C., Hartman, P.M., Bakker, R.M., Bakker, J.O., et al. (1998). Vaginal plethysmography in women with dyspareunia. *Journal of Sex Research, 35*, 141-147.

Wright, J.C. (1976). A comparison of systematic desensitization and social skill acquisition in the modification of social fear. *Behavior Therapy, 7*, 205-210.

Wright, M.J. (1991). Identifying child sexual abuse using the Personality Inventory for Children. *Dissertation Abstracts International, 52*, 1744.

Wulsin, L., Bachop, M., & Hoffman, D. (1988). Group therapy in manic-depressive illness. *American Journal of Psychotherapy, 2*, 263-271.

Wurtele, S.K., & Miller-Perrin, C.L. (1987). An evaluation of side-effects associated with participation in a child sexual abuse prevention program. *Journal of School Health, 57*, 228-231.

Wylie, K.R. (1997). Treatment outcome of brief couple therapy in psychogenic male erectile disorder. *Archives of Sexual Behavior, 26*, 527-545.

Wynne, L.C., & Singer, M.T. (1963). Thought disorder and family relations in schizophrenia. 2: A classification of forms of thinking. *Archives of General Psychiatry, 9*, 199-206.

Yaffe, K., Sawaya, G., Lieberburg, I., & Grady, D. (1998). Estrogen therapy in postmenopausal women. Effects on cognitive function and dementia. *JAMA, 279*, 688-695.

Yalom, I.D. (1980). *Existential psychotherapy*. New York: Basic Books.

Yalom, I.D. (1985). *The theory and practice of group psychotherapy* (3rd ed.). New York: Basic Books.

Yalom, I.D., Green, R., & Fisk, N. (1973). Prenatal exposure to female hormones: Effect on psychosexual development in boys. *Archives of General Psychiatry, 28*, 554-561.

Yates, A. (1989). Current perspectives on the eating disorders. *Journal of the American Academy of Child and Adolescent Psychiatry, 28*, 813-828.

Yetman, N.R. (1994). Race and ethnic inequality. In C. Calhoun & G. Ritzer (Eds.), *Social problems*. New York: McGraw-Hill.

Yirmiya, N., & Sigman, M. (1991). High functioning individuals with autism: Diagnosis, empirical findings, and theoretical issues. *Clinical Psychology Review, 11*, 669-683.

Yoshioka, R.B., Tashima, N., Chew, M., & Murase, K. (1981). *Mental health services for Pacific/Asian Americans*. San Francisco: Pacific American Mental Health Project.

Young, G.C. (1965). The aetiology of enuresis in terms of learning theory. *Medical Officer, 113*, 19-22.

Yurgelon-Todd, D., Waternaux, C.M., Cohen, B.N., Gruber, S.A., English, C.D., & Renshaw, P.F. (1996). Functional magnetic resonance imagery of schizophrenia patients and comparison subjects during word production. *American Journal of Psychiatry, 153*, 200-206.

Zakowski, S., Hall, M.H., & Baum, A. (1992). Stress, stress management, and the immune system. *Applied and Preventive Psychology, 1*, 1-13.

Zanarini, M. C., Frankenburg, F. R., Reich, D. et al. (2000b). Biparental failure in the childhood experiences of borderline patients. *Journal of Personality Disorders, 14*, 264-273.

Zanarini, M.C., Skodol, A.E., Bender, D. et al. (2000). The Collaborative Longitudinal Personality Disorders Study: Reliability of Axis I and Axis II Diagnoses. *Journal of Personality Disorders, 14*, 291-299.

Zanarini, M.C., Skodol, A.E., Bender, D. et al. (2000a). The Collaborative Longitudinal Study Personality Disorders Study: Reliability of axis I and II diagnoses. *Journal of Personality Disorders, 14*, 291-299.

Zanarini, M.C., Frankenberg, F.R., Dubo, E.D., Sickel, A.E., Tricka, A., & et al. (1998). Axis II comorbidity of borderline personality disorder. *Comprehensive Psychiatry, 39*, 296-302.

Zanarini, M.C., Frankenberg, F.R., Dubo, E.D., Sickel, A.E., Trikha, A., et al. (1998). Axis I comorbidity of borderline personality disorder. *American Journal of Psychiatry, 155*, 1733-1739.

Zanarini, M.C., Williams, A.A., Lewis, R.E., Reich, R.B., Vera, S.C., et al. (1997). Reported pathological childhood experiences associated with the development of borderline personality disorder. *American Journal of Psychiatry, 154*, 1101-1106.

Zane, M.D. (1984). Psychoanalysis and contextual analysis of phobias. *Journal of the American Academy of Psychoanalysis, 12*, 553-568.

Zarit, S.H., & Zarit, J.M. (1998). *Mental disorders in older adults: Fundamentals of assessment and treatment*. New York: Guilford Press.

Zarit, S.H., Dolan, M.M., & Leitsch, S.A. (1998). Interventions in nursing homes and other alternative living settings. In I.H. Nordhus, G.R. VandenBos, S. Berg, & P. Fromholt, (Eds.), *Clinical geropsychology* (pp. 329-343). Washington, D.C.: American Psychological Association.

Zarit, S.H. (1980). *Aging and mental disorders: Psychological approaches to assessment and treatment*. New York: Free Press.

Zarit, S.H. (1989). Issues and directions in family intervention research. In E. Light & B. Lebowitz (Eds.), *Alzheimer's Disease treatment and family stress: Directions for research* (Publication No. ADM 89-1569, pp. 458-486). Washington, DC: U.S. Department of Health and Human Services.

Zarit, S.H., Eiler, J., & Hassinger, M. (1985). Clinical assessment. In J.E. Birren & K.W. Schaie (Eds.), *Handbook of psychology of aging* (2nd ed.). New York: Van Nostrand-Reinhold.

Zarit, S.H., Todd, P.A., & Zarit, I.M. (1986). Subjective burden of husbands and wives as caregivers: A longitudinal study. *The Gerontologist, 26*, 260-266.

Zatzick, D.F., Marmer, C.R., Weiss, D.S., Browner, W.S., Metzler, T.J., et al. (1997). Posttraumatic stress disorder and functioning and quality of life in a nationally representative sample of male Vietnam veterans. *American Journal of Psychiatry, 154*, 1690-1695.

Zeaman, D., & Hanley, P. (1983). Stimulus preferences as structural features. In T.J. Tighe & B.E. Shepp (Eds.), *Perception, cognition, and development*. Hillsdale, NJ: Erlbaum.

Zeiss, A.M., & Steffen, A.M. (1996). Interdisciplinary health care teams: The basic unit of geriatric care. In L.L. Carstensen, B.A. Edelstein, & L. Dornbrand (Eds.), *The practical handbook of clinical gerontology* (pp. 423-450). Thousand Oaks, CA: Sage.

Zeiss, A.M., Zeiss, R.A., & Dornbrand, L. (1988, November). *Assessing and treating sexual problems in older couples*. Paper presented at the meeting of the Gerontological Society of America, San Francisco.

Zellner, D.A., Harner, D.E., & Adler, R.L. (1989). Effects of eating abnormalities and gender on perceptions of desirable body shape. *Journal of Abnormal Psychology, 98*, 93-96.

Ziegler, F.J., Imboden, J.B., & Meyer, E. (1960). Contemporary conversion reactions: A clinical study. *American Journal of Psychiatry, 116*, 901-910.

Zigler, E. (1967). Familial mental retardation: A continuing dilemma. *Science, 155*, 292-298.

Zigler, E., Hodapp, R.M., & Edison, M.R. (1990). From theory to practice in the care and education of mentally retarded individuals. *American Journal on Mental Retardation, 95*, 1-12.

Zilboorg, G., & Henry, G.W. (1941). *A history of medical psychology*. New York: Norton.

Zimbardo, P.G., Andersen, S.M., & Kabat, L.G. (1981). Paranoia and deafness: An experimental investigation. *Science, 212*, 1529-1531.

Zimbardo, P.G., LaBerge, S., & Butler, L.D. (1993). Psychophysiological consequences of unexplained arousal: A post-hypnotic suggestion paradigm. *Journal of Abnormal Psychology, 102*, 466-473.

Zimmer, L., & Morgan, J.P. (1995). *Exposing marijuana myths: A review of the scientific evidence*. New York: The Lindemith Center.

Zimmerman, M. (1994). Diagnosing personality disorders: A review of issues and research methods. *Archives of General Psychiatry, 51*, 225-245.

Zimmerman, M., & Coryell, W. (1989). DSM-III personality disorder diagnoses in a nonpatient sample. *Archives of General Psychiatry, 46*, 682-689.

Zimmerman, M., Coryell, W., Pfohl, B., & Staid, D. (1986). The validity of four types of endogenous depression. *Archives of General Psychiatry, 43*, 234-245.

Zinbarg, R E., Brown, T.A., Barlow, D.H., & Rapee, R.M. (2001). Anxiety sensitivity, panic, and depressed mood: A reanalysis teasing apart the contributions of the two levels in the hierarchical structure of the Anxiety Sensitivity Index. *Journal of Abnormal Psychology, 110*, 372-377.

Zoccolillo, M., & Rogers, K. (1991). Characteristics and outcome of hospitalized adolescent girls with conduct disorder. *Journal of the American Academy of Child and Adolescent Psychiatry, 30*, 973-981.

Zoccolillo, M., Pickles, A., Quinton, D., & Rutter, M. (1992). The outcome of childhood conduct disorder: Implications for defining antisocial personality disorder and conduct disorder. *Psychological Medicine, 22*, 971-986.

Zucker, K.J., & Bradley, S.J. (1995). *Gender identity disorder and psychosexual problems in children and adolescents*. New York: Guilford Press.

Zucker, K.J., & Blanchard, R. (1997). Transvestic fetishism: Psychopathology and theory. In D.R. Laws & W. O'Donohue (Eds.), *Sexual deviance* (pp. 280-296). NY: Guilford Press.

Zucker, K.J., Bradley, S.J., & Sanikhana, M. (1997). Sex difference in referral rates of children with gender identity disorder: Some hypotheses. *Journal of Abnormal Child Psychology, 25*, 217-227.

Zucker, K.J., Finegan, J.K., Deering, R.W., & Bradley, S.J. (1984). Two subgroups of gender-problem children. *Archives of Sexual Behavior, 13*, 27-39.

Zucker, K.J., Green, R., Garofano, C., Bradley, S.J., et al. (1994). Prenatal gender preference of mothers of feminine and masculine boys: Relation to sibling sex composition and birth order. *Journal of Abnormal Child Psychology, 22*, 1-13.

Zucker, K.J., Wild, J., Bradley, S.J., & Stern, A. (1993). Physical attractiveness of boys with gender identity disorder. *Archives of Sexual Behavior, 22*, 23-36.

Case References

Abouesh, A., & Clayton, A. (2000). Compulsive voyeurism and exhibitionism: A clinical response to paroxetine. *Archives of Sexual Behavior, 28*, 23-30.

Abramowitz, J. S. (1997). Effectiveness of psychological and pharmacological treatments for obsessive-compulsive disorder: A quantitative review. *Journal of Consulting and Clinical Psychology, 65*, 44-52.

Abramowitz, J. S. (1998). Does cognitive-behavioral therapy cure obsessive-compulsive disorder? A meta-analytic evaluation of clinical significance. *Behavior Therapy, 29*, 339-355.

Abramowitz, J. S., Franklin, M. E., Street, G. P., Kozak, J. M., & Foa, E. B. (2000). Effects of comorbid depression on response to treatment for obsessive-compulsive disorder. *Behavior Therapy, 31*, 517-528.

Abramson, L. Y., Metalsky, G. I., & Alloy, L. B. (1989). Hopelessness depression: A theory-based subtype of depression. *Psychological Review, 96*, 358-372.

Abramson, L. Y., Seligman, M. E. P., & Teasdale, J. (1978). Learned helplessness in humans: Critique and reformulation. *Journal of Abnormal Psychology, 87*, 49-74.

Acocella, J. (1999). *Creating hysteria: Women and multiple personality disorder.* San Francisco, CA: Jossey-Bass.

Adams, W. A. (1950). The Negro patient in psychiatric treatment. *American Journal of Orthopsychiatry, 20*, 305-310.

Agras, W. S., Schneider, J. A., Arnow, B., Raeburm, S. D., & Telch, C. F. (1989). Cognitive-behavioral and response prevention treatments for bulimia nervosa. *Journal of Consulting and Clinical Psychology, 57*, 215-221.

Ainsworth, M. D. S. (1989). Attachments beyond infancy. *American Psychologist, 44*, 709-716.

Akhtar, S. (1990). Paranoid personality disorder: A synthesis of developmental, dynamic and descriptive features. *American Journal of Psychotherapy, 44*, 5-25.

Akhtar, S. (1992). *Broken structures: Severe personality disorders and their treatment.* Northvale, NJ: Jason Aronson.

Akiskal, H. S. (1981). Subaffective disorders: Dysthymic, cyclothymic, and bipolar II Disorders in the "borderline" realm. *Psychiatric Clinics of North America, 4*, 25-46.

Akyuez, G., Dogan, O., Sar, V., Yargic, L. I., & Tutkun, J. (1999). Frequency of dissociative identity disorder in the general population in Turkey. *Comprehensive Psychiatry, 40*, 151-159.

Allen, J. J. B., & Iacono, W. G. (2001). Assessing the validity of amnesia in dissociative identity disorder. *Psychology, Public Policy, and Law, 7*, 311-344.

Alexander, F. (1950). Psychosomatic medicine. New York: Norton.

Alexander, F., & French, T. M. (1946). *Psychoanalytic therapy.* New York: Ronald Press.

Alloy, L. B., Reilly-Harrington, N., Fresco, D. M., Whitehouse, W. G., & Zechmeister, J. S. (1999). Cognitive styles and life events in subsyndromal unipolar and bipolar disorders. *Journal of Cognitive Psychotherapy, 13*, 21-40.

Althof, S. E. (1995). Pharmacologic treatment of rapid ejaculation. *Psychiatric Clinics of North America, 18*, 85-94.

American Psychiatric Association. (1952). *Diagnostic and statistical manual of mental disorders: First edition (DSM-I).* Washington, DC: American Psychiatric Association.

American Psychiatric Association. (1968). *Diagnostic and statistical manual of mental disorders: Second edition (DSM-II).* Washington, DC: American Psychiatric Association.

American Psychiatric Association. (1980). *Diagnostic and statistical manual of mental disorders: Third edition (DSM-III).* Washington, DC: American Psychiatric Association.

American Psychiatric Association. (1987). *Diagnostic and statistical manual of mental disorders: Third edition revised (DSM-III-R).* Washington, DC: American Psychiatric Association.

American Psychiatric Association. (1994). *Diagnostic and statistical manual of mental disorders: Fourth edition (DSM-IV).* Washington, DC: American Psychiatric Association.

American Psychiatric Association. (2000). *Diagnostic and statistical manual of mental disorders: Fourth edition, Text revision (DSM-IV-TR).* Washington, DC: American Psychiatric Association.

Andersen, A. E. (1997). Inpatient treatment of anorexia nervosa. In D. M. Garner & P. E. Garfinkel (Eds.), *Handbook of treatment for eating disorders* (2nd ed., pp. 327-353). New York: Guilford.

Andersen, B. L., & Cyranowski, J. C. (1995). Women's sexuality: Behaviors, responses, and individual differences. *Journal of Consulting and Clinical Psychology, 63*, 891-906.

Anderson, D. A., & Maloney, K. C. (2001). The efficacy of cognitive-behavioral therapy on the core symptoms of bulimia nervosa. *Clinical Psychology Review, 21*, 971-988.

Anderson, K. B., Cooper, H., & Okamura, L. (1997). Individual differences and attitudes toward rape: A meta-analytic review. *Personality and Social Psychology Bulletin, 23*, 295-315.

Anderson, N. B., & Armstead, C. A. (1995). Toward understanding the association of socioeconomic status and health: A new challenge for the biopsychosocial approach. *Psychosomatic Medicine, 57*, 213-225.

Anderson, N. B., McNeilly, M., & Myers, H. F. (1993). A biopsychosocial model of race differences in vascular reactivity. In J. J. Blascovich & E. S. Katkin (Eds.), *Cardiovascular reactivity to psychological stress and disease* (pp. 83-108). Washington, DC: American Psychological Association.

Andreasen, N. C., Arndt, S., Alliger, R., Miller, D., & Flaum, M. (1995). Symptoms of schizophrenia: Methods, meanings, and mechanisms. *Archives of General Psychiatry, 52*, 341-351.

Andreasen, N. C., Ehrhardt, J. C., Swayze, V. W., Alliger, R. J., Yuh, W. T. C., Cohen, G., & Ziebell, S. (1990). Magnetic resonance imaging of the brain in schizophrenia: The pathophysiologic significance of structural abnormalities. *Archives of General Psychiatry, 47*, 35-44.

Angst, J., Sellaro, R., & Angst, F. (1998). Long-term outcome and mortality of treated versus untreated bipolar and depressed patients: A preliminary report. *International Journal of Psychiatry in Clinical Practice, 2*, 115-119.

Anthony, J. C., & Aboraya, A. (1992). The epidemiology of selected mental disorders in later life. In J. E. Birren, R. B. Sloane, & G. D. Cohen (Eds.), *Handbook of mental health and aging* (2nd ed., pp. 27-73). San Diego: Academic Press.

Appelbaum, P. S., Robbins, P. C., & Monahan, J. (2000). Violence and delusions: Data from the MacArthur Violence Risk Assessment Study. *American Journal of Psychiatry, 157*, 566-572.

Arieti, S. (1979). New views on the psychodynamics of phobias. *American Journal of Psychotherapy, 33*, 82-95.

Atkinson, D. R. (1983). Ethnic similarity in counseling psychology: A review of research. *The Counseling Psychologist, 11*, 79-92.

Atkinson, D. R. (1985). A meta-review of research on cross-cultural counseling and psychotherapy. *Journal of Multicultural Counseling and Development, 13*, 138-153.

Atkinson, D. R., Maruyama, M., & Matsui, S. (1978). The effects of counselor race and counseling approach on Asian Americans' perception of counselor credibility and utility. *Journal of Counseling Psychology, 25*, 76-83.

August, G. J., Realmuto, G. M., MacDonald, A. W., et al. (1996). Prevalence of ADHD and comorbid disorders among elementary school children screened for disruptive behavior. *Journal of Abnormal Child Psychology, 24*, 555-569.

August, G. J., Stewart, M. A., & Tsai, L. (1981). The incidence of cognitive disabilities in the siblings of autistic children. *British Journal of Psychiatry, 138*, 416-422.

Austin, S. B. (2001). Population-based prevention of eating disorders: An application of the Rose prevention model. *Preventive Medicine, 32*, 268-283.

Axline, V. M. (1964). *Dibs: In search of self.* New York: Ballantine.

Baastrup, P. D., & Schou, M. (1967). Lithium as a prophylactic agent against recurrent depressions and manic-depressive psychosis. *Archives of General Psychiatry, 16*, 162-172.

Bach, A. K., Wincze, J. P., & Barlow, D. H. (2001). Sexual dysfunction. In D. H. Barlow (Ed.). *Clinical handbook of psychological disorders: A step-by-step treatment manual* (3rd ed., pp. 562-608). New York: Guilford.

Baer, L., & Jenike, M. A. (1992). Personality disorders in obsessive-compulsive disorder. *Psychiatric Clinics of North America, 15*, 803-812.

Bailey, A., LeCouteur, A., Gottesman, I., Bolton, P., Simonoff, E., et al. (1995). Autism as a strongly genetic disorder: Evidence from a British twin study. *Psychological Medicine, 25*, 63-77.

Baker, C. A., & Morrison, A. P. (1998). Cognitive processes in auditory hallucinations: Attributional biases and metacognition. *Psychological Medicine, 28*, 1199-1208.

Bakker, A., van Kesteren, P. J. M., Gooren, L. J. G., & Bezemer, P. D. (1993). The prevalence of transsexualism in the Netherlands. *Acta Psychiatrica Scandinavica, 87*, 237-238.

Ball, S. G., Baer, L., & Otto, M. W. (1996). Symptom subtypes of obsessive-compulsive disorder in behavioral treatment studies: A quantitative review. *Behaviour Research and Therapy, 34*, 47-51.

Ballenger, J. C. (1997). Panic disorder in the medical setting. *Journal of Clinical Psychiatry, 58* (Suppl. 2), 13-17.

Ballenger, J. C. (1999). Current treatments of the anxiety disorders in adults. *Biological Psychiatry, 46*, 1579-1594.

Ballenger, J. C., Davidson, J. R. T., Lecrubier, Y., Nutt, D. J., Borkovec, T. D., Rickels, K., Stein, D. J., & Wittchen, H. U. (2001). Consensus statement on generalized anxiety disorder from the International Consensus Group on Depression and Anxiety. *Journal of Clinical Psychiatry, 62*, 53-58.

Ballenger, J. C., Davidson, J. R. T., Lecrubier, Y., Nutt, D. J., Foa, E. B., Kessler, R. C. & McFarlane, A. C. (2000). Consensus statement on posttraumatic stress disorder from the international consensus group on depression and anxiety. *Journal of Clinical Psychiatry, 61* (Suppl. 5), 60-66.

Bancroft, J. (1997). Sexual problems. In D. M. Millar & C. G. Fairburn (Eds.), *Science and practice of cognitive behaviour therapy* (pp. 243-257). New York: Oxford University Press.

Bandura, A. (1986). *Social foundations of thought and action: A social cognitive theory.* Englewood Cliffs, NJ: Prentice-Hall.

Bandura, A., & Rosenthal, T. L. (1966). Vicarious classical conditioning as a function of arousal level. *Journal of Personality and Social Psychology, 3,* 54-62.

Barkley, R. A. (1990). *Attention-deficit hyperactivity disorder: A handbook for diagnosis and treatment.* New York: Guilford.

Barkley, R. A., DuPaul, G. J., & McMurray, M. B. (1990). A comprehensive evaluation of attention deficit disorder with and without hyperactivity defined by research criteria. *Journal of Consulting and Clinical Psychology, 58,* 775-789.

Barkley, R. A., Fischer, M., Edelbrock, C. S., & Smallish, L. (1990). The adolescent outcome of hyperactive children diagnosed by research criteria: I. An 8-year prospective follow-up. *Journal of the American Academy of Child and Adolescent Psychiatry, 29,* 546-557.

Barkley, R. A., Karlsson, J., & Pollard, S. (1985). Effects of age on the mother-child interactions of hyperactive children. *Journal of Abnormal Child Psychology, 13,* 631-638.

Barlow, D. H. (1986). Causes of sexual dysfunction: The role of anxiety and cognitive interference. *Journal of Consulting and Clinical Psychology, 54,* 140-148.

Barlow, D. H. (1997). Cognitive-behavioral therapy for panic disorder: Current status. *Journal of Clinical Psychiatry, 58* (Suppl. 2), 32-35.

Barlow, D. H., Abel, G. G., & Blanchard, E. B. (1979). Gender identity change in transsexuals: Follow-up and replications. *Archives of General Psychiatry, 36,* 1001-1007.

Barlow, D. H., Craske, M. G., Cerny, J. A., & Klosko, J. S. (1989). Behavioral treatment of panic disorder. *Behavior Therapy, 20,* 261-282.

Barlow, D. H., Gorman, J. M., Shear, M. K., & Woods, S. W. (2000). Cognitive-behavioral therapy, imipramine, or their combination for panic disorder: A randomized controlled trial. *Journal of the American Medical Association, 283,* 2529-2536.

Barlow, D. H., Raffa, S. D., & Cohen, E. M. (2002). Psychosocial treatments for panic disorders, phobias, and generalized anxiety disorder. In P. E. Nathan & J. M. Gorman (Eds.), *A guide to treatments that work* (2nd ed., pp. 301-335). London, England: Oxford University Press.

Barnes, M. F. (1995). Sex therapy in the couples context: Therapy issues of victims of sexual trauma. *American Journal of Family Therapy, 23,* 351-360.

Baron, M. (1995). Genes and psychosis: Old wine in new bottles? *Acta Psychiatrica Scandinavica, 92,* 81-86.

Baron, M., Risch, N., Hamburger, R., et al. (1987). Genetic linkage between X chromosome markers and manic depression. *Nature, 326,* 806-808.

Baron, M., Risch, N., Levitt, M., & Gruen, R. (1985). Familial transmission of schizotypal and borderline personality disorders. *American Journal of Psychiatry, 142,* 927-934.

Barrett, C. L., Hampe, E., & Miller, L. (1978). Research on psychotherapy with children. In S. L. Garfield & A. E. Bergin (Eds.), *Handbook of psychotherapy and behavior change: An empirical analysis* (2nd ed.). New York: Wiley.

Bartak, L., Rutter, M., & Cox, A. (1975). A comparative study of infantile autism and specific developmental language disorders: I. The children. *British Journal of Psychiatry, 126,* 127-145.

Basoglu, M., & Mineka, S. (1992). The role of uncontrollable and unpredictable stress in post-traumatic stress responses in torture survivors. In M. Basoglu (Ed.), *Torture and its consequences: Current treatment approaches* (pp. 182-225). Cambridge, England: Cambridge University Press.

Basoglu, M., & Paker, M. (1995). Severity of trauma as predictor of long-term psychological status in survivors of torture. *Journal of Anxiety Disorders, 9,* 339-350.

Basson, R., Berman, J., Burnett, A., Derogatis, L., Ferguson, D., Fourcroy, J., et al. (2000). Report of the international consensus development conference on female sexual dysfunction: Definitions and classifications. *Journal of Urology, 163,* 888-899.

Battle, E. S., & Lacey, B. (1972). A context for hyperactivity in children over time. *Child Development, 43,* 757-773.

Bebbington, P. E. (1998). Epidemiology of obsessive-compulsive disorder. *British Journal of Psychiatry, 173* (Suppl. 35), 2-6.

Bebbington, P. E., Brugha, T., MacCarthy, B., Potter, J., et al. (1988). The Camberwell Collaborative Depression Study: I. Depressed probands: Adversity and the form of depression. *British Journal of Psychiatry, 152,* 754-765.

Bebbington, P., & Ramana, R. (1995). The epidemiology of bipolar affective disorder. *Social Psychiatry and Psychiatric Epidemiology, 30,* 279-292.

Beck, A. T. (1967). *Depression: Causes and treatment.* Philadelphia: University of Pennsylvania Press.

Beck, A. T. (1987). Cognitive models of depression. *Journal of Cognitive Psychotherapy, 1,* 5-37.

Beck, A. T., Butler, A. C., Brown, G. K., Dahlsgaard, K. K., Newman, C. F., & Beck, J. S. (2001). Dysfunctional beliefs discriminate personality disorders. *Behaviour Research and Therapy, 39,* 1213-1225.

Beck, A. T., & Emery, G. (1985). *Anxiety disorders and phobias: A cognitive perspective.* New York: Basic Books.

Beck, A. T., Rush, A. J., Shaw, B. F., & Emery, G. (1979). *Cognitive therapy of depression.* New York: Guilford.

Becker, D. F., Grilo, C. M., Edell, W. S., & McGlashen, T. H. (2000). Comorbidity of borderline personality disorder with other personality disorders in hospitalized adolescents and adults. *American Journal of Psychiatry, 157,* 2011-2016.

Becker, J. V., & Kaplan, M. S. (1991). Rape victims: Issues, theories, and treatment. *Annual Review of Sex Research, 2,* 267-292.

Bellack, A. S., Mueser, K. T., Gingerich, S., & Agresta, J. (1997). *Social skills training for schizophrenia: A step-by-step guide.* New York: Guilford.

Benjamin, H. (1953). Transvestism and transsexualism. *International Journal of Sexology, 7,* 12-14.

Benjamin, H. (1966). *The transsexual phenomenon.* New York: Julian Press.

Benjamin, J., Ben-Zion, I. K., Karbofsky, E., & Dannon, P. (2000). Double-blind-placebo-controlled pilot study of paroxetine for specific phobia. *Psychopharmacology, 149,* 194(196.

Bennet, I. (1960). *Delinquent and neurotic children.* London: Tavistock Publications.

Benson, H. (1975). *The relaxation response.* New York: Morrow.

Bentall, R., & Kinderman, P. (1998). Psychological processes and delusional beliefs: Implications for the treatment of paranoid states. In T. Wykes & N. Tarrier (Eds.), *Outcome and innovation in psychological treatment of schizophrenia* (pp. 119-144). New York: Wiley.

Bernard, M. E. (1990). Rational-emotive therapy with children and adolescents. *School Psychology Review, 19,* 294-303.

Bernstein, A. (2001). Problems in treating paranoia: A case illustration. *Modern Psychoanalysis, 26,* 237-247.

Bernstein, D. P., Useda, D., & Siever, L. J. (1993). Paranoid personality disorder: Review of the literature and recommendations for DSM-IV. *Journal of Personality Disorders, 7,* 53-62.

Bernstein, D. P., Useda, D., & Siever, L. J. (1995). Paranoid personality disorder. In W. J. Livesley (Ed.), *The DSM-IV personality disorders* (pp. 45-57). New York: Guilford.

Bernstein, G. A., & Garfinkle, B. D. (1988). Pedigrees, functioning, and psychopathology in families of school phobic children. *American Journal of Psychiatry, 145,* 70-74.

Berrettini, W. H. (2000). Genetics of psychiatric disease. *Annual Review of Medicine, 51,* 465-479.

Berrios, G. E., & Chiu, H. (1989). Obsessive-compulsive disorders in Cambridgeshire: A follow-up study of up to 20 years. *British Journal of Psychiatry, 154* (Suppl. 4), 17-20.

Bertelsen, A., & Gottesman, I. I. (1995). Schizoaffective psychoses: Genetical clues to classification. *American Journal of Medical Genetics, 60,* 7-11.

Bettelheim, B. (1967). The empty fortress. New York: Free Press.

Bettelheim, B. (1973). Bringing up children. *Ladies Home Journal, 90,* 28.

Beutler, L. E., Machado, P. P. P., & Neufeldt, S. A. (1994). Therapist variables. In A. E. Bergin & S. L. Garfield (Eds.), *Handbook of psychotherapy and behavior change* (4th ed., pp. 229-269). New York: Wiley.

Biederman, J., Faraone, S. V., Keenan, K., et al. (1992). Further evidence for family-genetic risk factors in attention deficit hyperactivity disorder: Patterns of comorbidity in probands and relatives in psychiatrically and pediatrically referred samples. *Archives of General Psychiatry, 49,* 728-738.

Biederman, J., Faraone, S., Mick, E., et al. (1995). High risk for attention deficit hyperactivity disorder among children of parents with childhood onset of the disorder. *American Journal of Psychiatry, 152,* 431-435.

Biederman, J., Mick, E., Faraone, S. V., et al. (2002). Influence of gender on attention deficit hyperactivity disorder in children referred to a psychiatric clinic. *American Journal of Psychiatry, 159,* 36-42.

Biederman, J., Rosenbaum, J., Hirschfeld, D., Faraone, S., Bolduc, E., et al. (1990). Psychiatric correlates of behavioral inhibition in young children of parents with and without psychiatric disorders. *Archives of General Psychiatry, 47,* 21-26.

Black, D. W., & Noyes, R. (1997). Obsessive-compulsive disorder and axis II. *International Review of Psychiatry, 9,* 111-118.

Blackwood, D. H. R., Visscher, P. M., & Muir, W. J. (2001). Genetic studies of bipolar affective disorder in large families. *British Journal of Psychiatry, 178* (Suppl. 41), S134-S136.

Blair, C., Freeman, C., & Cull, A. (1995). The families of anorexia nervosa and cystic fibrosis patients. *Psychological Medicine, 25,* 985-993.

Blair, R. J. D., Jones, L., Clark, F., & Smith, M. (1997). The psychopathic individual: A lack of responsiveness to distress cues. *Psychophysiology, 34,* 192-198.

Blais, M. A., Hilsenroth, M. J., & Castlebury, F. D. (1997). Content validity of the newly revised Diagnostic and Statistical Manual of Mental Disorders-IV (DSM-IV) narcissistic personality (NPD) and borderline personality disorder (BPD) criteria sets. *Comprehensive Psychiatry, 38,* 31-47.

Blanchard, E. (1990). Biofeedback treatments of essential hypertension. *Biofeedback and Self-Regulation 15,* 209-228.

Blanchard, E. E., Eisele, G., Vollmer, A., Payne, A., et al. (1996). Controlled evaluation of thermal biofeedback in treatment of elevated blood pressure in unmedicated mild hypertension. *Biofeedback and Self-Regulation, 21,* 167-190.

Blanchard, R., & Clemmensen, L. H. (1988). A test of the DSM-III-R's implicit assumption that fetishistic arousal and gender dysphoria are mutually exclusive. *Journal of Sex Research, 25,* 426-432.

Bleuler, E. (1950). *Dementia praecox or the group of schizophrenias.* New York: International Universities Press. (Originally published 1911.)

Bliss, E. L. (1986). *Multiple personality, allied disorders and hypnosis.* Oxford: Oxford University Press.

Bodlund, O., & Kullgren, G. (1996). Transsexualism-general outcome and prognostic factors: A-five-year follow-up study of nineteen transsexuals in the process of changing sex. *Archives of Sexual Behavior, 25,* 303-316.

Boon, S., & Draijer, N. (1993). Multiple personality disorder in the Netherlands: A clinical investigation of 71 patients. *American Journal of Psychiatry, 150,* 489-494.

Bootzin, R. R. (1997). Examining the theory and clinical utility of writing about emotional experiences. *Psychological Science, 8,* 167-169.

Bordo, S. (1997). Anorexia nervosa: Psychopathology as the crystallization of culture. In M. M. Gergen & S. N. Davis (Eds.), *Toward a new psychology of gender* (pp. 423-453). New York: Routledge.

Borkovec, T. D., & Costello, E. (1993). Efficacy of applied relaxation and cognitive-behavioral therapy in the treatment of generalized anxiety disorder. *Journal of Consulting and Clinical Psychology, 61,* 611-619.

Bower, H. (2001). The gender identity disorder in the DSM-IV classification: A critical evaluation. *Australian and New Zealand Journal of Psychiatry, 35,* 1-8.

Bowlby, J. (1973). *Separation: Anxiety and anger.* New York: Basic Books.

Bradford, D., Stroup, S., & Lieberman, J. (2002). Pharmacological treatments for schizophrenia. In P. E. Nathan & J .M. Gorman (Eds.), *A guide to treatments that work* (2nd ed., pp. 169-199). London: Oxford University Press.

Bradley, S. J., & Zucker, K. J. (1997). Gender identity disorder: A review of the past 10 years. *Journal of the American Academy of Child and Adolescent Psychiatry, 36,* 872-880.

Bretschneider, J. G., & McCoy, N. L. (1988). Sexual interest and behavior in healthy 80-to 102-year-olds. *Archives of Sexual Behavior,* 17, 109-129.

Brewerton, T. D., Dansky, B. S., Kilpatrick, D. G., & O'Neil, P. M. (2000). Which comes first in the pathogenesis of bulimia nervosa: Dieting or bingeing? *International Journal of Eating Disorders, 20,* 259-264.

Brewin, C. R., Andrews, B., & Gotlib, I. H. (1993). Psychopathology and early experience: A reappraisal of retrospective reports. *Psychological Bulletin, 113,* 82-98.

Brewin, C. R., Andrews, B., & Valentine, J. D. (2000). Meta-analysis of risk factors for postraumatic stress disorder in trauma-exposed adults. *Journal of Consulting and Clinical Psychology, 68,* 748-766.

Brooks, F. (2001). Substance abuse and violence: A coexisting issue. In D. S. Sandhu (Ed.). *Faces of violence: Psychological correlates, concepts, and intervention strategies* (pp. 171-190). Huntington, NY: Nova Science Publishers.

Brown, A. S., & Susser, E. S. (2002). In utero infection and adult schizophrenia. *Mental Retardation and Developmental Disabilities Research Reviews, 8,* 51-57.

Brown, D., Frischholz, E. J., & Scheflin, A. W. (1999). Iatrogenic dissociative identity disorder-An evaluation of the scientific evidence. *Journal of Psychiatry and Law, 27,* 549-637.

Brown, G. W. (1993). Life events and affective disorder: Replications and limitations. *Psychosomatic Medicine, 55,* 248-259.

Brown, G. W., Bifulco, A., & Harris, T. O. (1987). Life events, vulnerability and onset of depression: Some refinements. *British Journal of Psychiatry, 150,* 30-42.

Brown, G. W., & Harris, T. (1978). *Social origins of depression: A study of psychiatric disorder in women.* New York: Free Press.

Brown, T. A. (1996). Validity of the DSM-III-R and DSM-IV classification systems for anxiety disorders. In R. M. Rapee (Ed.), *Current controversies in the anxiety disorders* (pp. 21-45). New York: Guilford.

Bruch, H. (1973). *Eating disorders: Obesity, anorexia nervosa, and the person within.* New York: Basic Books.

Bruch, H. (1981). Developmental considerations of anorexia nervosa and obesity. *Canadian Journal of Psychiatry, 26,* 212-217.

Bryant, R. A. (1995). Autobiographical memory across personalities in dissociative identity disorder: A case report. *Journal of Abnormal Psychology, 104,* 625-631.

Bryant, R. A., & Friedman, M. (2001). Medication and non-medication treatments of post-traumatic stress disorder. *Current Opinion in Psychiatry, 14,* 119-123

Bulik, C. M., Sullivan, P. F., & Kendler, K. S. (1998). Heritability of binge eating and broadly defined bulimia nervosa. *Biological Psychiatry, 44,* 1210-1218.

Bullough, V. L. (1999). Medicine and gender dysphoria: A brief overview. *Journal of Sex Education and Therapy, 24,* 110-116.

Bullough, V. L., & Bullough, B. (1993). *Cross dressing, sex, and gender.* Philadelphia: University of Pennsylvania Press.

Burns, A. S., Rivas, D. A., & Ditunno, J. F. (2001). The management of neurogenic bladder and sexual dysfunction after spinal cord injury. *Spine, 26,* S129-S136.

Burns, D. D. (1992). *Feeling good: The new mood therapy.* New York: Avon.

Bustillo, J. R., Lauriello, J., Horan, W. P., & Keith, S. J. (2001). The psychosocial treatment of schizophrenia: An update. *American Journal of Psychiatry, 158,* 163-175.

Butler, R. N., & Lewis, M. (1977). *Aging and mental health* (2nd ed.). St. Louis: Mosby.

Butzlaff, R. L., & Hooley, J. M. (1998). Expressed emotion and psychiatric relapse. *Archives of General Psychiatry, 55,* 547-552.

Byrne, S. M., & McLean, N. J. (2002). The cognitive-behavioral model of bulimia nervosa: A direct evaluation. *International Journal of Eating Disorders.*

Cade, J. F. J. (1949). Lithium salts in the treatment of psychotic excitement. *Medical Journal of Australia, 36,* 349-352.

Cadoret, R. J., Yates, W. R., Troughton, E., Woodworth, G., & Stewart, M. A. (1995a). Adoption study demonstrating two genetic pathways to drug abuse. *Archives of General Psychiatry, 52,* 42-52.

Cadoret, R. J., Yates, W. R., Troughton, E., Woodworth, G., & Stewart, M. A. (1995b). Genetic-environment interaction in the genesis of aggressivity and conduct disorders. *Archives of General Psychiatry, 52,* 916-924.

Caldwell, D. (1949). Psychopathia transsexualis. *Sexology, 16,* 274-280.

Calev, A., Guadino, E. A., Squires, N. K., Zervas, I. M., et al. (1995). ECT and memory cognition: A review. *British Journal of Clinical Psychology, 34,* 505-515.

Calhoun, K. S., & Wilson, A. E. (2000). Rape and sexual aggression. In L. T. Szuchman & F. Muscarella (Eds.), *Psychological perspectives on human sexuality* (pp. 573-602). New York: Wiley.

Cameron, N. (1959). The paranoid pseudo-community revisited. *American Journal of Sociology, 65,* 52-58.

Campbell, M. (1988). Fenfluramine treatment of autism. *Journal of Child Psychology and Psychiatry, 29,* 1-10.

Campbell, M., Anderson, L. T., & Small, A. M. (1990). Pharmacotherapy in autism: A summary of research at Bellevue/New York University. *Brain Dysfunction, 3,* 299-307.

Campbell, M., Anderson, L. T., Small, A. M., Locascio, L. L., Lynch, N. S., & Choroco, M. C. (1990). Naltrexone in autistic children: A double-blind and placebo controlled study. *Psychopharmacology Bulletin, 26,* 130-135.

Cannon, T. D., Kaprio, J., Loennqvist, J., Huttunen, M., & Koskenvuo, M. (1998). The genetic epidemiology of schizophrenia in a Finnish twin cohort: A population-based modeling study. *Archives of General Psychiatry, 55,* 67-74.

Cantwell, D. P., Baker, L., & Rutter, M. (1978). Family factors. In M. Rutter & E. Schopler (Eds.), *Autism: A reappraisal of concepts and treatment.* New York: Plenum.

Cappeliez, P. (1988). Some thoughts on the prevalence and etiology of depressive conditions in the elderly. Special Issue: Francophone research in gerontology in Canada. *Canadian Journal on Aging, 7,* 431-440.

Carroll, J. M., Touyz, S. M., & Beaumont, P. J. (1996). Specific comorbidity between bulimia nervosa and personality disorders. *International Journal of Eating Disorders, 19,* 159-170.

Casper, R. C., Eckert, H. A., Halmi, S. C., Goldberg, S. C., & Davis, J. M. (1980). Bulimia. *Archives of General Psychiatry, 37,* 1030-1035.

Casper, R. C., & Troiani, M. (2001). Family functioning in anorexia nervosa differs by subtypes. *International Journal of Eating Disorders, 20,* 338-342.

Cassell, S. (1965). Effect of brief puppet therapy upon the emotional responses of children undergoing cardiac catheterization. *Journal of Consulting Psychology, 29,* 1-8.

Castellanos, F. X., Giedd, J. N., Marsh, W. L., Hamburger, S. D., Vaituzis, A. C., et al. (1996). Quantitative brain magnetic resonance imaging in attention-deficit/hyperactivity disorder. *Archives of General Psychiatry, 53,* 607-616.

Castle, D. J., Scott, K., Wessely, S., & Murray, R. M. (1993). Does social deprivation during gestation and early life predispose to later schizophrenia? *Social Psychiatry and Psychiatric Epidemiology, 28,* 1-4.

Chakos, M., Lieberman, J., Hoffman, E., Bradford, D., & Sheitman, B. (2001). Effectiveness of second-generation antipsychotics in patients with treatment-resistant schizophrenia: A review and meta-analysis of randomized trials. *American Journal of Psychiatry, 158,* 518-526.

Chambers, K. C., and Bernstein, I. L. (in press). Conditioned flavor aversions. In R. L. Doty (Ed.), *Handbook of Clinical Olfaction and Gustation* (2nd ed.). New York: Marcel Dekker.

Chambless, D. L., Cherney, J., Caputo, G. C., & Rheinstein, B. J. (1987). Anxiety disorders and alcoholism: A study with inpatient alcoholics. *Journal of Anxiety Disorders, 1*, 29-40.

Chassin, L., Pitts, S. C., DeLucia, C., & Todd, M. (1999). A longitudinal study of children of alcoholics: Predicting young adult substance use disorders, anxiety, and depression. *Journal of Abnormal Psychology, 108*, 106-119.

Cheung, P., Schweitzer, I., Crowley, K., & Tuckwell, V. (1997). Violence in schizophrenia: Role of hallucinations and delusions. *Schizophrenia Research, 26*, 181-190.

Chivers, M. L., & Bailey, J. M. (2000). Sexual orientation of female-to-male transsexuals: A comparison of homosexual and nonhomosexual types. *Archives of Sexual Behavior, 29*, 259-278.

Chorpita, B. F., Albano, A. M., Heimberg, R. G., & Barlow, D. H. (1996). A systematic replication of the prescriptive treatment of school refusal behavior in a single subject. *Journal of Behavior Therapy and Experimental Psychiatry, 27*, 281-290.

Chrichton, P. (1996). First-rank symptoms or rank-and-file symptoms? *British Journal of Psychiatry, 169*, 537-540.

Churchill, D. W. (1969). Psychotic children and behavior modification. *American Journal of Psychiatry, 125*, 1585-1590.

Citronme, L., & Volavka, J. (2000). Management of violence in schizophrenia. *Psychiatric Annals, 30*, 41-52.

Clark, D. M., & Ehlers, A. (1993). An overview of the cognitive theory and treatment of panic disorder. *Applied and Preventive Psychology, 2*, 131-139.

Clark, L. A., & Harrison, J. A. (2001). Assessment instruments. In W. J. Livesley (Ed.), *Handbook of personality disorders: Theory, research, and treatment* (pp 277-306). New York: Guilford.

Clark, L. A., Livesley, W. J., & Morey, L. (1997). Personality disorder assessment: The challenge of construct validity. *Journal of Personality Disorders, 11*, 205-231.

Clark, R. E., Bartels, S. J., Mellman, T. A., Peacock, W. J. (2002). Recent trends in anti-psychotic combination therapy of schizophrenia and schizoaffective disorders: Implications for state mental health policy. *Schizophrenia Bulletin, 28*, 75-84.

Cleckley, H. E. (1976). *The mask of sanity*. St. Louis: Mosby.

Cloninger, C. R., Bohman, M., & Sigvardsson, S. (1981). Inheritance of alcohol abuse: Cross-fostering analysis of adopted men. *Archives of General Psychiatry, 38*, 861-868.

Cloninger, C. R., Sigvardsson, S., Gilligan, S. B., von Knorring, A., et al. (1988). Genetic heterogeneity and the classification of alcoholism. *Advances in Alcohol and Substance Abuse, 7*, 3-16.

Cohen, C. I. (1993). Poverty and the course of schizophrenia: Implications for research and policy. *Hospital and Community Psychiatry, 44*, 951-958.

Cohen, S., & Herbert, T. B. (1996). Health psychology: Psychological factors and physical disease from the perspective of human psychoneuroimmunology. In J. T. Spence, J. M. Darley, & D. J. Foss (Eds.), *Annual review of psychology* (pp. 123-142). Stanford, CA: Stanford University Press.

Cohen-Kettenis, P. T., & Arrindell, W. A. (1990). Perceived parental rearing style, parental divorce and transsexualism: A controlled study. *Psychological Medicine, 20*, 613-620.

Cohen-Kettenis, P. T., & van Goozen, S. H. (1997). Sex reassignment of adolescent transsexuals: A follow-up study. *Journal of the American Academy of Child and Adolescent Psychiatry, 36*, 263-271.

Colby, K. M. (1975). *Artificial paranoia: A computer simulation of paranoid processes*. New York: Pergamon.

Colby, K. M. (1977). Appraisal of four psychological theories of paranoid phenomena. *Journal of Abnormal Psychology, 86*, 54-59.

Cole, J. O., & Davis, J. M. (1969). Antipsychotic drugs. In L. Bellak & L. Loeb (Eds.), *The schizophrenic syndrome*. New York: Grune and Stratton.

Comas-Diaz, L. (1992). The future of psychotherapy with ethnic minorities. *Psychotherapy, 29*, 88-94.

Compton, A. (1992). The psychoanalytic view of phobias: III. Agoraphobia and other phobias of adults. *Psychoanalytic Quarterly, 61*, 400-425.

Conger, J. J. (1951). The effects of alcohol on conflict behavior in the albino rat. *Quarterly Journal of Studies on Alcohol, 12*, 129-145.

Conwell, Y. (1994). Suicide in elderly patients. In T. S. Schneider, C. F. Reynolds, III, B. D. Lebowitz, & A. J. Friedhoff (Eds.), *Diagnosis and treatment of depression in late life* (pp. 397-418). Washington, DC: American Psychiatric Press.

Cook, M., & Mineka, S. (1989). Observational conditioning of fear to fear-relevant versus fear-irrelevant stimuli in rhesus monkeys. *Journal of Abnormal Psychology, 98*, 448-459.

Cooks, J., Schotte, D. E., & McNally, R. J. (1992). Emotional arousal and overeating in restrained eaters. *Journal of Abnormal Psychology, 101*, 348-351.

Coolidge, F. L., Thded, L. L., & Young, S. E. (2002). The heritability of gender identity disorder in a child and adolescent twin sample. *Behavior Genetics, 32*, 251-257.

Coons, P. M., Bowman, E. S., & Milstein, V. (1988). Multiple personality disorder: A clinical investigation of 50 cases. *Journal of Nervous and Mental Disease, 176*, 519-527.

Cooper, M. J., Todd, G., & Wells, A. (2002). Content, origins, and consequences of dysfunctional beliefs in anorexia nervosa and bulimia nervosa. In R. L. Leahy & E. T. Dowd (Eds.). *Clinical advances in cognitive psychotherapy: Theory and application* (pp. 399-417). New York: Springer.

Cooper, M. L., Frone, M. R., Russell, M., & Mudar, P. (1995). Drinking to regulate positive and negative emotion: A motivational model of alcoholism. *Journal of Personality and Social Psychology, 69*, 961-971.

Coryell, W., Scheftner, W., Keller, M., Endicott, J., et al. (1993). The enduring psychosocial consequences of mania and depression. *American Journal of Psychiatry, 150*, 720-727.

Courchesne, E., Yeung-Courchesne, R., Press, G. A., Hesselink, J. R., & Jernigan, T. L. (1988). Hypoplasia of cerebellar vermal lobules VI and VII in autism. *New England Journal of Medicine, 318*, 1349-1354.

Cowan, P. A., Hoddinott, G. A., & Wright, B. A. (1965). Compliance and resistance in the conditioning of autistic children: An exploratory study. *Child Development, 36*, 913-923.

Cox, A., Rutter, M., Newman, S., & Bartak, L. (1975). A comparative study of autism and specific developmental language disorders: II. Parental characteristics. *British Journal of Psychiatry, 126*, 145-159.

Coyne, J. C. (1992). Cognition in depression: A paradigm in crisis. *Psychological Inquiry, 3*, 232-235.

Coyne, J. C. (1999). Thinking interactionally about depression: A radical restatement. In T. Joiner & J. C. Coyne (Eds.). *The interactional nature of depression* (pp. 365-392). Washington, DC: American Psychological Association.

Coyne, J. C., Downey, G., & Boergers, J. (1993). Depression in families: A systems perspective. In D. Cichetti & S. L. Toth (Eds.), *Rochester symposium on developmental psychopathology: Vol. 4 Developmental approaches to the affective disorders*. Rochester, NY: University of Rochester.

Coyne, J. C., & Gotlib, I. H. (1983). The role of cognition in depression: A critical appraisal. *Psychological Bulletin, 94*, 472-505.

Craighead, W. E., & Miklowitz, D. J. (2000). Psychosocial interventions for bipolar disorder. *Journal of Clinical Psychiatry, 61 (Supp.13)*, 58-64.

Craske, M. G., & Barlow, D. H. (2001). Panic disorder and agoraphobia. In D. H. Barlow (Ed.), *Clinical handbook of psychological disorders: A step-by-step treatment manual.* (3rd ed., pp. 1-59). New York: Guilford.

Craske, M. G., & Lewin, M. R. (1998). Cognitive-behavioral treatment of panic disorders. In V. E. Caballo (Ed.), *International handbook of cognitive and behavioural treatments for psychological disorders* (pp. 105-128). Oxford, England: Pergamon/Elsevier.

Craske, M. G., Rapee, R. M., & Barlow, D. H. (1992). Cognitive-behavioral treatment of panic disorder, agoraphobia, and generalized anxiety disorder. In S. M. Turner, K. S. Calhoun, & H. E. Adams (Eds.), *Handbook of clinical behavior therapy* (2nd ed., 39-65). New York: Wiley.

Crow, T. J., Ferrier, I. N., & Johnstone, E. C. (1986). The two-syndrome concept and neuroendocrinology of schizophrenia. *Psychiatric Clinics of North America, 9*, 99-113.

Crowe, R. R. (1984). Current concepts: Electroconvulsive therapy-A current perspective. *New England Journal of Medicine, 311*, 163-167.

Crowther, J. H., Kichler, J. C., Sherwood, N. E., & Kuhnert, J. E. (2002). The role of familial factors in bulimia nervosa. *Eating Disorders: The Journal of Treatment and Prevention, 10*, 141-151.

DaCosta, M., & Halmi, K. A. (1992). Classifications of anorexia nervosa: Question of subtypes. *International Journal of Eating Disorders, 11*, 305-313.

Dalal, B., Larkin, E., Leese, M., & Taylor, P. J. (1999). Clozapine treatment of long-standing schizophrenia and serious violence: A two-year follow-up study of the first 50 patients treated with clozapine in Rampton high security hospital. *Criminal Behaviour and Mental Health, 9*, 168-178.

Davison, G. C. (1968). Elimination of a sadistic fantasy by a client-controlled counter-conditioning technique. *Journal of Abnormal Psychology, 73*, 84-90.

Davison, G. C., & Lazarus, A. A. (1994). Clinical innovation and evaluation: Integrating practice with inquiry. *Clinical psychology: Science and Practice, 1*, 157-168.

Davison, G. C., & Neale, J. M. (1994). *Abnormal psychology* (6th ed.). New York: Wiley.

Davison, G. C., & Neale, J. M. (1998). *Abnormal psychology* (7th ed.). New York: Wiley.

Davison, G. C., Neale, J. M., & Kring, A. (2004). *Abnormal psychology* (9th ed.). New York: Wiley.

Davison, G. C., Robins, C., & Johnson, M. K. (1983). Articulated thoughts during simulated situations: A paradigm for studying cognition in emotion and behavior. *Cognitive Therapy and Research, 7*, 17-40.

Davison, G. C., Vogel, R. S., & Coffman, S. G. (1997). Think-aloud approaches to cognitive assessment and the Articulated Thoughts in Simulated Situations paradigm. *Journal of Consulting and Clinical Psychology, 65*, 950-958.

Davison, G. C., Williams, M. E., Nezami, E., Bice, T. L., & DeQuattro, V. (1991). Relaxation, reduction in angry articulated thoughts, and improvements in borderline essential hypertension and heart rate. *Journal of Behavioral Medicine, 14*, 453-468.

Davison, G. C., & Zighelboim, V. (1987). Irrational beliefs in the articulated thoughts of college students with social anxiety. *Journal of Rational-Emotive Therapy, 5*, 238-254.

Davison, J. R. T. (1997). Use of benzodiazepines in panic disorder. *Journal of Clinical Psychiatry, 58* (Suppl. 2), 26-28.

Dell, P. F. (2001). Why the diagnostic criteria for dissociative identity disorder should be changed. *Journal of Trauma and Dissociation, 2*, 7-37.

DeMyer, M. K., Pontius, W., Norton, J. A., Barton, S., Allen, J., & Denhoff, E. (1973). The natural history of children with minimal brain dysfunction. *Annals of the New York Academy of Sciences, 205*, 188-205.

Deniker, P. (1970). Introduction of neuroleptic chemotherapy into psychiatry. In F. J. Ayd & B. Blackwell (Eds.), *Discoveries in biological psychiatry*. Philadelphia: Lippincott.

De Silva, P. (1999). Sexual consequences of non-sexual trauma. *Sexual and Marital Therapy, 14*, 143-150.

Devanand, D. P., Dwork, A. J., Hutchinson, E. R., Bolwig, T. G., et al. (1994). Does ECT alter brain structure? *American Journal of Psychiatry, 151*, 957-970.

Diamond, M., & Sigmundson, H. K. (1997). Sex reassignment at birth. Long-term review and clinical implications. *Archives of Pediatrics and Adolescent Medicine, 151*, 298-304.

Dimsdale, J. E., Pierce, C., Schoefeld, D., Brown, A., Zusmann R., & Graham, R. (1986). Suppressed anger and blood pressure: The effects of race, sex, social class, and age. *Psychosomatic Medicine, 48*, 430-436.

DiTomasso, R. A. (1987). Essential hypertension: A methodological review. In L. Michelson & L. M. Ascher (Eds.), *Anxiety and stress disorders: Cognitive-behavioral assessment and treatment* (pp. 520-582). New York: Guilford.

Dohrenwend, B. P., Levav, I., Shrout, P. E., Schwartz, S., Naveh, G., Link, B. G., Skodol, A. E., & Stueve, A. (1992). Socioeconomic status and psychiatric disorders: The causation-selection issue. *Science, 255*, 946-952.

Dorahy, M. J. (2001). Dissociative identity disorder and memory dysfunction: The current state of experimental research and its future directions. *Clinical Psychology Review, 21*, 771-795.

Drake, R. E., & Mueser, K. T. (2000). Psychosocial approaches to dual diagnosis. *Schizophrenia Bulletin, 26*, 105-118.

Dubbert, P. (1995). Behavioral (life style) modification in the prevention and treatment of hypertension: *Clinical Psychology Review, 15*, 187-216.

Eaton, W., & Harrison, G. (2001). Life chances, life planning, and schizophrenia: A review and interpretation of research on social deprivation. *International Journal of Mental Health, 30*, 58-81.

Eaton, W. W., Anthony, J. C., Romanoski, A., Tien, A., Gallo, J., Cai, G., Neufeld, K., Schlaepfer, T., Laugharne, J., & Chen, L. S. (1998). Onset and recovery from panic disorder in the Baltimore Epidemiologic Catchment Area follow-up. *British Journal of Psychiatry, 173*, 501-507.

Eaton, W. W., Kramer, M., Anthony, J. C., Dryman, A., Shapiro, S., et al. (1989). The incidence of specific DIS/DSM-III mental disorders: Data from the NIMH Epidemiologic Catchment Area Programs. *Acta Psychiatrica Scandinavica, 79*, 163-178.

Eckert, E. D., Halmi, K. A., Marchi, P., Grove, W., et al. (1995). Ten-year-follow-up of anorexia nervosa: Clinical course and outcome. *Psychological Medicine, 25*, 143-156.

Eddy, K. T., Keel, P. K., Dorer, D. J., Delinsky, S. S., Franko, D. L., & Herzog, D. B. (2002). Longitudinal comparison of anorexia nervosa subtypes. *International Journal of Eating Disorders, 20*, 191-201.

Egan, G. (1975). *The skilled helper*. Monterey, CA: Brooks/Cole.

Egan, T. (1990, June 7). As memory of music faded, Alzheimer patient met death. *New York Times*, pp. A1, A1b.

Egeland, J. A., Gerhard, D. S., Pauls, D. L., Sussex, J. N., et al. (1987). Bipolar affective disorders linked to DNA markers on chromosome 11. *Nature, 325*, 783-787.

Eich, E., Macaulay, D., Loewenstein, R. J., & Dihle, P. H. (1997). Memory, amnesia, and dissociative identity disorder. *Psychological Science, 8*, 417-422.

Eisen, J. L., Phillips, K. A., & Rasmussen, S. A. (1999). Obsessions and delusions: The relationship between obsessive-compulsive disorder and the psychotic disorders. *Psychiatric Annals, 29*, 515-522.

Eisenberg, L., & Kanner, L. (1956). Early infantile autism. *American Journal of Orthopsychiatry, 26*, 556-566.

Elkin, I. (1994). The NIMH Treatment of Depression Collaborative Research Program: Where we began and where we are. In A. E. Bergin & S. L. Garfield (Eds.), *Handbook of psychotherapy and behavior change* (4th ed., pp. 114-139). New York: Wiley.

Elkin, I., Gibbons, R. D., Shea, M. T., & Shaw, B. F. (1996). Science is not a trial (but it can sometimes be a tribulation). *Journal of Consulting and Clinical Psychology, 64*, 92-103.

Ellason, J. W., & Ross, C. A. (1997). Two-year follow-up of inpatients with dissociative disorder. *American Journal of Psychiatry, 154*, 832-839.

Elliott, M. L., & Biever, L. S. (1996). Head injury and sexual dysfunction. *Brain Injury, 10*, 703-717.

Ellis, A. (1962). *Reason and emotion in psychotherapy*. New York: Lyle Stuart.

Ellis, A. (1993). Fundamentals of rational-emotive therapy for the 1990s. In W. Dryden & L. Hill (Eds.), *Innovations in rational-emotive therapy*. Newbury Park, CA: Sage Publications.

Ellis, A., & Bernard, M. E. (Eds.). (1983). *Rational-emotive approaches to the problems of childhood*. New York: Plenum.

Ellison, J. M. (1998). Antidepressant-induced sexual dysfunction: Review, classification, and suggestions for treatment. *Harvard Review of Psychiatry, 6*, 177-189.

Emrick, C. D., Tonigan, J. S., Montgomery, H. & Little, L. (1993). Alcoholics Anonymous: What is currently known? In B. S. McCrady & W. R. Miller (Eds.), Research on Alcoholics Anonymous: Opportunities and alternatives (pp. 41-76). New Brunswick, NJ: Rutgers Center of Alcohol Studies.

English, H. B. (1929). Three cases of the "conditioned fear response." *Journal of Abnormal and Social Psychology, 34*, 221-225.

Eronen, M. (1995). Mental disorders and homicidal behavior in female subjects. *American Journal of Psychiatry, 152*, 1216-1218.

Eronen, M., Angermeyer, M. C., & Schulze, B. (1998). The psychiatric epidemiology of violent behaviour. *Social Psychiatry and Psychiatric Epidemiology, 33* (Suppl. 1), S13-S23.

Esler, J., Julius, S., Sweifler, A., Randall, O., Harburg, E., Gardiner, H., & DeQuattro, V. (1977). Mild high-renin essential hypertension: A neurogenic human hypertension. *New England Journal of Medicine, 296*, 405-411.

Evans, J. D., Heaton, R. K., Paulsen, J. S., McAdams, L. A., Heaton, S. C., & Jeste, D. V. (1999). Schizoaffective disorder: A form of schizophrenia or affective disorder? *Journal of Clinical Psychiatry, 60*, 874-882.

Faber, S. D., & Burns, J. W. (1996). Anger management style, degree of expressed anger, and gender influence cardiovascular recovery from interpersonal harassment. *Journal of Behavioral Medicine, 19*, 31-53.

Fahy, T. A. (1988). The diagnosis of multiple personality disorder: A critical review. *British Journal of Psychiatry, 153*, 597-606.

Fahy, T. A., Abas, M., & Brown, J. C. (1989). Multiple personality: A symptom of psychiatric disorder. *British Journal of Psychiatry, 154*, 99-101.

Fairburn, C. (1981). A cognitive-behavioral approach to the treatment of bulimia. *Psychological Medicine, 11*, 707-711.

Fairburn, C. (1995). *Overcoming binge eating*. New York: Guilford.

Fairburn, C. G., & Beglin, S. J. (1990). Studies of the epidemiology of bulimia nervosa. *American Journal of Psychiatry, 147*, 401-498.

Fairburn, C. G., Jones, R., Peveler, R. C., Hope, R. A., & O'Connor, M. (1993). Psychotherapy and bulimia nervosa: Longer term effects of interpersonal psychotherapy, behavior therapy, and cognitive therapy. *Archives of General Psychiatry, 50*, 419-428.

Fairburn, C. G., Peveler, R. C., Jones, R., Hope, R. A., & Doll, H. A. (1993). Predictors of twelve-month outcome in bulimia nervosa and the influence of attitudes to shape and weight. *Journal of Consulting and Clinical Psychology, 61*, 696-698.

Fairburn, C. G., Welch, S. L., Doll, H. A., Davies, B. A., & O'Connor, M. E. (1997). Risk factors for bulimia nervosa: A community-based case-control study. *Archives of General Psychiatry, 54*, 509-517.

Fairburn, C. G., Welch, S. L., Norman, P. A., O'Connor, M. E., et al. (1996). Bias and bulimia nervosa: How typical are clinic cases? *American Journal of Psychiatry, 153*, 386-391.

Falloon, I. R. H., Held, T., Coverdale, J. H., Roncone, R., & Laidlaw, T. M. (1999). Family interventions for schizophrenia: A review of long-term benefits of international studies. *Psychiatric Rehabilitation Skills, 3*, 268-290.

Fazel, S., & Danesh, J. (2002). Serious mental disorder in 23,000 prisoners: A systematic review of 62 surveys. *Lancet, 359*, 545-550.

Fedora, O., Reddon, J. R., & Yeudall, L. T. (1986). Stimuli eliciting sexual arousal in genital exhibitionists: A possible clinical application. *Archives of Sexual Behavior, 15*, 417-427.

Feeny, N. C. (2000). Exploring the roles of emotional numbing, depression, and dissociation in PTSD. *Journal of Traumatic Stress, 13,* 489-498.

Feldman, P. J., Ullman, J. B., & Dunkel-Schetter, C. (1998). Women's reactions to rape victims: Motivational processes associated with blame and social support. Journal of Applied Social Psychology, 28, 469-503.

Fenichel, O. (1945). *The psychoanalytic theory of neuroses.* New York: Norton.

Fenigstein, A. (1996). Paranoia. In C. G. Costello (Ed.), *Personality characteristics of the personality disordered* (pp. 242-275). New York: Wiley.

Ferguson, C. P., & Pigott, T. A. (2000). Anorexia and bulimia nervosa: Neurobiology and pharmacotherapy. *Behavior Therapy, 31,* 237-263.

Ferster, C. B. (1961). Positive reinforcement and behavior deficits in autistic children. *Child Development, 32,* 437-456.

Fine, C. G. (1999). The tactical-integration model for the treatment of dissociative identity disorder and allied dissociative disorders. *American Journal of Psychotherapy, 53,* 361-376.

Finney, J. W., & Moos, R. H. (1998). Psychosocial treatments for alcohol use disorders. In P. E. Nathan & J. M. Gorman (Eds.), A guide to treatments that work (pp. 156-166). New York: Oxford University Press.

Fischer, M. (1973). Genetic and environmental factors in schizophrenia: A study of schizophrenic twins and their families. *Acta Psychiatrica Scandinavica (Suppl.* 238).

Fischetti, M., Curran, J. P., & Wessberg, H. W. (1977). Sense of timing. *Behavior Modification, 1,* 179-194.

Foa, E. B., Dancu, C. V., Hembree, E. A., Jaycox, L. H., Meadows, E. A., & Street, G. P. (1999). A comparison of exposure therapy, stress inoculation training, and their combination for reducing posttraumatic stress disorder in female assault victims. *Journal of Consulting and Clinical Psychology, 67,* 194-200.

Foa, E. B., & Kozak, M. J. (1995). DSM-IV field trial: Obsessive-compulsive disorder. *American Journal of Psychiatry, 152,* 90-96.

Foa, E. B., & Kozak, M. J. (1996). Psychological treatment for obsessive-compulsive disorder. In M. R. Mavissakalian & R. F. Prien (Eds.), *Long-term treatments of anxiety disorders* (pp. 285-309). Washington, DC: American Psychiatric Press.

Foa, F. B., Kozak, M. J., Steketee, G. S., & McCarthy, P. R. (1992). Treatment of depressive and obsessive-compulsive symptoms in OCD by imipramine and behaviour therapy. *British Journal of Clinical Psychology, 31,* 279-292.

Foa, E. B., & Riggs, D. S. (1995). Posttraumatic stress disorder following assault: Theoretical considerations and empirical findings. *Current Directions in Psychological Science, 4,* 61-65.

Foa, E. B., Riggs, D. S., & Gershuny, B. S. (1995). Arousal, numbing, and intrusion: Symptom structure of PTSD following assault. *American Journal of Psychiatry, 152,* 116-120.

Foa, E. B., & Rothbaum, B. O. (1997). *Treating the trauma of rape: Cognitive-behavioral therapy for PTSD.* New York: Guilford.

Foa, E. B., Rothbaum, B. O., Riggs, D. S., & Murdock, T. B. (1991). Treatment of posttraumatic stress disorder in rape victims: A comparison between cognitive-behavioral procedures and counseling. *Journal of Consulting and Clinical Psychology, 59,* 715-723.

Foa, E. B., & Steketee, G. (1989). Behavioral/cognitive conceptualization of posttraumatic stress disorder. *Behavior Therapy, 20,* 155-176.

Folstein, M. F., Marshal, F., Bassett, S. S., et al. (1991). Dementia: A case ascertainment in a community survey. *Journal of Gerontology, 46,* 132-138.

Folstein, S., & Rutter, M. (1978). A twin study of individuals with infantile autism. In M. Rutter & E. Schopler (Eds.), *Autism: A reappraisal of concepts and treatment.* New York: Plenum.

Fontana, A. F. (1966). Familial etiology of schizophrenia: Is a scientific methodology possible? *Psychological Bulletin, 66,* 214-227.

Forgac, G. E., & Michaels, E. J. (1982). Personality characteristics of two types of male exhibitionists. *Journal of Abnormal Psychology, 91,* 287-293.

Forrest, K. A. (2001). Toward an etiology of dissociative identity disorder: A neurodevelopmental approach. *Consciousness and Cognition, 10,* 259-293.

Forth, A. E., & Hare, R. D. (1989). The contingent negative variation in psychopaths. *Psychophysiology, 26,* 676-682.

Frank, E. (1996). Long-term treatment of depression: Interpersonal psychotherapy with and without medication. In C. Mundt, M. J. Goldstein, K. Hahlweg & P. Fiedler (Eds.), *Interpersonal factors in the origin and course of affective disorders* (pp. 303-315). London: Gaskell/Royal College of Psychiatrists.

Frank, E., Swartz, H. A., & Kupfer, D. J. (2000). Interpersonal and social rhythm therapy: Managing the chaos of bipolar disorder. *Biological Psychiatry, 48,* 593-604.

Freeman, C., Sinclair, F., Turnbull, J., & Annandale, A. (1985). Psychotherapy for bulimia: A controlled study. Conference on Anorexia Nervosa and Related Disorders. *Journal of Psychiatric Research, 19,* 473-478.

Freud, A. (1946). *The psychoanalytic treatment of children: Lectures and essays.* London: Imago.

Freud, S. (1925). Mourning and melancholia. In *Sigmund Freud, Collected Papers, Volume IV* (Alix and James Strachey, trans.). London: Hogarth Press. (Originally published in Zeitschrift, 1917.)

Freud, S. (1925). Psycho-analytic notes upon an autobiographical account of a case of paranoia (dementia paranoides). In *Sigmund Freud, Collected Papers, Volume III* (Alix and James Strachey, trans.). London: Hogarth Press. (Originally published in *Jahrbuch für psychoanalytische und psychopathologische Forschungen,* 1909.)

Freund, K., & Watson, R. (1990). Mapping the boundaries of courtship disorder. *Journal of Sex Research, 27,* 589-606.

Friedman, R. A., & Kocsis, J. H. (1996). Pharmacotherapy for chronic depression. *Psychiatric Clinics of North America, 19,* 121-132.

Frost, R. O., Steketee, G., Cohn, L., & Griess, K. (1994). Personality traits in subclinical and non-obsessive-compulsive volunteers and their parents. *Behaviour Research and Therapy, 32,* 47-56.

Funder, D. C. (1999). *Personality judgment: A realistic approach to person perception.* San Diego, CA: Academic Press.

Gallagher-Thompson, D., & Thompson, L. W. (1995). Psychotherapy with older adults in theory and practice. In B. Bongar & L. E. Beutler (Eds.), *Comprehensive textbook of psychotherapy: Theory and practice* (pp. 359-379). New York: Oxford University Press.

Gangestad, S. W., Bailey, J. M., & Martin, N. G. (2000). Taxometric analyses of sexual orientation and gender identity. *Journal of Personality and Social Psychology, 78,* 1109-1121.

Garcia, J., McGowan, B. K., & Green, K. F. (1972). Biological constraints on conditioning. In A. H. Black & W. F. Prokasy (Eds.), *Classical conditioning: II. Current research and theory.* New York: Appleton-Century-Crofts.

Garden, G. M., & Rothery, D. J. (1992). A female monozygotic twin pair discordant for transsexualism: Some theoretical implications. *British Journal of Psychiatry, 161,* 852-854.

Gardner, H. (1997, January 19). Review of the creation of Dr. B. *Los Angeles Times Book Review,* p. 3

Garfinkel, P. E., & Kaplan, A. S. (1986). Anorexia nervosa: Diagnostic conceptualizations. In K. D. Brownell & J. P. Foreyt (Eds.), *Handbook of eating disorders.* New York: Basic Books.

Garfinkel, P. E., Moldofsky, H., & Garner, D. M. (1980). The heterogeneity of anorexia nervosa. *Archives of General Psychiatry, 37,* 1036-1040.

Garner, D. M. (1986). Cognitive therapy for anorexia nervosa. In K. D. Brownell & J. P. Foreyt (Eds.), *Handbook of eating disorders.* New York: Basic Books.

Garner, D. M., & Magana, C. (2002). Bulimia nervosa. In M. Hersen & L. K. Porzelius (Eds.). *Diagnosis, conceptualization, and treatment planning for adults: A step by step guide* (pp. 251-269). Mahwah, NJ: Erlbaum.

Garvin, V., & Streigel-Moore, R. H. (2001). Health services research for eating disorders in the United States: A status report and a call to action. In R. H. Striegel-Moore & L. Smolak (Eds.). *Eating disorders: Innovative direction in research and practice* (pp. 135-152). Washington, DC: American Psychological Association.

Gatz, M., & Hurwicz, M. L. (1990). Are old people more depressed? Cross-sectional data on CES-D factors. *Psychology and Aging, 5,* 284-290.

Gatz, M., Kasl-Godley, J. E., & Karel, M. J. (1996). Aging and mental disorders. In J. E. Birren & K. W. Schaie (Eds.), *Handbook of the psychology of aging* (pp. 365-382). San Diego, CA: Academic Press.

Gatz, M., Kasl-Godley, J. E., & Karel, M. (in press). Aging and mental disorders. In J. E. Birren & K. W. Schaie (Eds.), *Handbook of the psychology of aging* (4th ed.). San Diego, CA: Academic Press.

Gatz, M., & Smyer, M. A. (1992). The mental health system and older adults in the 1990s. *American Psychologist, 47,* 741-751.

Gelernter, C. S., Uhde, T. W., Cimbolic, P., Arnkoff, D. B., Vittone, B. J., et al. (1991). Cognitive behavioral and pharmacological treatments of social phobia: A controlled study. *Archives of General Psychiatry, 48,* 938-945.

Gentry, W. D., Chesney, A. P., Gary, H. G., Hall, R. P., & Harburg, E. (1982). Habitual anger-coping styles: I. Effect on mean blood pressure and risk for essential hypertension. *Psychosomatic Medicine, 44,* 195-202.

Gentry, W. D., Chesney, A. P., Hall, R. P., & Harburg, E. (1981). Effect of habitual anger-coping pattern on blood pressure in black/white, high/low stress area respondents. *Psychosomatic Medicine, 43,* 88.

Gerlach, A. L., Wilhelm, F. H., Gruber, K., & Roth, W. T. (2001). Blushing and physiological arousability in social phobia. *Journal of Abnormal Psychology, 110,* 247-258.

Ghizzani, A., & Montomoli, M. (2000). Anorexia nervosa and sexuality in women: A revew. *Journal of Sex Education and Therapy, 25,* 80-88.

Gibbs, N. A., & Oltmanns, T. F. (1995). The relation between obsessive-compulsive personality traits and subtypes of compulsive behavior. *Journal of Anxiety Disorders, 9*, 397-410.

Gillberg, C. (1991). Outcome in autism and autistic-like conditions. *Journal of the American Academy of Child and Adolescent Psychiatry, 30*, 375-382.

Gillberg, C., Melander, H., von Knorring, A. L., Janols, L. A., Thernlund, G., et al. (1997). Long-term stimulant treatment of children with attention-deficit hyperactivity disorder symptoms: A randomized, double-blind, placebo-control trial. *Archives of General Psychiatry, 54*, 85-864.

Gillberg, C., & Svendsen, P. (1983). Childhood psychosis and computed tomographic brain scan findings. *Journal of Autism and Developmental Disorders, 13*, 19-32.

Gilligan, C. (1982). *In a different voice: Psychological theory and women's development*. Cambridge, MA: Harvard University Press.

Gittelman, R., Mannuzza, S., Shenker, R., & Bonagura, N. (1985). Hyperactive boys almost grown up: I. Psychiatric status. *Archives of General Psychiatry, 42*, 937-947.

Gleaves, D. H. (1996). The sociocognitive model of dissociative identity disorder: A reexamination of the evidence. *Psychological Bulletin, 120*, 42-59.

Gleaves, D. H., May, M. C., & Cardena, E. (2001). An examination of the diagnostic validity of dissociative identity disorder. *Clinical Psychology Review, 21*, 577-608.

Godart, N. T., Flament, M. F., Perdereau, F., & Jeammet, P. (2002). Comorbidity between eating disorders and anxiety disorders: A review. *International Journal of Eating Disorders, 32*, 253-270.

Goldfried, M. R. (1971). Systematic desensitization as training in self-control. *Journal of Consulting and Clinical Psychology, 46*, 1258-1265.

Goldfried, M. R., & Davison, G. C. (1976). *Clinical behavior therapy*. New York: Holt, Rinehart, & Winston.

Goldfried, M. R., & Davison, G. C. (1994). *Clinical behavior therapy*. Expanded edition. New York: Wiley.

Goldfried, M. R., Padawer, W., & Robins, C. (1984). Social anxiety and the semantic structure of heterosocial interactions. *Journal of Abnormal Psychology, 93*, 87-97.

Goldman, D., & Mazzanti, C. (2002). From phenotype to gene and back: A critical appraisal of progress so far. In J. Benjamin & R. P. Ebstein (Eds.). *Molecular genetics and the human personality* (pp. 273-291). Washington, DC: American Psychiatric Press.

Goodman, L. A., & Dutton, M. A. (1996). The relationship between victimization and cognitive schemata among episodically homeless, seriously mentally ill women. *Violence and Victims, 11*, 159-174.

Goodman, R., & Stevenson, J. (1989). A twin study of hyperactivity: II. The aetiological role of genes, family relationships, and perinatal adversity. *Journal of Child Psychology and Psychiatry, 30*, 691-709.

Goodwin, D. W. (1979). Alcoholism and heredity: A review and hypothesis. *Archives of General Psychiatry, 36*, 57-61.

Gordon, C., & Beresin, E. (1983). Conflicting treatment models for the inpatient management of borderline patients. *American Journal of Psychiatry, 140*, 979-983.

Gordon, C. T., State, R. C., Nelson, J. E., Hamburger, S. D., & Rapoport, J. L. (1993). A double-blind comparison of clomipramine, desipramine, and placebo in the treatment of autistic disorder. *Archives of General Psychiatry, 50*, 441-447.

Gordon, P., & Ahmed, W. (1988). A comparison of two group therapies for bulimia. *British Review of Bulimia and Anorexia Nervosa, 3*, 17-31.

Gore, S., Aseltine, R. H., Jr., & Colten, M. E. (1993). Gender, social-relational involvement, and depression. *Journal of Research on Adolescence, 3*, 101-125.

Gorenstein, E. E., & Newman, J. P. (1980). Disinhibitory psychopathology: A new perspective and a model for research. *Psychological Review, 87*, 301-315.

Gotlib, I. H., & Neubauer, D. L. (2000). Information-processing approaches to the study of cognitive biases in depression. In S. L. Johnson & A. M. Hayes (Eds.), *Stress, coping, and depression* (pp. 117-143). Mahwah, NJ: Erlbaum Associates.

Gottesman, I. I. (1991). *Schizophrenia genesis: The origins of madness*. New York: Freeman.

Gottesman, I. I., & Goldsmith, H. H. (1994). Developmental psychopathology of antisocial behavior: Inserting genes into its ontogenesis and epigenesis. In C. A. Nelson (Ed.), *Threats to optimal development*. Hillsdale, NJ: Erlbaum Associates.

Goyette, C. H., & Conners, C. K. (1977). *Food additives and hyperactivity*. Paper presented at the 85th annual convention of the American Psychological Association.

Greaves, G. B. (1980). Multiple personality: 165 years after Mary Reynolds. *Journal of Nervous and Mental Disease, 168*, 577-596.

Green, R. (1974). *Sexual identity conflict in children and adults*. New York: Basic Books.

Green, R. (1987). *The "sissy boy syndrome" and the development of homosexuality*. New Haven, CT: Yale University Press.

Green, R. (1994). Transsexualism and the law. *Bulletin of the American Academy of Psychiatry and the Law, 22*, 511-517.

Greene, B. A. (1985). Considerations in the treatment of black patients by white therapists. *Psychotherapy, 22*, 115-122.

Greist, J. H., & Jefferson, J. W. (1998). Pharmacotherapy for obsessive-compulsive disorder. *British Journal of Psychiatry, 173* (Suppl. 35), 64-70.

Grenier, G., & Byers, E. S. (1995). Rapid ejaculation: A review of conceptual, etiological, and treatment issues. *Archives of Sexual Behavior, 24*, 447-472.

Grove, W. R., Eckert, E. D., Heston, L., Bouchard, T., et al. (1990). Heritability of substance abuse and antisocial behavior in monozygotic twins reared apart. *Biological Psychiatry, 27*, 1293-1304.

Gruenewald, D. (1984). On the nature of multiple personality. Comparisons with hypnosis. *International Journal of Clinical and Experimental Hypnosis, 32*, 170-190.

Gunderson, J. G., & Sabo, A. N. (1993). The phenomenological and conceptual interface between borderline personality disorder and PTSD. *American Journal of Psychiatry, 150*, 19-27.

Gunderson, J. G., & Singer, M. T. (1975). Defining borderline patients: An overview. *American Journal of Psychiatry, 132*, 1-10.

Gurland, B. J. (1976). The comparative frequency of depression in various adult age groups. *Journal of Gerontology, 31*, 283-292.

Haaga, D. A., & Davison, G. C. (1989). Outcome studies of rational-emotive therapy. In M. E. Bernard & R. DiGiuseppe (Eds.), *Inside rational-emotive therapy*. New York: Academic Press.

Hacking, I. (1995). *Rewriting the soul: Multiple personality and the sciences of memory*. Princeton, NJ: Princeton University Press.

Haffey, M., & Cohen, P. M. (1992). Treatment issues for divorcing women. *Families in Society, 73*, 142-148.

Halmi, K. A. (1996). The psychobiology of eating behavior in anorexia nervosa. *Psychiatry Research, 62*, 23-29.

Halmi, K. A. (1997). Models to conceptualize risk factors for bulimia nervosa. *Archives of General Psychiatry, 54*, 507-508.

Hamburger, C., Sturup, G. K., & Dahl-Iverson, E. (1953). Transvestism: Hormonal, psychiatric and surgical treatment. *Journal of the American Medical Association, 152*, 391-396.

Hamilton, J. A., & Jensvold, M. (1992). Personality, psychopathology, and depression in women. In L. S. Brown & M. Ballou (Eds.), *Personality and psychopathology: Feminist reappraisals* (pp. 116-143). New York: Guilford.

Hammen, C. (1997). *Depression*. East Sussex, UK: Psychology Press.

Hammen, C. (2002). Context of stress in families of children with depressed parents. In S. H. Goodman & I. H. Gotlib (Eds.), *Children of depressed parents: Mechanisms of risk and implications for treatment* (pp. 175-199). Washington, DC: American Psychological Association.

Harburg, E., Erfurt, J. C., Hauenstein, L. S., Chape, C., Schull, W. J., & Schork, M. A. (1973). Socioecological stress, suppressed hostility, skin color and black-white male blood pressure: Detroit. *Psychosomatic Medicine, 35*, 276-296.

Hardy, K. V., & Laszloffy, T. A. (1995). Therapy with African-Americans and the phenomenon of rage. *In Session: Psychotherapy in Practice, 1*, 57-70.

Hare, R. D. (1978). Electrodermal and cardiovascular correlates of sociopathy. In R. D. Hare & D. Schalling (Eds.), *Psychopathic behaviour: Approaches to research*. New York: Wiley.

Hare, R. D., Harpur, T. J., Hakstian, R. A., et al. (1990). The revised psychopathy checklist: Reliability and factor structure. *Psychological Assessment, 2*, 338-341.

Hare, R. D., McPherson, L. M., & Forth, A. E. (1988). Male psychopaths and their criminal careers. *Journal of Consulting and Clinical Psychology, 56*, 710-714.

Harris, B. (1979). Whatever happened to Little Albert? *American Psychologist, 34*, 151-160.

Harrow, M., Grossman, L. S., Herbener, E. S., & Davies, E. W. (2000). Ten-year outcome: Patients with schizoaffective disorders, schizophrenia, affective disorders and mood-incongruent psychotic symptoms. *British Journal of Psychiatry, 177*, 421-426.

Hart, S. D., & Hare, R. D. (1989). Discriminant validity of the Psychopathy Checklist in a forensic psychiatric population. *Psychological Assessment, 1*, 211-218.

Hastrup, J. L., Light, K. C., & Obrist, P. A. (1982). Parental hypertension and cardiovascular response to stress in healthy young adults. *Psychophysiology, 19*, 615-622.

Hawley, C., & Buckley, R. (1974). Food dyes and the hyperkinetic child. *Academic Therapy, 10*, 27-32.

Hay, P. J., Sachdev, P. S., Cumming, S., Smith, J. S., et al. (1993). Treatment of obsessive-compulsive disorder by psychosurgery. *Acta Psychiatrica Scandinavica, 87*, 197-207.

Heatherton, T. F., & Polivy, J. (1992). Chronic dieting and eating disorders: A spiral model. In J. Crowther, E. Hobfall, M. A. P. Stephens, & D. L. Tennenbaum (Eds.), *The etiology of bulimia: The individual and familial context* (pp. 135-155). Washington, DC: Hemisphere.

Heberbrand, J. (1992). A critical appraisal of X-linked bipolar illness. Evidence for the assumed mode of transmission is lacking. *British Journal of Psychiatry, 160*, 7-11.

Heiden, W., & Hafner, H. (2000). The epidemiology of onset and course of schizophrenia. *European Archives of Psychiatry and Clinical Neuroscience, 250*, 292-303.

Heiman, J., LoPiccolo, L., & LoPiccolo, J. (1988). *Becoming orgasmic: A sexual growth program for women*. Englewood Cliffs, NJ: Prentice-Hall.

Heiman, J. R., & Verhulst, J. (1990). Sexual dysfunction and marriage. In F.D. Fincham & T. N. Bradbury (Eds.), *The psychology of marriage: Basic issues and applications* (pp. 299-322). New York: Guilford.

Heimberg, R. G., & Juster, H. R. (1994). Treatment of social phobia in cognitive-behavioral groups. *Journal of Clinical Psychiatry, 55*, 38-46.

Heimberg, R. G., Salzman, D. G., Holt, C. S., & Blendell, K. (1993). Cognitive-behavioral group treatment for social phobia: Effectiveness at five-year follow-up. *Cognitive Therapy and Research, 17*, 325-339.

Heinssen, R. K., Liberman, R. P., & Kopelowicz, A. (2000). Psychosocial skills training for schizophrenia: Lessons from the laboratory. *Schizophrenia Bulletin, 26*, 21-46.

Helzer, J. E., Robins, L., & McEvoy, L. (1987). Post-traumatic stress disorder in the general population: Findings of the Epidemiological Catchment Area Survey. *New England Journal of Medicine, 317*, 1630-1634.

Henker, B., & Whalen, C. K. (1989). Hyperactivity and attention deficits. Special Issue: Children and their development: Knowledge base, research agenda, and social policy application. *American Psychologist, 44*, 216-223.

Herbert, J. D. (1995). An overview of the current status of social phobia. *Applied and Preventive Psychology, 4*, 39-51.

Herpetz, S. C., Werth, U., Lukas, G., et al. (2001). Emotion in criminal offenders with psychopathic personality disorder. *Archives of General Psychiatry, 58*, 737-745.

Herzog, D. B. (1982). Bulimia: The secretive syndrome. *Psychosomatics, 23*, 481-483.

Heston, L. L. (1966). Psychiatric disorders in foster home reared children of schizophrenic mothers. *British Journal of Psychiatry, 112*, 819-825.

Hettema, J. M., Neale, M. C., & Kendler, K. S. (2001). A review and meta-analysis of the genetic epidemiology of the anxiety disorders. *American Journal of Psychiatry, 158*, 1568(1578.

Hewett, F. M. (1965). Teaching speech to an autistic child through operant conditioning. *American Journal of Orthopsychiatry, 33*, 927-936.

Hibbett, A., & Fogelman, K. (1990). Future lives of truants: Family formation and health-related behavior. *British Journal of Educational Psychology, 60*, 171-179.

Hibbett, A., Fogelman, K., & Manor, O. (1990). Occupational outcomes of truancy. *British Journal of Educational Psychology, 60*, 23-26.

Hirschfeld, R. M. A. (2001). Antidepressants in the United States: Current status and future needs. In M. M. Weissman (Ed.), *Treatment of depression: Bridging the 21st century* (pp. 123-134). Washington, DC: American Psychiatric Press.

Hlastala, S. A., Frank, E., Kowalski, J., Tu, X. M., Anderson, B., & Kupfer, D. J. (2000). Stressful life events, bipolar disorder, and the "kindling model." *Journal of Abnormal Psychology, 109*, 777-786.

Hoch, P., & Polatin, P. (1949). Pseudoneurotic forms of schizophrenia. *Psychiatric Quarterly, 23*, 248-276.

Hodapp, V., Weyer, G., & Becker, J. (1976). Situational stereotypy in essential hypertension patients. *Journal of Psychosomatic Research, 19*, 113-121.

Hodgins, S., Lapalme, M., & Toupin, J. (1999). Criminal activities and substance use of patients with major affective disorders and schizophrenia: A 2-year follow-up. *Journal of Affective Disorders, 55*, 187-202.

Hoek, H. W. (1993). Review of the epidemiological studies of eating disorders. *International Review of Psychiatry, 5*, 61-74.

Hofland, B. F. (1988). Autonomy in long term care: Background issues and a programmatic response. *The Gerontologist, 28* (Suppl.), 3-9.

Hokanson, J. E., & Burgess, M. (1962). The effects of three types of aggression on vascular processes. *Journal of Abnormal and Social Psychology, 65*, 446-449.

Holder, H., Longabaugh, R., Miller, W. R., & Rubonis, A. V. (1991). The cost-effectiveness of treatment for alcoholism: A first approximation. *Journal of Studies on Alcohol, 52*, 517-540.

Hollander, E., Stein, D. J., Decaria, D. M., Cohen, L. J., Saond, J. B., et al. (1994). Serotonergic sensitivity in borderline personality disorder. *American Journal of Psychiatry, 151*, 277-280.

Holm, V. A., & Varley, C. K. (1989). Pharmacological treatment of autistic children. In G. Dawson (Ed.), *Autism: Nature, diagnosis, treatment* (pp. 386-404). New York: Guilford.

Hooley, J. M. (1985). Expressed emotion: A review of the critical literature. *Clinical Psychology Review, 5*, 119-139.

Hooley, J. M., & Gotlib, I. H. (2000). A diathesis-stress conceptualization of expressed emotion and clinical outcome. *Applied and Preventive Psychology, 9*, 135-151.

Hoover, C. F., & Insel, T. R. (1984). Families of origin in obsessive-compulsive disorder. *Journal of Nervous and Mental Disease, 172*, 207-215.

Hope, D. A., Heimberg, R. G., & Bruch, M. A. (1995). Dismantling cognitive-behavioral group therapy for social phobia. *Behaviour Research and Therapy, 33*, 637-650.

Hornstein, N. L., & Putnam, F. W. (1996). Abuse and the development of dissociative symptoms and dissociative identity disorder. In C. R. Pfeffer (Ed.), *Severe stress and mental disturbance in children* (pp. 449-473). Washington, DC: American Psychiatric Press.

Hsu, L. K. G. (1987). Are eating disorders becoming more common in blacks? *International Journal of Eating Disorders, 6*, 113-124.

Hsu, L. K. G. (1990). Eating disorders. New York: Guilford.

Hsu, L. K. G. (1996). Epidemiology of the eating disorders. *Psychiatric Clinics of North America, 19*, 681-700.

Hsu, L. K. G., Crisp, A. H., & Callender, J. S. (1992). Recovery in anorexia nervosa: The patient's perspective. *International Journal of Eating Disorders, 11*, 341-350.

Hsu, L.K.G., Rand, W., Sullivan, S., Liu, D.W., Mulliken, B., McDonagh, B., & Kaye, W. H. (2001). Cognitive therapy, nutritional therapy and their combination in the treatment of bulimia nervosa. *Psychological Medicine, 31*, 871-879.

Hughlings-Jackson, J. (1931). In J. Taylor (Ed.), *Selected writings*. London: Hodder & Stoughton.

Hussong, A. M., Hicks, R. E., Levy, S. A., & Curran, P. J. (2001). Specifying the relations between affect and heavy alcohol use among young adults. *Journal of Abnormal Psychology, 110*, 449-461.

Imperato-McGinley, J., Guerrero, L., Gautier, T., & Peterson, R. E. (1974). Steroid 5a-reductase deficiency in man: An inherited form of male pseudohermaphroditism. *Science, 186*, 1213-1215.

Iwamasa, G. Y. (1993). Asian Americans and cognitive-behavioral therapy. *The Behavior Therapist, 16*, 233-235.

Jackson, A. M. (1973). Psychotherapy: Factors associated with the race of the therapist. *Psychotherapy: Theory, Research, and Practice, 10*, 273-277.

Jacobson, E. (1938). *Progressive relaxation*. Chicago: University of Chicago Press.

Jacobson, N. S., & Hollon, S. D. (1996). Cognitive-behavior therapy versus pharmacotherapy: Now that the jury's returned its verdict, it's time to present the rest of the evidence. *Journal of Consulting and Clinical Psychology, 64*, 74-80.

James, D. (1998). Multiple personality disorder in the courts: A review of the North American experience. *Journal of Forensic Psychiatry, 9*, 339-361.

Janicak, P. G., Keck, P. E., Davis, J. M., Kasckow, J. W., Tugrul, K., Dowd, S. M., Strong, J., Sharma, R. P., & Strakowski, S. M. (2001). A double-blind, randomized, prospective evaluation of the efficacy and safety of risperidone versus haloperidol in the treatment of schizoaffective disorder. *Journal of Clinical Psychopharmacology, 21*, 360-368.

Jansen, M. A., Arntz, A., Merckelbach, H., & Mersch, P. P. A. (1994). Personality disorders and features in social phobia and panic disorder. *Journal of Abnormal Psychology, 103*, 391-395.

Jenike, J. A. (1998). Neurosurgical treatment of obsessive-compulsive disorder. *British Journal of Psychiatry, 173*, 79-90.

Jenike, M. A., Baer, L., & Minichiello, W. E. (Eds.) (1986). *Obsessive-compulsive disorders: Theory and management*. Littleton, MA: PSG.

Jimerson, D. C., Wolfe, B. E., Metzger, E. D., Finkelstein, D. M., Cooper, T. B., & Levine, J. M. (1997). Decreased serotonin function in bulimia nervosa. *Archives of General Psychiatry, 54*, 529-534.

Johns, L. C., Hemsley, D., & Kuipers, E. (2002). A comparison of auditory hallucinations in a psychiatric and non-psychiatric group. *British Journal of Clinical Psychology, 41*, 81-86.

Johns, L. C., Rossell, S., Frith, C., Ahmad, F., Hemsley, D., Kuipers, E., & McGuire, P. K. (2001). Verbal self-monitoring and auditory verbal hallucinations in patients with schizophrenia. *Psychological Medicine, 31*, 705-715.

Johnson, J. G., Cohen, P., Brown, J., Smailes, E. M., & Bernstein, D. P. (1999). Childhood maltreatment increases risk for personality disorders during early childhood. *Archives of General Psychiatry, 56*, 600-606.

Johnson, J. G., Spitzer, R. L., & Williams, J. B. W. (2001). Health problems, impairment and illnesses associated with bulimia nervosa and binge eating disorder among primary care and obstetric gynaecology patients. *Psychological Medicine, 31*, 1455-1466.

Johnson, S. L., & Roberts, J. E. (1995). Life events and bipolar disorder: Implications from biological theories. *Psychological Bulletin, 117*, 434-449.

Johnson, S. L., Sandrow, D., Meyter, B., Winters, R., Miller, I., Solomon, D., & Keitner, G. (2000). Increases in manic symptoms after life events involving goal attainment. *Journal of Abnormal Psychology, 109*, 721-727.

Johnson, W. G., Schlundt, D. G., Barclay, D. R., Carr-Nangle, R. E., et al. (1995). A naturalistic functional analysis of binge eating. *Behavior Therapy, 26*, 101-118.

Jones, M. C. (1924). A laboratory study of fear: The case of Peter. *Pedagogical Seminary, 31*, 308-315.

Jones, P., & Cannon, M. (1998). The new epidemiology of schizophrenia. *Psychiatric Clinics of North America, 21*, 1-25.

Jutai, J. W., & Hare, R. D. (1983). Psychopathy and selective attention during performance of a complex perceptual-motor task. *Psychophysiology, 20*, 140-151.

Kagan, J., Snidman, N., Zentner, M., & Peterson, E. (1999).Infant temperament and anxious symptoms in school age children. *Development & Psychopathology, 11*, 209-224.

Kane, J. M. (1996). Treatment-resistant schizophrenic patients. *Journal of Clinical Psychiatry, 57* (*Suppl.* 9), 35-40.

Kane, J. M. (2001). Long-term therapeutic management in schizophrenia. In A. Breier & P.V. Tran (Eds.), *Current issues in the psychopharmacology of schizophrenia* (pp. 430-446). Philadelphia, PA: Lippincott Williams and Wilkins.

Kanner, L. (1943). Autistic disturbances of affective contact. *Nervous Child, 2*, 217-250.

Kanner, L. (1973). Follow-up of eleven autistic children originally reported in 1943. In L. Kanner (Ed.), *Childhood psychosis: Initial studies and new insights*. Washington, DC: Winston/Wiley.

Kanner, L., & Eisenberg, L. (1955). Notes on the follow-up studies of autistic children. In P. Hoch & J. Zubin (Eds.), *Psychopathology of childhood*. New York: Grune and Stratton.

Kano, S. (1989). *Making peace with food*. New York: HarperCollins.

Kapur, S., & Remington, G. (2001). Atypical antipsychotics: New directions and new challenges in the treatment of schizophrenia. *Annual Review of Medicine, 52*, 503-517.

Karno, M., & Golding, J. M. (1991). Obsessive compulsive disorder. In L. N. Robins & D. A. Regier (Eds.), *Psychiatric disorders in America: The Epidemiologic Catchment Area Study* (pp. 204-219). New York: Free Press.

Karpman, B. (1954). *The sexual offender and his offenses*. New York: Julian Press.

Kasen, S., Cohen, P., Skodol, A. E., Johnson, J. G., Smailes, E., & Brook, J. S. (2001). Childhood depression and adult personality disorder: Alternative pathways of continuity. *Archives of General Psychiatry, 58*, 231-236.

Kasl, S. V., & Cobb, S. (1970). Blood pressure changes in men undergoing job loss: A preliminary report. *Psychosomatic Medicine, 6*, 95-106.

Katon, W. (1996). Panic disorder: Relationship to high medical utilization, unexplained physical symptoms, and medical costs. *Journal of Clinical Psychiatry, 57* (*Suppl.* 10), 11-17.

Katz, R., & McGuffin, P. (1993). The genetics of affective disorders. In D. Fowles (Ed.), *Progress in experimental personality and psychopathology research*. New York: Springer.

Kavahagh, D. J., McGrath, J., Saunders, J. B., Dore, G., & Clark, D. (2002). Substance misuse in patients with schizophrenia: Epidemiology and management. *Drugs, 62*, 743-755.

Kaye, W. H., Strober, M., & Klump, K. L. (2002). Serotonin neuronal function in anorexia nervosa and bulimia nervosa. In F. Lewis-Hall & T. S. Williams (Eds.), *Psychiatric illness in women: Emerging treatments and research* (pp. 557-575). Washington, DC: American Psychiatric Publishing.

Kaye, W. H., Strober, M., & Rhodes, L. (2002). Body image disturbance and other core symptoms in anorexia and bulimia nervosa. In D. J. Castle & K. A. Phillips (Eds.). *Disorders of body image* (pp. 67-82). Petersfield, England: Wrightson Biomedical Publishing.

Keane, T. M. (1985). Defining traumatic stress: Some comments on the current terminological confusion [Letter to the editor]. *Behavior Therapy, 16*, 419-423.

Keane, T. M., Fisher, L. M., Krinsley, K. E., & Niles, B. L. (1994). Posttraumatic stress disorder. In M. Hersen & R. T. Ammerman (Eds.), *Handbook of prescriptive treatments for adults* (pp. 237-260). New York: Plenum.

Kearney, C. A. (1992). Prescriptive treatment for school refusal behavior. Symposium at annual meeting of the Association for Advancement of Behavior Therapy, Boston.

Kearney, C. A., & Silverman, W. K. (1996). The evolution and reconciliation of taxonomic strategies for school refusal behavior. *Clinical Psychology: Science and Practice, 3*, 339-354.

Keel, P. K., & Mitchell, J. E. (1997). Outcome in bulimia nervosa. *American Journal of Psychiatry, 154*, 313-321.

Keith, S. J., Regier, D. A., & Rae, D. S. (1991). Schizophrenic disorders. In L. N. Robins & D. A. Regier (Eds.), *Psychiatric disorders in America: The Epidemiologic Catchment Area Study* (pp. 33-52). New York: Free Press.

Kellner, R. (1982). Disorders of impulse control (not elsewhere classified). In J. Griest, J. W. Jefferson, & R. L. Spitzer (Eds.), *Treatment of mental disorders*. New York: Oxford University Press.

Kelly, M. P., Strassberg, D. S., & Kircher, J. R. (1990). Attitudinal and experiential correlates of anorgasmia. *Archives of Sexual Behavior, 19*, 165-177.

Kendell, R. E. (2002) The distinction between personality disorder and mental illness. *British Journal of Psychiatry, 180*, 110-115.

Kendler, K. S., & Diehl, S. R. (1993). The genetics of schizophrenia: A current, genetic-epidemiologic perspective. *Schizophrenia Bulletin, 19*, 261-285.

Kendler, K. S., & Hays, P. (1981). Paranoid psychosis (delusional disorder) and schizophrenia: A family history study. *Archives of General Psychiatry, 38*, 547-551.

Kendler, K. S., McGuire, J., Gruenberg, A. M., & Walsh, D. (1994). Outcome and family study of the subtypes of schizophrenia in the west of Ireland. *American Journal of Psychiatry, 151*, 849-856.

Kendler, K. S., Neale, M. C., Kessler, R. C., Heath, A. C., & Eaves, L. J. (1992). The genetic epidemiology of phobias in women: The interrelationship of agoraphobia, social phobia, situational phobia, and simple phobia. *Archives of General Psychiatry, 49*, 273-281.

Kendler, K. S., Neale, M. C., Kessler, R. C., Heath, A. C., et al. (1993). Panic disorder in women: A population-based twin study. *Psychological Medicine, 23*, 397-406.

Kennedy, J. A. (1952). Problems posed in the analysis of Negro patients. *Psychiatry, 15*, 313-327.

Kernberg, O. F. (1985). *Borderline conditions and pathological narcissism*. Northvale, NJ: Jason Aronson.

Kessler, R. C. (1997). The effects of stressful life events on depression. *Annual Review of Psychology, 48*, 191-214.

Kessler, R. C., McGonagle, K. A., Zhao, S., Nelson, C. B., Hughes, M., Eshleman, S., Wittchen, H., & Kendler, K. S. (1994). Lifetime and 12-month prevalence of DSM-III-R psychiatric disorders in the United States. *Archives of General Psychiatry, 51*, 8-19.

Kessler, S., & McKenna, W. (2000). Who put the "trans" in transgender? Gender theory and everyday life. *International Journal of Transgenderism, 4*.

Kessler, R., Sonnega, A., Bromet, E., et al. (1995). Posttraumatic stress disorder in the National Comorbidity Survey. *Archives of General Psychiatry, 52*, 1048-1060.

Kessler, R. C., Sonnega, A., Bromet, E., Hughes, M., Nelson, D. B., & Breslau, N. (1999). Epidemiological risk factors for trauma and PTSD. In R. Yehuda (Ed.), *Risk factors for posttraumatic stress disorder* (pp. 23-59). Washington, DC: American Psychiatric Press.

Kety, S. S., Rosenthal, D., Wender, P. H., & Schulsinger, F. (1971). Mental illness in the biological and adoptive families of adopted schizophrenics. *American Journal of Psychiatry, 128*, 82-86.

Kilpatrick, D. G., Saunders, B. E., Veronen, L. J., Best, C. L., & Von, J. M. (1987). Criminal victimization: Lifetime prevalence, reporting to police, and psychological impact. *Crime and Delinquency, 33*, 479-489.

Kilpatrick, D. G., Veronen, L. J., & Resick, P. A. (1979). Assessment of the aftermath of rape: Changing patterns of fear. *Journal of Behavioral Assessment, 1*, 133-148.

Kinderman, P. (2001). Changing causal attributions In P. W. Corrigan & D. L. Penn (Eds.), *Social cognition and schizophrenia* (pp. 195-215). Washington, DC: American Psychological Association.

Kinzie, J. D. (1985). Overview of clinical issues in the treatment of Southeast Asian refugees. In T. C. Owan (Ed.), *Southeast Asian mental health treatment, prevention services, training, and research*. Washington, DC: National Institute of Mental Health.

Kleifield, E. I., Wagner, S., & Halmi, K. A. (1996). Cognitive-behavioral treatment of anorexia nervosa. *Psychiatric Clinics of North America, 19*, 715-737.

Klein, D. F. (1981). Anxiety reconceptualized. In D. F. Klein & J. Rabkin (Eds.), *Anxiety: New directions and changing concepts*. New York: Raven Press.

Klein, D. F. (1993). False suffocation alarms, spontaneous panics, and related conditions: An integrative hypothesis. *Archives of General Psychiatry, 50*, 306-317.

Klein, D. F., & Ross, D. C. (1993). Reanalysis of the National Institute of Mental Health Treatment of Depression Collaborative Research Program general effectiveness report. *Neuropsychopharmacology, 8*, 241-251.

Klein, M. (1932). *The psychoanalysis of children*. London: Hogarth Press.

Kleindienst, N., & Greil, W. (2000). Differential efficacy of lithium and carbamazepine in the prophylaxis of bipolar disorder. *Neuropsychobiology, 42*, 2-10.

Klerman, G. L., Weissman, M. M., Rounsaville, B. J., & Chevron, E. S. (1984). *Interpersonal psychotherapy of depression*. New York: Basic Books.

Klonsky, E. D., Oltmanns, T. F., Turkheimer, E., & Fiedler, E. R. (2000). Recollections of conflict with parents and family support in the personality disorders. *Journal of Personality Disorders, 14*, 327-338.

Kluft, R. P. (1991). Clinical presentations of multiple personality disorder. *Psychiatric Clinics of North America, 14*, 605-629.

Kluft, R. P. (1995). The confirmation and disconfirmation of memories of abuse in DID patients: A naturalistic clinical study. *Dissociation: Progress in the Dissociative Disorders, 8*, 253-258.

Kluft, R. P. (1996). Treating the traumatic memories of patients with dissociative identity disorder. *American Journal of Psychiatry, 153* (*Suppl.*), 103-110.

Kluft, R. P. (1999). An overview of the psychotherapy of dissociative identity disorder. *American Journal of Psychotherapy, 53*, 289-319.

Knight, R. (1953). Borderline states. *Bulletin of the Menninger Clinic, 17*, 1-12.

Koegel, R. L., Schreibman, L., Britten, K. R., Burke, J. C., & O'Neill, R. E. (1982). A comparison of parent training to direct child treatment. In R. L. Koegel, A.

Rincover, & A. L. Egel (Eds.), *Educating and understanding autistic children*. San Diego, CA: College-Hill.

Koenig, H. G., & Blazer, D. G. (1992). Mood disorders and suicide. In J. E. Birren, R. B. Sloane, & G. D. Cohen (Eds.), *Handbook of mental health and aging* (2nd ed., pp. 379-407). San Diego, CA: Academic Press.

Koenigsberg, H. W. (1982). A comparison of hospitalized and nonhospitalized borderline patients. *American Journal of Psychiatry, 139*, 1292-1297.

Kohn, M. L. (1968). Social class and schizophrenia: A critical review. In D. Rosenthal & S. S. Kety (Eds.), *The transmission of schizophrenia*. New York: Pergamon.

Kolarsky, A., & Madlafousek, J. (1983). The inverse role of preparatory erotic stimulation in exhibitionists: Phallometric studies. *Archives of Sexual Behavior, 12*, 123-148.

Kolmen, B. K., Feldman, H. E., Handen, B. L., & Janosky, H. E. (1995). Naltrexone in young autistic children: A double-blind, placebo-controlled crossover study. *Journal of the American Academy of Child and Adolescent Psychiatry, 34*, 223-231.

Kopelowicz, A., Liberman, R. P., Mintz, J., & Zarate, R. (1997). Comparison of efficacy of social skills training for deficit and nondeficit negative symptoms in schizophrenia. *American Journal of Psychiatry, 154*, 424-425.

Koss, M. P. (1998). Hidden rape: Sexual aggression and victimization in a national sample of students in higher education. In M. E. Odem & J. Clay-Warner (Eds.), *Confronting rape and sexual assault. Worlds of women* (pp. 51-69).Wilmington, DE: SR Books/Scholarly Resources.

Koss, M. P., & Burkhart, B. R. (1989). A conceptual analysis of rape victimization. *Psychology of Women Quarterly, 13*, 27-40.

Koss, M. P., Gidycz, C. A., & Wisniewski, N. (1987). The scope of rape: Incidence and prevalence of sexual aggression and victimization in a national sample of higher education students. *Journal of Consulting and Clinical Psychology, 55*, 162-170.

Kraepelin, E. (1971). *Dementia praecox and paraphrenia* (R. M. Barclay, trans.). Huntington, NY: Krieger. (Originally published in 1919.)

Kreuger, R. B., & Kaplan, M. S. (1997). Frotteurism: Assessment and treatment. In D. R. Laws & W. O'Donohue (Eds.), *Sexual deviance*. New York: Guilford.

Kringlen, E. (1970). Natural history of obsessional neurosis. *Seminars in Psychiatry, 2*, 403-419.

Krueger, S., & Kennedy, S. H. (2000). Psychopharmacotherapy of anorexia nervosa, bulimia nervosa and binge-eating disorder. *Journal of Psychiatry and Neuroscience, 25*, 497-508.

Krystal, A. D., & Coffey, C. E. (1997). Neuropsychiatric considerations in the use of electroconvulsive therapy. *Journal of Neuropsychiatry and Clinical Neurosciences, 9*, 283-292.

Kuiper, B., & Cohen-Kettenis, P. (1988). Sex reassignment surgery: A study of 141 Dutch transsexuals. *Archives of Sexual Behavior, 17*, 439-457.

Kuipers, L., & Bebbington, P. (1988). Expressed emotion research in schizophrenia: Theoretical and clinical implications. *Psychological Medicine, 18*, 893-909.

Kushner, M. G., Abrams, K., & Borchardt, C. (2000). The relationship between anxiety disorders and alcohol use disorders: A review of major perspectives and findings. *Clinical Psychology Review, 20*, 149-171.

Kushner, M. G., Riggs, D. S., Foa, E. B., & Miller, S. M. (1992). Perceived controllability and the development of posttraumatic stress disorder (PTSD) in crime victims. *Behaviour Research and Therapy, 31*, 105-110.

Lambert, D., & Waters, C. H. (1998). Sexual dysfunction in Parkinson's disease. *Clinical Neuroscience, 5*, 73-77.

LaRue, A., Dessonville, C., & Jarvik, L. F. (1985). Aging and mental disorders. In J. E. Birren & K. W. Schaie (Eds.), *Handbook of psychology of aging* (2nd ed.). New York: Van Nostrand Reinhold.

Last, C. G., & Strauss, C. C. (1990). School refusal in anxiety-disordered children and adolescents. *Journal of the American Academy of Child and Adolescent Psychiatry, 29*, 31-35.

Latimer, P. R. (1995). Tardive dyskinesia: A review. *Canadian Journal of Psychiatry, 40* (Suppl. 2), S49-S54.

Lauer, J., Black, D. W., & Keen, P. (1993). Multiple personality disorder and borderline personality disorder: Distinct entities or variations on a common theme? *Annals of Clinical Psychiatry, 5*, 129-134.

Laumann, E. O., Gagnon, J. H., Michael, R. T., & Michaels, S. (1994). *The social organization of sexuality: Sexual practices in the United States*. Chicago: University of Chicago Press.

Lazarus, A. A. (1971). *Behavior therapy and beyond*. New York: McGraw-Hill.

Lazarus, A. A., Davison, G. C., & Polefka, D. (1965). Classical and operant factors in the treatment of a school phobia. *Journal of Abnormal Psychology, 70*, 225-229.

Lazarus, R. S., & Folkman, S. (1984). *Stress, appraisal, and coping*. New York: Springer.

Lecrubier, Y., & Weiller, E. (1997). Comorbidities in social phobia. *International Clinical Psychopharmacology, 12*, S17-S21.

Lee, D., DeQuattro, V., Cox, T., Pyter, L., Foti, A., Allen, J., Barndt, R., Azen, S., & Davison, G. C. (1987). Neurohormonal mechanisms and left ventricular hypertrophy: Effects of hygienic therapy. *Journal of Human Hypertension, 1*, 147-151.

LeFever, G. B., Dawson, K. V., & Morrow, A. L. (1999). The extent of drug therapy for attention deficit-hyperactivity disorder among children in public schools. *American Journal of Public Health, 89*, 1359-1364.

Leff, J., Sartorius, N., Jablonsky, A., Korten, A., & Ernberg, G. (1992). The International Pilot Study of Schizophrenia: Five-year follow-up findings. *Psychological Medicine, 22*, 131-145.

Lennox, B. R., Park, S. B. G., Medley, I., Morris, P. G., & Jones, P. B. (2000). The functional anatomy of auditory hallucinations in schizophrenia. *Psychiatry Research: Neuroimaging, 100*, 13-20.

Leonard, H. L., Swedo, S. E., Rapoport, J. L., Koby, E. V., Lenane, M. C., Cheslow, D. L., & Hamburger, S. D. (1989). Treatment of obsessive-compulsive disorder with clomipramine and desipramine in children and adolescents: A double-blind cross-over comparison. *Archives of General Psychiatry, 46*, 1088-1092.

Letourneau, E. J., & O'Donohue, W. (1997). Classical conditioning of female sexual arousal. *Archives of Sexual Behavior, 26*, 63-78.

Letourneau, E. J., Resnick, H. S., Kilpatrick, D. G., Saunders, B. E., et al. (1996). Comorbidity of sexual problems and posttraumatic stress disorder in female crime victims. *Behavior Therapy, 27*, 321-336.

Leung, F. (1996). Testing a dual-process family model in understanding the development of eating pathology: A structural equation modeling analysis. *International Journal of Eating Disorders, 20*, 367-375.

Levine, S. B. (1999). The newly revised standards of care for gender identity disorders. *Journal of Sex Education and Therapy, 24*, 117-127.

Levinson, D. F., Umapathy, C., & Musthaq, M. (1999). Treatment of schizoaffective disorder and schizophrenia with mood symptoms. *American Journal of Psychiatry, 156*, 1138-1148.

Lewins, F. (2002). Explaining stable partnerships among FTMs and MTFs: A significant difference? *Journal of Sociology, 38*, 76-88.

Lewinsohn, P. M., Rohde, P., Fischer, S. A., & Seeley, J. R. (1991). Age and depression. Unique and shared effects. *Psychology and Aging, 6*, 247-260.

Lewis, C. E. (2002). Impact of substance abuse and dependence on patients with schizophrenia. In J. G. Csernansky (Ed.), *Schizophrenia: A new guide for clinicians* (pp. 267-283). New York: Marcel Dekker.

Light, K. C., Dolan, C. A., Davis, M. R., & Sherwood, A. (1992). Cardiovascular responses to an active coping challenge as predictors of blood pressure patterns 10 to 15 years later. *Psychosomatic Medicine, 54*, 217-230.

Lilienfeld, S. O., Lynn, S. J., Kirsch, I., Chaves, J. F., Sarbin, T. R., & Powell, R. A. (1999). Dissociative identity disorder and the sociocognitive model: Recalling the lessons of the past. *Psychological Bulletin, 125*, 507-523.

Lindemaim, G., Korlin, D., & Uddenberg, N. (1986). Long-term follow-up of sex change in thirteen male-to-female transsexuals. *Archives of Sexual Behavior, 15*, 187-210.

Linehan, M. M. (1993). *Cognitive behavioral treatment of borderline personality disorder: The dialectics of effective treatment*. New York: Guilford.

Linehan, M. M., Armstrong, H. E., Suarez, R. A., Allmon, D., & Heard, H. L. (1991). Cognitive-behavioral treatment of chronically parasuicidal borderline patients. *Archives of General Psychiatry, 48*, 1060-1064.

Linehan, M. M., Heard, H. L., & Armstrong, H. E. (1992). Naturalistic follow-up of a behavioral treatment for chronically parasuicidal borderline patients. Unpublished manuscript, University of Washington.

Link, B. G., Monahan, J., Stueve, A., & Cullen, F. T. (1999). Real in their consequences: A sociological approach to understanding the association between psychotic symptoms and violence. *American Sociological Review, 64*, 316-332.

Link, G., Phelan, J. C., Bresnahan, M., Stueve, A., & Pescosolido, B. A. (1999). Public conceptions of mental illness: Labels, causes, dangerousness, and social distance. *American Journal of Public Health, 89*, 1328-1333.

Lion, J. R. (1978). Outpatient treatment of psychopaths. In W. H. Reid (Ed.), *The psychopath: A comprehensive study of antisocial disorders and behaviors*. New York: Brunner/Mazel.

Lipowski, Z. J. (1983). Transient cognitive disorders (delirium and acute confusional states) in the elderly. *American Journal of Psychiatry, 140*, 1426-1436.

Locke, H. J., & Wallace, K. M. (1959). Short marital adjustment and prediction tests: Their reliability and validity. *Marriage and Family Living, 21*, 251-255.

London, P. (1964). *Modes and morals of psychotherapy*. New York: Holt, Rinehart, & Winston.

LoPiccolo, J., & Stock, W. E. (1986). Treatment of sexual dysfunction. *Journal of Consulting and Clinical Psychology, 54*, 158-167.

Loranger, A. W., Oldham, J. M., & Tulis, E. H. (1983). Familial transmission of DSM-III borderline personality disorder. *Archives of General Psychiatry, 40*, 795-799.

Lotter, V. (1978). Follow-up studies. In M. Rutter & E. Schopler (Eds.), *Autism: A reappraisal of concepts and treatment*. New York: Plenum.

Lovaas, O. I. (1987). Behavioral treatment and normal educational and intellectual functioning in young autistic children. *Journal of Consulting and Clinical Psychology, 55*, 3-9.

Lovell, K., Marks, I. M., Noshirvani, H., Thrasher, S., & Livanou, M. (2001). Do cognitive and exposure treatments improve various PTSD symptoms differently? A randomized controlled trial. *Behavioural and Cognitive Psychotherapy, 29*, 107-112.

Lowe, M. R. (1996). Restraint, dieting, and the continuum model of bulimia nervosa. *Journal of Abnormal Psychology, 105*, 508-517.

Lykken, D. T. (1957). A study of anxiety in the sociopathic personality. *Journal of Abnormal and Social Psychology, 55*, 6-10.

Lyons, M. J., True, W. S., Eisen, A., Goldberg, J., Meyer, J. M., et al. (1995). Differential heritability of adult and juvenile traits. *Archives of General Psychiatry, 52*, 906-915.

Magee, W. J., Eaton, W. W., Wittchen, H. U., McGonagle, K. A., & Kessler, R. C. (1996). Agoraphobia, simple phobia and social phobia in the National Comorbidity Survey. *Archives of General Psychiatry, 53*, 159-168.

Maldonado, J. R., Butler, L. D., & Spiegel, D. (2002). Treatments for dissociative disorders. In P. E. Nathan J. M. Gorman (Eds.), *A guide to treatments that work* (2nd ed., pp. 463-496). London, England: Oxford University Press.

Maletzky, B. M. (1997). Exhibitionism: Assessment and treatment. In D. R. Laws & W. O'Donohue (Eds.), *Sexual deviance*. New York: Guilford.

Mannuzza, S., Klein, R. G., Bessler, A., Malloy, P., & LaPadula, M. (1993). Adult outcome of hyperactive boys: Educational achievement, occupational rank, and psychiatric status. *Archives of General Psychiatry, 50*, 563-551.

Mannuzza, S., Schneier, F. R., Chapman, T. F., Liebowitz, M. R., et al. (1995). Generalized social phobia: Reliability and validity. *Archives of General Psychiatry, 52(3)*, 230-237.

Manos, N., Vasilopoulou, E., & Sotiriou, M. (1987). DSM-III diagnoses borderline disorder and depression. *Journal of Personality Disorders, 1*, 263-268.

Manschreck, T. C. (1992). Delusional disorders: Clinical concepts and diagnostic strategies. *Psychiatric Annals, 22*, 241-251.

Manton, K. G., Blazer, D. G., & Woodbury, M. A. (1987). Suicide in middle age and later life: Sex and race specific life table and cohort analyses. *Journal of Gerontology, 42*, 219-227.

Marks, I. M. (1969). *Fears and phobias*. New York: Academic Press.

Marks, I. M. (1970). The classification of phobic disorders. *British Journal of Psychiatry, 116*, 377-386.

Marks, I. M. (1986). Epidemiology of anxiety. *Social Psychiatry, 21*, 167-171.

Marks, I. M. (1987). *Fears, phobias, and rituals: Panic, anxiety, and their disorders*. New York: Oxford University Press.

Marks, I. M. (1995). Advances in behavioral-cognitive therapy of social phobia. *Journal of Clinical Psychiatry, 56*, 25-31.

Marlatt, G. A. (1996). Taxonomy of high-risk situations for alcohol relapse: Evolution and development of a cognitive-behavioral model. *Addiction, 91* (Suppl.), S37-S49.

Marshall, J. (1998). Dual-diagnosis: co-morbidity of severe mental illness and substance misuse. *Journal of Forensic Psychiatry, 9*, 9-15.

Marshall, J. R. (1996). Comorbidity and its effects on panic disorder. *Bulletin of the Menninger Clinic, 60* (Suppl. A), A39-A52.

Marshall, W. L., Eccles, A., & Barbaree, H. E. (1991). The treatment of exhibitionism: A focus on sexual deviance versus cognitive and relationship factors. *Behavior Research and Therapy, 29*, 129-135.

Marshall, W. L., Jones, R., Ward, T., Johnston, P. & Barabee, H. E. (1991). Treatment outcomes with sex offenders. *Clinical Psychology Review, 11*, 465-485.

Masters, W. H., & Johnson, V. E. (1966). *Human sexual response*. Boston: Little, Brown.

Masters, W. H., & Johnson, V. E. (1970). *Human sexual inadequacy*. Boston: Little, Brown.

Masters, W. H., & Johnson, V. E. & Kolodny, R. C. (1985). *Human sexuality* (2nd ed.). Boston: Little, Brown.

Mathew, S. J., Yudofsky, S. C., McCullough, L. B., Teasdale, T. A., & Jankovic, J. (1999). Attitudes toward neurosurgical procedures for Parkinson's disease and obsessive-compulsive disorder. *Journal of Neuropsychiatry and Clinical Neurosciences, 11*, 259-267.

Matthews, A., & MacLeod, C. (1994). Cognitive approaches to emotion and emotional disorders. In L. W. Porter & M. Rosenzweig (Eds.), *Annual Review of Psychology* (pp. 25-50). Stanford, CA: Stanford University Press.

Matthews, K. A., & Rakacky, C. J. (1987). Familial aspects of type A behavior and physiologic reactivity to stress. In T. Dembroski & T. Schmidt (Eds.), *Behavioral factors in coronary heart disease*. Heidelberg: Springer-Verlag.

Mattia, J. I., & Zimmerman, M. (2001). Epidemiology. In W. J. Livesley (Ed.), *Handbook of personality disorders: Theory, research, and treatment* (pp. 107-123). New York: Guilford.

Mattick, R. P., & Andrews, G. (1994). Social phobia. In M. Hersen & R. T. Ammerman (Eds.), *Handbook of prescriptive treatments for adults* (pp. 157-177). New York: Plenum.

May, P. R. A., Van Putten, T., Yale, C., Potepan, P., Jenden, D. J., Fairchild, M. D., Goldstein, M. J., & Dixon, W. J. (1976). Predicting individual responses to drug treatment in schizophrenia: A test dose model. *Journal of Nervous and Mental Disease, 162*, 177-183.

Mayer, E. A., Craske, M., & Naliboff, B. D. (2001). Depression, anxiety, and the gastrointestinal system. *Journal of Clinical Psychiatry, 62* (Suppl. 8), 28-36.

McAdoo, W. G., & DeMyer, M. K. (1978). Personality characteristics of parents. In M. Rutter & E. Schopler (Eds.), *Autism: A reappraisal of concepts and treatment*. New York: Plenum.

McBride, P. A., Anderson, G. M., Hertzig, M. E., Sweeney, J. A., et al. (1989). Serotonergic responsivity in male young adults with autistic disorder: Results of a pilot study. *Archives of General Psychiatry, 46*, 213-221.

McBride, P. A., Anderson, G. M., & Shapiro, T. (1996). Autism research: Bringing together approaches to pull apart the disorder. *Archives of General Psychiatry, 53*, 980-983.

McCabe, M. P. (2001). Evaluation of a cognitive behavior therapy program for people with sexual dysfunction. *Journal of Sex and Marital Therapy, 27*, 259-271.

McCord, W., & McCord, J. (1964). *The psychopath: An essay on the criminal mind*. New York: Van Nostrand Reinhold.

McDougle, C. J. Price, L. H., Volkmar, F. R., Goodman, W. K., et al. (1992). Clomipramine in autism: Preliminary evidence of efficacy. *Journal of the American Academy of Child and Adolescent Psychiatry, 31*, 746-750.

McEachin, J. J., Smith, T., & Lovaas, O. I. (1993). Long-term outcome for children with autism who receive early intensive behavioral treatment. *American Journal on Mental Retardation, 97*, 359-372.

McElroy, S. L., Keck, P. E., & Strakowski, S. M. (1999). An overview of the treatment of schizoaffective disorder. *Journal of Clinical Psychiatry, 60* (Suppl. 5), 16-21.

McEwen, B. S. (1998). Protective and damaging effects of stress mediators. *New England Journal of Medicine, 338*, 171-179.

McGlashan, T. H. (1986). Schizotypal personality disorder: Chestnut Lodge follow-up study. *Archives of General Psychiatry, 43*, 329-334.

McGlashan, T. H., & Williams, P. V. (1990). Predicting outcome in schizoaffective psychosis. *Journal of Nervous and Mental Disease, 178*, 518-520.

McGlashan, T. M. (1983). The borderline syndrome: I. Testing three diagnostic systems. *Archives of General Psychiatry, 40*, 1311-1318.

McGrady, A., Nadsady, P. A., & Schumann-Brzezinski, C. (1991). Sustained effects of biofeedback-assisted relaxation in essential hypertension. *Biofeedback and Self-Regulation, 16*, 399-411.

McGue, M., & Gottesman, I. I. (1989). A single dominant gene still cannot account for the transmission of schizophrenia. *Archives of General Psychiatry, 46*, 478-480.

McGue, M., Pickens, R. W., & Suikis, D. S. (1992). Sex and age effects on the inheritance of alcohol problems: A twin study. *Journal of Abnormal Psychology, 101*, 3-17.

McIntosh, J. L. (1995). Suicide prevention in the elderly. In M. M. Silverman & R. W. Maris (Eds.), *Suicide prevention toward the year 2000* (pp. 180-192). New York: Guilford.

McLean, P. D., Whittal, J. L., Thordarson, D. S., Taylor, S., Sochting, I., Koch, W. J., Paterson, R.. & Anderson, K. W. (2001). Cognitive versus behavior therapy in the group treatment of obsessive-compulsive disorder. *Journal of Consulting and Clinical Psychology, 69*, 205-214

McMahon, F. J., Simpson, S. G., McInnis, M. G., Badner, J. A., MacKinnon, D. F., & DePaulo, J. R. (2001). Linkage of bipolar disorder to chromosome 18q and the validity of bipolar II disorder. *Archives of General Psychiatry, 58*, 1025-1031.

McNally, R. J. (1994a). *Panic disorder: A critical analysis*. New York: Guilford.

McNally, R. J. (1994b). Preparedness and phobias: A review. *Psychological Bulletin, 101*, 283-303.

McNeil, D. E. (1994). Hallucinations and violence. In J. Monahan & H. J. Steadman (Eds.). *Violence and mental disorder: Developments in risk assessment* (pp. 183-202). Chicago, IL: University of Chicago Press.

McNeil, D. E., Eisner, J. P., & Binder, R. L. (2000). The relationship between command hallucinations and violence. *Psychiatric Services, 51*, 1288-1292.

Meehl, P. E. (1964). Manual for use with checklist of schizotypic signs. Unpublished manuscript, University of Minnesota Medical School, Minneapolis.

Merckelbach, H., de Ruiter, C., van den Hout, M. A., & Hoekstra, R. (1989).

Conditioning experiences and phobias. *Behaviour Research and Therapy, 27,* 657-662.

Merskey, H. (1992). The manufacture of personalities: The production of multiple personality disorder. *British Journal of Psychiatry, 160,* 327-340.

Meyer, J. K. (1974). Clinical variants among sex reassignment applicants. *Archives of Sexual Behavior, 3,* 527-558.

Meyer, J. K., & Reter, D. J. (1979). Sex reassignment: Follow-up. *Archives of General Psychiatry, 36,* 1010-1015.

Meyer, W. J., Cole, C., & Emory, E. (1992). Depo provera treatment for sex offending behavior: An evaluation of outcome. *Bulletin of the American Academy of Psychiatry and the Law, 20,* 249-259.

Mickley, D. W. (2001). Medical aspects of anorexia and bulimia. In B. P. Kinoy (Ed.), *Eating disorders: New directions in treatment and recovery* (2nd ed., pp. 7-16). New York: Columbia University Press.

Miklowitz, D. J. (1996). Psychotherapy in combination with drug treatment for bipolar disorder. *Journal of Clinical Psychopharmacology, 16* (Suppl. 1), 56S-66S.

Miklowitz, D. J., Frank, E., & George, E. L. (1996). New psychosocial treatments for the outpatient management of bipolar disorder. *Psychopharmacology Bulletin, 32,* 613-621.

Miklowitz, D. J., Goldstein, M. J., & Nuechterlein, K. H. (1995). Verbal interactions in the families of schizophrenic and bipolar affective patients. *Journal of Abnormal Psychology, 104,* 268-276.

Miklowitz, D. J., Goldstein, J. J., Nuechterlein, K. H., Snyder, K. S., & Mintz, J. (1988). Family factors and the course of bipolar affective disorder. *Archives of General Psychiatry, 45,* 225-231.

Millberger, S., Biederman, J., Faraone, S. V., Chen, L., & Jones, J. (1996). Is maternal smoking during pregnancy a risk factor for attention deficit hyperactivity in children? *American Journal of Psychiatry, 153,* 1138-1142.

Miller, M. B., Useda, J. D., Trull, T. J., Burr, R. M., & Minks-Brown, C. (2001). Paranoid, schizoid, and schizotypal personality disorders. In P. B. Sutker & H. E. Adams (Eds.), *Comprehensive handbook of psychopathology* (3rd ed., pp. 535-559.). New York: Kluwer Academic/Plenum.

Miller, R. G., Palkes, H. S., & Stewart, M. A. (1973). Hyperactive children in suburban elementary schools. *Child Psychiatry and Human Development, 4,* 121-127.

Miller, W. R., Zweben, A., DiClemente, C. C., & Rychatarik, R. G. (1992). Motivational Enhancement Therapy manual: A clinical research guide for therapists treating individual with alcohol abuse and dependence. NIAA Project Match monograph, Vol. 2. Washington, DC: U.S. Department of Health and Human Services.

Millon, T. (1981). *Disorders of personality: DSM-III, Axis II.* New York: Wiley.

Mineka, S., & Zinbarg, R. (1995). Conditioning and ethological models of social phobia. In R. G. Heimberg, M. R. Liebowitz, D. A. Hope, & F. R. Schneier (Eds.), *Social phobia: Diagnosis, assessment, and treatment* (pp. 134-162). New York: Guilford.

Mineka, S., & Zinbarg, R. (1996). Conditioning and ethological models of anxiety disorders: Stress-in-dynamic-context anxiety models. In D. A. Hope (Ed.). *Nebraska Symposium on Motivation,* pp. 135-210. Lincoln: University of Nebraska Press.

Mischel, W., & Peake, P. K. (1982). Beyond déjà vu in the search for cross-situational consistency. *Psychological Review, 89,* 730-735.

Mishler, E. G., & Waxler, N. E. (1968). *Interaction in families: An experimental study of family processes and schizophrenia.* New York: Wiley.

Modestin, J. (1992). Multiple personality disorder in Switzerland. *American Journal of Psychiatry, 149,* 88-92.

Moffitt, T. E. (1993). Adolescence-limited and life-course-persistent antisocial behavior: A developmental taxonomy. *Psychological Review, 100,* 674-701.

Mohr, J. W., Turner, R. E., & Jerry, M. B. (1964). *Pedophilia and exhibitionism.* Toronto: University of Toronto Press.

Monahan, J. (2001). Major mental disorders and violence: Epidemiology and risk assessment. In G. Pinard & L. Pagani (Eds.), *Clinical assessment of dangerousness: Empirical contributions* (pp. 89-102). New York: Cambridge University Press.

Monroe, S. M., Rhode, P., Seeley, J. R., & Lewinsohn, P. M. (1999). Life events and depression in adolescence: Relationship loss as a prospective risk factor for first onset of major depressive disorder. *Journal of Abnormal Psychology, 108,* 606-614.

Morey, L. C. & Zanarini, M. C. (2000). Borderline personality: Traits and disorder. *Journal of Abnormal Psychology, 109,* 733-737.

Morrison, A. P., Wells, A., & Nothard, S. (2000). Cognitive factors in predisposition to auditory and visual hallucinations. *British Journal of Clinical Psychology, 39,* 67-78.

Mowrer, O. H. (1947). On the dual nature of learning: A reinterpretation of "conditioning" and "problem-solving." *Harvard Educational Review, 17,* 102-148.

MTA Cooperative Group. (1999). Moderators and mediators of treatment response for children with attention-deficit-hyperactivity disorder. *Archives of General Psychiatry, 56,* 1088-1096.

Munjack, D. J. (1984). The onset of driving phobias. *Journal of Behavior Therapy and Experimental Psychiatry, 15,* 305-308.

Murphy, J. K., Stoney, C. M., Alpert, B. S., & Walker, S. S. (1995). Gender and ethnicity in children's cardiovascular reactivity: 7 years of study. *Health Psychology, 14,* 48-55.

Murphy, W. D. (1997). Exhibitionism: Psychopathology and theory. In D. R. Laws & W. O'Donohue (Eds.), *Sexual deviance.* New York: Guilford.

Myers, J. K., Weissman, M. M., Tishler, G. L., Holzer, C. E., Leaf, P. J., Orvaschel, J., Anthony, J. C., Boyd, J. H., Burke, J. D., Kramer, M., & Stolzman, R. (1984). Six-month prevalence of psychiatric disorders in three communities. *Archives of General Psychiatry, 41,* 959-970.

Nageotte, C., Sullivan, G., Duan, N., & Camp., P. L. (1997). Medication compliance among the seriously mentally ill in a public mental health system. *Social Psychiatry and Psychiatric Epidemiology, 32,* 49-56.

Narash-Eisikovits, O., Dierberger, A., & Westen, D. (2002). A multidimensional meta-analysis of pharmacotherapy for bulimia nervosa: Summarizing the range of outcomes in controlled clinical trials. *Harvard Review of Psychiatry, 10,* 193-211.

Nassir, G. S., & Goodwin, F. K. (1999). Use of atypical antipsychotic agents in bipolar and schizoaffective disorders: Review of the empirical literature. *Journal of Clinical Psychopharmacology, 19,* 354-361.

Neighbors, H. W., & Jackson, J. S. (1996). *Mental health in black America.* Thousand Oaks, CA: Sage Publications.

Nelson, E., & Rice, J. (1997). Stability of diagnosis of obsessive-compulsive disorder in the Epidemiologic Catchment Area Study. *American Journal of Psychiatry, 154,* 826-831.

Netter, P., & Neuhauser-Metternich, S. (1991). Types of aggressiveness and catecholamine response in essential hypertensives and healthy controls. *Journal of Psychosomatic Research, 35,* 409-419.

Neugarten, B. L. (1977). Personality and aging. In J. W. Birren & K. W. Schaie (Eds.), *Handbook of the psychology of aging.* New York: Van Nostrand.

Neumann, C. S., Grimes, K., Walker, E. F., & Baum, K. (1995). Developmental pathways to schizophrenia: Behavioral stereotypes. *Journal of Abnormal Psychology, 104,* 558-566.

Newlin, D. B. & Thompson, J. B. (1990). Alcohol challenge with the sons of alcoholics: A review and analysis. *Psychological Bulletin, 108,* 383-402.

Newman, J. P., & Kosson, D. S. (1986). Passive avoidance learning in psychopathic and nonpsychopathic offenders. *Journal of Abnormal Psychology, 95,* 257-263.

Newman, J. P., Kosson, D. S., & Patterson, D. S. (1992). Delay of gratification in psychopathic and nonpsychopathic offenders. *Journal of Abnormal Psychology, 101,* 630-636.

Newman, J. P., Patterson, C. M., & Kosson, D. S. (1987). Response perseveration in psychopaths. *Journal of Abnormal Psychology, 96,* 145-149.

Newman, L. K. (1991). Sex, gender and culture: Issues in the definition, assessment and treatment of gender identity disorder. *Clinical Child Psychology and Psychiatry, 7,* 352-359.

Nguyen, S. D. (1985). Mental health services for refugees and immigrants in Canada. In T. C. Owen (Ed.), *Southeast Asian mental health: Treatment, prevention, services, training, and research* (pp. 261-282). Washington, DC: National Institute of Mental Health.

Nielsen, S. (2001). Epidemiology and mortality of eating disorders. *Psychiatric Clinics of North America, 24,* 201-214.

Nigg, J. T. (2001). Is ADHD an inhibitory disorder? *Psychological Bulletin, 127,* 571-598.

Nigg, J. T. & Goldsmith, H. H. (1994). Genetics of personality disorders: Perspectives from personality and psychopathology research. *Psychological Bulletin, 115,* 346-380.

Nigg, J. T., Lohr, N. E., Westen, D., Gold, L. J., & Silk, K. R. (1992). Malevolent object representations in borderline personality and major depression. *Journal of Abnormal Psychology, 101,* 61-67.

Nolen-Hoeksema, S. (1995). Epidemiology and theories of gender differences in unipolar depression. In M. V. Seeman (Ed.), *Gender and psychopathology* (pp. 63-88). Washington, DC: American Psychiatric Press.

Nolen-Hoeksema, S. (2000). The role of rumination in depressive disorders and mixed anxiety/depressive symptoms. *Journal of Abnormal Psychology, 109,* 504-511.

North, C. S., Thompson, S. J., Pollio, D. E., Ricci, D. A., et al. (1997). A diagnostic comparison of homeless and nonhomeless patients in an urban mental health clinic. *Social Psychiatry and Psychiatric Epidemiology, 32,* 236-240.

Norton, G. R., Cox, B. J., & Malan, J. (1992). Nonclinical panickers: A critical review. *Clinical Psychology Review, 12*(2), 121-139.

Notman, M. T., & Nadelson, C. C. (1995). Gender, development, and psychopathology: A revised psychodynamic view. In M. V. Seeman (Ed.), *Gender and psychopathology* (pp. 1-16). Washington, DC: American Psychiatric Press.

Novaco, R. W. (1995). Clinical problems of anger and its assessment and regulation though a stress coping skills approach. In W. O'Donohue & L. Krasner (Eds.), *Handbook of psychological skills training: Clinical techniques and applications* (pp. 320-338). Boston, MA: Allyn & Bacon.

O'Donohue, W., & Geer, J. H. (1993). *Handbook of sexual dysfunctions: Assessment and treatment*. Boston: Allyn & Bacon.

O'Donohue, W., & Plaud, J. J. (1994). The conditioning of human sexual arousal. *Archives of Sexual Behavior, 23*, 321-344.

O'Donohue, W. T., Swingen, D. N., Dopke, C. A., & Regev, L. G. (1999). Psychotherapy for male sexual dysfunction: A review. *Clinical Psychology Review, 18*, 591-630.

Ogata, S. N., Silk, K. R., Goodrich, S., et al. (1990). Childhood sexual and physical abuse in adult patients with borderline personality disorder. *American Journal of Psychiatry, 147*, 1008-1013.

Ogloff, J. R., & Wong, S. (1990). Electrodermal and cardiovascular evidence of a coping response in psychopaths. *Criminal Justice and Behavior, 17*, 231-245.

Ohayon, M. M. (2000). Prevalence of hallucinations and their pathological associations in the general population. *Psychiatry Research, 97*, 153-164.

Öhman, A. (1996). Preferential preattentive processing of threat in anxiety: Preparedness and attentional biases. In Ronald M. Rapee (Ed.), *Current controversies in the anxiety disorders* (pp. 253-290). New York: Guilford.

Öhman, A., Erixon, G., & Löfberg, I. (1975). Phobias and preparedness: Phobic versus neutral pictures as conditioned stimuli for human autonomic responses. *Journal of Abnormal Psychology, 84*, 41-45.

O'Leary, D. S., Flaum, M., Kesler, M. L., Flashman, L. A., Arndt, S., & Andreasen, N. C. (2000). Cognitive correlates of the negative, disorganized, and psychotic symptom dimensions of schizophrenia. *Journal of Neuropsychiatry and Clinical Neuroscience, 12*, 4-14.

O'Leary, K. D. (1980). Pills or skills for hyperactive children? *Journal of Applied Behavior Analysis, 13*, 193-204.

Opler, L. A., White, L., Caton, C. L. M., Dominguez, B., Hirshfield, S., & Shrout, P. E. (2001). Gender differences in the relationship of homelessness to symptom severity, substance abuse, and neuroleptic noncompliance in schizophrenia. *Journal of Nervous and Mental Disease, 189*, 449-456.

Orne, M. T., Dinges, D. F., & Orne, E. C. (1984). On the differential diagnosis of multiple personality in the forensic case. *International Journal of Clinical and Experimental Hypnosis, 32*, 118-169.

Osborn, I. (1998). *Tormenting thoughts and secret rituals*. New York: Dell Publishing.

Ost, L. G. (1987). Age of onset in different phobias. *Journal of Abnormal Psychology, 96*, 223-229.

Ost, L. G. (1992). Blood and injection phobia: Background and cognitive, physiological, and behavioral correlates. *Journal of Abnormal Psychology, 101*, 68-74.

Ouimette, P. C., Finney, J. W., & Moos, R. H. (1997). Twelve-step and cognitive-behavioral treatment for substance abuse: A comparison of treatment effectiveness. *Journal of Consulting and Clinical Psychology, 65*, 230-240.

Palmer, T. (1984). Treatment and the role of classification: Review of basics. *Crime and Delinquency, 30*, 245-267.

Paris, J. (1990). Completed suicide in borderline personality disorder. *Psychiatric Annals, 20*, 19-21.

Paris J., Zweig, F. M., & Gudzer. J. (1994). Psychological risk factors for borderline personality disorder in female patients. *Comprehensive Psychiatry, 35*, 301-305.

Patel, C., Marmot, M. G., Terry, D. J., Carruthers, M., Hunt, B., & Patel, M. (1985). Trial of relaxation in reducing coronary risk: Four-year follow-up. *British Medical Journal, 290*, 1103-1106.

Paternite, C. E., & Loney, J. (1980). Childhood hyperkinesis: Relationships between symptomatology and home environment. In C. K. Whalen & B. Henker (Eds.), *Hyperactive children*. New York: Academic Press.

Patrick, C. J., Bradley, M. M., & Lang, P. J. (1993). Emotion in the criminal psychopath: Startle reflex modulation. *Journal of Abnormal Psychology, 102*, 82-92.

Paul, R. (1987). Communication. In D. J. Cohen, A. M. Donellan, & R. Paul (Eds.), *Handbook of autism and pervasive developmental disorders* (pp. 61-84). New York: Wiley.

Pauls, D. L., Alsobrook, J. P., Goodman, W., Rasmussen, S., et al. (1995). A family study of obsessive-compulsive disorder. *American Journal of Psychiatry, 152*, 76-84.

Pearson, H. J., Marshall, W. L., Barbaree, H. E., & Southmayd, S. (1992). Treatment of a compulsive paraphiliac with buspirone. Annals of Sex Research, 5, 239-246.

Pelham, W. E., McBurnett, K., Harper, G. W., Milich, R., Murphy, D. A., Clinton, J., & Thiele, C. (1990). Methylphenidate and baseball playing in ADHD children: Who's on first? *Journal of Consulting and Clinical Psychology, 58*, 130-133.

Pennebaker, J. W. (1989). Confession, inhibition, and disease. In L. Berkowitz (Ed.), *Advances in experimental social psychology* (pp. 211-244), New York: Academic Press.

Pennebaker, J. W. (1997). Writing about emotional experiences as a therapeutic process. *Psychological Science, 8*, 162-166.

Pennebaker, J. W., Mayne, T. J., & Francis, M. E. (1997). Linguistic predictors of adaptive bereavement. *Journal of Personality and Social Psychology, 72*, 863-871.

Perris, C. (1992). Bipolar-unipolar distinction. In E. S. Paykel (Ed.), *Handbook of affective disorders* (2nd ed., pp. 57-75). New York: Guilford.

Perry, J. C., Banon, E., & Ianni, F. (1999). Effectiveness of psychotherapy for personality disorders. *American Journal of Psychiatry, 156*, 1312-1321.

Pescosolida, B. A., Monahan, J., Link, B., Stueve, A., & Kikuzawa, S. (1999). The public's view of the competence, dangerousness, and need for legal coercion of persons with mental health problems. *American Journal of Public Health, 89*, 1339-1345.

Peterson, C. B., & Mitchell, J. E. (1999). Psychosocial and pharmacological treatment of eating disorders: A review of research findings. *Journal of Clinical Psychology, 55*, 685-697.

Peterson, D. R. (1954). The diagnosis of subclinical schizophrenia. *Journal of Consulting Psychology, 18*, 198-200.

Petersen, M. E., & Dickey, R. (1995). Surgical sex reassignment: A comparative survey of international centers. *Archives of Sexual Behavior, 24*, 135-156.

Pfohl, B., Coryell, W., Zimmerman, M., & Stangl, D. (1986). DSM-III personality disorder: Diagnostic overlap and internal consistency of individual DSM-III criteria. *Comprehensive Psychiatry, 27*, 21-34.

Phillips, R. D. (1985). Whistling in the dark? A review of play therapy research. *Psychotherapy, 22*, 752-760.

Piren J., Palmer, P., Jacobi, D., Childress, D., & Arndt, S. (1997). Broader autism phenotype: Evidence from a family history study of multiple-incidence autism families. *American Journal of Psychiatry, 154*, 185-190.

Polivy, J., & Herman, C. P. (2002). Causes of eating disorders. *Annual Review of Psychology, 53*, 187-213.

Powers, P. S., Schulman, R. G., Gleghorn, A. A., & Prange, M. E. (1987). Perceptual and cognitive abnormalities in bulimia. *American Journal of Psychiatry, 144*, 1456-1460.

Putnam, F. W. (1989). *Diagnosis and treatment of multiple personality disorder*. New York: Guilford.

Putnam, F. W. (1991). Recent research on multiple personality disorder. *Psychiatric Clinics of North America, 14*, 489-502.

Putnam, F. W. (1993). Diagnosis and clinical phenomenology of multiple personality disorder: A North American perspective. *Dissociation, 6*, 80-86.

Putnam, F. W., Guroff, J. J., Silberman, E. K., Barban, L., & Post, R. M. (1986). The clinical phenomenology of multiple personality disorder: Review of 100 recent cases. *Journal of Clinical Psychiatry, 47*, 285-293.

Pyle, R. L., Mitchell, J. E., & Eckert, E. D. (1981). Bulimia: A report of 34 cases. *Journal of Clinical Psychology, 42*, 60-64.

Quay, H. C. (1997). Inhibition and attention deficit hyperactivity disorder. *Journal of Abnormal Child Psychology, 25*, 7-13.

Rabins, P. V., & Folstein, M. F. (1982). Delirium and dementia: Diagnostic criteria and fatality rates. *British Journal of Psychiatry, 140*, 149-153.

Rachman, S. J. (1976). The modification of obsessions: A new formulation. *Behavior Research and Therapy, 14*, 437-443.

Rachman, S. J., & Hodgson, R. J. (1980). *Obsessions and compulsions*. Englewood, Cliffs, NJ: Prentice-Hall.

Raine, A., O'Brien, M., Chan, C. J., et al. (1990). Reward learning in adolescent psychopaths. *Journal of Abnormal Child Psychology, 18*, 451-463.

Raine, A., & Venables, P. H. (1987). Contingent negative variation, P3 evoked potentials, and antisocial behavior. *Psychophysiology, 24*, 191-199.

Rapee, R. M., & Barlow, D. H. (1988). Cognitive-behavioral treatment of panic disorder. *Psychiatric Annals, 18*, 473-477.

Rapoport, J. L., Buchsbaum, M. S., Weingartner, H., Zahn, T. P., Ludlow, C., & Mikkelsen, E. J. (1980). Dextroamphetamine: Its cognitive and behavioral effects in normal and hyperactive boys and normal men. *Archives of General Psychiatry, 37*, 933-943.

Rasmussen, A. M., & Charney, D. S. (1997). Animal models of relevance to PTSD. *Annals of the New York Academy of Sciences, 821*, 332-351.

Rasmussen, S. A., & Eisen, J. L. (1992). The epidemiology and clinical features of obsessive compulsive disorder. *Psychiatric Clinics of North America, 15*, 743-758.

Regier, D. A., Boyd, J. H., Burke, J. D., Rae, D. S., et al. (1988). One-month prevalence of mental disorders in the United States: Based on five epidemiologic catchment area sites. *Archives of General Psychiatry, 45*, 977-986.

Regier, D. A., Rae, D. S., Narrow, W. E., Kaelber, C. T., & Schatzberg, A. F. (1998). Prevalence of anxiety disorders and their comorbidity with mood and addictive disorders. *British Journal of Psychiatry, 173* (Suppl. 34), 24-28.

Rehman, J., Lazer, S., Benet, A. E., Schaefer, L. C., & Melman, A. (1999). The reported sex and surgery satisfactions of 28 postoperative male-to-female transsexual patients. *Archives of Sexual Behavior, 28,* 71-89.

Reiser, W. F., Brust, A. A., Shapiro, A. P., Baker, H. M., Ransohoff, W., & Ferris, E. B. (1951). Life situations, emotions, and the course of patients with arterial hypertension. *Psychosomatic Medicine, 13,* 133-139.

Rekers, G. A., Kilgus, M., & Rosen, A. C. (1990). Long-term effects of treatment for gender identity disorder of childhood. *Journal of Psychology and Human Sexuality, 3,* 121-153.

Resick, P. A. (1993). The psychological impact of rape. *Journal of Interpersonal Violence, 8,* 223-255

Resick, P. A., & Calhoun, K. S. (1996). Post-traumatic stress disorder. In C. G Lindemann (Ed.), *Handbook of the treatment of the anxiety disorders* (2nd ed., pp. 191-216). Northvale, NJ: Jason Aronson.

Resick, P. A., & Schnicke, M. K. (1992). Cognitive processing therapy for sexual assault victims. *Journal of Consulting and Clinical Psychology, 60,* 748-756.

Resnick, H. S., Kilpatrick, D. G., Best, C. L., & Kramer, T. L. (1992). Vulnerability-stress factors in development of posttraumatic stress disorder. *Journal of Nervous and Mental Disease, 180,* 424-430.

Restak, R. M. (1979). The sex-change conspiracy. *Psychology Today, 13,* 20-24.

Ricca, V., Mannucci, E., Zucchi, T., Rotella, C. M., & Faravelli, C. (2000). Cognitive-behavioural therapy for bulimia nervosa and binge eating disorder: A review. *Psychotherapy and Psychosomatics, 69,* 287-295.

Rice, M. E., Harris, G. T., & Cormier, C. A. (1992). An evaluation of a maximum security therapeutic community for psychopaths and other mentally disordered offenders. *Law and Human Behavior, 16,* 399-412.

Ricks, D. M. (1972). The beginning of vocal communication in infants and autistic children. Unpublished dissertation, University of London.

Ridley, C. R. (1984). Clinical treatment of the nondisclosing black client. *American Psychologist, 39,* 1234-1244.

Rieber, R. W. (1999). Hypnosis, false memory and multiple personality: A trinity of affinity. *History of Psychiatry, 10,* 3-11.

Riggs, D. S., Dancu, C. V., Gershuny, B. S., Greenberg, D., & Foa, E. B. (1992). Anger and post-traumatic stress disorder in female crime victims. *Journal of Traumatic Stress, 5,* 613-625.

Rimland, B. (1964). *Infantile autism.* New York: Appleton-Century-Crofts.

Ritvo, E. R., Freeman, B. J., Geller, E., & Yuwiler, A. (1983). Effects of fenfluramine on 14 outpatients with the syndrome of autism. *Journal of the American Academy of Child Psychiatry, 22,* 549-558.

Robins, L. N. (1966). *Deviant children grown up.* Baltimore: Williams and Wilkins.

Robins, L. N., Helzer, J. E., Weissman, M. M., et al. (1984). Lifetime prevalence of specific psychiatric disorders in three sites. *Archives of General Psychiatry, 41,* 942-949.

Robins, L. N., & Ratcliffe, K. S. (1980). The long-term outcome of truancy. In L. Fersov & I. Berg (Eds.), *Out of school* (pp. 65-83). New York: Wiley.

Robins, L. N., & Regier, D. A. (Eds.). (1991). *Psychiatric disorders in America: The Epidemiologic Catchment Area Study.* New York: Free Press.

Rodin, J., & Langer, E. J. (1977). Long-term effects of a control-relevant intervention with the institutionalized aged. *Journal of Personality and Social Psychology, 35,* 897-902.

Rogers, C. R. (1951). *Client-centered therapy.* Boston: Houghton Mifflin.

Romano, S. J., Halmi, K. A., Sarkar, N. P., Koke, S., & Lee, J. S. (2002). A placebo-controlled study of fluoxetine in continued treatment of bulimia nervosa after successful acute fluoxetine treatment. *American Journal of Psychiatry, 159,* 96-102.

Rosen, R. C., & Leiblum, S. R. (1995). Treatment of sexual disorders in the 1990s: An integrated approach. *Journal of Consulting and Clinical Psychology, 63,* 877-890.

Rosenblatt, R. A., & Spiegel, C. (1988, December 2). Half of state's nursing homes fall short in federal study. *Los Angeles Times,* Part I, pp. 3-34.

Rosenthal, T. L., & Bandura, A. (1978). Psychological modeling: Theory and practice. In S. L. Garfield & A. E. Bergin (Eds.), *Handbook of psychotherapy and behavior change: An empirical analysis* (2nd ed.). New York: Wiley.

Ross, A. O., & Nelson, R. (1979). Behavior therapy. In H. S. Quay & J. S. Werry (Eds.), *Psychopathological disorders of childhood.* New York: Wiley.

Ross, C. A. (1991). Epidemiology of multiple personality disorder and dissociation. *Psychiatric Clinics of North America, 14,* 503-517.

Ross, C. A. (1997a). *Dissociative identity disorder: Diagnosis, clinical features, and treatment of multiple personality* (2nd ed.). New York: Wiley.

Ross, C. A. (1997b). Cognitive therapy of dissociative identity disorder. In P.S. Appelbaum & L.A. Uyehara (Eds.), *Trauma and memory: Clinical and legal controversies* (pp. 360-377). New York: Oxford University Press.

Rothbard, A. B., Schinnar, A. P., Hadley, T. P., Foley, K. A., & Kuno, E. (1998). Cost comparison of state hospital and community-based care for seriously mentally ill adults. *American Journal of Psychiatry, 155,* 523-529.

Rothbaum, B. O., Foa, E. B., Riggs, D. S., Murdock, T., & Walsh, W. (1992). A prospective examination of post-traumatic stress disorder in rape victims. *Journal of Traumatic Stress, 5,* 455-475.

Routh, D. K., & Bernholtz, J. E. (1991). Attachment, separation, and phobias. In J. L. Gewirtz & W. M. Kurtines (Eds.), *Intersections with attachment* (pp. 295-309). Hillsdale, N J: Erlbaum Associates.

Royal College of Psychiatrists (1989). *The practical administration of electroconvulsive therapy (ECT)* . London: Gaskell.

Russell, G. (1979). Bulimia nervosa: An ominous variant of anorexia nervosa. *Psychological Medicine, 9,* 429-448.

Rutter, M. (1967). Psychotic disorders in early childhood. In A. J. Cooper (Ed.), Recent developments in schizophrenia. *British Journal of Psychiatry, 1,* Special Publication.

Rutter, M. (1974). The development of infantile autism. *Psychological Medicine, 4,* 147-163.

Sachdev, P., & Hay, P. (1995). Does neurosurgery for obsessive-compulsive disorder produce personality change? *Journal of Nervous and Mental Disease, 183,* 408-413.

Salkovskis, P. M. (1999). Understanding and treating obsessive-compulsive disorder. *Behaviour Research and Therapy, 37,* S29-S52.

Salter, A. (1949). *Conditioned reflex therapy.* New York: Farrar, Straus.

Samelson, F. (1980). J. B. Watson's Little Albert, Cyril Burt's twins, and the need for a critical science. *American Psychologist, 35,* 619-625.

Sanislow, C. A., Grilo, C. M. & McGlashan, T. H. (2000). Factor analysis of the DSM-III-R borderline personality criteria in psychiatric inpatients. *American Journal of Psychiatry, 157,* 1629-1633.

Sanislow, C. A., & McGlashan, T. (1998). Treatment outcome of personality disorders. *Canadian Journal of Psychiatry, 43,* 237-250.

Scheel, K. R. (2000). The empirical basis of dialectical behavior therapy: Summary and critique and implications. *Clinical Psychology—Science and Practice, 17,* 68-86.

Schiffman, J., Abrahamson, A., Cannon, T, LaBrie, J., Parnas, J., Schulsinger, F., & Mednick, S. (2001). Early rearing factors in schizophrenia. *International Journal of Mental Health, 30,* 3-16.

Schneider, K. (1959). *Clinical psychopathology.* New York: Grune and Stratton.

Schooler, N. R., Keith, S. J., Severe, J. B., Matthews, S. M., Bellack, A. S., Glick, I. D., Hargreaves, W. A., Kane, J. M., Ninan, P. T., Frances, A., Jacobs, M., Lieberman, J. A., Mance, R., Simpson, G. M., & Woerner, M. G. (1997). Relapse and rehospitalization during maintenance treatment of schizophrenia. The effects of dose reduction and family treatment. *Archives of General Psychiatry, 54,* 453-463.

Schreiber, F. (1973). *Sybil.* Chicago: Henry Regnery. (Reprinted by Warner Paperback Library, New York, 1974)

Schuckit, M. A. (1994). Low level of response to alcohol as a predictor of future alcoholism. *American Journal of Psychiatry, 151,* 41-49.

Schuckit, M. A., & Smith, T. L. (1996). An 8-year follow-up of 450 sons of alcoholic, and control subjects. *Archives of General Psychiatry, 53,* 202-210.

Schuckit, M. A., Smith, T. L., Danko, G. P., Bucholz, K. K., Reich, T., & Bierut, L. (2001). Five-year clinical course associated with DSM-IV alcohol abuse or dependence in a large group of men and women. *American Journal of Psychiatry, 158,* 1084-1090.

Schulsinger, F. (1972). Psychopathy: Heredity and environment. *International Journal of Mental Health, 1,* 190-206.

Schulz, R., & Williamson, G. M. (1991). A 2-year longitudinal study of depression among Alzheimer's caregivers. *Psychology and Aging, 6,* 569-578.

Schwab, J. J., Fennell, E. B., & Warheit, G. J. (1974). The epidemiology of psychosomatic disorders. *Psychosomatics, 15,* 88-93.

Schwalberg, M. D., Barlow, D. H., Alger, S. A., & Howard, L. J. (1992). Comparison of bulimics, obese binge eaters, social phobics, and individuals with panic disorder on comorbidity across DSM-III anxiety disorders. *Journal of Abnormal Psychology, 101,* 675-682.

Schweizer, E., Rickels, K., Case, G., & Greenblatt, D. J. (1990). Long-term therapeutic use of benzodiazepines: Effects of gradual taper. *Archives of General Psychiatry, 47,* 908-915.

Seligman, M. E. P. (1971). Phobias and preparedness. *Behavior Therapy, 2,* 307-320.

Seligman, M. E. P. (1975). *Helplessness: On depression, development, and death.* San Francisco: Freeman.

Seto, M. C., & Kuban, M. (1996). Criterion related validity of phallometric tests for paraphilic rape and sadism, *Behaviour Research and Therapy, 34,* 175-183.

Shaner, R. (2000). Benzodiazepines in psychiatric emergency settings. *Psychiatric Annals, 30,* 268-275.

Shea, M. T., & Elkin, I. (1996). The NIMH Treatment of Depression Collaborative Research Program. In C. Mundt, M. J. Goldstein, K. Hahlweg, & P. Fiedler (Eds.), *Interpersonal factors in the origin and course of affective disorders* (pp. 316-328). London: Gaskell/Royal College of Psychiatrists.

Sher, K. J., & Levenson, R. W. (1982). Risk for alcoholism and individual differences in the stress-response-dampening effect of alcohol. *Journal of Abnormal Psychology, 91*, 350-367.

Sher, K. J., Walitzer, K. S., Wood, P. K., & Brent, E. F. (1991). Characteristics of children of alcoholics: Putative risk factors, substance use and abuse, and psychopathology. *Journal of Abnormal Psychology, 100*, 427-448.

Shergill, S. S., Brammer, M. J., Williams, S. C. R., Murray, R. M., & McGuire, P. K. (2000). Mapping auditory hallucinations in schizophrenia using functional magnetic imaging. *Archives of General Psychiatry, 57*, 1033-1038.

Sherman, J. A. (1994). John Henryism and the health of African-Americans. *Cultures, Medicine, and Psychiatry, 18*, 163-182.

Shoebridge, P. J., & Gowers, S. G. (2000). Parental high concern and adolescent-onset anorexia nervosa: A case-control study to investigate direction of causality. *British Journal of Psychiatry, 176*, 132-137.

Siegel, D. J. (1996). Cognition, memory, and dissociation. *Child and Adolescent Psychiatric Clinics of North America, 5*, 509-536.

Sigman, M., Ungerer, J. A., Mundy, P., & Sherman, T. (1987). Cognition in autistic children. In D. J. Cohen, A. M. Donellan, & R. Paul (Eds.). *Handbook of autism and pervasive developmental disorders*. New York: Wiley.

Silk, K. R., Lee, S., Hill, E. M., & Lohr, N. (1995). Borderline personality disorder symptoms and severity of sexual abuse. *American Journal of Psychiatry, 152*, 1053-1057.

Simon, N. M., & Pollack, M. H. (2000). The current status of the treatment of panic disorder: pharmacotherapy and cognitive-behavioral therapy. *Psychiatric Annals, 30*, 689-696.

Simons, J. S., & Carey, M. P. (2001). Prevalence of the sexual dysfunctions: Results from a decade of research. *Archives of Sexual Behavior, 30*, 177-219.

Simpson, K. J. (2002). Anorexia nervosa and culture. *Journal of Psychiatric and Mental Health Nursing, 9*, 65-71.

Singer, M., & Wynne, L. C. (1963). Differentiating characteristics of the parents of childhood schizophrenics, childhood neurotics, and young adult schizophrenics. *American Journal of Psychiatry, 120*, 234-243.

Smith, S. S., & Newman, J. P. (1990). Alcohol and drug dependence in psychopathic and nonpsychopathic criminal offenders. *Journal of Abnormal Psychology, 99*, 430-439.

Smith, Y. L. S., van Goozen, S. H. M., & Cohen-Kettenis, P. T. (2001). Adolescents with gender identity disorder who were accepted or rejected for sex reassignment surgery: A prospective follow-up study. *Journal of the American Academy of Child and Adolescent Psychiatry, 40*, 472-481.

Snyder, S. H. (1974). Madness and the brain. New York: McGraw-Hill.

Sobell, M. B., & Sobell, L. C. (1976). Second-year treatment outcome of alcoholics treated by individualized behavior therapy: Results. *Behavior Research and Therapy, 14*, 195-215.

Sobell, M. B. & Sobell, L. C. (1993). *Problem drinkers: Guided self-change treatment.* New York: Guilford.

Soloff, P. H., Cornelius, J., George, A., Nathan, S., Perel, J. M., & Ulrich, R. F. (1993). Efficacy of phenelzine and haloperidol in borderline personality disorder. *Archives of General Psychiatry, 50*, 377-386.

Spanos, N. P. (1996). *Multiple identities and false memories: A sociocognitive perspective.* Washington, DC: American Psychological Association.

Spanos, N. P., Weekes, J. R., & Bertrand, L. D. (1985). Multiple personality: A social psychological perspective. *Journal of Abnormal Psychology, 94*, 362-376.

Speilberger, C. D., Johnson, E. H., Russell, S. F., Crane, F. J., & Worden, T. J. (1985). The experience and expression of anger. In M. A. Chesney & R. H. Rosenman (Eds.), *Anger and hostility in cardiovascular and behavioral disorders*. New York: Hemisphere.

Spencer, G. (1989). *Projections of the population of the United States, by age, sex, and race: 1988 to 2080.* Washington, DC: U.S. Department of Commerce.

Spencer, T., Biederman, J., Wilens, T., et al. (1996). Pharmacotherapy of attention-deficit hyperactivity disorder across the life cycle. *Journal of the American Academy of Child and Adolescent Psychiatry, 35*, 389-408.

Spiegel, D. (2001). Deconstructing the dissociative disorders: For whom the Dell tolls. *Journal of Trauma and Dissociation, 2*, 51-57

Spitzberg, B. H. (1999). An analysis of empirical estimates of sexual aggression victimization and perpetration. *Violence and Victims, 14*, 241-260.

Spitzer, R. L., Endicott, J., & Gibbons, M. (1979). Crossing the border into borderline personality and borderline schizophrenia: The development of criteria. *Archives of General Psychiatry, 36*, 17-24.

Sprague, R. L., Cohen, M., & Werry, J. S. (1974). *Normative data on the Conners Teacher Rating Sale and abbreviated scale.* Technical Report. Children's Research Center, University of Illinois, Urbana.

Stanley, M. A., & Turner, S. M. (1995). Current status of pharmacological and behavioral treatment of obsessive-compulsive disorder. *Behavior Therapy, 26*, 163-186.

St. Clair, H. R. (1951). Psychiatric interview experience with Negroes. *American Journal of Psychiatry, 108*, 113-119.

Steadman, H. J., Mulvey, E. P., Monahan, J., Robbins, P. C., Appelbaum, P. S., Grisso, T., Roth, L., & Silver, E. (1998). Violence by people discharged from acute psychiatric inpatient facilities and by others in the same neighborhoods. *Archives of General Psychiatry, 55*, 393-401.

Steele, C. M., & Josephs, R. A. (1988). Drinking your troubles away: II. An attention-allocation model of alcohol's effects on psychological stress. *Journal of Abnormal Psychology, 97*, 196-205.

Steffenburg, S. (1991). Neuropsychological assessment of children with autism: A population-based study. *Developmental Medicine and Child Neurology, 33*, 495-511.

Steffenburg, S., Gillberg, C., Hellgren, L., Andersson, L., et al. (1989). A twin study of autism in Denmark, Finland, Iceland, Norway and Sweden. *Journal of Child Psychology and Psychiatry and Allied Disciplines, 30*, 405-416.

Steiger, H., Gauvin, L., Israel, M., Koerner, N., Ng Ying Kin, N. M. K., Paris, J., & Young, S. N. (2001). Association of serotonin and cortisol indices with childhood abuse in bulimia nervosa. *Archives of General Psychiatry, 58*, 837-843.

Steinhausen, H. (2002). The outcome of anorexia nervosa in the 20th century. *American Journal of Psychiatry, 159*, 1284-1293.

Steketee, G. (1994). Behavioral assessment and treatment planning with obsessive compulsive disorder: A review emphasizing clinical application. *Behavior Therapy, 25*, 613-633.

Stephens, J. H., Pascal, R., & McHugh, P. R. (2000). Long-term follow-up of patients with a diagnosis of paranoid state and hospitalized, 1913 to 1940. *Journal of Nervous and Mental Disease, 188*, 202-208.

Stevens, A., Fischer, A., Bartels, M., & Buchkremer, G. (1996). Electroconvulsive therapy: A review on indications, methods, risks and medication. *European Psychiatry, 11*, 165-174.

Stock, W. (1993). Inhibited female orgasm. In W. O'Donohue & J. H. Geer (Eds.), *Handbook of sexual dysfunctions: Assessment and treatment* (pp. 253-277). Needham Heights, MA: Allyn & Bacon.

Stoller, R. J. (1985). *Presentations of gender.* New Haven, CT: Yale University Press.

Stoller, R. J., & Herdt, G. H. (1985). Theories of the origin of male homosexuality: A cross-cultural look. *Archives of General Psychiatry, 42*, 399-404.

Stone, H. H. (1987). Psychotherapy of borderline patients in light of long-term follow-up. *Bulletin of the Menninger Clinic, 51*, 231-247.

Stone, L. J., & Hokanson, J. E. (1969). Arousal reduction via self-punitive behavior. *Journal of Personality and Social Psychology, 12*, 72-79.

Stoving, R. K., Hangaard, J., Hansen-Nord, M., & Hagen, C. (1999). A review of endocrine changes in anorexia nervosa. *Journal of Psychiatric Research, 33*, 139-152.

Striegel-Moore, R. H., Silberstein, L. R., & Rodin, J. (1993). The social self in bulimia nervosa: Public self-consciousness, social anxiety, and perceived fraudulence. *Journal of Abnormal Psychology, 102*, 297-304.

Stringer, A. Y., & Joseph, N. C. (1983). Methylphenidate in the treatment of aggression in two adults with antisocial personality disorder. *American Journal of Psychiatry, 140*, 1340-1342.

Strober, M. (1986). Anorexia nervosa: History and psychological concepts. In K. D. Brownell & J. P. Foreyt (Eds.), *Handbook of eating disorders*. New York: Basic Books.

Strober, M. (1997). Consultation and therapeutic engagement in severe anorexia nervosa. In D. M. Garner & P. E. Garfinkel (Eds.), *Handbook of treatment for eating disorders* (2nd ed., pp. 229-247). New York: Guilford.

Strober, M., & Katz, J. L. (1987). Do eating disorders and affective disorders share a common etiology? A dissenting opinion. *International Journal of Eating Disorders, 6*, 171-180.

Stuart, H. L., & Arboleda-Florez, J. E. (2001). A public health perspective on violent offenses among persons with mental illness. *Psychiatric Services, 52*, 654-659.

Suddath, R. L., Christison, G. W., Torrey, E. F., Casanova, M. R., & Weinberger, D. R. (1990). Anatomical abnormalities in the brains of monozygotic twins discordant for schizophrenia. *New England Journal of Medicine, 322*, 789-794.

Sue, D. W., & Sue, D. (1992). *Counselling the culturally different.* New York: Wiley.

Suedfeld, P., & Landon, P. B. (1978). Approaches to treatment. In R. D. Hare & D. Schalling (Eds.), *Psychopathic behavior: Approaches to research*. New York: Wiley.

Sugarman, P., Dumughn, C., Saad, K., Hinder, S., & Bluglass, S. (1994). Dangerousness in exhibitionists. *Journal of Forensic Psychiatry, 5*, 287-296.

Sullivan, P. A., Procci, W. R., DeQuattro, V., Schoentgen, S., Levine, D., Van der Meulen, J., & Bornheimer, J. F. (1981). Anger, anxiety, guilt and increased basal and stress-induced neurogenic tone: Causes or effects in primary hypertension? *Clinical Science, 61*, 389-392.

Sullivan, P. A., Schoentgen, S., DeQuattro, V., Procci, W., Levine, D., Van der Meulen, J., & Bornheimer, J. F. (1981). Anxiety, anger, and neurogenic tone at rest and in stress, in patients with primary hypertension. *Hypertension, 3*, 119-123.

Sullivan, P. F., Bulik, C. M., & Kendler, K. S. (1998). The genetic epidemiology of binging and vomiting. *British Journal of Psychiatry, 173*, 75-79.

Summerfield, D. (2001). The invention of post-traumatic stress disorder and the social usefulness of a psychiatric category. *British Medical Journal, 322*, 95-98.

Susser, E., Neugebauer, R., Hoek, H. W., Brown, A. S., et al. (1996). Schizophrenia after prenatal famine: Further evidence. *Archives of General Psychiatry, 53*, 25-31.

Sussman, N., & Chou, J. C. Y. (1988). Current issues in benzodiazepine use for anxiety disorders. *Psychiatric Annals, 18*, 139-145.

Swanson, J. W., Borum, R., Swartz, M. S., & Monahan, J. (1996). Psychotic symptoms and disorders and the risk of violent behaviour in the community. *Criminal Behaviour and Mental Health, 6*, 309-3269.

Swanson, J., Estroff, S., Swartz, M., Borum, R., et al. (1997). Violence and severe mental disorder in clinical and community populations: The effects of psychotic symptoms. *Psychiatry: Interpersonal and Biological Processes, 60*, 1-22.

Swartz, M., Blazer, D., George, L., & Winfield, I. (1990). Estimating the prevalence of borderline personality in the community. *Journal of Personality Disorders*, 257-272.

Swendsen, E. J., King, D. W., King, L. A., Wolfe, J., Erickson, D. J., & Stokes, L. R. (2000). Mood and alcohol consumption: An experience sampling test of the self-medication hypothesis. *Journal of Abnormal Psychology, 109*, 198-204.

Szatmari, P., Offord, D. R., & Boyle, M. H. (1989). Ontario Child Health Study: Prevalence of attention deficit disorder with hyperactivity. *Journal of Child Psychology and Psychiatry and Allied Disciplines, 30*, 219-230.

Tallmadge, J., & Barkley, R. A. (1983). The interactions of hyperactive and normal boys with their mothers and fathers. *Journal of Abnormal Child Psychology, 11*, 565-579.

Tannock, R. (1998). Attention deficit hyperactivity disorder: Advances in cognitive, neurobiological, and genetic research. *Journal of Child Psychology and Psychiatry, 39*, 65-69.

Tardiff, K. (2001). Axis II disorders and dangerousness. In G. Pinard & I. Pagani (Eds.), *Clinical assessment of dangerousness: Empirical contributions* (pp. 103-120). New York: Cambridge University Press.

Tarrier, N., Pilgrim, H., Sommerfield, C., Faragher, B., Reynolds, M., Graham, E., & Barrowclough, C. (1999). A randomized trial of cognitive therapy and imaginal exposure in the treatment of chronic posttraumatic stress disorder. *Journal of Consulting and Clinical Psychology, 67*, 13-18.

Teasdale, J. D. (1974). Learning models of obsessional-compulsive disorder. In H. R. Beech (Ed.), *Obsessional states*. London: Methuen.

Tennant, C. (1988). Parental loss in childhood: Its effect in adult life. *Archives of General Psychiatry, 45*, 1045-1050.

Teplin, L. A., Abram, K. M., & McClelland, G. M. (1996). Prevalence of psychiatric disorders among incarcerated women: Pretrial jail detainees. *Archives of General Psychiatry, 53*, 505-512.

Thigpen, C. H., & Cleckley, H. M. (1957). *The three faces of Eve*. New York: McGraw-Hill.

Thigpen, C. H., & Cleckley, H. M. (1984). On the incidence of multiple personality disorder. *International Journal of Clinical and Experimental Hypnosis, 32*, 63-66.

Thomas, J. A., & Dobbins, J. E. (1986). The color line and social distance in the genesis of essential hypertension. *Journal of the National Medical Association, 78*, 532-536.

Thomson, L. D. G., Bogue, J. P., Humphreys, M. S., & Johnstone, E. C. (2001). A survey of female patients in high security psychiatric care in Scotland. *Criminal Behaviour and Mental Health, 11*, 86-93.

Thornton, C., & Russell, J. (1997). Obsessive compulsive comorbidity in the dieting disorders. *International Journal of Eating Disorders, 21*, 83-87.

Thyer, B. A. (1991). Diagnosis and treatment of child and adolescent anxiety disorders. *Behavior Modification, 15*, 310-325.

Thyer, B. A., & Curtis, G. C. (1984). The effects of ethanol on phobic anxiety. *Behaviour Research and Therapy, 22*, 599-610.

Tollison, C. D., & Adams, H. E. (1979). *Sexual disorders: Treatment, theory, research*. New York: Gardner.

Tondo, L., Baldessarini, R. J., & Floris, G. (2001). Long-term clinical effectiveness of lithium maintenance treatment in types I and II bipolar disorders. *British Journal of Psychiatry, 178* (Suppl. 141), S184-S190.

Torgersen, S., Kringlen, E., & Cramer, V. (2001). The prevalence of personality disorders in a community sample. *Archives of General Psychiatry, 58*, 590-596.

Tsuang, M. T. (1991). Morbidity risks of schizophrenia and affective disorders among first-degree relatives of patients with schizoaffective disorders. *British Journal of Psychiatry, 158*, 165-170.

Tsuang, M. T., Stone, W. S., & Faraone, S. V. (1999). Schizophrenia: A review of genetic studies. *Harvard Review of Psychiatry, 7*, 185-207.

Turk, C. L., Heimberg, R. G., & Hope, D. A. (2001). Social anxiety disorder. In D. H. Barlow (Ed.), *Clinical handbook of psychological disorders* (pp. 114(153). New York: Guilford.

Turner, S. M., Beidel, D. C., & Cooley-Quille, M. R. (1995). Two-year follow-up of social phobics treated with Social Effectiveness Therapy. *Behaviour Research and Therapy, 33*, 553-555.

Twentyman, C. T., & McFall, R. M. (1975). Behavioral training of social skills in shy males. *Journal of Consulting and Clinical Psychology, 43*, 384-395.

Tyrer, P., & Tyrer, S. (1974). School refusal, truancy, and adult neurotic illness. *Psychological Medicine, 6*, 313-332.

Van Amerigen, M. A., Lane, R. M., Walker, J. R., et al. (2001). Sertreline treatment of generalized social phobia: A 20-week, double-blind, placebo-controlled study. *American Journal of Psychiatry, 158*, 275(281.

Van den Heuvel, O. A., van de Wetering, B. J. M., Veltman, D. J. & Pauls, D. L. (2000). Genetic studies of panic disorder: A review. *Journal of Clinical Psychiatry, 61*, 756-766.

Van den Oord, E. J., Boomsma, D. I., & Verhulst, F. C. (1994). A study of problem behaviors in 10- to 15-year old biologically related and unrelated international adoptees. *Behavior Genetics, 24*, 193-205.

Van der Ham, T. (1997). Empirically based subgrouping of eating disorders in adolescents: A longitudinal perspective. *British Journal of Psychiatry, 170*, 363-368.

Verschoor, A. M., & Poortinga, J. (1988). Psychosocial differences between Dutch male and female transsexuals. *Archives of Sexual Behavior, 17*, 173-178.

Vice, C. M., & Cooper, P. J. (1995). Sexual abuse in patients with eating disorder, patients with depression, and normal controls. *British Journal of Psychiatry, 167*, 80-85.

Vitousek, K., & Manke, F. (1994). Personality variables and disorders in anorexia nervosa and bulimia nervosa. *Journal of Abnormal Psychology, 103*, 137-147.

Wade, T. D., Treloar, S, A. & Martin, N. G. (2001). A comparison of family functioning, temperament, and childhood conditions in monozygotic twin pairs discordant for lifetime bulimia nervosa. *American Journal of Psychiatry, 158*, 1155-1157.

Walden, J., Mormann, C. L., Langosch, J., Berger, J, & Grunze, H. (1998). Differential treatment of bipolar disorder with old and new antiepileptic drugs. *Neuropsychobiology, 38*, 181-184.

Waldinger, M. D., Zwinderman, A. H., & Olivier, B. (2001). Antidepressants and ejaculation: A double-blind, randomized, placebo-controlled, fixed dose study with paroxetine, sertraline, and nefazodone. *Journal of Clinical Psychopharmacology, 21*, 293-297.

Waldinger, R. J., & Gunderson, J. G. (1984). Completed psychotherapies with borderline patients. *American Journal of Psychotherapy, 38*, 190-202.

Walker, E. F., Lewine, R. R. J., & Newmann, C. (1996). Childhood behavioral characteristics and adult brain morphology in schizophrenia. *Schizophrenia Research, 22*, 93-101.

Wallace, S. T., & Alden, L. E. (1997) Social phobia and positive social events: The price of success. *Journal of Abnormal Psychology, 106(3)* , 416-424.

Walters, E., & Kendler, K. S. (1994). Anorexia nervosa and anorexia-like symptoms in a population based twin sample. *American Journal of Psychiatry, 152*, 62-71.

Warshaw, R. (1988). *I never called it rape: The Ms. report on recognizing, fighting, and surviving acquaintance rape*. New York: Harper & Row.

Watson, J. B., & Rayner, R. (1920). Conditioned emotional reactions. *Journal of Experimental Psychology, 3*, 1-14.

Watt, N. F., & Lubensky, A. (1976). Childhood roots of schizophrenia. *Journal of Consulting and Clinical Psychology, 44*, 363-375.

Wearden, A. J., Tarrier, N., Barrowclough, C., Zastowny, T. R., & Rahill, A. A. (2000). A review of expressed emotion research in health care. *Clinical Psychology Review, 20*, 633-666.

Webb, C. T., & Levinson, D. F. (1993). Schizotypal and paranoid personality disorder in the relatives of patients with schizophrenia and affective disorders: A review. *Schizophrenia Research, 11*, 81-92.

Wegner, D. M. (1994). Ironic processes of mental control. *Psychological Review, 101*, 34-52.

Weiner, H. (1977). *Psychobiology and human disease*. New York: Elsevier.

Weiss, A. P., & Heckers, S. (1999). Neuroimaging of hallucinations: A review of the literature. *Psychiatry Research: Neuroimaging. 92*, 61-74.

Weissberg, M. (1993). Multiple personality disorder and iatrogenesis: The cautionary tale of Anna O. *International Journal of Clinical and Experimental Hypnosis, 41*, 15-34.

Weissman, M. M. (1985). The epidemiology of anxiety disorders: Rates, risks, and familial patterns. In A. H. Tuma & J. D. Maser (Eds.), *Anxiety and the anxiety disorders*. Hillsdale, NJ: Erlbaum.

Weissman, M. M., Bland, R. C., Canino, G. J., Greenwald, S., Hwu, H., et al. (1994).

The crossnational epidemiology of obsessive compulsive disorder. *Journal of Clinical Psychiatry, 55* (Suppl. 3), 5-10.

Weissman, M. M., Bruce, M. L., Leaf, P. J., Florio, L. P., & Holzer, C. (1991). Affective disorders. In L. N. Robins & D. A. Regier (Eds.), *Psychiatric disorders in America: The Epidemiologic Catchment Area Study* (pp. 53-80). New York: Free Press.

Weissman, M. M., & Markowitz, J. C. (1994). Interpersonal psychotherapy: Current status. *Archives of General Psychiatry, 51*, 599-606.

Werry, J. S., Weiss, G., & Douglas, V. (1964). Studies on the hyperactive child: I. Some preliminary findings. *Canadian Psychiatric Association Journal, 9*, 120-130.

Whalen, C. K., Henker, B., Buhrmester, D., Hinshaw, S. P., Huber, A., & Laski, K. (1989). Does stimulant medication improve the peer status of hyperactive children? *Journal of Consulting and Clinical Psychology, 57*, 545-549.

Whitaker, A. H., Van Rossen, R., Feldman, J. F., et al. (1997). Psychiatric outcomes in low birth weight children at age 6 years: Relation to neonatal cranial ultrasound abnormalities. *Archives of General Psychiatry, 54*, 847-856.

Wickramsekara, I. (1977). The application of learning theory to the treatment of a case of exhibitionism. In J. Fischer & H. Gochros (Eds.), *Handbook of behavior therapy with sexual problems*. New York: Pergamon.

Widiger, T. A. (2001). Official classification systems. In W. J. Livesley (Ed.), *Handbook of personality disorders: Theory, research, and treatment* (pp. 60-83). New York: Guilford.

Widiger, T. A., Frances, A., Spitzer, R., & Williams, J. (1988). The DSM-III-R personality disorders: An overview. *American Journal of Psychiatry, 145*, 786-795.

Widiger, T. A., Frances, A., & Trull, T. J. (1987). A psychometric analysis of the social-interpersonal and cognitive-perceptual items for the schizotypal personality disorder. *Archives of General Psychiatry, 44*, 741-745.

Widiger, T. A., Trull, T. J., Hurt, S., Clarkin, J., & Francis, A. (1987). A multidimensional scaling of the DMS-III personality disorders. *Archives of General Psychiatry, 44*, 557-566.

Wiederman, M. W. (1996). Women, sex, and food: A review of research on eating disorders and sexuality. *Journal of Sex Research, 33*, 301-311.

Wiegel, M., Wincze, J. P., & Barlow, D. H. (2002). Sexual dysfunction. In M. M. Antony & D. H. Barlow (Eds.), *Handbook of assessment and treatment planning for psychological disorders* (pp. 481-522). New York: Guilford.

Wilkerson, I. (1990, June 7). Physician fulfills a goal: Aiding a person in suicide. *New York Times*, p. A16.

Williams, S. L., & Rappoport, A. (1983). Cognitive treatment in the natural environment for agoraphobics. *Behavior Therapy, 19*, 1-9.

Williamson, D. A., Cubic, B. A., & Gleaves, D. H. (1993). Equivalence of body image disturbance in anorexia and bulimia nervosa. *Journal of Abnormal Psychology, 120*, 173-176.

Wilson, G. T., & Davison, G. C. (1971). Processes of fear-reduction in systematic desensitization: Animal studies. *Psychological Bulletin, 76*, 1-14.

Wilson, G. T., Fairburn, C. C., Agras, W. S., Walsh, B. T., & Kraemer, H. (2002). Cognitive-behavioral therapy for bulimia nervosa: Time course and mechanisms of change. *Journal of Consulting and Clinical Psychology, 70*, 267-274.

Winokur, G., Black, D. W., & Nasrallah, A. (1992). The schizoaffective continuum. In D. J. Kupfer (Ed.), *Reflections on modern psychiatry* (pp. 25-34). Washington, DC: American Psychiatric Press.

Wise, T. N., & Meyer, J. K. (1980). The border area between transvestism and gender dysphoria: Transvestitic applicants for sex reassignment. *Archives of Sexual Behavior, 9*, 327-342.

Wiseman, C. V., Gray, J. J., Moismann, J. E., & Arhens, A. H. (1992). Cultural expectations of thinness in women: An up-date. *International Journal of Eating Disorders, 11*, 85-89.

Wittchen, H., Schuster, P., & Lieb, R. (2001). Comorbidity and mixed anxiety-depressive disorder: Clinical curiosity or pathophysiological need? *Human Psychopharmacology, 16* (Suppl. 1), S21-S30.

Witzig, J. S. (1968). The group treatment of male exhibitionists. *American Journal of Psychiatry, 125*, 75-81.

Wolff, M., Alsobrook, J. P., & Pauls, D. L. (2000). Genetic aspects of obsessive-compulsive disorder. *Psychiatric Clinics of North America, 23*, 535-544.

Wolpe, J., & Rowan, V. C. (1988). Panic disorder: A product of classical conditioning: *Behavior Research and Therapy, 26*, 441-450.

Wolpe, J. P. (1958). *Psychotherapy by reciprocal inhibition*. Stanford, CA: Stanford University Press.

Wonderlich, S. A., Brewerton, T. D., Jocic, Z., Dansky, B. S., et al. (1997). Relationship of childhood sexual abuse and eating disorders. *Journal of the American Academy of Child and Adolescent Psychiatry, 36*, 1107-1115.

Wood, D. L., Sheps, S. G., et al. (1984). Cold pressor test as a predictor of hypertension. *Hypertension, 6*, 301-306.

Wooley, S. C. (1995). Sexual abuse and eating disorders: The concealed debate. In P. Fallon, M. A. Katzman, & S. C. Wooely (Eds.), *Feminist perspectives on eating disorders*. New York: Guilford.

World Almanac and Book of Facts 1993. (1992). New York: Pharos Books.

World Health Organization. (1990). *International classification of diseases and related health care problems* (10th ed.). Geneva.

Yalom, I. D., & Lieberman, M. A. (1971). A study of encounter group casualties. *Archives of General Psychiatry, 25*, 16-30.

Yates, A. (1990). Current perspectives on the eating disorders: II. Treatment, outcome, and research directions. *Journal of the American Academy of Child and Adolescent Psychiatry, 29*, 1-9.

Yeager, C. A., & Lewis, D. O. (1997). False memories of cult abuse. *American Journal of Psychiatry, 154*, 435.

Yehuda, R. (2002). Current concepts: Post-traumatic stress disorder. *New England Journal of Medicine, 346*, 108-114.

Yung, P. M., & Keltner, A. A. (1996). A controlled comparison of the effects of muscle and cognitive relaxation procedures on blood pressure: Implications for the behavioural treatment of borderline hypertensives. *Behaviour Research and Therapy, 34*, 821-826.

Zanarini, M. C., & Frankenburg, F. R. (1997). Pathways to the development of borderline personality disorder. *Journal of Personality Disorders, 11*, 93-104.

Zanarini, M. C., Gunderson, J. G., Marino, M. F., et al. (1988). DSM-III disorders in the families of borderline outpatients. *Journal of Personality Disorders, 2*, 292-302.

Zanarini, M. C., Skodol, A. E., Bender, D., Dolan, R., Sanislow, C., Schaefer, E., Morey, L. C., Grilo, C. M., Shea, M. T., McGlashan, T. H., & Gunderson, J. C. (2000). The Collaborative Longitudinal Personality Disorders Study: Reliability of axis I and II diagnoses. *Journal of Personality Disorders, 14*, 291-299.

Zarit, S. H. (1980). *Aging and mental disorders: Psychological approaches to assessment and treatment*. New York: Free Press.

Zaubler, T. S., & Katon, W. (1998). Panic disorder in the general medical setting. *Journal of Psychosomatic Research, 44*, 25-42.

Zimmerman, M. (1994). Diagnosing personality disorders: A review of issues and research methods. *Archives of General Psychiatry, 51*, 225-245.

Zito, J. M., Safer, D. J., dosReis, S., et al. (2000). Trends in the prescribing of psychotropic medication to preschoolers. *JAMA, 283*, 1025-1030.

Zohar, J., Kaplan, Z., & Benjamin, J. (1994). Compulsive exhibitionism successfully treated with fluvoxamine: A controlled case study. *Journal of Clinical Psychiatry, 55*, 86-88.

Zolar, A. H., Apter, A., King, R. A., Pauls, D. L., Leckman, J. F., & Cohen, D. J. (1999). Epidemiological studies. In J. F. Leckman & D. J. Cohen (Eds.). *Tourette's syndrome-tics, obsessions, compulsions: Developmental psychopathology and clinical care* (pp. 177-193). New York: Wiley.

Zucker, K. J., & Bradley, S. J. (1995). *Gender identity disorder and psychosexual problems in children and adolescents*. New York: Guilford.

Zucker, K. J., & Bradley, S. J. (2000). Gender identity disorder. In C. H. Zeanah (Ed.), *Handbook of infant mental health* (2nd ed., pp. 412-424). New York: Guilford.

Zucker, K. J., & Green, R. (1992). Psychosexual disorders in children and adolescents. *Journal of Child Psychology and Psychiatry, 33*, 107-151.

Quotation and Illustration Credits

Page 323, quotation: McGhie, A. & Chapman, J. S. (1961). Disorders of attention and perception in early schizophrenia. *British Journal of Medical Psychology, 34,* 103–116. Reprinted by permission of British Psychological Society.

Page 330, Table 11.2: Gottesman, I. I., McGuffin, P., & Farmer, A. E. (1987). Summary of major European family and twin studies of the genetics of schizophrenia. *Schizophrenia Bulletin, 13,* 23–47. Reprinted by permission.

Page 331, Table 11.3: Heston, L.L. (1966). Subjects separated from their schizophrenic mothers in early infancy. *British Journal of Psychiatry, 112,* 819–825. Reproduced by permission of the Royal College of Psychiatrists.

Pages 364-265, quotation: Rosen, E., Fox, R., & Gregory, I. (1972). Case history of long-term effects of prolonged alcohol abuse. *Abnormal psychology* (2nd ed.). Reprinted by permission of W. B. Saunders Company.

Page 391, Table 12.2: The Twelve Steps. Copyright © 1952. Reprinted with permission of Alcoholics Anonymous World Services, Inc. Permission to reprint this material does not mean that AA has reviewed or approved the contents of this publication nor that AA agrees with the views expressed herein. AA is a program of recovery from alcoholism *only*—use of the Steps in connection with programs and activity patterned after AA, but which address other problems, does not imply otherwise.

Pages 420, quotation: McNeill, E. (1967). The case of Dan in *The quiet furies: Man and disorder,* 84, 85, 87. Copyright © 1967. Adapted by permission of Prentice-Hall.

Page 426, Table 13.2: Costa, P. T., Jr. & McCrae, R. R. (1992). *NEO-PI-R.* Odessa, FL. Psychological Assessment Resources. Reprinted by permission.

Page 431, quotation: Linehan, M. M. (1992). Personal communication, 18 September and 16 November 1992. Reprinted by permission of the author.

Page 434, quotation: Rosen, R. C. & Rosen, L. (1981). Case study on William V. and his voyeuristic fantasies in *Human Sexuality,* 452–453. Reprinted by permission of McGraw-Hill Book Company.

Page 436, Table 14.1: Reprinted with permission from the American Psychiatric Association: *Diagnostic and Statistical Manual of Mental Disorders, Fourth Edition.* Copyright © 1994.

Page 467, Figure 14.2: Masters, W. H. & Johnson, V. E. (1970). *Human sexual inadequacy.* Reprinted by permission of Masters & Johnson Institute.

Page 481, Table 15.2: Barkley et al. (1990). Adapted from The adolescent outcome of hyperactive children diagnosed by research criteria, I: An 8-year prospective follow-up study. *Journal of the American Academy of Child and Adolescent Psychiatry.* Copyright © 1990 Williams & Wilkins. Reprinted by permission.

Page 486, Figure 15.1: From Blumstein, A., Cohen, J., & Farrington, D. P. *Criminology, 26,* 11. Copyright © 1988. The American Society of Criminology.

Page 495, Figure 15.3a: Mowrer, H. O. & Mowrer W. M. (1938). Enuresis: A method for its study and treatment. *American Journal of Orthopsychiatry, 8,* 436–459. Copyright © 1938 by the American Orthopsychiatric Association, Inc. Reprinted with permission from the American Journal of Orthopsychiatry.

Page 498, Table 15.3: Sparrow, S. S., Ballo, D. A., & Cicchetti, D. V. (1984). Sample items from the Vineland Adaptive Behavior Scales. Copyright © 1984, 1985 American Guidance Service, Inc.

Page 508, Table 15.4: Volkmar, F. R., Cohen, D. J., & Paul, R. (1986). Adapted from An evaluation of DSM-III criteria for infantile autism. *Journal of the American Academy of Child and Adolescent Psychiatry, 25,* 193. Copyright © 1986 Williams & Wilkins. Reprinted by permission.

Pages 512–513, Focus on Discovery 15.5, quotation: Grandin, T. (1995). Excerpts from *Thinking in pictures,* 132-135. Copyright © 1995. Used by permission of Doubleday, a division of Bantam Doubleday Dell Publishing Group, Inc.

Page 519, quotation: Strub, R. L. & Black, C. C. (1987). Growing out of autism. In E. Schopler & G. B. Mesibov (Eds.), *Autism in adolescents and adults.* Reprinted by permission of Plenum Publishing Corporation.

Page 558, Figure 16.a: Zeiss, A. M. & Steffan, A. M. (1996). Interdisciplinary health care teams: The basic unit of geriatric care. In L. L. Carstenson, D. A. Edelstein, & L. Dornbrand (Eds.). *The practical handbook of clinical gerontology.* Thousand Oaks, CA: Sage. Reprinted by permission.

Page 590, quotation: Safran, J. D., Vallis, T. M., Segal, Z. V., & Shaw, B. F. (1986). Assessment of core cognitive processes in cognitive therapy. *Cognitive Therapy and Research, 10,* 515. Reprinted by permission.

Page 396, Figure 12.a: Project Match Research Group. (1997). Matching alcoholism treatments to client heterogeneity: Project MATCH posttreatment drinking outcomes. *Journal of Studies of Alcohol, 58,* 7–29. Copyright © 1997 by Project Match Research Group. Reprinted by permission.

Page 612-613, quotation: Morse, S. J. (1982). A preference for liberty: The case against involuntary commitment of mentally disordered. *California Law Review, 70,* 98. Copyright © 1982 by California Law Review Inc. Reprinted by permission.

Pages 625, quotation: Clayton, E. W. (1988). From Rogers to Rivers: The rights of the mentally ill to refuse medications. *American Journal of Law and Medicine, 13,* 19–20. Copyright © 1987 by American Journal of Law & Medicine, XIII. Reprinted with the permission of the American Society of Law, Medicine & Ethics and Boston University School of Law.

Page 636, quotation: Baxter, E. & Hopper, K. (1981). Private lives/public places: Homeless adults on the streets of New York City. Reprinted by permission of Community Service Society.

Photo Credits

Name Index

Subject Index